Profiles of Illinois

2008

Second Edition

Profiles of Illinois

A Universal Reference Book

Grey House Publishing

PUBLISHER: Leslie Mackenzie
EDITORIAL DIRECTOR: Laura Mars-Proietti
EDITOR: David Garoogian
RESEARCH ASSISTANT: Michael Marturana; Alyssa Garoogian

PRODUCTION MANAGER: Karen Stevens
MARKETING DIRECTOR: Jessica Moody

Grey House Publishing, Inc.
185 Millerton Road
Millerton, NY 12546
518.789.8700
FAX 518.789.0545
www.greyhouse.com
e-mail: books @greyhouse.com

First edition published 2005
Printed in the U.S.A.

ISBN: 978-1-59237-366-6

Table of Contents

Introduction

Welcome to the second edition of *Profiles of Illinois - Facts, Figures & Statistics for 1,427 Populated Places in Illinois.* As with the other titles in our *State Profiles* series, we built this work using content from Grey House Publishing's award-winning *Profiles of America* - a 4-volume compilation of data on more than 42,000 places in the United States. We have updated and included the Illinois chapter from *Profiles of America,* and added entire fresh chapters of demographic information and ranking sections, so that *Profiles of Illinois* is the most comprehensive portrait of the state of Illinois ever published.

This second edition provides data on all populated communities and counties in the state of Illinois for which the US Census provides individual statistics. It includes seven major sections that cover everything from **Education** to **Ethnic Backgrounds** to **Climate**. All sections include **Comparative Statistics** or **Rankings**, and full-color **Maps** at the back of the book provide valuable information in a quickly processed, visual format. Here's an overview of each section:

1. Profiles

This section, organized by county, gives detailed profiles of 1,427 places plus 102 counties, and is based on the 2000 Census. This core Census data has been so extensively updated, however, that nearly 80% of this section has 2007 numbers. In addition, we have added current government statistics and original research, so that these profiles pull together statistical and descriptive information on every Census-recognized place in the state. Major fields of information include:

Geography	Housing	Education	Religion
Ancestry	Transportation	Population	Climate
Economy	Industry	Health	

In addition to place profiles, this section includes an **Alphabetical Place Index** and **Comparative Statistics** that compare Illinois' 100 largest communities by dozens of data points.

2. Education

This section begins with an **Educational State Profile,** summarizing number of schools, students, diplomas granted and educational dollars spent. Following the state profile are **School District Rankings** on 16 topics ranging from *Teacher/Student Ratios* to *High School Drop-Out Rates.* Following these rankings are statewide *National Assessment of Educational Progress (NAEP)* results and data from the *Illinois Standards Achievement Test (ISAT), Prairie State Achievement Examination (PSAE), Illinois Measure of Annual Growth in English (IMAGE), and Illinois Alternate Assessment (IAA).*

3. Ancestry

This section provides a detailed look at the ancestral and racial makeup of Illinois. 217 ethnic categories are ranked three ways: 1) by number, based on all places regardless of population; 2) by percent, based on all places regardless of population; 3) by percent, based on places with populations of 10,000 or more. You will discover, for example, that Moline has the greatest number of *Belgians* in the state (2,686), and that 37.3% of the population of Fulton are of *Dutch* ancestry.

4. Hispanic Population

This section defines Illinois' Hispanic population by 23 Hispanic backgrounds from *Argentinian* to *Venezuelan.* It ranks each of 15 categories, from Median Age to Median Home Value, by each Hispanic background. For example, you'll see that New Lennox has the highest percentage of *Mexicans* who speak English-only at home (76.3%), and that Naperville has the highest percentage of *Puerto Ricans* who are four-year college graduates (46.6%).

5. Asian Population

Similar in format to the section on Hispanic Population, this section defines Illinois' Asian population by 21 Asian backgrounds from *Bangladeshi* to *Vietnamese.* It ranks each of 14 categories, from Median Age to Median Home Value, by each Asian background. You will learn that *Koreans* in Buffalo Grove have a median household income of $83,219 and that 93.6% of *Thais* in Chicago are high-school graduates.

6. Climate
This important topic is explored in detail in this section, which includes a *State Summary,* a *map* of the state's weather stations, and profiles of both *National and Cooperative Weather Stations.* In addition, you'll find *Weather Station Rankings,* where you'll see that, over the 30-year recorded period, Chicago Midway Airport reported the highest annual snowfall with 42.8 inches.

This section also includes current *Storm* data, with the most destructive weather events ranked by both fatalities and property damage, from 1983-2008. Here you will learn that a flood caused $16.8 million in property damage in Galatia in March 2008 and that extreme cold was responsible for 10 fatalities in Cook County in February 2007.

7. Maps
For a more visual point of view, there are 16 full-color maps of Illinois at the back of the book. They provide information on topics such as Populated Places, Transportation and Physical Features, Core-Based Statistical Areas and Counties, Population Demographics, Household Size, Median Age, Income, Median Home Values, Educational Attainment, and another look at who voted for George Bush in 2004.

Note: The extensive **User's Guide** that follows this Introduction is segmented into six sections and examines, in some detail, each data field in the individual profiles and comparative sections for all chapters. It provides sources for all data points and statistical definitions as necessary.

User's Guide: Profiles

Places Covered

All 102 counties.

1,285 incorporated municipalities. Municipalities are incorporated as either cities, towns or villages.

26 census designated places (CDP). The U.S. Bureau of the Census defines a CDP as "a statistical entity, defined for each decennial census according to Census Bureau guidelines, comprising a densely settled concentration of population that is not within an incorporated place, but is locally identified by a name. CDPs are delineated cooperatively by state and local officials and the Census Bureau, following Census Bureau guidelines. Beginning with Census 2000 there are no size limits."

116 unincorporated communities. The communities included have both their own zip code and statistics for their ZIP Code Tabulation Area (ZCTA) available from the Census Bureau. They are referred to as "postal areas." A ZCTA is a statistical entity developed by the Census Bureau to approximate the delivery area for a US Postal Service 5-digit or 3-digit ZIP Code in the US and Puerto Rico. A ZCTA is an aggregation of census blocks that have the same predominant ZIP Code associated with the mailing addresses in the Census Bureau's Master Address File. Thus, the Postal Service's delivery areas have been adjusted to encompass whole census blocks so that the Census Bureau can tabulate census data for the ZCTAs. ZCTAs do not include all ZIP Codes used for mail delivery and therefore do not precisely depict the area within which mail deliveries associated with that ZIP Code occur. Additionally, some areas that are known by a unique name, although they are part of a larger incorporated place, are also included as "postal areas."

Important Notes

- *Profiles of Illinois* uses the term "community" to refer to all places except counties. The term "county" is used to refer to counties and county-equivalents. All places are defined as of the 2000 Census.
- In each community profile, only school districts that have schools that are physically located within the community are shown. In addition, statistics for each school district cover the entire district, regardless of the physical location of the schools within the district.
- Special care should be taken when interpreting certain statistics for communities containing large colleges or universities. College students were counted as residents of the area in which they were living while attending college (as they have been since the 1950 census). One effect this may have is skewing the figures for population, income, housing, and educational attainment.
- Some information (e.g. unemployment rates) is available for both counties and individual communities. Other information is available for just counties (e.g. election results), or just individual communities (e.g. local newspapers).
- Some statistical information is available only for larger communities. In addition, the larger places are more apt to have services such as newspapers, airports, school districts, etc.
- For the most complete information on any community, you should also check the entry for the county in which the community is located. In addition, more information and services will be listed under the larger places in the county.
- For a more in-depth discussion of geographic areas, please refer to the Census Bureau's Geographic Areas Reference Manual at http://www.census.gov/geo/www/garm.html.

Data Sources

CENSUS 2000

The parts of the data which are from the 2000 Decennial Census are from the following sources: *U.S. Bureau of the Census, Census of Population and Housing, 2000: Summary Files 1 and 3.* Summary File 3 (SF 3) consists of 813 detailed tables of Census 2000 social, economic and housing characteristics compiled from a sample of approximately 19 million housing units (about 1 in 6 households) that received the Census 2000 long-form questionnaire. Summary File 1 (SF 1) contains 286 tables focusing on age, sex, households, families, and housing units. This file presents 100-percent population and housing figures for the total population, for 63 race categories, and for many other race and Hispanic or Latino categories.

Comparing SF 3 Estimates with Corresponding Values in SF 1

As in earlier censuses, the responses from the sample of households reporting on long forms must be weighted to reflect the entire population. Specifically, each responding household represents, on average, six or seven other households who reported using short forms.

One consequence of the weighting procedures is that each estimate based on the long form responses has an associated confidence interval. These confidence intervals are wider (as a percentage of the estimate) for geographic areas with smaller populations and for characteristics that occur less frequently in the area being examined (such as the proportion of people in poverty in a middle-income neighborhood).

In order to release as much useful information as possible, statisticians must balance a number of factors. In particular, for Census 2000, the Bureau of the Census created weighting areas—geographic areas from which about two hundred or more long forms were completed—which are large enough to produce good quality estimates. If smaller weighting areas had been used, the confidence intervals around the estimates would have been significantly wider, rendering many estimates less useful due to their lower reliability.

The disadvantage of using weighting areas this large is that, for smaller geographic areas within them, the estimates of characteristics that are also reported on the short form will not match the counts reported in SF 1. Examples of these characteristics are the total number of people, the number of people reporting specific racial categories, and the number of housing units. The official values for items reported on the short form come from SF 1 and SF 2.

The differences between the long form estimates in SF 3 and values in SF 1 are particularly noticeable for the smallest places, tracts, and block groups. The long form estimates of total population and total housing units in SF 3 will, however, match the SF 1 counts for larger geographic areas such as counties and states, and will be essentially the same for medium and large cities.

SF 1 gives exact numbers even for very small groups and areas, whereas SF 3 gives estimates for small groups and areas such as tracts and small places that are less exact. The goal of SF 3 is to identify large differences among areas or large changes over time. Estimates for small areas and small population groups often do exhibit large changes from one census to the next, so having the capability to measure them is worthwhile.

2007 Estimates and 2012 Projections

Some 2000 Census data has been updated with data provided by Claritas. Founded in 1971, Claritas is the industry leader in applied demography and the preeminent provider of small-area demographic estimates.

Information for Communities

PHYSICAL CHARACTERISTICS

Place Type: Lists the type of place (city, town, village, borough, special city, CDP, township, plantation, gore, district, grant, location, reservation, or postal area). *Source: U.S. Bureau of the Census, Census of Population and Housing, 2000: Summary File 1 and U.S. Postal Service, City State File.*

Land and Water Area: Land and water area in square miles. *Source: U.S. Bureau of the Census, Census of Population and Housing, 2000: Summary File 1.*

Latitude and Longitude: Latitude and longitude in degrees. *Source: U.S. Bureau of the Census, Census of Population and Housing, 2000: Summary File 1.*

Elevation: Elevation in feet. *Source: U.S. Geological Survey, Geographic Names Information System (GNIS).*

HISTORY

History: Historical information. *Source: Columbia University Press, The Columbia Gazetteer of North America; Original research.*

POPULATION

Population: 1990 and 2000 figures are a 100% count of population. 2007 estimates and 2012 projections were provided by Claritas. *Source: Claritas; U.S. Bureau of the Census, Census of Population and Housing, 2000: Summary File 1.*

Population by Race: 2007 estimates includes the U.S. Bureau of the Census categories of White alone; Black alone; Asian alone; and Hispanic of any race. Alone refers to the fact that these figures are not in combination with any other race. 2007 data for American Indian/Alaska Native and Native Hawaiian/Other Pacific Islander was not available.

The concept of race, as used by the Census Bureau, reflects self-identification by people according to the race or races with which they most closely identify. These categories are socio-political constructs and should not be interpreted as being scientific or anthropological in nature. Furthermore, the race categories include both racial and national-origin groups.

- **White.** A person having origins in any of the original peoples of Europe, the Middle East, or North Africa. It includes people who indicate their race as "White" or report entries such as Irish, German, Italian, Lebanese, Near Easterner, Arab, or Polish.
- **Black or African American.** A person having origins in any of the Black racial groups of Africa. It includes people who indicate their race as "Black, African American, or Negro," or provide written entries such as African American, Afro-American, Kenyan, Nigerian, or Haitian.
- **Asian.** A person having origins in any of the original peoples of the Far East, Southeast Asia, or the Indian subcontinent including, for example, Cambodia, China, India, Japan, Korea, Malaysia, Pakistan, the Philippine Islands, Thailand, and Vietnam. It includes "Asian Indian," "Chinese," "Filipino," "Korean," "Japanese," "Vietnamese," and "Other Asian."
- **Hispanic.** The data on the Hispanic or Latino population, which was asked of all people, were derived from answers to long-form questionnaire Item 5, and short-form questionnaire Item 7. The terms "Spanish," "Hispanic origin," and "Latino" are used interchangeably. Some respondents identify with all three terms, while others may identify with only one of these three specific terms. Hispanics or Latinos who identify with the terms "Spanish," "Hispanic," or "Latino" are those who classify themselves in one of the specific Hispanic or Latino categories listed on the questionnaire — "Mexican," "Puerto Rican," or "Cuban" — as well as those who indicate that they are "other Spanish, Hispanic, or Latino." People who do not identify with one of the specific origins listed on the questionnaire but indicate that they are "other Spanish, Hispanic, or Latino" are those whose origins are from Spain, the Spanish-speaking countries of Central or South America, the Dominican Republic, or people identifying themselves generally as Spanish, Spanish-American, Hispanic, Hispano, Latino, and so on. All write-in responses to the "other Spanish/Hispanic/Latino" category were coded. Origin can be viewed as the heritage, nationality group, lineage, or country of birth of the person or the person's parents or ancestors before their arrival in the United States. People who identify their origin as Spanish, Hispanic, or Latino may be of any race.

Population Density: 2007 population estimate divided by the land area in square miles. *Source: Claritas; U.S. Bureau of the Census, Census of Population and Housing, 2000: Summary File 1.*

Average Household Size: Average household size was calculated by dividing the total population by the total number of households. Figures are 2007 estimates. *Source: Claritas.*

Median Age: Figures are 2007 estimates. *Source: Claritas.*

Male/Female Ratio: Number of males per 100 females. Figures are 2007 estimates. *Source: Claritas.*

Marital Status: Percentage of population never married, now married, widowed, or divorced. *Source: U.S. Bureau of the Census, Census of Population and Housing, 2000: Summary File 3.*

The marital status classification refers to the status at the time of enumeration. Data on marital status are tabulated only for the population 15 years old and over. Each person was asked whether they were "Now married," "Widowed," "Divorced," or "Never married." Couples who live together (for example, people in common-law marriages) were able to report the marital status they considered to be the most appropriate.

- **Never married**. Never married includes all people who have never been married, including people whose only marriage(s) was annulled.
- **Now married.** All people whose current marriage has not ended by widowhood or divorce. This category includes people defined as "separated."
- **Widowed**. This category includes widows and widowers who have not remarried.
- **Divorced.** This category includes people who are legally divorced and who have not remarried.

Foreign Born: Percentage of population who were not U.S. citizens at birth. Foreign-born people are those who indicated they were either a U.S. citizen by naturalization or they were not a citizen of the United States. *Source: U.S. Bureau of the Census, Census of Population and Housing, 2000: Summary File 3.*

Ancestry: Largest ancestry groups reported (up to five). Includes multiple ancestries. *Source: U.S. Bureau of the Census, Census of Population and Housing, 2000: Summary File 3.*

The data represent self-classification by people according to the ancestry group or groups with which they most closely identify. Ancestry refers to a person's ethnic origin or descent, "roots," heritage, or the place of birth of the person, the person's parents, or their ancestors before their arrival in the United States. Some ethnic identities, such as Egyptian or Polish, can be traced to geographic areas outside the United States, while other ethnicities such as Pennsylvania German or Cajun evolved in the United States.

The ancestry question was intended to provide data for groups that were not included in the Hispanic origin and race questions. Therefore, although data on all groups are collected, the ancestry data shown in these tabulations are for non-Hispanic and non-race groups. Hispanic and race groups are included in the "Other groups" category for the ancestry tables in these tabulations.

The ancestry question allowed respondents to report one or more ancestry groups, although only the first two were coded. If a response was in terms of a dual ancestry, for example, "Irish English," the person was assigned two codes, in this case one for Irish and another for English. However, in certain cases, multiple responses such as "French Canadian," "Greek Cypriote," and "Scotch Irish" were assigned a single code reflecting their status as unique groups. If a person reported one of these unique groups in addition to another group, for example, "Scotch Irish English," resulting in three terms, that person received one code for the unique group (Scotch-Irish) and another one for the remaining group (English). If a person reported "English Irish French," only English and Irish were coded. Certain combinations of ancestries where the ancestry group is a part of another, such as "German-Bavarian," were coded as a single ancestry using the more specific group (Bavarian). Also, responses such as "Polish-American" or "Italian-American" were coded and tabulated as a single entry (Polish or Italian).

The Census Bureau accepted "American" as a unique ethnicity if it was given alone, with an ambiguous response, or with state names. If the respondent listed any other ethnic identity such as "Italian-American," generally the "American" portion of the response was not coded. However, distinct groups such as "American Indian," "Mexican American," and "African American" were coded and identified separately because they represented groups who considered themselves different from those who reported as "Indian," "Mexican," or "African," respectively.

The data is based on the total number of ancestries reported and coded. Thus, the sum of the counts in this type of presentation is not the total population but the total of all responses.

ECONOMY

Unemployment Rate: April 2008. Includes all civilians age 16 or over who were unemployed and looking for work. *Source: U.S. Department of Labor, Bureau of Labor Statistics, Local Area Unemployment Statistics (http://www.bls.gov/lau/home.htm).*

Total Civilian Labor Force: April 2008. Includes all civilians age 16 or over who were either employed, or unemployed and looking for work. *Source: U.S. Department of Labor, Bureau of Labor Statistics, Local Area Unemployment Statistics (http://www.bls.gov/lau/home.htm).*

Single-Family Building Permits Issued: Building permits issued for new single-family housing units in 2007. *Source: U.S. Census Bureau, Manufacturing and Construction Division (http://www.census.gov/const/www/permitsindex.html).*

Multi-Family Building Permits Issued: Building permits issued for new multi-family housing units in 2007. *Source: U.S. Census Bureau, Manufacturing and Construction Division (http://www.census.gov/const/www/permitsindex.html).*

Statistics on housing units authorized by building permits include housing units issued in local permit-issuing jurisdictions by a building or zoning permit. Not all areas of the country require a building or zoning permit. The statistics only represent those areas that do require a permit. Current surveys indicate that construction is undertaken for all but a very small percentage of housing units authorized by building permits. A major portion typically get under way during the month of permit issuance and most of the remainder begin within the three following months. Because of this lag, the housing unit authorization statistics do not represent the number of units actually put into construction for the period shown, and should therefore not be directly interpreted as "housing starts."

Statistics are based upon reports submitted by local building permit officials in response to a mail survey. They are obtained using Form C-404 const/www/c404.pdf, "Report of New Privately-Owned Residential Building or Zoning Permits Issued." When a report is not received, missing data are either (1) obtained from the Survey of Use of Permits (SUP) which is used to collect information on housing starts, or (2) imputed based on the assumption that the ratio of current month authorizations to those of a year ago should be the same for reporting and non-reporting places.

Employment by Occupation: Percentage of the employed civilian population 16 years and over in management, professional, service, sales, farming, construction, and production occupations. *Source: U.S. Bureau of the Census, Census of Population and Housing, 2000: Summary File 3.*

- **Management** includes management, business, and financial operations occupations:
  - Management occupations, except farmers and farm managers
  - Farmers and farm managers
  - Business and financial operations occupations:
    - Business operations specialists
    - Financial specialists

- **Professional** includes professional and related occupations:
  - Computer and mathematical occupations
  - Architecture and engineering occupations:
    - Architects, surveyors, cartographers, and engineers
    - Drafters, engineering, and mapping technicians
  - Life, physical, and social science occupations
  - Community and social services occupations
  - Legal occupations
  - Education, training, and library occupations
  - Arts, design, entertainment, sports, and media occupations
  - Healthcare practitioners and technical occupations:
    - Health diagnosing and treating practitioners and technical occupations
    - Health technologists and technicians

- **Service** occupations include:
  - Healthcare support occupations
  - Protective service occupations:
    - Fire fighting, prevention, and law enforcement workers, including supervisors

Other protective service workers, including supervisors
Food preparation and serving related occupations
Building and grounds cleaning and maintenance occupations
Personal care and service occupations

- **Sales** and office occupations include:
  Sales and related occupations
  Office and administrative support occupations

- **Farming,** fishing, and forestry occupations

- **Construction,** extraction, and maintenance occupations include:
  Construction and extraction occupations:
    Supervisors, construction, and extraction workers
    Construction trades workers
    Extraction workers
  Installation, maintenance, and repair occupations

- **Production,** transportation, and material moving occupations include:
  Production occupations
  Transportation and material moving occupations:
    Supervisors, transportation, and material moving workers
    Aircraft and traffic control occupations
    Motor vehicle operators
    Rail, water, and other transportation occupations
    Material moving workers

INCOME

Per Capita Income: Per capita income is the mean income computed for every man, woman, and child in a particular group. It is derived by dividing the total income of a particular group by the total population in that group. Per capita income is rounded to the nearest whole dollar. Figures shown are 2007 estimates. *Source: Claritas.*

Median Household Income: Includes the income of the householder and all other individuals 15 years old and over in the household, whether they are related to the householder or not. The median divides the income distribution into two equal parts: one-half of the cases falling below the median income and one-half above the median. For households, the median income is based on the distribution of the total number of households including those with no income. Median income for households is computed on the basis of a standard distribution and is rounded to the nearest whole dollar. Figures shown are 2007 estimates. *Source: Claritas.*

Average Household Income: Average household income is obtained by dividing total household income by the total number of households. Figures shown are 2007 estimates. *Source: Claritas.*

Percent of Households with Income of $100,000 or more: Figures shown are 2007 estimates. *Source: Claritas.*

Poverty Rate: Percentage of population with income in 1999 below the poverty level. Based on individuals for whom poverty status is determined. Poverty status was determined for all people except institutionalized people, people in military group quarters, people in college dormitories, and unrelated individuals under 15 years old. *Source: U.S. Bureau of the Census, Census of Population and Housing, 2000: Summary File 3.*

The poverty status of families and unrelated individuals in 1999 was determined using 48 thresholds (income cutoffs) arranged in a two-dimensional matrix. The matrix consists of family size (from 1 person to 9 or more people) cross-classified by presence and number of family members under 18 years old (from no children present to 8 or more children present). Unrelated individuals and 2-person families were further differentiated by the age of the reference person (RP) (under 65 years old and 65 years old and over).

To determine a person's poverty status, one compares the person's total family income with the poverty threshold appropriate for that person's family size and composition. If the total income of that person's family is less than the threshold appropriate for that family, then the person is considered poor, together with every member of his or her family. If a person is not living with anyone related by birth, marriage, or adoption, then the person's own income is compared with his or her poverty threshold.

TAXES

Total City Taxes Per Capita: Total city taxes collected divided by the population of the city. *Source: U.S. Bureau of the Census, State and Local Government Finances, 2005-06 (http://www.census.gov/govs/www/estimate.html).*

Taxes include:

- Property Taxes
- Sales and Gross Receipts Taxes
- Federal Customs Duties
- General Sales and Gross Receipts Taxes
- Selective Sales Taxes (alcoholic beverages; amusements; insurance premiums; motor fuels; pari-mutuels; public utilities; tobacco products; other)
- License Taxes (alcoholic beverages; amusements; corporations in general; hunting and fishing; motor vehicles motor vehicle operators; public utilities; occupation and business, NEC; other)
- Income Taxes (individual income; corporation net income; other)
- Death and Gift
- Documentary & Stock Transfer
- Severance
- Taxes, NEC

Total City Property Taxes Per Capita: Total city property taxes collected divided by the population of the city. *Source: U.S. Bureau of the Census, State and Local Government Finances, 2005-06 (http://www.census.gov/govs/www/estimate.html).*

Property Taxes include general property taxes, relating to property as a whole, taxed at a single rate or at classified rates according to the class of property. Property refers to real property (e.g. land and structures) as well as personal property; personal property can be either tangible (e.g. automobiles and boats) or intangible (e.g. bank accounts and stocks and bonds). Special property taxes, levied on selected types of property (e.g. oil and gas properties, house trailers, motor vehicles, and intangibles) and subject to rates not directly related to general property tax rates. Taxes based on income produced by property as a measure of its value on the assessment date.

EDUCATION

Educational Attainment: Figures shown are 2007 estimates and show the percent of population age 25 and over with a:

- **High school diploma (including GED) or higher:** includes people whose highest degree was a high school diploma or its equivalent, people who attended college but did not receive a degree, and people who received a college, university, or professional degree. People who reported completing the 12th grade but not receiving a diploma are not high school graduates.
- **Bachelor's degree or higher**
- **Master's degree or higher:** Master's degrees include the traditional MA and MS degrees and field-specific degrees, such as MSW, MEd, MBA, MLS, and Meng. *Source: Claritas.*

School Districts: Lists the name of each school district, the grade range (PK=pre-kindergarten; KG=kindergarten), the student enrollment, and the district headquarters' phone number. In each community profile, only school districts that have schools that are physically located within the community are shown. In addition, statistics for each school district cover the entire district, regardless of the physical location of the schools within the district. *Source: U.S. Department of Education, National Center for Educational Statistics, Directory of Public Elementary and Secondary Education Agencies, 2005-06.*

Four-year Colleges: Lists the name of each four-year college, the type of institution (private or public; for-profit or non-profit; religious affiliation; historically black), the total student enrollment (Fall 2007 estimate), the general telephone number, and the annual tuition (including fees) for full-time, first-time undergraduate students (in-state and out-of-state). *Source: U.S. Department of Education, National Center for Educational Statistics, IPEDS College Data, 2007-08.*

Two-year Colleges: Lists the name of each two-year college, the type of institution (private or public; for-profit or non-profit; religious affiliation; historically black), the total student enrollment (Fall 2007 estimate), the general telephone number, and the annual tuition (including fees) for full-time, first-time undergraduate students (in-state and out-of-state). *Source: U.S. Department of Education, National Center for Educational Statistics, IPEDS College Data, 2007-08.*

Vocational/Technical Schools: Lists the name of each vocational/technical school, the type of institution (private or public; for-profit or non-profit; religious affiliation; historically black), the total student enrollment (Fall 2007 estimate), the general telephone number, and the annual tuition and fees for full-time students. *Source: U.S. Department of Education, National Center for Educational Statistics, IPEDS College Data, 2007-08.*

HOUSING

Homeownership Rate: Percentage of housing units that are owner-occupied. Figures shown are 2007 estimates. *Source: Claritas.*

Median Home Value: Median value of all owner-occupied housing units as reported by the owner. Figures shown are 2007 estimates. *Source: Claritas.*

Median Rent: Median monthly contract rent on specified renter-occupied and specified vacant-for-rent units. Specified renter-occupied and specified vacant-for-rent units exclude 1-family houses on 10 acres or more. Contract rent is the monthly rent agreed to or contracted for, regardless of any furnishings, utilities, fees, meals, or services that may be included. For vacant units, it is the monthly rent asked for the rental unit at the time of enumeration. *Source: U.S. Bureau of the Census, Census of Population and Housing, 2000: Summary File 3.*

Median Age of Housing: Median age of housing was calculated by subtracting median year structure built from 2000 (e.g. if the median year structure built is 1967, the median age of housing in that area is 33 years—2000 minus 1967). Year structure built refers to when the building was first constructed, not when it was remodeled, added to, or converted. For housing units under construction that met the housing unit definition—that is, all exterior windows, doors, and final usable floors were in place—the category "1999 or 2000" was used for tabulations. For mobile homes, houseboats, RVs, etc, the manufacturer's model year was assumed to be the year built. The data relate to the number of units built during the specified periods that were still in existence at the time of enumeration. *Source: U.S. Bureau of the Census, Census of Population and Housing, 2000: Summary File 3.*

HOSPITALS

Lists the hospital name and the number of licensed beds. *Source: Grey House Publishing, Directory of Hospital Personnel, 2007.*

SAFETY

Violent Crime Rate: Number of violent crimes reported per 10,000 population. Violent crimes include murder, forcible rape, robbery, and aggravated assault. *Source: Illinois State Police, Crime in Illinois 2006 (http://www.isp.state.il.us/crime/).*

Property Crime Rate: Number of property crimes reported per 10,000 population. Property crimes include burglary, larceny-theft, and motor vehicle theft. *Source: Illinois State Police, Crime in Illinois 2006 (http://www.isp.state.il.us/crime/).*

NEWSPAPERS

Lists the name, circulation and news focus of daily and weekly newspapers. Includes newspapers with offices located in the community profiled. *Source: MediaContactsPro 2008*

TRANSPORTATION

Commute to Work: Percentage of workers 16 years old and over that use the following means of transportation to commute to work: car; public transportation; walk; work from home. *Source: U.S. Bureau of the Census, Census of Population and Housing, 2000: Summary File 3.*

The means of transportation data for some areas may show workers using modes of public transportation that are not available in those areas (e.g. subway or elevated riders in a metropolitan area where there actually is no subway or elevated service). This result is largely due to people who worked during the reference week at a location that was different from their usual place of work (such as people away from home on business in an area where subway service was available) and people who used more than one means of transportation each day but whose principal means was unavailable where they lived (e.g. residents of non-metropolitan areas who drove to the fringe of a metropolitan area and took the commuter railroad most of the distance to work).

Travel Time to Work: Travel time to work for workers 16 years old and over. Reported for the following intervals: less than 15 minutes; 15 to 30 minutes; 30 to 45 minutes; 45 to 60 minutes; 60 minutes or more. *Source: U.S. Bureau of the Census, Census of Population and Housing, 2000: Summary File 3.*

Travel time to work refers to the total number of minutes that it usually took the person to get from home to work each day during the reference week. The elapsed time includes time spent waiting for public transportation, picking up passengers in carpools, and time spent in other activities related to getting to work.

Amtrak: Indicates if Amtrak service is available. Please note that the cities being served continually change. *Source: National Railroad Passenger Corporation, Amtrak National Timetable, 2008 (www.amtrak.com).*

AIRPORTS

Lists the local airport(s) along with type of service and hub size. *Source: U.S. Department of Transportation, Bureau of Transportation Statistics (http://www.bts.gov).*

ADDITIONAL INFORMATION CONTACTS

The following phone numbers are provided as sources of additional information: Chambers of Commerce; Economic Development Agencies; and Convention & Visitors Bureaus. Efforts have been made to provide the most recent area codes. However, area code changes may have occurred in listed numbers. *Source: Original research.*

Information for Counties

PHYSICAL CHARACTERISTICS

Physical Location: Describes the physical location of the county. *Source: Columbia University Press, The Columbia Gazetteer of North America and original research.*

Land and Water Area: Land and water area in square miles. *Source: U.S. Bureau of the Census, Census of Population and Housing, 2000: Summary File 1.*

Time Zone: Lists the time zone. *Source: Original research.*

Year Organized: Year the county government was organized. *Source: National Association of Counties (www.naco.org).*

County Seat: Lists the county seat. If a county has more than one seat, then both are listed. *Source: National Association of Counties (www.naco.org).*

Metropolitan Area: Indicates the metropolitan area the county is located in. Also lists all the component counties of that metropolitan area. The Office of Management and Budget (OMB) defines metropolitan and micropolitan statistical areas. The most current definitions are as of November 2007. *Source: U.S. Bureau of the Census (http://www.census.gov/population/www/estimates/metrodef.html).*

Climate: Includes all weather stations located within the county. Indicates the station name and elevation as well as the monthly average high and low temperatures, average precipitation, and average snowfall. The period of record is generally 1970-1999, however, certain weather stations contain averages going back as far as 1900. *Source: Grey House Publishing, Weather America: A Thirty-Year Summary of Statistical Weather Data and Rankings, 2001.*

POPULATION

Population: 1990 and 2000 figures are a 100% count of population. 2007 estimates and 2012 projections were provided by Claritas. *Source: Claritas; U.S. Bureau of the Census, Census of Population and Housing, 2000: Summary File 1.*

Population by Race: 2007 estimates includes the U.S. Bureau of the Census categories of White alone; Black alone; Asian alone; and Hispanic of any race. Alone refers to the fact that these figures are not in combination with any other race. 2007 data for American Indian/Alaska Native and Native Hawaiian/Other Pacific Islander was not available.

The concept of race, as used by the Census Bureau, reflects self-identification by people according to the race or races with which they most closely identify. These categories are socio-political constructs and should not be interpreted as being scientific or anthropological in nature. Furthermore, the race categories include both racial and national-origin groups.

- **White.** A person having origins in any of the original peoples of Europe, the Middle East, or North Africa. It includes people who indicate their race as "White" or report entries such as Irish, German, Italian, Lebanese, Near Easterner, Arab, or Polish.
- **Black or African American.** A person having origins in any of the Black racial groups of Africa. It includes people who indicate their race as "Black, African American, or Negro," or provide written entries such as African American, Afro-American, Kenyan, Nigerian, or Haitian.
- **Asian.** A person having origins in any of the original peoples of the Far East, Southeast Asia, or the Indian subcontinent including, for example, Cambodia, China, India, Japan, Korea, Malaysia, Pakistan, the Philippine Islands, Thailand, and Vietnam. It includes "Asian Indian," "Chinese," "Filipino," "Korean," "Japanese," "Vietnamese," and "Other Asian."
- **Hispanic.** The data on the Hispanic or Latino population, which was asked of all people, were derived from answers to long-form questionnaire Item 5, and short-form questionnaire Item 7. The terms "Spanish," "Hispanic origin," and "Latino" are used interchangeably. Some respondents identify with all three terms, while others may identify with only one of these three specific terms. Hispanics or Latinos who identify with the terms "Spanish," "Hispanic," or "Latino" are those who classify themselves in one of the specific Hispanic or Latino categories listed on the questionnaire — "Mexican," "Puerto Rican," or "Cuban" — as well as those who indicate that they are "other Spanish, Hispanic, or Latino." People who do not identify with one of the specific origins listed on the questionnaire but indicate that they are "other

Spanish, Hispanic, or Latino" are those whose origins are from Spain, the Spanish-speaking countries of Central or South America, the Dominican Republic, or people identifying themselves generally as Spanish, Spanish-American, Hispanic, Hispano, Latino, and so on. All write-in responses to the "other Spanish/Hispanic/Latino" category were coded. Origin can be viewed as the heritage, nationality group, lineage, or country of birth of the person or the person's parents or ancestors before their arrival in the United States. People who identify their origin as Spanish, Hispanic, or Latino may be of any race.

Population Density: 2007 population estimate divided by the land area in square miles. *Source: Claritas; U.S. Bureau of the Census, Census of Population and Housing, 2000: Summary File 1.*

Average Household Size: Average household size was calculated by dividing the total population by the total number of households. Figures are 2007 estimates. *Source: Claritas.*

Median Age: Figures are 2007 estimates. *Source: Claritas.*

Male/Female Ratio: Number of males per 100 females. Figures are 2007 estimates. *Source: Claritas.*

RELIGION

Religion: Lists the largest religious groups (up to five) based on the number of adherents divided by the population of the county. Adherents are defined as "all members, including full members, their children and the estimated number of other regular participants who are not considered as communicant, confirmed or full members." The data is based on a study of 149 religious bodies sponsored by the Association of Statisticians of American Religious Bodies. The 149 bodies reported 268,254 congregations and 141,371,963 adherents. *Source: Glenmary Research Center, Religious Congregations & Membership in the United States 2000.*

ECONOMY

Unemployment Rate: April 2008. Includes all civilians age 16 or over who were unemployed and looking for work. *Source: U.S. Department of Labor, Bureau of Labor Statistics, Local Area Unemployment Statistics (http://www.bls.gov/lau/home.htm).*

Total Civilian Labor Force: April 2008. Includes all civilians age 16 or over who were either employed, or unemployed and looking for work. *Source: U.S. Department of Labor, Bureau of Labor Statistics, Local Area Unemployment Statistics (http://www.bls.gov/lau/home.htm).*

Leading Industries: Lists the three largest industries (excluding government) based on the number of employees. *Source: U.S. Bureau of the Census, County Business Patterns 2006 (http://www.census.gov/epcd/cbp/view/cbpview.html).*

Farms: The total number of farms and the total acreage they occupy. *Source: U.S. Department of Agriculture, National Agricultural Statistics Service, 2002 Census of Agriculture (http://www.nass.usda.gov/census).*

Companies that Employ 500 or more persons: The numbers of companies that employ 500 or more persons. Includes private employers only. *Source: U.S. Bureau of the Census, County Business Patterns 2006 (http://www.census.gov/epcd/cbp/view/cbpview.html).*

Companies that Employ 100 - 499 persons: The numbers of companies that employ 100 - 499 persons. Includes private employers only. *Source: U.S. Bureau of the Census, County Business Patterns 2006 (http://www.census.gov/epcd/cbp/view/cbpview.html).*

Companies that Employ 1 - 99 persons: The numbers of companies that employ 1 - 99 persons. Includes private employers only. *Source: U.S. Bureau of the Census, County Business Patterns 2006 (http://www.census.gov/epcd/cbp/view/cbpview.html)*

Black-Owned Businesses: Number of businesses that are majority-owned by a Black or African-American person(s). Majority ownership is defined as having 51 percent or more of the stock or equity in the business. Black or African American is defined as a person having origins in any of the black racial groups of Africa, including those who consider themselves to be "Haitian." *Source: U.S. Bureau of the Census, 2002 Economic Census, Survey of Business Owners: Black-Owned Firms, 2002 (http://www.census.gov/csd/sbo/index.html).*

Asian-Owned Businesses: Number of businesses that are majority-owned by an Asian person(s). Majority ownership is defined as having 51 percent or more of the stock or equity in the business. *Source: U.S. Bureau of the Census, 2002 Economic Census, Survey of Business Owners: Black-Owned Firms, 2002 (http://www.census.gov/csd/sbo/index.html).*

Hispanic-Owned Businesses: Number of businesses that are majority-owned by a person(s) of Hispanic or Latino origin. Majority ownership is defined as having 51 percent or more of the stock or equity in the business. Hispanic or Latino origin is defined as a person of Cuban, Mexican, Puerto Rican, South or Central American, or other Spanish culture or origin, regardless of race. *Source: U.S. Bureau of the Census, 2002 Economic Census, Survey of Business Owners: Hispanic-Owned Firms, 2002 (http://www.census.gov/csd/sbo/index.html).*

Women-Owned Businesses: Number of businesses that are majority-owned by a woman. Majority ownership is defined as having 51 percent or more of the stock or equity in the business. *Source: U.S. Bureau of the Census, 2002 Economic Census, Survey of Business Owners: Women-Owned Firms, 2002 (http://www.census.gov/csd/sbo/index.html).*

The Survey of Business Owners (SBO), formerly known as the Surveys of Minority- and Women-Owned Business Enterprises (SMOBE/SWOBE), provides statistics that describe the composition of U.S. businesses by gender, Hispanic or Latino origin, and race. Additional statistics include owner's age, education level, veteran status, and primary function in the business; family- and home-based businesses; types of customers and workers; and sources of financing for expansion, capital improvements, or start-up. Economic policymakers in federal, state and local governments use the SBO data to understand conditions of business success and failure by comparing census-to-census changes in business performances and by comparing minority-/nonminority- and women-/men-owned businesses.

Retail Sales per Capita: Total dollar amount of estimated retail sales divided by the estimated population of the county in 2008. *Source: Editor & Publisher Market Guide 2008*

Single-Family Building Permits Issued: Building permits issued for new, single-family housing units in 2007. *Source: U.S. Census Bureau, Manufacturing and Construction Division (http://www.census.gov/const/www/permitsindex.html).*

Multi-Family Building Permits Issued: Building permits issued for new, multi-family housing units in 2007. *Source: U.S. Census Bureau, Manufacturing and Construction Division (http://www.census.gov/const/www/permitsindex.html).*

Statistics on housing units authorized by building permits include housing units issued in local permit-issuing jurisdictions by a building or zoning permit. Not all areas of the country require a building or zoning permit. The statistics only represent those areas that do require a permit. Current surveys indicate that construction is undertaken for all but a very small percentage of housing units authorized by building permits. A major portion typically get under way during the month of permit issuance and most of the remainder begin within the three following months. Because of this lag, the housing unit authorization statistics do not represent the number of units actually put into construction for the period shown, and should therefore not be directly interpreted as "housing starts."

Statistics are based upon reports submitted by local building permit officials in response to a mail survey. They are obtained using Form C-404 const/www/c404.pdf, "Report of New Privately-Owned Residential Building or Zoning Permits Issued." When a report is not received, missing data are either (1) obtained from the Survey of Use of Permits (SUP) which is used to collect information on housing starts, or (2) imputed based on the assumption that the ratio of current month authorizations to those of a year ago should be the same for reporting and non-reporting places.

INCOME

Per Capita Income: Per capita income is the mean income computed for every man, woman, and child in a particular group. It is derived by dividing the total income of a particular group by the total population in that group. Per capita income is rounded to the nearest whole dollar. Figures shown are 2007 estimates. *Source: Claritas.*

Median Household Income: Includes the income of the householder and all other individuals 15 years old and over in the household, whether they are related to the householder or not. The median divides the income distribution into two equal parts: one-half of the cases falling below the median income and one-half above the median. For households, the median income is based on the distribution of the total number of households including those with no income. Median income for households is computed on the basis of a standard distribution and is rounded to the nearest whole dollar. Figures shown are 2007 estimates. *Source: Claritas.*

Average Household Income: Average household income is obtained by dividing total household income by the total number of households. Figures shown are 2007 estimates. *Source: Claritas.*

Percent of Households with Income of $100,000 or more: Figures shown are 2007 estimates. *Source: Claritas.*

Poverty Rate: Estimated percentage of population with income in 2005 below the poverty level. *Source: U.S. Bureau of the Census, Small Area Income & Poverty Estimates.*

Bankruptcy Rate: The personal bankruptcy filing rate is the number of bankruptcies per thousand residents in 2007. Personal bankruptcy filings include both Chapter 7 (liquidations) and Chapter 13 (reorganizations) based on the county of residence of the filer. *Source: Federal Deposit Insurance Corporation, Regional Economic Conditions (http://www2.fdic.gov/recon/index.html).*

TAXES

Total County Taxes Per Capita: Total county taxes collected divided by the population of the county. *Source: U.S. Bureau of the Census, State and Local Government Finances, 2005-06 (http://www.census.gov/govs/www/estimate.html).*

Taxes include:

- Property Taxes
- Sales and Gross Receipts Taxes
- Federal Customs Duties
- General Sales and Gross Receipts Taxes
- Selective Sales Taxes (alcoholic beverages; amusements; insurance premiums; motor fuels; pari-mutuels; public utilities; tobacco products; other)
- License Taxes (alcoholic beverages; amusements; corporations in general; hunting and fishing; motor vehicles motor vehicle operators; public utilities; occupation and business, NEC; other)
- Income Taxes (individual income; corporation net income; other)
- Death and Gift
- Documentary & Stock Transfer
- Severance
- Taxes, NEC

Total County Property Taxes Per Capita: Total county property taxes collected divided by the population of the county. *Source: U.S. Bureau of the Census, State and Local Government Finances, 2005-06 (http://www.census.gov/govs/www/estimate.html).*

Property Taxes include general property taxes, relating to property as a whole, taxed at a single rate or at classified rates according to the class of property. Property refers to real property (e.g. land and structures) as well as personal property; personal property can be either tangible (e.g. automobiles and boats) or intangible (e.g. bank accounts and stocks and bonds). Special property taxes, levied on selected types of property (e.g. oil and gas properties, house trailers, motor vehicles, and intangibles) and subject to rates not directly related to general property tax rates. Taxes based on income produced by property as a measure of its value on the assessment date.

EDUCATION

Educational Attainment: Figures shown are 2007 estimates and show the percent of population age 25 and over with a:

- **High school diploma (including GED) or higher:** includes people whose highest degree was a high school diploma or its equivalent, people who attended college but did not receive a degree, and people who received a college, university, or professional degree. People who reported completing the 12th grade but not receiving a diploma are not high school graduates.
- **Bachelor's degree or higher**
- **Master's degree or higher:** Master's degrees include the traditional MA and MS degrees and field-specific degrees, such as MSW, MEd, MBA, MLS, and Meng. *Source: Claritas.*

HOUSING

Homeownership Rate: Percentage of housing units that are owner-occupied. Figures shown are 2007 estimates. *Source: Claritas.*

Median Home Value: Median value of all owner-occupied housing units as reported by the owner. Figures shown are 2007 estimates. *Source: Claritas.*

Median Rent: Median monthly contract rent on specified renter-occupied and specified vacant-for-rent units. Specified renter-occupied and specified vacant-for-rent units exclude 1-family houses on 10 acres or more. Contract rent is the monthly rent agreed to or contracted for, regardless of any furnishings, utilities, fees, meals, or services that may be included. For vacant units, it is the monthly rent asked for the rental unit at the time of enumeration. *Source: U.S. Bureau of the Census, Census of Population and Housing, 2000: Summary File 3.*

Median Age of Housing: Median age of housing was calculated by subtracting median year structure built from 2000 (e.g. if the median year structure built is 1967, the median age of housing in that area is 33 years — 2000 minus 1967). Year structure built refers to when the building was first constructed, not when it was remodeled, added to, or converted. For housing units under construction that met the housing unit definition—that is, all exterior windows, doors, and final usable floors were in place—the category "1999 or 2000" was used for tabulations. For mobile homes, houseboats, RVs, etc, the manufacturer's model year was assumed to be the year built. The data relate to the number of units built during the specified periods that were still in existence at the time of enumeration. *Source: U.S. Bureau of the Census, Census of Population and Housing, 2000: Summary File 3.*

HEALTH AND VITAL STATISTICS

Birth Rate: Estimated number of births per 10,000 population in 2007. *Source: U.S. Census Bureau, Annual Components of Population Change, July 1, 2006 - July 1 , 2007 (http://www.census.gov/popest/births.html).*

Death Rate: Estimated number of deaths per 10,000 population in 2007. *Source: U.S. Census Bureau, Annual Components of Population Change, July 1, 2006 - July 1 , 2007 (http://www.census.gov/popest/births.html).*

Age-adjusted Cancer Mortality Rate: Number of age-adjusted deaths from cancer per 100,000 population in 2005. Cancer is defined as International Classification of Disease (ICD) codes C00 - D48.9 Neoplasms. *Source: Centers for Disease Control, CDC Wonder (http://wonder.cdc.gov).*

Age-adjusted death rates are weighted averages of the age-specific death rates, where the weights represent a fixed population by age. They are used because the rates of almost all causes of death vary by age. Age adjustment is a technique for "removing" the effects of age from crude rates, so as to allow meaningful comparisons across populations with different underlying age structures. For example, comparing the crude rate of heart disease in New York to that of California is misleading, because the relatively older population in New York will lead to a higher crude death rate, even if the age-specific rates of heart disease in New York and California are the same. For such a comparison, age-adjusted rates would be preferable. Age-adjusted rates should be viewed as relative indexes rather than as direct or actual measures of mortality risk.

Death rates based on counts of twenty or less (<=20) are flagged as "Unreliable". Death rates based on fewer than three years of data for counties with populations of less than 100,000 in the 1990 Census counts, are also flagged as "Unreliable" if the number of deaths is five or less (<=5).

Air Quality Index: The percentage of days in 2007 the AQI fell into the Good (0-50), Moderate (51-100), Unhealthy for Sensitive Groups (101-150), and Unhealthy (151+) ranges. Data covers January 2007 through December 2007. Counties with less than 100 days of air quality data were excluded. *Source: AirData: Access to Air Pollution Data , U.S. Environmental Protection Agency, Office of Air and Radiation (http://www.epa.gov/air/data/index.html).*

The AQI is an index for reporting daily air quality. It tells you how clean or polluted your air is, and what associated health concerns you should be aware of. The AQI focuses on health effects that can happen within a few hours or days after breathing polluted air. EPA uses the AQI for five major air pollutants regulated by the Clean Air Act: ground-level ozone, particulate matter, carbon monoxide, sulfur dioxide, and nitrogen dioxide. For each of these pollutants, EPA has established national air quality standards to protect against harmful health effects.

The AQI runs from 0 to 500. The higher the AQI value, the greater the level of air pollution and the greater the health danger. For example, an AQI value of 50 represents good air quality and little potential to affect public health, while an AQI value over 300 represents hazardous air quality. An AQI value of 100 generally corresponds to the national air quality standard for the pollutant, which is the level EPA has set to protect public health. So, AQI values below 100 are generally thought of as satisfactory. When AQI values are above 100, air quality is considered to be unhealthy—at first for certain sensitive groups of people, then for everyone as AQI values get higher. Each category corresponds to a different level of health concern. For example, when the AQI for a pollutant is between 51 and 100, the health concern is "Moderate." Here are the six levels of health concern and what they mean:

- "Good" The AQI value for your community is between 0 and 50. Air quality is considered satisfactory and air pollution poses little or no risk.
- "Moderate" The AQI for your community is between 51 and 100. Air quality is acceptable; however, for some pollutants there may be a moderate health concern for a very small number of individuals. For example, people who are unusually sensitive to ozone may experience respiratory symptoms.
- "Unhealthy for Sensitive Groups" Certain groups of people are particularly sensitive to the harmful effects of certain air pollutants. This means they are likely to be affected at lower levels than the general public. For example, children and adults who are active outdoors and people with respiratory disease are at greater risk from exposure to ozone, while people with heart disease are at greater risk from carbon monoxide. Some people may be sensitive to more than one pollutant. When AQI values are between 101 and 150, members of sensitive groups may experience health effects. The general public is not likely to be affected when the AQI is in this range.
- "Unhealthy" AQI values are between 151 and 200. Everyone may begin to experience health effects. Members of sensitive groups may experience more serious health effects.
- "Very Unhealthy" AQI values between 201 and 300 trigger a health alert, meaning everyone may experience more serious health effects.
- "Hazardous" AQI values over 300 trigger health warnings of emergency conditions. The entire population is more likely to be affected.

Number of Physicians: The number of active, non-federal physicians per 10,000 population in 2005. *Source: Area Resource File (ARF). 2006 Release. U.S. Department of Health and Human Services, Health Resources and Services Administration, Bureau of Health Professions, Rockville, MD, June 2007.*

Number of Hospital Beds: The number of hospital beds per 10,000 population in 2004. *Source: Area Resource File (ARF). 2006 Release. U.S. Department of Health and Human Services, Health Resources and Services Administration, Bureau of Health Professions, Rockville, MD, June 2007.*

Number of Hospital Admissions: The number of hospital admissions per 10,000 population in 2004. *Source: Area Resource File (ARF). 2006 Release. U.S. Department of Health and Human Services, Health Resources and Services Administration, Bureau of Health Professions, Rockville, MD, June 2007.*

ELECTIONS

Elections: 2004 Presidential election results. *Source: Dave Leip's Atlas of U.S. Presidential Elections (http://www.uselectionatlas.org).*

NATIONAL AND STATE PARKS

Lists National and State parks located in the area. *Source: U.S. Geological Survey, Geographic Names Information System.*

ADDITIONAL INFORMATION CONTACTS

The following phone numbers are provided as sources of additional information: Chambers of Commerce; Economic Development Agencies; and Convention & Visitors Bureaus. Efforts have been made to provide the most recent area codes. However, area code changes may have occurred in listed numbers. *Source: Original research.*

User's Guide: Education

School District Rankings

Number of Schools: Total number of schools in the district. *Source: U.S. Department of Education, National Center for Education Statistics, Common Core of Data, Public Elementary/Secondary School Universe Survey: School Year 2005-2006.*

Number of Teachers: Teachers are defined as individuals who provide instruction to pre-kindergarten, kindergarten, grades 1 through 12, or ungraded classes, or individuals who teach in an environment other than a classroom setting, and who maintain daily student attendance records. Numbers reported are full-time equivalents (FTE). *Source: U.S. Department of Education, National Center for Education Statistics, Common Core of Data, Local Education Agency (School District) Universe Survey: School Year 2005-2006.*

Number of Students: A student is an individual for whom instruction is provided in an elementary or secondary education program that is not an adult education program and is under the jurisdiction of a school, school system, or other education institution. *Sources: U.S. Department of Education, National Center for Education Statistics, Common Core of Data, Local Education Agency (School District) Universe Survey: School Year 2005-2006 and Public Elementary/Secondary School Universe Survey: School Year 2005-2006*

Individual Education Program (IEP) Students: A written instructional plan for students with disabilities designated as special education students under IDEA-Part B. The written instructional plan includes a statement of present levels of educational performance of a child; statement of annual goals, including short-term instructional objectives; statement of specific educational services to be provided and the extent to which the child will be able to participate in regular educational programs; the projected date for initiation and anticipated duration of services; the appropriate objectives, criteria and evaluation procedures; and the schedules for determining, on at least an annual basis, whether instructional objectives are being achieved. *Source: U.S. Department of Education, National Center for Education Statistics, Common Core of Data, Local Education Agency (School District) Universe Survey: School Year 2005-2006*

English Language Learner (ELL) Students: Formerly referred to as Limited English Proficient (LEP). Students being served in appropriate programs of language assistance (e.g., English as a Second Language, High Intensity Language Training, bilingual education). Does not include pupils enrolled in a class to learn a language other than English. Also Limited-English-Proficient students are individuals who were not born in the United States or whose native language is a language other than English; or individuals who come from environments where a language other than English is dominant; or individuals who are American Indians and Alaskan Natives and who come from environments where a language other than English has had a significant impact on their level of English language proficiency; and who, by reason thereof, have sufficient difficulty speaking, reading, writing, or understanding the English language, to deny such individuals the opportunity to learn successfully in classrooms where the language of instruction is English or to participate fully in our society. *Source: U.S. Department of Education, National Center for Education Statistics, Common Core of Data, Local Education Agency (School District) Universe Survey: School Year 2005-2006*

Migrant Students: A migrant student as defined under federal regulation 34 CFR 200.40: 1) (a) Is younger than 22 (and has not graduated from high school or does not hold a high school equivalency certificate), but (b), if the child is too young to attend school-sponsored educational programs, is old enough to benefit from an organized instructional program; and 2) A migrant agricultural worker or a migrant fisher or has a parent, spouse, or guardian who is a migrant agricultural worker or a migrant fisher; and 3) Performs, or has a parent, spouse, or guardian who performs qualifying agricultural or fishing employment as a principal means of livelihood; and 4) Has moved within the preceding 36 months to obtain or to accompany or join a parent, spouse, or guardian to obtain, temporary or seasonal employment in agricultural or fishing work; and 5) Has moved from one school district to another; or in a state that is comprised of a single school district, has moved from one administrative area to another within such district; or resides in a school district of more than 15,000 square miles, and migrates a distance of 20 miles or more to a temporary residence to engage in a fishing activity. Provision 5 currently applies only to Alaska. *Note: Data covers the 2004-2005 school year. Source: U.S. Department of Education, National Center for Education Statistics, Common Core of Data, Public Elementary/Secondary School Universe Survey: School Year 2005-2006*

Students Eligible for Free Lunch Program: The free lunch program is defined as a program under the National School Lunch Act that provides cash subsidies for free lunches to students based on family size and income criteria. *Source: U.S. Department of Education, National Center for Education Statistics, Common Core of Data, Public Elementary/Secondary School Universe Survey: School Year 2005-2006*

Students Eligible for Reduced-Price Lunch Program: A student who is eligible to participate in the Reduced-Price Lunch Program under the National School Lunch Act. *Source: U.S. Department of Education, National Center for Education Statistics, Common Core of Data, Public Elementary/Secondary School Universe Survey: School Year 2005-2006*

Student/Teacher Ratio: The number of students divided by the number of teachers (FTE). See Number of Students and Number of Teachers above for for information.

Student/Librarian Ratio: The number of students divided by the number of library and media support staff. Library and media support staff are defined as staff members who render other professional library and media services; also includes library aides and those involved in library/media support. Their duties include selecting, preparing, caring for, and making available to instructional staff, equipment, films, filmstrips, transparencies, tapes, TV programs, and similar materials maintained separately or as part of an instructional materials center. Also included are activities in the audio-visual center, TV studio, related-work-study areas, and services provided by audio-visual personnel. Numbers are based on full-time equivalents. *Source: U.S. Department of Education, National Center for Education Statistics, Common Core of Data, Local Education Agency (School District) Universe Survey: School Year 2005-2006.*

Student/Counselor Ratio: The number of students divided by the number of guidance counselors. Guidance counselors are professional staff assigned specific duties and school time for any of the following activities in an elementary or secondary setting: counseling with students and parents; consulting with other staff members on learning problems; evaluating student abilities; assisting students in making educational and career choices; assisting students in personal and social development; providing referral assistance; and/or working with other staff members in planning and conducting guidance programs for students. The state applies its own standards in apportioning the aggregate of guidance counselors/directors into the elementary and secondary level components. Numbers reported are full-time equivalents. *Source: U.S. Department of Education, National Center for Education Statistics, Common Core of Data, Local Education Agency (School District) Universe Survey: School Year 2005-2006.*

Current Spending per Student: Expenditure for Instruction, Support Services, and Other Elementary/Secondary Programs. Includes salaries, employee benefits, purchased services, and supplies, as well as payments made by states on behalf of school districts. Also includes transfers made by school districts into their own retirement system. Excludes expenditure for Non-Elementary/Secondary Programs, debt service, capital outlay, and transfers to other governments or school districts. This item is formally called "Current Expenditures for Public Elementary/Secondary Education."

Instruction: Includes payments from all funds for salaries, employee benefits, supplies, materials, and contractual services for elementary/secondary instruction. It excludes capital outlay, debt service, and interfund transfers for elementary/secondary instruction. Instruction covers regular, special, and vocational programs offered in both the regular school year and summer school. It excludes instructional support activities as well as adult education and community services. Instruction salaries includes salaries for teachers and teacher aides and assistants.

Support Services: Relates to support services functions (series 2000) defined in Financial Accounting for Local and State School Systems (National Center for Education Statistics 2000). Includes payments from all funds for salaries, employee benefits, supplies, materials, and contractual services. It excludes capital outlay, debt service, and interfund transfers. It includes expenditure for the following functions:

- Business/Central/Other Support Services
- General Administration
- Instructional Staff Support
- Operation and Maintenance
- Pupil Support Services
- Pupil Transportation Services
- School Administration
- Nonspecified Support Services

Values shown are dollars per pupil per year. They were calculated by dividing the total dollar amounts by the fall membership. Fall membership is comprised of the total student enrollment on October 1 (or the closest school day to October 1) for all grade levels (including prekindergarten and kindergarten) and ungraded pupils. Membership includes students both present and absent on the measurement day. *Source: U.S. Department of Education, National Center for Education Statistics, Common Core of Data, School District Finance Survey (F-33), Fiscal Year 2005.*

Number of Diploma Recipients: A student who has received a diploma during the previous school year or subsequent summer school. This category includes regular diploma recipients and other diploma recipients. A High School Diploma is a formal document certifying the successful completion of a secondary school program prescribed by the state education agency or other appropriate body. *Note: The National Center for Education Statistics has not released more current district level data due to privacy issues. Source: U.S. Department of Education, National Center for Education Statistics, Common Core of Data, Local Education Agency (School District) Universe Survey: School Year 2002-2003. State data covers the 2004-2005 school year and comes from the Common Core of Data, State Nonfiscal Survey of Public Elementary/Secondary Education, 2005-06.*

High School Drop-out Rate: A dropout is a student who was enrolled in school at some time during the previous school year; was not enrolled at the beginning of the current school year; has not graduated from high school or completed a state or district approved educational program; and does not meet any of the following exclusionary conditions: has transferred to another public school district, private school, or state- or district-approved educational program; is temporarily absent due to suspension or school-approved illness; or has died. The values shown cover grades 9 through 12. *Note: The National Center for Education Statistics has not released more current district level data due to privacy issues. Source: U.S. Department of Education, National Center for Education Statistics, Common Core of Data, Local Education Agency Universe Dropout File: School Year 2001-2002*

Note: n/a indicates data not available.

State Educational Profile

Please refer to the District Rankings section in the front of this User's Guide for an explanation of data for all items except for the following:

Average Salary: The average teacher salary in 2004-2005. *Source: American Federation of Teachers, Survey & Analysis of Teacher Salary Trends 2005*

College Entrance Exam Scores:

Scholastic Aptitude Test (SAT). *Note: The College Board strongly discourages the comparison or ranking of states on the basis of SAT scores alone. Source: The College Board, Mean SAT Reasoning Test™ Critical Reading, Math, and Writing Scores by State, with Changes for Selected Years, 2006*

American College Testing Program (ACT). *ACT, 2006 Average ACT Scores by State*

National Assessment of Educational Progress (NAEP)

The National Assessment of Educational Progress (NAEP), also known as "the Nation's Report Card," is the only nationally representative and continuing assessment of what America's students know and can do in various subject areas. As a result of the "No Child Left Behind" legislation, all states are required to participate in NAEP.

For more information, visit the U.S. Department of Education, National Center for Education Statistics at http://nces.ed.gov/nationsreportcard.

Illinois State Assessments

Federal law requires that student achievement results for reading, mathematics and science for schools providing Title I services be reported to the general public.

The *Illinois Standards Achievement Test (ISAT)* is administered to students in grades 3 through 8. The *Prairie State Achievement Examination (PSAE)* is administered to students in grade 11. The *Illinois Measure of Annual Growth in English (IMAGE)* is administered to limited-English-proficient students. The *Illinois Alternate Assessment (IAA)* is administered to students with disabilities whose Individualized Education Programs (IEPs) indicate that participation in the ISAT or PSAE would not be appropriate. Students with disabilities have an IEP (No Child Left Behind Act). An IEP is a written plan for a child with a disability who is eligible to receive special education services under the Individuals with Disabilities Education Act. In order to protect students' identities, test data for groups of fewer than ten students are not reported.

For more information please visit the Illinois State Board of Education at http://www.isbe.state.il.us/assessment.

User's Guide: Ancestry

Places Covered

The ranking tables are based on 1,311 places in Illinois. Places covered fall into one of the following categories:

1,285 incorporated municipalities. Municipalities are incorporated as either cities, towns, or villages.

26 census designated places (CDP). The U.S. Bureau of the Census defines a CDP as "a statistical entity, defined for each decennial census according to Census Bureau guidelines, comprising a densely settled concentration of population that is not within an incorporated place, but is locally identified by a name. CDPs are delineated cooperatively by state and local officials and the Census Bureau, following Census Bureau guidelines. Beginning with Census 2000 there are no size limits."

Source of Data

The ancestries shown in this chapter were compiled from three different sections of the 2000 Census: Race; Hispanic Origin; and Ancestry. While the ancestries are sorted alphabetically for ease-of-use, it's important to note the origin of each piece of data. Data for Race and Hispanic Origin was taken from Summary File 1 (SF1) while Ancestry data was taken from Summary File 3 (SF3). The distinction is important because SF1 contains the 100-percent data, which is the information compiled from the questions asked of all people and about every housing unit. SF3 was compiled from a sample of approximately 19 million housing units (about 1 in 6 households) that received the Census 2000 long-form questionnaire.

Ancestries Based on Race

The data on race were derived from answers to the question on race that was asked of all people. The concept of race, as used by the Census Bureau, reflects self-identification by people according to the race or races with which they most closely identify. These categories are sociopolitical constructs and should not be interpreted as being scientific or anthropological in nature. Furthermore, the race categories include both racial and national-origin groups.

If an individual did not provide a race response, the race or races of the householder or other household members were assigned using specific rules of precedence of household relationship. For example, if race was missing for a natural-born child in the household, then either the race or races of the householder, another natural-born child, or the spouse of the householder were assigned. If race was not reported for anyone in the household, the race or races of a householder in a previously processed household were assigned.

- African-American/Black:
  - Not Hispanic
  - Hispanic
- Alaska Native tribes, specified:
  - Alaska Athabascan
  - Aleut
  - Eskimo
  - Tlingit-Haida
  - All other tribes
- Alaska Native tribes, not specified
- American Indian or Alaska Native tribes, not specified
- American Indian tribes, specified:
  - Apache
  - Blackfeet
  - Cherokee
  - Cheyenne
  - Chickasaw
  - Chippewa
  - Choctaw
  - Colville
  - Comanche
  - Cree
  - Creek
  - Crow
  - Delaware
  - Houma
  - Iroquois
  - Kiowa
  - Latin American Indians
  - Lumbee
  - Menominee
  - Navajo
  - Osage
  - Ottawa
  - Paiute
  - Pima
  - Potawatomi
  - Pueblo
  - Puget Sound Salish
  - Seminole
  - Shoshone
  - Sioux
  - Tohono O'Odham
  - Ute
  - Yakama
  - Yaqui
  - Yuman
  - All other tribes
- American Indian tribes, not specified
- Asian:
  - Bangladeshi
  - Cambodian
  - Chinese, except Taiwanese
  - Filipino
  - Hmong
  - Indian
  - Indonesian
  - Japanese
  - Korean
  - Laotian
  - Malaysian
  - Pakistani
  - Sri Lankan
  - Taiwanese
  - Thai
  - Vietnamese
  - Other Asian, specified
  - Other Asian, not specified
- Hawaii Native/Pacific Islander:
  - Melanesian:
    - Fijian
    - Other Melanesian
  - Micronesian:
    - Guamanian/Chamorro
    - Other Micronesian
  - Polynesian:
    - Native Hawaiian
    - Samoan
    - Tongan
    - Other Polynesian
  - Other Pacific Islander, specified
  - Other Pacific Islander, not specified
- White:
  - Not Hispanic
  - Hispanic

African American or Black: A person having origins in any of the Black racial groups of Africa. It includes people who indicate their race as "Black, African Am., or Negro," or provide written entries such as African American, Afro American, Kenyan, Nigerian, or Haitian.

American Indian or Alaska Native: A person having origins in any of the original peoples of North and South America (including Central America) and who maintain tribal affiliation or community attachment. It includes people who classified themselves as described below.

American Indian - Includes people who indicated their race as "American Indian," entered the name of an Indian tribe, or reported such entries as Canadian Indian, French American Indian, or Spanish-American Indian.

Respondents who identified themselves as American Indian were asked to report their enrolled or principal tribe. Therefore, tribal data in tabulations reflect the written entries reported on the questionnaires. Some of the entries (for example, Iroquois, Sioux, Colorado River, and Flathead) represent nations or reservations. The information on tribe is based on self identification and therefore does not reflect any designation of federally or state-recognized tribe. Information on American Indian tribes is presented in summary files. The information for Census 2000 is derived from the American Indian Tribal Classification List for the 1990 census that was updated based on a December 1997 Federal Register Notice, entitled "Indian Entities Recognized and Eligible to Receive Service From the United States Bureau of Indian Affairs," Department of the Interior, Bureau of Indian Affairs, issued by the Office of Management and Budget.

Alaska Native - Includes written responses of Eskimos, Aleuts, and Alaska Indians, as well as entries such as Arctic Slope, Inupiat, Yupik, Alutiiq, Egegik, and Pribilovian. The Alaska tribes are the Alaskan Athabascan, Tlingit, and Haida. The information for Census 2000 is based on the American Indian Tribal Classification List for the 1990 census, which was expanded to list the individual Alaska Native Villages when provided as a written response for race.

Asian: A person having origins in any of the original peoples of the Far East, Southeast Asia, or the Indian subcontinent including, for example, Cambodia, China, India, Japan, Korea, Malaysia, Pakistan, the Philippine Islands, Thailand, and Vietnam. It includes "Asian Indian," "Chinese," "Filipino," "Korean," "Japanese," "Vietnamese," and "Other Asian."

Asian Indian - Includes people who indicated their race as "Asian Indian" or identified themselves as Bengalese, Bharat, Dravidian, East Indian, or Goanese.

Chinese - Includes people who indicate their race as "Chinese" or who identify themselves as Cantonese, or Chinese American.

Filipino - Includes people who indicate their race as "Filipino" or who report entries such as Philipino, Philipine, or Filipino American.

Japanese - Includes people who indicate their race as "Japanese" or who report entries such as Nipponese or Japanese American.

Korean - Includes people who indicate their race as "Korean" or who provide a response of Korean American.

Vietnamese - Includes people who indicate their race as "Vietnamese" or who provide a response of Vietnamese American.

Cambodian - Includes people who provide a response such as Cambodian or Cambodia.

Hmong - Includes people who provide a response such as Hmong, Laohmong, or Mong.

Laotian - Includes people who provide a response such as Laotian, Laos, or Lao.

Thai - Includes people who provide a response such as Thai, Thailand, or Siamese.

Other Asian - Includes people who provide a response of Bangladeshi; Bhutanese; Burmese; Indochinese; Indonesian; Iwo Jiman; Madagascar; Malaysian; Maldivian; Nepalese; Okinawan; Pakistani; Singaporean; Sri Lankan; or Other Asian, specified and Other Asian, not specified.

Native Hawaiian or Other Pacific Islander: A person having origins in any of the original peoples of Hawaii, Guam, Samoa, or other Pacific Islands. It includes people who indicate their race as "Native Hawaiian," "Guamanian or Chamorro," "Samoan," and "Other Pacific Islander."

> *Native Hawaiian* - Includes people who indicate their race as "Native Hawaiian" or who identify themselves as "Part Hawaiian" or "Hawaiian."
>
> *Guamanian or Chamorro* - Includes people who indicate their race as such, including written entries of Chamorro or Guam.
>
> *Samoan* - Includes people who indicate their race as "Samoan" or who identify themselves as American Samoan or Western Samoan.
>
> *Other Pacific Islander* - Includes people who provide a write-in response of a Pacific Islander group, such as Carolinian, Chuukese (Trukese), Fijian, Kosraean, Melanesian, Micronesian, Northern Mariana Islander, Palauan, Papua New Guinean, Pohnpeian, Polynesian, Solomon Islander, Tahitian, Tokelauan, Tongan, Yapese, or Pacific Islander, not specified.

White: A person having origins in any of the original peoples of Europe, the Middle East, or North Africa. It includes people who indicate their race as "White" or report entries such as Irish, German, Italian, Lebanese, Near Easterner, Arab, or Polish.

Ancestries Based on Hispanic Origin

- Hispanic or Latino:
  - Central American:
    - Costa Rican
    - Guatemalan
    - Honduran
    - Nicaraguan
    - Panamanian
    - Salvadoran
    - Other Central American
  - Cuban
  - Dominican Republic
  - Mexican
  - Puerto Rican
  - South American:
    - Argentinean
    - Bolivian
    - Chilean
    - Colombian
    - Ecuadorian
    - Paraguayan
    - Peruvian
    - Uruguayan
    - Venezuelan
    - Other South American
  - Other Hispanic/Latino

The data on the Hispanic or Latino population were derived from answers to a question that was asked of all people. The terms "Spanish," "Hispanic origin," and "Latino" are used interchangeably. Some respondents identify with all three terms while others may identify with only one of these three specific terms. Hispanics or Latinos who identify with the terms "Spanish," "Hispanic," or "Latino" are those who classify themselves in one of the specific Spanish, Hispanic, or Latino categories listed on the questionnaire ("Mexican," "Puerto Rican," or "Cuban") as well as those who indicate that they are "other Spanish/Hispanic/Latino." People who do not identify with one of the specific origins listed on the questionnaire but indicate that they are "other Spanish, Hispanic, or Latino" are those whose origins are from Spain, the Spanish-speaking countries of Central or South America, the Dominican Republic, or people identifying themselves generally as Spanish, Spanish-American, Hispanic, Hispano, Latino, and so on. All write-in responses to the "other Spanish/Hispanic/Latino" category were coded.

Origin can be viewed as the heritage, nationality group, lineage, or country of birth of the person or the person's parents or ancestors before their arrival in the United States. People who identify their origin as Spanish, Hispanic, or Latino may be of any race.

In all cases where the origin of households, families, or occupied housing units is classified as Spanish, Hispanic, or Latino, the origin of the householder is used. If an individual could not provide a Hispanic origin response, their origin was assigned using specific rules of precedence of household relationship. For example, if origin was missing for a natural-born daughter in the household, then either the origin of the householder, another natural-born child, or spouse of the householder was assigned. If Hispanic origin was not reported for anyone in the household, the Hispanic origin of a householder in a previously processed household with the same race was assigned.

Other Ancestries

Acadian/Cajun
Afghan
African, Subsaharan:
- African
- Cape Verdean
- Ethiopian
- Ghanian
- Kenyan
- Liberian
- Nigerian
- Senegalese
- Sierra Leonean
- Somalian
- South African
- Sudanese
- Ugandan
- Zairian
- Zimbabwean
- Other Subsaharan African

Albanian
Alsatian
Arab:
- Arab/Arabic
- Egyptian
- Iraqi
- Jordanian
- Lebanese
- Moroccan
- Palestinian
- Syrian
- Other Arab

Armenian
Assyrian/Chaldean/Syriac
Australian
Austrian
Basque
Belgian
Brazilian
British
Bulgarian
Canadian
Carpatho Rusyn
Celtic
Croatian
Cypriot
Czech
Czechoslovakian
Danish
Dutch
Eastern European
English
Estonian
European
Finnish
French, except Basque
French Canadian
German
German Russian
Greek
Guyanese
Hungarian
Icelander
Iranian
Irish
Israeli
Italian
Latvian
Lithuanian
Luxemburger
Macedonian
Maltese
New Zealander
Northern European
Norwegian
Pennsylvania German
Polish
Portuguese
Romanian
Russian
Scandinavian
Scotch-Irish
Scottish
Serbian
Slavic
Slovak
Slovene
Soviet Union
Swedish
Swiss
Turkish
Ukrainian
United States or American
Welsh
West Indian, excluding Hispanic:
- Bahamian
- Barbadian
- Belizean
- Bermudan
- British West Indian
- Dutch West Indian
- Haitian
- Jamaican
- Trinidadian and Tobagonian
- U.S. Virgin Islander
- West Indian
- Other West Indian

Yugoslavian

The data on ancestry were derived from answers to long-form questionnaire Item 10, which was asked of a sample of the population. The data represent self-classification by people according to the ancestry group or groups with which they most closely identify. Ancestry refers to a person's ethnic origin or descent, "roots," heritage, or the place of birth of the person, the person's parents, or their ancestors before their arrival in the United States. Some ethnic identities, such as Egyptian or Polish, can be traced to geographic areas outside the United States, while other ethnicities, such as Pennsylvania German or Cajun, evolved in the United States.

The intent of the ancestry question was not to measure the degree of attachment the respondent had to a particular ethnicity. For example, a response of "Irish" might reflect total involvement in an Irish community or only a memory of ancestors several generations removed from the individual. Also, the question was intended to provide data for groups that were not included in the Hispanic origin and race questions. Official Hispanic origin data come from long-form questionnaire Item 5, and official race data come from long-form questionnaire Item 6. Therefore, although data on all groups are collected, the ancestry data shown in these tabulations are for non-Hispanic and non-race groups.

The ancestry question allowed respondents to report one or more ancestry groups, although only the first two were coded. If a response was in terms of a dual ancestry, for example, "Irish English," the person was assigned two codes, in this case one for Irish and another for English. However, in certain cases, multiple responses such as "French Canadian," "Greek Cypriote," and "Scotch Irish" were assigned a single code reflecting their status as unique groups. If a person reported one of these unique groups in addition to another group, for example, "Scotch Irish English," resulting in three terms, that person received one code for the unique group (Scotch-Irish) and another one for the remaining group (English). If a person reported "English Irish French," only English and Irish were coded. Certain combinations of ancestries where the ancestry group is a part of another, such as "German-Bavarian," were coded as a single ancestry using the more specific group (Bavarian). Also, responses such as "Polish-American" or "Italian-American" were coded and tabulated as a single entry (Polish or Italian).

The Census Bureau accepted "American" as a unique ethnicity if it was given alone, with an ambiguous response, or with state names. If the respondent listed any other ethnic identity such as "Italian-American," generally the "American" portion of the response was not coded. However, distinct groups such as "American Indian," "Mexican American," and "African American" were coded and identified separately because they represented groups who considered themselves different from those who reported as "Indian," "Mexican," or "African," respectively.

Census 2000 tabulations on ancestry are presented using two types of data presentations — one using total people as the base, and the other using total responses as the base. This chapter uses total responses as the base and includes the total number of ancestries reported and coded. If a person reported a multiple ancestry such as "French Danish," that response was counted twice in the tabulations — once in the French category and again in the Danish category. Thus, the sum of the counts in this type of presentation is not the total population but the total of all responses.

An automated coding system was used for coding ancestry in Census 2000. This greatly reduced the potential for error associated with a clerical review. Specialists with knowledge of the subject matter reviewed, edited, coded, and resolved inconsistent or incomplete responses. The code list used in Census 2000, containing over 1,000 categories, reflects the results of the Census Bureau's experience with the 1990 ancestry question, research, and consultation with many ethnic experts. Many decisions were made to determine the classification of responses. These decisions affected the grouping of the tabulated data. For example, the Italian category includes the responses of Sicilian and Tuscan, as well as a number of other responses.

Although some people consider religious affiliation a component of ethnic identity, the ancestry question was not designed to collect any information concerning religion. Thus, if a religion was given as an answer to the ancestry question, it was listed in the "Other groups" category which is not shown in this chapter.

Ancestry should not be confused with a person's place of birth, although a person's place of birth and ancestry may be the same.

Ranking Section

In the ranking section of this chapter, each ancestry has three tables. The first table shows the top 10 places sorted by number (based on all places, regardless of population), the second table shows the top 10 places sorted by percent (based on all places, regardless of population), the third table shows the top 10 places sorted by percent (based on places with populations of 10,000 or more).

Within each table, column one displays the place name, the state, and the county (if a place spans more than one county, the county that holds the majority of the population is shown). Column two displays the number of people reporting each ancestry, and column three is the percent of the total population reporting each ancestry. For tables representing ancestries based on race or Hispanic origin, the 100-percent population figure from SF1 is used to calculate the value in the "%" column. For all other ancestries the sample population figure from SF3 is used to calculate the value in the "%" column.

Alphabetical Ancestry Cross-Reference Guide

Acadian/Cajun
Afghan
African *See African, sub-Saharan: African*
African American/Black
African American/Black: Hispanic
African American/Black: Not Hispanic
African, sub-Saharan
African, sub-Saharan: African
African, sub-Saharan: Cape Verdean
African, sub-Saharan: Ethiopian
African, sub-Saharan: Ghanian
African, sub-Saharan: Kenyan
African, sub-Saharan: Liberian
African, sub-Saharan: Nigerian
African, sub-Saharan: Other
African, sub-Saharan: Senegalese
African, sub-Saharan: Sierra Leonean
African, sub-Saharan: Somalian
African, sub-Saharan: South African
African, sub-Saharan: Sudanese
African, sub-Saharan: Ugandan
African, sub-Saharan: Zairian
African, sub-Saharan: Zimbabwean
Alaska Athabascan *See Alaska Native: Alaska Athabascan*
Alaska Native tribes, not specified
Alaska Native tribes, specified
Alaska Native: Alaska Athabascan
Alaska Native: Aleut
Alaska Native: All other tribes
Alaska Native: Eskimo
Alaska Native: Tlingit-Haida
Albanian
Aleut *See Alaska Native: Aleut*
Alsatian
American *See United States or American*
American Indian or Alaska Native tribes, not specified
American Indian tribes, not specified
American Indian tribes, specified
American Indian: All other tribes
American Indian: Apache
American Indian: Blackfeet
American Indian: Cherokee
American Indian: Cheyenne
American Indian: Chickasaw
American Indian: Chippewa
American Indian: Choctaw
American Indian: Colville
American Indian: Comanche
American Indian: Cree
American Indian: Creek
American Indian: Crow
American Indian: Delaware
American Indian: Houma
American Indian: Iroquois
American Indian: Kiowa
American Indian: Latin American Indians
American Indian: Lumbee
American Indian: Menominee
American Indian: Navajo
American Indian: Osage
American Indian: Ottawa
American Indian: Paiute
American Indian: Pima
American Indian: Potawatomi
American Indian: Pueblo
American Indian: Puget Sound Salish
American Indian: Seminole
American Indian: Shoshone
American Indian: Sioux
American Indian: Tohono O'Odham
American Indian: Ute
American Indian: Yakama
American Indian: Yaqui
American Indian: Yuman
Apache *See American Indian: Apache*
Arab
Arab/Arabic *See Arab: Arab/Arabic*
Arab: Arab/Arabic
Arab: Egyptian
Arab: Iraqi
Arab: Jordanian
Arab: Lebanese
Arab: Moroccan
Arab: Other
Arab: Palestinian
Arab: Syrian
Argentinean *See Hispanic: Argentinean*
Armenian
Asian
Asian: Bangladeshi
Asian: Cambodian
Asian: Chinese, except Taiwanese
Asian: Filipino
Asian: Hmong
Asian: Indian
Asian: Indonesian
Asian: Japanese
Asian: Korean
Asian: Laotian
Asian: Malaysian
Asian: Other Asian, not specified
Asian: Other Asian, specified
Asian: Pakistani
Asian: Sri Lankan
Asian: Taiwanese
Asian: Thai
Asian: Vietnamese
Assyrian/Chaldean/Syriac
Australian
Austrian
Bahamian *See West Indian: Bahamian, excluding Hispanic*
Bangladeshi *See Asian: Bangladeshi*
Barbadian *See West Indian: Barbadian, excluding Hispanic*
Basque
Belgian
Belizean *See West Indian: Belizean, excluding Hispanic*
Bermudan *See West Indian: Bermudan, excluding Hispanic*
Blackfeet *See American Indian: Blackfeet*
Bolivian *See Hispanic: Bolivian*
Brazilian
British
British West Indian *See West Indian: British West Indian, excluding Hispanic*
Bulgarian
Cambodian *See Asian: Cambodian*
Canadian
Cape Verdean *See African, sub-Saharan: Cape Verdean*
Carpatho Rusyn
Celtic
Central American: *See Hispanic: Central American*
Cherokee *See American Indian: Cherokee*
Cheyenne *See American Indian: Cheyenne*
Chickasaw *See American Indian: Chickasaw*
Chilean *See Hispanic: Chilean*
Chinese, except Taiwanese *See Asian: Chinese, except Taiwanese*
Chippewa *See American Indian: Chippewa*
Choctaw *See American Indian: Choctaw*
Colombian *See Hispanic: Colombian*
Colville *See American Indian: Colville*
Comanche *See American Indian: Comanche*
Costa Rican *See Hispanic: Costa Rican*
Cree *See American Indian: Cree*
Creek *See American Indian: Creek*
Croatian
Crow *See American Indian: Crow*
Cuban *See Hispanic: Cuban*
Cypriot
Czech
Czechoslovakian
Danish
Delaware *See American Indian: Delaware*
Dominican Republic *See Hispanic: Dominican Republic*
Dutch
Dutch West Indian *See West Indian: Dutch West Indian, excluding Hispanic*
Eastern European
Ecuadorian *See Hispanic: Ecuadorian*
Egyptian *See Arab: Egyptian*
English
Eskimo *See Alaska Native: Eskimo*
Estonian
Ethiopian *See African, sub-Saharan: Ethiopian*
European
Fijian *See Hawaii Native/Pacific Islander: Fijian*
Filipino *See Asian: Filipino*
Finnish
French Canadian
French, except Basque
German
German Russian
Ghanian *See African, sub-Saharan: Ghanian*
Greek
Guamanian or Chamorro *See Hawaii Native/Pacific Islander: Guamanian or Chamorro*
Guatemalan *See Hispanic: Guatemalan*
Guyanese
Haitian *See West Indian: Haitian, excluding Hispanic*
Hawaii Native/Pacific Islander
Hawaii Native/Pacific Islander: Fijian
Hawaii Native/Pacific Islander: Guamanian or Chamorro
Hawaii Native/Pacific Islander: Melanesian
Hawaii Native/Pacific Islander: Micronesian
Hawaii Native/Pacific Islander: Native Hawaiian

Hawaii Native/Pacific Islander: Other Melanesian
Hawaii Native/Pacific Islander: Other Micronesian
Hawaii Native/Pacific Islander: Other Pacific Islander, not specified
Hawaii Native/Pacific Islander: Other Pacific Islander, specified
Hawaii Native/Pacific Islander: Other Polynesian
Hawaii Native/Pacific Islander: Polynesian
Hawaii Native/Pacific Islander: Samoan
Hawaii Native/Pacific Islander: Tongan
Hispanic or Latino
Hispanic: Argentinean
Hispanic: Bolivian
Hispanic: Central American
Hispanic: Chilean
Hispanic: Colombian
Hispanic: Costa Rican
Hispanic: Cuban
Hispanic: Dominican Republic
Hispanic: Ecuadorian
Hispanic: Guatemalan
Hispanic: Honduran
Hispanic: Mexican
Hispanic: Nicaraguan
Hispanic: Other
Hispanic: Other Central American
Hispanic: Other South American
Hispanic: Panamanian
Hispanic: Paraguayan
Hispanic: Peruvian
Hispanic: Puerto Rican
Hispanic: Salvadoran
Hispanic: South American
Hispanic: Uruguayan
Hispanic: Venezuelan
Hmong *See Asian: Hmong*
Honduran *See Hispanic: Honduran*
Houma *See American Indian: Houma*
Hungarian
Icelander
Indian, American *See American Indian*
Indian, Asian *See Asian: Indian*
Indonesian *See Asian: Indonesian*
Iranian
Iraqi *See Arab: Iraqi*
Irish
Iroquois *See American Indian: Iroquois*
Israeli
Italian
Jamaican *See West Indian: Jamaican, excluding Hispanic*
Japanese *See Asian: Japanese*
Jordanian *See Arab: Jordanian*
Kenyan *See African, sub-Saharan: Kenyan*
Kiowa *See American Indian: Kiowa*
Korean *See Asian: Korean*
Laotian *See Asian: Laotian*
Latin American Indians *See American Indian: Latin American Indians*
Latino *See Hispanic or Latino*
Latvian
Lebanese *See Arab: Lebanese*
Liberian *See African, sub-Saharan: Liberian*
Lithuanian
Lumbee *See American Indian: Lumbee*
Luxemburger
Macedonian
Malaysian *See Asian: Malaysian*
Maltese
Melanesian: *See Hawaii Native/Pacific Islander: Melanesian*
Menominee *See American Indian: Menominee*
Mexican *See Hispanic: Mexican*
Micronesian: *See Hawaii Native/Pacific Islander: Micronesian*
Moroccan *See Arab: Moroccan*
Native Hawaiian *See Hawaii Native/Pacific Islander: Native Hawaiian*
Navajo *See American Indian: Navajo*
New Zealander
Nicaraguan *See Hispanic: Nicaraguan*
Nigerian *See African, sub-Saharan: Nigerian*
Northern European
Norwegian
Osage *See American Indian: Osage*
Ottawa *See American Indian: Ottawa*
Paiute *See American Indian: Paiute*
Pakistani *See Asian: Pakistani*
Palestinian *See Arab: Palestinian*
Panamanian *See Hispanic: Panamanian*
Paraguayan *See Hispanic: Paraguayan*
Pennsylvania German
Peruvian *See Hispanic: Peruvian*
Pima *See American Indian: Pima*
Polish
Polynesian: *See Hawaii Native/Pacific Islander: Polynesian*
Portuguese
Potawatomi *See American Indian: Potawatomi*
Pueblo *See American Indian: Pueblo*
Puerto Rican *See Hispanic: Puerto Rican*
Puget Sound Salish *See American Indian: Puget Sound Salish*
Romanian
Russian
Salvadoran *See Hispanic: Salvadoran*
Samoan *See Hawaii Native/Pacific Islander: Samoan*
Scandinavian
Scotch-Irish
Scottish
Seminole *See American Indian: Seminole*
Senegalese *See African, sub-Saharan: Senegalese*
Serbian
Shoshone *See American Indian: Shoshone*
Sierra Leonean *See African, sub-Saharan: Sierra Leonean*
Sioux *See American Indian: Sioux*
Slavic
Slovak
Slovene
Somalian *See African, sub-Saharan: Somalian*
South African *See African, sub-Saharan: South African*
South American: *See Hispanic: South American*
Soviet Union
Sri Lankan *See Asian: Sri Lankan*
sub-Saharan African *See African, sub-Saharan*
Sudanese *See African, sub-Saharan: Sudanese*
Swedish
Swiss
Syrian *See Arab: Syrian*
Taiwanese *See Asian: Taiwanese*
Thai *See Asian: Thai*
Tlingit-Haida *See Alaska Native: Tlingit-Haida*
Tohono O'Odham *See American Indian: Tohono O'Odham*
Tongan *See Hawaii Native/Pacific Islander: Tongan*
Trinidadian and Tobagonian *See West Indian: Trinidadian and Tobagonian, excluding Hispanic*
Turkish
U.S. Virgin Islander *See West Indian: U.S. Virgin Islander, excluding Hispanic*
Ugandan *See African, sub-Saharan: Ugandan*
Ukrainian
United States or American
Uruguayan *See Hispanic: Uruguayan*
Ute *See American Indian: Ute*
Venezuelan *See Hispanic: Venezuelan*
Vietnamese *See Asian: Vietnamese*
Welsh
West Indian, excluding Hispanic
West Indian: Bahamian, excluding Hispanic
West Indian: Barbadian, excluding Hispanic
West Indian: Belizean, excluding Hispanic
West Indian: Bermudan, excluding Hispanic
West Indian: British West Indian, excluding Hispanic
West Indian: Dutch West Indian, excluding Hispanic
West Indian: Haitian, excluding Hispanic
West Indian: Jamaican, excluding Hispanic
West Indian: Other, excluding Hispanic
West Indian: Trinidadian and Tobagonian, excluding Hispanic
West Indian: U.S. Virgin Islander, excluding Hispanic
West Indian: West Indian, excluding Hispanic
White
White: Hispanic
White: Not Hispanic
Yakama *See American Indian: Yakama*
Yaqui *See American Indian: Yaqui*
Yugoslavian
Yuman *See American Indian: Yuman*
Zairian *See African, sub-Saharan: Zairian*
Zimbabwean *See African, sub-Saharan: Zimbabwean*

User's Guide: Hispanic Population

Places Covered

Ranking tables cover all counties and all places in Illinois with populations of 10,000 or more.

Source of Data

CENSUS 2000

Data for this chapter was derived from following source: *U.S. Bureau of the Census, Census of Population and Housing, 2000: Summary File 4.* Summary File 4 (SF 4) contains sample data, which is the information compiled from the questions asked of a sample (generally 1-in-6) of all people and housing units. Summary File 4 is repeated or iterated for the total population and 335 additional population groups. This chapter focuses on the following 24 population groups:

- Hispanic or Latino (of any race)
  - Central American
    - Costa Rican
    - Guatemalan
    - Honduran
    - Nicaraguan
    - Panamanian
    - Salvadoran
  - Cuban
  - Dominican (Dominican Republic)
  - Mexican
  - Puerto Rican
  - South American
    - Argentinian
    - Bolivian
    - Chilean
    - Colombian
    - Ecuadorian
    - Paraguayan
    - Peruvian
    - Uruguayan
    - Venezuelan
  - Spaniard
  - Other Hispanic or Latino

Please note that the above list only includes Spanish-speaking population groups. Groups such as Brazilian are not classified as Hispanic by the Bureau of the Census because they primarily speak Portugese.

In order for any of the tables for a specific group to be shown in Summary File 4, the data must meet a minimum population threshold. For Summary File 4, all tables are repeated for each race group, American Indian and Alaska Native tribe, and Hispanic or Latino group if the 100-percent count of people of that specific group in a particular geographic area is 100 or more. There also must be 50 or more unweighted people of that specific group in a particular geographic area. For example, if there are 100 or more 100-percent people tabulated as Chilean in County A, and there are 50 or more unweighted people, then all matrices for Chilean are shown in SF 4 for County A.

To maintain confidentiality, the Census Bureau applies statistical procedures that introduce some uncertainty into data for small geographic areas with small population groups. Therefore, tables may contain both sampling and nonsampling error.

In an iterated file such as SF 4, the universes *households, families,* and *occupied housing units* are classified by the race or ethnic group of the householder. In any population table where there is no note, the universe classification is always based on the race or ethnicity of the person. In all housing tables, the universe classification is based on the race or ethnicity of the householder.

Comparing SF 4 Estimates with Corresponding Values in SF 1 and SF 2

As in earlier censuses, the responses from the sample of households reporting on long forms must be weighted to reflect the entire population. Specifically, each responding household represents, on average, six or seven other households who reported using short forms. One consequence of the weighting procedures is that each estimate based on the long form responses has an associated confidence interval. These confidence intervals are wider (as a percentage of the estimate) for geographic areas with smaller populations and for characteristics that occur less frequently in the area being examined (such as the proportion of people in poverty in a middle-income neighborhood). In order to release as much useful information as possible, statisticians must balance a number of factors. In particular, for Census 2000, the Bureau of the Census created weighting areas—geographic areas from which about two hundred or more long forms were completed—which are large enough to produce good quality estimates. If smaller weighting areas had been used, the confidence intervals around the estimates would have been significantly wider, rendering many estimates less useful due to their lower reliability. The disadvantage of using weighting areas this large is that, for smaller geographic areas within them, the estimates of characteristics that are also reported on the short form will not match the counts reported in SF 1 or SF 2. Examples of these characteristics are the total number of people, the number of people reporting specific racial categories, and the number of housing units. The official values for items reported on the short form come from SF 1 and SF 2. The differences between the long form estimates in SF 4 and values in SF 1 or SF 2 are particularly noticeable for the smallest places, tracts, and block groups. The long form estimates of total population and total housing units in SF 4 will, however, match the SF 1 and SF 2 counts for larger geographic areas such as counties and states, and will be essentially the same for medium and large cities. This phenomenon also occurred for the 1990 Census, although in that case, the weighting areas included relatively small places. As a result, the long form estimates matched the short form counts for those places, but the confidence intervals around the estimates of characteristics collected only on the long form were often significantly wider (as a percentage of the estimate). SF 1 gives exact numbers even for very small groups and areas; whereas, SF 4 gives estimates for small groups and areas such as tracts and small places that are less exact. The goal of SF 4 is to identify large differences among areas or large changes over time. Estimates for small areas and small population groups often do exhibit large changes from one census to the next, so having the capability to measure them is worthwhile.

Topics

POPULATION

Total Population: Sample count of total population.

Hispanic Population: The data on the Hispanic or Latino population, which was asked of all people, were derived from answers to long-form questionnaire Item 5, and short-form questionnaire Item 7. The terms "Spanish," "Hispanic origin," and "Latino" are used interchangeably. Some respondents identify with all three terms, while others may identify with only one of these three specific terms. Hispanics or Latinos who identify with the terms "Spanish," "Hispanic," or "Latino" are those who classify themselves in one of the specific Hispanic or Latino categories listed on the questionnaire — "Mexican," "Puerto Rican," or "Cuban" — as well as those who indicate that they are "other Spanish, Hispanic, or Latino." People who do not identify with one of the specific origins listed on the questionnaire but indicate that they are "other Spanish, Hispanic, or Latino" are those whose origins are from Spain, the Spanish-speaking countries of Central or South America, the Dominican Republic, or people identifying themselves generally as Spanish, Spanish-American, Hispanic, Hispano, Latino, and so on. All write-in responses to the "other Spanish/Hispanic/Latino" category were coded. Origin can be viewed as the heritage, nationality group, lineage, or country of birth of the person or the person's parents or ancestors before their arrival in the United States. People who identify their origin as Spanish, Hispanic, or Latino may be of any race.

Population groups whose primary language is not Spanish are not classified as Hispanic by the Bureau of the Census and are not included in this chapter (eg. Brazilian).

AGE

Median Age: Divides the age distribution into two equal parts: one-half of the cases falling below the median age and one-half above the median. Median age is computed on the basis of a single year of age standard distribution.

The data on age, which was asked of all people, were derived from answers to the long-form questionnaire Item 4 and short-form questionnaire Item 6. The age classification is based on the age of the person in complete years as of April 1, 2000. The age of the person usually was derived from their date of birth information. Their reported age was used only when date of birth information was unavailable.

HOUSEHOLD SIZE

Average Household Size: A measure obtained by dividing the number of people in households by the total number of households (or householders). In cases where household members are tabulated by race or Hispanic origin, household members are classified by the race or Hispanic origin of the householder rather than the race or Hispanic origin of each individual. Average household size is rounded to the nearest hundredth.

LANGUAGE SPOKEN AT HOME

English Only: Number and percentage of population 5 years and over who report speaking English-only at home.

Spanish: Number and percentage of population 5 years and over who report speaking Spanish at home.

Language spoken at home data were derived from answers to long-form questionnaire Items 11a and 11b, which were asked of a sample of the population. Data were edited to include in tabulations only the population 5 years old and over. Questions 11a and 11b referred to languages spoken at home in an effort to measure the current use of languages other than English. People who knew languages other than English but did not use them at home or who only used them elsewhere were excluded. Most people who reported speaking a language other than English at home also speak English. The questions did not permit determination of the primary or dominant language of people who spoke both English and another language.

FOREIGN-BORN

Foreign Born: Number and percentage of population who were not U.S. citizens at birth. Foreign-born people are those who indicated they were either a U.S. citizen by naturalization or they were not a citizen of the United States.

Foreign-Born Naturalized Citizens: Number and percentage of population who were not U.S. citizens at birth but became U.S. citizens by naturalization.

The data on place of birth were derived from answers to long-form questionnaire Item 12 which was asked of a sample of the population. Respondents were asked to report the U.S. state, Puerto Rico, U.S. Island Area, or foreign country where they were born. People not reporting a place of birth were assigned the state or country of birth of another family member or their residence 5 years earlier, or were imputed the response of another person with similar characteristics. People born outside the United States were asked to report their place of birth according to current international boundaries. Since numerous changes in boundaries of foreign countries have occurred in the last century, some people may have reported their place of birth in terms of boundaries that existed at the time of their birth or emigration, or in accordance with their own national preference.

EDUCATIONAL ATTAINMENT

High School Graduates: Number and percentage of the population age 25 and over who have a high school diploma or higher. This category includes people whose highest degree was a high school diploma or its equivalent, people who attended college but did not receive a degree, and people who received a college, university, or professional degree. People who reported completing the 12th grade but not receiving a diploma are not high school graduates.

4-Years College Graduates: Number and percentage of the population age 25 and over who have a 4-year college, university, or professional degree.

Data on educational attainment were derived from answers to long-form questionnaire Item 9, which was asked of a sample of the population. Data on attainment are tabulated for the population 25 years old and over.

The order in which degrees were listed on the questionnaire suggested that doctorate degrees were "higher" than professional school degrees, which were "higher" than master's degrees. The question included instructions for people currently enrolled in school to report the level of the previous grade attended or the highest degree received. Respondents who did not report educational attainment or enrollment level were assigned the attainment of a person of the same age, race, Hispanic or Latino origin, occupation and sex, where possible, who resided in the same or a nearby area. Respondents who filled more than one box were edited to the highest level or degree reported.

The question included a response category that allowed respondents to report completing the 12th grade without receiving a high school diploma. It allowed people who received either a high school diploma or the equivalent (Test of General Educational Development—G.E.D.) and did not attend college, to be reported as "high school graduate(s)." The category "Associate degree" included people whose highest degree is an associate degree, which generally requires 2 years of college level work and is either in an occupational program that prepares them for a specific occupation, or an academic program primarily in the arts and sciences. The course work may or may not be transferable to a bachelor's degree. Master's degrees include the traditional MA and MS degrees and field-specific degrees, such as MSW, MEd, MBA, MLS, and MEng. Some examples of professional degrees include medicine, dentistry, chiropractic, optometry, osteopathic medicine, pharmacy, podiatry, veterinary medicine, law, and theology. Vocational and technical training such as barber school training; business, trade, technical, and vocational schools; or other training for a specific trade, are specifically excluded.

INCOME AND POVERTY

Median Household Income (in dollars): Includes the income of the householder and all other individuals 15 years old and over in the household, whether they are related to the householder or not. The median divides the income distribution into two equal parts: one-half of the cases falling below the median income and one-half above the median. For households, the median income is based on the distribution of the total number of households including those with no income. Median income for households is computed on the basis of a standard distribution and is rounded to the nearest whole dollar.

Per Capita Income (in dollars): Per capita income is the mean income computed for every man, woman, and child in a particular group. It is derived by dividing the total income of a particular group by the total population in that group. Per capita income is rounded to the nearest whole dollar.

The data on income in 1999 were derived from answers to long-form questionnaire Items 31 and 32, which were asked of a sample of the population 15 years old and over. "Total income" is the sum of the amounts reported separately for wage or salary income; net self-employment income; interest, dividends, or net rental or royalty income or income from estates and trusts; social security or railroad retirement income; Supplemental Security Income (SSI); public assistance or welfare payments; retirement, survivor, or disability pensions; and all other income.

Receipts from the following sources are not included as income: capital gains, money received from the sale of property (unless the recipient was engaged in the business of selling such property); the value of income "in kind" from food stamps, public housing subsidies, medical care, employer contributions for individuals, etc.; withdrawal of bank deposits; money borrowed; tax refunds; exchange of money between relatives living in the same household; and gifts and lump-sum inheritances, insurance payments, and other types of lump-sum receipts.

The eight types of income reported in the census are defined as follows:

Wage or salary income. Wage or salary income includes total money earnings received for work performed as an employee during the calendar year 1999. It includes wages, salary, armed forces pay, commissions, tips, piece-rate payments, and cash bonuses earned before deductions were made for taxes, bonds, pensions, union dues, etc.

Self-employment income. Self-employment income includes both farm and nonfarm self-employment income. Nonfarm self-employment income includes net money income (gross receipts minus expenses) from one's own business, professional enterprise, or partnership. Gross receipts include the value of all goods sold and services rendered. Expenses include costs of goods purchased, rent, heat, light, power, depreciation charges, wages and salaries paid, business taxes (not personal income taxes), etc. Farm self-employment income includes net money income (gross receipts minus operating expenses) from the operation of a farm by a person on his or her own account, as an owner, renter, or sharecropper. Gross receipts include the value of all products sold, government farm programs, money received from the rental of farm equipment to others, and incidental receipts from the sale of wood, sand, gravel, etc. Operating expenses include cost of feed, fertilizer, seed, and other farming supplies, cash wages paid to farmhands, depreciation charges, cash rent, interest on farm mortgages, farm building repairs, farm taxes (not state and federal personal income taxes), etc. The value of fuel, food, or other farm products used for family living is not included as part of net income.

Interest, dividends, or net rental income. Interest, dividends, or net rental income includes interest on savings or bonds, dividends from stockholdings or membership in associations, net income from rental of property to others and receipts from boarders or lodgers, net royalties, and periodic payments from an estate or trust fund.

Social Security income. Social security income includes social security pensions and survivors benefits, permanent disability insurance payments made by the Social Security Administration prior to deductions for medical insurance, and railroad retirement insurance checks from the U.S. government. Medicare reimbursements are not included.

Supplemental Security Income (SSI). Supplemental Security Income (SSI) is a nationwide U.S. assistance program administered by the Social Security Administration that guarantees a minimum level of income for needy aged, blind, or disabled individuals. The census questionnaire for Puerto Rico asked about the receipt of SSI; however, SSI is not a federally administered program in Puerto Rico. Therefore, it is probably not being interpreted by most respondents as the same as SSI in the United States. The only way a resident of Puerto Rico could have appropriately reported SSI would have been if they lived in the United States at any time during calendar year 1999 and received SSI.

Public assistance income. Public assistance income includes general assistance and Temporary Assistance to Needy Families (TANF). Separate payments received for hospital or other medical care (vendor payments) are excluded. This does not include Supplemental Security Income (SSI).

Retirement income. Retirement income includes: (1) retirement pensions and survivor benefits from a former employer; labor union; or federal, state, or local government; and the U.S. military; (2) income from workers' compensation; disability income from companies or unions; federal, state, or local government; and the U.S. military; (3) periodic receipts from annuities and insurance; and (4) regular income from IRA and KEOGH plans. This does not include social security income.

All other income. All other income includes unemployment compensation, Veterans' Administration (VA) payments, alimony and child support, contributions received periodically from people not living in the household, military family allotments, and other kinds of periodic income other than earnings.

Poverty Status: Number and percentage of population with income in 1999 below the poverty level. Based on individuals for whom poverty status is determined. Poverty status was determined for all people except institutionalized people, people in military group quarters, people in college dormitories, and unrelated individuals under 15 years old.

The poverty status of families and unrelated individuals in 1999 was determined using 48 thresholds (income cutoffs) arranged in a two dimensional matrix. The matrix consists of family size (from 1 person to 9 or more people) cross-classified by presence and number of family members under 18 years old (from no children present to 8 or more children present). Unrelated individuals and 2-person families were further differentiated by the age of the reference person (RP) (under 65 years old and 65 years old and over).

To determine a person's poverty status, one compares the person's total family income with the poverty threshold appropriate for that person's family size and composition. If the total income of that person's family is less than the threshold appropriate for that family, then the person is considered poor, together with every member of his or her family. If a person is not living with anyone related by birth, marriage, or adoption, then the person's own income is compared with his or her poverty threshold.

HOUSING

Homeownership: Number and percentage of housing units that are owner-occupied.

The data on tenure, which was asked at all occupied housing units, were obtained from answers to long-form questionnaire Item 33, and short-form questionnaire Item 2. All occupied housing units are classified as either owner occupied or renter occupied.

A housing unit is owner occupied if the owner or co-owner lives in the unit even if it is mortgaged or not fully paid for. The owner or co-owner must live in the unit and usually is Person 1 on the questionnaire. The unit is "Owned by you or someone in this household with a mortgage or loan" if it is being purchased with a mortgage or some other debt arrangement, such as a deed of trust, trust deed, contract to purchase, land contract, or purchase agreement. The unit is also considered owned with a mortgage if it is built on leased land and there is a mortgage on the unit. Mobile homes occupied by owners with installment loans balances are also included in this category.

Median Gross Rent (in dollars): Median monthly gross rent on specified renter-occupied and specified vacant-for-rent units. Specified renter-occupied and specified vacant-for-rent units exclude 1-family houses on 10 acres or more.

The data on gross rent were obtained from answers to long-form questionnaire Items 45a-d, which were asked on a sample basis. Gross rent is the contract rent plus the estimated average monthly cost of utilities (electricity, gas, water and sewer) and fuels (oil, coal, kerosene, wood, etc.) if these are paid by the renter (or paid for the renter by someone else). Gross rent is intended to eliminate differentials that result from varying practices with respect to the inclusion of utilities and fuels as part of the rental payment. The estimated costs of utilities and fuels are reported on an annual basis but are converted to monthly figures for the tabulations. Renter units occupied without payment of cash rent are shown separately as "No cash rent" in the tabulations.

Housing units that are renter occupied without payment of cash rent are shown separately as "No cash rent" in census data products. The unit may be owned by friends or relatives who live elsewhere and who allow occupancy without charge. Rent-free houses or apartments may be provided to compensate caretakers, ministers, tenant farmers, sharecroppers, or others.

Contract rent is the monthly rent agreed to or contracted for, regardless of any furnishings, utilities, fees, meals, or services that may be included. For vacant units, it is the monthly rent asked for the rental unit at the time of enumeration.

If the contract rent includes rent for a business unit or for living quarters occupied by another household, only that part of the rent estimated to be for the respondent's unit was included. Excluded was any rent paid for additional units or for business premises.

If a renter pays rent to the owner of a condominium or cooperative, and the condominium fee or cooperative carrying charge also is paid by the renter to the owner, the condominium fee or carrying charge was included as rent.

If a renter receives payments from lodgers or roomers who are listed as members of the household, the rent without deduction for any payments received from the lodgers or roomers was to be reported. The respondent was to report the rent agreed to or contracted for even if paid by someone else such as friends or relatives living elsewhere, a church or welfare agency, or the government through subsidies or vouchers.

The median divides the rent distribution into two equal parts: one-half of the cases falling below the median contract rent and one-half above the median. Median contract rents are computed on the basis of a standard distribution and are rounded to the nearest whole dollar. Units reported as "No cash rent" are excluded.

Median Home Value (in dollars): Reported by the owner of specified owner-occupied or specified vacant-for-sale housing units. Specified owner-occupied and specified vacant-for-sale housing units include only 1-family houses on less than 10 acres without a business or medical office on the property. The data for "specified units" exclude mobile homes, houses with a business or medical office, houses on 10 or more acres, and housing units in multi-unit buildings.

The data on value (also referred to as "price asked" for vacant units) were obtained from answers to long-form questionnaire Item 51, which was asked on a sample basis at owner-occupied housing units and units that were being bought, or vacant for sale at the time of enumeration. Value is the respondent's estimate of how much the property (house and lot, mobile home and lot, or condominium unit) would sell for if it were for sale. If the house or mobile home was owned or being bought, but the land on which it sits was not, the respondent was asked to estimate the combined value of the house or mobile home and the land. For vacant units, value was the price asked for the property. Value was tabulated separately for all owner-occupied and vacant-for-sale housing units, owner-occupied and vacant-for-sale mobile homes, and specified owner-occupied and specified vacant-for-sale housing units.

The median divides the value distribution into two equal parts: one-half of the cases falling below the median value of the property (house and lot, mobile home and lot, or condominium unit) and one-half above the median. Median values are computed on the basis of a standard distribution and are rounded to the nearest hundred dollars.

User's Guide: Asian Population

Places Covered

Ranking tables cover all counties and places in Illinois with Asian and/or Native Hawaiian and other Pacific Islander residents.

Source of Data

CENSUS 2000

Data for this chapter was derived from following source: *U.S. Bureau of the Census, Census of Population and Housing, 2000: Summary File 4.* Summary File 4 (SF 4) contains sample data, which is the information compiled from the questions asked of a sample (generally 1-in-6) of all people and housing units. Summary File 4 is repeated or iterated for the total population and 335 additional population groups. This chapter focuses on the following 23 population groups:

Asian
- Asian Indian
- Bangladeshi
- Cambodian
- Chinese (except Taiwanese)
- Filipino
- Hmong
- Indonesian
- Japanese
- Korean
- Laotian
- Malaysian
- Pakistani
- Sri Lankan
- Taiwanese
- Thai
- Vietnamese

Native Hawaiian and Other Pacific Islander
- Fijian
- Guamanian or Chamorro
- Hawaiian, Native
- Samoan
- Tongan

Please note that this chapter only includes people who responded to the question on race by indicating only one race. These people are classified by the Census Bureau as the race *alone* population. For example, respondents reporting a single detailed Asian group, such as Korean or Filipino, would be included in the Asian *alone* population. Respondents reporting more than one detailed Asian group, such as Chinese and Japanese or Asian Indian and Chinese and Vietnamese would also be included in the Asian *alone* population. This is because all of the detailed groups in these example combinations are part of the larger Asian race category. The same criteria apply to the Native Hawaiian and Other Pacific Islander groups.

In order for any of the tables for a specific group to be shown in Summary File 4, the data must meet a minimum population threshold. For Summary File 4, all tables are repeated for each race group, American Indian and Alaska Native tribe, and Hispanic or Latino group if the 100-percent count of people of that specific group in a particular geographic area is 100 or more. There also must be 50 or more unweighted people of that specific group in a particular geographic area. For example, if there are 100 or more 100-percent people tabulated as Korean in County A, and there are 50 or more unweighted people, then all matrices for Korean are shown in SF 4 for County A.

To maintain confidentiality, the Census Bureau applies statistical procedures that introduce some uncertainty into data for small geographic areas with small population groups. Therefore, tables may contain both sampling and nonsampling error.

In an iterated file such as SF 4, the universes *households, families,* and *occupied housing units* are classified by the race or ethnic group of the householder. In any population table where there is no note, the universe classification is always based on the race or ethnicity of the person. In all housing tables, the universe classification is based on the race or ethnicity of the householder.

Comparing SF 4 Estimates with Corresponding Values in SF 1 and SF 2

As in earlier censuses, the responses from the sample of households reporting on long forms must be weighted to reflect the entire population. Specifically, each responding household represents, on average, six or seven other households who reported using short forms. One consequence of the weighting procedures is that each estimate based on the long form responses has an associated confidence interval. These confidence intervals are wider (as a percentage of the estimate) for geographic areas with smaller populations and for characteristics that occur less frequently in the area being examined (such as the proportion of people in poverty in a middle-income neighborhood). In order to release as much useful information as possible, statisticians must balance a number of factors. In particular, for Census 2000, the Bureau of the Census created weighting areas—geographic areas from which about two hundred or more long forms were completed—which are large enough to produce good quality estimates. If smaller weighting areas had been used, the confidence intervals around the estimates would have been significantly wider, rendering many estimates less useful due to their lower reliability. The disadvantage of using weighting areas this large is that, for smaller geographic areas within them, the estimates of characteristics that are also reported on the short form will not match the counts reported in SF 1 or SF 2. Examples of these characteristics are the total number of people, the number of people reporting specific racial categories, and the number of housing units. The official values for items reported on the short form come from SF 1 and SF 2. The differences between the long form estimates in SF 4 and values in SF 1 or SF 2 are particularly noticeable for the smallest places, tracts, and block groups. The long form estimates of total population and total housing units in SF 4 will, however, match the SF 1 and SF 2 counts for larger geographic areas such as counties and states, and will be essentially the same for medium and large cities. This phenomenon also occurred for the 1990 Census, although in that case, the weighting areas included relatively small places. As a result, the long form estimates matched the short form counts for those places, but the confidence intervals around the estimates of characteristics collected only on the long form were often significantly wider (as a percentage of the estimate). SF 1 gives exact numbers even for very small groups and areas; whereas, SF 4 gives estimates for small groups and areas such as tracts and small places that are less exact. The goal of SF 4 is to identify large differences among areas or large changes over time. Estimates for small areas and small population groups often do exhibit large changes from one census to the next, so having the capability to measure them is worthwhile.

Topics

POPULATION

Total Population: Sample count of total population of all races.

Asian Population: A person having origins in any of the original peoples of the Far East, Southeast Asia, or the Indian subcontinent including, for example, Cambodia, China, India, Japan, Korea, Malaysia, Pakistan, the Philippine Islands, Thailand, and Vietnam. It includes Asian Indian, Bangladeshi, Cambodian, Chinese (except Taiwanese), Filipino, Hmong, Indonesian, Japanese, Korean, Laotian, Malaysian, Pakistani, Sri Lankan, Taiwanese, Thai, and Vietnamese.

Native Hawaiian or Other Pacific Islander (NHPI) Population: A person having origins in any of the original peoples of Hawaii, Guam, Samoa, or other Pacific Islands. It includes people who indicate their race as Fijian, Guamanian or Chamorro, Native Hawaiian, Samoan, and Tongan.

The data on race, which was asked of all people, were derived from answers to long-form questionnaire Item 6 and short-form questionnaire Item 8. The concept of race, as used by the Census Bureau, reflects self-identification by people according to the race or races with which they most closely identify. These categories are socio-political constructs and should not be interpreted as being scientific or anthropological in nature. Furthermore, the race categories include both racial and national-origin groups.

If an individual did not provide a race response, the race or races of the householder or other household members were assigned using specific rules of precedence of household relationship. For example, if race was missing for a natural-born child in the household, then either the race or races of the householder, another natural-born child, or the spouse of the householder were assigned. If race was not reported for anyone in the household, the race or races of a householder in a previously processed household were assigned.

AGE

Median Age: Divides the age distribution into two equal parts: one-half of the cases falling below the median age and one-half above the median. Median age is computed on the basis of a single year of age standard distribution.

The data on age, which was asked of all people, were derived from answers to the long-form questionnaire Item 4 and short-form questionnaire Item 6. The age classification is based on the age of the person in complete years as of April 1, 2000. The age of the person usually was derived from their date of birth information. Their reported age was used only when date of birth information was unavailable.

HOUSEHOLD SIZE

Average Household Size: A measure obtained by dividing the number of people in households by the total number of households (or householders). In cases where household members are tabulated by race or Hispanic origin, household members are classified by the race or Hispanic origin of the householder rather than the race or Hispanic origin of each individual. Average household size is rounded to the nearest hundredth.

LANGUAGE SPOKEN AT HOME

English Only: Number and percentage of population 5 years and over who report speaking English-only at home.

Language spoken at home data were derived from answers to long-form questionnaire Items 11a and 11b, which were asked of a sample of the population. Data were edited to include in tabulations only the population 5 years old and over. Questions 11a and 11b referred to languages spoken at home in an effort to measure the current use of languages other than English. People who knew languages other than English but did not use them at home or who only used them elsewhere were excluded. Most people who reported speaking a language other than English at home also speak English. The questions did not permit determination of the primary or dominant language of people who spoke both English and another language.

FOREIGN-BORN

Foreign Born: Number and percentage of population who were not U.S. citizens at birth. Foreign-born people are those who indicated they were either a U.S. citizen by naturalization or they were not a citizen of the United States.

Foreign-Born Naturalized Citizens: Number and percentage of population who were not U.S. citizens at birth but became U.S. citizens by naturalization.

The data on place of birth were derived from answers to long-form questionnaire Item 12 which was asked of a sample of the population. Respondents were asked to report the U.S. state, Puerto Rico, U.S. Island Area, or foreign country where they were born. People not reporting a place of birth were assigned the state or country of birth of another family member or their residence 5 years earlier, or were imputed the response of another person with similar characteristics. People born outside the United States were asked to report their place of birth according to current international boundaries. Since numerous changes in boundaries of foreign countries have occurred in the last century, some people may have reported their place of birth in terms of boundaries that existed at the time of their birth or emigration, or in accordance with their own national preference.

EDUCATIONAL ATTAINMENT

High School Graduates: Number and percentage of the population age 25 and over who have a high school diploma or higher. This category includes people whose highest degree was a high school diploma or its equivalent, people who attended college but did not receive a degree, and people who received a college, university, or professional degree. People who reported completing the 12th grade but not receiving a diploma are not high school graduates.

Four-Year College Graduates: Number and percentage of the population age 25 and over who have a 4-year college, university, or professional degree.

Data on educational attainment were derived from answers to long-form questionnaire Item 9, which was asked of a sample of the population. Data on attainment are tabulated for the population 25 years old and over.

The order in which degrees were listed on the questionnaire suggested that doctorate degrees were “higher” than professional school degrees, which were “higher” than master's degrees. The question included instructions for people currently enrolled in school to report the level of the previous grade attended or the highest degree received. Respondents who did not report educational attainment or enrollment level were assigned the attainment of a person of the same age, race, Hispanic or Latino origin, occupation and sex, where possible, who resided in the same or a nearby area. Respondents who filled more than one box were edited to the highest level or degree reported.

The question included a response category that allowed respondents to report completing the 12th grade without receiving a high school diploma. It allowed people who received either a high school diploma or the equivalent (Test of General Educational Development—G.E.D.) and did not attend college, to be reported as "high school graduate(s)." The category "Associate degree" included people whose highest degree is an associate degree, which generally requires 2 years of college level work and is either in an occupational program that prepares them for a specific occupation, or an academic program primarily in the arts and sciences. The course work may or may not be transferable to a bachelor's degree. Master's degrees include the traditional MA and MS degrees and field-specific degrees, such as MSW, MEd, MBA, MLS, and MEng. Some examples of professional degrees include medicine, dentistry, chiropractic, optometry, osteopathic medicine, pharmacy, podiatry, veterinary medicine, law, and theology. Vocational and technical training such as barber school training; business, trade, technical, and vocational schools; or other training for a specific trade, are specifically excluded.

INCOME AND POVERTY

Median Household Income (in dollars): Includes the income of the householder and all other individuals 15 years old and over in the household, whether they are related to the householder or not. The median divides the income distribution into two equal parts: one-half of the cases falling below the median income and one-half above the median. For households, the median income is based on the distribution of the total number of households including those with no income. Median income for households is computed on the basis of a standard distribution and is rounded to the nearest whole dollar.

Per Capita Income (in dollars): Per capita income is the mean income computed for every man, woman, and child in a particular group. It is derived by dividing the total income of a particular group by the total population in that group. Per capita income is rounded to the nearest whole dollar.

The data on income in 1999 were derived from answers to long-form questionnaire Items 31 and 32, which were asked of a sample of the population 15 years old and over. "Total income" is the sum of the amounts reported separately for wage or salary income; net self-employment income; interest, dividends, or net rental or royalty income or income from estates and trusts; social security or railroad retirement income; Supplemental Security Income (SSI); public assistance or welfare payments; retirement, survivor, or disability pensions; and all other income.

Receipts from the following sources are not included as income: capital gains, money received from the sale of property (unless the recipient was engaged in the business of selling such property); the value of income "in kind" from food stamps, public housing subsidies, medical care, employer contributions for individuals, etc.; withdrawal of bank deposits; money borrowed; tax refunds; exchange of money between relatives living in the same household; and gifts and lump-sum inheritances, insurance payments, and other types of lump-sum receipts.

The eight types of income reported in the census are defined as follows:

Wage or salary income. Wage or salary income includes total money earnings received for work performed as an employee during the calendar year 1999. It includes wages, salary, armed forces pay, commissions, tips, piece-rate payments, and cash bonuses earned before deductions were made for taxes, bonds, pensions, union dues, etc.

Self-employment income. Self-employment income includes both farm and nonfarm self-employment income. Nonfarm self-employment income includes net money income (gross receipts minus expenses) from one's own business, professional enterprise, or partnership. Gross receipts include the value of all goods sold and services rendered. Expenses include costs of goods purchased, rent, heat, light, power, depreciation charges, wages and salaries paid, business taxes (not personal income taxes), etc. Farm self-employment income includes net money income (gross receipts minus operating expenses) from the operation of a farm by a person on his or her own account, as an owner, renter, or sharecropper. Gross receipts include the value of all products sold, government farm programs, money received from the rental of farm equipment to others, and incidental receipts from the sale of wood, sand, gravel, etc. Operating expenses include cost of feed, fertilizer, seed, and other farming supplies, cash wages paid to farmhands, depreciation charges, cash rent, interest on farm mortgages, farm building repairs, farm taxes (not state and federal personal income taxes), etc. The value of fuel, food, or other farm products used for family living is not included as part of net income.

Interest, dividends, or net rental income. Interest, dividends, or net rental income includes interest on savings or bonds, dividends from stockholdings or membership in associations, net income from rental of property to others and receipts from boarders or lodgers, net royalties, and periodic payments from an estate or trust fund.

Social Security income. Social security income includes social security pensions and survivors benefits, permanent disability insurance payments made by the Social Security Administration prior to deductions for medical insurance, and railroad retirement insurance checks from the U.S. government. Medicare reimbursements are not included.

Supplemental Security Income (SSI). Supplemental Security Income (SSI) is a nationwide U.S. assistance program administered by the Social Security Administration that guarantees a minimum level of income for needy aged, blind, or disabled individuals. The census questionnaire for Puerto Rico asked about the receipt of SSI; however, SSI is not a federally administered program in Puerto Rico. Therefore, it is probably not being interpreted by most respondents as the same as SSI in the United States. The only way a resident of Puerto Rico could have appropriately reported SSI would have been if they lived in the United States at any time during calendar year 1999 and received SSI.

Public assistance income. Public assistance income includes general assistance and Temporary Assistance to Needy Families (TANF). Separate payments received for hospital or other medical care (vendor payments) are excluded. This does not include Supplemental Security Income (SSI).

Retirement income. Retirement income includes: (1) retirement pensions and survivor benefits from a former employer; labor union; or federal, state, or local government; and the U.S. military; (2) income from workers' compensation; disability income from companies or unions; federal, state, or local government; and the U.S. military; (3) periodic receipts from annuities and insurance; and (4) regular income from IRA and KEOGH plans. This does not include social security income.

All other income. All other income includes unemployment compensation, Veterans' Administration (VA) payments, alimony and child support, contributions received periodically from people not living in the household, military family allotments, and other kinds of periodic income other than earnings.

Poverty Status: Number and percentage of population with income in 1999 below the poverty level. Based on individuals for whom poverty status is determined. Poverty status was determined for all people except institutionalized people, people in military group quarters, people in college dormitories, and unrelated individuals under 15 years old.

The poverty status of families and unrelated individuals in 1999 was determined using 48 thresholds (income cutoffs) arranged in a two dimensional matrix. The matrix consists of family size (from 1 person to 9 or more people) cross-classified by presence and number of family members under 18 years old (from no children present to 8 or more children present). Unrelated individuals and 2-person families were further differentiated by the age of the reference person (RP) (under 65 years old and 65 years old and over).

To determine a person's poverty status, one compares the person's total family income with the poverty threshold appropriate for that person's family size and composition. If the total income of that person's family is less than the threshold appropriate for that family, then the person is considered poor, together with every member of his or her family. If a person is not living with anyone related by birth, marriage, or adoption, then the person's own income is compared with his or her poverty threshold.

HOUSING

Homeownership: Number and percentage of housing units that are owner-occupied.

The data on tenure, which was asked at all occupied housing units, were obtained from answers to long-form questionnaire Item 33, and short-form questionnaire Item 2. All occupied housing units are classified as either owner occupied or renter occupied.

A housing unit is owner occupied if the owner or co-owner lives in the unit even if it is mortgaged or not fully paid for. The owner or co-owner must live in the unit and usually is Person 1 on the questionnaire. The unit is "Owned by you or someone in this household with a mortgage or loan" if it is being purchased with a mortgage or some other debt arrangement, such as a deed of trust, trust deed, contract to purchase, land contract, or purchase agreement. The unit is also considered owned with a mortgage if it is built on leased land and there is a mortgage on the unit. Mobile homes occupied by owners with installment loans balances are also included in this category.

Median Gross Rent (in dollars): Median monthly gross rent on specified renter-occupied and specified vacant-for-rent units. Specified renter-occupied and specified vacant-for-rent units exclude 1-family houses on 10 acres or more.

The data on gross rent were obtained from answers to long-form questionnaire Items 45a-d, which were asked on a sample basis. Gross rent is the contract rent plus the estimated average monthly cost of utilities (electricity, gas, water and sewer) and fuels (oil, coal, kerosene, wood, etc.) if these are paid by the renter (or paid for the renter by someone else). Gross rent is intended to eliminate differentials that result from varying practices with respect to the inclusion of utilities and fuels as part of the rental payment. The estimated costs of utilities and fuels are reported on an annual basis but are converted to monthly figures for the tabulations. Renter units occupied without payment of cash rent are shown separately as "No cash rent" in the tabulations.

Housing units that are renter occupied without payment of cash rent are shown separately as "No cash rent" in census data products. The unit may be owned by friends or relatives who live elsewhere and who allow occupancy without charge. Rent-free houses or apartments may be provided to compensate caretakers, ministers, tenant farmers, sharecroppers, or others.

Contract rent is the monthly rent agreed to or contracted for, regardless of any furnishings, utilities, fees, meals, or services that may be included. For vacant units, it is the monthly rent asked for the rental unit at the time of enumeration.

If the contract rent includes rent for a business unit or for living quarters occupied by another household, only that part of the rent estimated to be for the respondent's unit was included. Excluded was any rent paid for additional units or for business premises.

If a renter pays rent to the owner of a condominium or cooperative, and the condominium fee or cooperative carrying charge also is paid by the renter to the owner, the condominium fee or carrying charge was included as rent.

If a renter receives payments from lodgers or roomers who are listed as members of the household, the rent without deduction for any payments received from the lodgers or roomers was to be reported. The respondent was to report the rent agreed to or contracted for even if paid by someone else such as friends or relatives living elsewhere, a church or welfare agency, or the government through subsidies or vouchers.

The median divides the rent distribution into two equal parts: one-half of the cases falling below the median contract rent and one-half above the median. Median contract rents are computed on the basis of a standard distribution and are rounded to the nearest whole dollar. Units reported as "No cash rent" are excluded.

Median Home Value (in dollars): Reported by the owner of specified owner-occupied or specified vacant-for-sale housing units. Specified owner-occupied and specified vacant-for-sale housing units include only 1-family houses on less than 10 acres without a business or medical office on the property. The data for "specified units" exclude mobile homes, houses with a business or medical office, houses on 10 or more acres, and housing units in multi-unit buildings.

The data on value (also referred to as "price asked" for vacant units) were obtained from answers to long-form questionnaire Item 51, which was asked on a sample basis at owner-occupied housing units and units that were being bought, or vacant for sale at the time of enumeration. Value is the respondent's estimate of how much the property (house and lot, mobile home and lot, or condominium unit) would sell for if it were for sale. If the house or mobile home was owned or being bought, but the land on which it sits was not, the respondent was asked to estimate the combined value of the house or mobile home and the land. For vacant units, value was the price asked for the property. Value was tabulated separately for all owner-occupied and vacant-for-sale housing units, owner-occupied and vacant-for-sale mobile homes, and specified owner-occupied and specified vacant-for-sale housing units.

The median divides the value distribution into two equal parts: one-half of the cases falling below the median value of the property (house and lot, mobile home and lot, or condominium unit) and one-half above the median. Median values are computed on the basis of a standard distribution and are rounded to the nearest hundred dollars.

User's Guide: Climate

Inclusion Criteria — How the Data and Stations Were Selected

There were two central goals in the preparation of the climate chapter. The first was to select those data elements which would have the broadest possible use by the greatest range of potential users. For most of the National Weather Service stations there is a substantial quantity and variety of climatological data that is collected, however for the majority of stations the data is more limited. After evaluating the available data set, the editors chose nine temperature measures, five precipitation measures, and heating and cooling degree days — sixteen key data elements that are widely requested and are believed to be of the greatest general interest.

The second goal was to provide data for as many weather stations as possible. Although there are over 10,000 stations in the United States, not every station collects data for both precipitation and temperature, and even among those that do, the data is not always complete for the last thirty years. As the editors used a different methodology than that of NCDC to compute data, a formal data sufficiency criteria was devised and applied to the source tapes in order to select stations for inclusion.

Sources of the Data

The data in the climate chapter is compiled from several sources. The majority comes from the original National Climactic Data Center computer tapes (TD-3220 Summary of Month Co-Operative). This data was used to create the entire table for each Cooperative station and part of each National Weather Service station. The remainder of the data for each NWS station comes from the International Station Meteorological Climate Summary, Version 4.0, September 1996, which is also available from the NCDC.

NCDC has two main classes or types of weather stations; first order stations which are staffed by professional meteorologists and cooperative stations which are staffed by volunteers. In the climate chapter all first order stations operated by the National Weather Service are included, as well as every cooperative station that met our selection criteria.

Potential cautions in using *Weather America*

First, as with any statistical reference work of this type, users need to be aware of the source of the data. The information here comes from NOAA, and it is the most comprehensive and reliable core data available. Although it is the best, it is not perfect. Most weather stations are staffed by volunteers, times of observation sometimes vary, stations occasionally are moved (especially over a thirty year period), equipment is changed or upgraded, and all of these factors affect the uniformity of the data. the climate chapter does not attempt to correct for these factors, and is not intended for either climatologists or atmospheric scientists. Users with concerns about data collection and reporting protocols are both referred to NCDC technical documentation, and also, they are perhaps better served by using the original computer tapes themselves as well.

Second, users need to be aware of the methodology used, which is described later in this User's Guide. Although this methodology has produced fully satisfactory results, it is not directly compatible with other methodologies, hence variances in the results published here and those which appear in other publications will doubtlessly arise.

Third, is the trap of that informal logical fallacy known as "hasty generalization," and its corollaries. This may involve presuming the future will be like the past (specifically, next year will be an average year), or it may involve misunderstanding the limitations of an arithmetic average, but more interestingly, it may involve those mistakes made most innocently by generalizing informally on too broad a basis. As weather is highly localized, the data should be taken in that context. A weather station collects data about climatic conditions at that spot, and that spot may or may not be an effective paradigm for an entire town or area. For example, the weather station in Burlington, Vermont is located at the airport about 3 miles east of the center of town. Most of Burlington is a lot closer to Lake Champlain, and that should mean to a careful user that there could be a significant difference between the temperature readings gathered at the weather station and readings that might be gathered at City Hall downtown. How much would this difference be? How could it be estimated? There are no answers here for these sorts of questions, but it is important for users of this book to raise them for themselves. (It is interesting to note that similar situations abound across the country. For example, compare different readings for the multiple stations in San Francisco, CA or for those around New York City.)

Our source of data has been consistent, so has our methodology. The data has been computed and reported consistently as well. As a result, the the climate chapter should prove valuable to the careful and informed reader.

Weather Station Tables

The weather station tables are grouped by type (National Weather Service and Cooperative) and then arranged alphabetically. The station name is almost always a place name, and is shown here just as it appears in NCDC data. The station name is followed by the county in which the station is located, the elevation of the station (at the time beginning of the thirty year period) and the latitude and longitude.

The National Weather Service Station tables contain 30 data elements which were compiled from two different sources, the International Station Meteorological Climate Summary (ISMCS) and NCDC TD-3220 data tapes. The following 14 elements are from the ISMCS: maximum precipitation, minimum precipitation, maximum 24-hour precipitation, maximum snowfall, maximum 24-hour snowfall, thunderstorm days, foggy days, predominant sky cover, relative humidity (morning and afternoon), dewpoint, wind speed and direction, and maximum wind gust. The remaining 16 elements come from the TD-3220 data tapes. The period of record (POR) for data from the TD-3220 data tapes is 1970-1999. The POR for ISMCS data varies from station to station.

Weather Elements (National Weather Service and Cooperative Stations)

The following elements were compiled by the editor from the NCDC TD-3220 data tapes using a period of record of 1970-1999.

The average temperatures (maximum, minimum, and mean) are the average (see Methodology below) of those temperatures for all available values for a given month. For example, for a given station the average maximum temperature for July is the arithmetic average of all available maximum July temperatures for that station. (Maximum means the highest recorded temperature, minimum means the lowest recorded temperature, and mean means an arithmetic average temperature.)

The extreme maximum temperature is the highest temperature recorded in each month over the period 1970-1999. The extreme minimum temperature is the lowest temperature recorded in each month over the same time period.

The days for maximum temperature and minimum temperature are the average number of days those criteria were met for all available instances. The symbol >= means greater than or equal to, the symbol <= means less than or equal to. For example, for a given station, the number of days the maximum temperature was greater than or equal to 90°F in July, is just an arithmetic average of the number of days in all the available Julys for that station.

Heating and cooling degree days are based on the median temperature for a given day and its variance from 65°F. For example, for a given station if the day's high temperature was 50°F and the day's low temperature was 30°F, the median (midpoint) temperature was 40°F. 40°F is 25 degrees below 65°F, hence on this day there would be 25 heating degree days. The also applies for cooling degree days. For example, for a given station if the day's high temperature was 80°F and the day's low temperature was 70°F, the median (midpoint) temperature was 75°F. 75°F is 10 degrees above 65°F, hence on this day there would be 10 cooling degree days. All heating and/or cooling degree days in a month are summed for the month giving respective totals for each element for that month. These sums for a given month for a given station over the past thirty years are again summed and then arithmetically averaged. It should be noted that the heating and cooling degree days do not cancel each other out. It is possible to have both for a given station in the same month.

Precipitation data is computed the same as heating and cooling degree days. Mean precipitation and mean snowfall are arithmetic averages of cumulative totals for the month. All available values for the thirty year period for a given month for a given station are summed and then divided by the number of values. The same is true for days of greater than or equal to 0.1" and 1.0" of precipitation, and days of greater than or equal to 1.0" of snow depth on the ground. The word trace appears for precipitation and snowfall amounts that are too small to measure.

Finally, remember that all values presented in the tables and the rankings are averages of available data (see Methodology below) for that specific data element for the last thirty years (1970-1999).

Weather Elements (National Weather Service Stations Only)

The following elements were taken directly from the International Station Meteorological Climate Summary. The periods of records vary per station.

Maximum precipitation, minimum precipitation, maximum 24-hour precipitation, maximum snowfall, maximum 24-hour snowfall, thunderstorm days, foggy days, relative humidity (morning and afternoon), dewpoint, prevailing wind speed and direction, and maximum wind gust are all self-explanatory.

The word trace appears for precipitation and snowfall amounts that are too small to measure.

Predominant sky cover contains four possible entries: CLR (clear); SCT (scattered); BRK (broken); and OVR (overcast).

How Cooperative Stations Were Selected

The basic criteria is that a station must have data for temperature, precipitation, heating and cooling degree days of sufficient quantity in order to create a meaningful average. More specifically, the definition of sufficiency here has two parts. First, there must be 22 values for a given data element (with the exception of cooling degree days which required only 14 values in order to be considered sufficient- more about this later), and second, eight of the sixteen elements included in the table must pass this sufficiency test. For example, in regard to average maximum temperature (the first element on every data table), a given station needs to have a value for every month of at least 22 of the last thirty years in order to meet the criteria, and, in addition, every station included must have at least eight of the sixteen elements at least this minimal level of completeness in order to fulfill the criteria. By using this procedure, 3,933 stations met these requirements and are included here.

Methodology

The following discussion applies only to data compiled from the NCDC TD-3220 data tapes.

the climate chapter is based on an arithmetic average of all available data for a specific data element at a given station. For example, the average maximum daily high temperature during July for Pontiac, New York was abstracted from NCDC source tapes for the thirty Julys, starting in July, 1970 and ending in July, 1999. These thirty figures were then summed and divided by thirty to produce an arithmetic average. As might be expected, there were not thirty values for every data element on every table. For a variety of reasons, NCDC data is sometimes incomplete. Thus the following standards were established.

For those data elements where there were 26-30 values, the data was taken to be essentially complete and an average was computed. For data elements where there were 22-25 values, the data was taken as being partly complete but still valid enough to use to compute an average. Such averages are shown in ***bold italic*** type to indicate that there was less than 26 values. For the few data elements where there were not even 22 values, no average was computed and 'na' appears in the space. If any of the twelve months for a given data element reported a value of 'na', no annual average was computed and the annual average was reported as 'na' as well.

This procedure was followed for 15 of the 16 data elements. The one exception is cooling degree days. The collection of this data began in 1980 so the following standards were adopted: for those data elements where there were 17-20 values, the data was taken to be essentially complete and an average was computed. For data elements where there were 14-16 values, the data was taken as being partly complete but still valid enough to use to compute an average. Such averages are shown in ***bold italic*** type to indicate that there was 14-16 values. For the few data elements where there were not even 14 values, no average was computed and 'na' appears in the space. If any of the twelve months for a given data element reported a value of 'na', no annual average was computed and the annual average was reported as 'na' as well.

Thus the basic computational methodology of the climate chapter is to provide an arithmetic average. Because of this, such a pure arithmetic average is somewhat different from the special type of average (called a "normal") which NCDC procedures produces and appears in federal publications.

Perhaps the best outline of the contrasting normalization methodology is found in the following paragraph (which appears as part of an NCDC technical document titled, CLIM81 1961-1990 NORMALS TD-9641 prepared by Lewis France of NCDC in May, 1992):

Normals have been defined as the arithmetic mean of a climatological element computed over a long time period. International agreements eventually led to the decision that the appropriate time period would be three consecutive decades (Guttman, 1989). The data record should be consistent (have no changes in location, instruments, observation practices, etc.; these are identified here as "exposure changes") and have no missing values so a normal will reflect the actual average climatic conditions. If any significant exposure changes have occurred, the data record is said to be "inhomogeneous," and the normal may not reflect a true climatic average. Such data need to be adjusted to remove the nonclimatic inhomogeneities. The resulting (adjusted) record is then said to be "homogeneous." If no exposure changes have occurred at a station, the normal is calculated simply by averaging the appropriate 30 values from the 1961-1990 record.

In the main, there are two "inhomogeneities" that NCDC is correcting for with normalization: adjusting for variances in time of day of observation (at the so-called First Order stations data is based on midnight to midnight observation times and this practice is not necessarily followed at cooperative stations which are staffed by volunteers), and second, estimating data that is either missing or incongruent.

A long discussion of the normalization process is not required here but a short note concerning comparative results of the two methodologies is appropriate.

When the editors first started compiling the climate chapter a concern arose because the normalization process would not be replicated: would our methodology produce strikingly different results than NCDC's? To allay concerns, results of the two processes were compared for the time period normalized results are available (1961-1990). In short, what was found was that the answer to this question is no. Never-the-less, users should be aware that because of both the time period covered (1970-1999) and the methodology used, data in the climate chapter is not compatible with data from other sources.

Adams County

Located in western Illinois; bounded on the west by the Mississippi River and the Missouri border. Covers a land area of 856.63 square miles, a water area of 14.64 square miles, and is located in the Central Time Zone. The county was founded in 1825. County seat is Quincy.

Adams County is part of the Quincy, IL-MO Micropolitan Statistical Area. The entire metro area includes: Adams County, IL; Lewis County, MO

Weather Station: Golden Elevation: 725 feet

	Jan	Feb	Mar	Apr	May	Jun	Jul	Aug	Sep	Oct	Nov	Dec
High	32	38	51	63	74	83	87	85	78	67	50	38
Low	15	20	31	41	52	62	65	63	55	44	32	21
Precip	1.2	1.5	2.7	3.6	5.0	3.7	4.3	3.7	3.9	3.1	3.0	2.1
Snow	6.0	4.9	2.0	0.6	0.0	0.0	0.0	0.0	0.0	tr	1.6	3.9

High and Low temperatures in degrees Fahrenheit; Precipitation and Snow in inches

Weather Station: Quincy Muni Baldwin Field Elevation: 761 feet

	Jan	Feb	Mar	Apr	May	Jun	Jul	Aug	Sep	Oct	Nov	Dec
High	32	38	50	63	73	82	87	84	77	65	50	37
Low	16	22	32	43	53	62	67	64	56	45	33	23
Precip	1.4	1.7	3.1	3.9	5.0	3.6	3.9	3.6	4.1	3.3	3.2	2.4
Snow	7.6	6.0	2.9	0.9	tr	tr	tr	tr	tr	tr	2.2	4.8

High and Low temperatures in degrees Fahrenheit; Precipitation and Snow in inches

Population: 66,090 (1990); 68,277 (2000); 66,839 (2007); 65,764 (2012 projected); Race: 94.6% White, 3.3% Black, 0.5% Asian, 1.0% Hispanic of any race (2007); Density: 78.0 persons per square mile (2007); Average household size: 2.51 (2007); Median age: 39.5 (2007); Males per 100 females: 93.2 (2007).
Religion: Five largest groups: 23.3% Catholic Church, 5.4% The United Methodist Church, 4.9% Christian Churches and Churches of Christ, 4.7% United Church of Christ, 4.3% Lutheran Church—Missouri Synod (2000).
Economy: Unemployment rate: 3.9% (4/2008); Total civilian labor force: 39,156 (4/2008); Leading industries: 20.1% manufacturing; 16.0% health care and social assistance; 15.9% retail trade (2005); Farms: 1,347 totaling 444,087 acres (2002); Companies that employ 500 or more persons: 6 (2006); Companies that employ 100 to 499 persons: 46 (2006); Companies that employ less than 100 persons: 1,865 (2006); Black-owned businesses: n/a (2002); Hispanic-owned businesses: n/a (2002); Asian-owned businesses: n/a (2002); Women-owned businesses: 1,533 (2002); Retail sales per capita: $16,893 (2008). Single-family building permits issued: 66 (2007); Multi-family building permits issued: 51 (2007).
Income: Per capita income: $21,834 (2007); Median household income: $41,887 (2007); Average household income: $53,487 (2007); Percent of households with income of $100,000 or more: 9.8% (2007); Poverty rate: 11.2% (2005); Bankruptcy rate: 2.77% (2007).
Taxes: Total county taxes per capita: $96 (2006); County property taxes per capita: $96 (2006).
Education: Percent of population age 25 and over with: High school diploma (including GED) or higher: 83.9% (2007); Bachelor's degree or higher: 17.9% (2007); Master's degree or higher: 6.0% (2007).
Housing: Homeownership rate: 74.5% (2007); Median home value: $94,046 (2007); Median rent: $314 per month (2000); Median age of housing: 44 years (2000).
Health: Birth rate: 130.8 per 10,000 population (2007); Death rate: 123.3 per 10,000 population (2007); Age-adjusted cancer mortality rate: 212.3 deaths per 100,000 population (2005); Air Quality Index: 86.0% good, 13.1% moderate, 0.9% unhealthy for sensitive individuals, 0.0% unhealthy (percent of days in 2007); Number of physicians: 23.7 per 10,000 population (2005); Hospital beds: 49.7 per 10,000 population (2004); Hospital admissions: 1,926.3 per 10,000 population (2004).
Elections: 2004 Presidential election results: 66.2% Bush, 33.4% Kerry, 0.0% Nader, 0.4% Badnarik
National and State Parks: Sid Simpson State Park; Siloam Springs State Park
Additional Information Contacts
Adams County Government. . . . . (217) 277-2150
http://www.co.adams.il.us
City of Quincy. . . . . (217) 228-4545
http://www.ci.quincy.il.us
Quincy Area Chamber of Commerce. . . . . (217) 222-7980
http://www.quincychamber.org

Adams County Communities

CAMP POINT (village). Covers a land area of 0.948 square miles and a water area of 0 square miles. Located at 40.04° N. Lat.; 91.06° W. Long. Elevation is 722 feet.
History: Camp Point was settled about 1870 by people of German ancestry.
Population: 1,230 (1990); 1,244 (2000); 1,210 (2007); 1,166 (2012 projected); Race: 99.1% White, 0.0% Black, 0.2% Asian, 0.4% Hispanic of any race (2007); Density: 1,276.2 persons per square mile (2007); Average household size: 2.69 (2007); Median age: 39.1 (2007); Males per 100 females: 90.0 (2007); Marriage status: 24.2% never married, 48.8% now married, 12.7% widowed, 14.3% divorced (2000); Foreign born: 0.0% (2000); Ancestry (includes multiple ancestries): 42.7% German, 13.1% Irish, 10.3% English, 7.5% United States or American, 4.0% Other groups (2000).
Economy: Single-family building permits issued: 4 (2007); Multi-family building permits issued: 0 (2007); Employment by occupation: 6.2% management, 15.3% professional, 13.4% services, 25.3% sales, 0.7% farming, 9.6% construction, 29.6% production (2000).
Income: Per capita income: $19,763 (2007); Median household income: $39,074 (2007); Average household income: $50,211 (2007); Percent of households with income of $100,000 or more: 9.3% (2007); Poverty rate: 11.7% (2000).
Education: Percent of population age 25 and over with: High school diploma (including GED) or higher: 84.4% (2007); Bachelor's degree or higher: 9.8% (2007); Master's degree or higher: 3.2% (2007).

School District(s)

Central CUSD 3 (PK-12)
2005-06 Enrollment: 1,053 . . . . (217) 593-7116
Housing: Homeownership rate: 71.8% (2007); Median home value: $70,238 (2007); Median rent: $261 per month (2000); Median age of housing: 46 years (2000).
Safety: Violent crime rate: 0.0 per 10,000 population; Property crime rate: 67.2 per 10,000 population (2006).
Newspapers: Camp Point Journal (Community news; Circulation 800); The Golden Clayton New Era (Community news; Circulation 300); Golden New Era (Community news; Circulation 600); Mendon Dispatch-Times (Community news; Circulation 875)
Transportation: Commute to work: 93.5% car, 0.4% public transportation, 3.9% walk, 1.4% work from home (2000); Travel time to work: 39.9% less than 15 minutes, 20.8% 15 to 30 minutes, 29.9% 30 to 45 minutes, 4.7% 45 to 60 minutes, 4.8% 60 minutes or more (2000)

CLAYTON (village). Covers a land area of 0.874 square miles and a water area of 0.002 square miles. Located at 40.02° N. Lat.; 90.95° W. Long. Elevation is 732 feet.
Population: 726 (1990); 904 (2000); 804 (2007); 796 (2012 projected); Race: 77.0% White, 20.8% Black, 0.0% Asian, 2.4% Hispanic of any race (2007); Density: 919.6 persons per square mile (2007); Average household size: 2.87 (2007); Median age: 36.4 (2007); Males per 100 females: 134.4 (2007); Marriage status: 17.3% never married, 64.3% now married, 7.7% widowed, 10.7% divorced (2000); Foreign born: 0.0% (2000); Ancestry (includes multiple ancestries): 23.2% German, 16.2% United States or American, 10.5% Irish, 8.6% English, 4.8% French (except Basque) (2000).
Economy: Single-family building permits issued: 0 (2007); Multi-family building permits issued: 0 (2007); Employment by occupation: 8.3% management, 8.0% professional, 19.3% services, 22.7% sales, 0.6% farming, 11.2% construction, 29.9% production (2000).
Income: Per capita income: $18,766 (2007); Median household income: $32,500 (2007); Average household income: $48,152 (2007); Percent of households with income of $100,000 or more: 10.0% (2007); Poverty rate: 14.7% (2000).
Education: Percent of population age 25 and over with: High school diploma (including GED) or higher: 59.6% (2007); Bachelor's degree or higher: 5.0% (2007); Master's degree or higher: 2.4% (2007).
Housing: Homeownership rate: 78.6% (2007); Median home value: $44,737 (2007); Median rent: $200 per month (2000); Median age of housing: 56 years (2000).
Safety: Violent crime rate: 0.0 per 10,000 population; Property crime rate: 0.0 per 10,000 population (2006).
Transportation: Commute to work: 85.5% car, 1.5% public transportation, 7.4% walk, 3.1% work from home (2000); Travel time to work: 36.0% less

than 15 minutes, 23.9% 15 to 30 minutes, 27.7% 30 to 45 minutes, 5.1% 45 to 60 minutes, 7.3% 60 minutes or more (2000)

COATSBURG (village). Covers a land area of 0.122 square miles and a water area of 0 square miles. Located at 40.03° N. Lat.; 91.16° W. Long. Elevation is 758 feet.

History: Coatsburg was surveyed by R.P. Coates in 1855, and developed as a shipping center for grain and livestock. Coatsburg was incorporated as a village in 1885.

Population: 201 (1990); 226 (2000); 248 (2007); 253 (2012 projected); Race: 98.8% White, 0.0% Black, 0.0% Asian, 4.8% Hispanic of any race (2007); Density: 2,036.4 persons per square mile (2007); Average household size: 2.51 (2007); Median age: 34.1 (2007); Males per 100 females: 71.0 (2007); Marriage status: 16.1% never married, 58.9% now married, 10.7% widowed, 14.3% divorced (2000); Foreign born: 0.0% (2000); Ancestry (includes multiple ancestries): 39.4% United States or American, 20.8% German, 6.9% English, 5.1% Other groups, 5.1% Irish (2000).

Economy: Employment by occupation: 9.9% management, 19.8% professional, 24.3% services, 10.8% sales, 2.7% farming, 9.9% construction, 22.5% production (2000).

Income: Per capita income: $16,593 (2007); Median household income: $40,833 (2007); Average household income: $41,566 (2007); Percent of households with income of $100,000 or more: 3.0% (2007); Poverty rate: 9.0% (2000).

Education: Percent of population age 25 and over with: High school diploma (including GED) or higher: 74.5% (2007); Bachelor's degree or higher: 2.5% (2007); Master's degree or higher: 0.0% (2007).

Housing: Homeownership rate: 85.9% (2007); Median home value: $52,500 (2007); Median rent: $325 per month (2000); Median age of housing: 44 years (2000).

Transportation: Commute to work: 95.3% car, 0.0% public transportation, 0.0% walk, 4.7% work from home (2000); Travel time to work: 14.9% less than 15 minutes, 46.5% 15 to 30 minutes, 30.7% 30 to 45 minutes, 4.0% 45 to 60 minutes, 4.0% 60 minutes or more (2000)

COLUMBUS (village). Covers a land area of 0.252 square miles and a water area of 0 square miles. Located at 39.98° N. Lat.; 91.14° W. Long. Elevation is 722 feet.

History: Vigorously competed with Quincy for seat of Adams county in 19th century.

Population: 88 (1990); 112 (2000); 111 (2007); 111 (2012 projected); Race: 91.9% White, 8.1% Black, 0.0% Asian, 0.0% Hispanic of any race (2007); Density: 440.5 persons per square mile (2007); Average household size: 2.64 (2007); Median age: 37.7 (2007); Males per 100 females: 105.6 (2007); Marriage status: 16.3% never married, 75.5% now married, 3.1% widowed, 5.1% divorced (2000); Foreign born: 0.0% (2000); Ancestry (includes multiple ancestries): 38.3% German, 15.0% Other groups, 14.2% Irish, 12.5% English, 10.0% Dutch (2000).

Economy: Employment by occupation: 11.8% management, 5.3% professional, 27.6% services, 28.9% sales, 0.0% farming, 9.2% construction, 17.1% production (2000).

Income: Per capita income: $22,297 (2007); Median household income: $44,000 (2007); Average household income: $58,929 (2007); Percent of households with income of $100,000 or more: 21.4% (2007); Poverty rate: 5.8% (2000).

Education: Percent of population age 25 and over with: High school diploma (including GED) or higher: 69.7% (2007); Bachelor's degree or higher: 6.6% (2007); Master's degree or higher: 1.3% (2007).

Housing: Homeownership rate: 88.1% (2007); Median home value: $59,000 (2007); Median rent: $325 per month (2000); Median age of housing: 34 years (2000).

Transportation: Commute to work: 93.4% car, 0.0% public transportation, 0.0% walk, 6.6% work from home (2000); Travel time to work: 9.9% less than 15 minutes, 45.1% 15 to 30 minutes, 33.8% 30 to 45 minutes, 8.5% 45 to 60 minutes, 2.8% 60 minutes or more (2000)

FOWLER (unincorporated postal area, zip code 62338). Covers a land area of 26.247 square miles and a water area of 0.076 square miles. Located at 39.98° N. Lat.; 91.25° W. Long. Elevation is 732 feet.

Population: 1,364 (2000); Race: 98.8% White, 0.0% Black, 0.0% Asian, 0.4% Hispanic of any race (2000); Density: 52.0 persons per square mile (2000); Age: 25.7% under 18, 11.3% over 64 (2000); Marriage status: 19.2% never married, 64.8% now married, 5.9% widowed, 10.1% divorced (2000); Foreign born: 0.1% (2000); Ancestry (includes multiple ancestries): 48.4% German, 17.9% Irish, 5.8% United States or American, 5.5% Other groups, 4.8% English (2000).

Economy: Employment by occupation: 10.9% management, 23.0% professional, 14.1% services, 25.8% sales, 0.7% farming, 9.3% construction, 16.2% production (2000).

Income: Per capita income: $18,181 (2000); Median household income: $45,192 (2000); Poverty rate: 3.3% (2000).

Education: Percent of population age 25 and over with: High school diploma (including GED) or higher: 86.9% (2000); Bachelor's degree or higher: 14.6% (2000).

Housing: Homeownership rate: 94.1% (2000); Median home value: $77,500 (2000); Median rent: $292 per month (2000); Median age of housing: 26 years (2000).

Transportation: Commute to work: 94.3% car, 0.7% public transportation, 0.0% walk, 5.0% work from home (2000); Travel time to work: 24.4% less than 15 minutes, 62.9% 15 to 30 minutes, 11.4% 30 to 45 minutes, 0.9% 45 to 60 minutes, 0.4% 60 minutes or more (2000)

GOLDEN (village). Covers a land area of 0.628 square miles and a water area of 0 square miles. Located at 40.11° N. Lat.; 91.01° W. Long. Elevation is 715 feet.

Population: 578 (1990); 629 (2000); 625 (2007); 602 (2012 projected); Race: 100.0% White, 0.0% Black, 0.0% Asian, 0.3% Hispanic of any race (2007); Density: 994.5 persons per square mile (2007); Average household size: 2.46 (2007); Median age: 41.5 (2007); Males per 100 females: 82.7 (2007); Marriage status: 15.5% never married, 64.9% now married, 12.5% widowed, 7.1% divorced (2000); Foreign born: 0.0% (2000); Ancestry (includes multiple ancestries): 53.8% German, 8.6% Irish, 7.1% United States or American, 6.1% English, 3.7% Scotch-Irish (2000).

Economy: Employment by occupation: 13.3% management, 12.3% professional, 17.2% services, 16.3% sales, 1.2% farming, 12.3% construction, 27.4% production (2000).

Income: Per capita income: $21,397 (2007); Median household income: $43,250 (2007); Average household income: $50,059 (2007); Percent of households with income of $100,000 or more: 8.3% (2007); Poverty rate: 3.5% (2000).

Taxes: Total city taxes per capita: $24 (2006); City property taxes per capita: $24 (2006).

Education: Percent of population age 25 and over with: High school diploma (including GED) or higher: 79.2% (2007); Bachelor's degree or higher: 8.7% (2007); Master's degree or higher: 1.2% (2007).

School District(s)

Central CUSD 3 (PK-12)
2005-06 Enrollment: 1,053 . . . . (217) 593-7116

Housing: Homeownership rate: 81.9% (2007); Median home value: $63,158 (2007); Median rent: $286 per month (2000); Median age of housing: 54 years (2000).

Transportation: Commute to work: 87.0% car, 0.0% public transportation, 4.9% walk, 4.9% work from home (2000); Travel time to work: 53.6% less than 15 minutes, 11.0% 15 to 30 minutes, 24.4% 30 to 45 minutes, 9.4% 45 to 60 minutes, 1.6% 60 minutes or more (2000)

LA PRAIRIE (village). Covers a land area of 0.224 square miles and a water area of 0 square miles. Located at 40.14° N. Lat.; 91.00° W. Long. Elevation is 709 feet.

Population: 68 (1990); 60 (2000); 60 (2007); 58 (2012 projected); Race: 100.0% White, 0.0% Black, 0.0% Asian, 0.0% Hispanic of any race (2007); Density: 268.4 persons per square mile (2007); Average household size: 2.40 (2007); Median age: 42.5 (2007); Males per 100 females: 93.5 (2007); Marriage status: 15.6% never married, 66.7% now married, 8.9% widowed, 8.9% divorced (2000); Foreign born: 3.6% (2000); Ancestry (includes multiple ancestries): 45.5% United States or American, 30.9% English, 25.5% Other groups, 16.4% German, 3.6% Welsh (2000).

Economy: Employment by occupation: 9.5% management, 9.5% professional, 52.4% services, 0.0% sales, 0.0% farming, 9.5% construction, 19.0% production (2000).

Income: Per capita income: $12,417 (2007); Median household income: $21,250 (2007); Average household income: $29,800 (2007); Percent of households with income of $100,000 or more: 0.0% (2007); Poverty rate: 50.9% (2000).

Education: Percent of population age 25 and over with: High school diploma (including GED) or higher: 61.0% (2007); Bachelor's degree or higher: 0.0% (2007); Master's degree or higher: 0.0% (2007).

Housing: Homeownership rate: 92.0% (2007); Median home value: $55,000 (2007); Median rent: $n/a per month (2000); Median age of housing: 60+ years (2000).
Transportation: Commute to work: 89.5% car, 0.0% public transportation, 10.5% walk, 0.0% work from home (2000); Travel time to work: 26.3% less than 15 minutes, 10.5% 15 to 30 minutes, 36.8% 30 to 45 minutes, 10.5% 45 to 60 minutes, 15.8% 60 minutes or more (2000)

LIBERTY (village). Covers a land area of 0.374 square miles and a water area of 0 square miles. Located at 39.88° N. Lat.; 91.10° W. Long. Elevation is 751 feet.
Population: 548 (1990); 519 (2000); 515 (2007); 504 (2012 projected); Race: 99.6% White, 0.0% Black, 0.0% Asian, 0.0% Hispanic of any race (2007); Density: 1,376.0 persons per square mile (2007); Average household size: 2.40 (2007); Median age: 37.9 (2007); Males per 100 females: 98.1 (2007); Marriage status: 22.9% never married, 62.4% now married, 6.9% widowed, 7.8% divorced (2000); Foreign born: 0.0% (2000); Ancestry (includes multiple ancestries): 38.3% German, 16.2% United States or American, 12.8% Irish, 7.5% English, 4.7% Scottish (2000).
Economy: Employment by occupation: 5.3% management, 16.0% professional, 12.2% services, 28.5% sales, 0.9% farming, 11.9% construction, 25.1% production (2000).
Income: Per capita income: $21,510 (2007); Median household income: $46,196 (2007); Average household income: $51,523 (2007); Percent of households with income of $100,000 or more: 7.9% (2007); Poverty rate: 12.2% (2000).
Education: Percent of population age 25 and over with: High school diploma (including GED) or higher: 77.6% (2007); Bachelor's degree or higher: 10.5% (2007); Master's degree or higher: 2.2% (2007).

School District(s)

Liberty CUSD 2 (PK-12)
2005-06 Enrollment: 626 . . . . (217) 645-3433
Housing: Homeownership rate: 79.1% (2007); Median home value: $87,143 (2007); Median rent: $275 per month (2000); Median age of housing: 28 years (2000).
Newspapers: Liberty Bee-Times (Community news; Circulation 1,400)
Transportation: Commute to work: 93.7% car, 0.0% public transportation, 5.7% walk, 0.0% work from home (2000); Travel time to work: 21.1% less than 15 minutes, 42.5% 15 to 30 minutes, 34.3% 30 to 45 minutes, 0.6% 45 to 60 minutes, 1.6% 60 minutes or more (2000)

LIMA (village). Covers a land area of 0.214 square miles and a water area of 0 square miles. Located at 40.17° N. Lat.; 91.37° W. Long. Elevation is 653 feet.
Population: 120 (1990); 159 (2000); 148 (2007); 146 (2012 projected); Race: 99.3% White, 0.0% Black, 0.0% Asian, 4.1% Hispanic of any race (2007); Density: 690.5 persons per square mile (2007); Average household size: 2.69 (2007); Median age: 36.2 (2007); Males per 100 females: 97.3 (2007); Marriage status: 28.0% never married, 55.9% now married, 4.2% widowed, 11.9% divorced (2000); Foreign born: 0.0% (2000); Ancestry (includes multiple ancestries): 23.1% German, 15.4% English, 14.0% Irish, 9.8% United States or American, 2.8% Other groups (2000).
Economy: Employment by occupation: 6.7% management, 8.3% professional, 13.3% services, 31.7% sales, 0.0% farming, 3.3% construction, 36.7% production (2000).
Income: Per capita income: $17,230 (2007); Median household income: $45,313 (2007); Average household income: $46,364 (2007); Percent of households with income of $100,000 or more: 0.0% (2007); Poverty rate: 0.7% (2000).
Education: Percent of population age 25 and over with: High school diploma (including GED) or higher: 77.2% (2007); Bachelor's degree or higher: 6.5% (2007); Master's degree or higher: 0.0% (2007).
Housing: Homeownership rate: 90.9% (2007); Median home value: $60,000 (2007); Median rent: $225 per month (2000); Median age of housing: 39 years (2000).
Transportation: Commute to work: 95.0% car, 0.0% public transportation, 1.7% walk, 3.3% work from home (2000); Travel time to work: 17.2% less than 15 minutes, 41.4% 15 to 30 minutes, 29.3% 30 to 45 minutes, 3.4% 45 to 60 minutes, 8.6% 60 minutes or more (2000)

LORAINE (village). Covers a land area of 0.846 square miles and a water area of 0 square miles. Located at 40.15° N. Lat.; 91.22° W. Long. Elevation is 643 feet.
Population: 390 (1990); 363 (2000); 373 (2007); 366 (2012 projected); Race: 99.2% White, 0.0% Black, 0.0% Asian, 0.0% Hispanic of any race (2007); Density: 440.9 persons per square mile (2007); Average household size: 2.57 (2007); Median age: 34.1 (2007); Males per 100 females: 98.4 (2007); Marriage status: 17.2% never married, 64.6% now married, 7.5% widowed, 10.8% divorced (2000); Foreign born: 0.0% (2000); Ancestry (includes multiple ancestries): 32.6% German, 16.7% Irish, 12.0% United States or American, 10.9% English, 9.5% Other groups (2000).
Economy: Employment by occupation: 9.1% management, 12.2% professional, 15.9% services, 20.7% sales, 1.2% farming, 11.0% construction, 29.9% production (2000).
Income: Per capita income: $23,881 (2007); Median household income: $55,750 (2007); Average household income: $61,431 (2007); Percent of households with income of $100,000 or more: 5.5% (2007); Poverty rate: 11.7% (2000).
Education: Percent of population age 25 and over with: High school diploma (including GED) or higher: 81.8% (2007); Bachelor's degree or higher: 4.4% (2007); Master's degree or higher: 0.0% (2007).
Housing: Homeownership rate: 81.4% (2007); Median home value: $54,000 (2007); Median rent: $235 per month (2000); Median age of housing: 60+ years (2000).
Transportation: Commute to work: 98.7% car, 0.0% public transportation, 0.0% walk, 1.3% work from home (2000); Travel time to work: 15.9% less than 15 minutes, 38.2% 15 to 30 minutes, 42.7% 30 to 45 minutes, 3.2% 45 to 60 minutes, 0.0% 60 minutes or more (2000)

MENDON (village). Covers a land area of 0.731 square miles and a water area of 0 square miles. Located at 40.08° N. Lat.; 91.28° W. Long. Elevation is 761 feet.
Population: 854 (1990); 883 (2000); 858 (2007); 835 (2012 projected); Race: 99.5% White, 0.2% Black, 0.0% Asian, 0.5% Hispanic of any race (2007); Density: 1,173.3 persons per square mile (2007); Average household size: 2.49 (2007); Median age: 33.7 (2007); Males per 100 females: 88.6 (2007); Marriage status: 21.0% never married, 60.7% now married, 10.1% widowed, 8.2% divorced (2000); Foreign born: 0.6% (2000); Ancestry (includes multiple ancestries): 42.7% German, 16.3% Irish, 9.2% English, 6.7% United States or American, 6.6% Other groups (2000).
Economy: Employment by occupation: 8.2% management, 14.3% professional, 22.3% services, 17.1% sales, 1.4% farming, 13.9% construction, 22.7% production (2000).
Income: Per capita income: $21,026 (2007); Median household income: $44,306 (2007); Average household income: $52,290 (2007); Percent of households with income of $100,000 or more: 9.0% (2007); Poverty rate: 8.0% (2000).
Education: Percent of population age 25 and over with: High school diploma (including GED) or higher: 80.7% (2007); Bachelor's degree or higher: 9.6% (2007); Master's degree or higher: 1.7% (2007).

School District(s)

CUSD 4 (PK-12)
2005-06 Enrollment: 786 . . . . (217) 936-2111
Housing: Homeownership rate: 77.1% (2007); Median home value: $85,111 (2007); Median rent: $245 per month (2000); Median age of housing: 40 years (2000).
Transportation: Commute to work: 96.7% car, 0.4% public transportation, 2.5% walk, 0.4% work from home (2000); Travel time to work: 22.2% less than 15 minutes, 56.3% 15 to 30 minutes, 15.4% 30 to 45 minutes, 2.3% 45 to 60 minutes, 3.9% 60 minutes or more (2000)

PALOMA (unincorporated postal area, zip code 62359). Covers a land area of 10.096 square miles and a water area of 0.003 square miles. Located at 40.02° N. Lat.; 91.21° W. Long. Elevation is 732 feet.
Population: 192 (2000); Race: 100.0% White, 0.0% Black, 0.0% Asian, 0.0% Hispanic of any race (2000); Density: 19.0 persons per square mile (2000); Age: 17.7% under 18, 14.2% over 64 (2000); Marriage status: 8.9% never married, 85.4% now married, 0.0% widowed, 5.7% divorced (2000); Foreign born: 0.0% (2000); Ancestry (includes multiple ancestries): 39.0% United States or American, 21.3% German, 15.6% English, 14.9% Irish, 4.3% Croatian (2000).
Economy: Employment by occupation: 6.7% management, 16.0% professional, 12.0% services, 28.0% sales, 8.0% farming, 0.0% construction, 29.3% production (2000).
Income: Per capita income: $18,310 (2000); Median household income: $43,295 (2000); Poverty rate: 0.0% (2000).
Education: Percent of population age 25 and over with: High school diploma (including GED) or higher: 85.0% (2000); Bachelor's degree or higher: 7.5% (2000).

Housing: Homeownership rate: 85.7% (2000); Median home value: $95,000 (2000); Median rent: $368 per month (2000); Median age of housing: 16 years (2000).
Transportation: Commute to work: 84.0% car, 0.0% public transportation, 0.0% walk, 16.0% work from home (2000); Travel time to work: 12.7% less than 15 minutes, 54.0% 15 to 30 minutes, 25.4% 30 to 45 minutes, 0.0% 45 to 60 minutes, 7.9% 60 minutes or more (2000)

PAYSON (village). Covers a land area of 1.147 square miles and a water area of 0 square miles. Located at 39.81° N. Lat.; 91.24° W. Long. Elevation is 761 feet.
Population: 1,114 (1990); 1,066 (2000); 1,024 (2007); 1,012 (2012 projected); Race: 98.5% White, 0.0% Black, 0.0% Asian, 0.5% Hispanic of any race (2007); Density: 892.8 persons per square mile (2007); Average household size: 2.67 (2007); Median age: 35.1 (2007); Males per 100 females: 96.9 (2007); Marriage status: 19.8% never married, 64.0% now married, 6.9% widowed, 9.3% divorced (2000); Foreign born: 0.6% (2000); Ancestry (includes multiple ancestries): 31.1% German, 18.2% United States or American, 10.3% Irish, 8.9% English, 7.0% Other groups (2000).
Economy: Employment by occupation: 10.7% management, 12.4% professional, 15.7% services, 25.4% sales, 1.4% farming, 10.9% construction, 23.5% production (2000).
Income: Per capita income: $19,116 (2007); Median household income: $47,431 (2007); Average household income: $51,110 (2007); Percent of households with income of $100,000 or more: 7.0% (2007); Poverty rate: 9.3% (2000).
Education: Percent of population age 25 and over with: High school diploma (including GED) or higher: 85.4% (2007); Bachelor's degree or higher: 9.2% (2007); Master's degree or higher: 3.4% (2007).

School District(s)

Payson CUSD 1 (PK-12)
2005-06 Enrollment: 599 .... (217) 656-3323
Housing: Homeownership rate: 82.2% (2007); Median home value: $78,026 (2007); Median rent: $270 per month (2000); Median age of housing: 28 years (2000).
Safety: Violent crime rate: 9.5 per 10,000 population; Property crime rate: 9.5 per 10,000 population (2006).
Transportation: Commute to work: 97.8% car, 0.0% public transportation, 0.4% walk, 1.8% work from home (2000); Travel time to work: 17.8% less than 15 minutes, 59.8% 15 to 30 minutes, 20.1% 30 to 45 minutes, 1.2% 45 to 60 minutes, 1.0% 60 minutes or more (2000)

PLAINVILLE (village). Covers a land area of 0.230 square miles and a water area of 0 square miles. Located at 39.78° N. Lat.; 91.18° W. Long. Elevation is 692 feet.
Population: 270 (1990); 248 (2000); 243 (2007); 241 (2012 projected); Race: 99.6% White, 0.0% Black, 0.0% Asian, 0.0% Hispanic of any race (2007); Density: 1,057.0 persons per square mile (2007); Average household size: 2.43 (2007); Median age: 38.6 (2007); Males per 100 females: 91.3 (2007); Marriage status: 12.6% never married, 69.9% now married, 6.6% widowed, 10.9% divorced (2000); Foreign born: 1.7% (2000); Ancestry (includes multiple ancestries): 28.0% United States or American, 23.7% German, 9.1% English, 3.9% Irish, 3.4% Scottish (2000).
Economy: Employment by occupation: 8.0% management, 18.8% professional, 15.2% services, 21.4% sales, 1.8% farming, 17.9% construction, 17.0% production (2000).
Income: Per capita income: $15,854 (2007); Median household income: $35,714 (2007); Average household income: $38,525 (2007); Percent of households with income of $100,000 or more: 0.0% (2007); Poverty rate: 6.9% (2000).
Education: Percent of population age 25 and over with: High school diploma (including GED) or higher: 79.2% (2007); Bachelor's degree or higher: 10.1% (2007); Master's degree or higher: 2.4% (2007).
Housing: Homeownership rate: 88.0% (2007); Median home value: $54,167 (2007); Median rent: $213 per month (2000); Median age of housing: 60+ years (2000).
Transportation: Commute to work: 94.5% car, 0.0% public transportation, 5.5% walk, 0.0% work from home (2000); Travel time to work: 16.4% less than 15 minutes, 40.9% 15 to 30 minutes, 37.3% 30 to 45 minutes, 0.0% 45 to 60 minutes, 5.5% 60 minutes or more (2000)

QUINCY (city). County seat. Covers a land area of 14.619 square miles and a water area of 0.027 square miles. Located at 39.93° N. Lat.; 91.38° W. Long. Elevation is 568 feet.
History: The first settlement at Quincy was called The Bluffs, and centered around the cabin of John Wood. Wood later served as lieutenant governor and governor of Illinois. When Adams County was created in 1825, Quincy was named as the county seat, and the town was platted. In the mid-1800's Quincy was an active shipping center.
Population: 41,151 (1990); 40,366 (2000); 39,073 (2007); 38,094 (2012 projected); Race: 92.4% White, 4.9% Black, 0.6% Asian, 1.2% Hispanic of any race (2007); Density: 2,672.8 persons per square mile (2007); Average household size: 2.41 (2007); Median age: 39.6 (2007); Males per 100 females: 89.3 (2007); Marriage status: 24.0% never married, 54.2% now married, 10.6% widowed, 11.2% divorced (2000); Foreign born: 1.0% (2000); Ancestry (includes multiple ancestries): 36.6% German, 12.1% Irish, 9.0% United States or American, 8.8% Other groups, 8.5% English (2000).
Economy: Unemployment rate: 4.1% (4/2008); Total civilian labor force: 22,632 (4/2008); Single-family building permits issued: 62 (2007); Multi-family building permits issued: 51 (2007); Employment by occupation: 9.9% management, 17.3% professional, 18.4% services, 28.4% sales, 0.1% farming, 7.5% construction, 18.4% production (2000).
Income: Per capita income: $20,626 (2007); Median household income: $36,676 (2007); Average household income: $47,997 (2007); Percent of households with income of $100,000 or more: 7.4% (2007); Poverty rate: 12.2% (2000).
Taxes: Total city taxes per capita: $287 (2006); City property taxes per capita: $71 (2006).
Education: Percent of population age 25 and over with: High school diploma (including GED) or higher: 82.9% (2007); Bachelor's degree or higher: 19.7% (2007); Master's degree or higher: 6.9% (2007).

School District(s)

Adams/Pike Roe
2005-06 Enrollment: n/a .... (217) 277-2080
Quincy Area Voc Ctr
2005-06 Enrollment: n/a .... (217) 224-3775
Quincy SD 172 (PK-12)
2005-06 Enrollment: 7,238 .... (217) 223-8700

Four-year College(s)

Blessing Rieman College of Nursing (Private, Not-for-profit)
Fall 2007 Enrollment: 219 .... (217) 228-5520
2007-08 Tuition: In-state $17,775; Out-of-state $17,775
Quincy University (Private, Not-for-profit, Roman Catholic)
Fall 2007 Enrollment: 1,323....................... (217) 222-8020
2007-08 Tuition: In-state $19,600; Out-of-state $19,600

Two-year College(s)

Blessing Hospital School of Radiologic Technology (Private, Not-for-profit)
Fall 2007 Enrollment: 22 .... (217) 223-8400
John Wood Community College (Public)
Fall 2007 Enrollment: 2,417....................... (217) 224-6500
2007-08 Tuition: In-state $5,880; Out-of-state $5,880
Vatterott College (Private, For-profit)
Fall 2007 Enrollment: 266 .... (800) 438-5621
2007-08 Tuition: In-state $9,419; Out-of-state $9,419

Vocational/Technical School(s)

Blessing Hospital School of Medical Laboratory Technology (Private, Not-for-profit)
Fall 2007 Enrollment: 6 .... (217) 223-8400
2007-08 Tuition: $1,270
Gem City College (Private, For-profit)
Fall 2007 Enrollment: 67 .... (217) 222-0391
2007-08 Tuition: $9,175
Housing: Homeownership rate: 67.3% (2007); Median home value: $87,283 (2007); Median rent: $323 per month (2000); Median age of housing: 50 years (2000).
Hospitals: Blessing Hospital (426 beds)
Safety: Violent crime rate: 75.8 per 10,000 population; Property crime rate: 397.8 per 10,000 population (2006).
Newspapers: Quincy Herald-Whig (Local news; Circulation 24,153)
Transportation: Commute to work: 92.3% car, 0.9% public transportation, 3.6% walk, 2.3% work from home (2000); Travel time to work: 68.6% less than 15 minutes, 23.5% 15 to 30 minutes, 4.0% 30 to 45 minutes, 1.8% 45 to 60 minutes, 2.0% 60 minutes or more (2000); Amtrak: Service available.
Airports: Quincy Regional-Baldwin Field (commercial service)
Additional Information Contacts
City of Quincy.................................... (217) 228-4545
http://www.ci.quincy.il.us

Quincy Area Chamber of Commerce. . . . . (217) 222-7980
http://www.quincychamber.org

URSA (village). Covers a land area of 0.682 square miles and a water area of 0 square miles. Located at 40.07° N. Lat.; 91.37° W. Long. Elevation is 610 feet.
Population: 578 (1990); 595 (2000); 567 (2007); 566 (2012 projected); Race: 98.4% White, 0.0% Black, 1.1% Asian, 2.5% Hispanic of any race (2007); Density: 831.8 persons per square mile (2007); Average household size: 2.30 (2007); Median age: 39.0 (2007); Males per 100 females: 80.0 (2007); Marriage status: 15.4% never married, 67.9% now married, 9.7% widowed, 7.0% divorced (2000); Foreign born: 0.3% (2000); Ancestry (includes multiple ancestries): 46.6% German, 13.9% Irish, 11.2% United States or American, 8.5% English, 5.8% Other groups (2000).
Economy: Employment by occupation: 8.7% management, 14.2% professional, 14.8% services, 29.4% sales, 0.3% farming, 12.9% construction, 19.7% production (2000).
Income: Per capita income: $21,583 (2007); Median household income: $42,917 (2007); Average household income: $49,746 (2007); Percent of households with income of $100,000 or more: 6.5% (2007); Poverty rate: 10.4% (2000).
Education: Percent of population age 25 and over with: High school diploma (including GED) or higher: 84.5% (2007); Bachelor's degree or higher: 14.4% (2007); Master's degree or higher: 4.5% (2007).

School District(s)

CUSD 4 (PK-12)
2005-06 Enrollment: 786 . . . . (217) 936-2111
Housing: Homeownership rate: 75.2% (2007); Median home value: $93,235 (2007); Median rent: $269 per month (2000); Median age of housing: 30 years (2000).
Transportation: Commute to work: 85.6% car, 0.0% public transportation, 5.6% walk, 8.2% work from home (2000); Travel time to work: 26.0% less than 15 minutes, 61.2% 15 to 30 minutes, 7.8% 30 to 45 minutes, 0.7% 45 to 60 minutes, 4.3% 60 minutes or more (2000)

Alexander County

Located in southern Illinois; bounded on the west and south by the Mississippi River and the Missouri border, and on the southeast by the Ohio River; includes part of Shawnee National Forest. Covers a land area of 236.38 square miles, a water area of 16.16 square miles, and is located in the Central Time Zone. The county was founded in 1819. County seat is Cairo.

Alexander County is part of the Cape Girardeau-Jackson, MO-IL Micropolitan Statistical Area. The entire metro area includes: Alexander County, IL; Bollinger County, MO; Cape Girardeau County, MO

Weather Station: Cairo WSO City Elevation: 311 feet

	Jan	Feb	Mar	Apr	May	Jun	Jul	Aug	Sep	Oct	Nov	Dec
High	41	47	57	69	78	86	90	87	81	70	57	46
Low	26	31	40	50	59	67	71	69	61	50	40	31
Precip	3.0	3.5	4.6	5.0	4.8	4.3	4.3	3.8	3.1	3.5	4.3	4.1
Snow	4.0	2.7	1.7	tr	0.0	0.0	0.0	0.0	0.0	0.1	0.2	0.9

High and Low temperatures in degrees Fahrenheit; Precipitation and Snow in inches

Population: 10,626 (1990); 9,590 (2000); 8,665 (2007); 7,949 (2012 projected); Race: 63.2% White, 34.7% Black, 0.5% Asian, 1.8% Hispanic of any race (2007); Density: 36.7 persons per square mile (2007); Average household size: 2.49 (2007); Median age: 38.7 (2007); Males per 100 females: 96.9 (2007).
Religion: Five largest groups: 21.4% Southern Baptist Convention, 3.6% American Baptist Churches in the USA, 3.4% Catholic Church, 2.5% The United Methodist Church, 1.5% Assemblies of God (2000).
Economy: Unemployment rate: 6.1% (4/2008); Total civilian labor force: 3,634 (4/2008); Leading industries: 25.6% health care and social assistance; 22.5% transportation & warehousing; 11.2% manufacturing (2005); Farms: 149 totaling 78,418 acres (2002); Companies that employ 500 or more persons: 0 (2006); Companies that employ 100 to 499 persons: 4 (2006); Companies that employ less than 100 persons: 126 (2006); Black-owned businesses: n/a (2002); Hispanic-owned businesses: n/a (2002); Asian-owned businesses: n/a (2002); Women-owned businesses: 291 (2002); Retail sales per capita: $4,247 (2008). Single-family building permits issued: 1 (2007); Multi-family building permits issued: 0 (2007).
Income: Per capita income: $18,026 (2007); Median household income: $30,176 (2007); Average household income: $42,074 (2007); Percent of households with income of $100,000 or more: 5.9% (2007); Poverty rate: 33.9% (2005); Bankruptcy rate: 7.45% (2007).
Taxes: Total county taxes per capita: $156 (2006); County property taxes per capita: $155 (2006).
Education: Percent of population age 25 and over with: High school diploma (including GED) or higher: 66.8% (2007); Bachelor's degree or higher: 7.0% (2007); Master's degree or higher: 2.6% (2007).
Housing: Homeownership rate: 72.0% (2007); Median home value: $44,027 (2007); Median rent: $185 per month (2000); Median age of housing: 39 years (2000).
Health: Birth rate: 138.3 per 10,000 population (2007); Death rate: 136.0 per 10,000 population (2007); Age-adjusted cancer mortality rate: 211.0 deaths per 100,000 population (2005); Number of physicians: 3.4 per 10,000 population (2005); Hospital beds: 0.0 per 10,000 population (2004); Hospital admissions: 0.0 per 10,000 population (2004).
Elections: 2004 Presidential election results: 47.3% Bush, 52.1% Kerry, 0.1% Nader, 0.6% Badnarik
National and State Parks: Fort Defiance State Park; Horseshoe Lake State Conservation Area
Additional Information Contacts
Alexander County Government . . . . (618) 734-7000

Cairo Chamber of Commerce . . . . (618) 734-2737
Horseshoe Lake Chamber of Commerce . . . . (618) 776-5198

Alexander County Communities

CAIRO (city). County seat. Covers a land area of 7.051 square miles and a water area of 2.081 square miles. Located at 37.01° N. Lat.; 89.18° W. Long. Elevation is 322 feet.
History: John G. Comegys, a St. Louis merchant, in 1818 secured the incorporation of the city of Cairo, named because he thought its site resembled Cairo, Egypt. Comegys died before he could carry out his plans, but the name Cairo remained when the Cairo City and Canal Company was formed in 1837 by Darius B. Holbrook. When the Illinois Central Railroad tracks were laid between Cairo and Chicago, Cairo's economy grew. Cairo was a Union headquarters during the Civil War, and received many thousands of Confederate prisoners.
Population: 4,873 (1990); 3,632 (2000); 3,247 (2007); 2,905 (2012 projected); Race: 35.6% White, 62.0% Black, 0.9% Asian, 0.9% Hispanic of any race (2007); Density: 460.5 persons per square mile (2007); Average household size: 2.29 (2007); Median age: 35.9 (2007); Males per 100 females: 78.5 (2007); Marriage status: 29.1% never married, 44.9% now married, 9.7% widowed, 16.2% divorced (2000); Foreign born: 1.4% (2000); Ancestry (includes multiple ancestries): 54.6% Other groups, 6.0% Irish, 6.0% German, 3.9% United States or American, 3.4% English (2000).
Economy: Single-family building permits issued: 0 (2007); Multi-family building permits issued: 0 (2007); Employment by occupation: 10.9% management, 14.9% professional, 22.7% services, 20.5% sales, 0.0% farming, 9.0% construction, 22.0% production (2000).
Income: Per capita income: $18,425 (2007); Median household income: $25,331 (2007); Average household income: $40,979 (2007); Percent of households with income of $100,000 or more: 6.1% (2007); Poverty rate: 33.5% (2000).
Education: Percent of population age 25 and over with: High school diploma (including GED) or higher: 67.7% (2007); Bachelor's degree or higher: 7.4% (2007); Master's degree or higher: 3.1% (2007).

School District(s)

Alxndr/John/Masc/Pulski/Union Roe (06-12)
2005-06 Enrollment: 191 . . . . (618) 634-2292
Cairo USD 1 (PK-12)
2005-06 Enrollment: 711 . . . . (618) 734-4102
Five County Reg Voc System
2005-06 Enrollment: n/a . . . . (618) 747-2703
Jamp Spec Educ Services (04-12)
2005-06 Enrollment: 34 . . . . (618) 742-6231
Housing: Homeownership rate: 55.8% (2007); Median home value: $33,956 (2007); Median rent: $176 per month (2000); Median age of housing: 48 years (2000).
Safety: Violent crime rate: 293.2 per 10,000 population; Property crime rate: 541.6 per 10,000 population (2006).
Newspapers: Cairo Citizen (Community news; Circulation 3,500)

Transportation: Commute to work: 89.9% car, 1.3% public transportation, 7.4% walk, 0.0% work from home (2000); Travel time to work: 61.4% less than 15 minutes, 18.0% 15 to 30 minutes, 10.2% 30 to 45 minutes, 7.2% 45 to 60 minutes, 3.2% 60 minutes or more (2000)

Additional Information Contacts

Cairo Chamber of Commerce . . . . (618) 734-2737

EAST CAPE GIRARDEAU (village). Covers a land area of 1.969 square miles and a water area of 0.034 square miles. Located at 37.29° N. Lat.; 89.49° W. Long. Elevation is 341 feet.

Population: 451 (1990); 437 (2000); 377 (2007); 358 (2012 projected); Race: 96.0% White, 1.1% Black, 0.8% Asian, 2.4% Hispanic of any race (2007); Density: 191.5 persons per square mile (2007); Average household size: 2.18 (2007); Median age: 41.9 (2007); Males per 100 females: 90.4 (2007); Marriage status: 18.2% never married, 61.3% now married, 5.9% widowed, 14.7% divorced (2000); Foreign born: 1.7% (2000); Ancestry (includes multiple ancestries): 25.2% United States or American, 17.6% Other groups, 17.4% German, 14.8% Irish, 3.8% English (2000).

Economy: Single-family building permits issued: 0 (2007); Multi-family building permits issued: 0 (2007); Employment by occupation: 8.1% management, 13.4% professional, 16.1% services, 23.7% sales, 0.0% farming, 7.5% construction, 31.2% production (2000).

Income: Per capita income: $15,822 (2007); Median household income: $30,109 (2007); Average household income: $34,480 (2007); Percent of households with income of $100,000 or more: 0.0% (2007); Poverty rate: 10.5% (2000).

Education: Percent of population age 25 and over with: High school diploma (including GED) or higher: 76.8% (2007); Bachelor's degree or higher: 9.0% (2007); Master's degree or higher: 0.0% (2007).

Housing: Homeownership rate: 75.7% (2007); Median home value: $44,583 (2007); Median rent: $255 per month (2000); Median age of housing: 29 years (2000).

Transportation: Commute to work: 95.1% car, 2.7% public transportation, 0.0% walk, 1.1% work from home (2000); Travel time to work: 42.6% less than 15 minutes, 36.1% 15 to 30 minutes, 11.5% 30 to 45 minutes, 5.5% 45 to 60 minutes, 4.4% 60 minutes or more (2000)

MCCLURE (unincorporated postal area, zip code 62957). Covers a land area of 50.471 square miles and a water area of 0.768 square miles. Located at 37.30° N. Lat.; 89.43° W. Long. Elevation is 341 feet.

Population: 1,174 (2000); Race: 98.8% White, 0.0% Black, 0.4% Asian, 0.6% Hispanic of any race (2000); Density: 23.3 persons per square mile (2000); Age: 26.6% under 18, 17.1% over 64 (2000); Marriage status: 19.6% never married, 61.3% now married, 8.0% widowed, 11.1% divorced (2000); Foreign born: 0.6% (2000); Ancestry (includes multiple ancestries): 24.9% United States or American, 16.3% German, 11.7% Other groups, 11.2% English, 9.0% Irish (2000).

Economy: Employment by occupation: 14.4% management, 9.2% professional, 19.0% services, 17.8% sales, 1.7% farming, 14.4% construction, 23.4% production (2000).

Income: Per capita income: $16,247 (2000); Median household income: $29,766 (2000); Poverty rate: 17.8% (2000).

Education: Percent of population age 25 and over with: High school diploma (including GED) or higher: 77.4% (2000); Bachelor's degree or higher: 9.8% (2000).

School District(s)

Shawnee CUSD 84 (KG-12)
2005-06 Enrollment: 481 . . . . (618) 833-5709

Housing: Homeownership rate: 82.8% (2000); Median home value: $45,600 (2000); Median rent: $236 per month (2000); Median age of housing: 30 years (2000).

Transportation: Commute to work: 95.3% car, 1.1% public transportation, 0.0% walk, 3.2% work from home (2000); Travel time to work: 30.5% less than 15 minutes, 38.7% 15 to 30 minutes, 20.4% 30 to 45 minutes, 5.5% 45 to 60 minutes, 4.8% 60 minutes or more (2000)

MILLER CITY (unincorporated postal area, zip code 62962). Covers a land area of 37.441 square miles and a water area of 0.523 square miles. Located at 37.09° N. Lat.; 89.33° W. Long. Elevation is 331 feet.

Population: 93 (2000); Race: 100.0% White, 0.0% Black, 0.0% Asian, 0.0% Hispanic of any race (2000); Density: 2.5 persons per square mile (2000); Age: 0.0% under 18, 14.5% over 64 (2000); Marriage status: 16.4% never married, 61.8% now married, 21.8% widowed, 0.0% divorced (2000); Foreign born: 0.0% (2000); Ancestry (includes multiple ancestries): 43.6% German, 9.1% United States or American, 9.1% Irish (2000).

Economy: Employment by occupation: 47.4% management, 0.0% professional, 0.0% services, 0.0% sales, 26.3% farming, 0.0% construction, 26.3% production (2000).

Income: Per capita income: $18,242 (2000); Median household income: $26,250 (2000); Poverty rate: 50.9% (2000).

Education: Percent of population age 25 and over with: High school diploma (including GED) or higher: 58.7% (2000); Bachelor's degree or higher: 30.4% (2000).

Housing: Homeownership rate: 36.8% (2000); Median home value: $45,000 (2000); Median rent: $150 per month (2000); Median age of housing: 28 years (2000).

Transportation: Commute to work: 100.0% car, 0.0% public transportation, 0.0% walk, 0.0% work from home (2000); Travel time to work: 0.0% less than 15 minutes, 73.7% 15 to 30 minutes, 0.0% 30 to 45 minutes, 0.0% 45 to 60 minutes, 26.3% 60 minutes or more (2000)

OLIVE BRANCH (unincorporated postal area, zip code 62969). Covers a land area of 25.996 square miles and a water area of 2.618 square miles. Located at 37.16° N. Lat.; 89.35° W. Long. Elevation is 341 feet.

Population: 879 (2000); Race: 98.4% White, 0.0% Black, 0.0% Asian, 0.0% Hispanic of any race (2000); Density: 33.8 persons per square mile (2000); Age: 26.0% under 18, 19.5% over 64 (2000); Marriage status: 13.9% never married, 66.5% now married, 11.0% widowed, 8.6% divorced (2000); Foreign born: 0.7% (2000); Ancestry (includes multiple ancestries): 10.1% Other groups, 10.0% German, 9.9% United States or American, 7.5% Irish, 7.0% English (2000).

Economy: Employment by occupation: 15.5% management, 14.7% professional, 16.6% services, 17.7% sales, 0.0% farming, 22.3% construction, 13.3% production (2000).

Income: Per capita income: $23,970 (2000); Median household income: $30,833 (2000); Poverty rate: 13.5% (2000).

Education: Percent of population age 25 and over with: High school diploma (including GED) or higher: 72.6% (2000); Bachelor's degree or higher: 12.4% (2000).

Housing: Homeownership rate: 88.3% (2000); Median home value: $59,600 (2000); Median rent: $144 per month (2000); Median age of housing: 27 years (2000).

Transportation: Commute to work: 88.3% car, 1.6% public transportation, 4.3% walk, 5.7% work from home (2000); Travel time to work: 18.7% less than 15 minutes, 48.4% 15 to 30 minutes, 20.7% 30 to 45 minutes, 2.0% 45 to 60 minutes, 10.1% 60 minutes or more (2000)

Additional Information Contacts

Horseshoe Lake Chamber of Commerce . . . . (618) 776-5198

TAMMS (village). Covers a land area of 2.340 square miles and a water area of 0 square miles. Located at 37.24° N. Lat.; 89.26° W. Long. Elevation is 341 feet.

Population: 731 (1990); 724 (2000); 710 (2007); 651 (2012 projected); Race: 72.1% White, 26.8% Black, 0.0% Asian, 2.3% Hispanic of any race (2007); Density: 303.5 persons per square mile (2007); Average household size: 2.54 (2007); Median age: 37.7 (2007); Males per 100 females: 83.9 (2007); Marriage status: 20.3% never married, 56.2% now married, 13.1% widowed, 10.5% divorced (2000); Foreign born: 0.0% (2000); Ancestry (includes multiple ancestries): 29.3% Other groups, 12.2% United States or American, 9.6% German, 9.0% Irish, 3.2% French (except Basque) (2000).

Economy: Employment by occupation: 11.9% management, 11.4% professional, 33.2% services, 15.3% sales, 0.0% farming, 8.4% construction, 19.8% production (2000).

Income: Per capita income: $11,603 (2007); Median household income: $19,840 (2007); Average household income: $27,849 (2007); Percent of households with income of $100,000 or more: 1.4% (2007); Poverty rate: 30.8% (2000).

Education: Percent of population age 25 and over with: High school diploma (including GED) or higher: 66.7% (2007); Bachelor's degree or higher: 1.1% (2007); Master's degree or higher: 0.2% (2007).

School District(s)

Dept of Corrections Sch Dist 428 (08-12)
2005-06 Enrollment: 2,271 . . . . (217) 522-2666

Egyptian CUSD 5 (PK-12)
2005-06 Enrollment: 610 . . . . (618) 776-5306

Five County Reg Voc Center
2005-06 Enrollment: n/a . . . . (618) 747-2703

Housing: Homeownership rate: 81.0% (2007); Median home value: $47,143 (2007); Median rent: $200 per month (2000); Median age of housing: 28 years (2000).
Transportation: Commute to work: 92.0% car, 1.0% public transportation, 3.0% walk, 1.0% work from home (2000); Travel time to work: 29.9% less than 15 minutes, 35.0% 15 to 30 minutes, 17.8% 30 to 45 minutes, 9.6% 45 to 60 minutes, 7.6% 60 minutes or more (2000)

THEBES (village). Covers a land area of 1.800 square miles and a water area of 0.513 square miles. Located at 37.21° N. Lat.; 89.45° W. Long. Elevation is 351 feet.
History: Thebes was laid out in 1844, and once served as the seat of Alexander County. The site was earlier known as Sparhawk's Landing.
Population: 461 (1990); 478 (2000); 453 (2007); 408 (2012 projected); Race: 90.7% White, 7.7% Black, 0.2% Asian, 0.0% Hispanic of any race (2007); Density: 251.7 persons per square mile (2007); Average household size: 2.73 (2007); Median age: 29.9 (2007); Males per 100 females: 95.3 (2007); Marriage status: 26.1% never married, 52.8% now married, 10.7% widowed, 10.4% divorced (2000); Foreign born: 0.0% (2000); Ancestry (includes multiple ancestries): 26.9% Other groups, 12.7% German, 9.6% Irish, 7.4% United States or American, 6.1% Scottish (2000).
Economy: Single-family building permits issued: 0 (2007); Multi-family building permits issued: 0 (2007); Employment by occupation: 5.7% management, 8.6% professional, 22.9% services, 19.3% sales, 2.1% farming, 12.9% construction, 28.6% production (2000).
Income: Per capita income: $15,933 (2007); Median household income: $30,455 (2007); Average household income: $43,479 (2007); Percent of households with income of $100,000 or more: 6.6% (2007); Poverty rate: 31.7% (2000).
Education: Percent of population age 25 and over with: High school diploma (including GED) or higher: 59.0% (2007); Bachelor's degree or higher: 4.0% (2007); Master's degree or higher: 4.0% (2007).
Housing: Homeownership rate: 63.9% (2007); Median home value: $33,947 (2007); Median rent: $213 per month (2000); Median age of housing: 29 years (2000).
Transportation: Commute to work: 97.8% car, 0.0% public transportation, 0.0% walk, 0.0% work from home (2000); Travel time to work: 5.1% less than 15 minutes, 48.6% 15 to 30 minutes, 37.0% 30 to 45 minutes, 2.9% 45 to 60 minutes, 6.5% 60 minutes or more (2000)

Bond County

Located in southwest central Illinois; drained by the Kaskaskia River. Covers a land area of 380.20 square miles, a water area of 2.46 square miles, and is located in the Central Time Zone. The county was founded in 1817. County seat is Greenville.

Bond County is part of the St. Louis, MO-IL Metropolitan Statistical Area. The entire metro area includes: Bond County, IL; Calhoun County, IL; Clinton County, IL; Jersey County, IL; Macoupin County, IL; Madison County, IL; Monroe County, IL; St. Clair County, IL; Crawford County, MO (pt.)*; Franklin County, MO; Jefferson County, MO; Lincoln County, MO; St. Charles County, MO; St. Louis County, MO; Warren County, MO; Washington County, MO; St. Louis city, MO

Population: 14,991 (1990); 17,633 (2000); 18,113 (2007); 18,378 (2012 projected); Race: 91.1% White, 6.9% Black, 0.4% Asian, 1.7% Hispanic of any race (2007); Density: 47.6 persons per square mile (2007); Average household size: 2.83 (2007); Median age: 36.7 (2007); Males per 100 females: 114.9 (2007).
Religion: Five largest groups: 10.6% Christian Churches and Churches of Christ, 10.0% Southern Baptist Convention, 8.2% Catholic Church, 5.1% The United Methodist Church, 3.6% Free Methodist Church of North America (2000).
Economy: Unemployment rate: 5.1% (4/2008); Total civilian labor force: 8,913 (4/2008); Leading industries: 22.5% health care and social assistance; 16.0% manufacturing; 10.7% retail trade (2005); Farms: 668 totaling 192,618 acres (2002); Companies that employ 500 or more persons: 2 (2006); Companies that employ 100 to 499 persons: 4 (2006); Companies that employ less than 100 persons: 330 (2006); Black-owned businesses: n/a (2002); Hispanic-owned businesses: n/a (2002); Asian-owned businesses: n/a (2002); Women-owned businesses: 428 (2002); Retail sales per capita: $9,137 (2008). Single-family building permits issued: 47 (2007); Multi-family building permits issued: 10 (2007).
Income: Per capita income: $21,006 (2007); Median household income: $45,095 (2007); Average household income: $54,382 (2007); Percent of households with income of $100,000 or more: 11.4% (2007); Poverty rate: 12.8% (2005); Bankruptcy rate: 3.42% (2007).
Taxes: Total county taxes per capita: $111 (2006); County property taxes per capita: $109 (2006).
Education: Percent of population age 25 and over with: High school diploma (including GED) or higher: 72.1% (2007); Bachelor's degree or higher: 14.7% (2007); Master's degree or higher: 5.0% (2007).
Housing: Homeownership rate: 80.1% (2007); Median home value: $97,216 (2007); Median rent: $271 per month (2000); Median age of housing: 35 years (2000).
Health: Birth rate: 123.2 per 10,000 population (2007); Death rate: 103.3 per 10,000 population (2007); Age-adjusted cancer mortality rate: 147.3 deaths per 100,000 population (2005); Number of physicians: 5.6 per 10,000 population (2005); Hospital beds: 78.0 per 10,000 population (2004); Hospital admissions: 1,062.4 per 10,000 population (2004).
Elections: 2004 Presidential election results: 55.2% Bush, 43.8% Kerry, 0.0% Nader, 0.9% Badnarik
Additional Information Contacts
Bond County Government . . . . (618) 664-1966

Greenville Chamber of Commerce . . . . (618) 664-9272
http://www.greenvilleusa.org

Bond County Communities

GREENVILLE (city). County seat. Covers a land area of 5.202 square miles and a water area of 0 square miles. Located at 38.89° N. Lat.; 89.40° W. Long. Elevation is 617 feet.
History: Greenville was settled in 1815, and developed as the seat of Bond County. Early industries were an evaporated milk plant, a glove plant, and a manufacturer of costumes and uniforms.
Population: 5,168 (1990); 6,955 (2000); 6,834 (2007); 6,735 (2012 projected); Race: 81.5% White, 16.0% Black, 0.8% Asian, 2.9% Hispanic of any race (2007); Density: 1,313.7 persons per square mile (2007); Average household size: 3.47 (2007); Median age: 33.8 (2007); Males per 100 females: 146.4 (2007); Marriage status: 21.6% never married, 65.4% now married, 7.7% widowed, 5.4% divorced (2000); Foreign born: 1.1% (2000); Ancestry (includes multiple ancestries): 24.5% German, 11.2% English, 8.1% Other groups, 7.4% Irish, 4.9% United States or American (2000).
Economy: Single-family building permits issued: 6 (2007); Multi-family building permits issued: 10 (2007); Employment by occupation: 9.2% management, 22.8% professional, 20.1% services, 27.1% sales, 0.6% farming, 5.8% construction, 14.3% production (2000).
Income: Per capita income: $19,298 (2007); Median household income: $42,120 (2007); Average household income: $50,777 (2007); Percent of households with income of $100,000 or more: 10.9% (2007); Poverty rate: 11.8% (2000).
Taxes: Total city taxes per capita: $99 (2006); City property taxes per capita: $64 (2006).
Education: Percent of population age 25 and over with: High school diploma (including GED) or higher: 62.2% (2007); Bachelor's degree or higher: 18.7% (2007); Master's degree or higher: 7.3% (2007).

School District(s)

Bond County CUSD 2 (PK-12)
2005-06 Enrollment: 1,895 . . . . (618) 664-0170

Four-year College(s)

Greenville College (Private, Not-for-profit, Free Methodist)
Fall 2007 Enrollment: 1,528. . . . . (618) 664-2800
2007-08 Tuition: In-state $18,672; Out-of-state $18,672

Housing: Homeownership rate: 69.4% (2007); Median home value: $93,209 (2007); Median rent: $270 per month (2000); Median age of housing: 43 years (2000).
Hospitals: Greenville Regional Hospital (50 beds)
Safety: Violent crime rate: 8.5 per 10,000 population; Property crime rate: 205.2 per 10,000 population (2006).
Newspapers: Greenville Advocate (Regional news; Circulation 5,100)
Transportation: Commute to work: 79.7% car, 0.4% public transportation, 14.8% walk, 4.3% work from home (2000); Travel time to work: 68.4% less than 15 minutes, 12.5% 15 to 30 minutes, 9.6% 30 to 45 minutes, 4.4% 45 to 60 minutes, 5.0% 60 minutes or more (2000)
Airports: Greenville (general aviation)
Additional Information Contacts
Greenville Chamber of Commerce . . . . (618) 664-9272
http://www.greenvilleusa.org

MULBERRY GROVE (village). Covers a land area of 0.986 square miles and a water area of 0.009 square miles. Located at 38.92° N. Lat.; 89.26° W. Long. Elevation is 561 feet.
Population: 660 (1990); 671 (2000); 615 (2007); 614 (2012 projected); Race: 97.2% White, 1.6% Black, 0.0% Asian, 0.5% Hispanic of any race (2007); Density: 623.9 persons per square mile (2007); Average household size: 2.29 (2007); Median age: 36.6 (2007); Males per 100 females: 89.8 (2007); Marriage status: 19.8% never married, 54.1% now married, 12.5% widowed, 13.5% divorced (2000); Foreign born: 0.3% (2000); Ancestry (includes multiple ancestries): 18.9% German, 12.9% Irish, 12.3% United States or American, 9.9% Other groups, 7.6% English (2000).
Economy: Single-family building permits issued: 0 (2007); Multi-family building permits issued: 0 (2007); Employment by occupation: 5.0% management, 9.0% professional, 19.3% services, 21.7% sales, 1.7% farming, 6.3% construction, 37.0% production (2000).
Income: Per capita income: $17,675 (2007); Median household income: $36,250 (2007); Average household income: $40,560 (2007); Percent of households with income of $100,000 or more: 2.6% (2007); Poverty rate: 14.8% (2000).
Education: Percent of population age 25 and over with: High school diploma (including GED) or higher: 74.9% (2007); Bachelor's degree or higher: 5.6% (2007); Master's degree or higher: 2.0% (2007).

School District(s)

Mulberry Grove CUSD 1 (KG-12)
2005-06 Enrollment: 448 . . . . (618) 326-8812
Housing: Homeownership rate: 75.0% (2007); Median home value: $63,611 (2007); Median rent: $274 per month (2000); Median age of housing: 45 years (2000).
Transportation: Commute to work: 92.4% car, 0.0% public transportation, 1.0% walk, 6.0% work from home (2000); Travel time to work: 30.7% less than 15 minutes, 41.0% 15 to 30 minutes, 9.5% 30 to 45 minutes, 5.7% 45 to 60 minutes, 13.1% 60 minutes or more (2000)

OLD RIPLEY (village). Covers a land area of 0.149 square miles and a water area of 0 square miles. Located at 38.89° N. Lat.; 89.57° W. Long. Elevation is 561 feet.
Population: 95 (1990); 127 (2000); 137 (2007); 140 (2012 projected); Race: 99.3% White, 0.7% Black, 0.0% Asian, 0.0% Hispanic of any race (2007); Density: 918.3 persons per square mile (2007); Average household size: 2.58 (2007); Median age: 37.5 (2007); Males per 100 females: 85.1 (2007); Marriage status: 24.1% never married, 65.5% now married, 5.7% widowed, 4.6% divorced (2000); Foreign born: 0.0% (2000); Ancestry (includes multiple ancestries): 22.2% German, 11.1% Irish, 9.3% English, 8.3% Dutch, 8.3% United States or American (2000).
Economy: Employment by occupation: 4.1% management, 8.2% professional, 20.4% services, 22.4% sales, 0.0% farming, 28.6% construction, 16.3% production (2000).
Income: Per capita income: $18,011 (2007); Median household income: $41,250 (2007); Average household income: $46,557 (2007); Percent of households with income of $100,000 or more: 3.8% (2007); Poverty rate: 3.7% (2000).
Education: Percent of population age 25 and over with: High school diploma (including GED) or higher: 75.9% (2007); Bachelor's degree or higher: 4.6% (2007); Master's degree or higher: 2.3% (2007).
Housing: Homeownership rate: 84.9% (2007); Median home value: $48,929 (2007); Median rent: $n/a per month (2000); Median age of housing: 49 years (2000).
Transportation: Commute to work: 95.9% car, 0.0% public transportation, 0.0% walk, 4.1% work from home (2000); Travel time to work: 4.3% less than 15 minutes, 42.6% 15 to 30 minutes, 29.8% 30 to 45 minutes, 12.8% 45 to 60 minutes, 10.6% 60 minutes or more (2000)

PIERRON (village). Covers a land area of 0.851 square miles and a water area of 0 square miles. Located at 38.77° N. Lat.; 89.55° W. Long. Elevation is 522 feet.
Population: 554 (1990); 653 (2000); 676 (2007); 674 (2012 projected); Race: 97.3% White, 0.0% Black, 0.3% Asian, 1.2% Hispanic of any race (2007); Density: 794.6 persons per square mile (2007); Average household size: 2.55 (2007); Median age: 35.0 (2007); Males per 100 females: 105.5 (2007); Marriage status: 22.1% never married, 55.2% now married, 7.4% widowed, 15.4% divorced (2000); Foreign born: 2.6% (2000); Ancestry (includes multiple ancestries): 41.7% German, 14.4% Other groups, 11.6% Irish, 10.0% United States or American, 9.5% English (2000).
Economy: Single-family building permits issued: 0 (2007); Multi-family building permits issued: 0 (2007); Employment by occupation: 11.3% management, 7.9% professional, 14.9% services, 16.9% sales, 0.0% farming, 14.9% construction, 34.1% production (2000).
Income: Per capita income: $19,826 (2007); Median household income: $39,722 (2007); Average household income: $50,575 (2007); Percent of households with income of $100,000 or more: 8.3% (2007); Poverty rate: 5.1% (2000).
Education: Percent of population age 25 and over with: High school diploma (including GED) or higher: 79.1% (2007); Bachelor's degree or higher: 8.7% (2007); Master's degree or higher: 3.0% (2007).
Housing: Homeownership rate: 89.1% (2007); Median home value: $67,857 (2007); Median rent: $370 per month (2000); Median age of housing: 22 years (2000).
Transportation: Commute to work: 93.6% car, 0.7% public transportation, 0.0% walk, 5.7% work from home (2000); Travel time to work: 19.0% less than 15 minutes, 47.3% 15 to 30 minutes, 15.1% 30 to 45 minutes, 7.5% 45 to 60 minutes, 11.1% 60 minutes or more (2000)

POCAHONTAS (village). Covers a land area of 0.751 square miles and a water area of 0.021 square miles. Located at 38.82° N. Lat.; 89.54° W. Long. Elevation is 561 feet.
History: Pocahontas, named for the legendary Indian princess, began as a stagecoach stop on the Cumberland Road.
Population: 837 (1990); 727 (2000); 637 (2007); 643 (2012 projected); Race: 98.4% White, 0.2% Black, 0.8% Asian, 0.0% Hispanic of any race (2007); Density: 848.4 persons per square mile (2007); Average household size: 2.31 (2007); Median age: 38.3 (2007); Males per 100 females: 99.7 (2007); Marriage status: 30.8% never married, 50.3% now married, 9.8% widowed, 9.0% divorced (2000); Foreign born: 0.0% (2000); Ancestry (includes multiple ancestries): 40.9% German, 13.1% United States or American, 11.7% English, 11.1% Irish, 9.7% Other groups (2000).
Economy: Single-family building permits issued: 2 (2007); Multi-family building permits issued: 0 (2007); Employment by occupation: 7.4% management, 6.2% professional, 20.5% services, 20.2% sales, 0.0% farming, 11.3% construction, 34.4% production (2000).
Income: Per capita income: $18,042 (2007); Median household income: $32,500 (2007); Average household income: $41,639 (2007); Percent of households with income of $100,000 or more: 4.0% (2007); Poverty rate: 13.8% (2000).
Education: Percent of population age 25 and over with: High school diploma (including GED) or higher: 77.9% (2007); Bachelor's degree or higher: 4.7% (2007); Master's degree or higher: 1.1% (2007).

School District(s)

Bond County CUSD 2 (PK-12)
2005-06 Enrollment: 1,895 . . . . (618) 664-0170
Housing: Homeownership rate: 78.6% (2007); Median home value: $68,478 (2007); Median rent: $258 per month (2000); Median age of housing: 45 years (2000).
Transportation: Commute to work: 92.8% car, 0.6% public transportation, 5.7% walk, 0.6% work from home (2000); Travel time to work: 20.2% less than 15 minutes, 43.1% 15 to 30 minutes, 11.4% 30 to 45 minutes, 14.2% 45 to 60 minutes, 11.1% 60 minutes or more (2000)

SMITHBORO (village). Covers a land area of 1.182 square miles and a water area of 0 square miles. Located at 38.89° N. Lat.; 89.34° W. Long. Elevation is 558 feet.
Population: 202 (1990); 200 (2000); 214 (2007); 217 (2012 projected); Race: 96.7% White, 1.9% Black, 0.0% Asian, 0.9% Hispanic of any race (2007); Density: 181.0 persons per square mile (2007); Average household size: 2.58 (2007); Median age: 35.0 (2007); Males per 100 females: 92.8 (2007); Marriage status: 19.7% never married, 59.1% now married, 8.3% widowed, 12.9% divorced (2000); Foreign born: 1.5% (2000); Ancestry (includes multiple ancestries): 24.1% German, 20.5% Other groups, 11.3% English, 9.7% Irish, 7.7% Italian (2000).
Economy: Single-family building permits issued: 0 (2007); Multi-family building permits issued: 0 (2007); Employment by occupation: 17.4% management, 2.9% professional, 26.1% services, 13.0% sales, 0.0% farming, 13.0% construction, 27.5% production (2000).
Income: Per capita income: $15,526 (2007); Median household income: $35,250 (2007); Average household income: $40,030 (2007); Percent of households with income of $100,000 or more: 6.0% (2007); Poverty rate: 26.4% (2000).

Education: Percent of population age 25 and over with: High school diploma (including GED) or higher: 67.9% (2007); Bachelor's degree or higher: 5.1% (2007); Master's degree or higher: 0.0% (2007).
Housing: Homeownership rate: 79.5% (2007); Median home value: $67,143 (2007); Median rent: $256 per month (2000); Median age of housing: 36 years (2000).
Transportation: Commute to work: 95.4% car, 0.0% public transportation, 0.0% walk, 0.0% work from home (2000); Travel time to work: 55.4% less than 15 minutes, 6.2% 15 to 30 minutes, 16.9% 30 to 45 minutes, 4.6% 45 to 60 minutes, 16.9% 60 minutes or more (2000)

SORENTO (village). Covers a land area of 0.541 square miles and a water area of 0 square miles. Located at 38.99° N. Lat.; 89.57° W. Long. Elevation is 584 feet.
Population: 596 (1990); 601 (2000); 561 (2007); 555 (2012 projected); Race: 98.6% White, 0.0% Black, 0.0% Asian, 1.1% Hispanic of any race (2007); Density: 1,036.6 persons per square mile (2007); Average household size: 2.48 (2007); Median age: 33.4 (2007); Males per 100 females: 87.0 (2007); Marriage status: 22.4% never married, 58.6% now married, 7.6% widowed, 11.5% divorced (2000); Foreign born: 0.5% (2000); Ancestry (includes multiple ancestries): 31.0% German, 16.1% Other groups, 13.5% English, 10.9% Irish, 10.8% United States or American (2000).
Economy: Single-family building permits issued: 6 (2007); Multi-family building permits issued: 0 (2007); Employment by occupation: 6.6% management, 9.1% professional, 23.7% services, 16.0% sales, 0.0% farming, 14.6% construction, 30.0% production (2000).
Income: Per capita income: $16,168 (2007); Median household income: $36,452 (2007); Average household income: $40,133 (2007); Percent of households with income of $100,000 or more: 4.4% (2007); Poverty rate: 14.2% (2000).
Education: Percent of population age 25 and over with: High school diploma (including GED) or higher: 77.2% (2007); Bachelor's degree or higher: 5.0% (2007); Master's degree or higher: 2.2% (2007).

School District(s)

Bond County CUSD 2 (PK-12)
2005-06 Enrollment: 1,895 . . . . (618) 664-0170
Housing: Homeownership rate: 85.8% (2007); Median home value: $45,263 (2007); Median rent: $153 per month (2000); Median age of housing: 47 years (2000).
Safety: Violent crime rate: 0.0 per 10,000 population; Property crime rate: 0.0 per 10,000 population (2006).
Transportation: Commute to work: 96.5% car, 0.0% public transportation, 1.4% walk, 1.8% work from home (2000); Travel time to work: 10.0% less than 15 minutes, 30.7% 15 to 30 minutes, 36.8% 30 to 45 minutes, 9.3% 45 to 60 minutes, 13.2% 60 minutes or more (2000)

Boone County

Located in northern Illinois; bounded on the north by Wisconsin. Covers a land area of 281.27 square miles, a water area of 0.68 square miles, and is located in the Central Time Zone. The county was founded in 1837. County seat is Belvidere.

Boone County is part of the Rockford, IL Metropolitan Statistical Area. The entire metro area includes: Boone County, IL; Winnebago County, IL

Population: 30,806 (1990); 41,786 (2000); 53,150 (2007); 61,121 (2012 projected); Race: 85.2% White, 1.6% Black, 1.0% Asian, 17.9% Hispanic of any race (2007); Density: 189.0 persons per square mile (2007); Average household size: 2.88 (2007); Median age: 34.1 (2007); Males per 100 females: 101.4 (2007).
Religion: Five largest groups: 19.1% Catholic Church, 6.0% Lutheran Church—Missouri Synod, 5.2% The United Methodist Church, 2.7% Evangelical Lutheran Church in America, 2.4% Presbyterian Church (U.S.A.) (2000).
Economy: Unemployment rate: 8.0% (4/2008); Total civilian labor force: 27,276 (4/2008); Leading industries: 36.1% manufacturing; 13.7% construction; 11.4% retail trade (2005); Farms: 476 totaling 146,940 acres (2002); Companies that employ 500 or more persons: 3 (2006); Companies that employ 100 to 499 persons: 14 (2006); Companies that employ less than 100 persons: 833 (2006); Black-owned businesses: n/a (2002); Hispanic-owned businesses: n/a (2002); Asian-owned businesses: n/a (2002); Women-owned businesses: 1,143 (2002); Retail sales per capita: $6,102 (2008). Single-family building permits issued: 250 (2007); Multi-family building permits issued: 34 (2007).
Income: Per capita income: $24,574 (2007); Median household income: $58,918 (2007); Average household income: $70,630 (2007); Percent of households with income of $100,000 or more: 19.1% (2007); Poverty rate: 8.0% (2005); Bankruptcy rate: 3.90% (2007).
Taxes: Total county taxes per capita: $177 (2006); County property taxes per capita: $143 (2006).
Education: Percent of population age 25 and over with: High school diploma (including GED) or higher: 80.5% (2007); Bachelor's degree or higher: 14.3% (2007); Master's degree or higher: 4.8% (2007).
Housing: Homeownership rate: 79.5% (2007); Median home value: $169,024 (2007); Median rent: $455 per month (2000); Median age of housing: 28 years (2000).
Health: Birth rate: 160.7 per 10,000 population (2007); Death rate: 60.3 per 10,000 population (2007); Age-adjusted cancer mortality rate: 199.7 deaths per 100,000 population (2005); Number of physicians: 14.1 per 10,000 population (2005); Hospital beds: 14.4 per 10,000 population (2004); Hospital admissions: 255.5 per 10,000 population (2004).
Elections: 2004 Presidential election results: 57.0% Bush, 42.4% Kerry, 0.1% Nader, 0.5% Badnarik

Additional Information Contacts

Boone County Government . . . . (815) 547-4770
http://www.boonecountyil.org
Belvidere Area Chamber of Commerce . . . . (815) 544-4357
http://www.belviderechamber.com
City of Belvidere . . . . (815) 544-2612
http://www.ci.belvidere.il.us

Boone County Communities

BELVIDERE (city). County seat. Covers a land area of 9.071 square miles and a water area of 0.053 square miles. Located at 42.25° N. Lat.; 88.84° W. Long. Elevation is 781 feet.
History: Belvidere was founded in 1836 as a stop on the Chicago-Galena stagecoach route. The National Sewing Machine Plant was founded here in 1879.
Population: 16,801 (1990); 20,820 (2000); 25,776 (2007); 29,322 (2012 projected); Race: 77.1% White, 2.0% Black, 0.9% Asian, 28.5% Hispanic of any race (2007); Density: 2,841.6 persons per square mile (2007); Average household size: 2.81 (2007); Median age: 32.9 (2007); Males per 100 females: 99.6 (2007); Marriage status: 23.9% never married, 58.6% now married, 6.8% widowed, 10.7% divorced (2000); Foreign born: 11.9% (2000); Ancestry (includes multiple ancestries): 30.6% German, 23.3% Other groups, 13.2% Irish, 9.0% English, 6.9% Swedish (2000).
Economy: Unemployment rate: 9.3% (4/2008); Total civilian labor force: 13,255 (4/2008); Single-family building permits issued: 106 (2007); Multi-family building permits issued: 32 (2007); Employment by occupation: 7.9% management, 10.6% professional, 14.9% services, 24.7% sales, 0.8% farming, 10.1% construction, 31.0% production (2000).
Income: Per capita income: $19,166 (2007); Median household income: $46,983 (2007); Average household income: $53,453 (2007); Percent of households with income of $100,000 or more: 9.0% (2007); Poverty rate: 10.0% (2000).
Education: Percent of population age 25 and over with: High school diploma (including GED) or higher: 74.1% (2007); Bachelor's degree or higher: 8.8% (2007); Master's degree or higher: 2.0% (2007).

School District(s)

Belvidere CUSD 100 (PK-12)
2005-06 Enrollment: 8,405 . . . . (815) 544-0301
Boone County Spec Educ Coop (PK-PK)
2005-06 Enrollment: 43 . . . . (815) 544-9851
Boone/Winnebago Roe (06-12)
2005-06 Enrollment: 267 . . . . (815) 636-3060
Housing: Homeownership rate: 68.2% (2007); Median home value: $135,076 (2007); Median rent: $451 per month (2000); Median age of housing: 37 years (2000).
Hospitals: Northwest Suburban Community Hospital (69 beds)
Safety: Violent crime rate: 20.7 per 10,000 population; Property crime rate: 276.9 per 10,000 population (2006).
Newspapers: Belvidere Daily Republican (Local news; Circulation 5,000); Boone County Shopper (Regional news; Circulation 18,364)
Transportation: Commute to work: 95.3% car, 0.4% public transportation, 1.9% walk, 1.9% work from home (2000); Travel time to work: 37.8% less than 15 minutes, 27.0% 15 to 30 minutes, 17.7% 30 to 45 minutes, 7.8% 45 to 60 minutes, 9.7% 60 minutes or more (2000)

Additional Information Contacts

Belvidere Area Chamber of Commerce . . . . (815) 544-4357
http://www.belviderechamber.com
City of Belvidere . . . . (815) 544-2612
http://www.ci.belvidere.il.us

CALEDONIA (village). Aka North Caledonia. Covers a land area of 0.533 square miles and a water area of 0 square miles. Located at 42.36° N. Lat.; 88.89° W. Long. Elevation is 928 feet.
Population: 67 (1990); 199 (2000); 303 (2007); 374 (2012 projected); Race: 100.0% White, 0.0% Black, 0.0% Asian, 0.0% Hispanic of any race (2007); Density: 568.0 persons per square mile (2007); Average household size: 2.81 (2007); Median age: 34.0 (2007); Males per 100 females: 103.4 (2007); Marriage status: 18.9% never married, 64.6% now married, 3.7% widowed, 12.8% divorced (2000); Foreign born: 0.9% (2000); Ancestry (includes multiple ancestries): 36.9% German, 16.4% Irish, 13.3% United States or American, 12.4% Norwegian, 9.8% English (2000).
Economy: Single-family building permits issued: 0 (2007); Multi-family building permits issued: 0 (2007); Employment by occupation: 17.1% management, 15.4% professional, 6.8% services, 17.9% sales, 0.0% farming, 15.4% construction, 27.4% production (2000).
Income: Per capita income: $22,079 (2007); Median household income: $58,125 (2007); Average household income: $61,944 (2007); Percent of households with income of $100,000 or more: 12.0% (2007); Poverty rate: 2.3% (2000).
Education: Percent of population age 25 and over with: High school diploma (including GED) or higher: 84.9% (2007); Bachelor's degree or higher: 11.6% (2007); Master's degree or higher: 5.0% (2007).

School District(s)

Belvidere CUSD 100 (PK-12)
2005-06 Enrollment: 8,405 . . . . (815) 544-0301
Housing: Homeownership rate: 87.0% (2007); Median home value: $138,636 (2007); Median rent: $575 per month (2000); Median age of housing: 60+ years (2000).
Transportation: Commute to work: 100.0% car, 0.0% public transportation, 0.0% walk, 0.0% work from home (2000); Travel time to work: 12.3% less than 15 minutes, 48.2% 15 to 30 minutes, 29.8% 30 to 45 minutes, 3.5% 45 to 60 minutes, 6.1% 60 minutes or more (2000)

CAPRON (village). Covers a land area of 0.728 square miles and a water area of 0 square miles. Located at 42.39° N. Lat.; 88.74° W. Long. Elevation is 909 feet.
Population: 862 (1990); 961 (2000); 1,045 (2007); 1,097 (2012 projected); Race: 87.2% White, 1.9% Black, 0.9% Asian, 21.9% Hispanic of any race (2007); Density: 1,434.8 persons per square mile (2007); Average household size: 2.90 (2007); Median age: 32.1 (2007); Males per 100 females: 103.3 (2007); Marriage status: 26.8% never married, 59.5% now married, 4.4% widowed, 9.4% divorced (2000); Foreign born: 5.2% (2000); Ancestry (includes multiple ancestries): 35.4% German, 20.8% Other groups, 11.5% Irish, 10.6% Polish, 6.3% Norwegian (2000).
Economy: Single-family building permits issued: 18 (2007); Multi-family building permits issued: 0 (2007); Employment by occupation: 8.2% management, 6.8% professional, 10.0% services, 25.4% sales, 1.1% farming, 10.0% construction, 38.5% production (2000).
Income: Per capita income: $21,522 (2007); Median household income: $53,421 (2007); Average household income: $62,472 (2007); Percent of households with income of $100,000 or more: 14.4% (2007); Poverty rate: 3.1% (2000).
Education: Percent of population age 25 and over with: High school diploma (including GED) or higher: 77.0% (2007); Bachelor's degree or higher: 7.4% (2007); Master's degree or higher: 1.4% (2007).

School District(s)

North Boone CUSD 200 (PK-12)
2005-06 Enrollment: 1,587 . . . . (815) 765-3322
Housing: Homeownership rate: 79.2% (2007); Median home value: $149,867 (2007); Median rent: $444 per month (2000); Median age of housing: 45 years (2000).
Transportation: Commute to work: 93.4% car, 0.7% public transportation, 3.2% walk, 2.5% work from home (2000); Travel time to work: 26.8% less than 15 minutes, 27.0% 15 to 30 minutes, 24.0% 30 to 45 minutes, 8.2% 45 to 60 minutes, 14.0% 60 minutes or more (2000)

GARDEN PRAIRIE (unincorporated postal area, zip code 61038). Covers a land area of 43.193 square miles and a water area of 0.010 square miles. Located at 42.25° N. Lat.; 88.74° W. Long. Elevation is 781 feet.
History: Garden Prairie began in 1849 when a station for the Galena & Chicago Union Railroad was built here.
Population: 1,371 (2000); Race: 97.3% White, 0.0% Black, 0.4% Asian, 1.3% Hispanic of any race (2000); Density: 31.7 persons per square mile (2000); Age: 28.4% under 18, 7.4% over 64 (2000); Marriage status: 20.7% never married, 64.7% now married, 3.0% widowed, 11.6% divorced (2000); Foreign born: 1.5% (2000); Ancestry (includes multiple ancestries): 41.7% German, 15.0% Irish, 9.2% Other groups, 8.9% Polish, 7.9% English (2000).
Economy: Employment by occupation: 16.1% management, 9.5% professional, 13.1% services, 15.3% sales, 1.7% farming, 18.3% construction, 26.1% production (2000).
Income: Per capita income: $17,987 (2000); Median household income: $52,833 (2000); Poverty rate: 3.7% (2000).
Education: Percent of population age 25 and over with: High school diploma (including GED) or higher: 81.0% (2000); Bachelor's degree or higher: 8.2% (2000).

School District(s)

Belvidere CUSD 100 (PK-12)
2005-06 Enrollment: 8,405 . . . . (815) 544-0301
Housing: Homeownership rate: 76.6% (2000); Median home value: $134,200 (2000); Median rent: $517 per month (2000); Median age of housing: 51 years (2000).
Transportation: Commute to work: 87.4% car, 0.0% public transportation, 1.7% walk, 7.8% work from home (2000); Travel time to work: 30.2% less than 15 minutes, 30.1% 15 to 30 minutes, 23.2% 30 to 45 minutes, 9.5% 45 to 60 minutes, 7.0% 60 minutes or more (2000)

POPLAR GROVE (village). Covers a land area of 4.495 square miles and a water area of <.001 square miles. Located at 42.35° N. Lat.; 88.83° W. Long. Elevation is 899 feet.
Population: 939 (1990); 1,368 (2000); 2,182 (2007); 2,742 (2012 projected); Race: 97.8% White, 0.0% Black, 0.2% Asian, 2.8% Hispanic of any race (2007); Density: 485.5 persons per square mile (2007); Average household size: 3.01 (2007); Median age: 32.0 (2007); Males per 100 females: 106.4 (2007); Marriage status: 18.5% never married, 68.3% now married, 4.9% widowed, 8.2% divorced (2000); Foreign born: 1.4% (2000); Ancestry (includes multiple ancestries): 35.6% German, 17.1% Irish, 10.2% Swedish, 9.9% English, 7.1% Other groups (2000).
Economy: Single-family building permits issued: 72 (2007); Multi-family building permits issued: 2 (2007); Employment by occupation: 10.6% management, 10.2% professional, 12.0% services, 27.1% sales, 0.7% farming, 11.5% construction, 27.9% production (2000).
Income: Per capita income: $22,500 (2007); Median household income: $60,550 (2007); Average household income: $67,811 (2007); Percent of households with income of $100,000 or more: 15.3% (2007); Poverty rate: 4.2% (2000).
Taxes: Total city taxes per capita: $131 (2006); City property taxes per capita: $53 (2006).
Education: Percent of population age 25 and over with: High school diploma (including GED) or higher: 87.9% (2007); Bachelor's degree or higher: 11.4% (2007); Master's degree or higher: 2.4% (2007).

School District(s)

North Boone CUSD 200 (PK-12)
2005-06 Enrollment: 1,587 . . . . (815) 765-3322
Housing: Homeownership rate: 84.8% (2007); Median home value: $172,059 (2007); Median rent: $481 per month (2000); Median age of housing: 24 years (2000).
Transportation: Commute to work: 89.8% car, 1.5% public transportation, 1.5% walk, 4.6% work from home (2000); Travel time to work: 16.5% less than 15 minutes, 37.6% 15 to 30 minutes, 21.3% 30 to 45 minutes, 9.8% 45 to 60 minutes, 14.9% 60 minutes or more (2000)

TIMBERLANE (village). Covers a land area of 1.295 square miles and a water area of 0.016 square miles. Located at 42.33° N. Lat.; 88.85° W. Long. Elevation is 840 feet.
Population: 88 (1990); 234 (2000); 358 (2007); 440 (2012 projected); Race: 96.6% White, 0.0% Black, 0.0% Asian, 2.8% Hispanic of any race (2007); Density: 276.5 persons per square mile (2007); Average household size: 2.98 (2007); Median age: 43.0 (2007); Males per 100 females: 93.5 (2007); Marriage status: 20.1% never married, 75.0% now married, 3.7% widowed, 1.2% divorced (2000); Foreign born: 0.0% (2000); Ancestry (includes multiple ancestries): 43.5% German, 13.5% Irish, 13.0% English, 11.0% Swedish, 9.0% Norwegian (2000).

Economy: Single-family building permits issued: 9 (2007); Multi-family building permits issued: 0 (2007); Employment by occupation: 16.2% management, 28.5% professional, 6.2% services, 27.7% sales, 0.0% farming, 10.0% construction, 11.5% production (2000).
Income: Per capita income: $35,656 (2007); Median household income: $94,000 (2007); Average household income: $106,375 (2007); Percent of households with income of $100,000 or more: 45.0% (2007); Poverty rate: 6.5% (2000).
Education: Percent of population age 25 and over with: High school diploma (including GED) or higher: 95.6% (2007); Bachelor's degree or higher: 32.9% (2007); Master's degree or higher: 16.1% (2007).
Housing: Homeownership rate: 100.0% (2007); Median home value: $242,453 (2007); Median rent: $n/a per month (2000); Median age of housing: 14 years (2000).
Transportation: Commute to work: 95.4% car, 1.5% public transportation, 0.0% walk, 3.1% work from home (2000); Travel time to work: 14.3% less than 15 minutes, 64.3% 15 to 30 minutes, 15.1% 30 to 45 minutes, 0.8% 45 to 60 minutes, 5.6% 60 minutes or more (2000)

Brown County

Located in western Illinois; bounded on the southeast by the Illinois River, and on the northeast by the La Moine River. Covers a land area of 305.65 square miles, a water area of 1.59 square miles, and is located in the Central Time Zone. The county was founded in 1839. County seat is Mount Sterling.
Population: 5,836 (1990); 6,950 (2000); 6,809 (2007); 6,696 (2012 projected); Race: 79.8% White, 18.7% Black, 0.2% Asian, 4.6% Hispanic of any race (2007); Density: 22.3 persons per square mile (2007); Average household size: 3.31 (2007); Median age: 35.4 (2007); Males per 100 females: 184.9 (2007).
Religion: Five largest groups: 11.9% Catholic Church, 9.0% American Baptist Churches in the USA, 5.0% Christian Churches and Churches of Christ, 4.3% Christian Church (Disciples of Christ), 4.2% The United Methodist Church (2000).
Economy: Unemployment rate: 3.6% (4/2008); Total civilian labor force: 3,443 (4/2008); Leading industries: 11.9% health care and social assistance; 5.8% retail trade; 4.3% other services (except public administration) (2005); Farms: 417 totaling 144,229 acres (2002); Companies that employ 500 or more persons: 1 (2006); Companies that employ 100 to 499 persons: 2 (2006); Companies that employ less than 100 persons: 127 (2006); Black-owned businesses: n/a (2002); Hispanic-owned businesses: n/a (2002); Asian-owned businesses: n/a (2002); Women-owned businesses: n/a (2002); Retail sales per capita: $3,474 (2008). Single-family building permits issued: 1 (2007); Multi-family building permits issued: 0 (2007).
Income: Per capita income: $17,973 (2007); Median household income: $43,665 (2007); Average household income: $50,373 (2007); Percent of households with income of $100,000 or more: 8.1% (2007); Poverty rate: 13.9% (2005); Bankruptcy rate: 2.13% (2007).
Education: Percent of population age 25 and over with: High school diploma (including GED) or higher: 62.3% (2007); Bachelor's degree or higher: 8.9% (2007); Master's degree or higher: 2.9% (2007).
Housing: Homeownership rate: 73.6% (2007); Median home value: $71,500 (2007); Median rent: $225 per month (2000); Median age of housing: 54 years (2000).
Health: Birth rate: 97.5 per 10,000 population (2007); Death rate: 76.1 per 10,000 population (2007); Age-adjusted cancer mortality rate: 319.9 deaths per 100,000 population (2005); Number of physicians: 6.0 per 10,000 population (2005); Hospital beds: 0.0 per 10,000 population (2004); Hospital admissions: 0.0 per 10,000 population (2004).
Elections: 2004 Presidential election results: 65.0% Bush, 34.6% Kerry, 0.0% Nader, 0.4% Badnarik
Additional Information Contacts
Brown County Government . . . . (217) 773-3421

Brown County Communities

MOUND STATION (village). Aka Timewell. Covers a land area of 0.518 square miles and a water area of 0 square miles. Located at 40.00° N. Lat.; 90.87° W. Long.
History: Also called Timewell.
Population: 147 (1990); 127 (2000); 117 (2007); 107 (2012 projected); Race: 99.1% White, 0.0% Black, 0.0% Asian, 0.0% Hispanic of any race (2007); Density: 226.0 persons per square mile (2007); Average household size: 2.49 (2007); Median age: 43.3 (2007); Males per 100 females: 91.8 (2007); Marriage status: 18.5% never married, 64.8% now married, 9.3% widowed, 7.4% divorced (2000); Foreign born: 0.6% (2000); Ancestry (includes multiple ancestries): 16.8% German, 13.7% United States or American, 11.8% English, 7.5% Other groups, 7.5% Irish (2000).
Economy: Employment by occupation: 4.5% management, 10.2% professional, 14.8% services, 33.0% sales, 0.0% farming, 4.5% construction, 33.0% production (2000).
Income: Per capita income: $24,829 (2007); Median household income: $56,875 (2007); Average household income: $61,809 (2007); Percent of households with income of $100,000 or more: 6.4% (2007); Poverty rate: 7.8% (2000).
Education: Percent of population age 25 and over with: High school diploma (including GED) or higher: 95.1% (2007); Bachelor's degree or higher: 3.7% (2007); Master's degree or higher: 0.0% (2007).
Housing: Homeownership rate: 85.1% (2007); Median home value: $40,000 (2007); Median rent: $263 per month (2000); Median age of housing: 60+ years (2000).
Transportation: Commute to work: 91.4% car, 0.0% public transportation, 3.7% walk, 0.0% work from home (2000); Travel time to work: 44.4% less than 15 minutes, 34.6% 15 to 30 minutes, 0.0% 30 to 45 minutes, 11.1% 45 to 60 minutes, 9.9% 60 minutes or more (2000)

MOUNT STERLING (city). County seat. Covers a land area of 1.076 square miles and a water area of 0 square miles. Located at 39.98° N. Lat.; 90.76° W. Long. Elevation is 725 feet.
History: Mount Sterling was settled in 1830 by Robert Curry, who named the village for the "sterling" quality of the soil. Mount Sterling developed as the seat of Brown County.
Population: 1,996 (1990); 2,070 (2000); 2,149 (2007); 2,196 (2012 projected); Race: 98.5% White, 0.1% Black, 0.5% Asian, 1.4% Hispanic of any race (2007); Density: 1,996.9 persons per square mile (2007); Average household size: 2.21 (2007); Median age: 39.0 (2007); Males per 100 females: 97.0 (2007); Marriage status: 23.5% never married, 54.5% now married, 11.6% widowed, 10.4% divorced (2000); Foreign born: 0.6% (2000); Ancestry (includes multiple ancestries): 26.9% German, 17.2% English, 15.6% United States or American, 14.4% Irish, 4.7% Other groups (2000).
Economy: Single-family building permits issued: 1 (2007); Multi-family building permits issued: 0 (2007); Employment by occupation: 7.6% management, 14.9% professional, 20.4% services, 27.5% sales, 1.3% farming, 4.0% construction, 24.2% production (2000).
Income: Per capita income: $19,440 (2007); Median household income: $33,827 (2007); Average household income: $41,608 (2007); Percent of households with income of $100,000 or more: 4.7% (2007); Poverty rate: 10.9% (2000).
Education: Percent of population age 25 and over with: High school diploma (including GED) or higher: 79.3% (2007); Bachelor's degree or higher: 13.3% (2007); Master's degree or higher: 5.9% (2007).

School District(s)
Brown County CUSD 1 (PK-12)
2005-06 Enrollment: 768 . . . . (217) 773-3359
Dept of Corrections Sch Dist 428 (08-12)
2005-06 Enrollment: 2,271 . . . . (217) 522-2666
Housing: Homeownership rate: 65.6% (2007); Median home value: $65,735 (2007); Median rent: $211 per month (2000); Median age of housing: 52 years (2000).
Safety: Violent crime rate: 24.9 per 10,000 population; Property crime rate: 19.9 per 10,000 population (2006).
Newspapers: Democrat Message (Community news; Circulation 2,800); Pennypincher (Community news; Circulation 10,000)
Transportation: Commute to work: 91.7% car, 0.0% public transportation, 3.6% walk, 2.7% work from home (2000); Travel time to work: 62.8% less than 15 minutes, 10.6% 15 to 30 minutes, 8.2% 30 to 45 minutes, 11.8% 45 to 60 minutes, 6.6% 60 minutes or more (2000)
Airports: Mount Sterling Municipal (general aviation)

RIPLEY (village). Covers a land area of 0.376 square miles and a water area of 0 square miles. Located at 40.02° N. Lat.; 90.63° W. Long. Elevation is 548 feet.
History: Ripley experienced prosperity in the 1830's and 1840's when its pottery kilns were producing.
Population: 103 (1990); 103 (2000); 92 (2007); 83 (2012 projected); Race: 100.0% White, 0.0% Black, 0.0% Asian, 0.0% Hispanic of any race (2007);

Density: 244.8 persons per square mile (2007); Average household size: 2.36 (2007); Median age: 46.9 (2007); Males per 100 females: 135.9 (2007); Marriage status: 15.9% never married, 73.9% now married, 2.3% widowed, 8.0% divorced (2000); Foreign born: 0.0% (2000); Ancestry (includes multiple ancestries): 33.3% German, 13.2% Irish, 11.4% United States or American, 6.1% Other groups, 4.4% English (2000).
Economy: Single-family building permits issued: 0 (2007); Multi-family building permits issued: 0 (2007); Employment by occupation: 4.8% management, 2.4% professional, 21.4% services, 38.1% sales, 4.8% farming, 7.1% construction, 21.4% production (2000).
Income: Per capita income: $19,076 (2007); Median household income: $42,500 (2007); Average household income: $45,000 (2007); Percent of households with income of $100,000 or more: 7.7% (2007); Poverty rate: 7.9% (2000).
Education: Percent of population age 25 and over with: High school diploma (including GED) or higher: 62.5% (2007); Bachelor's degree or higher: 4.2% (2007); Master's degree or higher: 4.2% (2007).
Housing: Homeownership rate: 94.9% (2007); Median home value: $27,500 (2007); Median rent: $n/a per month (2000); Median age of housing: 52 years (2000).
Transportation: Commute to work: 95.5% car, 4.5% public transportation, 0.0% walk, 0.0% work from home (2000); Travel time to work: 31.8% less than 15 minutes, 52.3% 15 to 30 minutes, 11.4% 30 to 45 minutes, 0.0% 45 to 60 minutes, 4.5% 60 minutes or more (2000)

TIMEWELL (unincorporated postal area, zip code 62375). Aka Mound Station. Covers a land area of 40.583 square miles and a water area of 0.018 square miles. Located at 40.00° N. Lat.; 90.87° W. Long. Elevation is 755 feet.
Population: 381 (2000); Race: 97.9% White, 0.0% Black, 0.3% Asian, 0.0% Hispanic of any race (2000); Density: 9.4 persons per square mile (2000); Age: 32.5% under 18, 6.9% over 64 (2000); Marriage status: 20.2% never married, 66.4% now married, 6.3% widowed, 7.1% divorced (2000); Foreign born: 2.1% (2000); Ancestry (includes multiple ancestries): 26.0% German, 17.3% United States or American, 14.3% English, 14.0% Irish, 6.6% Scotch-Irish (2000).
Economy: Employment by occupation: 15.1% management, 5.2% professional, 17.4% services, 29.7% sales, 0.0% farming, 10.5% construction, 22.1% production (2000).
Income: Per capita income: $15,507 (2000); Median household income: $42,679 (2000); Poverty rate: 8.3% (2000).
Education: Percent of population age 25 and over with: High school diploma (including GED) or higher: 97.0% (2000); Bachelor's degree or higher: 3.0% (2000).
Housing: Homeownership rate: 78.8% (2000); Median home value: $36,800 (2000); Median rent: $263 per month (2000); Median age of housing: 60+ years (2000).
Transportation: Commute to work: 94.5% car, 0.0% public transportation, 3.0% walk, 0.0% work from home (2000); Travel time to work: 47.3% less than 15 minutes, 39.4% 15 to 30 minutes, 0.0% 30 to 45 minutes, 5.5% 45 to 60 minutes, 7.9% 60 minutes or more (2000)

VERSAILLES (village). Covers a land area of 0.922 square miles and a water area of 0.005 square miles. Located at 39.88° N. Lat.; 90.65° W. Long. Elevation is 633 feet.
Population: 480 (1990); 567 (2000); 509 (2007); 468 (2012 projected); Race: 99.8% White, 0.2% Black, 0.0% Asian, 0.0% Hispanic of any race (2007); Density: 551.8 persons per square mile (2007); Average household size: 2.31 (2007); Median age: 38.6 (2007); Males per 100 females: 102.8 (2007); Marriage status: 21.8% never married, 52.1% now married, 13.4% widowed, 12.7% divorced (2000); Foreign born: 0.0% (2000); Ancestry (includes multiple ancestries): 20.4% United States or American, 16.3% German, 8.8% Irish, 7.3% English, 3.1% Other groups (2000).
Economy: Employment by occupation: 4.8% management, 4.8% professional, 31.2% services, 19.9% sales, 1.7% farming, 8.7% construction, 29.0% production (2000).
Income: Per capita income: $20,766 (2007); Median household income: $44,444 (2007); Average household income: $48,045 (2007); Percent of households with income of $100,000 or more: 7.7% (2007); Poverty rate: 12.5% (2000).
Education: Percent of population age 25 and over with: High school diploma (including GED) or higher: 73.3% (2007); Bachelor's degree or higher: 4.1% (2007); Master's degree or higher: 1.5% (2007).
Housing: Homeownership rate: 77.3% (2007); Median home value: $50,625 (2007); Median rent: $211 per month (2000); Median age of housing: 42 years (2000).
Transportation: Commute to work: 94.3% car, 0.0% public transportation, 3.0% walk, 1.3% work from home (2000); Travel time to work: 37.4% less than 15 minutes, 22.5% 15 to 30 minutes, 27.3% 30 to 45 minutes, 4.8% 45 to 60 minutes, 7.9% 60 minutes or more (2000)

Bureau County

Located in northern Illinois; bounded on the southeast by the Illinois River; includes Lake Depue. Covers a land area of 868.56 square miles, a water area of 4.74 square miles, and is located in the Central Time Zone. The county was founded in 1837. County seat is Princeton.

Bureau County is part of the Ottawa-Streator, IL Micropolitan Statistical Area. The entire metro area includes: Bureau County, IL; La Salle County, IL; Putnam County, IL

Weather Station: Walnut Elevation: 688 feet

	Jan	Feb	Mar	Apr	May	Jun	Jul	Aug	Sep	Oct	Nov	Dec
High	28	34	46	61	73	82	85	83	76	64	47	34
Low	11	17	28	38	50	59	63	61	52	41	30	18
Precip	1.3	1.3	2.7	3.5	4.4	4.6	3.6	4.4	3.6	2.9	2.6	2.0
Snow	10.8	6.7	4.3	1.3	tr	0.0	0.0	0.0	0.0	0.1	1.9	7.8

High and Low temperatures in degrees Fahrenheit; Precipitation and Snow in inches

Population: 35,688 (1990); 35,503 (2000); 35,388 (2007); 35,293 (2012 projected); Race: 96.0% White, 0.6% Black, 0.5% Asian, 6.3% Hispanic of any race (2007); Density: 40.7 persons per square mile (2007); Average household size: 2.47 (2007); Median age: 41.0 (2007); Males per 100 females: 95.4 (2007).
Religion: Five largest groups: 21.0% Catholic Church, 8.6% The United Methodist Church, 8.4% Evangelical Lutheran Church in America, 2.9% United Church of Christ, 2.5% American Baptist Churches in the USA (2000).
Economy: Unemployment rate: 5.2% (4/2008); Total civilian labor force: 19,612 (4/2008); Leading industries: 19.8% health care and social assistance; 16.8% manufacturing; 13.0% transportation & warehousing (2005); Farms: 1,091 totaling 491,180 acres (2002); Companies that employ 500 or more persons: 2 (2006); Companies that employ 100 to 499 persons: 16 (2006); Companies that employ less than 100 persons: 772 (2006); Black-owned businesses: n/a (2002); Hispanic-owned businesses: n/a (2002); Asian-owned businesses: n/a (2002); Women-owned businesses: n/a (2002); Retail sales per capita: $19,852 (2008). Single-family building permits issued: 43 (2007); Multi-family building permits issued: 50 (2007).
Income: Per capita income: $24,195 (2007); Median household income: $47,857 (2007); Average household income: $59,007 (2007); Percent of households with income of $100,000 or more: 12.8% (2007); Poverty rate: 10.1% (2005); Bankruptcy rate: 3.37% (2007).
Taxes: Total county taxes per capita: $118 (2006); County property taxes per capita: $115 (2006).
Education: Percent of population age 25 and over with: High school diploma (including GED) or higher: 84.2% (2007); Bachelor's degree or higher: 15.9% (2007); Master's degree or higher: 5.1% (2007).
Housing: Homeownership rate: 75.9% (2007); Median home value: $120,628 (2007); Median rent: $331 per month (2000); Median age of housing: 55 years (2000).
Health: Birth rate: 129.9 per 10,000 population (2007); Death rate: 110.5 per 10,000 population (2007); Age-adjusted cancer mortality rate: 185.5 deaths per 100,000 population (2005); Number of physicians: 10.9 per 10,000 population (2005); Hospital beds: 45.1 per 10,000 population (2004); Hospital admissions: 1,671.5 per 10,000 population (2004).
Elections: 2004 Presidential election results: 54.9% Bush, 44.5% Kerry, 0.1% Nader, 0.5% Badnarik
National and State Parks: Hennepin Canal Parkway State Park; Lake Depue State Fish and Wildlife Area; Miller-Anderson Woods State Nature Preserve
Additional Information Contacts
Bureau County Government . . . . (815) 875-2014

City of Princeton. . . . . (815) 875-2631
http://www.princeton-il.com/home/index.php?spl_1
City of Spring Valley. . . . . (815) 664-4221
http://www.spring-valley.il.us

Princeton Chamber of Commerce . . . . (815) 875-2616
http://www.visitprinceton-il.com
Walnut Chamber of Commerce . . . . (815) 379-2141
http://www.villageofwalnut.com

Bureau County Communities

ARLINGTON (village). Covers a land area of 0.428 square miles and a water area of 0 square miles. Located at 41.47° N. Lat.; 89.24° W. Long. Elevation is 751 feet.
Population: 200 (1990); 211 (2000); 203 (2007); 200 (2012 projected); Race: 88.2% White, 0.0% Black, 1.0% Asian, 10.3% Hispanic of any race (2007); Density: 474.7 persons per square mile (2007); Average household size: 2.71 (2007); Median age: 35.9 (2007); Males per 100 females: 103.0 (2007); Marriage status: 32.9% never married, 53.3% now married, 6.6% widowed, 7.2% divorced (2000); Foreign born: 1.9% (2000); Ancestry (includes multiple ancestries): 31.9% German, 21.1% Other groups, 12.2% Irish, 10.3% Norwegian, 8.5% English (2000).
Economy: Employment by occupation: 7.0% management, 9.3% professional, 29.1% services, 17.4% sales, 0.0% farming, 14.0% construction, 23.3% production (2000).
Income: Per capita income: $17,291 (2007); Median household income: $37,500 (2007); Average household income: $46,800 (2007); Percent of households with income of $100,000 or more: 10.7% (2007); Poverty rate: 13.7% (2000).
Education: Percent of population age 25 and over with: High school diploma (including GED) or higher: 78.3% (2007); Bachelor's degree or higher: 5.0% (2007); Master's degree or higher: 0.8% (2007).
Housing: Homeownership rate: 82.7% (2007); Median home value: $75,714 (2007); Median rent: $525 per month (2000); Median age of housing: 60+ years (2000).
Transportation: Commute to work: 91.7% car, 0.0% public transportation, 8.3% walk, 0.0% work from home (2000); Travel time to work: 23.8% less than 15 minutes, 44.0% 15 to 30 minutes, 8.3% 30 to 45 minutes, 13.1% 45 to 60 minutes, 10.7% 60 minutes or more (2000)

BUDA (village). Covers a land area of 1.008 square miles and a water area of 0 square miles. Located at 41.32° N. Lat.; 89.68° W. Long. Elevation is 768 feet.
Population: 563 (1990); 592 (2000); 592 (2007); 591 (2012 projected); Race: 99.3% White, 0.0% Black, 0.2% Asian, 1.5% Hispanic of any race (2007); Density: 587.3 persons per square mile (2007); Average household size: 2.48 (2007); Median age: 36.5 (2007); Males per 100 females: 84.4 (2007); Marriage status: 22.1% never married, 59.3% now married, 9.0% widowed, 9.6% divorced (2000); Foreign born: 1.3% (2000); Ancestry (includes multiple ancestries): 27.2% German, 17.2% English, 12.5% United States or American, 11.2% Irish, 5.5% Other groups (2000).
Economy: Employment by occupation: 3.6% management, 15.0% professional, 12.4% services, 21.2% sales, 1.5% farming, 9.9% construction, 36.5% production (2000).
Income: Per capita income: $20,076 (2007); Median household income: $42,969 (2007); Average household income: $49,728 (2007); Percent of households with income of $100,000 or more: 5.9% (2007); Poverty rate: 12.5% (2000).
Education: Percent of population age 25 and over with: High school diploma (including GED) or higher: 85.1% (2007); Bachelor's degree or higher: 7.5% (2007); Master's degree or higher: 1.9% (2007).

School District(s)

Bureau Valley CUSD 340 (PK-12)
2005-06 Enrollment: 1,305 . . . . (815) 445-3101
Housing: Homeownership rate: 84.9% (2007); Median home value: $79,286 (2007); Median rent: $308 per month (2000); Median age of housing: 60+ years (2000).
Safety: Violent crime rate: 0.0 per 10,000 population; Property crime rate: 34.4 per 10,000 population (2006).
Transportation: Commute to work: 92.3% car, 0.0% public transportation, 3.3% walk, 4.0% work from home (2000); Travel time to work: 30.4% less than 15 minutes, 43.0% 15 to 30 minutes, 19.0% 30 to 45 minutes, 2.3% 45 to 60 minutes, 5.3% 60 minutes or more (2000)

BUREAU JUNCTION (village). Aka Bureau. Covers a land area of 1.437 square miles and a water area of 0.066 square miles. Located at 41.28° N. Lat.; 89.36° W. Long. Elevation is 489 feet.
Population: 350 (1990); 368 (2000); 374 (2007); 368 (2012 projected); Race: 98.7% White, 0.0% Black, 0.0% Asian, 16.6% Hispanic of any race (2007); Density: 260.3 persons per square mile (2007); Average household size: 2.73 (2007); Median age: 33.5 (2007); Males per 100 females: 103.3 (2007); Marriage status: 29.7% never married, 51.4% now married, 5.6% widowed, 13.3% divorced (2000); Foreign born: 5.0% (2000); Ancestry (includes multiple ancestries): 25.2% German, 14.7% Irish, 11.9% English, 9.1% French (except Basque), 7.5% Polish (2000).
Economy: Employment by occupation: 4.2% management, 7.9% professional, 26.3% services, 16.3% sales, 0.5% farming, 14.2% construction, 30.5% production (2000).
Income: Per capita income: $20,194 (2007); Median household income: $52,250 (2007); Average household income: $55,128 (2007); Percent of households with income of $100,000 or more: 8.0% (2007); Poverty rate: 5.3% (2000).
Education: Percent of population age 25 and over with: High school diploma (including GED) or higher: 84.1% (2007); Bachelor's degree or higher: 7.9% (2007); Master's degree or higher: 4.8% (2007).

School District(s)

Leepertown CCSD 175 (PK-08)
2005-06 Enrollment: 50 . . . . (815) 659-3191
Housing: Homeownership rate: 78.1% (2007); Median home value: $78,500 (2007); Median rent: $217 per month (2000); Median age of housing: 60+ years (2000).
Transportation: Commute to work: 86.5% car, 0.0% public transportation, 8.1% walk, 2.7% work from home (2000); Travel time to work: 25.6% less than 15 minutes, 46.7% 15 to 30 minutes, 19.4% 30 to 45 minutes, 3.9% 45 to 60 minutes, 4.4% 60 minutes or more (2000)

CHERRY (village). Covers a land area of 0.538 square miles and a water area of 0 square miles. Located at 41.42° N. Lat.; 89.21° W. Long. Elevation is 679 feet.
History: Cherry was the scene of a mine fire in 1909 that killed 270 miners.
Population: 513 (1990); 509 (2000); 511 (2007); 508 (2012 projected); Race: 97.5% White, 0.4% Black, 0.0% Asian, 1.8% Hispanic of any race (2007); Density: 949.7 persons per square mile (2007); Average household size: 2.35 (2007); Median age: 40.6 (2007); Males per 100 females: 90.7 (2007); Marriage status: 18.2% never married, 64.1% now married, 8.1% widowed, 9.6% divorced (2000); Foreign born: 0.0% (2000); Ancestry (includes multiple ancestries): 32.9% German, 23.2% Italian, 15.2% Irish, 11.9% English, 11.9% Polish (2000).
Economy: Employment by occupation: 6.4% management, 11.1% professional, 11.8% services, 25.0% sales, 0.7% farming, 10.1% construction, 34.8% production (2000).
Income: Per capita income: $23,708 (2007); Median household income: $49,643 (2007); Average household income: $54,700 (2007); Percent of households with income of $100,000 or more: 6.5% (2007); Poverty rate: 1.8% (2000).
Education: Percent of population age 25 and over with: High school diploma (including GED) or higher: 80.6% (2007); Bachelor's degree or higher: 8.3% (2007); Master's degree or higher: 1.7% (2007).

School District(s)

Cherry SD 92 (KG-08)
2005-06 Enrollment: 83 . . . . (815) 894-2777
Housing: Homeownership rate: 84.3% (2007); Median home value: $110,887 (2007); Median rent: $394 per month (2000); Median age of housing: 60+ years (2000).
Safety: Violent crime rate: 0.0 per 10,000 population; Property crime rate: 0.0 per 10,000 population (2006).
Transportation: Commute to work: 95.9% car, 0.0% public transportation, 3.0% walk, 1.0% work from home (2000); Travel time to work: 30.0% less than 15 minutes, 50.2% 15 to 30 minutes, 8.9% 30 to 45 minutes, 1.4% 45 to 60 minutes, 9.6% 60 minutes or more (2000)

DALZELL (village). Covers a land area of 1.270 square miles and a water area of 0.010 square miles. Located at 41.35° N. Lat.; 89.17° W. Long. Elevation is 633 feet.
Population: 709 (1990); 717 (2000); 791 (2007); 839 (2012 projected); Race: 99.2% White, 0.3% Black, 0.0% Asian, 1.8% Hispanic of any race (2007); Density: 622.8 persons per square mile (2007); Average household size: 2.54 (2007); Median age: 39.9 (2007); Males per 100 females: 93.4 (2007); Marriage status: 21.0% never married, 65.5% now married, 6.3% widowed, 7.2% divorced (2000); Foreign born: 0.7% (2000); Ancestry (includes multiple ancestries): 35.7% Italian, 23.7% German, 19.1% Polish, 14.9% Irish, 7.6% English (2000).
Economy: Single-family building permits issued: 0 (2007); Multi-family building permits issued: 0 (2007); Employment by occupation: 5.6%

management, 17.0% professional, 13.4% services, 31.3% sales, 0.0% farming, 9.8% construction, 22.9% production (2000).
Income: Per capita income: $26,618 (2007); Median household income: $60,300 (2007); Average household income: $66,915 (2007); Percent of households with income of $100,000 or more: 11.9% (2007); Poverty rate: 3.5% (2000).
Education: Percent of population age 25 and over with: High school diploma (including GED) or higher: 85.9% (2007); Bachelor's degree or higher: 11.8% (2007); Master's degree or higher: 2.6% (2007).

School District(s)

Dalzell SD 98 (KG-08)
2005-06 Enrollment: 69 . . . . (815) 663-8821
Housing: Homeownership rate: 88.5% (2007); Median home value: $151,136 (2007); Median rent: $410 per month (2000); Median age of housing: 38 years (2000).
Transportation: Commute to work: 98.9% car, 0.0% public transportation, 0.0% walk, 1.1% work from home (2000); Travel time to work: 52.0% less than 15 minutes, 26.3% 15 to 30 minutes, 9.5% 30 to 45 minutes, 2.9% 45 to 60 minutes, 9.2% 60 minutes or more (2000)

DE PUE (village). Aka Depue. Covers a land area of 2.711 square miles and a water area of 0.259 square miles. Located at 41.32° N. Lat.; 89.30° W. Long.
Population: 1,774 (1990); 1,842 (2000); 1,787 (2007); 1,764 (2012 projected); Race: 80.1% White, 0.1% Black, 1.2% Asian, 56.1% Hispanic of any race (2007); Density: 659.1 persons per square mile (2007); Average household size: 2.79 (2007); Median age: 32.8 (2007); Males per 100 females: 111.2 (2007); Marriage status: 24.8% never married, 55.9% now married, 9.1% widowed, 10.2% divorced (2000); Foreign born: 20.6% (2000); Ancestry (includes multiple ancestries): 47.3% Other groups, 12.0% German, 7.9% English, 6.8% Irish, 6.8% United States or American (2000).
Economy: Single-family building permits issued: 1 (2007); Multi-family building permits issued: 0 (2007); Employment by occupation: 3.6% management, 7.5% professional, 11.3% services, 13.3% sales, 10.5% farming, 10.1% construction, 43.7% production (2000).
Income: Per capita income: $19,365 (2007); Median household income: $37,892 (2007); Average household income: $52,344 (2007); Percent of households with income of $100,000 or more: 8.6% (2007); Poverty rate: 13.1% (2000).
Education: Percent of population age 25 and over with: High school diploma (including GED) or higher: 60.0% (2007); Bachelor's degree or higher: 4.9% (2007); Master's degree or higher: 1.7% (2007).

School District(s)

Depue USD 103 (PK-12)
2005-06 Enrollment: 455 . . . . (815) 447-2121
Housing: Homeownership rate: 72.1% (2007); Median home value: $72,031 (2007); Median rent: $315 per month (2000); Median age of housing: 60+ years (2000).
Safety: Violent crime rate: 55.8 per 10,000 population; Property crime rate: 206.6 per 10,000 population (2006).
Transportation: Commute to work: 95.5% car, 0.4% public transportation, 2.2% walk, 0.7% work from home (2000); Travel time to work: 29.3% less than 15 minutes, 47.6% 15 to 30 minutes, 11.8% 30 to 45 minutes, 2.0% 45 to 60 minutes, 9.3% 60 minutes or more (2000)

DOVER (village). Covers a land area of 0.268 square miles and a water area of 0 square miles. Located at 41.43° N. Lat.; 89.39° W. Long. Elevation is 741 feet.
Population: 163 (1990); 172 (2000); 156 (2007); 155 (2012 projected); Race: 100.0% White, 0.0% Black, 0.0% Asian, 0.6% Hispanic of any race (2007); Density: 581.9 persons per square mile (2007); Average household size: 2.74 (2007); Median age: 42.1 (2007); Males per 100 females: 102.6 (2007); Marriage status: 22.5% never married, 65.8% now married, 4.5% widowed, 7.2% divorced (2000); Foreign born: 0.0% (2000); Ancestry (includes multiple ancestries): 24.7% German, 13.9% United States or American, 11.4% Irish, 7.0% Scottish, 6.3% Lithuanian (2000).
Economy: Employment by occupation: 1.3% management, 28.9% professional, 21.1% services, 18.4% sales, 0.0% farming, 15.8% construction, 14.5% production (2000).
Income: Per capita income: $18,510 (2007); Median household income: $52,692 (2007); Average household income: $50,658 (2007); Percent of households with income of $100,000 or more: 7.0% (2007); Poverty rate: 5.7% (2000).
Education: Percent of population age 25 and over with: High school diploma (including GED) or higher: 87.9% (2007); Bachelor's degree or higher: 25.3% (2007); Master's degree or higher: 8.1% (2007).
Housing: Homeownership rate: 89.5% (2007); Median home value: $85,000 (2007); Median rent: $n/a per month (2000); Median age of housing: 60+ years (2000).
Transportation: Commute to work: 98.7% car, 0.0% public transportation, 0.0% walk, 0.0% work from home (2000); Travel time to work: 56.6% less than 15 minutes, 27.6% 15 to 30 minutes, 6.6% 30 to 45 minutes, 1.3% 45 to 60 minutes, 7.9% 60 minutes or more (2000)

HOLLOWAYVILLE (village). Covers a land area of 0.049 square miles and a water area of 0 square miles. Located at 41.36° N. Lat.; 89.29° W. Long. Elevation is 659 feet.
Population: 37 (1990); 90 (2000); 86 (2007); 84 (2012 projected); Race: 100.0% White, 0.0% Black, 0.0% Asian, 0.0% Hispanic of any race (2007); Density: 1,755.0 persons per square mile (2007); Average household size: 3.07 (2007); Median age: 30.0 (2007); Males per 100 females: 91.1 (2007); Marriage status: 16.0% never married, 74.0% now married, 4.0% widowed, 6.0% divorced (2000); Foreign born: 0.0% (2000); Ancestry (includes multiple ancestries): 54.4% German, 29.1% Italian, 16.5% Irish, 12.7% Other groups, 5.1% English (2000).
Economy: Employment by occupation: 10.8% management, 32.4% professional, 16.2% services, 13.5% sales, 0.0% farming, 13.5% construction, 13.5% production (2000).
Income: Per capita income: $24,331 (2007); Median household income: $60,000 (2007); Average household income: $74,732 (2007); Percent of households with income of $100,000 or more: 28.6% (2007); Poverty rate: 0.0% (2000).
Education: Percent of population age 25 and over with: High school diploma (including GED) or higher: 93.8% (2007); Bachelor's degree or higher: 12.5% (2007); Master's degree or higher: 8.3% (2007).
Housing: Homeownership rate: 82.1% (2007); Median home value: $88,750 (2007); Median rent: $500 per month (2000); Median age of housing: 60+ years (2000).
Transportation: Commute to work: 94.6% car, 0.0% public transportation, 0.0% walk, 0.0% work from home (2000); Travel time to work: 18.9% less than 15 minutes, 59.5% 15 to 30 minutes, 5.4% 30 to 45 minutes, 5.4% 45 to 60 minutes, 10.8% 60 minutes or more (2000)

LA MOILLE (village). Covers a land area of 1.205 square miles and a water area of 0 square miles. Located at 41.52° N. Lat.; 89.28° W. Long. Elevation is 794 feet.
Population: 717 (1990); 773 (2000); 766 (2007); 761 (2012 projected); Race: 96.7% White, 0.3% Black, 0.0% Asian, 6.5% Hispanic of any race (2007); Density: 635.7 persons per square mile (2007); Average household size: 2.49 (2007); Median age: 35.5 (2007); Males per 100 females: 100.0 (2007); Marriage status: 19.0% never married, 61.7% now married, 7.8% widowed, 11.5% divorced (2000); Foreign born: 0.3% (2000); Ancestry (includes multiple ancestries): 45.0% German, 11.1% Irish, 10.2% English, 5.9% Other groups, 5.2% Italian (2000).
Economy: Employment by occupation: 11.3% management, 12.7% professional, 10.3% services, 27.2% sales, 0.8% farming, 11.1% construction, 26.6% production (2000).
Income: Per capita income: $20,473 (2007); Median household income: $43,056 (2007); Average household income: $50,917 (2007); Percent of households with income of $100,000 or more: 6.8% (2007); Poverty rate: 6.5% (2000).
Education: Percent of population age 25 and over with: High school diploma (including GED) or higher: 85.7% (2007); Bachelor's degree or higher: 9.5% (2007); Master's degree or higher: 3.6% (2007).

School District(s)

La Moille CUSD 303 (KG-12)
2005-06 Enrollment: 321 . . . . (815) 638-2018
Housing: Homeownership rate: 72.1% (2007); Median home value: $117,453 (2007); Median rent: $268 per month (2000); Median age of housing: 56 years (2000).
Safety: Violent crime rate: 0.0 per 10,000 population; Property crime rate: 26.3 per 10,000 population (2006).
Transportation: Commute to work: 94.1% car, 0.0% public transportation, 3.2% walk, 1.6% work from home (2000); Travel time to work: 25.3% less than 15 minutes, 56.3% 15 to 30 minutes, 8.0% 30 to 45 minutes, 3.8% 45 to 60 minutes, 6.6% 60 minutes or more (2000)

LADD (village). Covers a land area of 1.193 square miles and a water area of 0 square miles. Located at 41.38° N. Lat.; 89.21° W. Long. Elevation is 650 feet.
History: Incorporated 1890.
Population: 1,339 (1990); 1,313 (2000); 1,355 (2007); 1,391 (2012 projected); Race: 96.4% White, 0.1% Black, 0.1% Asian, 4.9% Hispanic of any race (2007); Density: 1,135.4 persons per square mile (2007); Average household size: 2.32 (2007); Median age: 39.1 (2007); Males per 100 females: 92.7 (2007); Marriage status: 18.8% never married, 61.9% now married, 8.7% widowed, 10.6% divorced (2000); Foreign born: 2.0% (2000); Ancestry (includes multiple ancestries): 30.2% German, 25.7% Italian, 17.3% Irish, 9.9% English, 9.4% Other groups (2000).
Economy: Single-family building permits issued: 0 (2007); Multi-family building permits issued: 0 (2007); Employment by occupation: 9.6% management, 19.6% professional, 16.4% services, 25.2% sales, 0.6% farming, 9.6% construction, 19.1% production (2000).
Income: Per capita income: $26,450 (2007); Median household income: $50,294 (2007); Average household income: $61,353 (2007); Percent of households with income of $100,000 or more: 15.6% (2007); Poverty rate: 4.9% (2000).
Education: Percent of population age 25 and over with: High school diploma (including GED) or higher: 82.6% (2007); Bachelor's degree or higher: 13.6% (2007); Master's degree or higher: 4.2% (2007).

School District(s)

Ladd CCSD 94 (KG-08)
2005-06 Enrollment: 188 . . . . (815) 894-2363
Housing: Homeownership rate: 76.7% (2007); Median home value: $126,111 (2007); Median rent: $351 per month (2000); Median age of housing: 57 years (2000).
Safety: Violent crime rate: 30.7 per 10,000 population; Property crime rate: 145.6 per 10,000 population (2006).
Transportation: Commute to work: 93.2% car, 0.0% public transportation, 3.7% walk, 2.6% work from home (2000); Travel time to work: 51.0% less than 15 minutes, 34.2% 15 to 30 minutes, 6.0% 30 to 45 minutes, 2.5% 45 to 60 minutes, 6.3% 60 minutes or more (2000)

MALDEN (village). Covers a land area of 0.274 square miles and a water area of 0 square miles. Located at 41.42° N. Lat.; 89.36° W. Long. Elevation is 705 feet.
Population: 381 (1990); 343 (2000); 308 (2007); 307 (2012 projected); Race: 96.8% White, 1.6% Black, 0.0% Asian, 0.0% Hispanic of any race (2007); Density: 1,125.8 persons per square mile (2007); Average household size: 2.63 (2007); Median age: 36.0 (2007); Males per 100 females: 113.9 (2007); Marriage status: 22.2% never married, 53.6% now married, 6.7% widowed, 17.5% divorced (2000); Foreign born: 0.8% (2000); Ancestry (includes multiple ancestries): 42.7% German, 15.5% English, 11.9% Irish, 10.0% Polish, 8.6% Other groups (2000).
Economy: Employment by occupation: 7.9% management, 8.5% professional, 15.2% services, 20.7% sales, 3.7% farming, 15.2% construction, 28.7% production (2000).
Income: Per capita income: $23,791 (2007); Median household income: $53,611 (2007); Average household income: $62,628 (2007); Percent of households with income of $100,000 or more: 8.5% (2007); Poverty rate: 3.1% (2000).
Education: Percent of population age 25 and over with: High school diploma (including GED) or higher: 90.1% (2007); Bachelor's degree or higher: 5.2% (2007); Master's degree or higher: 0.5% (2007).

School District(s)

Malden CCSD 84 (PK-08)
2005-06 Enrollment: 117 . . . . (815) 643-2436
Housing: Homeownership rate: 87.2% (2007); Median home value: $102,632 (2007); Median rent: $313 per month (2000); Median age of housing: 35 years (2000).
Transportation: Commute to work: 98.8% car, 0.0% public transportation, 0.6% walk, 0.6% work from home (2000); Travel time to work: 44.1% less than 15 minutes, 44.1% 15 to 30 minutes, 4.3% 30 to 45 minutes, 1.9% 45 to 60 minutes, 5.6% 60 minutes or more (2000)

MANLIUS (village). Covers a land area of 0.306 square miles and a water area of 0 square miles. Located at 41.45° N. Lat.; 89.67° W. Long. Elevation is 702 feet.
Population: 365 (1990); 355 (2000); 346 (2007); 339 (2012 projected); Race: 98.3% White, 0.6% Black, 0.0% Asian, 6.4% Hispanic of any race (2007); Density: 1,129.3 persons per square mile (2007); Average household size: 2.35 (2007); Median age: 36.7 (2007); Males per 100 females: 86.0 (2007); Marriage status: 23.1% never married, 55.3% now married, 10.6% widowed, 11.0% divorced (2000); Foreign born: 0.9% (2000); Ancestry (includes multiple ancestries): 33.5% German, 18.3% English, 8.1% Swedish, 6.8% Other groups, 6.2% Irish (2000).
Economy: Employment by occupation: 3.3% management, 14.7% professional, 20.7% services, 21.2% sales, 3.3% farming, 3.8% construction, 33.2% production (2000).
Income: Per capita income: $20,361 (2007); Median household income: $45,577 (2007); Average household income: $47,925 (2007); Percent of households with income of $100,000 or more: 4.1% (2007); Poverty rate: 7.1% (2000).
Education: Percent of population age 25 and over with: High school diploma (including GED) or higher: 90.1% (2007); Bachelor's degree or higher: 6.3% (2007); Master's degree or higher: 2.7% (2007).

School District(s)

Bureau Valley CUSD 340 (PK-12)
2005-06 Enrollment: 1,305 . . . . (815) 445-3101
Housing: Homeownership rate: 76.2% (2007); Median home value: $90,625 (2007); Median rent: $229 per month (2000); Median age of housing: 60+ years (2000).
Transportation: Commute to work: 89.6% car, 0.0% public transportation, 6.0% walk, 2.7% work from home (2000); Travel time to work: 35.4% less than 15 minutes, 41.0% 15 to 30 minutes, 11.8% 30 to 45 minutes, 8.4% 45 to 60 minutes, 3.4% 60 minutes or more (2000)

MINERAL (village). Covers a land area of 0.308 square miles and a water area of 0 square miles. Located at 41.38° N. Lat.; 89.83° W. Long. Elevation is 640 feet.
Population: 250 (1990); 272 (2000); 268 (2007); 268 (2012 projected); Race: 96.6% White, 1.5% Black, 0.0% Asian, 1.9% Hispanic of any race (2007); Density: 870.4 persons per square mile (2007); Average household size: 2.48 (2007); Median age: 37.6 (2007); Males per 100 females: 100.0 (2007); Marriage status: 23.0% never married, 55.8% now married, 10.1% widowed, 11.1% divorced (2000); Foreign born: 0.0% (2000); Ancestry (includes multiple ancestries): 28.2% German, 21.2% Belgian, 11.7% Irish, 10.6% English, 8.1% Swedish (2000).
Economy: Employment by occupation: 7.4% management, 3.0% professional, 13.3% services, 23.0% sales, 0.0% farming, 17.0% construction, 36.3% production (2000).
Income: Per capita income: $30,261 (2007); Median household income: $47,222 (2007); Average household income: $75,093 (2007); Percent of households with income of $100,000 or more: 13.9% (2007); Poverty rate: 8.4% (2000).
Education: Percent of population age 25 and over with: High school diploma (including GED) or higher: 78.8% (2007); Bachelor's degree or higher: 1.1% (2007); Master's degree or higher: 0.0% (2007).
Housing: Homeownership rate: 78.7% (2007); Median home value: $71,923 (2007); Median rent: $350 per month (2000); Median age of housing: 52 years (2000).
Transportation: Commute to work: 100.0% car, 0.0% public transportation, 0.0% walk, 0.0% work from home (2000); Travel time to work: 27.4% less than 15 minutes, 35.6% 15 to 30 minutes, 30.4% 30 to 45 minutes, 5.9% 45 to 60 minutes, 0.7% 60 minutes or more (2000)

NEPONSET (village). Covers a land area of 1.042 square miles and a water area of 0 square miles. Located at 41.29° N. Lat.; 89.79° W. Long. Elevation is 830 feet.
Population: 529 (1990); 519 (2000); 523 (2007); 525 (2012 projected); Race: 97.7% White, 0.6% Black, 1.0% Asian, 3.8% Hispanic of any race (2007); Density: 501.8 persons per square mile (2007); Average household size: 2.55 (2007); Median age: 43.8 (2007); Males per 100 females: 94.4 (2007); Marriage status: 20.8% never married, 62.3% now married, 9.5% widowed, 7.4% divorced (2000); Foreign born: 2.0% (2000); Ancestry (includes multiple ancestries): 30.6% English, 21.7% German, 16.7% Irish, 9.9% United States or American, 4.8% Scottish (2000).
Economy: Single-family building permits issued: 0 (2007); Multi-family building permits issued: 0 (2007); Employment by occupation: 9.2% management, 9.6% professional, 19.6% services, 19.6% sales, 0.8% farming, 5.6% construction, 35.6% production (2000).
Income: Per capita income: $22,495 (2007); Median household income: $49,643 (2007); Average household income: $57,390 (2007); Percent of households with income of $100,000 or more: 12.7% (2007); Poverty rate: 11.9% (2000).

Education: Percent of population age 25 and over with: High school diploma (including GED) or higher: 81.8% (2007); Bachelor's degree or higher: 9.6% (2007); Master's degree or higher: 3.2% (2007).

School District(s)

Neponset CCSD 307 (PK-08)
2005-06 Enrollment: 104 . . . . (309) 594-2306

Housing: Homeownership rate: 88.3% (2007); Median home value: $86,538 (2007); Median rent: $289 per month (2000); Median age of housing: 55 years (2000).

Safety: Violent crime rate: 0.0 per 10,000 population; Property crime rate: 19.8 per 10,000 population (2006).

Transportation: Commute to work: 86.2% car, 0.4% public transportation, 6.1% walk, 4.5% work from home (2000); Travel time to work: 37.4% less than 15 minutes, 36.6% 15 to 30 minutes, 11.9% 30 to 45 minutes, 4.3% 45 to 60 minutes, 9.8% 60 minutes or more (2000)

NEW BEDFORD (village). Covers a land area of 0.175 square miles and a water area of 0 square miles. Located at 41.51° N. Lat.; 89.71° W. Long. Elevation is 643 feet.

Population: 65 (1990); 95 (2000); 93 (2007); 89 (2012 projected); Race: 93.5% White, 0.0% Black, 1.1% Asian, 5.4% Hispanic of any race (2007); Density: 532.4 persons per square mile (2007); Average household size: 2.45 (2007); Median age: 42.5 (2007); Males per 100 females: 102.2 (2007); Marriage status: 14.9% never married, 75.7% now married, 8.1% widowed, 1.4% divorced (2000); Foreign born: 4.4% (2000); Ancestry (includes multiple ancestries): 37.4% German, 18.7% United States or American, 9.9% Danish, 9.9% Irish, 4.4% Scottish (2000).

Economy: Employment by occupation: 4.3% management, 13.0% professional, 28.3% services, 17.4% sales, 0.0% farming, 4.3% construction, 32.6% production (2000).

Income: Per capita income: $19,382 (2007); Median household income: $45,000 (2007); Average household income: $47,434 (2007); Percent of households with income of $100,000 or more: 2.6% (2007); Poverty rate: 3.3% (2000).

Education: Percent of population age 25 and over with: High school diploma (including GED) or higher: 75.8% (2007); Bachelor's degree or higher: 3.0% (2007); Master's degree or higher: 0.0% (2007).

Housing: Homeownership rate: 97.4% (2007); Median home value: $97,000 (2007); Median rent: $175 per month (2000); Median age of housing: 60+ years (2000).

Transportation: Commute to work: 100.0% car, 0.0% public transportation, 0.0% walk, 0.0% work from home (2000); Travel time to work: 0.0% less than 15 minutes, 54.3% 15 to 30 minutes, 28.3% 30 to 45 minutes, 4.3% 45 to 60 minutes, 13.0% 60 minutes or more (2000)

OHIO (village). Covers a land area of 0.753 square miles and a water area of 0 square miles. Located at 41.55° N. Lat.; 89.46° W. Long. Elevation is 902 feet.

Population: 449 (1990); 540 (2000); 534 (2007); 532 (2012 projected); Race: 99.1% White, 0.4% Black, 0.0% Asian, 4.1% Hispanic of any race (2007); Density: 709.3 persons per square mile (2007); Average household size: 2.42 (2007); Median age: 36.8 (2007); Males per 100 females: 92.8 (2007); Marriage status: 20.3% never married, 59.3% now married, 11.6% widowed, 8.7% divorced (2000); Foreign born: 0.8% (2000); Ancestry (includes multiple ancestries): 44.0% German, 21.4% Irish, 10.5% Swedish, 6.6% Polish, 6.0% English (2000).

Economy: Employment by occupation: 7.8% management, 13.4% professional, 15.6% services, 23.0% sales, 1.5% farming, 14.5% construction, 24.2% production (2000).

Income: Per capita income: $22,603 (2007); Median household income: $46,607 (2007); Average household income: $54,615 (2007); Percent of households with income of $100,000 or more: 10.4% (2007); Poverty rate: 3.6% (2000).

Education: Percent of population age 25 and over with: High school diploma (including GED) or higher: 92.9% (2007); Bachelor's degree or higher: 14.0% (2007); Master's degree or higher: 4.9% (2007).

School District(s)

Ohio CCSD 17 (KG-08)
2005-06 Enrollment: 100 . . . . (815) 376-4414

Ohio CHSD 505 (09-12)
2005-06 Enrollment: 57 . . . . (815) 376-2934

Housing: Homeownership rate: 78.3% (2007); Median home value: $113,141 (2007); Median rent: $217 per month (2000); Median age of housing: 60+ years (2000).

Transportation: Commute to work: 92.5% car, 0.0% public transportation, 2.6% walk, 3.4% work from home (2000); Travel time to work: 35.8% less than 15 minutes, 34.6% 15 to 30 minutes, 18.7% 30 to 45 minutes, 4.7% 45 to 60 minutes, 6.2% 60 minutes or more (2000)

PRINCETON (city). County seat. Covers a land area of 6.730 square miles and a water area of 0 square miles. Located at 41.37° N. Lat.; 89.46° W. Long. Elevation is 719 feet.

History: Princeton was laid out in 1833 by settlers from Massachusetts. The town grew as an orchard and farming center, and as the seat of Bureau County.

Population: 7,581 (1990); 7,501 (2000); 7,552 (2007); 7,531 (2012 projected); Race: 97.2% White, 0.7% Black, 0.8% Asian, 1.5% Hispanic of any race (2007); Density: 1,122.2 persons per square mile (2007); Average household size: 2.26 (2007); Median age: 44.0 (2007); Males per 100 females: 86.9 (2007); Marriage status: 20.8% never married, 58.3% now married, 10.0% widowed, 10.9% divorced (2000); Foreign born: 1.8% (2000); Ancestry (includes multiple ancestries): 32.0% German, 14.9% English, 14.4% Irish, 9.6% Swedish, 6.5% United States or American (2000).

Economy: Single-family building permits issued: 13 (2007); Multi-family building permits issued: 0 (2007); Employment by occupation: 12.9% management, 18.9% professional, 18.6% services, 22.1% sales, 0.5% farming, 7.8% construction, 19.1% production (2000).

Income: Per capita income: $25,991 (2007); Median household income: $46,149 (2007); Average household income: $57,767 (2007); Percent of households with income of $100,000 or more: 12.8% (2007); Poverty rate: 7.2% (2000).

Taxes: Total city taxes per capita: $156 (2006); City property taxes per capita: $151 (2006).

Education: Percent of population age 25 and over with: High school diploma (including GED) or higher: 88.9% (2007); Bachelor's degree or higher: 21.3% (2007); Master's degree or higher: 7.0% (2007).

School District(s)

Princeton ESD 115 (PK-08)
2005-06 Enrollment: 1,206 . . . . (815) 875-3162

Princeton HSD 500 (09-12)
2005-06 Enrollment: 673 . . . . (815) 875-3308

Housing: Homeownership rate: 68.5% (2007); Median home value: $133,795 (2007); Median rent: $335 per month (2000); Median age of housing: 47 years (2000).

Hospitals: Perry Memorial Hospital (87 beds)

Safety: Violent crime rate: 9.3 per 10,000 population; Property crime rate: 324.3 per 10,000 population (2006).

Newspapers: Bureau County Republican (Community news; Circulation 0); Illinois Valley Shopping News (Regional news; Circulation 13,298)

Transportation: Commute to work: 89.8% car, 0.0% public transportation, 2.7% walk, 4.2% work from home (2000); Travel time to work: 65.9% less than 15 minutes, 17.9% 15 to 30 minutes, 9.0% 30 to 45 minutes, 3.1% 45 to 60 minutes, 4.1% 60 minutes or more (2000); Amtrak: Service available.

Additional Information Contacts

City of Princeton. . . . . (815) 875-2631
http://www.princeton-il.com/home/index.php?spl_1

Princeton Chamber of Commerce . . . . (815) 875-2616
http://www.visitprinceton-il.com

SEATONVILLE (village). Covers a land area of 0.486 square miles and a water area of 0.015 square miles. Located at 41.36° N. Lat.; 89.27° W. Long. Elevation is 620 feet.

Population: 259 (1990); 303 (2000); 304 (2007); 297 (2012 projected); Race: 93.8% White, 0.0% Black, 2.0% Asian, 10.5% Hispanic of any race (2007); Density: 625.5 persons per square mile (2007); Average household size: 2.30 (2007); Median age: 42.9 (2007); Males per 100 females: 93.6 (2007); Marriage status: 17.5% never married, 63.3% now married, 12.4% widowed, 6.9% divorced (2000); Foreign born: 1.3% (2000); Ancestry (includes multiple ancestries): 32.9% German, 17.2% Italian, 13.8% Irish, 10.0% English, 9.7% Polish (2000).

Economy: Single-family building permits issued: 1 (2007); Multi-family building permits issued: 0 (2007); Employment by occupation: 8.3% management, 6.9% professional, 15.2% services, 28.3% sales, 1.4% farming, 8.3% construction, 31.7% production (2000).

Income: Per capita income: $22,821 (2007); Median household income: $39,118 (2007); Average household income: $52,557 (2007); Percent of households with income of $100,000 or more: 12.1% (2007); Poverty rate: 6.3% (2000).

Education: Percent of population age 25 and over with: High school diploma (including GED) or higher: 70.3% (2007); Bachelor's degree or higher: 6.3% (2007); Master's degree or higher: 2.3% (2007).
Housing: Homeownership rate: 90.9% (2007); Median home value: $102,778 (2007); Median rent: $350 per month (2000); Median age of housing: 60+ years (2000).
Transportation: Commute to work: 93.8% car, 1.4% public transportation, 1.4% walk, 3.4% work from home (2000); Travel time to work: 30.0% less than 15 minutes, 43.6% 15 to 30 minutes, 18.6% 30 to 45 minutes, 1.4% 45 to 60 minutes, 6.4% 60 minutes or more (2000)

SHEFFIELD (village). Covers a land area of 0.749 square miles and a water area of 0 square miles. Located at 41.35° N. Lat.; 89.73° W. Long. Elevation is 689 feet.
Population: 956 (1990); 946 (2000); 937 (2007); 937 (2012 projected); Race: 98.2% White, 0.3% Black, 0.1% Asian, 0.9% Hispanic of any race (2007); Density: 1,251.5 persons per square mile (2007); Average household size: 2.42 (2007); Median age: 41.6 (2007); Males per 100 females: 91.6 (2007); Marriage status: 19.0% never married, 62.1% now married, 7.2% widowed, 11.8% divorced (2000); Foreign born: 0.2% (2000); Ancestry (includes multiple ancestries): 22.6% German, 13.4% English, 12.2% Irish, 8.5% Belgian, 6.7% Other groups (2000).
Economy: Employment by occupation: 6.0% management, 18.1% professional, 19.0% services, 20.6% sales, 0.7% farming, 10.9% construction, 24.6% production (2000).
Income: Per capita income: $23,281 (2007); Median household income: $45,795 (2007); Average household income: $55,827 (2007); Percent of households with income of $100,000 or more: 10.9% (2007); Poverty rate: 10.6% (2000).
Education: Percent of population age 25 and over with: High school diploma (including GED) or higher: 82.8% (2007); Bachelor's degree or higher: 16.1% (2007); Master's degree or higher: 4.3% (2007).

School District(s)

Bureau Valley CUSD 340 (PK-12)
2005-06 Enrollment: 1,305 . . . . (815) 445-3101

Housing: Homeownership rate: 82.7% (2007); Median home value: $88,000 (2007); Median rent: $322 per month (2000); Median age of housing: 60+ years (2000).
Transportation: Commute to work: 93.1% car, 0.0% public transportation, 3.2% walk, 3.5% work from home (2000); Travel time to work: 26.6% less than 15 minutes, 39.0% 15 to 30 minutes, 20.8% 30 to 45 minutes, 5.5% 45 to 60 minutes, 8.1% 60 minutes or more (2000)

SPRING VALLEY (city). Covers a land area of 3.886 square miles and a water area of 0.019 square miles. Located at 41.32° N. Lat.; 89.20° W. Long. Elevation is 597 feet.
History: Spring Valley began as a mining operation, but later the economy was based on manufacturing.
Population: 5,246 (1990); 5,398 (2000); 5,272 (2007); 5,173 (2012 projected); Race: 94.3% White, 1.5% Black, 0.4% Asian, 9.3% Hispanic of any race (2007); Density: 1,356.8 persons per square mile (2007); Average household size: 2.47 (2007); Median age: 40.5 (2007); Males per 100 females: 93.1 (2007); Marriage status: 22.8% never married, 56.6% now married, 9.3% widowed, 11.3% divorced (2000); Foreign born: 2.9% (2000); Ancestry (includes multiple ancestries): 26.1% German, 22.9% Italian, 18.4% Irish, 12.4% Polish, 10.5% Other groups (2000).
Economy: Single-family building permits issued: 3 (2007); Multi-family building permits issued: 50 (2007); Employment by occupation: 6.7% management, 16.5% professional, 15.5% services, 28.6% sales, 0.3% farming, 9.5% construction, 22.9% production (2000).
Income: Per capita income: $23,616 (2007); Median household income: $46,096 (2007); Average household income: $57,177 (2007); Percent of households with income of $100,000 or more: 13.6% (2007); Poverty rate: 6.3% (2000).
Education: Percent of population age 25 and over with: High school diploma (including GED) or higher: 78.4% (2007); Bachelor's degree or higher: 17.5% (2007); Master's degree or higher: 6.2% (2007).

School District(s)

Hall HSD 502 (09-12)
2005-06 Enrollment: 439 . . . . (815) 664-2234
Spring Valley CCSD 99 (PK-08)
2005-06 Enrollment: 653 . . . . (815) 664-4242

Housing: Homeownership rate: 72.4% (2007); Median home value: $118,482 (2007); Median rent: $385 per month (2000); Median age of housing: 48 years (2000).
Hospitals: St. Margaret's Hospital (155 beds)
Safety: Violent crime rate: 24.2 per 10,000 population; Property crime rate: 239.8 per 10,000 population (2006).
Transportation: Commute to work: 95.7% car, 0.0% public transportation, 2.1% walk, 1.8% work from home (2000); Travel time to work: 42.3% less than 15 minutes, 40.8% 15 to 30 minutes, 7.4% 30 to 45 minutes, 2.1% 45 to 60 minutes, 7.4% 60 minutes or more (2000)

Additional Information Contacts

City of Spring Valley. . . . . (815) 664-4221
http://www.spring-valley.il.us

TISKILWA (village). Covers a land area of 0.479 square miles and a water area of 0 square miles. Located at 41.29° N. Lat.; 89.50° W. Long. Elevation is 522 feet.
Population: 833 (1990); 787 (2000); 713 (2007); 702 (2012 projected); Race: 97.9% White, 0.3% Black, 0.3% Asian, 1.4% Hispanic of any race (2007); Density: 1,488.3 persons per square mile (2007); Average household size: 2.43 (2007); Median age: 39.0 (2007); Males per 100 females: 94.8 (2007); Marriage status: 19.2% never married, 63.6% now married, 8.5% widowed, 8.8% divorced (2000); Foreign born: 0.9% (2000); Ancestry (includes multiple ancestries): 32.5% German, 16.1% English, 12.1% Irish, 9.9% Swedish, 6.6% United States or American (2000).
Economy: Single-family building permits issued: 1 (2007); Multi-family building permits issued: 0 (2007); Employment by occupation: 7.5% management, 9.6% professional, 16.0% services, 22.1% sales, 1.6% farming, 10.4% construction, 32.8% production (2000).
Income: Per capita income: $19,418 (2007); Median household income: $38,917 (2007); Average household income: $47,253 (2007); Percent of households with income of $100,000 or more: 4.1% (2007); Poverty rate: 8.0% (2000).
Education: Percent of population age 25 and over with: High school diploma (including GED) or higher: 84.8% (2007); Bachelor's degree or higher: 9.7% (2007); Master's degree or higher: 1.7% (2007).

School District(s)

Princeton ESD 115 (PK-08)
2005-06 Enrollment: 1,206 . . . . (815) 875-3162

Housing: Homeownership rate: 82.3% (2007); Median home value: $110,417 (2007); Median rent: $375 per month (2000); Median age of housing: 60+ years (2000).
Newspapers: Bureau Valley Chief (Community news; Circulation 2,800)
Transportation: Commute to work: 94.9% car, 0.0% public transportation, 1.9% walk, 1.6% work from home (2000); Travel time to work: 34.8% less than 15 minutes, 47.4% 15 to 30 minutes, 8.8% 30 to 45 minutes, 1.9% 45 to 60 minutes, 7.1% 60 minutes or more (2000)

WALNUT (village). Covers a land area of 0.833 square miles and a water area of 0 square miles. Located at 41.55° N. Lat.; 89.59° W. Long. Elevation is 705 feet.
Population: 1,522 (1990); 1,461 (2000); 1,445 (2007); 1,413 (2012 projected); Race: 99.1% White, 0.2% Black, 0.1% Asian, 0.6% Hispanic of any race (2007); Density: 1,735.0 persons per square mile (2007); Average household size: 2.50 (2007); Median age: 41.3 (2007); Males per 100 females: 87.9 (2007); Marriage status: 18.9% never married, 67.1% now married, 7.3% widowed, 6.7% divorced (2000); Foreign born: 1.2% (2000); Ancestry (includes multiple ancestries): 38.4% German, 13.5% Irish, 12.1% English, 8.5% Swedish, 7.2% United States or American (2000).
Economy: Single-family building permits issued: 0 (2007); Multi-family building permits issued: 0 (2007); Employment by occupation: 8.7% management, 15.4% professional, 16.2% services, 25.5% sales, 1.4% farming, 8.4% construction, 24.4% production (2000).
Income: Per capita income: $24,780 (2007); Median household income: $47,703 (2007); Average household income: $58,919 (2007); Percent of households with income of $100,000 or more: 11.1% (2007); Poverty rate: 6.6% (2000).
Education: Percent of population age 25 and over with: High school diploma (including GED) or higher: 87.6% (2007); Bachelor's degree or higher: 14.6% (2007); Master's degree or higher: 5.5% (2007).

School District(s)

Bureau Valley CUSD 340 (PK-12)
2005-06 Enrollment: 1,305 . . . . (815) 445-3101

Housing: Homeownership rate: 79.1% (2007); Median home value: $99,135 (2007); Median rent: $271 per month (2000); Median age of housing: 49 years (2000).
Safety: Violent crime rate: 56.3 per 10,000 population; Property crime rate: 77.4 per 10,000 population (2006).

Newspapers: Walnut Leader (Local news; Circulation 2,000)
Transportation: Commute to work: 87.0% car, 0.0% public transportation, 6.6% walk, 5.2% work from home (2000); Travel time to work: 52.4% less than 15 minutes, 20.7% 15 to 30 minutes, 18.9% 30 to 45 minutes, 4.0% 45 to 60 minutes, 4.0% 60 minutes or more (2000)
Additional Information Contacts
Walnut Chamber of Commerce . . . . (815) 379-2141
http://www.villageofwalnut.com

WYANET (village). Covers a land area of 1.000 square miles and a water area of 0 square miles. Located at 41.36° N. Lat.; 89.58° W. Long. Elevation is 659 feet.
Population: 1,016 (1990); 1,028 (2000); 942 (2007); 925 (2012 projected); Race: 99.0% White, 0.0% Black, 0.3% Asian, 0.8% Hispanic of any race (2007); Density: 942.0 persons per square mile (2007); Average household size: 2.47 (2007); Median age: 35.4 (2007); Males per 100 females: 95.0 (2007); Marriage status: 18.6% never married, 60.4% now married, 5.7% widowed, 15.3% divorced (2000); Foreign born: 0.8% (2000); Ancestry (includes multiple ancestries): 23.4% German, 16.6% Irish, 10.2% Swedish, 6.7% United States or American, 6.4% English (2000).
Economy: Employment by occupation: 6.6% management, 9.4% professional, 14.8% services, 19.5% sales, 2.1% farming, 8.8% construction, 38.8% production (2000).
Income: Per capita income: $19,493 (2007); Median household income: $42,308 (2007); Average household income: $48,069 (2007); Percent of households with income of $100,000 or more: 3.9% (2007); Poverty rate: 6.4% (2000).
Education: Percent of population age 25 and over with: High school diploma (including GED) or higher: 84.9% (2007); Bachelor's degree or higher: 6.5% (2007); Master's degree or higher: 1.0% (2007).

School District(s)

Bureau Valley CUSD 340 (PK-12)
2005-06 Enrollment: 1,305 . . . . (815) 445-3101
Bureau/Henry/Stark Roe (06-12)
2005-06 Enrollment: 21 . . . . (309) 936-7890
Housing: Homeownership rate: 77.7% (2007); Median home value: $104,613 (2007); Median rent: $327 per month (2000); Median age of housing: 56 years (2000).
Safety: Violent crime rate: 29.7 per 10,000 population; Property crime rate: 79.2 per 10,000 population (2006).
Transportation: Commute to work: 94.6% car, 0.0% public transportation, 1.3% walk, 2.7% work from home (2000); Travel time to work: 35.8% less than 15 minutes, 47.3% 15 to 30 minutes, 8.4% 30 to 45 minutes, 4.1% 45 to 60 minutes, 4.3% 60 minutes or more (2000)

Calhoun County

Located in western Illinois; bounded on the west and south by the Mississippi River and the Missouri border, and on the east by the Illinois River, which joins the Mississippi River at the southeastern tip of the county. Covers a land area of 253.82 square miles, a water area of 29.87 square miles, and is located in the Central Time Zone. The county was founded in 1825. County seat is Hardin.

Calhoun County is part of the St. Louis, MO-IL Metropolitan Statistical Area. The entire metro area includes: Bond County, IL; Calhoun County, IL; Clinton County, IL; Jersey County, IL; Macoupin County, IL; Madison County, IL; Monroe County, IL; St. Clair County, IL; Crawford County, MO (pt.)*; Franklin County, MO; Jefferson County, MO; Lincoln County, MO; St. Charles County, MO; St. Louis County, MO; Warren County, MO; Washington County, MO; St. Louis city, MO

Population: 5,322 (1990); 5,084 (2000); 5,198 (2007); 5,272 (2012 projected); Race: 98.7% White, 0.1% Black, 0.3% Asian, 0.9% Hispanic of any race (2007); Density: 20.5 persons per square mile (2007); Average household size: 2.44 (2007); Median age: 42.3 (2007); Males per 100 females: 99.8 (2007).
Religion: Five largest groups: 41.0% Catholic Church, 7.5% Lutheran Church—Missouri Synod, 5.3% New Testament Association of Independent Baptist Churches and other Fundamental Baptist Associations, 3.6% Presbyterian Church (U.S.A.), 3.6% Churches
Economy: Unemployment rate: 6.3% (4/2008); Total civilian labor force: 2,708 (4/2008); Leading industries: 25.4% accommodation & food services; 17.1% retail trade; 14.1% health care and social assistance (2005); Farms: 480 totaling 90,355 acres (2002); Companies that employ 500 or more persons: 0 (2006); Companies that employ 100 to 499 persons: 0 (2006); Companies that employ less than 100 persons: 97 (2006); Black-owned businesses: n/a (2002); Hispanic-owned businesses: n/a (2002); Asian-owned businesses: n/a (2002); Women-owned businesses: n/a (2002); Retail sales per capita: $8,203 (2008). Single-family building permits issued: 14 (2007); Multi-family building permits issued: 2 (2007).
Income: Per capita income: $20,620 (2007); Median household income: $41,761 (2007); Average household income: $50,164 (2007); Percent of households with income of $100,000 or more: 8.3% (2007); Poverty rate: 10.4% (2005); Bankruptcy rate: 0.77% (2007).
Education: Percent of population age 25 and over with: High school diploma (including GED) or higher: 80.0% (2007); Bachelor's degree or higher: 9.4% (2007); Master's degree or higher: 3.4% (2007).
Housing: Homeownership rate: 80.9% (2007); Median home value: $99,330 (2007); Median rent: $242 per month (2000); Median age of housing: 39 years (2000).
Health: Birth rate: 121.9 per 10,000 population (2007); Death rate: 110.3 per 10,000 population (2007); Age-adjusted cancer mortality rate: 201.7 (Unreliable) deaths per 100,000 population (2005); Number of physicians: 5.9 per 10,000 population (2005); Hospital beds: 0.0 per 10,000 population (2004); Hospital admissions: 0.0 per 10,000 population (2004).
Elections: 2004 Presidential election results: 48.7% Bush, 50.5% Kerry, 0.0% Nader, 0.8% Badnarik
National and State Parks: Batchtown State Fish and Waterfowl Management Area; Diamond-Hurricane Island State Fish and Waterfowl; Fuller Lake State Fish and Waterfowl Management Area; Mark Twain National Wildlife Refuge; Mortland Island State Fish And Waterfowl Man; Reds Landing State Fish And Waterfowl Manage; Rip Rap Landing State Fish and Waterfowl Management Area
Additional Information Contacts
Calhoun County Government . . . . (618) 576-2351

Calhoun County Communities

BATCHTOWN (village). Covers a land area of 1.881 square miles and a water area of 0 square miles. Located at 39.03° N. Lat.; 90.65° W. Long. Elevation is 581 feet.
Population: 225 (1990); 218 (2000); 228 (2007); 234 (2012 projected); Race: 99.6% White, 0.0% Black, 0.0% Asian, 0.0% Hispanic of any race (2007); Density: 121.2 persons per square mile (2007); Average household size: 2.51 (2007); Median age: 37.1 (2007); Males per 100 females: 109.2 (2007); Marriage status: 19.5% never married, 63.6% now married, 8.2% widowed, 8.7% divorced (2000); Foreign born: 0.8% (2000); Ancestry (includes multiple ancestries): 42.0% German, 14.0% English, 7.8% United States or American, 3.7% Irish, 3.3% Czech (2000).
Economy: Employment by occupation: 12.2% management, 16.5% professional, 13.9% services, 19.1% sales, 0.0% farming, 20.9% construction, 17.4% production (2000).
Income: Per capita income: $21,908 (2007); Median household income: $53,438 (2007); Average household income: $54,890 (2007); Percent of households with income of $100,000 or more: 9.9% (2007); Poverty rate: 2.5% (2000).
Education: Percent of population age 25 and over with: High school diploma (including GED) or higher: 85.5% (2007); Bachelor's degree or higher: 10.5% (2007); Master's degree or higher: 4.6% (2007).
Housing: Homeownership rate: 90.1% (2007); Median home value: $100,000 (2007); Median rent: $338 per month (2000); Median age of housing: 50 years (2000).
Transportation: Commute to work: 96.4% car, 0.0% public transportation, 0.0% walk, 3.6% work from home (2000); Travel time to work: 13.0% less than 15 minutes, 29.6% 15 to 30 minutes, 13.9% 30 to 45 minutes, 12.0% 45 to 60 minutes, 31.5% 60 minutes or more (2000)

BRUSSELS (village). Covers a land area of 0.607 square miles and a water area of 0 square miles. Located at 38.94° N. Lat.; 90.58° W. Long. Elevation is 522 feet.
Population: 136 (1990); 141 (2000); 145 (2007); 148 (2012 projected); Race: 100.0% White, 0.0% Black, 0.0% Asian, 4.8% Hispanic of any race (2007); Density: 239.0 persons per square mile (2007); Average household size: 2.30 (2007); Median age: 39.3 (2007); Males per 100 females: 126.6 (2007); Marriage status: 23.7% never married, 60.2% now married, 6.8% widowed, 9.3% divorced (2000); Foreign born: 0.0% (2000); Ancestry (includes multiple ancestries): 65.0% German, 7.9% United States or American, 2.9% Irish, 1.4% Czech, 1.4% Dutch (2000).

Economy: Employment by occupation: 5.8% management, 18.8% professional, 26.1% services, 21.7% sales, 2.9% farming, 17.4% construction, 7.2% production (2000).
Income: Per capita income: $21,672 (2007); Median household income: $51,364 (2007); Average household income: $49,881 (2007); Percent of households with income of $100,000 or more: 7.9% (2007); Poverty rate: 11.4% (2000).
Education: Percent of population age 25 and over with: High school diploma (including GED) or higher: 79.0% (2007); Bachelor's degree or higher: 13.0% (2007); Master's degree or higher: 9.0% (2007).

School District(s)

Brussels CUSD 42 (KG-12)
2005-06 Enrollment: 143 . . . . (618) 883-2131
Housing: Homeownership rate: 63.5% (2007); Median home value: $90,000 (2007); Median rent: $191 per month (2000); Median age of housing: 60+ years (2000).
Transportation: Commute to work: 92.4% car, 0.0% public transportation, 7.6% walk, 0.0% work from home (2000); Travel time to work: 39.4% less than 15 minutes, 10.6% 15 to 30 minutes, 16.7% 30 to 45 minutes, 19.7% 45 to 60 minutes, 13.6% 60 minutes or more (2000)

GOLDEN EAGLE (unincorporated postal area, zip code 62036). Covers a land area of 27.943 square miles and a water area of 0.008 square miles. Located at 38.91° N. Lat.; 90.57° W. Long. Elevation is 673 feet.
Population: 601 (2000); Race: 98.7% White, 0.0% Black, 0.9% Asian, 0.5% Hispanic of any race (2000); Density: 21.5 persons per square mile (2000); Age: 20.3% under 18, 19.9% over 64 (2000); Marriage status: 20.8% never married, 66.6% now married, 7.1% widowed, 5.5% divorced (2000); Foreign born: 2.0% (2000); Ancestry (includes multiple ancestries): 59.1% German, 10.4% Other groups, 9.9% Irish, 5.4% Dutch, 4.5% United States or American (2000).
Economy: Employment by occupation: 11.5% management, 14.3% professional, 15.5% services, 16.3% sales, 0.0% farming, 27.4% construction, 15.1% production (2000).
Income: Per capita income: $17,641 (2000); Median household income: $36,429 (2000); Poverty rate: 6.1% (2000).
Education: Percent of population age 25 and over with: High school diploma (including GED) or higher: 80.1% (2000); Bachelor's degree or higher: 7.8% (2000).
Housing: Homeownership rate: 83.9% (2000); Median home value: $83,800 (2000); Median rent: $220 per month (2000); Median age of housing: 47 years (2000).
Transportation: Commute to work: 89.8% car, 0.8% public transportation, 2.0% walk, 6.6% work from home (2000); Travel time to work: 24.1% less than 15 minutes, 10.5% 15 to 30 minutes, 14.5% 30 to 45 minutes, 15.8% 45 to 60 minutes, 35.1% 60 minutes or more (2000)

HAMBURG (village). Covers a land area of 0.522 square miles and a water area of 0.134 square miles. Located at 39.23° N. Lat.; 90.71° W. Long. Elevation is 443 feet.
Population: 150 (1990); 126 (2000); 127 (2007); 128 (2012 projected); Race: 99.2% White, 0.0% Black, 0.0% Asian, 0.0% Hispanic of any race (2007); Density: 243.4 persons per square mile (2007); Average household size: 2.05 (2007); Median age: 50.7 (2007); Males per 100 females: 89.6 (2007); Marriage status: 11.5% never married, 59.8% now married, 18.4% widowed, 10.3% divorced (2000); Foreign born: 0.0% (2000); Ancestry (includes multiple ancestries): 32.0% German, 18.6% Irish, 9.3% French (except Basque), 7.2% English, 6.2% Italian (2000).
Economy: Employment by occupation: 10.3% management, 28.2% professional, 10.3% services, 5.1% sales, 0.0% farming, 20.5% construction, 25.6% production (2000).
Income: Per capita income: $18,484 (2007); Median household income: $35,000 (2007); Average household income: $37,863 (2007); Percent of households with income of $100,000 or more: 0.0% (2007); Poverty rate: 7.2% (2000).
Education: Percent of population age 25 and over with: High school diploma (including GED) or higher: 62.5% (2007); Bachelor's degree or higher: 17.7% (2007); Master's degree or higher: 2.1% (2007).
Housing: Homeownership rate: 87.1% (2007); Median home value: $47,500 (2007); Median rent: $133 per month (2000); Median age of housing: 52 years (2000).
Transportation: Commute to work: 100.0% car, 0.0% public transportation, 0.0% walk, 0.0% work from home (2000); Travel time to work: 5.1% less than 15 minutes, 64.1% 15 to 30 minutes, 0.0% 30 to 45 minutes, 10.3% 45 to 60 minutes, 20.5% 60 minutes or more (2000)

HARDIN (village). County seat. Covers a land area of 2.097 square miles and a water area of 0.182 square miles. Located at 39.15° N. Lat.; 90.61° W. Long. Elevation is 443 feet.
History: Hardin developed as a distribution center for the surrounding apple-growing region, and as the seat of Calhoun County.
Population: 1,080 (1990); 959 (2000); 960 (2007); 961 (2012 projected); Race: 99.5% White, 0.0% Black, 0.2% Asian, 0.8% Hispanic of any race (2007); Density: 457.7 persons per square mile (2007); Average household size: 2.41 (2007); Median age: 40.8 (2007); Males per 100 females: 89.0 (2007); Marriage status: 17.6% never married, 55.3% now married, 17.1% widowed, 9.9% divorced (2000); Foreign born: 0.5% (2000); Ancestry (includes multiple ancestries): 42.4% German, 9.9% Irish, 9.6% French (except Basque), 7.3% United States or American, 6.2% Other groups (2000).
Economy: Employment by occupation: 7.5% management, 21.1% professional, 16.7% services, 23.2% sales, 0.5% farming, 13.6% construction, 17.4% production (2000).
Income: Per capita income: $19,669 (2007); Median household income: $37,411 (2007); Average household income: $46,861 (2007); Percent of households with income of $100,000 or more: 7.8% (2007); Poverty rate: 10.8% (2000).
Education: Percent of population age 25 and over with: High school diploma (including GED) or higher: 78.2% (2007); Bachelor's degree or higher: 9.8% (2007); Master's degree or higher: 1.9% (2007).

School District(s)

Calhoun CUSD 40 (PK-12)
2005-06 Enrollment: 548 . . . . (618) 576-2722
Housing: Homeownership rate: 69.4% (2007); Median home value: $78,958 (2007); Median rent: $251 per month (2000); Median age of housing: 34 years (2000).
Newspapers: Calhoun News-Herald (Community news; Circulation 4,000)
Transportation: Commute to work: 93.7% car, 0.0% public transportation, 4.8% walk, 1.0% work from home (2000); Travel time to work: 38.7% less than 15 minutes, 11.7% 15 to 30 minutes, 6.1% 30 to 45 minutes, 13.4% 45 to 60 minutes, 30.2% 60 minutes or more (2000)

KAMPSVILLE (village). Covers a land area of 1.020 square miles and a water area of 0.220 square miles. Located at 39.29° N. Lat.; 90.61° W. Long. Elevation is 433 feet.
Population: 380 (1990); 302 (2000); 312 (2007); 320 (2012 projected); Race: 95.2% White, 0.0% Black, 1.6% Asian, 1.3% Hispanic of any race (2007); Density: 306.0 persons per square mile (2007); Average household size: 2.21 (2007); Median age: 38.9 (2007); Males per 100 females: 91.4 (2007); Marriage status: 14.2% never married, 56.9% now married, 8.2% widowed, 20.7% divorced (2000); Foreign born: 0.0% (2000); Ancestry (includes multiple ancestries): 32.4% German, 15.5% Irish, 11.8% Other groups, 9.1% English, 4.4% United States or American (2000).
Economy: Employment by occupation: 8.2% management, 10.7% professional, 37.7% services, 16.4% sales, 1.6% farming, 15.6% construction, 9.8% production (2000).
Income: Per capita income: $16,579 (2007); Median household income: $30,500 (2007); Average household income: $36,684 (2007); Percent of households with income of $100,000 or more: 0.7% (2007); Poverty rate: 24.5% (2000).
Education: Percent of population age 25 and over with: High school diploma (including GED) or higher: 79.6% (2007); Bachelor's degree or higher: 10.7% (2007); Master's degree or higher: 1.9% (2007).
Housing: Homeownership rate: 66.7% (2007); Median home value: $62,857 (2007); Median rent: $257 per month (2000); Median age of housing: 42 years (2000).
Transportation: Commute to work: 91.7% car, 0.0% public transportation, 8.3% walk, 0.0% work from home (2000); Travel time to work: 29.2% less than 15 minutes, 18.3% 15 to 30 minutes, 13.3% 30 to 45 minutes, 16.7% 45 to 60 minutes, 22.5% 60 minutes or more (2000)

MICHAEL (unincorporated postal area, zip code 62065). Covers a land area of 8.873 square miles and a water area of 0.306 square miles. Located at 39.23° N. Lat.; 90.62° W. Long. Elevation is 446 feet.
Population: 114 (2000); Race: 96.9% White, 0.0% Black, 0.0% Asian, 0.0% Hispanic of any race (2000); Density: 12.8 persons per square mile (2000); Age: 29.8% under 18, 20.6% over 64 (2000); Marriage status: 19.4% never married, 69.4% now married, 6.1% widowed, 5.1% divorced

(2000); Foreign born: 6.9% (2000); Ancestry (includes multiple ancestries): 30.5% German, 10.7% United States or American, 6.1% Norwegian, 4.6% French (except Basque), 3.8% English (2000).
Economy: Employment by occupation: 7.4% management, 14.8% professional, 14.8% services, 40.7% sales, 0.0% farming, 7.4% construction, 14.8% production (2000).
Income: Per capita income: $10,806 (2000); Median household income: $24,583 (2000); Poverty rate: 2.3% (2000).
Education: Percent of population age 25 and over with: High school diploma (including GED) or higher: 71.1% (2000); Bachelor's degree or higher: 4.8% (2000).
Housing: Homeownership rate: 87.7% (2000); Median home value: $53,700 (2000); Median rent: $325 per month (2000); Median age of housing: 36 years (2000).
Transportation: Commute to work: 100.0% car, 0.0% public transportation, 0.0% walk, 0.0% work from home (2000); Travel time to work: 44.4% less than 15 minutes, 14.8% 15 to 30 minutes, 11.1% 30 to 45 minutes, 0.0% 45 to 60 minutes, 29.6% 60 minutes or more (2000)

MOZIER (unincorporated postal area, zip code 62070). Aka Baytown. Covers a land area of 10.423 square miles and a water area of 0.258 square miles. Located at 39.32° N. Lat.; 90.76° W. Long. Elevation is 446 feet.
Population: 63 (2000); Race: 100.0% White, 0.0% Black, 0.0% Asian, 0.0% Hispanic of any race (2000); Density: 6.0 persons per square mile (2000); Age: 21.9% under 18, 35.9% over 64 (2000); Marriage status: 4.0% never married, 72.0% now married, 20.0% widowed, 4.0% divorced (2000); Foreign born: 0.0% (2000); Ancestry (includes multiple ancestries): 39.1% United States or American, 10.9% German, 7.8% English (2000).
Economy: Employment by occupation: 8.3% management, 8.3% professional, 16.7% services, 12.5% sales, 0.0% farming, 16.7% construction, 37.5% production (2000).
Income: Per capita income: $14,966 (2000); Median household income: $33,750 (2000); Poverty rate: 7.8% (2000).
Education: Percent of population age 25 and over with: High school diploma (including GED) or higher: 62.0% (2000); Bachelor's degree or higher: 8.0% (2000).
Housing: Homeownership rate: 96.7% (2000); Median home value: $51,700 (2000); Median rent: $n/a per month (2000); Median age of housing: 42 years (2000).
Transportation: Commute to work: 100.0% car, 0.0% public transportation, 0.0% walk, 0.0% work from home (2000); Travel time to work: 20.8% less than 15 minutes, 37.5% 15 to 30 minutes, 8.3% 30 to 45 minutes, 16.7% 45 to 60 minutes, 16.7% 60 minutes or more (2000)

Carroll County

Located in northwestern Illinois; bounded on the west by the Mississippi River and the Iowa border; drained by the Plum River and Elkhorn Creek. Covers a land area of 444.21 square miles, a water area of 21.56 square miles, and is located in the Central Time Zone. The county was founded in 1839. County seat is Mount Carroll.

Weather Station: Mount Carroll Elevation: 639 feet

	Jan	Feb	Mar	Apr	May	Jun	Jul	Aug	Sep	Oct	Nov	Dec
High	28	34	46	60	72	81	85	82	75	63	47	34
Low	7	13	24	35	46	54	59	56	47	36	27	15
Precip	1.4	1.4	2.7	3.7	4.5	4.6	3.7	4.5	3.7	2.8	2.8	2.0
Snow	10.5	6.7	4.3	1.6	tr	0.0	0.0	0.0	tr	0.2	2.6	7.0

High and Low temperatures in degrees Fahrenheit; Precipitation and Snow in inches

Population: 16,805 (1990); 16,674 (2000); 15,933 (2007); 15,379 (2012 projected); Race: 96.5% White, 0.9% Black, 0.5% Asian, 2.6% Hispanic of any race (2007); Density: 35.9 persons per square mile (2007); Average household size: 2.42 (2007); Median age: 43.2 (2007); Males per 100 females: 97.2 (2007).
Religion: Five largest groups: 17.2% The United Methodist Church, 14.8% Catholic Church, 8.3% Evangelical Lutheran Church in America, 3.3% Church of the Brethren, 3.0% Churches of God, General Conference (2000).
Economy: Unemployment rate: 6.7% (4/2008); Total civilian labor force: 8,431 (4/2008); Leading industries: 27.8% manufacturing; 15.7% health care and social assistance; 13.0% retail trade (2005); Farms: 656 totaling 247,536 acres (2002); Companies that employ 500 or more persons: 0 (2006); Companies that employ 100 to 499 persons: 4 (2006); Companies that employ less than 100 persons: 428 (2006); Black-owned businesses: n/a (2002); Hispanic-owned businesses: n/a (2002); Asian-owned businesses: n/a (2002); Women-owned businesses: 565 (2002); Retail sales per capita: $7,129 (2008). Single-family building permits issued: 58 (2007); Multi-family building permits issued: 4 (2007).
Income: Per capita income: $21,665 (2007); Median household income: $42,074 (2007); Average household income: $52,049 (2007); Percent of households with income of $100,000 or more: 8.8% (2007); Poverty rate: 10.9% (2005); Bankruptcy rate: 2.45% (2007).
Education: Percent of population age 25 and over with: High school diploma (including GED) or higher: 83.1% (2007); Bachelor's degree or higher: 13.4% (2007); Master's degree or higher: 3.9% (2007).
Housing: Homeownership rate: 76.9% (2007); Median home value: $108,235 (2007); Median rent: $288 per month (2000); Median age of housing: 52 years (2000).
Health: Birth rate: 106.7 per 10,000 population (2007); Death rate: 118.7 per 10,000 population (2007); Age-adjusted cancer mortality rate: 202.8 deaths per 100,000 population (2005); Number of physicians: 5.0 per 10,000 population (2005); Hospital beds: 0.0 per 10,000 population (2004); Hospital admissions: 0.0 per 10,000 population (2004).
Elections: 2004 Presidential election results: 55.7% Bush, 43.5% Kerry, 0.1% Nader, 0.7% Badnarik
National and State Parks: Ayers Sand Prairie State Nature Preserve; Mississippi Palisades State Park
Additional Information Contacts
Carroll County Government . . . . (815) 244-0221

Mount Carroll Chamber of Commerce . . . . (815) 244-2255
http://www.mount-carroll.il.us
Savanna Chamber of Commerce . . . . (815) 273-2722
http://www.savanna-il.com
Shannon Chamber of Commerce . . . . (815) 864-2111
http://www.shannonillinois.com/Chamber_of_commerce.htm

Carroll County Communities

CHADWICK (village). Covers a land area of 0.317 square miles and a water area of 0 square miles. Located at 42.01° N. Lat.; 89.88° W. Long. Elevation is 801 feet.
Population: 566 (1990); 505 (2000); 452 (2007); 449 (2012 projected); Race: 97.8% White, 0.0% Black, 0.2% Asian, 1.5% Hispanic of any race (2007); Density: 1,428.0 persons per square mile (2007); Average household size: 2.35 (2007); Median age: 39.4 (2007); Males per 100 females: 95.7 (2007); Marriage status: 20.6% never married, 60.9% now married, 11.4% widowed, 7.1% divorced (2000); Foreign born: 0.0% (2000); Ancestry (includes multiple ancestries): 46.5% German, 10.1% Irish, 7.0% English, 5.4% Other groups, 5.2% Dutch (2000).
Economy: Employment by occupation: 9.9% management, 8.3% professional, 10.7% services, 26.6% sales, 0.0% farming, 13.5% construction, 31.0% production (2000).
Income: Per capita income: $20,354 (2007); Median household income: $45,500 (2007); Average household income: $47,917 (2007); Percent of households with income of $100,000 or more: 8.3% (2007); Poverty rate: 10.9% (2000).
Education: Percent of population age 25 and over with: High school diploma (including GED) or higher: 83.4% (2007); Bachelor's degree or higher: 9.5% (2007); Master's degree or higher: 3.7% (2007).

School District(s)

Chadwick-Milledgeville CUSD 399 (PK-12)
2005-06 Enrollment: 554 . . . . (815) 684-5191
Housing: Homeownership rate: 83.9% (2007); Median home value: $96,053 (2007); Median rent: $263 per month (2000); Median age of housing: 60+ years (2000).
Safety: Violent crime rate: 41.2 per 10,000 population; Property crime rate: 102.9 per 10,000 population (2006).
Transportation: Commute to work: 90.2% car, 0.0% public transportation, 6.9% walk, 0.8% work from home (2000); Travel time to work: 39.9% less than 15 minutes, 21.0% 15 to 30 minutes, 25.1% 30 to 45 minutes, 9.9% 45 to 60 minutes, 4.1% 60 minutes or more (2000)

LANARK (city). Covers a land area of 1.038 square miles and a water area of 0 square miles. Located at 42.10° N. Lat.; 89.83° W. Long. Elevation is 879 feet.
History: Lanark developed as a trading center and cannery operation for the surrounding farming community.

Population: 1,404 (1990); 1,584 (2000); 1,440 (2007); 1,386 (2012 projected); Race: 96.9% White, 0.1% Black, 1.6% Asian, 0.2% Hispanic of any race (2007); Density: 1,387.0 persons per square mile (2007); Average household size: 2.43 (2007); Median age: 42.0 (2007); Males per 100 females: 96.2 (2007); Marriage status: 20.9% never married, 60.2% now married, 8.8% widowed, 10.1% divorced (2000); Foreign born: 0.5% (2000); Ancestry (includes multiple ancestries): 54.1% German, 12.9% Irish, 10.0% English, 4.3% United States or American, 3.7% Other groups (2000).
Economy: Single-family building permits issued: 0 (2007); Multi-family building permits issued: 0 (2007); Employment by occupation: 11.9% management, 16.2% professional, 12.6% services, 21.5% sales, 1.6% farming, 9.9% construction, 26.4% production (2000).
Income: Per capita income: $20,202 (2007); Median household income: $39,545 (2007); Average household income: $49,029 (2007); Percent of households with income of $100,000 or more: 6.9% (2007); Poverty rate: 8.0% (2000).
Education: Percent of population age 25 and over with: High school diploma (including GED) or higher: 85.3% (2007); Bachelor's degree or higher: 12.1% (2007); Master's degree or higher: 3.5% (2007).

School District(s)

Eastland CUSD 308 (PK-12)
2005-06 Enrollment: 739 . . . . (815) 493-6301
Housing: Homeownership rate: 81.4% (2007); Median home value: $96,610 (2007); Median rent: $272 per month (2000); Median age of housing: 60+ years (2000).
Safety: Violent crime rate: 47.2 per 10,000 population; Property crime rate: 87.7 per 10,000 population (2006).
Newspapers: Prairie Advocate (Regional news; Circulation 12,500)
Transportation: Commute to work: 88.7% car, 0.0% public transportation, 5.1% walk, 5.1% work from home (2000); Travel time to work: 40.8% less than 15 minutes, 24.4% 15 to 30 minutes, 24.8% 30 to 45 minutes, 2.8% 45 to 60 minutes, 7.2% 60 minutes or more (2000)

MILLEDGEVILLE (village). Covers a land area of 0.708 square miles and a water area of 0 square miles. Located at 41.96° N. Lat.; 89.77° W. Long. Elevation is 761 feet.
Population: 1,102 (1990); 1,016 (2000); 1,060 (2007); 1,046 (2012 projected); Race: 98.5% White, 0.6% Black, 0.4% Asian, 1.5% Hispanic of any race (2007); Density: 1,496.4 persons per square mile (2007); Average household size: 2.23 (2007); Median age: 42.4 (2007); Males per 100 females: 94.1 (2007); Marriage status: 19.5% never married, 62.9% now married, 11.4% widowed, 6.2% divorced (2000); Foreign born: 1.1% (2000); Ancestry (includes multiple ancestries): 45.6% German, 11.2% Irish, 10.4% English, 7.3% Other groups, 6.6% Dutch (2000).
Economy: Single-family building permits issued: 1 (2007); Multi-family building permits issued: 0 (2007); Employment by occupation: 7.8% management, 15.8% professional, 9.4% services, 22.5% sales, 1.0% farming, 9.7% construction, 33.8% production (2000).
Income: Per capita income: $21,899 (2007); Median household income: $40,100 (2007); Average household income: $48,868 (2007); Percent of households with income of $100,000 or more: 6.3% (2007); Poverty rate: 5.2% (2000).
Education: Percent of population age 25 and over with: High school diploma (including GED) or higher: 89.0% (2007); Bachelor's degree or higher: 10.9% (2007); Master's degree or higher: 4.4% (2007).

School District(s)

Chadwick-Milledgeville CUSD 399 (PK-12)
2005-06 Enrollment: 554 . . . . (815) 684-5191
Housing: Homeownership rate: 81.7% (2007); Median home value: $109,000 (2007); Median rent: $283 per month (2000); Median age of housing: 54 years (2000).
Safety: Violent crime rate: 21.1 per 10,000 population; Property crime rate: 296.0 per 10,000 population (2006).
Transportation: Commute to work: 90.6% car, 0.0% public transportation, 7.5% walk, 1.2% work from home (2000); Travel time to work: 42.0% less than 15 minutes, 39.1% 15 to 30 minutes, 11.3% 30 to 45 minutes, 1.9% 45 to 60 minutes, 5.6% 60 minutes or more (2000)

MOUNT CARROLL (city). County seat. Covers a land area of 1.901 square miles and a water area of 0 square miles. Located at 42.09° N. Lat.; 89.97° W. Long. Elevation is 810 feet.
History: Founded 1843, incorporated 1867.
Population: 1,737 (1990); 1,832 (2000); 1,684 (2007); 1,584 (2012 projected); Race: 98.5% White, 0.1% Black, 0.3% Asian, 1.6% Hispanic of any race (2007); Density: 885.7 persons per square mile (2007); Average household size: 2.42 (2007); Median age: 40.9 (2007); Males per 100 females: 94.2 (2007); Marriage status: 18.6% never married, 63.3% now married, 7.6% widowed, 10.6% divorced (2000); Foreign born: 1.4% (2000); Ancestry (includes multiple ancestries): 44.4% German, 10.4% English, 9.5% Irish, 8.8% United States or American, 8.3% Dutch (2000).
Economy: Single-family building permits issued: 1 (2007); Multi-family building permits issued: 0 (2007); Employment by occupation: 9.4% management, 12.9% professional, 21.0% services, 18.8% sales, 1.1% farming, 10.5% construction, 26.3% production (2000).
Income: Per capita income: $18,901 (2007); Median household income: $38,409 (2007); Average household income: $44,989 (2007); Percent of households with income of $100,000 or more: 5.2% (2007); Poverty rate: 8.5% (2000).
Education: Percent of population age 25 and over with: High school diploma (including GED) or higher: 85.5% (2007); Bachelor's degree or higher: 12.1% (2007); Master's degree or higher: 4.6% (2007).

School District(s)

West Carroll CUSD 314 (PK-12)
2005-06 Enrollment: 1,541 . . . . (815) 259-2735
Housing: Homeownership rate: 77.5% (2007); Median home value: $108,871 (2007); Median rent: $293 per month (2000); Median age of housing: 60+ years (2000).
Safety: Violent crime rate: 64.6 per 10,000 population; Property crime rate: 187.8 per 10,000 population (2006).
Newspapers: Mirror-Democrat (Community news; Circulation 2,100); Northwestern Illinois Dispatch (Community news; Circulation 10,000)
Transportation: Commute to work: 91.0% car, 0.0% public transportation, 5.5% walk, 3.2% work from home (2000); Travel time to work: 50.6% less than 15 minutes, 24.5% 15 to 30 minutes, 13.3% 30 to 45 minutes, 5.8% 45 to 60 minutes, 5.8% 60 minutes or more (2000)

Additional Information Contacts

Mount Carroll Chamber of Commerce . . . . (815) 244-2255
http://www.mount-carroll.il.us

SAVANNA (city). Covers a land area of 2.609 square miles and a water area of 0.094 square miles. Located at 42.09° N. Lat.; 90.14° W. Long. Elevation is 600 feet.
History: Savanna was settled in 1828 as a farming center and river port. The coming of the railroad in 1850 made Savanna a trading town and shipping point for livestock and farm produce.
Population: 3,877 (1990); 3,542 (2000); 3,227 (2007); 2,999 (2012 projected); Race: 92.7% White, 2.6% Black, 0.1% Asian, 6.0% Hispanic of any race (2007); Density: 1,236.9 persons per square mile (2007); Average household size: 2.23 (2007); Median age: 42.3 (2007); Males per 100 females: 89.9 (2007); Marriage status: 22.2% never married, 50.6% now married, 12.6% widowed, 14.6% divorced (2000); Foreign born: 3.7% (2000); Ancestry (includes multiple ancestries): 29.8% German, 20.2% Irish, 10.7% Other groups, 10.4% United States or American, 9.9% English (2000).
Economy: Single-family building permits issued: 2 (2007); Multi-family building permits issued: 0 (2007); Employment by occupation: 6.9% management, 14.8% professional, 17.6% services, 17.7% sales, 1.4% farming, 8.5% construction, 33.2% production (2000).
Income: Per capita income: $17,857 (2007); Median household income: $31,572 (2007); Average household income: $38,811 (2007); Percent of households with income of $100,000 or more: 4.0% (2007); Poverty rate: 16.7% (2000).
Education: Percent of population age 25 and over with: High school diploma (including GED) or higher: 79.5% (2007); Bachelor's degree or higher: 11.6% (2007); Master's degree or higher: 3.1% (2007).

School District(s)

Carroll/Jo Daviess/Stephenson Roe (06-12)
2005-06 Enrollment: 80 . . . . (815) 947-3810
West Carroll CUSD 314 (PK-12)
2005-06 Enrollment: 1,541 . . . . (815) 259-2735
Housing: Homeownership rate: 67.7% (2007); Median home value: $68,058 (2007); Median rent: $272 per month (2000); Median age of housing: 57 years (2000).
Safety: Violent crime rate: 18.2 per 10,000 population; Property crime rate: 191.6 per 10,000 population (2006).
Newspapers: Savanna Times Journal (Community news; Circulation 2,500)
Transportation: Commute to work: 91.6% car, 0.9% public transportation, 3.9% walk, 2.3% work from home (2000); Travel time to work: 58.8% less

than 15 minutes, 12.7% 15 to 30 minutes, 14.5% 30 to 45 minutes, 4.6% 45 to 60 minutes, 9.3% 60 minutes or more (2000)
Additional Information Contacts
Savanna Chamber of Commerce .... (815) 273-2722
http://www.savanna-il.com

SHANNON (village). Covers a land area of 0.479 square miles and a water area of 0 square miles. Located at 42.15° N. Lat.; 89.74° W. Long. Elevation is 915 feet.
Population: 887 (1990); 854 (2000); 782 (2007); 755 (2012 projected); Race: 96.7% White, 0.5% Black, 1.7% Asian, 0.9% Hispanic of any race (2007); Density: 1,633.0 persons per square mile (2007); Average household size: 2.47 (2007); Median age: 44.5 (2007); Males per 100 females: 89.3 (2007); Marriage status: 18.7% never married, 62.5% now married, 9.3% widowed, 9.5% divorced (2000); Foreign born: 2.9% (2000); Ancestry (includes multiple ancestries): 51.9% German, 11.4% Irish, 6.5% English, 6.2% Dutch, 5.9% Other groups (2000).
Economy: Single-family building permits issued: 1 (2007); Multi-family building permits issued: 4 (2007); Employment by occupation: 10.5% management, 12.4% professional, 15.3% services, 27.7% sales, 1.0% farming, 9.8% construction, 23.4% production (2000).
Income: Per capita income: $24,323 (2007); Median household income: $49,286 (2007); Average household income: $59,620 (2007); Percent of households with income of $100,000 or more: 10.4% (2007); Poverty rate: 7.4% (2000).
Education: Percent of population age 25 and over with: High school diploma (including GED) or higher: 86.8% (2007); Bachelor's degree or higher: 17.8% (2007); Master's degree or higher: 3.8% (2007).
School District(s)
Eastland CUSD 308 (PK-12)
2005-06 Enrollment: 739 .... (815) 493-6301
Housing: Homeownership rate: 82.9% (2007); Median home value: $110,345 (2007); Median rent: $325 per month (2000); Median age of housing: 56 years (2000).
Transportation: Commute to work: 84.0% car, 0.0% public transportation, 10.7% walk, 3.6% work from home (2000); Travel time to work: 41.1% less than 15 minutes, 34.9% 15 to 30 minutes, 14.1% 30 to 45 minutes, 4.7% 45 to 60 minutes, 5.2% 60 minutes or more (2000)
Additional Information Contacts
Shannon Chamber of Commerce .... (815) 864-2111
http://www.shannonillinois.com/Chamber_of_commerce.htm

THOMSON (village). Covers a land area of 2.208 square miles and a water area of 0 square miles. Located at 41.96° N. Lat.; 90.10° W. Long. Elevation is 597 feet.
Population: 567 (1990); 559 (2000); 531 (2007); 520 (2012 projected); Race: 97.6% White, 0.0% Black, 0.8% Asian, 1.1% Hispanic of any race (2007); Density: 240.5 persons per square mile (2007); Average household size: 2.33 (2007); Median age: 42.3 (2007); Males per 100 females: 92.4 (2007); Marriage status: 24.8% never married, 58.0% now married, 6.7% widowed, 10.4% divorced (2000); Foreign born: 0.4% (2000); Ancestry (includes multiple ancestries): 30.0% German, 14.5% Irish, 10.2% English, 9.6% Other groups, 8.4% United States or American (2000).
Economy: Single-family building permits issued: 0 (2007); Multi-family building permits issued: 0 (2007); Employment by occupation: 6.9% management, 12.0% professional, 17.2% services, 18.6% sales, 0.0% farming, 9.5% construction, 35.8% production (2000).
Income: Per capita income: $23,390 (2007); Median household income: $40,333 (2007); Average household income: $54,474 (2007); Percent of households with income of $100,000 or more: 11.4% (2007); Poverty rate: 6.7% (2000).
Education: Percent of population age 25 and over with: High school diploma (including GED) or higher: 82.8% (2007); Bachelor's degree or higher: 10.5% (2007); Master's degree or higher: 3.8% (2007).
School District(s)
West Carroll CUSD 314 (PK-12)
2005-06 Enrollment: 1,541 .... (815) 259-2735
Housing: Homeownership rate: 70.6% (2007); Median home value: $108,468 (2007); Median rent: $295 per month (2000); Median age of housing: 50 years (2000).
Safety: Violent crime rate: 18.7 per 10,000 population; Property crime rate: 37.3 per 10,000 population (2006).
Newspapers: Carroll County Review (Regional news; Circulation 1,993)
Transportation: Commute to work: 92.2% car, 1.9% public transportation, 3.0% walk, 2.2% work from home (2000); Travel time to work: 32.6% less than 15 minutes, 40.5% 15 to 30 minutes, 13.6% 30 to 45 minutes, 7.2% 45 to 60 minutes, 6.1% 60 minutes or more (2000)

Cass County

Located in west central Illinois; bounded on the north by the Sangamon River, and on the west by the Illinois River. Covers a land area of 375.90 square miles, a water area of 7.83 square miles, and is located in the Central Time Zone. The county was founded in 1837. County seat is Virginia.
Population: 13,437 (1990); 13,695 (2000); 13,986 (2007); 14,174 (2012 projected); Race: 90.6% White, 1.3% Black, 0.6% Asian, 16.6% Hispanic of any race (2007); Density: 37.2 persons per square mile (2007); Average household size: 2.56 (2007); Median age: 37.7 (2007); Males per 100 females: 102.2 (2007).
Religion: Five largest groups: 27.6% Catholic Church, 10.8% The United Methodist Church, 9.4% Lutheran Church—Missouri Synod, 8.7% Evangelical Lutheran Church in America, 5.1% Christian Churches and Churches of Christ (2000).
Economy: Unemployment rate: 4.5% (4/2008); Total civilian labor force: 7,806 (4/2008); Leading industries: 47.5% manufacturing; 9.7% retail trade; 7.4% accommodation & food services (2005); Farms: 427 totaling 198,559 acres (2002); Companies that employ 500 or more persons: 1 (2006); Companies that employ 100 to 499 persons: 3 (2006); Companies that employ less than 100 persons: 287 (2006); Black-owned businesses: n/a (2002); Hispanic-owned businesses: n/a (2002); Asian-owned businesses: n/a (2002); Women-owned businesses: 408 (2002); Retail sales per capita: $8,242 (2008). Single-family building permits issued: 16 (2007); Multi-family building permits issued: 0 (2007).
Income: Per capita income: $19,692 (2007); Median household income: $41,494 (2007); Average household income: $49,573 (2007); Percent of households with income of $100,000 or more: 7.9% (2007); Poverty rate: 11.8% (2005); Bankruptcy rate: 2.62% (2007).
Education: Percent of population age 25 and over with: High school diploma (including GED) or higher: 79.4% (2007); Bachelor's degree or higher: 12.2% (2007); Master's degree or higher: 3.2% (2007).
Housing: Homeownership rate: 74.7% (2007); Median home value: $79,346 (2007); Median rent: $309 per month (2000); Median age of housing: 50 years (2000).
Health: Birth rate: 150.8 per 10,000 population (2007); Death rate: 105.6 per 10,000 population (2007); Age-adjusted cancer mortality rate: 149.1 deaths per 100,000 population (2005); Number of physicians: 2.9 per 10,000 population (2005); Hospital beds: 0.0 per 10,000 population (2004); Hospital admissions: 0.0 per 10,000 population (2004).
Elections: 2004 Presidential election results: 55.5% Bush, 43.7% Kerry, 0.0% Nader, 0.8% Badnarik
National and State Parks: Meredosia National Wildlife Refuge; Panther Creek State Conservation Area; Sanganois State Conservation Area; Toppers Hole State Conservation Area
Additional Information Contacts
Cass County Government .... (217) 452-2277

Beardstown Chamber of Commerce .... (217) 323-3271
http://www.beardstownil.org

Cass County Communities

ARENZVILLE (village). Covers a land area of 0.785 square miles and a water area of 0 square miles. Located at 39.87° N. Lat.; 90.37° W. Long. Elevation is 505 feet.
Population: 432 (1990); 419 (2000); 345 (2007); 347 (2012 projected); Race: 99.7% White, 0.0% Black, 0.0% Asian, 0.0% Hispanic of any race (2007); Density: 439.7 persons per square mile (2007); Average household size: 2.40 (2007); Median age: 40.1 (2007); Males per 100 females: 106.6 (2007); Marriage status: 15.2% never married, 68.1% now married, 10.7% widowed, 6.0% divorced (2000); Foreign born: 0.0% (2000); Ancestry (includes multiple ancestries): 45.2% German, 10.4% United States or American, 8.7% English, 7.6% Other groups, 6.1% Irish (2000).
Economy: Employment by occupation: 12.0% management, 12.4% professional, 17.1% services, 24.0% sales, 4.6% farming, 9.2% construction, 20.7% production (2000).
Income: Per capita income: $25,522 (2007); Median household income: $50,400 (2007); Average household income: $61,146 (2007); Percent of households with income of $100,000 or more: 11.1% (2007); Poverty rate: 2.1% (2000).

Education: Percent of population age 25 and over with: High school diploma (including GED) or higher: 86.0% (2007); Bachelor's degree or higher: 19.7% (2007); Master's degree or higher: 5.7% (2007).
Housing: Homeownership rate: 84.0% (2007); Median home value: $81,154 (2007); Median rent: $225 per month (2000); Median age of housing: 59 years (2000).
Transportation: Commute to work: 83.7% car, 0.0% public transportation, 4.7% walk, 9.8% work from home (2000); Travel time to work: 42.3% less than 15 minutes, 29.9% 15 to 30 minutes, 18.0% 30 to 45 minutes, 3.6% 45 to 60 minutes, 6.2% 60 minutes or more (2000)

ASHLAND (village). Covers a land area of 0.743 square miles and a water area of 0 square miles. Located at 39.88° N. Lat.; 90.00° W. Long. Elevation is 623 feet.
History: Incorporated 1869.
Population: 1,259 (1990); 1,361 (2000); 1,438 (2007); 1,489 (2012 projected); Race: 98.3% White, 0.4% Black, 0.4% Asian, 0.3% Hispanic of any race (2007); Density: 1,936.0 persons per square mile (2007); Average household size: 2.44 (2007); Median age: 38.2 (2007); Males per 100 females: 97.3 (2007); Marriage status: 20.2% never married, 62.8% now married, 7.5% widowed, 9.4% divorced (2000); Foreign born: 0.1% (2000); Ancestry (includes multiple ancestries): 29.1% German, 14.5% Irish, 13.7% English, 12.2% United States or American, 5.8% Other groups (2000).
Economy: Single-family building permits issued: 0 (2007); Multi-family building permits issued: 0 (2007); Employment by occupation: 13.3% management, 14.9% professional, 15.0% services, 28.8% sales, 1.3% farming, 10.4% construction, 16.3% production (2000).
Income: Per capita income: $24,967 (2007); Median household income: $52,015 (2007); Average household income: $60,955 (2007); Percent of households with income of $100,000 or more: 10.0% (2007); Poverty rate: 6.3% (2000).
Education: Percent of population age 25 and over with: High school diploma (including GED) or higher: 84.6% (2007); Bachelor's degree or higher: 17.1% (2007); Master's degree or higher: 4.1% (2007).

School District(s)

A-C Central CUSD 262 (PK-12)
2005-06 Enrollment: 490 . . . . (217) 476-8112
Housing: Homeownership rate: 80.6% (2007); Median home value: $104,617 (2007); Median rent: $348 per month (2000); Median age of housing: 39 years (2000).
Safety: Violent crime rate: 0.0 per 10,000 population; Property crime rate: 14.5 per 10,000 population (2006).
Newspapers: Ashland Sentinel (Community news; Circulation 800)
Transportation: Commute to work: 94.9% car, 0.6% public transportation, 2.5% walk, 1.6% work from home (2000); Travel time to work: 21.6% less than 15 minutes, 19.5% 15 to 30 minutes, 49.6% 30 to 45 minutes, 6.5% 45 to 60 minutes, 2.9% 60 minutes or more (2000)

BEARDSTOWN (city). Covers a land area of 3.408 square miles and a water area of 0.055 square miles. Located at 40.01° N. Lat.; 90.42° W. Long. Elevation is 449 feet.
History: Beardstown, first called Beard's Ferry, was settled in 1819 by Thomas Beard, who operated a ferry across the Illinois River. An early commercial fishing and clam industry gave way to farming and shipping. A 1922 flood covered Beardstown with a lake 18 miles wide, prompting the building of a cement sea wall when the waters receded.
Population: 5,379 (1990); 5,766 (2000); 6,028 (2007); 6,178 (2012 projected); Race: 82.6% White, 2.3% Black, 0.6% Asian, 34.2% Hispanic of any race (2007); Density: 1,769.0 persons per square mile (2007); Average household size: 2.69 (2007); Median age: 34.8 (2007); Males per 100 females: 103.0 (2007); Marriage status: 24.5% never married, 53.9% now married, 9.7% widowed, 12.0% divorced (2000); Foreign born: 17.9% (2000); Ancestry (includes multiple ancestries): 24.2% Other groups, 19.7% German, 12.3% United States or American, 10.7% Irish, 6.9% English (2000).
Economy: Single-family building permits issued: 4 (2007); Multi-family building permits issued: 0 (2007); Employment by occupation: 8.1% management, 12.9% professional, 17.2% services, 15.0% sales, 1.7% farming, 9.8% construction, 35.3% production (2000).
Income: Per capita income: $14,910 (2007); Median household income: $32,844 (2007); Average household income: $38,572 (2007); Percent of households with income of $100,000 or more: 3.2% (2007); Poverty rate: 19.8% (2000).
Education: Percent of population age 25 and over with: High school diploma (including GED) or higher: 72.7% (2007); Bachelor's degree or higher: 8.4% (2007); Master's degree or higher: 2.0% (2007).

School District(s)

Beardstown CUSD 15 (PK-12)
2005-06 Enrollment: 1,503 . . . . (217) 323-3099
Brown/Cass/Morgan/Scott Roe (07-12)
2005-06 Enrollment: 99 . . . . (217) 243-1804
Housing: Homeownership rate: 68.4% (2007); Median home value: $61,346 (2007); Median rent: $311 per month (2000); Median age of housing: 59 years (2000).
Safety: Violent crime rate: 39.1 per 10,000 population; Property crime rate: 275.7 per 10,000 population (2006).
Newspapers: Cass County Star-Gazette (Community news; Circulation 3,300); Star-Gazette Shopper (Community news; Circulation 9,600)
Transportation: Commute to work: 94.4% car, 0.0% public transportation, 2.6% walk, 2.8% work from home (2000); Travel time to work: 66.4% less than 15 minutes, 15.7% 15 to 30 minutes, 4.9% 30 to 45 minutes, 4.4% 45 to 60 minutes, 8.7% 60 minutes or more (2000)
Airports: Greater Beardstown (general aviation)

Additional Information Contacts

Beardstown Chamber of Commerce . . . . (217) 323-3271
http://www.beardstownil.org

CHANDLERVILLE (village). Covers a land area of 0.861 square miles and a water area of 0 square miles. Located at 40.04° N. Lat.; 90.15° W. Long. Elevation is 463 feet.
History: Chandlerville was named for its founder, Dr. Charles Chandler.
Population: 708 (1990); 704 (2000); 703 (2007); 690 (2012 projected); Race: 95.4% White, 1.1% Black, 0.7% Asian, 3.3% Hispanic of any race (2007); Density: 816.8 persons per square mile (2007); Average household size: 2.34 (2007); Median age: 39.0 (2007); Males per 100 females: 99.7 (2007); Marriage status: 20.0% never married, 60.5% now married, 7.3% widowed, 12.2% divorced (2000); Foreign born: 0.4% (2000); Ancestry (includes multiple ancestries): 22.0% English, 21.2% German, 10.7% United States or American, 8.1% Irish, 4.3% Other groups (2000).
Economy: Single-family building permits issued: 0 (2007); Multi-family building permits issued: 0 (2007); Employment by occupation: 6.9% management, 12.2% professional, 16.1% services, 23.9% sales, 4.5% farming, 10.4% construction, 26.0% production (2000).
Income: Per capita income: $20,349 (2007); Median household income: $38,370 (2007); Average household income: $47,525 (2007); Percent of households with income of $100,000 or more: 9.6% (2007); Poverty rate: 8.4% (2000).
Education: Percent of population age 25 and over with: High school diploma (including GED) or higher: 81.7% (2007); Bachelor's degree or higher: 9.0% (2007); Master's degree or higher: 1.4% (2007).

School District(s)

A-C Central CUSD 262 (PK-12)
2005-06 Enrollment: 490 . . . . (217) 476-8112
Housing: Homeownership rate: 81.1% (2007); Median home value: $62,143 (2007); Median rent: $260 per month (2000); Median age of housing: 60+ years (2000).
Safety: Violent crime rate: 69.8 per 10,000 population; Property crime rate: 0.0 per 10,000 population (2006).
Transportation: Commute to work: 93.5% car, 0.0% public transportation, 5.4% walk, 1.2% work from home (2000); Travel time to work: 31.0% less than 15 minutes, 27.4% 15 to 30 minutes, 23.2% 30 to 45 minutes, 8.7% 45 to 60 minutes, 9.6% 60 minutes or more (2000)

VIRGINIA (city). County seat. Covers a land area of 1.085 square miles and a water area of 0.012 square miles. Located at 39.94° N. Lat.; 90.21° W. Long. Elevation is 610 feet.
History: Virginia was platted in 1836 by Dr. Henry A. Hall, a former surgeon in the British Navy, and was incorporated as a village in 1842. It developed as a city after 1872.
Population: 1,863 (1990); 1,728 (2000); 1,790 (2007); 1,752 (2012 projected); Race: 98.3% White, 0.5% Black, 0.4% Asian, 1.5% Hispanic of any race (2007); Density: 1,650.3 persons per square mile (2007); Average household size: 2.34 (2007); Median age: 41.9 (2007); Males per 100 females: 92.9 (2007); Marriage status: 18.4% never married, 57.0% now married, 11.7% widowed, 12.9% divorced (2000); Foreign born: 0.3% (2000); Ancestry (includes multiple ancestries): 24.9% German, 19.5% English, 10.2% United States or American, 9.8% Irish, 5.6% Other groups (2000).

Economy: Single-family building permits issued: 0 (2007); Multi-family building permits issued: 0 (2007); Employment by occupation: 11.4% management, 12.5% professional, 13.9% services, 27.3% sales, 2.3% farming, 9.0% construction, 23.6% production (2000).
Income: Per capita income: $22,791 (2007); Median household income: $43,804 (2007); Average household income: $52,274 (2007); Percent of households with income of $100,000 or more: 8.6% (2007); Poverty rate: 7.7% (2000).
Education: Percent of population age 25 and over with: High school diploma (including GED) or higher: 79.6% (2007); Bachelor's degree or higher: 14.4% (2007); Master's degree or higher: 5.9% (2007).

School District(s)

Virginia CUSD 64 (KG-12)
2005-06 Enrollment: 320 . . . . (217) 452-3085
Housing: Homeownership rate: 72.6% (2007); Median home value: $77,159 (2007); Median rent: $311 per month (2000); Median age of housing: 47 years (2000).
Safety: Violent crime rate: 0.0 per 10,000 population; Property crime rate: 11.6 per 10,000 population (2006).
Transportation: Commute to work: 94.9% car, 0.0% public transportation, 1.6% walk, 3.0% work from home (2000); Travel time to work: 37.5% less than 15 minutes, 31.9% 15 to 30 minutes, 16.2% 30 to 45 minutes, 9.3% 45 to 60 minutes, 5.0% 60 minutes or more (2000)

Champaign County

Located in eastern Illinois; prairie region, drained by the Sangamon, Kaskaskia, and Embarrass Rivers, and by the South Fork of the Vermilion River. Covers a land area of 996.81 square miles, a water area of 0.73 square miles, and is located in the Central Time Zone. The county was founded in 1833. County seat is Urbana.

Champaign County is part of the Champaign-Urbana, IL Metropolitan Statistical Area. The entire metro area includes: Champaign County, IL; Ford County, IL; Piatt County, IL

Weather Station: Rantoul Chanute AFB — Elevation: 754 feet

	Jan	Feb	Mar	Apr	May	Jun	Jul	Aug	Sep	Oct	Nov	Dec
High	32	37	49	62	74	83	87	84	79	66	50	38
Low	14	19	29	39	50	60	64	61	53	41	31	21
Precip	1.7	1.8	3.1	3.9	4.2	3.9	4.5	4.3	3.2	2.9	3.1	2.6
Snow	na	na	1.9	0.4	tr	0.0	0.0	0.0	0.0	tr	0.5	na

High and Low temperatures in degrees Fahrenheit; Precipitation and Snow in inches

Weather Station: Urbana — Elevation: 741 feet

	Jan	Feb	Mar	Apr	May	Jun	Jul	Aug	Sep	Oct	Nov	Dec
High	32	37	49	62	74	83	85	83	78	65	50	37
Low	16	21	31	41	52	61	65	63	55	43	33	23
Precip	1.9	2.0	3.2	3.8	4.7	4.2	4.7	4.4	3.3	2.8	3.4	2.7
Snow	8.5	5.7	3.3	0.6	tr	0.0	0.0	0.0	0.0	0.1	2.1	5.6

High and Low temperatures in degrees Fahrenheit; Precipitation and Snow in inches

Population: 173,025 (1990); 179,669 (2000); 186,125 (2007); 189,896 (2012 projected); Race: 76.1% White, 11.0% Black, 8.1% Asian, 4.0% Hispanic of any race (2007); Density: 186.7 persons per square mile (2007); Average household size: 2.50 (2007); Median age: 28.8 (2007); Males per 100 females: 102.5 (2007).
Religion: Five largest groups: 10.9% Catholic Church, 4.9% The United Methodist Church, 4.4% Evangelical Lutheran Church in America, 2.3% Assemblies of God, 2.1% Christian Churches and Churches of Christ (2000).
Economy: Unemployment rate: 4.3% (4/2008); Total civilian labor force: 107,285 (4/2008); Leading industries: 16.5% retail trade; 14.6% health care and social assistance; 14.4% manufacturing (2005); Farms: 1,285 totaling 577,066 acres (2002); Companies that employ 500 or more persons: 10 (2006); Companies that employ 100 to 499 persons: 111 (2006); Companies that employ less than 100 persons: 4,143 (2006); Black-owned businesses: 993 (2002); Hispanic-owned businesses: 145 (2002); Asian-owned businesses: 469 (2002); Women-owned businesses: 4,316 (2002); Retail sales per capita: $14,291 (2008). Single-family building permits issued: 583 (2007); Multi-family building permits issued: 948 (2007).
Income: Per capita income: $23,626 (2007); Median household income: $43,788 (2007); Average household income: $57,972 (2007); Percent of households with income of $100,000 or more: 13.7% (2007); Poverty rate: 17.7% (2005); Bankruptcy rate: 2.42% (2007).
Taxes: Total county taxes per capita: $170 (2006); County property taxes per capita: $138 (2006).
Education: Percent of population age 25 and over with: High school diploma (including GED) or higher: 91.0% (2007); Bachelor's degree or higher: 38.7% (2007); Master's degree or higher: 19.7% (2007).
Housing: Homeownership rate: 56.4% (2007); Median home value: $124,192 (2007); Median rent: $455 per month (2000); Median age of housing: 29 years (2000).
Health: Birth rate: 128.9 per 10,000 population (2007); Death rate: 62.1 per 10,000 population (2007); Age-adjusted cancer mortality rate: 193.7 deaths per 100,000 population (2005); Air Quality Index: 89.0% good, 10.7% moderate, 0.3% unhealthy for sensitive individuals, 0.0% unhealthy (percent of days in 2007); Number of physicians: 31.2 per 10,000 population (2005); Hospital beds: 33.7 per 10,000 population (2004); Hospital admissions: 1,396.3 per 10,000 population (2004).
Elections: 2004 Presidential election results: 48.4% Bush, 50.4% Kerry, 0.1% Nader, 1.0% Badnarik

Additional Information Contacts

Champaign County Government . . . . (217) 384-3772
http://www.co.champaign.il.us
Champaign County Chamber of Commerce . . . . (217) 359-1791
http://www.ccchamber.org
Champaign Urbana Convention & Visitors Bureau . . . . (800) 369-6151
http://www.visitchampaigncounty.org
City of Champaign . . . . (217) 403-8700
http://www.city.champaign.il.us
City of Urbana . . . . (217) 384-2366
http://www.city.urbana.il.us/Urbana
Mahomet Chamber of Commerce . . . . (217) 586-3165
http://www.mahometchamberofcommerce.com
Rantoul Chamber of Commerce . . . . (217) 893-3323
http://www.rantoulchamber.com
Village of Rantoul . . . . (217) 893-1661
http://www.village.rantoul.il.us

Champaign County Communities

BONDVILLE (village). Covers a land area of 0.254 square miles and a water area of 0 square miles. Located at 40.11° N. Lat.; 88.36° W. Long. Elevation is 719 feet.
Population: 366 (1990); 455 (2000); 375 (2007); 374 (2012 projected); Race: 93.3% White, 0.0% Black, 0.5% Asian, 3.2% Hispanic of any race (2007); Density: 1,477.9 persons per square mile (2007); Average household size: 2.36 (2007); Median age: 33.1 (2007); Males per 100 females: 96.3 (2007); Marriage status: 24.0% never married, 53.5% now married, 1.7% widowed, 20.8% divorced (2000); Foreign born: 0.9% (2000); Ancestry (includes multiple ancestries): 27.4% German, 19.2% Irish, 9.6% English, 6.0% Italian, 6.0% Other groups (2000).
Economy: Single-family building permits issued: 0 (2007); Multi-family building permits issued: 0 (2007); Employment by occupation: 5.1% management, 13.6% professional, 18.7% services, 33.9% sales, 1.6% farming, 11.3% construction, 16.0% production (2000).
Income: Per capita income: $23,640 (2007); Median household income: $51,667 (2007); Average household income: $55,755 (2007); Percent of households with income of $100,000 or more: 6.9% (2007); Poverty rate: 11.9% (2000).
Education: Percent of population age 25 and over with: High school diploma (including GED) or higher: 89.3% (2007); Bachelor's degree or higher: 6.2% (2007); Master's degree or higher: 1.7% (2007).
Housing: Homeownership rate: 64.8% (2007); Median home value: $90,455 (2007); Median rent: $425 per month (2000); Median age of housing: 40 years (2000).
Transportation: Commute to work: 93.8% car, 0.0% public transportation, 0.0% walk, 6.2% work from home (2000); Travel time to work: 15.4% less than 15 minutes, 52.7% 15 to 30 minutes, 24.5% 30 to 45 minutes, 5.8% 45 to 60 minutes, 1.7% 60 minutes or more (2000)

BROADLANDS (village). Covers a land area of 0.271 square miles and a water area of 0 square miles. Located at 39.90° N. Lat.; 87.99° W. Long. Elevation is 679 feet.
Population: 340 (1990); 312 (2000); 297 (2007); 294 (2012 projected); Race: 96.6% White, 0.3% Black, 0.0% Asian, 0.0% Hispanic of any race (2007); Density: 1,097.2 persons per square mile (2007); Average household size: 2.56 (2007); Median age: 37.8 (2007); Males per 100 females: 106.3 (2007); Marriage status: 16.9% never married, 59.5% now

married, 13.2% widowed, 10.3% divorced (2000); Foreign born: 0.6% (2000); Ancestry (includes multiple ancestries): 31.0% German, 22.3% Irish, 19.0% United States or American, 6.6% English, 3.0% French (except Basque) (2000).
Economy: Single-family building permits issued: 0 (2007); Multi-family building permits issued: 0 (2007); Employment by occupation: 5.3% management, 14.0% professional, 17.3% services, 20.7% sales, 0.0% farming, 14.7% construction, 28.0% production (2000).
Income: Per capita income: $17,820 (2007); Median household income: $39,000 (2007); Average household income: $45,625 (2007); Percent of households with income of $100,000 or more: 7.8% (2007); Poverty rate: 6.3% (2000).
Education: Percent of population age 25 and over with: High school diploma (including GED) or higher: 86.7% (2007); Bachelor's degree or higher: 10.5% (2007); Master's degree or higher: 2.2% (2007).

School District(s)

Heritage CUSD 8 (PK-12)
2005-06 Enrollment: 562 . . . . (217) 834-3392
Housing: Homeownership rate: 87.9% (2007); Median home value: $76,667 (2007); Median rent: $414 per month (2000); Median age of housing: 49 years (2000).
Transportation: Commute to work: 91.2% car, 0.0% public transportation, 0.0% walk, 8.8% work from home (2000); Travel time to work: 14.8% less than 15 minutes, 20.7% 15 to 30 minutes, 43.0% 30 to 45 minutes, 16.3% 45 to 60 minutes, 5.2% 60 minutes or more (2000)

CHAMPAIGN (city). Covers a land area of 16.987 square miles and a water area of 0.023 square miles. Located at 40.11° N. Lat.; 88.26° W. Long. Elevation is 738 feet.
History: Champaign came into existence as West Urbana in 1854, built around the railroad station when the Illinois Central Railroad chose a route several miles west of the town of Urbana. Resisting a move to be annexed to Urbana, residents of West Urbana incorporated under the name of Champaign in 1860. Rivalry between the two cities was laid aside when they jointly founded a seminary, later to become the University of Illinois, between them.
Population: 65,449 (1990); 67,518 (2000); 69,618 (2007); 70,939 (2012 projected); Race: 69.7% White, 15.3% Black, 9.1% Asian, 5.8% Hispanic of any race (2007); Density: 4,098.3 persons per square mile (2007); Average household size: 2.46 (2007); Median age: 26.6 (2007); Males per 100 females: 104.0 (2007); Marriage status: 50.5% never married, 38.4% now married, 3.9% widowed, 7.2% divorced (2000); Foreign born: 9.4% (2000); Ancestry (includes multiple ancestries): 26.1% Other groups, 24.2% German, 13.4% Irish, 10.5% English, 4.6% Polish (2000).
Economy: Unemployment rate: 4.0% (4/2008); Total civilian labor force: 42,496 (4/2008); Single-family building permits issued: 206 (2007); Multi-family building permits issued: 593 (2007); Employment by occupation: 11.2% management, 33.9% professional, 16.3% services, 25.7% sales, 0.3% farming, 4.0% construction, 8.7% production (2000).
Income: Per capita income: $22,234 (2007); Median household income: $37,953 (2007); Average household income: $53,335 (2007); Percent of households with income of $100,000 or more: 12.0% (2007); Poverty rate: 22.1% (2000).
Taxes: Total city taxes per capita: $563 (2006); City property taxes per capita: $223 (2006).
Education: Percent of population age 25 and over with: High school diploma (including GED) or higher: 91.4% (2007); Bachelor's degree or higher: 44.5% (2007); Master's degree or higher: 22.4% (2007).

School District(s)

Champaign CUSD 4 (PK-12)
2005-06 Enrollment: 9,248 . . . . (217) 351-3800
Champaign/Ford Roe (05-12)
2005-06 Enrollment: 106 . . . . (217) 893-3219

Four-year College(s)

University of Illinois at Urbana-Champaign (Public)
Fall 2007 Enrollment: 42,326. . . . . (217) 333-1000
2007-08 Tuition: In-state $11,130; Out-of-state $25,216

Two-year College(s)

Parkland College (Public)
Fall 2007 Enrollment: 9,407. . . . . (217) 351-2200
2007-08 Tuition: In-state $6,570; Out-of-state $10,140

Vocational/Technical School(s)

Regency Beauty Institute (Private, For-profit)
Fall 2007 Enrollment: 71 . . . . (800) 787-6456
2007-08 Tuition: $14,200

Housing: Homeownership rate: 48.2% (2007); Median home value: $119,318 (2007); Median rent: $467 per month (2000); Median age of housing: 31 years (2000).
Hospitals: Pavilion Foundation Hospital (46 beds)
Safety: Violent crime rate: 93.6 per 10,000 population; Property crime rate: 357.6 per 10,000 population (2006).
Newspapers: News-Gazette (Local news; Circulation 46,048); Travel - The News-Gazette (Circulation 0)
Transportation: Commute to work: 75.3% car, 6.2% public transportation, 12.3% walk, 3.4% work from home (2000); Travel time to work: 57.1% less than 15 minutes, 34.0% 15 to 30 minutes, 5.1% 30 to 45 minutes, 1.7% 45 to 60 minutes, 2.1% 60 minutes or more (2000); Amtrak: Service available.

Additional Information Contacts

Champaign County Chamber of Commerce . . . . (217) 359-1791
http://www.ccchamber.org
Champaign Urbana Convention & Visitors Bureau . . . . (800) 369-6151
http://www.visitchampaigncounty.org
City of Champaign . . . . (217) 403-8700
http://www.city.champaign.il.us

DEWEY (unincorporated postal area, zip code 61840). Covers a land area of 33.901 square miles and a water area of 0.039 square miles. Located at 40.31° N. Lat.; 88.30° W. Long. Elevation is 732 feet.
Population: 709 (2000); Race: 97.6% White, 0.0% Black, 1.5% Asian, 2.0% Hispanic of any race (2000); Density: 20.9 persons per square mile (2000); Age: 25.9% under 18, 15.1% over 64 (2000); Marriage status: 16.8% never married, 66.4% now married, 5.6% widowed, 11.2% divorced (2000); Foreign born: 2.1% (2000); Ancestry (includes multiple ancestries): 32.7% German, 14.9% English, 9.8% United States or American, 9.8% Irish, 9.4% Italian (2000).
Economy: Employment by occupation: 21.5% management, 19.6% professional, 12.4% services, 24.0% sales, 1.4% farming, 6.4% construction, 14.6% production (2000).
Income: Per capita income: $24,557 (2000); Median household income: $52,381 (2000); Poverty rate: 1.8% (2000).
Education: Percent of population age 25 and over with: High school diploma (including GED) or higher: 96.3% (2000); Bachelor's degree or higher: 27.7% (2000).
Housing: Homeownership rate: 92.7% (2000); Median home value: $113,900 (2000); Median rent: $400 per month (2000); Median age of housing: 28 years (2000).
Transportation: Commute to work: 93.6% car, 0.0% public transportation, 0.0% walk, 6.4% work from home (2000); Travel time to work: 22.7% less than 15 minutes, 52.2% 15 to 30 minutes, 17.4% 30 to 45 minutes, 3.2% 45 to 60 minutes, 4.4% 60 minutes or more (2000)

FISHER (village). Covers a land area of 0.992 square miles and a water area of 0 square miles. Located at 40.31° N. Lat.; 88.34° W. Long. Elevation is 712 feet.
Population: 1,578 (1990); 1,647 (2000); 1,604 (2007); 1,590 (2012 projected); Race: 98.6% White, 0.0% Black, 0.0% Asian, 0.4% Hispanic of any race (2007); Density: 1,617.0 persons per square mile (2007); Average household size: 2.55 (2007); Median age: 34.4 (2007); Males per 100 females: 98.8 (2007); Marriage status: 21.6% never married, 64.4% now married, 6.1% widowed, 8.0% divorced (2000); Foreign born: 1.7% (2000); Ancestry (includes multiple ancestries): 32.1% German, 17.7% English, 11.8% United States or American, 10.2% Irish, 7.0% Other groups (2000).
Economy: Single-family building permits issued: 15 (2007); Multi-family building permits issued: 0 (2007); Employment by occupation: 12.0% management, 15.4% professional, 12.8% services, 26.8% sales, 0.2% farming, 11.2% construction, 21.5% production (2000).
Income: Per capita income: $22,820 (2007); Median household income: $48,942 (2007); Average household income: $58,099 (2007); Percent of households with income of $100,000 or more: 10.2% (2007); Poverty rate: 3.6% (2000).
Education: Percent of population age 25 and over with: High school diploma (including GED) or higher: 87.7% (2007); Bachelor's degree or higher: 14.6% (2007); Master's degree or higher: 4.8% (2007).

School District(s)

Fisher CUSD 1 (KG-12)
2005-06 Enrollment: 600 . . . . (217) 897-6125
Housing: Homeownership rate: 77.1% (2007); Median home value: $110,039 (2007); Median rent: $335 per month (2000); Median age of housing: 34 years (2000).

Safety: Violent crime rate: 90.7 per 10,000 population; Property crime rate: 175.3 per 10,000 population (2006).
Newspapers: Fisher Reporter (Community news; Circulation 1,150)
Transportation: Commute to work: 93.9% car, 0.0% public transportation, 2.3% walk, 2.9% work from home (2000); Travel time to work: 27.3% less than 15 minutes, 40.7% 15 to 30 minutes, 27.5% 30 to 45 minutes, 1.8% 45 to 60 minutes, 2.8% 60 minutes or more (2000)

FOOSLAND (village). Covers a land area of 0.072 square miles and a water area of 0 square miles. Located at 40.36° N. Lat.; 88.42° W. Long. Elevation is 735 feet.
Population: 132 (1990); 90 (2000); 87 (2007); 86 (2012 projected); Race: 100.0% White, 0.0% Black, 0.0% Asian, 0.0% Hispanic of any race (2007); Density: 1,205.1 persons per square mile (2007); Average household size: 2.17 (2007); Median age: 37.5 (2007); Males per 100 females: 123.1 (2007); Marriage status: 24.6% never married, 63.8% now married, 5.8% widowed, 5.8% divorced (2000); Foreign born: 0.0% (2000); Ancestry (includes multiple ancestries): 27.4% German, 22.6% Irish, 22.6% English, 4.8% French (except Basque), 3.6% Scottish (2000).
Economy: Employment by occupation: 7.0% management, 2.3% professional, 7.0% services, 18.6% sales, 4.7% farming, 2.3% construction, 58.1% production (2000).
Income: Per capita income: $23,937 (2007); Median household income: $37,500 (2007); Average household income: $52,063 (2007); Percent of households with income of $100,000 or more: 7.5% (2007); Poverty rate: 15.5% (2000).
Education: Percent of population age 25 and over with: High school diploma (including GED) or higher: 72.9% (2007); Bachelor's degree or higher: 5.1% (2007); Master's degree or higher: 0.0% (2007).
Housing: Homeownership rate: 87.5% (2007); Median home value: $80,714 (2007); Median rent: $292 per month (2000); Median age of housing: 53 years (2000).
Transportation: Commute to work: 88.4% car, 0.0% public transportation, 11.6% walk, 0.0% work from home (2000); Travel time to work: 23.3% less than 15 minutes, 34.9% 15 to 30 minutes, 27.9% 30 to 45 minutes, 0.0% 45 to 60 minutes, 14.0% 60 minutes or more (2000)

GIFFORD (village). Covers a land area of 0.633 square miles and a water area of 0 square miles. Located at 40.30° N. Lat.; 88.02° W. Long. Elevation is 797 feet.
Population: 852 (1990); 815 (2000); 750 (2007); 749 (2012 projected); Race: 97.5% White, 1.2% Black, 0.5% Asian, 0.5% Hispanic of any race (2007); Density: 1,185.5 persons per square mile (2007); Average household size: 2.67 (2007); Median age: 43.4 (2007); Males per 100 females: 86.1 (2007); Marriage status: 17.8% never married, 60.1% now married, 15.8% widowed, 6.3% divorced (2000); Foreign born: 1.8% (2000); Ancestry (includes multiple ancestries): 38.0% German, 12.1% Irish, 10.3% English, 6.8% Other groups, 4.8% United States or American (2000).
Economy: Single-family building permits issued: 4 (2007); Multi-family building permits issued: 0 (2007); Employment by occupation: 13.4% management, 11.7% professional, 9.9% services, 30.5% sales, 0.0% farming, 10.4% construction, 24.1% production (2000).
Income: Per capita income: $26,870 (2007); Median household income: $55,571 (2007); Average household income: $62,447 (2007); Percent of households with income of $100,000 or more: 9.3% (2007); Poverty rate: 1.8% (2000).
Education: Percent of population age 25 and over with: High school diploma (including GED) or higher: 77.4% (2007); Bachelor's degree or higher: 16.0% (2007); Master's degree or higher: 4.2% (2007).

School District(s)

Gifford CCSD 188 (KG-08)
2005-06 Enrollment: 202 . . . . (217) 568-7733
Housing: Homeownership rate: 87.5% (2007); Median home value: $117,692 (2007); Median rent: $300 per month (2000); Median age of housing: 37 years (2000).
Safety: Violent crime rate: 0.0 per 10,000 population; Property crime rate: 10.0 per 10,000 population (2006).
Transportation: Commute to work: 93.7% car, 0.0% public transportation, 4.0% walk, 0.5% work from home (2000); Travel time to work: 33.0% less than 15 minutes, 26.4% 15 to 30 minutes, 26.7% 30 to 45 minutes, 8.8% 45 to 60 minutes, 5.0% 60 minutes or more (2000)

HOMER (village). Covers a land area of 1.026 square miles and a water area of 0 square miles. Located at 40.03° N. Lat.; 87.95° W. Long. Elevation is 676 feet.
History: Village formerly on Salt Creek to North but moved in 19th century to be on railroad.
Population: 1,265 (1990); 1,200 (2000); 1,282 (2007); 1,308 (2012 projected); Race: 98.6% White, 0.1% Black, 0.6% Asian, 0.4% Hispanic of any race (2007); Density: 1,249.2 persons per square mile (2007); Average household size: 2.40 (2007); Median age: 36.0 (2007); Males per 100 females: 100.9 (2007); Marriage status: 17.4% never married, 61.6% now married, 8.4% widowed, 12.6% divorced (2000); Foreign born: 0.3% (2000); Ancestry (includes multiple ancestries): 24.2% German, 15.7% English, 15.3% Irish, 14.7% United States or American, 4.9% Other groups (2000).
Economy: Single-family building permits issued: 0 (2007); Multi-family building permits issued: 0 (2007); Employment by occupation: 7.9% management, 15.8% professional, 15.6% services, 27.4% sales, 0.4% farming, 11.1% construction, 21.9% production (2000).
Income: Per capita income: $20,293 (2007); Median household income: $42,009 (2007); Average household income: $48,626 (2007); Percent of households with income of $100,000 or more: 5.4% (2007); Poverty rate: 9.1% (2000).
Education: Percent of population age 25 and over with: High school diploma (including GED) or higher: 87.6% (2007); Bachelor's degree or higher: 11.8% (2007); Master's degree or higher: 3.5% (2007).

School District(s)

Heritage CUSD 8 (PK-12)
2005-06 Enrollment: 562 . . . . (217) 834-3392
Housing: Homeownership rate: 85.6% (2007); Median home value: $90,192 (2007); Median rent: $328 per month (2000); Median age of housing: 48 years (2000).
Safety: Violent crime rate: 0.0 per 10,000 population; Property crime rate: 34.6 per 10,000 population (2006).
Transportation: Commute to work: 92.3% car, 0.0% public transportation, 2.9% walk, 3.8% work from home (2000); Travel time to work: 24.2% less than 15 minutes, 30.3% 15 to 30 minutes, 39.4% 30 to 45 minutes, 4.4% 45 to 60 minutes, 1.7% 60 minutes or more (2000)

IVESDALE (village). Covers a land area of 0.749 square miles and a water area of 0 square miles. Located at 39.94° N. Lat.; 88.45° W. Long. Elevation is 682 feet.
Population: 339 (1990); 288 (2000); 261 (2007); 259 (2012 projected); Race: 99.2% White, 0.0% Black, 0.0% Asian, 0.0% Hispanic of any race (2007); Density: 348.4 persons per square mile (2007); Average household size: 2.39 (2007); Median age: 40.2 (2007); Males per 100 females: 96.2 (2007); Marriage status: 24.1% never married, 57.7% now married, 5.8% widowed, 12.4% divorced (2000); Foreign born: 1.3% (2000); Ancestry (includes multiple ancestries): 39.6% Irish, 24.8% German, 16.0% United States or American, 9.4% Other groups, 9.1% French (except Basque) (2000).
Economy: Single-family building permits issued: 1 (2007); Multi-family building permits issued: 0 (2007); Employment by occupation: 9.6% management, 10.2% professional, 11.8% services, 30.5% sales, 0.0% farming, 19.3% construction, 18.7% production (2000).
Income: Per capita income: $24,684 (2007); Median household income: $56,429 (2007); Average household income: $59,106 (2007); Percent of households with income of $100,000 or more: 11.9% (2007); Poverty rate: 3.5% (2000).
Education: Percent of population age 25 and over with: High school diploma (including GED) or higher: 88.8% (2007); Bachelor's degree or higher: 10.7% (2007); Master's degree or higher: 1.6% (2007).
Housing: Homeownership rate: 91.7% (2007); Median home value: $90,000 (2007); Median rent: $335 per month (2000); Median age of housing: 60+ years (2000).
Transportation: Commute to work: 96.1% car, 0.0% public transportation, 0.0% walk, 2.2% work from home (2000); Travel time to work: 25.7% less than 15 minutes, 15.4% 15 to 30 minutes, 49.1% 30 to 45 minutes, 4.0% 45 to 60 minutes, 5.7% 60 minutes or more (2000)

LAKE OF THE WOODS (CDP). Covers a land area of 2.101 square miles and a water area of 0.014 square miles. Located at 40.20° N. Lat.; 88.36° W. Long. Elevation is 748 feet.
History: Covered bridge.

Population: 2,718 (1990); 3,026 (2000); 3,297 (2007); 3,424 (2012 projected); Race: 96.9% White, 0.9% Black, 0.0% Asian, 1.0% Hispanic of any race (2007); Density: 1,569.0 persons per square mile (2007); Average household size: 2.59 (2007); Median age: 31.8 (2007); Males per 100 females: 98.9 (2007); Marriage status: 19.6% never married, 62.6% now married, 4.3% widowed, 13.4% divorced (2000); Foreign born: 0.3% (2000); Ancestry (includes multiple ancestries): 25.8% German, 15.1% United States or American, 14.4% Irish, 14.0% English, 8.6% Other groups (2000).
Economy: Employment by occupation: 10.4% management, 15.5% professional, 19.6% services, 24.4% sales, 1.2% farming, 11.3% construction, 17.6% production (2000).
Income: Per capita income: $24,178 (2007); Median household income: $51,376 (2007); Average household income: $62,571 (2007); Percent of households with income of $100,000 or more: 16.1% (2007); Poverty rate: 8.7% (2000).
Education: Percent of population age 25 and over with: High school diploma (including GED) or higher: 93.4% (2007); Bachelor's degree or higher: 27.9% (2007); Master's degree or higher: 10.3% (2007).
Housing: Homeownership rate: 80.8% (2007); Median home value: $104,508 (2007); Median rent: $486 per month (2000); Median age of housing: 17 years (2000).
Transportation: Commute to work: 97.2% car, 0.0% public transportation, 0.3% walk, 1.6% work from home (2000); Travel time to work: 27.5% less than 15 minutes, 58.1% 15 to 30 minutes, 9.1% 30 to 45 minutes, 1.9% 45 to 60 minutes, 3.4% 60 minutes or more (2000)

LONGVIEW (village). Aka Long View. Covers a land area of 0.251 square miles and a water area of 0 square miles. Located at 39.88° N. Lat.; 88.06° W. Long. Elevation is 679 feet.
Population: 180 (1990); 153 (2000); 155 (2007); 153 (2012 projected); Race: 98.1% White, 0.0% Black, 0.0% Asian, 1.3% Hispanic of any race (2007); Density: 618.6 persons per square mile (2007); Average household size: 2.63 (2007); Median age: 30.3 (2007); Males per 100 females: 82.4 (2007); Marriage status: 31.4% never married, 47.1% now married, 8.3% widowed, 13.2% divorced (2000); Foreign born: 0.0% (2000); Ancestry (includes multiple ancestries): 20.0% German, 15.8% United States or American, 13.3% Other groups, 9.7% Italian, 5.5% English (2000).
Economy: Employment by occupation: 4.5% management, 4.5% professional, 17.9% services, 31.3% sales, 0.0% farming, 25.4% construction, 16.4% production (2000).
Income: Per capita income: $14,306 (2007); Median household income: $35,417 (2007); Average household income: $37,585 (2007); Percent of households with income of $100,000 or more: 1.7% (2007); Poverty rate: 15.2% (2000).
Education: Percent of population age 25 and over with: High school diploma (including GED) or higher: 70.8% (2007); Bachelor's degree or higher: 0.0% (2007); Master's degree or higher: 0.0% (2007).

School District(s)

Rural Champaign Co Spec Ed Coop
2005-06 Enrollment: n/a . . . . (217) 892-8877
Housing: Homeownership rate: 79.7% (2007); Median home value: $53,125 (2007); Median rent: $500 per month (2000); Median age of housing: 60+ years (2000).
Transportation: Commute to work: 100.0% car, 0.0% public transportation, 0.0% walk, 0.0% work from home (2000); Travel time to work: 7.5% less than 15 minutes, 20.9% 15 to 30 minutes, 43.3% 30 to 45 minutes, 23.9% 45 to 60 minutes, 4.5% 60 minutes or more (2000)

LUDLOW (village). Covers a land area of 0.348 square miles and a water area of 0 square miles. Located at 40.38° N. Lat.; 88.12° W. Long. Elevation is 774 feet.
Population: 323 (1990); 324 (2000); 313 (2007); 305 (2012 projected); Race: 95.8% White, 2.9% Black, 0.0% Asian, 0.6% Hispanic of any race (2007); Density: 900.5 persons per square mile (2007); Average household size: 2.22 (2007); Median age: 33.9 (2007); Males per 100 females: 104.6 (2007); Marriage status: 22.1% never married, 51.2% now married, 10.0% widowed, 16.7% divorced (2000); Foreign born: 1.7% (2000); Ancestry (includes multiple ancestries): 29.6% German, 15.8% Irish, 14.5% Other groups, 8.8% English, 5.7% United States or American (2000).
Economy: Single-family building permits issued: 0 (2007); Multi-family building permits issued: 0 (2007); Employment by occupation: 1.2% management, 6.7% professional, 11.0% services, 25.2% sales, 0.0% farming, 14.7% construction, 41.1% production (2000).
Income: Per capita income: $24,457 (2007); Median household income: $40,357 (2007); Average household income: $54,291 (2007); Percent of households with income of $100,000 or more: 9.9% (2007); Poverty rate: 15.0% (2000).
Education: Percent of population age 25 and over with: High school diploma (including GED) or higher: 84.8% (2007); Bachelor's degree or higher: 3.0% (2007); Master's degree or higher: 1.0% (2007).

School District(s)

Ludlow CCSD 142 (KG-08)
2005-06 Enrollment: 98 . . . . (217) 396-5261
Housing: Homeownership rate: 62.4% (2007); Median home value: $67,500 (2007); Median rent: $262 per month (2000); Median age of housing: 41 years (2000).
Safety: Violent crime rate: 27.0 per 10,000 population; Property crime rate: 189.2 per 10,000 population (2006).
Transportation: Commute to work: 94.5% car, 1.2% public transportation, 2.5% walk, 0.0% work from home (2000); Travel time to work: 31.9% less than 15 minutes, 30.1% 15 to 30 minutes, 35.0% 30 to 45 minutes, 0.6% 45 to 60 minutes, 2.5% 60 minutes or more (2000)

MAHOMET (village). Covers a land area of 6.854 square miles and a water area of 0 square miles. Located at 40.19° N. Lat.; 88.40° W. Long. Elevation is 732 feet.
Population: 3,980 (1990); 4,877 (2000); 5,418 (2007); 5,656 (2012 projected); Race: 97.6% White, 0.2% Black, 0.8% Asian, 1.4% Hispanic of any race (2007); Density: 790.5 persons per square mile (2007); Average household size: 2.89 (2007); Median age: 30.3 (2007); Males per 100 females: 95.2 (2007); Marriage status: 19.1% never married, 70.5% now married, 3.9% widowed, 6.5% divorced (2000); Foreign born: 0.4% (2000); Ancestry (includes multiple ancestries): 32.3% German, 19.0% English, 11.1% Irish, 7.4% United States or American, 4.2% Other groups (2000).
Economy: Single-family building permits issued: 85 (2007); Multi-family building permits issued: 16 (2007); Employment by occupation: 15.5% management, 30.6% professional, 11.7% services, 29.0% sales, 0.0% farming, 7.7% construction, 5.4% production (2000).
Income: Per capita income: $26,742 (2007); Median household income: $66,075 (2007); Average household income: $77,394 (2007); Percent of households with income of $100,000 or more: 22.6% (2007); Poverty rate: 5.1% (2000).
Education: Percent of population age 25 and over with: High school diploma (including GED) or higher: 96.6% (2007); Bachelor's degree or higher: 37.9% (2007); Master's degree or higher: 12.5% (2007).

School District(s)

Mahomet-Seymour CUSD 3 (PK-12)
2005-06 Enrollment: 2,776 . . . . (217) 586-4995
Housing: Homeownership rate: 82.7% (2007); Median home value: $157,161 (2007); Median rent: $525 per month (2000); Median age of housing: 19 years (2000).
Safety: Violent crime rate: 8.8 per 10,000 population; Property crime rate: 136.5 per 10,000 population (2006).
Newspapers: Mahomet Citizen (Local news; Circulation 3,000)
Transportation: Commute to work: 92.6% car, 0.5% public transportation, 0.4% walk, 5.4% work from home (2000); Travel time to work: 23.0% less than 15 minutes, 59.3% 15 to 30 minutes, 9.0% 30 to 45 minutes, 3.4% 45 to 60 minutes, 5.3% 60 minutes or more (2000)
Additional Information Contacts
Mahomet Chamber of Commerce . . . . (217) 586-3165
http://www.mahometchamberofcommerce.com

OGDEN (village). Covers a land area of 0.567 square miles and a water area of 0 square miles. Located at 40.11° N. Lat.; 87.95° W. Long. Elevation is 669 feet.
Population: 708 (1990); 743 (2000); 728 (2007); 718 (2012 projected); Race: 98.9% White, 0.4% Black, 0.0% Asian, 1.5% Hispanic of any race (2007); Density: 1,284.7 persons per square mile (2007); Average household size: 2.63 (2007); Median age: 31.6 (2007); Males per 100 females: 102.8 (2007); Marriage status: 21.3% never married, 59.0% now married, 10.6% widowed, 9.1% divorced (2000); Foreign born: 2.0% (2000); Ancestry (includes multiple ancestries): 37.8% German, 19.3% Irish, 11.8% English, 10.0% Other groups, 6.9% United States or American (2000).
Economy: Single-family building permits issued: 0 (2007); Multi-family building permits issued: 0 (2007); Employment by occupation: 7.9% management, 11.8% professional, 18.4% services, 34.7% sales, 0.8% farming, 9.5% construction, 16.8% production (2000).

Income: Per capita income: $25,996 (2007); Median household income: $53,462 (2007); Average household income: $68,321 (2007); Percent of households with income of $100,000 or more: 11.9% (2007); Poverty rate: 3.0% (2000).
Education: Percent of population age 25 and over with: High school diploma (including GED) or higher: 90.8% (2007); Bachelor's degree or higher: 15.1% (2007); Master's degree or higher: 3.2% (2007).

School District(s)

Ogden CCSD 212 (KG-08)
2005-06 Enrollment: 139 . . . . (217) 582-2725
Housing: Homeownership rate: 88.1% (2007); Median home value: $113,750 (2007); Median rent: $450 per month (2000); Median age of housing: 29 years (2000).
Safety: Violent crime rate: 0.0 per 10,000 population; Property crime rate: 13.6 per 10,000 population (2006).
Newspapers: Ogden Leader (Community news; Circulation 8,000)
Transportation: Commute to work: 93.6% car, 0.0% public transportation, 1.3% walk, 4.3% work from home (2000); Travel time to work: 14.8% less than 15 minutes, 61.6% 15 to 30 minutes, 18.9% 30 to 45 minutes, 3.9% 45 to 60 minutes, 0.8% 60 minutes or more (2000)

PENFIELD (unincorporated postal area, zip code 61862). Covers a land area of 36.908 square miles and a water area of 0 square miles. Located at 40.29° N. Lat.; 87.95° W. Long. Elevation is 712 feet.
Population: 511 (2000); Race: 96.5% White, 0.7% Black, 0.0% Asian, 0.9% Hispanic of any race (2000); Density: 13.8 persons per square mile (2000); Age: 33.2% under 18, 10.4% over 64 (2000); Marriage status: 16.8% never married, 74.6% now married, 2.3% widowed, 6.4% divorced (2000); Foreign born: 0.4% (2000); Ancestry (includes multiple ancestries): 49.8% German, 21.4% Irish, 9.7% English, 7.5% Other groups, 5.5% Swedish (2000).
Economy: Employment by occupation: 10.5% management, 13.9% professional, 22.4% services, 18.4% sales, 1.7% farming, 10.9% construction, 22.1% production (2000).
Income: Per capita income: $18,170 (2000); Median household income: $47,000 (2000); Poverty rate: 3.9% (2000).
Education: Percent of population age 25 and over with: High school diploma (including GED) or higher: 92.5% (2000); Bachelor's degree or higher: 14.6% (2000).
Housing: Homeownership rate: 79.6% (2000); Median home value: $75,600 (2000); Median rent: $278 per month (2000); Median age of housing: 56 years (2000).
Transportation: Commute to work: 86.7% car, 0.7% public transportation, 1.7% walk, 10.9% work from home (2000); Travel time to work: 18.3% less than 15 minutes, 23.3% 15 to 30 minutes, 43.9% 30 to 45 minutes, 10.3% 45 to 60 minutes, 4.2% 60 minutes or more (2000)

PESOTUM (village). Covers a land area of 0.555 square miles and a water area of 0.005 square miles. Located at 39.91° N. Lat.; 88.27° W. Long. Elevation is 715 feet.
History: Pesotum developed as a grain storage and shipping center.
Population: 558 (1990); 521 (2000); 507 (2007); 496 (2012 projected); Race: 98.8% White, 0.0% Black, 0.4% Asian, 0.4% Hispanic of any race (2007); Density: 912.8 persons per square mile (2007); Average household size: 2.33 (2007); Median age: 39.9 (2007); Males per 100 females: 97.3 (2007); Marriage status: 19.3% never married, 64.9% now married, 9.5% widowed, 6.3% divorced (2000); Foreign born: 0.4% (2000); Ancestry (includes multiple ancestries): 45.4% German, 19.5% Irish, 18.9% English, 11.2% Other groups, 10.0% United States or American (2000).
Economy: Single-family building permits issued: 3 (2007); Multi-family building permits issued: 0 (2007); Employment by occupation: 5.5% management, 21.5% professional, 16.1% services, 29.2% sales, 0.0% farming, 13.5% construction, 14.2% production (2000).
Income: Per capita income: $26,603 (2007); Median household income: $59,667 (2007); Average household income: $61,869 (2007); Percent of households with income of $100,000 or more: 13.3% (2007); Poverty rate: 2.8% (2000).
Education: Percent of population age 25 and over with: High school diploma (including GED) or higher: 96.0% (2007); Bachelor's degree or higher: 14.0% (2007); Master's degree or higher: 6.0% (2007).
Housing: Homeownership rate: 94.5% (2007); Median home value: $97,027 (2007); Median rent: $323 per month (2000); Median age of housing: 51 years (2000).
Transportation: Commute to work: 97.4% car, 0.0% public transportation, 2.2% walk, 0.0% work from home (2000); Travel time to work: 15.4% less than 15 minutes, 55.5% 15 to 30 minutes, 25.0% 30 to 45 minutes, 2.2% 45 to 60 minutes, 1.8% 60 minutes or more (2000)

PHILO (village). Covers a land area of 0.762 square miles and a water area of 0 square miles. Located at 40.00° N. Lat.; 88.15° W. Long. Elevation is 735 feet.
Population: 1,073 (1990); 1,314 (2000); 1,335 (2007); 1,372 (2012 projected); Race: 98.3% White, 0.5% Black, 0.0% Asian, 0.4% Hispanic of any race (2007); Density: 1,751.0 persons per square mile (2007); Average household size: 2.72 (2007); Median age: 33.3 (2007); Males per 100 females: 102.6 (2007); Marriage status: 21.7% never married, 68.3% now married, 4.7% widowed, 5.2% divorced (2000); Foreign born: 0.5% (2000); Ancestry (includes multiple ancestries): 34.0% German, 24.5% Irish, 14.6% United States or American, 7.9% English, 4.0% Other groups (2000).
Economy: Single-family building permits issued: 11 (2007); Multi-family building permits issued: 0 (2007); Employment by occupation: 16.1% management, 18.2% professional, 14.1% services, 30.8% sales, 0.0% farming, 12.5% construction, 8.4% production (2000).
Income: Per capita income: $26,459 (2007); Median household income: $65,862 (2007); Average household income: $72,087 (2007); Percent of households with income of $100,000 or more: 16.9% (2007); Poverty rate: 3.4% (2000).
Education: Percent of population age 25 and over with: High school diploma (including GED) or higher: 91.9% (2007); Bachelor's degree or higher: 23.2% (2007); Master's degree or higher: 8.7% (2007).

School District(s)

Tolono CUSD 7 (PK-12)
2005-06 Enrollment: 1,514 . . . . (217) 485-6510
Housing: Homeownership rate: 91.2% (2007); Median home value: $133,460 (2007); Median rent: $425 per month (2000); Median age of housing: 32 years (2000).
Transportation: Commute to work: 96.8% car, 0.6% public transportation, 0.9% walk, 1.2% work from home (2000); Travel time to work: 19.7% less than 15 minutes, 61.7% 15 to 30 minutes, 11.6% 30 to 45 minutes, 2.1% 45 to 60 minutes, 4.9% 60 minutes or more (2000)

RANTOUL (village). Covers a land area of 7.237 square miles and a water area of 0.113 square miles. Located at 40.30° N. Lat.; 88.15° W. Long. Elevation is 745 feet.
History: Rantoul was named for Robert Rantoul who was a director of the Illinois Central Railroad.
Population: 17,218 (1990); 12,857 (2000); 12,145 (2007); 11,637 (2012 projected); Race: 75.1% White, 17.6% Black, 1.7% Asian, 3.2% Hispanic of any race (2007); Density: 1,678.2 persons per square mile (2007); Average household size: 2.34 (2007); Median age: 31.4 (2007); Males per 100 females: 92.8 (2007); Marriage status: 24.9% never married, 53.0% now married, 6.0% widowed, 16.1% divorced (2000); Foreign born: 3.4% (2000); Ancestry (includes multiple ancestries): 23.5% Other groups, 22.2% German, 11.4% Irish, 9.5% United States or American, 7.3% English (2000).
Economy: Single-family building permits issued: 4 (2007); Multi-family building permits issued: 0 (2007); Employment by occupation: 9.9% management, 13.3% professional, 14.7% services, 27.7% sales, 0.4% farming, 7.6% construction, 26.5% production (2000).
Income: Per capita income: $20,846 (2007); Median household income: $40,189 (2007); Average household income: $48,765 (2007); Percent of households with income of $100,000 or more: 7.5% (2007); Poverty rate: 10.7% (2000).
Taxes: Total city taxes per capita: $456 (2006); City property taxes per capita: $200 (2006).
Education: Percent of population age 25 and over with: High school diploma (including GED) or higher: 88.4% (2007); Bachelor's degree or higher: 15.8% (2007); Master's degree or higher: 5.3% (2007).

School District(s)

Educ for Employment Sys 330
2005-06 Enrollment: n/a . . . . (217) 893-1353
Rantoul City SD 137 (PK-08)
2005-06 Enrollment: 1,713 . . . . (217) 893-4171
Rantoul Township HSD 193 (09-12)
2005-06 Enrollment: 786 . . . . (217) 892-2151
Rural Champaign Co Spec Ed Coop
2005-06 Enrollment: n/a . . . . (217) 892-8877
Housing: Homeownership rate: 51.6% (2007); Median home value: $91,901 (2007); Median rent: $397 per month (2000); Median age of housing: 38 years (2000).

Safety: Violent crime rate: 106.5 per 10,000 population; Property crime rate: 292.4 per 10,000 population (2006).
Newspapers: Rantoul Press (Community news; Circulation 11,000)
Transportation: Commute to work: 93.6% car, 0.9% public transportation, 1.7% walk, 2.0% work from home (2000); Travel time to work: 51.0% less than 15 minutes, 30.9% 15 to 30 minutes, 13.0% 30 to 45 minutes, 2.0% 45 to 60 minutes, 3.1% 60 minutes or more (2000); Amtrak: Service available.
Additional Information Contacts
Rantoul Chamber of Commerce . . . . (217) 893-3323
http://www.rantoulchamber.com
Village of Rantoul. . . . . (217) 893-1661
http://www.village.rantoul.il.us

ROYAL (village). Covers a land area of 0.225 square miles and a water area of 0 square miles. Located at 40.19° N. Lat.; 87.97° W. Long. Elevation is 682 feet.
Population: 290 (1990); 279 (2000); 284 (2007); 284 (2012 projected); Race: 100.0% White, 0.0% Black, 0.0% Asian, 0.0% Hispanic of any race (2007); Density: 1,262.1 persons per square mile (2007); Average household size: 2.12 (2007); Median age: 45.4 (2007); Males per 100 females: 89.3 (2007); Marriage status: 18.1% never married, 67.3% now married, 9.3% widowed, 5.2% divorced (2000); Foreign born: 0.0% (2000); Ancestry (includes multiple ancestries): 62.8% German, 14.1% Irish, 8.8% English, 5.0% Other groups, 4.4% Italian (2000).
Economy: Single-family building permits issued: 0 (2007); Multi-family building permits issued: 0 (2007); Employment by occupation: 15.7% management, 19.7% professional, 6.2% services, 28.7% sales, 0.0% farming, 13.5% construction, 16.3% production (2000).
Income: Per capita income: $32,033 (2007); Median household income: $57,000 (2007); Average household income: $67,892 (2007); Percent of households with income of $100,000 or more: 14.2% (2007); Poverty rate: 0.6% (2000).
Education: Percent of population age 25 and over with: High school diploma (including GED) or higher: 85.2% (2007); Bachelor's degree or higher: 18.1% (2007); Master's degree or higher: 7.6% (2007).
School District(s)
Prairieview Ccd 192 (KG-08)
2005-06 Enrollment: 140 . . . . (217) 583-3300
Housing: Homeownership rate: 85.8% (2007); Median home value: $115,160 (2007); Median rent: $331 per month (2000); Median age of housing: 39 years (2000).
Transportation: Commute to work: 89.3% car, 0.0% public transportation, 2.8% walk, 7.3% work from home (2000); Travel time to work: 23.0% less than 15 minutes, 46.1% 15 to 30 minutes, 20.0% 30 to 45 minutes, 9.1% 45 to 60 minutes, 1.8% 60 minutes or more (2000)

SADORUS (village). Covers a land area of 0.846 square miles and a water area of 0 square miles. Located at 39.96° N. Lat.; 88.34° W. Long. Elevation is 692 feet.
Population: 469 (1990); 426 (2000); 405 (2007); 399 (2012 projected); Race: 97.3% White, 0.0% Black, 0.0% Asian, 0.0% Hispanic of any race (2007); Density: 479.0 persons per square mile (2007); Average household size: 2.56 (2007); Median age: 38.9 (2007); Males per 100 females: 127.5 (2007); Marriage status: 21.5% never married, 63.2% now married, 5.3% widowed, 10.0% divorced (2000); Foreign born: 2.3% (2000); Ancestry (includes multiple ancestries): 34.2% German, 14.6% Irish, 13.1% United States or American, 10.8% English, 3.5% Other groups (2000).
Economy: Single-family building permits issued: 1 (2007); Multi-family building permits issued: 0 (2007); Employment by occupation: 12.2% management, 8.7% professional, 16.1% services, 27.0% sales, 0.0% farming, 16.5% construction, 19.6% production (2000).
Income: Per capita income: $22,753 (2007); Median household income: $53,235 (2007); Average household income: $58,323 (2007); Percent of households with income of $100,000 or more: 10.8% (2007); Poverty rate: 3.6% (2000).
Education: Percent of population age 25 and over with: High school diploma (including GED) or higher: 81.9% (2007); Bachelor's degree or higher: 10.6% (2007); Master's degree or higher: 4.6% (2007).
Housing: Homeownership rate: 86.7% (2007); Median home value: $88,542 (2007); Median rent: $375 per month (2000); Median age of housing: 48 years (2000).
Transportation: Commute to work: 93.3% car, 0.0% public transportation, 2.2% walk, 3.6% work from home (2000); Travel time to work: 14.7% less than 15 minutes, 49.8% 15 to 30 minutes, 30.0% 30 to 45 minutes, 2.8% 45 to 60 minutes, 2.8% 60 minutes or more (2000)

SAINT JOSEPH (village). Covers a land area of 1.132 square miles and a water area of 0.004 square miles. Located at 40.11° N. Lat.; 88.03° W. Long. Elevation is 673 feet.
Population: 2,214 (1990); 2,912 (2000); 3,308 (2007); 3,560 (2012 projected); Race: 98.5% White, 0.1% Black, 0.3% Asian, 1.3% Hispanic of any race (2007); Density: 2,922.1 persons per square mile (2007); Average household size: 2.52 (2007); Median age: 35.0 (2007); Males per 100 females: 96.7 (2007); Marriage status: 16.9% never married, 69.2% now married, 7.1% widowed, 6.8% divorced (2000); Foreign born: 1.7% (2000); Ancestry (includes multiple ancestries): 36.9% German, 15.8% English, 13.3% Irish, 7.6% United States or American, 5.2% Other groups (2000).
Economy: Single-family building permits issued: 52 (2007); Multi-family building permits issued: 0 (2007); Employment by occupation: 14.6% management, 19.6% professional, 14.1% services, 29.9% sales, 0.8% farming, 11.0% construction, 9.9% production (2000).
Income: Per capita income: $26,652 (2007); Median household income: $62,588 (2007); Average household income: $66,648 (2007); Percent of households with income of $100,000 or more: 15.6% (2007); Poverty rate: 4.3% (2000).
Education: Percent of population age 25 and over with: High school diploma (including GED) or higher: 92.4% (2007); Bachelor's degree or higher: 26.7% (2007); Master's degree or higher: 10.4% (2007).
School District(s)
St Joseph CCSD 169 (PK-08)
2005-06 Enrollment: 795 . . . . (217) 469-2291
St Joseph Ogden CHSD 305 (09-12)
2005-06 Enrollment: 483 . . . . (217) 469-2586
Housing: Homeownership rate: 82.7% (2007); Median home value: $145,040 (2007); Median rent: $367 per month (2000); Median age of housing: 24 years (2000).
Transportation: Commute to work: 94.5% car, 0.4% public transportation, 1.1% walk, 3.3% work from home (2000); Travel time to work: 23.7% less than 15 minutes, 58.9% 15 to 30 minutes, 12.8% 30 to 45 minutes, 0.3% 45 to 60 minutes, 4.3% 60 minutes or more (2000)

SAVOY (village). Covers a land area of 1.543 square miles and a water area of 0.016 square miles. Located at 40.06° N. Lat.; 88.25° W. Long. Elevation is 735 feet.
Population: 3,097 (1990); 4,476 (2000); 5,164 (2007); 5,585 (2012 projected); Race: 77.5% White, 4.3% Black, 13.8% Asian, 2.7% Hispanic of any race (2007); Density: 3,345.7 persons per square mile (2007); Average household size: 2.14 (2007); Median age: 34.2 (2007); Males per 100 females: 87.4 (2007); Marriage status: 24.5% never married, 60.0% now married, 8.2% widowed, 7.3% divorced (2000); Foreign born: 11.5% (2000); Ancestry (includes multiple ancestries): 25.6% German, 15.5% English, 15.1% Other groups, 10.9% Irish, 10.5% United States or American (2000).
Economy: Single-family building permits issued: 46 (2007); Multi-family building permits issued: 2 (2007); Employment by occupation: 16.1% management, 41.5% professional, 11.2% services, 21.1% sales, 0.2% farming, 5.0% construction, 5.0% production (2000).
Income: Per capita income: $32,767 (2007); Median household income: $57,892 (2007); Average household income: $69,266 (2007); Percent of households with income of $100,000 or more: 20.8% (2007); Poverty rate: 9.1% (2000).
Education: Percent of population age 25 and over with: High school diploma (including GED) or higher: 96.5% (2007); Bachelor's degree or higher: 58.6% (2007); Master's degree or higher: 30.6% (2007).
Housing: Homeownership rate: 45.3% (2007); Median home value: $191,964 (2007); Median rent: $588 per month (2000); Median age of housing: 13 years (2000).
Transportation: Commute to work: 89.2% car, 5.4% public transportation, 0.3% walk, 4.0% work from home (2000); Travel time to work: 44.0% less than 15 minutes, 45.9% 15 to 30 minutes, 4.9% 30 to 45 minutes, 1.9% 45 to 60 minutes, 3.3% 60 minutes or more (2000)
Airports: University of Illinois-Willard (primary service)

SEYMOUR (unincorporated postal area, zip code 61875). Covers a land area of 30.015 square miles and a water area of 0 square miles. Located at 40.10° N. Lat.; 88.42° W. Long. Elevation is 699 feet.
Population: 795 (2000); Race: 100.0% White, 0.0% Black, 0.0% Asian, 0.0% Hispanic of any race (2000); Density: 26.5 persons per square mile

(2000); Age: 30.3% under 18, 6.7% over 64 (2000); Marriage status: 24.0% never married, 68.7% now married, 1.5% widowed, 5.8% divorced (2000); Foreign born: 1.1% (2000); Ancestry (includes multiple ancestries): 31.6% German, 31.2% Irish, 14.1% English, 6.6% Scottish, 5.2% United States or American (2000).
Economy: Employment by occupation: 20.8% management, 13.7% professional, 16.5% services, 20.6% sales, 0.0% farming, 7.3% construction, 21.1% production (2000).
Income: Per capita income: $29,477 (2000); Median household income: $68,750 (2000); Poverty rate: 1.2% (2000).
Education: Percent of population age 25 and over with: High school diploma (including GED) or higher: 98.9% (2000); Bachelor's degree or higher: 30.0% (2000).
Housing: Homeownership rate: 81.7% (2000); Median home value: $118,800 (2000); Median rent: $298 per month (2000); Median age of housing: 39 years (2000).
Transportation: Commute to work: 88.1% car, 3.8% public transportation, 3.1% walk, 5.0% work from home (2000); Travel time to work: 17.8% less than 15 minutes, 50.6% 15 to 30 minutes, 17.8% 30 to 45 minutes, 8.8% 45 to 60 minutes, 5.0% 60 minutes or more (2000)

SIDNEY (village). Covers a land area of 0.532 square miles and a water area of 0 square miles. Located at 40.02° N. Lat.; 88.07° W. Long. Elevation is 656 feet.
Population: 1,027 (1990); 1,062 (2000); 992 (2007); 999 (2012 projected); Race: 97.0% White, 0.3% Black, 0.5% Asian, 0.3% Hispanic of any race (2007); Density: 1,864.2 persons per square mile (2007); Average household size: 2.46 (2007); Median age: 34.8 (2007); Males per 100 females: 95.7 (2007); Marriage status: 18.6% never married, 64.2% now married, 8.0% widowed, 9.1% divorced (2000); Foreign born: 0.0% (2000); Ancestry (includes multiple ancestries): 34.5% German, 15.8% United States or American, 12.2% Irish, 11.8% English, 4.7% Other groups (2000).
Economy: Single-family building permits issued: 4 (2007); Multi-family building permits issued: 4 (2007); Employment by occupation: 11.2% management, 19.2% professional, 13.7% services, 31.1% sales, 0.0% farming, 11.6% construction, 13.2% production (2000).
Income: Per capita income: $27,467 (2007); Median household income: $60,462 (2007); Average household income: $67,444 (2007); Percent of households with income of $100,000 or more: 18.6% (2007); Poverty rate: 0.9% (2000).
Education: Percent of population age 25 and over with: High school diploma (including GED) or higher: 87.8% (2007); Bachelor's degree or higher: 20.8% (2007); Master's degree or higher: 7.6% (2007).
Housing: Homeownership rate: 80.2% (2007); Median home value: $125,000 (2007); Median rent: $421 per month (2000); Median age of housing: 34 years (2000).
Transportation: Commute to work: 93.3% car, 0.0% public transportation, 0.7% walk, 5.0% work from home (2000); Travel time to work: 9.6% less than 15 minutes, 60.5% 15 to 30 minutes, 22.6% 30 to 45 minutes, 3.3% 45 to 60 minutes, 3.9% 60 minutes or more (2000)

THOMASBORO (village). Covers a land area of 1.035 square miles and a water area of 0 square miles. Located at 40.24° N. Lat.; 88.18° W. Long. Elevation is 732 feet.
Population: 1,250 (1990); 1,233 (2000); 1,197 (2007); 1,163 (2012 projected); Race: 95.7% White, 0.7% Black, 0.7% Asian, 1.3% Hispanic of any race (2007); Density: 1,156.4 persons per square mile (2007); Average household size: 2.41 (2007); Median age: 34.0 (2007); Males per 100 females: 96.9 (2007); Marriage status: 18.5% never married, 60.2% now married, 7.1% widowed, 14.2% divorced (2000); Foreign born: 2.6% (2000); Ancestry (includes multiple ancestries): 30.8% German, 10.7% English, 10.2% Irish, 9.8% United States or American, 8.2% Other groups (2000).
Economy: Single-family building permits issued: 4 (2007); Multi-family building permits issued: 0 (2007); Employment by occupation: 9.0% management, 9.0% professional, 18.0% services, 25.1% sales, 0.3% farming, 11.6% construction, 27.0% production (2000).
Income: Per capita income: $20,631 (2007); Median household income: $43,485 (2007); Average household income: $49,788 (2007); Percent of households with income of $100,000 or more: 5.2% (2007); Poverty rate: 4.8% (2000).
Education: Percent of population age 25 and over with: High school diploma (including GED) or higher: 80.2% (2007); Bachelor's degree or higher: 9.2% (2007); Master's degree or higher: 3.2% (2007).

School District(s)

Prairieview Ccd 192 (KG-08)
2005-06 Enrollment: 140 . . . . (217) 583-3300
Thomasboro CCSD 130 (KG-08)
2005-06 Enrollment: 185 . . . . (217) 643-3275

Housing: Homeownership rate: 74.2% (2007); Median home value: $96,190 (2007); Median rent: $342 per month (2000); Median age of housing: 29 years (2000).
Safety: Violent crime rate: 57.3 per 10,000 population; Property crime rate: 171.8 per 10,000 population (2006).
Transportation: Commute to work: 94.9% car, 0.0% public transportation, 0.7% walk, 1.9% work from home (2000); Travel time to work: 24.0% less than 15 minutes, 57.8% 15 to 30 minutes, 15.9% 30 to 45 minutes, 1.6% 45 to 60 minutes, 0.7% 60 minutes or more (2000)

TOLONO (village). Covers a land area of 1.869 square miles and a water area of 0 square miles. Located at 39.98° N. Lat.; 88.26° W. Long. Elevation is 735 feet.
History: The name of Tolono was made up by J.B. Calhoun of the Illinois Central Railroad.
Population: 2,619 (1990); 2,700 (2000); 2,971 (2007); 3,113 (2012 projected); Race: 97.4% White, 0.3% Black, 0.1% Asian, 1.2% Hispanic of any race (2007); Density: 1,589.4 persons per square mile (2007); Average household size: 2.44 (2007); Median age: 34.9 (2007); Males per 100 females: 102.9 (2007); Marriage status: 20.8% never married, 61.7% now married, 6.4% widowed, 11.1% divorced (2000); Foreign born: 0.6% (2000); Ancestry (includes multiple ancestries): 27.6% German, 11.2% English, 10.4% Irish, 8.2% United States or American, 5.4% Other groups (2000).
Economy: Single-family building permits issued: 12 (2007); Multi-family building permits issued: 5 (2007); Employment by occupation: 11.1% management, 15.5% professional, 19.9% services, 29.4% sales, 0.3% farming, 13.4% construction, 10.4% production (2000).
Income: Per capita income: $25,184 (2007); Median household income: $54,379 (2007); Average household income: $61,330 (2007); Percent of households with income of $100,000 or more: 14.0% (2007); Poverty rate: 5.6% (2000).
Education: Percent of population age 25 and over with: High school diploma (including GED) or higher: 89.5% (2007); Bachelor's degree or higher: 15.7% (2007); Master's degree or higher: 5.1% (2007).

School District(s)

Tolono CUSD 7 (PK-12)
2005-06 Enrollment: 1,514 . . . . (217) 485-6510

Housing: Homeownership rate: 79.0% (2007); Median home value: $108,273 (2007); Median rent: $358 per month (2000); Median age of housing: 30 years (2000).
Safety: Violent crime rate: 21.6 per 10,000 population; Property crime rate: 169.3 per 10,000 population (2006).
Transportation: Commute to work: 94.2% car, 0.0% public transportation, 1.3% walk, 3.3% work from home (2000); Travel time to work: 22.7% less than 15 minutes, 60.4% 15 to 30 minutes, 11.1% 30 to 45 minutes, 3.8% 45 to 60 minutes, 2.0% 60 minutes or more (2000)

URBANA (city). County seat. Covers a land area of 10.494 square miles and a water area of 0.012 square miles. Located at 40.11° N. Lat.; 88.20° W. Long. Elevation is 728 feet.
History: Urbana was settled in 1822 by Willard Tompkins. Although designated as the county seat in 1833, the loss of the railroad to nearby Champaign in 1854 slowed Urbana's development. When the Illinois Industrial College, later to become the University of Illinois, was sited between Urbana and Champaign in 1867, the character of Urbana was determined.
Population: 37,214 (1990); 36,395 (2000); 37,654 (2007); 38,297 (2012 projected); Race: 63.8% White, 14.1% Black, 16.4% Asian, 4.6% Hispanic of any race (2007); Density: 3,588.3 persons per square mile (2007); Average household size: 2.51 (2007); Median age: 26.0 (2007); Males per 100 females: 113.3 (2007); Marriage status: 53.6% never married, 35.6% now married, 4.1% widowed, 6.7% divorced (2000); Foreign born: 15.8% (2000); Ancestry (includes multiple ancestries): 32.6% Other groups, 20.5% German, 10.9% Irish, 9.8% English, 4.1% Polish (2000).
Economy: Unemployment rate: 4.4% (4/2008); Total civilian labor force: 21,369 (4/2008); Single-family building permits issued: 83 (2007); Multi-family building permits issued: 328 (2007); Employment by occupation: 7.3% management, 45.6% professional, 14.8% services, 21.7% sales, 0.3% farming, 3.6% construction, 6.7% production (2000).

Income: Per capita income: $18,796 (2007); Median household income: $31,331 (2007); Average household income: $44,979 (2007); Percent of households with income of $100,000 or more: 8.7% (2007); Poverty rate: 27.3% (2000).
Education: Percent of population age 25 and over with: High school diploma (including GED) or higher: 91.2% (2007); Bachelor's degree or higher: 54.3% (2007); Master's degree or higher: 33.1% (2007).

School District(s)

Champaign/Ford Roe (05-12)
2005-06 Enrollment: 106 . . . . (217) 893-3219
University of Illinois Lab School (08-12)
2005-06 Enrollment: 306 . . . . (217) 333-2870
Urbana SD 116 (PK-12)
2005-06 Enrollment: 4,370 . . . . (217) 384-3636

Two-year College(s)

Mr John's School of Cosmetology & Nails (Private, For-profit)
Fall 2007 Enrollment: 33 . . . . (217) 328-2590

Vocational/Technical School(s)

Concept College of Cosmetology (Private, For-profit)
Fall 2007 Enrollment: 115 . . . . (217) 344-7550
2007-08 Tuition: $8,950

Housing: Homeownership rate: 37.5% (2007); Median home value: $121,474 (2007); Median rent: $463 per month (2000); Median age of housing: 31 years (2000).
Hospitals: Carle Foundation Hospital (305 beds); Provena Covenant Medical Center (268 beds)
Safety: Violent crime rate: 84.0 per 10,000 population; Property crime rate: 395.4 per 10,000 population (2006).
Transportation: Commute to work: 63.8% car, 10.9% public transportation, 17.0% walk, 3.2% work from home (2000); Travel time to work: 57.3% less than 15 minutes, 34.0% 15 to 30 minutes, 5.1% 30 to 45 minutes, 1.7% 45 to 60 minutes, 2.0% 60 minutes or more (2000); Amtrak: Service available.

Additional Information Contacts

City of Urbana . . . . (217) 384-2366
http://www.city.urbana.il.us/Urbana

Christian County

Located in central Illinois; bounded on the north by the Sangamon River; drained by the South Fork of the Sangamon River. Covers a land area of 709.06 square miles, a water area of 6.65 square miles, and is located in the Central Time Zone. The county was founded in 1839. County seat is Taylorville.

Christian County is part of the Taylorville, IL Micropolitan Statistical Area. The entire metro area includes: Christian County, IL

Weather Station: Pana 3 E — Elevation: 698 feet

	Jan	Feb	Mar	Apr	May	Jun	Jul	Aug	Sep	Oct	Nov	Dec
High	35	41	53	65	75	84	87	85	79	67	53	40
Low	18	23	33	43	53	62	66	63	56	45	35	24
Precip	2.2	2.2	3.5	4.0	4.0	4.5	3.9	3.0	3.1	2.9	3.8	3.2
Snow	7.4	5.0	4.2	0.9	tr	0.0	0.0	0.0	0.0	0.1	1.8	5.4

High and Low temperatures in degrees Fahrenheit; Precipitation and Snow in inches

Population: 34,418 (1990); 35,372 (2000); 35,163 (2007); 34,950 (2012 projected); Race: 95.7% White, 2.5% Black, 0.6% Asian, 1.1% Hispanic of any race (2007); Density: 49.6 persons per square mile (2007); Average household size: 2.51 (2007); Median age: 39.9 (2007); Males per 100 females: 101.8 (2007).
Religion: Five largest groups: 16.5% Catholic Church, 9.0% The United Methodist Church, 5.0% Christian Churches and Churches of Christ, 4.1% Lutheran Church—Missouri Synod, 2.9% American Baptist Churches in the USA (2000).
Economy: Unemployment rate: 5.3% (4/2008); Total civilian labor force: 17,862 (4/2008); Leading industries: 35.5% professional, scientific & technical services; 12.8% health care and social assistance; 11.4% retail trade (2005); Farms: 796 totaling 410,549 acres (2002); Companies that employ 500 or more persons: 2 (2006); Companies that employ 100 to 499 persons: 13 (2006); Companies that employ less than 100 persons: 782 (2006); Black-owned businesses: n/a (2002); Hispanic-owned businesses: n/a (2002); Asian-owned businesses: n/a (2002); Women-owned businesses: n/a (2002); Retail sales per capita: $13,328 (2008). Single-family building permits issued: 48 (2007); Multi-family building permits issued: 0 (2007).
Income: Per capita income: $21,501 (2007); Median household income: $42,530 (2007); Average household income: $52,116 (2007); Percent of households with income of $100,000 or more: 9.4% (2007); Poverty rate: 11.4% (2005); Bankruptcy rate: 3.97% (2007).
Taxes: Total county taxes per capita: $81 (2006); County property taxes per capita: $79 (2006).
Education: Percent of population age 25 and over with: High school diploma (including GED) or higher: 81.2% (2007); Bachelor's degree or higher: 10.8% (2007); Master's degree or higher: 3.5% (2007).
Housing: Homeownership rate: 76.6% (2007); Median home value: $88,942 (2007); Median rent: $297 per month (2000); Median age of housing: 47 years (2000).
Health: Birth rate: 120.7 per 10,000 population (2007); Death rate: 117.2 per 10,000 population (2007); Age-adjusted cancer mortality rate: 260.3 deaths per 100,000 population (2005); Number of physicians: 7.7 per 10,000 population (2005); Hospital beds: 49.7 per 10,000 population (2004); Hospital admissions: 877.2 per 10,000 population (2004).
Elections: 2004 Presidential election results: 59.2% Bush, 40.0% Kerry, 0.0% Nader, 0.7% Badnarik

Additional Information Contacts

Christian County Government . . . . (217) 824-4969

City of Taylorville . . . . (217) 824-2101
http://www.taylorville.net
Pana Chamber of Commerce . . . . (217) 562-4240
http://www.panachamber.com
The Greater Taylorville Chamber of Commerce . . . . (217) 824-4919
http://www.taylorvillechamber.com

Christian County Communities

ASSUMPTION (city). Covers a land area of 0.880 square miles and a water area of 0 square miles. Located at 39.52° N. Lat.; 89.04° W. Long. Elevation is 646 feet.
History: Incorporated 1902.
Population: 1,244 (1990); 1,261 (2000); 1,254 (2007); 1,258 (2012 projected); Race: 99.8% White, 0.0% Black, 0.2% Asian, 0.2% Hispanic of any race (2007); Density: 1,425.2 persons per square mile (2007); Average household size: 2.26 (2007); Median age: 40.0 (2007); Males per 100 females: 85.0 (2007); Marriage status: 18.5% never married, 60.6% now married, 11.4% widowed, 9.5% divorced (2000); Foreign born: 0.7% (2000); Ancestry (includes multiple ancestries): 21.3% German, 14.9% Irish, 10.5% United States or American, 9.3% English, 3.8% French (except Basque) (2000).
Economy: Single-family building permits issued: 1 (2007); Multi-family building permits issued: 0 (2007); Employment by occupation: 10.2% management, 14.9% professional, 16.8% services, 20.5% sales, 1.0% farming, 10.6% construction, 26.0% production (2000).
Income: Per capita income: $20,534 (2007); Median household income: $40,930 (2007); Average household income: $46,313 (2007); Percent of households with income of $100,000 or more: 5.2% (2007); Poverty rate: 9.5% (2000).
Education: Percent of population age 25 and over with: High school diploma (including GED) or higher: 84.6% (2007); Bachelor's degree or higher: 11.1% (2007); Master's degree or higher: 3.4% (2007).

School District(s)

Central A & M Cud 21 (PK-12)
2005-06 Enrollment: 965 . . . . (217) 226-4042

Housing: Homeownership rate: 77.7% (2007); Median home value: $65,714 (2007); Median rent: $269 per month (2000); Median age of housing: 59 years (2000).
Safety: Violent crime rate: 8.1 per 10,000 population; Property crime rate: 24.4 per 10,000 population (2006).
Newspapers: Golden Prairie News (Community news; Circulation 2,200)
Transportation: Commute to work: 95.4% car, 0.7% public transportation, 2.7% walk, 0.5% work from home (2000); Travel time to work: 46.9% less than 15 minutes, 16.2% 15 to 30 minutes, 21.7% 30 to 45 minutes, 5.7% 45 to 60 minutes, 9.6% 60 minutes or more (2000)

BULPITT (village). Covers a land area of 0.071 square miles and a water area of 0 square miles. Located at 39.59° N. Lat.; 89.42° W. Long. Elevation is 600 feet.
Population: 206 (1990); 206 (2000); 210 (2007); 210 (2012 projected); Race: 100.0% White, 0.0% Black, 0.0% Asian, 0.0% Hispanic of any race (2007); Density: 2,965.4 persons per square mile (2007); Average

household size: 2.12 (2007); Median age: 48.6 (2007); Males per 100 females: 87.5 (2007); Marriage status: 24.6% never married, 42.5% now married, 18.4% widowed, 14.5% divorced (2000); Foreign born: 0.0% (2000); Ancestry (includes multiple ancestries): 24.9% United States or American, 15.1% English, 14.6% Irish, 13.2% German, 5.9% Lithuanian (2000).
Economy: Single-family building permits issued: 0 (2007); Multi-family building permits issued: 0 (2007); Employment by occupation: 13.8% management, 7.5% professional, 22.5% services, 26.3% sales, 0.0% farming, 22.5% construction, 7.5% production (2000).
Income: Per capita income: $19,298 (2007); Median household income: $33,654 (2007); Average household income: $40,934 (2007); Percent of households with income of $100,000 or more: 4.0% (2007); Poverty rate: 8.3% (2000).
Education: Percent of population age 25 and over with: High school diploma (including GED) or higher: 69.0% (2007); Bachelor's degree or higher: 7.0% (2007); Master's degree or higher: 3.2% (2007).
Housing: Homeownership rate: 82.8% (2007); Median home value: $58,571 (2007); Median rent: $225 per month (2000); Median age of housing: 60+ years (2000).
Transportation: Commute to work: 97.5% car, 0.0% public transportation, 0.0% walk, 2.5% work from home (2000); Travel time to work: 30.8% less than 15 minutes, 21.8% 15 to 30 minutes, 30.8% 30 to 45 minutes, 16.7% 45 to 60 minutes, 0.0% 60 minutes or more (2000)

EDINBURG (village). Covers a land area of 0.581 square miles and a water area of 0 square miles. Located at 39.65° N. Lat.; 89.39° W. Long. Elevation is 591 feet.
Population: 1,074 (1990); 1,135 (2000); 1,152 (2007); 1,144 (2012 projected); Race: 99.0% White, 0.1% Black, 0.2% Asian, 0.6% Hispanic of any race (2007); Density: 1,981.7 persons per square mile (2007); Average household size: 2.29 (2007); Median age: 39.7 (2007); Males per 100 females: 92.0 (2007); Marriage status: 16.7% never married, 62.6% now married, 8.7% widowed, 12.0% divorced (2000); Foreign born: 0.8% (2000); Ancestry (includes multiple ancestries): 24.2% German, 13.0% Irish, 12.9% English, 11.7% United States or American, 7.2% Other groups (2000).
Economy: Single-family building permits issued: 1 (2007); Multi-family building permits issued: 0 (2007); Employment by occupation: 8.4% management, 12.0% professional, 13.9% services, 37.2% sales, 1.0% farming, 10.8% construction, 16.5% production (2000).
Income: Per capita income: $21,497 (2007); Median household income: $42,738 (2007); Average household income: $49,333 (2007); Percent of households with income of $100,000 or more: 7.8% (2007); Poverty rate: 8.5% (2000).
Education: Percent of population age 25 and over with: High school diploma (including GED) or higher: 88.2% (2007); Bachelor's degree or higher: 10.8% (2007); Master's degree or higher: 2.4% (2007).

School District(s)

Edinburg CUSD 4 (PK-12)
2005-06 Enrollment: 386 . . . . (217) 623-5603
Housing: Homeownership rate: 75.5% (2007); Median home value: $93,788 (2007); Median rent: $348 per month (2000); Median age of housing: 46 years (2000).
Newspapers: Herald Star (Community news; Circulation 750)
Transportation: Commute to work: 91.4% car, 0.7% public transportation, 2.3% walk, 3.8% work from home (2000); Travel time to work: 14.3% less than 15 minutes, 27.2% 15 to 30 minutes, 47.7% 30 to 45 minutes, 5.6% 45 to 60 minutes, 5.1% 60 minutes or more (2000)

JEISYVILLE (village). Covers a land area of 0.058 square miles and a water area of 0 square miles. Located at 39.57° N. Lat.; 89.40° W. Long. Elevation is 581 feet.
Population: 126 (1990); 128 (2000); 125 (2007); 123 (2012 projected); Race: 98.4% White, 1.6% Black, 0.0% Asian, 0.0% Hispanic of any race (2007); Density: 2,153.8 persons per square mile (2007); Average household size: 2.55 (2007); Median age: 34.5 (2007); Males per 100 females: 111.9 (2007); Marriage status: 4.4% never married, 64.7% now married, 23.5% widowed, 7.4% divorced (2000); Foreign born: 0.0% (2000); Ancestry (includes multiple ancestries): 22.2% Irish, 21.1% English, 15.6% Italian, 14.4% United States or American, 13.3% Other groups (2000).
Economy: Employment by occupation: 0.0% management, 15.0% professional, 10.0% services, 40.0% sales, 0.0% farming, 15.0% construction, 20.0% production (2000).
Income: Per capita income: $15,640 (2007); Median household income: $36,250 (2007); Average household income: $39,898 (2007); Percent of households with income of $100,000 or more: 4.1% (2007); Poverty rate: 4.4% (2000).
Education: Percent of population age 25 and over with: High school diploma (including GED) or higher: 62.5% (2007); Bachelor's degree or higher: 8.0% (2007); Master's degree or higher: 0.0% (2007).
Housing: Homeownership rate: 83.7% (2007); Median home value: $51,667 (2007); Median rent: $188 per month (2000); Median age of housing: 60+ years (2000).
Transportation: Commute to work: 100.0% car, 0.0% public transportation, 0.0% walk, 0.0% work from home (2000); Travel time to work: 30.0% less than 15 minutes, 45.0% 15 to 30 minutes, 25.0% 30 to 45 minutes, 0.0% 45 to 60 minutes, 0.0% 60 minutes or more (2000)

KINCAID (village). Covers a land area of 0.624 square miles and a water area of 0 square miles. Located at 39.58° N. Lat.; 89.41° W. Long. Elevation is 600 feet.
History: Incorporated 1915.
Population: 1,381 (1990); 1,441 (2000); 1,430 (2007); 1,427 (2012 projected); Race: 99.0% White, 0.0% Black, 0.0% Asian, 0.6% Hispanic of any race (2007); Density: 2,292.2 persons per square mile (2007); Average household size: 2.35 (2007); Median age: 36.5 (2007); Males per 100 females: 96.7 (2007); Marriage status: 17.9% never married, 57.2% now married, 11.5% widowed, 13.4% divorced (2000); Foreign born: 0.5% (2000); Ancestry (includes multiple ancestries): 16.8% German, 13.1% Irish, 11.6% Italian, 11.4% United States or American, 6.9% English (2000).
Economy: Single-family building permits issued: 6 (2007); Multi-family building permits issued: 0 (2007); Employment by occupation: 9.5% management, 13.6% professional, 17.7% services, 25.5% sales, 1.0% farming, 13.3% construction, 19.4% production (2000).
Income: Per capita income: $20,505 (2007); Median household income: $42,111 (2007); Average household income: $48,228 (2007); Percent of households with income of $100,000 or more: 6.9% (2007); Poverty rate: 10.5% (2000).
Education: Percent of population age 25 and over with: High school diploma (including GED) or higher: 78.8% (2007); Bachelor's degree or higher: 6.2% (2007); Master's degree or higher: 2.1% (2007).

School District(s)

South Fork SD 14 (PK-12)
2005-06 Enrollment: 426 . . . . (217) 237-4333
Housing: Homeownership rate: 81.1% (2007); Median home value: $69,044 (2007); Median rent: $269 per month (2000); Median age of housing: 54 years (2000).
Safety: Violent crime rate: 20.4 per 10,000 population; Property crime rate: 54.5 per 10,000 population (2006).
Transportation: Commute to work: 95.6% car, 0.5% public transportation, 1.8% walk, 1.3% work from home (2000); Travel time to work: 28.6% less than 15 minutes, 22.7% 15 to 30 minutes, 30.6% 30 to 45 minutes, 12.8% 45 to 60 minutes, 5.3% 60 minutes or more (2000)

MORRISONVILLE (village). Covers a land area of 1.031 square miles and a water area of 0 square miles. Located at 39.41° N. Lat.; 89.45° W. Long. Elevation is 630 feet.
History: Incorporated 1872.
Population: 1,113 (1990); 1,068 (2000); 912 (2007); 902 (2012 projected); Race: 98.6% White, 0.1% Black, 1.0% Asian, 0.7% Hispanic of any race (2007); Density: 884.2 persons per square mile (2007); Average household size: 2.39 (2007); Median age: 41.8 (2007); Males per 100 females: 102.7 (2007); Marriage status: 17.5% never married, 68.5% now married, 6.3% widowed, 7.7% divorced (2000); Foreign born: 0.8% (2000); Ancestry (includes multiple ancestries): 24.3% German, 19.8% Irish, 12.7% United States or American, 12.6% English, 5.5% Other groups (2000).
Economy: Employment by occupation: 12.3% management, 11.5% professional, 17.6% services, 29.1% sales, 1.2% farming, 13.0% construction, 15.4% production (2000).
Income: Per capita income: $22,453 (2007); Median household income: $42,763 (2007); Average household income: $53,747 (2007); Percent of households with income of $100,000 or more: 11.5% (2007); Poverty rate: 6.2% (2000).
Education: Percent of population age 25 and over with: High school diploma (including GED) or higher: 83.3% (2007); Bachelor's degree or higher: 12.2% (2007); Master's degree or higher: 4.5% (2007).

School District(s)

Christian/Montgomery Roe (06-11)
2005-06 Enrollment: 23 . . . . (217) 532-9591
Morrisonville CUSD 1 (PK-12)
2005-06 Enrollment: 357 . . . . (217) 526-4431

Housing: Homeownership rate: 83.5% (2007); Median home value: $76,750 (2007); Median rent: $278 per month (2000); Median age of housing: 59 years (2000).
Newspapers: Morrisonville Times (Community news; Circulation 1,000)
Transportation: Commute to work: 93.8% car, 0.0% public transportation, 1.0% walk, 4.2% work from home (2000); Travel time to work: 30.8% less than 15 minutes, 23.0% 15 to 30 minutes, 17.6% 30 to 45 minutes, 18.4% 45 to 60 minutes, 10.3% 60 minutes or more (2000)

MOUNT AUBURN (village). Covers a land area of 0.991 square miles and a water area of 0.001 square miles. Located at 39.76° N. Lat.; 89.26° W. Long. Elevation is 699 feet.
Population: 544 (1990); 515 (2000); 485 (2007); 485 (2012 projected); Race: 98.1% White, 0.0% Black, 0.0% Asian, 0.6% Hispanic of any race (2007); Density: 489.4 persons per square mile (2007); Average household size: 2.26 (2007); Median age: 43.2 (2007); Males per 100 females: 88.7 (2007); Marriage status: 21.4% never married, 61.4% now married, 6.4% widowed, 10.8% divorced (2000); Foreign born: 1.6% (2000); Ancestry (includes multiple ancestries): 24.4% United States or American, 23.4% German, 11.5% Irish, 6.8% Other groups, 6.4% English (2000).
Economy: Single-family building permits issued: 3 (2007); Multi-family building permits issued: 0 (2007); Employment by occupation: 7.8% management, 10.1% professional, 14.7% services, 30.4% sales, 3.3% farming, 11.1% construction, 22.5% production (2000).
Income: Per capita income: $25,773 (2007); Median household income: $53,214 (2007); Average household income: $58,140 (2007); Percent of households with income of $100,000 or more: 11.6% (2007); Poverty rate: 2.4% (2000).
Education: Percent of population age 25 and over with: High school diploma (including GED) or higher: 84.3% (2007); Bachelor's degree or higher: 7.2% (2007); Master's degree or higher: 1.9% (2007).

School District(s)

Taylorville CUSD 3 (PK-12)
2005-06 Enrollment: 3,095 . . . . (217) 824-4951

Housing: Homeownership rate: 84.2% (2007); Median home value: $71,316 (2007); Median rent: $283 per month (2000); Median age of housing: 36 years (2000).
Transportation: Commute to work: 94.4% car, 0.0% public transportation, 1.3% walk, 3.6% work from home (2000); Travel time to work: 13.4% less than 15 minutes, 29.8% 15 to 30 minutes, 41.8% 30 to 45 minutes, 12.0% 45 to 60 minutes, 3.1% 60 minutes or more (2000)

OWANECO (village). Covers a land area of 0.458 square miles and a water area of 0 square miles. Located at 39.48° N. Lat.; 89.19° W. Long. Elevation is 620 feet.
Population: 260 (1990); 256 (2000); 276 (2007); 287 (2012 projected); Race: 99.6% White, 0.0% Black, 0.0% Asian, 0.0% Hispanic of any race (2007); Density: 602.9 persons per square mile (2007); Average household size: 2.58 (2007); Median age: 35.3 (2007); Males per 100 females: 100.0 (2007); Marriage status: 12.8% never married, 72.3% now married, 8.2% widowed, 6.7% divorced (2000); Foreign born: 0.0% (2000); Ancestry (includes multiple ancestries): 33.2% German, 12.9% United States or American, 12.1% Irish, 9.0% English, 8.2% Italian (2000).
Economy: Employment by occupation: 2.5% management, 15.8% professional, 22.5% services, 27.5% sales, 1.7% farming, 10.0% construction, 20.0% production (2000).
Income: Per capita income: $17,899 (2007); Median household income: $42,500 (2007); Average household income: $46,168 (2007); Percent of households with income of $100,000 or more: 4.7% (2007); Poverty rate: 10.2% (2000).
Education: Percent of population age 25 and over with: High school diploma (including GED) or higher: 77.7% (2007); Bachelor's degree or higher: 8.6% (2007); Master's degree or higher: 2.9% (2007).
Housing: Homeownership rate: 81.3% (2007); Median home value: $78,929 (2007); Median rent: $254 per month (2000); Median age of housing: 57 years (2000).
Transportation: Commute to work: 92.5% car, 0.0% public transportation, 2.5% walk, 0.0% work from home (2000); Travel time to work: 22.5% less than 15 minutes, 35.0% 15 to 30 minutes, 10.8% 30 to 45 minutes, 23.3% 45 to 60 minutes, 8.3% 60 minutes or more (2000)

PALMER (village). Covers a land area of 0.998 square miles and a water area of 0 square miles. Located at 39.45° N. Lat.; 89.40° W. Long. Elevation is 623 feet.
Population: 275 (1990); 248 (2000); 222 (2007); 217 (2012 projected); Race: 96.8% White, 0.0% Black, 0.0% Asian, 0.0% Hispanic of any race (2007); Density: 222.5 persons per square mile (2007); Average household size: 2.71 (2007); Median age: 37.9 (2007); Males per 100 females: 89.7 (2007); Marriage status: 25.7% never married, 63.9% now married, 7.3% widowed, 3.1% divorced (2000); Foreign born: 0.4% (2000); Ancestry (includes multiple ancestries): 23.9% United States or American, 12.3% Irish, 11.9% Other groups, 6.2% German, 5.8% English (2000).
Economy: Single-family building permits issued: 0 (2007); Multi-family building permits issued: 0 (2007); Employment by occupation: 10.7% management, 12.6% professional, 26.2% services, 19.4% sales, 3.9% farming, 10.7% construction, 16.5% production (2000).
Income: Per capita income: $22,680 (2007); Median household income: $42,778 (2007); Average household income: $61,402 (2007); Percent of households with income of $100,000 or more: 9.8% (2007); Poverty rate: 5.3% (2000).
Education: Percent of population age 25 and over with: High school diploma (including GED) or higher: 72.0% (2007); Bachelor's degree or higher: 2.8% (2007); Master's degree or higher: 0.0% (2007).
Housing: Homeownership rate: 84.1% (2007); Median home value: $63,000 (2007); Median rent: $268 per month (2000); Median age of housing: 54 years (2000).
Transportation: Commute to work: 91.3% car, 0.0% public transportation, 1.0% walk, 7.8% work from home (2000); Travel time to work: 37.9% less than 15 minutes, 43.2% 15 to 30 minutes, 5.3% 30 to 45 minutes, 6.3% 45 to 60 minutes, 7.4% 60 minutes or more (2000)

PANA (city). Covers a land area of 2.671 square miles and a water area of 0 square miles. Located at 39.38° N. Lat.; 89.08° W. Long. Elevation is 699 feet.
History: Pana developed as a center for rose cultivation, with acres of greenhouses warmed by steam heat.
Population: 5,903 (1990); 5,614 (2000); 5,479 (2007); 5,348 (2012 projected); Race: 99.1% White, 0.1% Black, 0.3% Asian, 0.5% Hispanic of any race (2007); Density: 2,051.1 persons per square mile (2007); Average household size: 2.40 (2007); Median age: 40.5 (2007); Males per 100 females: 88.7 (2007); Marriage status: 20.5% never married, 59.3% now married, 9.8% widowed, 10.4% divorced (2000); Foreign born: 0.8% (2000); Ancestry (includes multiple ancestries): 23.0% German, 13.1% United States or American, 11.0% Irish, 9.8% English, 7.1% Other groups (2000).
Economy: Single-family building permits issued: 7 (2007); Multi-family building permits issued: 0 (2007); Employment by occupation: 3.6% management, 14.8% professional, 23.5% services, 19.7% sales, 0.7% farming, 10.2% construction, 27.5% production (2000).
Income: Per capita income: $17,961 (2007); Median household income: $34,408 (2007); Average household income: $41,640 (2007); Percent of households with income of $100,000 or more: 4.7% (2007); Poverty rate: 17.6% (2000).
Education: Percent of population age 25 and over with: High school diploma (including GED) or higher: 75.5% (2007); Bachelor's degree or higher: 7.1% (2007); Master's degree or higher: 2.0% (2007).

School District(s)

Pana CUSD 8 (PK-12)
2005-06 Enrollment: 1,565 . . . . (217) 562-1500

Housing: Homeownership rate: 70.5% (2007); Median home value: $66,244 (2007); Median rent: $277 per month (2000); Median age of housing: 53 years (2000).
Hospitals: Pana Community Hospital (25 beds)
Safety: Violent crime rate: 18.1 per 10,000 population; Property crime rate: 157.4 per 10,000 population (2006).
Newspapers: Pana News Palladium (Local news; Circulation 4,600)
Transportation: Commute to work: 92.8% car, 1.9% public transportation, 2.4% walk, 1.1% work from home (2000); Travel time to work: 51.5% less than 15 minutes, 17.9% 15 to 30 minutes, 9.8% 30 to 45 minutes, 10.8% 45 to 60 minutes, 10.0% 60 minutes or more (2000)

Additional Information Contacts

Pana Chamber of Commerce . . . . (217) 562-4240
http://www.panachamber.com

ROSAMOND (unincorporated postal area, zip code 62083). Covers a land area of 22.766 square miles and a water area of 0 square miles. Located at 39.35° N. Lat.; 89.20° W. Long. Elevation is 709 feet.
Population: 317 (2000); Race: 100.0% White, 0.0% Black, 0.0% Asian, 0.0% Hispanic of any race (2000); Density: 13.9 persons per square mile (2000); Age: 32.2% under 18, 12.6% over 64 (2000); Marriage status: 25.7% never married, 37.7% now married, 15.4% widowed, 21.1% divorced (2000); Foreign born: 0.0% (2000); Ancestry (includes multiple ancestries): 54.8% German, 16.7% Irish, 13.0% French (except Basque), 7.5% United States or American, 3.8% Other groups (2000).
Economy: Employment by occupation: 4.3% management, 0.0% professional, 34.0% services, 7.4% sales, 11.7% farming, 19.1% construction, 23.4% production (2000).
Income: Per capita income: $16,027 (2000); Median household income: $27,750 (2000); Poverty rate: 22.5% (2000).
Education: Percent of population age 25 and over with: High school diploma (including GED) or higher: 91.9% (2000); Bachelor's degree or higher: 7.4% (2000).
Housing: Homeownership rate: 93.2% (2000); Median home value: $48,600 (2000); Median rent: $n/a per month (2000); Median age of housing: 51 years (2000).
Transportation: Commute to work: 95.7% car, 0.0% public transportation, 4.3% walk, 0.0% work from home (2000); Travel time to work: 17.0% less than 15 minutes, 31.9% 15 to 30 minutes, 16.0% 30 to 45 minutes, 12.8% 45 to 60 minutes, 22.3% 60 minutes or more (2000)

STONINGTON (village). Covers a land area of 0.454 square miles and a water area of 0 square miles. Located at 39.63° N. Lat.; 89.19° W. Long. Elevation is 610 feet.
History: Incorporated 1885.
Population: 1,010 (1990); 960 (2000); 819 (2007); 813 (2012 projected); Race: 99.8% White, 0.0% Black, 0.0% Asian, 0.5% Hispanic of any race (2007); Density: 1,803.8 persons per square mile (2007); Average household size: 2.39 (2007); Median age: 36.4 (2007); Males per 100 females: 94.1 (2007); Marriage status: 16.2% never married, 64.1% now married, 9.7% widowed, 10.0% divorced (2000); Foreign born: 0.3% (2000); Ancestry (includes multiple ancestries): 19.6% German, 14.9% Irish, 11.8% English, 10.1% United States or American, 6.8% Other groups (2000).
Economy: Single-family building permits issued: 1 (2007); Multi-family building permits issued: 0 (2007); Employment by occupation: 5.1% management, 13.2% professional, 15.4% services, 31.4% sales, 1.5% farming, 10.4% construction, 23.0% production (2000).
Income: Per capita income: $18,999 (2007); Median household income: $41,563 (2007); Average household income: $45,364 (2007); Percent of households with income of $100,000 or more: 6.1% (2007); Poverty rate: 11.3% (2000).
Education: Percent of population age 25 and over with: High school diploma (including GED) or higher: 81.2% (2007); Bachelor's degree or higher: 11.3% (2007); Master's degree or higher: 2.9% (2007).

School District(s)

Taylorville CUSD 3 (PK-12)
2005-06 Enrollment: 3,095 . . . . (217) 824-4951

Housing: Homeownership rate: 81.0% (2007); Median home value: $79,130 (2007); Median rent: $265 per month (2000); Median age of housing: 60+ years (2000).
Safety: Violent crime rate: 64.9 per 10,000 population; Property crime rate: 119.0 per 10,000 population (2006).
Transportation: Commute to work: 95.7% car, 0.5% public transportation, 1.8% walk, 2.0% work from home (2000); Travel time to work: 31.5% less than 15 minutes, 27.3% 15 to 30 minutes, 22.7% 30 to 45 minutes, 14.3% 45 to 60 minutes, 4.2% 60 minutes or more (2000)

TAYLORVILLE (city). County seat. Covers a land area of 8.067 square miles and a water area of 1.952 square miles. Located at 39.54° N. Lat.; 89.28° W. Long. Elevation is 627 feet.
History: Incorporated 1881.
Population: 11,332 (1990); 11,427 (2000); 11,198 (2007); 10,960 (2012 projected); Race: 97.6% White, 0.6% Black, 0.8% Asian, 0.8% Hispanic of any race (2007); Density: 1,388.2 persons per square mile (2007); Average household size: 2.34 (2007); Median age: 40.4 (2007); Males per 100 females: 91.8 (2007); Marriage status: 19.6% never married, 56.6% now married, 10.9% widowed, 12.9% divorced (2000); Foreign born: 2.0% (2000); Ancestry (includes multiple ancestries): 20.5% German, 12.0% United States or American, 11.5% Irish, 11.2% English, 8.5% Other groups (2000).
Economy: Single-family building permits issued: 9 (2007); Multi-family building permits issued: 0 (2007); Employment by occupation: 8.7% management, 18.3% professional, 16.1% services, 27.9% sales, 0.4% farming, 10.6% construction, 17.9% production (2000).
Income: Per capita income: $21,463 (2007); Median household income: $38,620 (2007); Average household income: $48,974 (2007); Percent of households with income of $100,000 or more: 8.2% (2007); Poverty rate: 10.1% (2000).
Education: Percent of population age 25 and over with: High school diploma (including GED) or higher: 82.1% (2007); Bachelor's degree or higher: 14.0% (2007); Master's degree or higher: 4.8% (2007).

School District(s)

Dept of Corrections Sch Dist 428 (08-12)
2005-06 Enrollment: 2,271 . . . . (217) 522-2666
Mid-State Spec Educ Jnt Agr
2005-06 Enrollment: n/a . . . . (217) 824-8121
Taylorville CUSD 3 (PK-12)
2005-06 Enrollment: 3,095 . . . . (217) 824-4951

Housing: Homeownership rate: 69.9% (2007); Median home value: $90,607 (2007); Median rent: $315 per month (2000); Median age of housing: 45 years (2000).
Hospitals: Taylorville Memorial Hospital
Safety: Violent crime rate: 108.5 per 10,000 population; Property crime rate: 425.3 per 10,000 population (2006).
Newspapers: The Breeze-Courier (Local news; Circulation 6,770)
Transportation: Commute to work: 93.7% car, 0.7% public transportation, 2.5% walk, 2.3% work from home (2000); Travel time to work: 55.9% less than 15 minutes, 9.7% 15 to 30 minutes, 16.5% 30 to 45 minutes, 13.5% 45 to 60 minutes, 4.4% 60 minutes or more (2000)

Additional Information Contacts

City of Taylorville . . . . (217) 824-2101
http://www.taylorville.net
The Greater Taylorville Chamber of Commerce . . . . (217) 824-4919
http://www.taylorvillechamber.com

TOVEY (village). Aka Humphrey. Covers a land area of 0.185 square miles and a water area of 0 square miles. Located at 39.58° N. Lat.; 89.44° W. Long. Elevation is 600 feet.
History: Also known as Humphrey.
Population: 533 (1990); 516 (2000); 527 (2007); 529 (2012 projected); Race: 99.1% White, 0.4% Black, 0.0% Asian, 0.0% Hispanic of any race (2007); Density: 2,850.7 persons per square mile (2007); Average household size: 2.38 (2007); Median age: 41.3 (2007); Males per 100 females: 95.2 (2007); Marriage status: 21.3% never married, 62.1% now married, 8.0% widowed, 8.7% divorced (2000); Foreign born: 0.4% (2000); Ancestry (includes multiple ancestries): 19.7% Italian, 19.5% Irish, 15.6% German, 14.2% English, 6.1% French (except Basque) (2000).
Economy: Single-family building permits issued: 0 (2007); Multi-family building permits issued: 0 (2007); Employment by occupation: 6.8% management, 11.3% professional, 11.3% services, 35.3% sales, 3.2% farming, 16.7% construction, 15.4% production (2000).
Income: Per capita income: $17,960 (2007); Median household income: $35,227 (2007); Average household income: $42,828 (2007); Percent of households with income of $100,000 or more: 5.4% (2007); Poverty rate: 11.4% (2000).
Education: Percent of population age 25 and over with: High school diploma (including GED) or higher: 75.6% (2007); Bachelor's degree or higher: 7.0% (2007); Master's degree or higher: 2.8% (2007).
Housing: Homeownership rate: 86.4% (2007); Median home value: $73,261 (2007); Median rent: $263 per month (2000); Median age of housing: 46 years (2000).
Transportation: Commute to work: 94.8% car, 0.0% public transportation, 1.9% walk, 0.9% work from home (2000); Travel time to work: 17.6% less than 15 minutes, 23.3% 15 to 30 minutes, 42.4% 30 to 45 minutes, 9.0% 45 to 60 minutes, 7.6% 60 minutes or more (2000)

Clark County

Located in eastern Illinois; bounded on the southeast by the Wabash River and the Indiana border; drained by the North Fork Embarrass River. Covers a land area of 501.50 square miles, a water area of 3.38 square miles, and is located in the Central Time Zone. The county was founded in 1819. County seat is Marshall.

Population: 15,921 (1990); 17,008 (2000); 16,991 (2007); 16,949 (2012 projected); Race: 98.6% White, 0.4% Black, 0.2% Asian, 0.6% Hispanic of any race (2007); Density: 33.9 persons per square mile (2007); Average household size: 2.42 (2007); Median age: 40.4 (2007); Males per 100 females: 96.1 (2007).
Religion: Five largest groups: 19.8% Southern Baptist Convention, 13.1% The United Methodist Church, 6.3% Christian Churches and Churches of Christ, 4.4% Church of the Nazarene, 3.9% Catholic Church (2000).
Economy: Unemployment rate: 6.4% (4/2008); Total civilian labor force: 8,944 (4/2008); Leading industries: 40.1% manufacturing; 11.4% retail trade; 10.4% accommodation & food services (2005); Farms: 581 totaling 275,318 acres (2002); Companies that employ 500 or more persons: 1 (2006); Companies that employ 100 to 499 persons: 3 (2006); Companies that employ less than 100 persons: 363 (2006); Black-owned businesses: n/a (2002); Hispanic-owned businesses: n/a (2002); Asian-owned businesses: n/a (2002); Women-owned businesses: n/a (2002); Retail sales per capita: $9,852 (2008). Single-family building permits issued: 7 (2007); Multi-family building permits issued: 0 (2007).
Income: Per capita income: $21,570 (2007); Median household income: $42,789 (2007); Average household income: $51,681 (2007); Percent of households with income of $100,000 or more: 8.9% (2007); Poverty rate: 11.9% (2005); Bankruptcy rate: 4.09% (2007).
Education: Percent of population age 25 and over with: High school diploma (including GED) or higher: 79.9% (2007); Bachelor's degree or higher: 13.6% (2007); Master's degree or higher: 4.2% (2007).
Housing: Homeownership rate: 77.9% (2007); Median home value: $97,452 (2007); Median rent: $300 per month (2000); Median age of housing: 42 years (2000).
Health: Birth rate: 121.4 per 10,000 population (2007); Death rate: 130.3 per 10,000 population (2007); Age-adjusted cancer mortality rate: 168.6 deaths per 100,000 population (2005); Air Quality Index: 86.7% good, 12.4% moderate, 1.0% unhealthy for sensitive individuals, 0.0% unhealthy (percent of days in 2007); Number of physicians: 3.0 per 10,000 population (2005); Hospital beds: 0.0 per 10,000 population (2004); Hospital admissions: 0.0 per 10,000 population (2004).
Elections: 2004 Presidential election results: 63.5% Bush, 35.9% Kerry, 0.1% Nader, 0.5% Badnarik
National and State Parks: Lincoln Trail State Park
Additional Information Contacts
Clark County Government . . . . (217) 826-8311
http://www.clarkcountyil.org
City of Casey . . . . (217) 932-2700
http://www.clarkcountyil.org/Communities/casey.htm
Marshall Area Chamber of Commerce . . . . (217) 826-2034
http://www.marshall-il.com
Martinsville Chamber of Commerce. . . . . (217) 382-4323
http://www.martinsvilleilcity.com

Clark County Communities

CASEY (city). Covers a land area of 2.124 square miles and a water area of 0 square miles. Located at 39.30° N. Lat.; 87.99° W. Long. Elevation is 646 feet.
History: Incorporated 1896. Had oil boom in early 20th cent.
Population: 2,914 (1990); 2,942 (2000); 3,029 (2007); 3,026 (2012 projected); Race: 98.3% White, 1.1% Black, 0.0% Asian, 0.3% Hispanic of any race (2007); Density: 1,425.9 persons per square mile (2007); Average household size: 2.32 (2007); Median age: 40.3 (2007); Males per 100 females: 83.8 (2007); Marriage status: 20.5% never married, 53.3% now married, 14.8% widowed, 11.4% divorced (2000); Foreign born: 0.5% (2000); Ancestry (includes multiple ancestries): 22.9% United States or American, 15.2% German, 12.8% English, 7.0% Other groups, 5.7% Irish (2000).
Economy: Employment by occupation: 9.9% management, 18.7% professional, 18.8% services, 16.3% sales, 0.9% farming, 9.0% construction, 26.4% production (2000).
Income: Per capita income: $19,507 (2007); Median household income: $35,625 (2007); Average household income: $44,265 (2007); Percent of households with income of $100,000 or more: 7.1% (2007); Poverty rate: 15.4% (2000).
Education: Percent of population age 25 and over with: High school diploma (including GED) or higher: 73.4% (2007); Bachelor's degree or higher: 11.1% (2007); Master's degree or higher: 4.6% (2007).

School District(s)
Casey-Westfield CUSD 4C (PK-12)
2005-06 Enrollment: 1,210 . . . . (217) 932-2184
Housing: Homeownership rate: 71.0% (2007); Median home value: $73,795 (2007); Median rent: $318 per month (2000); Median age of housing: 50 years (2000).
Safety: Violent crime rate: 33.9 per 10,000 population; Property crime rate: 145.9 per 10,000 population (2006).
Transportation: Commute to work: 93.6% car, 0.4% public transportation, 3.0% walk, 3.0% work from home (2000); Travel time to work: 54.9% less than 15 minutes, 16.7% 15 to 30 minutes, 16.9% 30 to 45 minutes, 7.9% 45 to 60 minutes, 3.5% 60 minutes or more (2000)
Additional Information Contacts
City of Casey . . . . (217) 932-2700
http://www.clarkcountyil.org/Communities/casey.htm

DENNISON (unincorporated postal area, zip code 62423). Covers a land area of 26.547 square miles and a water area of 0.016 square miles. Located at 39.45° N. Lat.; 87.57° W. Long. Elevation is 581 feet.
Population: 738 (2000); Race: 98.7% White, 0.0% Black, 1.3% Asian, 0.0% Hispanic of any race (2000); Density: 27.8 persons per square mile (2000); Age: 24.9% under 18, 12.7% over 64 (2000); Marriage status: 18.5% never married, 69.6% now married, 4.1% widowed, 7.8% divorced (2000); Foreign born: 0.0% (2000); Ancestry (includes multiple ancestries): 14.9% English, 14.5% United States or American, 13.2% Irish, 11.3% German, 8.8% Other groups (2000).
Economy: Employment by occupation: 4.7% management, 7.9% professional, 22.9% services, 20.5% sales, 0.0% farming, 14.4% construction, 29.6% production (2000).
Income: Per capita income: $17,058 (2000); Median household income: $34,659 (2000); Poverty rate: 4.5% (2000).
Education: Percent of population age 25 and over with: High school diploma (including GED) or higher: 84.7% (2000); Bachelor's degree or higher: 5.8% (2000).
Housing: Homeownership rate: 85.5% (2000); Median home value: $91,700 (2000); Median rent: $353 per month (2000); Median age of housing: 25 years (2000).
Transportation: Commute to work: 100.0% car, 0.0% public transportation, 0.0% walk, 0.0% work from home (2000); Travel time to work: 13.2% less than 15 minutes, 49.9% 15 to 30 minutes, 18.5% 30 to 45 minutes, 8.8% 45 to 60 minutes, 9.7% 60 minutes or more (2000)

MARSHALL (city). County seat. Covers a land area of 3.135 square miles and a water area of 0.010 square miles. Located at 39.39° N. Lat.; 87.69° W. Long. Elevation is 640 feet.
History: Marshall was founded by William B. Archer and named by him for Chief Justice John Marshall. The town developed as the seat of Clark County.
Population: 3,693 (1990); 3,771 (2000); 3,527 (2007); 3,384 (2012 projected); Race: 97.9% White, 0.7% Black, 0.2% Asian, 1.0% Hispanic of any race (2007); Density: 1,124.9 persons per square mile (2007); Average household size: 2.24 (2007); Median age: 39.5 (2007); Males per 100 females: 86.5 (2007); Marriage status: 21.2% never married, 52.7% now married, 14.0% widowed, 12.1% divorced (2000); Foreign born: 0.9% (2000); Ancestry (includes multiple ancestries): 22.8% German, 17.0% Irish, 13.1% United States or American, 10.7% English, 6.4% Other groups (2000).
Economy: Single-family building permits issued: 7 (2007); Multi-family building permits issued: 0 (2007); Employment by occupation: 7.2% management, 16.1% professional, 14.7% services, 29.0% sales, 0.3% farming, 8.1% construction, 24.6% production (2000).
Income: Per capita income: $24,721 (2007); Median household income: $42,126 (2007); Average household income: $53,978 (2007); Percent of households with income of $100,000 or more: 10.3% (2007); Poverty rate: 6.2% (2000).
Education: Percent of population age 25 and over with: High school diploma (including GED) or higher: 74.2% (2007); Bachelor's degree or higher: 14.9% (2007); Master's degree or higher: 4.4% (2007).

School District(s)
Eastern Ill Area of Spec Educ (PK-12)
2005-06 Enrollment: 577 . . . . (217) 348-7700
Marshall CUSD 2c (PK-12)
2005-06 Enrollment: 1,412 . . . . (217) 826-5912

Housing: Homeownership rate: 63.9% (2007); Median home value: $101,098 (2007); Median rent: $311 per month (2000); Median age of housing: 39 years (2000).
Safety: Violent crime rate: 29.5 per 10,000 population; Property crime rate: 83.2 per 10,000 population (2006).
Transportation: Commute to work: 92.3% car, 0.4% public transportation, 3.6% walk, 1.9% work from home (2000); Travel time to work: 49.6% less than 15 minutes, 25.6% 15 to 30 minutes, 17.9% 30 to 45 minutes, 2.9% 45 to 60 minutes, 3.9% 60 minutes or more (2000)
Additional Information Contacts
Marshall Area Chamber of Commerce .... (217) 826-2034
http://www.marshall-il.com

MARTINSVILLE (city). Covers a land area of 2.056 square miles and a water area of 0.030 square miles. Located at 39.33° N. Lat.; 87.88° W. Long. Elevation is 610 feet.
History: Martinsville was platted in 1833 by Joseph Martin, and operated as a trading post, stagecoach station, and tavern. A period of growth came in 1904 when oil and gas were discovered, but by 1916 the wells were dry.
Population: 1,207 (1990); 1,225 (2000); 1,091 (2007); 1,093 (2012 projected); Race: 99.3% White, 0.0% Black, 0.1% Asian, 0.5% Hispanic of any race (2007); Density: 530.8 persons per square mile (2007); Average household size: 2.37 (2007); Median age: 38.4 (2007); Males per 100 females: 96.9 (2007); Marriage status: 18.5% never married, 62.1% now married, 7.7% widowed, 11.7% divorced (2000); Foreign born: 0.0% (2000); Ancestry (includes multiple ancestries): 20.0% United States or American, 15.8% German, 14.1% English, 10.6% Irish, 5.7% Other groups (2000).
Economy: Employment by occupation: 7.1% management, 11.9% professional, 10.8% services, 25.7% sales, 0.7% farming, 12.9% construction, 30.9% production (2000).
Income: Per capita income: $17,616 (2007); Median household income: $33,929 (2007); Average household income: $41,649 (2007); Percent of households with income of $100,000 or more: 5.0% (2007); Poverty rate: 12.3% (2000).
Education: Percent of population age 25 and over with: High school diploma (including GED) or higher: 82.7% (2007); Bachelor's degree or higher: 9.3% (2007); Master's degree or higher: 2.7% (2007).

School District(s)

Martinsville CUSD 3c (PK-12)
2005-06 Enrollment: 393 .... (217) 382-4321
Housing: Homeownership rate: 74.2% (2007); Median home value: $64,118 (2007); Median rent: $242 per month (2000); Median age of housing: 50 years (2000).
Safety: Violent crime rate: 0.0 per 10,000 population; Property crime rate: 430.9 per 10,000 population (2006).
Transportation: Commute to work: 91.3% car, 0.0% public transportation, 4.3% walk, 4.1% work from home (2000); Travel time to work: 49.8% less than 15 minutes, 17.5% 15 to 30 minutes, 13.9% 30 to 45 minutes, 11.6% 45 to 60 minutes, 7.1% 60 minutes or more (2000)
Additional Information Contacts
Martinsville Chamber of Commerce................... (217) 382-4323
http://www.martinsvilleilcity.com

WEST UNION (unincorporated postal area, zip code 62477). Aka Hatton. Covers a land area of 64.596 square miles and a water area of 0.113 square miles. Located at 39.23° N. Lat.; 87.66° W. Long. Elevation is 472 feet.
Population: 1,131 (2000); Race: 99.4% White, 0.0% Black, 0.0% Asian, 0.0% Hispanic of any race (2000); Density: 17.5 persons per square mile (2000); Age: 30.0% under 18, 11.6% over 64 (2000); Marriage status: 22.7% never married, 57.1% now married, 6.1% widowed, 14.1% divorced (2000); Foreign born: 0.0% (2000); Ancestry (includes multiple ancestries): 22.8% German, 15.6% United States or American, 13.6% English, 7.9% Irish, 5.2% French (except Basque) (2000).
Economy: Employment by occupation: 13.2% management, 13.0% professional, 9.6% services, 19.3% sales, 1.3% farming, 16.5% construction, 27.0% production (2000).
Income: Per capita income: $14,453 (2000); Median household income: $33,000 (2000); Poverty rate: 14.1% (2000).
Education: Percent of population age 25 and over with: High school diploma (including GED) or higher: 85.1% (2000); Bachelor's degree or higher: 11.8% (2000).
Housing: Homeownership rate: 85.6% (2000); Median home value: $40,800 (2000); Median rent: $253 per month (2000); Median age of housing: 53 years (2000).
Transportation: Commute to work: 89.9% car, 0.0% public transportation, 2.9% walk, 3.7% work from home (2000); Travel time to work: 17.2% less than 15 minutes, 47.8% 15 to 30 minutes, 19.4% 30 to 45 minutes, 8.3% 45 to 60 minutes, 7.3% 60 minutes or more (2000)

WESTFIELD (village). Covers a land area of 1.004 square miles and a water area of 0 square miles. Located at 39.45° N. Lat.; 87.99° W. Long. Elevation is 755 feet.
Population: 676 (1990); 678 (2000); 646 (2007); 629 (2012 projected); Race: 97.5% White, 0.9% Black, 0.5% Asian, 0.9% Hispanic of any race (2007); Density: 643.4 persons per square mile (2007); Average household size: 2.40 (2007); Median age: 38.5 (2007); Males per 100 females: 98.8 (2007); Marriage status: 16.7% never married, 68.7% now married, 6.3% widowed, 8.3% divorced (2000); Foreign born: 0.3% (2000); Ancestry (includes multiple ancestries): 19.0% German, 15.7% United States or American, 11.0% Other groups, 7.1% English, 6.7% Irish (2000).
Economy: Single-family building permits issued: 0 (2007); Multi-family building permits issued: 0 (2007); Employment by occupation: 6.7% management, 15.1% professional, 19.4% services, 18.1% sales, 0.7% farming, 17.4% construction, 22.7% production (2000).
Income: Per capita income: $19,056 (2007); Median household income: $41,528 (2007); Average household income: $45,762 (2007); Percent of households with income of $100,000 or more: 6.3% (2007); Poverty rate: 11.2% (2000).
Education: Percent of population age 25 and over with: High school diploma (including GED) or higher: 85.1% (2007); Bachelor's degree or higher: 7.5% (2007); Master's degree or higher: 0.7% (2007).
Housing: Homeownership rate: 79.6% (2007); Median home value: $70,000 (2007); Median rent: $258 per month (2000); Median age of housing: 60+ years (2000).
Transportation: Commute to work: 93.2% car, 2.0% public transportation, 1.4% walk, 3.4% work from home (2000); Travel time to work: 21.8% less than 15 minutes, 47.0% 15 to 30 minutes, 17.5% 30 to 45 minutes, 11.2% 45 to 60 minutes, 2.5% 60 minutes or more (2000)

Clay County

Located in south central Illinois; drained by the Little Wabash River. Covers a land area of 469.25 square miles, a water area of 0.59 square miles, and is located in the Central Time Zone. The county was founded in 1824. County seat is Louisville.

Weather Station: Flora 5 NW Elevation: 498 feet

	Jan	Feb	Mar	Apr	May	Jun	Jul	Aug	Sep	Oct	Nov	Dec
High	38	44	55	67	77	85	89	88	81	70	55	43
Low	21	25	34	43	53	62	65	63	56	45	35	26
Precip	2.6	2.4	4.0	4.3	4.2	4.2	3.8	3.2	3.2	3.0	4.0	3.3
Snow	2.5	2.1	1.2	0.2	tr	0.0	0.0	0.0	0.0	tr	0.8	1.5

High and Low temperatures in degrees Fahrenheit; Precipitation and Snow in inches

Population: 14,460 (1990); 14,560 (2000); 14,041 (2007); 13,672 (2012 projected); Race: 98.1% White, 0.2% Black, 0.8% Asian, 0.9% Hispanic of any race (2007); Density: 29.9 persons per square mile (2007); Average household size: 2.47 (2007); Median age: 40.9 (2007); Males per 100 females: 92.1 (2007).
Religion: Five largest groups: 20.6% Christian Churches and Churches of Christ, 16.2% Southern Baptist Convention, 10.5% Catholic Church, 9.3% The United Methodist Church, 2.4% Church of the Nazarene (2000).
Economy: Unemployment rate: 6.4% (4/2008); Total civilian labor force: 6,997 (4/2008); Leading industries: 41.2% manufacturing; 13.6% health care and social assistance; 9.2% retail trade (2005); Farms: 703 totaling 243,154 acres (2002); Companies that employ 500 or more persons: 1 (2006); Companies that employ 100 to 499 persons: 6 (2006); Companies that employ less than 100 persons: 369 (2006); Black-owned businesses: n/a (2002); Hispanic-owned businesses: n/a (2002); Asian-owned businesses: n/a (2002); Women-owned businesses: n/a (2002); Retail sales per capita: $10,871 (2008). Single-family building permits issued: 8 (2007); Multi-family building permits issued: 0 (2007).
Income: Per capita income: $19,223 (2007); Median household income: $36,633 (2007); Average household income: $46,465 (2007); Percent of households with income of $100,000 or more: 7.0% (2007); Poverty rate: 13.3% (2005); Bankruptcy rate: 2.02% (2007).

Education: Percent of population age 25 and over with: High school diploma (including GED) or higher: 75.9% (2007); Bachelor's degree or higher: 9.8% (2007); Master's degree or higher: 3.5% (2007).
Housing: Homeownership rate: 79.9% (2007); Median home value: $72,304 (2007); Median rent: $242 per month (2000); Median age of housing: 37 years (2000).
Health: Birth rate: 128.1 per 10,000 population (2007); Death rate: 134.6 per 10,000 population (2007); Age-adjusted cancer mortality rate: 157.1 deaths per 100,000 population (2005); Number of physicians: 5.7 per 10,000 population (2005); Hospital beds: 15.6 per 10,000 population (2004); Hospital admissions: 956.6 per 10,000 population (2004).
Elections: 2004 Presidential election results: 67.4% Bush, 32.1% Kerry, 0.0% Nader, 0.5% Badnarik
Additional Information Contacts
Clay County Government. . . . . (618) 665-3626

City of Flora . . . . (618) 662-8313
http://www.florail.us
Flora Chamber of Commerce . . . . (618) 662-5646
http://www.florachamber.com

Clay County Communities

CLAY CITY (village). Covers a land area of 1.782 square miles and a water area of 0 square miles. Located at 38.68° N. Lat.; 88.35° W. Long. Elevation is 433 feet.
History: Clay City developed as a shipping and trading center for the surrounding agricultural area when the railroad arrived here. It was built on the site of the first seat of Clay County, called Maysville. Oil was discovered near Clay City in 1937.
Population: 948 (1990); 1,000 (2000); 966 (2007); 943 (2012 projected); Race: 99.4% White, 0.0% Black, 0.1% Asian, 0.9% Hispanic of any race (2007); Density: 541.9 persons per square mile (2007); Average household size: 2.28 (2007); Median age: 39.1 (2007); Males per 100 females: 88.7 (2007); Marriage status: 23.5% never married, 50.3% now married, 11.3% widowed, 15.0% divorced (2000); Foreign born: 0.4% (2000); Ancestry (includes multiple ancestries): 27.6% United States or American, 25.1% German, 11.2% Irish, 7.7% English, 5.1% Other groups (2000).
Economy: Single-family building permits issued: 0 (2007); Multi-family building permits issued: 0 (2007); Employment by occupation: 6.3% management, 10.9% professional, 16.0% services, 17.4% sales, 2.3% farming, 10.7% construction, 36.4% production (2000).
Income: Per capita income: $15,844 (2007); Median household income: $30,000 (2007); Average household income: $36,097 (2007); Percent of households with income of $100,000 or more: 2.4% (2007); Poverty rate: 16.4% (2000).
Education: Percent of population age 25 and over with: High school diploma (including GED) or higher: 80.3% (2007); Bachelor's degree or higher: 7.1% (2007); Master's degree or higher: 0.5% (2007).

School District(s)

Clay City CUSD 10 (PK-12)
2005-06 Enrollment: 396 . . . . (618) 676-1431
Housing: Homeownership rate: 74.3% (2007); Median home value: $53,519 (2007); Median rent: $224 per month (2000); Median age of housing: 37 years (2000).
Transportation: Commute to work: 95.3% car, 0.0% public transportation, 4.2% walk, 0.5% work from home (2000); Travel time to work: 58.2% less than 15 minutes, 27.4% 15 to 30 minutes, 6.4% 30 to 45 minutes, 2.6% 45 to 60 minutes, 5.4% 60 minutes or more (2000)

FLORA (city). Covers a land area of 4.437 square miles and a water area of <.001 square miles. Located at 38.67° N. Lat.; 88.48° W. Long. Elevation is 492 feet.
History: Flora was named for the daughter of one of its founders. It developed as an industrial center with a diversity of manufacturing.
Population: 5,206 (1990); 5,086 (2000); 4,814 (2007); 4,626 (2012 projected); Race: 96.7% White, 0.3% Black, 1.9% Asian, 0.9% Hispanic of any race (2007); Density: 1,084.9 persons per square mile (2007); Average household size: 2.37 (2007); Median age: 40.6 (2007); Males per 100 females: 83.5 (2007); Marriage status: 17.7% never married, 56.9% now married, 11.9% widowed, 13.6% divorced (2000); Foreign born: 1.2% (2000); Ancestry (includes multiple ancestries): 23.7% United States or American, 17.8% German, 11.6% Irish, 8.8% English, 6.6% Other groups (2000).
Economy: Single-family building permits issued: 8 (2007); Multi-family building permits issued: 0 (2007); Employment by occupation: 7.8% management, 15.7% professional, 16.8% services, 24.3% sales, 0.0% farming, 9.3% construction, 26.2% production (2000).
Income: Per capita income: $19,349 (2007); Median household income: $34,320 (2007); Average household income: $44,404 (2007); Percent of households with income of $100,000 or more: 6.7% (2007); Poverty rate: 11.3% (2000).
Education: Percent of population age 25 and over with: High school diploma (including GED) or higher: 76.1% (2007); Bachelor's degree or higher: 10.8% (2007); Master's degree or higher: 4.3% (2007).

School District(s)

Flora CUSD 35 (PK-12)
2005-06 Enrollment: 1,539 . . . . (618) 662-2412
Housing: Homeownership rate: 71.0% (2007); Median home value: $70,960 (2007); Median rent: $253 per month (2000); Median age of housing: 41 years (2000).
Hospitals: Clay County Hospital (18 beds)
Safety: Violent crime rate: 10.3 per 10,000 population; Property crime rate: 203.9 per 10,000 population (2006).
Newspapers: Daily Clay County Advocate-Press (Local news; Circulation 2,850)
Transportation: Commute to work: 92.2% car, 1.0% public transportation, 2.4% walk, 3.6% work from home (2000); Travel time to work: 74.0% less than 15 minutes, 11.2% 15 to 30 minutes, 8.2% 30 to 45 minutes, 3.5% 45 to 60 minutes, 3.1% 60 minutes or more (2000)
Additional Information Contacts
City of Flora . . . . (618) 662-8313
http://www.florail.us
Flora Chamber of Commerce . . . . (618) 662-5646
http://www.florachamber.com

INGRAHAM (unincorporated postal area, zip code 62434). Covers a land area of 30.716 square miles and a water area of 0.043 square miles. Located at 38.83° N. Lat.; 88.33° W. Long. Elevation is 486 feet.
Population: 540 (2000); Race: 100.0% White, 0.0% Black, 0.0% Asian, 0.0% Hispanic of any race (2000); Density: 17.6 persons per square mile (2000); Age: 10.0% under 18, 45.0% over 64 (2000); Marriage status: 22.0% never married, 36.2% now married, 28.0% widowed, 13.8% divorced (2000); Foreign born: 0.0% (2000); Ancestry (includes multiple ancestries): 40.5% German, 16.2% United States or American, 10.2% English, 4.9% Other groups, 4.1% Irish (2000).
Economy: Employment by occupation: 11.0% management, 14.4% professional, 9.9% services, 15.5% sales, 5.5% farming, 10.5% construction, 33.1% production (2000).
Income: Per capita income: $15,245 (2000); Median household income: $30,625 (2000); Poverty rate: 8.2% (2000).
Education: Percent of population age 25 and over with: High school diploma (including GED) or higher: 58.4% (2000); Bachelor's degree or higher: 11.8% (2000).
Housing: Homeownership rate: 89.0% (2000); Median home value: $31,300 (2000); Median rent: $375 per month (2000); Median age of housing: 59 years (2000).
Transportation: Commute to work: 97.2% car, 0.0% public transportation, 2.8% walk, 0.0% work from home (2000); Travel time to work: 23.9% less than 15 minutes, 40.3% 15 to 30 minutes, 15.3% 30 to 45 minutes, 15.9% 45 to 60 minutes, 4.5% 60 minutes or more (2000)

IOLA (village). Covers a land area of 0.969 square miles and a water area of 0 square miles. Located at 38.83° N. Lat.; 88.62° W. Long. Elevation is 525 feet.
History: Incorporated 1914.
Population: 163 (1990); 171 (2000); 171 (2007); 165 (2012 projected); Race: 97.1% White, 0.0% Black, 0.0% Asian, 0.0% Hispanic of any race (2007); Density: 176.6 persons per square mile (2007); Average household size: 2.71 (2007); Median age: 33.4 (2007); Males per 100 females: 96.6 (2007); Marriage status: 28.8% never married, 59.8% now married, 6.1% widowed, 5.3% divorced (2000); Foreign born: 0.0% (2000); Ancestry (includes multiple ancestries): 39.3% United States or American, 23.0% German, 9.6% Irish, 4.5% Italian, 3.4% English (2000).
Economy: Employment by occupation: 0.0% management, 26.6% professional, 15.6% services, 14.1% sales, 3.1% farming, 7.8% construction, 32.8% production (2000).
Income: Per capita income: $13,187 (2007); Median household income: $32,500 (2007); Average household income: $35,794 (2007); Percent of

households with income of $100,000 or more: 3.2% (2007); Poverty rate: 17.4% (2000).
Education: Percent of population age 25 and over with: High school diploma (including GED) or higher: 58.7% (2007); Bachelor's degree or higher: 2.9% (2007); Master's degree or higher: 2.9% (2007).
Housing: Homeownership rate: 81.0% (2007); Median home value: $49,375 (2007); Median rent: $164 per month (2000); Median age of housing: 47 years (2000).
Transportation: Commute to work: 93.3% car, 0.0% public transportation, 6.7% walk, 0.0% work from home (2000); Travel time to work: 20.0% less than 15 minutes, 20.0% 15 to 30 minutes, 45.0% 30 to 45 minutes, 15.0% 45 to 60 minutes, 0.0% 60 minutes or more (2000)

LOUISVILLE (village). Aka Louis. County seat. Covers a land area of 0.692 square miles and a water area of 0 square miles. Located at 38.77° N. Lat.; 88.50° W. Long. Elevation is 479 feet.
Population: 1,110 (1990); 1,242 (2000); 1,245 (2007); 1,225 (2012 projected); Race: 99.0% White, 0.2% Black, 0.1% Asian, 0.7% Hispanic of any race (2007); Density: 1,798.5 persons per square mile (2007); Average household size: 2.46 (2007); Median age: 39.6 (2007); Males per 100 females: 94.2 (2007); Marriage status: 22.6% never married, 54.2% now married, 13.0% widowed, 10.2% divorced (2000); Foreign born: 0.3% (2000); Ancestry (includes multiple ancestries): 33.9% United States or American, 15.4% German, 9.1% English, 6.9% Irish, 3.3% Other groups (2000).
Economy: Employment by occupation: 11.0% management, 17.7% professional, 14.4% services, 21.3% sales, 0.0% farming, 8.0% construction, 27.6% production (2000).
Income: Per capita income: $16,298 (2007); Median household income: $29,847 (2007); Average household income: $37,811 (2007); Percent of households with income of $100,000 or more: 4.1% (2007); Poverty rate: 18.9% (2000).
Education: Percent of population age 25 and over with: High school diploma (including GED) or higher: 70.0% (2007); Bachelor's degree or higher: 11.1% (2007); Master's degree or higher: 3.4% (2007).

School District(s)

Clay/Cwford/Jsper/Lwrnce/Rhland
2005-06 Enrollment: n/a . . . . (618) 392-4631
North Clay CUSD 25 (PK-12)
2005-06 Enrollment: 720 . . . . (618) 665-3358

Housing: Homeownership rate: 74.4% (2007); Median home value: $58,143 (2007); Median rent: $184 per month (2000); Median age of housing: 35 years (2000).
Newspapers: Clay County Republican (Community news; Circulation 2,250)
Transportation: Commute to work: 92.8% car, 0.2% public transportation, 3.1% walk, 3.1% work from home (2000); Travel time to work: 43.1% less than 15 minutes, 31.8% 15 to 30 minutes, 12.4% 30 to 45 minutes, 9.5% 45 to 60 minutes, 3.2% 60 minutes or more (2000)

SAILOR SPRINGS (village). Covers a land area of 0.254 square miles and a water area of 0 square miles. Located at 38.76° N. Lat.; 88.36° W. Long. Elevation is 440 feet.
Population: 136 (1990); 128 (2000); 123 (2007); 120 (2012 projected); Race: 99.2% White, 0.0% Black, 0.0% Asian, 0.0% Hispanic of any race (2007); Density: 484.4 persons per square mile (2007); Average household size: 2.51 (2007); Median age: 37.1 (2007); Males per 100 females: 92.2 (2007); Marriage status: 25.2% never married, 58.9% now married, 13.1% widowed, 2.8% divorced (2000); Foreign born: 0.0% (2000); Ancestry (includes multiple ancestries): 29.2% United States or American, 20.0% German, 18.5% Irish, 10.0% Other groups, 4.6% French (except Basque) (2000).
Economy: Employment by occupation: 0.0% management, 0.0% professional, 22.4% services, 18.4% sales, 0.0% farming, 6.1% construction, 53.1% production (2000).
Income: Per capita income: $11,565 (2007); Median household income: $23,438 (2007); Average household income: $29,031 (2007); Percent of households with income of $100,000 or more: 4.1% (2007); Poverty rate: 22.3% (2000).
Education: Percent of population age 25 and over with: High school diploma (including GED) or higher: 62.3% (2007); Bachelor's degree or higher: 6.5% (2007); Master's degree or higher: 3.9% (2007).
Housing: Homeownership rate: 89.8% (2007); Median home value: $24,167 (2007); Median rent: $n/a per month (2000); Median age of housing: 60+ years (2000).
Transportation: Commute to work: 95.9% car, 0.0% public transportation, 0.0% walk, 4.1% work from home (2000); Travel time to work: 27.7% less than 15 minutes, 34.0% 15 to 30 minutes, 34.0% 30 to 45 minutes, 4.3% 45 to 60 minutes, 0.0% 60 minutes or more (2000)

XENIA (village). Covers a land area of 0.519 square miles and a water area of 0 square miles. Located at 38.63° N. Lat.; 88.63° W. Long. Elevation is 541 feet.
Population: 414 (1990); 407 (2000); 396 (2007); 386 (2012 projected); Race: 96.0% White, 0.0% Black, 0.0% Asian, 7.1% Hispanic of any race (2007); Density: 763.6 persons per square mile (2007); Average household size: 2.25 (2007); Median age: 39.6 (2007); Males per 100 females: 100.0 (2007); Marriage status: 16.8% never married, 60.4% now married, 9.1% widowed, 13.7% divorced (2000); Foreign born: 1.8% (2000); Ancestry (includes multiple ancestries): 27.8% German, 19.0% United States or American, 15.3% Irish, 9.5% Other groups, 8.5% English (2000).
Economy: Employment by occupation: 7.9% management, 13.6% professional, 22.5% services, 13.1% sales, 0.0% farming, 9.9% construction, 33.0% production (2000).
Income: Per capita income: $17,563 (2007); Median household income: $30,750 (2007); Average household income: $39,517 (2007); Percent of households with income of $100,000 or more: 5.1% (2007); Poverty rate: 14.5% (2000).
Education: Percent of population age 25 and over with: High school diploma (including GED) or higher: 71.0% (2007); Bachelor's degree or higher: 10.4% (2007); Master's degree or higher: 1.9% (2007).

School District(s)

Flora CUSD 35 (PK-12)
2005-06 Enrollment: 1,539 . . . . (618) 662-2412

Housing: Homeownership rate: 75.6% (2007); Median home value: $64,773 (2007); Median rent: $305 per month (2000); Median age of housing: 47 years (2000).
Transportation: Commute to work: 93.7% car, 1.1% public transportation, 2.1% walk, 1.6% work from home (2000); Travel time to work: 26.9% less than 15 minutes, 48.9% 15 to 30 minutes, 10.8% 30 to 45 minutes, 2.7% 45 to 60 minutes, 10.8% 60 minutes or more (2000)

Clinton County

Located in southern Illinois; bounded on the south by the Kaskaskia River. Covers a land area of 474.23 square miles, a water area of 29.25 square miles, and is located in the Central Time Zone. The county was founded in 1824. County seat is Carlyle.

Clinton County is part of the St. Louis, MO-IL Metropolitan Statistical Area. The entire metro area includes: Bond County, IL; Calhoun County, IL; Clinton County, IL; Jersey County, IL; Macoupin County, IL; Madison County, IL; Monroe County, IL; St. Clair County, IL; Crawford County, MO (pt.)*; Franklin County, MO; Jefferson County, MO; Lincoln County, MO; St. Charles County, MO; St. Louis County, MO; Warren County, MO; Washington County, MO; St. Louis city, MO

Population: 33,944 (1990); 35,535 (2000); 36,204 (2007); 36,531 (2012 projected); Race: 93.9% White, 3.9% Black, 0.4% Asian, 2.1% Hispanic of any race (2007); Density: 76.3 persons per square mile (2007); Average household size: 2.71 (2007); Median age: 38.1 (2007); Males per 100 females: 106.2 (2007).
Religion: Five largest groups: 56.0% Catholic Church, 5.0% Southern Baptist Convention, 4.0% Lutheran Church—Missouri Synod, 3.6% United Church of Christ, 3.5% The United Methodist Church (2000).
Economy: Unemployment rate: 4.8% (4/2008); Total civilian labor force: 19,872 (4/2008); Leading industries: 18.1% retail trade; 17.1% health care and social assistance; 12.8% manufacturing (2005); Farms: 915 totaling 254,629 acres (2002); Companies that employ 500 or more persons: 0 (2006); Companies that employ 100 to 499 persons: 12 (2006); Companies that employ less than 100 persons: 882 (2006); Black-owned businesses: n/a (2002); Hispanic-owned businesses: n/a (2002); Asian-owned businesses: n/a (2002); Women-owned businesses: 577 (2002); Retail sales per capita: $12,068 (2008). Single-family building permits issued: 139 (2007); Multi-family building permits issued: 10 (2007).
Income: Per capita income: $23,849 (2007); Median household income: $53,802 (2007); Average household income: $62,164 (2007); Percent of households with income of $100,000 or more: 15.2% (2007); Poverty rate: 7.5% (2005); Bankruptcy rate: 2.03% (2007).
Taxes: Total county taxes per capita: $123 (2006); County property taxes per capita: $120 (2006).

Education: Percent of population age 25 and over with: High school diploma (including GED) or higher: 77.8% (2007); Bachelor's degree or higher: 13.6% (2007); Master's degree or higher: 3.5% (2007).
Housing: Homeownership rate: 80.4% (2007); Median home value: $113,035 (2007); Median rent: $321 per month (2000); Median age of housing: 31 years (2000).
Health: Birth rate: 127.8 per 10,000 population (2007); Death rate: 95.2 per 10,000 population (2007); Age-adjusted cancer mortality rate: 174.7 deaths per 100,000 population (2005); Number of physicians: 8.3 per 10,000 population (2005); Hospital beds: 16.7 per 10,000 population (2004); Hospital admissions: 578.5 per 10,000 population (2004).
Elections: 2004 Presidential election results: 59.7% Bush, 39.7% Kerry, 0.1% Nader, 0.6% Badnarik
National and State Parks: Hazlet State Park; South Shore State Park
Additional Information Contacts
Clinton County Government. . . . . (618) 594-2464
http://www.clintonco.org
City of Carlyle. . . . . (618) 594-2468
http://www.playandstaycarlyle.com
Trenton Chamber of Commerce . . . . (618) 224-9329
http://www.trenton-ilchamber.com

Clinton County Communities

ALBERS (village). Covers a land area of 0.725 square miles and a water area of 0 square miles. Located at 38.54° N. Lat.; 89.61° W. Long. Elevation is 440 feet.
Population: 722 (1990); 878 (2000); 825 (2007); 815 (2012 projected); Race: 99.0% White, 0.2% Black, 0.0% Asian, 0.5% Hispanic of any race (2007); Density: 1,138.0 persons per square mile (2007); Average household size: 2.70 (2007); Median age: 35.0 (2007); Males per 100 females: 95.0 (2007); Marriage status: 26.8% never married, 61.5% now married, 6.9% widowed, 4.8% divorced (2000); Foreign born: 0.6% (2000); Ancestry (includes multiple ancestries): 59.0% German, 8.7% Irish, 6.8% United States or American, 5.0% Other groups, 2.3% French (except Basque) (2000).
Economy: Single-family building permits issued: 7 (2007); Multi-family building permits issued: 0 (2007); Employment by occupation: 17.6% management, 14.1% professional, 13.6% services, 23.3% sales, 0.0% farming, 13.9% construction, 17.6% production (2000).
Income: Per capita income: $23,573 (2007); Median household income: $56,667 (2007); Average household income: $63,554 (2007); Percent of households with income of $100,000 or more: 17.0% (2007); Poverty rate: 4.0% (2000).
Education: Percent of population age 25 and over with: High school diploma (including GED) or higher: 78.8% (2007); Bachelor's degree or higher: 13.4% (2007); Master's degree or higher: 2.3% (2007).
School District(s)
Albers SD 63 (KG-08)
2005-06 Enrollment: 169 . . . . (618) 248-5146
Housing: Homeownership rate: 81.0% (2007); Median home value: $137,097 (2007); Median rent: $377 per month (2000); Median age of housing: 26 years (2000).
Safety: Violent crime rate: 10.1 per 10,000 population; Property crime rate: 30.2 per 10,000 population (2006).
Transportation: Commute to work: 93.2% car, 0.5% public transportation, 5.2% walk, 0.5% work from home (2000); Travel time to work: 21.7% less than 15 minutes, 28.1% 15 to 30 minutes, 20.8% 30 to 45 minutes, 19.5% 45 to 60 minutes, 9.8% 60 minutes or more (2000)

AVISTON (village). Covers a land area of 1.103 square miles and a water area of 0 square miles. Located at 38.60° N. Lat.; 89.60° W. Long. Elevation is 469 feet.
Population: 1,164 (1990); 1,231 (2000); 1,264 (2007); 1,275 (2012 projected); Race: 98.7% White, 0.4% Black, 0.2% Asian, 1.2% Hispanic of any race (2007); Density: 1,145.7 persons per square mile (2007); Average household size: 2.61 (2007); Median age: 39.0 (2007); Males per 100 females: 96.0 (2007); Marriage status: 22.7% never married, 63.6% now married, 8.0% widowed, 5.7% divorced (2000); Foreign born: 0.5% (2000); Ancestry (includes multiple ancestries): 69.1% German, 5.0% English, 3.6% United States or American, 3.5% Irish, 2.7% Other groups (2000).
Economy: Single-family building permits issued: 15 (2007); Multi-family building permits issued: 4 (2007); Employment by occupation: 13.1% management, 21.2% professional, 13.4% services, 25.5% sales, 0.0% farming, 12.8% construction, 14.0% production (2000).
Income: Per capita income: $24,359 (2007); Median household income: $55,400 (2007); Average household income: $61,023 (2007); Percent of households with income of $100,000 or more: 15.1% (2007); Poverty rate: 2.8% (2000).
Education: Percent of population age 25 and over with: High school diploma (including GED) or higher: 81.6% (2007); Bachelor's degree or higher: 18.9% (2007); Master's degree or higher: 4.7% (2007).
School District(s)
Aviston SD 21 (PK-08)
2005-06 Enrollment: 342 . . . . (618) 228-7245
Housing: Homeownership rate: 76.7% (2007); Median home value: $130,469 (2007); Median rent: $362 per month (2000); Median age of housing: 27 years (2000).
Safety: Violent crime rate: 0.0 per 10,000 population; Property crime rate: 0.0 per 10,000 population (2006).
Transportation: Commute to work: 92.1% car, 0.3% public transportation, 3.5% walk, 4.1% work from home (2000); Travel time to work: 31.1% less than 15 minutes, 27.2% 15 to 30 minutes, 19.5% 30 to 45 minutes, 16.2% 45 to 60 minutes, 5.9% 60 minutes or more (2000)

BARTELSO (village). Covers a land area of 0.349 square miles and a water area of 0 square miles. Located at 38.53° N. Lat.; 89.46° W. Long. Elevation is 449 feet.
Population: 561 (1990); 593 (2000); 624 (2007); 623 (2012 projected); Race: 98.6% White, 0.0% Black, 0.3% Asian, 0.0% Hispanic of any race (2007); Density: 1,788.4 persons per square mile (2007); Average household size: 2.76 (2007); Median age: 35.4 (2007); Males per 100 females: 98.1 (2007); Marriage status: 28.0% never married, 61.6% now married, 8.6% widowed, 1.8% divorced (2000); Foreign born: 0.0% (2000); Ancestry (includes multiple ancestries): 66.0% German, 8.1% United States or American, 4.4% Irish, 1.6% French (except Basque), 1.6% Polish (2000).
Economy: Employment by occupation: 13.1% management, 16.1% professional, 14.6% services, 17.9% sales, 0.6% farming, 14.6% construction, 23.2% production (2000).
Income: Per capita income: $24,058 (2007); Median household income: $64,432 (2007); Average household income: $66,427 (2007); Percent of households with income of $100,000 or more: 14.2% (2007); Poverty rate: 1.3% (2000).
Education: Percent of population age 25 and over with: High school diploma (including GED) or higher: 77.5% (2007); Bachelor's degree or higher: 13.8% (2007); Master's degree or higher: 2.0% (2007).
School District(s)
Bartelso SD 57 (KG-08)
2005-06 Enrollment: 160 . . . . (618) 765-2164
Housing: Homeownership rate: 90.7% (2007); Median home value: $110,833 (2007); Median rent: $320 per month (2000); Median age of housing: 37 years (2000).
Transportation: Commute to work: 93.2% car, 0.6% public transportation, 2.4% walk, 3.8% work from home (2000); Travel time to work: 24.2% less than 15 minutes, 38.8% 15 to 30 minutes, 18.3% 30 to 45 minutes, 10.4% 45 to 60 minutes, 8.3% 60 minutes or more (2000)

BECKEMEYER (village). Covers a land area of 0.492 square miles and a water area of 0 square miles. Located at 38.60° N. Lat.; 89.43° W. Long. Elevation is 459 feet.
Population: 1,085 (1990); 1,043 (2000); 884 (2007); 890 (2012 projected); Race: 98.9% White, 0.0% Black, 0.7% Asian, 1.0% Hispanic of any race (2007); Density: 1,798.5 persons per square mile (2007); Average household size: 2.49 (2007); Median age: 34.1 (2007); Males per 100 females: 94.7 (2007); Marriage status: 27.8% never married, 54.3% now married, 8.0% widowed, 9.9% divorced (2000); Foreign born: 0.5% (2000); Ancestry (includes multiple ancestries): 50.1% German, 13.1% United States or American, 11.6% Other groups, 10.7% Irish, 3.2% French (except Basque) (2000).
Economy: Single-family building permits issued: 1 (2007); Multi-family building permits issued: 0 (2007); Employment by occupation: 7.8% management, 9.7% professional, 21.9% services, 17.6% sales, 0.2% farming, 11.0% construction, 31.8% production (2000).
Income: Per capita income: $20,953 (2007); Median household income: $43,750 (2007); Average household income: $52,176 (2007); Percent of households with income of $100,000 or more: 8.7% (2007); Poverty rate: 8.2% (2000).

Education: Percent of population age 25 and over with: High school diploma (including GED) or higher: 77.4% (2007); Bachelor's degree or higher: 5.3% (2007); Master's degree or higher: 0.0% (2007).

School District(s)

Breese SD 12 (PK-08)
2005-06 Enrollment: 687 . . . . (618) 526-7128

Housing: Homeownership rate: 85.1% (2007); Median home value: $73,143 (2007); Median rent: $266 per month (2000); Median age of housing: 47 years (2000).

Safety: Violent crime rate: 0.0 per 10,000 population; Property crime rate: 28.0 per 10,000 population (2006).

Transportation: Commute to work: 96.3% car, 0.2% public transportation, 0.4% walk, 2.0% work from home (2000); Travel time to work: 41.0% less than 15 minutes, 25.5% 15 to 30 minutes, 19.1% 30 to 45 minutes, 6.8% 45 to 60 minutes, 7.6% 60 minutes or more (2000)

BREESE (city). Covers a land area of 2.275 square miles and a water area of 0.025 square miles. Located at 38.61° N. Lat.; 89.52° W. Long. Elevation is 453 feet.

History: Breese was named for Judge Sidney Breese (1800-1876), an Illinois jurist and resident of the city. King Edward VII, then Prince of Wales, visited Breese in 1860.

Population: 3,749 (1990); 4,048 (2000); 4,327 (2007); 4,418 (2012 projected); Race: 98.3% White, 0.1% Black, 0.6% Asian, 1.4% Hispanic of any race (2007); Density: 1,901.7 persons per square mile (2007); Average household size: 2.60 (2007); Median age: 37.3 (2007); Males per 100 females: 94.9 (2007); Marriage status: 23.3% never married, 63.0% now married, 8.2% widowed, 5.5% divorced (2000); Foreign born: 1.0% (2000); Ancestry (includes multiple ancestries): 60.8% German, 6.5% United States or American, 5.9% Irish, 4.6% Other groups, 2.3% Dutch (2000).

Economy: Single-family building permits issued: 18 (2007); Multi-family building permits issued: 2 (2007); Employment by occupation: 11.5% management, 19.4% professional, 15.8% services, 24.3% sales, 0.2% farming, 7.1% construction, 21.6% production (2000).

Income: Per capita income: $24,936 (2007); Median household income: $57,711 (2007); Average household income: $63,988 (2007); Percent of households with income of $100,000 or more: 12.9% (2007); Poverty rate: 3.2% (2000).

Education: Percent of population age 25 and over with: High school diploma (including GED) or higher: 82.8% (2007); Bachelor's degree or higher: 20.7% (2007); Master's degree or higher: 3.7% (2007).

School District(s)

Breese SD 12 (PK-08)
2005-06 Enrollment: 687 . . . . (618) 526-7128
Central CHSD 71 (09-12)
2005-06 Enrollment: 608 . . . . (618) 526-4578

Housing: Homeownership rate: 77.6% (2007); Median home value: $127,060 (2007); Median rent: $353 per month (2000); Median age of housing: 33 years (2000).

Hospitals: St. Joseph's Hospital (85 beds)

Safety: Violent crime rate: 9.5 per 10,000 population; Property crime rate: 102.3 per 10,000 population (2006).

Newspapers: Breese Journal (Local news; Circulation 6,185)

Transportation: Commute to work: 94.2% car, 0.5% public transportation, 1.2% walk, 3.5% work from home (2000); Travel time to work: 39.8% less than 15 minutes, 21.5% 15 to 30 minutes, 15.1% 30 to 45 minutes, 7.6% 45 to 60 minutes, 16.0% 60 minutes or more (2000)

CARLYLE (city). County seat. Covers a land area of 2.993 square miles and a water area of 0.004 square miles. Located at 38.61° N. Lat.; 89.37° W. Long. Elevation is 456 feet.

History: Carlyle was sited on the location of John Hill's Fort, built in the early 1800's. Carlyle developed as the seat of Clinton County.

Population: 3,528 (1990); 3,406 (2000); 3,433 (2007); 3,442 (2012 projected); Race: 95.6% White, 3.1% Black, 0.5% Asian, 1.3% Hispanic of any race (2007); Density: 1,146.9 persons per square mile (2007); Average household size: 2.42 (2007); Median age: 42.0 (2007); Males per 100 females: 89.4 (2007); Marriage status: 24.6% never married, 50.8% now married, 14.9% widowed, 9.8% divorced (2000); Foreign born: 1.7% (2000); Ancestry (includes multiple ancestries): 41.6% German, 12.4% United States or American, 8.9% Other groups, 8.8% Irish, 8.3% English (2000).

Economy: Single-family building permits issued: 1 (2007); Multi-family building permits issued: 4 (2007); Employment by occupation: 7.4% management, 19.1% professional, 17.0% services, 20.1% sales, 0.6% farming, 11.1% construction, 24.7% production (2000).

Income: Per capita income: $23,596 (2007); Median household income: $44,764 (2007); Average household income: $55,586 (2007); Percent of households with income of $100,000 or more: 13.6% (2007); Poverty rate: 6.7% (2000).

Education: Percent of population age 25 and over with: High school diploma (including GED) or higher: 76.0% (2007); Bachelor's degree or higher: 12.5% (2007); Master's degree or higher: 2.3% (2007).

School District(s)

Carlyle CUSD 1 (PK-12)
2005-06 Enrollment: 1,302 . . . . (618) 594-8283

Housing: Homeownership rate: 72.5% (2007); Median home value: $102,984 (2007); Median rent: $281 per month (2000); Median age of housing: 41 years (2000).

Safety: Violent crime rate: 44.4 per 10,000 population; Property crime rate: 310.9 per 10,000 population (2006).

Newspapers: Union Banner (Community news; Circulation 6,500)

Transportation: Commute to work: 95.0% car, 1.0% public transportation, 1.0% walk, 1.9% work from home (2000); Travel time to work: 40.2% less than 15 minutes, 31.6% 15 to 30 minutes, 12.0% 30 to 45 minutes, 5.7% 45 to 60 minutes, 10.4% 60 minutes or more (2000)

Additional Information Contacts

City of Carlyle. . . . . (618) 594-2468
http://www.playandstaycarlyle.com

DAMIANSVILLE (village). Covers a land area of 0.242 square miles and a water area of 0 square miles. Located at 38.51° N. Lat.; 89.62° W. Long. Elevation is 430 feet.

Population: 383 (1990); 368 (2000); 377 (2007); 376 (2012 projected); Race: 96.3% White, 0.0% Black, 1.6% Asian, 0.8% Hispanic of any race (2007); Density: 1,560.0 persons per square mile (2007); Average household size: 2.86 (2007); Median age: 35.1 (2007); Males per 100 females: 99.5 (2007); Marriage status: 22.8% never married, 63.9% now married, 5.6% widowed, 7.7% divorced (2000); Foreign born: 1.9% (2000); Ancestry (includes multiple ancestries): 63.6% German, 8.1% Irish, 8.1% Other groups, 3.3% United States or American, 2.2% Italian (2000).

Economy: Single-family building permits issued: 5 (2007); Multi-family building permits issued: 0 (2007); Employment by occupation: 14.0% management, 21.5% professional, 14.5% services, 23.7% sales, 0.0% farming, 8.1% construction, 18.3% production (2000).

Income: Per capita income: $24,430 (2007); Median household income: $65,714 (2007); Average household income: $69,773 (2007); Percent of households with income of $100,000 or more: 22.0% (2007); Poverty rate: 5.8% (2000).

Education: Percent of population age 25 and over with: High school diploma (including GED) or higher: 84.3% (2007); Bachelor's degree or higher: 20.1% (2007); Master's degree or higher: 2.4% (2007).

School District(s)

Damiansville SD 62 (PK-08)
2005-06 Enrollment: 128 . . . . (618) 248-5188

Housing: Homeownership rate: 84.1% (2007); Median home value: $107,212 (2007); Median rent: $279 per month (2000); Median age of housing: 25 years (2000).

Transportation: Commute to work: 94.6% car, 1.1% public transportation, 3.8% walk, 0.5% work from home (2000); Travel time to work: 14.1% less than 15 minutes, 27.0% 15 to 30 minutes, 25.4% 30 to 45 minutes, 11.4% 45 to 60 minutes, 22.2% 60 minutes or more (2000)

GERMANTOWN (village). Covers a land area of 0.794 square miles and a water area of 0 square miles. Located at 38.55° N. Lat.; 89.53° W. Long. Elevation is 430 feet.

Population: 1,222 (1990); 1,118 (2000); 965 (2007); 971 (2012 projected); Race: 99.3% White, 0.0% Black, 0.3% Asian, 0.3% Hispanic of any race (2007); Density: 1,216.0 persons per square mile (2007); Average household size: 2.45 (2007); Median age: 40.8 (2007); Males per 100 females: 97.3 (2007); Marriage status: 27.4% never married, 59.1% now married, 7.4% widowed, 6.1% divorced (2000); Foreign born: 0.6% (2000); Ancestry (includes multiple ancestries): 68.9% German, 7.0% United States or American, 5.1% Irish, 1.9% French (except Basque), 1.8% English (2000).

Economy: Employment by occupation: 11.3% management, 13.0% professional, 15.2% services, 24.1% sales, 0.3% farming, 14.4% construction, 21.6% production (2000).

Income: Per capita income: $27,323 (2007); Median household income: $59,667 (2007); Average household income: $66,612 (2007); Percent of households with income of $100,000 or more: 19.8% (2007); Poverty rate: 6.0% (2000).
Education: Percent of population age 25 and over with: High school diploma (including GED) or higher: 76.7% (2007); Bachelor's degree or higher: 8.4% (2007); Master's degree or higher: 1.7% (2007).

School District(s)

Germantown SD 60 (PK-08)
2005-06 Enrollment: 304 . . . . (618) 523-4253
Housing: Homeownership rate: 83.0% (2007); Median home value: $114,261 (2007); Median rent: $366 per month (2000); Median age of housing: 38 years (2000).
Safety: Violent crime rate: 0.0 per 10,000 population; Property crime rate: 18.1 per 10,000 population (2006).
Transportation: Commute to work: 93.0% car, 0.3% public transportation, 3.4% walk, 2.8% work from home (2000); Travel time to work: 33.4% less than 15 minutes, 23.0% 15 to 30 minutes, 17.6% 30 to 45 minutes, 13.1% 45 to 60 minutes, 12.8% 60 minutes or more (2000)

HOFFMAN (village). Covers a land area of 0.362 square miles and a water area of 0 square miles. Located at 38.54° N. Lat.; 89.26° W. Long. Elevation is 456 feet.
Population: 511 (1990); 460 (2000); 419 (2007); 409 (2012 projected); Race: 97.9% White, 0.5% Black, 0.7% Asian, 0.7% Hispanic of any race (2007); Density: 1,157.2 persons per square mile (2007); Average household size: 2.46 (2007); Median age: 39.3 (2007); Males per 100 females: 92.2 (2007); Marriage status: 19.0% never married, 64.5% now married, 9.1% widowed, 7.4% divorced (2000); Foreign born: 0.2% (2000); Ancestry (includes multiple ancestries): 56.8% German, 7.7% United States or American, 7.7% English, 7.5% Irish, 7.0% Other groups (2000).
Economy: Single-family building permits issued: 0 (2007); Multi-family building permits issued: 0 (2007); Employment by occupation: 6.9% management, 13.0% professional, 16.9% services, 30.7% sales, 0.0% farming, 4.8% construction, 27.7% production (2000).
Income: Per capita income: $24,827 (2007); Median household income: $52,593 (2007); Average household income: $61,191 (2007); Percent of households with income of $100,000 or more: 14.1% (2007); Poverty rate: 2.5% (2000).
Education: Percent of population age 25 and over with: High school diploma (including GED) or higher: 84.8% (2007); Bachelor's degree or higher: 8.2% (2007); Master's degree or higher: 2.5% (2007).
Housing: Homeownership rate: 82.9% (2007); Median home value: $72,500 (2007); Median rent: $338 per month (2000); Median age of housing: 28 years (2000).
Transportation: Commute to work: 94.7% car, 0.0% public transportation, 1.8% walk, 1.8% work from home (2000); Travel time to work: 36.2% less than 15 minutes, 40.2% 15 to 30 minutes, 7.1% 30 to 45 minutes, 6.3% 45 to 60 minutes, 10.3% 60 minutes or more (2000)

HUEY (village). Covers a land area of 0.165 square miles and a water area of 0 square miles. Located at 38.60° N. Lat.; 89.29° W. Long. Elevation is 453 feet.
Population: 210 (1990); 196 (2000); 183 (2007); 182 (2012 projected); Race: 98.4% White, 0.5% Black, 0.0% Asian, 2.7% Hispanic of any race (2007); Density: 1,106.7 persons per square mile (2007); Average household size: 2.51 (2007); Median age: 36.3 (2007); Males per 100 females: 96.8 (2007); Marriage status: 21.7% never married, 62.7% now married, 2.5% widowed, 13.0% divorced (2000); Foreign born: 0.0% (2000); Ancestry (includes multiple ancestries): 40.4% German, 15.2% United States or American, 13.6% English, 8.1% Other groups, 7.6% Scotch-Irish (2000).
Economy: Single-family building permits issued: 0 (2007); Multi-family building permits issued: 0 (2007); Employment by occupation: 7.3% management, 9.7% professional, 10.5% services, 17.7% sales, 0.8% farming, 3.2% construction, 50.8% production (2000).
Income: Per capita income: $20,137 (2007); Median household income: $46,250 (2007); Average household income: $50,479 (2007); Percent of households with income of $100,000 or more: 11.0% (2007); Poverty rate: 7.6% (2000).
Education: Percent of population age 25 and over with: High school diploma (including GED) or higher: 77.6% (2007); Bachelor's degree or higher: 9.5% (2007); Master's degree or higher: 2.6% (2007).
Housing: Homeownership rate: 87.7% (2007); Median home value: $63,333 (2007); Median rent: $238 per month (2000); Median age of housing: 30 years (2000).
Transportation: Commute to work: 96.7% car, 0.0% public transportation, 0.0% walk, 1.7% work from home (2000); Travel time to work: 35.6% less than 15 minutes, 35.6% 15 to 30 minutes, 18.6% 30 to 45 minutes, 6.8% 45 to 60 minutes, 3.4% 60 minutes or more (2000)

KEYESPORT (village). Covers a land area of 0.403 square miles and a water area of 0.017 square miles. Located at 38.74° N. Lat.; 89.27° W. Long. Elevation is 453 feet.
Population: 440 (1990); 481 (2000); 516 (2007); 529 (2012 projected); Race: 99.0% White, 0.0% Black, 0.2% Asian, 0.6% Hispanic of any race (2007); Density: 1,280.5 persons per square mile (2007); Average household size: 2.21 (2007); Median age: 42.9 (2007); Males per 100 females: 105.6 (2007); Marriage status: 13.3% never married, 61.4% now married, 12.1% widowed, 13.3% divorced (2000); Foreign born: 0.4% (2000); Ancestry (includes multiple ancestries): 27.2% German, 24.5% United States or American, 11.4% Irish, 7.7% Other groups, 5.8% English (2000).
Economy: Employment by occupation: 11.1% management, 11.1% professional, 17.2% services, 18.7% sales, 0.0% farming, 18.7% construction, 23.2% production (2000).
Income: Per capita income: $17,204 (2007); Median household income: $27,083 (2007); Average household income: $38,101 (2007); Percent of households with income of $100,000 or more: 5.6% (2007); Poverty rate: 17.0% (2000).
Education: Percent of population age 25 and over with: High school diploma (including GED) or higher: 63.1% (2007); Bachelor's degree or higher: 5.8% (2007); Master's degree or higher: 0.8% (2007).
Housing: Homeownership rate: 67.4% (2007); Median home value: $53,095 (2007); Median rent: $275 per month (2000); Median age of housing: 27 years (2000).
Transportation: Commute to work: 88.8% car, 0.0% public transportation, 4.6% walk, 3.6% work from home (2000); Travel time to work: 18.5% less than 15 minutes, 30.2% 15 to 30 minutes, 16.9% 30 to 45 minutes, 15.3% 45 to 60 minutes, 19.0% 60 minutes or more (2000)

NEW BADEN (village). Covers a land area of 1.337 square miles and a water area of 0 square miles. Located at 38.53° N. Lat.; 89.70° W. Long. Elevation is 459 feet.
Population: 2,755 (1990); 3,001 (2000); 3,226 (2007); 3,284 (2012 projected); Race: 96.0% White, 1.3% Black, 1.0% Asian, 1.7% Hispanic of any race (2007); Density: 2,413.7 persons per square mile (2007); Average household size: 2.58 (2007); Median age: 38.3 (2007); Males per 100 females: 95.5 (2007); Marriage status: 26.3% never married, 58.5% now married, 7.1% widowed, 8.2% divorced (2000); Foreign born: 1.7% (2000); Ancestry (includes multiple ancestries): 46.7% German, 12.0% Irish, 9.6% United States or American, 9.0% English, 7.9% Other groups (2000).
Economy: Single-family building permits issued: 33 (2007); Multi-family building permits issued: 0 (2007); Employment by occupation: 11.7% management, 17.5% professional, 18.4% services, 25.8% sales, 1.4% farming, 9.7% construction, 15.5% production (2000).
Income: Per capita income: $23,600 (2007); Median household income: $54,158 (2007); Average household income: $60,220 (2007); Percent of households with income of $100,000 or more: 13.2% (2007); Poverty rate: 5.8% (2000).
Education: Percent of population age 25 and over with: High school diploma (including GED) or higher: 81.8% (2007); Bachelor's degree or higher: 17.5% (2007); Master's degree or higher: 5.5% (2007).

School District(s)

Wesclin CUSD 3 (PK-12)
2005-06 Enrollment: 1,416 . . . . (618) 224-7583
Housing: Homeownership rate: 75.2% (2007); Median home value: $113,797 (2007); Median rent: $364 per month (2000); Median age of housing: 31 years (2000).
Safety: Violent crime rate: 13.1 per 10,000 population; Property crime rate: 95.1 per 10,000 population (2006).
Transportation: Commute to work: 93.2% car, 2.1% public transportation, 2.2% walk, 0.7% work from home (2000); Travel time to work: 23.9% less than 15 minutes, 34.7% 15 to 30 minutes, 24.6% 30 to 45 minutes, 8.9% 45 to 60 minutes, 8.0% 60 minutes or more (2000)

SHATTUC (unincorporated postal area, zip code 62283). Covers a land area of 45.974 square miles and a water area of 0.009 square miles. Located at 38.64° N. Lat.; 89.20° W. Long. Elevation is 476 feet.
Population: 721 (2000); Race: 99.0% White, 0.0% Black, 0.0% Asian, 0.0% Hispanic of any race (2000); Density: 15.7 persons per square mile (2000); Age: 26.8% under 18, 20.2% over 64 (2000); Marriage status: 18.5% never married, 63.3% now married, 6.9% widowed, 11.2% divorced (2000); Foreign born: 0.0% (2000); Ancestry (includes multiple ancestries): 57.0% German, 18.3% United States or American, 11.7% English, 10.0% Italian, 3.2% Irish (2000).
Economy: Employment by occupation: 6.8% management, 15.3% professional, 9.1% services, 26.8% sales, 1.5% farming, 20.6% construction, 19.8% production (2000).
Income: Per capita income: $15,889 (2000); Median household income: $35,694 (2000); Poverty rate: 13.6% (2000).
Education: Percent of population age 25 and over with: High school diploma (including GED) or higher: 83.1% (2000); Bachelor's degree or higher: 8.5% (2000).
Housing: Homeownership rate: 84.2% (2000); Median home value: $63,800 (2000); Median rent: $313 per month (2000); Median age of housing: 39 years (2000).
Transportation: Commute to work: 94.3% car, 0.0% public transportation, 0.0% walk, 5.7% work from home (2000); Travel time to work: 16.4% less than 15 minutes, 36.2% 15 to 30 minutes, 31.9% 30 to 45 minutes, 11.7% 45 to 60 minutes, 3.7% 60 minutes or more (2000)

TRENTON (city). Covers a land area of 0.983 square miles and a water area of 0 square miles. Located at 38.60° N. Lat.; 89.68° W. Long. Elevation is 495 feet.
History: Incorporated 1865.
Population: 2,555 (1990); 2,610 (2000); 2,966 (2007); 3,193 (2012 projected); Race: 98.6% White, 0.4% Black, 0.4% Asian, 2.1% Hispanic of any race (2007); Density: 3,018.4 persons per square mile (2007); Average household size: 2.43 (2007); Median age: 39.4 (2007); Males per 100 females: 94.1 (2007); Marriage status: 21.5% never married, 61.4% now married, 9.0% widowed, 8.1% divorced (2000); Foreign born: 1.3% (2000); Ancestry (includes multiple ancestries): 51.6% German, 14.6% Irish, 13.6% English, 7.2% Other groups, 5.6% United States or American (2000).
Economy: Single-family building permits issued: 8 (2007); Multi-family building permits issued: 0 (2007); Employment by occupation: 12.0% management, 22.9% professional, 13.3% services, 28.6% sales, 0.4% farming, 7.4% construction, 15.4% production (2000).
Income: Per capita income: $26,124 (2007); Median household income: $56,612 (2007); Average household income: $63,194 (2007); Percent of households with income of $100,000 or more: 16.8% (2007); Poverty rate: 6.2% (2000).
Education: Percent of population age 25 and over with: High school diploma (including GED) or higher: 88.6% (2007); Bachelor's degree or higher: 24.5% (2007); Master's degree or higher: 8.7% (2007).

School District(s)

Wesclin CUSD 3 (PK-12)
2005-06 Enrollment: 1,416 . . . . (618) 224-7583
Housing: Homeownership rate: 80.4% (2007); Median home value: $121,121 (2007); Median rent: $394 per month (2000); Median age of housing: 38 years (2000).
Safety: Violent crime rate: 18.9 per 10,000 population; Property crime rate: 60.4 per 10,000 population (2006).
Newspapers: Trenton Sun (Local news; Circulation 1,400)
Transportation: Commute to work: 93.9% car, 0.4% public transportation, 1.5% walk, 3.4% work from home (2000); Travel time to work: 29.0% less than 15 minutes, 27.1% 15 to 30 minutes, 20.3% 30 to 45 minutes, 15.4% 45 to 60 minutes, 8.1% 60 minutes or more (2000)
Additional Information Contacts
Trenton Chamber of Commerce . . . . (618) 224-9329
http://www.trenton-ilchamber.com

Coles County

Located in east central Illinois; drained by the Kaskaskia, Embarrass, and Little Wabash Rivers; includes Paradise Lake. Covers a land area of 508.29 square miles, a water area of 1.78 square miles, and is located in the Central Time Zone. The county was founded in 1830. County seat is Charleston.

Coles County is part of the Charleston-Mattoon, IL Micropolitan Statistical Area. The entire metro area includes: Coles County, IL; Cumberland County, IL

Weather Station: Charleston — Elevation: 679 feet

	Jan	Feb	Mar	Apr	May	Jun	Jul	Aug	Sep	Oct	Nov	Dec
High	35	41	52	65	75	83	86	84	78	67	52	40
Low	19	23	33	43	53	62	66	64	57	45	35	25
Precip	2.2	2.4	3.4	4.1	4.2	3.7	4.5	3.3	3.1	3.2	3.8	3.2
Snow	9.3	4.1	2.7	0.2	tr	0.0	0.0	0.0	0.0	tr	1.6	4.2

High and Low temperatures in degrees Fahrenheit; Precipitation and Snow in inches

Weather Station: Mattoon — Elevation: 715 feet

	Jan	Feb	Mar	Apr	May	Jun	Jul	Aug	Sep	Oct	Nov	Dec
High	33	39	51	63	74	83	87	85	79	66	51	39
Low	17	22	32	42	53	62	66	64	56	44	34	23
Precip	2.0	2.0	3.1	4.0	3.9	4.1	4.1	3.1	3.1	3.0	3.7	2.7
Snow	6.9	3.4	1.9	0.1	tr	0.0	0.0	0.0	0.0	tr	1.0	4.4

High and Low temperatures in degrees Fahrenheit; Precipitation and Snow in inches

Population: 51,644 (1990); 53,196 (2000); 50,605 (2007); 48,762 (2012 projected); Race: 94.6% White, 2.4% Black, 1.1% Asian, 1.9% Hispanic of any race (2007); Density: 99.6 persons per square mile (2007); Average household size: 2.44 (2007); Median age: 31.9 (2007); Males per 100 females: 92.1 (2007).
Religion: Five largest groups: 6.3% Catholic Church, 5.9% Christian Churches and Churches of Christ, 5.0% The United Methodist Church, 3.8% Lutheran Church—Missouri Synod, 3.7% Southern Baptist Convention (2000).
Economy: Unemployment rate: 4.9% (4/2008); Total civilian labor force: 28,416 (4/2008); Leading industries: 21.5% health care and social assistance; 18.5% manufacturing; 17.4% retail trade (2005); Farms: 684 totaling 261,138 acres (2002); Companies that employ 500 or more persons: 2 (2006); Companies that employ 100 to 499 persons: 26 (2006); Companies that employ less than 100 persons: 1,228 (2006); Black-owned businesses: n/a (2002); Hispanic-owned businesses: n/a (2002); Asian-owned businesses: n/a (2002); Women-owned businesses: 637 (2002); Retail sales per capita: $16,725 (2008). Single-family building permits issued: 38 (2007); Multi-family building permits issued: 102 (2007).
Income: Per capita income: $20,379 (2007); Median household income: $36,801 (2007); Average household income: $48,547 (2007); Percent of households with income of $100,000 or more: 9.3% (2007); Poverty rate: 18.8% (2005); Bankruptcy rate: 3.59% (2007).
Taxes: Total county taxes per capita: $124 (2006); County property taxes per capita: $124 (2006).
Education: Percent of population age 25 and over with: High school diploma (including GED) or higher: 83.1% (2007); Bachelor's degree or higher: 21.5% (2007); Master's degree or higher: 10.1% (2007).
Housing: Homeownership rate: 62.1% (2007); Median home value: $101,373 (2007); Median rent: $351 per month (2000); Median age of housing: 37 years (2000).
Health: Birth rate: 113.5 per 10,000 population (2007); Death rate: 96.6 per 10,000 population (2007); Age-adjusted cancer mortality rate: 240.3 deaths per 100,000 population (2005); Number of physicians: 19.1 per 10,000 population (2005); Hospital beds: 25.6 per 10,000 population (2004); Hospital admissions: 1,601.0 per 10,000 population (2004).
Elections: 2004 Presidential election results: 57.1% Bush, 42.0% Kerry, 0.1% Nader, 0.7% Badnarik
National and State Parks: Fox Ridge State Park; Lincoln Log Cabin State Historic Site
Additional Information Contacts
Coles County Government. . . . . (217) 348-0501
http://www.co.coles.il.us
Charleston Area Chamber of Commerce. . . . . (217) 345-7041
http://www.charlestonchamber.com
City of Charleston . . . . (217) 345-5650
http://www.charlestonillinois.org
City of Mattoon. . . . . (217) 235-5654
http://www.mattoonillinois.org
Mattoon Chamber of Commerce . . . . (217) 235-5661
http://www.mattoonchamber.com
Oakland Chamber of Commerce . . . . (217) 346-2050
http://www.oaklandil.com

Coles County Communities

ASHMORE (village). Covers a land area of 0.834 square miles and a water area of 0 square miles. Located at 39.53° N. Lat.; 88.02° W. Long. Elevation is 699 feet.

Population: 888 (1990); 809 (2000); 738 (2007); 711 (2012 projected); Race: 96.2% White, 0.4% Black, 2.2% Asian, 0.9% Hispanic of any race (2007); Density: 885.2 persons per square mile (2007); Average household size: 2.57 (2007); Median age: 33.9 (2007); Males per 100 females: 94.7 (2007); Marriage status: 20.3% never married, 61.9% now married, 7.3% widowed, 10.5% divorced (2000); Foreign born: 0.7% (2000); Ancestry (includes multiple ancestries): 19.3% United States or American, 15.5% German, 13.4% Irish, 8.3% Other groups, 7.9% English (2000).

Economy: Single-family building permits issued: 0 (2007); Multi-family building permits issued: 0 (2007); Employment by occupation: 8.1% management, 10.6% professional, 16.6% services, 27.2% sales, 3.3% farming, 10.8% construction, 23.4% production (2000).

Income: Per capita income: $18,618 (2007); Median household income: $46,618 (2007); Average household income: $47,875 (2007); Percent of households with income of $100,000 or more: 4.2% (2007); Poverty rate: 9.4% (2000).

Education: Percent of population age 25 and over with: High school diploma (including GED) or higher: 81.2% (2007); Bachelor's degree or higher: 12.0% (2007); Master's degree or higher: 4.5% (2007).

School District(s)

Charleston CUSD 1 (PK-12)
2005-06 Enrollment: 2,902 . . . . (217) 639-1000

Housing: Homeownership rate: 82.2% (2007); Median home value: $87,568 (2007); Median rent: $316 per month (2000); Median age of housing: 31 years (2000).

Transportation: Commute to work: 95.1% car, 0.0% public transportation, 2.6% walk, 1.8% work from home (2000); Travel time to work: 29.5% less than 15 minutes, 44.5% 15 to 30 minutes, 20.8% 30 to 45 minutes, 2.6% 45 to 60 minutes, 2.6% 60 minutes or more (2000)

CHARLESTON (city). County seat. Covers a land area of 7.993 square miles and a water area of 0.680 square miles. Located at 39.48° N. Lat.; 88.17° W. Long. Elevation is 669 feet.

History: Charleston was the site of the fourth Lincoln-Douglas debate in 1858, when 12,000 people gathered to hear Abraham Lincoln state his views on equality of all people.

Population: 20,625 (1990); 21,039 (2000); 19,570 (2007); 18,826 (2012 projected); Race: 90.9% White, 4.8% Black, 2.0% Asian, 2.4% Hispanic of any race (2007); Density: 2,448.4 persons per square mile (2007); Average household size: 2.59 (2007); Median age: 24.5 (2007); Males per 100 females: 87.5 (2007); Marriage status: 55.2% never married, 32.8% now married, 4.9% widowed, 7.0% divorced (2000); Foreign born: 2.2% (2000); Ancestry (includes multiple ancestries): 27.9% German, 17.1% Irish, 11.1% English, 10.3% Other groups, 7.0% United States or American (2000).

Economy: Single-family building permits issued: 20 (2007); Multi-family building permits issued: 102 (2007); Employment by occupation: 8.8% management, 24.0% professional, 23.1% services, 27.3% sales, 0.1% farming, 5.7% construction, 10.9% production (2000).

Income: Per capita income: $16,777 (2007); Median household income: $26,695 (2007); Average household income: $40,947 (2007); Percent of households with income of $100,000 or more: 8.6% (2007); Poverty rate: 30.1% (2000).

Education: Percent of population age 25 and over with: High school diploma (including GED) or higher: 84.3% (2007); Bachelor's degree or higher: 34.5% (2007); Master's degree or higher: 18.1% (2007).

School District(s)

Charleston CUSD 1 (PK-12)
2005-06 Enrollment: 2,902 . . . . (217) 639-1000
Clk Cls Cmbn Dglas Edgr Mltr Shlb (06-12)
2005-06 Enrollment: 103 . . . . (217) 348-0151
Eastern Il Efe System
2005-06 Enrollment: n/a . . . . (217) 348-0151

Four-year College(s)

Eastern Illinois University (Public)
Fall 2007 Enrollment: 12,179. . . . . (217) 581-5000
2007-08 Tuition: In-state $7,990; Out-of-state $19,654

Housing: Homeownership rate: 45.6% (2007); Median home value: $105,815 (2007); Median rent: $361 per month (2000); Median age of housing: 31 years (2000).

Safety: Violent crime rate: 20.8 per 10,000 population; Property crime rate: 216.9 per 10,000 population (2006).

Newspapers: Times-Courier (Community news; Circulation 6,897)

Transportation: Commute to work: 79.3% car, 0.5% public transportation, 16.2% walk, 2.0% work from home (2000); Travel time to work: 64.5% less than 15 minutes, 25.4% 15 to 30 minutes, 4.9% 30 to 45 minutes, 1.6% 45 to 60 minutes, 3.6% 60 minutes or more (2000)

Additional Information Contacts

Charleston Area Chamber of Commerce. . . . . (217) 345-7041
http://www.charlestonchamber.com
City of Charleston . . . . (217) 345-5650
http://www.charlestonillinois.org

HUMBOLDT (village). Covers a land area of 0.562 square miles and a water area of 0 square miles. Located at 39.60° N. Lat.; 88.32° W. Long. Elevation is 663 feet.

Population: 470 (1990); 481 (2000); 432 (2007); 421 (2012 projected); Race: 98.8% White, 0.0% Black, 0.0% Asian, 6.3% Hispanic of any race (2007); Density: 768.9 persons per square mile (2007); Average household size: 2.59 (2007); Median age: 34.2 (2007); Males per 100 females: 94.6 (2007); Marriage status: 20.2% never married, 64.5% now married, 7.4% widowed, 8.0% divorced (2000); Foreign born: 0.8% (2000); Ancestry (includes multiple ancestries): 40.5% United States or American, 15.2% Irish, 11.5% German, 11.5% English, 6.2% Other groups (2000).

Economy: Employment by occupation: 2.2% management, 8.9% professional, 13.3% services, 20.9% sales, 0.0% farming, 9.3% construction, 45.3% production (2000).

Income: Per capita income: $21,406 (2007); Median household income: $47,188 (2007); Average household income: $55,374 (2007); Percent of households with income of $100,000 or more: 6.0% (2007); Poverty rate: 6.7% (2000).

Education: Percent of population age 25 and over with: High school diploma (including GED) or higher: 84.1% (2007); Bachelor's degree or higher: 5.9% (2007); Master's degree or higher: 3.0% (2007).

School District(s)

Eastern Ill Area of Spec Educ (PK-12)
2005-06 Enrollment: 577 . . . . (217) 348-7700

Housing: Homeownership rate: 82.0% (2007); Median home value: $74,333 (2007); Median rent: $338 per month (2000); Median age of housing: 41 years (2000).

Transportation: Commute to work: 97.7% car, 0.0% public transportation, 0.9% walk, 1.4% work from home (2000); Travel time to work: 27.5% less than 15 minutes, 48.6% 15 to 30 minutes, 20.6% 30 to 45 minutes, 2.3% 45 to 60 minutes, 0.9% 60 minutes or more (2000)

LERNA (village). Covers a land area of 0.117 square miles and a water area of 0 square miles. Located at 39.41° N. Lat.; 88.28° W. Long. Elevation is 751 feet.

Population: 295 (1990); 322 (2000); 375 (2007); 393 (2012 projected); Race: 98.7% White, 0.0% Black, 0.0% Asian, 0.8% Hispanic of any race (2007); Density: 3,215.6 persons per square mile (2007); Average household size: 2.82 (2007); Median age: 28.4 (2007); Males per 100 females: 97.4 (2007); Marriage status: 22.3% never married, 54.9% now married, 9.2% widowed, 13.6% divorced (2000); Foreign born: 0.0% (2000); Ancestry (includes multiple ancestries): 32.3% United States or American, 9.9% English, 9.6% German, 5.9% Irish, 3.1% Other groups (2000).

Economy: Employment by occupation: 9.3% management, 11.0% professional, 9.9% services, 32.6% sales, 0.0% farming, 11.0% construction, 26.2% production (2000).

Income: Per capita income: $16,927 (2007); Median household income: $36,563 (2007); Average household income: $47,726 (2007); Percent of households with income of $100,000 or more: 8.3% (2007); Poverty rate: 2.5% (2000).

Education: Percent of population age 25 and over with: High school diploma (including GED) or higher: 72.6% (2007); Bachelor's degree or higher: 6.1% (2007); Master's degree or higher: 2.4% (2007).

School District(s)

Clk Cls Cmbn Dglas Edgr Mltr Shlb (06-12)
2005-06 Enrollment: 103 . . . . (217) 348-0151

Housing: Homeownership rate: 82.7% (2007); Median home value: $67,000 (2007); Median rent: $238 per month (2000); Median age of housing: 42 years (2000).

Transportation: Commute to work: 98.8% car, 0.0% public transportation, 1.2% walk, 0.0% work from home (2000); Travel time to work: 26.0% less

than 15 minutes, 59.8% 15 to 30 minutes, 8.9% 30 to 45 minutes, 0.0% 45 to 60 minutes, 5.3% 60 minutes or more (2000)

MATTOON (city). Covers a land area of 9.309 square miles and a water area of 0.004 square miles. Located at 39.47° N. Lat.; 88.37° W. Long. Elevation is 735 feet.
History: Mattoon was named for William Mattoon of the Illinois Central Railroad. The town was established in the early 1850's as a railroad station and shipping center.
Population: 18,783 (1990); 18,291 (2000); 17,211 (2007); 16,287 (2012 projected); Race: 96.4% White, 1.3% Black, 0.5% Asian, 1.7% Hispanic of any race (2007); Density: 1,848.8 persons per square mile (2007); Average household size: 2.20 (2007); Median age: 37.5 (2007); Males per 100 females: 91.4 (2007); Marriage status: 25.8% never married, 52.0% now married, 9.2% widowed, 13.0% divorced (2000); Foreign born: 1.3% (2000); Ancestry (includes multiple ancestries): 20.6% German, 15.9% United States or American, 12.4% Irish, 11.7% English, 8.6% Other groups (2000).
Economy: Single-family building permits issued: 15 (2007); Multi-family building permits issued: 0 (2007); Employment by occupation: 7.0% management, 12.4% professional, 17.0% services, 25.6% sales, 0.4% farming, 10.5% construction, 27.0% production (2000).
Income: Per capita income: $21,125 (2007); Median household income: $35,890 (2007); Average household income: $46,171 (2007); Percent of households with income of $100,000 or more: 7.0% (2007); Poverty rate: 13.4% (2000).
Education: Percent of population age 25 and over with: High school diploma (including GED) or higher: 79.7% (2007); Bachelor's degree or higher: 12.8% (2007); Master's degree or higher: 4.8% (2007).

School District(s)

Clk Cls Cmbn Dglas Edgr Mltr Shlb (06-12)
2005-06 Enrollment: 103 . . . . (217) 348-0151
Eastern Ill Area of Spec Educ (PK-12)
2005-06 Enrollment: 577 . . . . (217) 348-7700
Mattoon CUSD 2 (PK-12)
2005-06 Enrollment: 3,361 . . . . (217) 238-8850

Two-year College(s)

Lake Land College (Public)
Fall 2007 Enrollment: 7,177. . . . . (217) 234-5253
2007-08 Tuition: In-state $4,732; Out-of-state $10,321
Housing: Homeownership rate: 61.8% (2007); Median home value: $89,915 (2007); Median rent: $343 per month (2000); Median age of housing: 47 years (2000).
Hospitals: Sarah Bush Lincoln Health Center (202 beds)
Safety: Violent crime rate: 43.7 per 10,000 population; Property crime rate: 329.0 per 10,000 population (2006).
Newspapers: Journal Gazette (Local news; Circulation 11,278)
Transportation: Commute to work: 95.1% car, 0.5% public transportation, 1.3% walk, 1.9% work from home (2000); Travel time to work: 60.5% less than 15 minutes, 26.4% 15 to 30 minutes, 8.4% 30 to 45 minutes, 2.2% 45 to 60 minutes, 2.5% 60 minutes or more (2000); Amtrak: Service available.
Airports: Coles County Memorial (general aviation)
Additional Information Contacts
City of Mattoon. . . . . (217) 235-5654
http://www.mattoonillinois.org
Mattoon Chamber of Commerce . . . . (217) 235-5661
http://www.mattoonchamber.com

OAKLAND (city). Covers a land area of 0.819 square miles and a water area of 0.043 square miles. Located at 39.65° N. Lat.; 88.02° W. Long. Elevation is 659 feet.
History: Incorporated 1855.
Population: 996 (1990); 996 (2000); 901 (2007); 884 (2012 projected); Race: 98.9% White, 0.3% Black, 0.0% Asian, 1.0% Hispanic of any race (2007); Density: 1,099.9 persons per square mile (2007); Average household size: 2.36 (2007); Median age: 41.8 (2007); Males per 100 females: 95.4 (2007); Marriage status: 16.8% never married, 60.9% now married, 10.0% widowed, 12.3% divorced (2000); Foreign born: 1.5% (2000); Ancestry (includes multiple ancestries): 15.7% German, 14.3% United States or American, 14.2% Irish, 13.6% English, 4.5% Other groups (2000).
Economy: Single-family building permits issued: 3 (2007); Multi-family building permits issued: 0 (2007); Employment by occupation: 8.5% management, 13.0% professional, 13.4% services, 21.3% sales, 1.3% farming, 11.1% construction, 31.3% production (2000).
Income: Per capita income: $19,195 (2007); Median household income: $39,737 (2007); Average household income: $45,275 (2007); Percent of households with income of $100,000 or more: 4.7% (2007); Poverty rate: 10.8% (2000).
Education: Percent of population age 25 and over with: High school diploma (including GED) or higher: 82.4% (2007); Bachelor's degree or higher: 15.0% (2007); Master's degree or higher: 3.8% (2007).

School District(s)

Oakland CUSD 5 (KG-12)
2005-06 Enrollment: 360 . . . . (217) 346-2555
Housing: Homeownership rate: 81.4% (2007); Median home value: $77,679 (2007); Median rent: $279 per month (2000); Median age of housing: 47 years (2000).
Transportation: Commute to work: 97.1% car, 0.0% public transportation, 1.1% walk, 1.8% work from home (2000); Travel time to work: 26.3% less than 15 minutes, 32.8% 15 to 30 minutes, 27.7% 30 to 45 minutes, 7.1% 45 to 60 minutes, 6.0% 60 minutes or more (2000)
Additional Information Contacts
Oakland Chamber of Commerce . . . . (217) 346-2050
http://www.oaklandil.com

TRILLA (unincorporated postal area, zip code 62469). Covers a land area of 19.320 square miles and a water area of 0.023 square miles. Located at 39.35° N. Lat.; 88.33° W. Long. Elevation is 653 feet.
Population: 322 (2000); Race: 100.0% White, 0.0% Black, 0.0% Asian, 0.0% Hispanic of any race (2000); Density: 16.7 persons per square mile (2000); Age: 28.0% under 18, 20.8% over 64 (2000); Marriage status: 19.0% never married, 66.7% now married, 5.0% widowed, 9.3% divorced (2000); Foreign born: 0.0% (2000); Ancestry (includes multiple ancestries): 36.1% German, 19.1% United States or American, 11.6% Irish, 10.0% Other groups, 7.3% Slovak (2000).
Economy: Employment by occupation: 9.3% management, 16.7% professional, 5.6% services, 34.6% sales, 0.0% farming, 14.8% construction, 19.1% production (2000).
Income: Per capita income: $13,517 (2000); Median household income: $40,375 (2000); Poverty rate: 3.8% (2000).
Education: Percent of population age 25 and over with: High school diploma (including GED) or higher: 82.6% (2000); Bachelor's degree or higher: 14.0% (2000).
Housing: Homeownership rate: 89.4% (2000); Median home value: $81,300 (2000); Median rent: $350 per month (2000); Median age of housing: 39 years (2000).
Transportation: Commute to work: 100.0% car, 0.0% public transportation, 0.0% walk, 0.0% work from home (2000); Travel time to work: 21.0% less than 15 minutes, 69.1% 15 to 30 minutes, 6.2% 30 to 45 minutes, 0.0% 45 to 60 minutes, 3.7% 60 minutes or more (2000)

Cook County

Located in northeastern Illinois; bounded on the east by Lake Michigan and Indiana; crossed by the Chicago and Des Plaines Rivers. Covers a land area of 945.68 square miles, a water area of 689.36 square miles, and is located in the Central Time Zone. The county was founded in 1831. County seat is Chicago.

Cook County is part of the Chicago-Naperville-Joliet, IL-IN-WI Metropolitan Statistical Area. The entire metro area includes: Chicago-Naperville-Joliet, IL Metropolitan Division (Cook County, IL; DeKalb County, IL; DuPage County, IL; Grundy County, IL; Kane County, IL; Kendall County, IL; McHenry County, IL; Will County, IL); Gary, IN Metropolitan Division (Jasper County, IN; Lake County, IN; Newton County, IN; Porter County, IN); Lake County-Kenosha County, IL-WI Metropolitan Division (Lake County, IL; Kenosha County, WI)

Weather Station: Chicago Midway Airport Elevation: 610 feet

	Jan	Feb	Mar	Apr	May	Jun	Jul	Aug	Sep	Oct	Nov	Dec
High	30	36	47	59	71	81	85	83	75	63	48	36
Low	16	21	30	40	51	61	66	65	57	45	34	23
Precip	1.9	1.8	2.9	3.9	3.8	4.2	3.8	3.9	3.5	2.9	3.3	2.7
Snow	13.0	10.2	6.6	1.8	tr	0.0	tr	0.0	tr	0.1	2.4	8.7

High and Low temperatures in degrees Fahrenheit; Precipitation and Snow in inches

Weather Station: Chicago O'Hare Int'l Airport Elevation: 656 feet

	Jan	Feb	Mar	Apr	May	Jun	Jul	Aug	Sep	Oct	Nov	Dec
High	30	35	46	58	70	80	84	82	75	63	48	35
Low	14	19	29	38	48	58	64	63	54	42	32	21
Precip	1.7	1.6	2.7	3.7	3.5	3.7	3.5	4.6	3.4	2.8	3.0	2.4
Snow	11.1	8.1	6.4	1.8	tr	tr	tr	tr	0.0	0.3	1.8	7.8

High and Low temperatures in degrees Fahrenheit; Precipitation and Snow in inches

Weather Station: Chicago University Elevation: 593 feet

	Jan	Feb	Mar	Apr	May	Jun	Jul	Aug	Sep	Oct	Nov	Dec
High	31	36	47	59	70	80	85	83	76	64	49	37
Low	18	22	32	42	51	61	67	66	58	47	36	24
Precip	1.9	1.7	3.1	3.7	3.5	4.2	3.5	4.1	3.4	2.8	3.5	2.9
Snow	na	na	na	na	na	na	na	na	na	na	na	na

High and Low temperatures in degrees Fahrenheit; Precipitation and Snow in inches

Weather Station: Park Forest Elevation: 708 feet

	Jan	Feb	Mar	Apr	May	Jun	Jul	Aug	Sep	Oct	Nov	Dec
High	29	35	45	58	70	80	84	82	75	63	48	35
Low	13	18	28	38	49	59	64	62	54	42	32	20
Precip	1.8	1.6	2.8	3.9	4.2	4.6	4.2	3.9	3.3	2.8	3.4	2.5
Snow	10.6	7.6	4.7	1.0	tr	0.0	0.0	0.0	0.0	0.2	1.0	5.7

High and Low temperatures in degrees Fahrenheit; Precipitation and Snow in inches

Population: 5,105,067 (1990); 5,376,741 (2000); 5,278,157 (2007); 5,187,690 (2012 projected); Race: 54.1% White, 26.1% Black, 5.4% Asian, 22.7% Hispanic of any race (2007); Density: 5,581.3 persons per square mile (2007); Average household size: 2.73 (2007); Median age: 35.6 (2007); Males per 100 females: 94.6 (2007).
Religion: Five largest groups: 39.9% Catholic Church, 4.4% Jewish Estimate, 1.8% Muslim Estimate, 1.2% Lutheran Church—Missouri Synod, 1.2% Evangelical Lutheran Church in America (2000).
Economy: Unemployment rate: 5.5% (4/2008); Total civilian labor force: 2,672,268 (4/2008); Leading industries: 13.6% health care and social assistance; 10.4% retail trade; 10.1% manufacturing (2005); Farms: 211 totaling 23,836 acres (2002); Companies that employ 500 or more persons: 448 (2006); Companies that employ 100 to 499 persons: 3,451 (2006); Companies that employ less than 100 persons: 127,534 (2006); Black-owned businesses: 54,753 (2002); Hispanic-owned businesses: 27,030 (2002); Asian-owned businesses: 27,776 (2002); Women-owned businesses: 130,422 (2002); Retail sales per capita: $13,109 (2008). Single-family building permits issued: 3,318 (2007); Multi-family building permits issued: 13,801 (2007).
Income: Per capita income: $26,567 (2007); Median household income: $52,477 (2007); Average household income: $71,841 (2007); Percent of households with income of $100,000 or more: 20.5% (2007); Poverty rate: 15.0% (2005); Bankruptcy rate: 3.19% (2007).
Taxes: Total county taxes per capita: $291 (2006); County property taxes per capita: $153 (2006).
Education: Percent of population age 25 and over with: High school diploma (including GED) or higher: 77.6% (2007); Bachelor's degree or higher: 28.2% (2007); Master's degree or higher: 10.9% (2007).
Housing: Homeownership rate: 58.0% (2007); Median home value: $241,923 (2007); Median rent: $582 per month (2000); Median age of housing: 44 years (2000).
Health: Birth rate: 148.0 per 10,000 population (2007); Death rate: 80.0 per 10,000 population (2007); Age-adjusted cancer mortality rate: 194.3 deaths per 100,000 population (2005); Air Quality Index: 42.2% good, 51.0% moderate, 6.3% unhealthy for sensitive individuals, 0.5% unhealthy (percent of days in 2007); Number of physicians: 38.6 per 10,000 population (2005); Hospital beds: 36.0 per 10,000 population (2004); Hospital admissions: 1,622.3 per 10,000 population (2004).
Elections: 2004 Presidential election results: 29.1% Bush, 70.2% Kerry, 0.0% Nader, 0.6% Badnarik
National and State Parks: Chicago Portage National Historic Site; Illinois and Michigan Canal State Trail

Additional Information Contacts

Cook County Government . . . . (312) 603-5500
http://www.co.cook.il.us
Alsip Chamber of Commerce. . . . . (708) 597-2668
http://www.alsipchamber.org
America - Israel Chamber of Commerce Chicago . . . . (312) 235-0586
http://www.americaisrael.org
Andersonville Chamber of Commerce. . . . . (773) 728-2995
http://www.andersonville.org
Argo-Summit Chamber of Commerce . . . . (708) 458-3033
Arlington Heights Chamber of Commerce . . . . (847) 253-1703
http://www.arlingtonhtschamber.com
Barrington Chamber of Commerce . . . . (847) 381-2525
http://www.barringtonchamber.com
Blue Island Area Chamber of Commerce . . . . (708) 388-1000
http://www.blueislandchamber.org
Bridgeview Chamber of Commerce. . . . . (708) 598-1700
http://www.bridgeviewchamber.com
Broadview Chamber of Commerce . . . . (708) 345-3011
Brookfield Chamber of Commerce. . . . . (708) 485-1434
Burbank Chamber of Commerce . . . . (708) 425-4668
Calumet City Chamber of Commerce . . . . (708) 891-5888
http://www.calumetcitychamber.com
Chicago Area Gay & Lesbian Chamber of Commerce . . . . (773) 303-0167
http://www.glchamber.org
Chicago Chinatown Chamber of Commerce . . . . (312) 326-5320
http://www.chicagochinatown.org
Chicago Convention & Visitors Bureau . . . . (312) 567-8500
http://www.choosechicago.com
Chicago Ridge-Worth Chamber of Commerce . . . . (708) 728-7691
http://www.crwchamber.com
Chicago Southland Convention & Visitors Bureau. . . . . (708) 895-8200
Chicagoland Chamber of Commerce. . . . . (312) 494-6700
http://www.chicagolandchamber.org
Cicero Chamber of Commerce . . . . (708) 863-6000
http://www.cicerochamber.org
City of Berwyn . . . . (708) 788-2660
http://www.berwyn-il.gov
City of Blue Island . . . . (708) 597-8603
http://www.blueisland.org
City of Burbank . . . . (708) 599-5500
http://www.burbankil.gov
City of Calumet City. . . . . (708) 891-8105
http://www.calumetcity.org
City of Chicago. . . . . (312) 744-5000
http://www.cityofchicago.org
City of Chicago Heights . . . . (708) 756-5315
http://www.chicagoheights.net
City of Country Club Hills. . . . . (708) 798-2616
http://www.countryclubhills.org
City of Countryside. . . . . (708) 354-7270
http://www.countryside-il.org
City of Des Plaines. . . . . (847) 391-5300
http://www.desplaines.org
City of Evanston. . . . . (847) 866-2925
http://www.cityofevanston.org
City of Harvey . . . . (708) 210-5366
http://www.cityofharvey.org
City of Hickory Hills . . . . (708) 598-4800
http://www.hickoryhillsil.org
City of Northlake . . . . (708) 343-8700
http://www.northlakecity.com
City of Oak Forest . . . . (708) 687-4050
http://www.oak-forest.org
City of Palos Heights . . . . (708) 361-1800
http://www.palosheights.org
City of Palos Hills. . . . . (708) 598-3400
http://www.paloshillsweb.org
City of Park Ridge . . . . (847) 318-5200
http://www.parkridge.us
City of Prospect Heights . . . . (847) 398-6070
http://www.prospect-heights.il.us
City of Rolling Meadows . . . . (847) 394-8500
http://www.ci.rolling-meadows.il.us
Des Plaines Chamber of Commerce & Industry . . . . (847) 824-4200
http://www.dpchamber.com
Dolton Chamber of Commerce . . . . (708) 841-4810
Evergreen Park Chamber of Commerce . . . . (708) 423-1118
http://www.evergreenparkchamber.org
Forest Park Chamber of Commerce . . . . (708) 366-2543
http://www.forestparkchamber.org
Franklin Park/Schiller Park Chamber of Commerce . . . . . . (708) 865-9510
http://www.chamberbyohare.org
German American Chamber of Commerce of the Midwest . (312) 644-2662
http://www.gaccom.org
Glencoe Chamber of Commerce . . . . (847) 835-3333

Glenview Chamber of Commerce . . . . . (847) 724-0900
http://www.glenviewchamber.com
Hanover Park Chamber of Commerce & Industry . . . . . (630) 372-2009
http://www.hanoverparkchamber.com
Hazel Crest Chamber of Commerce . . . . . (708) 335-4699
Hillside Chamber of Commerce & Industry . . . . . (708) 449-2449
http://www.hillsidechamberofcommerce.com
Hoffman Estates Chamber of Commerce & Industry . . . . . (847) 781-9100
http://www.hechamber.com
Homewood Area Chamber of Commerce . . . . . (708) 206-3384
http://www.homewoodareachamber.com
Illinois Chamber of Commerce . . . . . (312) 983-7100
http://www.ilchamber.org
Italian American Chamber of Commerce - Midwest . . . . . (312) 553-9137
http://www.italianchamber.us
Lake View East Chamber of Commerce . . . . . (773) 348-8608
http://www.lakevieweast.com
Lansing Chamber of Commerce . . . . . (708) 474-4170
http://www.communitylink.com/lansing/chamber.htm
Latin American Chamber of Commerce . . . . . (773) 252-5211
http://www.latinamericanchamberofcommerce.com
Lemont Area Chamber of Commerce . . . . . (630) 257-5997
http://www.lemontchamber.com
Lincoln Park Chamber of Commerce . . . . . (773) 880-5200
http://www.lincolnparkchamber.com
Lincolnwood Chamber of Commerce & Industry . . . . . (847) 679-5760
http://www.lincolnwoodchamber.org
Logan Square Chamber of Commerce . . . . . (773) 489-3222
http://www.loganchamber.org
Lynwood Chamber of Commerce . . . . . (708) 758-6101
http://www.ynns.com/lcc/location.php
Matteson Area Chamber of Commerce . . . . . (708) 747-6000
http://www.macclink.com
Matteson Chamber of Commerce . . . . . (708) 747-6000
Maywood Chamber of Commerce . . . . . (708) 345-7077
http://www.souari.forest.net/~maywood
Melrose Park Chamber of Commerce & Industry . . . . . (708) 338-1007
http://www.melroseparkchamber.org
Midlothian Chamber of Commerce . . . . . (708) 389-0020
http://www.villageprofile.com/illinois/midlothian
Mont Clare-Elmwood Park Chamber of Commerce . . . . . (708) 456-8000
http://www.mcepchamber.org
Morton Grove Chamber of Commerce & Industry . . . . . (847) 965-0330
http://www.mgcci.org
Mount Prospect Chamber of Commerce . . . . . (847) 398-6616
http://www.mountprospectchamber.org
Niles Chamber of Commerce . . . . . (847) 268-8180
http://www.nileschamber.org
Northbrook Chamber of Commerce & Industry . . . . . (847) 498-5555
http://www.northbrookchamber.org
Northfield Chamber of Commerce . . . . . (847) 441-1848
http://www.northfieldchamber.org
Northlake Chamber of Commerce . . . . . (708) 562-3110
http://www.northlakecity.com/links_chamber.htm
Oak Forest Chamber of Commerce . . . . . (708) 687-4600
http://www.oakforestchamber.org
Oak Lawn Chamber of Commerce . . . . . (708) 424-8300
http://www.oaklawnchamber.com
Oak Park Chamber of Commerce . . . . . (708) 848-8151
http://www.oprfchamber.org
Old Town Merchants & Residents Association . . . . . (312) 951-6106
http://www.oldtownchicago.org
Orland Park Chamber of Commerce . . . . . (708) 349-2972
http://www.orlandparkchamber.org
Palatine Area Chamber of Commerce . . . . . (847) 359-7200
http://www.palatinechamber.com
Palos Heights Chamber of Commerce . . . . . (708) 923-2300
http://www.paloschamber.org
Palos Park Business Association . . . . . (708) 448-2700
http://www.palospark.org
Park Ridge Chamber of Commerce . . . . . (847) 825-3121
http://www.parkridgechamber.com
Portgage Park Chamber of Commerce . . . . . (773) 777-2020
http://www.portageparkchamber.org
Puerto Rico Convention Bureau . . . . . (312) 840-8090
http://www.meetpuertorico.com
River Grove Area Chamber of Commerce . . . . . (708) 452-8259
http://www.vorg.us/org/cham.htm
Riverdale Chamber of Commerce . . . . . (708) 841-3311
http://www.district148.net/rcoc
Riverside Chamber of Commerce . . . . . (708) 802-1631
http://www.riversidechamberofcommerce.com
Rolling Meadows Chamber of Commerce . . . . . (847) 398-3730
http://www.rmchamber.org
Rosemont Chamber of Commerce . . . . . (847) 698-1190
http://www.rosemontchamber.com
Schaumburg Business Association . . . . . (847) 413-1010
http://www.schaumburgbusiness.com
Schiller Park Chamber of Commerce . . . . . (847) 671-3040
Skokie Chamber of Commerce . . . . . (847) 673-0240
http://www.skokiechamber.org
South Holland Business Association . . . . . (708) 596-0065
http://www.shba.org
South Shore Chamber Inc. . . . . . (773) 643-1652
http://www.southshorechamber.biz
Streamwood Chamber of Commerce . . . . . (630) 837-5200
http://www.streamwoodchamber.com
Streeterville Chamber of Commerce . . . . . (312) 664-2560
http://www.streetervillechamber.org
The 87th Street Stoney Island Chamber of Commerce . . . . (773) 734-0626
http://87thchamberofcommerce.com
Tinley Park Chamber of Commerce . . . . . (708) 532-5700
http://www.tinleychamber.org
Town of Cicero . . . . . (708) 656-3600
http://www.thetownofcicero.com
Turkish American Chamber of Commerce . . . . . (773) 251-8242
http://www.turkishchamber.org
Village of Alsip . . . . . (708) 385-6902
http://www.alsip.org.il
Village of Arlington Heights . . . . . (847) 368-5000
http://www.vah.com
Village of Barrington . . . . . (647) 304-3400
http://www.ci.barrington.il.us
Village of Bellwood . . . . . (708) 547-3500
http://www.vil.bellwood.il.us
Village of Berkeley . . . . . (708) 449-8840
http://www.berkeley.il.us
Village of Broadview . . . . . (708) 681-3600
http://www.villageofbroadview.com
Village of Brookfield . . . . . (708) 485-7344
http://www.villageofbrookfield.com
Village of Chicago Ridge . . . . . (708) 425-7700
http://www.chicagoridge.org
Village of Crestwood . . . . . (708) 371-4800
http://www.villageofcrestwood.com
Village of Dolton . . . . . (708) 849-4000
http://www.villageofdolton.com
Village of Elk Grove Village . . . . . (847) 437-0300
Village of Elmwood Park . . . . . (708) 452-7300
http://www.elmwoodpark.org
Village of Evergreen Park . . . . . (708) 422-1551
http://www.evergreenpark-ill.com
Village of Flossmoor . . . . . (708) 798-2300
http://www.flossmoor.org
Village of Forest Park . . . . . (708) 366-2323
http://www.forestpark.net
Village of Glencoe . . . . . (847) 835-4114
http://www.goglencoe.com
Village of Glenview . . . . . (847) 904-4370
http://www.glenview.il.us
Village of Glenwood . . . . . (708) 753-2308
http://www.villageofglenwood.com
Village of Hanover Park . . . . . (630) 372-4200
http://www.hanoverparkillinois.org
Village of Harwood Heights . . . . . (708) 867-7200
http://www.harwoodheights.org
Village of Hazel Crest . . . . . (708) 335-9600
http://www.villageofhazelcrest.com
Village of Hillside . . . . . (708) 449-6450
http://www.hillside-il.org
Village of Hoffman Estates . . . . . (847) 781-2605
http://www.hoffmanestates.com

Village of Homewood . . . . (708) 798-3000
http://village.homewood.il.us
Village of Inverness . . . . (847) 358-7740
http://www.villageofinverness.org
Village of Justice . . . . (708) 458-2520
http://www.villageofjustice.com
Village of La Grange . . . . (708) 579-2300
http://www.villageoflagrange.com
Village of La Grange Park . . . . (708) 354-0225
http://www.lagrangepark.org
Village of Lansing . . . . (708) 895-7200
http://www.villageoflansing.com
Village of Lemont . . . . (630) 257-1550
http://www.lemont.il.us
Village of Lincolnwood . . . . (847) 673-1540
http://www.lincolnwoodil.org
Village of Lynwood . . . . (708) 758-6101
http://www.lynwoodil.us
Village of Lyons . . . . (708) 780-5200
http://www.lyonspolice.org
Village of Matteson . . . . (708) 283-4900
http://www.vil.matteson.il.us
Village of Maywood . . . . (708) 344-1200
http://www.maywood-il.org
Village of Melrose Park . . . . (703) 343-4000
http://www.melrosepark.org
Village of Midlothian . . . . (708) 389-0200
http://www.villageofmidlothian.net
Village of Morton Grove . . . . (847) 965-4100
http://www.mortongroveil.org
Village of Mount Prospect . . . . (847) 392-6000
http://www.mountprospect.org
Village of Niles . . . . (847) 588-8000
http://www.vniles.com
Village of Norridge . . . . (708) 453-0800
http://www.villageofnorridge.com
Village of North Riverside . . . . (708) 447-4211
http://www.northriverside-il.org
Village of Northbrook . . . . (847) 272-5050
http://www.northbrook.il.us
Village of Northfield . . . . (847) 446-9200
http://www.northfieldil.org
Village of Oak Lawn . . . . (708) 636-4400
http://www.villageofoaklawn.com
Village of Oak Park . . . . (708) 445-3340
http://www.vil.oak-park.il.us
Village of Orland Hills . . . . (708) 349-6865
http://www.orlandhills.org
Village of Orland Park . . . . (708) 403-6100
http://www.orland-park.il.us
Village of Palatine . . . . (847) 358-6700
http://www.palatine.il.us
Village of Park Forest . . . . (708) 748-1112
http://www.villageofparkforest.com
Village of Richton Park . . . . (708) 481-8950
http://www.richtonpark.org
Village of River Grove . . . . (708) 453-8000
http://www.villageofrivergrove.org
Village of Riverdale . . . . (708) 841-2200
http://www.villageofriverdale.org
Village of Riverside . . . . (708) 447-2700
http://riverside.il.us
Village of Sauk Village . . . . (708) 758-3330
http://www.saukvillage.org
Village of Schaumburg . . . . (847) 895-4500
http://www.ci.schaumburg.il.us
Village of Schiller Park . . . . (847) 678-2550
http://www.villageofschillerpark.com
Village of Skokie . . . . (847) 673-0500
http://www.skokie.com
Village of South Holland . . . . (708) 210-2900
http://www.southholland.org
Village of Stickney . . . . (708) 749-4400
http://www.villageofstickney.com
Village of Streamwood . . . . (630) 837-0200
http://www.streamwood.org
Village of Tinley Park . . . . (704) 444-5000
http://www.tinleypark.org
Village of Westchester . . . . (708) 345-0020
http://www.westchester-il.org
Village of Western Springs . . . . (708) 246-1800
http://www.wsprings.com
Village of Wheeling . . . . (847) 459-2600
http://vi.wheeling.il.us
Village of Willow Springs . . . . (708) 467-3700
http://www.willowsprings-il.gov
Village of Wilmette . . . . (847) 251-2700
http://www.wilmette.com
Village of Winnetka . . . . (847) 501-6000
http://www.villageofwinnetka.org
Village of Worth . . . . (708) 448-1181
http://www.villageofworth.com
West Lawn Chamber of Commerce . . . . (773) 735-7690
http://www.westlawnchamber.org
West Suburban Chamber of Commerce . . . . (708) 352-0494
West Suburban Chamber of Commerce . . . . (708) 352-0494
http://www.westsuburbanchamber.org
Westchester Chamber of Commerce . . . . (708) 343-4300
http://www.westchesterchamber.org
Wheeling/Prospect Heights Area Chamber of Commerce & Industr . . (847) 541-0170
http://www.wphchamber.com
Wicker Park & Bucktown Chamber of Commerce . . . . (773) 384-2672
http://www.wickerparkbucktown.com
Wilmette Chamber of Commerce . . . . (847) 251-3800
http://www.wilmettechamber.org
Winnetka Chamber of Commerce . . . . (847) 446-4451
http://www.winnetkachamber.com

Cook County Communities

ALSIP (village). Covers a land area of 6.366 square miles and a water area of 0.159 square miles. Located at 41.67° N. Lat.; 87.73° W. Long. Elevation is 623 feet.

Population: 18,215 (1990); 19,725 (2000); 19,208 (2007); 18,674 (2012 projected); Race: 76.9% White, 12.2% Black, 2.4% Asian, 11.9% Hispanic of any race (2007); Density: 3,017.3 persons per square mile (2007); Average household size: 2.59 (2007); Median age: 36.1 (2007); Males per 100 females: 94.2 (2007); Marriage status: 30.1% never married, 52.7% now married, 7.6% widowed, 9.6% divorced (2000); Foreign born: 8.9% (2000); Ancestry (includes multiple ancestries): 24.2% Irish, 20.7% German, 20.1% Other groups, 17.3% Polish, 11.8% Italian (2000).

Economy: Single-family building permits issued: 8 (2007); Multi-family building permits issued: 2 (2007); Employment by occupation: 11.0% management, 14.1% professional, 12.9% services, 32.2% sales, 0.1% farming, 13.0% construction, 16.7% production (2000).

Income: Per capita income: $24,061 (2007); Median household income: $54,202 (2007); Average household income: $62,178 (2007); Percent of households with income of $100,000 or more: 15.2% (2007); Poverty rate: 6.6% (2000).

Education: Percent of population age 25 and over with: High school diploma (including GED) or higher: 84.4% (2007); Bachelor's degree or higher: 13.9% (2007); Master's degree or higher: 3.7% (2007).

School District(s)

Alsip-Hazlgrn-Oaklwn SD 126 (PK-08)
2005-06 Enrollment: 1,653 . . . . (708) 389-1900
Atwood Heights SD 125 (PK-08)
2005-06 Enrollment: 694 . . . . (708) 371-0080
Cook County SD 130 (PK-08)
2005-06 Enrollment: 3,948 . . . . (708) 385-6800

Housing: Homeownership rate: 65.5% (2007); Median home value: $206,188 (2007); Median rent: $601 per month (2000); Median age of housing: 28 years (2000).

Safety: Violent crime rate: 38.8 per 10,000 population; Property crime rate: 387.5 per 10,000 population (2006).

Transportation: Commute to work: 89.5% car, 6.7% public transportation, 1.2% walk, 1.7% work from home (2000); Travel time to work: 22.7% less than 15 minutes, 28.2% 15 to 30 minutes, 20.6% 30 to 45 minutes, 13.2% 45 to 60 minutes, 15.2% 60 minutes or more (2000)

Additional Information Contacts

Alsip Chamber of Commerce. . . . . (708) 597-2668
http://www.alsipchamber.org
Village of Alsip . . . . (708) 385-6902
http://www.alsip.org.il

ARLINGTON HEIGHTS (village). Covers a land area of 16.410 square miles and a water area of 0.031 square miles. Located at 42.09° N. Lat.; 87.98° W. Long. Elevation is 702 feet.
History: Named for Henry Bennet (1618-1685), 1st Earl of Arlington. Arlington Heights was settled in the 1830's. The Arlington Park Race Track opened here in 1929, drawing many visitors from Chicago.
Population: 75,201 (1990); 76,031 (2000); 73,135 (2007); 70,926 (2012 projected); Race: 89.0% White, 1.1% Black, 7.0% Asian, 5.3% Hispanic of any race (2007); Density: 4,456.9 persons per square mile (2007); Average household size: 2.45 (2007); Median age: 41.8 (2007); Males per 100 females: 92.8 (2007); Marriage status: 22.0% never married, 62.6% now married, 7.6% widowed, 7.8% divorced (2000); Foreign born: 13.9% (2000); Ancestry (includes multiple ancestries): 27.5% German, 19.2% Irish, 14.5% Polish, 12.0% Other groups, 11.1% Italian (2000).
Economy: Unemployment rate: 3.6% (4/2008); Total civilian labor force: 42,699 (4/2008); Single-family building permits issued: 109 (2007); Multi-family building permits issued: 0 (2007); Employment by occupation: 23.5% management, 27.0% professional, 7.5% services, 29.8% sales, 0.0% farming, 4.8% construction, 7.3% production (2000).
Income: Per capita income: $38,916 (2007); Median household income: $76,227 (2007); Average household income: $94,470 (2007); Percent of households with income of $100,000 or more: 35.5% (2007); Poverty rate: 2.5% (2000).
Taxes: Total city taxes per capita: $762 (2006); City property taxes per capita: $483 (2006).
Education: Percent of population age 25 and over with: High school diploma (including GED) or higher: 92.5% (2007); Bachelor's degree or higher: 46.3% (2007); Master's degree or higher: 16.2% (2007).

School District(s)

Arlington Heights SD 25 (PK-08)
2005-06 Enrollment: 4,970 . . . . (847) 758-4900
Comm Cons SD 59 (PK-08)
2005-06 Enrollment: 6,065 . . . . (847) 593-4300
Northwest Suburban Ed To Careers
2005-06 Enrollment: n/a . . . . (847) 718-6801
Nw Suburban Spec Educ Org (PK-12)
2005-06 Enrollment: 601 . . . . (847) 463-8100
Township HSD 214 (09-12)
2005-06 Enrollment: 12,542 . . . . (847) 718-7600
Wheeling CCSD 21 (PK-08)
2005-06 Enrollment: 6,725 . . . . (847) 537-8270

Vocational/Technical School(s)

Empire Beauty School-Arlington Heights (Private, For-profit)
Fall 2007 Enrollment: 189 . . . . (847) 394-8359
2007-08 Tuition: $17,595
Housing: Homeownership rate: 76.5% (2007); Median home value: $340,158 (2007); Median rent: $876 per month (2000); Median age of housing: 30 years (2000).
Hospitals: Northwest Community Hospital (488 beds)
Safety: Violent crime rate: 6.1 per 10,000 population; Property crime rate: 185.8 per 10,000 population (2006).
Newspapers: Arlington Heights Post (Community news; Circulation 6,231); Barrington Courier-Review (Community news; Circulation 7,604); Beep (Regional news; Circulation 0); Buffalo Grove Countryside (Community news; Circulation 6,020); Daily Herald (Local news; Circulation 148,375); Elk Grove Times (Community news; Circulation 2,547); Glencoe News (Community news; Circulation 2,345); Hoffman Estates Review (Community news; Circulation 2,281); Palatine Countryside (Community news; Circulation 6,231); Pioneer Press - Northwest/Arlington Heights Bureau (Local news; Circulation 0); Rolling Meadows Review (Community news; Circulation 1,756); Schaumburg Review (Local news; Circulation 5,089)
Transportation: Commute to work: 86.3% car, 7.8% public transportation, 1.7% walk, 3.7% work from home (2000); Travel time to work: 22.5% less than 15 minutes, 34.1% 15 to 30 minutes, 22.3% 30 to 45 minutes, 9.4% 45 to 60 minutes, 11.7% 60 minutes or more (2000)

Additional Information Contacts

Arlington Heights Chamber of Commerce . . . . (847) 253-1703
http://www.arlingtonhtschamber.com
Village of Arlington Heights . . . . (847) 368-5000
http://www.vah.com

BARRINGTON (village). Covers a land area of 4.597 square miles and a water area of 0.171 square miles. Located at 42.15° N. Lat.; 88.13° W. Long. Elevation is 827 feet.
History: Named for Great Barrington, Massachusetts. Barrington was founded in the 1850's and developed as an agricultural community.
Population: 9,741 (1990); 10,168 (2000); 10,541 (2007); 10,667 (2012 projected); Race: 95.0% White, 0.8% Black, 2.7% Asian, 3.0% Hispanic of any race (2007); Density: 2,292.9 persons per square mile (2007); Average household size: 2.70 (2007); Median age: 39.3 (2007); Males per 100 females: 91.3 (2007); Marriage status: 20.2% never married, 65.6% now married, 6.4% widowed, 7.9% divorced (2000); Foreign born: 6.6% (2000); Ancestry (includes multiple ancestries): 28.5% German, 23.3% Irish, 12.2% English, 8.7% Italian, 8.0% Polish (2000).
Economy: Single-family building permits issued: 16 (2007); Multi-family building permits issued: 7 (2007); Employment by occupation: 28.8% management, 26.3% professional, 6.6% services, 30.5% sales, 0.0% farming, 3.7% construction, 4.1% production (2000).
Income: Per capita income: $48,106 (2007); Median household income: $91,124 (2007); Average household income: $129,727 (2007); Percent of households with income of $100,000 or more: 46.0% (2007); Poverty rate: 3.1% (2000).
Education: Percent of population age 25 and over with: High school diploma (including GED) or higher: 94.5% (2007); Bachelor's degree or higher: 57.7% (2007); Master's degree or higher: 23.7% (2007).

School District(s)

Barrington CUSD 220 (PK-12)
2005-06 Enrollment: 9,135 . . . . (847) 381-6300
Housing: Homeownership rate: 78.0% (2007); Median home value: $457,576 (2007); Median rent: $839 per month (2000); Median age of housing: 35 years (2000).
Hospitals: Advocate Good Shephard Hospital (154 beds)
Transportation: Commute to work: 78.7% car, 9.6% public transportation, 2.4% walk, 8.6% work from home (2000); Travel time to work: 25.6% less than 15 minutes, 26.4% 15 to 30 minutes, 22.7% 30 to 45 minutes, 8.7% 45 to 60 minutes, 16.6% 60 minutes or more (2000)

Additional Information Contacts

Barrington Chamber of Commerce . . . . (847) 381-2525
http://www.barringtonchamber.com
Village of Barrington. . . . . (647) 304-3400
http://www.ci.barrington.il.us

BARRINGTON HILLS (village). Covers a land area of 27.879 square miles and a water area of 0.520 square miles. Located at 42.14° N. Lat.; 88.20° W. Long. Elevation is 846 feet.
Population: 4,069 (1990); 3,915 (2000); 4,213 (2007); 4,398 (2012 projected); Race: 92.7% White, 0.7% Black, 4.7% Asian, 2.6% Hispanic of any race (2007); Density: 151.1 persons per square mile (2007); Average household size: 2.81 (2007); Median age: 46.8 (2007); Males per 100 females: 96.0 (2007); Marriage status: 18.8% never married, 76.0% now married, 1.8% widowed, 3.4% divorced (2000); Foreign born: 5.1% (2000); Ancestry (includes multiple ancestries): 28.9% German, 20.4% Irish, 17.5% Italian, 14.2% English, 6.5% Other groups (2000).
Economy: Single-family building permits issued: 11 (2007); Multi-family building permits issued: 0 (2007); Employment by occupation: 34.2% management, 25.5% professional, 6.0% services, 27.3% sales, 0.5% farming, 2.1% construction, 4.4% production (2000).
Income: Per capita income: $77,756 (2007); Median household income: $162,252 (2007); Average household income: $218,390 (2007); Percent of households with income of $100,000 or more: 70.6% (2007); Poverty rate: 3.1% (2000).
Education: Percent of population age 25 and over with: High school diploma (including GED) or higher: 95.0% (2007); Bachelor's degree or higher: 67.4% (2007); Master's degree or higher: 28.8% (2007).
Housing: Homeownership rate: 93.5% (2007); Median home value: $911,388 (2007); Median rent: $1,375 per month (2000); Median age of housing: 31 years (2000).
Safety: Violent crime rate: 7.0 per 10,000 population; Property crime rate: 96.3 per 10,000 population (2006).
Transportation: Commute to work: 77.2% car, 9.8% public transportation, 0.3% walk, 11.7% work from home (2000); Travel time to work: 24.8% less than 15 minutes, 28.2% 15 to 30 minutes, 15.0% 30 to 45 minutes, 9.5% 45 to 60 minutes, 22.4% 60 minutes or more (2000)

BEDFORD PARK (village). Covers a land area of 5.965 square miles and a water area of 0.109 square miles. Located at 41.76° N. Lat.; 87.78° W. Long. Elevation is 617 feet.
Population: 566 (1990); 574 (2000); 523 (2007); 516 (2012 projected); Race: 96.7% White, 1.0% Black, 0.4% Asian, 9.0% Hispanic of any race (2007); Density: 87.7 persons per square mile (2007); Average household size: 2.68 (2007); Median age: 41.4 (2007); Males per 100 females: 90.9 (2007); Marriage status: 22.9% never married, 62.4% now married, 8.1% widowed, 6.6% divorced (2000); Foreign born: 4.6% (2000); Ancestry (includes multiple ancestries): 26.2% Irish, 24.9% German, 19.6% Polish, 13.5% Italian, 8.4% English (2000).
Economy: Single-family building permits issued: 0 (2007); Multi-family building permits issued: 0 (2007); Employment by occupation: 15.7% management, 15.7% professional, 13.8% services, 26.9% sales, 0.0% farming, 17.9% construction, 9.9% production (2000).
Income: Per capita income: $24,871 (2007); Median household income: $58,200 (2007); Average household income: $66,705 (2007); Percent of households with income of $100,000 or more: 17.4% (2007); Poverty rate: 2.1% (2000).
Education: Percent of population age 25 and over with: High school diploma (including GED) or higher: 83.5% (2007); Bachelor's degree or higher: 14.2% (2007); Master's degree or higher: 4.5% (2007).

School District(s)

Summit SD 104 (PK-08)
2005-06 Enrollment: 1,697 . . . . (708) 458-0505
Housing: Homeownership rate: 92.8% (2007); Median home value: $213,603 (2007); Median rent: $444 per month (2000); Median age of housing: 57 years (2000).
Transportation: Commute to work: 90.0% car, 4.2% public transportation, 5.8% walk, 0.0% work from home (2000); Travel time to work: 37.7% less than 15 minutes, 27.1% 15 to 30 minutes, 21.3% 30 to 45 minutes, 5.8% 45 to 60 minutes, 8.1% 60 minutes or more (2000)

BELLWOOD (village). Covers a land area of 2.386 square miles and a water area of 0 square miles. Located at 41.88° N. Lat.; 87.87° W. Long. Elevation is 633 feet.
History: Derived from its original name of Bell's Wood, which was probably named for a landowner. Incorporated 1900.
Population: 20,241 (1990); 20,535 (2000); 19,191 (2007); 18,248 (2012 projected); Race: 10.5% White, 82.4% Black, 0.9% Asian, 9.5% Hispanic of any race (2007); Density: 8,044.6 persons per square mile (2007); Average household size: 3.19 (2007); Median age: 33.6 (2007); Males per 100 females: 88.7 (2007); Marriage status: 36.5% never married, 48.1% now married, 6.0% widowed, 9.4% divorced (2000); Foreign born: 6.1% (2000); Ancestry (includes multiple ancestries): 79.6% Other groups, 3.2% German, 1.9% Italian, 1.8% Irish, 1.7% African (2000).
Economy: Single-family building permits issued: 0 (2007); Multi-family building permits issued: 0 (2007); Employment by occupation: 8.0% management, 12.0% professional, 13.4% services, 34.6% sales, 0.0% farming, 6.0% construction, 26.0% production (2000).
Income: Per capita income: $20,994 (2007); Median household income: $57,428 (2007); Average household income: $66,650 (2007); Percent of households with income of $100,000 or more: 16.7% (2007); Poverty rate: 7.2% (2000).
Taxes: Total city taxes per capita: $835 (2006); City property taxes per capita: $650 (2006).
Education: Percent of population age 25 and over with: High school diploma (including GED) or higher: 76.6% (2007); Bachelor's degree or higher: 11.9% (2007); Master's degree or higher: 3.6% (2007).

School District(s)

Bellwood SD 88 (PK-08)
2005-06 Enrollment: 3,239 . . . . (708) 344-9344
Berkeley SD 87 (PK-08)
2005-06 Enrollment: 2,886 . . . . (708) 449-3350
Intermediate Service Center 2 (07-12)
2005-06 Enrollment: 65 . . . . (708) 482-4350
Housing: Homeownership rate: 75.4% (2007); Median home value: $177,659 (2007); Median rent: $604 per month (2000); Median age of housing: 45 years (2000).
Safety: Violent crime rate: 54.8 per 10,000 population; Property crime rate: 280.8 per 10,000 population (2006).
Transportation: Commute to work: 86.8% car, 9.2% public transportation, 1.3% walk, 2.2% work from home (2000); Travel time to work: 17.1% less than 15 minutes, 36.0% 15 to 30 minutes, 27.6% 30 to 45 minutes, 9.7% 45 to 60 minutes, 9.6% 60 minutes or more (2000)
Additional Information Contacts
Village of Bellwood. . . . . (708) 547-3500
http://www.vil.bellwood.il.us

BERKELEY (village). Covers a land area of 1.393 square miles and a water area of 0 square miles. Located at 41.88° N. Lat.; 87.91° W. Long. Elevation is 650 feet.
Population: 5,137 (1990); 5,245 (2000); 4,949 (2007); 4,720 (2012 projected); Race: 46.0% White, 38.0% Black, 3.3% Asian, 20.9% Hispanic of any race (2007); Density: 3,552.9 persons per square mile (2007); Average household size: 2.85 (2007); Median age: 38.9 (2007); Males per 100 females: 96.9 (2007); Marriage status: 25.7% never married, 58.0% now married, 8.3% widowed, 8.0% divorced (2000); Foreign born: 13.4% (2000); Ancestry (includes multiple ancestries): 45.2% Other groups, 13.9% German, 13.7% Irish, 10.5% Italian, 6.0% English (2000).
Economy: Single-family building permits issued: 6 (2007); Multi-family building permits issued: 0 (2007); Employment by occupation: 9.8% management, 17.2% professional, 10.4% services, 33.6% sales, 0.0% farming, 8.0% construction, 21.0% production (2000).
Income: Per capita income: $26,534 (2007); Median household income: $65,000 (2007); Average household income: $75,443 (2007); Percent of households with income of $100,000 or more: 23.6% (2007); Poverty rate: 6.4% (2000).
Education: Percent of population age 25 and over with: High school diploma (including GED) or higher: 82.3% (2007); Bachelor's degree or higher: 19.5% (2007); Master's degree or higher: 6.0% (2007).

School District(s)

Berkeley SD 87 (PK-08)
2005-06 Enrollment: 2,886 . . . . (708) 449-3350
Housing: Homeownership rate: 86.0% (2007); Median home value: $209,564 (2007); Median rent: $674 per month (2000); Median age of housing: 44 years (2000).
Safety: Violent crime rate: 14.0 per 10,000 population; Property crime rate: 197.8 per 10,000 population (2006).
Transportation: Commute to work: 89.4% car, 5.3% public transportation, 2.7% walk, 2.5% work from home (2000); Travel time to work: 22.0% less than 15 minutes, 37.4% 15 to 30 minutes, 20.9% 30 to 45 minutes, 10.1% 45 to 60 minutes, 9.5% 60 minutes or more (2000)
Additional Information Contacts
Village of Berkeley . . . . (708) 449-8840
http://www.berkeley.il.us

BERWYN (city). Covers a land area of 3.893 square miles and a water area of 0 square miles. Located at 41.84° N. Lat.; 87.79° W. Long. Elevation is 617 feet.
History: Named for Berwyn, Pennsylvania. Berwyn was organized in 1890 by Charles E. Piper and Wilbur J. Andrews, realtors who felt that a town would be populated if they built it. Berwyn was incorporated as a village in 1891 and chartered as a city in 1908. It grew as a residential suburb, with many of the people employed in neighboring Cicero, where the Western Electric Company had a plant.
Population: 45,426 (1990); 54,016 (2000); 50,557 (2007); 47,963 (2012 projected); Race: 63.3% White, 1.7% Black, 2.8% Asian, 52.8% Hispanic of any race (2007); Density: 12,987.6 persons per square mile (2007); Average household size: 2.81 (2007); Median age: 35.4 (2007); Males per 100 females: 96.1 (2007); Marriage status: 31.1% never married, 51.4% now married, 8.1% widowed, 9.4% divorced (2000); Foreign born: 25.1% (2000); Ancestry (includes multiple ancestries): 39.4% Other groups, 12.0% Polish, 11.8% German, 11.1% Irish, 10.4% Italian (2000).
Economy: Unemployment rate: 5.8% (4/2008); Total civilian labor force: 26,230 (4/2008); Single-family building permits issued: 1 (2007); Multi-family building permits issued: 12 (2007); Employment by occupation: 10.3% management, 15.9% professional, 14.1% services, 30.0% sales, 0.0% farming, 9.6% construction, 20.1% production (2000).
Income: Per capita income: $21,008 (2007); Median household income: $48,723 (2007); Average household income: $58,902 (2007); Percent of households with income of $100,000 or more: 13.6% (2007); Poverty rate: 7.9% (2000).
Taxes: Total city taxes per capita: $727 (2006); City property taxes per capita: $440 (2006).
Education: Percent of population age 25 and over with: High school diploma (including GED) or higher: 74.6% (2007); Bachelor's degree or higher: 17.2% (2007); Master's degree or higher: 6.0% (2007).

School District(s)

Berwyn North SD 98 (PK-08)
2005-06 Enrollment: 3,272 . . . . (708) 484-6200
Berwyn South SD 100 (PK-08)
2005-06 Enrollment: 3,506 . . . . (708) 795-2300
J S Morton HSD 201 (09-12)
2005-06 Enrollment: 8,203 . . . . (708) 222-5702

Vocational/Technical School(s)

American Career College (Private, For-profit)
Fall 2007 Enrollment: 90 . . . . (708) 795-1500
2007-08 Tuition: $8,150

Housing: Homeownership rate: 61.4% (2007); Median home value: $217,773 (2007); Median rent: $545 per month (2000); Median age of housing: 60 years (2000).
Hospitals: MacNeal Hospital (427 beds)
Safety: Violent crime rate: 23.1 per 10,000 population; Property crime rate: 277.6 per 10,000 population (2006).
Newspapers: Chicago Deportivo (Local news; Circulation 75,000)
Transportation: Commute to work: 83.7% car, 10.8% public transportation, 3.2% walk, 1.6% work from home (2000); Travel time to work: 17.8% less than 15 minutes, 28.8% 15 to 30 minutes, 27.5% 30 to 45 minutes, 15.3% 45 to 60 minutes, 10.6% 60 minutes or more (2000)
Additional Information Contacts
City of Berwyn . . . . (708) 788-2660
http://www.berwyn-il.gov

BLUE ISLAND (city). Covers a land area of 4.030 square miles and a water area of 0.095 square miles. Located at 41.65° N. Lat.; 87.67° W. Long. Elevation is 640 feet.
History: Blue Island was named because it looked like an island surrounded by marshes, and a blue haze often hung over its woods. Settlers first came in 1835, and the village was laid out in 1872. Many of the early residents were of German and Italian ancestry.
Population: 21,203 (1990); 23,463 (2000); 22,461 (2007); 21,659 (2012 projected); Race: 45.2% White, 26.8% Black, 0.4% Asian, 45.1% Hispanic of any race (2007); Density: 5,573.8 persons per square mile (2007); Average household size: 2.91 (2007); Median age: 32.3 (2007); Males per 100 females: 96.6 (2007); Marriage status: 35.5% never married, 48.5% now married, 6.2% widowed, 9.9% divorced (2000); Foreign born: 22.1% (2000); Ancestry (includes multiple ancestries): 57.4% Other groups, 11.7% German, 10.4% Irish, 6.7% Polish, 6.6% Italian (2000).
Economy: Single-family building permits issued: 49 (2007); Multi-family building permits issued: 0 (2007); Employment by occupation: 7.0% management, 12.2% professional, 18.0% services, 27.2% sales, 0.0% farming, 12.5% construction, 23.0% production (2000).
Income: Per capita income: $16,308 (2007); Median household income: $38,574 (2007); Average household income: $47,290 (2007); Percent of households with income of $100,000 or more: 7.0% (2007); Poverty rate: 13.3% (2000).
Taxes: Total city taxes per capita: $388 (2006); City property taxes per capita: $274 (2006).
Education: Percent of population age 25 and over with: High school diploma (including GED) or higher: 65.8% (2007); Bachelor's degree or higher: 11.5% (2007); Master's degree or higher: 3.4% (2007).

School District(s)

CHSD 218 (09-12)
2005-06 Enrollment: 5,329 . . . . (708) 424-2000
Cook County SD 130 (PK-08)
2005-06 Enrollment: 3,948 . . . . (708) 385-6800
Exc Children Have Opportunities (PK-12)
2005-06 Enrollment: 649 . . . . (708) 333-7880

Vocational/Technical School(s)

Cannella School of Hair Design (Private, For-profit)
Fall 2007 Enrollment: 61 . . . . (708) 388-4949
2007-08 Tuition: $9,350
Environmental Technical Institute (Private, For-profit)
Fall 2007 Enrollment: 209 . . . . (630) 285-9100
2007-08 Tuition: $11,850

Housing: Homeownership rate: 53.9% (2007); Median home value: $155,554 (2007); Median rent: $521 per month (2000); Median age of housing: 46 years (2000).
Hospitals: St. Francis Hospital & Health Center (410 beds)
Safety: Violent crime rate: 106.6 per 10,000 population; Property crime rate: 378.7 per 10,000 population (2006).
Transportation: Commute to work: 80.8% car, 12.6% public transportation, 4.8% walk, 1.0% work from home (2000); Travel time to work: 23.7% less than 15 minutes, 28.2% 15 to 30 minutes, 18.9% 30 to 45 minutes, 11.9% 45 to 60 minutes, 17.3% 60 minutes or more (2000)
Additional Information Contacts
Blue Island Area Chamber of Commerce . . . . (708) 388-1000
http://www.blueislandchamber.org
City of Blue Island . . . . (708) 597-8603
http://www.blueisland.org

BRIDGEVIEW (village). Covers a land area of 4.126 square miles and a water area of 0 square miles. Located at 41.74° N. Lat.; 87.80° W. Long. Elevation is 620 feet.
History: Named for the city's many bridges. Incorporated 1947.
Population: 14,346 (1990); 15,335 (2000); 15,204 (2007); 14,896 (2012 projected); Race: 83.6% White, 1.2% Black, 2.8% Asian, 12.3% Hispanic of any race (2007); Density: 3,684.7 persons per square mile (2007); Average household size: 2.71 (2007); Median age: 37.9 (2007); Males per 100 females: 98.1 (2007); Marriage status: 25.1% never married, 54.3% now married, 11.0% widowed, 9.6% divorced (2000); Foreign born: 18.9% (2000); Ancestry (includes multiple ancestries): 25.7% Polish, 17.2% Irish, 15.1% German, 13.2% Other groups, 9.0% Italian (2000).
Economy: Single-family building permits issued: 54 (2007); Multi-family building permits issued: 5 (2007); Employment by occupation: 8.2% management, 10.2% professional, 13.5% services, 32.7% sales, 0.1% farming, 13.2% construction, 22.1% production (2000).
Income: Per capita income: $20,621 (2007); Median household income: $45,697 (2007); Average household income: $55,195 (2007); Percent of households with income of $100,000 or more: 12.0% (2007); Poverty rate: 7.2% (2000).
Education: Percent of population age 25 and over with: High school diploma (including GED) or higher: 72.6% (2007); Bachelor's degree or higher: 9.1% (2007); Master's degree or higher: 2.3% (2007).

School District(s)

Indian Springs SD 109 (PK-08)
2005-06 Enrollment: 2,895 . . . . (708) 496-8700
Ridgeland SD 122 (PK-08)
2005-06 Enrollment: 2,144 . . . . (708) 599-5550

Two-year College(s)

Northwestern Business College-Southwestern Campus (Private, For-profit)
Fall 2007 Enrollment: 1,050. . . . . (708) 237-5050
2007-08 Tuition: In-state $17,415; Out-of-state $17,415

Housing: Homeownership rate: 75.3% (2007); Median home value: $204,388 (2007); Median rent: $628 per month (2000); Median age of housing: 30 years (2000).
Safety: Violent crime rate: 13.4 per 10,000 population; Property crime rate: 292.0 per 10,000 population (2006).
Transportation: Commute to work: 90.4% car, 4.4% public transportation, 2.9% walk, 1.8% work from home (2000); Travel time to work: 26.2% less than 15 minutes, 29.8% 15 to 30 minutes, 22.2% 30 to 45 minutes, 8.6% 45 to 60 minutes, 13.2% 60 minutes or more (2000)
Additional Information Contacts
Bridgeview Chamber of Commerce . . . . (708) 598-1700
http://www.bridgeviewchamber.com

BROADVIEW (village). Covers a land area of 1.779 square miles and a water area of 0 square miles. Located at 41.85° N. Lat.; 87.85° W. Long. Elevation is 630 feet.
History: Broadview was incorporated as a village in 1910, and developed as a residential community.
Population: 8,713 (1990); 8,264 (2000); 7,823 (2007); 7,452 (2012 projected); Race: 17.6% White, 76.9% Black, 1.1% Asian, 5.2% Hispanic of any race (2007); Density: 4,397.0 persons per square mile (2007); Average household size: 2.60 (2007); Median age: 38.0 (2007); Males per 100 females: 86.4 (2007); Marriage status: 30.9% never married, 48.0% now married, 7.8% widowed, 13.3% divorced (2000); Foreign born: 3.9% (2000); Ancestry (includes multiple ancestries): 70.4% Other groups, 6.7% German, 3.8% Irish, 3.5% Polish, 2.7% Italian (2000).
Economy: Single-family building permits issued: 0 (2007); Multi-family building permits issued: 0 (2007); Employment by occupation: 15.1% management, 15.3% professional, 13.2% services, 34.1% sales, 0.0% farming, 3.8% construction, 18.6% production (2000).
Income: Per capita income: $23,379 (2007); Median household income: $51,327 (2007); Average household income: $60,783 (2007); Percent of

households with income of $100,000 or more: 14.6% (2007); Poverty rate: 6.4% (2000).
Education: Percent of population age 25 and over with: High school diploma (including GED) or higher: 82.8% (2007); Bachelor's degree or higher: 16.4% (2007); Master's degree or higher: 4.7% (2007).

School District(s)

Lindop SD 92 (PK-08)
2005-06 Enrollment: 505 . . . . (708) 345-3110
Maywood-Melrose Park-Broadview 89 (PK-08)
2005-06 Enrollment: 5,586 . . . . (708) 450-2460

Housing: Homeownership rate: 69.0% (2007); Median home value: $184,813 (2007); Median rent: $572 per month (2000); Median age of housing: 45 years (2000).
Safety: Violent crime rate: 75.1 per 10,000 population; Property crime rate: 530.8 per 10,000 population (2006).
Transportation: Commute to work: 85.8% car, 8.8% public transportation, 2.2% walk, 1.8% work from home (2000); Travel time to work: 17.4% less than 15 minutes, 35.1% 15 to 30 minutes, 27.7% 30 to 45 minutes, 10.6% 45 to 60 minutes, 9.2% 60 minutes or more (2000)

Additional Information Contacts

Broadview Chamber of Commerce . . . . (708) 345-3011
Village of Broadview . . . . (708) 681-3600
http://www.villageofbroadview.com

BROOKFIELD (village). Covers a land area of 3.052 square miles and a water area of 0.004 square miles. Located at 41.82° N. Lat.; 87.84° W. Long. Elevation is 623 feet.
History: Named for the many local brooks. Incorporated 1893.
Population: 18,861 (1990); 19,085 (2000); 18,243 (2007); 17,590 (2012 projected); Race: 91.3% White, 1.2% Black, 1.4% Asian, 11.1% Hispanic of any race (2007); Density: 5,976.5 persons per square mile (2007); Average household size: 2.54 (2007); Median age: 40.2 (2007); Males per 100 females: 91.5 (2007); Marriage status: 25.4% never married, 55.9% now married, 9.1% widowed, 9.6% divorced (2000); Foreign born: 9.2% (2000); Ancestry (includes multiple ancestries): 23.2% German, 20.1% Irish, 18.0% Polish, 13.0% Italian, 11.1% Other groups (2000).
Economy: Single-family building permits issued: 18 (2007); Multi-family building permits issued: 0 (2007); Employment by occupation: 14.0% management, 22.3% professional, 9.8% services, 33.0% sales, 0.0% farming, 8.7% construction, 12.2% production (2000).
Income: Per capita income: $28,890 (2007); Median household income: $61,519 (2007); Average household income: $73,061 (2007); Percent of households with income of $100,000 or more: 22.8% (2007); Poverty rate: 4.3% (2000).
Education: Percent of population age 25 and over with: High school diploma (including GED) or higher: 87.6% (2007); Bachelor's degree or higher: 26.1% (2007); Master's degree or higher: 8.0% (2007).

School District(s)

Brookfield Lagrange Park SD 95 (PK-08)
2005-06 Enrollment: 935 . . . . (708) 485-0606
La Grange SD 102 (PK-08)
2005-06 Enrollment: 2,681 . . . . (708) 482-2400
Lyons SD 103 (PK-08)
2005-06 Enrollment: 2,317 . . . . (708) 783-4100
Riverside SD 96 (PK-08)
2005-06 Enrollment: 1,300 . . . . (708) 447-5007

Housing: Homeownership rate: 74.2% (2007); Median home value: $236,533 (2007); Median rent: $678 per month (2000); Median age of housing: 50 years (2000).
Safety: Violent crime rate: 9.7 per 10,000 population; Property crime rate: 208.5 per 10,000 population (2006).
Transportation: Commute to work: 84.3% car, 9.1% public transportation, 2.3% walk, 3.8% work from home (2000); Travel time to work: 24.9% less than 15 minutes, 31.7% 15 to 30 minutes, 23.0% 30 to 45 minutes, 10.7% 45 to 60 minutes, 9.7% 60 minutes or more (2000)

Additional Information Contacts

Brookfield Chamber of Commerce. . . . . (708) 485-1434
Village of Brookfield . . . . (708) 485-7344
http://www.villageofbrookfield.com

BURBANK (city). Aka South Stickney. Covers a land area of 4.173 square miles and a water area of 0 square miles. Located at 41.74° N. Lat.; 87.77° W. Long. Elevation is 620 feet.
Population: 27,600 (1990); 27,902 (2000); 27,478 (2007); 27,015 (2012 projected); Race: 87.7% White, 0.4% Black, 2.0% Asian, 15.0% Hispanic of any race (2007); Density: 6,585.0 persons per square mile (2007); Average household size: 3.01 (2007); Median age: 38.1 (2007); Males per 100 females: 96.0 (2007); Marriage status: 28.4% never married, 55.1% now married, 9.1% widowed, 7.5% divorced (2000); Foreign born: 21.8% (2000); Ancestry (includes multiple ancestries): 30.3% Polish, 18.7% Irish, 16.1% German, 13.4% Other groups, 9.3% Italian (2000).
Economy: Unemployment rate: 5.2% (4/2008); Total civilian labor force: 14,753 (4/2008); Single-family building permits issued: 56 (2007); Multi-family building permits issued: 0 (2007); Employment by occupation: 8.5% management, 8.3% professional, 15.1% services, 30.5% sales, 0.0% farming, 12.2% construction, 25.4% production (2000).
Income: Per capita income: $20,638 (2007); Median household income: $53,130 (2007); Average household income: $61,395 (2007); Percent of households with income of $100,000 or more: 14.5% (2007); Poverty rate: 5.1% (2000).
Education: Percent of population age 25 and over with: High school diploma (including GED) or higher: 73.7% (2007); Bachelor's degree or higher: 9.5% (2007); Master's degree or higher: 3.1% (2007).

School District(s)

A E R O Spec Educ Coop (PK-12)
2005-06 Enrollment: 237 . . . . (708) 496-3330
Burbank SD 111 (PK-08)
2005-06 Enrollment: 3,240 . . . . (708) 496-0500
Reavis Twp HSD 220 (09-12)
2005-06 Enrollment: 1,780 . . . . (708) 599-7200

Housing: Homeownership rate: 83.3% (2007); Median home value: $215,268 (2007); Median rent: $629 per month (2000); Median age of housing: 38 years (2000).
Safety: Violent crime rate: 34.4 per 10,000 population; Property crime rate: 301.4 per 10,000 population (2006).
Transportation: Commute to work: 90.4% car, 5.6% public transportation, 2.0% walk, 0.9% work from home (2000); Travel time to work: 22.2% less than 15 minutes, 30.4% 15 to 30 minutes, 23.4% 30 to 45 minutes, 11.2% 45 to 60 minutes, 12.8% 60 minutes or more (2000)

Additional Information Contacts

Burbank Chamber of Commerce. . . . . (708) 425-4668
City of Burbank . . . . (708) 599-5500
http://www.burbankil.gov

BURNHAM (village). Covers a land area of 1.858 square miles and a water area of 0.093 square miles. Located at 41.63° N. Lat.; 87.55° W. Long. Elevation is 584 feet.
Population: 3,916 (1990); 4,170 (2000); 4,072 (2007); 3,984 (2012 projected); Race: 25.9% White, 60.3% Black, 1.1% Asian, 16.4% Hispanic of any race (2007); Density: 2,192.0 persons per square mile (2007); Average household size: 2.92 (2007); Median age: 38.1 (2007); Males per 100 females: 92.7 (2007); Marriage status: 28.0% never married, 50.1% now married, 8.5% widowed, 13.4% divorced (2000); Foreign born: 6.8% (2000); Ancestry (includes multiple ancestries): 66.2% Other groups, 12.8% Polish, 5.7% Irish, 4.5% German, 2.8% Italian (2000).
Economy: Single-family building permits issued: 10 (2007); Multi-family building permits issued: 0 (2007); Employment by occupation: 10.3% management, 13.6% professional, 16.7% services, 30.1% sales, 0.2% farming, 10.4% construction, 18.6% production (2000).
Income: Per capita income: $18,112 (2007); Median household income: $41,276 (2007); Average household income: $50,163 (2007); Percent of households with income of $100,000 or more: 8.7% (2007); Poverty rate: 9.8% (2000).
Education: Percent of population age 25 and over with: High school diploma (including GED) or higher: 74.7% (2007); Bachelor's degree or higher: 12.6% (2007); Master's degree or higher: 3.1% (2007).

School District(s)

Burnham SD 154-5 (PK-08)
2005-06 Enrollment: 198 . . . . (708) 862-8636

Housing: Homeownership rate: 74.3% (2007); Median home value: $131,898 (2007); Median rent: $554 per month (2000); Median age of housing: 36 years (2000).
Safety: Violent crime rate: 127.5 per 10,000 population; Property crime rate: 269.6 per 10,000 population (2006).
Transportation: Commute to work: 86.1% car, 12.8% public transportation, 0.6% walk, 0.1% work from home (2000); Travel time to work: 15.4% less than 15 minutes, 27.9% 15 to 30 minutes, 22.4% 30 to 45 minutes, 11.6% 45 to 60 minutes, 22.8% 60 minutes or more (2000)

CALUMET CITY (city). Covers a land area of 7.265 square miles and a water area of 0.117 square miles. Located at 41.61° N. Lat.; 87.54° W. Long. Elevation is 591 feet.

History: Named for the French translation of "straw". Calumet City was platted in 1833, and developed in the 1920's as a residential outgrowth of Hammond, Indiana. Calumet is the French name for the Indian peace-pipe.

Population: 37,803 (1990); 39,071 (2000); 37,397 (2007); 36,047 (2012 projected); Race: 29.6% White, 59.9% Black, 0.6% Asian, 13.3% Hispanic of any race (2007); Density: 5,147.6 persons per square mile (2007); Average household size: 2.63 (2007); Median age: 35.0 (2007); Males per 100 females: 87.9 (2007); Marriage status: 31.7% never married, 47.6% now married, 9.0% widowed, 11.7% divorced (2000); Foreign born: 7.3% (2000); Ancestry (includes multiple ancestries): 58.6% Other groups, 12.7% Polish, 6.5% German, 5.1% Irish, 3.8% Italian (2000).

Economy: Unemployment rate: 7.3% (4/2008); Total civilian labor force: 18,565 (4/2008); Single-family building permits issued: 12 (2007); Multi-family building permits issued: 0 (2007); Employment by occupation: 9.5% management, 15.1% professional, 14.0% services, 32.7% sales, 0.1% farming, 8.9% construction, 19.7% production (2000).

Income: Per capita income: $19,446 (2007); Median household income: $42,569 (2007); Average household income: $51,109 (2007); Percent of households with income of $100,000 or more: 9.3% (2007); Poverty rate: 12.2% (2000).

Education: Percent of population age 25 and over with: High school diploma (including GED) or higher: 80.8% (2007); Bachelor's degree or higher: 14.1% (2007); Master's degree or higher: 3.8% (2007).

School District(s)

Calumet City SD 155 (PK-08)
2005-06 Enrollment: 1,433 .... (708) 862-7665
Dolton SD 149 (PK-08)
2005-06 Enrollment: 3,732 .... (708) 868-7861
Hoover-Schrum Memorial SD 157 (PK-08)
2005-06 Enrollment: 945 .... (708) 868-7500
Lincoln ESD 156 (PK-08)
2005-06 Enrollment: 1,119 .... (708) 862-6625
Thornton Fractional Twp HSD 215 (09-12)
2005-06 Enrollment: 3,402 .... (708) 585-2309

Four-year College(s)

Westwood College-River Oaks
Fall 2007 Enrollment: 629 .... (708) 832-9760
2007-08 Tuition: In-state $13,000; Out-of-state $13,000

Housing: Homeownership rate: 63.5% (2007); Median home value: $134,992 (2007); Median rent: $552 per month (2000); Median age of housing: 35 years (2000).

Safety: Violent crime rate: 82.8 per 10,000 population; Property crime rate: 607.2 per 10,000 population (2006).

Transportation: Commute to work: 85.1% car, 10.9% public transportation, 2.3% walk, 0.8% work from home (2000); Travel time to work: 18.3% less than 15 minutes, 25.4% 15 to 30 minutes, 23.1% 30 to 45 minutes, 11.8% 45 to 60 minutes, 21.4% 60 minutes or more (2000)

Additional Information Contacts

Calumet City Chamber of Commerce .... (708) 891-5888
http://www.calumetcitychamber.com
City of Calumet City .... (708) 891-8105
http://www.calumetcity.org

CALUMET PARK (village). Covers a land area of 1.107 square miles and a water area of 0.039 square miles. Located at 41.66° N. Lat.; 87.65° W. Long. Elevation is 604 feet.

History: Incorporated 1912; name changed from Burr Oak in 1925.

Population: 8,418 (1990); 8,516 (2000); 7,982 (2007); 7,570 (2012 projected); Race: 10.9% White, 83.8% Black, 0.1% Asian, 8.6% Hispanic of any race (2007); Density: 7,212.8 persons per square mile (2007); Average household size: 2.87 (2007); Median age: 33.6 (2007); Males per 100 females: 88.9 (2007); Marriage status: 36.9% never married, 44.9% now married, 6.3% widowed, 11.9% divorced (2000); Foreign born: 4.0% (2000); Ancestry (includes multiple ancestries): 77.9% Other groups, 2.3% Polish, 2.3% African, 2.1% German, 1.1% United States or American (2000).

Economy: Single-family building permits issued: 7 (2007); Multi-family building permits issued: 0 (2007); Employment by occupation: 10.2% management, 14.9% professional, 14.1% services, 34.4% sales, 0.0% farming, 7.3% construction, 19.2% production (2000).

Income: Per capita income: $20,089 (2007); Median household income: $49,459 (2007); Average household income: $57,575 (2007); Percent of households with income of $100,000 or more: 13.6% (2007); Poverty rate: 11.5% (2000).

Taxes: Total city taxes per capita: $926 (2006); City property taxes per capita: $635 (2006).

Education: Percent of population age 25 and over with: High school diploma (including GED) or higher: 79.3% (2007); Bachelor's degree or higher: 13.1% (2007); Master's degree or higher: 3.9% (2007).

School District(s)

Calumet Public SD 132 (PK-08)
2005-06 Enrollment: 1,210 .... (708) 388-8920
Exc Children Have Opportunities (PK-12)
2005-06 Enrollment: 649 .... (708) 333-7880

Housing: Homeownership rate: 67.8% (2007); Median home value: $135,633 (2007); Median rent: $576 per month (2000); Median age of housing: 39 years (2000).

Safety: Violent crime rate: 113.2 per 10,000 population; Property crime rate: 493.6 per 10,000 population (2006).

Transportation: Commute to work: 79.9% car, 16.0% public transportation, 2.3% walk, 0.5% work from home (2000); Travel time to work: 11.5% less than 15 minutes, 27.9% 15 to 30 minutes, 19.8% 30 to 45 minutes, 18.1% 45 to 60 minutes, 22.7% 60 minutes or more (2000)

CHICAGO (city). County seat. Covers a land area of 227.133 square miles and a water area of 6.869 square miles. Located at 41.84° N. Lat.; 87.67° W. Long. Elevation is 587 feet.

History: The river here was called Checagou by the Indians, meaning something big, strong, or powerful. In 1803 Captain John Whistler and his men built Fort Dearborn on the site that was to become Chicago, where a few cabins occupied by Frenchmen and the Sable trading post already existed. John Kinzie, a Scotch-Canadian trader who took over the trading post, was the first English settler in the community that developed around Fort Dearborn. When Chicago was incorporated as a town in 1833, the population numbered under 200. The projected Illinois & Michigan Canal brought speculators; Chicago was incorporated as a city in 1837 and soon became the world's largest grain market and a major slaughterhouse. The completion of the Illinois & Michigan Canal in 1848 increased the commercial importance of Chicago, as did the many railroad lines that soon radiated from it. The quick ramshackle building of Chicago was halted in 1871 when the fire started in Patrick O'Leary's cow barn destroyed 17,450 buildings in 27 hours. Rebuilding was fast and more permanent.

Population: 2,783,726 (1990); 2,896,016 (2000); 2,823,257 (2007); 2,761,878 (2012 projected); Race: 40.8% White, 36.0% Black, 4.6% Asian, 28.9% Hispanic of any race (2007); Density: 12,430.0 persons per square mile (2007); Average household size: 2.73 (2007); Median age: 33.8 (2007); Males per 100 females: 95.3 (2007); Marriage status: 40.9% never married, 43.3% now married, 7.0% widowed, 8.8% divorced (2000); Foreign born: 21.7% (2000); Ancestry (includes multiple ancestries): 56.8% Other groups, 7.3% Polish, 6.6% Irish, 6.5% German, 3.5% Italian (2000).

Economy: Unemployment rate: 5.9% (4/2008); Total civilian labor force: 1,343,803 (4/2008); Single-family building permits issued: 870 (2007); Multi-family building permits issued: 12,591 (2007); Employment by occupation: 13.3% management, 20.2% professional, 16.6% services, 27.0% sales, 0.1% farming, 6.6% construction, 16.2% production (2000).

Income: Per capita income: $23,243 (2007); Median household income: $44,461 (2007); Average household income: $62,748 (2007); Percent of households with income of $100,000 or more: 16.3% (2007); Poverty rate: 19.6% (2000).

Taxes: Total city taxes per capita: $769 (2006); City property taxes per capita: $151 (2006).

Education: Percent of population age 25 and over with: High school diploma (including GED) or higher: 71.7% (2007); Bachelor's degree or higher: 25.9% (2007); Master's degree or higher: 10.2% (2007).

School District(s)

Central Stickney SD 110 (PK-08)
2005-06 Enrollment: 470 .... (708) 458-1152
City of Chicago SD 299 (PK-12)
2005-06 Enrollment: 420,982 .... (773) 553-1000
Dept of Corrections Sch Dist 428 (08-12)
2005-06 Enrollment: 2,271 .... (217) 522-2666
Dept of Human Services (PK-12)
2005-06 Enrollment: 298 .... (217) 524-1379
Intermediate Service Center 3
2005-06 Enrollment: n/a .... (312) 263-7767

Four-year College(s)

Adler School of Professional Psychology (Private, Not-for-profit)
Fall 2007 Enrollment: 549 . . . . (312) 201-5900
American Academy of Art (Private, For-profit)
Fall 2007 Enrollment: 387 . . . . (312) 461-0600
2007-08 Tuition: In-state $22,050; Out-of-state $22,050
Argosy University-Chicago (Private, For-profit)
Fall 2007 Enrollment: 2,061. . . . . (312) 777-7600
2007-08 Tuition: In-state $16,752; Out-of-state $16,752
Catholic Theological Union at Chicago (Private, Not-for-profit, Roman Catholic)
Fall 2007 Enrollment: 477 . . . . (773) 324-8000
Chicago School of Professional Psychology (Private, Not-for-profit)
Fall 2007 Enrollment: 1,327. . . . . (312) 329-6600
Chicago State University (Public)
Fall 2007 Enrollment: 6,810. . . . . (773) 995-2000
2007-08 Tuition: In-state $7,730; Out-of-state $13,850
Chicago Theological Seminary (Private, Not-for-profit, United Church of Christ)
Fall 2007 Enrollment: 236 . . . . (773) 752-5757
Columbia College Chicago (Private, Not-for-profit)
Fall 2007 Enrollment: 12,021. . . . . (312) 663-1600
2007-08 Tuition: In-state $17,584; Out-of-state $17,584
DePaul University (Private, Not-for-profit, Roman Catholic)
Fall 2007 Enrollment: 23,401. . . . . (312) 362-8000
2007-08 Tuition: In-state $24,394; Out-of-state $24,394
East-West University (Private, Not-for-profit)
Fall 2007 Enrollment: 1,144. . . . . (312) 939-0111
2007-08 Tuition: In-state $12,825; Out-of-state $12,825
Erikson Institute (Private, Not-for-profit)
Fall 2007 Enrollment: 314 . . . . (312) 755-2250
Harrington College of Design (Private, For-profit)
Fall 2007 Enrollment: 1,418. . . . . (312) 939-4975
2007-08 Tuition: In-state $15,800; Out-of-state $15,800
Illinois College of Optometry (Private, Not-for-profit)
Fall 2007 Enrollment: 614 . . . . (312) 949-7400
Illinois Institute of Technology (Private, Not-for-profit)
Fall 2007 Enrollment: 7,277. . . . . (312) 567-3000
2007-08 Tuition: In-state $26,756; Out-of-state $26,756
Institute for Clinical Social Work (Private, Not-for-profit)
Fall 2007 Enrollment: 85 . . . . (312) 726-8480
International Academy of Design and Technology (Private, For-profit)
Fall 2007 Enrollment: 2,335. . . . . (312) 980-9200
2007-08 Tuition: In-state $17,250; Out-of-state $17,250
Kendall College (Private, Not-for-profit, United Methodist)
Fall 2007 Enrollment: 1,448. . . . . (312) 752-2000
2007-08 Tuition: In-state $22,125; Out-of-state $22,125
Lexington College (Private, Not-for-profit, Roman Catholic)
Fall 2007 Enrollment: 57 . . . . (312) 226-6294
2007-08 Tuition: In-state $20,325; Out-of-state $20,325
Loyola University Chicago (Private, Not-for-profit, Roman Catholic)
Fall 2007 Enrollment: 15,545. . . . . (312) 915-6000
2007-08 Tuition: In-state $27,966; Out-of-state $27,966
Lutheran School of Theology at Chicago (Private, Not-for-profit, Evangelical Lutheran Church)
Fall 2007 Enrollment: 365 . . . . (773) 256-0700
McCormick Theological Seminary (Private, Not-for-profit, Presbyterian Church (USA))
Fall 2007 Enrollment: 251 . . . . (773) 947-6300
Meadville-Lombard Theological School (Private, Not-for-profit, Unitarian Universalist)
Fall 2007 Enrollment: 68 . . . . (773) 256-3000
Midwest College of Oriental Medicine (Private, For-profit)
Fall 2007 Enrollment: 151 . . . . (800) 593-2320
National-Louis University (Private, Not-for-profit)
Fall 2007 Enrollment: 7,405. . . . . (847) 475-1100
2007-08 Tuition: In-state $17,725; Out-of-state $17,725
New York Institute of Technology-Ellis College (Private, Not-for-profit)
Fall 2007 Enrollment: 2,416. . . . . (800) 405-5844
North Park University (Private, Not-for-profit, Evangelical Covenant Church of America)
Fall 2007 Enrollment: 3,200. . . . . (773) 244-6200
2007-08 Tuition: In-state $20,015; Out-of-state $20,015
Northeastern Illinois University (Public)
Fall 2007 Enrollment: 12,814. . . . . (773) 583-4050
2007-08 Tuition: In-state $5,641; Out-of-state $10,321
Pacific College of Oriental Medicine (Private, For-profit)
Fall 2007 Enrollment: 249 . . . . (773) 477-4822
2007-08 Tuition: In-state $9,133; Out-of-state $9,133
Robert Morris College (Private, Not-for-profit)
Fall 2007 Enrollment: 4,824. . . . . (312) 935-6800
2007-08 Tuition: In-state $16,800; Out-of-state $16,800
Roosevelt University (Private, Not-for-profit)
Fall 2007 Enrollment: 7,163. . . . . (312) 341-3500
2007-08 Tuition: In-state $16,980; Out-of-state $16,980
Rush University (Private, Not-for-profit)
Fall 2007 Enrollment: 1,596. . . . . (312) 942-7100
Saint Augustine College (Private, Not-for-profit)
Fall 2007 Enrollment: 1,289. . . . . (773) 878-8756
2007-08 Tuition: In-state $7,272; Out-of-state $7,272
Saint Xavier University (Private, Not-for-profit, Roman Catholic)
Fall 2007 Enrollment: 5,675. . . . . (773) 298-3000
2007-08 Tuition: In-state $21,236; Out-of-state $21,236
School of the Art Institute of Chicago (Private, Not-for-profit)
Fall 2007 Enrollment: 3,006. . . . . (312) 629-6100
2007-08 Tuition: In-state $31,040; Out-of-state $31,040
Shimer College (Private, Not-for-profit)
Fall 2007 Enrollment: 76 . . . . (312) 235-3500
2007-08 Tuition: In-state $24,890; Out-of-state $24,890
Spertus College (Private, Not-for-profit)
Fall 2007 Enrollment: 288 . . . . (312) 922-9012
Telshe Yeshiva-Chicago (Private, Not-for-profit)
Fall 2007 Enrollment: 77 . . . . (773) 463-7738
2007-08 Tuition: In-state $11,000; Out-of-state $11,000
The Illinois Institute of Art-Chicago (Private, For-profit)
Fall 2007 Enrollment: 2,867. . . . . (312) 280-3500
2007-08 Tuition: In-state $19,968; Out-of-state $19,968
The John Marshall Law School (Private, Not-for-profit)
Fall 2007 Enrollment: 1,530. . . . . (312) 427-2737
Toyota Technological Institute at Chicago (Private, Not-for-profit)
Fall 2007 Enrollment: 9 . . . . (773) 834-2500
University of Chicago (Private, Not-for-profit)
Fall 2007 Enrollment: 14,538. . . . . (773) 702-1234
2007-08 Tuition: In-state $35,868; Out-of-state $35,868
University of Illinois at Chicago (Public)
Fall 2007 Enrollment: 25,747. . . . . (312) 996-3000
2007-08 Tuition: In-state $10,546; Out-of-state $22,936
VanderCook College of Music (Private, Not-for-profit)
Fall 2007 Enrollment: 320 . . . . (312) 225-6288
2007-08 Tuition: In-state $18,800; Out-of-state $18,800
Westwood College-Chicago Loop (Private, For-profit)
Fall 2007 Enrollment: 831 . . . . (312) 578-3860
2007-08 Tuition: In-state $13,600; Out-of-state $13,600
Westwood College-O'Hare Airport (Private, For-profit)
Fall 2007 Enrollment: 560 . . . . (773) 380-6800
2007-08 Tuition: In-state $13,263; Out-of-state $13,263

Two-year College(s)

Advocate Illinois Masonic School of Radiologic Technology (Private, Not-for-profit, Evangelical Lutheran Church)
Fall 2007 Enrollment: 16 . . . . (773) 296-8950
2007-08 Tuition: In-state $3,300; Out-of-state $3,300
Advocate Trinity Hospital School of Radiologic Technology (Private, Not-for-profit, United Church of Christ)
Fall 2007 Enrollment: 31 . . . . (773) 967-5292
2007-08 Tuition: In-state $3,000; Out-of-state $3,000
City Colleges of Chicago-Harold Washington College (Public)
Fall 2007 Enrollment: 8,633. . . . . (312) 553-5600
2007-08 Tuition: In-state $5,949; Out-of-state $9,543
City Colleges of Chicago-Harry S Truman College (Public)
Fall 2007 Enrollment: 11,354. . . . . (773) 907-4700
2007-08 Tuition: In-state $5,949; Out-of-state $9,543
City Colleges of Chicago-Kennedy-King College (Public)
Fall 2007 Enrollment: 6,140. . . . . (773) 602-5000
2007-08 Tuition: In-state $5,949; Out-of-state $9,543
City Colleges of Chicago-Malcolm X College (Public)
Fall 2007 Enrollment: 6,031. . . . . (312) 850-7000
2007-08 Tuition: In-state $5,949; Out-of-state $9,543
City Colleges of Chicago-Olive-Harvey College (Public)
Fall 2007 Enrollment: 4,078. . . . . (773) 291-6100
2007-08 Tuition: In-state $5,949; Out-of-state $9,543

City Colleges of Chicago-Richard J Daley College (Public)
Fall 2007 Enrollment: 9,679. . . . . (773) 838-7500
2007-08 Tuition: In-state $5,949; Out-of-state $9,543
City Colleges of Chicago-Wilbur Wright College (Public)
Fall 2007 Enrollment: 10,993. . . . . (773) 777-7900
2007-08 Tuition: In-state $5,949; Out-of-state $9,543
Coyne American Institute Inc (Private, For-profit)
Fall 2007 Enrollment: 728 . . . . (773) 577-8100
MacCormac College (Private, Not-for-profit)
Fall 2007 Enrollment: 171 . . . . (312) 922-1884
2007-08 Tuition: In-state $10,600; Out-of-state $10,600
Northwestern Business College (Private, For-profit)
Fall 2007 Enrollment: 937 . . . . (773) 777-4220
2007-08 Tuition: In-state $17,575; Out-of-state $17,575
Taylor Business Institute (Private, For-profit)
Fall 2007 Enrollment: 250 . . . . (312) 658-5100
2007-08 Tuition: In-state $11,250; Out-of-state $11,250
The College of Office Technology (Private, For-profit)
Fall 2007 Enrollment: 368 . . . . (773) 278-0042
The Cooking and Hospitality Institute of Chicago (Private, For-profit)
Fall 2007 Enrollment: 988 . . . . (312) 944-0882
2007-08 Tuition: In-state $20,375; Out-of-state $20,375

Vocational/Technical School(s)

BIR Training Center (Private, For-profit)
Fall 2007 Enrollment: 294 . . . . (773) 866-0111
2007-08 Tuition: $11,380
Banner Institute-Chicago (Private, For-profit)
Fall 2007 Enrollment: 285 . . . . (312) 821-7561
CET-Chicago (Private, Not-for-profit)
Fall 2007 Enrollment: 412 . . . . (408) 287-7924
2007-08 Tuition: $8,132
Cain's Barber College Inc (Private, For-profit)
Fall 2007 Enrollment: 134 . . . . (773) 536-4441
2007-08 Tuition: $7,650
Cannella School of Hair Design (Private, For-profit)
Fall 2007 Enrollment: 183 . . . . (773) 890-0412
2007-08 Tuition: $8,500
Cannella School of Hair Design (Private, For-profit)
Fall 2007 Enrollment: 64 . . . . (773) 278-4477
2007-08 Tuition: $8,500
Cannella School of Hair Design (Private, For-profit)
Fall 2007 Enrollment: 85 . . . . (773) 221-4700
2007-08 Tuition: $9,350
Capri Garfield Ridge School of Beauty Culture (Private, For-profit)
Fall 2007 Enrollment: 159 . . . . (773) 778-0882
2007-08 Tuition: $13,475
Chicago Urban League Computer Training Center (Private, Not-for-profit)
Fall 2007 Enrollment: 15 . . . . (773) 483-0590
2007-08 Tuition: $4,693
Cortiva Institute-Chicago (Private, For-profit)
Fall 2007 Enrollment: 374 . . . . (312) 753-7900
Everest College-Chicago (Private, For-profit)
Fall 2007 Enrollment: 486 . . . . (312) 913-1616
2007-08 Tuition: $11,225
Illinois Careerpath Institute (Private, Not-for-profit)
Fall 2007 Enrollment: n/a. . . . . (312) 464-1629
Illinois School of Health Careers (Private, For-profit)
Fall 2007 Enrollment: 290 . . . . (312) 913-1230
2007-08 Tuition: $11,700
Illinois School of Health Careers-O'Hare Campus (Private, For-profit)
Fall 2007 Enrollment: 144 . . . . (773) 444-0300
2007-08 Tuition: $11,700
Mac Daniels Beauty School (Private, For-profit)
Fall 2007 Enrollment: 77 . . . . (773) 561-2376
2007-08 Tuition: $11,400
Pivot Point Beauty School (Private, For-profit)
Fall 2007 Enrollment: 93 . . . . (773) 463-3121
2007-08 Tuition: $16,460
Pyramid Career Institute (Private, For-profit)
Fall 2007 Enrollment: 9 . . . . (773) 975-9898
2007-08 Tuition: $4,500
Rosel School of Cosmetology (Private, For-profit)
Fall 2007 Enrollment: 114 . . . . (773) 508-5600
2007-08 Tuition: $7,600
Soma Institute-The National School of Clinical Massage Therapy (Private, For-profit)
Fall 2007 Enrollment: 308 . . . . (312) 939-2723
Spanish Coalition for Jobs Inc (Private, Not-for-profit)
Fall 2007 Enrollment: 64 . . . . (773) 247-0707
2007-08 Tuition: $7,600
Your School of Beauty Culture (Private, For-profit)
Fall 2007 Enrollment: n/a. . . . . (773) 538-4886

Housing: Homeownership rate: 43.6% (2007); Median home value: $234,398 (2007); Median rent: $543 per month (2000); Median age of housing: 52 years (2000).

Hospitals: Advocate Bethany Hospital (240 beds); Advocate Illinois Masonic Medical Center (370 beds); Advocate Trinity Hospital; Chicago Lakeshore Hospital (150 beds); Chicago Read Mental Health Center (26 beds); Children's Memorial Hospital (270 beds); Hartgrove Hospital (119 beds); Hazelden Chicago (22 beds); Holy Cross Hospital (244 beds); Jackson Park Hospital & Medical Center (336 beds); John H Stroger, Jr Hospital of Cook County (464 beds); Kindred Chicago Lakeshore (103 beds); La Rabida Childrens Hospital (49 beds); Lincoln Park Hospital (191 beds); Loretto Hospital (189 beds); Mercy Hospital (507 beds); Methodist Hospital of Chicago (198 beds); Michael Reese Hospital (565 beds); Mount Sinai Hospital (432 beds); Neurologic and Orthopedic Insitute of Chicago (78 beds); Northwestern Memorial Hospital (744 beds); Norwegian-American Hospital (200 beds); Our Lady of the Resurrection Medical Center (264 beds); Provident Hospital (243 beds); Ravenswood Hospital Medical Center (306 beds); Rehabilitation Institute of Chicago (155 beds); Resurrection Medical Center (434 beds); Roseland Community Hospital (162 beds); Rush-Presbyterian-St. Luke's Medical Center (809 beds); Sacred Heart Hospital (119 beds); Saint Anthony Hospital (166 beds); Saint Bernard Hospital and Health Care Center (183 beds); Saints Mary & Elizabeth Medical Center (387 beds); Schwab Rehabilitation Hospital (85 beds); Shriners Hospital for Children (60 beds); South Shore Hospital (170 beds); St. Elizabeth's Hospital (276 beds); St. Joseph Hospital (492 beds); Swedish Covenant Hospital (330 beds); Thorek Memorial Hospital (218 beds); University of Chicago Comer Children's Hospital (155 beds); University of Chicago Hospitals (662 beds); University of Illinois at Chicago Medical Center (570 beds); Veterans Affairs Lakeside Medical Center (337 beds); Veterans Affairs West Side Medical Center (435 beds); Weiss Memorial Hospital (357 beds)

Safety: Violent crime rate: 124.2 per 10,000 population; Property crime rate: 455.5 per 10,000 population (2006).

Newspapers: AHA News (National news; Circulation 23,681); African American Times (Local news; Circulation 0); Beverly Review (Community news; Circulation 6,400); The Bond Buyer - Chicago Bureau (Regional news; Circulation 0); Bridgeport News (Community news; Circulation 25,300); Brighton Park Life-McKinley Park Life (Local news; Circulation 30,000); Central Newspaper (Local news; Circulation 25,000); Chicago Catolico (Local news; Circulation 20,000); Chicago Chinese News (Local news; Circulation 10,000); Chicago Daily Law Bulletin (Regional news; Circulation 7,000); Chicago Defender (Local news; Circulation 525,000); Chicago Free Press (Community news; Circulation 26,000); Chicago Hospital News (Regional news; Circulation 0); Chicago Independent Bulletin (Local news; Circulation 64,000); Chicago Post (Community news; Circulation 38,000); Chicago Sun-Times (Local news; Circulation 487,480); Chicago Tribune (National news; Circulation 579,079); Chicago Woman Newspaper (Local news; Circulation 0); Chicago's Northwest Side Press (Community news; Circulation 49,000); China Journal (International news; Circulation 20,000); China Star Weekly (Circulation 5,000); Chinese American News (Local news; Circulation 10,000); Citizen Newspapers (Community news; Circulation 0); Clear Ridge Reporter (Local news; Circulation 0); DSN Retailing Today - Chicago Bureau (National news; Circulation 25,241); Draugas (International news; Circulation 6,000); El Heraldo De Chicago (Local news; Circulation 20,000); Environment & Climate News (National news; Circulation 0); Extra (Local news; Circulation 71,205); Financial Times - Chicago Bureau (Local news; Circulation 0); Greek Star (Local news; Circulation 7,800); The Herald Extra (Community news; Circulation 20,967); Hoy - Chicago Edition (Local news; Circulation 86,500); Hyde Park Herald (Community news; Circulation 6,738); India Bulletin (Local news; Circulation 26,000); Inside (Community news; Circulation 50,000); Journal (Local news; Circulation 1,500); Journal News (Community news; Circulation 48,000); Korea Times (Local news; Circulation 40,000); La Raza (Local news; Circulation 190,000); Los Angeles Times - Chicago Bureau (Local news; Circulation 0); Metro Extra (Local news; Circulation 72,000); Near West Gazette (Local news; Circulation 17,000); The New York Times - Chicago Bureau (Regional news; Circulation 0); Nitty Gritty News (Local news; Circulation 0); Nuevo

Siglo Newspaper (Local news; Circulation 20,000); Polish Daily News (National news; Circulation 28,400); RedEye (Local news; Circulation 200,000); Sauganash Sounds (Community news; Circulation 6,300); School Reform News (Regional news; Circulation 0); Sing Tao Daily - Chicago Bureau (Local news; Circulation 8,000); South End Citizen (Local news; Circulation 28,707); South Suburban Citizen (Local news; Circulation 21,500); Southeast Chicago Observer (Local news; Circulation 15,000); Southeast Extra (Local news; Circulation 71,205); Southwest Extra (Local news; Circulation 5,000); Southwest News Herald (Local news; Circulation 26,996); Southwest News-Herald (Community news; Circulation 25,000); Southwest Shopper (Community news; Circulation 27,000); Suburban Extra (Local news; Circulation 5,580); UIC Today (Local news; Circulation 0); USA Today - Chicago Bureau (National news; Circulation 0); Villager (Community news; Circulation 50,000); The Wall Street Journal - Chicago Bureau (Regional news; Circulation 0); The Washington Post - Chicago Bureau (Local news; Circulation 0); Windy City Times (Local news; Circulation 24,000)
Transportation: Commute to work: 64.6% car, 26.1% public transportation, 5.7% walk, 2.4% work from home (2000); Travel time to work: 13.2% less than 15 minutes, 27.9% 15 to 30 minutes, 28.3% 30 to 45 minutes, 14.7% 45 to 60 minutes, 16.0% 60 minutes or more (2000); Amtrak: Service available.
Airports: Chicago Midway International (primary service/large hub); Chicago O'Hare International (primary service/large hub); Lansing Municipal (general aviation)
Additional Information Contacts
America - Israel Chamber of Commerce Chicago . . . . (312) 235-0586
http://www.americaisrael.org
Andersonville Chamber of Commerce . . . . (773) 728-2995
http://www.andersonville.org
Chicago Area Gay & Lesbian Chamber of Commerce . . . . (773) 303-0167
http://www.glchamber.org
Chicago Chinatown Chamber of Commerce . . . . (312) 326-5320
http://www.chicagochinatown.org
Chicago Convention & Visitors Bureau . . . . (312) 567-8500
http://www.choosechicago.com
Chicagoland Chamber of Commerce . . . . (312) 494-6700
http://www.chicagolandchamber.org
City of Chicago . . . . (312) 744-5000
http://www.cityofchicago.org
German American Chamber of Commerce of the Midwest . (312) 644-2662
http://www.gaccom.org
Illinois Chamber of Commerce . . . . (312) 983-7100
http://www.ilchamber.org
Italian American Chamber of Commerce - Midwest . . . . . . (312) 553-9137
http://www.italianchamber.us
Lake View East Chamber of Commerce . . . . (773) 348-8608
http://www.lakevieweast.com
Latin American Chamber of Commerce . . . . (773) 252-5211
http://www.latinamericanchamberofcommerce.com
Lincoln Park Chamber of Commerce . . . . (773) 880-5200
http://www.lincolnparkchamber.com
Logan Square Chamber of Commerce . . . . (773) 489-3222
http://www.loganchamber.org
Old Town Merchants & Residents Association . . . . (312) 951-6106
http://www.oldtownchicago.org
Portgage Park Chamber of Commerce . . . . (773) 777-2020
http://www.portageparkchamber.org
Puerto Rico Convention Bureau . . . . (312) 840-8090
http://www.meetpuertorico.com
South Shore Chamber Inc. . . . . (773) 643-1652
http://www.southshorechamber.biz
Streeterville Chamber of Commerce . . . . (312) 664-2560
http://www.streetervillechamber.org
The 87th Street Stoney Island Chamber of Commerce . . . . (773) 734-0626
http://87thchamberofcommerce.com
West Lawn Chamber of Commerce . . . . (773) 735-7690
http://www.westlawnchamber.org
Wicker Park & Bucktown Chamber of Commerce . . . . (773) 384-2672
http://www.wickerparkbucktown.com

CHICAGO HEIGHTS (city). Covers a land area of 9.571 square miles and a water area of 0.011 square miles. Located at 41.51° N. Lat.; 87.64° W. Long. Elevation is 659 feet.
History: Chicago Heights developed at the point where the Hubbard Trail crossed the Sauk Trail, a heavily traveled junction. The first settlement here in the 1830's was called Thorn Grove, but it was renamed Bloom in 1849 by German settlers. In 1890 the Chicago Heights Land Association began encouraging settlers and industry to come here, and the name of the town was changed.
Population: 33,156 (1990); 32,776 (2000); 30,934 (2007); 29,641 (2012 projected); Race: 40.9% White, 38.8% Black, 0.5% Asian, 28.4% Hispanic of any race (2007); Density: 3,232.0 persons per square mile (2007); Average household size: 3.09 (2007); Median age: 31.9 (2007); Males per 100 females: 95.6 (2007); Marriage status: 35.2% never married, 48.7% now married, 7.8% widowed, 8.2% divorced (2000); Foreign born: 11.2% (2000); Ancestry (includes multiple ancestries): 55.9% Other groups, 11.4% Italian, 10.2% German, 6.6% Irish, 6.2% Polish (2000).
Economy: Unemployment rate: 9.4% (4/2008); Total civilian labor force: 13,761 (4/2008); Single-family building permits issued: 5 (2007); Multi-family building permits issued: 2 (2007); Employment by occupation: 8.1% management, 15.9% professional, 20.0% services, 26.4% sales, 0.1% farming, 7.6% construction, 21.9% production (2000).
Income: Per capita income: $16,677 (2007); Median household income: $40,904 (2007); Average household income: $50,859 (2007); Percent of households with income of $100,000 or more: 10.7% (2007); Poverty rate: 17.5% (2000).
Education: Percent of population age 25 and over with: High school diploma (including GED) or higher: 71.6% (2007); Bachelor's degree or higher: 12.2% (2007); Master's degree or higher: 3.9% (2007).

School District(s)

Bloom Twp HSD 206 (09-12)
2005-06 Enrollment: 3,558 . . . . (708) 755-7010
Chicago Heights SD 170 (PK-08)
2005-06 Enrollment: 3,517 . . . . (708) 756-4165
Flossmoor SD 161 (PK-08)
2005-06 Enrollment: 2,616 . . . . (708) 647-7000
Intermediate Service Center 4 (06-12)
2005-06 Enrollment: 137 . . . . (708) 754-6600
Park Forest SD 163 (PK-08)
2005-06 Enrollment: 2,202 . . . . (708) 668-9400
Speed Seja #802 (PK-12)
2005-06 Enrollment: 385 . . . . (708) 481-6100

Two-year College(s)

Prairie State College (Public)
Fall 2007 Enrollment: 5,507 . . . . (708) 709-3500
2007-08 Tuition: In-state $5,876; Out-of-state $7,988
Housing: Homeownership rate: 63.5% (2007); Median home value: $141,540 (2007); Median rent: $500 per month (2000); Median age of housing: 44 years (2000).
Hospitals: St. James Hospital and Health Center (587 beds)
Safety: Violent crime rate: 131.6 per 10,000 population; Property crime rate: 498.8 per 10,000 population (2006).
Newspapers: Chicago Standard News (Community news; Circulation 15,000); South Suburban Standard (Community news; Circulation 25,000)
Transportation: Commute to work: 87.8% car, 6.5% public transportation, 2.7% walk, 1.4% work from home (2000); Travel time to work: 33.9% less than 15 minutes, 33.5% 15 to 30 minutes, 12.9% 30 to 45 minutes, 7.9% 45 to 60 minutes, 11.8% 60 minutes or more (2000)
Additional Information Contacts
City of Chicago Heights . . . . (708) 756-5315
http://www.chicagoheights.net

CHICAGO RIDGE (village). Covers a land area of 2.230 square miles and a water area of 0 square miles. Located at 41.70° N. Lat.; 87.77° W. Long. Elevation is 594 feet.
Population: 13,556 (1990); 14,127 (2000); 13,682 (2007); 13,327 (2012 projected); Race: 86.1% White, 3.3% Black, 1.9% Asian, 7.7% Hispanic of any race (2007); Density: 6,136.7 persons per square mile (2007); Average household size: 2.45 (2007); Median age: 34.9 (2007); Males per 100 females: 95.4 (2007); Marriage status: 31.1% never married, 51.8% now married, 7.8% widowed, 9.2% divorced (2000); Foreign born: 13.8% (2000); Ancestry (includes multiple ancestries): 25.5% Irish, 20.3% Polish, 19.1% German, 13.6% Other groups, 11.2% Italian (2000).
Economy: Single-family building permits issued: 12 (2007); Multi-family building permits issued: 0 (2007); Employment by occupation: 11.3% management, 11.4% professional, 11.1% services, 34.3% sales, 0.0% farming, 12.4% construction, 19.5% production (2000).

Income: Per capita income: $24,783 (2007); Median household income: $52,380 (2007); Average household income: $60,443 (2007); Percent of households with income of $100,000 or more: 14.0% (2007); Poverty rate: 10.0% (2000).
Taxes: Total city taxes per capita: $741 (2006); City property taxes per capita: $464 (2006).
Education: Percent of population age 25 and over with: High school diploma (including GED) or higher: 81.6% (2007); Bachelor's degree or higher: 13.9% (2007); Master's degree or higher: 3.7% (2007).

School District(s)

Chicago Ridge SD 127-5 (PK-08)
2005-06 Enrollment: 1,271 . . . . (708) 636-2000
Housing: Homeownership rate: 52.3% (2007); Median home value: $182,041 (2007); Median rent: $633 per month (2000); Median age of housing: 28 years (2000).
Safety: Violent crime rate: 19.8 per 10,000 population; Property crime rate: 438.2 per 10,000 population (2006).
Transportation: Commute to work: 89.6% car, 7.1% public transportation, 1.8% walk, 0.6% work from home (2000); Travel time to work: 22.6% less than 15 minutes, 28.2% 15 to 30 minutes, 21.8% 30 to 45 minutes, 11.0% 45 to 60 minutes, 16.4% 60 minutes or more (2000)
Additional Information Contacts
Village of Chicago Ridge . . . . (708) 425-7700
http://www.chicagoridge.org

CICERO (town). Covers a land area of 5.846 square miles and a water area of 0 square miles. Located at 41.84° N. Lat.; 87.76° W. Long. Elevation is 604 feet.
History: Named for Marcus Tullius Cicero, a Roman orator. Cicero was settled in the mid-1800's. The first township election was held in 1857, and Cicero was incorporated as a town in 1867 and as a city in 1869, following an influx of homesteaders during the Civil War. Cicero shrank when parts of it were annexed to Chicago in 1892. During the industrial boom that followed the turn of the century, Al Capone was the proprietor of a row of gambling houses here.
Population: 67,436 (1990); 85,616 (2000); 82,072 (2007); 79,277 (2012 projected); Race: 43.3% White, 1.3% Black, 0.6% Asian, 85.4% Hispanic of any race (2007); Density: 14,039.0 persons per square mile (2007); Average household size: 3.80 (2007); Median age: 28.0 (2007); Males per 100 females: 105.5 (2007); Marriage status: 32.5% never married, 56.1% now married, 5.3% widowed, 6.1% divorced (2000); Foreign born: 43.6% (2000); Ancestry (includes multiple ancestries): 72.6% Other groups, 4.7% Polish, 3.7% Irish, 3.7% German, 3.0% Italian (2000).
Economy: Unemployment rate: 7.4% (4/2008); Total civilian labor force: 33,398 (4/2008); Single-family building permits issued: 0 (2007); Multi-family building permits issued: 0 (2007); Employment by occupation: 4.9% management, 6.3% professional, 16.6% services, 24.2% sales, 0.5% farming, 12.0% construction, 35.5% production (2000).
Income: Per capita income: $13,475 (2007); Median household income: $42,640 (2007); Average household income: $51,025 (2007); Percent of households with income of $100,000 or more: 8.4% (2007); Poverty rate: 15.5% (2000).
Education: Percent of population age 25 and over with: High school diploma (including GED) or higher: 48.0% (2007); Bachelor's degree or higher: 6.1% (2007); Master's degree or higher: 2.2% (2007).

School District(s)

Cicero SD 99 (PK-08)
2005-06 Enrollment: 13,528 . . . . (708) 863-4856
Intermediate Service Center 2 (07-12)
2005-06 Enrollment: 65 . . . . (708) 482-4350
J S Morton HSD 201 (09-12)
2005-06 Enrollment: 8,203 . . . . (708) 222-5702

Two-year College(s)

Morton College (Public)
Fall 2007 Enrollment: 5,057. . . . . (708) 656-8000
2007-08 Tuition: In-state $6,676; Out-of-state $8,724

Vocational/Technical School(s)

Bell Mar Beauty College (Private, For-profit)
Fall 2007 Enrollment: 126 . . . . (708) 863-6644
Housing: Homeownership rate: 55.2% (2007); Median home value: $188,039 (2007); Median rent: $498 per month (2000); Median age of housing: 55 years (2000).
Safety: Violent crime rate: 43.5 per 10,000 population; Property crime rate: 281.8 per 10,000 population (2006).
Newspapers: Cicero/Berwyn Suburban Edition (Local news; Circulation 200,000); Czechoslovak Herald - Nedelni Hlasatel (Local news; Circulation 10,000); El Dia Newspaper (Local news; Circulation 45,000); El Impercial (Local news; Circulation 20,000); Lawndale News (Regional news; Circulation 200,000)
Transportation: Commute to work: 83.9% car, 9.7% public transportation, 3.7% walk, 1.1% work from home (2000); Travel time to work: 14.7% less than 15 minutes, 30.7% 15 to 30 minutes, 27.6% 30 to 45 minutes, 13.5% 45 to 60 minutes, 13.5% 60 minutes or more (2000)
Additional Information Contacts
Cicero Chamber of Commerce . . . . (708) 863-6000
http://www.cicerochamber.org
Town of Cicero. . . . . (708) 656-3600
http://www.thetownofcicero.com

COUNTRY CLUB HILLS (city). Covers a land area of 4.614 square miles and a water area of 0.024 square miles. Located at 41.56° N. Lat.; 87.72° W. Long. Elevation is 682 feet.
Population: 15,435 (1990); 16,169 (2000); 16,732 (2007); 17,101 (2012 projected); Race: 9.1% White, 87.8% Black, 0.8% Asian, 1.7% Hispanic of any race (2007); Density: 3,626.5 persons per square mile (2007); Average household size: 3.05 (2007); Median age: 35.0 (2007); Males per 100 females: 86.0 (2007); Marriage status: 30.7% never married, 51.1% now married, 6.3% widowed, 11.9% divorced (2000); Foreign born: 2.4% (2000); Ancestry (includes multiple ancestries): 74.2% Other groups, 4.0% German, 3.9% Irish, 3.1% African, 2.5% Polish (2000).
Economy: Single-family building permits issued: 28 (2007); Multi-family building permits issued: 0 (2007); Employment by occupation: 14.6% management, 19.5% professional, 12.4% services, 33.1% sales, 0.0% farming, 5.2% construction, 15.2% production (2000).
Income: Per capita income: $24,308 (2007); Median household income: $64,869 (2007); Average household income: $74,106 (2007); Percent of households with income of $100,000 or more: 22.7% (2007); Poverty rate: 5.5% (2000).
Education: Percent of population age 25 and over with: High school diploma (including GED) or higher: 89.9% (2007); Bachelor's degree or higher: 22.8% (2007); Master's degree or higher: 7.1% (2007).

School District(s)

Bremen CHSD 228 (09-12)
2005-06 Enrollment: 5,194 . . . . (708) 389-1175
Country Club Hills SD 160 (PK-08)
2005-06 Enrollment: 1,639 . . . . (708) 957-6200
Prairie-Hills ESD 144 (PK-08)
2005-06 Enrollment: 2,955 . . . . (708) 210-2888
Speed Seja #802 (PK-12)
2005-06 Enrollment: 385 . . . . (708) 481-6100
Housing: Homeownership rate: 92.1% (2007); Median home value: $162,023 (2007); Median rent: $799 per month (2000); Median age of housing: 25 years (2000).
Safety: Violent crime rate: 62.3 per 10,000 population; Property crime rate: 332.0 per 10,000 population (2006).
Transportation: Commute to work: 86.4% car, 9.8% public transportation, 0.8% walk, 2.1% work from home (2000); Travel time to work: 15.6% less than 15 minutes, 22.8% 15 to 30 minutes, 21.0% 30 to 45 minutes, 16.3% 45 to 60 minutes, 24.2% 60 minutes or more (2000)
Additional Information Contacts
City of Country Club Hills. . . . . (708) 798-2616
http://www.countryclubhills.org

COUNTRYSIDE (city). Covers a land area of 2.690 square miles and a water area of 0 square miles. Located at 41.77° N. Lat.; 87.87° W. Long. Elevation is 663 feet.
Population: 6,002 (1990); 5,991 (2000); 5,666 (2007); 5,441 (2012 projected); Race: 90.5% White, 2.6% Black, 1.7% Asian, 8.8% Hispanic of any race (2007); Density: 2,105.9 persons per square mile (2007); Average household size: 2.23 (2007); Median age: 43.6 (2007); Males per 100 females: 90.6 (2007); Marriage status: 26.0% never married, 52.2% now married, 8.5% widowed, 13.3% divorced (2000); Foreign born: 16.1% (2000); Ancestry (includes multiple ancestries): 19.4% Polish, 17.9% German, 15.7% Irish, 12.1% Other groups, 10.2% Italian (2000).
Economy: Single-family building permits issued: 12 (2007); Multi-family building permits issued: 0 (2007); Employment by occupation: 13.4% management, 21.4% professional, 11.6% services, 30.6% sales, 0.0% farming, 9.7% construction, 13.2% production (2000).

Income: Per capita income: $29,227 (2007); Median household income: $50,990 (2007); Average household income: $65,141 (2007); Percent of households with income of $100,000 or more: 19.9% (2007); Poverty rate: 3.7% (2000).
Education: Percent of population age 25 and over with: High school diploma (including GED) or higher: 84.1% (2007); Bachelor's degree or higher: 22.8% (2007); Master's degree or higher: 9.2% (2007).

School District(s)

La Grange SD 105 South (PK-08)
2005-06 Enrollment: 1,184 . . . . (708) 482-2700
Housing: Homeownership rate: 71.8% (2007); Median home value: $270,511 (2007); Median rent: $667 per month (2000); Median age of housing: 29 years (2000).
Safety: Violent crime rate: 12.0 per 10,000 population; Property crime rate: 312.1 per 10,000 population (2006).
Transportation: Commute to work: 87.1% car, 5.3% public transportation, 2.0% walk, 4.1% work from home (2000); Travel time to work: 25.4% less than 15 minutes, 35.1% 15 to 30 minutes, 21.8% 30 to 45 minutes, 9.7% 45 to 60 minutes, 8.1% 60 minutes or more (2000)
Additional Information Contacts
City of Countryside. . . . . (708) 354-7270
http://www.countryside-il.org

CRESTWOOD (village). Covers a land area of 3.055 square miles and a water area of 0.053 square miles. Located at 41.64° N. Lat.; 87.74° W. Long. Elevation is 597 feet.
Population: 11,073 (1990); 11,251 (2000); 11,254 (2007); 11,344 (2012 projected); Race: 91.2% White, 5.3% Black, 0.6% Asian, 4.4% Hispanic of any race (2007); Density: 3,683.3 persons per square mile (2007); Average household size: 2.38 (2007); Median age: 40.9 (2007); Males per 100 females: 86.8 (2007); Marriage status: 28.2% never married, 49.6% now married, 11.4% widowed, 10.8% divorced (2000); Foreign born: 3.4% (2000); Ancestry (includes multiple ancestries): 29.4% Irish, 23.8% German, 19.8% Polish, 12.0% Italian, 9.5% Other groups (2000).
Economy: Single-family building permits issued: 3 (2007); Multi-family building permits issued: 0 (2007); Employment by occupation: 8.9% management, 17.6% professional, 11.4% services, 32.2% sales, 0.0% farming, 12.6% construction, 17.4% production (2000).
Income: Per capita income: $25,287 (2007); Median household income: $51,421 (2007); Average household income: $58,825 (2007); Percent of households with income of $100,000 or more: 13.1% (2007); Poverty rate: 4.6% (2000).
Education: Percent of population age 25 and over with: High school diploma (including GED) or higher: 84.1% (2007); Bachelor's degree or higher: 14.8% (2007); Master's degree or higher: 3.5% (2007).

School District(s)

Cook County SD 130 (PK-08)
2005-06 Enrollment: 3,948 . . . . (708) 385-6800
Midlothian SD 143 (PK-08)
2005-06 Enrollment: 1,881 . . . . (708) 388-6450
Housing: Homeownership rate: 80.4% (2007); Median home value: $184,676 (2007); Median rent: $606 per month (2000); Median age of housing: 26 years (2000).
Safety: Violent crime rate: 17.0 per 10,000 population; Property crime rate: 248.1 per 10,000 population (2006).
Transportation: Commute to work: 90.5% car, 7.1% public transportation, 0.5% walk, 1.2% work from home (2000); Travel time to work: 24.3% less than 15 minutes, 29.8% 15 to 30 minutes, 17.3% 30 to 45 minutes, 14.7% 45 to 60 minutes, 13.9% 60 minutes or more (2000)
Additional Information Contacts
Village of Crestwood . . . . (708) 371-4800
http://www.villageofcrestwood.com

DES PLAINES (city). Covers a land area of 14.423 square miles and a water area of 0.111 square miles. Located at 42.03° N. Lat.; 87.90° W. Long. Elevation is 633 feet.
History: Named for the French translation of "the maples," which are abundant along the nearby river. When Des Plaines was founded in the 1830's it was known as Rand, for its first settler, Socrates Rand. The name was changed in 1869 to that of the river which transverses the town.
Population: 54,783 (1990); 58,720 (2000); 58,126 (2007); 57,352 (2012 projected); Race: 80.6% White, 1.3% Black, 9.1% Asian, 18.5% Hispanic of any race (2007); Density: 4,030.0 persons per square mile (2007); Average household size: 2.64 (2007); Median age: 41.4 (2007); Males per 100 females: 94.0 (2007); Marriage status: 24.9% never married, 58.0% now married, 9.2% widowed, 8.0% divorced (2000); Foreign born: 23.9% (2000); Ancestry (includes multiple ancestries): 22.7% Other groups, 21.5% German, 18.2% Polish, 13.8% Irish, 10.6% Italian (2000).
Economy: Unemployment rate: 5.2% (4/2008); Total civilian labor force: 31,067 (4/2008); Single-family building permits issued: 32 (2007); Multi-family building permits issued: 180 (2007); Employment by occupation: 14.3% management, 17.9% professional, 12.3% services, 31.5% sales, 0.1% farming, 9.1% construction, 14.7% production (2000).
Income: Per capita income: $27,574 (2007); Median household income: $60,467 (2007); Average household income: $72,137 (2007); Percent of households with income of $100,000 or more: 20.7% (2007); Poverty rate: 4.6% (2000).
Taxes: Total city taxes per capita: $751 (2006); City property taxes per capita: $440 (2006).
Education: Percent of population age 25 and over with: High school diploma (including GED) or higher: 82.0% (2007); Bachelor's degree or higher: 24.7% (2007); Master's degree or higher: 8.1% (2007).

School District(s)

CCSD 62 (PK-08)
2005-06 Enrollment: 4,771 . . . . (847) 824-1136
Comm Cons SD 59 (PK-08)
2005-06 Enrollment: 6,065 . . . . (847) 593-4300
East Maine SD 63 (PK-08)
2005-06 Enrollment: 3,498 . . . . (847) 299-1900
Intermediate Service Center 1 (06-12)
2005-06 Enrollment: 126 . . . . (847) 824-8300
Maine Township HSD 207 (08-12)
2005-06 Enrollment: 6,993 . . . . (847) 696-3600

Two-year College(s)

Oakton Community College (Public)
Fall 2007 Enrollment: 10,805. . . . . (847) 635-1600
2007-08 Tuition: In-state $6,651; Out-of-state $8,407
Housing: Homeownership rate: 78.8% (2007); Median home value: $266,338 (2007); Median rent: $710 per month (2000); Median age of housing: 37 years (2000).
Hospitals: Holy Family Medical Center (184 beds)
Safety: Violent crime rate: 11.1 per 10,000 population; Property crime rate: 199.1 per 10,000 population (2006).
Newspapers: Arlington Heights Journal & Topics (Local news; Circulation 3,923); Buffalo Grove Journal & Topics (Local news; Circulation 3,217); Des Plaines Journal (Local news; Circulation 12,396); Elk Grove Journal (Local news; Circulation 4,689); Golf Mill Park Ridge Journal (Local news; Circulation 43,724); Mount Prospect Family Journal (Local news; Circulation 5,000); Mount Prospect Journal (Local news; Circulation 6,400); Niles Journal (Local news; Circulation 5,759); Northwest Journal (Local news; Circulation 5,637); Palatine Journal & Topics (Local news; Circulation 3,016); Prospect Heights Journal (Local news; Circulation 1,700); Rolling Meadows Journal & Topics (Local news; Circulation 3,171); Rosemont Journal (Local news; Circulation 604); Suburban Journal (Community news; Circulation 5,721); Wheeling Journal & Topics (Local news; Circulation 3,418)
Transportation: Commute to work: 88.8% car, 6.7% public transportation, 1.5% walk, 2.5% work from home (2000); Travel time to work: 24.3% less than 15 minutes, 34.9% 15 to 30 minutes, 23.3% 30 to 45 minutes, 8.5% 45 to 60 minutes, 9.0% 60 minutes or more (2000)
Additional Information Contacts
City of Des Plaines. . . . . (847) 391-5300
http://www.desplaines.org
Des Plaines Chamber of Commerce & Industry . . . . (847) 824-4200
http://www.dpchamber.com

DIXMOOR (village). Covers a land area of 1.243 square miles and a water area of 0 square miles. Located at 41.63° N. Lat.; 87.66° W. Long. Elevation is 600 feet.
History: Incorporated 1922.
Population: 3,647 (1990); 3,934 (2000); 3,687 (2007); 3,581 (2012 projected); Race: 27.5% White, 56.6% Black, 0.2% Asian, 24.5% Hispanic of any race (2007); Density: 2,965.9 persons per square mile (2007); Average household size: 2.97 (2007); Median age: 32.3 (2007); Males per 100 females: 91.9 (2007); Marriage status: 34.5% never married, 43.5% now married, 10.0% widowed, 12.0% divorced (2000); Foreign born: 9.2% (2000); Ancestry (includes multiple ancestries): 68.4% Other groups, 6.6% German, 6.0% Irish, 4.8% Polish, 1.7% Dutch (2000).
Economy: Single-family building permits issued: 15 (2007); Multi-family building permits issued: 0 (2007); Employment by occupation: 5.1%

management, 10.0% professional, 24.1% services, 28.9% sales, 0.0% farming, 9.0% construction, 23.0% production (2000).
Income: Per capita income: $12,038 (2007); Median household income: $28,947 (2007); Average household income: $35,658 (2007); Percent of households with income of $100,000 or more: 5.1% (2007); Poverty rate: 30.3% (2000).
Education: Percent of population age 25 and over with: High school diploma (including GED) or higher: 62.3% (2007); Bachelor's degree or higher: 7.1% (2007); Master's degree or higher: 1.9% (2007).

School District(s)

West Harvey-Dixmoor PSD 147 (PK-08)
2005-06 Enrollment: 1,667 . . . . (708) 339-9500
Housing: Homeownership rate: 81.4% (2007); Median home value: $54,375 (2007); Median rent: $501 per month (2000); Median age of housing: 32 years (2000).
Safety: Violent crime rate: 36.7 per 10,000 population; Property crime rate: 498.3 per 10,000 population (2006).
Transportation: Commute to work: 86.7% car, 9.2% public transportation, 1.2% walk, 1.6% work from home (2000); Travel time to work: 14.8% less than 15 minutes, 36.7% 15 to 30 minutes, 26.2% 30 to 45 minutes, 3.8% 45 to 60 minutes, 18.5% 60 minutes or more (2000)

DOLTON (village). Covers a land area of 4.551 square miles and a water area of 0.116 square miles. Located at 41.62° N. Lat.; 87.59° W. Long. Elevation is 604 feet.
History: Named for Andrew H. Dolton, town founder. Settled 1832. Incorporated 1892.
Population: 24,035 (1990); 25,614 (2000); 24,145 (2007); 23,080 (2012 projected); Race: 11.3% White, 85.7% Black, 0.5% Asian, 2.9% Hispanic of any race (2007); Density: 5,304.9 persons per square mile (2007); Average household size: 3.06 (2007); Median age: 34.3 (2007); Males per 100 females: 87.9 (2007); Marriage status: 33.4% never married, 49.0% now married, 6.4% widowed, 11.2% divorced (2000); Foreign born: 3.7% (2000); Ancestry (includes multiple ancestries): 74.3% Other groups, 3.6% German, 2.6% Polish, 2.4% Irish, 1.6% African (2000).
Economy: Unemployment rate: 7.2% (4/2008); Total civilian labor force: 12,497 (4/2008); Single-family building permits issued: 16 (2007); Multi-family building permits issued: 0 (2007); Employment by occupation: 11.0% management, 16.2% professional, 14.4% services, 33.5% sales, 0.0% farming, 6.2% construction, 18.6% production (2000).
Income: Per capita income: $19,360 (2007); Median household income: $51,589 (2007); Average household income: $58,958 (2007); Percent of households with income of $100,000 or more: 12.1% (2007); Poverty rate: 8.4% (2000).
Education: Percent of population age 25 and over with: High school diploma (including GED) or higher: 82.7% (2007); Bachelor's degree or higher: 15.3% (2007); Master's degree or higher: 3.2% (2007).

School District(s)

Dolton SD 148 (PK-08)
2005-06 Enrollment: 3,194 . . . . (708) 841-2290
Dolton SD 149 (PK-08)
2005-06 Enrollment: 3,732 . . . . (708) 868-7861
Thornton Twp HSD 205 (09-12)
2005-06 Enrollment: 6,554 . . . . (708) 225-4000
Housing: Homeownership rate: 81.1% (2007); Median home value: $140,423 (2007); Median rent: $623 per month (2000); Median age of housing: 37 years (2000).
Safety: Violent crime rate: 28.2 per 10,000 population; Property crime rate: 481.6 per 10,000 population (2006).
Transportation: Commute to work: 81.8% car, 13.0% public transportation, 1.4% walk, 2.6% work from home (2000); Travel time to work: 16.9% less than 15 minutes, 21.0% 15 to 30 minutes, 21.6% 30 to 45 minutes, 16.1% 45 to 60 minutes, 24.4% 60 minutes or more (2000)
Additional Information Contacts
Dolton Chamber of Commerce . . . . (708) 841-4810
Village of Dolton. . . . . (708) 849-4000
http://www.villageofdolton.com

EAST HAZEL CREST (village). Covers a land area of 0.767 square miles and a water area of 0 square miles. Located at 41.57° N. Lat.; 87.65° W. Long. Elevation is 620 feet.
Population: 1,570 (1990); 1,607 (2000); 1,533 (2007); 1,505 (2012 projected); Race: 50.1% White, 42.7% Black, 0.7% Asian, 8.0% Hispanic of any race (2007); Density: 1,998.1 persons per square mile (2007); Average household size: 2.71 (2007); Median age: 38.1 (2007); Males per 100 females: 89.7 (2007); Marriage status: 25.7% never married, 51.8% now married, 7.1% widowed, 15.4% divorced (2000); Foreign born: 4.8% (2000); Ancestry (includes multiple ancestries): 45.6% Other groups, 15.6% Irish, 11.3% Polish, 10.9% German, 6.3% Italian (2000).
Economy: Single-family building permits issued: 1 (2007); Multi-family building permits issued: 0 (2007); Employment by occupation: 9.9% management, 12.5% professional, 14.5% services, 28.3% sales, 0.0% farming, 14.1% construction, 20.8% production (2000).
Income: Per capita income: $21,192 (2007); Median household income: $48,041 (2007); Average household income: $55,872 (2007); Percent of households with income of $100,000 or more: 8.8% (2007); Poverty rate: 8.7% (2000).
Education: Percent of population age 25 and over with: High school diploma (including GED) or higher: 81.3% (2007); Bachelor's degree or higher: 11.3% (2007); Master's degree or higher: 3.6% (2007).
Housing: Homeownership rate: 64.2% (2007); Median home value: $158,705 (2007); Median rent: $605 per month (2000); Median age of housing: 37 years (2000).
Safety: Violent crime rate: 12.7 per 10,000 population; Property crime rate: 458.6 per 10,000 population (2006).
Transportation: Commute to work: 82.9% car, 12.1% public transportation, 0.9% walk, 3.0% work from home (2000); Travel time to work: 29.1% less than 15 minutes, 22.1% 15 to 30 minutes, 18.1% 30 to 45 minutes, 15.7% 45 to 60 minutes, 15.1% 60 minutes or more (2000)

ELK GROVE VILLAGE (village). Aka Elk Grove. Covers a land area of 11.039 square miles and a water area of 0.061 square miles. Located at 42.00° N. Lat.; 87.99° W. Long. Elevation is 686 feet.
Population: 33,624 (1990); 34,727 (2000); 33,526 (2007); 32,690 (2012 projected); Race: 83.6% White, 1.7% Black, 9.7% Asian, 8.0% Hispanic of any race (2007); Density: 3,037.0 persons per square mile (2007); Average household size: 2.58 (2007); Median age: 40.2 (2007); Males per 100 females: 95.0 (2007); Marriage status: 23.6% never married, 61.2% now married, 6.3% widowed, 8.9% divorced (2000); Foreign born: 14.3% (2000); Ancestry (includes multiple ancestries): 25.5% German, 19.3% Polish, 17.3% Other groups, 17.1% Irish, 14.7% Italian (2000).
Economy: Unemployment rate: 4.0% (4/2008); Total civilian labor force: 20,783 (4/2008); Single-family building permits issued: 3 (2007); Multi-family building permits issued: 0 (2007); Employment by occupation: 17.4% management, 19.3% professional, 9.2% services, 34.9% sales, 0.0% farming, 7.4% construction, 11.8% production (2000).
Income: Per capita income: $32,641 (2007); Median household income: $69,932 (2007); Average household income: $83,332 (2007); Percent of households with income of $100,000 or more: 27.4% (2007); Poverty rate: 2.0% (2000).
Education: Percent of population age 25 and over with: High school diploma (including GED) or higher: 90.3% (2007); Bachelor's degree or higher: 31.9% (2007); Master's degree or higher: 8.8% (2007).

School District(s)

Comm Cons SD 59 (PK-08)
2005-06 Enrollment: 6,065 . . . . (847) 593-4300
Schaumburg CCSD 54 (PK-08)
2005-06 Enrollment: 14,471 . . . . (847) 357-5000
Township HSD 214 (09-12)
2005-06 Enrollment: 12,542 . . . . (847) 718-7600
Housing: Homeownership rate: 75.7% (2007); Median home value: $273,541 (2007); Median rent: $776 per month (2000); Median age of housing: 27 years (2000).
Hospitals: Alexian Brothers Medical Center (473 beds)
Safety: Violent crime rate: 11.8 per 10,000 population; Property crime rate: 286.0 per 10,000 population (2006).
Transportation: Commute to work: 93.0% car, 3.5% public transportation, 0.9% walk, 2.4% work from home (2000); Travel time to work: 28.2% less than 15 minutes, 36.7% 15 to 30 minutes, 18.8% 30 to 45 minutes, 8.0% 45 to 60 minutes, 8.3% 60 minutes or more (2000)
Additional Information Contacts
Village of Elk Grove Village . . . . (847) 437-0300

ELMWOOD PARK (village). Covers a land area of 1.906 square miles and a water area of 0 square miles. Located at 41.92° N. Lat.; 87.81° W. Long. Elevation is 643 feet.
Population: 23,206 (1990); 25,405 (2000); 24,254 (2007); 23,427 (2012 projected); Race: 88.6% White, 0.7% Black, 2.6% Asian, 15.3% Hispanic of any race (2007); Density: 12,724.6 persons per square mile (2007); Average household size: 2.62 (2007); Median age: 40.6 (2007); Males per

100 females: 91.7 (2007); Marriage status: 27.2% never married, 52.8% now married, 10.1% widowed, 10.0% divorced (2000); Foreign born: 24.3% (2000); Ancestry (includes multiple ancestries): 28.7% Italian, 24.7% Polish, 13.5% Other groups, 12.3% Irish, 12.0% German (2000).
Economy: Unemployment rate: 4.8% (4/2008); Total civilian labor force: 13,542 (4/2008); Single-family building permits issued: 11 (2007); Multi-family building permits issued: 38 (2007); Employment by occupation: 13.7% management, 13.4% professional, 12.9% services, 33.3% sales, 0.1% farming, 10.0% construction, 16.4% production (2000).
Income: Per capita income: $25,202 (2007); Median household income: $53,828 (2007); Average household income: $65,756 (2007); Percent of households with income of $100,000 or more: 17.8% (2007); Poverty rate: 5.2% (2000).
Education: Percent of population age 25 and over with: High school diploma (including GED) or higher: 79.7% (2007); Bachelor's degree or higher: 19.2% (2007); Master's degree or higher: 6.3% (2007).

School District(s)

Elmwood Park CUSD 401 (PK-12)
2005-06 Enrollment: 2,766 . . . . (708) 583-5830
Housing: Homeownership rate: 64.8% (2007); Median home value: $271,791 (2007); Median rent: $625 per month (2000); Median age of housing: 46 years (2000).
Safety: Violent crime rate: 11.8 per 10,000 population; Property crime rate: 142.9 per 10,000 population (2006).
Transportation: Commute to work: 86.6% car, 8.8% public transportation, 2.3% walk, 1.5% work from home (2000); Travel time to work: 19.3% less than 15 minutes, 27.8% 15 to 30 minutes, 31.7% 30 to 45 minutes, 12.3% 45 to 60 minutes, 8.9% 60 minutes or more (2000)
Additional Information Contacts
Mont Clare-Elmwood Park Chamber of Commerce. . . . . . . (708) 456-8000
http://www.mcepchamber.org
Village of Elmwood Park . . . . (708) 452-7300
http://www.elmwoodpark.org

EVANSTON (city). Covers a land area of 7.746 square miles and a water area of 0.023 square miles. Located at 42.04° N. Lat.; 87.69° W. Long. Elevation is 614 feet.
History: Named for John Evans, founder of Northwestern University. Settlement at Evanston began around the harbor formed by the Grosse Pointe bluffs. The town was platted in 1854, and in 1855 Northwestern University was founded by the Methodist Episcopal Church. One of the first professors here was Frances E. Willard, who later founded the Women's Christian Temperance Union. In 1892 Evanston annexed the community of South Evanston and was incorporated as a city. The city was named for John Evans, one of the university founders.
Population: 73,233 (1990); 74,239 (2000); 76,344 (2007); 77,360 (2012 projected); Race: 64.2% White, 21.2% Black, 7.1% Asian, 7.9% Hispanic of any race (2007); Density: 9,855.8 persons per square mile (2007); Average household size: 2.49 (2007); Median age: 34.7 (2007); Males per 100 females: 90.1 (2007); Marriage status: 39.2% never married, 47.2% now married, 5.4% widowed, 8.2% divorced (2000); Foreign born: 15.4% (2000); Ancestry (includes multiple ancestries): 29.7% Other groups, 16.2% German, 12.5% Irish, 9.0% English, 5.6% Polish (2000).
Economy: Unemployment rate: 3.9% (4/2008); Total civilian labor force: 42,846 (4/2008); Single-family building permits issued: 16 (2007); Multi-family building permits issued: 402 (2007); Employment by occupation: 19.8% management, 40.9% professional, 9.1% services, 22.3% sales, 0.0% farming, 2.8% construction, 5.1% production (2000).
Income: Per capita income: $37,924 (2007); Median household income: $63,251 (2007); Average household income: $93,085 (2007); Percent of households with income of $100,000 or more: 30.8% (2007); Poverty rate: 11.1% (2000).
Taxes: Total city taxes per capita: $990 (2006); City property taxes per capita: $527 (2006).
Education: Percent of population age 25 and over with: High school diploma (including GED) or higher: 91.4% (2007); Bachelor's degree or higher: 62.6% (2007); Master's degree or higher: 33.2% (2007).

School District(s)

Evanston CCSD 65 (PK-08)
2005-06 Enrollment: 6,468 . . . . (847) 859-8010
Evanston Dists 65/202 Jnt Agr (PK-12)
2005-06 Enrollment: 73. . . . . (847) 492-5986
Evanston Twp HSD 202 (09-12)
2005-06 Enrollment: 3,164 . . . . (847) 424-7220

Four-year College(s)

Evanston Northwestern Healthcare School of Anesthesia (Private, Not-for-profit)
Fall 2007 Enrollment: 60 . . . . (847) 570-1959
Garrett-Evangelical Theological Seminary (Private, Not-for-profit, United Methodist)
Fall 2007 Enrollment: 315 . . . . (847) 866-3900
Northwestern University (Private, Not-for-profit)
Fall 2007 Enrollment: 19,005. . . . . (312) 491-3741
2007-08 Tuition: In-state $35,429; Out-of-state $35,429
Seabury-Western Theological Seminary (Private, Not-for-profit, Protestant Episcopal)
Fall 2007 Enrollment: 108 . . . . (847) 328-9300

Vocational/Technical School(s)

Pivot Point Beauty School (Private, For-profit)
Fall 2007 Enrollment: 211 . . . . (800) 886-0500
2007-08 Tuition: $16,463
Housing: Homeownership rate: 51.8% (2007); Median home value: $358,144 (2007); Median rent: $813 per month (2000); Median age of housing: 57 years (2000).
Hospitals: Evanston Hospital (635 beds); St. Francis Hospital (445 beds)
Safety: Violent crime rate: 32.4 per 10,000 population; Property crime rate: 389.3 per 10,000 population (2006).
Newspapers: National News Reporter (Local news; Circulation 0); Tribune Media Services - Evanston Bureau (Local news; Circulation 0)
Transportation: Commute to work: 61.7% car, 18.4% public transportation, 11.7% walk, 6.1% work from home (2000); Travel time to work: 26.4% less than 15 minutes, 23.6% 15 to 30 minutes, 22.5% 30 to 45 minutes, 15.6% 45 to 60 minutes, 11.9% 60 minutes or more (2000)
Additional Information Contacts
City of Evanston. . . . . (847) 866-2925
http://www.cityofevanston.org

EVERGREEN PARK (village). Covers a land area of 3.174 square miles and a water area of 0 square miles. Located at 41.72° N. Lat.; 87.70° W. Long. Elevation is 623 feet.
History: Named for the evergreen trees in the area. Incorporated 1893. St. Xavier College nearby.
Population: 20,874 (1990); 20,821 (2000); 19,607 (2007); 18,672 (2012 projected); Race: 83.6% White, 11.7% Black, 1.4% Asian, 5.2% Hispanic of any race (2007); Density: 6,177.5 persons per square mile (2007); Average household size: 2.82 (2007); Median age: 38.4 (2007); Males per 100 females: 91.5 (2007); Marriage status: 27.5% never married, 54.6% now married, 10.1% widowed, 7.8% divorced (2000); Foreign born: 4.2% (2000); Ancestry (includes multiple ancestries): 39.6% Irish, 21.4% German, 13.4% Other groups, 13.2% Polish, 10.2% Italian (2000).
Economy: Single-family building permits issued: 7 (2007); Multi-family building permits issued: 0 (2007); Employment by occupation: 14.6% management, 21.8% professional, 10.8% services, 30.4% sales, 0.1% farming, 10.5% construction, 11.8% production (2000).
Income: Per capita income: $26,012 (2007); Median household income: $61,407 (2007); Average household income: $72,829 (2007); Percent of households with income of $100,000 or more: 22.9% (2007); Poverty rate: 4.2% (2000).
Education: Percent of population age 25 and over with: High school diploma (including GED) or higher: 88.2% (2007); Bachelor's degree or higher: 27.8% (2007); Master's degree or higher: 8.4% (2007).

School District(s)

Evergreen Park CHSD 231 (09-12)
2005-06 Enrollment: 929 . . . . (708) 424-7400
Evergreen Park ESD 124 (PK-08)
2005-06 Enrollment: 2,004 . . . . (708) 423-0950
Housing: Homeownership rate: 85.5% (2007); Median home value: $206,037 (2007); Median rent: $567 per month (2000); Median age of housing: 46 years (2000).
Hospitals: Little Company of Mary Hospital & Health Care Centers (477 beds)
Safety: Violent crime rate: 15.1 per 10,000 population; Property crime rate: 366.8 per 10,000 population (2006).
Transportation: Commute to work: 82.5% car, 11.7% public transportation, 3.1% walk, 2.3% work from home (2000); Travel time to work: 25.0% less than 15 minutes, 22.0% 15 to 30 minutes, 22.9% 30 to 45 minutes, 14.2% 45 to 60 minutes, 15.8% 60 minutes or more (2000)
Additional Information Contacts

Evergreen Park Chamber of Commerce . . . . (708) 423-1118
http://www.evergreenparkchamber.org
Village of Evergreen Park . . . . (708) 422-1551
http://www.evergreenpark-ill.com

FLOSSMOOR (village). Covers a land area of 3.553 square miles and a water area of 0 square miles. Located at 41.54° N. Lat.; 87.68° W. Long. Elevation is 676 feet.
History: Incorporated 1924.
Population: 8,759 (1990); 9,301 (2000); 9,140 (2007); 8,979 (2012 projected); Race: 59.3% White, 34.5% Black, 3.6% Asian, 3.0% Hispanic of any race (2007); Density: 2,572.3 persons per square mile (2007); Average household size: 2.76 (2007); Median age: 43.9 (2007); Males per 100 females: 91.6 (2007); Marriage status: 20.3% never married, 66.5% now married, 6.3% widowed, 7.0% divorced (2000); Foreign born: 10.0% (2000); Ancestry (includes multiple ancestries): 29.8% Other groups, 13.8% German, 13.8% Irish, 9.7% Italian, 7.6% English (2000).
Economy: Single-family building permits issued: 11 (2007); Multi-family building permits issued: 0 (2007); Employment by occupation: 23.4% management, 38.5% professional, 5.2% services, 23.7% sales, 0.0% farming, 4.6% construction, 4.6% production (2000).
Income: Per capita income: $45,539 (2007); Median household income: $101,371 (2007); Average household income: $125,787 (2007); Percent of households with income of $100,000 or more: 50.8% (2007); Poverty rate: 2.8% (2000).
Taxes: Total city taxes per capita: $706 (2006); City property taxes per capita: $503 (2006).
Education: Percent of population age 25 and over with: High school diploma (including GED) or higher: 96.9% (2007); Bachelor's degree or higher: 61.4% (2007); Master's degree or higher: 32.3% (2007).

School District(s)

Flossmoor SD 161 (PK-08)
2005-06 Enrollment: 2,616 . . . . (708) 647-7000
Homewood Flossmoor CHSD 233 (09-12)
2005-06 Enrollment: 2,920 . . . . (708) 799-3000
Housing: Homeownership rate: 95.6% (2007); Median home value: $301,451 (2007); Median rent: $890 per month (2000); Median age of housing: 35 years (2000).
Safety: Violent crime rate: 12.8 per 10,000 population; Property crime rate: 171.5 per 10,000 population (2006).
Transportation: Commute to work: 80.0% car, 13.7% public transportation, 1.7% walk, 3.9% work from home (2000); Travel time to work: 27.8% less than 15 minutes, 20.9% 15 to 30 minutes, 13.7% 30 to 45 minutes, 18.1% 45 to 60 minutes, 19.5% 60 minutes or more (2000)
Additional Information Contacts
Village of Flossmoor . . . . (708) 798-2300
http://www.flossmoor.org

FORD HEIGHTS (village). Aka East Chicago Heights. Covers a land area of 1.768 square miles and a water area of 0 square miles. Located at 41.50° N. Lat.; 87.58° W. Long. Elevation is 663 feet.
Population: 4,271 (1990); 3,456 (2000); 3,090 (2007); 2,965 (2012 projected); Race: 2.2% White, 94.3% Black, 0.1% Asian, 3.7% Hispanic of any race (2007); Density: 1,747.8 persons per square mile (2007); Average household size: 3.51 (2007); Median age: 20.8 (2007); Males per 100 females: 88.1 (2007); Marriage status: 57.5% never married, 30.7% now married, 5.7% widowed, 6.1% divorced (2000); Foreign born: 0.6% (2000); Ancestry (includes multiple ancestries): 79.6% Other groups, 1.5% United States or American, 0.6% African, 0.3% Irish, 0.2% German (2000).
Economy: Single-family building permits issued: 0 (2007); Multi-family building permits issued: 0 (2007); Employment by occupation: 4.6% management, 11.6% professional, 29.3% services, 27.7% sales, 0.0% farming, 4.0% construction, 22.9% production (2000).
Income: Per capita income: $8,464 (2007); Median household income: $19,000 (2007); Average household income: $29,719 (2007); Percent of households with income of $100,000 or more: 3.3% (2007); Poverty rate: 49.0% (2000).
Education: Percent of population age 25 and over with: High school diploma (including GED) or higher: 69.6% (2007); Bachelor's degree or higher: 4.3% (2007); Master's degree or higher: 1.1% (2007).

School District(s)

Ford Heights SD 169 (PK-08)
2005-06 Enrollment: 738 . . . . (708) 758-1370
Housing: Homeownership rate: 32.3% (2007); Median home value: $70,000 (2007); Median rent: $369 per month (2000); Median age of housing: 35 years (2000).
Safety: Violent crime rate: 1,520.9 per 10,000 population; Property crime rate: 1,001.8 per 10,000 population (2006).
Transportation: Commute to work: 76.2% car, 14.6% public transportation, 5.1% walk, 2.6% work from home (2000); Travel time to work: 26.0% less than 15 minutes, 35.6% 15 to 30 minutes, 22.7% 30 to 45 minutes, 8.0% 45 to 60 minutes, 7.7% 60 minutes or more (2000)

FOREST PARK (village). Covers a land area of 2.421 square miles and a water area of 0 square miles. Located at 41.87° N. Lat.; 87.81° W. Long. Elevation is 623 feet.
Population: 14,918 (1990); 15,688 (2000); 15,066 (2007); 14,586 (2012 projected); Race: 46.3% White, 40.6% Black, 6.0% Asian, 9.9% Hispanic of any race (2007); Density: 6,223.8 persons per square mile (2007); Average household size: 2.10 (2007); Median age: 38.3 (2007); Males per 100 females: 91.3 (2007); Marriage status: 36.0% never married, 44.1% now married, 6.8% widowed, 13.1% divorced (2000); Foreign born: 14.8% (2000); Ancestry (includes multiple ancestries): 42.3% Other groups, 15.9% German, 14.6% Irish, 8.1% Italian, 5.9% English (2000).
Economy: Single-family building permits issued: 8 (2007); Multi-family building permits issued: 8 (2007); Employment by occupation: 12.8% management, 27.0% professional, 14.0% services, 29.1% sales, 0.0% farming, 6.3% construction, 10.8% production (2000).
Income: Per capita income: $30,611 (2007); Median household income: $51,775 (2007); Average household income: $63,467 (2007); Percent of households with income of $100,000 or more: 14.1% (2007); Poverty rate: 7.0% (2000).
Education: Percent of population age 25 and over with: High school diploma (including GED) or higher: 88.3% (2007); Bachelor's degree or higher: 36.4% (2007); Master's degree or higher: 14.8% (2007).

School District(s)

Forest Park SD 91 (PK-08)
2005-06 Enrollment: 1,078 . . . . (708) 366-5700
Proviso Twp HSD 209 (09-12)
2005-06 Enrollment: 4,873 . . . . (708) 338-5933
Housing: Homeownership rate: 44.4% (2007); Median home value: $209,436 (2007); Median rent: $621 per month (2000); Median age of housing: 49 years (2000).
Hospitals: Riveredge Hospital (210 beds)
Safety: Violent crime rate: 58.6 per 10,000 population; Property crime rate: 425.7 per 10,000 population (2006).
Transportation: Commute to work: 75.5% car, 17.0% public transportation, 5.3% walk, 1.7% work from home (2000); Travel time to work: 20.8% less than 15 minutes, 26.8% 15 to 30 minutes, 28.0% 30 to 45 minutes, 15.7% 45 to 60 minutes, 8.8% 60 minutes or more (2000)
Additional Information Contacts
Forest Park Chamber of Commerce . . . . (708) 366-2543
http://www.forestparkchamber.org
Village of Forest Park. . . . . (708) 366-2323
http://www.forestpark.net

FOREST VIEW (village). Covers a land area of 1.037 square miles and a water area of 0.132 square miles. Located at 41.80° N. Lat.; 87.78° W. Long. Elevation is 594 feet.
Population: 743 (1990); 778 (2000); 771 (2007); 749 (2012 projected); Race: 89.5% White, 0.4% Black, 0.0% Asian, 15.6% Hispanic of any race (2007); Density: 743.2 persons per square mile (2007); Average household size: 2.64 (2007); Median age: 45.0 (2007); Males per 100 females: 99.2 (2007); Marriage status: 25.9% never married, 55.2% now married, 12.4% widowed, 6.5% divorced (2000); Foreign born: 5.0% (2000); Ancestry (includes multiple ancestries): 25.9% Polish, 16.3% Czech, 15.1% Irish, 14.2% German, 13.4% Italian (2000).
Economy: Single-family building permits issued: 0 (2007); Multi-family building permits issued: 0 (2007); Employment by occupation: 8.9% management, 11.6% professional, 11.4% services, 38.2% sales, 0.0% farming, 9.9% construction, 20.0% production (2000).
Income: Per capita income: $23,765 (2007); Median household income: $53,158 (2007); Average household income: $62,748 (2007); Percent of households with income of $100,000 or more: 17.1% (2007); Poverty rate: 5.2% (2000).
Education: Percent of population age 25 and over with: High school diploma (including GED) or higher: 82.5% (2007); Bachelor's degree or higher: 8.7% (2007); Master's degree or higher: 2.5% (2007).

Housing: Homeownership rate: 90.4% (2007); Median home value: $226,768 (2007); Median rent: $567 per month (2000); Median age of housing: 45 years (2000).
Safety: Violent crime rate: 27.1 per 10,000 population; Property crime rate: 527.7 per 10,000 population (2006).
Transportation: Commute to work: 89.5% car, 7.2% public transportation, 2.8% walk, 0.0% work from home (2000); Travel time to work: 30.8% less than 15 minutes, 30.3% 15 to 30 minutes, 21.8% 30 to 45 minutes, 10.3% 45 to 60 minutes, 6.9% 60 minutes or more (2000)

FRANKLIN PARK (village). Covers a land area of 4.658 square miles and a water area of 0 square miles. Located at 41.93° N. Lat.; 87.87° W. Long. Elevation is 643 feet.
Population: 18,473 (1990); 19,434 (2000); 18,150 (2007); 17,274 (2012 projected); Race: 74.9% White, 1.0% Black, 3.1% Asian, 49.0% Hispanic of any race (2007); Density: 3,896.5 persons per square mile (2007); Average household size: 3.07 (2007); Median age: 35.9 (2007); Males per 100 females: 100.4 (2007); Marriage status: 27.4% never married, 56.3% now married, 8.6% widowed, 7.6% divorced (2000); Foreign born: 32.8% (2000); Ancestry (includes multiple ancestries): 38.4% Other groups, 19.6% Polish, 14.4% German, 13.0% Italian, 8.2% Irish (2000).
Economy: Single-family building permits issued: 0 (2007); Multi-family building permits issued: 0 (2007); Employment by occupation: 8.7% management, 12.2% professional, 11.3% services, 29.6% sales, 0.1% farming, 9.6% construction, 28.5% production (2000).
Income: Per capita income: $19,397 (2007); Median household income: $51,867 (2007); Average household income: $59,245 (2007); Percent of households with income of $100,000 or more: 13.9% (2007); Poverty rate: 7.1% (2000).
Education: Percent of population age 25 and over with: High school diploma (including GED) or higher: 67.0% (2007); Bachelor's degree or higher: 11.3% (2007); Master's degree or higher: 3.1% (2007).

School District(s)

Franklin Park SD 84 (PK-08)
2005-06 Enrollment: 1,333 . . . . (847) 455-4230
Leyden CHSD 212 (09-12)
2005-06 Enrollment: 3,537 . . . . (847) 451-3000
Mannheim SD 83 (PK-12)
2005-06 Enrollment: 2,757 . . . . (847) 455-4413

Housing: Homeownership rate: 72.9% (2007); Median home value: $223,121 (2007); Median rent: $536 per month (2000); Median age of housing: 45 years (2000).
Safety: Violent crime rate: 24.3 per 10,000 population; Property crime rate: 319.1 per 10,000 population (2006).
Transportation: Commute to work: 90.5% car, 4.9% public transportation, 3.1% walk, 1.0% work from home (2000); Travel time to work: 27.1% less than 15 minutes, 32.6% 15 to 30 minutes, 23.1% 30 to 45 minutes, 10.6% 45 to 60 minutes, 6.5% 60 minutes or more (2000)

Additional Information Contacts

Franklin Park/Schiller Park Chamber of Commerce . . . . . . (708) 865-9510
http://www.chamberbyohare.org

GLENCOE (village). Covers a land area of 3.777 square miles and a water area of 0.071 square miles. Located at 42.13° N. Lat.; 87.76° W. Long. Elevation is 673 feet.
History: One of the founders of Glencoe was Walter S. Gurnee, and the "coe" part of the town's name came from his wife's maiden name. Glencoe was incorporated as a village in 1869.
Population: 8,499 (1990); 8,762 (2000); 9,007 (2007); 9,154 (2012 projected); Race: 96.0% White, 1.4% Black, 1.3% Asian, 1.2% Hispanic of any race (2007); Density: 2,384.6 persons per square mile (2007); Average household size: 2.91 (2007); Median age: 42.7 (2007); Males per 100 females: 95.4 (2007); Marriage status: 14.7% never married, 75.8% now married, 4.8% widowed, 4.7% divorced (2000); Foreign born: 6.5% (2000); Ancestry (includes multiple ancestries): 16.0% German, 13.6% Irish, 11.8% Russian, 11.6% Other groups, 10.7% English (2000).
Economy: Single-family building permits issued: 34 (2007); Multi-family building permits issued: 0 (2007); Employment by occupation: 34.7% management, 33.9% professional, 4.4% services, 23.5% sales, 0.0% farming, 2.2% construction, 1.3% production (2000).
Income: Per capita income: $88,038 (2007); Median household income: $184,818 (2007); Average household income: $256,578 (2007); Percent of households with income of $100,000 or more: 70.3% (2007); Poverty rate: 2.3% (2000).
Education: Percent of population age 25 and over with: High school diploma (including GED) or higher: 97.7% (2007); Bachelor's degree or higher: 80.0% (2007); Master's degree or higher: 40.3% (2007).

School District(s)

Glencoe SD 35 (KG-08)
2005-06 Enrollment: 1,376 . . . . (847) 835-7800

Housing: Homeownership rate: 92.8% (2007); Median home value: $937,500 (2007); Median rent: $983 per month (2000); Median age of housing: 49 years (2000).
Safety: Violent crime rate: 1.1 per 10,000 population; Property crime rate: 104.7 per 10,000 population (2006).
Transportation: Commute to work: 64.7% car, 20.2% public transportation, 1.9% walk, 12.4% work from home (2000); Travel time to work: 18.6% less than 15 minutes, 24.1% 15 to 30 minutes, 24.5% 30 to 45 minutes, 16.5% 45 to 60 minutes, 16.3% 60 minutes or more (2000)

Additional Information Contacts

Glencoe Chamber of Commerce . . . . (847) 835-3333
Village of Glencoe . . . . (847) 835-4114
http://www.goglencoe.com

GLENVIEW (village). Covers a land area of 13.450 square miles and a water area of 0.041 square miles. Located at 42.07° N. Lat.; 87.81° W. Long. Elevation is 653 feet.
History: Named to promote the town as a good place to live. Settled 1833. Incorporated 1899.
Population: 40,177 (1990); 41,847 (2000); 44,617 (2007); 46,149 (2012 projected); Race: 81.8% White, 3.6% Black, 10.8% Asian, 5.5% Hispanic of any race (2007); Density: 3,317.2 persons per square mile (2007); Average household size: 2.71 (2007); Median age: 41.8 (2007); Males per 100 females: 92.7 (2007); Marriage status: 19.2% never married, 67.8% now married, 6.3% widowed, 6.8% divorced (2000); Foreign born: 19.5% (2000); Ancestry (includes multiple ancestries): 20.6% German, 18.6% Other groups, 17.0% Irish, 9.3% Polish, 7.5% English (2000).
Economy: Unemployment rate: 3.4% (4/2008); Total civilian labor force: 24,906 (4/2008); Single-family building permits issued: 82 (2007); Multi-family building permits issued: 0 (2007); Employment by occupation: 24.8% management, 28.8% professional, 8.0% services, 28.1% sales, 0.1% farming, 4.0% construction, 6.1% production (2000).
Income: Per capita income: $47,455 (2007); Median household income: $89,312 (2007); Average household income: $128,117 (2007); Percent of households with income of $100,000 or more: 44.2% (2007); Poverty rate: 2.0% (2000).
Taxes: Total city taxes per capita: $978 (2006); City property taxes per capita: $694 (2006).
Education: Percent of population age 25 and over with: High school diploma (including GED) or higher: 94.0% (2007); Bachelor's degree or higher: 54.2% (2007); Master's degree or higher: 23.3% (2007).

School District(s)

Avoca SD 37 (KG-08)
2005-06 Enrollment: 676 . . . . (847) 251-3587
East Maine SD 63 (PK-08)
2005-06 Enrollment: 3,498 . . . . (847) 299-1900
Glenview CCSD 34 (PK-08)
2005-06 Enrollment: 4,253 . . . . (847) 998-5000
Northbrook/Glenview SD 30 (PK-08)
2005-06 Enrollment: 1,081 . . . . (847) 498-4190
Northern Suburban Spec Ed Dist (KG-12)
2005-06 Enrollment: 127 . . . . (847) 831-5100
Northfield Twp HSD 225 (09-12)
2005-06 Enrollment: 4,868 . . . . (847) 486-4700
West Northfield SD 31 (KG-08)
2005-06 Enrollment: 857 . . . . (847) 272-6880

Housing: Homeownership rate: 85.0% (2007); Median home value: $464,460 (2007); Median rent: $783 per month (2000); Median age of housing: 33 years (2000).
Hospitals: Glenbrook Hospital (144 beds)
Safety: Violent crime rate: 6.3 per 10,000 population; Property crime rate: 182.7 per 10,000 population (2006).
Newspapers: Lincolnwood Review (Community news; Circulation 1,475); Mount Prospect Times (Local news; Circulation 2,294); Northbrook Star (Community news; Circulation 7,807); Pioneer Press - North Shore Bureau (Community news; Circulation 0); Pioneer Press Newspapers (Community news; Circulation 3,900); Skokie Review (Community news; Circulation 7,116); Wilmette Life (Community news; Circulation 7,309)

Transportation: Commute to work: 84.7% car, 8.1% public transportation, 1.5% walk, 5.0% work from home (2000); Travel time to work: 19.9% less than 15 minutes, 33.0% 15 to 30 minutes, 25.6% 30 to 45 minutes, 11.5% 45 to 60 minutes, 10.0% 60 minutes or more (2000); Amtrak: Service available.

Additional Information Contacts

Glenview Chamber of Commerce .... (847) 724-0900
http://www.glenviewchamber.com

Village of Glenview .... (847) 904-4370
http://www.glenview.il.us

GLENWOOD (village). Covers a land area of 2.687 square miles and a water area of 0 square miles. Located at 41.54° N. Lat.; 87.61° W. Long. Elevation is 620 feet.

Population: 9,402 (1990); 9,000 (2000); 8,647 (2007); 8,310 (2012 projected); Race: 41.3% White, 53.5% Black, 0.6% Asian, 6.3% Hispanic of any race (2007); Density: 3,218.7 persons per square mile (2007); Average household size: 2.66 (2007); Median age: 40.4 (2007); Males per 100 females: 87.4 (2007); Marriage status: 27.9% never married, 54.4% now married, 8.1% widowed, 9.6% divorced (2000); Foreign born: 3.5% (2000); Ancestry (includes multiple ancestries): 41.4% Other groups, 14.9% German, 10.0% Irish, 7.6% Polish, 7.4% Italian (2000).

Economy: Single-family building permits issued: 0 (2007); Multi-family building permits issued: 0 (2007); Employment by occupation: 13.7% management, 22.9% professional, 11.3% services, 30.7% sales, 0.0% farming, 7.2% construction, 14.1% production (2000).

Income: Per capita income: $26,804 (2007); Median household income: $59,290 (2007); Average household income: $71,248 (2007); Percent of households with income of $100,000 or more: 19.8% (2007); Poverty rate: 3.7% (2000).

Education: Percent of population age 25 and over with: High school diploma (including GED) or higher: 90.9% (2007); Bachelor's degree or higher: 27.8% (2007); Master's degree or higher: 9.5% (2007).

School District(s)

Brookwood SD 167 (PK-08)
2005-06 Enrollment: 1,324 .... (708) 758-5190

Housing: Homeownership rate: 86.4% (2007); Median home value: $176,815 (2007); Median rent: $657 per month (2000); Median age of housing: 30 years (2000).

Safety: Violent crime rate: 32.3 per 10,000 population; Property crime rate: 360.2 per 10,000 population (2006).

Transportation: Commute to work: 89.4% car, 7.3% public transportation, 0.2% walk, 2.3% work from home (2000); Travel time to work: 24.0% less than 15 minutes, 28.4% 15 to 30 minutes, 17.9% 30 to 45 minutes, 13.2% 45 to 60 minutes, 16.5% 60 minutes or more (2000)

Additional Information Contacts

Village of Glenwood.............................. (708) 753-2308
http://www.villageofglenwood.com

GOLF (village). Covers a land area of 0.445 square miles and a water area of 0 square miles. Located at 42.05° N. Lat.; 87.79° W. Long. Elevation is 636 feet.

Population: 454 (1990); 451 (2000); 494 (2007); 521 (2012 projected); Race: 99.6% White, 0.0% Black, 0.4% Asian, 0.6% Hispanic of any race (2007); Density: 1,111.2 persons per square mile (2007); Average household size: 2.89 (2007); Median age: 40.9 (2007); Males per 100 females: 96.8 (2007); Marriage status: 20.7% never married, 70.3% now married, 4.3% widowed, 4.6% divorced (2000); Foreign born: 3.8% (2000); Ancestry (includes multiple ancestries): 33.2% Irish, 24.6% English, 22.6% German, 10.8% Italian, 6.4% United States or American (2000).

Economy: Single-family building permits issued: 0 (2007); Multi-family building permits issued: 0 (2007); Employment by occupation: 27.3% management, 28.7% professional, 6.5% services, 32.4% sales, 0.0% farming, 2.8% construction, 2.3% production (2000).

Income: Per capita income: $81,270 (2007); Median household income: $140,441 (2007); Average household income: $234,781 (2007); Percent of households with income of $100,000 or more: 66.1% (2007); Poverty rate: 0.9% (2000).

Education: Percent of population age 25 and over with: High school diploma (including GED) or higher: 100.0% (2007); Bachelor's degree or higher: 82.4% (2007); Master's degree or higher: 33.2% (2007).

Housing: Homeownership rate: 95.9% (2007); Median home value: $924,107 (2007); Median rent: $n/a per month (2000); Median age of housing: 49 years (2000).

Safety: Violent crime rate: 0.0 per 10,000 population; Property crime rate: 0.0 per 10,000 population (2006).

Transportation: Commute to work: 67.6% car, 26.8% public transportation, 0.0% walk, 5.6% work from home (2000); Travel time to work: 21.4% less than 15 minutes, 13.4% 15 to 30 minutes, 42.3% 30 to 45 minutes, 12.9% 45 to 60 minutes, 10.0% 60 minutes or more (2000)

HANOVER PARK (village). Covers a land area of 6.794 square miles and a water area of 0 square miles. Located at 41.97° N. Lat.; 88.14° W. Long.

Population: 32,993 (1990); 38,278 (2000); 37,563 (2007); 37,096 (2012 projected); Race: 60.0% White, 7.6% Black, 14.3% Asian, 33.9% Hispanic of any race (2007); Density: 5,529.1 persons per square mile (2007); Average household size: 3.44 (2007); Median age: 32.1 (2007); Males per 100 females: 105.3 (2007); Marriage status: 29.7% never married, 58.9% now married, 3.2% widowed, 8.2% divorced (2000); Foreign born: 28.4% (2000); Ancestry (includes multiple ancestries): 40.7% Other groups, 15.5% German, 12.6% Irish, 11.0% Polish, 8.7% Italian (2000).

Economy: Unemployment rate: 6.1% (4/2008); Total civilian labor force: 21,564 (4/2008); Single-family building permits issued: 19 (2007); Multi-family building permits issued: 0 (2007); Employment by occupation: 12.2% management, 14.1% professional, 13.4% services, 31.5% sales, 0.1% farming, 8.8% construction, 19.9% production (2000).

Income: Per capita income: $24,129 (2007); Median household income: $73,312 (2007); Average household income: $82,959 (2007); Percent of households with income of $100,000 or more: 27.3% (2007); Poverty rate: 6.1% (2000).

Education: Percent of population age 25 and over with: High school diploma (including GED) or higher: 78.7% (2007); Bachelor's degree or higher: 20.0% (2007); Master's degree or higher: 3.9% (2007).

School District(s)

CCSD 93 (PK-08)
2005-06 Enrollment: 4,517 .... (630) 893-9393

Keeneyville SD 20 (PK-08)
2005-06 Enrollment: 1,708 .... (630) 894-2250

SD U-46 (PK-12)
2005-06 Enrollment: 39,656 .... (847) 888-5000

Schaumburg CCSD 54 (PK-08)
2005-06 Enrollment: 14,471 .... (847) 357-5000

Vocational/Technical School(s)

Empire Beauty School-Hanover Park (Private, For-profit)
Fall 2007 Enrollment: 87 .... (800) 223-3271
2007-08 Tuition: $17,595

Housing: Homeownership rate: 82.7% (2007); Median home value: $210,018 (2007); Median rent: $696 per month (2000); Median age of housing: 25 years (2000).

Safety: Violent crime rate: 21.0 per 10,000 population; Property crime rate: 156.9 per 10,000 population (2006).

Transportation: Commute to work: 92.0% car, 3.7% public transportation, 1.8% walk, 1.5% work from home (2000); Travel time to work: 19.6% less than 15 minutes, 34.5% 15 to 30 minutes, 24.8% 30 to 45 minutes, 11.0% 45 to 60 minutes, 10.1% 60 minutes or more (2000)

Additional Information Contacts

Hanover Park Chamber of Commerce & Industry .... (630) 372-2009
http://www.hanoverparkchamber.com

Village of Hanover Park .... (630) 372-4200
http://www.hanoverparkillinois.org

HARVEY (city). Covers a land area of 6.196 square miles and a water area of 0 square miles. Located at 41.61° N. Lat.; 87.65° W. Long. Elevation is 604 feet.

History: Named for Turlington W. Harvey, town founder. The site of Harvey was purchased in 1889 by Turlington W. Harvey, a Chicago lumberman, who organized a village that attracted other settlers and industries.

Population: 29,771 (1990); 30,000 (2000); 28,493 (2007); 27,347 (2012 projected); Race: 9.7% White, 76.8% Black, 0.5% Asian, 17.1% Hispanic of any race (2007); Density: 4,598.9 persons per square mile (2007); Average household size: 3.36 (2007); Median age: 29.1 (2007); Males per 100 females: 93.1 (2007); Marriage status: 38.8% never married, 44.5% now married, 7.6% widowed, 9.1% divorced (2000); Foreign born: 8.2% (2000); Ancestry (includes multiple ancestries): 77.7% Other groups, 2.5% African, 1.6% Polish, 1.2% German, 1.1% United States or American (2000).

Economy: Unemployment rate: 9.0% (4/2008); Total civilian labor force: 11,288 (4/2008); Single-family building permits issued: 13 (2007);

Multi-family building permits issued: 4 (2007); Employment by occupation: 5.9% management, 14.1% professional, 21.9% services, 28.5% sales, 0.3% farming, 7.3% construction, 22.0% production (2000).
Income: Per capita income: $13,107 (2007); Median household income: $34,210 (2007); Average household income: $43,140 (2007); Percent of households with income of $100,000 or more: 6.4% (2007); Poverty rate: 21.7% (2000).
Education: Percent of population age 25 and over with: High school diploma (including GED) or higher: 69.5% (2007); Bachelor's degree or higher: 8.2% (2007); Master's degree or higher: 2.4% (2007).

School District(s)

Harvey SD 152 (PK-08)
2005-06 Enrollment: 2,924 . . . . (708) 333-0300
South Holland SD 151 (PK-08)
2005-06 Enrollment: 1,594 . . . . (708) 339-1516
Thornton Twp HSD 205 (09-12)
2005-06 Enrollment: 6,554 . . . . (708) 225-4000
West Harvey-Dixmoor PSD 147 (PK-08)
2005-06 Enrollment: 1,667 . . . . (708) 339-9500

Four-year College(s)

Ingalls Memorial Hospital Dietetic Internship (Private, Not-for-profit)
Fall 2007 Enrollment: 6 . . . . (708) 915-5723

Housing: Homeownership rate: 56.8% (2007); Median home value: $102,823 (2007); Median rent: $490 per month (2000); Median age of housing: 41 years (2000).
Hospitals: Ingalls Memorial Hospital (326 beds)
Safety: Violent crime rate: 199.9 per 10,000 population; Property crime rate: 719.8 per 10,000 population (2006).
Transportation: Commute to work: 80.6% car, 13.1% public transportation, 3.6% walk, 2.2% work from home (2000); Travel time to work: 19.4% less than 15 minutes, 31.4% 15 to 30 minutes, 20.3% 30 to 45 minutes, 10.8% 45 to 60 minutes, 18.2% 60 minutes or more (2000)

Additional Information Contacts

City of Harvey . . . . (708) 210-5366
http://www.cityofharvey.org

HARWOOD HEIGHTS (village).

Covers a land area of 0.822 square miles and a water area of 0 square miles. Located at 41.96° N. Lat.; 87.80° W. Long. Elevation is 650 feet.
Population: 7,680 (1990); 8,297 (2000); 8,102 (2007); 7,888 (2012 projected); Race: 90.2% White, 0.4% Black, 5.2% Asian, 7.3% Hispanic of any race (2007); Density: 9,857.1 persons per square mile (2007); Average household size: 2.40 (2007); Median age: 44.7 (2007); Males per 100 females: 89.4 (2007); Marriage status: 25.1% never married, 53.5% now married, 13.8% widowed, 7.7% divorced (2000); Foreign born: 34.1% (2000); Ancestry (includes multiple ancestries): 37.4% Polish, 17.8% Italian, 14.5% German, 12.7% Other groups, 9.8% Irish (2000).
Economy: Single-family building permits issued: 20 (2007); Multi-family building permits issued: 0 (2007); Employment by occupation: 11.4% management, 12.9% professional, 13.9% services, 34.3% sales, 0.0% farming, 11.4% construction, 16.2% production (2000).
Income: Per capita income: $25,430 (2007); Median household income: $49,780 (2007); Average household income: $60,720 (2007); Percent of households with income of $100,000 or more: 14.9% (2007); Poverty rate: 4.6% (2000).
Education: Percent of population age 25 and over with: High school diploma (including GED) or higher: 77.6% (2007); Bachelor's degree or higher: 16.5% (2007); Master's degree or higher: 4.3% (2007).

School District(s)

Ridgewood CHSD 234 (09-12)
2005-06 Enrollment: 952 . . . . (708) 456-4242
Union Ridge SD 86 (PK-08)
2005-06 Enrollment: 612 . . . . (708) 867-5822

Housing: Homeownership rate: 60.7% (2007); Median home value: $305,195 (2007); Median rent: $664 per month (2000); Median age of housing: 37 years (2000).
Safety: Violent crime rate: 9.8 per 10,000 population; Property crime rate: 244.3 per 10,000 population (2006).
Transportation: Commute to work: 83.6% car, 9.3% public transportation, 3.3% walk, 2.7% work from home (2000); Travel time to work: 21.2% less than 15 minutes, 33.6% 15 to 30 minutes, 25.3% 30 to 45 minutes, 10.3% 45 to 60 minutes, 9.6% 60 minutes or more (2000)

Additional Information Contacts

Village of Harwood Heights . . . . (708) 867-7200
http://www.harwoodheights.org

HAZEL CREST (village).

Covers a land area of 3.381 square miles and a water area of 0.023 square miles. Located at 41.57° N. Lat.; 87.68° W. Long. Elevation is 646 feet.
Population: 13,438 (1990); 14,816 (2000); 14,358 (2007); 14,015 (2012 projected); Race: 14.9% White, 80.9% Black, 0.7% Asian, 3.7% Hispanic of any race (2007); Density: 4,246.0 persons per square mile (2007); Average household size: 2.92 (2007); Median age: 35.7 (2007); Males per 100 females: 84.6 (2007); Marriage status: 32.3% never married, 48.3% now married, 6.9% widowed, 12.5% divorced (2000); Foreign born: 3.4% (2000); Ancestry (includes multiple ancestries): 70.6% Other groups, 4.3% German, 4.0% Irish, 3.1% English, 2.2% Polish (2000).
Economy: Single-family building permits issued: 6 (2007); Multi-family building permits issued: 0 (2007); Employment by occupation: 12.8% management, 19.8% professional, 13.9% services, 31.4% sales, 0.0% farming, 6.6% construction, 15.5% production (2000).
Income: Per capita income: $21,479 (2007); Median household income: $53,675 (2007); Average household income: $62,390 (2007); Percent of households with income of $100,000 or more: 14.7% (2007); Poverty rate: 8.4% (2000).
Education: Percent of population age 25 and over with: High school diploma (including GED) or higher: 88.4% (2007); Bachelor's degree or higher: 22.5% (2007); Master's degree or higher: 7.8% (2007).

School District(s)

Hazel Crest SD 152-5 (PK-08)
2005-06 Enrollment: 1,084 . . . . (708) 335-0790
Prairie-Hills ESD 144 (PK-08)
2005-06 Enrollment: 2,955 . . . . (708) 210-2888

Housing: Homeownership rate: 81.5% (2007); Median home value: $146,410 (2007); Median rent: $763 per month (2000); Median age of housing: 31 years (2000).
Hospitals: Advocate South Suburban Hospital (291 beds)
Safety: Violent crime rate: 31.2 per 10,000 population; Property crime rate: 308.7 per 10,000 population (2006).
Transportation: Commute to work: 84.8% car, 9.5% public transportation, 1.2% walk, 2.9% work from home (2000); Travel time to work: 18.1% less than 15 minutes, 24.2% 15 to 30 minutes, 24.2% 30 to 45 minutes, 15.9% 45 to 60 minutes, 17.7% 60 minutes or more (2000)

Additional Information Contacts

Hazel Crest Chamber of Commerce . . . . (708) 335-4699
Village of Hazel Crest . . . . (708) 335-9600
http://www.villageofhazelcrest.com

HICKORY HILLS (city).

Covers a land area of 2.834 square miles and a water area of 0 square miles. Located at 41.72° N. Lat.; 87.82° W. Long. Elevation is 679 feet.
Population: 13,021 (1990); 13,926 (2000); 13,261 (2007); 12,924 (2012 projected); Race: 88.4% White, 1.8% Black, 2.3% Asian, 10.8% Hispanic of any race (2007); Density: 4,678.4 persons per square mile (2007); Average household size: 2.67 (2007); Median age: 38.4 (2007); Males per 100 females: 98.8 (2007); Marriage status: 26.5% never married, 56.8% now married, 8.0% widowed, 8.7% divorced (2000); Foreign born: 16.8% (2000); Ancestry (includes multiple ancestries): 26.9% Polish, 19.9% Irish, 17.2% German, 11.8% Other groups, 10.7% Italian (2000).
Economy: Single-family building permits issued: 18 (2007); Multi-family building permits issued: 0 (2007); Employment by occupation: 11.7% management, 17.0% professional, 11.2% services, 31.3% sales, 0.0% farming, 11.8% construction, 16.9% production (2000).
Income: Per capita income: $25,471 (2007); Median household income: $59,409 (2007); Average household income: $67,823 (2007); Percent of households with income of $100,000 or more: 17.4% (2007); Poverty rate: 5.5% (2000).
Education: Percent of population age 25 and over with: High school diploma (including GED) or higher: 81.8% (2007); Bachelor's degree or higher: 21.5% (2007); Master's degree or higher: 5.8% (2007).

School District(s)

North Palos SD 117 (PK-08)
2005-06 Enrollment: 2,790 . . . . (708) 598-5500

Vocational/Technical School(s)

Star Truck Driving School (Private, For-profit)
Fall 2007 Enrollment: 50 . . . . (630) 236-7200
2007-08 Tuition: $4,595

Housing: Homeownership rate: 72.7% (2007); Median home value: $242,141 (2007); Median rent: $613 per month (2000); Median age of housing: 32 years (2000).

Safety: Violent crime rate: 9.6 per 10,000 population; Property crime rate: 179.4 per 10,000 population (2006).
Transportation: Commute to work: 92.0% car, 2.4% public transportation, 2.1% walk, 3.0% work from home (2000); Travel time to work: 18.8% less than 15 minutes, 33.8% 15 to 30 minutes, 21.6% 30 to 45 minutes, 13.1% 45 to 60 minutes, 12.7% 60 minutes or more (2000)
Additional Information Contacts
City of Hickory Hills . . . . (708) 598-4800
http://www.hickoryhillsil.org

HILLSIDE (village). Covers a land area of 2.148 square miles and a water area of 0 square miles. Located at 41.87° N. Lat.; 87.90° W. Long. Elevation is 656 feet.
History: Incorporated 1905.
Population: 7,672 (1990); 8,155 (2000); 7,706 (2007); 7,343 (2012 projected); Race: 37.7% White, 46.3% Black, 5.0% Asian, 16.8% Hispanic of any race (2007); Density: 3,588.3 persons per square mile (2007); Average household size: 2.77 (2007); Median age: 38.5 (2007); Males per 100 females: 93.1 (2007); Marriage status: 30.5% never married, 52.1% now married, 6.7% widowed, 10.7% divorced (2000); Foreign born: 13.5% (2000); Ancestry (includes multiple ancestries): 46.7% Other groups, 11.4% German, 9.3% Italian, 9.3% Irish, 5.3% Polish (2000).
Economy: Single-family building permits issued: 1 (2007); Multi-family building permits issued: 0 (2007); Employment by occupation: 12.4% management, 20.1% professional, 12.2% services, 27.7% sales, 0.0% farming, 6.0% construction, 21.7% production (2000).
Income: Per capita income: $23,735 (2007); Median household income: $56,605 (2007); Average household income: $64,975 (2007); Percent of households with income of $100,000 or more: 15.0% (2007); Poverty rate: 6.3% (2000).
Taxes: Total city taxes per capita: $1,559 (2006); City property taxes per capita: $1,210 (2006).
Education: Percent of population age 25 and over with: High school diploma (including GED) or higher: 81.6% (2007); Bachelor's degree or higher: 20.2% (2007); Master's degree or higher: 6.1% (2007).

School District(s)

Hillside SD 93 (KG-08)
2005-06 Enrollment: 528 . . . . (708) 449-7280
Proviso Twp HSD 209 (09-12)
2005-06 Enrollment: 4,873 . . . . (708) 338-5933
Housing: Homeownership rate: 68.5% (2007); Median home value: $199,122 (2007); Median rent: $659 per month (2000); Median age of housing: 43 years (2000).
Safety: Violent crime rate: 73.3 per 10,000 population; Property crime rate: 306.3 per 10,000 population (2006).
Transportation: Commute to work: 92.0% car, 3.5% public transportation, 2.7% walk, 1.8% work from home (2000); Travel time to work: 19.4% less than 15 minutes, 36.8% 15 to 30 minutes, 22.5% 30 to 45 minutes, 11.2% 45 to 60 minutes, 10.1% 60 minutes or more (2000)
Additional Information Contacts
Hillside Chamber of Commerce & Industry . . . . (708) 449-2449
http://www.hillsidechamberofcommerce.com
Village of Hillside . . . . (708) 449-6450
http://www.hillside-il.org

HODGKINS (village). Covers a land area of 2.572 square miles and a water area of 0.065 square miles. Located at 41.76° N. Lat.; 87.85° W. Long. Elevation is 604 feet.
Population: 1,963 (1990); 2,134 (2000); 2,172 (2007); 2,186 (2012 projected); Race: 84.3% White, 0.1% Black, 0.0% Asian, 52.3% Hispanic of any race (2007); Density: 844.4 persons per square mile (2007); Average household size: 2.61 (2007); Median age: 35.7 (2007); Males per 100 females: 121.4 (2007); Marriage status: 26.3% never married, 50.5% now married, 8.8% widowed, 14.4% divorced (2000); Foreign born: 32.9% (2000); Ancestry (includes multiple ancestries): 42.8% Other groups, 12.7% Irish, 12.4% German, 8.0% Polish, 7.0% English (2000).
Economy: Single-family building permits issued: 0 (2007); Multi-family building permits issued: 0 (2007); Employment by occupation: 7.1% management, 7.3% professional, 31.3% services, 23.5% sales, 0.0% farming, 10.6% construction, 20.2% production (2000).
Income: Per capita income: $19,909 (2007); Median household income: $41,042 (2007); Average household income: $51,912 (2007); Percent of households with income of $100,000 or more: 9.8% (2007); Poverty rate: 15.5% (2000).
Education: Percent of population age 25 and over with: High school diploma (including GED) or higher: 59.9% (2007); Bachelor's degree or higher: 6.4% (2007); Master's degree or higher: 2.0% (2007).

School District(s)

La Grange SD 105 South (PK-08)
2005-06 Enrollment: 1,184 . . . . (708) 482-2700
Housing: Homeownership rate: 64.8% (2007); Median home value: $46,538 (2007); Median rent: $526 per month (2000); Median age of housing: 22 years (2000).
Safety: Violent crime rate: 38.6 per 10,000 population; Property crime rate: 1,056.4 per 10,000 population (2006).
Transportation: Commute to work: 77.8% car, 3.1% public transportation, 9.7% walk, 0.2% work from home (2000); Travel time to work: 34.8% less than 15 minutes, 40.3% 15 to 30 minutes, 12.0% 30 to 45 minutes, 6.4% 45 to 60 minutes, 6.4% 60 minutes or more (2000)
Additional Information Contacts
West Suburban Chamber of Commerce . . . . (708) 352-0494
http://www.westsuburbanchamber.org

HOFFMAN ESTATES (village). Covers a land area of 19.710 square miles and a water area of 0.158 square miles. Located at 42.06° N. Lat.; 88.11° W. Long. Elevation is 784 feet.
Population: 46,320 (1990); 49,495 (2000); 48,855 (2007); 49,104 (2012 projected); Race: 68.5% White, 5.0% Black, 18.5% Asian, 13.8% Hispanic of any race (2007); Density: 2,478.7 persons per square mile (2007); Average household size: 2.92 (2007); Median age: 35.8 (2007); Males per 100 females: 98.7 (2007); Marriage status: 27.6% never married, 59.9% now married, 4.5% widowed, 8.0% divorced (2000); Foreign born: 23.1% (2000); Ancestry (includes multiple ancestries): 29.4% Other groups, 21.9% German, 14.7% Irish, 13.3% Polish, 10.8% Italian (2000).
Economy: Unemployment rate: 4.1% (4/2008); Total civilian labor force: 31,315 (4/2008); Single-family building permits issued: 198 (2007); Multi-family building permits issued: 0 (2007); Employment by occupation: 18.3% management, 22.8% professional, 9.6% services, 31.2% sales, 0.1% farming, 6.1% construction, 11.9% production (2000).
Income: Per capita income: $31,420 (2007); Median household income: $76,350 (2007); Average household income: $91,156 (2007); Percent of households with income of $100,000 or more: 33.8% (2007); Poverty rate: 4.4% (2000).
Taxes: Total city taxes per capita: $603 (2006); City property taxes per capita: $334 (2006).
Education: Percent of population age 25 and over with: High school diploma (including GED) or higher: 89.6% (2007); Bachelor's degree or higher: 36.0% (2007); Master's degree or higher: 11.7% (2007).

School District(s)

Palatine CCSD 15 (PK-08)
2005-06 Enrollment: 12,794 . . . . (847) 963-3000
SD U-46 (PK-12)
2005-06 Enrollment: 39,656 . . . . (847) 888-5000
Schaumburg CCSD 54 (PK-08)
2005-06 Enrollment: 14,471 . . . . (847) 357-5000
Township HSD 211 (09-12)
2005-06 Enrollment: 13,026 . . . . (847) 755-6600

Four-year College(s)

American Intercontinental University Online (Private, For-profit)
Fall 2007 Enrollment: 22,173. . . . . (877) 701-3800
2007-08 Tuition: In-state $12,258; Out-of-state $12,258
Housing: Homeownership rate: 78.0% (2007); Median home value: $262,113 (2007); Median rent: $845 per month (2000); Median age of housing: 25 years (2000).
Hospitals: Saint Alexius Medical Center (331 beds)
Safety: Violent crime rate: 9.2 per 10,000 population; Property crime rate: 173.1 per 10,000 population (2006).
Transportation: Commute to work: 91.8% car, 3.3% public transportation, 1.3% walk, 2.7% work from home (2000); Travel time to work: 18.5% less than 15 minutes, 37.8% 15 to 30 minutes, 24.9% 30 to 45 minutes, 9.8% 45 to 60 minutes, 9.0% 60 minutes or more (2000)
Additional Information Contacts
Hoffman Estates Chamber of Commerce & Industry. . . . . . (847) 781-9100
http://www.hechamber.com
Village of Hoffman Estates. . . . . (847) 781-2605
http://www.hoffmanestates.com

HOMETOWN (city). Covers a land area of 0.478 square miles and a water area of 0 square miles. Located at 41.73° N. Lat.; 87.73° W. Long. Elevation is 620 feet.

Population: 4,769 (1990); 4,467 (2000); 4,168 (2007); 3,940 (2012 projected); Race: 96.6% White, 0.0% Black, 0.2% Asian, 5.1% Hispanic of any race (2007); Density: 8,728.5 persons per square mile (2007); Average household size: 2.32 (2007); Median age: 39.9 (2007); Males per 100 females: 85.0 (2007); Marriage status: 25.3% never married, 49.8% now married, 14.0% widowed, 10.9% divorced (2000); Foreign born: 2.9% (2000); Ancestry (includes multiple ancestries): 33.6% Irish, 28.7% German, 18.8% Polish, 13.0% Italian, 7.7% Other groups (2000).

Economy: Single-family building permits issued: 0 (2007); Multi-family building permits issued: 0 (2007); Employment by occupation: 8.9% management, 11.1% professional, 13.9% services, 35.6% sales, 0.0% farming, 16.0% construction, 14.6% production (2000).

Income: Per capita income: $22,088 (2007); Median household income: $43,981 (2007); Average household income: $51,288 (2007); Percent of households with income of $100,000 or more: 10.3% (2007); Poverty rate: 3.0% (2000).

Education: Percent of population age 25 and over with: High school diploma (including GED) or higher: 82.0% (2007); Bachelor's degree or higher: 8.6% (2007); Master's degree or higher: 1.6% (2007).

School District(s)

Oak Lawn-Hometown SD 123 (PK-08)
2005-06 Enrollment: 2,885 . . . . (708) 423-0150

Housing: Homeownership rate: 77.5% (2007); Median home value: $142,164 (2007); Median rent: $233 per month (2000); Median age of housing: 46 years (2000).

Safety: Violent crime rate: 4.7 per 10,000 population; Property crime rate: 165.1 per 10,000 population (2006).

Transportation: Commute to work: 91.3% car, 5.1% public transportation, 1.7% walk, 1.7% work from home (2000); Travel time to work: 26.3% less than 15 minutes, 27.3% 15 to 30 minutes, 25.2% 30 to 45 minutes, 9.5% 45 to 60 minutes, 11.7% 60 minutes or more (2000)

HOMEWOOD (village). Covers a land area of 5.204 square miles and a water area of 0.052 square miles. Located at 41.55° N. Lat.; 87.66° W. Long. Elevation is 659 feet.

History: Named for Homewood, Pennsylvania. The site of Homewood was laid out in 1852 by James Hart and was first known as Hartford.

Population: 19,278 (1990); 19,543 (2000); 18,825 (2007); 18,172 (2012 projected); Race: 71.7% White, 23.2% Black, 1.5% Asian, 4.1% Hispanic of any race (2007); Density: 3,617.5 persons per square mile (2007); Average household size: 2.59 (2007); Median age: 41.6 (2007); Males per 100 females: 86.4 (2007); Marriage status: 23.7% never married, 59.2% now married, 8.5% widowed, 8.6% divorced (2000); Foreign born: 4.4% (2000); Ancestry (includes multiple ancestries): 22.7% German, 21.7% Other groups, 19.0% Irish, 10.3% Polish, 9.7% Italian (2000).

Economy: Single-family building permits issued: 5 (2007); Multi-family building permits issued: 0 (2007); Employment by occupation: 17.0% management, 31.9% professional, 8.9% services, 27.4% sales, 0.0% farming, 7.7% construction, 7.0% production (2000).

Income: Per capita income: $29,438 (2007); Median household income: $62,717 (2007); Average household income: $76,166 (2007); Percent of households with income of $100,000 or more: 24.0% (2007); Poverty rate: 4.3% (2000).

Education: Percent of population age 25 and over with: High school diploma (including GED) or higher: 93.3% (2007); Bachelor's degree or higher: 41.0% (2007); Master's degree or higher: 16.3% (2007).

School District(s)

Homewood SD 153 (PK-08)
2005-06 Enrollment: 2,066 . . . . (708) 799-5661

Housing: Homeownership rate: 85.0% (2007); Median home value: $191,626 (2007); Median rent: $669 per month (2000); Median age of housing: 38 years (2000).

Safety: Violent crime rate: 28.0 per 10,000 population; Property crime rate: 501.7 per 10,000 population (2006).

Transportation: Commute to work: 79.0% car, 15.9% public transportation, 0.9% walk, 3.7% work from home (2000); Travel time to work: 26.4% less than 15 minutes, 25.4% 15 to 30 minutes, 14.1% 30 to 45 minutes, 14.1% 45 to 60 minutes, 20.0% 60 minutes or more (2000); Amtrak: Service available.

Additional Information Contacts

Homewood Area Chamber of Commerce . . . . (708) 206-3384
http://www.homewoodareachamber.com
Village of Homewood . . . . (708) 798-3000
http://village.homewood.il.us

INDIAN HEAD PARK (village). Covers a land area of 0.842 square miles and a water area of 0 square miles. Located at 41.76° N. Lat.; 87.89° W. Long. Elevation is 653 feet.

Population: 3,628 (1990); 3,685 (2000); 3,794 (2007); 3,882 (2012 projected); Race: 95.5% White, 1.0% Black, 2.1% Asian, 2.0% Hispanic of any race (2007); Density: 4,506.0 persons per square mile (2007); Average household size: 2.14 (2007); Median age: 56.0 (2007); Males per 100 females: 79.5 (2007); Marriage status: 17.2% never married, 58.3% now married, 13.3% widowed, 11.2% divorced (2000); Foreign born: 6.6% (2000); Ancestry (includes multiple ancestries): 26.4% German, 22.8% Irish, 14.3% Polish, 8.4% English, 7.7% Italian (2000).

Economy: Single-family building permits issued: 0 (2007); Multi-family building permits issued: 0 (2007); Employment by occupation: 22.2% management, 22.8% professional, 6.5% services, 37.6% sales, 0.0% farming, 4.8% construction, 6.1% production (2000).

Income: Per capita income: $49,062 (2007); Median household income: $73,905 (2007); Average household income: $102,393 (2007); Percent of households with income of $100,000 or more: 33.8% (2007); Poverty rate: 2.3% (2000).

Education: Percent of population age 25 and over with: High school diploma (including GED) or higher: 93.3% (2007); Bachelor's degree or higher: 37.7% (2007); Master's degree or higher: 15.2% (2007).

Housing: Homeownership rate: 95.3% (2007); Median home value: $295,843 (2007); Median rent: $891 per month (2000); Median age of housing: 22 years (2000).

Safety: Violent crime rate: 0.0 per 10,000 population; Property crime rate: 62.9 per 10,000 population (2006).

Transportation: Commute to work: 88.5% car, 6.2% public transportation, 0.0% walk, 5.3% work from home (2000); Travel time to work: 20.8% less than 15 minutes, 32.2% 15 to 30 minutes, 26.2% 30 to 45 minutes, 14.7% 45 to 60 minutes, 6.2% 60 minutes or more (2000)

INVERNESS (village). Covers a land area of 6.318 square miles and a water area of 0.151 square miles. Located at 42.11° N. Lat.; 88.09° W. Long. Elevation is 843 feet.

History: Incorporated 1962.

Population: 6,541 (1990); 6,749 (2000); 7,302 (2007); 7,570 (2012 projected); Race: 90.6% White, 0.8% Black, 7.2% Asian, 2.4% Hispanic of any race (2007); Density: 1,155.8 persons per square mile (2007); Average household size: 2.89 (2007); Median age: 47.0 (2007); Males per 100 females: 98.7 (2007); Marriage status: 18.3% never married, 74.2% now married, 4.4% widowed, 3.1% divorced (2000); Foreign born: 11.1% (2000); Ancestry (includes multiple ancestries): 29.1% German, 21.8% Irish, 14.0% Italian, 13.1% Polish, 11.2% English (2000).

Economy: Single-family building permits issued: 71 (2007); Multi-family building permits issued: 0 (2007); Employment by occupation: 37.2% management, 18.2% professional, 4.4% services, 31.0% sales, 0.0% farming, 4.2% construction, 5.1% production (2000).

Income: Per capita income: $77,021 (2007); Median household income: $152,903 (2007); Average household income: $221,941 (2007); Percent of households with income of $100,000 or more: 69.5% (2007); Poverty rate: 1.5% (2000).

Education: Percent of population age 25 and over with: High school diploma (including GED) or higher: 93.9% (2007); Bachelor's degree or higher: 53.8% (2007); Master's degree or higher: 22.7% (2007).

Housing: Homeownership rate: 97.8% (2007); Median home value: $654,831 (2007); Median rent: $908 per month (2000); Median age of housing: 20 years (2000).

Transportation: Commute to work: 86.0% car, 7.5% public transportation, 0.5% walk, 5.7% work from home (2000); Travel time to work: 16.4% less than 15 minutes, 34.2% 15 to 30 minutes, 23.8% 30 to 45 minutes, 13.2% 45 to 60 minutes, 12.4% 60 minutes or more (2000)

Additional Information Contacts

Village of Inverness . . . . (847) 358-7740
http://www.villageofinverness.org

JUSTICE (village). Covers a land area of 2.912 square miles and a water area of 0.042 square miles. Located at 41.74° N. Lat.; 87.83° W. Long. Elevation is 617 feet.

Population: 11,201 (1990); 12,193 (2000); 12,714 (2007); 12,971 (2012 projected); Race: 66.9% White, 22.4% Black, 1.9% Asian, 9.3% Hispanic of any race (2007); Density: 4,366.4 persons per square mile (2007); Average household size: 2.83 (2007); Median age: 33.6 (2007); Males per 100 females: 97.4 (2007); Marriage status: 33.1% never married, 53.3% now married, 4.6% widowed, 9.0% divorced (2000); Foreign born: 19.3% (2000); Ancestry (includes multiple ancestries): 26.7% Other groups, 24.2% Polish, 13.1% German, 11.8% Irish, 5.7% Italian (2000).
Economy: Single-family building permits issued: 9 (2007); Multi-family building permits issued: 0 (2007); Employment by occupation: 10.1% management, 12.4% professional, 13.0% services, 29.5% sales, 0.0% farming, 12.2% construction, 22.8% production (2000).
Income: Per capita income: $23,565 (2007); Median household income: $57,826 (2007); Average household income: $66,555 (2007); Percent of households with income of $100,000 or more: 15.6% (2007); Poverty rate: 7.3% (2000).
Education: Percent of population age 25 and over with: High school diploma (including GED) or higher: 78.7% (2007); Bachelor's degree or higher: 12.9% (2007); Master's degree or higher: 2.6% (2007).

School District(s)

Indian Springs SD 109 (PK-08)
2005-06 Enrollment: 2,895 . . . . (708) 496-8700
Housing: Homeownership rate: 53.5% (2007); Median home value: $219,132 (2007); Median rent: $670 per month (2000); Median age of housing: 28 years (2000).
Safety: Violent crime rate: 24.4 per 10,000 population; Property crime rate: 178.1 per 10,000 population (2006).
Transportation: Commute to work: 91.8% car, 5.2% public transportation, 0.9% walk, 0.6% work from home (2000); Travel time to work: 18.5% less than 15 minutes, 30.2% 15 to 30 minutes, 25.8% 30 to 45 minutes, 12.2% 45 to 60 minutes, 13.2% 60 minutes or more (2000)
Additional Information Contacts
Village of Justice . . . . (708) 458-2520
http://www.villageofjustice.com

KENILWORTH (village). Covers a land area of 0.595 square miles and a water area of 0 square miles. Located at 42.08° N. Lat.; 87.71° W. Long. Elevation is 617 feet.
History: Kenilworth was named for the novel by Sir Walter Scott. Many streets in the town are named for places or characters in the book. Kenilworth is the burial place of poet Eugene Field.
Population: 2,402 (1990); 2,494 (2000); 2,430 (2007); 2,378 (2012 projected); Race: 97.3% White, 0.1% Black, 2.3% Asian, 1.6% Hispanic of any race (2007); Density: 4,083.3 persons per square mile (2007); Average household size: 3.23 (2007); Median age: 39.7 (2007); Males per 100 females: 90.1 (2007); Marriage status: 18.1% never married, 75.5% now married, 3.8% widowed, 2.5% divorced (2000); Foreign born: 8.5% (2000); Ancestry (includes multiple ancestries): 26.3% Irish, 22.1% English, 20.6% German, 8.9% Italian, 8.0% Other groups (2000).
Economy: Single-family building permits issued: 7 (2007); Multi-family building permits issued: 0 (2007); Employment by occupation: 39.2% management, 31.8% professional, 4.5% services, 23.4% sales, 0.0% farming, 0.7% construction, 0.3% production (2000).
Income: Per capita income: $92,515 (2007); Median household income: $244,718 (2007); Average household income: $298,556 (2007); Percent of households with income of $100,000 or more: 84.7% (2007); Poverty rate: 1.1% (2000).
Education: Percent of population age 25 and over with: High school diploma (including GED) or higher: 99.8% (2007); Bachelor's degree or higher: 89.5% (2007); Master's degree or higher: 49.3% (2007).

School District(s)

Kenilworth SD 38 (PK-08)
2005-06 Enrollment: 594 . . . . (847) 256-5006
Housing: Homeownership rate: 96.0% (2007); Median home value: $1 million+ (2007); Median rent: $1,031 per month (2000); Median age of housing: 60+ years (2000).
Safety: Violent crime rate: 0.0 per 10,000 population; Property crime rate: 90.0 per 10,000 population (2006).
Transportation: Commute to work: 61.8% car, 24.9% public transportation, 1.0% walk, 11.1% work from home (2000); Travel time to work: 14.5% less than 15 minutes, 20.2% 15 to 30 minutes, 23.1% 30 to 45 minutes, 22.2% 45 to 60 minutes, 20.0% 60 minutes or more (2000)

LA GRANGE (village). Covers a land area of 2.509 square miles and a water area of 0 square miles. Located at 41.80° N. Lat.; 87.87° W. Long. Elevation is 646 feet.
History: La Grange was founded by W.D. Cossitt and named for Marquis de Lafayette's home in France. An early settlement along the Chicago, Burlington & Quincy Railroad, La Grange was incorporated in 1879.
Population: 15,352 (1990); 15,608 (2000); 15,426 (2007); 15,202 (2012 projected); Race: 90.3% White, 6.1% Black, 1.0% Asian, 5.0% Hispanic of any race (2007); Density: 6,148.2 persons per square mile (2007); Average household size: 2.78 (2007); Median age: 39.4 (2007); Males per 100 females: 94.6 (2007); Marriage status: 22.3% never married, 63.0% now married, 7.4% widowed, 7.3% divorced (2000); Foreign born: 5.6% (2000); Ancestry (includes multiple ancestries): 25.2% Irish, 24.8% German, 10.5% Polish, 10.3% Other groups, 10.2% Italian (2000).
Economy: Single-family building permits issued: 27 (2007); Multi-family building permits issued: 0 (2007); Employment by occupation: 28.1% management, 28.0% professional, 6.8% services, 27.7% sales, 0.1% farming, 3.6% construction, 5.8% production (2000).
Income: Per capita income: $42,159 (2007); Median household income: $91,551 (2007); Average household income: $115,597 (2007); Percent of households with income of $100,000 or more: 45.8% (2007); Poverty rate: 4.0% (2000).
Education: Percent of population age 25 and over with: High school diploma (including GED) or higher: 92.1% (2007); Bachelor's degree or higher: 54.1% (2007); Master's degree or higher: 20.6% (2007).

School District(s)

La Grange SD 102 (PK-08)
2005-06 Enrollment: 2,681 . . . . (708) 482-2400
La Grange SD 105 South (PK-08)
2005-06 Enrollment: 1,184 . . . . (708) 482-2700
Lagrange Area Dept Spec Ed-Ladse
2005-06 Enrollment: n/a . . . . (708) 354-5730
Lagrange Highlands SD 106 (PK-08)
2005-06 Enrollment: 873 . . . . (708) 246-3085
Lyons Twp HSD 204 (09-12)
2005-06 Enrollment: 3,826 . . . . (708) 579-6451
Pleasantdale SD 107 (PK-08)
2005-06 Enrollment: 830 . . . . (708) 784-2013
Housing: Homeownership rate: 80.7% (2007); Median home value: $406,897 (2007); Median rent: $677 per month (2000); Median age of housing: 50 years (2000).
Hospitals: Adventist LaGrange Memorial Hospital (274 beds)
Safety: Violent crime rate: 7.1 per 10,000 population; Property crime rate: 103.3 per 10,000 population (2006).
Transportation: Commute to work: 74.6% car, 17.6% public transportation, 2.6% walk, 4.6% work from home (2000); Travel time to work: 22.8% less than 15 minutes, 25.3% 15 to 30 minutes, 26.3% 30 to 45 minutes, 13.1% 45 to 60 minutes, 12.5% 60 minutes or more (2000); Amtrak: Service available.
Additional Information Contacts
Village of La Grange . . . . (708) 579-2300
http://www.villageoflagrange.com
West Suburban Chamber of Commerce . . . . (708) 352-0494

LA GRANGE PARK (village). Covers a land area of 2.253 square miles and a water area of 0 square miles. Located at 41.83° N. Lat.; 87.86° W. Long. Elevation is 623 feet.
History: Named for the French translation of "the barn". Incorporated 1892.
Population: 12,861 (1990); 13,295 (2000); 12,636 (2007); 12,101 (2012 projected); Race: 91.4% White, 4.4% Black, 1.7% Asian, 4.6% Hispanic of any race (2007); Density: 5,607.3 persons per square mile (2007); Average household size: 2.48 (2007); Median age: 42.4 (2007); Males per 100 females: 85.6 (2007); Marriage status: 22.4% never married, 58.1% now married, 12.7% widowed, 6.8% divorced (2000); Foreign born: 7.1% (2000); Ancestry (includes multiple ancestries): 22.6% Irish, 22.0% German, 16.1% Polish, 11.7% Italian, 9.5% Other groups (2000).
Economy: Single-family building permits issued: 5 (2007); Multi-family building permits issued: 0 (2007); Employment by occupation: 17.8% management, 25.4% professional, 10.1% services, 33.7% sales, 0.3% farming, 5.5% construction, 7.2% production (2000).
Income: Per capita income: $34,509 (2007); Median household income: $67,181 (2007); Average household income: $84,995 (2007); Percent of households with income of $100,000 or more: 28.6% (2007); Poverty rate: 2.6% (2000).

Education: Percent of population age 25 and over with: High school diploma (including GED) or higher: 92.1% (2007); Bachelor's degree or higher: 41.3% (2007); Master's degree or higher: 14.2% (2007).

School District(s)

Brookfield Lagrange Park SD 95 (PK-08)
2005-06 Enrollment: 935 . . . . (708) 485-0606
La Grange SD 102 (PK-08)
2005-06 Enrollment: 2,681 . . . . (708) 482-2400

Housing: Homeownership rate: 72.0% (2007); Median home value: $319,556 (2007); Median rent: $727 per month (2000); Median age of housing: 46 years (2000).
Safety: Violent crime rate: 12.6 per 10,000 population; Property crime rate: 124.2 per 10,000 population (2006).
Transportation: Commute to work: 83.3% car, 9.8% public transportation, 2.2% walk, 4.1% work from home (2000); Travel time to work: 21.3% less than 15 minutes, 29.2% 15 to 30 minutes, 27.4% 30 to 45 minutes, 13.9% 45 to 60 minutes, 8.2% 60 minutes or more (2000); Amtrak: Service available.

Additional Information Contacts

Village of La Grange Park . . . . (708) 354-0225
http://www.lagrangepark.org

LANSING (village). Covers a land area of 6.764 square miles and a water area of 0.064 square miles. Located at 41.56° N. Lat.; 87.54° W. Long. Elevation is 630 feet.
History: Named for John Lansing (1754-1829), hero of the American Revolution. Lansing was settled in the 1860's by Dutch and German farmers.
Population: 28,446 (1990); 28,332 (2000); 26,962 (2007); 25,969 (2012 projected); Race: 80.5% White, 14.8% Black, 0.9% Asian, 7.6% Hispanic of any race (2007); Density: 3,986.2 persons per square mile (2007); Average household size: 2.46 (2007); Median age: 39.6 (2007); Males per 100 females: 91.1 (2007); Marriage status: 25.7% never married, 56.7% now married, 8.5% widowed, 9.1% divorced (2000); Foreign born: 5.6% (2000); Ancestry (includes multiple ancestries): 20.4% German, 17.2% Other groups, 15.7% Polish, 15.5% Irish, 13.7% Dutch (2000).
Economy: Unemployment rate: 6.2% (4/2008); Total civilian labor force: 14,803 (4/2008); Single-family building permits issued: 11 (2007); Multi-family building permits issued: 0 (2007); Employment by occupation: 12.4% management, 17.5% professional, 13.3% services, 29.2% sales, 0.1% farming, 12.6% construction, 15.0% production (2000).
Income: Per capita income: $25,225 (2007); Median household income: $52,669 (2007); Average household income: $62,099 (2007); Percent of households with income of $100,000 or more: 14.0% (2007); Poverty rate: 5.4% (2000).
Taxes: Total city taxes per capita: $735 (2006); City property taxes per capita: $587 (2006).
Education: Percent of population age 25 and over with: High school diploma (including GED) or higher: 86.7% (2007); Bachelor's degree or higher: 18.4% (2007); Master's degree or higher: 5.2% (2007).

School District(s)

Lansing SD 158 (PK-08)
2005-06 Enrollment: 2,313 . . . . (708) 474-6700
Sunnybrook SD 171 (PK-08)
2005-06 Enrollment: 1,119 . . . . (708) 895-0750
Thornton Fractional Twp HSD 215 (09-12)
2005-06 Enrollment: 3,402 . . . . (708) 585-2309

Housing: Homeownership rate: 75.2% (2007); Median home value: $173,999 (2007); Median rent: $612 per month (2000); Median age of housing: 36 years (2000).
Safety: Violent crime rate: 20.5 per 10,000 population; Property crime rate: 425.6 per 10,000 population (2006).
Transportation: Commute to work: 89.2% car, 6.1% public transportation, 2.3% walk, 2.1% work from home (2000); Travel time to work: 29.1% less than 15 minutes, 29.9% 15 to 30 minutes, 16.6% 30 to 45 minutes, 9.7% 45 to 60 minutes, 14.8% 60 minutes or more (2000)

Additional Information Contacts

Chicago Southland Convention & Visitors Bureau. . . . . (708) 895-8200
Lansing Chamber of Commerce . . . . (708) 474-4170
http://www.communitylink.com/lansing/chamber.htm
Village of Lansing. . . . . (708) 895-7200
http://www.villageoflansing.com

LEMONT (village). Covers a land area of 6.453 square miles and a water area of 0.348 square miles. Located at 41.66° N. Lat.; 87.98° W. Long. Elevation is 607 feet.
History: Named for the French translation of "the mount". Incorporated 1873.
Population: 8,610 (1990); 13,098 (2000); 14,599 (2007); 15,502 (2012 projected); Race: 97.0% White, 0.4% Black, 0.9% Asian, 3.4% Hispanic of any race (2007); Density: 2,262.5 persons per square mile (2007); Average household size: 2.96 (2007); Median age: 40.2 (2007); Males per 100 females: 90.6 (2007); Marriage status: 21.3% never married, 63.9% now married, 9.0% widowed, 5.8% divorced (2000); Foreign born: 9.7% (2000); Ancestry (includes multiple ancestries): 32.8% Polish, 25.5% German, 20.6% Irish, 12.1% Italian, 5.3% Other groups (2000).
Economy: Single-family building permits issued: 130 (2007); Multi-family building permits issued: 0 (2007); Employment by occupation: 19.5% management, 24.5% professional, 10.0% services, 26.0% sales, 0.0% farming, 9.0% construction, 11.0% production (2000).
Income: Per capita income: $34,754 (2007); Median household income: $87,242 (2007); Average household income: $102,106 (2007); Percent of households with income of $100,000 or more: 41.5% (2007); Poverty rate: 3.6% (2000).
Education: Percent of population age 25 and over with: High school diploma (including GED) or higher: 86.3% (2007); Bachelor's degree or higher: 31.9% (2007); Master's degree or higher: 10.9% (2007).

School District(s)

Lemont Twp HSD 210 (09-12)
2005-06 Enrollment: 1,331 . . . . (630) 257-5838
Lemont-Bromberek CSD 113a (PK-08)
2005-06 Enrollment: 2,591 . . . . (630) 257-2286

Housing: Homeownership rate: 82.5% (2007); Median home value: $354,921 (2007); Median rent: $669 per month (2000); Median age of housing: 17 years (2000).
Safety: Violent crime rate: 4.0 per 10,000 population; Property crime rate: 119.5 per 10,000 population (2006).
Newspapers: Oak Forest-Palos Heights Villager (Local news; Circulation 1,000); Palos Hills-Palos Park Villager (Local news; Circulation 900); Tinley Park-Crestwood Villager (Local news; Circulation 1,100)
Transportation: Commute to work: 88.0% car, 6.3% public transportation, 1.0% walk, 3.9% work from home (2000); Travel time to work: 19.2% less than 15 minutes, 23.9% 15 to 30 minutes, 28.8% 30 to 45 minutes, 11.3% 45 to 60 minutes, 16.6% 60 minutes or more (2000)

Additional Information Contacts

Lemont Area Chamber of Commerce . . . . (630) 257-5997
http://www.lemontchamber.com
Village of Lemont. . . . . (630) 257-1550
http://www.lemont.il.us

LINCOLNWOOD (village). Covers a land area of 2.687 square miles and a water area of 0 square miles. Located at 42.00° N. Lat.; 87.73° W. Long. Elevation is 604 feet.
History: Named for Abraham Lincoln, 16th President of the U.S. Until 1935 called Tessville.
Population: 11,365 (1990); 12,359 (2000); 11,922 (2007); 11,570 (2012 projected); Race: 71.3% White, 0.5% Black, 23.5% Asian, 4.9% Hispanic of any race (2007); Density: 4,437.0 persons per square mile (2007); Average household size: 2.75 (2007); Median age: 46.6 (2007); Males per 100 females: 89.6 (2007); Marriage status: 19.2% never married, 65.5% now married, 11.4% widowed, 3.9% divorced (2000); Foreign born: 34.1% (2000); Ancestry (includes multiple ancestries): 32.8% Other groups, 8.7% Russian, 7.8% Greek, 7.0% Polish, 6.7% German (2000).
Economy: Single-family building permits issued: 13 (2007); Multi-family building permits issued: 0 (2007); Employment by occupation: 20.4% management, 30.7% professional, 7.1% services, 30.3% sales, 0.0% farming, 4.1% construction, 7.3% production (2000).
Income: Per capita income: $40,495 (2007); Median household income: $79,775 (2007); Average household income: $111,417 (2007); Percent of households with income of $100,000 or more: 37.7% (2007); Poverty rate: 2.9% (2000).
Education: Percent of population age 25 and over with: High school diploma (including GED) or higher: 89.3% (2007); Bachelor's degree or higher: 48.2% (2007); Master's degree or higher: 21.1% (2007).

School District(s)

Lincolnwood SD 74 (PK-08)
2005-06 Enrollment: 1,252 . . . . (847) 675-8234

Housing: Homeownership rate: 90.5% (2007); Median home value: $462,474 (2007); Median rent: $2,000+ per month (2000); Median age of housing: 43 years (2000).
Safety: Violent crime rate: 12.5 per 10,000 population; Property crime rate: 465.7 per 10,000 population (2006).
Newspapers: Elmwood Park/River Grove Times (Community news; Circulation 2,497); Evanston Review (Community news; Circulation 4,500); Glenview Announcements (Community news; Circulation 4,500); Harlem/Foster Times (Community news; Circulation 4,252); Niles Herald-Spectator (Local news; Circulation 4,500); North Center/Lincoln Belmont/Lakeview Booster (Community news; Circulation 4,500); North Town/Rogers Park/Edgewater/Ravenswood News-Star (Community news; Circulation 4,500); Park Ridge Advocate (Local news; Circulation 4,500); Wheeling Countryside (Community news; Circulation 4,500); Winnetka Talk (Community news; Circulation 4,500)
Transportation: Commute to work: 89.0% car, 5.1% public transportation, 1.1% walk, 4.6% work from home (2000); Travel time to work: 23.8% less than 15 minutes, 31.1% 15 to 30 minutes, 27.2% 30 to 45 minutes, 9.7% 45 to 60 minutes, 8.2% 60 minutes or more (2000)
Additional Information Contacts
Lincolnwood Chamber of Commerce & Industry . . . . (847) 679-5760
http://www.lincolnwoodchamber.org
Village of Lincolnwood . . . . (847) 673-1540
http://www.lincolnwoodil.org

LYNWOOD (village). Covers a land area of 4.925 square miles and a water area of 0.070 square miles. Located at 41.52° N. Lat.; 87.54° W. Long. Elevation is 617 feet.
Population: 6,721 (1990); 7,377 (2000); 7,636 (2007); 7,743 (2012 projected); Race: 35.4% White, 59.6% Black, 1.0% Asian, 4.7% Hispanic of any race (2007); Density: 1,550.4 persons per square mile (2007); Average household size: 2.80 (2007); Median age: 35.5 (2007); Males per 100 females: 91.4 (2007); Marriage status: 28.3% never married, 55.4% now married, 5.4% widowed, 10.9% divorced (2000); Foreign born: 5.1% (2000); Ancestry (includes multiple ancestries): 48.4% Other groups, 12.3% Polish, 10.3% German, 8.8% Irish, 6.1% Italian (2000).
Economy: Single-family building permits issued: 41 (2007); Multi-family building permits issued: 16 (2007); Employment by occupation: 13.0% management, 18.0% professional, 13.5% services, 30.8% sales, 0.0% farming, 10.1% construction, 14.5% production (2000).
Income: Per capita income: $26,021 (2007); Median household income: $64,893 (2007); Average household income: $72,942 (2007); Percent of households with income of $100,000 or more: 23.6% (2007); Poverty rate: 5.8% (2000).
Education: Percent of population age 25 and over with: High school diploma (including GED) or higher: 89.5% (2007); Bachelor's degree or higher: 22.6% (2007); Master's degree or higher: 7.8% (2007).
School District(s)
Sandridge SD 172 (PK-08)
2005-06 Enrollment: 409 . . . . (708) 895-2450
Housing: Homeownership rate: 88.0% (2007); Median home value: $183,956 (2007); Median rent: $598 per month (2000); Median age of housing: 19 years (2000).
Safety: Violent crime rate: 35.3 per 10,000 population; Property crime rate: 312.2 per 10,000 population (2006).
Transportation: Commute to work: 88.3% car, 8.3% public transportation, 0.0% walk, 2.4% work from home (2000); Travel time to work: 17.7% less than 15 minutes, 30.4% 15 to 30 minutes, 21.5% 30 to 45 minutes, 10.5% 45 to 60 minutes, 19.8% 60 minutes or more (2000)
Additional Information Contacts
Lynwood Chamber of Commerce . . . . (708) 758-6101
http://www.ynns.com/lcc/location.php
Village of Lynwood. . . . . (708) 758-6101
http://www.lynwoodil.us

LYONS (village). Covers a land area of 2.207 square miles and a water area of 0.048 square miles. Located at 41.81° N. Lat.; 87.82° W. Long. Elevation is 620 feet.
History: Lyons was established near the portage between the Chicago and Des Plaines Rivers, used by Marquette and Jolliet. Lyons developed as a residential community.
Population: 9,828 (1990); 10,255 (2000); 10,452 (2007); 10,537 (2012 projected); Race: 81.7% White, 1.4% Black, 1.6% Asian, 22.9% Hispanic of any race (2007); Density: 4,736.1 persons per square mile (2007); Average household size: 2.59 (2007); Median age: 37.2 (2007); Males per 100 females: 100.0 (2007); Marriage status: 26.3% never married, 53.1% now married, 9.1% widowed, 11.5% divorced (2000); Foreign born: 17.7% (2000); Ancestry (includes multiple ancestries): 17.7% Other groups, 15.6% Polish, 15.0% German, 14.0% Irish, 11.3% Italian (2000).
Economy: Single-family building permits issued: 0 (2007); Multi-family building permits issued: 0 (2007); Employment by occupation: 9.4% management, 13.8% professional, 12.0% services, 32.7% sales, 0.0% farming, 11.0% construction, 21.0% production (2000).
Income: Per capita income: $22,198 (2007); Median household income: $49,054 (2007); Average household income: $57,473 (2007); Percent of households with income of $100,000 or more: 10.9% (2007); Poverty rate: 6.3% (2000).
Education: Percent of population age 25 and over with: High school diploma (including GED) or higher: 78.7% (2007); Bachelor's degree or higher: 14.4% (2007); Master's degree or higher: 4.9% (2007).
School District(s)
Intermediate Service Center 2 (07-12)
2005-06 Enrollment: 65 . . . . (708) 482-4350
Lyons SD 103 (PK-08)
2005-06 Enrollment: 2,317 . . . . (708) 783-4100
Housing: Homeownership rate: 60.2% (2007); Median home value: $195,713 (2007); Median rent: $605 per month (2000); Median age of housing: 46 years (2000).
Safety: Violent crime rate: 31.5 per 10,000 population; Property crime rate: 288.6 per 10,000 population (2006).
Transportation: Commute to work: 90.0% car, 3.7% public transportation, 4.2% walk, 1.4% work from home (2000); Travel time to work: 25.6% less than 15 minutes, 33.4% 15 to 30 minutes, 23.7% 30 to 45 minutes, 8.5% 45 to 60 minutes, 8.9% 60 minutes or more (2000)
Additional Information Contacts
Village of Lyons . . . . (708) 780-5200
http://www.lyonspolice.org

MARKHAM (city). Covers a land area of 5.214 square miles and a water area of 0 square miles. Located at 41.59° N. Lat.; 87.69° W. Long. Elevation is 620 feet.
History: Named for Charles H. Markham, president of the Illinois Central railroad. Native prairie preserved at Indian Boundaries Prairies. Incorporated 1925.
Population: 13,126 (1990); 12,620 (2000); 12,213 (2007); 11,877 (2012 projected); Race: 15.4% White, 79.6% Black, 0.7% Asian, 4.4% Hispanic of any race (2007); Density: 2,342.5 persons per square mile (2007); Average household size: 3.23 (2007); Median age: 33.0 (2007); Males per 100 females: 87.5 (2007); Marriage status: 35.9% never married, 44.7% now married, 9.0% widowed, 10.4% divorced (2000); Foreign born: 2.8% (2000); Ancestry (includes multiple ancestries): 68.5% Other groups, 5.5% Irish, 5.1% German, 3.1% Polish, 1.8% Italian (2000).
Economy: Single-family building permits issued: 15 (2007); Multi-family building permits issued: 0 (2007); Employment by occupation: 7.3% management, 15.8% professional, 18.0% services, 30.0% sales, 0.0% farming, 8.4% construction, 20.4% production (2000).
Income: Per capita income: $16,564 (2007); Median household income: $45,194 (2007); Average household income: $53,031 (2007); Percent of households with income of $100,000 or more: 9.2% (2007); Poverty rate: 16.9% (2000).
Education: Percent of population age 25 and over with: High school diploma (including GED) or higher: 77.7% (2007); Bachelor's degree or higher: 10.6% (2007); Master's degree or higher: 3.3% (2007).
School District(s)
Hazel Crest SD 152-5 (PK-08)
2005-06 Enrollment: 1,084 . . . . (708) 335-0790
Prairie-Hills ESD 144 (PK-08)
2005-06 Enrollment: 2,955 . . . . (708) 210-2888
Speed Seja #802 (PK-12)
2005-06 Enrollment: 385 . . . . (708) 481-6100
Housing: Homeownership rate: 84.5% (2007); Median home value: $115,492 (2007); Median rent: $633 per month (2000); Median age of housing: 41 years (2000).
Safety: Violent crime rate: 64.2 per 10,000 population; Property crime rate: 256.8 per 10,000 population (2006).
Newspapers: Westside Journal (Local news; Circulation 37,000)
Transportation: Commute to work: 84.6% car, 9.5% public transportation, 1.6% walk, 2.3% work from home (2000); Travel time to work: 21.5% less than 15 minutes, 31.1% 15 to 30 minutes, 22.8% 30 to 45 minutes, 12.5% 45 to 60 minutes, 12.1% 60 minutes or more (2000)

MATTESON (village). Covers a land area of 7.138 square miles and a water area of 0.069 square miles. Located at 41.51° N. Lat.; 87.73° W. Long. Elevation is 692 feet.
Population: 11,920 (1990); 12,928 (2000); 16,326 (2007); 18,343 (2012 projected); Race: 25.7% White, 69.9% Black, 1.3% Asian, 3.8% Hispanic of any race (2007); Density: 2,287.3 persons per square mile (2007); Average household size: 2.82 (2007); Median age: 38.7 (2007); Males per 100 females: 86.7 (2007); Marriage status: 27.8% never married, 57.8% now married, 5.8% widowed, 8.7% divorced (2000); Foreign born: 3.9% (2000); Ancestry (includes multiple ancestries): 60.7% Other groups, 11.2% German, 8.2% Irish, 4.4% Polish, 2.9% English (2000).
Economy: Single-family building permits issued: 112 (2007); Multi-family building permits issued: 74 (2007); Employment by occupation: 15.8% management, 20.8% professional, 14.0% services, 29.5% sales, 0.0% farming, 6.9% construction, 13.1% production (2000).
Income: Per capita income: $28,604 (2007); Median household income: $66,913 (2007); Average household income: $80,167 (2007); Percent of households with income of $100,000 or more: 26.2% (2007); Poverty rate: 4.4% (2000).
Education: Percent of population age 25 and over with: High school diploma (including GED) or higher: 89.5% (2007); Bachelor's degree or higher: 25.7% (2007); Master's degree or higher: 8.8% (2007).

School District(s)

ESD 159 (PK-08)
2005-06 Enrollment: 2,025 . . . . (708) 720-1300
Matteson ESD 162 (PK-08)
2005-06 Enrollment: 3,399 . . . . (708) 748-0100

Housing: Homeownership rate: 82.9% (2007); Median home value: $205,671 (2007); Median rent: $643 per month (2000); Median age of housing: 23 years (2000).
Safety: Violent crime rate: 38.3 per 10,000 population; Property crime rate: 626.5 per 10,000 population (2006).
Transportation: Commute to work: 87.4% car, 9.8% public transportation, 1.1% walk, 1.4% work from home (2000); Travel time to work: 17.9% less than 15 minutes, 27.9% 15 to 30 minutes, 19.1% 30 to 45 minutes, 14.0% 45 to 60 minutes, 21.1% 60 minutes or more (2000)

Additional Information Contacts

Matteson Chamber of Commerce . . . . (708) 747-6000
Village of Matteson . . . . (708) 283-4900
http://www.vil.matteson.il.us

MAYWOOD (village). Covers a land area of 2.708 square miles and a water area of 0 square miles. Located at 41.88° N. Lat.; 87.84° W. Long. Elevation is 627 feet.
History: Named for May, the daugher of W. T. Nichols, owner of the town site. Maywood developed in the 1880's, when industrial growth in the Chicago area created a need for more residential areas.
Population: 27,139 (1990); 26,987 (2000); 25,378 (2007); 24,198 (2012 projected); Race: 9.7% White, 80.9% Black, 0.3% Asian, 13.4% Hispanic of any race (2007); Density: 9,371.5 persons per square mile (2007); Average household size: 3.42 (2007); Median age: 32.1 (2007); Males per 100 females: 88.8 (2007); Marriage status: 42.0% never married, 41.4% now married, 7.2% widowed, 9.5% divorced (2000); Foreign born: 7.2% (2000); Ancestry (includes multiple ancestries): 79.1% Other groups, 1.4% German, 1.1% Irish, 1.1% African, 0.8% Italian (2000).
Economy: Unemployment rate: 8.2% (4/2008); Total civilian labor force: 11,916 (4/2008); Single-family building permits issued: 0 (2007); Multi-family building permits issued: 0 (2007); Employment by occupation: 7.9% management, 12.8% professional, 17.9% services, 33.2% sales, 0.3% farming, 4.7% construction, 23.3% production (2000).
Income: Per capita income: $16,816 (2007); Median household income: $46,833 (2007); Average household income: $57,063 (2007); Percent of households with income of $100,000 or more: 13.2% (2007); Poverty rate: 13.4% (2000).
Taxes: Total city taxes per capita: $821 (2006); City property taxes per capita: $672 (2006).
Education: Percent of population age 25 and over with: High school diploma (including GED) or higher: 74.5% (2007); Bachelor's degree or higher: 10.6% (2007); Master's degree or higher: 3.8% (2007).

School District(s)

Intermediate Service Center 2 (07-12)
2005-06 Enrollment: 65 . . . . (708) 482-4350
Maywood-Melrose Park-Broadview 89 (PK-08)
2005-06 Enrollment: 5,586 . . . . (708) 450-2460
Proviso Area Exceptional Child (PK-12)
2005-06 Enrollment: 391 . . . . (708) 450-2100
Proviso Twp HSD 209 (09-12)
2005-06 Enrollment: 4,873 . . . . (708) 338-5933

Housing: Homeownership rate: 62.9% (2007); Median home value: $166,627 (2007); Median rent: $543 per month (2000); Median age of housing: 54 years (2000).
Hospitals: Loyola University Medical Center (589 beds)
Safety: Violent crime rate: 133.8 per 10,000 population; Property crime rate: 554.8 per 10,000 population (2006).
Transportation: Commute to work: 83.9% car, 9.4% public transportation, 3.2% walk, 1.7% work from home (2000); Travel time to work: 22.7% less than 15 minutes, 30.9% 15 to 30 minutes, 25.5% 30 to 45 minutes, 9.6% 45 to 60 minutes, 11.3% 60 minutes or more (2000)

Additional Information Contacts

Maywood Chamber of Commerce . . . . (708) 345-7077
http://www.souari.forest.net/~maywood
Village of Maywood . . . . (708) 344-1200
http://www.maywood-il.org

MCCOOK (village). Covers a land area of 2.603 square miles and a water area of 0.018 square miles. Located at 41.79° N. Lat.; 87.83° W. Long. Elevation is 617 feet.
Population: 235 (1990); 254 (2000); 262 (2007); 264 (2012 projected); Race: 93.9% White, 0.0% Black, 0.0% Asian, 12.6% Hispanic of any race (2007); Density: 100.6 persons per square mile (2007); Average household size: 2.18 (2007); Median age: 42.1 (2007); Males per 100 females: 92.6 (2007); Marriage status: 21.2% never married, 53.4% now married, 12.7% widowed, 12.7% divorced (2000); Foreign born: 0.0% (2000); Ancestry (includes multiple ancestries): 18.9% Polish, 16.3% Irish, 16.3% Croatian, 16.3% Italian, 11.5% German (2000).
Economy: Single-family building permits issued: 0 (2007); Multi-family building permits issued: 0 (2007); Employment by occupation: 15.1% management, 14.3% professional, 15.1% services, 27.0% sales, 0.0% farming, 9.5% construction, 19.0% production (2000).
Income: Per capita income: $29,313 (2007); Median household income: $50,000 (2007); Average household income: $64,000 (2007); Percent of households with income of $100,000 or more: 22.5% (2007); Poverty rate: 1.8% (2000).
Education: Percent of population age 25 and over with: High school diploma (including GED) or higher: 85.9% (2007); Bachelor's degree or higher: 10.6% (2007); Master's degree or higher: 6.1% (2007).
Housing: Homeownership rate: 50.0% (2007); Median home value: $246,154 (2007); Median rent: $552 per month (2000); Median age of housing: 46 years (2000).
Safety: Violent crime rate: 164.6 per 10,000 population; Property crime rate: 1,070.0 per 10,000 population (2006).
Transportation: Commute to work: 84.1% car, 6.3% public transportation, 4.8% walk, 4.8% work from home (2000); Travel time to work: 40.8% less than 15 minutes, 24.2% 15 to 30 minutes, 20.8% 30 to 45 minutes, 5.8% 45 to 60 minutes, 8.3% 60 minutes or more (2000)

MELROSE PARK (village). Covers a land area of 4.239 square miles and a water area of 0 square miles. Located at 41.90° N. Lat.; 87.86° W. Long. Elevation is 633 feet.
History: Named for Melrose in Roxburghshire, Scotland. Incorporated 1893.
Population: 20,859 (1990); 23,171 (2000); 22,256 (2007); 21,570 (2012 projected); Race: 65.5% White, 3.9% Black, 1.7% Asian, 64.0% Hispanic of any race (2007); Density: 5,249.8 persons per square mile (2007); Average household size: 3.10 (2007); Median age: 32.8 (2007); Males per 100 females: 100.9 (2007); Marriage status: 31.9% never married, 53.9% now married, 6.0% widowed, 8.2% divorced (2000); Foreign born: 35.3% (2000); Ancestry (includes multiple ancestries): 53.2% Other groups, 18.8% Italian, 7.8% German, 5.4% Irish, 4.0% Polish (2000).
Economy: Single-family building permits issued: 4 (2007); Multi-family building permits issued: 0 (2007); Employment by occupation: 8.8% management, 7.9% professional, 15.6% services, 28.0% sales, 0.2% farming, 8.5% construction, 31.0% production (2000).
Income: Per capita income: $17,870 (2007); Median household income: $44,746 (2007); Average household income: $55,366 (2007); Percent of households with income of $100,000 or more: 11.7% (2007); Poverty rate: 10.2% (2000).

Education: Percent of population age 25 and over with: High school diploma (including GED) or higher: 60.3% (2007); Bachelor's degree or higher: 9.6% (2007); Master's degree or higher: 4.3% (2007).

School District(s)

Bellwood SD 88 (PK-08)
2005-06 Enrollment: 3,239 . . . . (708) 344-9344
Mannheim SD 83 (PK-12)
2005-06 Enrollment: 2,757 . . . . (847) 455-4413
Maywood-Melrose Park-Broadview 89 (PK-08)
2005-06 Enrollment: 5,586 . . . . (708) 450-2460

Two-year College(s)

Lincoln College of Technology (Private, For-profit)
Fall 2007 Enrollment: 978 . . . . (708) 344-4700

Housing: Homeownership rate: 54.7% (2007); Median home value: $241,221 (2007); Median rent: $549 per month (2000); Median age of housing: 44 years (2000).

Hospitals: Gottlieb Memorial Hospital (250 beds); Westlake Community Hospital (326 beds)

Safety: Violent crime rate: 7.1 per 10,000 population; Property crime rate: 326.9 per 10,000 population (2006).

Transportation: Commute to work: 91.7% car, 2.8% public transportation, 3.0% walk, 1.2% work from home (2000); Travel time to work: 30.0% less than 15 minutes, 33.0% 15 to 30 minutes, 22.2% 30 to 45 minutes, 8.9% 45 to 60 minutes, 6.0% 60 minutes or more (2000)

Additional Information Contacts

Melrose Park Chamber of Commerce & Industry . . . . (708) 338-1007
http://www.melroseparkchamber.org
Village of Melrose Park . . . . (703) 343-4000
http://www.melrosepark.org

MERRIONETTE PARK (village). Covers a land area of 0.377 square miles and a water area of 0 square miles. Located at 41.68° N. Lat.; 87.69° W. Long. Elevation is 620 feet.

History: Incorporated 1947.

Population: 2,065 (1990); 1,999 (2000); 1,881 (2007); 1,793 (2012 projected); Race: 88.0% White, 8.2% Black, 0.4% Asian, 5.6% Hispanic of any race (2007); Density: 4,995.9 persons per square mile (2007); Average household size: 2.06 (2007); Median age: 42.1 (2007); Males per 100 females: 92.9 (2007); Marriage status: 30.2% never married, 44.4% now married, 11.9% widowed, 13.6% divorced (2000); Foreign born: 2.6% (2000); Ancestry (includes multiple ancestries): 34.5% Irish, 23.8% German, 17.2% Polish, 11.4% Other groups, 11.0% Italian (2000).

Economy: Single-family building permits issued: 0 (2007); Multi-family building permits issued: 0 (2007); Employment by occupation: 10.2% management, 22.0% professional, 9.6% services, 34.4% sales, 0.0% farming, 9.2% construction, 14.5% production (2000).

Income: Per capita income: $23,159 (2007); Median household income: $39,577 (2007); Average household income: $47,661 (2007); Percent of households with income of $100,000 or more: 7.1% (2007); Poverty rate: 7.5% (2000).

Education: Percent of population age 25 and over with: High school diploma (including GED) or higher: 86.0% (2007); Bachelor's degree or higher: 15.1% (2007); Master's degree or higher: 3.3% (2007).

School District(s)

Atwood Heights SD 125 (PK-08)
2005-06 Enrollment: 694 . . . . (708) 371-0080

Vocational/Technical School(s)

Everest College-Merrionette Park (Private, For-profit)
Fall 2007 Enrollment: 268 . . . . (708) 239-0055
2007-08 Tuition: $11,225

Housing: Homeownership rate: 75.2% (2007); Median home value: $147,901 (2007); Median rent: $555 per month (2000); Median age of housing: 39 years (2000).

Safety: Violent crime rate: 19.5 per 10,000 population; Property crime rate: 512.9 per 10,000 population (2006).

Transportation: Commute to work: 86.1% car, 9.2% public transportation, 3.7% walk, 0.0% work from home (2000); Travel time to work: 21.2% less than 15 minutes, 31.8% 15 to 30 minutes, 20.7% 30 to 45 minutes, 12.8% 45 to 60 minutes, 13.4% 60 minutes or more (2000)

MIDLOTHIAN (village). Covers a land area of 2.829 square miles and a water area of 0 square miles. Located at 41.62° N. Lat.; 87.72° W. Long. Elevation is 614 feet.

History: Named for the title of a novel by Sir Walter Scott. Incorporated 1927.

Population: 14,413 (1990); 14,315 (2000); 13,836 (2007); 13,462 (2012 projected); Race: 85.0% White, 7.8% Black, 2.1% Asian, 8.8% Hispanic of any race (2007); Density: 4,890.2 persons per square mile (2007); Average household size: 2.73 (2007); Median age: 36.2 (2007); Males per 100 females: 95.4 (2007); Marriage status: 27.8% never married, 54.2% now married, 7.7% widowed, 10.4% divorced (2000); Foreign born: 3.8% (2000); Ancestry (includes multiple ancestries): 27.5% German, 26.5% Irish, 15.4% Polish, 14.6% Other groups, 10.4% Italian (2000).

Economy: Single-family building permits issued: 8 (2007); Multi-family building permits issued: 0 (2007); Employment by occupation: 10.4% management, 13.7% professional, 15.3% services, 32.7% sales, 0.0% farming, 13.1% construction, 14.8% production (2000).

Income: Per capita income: $23,901 (2007); Median household income: $56,722 (2007); Average household income: $64,813 (2007); Percent of households with income of $100,000 or more: 16.6% (2007); Poverty rate: 7.0% (2000).

Education: Percent of population age 25 and over with: High school diploma (including GED) or higher: 85.4% (2007); Bachelor's degree or higher: 14.6% (2007); Master's degree or higher: 4.6% (2007).

School District(s)

Bremen CHSD 228 (09-12)
2005-06 Enrollment: 5,194 . . . . (708) 389-1175
Eisenhower Cooperative (PK-08)
2005-06 Enrollment: 141 . . . . (708) 424-9900
Midlothian SD 143 (PK-08)
2005-06 Enrollment: 1,881 . . . . (708) 388-6450

Housing: Homeownership rate: 79.9% (2007); Median home value: $171,296 (2007); Median rent: $559 per month (2000); Median age of housing: 36 years (2000).

Safety: Violent crime rate: 50.2 per 10,000 population; Property crime rate: 350.6 per 10,000 population (2006).

Newspapers: Alsip Express (Community news; Circulation 4,460); Beverly News (Community news; Circulation 4,080); Bridgeview Independent (Community news; Circulation 2,740); Burbank/Stickney Independent (Community news; Circulation 6,110); Chicago Ridge Citizen (Community news; Circulation 2,915); Evergreen Park Courier (Community news; Circulation 4,410); Hickory Hills Citizen (Community news; Circulation 3,530); Midlothian/Bremen Messenger (Community news; Circulation 10,200); Mount Greenwood Express (Community news; Circulation 7,471); Oak Lawn Independent (Community news; Circulation 10,880); Orland Township Messenger (Community news; Circulation 3,788); Palos Citizen (Community news; Circulation 4,610); Scottsdale-Ashburn Independent (Community news; Circulation 5,975); Worth Citizen (Community news; Circulation 2,660)

Transportation: Commute to work: 88.3% car, 7.2% public transportation, 1.2% walk, 2.2% work from home (2000); Travel time to work: 24.9% less than 15 minutes, 31.7% 15 to 30 minutes, 19.5% 30 to 45 minutes, 9.3% 45 to 60 minutes, 14.6% 60 minutes or more (2000)

Additional Information Contacts

Midlothian Chamber of Commerce . . . . (708) 389-0020
http://www.villageprofile.com/illinois/midlothian
Village of Midlothian. . . . . (708) 389-0200
http://www.villageofmidlothian.net

MORTON GROVE (village). Covers a land area of 5.095 square miles and a water area of 0 square miles. Located at 42.04° N. Lat.; 87.78° W. Long. Elevation is 623 feet.

History: Named for Marcus Morton, governor of Massachusetts (1840-1843). Incorporated 1895.

Population: 22,435 (1990); 22,451 (2000); 22,038 (2007); 21,654 (2012 projected); Race: 70.0% White, 0.8% Black, 25.3% Asian, 5.5% Hispanic of any race (2007); Density: 4,325.4 persons per square mile (2007); Average household size: 2.73 (2007); Median age: 46.7 (2007); Males per 100 females: 90.6 (2007); Marriage status: 21.0% never married, 64.7% now married, 9.1% widowed, 5.2% divorced (2000); Foreign born: 33.6% (2000); Ancestry (includes multiple ancestries): 29.2% Other groups, 16.0% German, 11.9% Polish, 8.7% Irish, 5.9% Italian (2000).

Economy: Single-family building permits issued: 60 (2007); Multi-family building permits issued: 0 (2007); Employment by occupation: 13.8% management, 25.4% professional, 8.9% services, 34.9% sales, 0.2% farming, 6.2% construction, 10.6% production (2000).

Income: Per capita income: $31,206 (2007); Median household income: $71,951 (2007); Average household income: $84,355 (2007); Percent of households with income of $100,000 or more: 30.8% (2007); Poverty rate: 2.7% (2000).

Education: Percent of population age 25 and over with: High school diploma (including GED) or higher: 87.4% (2007); Bachelor's degree or higher: 34.3% (2007); Master's degree or higher: 11.3% (2007).

School District(s)

East Maine SD 63 (PK-08)
2005-06 Enrollment: 3,498 . . . . (847) 299-1900
Golf ESD 67 (PK-08)
2005-06 Enrollment: 557 . . . . (847) 966-8200
Morton Grove SD 70 (KG-08)
2005-06 Enrollment: 765 . . . . (847) 965-6200
Niles Twp District for Spec Educ (PK-12)
2005-06 Enrollment: 102 . . . . (847) 965-9040
Skokie SD 69 (PK-08)
2005-06 Enrollment: 1,501 . . . . (847) 675-7666

Housing: Homeownership rate: 94.0% (2007); Median home value: $322,585 (2007); Median rent: $640 per month (2000); Median age of housing: 42 years (2000).
Safety: Violent crime rate: 5.0 per 10,000 population; Property crime rate: 179.3 per 10,000 population (2006).
Transportation: Commute to work: 88.5% car, 6.0% public transportation, 1.5% walk, 3.4% work from home (2000); Travel time to work: 22.5% less than 15 minutes, 33.2% 15 to 30 minutes, 25.7% 30 to 45 minutes, 10.9% 45 to 60 minutes, 7.6% 60 minutes or more (2000)

Additional Information Contacts

Morton Grove Chamber of Commerce & Industry . . . . (847) 965-0330
http://www.mgcci.org
Village of Morton Grove . . . . (847) 965-4100
http://www.mortongroveil.org

MOUNT PROSPECT (village). Covers a land area of 10.206 square miles and a water area of 0.036 square miles. Located at 42.06° N. Lat.; 87.93° W. Long. Elevation is 669 feet.
History: Named for its high location, and for the hope that newcomers would view the town as a good place to settle. Incorporated 1917.
Population: 53,114 (1990); 56,265 (2000); 54,082 (2007); 52,523 (2012 projected); Race: 76.6% White, 2.1% Black, 13.2% Asian, 14.8% Hispanic of any race (2007); Density: 5,299.2 persons per square mile (2007); Average household size: 2.62 (2007); Median age: 38.9 (2007); Males per 100 females: 99.0 (2007); Marriage status: 25.4% never married, 61.8% now married, 6.1% widowed, 6.7% divorced (2000); Foreign born: 26.7% (2000); Ancestry (includes multiple ancestries): 25.0% Other groups, 21.1% German, 16.3% Polish, 13.4% Irish, 10.9% Italian (2000).
Economy: Unemployment rate: 3.7% (4/2008); Total civilian labor force: 31,335 (4/2008); Single-family building permits issued: 12 (2007); Multi-family building permits issued: 0 (2007); Employment by occupation: 17.5% management, 21.9% professional, 10.4% services, 31.3% sales, 0.1% farming, 5.9% construction, 12.9% production (2000).
Income: Per capita income: $30,277 (2007); Median household income: $64,474 (2007); Average household income: $79,018 (2007); Percent of households with income of $100,000 or more: 25.5% (2007); Poverty rate: 4.6% (2000).
Taxes: Total city taxes per capita: $699 (2006); City property taxes per capita: $435 (2006).
Education: Percent of population age 25 and over with: High school diploma (including GED) or higher: 85.4% (2007); Bachelor's degree or higher: 35.3% (2007); Master's degree or higher: 11.9% (2007).

School District(s)

Comm Cons SD 59 (PK-08)
2005-06 Enrollment: 6,065 . . . . (847) 593-4300
Mount Prospect SD 57 (PK-08)
2005-06 Enrollment: 2,064 . . . . (847) 394-7300
Nw Suburban Spec Educ Org (PK-12)
2005-06 Enrollment: 601 . . . . (847) 463-8100
River Trails SD 26 (PK-08)
2005-06 Enrollment: 1,636 . . . . (847) 297-4120
Township HSD 214 (09-12)
2005-06 Enrollment: 12,542 . . . . (847) 718-7600
Wheeling CCSD 21 (PK-08)
2005-06 Enrollment: 6,725 . . . . (847) 537-8270

Four-year College(s)

Christian Life College (Private, Not-for-profit, Other Protestant)
Fall 2007 Enrollment: 40 . . . . (847) 259-1840
2007-08 Tuition: In-state $9,430; Out-of-state $9,430
ITT Technical Institute-Mount Prospect (Private, For-profit)
Fall 2007 Enrollment: 523 . . . . (847) 375-8800
2007-08 Tuition: In-state $15,600; Out-of-state $15,600

Housing: Homeownership rate: 71.7% (2007); Median home value: $311,959 (2007); Median rent: $738 per month (2000); Median age of housing: 32 years (2000).
Safety: Violent crime rate: 7.9 per 10,000 population; Property crime rate: 153.1 per 10,000 population (2006).
Transportation: Commute to work: 88.6% car, 6.0% public transportation, 2.1% walk, 2.2% work from home (2000); Travel time to work: 23.4% less than 15 minutes, 35.6% 15 to 30 minutes, 23.6% 30 to 45 minutes, 8.4% 45 to 60 minutes, 8.9% 60 minutes or more (2000)

Additional Information Contacts

Mount Prospect Chamber of Commerce . . . . (847) 398-6616
http://www.mountprospectchamber.org
Village of Mount Prospect . . . . (847) 392-6000
http://www.mountprospect.org

NILES (village). Covers a land area of 5.875 square miles and a water area of 0 square miles. Located at 42.03° N. Lat.; 87.81° W. Long. Elevation is 636 feet.
History: Named for Niles, New York. Settled 1832. Incorporated 1899. The village has a half size replica of the leaning tower of Pisa. Niles College of Loyola University is here.
Population: 28,533 (1990); 30,068 (2000); 29,151 (2007); 28,382 (2012 projected); Race: 79.4% White, 0.5% Black, 15.5% Asian, 6.0% Hispanic of any race (2007); Density: 4,961.8 persons per square mile (2007); Average household size: 2.50 (2007); Median age: 49.1 (2007); Males per 100 females: 87.1 (2007); Marriage status: 24.3% never married, 55.5% now married, 13.0% widowed, 7.2% divorced (2000); Foreign born: 33.7% (2000); Ancestry (includes multiple ancestries): 22.8% Polish, 19.3% Other groups, 14.2% German, 9.8% Irish, 8.9% Italian (2000).
Economy: Unemployment rate: 4.5% (4/2008); Total civilian labor force: 14,720 (4/2008); Single-family building permits issued: 13 (2007); Multi-family building permits issued: 0 (2007); Employment by occupation: 12.6% management, 18.7% professional, 13.2% services, 32.4% sales, 0.1% farming, 8.2% construction, 14.9% production (2000).
Income: Per capita income: $27,415 (2007); Median household income: $55,153 (2007); Average household income: $66,624 (2007); Percent of households with income of $100,000 or more: 18.6% (2007); Poverty rate: 5.4% (2000).
Taxes: Total city taxes per capita: $863 (2006); City property taxes per capita: $303 (2006).
Education: Percent of population age 25 and over with: High school diploma (including GED) or higher: 81.4% (2007); Bachelor's degree or higher: 25.0% (2007); Master's degree or higher: 8.9% (2007).

School District(s)

East Maine SD 63 (PK-08)
2005-06 Enrollment: 3,498 . . . . (847) 299-1900
Niles ESD 71 (KG-08)
2005-06 Enrollment: 520 . . . . (847) 966-9280
Park Ridge CCSD 64 (PK-08)
2005-06 Enrollment: 4,307 . . . . (847) 318-4300

Vocational/Technical School(s)

Niles School of Cosmetology (Private, For-profit)
Fall 2007 Enrollment: 125 . . . . (847) 965-8061
2007-08 Tuition: $7,400

Housing: Homeownership rate: 76.2% (2007); Median home value: $309,676 (2007); Median rent: $707 per month (2000); Median age of housing: 37 years (2000).
Safety: Violent crime rate: 18.1 per 10,000 population; Property crime rate: 276.8 per 10,000 population (2006).
Newspapers: Niles Bugle (Community news; Circulation 34,000)
Transportation: Commute to work: 88.9% car, 6.1% public transportation, 2.0% walk, 2.0% work from home (2000); Travel time to work: 20.6% less than 15 minutes, 32.0% 15 to 30 minutes, 26.7% 30 to 45 minutes, 10.5% 45 to 60 minutes, 10.2% 60 minutes or more (2000)

Additional Information Contacts

Niles Chamber of Commerce. . . . . (847) 268-8180
http://www.nileschamber.org
Village of Niles . . . . (847) 588-8000
http://www.vniles.com

NORRIDGE (village). Covers a land area of 1.820 square miles and a water area of 0 square miles. Located at 41.96° N. Lat.; 87.82° W. Long. Elevation is 640 feet.
History: Named for two nearby residential areas, Norwood and Park Ridge. Incorporated 1948.
Population: 14,463 (1990); 14,582 (2000); 13,895 (2007); 13,441 (2012 projected); Race: 93.4% White, 0.2% Black, 3.3% Asian, 4.9% Hispanic of any race (2007); Density: 7,636.1 persons per square mile (2007); Average household size: 2.54 (2007); Median age: 49.0 (2007); Males per 100 females: 86.6 (2007); Marriage status: 25.5% never married, 56.3% now married, 11.7% widowed, 6.5% divorced (2000); Foreign born: 32.5% (2000); Ancestry (includes multiple ancestries): 31.8% Polish, 25.5% Italian, 13.3% German, 7.9% Other groups, 7.5% Irish (2000).
Economy: Single-family building permits issued: 14 (2007); Multi-family building permits issued: 0 (2007); Employment by occupation: 12.7% management, 12.6% professional, 14.2% services, 32.7% sales, 0.1% farming, 11.4% construction, 16.4% production (2000).
Income: Per capita income: $26,455 (2007); Median household income: $54,236 (2007); Average household income: $66,104 (2007); Percent of households with income of $100,000 or more: 17.7% (2007); Poverty rate: 3.9% (2000).
Education: Percent of population age 25 and over with: High school diploma (including GED) or higher: 74.0% (2007); Bachelor's degree or higher: 15.6% (2007); Master's degree or higher: 4.9% (2007).

School District(s)

Norridge SD 80 (KG-08)
2005-06 Enrollment: 1,016 . . . . (708) 583-2068
Pennoyer SD 79 (PK-08)
2005-06 Enrollment: 383 . . . . (708) 456-9094
Ridgewood CHSD 234 (09-12)
2005-06 Enrollment: 952 . . . . (708) 456-4242

Housing: Homeownership rate: 83.7% (2007); Median home value: $320,808 (2007); Median rent: $629 per month (2000); Median age of housing: 41 years (2000).
Safety: Violent crime rate: 11.4 per 10,000 population; Property crime rate: 421.2 per 10,000 population (2006).
Transportation: Commute to work: 90.7% car, 5.6% public transportation, 1.7% walk, 1.5% work from home (2000); Travel time to work: 24.2% less than 15 minutes, 27.7% 15 to 30 minutes, 27.9% 30 to 45 minutes, 8.9% 45 to 60 minutes, 11.2% 60 minutes or more (2000)

Additional Information Contacts

Village of Norridge . . . . (708) 453-0800
http://www.villageofnorridge.com

NORTH RIVERSIDE (village). Covers a land area of 1.544 square miles and a water area of 0 square miles. Located at 41.84° N. Lat.; 87.83° W. Long. Elevation is 617 feet.
Population: 6,005 (1990); 6,688 (2000); 6,260 (2007); 5,960 (2012 projected); Race: 86.8% White, 4.4% Black, 3.3% Asian, 11.5% Hispanic of any race (2007); Density: 4,054.1 persons per square mile (2007); Average household size: 2.32 (2007); Median age: 48.0 (2007); Males per 100 females: 90.7 (2007); Marriage status: 22.7% never married, 55.8% now married, 11.9% widowed, 9.6% divorced (2000); Foreign born: 14.4% (2000); Ancestry (includes multiple ancestries): 17.7% Polish, 16.2% German, 14.0% Italian, 13.1% Irish, 12.5% Other groups (2000).
Economy: Single-family building permits issued: 0 (2007); Multi-family building permits issued: 0 (2007); Employment by occupation: 14.0% management, 23.0% professional, 10.8% services, 32.4% sales, 0.0% farming, 7.4% construction, 12.3% production (2000).
Income: Per capita income: $26,607 (2007); Median household income: $50,758 (2007); Average household income: $61,072 (2007); Percent of households with income of $100,000 or more: 14.2% (2007); Poverty rate: 4.7% (2000).
Education: Percent of population age 25 and over with: High school diploma (including GED) or higher: 80.8% (2007); Bachelor's degree or higher: 24.0% (2007); Master's degree or higher: 8.2% (2007).

School District(s)

Komarek SD 94 (KG-08)
2005-06 Enrollment: 448 . . . . (708) 447-8030

Housing: Homeownership rate: 71.4% (2007); Median home value: $232,396 (2007); Median rent: $601 per month (2000); Median age of housing: 45 years (2000).
Safety: Violent crime rate: 40.7 per 10,000 population; Property crime rate: 1,291.1 per 10,000 population (2006).
Newspapers: Berwyn-Stickney-Forest View Life (Local news; Circulation 30,000); Cicero Life (Local news; Circulation 30,000)
Transportation: Commute to work: 89.8% car, 7.5% public transportation, 0.8% walk, 1.8% work from home (2000); Travel time to work: 25.9% less than 15 minutes, 30.8% 15 to 30 minutes, 23.8% 30 to 45 minutes, 9.6% 45 to 60 minutes, 10.0% 60 minutes or more (2000)

Additional Information Contacts

Village of North Riverside . . . . (708) 447-4211
http://www.northriverside-il.org

NORTHBROOK (village). Covers a land area of 12.919 square miles and a water area of 0.049 square miles. Located at 42.12° N. Lat.; 87.84° W. Long. Elevation is 646 feet.
History: Named for the middle forks of the north branch of the Chicago River. It was incorporated as Shermerville in 1901 and was reincorporated as Northbrook in 1923. Once a farming community, Northbrook developed industry after the coming of a railroad in 1871. Settled 1836.
Population: 33,020 (1990); 33,435 (2000); 34,279 (2007); 34,626 (2012 projected); Race: 87.9% White, 0.7% Black, 9.8% Asian, 2.1% Hispanic of any race (2007); Density: 2,653.5 persons per square mile (2007); Average household size: 2.73 (2007); Median age: 46.0 (2007); Males per 100 females: 93.4 (2007); Marriage status: 17.5% never married, 70.1% now married, 6.7% widowed, 5.6% divorced (2000); Foreign born: 15.2% (2000); Ancestry (includes multiple ancestries): 18.3% German, 15.6% Other groups, 12.3% Russian, 12.1% Irish, 10.0% Polish (2000).
Economy: Unemployment rate: 3.4% (4/2008); Total civilian labor force: 17,850 (4/2008); Single-family building permits issued: 59 (2007); Multi-family building permits issued: 0 (2007); Employment by occupation: 26.4% management, 31.3% professional, 4.7% services, 31.6% sales, 0.0% farming, 2.6% construction, 3.3% production (2000).
Income: Per capita income: $52,489 (2007); Median household income: $101,455 (2007); Average household income: $142,153 (2007); Percent of households with income of $100,000 or more: 50.7% (2007); Poverty rate: 2.3% (2000).
Taxes: Total city taxes per capita: $721 (2006); City property taxes per capita: $396 (2006).
Education: Percent of population age 25 and over with: High school diploma (including GED) or higher: 95.5% (2007); Bachelor's degree or higher: 62.2% (2007); Master's degree or higher: 27.7% (2007).

School District(s)

Northbrook ESD 27 (KG-08)
2005-06 Enrollment: 1,293 . . . . (847) 498-2610
Northbrook SD 28 (PK-08)
2005-06 Enrollment: 1,736 . . . . (847) 498-7900
Northbrook/Glenview SD 30 (PK-08)
2005-06 Enrollment: 1,081 . . . . (847) 498-4190
Northern Suburban Spec Ed Dist (KG-12)
2005-06 Enrollment: 127 . . . . (847) 831-5100
Northfield Twp HSD 225 (09-12)
2005-06 Enrollment: 4,868 . . . . (847) 486-4700
West Northfield SD 31 (KG-08)
2005-06 Enrollment: 857 . . . . (847) 272-6880

Housing: Homeownership rate: 91.6% (2007); Median home value: $531,141 (2007); Median rent: $1,215 per month (2000); Median age of housing: 31 years (2000).
Safety: Violent crime rate: 4.7 per 10,000 population; Property crime rate: 193.6 per 10,000 population (2006).
Newspapers: Gardner Chronicle (Local news; Circulation 847)
Transportation: Commute to work: 81.5% car, 9.9% public transportation, 1.3% walk, 6.6% work from home (2000); Travel time to work: 24.2% less than 15 minutes, 29.8% 15 to 30 minutes, 21.9% 30 to 45 minutes, 12.1% 45 to 60 minutes, 12.0% 60 minutes or more (2000)

Additional Information Contacts

Northbrook Chamber of Commerce & Industry . . . . (847) 498-5555
http://www.northbrookchamber.org
Village of Northbrook . . . . (847) 272-5050
http://www.northbrook.il.us

NORTHFIELD (village). Covers a land area of 2.957 square miles and a water area of 0 square miles. Located at 42.10° N. Lat.; 87.77° W. Long. Elevation is 633 feet.
Population: 4,913 (1990); 5,389 (2000); 5,441 (2007); 5,432 (2012 projected); Race: 91.7% White, 0.6% Black, 6.1% Asian, 1.9% Hispanic of any race (2007); Density: 1,840.0 persons per square mile (2007); Average household size: 2.48 (2007); Median age: 46.2 (2007); Males per 100

females: 91.4 (2007); Marriage status: 17.0% never married, 68.1% now married, 8.3% widowed, 6.5% divorced (2000); Foreign born: 12.2% (2000); Ancestry (includes multiple ancestries): 21.4% German, 20.0% Irish, 18.8% English, 7.3% Other groups, 6.8% Polish (2000).
Economy: Single-family building permits issued: 1 (2007); Multi-family building permits issued: 0 (2007); Employment by occupation: 21.9% management, 29.9% professional, 8.5% services, 31.3% sales, 0.0% farming, 3.6% construction, 4.9% production (2000).
Income: Per capita income: $56,866 (2007); Median household income: $100,056 (2007); Average household income: $140,743 (2007); Percent of households with income of $100,000 or more: 50.0% (2007); Poverty rate: 1.6% (2000).
Taxes: Total city taxes per capita: $1,005 (2006); City property taxes per capita: $556 (2006).
Education: Percent of population age 25 and over with: High school diploma (including GED) or higher: 96.4% (2007); Bachelor's degree or higher: 67.7% (2007); Master's degree or higher: 27.8% (2007).

School District(s)

New Trier Twp HSD 203 (09-12)
2005-06 Enrollment: 4,044 . . . . (847) 446-7000
Sunset Ridge SD 29 (KG-08)
2005-06 Enrollment: 529 . . . . (847) 881-9401

Housing: Homeownership rate: 91.9% (2007); Median home value: $601,269 (2007); Median rent: $917 per month (2000); Median age of housing: 41 years (2000).
Safety: Violent crime rate: 3.6 per 10,000 population; Property crime rate: 212.9 per 10,000 population (2006).
Transportation: Commute to work: 85.7% car, 8.2% public transportation, 0.8% walk, 4.9% work from home (2000); Travel time to work: 33.0% less than 15 minutes, 29.9% 15 to 30 minutes, 15.7% 30 to 45 minutes, 8.4% 45 to 60 minutes, 13.1% 60 minutes or more (2000)

Additional Information Contacts

Northfield Chamber of Commerce . . . . (847) 441-1848
http://www.northfieldchamber.org
Village of Northfield . . . . (847) 446-9200
http://www.northfieldil.org

NORTHLAKE (city). Aka North Lake. Covers a land area of 3.015 square miles and a water area of 0 square miles. Located at 41.91° N. Lat.; 87.90° W. Long. Elevation is 646 feet.
History: St. John Vianney Roman Catholic Church, which is shaped like a fish, has the largest mosaic-tile mural in the Western Hemisphere. Incorporated 1949.
Population: 12,583 (1990); 11,878 (2000); 11,038 (2007); 10,489 (2012 projected); Race: 69.8% White, 2.8% Black, 3.5% Asian, 45.4% Hispanic of any race (2007); Density: 3,660.7 persons per square mile (2007); Average household size: 3.14 (2007); Median age: 37.5 (2007); Males per 100 females: 96.0 (2007); Marriage status: 26.6% never married, 56.5% now married, 8.4% widowed, 8.4% divorced (2000); Foreign born: 24.6% (2000); Ancestry (includes multiple ancestries): 36.9% Other groups, 17.7% German, 14.2% Irish, 11.9% Italian, 11.8% Polish (2000).
Economy: Single-family building permits issued: 11 (2007); Multi-family building permits issued: 0 (2007); Employment by occupation: 9.6% management, 6.9% professional, 11.0% services, 33.6% sales, 0.2% farming, 10.0% construction, 28.7% production (2000).
Income: Per capita income: $20,465 (2007); Median household income: $54,698 (2007); Average household income: $62,420 (2007); Percent of households with income of $100,000 or more: 15.1% (2007); Poverty rate: 8.4% (2000).
Education: Percent of population age 25 and over with: High school diploma (including GED) or higher: 67.1% (2007); Bachelor's degree or higher: 7.7% (2007); Master's degree or higher: 2.6% (2007).

School District(s)

Berkeley SD 87 (PK-08)
2005-06 Enrollment: 2,886 . . . . (708) 449-3350
Leyden CHSD 212 (09-12)
2005-06 Enrollment: 3,537 . . . . (847) 451-3000
Mannheim SD 83 (PK-12)
2005-06 Enrollment: 2,757 . . . . (847) 455-4413

Housing: Homeownership rate: 78.4% (2007); Median home value: $210,880 (2007); Median rent: $558 per month (2000); Median age of housing: 44 years (2000).
Hospitals: Kindred Hospital-Northlake (94 beds)
Safety: Violent crime rate: 18.5 per 10,000 population; Property crime rate: 347.8 per 10,000 population (2006).
Transportation: Commute to work: 93.5% car, 2.7% public transportation, 1.7% walk, 0.5% work from home (2000); Travel time to work: 28.6% less than 15 minutes, 38.0% 15 to 30 minutes, 21.1% 30 to 45 minutes, 7.0% 45 to 60 minutes, 5.3% 60 minutes or more (2000)

Additional Information Contacts

City of Northlake . . . . (708) 343-8700
http://www.northlakecity.com
Northlake Chamber of Commerce . . . . (708) 562-3110
http://www.northlakecity.com/links_chamber.htm

OAK FOREST (city). Covers a land area of 5.649 square miles and a water area of 0.053 square miles. Located at 41.60° N. Lat.; 87.75° W. Long. Elevation is 673 feet.
History: Named for the many oak trees in the area. In 1911 the Oak Forest Infirmary and Tuberculosis Hospital was established in the town of Oak Forest.
Population: 26,662 (1990); 28,051 (2000); 28,382 (2007); 28,500 (2012 projected); Race: 87.6% White, 4.8% Black, 3.3% Asian, 7.9% Hispanic of any race (2007); Density: 5,024.0 persons per square mile (2007); Average household size: 2.84 (2007); Median age: 37.5 (2007); Males per 100 females: 99.0 (2007); Marriage status: 26.7% never married, 60.0% now married, 5.6% widowed, 7.6% divorced (2000); Foreign born: 5.8% (2000); Ancestry (includes multiple ancestries): 26.3% Irish, 25.1% German, 18.3% Polish, 13.0% Italian, 11.2% Other groups (2000).
Economy: Unemployment rate: 5.1% (4/2008); Total civilian labor force: 16,335 (4/2008); Single-family building permits issued: 4 (2007); Multi-family building permits issued: 12 (2007); Employment by occupation: 12.6% management, 19.6% professional, 11.4% services, 31.6% sales, 0.1% farming, 12.0% construction, 12.8% production (2000).
Income: Per capita income: $27,426 (2007); Median household income: $68,813 (2007); Average household income: $77,505 (2007); Percent of households with income of $100,000 or more: 25.1% (2007); Poverty rate: 3.6% (2000).
Education: Percent of population age 25 and over with: High school diploma (including GED) or higher: 89.2% (2007); Bachelor's degree or higher: 22.5% (2007); Master's degree or higher: 6.7% (2007).

School District(s)

Arbor Park SD 145 (PK-08)
2005-06 Enrollment: 1,503 . . . . (708) 687-8040
Bremen CHSD 228 (09-12)
2005-06 Enrollment: 5,194 . . . . (708) 389-1175
Forest Ridge SD 142 (PK-08)
2005-06 Enrollment: 1,698 . . . . (708) 687-3334
Prairie-Hills ESD 144 (PK-08)
2005-06 Enrollment: 2,955 . . . . (708) 210-2888
Southwest Cook Coop Sped Ed
2005-06 Enrollment: n/a . . . . (708) 687-0900
Tinley Park CCSD 146 (PK-08)
2005-06 Enrollment: 2,407 . . . . (708) 614-4500

Vocational/Technical School(s)

Capri Oak Forest Beauty College (Private, For-profit)
Fall 2007 Enrollment: 190 . . . . (708) 687-3020
2007-08 Tuition: $15,600
John Amico School of Hair Design (Private, For-profit)
Fall 2007 Enrollment: n/a. . . . . (708) 687-7800
2007-08 Tuition: $6,200

Housing: Homeownership rate: 81.5% (2007); Median home value: $216,553 (2007); Median rent: $629 per month (2000); Median age of housing: 28 years (2000).
Hospitals: Oak Forest Hospital of Cook County (550 beds)
Safety: Violent crime rate: 22.1 per 10,000 population; Property crime rate: 220.9 per 10,000 population (2006).
Transportation: Commute to work: 87.2% car, 8.8% public transportation, 1.0% walk, 2.4% work from home (2000); Travel time to work: 22.5% less than 15 minutes, 29.2% 15 to 30 minutes, 19.8% 30 to 45 minutes, 11.8% 45 to 60 minutes, 16.7% 60 minutes or more (2000)

Additional Information Contacts

City of Oak Forest . . . . (708) 687-4050
http://www.oak-forest.org
Oak Forest Chamber of Commerce. . . . . (708) 687-4600
http://www.oakforestchamber.org

OAK LAWN (village). Covers a land area of 8.595 square miles and a water area of <.001 square miles. Located at 41.71° N. Lat.; 87.75° W. Long. Elevation is 597 feet.

History: Named for its many oak trees. Incorporated 1909.
Population: 56,325 (1990); 55,245 (2000); 53,463 (2007); 52,051 (2012 projected); Race: 91.2% White, 1.8% Black, 2.1% Asian, 7.2% Hispanic of any race (2007); Density: 6,219.9 persons per square mile (2007); Average household size: 2.45 (2007); Median age: 43.1 (2007); Males per 100 females: 89.2 (2007); Marriage status: 24.7% never married, 55.9% now married, 11.6% widowed, 7.8% divorced (2000); Foreign born: 11.5% (2000); Ancestry (includes multiple ancestries): 30.4% Irish, 19.5% German, 19.3% Polish, 9.7% Italian, 8.9% Other groups (2000).
Economy: Unemployment rate: 5.6% (4/2008); Total civilian labor force: 27,345 (4/2008); Single-family building permits issued: 30 (2007); Multi-family building permits issued: 80 (2007); Employment by occupation: 13.0% management, 18.9% professional, 10.7% services, 31.2% sales, 0.1% farming, 12.0% construction, 14.1% production (2000).
Income: Per capita income: $27,423 (2007); Median household income: $53,414 (2007); Average household income: $66,748 (2007); Percent of households with income of $100,000 or more: 18.8% (2007); Poverty rate: 5.4% (2000).
Taxes: Total city taxes per capita: $451 (2006); City property taxes per capita: $315 (2006).
Education: Percent of population age 25 and over with: High school diploma (including GED) or higher: 83.4% (2007); Bachelor's degree or higher: 21.0% (2007); Master's degree or higher: 6.9% (2007).

School District(s)

Atwood Heights SD 125 (PK-08)
2005-06 Enrollment: 694 .... (708) 371-0080
CHSD 218 (09-12)
2005-06 Enrollment: 5,329 .... (708) 424-2000
Eisenhower Cooperative (PK-08)
2005-06 Enrollment: 141 .... (708) 424-9900
Oak Lawn CHSD 229 (09-12)
2005-06 Enrollment: 1,769 .... (708) 424-5200
Oak Lawn-Hometown SD 123 (PK-08)
2005-06 Enrollment: 2,885 .... (708) 423-0150
Ridgeland SD 122 (PK-08)
2005-06 Enrollment: 2,144 .... (708) 599-5550

Two-year College(s)

Fox College Inc (Private, For-profit)
Fall 2007 Enrollment: 256 .... (708) 636-7700
2007-08 Tuition: In-state $13,820; Out-of-state $13,820

Vocational/Technical School(s)

Cameo Beauty Academy (Private, For-profit)
Fall 2007 Enrollment: 126 .... (708) 636-4660
2007-08 Tuition: $15,475

Housing: Homeownership rate: 82.8% (2007); Median home value: $222,650 (2007); Median rent: $639 per month (2000); Median age of housing: 35 years (2000).
Hospitals: Advocate Christ Medical Center and Hope Children's Hospital (64 beds)
Safety: Violent crime rate: 10.4 per 10,000 population; Property crime rate: 208.7 per 10,000 population (2006).
Transportation: Commute to work: 87.5% car, 8.2% public transportation, 1.8% walk, 2.1% work from home (2000); Travel time to work: 24.5% less than 15 minutes, 26.1% 15 to 30 minutes, 21.5% 30 to 45 minutes, 13.9% 45 to 60 minutes, 14.0% 60 minutes or more (2000)

Additional Information Contacts

Oak Lawn Chamber of Commerce .... (708) 424-8300
http://www.oaklawnchamber.com
Village of Oak Lawn .... (708) 636-4400
http://www.villageofoaklawn.com

OAK PARK (village). Covers a land area of 4.701 square miles and a water area of 0 square miles. Located at 41.88° N. Lat.; 87.79° W. Long. Elevation is 620 feet.
History: Oak Park was settled in 1833 by Joseph Kettlestrings, who came with his wife from Maryland. They named the village for the oak trees growing there. In the 1890's Oak Park was known as Saints' Rest because of its many churches. This was the site of one of Frank Lloyd Wright's early workshops and examples of his architecture graced the village.
Population: 53,648 (1990); 52,524 (2000); 50,355 (2007); 48,665 (2012 projected); Race: 65.9% White, 24.2% Black, 4.6% Asian, 5.3% Hispanic of any race (2007); Density: 10,712.0 persons per square mile (2007); Average household size: 2.24 (2007); Median age: 38.5 (2007); Males per 100 females: 88.1 (2007); Marriage status: 33.5% never married, 51.1% now married, 5.3% widowed, 10.0% divorced (2000); Foreign born: 9.8% (2000); Ancestry (includes multiple ancestries): 29.3% Other groups, 18.0% German, 17.4% Irish, 8.7% English, 7.5% Italian (2000).
Economy: Unemployment rate: 3.6% (4/2008); Total civilian labor force: 31,517 (4/2008); Single-family building permits issued: 35 (2007); Multi-family building permits issued: 32 (2007); Employment by occupation: 19.6% management, 40.9% professional, 7.9% services, 23.8% sales, 0.0% farming, 2.8% construction, 5.1% production (2000).
Income: Per capita income: $43,709 (2007); Median household income: $68,371 (2007); Average household income: $97,457 (2007); Percent of households with income of $100,000 or more: 32.5% (2007); Poverty rate: 5.6% (2000).
Taxes: Total city taxes per capita: $904 (2006); City property taxes per capita: $586 (2006).
Education: Percent of population age 25 and over with: High school diploma (including GED) or higher: 94.3% (2007); Bachelor's degree or higher: 61.8% (2007); Master's degree or higher: 30.6% (2007).

School District(s)

Intermediate Service Center 2 (07-12)
2005-06 Enrollment: 65 .... (708) 482-4350
Oak Park - River Forest SD 200 (09-12)
2005-06 Enrollment: 3,076 .... (708) 383-0700
Oak Park ESD 97 (PK-08)
2005-06 Enrollment: 4,973 .... (708) 524-3000

Four-year College(s)

West Suburban College of Nursing (Private, Not-for-profit, Roman Catholic)
Fall 2007 Enrollment: 213 .... (708) 763-6530

Housing: Homeownership rate: 55.9% (2007); Median home value: $332,968 (2007); Median rent: $674 per month (2000); Median age of housing: 60+ years (2000).
Hospitals: Rush Oak Park Hospital (296 beds); West Suburban Medical Center (245 beds)
Safety: Violent crime rate: 40.6 per 10,000 population; Property crime rate: 357.4 per 10,000 population (2006).
Newspapers: Austin Weekly News (Community news; Circulation 10,000); Chicago Journal (Local news; Circulation 3,600); Elm Leaves (Community news; Circulation 3,592); Forest Leaves (Community news; Circulation 2,403); Forest Park Review (Community news; Circulation 3,200); Franklin Park Herald-Journal (Local news; Circulation 3,010); Maywood Herald (Community news; Circulation 2,856); Melrose Park Herald (Community news; Circulation 1,775); Northlake Herald-Journal (Community news; Circulation 1,583); Oak Leaves (Community news; Circulation 10,031); River Grove Messenger (Community news; Circulation 1,177); Skyline (Community news; Circulation 28,503); Wednesday Journal (Community news; Circulation 14,500); West Proviso Herald (Community news; Circulation 2,292); Westchester Herald (Community news; Circulation 1,100); Wicker Park Booster (Local news; Circulation 10,064)
Transportation: Commute to work: 68.4% car, 21.8% public transportation, 4.0% walk, 5.1% work from home (2000); Travel time to work: 16.9% less than 15 minutes, 26.4% 15 to 30 minutes, 34.6% 30 to 45 minutes, 14.2% 45 to 60 minutes, 7.8% 60 minutes or more (2000)

Additional Information Contacts

Oak Park Chamber of Commerce .... (708) 848-8151
http://www.oprfchamber.org
Village of Oak Park .... (708) 445-3340
http://www.vil.oak-park.il.us

OLYMPIA FIELDS (village). Covers a land area of 2.842 square miles and a water area of 0.004 square miles. Located at 41.51° N. Lat.; 87.69° W. Long. Elevation is 692 feet.
History: Olympia Fields was developed in 1926 as a residential community centered around the Olympia Fields Country Club and Golf Course.
Population: 4,245 (1990); 4,732 (2000); 4,631 (2007); 4,531 (2012 projected); Race: 33.5% White, 61.7% Black, 2.7% Asian, 2.3% Hispanic of any race (2007); Density: 1,629.7 persons per square mile (2007); Average household size: 2.75 (2007); Median age: 47.9 (2007); Males per 100 females: 91.3 (2007); Marriage status: 20.6% never married, 68.2% now married, 6.2% widowed, 5.0% divorced (2000); Foreign born: 8.3% (2000); Ancestry (includes multiple ancestries): 45.2% Other groups, 9.6% German, 7.8% Irish, 6.6% Italian, 4.8% English (2000).
Economy: Single-family building permits issued: 32 (2007); Multi-family building permits issued: 0 (2007); Employment by occupation: 26.8% management, 31.6% professional, 6.2% services, 27.7% sales, 0.0% farming, 2.9% construction, 4.9% production (2000).
Income: Per capita income: $46,191 (2007); Median household income: $96,066 (2007); Average household income: $125,491 (2007); Percent of

households with income of $100,000 or more: 47.2% (2007); Poverty rate: 4.6% (2000).
Education: Percent of population age 25 and over with: High school diploma (including GED) or higher: 94.6% (2007); Bachelor's degree or higher: 55.6% (2007); Master's degree or higher: 24.9% (2007).

School District(s)

Career Preparation Network
2005-06 Enrollment: n/a . . . . (708) 679-5716
Matteson ESD 162 (PK-08)
2005-06 Enrollment: 3,399 . . . . (708) 748-0100
Rich Twp HSD 227 (09-12)
2005-06 Enrollment: 3,962 . . . . (708) 679-5800

Housing: Homeownership rate: 94.5% (2007); Median home value: $348,619 (2007); Median rent: $2,000+ per month (2000); Median age of housing: 24 years (2000).
Hospitals: St. James Hospital and Health Center (201 beds)
Safety: Violent crime rate: 62.1 per 10,000 population; Property crime rate: 490.0 per 10,000 population (2006).
Transportation: Commute to work: 80.6% car, 11.6% public transportation, 1.3% walk, 4.0% work from home (2000); Travel time to work: 19.7% less than 15 minutes, 19.8% 15 to 30 minutes, 22.5% 30 to 45 minutes, 14.1% 45 to 60 minutes, 24.0% 60 minutes or more (2000)

ORLAND HILLS (village). Aka Westhaven. Covers a land area of 1.090 square miles and a water area of 0.008 square miles. Located at 41.58° N. Lat.; 87.84° W. Long. Elevation is 702 feet.
Population: 5,547 (1990); 6,779 (2000); 7,074 (2007); 7,226 (2012 projected); Race: 84.0% White, 5.6% Black, 4.5% Asian, 7.0% Hispanic of any race (2007); Density: 6,487.8 persons per square mile (2007); Average household size: 3.10 (2007); Median age: 31.2 (2007); Males per 100 females: 97.8 (2007); Marriage status: 26.5% never married, 62.3% now married, 3.4% widowed, 7.8% divorced (2000); Foreign born: 8.7% (2000); Ancestry (includes multiple ancestries): 22.9% Irish, 21.9% German, 21.7% Polish, 14.1% Other groups, 13.4% Italian (2000).
Economy: Single-family building permits issued: 0 (2007); Multi-family building permits issued: 0 (2007); Employment by occupation: 12.3% management, 18.6% professional, 12.3% services, 32.1% sales, 0.0% farming, 13.9% construction, 10.8% production (2000).
Income: Per capita income: $28,143 (2007); Median household income: $82,107 (2007); Average household income: $86,312 (2007); Percent of households with income of $100,000 or more: 31.2% (2007); Poverty rate: 5.3% (2000).
Education: Percent of population age 25 and over with: High school diploma (including GED) or higher: 92.2% (2007); Bachelor's degree or higher: 19.4% (2007); Master's degree or higher: 3.6% (2007).
Housing: Homeownership rate: 78.0% (2007); Median home value: $238,732 (2007); Median rent: $734 per month (2000); Median age of housing: 16 years (2000).
Safety: Violent crime rate: 9.6 per 10,000 population; Property crime rate: 104.5 per 10,000 population (2006).
Transportation: Commute to work: 89.6% car, 6.8% public transportation, 0.8% walk, 2.4% work from home (2000); Travel time to work: 19.3% less than 15 minutes, 22.7% 15 to 30 minutes, 22.0% 30 to 45 minutes, 14.7% 45 to 60 minutes, 21.4% 60 minutes or more (2000)

Additional Information Contacts

Village of Orland Hills. . . . . (708) 349-6865
http://www.orlandhills.org

ORLAND PARK (village). Covers a land area of 19.141 square miles and a water area of 0.295 square miles. Located at 41.61° N. Lat.; 87.85° W. Long. Elevation is 705 feet.
Population: 38,946 (1990); 51,077 (2000); 57,385 (2007); 61,118 (2012 projected); Race: 92.9% White, 0.9% Black, 3.6% Asian, 4.3% Hispanic of any race (2007); Density: 2,998.0 persons per square mile (2007); Average household size: 2.70 (2007); Median age: 42.9 (2007); Males per 100 females: 91.9 (2007); Marriage status: 22.8% never married, 63.6% now married, 7.6% widowed, 6.1% divorced (2000); Foreign born: 9.4% (2000); Ancestry (includes multiple ancestries): 26.5% Irish, 19.5% German, 18.5% Polish, 14.8% Italian, 9.3% Other groups (2000).
Economy: Unemployment rate: 4.2% (4/2008); Total civilian labor force: 29,786 (4/2008); Single-family building permits issued: 45 (2007); Multi-family building permits issued: 24 (2007); Employment by occupation: 18.7% management, 21.8% professional, 9.4% services, 32.1% sales, 0.0% farming, 8.1% construction, 9.9% production (2000).
Income: Per capita income: $36,347 (2007); Median household income: $80,413 (2007); Average household income: $97,954 (2007); Percent of households with income of $100,000 or more: 36.6% (2007); Poverty rate: 3.1% (2000).
Education: Percent of population age 25 and over with: High school diploma (including GED) or higher: 90.0% (2007); Bachelor's degree or higher: 31.5% (2007); Master's degree or higher: 11.9% (2007).

School District(s)

Cons HSD 230 (09-12)
2005-06 Enrollment: 8,805 . . . . (708) 745-5210
Kirby SD 140 (PK-08)
2005-06 Enrollment: 4,485 . . . . (708) 532-6462
Orland SD 135 (PK-08)
2005-06 Enrollment: 5,933 . . . . (708) 364-3306
Tinley Park CCSD 146 (PK-08)
2005-06 Enrollment: 2,407 . . . . (708) 614-4500

Four-year College(s)

ITT Technnical Institute-Orland Park (Private, For-profit)
Fall 2007 Enrollment: 383 . . . . (708) 326-3200
2007-08 Tuition: In-state $15,600; Out-of-state $15,600

Housing: Homeownership rate: 91.6% (2007); Median home value: $291,438 (2007); Median rent: $710 per month (2000); Median age of housing: 15 years (2000).
Safety: Violent crime rate: 2.8 per 10,000 population; Property crime rate: 196.5 per 10,000 population (2006).
Transportation: Commute to work: 89.7% car, 6.5% public transportation, 1.1% walk, 2.1% work from home (2000); Travel time to work: 19.5% less than 15 minutes, 26.0% 15 to 30 minutes, 21.7% 30 to 45 minutes, 12.5% 45 to 60 minutes, 20.3% 60 minutes or more (2000)

Additional Information Contacts

Orland Park Chamber of Commerce . . . . (708) 349-2972
http://www.orlandparkchamber.org
Village of Orland Park . . . . (708) 403-6100
http://www.orland-park.il.us

PALATINE (village). Covers a land area of 12.973 square miles and a water area of 0.134 square miles. Located at 42.11° N. Lat.; 88.04° W. Long. Elevation is 741 feet.
History: Named for the Rhenish Palatinate, Germany, as "palatine" designates a high official. William Rainey Harper College is in Palatine. Incorporated 1869.
Population: 58,182 (1990); 65,479 (2000); 66,680 (2007); 67,391 (2012 projected); Race: 80.4% White, 2.1% Black, 9.0% Asian, 17.5% Hispanic of any race (2007); Density: 5,139.8 persons per square mile (2007); Average household size: 2.56 (2007); Median age: 36.7 (2007); Males per 100 females: 98.9 (2007); Marriage status: 27.4% never married, 59.2% now married, 5.0% widowed, 8.5% divorced (2000); Foreign born: 21.9% (2000); Ancestry (includes multiple ancestries): 25.2% Other groups, 25.1% German, 14.8% Irish, 12.0% Polish, 9.1% Italian (2000).
Economy: Unemployment rate: 4.2% (4/2008); Total civilian labor force: 42,021 (4/2008); Single-family building permits issued: 40 (2007); Multi-family building permits issued: 56 (2007); Employment by occupation: 19.4% management, 24.4% professional, 10.5% services, 30.0% sales, 0.1% farming, 5.7% construction, 10.0% production (2000).
Income: Per capita income: $36,125 (2007); Median household income: $73,750 (2007); Average household income: $92,274 (2007); Percent of households with income of $100,000 or more: 32.2% (2007); Poverty rate: 4.8% (2000).
Taxes: Total city taxes per capita: $537 (2006); City property taxes per capita: $373 (2006).
Education: Percent of population age 25 and over with: High school diploma (including GED) or higher: 88.8% (2007); Bachelor's degree or higher: 41.2% (2007); Master's degree or higher: 13.9% (2007).

School District(s)

Lake Zurich CUSD 95 (PK-12)
2005-06 Enrollment: 6,557 . . . . (847) 438-2831
Nw Suburban Spec Educ Org (PK-12)
2005-06 Enrollment: 601 . . . . (847) 463-8100
Palatine CCSD 15 (PK-08)
2005-06 Enrollment: 12,794 . . . . (847) 963-3000
Township HSD 211 (09-12)
2005-06 Enrollment: 13,026 . . . . (847) 755-6600

Two-year College(s)

Harper College (Public)
Fall 2007 Enrollment: 15,156. . . . . (847) 925-6000
2007-08 Tuition: In-state $9,834; Out-of-state $12,174

Housing: Homeownership rate: 68.8% (2007); Median home value: $276,121 (2007); Median rent: $817 per month (2000); Median age of housing: 24 years (2000).

Safety: Violent crime rate: 8.6 per 10,000 population; Property crime rate: 192.3 per 10,000 population (2006).

Transportation: Commute to work: 90.3% car, 4.7% public transportation, 1.4% walk, 2.5% work from home (2000); Travel time to work: 21.8% less than 15 minutes, 36.4% 15 to 30 minutes, 24.4% 30 to 45 minutes, 8.5% 45 to 60 minutes, 8.9% 60 minutes or more (2000)

Additional Information Contacts

Palatine Area Chamber of Commerce . . . . (847) 359-7200
http://www.palatinechamber.com

Village of Palatine . . . . (847) 358-6700
http://www.palatine.il.us

PALOS HEIGHTS (city). Covers a land area of 3.780 square miles and a water area of 0.086 square miles. Located at 41.66° N. Lat.; 87.79° W. Long. Elevation is 623 feet.

History: Named for Palos, Spain. Trinity Christian College is here.

Population: 11,513 (1990); 11,260 (2000); 12,513 (2007); 13,271 (2012 projected); Race: 96.5% White, 0.5% Black, 1.8% Asian, 1.6% Hispanic of any race (2007); Density: 3,310.1 persons per square mile (2007); Average household size: 2.69 (2007); Median age: 49.2 (2007); Males per 100 females: 86.1 (2007); Marriage status: 19.6% never married, 64.5% now married, 11.2% widowed, 4.7% divorced (2000); Foreign born: 6.4% (2000); Ancestry (includes multiple ancestries): 27.2% Irish, 20.5% German, 14.1% Polish, 10.5% Italian, 9.1% Dutch (2000).

Economy: Single-family building permits issued: 9 (2007); Multi-family building permits issued: 20 (2007); Employment by occupation: 20.2% management, 25.6% professional, 8.9% services, 27.5% sales, 0.2% farming, 8.7% construction, 8.9% production (2000).

Income: Per capita income: $38,406 (2007); Median household income: $78,959 (2007); Average household income: $102,128 (2007); Percent of households with income of $100,000 or more: 35.1% (2007); Poverty rate: 3.2% (2000).

Education: Percent of population age 25 and over with: High school diploma (including GED) or higher: 90.7% (2007); Bachelor's degree or higher: 38.9% (2007); Master's degree or higher: 16.3% (2007).

School District(s)

CHSD 218 (09-12)
2005-06 Enrollment: 5,329 . . . . (708) 424-2000

Palos CCSD 118 (PK-08)
2005-06 Enrollment: 1,986 . . . . (708) 448-4800

Palos Heights SD 128 (PK-08)
2005-06 Enrollment: 743 . . . . (708) 597-9040

Four-year College(s)

Trinity Christian College (Private, Not-for-profit, Interdenominational)
Fall 2007 Enrollment: 1,367. . . . . (708) 597-3000
2007-08 Tuition: In-state $19,241; Out-of-state $19,241

Housing: Homeownership rate: 97.5% (2007); Median home value: $317,113 (2007); Median rent: $925 per month (2000); Median age of housing: 29 years (2000).

Hospitals: Palos Community Hospital (436 beds)

Safety: Violent crime rate: 20.7 per 10,000 population; Property crime rate: 104.3 per 10,000 population (2006).

Newspapers: Oak Lawn/Evergreen Park Reporter (Community news; Circulation 17,424); Palos Hills/Hickory Hills Reporter (Community news; Circulation 18,912); Regional News (Community news; Circulation 18,590)

Transportation: Commute to work: 87.7% car, 5.2% public transportation, 3.2% walk, 3.0% work from home (2000); Travel time to work: 23.2% less than 15 minutes, 31.0% 15 to 30 minutes, 16.2% 30 to 45 minutes, 12.5% 45 to 60 minutes, 17.1% 60 minutes or more (2000)

Additional Information Contacts

City of Palos Heights . . . . (708) 361-1800
http://www.palosheights.org

Palos Heights Chamber of Commerce . . . . (708) 923-2300
http://www.paloschamber.org

PALOS HILLS (city). Covers a land area of 4.167 square miles and a water area of 0.070 square miles. Located at 41.69° N. Lat.; 87.82° W. Long. Elevation is 597 feet.

Population: 17,800 (1990); 17,665 (2000); 16,964 (2007); 16,415 (2012 projected); Race: 84.3% White, 6.8% Black, 2.9% Asian, 5.9% Hispanic of any race (2007); Density: 4,071.5 persons per square mile (2007); Average household size: 2.39 (2007); Median age: 43.2 (2007); Males per 100 females: 88.6 (2007); Marriage status: 27.4% never married, 54.4% now married, 8.9% widowed, 9.3% divorced (2000); Foreign born: 16.4% (2000); Ancestry (includes multiple ancestries): 19.1% Irish, 18.9% Polish, 16.3% German, 12.9% Other groups, 10.5% Italian (2000).

Economy: Single-family building permits issued: 6 (2007); Multi-family building permits issued: 0 (2007); Employment by occupation: 13.8% management, 20.4% professional, 11.9% services, 29.4% sales, 0.0% farming, 10.6% construction, 13.9% production (2000).

Income: Per capita income: $29,272 (2007); Median household income: $61,141 (2007); Average household income: $69,646 (2007); Percent of households with income of $100,000 or more: 20.1% (2007); Poverty rate: 3.4% (2000).

Education: Percent of population age 25 and over with: High school diploma (including GED) or higher: 85.2% (2007); Bachelor's degree or higher: 24.1% (2007); Master's degree or higher: 8.0% (2007).

School District(s)

Cons HSD 230 (09-12)
2005-06 Enrollment: 8,805 . . . . (708) 745-5210

North Palos SD 117 (PK-08)
2005-06 Enrollment: 2,790 . . . . (708) 598-5500

Southwest Cook Coop Sped Ed
2005-06 Enrollment: n/a . . . . (708) 687-0900

Two-year College(s)

Moraine Valley Community College (Public)
Fall 2007 Enrollment: 15,859. . . . . (708) 974-4300
2007-08 Tuition: In-state $6,272; Out-of-state $7,562

Vocational/Technical School(s)

Hair Professionals Career College (Private, For-profit)
Fall 2007 Enrollment: 179 . . . . (708) 430-1755
2007-08 Tuition: $16,400

Housing: Homeownership rate: 78.3% (2007); Median home value: $236,172 (2007); Median rent: $718 per month (2000); Median age of housing: 25 years (2000).

Safety: Violent crime rate: 6.4 per 10,000 population; Property crime rate: 96.8 per 10,000 population (2006).

Transportation: Commute to work: 93.6% car, 3.9% public transportation, 0.6% walk, 1.4% work from home (2000); Travel time to work: 18.8% less than 15 minutes, 26.0% 15 to 30 minutes, 26.5% 30 to 45 minutes, 13.1% 45 to 60 minutes, 15.5% 60 minutes or more (2000)

Additional Information Contacts

City of Palos Hills . . . . (708) 598-3400
http://www.paloshillsweb.org

PALOS PARK (village). Covers a land area of 3.776 square miles and a water area of 0.039 square miles. Located at 41.66° N. Lat.; 87.83° W. Long. Elevation is 689 feet.

Population: 4,454 (1990); 4,689 (2000); 4,760 (2007); 4,795 (2012 projected); Race: 97.3% White, 0.3% Black, 1.5% Asian, 2.3% Hispanic of any race (2007); Density: 1,260.6 persons per square mile (2007); Average household size: 2.56 (2007); Median age: 48.9 (2007); Males per 100 females: 93.0 (2007); Marriage status: 18.8% never married, 64.2% now married, 9.5% widowed, 7.6% divorced (2000); Foreign born: 8.6% (2000); Ancestry (includes multiple ancestries): 25.0% Irish, 21.7% German, 14.4% Polish, 8.0% Italian, 6.8% English (2000).

Economy: Single-family building permits issued: 14 (2007); Multi-family building permits issued: 0 (2007); Employment by occupation: 18.9% management, 28.5% professional, 7.9% services, 30.2% sales, 0.6% farming, 7.4% construction, 6.5% production (2000).

Income: Per capita income: $43,399 (2007); Median household income: $89,118 (2007); Average household income: $111,101 (2007); Percent of households with income of $100,000 or more: 44.0% (2007); Poverty rate: 4.5% (2000).

Education: Percent of population age 25 and over with: High school diploma (including GED) or higher: 94.2% (2007); Bachelor's degree or higher: 45.2% (2007); Master's degree or higher: 19.5% (2007).

School District(s)

Palos CCSD 118 (PK-08)
2005-06 Enrollment: 1,986 . . . . (708) 448-4800

Housing: Homeownership rate: 97.1% (2007); Median home value: $412,833 (2007); Median rent: $607 per month (2000); Median age of housing: 32 years (2000).

Safety: Violent crime rate: 2.1 per 10,000 population; Property crime rate: 69.4 per 10,000 population (2006).
Transportation: Commute to work: 88.3% car, 6.6% public transportation, 0.9% walk, 4.2% work from home (2000); Travel time to work: 17.5% less than 15 minutes, 25.9% 15 to 30 minutes, 25.5% 30 to 45 minutes, 13.4% 45 to 60 minutes, 17.7% 60 minutes or more (2000)
Additional Information Contacts
Palos Park Business Association. . . . . (708) 448-2700
http://www.palospark.org

PARK FOREST (village). Covers a land area of 4.925 square miles and a water area of 0 square miles. Located at 41.48° N. Lat.; 87.68° W. Long. Elevation is 712 feet.
Population: 24,770 (1990); 23,462 (2000); 22,909 (2007); 22,523 (2012 projected); Race: 46.5% White, 47.4% Black, 0.8% Asian, 6.6% Hispanic of any race (2007); Density: 4,651.3 persons per square mile (2007); Average household size: 2.53 (2007); Median age: 36.5 (2007); Males per 100 females: 88.0 (2007); Marriage status: 30.3% never married, 49.7% now married, 7.3% widowed, 12.7% divorced (2000); Foreign born: 3.1% (2000); Ancestry (includes multiple ancestries): 42.0% Other groups, 19.4% German, 11.9% Irish, 8.2% English, 6.7% Italian (2000).
Economy: Unemployment rate: 6.1% (4/2008); Total civilian labor force: 12,731 (4/2008); Single-family building permits issued: 24 (2007); Multi-family building permits issued: 0 (2007); Employment by occupation: 12.0% management, 24.1% professional, 14.9% services, 28.8% sales, 0.1% farming, 7.0% construction, 13.1% production (2000).
Income: Per capita income: $24,105 (2007); Median household income: $52,079 (2007); Average household income: $60,179 (2007); Percent of households with income of $100,000 or more: 12.4% (2007); Poverty rate: 6.7% (2000).
Education: Percent of population age 25 and over with: High school diploma (including GED) or higher: 88.1% (2007); Bachelor's degree or higher: 27.0% (2007); Master's degree or higher: 10.3% (2007).

School District(s)

Crete Monee CUSD 201u (PK-12)
2005-06 Enrollment: 4,774 . . . . (708) 367-8300
Matteson ESD 162 (PK-08)
2005-06 Enrollment: 3,399 . . . . (708) 748-0100
Park Forest SD 163 (PK-08)
2005-06 Enrollment: 2,202 . . . . (708) 668-9400
Rich Twp HSD 227 (09-12)
2005-06 Enrollment: 3,962 . . . . (708) 679-5800
Speed Seja #802 (PK-12)
2005-06 Enrollment: 385. . . . . (708) 481-6100

Housing: Homeownership rate: 73.0% (2007); Median home value: $121,677 (2007); Median rent: $606 per month (2000); Median age of housing: 44 years (2000).
Safety: Violent crime rate: 41.7 per 10,000 population; Property crime rate: 257.4 per 10,000 population (2006).
Transportation: Commute to work: 86.8% car, 10.1% public transportation, 0.8% walk, 1.7% work from home (2000); Travel time to work: 25.2% less than 15 minutes, 29.2% 15 to 30 minutes, 16.4% 30 to 45 minutes, 10.7% 45 to 60 minutes, 18.6% 60 minutes or more (2000)
Additional Information Contacts
Matteson Area Chamber of Commerce . . . . (708) 747-6000
http://www.macclink.com
Village of Park Forest. . . . . (708) 748-1112
http://www.villageofparkforest.com

PARK RIDGE (city). Covers a land area of 7.028 square miles and a water area of 0.042 square miles. Located at 42.01° N. Lat.; 87.84° W. Long. Elevation is 643 feet.
History: Named for its location on a mountain ridge, and the pleasant parklike surroundings. Park Ridge began in 1853 when George Penny started a brickyard and lumberyard. Residents called the town Pennyville, but changed it to Brickton when Penny protested. When the clay from which the bricks were produced was gone and the Chicago & North Western Railway had arrived, Brickton became a commuting suburb and changed its name to Park Ridge.
Population: 37,075 (1990); 37,775 (2000); 36,376 (2007); 35,280 (2012 projected); Race: 94.6% White, 0.3% Black, 2.9% Asian, 3.9% Hispanic of any race (2007); Density: 5,175.5 persons per square mile (2007); Average household size: 2.65 (2007); Median age: 44.4 (2007); Males per 100 females: 90.4 (2007); Marriage status: 21.9% never married, 63.5% now married, 8.8% widowed, 5.8% divorced (2000); Foreign born: 12.7% (2000); Ancestry (includes multiple ancestries): 24.1% German, 22.4% Irish, 20.8% Polish, 16.3% Italian, 7.1% Other groups (2000).
Economy: Unemployment rate: 3.5% (4/2008); Total civilian labor force: 19,705 (4/2008); Single-family building permits issued: 48 (2007); Multi-family building permits issued: 114 (2007); Employment by occupation: 23.0% management, 27.3% professional, 8.3% services, 29.5% sales, 0.0% farming, 5.2% construction, 6.7% production (2000).
Income: Per capita income: $40,699 (2007); Median household income: $82,842 (2007); Average household income: $106,882 (2007); Percent of households with income of $100,000 or more: 39.0% (2007); Poverty rate: 2.4% (2000).
Education: Percent of population age 25 and over with: High school diploma (including GED) or higher: 92.3% (2007); Bachelor's degree or higher: 46.2% (2007); Master's degree or higher: 18.2% (2007).

School District(s)

Maine Township HSD 207 (08-12)
2005-06 Enrollment: 6,993 . . . . (847) 696-3600
Park Ridge CCSD 64 (PK-08)
2005-06 Enrollment: 4,307 . . . . (847) 318-4300

Housing: Homeownership rate: 87.1% (2007); Median home value: $459,543 (2007); Median rent: $797 per month (2000); Median age of housing: 44 years (2000).
Hospitals: Advocate Lutheran General Children's Hospital
Safety: Violent crime rate: 4.9 per 10,000 population; Property crime rate: 167.6 per 10,000 population (2006).
Newspapers: Des Plaines Times (Local news; Circulation 3,503); Edgebrook Times Review (Local news; Circulation 1,465); Edison-Norwood Times Review (Local news; Circulation 3,405); Harlem-Irving Times (Community news; Circulation 4,457); Morton Grove Champion (Community news; Circulation 3,070); Norridge-Harwood Heights News (Local news; Circulation 3,813); Portage Park Times (Community news; Circulation 3,016); Rosemont Times (Local news; Circulation 1,370)
Transportation: Commute to work: 83.6% car, 10.1% public transportation, 1.8% walk, 4.0% work from home (2000); Travel time to work: 26.3% less than 15 minutes, 29.3% 15 to 30 minutes, 26.6% 30 to 45 minutes, 9.3% 45 to 60 minutes, 8.5% 60 minutes or more (2000)
Additional Information Contacts
City of Park Ridge . . . . (847) 318-5200
http://www.parkridge.us
Park Ridge Chamber of Commerce. . . . . (847) 825-3121
http://www.parkridgechamber.com

PHOENIX (village). Covers a land area of 0.451 square miles and a water area of 0 square miles. Located at 41.61° N. Lat.; 87.63° W. Long. Elevation is 600 feet.
History: Phoenix developed as a residential outgrowth of its neighbor, Harvey.
Population: 2,217 (1990); 2,157 (2000); 2,078 (2007); 2,081 (2012 projected); Race: 4.2% White, 91.4% Black, 0.0% Asian, 6.3% Hispanic of any race (2007); Density: 4,610.2 persons per square mile (2007); Average household size: 2.75 (2007); Median age: 35.4 (2007); Males per 100 females: 88.2 (2007); Marriage status: 37.6% never married, 36.8% now married, 12.8% widowed, 12.8% divorced (2000); Foreign born: 2.7% (2000); Ancestry (includes multiple ancestries): 82.6% Other groups, 3.2% African, 1.0% United States or American, 0.7% German, 0.6% Polish (2000).
Economy: Single-family building permits issued: 2 (2007); Multi-family building permits issued: 0 (2007); Employment by occupation: 7.5% management, 14.6% professional, 25.7% services, 26.5% sales, 0.0% farming, 5.6% construction, 20.2% production (2000).
Income: Per capita income: $15,469 (2007); Median household income: $31,154 (2007); Average household income: $42,520 (2007); Percent of households with income of $100,000 or more: 7.3% (2007); Poverty rate: 22.9% (2000).
Education: Percent of population age 25 and over with: High school diploma (including GED) or higher: 69.0% (2007); Bachelor's degree or higher: 6.8% (2007); Master's degree or higher: 1.5% (2007).

School District(s)

South Holland SD 151 (PK-08)
2005-06 Enrollment: 1,594 . . . . (708) 339-1516

Housing: Homeownership rate: 61.2% (2007); Median home value: $100,841 (2007); Median rent: $423 per month (2000); Median age of housing: 43 years (2000).
Safety: Violent crime rate: 116.0 per 10,000 population; Property crime rate: 227.2 per 10,000 population (2006).

Transportation: Commute to work: 87.8% car, 8.8% public transportation, 1.9% walk, 0.0% work from home (2000); Travel time to work: 25.6% less than 15 minutes, 29.2% 15 to 30 minutes, 19.2% 30 to 45 minutes, 11.9% 45 to 60 minutes, 14.2% 60 minutes or more (2000)

POSEN (village). Covers a land area of 1.179 square miles and a water area of 0 square miles. Located at 41.62° N. Lat.; 87.68° W. Long. Elevation is 600 feet.

History: Posen was settled in 1893 when a Chicago realtor sold 12,000 lots, mostly to Polish immigrants. Posen was incorporated in 1901.

Population: 4,246 (1990); 4,730 (2000); 4,865 (2007); 4,953 (2012 projected); Race: 68.6% White, 12.3% Black, 0.1% Asian, 34.4% Hispanic of any race (2007); Density: 4,125.0 persons per square mile (2007); Average household size: 2.98 (2007); Median age: 34.6 (2007); Males per 100 females: 101.3 (2007); Marriage status: 29.3% never married, 54.6% now married, 7.4% widowed, 8.8% divorced (2000); Foreign born: 10.7% (2000); Ancestry (includes multiple ancestries): 28.4% Other groups, 25.7% Polish, 22.2% German, 17.4% Irish, 7.8% Italian (2000).

Economy: Single-family building permits issued: 6 (2007); Multi-family building permits issued: 0 (2007); Employment by occupation: 6.6% management, 10.3% professional, 14.8% services, 30.5% sales, 0.0% farming, 15.9% construction, 21.9% production (2000).

Income: Per capita income: $19,393 (2007); Median household income: $54,036 (2007); Average household income: $57,846 (2007); Percent of households with income of $100,000 or more: 12.0% (2007); Poverty rate: 7.1% (2000).

Education: Percent of population age 25 and over with: High school diploma (including GED) or higher: 69.1% (2007); Bachelor's degree or higher: 8.1% (2007); Master's degree or higher: 1.3% (2007).

School District(s)

Posen-Robbins ESD 143-5 (PK-08)
2005-06 Enrollment: 1,697 . . . . (708) 388-7200

Housing: Homeownership rate: 79.2% (2007); Median home value: $144,332 (2007); Median rent: $491 per month (2000); Median age of housing: 41 years (2000).

Safety: Violent crime rate: 64.9 per 10,000 population; Property crime rate: 442.3 per 10,000 population (2006).

Transportation: Commute to work: 93.9% car, 3.4% public transportation, 0.9% walk, 0.4% work from home (2000); Travel time to work: 28.3% less than 15 minutes, 29.0% 15 to 30 minutes, 20.6% 30 to 45 minutes, 9.5% 45 to 60 minutes, 12.6% 60 minutes or more (2000)

PROSPECT HEIGHTS (city). Covers a land area of 4.258 square miles and a water area of 0.024 square miles. Located at 42.10° N. Lat.; 87.92° W. Long. Elevation is 669 feet.

Population: 15,240 (1990); 17,081 (2000); 16,282 (2007); 15,857 (2012 projected); Race: 71.9% White, 1.7% Black, 4.4% Asian, 35.4% Hispanic of any race (2007); Density: 3,823.5 persons per square mile (2007); Average household size: 2.71 (2007); Median age: 36.8 (2007); Males per 100 females: 103.0 (2007); Marriage status: 23.4% never married, 63.6% now married, 6.7% widowed, 6.3% divorced (2000); Foreign born: 36.5% (2000); Ancestry (includes multiple ancestries): 30.6% Other groups, 20.4% Polish, 19.7% German, 8.6% Irish, 6.8% Italian (2000).

Economy: Single-family building permits issued: 9 (2007); Multi-family building permits issued: 0 (2007); Employment by occupation: 15.6% management, 20.5% professional, 12.2% services, 23.8% sales, 0.0% farming, 9.7% construction, 18.2% production (2000).

Income: Per capita income: $31,309 (2007); Median household income: $63,119 (2007); Average household income: $84,563 (2007); Percent of households with income of $100,000 or more: 25.4% (2007); Poverty rate: 4.3% (2000).

Education: Percent of population age 25 and over with: High school diploma (including GED) or higher: 77.0% (2007); Bachelor's degree or higher: 28.4% (2007); Master's degree or higher: 9.1% (2007).

School District(s)

Prospect Heights SD 23 (PK-08)
2005-06 Enrollment: 1,482 . . . . (847) 870-3850

Housing: Homeownership rate: 73.6% (2007); Median home value: $292,341 (2007); Median rent: $650 per month (2000); Median age of housing: 27 years (2000).

Safety: Violent crime rate: 14.0 per 10,000 population; Property crime rate: 122.7 per 10,000 population (2006).

Transportation: Commute to work: 89.0% car, 4.6% public transportation, 1.3% walk, 2.5% work from home (2000); Travel time to work: 22.1% less than 15 minutes, 38.3% 15 to 30 minutes, 24.4% 30 to 45 minutes, 6.6% 45 to 60 minutes, 8.6% 60 minutes or more (2000)

Additional Information Contacts

City of Prospect Heights . . . . (847) 398-6070
http://www.prospect-heights.il.us

RICHTON PARK (village). Aka Richton. Covers a land area of 3.374 square miles and a water area of 0.021 square miles. Located at 41.48° N. Lat.; 87.72° W. Long. Elevation is 725 feet.

Population: 10,653 (1990); 12,533 (2000); 13,174 (2007); 13,558 (2012 projected); Race: 27.3% White, 67.3% Black, 1.5% Asian, 4.3% Hispanic of any race (2007); Density: 3,904.7 persons per square mile (2007); Average household size: 2.73 (2007); Median age: 35.5 (2007); Males per 100 females: 85.4 (2007); Marriage status: 29.4% never married, 50.5% now married, 5.8% widowed, 14.3% divorced (2000); Foreign born: 4.6% (2000); Ancestry (includes multiple ancestries): 59.0% Other groups, 10.6% German, 7.7% Irish, 4.8% Polish, 4.8% English (2000).

Economy: Single-family building permits issued: 18 (2007); Multi-family building permits issued: 0 (2007); Employment by occupation: 11.9% management, 23.2% professional, 10.7% services, 32.5% sales, 0.0% farming, 9.5% construction, 12.3% production (2000).

Income: Per capita income: $23,930 (2007); Median household income: $50,911 (2007); Average household income: $64,441 (2007); Percent of households with income of $100,000 or more: 17.6% (2007); Poverty rate: 7.0% (2000).

Education: Percent of population age 25 and over with: High school diploma (including GED) or higher: 90.4% (2007); Bachelor's degree or higher: 25.2% (2007); Master's degree or higher: 6.8% (2007).

School District(s)

ESD 159 (PK-08)
2005-06 Enrollment: 2,025 . . . . (708) 720-1300
Matteson ESD 162 (PK-08)
2005-06 Enrollment: 3,399 . . . . (708) 748-0100
Rich Twp HSD 227 (09-12)
2005-06 Enrollment: 3,962 . . . . (708) 679-5800

Housing: Homeownership rate: 65.1% (2007); Median home value: $183,033 (2007); Median rent: $621 per month (2000); Median age of housing: 24 years (2000).

Safety: Violent crime rate: 42.3 per 10,000 population; Property crime rate: 265.4 per 10,000 population (2006).

Transportation: Commute to work: 80.9% car, 13.4% public transportation, 1.8% walk, 2.0% work from home (2000); Travel time to work: 19.9% less than 15 minutes, 20.3% 15 to 30 minutes, 16.2% 30 to 45 minutes, 16.2% 45 to 60 minutes, 27.4% 60 minutes or more (2000)

Additional Information Contacts

Village of Richton Park. . . . . (708) 481-8950
http://www.richtonpark.org

RIVER FOREST (village). Covers a land area of 2.509 square miles and a water area of 0.001 square miles. Located at 41.89° N. Lat.; 87.81° W. Long. Elevation is 630 feet.

History: Named for the forest along the Des Plaines River. River Forest was settled in 1836 by the Ashbel Steele family. Another early resident was Daniel Cunningham Thatcher, a Chicago businessman who retired to River Forest in 1854. In 1862 Thatcher persuaded the Chicago & North Western Railway to build a station on his property, which was called Thatcher. For ten years, River Forest was known as Thatcher, but in 1880 the community was organized as the Village of River Forest.

Population: 11,669 (1990); 11,635 (2000); 11,233 (2007); 10,908 (2012 projected); Race: 87.3% White, 6.2% Black, 3.4% Asian, 5.0% Hispanic of any race (2007); Density: 4,477.9 persons per square mile (2007); Average household size: 2.88 (2007); Median age: 38.1 (2007); Males per 100 females: 86.0 (2007); Marriage status: 28.6% never married, 58.9% now married, 7.0% widowed, 5.6% divorced (2000); Foreign born: 7.6% (2000); Ancestry (includes multiple ancestries): 30.8% Irish, 24.9% German, 11.8% Other groups, 10.7% English, 10.5% Italian (2000).

Economy: Single-family building permits issued: 2 (2007); Multi-family building permits issued: 0 (2007); Employment by occupation: 20.7% management, 39.0% professional, 7.3% services, 25.7% sales, 0.2% farming, 2.3% construction, 4.7% production (2000).

Income: Per capita income: $53,977 (2007); Median household income: $101,622 (2007); Average household income: $152,677 (2007); Percent of households with income of $100,000 or more: 50.5% (2007); Poverty rate: 2.7% (2000).

Education: Percent of population age 25 and over with: High school diploma (including GED) or higher: 96.7% (2007); Bachelor's degree or higher: 69.4% (2007); Master's degree or higher: 38.1% (2007).

School District(s)

River Forest SD 90 (PK-08)
2005-06 Enrollment: 1,375 . . . . (708) 771-8282

Four-year College(s)

Concordia University (Private, Not-for-profit, Lutheran Church - Missouri Synod)
Fall 2007 Enrollment: 4,126. . . . . (708) 771-8300
2007-08 Tuition: In-state $21,320; Out-of-state $21,320
Dominican University (Private, Not-for-profit, Roman Catholic)
Fall 2007 Enrollment: 3,338. . . . . (708) 366-2490
2007-08 Tuition: In-state $22,450; Out-of-state $22,450

Housing: Homeownership rate: 86.6% (2007); Median home value: $534,123 (2007); Median rent: $665 per month (2000); Median age of housing: 59 years (2000).

Safety: Violent crime rate: 16.8 per 10,000 population; Property crime rate: 328.6 per 10,000 population (2006).

Transportation: Commute to work: 68.0% car, 16.3% public transportation, 9.8% walk, 5.4% work from home (2000); Travel time to work: 27.0% less than 15 minutes, 20.8% 15 to 30 minutes, 34.1% 30 to 45 minutes, 12.7% 45 to 60 minutes, 5.4% 60 minutes or more (2000)

RIVER GROVE (village). Covers a land area of 2.386 square miles and a water area of 0 square miles. Located at 41.92° N. Lat.; 87.84° W. Long. Elevation is 627 feet.

History: Triton College. Incorporated 1888.

Population: 9,961 (1990); 10,668 (2000); 10,100 (2007); 9,630 (2012 projected); Race: 89.5% White, 0.5% Black, 2.4% Asian, 13.3% Hispanic of any race (2007); Density: 4,232.3 persons per square mile (2007); Average household size: 2.47 (2007); Median age: 39.4 (2007); Males per 100 females: 94.9 (2007); Marriage status: 27.7% never married, 51.6% now married, 10.1% widowed, 10.6% divorced (2000); Foreign born: 25.1% (2000); Ancestry (includes multiple ancestries): 31.8% Polish, 17.6% Italian, 17.1% German, 14.4% Irish, 12.5% Other groups (2000).

Economy: Single-family building permits issued: 4 (2007); Multi-family building permits issued: 0 (2007); Employment by occupation: 8.3% management, 11.5% professional, 12.4% services, 34.8% sales, 0.0% farming, 12.3% construction, 20.8% production (2000).

Income: Per capita income: $23,672 (2007); Median household income: $45,472 (2007); Average household income: $57,953 (2007); Percent of households with income of $100,000 or more: 11.3% (2007); Poverty rate: 5.9% (2000).

Education: Percent of population age 25 and over with: High school diploma (including GED) or higher: 77.4% (2007); Bachelor's degree or higher: 14.4% (2007); Master's degree or higher: 4.0% (2007).

School District(s)

Rhodes SD 84-5 (PK-08)
2005-06 Enrollment: 645 . . . . (708) 453-1266
River Grove SD 85-5 (KG-08)
2005-06 Enrollment: 594 . . . . (708) 453-6172

Two-year College(s)

Triton College (Public)
Fall 2007 Enrollment: 15,658. . . . . (708) 456-0300
2007-08 Tuition: In-state $5,498; Out-of-state $6,924

Housing: Homeownership rate: 57.6% (2007); Median home value: $224,741 (2007); Median rent: $631 per month (2000); Median age of housing: 42 years (2000).

Safety: Violent crime rate: 23.5 per 10,000 population; Property crime rate: 287.8 per 10,000 population (2006).

Transportation: Commute to work: 90.2% car, 5.4% public transportation, 3.3% walk, 0.6% work from home (2000); Travel time to work: 21.5% less than 15 minutes, 27.3% 15 to 30 minutes, 27.8% 30 to 45 minutes, 14.3% 45 to 60 minutes, 9.1% 60 minutes or more (2000)

Additional Information Contacts

River Grove Area Chamber of Commerce. . . . . (708) 452-8259
http://www.vorg.us/org/cham.htm
Village of River Grove . . . . (708) 453-8000
http://www.villageofrivergrove.org

RIVERDALE (village). Covers a land area of 3.638 square miles and a water area of 0.148 square miles. Located at 41.64° N. Lat.; 87.63° W. Long. Elevation is 600 feet.

History: Named for its location along the Calumet River, by Frederick C. Schmidt. Riverdale began when George Dolton and J.C. Matthews established a ferry across the Little Calumet River in 1836. The town later became a railroad center and a steel manufacturing area.

Population: 13,671 (1990); 15,055 (2000); 14,466 (2007); 14,015 (2012 projected); Race: 8.9% White, 88.4% Black, 0.2% Asian, 2.6% Hispanic of any race (2007); Density: 3,976.7 persons per square mile (2007); Average household size: 3.10 (2007); Median age: 28.5 (2007); Males per 100 females: 86.4 (2007); Marriage status: 38.8% never married, 44.9% now married, 5.4% widowed, 10.9% divorced (2000); Foreign born: 3.3% (2000); Ancestry (includes multiple ancestries): 77.8% Other groups, 2.7% German, 2.3% Polish, 1.8% African, 1.5% Irish (2000).

Economy: Single-family building permits issued: 0 (2007); Multi-family building permits issued: 0 (2007); Employment by occupation: 8.2% management, 15.0% professional, 20.6% services, 33.4% sales, 0.0% farming, 3.7% construction, 19.0% production (2000).

Income: Per capita income: $14,589 (2007); Median household income: $39,672 (2007); Average household income: $45,029 (2007); Percent of households with income of $100,000 or more: 5.5% (2007); Poverty rate: 18.4% (2000).

Education: Percent of population age 25 and over with: High school diploma (including GED) or higher: 82.3% (2007); Bachelor's degree or higher: 11.9% (2007); Master's degree or higher: 2.1% (2007).

School District(s)

Dolton SD 148 (PK-08)
2005-06 Enrollment: 3,194 . . . . (708) 841-2290
Gen George Patton SD 133 (PK-08)
2005-06 Enrollment: 460 . . . . (708) 841-3955

Housing: Homeownership rate: 58.1% (2007); Median home value: $124,288 (2007); Median rent: $595 per month (2000); Median age of housing: 42 years (2000).

Safety: Violent crime rate: 137.1 per 10,000 population; Property crime rate: 330.4 per 10,000 population (2006).

Transportation: Commute to work: 78.0% car, 18.5% public transportation, 1.0% walk, 1.4% work from home (2000); Travel time to work: 9.6% less than 15 minutes, 23.6% 15 to 30 minutes, 25.4% 30 to 45 minutes, 17.8% 45 to 60 minutes, 23.6% 60 minutes or more (2000)

Additional Information Contacts

Riverdale Chamber of Commerce . . . . (708) 841-3311
http://www.district148.net/rcoc
Village of Riverdale . . . . (708) 841-2200
http://www.villageofriverdale.org

RIVERSIDE (village). Covers a land area of 1.973 square miles and a water area of 0.015 square miles. Located at 41.83° N. Lat.; 87.81° W. Long. Elevation is 617 feet.

History: Riverside originated in 1866 with the plan of the Riverside Improvement Company to create an ideal suburb. They commissioned Olmsted and Vaux, New York landscape architects who had designed Central Park. The site for Riverside was selected for its forested terrain, the railroad facilities, and the Des Plaines River whose winding course determined the layout of the town. Incorporated 1923.

Population: 8,774 (1990); 8,895 (2000); 8,390 (2007); 7,983 (2012 projected); Race: 94.0% White, 0.4% Black, 1.9% Asian, 7.1% Hispanic of any race (2007); Density: 4,253.1 persons per square mile (2007); Average household size: 2.52 (2007); Median age: 42.3 (2007); Males per 100 females: 93.4 (2007); Marriage status: 24.5% never married, 60.0% now married, 8.3% widowed, 7.2% divorced (2000); Foreign born: 9.0% (2000); Ancestry (includes multiple ancestries): 20.8% Irish, 18.4% Polish, 17.7% German, 13.8% Italian, 8.9% Other groups (2000).

Economy: Single-family building permits issued: 9 (2007); Multi-family building permits issued: 0 (2007); Employment by occupation: 18.9% management, 32.5% professional, 8.3% services, 30.6% sales, 0.3% farming, 3.3% construction, 6.2% production (2000).

Income: Per capita income: $39,302 (2007); Median household income: $73,302 (2007); Average household income: $98,758 (2007); Percent of households with income of $100,000 or more: 34.4% (2007); Poverty rate: 3.0% (2000).

Education: Percent of population age 25 and over with: High school diploma (including GED) or higher: 93.5% (2007); Bachelor's degree or higher: 51.2% (2007); Master's degree or higher: 22.7% (2007).

School District(s)

Intermediate Service Center 2 (07-12)
2005-06 Enrollment: 65 . . . . (708) 482-4350

Riverside SD 96 (PK-08)
2005-06 Enrollment: 1,300 . . . . (708) 447-5007
Riverside-Brookfield Twp SD 208 (09-12)
2005-06 Enrollment: 1,407 . . . . (708) 442-7500
Housing: Homeownership rate: 78.5% (2007); Median home value: $403,345 (2007); Median rent: $620 per month (2000); Median age of housing: 60+ years (2000).
Safety: Violent crime rate: 70.7 per 10,000 population; Property crime rate: 130.8 per 10,000 population (2006).
Transportation: Commute to work: 80.5% car, 13.5% public transportation, 1.9% walk, 3.7% work from home (2000); Travel time to work: 18.6% less than 15 minutes, 27.2% 15 to 30 minutes, 31.2% 30 to 45 minutes, 13.9% 45 to 60 minutes, 9.1% 60 minutes or more (2000)
Additional Information Contacts
Riverside Chamber of Commerce . . . . (708) 802-1631
http://www.riversidechamberofcommerce.com
Village of Riverside . . . . (708) 447-2700
http://riverside.il.us

ROBBINS (village). Covers a land area of 1.469 square miles and a water area of 0 square miles. Located at 41.64° N. Lat.; 87.70° W. Long. Elevation is 600 feet.
History: Robbins, named for realtor and developer Eugene S. Robbins, was organized as a residential area and incorporated in 1917.
Population: 7,498 (1990); 6,635 (2000); 6,308 (2007); 6,050 (2012 projected); Race: 4.4% White, 92.3% Black, 0.1% Asian, 3.9% Hispanic of any race (2007); Density: 4,293.4 persons per square mile (2007); Average household size: 3.33 (2007); Median age: 32.2 (2007); Males per 100 females: 91.3 (2007); Marriage status: 47.2% never married, 32.3% now married, 11.1% widowed, 9.4% divorced (2000); Foreign born: 0.6% (2000); Ancestry (includes multiple ancestries): 82.8% Other groups, 1.3% African, 0.7% United States or American, 0.5% Irish, 0.5% English (2000).
Economy: Single-family building permits issued: 23 (2007); Multi-family building permits issued: 2 (2007); Employment by occupation: 6.1% management, 12.5% professional, 29.0% services, 25.1% sales, 0.0% farming, 8.5% construction, 18.8% production (2000).
Income: Per capita income: $10,863 (2007); Median household income: $27,152 (2007); Average household income: $34,212 (2007); Percent of households with income of $100,000 or more: 4.1% (2007); Poverty rate: 35.5% (2000).
Education: Percent of population age 25 and over with: High school diploma (including GED) or higher: 67.3% (2007); Bachelor's degree or higher: 8.5% (2007); Master's degree or higher: 2.0% (2007).
School District(s)
CHSD 218 (09-12)
2005-06 Enrollment: 5,329 . . . . (708) 424-2000
Posen-Robbins ESD 143-5 (PK-08)
2005-06 Enrollment: 1,697 . . . . (708) 388-7200
Housing: Homeownership rate: 55.9% (2007); Median home value: $85,649 (2007); Median rent: $365 per month (2000); Median age of housing: 39 years (2000).
Safety: Violent crime rate: 149.0 per 10,000 population; Property crime rate: 235.3 per 10,000 population (2006).
Transportation: Commute to work: 85.5% car, 4.1% public transportation, 4.9% walk, 2.3% work from home (2000); Travel time to work: 21.2% less than 15 minutes, 33.2% 15 to 30 minutes, 15.4% 30 to 45 minutes, 16.1% 45 to 60 minutes, 14.1% 60 minutes or more (2000)

ROLLING MEADOWS (city). Covers a land area of 5.455 square miles and a water area of 0.005 square miles. Located at 42.07° N. Lat.; 88.02° W. Long. Elevation is 719 feet.
History: Named to promote the town as a pleasant place to live. Incorporated 1955.
Population: 23,056 (1990); 24,604 (2000); 23,873 (2007); 23,249 (2012 projected); Race: 77.6% White, 3.3% Black, 8.1% Asian, 23.1% Hispanic of any race (2007); Density: 4,376.4 persons per square mile (2007); Average household size: 2.77 (2007); Median age: 36.5 (2007); Males per 100 females: 102.0 (2007); Marriage status: 27.2% never married, 60.3% now married, 4.8% widowed, 7.7% divorced (2000); Foreign born: 21.3% (2000); Ancestry (includes multiple ancestries): 27.7% Other groups, 26.5% German, 14.9% Irish, 11.7% Polish, 9.4% Italian (2000).
Economy: Single-family building permits issued: 3 (2007); Multi-family building permits issued: 0 (2007); Employment by occupation: 17.5% management, 18.2% professional, 14.7% services, 29.9% sales, 0.0% farming, 6.9% construction, 12.8% production (2000).
Income: Per capita income: $29,829 (2007); Median household income: $66,630 (2007); Average household income: $81,906 (2007); Percent of households with income of $100,000 or more: 26.3% (2007); Poverty rate: 5.1% (2000).
Education: Percent of population age 25 and over with: High school diploma (including GED) or higher: 83.3% (2007); Bachelor's degree or higher: 31.6% (2007); Master's degree or higher: 9.6% (2007).
School District(s)
Palatine CCSD 15 (PK-08)
2005-06 Enrollment: 12,794 . . . . (847) 963-3000
Township HSD 214 (09-12)
2005-06 Enrollment: 12,542 . . . . (847) 718-7600
Housing: Homeownership rate: 76.3% (2007); Median home value: $245,515 (2007); Median rent: $822 per month (2000); Median age of housing: 31 years (2000).
Safety: Violent crime rate: 18.0 per 10,000 population; Property crime rate: 220.0 per 10,000 population (2006).
Transportation: Commute to work: 87.5% car, 4.4% public transportation, 2.7% walk, 3.0% work from home (2000); Travel time to work: 28.8% less than 15 minutes, 37.0% 15 to 30 minutes, 19.8% 30 to 45 minutes, 6.5% 45 to 60 minutes, 7.9% 60 minutes or more (2000)
Additional Information Contacts
City of Rolling Meadows . . . . (847) 394-8500
http://www.ci.rolling-meadows.il.us
Rolling Meadows Chamber of Commerce . . . . (847) 398-3730
http://www.rmchamber.org

ROSEMONT (village). Covers a land area of 1.743 square miles and a water area of 0 square miles. Located at 41.99° N. Lat.; 87.87° W. Long. Elevation is 636 feet.
Population: 3,995 (1990); 4,224 (2000); 4,123 (2007); 4,020 (2012 projected); Race: 80.7% White, 1.5% Black, 3.9% Asian, 41.9% Hispanic of any race (2007); Density: 2,365.6 persons per square mile (2007); Average household size: 2.50 (2007); Median age: 35.8 (2007); Males per 100 females: 109.6 (2007); Marriage status: 29.6% never married, 53.9% now married, 6.9% widowed, 9.5% divorced (2000); Foreign born: 37.3% (2000); Ancestry (includes multiple ancestries): 33.7% Other groups, 15.9% German, 13.4% Polish, 12.5% Italian, 5.8% Irish (2000).
Economy: Single-family building permits issued: 0 (2007); Multi-family building permits issued: 0 (2007); Employment by occupation: 11.6% management, 10.3% professional, 21.7% services, 27.3% sales, 0.0% farming, 6.5% construction, 22.5% production (2000).
Income: Per capita income: $20,938 (2007); Median household income: $37,212 (2007); Average household income: $52,447 (2007); Percent of households with income of $100,000 or more: 10.9% (2007); Poverty rate: 14.9% (2000).
Education: Percent of population age 25 and over with: High school diploma (including GED) or higher: 70.9% (2007); Bachelor's degree or higher: 17.3% (2007); Master's degree or higher: 5.7% (2007).
School District(s)
Rosemont ESD 78 (PK-08)
2005-06 Enrollment: 247 . . . . (847) 825-0144
Housing: Homeownership rate: 27.9% (2007); Median home value: $378,395 (2007); Median rent: $561 per month (2000); Median age of housing: 33 years (2000).
Safety: Violent crime rate: 29.7 per 10,000 population; Property crime rate: 743.1 per 10,000 population (2006).
Transportation: Commute to work: 76.3% car, 10.1% public transportation, 11.5% walk, 1.1% work from home (2000); Travel time to work: 35.6% less than 15 minutes, 31.7% 15 to 30 minutes, 18.9% 30 to 45 minutes, 8.5% 45 to 60 minutes, 5.4% 60 minutes or more (2000)
Additional Information Contacts
Rosemont Chamber of Commerce . . . . (847) 698-1190
http://www.rosemontchamber.com
Turkish American Chamber of Commerce. . . . . (773) 251-8242
http://www.turkishchamber.org

SAUK VILLAGE (village). Covers a land area of 3.804 square miles and a water area of 0.044 square miles. Located at 41.48° N. Lat.; 87.56° W. Long. Elevation is 653 feet.
Population: 10,770 (1990); 10,411 (2000); 10,491 (2007); 10,504 (2012 projected); Race: 52.0% White, 40.2% Black, 0.7% Asian, 13.5% Hispanic of any race (2007); Density: 2,758.2 persons per square mile (2007); Average household size: 3.07 (2007); Median age: 31.4 (2007); Males per 100 females: 97.8 (2007); Marriage status: 28.9% never married, 56.1%

now married, 6.0% widowed, 9.0% divorced (2000); Foreign born: 4.0% (2000); Ancestry (includes multiple ancestries): 43.4% Other groups, 18.1% German, 12.8% Irish, 8.1% Polish, 5.5% English (2000).
Economy: Single-family building permits issued: 0 (2007); Multi-family building permits issued: 0 (2007); Employment by occupation: 9.5% management, 10.8% professional, 15.6% services, 27.2% sales, 0.1% farming, 11.1% construction, 25.7% production (2000).
Income: Per capita income: $17,709 (2007); Median household income: $49,080 (2007); Average household income: $54,417 (2007); Percent of households with income of $100,000 or more: 7.3% (2007); Poverty rate: 9.6% (2000).
Education: Percent of population age 25 and over with: High school diploma (including GED) or higher: 79.5% (2007); Bachelor's degree or higher: 8.8% (2007); Master's degree or higher: 2.0% (2007).

School District(s)

CCSD 168 (PK-08)
2005-06 Enrollment: 1,797 . . . . (708) 758-1610
Housing: Homeownership rate: 81.4% (2007); Median home value: $116,036 (2007); Median rent: $648 per month (2000); Median age of housing: 30 years (2000).
Safety: Violent crime rate: 66.8 per 10,000 population; Property crime rate: 480.6 per 10,000 population (2006).
Transportation: Commute to work: 92.0% car, 3.1% public transportation, 2.2% walk, 1.8% work from home (2000); Travel time to work: 17.8% less than 15 minutes, 32.9% 15 to 30 minutes, 22.8% 30 to 45 minutes, 9.9% 45 to 60 minutes, 16.6% 60 minutes or more (2000)
Additional Information Contacts
Village of Sauk Village . . . . (708) 758-3330
http://www.saukvillage.org

SCHAUMBURG (village). Aka Schaumburg Center. Covers a land area of 19.003 square miles and a water area of 0.121 square miles. Located at 42.03° N. Lat.; 88.08° W. Long. Elevation is 794 feet.
Population: 68,706 (1990); 75,386 (2000); 74,400 (2007); 72,641 (2012 projected); Race: 73.3% White, 3.9% Black, 18.0% Asian, 7.1% Hispanic of any race (2007); Density: 3,915.2 persons per square mile (2007); Average household size: 2.37 (2007); Median age: 38.2 (2007); Males per 100 females: 95.3 (2007); Marriage status: 29.5% never married, 54.9% now married, 6.0% widowed, 9.6% divorced (2000); Foreign born: 19.1% (2000); Ancestry (includes multiple ancestries): 24.8% German, 23.2% Other groups, 15.0% Irish, 14.9% Polish, 12.6% Italian (2000).
Economy: Unemployment rate: 4.1% (4/2008); Total civilian labor force: 46,859 (4/2008); Single-family building permits issued: 25 (2007); Multi-family building permits issued: 0 (2007); Employment by occupation: 19.3% management, 25.0% professional, 8.6% services, 32.2% sales, 0.0% farming, 5.3% construction, 9.6% production (2000).
Income: Per capita income: $35,119 (2007); Median household income: $68,798 (2007); Average household income: $82,609 (2007); Percent of households with income of $100,000 or more: 26.8% (2007); Poverty rate: 3.0% (2000).
Taxes: Total city taxes per capita: $698 (2006); City property taxes per capita: $31 (2006).
Education: Percent of population age 25 and over with: High school diploma (including GED) or higher: 91.9% (2007); Bachelor's degree or higher: 39.4% (2007); Master's degree or higher: 12.6% (2007).

School District(s)

Schaumburg CCSD 54 (PK-08)
2005-06 Enrollment: 14,471 . . . . (847) 357-5000
Township HSD 211 (09-12)
2005-06 Enrollment: 13,026 . . . . (847) 755-6600

Four-year College(s)

Argosy University-Schaumburg (Private, For-profit)
Fall 2007 Enrollment: 605 . . . . (847) 969-4900
2007-08 Tuition: In-state $16,752; Out-of-state $16,752
The Illinois Institute of Art-Schaumburg (Private, For-profit)
Fall 2007 Enrollment: 1,268. . . . . (847) 619-3450
2007-08 Tuition: In-state $20,934; Out-of-state $20,934
University of Phoenix-Chicago Campus (Private, For-profit)
Fall 2007 Enrollment: 1,351. . . . . (847) 413-1922
2007-08 Tuition: In-state $12,270; Out-of-state $12,270
Housing: Homeownership rate: 69.3% (2007); Median home value: $238,449 (2007); Median rent: $918 per month (2000); Median age of housing: 22 years (2000).
Safety: Violent crime rate: 12.1 per 10,000 population; Property crime rate: 432.1 per 10,000 population (2006).
Newspapers: Chicago Tribune - Schaumburg Bureau (Local news; Circulation 0)
Transportation: Commute to work: 91.9% car, 4.1% public transportation, 0.9% walk, 2.7% work from home (2000); Travel time to work: 22.1% less than 15 minutes, 33.7% 15 to 30 minutes, 24.0% 30 to 45 minutes, 9.9% 45 to 60 minutes, 10.3% 60 minutes or more (2000)
Airports: Schaumburg Regional (general aviation)
Additional Information Contacts
Schaumburg Business Association . . . . (847) 413-1010
http://www.schaumburgbusiness.com
Village of Schaumburg. . . . . (847) 895-4500
http://www.ci.schaumburg.il.us

SCHILLER PARK (village). Covers a land area of 2.766 square miles and a water area of 0 square miles. Located at 41.95° N. Lat.; 87.87° W. Long. Elevation is 640 feet.
History: Named for Johann Christopher Friedrich von Schiller (1759-1805), a German poet. Incorporated 1914.
Population: 11,266 (1990); 11,850 (2000); 11,515 (2007); 11,245 (2012 projected); Race: 77.0% White, 2.4% Black, 5.7% Asian, 27.9% Hispanic of any race (2007); Density: 4,162.4 persons per square mile (2007); Average household size: 2.86 (2007); Median age: 36.3 (2007); Males per 100 females: 103.6 (2007); Marriage status: 27.7% never married, 58.3% now married, 6.4% widowed, 7.5% divorced (2000); Foreign born: 39.1% (2000); Ancestry (includes multiple ancestries): 29.8% Other groups, 22.2% Polish, 18.7% Italian, 13.0% German, 9.3% Irish (2000).
Economy: Single-family building permits issued: 24 (2007); Multi-family building permits issued: 41 (2007); Employment by occupation: 10.5% management, 8.7% professional, 16.7% services, 29.4% sales, 0.0% farming, 10.5% construction, 24.2% production (2000).
Income: Per capita income: $19,232 (2007); Median household income: $45,171 (2007); Average household income: $55,042 (2007); Percent of households with income of $100,000 or more: 10.8% (2007); Poverty rate: 9.2% (2000).
Education: Percent of population age 25 and over with: High school diploma (including GED) or higher: 72.3% (2007); Bachelor's degree or higher: 14.3% (2007); Master's degree or higher: 4.6% (2007).

School District(s)

Schiller Park SD 81 (PK-08)
2005-06 Enrollment: 1,286 . . . . (847) 671-1816
Housing: Homeownership rate: 53.4% (2007); Median home value: $247,774 (2007); Median rent: $594 per month (2000); Median age of housing: 36 years (2000).
Safety: Violent crime rate: 24.1 per 10,000 population; Property crime rate: 268.2 per 10,000 population (2006).
Transportation: Commute to work: 88.2% car, 4.2% public transportation, 4.8% walk, 1.8% work from home (2000); Travel time to work: 26.7% less than 15 minutes, 34.7% 15 to 30 minutes, 26.4% 30 to 45 minutes, 5.5% 45 to 60 minutes, 6.8% 60 minutes or more (2000)
Additional Information Contacts
Schiller Park Chamber of Commerce . . . . (847) 671-3040
Village of Schiller Park. . . . . (847) 678-2550
http://www.villageofschillerpark.com

SKOKIE (village). Aka Niles Center. Covers a land area of 10.041 square miles and a water area of 0 square miles. Located at 42.03° N. Lat.; 87.74° W. Long. Elevation is 607 feet.
History: Named for the Potawatomi translation of "marsh". Hebrew Theological College (1922) was moved here from Chicago in 1958. National Jewish Theater. Incorporated 1888.
Population: 59,432 (1990); 63,348 (2000); 65,302 (2007); 66,332 (2012 projected); Race: 63.7% White, 5.7% Black, 24.1% Asian, 6.9% Hispanic of any race (2007); Density: 6,503.3 persons per square mile (2007); Average household size: 2.78 (2007); Median age: 43.6 (2007); Males per 100 females: 90.4 (2007); Marriage status: 24.2% never married, 59.6% now married, 9.7% widowed, 6.5% divorced (2000); Foreign born: 37.0% (2000); Ancestry (includes multiple ancestries): 35.9% Other groups, 9.3% German, 8.9% Russian, 6.7% Polish, 6.1% Irish (2000).
Economy: Unemployment rate: 4.1% (4/2008); Total civilian labor force: 34,960 (4/2008); Single-family building permits issued: 38 (2007); Multi-family building permits issued: 0 (2007); Employment by occupation: 16.1% management, 30.2% professional, 10.5% services, 29.1% sales, 0.0% farming, 4.3% construction, 9.7% production (2000).
Income: Per capita income: $30,254 (2007); Median household income: $64,977 (2007); Average household income: $83,480 (2007); Percent of

households with income of $100,000 or more: 27.5% (2007); Poverty rate: 5.4% (2000).
Taxes: Total city taxes per capita: $647 (2006); City property taxes per capita: $390 (2006).
Education: Percent of population age 25 and over with: High school diploma (including GED) or higher: 87.3% (2007); Bachelor's degree or higher: 42.3% (2007); Master's degree or higher: 17.4% (2007).

School District(s)

East Prairie SD 73 (PK-08)
2005-06 Enrollment: 467 . . . . (847) 673-1141
Evanston CCSD 65 (PK-08)
2005-06 Enrollment: 6,468 . . . . (847) 859-8010
Fairview SD 72 (KG-08)
2005-06 Enrollment: 604 . . . . (847) 929-1050
Niles Twp CHSD 219 (09-12)
2005-06 Enrollment: 4,772 . . . . (847) 626-3000
Skokie SD 68 (KG-08)
2005-06 Enrollment: 1,616 . . . . (847) 676-9000
Skokie SD 69 (PK-08)
2005-06 Enrollment: 1,501 . . . . (847) 675-7666
Skokie SD 73-5 (PK-08)
2005-06 Enrollment: 1,068 . . . . (847) 324-0509

Four-year College(s)

Hebrew Theological College (Private, Not-for-profit, Jewish)
Fall 2007 Enrollment: 422 . . . . (847) 982-2500
2007-08 Tuition: In-state $16,935; Out-of-state $16,935
Knowledge Systems Institute (Private, Not-for-profit)
Fall 2007 Enrollment: 80 . . . . (847) 679-3135

Two-year College(s)

Computer Systems Institute (Private, For-profit)
Fall 2007 Enrollment: 277 . . . . (847) 967-5030
Zarem Golde ORT Technical Institute (Private, Not-for-profit)
Fall 2007 Enrollment: 311 . . . . (847) 324-5588

Vocational/Technical School(s)

European Massage Therapy School (Private, For-profit)
Fall 2007 Enrollment: 72 . . . . (847) 673-7595
Everest College-Skokie (Private, For-profit)
Fall 2007 Enrollment: 171 . . . . (847) 470-0277
2007-08 Tuition: $11,225

Housing: Homeownership rate: 74.7% (2007); Median home value: $328,708 (2007); Median rent: $748 per month (2000); Median age of housing: 42 years (2000).
Hospitals: Rush North Shore Medical Center (265 beds)
Safety: Violent crime rate: 17.0 per 10,000 population; Property crime rate: 299.2 per 10,000 population (2006).
Newspapers: Chicago Jewish News (Regional news; Circulation 13,500); India Abroad-Midwestern Edition (Regional news; Circulation 95,000)
Transportation: Commute to work: 85.3% car, 8.1% public transportation, 2.2% walk, 3.5% work from home (2000); Travel time to work: 22.8% less than 15 minutes, 30.9% 15 to 30 minutes, 23.3% 30 to 45 minutes, 13.2% 45 to 60 minutes, 9.9% 60 minutes or more (2000)

Additional Information Contacts

Skokie Chamber of Commerce . . . . (847) 673-0240
http://www.skokiechamber.org
Village of Skokie . . . . (847) 673-0500
http://www.skokie.com

SOUTH BARRINGTON (village). Covers a land area of 6.555 square miles and a water area of 0.309 square miles. Located at 42.08° N. Lat.; 88.15° W. Long. Elevation is 853 feet.
Population: 2,960 (1990); 3,760 (2000); 4,177 (2007); 4,447 (2012 projected); Race: 79.5% White, 1.0% Black, 16.7% Asian, 2.4% Hispanic of any race (2007); Density: 637.2 persons per square mile (2007); Average household size: 3.21 (2007); Median age: 42.7 (2007); Males per 100 females: 96.9 (2007); Marriage status: 22.6% never married, 73.8% now married, 1.4% widowed, 2.1% divorced (2000); Foreign born: 19.4% (2000); Ancestry (includes multiple ancestries): 22.0% German, 19.3% Other groups, 16.4% Italian, 11.5% Polish, 11.3% Irish (2000).
Economy: Single-family building permits issued: 71 (2007); Multi-family building permits issued: 0 (2007); Employment by occupation: 32.2% management, 27.3% professional, 3.5% services, 30.4% sales, 0.0% farming, 2.7% construction, 3.9% production (2000).
Income: Per capita income: $78,750 (2007); Median household income: $199,819 (2007); Average household income: $252,836 (2007); Percent of households with income of $100,000 or more: 77.8% (2007); Poverty rate: 2.6% (2000).
Education: Percent of population age 25 and over with: High school diploma (including GED) or higher: 97.4% (2007); Bachelor's degree or higher: 62.6% (2007); Master's degree or higher: 30.1% (2007).

School District(s)

Barrington CUSD 220 (PK-12)
2005-06 Enrollment: 9,135 . . . . (847) 381-6300

Housing: Homeownership rate: 98.7% (2007); Median home value: $933,511 (2007); Median rent: $2,000+ per month (2000); Median age of housing: 14 years (2000).
Safety: Violent crime rate: 0.0 per 10,000 population; Property crime rate: 139.8 per 10,000 population (2006).
Transportation: Commute to work: 86.9% car, 5.2% public transportation, 0.4% walk, 7.0% work from home (2000); Travel time to work: 15.7% less than 15 minutes, 35.8% 15 to 30 minutes, 23.1% 30 to 45 minutes, 11.2% 45 to 60 minutes, 14.2% 60 minutes or more (2000)

SOUTH CHICAGO HEIGHTS (village). Covers a land area of 1.535 square miles and a water area of 0.016 square miles. Located at 41.48° N. Lat.; 87.63° W. Long. Elevation is 591 feet.
History: Incorporated 1907.
Population: 3,544 (1990); 3,970 (2000); 3,857 (2007); 3,755 (2012 projected); Race: 72.5% White, 10.2% Black, 1.5% Asian, 21.1% Hispanic of any race (2007); Density: 2,512.5 persons per square mile (2007); Average household size: 2.50 (2007); Median age: 39.6 (2007); Males per 100 females: 95.8 (2007); Marriage status: 25.8% never married, 54.6% now married, 8.8% widowed, 10.8% divorced (2000); Foreign born: 7.9% (2000); Ancestry (includes multiple ancestries): 30.1% Other groups, 19.4% German, 18.3% Italian, 14.2% Irish, 11.3% Polish (2000).
Economy: Single-family building permits issued: 0 (2007); Multi-family building permits issued: 3 (2007); Employment by occupation: 7.3% management, 10.8% professional, 14.4% services, 31.6% sales, 0.4% farming, 12.5% construction, 23.0% production (2000).
Income: Per capita income: $21,784 (2007); Median household income: $45,556 (2007); Average household income: $53,210 (2007); Percent of households with income of $100,000 or more: 10.7% (2007); Poverty rate: 6.7% (2000).
Education: Percent of population age 25 and over with: High school diploma (including GED) or higher: 71.7% (2007); Bachelor's degree or higher: 6.5% (2007); Master's degree or higher: 2.5% (2007).

School District(s)

Chicago Heights SD 170 (PK-08)
2005-06 Enrollment: 3,517 . . . . (708) 756-4165
Steger SD 194 (PK-08)
2005-06 Enrollment: 1,613 . . . . (708) 755-0022

Housing: Homeownership rate: 70.8% (2007); Median home value: $143,036 (2007); Median rent: $484 per month (2000); Median age of housing: 43 years (2000).
Safety: Violent crime rate: 43.9 per 10,000 population; Property crime rate: 694.6 per 10,000 population (2006).
Transportation: Commute to work: 84.9% car, 6.5% public transportation, 6.4% walk, 0.7% work from home (2000); Travel time to work: 35.4% less than 15 minutes, 29.8% 15 to 30 minutes, 12.4% 30 to 45 minutes, 8.7% 45 to 60 minutes, 13.6% 60 minutes or more (2000)

SOUTH HOLLAND (village). Covers a land area of 7.280 square miles and a water area of 0.015 square miles. Located at 41.59° N. Lat.; 87.59° W. Long. Elevation is 600 feet.
History: Named for the province of South Holland, Netherlands, home of early settlers. South Holland was settled in 1840 by immigrants from the Netherlands. An early industry was the raising of onions.
Population: 22,035 (1990); 22,147 (2000); 21,323 (2007); 20,639 (2012 projected); Race: 35.1% White, 59.6% Black, 0.7% Asian, 5.1% Hispanic of any race (2007); Density: 2,928.9 persons per square mile (2007); Average household size: 2.90 (2007); Median age: 41.4 (2007); Males per 100 females: 89.5 (2007); Marriage status: 23.1% never married, 61.6% now married, 8.6% widowed, 6.7% divorced (2000); Foreign born: 5.1% (2000); Ancestry (includes multiple ancestries): 48.3% Other groups, 12.2% Dutch, 8.6% German, 6.4% Irish, 6.3% Polish (2000).
Economy: Single-family building permits issued: 2 (2007); Multi-family building permits issued: 0 (2007); Employment by occupation: 13.9% management, 22.7% professional, 10.9% services, 30.9% sales, 0.0% farming, 9.1% construction, 12.5% production (2000).

Income: Per capita income: $27,189 (2007); Median household income: $64,879 (2007); Average household income: $77,231 (2007); Percent of households with income of $100,000 or more: 23.7% (2007); Poverty rate: 4.6% (2000).
Taxes: Total city taxes per capita: $739 (2006); City property taxes per capita: $526 (2006).
Education: Percent of population age 25 and over with: High school diploma (including GED) or higher: 87.7% (2007); Bachelor's degree or higher: 25.7% (2007); Master's degree or higher: 9.5% (2007).

School District(s)

Dolton SD 149 (PK-08)
2005-06 Enrollment: 3,732 . . . . (708) 868-7861
Exc Children Have Opportunities (PK-12)
2005-06 Enrollment: 649 . . . . (708) 333-7880
South Holland SD 150 (PK-08)
2005-06 Enrollment: 1,136 . . . . (708) 339-4240
South Holland SD 151 (PK-08)
2005-06 Enrollment: 1,594 . . . . (708) 339-1516
Thornton Twp HSD 205 (09-12)
2005-06 Enrollment: 6,554 . . . . (708) 225-4000

Two-year College(s)

South Suburban College (Public)
Fall 2007 Enrollment: 6,260. . . . . (708) 596-2000
2007-08 Tuition: In-state $8,452; Out-of-state $10,102
Housing: Homeownership rate: 93.1% (2007); Median home value: $199,859 (2007); Median rent: $539 per month (2000); Median age of housing: 35 years (2000).
Safety: Violent crime rate: 33.9 per 10,000 population; Property crime rate: 261.2 per 10,000 population (2006).
Newspapers: Calumet City Shopper (Local news; Circulation 0); Lansing Shopper (Local news; Circulation 0); Munster Shopper (Local news; Circulation 0); Riverdale-Dolton Shopper (Local news; Circulation 0); South Holland Shopper (Local news; Circulation 0)
Transportation: Commute to work: 85.5% car, 9.4% public transportation, 1.2% walk, 3.1% work from home (2000); Travel time to work: 20.2% less than 15 minutes, 23.6% 15 to 30 minutes, 23.4% 30 to 45 minutes, 13.7% 45 to 60 minutes, 19.1% 60 minutes or more (2000)

Additional Information Contacts

South Holland Business Association . . . . (708) 596-0065
http://www.shba.org
Village of South Holland. . . . . (708) 210-2900
http://www.southholland.org

STICKNEY (village). Covers a land area of 1.928 square miles and a water area of 0.033 square miles. Located at 41.81° N. Lat.; 87.78° W. Long. Elevation is 604 feet.
History: Incorporated 1913.
Population: 5,678 (1990); 6,148 (2000); 5,856 (2007); 5,658 (2012 projected); Race: 88.5% White, 0.5% Black, 1.3% Asian, 30.3% Hispanic of any race (2007); Density: 3,038.0 persons per square mile (2007); Average household size: 2.77 (2007); Median age: 39.0 (2007); Males per 100 females: 99.0 (2007); Marriage status: 25.8% never married, 55.5% now married, 9.2% widowed, 9.5% divorced (2000); Foreign born: 16.2% (2000); Ancestry (includes multiple ancestries): 21.2% Other groups, 19.5% Polish, 14.0% German, 12.9% Czech, 9.2% Italian (2000).
Economy: Single-family building permits issued: 5 (2007); Multi-family building permits issued: 0 (2007); Employment by occupation: 6.4% management, 11.2% professional, 21.7% services, 33.3% sales, 0.5% farming, 11.9% construction, 14.9% production (2000).
Income: Per capita income: $20,580 (2007); Median household income: $47,861 (2007); Average household income: $54,183 (2007); Percent of households with income of $100,000 or more: 9.2% (2007); Poverty rate: 5.8% (2000).
Education: Percent of population age 25 and over with: High school diploma (including GED) or higher: 76.4% (2007); Bachelor's degree or higher: 8.9% (2007); Master's degree or higher: 2.2% (2007).

School District(s)

Lyons SD 103 (PK-08)
2005-06 Enrollment: 2,317 . . . . (708) 783-4100
Housing: Homeownership rate: 77.1% (2007); Median home value: $207,839 (2007); Median rent: $558 per month (2000); Median age of housing: 45 years (2000).
Safety: Violent crime rate: 4.9 per 10,000 population; Property crime rate: 257.0 per 10,000 population (2006).
Transportation: Commute to work: 76.9% car, 6.8% public transportation, 13.0% walk, 2.6% work from home (2000); Travel time to work: 27.3% less than 15 minutes, 28.5% 15 to 30 minutes, 25.5% 30 to 45 minutes, 9.3% 45 to 60 minutes, 9.4% 60 minutes or more (2000)

Additional Information Contacts

Village of Stickney . . . . (708) 749-4400
http://www.villageofstickney.com

STONE PARK (village). Covers a land area of 0.333 square miles and a water area of 0 square miles. Located at 41.90° N. Lat.; 87.88° W. Long. Elevation is 640 feet.
History: Incorporated 1939.
Population: 4,383 (1990); 5,127 (2000); 4,821 (2007); 4,587 (2012 projected); Race: 53.2% White, 2.2% Black, 1.3% Asian, 84.6% Hispanic of any race (2007); Density: 14,460.3 persons per square mile (2007); Average household size: 4.15 (2007); Median age: 28.4 (2007); Males per 100 females: 113.6 (2007); Marriage status: 34.5% never married, 55.1% now married, 4.0% widowed, 6.4% divorced (2000); Foreign born: 50.3% (2000); Ancestry (includes multiple ancestries): 74.8% Other groups, 3.6% German, 3.0% Italian, 2.9% United States or American, 2.3% Irish (2000).
Economy: Single-family building permits issued: 3 (2007); Multi-family building permits issued: 0 (2007); Employment by occupation: 0.8% management, 7.9% professional, 11.8% services, 18.9% sales, 0.5% farming, 10.2% construction, 49.9% production (2000).
Income: Per capita income: $12,301 (2007); Median household income: $39,712 (2007); Average household income: $51,079 (2007); Percent of households with income of $100,000 or more: 5.0% (2007); Poverty rate: 15.2% (2000).
Education: Percent of population age 25 and over with: High school diploma (including GED) or higher: 43.9% (2007); Bachelor's degree or higher: 4.1% (2007); Master's degree or higher: 2.1% (2007).

School District(s)

Bellwood SD 88 (PK-08)
2005-06 Enrollment: 3,239 . . . . (708) 344-9344
Housing: Homeownership rate: 60.7% (2007); Median home value: $188,407 (2007); Median rent: $583 per month (2000); Median age of housing: 36 years (2000).
Safety: Violent crime rate: 104.0 per 10,000 population; Property crime rate: 295.6 per 10,000 population (2006).
Transportation: Commute to work: 91.4% car, 3.3% public transportation, 1.6% walk, 2.1% work from home (2000); Travel time to work: 24.5% less than 15 minutes, 34.3% 15 to 30 minutes, 25.5% 30 to 45 minutes, 9.1% 45 to 60 minutes, 6.6% 60 minutes or more (2000)

STREAMWOOD (village). Covers a land area of 7.297 square miles and a water area of 0.027 square miles. Located at 42.02° N. Lat.; 88.17° W. Long. Elevation is 807 feet.
Population: 31,724 (1990); 36,407 (2000); 36,151 (2007); 35,833 (2012 projected); Race: 69.9% White, 4.8% Black, 11.4% Asian, 22.7% Hispanic of any race (2007); Density: 4,954.0 persons per square mile (2007); Average household size: 3.00 (2007); Median age: 34.9 (2007); Males per 100 females: 99.9 (2007); Marriage status: 24.8% never married, 61.6% now married, 4.5% widowed, 9.1% divorced (2000); Foreign born: 19.9% (2000); Ancestry (includes multiple ancestries): 30.3% Other groups, 21.2% German, 14.6% Polish, 13.7% Irish, 10.5% Italian (2000).
Economy: Unemployment rate: 5.4% (4/2008); Total civilian labor force: 22,864 (4/2008); Single-family building permits issued: 26 (2007); Multi-family building permits issued: 0 (2007); Employment by occupation: 14.7% management, 18.3% professional, 11.3% services, 32.1% sales, 0.1% farming, 9.3% construction, 14.1% production (2000).
Income: Per capita income: $28,337 (2007); Median household income: $74,099 (2007); Average household income: $84,688 (2007); Percent of households with income of $100,000 or more: 27.4% (2007); Poverty rate: 3.0% (2000).
Education: Percent of population age 25 and over with: High school diploma (including GED) or higher: 85.6% (2007); Bachelor's degree or higher: 27.1% (2007); Master's degree or higher: 6.8% (2007).

School District(s)

SD U-46 (PK-12)
2005-06 Enrollment: 39,656 . . . . (847) 888-5000
Township HSD 211 (09-12)
2005-06 Enrollment: 13,026 . . . . (847) 755-6600
Housing: Homeownership rate: 89.6% (2007); Median home value: $214,880 (2007); Median rent: $970 per month (2000); Median age of housing: 20 years (2000).

Safety: Violent crime rate: 12.9 per 10,000 population; Property crime rate: 223.3 per 10,000 population (2006).
Transportation: Commute to work: 93.0% car, 3.3% public transportation, 0.7% walk, 2.3% work from home (2000); Travel time to work: 14.9% less than 15 minutes, 34.3% 15 to 30 minutes, 26.8% 30 to 45 minutes, 12.6% 45 to 60 minutes, 11.3% 60 minutes or more (2000)
Additional Information Contacts
Streamwood Chamber of Commerce . . . . (630) 837-5200
http://www.streamwoodchamber.com
Village of Streamwood . . . . (630) 837-0200
http://www.streamwood.org

SUMMIT (village). Covers a land area of 2.124 square miles and a water area of 0.154 square miles. Located at 41.78° N. Lat.; 87.81° W. Long. Elevation is 614 feet.
History: Summit developed around the Corn Products Company Plant, a corn refinery. It was named for its location at the crest of the watershed between the Great Lakes and the Mississippi drainage systems. Rain falling on the east side of town drains into the Atlantic Ocean; that falling on the west side into the Gulf of Mexico.
Population: 9,971 (1990); 10,637 (2000); 10,263 (2007); 9,962 (2012 projected); Race: 62.1% White, 10.3% Black, 1.1% Asian, 58.9% Hispanic of any race (2007); Density: 4,832.6 persons per square mile (2007); Average household size: 3.25 (2007); Median age: 31.8 (2007); Males per 100 females: 106.2 (2007); Marriage status: 33.6% never married, 49.7% now married, 8.7% widowed, 8.0% divorced (2000); Foreign born: 34.1% (2000); Ancestry (includes multiple ancestries): 58.0% Other groups, 11.7% Polish, 5.2% German, 4.4% Irish, 3.0% Italian (2000).
Economy: Single-family building permits issued: 5 (2007); Multi-family building permits issued: 4 (2007); Employment by occupation: 6.3% management, 10.1% professional, 17.8% services, 24.6% sales, 0.4% farming, 10.4% construction, 30.4% production (2000).
Income: Per capita income: $16,320 (2007); Median household income: $43,350 (2007); Average household income: $52,206 (2007); Percent of households with income of $100,000 or more: 11.7% (2007); Poverty rate: 16.2% (2000).
Education: Percent of population age 25 and over with: High school diploma (including GED) or higher: 58.8% (2007); Bachelor's degree or higher: 7.5% (2007); Master's degree or higher: 1.8% (2007).
School District(s)
Argo CHSD 217 (09-12)
2005-06 Enrollment: 1,744 . . . . (708) 728-3200
Summit SD 104 (PK-08)
2005-06 Enrollment: 1,697 . . . . (708) 458-0505
Housing: Homeownership rate: 52.8% (2007); Median home value: $182,104 (2007); Median rent: $499 per month (2000); Median age of housing: 45 years (2000).
Safety: Violent crime rate: 44.5 per 10,000 population; Property crime rate: 315.0 per 10,000 population (2006).
Newspapers: Des Plaines Valley News (Regional news; Circulation 8,000)
Transportation: Commute to work: 85.0% car, 6.3% public transportation, 5.7% walk, 1.0% work from home (2000); Travel time to work: 27.0% less than 15 minutes, 34.2% 15 to 30 minutes, 21.7% 30 to 45 minutes, 9.1% 45 to 60 minutes, 8.0% 60 minutes or more (2000); Amtrak: Service available.
Additional Information Contacts
Argo-Summit Chamber of Commerce . . . . (708) 458-3033

THORNTON (village). Covers a land area of 2.334 square miles and a water area of 0.044 square miles. Located at 41.57° N. Lat.; 87.61° W. Long. Elevation is 597 feet.
History: Incorporated 1900.
Population: 2,763 (1990); 2,582 (2000); 2,394 (2007); 2,285 (2012 projected); Race: 95.6% White, 1.1% Black, 0.3% Asian, 4.9% Hispanic of any race (2007); Density: 1,025.7 persons per square mile (2007); Average household size: 2.53 (2007); Median age: 41.9 (2007); Males per 100 females: 89.1 (2007); Marriage status: 22.0% never married, 58.3% now married, 9.4% widowed, 10.3% divorced (2000); Foreign born: 1.4% (2000); Ancestry (includes multiple ancestries): 26.4% German, 20.3% Irish, 15.7% Polish, 9.5% Italian, 9.1% Dutch (2000).
Economy: Single-family building permits issued: 0 (2007); Multi-family building permits issued: 0 (2007); Employment by occupation: 6.0% management, 14.4% professional, 13.7% services, 32.6% sales, 0.0% farming, 16.1% construction, 17.2% production (2000).
Income: Per capita income: $26,004 (2007); Median household income: $53,859 (2007); Average household income: $65,737 (2007); Percent of households with income of $100,000 or more: 17.6% (2007); Poverty rate: 2.9% (2000).
Taxes: Total city taxes per capita: $894 (2006); City property taxes per capita: $737 (2006).
Education: Percent of population age 25 and over with: High school diploma (including GED) or higher: 87.1% (2007); Bachelor's degree or higher: 12.2% (2007); Master's degree or higher: 2.2% (2007).
School District(s)
Thornton SD 154 (PK-08)
2005-06 Enrollment: 282 . . . . (708) 877-5160
Housing: Homeownership rate: 85.2% (2007); Median home value: $156,890 (2007); Median rent: $548 per month (2000); Median age of housing: 44 years (2000).
Safety: Violent crime rate: 12.2 per 10,000 population; Property crime rate: 305.1 per 10,000 population (2006).
Transportation: Commute to work: 90.3% car, 6.6% public transportation, 2.2% walk, 1.0% work from home (2000); Travel time to work: 36.0% less than 15 minutes, 31.1% 15 to 30 minutes, 13.5% 30 to 45 minutes, 6.1% 45 to 60 minutes, 13.4% 60 minutes or more (2000)

TINLEY PARK (village). Covers a land area of 14.953 square miles and a water area of 0.036 square miles. Located at 41.57° N. Lat.; 87.80° W. Long. Elevation is 699 feet.
Population: 38,640 (1990); 48,401 (2000); 56,060 (2007); 60,560 (2012 projected); Race: 91.7% White, 2.2% Black, 2.9% Asian, 5.2% Hispanic of any race (2007); Density: 3,749.1 persons per square mile (2007); Average household size: 2.74 (2007); Median age: 38.3 (2007); Males per 100 females: 94.4 (2007); Marriage status: 25.2% never married, 60.3% now married, 7.1% widowed, 7.4% divorced (2000); Foreign born: 5.8% (2000); Ancestry (includes multiple ancestries): 25.4% Irish, 23.1% German, 19.7% Polish, 14.3% Italian, 8.6% Other groups (2000).
Economy: Unemployment rate: 4.0% (4/2008); Total civilian labor force: 33,403 (4/2008); Single-family building permits issued: 94 (2007); Multi-family building permits issued: 0 (2007); Employment by occupation: 15.8% management, 20.4% professional, 11.0% services, 30.2% sales, 0.1% farming, 11.4% construction, 11.3% production (2000).
Income: Per capita income: $30,845 (2007); Median household income: $73,656 (2007); Average household income: $83,701 (2007); Percent of households with income of $100,000 or more: 29.9% (2007); Poverty rate: 2.5% (2000).
Education: Percent of population age 25 and over with: High school diploma (including GED) or higher: 89.4% (2007); Bachelor's degree or higher: 25.0% (2007); Master's degree or higher: 7.5% (2007).
School District(s)
Arbor Park SD 145 (PK-08)
2005-06 Enrollment: 1,503 . . . . (708) 687-8040
Bremen CHSD 228 (09-12)
2005-06 Enrollment: 5,194 . . . . (708) 389-1175
Cons HSD 230 (09-12)
2005-06 Enrollment: 8,805 . . . . (708) 745-5210
Kirby SD 140 (PK-08)
2005-06 Enrollment: 4,485 . . . . (708) 532-6462
Southwest Cook Coop Sped Ed
2005-06 Enrollment: n/a . . . . (708) 687-0900
Summit Hill SD 161 (PK-08)
2005-06 Enrollment: 3,583 . . . . (815) 469-9103
Tinley Park CCSD 146 (PK-08)
2005-06 Enrollment: 2,407 . . . . (708) 614-4500
Housing: Homeownership rate: 85.1% (2007); Median home value: $239,889 (2007); Median rent: $661 per month (2000); Median age of housing: 18 years (2000).
Hospitals: Tinley Park Mental Health Center (100 beds)
Safety: Violent crime rate: 12.0 per 10,000 population; Property crime rate: 214.3 per 10,000 population (2006).
Newspapers: Alsip/Blue Island Star (Local news; Circulation 2,350); Calumet City Star (Local news; Circulation 2,975); Chicago Heights Star (Local news; Circulation 14,640); Chicago Tribune - Tinley Park Bureau (Local news; Circulation 0); Crete/University Park Star (Local news; Circulation 3,840); Daily Southtown (Community news; Circulation 56,305); Frankfort Mokena Star (Local news; Circulation 5,300); Harvey Markham Star (Local news; Circulation 5,150); Hazel Crest/Country Club Hills Star (Local news; Circulation 4,560); Homer Township Star (Local news; Circulation 2,075); Homewood/Flossmoor Star (Local news; Circulation

8,220); Lansing/Lynwood Star (Local news; Circulation 3,200); Matteson/Richton Park Star (Local news; Circulation 5,300); New Lenox/Manhattan Star (Local news; Circulation 5,500); Oak Forest/Crestwood/Midlothian Star (Local news; Circulation 4,950); Oak Lawn Star (Local news; Circulation 2,535); Orland Park Star (Local news; Circulation 4,325); Palos Area Star (Local news; Circulation 3,050); Park Forest Star (Local news; Circulation 7,040); South Holland/Dolton Star (Local news; Circulation 0); Tinley Park Star (Local news; Circulation 0)
Transportation: Commute to work: 86.9% car, 10.2% public transportation, 0.8% walk, 1.7% work from home (2000); Travel time to work: 20.3% less than 15 minutes, 27.7% 15 to 30 minutes, 19.4% 30 to 45 minutes, 14.0% 45 to 60 minutes, 18.5% 60 minutes or more (2000)
Additional Information Contacts
Tinley Park Chamber of Commerce. . . . . (708) 532-5700
http://www.tinleychamber.org
Village of Tinley Park . . . . (704) 444-5000
http://www.tinleypark.org

WESTCHESTER (village). Covers a land area of 3.195 square miles and a water area of 0 square miles. Located at 41.85° N. Lat.; 87.88° W. Long. Elevation is 636 feet.
Population: 17,309 (1990); 16,824 (2000); 15,936 (2007); 15,250 (2012 projected); Race: 81.0% White, 10.6% Black, 3.8% Asian, 8.2% Hispanic of any race (2007); Density: 4,987.3 persons per square mile (2007); Average household size: 2.38 (2007); Median age: 46.6 (2007); Males per 100 females: 88.2 (2007); Marriage status: 20.4% never married, 60.4% now married, 11.9% widowed, 7.4% divorced (2000); Foreign born: 9.5% (2000); Ancestry (includes multiple ancestries): 20.9% Italian, 19.9% German, 17.1% Irish, 16.0% Other groups, 15.0% Polish (2000).
Economy: Single-family building permits issued: 0 (2007); Multi-family building permits issued: 0 (2007); Employment by occupation: 17.3% management, 24.1% professional, 9.3% services, 33.1% sales, 0.1% farming, 5.7% construction, 10.4% production (2000).
Income: Per capita income: $33,842 (2007); Median household income: $67,765 (2007); Average household income: $80,523 (2007); Percent of households with income of $100,000 or more: 27.3% (2007); Poverty rate: 2.5% (2000).
Taxes: Total city taxes per capita: $521 (2006); City property taxes per capita: $359 (2006).
Education: Percent of population age 25 and over with: High school diploma (including GED) or higher: 89.0% (2007); Bachelor's degree or higher: 30.9% (2007); Master's degree or higher: 10.8% (2007).

School District(s)

Westchester SD 92-5 (PK-08)
2005-06 Enrollment: 1,101 . . . . (708) 450-2700
Housing: Homeownership rate: 93.6% (2007); Median home value: $254,967 (2007); Median rent: $776 per month (2000); Median age of housing: 43 years (2000).
Safety: Violent crime rate: 6.2 per 10,000 population; Property crime rate: 157.0 per 10,000 population (2006).
Transportation: Commute to work: 90.1% car, 5.5% public transportation, 1.9% walk, 2.4% work from home (2000); Travel time to work: 23.7% less than 15 minutes, 35.6% 15 to 30 minutes, 25.8% 30 to 45 minutes, 8.2% 45 to 60 minutes, 6.7% 60 minutes or more (2000)
Additional Information Contacts
Village of Westchester . . . . (708) 345-0020
http://www.westchester-il.org
Westchester Chamber of Commerce. . . . . (708) 343-4300
http://www.westchesterchamber.org

WESTERN SPRINGS (village). Covers a land area of 2.626 square miles and a water area of 0 square miles. Located at 41.80° N. Lat.; 87.90° W. Long. Elevation is 673 feet.
History: Western Springs was named for the mineral springs, believed to be medicinal when the community was settled by the Quakers in 1866.
Population: 11,993 (1990); 12,493 (2000); 12,484 (2007); 12,448 (2012 projected); Race: 98.1% White, 0.2% Black, 0.8% Asian, 2.0% Hispanic of any race (2007); Density: 4,753.2 persons per square mile (2007); Average household size: 2.94 (2007); Median age: 40.6 (2007); Males per 100 females: 93.6 (2007); Marriage status: 17.1% never married, 72.8% now married, 6.1% widowed, 4.0% divorced (2000); Foreign born: 3.8% (2000); Ancestry (includes multiple ancestries): 29.9% Irish, 27.8% German, 13.8% Polish, 13.5% Italian, 9.0% English (2000).
Economy: Single-family building permits issued: 64 (2007); Multi-family building permits issued: 0 (2007); Employment by occupation: 27.1% management, 34.9% professional, 4.3% services, 28.0% sales, 0.0% farming, 2.8% construction, 2.9% production (2000).
Income: Per capita income: $50,159 (2007); Median household income: $113,218 (2007); Average household income: $147,373 (2007); Percent of households with income of $100,000 or more: 56.7% (2007); Poverty rate: 0.9% (2000).
Education: Percent of population age 25 and over with: High school diploma (including GED) or higher: 97.3% (2007); Bachelor's degree or higher: 67.2% (2007); Master's degree or higher: 27.2% (2007).

School District(s)

Western Springs SD 101 (PK-08)
2005-06 Enrollment: 1,449 . . . . (708) 246-3700
Housing: Homeownership rate: 95.4% (2007); Median home value: $515,250 (2007); Median rent: $650 per month (2000); Median age of housing: 46 years (2000).
Safety: Violent crime rate: 2.4 per 10,000 population; Property crime rate: 81.4 per 10,000 population (2006).
Transportation: Commute to work: 77.0% car, 16.1% public transportation, 1.2% walk, 5.5% work from home (2000); Travel time to work: 25.3% less than 15 minutes, 23.9% 15 to 30 minutes, 22.2% 30 to 45 minutes, 16.5% 45 to 60 minutes, 12.1% 60 minutes or more (2000)
Additional Information Contacts
Village of Western Springs. . . . . (708) 246-1800
http://www.wsprings.com

WHEELING (village). Covers a land area of 8.400 square miles and a water area of 0.036 square miles. Located at 42.13° N. Lat.; 87.93° W. Long. Elevation is 650 feet.
History: Named for Wheeling, West Virginia. The first building in Wheeling was a country store established in 1830 on the Chicago-Milwaukee stage route.
Population: 30,008 (1990); 34,496 (2000); 34,696 (2007); 34,559 (2012 projected); Race: 69.3% White, 2.7% Black, 11.3% Asian, 29.1% Hispanic of any race (2007); Density: 4,130.3 persons per square mile (2007); Average household size: 2.64 (2007); Median age: 37.1 (2007); Males per 100 females: 97.3 (2007); Marriage status: 27.6% never married, 57.8% now married, 5.5% widowed, 9.1% divorced (2000); Foreign born: 31.4% (2000); Ancestry (includes multiple ancestries): 33.6% Other groups, 16.7% German, 10.8% Polish, 9.7% Irish, 6.8% Russian (2000).
Economy: Unemployment rate: 4.3% (4/2008); Total civilian labor force: 22,596 (4/2008); Single-family building permits issued: 14 (2007); Multi-family building permits issued: 72 (2007); Employment by occupation: 13.4% management, 21.7% professional, 12.4% services, 31.3% sales, 0.1% farming, 6.2% construction, 14.8% production (2000).
Income: Per capita income: $28,656 (2007); Median household income: $62,720 (2007); Average household income: $75,240 (2007); Percent of households with income of $100,000 or more: 21.5% (2007); Poverty rate: 5.3% (2000).
Education: Percent of population age 25 and over with: High school diploma (including GED) or higher: 82.5% (2007); Bachelor's degree or higher: 32.3% (2007); Master's degree or higher: 10.5% (2007).

School District(s)

Township HSD 214 (09-12)
2005-06 Enrollment: 12,542 . . . . (847) 718-7600
Wheeling CCSD 21 (PK-08)
2005-06 Enrollment: 6,725 . . . . (847) 537-8270

Two-year College(s)

Worsham College of Mortuary Science (Private, For-profit)
Fall 2007 Enrollment: 104 . . . . (847) 808-8444
Housing: Homeownership rate: 65.9% (2007); Median home value: $226,132 (2007); Median rent: $824 per month (2000); Median age of housing: 24 years (2000).
Safety: Violent crime rate: 12.3 per 10,000 population; Property crime rate: 184.5 per 10,000 population (2006).
Transportation: Commute to work: 92.3% car, 3.3% public transportation, 1.8% walk, 1.9% work from home (2000); Travel time to work: 24.6% less than 15 minutes, 38.5% 15 to 30 minutes, 22.4% 30 to 45 minutes, 6.9% 45 to 60 minutes, 7.5% 60 minutes or more (2000)
Airports: Chicago Executive (general aviation)
Additional Information Contacts
Village of Wheeling . . . . (847) 459-2600
http://vi.wheeling.il.us
Wheeling/Prospect Heights Area Chamber of Commerce & Industr . . (847) 541-0170
http://www.wphchamber.com

WILLOW SPRINGS (village). Covers a land area of 3.868 square miles and a water area of 0.110 square miles. Located at 41.73° N. Lat.; 87.87° W. Long. Elevation is 617 feet.
Population: 4,660 (1990); 5,027 (2000); 5,767 (2007); 6,182 (2012 projected); Race: 92.3% White, 0.9% Black, 2.2% Asian, 7.0% Hispanic of any race (2007); Density: 1,491.1 persons per square mile (2007); Average household size: 2.61 (2007); Median age: 43.3 (2007); Males per 100 females: 100.0 (2007); Marriage status: 23.3% never married, 62.0% now married, 6.4% widowed, 8.3% divorced (2000); Foreign born: 13.3% (2000); Ancestry (includes multiple ancestries): 25.3% Polish, 19.6% German, 12.6% Irish, 11.3% Italian, 6.1% Other groups (2000).
Economy: Single-family building permits issued: 2 (2007); Multi-family building permits issued: 0 (2007); Employment by occupation: 15.0% management, 15.9% professional, 10.3% services, 29.0% sales, 0.0% farming, 12.0% construction, 17.8% production (2000).
Income: Per capita income: $33,257 (2007); Median household income: $67,635 (2007); Average household income: $86,745 (2007); Percent of households with income of $100,000 or more: 26.9% (2007); Poverty rate: 6.2% (2000).
Taxes: Total city taxes per capita: $735 (2006); City property taxes per capita: $548 (2006).
Education: Percent of population age 25 and over with: High school diploma (including GED) or higher: 85.7% (2007); Bachelor's degree or higher: 24.4% (2007); Master's degree or higher: 10.7% (2007).

School District(s)

Willow Springs SD 108 (KG-08)
2005-06 Enrollment: 377 . . . . (708) 839-6828
Housing: Homeownership rate: 86.7% (2007); Median home value: $327,160 (2007); Median rent: $613 per month (2000); Median age of housing: 27 years (2000).
Safety: Violent crime rate: 13.3 per 10,000 population; Property crime rate: 173.0 per 10,000 population (2006).
Transportation: Commute to work: 90.7% car, 3.8% public transportation, 0.8% walk, 3.7% work from home (2000); Travel time to work: 16.3% less than 15 minutes, 26.7% 15 to 30 minutes, 29.3% 30 to 45 minutes, 12.8% 45 to 60 minutes, 14.9% 60 minutes or more (2000)

Additional Information Contacts

Village of Willow Springs . . . . (708) 467-3700
http://www.willowsprings-il.gov

WILMETTE (village). Covers a land area of 5.384 square miles and a water area of 0.006 square miles. Located at 42.07° N. Lat.; 87.72° W. Long. Elevation is 636 feet.
History: Wilmette was named for Antoine Ouilmette, a French-Canadian who settled here when his wife received the land under a government treaty in 1829.
Population: 26,685 (1990); 27,651 (2000); 26,704 (2007); 25,966 (2012 projected); Race: 88.8% White, 0.6% Black, 8.7% Asian, 2.4% Hispanic of any race (2007); Density: 4,959.9 persons per square mile (2007); Average household size: 2.78 (2007); Median age: 43.6 (2007); Males per 100 females: 92.1 (2007); Marriage status: 18.4% never married, 69.5% now married, 6.4% widowed, 5.7% divorced (2000); Foreign born: 13.2% (2000); Ancestry (includes multiple ancestries): 20.2% German, 19.4% Irish, 15.1% Other groups, 11.5% English, 7.2% Polish (2000).
Economy: Unemployment rate: 3.2% (4/2008); Total civilian labor force: 13,268 (4/2008); Single-family building permits issued: 30 (2007); Multi-family building permits issued: 0 (2007); Employment by occupation: 27.4% management, 39.5% professional, 4.5% services, 24.6% sales, 0.0% farming, 1.8% construction, 2.1% production (2000).
Income: Per capita income: $59,894 (2007); Median household income: $117,848 (2007); Average household income: $166,273 (2007); Percent of households with income of $100,000 or more: 57.7% (2007); Poverty rate: 2.3% (2000).
Education: Percent of population age 25 and over with: High school diploma (including GED) or higher: 96.8% (2007); Bachelor's degree or higher: 72.4% (2007); Master's degree or higher: 38.2% (2007).

School District(s)

Avoca SD 37 (KG-08)
2005-06 Enrollment: 676 . . . . (847) 251-3587
Wilmette SD 39 (PK-08)
2005-06 Enrollment: 3,615 . . . . (847) 256-2450
Housing: Homeownership rate: 86.7% (2007); Median home value: $654,021 (2007); Median rent: $958 per month (2000); Median age of housing: 48 years (2000).
Safety: Violent crime rate: 1.9 per 10,000 population; Property crime rate: 140.0 per 10,000 population (2006).
Transportation: Commute to work: 72.1% car, 18.7% public transportation, 1.3% walk, 7.1% work from home (2000); Travel time to work: 21.1% less than 15 minutes, 23.6% 15 to 30 minutes, 21.7% 30 to 45 minutes, 19.9% 45 to 60 minutes, 13.7% 60 minutes or more (2000)

Additional Information Contacts

Village of Wilmette . . . . (847) 251-2700
http://www.wilmette.com
Wilmette Chamber of Commerce. . . . . (847) 251-3800
http://www.wilmettechamber.org

WINNETKA (village). Covers a land area of 3.830 square miles and a water area of 0.086 square miles. Located at 42.10° N. Lat.; 87.73° W. Long. Elevation is 653 feet.
History: Named for a variation of the Algonquian translation of "beautiful". Winnetka was incorporated in 1869. The Winnetka public school system, organized in 1919 with Carleton Washburne as superintendent, gained recognition for innovative eucation.
Population: 12,174 (1990); 12,419 (2000); 12,428 (2007); 12,396 (2012 projected); Race: 96.4% White, 0.2% Black, 2.2% Asian, 1.5% Hispanic of any race (2007); Density: 3,245.0 persons per square mile (2007); Average household size: 3.05 (2007); Median age: 38.5 (2007); Males per 100 females: 94.1 (2007); Marriage status: 15.1% never married, 75.1% now married, 4.3% widowed, 5.5% divorced (2000); Foreign born: 5.1% (2000); Ancestry (includes multiple ancestries): 23.1% German, 22.4% Irish, 18.3% English, 6.3% Other groups, 5.7% Italian (2000).
Economy: Single-family building permits issued: 24 (2007); Multi-family building permits issued: 0 (2007); Employment by occupation: 37.0% management, 32.0% professional, 4.4% services, 24.1% sales, 0.0% farming, 1.5% construction, 0.8% production (2000).
Income: Per capita income: $82,768 (2007); Median household income: $188,129 (2007); Average household income: $252,123 (2007); Percent of households with income of $100,000 or more: 73.7% (2007); Poverty rate: 1.4% (2000).
Education: Percent of population age 25 and over with: High school diploma (including GED) or higher: 99.0% (2007); Bachelor's degree or higher: 84.5% (2007); Master's degree or higher: 44.2% (2007).

School District(s)

New Trier Twp HSD 203 (09-12)
2005-06 Enrollment: 4,044 . . . . (847) 446-7000
Winnetka SD 36 (PK-08)
2005-06 Enrollment: 2,105 . . . . (847) 446-9400
Housing: Homeownership rate: 89.5% (2007); Median home value: $1 million+ (2007); Median rent: $1,018 per month (2000); Median age of housing: 60+ years (2000).
Safety: Violent crime rate: 4.8 per 10,000 population; Property crime rate: 83.5 per 10,000 population (2006).
Transportation: Commute to work: 62.5% car, 26.6% public transportation, 2.0% walk, 7.6% work from home (2000); Travel time to work: 19.2% less than 15 minutes, 20.1% 15 to 30 minutes, 24.0% 30 to 45 minutes, 19.8% 45 to 60 minutes, 16.8% 60 minutes or more (2000)

Additional Information Contacts

Village of Winnetka . . . . (847) 501-6000
http://www.villageofwinnetka.org
Winnetka Chamber of Commerce . . . . (847) 446-4451
http://www.winnetkachamber.com

WORTH (village). Covers a land area of 2.384 square miles and a water area of 0.022 square miles. Located at 41.68° N. Lat.; 87.79° W. Long. Elevation is 610 feet.
Population: 11,211 (1990); 11,047 (2000); 10,623 (2007); 10,290 (2012 projected); Race: 90.0% White, 2.2% Black, 1.5% Asian, 8.0% Hispanic of any race (2007); Density: 4,456.6 persons per square mile (2007); Average household size: 2.48 (2007); Median age: 38.5 (2007); Males per 100 females: 97.3 (2007); Marriage status: 28.7% never married, 49.5% now married, 10.6% widowed, 11.1% divorced (2000); Foreign born: 9.1% (2000); Ancestry (includes multiple ancestries): 23.4% German, 22.7% Irish, 20.3% Polish, 11.9% Other groups, 10.1% Italian (2000).
Economy: Single-family building permits issued: 4 (2007); Multi-family building permits issued: 0 (2007); Employment by occupation: 7.7% management, 10.9% professional, 15.3% services, 32.6% sales, 0.0% farming, 15.8% construction, 17.7% production (2000).
Income: Per capita income: $22,510 (2007); Median household income: $46,447 (2007); Average household income: $55,376 (2007); Percent of

households with income of $100,000 or more: 11.7% (2007); Poverty rate: 9.3% (2000).
Education: Percent of population age 25 and over with: High school diploma (including GED) or higher: 81.4% (2007); Bachelor's degree or higher: 11.2% (2007); Master's degree or higher: 3.3% (2007).

School District(s)

Worth SD 127 (PK-08)
2005-06 Enrollment: 1,086 . . . . (708) 448-2800
Housing: Homeownership rate: 68.6% (2007); Median home value: $197,354 (2007); Median rent: $609 per month (2000); Median age of housing: 37 years (2000).
Safety: Violent crime rate: 8.4 per 10,000 population; Property crime rate: 114.5 per 10,000 population (2006).
Transportation: Commute to work: 90.6% car, 5.0% public transportation, 2.0% walk, 1.3% work from home (2000); Travel time to work: 25.1% less than 15 minutes, 31.7% 15 to 30 minutes, 20.1% 30 to 45 minutes, 11.9% 45 to 60 minutes, 11.2% 60 minutes or more (2000)
Additional Information Contacts
Chicago Ridge-Worth Chamber of Commerce . . . . (708) 728-7691
http://www.crwchamber.com
Village of Worth . . . . (708) 448-1181
http://www.villageofworth.com

Crawford County

Located in southeastern Illinois; bounded on the east by the Wabash River and the Indiana border; drained by the Embarrass River. Covers a land area of 443.53 square miles, a water area of 2.20 square miles, and is located in the Central Time Zone. The county was founded in 1816. County seat is Robinson.

Weather Station: Palestine 2 W — Elevation: 469 feet

	Jan	Feb	Mar	Apr	May	Jun	Jul	Aug	Sep	Oct	Nov	Dec
High	37	43	54	66	76	85	88	86	80	68	54	42
Low	20	25	35	44	54	62	66	65	56	45	36	26
Precip	2.5	2.5	3.8	4.1	4.6	3.8	3.9	3.7	3.3	2.9	3.9	3.1
Snow	6.4	4.5	2.6	0.2	0.0	0.0	0.0	0.0	0.0	tr	1.0	3.8

High and Low temperatures in degrees Fahrenheit; Precipitation and Snow in inches

Population: 19,464 (1990); 20,452 (2000); 19,778 (2007); 19,279 (2012 projected); Race: 93.2% White, 4.8% Black, 0.4% Asian, 2.1% Hispanic of any race (2007); Density: 44.6 persons per square mile (2007); Average household size: 2.60 (2007); Median age: 40.0 (2007); Males per 100 females: 109.9 (2007).
Religion: Five largest groups: 10.5% The United Methodist Church, 10.3% Christian Churches and Churches of Christ, 8.9% Southern Baptist Convention, 6.9% Christian Church (Disciples of Christ), 4.2% Catholic Church (2000).
Economy: Unemployment rate: 4.8% (4/2008); Total civilian labor force: 9,715 (4/2008); Leading industries: 34.7% manufacturing; 11.9% health care and social assistance; 11.9% retail trade (2005); Farms: 567 totaling 213,661 acres (2002); Companies that employ 500 or more persons: 2 (2006); Companies that employ 100 to 499 persons: 11 (2006); Companies that employ less than 100 persons: 435 (2006); Black-owned businesses: n/a (2002); Hispanic-owned businesses: n/a (2002); Asian-owned businesses: n/a (2002); Women-owned businesses: 330 (2002); Retail sales per capita: $16,422 (2008). Single-family building permits issued: 2 (2007); Multi-family building permits issued: 2 (2007).
Income: Per capita income: $20,589 (2007); Median household income: $39,423 (2007); Average household income: $50,281 (2007); Percent of households with income of $100,000 or more: 9.2% (2007); Poverty rate: 13.7% (2005); Bankruptcy rate: 4.28% (2007).
Education: Percent of population age 25 and over with: High school diploma (including GED) or higher: 79.5% (2007); Bachelor's degree or higher: 10.5% (2007); Master's degree or higher: 3.7% (2007).
Housing: Homeownership rate: 80.6% (2007); Median home value: $73,953 (2007); Median rent: $280 per month (2000); Median age of housing: 44 years (2000).
Health: Birth rate: 98.4 per 10,000 population (2007); Death rate: 121.4 per 10,000 population (2007); Age-adjusted cancer mortality rate: 181.2 deaths per 100,000 population (2005); Number of physicians: 9.1 per 10,000 population (2005); Hospital beds: 46.8 per 10,000 population (2004); Hospital admissions: 900.2 per 10,000 population (2004).
Elections: 2004 Presidential election results: 65.2% Bush, 34.2% Kerry, 0.1% Nader, 0.5% Badnarik
National and State Parks: Crawford County State Fish and Wildlife Area
Additional Information Contacts
Crawford County Government . . . . (618) 546-1212
http://www.crawfordcountycentral.com
City of Robinson. . . . . (618) 544-7616
http://www.cityofrobinson.com
Oblong Chamber of Commerce . . . . (618) 592-4355
http://www.theonlyoblong.com
Palestine Chamber of Commerce . . . . (618) 586-2222
http://www.pioneercity.com
Robinson Chamber of Commerce . . . . (618) 546-1557
http://www.robinsonchamber.org

Crawford County Communities

ANNAPOLIS (unincorporated postal area, zip code 62413). Covers a land area of 34.895 square miles and a water area of 0.042 square miles. Located at 39.13° N. Lat.; 87.83° W. Long. Elevation is 584 feet.
Population: 441 (2000); Race: 99.3% White, 0.0% Black, 0.0% Asian, 2.0% Hispanic of any race (2000); Density: 12.6 persons per square mile (2000); Age: 26.5% under 18, 14.7% over 64 (2000); Marriage status: 25.9% never married, 65.2% now married, 6.3% widowed, 2.6% divorced (2000); Foreign born: 0.0% (2000); Ancestry (includes multiple ancestries): 12.5% German, 12.5% United States or American, 10.3% Irish, 9.6% English, 8.1% Other groups (2000).
Economy: Employment by occupation: 9.0% management, 8.5% professional, 22.8% services, 17.5% sales, 1.6% farming, 11.6% construction, 29.1% production (2000).
Income: Per capita income: $17,743 (2000); Median household income: $41,827 (2000); Poverty rate: 14.7% (2000).
Education: Percent of population age 25 and over with: High school diploma (including GED) or higher: 86.2% (2000); Bachelor's degree or higher: 7.4% (2000).
Housing: Homeownership rate: 88.4% (2000); Median home value: $34,800 (2000); Median rent: $325 per month (2000); Median age of housing: 41 years (2000).
Transportation: Commute to work: 89.4% car, 0.0% public transportation, 1.6% walk, 9.0% work from home (2000); Travel time to work: 12.2% less than 15 minutes, 63.4% 15 to 30 minutes, 15.1% 30 to 45 minutes, 1.7% 45 to 60 minutes, 7.6% 60 minutes or more (2000)

FLAT ROCK (village). Covers a land area of 0.856 square miles and a water area of 0 square miles. Located at 38.90° N. Lat.; 87.67° W. Long. Elevation is 502 feet.
Population: 426 (1990); 415 (2000); 351 (2007); 356 (2012 projected); Race: 96.6% White, 1.7% Black, 1.1% Asian, 0.0% Hispanic of any race (2007); Density: 410.2 persons per square mile (2007); Average household size: 2.49 (2007); Median age: 37.2 (2007); Males per 100 females: 87.7 (2007); Marriage status: 19.1% never married, 61.4% now married, 10.4% widowed, 9.0% divorced (2000); Foreign born: 0.5% (2000); Ancestry (includes multiple ancestries): 27.7% United States or American, 17.1% German, 11.8% English, 6.3% Irish, 3.6% Other groups (2000).
Economy: Employment by occupation: 3.7% management, 13.9% professional, 16.0% services, 19.8% sales, 0.0% farming, 11.8% construction, 34.8% production (2000).
Income: Per capita income: $19,779 (2007); Median household income: $47,031 (2007); Average household income: $49,238 (2007); Percent of households with income of $100,000 or more: 3.5% (2007); Poverty rate: 12.6% (2000).
Education: Percent of population age 25 and over with: High school diploma (including GED) or higher: 81.3% (2007); Bachelor's degree or higher: 5.4% (2007); Master's degree or higher: 2.1% (2007).
Housing: Homeownership rate: 92.9% (2007); Median home value: $58,684 (2007); Median rent: $188 per month (2000); Median age of housing: 59 years (2000).
Transportation: Commute to work: 94.1% car, 1.6% public transportation, 1.6% walk, 2.7% work from home (2000); Travel time to work: 33.5% less than 15 minutes, 44.5% 15 to 30 minutes, 17.6% 30 to 45 minutes, 1.6% 45 to 60 minutes, 2.7% 60 minutes or more (2000)

HUTSONVILLE (village). Covers a land area of 0.693 square miles and a water area of 0 square miles. Located at 39.10° N. Lat.; 87.65° W. Long. Elevation is 436 feet.
Population: 627 (1990); 568 (2000); 480 (2007); 478 (2012 projected); Race: 98.8% White, 0.0% Black, 0.0% Asian, 0.6% Hispanic of any race (2007); Density: 692.7 persons per square mile (2007); Average household

size: 2.32 (2007); Median age: 42.1 (2007); Males per 100 females: 94.3 (2007); Marriage status: 22.5% never married, 54.8% now married, 10.4% widowed, 12.3% divorced (2000); Foreign born: 0.4% (2000); Ancestry (includes multiple ancestries): 17.0% German, 13.5% Irish, 9.3% English, 7.6% Other groups, 3.7% United States or American (2000).
Economy: Single-family building permits issued: 0 (2007); Multi-family building permits issued: 2 (2007); Employment by occupation: 5.4% management, 12.4% professional, 22.0% services, 17.0% sales, 0.8% farming, 8.9% construction, 33.6% production (2000).
Income: Per capita income: $17,859 (2007); Median household income: $38,125 (2007); Average household income: $41,413 (2007); Percent of households with income of $100,000 or more: 4.3% (2007); Poverty rate: 15.6% (2000).
Education: Percent of population age 25 and over with: High school diploma (including GED) or higher: 81.4% (2007); Bachelor's degree or higher: 9.0% (2007); Master's degree or higher: 2.9% (2007).

School District(s)

Hutsonville CUSD 1 (PK-12)
2005-06 Enrollment: 395 . . . . (618) 563-4912

Housing: Homeownership rate: 75.8% (2007); Median home value: $56,304 (2007); Median rent: $225 per month (2000); Median age of housing: 52 years (2000).
Safety: Violent crime rate: 49.5 per 10,000 population; Property crime rate: 49.5 per 10,000 population (2006).
Transportation: Commute to work: 90.1% car, 0.8% public transportation, 7.5% walk, 0.8% work from home (2000); Travel time to work: 43.8% less than 15 minutes, 28.3% 15 to 30 minutes, 11.2% 30 to 45 minutes, 7.6% 45 to 60 minutes, 9.2% 60 minutes or more (2000)

OBLONG (village). Covers a land area of 0.950 square miles and a water area of 0.009 square miles. Located at 39.00° N. Lat.; 87.90° W. Long. Elevation is 512 feet.
History: Incorporated 1883.
Population: 1,621 (1990); 1,580 (2000); 1,528 (2007); 1,507 (2012 projected); Race: 99.0% White, 0.3% Black, 0.1% Asian, 0.3% Hispanic of any race (2007); Density: 1,608.1 persons per square mile (2007); Average household size: 2.31 (2007); Median age: 42.2 (2007); Males per 100 females: 85.0 (2007); Marriage status: 17.0% never married, 55.7% now married, 13.4% widowed, 13.8% divorced (2000); Foreign born: 0.4% (2000); Ancestry (includes multiple ancestries): 23.3% United States or American, 14.5% German, 10.1% English, 6.6% Irish, 6.2% Other groups (2000).
Economy: Employment by occupation: 5.7% management, 13.3% professional, 18.3% services, 17.9% sales, 1.1% farming, 8.5% construction, 35.2% production (2000).
Income: Per capita income: $17,538 (2007); Median household income: $32,675 (2007); Average household income: $39,985 (2007); Percent of households with income of $100,000 or more: 4.2% (2007); Poverty rate: 9.9% (2000).
Education: Percent of population age 25 and over with: High school diploma (including GED) or higher: 77.4% (2007); Bachelor's degree or higher: 11.7% (2007); Master's degree or higher: 5.2% (2007).

School District(s)

Oblong CUSD 4 (PK-12)
2005-06 Enrollment: 749 . . . . (618) 592-3933

Housing: Homeownership rate: 79.0% (2007); Median home value: $63,559 (2007); Median rent: $246 per month (2000); Median age of housing: 46 years (2000).
Safety: Violent crime rate: 51.5 per 10,000 population; Property crime rate: 167.3 per 10,000 population (2006).
Newspapers: Oblong Gem (Community news; Circulation 2,000)
Transportation: Commute to work: 93.8% car, 0.2% public transportation, 2.5% walk, 2.8% work from home (2000); Travel time to work: 33.9% less than 15 minutes, 42.8% 15 to 30 minutes, 13.8% 30 to 45 minutes, 4.1% 45 to 60 minutes, 5.4% 60 minutes or more (2000)

Additional Information Contacts

Oblong Chamber of Commerce . . . . (618) 592-4355
http://www.theonlyoblong.com

PALESTINE (village). Covers a land area of 0.746 square miles and a water area of 0 square miles. Located at 39.00° N. Lat.; 87.61° W. Long. Elevation is 449 feet.
History: Palestine was the location in 1830 of one of the six land offices in Illinois, where settlers came to register their land claims.
Population: 1,619 (1990); 1,366 (2000); 1,305 (2007); 1,280 (2012 projected); Race: 99.5% White, 0.1% Black, 0.1% Asian, 0.9% Hispanic of any race (2007); Density: 1,750.4 persons per square mile (2007); Average household size: 2.14 (2007); Median age: 42.2 (2007); Males per 100 females: 90.0 (2007); Marriage status: 16.6% never married, 60.6% now married, 9.9% widowed, 13.0% divorced (2000); Foreign born: 0.7% (2000); Ancestry (includes multiple ancestries): 19.2% United States or American, 14.7% German, 12.9% Irish, 10.2% English, 9.6% Other groups (2000).
Economy: Employment by occupation: 5.0% management, 10.5% professional, 12.5% services, 22.8% sales, 0.0% farming, 12.5% construction, 36.8% production (2000).
Income: Per capita income: $18,707 (2007); Median household income: $33,444 (2007); Average household income: $40,020 (2007); Percent of households with income of $100,000 or more: 4.9% (2007); Poverty rate: 15.8% (2000).
Education: Percent of population age 25 and over with: High school diploma (including GED) or higher: 78.9% (2007); Bachelor's degree or higher: 9.6% (2007); Master's degree or higher: 4.3% (2007).

School District(s)

Palestine CUSD 3 (PK-12)
2005-06 Enrollment: 443 . . . . (618) 586-2713

Housing: Homeownership rate: 78.0% (2007); Median home value: $58,727 (2007); Median rent: $256 per month (2000); Median age of housing: 53 years (2000).
Safety: Violent crime rate: 74.5 per 10,000 population; Property crime rate: 260.8 per 10,000 population (2006).
Transportation: Commute to work: 93.0% car, 0.3% public transportation, 2.7% walk, 3.3% work from home (2000); Travel time to work: 38.9% less than 15 minutes, 43.8% 15 to 30 minutes, 12.5% 30 to 45 minutes, 2.2% 45 to 60 minutes, 2.6% 60 minutes or more (2000)

Additional Information Contacts

Palestine Chamber of Commerce . . . . (618) 586-2222
http://www.pioneercity.com

ROBINSON (city). County seat. Covers a land area of 3.625 square miles and a water area of 0.063 square miles. Located at 39.00° N. Lat.; 87.73° W. Long. Elevation is 531 feet.
History: Lincoln Trail College here. Incorporated 1875.
Population: 6,951 (1990); 6,822 (2000); 6,393 (2007); 6,067 (2012 projected); Race: 96.2% White, 0.9% Black, 0.8% Asian, 1.9% Hispanic of any race (2007); Density: 1,763.5 persons per square mile (2007); Average household size: 2.33 (2007); Median age: 40.3 (2007); Males per 100 females: 90.6 (2007); Marriage status: 21.6% never married, 54.8% now married, 11.6% widowed, 11.9% divorced (2000); Foreign born: 0.9% (2000); Ancestry (includes multiple ancestries): 21.8% United States or American, 18.7% German, 10.2% English, 9.4% Irish, 8.6% Other groups (2000).
Economy: Single-family building permits issued: 2 (2007); Multi-family building permits issued: 0 (2007); Employment by occupation: 8.4% management, 14.8% professional, 18.7% services, 19.9% sales, 0.5% farming, 10.0% construction, 27.7% production (2000).
Income: Per capita income: $19,743 (2007); Median household income: $35,680 (2007); Average household income: $45,337 (2007); Percent of households with income of $100,000 or more: 7.2% (2007); Poverty rate: 11.1% (2000).
Education: Percent of population age 25 and over with: High school diploma (including GED) or higher: 82.9% (2007); Bachelor's degree or higher: 13.1% (2007); Master's degree or higher: 4.0% (2007).

School District(s)

Clay/Cwford/Jsper/Lwrnce/Rhland
2005-06 Enrollment: n/a . . . . (618) 392-4631
Dept of Corrections Sch Dist 428 (08-12)
2005-06 Enrollment: 2,271 . . . . (217) 522-2666
Robinson CUSD 2 (PK-12)
2005-06 Enrollment: 1,751 . . . . (618) 544-7511
Twin Rivers Career & Tech Ed Sys
2005-06 Enrollment: n/a . . . . (618) 544-8664

Two-year College(s)

Illinois Eastern Community Colleges-Lincoln Trail College (Public)
Fall 2007 Enrollment: 1,445. . . . . (618) 393-2982
2007-08 Tuition: In-state $6,117; Out-of-state $7,615

Housing: Homeownership rate: 72.6% (2007); Median home value: $71,088 (2007); Median rent: $300 per month (2000); Median age of housing: 46 years (2000).

Hospitals: Crawford Memorial Hospital (93 beds)
Safety: Violent crime rate: 32.5 per 10,000 population; Property crime rate: 296.7 per 10,000 population (2006).
Newspapers: Robinson Constitution (Community news; Circulation 700); Robinson Daily News (Community news; Circulation 7,059)
Transportation: Commute to work: 93.1% car, 0.4% public transportation, 2.2% walk, 3.3% work from home (2000); Travel time to work: 73.8% less than 15 minutes, 10.2% 15 to 30 minutes, 8.9% 30 to 45 minutes, 3.5% 45 to 60 minutes, 3.8% 60 minutes or more (2000)
Airports: Robinson Municipal (general aviation)
Additional Information Contacts
City of Robinson. . . . . (618) 544-7616
http://www.cityofrobinson.com
Robinson Chamber of Commerce . . . . (618) 546-1557
http://www.robinsonchamber.org

STOY (village). Covers a land area of 0.889 square miles and a water area of 0 square miles. Located at 38.99° N. Lat.; 87.83° W. Long. Elevation is 489 feet.
Population: 135 (1990); 119 (2000); 120 (2007); 117 (2012 projected); Race: 100.0% White, 0.0% Black, 0.0% Asian, 0.0% Hispanic of any race (2007); Density: 135.0 persons per square mile (2007); Average household size: 2.31 (2007); Median age: 40.7 (2007); Males per 100 females: 100.0 (2007); Marriage status: 16.5% never married, 70.6% now married, 4.7% widowed, 8.2% divorced (2000); Foreign born: 0.0% (2000); Ancestry (includes multiple ancestries): 33.3% United States or American, 27.1% German, 13.5% Other groups, 6.3% Irish, 5.2% French (except Basque) (2000).
Economy: Employment by occupation: 4.1% management, 8.2% professional, 12.2% services, 16.3% sales, 0.0% farming, 8.2% construction, 51.0% production (2000).
Income: Per capita income: $21,958 (2007); Median household income: $50,000 (2007); Average household income: $50,673 (2007); Percent of households with income of $100,000 or more: 5.8% (2007); Poverty rate: 1.0% (2000).
Education: Percent of population age 25 and over with: High school diploma (including GED) or higher: 83.1% (2007); Bachelor's degree or higher: 0.0% (2007); Master's degree or higher: 0.0% (2007).
Housing: Homeownership rate: 86.5% (2007); Median home value: $82,778 (2007); Median rent: $213 per month (2000); Median age of housing: 43 years (2000).
Transportation: Commute to work: 100.0% car, 0.0% public transportation, 0.0% walk, 0.0% work from home (2000); Travel time to work: 75.5% less than 15 minutes, 24.5% 15 to 30 minutes, 0.0% 30 to 45 minutes, 0.0% 45 to 60 minutes, 0.0% 60 minutes or more (2000)

WEST YORK (unincorporated postal area, zip code 62478). Covers a land area of 23.200 square miles and a water area of 0.037 square miles. Located at 39.17° N. Lat.; 87.72° W. Long. Elevation is 508 feet.
Population: 414 (2000); Race: 100.0% White, 0.0% Black, 0.0% Asian, 4.1% Hispanic of any race (2000); Density: 17.8 persons per square mile (2000); Age: 23.7% under 18, 12.5% over 64 (2000); Marriage status: 8.0% never married, 80.3% now married, 6.3% widowed, 5.3% divorced (2000); Foreign born: 1.0% (2000); Ancestry (includes multiple ancestries): 18.1% United States or American, 13.5% German, 9.9% English, 5.9% Other groups, 2.3% Norwegian (2000).
Economy: Employment by occupation: 19.6% management, 9.5% professional, 4.8% services, 21.4% sales, 5.4% farming, 8.3% construction, 31.0% production (2000).
Income: Per capita income: $18,541 (2000); Median household income: $32,125 (2000); Poverty rate: 7.9% (2000).
Education: Percent of population age 25 and over with: High school diploma (including GED) or higher: 91.2% (2000); Bachelor's degree or higher: 9.2% (2000).
Housing: Homeownership rate: 82.9% (2000); Median home value: $37,300 (2000); Median rent: $153 per month (2000); Median age of housing: 44 years (2000).
Transportation: Commute to work: 84.4% car, 0.0% public transportation, 3.1% walk, 12.5% work from home (2000); Travel time to work: 21.4% less than 15 minutes, 46.4% 15 to 30 minutes, 10.7% 30 to 45 minutes, 15.7% 45 to 60 minutes, 5.7% 60 minutes or more (2000)

Cumberland County

Located in southeast central Illinois; drained by the Embarrass River. Covers a land area of 346.02 square miles, a water area of 0.98 square miles, and is located in the Central Time Zone. The county was founded in 1843. County seat is Toledo.

Cumberland County is part of the Charleston-Mattoon, IL Micropolitan Statistical Area. The entire metro area includes: Coles County, IL; Cumberland County, IL

Population: 10,670 (1990); 11,253 (2000); 10,905 (2007); 10,638 (2012 projected); Race: 98.6% White, 0.4% Black, 0.2% Asian, 0.6% Hispanic of any race (2007); Density: 31.5 persons per square mile (2007); Average household size: 2.54 (2007); Median age: 39.7 (2007); Males per 100 females: 96.8 (2007).
Religion: Five largest groups: 8.5% Christian Churches and Churches of Christ, 8.3% Catholic Church, 7.4% Southern Baptist Convention, 6.9% The United Methodist Church, 2.0% Churches of God, General Conference (2000).
Economy: Unemployment rate: 5.5% (4/2008); Total civilian labor force: 5,988 (4/2008); Leading industries: 24.3% manufacturing; 18.3% health care and social assistance; 13.0% retail trade (2005); Farms: 583 totaling 173,363 acres (2002); Companies that employ 500 or more persons: 0 (2006); Companies that employ 100 to 499 persons: 1 (2006); Companies that employ less than 100 persons: 187 (2006); Black-owned businesses: n/a (2002); Hispanic-owned businesses: n/a (2002); Asian-owned businesses: n/a (2002); Women-owned businesses: n/a (2002); Retail sales per capita: $5,167 (2008). Single-family building permits issued: 3 (2007); Multi-family building permits issued: 0 (2007).
Income: Per capita income: $20,227 (2007); Median household income: $42,519 (2007); Average household income: $50,326 (2007); Percent of households with income of $100,000 or more: 7.4% (2007); Poverty rate: 10.9% (2005); Bankruptcy rate: 3.69% (2007).
Education: Percent of population age 25 and over with: High school diploma (including GED) or higher: 79.9% (2007); Bachelor's degree or higher: 10.2% (2007); Master's degree or higher: 3.2% (2007).
Housing: Homeownership rate: 82.3% (2007); Median home value: $103,607 (2007); Median rent: $275 per month (2000); Median age of housing: 34 years (2000).
Health: Birth rate: 126.4 per 10,000 population (2007); Death rate: 122.7 per 10,000 population (2007); Age-adjusted cancer mortality rate: 175.0 deaths per 100,000 population (2005); Number of physicians: 0.9 per 10,000 population (2005); Hospital beds: 0.0 per 10,000 population (2004); Hospital admissions: 0.0 per 10,000 population (2004).
Elections: 2004 Presidential election results: 64.6% Bush, 34.4% Kerry, 0.1% Nader, 0.9% Badnarik
Additional Information Contacts
Cumberland County Government . . . . (217) 849-2631

Neoga Area Chamber of Commerce . . . . (217) 895-3237

Cumberland County Communities

GREENUP (village). Covers a land area of 1.700 square miles and a water area of 0.002 square miles. Located at 39.24° N. Lat.; 88.16° W. Long. Elevation is 591 feet.
History: Greenup was named for William C. Greenup, the first clerk of the Illinois Territorial Legislature, who donated the townsite. The village was incorporated in 1836, and served for a time as the seat of Cumberland County.
Population: 1,637 (1990); 1,532 (2000); 1,434 (2007); 1,403 (2012 projected); Race: 98.5% White, 0.2% Black, 0.3% Asian, 0.1% Hispanic of any race (2007); Density: 843.5 persons per square mile (2007); Average household size: 2.18 (2007); Median age: 44.6 (2007); Males per 100 females: 83.8 (2007); Marriage status: 18.7% never married, 52.9% now married, 15.3% widowed, 13.1% divorced (2000); Foreign born: 1.4% (2000); Ancestry (includes multiple ancestries): 18.4% German, 18.1% United States or American, 9.4% Irish, 9.0% English, 5.0% Other groups (2000).
Economy: Employment by occupation: 8.5% management, 9.3% professional, 15.9% services, 24.9% sales, 0.3% farming, 10.5% construction, 30.6% production (2000).
Income: Per capita income: $20,832 (2007); Median household income: $34,628 (2007); Average household income: $42,709 (2007); Percent of

households with income of $100,000 or more: 4.6% (2007); Poverty rate: 13.2% (2000).
Education: Percent of population age 25 and over with: High school diploma (including GED) or higher: 74.0% (2007); Bachelor's degree or higher: 9.7% (2007); Master's degree or higher: 3.3% (2007).
Housing: Homeownership rate: 75.5% (2007); Median home value: $85,593 (2007); Median rent: $272 per month (2000); Median age of housing: 44 years (2000).
Safety: Violent crime rate: 113.8 per 10,000 population; Property crime rate: 301.2 per 10,000 population (2006).
Newspapers: Greenup Press (National news; Circulation 1,700)
Transportation: Commute to work: 93.4% car, 0.0% public transportation, 1.2% walk, 3.6% work from home (2000); Travel time to work: 44.0% less than 15 minutes, 20.5% 15 to 30 minutes, 25.0% 30 to 45 minutes, 4.9% 45 to 60 minutes, 5.6% 60 minutes or more (2000)

JEWETT (village). Covers a land area of 1.006 square miles and a water area of 0 square miles. Located at 39.20° N. Lat.; 88.24° W. Long. Elevation is 584 feet.
History: The village of Jewett grew from the town of Pleasantville, which had been a stagecoach stop in the mid-1800's.
Population: 194 (1990); 232 (2000); 214 (2007); 208 (2012 projected); Race: 100.0% White, 0.0% Black, 0.0% Asian, 0.0% Hispanic of any race (2007); Density: 212.8 persons per square mile (2007); Average household size: 2.74 (2007); Median age: 36.0 (2007); Males per 100 females: 92.8 (2007); Marriage status: 29.2% never married, 51.7% now married, 11.2% widowed, 7.9% divorced (2000); Foreign born: 0.0% (2000); Ancestry (includes multiple ancestries): 21.4% United States or American, 14.5% German, 8.6% Irish, 3.2% English, 2.7% Other groups (2000).
Economy: Employment by occupation: 2.2% management, 4.4% professional, 10.0% services, 23.3% sales, 2.2% farming, 8.9% construction, 48.9% production (2000).
Income: Per capita income: $15,164 (2007); Median household income: $33,571 (2007); Average household income: $41,603 (2007); Percent of households with income of $100,000 or more: 5.1% (2007); Poverty rate: 19.5% (2000).
Education: Percent of population age 25 and over with: High school diploma (including GED) or higher: 69.0% (2007); Bachelor's degree or higher: 4.2% (2007); Master's degree or higher: 2.8% (2007).
Housing: Homeownership rate: 89.7% (2007); Median home value: $59,091 (2007); Median rent: $313 per month (2000); Median age of housing: 37 years (2000).
Transportation: Commute to work: 100.0% car, 0.0% public transportation, 0.0% walk, 0.0% work from home (2000); Travel time to work: 8.9% less than 15 minutes, 33.3% 15 to 30 minutes, 52.2% 30 to 45 minutes, 5.6% 45 to 60 minutes, 0.0% 60 minutes or more (2000)

NEOGA (city). Covers a land area of 1.350 square miles and a water area of 0 square miles. Located at 39.32° N. Lat.; 88.45° W. Long. Elevation is 659 feet.
History: The name of Neoga is of Indian origin, meaning "place of the Deity."
Population: 1,674 (1990); 1,854 (2000); 1,760 (2007); 1,725 (2012 projected); Race: 97.0% White, 0.9% Black, 0.4% Asian, 1.4% Hispanic of any race (2007); Density: 1,303.3 persons per square mile (2007); Average household size: 2.78 (2007); Median age: 34.2 (2007); Males per 100 females: 89.9 (2007); Marriage status: 21.7% never married, 61.7% now married, 5.2% widowed, 11.5% divorced (2000); Foreign born: 0.3% (2000); Ancestry (includes multiple ancestries): 25.7% German, 20.5% United States or American, 9.3% Irish, 9.0% English, 8.9% Other groups (2000).
Economy: Single-family building permits issued: 2 (2007); Multi-family building permits issued: 0 (2007); Employment by occupation: 5.0% management, 13.5% professional, 16.4% services, 25.9% sales, 0.3% farming, 10.6% construction, 28.3% production (2000).
Income: Per capita income: $19,216 (2007); Median household income: $42,222 (2007); Average household income: $49,834 (2007); Percent of households with income of $100,000 or more: 7.4% (2007); Poverty rate: 11.8% (2000).
Education: Percent of population age 25 and over with: High school diploma (including GED) or higher: 80.9% (2007); Bachelor's degree or higher: 12.1% (2007); Master's degree or higher: 4.3% (2007).

School District(s)

Neoga CUSD 3 (PK-12)
2005-06 Enrollment: 827 . . . . (217) 895-2201

Housing: Homeownership rate: 76.0% (2007); Median home value: $101,613 (2007); Median rent: $281 per month (2000); Median age of housing: 31 years (2000).
Safety: Violent crime rate: 79.1 per 10,000 population; Property crime rate: 186.4 per 10,000 population (2006).
Newspapers: Neoga News (Community news; Circulation 800)
Transportation: Commute to work: 94.4% car, 0.5% public transportation, 3.1% walk, 1.7% work from home (2000); Travel time to work: 24.2% less than 15 minutes, 46.4% 15 to 30 minutes, 19.6% 30 to 45 minutes, 4.2% 45 to 60 minutes, 5.6% 60 minutes or more (2000)
Additional Information Contacts
Neoga Area Chamber of Commerce . . . . (217) 895-3237

TOLEDO (village). County seat. Covers a land area of 0.798 square miles and a water area of 0 square miles. Located at 39.27° N. Lat.; 88.24° W. Long. Elevation is 597 feet.
Population: 1,272 (1990); 1,166 (2000); 1,090 (2007); 1,052 (2012 projected); Race: 99.1% White, 0.0% Black, 0.0% Asian, 0.2% Hispanic of any race (2007); Density: 1,365.7 persons per square mile (2007); Average household size: 2.26 (2007); Median age: 38.1 (2007); Males per 100 females: 91.6 (2007); Marriage status: 22.6% never married, 46.7% now married, 13.3% widowed, 17.3% divorced (2000); Foreign born: 0.4% (2000); Ancestry (includes multiple ancestries): 28.8% United States or American, 19.4% German, 10.3% Irish, 6.3% English, 5.9% Other groups (2000).
Economy: Employment by occupation: 6.6% management, 12.8% professional, 19.6% services, 19.5% sales, 1.4% farming, 5.8% construction, 34.2% production (2000).
Income: Per capita income: $16,122 (2007); Median household income: $29,432 (2007); Average household income: $35,757 (2007); Percent of households with income of $100,000 or more: 1.9% (2007); Poverty rate: 16.8% (2000).
Taxes: Total city taxes per capita: $68 (2006); City property taxes per capita: $66 (2006).
Education: Percent of population age 25 and over with: High school diploma (including GED) or higher: 76.9% (2007); Bachelor's degree or higher: 11.5% (2007); Master's degree or higher: 4.5% (2007).

School District(s)

Cumberland CUSD 77 (PK-12)
2005-06 Enrollment: 1,052 . . . . (217) 923-3132

Housing: Homeownership rate: 69.9% (2007); Median home value: $83,571 (2007); Median rent: $264 per month (2000); Median age of housing: 38 years (2000).
Safety: Violent crime rate: 17.5 per 10,000 population; Property crime rate: 262.5 per 10,000 population (2006).
Newspapers: Toledo Democrat (Community news; Circulation 1,860)
Transportation: Commute to work: 95.1% car, 0.0% public transportation, 1.0% walk, 3.0% work from home (2000); Travel time to work: 32.1% less than 15 minutes, 22.8% 15 to 30 minutes, 31.1% 30 to 45 minutes, 5.7% 45 to 60 minutes, 8.3% 60 minutes or more (2000)

De Witt County

Located in central Illinois; drained by Salt Creek. Covers a land area of 397.58 square miles, a water area of 7.58 square miles, and is located in the Central Time Zone. The county was founded in 1839. County seat is Clinton.
Population: 16,516 (1990); 16,798 (2000); 16,614 (2007); 16,477 (2012 projected); Race: 97.4% White, 0.8% Black, 0.4% Asian, 1.6% Hispanic of any race (2007); Density: 41.8 persons per square mile (2007); Average household size: 2.45 (2007); Median age: 40.1 (2007); Males per 100 females: 95.5 (2007).
Religion: Five largest groups: 19.7% Christian Churches and Churches of Christ, 10.2% Catholic Church, 9.2% The United Methodist Church, 2.1% Assemblies of God, 1.6% New Testament Association of Independent Baptist Churches and other Fundamental Ba
Economy: Unemployment rate: 5.3% (4/2008); Total civilian labor force: 8,568 (4/2008); Leading industries: 18.2% retail trade; 11.9% manufacturing; 11.6% health care and social assistance (2005); Farms: 459 totaling 202,699 acres (2002); Companies that employ 500 or more persons: 1 (2006); Companies that employ 100 to 499 persons: 4 (2006); Companies that employ less than 100 persons: 386 (2006); Black-owned businesses: n/a (2002); Hispanic-owned businesses: n/a (2002); Asian-owned businesses: n/a (2002); Women-owned businesses: 513

(2002); Retail sales per capita: $13,185 (2008). Single-family building permits issued: 31 (2007); Multi-family building permits issued: 3 (2007).
Income: Per capita income: $24,110 (2007); Median household income: $46,991 (2007); Average household income: $58,590 (2007); Percent of households with income of $100,000 or more: 13.6% (2007); Poverty rate: 9.8% (2005); Bankruptcy rate: 3.89% (2007).
Taxes: Total county taxes per capita: $204 (2006); County property taxes per capita: $204 (2006).
Education: Percent of population age 25 and over with: High school diploma (including GED) or higher: 83.6% (2007); Bachelor's degree or higher: 13.7% (2007); Master's degree or higher: 3.2% (2007).
Housing: Homeownership rate: 75.4% (2007); Median home value: $110,370 (2007); Median rent: $307 per month (2000); Median age of housing: 46 years (2000).
Health: Birth rate: 127.2 per 10,000 population (2007); Death rate: 130.8 per 10,000 population (2007); Age-adjusted cancer mortality rate: 221.5 deaths per 100,000 population (2005); Number of physicians: 7.9 per 10,000 population (2005); Hospital beds: 15.2 per 10,000 population (2004); Hospital admissions: 377.8 per 10,000 population (2004).
Elections: 2004 Presidential election results: 63.1% Bush, 36.4% Kerry, 0.0% Nader, 0.5% Badnarik
National and State Parks: Clinton Lake State Recreational Area; Weldon Springs State Park
Additional Information Contacts
De Witt County Government . . . . (217) 935-2119
http://www.dewittcountyill.com
City of Clinton. . . . . (217) 935-9438
http://www.clintonillinois.com
Clinton Area Chamber of Commerce & Tourism Bureau . . . (217) 935-3364
http://www.clintonilchamber.com

De Witt County Communities

CLINTON (city). County seat. Covers a land area of 2.653 square miles and a water area of <.001 square miles. Located at 40.15° N. Lat.; 88.95° W. Long. Elevation is 732 feet.
History: Clinton was the site of Abraham's Lincoln speech in which he gave the oft-quoted lines of "you can fool all the people part of the time and part of the people all of the time, but you cannot fool all the people all the time."
Population: 7,437 (1990); 7,485 (2000); 7,206 (2007); 7,009 (2012 projected); Race: 96.3% White, 1.5% Black, 0.2% Asian, 2.9% Hispanic of any race (2007); Density: 2,716.0 persons per square mile (2007); Average household size: 2.35 (2007); Median age: 38.1 (2007); Males per 100 females: 91.5 (2007); Marriage status: 21.1% never married, 58.1% now married, 8.8% widowed, 12.0% divorced (2000); Foreign born: 1.8% (2000); Ancestry (includes multiple ancestries): 17.7% German, 13.0% English, 12.1% United States or American, 11.2% Irish, 9.0% Other groups (2000).
Economy: Single-family building permits issued: 7 (2007); Multi-family building permits issued: 3 (2007); Employment by occupation: 9.9% management, 13.2% professional, 18.3% services, 27.3% sales, 0.4% farming, 9.9% construction, 21.0% production (2000).
Income: Per capita income: $21,610 (2007); Median household income: $40,269 (2007); Average household income: $50,403 (2007); Percent of households with income of $100,000 or more: 10.0% (2007); Poverty rate: 10.8% (2000).
Education: Percent of population age 25 and over with: High school diploma (including GED) or higher: 81.7% (2007); Bachelor's degree or higher: 11.9% (2007); Master's degree or higher: 2.9% (2007).

School District(s)

Clinton CUSD 15 (PK-12)
2005-06 Enrollment: 2,161 . . . . (217) 935-8321
Housing: Homeownership rate: 68.5% (2007); Median home value: $102,734 (2007); Median rent: $314 per month (2000); Median age of housing: 50 years (2000).
Hospitals: Dr. John Warner Hospital (43 beds)
Safety: Violent crime rate: 26.2 per 10,000 population; Property crime rate: 538.5 per 10,000 population (2006).
Newspapers: Clinton Daily Journal (Regional news; Circulation 4,000)
Transportation: Commute to work: 94.3% car, 0.2% public transportation, 3.9% walk, 1.5% work from home (2000); Travel time to work: 54.1% less than 15 minutes, 14.9% 15 to 30 minutes, 20.9% 30 to 45 minutes, 6.1% 45 to 60 minutes, 4.0% 60 minutes or more (2000)
Additional Information Contacts
City of Clinton. . . . . (217) 935-9438
http://www.clintonillinois.com
Clinton Area Chamber of Commerce & Tourism Bureau . . . (217) 935-3364
http://www.clintonilchamber.com

DE WITT (village). Covers a land area of 0.254 square miles and a water area of 0 square miles. Located at 40.18° N. Lat.; 88.78° W. Long. Elevation is 735 feet.
Population: 122 (1990); 188 (2000); 207 (2007); 218 (2012 projected); Race: 97.1% White, 1.0% Black, 0.0% Asian, 0.0% Hispanic of any race (2007); Density: 815.5 persons per square mile (2007); Average household size: 2.41 (2007); Median age: 46.0 (2007); Males per 100 females: 84.8 (2007); Marriage status: 14.0% never married, 61.5% now married, 10.5% widowed, 14.0% divorced (2000); Foreign born: 0.0% (2000); Ancestry (includes multiple ancestries): 17.8% United States or American, 11.1% English, 11.1% Irish, 8.9% German, 7.8% Other groups (2000).
Economy: Employment by occupation: 9.3% management, 6.7% professional, 26.7% services, 16.0% sales, 0.0% farming, 18.7% construction, 22.7% production (2000).
Income: Per capita income: $22,669 (2007); Median household income: $48,000 (2007); Average household income: $54,564 (2007); Percent of households with income of $100,000 or more: 12.8% (2007); Poverty rate: 1.1% (2000).
Education: Percent of population age 25 and over with: High school diploma (including GED) or higher: 74.4% (2007); Bachelor's degree or higher: 3.2% (2007); Master's degree or higher: 0.0% (2007).
Housing: Homeownership rate: 88.4% (2007); Median home value: $84,286 (2007); Median rent: $275 per month (2000); Median age of housing: 60+ years (2000).
Transportation: Commute to work: 98.7% car, 0.0% public transportation, 0.0% walk, 0.0% work from home (2000); Travel time to work: 30.7% less than 15 minutes, 49.3% 15 to 30 minutes, 9.3% 30 to 45 minutes, 8.0% 45 to 60 minutes, 2.7% 60 minutes or more (2000)

DEWITT (unincorporated postal area, zip code 61735). Aka De Witt. Covers a land area of 31.520 square miles and a water area of 0.043 square miles. Located at 40.20° N. Lat.; 88.80° W. Long.
Population: 408 (2000); Race: 97.7% White, 0.0% Black, 0.3% Asian, 0.0% Hispanic of any race (2000); Density: 12.9 persons per square mile (2000); Age: 22.8% under 18, 14.8% over 64 (2000); Marriage status: 11.7% never married, 75.1% now married, 4.9% widowed, 8.4% divorced (2000); Foreign born: 0.0% (2000); Ancestry (includes multiple ancestries): 14.0% German, 10.9% Irish, 9.8% English, 7.8% United States or American, 7.0% Scottish (2000).
Economy: Employment by occupation: 28.4% management, 17.3% professional, 9.6% services, 8.2% sales, 0.0% farming, 13.0% construction, 23.6% production (2000).
Income: Per capita income: $23,504 (2000); Median household income: $45,972 (2000); Poverty rate: 0.5% (2000).
Education: Percent of population age 25 and over with: High school diploma (including GED) or higher: 81.2% (2000); Bachelor's degree or higher: 17.3% (2000).
Housing: Homeownership rate: 87.7% (2000); Median home value: $67,100 (2000); Median rent: $275 per month (2000); Median age of housing: 47 years (2000).
Transportation: Commute to work: 90.9% car, 0.0% public transportation, 1.0% walk, 7.7% work from home (2000); Travel time to work: 26.6% less than 15 minutes, 30.2% 15 to 30 minutes, 29.2% 30 to 45 minutes, 10.4% 45 to 60 minutes, 3.6% 60 minutes or more (2000)

FARMER CITY (city). Covers a land area of 2.302 square miles and a water area of 0.049 square miles. Located at 40.24° N. Lat.; 88.64° W. Long. Elevation is 725 feet.
History: Incorporated 1869.
Population: 2,169 (1990); 2,055 (2000); 2,048 (2007); 2,029 (2012 projected); Race: 99.7% White, 0.0% Black, 0.0% Asian, 0.3% Hispanic of any race (2007); Density: 889.7 persons per square mile (2007); Average household size: 2.47 (2007); Median age: 41.0 (2007); Males per 100 females: 94.1 (2007); Marriage status: 21.0% never married, 53.6% now married, 12.2% widowed, 13.1% divorced (2000); Foreign born: 0.3% (2000); Ancestry (includes multiple ancestries): 24.2% German, 12.2% United States or American, 12.1% English, 10.6% Irish, 3.9% Other groups (2000).

Economy: Employment by occupation: 9.9% management, 14.0% professional, 15.0% services, 29.2% sales, 0.5% farming, 13.0% construction, 18.5% production (2000).
Income: Per capita income: $23,133 (2007); Median household income: $45,682 (2007); Average household income: $56,102 (2007); Percent of households with income of $100,000 or more: 12.7% (2007); Poverty rate: 8.3% (2000).
Education: Percent of population age 25 and over with: High school diploma (including GED) or higher: 82.7% (2007); Bachelor's degree or higher: 14.3% (2007); Master's degree or higher: 2.5% (2007).

School District(s)

Blue Ridge CUSD 18 (PK-12)
2005-06 Enrollment: 943 . . . . (309) 928-9141
Housing: Homeownership rate: 76.1% (2007); Median home value: $100,202 (2007); Median rent: $293 per month (2000); Median age of housing: 54 years (2000).
Safety: Violent crime rate: 0.0 per 10,000 population; Property crime rate: 69.8 per 10,000 population (2006).
Newspapers: Farmer City Journal (Local news; Circulation 1,900)
Transportation: Commute to work: 90.9% car, 0.0% public transportation, 5.0% walk, 3.1% work from home (2000); Travel time to work: 41.3% less than 15 minutes, 23.5% 15 to 30 minutes, 28.5% 30 to 45 minutes, 3.9% 45 to 60 minutes, 2.7% 60 minutes or more (2000)

KENNEY (village). Covers a land area of 0.301 square miles and a water area of 0 square miles. Located at 40.09° N. Lat.; 89.08° W. Long. Elevation is 650 feet.
Population: 390 (1990); 374 (2000); 383 (2007); 383 (2012 projected); Race: 98.4% White, 0.5% Black, 0.5% Asian, 0.8% Hispanic of any race (2007); Density: 1,272.6 persons per square mile (2007); Average household size: 2.29 (2007); Median age: 41.4 (2007); Males per 100 females: 92.5 (2007); Marriage status: 16.6% never married, 62.5% now married, 11.2% widowed, 9.7% divorced (2000); Foreign born: 0.8% (2000); Ancestry (includes multiple ancestries): 21.4% German, 18.8% English, 15.7% United States or American, 9.1% Irish, 6.8% Other groups (2000).
Economy: Employment by occupation: 13.0% management, 14.1% professional, 14.1% services, 20.5% sales, 0.5% farming, 14.1% construction, 23.8% production (2000).
Income: Per capita income: $22,728 (2007); Median household income: $41,607 (2007); Average household income: $52,126 (2007); Percent of households with income of $100,000 or more: 11.4% (2007); Poverty rate: 6.5% (2000).
Education: Percent of population age 25 and over with: High school diploma (including GED) or higher: 83.6% (2007); Bachelor's degree or higher: 6.8% (2007); Master's degree or higher: 0.4% (2007).
Housing: Homeownership rate: 81.4% (2007); Median home value: $73,636 (2007); Median rent: $288 per month (2000); Median age of housing: 60+ years (2000).
Transportation: Commute to work: 98.4% car, 0.0% public transportation, 1.6% walk, 0.0% work from home (2000); Travel time to work: 30.1% less than 15 minutes, 37.2% 15 to 30 minutes, 19.1% 30 to 45 minutes, 10.4% 45 to 60 minutes, 3.3% 60 minutes or more (2000)

WAPELLA (village). Covers a land area of 0.545 square miles and a water area of 0 square miles. Located at 40.22° N. Lat.; 88.96° W. Long. Elevation is 745 feet.
Population: 612 (1990); 651 (2000); 662 (2007); 661 (2012 projected); Race: 98.9% White, 0.0% Black, 0.0% Asian, 1.2% Hispanic of any race (2007); Density: 1,213.8 persons per square mile (2007); Average household size: 2.51 (2007); Median age: 33.3 (2007); Males per 100 females: 106.2 (2007); Marriage status: 19.3% never married, 64.8% now married, 7.9% widowed, 7.9% divorced (2000); Foreign born: 0.5% (2000); Ancestry (includes multiple ancestries): 16.7% German, 14.4% English, 8.3% Irish, 6.2% United States or American, 6.2% Other groups (2000).
Economy: Single-family building permits issued: 0 (2007); Multi-family building permits issued: 0 (2007); Employment by occupation: 12.1% management, 10.2% professional, 16.5% services, 24.2% sales, 3.1% farming, 13.0% construction, 20.8% production (2000).
Income: Per capita income: $20,242 (2007); Median household income: $40,000 (2007); Average household income: $50,758 (2007); Percent of households with income of $100,000 or more: 6.8% (2007); Poverty rate: 8.1% (2000).
Education: Percent of population age 25 and over with: High school diploma (including GED) or higher: 78.0% (2007); Bachelor's degree or higher: 4.9% (2007); Master's degree or higher: 0.7% (2007).
Housing: Homeownership rate: 84.1% (2007); Median home value: $96,471 (2007); Median rent: $328 per month (2000); Median age of housing: 37 years (2000).
Transportation: Commute to work: 97.4% car, 0.0% public transportation, 0.6% walk, 1.0% work from home (2000); Travel time to work: 33.9% less than 15 minutes, 31.9% 15 to 30 minutes, 25.2% 30 to 45 minutes, 2.3% 45 to 60 minutes, 6.8% 60 minutes or more (2000)

WAYNESVILLE (village). Covers a land area of 0.322 square miles and a water area of 0 square miles. Located at 40.24° N. Lat.; 89.12° W. Long. Elevation is 735 feet.
Population: 440 (1990); 452 (2000); 423 (2007); 424 (2012 projected); Race: 98.8% White, 0.7% Black, 0.0% Asian, 0.0% Hispanic of any race (2007); Density: 1,314.0 persons per square mile (2007); Average household size: 2.40 (2007); Median age: 39.5 (2007); Males per 100 females: 102.4 (2007); Marriage status: 15.3% never married, 62.9% now married, 8.3% widowed, 13.5% divorced (2000); Foreign born: 0.0% (2000); Ancestry (includes multiple ancestries): 28.1% German, 15.6% English, 15.1% Irish, 11.6% United States or American, 4.7% French (except Basque) (2000).
Economy: Employment by occupation: 9.7% management, 7.2% professional, 17.9% services, 28.2% sales, 2.1% farming, 12.3% construction, 22.6% production (2000).
Income: Per capita income: $20,053 (2007); Median household income: $45,952 (2007); Average household income: $48,196 (2007); Percent of households with income of $100,000 or more: 3.4% (2007); Poverty rate: 7.8% (2000).
Education: Percent of population age 25 and over with: High school diploma (including GED) or higher: 76.3% (2007); Bachelor's degree or higher: 3.8% (2007); Master's degree or higher: 1.7% (2007).
Housing: Homeownership rate: 88.6% (2007); Median home value: $73,913 (2007); Median rent: $245 per month (2000); Median age of housing: 58 years (2000).
Transportation: Commute to work: 94.2% car, 0.0% public transportation, 1.6% walk, 3.7% work from home (2000); Travel time to work: 7.1% less than 15 minutes, 30.4% 15 to 30 minutes, 47.3% 30 to 45 minutes, 9.8% 45 to 60 minutes, 5.4% 60 minutes or more (2000)

WELDON (village). Covers a land area of 0.269 square miles and a water area of 0 square miles. Located at 40.12° N. Lat.; 88.75° W. Long. Elevation is 712 feet.
Population: 366 (1990); 440 (2000); 427 (2007); 425 (2012 projected); Race: 96.0% White, 0.0% Black, 1.2% Asian, 0.2% Hispanic of any race (2007); Density: 1,587.2 persons per square mile (2007); Average household size: 2.32 (2007); Median age: 39.9 (2007); Males per 100 females: 91.5 (2007); Marriage status: 19.9% never married, 59.4% now married, 11.8% widowed, 8.9% divorced (2000); Foreign born: 0.5% (2000); Ancestry (includes multiple ancestries): 16.0% English, 13.1% German, 8.8% Irish, 7.4% Other groups, 6.5% United States or American (2000).
Economy: Employment by occupation: 4.7% management, 5.1% professional, 14.0% services, 27.9% sales, 1.9% farming, 19.5% construction, 27.0% production (2000).
Income: Per capita income: $23,624 (2007); Median household income: $46,000 (2007); Average household income: $54,823 (2007); Percent of households with income of $100,000 or more: 10.9% (2007); Poverty rate: 5.7% (2000).
Education: Percent of population age 25 and over with: High school diploma (including GED) or higher: 78.3% (2007); Bachelor's degree or higher: 10.0% (2007); Master's degree or higher: 2.1% (2007).

School District(s)

Deland-Weldon CUSD 57 (PK-12)
2005-06 Enrollment: 194 . . . . (217) 736-2311
Housing: Homeownership rate: 87.5% (2007); Median home value: $84,167 (2007); Median rent: $310 per month (2000); Median age of housing: 53 years (2000).
Transportation: Commute to work: 89.0% car, 0.5% public transportation, 5.2% walk, 4.8% work from home (2000); Travel time to work: 24.5% less than 15 minutes, 25.0% 15 to 30 minutes, 37.0% 30 to 45 minutes, 10.5% 45 to 60 minutes, 3.0% 60 minutes or more (2000)

De Kalb County

Located in northern Illinois; drained by branches of the Kishwaukee River. Covers a land area of 634.16 square miles, a water area of 0.81 square miles, and is located in the Central Time Zone. The county was founded in 1837. County seat is Sycamore.

De Kalb County is part of the Chicago-Naperville-Joliet, IL-IN-WI Metropolitan Statistical Area. The entire metro area includes: Chicago-Naperville-Joliet, IL Metropolitan Division (Cook County, IL; DeKalb County, IL; DuPage County, IL; Grundy County, IL; Kane County, IL; Kendall County, IL; McHenry County, IL; Will County, IL); Gary, IN Metropolitan Division (Jasper County, IN; Lake County, IN; Newton County, IN; Porter County, IN); Lake County-Kenosha County, IL-WI Metropolitan Division (Lake County, IL; Kenosha County, WI)

Weather Station: De Kalb Elevation: 872 feet

	Jan	Feb	Mar	Apr	May	Jun	Jul	Aug	Sep	Oct	Nov	Dec
High	27	33	45	59	72	81	84	82	76	63	46	34
Low	11	17	27	38	48	59	63	61	53	41	30	19
Precip	1.5	1.4	2.5	3.5	4.3	4.5	4.4	4.5	3.7	2.7	2.8	2.2
Snow	9.7	7.1	5.1	1.3	tr	0.0	0.0	0.0	0.0	0.1	2.1	8.6

High and Low temperatures in degrees Fahrenheit; Precipitation and Snow in inches

Population: 77,932 (1990); 88,969 (2000); 100,470 (2007); 108,517 (2012 projected); Race: 86.4% White, 5.0% Black, 2.7% Asian, 8.9% Hispanic of any race (2007); Density: 158.4 persons per square mile (2007); Average household size: 2.80 (2007); Median age: 28.9 (2007); Males per 100 females: 99.2 (2007).
Religion: Five largest groups: 19.2% Catholic Church, 6.5% Evangelical Lutheran Church in America, 5.6% The United Methodist Church, 3.5% United Church of Christ, 3.3% Lutheran Church—Missouri Synod (2000).
Economy: Unemployment rate: 5.6% (4/2008); Total civilian labor force: 58,042 (4/2008); Leading industries: 19.4% retail trade; 17.2% manufacturing; 15.9% health care and social assistance (2005); Farms: 816 totaling 359,352 acres (2002); Companies that employ 500 or more persons: 2 (2006); Companies that employ 100 to 499 persons: 50 (2006); Companies that employ less than 100 persons: 2,050 (2006); Black-owned businesses: n/a (2002); Hispanic-owned businesses: n/a (2002); Asian-owned businesses: n/a (2002); Women-owned businesses: n/a (2002); Retail sales per capita: $12,307 (2008). Single-family building permits issued: 464 (2007); Multi-family building permits issued: 120 (2007).
Income: Per capita income: $22,259 (2007); Median household income: $51,493 (2007); Average household income: $60,742 (2007); Percent of households with income of $100,000 or more: 15.4% (2007); Poverty rate: 14.6% (2005); Bankruptcy rate: 2.42% (2007).
Taxes: Total county taxes per capita: $146 (2006); County property taxes per capita: $138 (2006).
Education: Percent of population age 25 and over with: High school diploma (including GED) or higher: 87.8% (2007); Bachelor's degree or higher: 27.6% (2007); Master's degree or higher: 11.0% (2007).
Housing: Homeownership rate: 60.2% (2007); Median home value: $186,822 (2007); Median rent: $504 per month (2000); Median age of housing: 32 years (2000).
Health: Birth rate: 131.9 per 10,000 population (2007); Death rate: 58.7 per 10,000 population (2007); Age-adjusted cancer mortality rate: 209.5 deaths per 100,000 population (2005); Number of physicians: 9.1 per 10,000 population (2005); Hospital beds: 20.3 per 10,000 population (2004); Hospital admissions: 684.7 per 10,000 population (2004).
Elections: 2004 Presidential election results: 51.7% Bush, 47.3% Kerry, 0.2% Nader, 0.8% Badnarik
National and State Parks: Shabbona Lake State Recreational Area
Additional Information Contacts
De Kalb County Government. . . . . (815) 895-7189
http://www.dekalbcounty.org
City of De Kalb. . . . . (815) 748-2095
http://www.cityofdekalb.com
City of Sandwich . . . . (815) 786-9321
http://www.sandwich.il.us
City of Sycamore . . . . (815) 895-4515
http://www.cityofsycamore.com
De Kalb Chamber of Commerce . . . . (815) 756-6306
http://www.dekalb.org
Genoa Area Chamber of Commerce . . . . (815) 784-2212
http://www.genoa-il-chamberofcommerce.com
Sandwich Chamber of Commerce. (815) 786-9075
http://www.sandwich-il.org
Sycamore Chamber of Commerce . . . . (815) 895-3456
http://www.sycamorechamber.com
Town of Cortland . . . . (815) 756-9041
http://www.cortlandil.org

De Kalb County Communities

CLARE (unincorporated postal area, zip code 60111). Covers a land area of 23.578 square miles and a water area of 0 square miles. Located at 41.99° N. Lat.; 88.84° W. Long. Elevation is 869 feet.
Population: 305 (2000); Race: 98.9% White, 0.0% Black, 0.0% Asian, 0.0% Hispanic of any race (2000); Density: 12.9 persons per square mile (2000); Age: 30.1% under 18, 13.0% over 64 (2000); Marriage status: 22.5% never married, 67.2% now married, 6.4% widowed, 3.9% divorced (2000); Foreign born: 1.5% (2000); Ancestry (includes multiple ancestries): 31.6% German, 20.1% United States or American, 17.1% English, 14.5% Swedish, 7.4% Irish (2000).
Economy: Employment by occupation: 16.9% management, 19.5% professional, 2.6% services, 26.0% sales, 0.0% farming, 18.8% construction, 16.2% production (2000).
Income: Per capita income: $27,141 (2000); Median household income: $58,750 (2000); Poverty rate: 1.9% (2000).
Education: Percent of population age 25 and over with: High school diploma (including GED) or higher: 87.8% (2000); Bachelor's degree or higher: 27.1% (2000).
Housing: Homeownership rate: 70.4% (2000); Median home value: $146,300 (2000); Median rent: $438 per month (2000); Median age of housing: 60+ years (2000).
Transportation: Commute to work: 90.3% car, 1.9% public transportation, 3.2% walk, 4.5% work from home (2000); Travel time to work: 36.7% less than 15 minutes, 53.1% 15 to 30 minutes, 0.0% 30 to 45 minutes, 7.5% 45 to 60 minutes, 2.7% 60 minutes or more (2000)

CORTLAND (town). Covers a land area of 1.756 square miles and a water area of 0 square miles. Located at 41.92° N. Lat.; 88.69° W. Long. Elevation is 902 feet.
Population: 1,079 (1990); 2,066 (2000); 3,016 (2007); 3,624 (2012 projected); Race: 93.9% White, 1.4% Black, 1.6% Asian, 6.1% Hispanic of any race (2007); Density: 1,717.2 persons per square mile (2007); Average household size: 3.02 (2007); Median age: 30.0 (2007); Males per 100 females: 97.5 (2007); Marriage status: 21.2% never married, 67.1% now married, 3.7% widowed, 8.0% divorced (2000); Foreign born: 3.8% (2000); Ancestry (includes multiple ancestries): 31.0% German, 15.3% Irish, 9.2% Other groups, 8.4% English, 7.0% United States or American (2000).
Economy: Single-family building permits issued: 88 (2007); Multi-family building permits issued: 5 (2007); Employment by occupation: 11.0% management, 17.6% professional, 14.4% services, 25.9% sales, 0.2% farming, 12.0% construction, 19.0% production (2000).
Income: Per capita income: $21,961 (2007); Median household income: $60,959 (2007); Average household income: $66,235 (2007); Percent of households with income of $100,000 or more: 16.5% (2007); Poverty rate: 3.7% (2000).
Education: Percent of population age 25 and over with: High school diploma (including GED) or higher: 87.2% (2007); Bachelor's degree or higher: 22.0% (2007); Master's degree or higher: 6.9% (2007).

School District(s)

Dekalb CUSD 428 (PK-12)
2005-06 Enrollment: 5,694 . . . . (815) 754-2350
Housing: Homeownership rate: 72.3% (2007); Median home value: $191,037 (2007); Median rent: $654 per month (2000); Median age of housing: 9 years (2000).
Safety: Violent crime rate: 6.4 per 10,000 population; Property crime rate: 108.5 per 10,000 population (2006).
Transportation: Commute to work: 95.9% car, 0.0% public transportation, 0.7% walk, 2.9% work from home (2000); Travel time to work: 39.6% less than 15 minutes, 27.1% 15 to 30 minutes, 15.7% 30 to 45 minutes, 7.9% 45 to 60 minutes, 9.7% 60 minutes or more (2000)
Additional Information Contacts
Town of Cortland . . . . (815) 756-9041
http://www.cortlandil.org

DE KALB (city). Covers a land area of 12.611 square miles and a water area of 0.008 square miles. Located at 41.93° N. Lat.; 88.75° W. Long. Elevation is 880 feet.

History: De Kalb was named for Baron Johann De Kalb, a major general in the Revolutionary Army. In 1874 Joseph E. Glidden patented an improved barbed wire, and Jacob Haish patented a barbed wire manufacturing process. The two patents overlapped and caused a long legal battle, but until 1938 De Kalb was known as the barbed wire capital of the world.

Population: 36,443 (1990); 39,018 (2000); 42,793 (2007); 45,506 (2012 projected); Race: 75.3% White, 10.2% Black, 5.3% Asian, 12.6% Hispanic of any race (2007); Density: 3,393.3 persons per square mile (2007); Average household size: 2.98 (2007); Median age: 24.5 (2007); Males per 100 females: 98.4 (2007); Marriage status: 52.5% never married, 38.2% now married, 3.6% widowed, 5.7% divorced (2000); Foreign born: 9.1% (2000); Ancestry (includes multiple ancestries): 24.5% German, 21.9% Other groups, 14.5% Irish, 7.5% English, 6.1% Polish (2000).

Economy: Unemployment rate: 4.7% (4/2008); Total civilian labor force: 23,628 (4/2008); Single-family building permits issued: 111 (2007); Multi-family building permits issued: 15 (2007); Employment by occupation: 10.3% management, 26.7% professional, 18.1% services, 27.5% sales, 0.2% farming, 5.5% construction, 11.7% production (2000).

Income: Per capita income: $17,428 (2007); Median household income: $38,061 (2007); Average household income: $48,556 (2007); Percent of households with income of $100,000 or more: 9.6% (2007); Poverty rate: 21.3% (2000).

Education: Percent of population age 25 and over with: High school diploma (including GED) or higher: 87.9% (2007); Bachelor's degree or higher: 38.7% (2007); Master's degree or higher: 18.2% (2007).

School District(s)

Dekalb CUSD 428 (PK-12)
2005-06 Enrollment: 5,694 . . . . (815) 754-2350
Dekalb Roe (07-12)
2005-06 Enrollment: 32 . . . . (815) 895-3096
KEC Area Voc Center
2005-06 Enrollment: n/a . . . . (815) 754-2400
Kishwaukee Educ Consortium
2005-06 Enrollment: n/a . . . . (815) 754-2400

Four-year College(s)

Northern Illinois University (Public)
Fall 2007 Enrollment: 25,254. . . . . (800) 892-3050
2007-08 Tuition: In-state $8,588; Out-of-state $14,738

Housing: Homeownership rate: 42.4% (2007); Median home value: $173,225 (2007); Median rent: $499 per month (2000); Median age of housing: 29 years (2000).

Hospitals: Kishwaukee Community Hospital (172 beds)

Safety: Violent crime rate: 45.6 per 10,000 population; Property crime rate: 302.7 per 10,000 population (2006).

Newspapers: Daily Chronicle (Local news; Circulation 12,300); Midweek (Local news; Circulation 30,000)

Transportation: Commute to work: 80.0% car, 2.5% public transportation, 12.8% walk, 2.4% work from home (2000); Travel time to work: 55.9% less than 15 minutes, 18.7% 15 to 30 minutes, 10.5% 30 to 45 minutes, 7.2% 45 to 60 minutes, 7.7% 60 minutes or more (2000)

Airports: De Kalb Taylor Municipal (general aviation)

Additional Information Contacts

City of De Kalb . . . . (815) 748-2095
http://www.cityofdekalb.com
De Kalb Chamber of Commerce . . . . (815) 756-6306
http://www.dekalb.org

ESMOND (unincorporated postal area, zip code 60129). Covers a land area of 22.108 square miles and a water area of 0 square miles. Located at 42.03° N. Lat.; 88.97° W. Long. Elevation is 820 feet.

Population: 291 (2000); Race: 95.3% White, 0.0% Black, 0.0% Asian, 5.7% Hispanic of any race (2000); Density: 13.2 persons per square mile (2000); Age: 28.3% under 18, 7.7% over 64 (2000); Marriage status: 21.4% never married, 69.4% now married, 3.1% widowed, 6.1% divorced (2000); Foreign born: 3.4% (2000); Ancestry (includes multiple ancestries): 36.7% German, 10.4% Irish, 9.1% English, 7.4% United States or American, 5.4% Dutch (2000).

Economy: Employment by occupation: 14.0% management, 14.5% professional, 12.2% services, 17.4% sales, 1.2% farming, 17.4% construction, 23.3% production (2000).

Income: Per capita income: $17,101 (2000); Median household income: $43,438 (2000); Poverty rate: 4.8% (2000).

Education: Percent of population age 25 and over with: High school diploma (including GED) or higher: 85.6% (2000); Bachelor's degree or higher: 20.3% (2000).

Housing: Homeownership rate: 62.5% (2000); Median home value: $126,100 (2000); Median rent: $392 per month (2000); Median age of housing: 60+ years (2000).

Transportation: Commute to work: 89.5% car, 1.2% public transportation, 0.0% walk, 8.1% work from home (2000); Travel time to work: 9.5% less than 15 minutes, 54.4% 15 to 30 minutes, 20.3% 30 to 45 minutes, 8.9% 45 to 60 minutes, 7.0% 60 minutes or more (2000)

GENOA (city). Covers a land area of 1.913 square miles and a water area of 0 square miles. Located at 42.09° N. Lat.; 88.69° W. Long. Elevation is 833 feet.

Population: 3,287 (1990); 4,169 (2000); 4,358 (2007); 4,549 (2012 projected); Race: 94.4% White, 0.2% Black, 0.4% Asian, 15.3% Hispanic of any race (2007); Density: 2,277.6 persons per square mile (2007); Average household size: 2.69 (2007); Median age: 31.7 (2007); Males per 100 females: 99.2 (2007); Marriage status: 19.8% never married, 63.8% now married, 5.6% widowed, 10.8% divorced (2000); Foreign born: 8.1% (2000); Ancestry (includes multiple ancestries): 28.4% German, 15.5% Irish, 15.0% Other groups, 9.7% English, 7.0% Polish (2000).

Economy: Single-family building permits issued: 41 (2007); Multi-family building permits issued: 0 (2007); Employment by occupation: 9.0% management, 16.3% professional, 12.4% services, 21.1% sales, 0.3% farming, 16.2% construction, 24.7% production (2000).

Income: Per capita income: $23,279 (2007); Median household income: $54,798 (2007); Average household income: $62,701 (2007); Percent of households with income of $100,000 or more: 15.8% (2007); Poverty rate: 3.3% (2000).

Education: Percent of population age 25 and over with: High school diploma (including GED) or higher: 79.1% (2007); Bachelor's degree or higher: 10.9% (2007); Master's degree or higher: 2.2% (2007).

School District(s)

Genoa Kingston CUSD 424 (PK-12)
2005-06 Enrollment: 1,940 . . . . (815) 784-6222

Housing: Homeownership rate: 72.2% (2007); Median home value: $166,366 (2007); Median rent: $485 per month (2000); Median age of housing: 37 years (2000).

Safety: Violent crime rate: 17.1 per 10,000 population; Property crime rate: 199.1 per 10,000 population (2006).

Transportation: Commute to work: 92.2% car, 0.0% public transportation, 3.6% walk, 2.5% work from home (2000); Travel time to work: 28.5% less than 15 minutes, 30.7% 15 to 30 minutes, 22.3% 30 to 45 minutes, 8.6% 45 to 60 minutes, 9.9% 60 minutes or more (2000)

Additional Information Contacts

Genoa Area Chamber of Commerce . . . . (815) 784-2212
http://www.genoa-il-chamberofcommerce.com

HINCKLEY (village). Covers a land area of 0.949 square miles and a water area of 0.006 square miles. Located at 41.77° N. Lat.; 88.64° W. Long. Elevation is 745 feet.

Population: 1,795 (1990); 1,994 (2000); 1,983 (2007); 1,997 (2012 projected); Race: 97.6% White, 0.2% Black, 0.1% Asian, 3.0% Hispanic of any race (2007); Density: 2,089.1 persons per square mile (2007); Average household size: 2.69 (2007); Median age: 35.5 (2007); Males per 100 females: 99.5 (2007); Marriage status: 18.9% never married, 68.5% now married, 4.1% widowed, 8.5% divorced (2000); Foreign born: 1.1% (2000); Ancestry (includes multiple ancestries): 35.2% German, 15.7% Irish, 10.0% English, 6.9% Norwegian, 6.9% Other groups (2000).

Economy: Single-family building permits issued: 6 (2007); Multi-family building permits issued: 0 (2007); Employment by occupation: 12.4% management, 17.2% professional, 13.2% services, 27.2% sales, 0.4% farming, 14.3% construction, 15.4% production (2000).

Income: Per capita income: $27,284 (2007); Median household income: $67,331 (2007); Average household income: $73,512 (2007); Percent of households with income of $100,000 or more: 22.1% (2007); Poverty rate: 4.4% (2000).

Education: Percent of population age 25 and over with: High school diploma (including GED) or higher: 90.7% (2007); Bachelor's degree or higher: 21.0% (2007); Master's degree or higher: 5.6% (2007).

School District(s)

Hinckley Big Rock CUSD 429 (PK-12)
2005-06 Enrollment: 875 . . . . (815) 286-7575

Housing: Homeownership rate: 75.5% (2007); Median home value: $206,316 (2007); Median rent: $577 per month (2000); Median age of housing: 29 years (2000).

Safety: Violent crime rate: 53.7 per 10,000 population; Property crime rate: 141.5 per 10,000 population (2006).

Transportation: Commute to work: 92.4% car, 0.5% public transportation, 1.6% walk, 5.0% work from home (2000); Travel time to work: 21.8% less than 15 minutes, 25.5% 15 to 30 minutes, 31.8% 30 to 45 minutes, 11.5% 45 to 60 minutes, 9.3% 60 minutes or more (2000)

KINGSTON (village). Covers a land area of 1.003 square miles and a water area of 0 square miles. Located at 42.10° N. Lat.; 88.76° W. Long. Elevation is 794 feet.

Population: 745 (1990); 980 (2000); 1,287 (2007); 1,496 (2012 projected); Race: 97.7% White, 0.1% Black, 0.2% Asian, 4.0% Hispanic of any race (2007); Density: 1,282.9 persons per square mile (2007); Average household size: 2.97 (2007); Median age: 31.7 (2007); Males per 100 females: 106.9 (2007); Marriage status: 26.9% never married, 59.9% now married, 2.7% widowed, 10.4% divorced (2000); Foreign born: 1.6% (2000); Ancestry (includes multiple ancestries): 29.5% German, 15.8% Irish, 13.8% Other groups, 8.0% Italian, 7.4% Polish (2000).

Economy: Single-family building permits issued: 1 (2007); Multi-family building permits issued: 0 (2007); Employment by occupation: 9.4% management, 9.9% professional, 14.5% services, 18.1% sales, 0.0% farming, 20.3% construction, 27.8% production (2000).

Income: Per capita income: $24,966 (2007); Median household income: $62,799 (2007); Average household income: $70,901 (2007); Percent of households with income of $100,000 or more: 20.8% (2007); Poverty rate: 4.8% (2000).

Education: Percent of population age 25 and over with: High school diploma (including GED) or higher: 86.9% (2007); Bachelor's degree or higher: 17.1% (2007); Master's degree or higher: 4.8% (2007).

School District(s)

Genoa Kingston CUSD 424 (PK-12)
2005-06 Enrollment: 1,940 . . . . (815) 784-6222

Housing: Homeownership rate: 83.4% (2007); Median home value: $175,647 (2007); Median rent: $512 per month (2000); Median age of housing: 29 years (2000).

Transportation: Commute to work: 93.2% car, 0.9% public transportation, 1.7% walk, 3.5% work from home (2000); Travel time to work: 28.0% less than 15 minutes, 30.1% 15 to 30 minutes, 23.8% 30 to 45 minutes, 6.1% 45 to 60 minutes, 12.0% 60 minutes or more (2000)

KIRKLAND (village). Covers a land area of 1.125 square miles and a water area of 0 square miles. Located at 42.09° N. Lat.; 88.85° W. Long. Elevation is 768 feet.

Population: 1,082 (1990); 1,166 (2000); 1,173 (2007); 1,172 (2012 projected); Race: 98.3% White, 0.3% Black, 0.0% Asian, 2.1% Hispanic of any race (2007); Density: 1,042.2 persons per square mile (2007); Average household size: 2.70 (2007); Median age: 32.2 (2007); Males per 100 females: 106.5 (2007); Marriage status: 26.2% never married, 57.9% now married, 6.9% widowed, 9.0% divorced (2000); Foreign born: 1.9% (2000); Ancestry (includes multiple ancestries): 35.0% German, 14.2% Irish, 12.9% English, 9.3% Swedish, 7.8% Other groups (2000).

Economy: Single-family building permits issued: 3 (2007); Multi-family building permits issued: 0 (2007); Employment by occupation: 9.8% management, 14.7% professional, 11.9% services, 21.0% sales, 0.0% farming, 15.5% construction, 27.2% production (2000).

Income: Per capita income: $21,797 (2007); Median household income: $53,333 (2007); Average household income: $58,911 (2007); Percent of households with income of $100,000 or more: 10.8% (2007); Poverty rate: 6.0% (2000).

Education: Percent of population age 25 and over with: High school diploma (including GED) or higher: 81.6% (2007); Bachelor's degree or higher: 15.9% (2007); Master's degree or higher: 3.2% (2007).

School District(s)

Hiawatha CUSD 426 (PK-12)
2005-06 Enrollment: 638 . . . . (815) 522-6676

Housing: Homeownership rate: 76.7% (2007); Median home value: $155,227 (2007); Median rent: $465 per month (2000); Median age of housing: 46 years (2000).

Safety: Violent crime rate: 6.2 per 10,000 population; Property crime rate: 236.5 per 10,000 population (2006).

Transportation: Commute to work: 90.0% car, 0.9% public transportation, 7.1% walk, 2.0% work from home (2000); Travel time to work: 23.2% less than 15 minutes, 36.9% 15 to 30 minutes, 17.6% 30 to 45 minutes, 11.3% 45 to 60 minutes, 10.9% 60 minutes or more (2000)

MALTA (village). Covers a land area of 0.375 square miles and a water area of 0 square miles. Located at 41.92° N. Lat.; 88.86° W. Long. Elevation is 909 feet.

Population: 877 (1990); 969 (2000); 908 (2007); 909 (2012 projected); Race: 95.9% White, 0.3% Black, 0.3% Asian, 2.4% Hispanic of any race (2007); Density: 2,421.3 persons per square mile (2007); Average household size: 2.56 (2007); Median age: 33.4 (2007); Males per 100 females: 94.8 (2007); Marriage status: 19.9% never married, 64.0% now married, 6.6% widowed, 9.5% divorced (2000); Foreign born: 0.9% (2000); Ancestry (includes multiple ancestries): 26.6% German, 13.4% English, 12.6% Swedish, 10.9% Irish, 9.1% United States or American (2000).

Economy: Single-family building permits issued: 7 (2007); Multi-family building permits issued: 0 (2007); Employment by occupation: 11.6% management, 13.3% professional, 17.0% services, 25.8% sales, 0.6% farming, 9.6% construction, 22.2% production (2000).

Income: Per capita income: $23,720 (2007); Median household income: $51,061 (2007); Average household income: $60,669 (2007); Percent of households with income of $100,000 or more: 13.8% (2007); Poverty rate: 6.8% (2000).

Education: Percent of population age 25 and over with: High school diploma (including GED) or higher: 86.9% (2007); Bachelor's degree or higher: 17.1% (2007); Master's degree or higher: 6.1% (2007).

School District(s)

Dekalb CUSD 428 (PK-12)
2005-06 Enrollment: 5,694 . . . . (815) 754-2350

Two-year College(s)

Kishwaukee College (Public)
Fall 2007 Enrollment: 4,466. . . . . (815) 825-2086
2007-08 Tuition: In-state $7,975; Out-of-state $7,975

Housing: Homeownership rate: 72.1% (2007); Median home value: $154,435 (2007); Median rent: $482 per month (2000); Median age of housing: 45 years (2000).

Safety: Violent crime rate: 0.0 per 10,000 population; Property crime rate: 0.0 per 10,000 population (2006).

Transportation: Commute to work: 93.3% car, 0.2% public transportation, 1.6% walk, 4.5% work from home (2000); Travel time to work: 25.8% less than 15 minutes, 46.7% 15 to 30 minutes, 8.6% 30 to 45 minutes, 10.2% 45 to 60 minutes, 8.6% 60 minutes or more (2000)

SANDWICH (city). Covers a land area of 3.014 square miles and a water area of 0 square miles. Located at 41.64° N. Lat.; 88.62° W. Long. Elevation is 666 feet.

History: Sandwich was named for Sandwich, Massachusetts. Early industries were the manufacture of plows, reapers, windmills, and cornshellers.

Population: 5,662 (1990); 6,509 (2000); 6,978 (2007); 7,347 (2012 projected); Race: 94.7% White, 0.2% Black, 0.4% Asian, 11.1% Hispanic of any race (2007); Density: 2,315.1 persons per square mile (2007); Average household size: 2.75 (2007); Median age: 35.2 (2007); Males per 100 females: 98.5 (2007); Marriage status: 22.1% never married, 57.8% now married, 8.1% widowed, 11.9% divorced (2000); Foreign born: 5.6% (2000); Ancestry (includes multiple ancestries): 31.2% German, 15.7% Irish, 11.6% Other groups, 11.1% English, 9.2% Norwegian (2000).

Economy: Single-family building permits issued: 20 (2007); Multi-family building permits issued: 0 (2007); Employment by occupation: 9.5% management, 12.0% professional, 12.5% services, 29.6% sales, 0.6% farming, 15.4% construction, 20.5% production (2000).

Income: Per capita income: $22,618 (2007); Median household income: $56,095 (2007); Average household income: $60,874 (2007); Percent of households with income of $100,000 or more: 15.5% (2007); Poverty rate: 5.5% (2000).

Education: Percent of population age 25 and over with: High school diploma (including GED) or higher: 78.5% (2007); Bachelor's degree or higher: 11.4% (2007); Master's degree or higher: 4.1% (2007).

School District(s)

Indian Valley Area Voc Ctr
2005-06 Enrollment: n/a . . . . (815) 786-9873

Sandwich CUSD 430 (PK-12)
2005-06 Enrollment: 2,566 . . . . (815) 786-2187

Housing: Homeownership rate: 69.9% (2007); Median home value: $181,984 (2007); Median rent: $510 per month (2000); Median age of housing: 38 years (2000).

Safety: Violent crime rate: 11.4 per 10,000 population; Property crime rate: 182.4 per 10,000 population (2006).

Transportation: Commute to work: 90.4% car, 1.3% public transportation, 2.9% walk, 1.9% work from home (2000); Travel time to work: 38.9% less than 15 minutes, 16.6% 15 to 30 minutes, 25.0% 30 to 45 minutes, 10.1% 45 to 60 minutes, 9.4% 60 minutes or more (2000)

Additional Information Contacts

City of Sandwich . . . . (815) 786-9321
http://www.sandwich.il.us

Sandwich Chamber of Commerce . . . . (815) 786-9075
http://www.sandwich-il.org

SHABBONA (village). Covers a land area of 0.742 square miles and a water area of 0 square miles. Located at 41.76° N. Lat.; 88.87° W. Long. Elevation is 899 feet.

Population: 850 (1990); 929 (2000); 900 (2007); 901 (2012 projected); Race: 98.6% White, 0.1% Black, 0.0% Asian, 1.7% Hispanic of any race (2007); Density: 1,213.6 persons per square mile (2007); Average household size: 2.77 (2007); Median age: 39.3 (2007); Males per 100 females: 82.2 (2007); Marriage status: 18.8% never married, 54.4% now married, 16.8% widowed, 10.0% divorced (2000); Foreign born: 1.3% (2000); Ancestry (includes multiple ancestries): 29.6% German, 18.6% Irish, 12.3% Norwegian, 11.8% English, 9.2% Other groups (2000).

Economy: Single-family building permits issued: 0 (2007); Multi-family building permits issued: 0 (2007); Employment by occupation: 11.2% management, 14.0% professional, 12.4% services, 25.5% sales, 2.6% farming, 17.4% construction, 16.9% production (2000).

Income: Per capita income: $26,134 (2007); Median household income: $54,070 (2007); Average household income: $68,231 (2007); Percent of households with income of $100,000 or more: 18.8% (2007); Poverty rate: 5.3% (2000).

Education: Percent of population age 25 and over with: High school diploma (including GED) or higher: 86.0% (2007); Bachelor's degree or higher: 11.6% (2007); Master's degree or higher: 3.0% (2007).

School District(s)

Indian Creek CUSD 425 (PK-12)
2005-06 Enrollment: 863 . . . . (815) 824-2197

Housing: Homeownership rate: 72.6% (2007); Median home value: $159,746 (2007); Median rent: $518 per month (2000); Median age of housing: 47 years (2000).

Transportation: Commute to work: 92.6% car, 0.0% public transportation, 2.7% walk, 3.9% work from home (2000); Travel time to work: 19.7% less than 15 minutes, 32.6% 15 to 30 minutes, 24.9% 30 to 45 minutes, 12.1% 45 to 60 minutes, 10.8% 60 minutes or more (2000)

SOMONAUK (village). Covers a land area of 0.613 square miles and a water area of 0 square miles. Located at 41.63° N. Lat.; 88.68° W. Long. Elevation is 686 feet.

Population: 1,263 (1990); 1,295 (2000); 1,375 (2007); 1,429 (2012 projected); Race: 96.7% White, 0.0% Black, 0.1% Asian, 3.2% Hispanic of any race (2007); Density: 2,244.0 persons per square mile (2007); Average household size: 2.52 (2007); Median age: 34.4 (2007); Males per 100 females: 93.4 (2007); Marriage status: 22.3% never married, 62.7% now married, 7.3% widowed, 7.7% divorced (2000); Foreign born: 1.0% (2000); Ancestry (includes multiple ancestries): 31.7% German, 15.0% Irish, 13.3% English, 8.8% French (except Basque), 8.3% United States or American (2000).

Economy: Single-family building permits issued: 5 (2007); Multi-family building permits issued: 0 (2007); Employment by occupation: 9.9% management, 15.8% professional, 12.8% services, 28.6% sales, 0.3% farming, 14.2% construction, 18.4% production (2000).

Income: Per capita income: $22,882 (2007); Median household income: $51,532 (2007); Average household income: $57,729 (2007); Percent of households with income of $100,000 or more: 11.4% (2007); Poverty rate: 5.4% (2000).

Education: Percent of population age 25 and over with: High school diploma (including GED) or higher: 90.0% (2007); Bachelor's degree or higher: 13.7% (2007); Master's degree or higher: 5.0% (2007).

School District(s)

Somonauk CUSD 432 (PK-12)
2005-06 Enrollment: 1,029 . . . . (815) 498-2314

Housing: Homeownership rate: 69.5% (2007); Median home value: $175,833 (2007); Median rent: $568 per month (2000); Median age of housing: 48 years (2000).

Safety: Violent crime rate: 46.9 per 10,000 population; Property crime rate: 194.4 per 10,000 population (2006).

Transportation: Commute to work: 94.3% car, 0.3% public transportation, 2.1% walk, 1.7% work from home (2000); Travel time to work: 30.7% less than 15 minutes, 17.9% 15 to 30 minutes, 27.5% 30 to 45 minutes, 15.1% 45 to 60 minutes, 8.7% 60 minutes or more (2000)

SYCAMORE (city). County seat. Covers a land area of 5.485 square miles and a water area of 0.018 square miles. Located at 41.98° N. Lat.; 88.69° W. Long. Elevation is 869 feet.

Population: 10,107 (1990); 12,020 (2000); 14,730 (2007); 16,527 (2012 projected); Race: 93.0% White, 2.2% Black, 0.9% Asian, 5.8% Hispanic of any race (2007); Density: 2,685.7 persons per square mile (2007); Average household size: 2.56 (2007); Median age: 34.1 (2007); Males per 100 females: 97.6 (2007); Marriage status: 22.7% never married, 60.9% now married, 6.0% widowed, 10.4% divorced (2000); Foreign born: 4.0% (2000); Ancestry (includes multiple ancestries): 30.9% German, 16.0% Irish, 10.4% Other groups, 10.4% English, 8.5% Swedish (2000).

Economy: Single-family building permits issued: 124 (2007); Multi-family building permits issued: 100 (2007); Employment by occupation: 13.8% management, 20.1% professional, 13.6% services, 24.0% sales, 0.1% farming, 9.1% construction, 19.3% production (2000).

Income: Per capita income: $26,126 (2007); Median household income: $58,105 (2007); Average household income: $66,402 (2007); Percent of households with income of $100,000 or more: 16.3% (2007); Poverty rate: 3.7% (2000).

Taxes: Total city taxes per capita: $841 (2006); City property taxes per capita: $182 (2006).

Education: Percent of population age 25 and over with: High school diploma (including GED) or higher: 90.7% (2007); Bachelor's degree or higher: 28.2% (2007); Master's degree or higher: 10.0% (2007).

School District(s)

Sycamore CUSD 427 (KG-12)
2005-06 Enrollment: 3,441 . . . . (815) 899-8103

Vocational/Technical School(s)

Hair Professionals Career College Inc (Private, For-profit)
Fall 2007 Enrollment: 182 . . . . (815) 756-3596
2007-08 Tuition: $16,400

Housing: Homeownership rate: 69.0% (2007); Median home value: $177,565 (2007); Median rent: $529 per month (2000); Median age of housing: 33 years (2000).

Hospitals: Kindred Hospital - Sycamore (77 beds)

Safety: Violent crime rate: 13.5 per 10,000 population; Property crime rate: 303.4 per 10,000 population (2006).

Newspapers: Genoa/Kingston/Kirkland News (Local news; Circulation 2,000); Hampshire Register (Community news; Circulation 1,700); Hampshire Register News (Local news; Circulation 1,700); Sycamore News (Local news; Circulation 10,221)

Transportation: Commute to work: 94.1% car, 0.1% public transportation, 2.2% walk, 2.3% work from home (2000); Travel time to work: 46.6% less than 15 minutes, 25.2% 15 to 30 minutes, 13.6% 30 to 45 minutes, 7.2% 45 to 60 minutes, 7.4% 60 minutes or more (2000)

Additional Information Contacts

City of Sycamore . . . . (815) 895-4515
http://www.cityofsycamore.com

Sycamore Chamber of Commerce . . . . (815) 895-3456
http://www.sycamorechamber.com

WATERMAN (village). Covers a land area of 1.002 square miles and a water area of 0 square miles. Located at 41.77° N. Lat.; 88.77° W. Long. Elevation is 823 feet.

Population: 1,073 (1990); 1,224 (2000); 1,371 (2007); 1,455 (2012 projected); Race: 98.2% White, 0.1% Black, 0.1% Asian, 1.5% Hispanic of any race (2007); Density: 1,368.1 persons per square mile (2007); Average household size: 2.63 (2007); Median age: 32.0 (2007); Males per 100 females: 93.9 (2007); Marriage status: 21.6% never married, 64.3% now married, 6.3% widowed, 7.8% divorced (2000); Foreign born: 1.6% (2000); Ancestry (includes multiple ancestries): 33.2% German, 11.7% English, 10.3% Irish, 10.1% Norwegian, 8.0% Polish (2000).

Economy: Single-family building permits issued: 38 (2007); Multi-family building permits issued: 0 (2007); Employment by occupation: 14.0% management, 12.6% professional, 15.9% services, 25.4% sales, 1.0% farming, 11.4% construction, 19.6% production (2000).
Income: Per capita income: $24,579 (2007); Median household income: $58,367 (2007); Average household income: $64,555 (2007); Percent of households with income of $100,000 or more: 15.9% (2007); Poverty rate: 6.2% (2000).
Education: Percent of population age 25 and over with: High school diploma (including GED) or higher: 90.2% (2007); Bachelor's degree or higher: 19.3% (2007); Master's degree or higher: 3.3% (2007).

School District(s)

Indian Creek CUSD 425 (PK-12)
2005-06 Enrollment: 863 . . . . (815) 824-2197

Housing: Homeownership rate: 76.1% (2007); Median home value: $180,030 (2007); Median rent: $500 per month (2000); Median age of housing: 45 years (2000).
Safety: Violent crime rate: 16.5 per 10,000 population; Property crime rate: 469.5 per 10,000 population (2006).
Transportation: Commute to work: 90.6% car, 0.0% public transportation, 4.0% walk, 5.1% work from home (2000); Travel time to work: 23.3% less than 15 minutes, 36.0% 15 to 30 minutes, 20.9% 30 to 45 minutes, 6.8% 45 to 60 minutes, 13.0% 60 minutes or more (2000)

Douglas County

Located in east central Illinois; drained by the Embarrass and Kaskaskia Rivers. Covers a land area of 416.86 square miles, a water area of 0.56 square miles, and is located in the Central Time Zone. The county was founded in 1859. County seat is Tuscola.

Weather Station: Tuscola — Elevation: 652 feet

	Jan	Feb	Mar	Apr	May	Jun	Jul	Aug	Sep	Oct	Nov	Dec
High	34	40	52	66	77	85	88	86	81	68	52	40
Low	17	22	32	42	52	62	65	63	55	44	33	24
Precip	2.1	2.1	3.2	4.0	4.0	4.1	4.7	3.7	3.2	2.9	3.8	3.0
Snow	8.0	4.8	2.5	0.3	tr	0.0	0.0	0.0	0.0	tr	1.7	4.8

High and Low temperatures in degrees Fahrenheit; Precipitation and Snow in inches

Population: 19,464 (1990); 19,922 (2000); 19,963 (2007); 19,940 (2012 projected); Race: 96.0% White, 0.5% Black, 0.6% Asian, 5.3% Hispanic of any race (2007); Density: 47.9 persons per square mile (2007); Average household size: 2.60 (2007); Median age: 38.1 (2007); Males per 100 females: 96.4 (2007).
Religion: Five largest groups: 12.4% The United Methodist Church, 11.3% Catholic Church, 8.1% Christian Churches and Churches of Christ, 7.3% Old Order Amish Church, 5.3% Christian Church (Disciples of Christ) (2000).
Economy: Unemployment rate: 5.2% (4/2008); Total civilian labor force: 10,484 (4/2008); Leading industries: 39.2% manufacturing; 19.2% retail trade; 8.7% accommodation & food services (2005); Farms: 576 totaling 232,690 acres (2002); Companies that employ 500 or more persons: 0 (2006); Companies that employ 100 to 499 persons: 9 (2006); Companies that employ less than 100 persons: 649 (2006); Black-owned businesses: n/a (2002); Hispanic-owned businesses: n/a (2002); Asian-owned businesses: n/a (2002); Women-owned businesses: 443 (2002); Retail sales per capita: $10,710 (2008). Single-family building permits issued: 40 (2007); Multi-family building permits issued: 2 (2007).
Income: Per capita income: $22,355 (2007); Median household income: $46,724 (2007); Average household income: $57,546 (2007); Percent of households with income of $100,000 or more: 11.7% (2007); Poverty rate: 7.5% (2005); Bankruptcy rate: 4.34% (2007).
Education: Percent of population age 25 and over with: High school diploma (including GED) or higher: 79.0% (2007); Bachelor's degree or higher: 13.8% (2007); Master's degree or higher: 4.5% (2007).
Housing: Homeownership rate: 76.9% (2007); Median home value: $101,321 (2007); Median rent: $317 per month (2000); Median age of housing: 42 years (2000).
Health: Birth rate: 156.1 per 10,000 population (2007); Death rate: 99.5 per 10,000 population (2007); Age-adjusted cancer mortality rate: 238.8 deaths per 100,000 population (2005); Number of physicians: 5.6 per 10,000 population (2005); Hospital beds: 0.0 per 10,000 population (2004); Hospital admissions: 0.0 per 10,000 population (2004).
Elections: 2004 Presidential election results: 66.8% Bush, 32.4% Kerry, 0.0% Nader, 0.8% Badnarik
National and State Parks: Walnut Point State Park

Additional Information Contacts

Douglas County Government. . . . . (217) 253-2411

Arcola Chamber of Commerce . . . . (800) 336-5456
http://www.arcolachamber.com
City of Arcola . . . . (217) 268-4966
http://www.arcolaillinois.org
Tuscola Chamber of Commerce . . . . (217) 253-5013
http://www.tuscola.org

Douglas County Communities

ARCOLA (city). Covers a land area of 1.368 square miles and a water area of 0.017 square miles. Located at 39.68° N. Lat.; 88.30° W. Long. Elevation is 679 feet.
History: Arcola was laid out in 1855 and named for a town in Italy. Broom corn was grown here, some for the local manufacture of brooms and some for export.
Population: 2,678 (1990); 2,652 (2000); 2,679 (2007); 2,691 (2012 projected); Race: 84.8% White, 0.2% Black, 1.7% Asian, 29.2% Hispanic of any race (2007); Density: 1,958.6 persons per square mile (2007); Average household size: 2.59 (2007); Median age: 37.5 (2007); Males per 100 females: 95.7 (2007); Marriage status: 20.9% never married, 63.1% now married, 6.4% widowed, 9.5% divorced (2000); Foreign born: 12.3% (2000); Ancestry (includes multiple ancestries): 20.2% Other groups, 17.4% German, 15.2% United States or American, 9.8% English, 7.3% Irish (2000).
Economy: Single-family building permits issued: 3 (2007); Multi-family building permits issued: 2 (2007); Employment by occupation: 10.1% management, 10.2% professional, 13.8% services, 24.5% sales, 1.8% farming, 5.5% construction, 34.1% production (2000).
Income: Per capita income: $21,631 (2007); Median household income: $43,263 (2007); Average household income: $55,774 (2007); Percent of households with income of $100,000 or more: 10.7% (2007); Poverty rate: 3.7% (2000).
Education: Percent of population age 25 and over with: High school diploma (including GED) or higher: 77.0% (2007); Bachelor's degree or higher: 12.9% (2007); Master's degree or higher: 4.6% (2007).

School District(s)

Arcola CUSD 306 (PK-12)
2005-06 Enrollment: 705 . . . . (217) 268-4963
Eastern Ill Area of Spec Educ (PK-12)
2005-06 Enrollment: 577 . . . . (217) 348-7700

Housing: Homeownership rate: 75.2% (2007); Median home value: $97,037 (2007); Median rent: $322 per month (2000); Median age of housing: 39 years (2000).
Safety: Violent crime rate: 15.0 per 10,000 population; Property crime rate: 48.8 per 10,000 population (2006).
Newspapers: Arcola Record-Herald (Community news; Circulation 2,200)
Transportation: Commute to work: 87.0% car, 0.6% public transportation, 7.7% walk, 4.3% work from home (2000); Travel time to work: 60.4% less than 15 minutes, 24.7% 15 to 30 minutes, 8.8% 30 to 45 minutes, 4.0% 45 to 60 minutes, 2.1% 60 minutes or more (2000)

Additional Information Contacts

Arcola Chamber of Commerce . . . . (800) 336-5456
http://www.arcolachamber.com
City of Arcola . . . . (217) 268-4966
http://www.arcolaillinois.org

ARTHUR (village). Covers a land area of 1.276 square miles and a water area of 0 square miles. Located at 39.71° N. Lat.; 88.47° W. Long. Elevation is 663 feet.
History: Arthur was settled in 1864 by a group of Amish colonists. The village was platted in 1873 by the Paris & Decatur Railroad Company. An early industry was the production of brooms.
Population: 2,268 (1990); 2,203 (2000); 2,249 (2007); 2,242 (2012 projected); Race: 99.7% White, 0.0% Black, 0.0% Asian, 0.5% Hispanic of any race (2007); Density: 1,762.8 persons per square mile (2007); Average household size: 2.41 (2007); Median age: 40.7 (2007); Males per 100 females: 90.9 (2007); Marriage status: 18.9% never married, 66.1% now married, 9.8% widowed, 5.2% divorced (2000); Foreign born: 0.4% (2000); Ancestry (includes multiple ancestries): 29.6% German, 15.0% United States or American, 11.5% English, 8.6% Irish, 4.8% Other groups (2000).
Economy: Single-family building permits issued: 4 (2007); Multi-family building permits issued: 0 (2007); Employment by occupation: 11.0%

management, 11.0% professional, 13.6% services, 29.7% sales, 0.3% farming, 10.8% construction, 23.7% production (2000).
Income: Per capita income: $22,503 (2007); Median household income: $44,574 (2007); Average household income: $51,999 (2007); Percent of households with income of $100,000 or more: 9.5% (2007); Poverty rate: 6.0% (2000).
Education: Percent of population age 25 and over with: High school diploma (including GED) or higher: 81.1% (2007); Bachelor's degree or higher: 16.3% (2007); Master's degree or higher: 3.7% (2007).

School District(s)

Arthur CUSD 305 (PK-12)
2005-06 Enrollment: 504 . . . . (217) 543-2511
Housing: Homeownership rate: 74.4% (2007); Median home value: $102,083 (2007); Median rent: $326 per month (2000); Median age of housing: 40 years (2000).
Safety: Violent crime rate: 9.2 per 10,000 population; Property crime rate: 151.4 per 10,000 population (2006).
Newspapers: Arthur Graphic Clarion (Local news; Circulation 3,100)
Transportation: Commute to work: 90.1% car, 0.0% public transportation, 4.5% walk, 2.9% work from home (2000); Travel time to work: 68.9% less than 15 minutes, 12.3% 15 to 30 minutes, 11.8% 30 to 45 minutes, 4.5% 45 to 60 minutes, 2.5% 60 minutes or more (2000)

CAMARGO (village). Covers a land area of 1.263 square miles and a water area of 0.013 square miles. Located at 39.79° N. Lat.; 88.16° W. Long. Elevation is 663 feet.
Population: 372 (1990); 469 (2000); 490 (2007); 498 (2012 projected); Race: 99.4% White, 0.0% Black, 0.0% Asian, 0.0% Hispanic of any race (2007); Density: 387.9 persons per square mile (2007); Average household size: 2.46 (2007); Median age: 40.4 (2007); Males per 100 females: 104.2 (2007); Marriage status: 19.3% never married, 60.9% now married, 8.5% widowed, 11.3% divorced (2000); Foreign born: 0.0% (2000); Ancestry (includes multiple ancestries): 19.2% United States or American, 17.5% German, 10.9% Irish, 10.9% English, 3.4% French (except Basque) (2000).
Economy: Single-family building permits issued: 4 (2007); Multi-family building permits issued: 0 (2007); Employment by occupation: 10.0% management, 15.4% professional, 12.9% services, 15.8% sales, 0.0% farming, 14.2% construction, 31.7% production (2000).
Income: Per capita income: $23,087 (2007); Median household income: $49,833 (2007); Average household income: $56,847 (2007); Percent of households with income of $100,000 or more: 12.6% (2007); Poverty rate: 6.9% (2000).
Education: Percent of population age 25 and over with: High school diploma (including GED) or higher: 84.6% (2007); Bachelor's degree or higher: 8.2% (2007); Master's degree or higher: 0.9% (2007).
Housing: Homeownership rate: 83.9% (2007); Median home value: $92,500 (2007); Median rent: $275 per month (2000); Median age of housing: 29 years (2000).
Transportation: Commute to work: 90.8% car, 0.0% public transportation, 3.3% walk, 5.4% work from home (2000); Travel time to work: 37.0% less than 15 minutes, 12.8% 15 to 30 minutes, 39.2% 30 to 45 minutes, 7.5% 45 to 60 minutes, 3.5% 60 minutes or more (2000)

GARRETT (village). Covers a land area of 0.139 square miles and a water area of 0 square miles. Located at 39.79° N. Lat.; 88.42° W. Long. Elevation is 669 feet.
Population: 169 (1990); 198 (2000); 203 (2007); 199 (2012 projected); Race: 98.5% White, 0.0% Black, 0.0% Asian, 4.4% Hispanic of any race (2007); Density: 1,458.9 persons per square mile (2007); Average household size: 2.60 (2007); Median age: 33.6 (2007); Males per 100 females: 99.0 (2007); Marriage status: 26.8% never married, 42.8% now married, 7.2% widowed, 23.2% divorced (2000); Foreign born: 0.0% (2000); Ancestry (includes multiple ancestries): 31.5% English, 22.7% German, 18.7% United States or American, 6.9% Other groups, 4.4% Irish (2000).
Economy: Employment by occupation: 1.4% management, 5.6% professional, 22.2% services, 13.9% sales, 2.8% farming, 16.7% construction, 37.5% production (2000).
Income: Per capita income: $15,665 (2007); Median household income: $36,000 (2007); Average household income: $40,769 (2007); Percent of households with income of $100,000 or more: 2.6% (2007); Poverty rate: 14.0% (2000).
Education: Percent of population age 25 and over with: High school diploma (including GED) or higher: 80.8% (2007); Bachelor's degree or higher: 1.7% (2007); Master's degree or higher: 1.7% (2007).
Housing: Homeownership rate: 85.9% (2007); Median home value: $30,313 (2007); Median rent: $240 per month (2000); Median age of housing: 50 years (2000).
Transportation: Commute to work: 100.0% car, 0.0% public transportation, 0.0% walk, 0.0% work from home (2000); Travel time to work: 23.6% less than 15 minutes, 54.2% 15 to 30 minutes, 18.1% 30 to 45 minutes, 1.4% 45 to 60 minutes, 2.8% 60 minutes or more (2000)

HINDSBORO (village). Covers a land area of 0.308 square miles and a water area of 0 square miles. Located at 39.68° N. Lat.; 88.13° W. Long. Elevation is 650 feet.
Population: 359 (1990); 361 (2000); 294 (2007); 296 (2012 projected); Race: 100.0% White, 0.0% Black, 0.0% Asian, 4.4% Hispanic of any race (2007); Density: 955.3 persons per square mile (2007); Average household size: 2.58 (2007); Median age: 36.4 (2007); Males per 100 females: 94.7 (2007); Marriage status: 20.1% never married, 57.3% now married, 9.9% widowed, 12.8% divorced (2000); Foreign born: 0.8% (2000); Ancestry (includes multiple ancestries): 28.4% German, 17.1% Irish, 15.4% English, 12.1% Other groups, 7.9% United States or American (2000).
Economy: Single-family building permits issued: 0 (2007); Multi-family building permits issued: 0 (2007); Employment by occupation: 8.4% management, 16.2% professional, 10.4% services, 20.1% sales, 1.3% farming, 7.8% construction, 35.7% production (2000).
Income: Per capita income: $19,255 (2007); Median household income: $36,429 (2007); Average household income: $48,487 (2007); Percent of households with income of $100,000 or more: 7.9% (2007); Poverty rate: 16.0% (2000).
Education: Percent of population age 25 and over with: High school diploma (including GED) or higher: 74.7% (2007); Bachelor's degree or higher: 15.1% (2007); Master's degree or higher: 7.5% (2007).
Housing: Homeownership rate: 87.7% (2007); Median home value: $66,500 (2007); Median rent: $263 per month (2000); Median age of housing: 58 years (2000).
Transportation: Commute to work: 94.1% car, 0.0% public transportation, 3.3% walk, 2.6% work from home (2000); Travel time to work: 35.6% less than 15 minutes, 43.0% 15 to 30 minutes, 16.8% 30 to 45 minutes, 2.0% 45 to 60 minutes, 2.7% 60 minutes or more (2000)

NEWMAN (city). Covers a land area of 0.624 square miles and a water area of 0 square miles. Located at 39.79° N. Lat.; 87.98° W. Long. Elevation is 653 feet.
History: Newman was founded in 1857 and named for B. Newman, son-in-law of the Methodist circuit-rider Peter Cartwright. Early industries included tile factories, and later a corn cannery and dairy products plant.
Population: 988 (1990); 956 (2000); 959 (2007); 918 (2012 projected); Race: 98.1% White, 1.3% Black, 0.0% Asian, 0.1% Hispanic of any race (2007); Density: 1,536.5 persons per square mile (2007); Average household size: 2.34 (2007); Median age: 44.6 (2007); Males per 100 females: 87.3 (2007); Marriage status: 19.4% never married, 56.1% now married, 14.3% widowed, 10.2% divorced (2000); Foreign born: 0.5% (2000); Ancestry (includes multiple ancestries): 16.8% German, 15.5% United States or American, 12.7% Irish, 10.9% English, 6.5% Other groups (2000).
Economy: Single-family building permits issued: 1 (2007); Multi-family building permits issued: 0 (2007); Employment by occupation: 11.1% management, 12.0% professional, 18.9% services, 22.7% sales, 1.8% farming, 9.1% construction, 24.3% production (2000).
Income: Per capita income: $22,292 (2007); Median household income: $38,500 (2007); Average household income: $50,927 (2007); Percent of households with income of $100,000 or more: 9.3% (2007); Poverty rate: 16.7% (2000).
Education: Percent of population age 25 and over with: High school diploma (including GED) or higher: 84.5% (2007); Bachelor's degree or higher: 11.7% (2007); Master's degree or higher: 2.9% (2007).

School District(s)

Shiloh CUSD 1 (PK-12)
2005-06 Enrollment: 489 . . . . (217) 887-2364
Housing: Homeownership rate: 77.6% (2007); Median home value: $59,302 (2007); Median rent: $266 per month (2000); Median age of housing: 59 years (2000).
Safety: Violent crime rate: 42.7 per 10,000 population; Property crime rate: 213.7 per 10,000 population (2006).
Newspapers: Newman Independent (Community news; Circulation 850)
Transportation: Commute to work: 93.6% car, 0.7% public transportation, 3.2% walk, 1.6% work from home (2000); Travel time to work: 23.8% less

than 15 minutes, 26.3% 15 to 30 minutes, 24.0% 30 to 45 minutes, 21.0% 45 to 60 minutes, 4.8% 60 minutes or more (2000)

TUSCOLA (city). County seat. Covers a land area of 2.133 square miles and a water area of 0.007 square miles. Located at 39.79° N. Lat.; 88.28° W. Long. Elevation is 653 feet.
History: The extension of the Illinois Central Railroad across the prairies in 1855 opened the land to cultivation and resulted in the settling of Tuscola in 1857. The name is of Indian origin and means "a level plain."
Population: 4,298 (1990); 4,448 (2000); 4,583 (2007); 4,662 (2012 projected); Race: 96.7% White, 0.6% Black, 1.4% Asian, 1.7% Hispanic of any race (2007); Density: 2,148.2 persons per square mile (2007); Average household size: 2.32 (2007); Median age: 39.0 (2007); Males per 100 females: 94.0 (2007); Marriage status: 20.3% never married, 61.9% now married, 7.9% widowed, 9.9% divorced (2000); Foreign born: 1.9% (2000); Ancestry (includes multiple ancestries): 27.9% German, 12.0% English, 11.8% Irish, 11.7% United States or American, 7.6% Other groups (2000).
Economy: Single-family building permits issued: 9 (2007); Multi-family building permits issued: 0 (2007); Employment by occupation: 13.2% management, 16.5% professional, 16.9% services, 26.5% sales, 0.3% farming, 10.1% construction, 16.5% production (2000).
Income: Per capita income: $23,115 (2007); Median household income: $45,401 (2007); Average household income: $53,470 (2007); Percent of households with income of $100,000 or more: 8.2% (2007); Poverty rate: 4.1% (2000).
Education: Percent of population age 25 and over with: High school diploma (including GED) or higher: 89.8% (2007); Bachelor's degree or higher: 18.2% (2007); Master's degree or higher: 6.4% (2007).

School District(s)

Tuscola CUSD 301 (PK-12)
2005-06 Enrollment: 994 . . . . (217) 253-4241
Housing: Homeownership rate: 72.3% (2007); Median home value: $109,695 (2007); Median rent: $353 per month (2000); Median age of housing: 44 years (2000).
Safety: Violent crime rate: 78.6 per 10,000 population; Property crime rate: 242.2 per 10,000 population (2006).
Newspapers: Tuscola Review (Local news; Circulation 3,600)
Transportation: Commute to work: 93.5% car, 0.0% public transportation, 1.8% walk, 4.4% work from home (2000); Travel time to work: 53.9% less than 15 minutes, 14.8% 15 to 30 minutes, 25.2% 30 to 45 minutes, 3.9% 45 to 60 minutes, 2.2% 60 minutes or more (2000)
Additional Information Contacts
Tuscola Chamber of Commerce . . . . (217) 253-5013
http://www.tuscola.org

VILLA GROVE (city). Covers a land area of 1.492 square miles and a water area of 0.007 square miles. Located at 39.86° N. Lat.; 88.16° W. Long. Elevation is 653 feet.
Population: 2,778 (1990); 2,553 (2000); 2,510 (2007); 2,490 (2012 projected); Race: 97.8% White, 0.5% Black, 0.2% Asian, 1.4% Hispanic of any race (2007); Density: 1,682.3 persons per square mile (2007); Average household size: 2.43 (2007); Median age: 38.8 (2007); Males per 100 females: 97.0 (2007); Marriage status: 20.3% never married, 58.5% now married, 8.3% widowed, 12.9% divorced (2000); Foreign born: 0.8% (2000); Ancestry (includes multiple ancestries): 29.8% German, 15.7% United States or American, 13.2% Irish, 12.5% Other groups, 10.8% English (2000).
Economy: Single-family building permits issued: 5 (2007); Multi-family building permits issued: 0 (2007); Employment by occupation: 8.9% management, 10.7% professional, 19.7% services, 28.6% sales, 0.7% farming, 8.0% construction, 23.4% production (2000).
Income: Per capita income: $20,815 (2007); Median household income: $43,920 (2007); Average household income: $50,232 (2007); Percent of households with income of $100,000 or more: 7.5% (2007); Poverty rate: 7.1% (2000).
Education: Percent of population age 25 and over with: High school diploma (including GED) or higher: 83.8% (2007); Bachelor's degree or higher: 10.7% (2007); Master's degree or higher: 2.7% (2007).

School District(s)

Villa Grove CUSD 302 (PK-12)
2005-06 Enrollment: 669 . . . . (217) 832-2261
Housing: Homeownership rate: 75.7% (2007); Median home value: $89,766 (2007); Median rent: $317 per month (2000); Median age of housing: 45 years (2000).
Safety: Violent crime rate: 23.9 per 10,000 population; Property crime rate: 167.5 per 10,000 population (2006).
Newspapers: Southern Champaign County Today (Local news; Circulation 2,850); Villa Grove News (Local news; Circulation 1,700)
Transportation: Commute to work: 94.8% car, 0.0% public transportation, 3.2% walk, 1.2% work from home (2000); Travel time to work: 22.9% less than 15 minutes, 29.2% 15 to 30 minutes, 37.7% 30 to 45 minutes, 6.7% 45 to 60 minutes, 3.5% 60 minutes or more (2000)

Du Page County

Located in northeastern Illinois; drained by the Du Page River. Covers a land area of 333.61 square miles, a water area of 2.95 square miles, and is located in the Central Time Zone. The county was founded in 1939. County seat is Wheaton.

Du Page County is part of the Chicago-Naperville-Joliet, IL-IN-WI Metropolitan Statistical Area. The entire metro area includes: Chicago-Naperville-Joliet, IL Metropolitan Division (Cook County, IL; DeKalb County, IL; DuPage County, IL; Grundy County, IL; Kane County, IL; Kendall County, IL; McHenry County, IL; Will County, IL); Gary, IN Metropolitan Division (Jasper County, IN; Lake County, IN; Newton County, IN; Porter County, IN); Lake County-Kenosha County, IL-WI Metropolitan Division (Lake County, IL; Kenosha County, WI)

Weather Station: Wheaton 3 SE Elevation: 679 feet

	Jan	Feb	Mar	Apr	May	Jun	Jul	Aug	Sep	Oct	Nov	Dec
High	31	37	49	62	74	83	87	85	78	66	49	37
Low	14	18	28	37	47	57	63	61	53	42	31	21
Precip	1.8	1.6	2.7	3.8	4.0	3.9	3.9	4.7	3.5	2.7	3.2	2.4
Snow	11.1	7.8	4.8	0.8	tr	0.0	0.0	0.0	0.0	tr	1.9	6.1

High and Low temperatures in degrees Fahrenheit; Precipitation and Snow in inches

Population: 781,666 (1990); 904,161 (2000); 933,488 (2007); 949,144 (2012 projected); Race: 79.4% White, 4.2% Black, 9.9% Asian, 11.9% Hispanic of any race (2007); Density: 2,798.2 persons per square mile (2007); Average household size: 2.76 (2007); Median age: 37.5 (2007); Males per 100 females: 98.0 (2007).
Religion: Five largest groups: 38.6% Catholic Church, 3.0% Lutheran Church—Missouri Synod, 3.0% Evangelical Lutheran Church in America, 2.2% The United Methodist Church, 1.7% Muslim Estimate (2000).
Economy: Unemployment rate: 4.3% (4/2008); Total civilian labor force: 544,189 (4/2008); Leading industries: 11.1% retail trade; 11.0% administration, support, waste management, remediation services; 10.3% manufacturing (2005); Farms: 79 totaling 7,683 acres (2002); Companies that employ 500 or more persons: 101 (2006); Companies that employ 100 to 499 persons: 981 (2006); Companies that employ less than 100 persons: 32,989 (2006); Black-owned businesses: n/a (2002); Hispanic-owned businesses: n/a (2002); Asian-owned businesses: n/a (2002); Women-owned businesses: n/a (2002); Retail sales per capita: $21,521 (2008). Single-family building permits issued: 1,516 (2007); Multi-family building permits issued: 350 (2007).
Income: Per capita income: $35,148 (2007); Median household income: $74,975 (2007); Average household income: $96,470 (2007); Percent of households with income of $100,000 or more: 33.4% (2007); Poverty rate: 5.0% (2005); Bankruptcy rate: 1.93% (2007).
Taxes: Total county taxes per capita: $160 (2006); County property taxes per capita: $117 (2006).
Education: Percent of population age 25 and over with: High school diploma (including GED) or higher: 89.9% (2007); Bachelor's degree or higher: 41.6% (2007); Master's degree or higher: 14.8% (2007).
Housing: Homeownership rate: 76.3% (2007); Median home value: $291,753 (2007); Median rent: $775 per month (2000); Median age of housing: 25 years (2000).
Health: Birth rate: 130.2 per 10,000 population (2007); Death rate: 61.9 per 10,000 population (2007); Age-adjusted cancer mortality rate: 175.5 deaths per 100,000 population (2005); Air Quality Index: 68.5% good, 30.7% moderate, 0.8% unhealthy for sensitive individuals, 0.0% unhealthy (percent of days in 2007); Number of physicians: 44.0 per 10,000 population (2005); Hospital beds: 23.2 per 10,000 population (2004); Hospital admissions: 1,185.1 per 10,000 population (2004).
Elections: 2004 Presidential election results: 54.4% Bush, 44.8% Kerry, 0.2% Nader, 0.6% Badnarik
Additional Information Contacts
Du Page County Government . . . . (630) 407-8700
http://www.co.dupage.il.us

Bartlett Chamber of Commerce . . . . (630) 830-0324
http://www.bartlettchamber.com
Bloomingdale Chamber of Commerce . . . . (630) 980-9082
http://www.bloomingdalechamber.com
Carol Stream Chamber of Commerce . . . . (630) 665-3325
http://www.carolstreamchamber.com
City of Darien . . . . (630) 852-5000
http://www.darien.il.us
City of Elmhurst . . . . (630) 530-3000
http://www.elmhurst.org
City of Naperville . . . . (630) 420-6111
http://www.naperville.il.us
City of Warrenville . . . . (630) 393-9427
http://www.warrenville.il.us
City of West Chicago . . . . (630) 393-9427
http://www.westchicago.org
City of Wheaton . . . . (630) 260-2012
http://www.wheaton.il.us
City of Wood Dale . . . . (630) 766-4900
http://www.wooddale.com
Clarendon Hills Chamber of Commerce . . . . (630) 654-3030
Darien Chamber of Commerce . . . . (630) 968-0004
http://www.darienchamber.com
Downers Grove Area Chamber of Commerce . . . . (630) 968-4050
http://www.downersgrove.org
Elmhurst Chamber of Commerce . . . . (630) 834-6060
http://www.elmhurstchamber.org
Glen Ellyn Chamber of Commerce . . . . (630) 469-0907
http://www.glenellynchamber.com
Glendale Heights Chamber of Commerce . . . . (630) 545-1099
http://www.glendaleheightschamber.com
Greater Oak Brook Chamber of Commerce . . . . (630) 472-9377
http://www.obchamber.com
Hinsdale Chamber of Commerce . . . . (630) 323-3952
http://www.hinsdalechamber.com
Lisle Area Chamber of Commerce . . . . (630) 964-0052
http://www.lislechamber.com
Lisle Convention & Visitors Bureau . . . . (800) 733-9811
http://www.lislecvb.com
Lombard Chamber of Commerce . . . . (630) 627-5040
http://www.lombardchamber.com
Naperville Area Chamber of Commerce . . . . (630) 355-4141
http://www.naperville.net
Roselle Chamber of Commerce & Industry . . . . (630) 894-3010
http://www.rosellechamber.com
Villa Park Chamber of Commerce . . . . (630) 941-9133
http://www.villaparkchamber.org
Village of Addison . . . . (630) 543-4100
http://www.addisonadvantage.org
Village of Bartlett . . . . (630) 837-0800
http://www.village.bartlett.il.us
Village of Bensenville . . . . (630) 766-8200
http://www.bensenville.il.us
Village of Bloomingdale . . . . (630) 893-7000
http://www.villageofbloomingdale.org
Village of Burr Ridge . . . . (630) 654-8181
http://www.burr-ridge.gov
Village of Carol Stream . . . . (630) 665-7050
http://www.carolstream.org
Village of Downers Grove . . . . (630) 434-5500
http://www.downers.us
Village of Glen Ellyn . . . . (630) 469-3000
http://www.glen-ellyn.com/gov/index.html
Village of Glendale Heights . . . . (630) 260-6000
http://www.glendaleheights.org
Village of Hinsdale . . . . (630) 789-7011
http://www.villageofhinsdale.org
Village of Itasca . . . . (630) 773-0835
http://www.itasca.com
Village of Lisle . . . . (630) 271-4100
http://www.vil.lisle.il.us
Village of Lombard . . . . (630) 620-5700
http://www.villageoflombard.org
Village of Oak Brook . . . . (630) 368-5000
http://www.oak-brook.org
Village of Roselle . . . . (630) 980-2000
http://www.roselle.il.us
Village of Villa Park . . . . (630) 834-8500
http://www.invillapark.com
Village of Westmont . . . . (630) 981-6200
http://www.westmont.il.gov
Village of Willowbrook . . . . (630) 323-8215
http://www.willowbrookil.org
Village of Winfield . . . . (630) 933-7100
http://www.villageofwinfield.com
Village of Woodridge . . . . (630) 719-4712
http://www.vil.woodridge.il.us
Warrenville Chamber of Commerce . . . . (630) 393-9080
http://www.warrenvillechamber.com
West Chicago Chamber of Commerce & Industry . . . . (630) 231-3003
http://www.wegochamber.org
Westmont Chamber of Commerce & Tourism Bureau . . . . (630) 960-5553
http://www.westmontchamber.com
Wheaton Chamber of Commerce . . . . (630) 668-6464
http://www.ewheaton.com
Willowbrook-Burr Ridge Chamber of Commerce . . . . (630) 654-0909
http://www.wbbrchamber.org
Winfield Chamber of Commerce . . . . (630) 682-3712
http://www.winfieldchamber.biz
Wood Dale Chamber of Commerce . . . . (630) 595-0505
http://www.wooddalechamber.com
Woodridge Area Chamber of Commerce . . . . (630) 960-7080
http://www.woodridgechamber.org

Du Page County Communities

ADDISON (village). Covers a land area of 9.432 square miles and a water area of 0.054 square miles. Located at 41.93° N. Lat.; 88.00° W. Long. Elevation is 689 feet.

History: Addison developed as a community of German Lutherans in the 1840's. It was named for the 18th-century essayist, Joseph Addison.

Population: 33,723 (1990); 35,914 (2000); 36,750 (2007); 37,213 (2012 projected); Race: 68.3% White, 3.4% Black, 9.4% Asian, 37.8% Hispanic of any race (2007); Density: 3,896.2 persons per square mile (2007); Average household size: 3.09 (2007); Median age: 34.8 (2007); Males per 100 females: 103.6 (2007); Marriage status: 28.1% never married, 60.0% now married, 4.8% widowed, 7.2% divorced (2000); Foreign born: 34.3% (2000); Ancestry (includes multiple ancestries): 36.9% Other groups, 16.3% Italian, 14.3% German, 13.0% Polish, 8.8% Irish (2000).

Economy: Unemployment rate: 6.3% (4/2008); Total civilian labor force: 20,489 (4/2008); Single-family building permits issued: 29 (2007); Multi-family building permits issued: 5 (2007); Employment by occupation: 12.5% management, 14.4% professional, 11.5% services, 29.6% sales, 0.1% farming, 10.2% construction, 21.7% production (2000).

Income: Per capita income: $23,443 (2007); Median household income: $58,071 (2007); Average household income: $72,241 (2007); Percent of households with income of $100,000 or more: 20.9% (2007); Poverty rate: 9.6% (2000).

Taxes: Total city taxes per capita: $485 (2006); City property taxes per capita: $237 (2006).

Education: Percent of population age 25 and over with: High school diploma (including GED) or higher: 73.0% (2007); Bachelor's degree or higher: 19.3% (2007); Master's degree or higher: 5.1% (2007).

School District(s)

Addison SD 4 (PK-08)
2005-06 Enrollment: 3,968 . . . . (630) 628-2500
Du Page HSD 88 (09-12)
2005-06 Enrollment: 4,057 . . . . (630) 530-3980
Dupage Roe (06-12)
2005-06 Enrollment: 70 . . . . (630) 407-5800
Technology Center of Dupage
2005-06 Enrollment: n/a . . . . (630) 620-8770

Four-year College(s)

DeVry University-Illinois (Private, For-profit)
Fall 2007 Enrollment: 19,417 . . . . (630) 953-1300
2007-08 Tuition: In-state $13,220; Out-of-state $13,220

Housing: Homeownership rate: 68.0% (2007); Median home value: $270,821 (2007); Median rent: $644 per month (2000); Median age of housing: 29 years (2000).

Safety: Violent crime rate: 23.4 per 10,000 population; Property crime rate: 236.1 per 10,000 population (2006).
Transportation: Commute to work: 92.2% car, 2.6% public transportation, 2.4% walk, 1.7% work from home (2000); Travel time to work: 27.4% less than 15 minutes, 38.2% 15 to 30 minutes, 20.5% 30 to 45 minutes, 6.5% 45 to 60 minutes, 7.4% 60 minutes or more (2000)
Additional Information Contacts
Village of Addison . . . . (630) 543-4100
http://www.addisonadvantage.org

BARTLETT (village). Covers a land area of 14.814 square miles and a water area of 0.144 square miles. Located at 41.97° N. Lat.; 88.19° W. Long.
Population: 19,814 (1990); 36,706 (2000); 39,234 (2007); 40,643 (2012 projected); Race: 82.7% White, 2.6% Black, 10.9% Asian, 7.4% Hispanic of any race (2007); Density: 2,648.5 persons per square mile (2007); Average household size: 3.01 (2007); Median age: 35.3 (2007); Males per 100 females: 97.8 (2007); Marriage status: 19.5% never married, 70.3% now married, 3.2% widowed, 7.1% divorced (2000); Foreign born: 10.9% (2000); Ancestry (includes multiple ancestries): 28.5% German, 17.2% Italian, 16.4% Other groups, 16.3% Irish, 15.3% Polish (2000).
Economy: Unemployment rate: 4.4% (4/2008); Total civilian labor force: 23,752 (4/2008); Single-family building permits issued: 252 (2007); Multi-family building permits issued: 144 (2007); Employment by occupation: 23.3% management, 19.9% professional, 7.9% services, 31.9% sales, 0.0% farming, 7.2% construction, 9.8% production (2000).
Income: Per capita income: $34,982 (2007); Median household income: $92,120 (2007); Average household income: $105,128 (2007); Percent of households with income of $100,000 or more: 43.7% (2007); Poverty rate: 1.9% (2000).
Education: Percent of population age 25 and over with: High school diploma (including GED) or higher: 92.3% (2007); Bachelor's degree or higher: 38.8% (2007); Master's degree or higher: 10.9% (2007).
School District(s)
SD U-46 (PK-12)
2005-06 Enrollment: 39,656 . . . . (847) 888-5000
Housing: Homeownership rate: 93.6% (2007); Median home value: $302,478 (2007); Median rent: $691 per month (2000); Median age of housing: 11 years (2000).
Safety: Violent crime rate: 3.9 per 10,000 population; Property crime rate: 124.2 per 10,000 population (2006).
Newspapers: Bartlett Examiner (Community news; Circulation 10,000); Carol Stream Examiner (Community news; Circulation 7,700); Hanover Park Examiner (Community news; Circulation 5,800); Streamwood Examiner (Community news; Circulation 7,000); Wayne Examiner (Community news; Circulation 9,000)
Transportation: Commute to work: 90.1% car, 5.4% public transportation, 0.3% walk, 3.4% work from home (2000); Travel time to work: 15.3% less than 15 minutes, 29.3% 15 to 30 minutes, 27.8% 30 to 45 minutes, 12.6% 45 to 60 minutes, 15.0% 60 minutes or more (2000)
Additional Information Contacts
Bartlett Chamber of Commerce . . . . (630) 830-0324
http://www.bartlettchamber.com
Village of Bartlett . . . . (630) 837-0800
http://www.village.bartlett.il.us

BENSENVILLE (village). Covers a land area of 6.006 square miles and a water area of 0 square miles. Located at 41.95° N. Lat.; 87.94° W. Long. Elevation is 679 feet.
Population: 17,957 (1990); 20,703 (2000); 20,638 (2007); 20,523 (2012 projected); Race: 61.7% White, 4.4% Black, 6.7% Asian, 48.1% Hispanic of any race (2007); Density: 3,436.4 persons per square mile (2007); Average household size: 3.05 (2007); Median age: 35.1 (2007); Males per 100 females: 106.7 (2007); Marriage status: 28.0% never married, 56.9% now married, 6.8% widowed, 8.3% divorced (2000); Foreign born: 31.5% (2000); Ancestry (includes multiple ancestries): 43.8% Other groups, 17.6% German, 10.7% Polish, 9.8% Irish, 9.3% Italian (2000).
Economy: Single-family building permits issued: 5 (2007); Multi-family building permits issued: 0 (2007); Employment by occupation: 9.6% management, 13.7% professional, 10.7% services, 30.6% sales, 0.3% farming, 8.1% construction, 26.8% production (2000).
Income: Per capita income: $21,970 (2007); Median household income: $57,968 (2007); Average household income: $65,679 (2007); Percent of households with income of $100,000 or more: 15.6% (2007); Poverty rate: 6.5% (2000).
Education: Percent of population age 25 and over with: High school diploma (including GED) or higher: 71.1% (2007); Bachelor's degree or higher: 18.5% (2007); Master's degree or higher: 4.4% (2007).
School District(s)
Bensenville SD 2 (PK-08)
2005-06 Enrollment: 2,403 . . . . (630) 766-5940
Fenton CHSD 100 (09-12)
2005-06 Enrollment: 1,563 . . . . (630) 860-6257
Vocational/Technical School(s)
Star Truck Driving School (Private, For-profit)
Fall 2007 Enrollment: 71 . . . . (630) 236-7200
2007-08 Tuition: $4,595
Housing: Homeownership rate: 54.9% (2007); Median home value: $242,535 (2007); Median rent: $731 per month (2000); Median age of housing: 32 years (2000).
Safety: Violent crime rate: 22.4 per 10,000 population; Property crime rate: 249.6 per 10,000 population (2006).
Newspapers: KJT International & Polish News (International news; Circulation 10,000)
Transportation: Commute to work: 89.0% car, 4.2% public transportation, 3.2% walk, 2.2% work from home (2000); Travel time to work: 28.6% less than 15 minutes, 39.5% 15 to 30 minutes, 17.4% 30 to 45 minutes, 8.6% 45 to 60 minutes, 6.0% 60 minutes or more (2000)
Additional Information Contacts
Village of Bensenville. . . . . (630) 766-8200
http://www.bensenville.il.us

BLOOMINGDALE (village). Covers a land area of 6.765 square miles and a water area of 0.042 square miles. Located at 41.95° N. Lat.; 88.08° W. Long. Elevation is 764 feet.
Population: 16,990 (1990); 21,675 (2000); 22,133 (2007); 22,280 (2012 projected); Race: 80.4% White, 3.6% Black, 11.5% Asian, 6.5% Hispanic of any race (2007); Density: 3,271.8 persons per square mile (2007); Average household size: 2.59 (2007); Median age: 41.1 (2007); Males per 100 females: 94.1 (2007); Marriage status: 24.6% never married, 58.0% now married, 8.2% widowed, 9.2% divorced (2000); Foreign born: 13.2% (2000); Ancestry (includes multiple ancestries): 21.0% German, 20.7% Italian, 16.8% Other groups, 15.9% Irish, 12.5% Polish (2000).
Economy: Single-family building permits issued: 15 (2007); Multi-family building permits issued: 0 (2007); Employment by occupation: 22.4% management, 19.2% professional, 8.3% services, 33.8% sales, 0.0% farming, 5.8% construction, 10.6% production (2000).
Income: Per capita income: $35,371 (2007); Median household income: $73,457 (2007); Average household income: $90,550 (2007); Percent of households with income of $100,000 or more: 30.2% (2007); Poverty rate: 2.7% (2000).
Taxes: Total city taxes per capita: $498 (2006); City property taxes per capita: $261 (2006).
Education: Percent of population age 25 and over with: High school diploma (including GED) or higher: 89.4% (2007); Bachelor's degree or higher: 34.7% (2007); Master's degree or higher: 10.4% (2007).
School District(s)
Bloomingdale SD 13 (PK-08)
2005-06 Enrollment: 1,412 . . . . (630) 893-9590
CCSD 93 (PK-08)
2005-06 Enrollment: 4,517 . . . . (630) 893-9393
Marquardt SD 15 (PK-08)
2005-06 Enrollment: 2,622 . . . . (630) 469-7615
North Dupage Sp Ed Cooperative (03-12)
2005-06 Enrollment: 42 . . . . (630) 894-0490
Vocational/Technical School(s)
Pivot Point Beauty School (Private, For-profit)
Fall 2007 Enrollment: 263 . . . . (847) 985-5900
2007-08 Tuition: $16,482
Housing: Homeownership rate: 71.8% (2007); Median home value: $317,426 (2007); Median rent: $912 per month (2000); Median age of housing: 18 years (2000).
Safety: Violent crime rate: 9.6 per 10,000 population; Property crime rate: 399.6 per 10,000 population (2006).
Transportation: Commute to work: 90.5% car, 5.4% public transportation, 0.8% walk, 2.7% work from home (2000); Travel time to work: 18.5% less than 15 minutes, 32.9% 15 to 30 minutes, 27.8% 30 to 45 minutes, 8.7% 45 to 60 minutes, 12.0% 60 minutes or more (2000)
Additional Information Contacts

Bloomingdale Chamber of Commerce . . . . (630) 980-9082
http://www.bloomingdalechamber.com
Village of Bloomingdale . . . . (630) 893-7000
http://www.villageofbloomingdale.org

BURR RIDGE (village). Covers a land area of 6.424 square miles and a water area of 0.112 square miles. Located at 41.75° N. Lat.; 87.92° W. Long. Elevation is 702 feet.

Population: 8,340 (1990); 10,408 (2000); 10,867 (2007); 11,080 (2012 projected); Race: 82.2% White, 1.3% Black, 13.3% Asian, 3.7% Hispanic of any race (2007); Density: 1,691.5 persons per square mile (2007); Average household size: 2.88 (2007); Median age: 46.4 (2007); Males per 100 females: 95.6 (2007); Marriage status: 20.2% never married, 69.7% now married, 6.0% widowed, 4.1% divorced (2000); Foreign born: 13.2% (2000); Ancestry (includes multiple ancestries): 21.2% German, 17.4% Irish, 15.0% Other groups, 12.2% Italian, 9.8% Polish (2000).

Economy: Single-family building permits issued: 30 (2007); Multi-family building permits issued: 0 (2007); Employment by occupation: 28.3% management, 34.0% professional, 5.7% services, 26.8% sales, 0.1% farming, 2.9% construction, 2.1% production (2000).

Income: Per capita income: $72,973 (2007); Median household income: $148,965 (2007); Average household income: $208,526 (2007); Percent of households with income of $100,000 or more: 65.9% (2007); Poverty rate: 2.8% (2000).

Education: Percent of population age 25 and over with: High school diploma (including GED) or higher: 95.3% (2007); Bachelor's degree or higher: 58.4% (2007); Master's degree or higher: 26.0% (2007).

School District(s)

CCSD 180 (PK-08)
2005-06 Enrollment: 769 . . . . (630) 734-6600
Gower SD 62 (PK-08)
2005-06 Enrollment: 956 . . . . (630) 986-5383
Hinsdale CCSD 181 (PK-08)
2005-06 Enrollment: 4,059 . . . . (630) 887-1070
Pleasantdale SD 107 (PK-08)
2005-06 Enrollment: 830 . . . . (708) 784-2013

Four-year College(s)

ITT Technical Institute-Burr Ridge (Private, For-profit)
Fall 2007 Enrollment: 287 . . . . (630) 455-6470
2007-08 Tuition: In-state $15,600; Out-of-state $15,600

Vocational/Technical School(s)

Everest College-Burr Ridge (Private, For-profit)
Fall 2007 Enrollment: 362 . . . . (630) 920-1102
2007-08 Tuition: $11,225

Housing: Homeownership rate: 94.8% (2007); Median home value: $685,244 (2007); Median rent: $1,130 per month (2000); Median age of housing: 16 years (2000).

Safety: Violent crime rate: 1.8 per 10,000 population; Property crime rate: 151.9 per 10,000 population (2006).

Transportation: Commute to work: 86.2% car, 8.9% public transportation, 0.0% walk, 4.6% work from home (2000); Travel time to work: 16.2% less than 15 minutes, 29.1% 15 to 30 minutes, 25.9% 30 to 45 minutes, 14.9% 45 to 60 minutes, 13.9% 60 minutes or more (2000)

Additional Information Contacts

Village of Burr Ridge . . . . (630) 654-8181
http://www.burr-ridge.gov
Willowbrook-Burr Ridge Chamber of Commerce . . . . (630) 654-0909
http://www.wbbrchamber.org

CAROL STREAM (village). Covers a land area of 8.896 square miles and a water area of 0.028 square miles. Located at 41.92° N. Lat.; 88.14° W. Long. Elevation is 758 feet.

Population: 32,079 (1990); 40,438 (2000); 40,037 (2007); 39,694 (2012 projected); Race: 72.6% White, 5.2% Black, 14.6% Asian, 12.7% Hispanic of any race (2007); Density: 4,500.7 persons per square mile (2007); Average household size: 2.95 (2007); Median age: 33.7 (2007); Males per 100 females: 98.2 (2007); Marriage status: 25.7% never married, 61.8% now married, 4.9% widowed, 7.5% divorced (2000); Foreign born: 16.8% (2000); Ancestry (includes multiple ancestries): 24.5% Other groups, 24.3% German, 14.3% Irish, 14.2% Italian, 12.7% Polish (2000).

Economy: Unemployment rate: 4.5% (4/2008); Total civilian labor force: 23,708 (4/2008); Single-family building permits issued: 148 (2007); Multi-family building permits issued: 0 (2007); Employment by occupation: 17.8% management, 19.9% professional, 9.0% services, 33.4% sales, 0.0% farming, 6.8% construction, 13.1% production (2000).

Income: Per capita income: $28,369 (2007); Median household income: $73,572 (2007); Average household income: $83,163 (2007); Percent of households with income of $100,000 or more: 30.7% (2007); Poverty rate: 3.4% (2000).

Education: Percent of population age 25 and over with: High school diploma (including GED) or higher: 89.7% (2007); Bachelor's degree or higher: 31.9% (2007); Master's degree or higher: 8.4% (2007).

School District(s)

Benjamin SD 25 (PK-08)
2005-06 Enrollment: 919 . . . . (630) 876-7800
CCSD 93 (PK-08)
2005-06 Enrollment: 4,517 . . . . (630) 893-9393
Glenbard Twp HSD 87 (09-12)
2005-06 Enrollment: 8,998 . . . . (630) 469-9100
SD U-46 (PK-12)
2005-06 Enrollment: 39,656 . . . . (847) 888-5000

Housing: Homeownership rate: 70.5% (2007); Median home value: $246,507 (2007); Median rent: $750 per month (2000); Median age of housing: 17 years (2000).

Safety: Violent crime rate: 20.0 per 10,000 population; Property crime rate: 179.3 per 10,000 population (2006).

Transportation: Commute to work: 91.9% car, 3.7% public transportation, 0.9% walk, 2.9% work from home (2000); Travel time to work: 24.1% less than 15 minutes, 29.1% 15 to 30 minutes, 25.5% 30 to 45 minutes, 10.0% 45 to 60 minutes, 11.3% 60 minutes or more (2000)

Additional Information Contacts

Carol Stream Chamber of Commerce . . . . (630) 665-3325
http://www.carolstreamchamber.com
Village of Carol Stream . . . . (630) 665-7050
http://www.carolstream.org

CLARENDON HILLS (village). Covers a land area of 1.739 square miles and a water area of 0.003 square miles. Located at 41.79° N. Lat.; 87.95° W. Long. Elevation is 728 feet.

Population: 7,174 (1990); 7,610 (2000); 8,344 (2007); 8,763 (2012 projected); Race: 92.2% White, 1.2% Black, 4.4% Asian, 2.8% Hispanic of any race (2007); Density: 4,799.2 persons per square mile (2007); Average household size: 2.73 (2007); Median age: 37.8 (2007); Males per 100 females: 93.5 (2007); Marriage status: 20.3% never married, 67.0% now married, 5.3% widowed, 7.5% divorced (2000); Foreign born: 8.1% (2000); Ancestry (includes multiple ancestries): 26.9% German, 21.7% Irish, 13.4% Polish, 10.0% Italian, 8.5% English (2000).

Economy: Single-family building permits issued: 26 (2007); Multi-family building permits issued: 0 (2007); Employment by occupation: 29.2% management, 28.4% professional, 7.2% services, 28.1% sales, 0.0% farming, 2.7% construction, 4.4% production (2000).

Income: Per capita income: $48,616 (2007); Median household income: $96,224 (2007); Average household income: $132,405 (2007); Percent of households with income of $100,000 or more: 47.9% (2007); Poverty rate: 0.6% (2000).

Education: Percent of population age 25 and over with: High school diploma (including GED) or higher: 96.0% (2007); Bachelor's degree or higher: 65.2% (2007); Master's degree or higher: 27.5% (2007).

School District(s)

Hinsdale CCSD 181 (PK-08)
2005-06 Enrollment: 4,059 . . . . (630) 887-1070
Maercker SD 60 (PK-08)
2005-06 Enrollment: 1,413 . . . . (630) 323-2086

Housing: Homeownership rate: 82.3% (2007); Median home value: $511,897 (2007); Median rent: $688 per month (2000); Median age of housing: 41 years (2000).

Safety: Violent crime rate: 6.0 per 10,000 population; Property crime rate: 91.7 per 10,000 population (2006).

Transportation: Commute to work: 73.7% car, 18.2% public transportation, 3.5% walk, 3.3% work from home (2000); Travel time to work: 27.4% less than 15 minutes, 24.4% 15 to 30 minutes, 21.8% 30 to 45 minutes, 13.9% 45 to 60 minutes, 12.5% 60 minutes or more (2000)

Additional Information Contacts

Clarendon Hills Chamber of Commerce . . . . (630) 654-3030

DARIEN (city). Covers a land area of 6.043 square miles and a water area of 0.073 square miles. Located at 41.74° N. Lat.; 87.98° W. Long. Elevation is 751 feet.

Population: 21,678 (1990); 22,860 (2000); 22,593 (2007); 22,349 (2012 projected); Race: 80.6% White, 2.9% Black, 13.3% Asian, 4.9% Hispanic of

any race (2007); Density: 3,738.5 persons per square mile (2007); Average household size: 2.56 (2007); Median age: 43.2 (2007); Males per 100 females: 96.6 (2007); Marriage status: 21.6% never married, 64.3% now married, 5.8% widowed, 8.3% divorced (2000); Foreign born: 15.2% (2000); Ancestry (includes multiple ancestries): 19.9% German, 19.2% Polish, 19.1% Other groups, 16.1% Irish, 14.8% Italian (2000).
Economy: Single-family building permits issued: 9 (2007); Multi-family building permits issued: 0 (2007); Employment by occupation: 23.1% management, 26.1% professional, 8.2% services, 29.9% sales, 0.1% farming, 5.3% construction, 7.4% production (2000).
Income: Per capita income: $39,472 (2007); Median household income: $81,989 (2007); Average household income: $101,170 (2007); Percent of households with income of $100,000 or more: 37.7% (2007); Poverty rate: 2.2% (2000).
Education: Percent of population age 25 and over with: High school diploma (including GED) or higher: 93.5% (2007); Bachelor's degree or higher: 43.6% (2007); Master's degree or higher: 16.6% (2007).

School District(s)

Cass SD 63 (PK-08)
2005-06 Enrollment: 915 . . . . (630) 985-2000
Center Cass SD 66 (PK-08)
2005-06 Enrollment: 1,303 . . . . (630) 783-5000
Darien SD 61 (PK-08)
2005-06 Enrollment: 1,651 . . . . (630) 968-7505
Hinsdale Twp HSD 86 (09-12)
2005-06 Enrollment: 4,480 . . . . (630) 655-6100

Vocational/Technical School(s)

Regency Beauty Institute (Private, For-profit)
Fall 2007 Enrollment: 39 . . . . (630) 824-4022
2007-08 Tuition: $14,200

Housing: Homeownership rate: 85.5% (2007); Median home value: $316,176 (2007); Median rent: $730 per month (2000); Median age of housing: 22 years (2000).
Safety: Violent crime rate: 7.5 per 10,000 population; Property crime rate: 117.9 per 10,000 population (2006).
Transportation: Commute to work: 88.6% car, 6.3% public transportation, 1.0% walk, 3.7% work from home (2000); Travel time to work: 19.1% less than 15 minutes, 31.2% 15 to 30 minutes, 23.0% 30 to 45 minutes, 11.7% 45 to 60 minutes, 15.1% 60 minutes or more (2000)

Additional Information Contacts

City of Darien . . . . (630) 852-5000
http://www.darien.il.us
Darien Chamber of Commerce . . . . (630) 968-0004
http://www.darienchamber.com

DOWNERS GROVE (village). Covers a land area of 14.246 square miles and a water area of 0.010 square miles. Located at 41.79° N. Lat.; 88.01° W. Long. Elevation is 741 feet.
History: Named for Pierce Downer, an eary settler. Downers Grove was settled in 1832 by Pierce Downer at the intersection of two trails. The town was incorporated in 1873.
Population: 48,477 (1990); 48,724 (2000); 48,433 (2007); 47,958 (2012 projected); Race: 87.5% White, 2.4% Black, 7.3% Asian, 4.5% Hispanic of any race (2007); Density: 3,399.8 persons per square mile (2007); Average household size: 2.55 (2007); Median age: 41.3 (2007); Males per 100 females: 93.6 (2007); Marriage status: 23.1% never married, 62.0% now married, 8.1% widowed, 6.9% divorced (2000); Foreign born: 9.8% (2000); Ancestry (includes multiple ancestries): 25.5% German, 20.3% Irish, 14.9% Polish, 12.4% Other groups, 10.8% Italian (2000).
Economy: Unemployment rate: 3.6% (4/2008); Total civilian labor force: 28,041 (4/2008); Single-family building permits issued: 86 (2007); Multi-family building permits issued: 4 (2007); Employment by occupation: 21.5% management, 27.5% professional, 8.1% services, 30.2% sales, 0.0% farming, 5.0% construction, 7.7% production (2000).
Income: Per capita income: $35,674 (2007); Median household income: $72,555 (2007); Average household income: $90,201 (2007); Percent of households with income of $100,000 or more: 32.7% (2007); Poverty rate: 2.3% (2000).
Taxes: Total city taxes per capita: $567 (2006); City property taxes per capita: $292 (2006).
Education: Percent of population age 25 and over with: High school diploma (including GED) or higher: 93.0% (2007); Bachelor's degree or higher: 46.3% (2007); Master's degree or higher: 18.0% (2007).

School District(s)

CHSD 99 (09-12)
2005-06 Enrollment: 5,559 . . . . (630) 795-7100
Center Cass SD 66 (PK-08)
2005-06 Enrollment: 1,303 . . . . (630) 783-5000
Downers Grove Gsd 58 (PK-08)
2005-06 Enrollment: 5,023 . . . . (630) 719-5800
Sch Assoc Sped Educ Dupage Sased (02-12)
2005-06 Enrollment: 146 . . . . (630) 778-4500

Four-year College(s)

Midwestern University (Private, Not-for-profit)
Fall 2007 Enrollment: 1,978. . . . . (630) 969-4400

Housing: Homeownership rate: 79.2% (2007); Median home value: $311,347 (2007); Median rent: $718 per month (2000); Median age of housing: 32 years (2000).
Hospitals: Advocate Good Samaritan Hospital (327 beds)
Safety: Violent crime rate: 14.1 per 10,000 population; Property crime rate: 225.5 per 10,000 population (2006).
Newspapers: Bolingbrook Metropolitan (Local news; Circulation 5,000); Downers Grove Reporter (Local news; Circulation 24,431); Lemont Metropolitan (Community news; Circulation 4,500); Lemont Reporter (Community news; Circulation 7,448); Liberty Suburban Chicago Newspapers (Regional news; Circulation 0); Lisle Reporter (Community news; Circulation 7,174); Mokena-Frankfort Villager (Local news; Circulation 0); Reporter Metropolitian (Community news; Circulation 2,500); Romeoville Reporter (Community news; Circulation 5,000); Suburban Life (Community news; Circulation 6,400); Suburban Life - Lombard, Oakbrook Terrace, Villa Park (Regional news; Circulation 0); Westmont Progress (Community news; Circulation 8,440); Woodridge Progress (Community news; Circulation 8,987)
Transportation: Commute to work: 82.8% car, 10.7% public transportation, 1.6% walk, 4.3% work from home (2000); Travel time to work: 23.4% less than 15 minutes, 31.6% 15 to 30 minutes, 20.6% 30 to 45 minutes, 11.9% 45 to 60 minutes, 12.5% 60 minutes or more (2000)

Additional Information Contacts

Downers Grove Area Chamber of Commerce. . . . . (630) 968-4050
http://www.downersgrove.org
Village of Downers Grove . . . . (630) 434-5500
http://www.downers.us

ELMHURST (city). Covers a land area of 10.265 square miles and a water area of 0.004 square miles. Located at 41.89° N. Lat.; 87.94° W. Long. Elevation is 686 feet.
History: Elmhurst was first known as Cottage Hill, named for the home built in 1843 by J.L. Hovey. The later name of Elmhurst referred to a double row of elm trees that grew along Cottage Hill Avenue. Poet Carl Sandburg lived in Elmhurst at one time.
Population: 42,108 (1990); 42,762 (2000); 45,584 (2007); 47,237 (2012 projected); Race: 91.6% White, 1.4% Black, 4.4% Asian, 4.9% Hispanic of any race (2007); Density: 4,440.9 persons per square mile (2007); Average household size: 2.71 (2007); Median age: 40.9 (2007); Males per 100 females: 93.8 (2007); Marriage status: 22.8% never married, 63.2% now married, 7.6% widowed, 6.4% divorced (2000); Foreign born: 8.0% (2000); Ancestry (includes multiple ancestries): 26.5% German, 21.5% Irish, 14.2% Italian, 13.2% Polish, 9.5% Other groups (2000).
Economy: Unemployment rate: 3.5% (4/2008); Total civilian labor force: 25,227 (4/2008); Single-family building permits issued: 108 (2007); Multi-family building permits issued: 32 (2007); Employment by occupation: 20.9% management, 26.5% professional, 7.8% services, 31.6% sales, 0.0% farming, 5.7% construction, 7.5% production (2000).
Income: Per capita income: $37,477 (2007); Median household income: $78,865 (2007); Average household income: $100,114 (2007); Percent of households with income of $100,000 or more: 36.4% (2007); Poverty rate: 2.5% (2000).
Education: Percent of population age 25 and over with: High school diploma (including GED) or higher: 91.2% (2007); Bachelor's degree or higher: 44.6% (2007); Master's degree or higher: 17.0% (2007).

School District(s)

Elmhurst SD 205 (PK-12)
2005-06 Enrollment: 7,648 . . . . (630) 834-4530
Salt Creek SD 48 (PK-08)
2005-06 Enrollment: 536 . . . . (630) 279-8400

Four-year College(s)

Elmhurst College (Private, Not-for-profit, United Church of Christ)
Fall 2007 Enrollment: 3,184. . . . . (630) 617-3500
2007-08 Tuition: In-state $24,660; Out-of-state $24,660

Housing: Homeownership rate: 82.7% (2007); Median home value: $343,811 (2007); Median rent: $780 per month (2000); Median age of housing: 44 years (2000).

Hospitals: Elmhurst Memorial Hospital (427 beds)

Safety: Violent crime rate: 6.4 per 10,000 population; Property crime rate: 197.2 per 10,000 population (2006).

Newspapers: La Grange Suburban Life (Community news; Circulation 3,000); Roselle Press (Community news; Circulation 1,551)

Transportation: Commute to work: 85.3% car, 7.5% public transportation, 3.1% walk, 3.2% work from home (2000); Travel time to work: 27.9% less than 15 minutes, 32.4% 15 to 30 minutes, 21.7% 30 to 45 minutes, 9.2% 45 to 60 minutes, 8.8% 60 minutes or more (2000)

Additional Information Contacts

City of Elmhurst . . . . (630) 530-3000
http://www.elmhurst.org
Elmhurst Chamber of Commerce . . . . (630) 834-6060
http://www.elmhurstchamber.org

GLEN ELLYN (village). Covers a land area of 6.616 square miles and a water area of 0.021 square miles. Located at 41.87° N. Lat.; 88.06° W. Long. Elevation is 741 feet.

History: Glen Ellyn was named when the town was platted by Thomas E. Hill for his wife Ellyn. When the Galena & Chicago Union Railroad was constructed south of town in 1849, the residents transplanted their town to the present site, platted in 1851.

Population: 26,153 (1990); 26,999 (2000); 26,767 (2007); 26,514 (2012 projected); Race: 86.8% White, 2.5% Black, 5.8% Asian, 6.1% Hispanic of any race (2007); Density: 4,045.6 persons per square mile (2007); Average household size: 2.65 (2007); Median age: 38.9 (2007); Males per 100 females: 96.3 (2007); Marriage status: 22.0% never married, 65.7% now married, 5.6% widowed, 6.8% divorced (2000); Foreign born: 10.7% (2000); Ancestry (includes multiple ancestries): 27.8% German, 22.5% Irish, 13.3% English, 13.0% Other groups, 10.3% Italian (2000).

Economy: Unemployment rate: 3.6% (4/2008); Total civilian labor force: 15,057 (4/2008); Single-family building permits issued: 41 (2007); Multi-family building permits issued: 4 (2007); Employment by occupation: 24.3% management, 29.1% professional, 8.0% services, 29.2% sales, 0.0% farming, 3.3% construction, 6.2% production (2000).

Income: Per capita income: $42,271 (2007); Median household income: $82,487 (2007); Average household income: $111,474 (2007); Percent of households with income of $100,000 or more: 40.8% (2007); Poverty rate: 2.8% (2000).

Education: Percent of population age 25 and over with: High school diploma (including GED) or higher: 94.3% (2007); Bachelor's degree or higher: 58.5% (2007); Master's degree or higher: 22.5% (2007).

School District(s)

CCSD 89 (PK-08)
2005-06 Enrollment: 2,250 . . . . (630) 469-8900
Glen Ellyn SD 41 (PK-08)
2005-06 Enrollment: 3,549 . . . . (630) 790-6400
Glenbard Twp HSD 87 (09-12)
2005-06 Enrollment: 8,998 . . . . (630) 469-9100
Philip J Rock Center and School (03-12)
2005-06 Enrollment: 16 . . . . (630) 790-2474

Two-year College(s)

College of DuPage (Public)
Fall 2007 Enrollment: 25,768. . . . . (630) 942-2800
2007-08 Tuition: In-state $9,344; Out-of-state $11,200

Housing: Homeownership rate: 77.5% (2007); Median home value: $410,936 (2007); Median rent: $687 per month (2000); Median age of housing: 35 years (2000).

Safety: Violent crime rate: 14.0 per 10,000 population; Property crime rate: 180.9 per 10,000 population (2006).

Newspapers: Addison Press (Local news; Circulation 0); Elmhurst Press (Community news; Circulation 0); Glen Ellyn News (Community news; Circulation 0); Itasca Press (Community news; Circulation 0); Lombard Spectator (Community news; Circulation 0); Villa Park Argus (Community news; Circulation 4,019); Warrenville Post (Community news; Circulation 3,400); Wheaton Leader (Local news; Circulation 480)

Transportation: Commute to work: 78.6% car, 11.7% public transportation, 2.8% walk, 5.7% work from home (2000); Travel time to work: 25.3% less than 15 minutes, 31.3% 15 to 30 minutes, 17.0% 30 to 45 minutes, 10.3% 45 to 60 minutes, 16.2% 60 minutes or more (2000)

Additional Information Contacts

Glen Ellyn Chamber of Commerce . . . . (630) 469-0907
http://www.glenellynchamber.com
Village of Glen Ellyn. . . . . (630) 469-3000
http://www.glen-ellyn.com/gov/index.html

GLENDALE HEIGHTS (village). Covers a land area of 5.404 square miles and a water area of 0.003 square miles. Located at 41.92° N. Lat.; 88.07° W. Long. Elevation is 761 feet.

Population: 28,241 (1990); 31,765 (2000); 32,433 (2007); 32,656 (2012 projected); Race: 52.7% White, 6.9% Black, 24.6% Asian, 25.8% Hispanic of any race (2007); Density: 6,001.4 persons per square mile (2007); Average household size: 2.93 (2007); Median age: 33.7 (2007); Males per 100 females: 104.2 (2007); Marriage status: 31.0% never married, 56.8% now married, 3.6% widowed, 8.6% divorced (2000); Foreign born: 30.3% (2000); Ancestry (includes multiple ancestries): 40.0% Other groups, 16.8% German, 11.4% Polish, 10.1% Italian, 9.5% Irish (2000).

Economy: Unemployment rate: 5.4% (4/2008); Total civilian labor force: 19,724 (4/2008); Single-family building permits issued: 5 (2007); Multi-family building permits issued: 0 (2007); Employment by occupation: 13.3% management, 17.4% professional, 10.1% services, 31.8% sales, 0.1% farming, 8.0% construction, 19.3% production (2000).

Income: Per capita income: $23,763 (2007); Median household income: $60,776 (2007); Average household income: $69,619 (2007); Percent of households with income of $100,000 or more: 17.6% (2007); Poverty rate: 6.1% (2000).

Education: Percent of population age 25 and over with: High school diploma (including GED) or higher: 81.7% (2007); Bachelor's degree or higher: 26.9% (2007); Master's degree or higher: 6.8% (2007).

School District(s)

Coop Assoc for Spec Educ (02-12)
2005-06 Enrollment: 90 . . . . (630) 942-5600
Marquardt SD 15 (PK-08)
2005-06 Enrollment: 2,622 . . . . (630) 469-7615
Queen Bee SD 16 (PK-08)
2005-06 Enrollment: 2,053 . . . . (630) 260-6100

Two-year College(s)

UTI of Illinois Inc (Private, For-profit)
Fall 2007 Enrollment: 2,320. . . . . (630) 529-2662

Housing: Homeownership rate: 69.7% (2007); Median home value: $217,033 (2007); Median rent: $764 per month (2000); Median age of housing: 23 years (2000).

Hospitals: Adventist GlenOaks Hospital (186 beds)

Safety: Violent crime rate: 16.0 per 10,000 population; Property crime rate: 194.7 per 10,000 population (2006).

Transportation: Commute to work: 93.9% car, 2.6% public transportation, 1.1% walk, 1.5% work from home (2000); Travel time to work: 23.0% less than 15 minutes, 33.9% 15 to 30 minutes, 25.7% 30 to 45 minutes, 8.4% 45 to 60 minutes, 9.0% 60 minutes or more (2000)

Additional Information Contacts

Glendale Heights Chamber of Commerce. . . . . (630) 545-1099
http://www.glendaleheightschamber.com
Village of Glendale Heights . . . . (630) 260-6000
http://www.glendaleheights.org

HINSDALE (village). Covers a land area of 4.636 square miles and a water area of 0.005 square miles. Located at 41.80° N. Lat.; 87.92° W. Long. Elevation is 699 feet.

History: Hinsdale developed along the route of the Chicago, Burlington & Quincy Railroad, and was named for railroad director H.W. Hinsdale. In 1923 Hinsdale annexed nearby Fullersburg, which had been settled in 1835 by Jacob Fuller and his family.

Population: 16,054 (1990); 17,349 (2000); 17,807 (2007); 18,074 (2012 projected); Race: 92.3% White, 0.9% Black, 4.9% Asian, 3.0% Hispanic of any race (2007); Density: 3,841.1 persons per square mile (2007); Average household size: 2.94 (2007); Median age: 40.3 (2007); Males per 100 females: 92.8 (2007); Marriage status: 18.4% never married, 70.6% now married, 5.7% widowed, 5.4% divorced (2000); Foreign born: 9.0% (2000); Ancestry (includes multiple ancestries): 24.5% German, 23.5% Irish, 13.9% English, 9.9% Italian, 9.3% Other groups (2000).

Economy: Single-family building permits issued: 43 (2007); Multi-family building permits issued: 0 (2007); Employment by occupation: 32.0%

management, 29.9% professional, 4.9% services, 26.8% sales, 0.0% farming, 2.6% construction, 3.9% production (2000).
Income: Per capita income: $62,874 (2007); Median household income: $118,336 (2007); Average household income: $183,834 (2007); Percent of households with income of $100,000 or more: 56.4% (2007); Poverty rate: 3.2% (2000).
Education: Percent of population age 25 and over with: High school diploma (including GED) or higher: 97.2% (2007); Bachelor's degree or higher: 68.6% (2007); Master's degree or higher: 31.3% (2007).

School District(s)

Hinsdale CCSD 181 (PK-08)
2005-06 Enrollment: 4,059 . . . . (630) 887-1070
Hinsdale Twp HSD 86 (09-12)
2005-06 Enrollment: 4,480 . . . . (630) 655-6100

Housing: Homeownership rate: 83.2% (2007); Median home value: $796,988 (2007); Median rent: $765 per month (2000); Median age of housing: 40 years (2000).
Hospitals: Hinsdale Hospital (426 beds)
Safety: Violent crime rate: 10.6 per 10,000 population; Property crime rate: 149.7 per 10,000 population (2006).
Newspapers: Darien Doings (Community news; Circulation 300); Doings (Community news; Circulation 5,443); Doings - Clarendon Hills Edition (Local news; Circulation 1,597); Indian Head Park Doings (Local news; Circulation 200); La Grange Doings (Local news; Circulation 4,068); Oak Brook Doings (Community news; Circulation 1,362); Weekly Doings - Burr Ridge/Willowbrook/Darien Edition (Local news; Circulation 3,442); Western Springs Doings with News of Indian Head Park (Local news; Circulation 2,259); Willowbrook Doings (Local news; Circulation 500)
Transportation: Commute to work: 71.3% car, 18.3% public transportation, 3.1% walk, 6.1% work from home (2000); Travel time to work: 29.6% less than 15 minutes, 20.8% 15 to 30 minutes, 25.0% 30 to 45 minutes, 13.6% 45 to 60 minutes, 10.9% 60 minutes or more (2000)

Additional Information Contacts

Hinsdale Chamber of Commerce. . . . . (630) 323-3952
http://www.hinsdalechamber.com
Village of Hinsdale . . . . (630) 789-7011
http://www.villageofhinsdale.org

ITASCA (village). Covers a land area of 4.916 square miles and a water area of 0.069 square miles. Located at 41.97° N. Lat.; 88.01° W. Long. Elevation is 702 feet.
Population: 7,247 (1990); 8,302 (2000); 8,384 (2007); 8,466 (2012 projected); Race: 84.2% White, 2.1% Black, 7.7% Asian, 8.6% Hispanic of any race (2007); Density: 1,705.4 persons per square mile (2007); Average household size: 2.56 (2007); Median age: 40.2 (2007); Males per 100 females: 94.2 (2007); Marriage status: 26.9% never married, 59.6% now married, 7.2% widowed, 6.4% divorced (2000); Foreign born: 18.8% (2000); Ancestry (includes multiple ancestries): 24.9% German, 17.7% Polish, 17.1% Italian, 16.3% Other groups, 15.5% Irish (2000).
Economy: Single-family building permits issued: 11 (2007); Multi-family building permits issued: 10 (2007); Employment by occupation: 18.9% management, 20.4% professional, 8.8% services, 32.1% sales, 0.0% farming, 7.0% construction, 12.8% production (2000).
Income: Per capita income: $39,728 (2007); Median household income: $79,604 (2007); Average household income: $100,563 (2007); Percent of households with income of $100,000 or more: 36.0% (2007); Poverty rate: 4.7% (2000).
Education: Percent of population age 25 and over with: High school diploma (including GED) or higher: 88.2% (2007); Bachelor's degree or higher: 33.1% (2007); Master's degree or higher: 11.7% (2007).

School District(s)

Itasca SD 10 (PK-08)
2005-06 Enrollment: 863 . . . . (630) 773-1232

Vocational/Technical School(s)

Environmental Technical Institute (Private, For-profit)
Fall 2007 Enrollment: 258 . . . . (630) 285-9100
2007-08 Tuition: $11,850

Housing: Homeownership rate: 76.7% (2007); Median home value: $314,782 (2007); Median rent: $827 per month (2000); Median age of housing: 26 years (2000).
Safety: Violent crime rate: 5.9 per 10,000 population; Property crime rate: 304.4 per 10,000 population (2006).
Transportation: Commute to work: 88.6% car, 5.1% public transportation, 1.9% walk, 4.1% work from home (2000); Travel time to work: 22.8% less than 15 minutes, 39.1% 15 to 30 minutes, 23.8% 30 to 45 minutes, 6.6% 45 to 60 minutes, 7.8% 60 minutes or more (2000)

Additional Information Contacts

Village of Itasca . . . . (630) 773-0835
http://www.itasca.com

LISLE (village). Covers a land area of 6.373 square miles and a water area of 0.045 square miles. Located at 41.79° N. Lat.; 88.08° W. Long. Elevation is 673 feet.
Population: 19,275 (1990); 21,182 (2000); 21,855 (2007); 22,140 (2012 projected); Race: 78.9% White, 4.4% Black, 12.3% Asian, 7.1% Hispanic of any race (2007); Density: 3,429.3 persons per square mile (2007); Average household size: 2.41 (2007); Median age: 38.0 (2007); Males per 100 females: 101.2 (2007); Marriage status: 28.8% never married, 57.0% now married, 5.2% widowed, 9.0% divorced (2000); Foreign born: 13.1% (2000); Ancestry (includes multiple ancestries): 22.3% German, 20.2% Other groups, 16.0% Irish, 12.8% Polish, 10.3% Italian (2000).
Economy: Single-family building permits issued: 28 (2007); Multi-family building permits issued: 0 (2007); Employment by occupation: 23.4% management, 28.2% professional, 8.7% services, 27.1% sales, 0.0% farming, 5.1% construction, 7.5% production (2000).
Income: Per capita income: $38,569 (2007); Median household income: $70,026 (2007); Average household income: $92,787 (2007); Percent of households with income of $100,000 or more: 31.5% (2007); Poverty rate: 3.6% (2000).
Education: Percent of population age 25 and over with: High school diploma (including GED) or higher: 95.3% (2007); Bachelor's degree or higher: 50.0% (2007); Master's degree or higher: 20.0% (2007).

School District(s)

Lisle CUSD 202 (PK-12)
2005-06 Enrollment: 1,713 . . . . (630) 493-8001
Naperville CUSD 203 (PK-12)
2005-06 Enrollment: 18,697 . . . . (630) 420-6300

Four-year College(s)

Benedictine University (Private, Not-for-profit, Roman Catholic)
Fall 2007 Enrollment: 4,573. . . . . (630) 829-6000
2007-08 Tuition: In-state $21,310; Out-of-state $21,310

Vocational/Technical School(s)

Empire Beauty School-Lisle (Private, For-profit)
Fall 2007 Enrollment: 81 . . . . (570) 429-4321
2007-08 Tuition: $17,595

Housing: Homeownership rate: 57.0% (2007); Median home value: $312,421 (2007); Median rent: $832 per month (2000); Median age of housing: 21 years (2000).
Safety: Violent crime rate: 11.6 per 10,000 population; Property crime rate: 206.2 per 10,000 population (2006).
Transportation: Commute to work: 84.8% car, 9.8% public transportation, 1.6% walk, 3.4% work from home (2000); Travel time to work: 25.0% less than 15 minutes, 31.2% 15 to 30 minutes, 19.7% 30 to 45 minutes, 10.5% 45 to 60 minutes, 13.6% 60 minutes or more (2000)

Additional Information Contacts

Lisle Area Chamber of Commerce. (630) 964-0052
http://www.lislechamber.com
Lisle Convention & Visitors Bureau . . . . (800) 733-9811
http://www.lislecvb.com
Village of Lisle . . . . (630) 271-4100
http://www.vil.lisle.il.us

LOMBARD (village). Covers a land area of 9.685 square miles and a water area of 0.014 square miles. Located at 41.87° N. Lat.; 88.01° W. Long. Elevation is 719 feet.
History: Lombard was settled in 1834 by Winslow Churchill. The town was platted in 1868 by Joseph Lombard of Chicago, for whom it was named. Lombard has been known for its many varieties of lilacs, displayed in Lilacia Park, the gift of Colonel William Plum who collected lilacs from around the world.
Population: 40,229 (1990); 42,322 (2000); 42,350 (2007); 42,094 (2012 projected); Race: 82.6% White, 4.0% Black, 9.0% Asian, 6.2% Hispanic of any race (2007); Density: 4,372.7 persons per square mile (2007); Average household size: 2.52 (2007); Median age: 39.5 (2007); Males per 100 females: 95.5 (2007); Marriage status: 26.1% never married, 58.0% now married, 7.5% widowed, 8.5% divorced (2000); Foreign born: 11.6% (2000); Ancestry (includes multiple ancestries): 27.1% German, 19.7% Irish, 15.3% Other groups, 14.4% Italian, 11.0% Polish (2000).

Economy: Unemployment rate: 4.6% (4/2008); Total civilian labor force: 25,065 (4/2008); Single-family building permits issued: 33 (2007); Multi-family building permits issued: 80 (2007); Employment by occupation: 17.0% management, 22.9% professional, 8.0% services, 35.4% sales, 0.0% farming, 7.4% construction, 9.2% production (2000).
Income: Per capita income: $31,104 (2007); Median household income: $65,375 (2007); Average household income: $77,507 (2007); Percent of households with income of $100,000 or more: 23.8% (2007); Poverty rate: 3.8% (2000).
Taxes: Total city taxes per capita: $409 (2006); City property taxes per capita: $156 (2006).
Education: Percent of population age 25 and over with: High school diploma (including GED) or higher: 90.4% (2007); Bachelor's degree or higher: 36.3% (2007); Master's degree or higher: 10.9% (2007).

School District(s)

Glenbard Twp HSD 87 (09-12)
2005-06 Enrollment: 8,998 . . . . (630) 469-9100
Lombard SD 44 (PK-08)
2005-06 Enrollment: 3,144 . . . . (630) 827-4400
SD 45 Dupage County (PK-08)
2005-06 Enrollment: 3,595 . . . . (630) 530-6200
Sch Assoc Sped Educ Dupage Sased (02-12)
2005-06 Enrollment: 146 . . . . (630) 778-4500

Four-year College(s)

National University of Health Sciences (Private, Not-for-profit)
Fall 2007 Enrollment: 651 . . . . (630) 629-2000
Northern Baptist Theological Seminary (Private, Not-for-profit)
Fall 2007 Enrollment: n/a. . . . . (630) 620-2180

Vocational/Technical School(s)

The Illinois Center for Broadcasting (Private, For-profit)
Fall 2007 Enrollment: 205 . . . . (630) 916-1700
2007-08 Tuition: $14,237

Housing: Homeownership rate: 74.5% (2007); Median home value: $255,701 (2007); Median rent: $845 per month (2000); Median age of housing: 33 years (2000).
Safety: Violent crime rate: 9.1 per 10,000 population; Property crime rate: 271.9 per 10,000 population (2006).
Newspapers: Lombardian (Community news; Circulation 13,500); Villa Park Review (Community news; Circulation 8,000)
Transportation: Commute to work: 88.7% car, 6.4% public transportation, 1.6% walk, 2.7% work from home (2000); Travel time to work: 24.4% less than 15 minutes, 32.5% 15 to 30 minutes, 23.4% 30 to 45 minutes, 9.3% 45 to 60 minutes, 10.4% 60 minutes or more (2000)

Additional Information Contacts

Lombard Chamber of Commerce . . . . (630) 627-5040
http://www.lombardchamber.com
Village of Lombard . . . . (630) 620-5700
http://www.villageoflombard.org

MEDINAH (unincorporated postal area, zip code 60157). Covers a land area of 1.467 square miles and a water area of 0.007 square miles. Located at 41.84° N. Lat.; 88.08° W. Long. Elevation is 732 feet.
Population: 2,111 (2000); Race: 91.2% White, 0.5% Black, 5.8% Asian, 4.5% Hispanic of any race (2000); Density: 1,439.0 persons per square mile (2000); Age: 20.0% under 18, 17.7% over 64 (2000); Marriage status: 16.4% never married, 73.3% now married, 8.0% widowed, 2.3% divorced (2000); Foreign born: 13.8% (2000); Ancestry (includes multiple ancestries): 35.7% German, 19.8% Polish, 18.6% Italian, 12.3% Irish, 11.5% Other groups (2000).
Economy: Employment by occupation: 25.6% management, 15.2% professional, 3.1% services, 31.6% sales, 0.0% farming, 13.3% construction, 11.1% production (2000).
Income: Per capita income: $36,250 (2000); Median household income: $81,251 (2000); Poverty rate: 3.6% (2000).
Education: Percent of population age 25 and over with: High school diploma (including GED) or higher: 91.8% (2000); Bachelor's degree or higher: 35.3% (2000).

School District(s)

Medinah SD 11 (KG-08)
2005-06 Enrollment: 736 . . . . (630) 893-3737

Housing: Homeownership rate: 98.1% (2000); Median home value: $254,100 (2000); Median rent: $544 per month (2000); Median age of housing: 38 years (2000).
Transportation: Commute to work: 90.5% car, 8.1% public transportation, 0.0% walk, 0.7% work from home (2000); Travel time to work: 18.4% less than 15 minutes, 39.5% 15 to 30 minutes, 20.3% 30 to 45 minutes, 14.7% 45 to 60 minutes, 7.0% 60 minutes or more (2000)

NAPERVILLE (city). Covers a land area of 35.377 square miles and a water area of 0.145 square miles. Located at 41.75° N. Lat.; 88.15° W. Long. Elevation is 709 feet.
History: Named for Captain Joseph Naper, founder. The first settlement at Naperville was Fort Payne, built in 1832. That same year, Joseph Naper built a saw mill and platted the town site. From 1839 to 1868 Naperville was the seat of DuPage County.
Population: 90,506 (1990); 128,358 (2000); 143,591 (2007); 153,513 (2012 projected); Race: 78.2% White, 4.3% Black, 14.6% Asian, 4.6% Hispanic of any race (2007); Density: 4,058.9 persons per square mile (2007); Average household size: 2.94 (2007); Median age: 35.4 (2007); Males per 100 females: 96.3 (2007); Marriage status: 22.2% never married, 68.4% now married, 3.5% widowed, 6.0% divorced (2000); Foreign born: 11.7% (2000); Ancestry (includes multiple ancestries): 27.0% German, 18.5% Irish, 16.8% Other groups, 10.9% Polish, 10.6% Italian (2000).
Economy: Unemployment rate: 3.6% (4/2008); Total civilian labor force: 78,872 (4/2008); Single-family building permits issued: 281 (2007); Multi-family building permits issued: 62 (2007); Employment by occupation: 26.9% management, 29.1% professional, 7.5% services, 28.2% sales, 0.0% farming, 3.6% construction, 4.7% production (2000).
Income: Per capita income: $40,965 (2007); Median household income: $99,200 (2007); Average household income: $119,817 (2007); Percent of households with income of $100,000 or more: 49.5% (2007); Poverty rate: 2.2% (2000).
Taxes: Total city taxes per capita: $469 (2006); City property taxes per capita: $280 (2006).
Education: Percent of population age 25 and over with: High school diploma (including GED) or higher: 96.4% (2007); Bachelor's degree or higher: 61.0% (2007); Master's degree or higher: 23.7% (2007).

School District(s)

Indian Prairie CUSD 204 (PK-12)
2005-06 Enrollment: 28,510 . . . . (630) 375-3000
Naperville CUSD 203 (PK-12)
2005-06 Enrollment: 18,697 . . . . (630) 420-6300
Sch Assoc Sped Educ Dupage Sased (02-12)
2005-06 Enrollment: 146 . . . . (630) 778-4500

Four-year College(s)

North Central College (Private, Not-for-profit, United Methodist)
Fall 2007 Enrollment: 2,559. . . . . (630) 637-5100
2007-08 Tuition: In-state $24,564; Out-of-state $24,564

Housing: Homeownership rate: 80.4% (2007); Median home value: $383,602 (2007); Median rent: $865 per month (2000); Median age of housing: 14 years (2000).
Hospitals: Edward Hospital (179 beds)
Safety: Violent crime rate: 6.7 per 10,000 population; Property crime rate: 167.1 per 10,000 population (2006).
Newspapers: Bolingbrook Sun (Local news; Circulation 17,000); Bolingbrook/Romeoville Sun (Community news; Circulation 7,300); Hollywood Reporter - New York Bureau (Circulation 0); Homer Township Sun (Community news; Circulation 1,750); Lisle Sun (Community news; Circulation 13,000); Newsday - United Nations Bureau (Local news; Circulation 0); Rockland Edition (Local news; Circulation 0); Victoria Advocate - Cuero Bureau (Local news; Circulation 0); Wheaton Sun (Local news; Circulation 5,600)
Transportation: Commute to work: 83.4% car, 9.0% public transportation, 1.4% walk, 5.6% work from home (2000); Travel time to work: 21.3% less than 15 minutes, 29.8% 15 to 30 minutes, 19.0% 30 to 45 minutes, 11.8% 45 to 60 minutes, 17.9% 60 minutes or more (2000); Amtrak: Service available.

Additional Information Contacts

City of Naperville . . . . (630) 420-6111
http://www.naperville.il.us
Naperville Area Chamber of Commerce . . . . (630) 355-4141
http://www.naperville.net

OAK BROOK (village). Covers a land area of 8.161 square miles and a water area of 0.097 square miles. Located at 41.84° N. Lat.; 87.95° W. Long. Elevation is 663 feet.
Population: 9,178 (1990); 8,702 (2000); 8,814 (2007); 8,879 (2012 projected); Race: 73.5% White, 2.0% Black, 22.2% Asian, 2.5% Hispanic of any race (2007); Density: 1,080.1 persons per square mile (2007); Average household size: 2.73 (2007); Median age: 52.5 (2007); Males per 100

females: 91.5 (2007); Marriage status: 20.3% never married, 69.5% now married, 6.9% widowed, 3.3% divorced (2000); Foreign born: 22.2% (2000); Ancestry (includes multiple ancestries): 25.7% Other groups, 16.8% German, 13.0% Irish, 12.6% Italian, 5.9% Polish (2000).
Economy: Single-family building permits issued: 17 (2007); Multi-family building permits issued: 0 (2007); Employment by occupation: 26.8% management, 35.9% professional, 6.6% services, 25.9% sales, 0.0% farming, 2.6% construction, 2.2% production (2000).
Income: Per capita income: $76,647 (2007); Median household income: $146,176 (2007); Average household income: $209,004 (2007); Percent of households with income of $100,000 or more: 63.7% (2007); Poverty rate: 2.1% (2000).
Education: Percent of population age 25 and over with: High school diploma (including GED) or higher: 96.1% (2007); Bachelor's degree or higher: 61.1% (2007); Master's degree or higher: 35.0% (2007).

School District(s)

Butler SD 53 (KG-08)
2005-06 Enrollment: 488 . . . . (630) 573-2887
Housing: Homeownership rate: 97.0% (2007); Median home value: $821,549 (2007); Median rent: $894 per month (2000); Median age of housing: 23 years (2000).
Safety: Violent crime rate: 7.9 per 10,000 population; Property crime rate: 697.2 per 10,000 population (2006).
Newspapers: Bensenville Press (Local news; Circulation 1,142); Chicago Tribune - Oak Brook Bureau (Local news; Circulation 0); La Grange Park Press (Local news; Circulation 880); Suburban Life - DuPage (Regional news; Circulation 8,370); Suburban Life - Elmhurst (Community news; Circulation 14,800); Suburban Life Citizen (Regional news; Circulation 31,500)
Transportation: Commute to work: 91.1% car, 4.0% public transportation, 0.9% walk, 3.9% work from home (2000); Travel time to work: 21.4% less than 15 minutes, 27.5% 15 to 30 minutes, 28.3% 30 to 45 minutes, 15.3% 45 to 60 minutes, 7.5% 60 minutes or more (2000)

Additional Information Contacts

Greater Oak Brook Chamber of Commerce . . . . (630) 472-9377
http://www.obchamber.com
Village of Oak Brook . . . . (630) 368-5000
http://www.oak-brook.org

OAKBROOK TERRACE (city). Covers a land area of 1.393 square miles and a water area of 0 square miles. Located at 41.85° N. Lat.; 87.96° W. Long. Elevation is 686 feet.
Population: 2,218 (1990); 2,300 (2000); 2,146 (2007); 2,093 (2012 projected); Race: 71.4% White, 6.8% Black, 17.6% Asian, 5.5% Hispanic of any race (2007); Density: 1,540.6 persons per square mile (2007); Average household size: 1.90 (2007); Median age: 43.0 (2007); Males per 100 females: 93.0 (2007); Marriage status: 19.9% never married, 58.6% now married, 11.8% widowed, 9.7% divorced (2000); Foreign born: 14.9% (2000); Ancestry (includes multiple ancestries): 20.9% German, 20.5% Other groups, 19.9% Italian, 13.8% Irish, 13.2% Polish (2000).
Economy: Single-family building permits issued: 7 (2007); Multi-family building permits issued: 0 (2007); Employment by occupation: 23.3% management, 38.6% professional, 3.3% services, 24.1% sales, 0.0% farming, 6.2% construction, 4.5% production (2000).
Income: Per capita income: $43,255 (2007); Median household income: $63,834 (2007); Average household income: $82,073 (2007); Percent of households with income of $100,000 or more: 24.0% (2007); Poverty rate: 3.3% (2000).
Education: Percent of population age 25 and over with: High school diploma (including GED) or higher: 91.7% (2007); Bachelor's degree or higher: 43.1% (2007); Master's degree or higher: 21.4% (2007).

School District(s)

Salt Creek SD 48 (PK-08)
2005-06 Enrollment: 536 . . . . (630) 279-8400
Housing: Homeownership rate: 40.4% (2007); Median home value: $251,645 (2007); Median rent: $943 per month (2000); Median age of housing: 26 years (2000).
Safety: Violent crime rate: 62.2 per 10,000 population; Property crime rate: 760.3 per 10,000 population (2006).
Transportation: Commute to work: 90.0% car, 4.7% public transportation, 2.1% walk, 1.8% work from home (2000); Travel time to work: 25.7% less than 15 minutes, 27.8% 15 to 30 minutes, 23.7% 30 to 45 minutes, 16.3% 45 to 60 minutes, 6.5% 60 minutes or more (2000)

ROSELLE (village). Covers a land area of 5.374 square miles and a water area of 0.017 square miles. Located at 41.98° N. Lat.; 88.08° W. Long. Elevation is 771 feet.
Population: 21,424 (1990); 23,115 (2000); 23,122 (2007); 22,972 (2012 projected); Race: 85.1% White, 2.2% Black, 8.5% Asian, 6.8% Hispanic of any race (2007); Density: 4,302.4 persons per square mile (2007); Average household size: 2.70 (2007); Median age: 38.1 (2007); Males per 100 females: 96.4 (2007); Marriage status: 24.9% never married, 62.2% now married, 4.7% widowed, 8.2% divorced (2000); Foreign born: 15.1% (2000); Ancestry (includes multiple ancestries): 28.3% German, 17.1% Polish, 17.0% Irish, 16.1% Other groups, 16.0% Italian (2000).
Economy: Single-family building permits issued: 18 (2007); Multi-family building permits issued: 0 (2007); Employment by occupation: 19.4% management, 20.2% professional, 9.8% services, 33.9% sales, 0.0% farming, 6.2% construction, 10.5% production (2000).
Income: Per capita income: $32,095 (2007); Median household income: $72,271 (2007); Average household income: $86,608 (2007); Percent of households with income of $100,000 or more: 28.8% (2007); Poverty rate: 2.0% (2000).
Education: Percent of population age 25 and over with: High school diploma (including GED) or higher: 90.8% (2007); Bachelor's degree or higher: 33.9% (2007); Master's degree or higher: 9.6% (2007).

School District(s)

Keeneyville SD 20 (PK-08)
2005-06 Enrollment: 1,708 . . . . (630) 894-2250
Lake Park CHSD 108 (09-12)
2005-06 Enrollment: 3,026 . . . . (630) 529-4500
Medinah SD 11 (KG-08)
2005-06 Enrollment: 736 . . . . (630) 893-3737
North Dupage Sp Ed Cooperative (03-12)
2005-06 Enrollment: 42 . . . . (630) 894-0490
Roselle SD 12 (KG-08)
2005-06 Enrollment: 688 . . . . (630) 529-2091
Schaumburg CCSD 54 (PK-08)
2005-06 Enrollment: 14,471 . . . . (847) 357-5000
Housing: Homeownership rate: 81.3% (2007); Median home value: $258,338 (2007); Median rent: $842 per month (2000); Median age of housing: 23 years (2000).
Safety: Violent crime rate: 5.6 per 10,000 population; Property crime rate: 148.9 per 10,000 population (2006).
Transportation: Commute to work: 89.0% car, 6.1% public transportation, 1.1% walk, 3.4% work from home (2000); Travel time to work: 18.5% less than 15 minutes, 33.9% 15 to 30 minutes, 25.0% 30 to 45 minutes, 11.4% 45 to 60 minutes, 11.1% 60 minutes or more (2000)

Additional Information Contacts

Roselle Chamber of Commerce & Industry . . . . (630) 894-3010
http://www.rosellechamber.com
Village of Roselle . . . . (630) 980-2000
http://www.roselle.il.us

VILLA PARK (village). Covers a land area of 4.702 square miles and a water area of 0.004 square miles. Located at 41.88° N. Lat.; 87.97° W. Long. Elevation is 702 feet.
Population: 22,214 (1990); 22,075 (2000); 22,531 (2007); 22,707 (2012 projected); Race: 86.2% White, 2.4% Black, 3.9% Asian, 16.9% Hispanic of any race (2007); Density: 4,792.2 persons per square mile (2007); Average household size: 2.83 (2007); Median age: 37.2 (2007); Males per 100 females: 102.4 (2007); Marriage status: 26.4% never married, 59.7% now married, 5.6% widowed, 8.3% divorced (2000); Foreign born: 14.4% (2000); Ancestry (includes multiple ancestries): 27.2% German, 19.2% Irish, 18.3% Other groups, 12.9% Italian, 11.8% Polish (2000).
Economy: Single-family building permits issued: 8 (2007); Multi-family building permits issued: 0 (2007); Employment by occupation: 12.6% management, 15.8% professional, 14.1% services, 31.5% sales, 0.0% farming, 11.1% construction, 14.9% production (2000).
Income: Per capita income: $24,599 (2007); Median household income: $60,924 (2007); Average household income: $69,450 (2007); Percent of households with income of $100,000 or more: 18.5% (2007); Poverty rate: 4.8% (2000).
Education: Percent of population age 25 and over with: High school diploma (including GED) or higher: 85.2% (2007); Bachelor's degree or higher: 23.4% (2007); Master's degree or higher: 7.9% (2007).

School District(s)

Du Page HSD 88 (09-12)
2005-06 Enrollment: 4,057 . . . . (630) 530-3980
SD 45 Dupage County (PK-08)
2005-06 Enrollment: 3,595 . . . . (630) 530-6200
Salt Creek SD 48 (PK-08)
2005-06 Enrollment: 536 . . . . (630) 279-8400

Vocational/Technical School(s)

Cannella School of Hair Design (Private, For-profit)
Fall 2007 Enrollment: 42 . . . . (708) 833-6118
2007-08 Tuition: $8,500
Ms Roberts Academy of Beauty Culture-Villa Park (Private, For-profit)
Fall 2007 Enrollment: 107 . . . . (630) 941-3880
2007-08 Tuition: $10,340

Housing: Homeownership rate: 77.0% (2007); Median home value: $243,999 (2007); Median rent: $664 per month (2000); Median age of housing: 44 years (2000).
Safety: Violent crime rate: 23.9 per 10,000 population; Property crime rate: 230.4 per 10,000 population (2006).
Transportation: Commute to work: 89.0% car, 4.3% public transportation, 2.8% walk, 2.4% work from home (2000); Travel time to work: 27.6% less than 15 minutes, 34.6% 15 to 30 minutes, 21.7% 30 to 45 minutes, 8.0% 45 to 60 minutes, 8.1% 60 minutes or more (2000)

Additional Information Contacts

Villa Park Chamber of Commerce . . . . (630) 941-9133
http://www.villaparkchamber.org
Village of Villa Park . . . . (630) 834-8500
http://www.invillapark.com

WARRENVILLE (city). Covers a land area of 5.498 square miles and a water area of 0.119 square miles. Located at 41.82° N. Lat.; 88.18° W. Long. Elevation is 696 feet.
History: Named for Daniel Warren (1780-1866), town founder. Warrenville was settled in the 1830's around a tannery and gristmill.
Population: 11,409 (1990); 13,363 (2000); 13,568 (2007); 13,711 (2012 projected); Race: 85.6% White, 3.0% Black, 3.6% Asian, 16.1% Hispanic of any race (2007); Density: 2,467.9 persons per square mile (2007); Average household size: 2.69 (2007); Median age: 36.2 (2007); Males per 100 females: 98.2 (2007); Marriage status: 26.3% never married, 60.4% now married, 2.6% widowed, 10.7% divorced (2000); Foreign born: 9.4% (2000); Ancestry (includes multiple ancestries): 27.3% German, 16.8% Irish, 16.1% Other groups, 10.1% English, 9.7% Italian (2000).
Economy: Single-family building permits issued: 12 (2007); Multi-family building permits issued: 0 (2007); Employment by occupation: 15.1% management, 27.7% professional, 10.4% services, 28.1% sales, 0.0% farming, 9.4% construction, 9.2% production (2000).
Income: Per capita income: $31,209 (2007); Median household income: $70,019 (2007); Average household income: $83,535 (2007); Percent of households with income of $100,000 or more: 24.0% (2007); Poverty rate: 1.6% (2000).
Education: Percent of population age 25 and over with: High school diploma (including GED) or higher: 93.0% (2007); Bachelor's degree or higher: 40.1% (2007); Master's degree or higher: 11.5% (2007).

School District(s)

CUSD 200 (PK-12)
2005-06 Enrollment: 14,076 . . . . (630) 682-2002
Dept of Corrections Sch Dist 428 (08-12)
2005-06 Enrollment: 2,271 . . . . (217) 522-2666

Housing: Homeownership rate: 81.9% (2007); Median home value: $219,190 (2007); Median rent: $934 per month (2000); Median age of housing: 22 years (2000).
Safety: Violent crime rate: 6.1 per 10,000 population; Property crime rate: 184.6 per 10,000 population (2006).
Transportation: Commute to work: 88.8% car, 4.1% public transportation, 1.1% walk, 5.2% work from home (2000); Travel time to work: 24.8% less than 15 minutes, 35.9% 15 to 30 minutes, 20.7% 30 to 45 minutes, 8.0% 45 to 60 minutes, 10.6% 60 minutes or more (2000)

Additional Information Contacts

City of Warrenville . . . . (630) 393-9427
http://www.warrenville.il.us
Warrenville Chamber of Commerce. . . . . (630) 393-9080
http://www.warrenvillechamber.com

WAYNE (village). Covers a land area of 5.816 square miles and a water area of 0 square miles. Located at 41.95° N. Lat.; 88.25° W. Long. Elevation is 758 feet.
Population: 1,461 (1990); 2,137 (2000); 2,849 (2007); 3,297 (2012 projected); Race: 92.2% White, 0.7% Black, 4.5% Asian, 7.1% Hispanic of any race (2007); Density: 489.8 persons per square mile (2007); Average household size: 3.01 (2007); Median age: 42.9 (2007); Males per 100 females: 94.1 (2007); Marriage status: 17.3% never married, 71.7% now married, 4.7% widowed, 6.3% divorced (2000); Foreign born: 5.0% (2000); Ancestry (includes multiple ancestries): 20.2% German, 18.6% Irish, 17.6% Italian, 15.2% Polish, 9.3% English (2000).
Economy: Employment by occupation: 29.7% management, 18.2% professional, 6.5% services, 33.2% sales, 1.0% farming, 7.2% construction, 4.2% production (2000).
Income: Per capita income: $61,842 (2007); Median household income: $135,677 (2007); Average household income: $185,852 (2007); Percent of households with income of $100,000 or more: 65.1% (2007); Poverty rate: 0.6% (2000).
Education: Percent of population age 25 and over with: High school diploma (including GED) or higher: 95.6% (2007); Bachelor's degree or higher: 54.1% (2007); Master's degree or higher: 18.7% (2007).

School District(s)

SD U-46 (PK-12)
2005-06 Enrollment: 39,656 . . . . (847) 888-5000

Housing: Homeownership rate: 97.5% (2007); Median home value: $642,663 (2007); Median rent: $550 per month (2000); Median age of housing: 20 years (2000).
Safety: Violent crime rate: 0.0 per 10,000 population; Property crime rate: 46.7 per 10,000 population (2006).
Transportation: Commute to work: 90.2% car, 4.4% public transportation, 0.4% walk, 5.0% work from home (2000); Travel time to work: 13.8% less than 15 minutes, 30.7% 15 to 30 minutes, 20.1% 30 to 45 minutes, 18.3% 45 to 60 minutes, 17.1% 60 minutes or more (2000)

WEST CHICAGO (city). Covers a land area of 13.839 square miles and a water area of 0.004 square miles. Located at 41.88° N. Lat.; 88.21° W. Long. Elevation is 784 feet.
Population: 15,874 (1990); 23,469 (2000); 26,258 (2007); 27,875 (2012 projected); Race: 75.4% White, 1.7% Black, 2.4% Asian, 59.7% Hispanic of any race (2007); Density: 1,897.4 persons per square mile (2007); Average household size: 3.75 (2007); Median age: 30.6 (2007); Males per 100 females: 112.6 (2007); Marriage status: 29.7% never married, 61.8% now married, 2.8% widowed, 5.8% divorced (2000); Foreign born: 34.1% (2000); Ancestry (includes multiple ancestries): 45.3% Other groups, 17.2% German, 9.7% Irish, 6.4% Italian, 6.4% Polish (2000).
Economy: Unemployment rate: 5.9% (4/2008); Total civilian labor force: 14,978 (4/2008); Single-family building permits issued: 9 (2007); Multi-family building permits issued: 0 (2007); Employment by occupation: 11.3% management, 14.4% professional, 17.6% services, 23.3% sales, 0.5% farming, 10.5% construction, 22.5% production (2000).
Income: Per capita income: $21,848 (2007); Median household income: $70,449 (2007); Average household income: $81,536 (2007); Percent of households with income of $100,000 or more: 27.7% (2007); Poverty rate: 9.3% (2000).
Taxes: Total city taxes per capita: $256 (2006); City property taxes per capita: $127 (2006).
Education: Percent of population age 25 and over with: High school diploma (including GED) or higher: 66.9% (2007); Bachelor's degree or higher: 21.8% (2007); Master's degree or higher: 5.1% (2007).

School District(s)

Benjamin SD 25 (PK-08)
2005-06 Enrollment: 919 . . . . (630) 876-7800
CHSD 94 (09-12)
2005-06 Enrollment: 2,132 . . . . (630) 876-6200
St Charles CUSD 303 (PK-12)
2005-06 Enrollment: 13,443 . . . . (630) 513-3030
West Chicago ESD 33 (PK-08)
2005-06 Enrollment: 3,944 . . . . (630) 293-6000

Housing: Homeownership rate: 69.2% (2007); Median home value: $250,494 (2007); Median rent: $715 per month (2000); Median age of housing: 27 years (2000).
Safety: Violent crime rate: 18.8 per 10,000 population; Property crime rate: 221.4 per 10,000 population (2006).
Newspapers: Warrenville Press (Local news; Circulation 2,200)

Transportation: Commute to work: 89.7% car, 3.1% public transportation, 3.0% walk, 2.0% work from home (2000); Travel time to work: 30.0% less than 15 minutes, 37.8% 15 to 30 minutes, 17.0% 30 to 45 minutes, 7.1% 45 to 60 minutes, 8.1% 60 minutes or more (2000)
Airports: Dupage (general aviation)
Additional Information Contacts
City of West Chicago . . . . (630) 393-9427
http://www.westchicago.org
West Chicago Chamber of Commerce & Industry . . . . (630) 231-3003
http://www.wegochamber.org

WESTMONT (village). Covers a land area of 4.897 square miles and a water area of 0.010 square miles. Located at 41.79° N. Lat.; 87.97° W. Long. Elevation is 748 feet.
Population: 22,443 (1990); 24,554 (2000); 24,666 (2007); 24,563 (2012 projected); Race: 71.7% White, 7.5% Black, 14.7% Asian, 9.1% Hispanic of any race (2007); Density: 5,037.2 persons per square mile (2007); Average household size: 2.45 (2007); Median age: 39.1 (2007); Males per 100 females: 89.7 (2007); Marriage status: 26.0% never married, 55.9% now married, 8.2% widowed, 9.9% divorced (2000); Foreign born: 19.7% (2000); Ancestry (includes multiple ancestries): 25.3% Other groups, 17.6% German, 15.3% Irish, 13.7% Polish, 8.7% Italian (2000).
Economy: Unemployment rate: 4.3% (4/2008); Total civilian labor force: 13,969 (4/2008); Single-family building permits issued: 35 (2007); Multi-family building permits issued: 0 (2007); Employment by occupation: 15.9% management, 22.4% professional, 13.7% services, 30.7% sales, 0.1% farming, 7.0% construction, 10.2% production (2000).
Income: Per capita income: $30,456 (2007); Median household income: $57,560 (2007); Average household income: $72,935 (2007); Percent of households with income of $100,000 or more: 21.0% (2007); Poverty rate: 5.8% (2000).
Education: Percent of population age 25 and over with: High school diploma (including GED) or higher: 86.5% (2007); Bachelor's degree or higher: 35.2% (2007); Master's degree or higher: 12.2% (2007).

School District(s)

CUSD 201 (PK-12)
2005-06 Enrollment: 1,705 . . . . (630) 468-8004
Maercker SD 60 (PK-08)
2005-06 Enrollment: 1,413 . . . . (630) 323-2086
Sch Assoc Sped Educ Dupage Sased (02-12)
2005-06 Enrollment: 146 . . . . (630) 778-4500
Housing: Homeownership rate: 54.2% (2007); Median home value: $276,709 (2007); Median rent: $711 per month (2000); Median age of housing: 26 years (2000).
Safety: Violent crime rate: 16.1 per 10,000 population; Property crime rate: 222.4 per 10,000 population (2006).
Transportation: Commute to work: 86.2% car, 7.6% public transportation, 1.9% walk, 2.7% work from home (2000); Travel time to work: 24.8% less than 15 minutes, 31.6% 15 to 30 minutes, 21.2% 30 to 45 minutes, 9.9% 45 to 60 minutes, 12.6% 60 minutes or more (2000)
Additional Information Contacts
Village of Westmont . . . . (630) 981-6200
http://www.westmont.il.gov
Westmont Chamber of Commerce & Tourism Bureau . . . . (630) 960-5553
http://www.westmontchamber.com

WHEATON (city). County seat. Covers a land area of 11.221 square miles and a water area of 0.045 square miles. Located at 41.86° N. Lat.; 88.10° W. Long. Elevation is 758 feet.
History: Named for the Wheaton family, early settlers. Wheaton was settled in 1838 by Warren and Jesse Wheaton, who were instrumental in bringing to the town the railroad, a college, and the county courthouse. In 1853, Warren Wheaton donated the land for the Illinois Institute, which seven years later became Wheaton College. In 1867 the seat of DuPage County was moved from Naperville to Wheaton, and the courthouse was built on land donated by Warren Wheaton.
Population: 52,280 (1990); 55,416 (2000); 54,541 (2007); 53,881 (2012 projected); Race: 87.6% White, 3.5% Black, 5.7% Asian, 4.7% Hispanic of any race (2007); Density: 4,860.6 persons per square mile (2007); Average household size: 2.84 (2007); Median age: 37.8 (2007); Males per 100 females: 95.5 (2007); Marriage status: 26.9% never married, 61.3% now married, 4.9% widowed, 6.8% divorced (2000); Foreign born: 9.5% (2000); Ancestry (includes multiple ancestries): 28.1% German, 18.4% Irish, 12.9% English, 12.0% Other groups, 9.4% Italian (2000).
Economy: Unemployment rate: 3.4% (4/2008); Total civilian labor force: 30,324 (4/2008); Single-family building permits issued: 68 (2007); Multi-family building permits issued: 0 (2007); Employment by occupation: 22.7% management, 31.1% professional, 8.8% services, 28.0% sales, 0.0% farming, 4.2% construction, 5.2% production (2000).
Income: Per capita income: $39,052 (2007); Median household income: $80,083 (2007); Average household income: $108,565 (2007); Percent of households with income of $100,000 or more: 37.9% (2007); Poverty rate: 3.6% (2000).
Education: Percent of population age 25 and over with: High school diploma (including GED) or higher: 94.1% (2007); Bachelor's degree or higher: 57.2% (2007); Master's degree or higher: 22.0% (2007).

School District(s)

CCSD 89 (PK-08)
2005-06 Enrollment: 2,250 . . . . (630) 469-8900
CUSD 200 (PK-12)
2005-06 Enrollment: 14,076 . . . . (630) 682-2002
Sch Assoc Sped Educ Dupage Sased (02-12)
2005-06 Enrollment: 146 . . . . (630) 778-4500

Four-year College(s)

Wheaton College (Private, Not-for-profit, Undenominational)
Fall 2007 Enrollment: 2,895. . . . . (630) 752-5000
2007-08 Tuition: In-state $23,730; Out-of-state $23,730

Vocational/Technical School(s)

Hair Professionals Academy of Cosmetology (Private, For-profit)
Fall 2007 Enrollment: 188 . . . . (630) 653-6630
2007-08 Tuition: $15,588
Housing: Homeownership rate: 73.9% (2007); Median home value: $333,929 (2007); Median rent: $834 per month (2000); Median age of housing: 27 years (2000).
Hospitals: Marianjoy Rehabilitation Hospital (120 beds)
Safety: Violent crime rate: 12.1 per 10,000 population; Property crime rate: 153.0 per 10,000 population (2006).
Transportation: Commute to work: 81.7% car, 8.5% public transportation, 4.2% walk, 4.5% work from home (2000); Travel time to work: 32.6% less than 15 minutes, 28.1% 15 to 30 minutes, 17.2% 30 to 45 minutes, 8.5% 45 to 60 minutes, 13.7% 60 minutes or more (2000)
Additional Information Contacts
City of Wheaton . . . . (630) 260-2012
http://www.wheaton.il.us
Wheaton Chamber of Commerce . . . . (630) 668-6464
http://www.ewheaton.com

WILLOWBROOK (village). Covers a land area of 2.601 square miles and a water area of 0.025 square miles. Located at 41.76° N. Lat.; 87.94° W. Long. Elevation is 732 feet.
Population: 8,791 (1990); 8,967 (2000); 8,841 (2007); 8,691 (2012 projected); Race: 82.0% White, 3.4% Black, 10.7% Asian, 5.5% Hispanic of any race (2007); Density: 3,399.4 persons per square mile (2007); Average household size: 2.13 (2007); Median age: 45.7 (2007); Males per 100 females: 86.2 (2007); Marriage status: 27.3% never married, 54.4% now married, 9.4% widowed, 8.8% divorced (2000); Foreign born: 16.8% (2000); Ancestry (includes multiple ancestries): 19.9% German, 17.5% Irish, 17.2% Other groups, 12.7% Italian, 11.4% Polish (2000).
Economy: Single-family building permits issued: 9 (2007); Multi-family building permits issued: 0 (2007); Employment by occupation: 20.1% management, 30.5% professional, 9.1% services, 28.8% sales, 0.0% farming, 3.8% construction, 7.7% production (2000).
Income: Per capita income: $40,175 (2007); Median household income: $58,736 (2007); Average household income: $85,103 (2007); Percent of households with income of $100,000 or more: 22.9% (2007); Poverty rate: 2.0% (2000).
Education: Percent of population age 25 and over with: High school diploma (including GED) or higher: 91.8% (2007); Bachelor's degree or higher: 43.8% (2007); Master's degree or higher: 17.7% (2007).

School District(s)

CCSD 180 (PK-08)
2005-06 Enrollment: 769 . . . . (630) 734-6600
Gower SD 62 (PK-08)
2005-06 Enrollment: 956 . . . . (630) 986-5383
Maercker SD 60 (PK-08)
2005-06 Enrollment: 1,413 . . . . (630) 323-2086
Housing: Homeownership rate: 77.2% (2007); Median home value: $252,477 (2007); Median rent: $890 per month (2000); Median age of housing: 22 years (2000).

Safety: Violent crime rate: 13.5 per 10,000 population; Property crime rate: 218.1 per 10,000 population (2006).
Transportation: Commute to work: 88.0% car, 6.1% public transportation, 2.2% walk, 3.4% work from home (2000); Travel time to work: 18.8% less than 15 minutes, 29.7% 15 to 30 minutes, 26.7% 30 to 45 minutes, 13.0% 45 to 60 minutes, 11.8% 60 minutes or more (2000)
Additional Information Contacts
Village of Willowbrook .... (630) 323-8215
http://www.willowbrookil.org

WINFIELD (village). Covers a land area of 2.700 square miles and a water area of 0.006 square miles. Located at 41.87° N. Lat.; 88.15° W. Long. Elevation is 771 feet.
Population: 7,629 (1990); 8,718 (2000); 9,502 (2007); 9,919 (2012 projected); Race: 91.6% White, 1.5% Black, 3.9% Asian, 3.4% Hispanic of any race (2007); Density: 3,518.6 persons per square mile (2007); Average household size: 2.90 (2007); Median age: 39.9 (2007); Males per 100 females: 95.5 (2007); Marriage status: 18.8% never married, 71.4% now married, 3.7% widowed, 6.1% divorced (2000); Foreign born: 6.3% (2000); Ancestry (includes multiple ancestries): 28.5% German, 18.4% Irish, 13.7% English, 12.7% Italian, 11.7% Polish (2000).
Economy: Single-family building permits issued: 6 (2007); Multi-family building permits issued: 9 (2007); Employment by occupation: 22.8% management, 26.7% professional, 7.6% services, 28.1% sales, 0.0% farming, 7.4% construction, 7.4% production (2000).
Income: Per capita income: $42,223 (2007); Median household income: $96,343 (2007); Average household income: $121,941 (2007); Percent of households with income of $100,000 or more: 47.6% (2007); Poverty rate: 3.0% (2000).
Education: Percent of population age 25 and over with: High school diploma (including GED) or higher: 92.6% (2007); Bachelor's degree or higher: 45.6% (2007); Master's degree or higher: 15.7% (2007).

School District(s)

CUSD 200 (PK-12)
2005-06 Enrollment: 14,076 .... (630) 682-2002
Winfield SD 34 (PK-08)
2005-06 Enrollment: 380 .... (630) 909-4900
Housing: Homeownership rate: 95.6% (2007); Median home value: $306,980 (2007); Median rent: $837 per month (2000); Median age of housing: 17 years (2000).
Hospitals: Behavioral Health Service of Winfield (52 beds); Central DuPage Hospital Behavioral Health Services (20 beds)
Safety: Violent crime rate: 9.1 per 10,000 population; Property crime rate: 54.9 per 10,000 population (2006).
Transportation: Commute to work: 84.7% car, 10.8% public transportation, 0.5% walk, 3.5% work from home (2000); Travel time to work: 23.7% less than 15 minutes, 27.8% 15 to 30 minutes, 21.2% 30 to 45 minutes, 11.7% 45 to 60 minutes, 15.7% 60 minutes or more (2000)
Additional Information Contacts
Village of Winfield .... (630) 933-7100
http://www.villageofwinfield.com
Winfield Chamber of Commerce .... (630) 682-3712
http://www.winfieldchamber.biz

WOOD DALE (city). Covers a land area of 4.671 square miles and a water area of 0 square miles. Located at 41.96° N. Lat.; 87.97° W. Long. Elevation is 692 feet.
Population: 12,974 (1990); 13,535 (2000); 13,159 (2007); 12,943 (2012 projected); Race: 85.8% White, 0.9% Black, 3.7% Asian, 17.1% Hispanic of any race (2007); Density: 2,817.3 persons per square mile (2007); Average household size: 2.62 (2007); Median age: 42.1 (2007); Males per 100 females: 98.9 (2007); Marriage status: 23.6% never married, 60.3% now married, 7.8% widowed, 8.4% divorced (2000); Foreign born: 21.2% (2000); Ancestry (includes multiple ancestries): 20.6% Polish, 19.3% German, 18.8% Italian, 18.5% Other groups, 12.0% Irish (2000).
Economy: Single-family building permits issued: 46 (2007); Multi-family building permits issued: 0 (2007); Employment by occupation: 16.4% management, 17.3% professional, 10.2% services, 28.7% sales, 0.1% farming, 10.4% construction, 16.9% production (2000).
Income: Per capita income: $28,699 (2007); Median household income: $63,449 (2007); Average household income: $74,939 (2007); Percent of households with income of $100,000 or more: 22.9% (2007); Poverty rate: 4.1% (2000).
Education: Percent of population age 25 and over with: High school diploma (including GED) or higher: 82.8% (2007); Bachelor's degree or higher: 19.7% (2007); Master's degree or higher: 5.7% (2007).

School District(s)

Wood Dale SD 7 (PK-08)
2005-06 Enrollment: 1,274 .... (630) 595-9510
Housing: Homeownership rate: 84.8% (2007); Median home value: $258,762 (2007); Median rent: $801 per month (2000); Median age of housing: 28 years (2000).
Safety: Violent crime rate: 10.4 per 10,000 population; Property crime rate: 218.3 per 10,000 population (2006).
Transportation: Commute to work: 92.4% car, 3.3% public transportation, 1.4% walk, 2.4% work from home (2000); Travel time to work: 24.7% less than 15 minutes, 39.1% 15 to 30 minutes, 20.9% 30 to 45 minutes, 7.3% 45 to 60 minutes, 8.1% 60 minutes or more (2000)
Additional Information Contacts
City of Wood Dale .... (630) 766-4900
http://www.wooddale.com
Wood Dale Chamber of Commerce .... (630) 595-0505
http://www.wooddalechamber.com

WOODRIDGE (village). Covers a land area of 8.323 square miles and a water area of 0.023 square miles. Located at 41.74° N. Lat.; 88.04° W. Long. Elevation is 732 feet.
Population: 27,524 (1990); 30,934 (2000); 34,123 (2007); 36,006 (2012 projected); Race: 67.7% White, 10.4% Black, 14.8% Asian, 12.2% Hispanic of any race (2007); Density: 4,099.9 persons per square mile (2007); Average household size: 2.68 (2007); Median age: 35.8 (2007); Males per 100 females: 99.7 (2007); Marriage status: 28.2% never married, 59.3% now married, 3.6% widowed, 8.8% divorced (2000); Foreign born: 17.3% (2000); Ancestry (includes multiple ancestries): 27.4% Other groups, 21.6% German, 17.4% Irish, 12.0% Polish, 10.0% Italian (2000).
Economy: Unemployment rate: 4.2% (4/2008); Total civilian labor force: 20,836 (4/2008); Single-family building permits issued: 38 (2007); Multi-family building permits issued: 0 (2007); Employment by occupation: 18.4% management, 24.8% professional, 10.3% services, 29.6% sales, 0.0% farming, 6.9% construction, 10.0% production (2000).
Income: Per capita income: $31,809 (2007); Median household income: $69,903 (2007); Average household income: $85,206 (2007); Percent of households with income of $100,000 or more: 28.7% (2007); Poverty rate: 3.8% (2000).
Education: Percent of population age 25 and over with: High school diploma (including GED) or higher: 90.0% (2007); Bachelor's degree or higher: 39.4% (2007); Master's degree or higher: 12.5% (2007).

School District(s)

Woodridge SD 68 (PK-08)
2005-06 Enrollment: 2,854 .... (630) 985-7925

Four-year College(s)

Westwood College-Dupage (Private, For-profit)
Fall 2007 Enrollment: 519 .... (630) 434-8250
2007-08 Tuition: In-state $12,753; Out-of-state $12,753
Housing: Homeownership rate: 66.2% (2007); Median home value: $243,967 (2007); Median rent: $719 per month (2000); Median age of housing: 24 years (2000).
Safety: Violent crime rate: 14.1 per 10,000 population; Property crime rate: 176.5 per 10,000 population (2006).
Transportation: Commute to work: 88.2% car, 7.0% public transportation, 1.4% walk, 2.7% work from home (2000); Travel time to work: 18.5% less than 15 minutes, 35.2% 15 to 30 minutes, 23.1% 30 to 45 minutes, 10.1% 45 to 60 minutes, 13.0% 60 minutes or more (2000)
Additional Information Contacts
Village of Woodridge .... (630) 719-4712
http://www.vil.woodridge.il.us
Woodridge Area Chamber of Commerce............... (630) 960-7080
http://www.woodridgechamber.org

Edgar County

Located in eastern Illinois; bounded on the east by Indiana; drained by tributaries of the Wabash River. Covers a land area of 623.55 square miles, a water area of 0.63 square miles, and is located in the Central Time Zone. The county was founded in 1823. County seat is Paris.

Weather Station: Paris Waterworks Elevation: 679 feet

	Jan	Feb	Mar	Apr	May	Jun	Jul	Aug	Sep	Oct	Nov	Dec
High	34	40	51	64	75	83	86	84	79	66	52	40
Low	18	23	33	43	53	62	66	64	57	45	35	24
Precip	2.2	2.2	3.3	4.1	4.2	4.1	4.4	4.4	3.0	2.8	3.6	3.1
Snow	10.4	6.6	3.6	0.3	0.0	0.0	0.0	0.0	0.0	0.1	1.3	5.9

High and Low temperatures in degrees Fahrenheit; Precipitation and Snow in inches

Population: 19,595 (1990); 19,704 (2000); 19,031 (2007); 18,529 (2012 projected); Race: 96.7% White, 2.0% Black, 0.3% Asian, 1.0% Hispanic of any race (2007); Density: 30.5 persons per square mile (2007); Average household size: 2.49 (2007); Median age: 40.9 (2007); Males per 100 females: 96.6 (2007).
Religion: Five largest groups: 15.0% Christian Churches and Churches of Christ, 10.9% The United Methodist Church, 7.2% Catholic Church, 4.4% Christian Church (Disciples of Christ), 2.8% New Testament Association of Independent Baptist Churches and
Economy: Unemployment rate: 5.5% (4/2008); Total civilian labor force: 10,582 (4/2008); Leading industries: 37.7% manufacturing; 13.9% retail trade; 13.0% health care and social assistance (2005); Farms: 667 totaling 355,035 acres (2002); Companies that employ 500 or more persons: 1 (2006); Companies that employ 100 to 499 persons: 9 (2006); Companies that employ less than 100 persons: 387 (2006); Black-owned businesses: n/a (2002); Hispanic-owned businesses: n/a (2002); Asian-owned businesses: n/a (2002); Women-owned businesses: n/a (2002); Retail sales per capita: $8,877 (2008). Single-family building permits issued: 15 (2007); Multi-family building permits issued: 0 (2007).
Income: Per capita income: $21,147 (2007); Median household income: $41,354 (2007); Average household income: $51,407 (2007); Percent of households with income of $100,000 or more: 8.4% (2007); Poverty rate: 13.2% (2005); Bankruptcy rate: 4.02% (2007).
Education: Percent of population age 25 and over with: High school diploma (including GED) or higher: 81.3% (2007); Bachelor's degree or higher: 13.2% (2007); Master's degree or higher: 4.1% (2007).
Housing: Homeownership rate: 74.7% (2007); Median home value: $81,542 (2007); Median rent: $282 per month (2000); Median age of housing: 49 years (2000).
Health: Birth rate: 122.1 per 10,000 population (2007); Death rate: 131.1 per 10,000 population (2007); Age-adjusted cancer mortality rate: 194.0 deaths per 100,000 population (2005); Number of physicians: 6.8 per 10,000 population (2005); Hospital beds: 13.1 per 10,000 population (2004); Hospital admissions: 432.1 per 10,000 population (2004).
Elections: 2004 Presidential election results: 62.4% Bush, 36.7% Kerry, 0.0% Nader, 0.9% Badnarik

Additional Information Contacts

Edgar County Government . . . . (217) 466-7433
http://www.edgarcounty-il.gov
City of Paris . . . . (217) 465-7601
http://parisillinois.org
Paris Area Chamber of Commerce & Tourism . . . . (217) 465-4179
http://www.parisilchamber.com

Edgar County Communities

BROCTON (village). Covers a land area of 0.579 square miles and a water area of 0 square miles. Located at 39.71° N. Lat.; 87.93° W. Long. Elevation is 663 feet.
Population: 322 (1990); 322 (2000); 307 (2007); 290 (2012 projected); Race: 99.7% White, 0.0% Black, 0.0% Asian, 0.0% Hispanic of any race (2007); Density: 530.6 persons per square mile (2007); Average household size: 2.38 (2007); Median age: 39.4 (2007); Males per 100 females: 95.5 (2007); Marriage status: 14.3% never married, 57.9% now married, 10.0% widowed, 17.8% divorced (2000); Foreign born: 0.0% (2000); Ancestry (includes multiple ancestries): 25.4% United States or American, 11.5% German, 6.5% Other groups, 6.2% Irish, 3.8% English (2000).
Economy: Single-family building permits issued: 0 (2007); Multi-family building permits issued: 0 (2007); Employment by occupation: 5.4% management, 4.0% professional, 12.8% services, 20.1% sales, 3.4% farming, 4.7% construction, 49.7% production (2000).
Income: Per capita income: $22,093 (2007); Median household income: $39,167 (2007); Average household income: $52,578 (2007); Percent of households with income of $100,000 or more: 7.8% (2007); Poverty rate: 16.5% (2000).
Education: Percent of population age 25 and over with: High school diploma (including GED) or higher: 74.9% (2007); Bachelor's degree or higher: 4.9% (2007); Master's degree or higher: 0.0% (2007).
Housing: Homeownership rate: 81.4% (2007); Median home value: $44,167 (2007); Median rent: $208 per month (2000); Median age of housing: 60+ years (2000).
Transportation: Commute to work: 93.2% car, 0.0% public transportation, 4.8% walk, 0.0% work from home (2000); Travel time to work: 12.3% less than 15 minutes, 37.0% 15 to 30 minutes, 26.7% 30 to 45 minutes, 11.0% 45 to 60 minutes, 13.0% 60 minutes or more (2000)

CHRISMAN (city). Covers a land area of 0.732 square miles and a water area of 0 square miles. Located at 39.80° N. Lat.; 87.67° W. Long. Elevation is 650 feet.
History: Chrisman was platted in 1872 by Matthias Chrisman, and grew as a trading center and shipping point.
Population: 1,228 (1990); 1,318 (2000); 1,248 (2007); 1,226 (2012 projected); Race: 99.2% White, 0.2% Black, 0.2% Asian, 0.3% Hispanic of any race (2007); Density: 1,705.9 persons per square mile (2007); Average household size: 2.43 (2007); Median age: 45.4 (2007); Males per 100 females: 85.4 (2007); Marriage status: 19.1% never married, 54.7% now married, 17.5% widowed, 8.7% divorced (2000); Foreign born: 0.6% (2000); Ancestry (includes multiple ancestries): 26.3% United States or American, 16.3% German, 12.1% English, 11.1% Irish, 4.4% Other groups (2000).
Economy: Single-family building permits issued: 5 (2007); Multi-family building permits issued: 0 (2007); Employment by occupation: 10.2% management, 17.6% professional, 20.8% services, 21.3% sales, 3.7% farming, 5.7% construction, 20.7% production (2000).
Income: Per capita income: $20,563 (2007); Median household income: $38,977 (2007); Average household income: $46,369 (2007); Percent of households with income of $100,000 or more: 6.4% (2007); Poverty rate: 10.7% (2000).
Education: Percent of population age 25 and over with: High school diploma (including GED) or higher: 82.3% (2007); Bachelor's degree or higher: 14.5% (2007); Master's degree or higher: 2.8% (2007).

School District(s)

Edgar County Cud 6 (KG-12)
2005-06 Enrollment: 379 . . . . (217) 269-2513
Housing: Homeownership rate: 71.7% (2007); Median home value: $79,667 (2007); Median rent: $247 per month (2000); Median age of housing: 48 years (2000).
Transportation: Commute to work: 93.8% car, 0.5% public transportation, 1.8% walk, 3.3% work from home (2000); Travel time to work: 32.3% less than 15 minutes, 29.7% 15 to 30 minutes, 25.0% 30 to 45 minutes, 8.4% 45 to 60 minutes, 4.5% 60 minutes or more (2000)

HUME (village). Covers a land area of 0.514 square miles and a water area of 0 square miles. Located at 39.79° N. Lat.; 87.86° W. Long. Elevation is 663 feet.
Population: 406 (1990); 382 (2000); 352 (2007); 337 (2012 projected); Race: 99.7% White, 0.0% Black, 0.0% Asian, 2.3% Hispanic of any race (2007); Density: 684.7 persons per square mile (2007); Average household size: 2.15 (2007); Median age: 45.8 (2007); Males per 100 females: 88.2 (2007); Marriage status: 16.4% never married, 58.4% now married, 12.8% widowed, 12.5% divorced (2000); Foreign born: 0.0% (2000); Ancestry (includes multiple ancestries): 19.5% United States or American, 17.2% German, 12.3% Irish, 9.4% English, 5.4% Other groups (2000).
Economy: Employment by occupation: 6.1% management, 12.2% professional, 14.9% services, 31.5% sales, 2.8% farming, 10.5% construction, 22.1% production (2000).
Income: Per capita income: $17,720 (2007); Median household income: $33,636 (2007); Average household income: $38,034 (2007); Percent of households with income of $100,000 or more: 1.8% (2007); Poverty rate: 10.9% (2000).
Education: Percent of population age 25 and over with: High school diploma (including GED) or higher: 81.9% (2007); Bachelor's degree or higher: 9.4% (2007); Master's degree or higher: 3.9% (2007).

School District(s)

Shiloh CUSD 1 (PK-12)
2005-06 Enrollment: 489 . . . . (217) 887-2364
Housing: Homeownership rate: 84.8% (2007); Median home value: $59,737 (2007); Median rent: $220 per month (2000); Median age of housing: 52 years (2000).
Transportation: Commute to work: 96.7% car, 0.0% public transportation, 1.7% walk, 1.7% work from home (2000); Travel time to work: 21.3% less than 15 minutes, 24.7% 15 to 30 minutes, 25.3% 30 to 45 minutes, 14.0% 45 to 60 minutes, 14.6% 60 minutes or more (2000)

KANSAS (village). Covers a land area of 1.028 square miles and a water area of 0 square miles. Located at 39.55° N. Lat.; 87.93° W. Long. Elevation is 712 feet.

Population: 887 (1990); 842 (2000); 835 (2007); 812 (2012 projected); Race: 97.8% White, 0.4% Black, 0.4% Asian, 1.6% Hispanic of any race (2007); Density: 812.1 persons per square mile (2007); Average household size: 2.46 (2007); Median age: 37.8 (2007); Males per 100 females: 92.8 (2007); Marriage status: 19.8% never married, 61.0% now married, 8.6% widowed, 10.7% divorced (2000); Foreign born: 1.4% (2000); Ancestry (includes multiple ancestries): 21.1% German, 19.7% United States or American, 10.7% Irish, 9.4% Other groups, 9.2% English (2000).

Economy: Employment by occupation: 10.6% management, 10.3% professional, 15.7% services, 21.5% sales, 2.7% farming, 11.5% construction, 27.8% production (2000).

Income: Per capita income: $17,512 (2007); Median household income: $31,917 (2007); Average household income: $43,134 (2007); Percent of households with income of $100,000 or more: 5.6% (2007); Poverty rate: 15.4% (2000).

Education: Percent of population age 25 and over with: High school diploma (including GED) or higher: 87.1% (2007); Bachelor's degree or higher: 13.4% (2007); Master's degree or higher: 6.0% (2007).

School District(s)

Eastern Ill Area of Spec Educ (PK-12)
2005-06 Enrollment: 577 . . . . (217) 348-7700

Kansas CUSD 3 (KG-12)
2005-06 Enrollment: 256 . . . . (217) 948-5174

Housing: Homeownership rate: 72.3% (2007); Median home value: $77,381 (2007); Median rent: $256 per month (2000); Median age of housing: 49 years (2000).

Safety: Violent crime rate: 12.1 per 10,000 population; Property crime rate: 48.4 per 10,000 population (2006).

Transportation: Commute to work: 92.1% car, 0.6% public transportation, 2.4% walk, 3.3% work from home (2000); Travel time to work: 28.5% less than 15 minutes, 41.4% 15 to 30 minutes, 21.9% 30 to 45 minutes, 3.4% 45 to 60 minutes, 4.7% 60 minutes or more (2000)

METCALF (village). Covers a land area of 0.552 square miles and a water area of 0 square miles. Located at 39.80° N. Lat.; 87.80° W. Long. Elevation is 689 feet.

Population: 227 (1990); 213 (2000); 197 (2007); 188 (2012 projected); Race: 99.0% White, 0.0% Black, 0.0% Asian, 1.0% Hispanic of any race (2007); Density: 356.8 persons per square mile (2007); Average household size: 2.59 (2007); Median age: 33.0 (2007); Males per 100 females: 84.1 (2007); Marriage status: 24.7% never married, 56.0% now married, 9.0% widowed, 10.2% divorced (2000); Foreign born: 0.0% (2000); Ancestry (includes multiple ancestries): 33.0% United States or American, 10.8% English, 9.8% Other groups, 9.3% German, 6.2% Irish (2000).

Economy: Employment by occupation: 8.7% management, 9.8% professional, 18.5% services, 20.7% sales, 8.7% farming, 9.8% construction, 23.9% production (2000).

Income: Per capita income: $15,431 (2007); Median household income: $33,333 (2007); Average household income: $40,000 (2007); Percent of households with income of $100,000 or more: 3.9% (2007); Poverty rate: 15.5% (2000).

Education: Percent of population age 25 and over with: High school diploma (including GED) or higher: 65.9% (2007); Bachelor's degree or higher: 3.3% (2007); Master's degree or higher: 1.6% (2007).

Housing: Homeownership rate: 76.3% (2007); Median home value: $22,500 (2007); Median rent: $245 per month (2000); Median age of housing: 57 years (2000).

Transportation: Commute to work: 97.8% car, 0.0% public transportation, 0.0% walk, 2.2% work from home (2000); Travel time to work: 26.1% less than 15 minutes, 23.9% 15 to 30 minutes, 12.5% 30 to 45 minutes, 22.7% 45 to 60 minutes, 14.8% 60 minutes or more (2000)

PARIS (city). County seat. Covers a land area of 4.815 square miles and a water area of 0.396 square miles. Located at 39.61° N. Lat.; 87.69° W. Long. Elevation is 722 feet.

History: Paris was the site of several speeches by Abraham Lincoln. The town was platted in 1853 and grew as the seat of Edgar County.

Population: 9,195 (1990); 9,077 (2000); 8,682 (2007); 8,341 (2012 projected); Race: 98.4% White, 0.4% Black, 0.4% Asian, 1.0% Hispanic of any race (2007); Density: 1,803.2 persons per square mile (2007); Average household size: 2.32 (2007); Median age: 40.1 (2007); Males per 100 females: 86.9 (2007); Marriage status: 19.0% never married, 56.4% now married, 11.9% widowed, 12.8% divorced (2000); Foreign born: 0.7% (2000); Ancestry (includes multiple ancestries): 21.6% United States or American, 16.9% German, 12.5% Irish, 10.2% English, 6.9% Other groups (2000).

Economy: Single-family building permits issued: 10 (2007); Multi-family building permits issued: 0 (2007); Employment by occupation: 7.5% management, 14.7% professional, 16.3% services, 19.4% sales, 0.4% farming, 8.2% construction, 33.5% production (2000).

Income: Per capita income: $20,698 (2007); Median household income: $36,686 (2007); Average household income: $47,214 (2007); Percent of households with income of $100,000 or more: 6.4% (2007); Poverty rate: 12.7% (2000).

Education: Percent of population age 25 and over with: High school diploma (including GED) or higher: 79.4% (2007); Bachelor's degree or higher: 11.1% (2007); Master's degree or higher: 3.7% (2007).

School District(s)

Clk Cls Cmbn Dglas Edgr Mltr Shlb (06-12)
2005-06 Enrollment: 103 . . . . (217) 348-0151

Paris CUSD 4 (PK-08)
2005-06 Enrollment: 568 . . . . (217) 465-5391

Paris-Union SD 95 (PK-12)
2005-06 Enrollment: 1,664 . . . . (217) 465-8448

Housing: Homeownership rate: 69.6% (2007); Median home value: $69,409 (2007); Median rent: $290 per month (2000); Median age of housing: 51 years (2000).

Hospitals: Paris Community Hospital (49 beds)

Safety: Violent crime rate: 73.6 per 10,000 population; Property crime rate: 172.1 per 10,000 population (2006).

Newspapers: Paris Daily Beacon News (Local news; Circulation 5,600)

Transportation: Commute to work: 95.3% car, 0.0% public transportation, 2.1% walk, 1.9% work from home (2000); Travel time to work: 66.8% less than 15 minutes, 12.4% 15 to 30 minutes, 11.3% 30 to 45 minutes, 4.2% 45 to 60 minutes, 5.3% 60 minutes or more (2000)

Airports: Edgar County (general aviation)

Additional Information Contacts

City of Paris . . . . (217) 465-7601
http://parisillinois.org

Paris Area Chamber of Commerce & Tourism . . . . (217) 465-4179
http://www.parisilchamber.com

REDMON (village). Covers a land area of 0.148 square miles and a water area of 0 square miles. Located at 39.64° N. Lat.; 87.86° W. Long. Elevation is 689 feet.

Population: 201 (1990); 199 (2000); 190 (2007); 178 (2012 projected); Race: 100.0% White, 0.0% Black, 0.0% Asian, 0.0% Hispanic of any race (2007); Density: 1,285.9 persons per square mile (2007); Average household size: 2.35 (2007); Median age: 43.3 (2007); Males per 100 females: 102.1 (2007); Marriage status: 19.5% never married, 57.9% now married, 6.1% widowed, 16.5% divorced (2000); Foreign born: 0.0% (2000); Ancestry (includes multiple ancestries): 12.3% United States or American, 10.2% German, 8.6% Other groups, 8.0% English, 4.3% Irish (2000).

Economy: Employment by occupation: 4.0% management, 18.2% professional, 9.1% services, 21.2% sales, 2.0% farming, 5.1% construction, 40.4% production (2000).

Income: Per capita income: $17,684 (2007); Median household income: $35,417 (2007); Average household income: $41,481 (2007); Percent of households with income of $100,000 or more: 6.2% (2007); Poverty rate: 19.4% (2000).

Education: Percent of population age 25 and over with: High school diploma (including GED) or higher: 81.6% (2007); Bachelor's degree or higher: 9.6% (2007); Master's degree or higher: 1.5% (2007).

Housing: Homeownership rate: 72.8% (2007); Median home value: $69,286 (2007); Median rent: $305 per month (2000); Median age of housing: 58 years (2000).

Transportation: Commute to work: 96.0% car, 2.0% public transportation, 0.0% walk, 2.0% work from home (2000); Travel time to work: 17.5% less than 15 minutes, 48.5% 15 to 30 minutes, 15.5% 30 to 45 minutes, 14.4% 45 to 60 minutes, 4.1% 60 minutes or more (2000)

VERMILION (village). Covers a land area of 0.762 square miles and a water area of 0 square miles. Located at 39.58° N. Lat.; 87.58° W. Long. Elevation is 692 feet.

History: Formerly Vermillion.

Population: 283 (1990); 239 (2000); 235 (2007); 228 (2012 projected); Race: 99.6% White, 0.0% Black, 0.0% Asian, 0.4% Hispanic of any race (2007); Density: 308.3 persons per square mile (2007); Average household size: 2.55 (2007); Median age: 42.1 (2007); Males per 100 females: 91.1 (2007); Marriage status: 22.0% never married, 57.8% now married, 7.5% widowed, 12.7% divorced (2000); Foreign born: 0.0% (2000); Ancestry (includes multiple ancestries): 30.9% United States or American, 14.4% German, 11.1% English, 6.2% Other groups, 3.7% Scottish (2000).
Economy: Single-family building permits issued: 0 (2007); Multi-family building permits issued: 0 (2007); Employment by occupation: 1.8% management, 10.0% professional, 8.2% services, 22.7% sales, 0.0% farming, 12.7% construction, 44.5% production (2000).
Income: Per capita income: $16,298 (2007); Median household income: $38,500 (2007); Average household income: $41,630 (2007); Percent of households with income of $100,000 or more: 2.2% (2007); Poverty rate: 17.3% (2000).
Education: Percent of population age 25 and over with: High school diploma (including GED) or higher: 79.7% (2007); Bachelor's degree or higher: 7.6% (2007); Master's degree or higher: 1.2% (2007).
Housing: Homeownership rate: 83.7% (2007); Median home value: $49,444 (2007); Median rent: $317 per month (2000); Median age of housing: 59 years (2000).
Transportation: Commute to work: 96.4% car, 0.0% public transportation, 0.9% walk, 2.7% work from home (2000); Travel time to work: 14.0% less than 15 minutes, 64.5% 15 to 30 minutes, 11.2% 30 to 45 minutes, 4.7% 45 to 60 minutes, 5.6% 60 minutes or more (2000)

Edwards County

Located in southeastern Illinois; drained by the Little Wabash River. Covers a land area of 222.35 square miles, a water area of 0.31 square miles, and is located in the Central Time Zone. The county was founded in 1814. County seat is Albion.

Weather Station: Albion — Elevation: 528 feet

	Jan	Feb	Mar	Apr	May	Jun	Jul	Aug	Sep	Oct	Nov	Dec
High	39	45	56	67	77	86	90	88	82	71	55	44
Low	23	27	36	45	55	64	68	66	59	47	37	27
Precip	2.6	2.8	4.2	5.3	4.7	4.2	3.8	3.1	3.0	3.5	4.3	3.3
Snow	2.7	2.7	2.0	0.1	0.0	0.0	0.0	0.0	0.0	0.1	0.2	2.5

High and Low temperatures in degrees Fahrenheit; Precipitation and Snow in inches

Population: 7,440 (1990); 6,971 (2000); 6,755 (2007); 6,605 (2012 projected); Race: 98.8% White, 0.1% Black, 0.5% Asian, 0.5% Hispanic of any race (2007); Density: 30.4 persons per square mile (2007); Average household size: 2.37 (2007); Median age: 42.2 (2007); Males per 100 females: 93.6 (2007).
Religion: Five largest groups: 23.3% Christian Churches and Churches of Christ, 14.4% Southern Baptist Convention, 14.2% The United Methodist Church, 9.7% Independent, Non-Charismatic Churches, 4.4% Christian Church (Disciples of Christ) (2000).
Economy: Unemployment rate: 5.9% (4/2008); Total civilian labor force: 3,374 (4/2008); Leading industries: 8.9% retail trade; 6.6% health care and social assistance; 5.1% wholesale trade (2005); Farms: 379 totaling 123,026 acres (2002); Companies that employ 500 or more persons: 1 (2006); Companies that employ 100 to 499 persons: 1 (2006); Companies that employ less than 100 persons: 161 (2006); Black-owned businesses: n/a (2002); Hispanic-owned businesses: n/a (2002); Asian-owned businesses: n/a (2002); Women-owned businesses: n/a (2002); Retail sales per capita: $7,850 (2008). Single-family building permits issued: n/a (2007); Multi-family building permits issued: n/a (2007).
Income: Per capita income: $20,729 (2007); Median household income: $40,311 (2007); Average household income: $48,827 (2007); Percent of households with income of $100,000 or more: 7.2% (2007); Poverty rate: 10.5% (2005); Bankruptcy rate: 1.83% (2007).
Education: Percent of population age 25 and over with: High school diploma (including GED) or higher: 82.4% (2007); Bachelor's degree or higher: 10.0% (2007); Master's degree or higher: 3.0% (2007).
Housing: Homeownership rate: 81.3% (2007); Median home value: $62,418 (2007); Median rent: $210 per month (2000); Median age of housing: 40 years (2000).
Health: Birth rate: 112.6 per 10,000 population (2007); Death rate: 121.7 per 10,000 population (2007); Age-adjusted cancer mortality rate: 192.3 (Unreliable) deaths per 100,000 population (2005); Number of physicians: 1.5 per 10,000 population (2005); Hospital beds: 0.0 per 10,000 population (2004); Hospital admissions: 0.0 per 10,000 population (2004).
Elections: 2004 Presidential election results: 71.7% Bush, 27.6% Kerry, 0.0% Nader, 0.6% Badnarik
Additional Information Contacts
Edwards County Government . . . . (618) 445-2115

Albion Chamber of Commerce. . . . . (618) 445-2303
http://www.albionchamber.com

Edwards County Communities

ALBION (city). County seat. Covers a land area of 2.139 square miles and a water area of 0.049 square miles. Located at 38.37° N. Lat.; 88.06° W. Long. Elevation is 522 feet.
History: In 1818 Morris Birkbeck and George Flower came from England to find a place that would provide a better life for the English working class. They settled on this section of prairie and led many English colonists here, who named the town Albion, remembering their former homeland.
Population: 2,150 (1990); 1,933 (2000); 1,891 (2007); 1,851 (2012 projected); Race: 98.5% White, 0.2% Black, 0.8% Asian, 0.6% Hispanic of any race (2007); Density: 884.2 persons per square mile (2007); Average household size: 2.23 (2007); Median age: 43.5 (2007); Males per 100 females: 85.2 (2007); Marriage status: 15.6% never married, 61.0% now married, 11.9% widowed, 11.5% divorced (2000); Foreign born: 0.5% (2000); Ancestry (includes multiple ancestries): 25.0% English, 23.5% United States or American, 18.5% German, 9.0% Irish, 4.8% Other groups (2000).
Economy: Employment by occupation: 5.6% management, 13.0% professional, 13.8% services, 23.9% sales, 0.2% farming, 10.5% construction, 32.9% production (2000).
Income: Per capita income: $19,278 (2007); Median household income: $36,920 (2007); Average household income: $42,403 (2007); Percent of households with income of $100,000 or more: 3.3% (2007); Poverty rate: 12.2% (2000).
Education: Percent of population age 25 and over with: High school diploma (including GED) or higher: 79.1% (2007); Bachelor's degree or higher: 9.4% (2007); Master's degree or higher: 3.3% (2007).

School District(s)

Edwards County CUSD 1 (PK-12)
2005-06 Enrollment: 974 . . . . (618) 445-2814
Housing: Homeownership rate: 74.4% (2007); Median home value: $56,364 (2007); Median rent: $210 per month (2000); Median age of housing: 42 years (2000).
Safety: Violent crime rate: 26.4 per 10,000 population; Property crime rate: 163.8 per 10,000 population (2006).
Newspapers: Navigator & Journal-Register (Community news; Circulation 3,600); Prairie Post (Community news; Circulation 12,750)
Transportation: Commute to work: 89.9% car, 0.0% public transportation, 5.2% walk, 4.7% work from home (2000); Travel time to work: 54.7% less than 15 minutes, 18.3% 15 to 30 minutes, 11.5% 30 to 45 minutes, 7.1% 45 to 60 minutes, 8.4% 60 minutes or more (2000)
Additional Information Contacts
Albion Chamber of Commerce. . . . . (618) 445-2303
http://www.albionchamber.com

BONE GAP (village). Covers a land area of 0.604 square miles and a water area of 0 square miles. Located at 38.44° N. Lat.; 87.99° W. Long. Elevation is 482 feet.
Population: 271 (1990); 272 (2000); 267 (2007); 257 (2012 projected); Race: 98.9% White, 0.0% Black, 0.7% Asian, 0.0% Hispanic of any race (2007); Density: 442.2 persons per square mile (2007); Average household size: 2.70 (2007); Median age: 32.0 (2007); Males per 100 females: 94.9 (2007); Marriage status: 24.8% never married, 57.5% now married, 8.9% widowed, 8.9% divorced (2000); Foreign born: 0.0% (2000); Ancestry (includes multiple ancestries): 23.9% German, 17.8% English, 13.1% United States or American, 8.5% Other groups, 4.6% Polish (2000).
Economy: Employment by occupation: 13.1% management, 1.9% professional, 15.0% services, 26.2% sales, 0.9% farming, 8.4% construction, 34.6% production (2000).
Income: Per capita income: $13,006 (2007); Median household income: $32,500 (2007); Average household income: $35,076 (2007); Percent of households with income of $100,000 or more: 3.0% (2007); Poverty rate: 25.1% (2000).
Education: Percent of population age 25 and over with: High school diploma (including GED) or higher: 83.4% (2007); Bachelor's degree or higher: 3.7% (2007); Master's degree or higher: 0.0% (2007).

Housing: Homeownership rate: 81.8% (2007); Median home value: $40,833 (2007); Median rent: $235 per month (2000); Median age of housing: 38 years (2000).
Transportation: Commute to work: 90.3% car, 0.0% public transportation, 1.9% walk, 7.8% work from home (2000); Travel time to work: 26.3% less than 15 minutes, 41.1% 15 to 30 minutes, 7.4% 30 to 45 minutes, 11.6% 45 to 60 minutes, 13.7% 60 minutes or more (2000)

BROWNS (village). Covers a land area of 0.292 square miles and a water area of 0 square miles. Located at 38.37° N. Lat.; 87.98° W. Long. Elevation is 407 feet.
Population: 207 (1990); 175 (2000); 187 (2007); 186 (2012 projected); Race: 96.3% White, 1.1% Black, 2.1% Asian, 2.7% Hispanic of any race (2007); Density: 640.6 persons per square mile (2007); Average household size: 2.56 (2007); Median age: 38.4 (2007); Males per 100 females: 98.9 (2007); Marriage status: 24.2% never married, 64.4% now married, 5.3% widowed, 6.1% divorced (2000); Foreign born: 0.6% (2000); Ancestry (includes multiple ancestries): 23.2% English, 19.0% German, 13.7% French (except Basque), 11.3% Irish, 7.7% United States or American (2000).
Economy: Employment by occupation: 0.0% management, 5.5% professional, 21.9% services, 30.1% sales, 1.4% farming, 2.7% construction, 38.4% production (2000).
Income: Per capita income: $14,144 (2007); Median household income: $30,313 (2007); Average household income: $36,233 (2007); Percent of households with income of $100,000 or more: 1.4% (2007); Poverty rate: 6.5% (2000).
Education: Percent of population age 25 and over with: High school diploma (including GED) or higher: 75.0% (2007); Bachelor's degree or higher: 5.6% (2007); Master's degree or higher: 0.0% (2007).
Housing: Homeownership rate: 87.7% (2007); Median home value: $24,000 (2007); Median rent: $175 per month (2000); Median age of housing: 57 years (2000).
Transportation: Commute to work: 98.6% car, 0.0% public transportation, 1.4% walk, 0.0% work from home (2000); Travel time to work: 56.2% less than 15 minutes, 15.1% 15 to 30 minutes, 11.0% 30 to 45 minutes, 9.6% 45 to 60 minutes, 8.2% 60 minutes or more (2000)

ELLERY (unincorporated postal area, zip code 62833). Covers a land area of 49.474 square miles and a water area of 0.244 square miles. Located at 38.36° N. Lat.; 88.16° W. Long.
Population: 376 (2000); Race: 96.5% White, 0.0% Black, 0.0% Asian, 0.0% Hispanic of any race (2000); Density: 7.6 persons per square mile (2000); Age: 22.1% under 18, 17.1% over 64 (2000); Marriage status: 13.7% never married, 76.3% now married, 3.0% widowed, 7.0% divorced (2000); Foreign born: 0.0% (2000); Ancestry (includes multiple ancestries): 32.8% English, 16.8% United States or American, 10.4% German, 8.0% Irish, 6.4% Other groups (2000).
Economy: Employment by occupation: 18.1% management, 4.8% professional, 22.9% services, 24.1% sales, 2.4% farming, 4.8% construction, 22.9% production (2000).
Income: Per capita income: $12,419 (2000); Median household income: $32,885 (2000); Poverty rate: 7.5% (2000).
Education: Percent of population age 25 and over with: High school diploma (including GED) or higher: 75.1% (2000); Bachelor's degree or higher: 7.1% (2000).
Housing: Homeownership rate: 91.7% (2000); Median home value: $54,700 (2000); Median rent: <$100 per month (2000); Median age of housing: 41 years (2000).
Transportation: Commute to work: 92.8% car, 0.0% public transportation, 6.0% walk, 1.2% work from home (2000); Travel time to work: 32.3% less than 15 minutes, 46.3% 15 to 30 minutes, 9.8% 30 to 45 minutes, 5.5% 45 to 60 minutes, 6.1% 60 minutes or more (2000)

WEST SALEM (village). Covers a land area of 1.559 square miles and a water area of <.001 square miles. Located at 38.52° N. Lat.; 88.00° W. Long. Elevation is 525 feet.
History: West Salem was settled in 1838 by German Moravians from North Carolina.
Population: 1,042 (1990); 1,001 (2000); 936 (2007); 919 (2012 projected); Race: 99.1% White, 0.2% Black, 0.0% Asian, 0.0% Hispanic of any race (2007); Density: 600.5 persons per square mile (2007); Average household size: 2.33 (2007); Median age: 40.8 (2007); Males per 100 females: 92.2 (2007); Marriage status: 16.1% never married, 63.2% now married, 7.3% widowed, 13.4% divorced (2000); Foreign born: 0.4% (2000); Ancestry (includes multiple ancestries): 23.7% German, 15.1% English, 14.9% United States or American, 8.7% Irish, 6.1% Other groups (2000).
Economy: Employment by occupation: 5.0% management, 12.3% professional, 9.5% services, 19.9% sales, 0.4% farming, 9.5% construction, 43.3% production (2000).
Income: Per capita income: $17,363 (2007); Median household income: $31,597 (2007); Average household income: $39,589 (2007); Percent of households with income of $100,000 or more: 5.0% (2007); Poverty rate: 11.2% (2000).
Education: Percent of population age 25 and over with: High school diploma (including GED) or higher: 84.3% (2007); Bachelor's degree or higher: 9.7% (2007); Master's degree or higher: 2.0% (2007).

School District(s)

Edwards County CUSD 1 (PK-12)
2005-06 Enrollment: 974 . . . . (618) 445-2814

Housing: Homeownership rate: 80.8% (2007); Median home value: $54,800 (2007); Median rent: $238 per month (2000); Median age of housing: 51 years (2000).
Safety: Violent crime rate: 30.7 per 10,000 population; Property crime rate: 92.1 per 10,000 population (2006).
Newspapers: Edwards County Times Advocate (Community news; Circulation 1,850); Times Advocate Shopping Messenger (Community news; Circulation 5,000); West Salem Times Advocate (Local news; Circulation 6,500)
Transportation: Commute to work: 90.2% car, 0.0% public transportation, 7.2% walk, 2.2% work from home (2000); Travel time to work: 45.9% less than 15 minutes, 35.6% 15 to 30 minutes, 8.9% 30 to 45 minutes, 3.6% 45 to 60 minutes, 6.0% 60 minutes or more (2000)

Effingham County

Located in southeast central Illinois; drained by the Little Wabash River. Covers a land area of 478.70 square miles, a water area of 1.20 square miles, and is located in the Central Time Zone. The county was founded in 1831. County seat is Effingham.

Effingham County is part of the Effingham, IL Micropolitan Statistical Area. The entire metro area includes: Effingham County, IL

Weather Station: Effingham — Elevation: 606 feet

	Jan	Feb	Mar	Apr	May	Jun	Jul	Aug	Sep	Oct	Nov	Dec
High	34	40	52	64	74	83	87	85	79	67	53	40
Low	17	21	32	42	52	61	66	63	55	43	34	23
Precip	2.1	2.4	3.7	4.0	4.2	4.2	4.3	2.9	3.2	3.0	4.0	3.4
Snow	7.3	5.2	2.9	0.2	0.0	0.0	0.0	0.0	0.0	tr	1.3	3.8

High and Low temperatures in degrees Fahrenheit; Precipitation and Snow in inches

Population: 31,704 (1990); 34,264 (2000); 34,635 (2007); 34,766 (2012 projected); Race: 98.2% White, 0.4% Black, 0.4% Asian, 1.2% Hispanic of any race (2007); Density: 72.4 persons per square mile (2007); Average household size: 2.58 (2007); Median age: 37.3 (2007); Males per 100 females: 97.5 (2007).
Religion: Five largest groups: 37.1% Catholic Church, 11.1% Lutheran Church—Missouri Synod, 9.3% Southern Baptist Convention, 6.6% The United Methodist Church, 4.0% Christian Churches and Churches of Christ (2000).
Economy: Unemployment rate: 4.6% (4/2008); Total civilian labor force: 18,818 (4/2008); Leading industries: 19.9% manufacturing; 17.3% retail trade; 15.3% health care and social assistance (2005); Farms: 1,134 totaling 278,199 acres (2002); Companies that employ 500 or more persons: 3 (2006); Companies that employ 100 to 499 persons: 28 (2006); Companies that employ less than 100 persons: 1,142 (2006); Black-owned businesses: n/a (2002); Hispanic-owned businesses: n/a (2002); Asian-owned businesses: n/a (2002); Women-owned businesses: 1,091 (2002); Retail sales per capita: $26,039 (2008). Single-family building permits issued: 36 (2007); Multi-family building permits issued: 6 (2007).
Income: Per capita income: $22,051 (2007); Median household income: $45,843 (2007); Average household income: $56,494 (2007); Percent of households with income of $100,000 or more: 10.8% (2007); Poverty rate: 9.2% (2005); Bankruptcy rate: 2.37% (2007).
Education: Percent of population age 25 and over with: High school diploma (including GED) or higher: 83.4% (2007); Bachelor's degree or higher: 15.2% (2007); Master's degree or higher: 4.6% (2007).
Housing: Homeownership rate: 76.3% (2007); Median home value: $118,322 (2007); Median rent: $348 per month (2000); Median age of housing: 28 years (2000).

Health: Birth rate: 140.2 per 10,000 population (2007); Death rate: 95.5 per 10,000 population (2007); Age-adjusted cancer mortality rate: 175.4 deaths per 100,000 population (2005); Air Quality Index: 79.5% good, 18.8% moderate, 1.8% unhealthy for sensitive individuals, 0.0% unhealthy (percent of days in 2007); Number of physicians: 22.1 per 10,000 population (2005); Hospital beds: 42.3 per 10,000 population (2004); Hospital admissions: 2,123.3 per 10,000 population (2004).
Elections: 2004 Presidential election results: 72.3% Bush, 27.0% Kerry, 0.0% Nader, 0.7% Badnarik
Additional Information Contacts
Effingham County Government . . . . (217) 342-4990
http://www.co.effingham.il.us
City of Altamont . . . . (618) 483-5212
http://www.altamontil.net
City of Effingham . . . . (217) 542-5301
http://www.effinghamil.com
The Greater Effingham Chamber of Commerce . . . . (217) 342-4147
http://www.effinghamchamber.org

Effingham County Communities

ALTAMONT (city). Covers a land area of 1.303 square miles and a water area of 0 square miles. Located at 39.06° N. Lat.; 88.74° W. Long. Elevation is 620 feet.
History: Altamont was organized in 1872 along the Pennsylvania and Baltimore & Ohio Railroads. Named for a nearby hill, Altamont developed as a wheat shipping center.
Population: 2,329 (1990); 2,283 (2000); 2,442 (2007); 2,448 (2012 projected); Race: 99.3% White, 0.2% Black, 0.0% Asian, 0.3% Hispanic of any race (2007); Density: 1,873.6 persons per square mile (2007); Average household size: 2.50 (2007); Median age: 39.9 (2007); Males per 100 females: 91.4 (2007); Marriage status: 20.3% never married, 59.2% now married, 10.5% widowed, 10.0% divorced (2000); Foreign born: 0.4% (2000); Ancestry (includes multiple ancestries): 34.2% German, 13.1% United States or American, 11.7% Irish, 7.8% English, 7.0% Other groups (2000).
Economy: Single-family building permits issued: 6 (2007); Multi-family building permits issued: 0 (2007); Employment by occupation: 9.0% management, 15.0% professional, 17.6% services, 26.4% sales, 0.1% farming, 9.1% construction, 22.8% production (2000).
Income: Per capita income: $18,439 (2007); Median household income: $39,432 (2007); Average household income: $45,259 (2007); Percent of households with income of $100,000 or more: 4.7% (2007); Poverty rate: 6.9% (2000).
Education: Percent of population age 25 and over with: High school diploma (including GED) or higher: 76.8% (2007); Bachelor's degree or higher: 12.4% (2007); Master's degree or higher: 2.7% (2007).
School District(s)
Altamont CUSD 10 (PK-12)
2005-06 Enrollment: 798 . . . . (618) 483-6195
Housing: Homeownership rate: 75.5% (2007); Median home value: $87,308 (2007); Median rent: $358 per month (2000); Median age of housing: 38 years (2000).
Safety: Violent crime rate: 62.0 per 10,000 population; Property crime rate: 212.5 per 10,000 population (2006).
Newspapers: Altamont Independent (Local news; Circulation 3,500); Altamont News (Local news; Circulation 1,600)
Transportation: Commute to work: 93.1% car, 0.0% public transportation, 2.0% walk, 3.9% work from home (2000); Travel time to work: 35.1% less than 15 minutes, 54.7% 15 to 30 minutes, 5.9% 30 to 45 minutes, 1.7% 45 to 60 minutes, 2.6% 60 minutes or more (2000)
Additional Information Contacts
City of Altamont . . . . (618) 483-5212
http://www.altamontil.net

BEECHER CITY (village). Covers a land area of 0.905 square miles and a water area of 0 square miles. Located at 39.18° N. Lat.; 88.78° W. Long. Elevation is 610 feet.
Population: 437 (1990); 493 (2000); 531 (2007); 553 (2012 projected); Race: 99.1% White, 0.0% Black, 0.0% Asian, 0.0% Hispanic of any race (2007); Density: 586.9 persons per square mile (2007); Average household size: 2.52 (2007); Median age: 33.1 (2007); Males per 100 females: 90.3 (2007); Marriage status: 21.0% never married, 56.6% now married, 10.4% widowed, 12.0% divorced (2000); Foreign born: 0.6% (2000); Ancestry (includes multiple ancestries): 23.5% German, 14.0% English, 10.2% United States or American, 10.0% Irish, 4.4% Other groups (2000).
Economy: Employment by occupation: 4.2% management, 8.9% professional, 8.4% services, 20.4% sales, 1.0% farming, 14.1% construction, 42.9% production (2000).
Income: Per capita income: $14,054 (2007); Median household income: $29,900 (2007); Average household income: $35,367 (2007); Percent of households with income of $100,000 or more: 2.4% (2007); Poverty rate: 18.4% (2000).
Education: Percent of population age 25 and over with: High school diploma (including GED) or higher: 77.3% (2007); Bachelor's degree or higher: 9.3% (2007); Master's degree or higher: 1.9% (2007).
School District(s)
Beecher City CUSD 20 (PK-12)
2005-06 Enrollment: 460 . . . . (618) 487-5100
Housing: Homeownership rate: 65.4% (2007); Median home value: $63,000 (2007); Median rent: $308 per month (2000); Median age of housing: 44 years (2000).
Newspapers: Beecher City Journal (Community news; Circulation 1,600)
Transportation: Commute to work: 92.4% car, 0.0% public transportation, 4.9% walk, 1.1% work from home (2000); Travel time to work: 20.3% less than 15 minutes, 56.0% 15 to 30 minutes, 12.1% 30 to 45 minutes, 1.6% 45 to 60 minutes, 9.9% 60 minutes or more (2000)

DIETERICH (village). Covers a land area of 1.185 square miles and a water area of 0 square miles. Located at 39.06° N. Lat.; 88.37° W. Long. Elevation is 587 feet.
Population: 606 (1990); 591 (2000); 575 (2007); 573 (2012 projected); Race: 99.1% White, 0.0% Black, 0.2% Asian, 0.7% Hispanic of any race (2007); Density: 485.1 persons per square mile (2007); Average household size: 2.65 (2007); Median age: 35.7 (2007); Males per 100 females: 92.3 (2007); Marriage status: 17.5% never married, 66.4% now married, 6.1% widowed, 10.0% divorced (2000); Foreign born: 0.7% (2000); Ancestry (includes multiple ancestries): 41.8% German, 20.2% United States or American, 8.1% Irish, 6.5% English, 3.3% Other groups (2000).
Economy: Employment by occupation: 8.4% management, 12.9% professional, 14.1% services, 22.8% sales, 1.5% farming, 11.1% construction, 29.1% production (2000).
Income: Per capita income: $20,048 (2007); Median household income: $51,458 (2007); Average household income: $53,122 (2007); Percent of households with income of $100,000 or more: 7.4% (2007); Poverty rate: 7.5% (2000).
Education: Percent of population age 25 and over with: High school diploma (including GED) or higher: 83.8% (2007); Bachelor's degree or higher: 11.9% (2007); Master's degree or higher: 2.4% (2007).
School District(s)
Dieterich CUSD 30 (PK-12)
2005-06 Enrollment: 506 . . . . (217) 925-5249
Teutopolis CUSD 50 (PK-12)
2005-06 Enrollment: 1,377 . . . . (217) 857-3535
Housing: Homeownership rate: 86.2% (2007); Median home value: $87,941 (2007); Median rent: $325 per month (2000); Median age of housing: 42 years (2000).
Transportation: Commute to work: 92.4% car, 0.9% public transportation, 1.8% walk, 4.3% work from home (2000); Travel time to work: 33.7% less than 15 minutes, 57.1% 15 to 30 minutes, 6.3% 30 to 45 minutes, 1.9% 45 to 60 minutes, 1.0% 60 minutes or more (2000)

EDGEWOOD (village). Covers a land area of 1.003 square miles and a water area of 0.011 square miles. Located at 38.92° N. Lat.; 88.66° W. Long. Elevation is 574 feet.
Population: 502 (1990); 527 (2000); 554 (2007); 572 (2012 projected); Race: 99.6% White, 0.0% Black, 0.0% Asian, 0.7% Hispanic of any race (2007); Density: 552.2 persons per square mile (2007); Average household size: 2.28 (2007); Median age: 37.7 (2007); Males per 100 females: 93.0 (2007); Marriage status: 22.2% never married, 53.8% now married, 10.5% widowed, 13.5% divorced (2000); Foreign born: 0.8% (2000); Ancestry (includes multiple ancestries): 27.5% German, 10.6% United States or American, 10.4% Irish, 5.2% Other groups, 4.1% English (2000).
Economy: Employment by occupation: 4.7% management, 4.3% professional, 15.1% services, 16.8% sales, 2.2% farming, 10.3% construction, 46.6% production (2000).
Income: Per capita income: $17,319 (2007); Median household income: $26,979 (2007); Average household income: $39,486 (2007); Percent of

households with income of $100,000 or more: 4.1% (2007); Poverty rate: 16.7% (2000).
Education: Percent of population age 25 and over with: High school diploma (including GED) or higher: 65.3% (2007); Bachelor's degree or higher: 2.9% (2007); Master's degree or higher: 1.9% (2007).

School District(s)

Effingham CUSD 40 (PK-12)
2005-06 Enrollment: 3,005 . . . . (217) 540-1501

Housing: Homeownership rate: 69.5% (2007); Median home value: $46,034 (2007); Median rent: $232 per month (2000); Median age of housing: 42 years (2000).
Transportation: Commute to work: 96.1% car, 0.9% public transportation, 0.4% walk, 2.6% work from home (2000); Travel time to work: 15.2% less than 15 minutes, 59.2% 15 to 30 minutes, 15.2% 30 to 45 minutes, 0.9% 45 to 60 minutes, 9.4% 60 minutes or more (2000)

EFFINGHAM (city). County seat. Covers a land area of 8.667 square miles and a water area of 0.058 square miles. Located at 39.12° N. Lat.; 88.54° W. Long. Elevation is 594 feet.
History: Effingham was settled by German immigrants, and was incorporated as a village in 1861.
Population: 12,261 (1990); 12,384 (2000); 12,228 (2007); 12,100 (2012 projected); Race: 96.8% White, 0.8% Black, 0.8% Asian, 1.8% Hispanic of any race (2007); Density: 1,410.9 persons per square mile (2007); Average household size: 2.27 (2007); Median age: 38.7 (2007); Males per 100 females: 89.3 (2007); Marriage status: 22.2% never married, 55.2% now married, 11.6% widowed, 11.0% divorced (2000); Foreign born: 1.7% (2000); Ancestry (includes multiple ancestries): 37.3% German, 10.3% Irish, 10.2% English, 9.0% United States or American, 6.2% Other groups (2000).
Economy: Single-family building permits issued: 24 (2007); Multi-family building permits issued: 6 (2007); Employment by occupation: 10.4% management, 17.4% professional, 18.1% services, 26.4% sales, 0.5% farming, 5.5% construction, 21.7% production (2000).
Income: Per capita income: $23,060 (2007); Median household income: $40,480 (2007); Average household income: $51,601 (2007); Percent of households with income of $100,000 or more: 9.6% (2007); Poverty rate: 9.6% (2000).
Education: Percent of population age 25 and over with: High school diploma (including GED) or higher: 81.8% (2007); Bachelor's degree or higher: 17.2% (2007); Master's degree or higher: 5.7% (2007).

School District(s)

Bond/Effingham/Fayette Roe (07-12)
2005-06 Enrollment: 70 . . . . (618) 283-5011
Eastern Ill Area of Spec Educ (PK-12)
2005-06 Enrollment: 577 . . . . (217) 348-7700
Effingham CUSD 40 (PK-12)
2005-06 Enrollment: 3,005 . . . . (217) 540-1501
Teutopolis CUSD 50 (PK-12)
2005-06 Enrollment: 1,377 . . . . (217) 857-3535

Housing: Homeownership rate: 63.3% (2007); Median home value: $115,082 (2007); Median rent: $358 per month (2000); Median age of housing: 30 years (2000).
Hospitals: St. Anthony's Memorial Hospital (146 beds)
Safety: Violent crime rate: 53.1 per 10,000 population; Property crime rate: 508.0 per 10,000 population (2006).
Newspapers: Effingham Daily News (Local news; Circulation 13,266)
Transportation: Commute to work: 93.0% car, 0.6% public transportation, 2.2% walk, 2.7% work from home (2000); Travel time to work: 70.4% less than 15 minutes, 19.8% 15 to 30 minutes, 5.0% 30 to 45 minutes, 1.4% 45 to 60 minutes, 3.4% 60 minutes or more (2000); Amtrak: Service available.
Airports: Effingham County Memorial (general aviation)

Additional Information Contacts

City of Effingham . . . . (217) 542-5301
http://www.effinghamil.com
The Greater Effingham Chamber of Commerce . . . . (217) 342-4147
http://www.effinghamchamber.org

MASON (town). Covers a land area of 1.137 square miles and a water area of 0.005 square miles. Located at 38.95° N. Lat.; 88.62° W. Long. Elevation is 581 feet.
Population: 387 (1990); 396 (2000); 416 (2007); 428 (2012 projected); Race: 97.8% White, 0.0% Black, 0.0% Asian, 3.4% Hispanic of any race (2007); Density: 365.9 persons per square mile (2007); Average household size: 2.63 (2007); Median age: 38.2 (2007); Males per 100 females: 114.4 (2007); Marriage status: 19.6% never married, 59.2% now married, 6.4% widowed, 14.7% divorced (2000); Foreign born: 0.0% (2000); Ancestry (includes multiple ancestries): 31.9% German, 12.7% English, 9.2% Other groups, 5.9% United States or American, 4.5% Irish (2000).
Economy: Employment by occupation: 2.5% management, 7.5% professional, 13.5% services, 21.5% sales, 0.0% farming, 13.0% construction, 42.0% production (2000).
Income: Per capita income: $18,984 (2007); Median household income: $49,545 (2007); Average household income: $49,984 (2007); Percent of households with income of $100,000 or more: 7.0% (2007); Poverty rate: 6.1% (2000).
Education: Percent of population age 25 and over with: High school diploma (including GED) or higher: 70.4% (2007); Bachelor's degree or higher: 4.3% (2007); Master's degree or higher: 0.7% (2007).
Housing: Homeownership rate: 88.0% (2007); Median home value: $55,667 (2007); Median rent: $275 per month (2000); Median age of housing: 45 years (2000).
Transportation: Commute to work: 96.5% car, 2.5% public transportation, 1.0% walk, 0.0% work from home (2000); Travel time to work: 10.1% less than 15 minutes, 70.7% 15 to 30 minutes, 12.6% 30 to 45 minutes, 1.5% 45 to 60 minutes, 5.1% 60 minutes or more (2000)

MONTROSE (village). Covers a land area of 0.710 square miles and a water area of 0 square miles. Located at 39.16° N. Lat.; 88.37° W. Long. Elevation is 600 feet.
Population: 306 (1990); 257 (2000); 274 (2007); 285 (2012 projected); Race: 100.0% White, 0.0% Black, 0.0% Asian, 0.0% Hispanic of any race (2007); Density: 385.9 persons per square mile (2007); Average household size: 2.36 (2007); Median age: 40.2 (2007); Males per 100 females: 98.6 (2007); Marriage status: 28.9% never married, 46.3% now married, 14.2% widowed, 10.5% divorced (2000); Foreign born: 0.0% (2000); Ancestry (includes multiple ancestries): 34.3% German, 18.0% Irish, 7.3% United States or American, 6.0% English, 5.6% Other groups (2000).
Economy: Employment by occupation: 1.8% management, 6.2% professional, 17.7% services, 20.4% sales, 1.8% farming, 13.3% construction, 38.9% production (2000).
Income: Per capita income: $18,777 (2007); Median household income: $30,000 (2007); Average household income: $44,353 (2007); Percent of households with income of $100,000 or more: 6.0% (2007); Poverty rate: 16.7% (2000).
Education: Percent of population age 25 and over with: High school diploma (including GED) or higher: 63.5% (2007); Bachelor's degree or higher: 5.7% (2007); Master's degree or higher: 3.6% (2007).

School District(s)

Jasper County Cud 1 (PK-12)
2005-06 Enrollment: 1,494 . . . . (618) 783-8459

Housing: Homeownership rate: 83.6% (2007); Median home value: $68,750 (2007); Median rent: $265 per month (2000); Median age of housing: 40 years (2000).
Transportation: Commute to work: 95.6% car, 0.0% public transportation, 0.0% walk, 2.7% work from home (2000); Travel time to work: 38.2% less than 15 minutes, 50.0% 15 to 30 minutes, 4.5% 30 to 45 minutes, 0.9% 45 to 60 minutes, 6.4% 60 minutes or more (2000)

SHUMWAY (village). Covers a land area of 0.312 square miles and a water area of 0 square miles. Located at 39.18° N. Lat.; 88.65° W. Long. Elevation is 656 feet.
Population: 243 (1990); 217 (2000); 222 (2007); 225 (2012 projected); Race: 100.0% White, 0.0% Black, 0.0% Asian, 0.0% Hispanic of any race (2007); Density: 712.2 persons per square mile (2007); Average household size: 2.58 (2007); Median age: 33.6 (2007); Males per 100 females: 111.4 (2007); Marriage status: 27.9% never married, 48.9% now married, 9.5% widowed, 13.7% divorced (2000); Foreign born: 0.8% (2000); Ancestry (includes multiple ancestries): 21.7% German, 14.1% Italian, 9.6% English, 6.0% United States or American, 6.0% Irish (2000).
Economy: Employment by occupation: 4.9% management, 6.8% professional, 25.2% services, 20.4% sales, 2.9% farming, 4.9% construction, 35.0% production (2000).
Income: Per capita income: $18,885 (2007); Median household income: $47,778 (2007); Average household income: $48,750 (2007); Percent of households with income of $100,000 or more: 3.5% (2007); Poverty rate: 8.0% (2000).
Education: Percent of population age 25 and over with: High school diploma (including GED) or higher: 84.5% (2007); Bachelor's degree or higher: 9.2% (2007); Master's degree or higher: 3.5% (2007).

School District(s)

Beecher City CUSD 20 (PK-12)
2005-06 Enrollment: 460 . . . . (618) 487-5100

Housing: Homeownership rate: 86.0% (2007); Median home value: $68,000 (2007); Median rent: $275 per month (2000); Median age of housing: 45 years (2000).

Transportation: Commute to work: 89.3% car, 0.0% public transportation, 0.0% walk, 10.7% work from home (2000); Travel time to work: 14.1% less than 15 minutes, 82.6% 15 to 30 minutes, 1.1% 30 to 45 minutes, 2.2% 45 to 60 minutes, 0.0% 60 minutes or more (2000)

TEUTOPOLIS (village). Covers a land area of 1.580 square miles and a water area of 0 square miles. Located at 39.13° N. Lat.; 88.47° W. Long. Elevation is 607 feet.

History: Teutopolis was established in 1839 by a group of German Catholics from Cincinnati, Ohio.

Population: 1,468 (1990); 1,559 (2000); 1,633 (2007); 1,673 (2012 projected); Race: 99.9% White, 0.0% Black, 0.1% Asian, 0.1% Hispanic of any race (2007); Density: 1,033.7 persons per square mile (2007); Average household size: 2.83 (2007); Median age: 34.4 (2007); Males per 100 females: 100.6 (2007); Marriage status: 26.7% never married, 60.6% now married, 6.1% widowed, 6.7% divorced (2000); Foreign born: 0.3% (2000); Ancestry (includes multiple ancestries): 71.1% German, 8.3% Irish, 6.5% United States or American, 2.8% English, 1.9% Other groups (2000).

Economy: Single-family building permits issued: 6 (2007); Multi-family building permits issued: 0 (2007); Employment by occupation: 12.2% management, 16.8% professional, 11.0% services, 28.4% sales, 0.0% farming, 13.8% construction, 17.8% production (2000).

Income: Per capita income: $27,447 (2007); Median household income: $55,764 (2007); Average household income: $77,613 (2007); Percent of households with income of $100,000 or more: 16.3% (2007); Poverty rate: 4.8% (2000).

Education: Percent of population age 25 and over with: High school diploma (including GED) or higher: 89.0% (2007); Bachelor's degree or higher: 21.9% (2007); Master's degree or higher: 5.3% (2007).

School District(s)

Teutopolis CUSD 50 (PK-12)
2005-06 Enrollment: 1,377 . . . . (217) 857-3535

Housing: Homeownership rate: 77.6% (2007); Median home value: $141,477 (2007); Median rent: $384 per month (2000); Median age of housing: 32 years (2000).

Newspapers: Teutopolis Press-Dieterich Special Gazette (Local news; Circulation 1,000)

Transportation: Commute to work: 94.0% car, 0.0% public transportation, 1.6% walk, 1.7% work from home (2000); Travel time to work: 72.3% less than 15 minutes, 18.9% 15 to 30 minutes, 3.3% 30 to 45 minutes, 2.8% 45 to 60 minutes, 2.7% 60 minutes or more (2000)

WATSON (village). Covers a land area of 0.977 square miles and a water area of 0 square miles. Located at 39.02° N. Lat.; 88.56° W. Long. Elevation is 561 feet.

Population: 712 (1990); 729 (2000); 727 (2007); 724 (2012 projected); Race: 97.9% White, 0.0% Black, 0.3% Asian, 1.8% Hispanic of any race (2007); Density: 743.9 persons per square mile (2007); Average household size: 2.90 (2007); Median age: 30.9 (2007); Males per 100 females: 94.4 (2007); Marriage status: 22.2% never married, 61.1% now married, 5.3% widowed, 11.5% divorced (2000); Foreign born: 1.2% (2000); Ancestry (includes multiple ancestries): 31.7% German, 18.1% Irish, 12.9% United States or American, 12.5% Other groups, 4.8% English (2000).

Economy: Employment by occupation: 5.9% management, 7.7% professional, 22.7% services, 19.7% sales, 0.3% farming, 9.9% construction, 33.9% production (2000).

Income: Per capita income: $18,181 (2007); Median household income: $48,167 (2007); Average household income: $52,659 (2007); Percent of households with income of $100,000 or more: 6.8% (2007); Poverty rate: 9.5% (2000).

Education: Percent of population age 25 and over with: High school diploma (including GED) or higher: 81.5% (2007); Bachelor's degree or higher: 5.4% (2007); Master's degree or higher: 0.7% (2007).

Housing: Homeownership rate: 88.0% (2007); Median home value: $89,342 (2007); Median rent: $300 per month (2000); Median age of housing: 21 years (2000).

Transportation: Commute to work: 94.4% car, 0.0% public transportation, 2.1% walk, 3.5% work from home (2000); Travel time to work: 27.5% less than 15 minutes, 56.7% 15 to 30 minutes, 7.5% 30 to 45 minutes, 5.3% 45 to 60 minutes, 3.1% 60 minutes or more (2000)

Fayette County

Located in south central Illinois; drained by the Kaskaskia River. Covers a land area of 716.49 square miles, a water area of 8.87 square miles, and is located in the Central Time Zone. The county was founded in 1821. County seat is Vandalia.

Population: 20,893 (1990); 21,802 (2000); 21,785 (2007); 21,789 (2012 projected); Race: 94.1% White, 4.8% Black, 0.2% Asian, 1.1% Hispanic of any race (2007); Density: 30.4 persons per square mile (2007); Average household size: 2.64 (2007); Median age: 38.4 (2007); Males per 100 females: 107.5 (2007).

Religion: Five largest groups: 19.5% Southern Baptist Convention, 7.9% Lutheran Church—Missouri Synod, 7.6% The United Methodist Church, 4.9% Christian Churches and Churches of Christ, 3.9% Catholic Church (2000).

Economy: Unemployment rate: 7.0% (4/2008); Total civilian labor force: 10,301 (4/2008); Leading industries: 19.1% health care and social assistance; 18.1% retail trade; 17.5% manufacturing (2005); Farms: 1,248 totaling 365,680 acres (2002); Companies that employ 500 or more persons: 0 (2006); Companies that employ 100 to 499 persons: 9 (2006); Companies that employ less than 100 persons: 475 (2006); Black-owned businesses: n/a (2002); Hispanic-owned businesses: n/a (2002); Asian-owned businesses: n/a (2002); Women-owned businesses: 343 (2002); Retail sales per capita: $11,965 (2008). Single-family building permits issued: 5 (2007); Multi-family building permits issued: 2 (2007).

Income: Per capita income: $18,298 (2007); Median household income: $37,118 (2007); Average household income: $45,597 (2007); Percent of households with income of $100,000 or more: 6.5% (2007); Poverty rate: 15.3% (2005); Bankruptcy rate: 2.84% (2007).

Education: Percent of population age 25 and over with: High school diploma (including GED) or higher: 72.5% (2007); Bachelor's degree or higher: 9.1% (2007); Master's degree or higher: 2.8% (2007).

Housing: Homeownership rate: 79.8% (2007); Median home value: $87,366 (2007); Median rent: $266 per month (2000); Median age of housing: 38 years (2000).

Health: Birth rate: 123.5 per 10,000 population (2007); Death rate: 107.6 per 10,000 population (2007); Age-adjusted cancer mortality rate: 143.7 deaths per 100,000 population (2005); Number of physicians: 3.3 per 10,000 population (2005); Hospital beds: 67.5 per 10,000 population (2004); Hospital admissions: 687.1 per 10,000 population (2004).

Elections: 2004 Presidential election results: 61.6% Bush, 37.4% Kerry, 0.1% Nader, 1.0% Badnarik

National and State Parks: Carlyle Lake State Wildlife Management Area; Ramsey Lake State Park; Vandalia State House Historic Site

Additional Information Contacts

Fayette County Government . . . . (618) 283-5000

Vandalia Chamber of Commerce. . . . . (618) 283-2728
http://www.vandaliaillinois.com/chamber

Fayette County Communities

BINGHAM (village). Covers a land area of 0.272 square miles and a water area of 0 square miles. Located at 39.11° N. Lat.; 89.21° W. Long. Elevation is 600 feet.

Population: 98 (1990); 117 (2000); 120 (2007); 122 (2012 projected); Race: 100.0% White, 0.0% Black, 0.0% Asian, 0.0% Hispanic of any race (2007); Density: 440.6 persons per square mile (2007); Average household size: 2.61 (2007); Median age: 32.5 (2007); Males per 100 females: 110.5 (2007); Marriage status: 24.6% never married, 40.0% now married, 4.6% widowed, 30.8% divorced (2000); Foreign born: 0.0% (2000); Ancestry (includes multiple ancestries): 36.1% German, 29.9% Other groups, 7.2% English, 7.2% Irish, 5.2% Scottish (2000).

Economy: Employment by occupation: 5.7% management, 20.0% professional, 0.0% services, 22.9% sales, 11.4% farming, 11.4% construction, 28.6% production (2000).

Income: Per capita income: $10,583 (2007); Median household income: $25,000 (2007); Average household income: $27,609 (2007); Percent of households with income of $100,000 or more: 0.0% (2007); Poverty rate: 39.2% (2000).

Education: Percent of population age 25 and over with: High school diploma (including GED) or higher: 64.0% (2007); Bachelor's degree or higher: 8.0% (2007); Master's degree or higher: 0.0% (2007).
Housing: Homeownership rate: 71.7% (2007); Median home value: $37,500 (2007); Median rent: $175 per month (2000); Median age of housing: 42 years (2000).
Transportation: Commute to work: 93.5% car, 0.0% public transportation, 0.0% walk, 6.5% work from home (2000); Travel time to work: 6.9% less than 15 minutes, 24.1% 15 to 30 minutes, 62.1% 30 to 45 minutes, 0.0% 45 to 60 minutes, 6.9% 60 minutes or more (2000)

BROWNSTOWN (village). Covers a land area of 0.628 square miles and a water area of 0 square miles. Located at 38.99° N. Lat.; 88.95° W. Long. Elevation is 594 feet.
Population: 733 (1990); 705 (2000); 687 (2007); 689 (2012 projected); Race: 98.0% White, 0.6% Black, 0.1% Asian, 0.9% Hispanic of any race (2007); Density: 1,094.4 persons per square mile (2007); Average household size: 2.35 (2007); Median age: 37.9 (2007); Males per 100 females: 73.0 (2007); Marriage status: 24.6% never married, 49.3% now married, 11.9% widowed, 14.3% divorced (2000); Foreign born: 0.3% (2000); Ancestry (includes multiple ancestries): 24.3% German, 16.9% United States or American, 13.9% English, 9.3% Irish, 5.6% Other groups (2000).
Economy: Employment by occupation: 4.0% management, 13.1% professional, 26.4% services, 21.3% sales, 2.7% farming, 9.7% construction, 22.8% production (2000).
Income: Per capita income: $16,600 (2007); Median household income: $32,069 (2007); Average household income: $38,870 (2007); Percent of households with income of $100,000 or more: 4.1% (2007); Poverty rate: 14.8% (2000).
Education: Percent of population age 25 and over with: High school diploma (including GED) or higher: 84.3% (2007); Bachelor's degree or higher: 9.1% (2007); Master's degree or higher: 3.8% (2007).

School District(s)

Brownstown CUSD 201 (PK-12)
2005-06 Enrollment: 434 . . . . (618) 427-3355
Housing: Homeownership rate: 78.8% (2007); Median home value: $65,294 (2007); Median rent: $237 per month (2000); Median age of housing: 47 years (2000).
Transportation: Commute to work: 88.5% car, 0.0% public transportation, 4.1% walk, 6.7% work from home (2000); Travel time to work: 43.3% less than 15 minutes, 29.7% 15 to 30 minutes, 15.0% 30 to 45 minutes, 2.4% 45 to 60 minutes, 9.6% 60 minutes or more (2000)

FARINA (village). Covers a land area of 1.440 square miles and a water area of 0.007 square miles. Located at 38.83° N. Lat.; 88.77° W. Long. Elevation is 581 feet.
Population: 575 (1990); 558 (2000); 536 (2007); 531 (2012 projected); Race: 99.4% White, 0.0% Black, 0.0% Asian, 0.0% Hispanic of any race (2007); Density: 372.3 persons per square mile (2007); Average household size: 2.30 (2007); Median age: 46.1 (2007); Males per 100 females: 84.8 (2007); Marriage status: 21.7% never married, 55.2% now married, 10.0% widowed, 13.0% divorced (2000); Foreign born: 0.2% (2000); Ancestry (includes multiple ancestries): 35.5% German, 11.0% Irish, 10.1% United States or American, 7.6% English, 6.7% Other groups (2000).
Economy: Employment by occupation: 10.9% management, 7.4% professional, 21.0% services, 20.2% sales, 1.9% farming, 8.6% construction, 30.0% production (2000).
Income: Per capita income: $20,508 (2007); Median household income: $37,167 (2007); Average household income: $46,448 (2007); Percent of households with income of $100,000 or more: 7.7% (2007); Poverty rate: 10.8% (2000).
Education: Percent of population age 25 and over with: High school diploma (including GED) or higher: 77.8% (2007); Bachelor's degree or higher: 8.3% (2007); Master's degree or higher: 2.0% (2007).

School District(s)

South Central Cud 401 (PK-12)
2005-06 Enrollment: 731 . . . . (618) 547-3414
Housing: Homeownership rate: 88.0% (2007); Median home value: $58,158 (2007); Median rent: $230 per month (2000); Median age of housing: 45 years (2000).
Newspapers: Farina News (Community news; Circulation 1,250)
Transportation: Commute to work: 88.2% car, 0.0% public transportation, 4.3% walk, 4.7% work from home (2000); Travel time to work: 44.4% less than 15 minutes, 14.4% 15 to 30 minutes, 33.3% 30 to 45 minutes, 3.7% 45 to 60 minutes, 4.1% 60 minutes or more (2000)

RAMSEY (village). Covers a land area of 1.007 square miles and a water area of 0 square miles. Located at 39.14° N. Lat.; 89.11° W. Long. Elevation is 610 feet.
Population: 963 (1990); 1,056 (2000); 1,083 (2007); 1,100 (2012 projected); Race: 99.6% White, 0.0% Black, 0.0% Asian, 0.3% Hispanic of any race (2007); Density: 1,075.5 persons per square mile (2007); Average household size: 2.34 (2007); Median age: 35.4 (2007); Males per 100 females: 96.2 (2007); Marriage status: 21.7% never married, 55.3% now married, 12.2% widowed, 10.8% divorced (2000); Foreign born: 0.7% (2000); Ancestry (includes multiple ancestries): 22.4% German, 10.5% English, 7.9% United States or American, 7.9% Irish, 5.6% Other groups (2000).
Economy: Employment by occupation: 3.4% management, 11.0% professional, 22.3% services, 21.6% sales, 2.5% farming, 6.9% construction, 32.2% production (2000).
Income: Per capita income: $18,093 (2007); Median household income: $36,731 (2007); Average household income: $42,413 (2007); Percent of households with income of $100,000 or more: 5.0% (2007); Poverty rate: 13.0% (2000).
Education: Percent of population age 25 and over with: High school diploma (including GED) or higher: 74.1% (2007); Bachelor's degree or higher: 7.1% (2007); Master's degree or higher: 2.4% (2007).

School District(s)

Ramsey CUSD 204 (PK-12)
2005-06 Enrollment: 540 . . . . (618) 423-2335
Housing: Homeownership rate: 72.3% (2007); Median home value: $60,857 (2007); Median rent: $235 per month (2000); Median age of housing: 32 years (2000).
Safety: Violent crime rate: 0.0 per 10,000 population; Property crime rate: 0.0 per 10,000 population (2006).
Newspapers: Ramsey News-Journal (National news; Circulation 2,000)
Transportation: Commute to work: 94.3% car, 0.5% public transportation, 2.4% walk, 2.8% work from home (2000); Travel time to work: 28.5% less than 15 minutes, 41.2% 15 to 30 minutes, 14.4% 30 to 45 minutes, 6.6% 45 to 60 minutes, 9.3% 60 minutes or more (2000)

SAINT ELMO (city). Covers a land area of 0.957 square miles and a water area of 0.024 square miles. Located at 39.02° N. Lat.; 88.85° W. Long. Elevation is 620 feet.
History: St. Elmo was settled in 1830 by a group of Kentucky Catholics, and developed as a railroad and brick manufacturing town. Later, oil was discovered and the economy boomed.
Population: 1,494 (1990); 1,456 (2000); 1,548 (2007); 1,555 (2012 projected); Race: 99.0% White, 0.1% Black, 0.1% Asian, 0.1% Hispanic of any race (2007); Density: 1,617.7 persons per square mile (2007); Average household size: 2.54 (2007); Median age: 38.0 (2007); Males per 100 females: 87.4 (2007); Marriage status: 17.1% never married, 65.1% now married, 9.3% widowed, 8.5% divorced (2000); Foreign born: 0.1% (2000); Ancestry (includes multiple ancestries): 18.3% German, 17.5% United States or American, 11.2% Irish, 9.2% English, 7.5% Other groups (2000).
Economy: Single-family building permits issued: 0 (2007); Multi-family building permits issued: 0 (2007); Employment by occupation: 6.2% management, 9.0% professional, 21.9% services, 20.1% sales, 3.7% farming, 8.0% construction, 31.1% production (2000).
Income: Per capita income: $17,172 (2007); Median household income: $36,604 (2007); Average household income: $43,012 (2007); Percent of households with income of $100,000 or more: 4.3% (2007); Poverty rate: 12.7% (2000).
Education: Percent of population age 25 and over with: High school diploma (including GED) or higher: 76.4% (2007); Bachelor's degree or higher: 8.5% (2007); Master's degree or higher: 2.7% (2007).

School District(s)

St Elmo CUSD 202 (PK-12)
2005-06 Enrollment: 553 . . . . (618) 829-3264
Housing: Homeownership rate: 79.7% (2007); Median home value: $62,500 (2007); Median rent: $260 per month (2000); Median age of housing: 46 years (2000).
Safety: Violent crime rate: 27.9 per 10,000 population; Property crime rate: 425.1 per 10,000 population (2006).
Newspapers: Saint Elmo Banner (Local news; Circulation 900)
Transportation: Commute to work: 91.2% car, 0.0% public transportation, 4.8% walk, 3.7% work from home (2000); Travel time to work: 31.6% less

than 15 minutes, 37.9% 15 to 30 minutes, 24.5% 30 to 45 minutes, 2.5% 45 to 60 minutes, 3.5% 60 minutes or more (2000)

SAINT PETER (village). Covers a land area of 0.535 square miles and a water area of 0 square miles. Located at 38.86° N. Lat.; 88.85° W. Long. Elevation is 597 feet.
Population: 353 (1990); 386 (2000); 371 (2007); 368 (2012 projected); Race: 99.5% White, 0.0% Black, 0.3% Asian, 0.0% Hispanic of any race (2007); Density: 693.3 persons per square mile (2007); Average household size: 2.42 (2007); Median age: 41.9 (2007); Males per 100 females: 93.2 (2007); Marriage status: 26.7% never married, 51.4% now married, 13.9% widowed, 8.1% divorced (2000); Foreign born: 0.0% (2000); Ancestry (includes multiple ancestries): 43.7% German, 10.9% United States or American, 7.5% Irish, 6.7% English, 3.4% Other groups (2000).
Economy: Employment by occupation: 10.5% management, 9.4% professional, 27.1% services, 24.9% sales, 0.0% farming, 12.2% construction, 16.0% production (2000).
Income: Per capita income: $17,035 (2007); Median household income: $35,227 (2007); Average household income: $41,307 (2007); Percent of households with income of $100,000 or more: 5.9% (2007); Poverty rate: 12.7% (2000).
Education: Percent of population age 25 and over with: High school diploma (including GED) or higher: 74.4% (2007); Bachelor's degree or higher: 8.5% (2007); Master's degree or higher: 2.7% (2007).
Housing: Homeownership rate: 89.5% (2007); Median home value: $70,357 (2007); Median rent: $206 per month (2000); Median age of housing: 46 years (2000).
Transportation: Commute to work: 87.4% car, 1.1% public transportation, 10.3% walk, 1.1% work from home (2000); Travel time to work: 41.3% less than 15 minutes, 18.0% 15 to 30 minutes, 30.8% 30 to 45 minutes, 5.2% 45 to 60 minutes, 4.7% 60 minutes or more (2000)

SHOBONIER (unincorporated postal area, zip code 62885). Covers a land area of 56.052 square miles and a water area of 0.065 square miles. Located at 38.86° N. Lat.; 89.05° W. Long. Elevation is 515 feet.
Population: 837 (2000); Race: 100.0% White, 0.0% Black, 0.0% Asian, 3.8% Hispanic of any race (2000); Density: 14.9 persons per square mile (2000); Age: 27.5% under 18, 14.8% over 64 (2000); Marriage status: 19.5% never married, 62.4% now married, 8.5% widowed, 9.5% divorced (2000); Foreign born: 0.0% (2000); Ancestry (includes multiple ancestries): 31.1% German, 13.4% Other groups, 12.7% United States or American, 5.5% English, 5.3% Scotch-Irish (2000).
Economy: Employment by occupation: 17.4% management, 7.1% professional, 24.0% services, 15.5% sales, 2.5% farming, 10.6% construction, 22.9% production (2000).
Income: Per capita income: $14,896 (2000); Median household income: $32,188 (2000); Poverty rate: 16.7% (2000).
Education: Percent of population age 25 and over with: High school diploma (including GED) or higher: 65.7% (2000); Bachelor's degree or higher: 1.6% (2000).
Housing: Homeownership rate: 80.1% (2000); Median home value: $60,600 (2000); Median rent: $225 per month (2000); Median age of housing: 43 years (2000).
Transportation: Commute to work: 89.4% car, 0.0% public transportation, 3.0% walk, 7.6% work from home (2000); Travel time to work: 32.4% less than 15 minutes, 39.5% 15 to 30 minutes, 18.3% 30 to 45 minutes, 3.8% 45 to 60 minutes, 5.9% 60 minutes or more (2000)

VANDALIA (city). County seat. Covers a land area of 5.665 square miles and a water area of 0.016 square miles. Located at 38.96° N. Lat.; 89.10° W. Long. Elevation is 518 feet.
History: Vandalia was laid out in 1819 at the direction of the Illinois State Legislature, and served until 1839 as the capital. Three capitol buildings were erected in Vandalia during its 20 years as the state capital.
Population: 6,335 (1990); 6,975 (2000); 6,866 (2007); 6,798 (2012 projected); Race: 83.5% White, 15.0% Black, 0.5% Asian, 2.3% Hispanic of any race (2007); Density: 1,212.1 persons per square mile (2007); Average household size: 2.98 (2007); Median age: 36.1 (2007); Males per 100 females: 135.5 (2007); Marriage status: 19.2% never married, 58.6% now married, 7.7% widowed, 14.5% divorced (2000); Foreign born: 0.7% (2000); Ancestry (includes multiple ancestries): 21.4% German, 10.3% United States or American, 9.9% English, 7.4% Irish, 5.4% Other groups (2000).
Economy: Single-family building permits issued: 5 (2007); Multi-family building permits issued: 2 (2007); Employment by occupation: 7.1% management, 13.7% professional, 23.3% services, 23.1% sales, 1.0% farming, 8.8% construction, 23.2% production (2000).
Income: Per capita income: $16,806 (2007); Median household income: $35,294 (2007); Average household income: $40,520 (2007); Percent of households with income of $100,000 or more: 4.4% (2007); Poverty rate: 15.6% (2000).
Education: Percent of population age 25 and over with: High school diploma (including GED) or higher: 61.1% (2007); Bachelor's degree or higher: 10.0% (2007); Master's degree or higher: 2.6% (2007).

School District(s)

Bond/Effingham/Fayette Roe (07-12)
2005-06 Enrollment: 70 . . . . (618) 283-5011
Dept of Corrections Sch Dist 428 (08-12)
2005-06 Enrollment: 2,271 . . . . (217) 522-2666
Okaw Area Vocational Center
2005-06 Enrollment: n/a . . . . (618) 283-5150
Vandalia CUSD 203 (PK-12)
2005-06 Enrollment: 1,773 . . . . (618) 283-4525

Housing: Homeownership rate: 67.7% (2007); Median home value: $87,809 (2007); Median rent: $282 per month (2000); Median age of housing: 47 years (2000).
Hospitals: Fayette County Hospital (160 beds)
Safety: Violent crime rate: 29.4 per 10,000 population; Property crime rate: 339.2 per 10,000 population (2006).
Newspapers: Vandalia Leader Union (Local news; Circulation 6,100)
Transportation: Commute to work: 95.5% car, 0.0% public transportation, 1.9% walk, 1.4% work from home (2000); Travel time to work: 75.9% less than 15 minutes, 9.1% 15 to 30 minutes, 7.0% 30 to 45 minutes, 3.2% 45 to 60 minutes, 4.8% 60 minutes or more (2000)
Airports: Vandalia Municipal (general aviation)

Additional Information Contacts

Vandalia Chamber of Commerce. . . . . (618) 283-2728
http://www.vandaliaillinois.com/chamber

Ford County

Located in east central Illinois; drained by the Mackinaw River. Covers a land area of 485.90 square miles, a water area of 0.52 square miles, and is located in the Central Time Zone. The county was founded in 1859. County seat is Paxton.

Ford County is part of the Champaign-Urbana, IL Metropolitan Statistical Area. The entire metro area includes: Champaign County, IL; Ford County, IL; Piatt County, IL

Weather Station: Piper City — Elevation: 669 feet

	Jan	Feb	Mar	Apr	May	Jun	Jul	Aug	Sep	Oct	Nov	Dec
High	31	37	49	63	75	84	86	84	78	66	49	37
Low	14	19	29	38	50	59	63	60	52	41	31	21
Precip	1.8	1.7	2.8	3.4	4.2	3.7	4.2	3.9	3.0	2.6	2.9	2.5
Snow	9.4	6.2	3.4	1.1	tr	0.0	0.0	0.0	0.0	0.2	2.0	5.8

High and Low temperatures in degrees Fahrenheit; Precipitation and Snow in inches

Population: 14,275 (1990); 14,241 (2000); 14,136 (2007); 14,024 (2012 projected); Race: 97.5% White, 0.6% Black, 0.6% Asian, 1.6% Hispanic of any race (2007); Density: 29.1 persons per square mile (2007); Average household size: 2.51 (2007); Median age: 40.6 (2007); Males per 100 females: 92.0 (2007).
Religion: Five largest groups: 18.0% The United Methodist Church, 12.8% Evangelical Lutheran Church in America, 11.1% Catholic Church, 3.9% New Testament Association of Independent Baptist Churches and other Fundamental Baptist Associations, 3.6% S
Economy: Unemployment rate: 5.0% (4/2008); Total civilian labor force: 7,705 (4/2008); Leading industries: 21.7% manufacturing; 20.9% health care and social assistance; 14.7% retail trade (2005); Farms: 530 totaling 286,069 acres (2002); Companies that employ 500 or more persons: 0 (2006); Companies that employ 100 to 499 persons: 6 (2006); Companies that employ less than 100 persons: 383 (2006); Black-owned businesses: n/a (2002); Hispanic-owned businesses: n/a (2002); Asian-owned businesses: n/a (2002); Women-owned businesses: 506 (2002); Retail sales per capita: $11,077 (2008). Single-family building permits issued: 14 (2007); Multi-family building permits issued: 8 (2007).
Income: Per capita income: $22,653 (2007); Median household income: $45,876 (2007); Average household income: $55,275 (2007); Percent of households with income of $100,000 or more: 11.9% (2007); Poverty rate: 9.1% (2005); Bankruptcy rate: 3.11% (2007).

Taxes: Total county taxes per capita: $203 (2006); County property taxes per capita: $146 (2006).
Education: Percent of population age 25 and over with: High school diploma (including GED) or higher: 85.9% (2007); Bachelor's degree or higher: 13.5% (2007); Master's degree or higher: 4.3% (2007).
Housing: Homeownership rate: 76.4% (2007); Median home value: $99,501 (2007); Median rent: $317 per month (2000); Median age of housing: 50 years (2000).
Health: Birth rate: 132.0 per 10,000 population (2007); Death rate: 144.7 per 10,000 population (2007); Age-adjusted cancer mortality rate: 234.2 deaths per 100,000 population (2005); Number of physicians: 12.1 per 10,000 population (2005); Hospital beds: 56.9 per 10,000 population (2004); Hospital admissions: 738.7 per 10,000 population (2004).
Elections: 2004 Presidential election results: 69.6% Bush, 29.5% Kerry, 0.1% Nader, 0.8% Badnarik

Additional Information Contacts

Ford County Government .... (217) 379-2721

Gibson City Chamber of Commerce .... (217) 784-5217
http://www.gibsoncityillinois.com
Paxton Chamber of Commerce .... (217) 379-4655
http://www.paxtonchamber.org

Ford County Communities

CABERY (village). Covers a land area of 0.350 square miles and a water area of 0 square miles. Located at 40.99° N. Lat.; 88.20° W. Long. Elevation is 699 feet.
Population: 268 (1990); 263 (2000); 245 (2007); 243 (2012 projected); Race: 96.3% White, 0.0% Black, 0.0% Asian, 3.7% Hispanic of any race (2007); Density: 699.7 persons per square mile (2007); Average household size: 2.66 (2007); Median age: 36.0 (2007); Males per 100 females: 82.8 (2007); Marriage status: 28.4% never married, 55.2% now married, 8.8% widowed, 7.7% divorced (2000); Foreign born: 0.8% (2000); Ancestry (includes multiple ancestries): 38.9% German, 13.4% English, 12.2% French (except Basque), 11.8% United States or American, 8.8% Irish (2000).
Economy: Employment by occupation: 19.1% management, 12.7% professional, 17.3% services, 17.3% sales, 0.0% farming, 5.5% construction, 28.2% production (2000).
Income: Per capita income: $22,735 (2007); Median household income: $49,286 (2007); Average household income: $60,543 (2007); Percent of households with income of $100,000 or more: 12.0% (2007); Poverty rate: 11.6% (2000).
Education: Percent of population age 25 and over with: High school diploma (including GED) or higher: 81.4% (2007); Bachelor's degree or higher: 12.8% (2007); Master's degree or higher: 4.5% (2007).
Housing: Homeownership rate: 83.7% (2007); Median home value: $104,464 (2007); Median rent: $400 per month (2000); Median age of housing: 60+ years (2000).
Transportation: Commute to work: 85.0% car, 0.0% public transportation, 10.3% walk, 4.7% work from home (2000); Travel time to work: 23.5% less than 15 minutes, 23.5% 15 to 30 minutes, 22.5% 30 to 45 minutes, 21.6% 45 to 60 minutes, 8.8% 60 minutes or more (2000)

ELLIOTT (village). Covers a land area of 0.484 square miles and a water area of 0 square miles. Located at 40.46° N. Lat.; 88.27° W. Long. Elevation is 781 feet.
Population: 309 (1990); 341 (2000); 322 (2007); 320 (2012 projected); Race: 98.8% White, 0.0% Black, 0.0% Asian, 0.6% Hispanic of any race (2007); Density: 664.9 persons per square mile (2007); Average household size: 2.66 (2007); Median age: 34.3 (2007); Males per 100 females: 91.7 (2007); Marriage status: 20.4% never married, 70.3% now married, 2.6% widowed, 6.7% divorced (2000); Foreign born: 0.0% (2000); Ancestry (includes multiple ancestries): 34.4% German, 20.1% Irish, 6.7% French (except Basque), 5.2% Norwegian, 5.2% English (2000).
Economy: Employment by occupation: 10.4% management, 11.4% professional, 12.8% services, 29.4% sales, 0.9% farming, 20.4% construction, 14.7% production (2000).
Income: Per capita income: $20,559 (2007); Median household income: $47,188 (2007); Average household income: $54,711 (2007); Percent of households with income of $100,000 or more: 7.4% (2007); Poverty rate: 8.5% (2000).
Education: Percent of population age 25 and over with: High school diploma (including GED) or higher: 88.7% (2007); Bachelor's degree or higher: 12.3% (2007); Master's degree or higher: 2.0% (2007).
Housing: Homeownership rate: 87.6% (2007); Median home value: $90,667 (2007); Median rent: $333 per month (2000); Median age of housing: 60+ years (2000).
Transportation: Commute to work: 91.3% car, 0.0% public transportation, 1.5% walk, 7.3% work from home (2000); Travel time to work: 45.5% less than 15 minutes, 17.3% 15 to 30 minutes, 29.8% 30 to 45 minutes, 7.3% 45 to 60 minutes, 0.0% 60 minutes or more (2000)

GIBSON (city). Aka Gibson City. Covers a land area of 2.103 square miles and a water area of 0.021 square miles. Located at 40.46° N. Lat.; 88.37° W. Long.
Population: 3,404 (1990); 3,373 (2000); 3,252 (2007); 3,157 (2012 projected); Race: 97.4% White, 1.1% Black, 1.0% Asian, 0.6% Hispanic of any race (2007); Density: 1,546.4 persons per square mile (2007); Average household size: 2.26 (2007); Median age: 43.2 (2007); Males per 100 females: 84.1 (2007); Marriage status: 17.7% never married, 60.9% now married, 11.7% widowed, 9.7% divorced (2000); Foreign born: 0.3% (2000); Ancestry (includes multiple ancestries): 32.0% German, 11.8% Irish, 11.0% English, 9.4% United States or American, 5.6% Other groups (2000).
Economy: Employment by occupation: 12.8% management, 14.1% professional, 16.0% services, 21.2% sales, 0.8% farming, 13.1% construction, 22.0% production (2000).
Income: Per capita income: $21,671 (2007); Median household income: $38,229 (2007); Average household income: $48,197 (2007); Percent of households with income of $100,000 or more: 8.6% (2007); Poverty rate: 9.4% (2000).
Education: Percent of population age 25 and over with: High school diploma (including GED) or higher: 80.1% (2007); Bachelor's degree or higher: 14.3% (2007); Master's degree or higher: 5.5% (2007).

School District(s)

Gibson City-Melvin-Sibley CUSD 5 (PK-12)
2005-06 Enrollment: 1,123 .... (217) 784-8296
Iroquois Special Education (04-12)
2005-06 Enrollment: 75 .... (815) 265-8601

Housing: Homeownership rate: 68.6% (2007); Median home value: $95,607 (2007); Median rent: $309 per month (2000); Median age of housing: 49 years (2000).
Hospitals: Gibson Area Hospital & Health Services (82 beds)
Safety: Violent crime rate: 21.3 per 10,000 population; Property crime rate: 225.5 per 10,000 population (2006).
Newspapers: Gibson City Courier (Community news; Circulation 2,000); Target (Community news; Circulation 13,875)
Transportation: Commute to work: 88.9% car, 0.0% public transportation, 6.4% walk, 3.7% work from home (2000); Travel time to work: 59.9% less than 15 minutes, 13.4% 15 to 30 minutes, 15.8% 30 to 45 minutes, 9.4% 45 to 60 minutes, 1.6% 60 minutes or more (2000)

Additional Information Contacts

Gibson City Chamber of Commerce .... (217) 784-5217
http://www.gibsoncityillinois.com

KEMPTON (village). Covers a land area of 0.212 square miles and a water area of 0 square miles. Located at 40.93° N. Lat.; 88.23° W. Long. Elevation is 735 feet.
Population: 219 (1990); 235 (2000); 229 (2007); 224 (2012 projected); Race: 98.7% White, 0.0% Black, 0.9% Asian, 2.6% Hispanic of any race (2007); Density: 1,082.7 persons per square mile (2007); Average household size: 2.97 (2007); Median age: 27.5 (2007); Males per 100 females: 102.7 (2007); Marriage status: 30.4% never married, 56.8% now married, 7.4% widowed, 5.4% divorced (2000); Foreign born: 0.4% (2000); Ancestry (includes multiple ancestries): 46.4% German, 24.2% Irish, 11.7% United States or American, 7.2% Italian, 7.2% English (2000).
Economy: Employment by occupation: 19.2% management, 8.7% professional, 10.6% services, 24.0% sales, 2.9% farming, 11.5% construction, 23.1% production (2000).
Income: Per capita income: $20,382 (2007); Median household income: $57,222 (2007); Average household income: $60,617 (2007); Percent of households with income of $100,000 or more: 15.6% (2007); Poverty rate: 18.9% (2000).
Education: Percent of population age 25 and over with: High school diploma (including GED) or higher: 90.2% (2007); Bachelor's degree or higher: 8.2% (2007); Master's degree or higher: 3.3% (2007).

School District(s)

Tri Point CUSD 6-J (PK-12)
2005-06 Enrollment: 583 . . . . (815) 253-6299

Housing: Homeownership rate: 75.3% (2007); Median home value: $92,000 (2007); Median rent: $367 per month (2000); Median age of housing: 60+ years (2000).

Transportation: Commute to work: 84.0% car, 0.0% public transportation, 13.0% walk, 3.0% work from home (2000); Travel time to work: 20.6% less than 15 minutes, 14.4% 15 to 30 minutes, 45.4% 30 to 45 minutes, 11.3% 45 to 60 minutes, 8.2% 60 minutes or more (2000)

MELVIN (village). Covers a land area of 0.339 square miles and a water area of 0 square miles. Located at 40.56° N. Lat.; 88.24° W. Long. Elevation is 814 feet.

Population: 466 (1990); 465 (2000); 449 (2007); 449 (2012 projected); Race: 99.6% White, 0.0% Black, 0.0% Asian, 2.2% Hispanic of any race (2007); Density: 1,325.0 persons per square mile (2007); Average household size: 2.41 (2007); Median age: 37.9 (2007); Males per 100 females: 95.2 (2007); Marriage status: 18.4% never married, 60.3% now married, 10.8% widowed, 10.5% divorced (2000); Foreign born: 1.5% (2000); Ancestry (includes multiple ancestries): 37.2% German, 12.1% English, 9.5% Irish, 9.1% Other groups, 8.0% United States or American (2000).

Economy: Employment by occupation: 7.4% management, 15.7% professional, 20.3% services, 17.5% sales, 0.0% farming, 15.7% construction, 23.5% production (2000).

Income: Per capita income: $22,990 (2007); Median household income: $50,435 (2007); Average household income: $55,497 (2007); Percent of households with income of $100,000 or more: 9.7% (2007); Poverty rate: 7.0% (2000).

Education: Percent of population age 25 and over with: High school diploma (including GED) or higher: 87.1% (2007); Bachelor's degree or higher: 15.0% (2007); Master's degree or higher: 5.8% (2007).

Housing: Homeownership rate: 85.5% (2007); Median home value: $65,000 (2007); Median rent: $270 per month (2000); Median age of housing: 60+ years (2000).

Newspapers: Ford County Press (Local news; Circulation 1,000)

Transportation: Commute to work: 92.1% car, 0.0% public transportation, 2.8% walk, 4.2% work from home (2000); Travel time to work: 32.9% less than 15 minutes, 33.3% 15 to 30 minutes, 13.5% 30 to 45 minutes, 12.1% 45 to 60 minutes, 8.2% 60 minutes or more (2000)

PAXTON (city). County seat. Covers a land area of 2.228 square miles and a water area of 0 square miles. Located at 40.45° N. Lat.; 88.09° W. Long. Elevation is 791 feet.

History: Paxton was settled in the 1850's by immigrants from Sweden.

Population: 4,408 (1990); 4,525 (2000); 4,462 (2007); 4,409 (2012 projected); Race: 96.6% White, 1.0% Black, 0.7% Asian, 2.2% Hispanic of any race (2007); Density: 2,003.1 persons per square mile (2007); Average household size: 2.53 (2007); Median age: 39.3 (2007); Males per 100 females: 92.6 (2007); Marriage status: 20.1% never married, 61.2% now married, 8.1% widowed, 10.6% divorced (2000); Foreign born: 1.2% (2000); Ancestry (includes multiple ancestries): 35.9% German, 13.1% Irish, 12.4% English, 9.7% Swedish, 7.0% Other groups (2000).

Economy: Single-family building permits issued: 3 (2007); Multi-family building permits issued: 8 (2007); Employment by occupation: 8.7% management, 11.8% professional, 15.9% services, 25.9% sales, 0.6% farming, 9.6% construction, 27.5% production (2000).

Income: Per capita income: $21,950 (2007); Median household income: $45,940 (2007); Average household income: $53,403 (2007); Percent of households with income of $100,000 or more: 10.5% (2007); Poverty rate: 4.8% (2000).

Education: Percent of population age 25 and over with: High school diploma (including GED) or higher: 88.0% (2007); Bachelor's degree or higher: 13.3% (2007); Master's degree or higher: 4.2% (2007).

School District(s)

Iroquois Special Education (04-12)
2005-06 Enrollment: 75 . . . . (815) 265-8601

Paxton-Buckley-Loda CUD 10 (PK-12)
2005-06 Enrollment: 1,500 . . . . (217) 379-3314

Housing: Homeownership rate: 78.2% (2007); Median home value: $92,873 (2007); Median rent: $330 per month (2000); Median age of housing: 49 years (2000).

Safety: Violent crime rate: 46.3 per 10,000 population; Property crime rate: 191.9 per 10,000 population (2006).

Newspapers: Loda Times (Community news; Circulation 360); Paxton Corporation (Community news; Circulation 2,180); Paxton Daily Record (Local news; Circulation 4,200)

Transportation: Commute to work: 95.0% car, 0.4% public transportation, 1.2% walk, 1.6% work from home (2000); Travel time to work: 46.6% less than 15 minutes, 21.8% 15 to 30 minutes, 22.3% 30 to 45 minutes, 5.0% 45 to 60 minutes, 4.3% 60 minutes or more (2000)

Additional Information Contacts

Paxton Chamber of Commerce . . . . (217) 379-4655
http://www.paxtonchamber.org

PIPER CITY (village). Covers a land area of 0.554 square miles and a water area of 0 square miles. Located at 40.75° N. Lat.; 88.19° W. Long. Elevation is 673 feet.

Population: 760 (1990); 781 (2000); 774 (2007); 763 (2012 projected); Race: 95.6% White, 0.1% Black, 1.8% Asian, 1.6% Hispanic of any race (2007); Density: 1,396.5 persons per square mile (2007); Average household size: 2.60 (2007); Median age: 42.8 (2007); Males per 100 females: 88.3 (2007); Marriage status: 21.2% never married, 57.3% now married, 15.5% widowed, 6.1% divorced (2000); Foreign born: 2.6% (2000); Ancestry (includes multiple ancestries): 36.8% German, 27.4% Irish, 13.1% English, 10.7% French (except Basque), 9.0% Other groups (2000).

Economy: Single-family building permits issued: 0 (2007); Multi-family building permits issued: 0 (2007); Employment by occupation: 14.1% management, 14.1% professional, 20.6% services, 20.6% sales, 1.4% farming, 12.2% construction, 17.1% production (2000).

Income: Per capita income: $26,077 (2007); Median household income: $47,308 (2007); Average household income: $62,416 (2007); Percent of households with income of $100,000 or more: 11.4% (2007); Poverty rate: 10.0% (2000).

Education: Percent of population age 25 and over with: High school diploma (including GED) or higher: 81.0% (2007); Bachelor's degree or higher: 12.7% (2007); Master's degree or higher: 5.9% (2007).

School District(s)

Tri Point CUSD 6-J (PK-12)
2005-06 Enrollment: 583 . . . . (815) 253-6299

Housing: Homeownership rate: 79.5% (2007); Median home value: $107,532 (2007); Median rent: $340 per month (2000); Median age of housing: 54 years (2000).

Safety: Violent crime rate: 0.0 per 10,000 population; Property crime rate: 93.5 per 10,000 population (2006).

Transportation: Commute to work: 92.8% car, 0.0% public transportation, 1.4% walk, 5.8% work from home (2000); Travel time to work: 35.2% less than 15 minutes, 20.7% 15 to 30 minutes, 15.7% 30 to 45 minutes, 13.0% 45 to 60 minutes, 15.4% 60 minutes or more (2000)

ROBERTS (village). Covers a land area of 0.518 square miles and a water area of 0 square miles. Located at 40.61° N. Lat.; 88.18° W. Long. Elevation is 781 feet.

Population: 413 (1990); 387 (2000); 379 (2007); 371 (2012 projected); Race: 98.9% White, 0.0% Black, 0.0% Asian, 1.8% Hispanic of any race (2007); Density: 731.4 persons per square mile (2007); Average household size: 2.24 (2007); Median age: 42.9 (2007); Males per 100 females: 78.8 (2007); Marriage status: 21.2% never married, 52.6% now married, 14.6% widowed, 11.5% divorced (2000); Foreign born: 0.8% (2000); Ancestry (includes multiple ancestries): 44.0% German, 19.0% English, 12.1% Irish, 9.0% Other groups, 8.5% French (except Basque) (2000).

Economy: Employment by occupation: 10.4% management, 10.9% professional, 13.3% services, 29.9% sales, 0.9% farming, 12.3% construction, 22.3% production (2000).

Income: Per capita income: $21,854 (2007); Median household income: $40,417 (2007); Average household income: $49,009 (2007); Percent of households with income of $100,000 or more: 8.3% (2007); Poverty rate: 7.5% (2000).

Education: Percent of population age 25 and over with: High school diploma (including GED) or higher: 89.7% (2007); Bachelor's degree or higher: 8.7% (2007); Master's degree or higher: 1.1% (2007).

Housing: Homeownership rate: 89.9% (2007); Median home value: $88,182 (2007); Median rent: $213 per month (2000); Median age of housing: 58 years (2000).

Transportation: Commute to work: 92.8% car, 0.0% public transportation, 7.2% walk, 0.0% work from home (2000); Travel time to work: 43.0% less than 15 minutes, 33.3% 15 to 30 minutes, 9.7% 30 to 45 minutes, 10.6% 45 to 60 minutes, 3.4% 60 minutes or more (2000)

SIBLEY (village). Covers a land area of 0.538 square miles and a water area of 0.013 square miles. Located at 40.58° N. Lat.; 88.38° W. Long. Elevation is 827 feet.
Population: 359 (1990); 329 (2000); 337 (2007); 341 (2012 projected); Race: 97.9% White, 0.0% Black, 0.0% Asian, 1.5% Hispanic of any race (2007); Density: 626.5 persons per square mile (2007); Average household size: 2.41 (2007); Median age: 42.4 (2007); Males per 100 females: 99.4 (2007); Marriage status: 19.1% never married, 64.8% now married, 10.5% widowed, 5.6% divorced (2000); Foreign born: 0.6% (2000); Ancestry (includes multiple ancestries): 39.5% German, 11.3% English, 8.4% United States or American, 5.8% French (except Basque), 4.8% Swedish (2000).
Economy: Employment by occupation: 9.1% management, 7.0% professional, 21.0% services, 21.0% sales, 2.8% farming, 14.7% construction, 24.5% production (2000).
Income: Per capita income: $21,958 (2007); Median household income: $42,500 (2007); Average household income: $52,857 (2007); Percent of households with income of $100,000 or more: 9.3% (2007); Poverty rate: 7.4% (2000).
Education: Percent of population age 25 and over with: High school diploma (including GED) or higher: 76.6% (2007); Bachelor's degree or higher: 6.0% (2007); Master's degree or higher: 2.1% (2007).
Housing: Homeownership rate: 85.7% (2007); Median home value: $53,333 (2007); Median rent: $304 per month (2000); Median age of housing: 60+ years (2000).
Transportation: Commute to work: 89.2% car, 2.2% public transportation, 3.6% walk, 2.9% work from home (2000); Travel time to work: 17.8% less than 15 minutes, 33.3% 15 to 30 minutes, 13.3% 30 to 45 minutes, 21.5% 45 to 60 minutes, 14.1% 60 minutes or more (2000)

Franklin County

Located in southern Illinois; bounded on the northwest by the Little Muddy River; drained by the Big Muddy River. Covers a land area of 412.08 square miles, a water area of 19.32 square miles, and is located in the Central Time Zone. The county was founded in 1818. County seat is Benton.
Population: 40,319 (1990); 39,018 (2000); 40,038 (2007); 40,726 (2012 projected); Race: 98.3% White, 0.3% Black, 0.2% Asian, 1.1% Hispanic of any race (2007); Density: 97.2 persons per square mile (2007); Average household size: 2.35 (2007); Median age: 40.6 (2007); Males per 100 females: 92.8 (2007).
Religion: Five largest groups: 30.8% Southern Baptist Convention, 5.9% Christian Churches and Churches of Christ, 3.9% Catholic Church, 3.6% Church of God (Cleveland, Tennessee), 3.6% The United Methodist Church (2000).
Economy: Unemployment rate: 7.1% (4/2008); Total civilian labor force: 18,318 (4/2008); Leading industries: 21.7% retail trade; 16.5% health care and social assistance; 14.1% accommodation & food services (2005); Farms: 727 totaling 179,694 acres (2002); Companies that employ 500 or more persons: 0 (2006); Companies that employ 100 to 499 persons: 7 (2006); Companies that employ less than 100 persons: 791 (2006); Black-owned businesses: n/a (2002); Hispanic-owned businesses: n/a (2002); Asian-owned businesses: n/a (2002); Women-owned businesses: 794 (2002); Retail sales per capita: $11,990 (2008). Single-family building permits issued: 28 (2007); Multi-family building permits issued: 6 (2007).
Income: Per capita income: $19,004 (2007); Median household income: $34,565 (2007); Average household income: $44,340 (2007); Percent of households with income of $100,000 or more: 7.0% (2007); Poverty rate: 16.7% (2005); Bankruptcy rate: 6.10% (2007).
Education: Percent of population age 25 and over with: High school diploma (including GED) or higher: 76.8% (2007); Bachelor's degree or higher: 11.4% (2007); Master's degree or higher: 3.7% (2007).
Housing: Homeownership rate: 78.0% (2007); Median home value: $63,637 (2007); Median rent: $264 per month (2000); Median age of housing: 45 years (2000).
Health: Birth rate: 129.1 per 10,000 population (2007); Death rate: 141.3 per 10,000 population (2007); Age-adjusted cancer mortality rate: 206.8 deaths per 100,000 population (2005); Number of physicians: 5.6 per 10,000 population (2005); Hospital beds: 6.4 per 10,000 population (2004); Hospital admissions: 180.2 per 10,000 population (2004).
Elections: 2004 Presidential election results: 53.7% Bush, 45.6% Kerry, 0.1% Nader, 0.7% Badnarik
National and State Parks: Wayne Fitzgerrell State Park
Additional Information Contacts
Franklin County Government . . . . (618) 438-3221

Benton/West City Area Chamber of Commerce . . . . (618) 438-2121
http://www.bentonwestcity.com/chamber
City of West Frankfort . . . . (618) 932-3262
http://www.westfrankfort-il.com
Sesser Area Chamber of Commerce. . . . . (618) 625-3611
http://www.sesserchamber.org
West Frankfort Chamber of Commerce. . . . . (618) 932-2181
http://www.westfrankfort.com

Franklin County Communities

BENTON (city). County seat. Covers a land area of 5.349 square miles and a water area of 0.141 square miles. Located at 38.00° N. Lat.; 88.91° W. Long. Elevation is 472 feet.
History: Incorporated 1841.
Population: 7,264 (1990); 6,880 (2000); 6,808 (2007); 6,765 (2012 projected); Race: 98.2% White, 0.7% Black, 0.3% Asian, 0.8% Hispanic of any race (2007); Density: 1,272.8 persons per square mile (2007); Average household size: 2.32 (2007); Median age: 42.2 (2007); Males per 100 females: 88.4 (2007); Marriage status: 18.2% never married, 59.9% now married, 10.8% widowed, 11.0% divorced (2000); Foreign born: 0.8% (2000); Ancestry (includes multiple ancestries): 16.4% German, 15.1% English, 15.0% United States or American, 12.6% Irish, 6.7% Other groups (2000).
Economy: Single-family building permits issued: 12 (2007); Multi-family building permits issued: 0 (2007); Employment by occupation: 6.9% management, 16.8% professional, 20.2% services, 29.4% sales, 0.3% farming, 8.4% construction, 18.0% production (2000).
Income: Per capita income: $18,934 (2007); Median household income: $34,500 (2007); Average household income: $43,196 (2007); Percent of households with income of $100,000 or more: 6.9% (2007); Poverty rate: 17.5% (2000).
Education: Percent of population age 25 and over with: High school diploma (including GED) or higher: 75.8% (2007); Bachelor's degree or higher: 13.4% (2007); Master's degree or higher: 4.9% (2007).
School District(s)
Benton CCSD 47 (PK-08)
2005-06 Enrollment: 1,079 . . . . (618) 439-3136
Benton Cons HSD 103 (09-12)
2005-06 Enrollment: 643 . . . . (618) 439-6415
Franklin/Williamson Roe (06-12)
2005-06 Enrollment: 166 . . . . (618) 438-9711
Housing: Homeownership rate: 70.2% (2007); Median home value: $64,608 (2007); Median rent: $287 per month (2000); Median age of housing: 46 years (2000).
Hospitals: Franklin Hospital (25 beds)
Safety: Violent crime rate: 82.3 per 10,000 population; Property crime rate: 489.2 per 10,000 population (2006).
Newspapers: Benton Evening News (Local news; Circulation 4,000); Benton Standard (Community news; Circulation 300)
Transportation: Commute to work: 93.2% car, 0.0% public transportation, 3.5% walk, 2.9% work from home (2000); Travel time to work: 49.8% less than 15 minutes, 23.4% 15 to 30 minutes, 17.1% 30 to 45 minutes, 4.7% 45 to 60 minutes, 4.9% 60 minutes or more (2000)
Additional Information Contacts
Benton/West City Area Chamber of Commerce . . . . (618) 438-2121
http://www.bentonwestcity.com/chamber

BUCKNER (village). Covers a land area of 0.887 square miles and a water area of 0.013 square miles. Located at 37.98° N. Lat.; 89.01° W. Long. Elevation is 404 feet.
Population: 478 (1990); 479 (2000); 498 (2007); 507 (2012 projected); Race: 99.2% White, 0.0% Black, 0.0% Asian, 2.4% Hispanic of any race (2007); Density: 561.8 persons per square mile (2007); Average household size: 2.16 (2007); Median age: 42.3 (2007); Males per 100 females: 96.1 (2007); Marriage status: 23.3% never married, 46.4% now married, 9.0% widowed, 21.2% divorced (2000); Foreign born: 1.0% (2000); Ancestry (includes multiple ancestries): 14.2% Irish, 13.4% United States or American, 10.0% German, 8.8% Other groups, 7.7% English (2000).
Economy: Employment by occupation: 2.6% management, 5.7% professional, 21.4% services, 25.0% sales, 0.0% farming, 10.4% construction, 34.9% production (2000).

Income: Per capita income: $15,070 (2007); Median household income: $28,900 (2007); Average household income: $32,489 (2007); Percent of households with income of $100,000 or more: 0.4% (2007); Poverty rate: 23.3% (2000).
Education: Percent of population age 25 and over with: High school diploma (including GED) or higher: 71.3% (2007); Bachelor's degree or higher: 4.4% (2007); Master's degree or higher: 0.0% (2007).
Housing: Homeownership rate: 81.4% (2007); Median home value: $31,750 (2007); Median rent: $272 per month (2000); Median age of housing: 60+ years (2000).
Transportation: Commute to work: 98.9% car, 0.0% public transportation, 1.1% walk, 0.0% work from home (2000); Travel time to work: 33.2% less than 15 minutes, 31.5% 15 to 30 minutes, 16.8% 30 to 45 minutes, 9.2% 45 to 60 minutes, 9.2% 60 minutes or more (2000)

CHRISTOPHER (city). Covers a land area of 1.410 square miles and a water area of 0 square miles. Located at 37.97° N. Lat.; 89.05° W. Long. Elevation is 440 feet.
History: Incorporated 1903.
Population: 2,882 (1990); 2,836 (2000); 2,806 (2007); 2,793 (2012 projected); Race: 98.2% White, 0.2% Black, 0.4% Asian, 0.8% Hispanic of any race (2007); Density: 1,989.7 persons per square mile (2007); Average household size: 2.15 (2007); Median age: 41.5 (2007); Males per 100 females: 88.1 (2007); Marriage status: 18.4% never married, 57.2% now married, 12.3% widowed, 12.1% divorced (2000); Foreign born: 0.3% (2000); Ancestry (includes multiple ancestries): 17.0% German, 13.5% English, 12.6% Irish, 11.6% Other groups, 9.5% United States or American (2000).
Economy: Single-family building permits issued: 2 (2007); Multi-family building permits issued: 0 (2007); Employment by occupation: 4.3% management, 16.4% professional, 19.9% services, 28.2% sales, 0.0% farming, 10.3% construction, 20.9% production (2000).
Income: Per capita income: $18,109 (2007); Median household income: $30,517 (2007); Average household income: $38,849 (2007); Percent of households with income of $100,000 or more: 4.2% (2007); Poverty rate: 19.8% (2000).
Education: Percent of population age 25 and over with: High school diploma (including GED) or higher: 73.6% (2007); Bachelor's degree or higher: 11.1% (2007); Master's degree or higher: 2.6% (2007).

School District(s)

Christopher USD 99 (PK-12)
2005-06 Enrollment: 790 . . . . (618) 724-9461
Housing: Homeownership rate: 72.6% (2007); Median home value: $49,728 (2007); Median rent: $228 per month (2000); Median age of housing: 52 years (2000).
Safety: Violent crime rate: 31.8 per 10,000 population; Property crime rate: 187.1 per 10,000 population (2006).
Newspapers: Franklin Press Shopper (Local news; Circulation 7,400); Progress (Community news; Circulation 900)
Transportation: Commute to work: 95.2% car, 0.0% public transportation, 0.7% walk, 3.3% work from home (2000); Travel time to work: 36.2% less than 15 minutes, 29.6% 15 to 30 minutes, 21.8% 30 to 45 minutes, 5.2% 45 to 60 minutes, 7.2% 60 minutes or more (2000)

EWING (village). Covers a land area of 1.014 square miles and a water area of 0 square miles. Located at 38.09° N. Lat.; 88.85° W. Long. Elevation is 469 feet.
Population: 264 (1990); 310 (2000); 327 (2007); 339 (2012 projected); Race: 100.0% White, 0.0% Black, 0.0% Asian, 2.8% Hispanic of any race (2007); Density: 322.6 persons per square mile (2007); Average household size: 2.57 (2007); Median age: 38.5 (2007); Males per 100 females: 91.2 (2007); Marriage status: 12.5% never married, 69.4% now married, 8.6% widowed, 9.5% divorced (2000); Foreign born: 0.7% (2000); Ancestry (includes multiple ancestries): 22.3% German, 17.3% United States or American, 16.9% English, 14.6% Irish, 8.6% Other groups (2000).
Economy: Employment by occupation: 0.0% management, 8.2% professional, 17.2% services, 32.0% sales, 0.0% farming, 13.9% construction, 28.7% production (2000).
Income: Per capita income: $17,393 (2007); Median household income: $36,563 (2007); Average household income: $44,783 (2007); Percent of households with income of $100,000 or more: 7.9% (2007); Poverty rate: 9.3% (2000).
Education: Percent of population age 25 and over with: High school diploma (including GED) or higher: 82.0% (2007); Bachelor's degree or higher: 8.1% (2007); Master's degree or higher: 4.7% (2007).

School District(s)

Ewing Northern CCSD 115 (PK-08)
2005-06 Enrollment: 232 . . . . (618) 629-2181
Housing: Homeownership rate: 85.8% (2007); Median home value: $51,786 (2007); Median rent: $275 per month (2000); Median age of housing: 29 years (2000).
Transportation: Commute to work: 92.5% car, 0.0% public transportation, 2.5% walk, 5.0% work from home (2000); Travel time to work: 18.4% less than 15 minutes, 46.5% 15 to 30 minutes, 32.5% 30 to 45 minutes, 1.8% 45 to 60 minutes, 0.9% 60 minutes or more (2000)

HANAFORD (village). Aka Logan. Covers a land area of 1.022 square miles and a water area of 0 square miles. Located at 37.95° N. Lat.; 88.83° W. Long. Elevation is 480 feet.
History: Also called Logan.
Population: 380 (1990); 55 (2000); 57 (2007); 58 (2012 projected); Race: 100.0% White, 0.0% Black, 0.0% Asian, 0.0% Hispanic of any race (2007); Density: 55.8 persons per square mile (2007); Average household size: 2.59 (2007); Median age: 36.3 (2007); Males per 100 females: 111.1 (2007); Marriage status: 0.0% never married, 0.0% now married, 100.0% widowed, 0.0% divorced (2000); Foreign born: 0.0% (2000); Ancestry (includes multiple ancestries): 100.0% German, 100.0% English (2000).
Economy: Employment by occupation: 0.0% management, 0.0% professional, 0.0% services, 100.0% sales, 0.0% farming, 0.0% construction, 0.0% production (2000).
Income: Per capita income: $23,421 (2007); Median household income: $59,167 (2007); Average household income: $60,682 (2007); Percent of households with income of $100,000 or more: 0.0% (2007); Poverty rate: 0.0% (2000).
Education: Percent of population age 25 and over with: High school diploma (including GED) or higher: 100.0% (2007); Bachelor's degree or higher: 0.0% (2007); Master's degree or higher: 0.0% (2007).
Housing: Homeownership rate: 81.8% (2007); Median home value: $120,455 (2007); Median rent: $n/a per month (2000); Median age of housing: 16 years (2000).
Transportation: Commute to work: 100.0% car, 0.0% public transportation, 0.0% walk, 0.0% work from home (2000); Travel time to work: 0.0% less than 15 minutes, 100.0% 15 to 30 minutes, 0.0% 30 to 45 minutes, 0.0% 45 to 60 minutes, 0.0% 60 minutes or more (2000)

MULKEYTOWN (unincorporated postal area, zip code 62865). Covers a land area of 50.295 square miles and a water area of 0.441 square miles. Located at 37.96° N. Lat.; 89.06° W. Long. Elevation is 446 feet.
Population: 1,879 (2000); Race: 96.5% White, 0.0% Black, 0.0% Asian, 2.5% Hispanic of any race (2000); Density: 37.4 persons per square mile (2000); Age: 25.5% under 18, 13.5% over 64 (2000); Marriage status: 18.5% never married, 67.0% now married, 6.4% widowed, 8.1% divorced (2000); Foreign born: 0.1% (2000); Ancestry (includes multiple ancestries): 16.4% English, 15.0% German, 12.4% Irish, 11.7% United States or American, 9.1% Other groups (2000).
Economy: Employment by occupation: 11.0% management, 17.8% professional, 20.6% services, 26.1% sales, 0.0% farming, 12.7% construction, 11.8% production (2000).
Income: Per capita income: $17,037 (2000); Median household income: $38,200 (2000); Poverty rate: 12.7% (2000).
Education: Percent of population age 25 and over with: High school diploma (including GED) or higher: 80.1% (2000); Bachelor's degree or higher: 12.4% (2000).
Housing: Homeownership rate: 91.3% (2000); Median home value: $54,000 (2000); Median rent: $181 per month (2000); Median age of housing: 27 years (2000).
Transportation: Commute to work: 95.1% car, 0.7% public transportation, 0.2% walk, 4.0% work from home (2000); Travel time to work: 25.4% less than 15 minutes, 38.8% 15 to 30 minutes, 27.8% 30 to 45 minutes, 5.4% 45 to 60 minutes, 2.6% 60 minutes or more (2000)

NORTH CITY (village). Aka Coello. Covers a land area of 2.193 square miles and a water area of 0.040 square miles. Located at 37.99° N. Lat.; 89.06° W. Long. Elevation is 469 feet.
Population: 627 (1990); 630 (2000); 711 (2007); 762 (2012 projected); Race: 95.6% White, 0.3% Black, 0.4% Asian, 3.1% Hispanic of any race (2007); Density: 324.3 persons per square mile (2007); Average household size: 2.39 (2007); Median age: 40.8 (2007); Males per 100 females: 102.6 (2007); Marriage status: 21.5% never married, 60.9% now married, 5.8% widowed, 11.7% divorced (2000); Foreign born: 1.9% (2000); Ancestry

(includes multiple ancestries): 16.8% English, 13.5% German, 12.6% Irish, 12.1% Italian, 11.0% Other groups (2000).
Economy: Single-family building permits issued: 8 (2007); Multi-family building permits issued: 0 (2007); Employment by occupation: 9.3% management, 11.5% professional, 18.5% services, 19.6% sales, 1.1% farming, 15.9% construction, 24.1% production (2000).
Income: Per capita income: $16,596 (2007); Median household income: $33,125 (2007); Average household income: $39,597 (2007); Percent of households with income of $100,000 or more: 2.7% (2007); Poverty rate: 19.6% (2000).
Education: Percent of population age 25 and over with: High school diploma (including GED) or higher: 75.0% (2007); Bachelor's degree or higher: 5.9% (2007); Master's degree or higher: 2.0% (2007).
Housing: Homeownership rate: 85.9% (2007); Median home value: $55,217 (2007); Median rent: $213 per month (2000); Median age of housing: 44 years (2000).
Transportation: Commute to work: 95.4% car, 0.0% public transportation, 2.3% walk, 2.3% work from home (2000); Travel time to work: 27.0% less than 15 minutes, 27.7% 15 to 30 minutes, 24.2% 30 to 45 minutes, 13.3% 45 to 60 minutes, 7.8% 60 minutes or more (2000)

ORIENT (city). Covers a land area of 0.750 square miles and a water area of 0.006 square miles. Located at 37.91° N. Lat.; 88.97° W. Long. Elevation is 482 feet.
Population: 457 (1990); 296 (2000); 260 (2007); 265 (2012 projected); Race: 99.2% White, 0.8% Black, 0.0% Asian, 0.0% Hispanic of any race (2007); Density: 346.7 persons per square mile (2007); Average household size: 2.22 (2007); Median age: 42.5 (2007); Males per 100 females: 89.8 (2007); Marriage status: 16.6% never married, 54.4% now married, 14.7% widowed, 14.3% divorced (2000); Foreign born: 0.0% (2000); Ancestry (includes multiple ancestries): 30.2% United States or American, 19.9% Other groups, 19.7% Irish, 6.0% German, 5.7% Italian (2000).
Economy: Employment by occupation: 6.9% management, 5.4% professional, 29.2% services, 12.3% sales, 0.0% farming, 10.8% construction, 35.4% production (2000).
Income: Per capita income: $12,990 (2007); Median household income: $26,346 (2007); Average household income: $28,868 (2007); Percent of households with income of $100,000 or more: 0.9% (2007); Poverty rate: 19.0% (2000).
Education: Percent of population age 25 and over with: High school diploma (including GED) or higher: 60.0% (2007); Bachelor's degree or higher: 4.3% (2007); Master's degree or higher: 0.0% (2007).
Housing: Homeownership rate: 89.7% (2007); Median home value: $40,217 (2007); Median rent: $225 per month (2000); Median age of housing: 60+ years (2000).
Transportation: Commute to work: 97.6% car, 0.0% public transportation, 0.0% walk, 2.4% work from home (2000); Travel time to work: 23.1% less than 15 minutes, 45.5% 15 to 30 minutes, 25.6% 30 to 45 minutes, 0.0% 45 to 60 minutes, 5.8% 60 minutes or more (2000)

ROYALTON (village). Covers a land area of 1.131 square miles and a water area of 0.001 square miles. Located at 37.88° N. Lat.; 89.11° W. Long. Elevation is 394 feet.
History: Incorporated 1907.
Population: 1,191 (1990); 1,130 (2000); 1,060 (2007); 1,057 (2012 projected); Race: 99.6% White, 0.0% Black, 0.0% Asian, 0.4% Hispanic of any race (2007); Density: 937.3 persons per square mile (2007); Average household size: 2.15 (2007); Median age: 40.7 (2007); Males per 100 females: 88.3 (2007); Marriage status: 19.2% never married, 53.1% now married, 12.2% widowed, 15.4% divorced (2000); Foreign born: 0.4% (2000); Ancestry (includes multiple ancestries): 19.5% United States or American, 14.3% German, 11.4% Irish, 10.6% Other groups, 9.8% English (2000).
Economy: Employment by occupation: 10.6% management, 14.9% professional, 17.2% services, 18.1% sales, 0.5% farming, 11.9% construction, 26.8% production (2000).
Income: Per capita income: $17,519 (2007); Median household income: $28,313 (2007); Average household income: $37,667 (2007); Percent of households with income of $100,000 or more: 4.9% (2007); Poverty rate: 20.3% (2000).
Education: Percent of population age 25 and over with: High school diploma (including GED) or higher: 75.8% (2007); Bachelor's degree or higher: 7.5% (2007); Master's degree or higher: 2.7% (2007).
Housing: Homeownership rate: 77.9% (2007); Median home value: $46,486 (2007); Median rent: $238 per month (2000); Median age of housing: 52 years (2000).
Safety: Violent crime rate: 0.0 per 10,000 population; Property crime rate: 179.3 per 10,000 population (2006).
Transportation: Commute to work: 93.2% car, 0.7% public transportation, 1.4% walk, 4.0% work from home (2000); Travel time to work: 17.6% less than 15 minutes, 51.0% 15 to 30 minutes, 21.0% 30 to 45 minutes, 4.4% 45 to 60 minutes, 6.1% 60 minutes or more (2000)

SESSER (city). Covers a land area of 1.021 square miles and a water area of 0 square miles. Located at 38.09° N. Lat.; 89.05° W. Long. Elevation is 479 feet.
History: Incorporated 1906.
Population: 2,155 (1990); 2,128 (2000); 2,221 (2007); 2,289 (2012 projected); Race: 98.2% White, 0.2% Black, 0.0% Asian, 1.0% Hispanic of any race (2007); Density: 2,176.0 persons per square mile (2007); Average household size: 2.28 (2007); Median age: 38.1 (2007); Males per 100 females: 87.0 (2007); Marriage status: 19.3% never married, 56.1% now married, 11.6% widowed, 12.9% divorced (2000); Foreign born: 0.5% (2000); Ancestry (includes multiple ancestries): 14.9% United States or American, 11.3% German, 9.8% English, 7.6% Irish, 6.6% Other groups (2000).
Economy: Single-family building permits issued: 2 (2007); Multi-family building permits issued: 0 (2007); Employment by occupation: 6.2% management, 14.7% professional, 19.9% services, 23.7% sales, 0.0% farming, 17.6% construction, 17.9% production (2000).
Income: Per capita income: $18,804 (2007); Median household income: $31,250 (2007); Average household income: $42,602 (2007); Percent of households with income of $100,000 or more: 5.5% (2007); Poverty rate: 20.4% (2000).
Education: Percent of population age 25 and over with: High school diploma (including GED) or higher: 73.9% (2007); Bachelor's degree or higher: 8.5% (2007); Master's degree or higher: 3.3% (2007).

School District(s)

Sesser-Valier CUSD 196 (PK-12)
2005-06 Enrollment: 778 . . . . (618) 625-5105

Housing: Homeownership rate: 77.9% (2007); Median home value: $58,257 (2007); Median rent: $259 per month (2000); Median age of housing: 44 years (2000).
Safety: Violent crime rate: 140.4 per 10,000 population; Property crime rate: 458.8 per 10,000 population (2006).
Transportation: Commute to work: 95.4% car, 0.0% public transportation, 1.3% walk, 2.8% work from home (2000); Travel time to work: 24.9% less than 15 minutes, 39.2% 15 to 30 minutes, 25.7% 30 to 45 minutes, 6.4% 45 to 60 minutes, 3.8% 60 minutes or more (2000)

Additional Information Contacts

Sesser Area Chamber of Commerce. . . . . (618) 625-3611
http://www.sesserchamber.org

THOMPSONVILLE (village). Covers a land area of 2.050 square miles and a water area of 0.013 square miles. Located at 37.91° N. Lat.; 88.76° W. Long. Elevation is 502 feet.
Population: 602 (1990); 571 (2000); 582 (2007); 590 (2012 projected); Race: 98.6% White, 0.0% Black, 0.0% Asian, 1.2% Hispanic of any race (2007); Density: 283.9 persons per square mile (2007); Average household size: 2.56 (2007); Median age: 37.1 (2007); Males per 100 females: 94.0 (2007); Marriage status: 22.3% never married, 60.7% now married, 9.2% widowed, 7.8% divorced (2000); Foreign born: 0.5% (2000); Ancestry (includes multiple ancestries): 19.5% United States or American, 14.9% Irish, 13.5% English, 13.0% German, 5.9% French (except Basque) (2000).
Economy: Employment by occupation: 7.7% management, 15.3% professional, 13.2% services, 19.1% sales, 4.3% farming, 12.3% construction, 28.1% production (2000).
Income: Per capita income: $16,349 (2007); Median household income: $37,083 (2007); Average household income: $41,916 (2007); Percent of households with income of $100,000 or more: 3.5% (2007); Poverty rate: 17.8% (2000).
Education: Percent of population age 25 and over with: High school diploma (including GED) or higher: 84.2% (2007); Bachelor's degree or higher: 8.5% (2007); Master's degree or higher: 2.3% (2007).

School District(s)

Thompsonville CHSD 112 (09-12)
2005-06 Enrollment: 103 . . . . (618) 627-2446

Thompsonville SD 62 (KG-08)
2005-06 Enrollment: 220 . . . . (618) 627-2446
Housing: Homeownership rate: 74.4% (2007); Median home value: $57,500 (2007); Median rent: $198 per month (2000); Median age of housing: 35 years (2000).
Transportation: Commute to work: 91.3% car, 0.0% public transportation, 0.0% walk, 7.4% work from home (2000); Travel time to work: 11.3% less than 15 minutes, 41.0% 15 to 30 minutes, 26.4% 30 to 45 minutes, 16.0% 45 to 60 minutes, 5.2% 60 minutes or more (2000)

VALIER (village). Covers a land area of 1.128 square miles and a water area of 0 square miles. Located at 38.01° N. Lat.; 89.04° W. Long. Elevation is 459 feet.
Population: 708 (1990); 662 (2000); 739 (2007); 788 (2012 projected); Race: 98.5% White, 0.0% Black, 0.0% Asian, 0.1% Hispanic of any race (2007); Density: 655.3 persons per square mile (2007); Average household size: 2.40 (2007); Median age: 38.2 (2007); Males per 100 females: 94.5 (2007); Marriage status: 25.1% never married, 56.3% now married, 7.0% widowed, 11.6% divorced (2000); Foreign born: 0.9% (2000); Ancestry (includes multiple ancestries): 15.7% United States or American, 12.8% Irish, 12.8% German, 9.6% English, 5.2% French (except Basque) (2000).
Economy: Single-family building permits issued: 0 (2007); Multi-family building permits issued: 0 (2007); Employment by occupation: 5.1% management, 15.9% professional, 15.2% services, 34.7% sales, 0.0% farming, 11.9% construction, 17.3% production (2000).
Income: Per capita income: $17,351 (2007); Median household income: $34,400 (2007); Average household income: $41,631 (2007); Percent of households with income of $100,000 or more: 3.6% (2007); Poverty rate: 7.3% (2000).
Education: Percent of population age 25 and over with: High school diploma (including GED) or higher: 85.0% (2007); Bachelor's degree or higher: 9.1% (2007); Master's degree or higher: 2.2% (2007).
Housing: Homeownership rate: 83.4% (2007); Median home value: $60,357 (2007); Median rent: $261 per month (2000); Median age of housing: 54 years (2000).
Transportation: Commute to work: 98.2% car, 0.0% public transportation, 0.0% walk, 0.7% work from home (2000); Travel time to work: 21.1% less than 15 minutes, 41.5% 15 to 30 minutes, 21.1% 30 to 45 minutes, 12.2% 45 to 60 minutes, 4.1% 60 minutes or more (2000)

WEST CITY (village). Covers a land area of 1.614 square miles and a water area of 0 square miles. Located at 37.99° N. Lat.; 88.94° W. Long. Elevation is 456 feet.
History: Incorporated 1911.
Population: 747 (1990); 716 (2000); 699 (2007); 668 (2012 projected); Race: 96.1% White, 1.4% Black, 0.3% Asian, 0.6% Hispanic of any race (2007); Density: 433.2 persons per square mile (2007); Average household size: 2.35 (2007); Median age: 40.7 (2007); Males per 100 females: 95.3 (2007); Marriage status: 19.9% never married, 51.6% now married, 13.9% widowed, 14.6% divorced (2000); Foreign born: 0.0% (2000); Ancestry (includes multiple ancestries): 14.4% United States or American, 13.9% Irish, 12.3% German, 8.6% English, 7.6% Other groups (2000).
Economy: Single-family building permits issued: 1 (2007); Multi-family building permits issued: 6 (2007); Employment by occupation: 5.9% management, 9.2% professional, 28.6% services, 29.7% sales, 1.1% farming, 8.8% construction, 16.8% production (2000).
Income: Per capita income: $13,677 (2007); Median household income: $24,483 (2007); Average household income: $31,871 (2007); Percent of households with income of $100,000 or more: 2.7% (2007); Poverty rate: 22.1% (2000).
Education: Percent of population age 25 and over with: High school diploma (including GED) or higher: 68.5% (2007); Bachelor's degree or higher: 5.8% (2007); Master's degree or higher: 2.2% (2007).
Housing: Homeownership rate: 69.8% (2007); Median home value: $48,974 (2007); Median rent: $222 per month (2000); Median age of housing: 46 years (2000).
Safety: Violent crime rate: 13.6 per 10,000 population; Property crime rate: 732.7 per 10,000 population (2006).
Transportation: Commute to work: 92.9% car, 0.0% public transportation, 3.0% walk, 3.0% work from home (2000); Travel time to work: 41.4% less than 15 minutes, 26.1% 15 to 30 minutes, 14.2% 30 to 45 minutes, 7.7% 45 to 60 minutes, 10.7% 60 minutes or more (2000)

WEST FRANKFORT (city). Covers a land area of 4.746 square miles and a water area of 0.013 square miles. Located at 37.89° N. Lat.; 88.92° W. Long. Elevation is 400 feet.
History: Incorporated 1901; annexed Frankfort Heights in 1923.
Population: 8,671 (1990); 8,196 (2000); 8,181 (2007); 8,201 (2012 projected); Race: 98.2% White, 0.3% Black, 0.4% Asian, 1.4% Hispanic of any race (2007); Density: 1,723.6 persons per square mile (2007); Average household size: 2.26 (2007); Median age: 40.0 (2007); Males per 100 females: 88.2 (2007); Marriage status: 19.8% never married, 54.1% now married, 10.4% widowed, 15.7% divorced (2000); Foreign born: 0.9% (2000); Ancestry (includes multiple ancestries): 20.6% United States or American, 13.3% German, 10.9% Irish, 10.7% English, 9.5% Other groups (2000).
Economy: Single-family building permits issued: 3 (2007); Multi-family building permits issued: 0 (2007); Employment by occupation: 8.1% management, 11.7% professional, 22.6% services, 25.8% sales, 0.0% farming, 8.7% construction, 23.0% production (2000).
Income: Per capita income: $17,621 (2007); Median household income: $29,778 (2007); Average household income: $39,454 (2007); Percent of households with income of $100,000 or more: 5.4% (2007); Poverty rate: 18.6% (2000).
Taxes: Total city taxes per capita: $136 (2006); City property taxes per capita: $92 (2006).
Education: Percent of population age 25 and over with: High school diploma (including GED) or higher: 75.2% (2007); Bachelor's degree or higher: 11.4% (2007); Master's degree or higher: 3.6% (2007).

School District(s)

Frankfort CUSD 168 (PK-12)
2005-06 Enrollment: 1,845 . . . . (618) 937-2421
Housing: Homeownership rate: 67.9% (2007); Median home value: $55,889 (2007); Median rent: $271 per month (2000); Median age of housing: 52 years (2000).
Safety: Violent crime rate: 30.2 per 10,000 population; Property crime rate: 271.6 per 10,000 population (2006).
Newspapers: Daily American (Local news; Circulation 4,200)
Transportation: Commute to work: 94.0% car, 0.0% public transportation, 1.9% walk, 2.3% work from home (2000); Travel time to work: 42.8% less than 15 minutes, 33.1% 15 to 30 minutes, 12.2% 30 to 45 minutes, 7.0% 45 to 60 minutes, 4.9% 60 minutes or more (2000)
Additional Information Contacts
City of West Frankfort . . . . (618) 932-3262
http://www.westfrankfort-il.com
West Frankfort Chamber of Commerce . . . . (618) 932-2181
http://www.westfrankfort.com

WHITTINGTON (unincorporated postal area, zip code 62897). Covers a land area of 14.931 square miles and a water area of 0.050 square miles. Located at 38.08° N. Lat.; 88.92° W. Long. Elevation is 443 feet.
Population: 335 (2000); Race: 100.0% White, 0.0% Black, 0.0% Asian, 0.0% Hispanic of any race (2000); Density: 22.4 persons per square mile (2000); Age: 26.3% under 18, 12.5% over 64 (2000); Marriage status: 16.5% never married, 62.6% now married, 7.1% widowed, 13.8% divorced (2000); Foreign born: 0.0% (2000); Ancestry (includes multiple ancestries): 19.9% English, 16.5% United States or American, 12.8% German, 9.8% Irish, 4.9% Other groups (2000).
Economy: Employment by occupation: 11.4% management, 8.3% professional, 20.5% services, 31.1% sales, 0.0% farming, 6.8% construction, 22.0% production (2000).
Income: Per capita income: $14,399 (2000); Median household income: $27,708 (2000); Poverty rate: 14.3% (2000).
Education: Percent of population age 25 and over with: High school diploma (including GED) or higher: 79.5% (2000); Bachelor's degree or higher: 10.5% (2000).
Housing: Homeownership rate: 88.0% (2000); Median home value: $63,100 (2000); Median rent: $325 per month (2000); Median age of housing: 34 years (2000).
Transportation: Commute to work: 80.8% car, 0.0% public transportation, 6.2% walk, 13.1% work from home (2000); Travel time to work: 46.0% less than 15 minutes, 23.9% 15 to 30 minutes, 11.5% 30 to 45 minutes, 15.0% 45 to 60 minutes, 3.5% 60 minutes or more (2000)

ZEIGLER (city). Covers a land area of 0.860 square miles and a water area of 0 square miles. Located at 37.90° N. Lat.; 89.05° W. Long. Elevation is 410 feet.

Population: 1,752 (1990); 1,669 (2000); 1,776 (2007); 1,817 (2012 projected); Race: 98.8% White, 0.3% Black, 0.1% Asian, 0.8% Hispanic of any race (2007); Density: 2,065.3 persons per square mile (2007); Average household size: 2.28 (2007); Median age: 39.1 (2007); Males per 100 females: 95.2 (2007); Marriage status: 20.2% never married, 55.4% now married, 12.1% widowed, 12.3% divorced (2000); Foreign born: 1.0% (2000); Ancestry (includes multiple ancestries): 21.3% United States or American, 14.4% German, 10.5% Irish, 9.4% English, 7.2% Other groups (2000).
Economy: Single-family building permits issued: 0 (2007); Multi-family building permits issued: 0 (2007); Employment by occupation: 6.1% management, 14.3% professional, 18.0% services, 22.1% sales, 0.0% farming, 15.1% construction, 24.4% production (2000).
Income: Per capita income: $16,782 (2007); Median household income: $28,629 (2007); Average household income: $36,388 (2007); Percent of households with income of $100,000 or more: 4.1% (2007); Poverty rate: 17.5% (2000).
Education: Percent of population age 25 and over with: High school diploma (including GED) or higher: 73.5% (2007); Bachelor's degree or higher: 8.5% (2007); Master's degree or higher: 1.4% (2007).

School District(s)

Zeigler-Royalton CUSD 188 (PK-12)
2005-06 Enrollment: 664 . . . . (618) 596-5841
Housing: Homeownership rate: 78.0% (2007); Median home value: $41,250 (2007); Median rent: $210 per month (2000); Median age of housing: 60+ years (2000).
Safety: Violent crime rate: 784.8 per 10,000 population; Property crime rate: 368.6 per 10,000 population (2006).
Transportation: Commute to work: 94.0% car, 0.0% public transportation, 3.6% walk, 1.7% work from home (2000); Travel time to work: 26.7% less than 15 minutes, 41.5% 15 to 30 minutes, 19.7% 30 to 45 minutes, 4.6% 45 to 60 minutes, 7.5% 60 minutes or more (2000)

Fulton County

Located in west central Illinois; bounded on the southeast by the Illinois River; drained by the Spoon River. Covers a land area of 865.62 square miles, a water area of 16.97 square miles, and is located in the Central Time Zone. The county was founded in 1823. County seat is Lewistown.

Fulton County is part of the Canton, IL Micropolitan Statistical Area. The entire metro area includes: Fulton County, IL

Population: 38,080 (1990); 38,250 (2000); 37,696 (2007); 37,317 (2012 projected); Race: 94.8% White, 3.9% Black, 0.3% Asian, 1.5% Hispanic of any race (2007); Density: 43.5 persons per square mile (2007); Average household size: 2.55 (2007); Median age: 40.4 (2007); Males per 100 females: 106.6 (2007).
Religion: Five largest groups: 10.2% The United Methodist Church, 5.2% Catholic Church, 4.4% Christian Church (Disciples of Christ), 2.9% Christian Churches and Churches of Christ, 2.3% Church of the Nazarene (2000).
Economy: Unemployment rate: 5.4% (4/2008); Total civilian labor force: 18,141 (4/2008); Leading industries: 23.4% health care and social assistance; 22.2% retail trade; 12.5% accommodation & food services (2005); Farms: 1,055 totaling 413,415 acres (2002); Companies that employ 500 or more persons: 1 (2006); Companies that employ 100 to 499 persons: 9 (2006); Companies that employ less than 100 persons: 711 (2006); Black-owned businesses: n/a (2002); Hispanic-owned businesses: n/a (2002); Asian-owned businesses: n/a (2002); Women-owned businesses: n/a (2002); Retail sales per capita: $9,765 (2008). Single-family building permits issued: 61 (2007); Multi-family building permits issued: 0 (2007).
Income: Per capita income: $20,920 (2007); Median household income: $40,889 (2007); Average household income: $51,427 (2007); Percent of households with income of $100,000 or more: 9.5% (2007); Poverty rate: 12.1% (2005); Bankruptcy rate: 3.77% (2007).
Taxes: Total county taxes per capita: $110 (2006); County property taxes per capita: $110 (2006).
Education: Percent of population age 25 and over with: High school diploma (including GED) or higher: 78.1% (2007); Bachelor's degree or higher: 11.5% (2007); Master's degree or higher: 3.7% (2007).
Housing: Homeownership rate: 76.5% (2007); Median home value: $89,313 (2007); Median rent: $282 per month (2000); Median age of housing: 51 years (2000).
Health: Birth rate: 113.2 per 10,000 population (2007); Death rate: 127.6 per 10,000 population (2007); Age-adjusted cancer mortality rate: 221.1 deaths per 100,000 population (2005); Number of physicians: 8.6 per 10,000 population (2005); Hospital beds: 33.2 per 10,000 population (2004); Hospital admissions: 839.9 per 10,000 population (2004).
Elections: 2004 Presidential election results: 45.9% Bush, 53.3% Kerry, 0.1% Nader, 0.7% Badnarik
National and State Parks: Anderson Lake State Conservation Area; Dickson Mounds State Park; Rice Lake State Conservation Area
Additional Information Contacts
Fulton County Government . . . . (309) 547-3041
http://www.fultonco.org
Canton Chamber of Commerce . . . . (309) 647-2677
City of Canton . . . . (309) 647-0065
http://www.cantonillinois.org
Lewistown Chamber of Commerce . . . . (309) 547-4300
http://www.lewistownillinois.us

Fulton County Communities

ASTORIA (village). Covers a land area of 0.590 square miles and a water area of 0 square miles. Located at 40.22° N. Lat.; 90.35° W. Long. Elevation is 712 feet.
History: The villages of Washington, laid out in 1836, and Vienna, platted in 1837, were later combined and named Astoria, for John Jacob Astor who owned land in the area. Astoria was a station on the stagecoach line between Peoria and Quincy.
Population: 1,228 (1990); 1,193 (2000); 1,185 (2007); 1,174 (2012 projected); Race: 98.6% White, 0.0% Black, 0.6% Asian, 0.9% Hispanic of any race (2007); Density: 2,007.2 persons per square mile (2007); Average household size: 2.35 (2007); Median age: 41.1 (2007); Males per 100 females: 92.1 (2007); Marriage status: 18.1% never married, 63.4% now married, 10.5% widowed, 8.0% divorced (2000); Foreign born: 0.2% (2000); Ancestry (includes multiple ancestries): 24.5% German, 16.0% United States or American, 12.5% English, 5.9% Irish, 5.6% Other groups (2000).
Economy: Single-family building permits issued: 0 (2007); Multi-family building permits issued: 0 (2007); Employment by occupation: 8.3% management, 14.5% professional, 21.6% services, 15.6% sales, 3.0% farming, 8.1% construction, 28.9% production (2000).
Income: Per capita income: $17,212 (2007); Median household income: $33,352 (2007); Average household income: $39,545 (2007); Percent of households with income of $100,000 or more: 3.8% (2007); Poverty rate: 11.3% (2000).
Education: Percent of population age 25 and over with: High school diploma (including GED) or higher: 79.3% (2007); Bachelor's degree or higher: 9.6% (2007); Master's degree or higher: 2.7% (2007).

School District(s)

Astoria CUSD 1 (KG-12)
2005-06 Enrollment: 344 . . . . (309) 329-2111
Housing: Homeownership rate: 76.4% (2007); Median home value: $49,167 (2007); Median rent: $226 per month (2000); Median age of housing: 60+ years (2000).
Safety: Violent crime rate: 34.5 per 10,000 population; Property crime rate: 163.8 per 10,000 population (2006).
Newspapers: South Fulton Argus (Regional news; Circulation 2,200)
Transportation: Commute to work: 90.7% car, 0.0% public transportation, 4.9% walk, 3.9% work from home (2000); Travel time to work: 38.4% less than 15 minutes, 17.4% 15 to 30 minutes, 15.9% 30 to 45 minutes, 14.4% 45 to 60 minutes, 13.9% 60 minutes or more (2000)

AVON (village). Covers a land area of 0.443 square miles and a water area of 0 square miles. Located at 40.66° N. Lat.; 90.43° W. Long. Elevation is 640 feet.
Population: 963 (1990); 915 (2000); 857 (2007); 858 (2012 projected); Race: 98.6% White, 0.0% Black, 0.2% Asian, 0.7% Hispanic of any race (2007); Density: 1,934.4 persons per square mile (2007); Average household size: 2.40 (2007); Median age: 40.9 (2007); Males per 100 females: 93.0 (2007); Marriage status: 20.1% never married, 57.8% now married, 8.3% widowed, 13.8% divorced (2000); Foreign born: 0.8% (2000); Ancestry (includes multiple ancestries): 20.9% German, 12.3% Irish, 10.1% English, 9.9% United States or American, 5.3% Swedish (2000).
Economy: Single-family building permits issued: 0 (2007); Multi-family building permits issued: 0 (2007); Employment by occupation: 8.0%

management, 12.7% professional, 22.4% services, 15.3% sales, 1.0% farming, 9.7% construction, 30.9% production (2000).
Income: Per capita income: $20,461 (2007); Median household income: $41,339 (2007); Average household income: $49,118 (2007); Percent of households with income of $100,000 or more: 8.1% (2007); Poverty rate: 11.7% (2000).
Education: Percent of population age 25 and over with: High school diploma (including GED) or higher: 81.5% (2007); Bachelor's degree or higher: 9.8% (2007); Master's degree or higher: 2.9% (2007).

School District(s)

Avon CUSD 176 (PK-12)
2005-06 Enrollment: 273 . . . . (309) 465-3708
Housing: Homeownership rate: 78.4% (2007); Median home value: $71,333 (2007); Median rent: $202 per month (2000); Median age of housing: 48 years (2000).
Transportation: Commute to work: 92.9% car, 0.0% public transportation, 3.9% walk, 2.0% work from home (2000); Travel time to work: 28.1% less than 15 minutes, 27.9% 15 to 30 minutes, 34.7% 30 to 45 minutes, 3.5% 45 to 60 minutes, 5.8% 60 minutes or more (2000)

BANNER (village). Covers a land area of 0.336 square miles and a water area of 0 square miles. Located at 40.51° N. Lat.; 89.91° W. Long. Elevation is 469 feet.
Population: 160 (1990); 149 (2000); 135 (2007); 132 (2012 projected); Race: 94.8% White, 0.0% Black, 0.0% Asian, 5.2% Hispanic of any race (2007); Density: 401.9 persons per square mile (2007); Average household size: 2.76 (2007); Median age: 36.5 (2007); Males per 100 females: 87.5 (2007); Marriage status: 30.0% never married, 53.6% now married, 7.3% widowed, 9.1% divorced (2000); Foreign born: 0.0% (2000); Ancestry (includes multiple ancestries): 26.2% United States or American, 20.6% German, 19.1% English, 5.7% Other groups, 5.0% Irish (2000).
Economy: Employment by occupation: 14.8% management, 9.3% professional, 25.9% services, 11.1% sales, 0.0% farming, 16.7% construction, 22.2% production (2000).
Income: Per capita income: $16,667 (2007); Median household income: $41,071 (2007); Average household income: $45,918 (2007); Percent of households with income of $100,000 or more: 8.2% (2007); Poverty rate: 19.1% (2000).
Education: Percent of population age 25 and over with: High school diploma (including GED) or higher: 77.7% (2007); Bachelor's degree or higher: 3.2% (2007); Master's degree or higher: 0.0% (2007).
Housing: Homeownership rate: 77.6% (2007); Median home value: $71,429 (2007); Median rent: $317 per month (2000); Median age of housing: 43 years (2000).
Transportation: Commute to work: 90.4% car, 0.0% public transportation, 0.0% walk, 9.6% work from home (2000); Travel time to work: 0.0% less than 15 minutes, 25.5% 15 to 30 minutes, 51.1% 30 to 45 minutes, 19.1% 45 to 60 minutes, 4.3% 60 minutes or more (2000)

BRYANT (village). Covers a land area of 0.256 square miles and a water area of 0 square miles. Located at 40.46° N. Lat.; 90.09° W. Long. Elevation is 607 feet.
Population: 273 (1990); 255 (2000); 252 (2007); 248 (2012 projected); Race: 97.6% White, 0.8% Black, 0.4% Asian, 1.2% Hispanic of any race (2007); Density: 982.9 persons per square mile (2007); Average household size: 2.60 (2007); Median age: 33.0 (2007); Males per 100 females: 93.8 (2007); Marriage status: 26.1% never married, 58.4% now married, 9.3% widowed, 6.2% divorced (2000); Foreign born: 0.0% (2000); Ancestry (includes multiple ancestries): 22.4% German, 17.7% Irish, 11.9% Other groups, 10.2% English, 9.5% United States or American (2000).
Economy: Employment by occupation: 8.8% management, 11.6% professional, 18.4% services, 29.3% sales, 3.4% farming, 3.4% construction, 25.2% production (2000).
Income: Per capita income: $15,774 (2007); Median household income: $29,423 (2007); Average household income: $40,979 (2007); Percent of households with income of $100,000 or more: 4.1% (2007); Poverty rate: 14.3% (2000).
Education: Percent of population age 25 and over with: High school diploma (including GED) or higher: 78.4% (2007); Bachelor's degree or higher: 8.0% (2007); Master's degree or higher: 1.2% (2007).
Housing: Homeownership rate: 81.4% (2007); Median home value: $56,818 (2007); Median rent: $267 per month (2000); Median age of housing: 49 years (2000).
Transportation: Commute to work: 100.0% car, 0.0% public transportation, 0.0% walk, 0.0% work from home (2000); Travel time to work: 23.1% less than 15 minutes, 39.2% 15 to 30 minutes, 9.8% 30 to 45 minutes, 14.0% 45 to 60 minutes, 14.0% 60 minutes or more (2000)

CANTON (city). Covers a land area of 7.849 square miles and a water area of 0.163 square miles. Located at 40.55° N. Lat.; 90.03° W. Long. Elevation is 646 feet.
History: Canton was founded in 1825 by Isaac Swan of New York. He selected the name for the town in the belief that the city of Canton in China was located directly opposite on the globe.
Population: 14,212 (1990); 15,288 (2000); 14,864 (2007); 14,570 (2012 projected); Race: 88.5% White, 9.7% Black, 0.5% Asian, 2.8% Hispanic of any race (2007); Density: 1,893.8 persons per square mile (2007); Average household size: 2.69 (2007); Median age: 37.9 (2007); Males per 100 females: 118.7 (2007); Marriage status: 17.2% never married, 56.7% now married, 9.0% widowed, 17.1% divorced (2000); Foreign born: 1.2% (2000); Ancestry (includes multiple ancestries): 17.4% German, 11.4% United States or American, 10.5% English, 7.7% Irish, 5.7% Other groups (2000).
Economy: Single-family building permits issued: 7 (2007); Multi-family building permits issued: 0 (2007); Employment by occupation: 7.3% management, 20.1% professional, 21.0% services, 27.6% sales, 0.6% farming, 10.3% construction, 13.1% production (2000).
Income: Per capita income: $19,217 (2007); Median household income: $36,071 (2007); Average household income: $47,258 (2007); Percent of households with income of $100,000 or more: 7.9% (2007); Poverty rate: 13.4% (2000).
Education: Percent of population age 25 and over with: High school diploma (including GED) or higher: 71.9% (2007); Bachelor's degree or higher: 11.8% (2007); Master's degree or higher: 3.7% (2007).

School District(s)

Canton Union SD 66 (PK-12)
2005-06 Enrollment: 2,685 . . . . (309) 647-9411
Dept of Corrections Sch Dist 428 (08-12)
2005-06 Enrollment: 2,271 . . . . (217) 522-2666
Fulton/Schuyler Roe (06-12)
2005-06 Enrollment: 37 . . . . (309) 547-3041

Two-year College(s)

Graham Hospital School of Nursing (Private, Not-for-profit)
Fall 2007 Enrollment: 62 . . . . (309) 647-4086
2007-08 Tuition: In-state $8,550; Out-of-state $8,550
Spoon River College (Public)
Fall 2007 Enrollment: 2,139. . . . . (309) 647-4645
2007-08 Tuition: In-state $4,410; Out-of-state $5,460
Housing: Homeownership rate: 69.1% (2007); Median home value: $91,201 (2007); Median rent: $317 per month (2000); Median age of housing: 48 years (2000).
Hospitals: Graham Hospital (124 beds)
Safety: Violent crime rate: 29.5 per 10,000 population; Property crime rate: 249.0 per 10,000 population (2006).
Newspapers: The Daily Ledger (Local news; Circulation 9,200)
Transportation: Commute to work: 94.2% car, 0.3% public transportation, 2.0% walk, 2.1% work from home (2000); Travel time to work: 52.0% less than 15 minutes, 13.1% 15 to 30 minutes, 12.4% 30 to 45 minutes, 16.5% 45 to 60 minutes, 5.9% 60 minutes or more (2000)
Airports: Ingersoll (general aviation)
Additional Information Contacts
Canton Chamber of Commerce. . . . . (309) 647-2677
City of Canton . . . . (309) 647-0065
http://www.cantonillinois.org

CUBA (city). Covers a land area of 0.542 square miles and a water area of 0 square miles. Located at 40.49° N. Lat.; 90.19° W. Long. Elevation is 682 feet.
History: Incorporated 1853.
Population: 1,440 (1990); 1,418 (2000); 1,379 (2007); 1,373 (2012 projected); Race: 98.7% White, 0.1% Black, 0.1% Asian, 0.6% Hispanic of any race (2007); Density: 2,544.7 persons per square mile (2007); Average household size: 2.54 (2007); Median age: 38.7 (2007); Males per 100 females: 86.1 (2007); Marriage status: 21.3% never married, 55.5% now married, 11.5% widowed, 11.7% divorced (2000); Foreign born: 0.8% (2000); Ancestry (includes multiple ancestries): 16.9% German, 14.2% United States or American, 12.7% English, 7.2% Irish, 4.6% Other groups (2000).
Economy: Single-family building permits issued: 0 (2007); Multi-family building permits issued: 0 (2007); Employment by occupation: 6.0%

management, 13.6% professional, 23.4% services, 28.0% sales, 0.4% farming, 10.2% construction, 18.4% production (2000).
Income: Per capita income: $16,805 (2007); Median household income: $34,643 (2007); Average household income: $40,852 (2007); Percent of households with income of $100,000 or more: 4.8% (2007); Poverty rate: 9.8% (2000).
Education: Percent of population age 25 and over with: High school diploma (including GED) or higher: 78.4% (2007); Bachelor's degree or higher: 9.0% (2007); Master's degree or higher: 3.2% (2007).

School District(s)

CUSD 3 Fulton County (PK-12)
2005-06 Enrollment: 539 . . . . (309) 785-5021
Housing: Homeownership rate: 78.3% (2007); Median home value: $71,827 (2007); Median rent: $286 per month (2000); Median age of housing: 58 years (2000).
Safety: Violent crime rate: 7.2 per 10,000 population; Property crime rate: 21.7 per 10,000 population (2006).
Transportation: Commute to work: 93.7% car, 0.0% public transportation, 4.3% walk, 1.2% work from home (2000); Travel time to work: 39.2% less than 15 minutes, 21.2% 15 to 30 minutes, 14.0% 30 to 45 minutes, 11.0% 45 to 60 minutes, 14.6% 60 minutes or more (2000)

DUNFERMLINE (village). Covers a land area of 0.131 square miles and a water area of 0 square miles. Located at 40.49° N. Lat.; 90.03° W. Long. Elevation is 633 feet.
Population: 259 (1990); 262 (2000); 251 (2007); 241 (2012 projected); Race: 94.0% White, 0.0% Black, 0.0% Asian, 0.0% Hispanic of any race (2007); Density: 1,916.0 persons per square mile (2007); Average household size: 2.41 (2007); Median age: 40.9 (2007); Males per 100 females: 100.8 (2007); Marriage status: 17.6% never married, 64.3% now married, 5.7% widowed, 12.4% divorced (2000); Foreign born: 0.0% (2000); Ancestry (includes multiple ancestries): 18.3% United States or American, 15.6% English, 11.7% German, 4.3% Croatian, 3.9% Other groups (2000).
Economy: Single-family building permits issued: 1 (2007); Multi-family building permits issued: 0 (2007); Employment by occupation: 5.0% management, 12.5% professional, 20.8% services, 24.2% sales, 0.0% farming, 20.0% construction, 17.5% production (2000).
Income: Per capita income: $20,398 (2007); Median household income: $43,125 (2007); Average household income: $49,231 (2007); Percent of households with income of $100,000 or more: 9.6% (2007); Poverty rate: 9.5% (2000).
Education: Percent of population age 25 and over with: High school diploma (including GED) or higher: 82.0% (2007); Bachelor's degree or higher: 1.1% (2007); Master's degree or higher: 0.0% (2007).
Housing: Homeownership rate: 86.5% (2007); Median home value: $79,231 (2007); Median rent: $260 per month (2000); Median age of housing: 46 years (2000).
Safety: Violent crime rate: 0.0 per 10,000 population; Property crime rate: 68.3 per 10,000 population (2006).
Transportation: Commute to work: 96.6% car, 0.0% public transportation, 0.0% walk, 3.4% work from home (2000); Travel time to work: 36.0% less than 15 minutes, 26.3% 15 to 30 minutes, 12.3% 30 to 45 minutes, 16.7% 45 to 60 minutes, 8.8% 60 minutes or more (2000)

ELLISVILLE (village). Covers a land area of 0.271 square miles and a water area of 0 square miles. Located at 40.62° N. Lat.; 90.30° W. Long. Elevation is 551 feet.
Population: 116 (1990); 87 (2000); 87 (2007); 87 (2012 projected); Race: 100.0% White, 0.0% Black, 0.0% Asian, 0.0% Hispanic of any race (2007); Density: 320.6 persons per square mile (2007); Average household size: 2.02 (2007); Median age: 47.5 (2007); Males per 100 females: 93.3 (2007); Marriage status: 23.1% never married, 58.2% now married, 14.3% widowed, 4.4% divorced (2000); Foreign born: 0.0% (2000); Ancestry (includes multiple ancestries): 17.6% German, 11.1% Irish, 8.3% United States or American, 7.4% English, 4.6% Other groups (2000).
Economy: Employment by occupation: 3.3% management, 6.7% professional, 15.0% services, 25.0% sales, 0.0% farming, 23.3% construction, 26.7% production (2000).
Income: Per capita income: $21,236 (2007); Median household income: $43,214 (2007); Average household income: $42,965 (2007); Percent of households with income of $100,000 or more: 4.7% (2007); Poverty rate: 3.7% (2000).
Education: Percent of population age 25 and over with: High school diploma (including GED) or higher: 81.2% (2007); Bachelor's degree or higher: 0.0% (2007); Master's degree or higher: 0.0% (2007).
Housing: Homeownership rate: 83.7% (2007); Median home value: $35,000 (2007); Median rent: $225 per month (2000); Median age of housing: 60+ years (2000).
Transportation: Commute to work: 91.2% car, 0.0% public transportation, 8.8% walk, 0.0% work from home (2000); Travel time to work: 12.3% less than 15 minutes, 64.9% 15 to 30 minutes, 12.3% 30 to 45 minutes, 0.0% 45 to 60 minutes, 10.5% 60 minutes or more (2000)

FAIRVIEW (village). Covers a land area of 4.162 square miles and a water area of 0.074 square miles. Located at 40.63° N. Lat.; 90.16° W. Long. Elevation is 735 feet.
Population: 510 (1990); 493 (2000); 475 (2007); 473 (2012 projected); Race: 99.2% White, 0.0% Black, 0.2% Asian, 0.2% Hispanic of any race (2007); Density: 114.1 persons per square mile (2007); Average household size: 2.44 (2007); Median age: 39.8 (2007); Males per 100 females: 107.4 (2007); Marriage status: 27.1% never married, 53.7% now married, 9.7% widowed, 9.5% divorced (2000); Foreign born: 0.4% (2000); Ancestry (includes multiple ancestries): 32.5% German, 17.7% English, 15.0% Irish, 8.1% Other groups, 4.7% United States or American (2000).
Economy: Single-family building permits issued: 0 (2007); Multi-family building permits issued: 0 (2007); Employment by occupation: 7.4% management, 20.3% professional, 14.7% services, 14.7% sales, 0.9% farming, 11.5% construction, 30.4% production (2000).
Income: Per capita income: $20,721 (2007); Median household income: $40,893 (2007); Average household income: $50,474 (2007); Percent of households with income of $100,000 or more: 8.7% (2007); Poverty rate: 10.9% (2000).
Education: Percent of population age 25 and over with: High school diploma (including GED) or higher: 88.4% (2007); Bachelor's degree or higher: 15.5% (2007); Master's degree or higher: 4.2% (2007).
Housing: Homeownership rate: 86.2% (2007); Median home value: $90,556 (2007); Median rent: $367 per month (2000); Median age of housing: 60+ years (2000).
Safety: Violent crime rate: 104.2 per 10,000 population; Property crime rate: 145.8 per 10,000 population (2006).
Transportation: Commute to work: 93.9% car, 0.0% public transportation, 4.2% walk, 1.9% work from home (2000); Travel time to work: 22.4% less than 15 minutes, 27.6% 15 to 30 minutes, 20.0% 30 to 45 minutes, 20.0% 45 to 60 minutes, 10.0% 60 minutes or more (2000)

FARMINGTON (city). Covers a land area of 1.241 square miles and a water area of 0 square miles. Located at 40.69° N. Lat.; 90.00° W. Long. Elevation is 745 feet.
History: Farmington was laid out in 1834, and grew as a mining town. In 1856 Farmington was the scene of a "whiskey war" when a group of women marched on the saloons, breaking windows and smashing bottles.
Population: 2,547 (1990); 2,601 (2000); 2,478 (2007); 2,391 (2012 projected); Race: 98.6% White, 0.1% Black, 0.1% Asian, 0.8% Hispanic of any race (2007); Density: 1,996.1 persons per square mile (2007); Average household size: 2.53 (2007); Median age: 40.4 (2007); Males per 100 females: 90.5 (2007); Marriage status: 20.8% never married, 59.8% now married, 11.7% widowed, 7.7% divorced (2000); Foreign born: 0.7% (2000); Ancestry (includes multiple ancestries): 27.5% German, 14.7% Irish, 14.1% English, 13.3% United States or American, 5.2% Italian (2000).
Economy: Single-family building permits issued: 3 (2007); Multi-family building permits issued: 0 (2007); Employment by occupation: 10.1% management, 13.8% professional, 20.5% services, 21.0% sales, 0.0% farming, 10.2% construction, 24.3% production (2000).
Income: Per capita income: $23,561 (2007); Median household income: $44,710 (2007); Average household income: $57,224 (2007); Percent of households with income of $100,000 or more: 10.8% (2007); Poverty rate: 7.0% (2000).
Education: Percent of population age 25 and over with: High school diploma (including GED) or higher: 84.7% (2007); Bachelor's degree or higher: 11.7% (2007); Master's degree or higher: 5.0% (2007).

School District(s)

Farmington Central CUSD 265 (PK-12)
2005-06 Enrollment: 1,404 . . . . (309) 245-1000
Housing: Homeownership rate: 80.0% (2007); Median home value: $93,500 (2007); Median rent: $263 per month (2000); Median age of housing: 60 years (2000).

Safety: Violent crime rate: 4.0 per 10,000 population; Property crime rate: 123.3 per 10,000 population (2006).
Transportation: Commute to work: 97.0% car, 0.0% public transportation, 2.0% walk, 1.0% work from home (2000); Travel time to work: 37.7% less than 15 minutes, 15.9% 15 to 30 minutes, 27.5% 30 to 45 minutes, 13.8% 45 to 60 minutes, 5.0% 60 minutes or more (2000)

IPAVA (village). Covers a land area of 0.270 square miles and a water area of 0 square miles. Located at 40.35° N. Lat.; 90.32° W. Long. Elevation is 659 feet.
History: Vestiges of Camp Ellis, a World War II prisoner-of-war camp, nearby.
Population: 483 (1990); 506 (2000); 458 (2007); 463 (2012 projected); Race: 100.0% White, 0.0% Black, 0.0% Asian, 0.4% Hispanic of any race (2007); Density: 1,698.9 persons per square mile (2007); Average household size: 2.23 (2007); Median age: 40.2 (2007); Males per 100 females: 100.0 (2007); Marriage status: 15.8% never married, 61.5% now married, 12.1% widowed, 10.6% divorced (2000); Foreign born: 1.0% (2000); Ancestry (includes multiple ancestries): 23.7% United States or American, 20.8% German, 9.3% English, 7.2% Other groups, 7.2% Irish (2000).
Economy: Single-family building permits issued: 1 (2007); Multi-family building permits issued: 0 (2007); Employment by occupation: 9.5% management, 11.3% professional, 13.5% services, 27.9% sales, 1.4% farming, 13.1% construction, 23.4% production (2000).
Income: Per capita income: $18,619 (2007); Median household income: $36,591 (2007); Average household income: $41,598 (2007); Percent of households with income of $100,000 or more: 3.4% (2007); Poverty rate: 10.1% (2000).
Education: Percent of population age 25 and over with: High school diploma (including GED) or higher: 75.7% (2007); Bachelor's degree or higher: 7.0% (2007); Master's degree or higher: 1.0% (2007).
Housing: Homeownership rate: 85.4% (2007); Median home value: $57,069 (2007); Median rent: $227 per month (2000); Median age of housing: 60+ years (2000).
Transportation: Commute to work: 94.0% car, 0.0% public transportation, 2.3% walk, 2.3% work from home (2000); Travel time to work: 17.5% less than 15 minutes, 25.6% 15 to 30 minutes, 40.3% 30 to 45 minutes, 5.7% 45 to 60 minutes, 10.9% 60 minutes or more (2000)

LEWISTOWN (city). County seat. Covers a land area of 1.838 square miles and a water area of 0 square miles. Located at 40.39° N. Lat.; 90.15° W. Long. Elevation is 591 feet.
History: Lewiston was founded in 1821 by Major Ossian M. Ross, who had received the land for his service in the War of 1812. The town was named for the Major's son, Lewis. In 1823 Ross organized Fulton County and had Lewiston named as the seat, with the courthouse built on land he donated.
Population: 2,592 (1990); 2,522 (2000); 2,458 (2007); 2,400 (2012 projected); Race: 98.9% White, 0.0% Black, 0.1% Asian, 1.0% Hispanic of any race (2007); Density: 1,337.4 persons per square mile (2007); Average household size: 2.30 (2007); Median age: 43.5 (2007); Males per 100 females: 89.5 (2007); Marriage status: 18.7% never married, 57.9% now married, 12.1% widowed, 11.4% divorced (2000); Foreign born: 0.5% (2000); Ancestry (includes multiple ancestries): 14.9% United States or American, 14.7% German, 10.5% English, 10.0% Irish, 6.0% Other groups (2000).
Economy: Single-family building permits issued: 3 (2007); Multi-family building permits issued: 0 (2007); Employment by occupation: 9.4% management, 16.4% professional, 21.6% services, 23.4% sales, 0.7% farming, 8.2% construction, 20.4% production (2000).
Income: Per capita income: $20,119 (2007); Median household income: $39,296 (2007); Average household income: $45,675 (2007); Percent of households with income of $100,000 or more: 6.8% (2007); Poverty rate: 7.1% (2000).
Education: Percent of population age 25 and over with: High school diploma (including GED) or higher: 80.0% (2007); Bachelor's degree or higher: 11.8% (2007); Master's degree or higher: 4.9% (2007).

School District(s)

Lewistown CUSD 97 (PK-12)
2005-06 Enrollment: 777 . . . . (309) 547-5826
West Central Ill Spec Educ Coop (07-12)
2005-06 Enrollment: 80 . . . . (309) 837-3911
Housing: Homeownership rate: 67.3% (2007); Median home value: $82,969 (2007); Median rent: $215 per month (2000); Median age of housing: 51 years (2000).
Safety: Violent crime rate: 122.5 per 10,000 population; Property crime rate: 183.8 per 10,000 population (2006).
Newspapers: Fulton Democrat (Local news; Circulation 5,300)
Transportation: Commute to work: 88.3% car, 0.7% public transportation, 6.3% walk, 2.7% work from home (2000); Travel time to work: 41.7% less than 15 minutes, 24.3% 15 to 30 minutes, 13.9% 30 to 45 minutes, 9.7% 45 to 60 minutes, 10.5% 60 minutes or more (2000)
Additional Information Contacts
Lewistown Chamber of Commerce . . . . (309) 547-4300
http://www.lewistownillinois.us

LIVERPOOL (village). Covers a land area of 0.081 square miles and a water area of 0.001 square miles. Located at 40.39° N. Lat.; 90.00° W. Long. Elevation is 446 feet.
History: Liverpool, named for the town in England, began as a river town and shipping center. Commercial fishing developed later.
Population: 129 (1990); 119 (2000); 108 (2007); 105 (2012 projected); Race: 100.0% White, 0.0% Black, 0.0% Asian, 0.9% Hispanic of any race (2007); Density: 1,339.3 persons per square mile (2007); Average household size: 2.51 (2007); Median age: 34.2 (2007); Males per 100 females: 103.8 (2007); Marriage status: 37.5% never married, 46.9% now married, 9.4% widowed, 6.3% divorced (2000); Foreign born: 0.0% (2000); Ancestry (includes multiple ancestries): 38.9% United States or American, 10.5% British, 9.5% Other groups, 4.2% English, 3.2% Austrian (2000).
Economy: Employment by occupation: 6.7% management, 0.0% professional, 30.0% services, 6.7% sales, 6.7% farming, 36.7% construction, 13.3% production (2000).
Income: Per capita income: $18,519 (2007); Median household income: $39,167 (2007); Average household income: $46,512 (2007); Percent of households with income of $100,000 or more: 9.3% (2007); Poverty rate: 2.1% (2000).
Education: Percent of population age 25 and over with: High school diploma (including GED) or higher: 60.6% (2007); Bachelor's degree or higher: 0.0% (2007); Master's degree or higher: 0.0% (2007).
Housing: Homeownership rate: 81.4% (2007); Median home value: $47,000 (2007); Median rent: $375 per month (2000); Median age of housing: 47 years (2000).
Transportation: Commute to work: 100.0% car, 0.0% public transportation, 0.0% walk, 0.0% work from home (2000); Travel time to work: 6.7% less than 15 minutes, 56.7% 15 to 30 minutes, 16.7% 30 to 45 minutes, 6.7% 45 to 60 minutes, 13.3% 60 minutes or more (2000)

LONDON MILLS (village). Covers a land area of 0.694 square miles and a water area of 0 square miles. Located at 40.71° N. Lat.; 90.26° W. Long. Elevation is 541 feet.
Population: 485 (1990); 447 (2000); 449 (2007); 442 (2012 projected); Race: 99.6% White, 0.0% Black, 0.0% Asian, 0.2% Hispanic of any race (2007); Density: 647.4 persons per square mile (2007); Average household size: 2.66 (2007); Median age: 36.0 (2007); Males per 100 females: 98.7 (2007); Marriage status: 18.0% never married, 65.5% now married, 2.2% widowed, 14.2% divorced (2000); Foreign born: 0.0% (2000); Ancestry (includes multiple ancestries): 23.6% German, 13.8% Irish, 8.4% Swedish, 6.3% English, 5.8% Other groups (2000).
Economy: Employment by occupation: 10.9% management, 12.2% professional, 17.9% services, 14.1% sales, 3.2% farming, 13.5% construction, 28.2% production (2000).
Income: Per capita income: $21,665 (2007); Median household income: $48,438 (2007); Average household income: $57,559 (2007); Percent of households with income of $100,000 or more: 12.4% (2007); Poverty rate: 9.3% (2000).
Education: Percent of population age 25 and over with: High school diploma (including GED) or higher: 80.1% (2007); Bachelor's degree or higher: 12.5% (2007); Master's degree or higher: 3.9% (2007).

School District(s)

Spoon River Valley CUSD 4 (PK-12)
2005-06 Enrollment: 451 . . . . (309) 778-2204
Housing: Homeownership rate: 90.5% (2007); Median home value: $71,154 (2007); Median rent: $234 per month (2000); Median age of housing: 60+ years (2000).
Safety: Violent crime rate: 0.0 per 10,000 population; Property crime rate: 90.9 per 10,000 population (2006).
Transportation: Commute to work: 95.3% car, 0.0% public transportation, 2.0% walk, 2.7% work from home (2000); Travel time to work: 20.5% less than 15 minutes, 22.6% 15 to 30 minutes, 34.2% 30 to 45 minutes, 8.9% 45 to 60 minutes, 13.7% 60 minutes or more (2000)

MARIETTA (village). Covers a land area of 0.269 square miles and a water area of 0 square miles. Located at 40.50° N. Lat.; 90.39° W. Long. Elevation is 650 feet.

Population: 142 (1990); 150 (2000); 167 (2007); 176 (2012 projected); Race: 97.0% White, 0.0% Black, 0.0% Asian, 0.0% Hispanic of any race (2007); Density: 620.2 persons per square mile (2007); Average household size: 2.61 (2007); Median age: 34.6 (2007); Males per 100 females: 114.1 (2007); Marriage status: 18.5% never married, 66.4% now married, 1.7% widowed, 13.4% divorced (2000); Foreign born: 0.0% (2000); Ancestry (includes multiple ancestries): 21.9% German, 17.8% United States or American, 14.4% Irish, 13.7% Other groups, 6.2% English (2000).

Economy: Employment by occupation: 7.5% management, 6.3% professional, 15.0% services, 7.5% sales, 0.0% farming, 12.5% construction, 51.2% production (2000).

Income: Per capita income: $21,452 (2007); Median household income: $48,333 (2007); Average household income: $55,977 (2007); Percent of households with income of $100,000 or more: 15.6% (2007); Poverty rate: 2.7% (2000).

Education: Percent of population age 25 and over with: High school diploma (including GED) or higher: 78.9% (2007); Bachelor's degree or higher: 4.4% (2007); Master's degree or higher: 0.0% (2007).

Housing: Homeownership rate: 84.4% (2007); Median home value: $37,000 (2007); Median rent: $300 per month (2000); Median age of housing: 58 years (2000).

Transportation: Commute to work: 93.6% car, 0.0% public transportation, 3.8% walk, 2.6% work from home (2000); Travel time to work: 13.2% less than 15 minutes, 43.4% 15 to 30 minutes, 15.8% 30 to 45 minutes, 2.6% 45 to 60 minutes, 25.0% 60 minutes or more (2000)

NORRIS (village). Covers a land area of 0.281 square miles and a water area of 0 square miles. Located at 40.62° N. Lat.; 90.03° W. Long. Elevation is 728 feet.

Population: 212 (1990); 194 (2000); 206 (2007); 212 (2012 projected); Race: 100.0% White, 0.0% Black, 0.0% Asian, 0.0% Hispanic of any race (2007); Density: 732.5 persons per square mile (2007); Average household size: 2.26 (2007); Median age: 44.0 (2007); Males per 100 females: 100.0 (2007); Marriage status: 22.7% never married, 64.3% now married, 6.5% widowed, 6.5% divorced (2000); Foreign born: 0.0% (2000); Ancestry (includes multiple ancestries): 20.5% German, 14.5% Other groups, 13.2% English, 9.1% Polish, 9.1% United States or American (2000).

Economy: Employment by occupation: 6.6% management, 15.1% professional, 16.0% services, 26.4% sales, 0.0% farming, 13.2% construction, 22.6% production (2000).

Income: Per capita income: $20,267 (2007); Median household income: $35,625 (2007); Average household income: $45,879 (2007); Percent of households with income of $100,000 or more: 12.1% (2007); Poverty rate: 4.6% (2000).

Education: Percent of population age 25 and over with: High school diploma (including GED) or higher: 74.7% (2007); Bachelor's degree or higher: 7.8% (2007); Master's degree or higher: 5.8% (2007).

Housing: Homeownership rate: 85.7% (2007); Median home value: $69,231 (2007); Median rent: $263 per month (2000); Median age of housing: 60+ years (2000).

Transportation: Commute to work: 95.3% car, 0.0% public transportation, 4.7% walk, 0.0% work from home (2000); Travel time to work: 36.8% less than 15 minutes, 32.1% 15 to 30 minutes, 17.9% 30 to 45 minutes, 13.2% 45 to 60 minutes, 0.0% 60 minutes or more (2000)

SAINT DAVID (village). Covers a land area of 0.296 square miles and a water area of 0 square miles. Located at 40.49° N. Lat.; 90.05° W. Long. Elevation is 627 feet.

Population: 621 (1990); 587 (2000); 561 (2007); 538 (2012 projected); Race: 99.8% White, 0.2% Black, 0.0% Asian, 0.0% Hispanic of any race (2007); Density: 1,894.3 persons per square mile (2007); Average household size: 2.41 (2007); Median age: 38.3 (2007); Males per 100 females: 109.3 (2007); Marriage status: 17.2% never married, 64.0% now married, 8.3% widowed, 10.6% divorced (2000); Foreign born: 0.7% (2000); Ancestry (includes multiple ancestries): 22.0% United States or American, 12.6% English, 12.4% German, 7.9% Irish, 7.1% Italian (2000).

Economy: Single-family building permits issued: 0 (2007); Multi-family building permits issued: 0 (2007); Employment by occupation: 8.6% management, 14.4% professional, 14.0% services, 25.5% sales, 0.8% farming, 14.0% construction, 22.6% production (2000).

Income: Per capita income: $18,574 (2007); Median household income: $38,594 (2007); Average household income: $44,721 (2007); Percent of households with income of $100,000 or more: 6.4% (2007); Poverty rate: 11.1% (2000).

Education: Percent of population age 25 and over with: High school diploma (including GED) or higher: 79.0% (2007); Bachelor's degree or higher: 4.3% (2007); Master's degree or higher: 1.1% (2007).

Housing: Homeownership rate: 83.7% (2007); Median home value: $65,000 (2007); Median rent: $300 per month (2000); Median age of housing: 59 years (2000).

Transportation: Commute to work: 93.7% car, 0.0% public transportation, 1.7% walk, 1.7% work from home (2000); Travel time to work: 39.3% less than 15 minutes, 21.4% 15 to 30 minutes, 12.4% 30 to 45 minutes, 12.0% 45 to 60 minutes, 15.0% 60 minutes or more (2000)

SMITHFIELD (village). Covers a land area of 0.476 square miles and a water area of 0 square miles. Located at 40.47° N. Lat.; 90.29° W. Long. Elevation is 646 feet.

Population: 277 (1990); 214 (2000); 236 (2007); 246 (2012 projected); Race: 99.6% White, 0.0% Black, 0.0% Asian, 0.0% Hispanic of any race (2007); Density: 496.3 persons per square mile (2007); Average household size: 2.23 (2007); Median age: 46.4 (2007); Males per 100 females: 103.4 (2007); Marriage status: 21.2% never married, 56.4% now married, 12.8% widowed, 9.5% divorced (2000); Foreign born: 1.0% (2000); Ancestry (includes multiple ancestries): 16.3% United States or American, 12.0% German, 9.6% Irish, 8.6% English, 7.2% Eastern European (2000).

Economy: Employment by occupation: 7.1% management, 15.2% professional, 17.2% services, 17.2% sales, 0.0% farming, 18.2% construction, 25.3% production (2000).

Income: Per capita income: $20,254 (2007); Median household income: $40,000 (2007); Average household income: $45,094 (2007); Percent of households with income of $100,000 or more: 2.8% (2007); Poverty rate: 3.8% (2000).

Education: Percent of population age 25 and over with: High school diploma (including GED) or higher: 88.3% (2007); Bachelor's degree or higher: 5.0% (2007); Master's degree or higher: 0.0% (2007).

Housing: Homeownership rate: 84.9% (2007); Median home value: $50,000 (2007); Median rent: $233 per month (2000); Median age of housing: 60+ years (2000).

Transportation: Commute to work: 86.9% car, 5.1% public transportation, 2.0% walk, 2.0% work from home (2000); Travel time to work: 19.6% less than 15 minutes, 37.1% 15 to 30 minutes, 16.5% 30 to 45 minutes, 17.5% 45 to 60 minutes, 9.3% 60 minutes or more (2000)

TABLE GROVE (village). Covers a land area of 0.280 square miles and a water area of 0 square miles. Located at 40.36° N. Lat.; 90.42° W. Long. Elevation is 725 feet.

Population: 408 (1990); 396 (2000); 413 (2007); 417 (2012 projected); Race: 99.5% White, 0.0% Black, 0.0% Asian, 0.0% Hispanic of any race (2007); Density: 1,474.5 persons per square mile (2007); Average household size: 2.31 (2007); Median age: 42.2 (2007); Males per 100 females: 92.1 (2007); Marriage status: 17.0% never married, 62.5% now married, 10.5% widowed, 9.9% divorced (2000); Foreign born: 0.0% (2000); Ancestry (includes multiple ancestries): 21.1% English, 20.1% German, 9.4% Irish, 6.0% United States or American, 4.7% Scottish (2000).

Economy: Employment by occupation: 8.8% management, 16.1% professional, 9.3% services, 23.9% sales, 2.0% farming, 13.2% construction, 26.8% production (2000).

Income: Per capita income: $22,778 (2007); Median household income: $45,357 (2007); Average household income: $52,556 (2007); Percent of households with income of $100,000 or more: 10.1% (2007); Poverty rate: 12.7% (2000).

Education: Percent of population age 25 and over with: High school diploma (including GED) or higher: 85.1% (2007); Bachelor's degree or higher: 11.4% (2007); Master's degree or higher: 3.1% (2007).

School District(s)

V I T CUSD 2 (PK-12)
2005-06 Enrollment: 425 . . . . (309) 758-5138

Housing: Homeownership rate: 87.7% (2007); Median home value: $57,174 (2007); Median rent: $208 per month (2000); Median age of housing: 60+ years (2000).

Transportation: Commute to work: 96.0% car, 0.0% public transportation, 3.0% walk, 1.0% work from home (2000); Travel time to work: 29.1% less

than 15 minutes, 39.2% 15 to 30 minutes, 15.6% 30 to 45 minutes, 3.0% 45 to 60 minutes, 13.1% 60 minutes or more (2000)

VERMONT (village). Covers a land area of 1.263 square miles and a water area of 0 square miles. Located at 40.29° N. Lat.; 90.42° W. Long. Elevation is 692 feet.
Population: 806 (1990); 792 (2000); 771 (2007); 762 (2012 projected); Race: 98.2% White, 0.0% Black, 0.1% Asian, 0.9% Hispanic of any race (2007); Density: 610.5 persons per square mile (2007); Average household size: 2.50 (2007); Median age: 36.7 (2007); Males per 100 females: 110.1 (2007); Marriage status: 23.0% never married, 61.9% now married, 4.9% widowed, 10.2% divorced (2000); Foreign born: 0.6% (2000); Ancestry (includes multiple ancestries): 17.6% German, 14.4% United States or American, 8.2% English, 7.9% Irish, 5.3% Other groups (2000).
Economy: Employment by occupation: 6.9% management, 14.1% professional, 16.2% services, 17.7% sales, 2.1% farming, 7.8% construction, 35.3% production (2000).
Income: Per capita income: $16,754 (2007); Median household income: $36,625 (2007); Average household income: $41,804 (2007); Percent of households with income of $100,000 or more: 4.9% (2007); Poverty rate: 14.2% (2000).
Education: Percent of population age 25 and over with: High school diploma (including GED) or higher: 79.1% (2007); Bachelor's degree or higher: 6.4% (2007); Master's degree or higher: 2.5% (2007).
Housing: Homeownership rate: 84.1% (2007); Median home value: $47,407 (2007); Median rent: $196 per month (2000); Median age of housing: 60+ years (2000).
Safety: Violent crime rate: 64.0 per 10,000 population; Property crime rate: 25.6 per 10,000 population (2006).
Transportation: Commute to work: 90.5% car, 0.0% public transportation, 5.5% walk, 1.8% work from home (2000); Travel time to work: 30.4% less than 15 minutes, 21.7% 15 to 30 minutes, 30.4% 30 to 45 minutes, 6.2% 45 to 60 minutes, 11.2% 60 minutes or more (2000)

Gallatin County

Located in southeastern Illinois, partly in the Ozarks; bounded on the northeast by the Wabash River and the Indiana border, and on the southeast by the Ohio River and the Kentucky border; includes part of Shawnee National Forest. Covers a land area of 323.73 square miles, a water area of 4.68 square miles, and is located in the Central Time Zone. The county was founded in 1812. County seat is Shawneetown.
Population: 6,909 (1990); 6,445 (2000); 6,102 (2007); 5,872 (2012 projected); Race: 98.6% White, 0.3% Black, 0.0% Asian, 0.8% Hispanic of any race (2007); Density: 18.8 persons per square mile (2007); Average household size: 2.33 (2007); Median age: 42.3 (2007); Males per 100 females: 91.9 (2007).
Religion: Five largest groups: 17.7% Catholic Church, 14.1% Southern Baptist Convention, 3.7% The United Methodist Church, 3.1% The Church of Jesus Christ of Latter-day Saints, 2.1% Presbyterian Church (U.S.A.) (2000).
Economy: Unemployment rate: 6.5% (4/2008); Total civilian labor force: 2,649 (4/2008); Leading industries: 16.5% transportation & warehousing; 8.5% retail trade; 4.1% wholesale trade (2005); Farms: 187 totaling 154,446 acres (2002); Companies that employ 500 or more persons: 0 (2006); Companies that employ 100 to 499 persons: 2 (2006); Companies that employ less than 100 persons: 116 (2006); Black-owned businesses: n/a (2002); Hispanic-owned businesses: n/a (2002); Asian-owned businesses: n/a (2002); Women-owned businesses: n/a (2002); Retail sales per capita: $4,686 (2008). Single-family building permits issued: n/a (2007); Multi-family building permits issued: n/a (2007).
Income: Per capita income: $18,106 (2007); Median household income: $30,576 (2007); Average household income: $42,024 (2007); Percent of households with income of $100,000 or more: 5.8% (2007); Poverty rate: 18.9% (2005); Bankruptcy rate: 2.66% (2007).
Education: Percent of population age 25 and over with: High school diploma (including GED) or higher: 73.7% (2007); Bachelor's degree or higher: 7.8% (2007); Master's degree or higher: 2.8% (2007).
Housing: Homeownership rate: 81.1% (2007); Median home value: $57,321 (2007); Median rent: $191 per month (2000); Median age of housing: 33 years (2000).
Health: Birth rate: 111.2 per 10,000 population (2007); Death rate: 149.4 per 10,000 population (2007); Age-adjusted cancer mortality rate: 289.3 deaths per 100,000 population (2005); Number of physicians: 1.6 per 10,000 population (2005); Hospital beds: 0.0 per 10,000 population (2004); Hospital admissions: 0.0 per 10,000 population (2004).
Elections: 2004 Presidential election results: 50.2% Bush, 48.8% Kerry, 0.0% Nader, 1.0% Badnarik
Additional Information Contacts
Gallatin County Government . . . . (618) 269-3025

Gallatin County Communities

EQUALITY (village). Covers a land area of 0.901 square miles and a water area of 0 square miles. Located at 37.73° N. Lat.; 88.34° W. Long. Elevation is 410 feet.
History: Formerly county seat and site of salt works.
Population: 748 (1990); 721 (2000); 706 (2007); 673 (2012 projected); Race: 99.4% White, 0.0% Black, 0.0% Asian, 1.6% Hispanic of any race (2007); Density: 783.6 persons per square mile (2007); Average household size: 2.26 (2007); Median age: 40.8 (2007); Males per 100 females: 92.9 (2007); Marriage status: 15.8% never married, 60.5% now married, 11.9% widowed, 11.9% divorced (2000); Foreign born: 0.3% (2000); Ancestry (includes multiple ancestries): 31.0% United States or American, 11.9% Irish, 11.5% German, 6.8% Other groups, 4.9% English (2000).
Economy: Employment by occupation: 5.6% management, 14.7% professional, 18.3% services, 28.2% sales, 0.8% farming, 14.3% construction, 18.3% production (2000).
Income: Per capita income: $14,023 (2007); Median household income: $25,268 (2007); Average household income: $31,629 (2007); Percent of households with income of $100,000 or more: 1.9% (2007); Poverty rate: 20.7% (2000).
Education: Percent of population age 25 and over with: High school diploma (including GED) or higher: 77.1% (2007); Bachelor's degree or higher: 5.9% (2007); Master's degree or higher: 3.1% (2007).
Housing: Homeownership rate: 78.0% (2007); Median home value: $45,000 (2007); Median rent: $188 per month (2000); Median age of housing: 40 years (2000).
Transportation: Commute to work: 95.2% car, 0.0% public transportation, 0.0% walk, 4.8% work from home (2000); Travel time to work: 34.6% less than 15 minutes, 41.3% 15 to 30 minutes, 9.6% 30 to 45 minutes, 4.2% 45 to 60 minutes, 10.4% 60 minutes or more (2000)

JUNCTION (village). Covers a land area of 0.887 square miles and a water area of 0 square miles. Located at 37.72° N. Lat.; 88.23° W. Long. Elevation is 361 feet.
Population: 201 (1990); 139 (2000); 131 (2007); 125 (2012 projected); Race: 97.7% White, 0.0% Black, 0.0% Asian, 3.1% Hispanic of any race (2007); Density: 147.7 persons per square mile (2007); Average household size: 2.05 (2007); Median age: 44.3 (2007); Males per 100 females: 77.0 (2007); Marriage status: 22.1% never married, 54.3% now married, 16.4% widowed, 7.1% divorced (2000); Foreign born: 3.1% (2000); Ancestry (includes multiple ancestries): 29.0% United States or American, 11.7% Italian, 11.1% Irish, 8.6% Other groups, 7.4% English (2000).
Economy: Employment by occupation: 7.2% management, 29.0% professional, 10.1% services, 15.9% sales, 0.0% farming, 2.9% construction, 34.8% production (2000).
Income: Per capita income: $18,588 (2007); Median household income: $38,000 (2007); Average household income: $38,047 (2007); Percent of households with income of $100,000 or more: 0.0% (2007); Poverty rate: 11.1% (2000).
Education: Percent of population age 25 and over with: High school diploma (including GED) or higher: 65.6% (2007); Bachelor's degree or higher: 9.4% (2007); Master's degree or higher: 3.1% (2007).

School District(s)

Gallatin CUSD 7 (PK-12)
2005-06 Enrollment: 915 . . . . (618) 272-3821
Housing: Homeownership rate: 89.1% (2007); Median home value: $36,500 (2007); Median rent: $175 per month (2000); Median age of housing: 32 years (2000).
Transportation: Commute to work: 100.0% car, 0.0% public transportation, 0.0% walk, 0.0% work from home (2000); Travel time to work: 40.6% less than 15 minutes, 7.2% 15 to 30 minutes, 17.4% 30 to 45 minutes, 2.9% 45 to 60 minutes, 31.9% 60 minutes or more (2000)

NEW HAVEN (village). Covers a land area of 1.205 square miles and a water area of 0.028 square miles. Located at 37.90° N. Lat.; 88.12° W. Long. Elevation is 367 feet.

Population: 459 (1990); 477 (2000); 455 (2007); 437 (2012 projected); Race: 100.0% White, 0.0% Black, 0.0% Asian, 1.3% Hispanic of any race (2007); Density: 377.5 persons per square mile (2007); Average household size: 2.32 (2007); Median age: 41.0 (2007); Males per 100 females: 97.0 (2007); Marriage status: 16.2% never married, 64.2% now married, 8.2% widowed, 11.4% divorced (2000); Foreign born: 0.5% (2000); Ancestry (includes multiple ancestries): 16.4% English, 13.2% Irish, 10.9% United States or American, 10.3% Other groups, 9.3% German (2000).
Economy: Employment by occupation: 5.7% management, 17.1% professional, 20.0% services, 12.0% sales, 3.4% farming, 16.0% construction, 25.7% production (2000).
Income: Per capita income: $15,082 (2007); Median household income: $31,750 (2007); Average household income: $35,013 (2007); Percent of households with income of $100,000 or more: 1.0% (2007); Poverty rate: 22.6% (2000).
Education: Percent of population age 25 and over with: High school diploma (including GED) or higher: 72.4% (2007); Bachelor's degree or higher: 0.6% (2007); Master's degree or higher: 0.6% (2007).
Housing: Homeownership rate: 86.2% (2007); Median home value: $41,250 (2007); Median rent: $158 per month (2000); Median age of housing: 34 years (2000).
Transportation: Commute to work: 95.3% car, 1.2% public transportation, 3.5% walk, 0.0% work from home (2000); Travel time to work: 17.0% less than 15 minutes, 30.4% 15 to 30 minutes, 18.1% 30 to 45 minutes, 12.3% 45 to 60 minutes, 22.2% 60 minutes or more (2000)

OLD SHAWNEETOWN (village). Covers a land area of 0.523 square miles and a water area of 0 square miles. Located at 37.69° N. Lat.; 88.13° W. Long. Elevation is 351 feet.
Population: 356 (1990); 278 (2000); 240 (2007); 237 (2012 projected); Race: 99.2% White, 0.0% Black, 0.0% Asian, 1.3% Hispanic of any race (2007); Density: 459.0 persons per square mile (2007); Average household size: 2.73 (2007); Median age: 31.4 (2007); Males per 100 females: 96.7 (2007); Marriage status: 22.5% never married, 46.9% now married, 4.7% widowed, 25.8% divorced (2000); Foreign born: 0.0% (2000); Ancestry (includes multiple ancestries): 37.9% Other groups, 10.8% United States or American, 8.9% English, 7.4% German, 6.7% Irish (2000).
Economy: Employment by occupation: 0.0% management, 8.3% professional, 25.0% services, 7.1% sales, 0.0% farming, 7.1% construction, 52.4% production (2000).
Income: Per capita income: $9,292 (2007); Median household income: $20,500 (2007); Average household income: $25,341 (2007); Percent of households with income of $100,000 or more: 2.3% (2007); Poverty rate: 39.4% (2000).
Education: Percent of population age 25 and over with: High school diploma (including GED) or higher: 50.4% (2007); Bachelor's degree or higher: 0.0% (2007); Master's degree or higher: 0.0% (2007).
Housing: Homeownership rate: 83.0% (2007); Median home value: $13,269 (2007); Median rent: $225 per month (2000); Median age of housing: 25 years (2000).
Safety: Violent crime rate: 37.3 per 10,000 population; Property crime rate: 149.3 per 10,000 population (2006).
Transportation: Commute to work: 97.6% car, 0.0% public transportation, 2.4% walk, 0.0% work from home (2000); Travel time to work: 25.6% less than 15 minutes, 28.0% 15 to 30 minutes, 4.9% 30 to 45 minutes, 18.3% 45 to 60 minutes, 23.2% 60 minutes or more (2000)

OMAHA (village). Covers a land area of 0.830 square miles and a water area of 0 square miles. Located at 37.89° N. Lat.; 88.30° W. Long. Elevation is 374 feet.
Population: 273 (1990); 263 (2000); 253 (2007); 243 (2012 projected); Race: 100.0% White, 0.0% Black, 0.0% Asian, 0.0% Hispanic of any race (2007); Density: 304.7 persons per square mile (2007); Average household size: 2.07 (2007); Median age: 42.6 (2007); Males per 100 females: 94.6 (2007); Marriage status: 17.4% never married, 57.0% now married, 12.1% widowed, 13.5% divorced (2000); Foreign born: 0.0% (2000); Ancestry (includes multiple ancestries): 17.6% Irish, 16.2% English, 16.2% United States or American, 10.7% French (except Basque), 9.6% German (2000).
Economy: Employment by occupation: 1.6% management, 15.3% professional, 16.1% services, 25.8% sales, 2.4% farming, 9.7% construction, 29.0% production (2000).
Income: Per capita income: $18,014 (2007); Median household income: $28,750 (2007); Average household income: $37,357 (2007); Percent of households with income of $100,000 or more: 4.1% (2007); Poverty rate: 18.8% (2000).
Education: Percent of population age 25 and over with: High school diploma (including GED) or higher: 76.4% (2007); Bachelor's degree or higher: 11.2% (2007); Master's degree or higher: 4.5% (2007).
Housing: Homeownership rate: 79.5% (2007); Median home value: $39,688 (2007); Median rent: $182 per month (2000); Median age of housing: 32 years (2000).
Transportation: Commute to work: 93.2% car, 3.4% public transportation, 0.0% walk, 1.7% work from home (2000); Travel time to work: 19.0% less than 15 minutes, 27.6% 15 to 30 minutes, 35.3% 30 to 45 minutes, 8.6% 45 to 60 minutes, 9.5% 60 minutes or more (2000)

RIDGWAY (village). Covers a land area of 0.900 square miles and a water area of 0 square miles. Located at 37.79° N. Lat.; 88.26° W. Long. Elevation is 371 feet.
History: Incorporated 1886.
Population: 1,103 (1990); 928 (2000); 872 (2007); 841 (2012 projected); Race: 99.4% White, 0.2% Black, 0.0% Asian, 0.3% Hispanic of any race (2007); Density: 968.4 persons per square mile (2007); Average household size: 2.07 (2007); Median age: 45.5 (2007); Males per 100 females: 88.3 (2007); Marriage status: 19.4% never married, 58.5% now married, 11.7% widowed, 10.4% divorced (2000); Foreign born: 0.0% (2000); Ancestry (includes multiple ancestries): 22.0% German, 13.9% Irish, 12.3% United States or American, 10.4% French (except Basque), 8.1% English (2000).
Economy: Employment by occupation: 9.4% management, 19.9% professional, 19.4% services, 18.0% sales, 2.1% farming, 11.7% construction, 19.4% production (2000).
Income: Per capita income: $21,347 (2007); Median household income: $33,533 (2007); Average household income: $44,216 (2007); Percent of households with income of $100,000 or more: 6.4% (2007); Poverty rate: 18.0% (2000).
Education: Percent of population age 25 and over with: High school diploma (including GED) or higher: 78.9% (2007); Bachelor's degree or higher: 11.5% (2007); Master's degree or higher: 2.8% (2007).
Housing: Homeownership rate: 78.9% (2007); Median home value: $57,442 (2007); Median rent: $206 per month (2000); Median age of housing: 34 years (2000).
Safety: Violent crime rate: 11.3 per 10,000 population; Property crime rate: 45.2 per 10,000 population (2006).
Transportation: Commute to work: 95.0% car, 0.0% public transportation, 1.9% walk, 2.6% work from home (2000); Travel time to work: 35.5% less than 15 minutes, 26.9% 15 to 30 minutes, 19.8% 30 to 45 minutes, 4.2% 45 to 60 minutes, 13.7% 60 minutes or more (2000)

SHAWNEETOWN (city). Aka New Shawneetown. County seat. Covers a land area of 1.193 square miles and a water area of 0.037 square miles. Located at 37.71° N. Lat.; 88.18° W. Long. Elevation is 400 feet.
History: Shawneetown, settled in the early 1800s, developed as a port on the Ohio River and as a financial center when Chicago was still a small village. Salt was an important export for the growing town, through which travelers and merchandise passed on the river. Shawneetown State Historical Site is here. Gallatin County Courthouse and most residents moved to (new) Shawneetown in late 1930s after disastrous Ohio River flood of 1937. The first state chartered bank opened here.
Population: 1,575 (1990); 1,410 (2000); 1,328 (2007); 1,280 (2012 projected); Race: 96.7% White, 0.2% Black, 0.0% Asian, 1.4% Hispanic of any race (2007); Density: 1,113.1 persons per square mile (2007); Average household size: 2.19 (2007); Median age: 41.7 (2007); Males per 100 females: 87.0 (2007); Marriage status: 17.5% never married, 56.9% now married, 12.9% widowed, 12.7% divorced (2000); Foreign born: 1.0% (2000); Ancestry (includes multiple ancestries): 13.0% German, 11.3% United States or American, 9.7% Irish, 9.1% Other groups, 7.4% English (2000).
Economy: Employment by occupation: 8.8% management, 13.7% professional, 24.3% services, 18.7% sales, 2.8% farming, 13.5% construction, 18.1% production (2000).
Income: Per capita income: $18,126 (2007); Median household income: $23,526 (2007); Average household income: $39,300 (2007); Percent of households with income of $100,000 or more: 6.6% (2007); Poverty rate: 27.8% (2000).
Education: Percent of population age 25 and over with: High school diploma (including GED) or higher: 64.4% (2007); Bachelor's degree or higher: 4.3% (2007); Master's degree or higher: 2.3% (2007).
Housing: Homeownership rate: 74.6% (2007); Median home value: $53,596 (2007); Median rent: $172 per month (2000); Median age of housing: 36 years (2000).

Safety: Violent crime rate: 59.5 per 10,000 population; Property crime rate: 252.8 per 10,000 population (2006).
Newspapers: Gallatin Democrat (Local news; Circulation 1,200); Ridgway News (Local news; Circulation 700)
Transportation: Commute to work: 91.9% car, 0.4% public transportation, 1.6% walk, 6.1% work from home (2000); Travel time to work: 37.8% less than 15 minutes, 16.8% 15 to 30 minutes, 15.9% 30 to 45 minutes, 11.0% 45 to 60 minutes, 18.5% 60 minutes or more (2000)

Greene County

Located in southwest central Illinois; bounded on the west by the Illinois River; drained by Macoupin and Apple Creeks. Covers a land area of 543.09 square miles, a water area of 3.25 square miles, and is located in the Central Time Zone. The county was founded in 1821. County seat is Carrollton.

Weather Station: White Hall 1 E — Elevation: 577 feet

	Jan	Feb	Mar	Apr	May	Jun	Jul	Aug	Sep	Oct	Nov	Dec
High	35	41	52	65	75	83	87	85	79	68	53	40
Low	17	21	31	42	52	61	65	63	55	44	33	23
Precip	1.6	1.7	3.3	3.8	4.5	3.6	3.3	3.0	3.1	2.6	3.2	2.5
Snow	na	na	2.0	0.5	0.0	0.0	0.0	0.0	0.0	tr	0.7	2.9

High and Low temperatures in degrees Fahrenheit; Precipitation and Snow in inches

Population: 15,317 (1990); 14,761 (2000); 14,552 (2007); 14,381 (2012 projected); Race: 97.9% White, 1.0% Black, 0.2% Asian, 0.8% Hispanic of any race (2007); Density: 26.8 persons per square mile (2007); Average household size: 2.55 (2007); Median age: 39.4 (2007); Males per 100 females: 96.0 (2007).
Religion: Five largest groups: 20.8% Southern Baptist Convention, 17.6% American Baptist Churches in the USA, 13.7% Catholic Church, 6.0% The United Methodist Church, 1.7% Lutheran Church—Missouri Synod (2000).
Economy: Unemployment rate: 5.3% (4/2008); Total civilian labor force: 6,888 (4/2008); Leading industries: 22.4% retail trade; 19.0% health care and social assistance; 13.0% accommodation & food services (2005); Farms: 678 totaling 314,772 acres (2002); Companies that employ 500 or more persons: 0 (2006); Companies that employ 100 to 499 persons: 1 (2006); Companies that employ less than 100 persons: 266 (2006); Black-owned businesses: n/a (2002); Hispanic-owned businesses: n/a (2002); Asian-owned businesses: n/a (2002); Women-owned businesses: n/a (2002); Retail sales per capita: $7,816 (2008). Single-family building permits issued: 17 (2007); Multi-family building permits issued: 2 (2007).
Income: Per capita income: $19,129 (2007); Median household income: $38,891 (2007); Average household income: $47,955 (2007); Percent of households with income of $100,000 or more: 7.5% (2007); Poverty rate: 13.7% (2005); Bankruptcy rate: 1.87% (2007).
Education: Percent of population age 25 and over with: High school diploma (including GED) or higher: 78.7% (2007); Bachelor's degree or higher: 9.9% (2007); Master's degree or higher: 3.6% (2007).
Housing: Homeownership rate: 76.0% (2007); Median home value: $71,913 (2007); Median rent: $257 per month (2000); Median age of housing: 56 years (2000).
Health: Birth rate: 124.6 per 10,000 population (2007); Death rate: 123.8 per 10,000 population (2007); Age-adjusted cancer mortality rate: 166.0 deaths per 100,000 population (2005); Number of physicians: 4.9 per 10,000 population (2005); Hospital beds: 45.4 per 10,000 population (2004); Hospital admissions: 533.1 per 10,000 population (2004).
Elections: 2004 Presidential election results: 58.7% Bush, 40.5% Kerry, 0.0% Nader, 0.9% Badnarik
Additional Information Contacts
Greene County Government . . . . (217) 942-5443

Greene County Communities

CARROLLTON (city). County seat. Covers a land area of 1.669 square miles and a water area of 0.002 square miles. Located at 39.29° N. Lat.; 90.40° W. Long. Elevation is 620 feet.
History: Carrollton was settled in 1818 and developed as the seat of Green County.
Population: 2,553 (1990); 2,605 (2000); 2,588 (2007); 2,567 (2012 projected); Race: 98.5% White, 0.0% Black, 0.5% Asian, 0.7% Hispanic of any race (2007); Density: 1,551.0 persons per square mile (2007); Average household size: 2.40 (2007); Median age: 40.9 (2007); Males per 100 females: 88.1 (2007); Marriage status: 19.1% never married, 59.0% now married, 12.9% widowed, 9.0% divorced (2000); Foreign born: 0.2% (2000); Ancestry (includes multiple ancestries): 31.0% German, 17.3% United States or American, 11.5% English, 11.1% Irish, 4.9% Other groups (2000).
Economy: Single-family building permits issued: 17 (2007); Multi-family building permits issued: 2 (2007); Employment by occupation: 8.8% management, 17.9% professional, 18.7% services, 25.0% sales, 0.0% farming, 8.3% construction, 21.3% production (2000).
Income: Per capita income: $20,466 (2007); Median household income: $37,273 (2007); Average household income: $48,142 (2007); Percent of households with income of $100,000 or more: 7.8% (2007); Poverty rate: 9.0% (2000).
Education: Percent of population age 25 and over with: High school diploma (including GED) or higher: 81.1% (2007); Bachelor's degree or higher: 16.0% (2007); Master's degree or higher: 6.0% (2007).

School District(s)

Carrollton CUSD 1 (PK-12)
2005-06 Enrollment: 700 . . . . (217) 942-5314
Housing: Homeownership rate: 75.3% (2007); Median home value: $86,949 (2007); Median rent: $269 per month (2000); Median age of housing: 56 years (2000).
Hospitals: Thomas H. Boyd Memorial Hospital (65 beds)
Safety: Violent crime rate: 115.1 per 10,000 population; Property crime rate: 182.6 per 10,000 population (2006).
Newspapers: Gazette Patriot (Regional news; Circulation 1,662)
Transportation: Commute to work: 90.9% car, 0.0% public transportation, 3.6% walk, 4.4% work from home (2000); Travel time to work: 49.0% less than 15 minutes, 16.0% 15 to 30 minutes, 5.9% 30 to 45 minutes, 14.2% 45 to 60 minutes, 15.0% 60 minutes or more (2000)

ELDRED (village). Covers a land area of 0.135 square miles and a water area of 0 square miles. Located at 39.28° N. Lat.; 90.55° W. Long. Elevation is 449 feet.
Population: 254 (1990); 211 (2000); 202 (2007); 193 (2012 projected); Race: 97.5% White, 0.0% Black, 1.5% Asian, 0.0% Hispanic of any race (2007); Density: 1,500.8 persons per square mile (2007); Average household size: 2.15 (2007); Median age: 47.2 (2007); Males per 100 females: 82.0 (2007); Marriage status: 33.0% never married, 36.9% now married, 8.0% widowed, 22.2% divorced (2000); Foreign born: 1.4% (2000); Ancestry (includes multiple ancestries): 49.8% United States or American, 25.1% German, 10.5% English, 6.4% Irish, 4.1% Other groups (2000).
Economy: Employment by occupation: 3.8% management, 10.4% professional, 23.6% services, 21.7% sales, 0.0% farming, 19.8% construction, 20.8% production (2000).
Income: Per capita income: $20,087 (2007); Median household income: $37,500 (2007); Average household income: $43,165 (2007); Percent of households with income of $100,000 or more: 4.3% (2007); Poverty rate: 37.2% (2000).
Education: Percent of population age 25 and over with: High school diploma (including GED) or higher: 75.2% (2007); Bachelor's degree or higher: 4.7% (2007); Master's degree or higher: 0.0% (2007).
Housing: Homeownership rate: 71.3% (2007); Median home value: $64,167 (2007); Median rent: $233 per month (2000); Median age of housing: 60+ years (2000).
Transportation: Commute to work: 93.4% car, 0.0% public transportation, 4.7% walk, 0.0% work from home (2000); Travel time to work: 34.0% less than 15 minutes, 33.0% 15 to 30 minutes, 11.3% 30 to 45 minutes, 2.8% 45 to 60 minutes, 18.9% 60 minutes or more (2000)

GREENFIELD (city). Covers a land area of 1.716 square miles and a water area of 0.063 square miles. Located at 39.34° N. Lat.; 90.21° W. Long. Elevation is 587 feet.
History: Incorporated 1837.
Population: 1,209 (1990); 1,179 (2000); 1,186 (2007); 1,172 (2012 projected); Race: 99.4% White, 0.2% Black, 0.0% Asian, 0.5% Hispanic of any race (2007); Density: 691.3 persons per square mile (2007); Average household size: 2.34 (2007); Median age: 39.6 (2007); Males per 100 females: 89.8 (2007); Marriage status: 24.9% never married, 50.6% now married, 14.1% widowed, 10.4% divorced (2000); Foreign born: 0.5% (2000); Ancestry (includes multiple ancestries): 19.4% German, 12.6% United States or American, 11.0% Irish, 10.1% English, 5.0% Other groups (2000).
Economy: Single-family building permits issued: 0 (2007); Multi-family building permits issued: 0 (2007); Employment by occupation: 9.2%

management, 17.8% professional, 22.2% services, 16.4% sales, 3.0% farming, 9.2% construction, 22.4% production (2000).
Income: Per capita income: $19,507 (2007); Median household income: $37,273 (2007); Average household income: $45,647 (2007); Percent of households with income of $100,000 or more: 5.3% (2007); Poverty rate: 10.2% (2000).
Education: Percent of population age 25 and over with: High school diploma (including GED) or higher: 84.0% (2007); Bachelor's degree or higher: 6.4% (2007); Master's degree or higher: 1.6% (2007).

School District(s)

Greenfield CUSD 10 (PK-12)
2005-06 Enrollment: 547 . . . . (217) 368-2447
Housing: Homeownership rate: 74.1% (2007); Median home value: $67,813 (2007); Median rent: $256 per month (2000); Median age of housing: 47 years (2000).
Safety: Violent crime rate: 52.5 per 10,000 population; Property crime rate: 70.1 per 10,000 population (2006).
Transportation: Commute to work: 93.2% car, 0.0% public transportation, 2.1% walk, 4.6% work from home (2000); Travel time to work: 30.3% less than 15 minutes, 6.9% 15 to 30 minutes, 30.7% 30 to 45 minutes, 18.5% 45 to 60 minutes, 13.6% 60 minutes or more (2000)

HILLVIEW (village). Covers a land area of 0.848 square miles and a water area of 0 square miles. Located at 39.45° N. Lat.; 90.53° W. Long. Elevation is 440 feet.
Population: 271 (1990); 179 (2000); 164 (2007); 158 (2012 projected); Race: 100.0% White, 0.0% Black, 0.0% Asian, 0.0% Hispanic of any race (2007); Density: 193.5 persons per square mile (2007); Average household size: 2.78 (2007); Median age: 38.2 (2007); Males per 100 females: 105.0 (2007); Marriage status: 23.1% never married, 66.9% now married, 5.8% widowed, 4.1% divorced (2000); Foreign born: 0.0% (2000); Ancestry (includes multiple ancestries): 16.0% United States or American, 14.8% Other groups, 11.7% Irish, 10.5% Swedish, 7.4% German (2000).
Economy: Employment by occupation: 2.1% management, 12.8% professional, 21.3% services, 19.1% sales, 4.3% farming, 0.0% construction, 40.4% production (2000).
Income: Per capita income: $13,095 (2007); Median household income: $27,500 (2007); Average household income: $36,398 (2007); Percent of households with income of $100,000 or more: 0.0% (2007); Poverty rate: 25.3% (2000).
Education: Percent of population age 25 and over with: High school diploma (including GED) or higher: 57.4% (2007); Bachelor's degree or higher: 0.0% (2007); Master's degree or higher: 0.0% (2007).
Housing: Homeownership rate: 84.7% (2007); Median home value: $31,250 (2007); Median rent: $238 per month (2000); Median age of housing: 60+ years (2000).
Transportation: Commute to work: 91.5% car, 0.0% public transportation, 0.0% walk, 6.4% work from home (2000); Travel time to work: 15.9% less than 15 minutes, 36.4% 15 to 30 minutes, 11.4% 30 to 45 minutes, 18.2% 45 to 60 minutes, 18.2% 60 minutes or more (2000)

KANE (village). Covers a land area of 0.541 square miles and a water area of 0 square miles. Located at 39.19° N. Lat.; 90.35° W. Long. Elevation is 561 feet.
Population: 456 (1990); 459 (2000); 449 (2007); 443 (2012 projected); Race: 98.9% White, 0.0% Black, 0.2% Asian, 0.2% Hispanic of any race (2007); Density: 829.3 persons per square mile (2007); Average household size: 2.63 (2007); Median age: 34.1 (2007); Males per 100 females: 96.9 (2007); Marriage status: 18.8% never married, 58.2% now married, 8.5% widowed, 14.5% divorced (2000); Foreign born: 0.7% (2000); Ancestry (includes multiple ancestries): 18.1% German, 12.7% United States or American, 5.9% English, 5.9% Other groups, 4.3% Irish (2000).
Economy: Employment by occupation: 6.7% management, 13.5% professional, 27.0% services, 20.2% sales, 2.2% farming, 14.6% construction, 15.7% production (2000).
Income: Per capita income: $14,104 (2007); Median household income: $35,167 (2007); Average household income: $37,032 (2007); Percent of households with income of $100,000 or more: 0.6% (2007); Poverty rate: 11.8% (2000).
Education: Percent of population age 25 and over with: High school diploma (including GED) or higher: 72.0% (2007); Bachelor's degree or higher: 3.5% (2007); Master's degree or higher: 1.7% (2007).
Housing: Homeownership rate: 78.9% (2007); Median home value: $55,938 (2007); Median rent: $244 per month (2000); Median age of housing: 56 years (2000).
Transportation: Commute to work: 97.7% car, 0.0% public transportation, 2.3% walk, 0.0% work from home (2000); Travel time to work: 26.1% less than 15 minutes, 30.7% 15 to 30 minutes, 16.5% 30 to 45 minutes, 11.9% 45 to 60 minutes, 14.8% 60 minutes or more (2000)

ROCKBRIDGE (village). Covers a land area of 0.739 square miles and a water area of 0 square miles. Located at 39.27° N. Lat.; 90.20° W. Long. Elevation is 541 feet.
Population: 197 (1990); 189 (2000); 185 (2007); 182 (2012 projected); Race: 100.0% White, 0.0% Black, 0.0% Asian, 0.5% Hispanic of any race (2007); Density: 250.3 persons per square mile (2007); Average household size: 2.23 (2007); Median age: 48.4 (2007); Males per 100 females: 101.1 (2007); Marriage status: 13.8% never married, 70.4% now married, 11.3% widowed, 4.4% divorced (2000); Foreign born: 0.0% (2000); Ancestry (includes multiple ancestries): 22.2% German, 16.1% United States or American, 9.4% Irish, 7.8% English, 7.2% Other groups (2000).
Economy: Employment by occupation: 9.5% management, 9.5% professional, 13.7% services, 27.4% sales, 2.1% farming, 3.2% construction, 34.7% production (2000).
Income: Per capita income: $19,216 (2007); Median household income: $38,750 (2007); Average household income: $42,831 (2007); Percent of households with income of $100,000 or more: 4.8% (2007); Poverty rate: 7.2% (2000).
Education: Percent of population age 25 and over with: High school diploma (including GED) or higher: 73.3% (2007); Bachelor's degree or higher: 3.4% (2007); Master's degree or higher: 0.0% (2007).
Housing: Homeownership rate: 86.7% (2007); Median home value: $62,000 (2007); Median rent: $271 per month (2000); Median age of housing: 49 years (2000).
Transportation: Commute to work: 95.7% car, 0.0% public transportation, 2.2% walk, 2.2% work from home (2000); Travel time to work: 29.7% less than 15 minutes, 12.1% 15 to 30 minutes, 30.8% 30 to 45 minutes, 14.3% 45 to 60 minutes, 13.2% 60 minutes or more (2000)

ROODHOUSE (city). Covers a land area of 1.132 square miles and a water area of 0 square miles. Located at 39.48° N. Lat.; 90.37° W. Long. Elevation is 656 feet.
History: Roodhouse was laid out by an early settler, John Roodhouse, and developed as a railroad center.
Population: 2,139 (1990); 2,214 (2000); 2,222 (2007); 2,222 (2012 projected); Race: 92.9% White, 5.9% Black, 0.1% Asian, 1.0% Hispanic of any race (2007); Density: 1,962.7 persons per square mile (2007); Average household size: 2.72 (2007); Median age: 33.1 (2007); Males per 100 females: 105.2 (2007); Marriage status: 20.5% never married, 56.9% now married, 9.5% widowed, 13.1% divorced (2000); Foreign born: 0.8% (2000); Ancestry (includes multiple ancestries): 15.8% United States or American, 13.3% English, 11.2% German, 10.3% Irish, 7.3% Other groups (2000).
Economy: Employment by occupation: 4.4% management, 10.4% professional, 17.3% services, 23.8% sales, 1.3% farming, 9.7% construction, 33.1% production (2000).
Income: Per capita income: $15,543 (2007); Median household income: $35,885 (2007); Average household income: $41,857 (2007); Percent of households with income of $100,000 or more: 4.5% (2007); Poverty rate: 16.8% (2000).
Education: Percent of population age 25 and over with: High school diploma (including GED) or higher: 73.9% (2007); Bachelor's degree or higher: 6.9% (2007); Master's degree or higher: 2.8% (2007).

School District(s)

North Greene USD 3 (PK-12)
2005-06 Enrollment: 1,117 . . . . (217) 374-2842
Housing: Homeownership rate: 74.8% (2007); Median home value: $57,533 (2007); Median rent: $260 per month (2000); Median age of housing: 54 years (2000).
Safety: Violent crime rate: 67.7 per 10,000 population; Property crime rate: 117.3 per 10,000 population (2006).
Transportation: Commute to work: 93.8% car, 0.4% public transportation, 2.8% walk, 1.8% work from home (2000); Travel time to work: 36.9% less than 15 minutes, 15.2% 15 to 30 minutes, 33.8% 30 to 45 minutes, 4.6% 45 to 60 minutes, 9.5% 60 minutes or more (2000)

WHITE HALL (city). Aka Whitehall. Covers a land area of 2.579 square miles and a water area of 0.057 square miles. Located at 39.43° N. Lat.; 90.39° W. Long. Elevation is 571 feet.

History: White Hall was founded in 1820 and developed around the manufacture of pottery from local clay.
Population: 2,843 (1990); 2,629 (2000); 2,610 (2007); 2,591 (2012 projected); Race: 98.2% White, 0.3% Black, 0.0% Asian, 1.4% Hispanic of any race (2007); Density: 1,011.9 persons per square mile (2007); Average household size: 2.40 (2007); Median age: 42.5 (2007); Males per 100 females: 85.9 (2007); Marriage status: 17.8% never married, 57.7% now married, 12.2% widowed, 12.3% divorced (2000); Foreign born: 0.3% (2000); Ancestry (includes multiple ancestries): 16.4% German, 15.4% United States or American, 13.6% English, 11.8% Irish, 7.8% Other groups (2000).
Economy: Employment by occupation: 7.6% management, 16.3% professional, 19.1% services, 18.7% sales, 2.2% farming, 14.8% construction, 21.3% production (2000).
Income: Per capita income: $18,351 (2007); Median household income: $32,220 (2007); Average household income: $41,228 (2007); Percent of households with income of $100,000 or more: 6.2% (2007); Poverty rate: 18.8% (2000).
Education: Percent of population age 25 and over with: High school diploma (including GED) or higher: 72.3% (2007); Bachelor's degree or higher: 8.9% (2007); Master's degree or higher: 4.3% (2007).

School District(s)

North Greene USD 3 (PK-12)
2005-06 Enrollment: 1,117 . . . . (217) 374-2842
Housing: Homeownership rate: 73.2% (2007); Median home value: $54,207 (2007); Median rent: $237 per month (2000); Median age of housing: 60 years (2000).
Safety: Violent crime rate: 76.7 per 10,000 population; Property crime rate: 122.7 per 10,000 population (2006).
Transportation: Commute to work: 88.8% car, 0.0% public transportation, 4.6% walk, 5.1% work from home (2000); Travel time to work: 41.5% less than 15 minutes, 8.2% 15 to 30 minutes, 29.1% 30 to 45 minutes, 9.2% 45 to 60 minutes, 12.0% 60 minutes or more (2000)

WILMINGTON (village). Aka Patterson. Covers a land area of 0.792 square miles and a water area of 0 square miles. Located at 39.48° N. Lat.; 90.49° W. Long.
Population: 129 (1990); 120 (2000); 110 (2007); 106 (2012 projected); Race: 96.4% White, 0.0% Black, 0.0% Asian, 0.0% Hispanic of any race (2007); Density: 138.9 persons per square mile (2007); Average household size: 2.68 (2007); Median age: 32.5 (2007); Males per 100 females: 74.6 (2007); Marriage status: 18.5% never married, 66.7% now married, 6.2% widowed, 8.6% divorced (2000); Foreign born: 0.0% (2000); Ancestry (includes multiple ancestries): 23.2% Dutch, 22.3% Irish, 19.6% German, 17.0% United States or American, 13.4% English (2000).
Economy: Employment by occupation: 1.9% management, 15.1% professional, 32.1% services, 9.4% sales, 3.8% farming, 22.6% construction, 15.1% production (2000).
Income: Per capita income: $17,432 (2007); Median household income: $39,167 (2007); Average household income: $46,768 (2007); Percent of households with income of $100,000 or more: 7.3% (2007); Poverty rate: 2.7% (2000).
Education: Percent of population age 25 and over with: High school diploma (including GED) or higher: 87.3% (2007); Bachelor's degree or higher: 6.3% (2007); Master's degree or higher: 4.8% (2007).
Housing: Homeownership rate: 85.4% (2007); Median home value: $33,125 (2007); Median rent: $n/a per month (2000); Median age of housing: 50 years (2000).
Transportation: Commute to work: 81.1% car, 0.0% public transportation, 1.9% walk, 0.0% work from home (2000); Travel time to work: 28.3% less than 15 minutes, 35.8% 15 to 30 minutes, 20.8% 30 to 45 minutes, 1.9% 45 to 60 minutes, 13.2% 60 minutes or more (2000)

Grundy County

Located in northeastern Illinois; drained by the Illinois, Des Plaines, and Kankakee Rivers. Covers a land area of 419.90 square miles, a water area of 10.52 square miles, and is located in the Central Time Zone. The county was founded in 1841. County seat is Morris.

Grundy County is part of the Chicago-Naperville-Joliet, IL-IN-WI Metropolitan Statistical Area. The entire metro area includes: Chicago-Naperville-Joliet, IL Metropolitan Division (Cook County, IL; DeKalb County, IL; DuPage County, IL; Grundy County, IL; Kane County, IL; Kendall County, IL; McHenry County, IL; Will County, IL); Gary, IN Metropolitan Division (Jasper County, IN; Lake County, IN; Newton County, IN; Porter County, IN); Lake County-Kenosha County, IL-WI Metropolitan Division (Lake County, IL; Kenosha County, WI)

Population: 32,337 (1990); 37,535 (2000); 46,438 (2007); 53,207 (2012 projected); Race: 94.2% White, 1.2% Black, 0.7% Asian, 6.6% Hispanic of any race (2007); Density: 110.6 persons per square mile (2007); Average household size: 2.59 (2007); Median age: 35.6 (2007); Males per 100 females: 100.1 (2007).
Religion: Five largest groups: 26.6% Catholic Church, 6.6% The United Methodist Church, 4.2% Christian Churches and Churches of Christ, 4.2% Evangelical Lutheran Church in America, 2.4% Presbyterian Church (U.S.A.) (2000).
Economy: Unemployment rate: 6.8% (4/2008); Total civilian labor force: 25,798 (4/2008); Leading industries: 15.1% retail trade; 12.3% manufacturing; 12.2% health care and social assistance (2005); Farms: 407 totaling 213,467 acres (2002); Companies that employ 500 or more persons: 4 (2006); Companies that employ 100 to 499 persons: 14 (2006); Companies that employ less than 100 persons: 1,111 (2006); Black-owned businesses: n/a (2002); Hispanic-owned businesses: n/a (2002); Asian-owned businesses: n/a (2002); Women-owned businesses: 744 (2002); Retail sales per capita: $14,196 (2008). Single-family building permits issued: 156 (2007); Multi-family building permits issued: 59 (2007).
Income: Per capita income: $27,041 (2007); Median household income: $60,594 (2007); Average household income: $69,683 (2007); Percent of households with income of $100,000 or more: 20.8% (2007); Poverty rate: 5.3% (2005); Bankruptcy rate: 5.15% (2007).
Taxes: Total county taxes per capita: $197 (2006); County property taxes per capita: $190 (2006).
Education: Percent of population age 25 and over with: High school diploma (including GED) or higher: 86.4% (2007); Bachelor's degree or higher: 14.6% (2007); Master's degree or higher: 4.0% (2007).
Housing: Homeownership rate: 74.3% (2007); Median home value: $200,076 (2007); Median rent: $508 per month (2000); Median age of housing: 29 years (2000).
Health: Birth rate: 172.0 per 10,000 population (2007); Death rate: 72.5 per 10,000 population (2007); Age-adjusted cancer mortality rate: 226.1 deaths per 100,000 population (2005); Number of physicians: 12.0 per 10,000 population (2005); Hospital beds: 20.0 per 10,000 population (2004); Hospital admissions: 1,089.8 per 10,000 population (2004).
Elections: 2004 Presidential election results: 56.5% Bush, 42.7% Kerry, 0.1% Nader, 0.7% Badnarik
National and State Parks: Gebhard Woods State Park; Goose Lake Prairie State Park; Heidecke State Fish and Wildlife Area; Mazonia State Fish and Wildlife Area; William Stratton State Access Area
Additional Information Contacts
Grundy County Government . . . . (815) 941-3400
http://www.grundyco.org
City of Morris . . . . (815) 942-0103
http://city.mornet.org
Greater Channahon-Minooka Area Chamber of Commerce (815) 521-9999
http://www.cmchamber.org
Grundy County Chamber of Commerce & Industry . . . . (815) 942-0113
http://www.grundychamber.com

Grundy County Communities

BRACEVILLE (village). Covers a land area of 1.316 square miles and a water area of 0.011 square miles. Located at 41.22° N. Lat.; 88.26° W. Long. Elevation is 577 feet.
History: Braceville boomed as a coal-mining town in the late 1800's, but declined when the mines closed.
Population: 590 (1990); 792 (2000); 918 (2007); 991 (2012 projected); Race: 98.1% White, 0.0% Black, 0.0% Asian, 1.2% Hispanic of any race (2007); Density: 697.5 persons per square mile (2007); Average household size: 2.72 (2007); Median age: 32.5 (2007); Males per 100 females: 95.7 (2007); Marriage status: 24.2% never married, 60.0% now married, 3.5% widowed, 12.3% divorced (2000); Foreign born: 0.2% (2000); Ancestry (includes multiple ancestries): 33.4% German, 18.8% Irish, 11.3% Other groups, 9.7% English, 8.2% Italian (2000).
Economy: Employment by occupation: 6.0% management, 10.5% professional, 18.4% services, 22.6% sales, 0.0% farming, 20.2% construction, 22.3% production (2000).
Income: Per capita income: $21,511 (2007); Median household income: $54,694 (2007); Average household income: $58,425 (2007); Percent of

households with income of $100,000 or more: 8.0% (2007); Poverty rate: 4.3% (2000).
Education: Percent of population age 25 and over with: High school diploma (including GED) or higher: 82.0% (2007); Bachelor's degree or higher: 6.6% (2007); Master's degree or higher: 1.5% (2007).

School District(s)

Braceville SD 75 (KG-08)
2005-06 Enrollment: 173 . . . . (815) 237-8040
Housing: Homeownership rate: 83.4% (2007); Median home value: $157,042 (2007); Median rent: $565 per month (2000); Median age of housing: 41 years (2000).
Transportation: Commute to work: 95.8% car, 0.5% public transportation, 1.3% walk, 1.9% work from home (2000); Travel time to work: 21.4% less than 15 minutes, 24.3% 15 to 30 minutes, 29.5% 30 to 45 minutes, 10.3% 45 to 60 minutes, 14.6% 60 minutes or more (2000)

CARBON HILL (village). Covers a land area of 0.176 square miles and a water area of 0 square miles. Located at 41.29° N. Lat.; 88.30° W. Long. Elevation is 561 feet.
Population: 362 (1990); 392 (2000); 433 (2007); 468 (2012 projected); Race: 97.0% White, 0.0% Black, 0.0% Asian, 3.7% Hispanic of any race (2007); Density: 2,459.8 persons per square mile (2007); Average household size: 2.55 (2007); Median age: 34.5 (2007); Males per 100 females: 91.6 (2007); Marriage status: 23.1% never married, 56.0% now married, 5.5% widowed, 15.3% divorced (2000); Foreign born: 1.8% (2000); Ancestry (includes multiple ancestries): 25.0% Irish, 24.7% German, 18.2% Italian, 12.1% Other groups, 7.4% English (2000).
Economy: Single-family building permits issued: 3 (2007); Multi-family building permits issued: 0 (2007); Employment by occupation: 8.2% management, 10.9% professional, 10.4% services, 27.9% sales, 0.0% farming, 24.6% construction, 18.0% production (2000).
Income: Per capita income: $26,622 (2007); Median household income: $62,143 (2007); Average household income: $67,809 (2007); Percent of households with income of $100,000 or more: 18.8% (2007); Poverty rate: 3.0% (2000).
Taxes: Total city taxes per capita: $140 (2006); City property taxes per capita: $96 (2006).
Education: Percent of population age 25 and over with: High school diploma (including GED) or higher: 78.5% (2007); Bachelor's degree or higher: 6.0% (2007); Master's degree or higher: 3.0% (2007).
Housing: Homeownership rate: 78.2% (2007); Median home value: $173,558 (2007); Median rent: $482 per month (2000); Median age of housing: 28 years (2000).
Transportation: Commute to work: 95.1% car, 0.0% public transportation, 0.5% walk, 4.4% work from home (2000); Travel time to work: 24.0% less than 15 minutes, 28.0% 15 to 30 minutes, 23.4% 30 to 45 minutes, 8.0% 45 to 60 minutes, 16.6% 60 minutes or more (2000)

COAL CITY (village). Covers a land area of 2.423 square miles and a water area of 0 square miles. Located at 41.28° N. Lat.; 88.28° W. Long. Elevation is 564 feet.
History: Coal City began when shaft mines were opened here in 1875. The shaft mines were followed by strip mining.
Population: 4,021 (1990); 4,797 (2000); 5,550 (2007); 6,170 (2012 projected); Race: 96.9% White, 1.0% Black, 0.0% Asian, 2.7% Hispanic of any race (2007); Density: 2,290.9 persons per square mile (2007); Average household size: 2.55 (2007); Median age: 34.7 (2007); Males per 100 females: 96.8 (2007); Marriage status: 23.2% never married, 59.8% now married, 8.3% widowed, 8.7% divorced (2000); Foreign born: 1.1% (2000); Ancestry (includes multiple ancestries): 27.5% German, 21.2% Irish, 19.6% Italian, 14.4% English, 5.3% Other groups (2000).
Economy: Single-family building permits issued: 45 (2007); Multi-family building permits issued: 0 (2007); Employment by occupation: 7.4% management, 18.0% professional, 14.7% services, 20.2% sales, 0.2% farming, 18.9% construction, 20.6% production (2000).
Income: Per capita income: $27,691 (2007); Median household income: $60,824 (2007); Average household income: $70,562 (2007); Percent of households with income of $100,000 or more: 22.7% (2007); Poverty rate: 3.1% (2000).
Education: Percent of population age 25 and over with: High school diploma (including GED) or higher: 90.3% (2007); Bachelor's degree or higher: 13.8% (2007); Master's degree or higher: 3.6% (2007).

School District(s)

Coal City CUSD 1 (PK-12)
2005-06 Enrollment: 2,018 . . . . (815) 634-2287
Housing: Homeownership rate: 73.0% (2007); Median home value: $184,352 (2007); Median rent: $501 per month (2000); Median age of housing: 33 years (2000).
Safety: Violent crime rate: 5.8 per 10,000 population; Property crime rate: 205.0 per 10,000 population (2006).
Newspapers: Coal City Courant (Local news; Circulation 2,400)
Transportation: Commute to work: 97.0% car, 0.0% public transportation, 1.3% walk, 1.0% work from home (2000); Travel time to work: 28.0% less than 15 minutes, 35.7% 15 to 30 minutes, 20.8% 30 to 45 minutes, 7.0% 45 to 60 minutes, 8.5% 60 minutes or more (2000)

DIAMOND (village). Covers a land area of 1.582 square miles and a water area of 0 square miles. Located at 41.28° N. Lat.; 88.25° W. Long. Elevation is 564 feet.
Population: 1,236 (1990); 1,393 (2000); 1,695 (2007); 1,939 (2012 projected); Race: 95.5% White, 0.0% Black, 0.1% Asian, 5.6% Hispanic of any race (2007); Density: 1,071.2 persons per square mile (2007); Average household size: 2.48 (2007); Median age: 34.0 (2007); Males per 100 females: 93.5 (2007); Marriage status: 23.2% never married, 55.2% now married, 5.5% widowed, 16.0% divorced (2000); Foreign born: 0.4% (2000); Ancestry (includes multiple ancestries): 24.6% German, 19.2% Italian, 17.5% Irish, 13.8% English, 7.7% Polish (2000).
Economy: Single-family building permits issued: 10 (2007); Multi-family building permits issued: 4 (2007); Employment by occupation: 9.8% management, 11.1% professional, 14.5% services, 28.4% sales, 0.0% farming, 16.0% construction, 20.3% production (2000).
Income: Per capita income: $25,715 (2007); Median household income: $53,700 (2007); Average household income: $63,818 (2007); Percent of households with income of $100,000 or more: 17.6% (2007); Poverty rate: 8.6% (2000).
Education: Percent of population age 25 and over with: High school diploma (including GED) or higher: 84.7% (2007); Bachelor's degree or higher: 8.9% (2007); Master's degree or higher: 2.8% (2007).
Housing: Homeownership rate: 75.4% (2007); Median home value: $165,733 (2007); Median rent: $596 per month (2000); Median age of housing: 22 years (2000).
Transportation: Commute to work: 95.7% car, 0.6% public transportation, 1.7% walk, 1.2% work from home (2000); Travel time to work: 20.8% less than 15 minutes, 33.0% 15 to 30 minutes, 23.5% 30 to 45 minutes, 8.9% 45 to 60 minutes, 13.8% 60 minutes or more (2000)

EAST BROOKLYN (village). Covers a land area of 0.052 square miles and a water area of 0 square miles. Located at 41.17° N. Lat.; 88.26° W. Long. Elevation is 584 feet.
Population: 88 (1990); 123 (2000); 101 (2007); 105 (2012 projected); Race: 88.1% White, 0.0% Black, 3.0% Asian, 5.0% Hispanic of any race (2007); Density: 1,945.6 persons per square mile (2007); Average household size: 2.59 (2007); Median age: 35.8 (2007); Males per 100 females: 62.9 (2007); Marriage status: 35.4% never married, 54.9% now married, 6.1% widowed, 3.7% divorced (2000); Foreign born: 0.0% (2000); Ancestry (includes multiple ancestries): 54.9% Italian, 16.7% German, 12.7% Irish, 9.8% Czech, 9.8% Norwegian (2000).
Economy: Single-family building permits issued: 1 (2007); Multi-family building permits issued: 0 (2007); Employment by occupation: 6.3% management, 27.1% professional, 6.3% services, 8.3% sales, 0.0% farming, 29.2% construction, 22.9% production (2000).
Income: Per capita income: $25,446 (2007); Median household income: $55,000 (2007); Average household income: $65,897 (2007); Percent of households with income of $100,000 or more: 17.9% (2007); Poverty rate: 12.7% (2000).
Education: Percent of population age 25 and over with: High school diploma (including GED) or higher: 80.3% (2007); Bachelor's degree or higher: 9.1% (2007); Master's degree or higher: 0.0% (2007).
Housing: Homeownership rate: 82.1% (2007); Median home value: $166,667 (2007); Median rent: $275 per month (2000); Median age of housing: 41 years (2000).
Transportation: Commute to work: 100.0% car, 0.0% public transportation, 0.0% walk, 0.0% work from home (2000); Travel time to work: 16.7% less than 15 minutes, 35.4% 15 to 30 minutes, 37.5% 30 to 45 minutes, 0.0% 45 to 60 minutes, 10.4% 60 minutes or more (2000)

GARDNER (village). Covers a land area of 1.040 square miles and a water area of 0.014 square miles. Located at 41.18° N. Lat.; 88.31° W. Long. Elevation is 587 feet.

Population: 1,237 (1990); 1,406 (2000); 1,566 (2007); 1,658 (2012 projected); Race: 96.5% White, 0.4% Black, 0.3% Asian, 6.4% Hispanic of any race (2007); Density: 1,505.2 persons per square mile (2007); Average household size: 2.47 (2007); Median age: 34.7 (2007); Males per 100 females: 97.7 (2007); Marriage status: 20.4% never married, 60.5% now married, 6.9% widowed, 12.2% divorced (2000); Foreign born: 2.5% (2000); Ancestry (includes multiple ancestries): 22.3% German, 18.5% Irish, 17.1% Italian, 11.5% English, 7.3% Norwegian (2000).
Economy: Single-family building permits issued: 6 (2007); Multi-family building permits issued: 0 (2007); Employment by occupation: 4.5% management, 18.0% professional, 14.5% services, 21.6% sales, 0.6% farming, 17.8% construction, 23.0% production (2000).
Income: Per capita income: $22,502 (2007); Median household income: $46,950 (2007); Average household income: $55,492 (2007); Percent of households with income of $100,000 or more: 11.5% (2007); Poverty rate: 6.8% (2000).
Education: Percent of population age 25 and over with: High school diploma (including GED) or higher: 83.8% (2007); Bachelor's degree or higher: 9.3% (2007); Master's degree or higher: 2.3% (2007).

School District(s)

Gardner CCSD 72c (PK-08)
2005-06 Enrollment: 264 . . . . (815) 237-2313
Gardner S Wilmington Twp HSD 73 (09-12)
2005-06 Enrollment: 245 . . . . (815) 237-2176

Housing: Homeownership rate: 74.2% (2007); Median home value: $153,397 (2007); Median rent: $435 per month (2000); Median age of housing: 47 years (2000).
Transportation: Commute to work: 95.0% car, 0.0% public transportation, 2.6% walk, 1.1% work from home (2000); Travel time to work: 25.3% less than 15 minutes, 23.9% 15 to 30 minutes, 26.1% 30 to 45 minutes, 12.8% 45 to 60 minutes, 11.9% 60 minutes or more (2000)

KINSMAN (village). Covers a land area of 0.067 square miles and a water area of 0 square miles. Located at 41.19° N. Lat.; 88.57° W. Long. Elevation is 659 feet.
Population: 112 (1990); 109 (2000); 128 (2007); 141 (2012 projected); Race: 94.5% White, 0.0% Black, 0.0% Asian, 19.5% Hispanic of any race (2007); Density: 1,923.5 persons per square mile (2007); Average household size: 2.29 (2007); Median age: 45.0 (2007); Males per 100 females: 109.8 (2007); Marriage status: 16.0% never married, 72.0% now married, 10.0% widowed, 2.0% divorced (2000); Foreign born: 4.1% (2000); Ancestry (includes multiple ancestries): 29.5% German, 22.1% United States or American, 21.3% Irish, 7.4% Norwegian, 6.6% Danish (2000).
Economy: Single-family building permits issued: 0 (2007); Multi-family building permits issued: 0 (2007); Employment by occupation: 6.5% management, 4.8% professional, 3.2% services, 38.7% sales, 0.0% farming, 9.7% construction, 37.1% production (2000).
Income: Per capita income: $26,836 (2007); Median household income: $50,000 (2007); Average household income: $61,339 (2007); Percent of households with income of $100,000 or more: 17.9% (2007); Poverty rate: 0.0% (2000).
Education: Percent of population age 25 and over with: High school diploma (including GED) or higher: 77.5% (2007); Bachelor's degree or higher: 9.0% (2007); Master's degree or higher: 0.0% (2007).
Housing: Homeownership rate: 89.3% (2007); Median home value: $125,000 (2007); Median rent: $425 per month (2000); Median age of housing: 56 years (2000).
Transportation: Commute to work: 88.7% car, 0.0% public transportation, 3.2% walk, 4.8% work from home (2000); Travel time to work: 16.9% less than 15 minutes, 37.3% 15 to 30 minutes, 18.6% 30 to 45 minutes, 18.6% 45 to 60 minutes, 8.5% 60 minutes or more (2000)

MAZON (village). Covers a land area of 0.598 square miles and a water area of 0 square miles. Located at 41.24° N. Lat.; 88.42° W. Long. Elevation is 587 feet.
History: Near the Mazon River, a classic source of fossils from a middle Pennsylvanian formation.
Population: 818 (1990); 904 (2000); 851 (2007); 894 (2012 projected); Race: 92.0% White, 2.2% Black, 0.1% Asian, 4.0% Hispanic of any race (2007); Density: 1,422.1 persons per square mile (2007); Average household size: 2.55 (2007); Median age: 34.2 (2007); Males per 100 females: 100.7 (2007); Marriage status: 16.7% never married, 69.5% now married, 5.3% widowed, 8.4% divorced (2000); Foreign born: 1.6% (2000); Ancestry (includes multiple ancestries): 22.3% German, 20.8% English, 19.1% Irish, 12.0% Other groups, 10.4% Norwegian (2000).
Economy: Single-family building permits issued: 0 (2007); Multi-family building permits issued: 2 (2007); Employment by occupation: 10.8% management, 18.0% professional, 12.2% services, 19.0% sales, 0.9% farming, 16.6% construction, 22.5% production (2000).
Income: Per capita income: $26,633 (2007); Median household income: $62,547 (2007); Average household income: $67,859 (2007); Percent of households with income of $100,000 or more: 17.7% (2007); Poverty rate: 3.4% (2000).
Education: Percent of population age 25 and over with: High school diploma (including GED) or higher: 90.7% (2007); Bachelor's degree or higher: 15.7% (2007); Master's degree or higher: 7.8% (2007).

School District(s)

Mazon-Verona-Kinsman ESD 2c (PK-08)
2005-06 Enrollment: 316 . . . . (815) 448-2200

Housing: Homeownership rate: 76.9% (2007); Median home value: $165,675 (2007); Median rent: $504 per month (2000); Median age of housing: 41 years (2000).
Transportation: Commute to work: 94.3% car, 0.5% public transportation, 2.2% walk, 2.9% work from home (2000); Travel time to work: 30.5% less than 15 minutes, 27.8% 15 to 30 minutes, 20.7% 30 to 45 minutes, 13.5% 45 to 60 minutes, 7.4% 60 minutes or more (2000)

MINOOKA (village). Covers a land area of 4.263 square miles and a water area of 0.071 square miles. Located at 41.45° N. Lat.; 88.26° W. Long. Elevation is 610 feet.
Population: 3,024 (1990); 3,971 (2000); 6,496 (2007); 8,150 (2012 projected); Race: 95.6% White, 1.2% Black, 0.7% Asian, 4.7% Hispanic of any race (2007); Density: 1,523.8 persons per square mile (2007); Average household size: 3.02 (2007); Median age: 33.1 (2007); Males per 100 females: 98.3 (2007); Marriage status: 23.7% never married, 65.9% now married, 2.9% widowed, 7.5% divorced (2000); Foreign born: 1.9% (2000); Ancestry (includes multiple ancestries): 34.2% German, 22.6% Irish, 11.0% Italian, 10.0% English, 7.8% Polish (2000).
Economy: Single-family building permits issued: 46 (2007); Multi-family building permits issued: 0 (2007); Employment by occupation: 14.7% management, 23.1% professional, 12.0% services, 23.1% sales, 0.6% farming, 12.5% construction, 14.0% production (2000).
Income: Per capita income: $31,727 (2007); Median household income: $89,952 (2007); Average household income: $95,816 (2007); Percent of households with income of $100,000 or more: 41.2% (2007); Poverty rate: 2.2% (2000).
Education: Percent of population age 25 and over with: High school diploma (including GED) or higher: 95.1% (2007); Bachelor's degree or higher: 28.4% (2007); Master's degree or higher: 10.0% (2007).

School District(s)

Minooka CCSD 201 (PK-08)
2005-06 Enrollment: 2,784 . . . . (815) 467-6121
Minooka CHSD 111 (09-12)
2005-06 Enrollment: 1,847 . . . . (815) 467-2557

Housing: Homeownership rate: 85.9% (2007); Median home value: $268,473 (2007); Median rent: $557 per month (2000); Median age of housing: 14 years (2000).
Safety: Violent crime rate: 15.5 per 10,000 population; Property crime rate: 177.3 per 10,000 population (2006).
Transportation: Commute to work: 96.0% car, 0.7% public transportation, 1.3% walk, 2.0% work from home (2000); Travel time to work: 27.2% less than 15 minutes, 38.9% 15 to 30 minutes, 17.8% 30 to 45 minutes, 7.1% 45 to 60 minutes, 9.1% 60 minutes or more (2000)

Additional Information Contacts

Greater Channahon-Minooka Area Chamber of Commerce (815) 521-9999
http://www.cmchamber.org

MORRIS (city). County seat. Covers a land area of 6.879 square miles and a water area of 0.281 square miles. Located at 41.36° N. Lat.; 88.42° W. Long. Elevation is 515 feet.
History: Morris was platted in 1842 and named for Isaac N. Morris, an Illinois & Michigan Canal commissioner, who negotiated to have the village named as the county seat. Morris grew as a shipping and paper manufacturing center.
Population: 10,429 (1990); 11,928 (2000); 12,826 (2007); 13,723 (2012 projected); Race: 89.9% White, 2.4% Black, 1.0% Asian, 11.4% Hispanic of any race (2007); Density: 1,864.5 persons per square mile (2007); Average household size: 2.41 (2007); Median age: 36.0 (2007); Males per 100

females: 97.5 (2007); Marriage status: 24.0% never married, 56.2% now married, 9.6% widowed, 10.2% divorced (2000); Foreign born: 3.9% (2000); Ancestry (includes multiple ancestries): 21.6% German, 20.1% Irish, 13.4% Norwegian, 12.3% Other groups, 8.9% English (2000).
Economy: Single-family building permits issued: 19 (2007); Multi-family building permits issued: 53 (2007); Employment by occupation: 9.8% management, 15.3% professional, 17.6% services, 26.7% sales, 0.0% farming, 11.3% construction, 19.3% production (2000).
Income: Per capita income: $26,869 (2007); Median household income: $51,019 (2007); Average household income: $63,645 (2007); Percent of households with income of $100,000 or more: 17.0% (2007); Poverty rate: 6.6% (2000).
Education: Percent of population age 25 and over with: High school diploma (including GED) or higher: 84.2% (2007); Bachelor's degree or higher: 18.9% (2007); Master's degree or higher: 5.2% (2007).

School District(s)

Grundy Area Vocational Center
2005-06 Enrollment: n/a . . . . (815) 942-4390
Grundy/Kendall Roe (09-12)
2005-06 Enrollment: 119 . . . . (815) 941-3247
Morris CHSD 101 (09-12)
2005-06 Enrollment: 984 . . . . (815) 941-5327
Morris SD 54 (PK-08)
2005-06 Enrollment: 1,235 . . . . (815) 942-0056
Nettle Creek CCSD 24c (KG-08)
2005-06 Enrollment: 101 . . . . (815) 942-0511
Saratoga CCSD 60c (PK-08)
2005-06 Enrollment: 642 . . . . (815) 942-2128

Housing: Homeownership rate: 57.5% (2007); Median home value: $202,837 (2007); Median rent: $500 per month (2000); Median age of housing: 32 years (2000).
Hospitals: Morris Hospital (82 beds)
Safety: Violent crime rate: 17.8 per 10,000 population; Property crime rate: 412.7 per 10,000 population (2006).
Newspapers: Morris Daily Herald (Local news; Circulation 7,500)
Transportation: Commute to work: 93.3% car, 1.1% public transportation, 2.4% walk, 2.5% work from home (2000); Travel time to work: 47.4% less than 15 minutes, 20.7% 15 to 30 minutes, 18.2% 30 to 45 minutes, 5.0% 45 to 60 minutes, 8.7% 60 minutes or more (2000)

Additional Information Contacts

City of Morris . . . . (815) 942-0103
http://city.mornet.org
Grundy County Chamber of Commerce & Industry . . . . (815) 942-0113
http://www.grundychamber.com

SOUTH WILMINGTON (village). Covers a land area of 0.570 square miles and a water area of 0 square miles. Located at 41.17° N. Lat.; 88.27° W. Long. Elevation is 587 feet.
Population: 710 (1990); 621 (2000); 516 (2007); 535 (2012 projected); Race: 96.7% White, 0.0% Black, 0.0% Asian, 4.8% Hispanic of any race (2007); Density: 905.5 persons per square mile (2007); Average household size: 2.35 (2007); Median age: 39.7 (2007); Males per 100 females: 93.3 (2007); Marriage status: 25.8% never married, 55.4% now married, 9.6% widowed, 9.2% divorced (2000); Foreign born: 0.0% (2000); Ancestry (includes multiple ancestries): 38.2% Italian, 19.7% Irish, 17.8% German, 14.9% English, 7.4% Polish (2000).
Economy: Single-family building permits issued: 0 (2007); Multi-family building permits issued: 0 (2007); Employment by occupation: 6.2% management, 14.1% professional, 12.4% services, 19.9% sales, 1.0% farming, 23.9% construction, 22.5% production (2000).
Income: Per capita income: $25,036 (2007); Median household income: $44,250 (2007); Average household income: $57,545 (2007); Percent of households with income of $100,000 or more: 13.2% (2007); Poverty rate: 7.9% (2000).
Education: Percent of population age 25 and over with: High school diploma (including GED) or higher: 83.9% (2007); Bachelor's degree or higher: 7.0% (2007); Master's degree or higher: 1.9% (2007).

School District(s)

South Wilmington CCSD 74 (KG-08)
2005-06 Enrollment: 86 . . . . (815) 237-2281

Housing: Homeownership rate: 85.0% (2007); Median home value: $140,890 (2007); Median rent: $500 per month (2000); Median age of housing: 55 years (2000).
Transportation: Commute to work: 96.0% car, 0.0% public transportation, 2.7% walk, 0.7% work from home (2000); Travel time to work: 20.7% less than 15 minutes, 25.4% 15 to 30 minutes, 36.8% 30 to 45 minutes, 8.7% 45 to 60 minutes, 8.4% 60 minutes or more (2000)

VERONA (village). Covers a land area of 0.146 square miles and a water area of 0 square miles. Located at 41.21° N. Lat.; 88.50° W. Long. Elevation is 630 feet.
Population: 242 (1990); 257 (2000); 283 (2007); 299 (2012 projected); Race: 95.1% White, 0.0% Black, 0.0% Asian, 15.5% Hispanic of any race (2007); Density: 1,941.1 persons per square mile (2007); Average household size: 2.86 (2007); Median age: 33.5 (2007); Males per 100 females: 103.6 (2007); Marriage status: 19.7% never married, 63.7% now married, 12.4% widowed, 4.1% divorced (2000); Foreign born: 4.0% (2000); Ancestry (includes multiple ancestries): 19.5% Irish, 16.3% Other groups, 16.3% German, 8.0% United States or American, 7.2% Italian (2000).
Economy: Single-family building permits issued: 0 (2007); Multi-family building permits issued: 0 (2007); Employment by occupation: 1.9% management, 8.7% professional, 18.3% services, 27.9% sales, 0.0% farming, 12.5% construction, 30.8% production (2000).
Income: Per capita income: $17,995 (2007); Median household income: $51,944 (2007); Average household income: $51,439 (2007); Percent of households with income of $100,000 or more: 6.1% (2007); Poverty rate: 5.2% (2000).
Education: Percent of population age 25 and over with: High school diploma (including GED) or higher: 70.9% (2007); Bachelor's degree or higher: 4.6% (2007); Master's degree or higher: 0.0% (2007).
Housing: Homeownership rate: 86.9% (2007); Median home value: $105,556 (2007); Median rent: $381 per month (2000); Median age of housing: 59 years (2000).
Transportation: Commute to work: 91.8% car, 0.0% public transportation, 0.0% walk, 8.2% work from home (2000); Travel time to work: 11.1% less than 15 minutes, 42.2% 15 to 30 minutes, 26.7% 30 to 45 minutes, 0.0% 45 to 60 minutes, 20.0% 60 minutes or more (2000)

Hamilton County

Located in southeastern Illinois; drained by the North Fork of the Saline River. Covers a land area of 435.16 square miles, a water area of 0.67 square miles, and is located in the Central Time Zone. The county was founded in 1821. County seat is McLeansboro.

Hamilton County is part of the Mount Vernon, IL Micropolitan Statistical Area. The entire metro area includes: Hamilton County, IL; Jefferson County, IL

Weather Station: McLeansboro 2 ENE Elevation: 479 feet

	Jan	Feb	Mar	Apr	May	Jun	Jul	Aug	Sep	Oct	Nov	Dec
High	38	44	54	66	76	85	89	88	81	69	55	44
Low	20	24	34	44	53	62	66	63	55	43	35	25
Precip	3.1	2.7	4.5	4.7	4.6	3.8	3.5	3.0	2.9	3.1	4.5	3.6
Snow	5.0	4.4	2.5	0.4	0.0	0.0	0.0	0.0	0.0	0.2	0.7	3.1

High and Low temperatures in degrees Fahrenheit; Precipitation and Snow in inches

Population: 8,499 (1990); 8,621 (2000); 8,227 (2007); 7,941 (2012 projected); Race: 98.1% White, 0.6% Black, 0.2% Asian, 1.2% Hispanic of any race (2007); Density: 18.9 persons per square mile (2007); Average household size: 2.50 (2007); Median age: 42.4 (2007); Males per 100 females: 93.3 (2007).
Religion: Five largest groups: 33.3% Southern Baptist Convention, 11.8% Catholic Church, 4.9% The United Methodist Church, 3.7% Christian Churches and Churches of Christ, 1.3% Church of God (Cleveland, Tennessee) (2000).
Economy: Unemployment rate: 6.1% (4/2008); Total civilian labor force: 4,344 (4/2008); Leading industries: 32.0% health care and social assistance; 16.5% retail trade; 8.5% accommodation & food services (2005); Farms: 694 totaling 234,314 acres (2002); Companies that employ 500 or more persons: 0 (2006); Companies that employ 100 to 499 persons: 1 (2006); Companies that employ less than 100 persons: 188 (2006); Black-owned businesses: n/a (2002); Hispanic-owned businesses: n/a (2002); Asian-owned businesses: n/a (2002); Women-owned businesses: n/a (2002); Retail sales per capita: $6,468 (2008). Single-family building permits issued: 0 (2007); Multi-family building permits issued: 0 (2007).
Income: Per capita income: $19,469 (2007); Median household income: $37,489 (2007); Average household income: $48,115 (2007); Percent of

households with income of $100,000 or more: 8.0% (2007); Poverty rate: 13.8% (2005); Bankruptcy rate: 2.67% (2007).
Education: Percent of population age 25 and over with: High school diploma (including GED) or higher: 74.5% (2007); Bachelor's degree or higher: 10.5% (2007); Master's degree or higher: 3.8% (2007).
Housing: Homeownership rate: 81.5% (2007); Median home value: $69,220 (2007); Median rent: $164 per month (2000); Median age of housing: 39 years (2000).
Health: Birth rate: 105.5 per 10,000 population (2007); Death rate: 118.9 per 10,000 population (2007); Age-adjusted cancer mortality rate: 183.8 deaths per 100,000 population (2005); Air Quality Index: 60.1% good, 38.3% moderate, 1.6% unhealthy for sensitive individuals, 0.0% unhealthy (percent of days in 2007); Number of physicians: 6.0 per 10,000 population (2005); Hospital beds: 108.5 per 10,000 population (2004); Hospital admissions: 1,097.1 per 10,000 population (2004).
Elections: 2004 Presidential election results: 58.8% Bush, 40.2% Kerry, 0.0% Nader, 1.0% Badnarik
National and State Parks: Hamilton County State Conservation Area
Additional Information Contacts
Hamilton County Government . . . . (618) 643-2721

Hamilton County Chamber of Commerce . . . . (618) 643-2351
http://www.mcleansboro.com

Hamilton County Communities

BELLE PRAIRIE CITY (town). Aka Belle Prairie. Covers a land area of 0.449 square miles and a water area of 0 square miles. Located at 38.22° N. Lat.; 88.55° W. Long. Elevation is 476 feet.
Population: 64 (1990); 60 (2000); 58 (2007); 57 (2012 projected); Race: 100.0% White, 0.0% Black, 0.0% Asian, 0.0% Hispanic of any race (2007); Density: 129.2 persons per square mile (2007); Average household size: 2.52 (2007); Median age: 44.2 (2007); Males per 100 females: 93.3 (2007); Marriage status: 13.6% never married, 70.5% now married, 13.6% widowed, 2.3% divorced (2000); Foreign born: 0.0% (2000); Ancestry (includes multiple ancestries): 17.2% German, 15.5% Italian, 15.5% English, 12.1% Irish, 5.2% Other groups (2000).
Economy: Employment by occupation: 19.2% management, 26.9% professional, 19.2% services, 19.2% sales, 0.0% farming, 7.7% construction, 7.7% production (2000).
Income: Per capita income: $24,095 (2007); Median household income: $43,056 (2007); Average household income: $60,761 (2007); Percent of households with income of $100,000 or more: 26.1% (2007); Poverty rate: 0.0% (2000).
Education: Percent of population age 25 and over with: High school diploma (including GED) or higher: 85.7% (2007); Bachelor's degree or higher: 14.3% (2007); Master's degree or higher: 0.0% (2007).
Housing: Homeownership rate: 95.7% (2007); Median home value: $93,333 (2007); Median rent: $n/a per month (2000); Median age of housing: 48 years (2000).
Transportation: Commute to work: 100.0% car, 0.0% public transportation, 0.0% walk, 0.0% work from home (2000); Travel time to work: 11.5% less than 15 minutes, 30.8% 15 to 30 minutes, 38.5% 30 to 45 minutes, 3.8% 45 to 60 minutes, 15.4% 60 minutes or more (2000)

BROUGHTON (village). Covers a land area of 1.918 square miles and a water area of 0 square miles. Located at 37.93° N. Lat.; 88.46° W. Long. Elevation is 377 feet.
Population: 218 (1990); 193 (2000); 180 (2007); 178 (2012 projected); Race: 98.9% White, 0.0% Black, 1.1% Asian, 0.6% Hispanic of any race (2007); Density: 93.9 persons per square mile (2007); Average household size: 2.28 (2007); Median age: 41.8 (2007); Males per 100 females: 81.8 (2007); Marriage status: 13.8% never married, 56.9% now married, 10.6% widowed, 18.8% divorced (2000); Foreign born: 0.5% (2000); Ancestry (includes multiple ancestries): 18.8% United States or American, 17.3% English, 8.9% German, 7.9% Irish, 5.4% Other groups (2000).
Economy: Employment by occupation: 9.3% management, 13.3% professional, 24.0% services, 24.0% sales, 8.0% farming, 14.7% construction, 6.7% production (2000).
Income: Per capita income: $11,444 (2007); Median household income: $22,045 (2007); Average household income: $26,076 (2007); Percent of households with income of $100,000 or more: 0.0% (2007); Poverty rate: 27.2% (2000).
Education: Percent of population age 25 and over with: High school diploma (including GED) or higher: 71.7% (2007); Bachelor's degree or higher: 5.0% (2007); Master's degree or higher: 0.0% (2007).
Housing: Homeownership rate: 86.1% (2007); Median home value: $33,000 (2007); Median rent: $125 per month (2000); Median age of housing: 44 years (2000).
Transportation: Commute to work: 92.0% car, 0.0% public transportation, 8.0% walk, 0.0% work from home (2000); Travel time to work: 26.7% less than 15 minutes, 29.3% 15 to 30 minutes, 24.0% 30 to 45 minutes, 9.3% 45 to 60 minutes, 10.7% 60 minutes or more (2000)

DAHLGREN (village). Covers a land area of 1.004 square miles and a water area of 0 square miles. Located at 38.19° N. Lat.; 88.68° W. Long. Elevation is 515 feet.
Population: 512 (1990); 514 (2000); 497 (2007); 486 (2012 projected); Race: 100.0% White, 0.0% Black, 0.0% Asian, 0.8% Hispanic of any race (2007); Density: 495.2 persons per square mile (2007); Average household size: 2.34 (2007); Median age: 42.3 (2007); Males per 100 females: 91.9 (2007); Marriage status: 23.6% never married, 57.1% now married, 11.0% widowed, 8.3% divorced (2000); Foreign born: 0.6% (2000); Ancestry (includes multiple ancestries): 23.4% German, 18.5% United States or American, 17.2% English, 14.4% Irish, 7.8% Other groups (2000).
Economy: Employment by occupation: 6.5% management, 8.9% professional, 23.8% services, 29.0% sales, 4.2% farming, 4.2% construction, 23.4% production (2000).
Income: Per capita income: $17,541 (2007); Median household income: $35,500 (2007); Average household income: $40,696 (2007); Percent of households with income of $100,000 or more: 1.9% (2007); Poverty rate: 13.5% (2000).
Education: Percent of population age 25 and over with: High school diploma (including GED) or higher: 79.1% (2007); Bachelor's degree or higher: 6.1% (2007); Master's degree or higher: 1.5% (2007).

School District(s)

Hamilton Co CUSD 10 (PK-12)
2005-06 Enrollment: 1,290 . . . . (618) 643-2328
Housing: Homeownership rate: 84.4% (2007); Median home value: $39,423 (2007); Median rent: $178 per month (2000); Median age of housing: 54 years (2000).
Transportation: Commute to work: 94.8% car, 0.0% public transportation, 0.5% walk, 2.8% work from home (2000); Travel time to work: 14.0% less than 15 minutes, 57.0% 15 to 30 minutes, 20.3% 30 to 45 minutes, 5.3% 45 to 60 minutes, 3.4% 60 minutes or more (2000)

DALE (unincorporated postal area, zip code 62829). Aka Dales. Covers a land area of 6.561 square miles and a water area of 0 square miles. Located at 38.00° N. Lat.; 88.50° W. Long. Elevation is 400 feet.
Population: 157 (2000); Race: 100.0% White, 0.0% Black, 0.0% Asian, 3.5% Hispanic of any race (2000); Density: 23.9 persons per square mile (2000); Age: 22.9% under 18, 5.3% over 64 (2000); Marriage status: 15.7% never married, 75.7% now married, 0.0% widowed, 8.6% divorced (2000); Foreign born: 1.8% (2000); Ancestry (includes multiple ancestries): 17.1% German, 11.2% United States or American, 11.2% Irish, 8.2% European, 4.7% Danish (2000).
Economy: Employment by occupation: 0.0% management, 28.0% professional, 22.6% services, 15.1% sales, 9.7% farming, 8.6% construction, 16.1% production (2000).
Income: Per capita income: $16,996 (2000); Median household income: $50,417 (2000); Poverty rate: 0.0% (2000).
Education: Percent of population age 25 and over with: High school diploma (including GED) or higher: 83.9% (2000); Bachelor's degree or higher: 11.9% (2000).
Housing: Homeownership rate: 90.2% (2000); Median home value: $58,600 (2000); Median rent: $n/a per month (2000); Median age of housing: 43 years (2000).
Transportation: Commute to work: 93.5% car, 0.0% public transportation, 0.0% walk, 6.5% work from home (2000); Travel time to work: 21.8% less than 15 minutes, 40.2% 15 to 30 minutes, 19.5% 30 to 45 minutes, 8.0% 45 to 60 minutes, 10.3% 60 minutes or more (2000)

MACEDONIA (village). Covers a land area of 0.271 square miles and a water area of 0 square miles. Located at 38.05° N. Lat.; 88.70° W. Long.
Population: 58 (1990); 51 (2000); 51 (2007); 49 (2012 projected); Race: 100.0% White, 0.0% Black, 0.0% Asian, 0.0% Hispanic of any race (2007); Density: 188.4 persons per square mile (2007); Average household size: 3.00 (2007); Median age: 34.2 (2007); Males per 100 females: 168.4

(2007); Marriage status: 31.7% never married, 61.0% now married, 4.9% widowed, 2.4% divorced (2000); Foreign born: 0.0% (2000); Ancestry (includes multiple ancestries): 18.2% United States or American, 7.3% German, 7.3% English, 3.6% Dutch, 3.6% Irish (2000).
Economy: Employment by occupation: 10.3% management, 6.9% professional, 20.7% services, 34.5% sales, 0.0% farming, 0.0% construction, 27.6% production (2000).
Income: Per capita income: $13,971 (2007); Median household income: $24,500 (2007); Average household income: $41,912 (2007); Percent of households with income of $100,000 or more: 0.0% (2007); Poverty rate: 23.6% (2000).
Education: Percent of population age 25 and over with: High school diploma (including GED) or higher: 71.9% (2007); Bachelor's degree or higher: 6.3% (2007); Master's degree or higher: 0.0% (2007).
Housing: Homeownership rate: 76.5% (2007); Median home value: $57,500 (2007); Median rent: $313 per month (2000); Median age of housing: 32 years (2000).
Transportation: Commute to work: 82.8% car, 0.0% public transportation, 0.0% walk, 17.2% work from home (2000); Travel time to work: 8.3% less than 15 minutes, 41.7% 15 to 30 minutes, 16.7% 30 to 45 minutes, 20.8% 45 to 60 minutes, 12.5% 60 minutes or more (2000)

MCLEANSBORO (city). County seat. Covers a land area of 2.290 square miles and a water area of 0 square miles. Located at 38.09° N. Lat.; 88.53° W. Long. Elevation is 502 feet.
History: Incorporated 1840.
Population: 2,851 (1990); 2,945 (2000); 2,770 (2007); 2,639 (2012 projected); Race: 98.2% White, 0.7% Black, 0.3% Asian, 0.6% Hispanic of any race (2007); Density: 1,209.9 persons per square mile (2007); Average household size: 2.39 (2007); Median age: 43.6 (2007); Males per 100 females: 81.3 (2007); Marriage status: 23.3% never married, 54.4% now married, 13.1% widowed, 9.2% divorced (2000); Foreign born: 0.2% (2000); Ancestry (includes multiple ancestries): 13.7% United States or American, 13.4% German, 11.0% English, 7.9% Irish, 6.0% Other groups (2000).
Economy: Single-family building permits issued: 0 (2007); Multi-family building permits issued: 0 (2007); Employment by occupation: 7.6% management, 18.9% professional, 23.2% services, 22.9% sales, 0.8% farming, 11.2% construction, 15.4% production (2000).
Income: Per capita income: $17,626 (2007); Median household income: $28,068 (2007); Average household income: $40,734 (2007); Percent of households with income of $100,000 or more: 7.3% (2007); Poverty rate: 19.7% (2000).
Education: Percent of population age 25 and over with: High school diploma (including GED) or higher: 68.2% (2007); Bachelor's degree or higher: 11.4% (2007); Master's degree or higher: 4.3% (2007).

School District(s)

Hamilton Co CUSD 10 (PK-12)
2005-06 Enrollment: 1,290 . . . . (618) 643-2328
Housing: Homeownership rate: 68.6% (2007); Median home value: $59,189 (2007); Median rent: $146 per month (2000); Median age of housing: 37 years (2000).
Hospitals: Hamilton Memorial Hospital
Safety: Violent crime rate: 75.6 per 10,000 population; Property crime rate: 133.3 per 10,000 population (2006).
Newspapers: Times Leader (Local news; Circulation 3,600)
Transportation: Commute to work: 96.1% car, 1.1% public transportation, 2.0% walk, 0.8% work from home (2000); Travel time to work: 43.8% less than 15 minutes, 11.8% 15 to 30 minutes, 30.1% 30 to 45 minutes, 8.6% 45 to 60 minutes, 5.7% 60 minutes or more (2000)
Additional Information Contacts
Hamilton County Chamber of Commerce . . . . (618) 643-2351
http://www.mcleansboro.com

Hancock County

Located in western Illinois; bounded on the west by Lake Keokuk (on the Mississippi River) and the Iowa and Missouri borders; drained by the La Moine River and Bear Creek. Covers a land area of 794.62 square miles, a water area of 19.92 square miles, and is located in the Central Time Zone. The county was founded in 1825. County seat is Carthage.

Weather Station: La Harpe Elevation: 698 feet

	Jan	Feb	Mar	Apr	May	Jun	Jul	Aug	Sep	Oct	Nov	Dec
High	32	38	50	63	74	83	87	85	78	66	50	37
Low	13	18	29	39	50	59	63	61	52	41	30	19
Precip	1.4	1.6	2.9	3.9	4.6	4.2	4.5	3.9	4.3	2.9	3.1	2.3
Snow	7.8	5.1	3.7	1.1	0.0	0.0	0.0	0.0	0.0	tr	1.9	5.5

High and Low temperatures in degrees Fahrenheit; Precipitation and Snow in inches

Population: 21,373 (1990); 20,121 (2000); 18,885 (2007); 17,968 (2012 projected); Race: 98.6% White, 0.4% Black, 0.2% Asian, 0.4% Hispanic of any race (2007); Density: 23.8 persons per square mile (2007); Average household size: 2.47 (2007); Median age: 42.8 (2007); Males per 100 females: 94.7 (2007).
Religion: Five largest groups: 12.9% Catholic Church, 9.9% The United Methodist Church, 6.4% Christian Churches and Churches of Christ, 5.7% Evangelical Lutheran Church in America, 3.4% Presbyterian Church (U.S.A.) (2000).
Economy: Unemployment rate: 5.6% (4/2008); Total civilian labor force: 10,079 (4/2008); Leading industries: 25.9% manufacturing; 18.1% retail trade; 14.1% health care and social assistance (2005); Farms: 1,095 totaling 431,823 acres (2002); Companies that employ 500 or more persons: 1 (2006); Companies that employ 100 to 499 persons: 1 (2006); Companies that employ less than 100 persons: 444 (2006); Black-owned businesses: n/a (2002); Hispanic-owned businesses: n/a (2002); Asian-owned businesses: n/a (2002); Women-owned businesses: 483 (2002); Retail sales per capita: $7,929 (2008). Single-family building permits issued: 9 (2007); Multi-family building permits issued: 10 (2007).
Income: Per capita income: $21,192 (2007); Median household income: $43,484 (2007); Average household income: $51,730 (2007); Percent of households with income of $100,000 or more: 8.1% (2007); Poverty rate: 11.0% (2005); Bankruptcy rate: 1.96% (2007).
Education: Percent of population age 25 and over with: High school diploma (including GED) or higher: 85.6% (2007); Bachelor's degree or higher: 15.6% (2007); Master's degree or higher: 4.4% (2007).
Housing: Homeownership rate: 80.5% (2007); Median home value: $86,426 (2007); Median rent: $260 per month (2000); Median age of housing: 49 years (2000).
Health: Birth rate: 109.9 per 10,000 population (2007); Death rate: 118.4 per 10,000 population (2007); Age-adjusted cancer mortality rate: 157.1 deaths per 100,000 population (2005); Number of physicians: 6.3 per 10,000 population (2005); Hospital beds: 7.8 per 10,000 population (2004); Hospital admissions: 335.1 per 10,000 population (2004).
Elections: 2004 Presidential election results: 59.0% Bush, 40.2% Kerry, 0.0% Nader, 0.9% Badnarik
National and State Parks: Montebello State Park; Nauvoo State Park
Additional Information Contacts
Hancock County Government . . . . (217) 357-3911

City of Carthage . . . . (217) 357-3119
http://www.carthage-il.com/government/maingov.htm
Nauvoo Chamber of Commerce . . . . (217) 453-6648
http://www.nauvoochamber.org
Warsaw Chamber of Commerce . . . . (217) 256-4235

Hancock County Communities

AUGUSTA (village). Covers a land area of 0.713 square miles and a water area of 0 square miles. Located at 40.23° N. Lat.; 90.95° W. Long. Elevation is 663 feet.
Population: 613 (1990); 657 (2000); 574 (2007); 556 (2012 projected); Race: 99.8% White, 0.0% Black, 0.0% Asian, 1.0% Hispanic of any race (2007); Density: 804.7 persons per square mile (2007); Average household size: 2.22 (2007); Median age: 45.3 (2007); Males per 100 females: 88.2 (2007); Marriage status: 20.3% never married, 55.8% now married, 12.7% widowed, 11.1% divorced (2000); Foreign born: 0.0% (2000); Ancestry (includes multiple ancestries): 23.6% United States or American, 20.7% German, 13.4% English, 7.0% Irish, 4.8% Other groups (2000).
Economy: Employment by occupation: 8.7% management, 16.5% professional, 15.2% services, 21.4% sales, 0.6% farming, 11.5% construction, 26.1% production (2000).
Income: Per capita income: $19,334 (2007); Median household income: $34,615 (2007); Average household income: $43,014 (2007); Percent of households with income of $100,000 or more: 5.8% (2007); Poverty rate: 9.7% (2000).

Education: Percent of population age 25 and over with: High school diploma (including GED) or higher: 81.7% (2007); Bachelor's degree or higher: 12.5% (2007); Master's degree or higher: 4.6% (2007).

School District(s)

Southeastern CUSD 337 (PK-12)
2005-06 Enrollment: 571 . . . . (217) 842-5236

Housing: Homeownership rate: 82.6% (2007); Median home value: $48,871 (2007); Median rent: $213 per month (2000); Median age of housing: 60+ years (2000).

Safety: Violent crime rate: 0.0 per 10,000 population; Property crime rate: 64.0 per 10,000 population (2006).

Newspapers: Eagle-Scribe (Local news; Circulation 1,225)

Transportation: Commute to work: 89.7% car, 0.9% public transportation, 5.0% walk, 3.1% work from home (2000); Travel time to work: 38.6% less than 15 minutes, 17.0% 15 to 30 minutes, 20.9% 30 to 45 minutes, 14.5% 45 to 60 minutes, 9.0% 60 minutes or more (2000)

BASCO (village). Covers a land area of 0.227 square miles and a water area of 0 square miles. Located at 40.32° N. Lat.; 91.19° W. Long. Elevation is 630 feet.

Population: 99 (1990); 107 (2000); 106 (2007); 101 (2012 projected); Race: 100.0% White, 0.0% Black, 0.0% Asian, 0.0% Hispanic of any race (2007); Density: 467.3 persons per square mile (2007); Average household size: 2.26 (2007); Median age: 36.9 (2007); Males per 100 females: 96.3 (2007); Marriage status: 27.8% never married, 47.4% now married, 13.4% widowed, 11.3% divorced (2000); Foreign born: 0.0% (2000); Ancestry (includes multiple ancestries): 41.0% German, 18.0% United States or American, 13.1% Irish, 10.7% English, 4.9% French (except Basque) (2000).

Economy: Employment by occupation: 8.3% management, 9.7% professional, 22.2% services, 23.6% sales, 0.0% farming, 12.5% construction, 23.6% production (2000).

Income: Per capita income: $22,642 (2007); Median household income: $34,773 (2007); Average household income: $51,064 (2007); Percent of households with income of $100,000 or more: 12.8% (2007); Poverty rate: 9.2% (2000).

Education: Percent of population age 25 and over with: High school diploma (including GED) or higher: 84.3% (2007); Bachelor's degree or higher: 18.6% (2007); Master's degree or higher: 0.0% (2007).

Housing: Homeownership rate: 93.6% (2007); Median home value: $65,000 (2007); Median rent: $188 per month (2000); Median age of housing: 60+ years (2000).

Transportation: Commute to work: 88.9% car, 0.0% public transportation, 8.3% walk, 2.8% work from home (2000); Travel time to work: 22.9% less than 15 minutes, 51.4% 15 to 30 minutes, 18.6% 30 to 45 minutes, 7.1% 45 to 60 minutes, 0.0% 60 minutes or more (2000)

BENTLEY (town). Aka Bently. Covers a land area of 0.142 square miles and a water area of 0 square miles. Located at 40.34° N. Lat.; 91.11° W. Long. Elevation is 676 feet.

Population: 36 (1990); 43 (2000); 44 (2007); 42 (2012 projected); Race: 100.0% White, 0.0% Black, 0.0% Asian, 0.0% Hispanic of any race (2007); Density: 308.8 persons per square mile (2007); Average household size: 2.44 (2007); Median age: 48.3 (2007); Males per 100 females: 100.0 (2007); Marriage status: 30.0% never married, 63.3% now married, 0.0% widowed, 6.7% divorced (2000); Foreign born: 0.0% (2000); Ancestry (includes multiple ancestries): 38.5% United States or American, 33.3% Irish, 23.1% German, 23.1% English, 7.7% Other groups (2000).

Economy: Employment by occupation: 15.0% management, 35.0% professional, 15.0% services, 15.0% sales, 0.0% farming, 10.0% construction, 10.0% production (2000).

Income: Per capita income: $13,523 (2007); Median household income: $28,750 (2007); Average household income: $33,056 (2007); Percent of households with income of $100,000 or more: 0.0% (2007); Poverty rate: 15.4% (2000).

Education: Percent of population age 25 and over with: High school diploma (including GED) or higher: 84.4% (2007); Bachelor's degree or higher: 34.4% (2007); Master's degree or higher: 18.8% (2007).

Housing: Homeownership rate: 94.4% (2007); Median home value: $17,500 (2007); Median rent: $n/a per month (2000); Median age of housing: 57 years (2000).

Transportation: Commute to work: 90.0% car, 0.0% public transportation, 10.0% walk, 0.0% work from home (2000); Travel time to work: 30.0% less than 15 minutes, 20.0% 15 to 30 minutes, 30.0% 30 to 45 minutes, 20.0% 45 to 60 minutes, 0.0% 60 minutes or more (2000)

BOWEN (village). Covers a land area of 0.431 square miles and a water area of 0 square miles. Located at 40.23° N. Lat.; 91.06° W. Long. Elevation is 689 feet.

Population: 462 (1990); 535 (2000); 490 (2007); 469 (2012 projected); Race: 99.8% White, 0.0% Black, 0.0% Asian, 0.2% Hispanic of any race (2007); Density: 1,137.2 persons per square mile (2007); Average household size: 2.63 (2007); Median age: 35.2 (2007); Males per 100 females: 94.4 (2007); Marriage status: 21.2% never married, 58.7% now married, 7.2% widowed, 12.8% divorced (2000); Foreign born: 0.4% (2000); Ancestry (includes multiple ancestries): 36.4% German, 12.1% United States or American, 11.7% English, 11.4% Irish, 6.8% Other groups (2000).

Economy: Employment by occupation: 4.3% management, 12.8% professional, 9.3% services, 25.7% sales, 1.2% farming, 12.5% construction, 34.2% production (2000).

Income: Per capita income: $14,827 (2007); Median household income: $30,455 (2007); Average household income: $39,059 (2007); Percent of households with income of $100,000 or more: 1.1% (2007); Poverty rate: 16.3% (2000).

Education: Percent of population age 25 and over with: High school diploma (including GED) or higher: 83.5% (2007); Bachelor's degree or higher: 11.7% (2007); Master's degree or higher: 3.2% (2007).

School District(s)

Southeastern CUSD 337 (PK-12)
2005-06 Enrollment: 571 . . . . (217) 842-5236

Housing: Homeownership rate: 81.2% (2007); Median home value: $58,750 (2007); Median rent: $272 per month (2000); Median age of housing: 60+ years (2000).

Transportation: Commute to work: 93.1% car, 0.0% public transportation, 2.8% walk, 4.0% work from home (2000); Travel time to work: 20.7% less than 15 minutes, 38.0% 15 to 30 minutes, 18.6% 30 to 45 minutes, 13.1% 45 to 60 minutes, 9.7% 60 minutes or more (2000)

BURNSIDE (unincorporated postal area, zip code 62318). Covers a land area of 40.074 square miles and a water area of 0 square miles. Located at 40.51° N. Lat.; 91.12° W. Long. Elevation is 646 feet.

Population: 358 (2000); Race: 100.0% White, 0.0% Black, 0.0% Asian, 0.0% Hispanic of any race (2000); Density: 8.9 persons per square mile (2000); Age: 22.6% under 18, 15.8% over 64 (2000); Marriage status: 25.5% never married, 58.2% now married, 5.6% widowed, 10.8% divorced (2000); Foreign born: 0.0% (2000); Ancestry (includes multiple ancestries): 24.2% English, 23.9% German, 13.9% United States or American, 8.4% Irish, 2.4% Scottish (2000).

Economy: Employment by occupation: 17.8% management, 22.3% professional, 8.1% services, 21.3% sales, 3.0% farming, 6.1% construction, 21.3% production (2000).

Income: Per capita income: $17,642 (2000); Median household income: $44,063 (2000); Poverty rate: 12.8% (2000).

Education: Percent of population age 25 and over with: High school diploma (including GED) or higher: 83.1% (2000); Bachelor's degree or higher: 14.1% (2000).

Housing: Homeownership rate: 71.4% (2000); Median home value: $48,500 (2000); Median rent: $225 per month (2000); Median age of housing: 60+ years (2000).

Transportation: Commute to work: 91.9% car, 0.0% public transportation, 1.0% walk, 7.1% work from home (2000); Travel time to work: 35.5% less than 15 minutes, 38.3% 15 to 30 minutes, 2.7% 30 to 45 minutes, 18.6% 45 to 60 minutes, 4.9% 60 minutes or more (2000)

CARTHAGE (city). County seat. Covers a land area of 1.605 square miles and a water area of 0 square miles. Located at 40.41° N. Lat.; 91.13° W. Long. Elevation is 669 feet.

History: Incorporated 1837. In 1844, Joseph Smith, Mormon leader, and his brother were killed in the city jail by a mob; the old jail is now property of the Mormon Church.

Population: 2,658 (1990); 2,725 (2000); 2,503 (2007); 2,343 (2012 projected); Race: 97.3% White, 1.1% Black, 0.7% Asian, 0.3% Hispanic of any race (2007); Density: 1,559.6 persons per square mile (2007); Average household size: 2.32 (2007); Median age: 43.1 (2007); Males per 100 females: 85.1 (2007); Marriage status: 18.9% never married, 58.9% now married, 9.9% widowed, 12.3% divorced (2000); Foreign born: 0.9% (2000); Ancestry (includes multiple ancestries): 28.6% German, 14.7% United States or American, 13.6% English, 10.7% Irish, 6.0% Other groups (2000).

Economy: Single-family building permits issued: 1 (2007); Multi-family building permits issued: 10 (2007); Employment by occupation: 9.9% management, 19.5% professional, 17.6% services, 22.0% sales, 1.8% farming, 7.0% construction, 22.2% production (2000).
Income: Per capita income: $22,755 (2007); Median household income: $42,321 (2007); Average household income: $52,044 (2007); Percent of households with income of $100,000 or more: 11.0% (2007); Poverty rate: 8.4% (2000).
Education: Percent of population age 25 and over with: High school diploma (including GED) or higher: 85.6% (2007); Bachelor's degree or higher: 20.1% (2007); Master's degree or higher: 10.0% (2007).

School District(s)

Carthage CUSD 338 (PK-12)
2005-06 Enrollment: 753 . . . . (217) 357-3922
Hancock/Mc Donough Roe (08-12)
2005-06 Enrollment: 40 . . . . (309) 837-4821

Housing: Homeownership rate: 69.8% (2007); Median home value: $95,190 (2007); Median rent: $278 per month (2000); Median age of housing: 46 years (2000).
Hospitals: Memorial Hospital (67 beds)
Safety: Violent crime rate: 0.0 per 10,000 population; Property crime rate: 102.0 per 10,000 population (2006).
Newspapers: Hancock County Journal Pilot (Regional news; Circulation 4,500)
Transportation: Commute to work: 94.0% car, 1.0% public transportation, 1.5% walk, 3.2% work from home (2000); Travel time to work: 63.4% less than 15 minutes, 14.9% 15 to 30 minutes, 14.1% 30 to 45 minutes, 3.7% 45 to 60 minutes, 3.9% 60 minutes or more (2000)

Additional Information Contacts

City of Carthage . . . . (217) 357-3119
http://www.carthage-il.com/government/maingov.htm

DALLAS CITY (city). Covers a land area of 2.375 square miles and a water area of 0.905 square miles. Located at 40.63° N. Lat.; 91.16° W. Long. Elevation is 545 feet.
Population: 1,037 (1990); 1,055 (2000); 973 (2007); 935 (2012 projected); Race: 99.7% White, 0.0% Black, 0.0% Asian, 0.5% Hispanic of any race (2007); Density: 409.6 persons per square mile (2007); Average household size: 2.22 (2007); Median age: 48.3 (2007); Males per 100 females: 85.7 (2007); Marriage status: 14.9% never married, 64.2% now married, 11.6% widowed, 9.3% divorced (2000); Foreign born: 0.0% (2000); Ancestry (includes multiple ancestries): 22.6% German, 16.7% United States or American, 13.0% English, 9.4% Irish, 5.0% Other groups (2000).
Economy: Employment by occupation: 5.5% management, 16.8% professional, 16.1% services, 22.5% sales, 1.4% farming, 12.0% construction, 25.7% production (2000).
Income: Per capita income: $18,562 (2007); Median household income: $35,952 (2007); Average household income: $41,113 (2007); Percent of households with income of $100,000 or more: 3.2% (2007); Poverty rate: 13.4% (2000).
Education: Percent of population age 25 and over with: High school diploma (including GED) or higher: 79.6% (2007); Bachelor's degree or higher: 8.6% (2007); Master's degree or higher: 2.2% (2007).

School District(s)

Dallas CUSD 336 (PK-08)
2005-06 Enrollment: 245 . . . . (217) 852-3204

Housing: Homeownership rate: 77.6% (2007); Median home value: $71,905 (2007); Median rent: $230 per month (2000); Median age of housing: 50 years (2000).
Safety: Violent crime rate: 49.5 per 10,000 population; Property crime rate: 148.4 per 10,000 population (2006).
Transportation: Commute to work: 88.5% car, 0.0% public transportation, 6.7% walk, 4.4% work from home (2000); Travel time to work: 34.5% less than 15 minutes, 34.9% 15 to 30 minutes, 17.1% 30 to 45 minutes, 2.7% 45 to 60 minutes, 10.8% 60 minutes or more (2000)

ELVASTON (village). Covers a land area of 0.797 square miles and a water area of 0 square miles. Located at 40.39° N. Lat.; 91.25° W. Long. Elevation is 659 feet.
Population: 198 (1990); 152 (2000); 153 (2007); 147 (2012 projected); Race: 98.0% White, 2.0% Black, 0.0% Asian, 0.0% Hispanic of any race (2007); Density: 192.1 persons per square mile (2007); Average household size: 2.19 (2007); Median age: 38.7 (2007); Males per 100 females: 93.7 (2007); Marriage status: 7.1% never married, 63.5% now married, 12.7% widowed, 16.7% divorced (2000); Foreign born: 0.0% (2000); Ancestry (includes multiple ancestries): 30.4% German, 13.9% Irish, 8.2% Dutch, 7.0% French (except Basque), 5.1% Scotch-Irish (2000).
Economy: Employment by occupation: 5.4% management, 6.5% professional, 19.6% services, 17.4% sales, 5.4% farming, 14.1% construction, 31.5% production (2000).
Income: Per capita income: $39,722 (2007); Median household income: $45,000 (2007); Average household income: $86,821 (2007); Percent of households with income of $100,000 or more: 18.6% (2007); Poverty rate: 12.7% (2000).
Education: Percent of population age 25 and over with: High school diploma (including GED) or higher: 84.6% (2007); Bachelor's degree or higher: 2.9% (2007); Master's degree or higher: 0.0% (2007).
Housing: Homeownership rate: 90.0% (2007); Median home value: $61,000 (2007); Median rent: $275 per month (2000); Median age of housing: 60+ years (2000).
Transportation: Commute to work: 100.0% car, 0.0% public transportation, 0.0% walk, 0.0% work from home (2000); Travel time to work: 63.6% less than 15 minutes, 27.3% 15 to 30 minutes, 6.8% 30 to 45 minutes, 2.3% 45 to 60 minutes, 0.0% 60 minutes or more (2000)

FERRIS (village). Covers a land area of 1.957 square miles and a water area of 0 square miles. Located at 40.46° N. Lat.; 91.16° W. Long. Elevation is 682 feet.
Population: 177 (1990); 168 (2000); 186 (2007); 187 (2012 projected); Race: 98.4% White, 0.5% Black, 0.0% Asian, 0.0% Hispanic of any race (2007); Density: 95.0 persons per square mile (2007); Average household size: 2.38 (2007); Median age: 41.7 (2007); Males per 100 females: 116.3 (2007); Marriage status: 17.8% never married, 61.2% now married, 15.1% widowed, 5.9% divorced (2000); Foreign born: 0.0% (2000); Ancestry (includes multiple ancestries): 35.0% German, 20.2% English, 10.9% Irish, 6.6% United States or American, 5.5% Scottish (2000).
Economy: Employment by occupation: 15.9% management, 11.4% professional, 15.9% services, 20.5% sales, 0.0% farming, 18.2% construction, 18.2% production (2000).
Income: Per capita income: $21,989 (2007); Median household income: $50,000 (2007); Average household income: $52,436 (2007); Percent of households with income of $100,000 or more: 3.8% (2007); Poverty rate: 2.7% (2000).
Education: Percent of population age 25 and over with: High school diploma (including GED) or higher: 87.9% (2007); Bachelor's degree or higher: 10.6% (2007); Master's degree or higher: 0.0% (2007).
Housing: Homeownership rate: 87.2% (2007); Median home value: $60,000 (2007); Median rent: $292 per month (2000); Median age of housing: 56 years (2000).
Transportation: Commute to work: 93.0% car, 0.0% public transportation, 0.0% walk, 3.5% work from home (2000); Travel time to work: 39.8% less than 15 minutes, 27.7% 15 to 30 minutes, 16.9% 30 to 45 minutes, 9.6% 45 to 60 minutes, 6.0% 60 minutes or more (2000)

HAMILTON (city). Covers a land area of 3.748 square miles and a water area of 1.611 square miles. Located at 40.39° N. Lat.; 91.34° W. Long. Elevation is 643 feet.
History: Incorporated 1859.
Population: 3,326 (1990); 3,029 (2000); 2,777 (2007); 2,604 (2012 projected); Race: 97.9% White, 1.2% Black, 0.4% Asian, 0.6% Hispanic of any race (2007); Density: 741.0 persons per square mile (2007); Average household size: 2.43 (2007); Median age: 43.0 (2007); Males per 100 females: 92.7 (2007); Marriage status: 17.4% never married, 61.0% now married, 8.8% widowed, 12.9% divorced (2000); Foreign born: 1.0% (2000); Ancestry (includes multiple ancestries): 27.9% German, 16.3% United States or American, 12.0% Irish, 11.9% English, 4.7% Other groups (2000).
Economy: Single-family building permits issued: 2 (2007); Multi-family building permits issued: 0 (2007); Employment by occupation: 11.0% management, 12.1% professional, 13.2% services, 23.1% sales, 0.9% farming, 11.8% construction, 27.9% production (2000).
Income: Per capita income: $21,625 (2007); Median household income: $44,375 (2007); Average household income: $50,827 (2007); Percent of households with income of $100,000 or more: 6.5% (2007); Poverty rate: 7.1% (2000).
Education: Percent of population age 25 and over with: High school diploma (including GED) or higher: 85.4% (2007); Bachelor's degree or higher: 14.2% (2007); Master's degree or higher: 1.4% (2007).

School District(s)

Hamilton CCSD 328 (PK-12)
2005-06 Enrollment: 644 . . . . (217) 847-3315

Housing: Homeownership rate: 81.0% (2007); Median home value: $88,462 (2007); Median rent: $352 per month (2000); Median age of housing: 34 years (2000).

Safety: Violent crime rate: 52.9 per 10,000 population; Property crime rate: 200.8 per 10,000 population (2006).

Transportation: Commute to work: 93.6% car, 0.0% public transportation, 1.9% walk, 3.5% work from home (2000); Travel time to work: 52.7% less than 15 minutes, 35.0% 15 to 30 minutes, 8.7% 30 to 45 minutes, 2.1% 45 to 60 minutes, 1.5% 60 minutes or more (2000)

LA HARPE (city). Covers a land area of 1.355 square miles and a water area of 0 square miles. Located at 40.58° N. Lat.; 90.96° W. Long. Elevation is 699 feet.

History: Incorporated 1859.

Population: 1,407 (1990); 1,385 (2000); 1,197 (2007); 1,153 (2012 projected); Race: 99.9% White, 0.0% Black, 0.0% Asian, 0.0% Hispanic of any race (2007); Density: 883.1 persons per square mile (2007); Average household size: 2.47 (2007); Median age: 44.2 (2007); Males per 100 females: 85.6 (2007); Marriage status: 20.4% never married, 61.9% now married, 10.4% widowed, 7.2% divorced (2000); Foreign born: 0.1% (2000); Ancestry (includes multiple ancestries): 18.1% German, 15.2% United States or American, 14.0% English, 9.2% Irish, 4.2% Other groups (2000).

Economy: Employment by occupation: 7.0% management, 14.5% professional, 21.5% services, 18.2% sales, 0.2% farming, 11.5% construction, 27.2% production (2000).

Income: Per capita income: $20,340 (2007); Median household income: $40,536 (2007); Average household income: $49,639 (2007); Percent of households with income of $100,000 or more: 8.7% (2007); Poverty rate: 7.4% (2000).

Education: Percent of population age 25 and over with: High school diploma (including GED) or higher: 83.4% (2007); Bachelor's degree or higher: 12.9% (2007); Master's degree or higher: 3.3% (2007).

School District(s)

La Harpe CUSD 335 (PK-12)
2005-06 Enrollment: 434 . . . . (217) 659-7739

Housing: Homeownership rate: 83.3% (2007); Median home value: $79,167 (2007); Median rent: $244 per month (2000); Median age of housing: 43 years (2000).

Safety: Violent crime rate: 7.6 per 10,000 population; Property crime rate: 75.6 per 10,000 population (2006).

Newspapers: Hancock County Quill (Community news; Circulation 1,250)

Transportation: Commute to work: 89.9% car, 0.0% public transportation, 5.9% walk, 3.5% work from home (2000); Travel time to work: 42.8% less than 15 minutes, 17.9% 15 to 30 minutes, 29.0% 30 to 45 minutes, 4.6% 45 to 60 minutes, 5.7% 60 minutes or more (2000)

NAUVOO (city). Covers a land area of 3.382 square miles and a water area of 1.441 square miles. Located at 40.54° N. Lat.; 91.38° W. Long. Elevation is 650 feet.

History: Joseph Smith built the city of Nauvoo in 1839 as the headquarters for the Mormon church, on the site of a small settlement called Commerce. The charter for Nauvoo gave it a measure of autonomy such as maintaining its own militia and courts. Internal discord and outside opposition troubled the church, and in 1845 the Nauvoo charter was repealed and Brigham Young soon led the members westward. In 1849 the deserted city became the scene of the Icarian colony attempt at a Utopian communistic society, which crumbled in 1856. The resettlement of Nauvoo, mostly by German immigrants, began in the 1860's. Joseph Smith and his brother Hyrum were buried in Nauvoo.

Population: 1,108 (1990); 1,063 (2000); 979 (2007); 966 (2012 projected); Race: 96.8% White, 0.6% Black, 0.2% Asian, 1.3% Hispanic of any race (2007); Density: 289.5 persons per square mile (2007); Average household size: 2.60 (2007); Median age: 45.3 (2007); Males per 100 females: 88.3 (2007); Marriage status: 23.2% never married, 63.4% now married, 8.0% widowed, 5.5% divorced (2000); Foreign born: 1.2% (2000); Ancestry (includes multiple ancestries): 40.0% German, 21.2% Irish, 17.0% English, 7.5% French (except Basque), 5.4% Other groups (2000).

Economy: Single-family building permits issued: 5 (2007); Multi-family building permits issued: 0 (2007); Employment by occupation: 11.2% management, 13.2% professional, 18.6% services, 23.2% sales, 0.4% farming, 10.8% construction, 22.6% production (2000).

Income: Per capita income: $24,724 (2007); Median household income: $50,294 (2007); Average household income: $58,484 (2007); Percent of households with income of $100,000 or more: 14.1% (2007); Poverty rate: 12.8% (2000).

Education: Percent of population age 25 and over with: High school diploma (including GED) or higher: 93.1% (2007); Bachelor's degree or higher: 23.2% (2007); Master's degree or higher: 11.5% (2007).

School District(s)

Nauvoo-Colusa CUSD 325 (PK-12)
2005-06 Enrollment: 403 . . . . (217) 453-6639

Housing: Homeownership rate: 81.1% (2007); Median home value: $119,556 (2007); Median rent: $236 per month (2000); Median age of housing: 37 years (2000).

Safety: Violent crime rate: 26.0 per 10,000 population; Property crime rate: 112.6 per 10,000 population (2006).

Newspapers: Nauvoo New Independent (Community news; Circulation 500)

Transportation: Commute to work: 86.8% car, 1.0% public transportation, 8.7% walk, 2.7% work from home (2000); Travel time to work: 45.9% less than 15 minutes, 28.8% 15 to 30 minutes, 20.1% 30 to 45 minutes, 1.0% 45 to 60 minutes, 4.2% 60 minutes or more (2000)

Additional Information Contacts

Nauvoo Chamber of Commerce . . . . (217) 453-6648
http://www.nauvoochamber.org

NIOTA (unincorporated postal area, zip code 62358). Covers a land area of 40.663 square miles and a water area of 0.018 square miles. Located at 40.58° N. Lat.; 91.26° W. Long. Elevation is 522 feet.

Population: 646 (2000); Race: 96.6% White, 0.0% Black, 0.6% Asian, 0.6% Hispanic of any race (2000); Density: 15.9 persons per square mile (2000); Age: 22.2% under 18, 17.3% over 64 (2000); Marriage status: 21.2% never married, 62.0% now married, 8.2% widowed, 8.6% divorced (2000); Foreign born: 1.0% (2000); Ancestry (includes multiple ancestries): 30.8% German, 18.2% Irish, 8.9% English, 7.7% United States or American, 5.1% Other groups (2000).

Economy: Employment by occupation: 16.6% management, 7.5% professional, 19.8% services, 15.8% sales, 2.4% farming, 8.8% construction, 29.1% production (2000).

Income: Per capita income: $16,672 (2000); Median household income: $41,630 (2000); Poverty rate: 5.2% (2000).

Education: Percent of population age 25 and over with: High school diploma (including GED) or higher: 87.2% (2000); Bachelor's degree or higher: 13.1% (2000).

Housing: Homeownership rate: 89.2% (2000); Median home value: $47,300 (2000); Median rent: $219 per month (2000); Median age of housing: 46 years (2000).

Transportation: Commute to work: 88.7% car, 1.9% public transportation, 2.5% walk, 5.8% work from home (2000); Travel time to work: 27.2% less than 15 minutes, 42.7% 15 to 30 minutes, 24.0% 30 to 45 minutes, 4.1% 45 to 60 minutes, 2.0% 60 minutes or more (2000)

PLYMOUTH (village). Covers a land area of 0.589 square miles and a water area of 0 square miles. Located at 40.29° N. Lat.; 90.91° W. Long. Elevation is 650 feet.

Population: 521 (1990); 562 (2000); 517 (2007); 494 (2012 projected); Race: 96.1% White, 0.2% Black, 1.4% Asian, 0.8% Hispanic of any race (2007); Density: 877.5 persons per square mile (2007); Average household size: 2.40 (2007); Median age: 36.5 (2007); Males per 100 females: 92.9 (2007); Marriage status: 18.0% never married, 59.1% now married, 11.0% widowed, 11.8% divorced (2000); Foreign born: 0.4% (2000); Ancestry (includes multiple ancestries): 32.7% United States or American, 17.5% German, 15.2% Irish, 6.3% Dutch, 5.6% Other groups (2000).

Economy: Employment by occupation: 6.6% management, 4.3% professional, 24.2% services, 12.3% sales, 8.1% farming, 11.4% construction, 33.2% production (2000).

Income: Per capita income: $15,309 (2007); Median household income: $27,935 (2007); Average household income: $36,814 (2007); Percent of households with income of $100,000 or more: 3.7% (2007); Poverty rate: 18.8% (2000).

Education: Percent of population age 25 and over with: High school diploma (including GED) or higher: 77.4% (2007); Bachelor's degree or higher: 6.3% (2007); Master's degree or higher: 1.5% (2007).

School District(s)

Southeastern CUSD 337 (PK-12)
2005-06 Enrollment: 571 . . . . (217) 842-5236

Housing: Homeownership rate: 74.4% (2007); Median home value: $30,769 (2007); Median rent: $220 per month (2000); Median age of housing: 60+ years (2000).
Safety: Violent crime rate: 0.0 per 10,000 population; Property crime rate: 0.0 per 10,000 population (2006).
Transportation: Commute to work: 93.3% car, 0.0% public transportation, 3.3% walk, 1.9% work from home (2000); Travel time to work: 31.7% less than 15 minutes, 26.3% 15 to 30 minutes, 27.8% 30 to 45 minutes, 6.8% 45 to 60 minutes, 7.3% 60 minutes or more (2000)

PONTOOSUC (village). Covers a land area of 1.409 square miles and a water area of 0.667 square miles. Located at 40.63° N. Lat.; 91.21° W. Long. Elevation is 525 feet.
Population: 264 (1990); 171 (2000); 155 (2007); 150 (2012 projected); Race: 98.7% White, 0.0% Black, 0.0% Asian, 0.0% Hispanic of any race (2007); Density: 110.0 persons per square mile (2007); Average household size: 2.28 (2007); Median age: 46.0 (2007); Males per 100 females: 89.0 (2007); Marriage status: 25.4% never married, 52.8% now married, 7.7% widowed, 14.1% divorced (2000); Foreign born: 0.0% (2000); Ancestry (includes multiple ancestries): 21.7% United States or American, 19.9% German, 15.5% Irish, 10.6% English, 6.2% Other groups (2000).
Economy: Employment by occupation: 10.5% management, 6.6% professional, 26.3% services, 9.2% sales, 2.6% farming, 6.6% construction, 38.2% production (2000).
Income: Per capita income: $17,468 (2007); Median household income: $31,250 (2007); Average household income: $39,816 (2007); Percent of households with income of $100,000 or more: 7.4% (2007); Poverty rate: 16.8% (2000).
Education: Percent of population age 25 and over with: High school diploma (including GED) or higher: 70.8% (2007); Bachelor's degree or higher: 4.2% (2007); Master's degree or higher: 2.5% (2007).
Housing: Homeownership rate: 85.3% (2007); Median home value: $50,000 (2007); Median rent: $182 per month (2000); Median age of housing: 29 years (2000).
Transportation: Commute to work: 92.1% car, 0.0% public transportation, 0.0% walk, 2.6% work from home (2000); Travel time to work: 24.3% less than 15 minutes, 31.1% 15 to 30 minutes, 23.0% 30 to 45 minutes, 2.7% 45 to 60 minutes, 18.9% 60 minutes or more (2000)

SUTTER (unincorporated postal area, zip code 62373). Covers a land area of 52.216 square miles and a water area of 0.210 square miles. Located at 40.24° N. Lat.; 91.35° W. Long. Elevation is 656 feet.
Population: 415 (2000); Race: 100.0% White, 0.0% Black, 0.0% Asian, 0.0% Hispanic of any race (2000); Density: 7.9 persons per square mile (2000); Age: 34.4% under 18, 12.4% over 64 (2000); Marriage status: 18.5% never married, 75.5% now married, 2.4% widowed, 3.6% divorced (2000); Foreign born: 0.0% (2000); Ancestry (includes multiple ancestries): 28.5% German, 11.5% Irish, 8.5% United States or American, 4.8% English, 4.8% Other groups (2000).
Economy: Employment by occupation: 31.8% management, 18.9% professional, 7.0% services, 14.4% sales, 7.5% farming, 4.0% construction, 16.4% production (2000).
Income: Per capita income: $15,697 (2000); Median household income: $46,250 (2000); Poverty rate: 2.4% (2000).
Education: Percent of population age 25 and over with: High school diploma (including GED) or higher: 88.5% (2000); Bachelor's degree or higher: 24.1% (2000).
Housing: Homeownership rate: 75.9% (2000); Median home value: $91,600 (2000); Median rent: $192 per month (2000); Median age of housing: 60+ years (2000).
Transportation: Commute to work: 72.6% car, 0.0% public transportation, 5.5% walk, 21.9% work from home (2000); Travel time to work: 34.4% less than 15 minutes, 22.3% 15 to 30 minutes, 40.8% 30 to 45 minutes, 0.0% 45 to 60 minutes, 2.5% 60 minutes or more (2000)

WARSAW (city). Covers a land area of 6.617 square miles and a water area of 0.871 square miles. Located at 40.35° N. Lat.; 91.43° W. Long. Elevation is 577 feet.
History: Laid out 1834, incorporated 1837. Two forts were established here in 1814.
Population: 1,882 (1990); 1,793 (2000); 1,668 (2007); 1,505 (2012 projected); Race: 99.0% White, 0.1% Black, 0.0% Asian, 0.8% Hispanic of any race (2007); Density: 252.1 persons per square mile (2007); Average household size: 2.41 (2007); Median age: 41.2 (2007); Males per 100 females: 98.3 (2007); Marriage status: 20.6% never married, 62.5% now married, 8.9% widowed, 8.0% divorced (2000); Foreign born: 0.3% (2000); Ancestry (includes multiple ancestries): 30.8% German, 13.8% United States or American, 12.0% Irish, 10.6% English, 5.5% Other groups (2000).
Economy: Single-family building permits issued: 1 (2007); Multi-family building permits issued: 0 (2007); Employment by occupation: 7.3% management, 16.3% professional, 13.1% services, 21.2% sales, 0.9% farming, 9.0% construction, 32.3% production (2000).
Income: Per capita income: $20,091 (2007); Median household income: $38,827 (2007); Average household income: $48,499 (2007); Percent of households with income of $100,000 or more: 6.2% (2007); Poverty rate: 8.0% (2000).
Education: Percent of population age 25 and over with: High school diploma (including GED) or higher: 83.6% (2007); Bachelor's degree or higher: 13.8% (2007); Master's degree or higher: 5.8% (2007).

School District(s)

Warsaw CUSD 316 (PK-12)
2005-06 Enrollment: 547 . . . . (217) 256-4282
Housing: Homeownership rate: 82.3% (2007); Median home value: $91,230 (2007); Median rent: $251 per month (2000); Median age of housing: 60+ years (2000).
Safety: Violent crime rate: 72.8 per 10,000 population; Property crime rate: 127.4 per 10,000 population (2006).
Transportation: Commute to work: 93.6% car, 0.2% public transportation, 2.6% walk, 3.1% work from home (2000); Travel time to work: 29.5% less than 15 minutes, 44.4% 15 to 30 minutes, 16.7% 30 to 45 minutes, 5.4% 45 to 60 minutes, 3.9% 60 minutes or more (2000)
Additional Information Contacts
Warsaw Chamber of Commerce . . . . (217) 256-4235

WEST POINT (village). Covers a land area of 0.168 square miles and a water area of 0 square miles. Located at 40.25° N. Lat.; 91.18° W. Long. Elevation is 669 feet.
Population: 214 (1990); 195 (2000); 174 (2007); 167 (2012 projected); Race: 100.0% White, 0.0% Black, 0.0% Asian, 0.0% Hispanic of any race (2007); Density: 1,033.3 persons per square mile (2007); Average household size: 2.81 (2007); Median age: 36.9 (2007); Males per 100 females: 102.3 (2007); Marriage status: 30.5% never married, 50.0% now married, 6.5% widowed, 13.0% divorced (2000); Foreign born: 1.5% (2000); Ancestry (includes multiple ancestries): 33.2% United States or American, 25.5% German, 15.8% Other groups, 15.3% English, 13.8% Irish (2000).
Economy: Employment by occupation: 2.3% management, 14.8% professional, 12.5% services, 11.4% sales, 3.4% farming, 18.2% construction, 37.5% production (2000).
Income: Per capita income: $14,195 (2007); Median household income: $34,000 (2007); Average household income: $39,839 (2007); Percent of households with income of $100,000 or more: 3.2% (2007); Poverty rate: 16.3% (2000).
Education: Percent of population age 25 and over with: High school diploma (including GED) or higher: 77.0% (2007); Bachelor's degree or higher: 8.0% (2007); Master's degree or higher: 0.0% (2007).
Housing: Homeownership rate: 95.2% (2007); Median home value: $27,500 (2007); Median rent: $325 per month (2000); Median age of housing: 60+ years (2000).
Transportation: Commute to work: 96.6% car, 0.0% public transportation, 0.0% walk, 3.4% work from home (2000); Travel time to work: 1.2% less than 15 minutes, 41.2% 15 to 30 minutes, 31.8% 30 to 45 minutes, 16.5% 45 to 60 minutes, 9.4% 60 minutes or more (2000)

Hardin County

Located in southeastern Illinois; bounded on the south and east by the Ohio River and the Kentucky border; drained by Big Creek; includes part of Shawnee National Forest. Covers a land area of 178.33 square miles, a water area of 3.20 square miles, and is located in the Central Time Zone. The county was founded in 1839. County seat is Elizabethtown.

Weather Station: Rosiclare 5 NW Elevation: 396 feet

	Jan	Feb	Mar	Apr	May	Jun	Jul	Aug	Sep	Oct	Nov	Dec
High	42	48	58	69	77	84	88	87	81	70	58	47
Low	22	26	35	43	53	61	66	64	56	44	36	27
Precip	3.3	3.6	4.8	5.0	5.0	4.3	4.2	3.5	3.2	3.4	4.3	4.3
Snow	4.3	3.3	1.4	0.1	0.0	0.0	0.0	0.0	0.0	0.2	0.1	1.3

High and Low temperatures in degrees Fahrenheit; Precipitation and Snow in inches

Population: 5,189 (1990); 4,800 (2000); 4,705 (2007); 4,632 (2012 projected); Race: 96.1% White, 2.1% Black, 0.6% Asian, 1.2% Hispanic of any race (2007); Density: 26.4 persons per square mile (2007); Average household size: 2.34 (2007); Median age: 43.5 (2007); Males per 100 females: 98.3 (2007).
Religion: Five largest groups: 15.3% Southern Baptist Convention, 4.4% Christian Churches and Churches of Christ, 3.3% Catholic Church, 2.9% Churches of Christ, 2.6% The United Methodist Church (2000).
Economy: Unemployment rate: 7.9% (4/2008); Total civilian labor force: 1,725 (4/2008); Leading industries: 46.6% health care and social assistance; 11.7% transportation & warehousing (2005); Farms: 179 totaling 39,752 acres (2002); Companies that employ 500 or more persons: 0 (2006); Companies that employ 100 to 499 persons: 2 (2006); Companies that employ less than 100 persons: 65 (2006); Black-owned businesses: n/a (2002); Hispanic-owned businesses: n/a (2002); Asian-owned businesses: n/a (2002); Women-owned businesses: n/a (2002); Retail sales per capita: $3,202 (2008). Single-family building permits issued: 0 (2007); Multi-family building permits issued: 0 (2007).
Income: Per capita income: $19,402 (2007); Median household income: $32,542 (2007); Average household income: $43,375 (2007); Percent of households with income of $100,000 or more: 6.7% (2007); Poverty rate: 19.0% (2005); Bankruptcy rate: 1.79% (2007).
Education: Percent of population age 25 and over with: High school diploma (including GED) or higher: 68.2% (2007); Bachelor's degree or higher: 9.8% (2007); Master's degree or higher: 2.9% (2007).
Housing: Homeownership rate: 80.8% (2007); Median home value: $61,029 (2007); Median rent: $185 per month (2000); Median age of housing: 39 years (2000).
Health: Birth rate: 100.7 per 10,000 population (2007); Death rate: 129.8 per 10,000 population (2007); Age-adjusted cancer mortality rate: 202.9 (Unreliable) deaths per 100,000 population (2005); Number of physicians: 8.7 per 10,000 population (2005); Hospital beds: 42.9 per 10,000 population (2004); Hospital admissions: 1,277.6 per 10,000 population (2004).
Elections: 2004 Presidential election results: 61.6% Bush, 37.9% Kerry, 0.0% Nader, 0.5% Badnarik
National and State Parks: Cave-In-Rock State Park
Additional Information Contacts
Hardin County Government . . . . (618) 287-2251

Hardin County Communities

CAVE-IN-ROCK (village). Covers a land area of 0.396 square miles and a water area of 0.029 square miles. Located at 37.47° N. Lat.; 88.16° W. Long. Elevation is 371 feet.
History: Cave-in-Rock was named for a natural cave above the water line in the Ohio River bluff, a landmark for boatmen. The cave served as a pirate's den for a number of thieves beginning with Samuel Mason, who in 1797 lured victims there by promises of liquor and entertainment, and then robbed them.
Population: 460 (1990); 346 (2000); 326 (2007); 322 (2012 projected); Race: 97.9% White, 0.0% Black, 0.0% Asian, 2.5% Hispanic of any race (2007); Density: 824.0 persons per square mile (2007); Average household size: 2.02 (2007); Median age: 39.7 (2007); Males per 100 females: 81.1 (2007); Marriage status: 14.5% never married, 49.0% now married, 23.7% widowed, 12.9% divorced (2000); Foreign born: 0.0% (2000); Ancestry (includes multiple ancestries): 23.6% Other groups, 12.8% United States or American, 12.8% English, 9.6% German, 8.3% Irish (2000).
Economy: Single-family building permits issued: 0 (2007); Multi-family building permits issued: 0 (2007); Employment by occupation: 2.8% management, 27.4% professional, 29.2% services, 12.3% sales, 1.9% farming, 7.5% construction, 18.9% production (2000).
Income: Per capita income: $13,213 (2007); Median household income: $21,346 (2007); Average household income: $26,755 (2007); Percent of households with income of $100,000 or more: 0.6% (2007); Poverty rate: 28.6% (2000).
Education: Percent of population age 25 and over with: High school diploma (including GED) or higher: 68.9% (2007); Bachelor's degree or higher: 9.0% (2007); Master's degree or higher: 2.8% (2007).
Housing: Homeownership rate: 62.1% (2007); Median home value: $45,556 (2007); Median rent: $190 per month (2000); Median age of housing: 37 years (2000).
Transportation: Commute to work: 85.8% car, 0.0% public transportation, 10.4% walk, 0.9% work from home (2000); Travel time to work: 51.4% less than 15 minutes, 26.7% 15 to 30 minutes, 11.4% 30 to 45 minutes, 7.6% 45 to 60 minutes, 2.9% 60 minutes or more (2000)

ELIZABETHTOWN (village). County seat. Covers a land area of 0.702 square miles and a water area of 0 square miles. Located at 37.44° N. Lat.; 88.30° W. Long. Elevation is 364 feet.
Population: 427 (1990); 348 (2000); 347 (2007); 347 (2012 projected); Race: 98.3% White, 1.2% Black, 0.0% Asian, 0.3% Hispanic of any race (2007); Density: 494.2 persons per square mile (2007); Average household size: 1.86 (2007); Median age: 51.8 (2007); Males per 100 females: 84.6 (2007); Marriage status: 16.8% never married, 50.2% now married, 15.9% widowed, 17.1% divorced (2000); Foreign born: 0.0% (2000); Ancestry (includes multiple ancestries): 18.7% German, 17.0% Irish, 13.5% English, 10.4% Other groups, 10.2% United States or American (2000).
Economy: Single-family building permits issued: 0 (2007); Multi-family building permits issued: 0 (2007); Employment by occupation: 5.1% management, 28.3% professional, 21.0% services, 19.6% sales, 0.0% farming, 10.9% construction, 15.2% production (2000).
Income: Per capita income: $20,259 (2007); Median household income: $20,227 (2007); Average household income: $37,594 (2007); Percent of households with income of $100,000 or more: 4.8% (2007); Poverty rate: 22.5% (2000).
Education: Percent of population age 25 and over with: High school diploma (including GED) or higher: 76.8% (2007); Bachelor's degree or higher: 10.5% (2007); Master's degree or higher: 4.1% (2007).

School District(s)

Hardin County CUSD 1 (PK-12)
2005-06 Enrollment: 683 . . . . (618) 287-2411
Housing: Homeownership rate: 64.2% (2007); Median home value: $49,412 (2007); Median rent: $174 per month (2000); Median age of housing: 37 years (2000).
Newspapers: Hardin County Independent (National news; Circulation 2,700)
Transportation: Commute to work: 93.5% car, 2.2% public transportation, 0.0% walk, 2.9% work from home (2000); Travel time to work: 45.5% less than 15 minutes, 26.9% 15 to 30 minutes, 9.0% 30 to 45 minutes, 9.7% 45 to 60 minutes, 9.0% 60 minutes or more (2000)

ROSICLARE (city). Covers a land area of 2.168 square miles and a water area of 0.116 square miles. Located at 37.42° N. Lat.; 88.34° W. Long. Elevation is 354 feet.
History: Incorporated as village 1874, as city 1932.
Population: 1,378 (1990); 1,213 (2000); 1,136 (2007); 1,109 (2012 projected); Race: 97.8% White, 0.4% Black, 0.4% Asian, 1.2% Hispanic of any race (2007); Density: 524.0 persons per square mile (2007); Average household size: 2.29 (2007); Median age: 43.5 (2007); Males per 100 females: 84.1 (2007); Marriage status: 18.3% never married, 58.2% now married, 12.9% widowed, 10.6% divorced (2000); Foreign born: 0.3% (2000); Ancestry (includes multiple ancestries): 12.9% Other groups, 12.3% Irish, 11.2% German, 8.8% United States or American, 8.6% English (2000).
Economy: Single-family building permits issued: 0 (2007); Multi-family building permits issued: 0 (2007); Employment by occupation: 6.4% management, 17.8% professional, 26.3% services, 17.3% sales, 0.0% farming, 13.9% construction, 18.2% production (2000).
Income: Per capita income: $18,358 (2007); Median household income: $28,682 (2007); Average household income: $38,999 (2007); Percent of households with income of $100,000 or more: 3.8% (2007); Poverty rate: 22.5% (2000).
Education: Percent of population age 25 and over with: High school diploma (including GED) or higher: 67.1% (2007); Bachelor's degree or higher: 9.5% (2007); Master's degree or higher: 3.8% (2007).
Housing: Homeownership rate: 73.0% (2007); Median home value: $49,464 (2007); Median rent: $177 per month (2000); Median age of housing: 49 years (2000).
Hospitals: Hardin County General Hospital (48 beds)
Transportation: Commute to work: 91.6% car, 1.8% public transportation, 4.9% walk, 0.4% work from home (2000); Travel time to work: 47.2% less than 15 minutes, 23.2% 15 to 30 minutes, 9.8% 30 to 45 minutes, 9.8% 45 to 60 minutes, 10.0% 60 minutes or more (2000)

Henderson County

Located in western Illinois; bounded on the west by the Mississippi River and the Iowa border; drained by Henderson Creek. Covers a land area of

378.81 square miles, a water area of 16.31 square miles, and is located in the Central Time Zone. The county was founded in 1841. County seat is Oquawka.

Henderson County is part of the Burlington, IA-IL Micropolitan Statistical Area. The entire metro area includes: Henderson County, IL; Des Moines County, IA

Population: 8,096 (1990); 8,213 (2000); 7,888 (2007); 7,626 (2012 projected); Race: 98.6% White, 0.4% Black, 0.1% Asian, 0.9% Hispanic of any race (2007); Density: 20.8 persons per square mile (2007); Average household size: 2.41 (2007); Median age: 43.5 (2007); Males per 100 females: 96.2 (2007).
Religion: Five largest groups: 11.2% The United Methodist Church, 4.4% Catholic Church, 4.0% Presbyterian Church (U.S.A.), 3.7% Christian Churches and Churches of Christ, 2.7% American Baptist Churches in the USA (2000).
Economy: Unemployment rate: 5.7% (4/2008); Total civilian labor force: 4,242 (4/2008); Leading industries: 23.2% retail trade; 19.6% health care and social assistance; 8.8% accommodation & food services (2005); Farms: 392 totaling 201,200 acres (2002); Companies that employ 500 or more persons: 0 (2006); Companies that employ 100 to 499 persons: 0 (2006); Companies that employ less than 100 persons: 104 (2006); Black-owned businesses: n/a (2002); Hispanic-owned businesses: n/a (2002); Asian-owned businesses: n/a (2002); Women-owned businesses: n/a (2002); Retail sales per capita: $3,749 (2008). Single-family building permits issued: 6 (2007); Multi-family building permits issued: 0 (2007).
Income: Per capita income: $21,491 (2007); Median household income: $43,042 (2007); Average household income: $51,494 (2007); Percent of households with income of $100,000 or more: 8.6% (2007); Poverty rate: 11.8% (2005); Bankruptcy rate: 1.85% (2007).
Education: Percent of population age 25 and over with: High school diploma (including GED) or higher: 82.3% (2007); Bachelor's degree or higher: 9.9% (2007); Master's degree or higher: 3.0% (2007).
Housing: Homeownership rate: 78.9% (2007); Median home value: $79,523 (2007); Median rent: $262 per month (2000); Median age of housing: 37 years (2000).
Health: Birth rate: 84.4 per 10,000 population (2007); Death rate: 110.7 per 10,000 population (2007); Age-adjusted cancer mortality rate: 278.3 deaths per 100,000 population (2005); Number of physicians: 7.7 per 10,000 population (2005); Hospital beds: 0.0 per 10,000 population (2004); Hospital admissions: 0.0 per 10,000 population (2004).
Elections: 2004 Presidential election results: 44.7% Bush, 54.6% Kerry, 0.1% Nader, 0.6% Badnarik
National and State Parks: Big River State Forest; Delabar State Park; Oquawka State Wildlife Refuge
Additional Information Contacts
Henderson County Government . . . . (309) 867-2911

Henderson County Communities

BIGGSVILLE (village). Covers a land area of 0.332 square miles and a water area of 0 square miles. Located at 40.85° N. Lat.; 90.86° W. Long. Elevation is 686 feet.
Population: 349 (1990); 343 (2000); 331 (2007); 322 (2012 projected); Race: 98.2% White, 1.8% Black, 0.0% Asian, 2.7% Hispanic of any race (2007); Density: 995.9 persons per square mile (2007); Average household size: 2.35 (2007); Median age: 41.4 (2007); Males per 100 females: 98.2 (2007); Marriage status: 26.8% never married, 56.4% now married, 7.5% widowed, 9.3% divorced (2000); Foreign born: 1.7% (2000); Ancestry (includes multiple ancestries): 24.9% German, 18.8% Irish, 14.7% United States or American, 10.1% English, 7.8% Dutch (2000).
Economy: Single-family building permits issued: 0 (2007); Multi-family building permits issued: 0 (2007); Employment by occupation: 5.4% management, 6.0% professional, 16.7% services, 25.6% sales, 1.2% farming, 17.3% construction, 28.0% production (2000).
Income: Per capita income: $21,488 (2007); Median household income: $43,542 (2007); Average household income: $50,443 (2007); Percent of households with income of $100,000 or more: 3.5% (2007); Poverty rate: 7.5% (2000).
Education: Percent of population age 25 and over with: High school diploma (including GED) or higher: 85.0% (2007); Bachelor's degree or higher: 10.7% (2007); Master's degree or higher: 3.0% (2007).

School District(s)
West Central CUSD 235 (PK-12)
2005-06 Enrollment: 1,106 . . . . (309) 627-2371
Housing: Homeownership rate: 81.6% (2007); Median home value: $62,333 (2007); Median rent: $284 per month (2000); Median age of housing: 50 years (2000).
Transportation: Commute to work: 94.0% car, 0.0% public transportation, 4.8% walk, 1.2% work from home (2000); Travel time to work: 26.2% less than 15 minutes, 49.4% 15 to 30 minutes, 15.2% 30 to 45 minutes, 6.7% 45 to 60 minutes, 2.4% 60 minutes or more (2000)

CARMAN (unincorporated postal area, zip code 61425). Covers a land area of 41.606 square miles and a water area of 1.316 square miles. Located at 40.77° N. Lat.; 91.05° W. Long. Elevation is 535 feet.
Population: 743 (2000); Race: 98.7% White, 0.0% Black, 1.0% Asian, 0.3% Hispanic of any race (2000); Density: 17.9 persons per square mile (2000); Age: 19.7% under 18, 11.6% over 64 (2000); Marriage status: 19.9% never married, 64.1% now married, 6.1% widowed, 9.9% divorced (2000); Foreign born: 1.0% (2000); Ancestry (includes multiple ancestries): 18.4% German, 13.0% Irish, 10.6% United States or American, 9.3% English, 5.0% Other groups (2000).
Economy: Employment by occupation: 10.2% management, 6.9% professional, 20.6% services, 19.1% sales, 0.0% farming, 12.7% construction, 30.5% production (2000).
Income: Per capita income: $20,071 (2000); Median household income: $42,639 (2000); Poverty rate: 7.2% (2000).
Education: Percent of population age 25 and over with: High school diploma (including GED) or higher: 84.2% (2000); Bachelor's degree or higher: 8.5% (2000).
Housing: Homeownership rate: 86.1% (2000); Median home value: $64,100 (2000); Median rent: $305 per month (2000); Median age of housing: 26 years (2000).
Transportation: Commute to work: 95.0% car, 0.0% public transportation, 0.8% walk, 2.6% work from home (2000); Travel time to work: 42.2% less than 15 minutes, 44.9% 15 to 30 minutes, 5.4% 30 to 45 minutes, 5.7% 45 to 60 minutes, 1.9% 60 minutes or more (2000)

GLADSTONE (village). Covers a land area of 0.393 square miles and a water area of 0 square miles. Located at 40.86° N. Lat.; 90.95° W. Long. Elevation is 551 feet.
History: Gladstone was platted in 1856 and settled by Irish, Swedish, and German immigrants. The town developed around the quarrying of limestone on nearby Henderson Creek.
Population: 272 (1990); 284 (2000); 289 (2007); 283 (2012 projected); Race: 99.0% White, 0.7% Black, 0.0% Asian, 0.3% Hispanic of any race (2007); Density: 734.8 persons per square mile (2007); Average household size: 2.01 (2007); Median age: 44.1 (2007); Males per 100 females: 90.1 (2007); Marriage status: 18.8% never married, 55.2% now married, 9.9% widowed, 16.1% divorced (2000); Foreign born: 0.0% (2000); Ancestry (includes multiple ancestries): 24.8% United States or American, 13.5% German, 10.9% Irish, 6.0% Swedish, 3.4% English (2000).
Economy: Single-family building permits issued: 0 (2007); Multi-family building permits issued: 0 (2007); Employment by occupation: 5.9% management, 13.6% professional, 20.3% services, 11.9% sales, 0.0% farming, 15.3% construction, 33.1% production (2000).
Income: Per capita income: $18,538 (2007); Median household income: $32,500 (2007); Average household income: $37,205 (2007); Percent of households with income of $100,000 or more: 1.4% (2007); Poverty rate: 10.5% (2000).
Education: Percent of population age 25 and over with: High school diploma (including GED) or higher: 78.2% (2007); Bachelor's degree or higher: 2.8% (2007); Master's degree or higher: 0.9% (2007).
Housing: Homeownership rate: 82.6% (2007); Median home value: $61,667 (2007); Median rent: $220 per month (2000); Median age of housing: 44 years (2000).
Transportation: Commute to work: 91.5% car, 0.0% public transportation, 0.0% walk, 6.8% work from home (2000); Travel time to work: 20.0% less than 15 minutes, 52.7% 15 to 30 minutes, 9.1% 30 to 45 minutes, 7.3% 45 to 60 minutes, 10.9% 60 minutes or more (2000)

GULF PORT (village). Aka Gulfport. Covers a land area of 1.505 square miles and a water area of 0.921 square miles. Located at 40.80° N. Lat.; 91.08° W. Long.
Population: 209 (1990); 207 (2000); 189 (2007); 186 (2012 projected); Race: 96.3% White, 0.0% Black, 0.0% Asian, 1.6% Hispanic of any race (2007); Density: 125.6 persons per square mile (2007); Average household

size: 2.28 (2007); Median age: 44.2 (2007); Males per 100 females: 83.5 (2007); Marriage status: 17.8% never married, 64.9% now married, 2.9% widowed, 14.4% divorced (2000); Foreign born: 0.0% (2000); Ancestry (includes multiple ancestries): 17.6% German, 14.6% English, 11.7% Irish, 11.2% United States or American, 9.8% Other groups (2000).
Economy: Single-family building permits issued: 1 (2007); Multi-family building permits issued: 0 (2007); Employment by occupation: 4.5% management, 0.0% professional, 29.5% services, 18.8% sales, 0.0% farming, 8.9% construction, 38.4% production (2000).
Income: Per capita income: $21,667 (2007); Median household income: $45,250 (2007); Average household income: $49,337 (2007); Percent of households with income of $100,000 or more: 6.0% (2007); Poverty rate: 5.4% (2000).
Education: Percent of population age 25 and over with: High school diploma (including GED) or higher: 83.4% (2007); Bachelor's degree or higher: 2.1% (2007); Master's degree or higher: 0.0% (2007).
Housing: Homeownership rate: 74.7% (2007); Median home value: $37,500 (2007); Median rent: $232 per month (2000); Median age of housing: 28 years (2000).
Transportation: Commute to work: 94.0% car, 0.0% public transportation, 3.0% walk, 0.0% work from home (2000); Travel time to work: 66.0% less than 15 minutes, 19.0% 15 to 30 minutes, 5.0% 30 to 45 minutes, 7.0% 45 to 60 minutes, 3.0% 60 minutes or more (2000)

LOMAX (village). Covers a land area of 1.043 square miles and a water area of 0 square miles. Located at 40.68° N. Lat.; 91.07° W. Long. Elevation is 548 feet.
Population: 473 (1990); 477 (2000); 453 (2007); 435 (2012 projected); Race: 98.7% White, 0.0% Black, 0.4% Asian, 2.6% Hispanic of any race (2007); Density: 434.3 persons per square mile (2007); Average household size: 2.41 (2007); Median age: 35.6 (2007); Males per 100 females: 88.8 (2007); Marriage status: 21.6% never married, 53.6% now married, 8.3% widowed, 16.5% divorced (2000); Foreign born: 0.4% (2000); Ancestry (includes multiple ancestries): 26.9% German, 18.6% United States or American, 11.3% Irish, 10.9% English, 4.0% Other groups (2000).
Economy: Single-family building permits issued: 0 (2007); Multi-family building permits issued: 0 (2007); Employment by occupation: 10.0% management, 12.8% professional, 13.7% services, 17.8% sales, 0.0% farming, 10.5% construction, 35.2% production (2000).
Income: Per capita income: $17,357 (2007); Median household income: $35,000 (2007); Average household income: $41,822 (2007); Percent of households with income of $100,000 or more: 2.7% (2007); Poverty rate: 11.4% (2000).
Education: Percent of population age 25 and over with: High school diploma (including GED) or higher: 72.1% (2007); Bachelor's degree or higher: 8.9% (2007); Master's degree or higher: 5.2% (2007).
Housing: Homeownership rate: 81.4% (2007); Median home value: $50,750 (2007); Median rent: $263 per month (2000); Median age of housing: 41 years (2000).
Transportation: Commute to work: 95.8% car, 0.0% public transportation, 2.3% walk, 1.9% work from home (2000); Travel time to work: 10.0% less than 15 minutes, 63.0% 15 to 30 minutes, 15.2% 30 to 45 minutes, 4.3% 45 to 60 minutes, 7.6% 60 minutes or more (2000)

MEDIA (village). Covers a land area of 1.698 square miles and a water area of 0 square miles. Located at 40.77° N. Lat.; 90.83° W. Long. Elevation is 709 feet.
Population: 146 (1990); 130 (2000); 120 (2007); 117 (2012 projected); Race: 97.5% White, 0.0% Black, 0.0% Asian, 2.5% Hispanic of any race (2007); Density: 70.7 persons per square mile (2007); Average household size: 2.31 (2007); Median age: 46.5 (2007); Males per 100 females: 100.0 (2007); Marriage status: 25.0% never married, 52.9% now married, 6.7% widowed, 15.4% divorced (2000); Foreign born: 0.0% (2000); Ancestry (includes multiple ancestries): 29.8% United States or American, 14.0% Dutch, 11.4% Irish, 7.9% German, 7.0% Swedish (2000).
Economy: Single-family building permits issued: 0 (2007); Multi-family building permits issued: 0 (2007); Employment by occupation: 15.4% management, 16.9% professional, 10.8% services, 23.1% sales, 0.0% farming, 13.8% construction, 20.0% production (2000).
Income: Per capita income: $26,688 (2007); Median household income: $41,875 (2007); Average household income: $61,587 (2007); Percent of households with income of $100,000 or more: 21.2% (2007); Poverty rate: 12.4% (2000).
Education: Percent of population age 25 and over with: High school diploma (including GED) or higher: 92.5% (2007); Bachelor's degree or higher: 6.5% (2007); Master's degree or higher: 0.0% (2007).

School District(s)

West Central CUSD 235 (PK-12)
2005-06 Enrollment: 1,106 . . . . (309) 627-2371
Housing: Homeownership rate: 76.9% (2007); Median home value: $82,500 (2007); Median rent: $265 per month (2000); Median age of housing: 47 years (2000).
Transportation: Commute to work: 96.9% car, 0.0% public transportation, 0.0% walk, 0.0% work from home (2000); Travel time to work: 27.7% less than 15 minutes, 47.7% 15 to 30 minutes, 18.5% 30 to 45 minutes, 6.2% 45 to 60 minutes, 0.0% 60 minutes or more (2000)

OQUAWKA (village). County seat. Covers a land area of 1.463 square miles and a water area of 0.389 square miles. Located at 40.93° N. Lat.; 90.94° W. Long. Elevation is 554 feet.
History: Oquawka began as a trading post built in 1827 by the Phelps brothers. The name is of Indian origin, a variation of Ozaukee meaning "yellow banks." An early industry was the manufacture of pearl button blanks from mussel shells.
Population: 1,442 (1990); 1,539 (2000); 1,480 (2007); 1,434 (2012 projected); Race: 98.9% White, 0.1% Black, 0.1% Asian, 0.4% Hispanic of any race (2007); Density: 1,011.5 persons per square mile (2007); Average household size: 2.34 (2007); Median age: 41.1 (2007); Males per 100 females: 93.0 (2007); Marriage status: 21.5% never married, 56.5% now married, 9.2% widowed, 12.8% divorced (2000); Foreign born: 0.0% (2000); Ancestry (includes multiple ancestries): 20.3% German, 16.0% United States or American, 12.9% English, 11.2% Irish, 7.2% Other groups (2000).
Economy: Single-family building permits issued: 1 (2007); Multi-family building permits issued: 0 (2007); Employment by occupation: 4.9% management, 9.9% professional, 14.5% services, 21.6% sales, 0.4% farming, 12.8% construction, 35.8% production (2000).
Income: Per capita income: $18,977 (2007); Median household income: $36,645 (2007); Average household income: $43,547 (2007); Percent of households with income of $100,000 or more: 6.0% (2007); Poverty rate: 12.8% (2000).
Education: Percent of population age 25 and over with: High school diploma (including GED) or higher: 73.3% (2007); Bachelor's degree or higher: 4.8% (2007); Master's degree or higher: 1.5% (2007).
Housing: Homeownership rate: 76.1% (2007); Median home value: $78,182 (2007); Median rent: $250 per month (2000); Median age of housing: 33 years (2000).
Newspapers: Oquawka Current (Community news; Circulation 2,000)
Transportation: Commute to work: 97.4% car, 0.0% public transportation, 0.3% walk, 2.0% work from home (2000); Travel time to work: 17.5% less than 15 minutes, 47.3% 15 to 30 minutes, 21.4% 30 to 45 minutes, 7.2% 45 to 60 minutes, 6.6% 60 minutes or more (2000)

RARITAN (village). Covers a land area of 0.099 square miles and a water area of 0 square miles. Located at 40.69° N. Lat.; 90.82° W. Long. Elevation is 761 feet.
Population: 146 (1990); 140 (2000); 131 (2007); 126 (2012 projected); Race: 99.2% White, 0.0% Black, 0.0% Asian, 0.0% Hispanic of any race (2007); Density: 1,321.0 persons per square mile (2007); Average household size: 2.34 (2007); Median age: 41.9 (2007); Males per 100 females: 98.5 (2007); Marriage status: 11.2% never married, 82.8% now married, 4.3% widowed, 1.7% divorced (2000); Foreign born: 0.0% (2000); Ancestry (includes multiple ancestries): 22.9% United States or American, 19.7% German, 13.4% Other groups, 12.7% Irish, 11.5% English (2000).
Economy: Single-family building permits issued: 0 (2007); Multi-family building permits issued: 0 (2007); Employment by occupation: 3.5% management, 10.6% professional, 10.6% services, 32.9% sales, 0.0% farming, 11.8% construction, 30.6% production (2000).
Income: Per capita income: $18,569 (2007); Median household income: $33,462 (2007); Average household income: $43,438 (2007); Percent of households with income of $100,000 or more: 5.4% (2007); Poverty rate: 0.0% (2000).
Education: Percent of population age 25 and over with: High school diploma (including GED) or higher: 90.3% (2007); Bachelor's degree or higher: 12.9% (2007); Master's degree or higher: 2.2% (2007).
Housing: Homeownership rate: 85.7% (2007); Median home value: $55,714 (2007); Median rent: $222 per month (2000); Median age of housing: 54 years (2000).

Transportation: Commute to work: 89.2% car, 0.0% public transportation, 8.4% walk, 0.0% work from home (2000); Travel time to work: 21.7% less than 15 minutes, 44.6% 15 to 30 minutes, 20.5% 30 to 45 minutes, 1.2% 45 to 60 minutes, 12.0% 60 minutes or more (2000)

STRONGHURST (village). Covers a land area of 0.887 square miles and a water area of 0 square miles. Located at 40.74° N. Lat.; 90.90° W. Long. Elevation is 676 feet.
Population: 824 (1990); 896 (2000); 858 (2007); 827 (2012 projected); Race: 99.3% White, 0.1% Black, 0.0% Asian, 0.1% Hispanic of any race (2007); Density: 967.0 persons per square mile (2007); Average household size: 2.51 (2007); Median age: 45.0 (2007); Males per 100 females: 84.9 (2007); Marriage status: 18.3% never married, 59.0% now married, 11.6% widowed, 11.1% divorced (2000); Foreign born: 0.4% (2000); Ancestry (includes multiple ancestries): 26.4% German, 14.8% Irish, 12.6% English, 9.8% United States or American, 8.4% Swedish (2000).
Economy: Single-family building permits issued: 0 (2007); Multi-family building permits issued: 0 (2007); Employment by occupation: 9.6% management, 15.4% professional, 12.8% services, 29.7% sales, 1.8% farming, 9.6% construction, 21.1% production (2000).
Income: Per capita income: $20,729 (2007); Median household income: $41,667 (2007); Average household income: $50,651 (2007); Percent of households with income of $100,000 or more: 6.1% (2007); Poverty rate: 6.9% (2000).
Education: Percent of population age 25 and over with: High school diploma (including GED) or higher: 85.7% (2007); Bachelor's degree or higher: 12.6% (2007); Master's degree or higher: 3.6% (2007).

School District(s)

West Central CUSD 235 (PK-12)
2005-06 Enrollment: 1,106 . . . . (309) 627-2371
Housing: Homeownership rate: 76.3% (2007); Median home value: $78,281 (2007); Median rent: $308 per month (2000); Median age of housing: 54 years (2000).
Newspapers: Henderson County Quill (Local news; Circulation 1,800)
Transportation: Commute to work: 88.7% car, 0.0% public transportation, 7.1% walk, 4.2% work from home (2000); Travel time to work: 35.2% less than 15 minutes, 34.2% 15 to 30 minutes, 21.0% 30 to 45 minutes, 3.8% 45 to 60 minutes, 5.7% 60 minutes or more (2000)

Henry County

Located in northwestern Illinois; bounded on the northwest by the Rock River; drained by the Green and Edwards Rivers. Covers a land area of 823.21 square miles, a water area of 2.38 square miles, and is located in the Central Time Zone. The county was founded in 1825. County seat is Cambridge.

Henry County is part of the Davenport-Moline-Rock Island, IA-IL Metropolitan Statistical Area. The entire metro area includes: Henry County, IL; Mercer County, IL; Rock Island County, IL; Scott County, IA

Weather Station: Galva Elevation: 807 feet

	Jan	Feb	Mar	Apr	May	Jun	Jul	Aug	Sep	Oct	Nov	Dec
High	28	34	46	60	72	81	85	83	76	63	47	34
Low	12	17	27	39	50	60	64	62	53	41	30	18
Precip	1.5	1.5	2.8	3.9	4.2	4.5	4.0	4.4	3.7	2.8	2.9	2.3
Snow	8.2	6.2	4.2	1.7	0.0	0.0	0.0	0.0	0.0	0.4	2.2	5.7

High and Low temperatures in degrees Fahrenheit; Precipitation and Snow in inches

Weather Station: Geneseo Elevation: 636 feet

	Jan	Feb	Mar	Apr	May	Jun	Jul	Aug	Sep	Oct	Nov	Dec
High	28	34	47	61	73	82	86	83	76	63	47	34
Low	12	18	29	40	51	61	65	62	54	42	30	19
Precip	1.5	1.5	2.7	3.8	4.4	4.2	4.0	4.3	3.2	3.0	2.9	2.2
Snow	7.8	5.1	3.7	1.7	0.0	0.0	0.0	0.0	0.0	tr	2.2	6.6

High and Low temperatures in degrees Fahrenheit; Precipitation and Snow in inches

Population: 51,159 (1990); 51,020 (2000); 50,573 (2007); 50,201 (2012 projected); Race: 95.5% White, 1.3% Black, 0.4% Asian, 3.5% Hispanic of any race (2007); Density: 61.4 persons per square mile (2007); Average household size: 2.51 (2007); Median age: 40.9 (2007); Males per 100 females: 97.4 (2007).
Religion: Five largest groups: 19.2% Catholic Church, 11.2% The United Methodist Church, 10.3% Evangelical Lutheran Church in America, 3.9% American Baptist Churches in the USA, 3.0% Lutheran Church—Missouri Synod (2000).
Economy: Unemployment rate: 5.4% (4/2008); Total civilian labor force: 28,551 (4/2008); Leading industries: 30.0% manufacturing; 16.3% retail trade; 10.8% health care and social assistance (2005); Farms: 1,284 totaling 481,311 acres (2002); Companies that employ 500 or more persons: 2 (2006); Companies that employ 100 to 499 persons: 14 (2006); Companies that employ less than 100 persons: 1,117 (2006); Black-owned businesses: n/a (2002); Hispanic-owned businesses: n/a (2002); Asian-owned businesses: n/a (2002); Women-owned businesses: 1,253 (2002); Retail sales per capita: $10,800 (2008). Single-family building permits issued: 76 (2007); Multi-family building permits issued: 2 (2007).
Income: Per capita income: $22,967 (2007); Median household income: $47,245 (2007); Average household income: $57,299 (2007); Percent of households with income of $100,000 or more: 12.9% (2007); Poverty rate: 10.3% (2005); Bankruptcy rate: 2.72% (2007).
Taxes: Total county taxes per capita: $114 (2006); County property taxes per capita: $113 (2006).
Education: Percent of population age 25 and over with: High school diploma (including GED) or higher: 84.5% (2007); Bachelor's degree or higher: 15.9% (2007); Master's degree or higher: 4.8% (2007).
Housing: Homeownership rate: 78.9% (2007); Median home value: $108,091 (2007); Median rent: $322 per month (2000); Median age of housing: 48 years (2000).
Health: Birth rate: 119.0 per 10,000 population (2007); Death rate: 105.5 per 10,000 population (2007); Age-adjusted cancer mortality rate: 183.9 deaths per 100,000 population (2005); Number of physicians: 5.0 per 10,000 population (2005); Hospital beds: 20.4 per 10,000 population (2004); Hospital admissions: 591.8 per 10,000 population (2004).
Elections: 2004 Presidential election results: 52.3% Bush, 47.1% Kerry, 0.1% Nader, 0.5% Badnarik
National and State Parks: Johnson Sauk Trail State Park
Additional Information Contacts
Henry County Government . . . . (309) 937-3574
http://www.co.henry.il.us
City of Colona . . . . (309) 792-0571
http://colona.govoffice.com
City of Geneseo . . . . (309) 944-6419
http://www.cityofgeneseo.com
Geneseo Chamber of Commerce . . . . (309) 944-2686
http://www.geneseo.org
Kewanee Chamber of Commerce . . . . (309) 852-2175
http://www.kewanee-il.com
Village of Cambridge . . . . (309) 937-2570
http://www.cambridgeil.org

Henry County Communities

ALPHA (village). Covers a land area of 0.322 square miles and a water area of 0 square miles. Located at 41.19° N. Lat.; 90.38° W. Long. Elevation is 801 feet.
Population: 809 (1990); 726 (2000); 748 (2007); 749 (2012 projected); Race: 98.4% White, 0.0% Black, 0.0% Asian, 1.5% Hispanic of any race (2007); Density: 2,323.1 persons per square mile (2007); Average household size: 2.36 (2007); Median age: 41.6 (2007); Males per 100 females: 101.1 (2007); Marriage status: 18.4% never married, 59.5% now married, 8.9% widowed, 13.2% divorced (2000); Foreign born: 0.8% (2000); Ancestry (includes multiple ancestries): 21.7% German, 19.6% Swedish, 12.3% English, 9.7% Irish, 8.5% United States or American (2000).
Economy: Single-family building permits issued: 0 (2007); Multi-family building permits issued: 0 (2007); Employment by occupation: 9.6% management, 11.5% professional, 16.9% services, 28.5% sales, 1.7% farming, 10.1% construction, 21.7% production (2000).
Income: Per capita income: $19,582 (2007); Median household income: $38,438 (2007); Average household income: $46,207 (2007); Percent of households with income of $100,000 or more: 4.1% (2007); Poverty rate: 5.8% (2000).
Education: Percent of population age 25 and over with: High school diploma (including GED) or higher: 87.3% (2007); Bachelor's degree or higher: 11.0% (2007); Master's degree or higher: 2.9% (2007).

School District(s)

Alwood CUSD 225 (PK-12)
2005-06 Enrollment: 517 . . . . (309) 334-2719
Housing: Homeownership rate: 86.8% (2007); Median home value: $86,875 (2007); Median rent: $306 per month (2000); Median age of housing: 50 years (2000).

Safety: Violent crime rate: 0.0 per 10,000 population; Property crime rate: 14.2 per 10,000 population (2006).
Transportation: Commute to work: 91.5% car, 0.0% public transportation, 5.1% walk, 3.4% work from home (2000); Travel time to work: 34.7% less than 15 minutes, 31.8% 15 to 30 minutes, 24.8% 30 to 45 minutes, 4.7% 45 to 60 minutes, 4.1% 60 minutes or more (2000)

ANDOVER (village). Covers a land area of 0.999 square miles and a water area of 0 square miles. Located at 41.29° N. Lat.; 90.29° W. Long. Elevation is 774 feet.
Population: 579 (1990); 594 (2000); 565 (2007); 551 (2012 projected); Race: 97.9% White, 0.0% Black, 1.4% Asian, 1.4% Hispanic of any race (2007); Density: 565.7 persons per square mile (2007); Average household size: 2.64 (2007); Median age: 43.0 (2007); Males per 100 females: 96.2 (2007); Marriage status: 18.1% never married, 69.9% now married, 4.0% widowed, 8.0% divorced (2000); Foreign born: 0.8% (2000); Ancestry (includes multiple ancestries): 26.8% German, 20.5% Swedish, 15.8% Irish, 10.4% English, 5.2% Other groups (2000).
Economy: Single-family building permits issued: 0 (2007); Multi-family building permits issued: 0 (2007); Employment by occupation: 5.3% management, 13.5% professional, 14.5% services, 25.7% sales, 0.0% farming, 15.2% construction, 25.7% production (2000).
Income: Per capita income: $22,774 (2007); Median household income: $53,667 (2007); Average household income: $60,129 (2007); Percent of households with income of $100,000 or more: 14.5% (2007); Poverty rate: 5.9% (2000).
Education: Percent of population age 25 and over with: High school diploma (including GED) or higher: 86.9% (2007); Bachelor's degree or higher: 12.3% (2007); Master's degree or higher: 0.5% (2007).
Housing: Homeownership rate: 87.9% (2007); Median home value: $105,469 (2007); Median rent: $325 per month (2000); Median age of housing: 32 years (2000).
Transportation: Commute to work: 94.6% car, 0.0% public transportation, 1.0% walk, 2.4% work from home (2000); Travel time to work: 11.1% less than 15 minutes, 24.6% 15 to 30 minutes, 49.5% 30 to 45 minutes, 8.3% 45 to 60 minutes, 6.6% 60 minutes or more (2000)

ANNAWAN (town). Covers a land area of 0.682 square miles and a water area of 0 square miles. Located at 41.39° N. Lat.; 89.90° W. Long. Elevation is 630 feet.
History: Annawan developed as the center of a stock farming and coal mining region.
Population: 817 (1990); 868 (2000); 806 (2007); 804 (2012 projected); Race: 99.8% White, 0.0% Black, 0.0% Asian, 1.4% Hispanic of any race (2007); Density: 1,182.6 persons per square mile (2007); Average household size: 2.39 (2007); Median age: 37.0 (2007); Males per 100 females: 93.3 (2007); Marriage status: 26.7% never married, 60.0% now married, 5.8% widowed, 7.4% divorced (2000); Foreign born: 0.2% (2000); Ancestry (includes multiple ancestries): 33.6% Belgian, 27.7% German, 8.8% Irish, 7.9% English, 6.8% Swedish (2000).
Economy: Single-family building permits issued: 0 (2007); Multi-family building permits issued: 0 (2007); Employment by occupation: 7.3% management, 17.4% professional, 13.0% services, 30.5% sales, 1.8% farming, 10.7% construction, 19.3% production (2000).
Income: Per capita income: $22,792 (2007); Median household income: $45,833 (2007); Average household income: $54,510 (2007); Percent of households with income of $100,000 or more: 9.2% (2007); Poverty rate: 9.7% (2000).
Education: Percent of population age 25 and over with: High school diploma (including GED) or higher: 86.3% (2007); Bachelor's degree or higher: 13.0% (2007); Master's degree or higher: 4.6% (2007).

School District(s)

Annawan CUSD 226 (PK-12)
2005-06 Enrollment: 423 . . . . (309) 935-6781
Housing: Homeownership rate: 80.4% (2007); Median home value: $107,176 (2007); Median rent: $294 per month (2000); Median age of housing: 48 years (2000).
Safety: Violent crime rate: 21.8 per 10,000 population; Property crime rate: 65.3 per 10,000 population (2006).
Transportation: Commute to work: 93.9% car, 0.0% public transportation, 3.9% walk, 1.3% work from home (2000); Travel time to work: 36.8% less than 15 minutes, 31.5% 15 to 30 minutes, 15.7% 30 to 45 minutes, 10.1% 45 to 60 minutes, 5.9% 60 minutes or more (2000)

ATKINSON (town). Covers a land area of 1.509 square miles and a water area of 0.004 square miles. Located at 41.41° N. Lat.; 90.01° W. Long. Elevation is 659 feet.
Population: 954 (1990); 1,001 (2000); 936 (2007); 925 (2012 projected); Race: 97.8% White, 0.9% Black, 0.3% Asian, 1.3% Hispanic of any race (2007); Density: 620.1 persons per square mile (2007); Average household size: 2.24 (2007); Median age: 42.0 (2007); Males per 100 females: 94.2 (2007); Marriage status: 25.3% never married, 57.0% now married, 10.1% widowed, 7.7% divorced (2000); Foreign born: 0.3% (2000); Ancestry (includes multiple ancestries): 33.9% Belgian, 26.0% German, 11.9% Irish, 9.6% Swedish, 8.5% English (2000).
Economy: Single-family building permits issued: 2 (2007); Multi-family building permits issued: 0 (2007); Employment by occupation: 8.1% management, 12.6% professional, 16.4% services, 28.9% sales, 2.2% farming, 16.4% construction, 15.5% production (2000).
Income: Per capita income: $21,816 (2007); Median household income: $43,194 (2007); Average household income: $48,969 (2007); Percent of households with income of $100,000 or more: 7.9% (2007); Poverty rate: 10.0% (2000).
Education: Percent of population age 25 and over with: High school diploma (including GED) or higher: 81.7% (2007); Bachelor's degree or higher: 13.3% (2007); Master's degree or higher: 3.2% (2007).

School District(s)

Geneseo CUSD 228 (PK-12)
2005-06 Enrollment: 2,826 . . . . (309) 945-0450
Henry-Stark County Spec Ed Dist (03-12)
2005-06 Enrollment: 50 . . . . (309) 852-5696
Housing: Homeownership rate: 78.4% (2007); Median home value: $94,844 (2007); Median rent: $320 per month (2000); Median age of housing: 55 years (2000).
Safety: Violent crime rate: 194.9 per 10,000 population; Property crime rate: 225.6 per 10,000 population (2006).
Transportation: Commute to work: 94.6% car, 0.0% public transportation, 3.4% walk, 1.6% work from home (2000); Travel time to work: 43.7% less than 15 minutes, 27.2% 15 to 30 minutes, 21.1% 30 to 45 minutes, 5.3% 45 to 60 minutes, 2.7% 60 minutes or more (2000)

BISHOP HILL (village). Covers a land area of 0.539 square miles and a water area of 0 square miles. Located at 41.20° N. Lat.; 90.11° W. Long. Elevation is 784 feet.
History: Bishop Hill was settled in 1846 by a group of Swedish emigrants led by Erik Jansson, who envisioned a communistic society based on religion. Jansson's leadership lasted only a few years, and by 1861 the communal property had been divided among individuals.
Population: 131 (1990); 125 (2000); 124 (2007); 122 (2012 projected); Race: 100.0% White, 0.0% Black, 0.0% Asian, 0.8% Hispanic of any race (2007); Density: 230.2 persons per square mile (2007); Average household size: 2.21 (2007); Median age: 51.8 (2007); Males per 100 females: 100.0 (2007); Marriage status: 8.0% never married, 77.9% now married, 7.1% widowed, 7.1% divorced (2000); Foreign born: 4.4% (2000); Ancestry (includes multiple ancestries): 26.3% Swedish, 22.6% German, 13.9% English, 13.1% United States or American, 6.6% Italian (2000).
Economy: Single-family building permits issued: 0 (2007); Multi-family building permits issued: 0 (2007); Employment by occupation: 15.9% management, 20.6% professional, 14.3% services, 30.2% sales, 0.0% farming, 4.8% construction, 14.3% production (2000).
Income: Per capita income: $30,141 (2007); Median household income: $53,333 (2007); Average household income: $66,741 (2007); Percent of households with income of $100,000 or more: 21.4% (2007); Poverty rate: 0.0% (2000).
Education: Percent of population age 25 and over with: High school diploma (including GED) or higher: 95.7% (2007); Bachelor's degree or higher: 34.0% (2007); Master's degree or higher: 3.2% (2007).
Housing: Homeownership rate: 94.6% (2007); Median home value: $103,676 (2007); Median rent: $325 per month (2000); Median age of housing: 60+ years (2000).
Transportation: Commute to work: 76.2% car, 0.0% public transportation, 11.1% walk, 12.7% work from home (2000); Travel time to work: 41.8% less than 15 minutes, 16.4% 15 to 30 minutes, 18.2% 30 to 45 minutes, 10.9% 45 to 60 minutes, 12.7% 60 minutes or more (2000)

CAMBRIDGE (village). County seat. Covers a land area of 1.415 square miles and a water area of 0.013 square miles. Located at 41.30° N. Lat.; 90.19° W. Long. Elevation is 810 feet.

History: Incorporated 1861.
Population: 2,153 (1990); 2,180 (2000); 2,111 (2007); 2,057 (2012 projected); Race: 97.4% White, 1.2% Black, 0.6% Asian, 0.7% Hispanic of any race (2007); Density: 1,491.4 persons per square mile (2007); Average household size: 2.49 (2007); Median age: 38.1 (2007); Males per 100 females: 103.8 (2007); Marriage status: 20.0% never married, 62.3% now married, 8.8% widowed, 8.9% divorced (2000); Foreign born: 0.9% (2000); Ancestry (includes multiple ancestries): 24.0% German, 20.5% Swedish, 15.2% English, 11.9% United States or American, 10.3% Irish (2000).
Economy: Single-family building permits issued: 4 (2007); Multi-family building permits issued: 0 (2007); Employment by occupation: 13.1% management, 16.6% professional, 18.4% services, 21.9% sales, 1.0% farming, 13.9% construction, 15.1% production (2000).
Income: Per capita income: $22,321 (2007); Median household income: $45,972 (2007); Average household income: $54,988 (2007); Percent of households with income of $100,000 or more: 11.0% (2007); Poverty rate: 10.3% (2000).
Education: Percent of population age 25 and over with: High school diploma (including GED) or higher: 83.1% (2007); Bachelor's degree or higher: 14.6% (2007); Master's degree or higher: 5.5% (2007).

School District(s)

Cambridge CUSD 227 (PK-12)
2005-06 Enrollment: 529 . . . . (309) 937-2144
Housing: Homeownership rate: 80.7% (2007); Median home value: $100,316 (2007); Median rent: $306 per month (2000); Median age of housing: 48 years (2000).
Safety: Violent crime rate: 28.3 per 10,000 population; Property crime rate: 61.3 per 10,000 population (2006).
Newspapers: Cambridge Chronicle (Local news; Circulation 1,500)
Transportation: Commute to work: 91.7% car, 0.0% public transportation, 4.4% walk, 1.8% work from home (2000); Travel time to work: 42.3% less than 15 minutes, 24.9% 15 to 30 minutes, 18.5% 30 to 45 minutes, 11.9% 45 to 60 minutes, 2.5% 60 minutes or more (2000)
Additional Information Contacts
Village of Cambridge . . . . (309) 937-2570
http://www.cambridgeil.org

CLEVELAND (village). Covers a land area of 0.361 square miles and a water area of 0.003 square miles. Located at 41.50° N. Lat.; 90.31° W. Long. Elevation is 571 feet.
Population: 283 (1990); 253 (2000); 240 (2007); 234 (2012 projected); Race: 98.8% White, 0.0% Black, 0.0% Asian, 6.7% Hispanic of any race (2007); Density: 664.2 persons per square mile (2007); Average household size: 2.67 (2007); Median age: 41.0 (2007); Males per 100 females: 93.5 (2007); Marriage status: 16.2% never married, 66.2% now married, 8.1% widowed, 9.6% divorced (2000); Foreign born: 0.0% (2000); Ancestry (includes multiple ancestries): 20.7% German, 13.9% Other groups, 13.5% Irish, 11.2% Swedish, 10.0% English (2000).
Economy: Single-family building permits issued: 0 (2007); Multi-family building permits issued: 0 (2007); Employment by occupation: 5.6% management, 16.1% professional, 7.0% services, 39.2% sales, 0.0% farming, 11.2% construction, 21.0% production (2000).
Income: Per capita income: $22,063 (2007); Median household income: $54,091 (2007); Average household income: $58,833 (2007); Percent of households with income of $100,000 or more: 10.0% (2007); Poverty rate: 6.4% (2000).
Education: Percent of population age 25 and over with: High school diploma (including GED) or higher: 79.5% (2007); Bachelor's degree or higher: 8.4% (2007); Master's degree or higher: 0.0% (2007).
Housing: Homeownership rate: 82.2% (2007); Median home value: $104,688 (2007); Median rent: $392 per month (2000); Median age of housing: 36 years (2000).
Transportation: Commute to work: 89.4% car, 0.0% public transportation, 2.1% walk, 3.5% work from home (2000); Travel time to work: 22.8% less than 15 minutes, 58.8% 15 to 30 minutes, 10.3% 30 to 45 minutes, 4.4% 45 to 60 minutes, 3.7% 60 minutes or more (2000)

COLONA (city). Covers a land area of 3.497 square miles and a water area of 0.061 square miles. Located at 41.47° N. Lat.; 90.34° W. Long. Elevation is 604 feet.
Population: 5,152 (1990); 5,173 (2000); 5,136 (2007); 5,115 (2012 projected); Race: 96.7% White, 0.4% Black, 0.2% Asian, 4.2% Hispanic of any race (2007); Density: 1,468.5 persons per square mile (2007); Average household size: 2.62 (2007); Median age: 36.2 (2007); Males per 100 females: 100.4 (2007); Marriage status: 23.3% never married, 62.9% now married, 4.2% widowed, 9.6% divorced (2000); Foreign born: 1.8% (2000); Ancestry (includes multiple ancestries): 22.6% German, 15.8% Irish, 11.8% Other groups, 8.8% United States or American, 7.5% English (2000).
Economy: Single-family building permits issued: 24 (2007); Multi-family building permits issued: 0 (2007); Employment by occupation: 7.9% management, 12.3% professional, 19.9% services, 26.6% sales, 0.3% farming, 10.3% construction, 22.7% production (2000).
Income: Per capita income: $21,813 (2007); Median household income: $49,283 (2007); Average household income: $57,071 (2007); Percent of households with income of $100,000 or more: 12.6% (2007); Poverty rate: 7.6% (2000).
Education: Percent of population age 25 and over with: High school diploma (including GED) or higher: 77.5% (2007); Bachelor's degree or higher: 9.1% (2007); Master's degree or higher: 2.4% (2007).

School District(s)

Colona SD 190 (PK-08)
2005-06 Enrollment: 570 . . . . (309) 792-1232
Housing: Homeownership rate: 83.4% (2007); Median home value: $99,360 (2007); Median rent: $355 per month (2000); Median age of housing: 33 years (2000).
Safety: Violent crime rate: 13.3 per 10,000 population; Property crime rate: 202.8 per 10,000 population (2006).
Transportation: Commute to work: 95.7% car, 0.0% public transportation, 2.1% walk, 1.9% work from home (2000); Travel time to work: 21.1% less than 15 minutes, 50.8% 15 to 30 minutes, 22.4% 30 to 45 minutes, 1.8% 45 to 60 minutes, 3.8% 60 minutes or more (2000)
Additional Information Contacts
City of Colona . . . . (309) 792-0571
http://colona.govoffice.com

GALVA (city). Covers a land area of 1.714 square miles and a water area of 0 square miles. Located at 41.16° N. Lat.; 90.04° W. Long. Elevation is 850 feet.
History: Galva was founded in 1854 by a group of Swedish settlers, who named it for their home in Sweden, Gefle. These first residents had been members of the religious colony at Bishop Hill.
Population: 2,761 (1990); 2,758 (2000); 2,688 (2007); 2,634 (2012 projected); Race: 98.3% White, 0.4% Black, 0.3% Asian, 2.2% Hispanic of any race (2007); Density: 1,568.6 persons per square mile (2007); Average household size: 2.38 (2007); Median age: 40.7 (2007); Males per 100 females: 91.7 (2007); Marriage status: 19.9% never married, 58.8% now married, 10.8% widowed, 10.4% divorced (2000); Foreign born: 1.4% (2000); Ancestry (includes multiple ancestries): 21.5% German, 18.3% Swedish, 15.5% English, 11.1% Irish, 10.6% United States or American (2000).
Economy: Single-family building permits issued: 1 (2007); Multi-family building permits issued: 0 (2007); Employment by occupation: 12.1% management, 15.6% professional, 16.0% services, 26.7% sales, 1.2% farming, 9.7% construction, 18.6% production (2000).
Income: Per capita income: $21,937 (2007); Median household income: $42,227 (2007); Average household income: $51,919 (2007); Percent of households with income of $100,000 or more: 9.5% (2007); Poverty rate: 7.2% (2000).
Education: Percent of population age 25 and over with: High school diploma (including GED) or higher: 86.1% (2007); Bachelor's degree or higher: 16.3% (2007); Master's degree or higher: 4.5% (2007).

School District(s)

Galva CUSD 224 (PK-12)
2005-06 Enrollment: 628 . . . . (309) 932-2108
Housing: Homeownership rate: 77.1% (2007); Median home value: $80,000 (2007); Median rent: $298 per month (2000); Median age of housing: 59 years (2000).
Safety: Violent crime rate: 25.9 per 10,000 population; Property crime rate: 203.3 per 10,000 population (2006).
Newspapers: Galva News (Local news; Circulation 2,314); Wrova Shopper (Local news; Circulation 1,283)
Transportation: Commute to work: 92.6% car, 0.0% public transportation, 3.5% walk, 2.4% work from home (2000); Travel time to work: 50.3% less than 15 minutes, 24.0% 15 to 30 minutes, 11.5% 30 to 45 minutes, 9.3% 45 to 60 minutes, 5.0% 60 minutes or more (2000)

GENESEO (city). Covers a land area of 4.032 square miles and a water area of 0.008 square miles. Located at 41.45° N. Lat.; 90.15° W. Long. Elevation is 650 feet.

History: Geneseo was settled in 1836 by people from New York, and named for Geneseo in that state. Early industries were a corn and pea cannery, and a bandage factory.
Population: 6,091 (1990); 6,480 (2000); 6,490 (2007); 6,500 (2012 projected); Race: 98.1% White, 0.3% Black, 0.6% Asian, 1.2% Hispanic of any race (2007); Density: 1,609.4 persons per square mile (2007); Average household size: 2.36 (2007); Median age: 43.0 (2007); Males per 100 females: 91.6 (2007); Marriage status: 20.6% never married, 60.8% now married, 11.5% widowed, 7.1% divorced (2000); Foreign born: 1.1% (2000); Ancestry (includes multiple ancestries): 31.9% German, 13.5% English, 13.4% Irish, 12.8% Swedish, 9.7% Belgian (2000).
Economy: Single-family building permits issued: 12 (2007); Multi-family building permits issued: 2 (2007); Employment by occupation: 14.9% management, 19.8% professional, 13.7% services, 26.0% sales, 0.8% farming, 10.1% construction, 14.7% production (2000).
Income: Per capita income: $24,177 (2007); Median household income: $47,224 (2007); Average household income: $56,610 (2007); Percent of households with income of $100,000 or more: 11.9% (2007); Poverty rate: 5.3% (2000).
Education: Percent of population age 25 and over with: High school diploma (including GED) or higher: 88.6% (2007); Bachelor's degree or higher: 23.8% (2007); Master's degree or higher: 6.0% (2007).

School District(s)

Bureau/Henry/Stark Roe (06-12)
2005-06 Enrollment: 21 . . . . (309) 936-7890
Geneseo CUSD 228 (PK-12)
2005-06 Enrollment: 2,826 . . . . (309) 945-0450

Housing: Homeownership rate: 76.3% (2007); Median home value: $137,914 (2007); Median rent: $380 per month (2000); Median age of housing: 45 years (2000).
Hospitals: Hammond-Henry Hospital (105 beds)
Safety: Violent crime rate: 15.3 per 10,000 population; Property crime rate: 191.6 per 10,000 population (2006).
Newspapers: Geneseo Republic (Community news; Circulation 4,300)
Transportation: Commute to work: 91.8% car, 0.0% public transportation, 4.0% walk, 2.5% work from home (2000); Travel time to work: 54.9% less than 15 minutes, 18.4% 15 to 30 minutes, 19.2% 30 to 45 minutes, 3.6% 45 to 60 minutes, 4.0% 60 minutes or more (2000)

Additional Information Contacts

City of Geneseo . . . . (309) 944-6419
http://www.cityofgeneseo.com
Geneseo Chamber of Commerce . . . . (309) 944-2686
http://www.geneseo.org

HOOPPOLE (village). Covers a land area of 0.347 square miles and a water area of 0 square miles. Located at 41.52° N. Lat.; 89.91° W. Long. Elevation is 623 feet.
History: In a grove of hickory trees near Hooppole, coopers cut bands to use in the crafting of their barrels, and from this the town was named.
Population: 196 (1990); 162 (2000); 155 (2007); 152 (2012 projected); Race: 95.5% White, 0.6% Black, 0.0% Asian, 10.3% Hispanic of any race (2007); Density: 446.6 persons per square mile (2007); Average household size: 2.58 (2007); Median age: 37.5 (2007); Males per 100 females: 124.6 (2007); Marriage status: 9.6% never married, 69.6% now married, 6.7% widowed, 14.1% divorced (2000); Foreign born: 0.0% (2000); Ancestry (includes multiple ancestries): 33.1% German, 20.9% Swedish, 14.1% Irish, 9.2% Belgian, 8.6% English (2000).
Economy: Single-family building permits issued: 0 (2007); Multi-family building permits issued: 0 (2007); Employment by occupation: 3.3% management, 13.3% professional, 27.8% services, 22.2% sales, 0.0% farming, 12.2% construction, 21.1% production (2000).
Income: Per capita income: $19,468 (2007); Median household income: $42,500 (2007); Average household income: $50,292 (2007); Percent of households with income of $100,000 or more: 6.7% (2007); Poverty rate: 4.3% (2000).
Education: Percent of population age 25 and over with: High school diploma (including GED) or higher: 84.8% (2007); Bachelor's degree or higher: 9.1% (2007); Master's degree or higher: 1.0% (2007).
Housing: Homeownership rate: 91.7% (2007); Median home value: $63,929 (2007); Median rent: $175 per month (2000); Median age of housing: 60+ years (2000).
Transportation: Commute to work: 88.9% car, 0.0% public transportation, 2.2% walk, 3.3% work from home (2000); Travel time to work: 8.0% less than 15 minutes, 46.0% 15 to 30 minutes, 13.8% 30 to 45 minutes, 18.4% 45 to 60 minutes, 13.8% 60 minutes or more (2000)

KEWANEE (city). Covers a land area of 6.277 square miles and a water area of 0.013 square miles. Located at 41.24° N. Lat.; 89.92° W. Long. Elevation is 850 feet.
History: Kewanee was established in 1836 by the Connecticut Association to promote Protestantism in Illinois. The town was first called Wethersfield after the town in Connecticut. When the railroad line was laid a mile north, a settlement developed around the depot. By 1857 the new settlement, named Kewanee, had surpassed the older Wethersfield, which was incorporated with Kewanee in 1924.
Population: 13,199 (1990); 12,944 (2000); 12,561 (2007); 12,267 (2012 projected); Race: 88.1% White, 3.9% Black, 0.5% Asian, 8.0% Hispanic of any race (2007); Density: 2,001.1 persons per square mile (2007); Average household size: 2.41 (2007); Median age: 39.0 (2007); Males per 100 females: 91.2 (2007); Marriage status: 21.3% never married, 53.1% now married, 12.9% widowed, 12.7% divorced (2000); Foreign born: 2.9% (2000); Ancestry (includes multiple ancestries): 23.2% German, 12.9% Other groups, 11.7% Irish, 10.9% English, 10.4% United States or American (2000).
Economy: Single-family building permits issued: 7 (2007); Multi-family building permits issued: 0 (2007); Employment by occupation: 8.6% management, 13.2% professional, 18.9% services, 26.2% sales, 0.5% farming, 9.8% construction, 22.9% production (2000).
Income: Per capita income: $18,785 (2007); Median household income: $34,988 (2007); Average household income: $44,579 (2007); Percent of households with income of $100,000 or more: 7.0% (2007); Poverty rate: 13.9% (2000).
Education: Percent of population age 25 and over with: High school diploma (including GED) or higher: 77.7% (2007); Bachelor's degree or higher: 10.0% (2007); Master's degree or higher: 3.5% (2007).

School District(s)

Dept of Corrections Sch Dist 428 (08-12)
2005-06 Enrollment: 2,271 . . . . (217) 522-2666
Kewanee CUSD 229 (PK-12)
2005-06 Enrollment: 1,841 . . . . (309) 853-3341
Wethersfield CUSD 230 (PK-12)
2005-06 Enrollment: 691 . . . . (309) 853-4860

Housing: Homeownership rate: 74.2% (2007); Median home value: $64,732 (2007); Median rent: $291 per month (2000); Median age of housing: 60+ years (2000).
Hospitals: Kewanee Hospital (25 beds)
Safety: Violent crime rate: 35.6 per 10,000 population; Property crime rate: 697.7 per 10,000 population (2006).
Newspapers: Kewanee Star-Courier (Local news; Circulation 5,800)
Transportation: Commute to work: 93.9% car, 0.3% public transportation, 2.5% walk, 1.6% work from home (2000); Travel time to work: 67.5% less than 15 minutes, 14.5% 15 to 30 minutes, 6.2% 30 to 45 minutes, 5.4% 45 to 60 minutes, 6.5% 60 minutes or more (2000); Amtrak: Service available.
Airports: Kewanee Municipal (general aviation)

Additional Information Contacts

Kewanee Chamber of Commerce . . . . (309) 852-2175
http://www.kewanee-il.com

LYNN CENTER (unincorporated postal area, zip code 61262). Covers a land area of 44.229 square miles and a water area of 0.029 square miles. Located at 41.28° N. Lat.; 90.36° W. Long. Elevation is 758 feet.
Population: 878 (2000); Race: 100.0% White, 0.0% Black, 0.0% Asian, 0.0% Hispanic of any race (2000); Density: 19.9 persons per square mile (2000); Age: 22.8% under 18, 13.3% over 64 (2000); Marriage status: 16.1% never married, 72.9% now married, 3.9% widowed, 7.1% divorced (2000); Foreign born: 0.2% (2000); Ancestry (includes multiple ancestries): 25.7% German, 25.0% Swedish, 14.7% English, 10.6% Irish, 8.5% Belgian (2000).
Economy: Employment by occupation: 16.1% management, 14.9% professional, 8.3% services, 20.9% sales, 0.2% farming, 14.9% construction, 24.8% production (2000).
Income: Per capita income: $20,088 (2000); Median household income: $51,518 (2000); Poverty rate: 1.1% (2000).
Education: Percent of population age 25 and over with: High school diploma (including GED) or higher: 90.8% (2000); Bachelor's degree or higher: 9.6% (2000).
Housing: Homeownership rate: 80.8% (2000); Median home value: $93,500 (2000); Median rent: $243 per month (2000); Median age of housing: 39 years (2000).

Transportation: Commute to work: 92.7% car, 0.0% public transportation, 3.8% walk, 3.5% work from home (2000); Travel time to work: 12.7% less than 15 minutes, 28.9% 15 to 30 minutes, 52.1% 30 to 45 minutes, 4.6% 45 to 60 minutes, 1.7% 60 minutes or more (2000)

OPHEIM (unincorporated postal area, zip code 61468). Covers a land area of 7.229 square miles and a water area of 0 square miles. Located at 41.25° N. Lat.; 90.40° W. Long.
Population: 143 (2000); Race: 92.5% White, 7.5% Black, 0.0% Asian, 0.0% Hispanic of any race (2000); Density: 19.8 persons per square mile (2000); Age: 48.5% under 18, 6.7% over 64 (2000); Marriage status: 31.7% never married, 51.2% now married, 6.1% widowed, 11.0% divorced (2000); Foreign born: 0.0% (2000); Ancestry (includes multiple ancestries): 19.4% Swedish, 14.2% United States or American, 11.9% Irish, 6.0% Other groups, 4.5% German (2000).
Economy: Employment by occupation: 3.4% management, 6.8% professional, 16.9% services, 23.7% sales, 0.0% farming, 15.3% construction, 33.9% production (2000).
Income: Per capita income: $10,793 (2000); Median household income: $40,750 (2000); Poverty rate: 5.3% (2000).
Education: Percent of population age 25 and over with: High school diploma (including GED) or higher: 88.1% (2000); Bachelor's degree or higher: 11.9% (2000).
Housing: Homeownership rate: 83.3% (2000); Median home value: $53,300 (2000); Median rent: $275 per month (2000); Median age of housing: 60+ years (2000).
Transportation: Commute to work: 100.0% car, 0.0% public transportation, 0.0% walk, 0.0% work from home (2000); Travel time to work: 7.8% less than 15 minutes, 9.8% 15 to 30 minutes, 62.7% 30 to 45 minutes, 19.6% 45 to 60 minutes, 0.0% 60 minutes or more (2000)

ORION (village). Covers a land area of 0.861 square miles and a water area of 0 square miles. Located at 41.35° N. Lat.; 90.37° W. Long. Elevation is 774 feet.
Population: 1,885 (1990); 1,713 (2000); 1,566 (2007); 1,534 (2012 projected); Race: 99.2% White, 0.0% Black, 0.1% Asian, 1.9% Hispanic of any race (2007); Density: 1,818.4 persons per square mile (2007); Average household size: 2.38 (2007); Median age: 41.6 (2007); Males per 100 females: 96.7 (2007); Marriage status: 20.2% never married, 64.3% now married, 8.6% widowed, 6.9% divorced (2000); Foreign born: 0.7% (2000); Ancestry (includes multiple ancestries): 31.8% German, 22.5% Swedish, 14.7% Irish, 12.0% English, 7.8% United States or American (2000).
Economy: Single-family building permits issued: 1 (2007); Multi-family building permits issued: 0 (2007); Employment by occupation: 10.6% management, 17.1% professional, 12.8% services, 31.8% sales, 0.5% farming, 9.9% construction, 17.4% production (2000).
Income: Per capita income: $27,130 (2007); Median household income: $58,786 (2007); Average household income: $64,665 (2007); Percent of households with income of $100,000 or more: 15.4% (2007); Poverty rate: 3.8% (2000).
Education: Percent of population age 25 and over with: High school diploma (including GED) or higher: 90.2% (2007); Bachelor's degree or higher: 17.5% (2007); Master's degree or higher: 5.4% (2007).

School District(s)

Orion CUSD 223 (PK-12)
2005-06 Enrollment: 1,100 . . . . (309) 526-3388
Housing: Homeownership rate: 81.9% (2007); Median home value: $129,455 (2007); Median rent: $365 per month (2000); Median age of housing: 39 years (2000).
Safety: Violent crime rate: 23.5 per 10,000 population; Property crime rate: 58.7 per 10,000 population (2006).
Newspapers: Orion Gazette (Community news; Circulation 2,500)
Transportation: Commute to work: 95.6% car, 0.0% public transportation, 2.1% walk, 2.2% work from home (2000); Travel time to work: 23.0% less than 15 minutes, 46.6% 15 to 30 minutes, 25.9% 30 to 45 minutes, 2.3% 45 to 60 minutes, 2.2% 60 minutes or more (2000)

OSCO (unincorporated postal area, zip code 61274). Covers a land area of 24.924 square miles and a water area of 0 square miles. Located at 41.37° N. Lat.; 90.27° W. Long. Elevation is 771 feet.
Population: 404 (2000); Race: 97.8% White, 0.0% Black, 0.0% Asian, 0.0% Hispanic of any race (2000); Density: 16.2 persons per square mile (2000); Age: 27.1% under 18, 10.4% over 64 (2000); Marriage status: 20.4% never married, 72.3% now married, 3.4% widowed, 3.9% divorced (2000); Foreign born: 0.0% (2000); Ancestry (includes multiple ancestries): 29.9% German, 29.3% Swedish, 19.1% English, 9.3% United States or American, 8.0% Belgian (2000).
Economy: Employment by occupation: 28.7% management, 0.0% professional, 15.0% services, 24.3% sales, 2.4% farming, 16.6% construction, 13.0% production (2000).
Income: Per capita income: $16,351 (2000); Median household income: $39,808 (2000); Poverty rate: 5.1% (2000).
Education: Percent of population age 25 and over with: High school diploma (including GED) or higher: 93.6% (2000); Bachelor's degree or higher: 0.0% (2000).
Housing: Homeownership rate: 74.5% (2000); Median home value: $85,800 (2000); Median rent: $325 per month (2000); Median age of housing: 60+ years (2000).
Transportation: Commute to work: 63.2% car, 0.0% public transportation, 9.3% walk, 27.5% work from home (2000); Travel time to work: 41.9% less than 15 minutes, 27.4% 15 to 30 minutes, 22.9% 30 to 45 minutes, 4.5% 45 to 60 minutes, 3.4% 60 minutes or more (2000)

WOODHULL (village). Covers a land area of 0.825 square miles and a water area of 0 square miles. Located at 41.17° N. Lat.; 90.31° W. Long. Elevation is 810 feet.
Population: 826 (1990); 809 (2000); 861 (2007); 876 (2012 projected); Race: 99.1% White, 0.3% Black, 0.2% Asian, 1.0% Hispanic of any race (2007); Density: 1,043.6 persons per square mile (2007); Average household size: 2.31 (2007); Median age: 41.7 (2007); Males per 100 females: 99.3 (2007); Marriage status: 16.1% never married, 63.8% now married, 11.0% widowed, 9.1% divorced (2000); Foreign born: 0.6% (2000); Ancestry (includes multiple ancestries): 28.7% Swedish, 16.9% German, 13.1% Irish, 10.4% English, 9.3% United States or American (2000).
Economy: Single-family building permits issued: 0 (2007); Multi-family building permits issued: 0 (2007); Employment by occupation: 6.9% management, 14.8% professional, 14.6% services, 25.9% sales, 0.8% farming, 13.0% construction, 24.1% production (2000).
Income: Per capita income: $18,403 (2007); Median household income: $36,848 (2007); Average household income: $42,480 (2007); Percent of households with income of $100,000 or more: 3.8% (2007); Poverty rate: 9.1% (2000).
Education: Percent of population age 25 and over with: High school diploma (including GED) or higher: 87.6% (2007); Bachelor's degree or higher: 16.6% (2007); Master's degree or higher: 2.5% (2007).

School District(s)

Alwood CUSD 225 (PK-12)
2005-06 Enrollment: 517 . . . . (309) 334-2719
Housing: Homeownership rate: 75.1% (2007); Median home value: $92,895 (2007); Median rent: $272 per month (2000); Median age of housing: 58 years (2000).
Safety: Violent crime rate: 12.3 per 10,000 population; Property crime rate: 209.9 per 10,000 population (2006).
Transportation: Commute to work: 91.3% car, 0.0% public transportation, 4.2% walk, 4.5% work from home (2000); Travel time to work: 29.1% less than 15 minutes, 25.5% 15 to 30 minutes, 28.0% 30 to 45 minutes, 10.5% 45 to 60 minutes, 6.9% 60 minutes or more (2000)

Iroquois County

Located in eastern Illinois; bounded on the east by Indiana; drained by the Iroquois River and Sugar Creek. Covers a land area of 1,116.43 square miles, a water area of 1.60 square miles, and is located in the Central Time Zone. The county was founded in 1833. County seat is Watseka.

Weather Station: Watseka 2 NW Elevation: 620 feet

	Jan	Feb	Mar	Apr	May	Jun	Jul	Aug	Sep	Oct	Nov	Dec
High	30	36	48	60	72	82	85	83	77	64	49	36
Low	14	18	29	38	49	59	62	60	52	40	31	21
Precip	1.7	1.6	3.5	4.1	4.2	4.7	4.2	3.8	3.6	2.8	3.3	2.6
Snow	6.9	4.6	2.5	0.9	0.0	0.0	0.0	0.0	0.0	tr	1.3	5.2

High and Low temperatures in degrees Fahrenheit; Precipitation and Snow in inches

Population: 30,787 (1990); 31,334 (2000); 30,638 (2007); 30,184 (2012 projected); Race: 94.5% White, 1.1% Black, 0.5% Asian, 5.1% Hispanic of any race (2007); Density: 27.4 persons per square mile (2007); Average household size: 2.54 (2007); Median age: 41.4 (2007); Males per 100 females: 96.3 (2007).
Religion: Five largest groups: 12.9% Catholic Church, 11.4% Lutheran Church—Missouri Synod, 9.7% The United Methodist Church, 7.0%

Evangelical Lutheran Church in America, 5.0% Christian Churches and Churches of Christ (2000).
Economy: Unemployment rate: 6.2% (4/2008); Total civilian labor force: 16,620 (4/2008); Leading industries: 24.4% health care and social assistance; 16.3% retail trade; 13.9% manufacturing (2005); Farms: 1,386 totaling 678,918 acres (2002); Companies that employ 500 or more persons: 0 (2006); Companies that employ 100 to 499 persons: 9 (2006); Companies that employ less than 100 persons: 740 (2006); Black-owned businesses: n/a (2002); Hispanic-owned businesses: n/a (2002); Asian-owned businesses: n/a (2002); Women-owned businesses: 721 (2002); Retail sales per capita: $9,556 (2008). Single-family building permits issued: 52 (2007); Multi-family building permits issued: 3 (2007).
Income: Per capita income: $22,269 (2007); Median household income: $45,422 (2007); Average household income: $55,907 (2007); Percent of households with income of $100,000 or more: 10.3% (2007); Poverty rate: 10.5% (2005); Bankruptcy rate: 2.84% (2007).
Education: Percent of population age 25 and over with: High school diploma (including GED) or higher: 80.3% (2007); Bachelor's degree or higher: 11.9% (2007); Master's degree or higher: 4.7% (2007).
Housing: Homeownership rate: 76.5% (2007); Median home value: $123,123 (2007); Median rent: $329 per month (2000); Median age of housing: 47 years (2000).
Health: Birth rate: 122.5 per 10,000 population (2007); Death rate: 135.7 per 10,000 population (2007); Age-adjusted cancer mortality rate: 177.6 deaths per 100,000 population (2005); Number of physicians: 8.6 per 10,000 population (2005); Hospital beds: 36.9 per 10,000 population (2004); Hospital admissions: 801.0 per 10,000 population (2004).
Elections: 2004 Presidential election results: 71.7% Bush, 27.7% Kerry, 0.1% Nader, 0.6% Badnarik
National and State Parks: Iroquois County State Conservation Area
Additional Information Contacts
Iroquois County Government . . . . (815) 432-6960
http://www.co.iroquois.il.us
City of Watseka . . . . (815) 432-2711
http://www.watsekacity.com
Gilman Chamber of Commerce . . . . (815) 265-4818
Onarga Chamber of Commerce. . . . . (815) 268-4471
http://www.onarga.net/OChamber.html
Watseka Area Chamber of Commerce . . . . (815) 432-2416
http://www.watsekachamber.org

Iroquois County Communities

ASHKUM (village). Covers a land area of 0.820 square miles and a water area of 0 square miles. Located at 40.88° N. Lat.; 87.95° W. Long. Elevation is 669 feet.
Population: 681 (1990); 724 (2000); 736 (2007); 723 (2012 projected); Race: 98.8% White, 0.0% Black, 0.0% Asian, 0.7% Hispanic of any race (2007); Density: 897.9 persons per square mile (2007); Average household size: 2.35 (2007); Median age: 39.9 (2007); Males per 100 females: 99.5 (2007); Marriage status: 22.3% never married, 61.1% now married, 8.9% widowed, 7.7% divorced (2000); Foreign born: 0.0% (2000); Ancestry (includes multiple ancestries): 35.1% German, 21.3% French (except Basque), 18.0% Irish, 9.8% English, 5.6% United States or American (2000).
Economy: Single-family building permits issued: 1 (2007); Multi-family building permits issued: 0 (2007); Employment by occupation: 7.0% management, 17.1% professional, 20.0% services, 23.2% sales, 1.2% farming, 10.4% construction, 21.2% production (2000).
Income: Per capita income: $25,279 (2007); Median household income: $43,167 (2007); Average household income: $59,441 (2007); Percent of households with income of $100,000 or more: 10.2% (2007); Poverty rate: 3.8% (2000).
Education: Percent of population age 25 and over with: High school diploma (including GED) or higher: 86.2% (2007); Bachelor's degree or higher: 11.6% (2007); Master's degree or higher: 4.1% (2007).

School District(s)

Central CUSD 4 (PK-12)
2005-06 Enrollment: 1,240 . . . . (815) 694-2231
Housing: Homeownership rate: 77.0% (2007); Median home value: $133,413 (2007); Median rent: $381 per month (2000); Median age of housing: 44 years (2000).
Transportation: Commute to work: 93.6% car, 0.0% public transportation, 2.0% walk, 4.4% work from home (2000); Travel time to work: 38.0% less than 15 minutes, 26.7% 15 to 30 minutes, 19.8% 30 to 45 minutes, 5.5% 45 to 60 minutes, 10.0% 60 minutes or more (2000)

BEAVERVILLE (village). Covers a land area of 0.262 square miles and a water area of 0.004 square miles. Located at 40.95° N. Lat.; 87.65° W. Long. Elevation is 676 feet.
Population: 287 (1990); 391 (2000); 384 (2007); 378 (2012 projected); Race: 99.0% White, 0.0% Black, 0.3% Asian, 0.8% Hispanic of any race (2007); Density: 1,464.7 persons per square mile (2007); Average household size: 2.59 (2007); Median age: 37.8 (2007); Males per 100 females: 100.0 (2007); Marriage status: 23.2% never married, 55.0% now married, 14.9% widowed, 7.0% divorced (2000); Foreign born: 0.0% (2000); Ancestry (includes multiple ancestries): 20.6% French (except Basque), 19.3% German, 12.0% French Canadian, 9.9% Irish, 8.9% United States or American (2000).
Economy: Single-family building permits issued: 3 (2007); Multi-family building permits issued: 0 (2007); Employment by occupation: 7.3% management, 6.0% professional, 18.0% services, 23.3% sales, 0.0% farming, 14.0% construction, 31.3% production (2000).
Income: Per capita income: $18,197 (2007); Median household income: $40,909 (2007); Average household income: $47,213 (2007); Percent of households with income of $100,000 or more: 8.1% (2007); Poverty rate: 9.7% (2000).
Education: Percent of population age 25 and over with: High school diploma (including GED) or higher: 74.6% (2007); Bachelor's degree or higher: 2.3% (2007); Master's degree or higher: 1.2% (2007).
Housing: Homeownership rate: 77.0% (2007); Median home value: $106,667 (2007); Median rent: $338 per month (2000); Median age of housing: 60+ years (2000).
Transportation: Commute to work: 89.8% car, 0.0% public transportation, 8.2% walk, 0.0% work from home (2000); Travel time to work: 23.8% less than 15 minutes, 29.9% 15 to 30 minutes, 36.1% 30 to 45 minutes, 4.1% 45 to 60 minutes, 6.1% 60 minutes or more (2000)

BUCKLEY (village). Covers a land area of 0.345 square miles and a water area of 0.006 square miles. Located at 40.59° N. Lat.; 88.03° W. Long. Elevation is 702 feet.
Population: 557 (1990); 593 (2000); 617 (2007); 634 (2012 projected); Race: 96.3% White, 0.5% Black, 0.3% Asian, 4.9% Hispanic of any race (2007); Density: 1,790.8 persons per square mile (2007); Average household size: 2.24 (2007); Median age: 42.1 (2007); Males per 100 females: 100.3 (2007); Marriage status: 19.3% never married, 66.5% now married, 8.6% widowed, 5.6% divorced (2000); Foreign born: 3.7% (2000); Ancestry (includes multiple ancestries): 50.9% German, 11.4% United States or American, 7.7% Other groups, 7.7% Irish, 6.3% English (2000).
Economy: Single-family building permits issued: 1 (2007); Multi-family building permits issued: 0 (2007); Employment by occupation: 14.2% management, 13.5% professional, 13.5% services, 18.1% sales, 0.6% farming, 20.0% construction, 20.0% production (2000).
Income: Per capita income: $28,258 (2007); Median household income: $44,464 (2007); Average household income: $63,400 (2007); Percent of households with income of $100,000 or more: 8.7% (2007); Poverty rate: 5.3% (2000).
Education: Percent of population age 25 and over with: High school diploma (including GED) or higher: 81.3% (2007); Bachelor's degree or higher: 11.2% (2007); Master's degree or higher: 3.5% (2007).
Housing: Homeownership rate: 79.3% (2007); Median home value: $98,857 (2007); Median rent: $345 per month (2000); Median age of housing: 46 years (2000).
Transportation: Commute to work: 93.5% car, 0.0% public transportation, 3.9% walk, 1.3% work from home (2000); Travel time to work: 38.2% less than 15 minutes, 28.8% 15 to 30 minutes, 19.9% 30 to 45 minutes, 8.2% 45 to 60 minutes, 4.9% 60 minutes or more (2000)

CHEBANSE (village). Covers a land area of 0.437 square miles and a water area of 0 square miles. Located at 41.00° N. Lat.; 87.91° W. Long. Elevation is 666 feet.
History: Chebanse developed as an agricultural community, settled by many people of German descent.
Population: 1,182 (1990); 1,148 (2000); 1,166 (2007); 1,159 (2012 projected); Race: 98.7% White, 0.2% Black, 0.1% Asian, 1.5% Hispanic of any race (2007); Density: 2,666.6 persons per square mile (2007); Average household size: 2.56 (2007); Median age: 39.3 (2007); Males per 100 females: 91.5 (2007); Marriage status: 19.4% never married, 66.1% now married, 6.8% widowed, 7.7% divorced (2000); Foreign born: 1.0% (2000);

Ancestry (includes multiple ancestries): 37.6% German, 17.3% French (except Basque), 15.2% Irish, 8.5% United States or American, 7.3% Other groups (2000).
Economy: Single-family building permits issued: 3 (2007); Multi-family building permits issued: 0 (2007); Employment by occupation: 6.6% management, 14.3% professional, 18.2% services, 29.2% sales, 0.7% farming, 13.9% construction, 17.2% production (2000).
Income: Per capita income: $23,582 (2007); Median household income: $56,316 (2007); Average household income: $60,132 (2007); Percent of households with income of $100,000 or more: 13.4% (2007); Poverty rate: 3.2% (2000).
Education: Percent of population age 25 and over with: High school diploma (including GED) or higher: 91.2% (2007); Bachelor's degree or higher: 10.2% (2007); Master's degree or higher: 2.8% (2007).

School District(s)

Central CUSD 4 (PK-12)
2005-06 Enrollment: 1,240 . . . . (815) 694-2231
Housing: Homeownership rate: 78.3% (2007); Median home value: $144,929 (2007); Median rent: $425 per month (2000); Median age of housing: 43 years (2000).
Safety: Violent crime rate: 9.1 per 10,000 population; Property crime rate: 81.7 per 10,000 population (2006).
Transportation: Commute to work: 96.2% car, 0.0% public transportation, 2.7% walk, 0.8% work from home (2000); Travel time to work: 26.0% less than 15 minutes, 49.0% 15 to 30 minutes, 13.6% 30 to 45 minutes, 1.8% 45 to 60 minutes, 9.6% 60 minutes or more (2000)

CISSNA PARK (village). Covers a land area of 0.719 square miles and a water area of 0 square miles. Located at 40.56° N. Lat.; 87.89° W. Long. Elevation is 666 feet.
History: Cissna Park developed as the center of a community of members of the Apostolic Church, known as New Amish, led by Samuel Frolich of Switzerland.
Population: 805 (1990); 811 (2000); 812 (2007); 803 (2012 projected); Race: 98.8% White, 0.5% Black, 0.4% Asian, 1.1% Hispanic of any race (2007); Density: 1,129.9 persons per square mile (2007); Average household size: 2.14 (2007); Median age: 46.3 (2007); Males per 100 females: 78.9 (2007); Marriage status: 23.6% never married, 54.5% now married, 14.1% widowed, 7.8% divorced (2000); Foreign born: 0.4% (2000); Ancestry (includes multiple ancestries): 53.0% German, 10.9% English, 7.1% Irish, 6.9% United States or American, 5.9% Swiss (2000).
Economy: Single-family building permits issued: 0 (2007); Multi-family building permits issued: 0 (2007); Employment by occupation: 8.3% management, 15.0% professional, 19.4% services, 32.5% sales, 0.0% farming, 11.1% construction, 13.8% production (2000).
Income: Per capita income: $22,955 (2007); Median household income: $42,833 (2007); Average household income: $48,763 (2007); Percent of households with income of $100,000 or more: 5.8% (2007); Poverty rate: 7.4% (2000).
Education: Percent of population age 25 and over with: High school diploma (including GED) or higher: 76.2% (2007); Bachelor's degree or higher: 14.6% (2007); Master's degree or higher: 3.7% (2007).

School District(s)

Cissna Park CUSD 6 (KG-12)
2005-06 Enrollment: 353 . . . . (815) 457-2171
Housing: Homeownership rate: 77.6% (2007); Median home value: $108,532 (2007); Median rent: $252 per month (2000); Median age of housing: 46 years (2000).
Newspapers: Cissna Park News (Community news; Circulation 1,554); Rankin Independent (Community news; Circulation 472)
Transportation: Commute to work: 84.2% car, 1.7% public transportation, 8.3% walk, 5.0% work from home (2000); Travel time to work: 48.1% less than 15 minutes, 16.9% 15 to 30 minutes, 21.8% 30 to 45 minutes, 7.9% 45 to 60 minutes, 5.2% 60 minutes or more (2000)

CLIFTON (village). Covers a land area of 0.887 square miles and a water area of 0 square miles. Located at 40.93° N. Lat.; 87.93° W. Long. Elevation is 669 feet.
Population: 1,364 (1990); 1,317 (2000); 1,270 (2007); 1,260 (2012 projected); Race: 99.1% White, 0.0% Black, 0.4% Asian, 0.8% Hispanic of any race (2007); Density: 1,432.1 persons per square mile (2007); Average household size: 2.48 (2007); Median age: 37.7 (2007); Males per 100 females: 91.6 (2007); Marriage status: 20.9% never married, 65.1% now married, 8.2% widowed, 5.8% divorced (2000); Foreign born: 1.0% (2000); Ancestry (includes multiple ancestries): 34.6% German, 17.2% French (except Basque), 14.3% United States or American, 11.6% Irish, 9.4% English (2000).
Economy: Single-family building permits issued: 2 (2007); Multi-family building permits issued: 0 (2007); Employment by occupation: 13.2% management, 15.7% professional, 13.5% services, 30.5% sales, 0.7% farming, 10.7% construction, 15.7% production (2000).
Income: Per capita income: $26,388 (2007); Median household income: $59,375 (2007); Average household income: $65,454 (2007); Percent of households with income of $100,000 or more: 18.0% (2007); Poverty rate: 4.5% (2000).
Education: Percent of population age 25 and over with: High school diploma (including GED) or higher: 86.4% (2007); Bachelor's degree or higher: 13.8% (2007); Master's degree or higher: 4.7% (2007).

School District(s)

Central CUSD 4 (PK-12)
2005-06 Enrollment: 1,240 . . . . (815) 694-2231
Housing: Homeownership rate: 78.1% (2007); Median home value: $146,392 (2007); Median rent: $349 per month (2000); Median age of housing: 43 years (2000).
Transportation: Commute to work: 90.2% car, 1.5% public transportation, 3.8% walk, 4.3% work from home (2000); Travel time to work: 27.7% less than 15 minutes, 40.2% 15 to 30 minutes, 17.5% 30 to 45 minutes, 3.2% 45 to 60 minutes, 11.4% 60 minutes or more (2000)

CRESCENT CITY (village). Aka Crescent. Covers a land area of 0.503 square miles and a water area of 0 square miles. Located at 40.77° N. Lat.; 87.85° W. Long. Elevation is 640 feet.
Population: 549 (1990); 631 (2000); 602 (2007); 592 (2012 projected); Race: 97.8% White, 0.0% Black, 0.0% Asian, 2.0% Hispanic of any race (2007); Density: 1,196.1 persons per square mile (2007); Average household size: 2.39 (2007); Median age: 38.7 (2007); Males per 100 females: 97.4 (2007); Marriage status: 16.1% never married, 66.5% now married, 9.4% widowed, 7.9% divorced (2000); Foreign born: 0.0% (2000); Ancestry (includes multiple ancestries): 44.9% German, 9.6% English, 8.0% United States or American, 8.0% Irish, 7.2% Other groups (2000).
Economy: Single-family building permits issued: 0 (2007); Multi-family building permits issued: 0 (2007); Employment by occupation: 9.9% management, 17.7% professional, 17.0% services, 23.0% sales, 1.4% farming, 10.3% construction, 20.6% production (2000).
Income: Per capita income: $20,108 (2007); Median household income: $42,609 (2007); Average household income: $48,036 (2007); Percent of households with income of $100,000 or more: 4.8% (2007); Poverty rate: 1.9% (2000).
Education: Percent of population age 25 and over with: High school diploma (including GED) or higher: 83.1% (2007); Bachelor's degree or higher: 9.4% (2007); Master's degree or higher: 3.2% (2007).

School District(s)

Crescent Iroquois CUSD 249 (KG-12)
2005-06 Enrollment: 197 . . . . (815) 683-2141
Housing: Homeownership rate: 80.2% (2007); Median home value: $131,410 (2007); Median rent: $372 per month (2000); Median age of housing: 36 years (2000).
Transportation: Commute to work: 90.4% car, 0.0% public transportation, 3.2% walk, 6.4% work from home (2000); Travel time to work: 41.2% less than 15 minutes, 32.4% 15 to 30 minutes, 19.5% 30 to 45 minutes, 4.2% 45 to 60 minutes, 2.7% 60 minutes or more (2000)

DANFORTH (village). Covers a land area of 0.477 square miles and a water area of 0 square miles. Located at 40.82° N. Lat.; 87.97° W. Long. Elevation is 653 feet.
History: Danforth was settled by immigrants from the Netherlands, on land purchased in the 1850's by A.H. and George Danforth. The swampy land was ditched and drained by the Dutch, who built windmills and established farms.
Population: 460 (1990); 587 (2000); 565 (2007); 559 (2012 projected); Race: 98.2% White, 0.0% Black, 0.4% Asian, 1.9% Hispanic of any race (2007); Density: 1,184.6 persons per square mile (2007); Average household size: 2.88 (2007); Median age: 50.3 (2007); Males per 100 females: 78.2 (2007); Marriage status: 15.4% never married, 67.1% now married, 9.4% widowed, 8.1% divorced (2000); Foreign born: 0.3% (2000); Ancestry (includes multiple ancestries): 39.0% German, 14.4% Other groups, 8.7% French (except Basque), 6.8% English, 6.1% Dutch (2000).
Economy: Single-family building permits issued: 0 (2007); Multi-family building permits issued: 0 (2007); Employment by occupation: 8.1%

management, 13.8% professional, 18.8% services, 27.3% sales, 2.7% farming, 12.7% construction, 16.5% production (2000).
Income: Per capita income: $19,368 (2007); Median household income: $39,333 (2007); Average household income: $49,656 (2007); Percent of households with income of $100,000 or more: 9.7% (2007); Poverty rate: 1.3% (2000).
Education: Percent of population age 25 and over with: High school diploma (including GED) or higher: 73.6% (2007); Bachelor's degree or higher: 15.5% (2007); Master's degree or higher: 8.7% (2007).

School District(s)

Iroquois West CUSD 10 (PK-12)
2005-06 Enrollment: 935 . . . . (815) 265-4642
Housing: Homeownership rate: 81.1% (2007); Median home value: $121,474 (2007); Median rent: $341 per month (2000); Median age of housing: 59 years (2000).
Transportation: Commute to work: 90.7% car, 0.0% public transportation, 2.3% walk, 5.8% work from home (2000); Travel time to work: 38.4% less than 15 minutes, 21.5% 15 to 30 minutes, 25.6% 30 to 45 minutes, 9.5% 45 to 60 minutes, 5.0% 60 minutes or more (2000)

DONOVAN (village). Covers a land area of 0.311 square miles and a water area of 0 square miles. Located at 40.88° N. Lat.; 87.61° W. Long. Elevation is 673 feet.
History: Donovan was settled by Swedish immigrants after the railroad was built here, and named for the operator of the Buckhorn Tavern.
Population: 361 (1990); 351 (2000); 331 (2007); 330 (2012 projected); Race: 95.2% White, 1.2% Black, 0.0% Asian, 5.4% Hispanic of any race (2007); Density: 1,063.2 persons per square mile (2007); Average household size: 2.69 (2007); Median age: 35.1 (2007); Males per 100 females: 88.1 (2007); Marriage status: 20.2% never married, 62.5% now married, 10.5% widowed, 6.9% divorced (2000); Foreign born: 0.0% (2000); Ancestry (includes multiple ancestries): 26.6% German, 18.5% French (except Basque), 13.2% Swedish, 10.6% English, 10.1% United States or American (2000).
Economy: Single-family building permits issued: 0 (2007); Multi-family building permits issued: 0 (2007); Employment by occupation: 8.4% management, 13.5% professional, 23.2% services, 13.5% sales, 0.0% farming, 8.4% construction, 32.9% production (2000).
Income: Per capita income: $24,252 (2007); Median household income: $50,333 (2007); Average household income: $65,264 (2007); Percent of households with income of $100,000 or more: 12.2% (2007); Poverty rate: 4.1% (2000).
Education: Percent of population age 25 and over with: High school diploma (including GED) or higher: 85.1% (2007); Bachelor's degree or higher: 14.9% (2007); Master's degree or higher: 4.5% (2007).

School District(s)

Donovan CUSD 3 (KG-12)
2005-06 Enrollment: 486 . . . . (815) 486-7397
Housing: Homeownership rate: 75.6% (2007); Median home value: $97,857 (2007); Median rent: $305 per month (2000); Median age of housing: 60+ years (2000).
Transportation: Commute to work: 87.7% car, 0.0% public transportation, 3.2% walk, 5.2% work from home (2000); Travel time to work: 22.4% less than 15 minutes, 34.7% 15 to 30 minutes, 21.8% 30 to 45 minutes, 10.9% 45 to 60 minutes, 10.2% 60 minutes or more (2000)

GILMAN (city). Covers a land area of 2.114 square miles and a water area of 0.020 square miles. Located at 40.76° N. Lat.; 87.99° W. Long. Elevation is 650 feet.
History: Incorporated 1867.
Population: 1,816 (1990); 1,793 (2000); 1,744 (2007); 1,698 (2012 projected); Race: 91.0% White, 0.4% Black, 0.3% Asian, 12.4% Hispanic of any race (2007); Density: 824.8 persons per square mile (2007); Average household size: 2.47 (2007); Median age: 42.2 (2007); Males per 100 females: 90.2 (2007); Marriage status: 22.2% never married, 56.1% now married, 11.3% widowed, 10.3% divorced (2000); Foreign born: 4.5% (2000); Ancestry (includes multiple ancestries): 34.2% German, 13.3% Other groups, 11.2% Irish, 10.2% United States or American, 9.7% English (2000).
Economy: Single-family building permits issued: 3 (2007); Multi-family building permits issued: 0 (2007); Employment by occupation: 7.9% management, 17.3% professional, 24.3% services, 18.1% sales, 0.7% farming, 10.7% construction, 21.0% production (2000).
Income: Per capita income: $20,848 (2007); Median household income: $42,806 (2007); Average household income: $50,781 (2007); Percent of households with income of $100,000 or more: 5.7% (2007); Poverty rate: 9.9% (2000).
Education: Percent of population age 25 and over with: High school diploma (including GED) or higher: 73.7% (2007); Bachelor's degree or higher: 9.4% (2007); Master's degree or higher: 2.5% (2007).

School District(s)

Iroquois West CUSD 10 (PK-12)
2005-06 Enrollment: 935 . . . . (815) 265-4642
Housing: Homeownership rate: 73.1% (2007); Median home value: $124,861 (2007); Median rent: $329 per month (2000); Median age of housing: 51 years (2000).
Safety: Violent crime rate: 55.9 per 10,000 population; Property crime rate: 106.3 per 10,000 population (2006).
Newspapers: Gilman Star (Local news; Circulation 2,900)
Transportation: Commute to work: 95.4% car, 0.2% public transportation, 1.1% walk, 1.9% work from home (2000); Travel time to work: 52.1% less than 15 minutes, 19.8% 15 to 30 minutes, 15.2% 30 to 45 minutes, 7.5% 45 to 60 minutes, 5.4% 60 minutes or more (2000); Amtrak: Service available.
Additional Information Contacts
Gilman Chamber of Commerce . . . . (815) 265-4818

IROQUOIS (village). Covers a land area of 0.598 square miles and a water area of 0 square miles. Located at 40.82° N. Lat.; 87.58° W. Long. Elevation is 659 feet.
History: Iroquois was the name given by the Big Four Railroad in 1871 to its station on the Iroquois River. In 1875 the town of Concord, on the other side of the river, was incorporated under the Iroquois name.
Population: 199 (1990); 207 (2000); 196 (2007); 195 (2012 projected); Race: 98.0% White, 0.0% Black, 0.5% Asian, 0.0% Hispanic of any race (2007); Density: 327.7 persons per square mile (2007); Average household size: 2.51 (2007); Median age: 42.5 (2007); Males per 100 females: 96.0 (2007); Marriage status: 19.9% never married, 67.9% now married, 2.6% widowed, 9.6% divorced (2000); Foreign born: 1.6% (2000); Ancestry (includes multiple ancestries): 35.5% German, 13.4% French (except Basque), 12.4% Irish, 11.8% United States or American, 10.8% English (2000).
Economy: Single-family building permits issued: 0 (2007); Multi-family building permits issued: 0 (2007); Employment by occupation: 6.4% management, 9.6% professional, 14.9% services, 19.1% sales, 2.1% farming, 8.5% construction, 39.4% production (2000).
Income: Per capita income: $19,120 (2007); Median household income: $44,000 (2007); Average household income: $48,045 (2007); Percent of households with income of $100,000 or more: 5.1% (2007); Poverty rate: 1.6% (2000).
Education: Percent of population age 25 and over with: High school diploma (including GED) or higher: 75.2% (2007); Bachelor's degree or higher: 10.2% (2007); Master's degree or higher: 5.8% (2007).
Housing: Homeownership rate: 83.3% (2007); Median home value: $78,846 (2007); Median rent: $263 per month (2000); Median age of housing: 60+ years (2000).
Transportation: Commute to work: 91.5% car, 0.0% public transportation, 6.4% walk, 2.1% work from home (2000); Travel time to work: 22.8% less than 15 minutes, 44.6% 15 to 30 minutes, 10.9% 30 to 45 minutes, 13.0% 45 to 60 minutes, 8.7% 60 minutes or more (2000)

LODA (village). Covers a land area of 1.448 square miles and a water area of 0.008 square miles. Located at 40.51° N. Lat.; 88.07° W. Long. Elevation is 778 feet.
Population: 390 (1990); 419 (2000); 431 (2007); 441 (2012 projected); Race: 92.8% White, 2.1% Black, 0.0% Asian, 8.4% Hispanic of any race (2007); Density: 297.7 persons per square mile (2007); Average household size: 2.51 (2007); Median age: 42.0 (2007); Males per 100 females: 94.1 (2007); Marriage status: 19.8% never married, 57.8% now married, 11.3% widowed, 11.0% divorced (2000); Foreign born: 2.4% (2000); Ancestry (includes multiple ancestries): 26.4% German, 14.4% United States or American, 11.3% Irish, 11.1% Other groups, 9.0% English (2000).
Economy: Single-family building permits issued: 1 (2007); Multi-family building permits issued: 0 (2007); Employment by occupation: 15.3% management, 7.7% professional, 18.4% services, 13.8% sales, 0.0% farming, 12.2% construction, 32.7% production (2000).
Income: Per capita income: $26,108 (2007); Median household income: $44,444 (2007); Average household income: $65,422 (2007); Percent of households with income of $100,000 or more: 12.8% (2007); Poverty rate: 16.0% (2000).

Education: Percent of population age 25 and over with: High school diploma (including GED) or higher: 81.2% (2007); Bachelor's degree or higher: 9.2% (2007); Master's degree or higher: 7.2% (2007).
Housing: Homeownership rate: 77.3% (2007); Median home value: $88,438 (2007); Median rent: $275 per month (2000); Median age of housing: 52 years (2000).
Transportation: Commute to work: 94.2% car, 0.0% public transportation, 2.6% walk, 3.2% work from home (2000); Travel time to work: 38.6% less than 15 minutes, 28.3% 15 to 30 minutes, 16.8% 30 to 45 minutes, 15.2% 45 to 60 minutes, 1.1% 60 minutes or more (2000)

MARTINTON (village). Covers a land area of 0.251 square miles and a water area of 0 square miles. Located at 40.91° N. Lat.; 87.72° W. Long. Elevation is 627 feet.
History: Martinton was founded in 1871 as a station on the Chicago & Eastern Illinois Railway, and named for Porter Martin, an early resident.
Population: 299 (1990); 375 (2000); 382 (2007); 378 (2012 projected); Race: 96.1% White, 2.4% Black, 0.3% Asian, 0.8% Hispanic of any race (2007); Density: 1,520.7 persons per square mile (2007); Average household size: 2.81 (2007); Median age: 33.8 (2007); Males per 100 females: 89.1 (2007); Marriage status: 14.9% never married, 74.3% now married, 4.1% widowed, 6.7% divorced (2000); Foreign born: 0.0% (2000); Ancestry (includes multiple ancestries): 16.9% German, 14.6% French (except Basque), 14.1% Irish, 10.8% United States or American, 8.7% French Canadian (2000).
Economy: Single-family building permits issued: 0 (2007); Multi-family building permits issued: 0 (2007); Employment by occupation: 5.4% management, 10.8% professional, 10.8% services, 24.7% sales, 2.2% farming, 11.8% construction, 34.4% production (2000).
Income: Per capita income: $20,969 (2007); Median household income: $53,000 (2007); Average household income: $58,897 (2007); Percent of households with income of $100,000 or more: 5.1% (2007); Poverty rate: 4.6% (2000).
Education: Percent of population age 25 and over with: High school diploma (including GED) or higher: 80.3% (2007); Bachelor's degree or higher: 2.6% (2007); Master's degree or higher: 0.0% (2007).
Housing: Homeownership rate: 78.7% (2007); Median home value: $123,707 (2007); Median rent: $331 per month (2000); Median age of housing: 53 years (2000).
Transportation: Commute to work: 98.4% car, 0.0% public transportation, 0.0% walk, 1.6% work from home (2000); Travel time to work: 17.1% less than 15 minutes, 43.6% 15 to 30 minutes, 30.4% 30 to 45 minutes, 5.5% 45 to 60 minutes, 3.3% 60 minutes or more (2000)

MILFORD (village). Covers a land area of 0.632 square miles and a water area of 0 square miles. Located at 40.62° N. Lat.; 87.69° W. Long. Elevation is 669 feet.
History: Milford, incorporated as a village in 1874, was first laid out in 1836 by William Pickerel who operated a mill near a ford on Sugar Creek.
Population: 1,512 (1990); 1,369 (2000); 1,372 (2007); 1,296 (2012 projected); Race: 99.3% White, 0.0% Black, 0.0% Asian, 2.0% Hispanic of any race (2007); Density: 2,171.6 persons per square mile (2007); Average household size: 2.18 (2007); Median age: 44.6 (2007); Males per 100 females: 98.0 (2007); Marriage status: 18.8% never married, 58.3% now married, 12.0% widowed, 11.0% divorced (2000); Foreign born: 0.7% (2000); Ancestry (includes multiple ancestries): 25.2% German, 9.2% English, 8.9% United States or American, 7.6% Irish, 5.1% Other groups (2000).
Economy: Single-family building permits issued: 1 (2007); Multi-family building permits issued: 0 (2007); Employment by occupation: 7.9% management, 12.1% professional, 17.9% services, 23.0% sales, 0.6% farming, 9.5% construction, 28.9% production (2000).
Income: Per capita income: $21,855 (2007); Median household income: $35,345 (2007); Average household income: $47,747 (2007); Percent of households with income of $100,000 or more: 7.8% (2007); Poverty rate: 7.2% (2000).
Taxes: Total city taxes per capita: $68 (2006); City property taxes per capita: $68 (2006).
Education: Percent of population age 25 and over with: High school diploma (including GED) or higher: 74.5% (2007); Bachelor's degree or higher: 7.8% (2007); Master's degree or higher: 2.6% (2007).

School District(s)

Iroquois Special Education (04-12)
2005-06 Enrollment: 75 . . . . (815) 265-8601
Milford CCSD 280 (PK-08)
2005-06 Enrollment: 454 . . . . (815) 889-5176
Milford Twp HSD 233 (09-12)
2005-06 Enrollment: 203 . . . . (815) 889-5176
Housing: Homeownership rate: 72.3% (2007); Median home value: $76,471 (2007); Median rent: $311 per month (2000); Median age of housing: 53 years (2000).
Transportation: Commute to work: 93.5% car, 0.8% public transportation, 2.3% walk, 1.8% work from home (2000); Travel time to work: 39.4% less than 15 minutes, 38.3% 15 to 30 minutes, 9.4% 30 to 45 minutes, 5.0% 45 to 60 minutes, 7.9% 60 minutes or more (2000)

ONARGA (village). Covers a land area of 1.310 square miles and a water area of 0 square miles. Located at 40.71° N. Lat.; 88.00° W. Long. Elevation is 669 feet.
History: Benjamin Hardy, the composer of the song "Darling Nellie Gray," lived in Onarga.
Population: 1,281 (1990); 1,438 (2000); 1,383 (2007); 1,355 (2012 projected); Race: 62.9% White, 4.2% Black, 0.3% Asian, 43.0% Hispanic of any race (2007); Density: 1,055.9 persons per square mile (2007); Average household size: 3.09 (2007); Median age: 31.6 (2007); Males per 100 females: 112.8 (2007); Marriage status: 25.7% never married, 58.4% now married, 8.1% widowed, 7.7% divorced (2000); Foreign born: 19.7% (2000); Ancestry (includes multiple ancestries): 44.3% Other groups, 18.6% German, 8.9% Irish, 8.3% English, 6.9% United States or American (2000).
Economy: Single-family building permits issued: 0 (2007); Multi-family building permits issued: 0 (2007); Employment by occupation: 8.1% management, 10.6% professional, 17.9% services, 15.3% sales, 7.6% farming, 9.8% construction, 30.6% production (2000).
Income: Per capita income: $17,153 (2007); Median household income: $41,900 (2007); Average household income: $52,858 (2007); Percent of households with income of $100,000 or more: 8.9% (2007); Poverty rate: 10.9% (2000).
Education: Percent of population age 25 and over with: High school diploma (including GED) or higher: 64.3% (2007); Bachelor's degree or higher: 4.4% (2007); Master's degree or higher: 1.6% (2007).

School District(s)

Iroquois Special Education (04-12)
2005-06 Enrollment: 75 . . . . (815) 265-8601
Iroquois West CUSD 10 (PK-12)
2005-06 Enrollment: 935 . . . . (815) 265-4642
Housing: Homeownership rate: 79.6% (2007); Median home value: $116,379 (2007); Median rent: $345 per month (2000); Median age of housing: 60+ years (2000).
Safety: Violent crime rate: 35.8 per 10,000 population; Property crime rate: 164.8 per 10,000 population (2006).
Transportation: Commute to work: 90.5% car, 0.0% public transportation, 5.4% walk, 2.9% work from home (2000); Travel time to work: 48.5% less than 15 minutes, 21.2% 15 to 30 minutes, 20.0% 30 to 45 minutes, 5.4% 45 to 60 minutes, 4.9% 60 minutes or more (2000)

Additional Information Contacts

Onarga Chamber of Commerce. . . . . (815) 268-4471
http://www.onarga.net/OChamber.html

PAPINEAU (village). Covers a land area of 0.226 square miles and a water area of 0 square miles. Located at 40.96° N. Lat.; 87.71° W. Long. Elevation is 630 feet.
Population: 147 (1990); 196 (2000); 200 (2007); 197 (2012 projected); Race: 94.0% White, 6.0% Black, 0.0% Asian, 0.0% Hispanic of any race (2007); Density: 885.4 persons per square mile (2007); Average household size: 3.33 (2007); Median age: 27.7 (2007); Males per 100 females: 108.3 (2007); Marriage status: 11.8% never married, 80.1% now married, 5.1% widowed, 2.9% divorced (2000); Foreign born: 2.7% (2000); Ancestry (includes multiple ancestries): 36.1% German, 18.0% United States or American, 13.1% Polish, 11.5% French (except Basque), 7.7% Irish (2000).
Economy: Single-family building permits issued: 0 (2007); Multi-family building permits issued: 0 (2007); Employment by occupation: 8.4% management, 13.7% professional, 13.7% services, 30.5% sales, 2.1% farming, 9.5% construction, 22.1% production (2000).
Income: Per capita income: $18,013 (2007); Median household income: $56,250 (2007); Average household income: $60,042 (2007); Percent of households with income of $100,000 or more: 6.7% (2007); Poverty rate: 1.6% (2000).

Education: Percent of population age 25 and over with: High school diploma (including GED) or higher: 81.3% (2007); Bachelor's degree or higher: 9.3% (2007); Master's degree or higher: 2.8% (2007).
Housing: Homeownership rate: 85.0% (2007); Median home value: $73,750 (2007); Median rent: $250 per month (2000); Median age of housing: 60+ years (2000).
Transportation: Commute to work: 97.9% car, 0.0% public transportation, 1.1% walk, 1.1% work from home (2000); Travel time to work: 26.6% less than 15 minutes, 37.2% 15 to 30 minutes, 20.2% 30 to 45 minutes, 6.4% 45 to 60 minutes, 9.6% 60 minutes or more (2000)

SHELDON (village). Covers a land area of 0.753 square miles and a water area of 0 square miles. Located at 40.77° N. Lat.; 87.56° W. Long. Elevation is 682 feet.
History: Sheldon was established in 1860 by the Toledo, Peoria & Western Railroad as a switching point, and named for a railroad director. The town was a grain shipping center.
Population: 1,109 (1990); 1,232 (2000); 1,127 (2007); 1,105 (2012 projected); Race: 97.1% White, 0.7% Black, 0.7% Asian, 1.7% Hispanic of any race (2007); Density: 1,495.9 persons per square mile (2007); Average household size: 2.63 (2007); Median age: 37.7 (2007); Males per 100 females: 97.4 (2007); Marriage status: 21.5% never married, 56.1% now married, 9.9% widowed, 12.5% divorced (2000); Foreign born: 1.1% (2000); Ancestry (includes multiple ancestries): 24.8% German, 11.9% Irish, 10.1% English, 5.6% Other groups, 4.6% United States or American (2000).
Economy: Single-family building permits issued: 1 (2007); Multi-family building permits issued: 0 (2007); Employment by occupation: 6.7% management, 12.2% professional, 16.5% services, 15.8% sales, 1.0% farming, 8.4% construction, 39.5% production (2000).
Income: Per capita income: $19,472 (2007); Median household income: $43,704 (2007); Average household income: $51,075 (2007); Percent of households with income of $100,000 or more: 10.0% (2007); Poverty rate: 10.7% (2000).
Education: Percent of population age 25 and over with: High school diploma (including GED) or higher: 74.2% (2007); Bachelor's degree or higher: 8.5% (2007); Master's degree or higher: 1.4% (2007).

School District(s)

Milford CCSD 280 (PK-08)
2005-06 Enrollment: 454 . . . . (815) 889-5176

Housing: Homeownership rate: 75.2% (2007); Median home value: $97,250 (2007); Median rent: $333 per month (2000); Median age of housing: 60 years (2000).
Transportation: Commute to work: 95.7% car, 0.0% public transportation, 1.2% walk, 2.1% work from home (2000); Travel time to work: 39.2% less than 15 minutes, 39.0% 15 to 30 minutes, 6.8% 30 to 45 minutes, 7.6% 45 to 60 minutes, 7.4% 60 minutes or more (2000)

THAWVILLE (village). Covers a land area of 0.324 square miles and a water area of 0 square miles. Located at 40.67° N. Lat.; 88.11° W. Long. Elevation is 689 feet.
Population: 241 (1990); 258 (2000); 270 (2007); 279 (2012 projected); Race: 93.7% White, 0.0% Black, 1.1% Asian, 8.1% Hispanic of any race (2007); Density: 834.5 persons per square mile (2007); Average household size: 2.50 (2007); Median age: 43.1 (2007); Males per 100 females: 90.1 (2007); Marriage status: 16.8% never married, 65.3% now married, 8.2% widowed, 9.7% divorced (2000); Foreign born: 0.0% (2000); Ancestry (includes multiple ancestries): 32.8% German, 11.5% Irish, 11.1% English, 9.8% Other groups, 5.5% French (except Basque) (2000).
Economy: Single-family building permits issued: 0 (2007); Multi-family building permits issued: 3 (2007); Employment by occupation: 11.5% management, 21.2% professional, 15.9% services, 20.4% sales, 3.5% farming, 8.8% construction, 18.6% production (2000).
Income: Per capita income: $25,398 (2007); Median household income: $47,692 (2007); Average household income: $63,495 (2007); Percent of households with income of $100,000 or more: 10.2% (2007); Poverty rate: 2.6% (2000).
Education: Percent of population age 25 and over with: High school diploma (including GED) or higher: 80.2% (2007); Bachelor's degree or higher: 11.8% (2007); Master's degree or higher: 4.8% (2007).

School District(s)

Iroquois West CUSD 10 (PK-12)
2005-06 Enrollment: 935 . . . . (815) 265-4642

Housing: Homeownership rate: 91.7% (2007); Median home value: $87,727 (2007); Median rent: $375 per month (2000); Median age of housing: 60+ years (2000).
Transportation: Commute to work: 92.9% car, 0.0% public transportation, 0.0% walk, 7.1% work from home (2000); Travel time to work: 23.8% less than 15 minutes, 41.0% 15 to 30 minutes, 22.9% 30 to 45 minutes, 7.6% 45 to 60 minutes, 4.8% 60 minutes or more (2000)

WATSEKA (city). County seat. Covers a land area of 2.618 square miles and a water area of 0 square miles. Located at 40.77° N. Lat.; 87.73° W. Long. Elevation is 633 feet.
History: Watseka was first called South Middleport when it was laid out in 1860. The name was changed in 1865 to honor the Potawatomi wife (Watch-e-kee) of Gurdon Hubbard of the American Fur Company. Watseka developed as the seat of Iroquois County.
Population: 5,453 (1990); 5,670 (2000); 5,653 (2007); 5,574 (2012 projected); Race: 95.3% White, 1.2% Black, 0.8% Asian, 3.4% Hispanic of any race (2007); Density: 2,158.9 persons per square mile (2007); Average household size: 2.42 (2007); Median age: 41.5 (2007); Males per 100 females: 90.7 (2007); Marriage status: 24.0% never married, 56.0% now married, 10.0% widowed, 10.1% divorced (2000); Foreign born: 2.2% (2000); Ancestry (includes multiple ancestries): 24.1% German, 10.8% United States or American, 10.2% Irish, 9.1% Other groups, 9.0% English (2000).
Economy: Single-family building permits issued: 8 (2007); Multi-family building permits issued: 0 (2007); Employment by occupation: 8.5% management, 11.8% professional, 19.4% services, 24.7% sales, 0.4% farming, 8.4% construction, 26.8% production (2000).
Income: Per capita income: $20,478 (2007); Median household income: $35,957 (2007); Average household income: $48,283 (2007); Percent of households with income of $100,000 or more: 7.9% (2007); Poverty rate: 15.4% (2000).
Education: Percent of population age 25 and over with: High school diploma (including GED) or higher: 74.8% (2007); Bachelor's degree or higher: 12.5% (2007); Master's degree or higher: 6.1% (2007).

School District(s)

Iroquois Area Reg Del System
2005-06 Enrollment: n/a . . . . (815) 432-5471
Iroquois County CUSD 9 (PK-12)
2005-06 Enrollment: 1,224 . . . . (815) 432-4931

Housing: Homeownership rate: 67.5% (2007); Median home value: $104,549 (2007); Median rent: $336 per month (2000); Median age of housing: 44 years (2000).
Hospitals: Iroquois Memorial Hospital & Resident Home (94 beds)
Safety: Violent crime rate: 32.4 per 10,000 population; Property crime rate: 342.5 per 10,000 population (2006).
Newspapers: Iroquois County's Times-Republic (Local news; Circulation 2,900)
Transportation: Commute to work: 89.7% car, 0.4% public transportation, 6.4% walk, 2.7% work from home (2000); Travel time to work: 67.3% less than 15 minutes, 12.8% 15 to 30 minutes, 8.2% 30 to 45 minutes, 5.3% 45 to 60 minutes, 6.4% 60 minutes or more (2000)

Additional Information Contacts

City of Watseka . . . . (815) 432-2711
http://www.watsekacity.com
Watseka Area Chamber of Commerce . . . . (815) 432-2416
http://www.watsekachamber.org

WELLINGTON (village). Covers a land area of 0.277 square miles and a water area of 0 square miles. Located at 40.54° N. Lat.; 87.68° W. Long. Elevation is 699 feet.
Population: 294 (1990); 264 (2000); 210 (2007); 206 (2012 projected); Race: 100.0% White, 0.0% Black, 0.0% Asian, 2.4% Hispanic of any race (2007); Density: 758.8 persons per square mile (2007); Average household size: 2.33 (2007); Median age: 42.9 (2007); Males per 100 females: 98.1 (2007); Marriage status: 9.8% never married, 71.2% now married, 4.9% widowed, 14.1% divorced (2000); Foreign born: 1.9% (2000); Ancestry (includes multiple ancestries): 25.6% German, 13.0% United States or American, 12.6% Irish, 10.7% English, 6.1% Other groups (2000).
Economy: Single-family building permits issued: 2 (2007); Multi-family building permits issued: 0 (2007); Employment by occupation: 11.1% management, 9.5% professional, 4.8% services, 17.5% sales, 0.0% farming, 25.4% construction, 31.7% production (2000).
Income: Per capita income: $20,738 (2007); Median household income: $36,667 (2007); Average household income: $48,389 (2007); Percent of

households with income of $100,000 or more: 6.7% (2007); Poverty rate: 3.9% (2000).
Education: Percent of population age 25 and over with: High school diploma (including GED) or higher: 82.3% (2007); Bachelor's degree or higher: 5.4% (2007); Master's degree or higher: 3.4% (2007).
Housing: Homeownership rate: 83.3% (2007); Median home value: $66,818 (2007); Median rent: $256 per month (2000); Median age of housing: 60+ years (2000).
Transportation: Commute to work: 84.4% car, 0.0% public transportation, 10.7% walk, 0.0% work from home (2000); Travel time to work: 50.8% less than 15 minutes, 22.1% 15 to 30 minutes, 9.8% 30 to 45 minutes, 10.7% 45 to 60 minutes, 6.6% 60 minutes or more (2000)

WOODLAND (village). Covers a land area of 0.449 square miles and a water area of 0 square miles. Located at 40.71° N. Lat.; 87.73° W. Long. Elevation is 633 feet.
Population: 333 (1990); 319 (2000); 303 (2007); 295 (2012 projected); Race: 90.1% White, 5.3% Black, 0.0% Asian, 7.3% Hispanic of any race (2007); Density: 674.1 persons per square mile (2007); Average household size: 2.55 (2007); Median age: 36.4 (2007); Males per 100 females: 96.8 (2007); Marriage status: 20.7% never married, 59.4% now married, 8.0% widowed, 12.0% divorced (2000); Foreign born: 1.5% (2000); Ancestry (includes multiple ancestries): 31.4% German, 11.7% Irish, 10.2% Other groups, 10.2% French (except Basque), 8.9% English (2000).
Economy: Single-family building permits issued: 0 (2007); Multi-family building permits issued: 0 (2007); Employment by occupation: 4.9% management, 7.0% professional, 18.2% services, 24.5% sales, 0.0% farming, 15.4% construction, 30.1% production (2000).
Income: Per capita income: $17,368 (2007); Median household income: $39,107 (2007); Average household income: $44,223 (2007); Percent of households with income of $100,000 or more: 5.9% (2007); Poverty rate: 21.2% (2000).
Taxes: Total city taxes per capita: $45 (2006); City property taxes per capita: $45 (2006).
Education: Percent of population age 25 and over with: High school diploma (including GED) or higher: 76.2% (2007); Bachelor's degree or higher: 4.9% (2007); Master's degree or higher: 0.0% (2007).

School District(s)

Iroquois County CUSD 9 (PK-12)
2005-06 Enrollment: 1,224 . . . . (815) 432-4931
Housing: Homeownership rate: 79.0% (2007); Median home value: $85,556 (2007); Median rent: $402 per month (2000); Median age of housing: 38 years (2000).
Transportation: Commute to work: 96.5% car, 0.0% public transportation, 3.5% walk, 0.0% work from home (2000); Travel time to work: 39.2% less than 15 minutes, 35.7% 15 to 30 minutes, 6.3% 30 to 45 minutes, 2.8% 45 to 60 minutes, 16.1% 60 minutes or more (2000)

Jackson County

Located in southwestern Illinois; bounded on the southwest by the Mississippi River and the Missouri border; drained by the Big Muddy and Little Muddy Rivers; includes part of Shawnee National Forest. Covers a land area of 588.12 square miles, a water area of 14.40 square miles, and is located in the Central Time Zone. The county was founded in 1816. County seat is Murphysboro.

Jackson County is part of the Carbondale, IL Micropolitan Statistical Area. The entire metro area includes: Jackson County, IL

Weather Station: Carbondale Sewage Plant — Elevation: 387 feet

	Jan	Feb	Mar	Apr	May	Jun	Jul	Aug	Sep	Oct	Nov	Dec
High	40	46	55	67	76	85	89	88	81	70	56	45
Low	21	24	34	44	53	62	66	63	55	42	35	26
Precip	3.0	2.8	4.4	4.6	4.7	4.5	3.3	4.0	3.1	2.8	4.5	3.7
Snow	4.9	3.8	2.0	0.3	0.0	0.0	0.0	0.0	0.0	0.1	0.5	2.2

High and Low temperatures in degrees Fahrenheit; Precipitation and Snow in inches

Population: 61,067 (1990); 59,612 (2000); 57,700 (2007); 56,367 (2012 projected); Race: 79.5% White, 12.3% Black, 4.4% Asian, 3.0% Hispanic of any race (2007); Density: 98.1 persons per square mile (2007); Average household size: 2.37 (2007); Median age: 30.9 (2007); Males per 100 females: 104.1 (2007).
Religion: Five largest groups: 10.9% Southern Baptist Convention, 4.7% Catholic Church, 3.9% The United Methodist Church, 3.8% American Baptist Churches in the USA, 3.7% Lutheran Church—Missouri Synod (2000).
Economy: Unemployment rate: 4.4% (4/2008); Total civilian labor force: 34,564 (4/2008); Leading industries: 23.0% retail trade; 19.8% health care and social assistance; 16.4% accommodation & food services (2005); Farms: 740 totaling 199,683 acres (2002); Companies that employ 500 or more persons: 1 (2006); Companies that employ 100 to 499 persons: 24 (2006); Companies that employ less than 100 persons: 1,345 (2006); Black-owned businesses: n/a (2002); Hispanic-owned businesses: n/a (2002); Asian-owned businesses: n/a (2002); Women-owned businesses: 1,070 (2002); Retail sales per capita: $15,410 (2008). Single-family building permits issued: 31 (2007); Multi-family building permits issued: 344 (2007).
Income: Per capita income: $19,274 (2007); Median household income: $29,529 (2007); Average household income: $44,460 (2007); Percent of households with income of $100,000 or more: 8.8% (2007); Poverty rate: 29.1% (2005); Bankruptcy rate: 3.20% (2007).
Taxes: Total county taxes per capita: $182 (2006); County property taxes per capita: $125 (2006).
Education: Percent of population age 25 and over with: High school diploma (including GED) or higher: 85.5% (2007); Bachelor's degree or higher: 32.7% (2007); Master's degree or higher: 15.2% (2007).
Housing: Homeownership rate: 54.1% (2007); Median home value: $86,013 (2007); Median rent: $332 per month (2000); Median age of housing: 29 years (2000).
Health: Birth rate: 119.6 per 10,000 population (2007); Death rate: 74.4 per 10,000 population (2007); Age-adjusted cancer mortality rate: 185.7 deaths per 100,000 population (2005); Air Quality Index: 98.3% good, 1.7% moderate, 0.0% unhealthy for sensitive individuals, 0.0% unhealthy (percent of days in 2007); Number of physicians: 30.6 per 10,000 population (2005); Hospital beds: 28.5 per 10,000 population (2004); Hospital admissions: 1,791.3 per 10,000 population (2004).
Elections: 2004 Presidential election results: 43.3% Bush, 55.4% Kerry, 0.1% Nader, 1.2% Badnarik
National and State Parks: Giant City State Park; Lake Murphysboro State Park
Additional Information Contacts
Jackson County Government. . . . . (618) 687-7360
http://www.co.jackson.il.us
Carbondale Chamber of Commerce . . . . (618) 529-2146
http://www.carbondalechamber.com
City of Carbondale . . . . (618) 549-5302
http://www.ci.carbondale.il.us
City of Murphysboro. . . . . (618) 684-4961
http://www.murphysboro.com
Murphysboro Chamber of Commerce . . . . (618) 684-6421
http://www.murphysboro.com/index.php?p=83

Jackson County Communities

AVA (city). Covers a land area of 1.064 square miles and a water area of 0.006 square miles. Located at 37.88° N. Lat.; 89.49° W. Long. Elevation is 604 feet.
Population: 674 (1990); 662 (2000); 681 (2007); 684 (2012 projected); Race: 99.1% White, 0.0% Black, 0.0% Asian, 1.0% Hispanic of any race (2007); Density: 639.9 persons per square mile (2007); Average household size: 2.31 (2007); Median age: 38.4 (2007); Males per 100 females: 94.6 (2007); Marriage status: 20.8% never married, 56.0% now married, 15.3% widowed, 7.9% divorced (2000); Foreign born: 0.3% (2000); Ancestry (includes multiple ancestries): 30.8% German, 18.0% Irish, 11.2% English, 8.9% United States or American, 7.4% Other groups (2000).
Economy: Employment by occupation: 2.8% management, 16.0% professional, 14.8% services, 26.8% sales, 0.0% farming, 17.6% construction, 22.0% production (2000).
Income: Per capita income: $18,326 (2007); Median household income: $28,917 (2007); Average household income: $42,305 (2007); Percent of households with income of $100,000 or more: 8.1% (2007); Poverty rate: 14.4% (2000).
Education: Percent of population age 25 and over with: High school diploma (including GED) or higher: 70.6% (2007); Bachelor's degree or higher: 9.1% (2007); Master's degree or higher: 2.4% (2007).
Housing: Homeownership rate: 78.3% (2007); Median home value: $60,357 (2007); Median rent: $183 per month (2000); Median age of housing: 45 years (2000).

Transportation: Commute to work: 92.9% car, 0.0% public transportation, 1.7% walk, 4.6% work from home (2000); Travel time to work: 25.2% less than 15 minutes, 33.5% 15 to 30 minutes, 30.0% 30 to 45 minutes, 5.2% 45 to 60 minutes, 6.1% 60 minutes or more (2000)

CAMPBELL HILL (village). Covers a land area of 0.408 square miles and a water area of 0 square miles. Located at 37.92° N. Lat.; 89.55° W. Long. Elevation is 561 feet.

Population: 351 (1990); 333 (2000); 313 (2007); 314 (2012 projected); Race: 99.7% White, 0.0% Black, 0.0% Asian, 0.3% Hispanic of any race (2007); Density: 766.4 persons per square mile (2007); Average household size: 2.28 (2007); Median age: 41.1 (2007); Males per 100 females: 103.2 (2007); Marriage status: 29.8% never married, 45.8% now married, 19.5% widowed, 5.0% divorced (2000); Foreign born: 2.9% (2000); Ancestry (includes multiple ancestries): 51.8% German, 6.8% Polish, 6.5% Irish, 4.9% Other groups, 4.6% Dutch (2000).

Economy: Single-family building permits issued: 0 (2007); Multi-family building permits issued: 0 (2007); Employment by occupation: 13.8% management, 10.8% professional, 7.7% services, 28.5% sales, 0.0% farming, 16.2% construction, 23.1% production (2000).

Income: Per capita income: $19,058 (2007); Median household income: $38,214 (2007); Average household income: $43,540 (2007); Percent of households with income of $100,000 or more: 5.1% (2007); Poverty rate: 5.5% (2000).

Education: Percent of population age 25 and over with: High school diploma (including GED) or higher: 69.1% (2007); Bachelor's degree or higher: 15.2% (2007); Master's degree or higher: 8.5% (2007).

School District(s)

Trico CUSD 176 (PK-12)
2005-06 Enrollment: 957 . . . . (618) 426-1111

Housing: Homeownership rate: 86.9% (2007); Median home value: $63,611 (2007); Median rent: $292 per month (2000); Median age of housing: 35 years (2000).

Transportation: Commute to work: 96.0% car, 0.0% public transportation, 4.0% walk, 0.0% work from home (2000); Travel time to work: 27.0% less than 15 minutes, 30.2% 15 to 30 minutes, 34.9% 30 to 45 minutes, 1.6% 45 to 60 minutes, 6.3% 60 minutes or more (2000)

CARBONDALE (city). Covers a land area of 11.895 square miles and a water area of 0.249 square miles. Located at 37.72° N. Lat.; 89.22° W. Long. Elevation is 413 feet.

History: Carbondale developed as a coal mining center and a division point on the Illinois Central Railroad. In 1874 the Southern Illinois State Normal University was founded here.

Population: 27,831 (1990); 20,681 (2000); 19,974 (2007); 19,344 (2012 projected); Race: 63.3% White, 22.7% Black, 9.2% Asian, 3.6% Hispanic of any race (2007); Density: 1,679.2 persons per square mile (2007); Average household size: 2.02 (2007); Median age: 27.3 (2007); Males per 100 females: 106.5 (2007); Marriage status: 58.8% never married, 28.5% now married, 5.0% widowed, 7.7% divorced (2000); Foreign born: 10.6% (2000); Ancestry (includes multiple ancestries): 32.7% Other groups, 18.4% German, 11.4% Irish, 9.1% English, 4.6% United States or American (2000).

Economy: Unemployment rate: 3.6% (4/2008); Total civilian labor force: 14,911 (4/2008); Single-family building permits issued: 28 (2007); Multi-family building permits issued: 340 (2007); Employment by occupation: 6.8% management, 34.3% professional, 21.1% services, 27.3% sales, 0.6% farming, 2.7% construction, 7.1% production (2000).

Income: Per capita income: $16,028 (2007); Median household income: $19,074 (2007); Average household income: $31,969 (2007); Percent of households with income of $100,000 or more: 4.9% (2007); Poverty rate: 41.4% (2000).

Taxes: Total city taxes per capita: $344 (2006); City property taxes per capita: $48 (2006).

Education: Percent of population age 25 and over with: High school diploma (including GED) or higher: 90.5% (2007); Bachelor's degree or higher: 47.2% (2007); Master's degree or higher: 23.0% (2007).

School District(s)

Carbondale CHSD 165 (09-12)
2005-06 Enrollment: 1,207 . . . . (618) 457-4722
Carbondale ESD 95 (PK-08)
2005-06 Enrollment: 1,384 . . . . (618) 457-2040
Giant City CCSD 130 (KG-08)
2005-06 Enrollment: 259 . . . . (618) 457-5391
Unity Point CCSD 140 (PK-08)
2005-06 Enrollment: 711 . . . . (618) 529-4151

Four-year College(s)

Southern Illinois University Carbondale (Public)
Fall 2007 Enrollment: 20,983. . . . . (618) 453-2121
2007-08 Tuition: In-state $8,899; Out-of-state $18,421

Housing: Homeownership rate: 29.6% (2007); Median home value: $95,257 (2007); Median rent: $341 per month (2000); Median age of housing: 29 years (2000).

Hospitals: Memorial Hospital Carbondale (150 beds)

Safety: Violent crime rate: 90.3 per 10,000 population; Property crime rate: 459.5 per 10,000 population (2006).

Newspapers: Southern Illinoisan (Local news; Circulation 32,000)

Transportation: Commute to work: 81.0% car, 3.1% public transportation, 10.6% walk, 2.4% work from home (2000); Travel time to work: 67.7% less than 15 minutes, 22.1% 15 to 30 minutes, 5.1% 30 to 45 minutes, 2.1% 45 to 60 minutes, 3.0% 60 minutes or more (2000); Amtrak: Service available.

Airports: Southern Illinois (general aviation)

Additional Information Contacts

Carbondale Chamber of Commerce . . . . (618) 529-2146
http://www.carbondalechamber.com
City of Carbondale . . . . (618) 549-5302
http://www.ci.carbondale.il.us

DE SOTO (village). Covers a land area of 0.943 square miles and a water area of 0 square miles. Located at 37.81° N. Lat.; 89.22° W. Long. Elevation is 400 feet.

Population: 1,551 (1990); 1,653 (2000); 1,649 (2007); 1,589 (2012 projected); Race: 97.3% White, 0.7% Black, 0.5% Asian, 1.9% Hispanic of any race (2007); Density: 1,748.2 persons per square mile (2007); Average household size: 2.40 (2007); Median age: 35.5 (2007); Males per 100 females: 94.9 (2007); Marriage status: 27.4% never married, 55.0% now married, 6.3% widowed, 11.3% divorced (2000); Foreign born: 1.3% (2000); Ancestry (includes multiple ancestries): 21.3% German, 14.9% Irish, 11.9% United States or American, 11.5% Other groups, 9.1% English (2000).

Economy: Single-family building permits issued: 0 (2007); Multi-family building permits issued: 0 (2007); Employment by occupation: 8.2% management, 18.2% professional, 22.5% services, 28.2% sales, 0.7% farming, 7.6% construction, 14.6% production (2000).

Income: Per capita income: $18,301 (2007); Median household income: $36,324 (2007); Average household income: $43,082 (2007); Percent of households with income of $100,000 or more: 3.8% (2007); Poverty rate: 14.3% (2000).

Education: Percent of population age 25 and over with: High school diploma (including GED) or higher: 83.3% (2007); Bachelor's degree or higher: 17.6% (2007); Master's degree or higher: 6.1% (2007).

School District(s)

Desoto Cons SD 86 (KG-08)
2005-06 Enrollment: 234 . . . . (618) 867-2317

Housing: Homeownership rate: 69.3% (2007); Median home value: $74,853 (2007); Median rent: $321 per month (2000); Median age of housing: 27 years (2000).

Safety: Violent crime rate: 19.0 per 10,000 population; Property crime rate: 94.8 per 10,000 population (2006).

Transportation: Commute to work: 94.9% car, 0.4% public transportation, 2.1% walk, 0.7% work from home (2000); Travel time to work: 32.1% less than 15 minutes, 49.4% 15 to 30 minutes, 10.6% 30 to 45 minutes, 2.2% 45 to 60 minutes, 5.6% 60 minutes or more (2000)

DOWELL (village). Covers a land area of 0.371 square miles and a water area of 0 square miles. Located at 37.94° N. Lat.; 89.24° W. Long. Elevation is 400 feet.

History: Dowell grew around the Kathleen Coal Company Mine in 1916, and was named for George Dowell, legal advisor for the Progressive Miners of America.

Population: 465 (1990); 441 (2000); 370 (2007); 376 (2012 projected); Race: 98.1% White, 0.3% Black, 0.0% Asian, 0.3% Hispanic of any race (2007); Density: 996.7 persons per square mile (2007); Average household size: 2.16 (2007); Median age: 41.7 (2007); Males per 100 females: 84.1 (2007); Marriage status: 24.9% never married, 50.7% now married, 11.3% widowed, 13.1% divorced (2000); Foreign born: 0.4% (2000); Ancestry (includes multiple ancestries): 13.9% Other groups, 12.7% German, 8.6% English, 7.9% United States or American, 7.7% Irish (2000).

Economy: Single-family building permits issued: 0 (2007); Multi-family building permits issued: 0 (2007); Employment by occupation: 6.6% management, 12.2% professional, 13.7% services, 22.8% sales, 1.0% farming, 11.7% construction, 32.0% production (2000).
Income: Per capita income: $14,932 (2007); Median household income: $27,237 (2007); Average household income: $32,310 (2007); Percent of households with income of $100,000 or more: 0.6% (2007); Poverty rate: 13.3% (2000).
Education: Percent of population age 25 and over with: High school diploma (including GED) or higher: 65.4% (2007); Bachelor's degree or higher: 4.6% (2007); Master's degree or higher: 0.4% (2007).
Housing: Homeownership rate: 83.0% (2007); Median home value: $44,286 (2007); Median rent: $313 per month (2000); Median age of housing: 51 years (2000).
Transportation: Commute to work: 98.4% car, 0.0% public transportation, 0.5% walk, 1.1% work from home (2000); Travel time to work: 31.7% less than 15 minutes, 30.6% 15 to 30 minutes, 24.7% 30 to 45 minutes, 4.8% 45 to 60 minutes, 8.1% 60 minutes or more (2000)

ELKVILLE (village). Covers a land area of 0.767 square miles and a water area of 0 square miles. Located at 37.91° N. Lat.; 89.23° W. Long. Elevation is 400 feet.
Population: 958 (1990); 1,001 (2000); 994 (2007); 957 (2012 projected); Race: 94.8% White, 2.8% Black, 0.0% Asian, 3.0% Hispanic of any race (2007); Density: 1,296.5 persons per square mile (2007); Average household size: 2.44 (2007); Median age: 35.5 (2007); Males per 100 females: 98.0 (2007); Marriage status: 21.7% never married, 65.2% now married, 5.5% widowed, 7.6% divorced (2000); Foreign born: 0.0% (2000); Ancestry (includes multiple ancestries): 21.3% German, 13.7% Other groups, 10.6% Irish, 8.6% United States or American, 8.5% English (2000).
Economy: Single-family building permits issued: 0 (2007); Multi-family building permits issued: 0 (2007); Employment by occupation: 4.0% management, 8.7% professional, 18.6% services, 24.4% sales, 0.0% farming, 13.2% construction, 31.1% production (2000).
Income: Per capita income: $15,571 (2007); Median household income: $29,904 (2007); Average household income: $36,783 (2007); Percent of households with income of $100,000 or more: 2.2% (2007); Poverty rate: 21.2% (2000).
Education: Percent of population age 25 and over with: High school diploma (including GED) or higher: 77.6% (2007); Bachelor's degree or higher: 9.2% (2007); Master's degree or higher: 3.0% (2007).

School District(s)

Elverado CUSD 196 (PK-12)
2005-06 Enrollment: 519 . . . . (618) 568-1321
Housing: Homeownership rate: 70.6% (2007); Median home value: $56,667 (2007); Median rent: $266 per month (2000); Median age of housing: 40 years (2000).
Transportation: Commute to work: 93.6% car, 0.0% public transportation, 3.3% walk, 1.4% work from home (2000); Travel time to work: 27.0% less than 15 minutes, 40.1% 15 to 30 minutes, 20.5% 30 to 45 minutes, 5.0% 45 to 60 minutes, 7.4% 60 minutes or more (2000)

GORHAM (village). Covers a land area of 1.218 square miles and a water area of 0.011 square miles. Located at 37.71° N. Lat.; 89.48° W. Long. Elevation is 361 feet.
Population: 290 (1990); 256 (2000); 240 (2007); 240 (2012 projected); Race: 98.3% White, 0.0% Black, 0.0% Asian, 0.0% Hispanic of any race (2007); Density: 197.1 persons per square mile (2007); Average household size: 2.53 (2007); Median age: 32.8 (2007); Males per 100 females: 92.0 (2007); Marriage status: 19.7% never married, 58.1% now married, 14.6% widowed, 7.6% divorced (2000); Foreign born: 0.0% (2000); Ancestry (includes multiple ancestries): 19.5% United States or American, 16.3% German, 12.1% Other groups, 11.3% Irish, 7.8% French (except Basque) (2000).
Economy: Employment by occupation: 2.1% management, 8.5% professional, 18.1% services, 28.7% sales, 2.1% farming, 10.6% construction, 29.8% production (2000).
Income: Per capita income: $16,018 (2007); Median household income: $25,833 (2007); Average household income: $38,947 (2007); Percent of households with income of $100,000 or more: 3.2% (2007); Poverty rate: 26.8% (2000).
Education: Percent of population age 25 and over with: High school diploma (including GED) or higher: 70.1% (2007); Bachelor's degree or higher: 2.7% (2007); Master's degree or higher: 1.4% (2007).
Housing: Homeownership rate: 83.2% (2007); Median home value: $30,625 (2007); Median rent: $225 per month (2000); Median age of housing: 51 years (2000).
Transportation: Commute to work: 100.0% car, 0.0% public transportation, 0.0% walk, 0.0% work from home (2000); Travel time to work: 14.1% less than 15 minutes, 35.9% 15 to 30 minutes, 21.7% 30 to 45 minutes, 15.2% 45 to 60 minutes, 13.0% 60 minutes or more (2000)

GRAND TOWER (city). Covers a land area of 1.258 square miles and a water area of 0.002 square miles. Located at 37.63° N. Lat.; 89.50° W. Long. Elevation is 361 feet.
History: Grand Tower was named for the 60-foot-high Tower Rock in the middle of the Mississippi River.
Population: 775 (1990); 624 (2000); 639 (2007); 639 (2012 projected); Race: 98.0% White, 0.3% Black, 0.0% Asian, 0.8% Hispanic of any race (2007); Density: 507.9 persons per square mile (2007); Average household size: 2.27 (2007); Median age: 38.7 (2007); Males per 100 females: 96.6 (2007); Marriage status: 17.2% never married, 65.1% now married, 6.1% widowed, 11.7% divorced (2000); Foreign born: 0.3% (2000); Ancestry (includes multiple ancestries): 15.7% Irish, 15.1% United States or American, 10.9% English, 10.4% Other groups, 7.3% German (2000).
Economy: Single-family building permits issued: 0 (2007); Multi-family building permits issued: 0 (2007); Employment by occupation: 9.4% management, 16.3% professional, 13.1% services, 15.5% sales, 0.4% farming, 18.8% construction, 26.5% production (2000).
Income: Per capita income: $19,562 (2007); Median household income: $34,375 (2007); Average household income: $44,484 (2007); Percent of households with income of $100,000 or more: 6.0% (2007); Poverty rate: 20.9% (2000).
Education: Percent of population age 25 and over with: High school diploma (including GED) or higher: 71.1% (2007); Bachelor's degree or higher: 8.7% (2007); Master's degree or higher: 3.0% (2007).

School District(s)

Shawnee CUSD 84 (KG-12)
2005-06 Enrollment: 481 . . . . (618) 833-5709
Housing: Homeownership rate: 75.4% (2007); Median home value: $45,952 (2007); Median rent: $170 per month (2000); Median age of housing: 40 years (2000).
Safety: Violent crime rate: 0.0 per 10,000 population; Property crime rate: 0.0 per 10,000 population (2006).
Transportation: Commute to work: 87.4% car, 0.0% public transportation, 3.5% walk, 2.6% work from home (2000); Travel time to work: 25.8% less than 15 minutes, 28.9% 15 to 30 minutes, 30.2% 30 to 45 minutes, 7.6% 45 to 60 minutes, 7.6% 60 minutes or more (2000)

JACOB (unincorporated postal area, zip code 62950). Covers a land area of 28.982 square miles and a water area of 0.074 square miles. Located at 37.75° N. Lat.; 89.56° W. Long. Elevation is 361 feet.
Population: 232 (2000); Race: 100.0% White, 0.0% Black, 0.0% Asian, 4.7% Hispanic of any race (2000); Density: 8.0 persons per square mile (2000); Age: 14.1% under 18, 32.3% over 64 (2000); Marriage status: 9.7% never married, 80.6% now married, 9.7% widowed, 0.0% divorced (2000); Foreign born: 4.7% (2000); Ancestry (includes multiple ancestries): 60.4% German, 6.3% Other groups, 4.7% Italian, 4.7% Lebanese, 3.1% Dutch (2000).
Economy: Employment by occupation: 26.4% management, 14.5% professional, 22.7% services, 24.5% sales, 0.0% farming, 5.5% construction, 6.4% production (2000).
Income: Per capita income: $20,713 (2000); Median household income: $23,750 (2000); Poverty rate: 14.1% (2000).
Education: Percent of population age 25 and over with: High school diploma (including GED) or higher: 65.5% (2000); Bachelor's degree or higher: 10.3% (2000).
Housing: Homeownership rate: 78.6% (2000); Median home value: $32,900 (2000); Median rent: $321 per month (2000); Median age of housing: 51 years (2000).
Transportation: Commute to work: 87.3% car, 0.0% public transportation, 0.0% walk, 6.4% work from home (2000); Travel time to work: 35.9% less than 15 minutes, 23.3% 15 to 30 minutes, 34.0% 30 to 45 minutes, 0.0% 45 to 60 minutes, 6.8% 60 minutes or more (2000)

MAKANDA (village). Covers a land area of 4.332 square miles and a water area of 0 square miles. Located at 37.61° N. Lat.; 89.23° W. Long. Elevation is 446 feet.

Population: 404 (1990); 419 (2000); 410 (2007); 405 (2012 projected); Race: 95.1% White, 3.4% Black, 0.5% Asian, 0.7% Hispanic of any race (2007); Density: 94.7 persons per square mile (2007); Average household size: 2.27 (2007); Median age: 43.0 (2007); Males per 100 females: 126.5 (2007); Marriage status: 23.6% never married, 61.1% now married, 4.3% widowed, 11.0% divorced (2000); Foreign born: 7.9% (2000); Ancestry (includes multiple ancestries): 25.1% German, 22.9% Irish, 9.6% English, 9.6% Other groups, 8.4% United States or American (2000).
Economy: Employment by occupation: 10.4% management, 29.0% professional, 13.4% services, 22.9% sales, 1.3% farming, 10.4% construction, 12.6% production (2000).
Income: Per capita income: $28,128 (2007); Median household income: $51,389 (2007); Average household income: $63,715 (2007); Percent of households with income of $100,000 or more: 17.1% (2007); Poverty rate: 10.8% (2000).
Education: Percent of population age 25 and over with: High school diploma (including GED) or higher: 91.8% (2007); Bachelor's degree or higher: 39.8% (2007); Master's degree or higher: 15.6% (2007).
Housing: Homeownership rate: 83.4% (2007); Median home value: $95,500 (2007); Median rent: $275 per month (2000); Median age of housing: 28 years (2000).
Transportation: Commute to work: 94.4% car, 0.0% public transportation, 1.3% walk, 4.3% work from home (2000); Travel time to work: 18.6% less than 15 minutes, 57.5% 15 to 30 minutes, 17.6% 30 to 45 minutes, 0.0% 45 to 60 minutes, 6.3% 60 minutes or more (2000)

MURPHYSBORO (city). County seat. Covers a land area of 4.832 square miles and a water area of 0.008 square miles. Located at 37.76° N. Lat.; 89.33° W. Long. Elevation is 420 feet.
History: A memorial to John A. Logan is in the city. Incorporated 1867.
Population: 9,325 (1990); 13,295 (2000); 11,840 (2007); 11,288 (2012 projected); Race: 79.6% White, 14.4% Black, 1.9% Asian, 3.6% Hispanic of any race (2007); Density: 2,450.2 persons per square mile (2007); Average household size: 3.34 (2007); Median age: 24.1 (2007); Males per 100 females: 104.9 (2007); Marriage status: 46.7% never married, 38.7% now married, 7.5% widowed, 7.2% divorced (2000); Foreign born: 2.8% (2000); Ancestry (includes multiple ancestries): 22.0% German, 21.2% Other groups, 13.3% Irish, 7.1% English, 4.9% Italian (2000).
Economy: Single-family building permits issued: 3 (2007); Multi-family building permits issued: 4 (2007); Employment by occupation: 7.6% management, 22.5% professional, 23.2% services, 28.7% sales, 0.0% farming, 8.2% construction, 9.7% production (2000).
Income: Per capita income: $16,127 (2007); Median household income: $29,439 (2007); Average household income: $46,433 (2007); Percent of households with income of $100,000 or more: 9.2% (2007); Poverty rate: 21.3% (2000).
Education: Percent of population age 25 and over with: High school diploma (including GED) or higher: 76.5% (2007); Bachelor's degree or higher: 19.0% (2007); Master's degree or higher: 7.1% (2007).

School District(s)

Dept of Corrections Sch Dist 428 (08-12)
2005-06 Enrollment: 2,271 . . . . (217) 522-2666
Jackson/Perry Roe (06-08)
2005-06 Enrollment: 8 . . . . (618) 687-7290
Murphysboro CUSD 186 (PK-12)
2005-06 Enrollment: 2,046 . . . . (618) 684-3781
Tri-County Sp Ed Jnt Agreement (PK-12)
2005-06 Enrollment: 149 . . . . (618) 684-2109

Housing: Homeownership rate: 59.7% (2007); Median home value: $63,638 (2007); Median rent: $325 per month (2000); Median age of housing: 44 years (2000).
Safety: Violent crime rate: 91.7 per 10,000 population; Property crime rate: 577.9 per 10,000 population (2006).
Newspapers: Murphysboro American (Regional news; Circulation 10,294)
Transportation: Commute to work: 75.4% car, 0.3% public transportation, 17.9% walk, 3.0% work from home (2000); Travel time to work: 53.9% less than 15 minutes, 31.0% 15 to 30 minutes, 8.4% 30 to 45 minutes, 3.5% 45 to 60 minutes, 3.2% 60 minutes or more (2000)

Additional Information Contacts

City of Murphysboro . . . . (618) 684-4961
http://www.murphysboro.com
Murphysboro Chamber of Commerce . . . . (618) 684-6421
http://www.murphysboro.com/index.php?p=83

POMONA (unincorporated postal area, zip code 62975). Covers a land area of 20.400 square miles and a water area of 0 square miles. Located at 37.61° N. Lat.; 89.36° W. Long. Elevation is 407 feet.
Population: 240 (2000); Race: 100.0% White, 0.0% Black, 0.0% Asian, 0.0% Hispanic of any race (2000); Density: 11.8 persons per square mile (2000); Age: 29.6% under 18, 5.2% over 64 (2000); Marriage status: 33.1% never married, 55.8% now married, 7.0% widowed, 4.1% divorced (2000); Foreign born: 0.0% (2000); Ancestry (includes multiple ancestries): 20.4% German, 17.0% Irish, 9.1% United States or American, 7.0% Polish, 6.5% Other groups (2000).
Economy: Employment by occupation: 21.1% management, 3.7% professional, 15.6% services, 23.9% sales, 0.0% farming, 22.0% construction, 13.8% production (2000).
Income: Per capita income: $19,845 (2000); Median household income: $41,250 (2000); Poverty rate: 16.1% (2000).
Education: Percent of population age 25 and over with: High school diploma (including GED) or higher: 60.9% (2000); Bachelor's degree or higher: 8.7% (2000).
Housing: Homeownership rate: 83.1% (2000); Median home value: $17,500 (2000); Median rent: $275 per month (2000); Median age of housing: 17 years (2000).
Transportation: Commute to work: 94.2% car, 0.0% public transportation, 0.0% walk, 0.0% work from home (2000); Travel time to work: 0.0% less than 15 minutes, 27.2% 15 to 30 minutes, 45.6% 30 to 45 minutes, 8.7% 45 to 60 minutes, 18.4% 60 minutes or more (2000)

VERGENNES (village). Covers a land area of 0.362 square miles and a water area of 0 square miles. Located at 37.90° N. Lat.; 89.34° W. Long. Elevation is 397 feet.
Population: 311 (1990); 491 (2000); 484 (2007); 473 (2012 projected); Race: 62.6% White, 31.6% Black, 0.8% Asian, 7.2% Hispanic of any race (2007); Density: 1,338.3 persons per square mile (2007); Average household size: 3.64 (2007); Median age: 19.0 (2007); Males per 100 females: 160.2 (2007); Marriage status: 42.4% never married, 47.3% now married, 4.7% widowed, 5.6% divorced (2000); Foreign born: 0.0% (2000); Ancestry (includes multiple ancestries): 16.6% German, 9.2% Other groups, 8.0% United States or American, 5.7% English, 3.1% Irish (2000).
Economy: Employment by occupation: 9.9% management, 11.1% professional, 17.5% services, 36.8% sales, 0.0% farming, 7.6% construction, 17.0% production (2000).
Income: Per capita income: $11,302 (2007); Median household income: $41,458 (2007); Average household income: $40,902 (2007); Percent of households with income of $100,000 or more: 0.8% (2007); Poverty rate: 19.1% (2000).
Education: Percent of population age 25 and over with: High school diploma (including GED) or higher: 79.7% (2007); Bachelor's degree or higher: 5.1% (2007); Master's degree or higher: 0.5% (2007).

School District(s)

Elverado CUSD 196 (PK-12)
2005-06 Enrollment: 519 . . . . (618) 568-1321

Housing: Homeownership rate: 79.7% (2007); Median home value: $62,857 (2007); Median rent: $260 per month (2000); Median age of housing: 37 years (2000).
Transportation: Commute to work: 90.6% car, 0.0% public transportation, 2.3% walk, 7.0% work from home (2000); Travel time to work: 17.0% less than 15 minutes, 47.8% 15 to 30 minutes, 24.5% 30 to 45 minutes, 3.1% 45 to 60 minutes, 7.5% 60 minutes or more (2000)

Jasper County

Located in southeast central Illinois; drained by the Embarrass River. Covers a land area of 494.40 square miles, a water area of 3.62 square miles, and is located in the Central Time Zone. The county was founded in 1831. County seat is Newton.

Weather Station: Newton 6 SSE Elevation: 508 feet

	Jan	Feb	Mar	Apr	May	Jun	Jul	Aug	Sep	Oct	Nov	Dec
High	35	41	52	63	74	83	87	85	79	67	53	41
Low	18	22	33	42	52	62	65	62	54	43	34	24
Precip	2.4	2.3	3.8	3.9	4.4	3.7	4.2	3.3	3.2	2.8	3.9	2.9
Snow	4.9	3.2	2.2	0.1	tr	0.0	0.0	0.0	0.0	0.1	0.9	3.4

High and Low temperatures in degrees Fahrenheit; Precipitation and Snow in inches

Population: 10,609 (1990); 10,117 (2000); 10,001 (2007); 9,899 (2012 projected); Race: 99.0% White, 0.2% Black, 0.2% Asian, 0.6% Hispanic of

any race (2007); Density: 20.2 persons per square mile (2007); Average household size: 2.53 (2007); Median age: 40.5 (2007); Males per 100 females: 96.2 (2007).
Religion: Five largest groups: 22.2% Catholic Church, 10.1% Christian Churches and Churches of Christ, 8.2% The United Methodist Church, 5.1% Southern Baptist Convention, 4.9% American Baptist Churches in the USA (2000).
Economy: Unemployment rate: 5.1% (4/2008); Total civilian labor force: 5,401 (4/2008); Leading industries: 18.8% manufacturing; 16.9% retail trade; 8.6% construction (2005); Farms: 791 totaling 271,329 acres (2002); Companies that employ 500 or more persons: 0 (2006); Companies that employ 100 to 499 persons: 2 (2006); Companies that employ less than 100 persons: 240 (2006); Black-owned businesses: n/a (2002); Hispanic-owned businesses: n/a (2002); Asian-owned businesses: n/a (2002); Women-owned businesses: 360 (2002); Retail sales per capita: $14,579 (2008). Single-family building permits issued: 1 (2007); Multi-family building permits issued: 0 (2007).
Income: Per capita income: $20,742 (2007); Median household income: $42,815 (2007); Average household income: $52,185 (2007); Percent of households with income of $100,000 or more: 8.5% (2007); Poverty rate: 10.8% (2005); Bankruptcy rate: 3.09% (2007).
Education: Percent of population age 25 and over with: High school diploma (including GED) or higher: 83.0% (2007); Bachelor's degree or higher: 11.2% (2007); Master's degree or higher: 3.2% (2007).
Housing: Homeownership rate: 83.2% (2007); Median home value: $95,425 (2007); Median rent: $256 per month (2000); Median age of housing: 35 years (2000).
Health: Birth rate: 126.7 per 10,000 population (2007); Death rate: 111.3 per 10,000 population (2007); Age-adjusted cancer mortality rate: 189.4 deaths per 100,000 population (2005); Number of physicians: 2.0 per 10,000 population (2005); Hospital beds: 0.0 per 10,000 population (2004); Hospital admissions: 0.0 per 10,000 population (2004).
Elections: 2004 Presidential election results: 66.1% Bush, 33.4% Kerry, 0.0% Nader, 0.5% Badnarik
National and State Parks: Newton Lake State Fish and Wildlife Area; Sam Parr State Park
Additional Information Contacts
Jasper County Government . . . . (618) 783-3124

Jasper County Chamber of Commerce . . . . (618) 783-3399
http://www.newtonillinois.com

Jasper County Communities

HIDALGO (village). Covers a land area of 0.343 square miles and a water area of 0 square miles. Located at 39.15° N. Lat.; 88.15° W. Long. Elevation is 587 feet.
Population: 122 (1990); 123 (2000); 118 (2007); 118 (2012 projected); Race: 100.0% White, 0.0% Black, 0.0% Asian, 0.0% Hispanic of any race (2007); Density: 343.6 persons per square mile (2007); Average household size: 2.41 (2007); Median age: 33.8 (2007); Males per 100 females: 84.4 (2007); Marriage status: 36.1% never married, 50.0% now married, 4.6% widowed, 9.3% divorced (2000); Foreign born: 0.0% (2000); Ancestry (includes multiple ancestries): 12.7% Irish, 12.7% German, 9.5% English, 8.7% Other groups, 4.0% Dutch (2000).
Economy: Employment by occupation: 7.4% management, 11.1% professional, 25.9% services, 25.9% sales, 0.0% farming, 13.0% construction, 16.7% production (2000).
Income: Per capita income: $17,309 (2007); Median household income: $31,250 (2007); Average household income: $41,684 (2007); Percent of households with income of $100,000 or more: 10.2% (2007); Poverty rate: 6.3% (2000).
Education: Percent of population age 25 and over with: High school diploma (including GED) or higher: 69.2% (2007); Bachelor's degree or higher: 6.4% (2007); Master's degree or higher: 3.8% (2007).
School District(s)
Jasper County Cud 1 (PK-12)
2005-06 Enrollment: 1,494 . . . . (618) 783-8459
Housing: Homeownership rate: 83.7% (2007); Median home value: $63,000 (2007); Median rent: $213 per month (2000); Median age of housing: 39 years (2000).
Transportation: Commute to work: 88.7% car, 0.0% public transportation, 3.8% walk, 3.8% work from home (2000); Travel time to work: 3.9% less than 15 minutes, 27.5% 15 to 30 minutes, 27.5% 30 to 45 minutes, 37.3% 45 to 60 minutes, 3.9% 60 minutes or more (2000)

NEWTON (city). County seat. Covers a land area of 1.863 square miles and a water area of 0 square miles. Located at 38.98° N. Lat.; 88.16° W. Long. Elevation is 535 feet.
History: Settled 1828, incorporated 1831.
Population: 3,234 (1990); 3,069 (2000); 3,019 (2007); 2,979 (2012 projected); Race: 98.9% White, 0.3% Black, 0.2% Asian, 0.7% Hispanic of any race (2007); Density: 1,620.5 persons per square mile (2007); Average household size: 2.29 (2007); Median age: 41.2 (2007); Males per 100 females: 84.8 (2007); Marriage status: 23.2% never married, 57.2% now married, 9.6% widowed, 10.0% divorced (2000); Foreign born: 0.2% (2000); Ancestry (includes multiple ancestries): 34.8% German, 10.4% Irish, 9.9% United States or American, 8.3% English, 5.2% Other groups (2000).
Economy: Employment by occupation: 9.1% management, 9.7% professional, 19.1% services, 29.1% sales, 0.0% farming, 8.4% construction, 24.7% production (2000).
Income: Per capita income: $19,962 (2007); Median household income: $36,250 (2007); Average household income: $44,941 (2007); Percent of households with income of $100,000 or more: 7.1% (2007); Poverty rate: 11.7% (2000).
Education: Percent of population age 25 and over with: High school diploma (including GED) or higher: 80.4% (2007); Bachelor's degree or higher: 12.5% (2007); Master's degree or higher: 4.4% (2007).
School District(s)
Clay/Cwford/Jsper/Lwrnce/Rhland
2005-06 Enrollment: n/a . . . . (618) 392-4631
Jasper County Cud 1 (PK-12)
2005-06 Enrollment: 1,494 . . . . (618) 783-8459
Housing: Homeownership rate: 73.5% (2007); Median home value: $78,789 (2007); Median rent: $255 per month (2000); Median age of housing: 41 years (2000).
Safety: Violent crime rate: 121.8 per 10,000 population; Property crime rate: 335.7 per 10,000 population (2006).
Newspapers: Newton Press-Mentor (Local news; Circulation 0)
Transportation: Commute to work: 89.7% car, 0.0% public transportation, 7.0% walk, 1.6% work from home (2000); Travel time to work: 66.4% less than 15 minutes, 12.2% 15 to 30 minutes, 17.9% 30 to 45 minutes, 2.0% 45 to 60 minutes, 1.5% 60 minutes or more (2000)
Additional Information Contacts
Jasper County Chamber of Commerce . . . . (618) 783-3399
http://www.newtonillinois.com

ROSE HILL (village). Covers a land area of 0.633 square miles and a water area of 0 square miles. Located at 39.10° N. Lat.; 88.14° W. Long. Elevation is 564 feet.
Population: 78 (1990); 79 (2000); 76 (2007); 74 (2012 projected); Race: 98.7% White, 0.0% Black, 1.3% Asian, 0.0% Hispanic of any race (2007); Density: 120.1 persons per square mile (2007); Average household size: 2.11 (2007); Median age: 49.3 (2007); Males per 100 females: 111.1 (2007); Marriage status: 29.5% never married, 50.0% now married, 15.4% widowed, 5.1% divorced (2000); Foreign born: 0.0% (2000); Ancestry (includes multiple ancestries): 17.6% English, 17.6% German, 15.4% Irish, 13.2% United States or American, 4.4% Scottish (2000).
Economy: Employment by occupation: 0.0% management, 27.8% professional, 0.0% services, 27.8% sales, 0.0% farming, 11.1% construction, 33.3% production (2000).
Income: Per capita income: $14,934 (2007); Median household income: $31,250 (2007); Average household income: $31,528 (2007); Percent of households with income of $100,000 or more: 0.0% (2007); Poverty rate: 2.2% (2000).
Education: Percent of population age 25 and over with: High school diploma (including GED) or higher: 74.2% (2007); Bachelor's degree or higher: 9.7% (2007); Master's degree or higher: 3.2% (2007).
Housing: Homeownership rate: 86.1% (2007); Median home value: $40,833 (2007); Median rent: $175 per month (2000); Median age of housing: 40 years (2000).
Transportation: Commute to work: 94.4% car, 0.0% public transportation, 0.0% walk, 5.6% work from home (2000); Travel time to work: 8.8% less than 15 minutes, 23.5% 15 to 30 minutes, 38.2% 30 to 45 minutes, 5.9% 45 to 60 minutes, 23.5% 60 minutes or more (2000)

SAINTE MARIE (village). Aka Saint Marie. Covers a land area of 1.112 square miles and a water area of 0 square miles. Located at 38.93° N. Lat.; 88.02° W. Long. Elevation is 486 feet.

Population: 281 (1990); 261 (2000); 217 (2007); 221 (2012 projected); Race: 100.0% White, 0.0% Black, 0.0% Asian, 0.0% Hispanic of any race (2007); Density: 195.1 persons per square mile (2007); Average household size: 2.19 (2007); Median age: 40.8 (2007); Males per 100 females: 76.4 (2007); Marriage status: 17.2% never married, 65.6% now married, 13.4% widowed, 3.8% divorced (2000); Foreign born: 0.0% (2000); Ancestry (includes multiple ancestries): 49.0% German, 9.6% Irish, 7.6% French (except Basque), 5.6% Other groups, 5.2% Dutch (2000).
Economy: Single-family building permits issued: 1 (2007); Multi-family building permits issued: 0 (2007); Employment by occupation: 16.2% management, 12.1% professional, 20.2% services, 18.2% sales, 3.0% farming, 8.1% construction, 22.2% production (2000).
Income: Per capita income: $19,770 (2007); Median household income: $41,563 (2007); Average household income: $43,333 (2007); Percent of households with income of $100,000 or more: 6.1% (2007); Poverty rate: 6.8% (2000).
Education: Percent of population age 25 and over with: High school diploma (including GED) or higher: 76.8% (2007); Bachelor's degree or higher: 11.3% (2007); Master's degree or higher: 1.3% (2007).

School District(s)

Jasper County Cud 1 (PK-12)
2005-06 Enrollment: 1,494 . . . . (618) 783-8459

Housing: Homeownership rate: 84.8% (2007); Median home value: $76,250 (2007); Median rent: $131 per month (2000); Median age of housing: 44 years (2000).
Transportation: Commute to work: 83.8% car, 0.0% public transportation, 3.0% walk, 10.1% work from home (2000); Travel time to work: 39.3% less than 15 minutes, 40.4% 15 to 30 minutes, 13.5% 30 to 45 minutes, 4.5% 45 to 60 minutes, 2.2% 60 minutes or more (2000)

WEST LIBERTY (unincorporated postal area, zip code 62475). Covers a land area of 28.531 square miles and a water area of 0.057 square miles. Located at 38.86° N. Lat.; 88.05° W. Long. Elevation is 482 feet.
Population: 416 (2000); Race: 100.0% White, 0.0% Black, 0.0% Asian, 0.0% Hispanic of any race (2000); Density: 14.6 persons per square mile (2000); Age: 29.1% under 18, 11.9% over 64 (2000); Marriage status: 26.3% never married, 72.5% now married, 1.2% widowed, 0.0% divorced (2000); Foreign born: 0.0% (2000); Ancestry (includes multiple ancestries): 55.5% German, 12.6% English, 8.3% Swiss, 7.6% United States or American, 6.7% Other groups (2000).
Economy: Employment by occupation: 24.9% management, 1.9% professional, 15.0% services, 36.6% sales, 4.2% farming, 0.0% construction, 17.4% production (2000).
Income: Per capita income: $14,590 (2000); Median household income: $40,179 (2000); Poverty rate: 8.9% (2000).
Education: Percent of population age 25 and over with: High school diploma (including GED) or higher: 89.2% (2000); Bachelor's degree or higher: 12.2% (2000).
Housing: Homeownership rate: 100.0% (2000); Median home value: $56,900 (2000); Median rent: $n/a per month (2000); Median age of housing: 50 years (2000).
Transportation: Commute to work: 83.6% car, 0.0% public transportation, 8.5% walk, 5.2% work from home (2000); Travel time to work: 37.1% less than 15 minutes, 52.5% 15 to 30 minutes, 9.4% 30 to 45 minutes, 1.0% 45 to 60 minutes, 0.0% 60 minutes or more (2000)

WHEELER (village). Covers a land area of 0.576 square miles and a water area of 0 square miles. Located at 39.04° N. Lat.; 88.31° W. Long. Elevation is 561 feet.
Population: 161 (1990); 119 (2000); 122 (2007); 120 (2012 projected); Race: 99.2% White, 0.0% Black, 0.0% Asian, 5.7% Hispanic of any race (2007); Density: 211.7 persons per square mile (2007); Average household size: 2.77 (2007); Median age: 29.4 (2007); Males per 100 females: 110.3 (2007); Marriage status: 28.9% never married, 50.6% now married, 6.0% widowed, 14.5% divorced (2000); Foreign born: 0.0% (2000); Ancestry (includes multiple ancestries): 32.7% German, 12.4% English, 8.0% Irish, 7.1% United States or American, 5.3% Dutch (2000).
Economy: Employment by occupation: 0.0% management, 4.5% professional, 27.3% services, 22.7% sales, 0.0% farming, 9.1% construction, 36.4% production (2000).
Income: Per capita income: $13,852 (2007); Median household income: $35,000 (2007); Average household income: $38,409 (2007); Percent of households with income of $100,000 or more: 0.0% (2007); Poverty rate: 27.4% (2000).
Education: Percent of population age 25 and over with: High school diploma (including GED) or higher: 55.1% (2007); Bachelor's degree or higher: 2.9% (2007); Master's degree or higher: 0.0% (2007).
Housing: Homeownership rate: 68.2% (2007); Median home value: $40,000 (2007); Median rent: $275 per month (2000); Median age of housing: 41 years (2000).
Transportation: Commute to work: 100.0% car, 0.0% public transportation, 0.0% walk, 0.0% work from home (2000); Travel time to work: 9.1% less than 15 minutes, 34.1% 15 to 30 minutes, 40.9% 30 to 45 minutes, 15.9% 45 to 60 minutes, 0.0% 60 minutes or more (2000)

WILLOW HILL (village). Covers a land area of 1.038 square miles and a water area of 0 square miles. Located at 38.99° N. Lat.; 88.02° W. Long. Elevation is 502 feet.
Population: 268 (1990); 250 (2000); 250 (2007); 240 (2012 projected); Race: 95.6% White, 0.0% Black, 4.4% Asian, 0.0% Hispanic of any race (2007); Density: 240.9 persons per square mile (2007); Average household size: 2.98 (2007); Median age: 31.1 (2007); Males per 100 females: 104.9 (2007); Marriage status: 21.5% never married, 56.9% now married, 4.1% widowed, 17.4% divorced (2000); Foreign born: 0.4% (2000); Ancestry (includes multiple ancestries): 18.3% German, 13.0% United States or American, 8.0% Other groups, 6.5% Irish, 4.2% English (2000).
Economy: Single-family building permits issued: 0 (2007); Multi-family building permits issued: 0 (2007); Employment by occupation: 4.0% management, 5.6% professional, 16.7% services, 6.3% sales, 0.0% farming, 7.9% construction, 59.5% production (2000).
Income: Per capita income: $13,970 (2007); Median household income: $34,286 (2007); Average household income: $41,577 (2007); Percent of households with income of $100,000 or more: 2.4% (2007); Poverty rate: 24.0% (2000).
Education: Percent of population age 25 and over with: High school diploma (including GED) or higher: 77.1% (2007); Bachelor's degree or higher: 0.0% (2007); Master's degree or higher: 0.0% (2007).

School District(s)

Jasper County Cud 1 (PK-12)
2005-06 Enrollment: 1,494 . . . . (618) 783-8459

Housing: Homeownership rate: 83.3% (2007); Median home value: $42,000 (2007); Median rent: $220 per month (2000); Median age of housing: 51 years (2000).
Transportation: Commute to work: 97.6% car, 0.0% public transportation, 2.4% walk, 0.0% work from home (2000); Travel time to work: 20.6% less than 15 minutes, 46.0% 15 to 30 minutes, 19.0% 30 to 45 minutes, 11.1% 45 to 60 minutes, 3.2% 60 minutes or more (2000)

YALE (village). Covers a land area of 0.575 square miles and a water area of 0 square miles. Located at 39.12° N. Lat.; 88.02° W. Long. Elevation is 558 feet.
Population: 94 (1990); 97 (2000); 93 (2007); 92 (2012 projected); Race: 100.0% White, 0.0% Black, 0.0% Asian, 2.2% Hispanic of any race (2007); Density: 161.8 persons per square mile (2007); Average household size: 2.58 (2007); Median age: 37.5 (2007); Males per 100 females: 106.7 (2007); Marriage status: 17.7% never married, 62.9% now married, 9.7% widowed, 9.7% divorced (2000); Foreign born: 0.0% (2000); Ancestry (includes multiple ancestries): 20.9% United States or American, 20.9% Other groups, 16.3% German, 11.6% Irish, 4.7% English (2000).
Economy: Employment by occupation: 0.0% management, 0.0% professional, 3.6% services, 32.1% sales, 7.1% farming, 7.1% construction, 50.0% production (2000).
Income: Per capita income: $19,758 (2007); Median household income: $25,833 (2007); Average household income: $51,042 (2007); Percent of households with income of $100,000 or more: 8.3% (2007); Poverty rate: 29.1% (2000).
Education: Percent of population age 25 and over with: High school diploma (including GED) or higher: 54.2% (2007); Bachelor's degree or higher: 3.4% (2007); Master's degree or higher: 3.4% (2007).
Housing: Homeownership rate: 83.3% (2007); Median home value: $45,000 (2007); Median rent: $200 per month (2000); Median age of housing: 60+ years (2000).
Transportation: Commute to work: 82.1% car, 0.0% public transportation, 10.7% walk, 3.6% work from home (2000); Travel time to work: 29.6% less than 15 minutes, 37.0% 15 to 30 minutes, 7.4% 30 to 45 minutes, 22.2% 45 to 60 minutes, 3.7% 60 minutes or more (2000)

Jefferson County

Located in southern Illinois; drained by the Big Muddy River. Covers a land area of 570.96 square miles, a water area of 12.76 square miles, and is located in the Central Time Zone. The county was founded in 1819. County seat is Mount Vernon.

Jefferson County is part of the Mount Vernon, IL Micropolitan Statistical Area. The entire metro area includes: Hamilton County, IL; Jefferson County, IL

Weather Station: Mount Vernon-Outland Airport Elevation: 465 feet

	Jan	Feb	Mar	Apr	May	Jun	Jul	Aug	Sep	Oct	Nov	Dec
High	37	43	54	65	75	84	88	87	80	68	54	43
Low	20	24	34	44	53	62	67	64	56	44	35	25
Precip	2.5	2.6	4.0	4.4	4.5	3.5	3.5	3.2	3.2	3.0	4.3	3.2
Snow	6.4	4.8	1.9	0.4	0.0	0.0	0.0	0.0	0.0	0.2	0.7	2.9

High and Low temperatures in degrees Fahrenheit; Precipitation and Snow in inches

Population: 37,020 (1990); 40,045 (2000); 40,562 (2007); 40,822 (2012 projected); Race: 89.0% White, 8.4% Black, 0.7% Asian, 1.6% Hispanic of any race (2007); Density: 71.0 persons per square mile (2007); Average household size: 2.57 (2007); Median age: 38.4 (2007); Males per 100 females: 104.7 (2007).
Religion: Five largest groups: 25.9% Southern Baptist Convention, 7.5% Christian Churches and Churches of Christ, 6.0% Catholic Church, 5.1% The United Methodist Church, 1.8% National Association of Free Will Baptists (2000).
Economy: Unemployment rate: 5.0% (4/2008); Total civilian labor force: 21,376 (4/2008); Leading industries: 18.4% health care and social assistance; 15.2% manufacturing; 13.7% transportation & warehousing (2005); Farms: 1,168 totaling 259,294 acres (2002); Companies that employ 500 or more persons: 3 (2006); Companies that employ 100 to 499 persons: 16 (2006); Companies that employ less than 100 persons: 1,034 (2006); Black-owned businesses: n/a (2002); Hispanic-owned businesses: n/a (2002); Asian-owned businesses: n/a (2002); Women-owned businesses: 833 (2002); Retail sales per capita: $13,943 (2008). Single-family building permits issued: 23 (2007); Multi-family building permits issued: 8 (2007).
Income: Per capita income: $20,103 (2007); Median household income: $39,848 (2007); Average household income: $50,418 (2007); Percent of households with income of $100,000 or more: 9.3% (2007); Poverty rate: 15.6% (2005); Bankruptcy rate: 2.99% (2007).
Education: Percent of population age 25 and over with: High school diploma (including GED) or higher: 77.1% (2007); Bachelor's degree or higher: 13.8% (2007); Master's degree or higher: 4.8% (2007).
Housing: Homeownership rate: 74.7% (2007); Median home value: $84,155 (2007); Median rent: $288 per month (2000); Median age of housing: 31 years (2000).
Health: Birth rate: 124.2 per 10,000 population (2007); Death rate: 98.1 per 10,000 population (2007); Age-adjusted cancer mortality rate: 186.1 deaths per 100,000 population (2005); Number of physicians: 18.4 per 10,000 population (2005); Hospital beds: 45.0 per 10,000 population (2004); Hospital admissions: 2,151.6 per 10,000 population (2004).
Elections: 2004 Presidential election results: 59.9% Bush, 39.6% Kerry, 0.1% Nader, 0.4% Badnarik
National and State Parks: Mount Vernon State Game Farm; Rend Lake State Waterfowl Management Area
Additional Information Contacts
Jefferson County Government . . . . (618) 244-8000

City of Mount Vernon . . . . (618) 242-0746
http://www.mtvernon.com
Jefferson County Chamber of Commerce . . . . (618) 242-5725
http://www.southernillinois.com

Jefferson County Communities

BELLE RIVE (village). Covers a land area of 1.026 square miles and a water area of 0 square miles. Located at 38.23° N. Lat.; 88.74° W. Long. Elevation is 479 feet.
Population: 396 (1990); 371 (2000); 375 (2007); 372 (2012 projected); Race: 97.6% White, 1.1% Black, 0.0% Asian, 0.0% Hispanic of any race (2007); Density: 365.4 persons per square mile (2007); Average household size: 2.53 (2007); Median age: 41.9 (2007); Males per 100 females: 94.3 (2007); Marriage status: 19.6% never married, 68.5% now married, 7.7% widowed, 4.2% divorced (2000); Foreign born: 1.3% (2000); Ancestry (includes multiple ancestries): 17.3% German, 10.9% Other groups, 10.6% English, 10.4% Irish, 8.0% United States or American (2000).
Economy: Employment by occupation: 3.4% management, 11.7% professional, 12.8% services, 30.7% sales, 1.1% farming, 11.7% construction, 28.5% production (2000).
Income: Per capita income: $19,793 (2007); Median household income: $46,500 (2007); Average household income: $50,152 (2007); Percent of households with income of $100,000 or more: 6.8% (2007); Poverty rate: 13.8% (2000).
Education: Percent of population age 25 and over with: High school diploma (including GED) or higher: 79.1% (2007); Bachelor's degree or higher: 3.0% (2007); Master's degree or higher: 0.8% (2007).

School District(s)

Opdyke-Belle-Rive CCSD 5 (KG-08)
2005-06 Enrollment: 174 . . . . (618) 756-2492
Housing: Homeownership rate: 81.8% (2007); Median home value: $49,545 (2007); Median rent: $281 per month (2000); Median age of housing: 32 years (2000).
Transportation: Commute to work: 92.4% car, 0.0% public transportation, 1.2% walk, 2.3% work from home (2000); Travel time to work: 24.4% less than 15 minutes, 57.1% 15 to 30 minutes, 13.7% 30 to 45 minutes, 1.2% 45 to 60 minutes, 3.6% 60 minutes or more (2000)

BLUFORD (village). Covers a land area of 1.456 square miles and a water area of 0.008 square miles. Located at 38.32° N. Lat.; 88.73° W. Long. Elevation is 522 feet.
Population: 747 (1990); 785 (2000); 693 (2007); 692 (2012 projected); Race: 97.7% White, 0.0% Black, 0.3% Asian, 1.3% Hispanic of any race (2007); Density: 475.9 persons per square mile (2007); Average household size: 2.73 (2007); Median age: 36.3 (2007); Males per 100 females: 99.1 (2007); Marriage status: 21.4% never married, 64.6% now married, 4.4% widowed, 9.5% divorced (2000); Foreign born: 0.3% (2000); Ancestry (includes multiple ancestries): 12.3% Irish, 11.8% German, 9.9% United States or American, 9.3% English, 8.3% Other groups (2000).
Economy: Single-family building permits issued: 0 (2007); Multi-family building permits issued: 0 (2007); Employment by occupation: 7.4% management, 5.0% professional, 18.9% services, 28.2% sales, 0.0% farming, 10.5% construction, 30.0% production (2000).
Income: Per capita income: $17,673 (2007); Median household income: $43,235 (2007); Average household income: $48,219 (2007); Percent of households with income of $100,000 or more: 6.3% (2007); Poverty rate: 7.9% (2000).
Education: Percent of population age 25 and over with: High school diploma (including GED) or higher: 78.8% (2007); Bachelor's degree or higher: 5.3% (2007); Master's degree or higher: 1.8% (2007).

School District(s)

Bluford CCSD 114 (PK-08)
2005-06 Enrollment: 293 . . . . (618) 732-8242
Farrington CCSD 99 (KG-08)
2005-06 Enrollment: 42 . . . . (618) 755-4414
Webber Twp HSD 204 (09-12)
2005-06 Enrollment: 202 . . . . (618) 732-6121
Housing: Homeownership rate: 84.3% (2007); Median home value: $62,174 (2007); Median rent: $320 per month (2000); Median age of housing: 30 years (2000).
Transportation: Commute to work: 96.5% car, 1.3% public transportation, 0.0% walk, 0.0% work from home (2000); Travel time to work: 11.6% less than 15 minutes, 57.9% 15 to 30 minutes, 18.2% 30 to 45 minutes, 9.4% 45 to 60 minutes, 2.8% 60 minutes or more (2000)

BONNIE (village). Covers a land area of 1.233 square miles and a water area of <.001 square miles. Located at 38.20° N. Lat.; 88.90° W. Long. Elevation is 427 feet.
Population: 410 (1990); 424 (2000); 385 (2007); 388 (2012 projected); Race: 97.4% White, 0.0% Black, 0.0% Asian, 1.0% Hispanic of any race (2007); Density: 312.2 persons per square mile (2007); Average household size: 2.41 (2007); Median age: 39.9 (2007); Males per 100 females: 91.5 (2007); Marriage status: 19.5% never married, 59.3% now married, 10.9% widowed, 10.3% divorced (2000); Foreign born: 0.9% (2000); Ancestry (includes multiple ancestries): 20.7% German, 18.1% Other groups, 13.8% United States or American, 13.4% Irish, 10.6% English (2000).
Economy: Single-family building permits issued: 0 (2007); Multi-family building permits issued: 0 (2007); Employment by occupation: 7.4%

management, 18.3% professional, 18.3% services, 23.8% sales, 0.0% farming, 11.9% construction, 20.3% production (2000).
Income: Per capita income: $16,143 (2007); Median household income: $32,667 (2007); Average household income: $38,844 (2007); Percent of households with income of $100,000 or more: 3.8% (2007); Poverty rate: 9.7% (2000).
Education: Percent of population age 25 and over with: High school diploma (including GED) or higher: 73.5% (2007); Bachelor's degree or higher: 4.8% (2007); Master's degree or higher: 1.5% (2007).
Housing: Homeownership rate: 82.5% (2007); Median home value: $59,048 (2007); Median rent: $244 per month (2000); Median age of housing: 28 years (2000).
Transportation: Commute to work: 99.0% car, 0.0% public transportation, 0.0% walk, 0.0% work from home (2000); Travel time to work: 27.8% less than 15 minutes, 50.0% 15 to 30 minutes, 10.6% 30 to 45 minutes, 4.0% 45 to 60 minutes, 7.6% 60 minutes or more (2000)

DIX (village). Aka Rome. Covers a land area of 2.094 square miles and a water area of 0.009 square miles. Located at 38.44° N. Lat.; 88.94° W. Long. Elevation is 600 feet.
Population: 430 (1990); 494 (2000); 488 (2007); 488 (2012 projected); Race: 97.5% White, 0.0% Black, 1.4% Asian, 0.8% Hispanic of any race (2007); Density: 233.0 persons per square mile (2007); Average household size: 1.77 (2007); Median age: 50.0 (2007); Males per 100 females: 80.7 (2007); Marriage status: 13.9% never married, 45.5% now married, 18.7% widowed, 22.0% divorced (2000); Foreign born: 0.2% (2000); Ancestry (includes multiple ancestries): 23.3% German, 19.9% United States or American, 16.3% English, 11.4% Irish, 3.2% Other groups (2000).
Economy: Employment by occupation: 11.2% management, 12.2% professional, 22.8% services, 23.4% sales, 3.0% farming, 9.6% construction, 17.8% production (2000).
Income: Per capita income: $14,744 (2007); Median household income: $15,288 (2007); Average household income: $26,164 (2007); Percent of households with income of $100,000 or more: 0.7% (2007); Poverty rate: 22.0% (2000).
Education: Percent of population age 25 and over with: High school diploma (including GED) or higher: 70.9% (2007); Bachelor's degree or higher: 8.4% (2007); Master's degree or higher: 1.9% (2007).

School District(s)

Rome CCSD 2 (KG-08)
2005-06 Enrollment: 323 . . . . (618) 266-7214
Housing: Homeownership rate: 45.8% (2007); Median home value: $90,769 (2007); Median rent: $144 per month (2000); Median age of housing: 20 years (2000).
Transportation: Commute to work: 85.6% car, 3.6% public transportation, 7.2% walk, 3.6% work from home (2000); Travel time to work: 27.1% less than 15 minutes, 62.8% 15 to 30 minutes, 2.1% 30 to 45 minutes, 1.6% 45 to 60 minutes, 6.4% 60 minutes or more (2000)

INA (village). Covers a land area of 2.405 square miles and a water area of 0 square miles. Located at 38.15° N. Lat.; 88.90° W. Long. Elevation is 430 feet.
Population: 722 (1990); 2,455 (2000); 2,494 (2007); 2,512 (2012 projected); Race: 38.5% White, 57.7% Black, 0.4% Asian, 8.3% Hispanic of any race (2007); Density: 1,036.8 persons per square mile (2007); Average household size: 12.41 (2007); Median age: 33.4 (2007); Males per 100 females: 905.6 (2007); Marriage status: 4.2% never married, 74.0% now married, 3.3% widowed, 18.6% divorced (2000); Foreign born: 1.8% (2000); Ancestry (includes multiple ancestries): 3.6% German, 2.6% Irish, 2.3% United States or American, 1.6% English, 1.6% Other groups (2000).
Economy: Single-family building permits issued: 0 (2007); Multi-family building permits issued: 0 (2007); Employment by occupation: 8.3% management, 7.8% professional, 22.5% services, 25.5% sales, 0.0% farming, 10.8% construction, 25.0% production (2000).
Income: Per capita income: $9,158 (2007); Median household income: $31,250 (2007); Average household income: $45,746 (2007); Percent of households with income of $100,000 or more: 10.9% (2007); Poverty rate: 19.2% (2000).
Education: Percent of population age 25 and over with: High school diploma (including GED) or higher: 33.4% (2007); Bachelor's degree or higher: 1.4% (2007); Master's degree or higher: 0.8% (2007).

School District(s)

Dept of Corrections Sch Dist 428 (08-12)
2005-06 Enrollment: 2,271 . . . . (217) 522-2666
Ina CCSD 8 (KG-08)
2005-06 Enrollment: 136 . . . . (618) 437-5361

Two-year College(s)

Rend Lake College (Public)
Fall 2007 Enrollment: 4,821 . . . . (618) 437-5321
2007-08 Tuition: In-state $3,264; Out-of-state $4,800
Housing: Homeownership rate: 71.6% (2007); Median home value: $60,000 (2007); Median rent: $188 per month (2000); Median age of housing: 38 years (2000).
Transportation: Commute to work: 93.5% car, 0.0% public transportation, 3.0% walk, 3.0% work from home (2000); Travel time to work: 31.3% less than 15 minutes, 48.2% 15 to 30 minutes, 9.7% 30 to 45 minutes, 2.1% 45 to 60 minutes, 8.7% 60 minutes or more (2000)

MOUNT VERNON (city). County seat. Covers a land area of 11.521 square miles and a water area of 0.099 square miles. Located at 38.31° N. Lat.; 88.90° W. Long. Elevation is 512 feet.
History: Mount Vernon was settled by people from the southern states. It grew slowly as the seat of Jefferson County after 1819.
Population: 17,465 (1990); 16,269 (2000); 16,182 (2007); 16,057 (2012 projected); Race: 84.7% White, 11.3% Black, 1.2% Asian, 1.7% Hispanic of any race (2007); Density: 1,404.5 persons per square mile (2007); Average household size: 2.30 (2007); Median age: 38.5 (2007); Males per 100 females: 86.3 (2007); Marriage status: 21.9% never married, 53.7% now married, 11.3% widowed, 13.0% divorced (2000); Foreign born: 1.1% (2000); Ancestry (includes multiple ancestries): 16.6% German, 16.3% Other groups, 16.0% United States or American, 10.8% English, 9.1% Irish (2000).
Economy: Single-family building permits issued: 23 (2007); Multi-family building permits issued: 8 (2007); Employment by occupation: 9.7% management, 19.7% professional, 18.4% services, 27.9% sales, 0.3% farming, 8.2% construction, 15.7% production (2000).
Income: Per capita income: $19,199 (2007); Median household income: $31,884 (2007); Average household income: $43,385 (2007); Percent of households with income of $100,000 or more: 7.1% (2007); Poverty rate: 17.1% (2000).
Education: Percent of population age 25 and over with: High school diploma (including GED) or higher: 78.0% (2007); Bachelor's degree or higher: 17.6% (2007); Master's degree or higher: 6.2% (2007).

School District(s)

Bethel SD 82 (KG-08)
2005-06 Enrollment: 117 . . . . (618) 244-8095
Dodds CCSD 7 (KG-08)
2005-06 Enrollment: 162 . . . . (618) 244-8070
Franklin-Jefferson Co Sp Ed Dist
2005-06 Enrollment: n/a . . . . (618) 439-7231
Hamilton/Jefferson Roe (06-12)
2005-06 Enrollment: 72 . . . . (618) 244-8040
Mcclellan CCSD 12 (KG-08)
2005-06 Enrollment: 71 . . . . (618) 244-8072
Mount Vernon SD 80 (PK-08)
2005-06 Enrollment: 1,814 . . . . (618) 244-8080
Mt Vernon Area Voc Center
2005-06 Enrollment: n/a . . . . (618) 246-5602
Mt Vernon Twp HSD 201 (09-12)
2005-06 Enrollment: 1,320 . . . . (618) 244-3700
Summersville SD 79 (PK-08)
2005-06 Enrollment: 298 . . . . (618) 244-8079
Housing: Homeownership rate: 60.0% (2007); Median home value: $72,260 (2007); Median rent: $303 per month (2000); Median age of housing: 40 years (2000).
Hospitals: Crossroads Community Hospital (55 beds); Good Samaritan Regional Health Center (175 beds)
Safety: Violent crime rate: 166.4 per 10,000 population; Property crime rate: 758.7 per 10,000 population (2006).
Newspapers: Health Watch - Register News (Local news; Circulation 0); Morning Sentinel (Regional news; Circulation 16,000); Mount Vernon Register-News (Local news; Circulation 15,000); Vernois News (Community news; Circulation 2,000)
Transportation: Commute to work: 92.1% car, 1.4% public transportation, 2.7% walk, 2.4% work from home (2000); Travel time to work: 60.7% less than 15 minutes, 24.4% 15 to 30 minutes, 8.8% 30 to 45 minutes, 1.7% 45 to 60 minutes, 4.5% 60 minutes or more (2000)
Additional Information Contacts

City of Mount Vernon . . . . (618) 242-0746
http://www.mtvernon.com
Jefferson County Chamber of Commerce . . . . (618) 242-5725
http://www.southernillinois.com

NASON (city). Covers a land area of 0.903 square miles and a water area of 0 square miles. Located at 38.17° N. Lat.; 88.96° W. Long. Elevation is 436 feet.

Population: 235 (1990); 234 (2000); 222 (2007); 216 (2012 projected); Race: 99.1% White, 0.0% Black, 0.0% Asian, 0.0% Hispanic of any race (2007); Density: 245.7 persons per square mile (2007); Average household size: 2.29 (2007); Median age: 43.1 (2007); Males per 100 females: 122.0 (2007); Marriage status: 20.1% never married, 51.7% now married, 8.6% widowed, 19.5% divorced (2000); Foreign born: 0.0% (2000); Ancestry (includes multiple ancestries): 26.8% Irish, 25.8% German, 9.6% United States or American, 9.6% English, 5.1% Other groups (2000).

Economy: Employment by occupation: 3.6% management, 6.3% professional, 27.7% services, 23.2% sales, 0.0% farming, 17.9% construction, 21.4% production (2000).

Income: Per capita income: $19,291 (2007); Median household income: $38,500 (2007); Average household income: $44,149 (2007); Percent of households with income of $100,000 or more: 5.2% (2007); Poverty rate: 4.6% (2000).

Education: Percent of population age 25 and over with: High school diploma (including GED) or higher: 78.4% (2007); Bachelor's degree or higher: 6.4% (2007); Master's degree or higher: 1.2% (2007).

Housing: Homeownership rate: 92.8% (2007); Median home value: $46,000 (2007); Median rent: $200 per month (2000); Median age of housing: 39 years (2000).

Transportation: Commute to work: 100.0% car, 0.0% public transportation, 0.0% walk, 0.0% work from home (2000); Travel time to work: 11.8% less than 15 minutes, 54.5% 15 to 30 minutes, 10.9% 30 to 45 minutes, 12.7% 45 to 60 minutes, 10.0% 60 minutes or more (2000)

OPDYKE (unincorporated postal area, zip code 62872). Covers a land area of 27.292 square miles and a water area of 0.033 square miles. Located at 38.28° N. Lat.; 88.79° W. Long. Elevation is 515 feet.

Population: 1,327 (2000); Race: 98.9% White, 0.2% Black, 0.1% Asian, 3.3% Hispanic of any race (2000); Density: 48.6 persons per square mile (2000); Age: 33.5% under 18, 8.7% over 64 (2000); Marriage status: 18.3% never married, 69.1% now married, 5.1% widowed, 7.5% divorced (2000); Foreign born: 0.3% (2000); Ancestry (includes multiple ancestries): 20.9% German, 15.4% United States or American, 10.4% Irish, 8.3% English, 7.6% Other groups (2000).

Economy: Employment by occupation: 10.8% management, 11.5% professional, 16.7% services, 22.3% sales, 0.7% farming, 12.5% construction, 25.6% production (2000).

Income: Per capita income: $14,881 (2000); Median household income: $38,854 (2000); Poverty rate: 12.7% (2000).

Education: Percent of population age 25 and over with: High school diploma (including GED) or higher: 76.8% (2000); Bachelor's degree or higher: 8.0% (2000).

School District(s)

Opdyke-Belle-Rive CCSD 5 (KG-08)
2005-06 Enrollment: 174 . . . . (618) 756-2492

Housing: Homeownership rate: 92.0% (2000); Median home value: $68,700 (2000); Median rent: $241 per month (2000); Median age of housing: 25 years (2000).

Transportation: Commute to work: 93.1% car, 0.7% public transportation, 2.0% walk, 2.9% work from home (2000); Travel time to work: 23.6% less than 15 minutes, 57.8% 15 to 30 minutes, 10.8% 30 to 45 minutes, 3.0% 45 to 60 minutes, 4.9% 60 minutes or more (2000)

SCHELLER (unincorporated postal area, zip code 62883). Covers a land area of 38.171 square miles and a water area of 0.082 square miles. Located at 38.16° N. Lat.; 89.11° W. Long. Elevation is 509 feet.

Population: 607 (2000); Race: 100.0% White, 0.0% Black, 0.0% Asian, 0.5% Hispanic of any race (2000); Density: 15.9 persons per square mile (2000); Age: 17.0% under 18, 20.5% over 64 (2000); Marriage status: 21.2% never married, 61.6% now married, 8.9% widowed, 8.3% divorced (2000); Foreign born: 0.0% (2000); Ancestry (includes multiple ancestries): 43.0% Polish, 24.3% German, 9.6% Irish, 8.9% United States or American, 8.4% English (2000).

Economy: Employment by occupation: 11.5% management, 17.5% professional, 10.5% services, 15.4% sales, 2.1% farming, 10.8% construction, 32.2% production (2000).

Income: Per capita income: $21,207 (2000); Median household income: $43,021 (2000); Poverty rate: 1.4% (2000).

Education: Percent of population age 25 and over with: High school diploma (including GED) or higher: 80.9% (2000); Bachelor's degree or higher: 5.9% (2000).

Housing: Homeownership rate: 86.0% (2000); Median home value: $68,700 (2000); Median rent: $186 per month (2000); Median age of housing: 28 years (2000).

Transportation: Commute to work: 88.8% car, 0.0% public transportation, 4.0% walk, 5.8% work from home (2000); Travel time to work: 27.5% less than 15 minutes, 24.8% 15 to 30 minutes, 28.6% 30 to 45 minutes, 14.5% 45 to 60 minutes, 4.6% 60 minutes or more (2000)

TEXICO (unincorporated postal area, zip code 62889). Covers a land area of 34.835 square miles and a water area of 0.062 square miles. Located at 38.45° N. Lat.; 88.82° W. Long. Elevation is 512 feet.

Population: 943 (2000); Race: 97.1% White, 1.8% Black, 0.0% Asian, 0.0% Hispanic of any race (2000); Density: 27.1 persons per square mile (2000); Age: 25.9% under 18, 13.4% over 64 (2000); Marriage status: 19.6% never married, 66.4% now married, 6.4% widowed, 7.7% divorced (2000); Foreign born: 0.4% (2000); Ancestry (includes multiple ancestries): 20.4% United States or American, 16.9% English, 12.3% Other groups, 10.7% German, 8.6% Irish (2000).

Economy: Employment by occupation: 8.9% management, 10.2% professional, 14.9% services, 23.1% sales, 0.0% farming, 12.2% construction, 30.7% production (2000).

Income: Per capita income: $17,291 (2000); Median household income: $38,452 (2000); Poverty rate: 16.0% (2000).

Education: Percent of population age 25 and over with: High school diploma (including GED) or higher: 83.3% (2000); Bachelor's degree or higher: 8.1% (2000).

School District(s)

Field CCSD 3 (PK-08)
2005-06 Enrollment: 313 . . . . (618) 755-4611

Housing: Homeownership rate: 89.7% (2000); Median home value: $43,200 (2000); Median rent: $341 per month (2000); Median age of housing: 28 years (2000).

Transportation: Commute to work: 94.4% car, 1.8% public transportation, 0.4% walk, 2.0% work from home (2000); Travel time to work: 9.1% less than 15 minutes, 58.1% 15 to 30 minutes, 15.9% 30 to 45 minutes, 4.6% 45 to 60 minutes, 12.3% 60 minutes or more (2000)

WALTONVILLE (village). Covers a land area of 0.958 square miles and a water area of 0.026 square miles. Located at 38.21° N. Lat.; 89.04° W. Long. Elevation is 463 feet.

Population: 396 (1990); 422 (2000); 491 (2007); 519 (2012 projected); Race: 98.8% White, 0.0% Black, 0.0% Asian, 1.2% Hispanic of any race (2007); Density: 512.6 persons per square mile (2007); Average household size: 2.36 (2007); Median age: 35.5 (2007); Males per 100 females: 86.7 (2007); Marriage status: 6.9% never married, 75.3% now married, 7.2% widowed, 10.5% divorced (2000); Foreign born: 0.7% (2000); Ancestry (includes multiple ancestries): 17.1% German, 15.4% Irish, 12.7% United States or American, 8.3% English, 6.6% Other groups (2000).

Economy: Employment by occupation: 12.2% management, 16.0% professional, 4.6% services, 22.9% sales, 0.0% farming, 14.5% construction, 29.8% production (2000).

Income: Per capita income: $14,715 (2007); Median household income: $29,130 (2007); Average household income: $34,736 (2007); Percent of households with income of $100,000 or more: 1.9% (2007); Poverty rate: 16.6% (2000).

Education: Percent of population age 25 and over with: High school diploma (including GED) or higher: 70.7% (2007); Bachelor's degree or higher: 6.4% (2007); Master's degree or higher: 0.0% (2007).

School District(s)

Waltonville CUSD 1 (PK-12)
2005-06 Enrollment: 368 . . . . (618) 279-7211

Housing: Homeownership rate: 73.1% (2007); Median home value: $65,000 (2007); Median rent: $218 per month (2000); Median age of housing: 52 years (2000).

Transportation: Commute to work: 89.9% car, 0.0% public transportation, 6.2% walk, 3.9% work from home (2000); Travel time to work: 25.0% less

than 15 minutes, 46.0% 15 to 30 minutes, 16.1% 30 to 45 minutes, 4.8% 45 to 60 minutes, 8.1% 60 minutes or more (2000)

WOODLAWN (village). Covers a land area of 0.714 square miles and a water area of 0 square miles. Located at 38.33° N. Lat.; 89.03° W. Long. Elevation is 492 feet.
Population: 582 (1990); 630 (2000); 683 (2007); 693 (2012 projected); Race: 98.4% White, 0.4% Black, 0.0% Asian, 0.0% Hispanic of any race (2007); Density: 956.5 persons per square mile (2007); Average household size: 2.57 (2007); Median age: 35.5 (2007); Males per 100 females: 88.2 (2007); Marriage status: 14.6% never married, 66.9% now married, 8.2% widowed, 10.4% divorced (2000); Foreign born: 0.6% (2000); Ancestry (includes multiple ancestries): 19.4% German, 13.6% United States or American, 9.1% English, 8.3% Polish, 8.0% Irish (2000).
Economy: Employment by occupation: 8.4% management, 16.8% professional, 14.2% services, 28.1% sales, 0.0% farming, 8.0% construction, 24.5% production (2000).
Income: Per capita income: $20,897 (2007); Median household income: $47,368 (2007); Average household income: $53,656 (2007); Percent of households with income of $100,000 or more: 8.3% (2007); Poverty rate: 11.4% (2000).
Education: Percent of population age 25 and over with: High school diploma (including GED) or higher: 90.2% (2007); Bachelor's degree or higher: 14.0% (2007); Master's degree or higher: 5.1% (2007).

School District(s)

Woodlawn CCSD 4 (KG-08)
2005-06 Enrollment: 314 . . . . (618) 735-2661
Woodlawn CHSD 205 (09-12)
2005-06 Enrollment: 205 . . . . (618) 735-2631

Housing: Homeownership rate: 78.9% (2007); Median home value: $76,875 (2007); Median rent: $148 per month (2000); Median age of housing: 20 years (2000).
Transportation: Commute to work: 93.0% car, 0.0% public transportation, 4.4% walk, 1.8% work from home (2000); Travel time to work: 41.4% less than 15 minutes, 39.5% 15 to 30 minutes, 15.8% 30 to 45 minutes, 1.9% 45 to 60 minutes, 1.5% 60 minutes or more (2000)

Jersey County

Located in western Illinois; bounded on the south by the Mississippi River and the Missouri border, and on the west by the Illinois River. Covers a land area of 369.16 square miles, a water area of 7.86 square miles, and is located in the Central Time Zone. The county was founded in 1839. County seat is Jerseyville.

Jersey County is part of the St. Louis, MO-IL Metropolitan Statistical Area. The entire metro area includes: Bond County, IL; Calhoun County, IL; Clinton County, IL; Jersey County, IL; Macoupin County, IL; Madison County, IL; Monroe County, IL; St. Clair County, IL; Crawford County, MO (pt.)*; Franklin County, MO; Jefferson County, MO; Lincoln County, MO; St. Charles County, MO; St. Louis County, MO; Warren County, MO; Washington County, MO; St. Louis city, MO

Weather Station: Jerseyville 2 SW — Elevation: 629 feet

	Jan	Feb	Mar	Apr	May	Jun	Jul	Aug	Sep	Oct	Nov	Dec
High	35	41	53	65	75	83	88	86	79	68	53	41
Low	17	22	32	42	52	61	65	63	54	43	33	23
Precip	1.9	2.0	3.5	4.3	3.9	3.7	3.4	2.9	3.4	2.9	3.7	2.8
Snow	5.1	3.7	2.8	0.5	0.0	0.0	0.0	0.0	0.0	tr	1.2	3.5

High and Low temperatures in degrees Fahrenheit; Precipitation and Snow in inches

Population: 20,539 (1990); 21,668 (2000); 22,686 (2007); 23,339 (2012 projected); Race: 97.4% White, 1.2% Black, 0.4% Asian, 1.0% Hispanic of any race (2007); Density: 61.5 persons per square mile (2007); Average household size: 2.62 (2007); Median age: 38.5 (2007); Males per 100 females: 95.9 (2007).
Religion: Five largest groups: 20.1% Catholic Church, 6.8% American Baptist Churches in the USA, 6.2% Southern Baptist Convention, 4.9% Assemblies of God, 3.7% The United Methodist Church (2000).
Economy: Unemployment rate: 5.1% (4/2008); Total civilian labor force: 12,158 (4/2008); Leading industries: 21.2% retail trade; 21.1% health care and social assistance; 16.1% accommodation & food services (2005); Farms: 520 totaling 173,144 acres (2002); Companies that employ 500 or more persons: 0 (2006); Companies that employ 100 to 499 persons: 5 (2006); Companies that employ less than 100 persons: 441 (2006); Black-owned businesses: n/a (2002); Hispanic-owned businesses: n/a (2002); Asian-owned businesses: n/a (2002); Women-owned businesses: n/a (2002); Retail sales per capita: $13,233 (2008). Single-family building permits issued: 72 (2007); Multi-family building permits issued: 23 (2007).
Income: Per capita income: $23,857 (2007); Median household income: $50,076 (2007); Average household income: $61,503 (2007); Percent of households with income of $100,000 or more: 14.2% (2007); Poverty rate: 8.2% (2005); Bankruptcy rate: 1.91% (2007).
Education: Percent of population age 25 and over with: High school diploma (including GED) or higher: 82.8% (2007); Bachelor's degree or higher: 12.6% (2007); Master's degree or higher: 4.3% (2007).
Housing: Homeownership rate: 77.6% (2007); Median home value: $119,708 (2007); Median rent: $319 per month (2000); Median age of housing: 32 years (2000).
Health: Birth rate: 122.0 per 10,000 population (2007); Death rate: 103.3 per 10,000 population (2007); Age-adjusted cancer mortality rate: 186.1 deaths per 100,000 population (2005); Air Quality Index: 81.4% good, 17.8% moderate, 0.8% unhealthy for sensitive individuals, 0.0% unhealthy (percent of days in 2007); Number of physicians: 9.9 per 10,000 population (2005); Hospital beds: 30.3 per 10,000 population (2004); Hospital admissions: 917.3 per 10,000 population (2004).
Elections: 2004 Presidential election results: 53.6% Bush, 45.3% Kerry, 0.0% Nader, 1.0% Badnarik
National and State Parks: Pere Marquette State Park; Stump Lake State Fish And Waterfowl Manageme; The Glades State Fish And Waterfowl Manageme

Additional Information Contacts

Jersey County Government . . . . (618) 498-5571

City of Jerseyville . . . . (618) 498-3312
http://www.jerseyville-il.us
Jersey County Business Association . . . . (618) 639-5222
http://www.jerseycounty.org

Jersey County Communities

DOW (unincorporated postal area, zip code 62022). Covers a land area of 17.512 square miles and a water area of 0.001 square miles. Located at 38.99° N. Lat.; 90.34° W. Long. Elevation is 673 feet.
Population: 962 (2000); Race: 97.8% White, 0.7% Black, 0.5% Asian, 0.0% Hispanic of any race (2000); Density: 54.9 persons per square mile (2000); Age: 16.5% under 18, 14.9% over 64 (2000); Marriage status: 15.9% never married, 68.1% now married, 4.4% widowed, 11.6% divorced (2000); Foreign born: 2.0% (2000); Ancestry (includes multiple ancestries): 32.9% German, 14.1% United States or American, 13.1% Irish, 8.0% English, 5.8% Other groups (2000).
Economy: Employment by occupation: 11.9% management, 22.2% professional, 15.9% services, 23.6% sales, 0.0% farming, 14.5% construction, 11.9% production (2000).
Income: Per capita income: $24,943 (2000); Median household income: $48,750 (2000); Poverty rate: 3.3% (2000).
Education: Percent of population age 25 and over with: High school diploma (including GED) or higher: 85.0% (2000); Bachelor's degree or higher: 11.5% (2000).

School District(s)

Jersey CUSD 100 (PK-12)
2005-06 Enrollment: 2,944 . . . . (618) 498-5561

Housing: Homeownership rate: 94.0% (2000); Median home value: $81,500 (2000); Median rent: $425 per month (2000); Median age of housing: 33 years (2000).
Transportation: Commute to work: 90.2% car, 1.2% public transportation, 0.0% walk, 8.6% work from home (2000); Travel time to work: 9.4% less than 15 minutes, 37.9% 15 to 30 minutes, 30.3% 30 to 45 minutes, 14.6% 45 to 60 minutes, 7.8% 60 minutes or more (2000)

ELSAH (village). Covers a land area of 1.062 square miles and a water area of 0 square miles. Located at 38.95° N. Lat.; 90.35° W. Long. Elevation is 433 feet.
History: The first settler in Elsah was Addision Greene in 1847, who chopped wood for the steamboats that came along the Mississippi River. The settlement of Jersey Landing developed and was purchased in 1853 by General James Semple, who changed its name to Elsah and built a distillery and two grist mills.
Population: 851 (1990); 635 (2000); 644 (2007); 649 (2012 projected); Race: 84.9% White, 9.0% Black, 1.2% Asian, 4.2% Hispanic of any race (2007); Density: 606.6 persons per square mile (2007); Average household

size: 8.59 (2007); Median age: 21.1 (2007); Males per 100 females: 73.1 (2007); Marriage status: 62.2% never married, 34.3% now married, 2.5% widowed, 1.0% divorced (2000); Foreign born: 13.3% (2000); Ancestry (includes multiple ancestries): 31.2% German, 19.7% English, 13.0% Other groups, 9.3% Scottish, 7.0% Irish (2000).
Economy: Single-family building permits issued: 0 (2007); Multi-family building permits issued: 0 (2007); Employment by occupation: 9.3% management, 24.0% professional, 16.9% services, 43.3% sales, 0.0% farming, 2.0% construction, 4.6% production (2000).
Income: Per capita income: $14,958 (2007); Median household income: $64,821 (2007); Average household income: $87,167 (2007); Percent of households with income of $100,000 or more: 29.3% (2007); Poverty rate: 0.0% (2000).
Education: Percent of population age 25 and over with: High school diploma (including GED) or higher: 97.0% (2007); Bachelor's degree or higher: 71.3% (2007); Master's degree or higher: 34.7% (2007).

Four-year College(s)

Principia College (Private, Not-for-profit)
Fall 2007 Enrollment: n/a. . . . . (618) 374-2131
2007-08 Tuition: In-state $22,080; Out-of-state $22,080
Housing: Homeownership rate: 66.7% (2007); Median home value: $204,545 (2007); Median rent: $380 per month (2000); Median age of housing: 60+ years (2000).
Transportation: Commute to work: 15.9% car, 0.5% public transportation, 71.6% walk, 3.7% work from home (2000); Travel time to work: 87.3% less than 15 minutes, 2.0% 15 to 30 minutes, 2.0% 30 to 45 minutes, 4.8% 45 to 60 minutes, 3.8% 60 minutes or more (2000)

FIDELITY (village). Covers a land area of 0.112 square miles and a water area of 0 square miles. Located at 39.15° N. Lat.; 90.16° W. Long. Elevation is 636 feet.
Population: 66 (1990); 105 (2000); 95 (2007); 95 (2012 projected); Race: 100.0% White, 0.0% Black, 0.0% Asian, 0.0% Hispanic of any race (2007); Density: 851.6 persons per square mile (2007); Average household size: 2.50 (2007); Median age: 38.7 (2007); Males per 100 females: 97.9 (2007); Marriage status: 15.2% never married, 65.8% now married, 6.3% widowed, 12.7% divorced (2000); Foreign born: 0.0% (2000); Ancestry (includes multiple ancestries): 35.9% Other groups, 10.7% United States or American, 9.7% German, 6.8% French (except Basque), 5.8% Irish (2000).
Economy: Employment by occupation: 7.1% management, 0.0% professional, 25.0% services, 17.9% sales, 0.0% farming, 28.6% construction, 21.4% production (2000).
Income: Per capita income: $10,684 (2007); Median household income: $20,000 (2007); Average household income: $26,711 (2007); Percent of households with income of $100,000 or more: 0.0% (2007); Poverty rate: 28.2% (2000).
Education: Percent of population age 25 and over with: High school diploma (including GED) or higher: 71.4% (2007); Bachelor's degree or higher: 4.8% (2007); Master's degree or higher: 0.0% (2007).
Housing: Homeownership rate: 63.2% (2007); Median home value: $22,500 (2007); Median rent: $283 per month (2000); Median age of housing: 40 years (2000).
Transportation: Commute to work: 100.0% car, 0.0% public transportation, 0.0% walk, 0.0% work from home (2000); Travel time to work: 15.4% less than 15 minutes, 26.9% 15 to 30 minutes, 30.8% 30 to 45 minutes, 0.0% 45 to 60 minutes, 26.9% 60 minutes or more (2000)

FIELDON (village). Covers a land area of 0.199 square miles and a water area of 0 square miles. Located at 39.10° N. Lat.; 90.50° W. Long. Elevation is 692 feet.
Population: 284 (1990); 271 (2000); 337 (2007); 378 (2012 projected); Race: 100.0% White, 0.0% Black, 0.0% Asian, 1.8% Hispanic of any race (2007); Density: 1,693.9 persons per square mile (2007); Average household size: 2.59 (2007); Median age: 39.0 (2007); Males per 100 females: 101.8 (2007); Marriage status: 18.8% never married, 70.8% now married, 5.4% widowed, 5.0% divorced (2000); Foreign born: 0.0% (2000); Ancestry (includes multiple ancestries): 41.7% German, 9.3% Irish, 6.2% Dutch, 3.5% United States or American, 2.7% French (except Basque) (2000).
Economy: Single-family building permits issued: 0 (2007); Multi-family building permits issued: 0 (2007); Employment by occupation: 4.8% management, 14.4% professional, 22.1% services, 13.5% sales, 1.0% farming, 15.4% construction, 28.8% production (2000).
Income: Per capita income: $18,887 (2007); Median household income: $44,545 (2007); Average household income: $48,962 (2007); Percent of households with income of $100,000 or more: 2.3% (2007); Poverty rate: 0.8% (2000).
Education: Percent of population age 25 and over with: High school diploma (including GED) or higher: 79.1% (2007); Bachelor's degree or higher: 6.5% (2007); Master's degree or higher: 1.3% (2007).

School District(s)

Jersey CUSD 100 (PK-12)
2005-06 Enrollment: 2,944 . . . . (618) 498-5561
Housing: Homeownership rate: 85.4% (2007); Median home value: $65,833 (2007); Median rent: $363 per month (2000); Median age of housing: 47 years (2000).
Transportation: Commute to work: 94.2% car, 0.0% public transportation, 1.9% walk, 3.9% work from home (2000); Travel time to work: 12.1% less than 15 minutes, 52.5% 15 to 30 minutes, 11.1% 30 to 45 minutes, 11.1% 45 to 60 minutes, 13.1% 60 minutes or more (2000)

GRAFTON (city). Covers a land area of 4.056 square miles and a water area of 0 square miles. Located at 38.97° N. Lat.; 90.43° W. Long. Elevation is 449 feet.
History: City suffered greatly during a devastating flood (1993). Incorporated 1837.
Population: 923 (1990); 609 (2000); 608 (2007); 638 (2012 projected); Race: 98.0% White, 1.0% Black, 0.0% Asian, 0.7% Hispanic of any race (2007); Density: 149.9 persons per square mile (2007); Average household size: 2.25 (2007); Median age: 45.4 (2007); Males per 100 females: 94.2 (2007); Marriage status: 21.3% never married, 53.6% now married, 9.3% widowed, 15.9% divorced (2000); Foreign born: 1.1% (2000); Ancestry (includes multiple ancestries): 25.2% German, 17.9% English, 13.2% Irish, 12.2% United States or American, 5.4% Other groups (2000).
Economy: Single-family building permits issued: 5 (2007); Multi-family building permits issued: 0 (2007); Employment by occupation: 15.8% management, 8.8% professional, 24.2% services, 16.9% sales, 0.8% farming, 9.2% construction, 24.2% production (2000).
Income: Per capita income: $29,391 (2007); Median household income: $46,053 (2007); Average household income: $66,185 (2007); Percent of households with income of $100,000 or more: 16.7% (2007); Poverty rate: 14.0% (2000).
Education: Percent of population age 25 and over with: High school diploma (including GED) or higher: 80.0% (2007); Bachelor's degree or higher: 12.0% (2007); Master's degree or higher: 2.6% (2007).

School District(s)

Dept of Corrections Sch Dist 428 (08-12)
2005-06 Enrollment: 2,271 . . . . (217) 522-2666
Jersey CUSD 100 (PK-12)
2005-06 Enrollment: 2,944 . . . . (618) 498-5561
Housing: Homeownership rate: 68.9% (2007); Median home value: $108,333 (2007); Median rent: $282 per month (2000); Median age of housing: 32 years (2000).
Safety: Violent crime rate: 144.5 per 10,000 population; Property crime rate: 332.4 per 10,000 population (2006).
Transportation: Commute to work: 93.1% car, 0.8% public transportation, 6.2% walk, 0.0% work from home (2000); Travel time to work: 36.2% less than 15 minutes, 17.7% 15 to 30 minutes, 20.4% 30 to 45 minutes, 12.7% 45 to 60 minutes, 13.1% 60 minutes or more (2000)

JERSEYVILLE (city). County seat. Covers a land area of 4.392 square miles and a water area of 0 square miles. Located at 39.12° N. Lat.; 90.32° W. Long. Elevation is 659 feet.
History: Plotted 1834, incorporated 1855.
Population: 7,637 (1990); 7,984 (2000); 8,453 (2007); 8,652 (2012 projected); Race: 98.8% White, 0.2% Black, 0.2% Asian, 0.8% Hispanic of any race (2007); Density: 1,924.7 persons per square mile (2007); Average household size: 2.40 (2007); Median age: 39.1 (2007); Males per 100 females: 87.0 (2007); Marriage status: 19.9% never married, 55.6% now married, 11.4% widowed, 13.0% divorced (2000); Foreign born: 0.2% (2000); Ancestry (includes multiple ancestries): 32.6% German, 12.2% Irish, 11.9% English, 11.1% United States or American, 6.0% Other groups (2000).
Economy: Single-family building permits issued: 22 (2007); Multi-family building permits issued: 23 (2007); Employment by occupation: 9.3% management, 18.2% professional, 18.1% services, 27.3% sales, 0.0% farming, 11.7% construction, 15.3% production (2000).
Income: Per capita income: $24,955 (2007); Median household income: $44,496 (2007); Average household income: $58,400 (2007); Percent of

households with income of $100,000 or more: 13.7% (2007); Poverty rate: 7.3% (2000).
Education: Percent of population age 25 and over with: High school diploma (including GED) or higher: 76.7% (2007); Bachelor's degree or higher: 11.3% (2007); Master's degree or higher: 4.2% (2007).

School District(s)

Calhoun/Greene/Jersey/Macoupn Roe (06-12)
2005-06 Enrollment: 73 . . . . (217) 854-4016
Jersey CUSD 100 (PK-12)
2005-06 Enrollment: 2,944 . . . . (618) 498-5561
Housing: Homeownership rate: 66.8% (2007); Median home value: $108,942 (2007); Median rent: $309 per month (2000); Median age of housing: 42 years (2000).
Hospitals: Jersey Community Hospital (67 beds)
Safety: Violent crime rate: 31.8 per 10,000 population; Property crime rate: 462.9 per 10,000 population (2006).
Newspapers: Jersey County Star (Local news; Circulation 1,500); Quad County Edition of the Telegraph (Community news; Circulation 9,000)
Transportation: Commute to work: 93.6% car, 0.3% public transportation, 2.1% walk, 2.9% work from home (2000); Travel time to work: 46.1% less than 15 minutes, 15.6% 15 to 30 minutes, 18.5% 30 to 45 minutes, 8.3% 45 to 60 minutes, 11.4% 60 minutes or more (2000)
Additional Information Contacts
City of Jerseyville . . . . (618) 498-3312
http://www.jerseyville-il.us
Jersey County Business Association . . . . (618) 639-5222
http://www.jerseycounty.org

OTTERVILLE (town). Covers a land area of 1.002 square miles and a water area of 0 square miles. Located at 39.05° N. Lat.; 90.39° W. Long. Elevation is 627 feet.
Population: 115 (1990); 120 (2000); 111 (2007); 110 (2012 projected); Race: 95.5% White, 0.0% Black, 0.0% Asian, 3.6% Hispanic of any race (2007); Density: 110.8 persons per square mile (2007); Average household size: 2.85 (2007); Median age: 35.5 (2007); Males per 100 females: 76.2 (2007); Marriage status: 28.6% never married, 59.2% now married, 2.0% widowed, 10.2% divorced (2000); Foreign born: 0.0% (2000); Ancestry (includes multiple ancestries): 50.7% German, 27.8% Other groups, 25.7% Irish, 13.2% United States or American, 4.2% Scottish (2000).
Economy: Employment by occupation: 5.6% management, 5.6% professional, 11.1% services, 42.6% sales, 0.0% farming, 7.4% construction, 27.8% production (2000).
Income: Per capita income: $16,441 (2007); Median household income: $46,875 (2007); Average household income: $46,795 (2007); Percent of households with income of $100,000 or more: 0.0% (2007); Poverty rate: 14.6% (2000).
Education: Percent of population age 25 and over with: High school diploma (including GED) or higher: 70.6% (2007); Bachelor's degree or higher: 1.5% (2007); Master's degree or higher: 1.5% (2007).
Housing: Homeownership rate: 92.3% (2007); Median home value: $80,000 (2007); Median rent: $175 per month (2000); Median age of housing: 35 years (2000).
Transportation: Commute to work: 82.7% car, 0.0% public transportation, 9.6% walk, 7.7% work from home (2000); Travel time to work: 18.8% less than 15 minutes, 41.7% 15 to 30 minutes, 14.6% 30 to 45 minutes, 8.3% 45 to 60 minutes, 16.7% 60 minutes or more (2000)

Jo Daviess County

Located in northwestern Illinois; bounded on the north by Wisconsin, and on the west by the Mississippi River and the Iowa border; drained by the Apple, Plum, and Galena Rivers; includes Charles Mound, highest point in the state (1,241 ft). Covers a land area of 601.08 square miles, a water area of 17.64 square miles, and is located in the Central Time Zone. The county was founded in 1827. County seat is Galena.

Weather Station: Stockton 3 NNE Elevation: 967 feet

	Jan	Feb	Mar	Apr	May	Jun	Jul	Aug	Sep	Oct	Nov	Dec
High	26	31	43	58	70	79	82	80	72	61	44	31
Low	9	15	25	37	48	57	62	59	51	40	28	16
Precip	1.2	1.3	2.4	3.5	3.8	4.6	3.2	4.3	3.9	2.8	2.7	1.6
Snow	8.8	6.5	4.8	2.0	tr	0.0	0.0	0.0	0.0	0.3	2.6	7.4

High and Low temperatures in degrees Fahrenheit; Precipitation and Snow in inches

Population: 21,821 (1990); 22,289 (2000); 22,641 (2007); 22,805 (2012 projected); Race: 98.2% White, 0.4% Black, 0.2% Asian, 2.7% Hispanic of any race (2007); Density: 37.7 persons per square mile (2007); Average household size: 2.33 (2007); Median age: 42.9 (2007); Males per 100 females: 102.1 (2007).
Religion: Five largest groups: 50.0% Catholic Church, 10.6% The United Methodist Church, 10.5% Evangelical Lutheran Church in America, 2.7% Presbyterian Church (U.S.A.), 1.3% Lutheran Church—Missouri Synod (2000).
Economy: Unemployment rate: 5.4% (4/2008); Total civilian labor force: 13,359 (4/2008); Leading industries: 21.1% accommodation & food services; 15.9% manufacturing; 14.6% retail trade (2005); Farms: 989 totaling 264,493 acres (2002); Companies that employ 500 or more persons: 0 (2006); Companies that employ 100 to 499 persons: 14 (2006); Companies that employ less than 100 persons: 772 (2006); Black-owned businesses: n/a (2002); Hispanic-owned businesses: n/a (2002); Asian-owned businesses: n/a (2002); Women-owned businesses: 510 (2002); Retail sales per capita: $10,598 (2008). Single-family building permits issued: 121 (2007); Multi-family building permits issued: 0 (2007).
Income: Per capita income: $25,453 (2007); Median household income: $47,357 (2007); Average household income: $59,069 (2007); Percent of households with income of $100,000 or more: 12.1% (2007); Poverty rate: 9.0% (2005); Bankruptcy rate: 1.12% (2007).
Education: Percent of population age 25 and over with: High school diploma (including GED) or higher: 83.7% (2007); Bachelor's degree or higher: 15.8% (2007); Master's degree or higher: 5.0% (2007).
Housing: Homeownership rate: 78.0% (2007); Median home value: $143,303 (2007); Median rent: $307 per month (2000); Median age of housing: 34 years (2000).
Health: Birth rate: 111.6 per 10,000 population (2007); Death rate: 103.1 per 10,000 population (2007); Age-adjusted cancer mortality rate: 201.7 deaths per 100,000 population (2005); Number of physicians: 8.1 per 10,000 population (2005); Hospital beds: 36.7 per 10,000 population (2004); Hospital admissions: 129.7 per 10,000 population (2004).
Elections: 2004 Presidential election results: 53.3% Bush, 45.8% Kerry, 0.0% Nader, 0.8% Badnarik
National and State Parks: Apple River Canyon State Park
Additional Information Contacts
Jo Daviess County Government . . . . (815) 777-0161
http://www.jodaviess.org
Galena Area Chamber of Commerce . . . . (815) 777-9050
http://www.galenachamber.com
Hanover Chamber of Commerce . . . . (815) 591-3800
http://www.hanover-il.com/biz/chamber.htm
Stockton Area Chamber of Commerce . . . . (815) 947-3963
http://www.stocktonil.com

Jo Daviess County Communities

APPLE RIVER (village). Covers a land area of 0.790 square miles and a water area of 0 square miles. Located at 42.50° N. Lat.; 90.09° W. Long. Elevation is 1,010 feet.
Population: 414 (1990); 379 (2000); 352 (2007); 351 (2012 projected); Race: 97.7% White, 2.3% Black, 0.0% Asian, 0.0% Hispanic of any race (2007); Density: 445.4 persons per square mile (2007); Average household size: 2.30 (2007); Median age: 39.8 (2007); Males per 100 females: 98.9 (2007); Marriage status: 24.2% never married, 53.7% now married, 10.4% widowed, 11.7% divorced (2000); Foreign born: 0.0% (2000); Ancestry (includes multiple ancestries): 38.8% German, 11.4% Irish, 9.7% English, 8.2% Belgian, 7.7% United States or American (2000).
Economy: Employment by occupation: 6.6% management, 8.1% professional, 16.2% services, 20.7% sales, 4.5% farming, 16.7% construction, 27.3% production (2000).
Income: Per capita income: $26,619 (2007); Median household income: $48,542 (2007); Average household income: $61,242 (2007); Percent of households with income of $100,000 or more: 12.4% (2007); Poverty rate: 10.2% (2000).
Education: Percent of population age 25 and over with: High school diploma (including GED) or higher: 74.4% (2007); Bachelor's degree or higher: 6.2% (2007); Master's degree or higher: 2.5% (2007).

School District(s)

Warren CUSD 205 (PK-12)
2005-06 Enrollment: 493 . . . . (815) 745-2653
Housing: Homeownership rate: 70.6% (2007); Median home value: $85,000 (2007); Median rent: $275 per month (2000); Median age of housing: 60+ years (2000).

Transportation: Commute to work: 86.4% car, 0.0% public transportation, 9.1% walk, 4.5% work from home (2000); Travel time to work: 35.4% less than 15 minutes, 22.8% 15 to 30 minutes, 13.8% 30 to 45 minutes, 9.5% 45 to 60 minutes, 18.5% 60 minutes or more (2000)

EAST DUBUQUE (city). Covers a land area of 2.062 square miles and a water area of 0.081 square miles. Located at 42.49° N. Lat.; 90.64° W. Long. Elevation is 610 feet.
History: Incorporated 1857.
Population: 2,130 (1990); 1,995 (2000); 1,894 (2007); 1,869 (2012 projected); Race: 98.7% White, 0.3% Black, 0.3% Asian, 2.0% Hispanic of any race (2007); Density: 918.4 persons per square mile (2007); Average household size: 2.22 (2007); Median age: 39.1 (2007); Males per 100 females: 109.7 (2007); Marriage status: 23.0% never married, 55.6% now married, 8.6% widowed, 12.8% divorced (2000); Foreign born: 0.4% (2000); Ancestry (includes multiple ancestries): 51.8% German, 18.7% Irish, 7.7% United States or American, 5.3% English, 5.0% French (except Basque) (2000).
Economy: Single-family building permits issued: 0 (2007); Multi-family building permits issued: 0 (2007); Employment by occupation: 5.9% management, 12.8% professional, 20.7% services, 27.7% sales, 0.4% farming, 7.9% construction, 24.5% production (2000).
Income: Per capita income: $21,583 (2007); Median household income: $41,050 (2007); Average household income: $47,810 (2007); Percent of households with income of $100,000 or more: 5.6% (2007); Poverty rate: 4.3% (2000).
Education: Percent of population age 25 and over with: High school diploma (including GED) or higher: 78.0% (2007); Bachelor's degree or higher: 8.2% (2007); Master's degree or higher: 1.3% (2007).

School District(s)

East Dubuque USD 119 (PK-12)
2005-06 Enrollment: 657 . . . . (815) 747-3180
Housing: Homeownership rate: 68.7% (2007); Median home value: $123,929 (2007); Median rent: $328 per month (2000); Median age of housing: 52 years (2000).
Safety: Violent crime rate: 146.1 per 10,000 population; Property crime rate: 110.8 per 10,000 population (2006).
Newspapers: East Dubuque Register (Local news; Circulation 1,300)
Transportation: Commute to work: 94.7% car, 0.6% public transportation, 2.3% walk, 1.9% work from home (2000); Travel time to work: 51.9% less than 15 minutes, 36.6% 15 to 30 minutes, 1.8% 30 to 45 minutes, 2.5% 45 to 60 minutes, 7.2% 60 minutes or more (2000)

ELIZABETH (village). Covers a land area of 0.439 square miles and a water area of 0 square miles. Located at 42.31° N. Lat.; 90.22° W. Long. Elevation is 801 feet.
History: Elizabeth was built on the site of the Apple River Fort, established during the Black Hawk War.
Population: 689 (1990); 682 (2000); 641 (2007); 617 (2012 projected); Race: 99.1% White, 0.5% Black, 0.0% Asian, 0.2% Hispanic of any race (2007); Density: 1,461.4 persons per square mile (2007); Average household size: 2.13 (2007); Median age: 49.6 (2007); Males per 100 females: 85.3 (2007); Marriage status: 21.5% never married, 48.8% now married, 17.6% widowed, 12.2% divorced (2000); Foreign born: 2.2% (2000); Ancestry (includes multiple ancestries): 50.1% German, 13.2% Irish, 13.1% English, 2.6% Dutch, 2.0% United States or American (2000).
Economy: Employment by occupation: 6.7% management, 13.7% professional, 22.5% services, 24.6% sales, 0.6% farming, 18.7% construction, 13.2% production (2000).
Income: Per capita income: $19,200 (2007); Median household income: $36,466 (2007); Average household income: $40,141 (2007); Percent of households with income of $100,000 or more: 2.7% (2007); Poverty rate: 8.2% (2000).
Education: Percent of population age 25 and over with: High school diploma (including GED) or higher: 79.1% (2007); Bachelor's degree or higher: 10.2% (2007); Master's degree or higher: 3.7% (2007).

School District(s)

Jo Daviess-Carroll Area Voc Ctr
2005-06 Enrollment: n/a . . . . (815) 858-2203
Housing: Homeownership rate: 73.4% (2007); Median home value: $107,008 (2007); Median rent: $354 per month (2000); Median age of housing: 60+ years (2000).
Safety: Violent crime rate: 0.0 per 10,000 population; Property crime rate: 14.9 per 10,000 population (2006).
Transportation: Commute to work: 83.6% car, 0.0% public transportation, 11.1% walk, 4.7% work from home (2000); Travel time to work: 43.3% less than 15 minutes, 31.0% 15 to 30 minutes, 11.0% 30 to 45 minutes, 9.8% 45 to 60 minutes, 4.9% 60 minutes or more (2000)

GALENA (city). County seat. Covers a land area of 3.735 square miles and a water area of <.001 square miles. Located at 42.41° N. Lat.; 90.43° W. Long. Elevation is 633 feet.
History: The lead deposits in the Galena area interested French explorers in the 1700's. The town of Galena was laid out in 1826 and named for the mineral galena, the principal ore of lead. By this time the government was controlling the mineral lands and issuing leases. Smelter operations were responsible for Galena's early growth, and traffic on the old Fever River made it a trading center until the middle of the 1800's, when the lead veins were exhausted and the river silted in. Ulysses S. Grant was a resident of Galena when he was chosen to lead the Federal troops in the Civil War.
Population: 3,680 (1990); 3,460 (2000); 3,390 (2007); 3,359 (2012 projected); Race: 96.3% White, 0.6% Black, 0.5% Asian, 9.3% Hispanic of any race (2007); Density: 907.7 persons per square mile (2007); Average household size: 2.12 (2007); Median age: 45.6 (2007); Males per 100 females: 96.5 (2007); Marriage status: 22.8% never married, 54.0% now married, 10.2% widowed, 13.1% divorced (2000); Foreign born: 4.0% (2000); Ancestry (includes multiple ancestries): 40.9% German, 16.8% Irish, 11.7% English, 8.1% United States or American, 7.4% Other groups (2000).
Economy: Single-family building permits issued: 4 (2007); Multi-family building permits issued: 0 (2007); Employment by occupation: 13.0% management, 16.1% professional, 27.5% services, 20.3% sales, 1.2% farming, 9.0% construction, 13.1% production (2000).
Income: Per capita income: $24,248 (2007); Median household income: $42,791 (2007); Average household income: $50,523 (2007); Percent of households with income of $100,000 or more: 7.5% (2007); Poverty rate: 9.9% (2000).
Education: Percent of population age 25 and over with: High school diploma (including GED) or higher: 78.6% (2007); Bachelor's degree or higher: 16.5% (2007); Master's degree or higher: 5.1% (2007).

School District(s)

Galena USD 120 (PK-12)
2005-06 Enrollment: 841 . . . . (815) 777-3086
Housing: Homeownership rate: 67.1% (2007); Median home value: $144,151 (2007); Median rent: $352 per month (2000); Median age of housing: 60+ years (2000).
Safety: Violent crime rate: 32.3 per 10,000 population; Property crime rate: 123.3 per 10,000 population (2006).
Newspapers: Galena Gazette (Local news; Circulation 5,800)
Transportation: Commute to work: 80.2% car, 0.5% public transportation, 12.2% walk, 7.1% work from home (2000); Travel time to work: 54.5% less than 15 minutes, 30.0% 15 to 30 minutes, 10.7% 30 to 45 minutes, 2.0% 45 to 60 minutes, 2.8% 60 minutes or more (2000)
Additional Information Contacts
Galena Area Chamber of Commerce . . . . (815) 777-9050
http://www.galenachamber.com

HANOVER (village). Covers a land area of 0.592 square miles and a water area of 0 square miles. Located at 42.25° N. Lat.; 90.28° W. Long. Elevation is 627 feet.
History: Hanover's early development depended on mining. When this declined, the town built a dam across the Apple River and established a grist mill. When a woolen mill was added in 1864, the town became a textile center.
Population: 911 (1990); 836 (2000); 699 (2007); 693 (2012 projected); Race: 96.7% White, 0.4% Black, 0.4% Asian, 1.3% Hispanic of any race (2007); Density: 1,179.9 persons per square mile (2007); Average household size: 2.03 (2007); Median age: 40.2 (2007); Males per 100 females: 99.7 (2007); Marriage status: 24.3% never married, 45.9% now married, 15.1% widowed, 14.8% divorced (2000); Foreign born: 0.8% (2000); Ancestry (includes multiple ancestries): 40.5% German, 20.1% Irish, 13.7% English, 6.4% French (except Basque), 6.3% Norwegian (2000).
Economy: Single-family building permits issued: 1 (2007); Multi-family building permits issued: 0 (2007); Employment by occupation: 6.5% management, 11.6% professional, 21.2% services, 23.7% sales, 2.3% farming, 14.1% construction, 20.6% production (2000).
Income: Per capita income: $18,441 (2007); Median household income: $32,241 (2007); Average household income: $37,471 (2007); Percent of

households with income of $100,000 or more: 3.5% (2007); Poverty rate: 14.4% (2000).
Education: Percent of population age 25 and over with: High school diploma (including GED) or higher: 81.4% (2007); Bachelor's degree or higher: 8.9% (2007); Master's degree or higher: 3.4% (2007).

School District(s)

River Ridge CUSD 210 (PK-12)
2005-06 Enrollment: 549 . . . . (815) 858-9005
Housing: Homeownership rate: 64.5% (2007); Median home value: $83,704 (2007); Median rent: $234 per month (2000); Median age of housing: 58 years (2000).
Safety: Violent crime rate: 25.1 per 10,000 population; Property crime rate: 87.8 per 10,000 population (2006).
Transportation: Commute to work: 87.2% car, 0.0% public transportation, 9.0% walk, 2.3% work from home (2000); Travel time to work: 44.2% less than 15 minutes, 28.1% 15 to 30 minutes, 9.0% 30 to 45 minutes, 11.3% 45 to 60 minutes, 7.5% 60 minutes or more (2000)

Additional Information Contacts

Hanover Chamber of Commerce . . . . (815) 591-3800
http://www.hanover-il.com/biz/chamber.htm

MENOMINEE (village). Covers a land area of 1.925 square miles and a water area of 0 square miles. Located at 42.47° N. Lat.; 90.54° W. Long. Elevation is 761 feet.
Population: 267 (1990); 237 (2000); 237 (2007); 231 (2012 projected); Race: 96.2% White, 2.1% Black, 0.0% Asian, 8.4% Hispanic of any race (2007); Density: 123.1 persons per square mile (2007); Average household size: 2.89 (2007); Median age: 32.3 (2007); Males per 100 females: 95.9 (2007); Marriage status: 33.7% never married, 57.5% now married, 5.5% widowed, 3.3% divorced (2000); Foreign born: 9.1% (2000); Ancestry (includes multiple ancestries): 38.4% German, 17.8% Irish, 10.7% United States or American, 5.8% European, 5.0% Italian (2000).
Economy: Employment by occupation: 6.7% management, 13.3% professional, 22.5% services, 18.3% sales, 1.7% farming, 11.7% construction, 25.8% production (2000).
Income: Per capita income: $18,270 (2007); Median household income: $52,941 (2007); Average household income: $52,805 (2007); Percent of households with income of $100,000 or more: 6.1% (2007); Poverty rate: 18.2% (2000).
Education: Percent of population age 25 and over with: High school diploma (including GED) or higher: 72.0% (2007); Bachelor's degree or higher: 14.7% (2007); Master's degree or higher: 1.4% (2007).
Housing: Homeownership rate: 79.3% (2007); Median home value: $151,250 (2007); Median rent: $263 per month (2000); Median age of housing: 42 years (2000).
Transportation: Commute to work: 98.3% car, 0.0% public transportation, 0.0% walk, 1.7% work from home (2000); Travel time to work: 24.1% less than 15 minutes, 57.8% 15 to 30 minutes, 16.4% 30 to 45 minutes, 1.7% 45 to 60 minutes, 0.0% 60 minutes or more (2000)

NORA (village). Covers a land area of 0.906 square miles and a water area of 0 square miles. Located at 42.45° N. Lat.; 89.94° W. Long. Elevation is 1,014 feet.
Population: 162 (1990); 118 (2000); 115 (2007); 114 (2012 projected); Race: 100.0% White, 0.0% Black, 0.0% Asian, 0.0% Hispanic of any race (2007); Density: 126.9 persons per square mile (2007); Average household size: 2.17 (2007); Median age: 43.1 (2007); Males per 100 females: 98.3 (2007); Marriage status: 17.9% never married, 44.0% now married, 11.9% widowed, 26.2% divorced (2000); Foreign born: 0.0% (2000); Ancestry (includes multiple ancestries): 36.0% German, 17.0% United States or American, 14.0% English, 8.0% Dutch, 7.0% French (except Basque) (2000).
Economy: Employment by occupation: 10.2% management, 4.1% professional, 6.1% services, 6.1% sales, 4.1% farming, 8.2% construction, 61.2% production (2000).
Income: Per capita income: $18,674 (2007); Median household income: $32,917 (2007); Average household income: $40,519 (2007); Percent of households with income of $100,000 or more: 1.9% (2007); Poverty rate: 11.0% (2000).
Education: Percent of population age 25 and over with: High school diploma (including GED) or higher: 80.2% (2007); Bachelor's degree or higher: 3.5% (2007); Master's degree or higher: 0.0% (2007).
Housing: Homeownership rate: 77.4% (2007); Median home value: $100,735 (2007); Median rent: $260 per month (2000); Median age of housing: 28 years (2000).
Transportation: Commute to work: 85.7% car, 0.0% public transportation, 0.0% walk, 12.2% work from home (2000); Travel time to work: 23.3% less than 15 minutes, 39.5% 15 to 30 minutes, 27.9% 30 to 45 minutes, 4.7% 45 to 60 minutes, 4.7% 60 minutes or more (2000)

SCALES MOUND (village). Covers a land area of 0.235 square miles and a water area of 0 square miles. Located at 42.47° N. Lat.; 90.25° W. Long. Elevation is 955 feet.
Population: 398 (1990); 401 (2000); 423 (2007); 428 (2012 projected); Race: 96.9% White, 0.0% Black, 0.5% Asian, 6.4% Hispanic of any race (2007); Density: 1,803.3 persons per square mile (2007); Average household size: 2.34 (2007); Median age: 37.3 (2007); Males per 100 females: 92.3 (2007); Marriage status: 28.4% never married, 47.4% now married, 12.2% widowed, 11.9% divorced (2000); Foreign born: 0.4% (2000); Ancestry (includes multiple ancestries): 57.3% German, 18.2% English, 12.7% Irish, 7.6% United States or American, 4.9% Other groups (2000).
Economy: Single-family building permits issued: 0 (2007); Multi-family building permits issued: 0 (2007); Employment by occupation: 9.1% management, 14.4% professional, 18.9% services, 15.2% sales, 3.3% farming, 13.2% construction, 25.9% production (2000).
Income: Per capita income: $18,913 (2007); Median household income: $40,357 (2007); Average household income: $44,199 (2007); Percent of households with income of $100,000 or more: 3.9% (2007); Poverty rate: 7.8% (2000).
Education: Percent of population age 25 and over with: High school diploma (including GED) or higher: 82.2% (2007); Bachelor's degree or higher: 8.9% (2007); Master's degree or higher: 3.1% (2007).

School District(s)

Scales Mound CUSD 211 (PK-12)
2005-06 Enrollment: 248 . . . . (815) 845-2215
Housing: Homeownership rate: 75.7% (2007); Median home value: $116,544 (2007); Median rent: $419 per month (2000); Median age of housing: 60+ years (2000).
Transportation: Commute to work: 81.9% car, 0.8% public transportation, 11.9% walk, 3.3% work from home (2000); Travel time to work: 31.1% less than 15 minutes, 40.0% 15 to 30 minutes, 13.6% 30 to 45 minutes, 10.2% 45 to 60 minutes, 5.1% 60 minutes or more (2000)

STOCKTON (village). Aka Plum River. Covers a land area of 0.852 square miles and a water area of 0 square miles. Located at 42.35° N. Lat.; 90.00° W. Long. Elevation is 994 feet.
History: Stockton was named by Alanson Parker, an early settler, who saw the prospects of this becoming a stock raising center, which it did near the end of the 1800's. Before the cattle came, Stockton was the home of lead smelters.
Population: 1,924 (1990); 1,926 (2000); 1,896 (2007); 1,887 (2012 projected); Race: 99.8% White, 0.0% Black, 0.1% Asian, 0.7% Hispanic of any race (2007); Density: 2,225.0 persons per square mile (2007); Average household size: 2.24 (2007); Median age: 41.7 (2007); Males per 100 females: 92.1 (2007); Marriage status: 20.6% never married, 56.8% now married, 11.3% widowed, 11.3% divorced (2000); Foreign born: 0.9% (2000); Ancestry (includes multiple ancestries): 47.8% German, 13.7% Irish, 10.5% English, 8.3% United States or American, 4.6% Dutch (2000).
Economy: Single-family building permits issued: 3 (2007); Multi-family building permits issued: 0 (2007); Employment by occupation: 6.8% management, 10.9% professional, 14.6% services, 22.0% sales, 1.7% farming, 13.7% construction, 30.3% production (2000).
Income: Per capita income: $20,891 (2007); Median household income: $40,255 (2007); Average household income: $45,734 (2007); Percent of households with income of $100,000 or more: 5.2% (2007); Poverty rate: 8.2% (2000).
Education: Percent of population age 25 and over with: High school diploma (including GED) or higher: 81.9% (2007); Bachelor's degree or higher: 9.1% (2007); Master's degree or higher: 1.9% (2007).

School District(s)

Stockton CUSD 206 (PK-12)
2005-06 Enrollment: 653 . . . . (815) 947-3321
Housing: Homeownership rate: 74.6% (2007); Median home value: $108,170 (2007); Median rent: $315 per month (2000); Median age of housing: 52 years (2000).
Safety: Violent crime rate: 60.4 per 10,000 population; Property crime rate: 368.1 per 10,000 population (2006).
Transportation: Commute to work: 88.3% car, 0.4% public transportation, 7.4% walk, 3.4% work from home (2000); Travel time to work: 54.0% less

than 15 minutes, 13.5% 15 to 30 minutes, 21.3% 30 to 45 minutes, 4.3% 45 to 60 minutes, 6.9% 60 minutes or more (2000)

Additional Information Contacts

Stockton Area Chamber of Commerce . . . . (815) 947-3963
http://www.stocktonil.com

WARREN (village). Covers a land area of 0.964 square miles and a water area of 0 square miles. Located at 42.49° N. Lat.; 89.99° W. Long. Elevation is 981 feet.

History: Warren began in 1850 with the name of Courtland, but was renamed in 1853 to honor the son of Alexander Burnett, who had founded the town in 1843. Warren was located at the crossing of the Old Sucker Trail with the Chicago-Galena Stagecoach Road, and later became a station on the railroad line between Galena and Chicago.

Population: 1,562 (1990); 1,496 (2000); 1,516 (2007); 1,538 (2012 projected); Race: 99.2% White, 0.5% Black, 0.0% Asian, 2.0% Hispanic of any race (2007); Density: 1,571.9 persons per square mile (2007); Average household size: 2.32 (2007); Median age: 40.9 (2007); Males per 100 females: 96.4 (2007); Marriage status: 23.1% never married, 58.2% now married, 9.3% widowed, 9.4% divorced (2000); Foreign born: 1.4% (2000); Ancestry (includes multiple ancestries): 48.1% German, 13.7% Irish, 13.5% English, 11.4% United States or American, 5.0% Norwegian (2000).

Economy: Single-family building permits issued: 0 (2007); Multi-family building permits issued: 0 (2007); Employment by occupation: 6.1% management, 12.4% professional, 12.0% services, 21.8% sales, 2.0% farming, 10.3% construction, 35.3% production (2000).

Income: Per capita income: $22,914 (2007); Median household income: $45,368 (2007); Average household income: $53,197 (2007); Percent of households with income of $100,000 or more: 10.4% (2007); Poverty rate: 6.4% (2000).

Education: Percent of population age 25 and over with: High school diploma (including GED) or higher: 82.5% (2007); Bachelor's degree or higher: 10.8% (2007); Master's degree or higher: 2.7% (2007).

School District(s)

Warren CUSD 205 (PK-12)
2005-06 Enrollment: 493 . . . . (815) 745-2653

Housing: Homeownership rate: 81.9% (2007); Median home value: $111,262 (2007); Median rent: $257 per month (2000); Median age of housing: 60+ years (2000).

Safety: Violent crime rate: 0.0 per 10,000 population; Property crime rate: 77.4 per 10,000 population (2006).

Transportation: Commute to work: 89.7% car, 0.3% public transportation, 7.0% walk, 2.6% work from home (2000); Travel time to work: 40.0% less than 15 minutes, 17.6% 15 to 30 minutes, 27.8% 30 to 45 minutes, 8.6% 45 to 60 minutes, 6.0% 60 minutes or more (2000)

Johnson County

Located in southern Illinois, in the Ozarks; drained by the Cache River; includes part of Shawnee National Forest. Covers a land area of 344.63 square miles, a water area of 4.25 square miles, and is located in the Central Time Zone. The county was founded in 1812. County seat is Vienna.

Population: 11,347 (1990); 12,878 (2000); 13,289 (2007); 13,569 (2012 projected); Race: 86.1% White, 11.8% Black, 0.2% Asian, 3.0% Hispanic of any race (2007); Density: 38.6 persons per square mile (2007); Average household size: 2.93 (2007); Median age: 37.2 (2007); Males per 100 females: 134.1 (2007).

Religion: Five largest groups: 21.5% Southern Baptist Convention, 5.2% The United Methodist Church, 1.5% Catholic Church, 1.1% Cumberland Presbyterian Church, 1.0% Churches of Christ (2000).

Economy: Unemployment rate: 6.1% (4/2008); Total civilian labor force: 5,428 (4/2008); Leading industries: 22.0% professional, scientific & technical services; 18.9% retail trade; 16.5% health care and social assistance (2005); Farms: 636 totaling 120,922 acres (2002); Companies that employ 500 or more persons: 0 (2006); Companies that employ 100 to 499 persons: 1 (2006); Companies that employ less than 100 persons: 193 (2006); Black-owned businesses: n/a (2002); Hispanic-owned businesses: n/a (2002); Asian-owned businesses: n/a (2002); Women-owned businesses: n/a (2002); Retail sales per capita: $5,402 (2008). Single-family building permits issued: 1 (2007); Multi-family building permits issued: 0 (2007).

Income: Per capita income: $20,737 (2007); Median household income: $39,769 (2007); Average household income: $51,876 (2007); Percent of households with income of $100,000 or more: 9.7% (2007); Poverty rate: 14.9% (2005); Bankruptcy rate: 3.83% (2007).

Education: Percent of population age 25 and over with: High school diploma (including GED) or higher: 68.3% (2007); Bachelor's degree or higher: 12.0% (2007); Master's degree or higher: 4.5% (2007).

Housing: Homeownership rate: 85.0% (2007); Median home value: $94,750 (2007); Median rent: $241 per month (2000); Median age of housing: 26 years (2000).

Health: Birth rate: 108.7 per 10,000 population (2007); Death rate: 90.3 per 10,000 population (2007); Age-adjusted cancer mortality rate: 230.7 deaths per 100,000 population (2005); Number of physicians: 1.5 per 10,000 population (2005); Hospital beds: 0.0 per 10,000 population (2004); Hospital admissions: 0.0 per 10,000 population (2004).

Elections: 2004 Presidential election results: 68.2% Bush, 30.9% Kerry, 0.1% Nader, 0.8% Badnarik

National and State Parks: Cache River State Natural Area; Ferne Clyffe State Park

Additional Information Contacts

Johnson County Government . . . . (618) 658-4751

Johnson County Communities

BELKNAP (village). Covers a land area of 1.035 square miles and a water area of 0 square miles. Located at 37.32° N. Lat.; 88.94° W. Long. Elevation is 404 feet.

Population: 125 (1990); 133 (2000); 139 (2007); 141 (2012 projected); Race: 90.6% White, 0.0% Black, 0.0% Asian, 0.7% Hispanic of any race (2007); Density: 134.4 persons per square mile (2007); Average household size: 2.62 (2007); Median age: 31.6 (2007); Males per 100 females: 67.5 (2007); Marriage status: 26.3% never married, 56.8% now married, 6.3% widowed, 10.5% divorced (2000); Foreign born: 0.0% (2000); Ancestry (includes multiple ancestries): 26.4% German, 20.7% English, 16.5% United States or American, 14.0% Irish, 10.7% Other groups (2000).

Economy: Employment by occupation: 3.8% management, 11.5% professional, 34.6% services, 38.5% sales, 0.0% farming, 7.7% construction, 3.8% production (2000).

Income: Per capita income: $13,525 (2007); Median household income: $28,750 (2007); Average household income: $35,472 (2007); Percent of households with income of $100,000 or more: 3.8% (2007); Poverty rate: 13.2% (2000).

Education: Percent of population age 25 and over with: High school diploma (including GED) or higher: 75.6% (2007); Bachelor's degree or higher: 3.7% (2007); Master's degree or higher: 0.0% (2007).

Housing: Homeownership rate: 96.2% (2007); Median home value: $19,500 (2007); Median rent: $n/a per month (2000); Median age of housing: 55 years (2000).

Transportation: Commute to work: 100.0% car, 0.0% public transportation, 0.0% walk, 0.0% work from home (2000); Travel time to work: 3.8% less than 15 minutes, 40.4% 15 to 30 minutes, 46.2% 30 to 45 minutes, 3.8% 45 to 60 minutes, 5.8% 60 minutes or more (2000)

BUNCOMBE (village). Covers a land area of 1.209 square miles and a water area of 0 square miles. Located at 37.47° N. Lat.; 88.97° W. Long. Elevation is 518 feet.

Population: 208 (1990); 186 (2000); 181 (2007); 179 (2012 projected); Race: 100.0% White, 0.0% Black, 0.0% Asian, 0.0% Hispanic of any race (2007); Density: 149.7 persons per square mile (2007); Average household size: 2.45 (2007); Median age: 39.0 (2007); Males per 100 females: 105.7 (2007); Marriage status: 16.3% never married, 69.3% now married, 5.4% widowed, 9.0% divorced (2000); Foreign born: 0.0% (2000); Ancestry (includes multiple ancestries): 26.1% Other groups, 17.7% Irish, 12.8% German, 9.4% English, 5.9% United States or American (2000).

Economy: Employment by occupation: 12.5% management, 5.7% professional, 23.9% services, 27.3% sales, 0.0% farming, 19.3% construction, 11.4% production (2000).

Income: Per capita income: $18,343 (2007); Median household income: $37,222 (2007); Average household income: $44,865 (2007); Percent of households with income of $100,000 or more: 9.5% (2007); Poverty rate: 8.5% (2000).

Education: Percent of population age 25 and over with: High school diploma (including GED) or higher: 74.2% (2007); Bachelor's degree or higher: 6.5% (2007); Master's degree or higher: 0.0% (2007).

School District(s)

Buncombe Cons SD 43 (KG-08)
2005-06 Enrollment: 64 . . . . (618) 658-8830
Lick Creek CCSD 16 (KG-08)
2005-06 Enrollment: 131 . . . . (618) 833-2545

Housing: Homeownership rate: 82.4% (2007); Median home value: $53,000 (2007); Median rent: $125 per month (2000); Median age of housing: 51 years (2000).

Transportation: Commute to work: 93.2% car, 0.0% public transportation, 2.3% walk, 1.1% work from home (2000); Travel time to work: 29.9% less than 15 minutes, 23.0% 15 to 30 minutes, 29.9% 30 to 45 minutes, 8.0% 45 to 60 minutes, 9.2% 60 minutes or more (2000)

CYPRESS (village). Aka Whitehill. Covers a land area of 0.747 square miles and a water area of 0 square miles. Located at 37.36° N. Lat.; 89.01° W. Long. Elevation is 390 feet.

Population: 275 (1990); 271 (2000); 280 (2007); 282 (2012 projected); Race: 99.3% White, 0.0% Black, 0.0% Asian, 0.0% Hispanic of any race (2007); Density: 374.7 persons per square mile (2007); Average household size: 2.31 (2007); Median age: 41.2 (2007); Males per 100 females: 100.0 (2007); Marriage status: 17.7% never married, 57.6% now married, 7.6% widowed, 17.2% divorced (2000); Foreign born: 0.0% (2000); Ancestry (includes multiple ancestries): 21.4% German, 16.0% English, 15.1% Irish, 13.9% Other groups, 12.6% Dutch (2000).

Economy: Employment by occupation: 6.4% management, 9.1% professional, 20.0% services, 15.5% sales, 0.0% farming, 10.0% construction, 39.1% production (2000).

Income: Per capita income: $16,777 (2007); Median household income: $35,208 (2007); Average household income: $38,822 (2007); Percent of households with income of $100,000 or more: 2.5% (2007); Poverty rate: 7.6% (2000).

Education: Percent of population age 25 and over with: High school diploma (including GED) or higher: 83.5% (2007); Bachelor's degree or higher: 1.9% (2007); Master's degree or higher: 0.0% (2007).

School District(s)

Cypress SD 64 (PK-08)
2005-06 Enrollment: 134 . . . . (618) 657-2525

Housing: Homeownership rate: 86.8% (2007); Median home value: $38,382 (2007); Median rent: $163 per month (2000); Median age of housing: 50 years (2000).

Transportation: Commute to work: 95.5% car, 2.7% public transportation, 1.8% walk, 0.0% work from home (2000); Travel time to work: 24.5% less than 15 minutes, 31.8% 15 to 30 minutes, 21.8% 30 to 45 minutes, 6.4% 45 to 60 minutes, 15.5% 60 minutes or more (2000)

GOREVILLE (village). Covers a land area of 1.630 square miles and a water area of 0.011 square miles. Located at 37.55° N. Lat.; 88.97° W. Long. Elevation is 735 feet.

Population: 900 (1990); 938 (2000); 1,006 (2007); 1,038 (2012 projected); Race: 98.7% White, 0.0% Black, 0.2% Asian, 0.9% Hispanic of any race (2007); Density: 617.0 persons per square mile (2007); Average household size: 2.37 (2007); Median age: 38.8 (2007); Males per 100 females: 84.9 (2007); Marriage status: 15.6% never married, 62.8% now married, 10.4% widowed, 11.2% divorced (2000); Foreign born: 0.4% (2000); Ancestry (includes multiple ancestries): 20.5% United States or American, 12.6% English, 12.1% German, 10.9% Irish, 6.8% Other groups (2000).

Economy: Single-family building permits issued: 1 (2007); Multi-family building permits issued: 0 (2007); Employment by occupation: 8.2% management, 16.7% professional, 23.3% services, 23.3% sales, 1.6% farming, 11.7% construction, 15.2% production (2000).

Income: Per capita income: $17,930 (2007); Median household income: $37,800 (2007); Average household income: $42,541 (2007); Percent of households with income of $100,000 or more: 4.7% (2007); Poverty rate: 12.2% (2000).

Education: Percent of population age 25 and over with: High school diploma (including GED) or higher: 81.8% (2007); Bachelor's degree or higher: 10.6% (2007); Master's degree or higher: 4.4% (2007).

School District(s)

Five County Reg Voc Center
2005-06 Enrollment: n/a . . . . (618) 747-2703
Goreville CUD 1 (PK-12)
2005-06 Enrollment: 605 . . . . (618) 995-9831

Housing: Homeownership rate: 76.9% (2007); Median home value: $87,273 (2007); Median rent: $250 per month (2000); Median age of housing: 32 years (2000).

Safety: Violent crime rate: 0.0 per 10,000 population; Property crime rate: 92.8 per 10,000 population (2006).

Newspapers: Goreville Gazette (Regional news; Circulation 800)

Transportation: Commute to work: 94.8% car, 0.0% public transportation, 2.3% walk, 2.9% work from home (2000); Travel time to work: 22.5% less than 15 minutes, 39.6% 15 to 30 minutes, 22.3% 30 to 45 minutes, 6.2% 45 to 60 minutes, 9.4% 60 minutes or more (2000)

GRANTSBURG (unincorporated postal area, zip code 62943). Covers a land area of 32.210 square miles and a water area of 0.135 square miles. Located at 37.34° N. Lat.; 88.73° W. Long. Elevation is 377 feet.

Population: 547 (2000); Race: 98.0% White, 0.0% Black, 0.0% Asian, 0.0% Hispanic of any race (2000); Density: 17.0 persons per square mile (2000); Age: 28.2% under 18, 21.0% over 64 (2000); Marriage status: 9.3% never married, 72.4% now married, 6.3% widowed, 12.0% divorced (2000); Foreign born: 0.9% (2000); Ancestry (includes multiple ancestries): 21.0% Other groups, 19.0% German, 17.3% Irish, 13.1% United States or American, 5.5% Dutch (2000).

Economy: Employment by occupation: 18.3% management, 16.7% professional, 30.4% services, 17.5% sales, 2.1% farming, 7.1% construction, 7.9% production (2000).

Income: Per capita income: $15,316 (2000); Median household income: $29,539 (2000); Poverty rate: 16.0% (2000).

Education: Percent of population age 25 and over with: High school diploma (including GED) or higher: 76.2% (2000); Bachelor's degree or higher: 8.4% (2000).

Housing: Homeownership rate: 91.6% (2000); Median home value: $53,900 (2000); Median rent: $288 per month (2000); Median age of housing: 38 years (2000).

Transportation: Commute to work: 86.1% car, 0.0% public transportation, 0.0% walk, 6.1% work from home (2000); Travel time to work: 22.7% less than 15 minutes, 38.0% 15 to 30 minutes, 15.7% 30 to 45 minutes, 21.4% 45 to 60 minutes, 2.2% 60 minutes or more (2000)

NEW BURNSIDE (village). Covers a land area of 1.055 square miles and a water area of 0 square miles. Located at 37.57° N. Lat.; 88.77° W. Long. Elevation is 541 feet.

History: New Burnside was founded in 1872 and named for Major General Ambrose E. Burnside, president of the Big Four Railroad. Fruit growing was an important industry.

Population: 259 (1990); 242 (2000); 241 (2007); 239 (2012 projected); Race: 100.0% White, 0.0% Black, 0.0% Asian, 1.7% Hispanic of any race (2007); Density: 228.4 persons per square mile (2007); Average household size: 2.54 (2007); Median age: 33.7 (2007); Males per 100 females: 94.4 (2007); Marriage status: 17.7% never married, 68.7% now married, 8.6% widowed, 5.1% divorced (2000); Foreign born: 1.9% (2000); Ancestry (includes multiple ancestries): 13.0% United States or American, 5.0% German, 4.6% Other groups, 4.6% Irish, 3.4% Dutch (2000).

Economy: Employment by occupation: 8.6% management, 17.3% professional, 27.2% services, 21.0% sales, 0.0% farming, 2.5% construction, 23.5% production (2000).

Income: Per capita income: $23,828 (2007); Median household income: $41,833 (2007); Average household income: $60,447 (2007); Percent of households with income of $100,000 or more: 11.6% (2007); Poverty rate: 15.4% (2000).

Education: Percent of population age 25 and over with: High school diploma (including GED) or higher: 74.7% (2007); Bachelor's degree or higher: 8.9% (2007); Master's degree or higher: 2.5% (2007).

Housing: Homeownership rate: 83.2% (2007); Median home value: $47,941 (2007); Median rent: $190 per month (2000); Median age of housing: 28 years (2000).

Transportation: Commute to work: 92.3% car, 0.0% public transportation, 1.3% walk, 6.4% work from home (2000); Travel time to work: 15.1% less than 15 minutes, 35.6% 15 to 30 minutes, 35.6% 30 to 45 minutes, 13.7% 45 to 60 minutes, 0.0% 60 minutes or more (2000)

OZARK (unincorporated postal area, zip code 62972). Covers a land area of 19.848 square miles and a water area of 0.112 square miles. Located at 37.54° N. Lat.; 88.74° W. Long. Elevation is 689 feet.

Population: 408 (2000); Race: 98.3% White, 0.0% Black, 0.0% Asian, 1.7% Hispanic of any race (2000); Density: 20.6 persons per square mile (2000); Age: 33.5% under 18, 7.4% over 64 (2000); Marriage status: 24.5% never married, 62.8% now married, 6.3% widowed, 6.3% divorced (2000); Foreign born: 1.7% (2000); Ancestry (includes multiple ancestries): 21.6%

English, 19.5% German, 12.5% Other groups, 9.5% United States or American, 7.2% Irish (2000).
Economy: Employment by occupation: 7.7% management, 6.5% professional, 10.7% services, 29.0% sales, 0.0% farming, 19.5% construction, 26.6% production (2000).
Income: Per capita income: $11,309 (2000); Median household income: $28,558 (2000); Poverty rate: 11.5% (2000).
Education: Percent of population age 25 and over with: High school diploma (including GED) or higher: 80.3% (2000); Bachelor's degree or higher: 3.9% (2000).
Housing: Homeownership rate: 91.6% (2000); Median home value: $52,900 (2000); Median rent: $265 per month (2000); Median age of housing: 25 years (2000).
Transportation: Commute to work: 95.1% car, 0.0% public transportation, 0.0% walk, 1.2% work from home (2000); Travel time to work: 11.7% less than 15 minutes, 27.2% 15 to 30 minutes, 10.5% 30 to 45 minutes, 19.1% 45 to 60 minutes, 31.5% 60 minutes or more (2000)

SIMPSON (village). Covers a land area of 0.522 square miles and a water area of 0 square miles. Located at 37.46° N. Lat.; 88.75° W. Long. Elevation is 390 feet.
Population: 61 (1990); 54 (2000); 58 (2007); 60 (2012 projected); Race: 89.7% White, 6.9% Black, 0.0% Asian, 10.3% Hispanic of any race (2007); Density: 111.1 persons per square mile (2007); Average household size: 2.64 (2007); Median age: 28.8 (2007); Males per 100 females: 141.7 (2007); Marriage status: 28.3% never married, 60.9% now married, 10.9% widowed, 0.0% divorced (2000); Foreign born: 0.0% (2000); Ancestry (includes multiple ancestries): 38.6% English, 17.5% German, 15.8% Irish, 10.5% Other groups, 10.5% Scottish (2000).
Economy: Employment by occupation: 0.0% management, 10.0% professional, 15.0% services, 40.0% sales, 0.0% farming, 5.0% construction, 30.0% production (2000).
Income: Per capita income: $16,034 (2007); Median household income: $29,000 (2007); Average household income: $42,273 (2007); Percent of households with income of $100,000 or more: 0.0% (2007); Poverty rate: 7.0% (2000).
Education: Percent of population age 25 and over with: High school diploma (including GED) or higher: 87.5% (2007); Bachelor's degree or higher: 12.5% (2007); Master's degree or higher: 6.3% (2007).
Housing: Homeownership rate: 90.9% (2007); Median home value: $102,500 (2007); Median rent: $225 per month (2000); Median age of housing: 30 years (2000).
Transportation: Commute to work: 90.0% car, 0.0% public transportation, 10.0% walk, 0.0% work from home (2000); Travel time to work: 20.0% less than 15 minutes, 5.0% 15 to 30 minutes, 25.0% 30 to 45 minutes, 20.0% 45 to 60 minutes, 30.0% 60 minutes or more (2000)

TUNNEL HILL (unincorporated postal area, zip code 62991). Covers a land area of 34.134 square miles and a water area of 0.038 square miles. Located at 37.54° N. Lat.; 88.86° W. Long. Elevation is 636 feet.
Population: 685 (2000); Race: 100.0% White, 0.0% Black, 0.0% Asian, 0.4% Hispanic of any race (2000); Density: 20.1 persons per square mile (2000); Age: 22.0% under 18, 10.2% over 64 (2000); Marriage status: 16.9% never married, 66.9% now married, 8.1% widowed, 8.1% divorced (2000); Foreign born: 0.0% (2000); Ancestry (includes multiple ancestries): 26.6% Irish, 21.3% German, 13.3% English, 13.0% Other groups, 10.3% United States or American (2000).
Economy: Employment by occupation: 13.6% management, 25.2% professional, 27.8% services, 17.7% sales, 1.0% farming, 7.0% construction, 7.7% production (2000).
Income: Per capita income: $20,884 (2000); Median household income: $40,893 (2000); Poverty rate: 11.2% (2000).
Education: Percent of population age 25 and over with: High school diploma (including GED) or higher: 84.6% (2000); Bachelor's degree or higher: 18.1% (2000).

School District(s)

New Simpson Hill SD 32 (PK-08)
2005-06 Enrollment: 293 . . . . (618) 658-8536
Housing: Homeownership rate: 94.1% (2000); Median home value: $96,700 (2000); Median rent: $318 per month (2000); Median age of housing: 12 years (2000).
Transportation: Commute to work: 94.4% car, 1.2% public transportation, 0.0% walk, 3.6% work from home (2000); Travel time to work: 16.3% less than 15 minutes, 43.7% 15 to 30 minutes, 24.1% 30 to 45 minutes, 12.1% 45 to 60 minutes, 3.8% 60 minutes or more (2000)

VIENNA (city). County seat. Covers a land area of 2.240 square miles and a water area of 0.011 square miles. Located at 37.41° N. Lat.; 88.89° W. Long. Elevation is 404 feet.
History: Incorporated 1837.
Population: 1,465 (1990); 1,234 (2000); 1,234 (2007); 1,236 (2012 projected); Race: 98.7% White, 0.1% Black, 0.0% Asian, 1.9% Hispanic of any race (2007); Density: 550.8 persons per square mile (2007); Average household size: 2.17 (2007); Median age: 39.2 (2007); Males per 100 females: 75.8 (2007); Marriage status: 23.2% never married, 47.6% now married, 16.1% widowed, 13.1% divorced (2000); Foreign born: 0.3% (2000); Ancestry (includes multiple ancestries): 26.4% United States or American, 20.9% Other groups, 11.5% German, 8.9% English, 8.9% Irish (2000).
Economy: Employment by occupation: 6.9% management, 16.3% professional, 33.9% services, 25.0% sales, 0.6% farming, 7.5% construction, 9.9% production (2000).
Income: Per capita income: $17,574 (2007); Median household income: $26,129 (2007); Average household income: $37,698 (2007); Percent of households with income of $100,000 or more: 5.1% (2007); Poverty rate: 20.0% (2000).
Education: Percent of population age 25 and over with: High school diploma (including GED) or higher: 67.8% (2007); Bachelor's degree or higher: 8.7% (2007); Master's degree or higher: 2.6% (2007).

School District(s)

Dept of Corrections Sch Dist 428 (08-12)
2005-06 Enrollment: 2,271 . . . . (217) 522-2666
Five County Reg Voc System
2005-06 Enrollment: n/a . . . . (618) 747-2703
Vienna HSD 133 (09-12)
2005-06 Enrollment: 375 . . . . (618) 658-4461
Vienna SD 55 (PK-08)
2005-06 Enrollment: 434 . . . . (618) 658-8638
Housing: Homeownership rate: 61.4% (2007); Median home value: $59,500 (2007); Median rent: $197 per month (2000); Median age of housing: 33 years (2000).
Safety: Violent crime rate: 130.4 per 10,000 population; Property crime rate: 406.4 per 10,000 population (2006).
Newspapers: Vienna Times (National news; Circulation 2,800)
Transportation: Commute to work: 92.1% car, 1.0% public transportation, 4.4% walk, 0.8% work from home (2000); Travel time to work: 46.3% less than 15 minutes, 18.2% 15 to 30 minutes, 25.8% 30 to 45 minutes, 6.1% 45 to 60 minutes, 3.6% 60 minutes or more (2000)

Kane County

Located in northeastern Illinois; drained by the Fox River and Mill Creek. Covers a land area of 520.44 square miles, a water area of 3.64 square miles, and is located in the Central Time Zone. The county was founded in 1836. County seat is Geneva.

Kane County is part of the Chicago-Naperville-Joliet, IL-IN-WI Metropolitan Statistical Area. The entire metro area includes: Chicago-Naperville-Joliet, IL Metropolitan Division (Cook County, IL; DeKalb County, IL; DuPage County, IL; Grundy County, IL; Kane County, IL; Kendall County, IL; McHenry County, IL; Will County, IL); Gary, IN Metropolitan Division (Jasper County, IN; Lake County, IN; Newton County, IN; Porter County, IN); Lake County-Kenosha County, IL-WI Metropolitan Division (Lake County, IL; Kenosha County, WI)

Weather Station: Aurora Elevation: 639 feet

	Jan	Feb	Mar	Apr	May	Jun	Jul	Aug	Sep	Oct	Nov	Dec
High	29	35	47	60	72	81	85	83	75	63	48	35
Low	11	17	27	38	48	57	62	60	52	40	30	18
Precip	1.6	1.5	2.6	4.0	4.0	4.4	4.3	4.4	3.6	2.7	3.2	2.4
Snow	9.9	6.9	3.8	0.9	0.0	0.0	0.0	0.0	0.0	tr	1.5	6.7

High and Low temperatures in degrees Fahrenheit; Precipitation and Snow in inches

Population: 317,471 (1990); 404,119 (2000); 500,408 (2007); 563,285 (2012 projected); Race: 76.1% White, 5.3% Black, 2.9% Asian, 28.3% Hispanic of any race (2007); Density: 961.5 persons per square mile (2007); Average household size: 3.04 (2007); Median age: 32.6 (2007); Males per 100 females: 102.2 (2007).
Religion: Five largest groups: 34.4% Catholic Church, 3.7% Lutheran Church—Missouri Synod, 3.5% Evangelical Lutheran Church in America, 3.3% The United Methodist Church, 1.9% United Church of Christ (2000).

Economy: Unemployment rate: 5.8% (4/2008); Total civilian labor force: 269,744 (4/2008); Leading industries: 17.5% manufacturing; 12.8% retail trade; 11.4% health care and social assistance (2005); Farms: 619 totaling 198,227 acres (2002); Companies that employ 500 or more persons: 24 (2006); Companies that employ 100 to 499 persons: 287 (2006); Companies that employ less than 100 persons: 12,004 (2006); Black-owned businesses: 708 (2002); Hispanic-owned businesses: 2,125 (2002); Asian-owned businesses: 1,021 (2002); Women-owned businesses: 8,989 (2002); Retail sales per capita: $13,894 (2008). Single-family building permits issued: 2,562 (2007); Multi-family building permits issued: 84 (2007).
Income: Per capita income: $28,030 (2007); Median household income: $67,388 (2007); Average household income: $84,633 (2007); Percent of households with income of $100,000 or more: 27.5% (2007); Poverty rate: 8.5% (2005); Bankruptcy rate: 2.29% (2007).
Taxes: Total county taxes per capita: $162 (2006); County property taxes per capita: $136 (2006).
Education: Percent of population age 25 and over with: High school diploma (including GED) or higher: 80.7% (2007); Bachelor's degree or higher: 27.9% (2007); Master's degree or higher: 9.0% (2007).
Housing: Homeownership rate: 77.2% (2007); Median home value: $232,983 (2007); Median rent: $615 per month (2000); Median age of housing: 29 years (2000).
Health: Birth rate: 181.2 per 10,000 population (2007); Death rate: 54.3 per 10,000 population (2007); Age-adjusted cancer mortality rate: 177.6 deaths per 100,000 population (2005); Air Quality Index: 87.1% good, 11.8% moderate, 1.1% unhealthy for sensitive individuals, 0.0% unhealthy (percent of days in 2007); Number of physicians: 14.2 per 10,000 population (2005); Hospital beds: 25.5 per 10,000 population (2004); Hospital admissions: 906.3 per 10,000 population (2004).
Elections: 2004 Presidential election results: 55.0% Bush, 44.1% Kerry, 0.0% Nader, 0.8% Badnarik

Additional Information Contacts

Kane County Government . . . . (630) 232-3400
http://www.countyofkane.org
Aurora Chamber of Commerce . . . . (630) 897-9214
http://www.aurorachamber.com
Aurora Hispanic Chamber of Commerce . . . . (630) 264-2422
http://www.ahcc-il.com
Batavia Chamber of Commerce . . . . (630) 879-7134
http://www.bataviachamber.org
Cardunal Area Chamber of Commerce . . . . (847) 426-8565
http://www.cardunal.com
City of Aurora . . . . (630) 264-4636
http://www.aurora-il.org
City of Batavia . . . . (630) 454-2000
http://www.cityofbatavia.net
City of Elgin . . . . (847) 931-6100
http://www.cityofelgin.org
City of Geneva . . . . (630) 232-7494
http://www.geneva.il.us
City of Saint Charles . . . . (630) 377-4400
http://www.ci.st-charles.il.us
Elgin Area Chamber of Commerce . . . . (847) 741-5660
http://www.elginchamber.com
Geneva Chamber of Commerce . . . . (630) 232-6060
http://www.genevachamber.com
Greater Montgomery Area Chamber of Commerce . . . . (630) 897-8137
http://www.chamberofmontgomeryil.org
Hampshire Chamber of Commerce . . . . (847) 683-1122
http://www.hampshirechamber.org
South Elgin Chamber of Commerce . . . . (847) 888-2287
http://www.southelginchamber.com
St. Charles Chamber of Commerce . . . . (630) 584-8384
http://www.stcharleschamber.com
Sugar Grove Chamber of Commerce & Industry . . . . (630) 466-7895
http://www.sugargrovechamber.org
Village of Carpentersville . . . . (847) 426-3439
http://vil.carpentersville.il.us
Village of Montgomery . . . . (630) 896-0791
http://ci.montgomery.il.us
Village of North Aurora . . . . (630) 897-8228
http://www.vil.north-aurora.il.us
Village of South Elgin . . . . (847) 741-2141
http://www.southelgin.com
Village of West Dundee . . . . (847) 551-3800
http://www.west-dundee.il.us

Kane County Communities

AURORA (city). Covers a land area of 38.526 square miles and a water area of 0.893 square miles. Located at 41.76° N. Lat.; 88.29° W. Long. Elevation is 679 feet.
History: Named for the Iroquoian translation of "constant dawn". Joseph McCarty of Elmira, New York, came to Illinois in 1834 and chose the site on the Fox River as superior to Chicago as a place to settle. Th e community of Aurora was platted in 1836 and a post office was soon established. Development along both sides of the river resulted in separate towns of East Aurora and West Aurora until 1857, when the two were joined in incorporation. Meanwhile, the Chicago, Burlington & Quincy Railroad had arrived with its tracks and shops, and with it a period of growth. Aurora, in 1881, was one of the first towns in the U.S. to have electric street lights.
Population: 102,513 (1990); 142,990 (2000); 176,446 (2007); 198,088 (2012 projected); Race: 63.0% White, 11.2% Black, 4.6% Asian, 38.5% Hispanic of any race (2007); Density: 4,579.9 persons per square mile (2007); Average household size: 3.11 (2007); Median age: 30.8 (2007); Males per 100 females: 102.4 (2007); Marriage status: 29.0% never married, 58.9% now married, 4.0% widowed, 8.2% divorced (2000); Foreign born: 21.5% (2000); Ancestry (includes multiple ancestries): 44.4% Other groups, 17.5% German, 9.7% Irish, 5.6% English, 4.7% Italian (2000).
Economy: Unemployment rate: 5.9% (4/2008); Total civilian labor force: 92,411 (4/2008); Single-family building permits issued: 338 (2007); Multi-family building permits issued: 0 (2007); Employment by occupation: 15.0% management, 18.3% professional, 12.4% services, 25.9% sales, 0.3% farming, 7.6% construction, 20.5% production (2000).
Income: Per capita income: $25,141 (2007); Median household income: $61,987 (2007); Average household income: $77,525 (2007); Percent of households with income of $100,000 or more: 24.1% (2007); Poverty rate: 8.5% (2000).
Taxes: Total city taxes per capita: $619 (2006); City property taxes per capita: $373 (2006).
Education: Percent of population age 25 and over with: High school diploma (including GED) or higher: 76.1% (2007); Bachelor's degree or higher: 30.5% (2007); Master's degree or higher: 9.4% (2007).

School District(s)

Aurora East Usd 131 (PK-12)
2005-06 Enrollment: 12,316 . . . . (630) 299-5554
Aurora West Usd 129 (PK-12)
2005-06 Enrollment: 12,491 . . . . (630) 301-5033
Illinois Mathematics & Science Academy (10-12)
2005-06 Enrollment: 634 . . . . (630) 907-5053
Indian Prairie CUSD 204 (PK-12)
2005-06 Enrollment: 28,510 . . . . (630) 375-3000
Oswego CUSD 308 (PK-12)
2005-06 Enrollment: 12,599 . . . . (630) 636-3080

Four-year College(s)

Aurora University (Private, Not-for-profit)
Fall 2007 Enrollment: 3,946 . . . . (630) 892-6431
2007-08 Tuition: In-state $16,850; Out-of-state $16,850

Vocational/Technical School(s)

Regency Beauty Institute (Private, For-profit)
Fall 2007 Enrollment: 57 . . . . (630) 723-5051
2007-08 Tuition: $14,200

Housing: Homeownership rate: 70.4% (2007); Median home value: $199,854 (2007); Median rent: $609 per month (2000); Median age of housing: 25 years (2000).
Hospitals: Provena Mercy Medical Center (356 beds); Rush-Copley Medical Center (183 beds)
Safety: Violent crime rate: 47.0 per 10,000 population; Property crime rate: 293.5 per 10,000 population (2006).
Newspapers: Aurora Beacon-News (Local news; Circulation 36,000)
Transportation: Commute to work: 88.9% car, 5.5% public transportation, 1.6% walk, 2.7% work from home (2000); Travel time to work: 23.5% less than 15 minutes, 35.6% 15 to 30 minutes, 19.5% 30 to 45 minutes, 9.3% 45 to 60 minutes, 12.1% 60 minutes or more (2000)
Airports: Aurora Municipal (general aviation)

Additional Information Contacts

Aurora Chamber of Commerce . . . . (630) 897-9214
http://www.aurorachamber.com

Aurora Hispanic Chamber of Commerce . . . . (630) 264-2422
http://www.ahcc-il.com
City of Aurora . . . . (630) 264-4636
http://www.aurora-il.org

BATAVIA (city). Covers a land area of 9.046 square miles and a water area of 0.140 square miles. Located at 41.84° N. Lat.; 88.30° W. Long. Elevation is 715 feet.
History: Batavia was settled in 1832 by people from New York, who chose the site for its water power, fertile soil, and surface limestone. They named the new town for their home in New York. Early Batavia had the nickname of Quarry City.
Population: 17,818 (1990); 23,866 (2000); 27,044 (2007); 29,193 (2012 projected); Race: 91.9% White, 2.4% Black, 1.9% Asian, 7.1% Hispanic of any race (2007); Density: 2,989.7 persons per square mile (2007); Average household size: 2.87 (2007); Median age: 34.8 (2007); Males per 100 females: 97.0 (2007); Marriage status: 21.4% never married, 64.8% now married, 5.7% widowed, 8.0% divorced (2000); Foreign born: 5.2% (2000); Ancestry (includes multiple ancestries): 31.6% German, 18.1% Irish, 11.5% English, 10.8% Other groups, 8.8% Italian (2000).
Economy: Unemployment rate: 4.3% (4/2008); Total civilian labor force: 15,427 (4/2008); Single-family building permits issued: 25 (2007); Multi-family building permits issued: 48 (2007); Employment by occupation: 20.5% management, 23.8% professional, 10.8% services, 28.0% sales, 0.0% farming, 7.1% construction, 9.7% production (2000).
Income: Per capita income: $32,049 (2007); Median household income: $80,155 (2007); Average household income: $91,494 (2007); Percent of households with income of $100,000 or more: 36.4% (2007); Poverty rate: 3.6% (2000).
Taxes: Total city taxes per capita: $317 (2006); City property taxes per capita: $193 (2006).
Education: Percent of population age 25 and over with: High school diploma (including GED) or higher: 93.8% (2007); Bachelor's degree or higher: 43.4% (2007); Master's degree or higher: 15.2% (2007).

School District(s)

Batavia Usd 101 (PK-12)
2005-06 Enrollment: 6,235 . . . . (630) 879-4600
Housing: Homeownership rate: 78.7% (2007); Median home value: $286,919 (2007); Median rent: $702 per month (2000); Median age of housing: 22 years (2000).
Safety: Violent crime rate: 8.8 per 10,000 population; Property crime rate: 223.4 per 10,000 population (2006).
Newspapers: Windmill Herald (Local news; Circulation 11,000)
Transportation: Commute to work: 90.2% car, 2.3% public transportation, 1.6% walk, 4.4% work from home (2000); Travel time to work: 31.9% less than 15 minutes, 31.3% 15 to 30 minutes, 18.1% 30 to 45 minutes, 7.9% 45 to 60 minutes, 10.8% 60 minutes or more (2000)
Additional Information Contacts
Batavia Chamber of Commerce . . . . (630) 879-7134
http://www.bataviachamber.org
City of Batavia . . . . (630) 454-2000
http://www.cityofbatavia.net

BIG ROCK (unincorporated postal area, zip code 60511). Covers a land area of 29.145 square miles and a water area of 0 square miles. Located at 41.75° N. Lat.; 88.54° W. Long. Elevation is 709 feet.
Population: 1,862 (2000); Race: 99.3% White, 0.0% Black, 0.0% Asian, 1.8% Hispanic of any race (2000); Density: 63.9 persons per square mile (2000); Age: 23.7% under 18, 9.5% over 64 (2000); Marriage status: 21.1% never married, 74.6% now married, 3.0% widowed, 1.3% divorced (2000); Foreign born: 0.8% (2000); Ancestry (includes multiple ancestries): 28.9% German, 13.5% Irish, 12.4% English, 8.5% United States or American, 6.7% French (except Basque) (2000).
Economy: Employment by occupation: 13.7% management, 9.9% professional, 11.9% services, 32.4% sales, 0.0% farming, 14.8% construction, 17.3% production (2000).
Income: Per capita income: $30,689 (2000); Median household income: $72,622 (2000); Poverty rate: 4.5% (2000).
Education: Percent of population age 25 and over with: High school diploma (including GED) or higher: 92.7% (2000); Bachelor's degree or higher: 20.2% (2000).

School District(s)

Hinckley Big Rock CUSD 429 (PK-12)
2005-06 Enrollment: 875 . . . . (815) 286-7575
Housing: Homeownership rate: 87.3% (2000); Median home value: $188,100 (2000); Median rent: $547 per month (2000); Median age of housing: 29 years (2000).
Transportation: Commute to work: 94.1% car, 0.0% public transportation, 0.0% walk, 5.9% work from home (2000); Travel time to work: 15.4% less than 15 minutes, 37.4% 15 to 30 minutes, 29.6% 30 to 45 minutes, 11.4% 45 to 60 minutes, 6.2% 60 minutes or more (2000)

BURLINGTON (village). Covers a land area of 0.354 square miles and a water area of 0 square miles. Located at 42.05° N. Lat.; 88.54° W. Long. Elevation is 925 feet.
Population: 431 (1990); 452 (2000); 574 (2007); 649 (2012 projected); Race: 94.6% White, 0.0% Black, 2.8% Asian, 1.0% Hispanic of any race (2007); Density: 1,621.9 persons per square mile (2007); Average household size: 2.61 (2007); Median age: 32.7 (2007); Males per 100 females: 86.4 (2007); Marriage status: 24.5% never married, 59.2% now married, 4.2% widowed, 12.1% divorced (2000); Foreign born: 6.1% (2000); Ancestry (includes multiple ancestries): 41.4% German, 14.8% Irish, 14.3% Polish, 8.0% Other groups, 6.9% English (2000).
Economy: Employment by occupation: 8.5% management, 18.4% professional, 11.1% services, 23.1% sales, 0.0% farming, 14.5% construction, 24.4% production (2000).
Income: Per capita income: $28,358 (2007); Median household income: $63,000 (2007); Average household income: $73,989 (2007); Percent of households with income of $100,000 or more: 24.5% (2007); Poverty rate: 5.7% (2000).
Education: Percent of population age 25 and over with: High school diploma (including GED) or higher: 93.7% (2007); Bachelor's degree or higher: 19.0% (2007); Master's degree or higher: 7.2% (2007).

School District(s)

Central CUSD 301 (PK-12)
2005-06 Enrollment: 2,594 . . . . (847) 464-6005
Housing: Homeownership rate: 68.2% (2007); Median home value: $213,542 (2007); Median rent: $610 per month (2000); Median age of housing: 43 years (2000).
Transportation: Commute to work: 92.1% car, 0.0% public transportation, 4.8% walk, 0.9% work from home (2000); Travel time to work: 21.1% less than 15 minutes, 38.3% 15 to 30 minutes, 23.8% 30 to 45 minutes, 8.4% 45 to 60 minutes, 8.4% 60 minutes or more (2000)

CARPENTERSVILLE (village). Covers a land area of 7.450 square miles and a water area of 0.148 square miles. Located at 42.12° N. Lat.; 88.27° W. Long. Elevation is 889 feet.
History: Named for D. G. Carpenter, an early settler. Carpentersville was settled in 1834 by Angelo Carpenter of Massachusetts and his father and uncle. Carpenter built several mills and a store, and in 1851 he platted the town. An early industry was the Illinois Iron and Bolt Company.
Population: 23,869 (1990); 30,586 (2000); 37,732 (2007); 42,348 (2012 projected); Race: 60.8% White, 4.0% Black, 3.3% Asian, 51.0% Hispanic of any race (2007); Density: 5,064.6 persons per square mile (2007); Average household size: 3.46 (2007); Median age: 30.1 (2007); Males per 100 females: 106.9 (2007); Marriage status: 28.2% never married, 60.4% now married, 3.8% widowed, 7.5% divorced (2000); Foreign born: 26.4% (2000); Ancestry (includes multiple ancestries): 43.0% Other groups, 17.9% German, 9.6% Irish, 7.7% Polish, 5.2% Italian (2000).
Economy: Unemployment rate: 7.8% (4/2008); Total civilian labor force: 19,009 (4/2008); Single-family building permits issued: 54 (2007); Multi-family building permits issued: 0 (2007); Employment by occupation: 9.2% management, 10.5% professional, 14.6% services, 29.4% sales, 0.4% farming, 11.1% construction, 24.7% production (2000).
Income: Per capita income: $20,197 (2007); Median household income: $60,330 (2007); Average household income: $69,854 (2007); Percent of households with income of $100,000 or more: 18.5% (2007); Poverty rate: 8.5% (2000).
Education: Percent of population age 25 and over with: High school diploma (including GED) or higher: 68.2% (2007); Bachelor's degree or higher: 13.6% (2007); Master's degree or higher: 3.1% (2007).

School District(s)

Barrington CUSD 220 (PK-12)
2005-06 Enrollment: 9,135 . . . . (847) 381-6300
CUSD 300 (PK-12)
2005-06 Enrollment: 18,670 . . . . (847) 426-1300
Housing: Homeownership rate: 81.5% (2007); Median home value: $170,189 (2007); Median rent: $618 per month (2000); Median age of housing: 34 years (2000).

Safety: Violent crime rate: 21.8 per 10,000 population; Property crime rate: 274.4 per 10,000 population (2006).
Transportation: Commute to work: 94.6% car, 1.1% public transportation, 1.1% walk, 1.4% work from home (2000); Travel time to work: 20.6% less than 15 minutes, 31.2% 15 to 30 minutes, 23.1% 30 to 45 minutes, 13.6% 45 to 60 minutes, 11.5% 60 minutes or more (2000)
Additional Information Contacts
Village of Carpentersville . . . . (847) 426-3439
http://vil.carpentersville.il.us

DUNDEE (unincorporated postal area, zip code 60118). Aka West Dundee. Covers a land area of 22.307 square miles and a water area of 0.373 square miles. Located at 42.02° N. Lat.; 88.41° W. Long. Elevation is 919 feet.
Population: 14,739 (2000); Race: 95.1% White, 0.6% Black, 1.0% Asian, 3.2% Hispanic of any race (2000); Density: 660.7 persons per square mile (2000); Age: 26.0% under 18, 9.3% over 64 (2000); Marriage status: 20.8% never married, 65.7% now married, 4.1% widowed, 9.4% divorced (2000); Foreign born: 7.9% (2000); Ancestry (includes multiple ancestries): 35.3% German, 15.8% Irish, 13.0% Polish, 9.7% Italian, 9.1% English (2000).
Economy: Employment by occupation: 22.8% management, 20.2% professional, 8.1% services, 30.9% sales, 0.3% farming, 8.5% construction, 9.2% production (2000).
Income: Per capita income: $31,260 (2000); Median household income: $72,500 (2000); Poverty rate: 3.0% (2000).
Education: Percent of population age 25 and over with: High school diploma (including GED) or higher: 91.4% (2000); Bachelor's degree or higher: 37.0% (2000).
School District(s)
CUSD 300 (PK-12)
2005-06 Enrollment: 18,670 . . . . (847) 426-1300
Housing: Homeownership rate: 82.4% (2000); Median home value: $214,000 (2000); Median rent: $679 per month (2000); Median age of housing: 29 years (2000).
Transportation: Commute to work: 90.4% car, 2.3% public transportation, 1.5% walk, 5.4% work from home (2000); Travel time to work: 25.5% less than 15 minutes, 27.5% 15 to 30 minutes, 23.9% 30 to 45 minutes, 12.6% 45 to 60 minutes, 10.6% 60 minutes or more (2000)
Additional Information Contacts
Cardunal Area Chamber of Commerce . . . . (847) 426-8565
http://www.cardunal.com

EAST DUNDEE (village). Covers a land area of 2.679 square miles and a water area of 0.235 square miles. Located at 42.10° N. Lat.; 88.27° W. Long. Elevation is 768 feet.
History: East Dundee was settled mainly by German immigrants who left their home country during the 1848 Revolution.
Population: 2,838 (1990); 2,955 (2000); 3,251 (2007); 3,463 (2012 projected); Race: 90.4% White, 1.5% Black, 3.6% Asian, 4.8% Hispanic of any race (2007); Density: 1,213.6 persons per square mile (2007); Average household size: 2.37 (2007); Median age: 39.6 (2007); Males per 100 females: 97.5 (2007); Marriage status: 21.5% never married, 62.5% now married, 5.1% widowed, 10.9% divorced (2000); Foreign born: 6.9% (2000); Ancestry (includes multiple ancestries): 37.9% German, 13.8% Irish, 11.5% English, 8.6% Italian, 7.4% Polish (2000).
Economy: Single-family building permits issued: 0 (2007); Multi-family building permits issued: 0 (2007); Employment by occupation: 17.7% management, 18.8% professional, 12.1% services, 29.4% sales, 0.0% farming, 11.2% construction, 10.8% production (2000).
Income: Per capita income: $38,328 (2007); Median household income: $66,927 (2007); Average household income: $90,886 (2007); Percent of households with income of $100,000 or more: 26.7% (2007); Poverty rate: 4.8% (2000).
Education: Percent of population age 25 and over with: High school diploma (including GED) or higher: 90.5% (2007); Bachelor's degree or higher: 32.6% (2007); Master's degree or higher: 11.9% (2007).
Housing: Homeownership rate: 85.6% (2007); Median home value: $228,529 (2007); Median rent: $660 per month (2000); Median age of housing: 41 years (2000).
Safety: Violent crime rate: 54.2 per 10,000 population; Property crime rate: 519.4 per 10,000 population (2006).
Transportation: Commute to work: 91.5% car, 1.2% public transportation, 2.3% walk, 4.4% work from home (2000); Travel time to work: 26.6% less than 15 minutes, 34.3% 15 to 30 minutes, 22.6% 30 to 45 minutes, 8.1% 45 to 60 minutes, 8.4% 60 minutes or more (2000)

ELBURN (village). Covers a land area of 2.727 square miles and a water area of 0 square miles. Located at 41.89° N. Lat.; 88.46° W. Long. Elevation is 853 feet.
History: Elburn began in 1854 when the Galena & Chicago Union Railroad line was laid, and developed as a farming center. It is said that when Lincoln visited Elburn in 1858, he was greeted by a group calling itself the Lincoln True Hearts, pledging support.
Population: 1,762 (1990); 2,756 (2000); 3,361 (2007); 3,725 (2012 projected); Race: 97.6% White, 0.1% Black, 0.5% Asian, 3.0% Hispanic of any race (2007); Density: 1,232.4 persons per square mile (2007); Average household size: 2.63 (2007); Median age: 34.5 (2007); Males per 100 females: 95.3 (2007); Marriage status: 18.2% never married, 64.9% now married, 7.8% widowed, 9.0% divorced (2000); Foreign born: 3.5% (2000); Ancestry (includes multiple ancestries): 31.7% German, 18.0% Irish, 11.8% Swedish, 11.1% Italian, 8.6% English (2000).
Economy: Single-family building permits issued: 36 (2007); Multi-family building permits issued: 12 (2007); Employment by occupation: 17.4% management, 20.0% professional, 12.4% services, 32.0% sales, 0.0% farming, 8.8% construction, 9.3% production (2000).
Income: Per capita income: $33,044 (2007); Median household income: $80,189 (2007); Average household income: $86,273 (2007); Percent of households with income of $100,000 or more: 33.6% (2007); Poverty rate: 4.1% (2000).
Education: Percent of population age 25 and over with: High school diploma (including GED) or higher: 92.6% (2007); Bachelor's degree or higher: 35.0% (2007); Master's degree or higher: 10.5% (2007).
School District(s)
Kaneland CUSD 302 (PK-12)
2005-06 Enrollment: 3,994 . . . . (630) 365-5111
Housing: Homeownership rate: 81.5% (2007); Median home value: $264,208 (2007); Median rent: $621 per month (2000); Median age of housing: 8 years (2000).
Safety: Violent crime rate: 2.1 per 10,000 population; Property crime rate: 105.9 per 10,000 population (2006).
Newspapers: Elburn Herald (Local news; Circulation 3,301)
Transportation: Commute to work: 89.7% car, 1.1% public transportation, 3.6% walk, 4.4% work from home (2000); Travel time to work: 29.3% less than 15 minutes, 34.6% 15 to 30 minutes, 18.8% 30 to 45 minutes, 8.2% 45 to 60 minutes, 9.0% 60 minutes or more (2000)

ELGIN (city). Covers a land area of 25.003 square miles and a water area of 0.386 square miles. Located at 42.03° N. Lat.; 88.28° W. Long. Elevation is 745 feet.
History: Named for a Scottish hymn, "Elgin," by James T. Gifford. Elgin was settled in 1835 by James and Hezekiah Gifford from New York, who dammed the river and built a sawmill and a gristmill. It was incorporated as a village in 1847 and as a town in 1854. An early industry here was the production of condensed milk, a process developed by Gail Borden. The Elgin watch industry, which made the name of Elgin known around the world, began in 1866, followed by the Elgin Watchmakers College which opened in the 1920's.
Population: 78,650 (1990); 94,487 (2000); 99,739 (2007); 103,587 (2012 projected); Race: 65.1% White, 6.2% Black, 5.3% Asian, 43.5% Hispanic of any race (2007); Density: 3,989.1 persons per square mile (2007); Average household size: 3.03 (2007); Median age: 32.0 (2007); Males per 100 females: 101.3 (2007); Marriage status: 28.6% never married, 57.5% now married, 5.0% widowed, 8.9% divorced (2000); Foreign born: 23.7% (2000); Ancestry (includes multiple ancestries): 41.2% Other groups, 22.0% German, 9.8% Irish, 6.3% Polish, 5.6% English (2000).
Economy: Unemployment rate: 7.5% (4/2008); Total civilian labor force: 57,058 (4/2008); Single-family building permits issued: 756 (2007); Multi-family building permits issued: 10 (2007); Employment by occupation: 12.3% management, 15.6% professional, 15.0% services, 25.5% sales, 0.3% farming, 8.6% construction, 22.6% production (2000).
Income: Per capita income: $23,049 (2007); Median household income: $58,569 (2007); Average household income: $69,048 (2007); Percent of households with income of $100,000 or more: 19.1% (2007); Poverty rate: 8.1% (2000).
Taxes: Total city taxes per capita: $458 (2006); City property taxes per capita: $369 (2006).
Education: Percent of population age 25 and over with: High school diploma (including GED) or higher: 73.8% (2007); Bachelor's degree or higher: 20.6% (2007); Master's degree or higher: 6.0% (2007).

School District(s)

Central CUSD 301 (PK-12)
2005-06 Enrollment: 2,594 . . . . (847) 464-6005
SD U-46 (PK-12)
2005-06 Enrollment: 39,656 . . . . (847) 888-5000

Four-year College(s)

Judson University (Private, Not-for-profit, Baptist)
Fall 2007 Enrollment: 1,236. . . . . (847) 628-2500
2007-08 Tuition: In-state $20,420; Out-of-state $20,420

Two-year College(s)

Elgin Community College (Public)
Fall 2007 Enrollment: 9,613. . . . . (847) 697-1000
2007-08 Tuition: In-state $8,633; Out-of-state $10,503

Vocational/Technical School(s)

Cannella School of Hair Design (Private, For-profit)
Fall 2007 Enrollment: 109 . . . . (708) 742-6611
2007-08 Tuition: $8,500

Housing: Homeownership rate: 70.9% (2007); Median home value: $199,837 (2007); Median rent: $611 per month (2000); Median age of housing: 31 years (2000).

Hospitals: Provena Saint Joseph Hospital (260 beds); Sherman Hospital (353 beds)

Safety: Violent crime rate: 31.0 per 10,000 population; Property crime rate: 275.0 per 10,000 population (2006).

Newspapers: Courier-News (Local news; Circulation 33,240)

Transportation: Commute to work: 92.6% car, 2.7% public transportation, 1.9% walk, 2.1% work from home (2000); Travel time to work: 29.5% less than 15 minutes, 32.7% 15 to 30 minutes, 19.8% 30 to 45 minutes, 9.3% 45 to 60 minutes, 8.6% 60 minutes or more (2000)

Additional Information Contacts

City of Elgin . . . . (847) 931-6100
http://www.cityofelgin.org
Elgin Area Chamber of Commerce . . . . (847) 741-5660
http://www.elginchamber.com

GENEVA (city). County seat. Covers a land area of 8.407 square miles and a water area of 0.176 square miles. Located at 41.88° N. Lat.; 88.31° W. Long. Elevation is 712 feet.

History: Named for Geneva, New York. Geneva was settled about 1832 by soldiers returning from the Black Hawk War and by pioneers heading west.

Population: 13,292 (1990); 19,515 (2000); 24,072 (2007); 27,090 (2012 projected); Race: 95.6% White, 1.0% Black, 1.9% Asian, 3.4% Hispanic of any race (2007); Density: 2,863.5 persons per square mile (2007); Average household size: 2.98 (2007); Median age: 35.2 (2007); Males per 100 females: 101.3 (2007); Marriage status: 20.4% never married, 67.0% now married, 5.2% widowed, 7.4% divorced (2000); Foreign born: 4.5% (2000); Ancestry (includes multiple ancestries): 29.7% German, 23.9% Irish, 11.0% Polish, 10.3% English, 9.8% Italian (2000).

Economy: Single-family building permits issued: 31 (2007); Multi-family building permits issued: 0 (2007); Employment by occupation: 24.5% management, 27.4% professional, 8.8% services, 27.7% sales, 0.3% farming, 4.5% construction, 6.8% production (2000).

Income: Per capita income: $37,599 (2007); Median household income: $90,279 (2007); Average household income: $111,162 (2007); Percent of households with income of $100,000 or more: 43.8% (2007); Poverty rate: 2.2% (2000).

Taxes: Total city taxes per capita: $413 (2006); City property taxes per capita: $287 (2006).

Education: Percent of population age 25 and over with: High school diploma (including GED) or higher: 95.7% (2007); Bachelor's degree or higher: 53.6% (2007); Master's degree or higher: 19.7% (2007).

School District(s)

Geneva CUSD 304 (PK-12)
2005-06 Enrollment: 5,814 . . . . (630) 463-3000
Kane Roe (07-12)
2005-06 Enrollment: 60 . . . . (630) 232-5955

Housing: Homeownership rate: 84.7% (2007); Median home value: $319,495 (2007); Median rent: $810 per month (2000); Median age of housing: 20 years (2000).

Hospitals: Delnor-Community Health System (118 beds)

Safety: Violent crime rate: 9.8 per 10,000 population; Property crime rate: 123.4 per 10,000 population (2006).

Newspapers: El Conquistador (Local news; Circulation 15,000); Kane County Chronicle (Local news; Circulation 14,000)

Transportation: Commute to work: 87.9% car, 5.8% public transportation, 2.0% walk, 4.0% work from home (2000); Travel time to work: 32.7% less than 15 minutes, 26.7% 15 to 30 minutes, 16.4% 30 to 45 minutes, 9.1% 45 to 60 minutes, 15.1% 60 minutes or more (2000)

Additional Information Contacts

City of Geneva . . . . (630) 232-7494
http://www.geneva.il.us
Geneva Chamber of Commerce . . . . (630) 232-6060
http://www.genevachamber.com

GILBERTS (village). Covers a land area of 3.214 square miles and a water area of 0.004 square miles. Located at 42.10° N. Lat.; 88.36° W. Long. Elevation is 899 feet.

Population: 1,039 (1990); 1,279 (2000); 2,387 (2007); 3,092 (2012 projected); Race: 93.8% White, 0.2% Black, 2.6% Asian, 4.0% Hispanic of any race (2007); Density: 742.7 persons per square mile (2007); Average household size: 3.21 (2007); Median age: 35.2 (2007); Males per 100 females: 100.4 (2007); Marriage status: 21.5% never married, 70.8% now married, 3.5% widowed, 4.2% divorced (2000); Foreign born: 2.4% (2000); Ancestry (includes multiple ancestries): 38.6% German, 16.5% Irish, 14.7% Polish, 13.2% Italian, 9.0% English (2000).

Economy: Single-family building permits issued: 87 (2007); Multi-family building permits issued: 0 (2007); Employment by occupation: 16.8% management, 20.1% professional, 9.9% services, 30.5% sales, 0.0% farming, 14.0% construction, 8.7% production (2000).

Income: Per capita income: $35,971 (2007); Median household income: $100,177 (2007); Average household income: $115,407 (2007); Percent of households with income of $100,000 or more: 50.1% (2007); Poverty rate: 0.6% (2000).

Education: Percent of population age 25 and over with: High school diploma (including GED) or higher: 93.2% (2007); Bachelor's degree or higher: 25.2% (2007); Master's degree or higher: 8.8% (2007).

Housing: Homeownership rate: 95.3% (2007); Median home value: $299,844 (2007); Median rent: $688 per month (2000); Median age of housing: 16 years (2000).

Safety: Violent crime rate: 16.4 per 10,000 population; Property crime rate: 88.3 per 10,000 population (2006).

Transportation: Commute to work: 92.9% car, 1.7% public transportation, 0.8% walk, 3.8% work from home (2000); Travel time to work: 22.4% less than 15 minutes, 30.1% 15 to 30 minutes, 22.0% 30 to 45 minutes, 14.2% 45 to 60 minutes, 11.3% 60 minutes or more (2000)

HAMPSHIRE (village). Covers a land area of 4.877 square miles and a water area of 0 square miles. Located at 42.09° N. Lat.; 88.52° W. Long. Elevation is 899 feet.

Population: 1,960 (1990); 2,900 (2000); 4,660 (2007); 5,722 (2012 projected); Race: 98.0% White, 0.1% Black, 0.2% Asian, 2.6% Hispanic of any race (2007); Density: 955.6 persons per square mile (2007); Average household size: 2.93 (2007); Median age: 30.7 (2007); Males per 100 females: 97.2 (2007); Marriage status: 23.5% never married, 62.0% now married, 6.4% widowed, 8.1% divorced (2000); Foreign born: 2.0% (2000); Ancestry (includes multiple ancestries): 45.8% German, 18.1% Irish, 11.2% Italian, 9.9% Polish, 9.1% English (2000).

Economy: Single-family building permits issued: 322 (2007); Multi-family building permits issued: 0 (2007); Employment by occupation: 13.6% management, 17.5% professional, 12.7% services, 27.2% sales, 0.3% farming, 12.7% construction, 16.1% production (2000).

Income: Per capita income: $25,415 (2007); Median household income: $67,105 (2007); Average household income: $74,394 (2007); Percent of households with income of $100,000 or more: 21.8% (2007); Poverty rate: 2.9% (2000).

Education: Percent of population age 25 and over with: High school diploma (including GED) or higher: 87.2% (2007); Bachelor's degree or higher: 19.1% (2007); Master's degree or higher: 4.4% (2007).

School District(s)

CUSD 300 (PK-12)
2005-06 Enrollment: 18,670 . . . . (847) 426-1300

Housing: Homeownership rate: 80.8% (2007); Median home value: $225,949 (2007); Median rent: $633 per month (2000); Median age of housing: 24 years (2000).

Safety: Violent crime rate: 4.9 per 10,000 population; Property crime rate: 98.1 per 10,000 population (2006).

Transportation: Commute to work: 90.6% car, 1.3% public transportation, 3.0% walk, 3.6% work from home (2000); Travel time to work: 29.5% less

than 15 minutes, 30.3% 15 to 30 minutes, 22.9% 30 to 45 minutes, 7.4% 45 to 60 minutes, 9.9% 60 minutes or more (2000)

Additional Information Contacts

Hampshire Chamber of Commerce . . . . (847) 683-1122
http://www.hampshirechamber.org

LILY LAKE (village). Covers a land area of 2.246 square miles and a water area of <.001 square miles. Located at 41.94° N. Lat.; 88.47° W. Long. Elevation is 961 feet.

Population: 714 (1990); 825 (2000); 968 (2007); 1,060 (2012 projected); Race: 97.5% White, 1.1% Black, 0.2% Asian, 2.7% Hispanic of any race (2007); Density: 431.0 persons per square mile (2007); Average household size: 3.27 (2007); Median age: 35.2 (2007); Males per 100 females: 114.2 (2007); Marriage status: 21.0% never married, 72.4% now married, 3.1% widowed, 3.5% divorced (2000); Foreign born: 3.5% (2000); Ancestry (includes multiple ancestries): 31.6% German, 14.6% Irish, 13.4% Polish, 9.2% Swedish, 7.4% Italian (2000).
Economy: Employment by occupation: 17.3% management, 20.7% professional, 6.1% services, 35.1% sales, 0.0% farming, 10.8% construction, 9.9% production (2000).
Income: Per capita income: $32,846 (2007); Median household income: $89,145 (2007); Average household income: $107,416 (2007); Percent of households with income of $100,000 or more: 38.9% (2007); Poverty rate: 0.6% (2000).
Taxes: Total city taxes per capita: $162 (2006); City property taxes per capita: $0 (2006).
Education: Percent of population age 25 and over with: High school diploma (including GED) or higher: 94.5% (2007); Bachelor's degree or higher: 27.2% (2007); Master's degree or higher: 7.2% (2007).
Housing: Homeownership rate: 95.6% (2007); Median home value: $282,500 (2007); Median rent: $675 per month (2000); Median age of housing: 22 years (2000).
Transportation: Commute to work: 91.6% car, 2.9% public transportation, 1.1% walk, 4.1% work from home (2000); Travel time to work: 13.7% less than 15 minutes, 36.1% 15 to 30 minutes, 25.2% 30 to 45 minutes, 11.6% 45 to 60 minutes, 13.4% 60 minutes or more (2000)

MAPLE PARK (village). Covers a land area of 0.594 square miles and a water area of 0 square miles. Located at 41.90° N. Lat.; 88.59° W. Long. Elevation is 863 feet.

Population: 690 (1990); 765 (2000); 1,264 (2007); 1,590 (2012 projected); Race: 96.4% White, 0.0% Black, 0.2% Asian, 3.5% Hispanic of any race (2007); Density: 2,128.3 persons per square mile (2007); Average household size: 2.72 (2007); Median age: 33.7 (2007); Males per 100 females: 107.2 (2007); Marriage status: 29.0% never married, 54.6% now married, 7.7% widowed, 8.7% divorced (2000); Foreign born: 0.4% (2000); Ancestry (includes multiple ancestries): 37.1% German, 13.2% Irish, 12.0% Norwegian, 11.8% United States or American, 9.4% English (2000).
Economy: Single-family building permits issued: 12 (2007); Multi-family building permits issued: 0 (2007); Employment by occupation: 10.0% management, 13.7% professional, 8.9% services, 28.3% sales, 1.9% farming, 15.9% construction, 21.3% production (2000).
Income: Per capita income: $26,264 (2007); Median household income: $58,043 (2007); Average household income: $71,546 (2007); Percent of households with income of $100,000 or more: 17.9% (2007); Poverty rate: 5.8% (2000).
Education: Percent of population age 25 and over with: High school diploma (including GED) or higher: 91.0% (2007); Bachelor's degree or higher: 15.6% (2007); Master's degree or higher: 5.5% (2007).

School District(s)

Central CUSD 301 (PK-12)
2005-06 Enrollment: 2,594 . . . . (847) 464-6005
Fox Valley Career Center
2005-06 Enrollment: n/a . . . . (630) 365-5113
Kaneland CUSD 302 (PK-12)
2005-06 Enrollment: 3,994 . . . . (630) 365-5111

Housing: Homeownership rate: 79.1% (2007); Median home value: $194,612 (2007); Median rent: $522 per month (2000); Median age of housing: 43 years (2000).
Safety: Violent crime rate: 0.0 per 10,000 population; Property crime rate: 88.3 per 10,000 population (2006).
Transportation: Commute to work: 93.3% car, 1.1% public transportation, 1.1% walk, 4.6% work from home (2000); Travel time to work: 16.7% less than 15 minutes, 45.2% 15 to 30 minutes, 23.2% 30 to 45 minutes, 9.0% 45 to 60 minutes, 5.9% 60 minutes or more (2000)

MONTGOMERY (village). Covers a land area of 6.415 square miles and a water area of 0.196 square miles. Located at 41.72° N. Lat.; 88.32° W. Long. Elevation is 640 feet.

Population: 4,644 (1990); 5,471 (2000); 8,324 (2007); 10,221 (2012 projected); Race: 83.5% White, 4.7% Black, 1.1% Asian, 21.7% Hispanic of any race (2007); Density: 1,297.7 persons per square mile (2007); Average household size: 2.56 (2007); Median age: 35.4 (2007); Males per 100 females: 96.7 (2007); Marriage status: 21.5% never married, 62.7% now married, 8.1% widowed, 7.7% divorced (2000); Foreign born: 5.8% (2000); Ancestry (includes multiple ancestries): 30.6% German, 14.9% Other groups, 12.1% Irish, 10.6% English, 6.0% Polish (2000).
Economy: Single-family building permits issued: 244 (2007); Multi-family building permits issued: 0 (2007); Employment by occupation: 14.2% management, 12.6% professional, 11.4% services, 32.5% sales, 0.2% farming, 11.9% construction, 17.1% production (2000).
Income: Per capita income: $25,874 (2007); Median household income: $58,380 (2007); Average household income: $66,147 (2007); Percent of households with income of $100,000 or more: 16.5% (2007); Poverty rate: 3.7% (2000).
Education: Percent of population age 25 and over with: High school diploma (including GED) or higher: 83.0% (2007); Bachelor's degree or higher: 19.0% (2007); Master's degree or higher: 4.9% (2007).

School District(s)

Aurora West Usd 129 (PK-12)
2005-06 Enrollment: 12,491 . . . . (630) 301-5033
Kaneland CUSD 302 (PK-12)
2005-06 Enrollment: 3,994 . . . . (630) 365-5111
Oswego CUSD 308 (PK-12)
2005-06 Enrollment: 12,599 . . . . (630) 636-3080

Housing: Homeownership rate: 76.6% (2007); Median home value: $190,278 (2007); Median rent: $578 per month (2000); Median age of housing: 32 years (2000).
Safety: Violent crime rate: 10.9 per 10,000 population; Property crime rate: 325.3 per 10,000 population (2006).
Transportation: Commute to work: 94.2% car, 1.9% public transportation, 0.4% walk, 3.2% work from home (2000); Travel time to work: 27.6% less than 15 minutes, 35.4% 15 to 30 minutes, 18.0% 30 to 45 minutes, 8.7% 45 to 60 minutes, 10.4% 60 minutes or more (2000)

Additional Information Contacts

Greater Montgomery Area Chamber of Commerce. . . . . . . (630) 897-8137
http://www.chamberofmontgomeryil.org
Village of Montgomery . . . . (630) 896-0791
http://ci.montgomery.il.us

NORTH AURORA (village). Covers a land area of 5.159 square miles and a water area of 0.147 square miles. Located at 41.80° N. Lat.; 88.32° W. Long. Elevation is 679 feet.

Population: 6,673 (1990); 10,585 (2000); 14,896 (2007); 17,673 (2012 projected); Race: 84.0% White, 4.5% Black, 3.5% Asian, 13.6% Hispanic of any race (2007); Density: 2,887.4 persons per square mile (2007); Average household size: 2.64 (2007); Median age: 34.5 (2007); Males per 100 females: 99.8 (2007); Marriage status: 22.0% never married, 64.4% now married, 5.8% widowed, 7.9% divorced (2000); Foreign born: 8.0% (2000); Ancestry (includes multiple ancestries): 32.8% German, 17.9% Other groups, 17.2% Irish, 9.1% Polish, 7.9% English (2000).
Economy: Single-family building permits issued: 97 (2007); Multi-family building permits issued: 0 (2007); Employment by occupation: 14.2% management, 19.4% professional, 10.5% services, 34.9% sales, 0.1% farming, 8.3% construction, 12.5% production (2000).
Income: Per capita income: $29,108 (2007); Median household income: $64,834 (2007); Average household income: $76,542 (2007); Percent of households with income of $100,000 or more: 24.8% (2007); Poverty rate: 3.0% (2000).
Education: Percent of population age 25 and over with: High school diploma (including GED) or higher: 87.9% (2007); Bachelor's degree or higher: 30.9% (2007); Master's degree or higher: 9.1% (2007).

School District(s)

Aurora West Usd 129 (PK-12)
2005-06 Enrollment: 12,491 . . . . (630) 301-5033

Vocational/Technical School(s)

Everest College-North Aurora (Private, For-profit)
Fall 2007 Enrollment: 103 . . . . (630) 896-2140
2007-08 Tuition: $10,700

Housing: Homeownership rate: 78.4% (2007); Median home value: $216,542 (2007); Median rent: $662 per month (2000); Median age of housing: 19 years (2000).
Safety: Violent crime rate: 38.2 per 10,000 population; Property crime rate: 253.6 per 10,000 population (2006).
Transportation: Commute to work: 94.5% car, 1.3% public transportation, 0.7% walk, 2.6% work from home (2000); Travel time to work: 24.7% less than 15 minutes, 39.3% 15 to 30 minutes, 18.7% 30 to 45 minutes, 9.2% 45 to 60 minutes, 8.1% 60 minutes or more (2000)
Additional Information Contacts
Village of North Aurora. . . . . (630) 897-8228
http://www.vil.north-aurora.il.us

PINGREE GROVE (village). Covers a land area of 0.616 square miles and a water area of 0 square miles. Located at 42.06° N. Lat.; 88.41° W. Long. Elevation is 912 feet.
Population: 130 (1990); 124 (2000); 251 (2007); 335 (2012 projected); Race: 99.6% White, 0.0% Black, 0.0% Asian, 4.8% Hispanic of any race (2007); Density: 407.5 persons per square mile (2007); Average household size: 2.51 (2007); Median age: 44.6 (2007); Males per 100 females: 90.2 (2007); Marriage status: 9.4% never married, 65.9% now married, 15.3% widowed, 9.4% divorced (2000); Foreign born: 0.0% (2000); Ancestry (includes multiple ancestries): 52.2% German, 13.0% French (except Basque), 9.8% Other groups, 7.6% English, 6.5% Irish (2000).
Economy: Single-family building permits issued: 202 (2007); Multi-family building permits issued: 0 (2007); Employment by occupation: 6.7% management, 24.4% professional, 13.3% services, 35.6% sales, 0.0% farming, 8.9% construction, 11.1% production (2000).
Income: Per capita income: $24,721 (2007); Median household income: $52,941 (2007); Average household income: $62,050 (2007); Percent of households with income of $100,000 or more: 18.0% (2007); Poverty rate: 0.0% (2000).
Education: Percent of population age 25 and over with: High school diploma (including GED) or higher: 66.7% (2007); Bachelor's degree or higher: 6.7% (2007); Master's degree or higher: 3.6% (2007).
Housing: Homeownership rate: 86.0% (2007); Median home value: $162,500 (2007); Median rent: $425 per month (2000); Median age of housing: 59 years (2000).
Transportation: Commute to work: 93.3% car, 0.0% public transportation, 6.7% walk, 0.0% work from home (2000); Travel time to work: 20.0% less than 15 minutes, 55.6% 15 to 30 minutes, 8.9% 30 to 45 minutes, 15.6% 45 to 60 minutes, 0.0% 60 minutes or more (2000)

SAINT CHARLES (city). Covers a land area of 13.990 square miles and a water area of 0.158 square miles. Located at 41.91° N. Lat.; 88.31° W. Long. Elevation is 732 feet.
History: Named for Saint Charles Borromeo (1538-1584), an Italian cardinal. The community of St. Charles developed around a mill in the mid-1800's, and became a residential area for people moving out from Chicago.
Population: 24,173 (1990); 27,896 (2000); 32,053 (2007); 34,834 (2012 projected); Race: 90.5% White, 2.0% Black, 3.1% Asian, 8.5% Hispanic of any race (2007); Density: 2,291.1 persons per square mile (2007); Average household size: 2.67 (2007); Median age: 36.3 (2007); Males per 100 females: 101.1 (2007); Marriage status: 24.3% never married, 61.6% now married, 5.4% widowed, 8.8% divorced (2000); Foreign born: 6.6% (2000); Ancestry (includes multiple ancestries): 29.7% German, 17.9% Irish, 12.2% English, 10.6% Polish, 9.6% Italian (2000).
Economy: Unemployment rate: 4.3% (4/2008); Total civilian labor force: 19,467 (4/2008); Single-family building permits issued: 30 (2007); Multi-family building permits issued: 0 (2007); Employment by occupation: 20.1% management, 22.7% professional, 9.8% services, 31.8% sales, 0.1% farming, 6.5% construction, 8.9% production (2000).
Income: Per capita income: $38,950 (2007); Median household income: $79,060 (2007); Average household income: $103,198 (2007); Percent of households with income of $100,000 or more: 36.7% (2007); Poverty rate: 3.4% (2000).
Taxes: Total city taxes per capita: $714 (2006); City property taxes per capita: $316 (2006).
Education: Percent of population age 25 and over with: High school diploma (including GED) or higher: 91.6% (2007); Bachelor's degree or higher: 43.0% (2007); Master's degree or higher: 14.6% (2007).

School District(s)

Dept of Corrections Sch Dist 428 (08-12)
2005-06 Enrollment: 2,271 . . . . (217) 522-2666
Mid-Valley Special Ed Coop (02-12)
2005-06 Enrollment: 58 . . . . (630) 513-4400
St Charles CUSD 303 (PK-12)
2005-06 Enrollment: 13,443 . . . . (630) 513-3030
Housing: Homeownership rate: 73.5% (2007); Median home value: $280,006 (2007); Median rent: $748 per month (2000); Median age of housing: 22 years (2000).
Safety: Violent crime rate: 19.5 per 10,000 population; Property crime rate: 268.2 per 10,000 population (2006).
Newspapers: Batavia Republican (Community news; Circulation 3,200); The Farmside (Regional news; Circulation 1,563); Geneva Republican (Local news; Circulation 25,000); Saint Charles Republican (Community news; Circulation 16,500); West Chicago Press (Local news; Circulation 4,000); Winfield Press (Local news; Circulation 3,700)
Transportation: Commute to work: 90.9% car, 3.2% public transportation, 1.6% walk, 3.8% work from home (2000); Travel time to work: 37.2% less than 15 minutes, 26.1% 15 to 30 minutes, 19.2% 30 to 45 minutes, 8.2% 45 to 60 minutes, 9.4% 60 minutes or more (2000)
Additional Information Contacts
City of Saint Charles . . . . (630) 377-4400
http://www.ci.st-charles.il.us
St. Charles Chamber of Commerce. . . . . (630) 584-8384
http://www.stcharleschamber.com

SLEEPY HOLLOW (village). Covers a land area of 2.011 square miles and a water area of 0.015 square miles. Located at 42.09° N. Lat.; 88.31° W. Long. Elevation is 738 feet.
Population: 3,311 (1990); 3,553 (2000); 4,270 (2007); 4,744 (2012 projected); Race: 89.6% White, 0.6% Black, 3.8% Asian, 5.6% Hispanic of any race (2007); Density: 2,122.8 persons per square mile (2007); Average household size: 2.97 (2007); Median age: 37.8 (2007); Males per 100 females: 103.0 (2007); Marriage status: 17.4% never married, 74.7% now married, 2.2% widowed, 5.7% divorced (2000); Foreign born: 8.8% (2000); Ancestry (includes multiple ancestries): 33.6% German, 17.5% Polish, 14.8% Irish, 12.0% Italian, 10.3% English (2000).
Economy: Single-family building permits issued: 0 (2007); Multi-family building permits issued: 0 (2007); Employment by occupation: 28.6% management, 20.6% professional, 5.6% services, 29.3% sales, 0.0% farming, 7.7% construction, 8.1% production (2000).
Income: Per capita income: $36,423 (2007); Median household income: $99,170 (2007); Average household income: $108,155 (2007); Percent of households with income of $100,000 or more: 49.4% (2007); Poverty rate: 1.8% (2000).
Education: Percent of population age 25 and over with: High school diploma (including GED) or higher: 94.3% (2007); Bachelor's degree or higher: 42.0% (2007); Master's degree or higher: 13.1% (2007).

School District(s)

CUSD 300 (PK-12)
2005-06 Enrollment: 18,670 . . . . (847) 426-1300
Housing: Homeownership rate: 90.3% (2007); Median home value: $344,052 (2007); Median rent: $752 per month (2000); Median age of housing: 24 years (2000).
Safety: Violent crime rate: 0.0 per 10,000 population; Property crime rate: 70.4 per 10,000 population (2006).
Transportation: Commute to work: 91.5% car, 2.2% public transportation, 0.4% walk, 5.1% work from home (2000); Travel time to work: 24.2% less than 15 minutes, 22.7% 15 to 30 minutes, 27.7% 30 to 45 minutes, 13.7% 45 to 60 minutes, 11.7% 60 minutes or more (2000)

SOUTH ELGIN (village). Covers a land area of 6.288 square miles and a water area of 0.123 square miles. Located at 41.99° N. Lat.; 88.30° W. Long. Elevation is 709 feet.
Population: 9,247 (1990); 16,100 (2000); 20,595 (2007); 23,511 (2012 projected); Race: 79.1% White, 2.9% Black, 9.9% Asian, 14.0% Hispanic of any race (2007); Density: 3,275.3 persons per square mile (2007); Average household size: 2.88 (2007); Median age: 32.5 (2007); Males per 100 females: 101.8 (2007); Marriage status: 21.2% never married, 64.5% now married, 4.5% widowed, 9.8% divorced (2000); Foreign born: 9.1% (2000); Ancestry (includes multiple ancestries): 29.6% German, 22.0% Other groups, 14.2% Irish, 11.8% Italian, 10.8% Polish (2000).
Economy: Single-family building permits issued: 28 (2007); Multi-family building permits issued: 14 (2007); Employment by occupation: 16.4% management, 16.3% professional, 11.8% services, 30.2% sales, 0.1% farming, 9.3% construction, 15.9% production (2000).

Income: Per capita income: $29,275 (2007); Median household income: $74,882 (2007); Average household income: $84,183 (2007); Percent of households with income of $100,000 or more: 26.5% (2007); Poverty rate: 3.0% (2000).
Education: Percent of population age 25 and over with: High school diploma (including GED) or higher: 90.7% (2007); Bachelor's degree or higher: 26.3% (2007); Master's degree or higher: 5.9% (2007).

School District(s)

SD U-46 (PK-12)
2005-06 Enrollment: 39,656 . . . . (847) 888-5000
St Charles CUSD 303 (PK-12)
2005-06 Enrollment: 13,443 . . . . (630) 513-3030

Housing: Homeownership rate: 90.1% (2007); Median home value: $218,722 (2007); Median rent: $675 per month (2000); Median age of housing: 8 years (2000).
Safety: Violent crime rate: 12.5 per 10,000 population; Property crime rate: 169.1 per 10,000 population (2006).
Transportation: Commute to work: 92.2% car, 2.6% public transportation, 0.8% walk, 4.1% work from home (2000); Travel time to work: 21.5% less than 15 minutes, 30.8% 15 to 30 minutes, 22.5% 30 to 45 minutes, 11.0% 45 to 60 minutes, 14.2% 60 minutes or more (2000)

Additional Information Contacts

South Elgin Chamber of Commerce . . . . (847) 888-2287
http://www.southelginchamber.com
Village of South Elgin. . . . . (847) 741-2141
http://www.southelgin.com

SUGAR GROVE (village). Covers a land area of 6.449 square miles and a water area of 0.015 square miles. Located at 41.77° N. Lat.; 88.44° W. Long. Elevation is 719 feet.
Population: 2,522 (1990); 3,909 (2000); 7,423 (2007); 9,648 (2012 projected); Race: 94.2% White, 1.7% Black, 0.8% Asian, 6.6% Hispanic of any race (2007); Density: 1,151.0 persons per square mile (2007); Average household size: 3.06 (2007); Median age: 34.4 (2007); Males per 100 females: 101.9 (2007); Marriage status: 17.3% never married, 70.6% now married, 3.0% widowed, 9.1% divorced (2000); Foreign born: 1.7% (2000); Ancestry (includes multiple ancestries): 30.5% German, 15.9% Irish, 11.8% Other groups, 11.7% Italian, 9.2% English (2000).
Economy: Single-family building permits issued: 64 (2007); Multi-family building permits issued: 0 (2007); Employment by occupation: 22.2% management, 20.3% professional, 6.1% services, 29.3% sales, 0.0% farming, 9.5% construction, 12.7% production (2000).
Income: Per capita income: $33,560 (2007); Median household income: $84,347 (2007); Average household income: $102,771 (2007); Percent of households with income of $100,000 or more: 35.4% (2007); Poverty rate: 1.8% (2000).
Education: Percent of population age 25 and over with: High school diploma (including GED) or higher: 97.4% (2007); Bachelor's degree or higher: 32.5% (2007); Master's degree or higher: 8.8% (2007).

School District(s)

Kaneland CUSD 302 (PK-12)
2005-06 Enrollment: 3,994 . . . . (630) 365-5111

Two-year College(s)

Waubonsee Community College (Public)
Fall 2007 Enrollment: 8,731. . . . . (630) 466-7900
2007-08 Tuition: In-state $5,391; Out-of-state $6,048

Housing: Homeownership rate: 88.1% (2007); Median home value: $256,774 (2007); Median rent: $694 per month (2000); Median age of housing: 12 years (2000).
Safety: Violent crime rate: 3.8 per 10,000 population; Property crime rate: 96.8 per 10,000 population (2006).
Transportation: Commute to work: 91.8% car, 1.8% public transportation, 0.3% walk, 5.3% work from home (2000); Travel time to work: 18.6% less than 15 minutes, 34.4% 15 to 30 minutes, 25.6% 30 to 45 minutes, 12.9% 45 to 60 minutes, 8.5% 60 minutes or more (2000)

Additional Information Contacts

Sugar Grove Chamber of Commerce & Industry. . . . . (630) 466-7895
http://www.sugargrovechamber.org

VIRGIL (village). Covers a land area of 1.882 square miles and a water area of 0 square miles. Located at 41.95° N. Lat.; 88.52° W. Long. Elevation is 869 feet.
Population: 263 (1990); 266 (2000); 380 (2007); 453 (2012 projected); Race: 96.8% White, 1.1% Black, 0.3% Asian, 3.2% Hispanic of any race (2007); Density: 201.9 persons per square mile (2007); Average household size: 3.06 (2007); Median age: 34.5 (2007); Males per 100 females: 100.0 (2007); Marriage status: 18.1% never married, 66.7% now married, 3.4% widowed, 11.9% divorced (2000); Foreign born: 0.0% (2000); Ancestry (includes multiple ancestries): 32.0% German, 19.9% Irish, 14.1% English, 11.2% Italian, 10.8% Other groups (2000).
Economy: Employment by occupation: 16.5% management, 12.8% professional, 15.8% services, 22.6% sales, 0.8% farming, 11.3% construction, 20.3% production (2000).
Income: Per capita income: $33,059 (2007); Median household income: $82,407 (2007); Average household income: $101,310 (2007); Percent of households with income of $100,000 or more: 34.7% (2007); Poverty rate: 0.4% (2000).
Education: Percent of population age 25 and over with: High school diploma (including GED) or higher: 85.0% (2007); Bachelor's degree or higher: 9.7% (2007); Master's degree or higher: 4.0% (2007).
Housing: Homeownership rate: 85.5% (2007); Median home value: $226,000 (2007); Median rent: $575 per month (2000); Median age of housing: 28 years (2000).
Transportation: Commute to work: 91.0% car, 3.0% public transportation, 3.8% walk, 2.3% work from home (2000); Travel time to work: 20.8% less than 15 minutes, 20.8% 15 to 30 minutes, 32.3% 30 to 45 minutes, 10.0% 45 to 60 minutes, 16.2% 60 minutes or more (2000)

WEST DUNDEE (village). Aka Dundee. Covers a land area of 2.660 square miles and a water area of 0.078 square miles. Located at 42.09° N. Lat.; 88.28° W. Long. Elevation is 761 feet.
History: West Dundee was settled by Scots and English in the 1830's, and named for Dundee, Scotland. Allan Pinkerton (1819-1884) operated a coopers trade in West Dundee, but found a second career as a detective when his evidence resulted in the capture of some counterfeiters.
Population: 3,794 (1990); 5,428 (2000); 7,306 (2007); 8,525 (2012 projected); Race: 90.3% White, 0.8% Black, 4.1% Asian, 5.6% Hispanic of any race (2007); Density: 2,746.5 persons per square mile (2007); Average household size: 2.68 (2007); Median age: 35.5 (2007); Males per 100 females: 96.6 (2007); Marriage status: 21.3% never married, 60.4% now married, 6.0% widowed, 12.2% divorced (2000); Foreign born: 6.9% (2000); Ancestry (includes multiple ancestries): 35.9% German, 19.7% Irish, 11.2% Polish, 8.3% English, 7.9% Italian (2000).
Economy: Single-family building permits issued: 6 (2007); Multi-family building permits issued: 0 (2007); Employment by occupation: 23.3% management, 21.4% professional, 7.0% services, 32.3% sales, 0.0% farming, 6.4% construction, 9.7% production (2000).
Income: Per capita income: $34,889 (2007); Median household income: $69,718 (2007); Average household income: $93,439 (2007); Percent of households with income of $100,000 or more: 34.5% (2007); Poverty rate: 3.7% (2000).
Education: Percent of population age 25 and over with: High school diploma (including GED) or higher: 91.2% (2007); Bachelor's degree or higher: 37.3% (2007); Master's degree or higher: 13.6% (2007).

School District(s)

CUSD 300 (PK-12)
2005-06 Enrollment: 18,670 . . . . (847) 426-1300

Vocational/Technical School(s)

Hair Professionals Academy of Cosmetology (Private, For-profit)
Fall 2007 Enrollment: 189 . . . . (847) 836-5900
2007-08 Tuition: $15,588

Housing: Homeownership rate: 72.5% (2007); Median home value: $292,120 (2007); Median rent: $669 per month (2000); Median age of housing: 32 years (2000).
Safety: Violent crime rate: 7.6 per 10,000 population; Property crime rate: 469.8 per 10,000 population (2006).
Transportation: Commute to work: 91.5% car, 2.8% public transportation, 1.0% walk, 4.8% work from home (2000); Travel time to work: 27.9% less than 15 minutes, 28.9% 15 to 30 minutes, 21.6% 30 to 45 minutes, 12.6% 45 to 60 minutes, 9.0% 60 minutes or more (2000)

Additional Information Contacts

Village of West Dundee . . . . (847) 551-3800
http://www.west-dundee.il.us

Kankakee County

Located in northeastern Illinois; bounded on the east by Indiana; drained by the Kankakee and Iroquois Rivers. Covers a land area of 676.75 square miles, a water area of 4.70 square miles, and is located in the Central Time Zone. The county was founded in 1853. County seat is Kankakee.

Kankakee County is part of the Kankakee-Bradley, IL Metropolitan Statistical Area. The entire metro area includes: Kankakee County, IL

Weather Station: Kankakee Metro Wastewater Elevation: 639 feet

	Jan	Feb	Mar	Apr	May	Jun	Jul	Aug	Sep	Oct	Nov	Dec
High	31	36	48	60	72	82	86	83	77	65	50	36
Low	13	18	28	38	49	59	63	61	52	40	31	20
Precip	1.9	1.7	2.8	3.8	4.6	4.4	4.3	3.2	3.3	2.7	3.4	2.5
Snow	8.9	6.4	2.9	1.0	tr	0.0	0.0	0.0	0.0	tr	1.0	5.6

High and Low temperatures in degrees Fahrenheit; Precipitation and Snow in inches

Population: 96,255 (1990); 103,833 (2000); 109,248 (2007); 112,812 (2012 projected); Race: 78.9% White, 14.9% Black, 0.9% Asian, 6.9% Hispanic of any race (2007); Density: 161.4 persons per square mile (2007); Average household size: 2.69 (2007); Median age: 35.4 (2007); Males per 100 females: 95.4 (2007).
Religion: Five largest groups: 21.4% Catholic Church, 5.2% Church of the Nazarene, 4.6% The United Methodist Church, 4.5% Lutheran Church—Missouri Synod, 1.4% Southern Baptist Convention (2000).
Economy: Unemployment rate: 7.0% (4/2008); Total civilian labor force: 56,922 (4/2008); Leading industries: 16.6% health care and social assistance; 16.2% retail trade; 15.0% manufacturing (2005); Farms: 722 totaling 347,161 acres (2002); Companies that employ 500 or more persons: 6 (2006); Companies that employ 100 to 499 persons: 57 (2006); Companies that employ less than 100 persons: 2,321 (2006); Black-owned businesses: n/a (2002); Hispanic-owned businesses: n/a (2002); Asian-owned businesses: n/a (2002); Women-owned businesses: 1,791 (2002); Retail sales per capita: $13,677 (2008). Single-family building permits issued: 382 (2007); Multi-family building permits issued: 26 (2007).
Income: Per capita income: $22,742 (2007); Median household income: $48,576 (2007); Average household income: $60,021 (2007); Percent of households with income of $100,000 or more: 14.1% (2007); Poverty rate: 13.1% (2005); Bankruptcy rate: 3.78% (2007).
Taxes: Total county taxes per capita: $114 (2006); County property taxes per capita: $110 (2006).
Education: Percent of population age 25 and over with: High school diploma (including GED) or higher: 80.2% (2007); Bachelor's degree or higher: 15.2% (2007); Master's degree or higher: 5.7% (2007).
Housing: Homeownership rate: 70.2% (2007); Median home value: $125,824 (2007); Median rent: $443 per month (2000); Median age of housing: 36 years (2000).
Health: Birth rate: 149.9 per 10,000 population (2007); Death rate: 96.1 per 10,000 population (2007); Age-adjusted cancer mortality rate: 211.9 deaths per 100,000 population (2005); Number of physicians: 17.0 per 10,000 population (2005); Hospital beds: 41.5 per 10,000 population (2004); Hospital admissions: 1,909.4 per 10,000 population (2004).
Elections: 2004 Presidential election results: 54.9% Bush, 44.4% Kerry, 0.0% Nader, 0.7% Badnarik

Additional Information Contacts

Kankakee County Government . . . . (815) 937-3642
http://www.co.kankakee.il.us
Bradley-Bourbonnais Regional Chamber of Commerce . . . (815) 932-2222
http://www.bbchamber.com
City of Kankakee . . . . (815) 933-0480
http://www.ci.kankakee.il.us
Grant Park Chamber of Commerce . . . . (815) 465-0604
http://www.grantparkchamber.com
Herscher Chamber of Commerce . . . . (815) 426-2131
http://www.herscher.net
Kankakee River Valley Chamber. . . . . (815) 933-7721
Manteno Chamber of Commerce. . . . . (815) 468-6226
http://www.mantenochamber.com
Momence Chamber of Commerce. (815) 472-4620
http://www.momence.net
Village of Bourbonnais. . . . . (815) 937-3570
http://www.villageofbourbonnais.com
Village of Bradley. . . . . (815) 932-2125
http://www.bradleyil.org
Village of Manteno . . . . (815) 929-4800
http://manteno.govoffice.com

Kankakee County Communities

AROMA PARK (village). Covers a land area of 1.200 square miles and a water area of 0.185 square miles. Located at 41.07° N. Lat.; 87.80° W. Long. Elevation is 617 feet.
Population: 801 (1990); 821 (2000); 744 (2007); 750 (2012 projected); Race: 89.7% White, 5.9% Black, 0.0% Asian, 9.9% Hispanic of any race (2007); Density: 620.0 persons per square mile (2007); Average household size: 2.62 (2007); Median age: 38.7 (2007); Males per 100 females: 100.0 (2007); Marriage status: 21.6% never married, 60.1% now married, 5.3% widowed, 13.0% divorced (2000); Foreign born: 4.5% (2000); Ancestry (includes multiple ancestries): 31.1% German, 15.7% Other groups, 14.4% French (except Basque), 10.3% Irish, 8.0% English (2000).
Economy: Single-family building permits issued: 1 (2007); Multi-family building permits issued: 2 (2007); Employment by occupation: 9.3% management, 12.5% professional, 16.2% services, 25.8% sales, 0.5% farming, 16.0% construction, 19.7% production (2000).
Income: Per capita income: $22,553 (2007); Median household income: $46,296 (2007); Average household income: $57,201 (2007); Percent of households with income of $100,000 or more: 11.3% (2007); Poverty rate: 6.9% (2000).
Education: Percent of population age 25 and over with: High school diploma (including GED) or higher: 82.7% (2007); Bachelor's degree or higher: 10.4% (2007); Master's degree or higher: 5.8% (2007).

School District(s)

Kankakee SD 111 (PK-12)
2005-06 Enrollment: 5,971 . . . . (815) 933-0700
Housing: Homeownership rate: 77.5% (2007); Median home value: $109,434 (2007); Median rent: $389 per month (2000); Median age of housing: 44 years (2000).
Transportation: Commute to work: 92.7% car, 1.1% public transportation, 1.1% walk, 4.6% work from home (2000); Travel time to work: 29.8% less than 15 minutes, 47.4% 15 to 30 minutes, 11.9% 30 to 45 minutes, 5.1% 45 to 60 minutes, 5.7% 60 minutes or more (2000)

BONFIELD (village). Covers a land area of 0.274 square miles and a water area of 0 square miles. Located at 41.14° N. Lat.; 88.05° W. Long. Elevation is 630 feet.
Population: 299 (1990); 364 (2000); 416 (2007); 434 (2012 projected); Race: 97.6% White, 0.0% Black, 0.0% Asian, 1.7% Hispanic of any race (2007); Density: 1,518.7 persons per square mile (2007); Average household size: 2.93 (2007); Median age: 32.8 (2007); Males per 100 females: 90.0 (2007); Marriage status: 17.8% never married, 76.3% now married, 4.1% widowed, 1.9% divorced (2000); Foreign born: 0.3% (2000); Ancestry (includes multiple ancestries): 36.8% German, 13.0% Irish, 11.6% French (except Basque), 9.5% United States or American, 9.0% Polish (2000).
Economy: Single-family building permits issued: 0 (2007); Multi-family building permits issued: 0 (2007); Employment by occupation: 7.3% management, 16.3% professional, 10.1% services, 26.4% sales, 1.7% farming, 21.3% construction, 16.9% production (2000).
Income: Per capita income: $23,359 (2007); Median household income: $59,375 (2007); Average household income: $68,433 (2007); Percent of households with income of $100,000 or more: 19.0% (2007); Poverty rate: 2.6% (2000).
Education: Percent of population age 25 and over with: High school diploma (including GED) or higher: 90.8% (2007); Bachelor's degree or higher: 10.8% (2007); Master's degree or higher: 3.8% (2007).

School District(s)

Herscher CUSD 2 (PK-12)
2005-06 Enrollment: 2,160 . . . . (815) 426-2162
Housing: Homeownership rate: 82.4% (2007); Median home value: $168,125 (2007); Median rent: $425 per month (2000); Median age of housing: 34 years (2000).
Transportation: Commute to work: 87.6% car, 0.0% public transportation, 5.6% walk, 5.1% work from home (2000); Travel time to work: 17.9% less than 15 minutes, 42.3% 15 to 30 minutes, 20.8% 30 to 45 minutes, 11.3% 45 to 60 minutes, 7.7% 60 minutes or more (2000)

BOURBONNAIS (village). Covers a land area of 4.620 square miles and a water area of 0 square miles. Located at 41.16° N. Lat.; 87.87° W. Long. Elevation is 650 feet.
History: Fur trader Noel La Vasseur established a trading post here in 1832, which drew French-Canadian settlers to the community named for Francois Bourbonnais. Bourbonnais was the first settlement on the Kankakee River.
Population: 14,215 (1990); 15,256 (2000); 16,544 (2007); 17,345 (2012 projected); Race: 88.9% White, 5.4% Black, 3.1% Asian, 3.0% Hispanic of any race (2007); Density: 3,580.9 persons per square mile (2007); Average household size: 2.82 (2007); Median age: 32.7 (2007); Males per 100

females: 90.9 (2007); Marriage status: 29.1% never married, 58.1% now married, 5.3% widowed, 7.4% divorced (2000); Foreign born: 4.0% (2000); Ancestry (includes multiple ancestries): 25.4% German, 14.7% Irish, 13.1% Other groups, 12.1% French (except Basque), 8.2% English (2000).
Economy: Single-family building permits issued: 106 (2007); Multi-family building permits issued: 0 (2007); Employment by occupation: 11.8% management, 22.5% professional, 14.7% services, 29.5% sales, 0.0% farming, 7.5% construction, 14.0% production (2000).
Income: Per capita income: $25,312 (2007); Median household income: $55,389 (2007); Average household income: $69,341 (2007); Percent of households with income of $100,000 or more: 17.0% (2007); Poverty rate: 6.5% (2000).
Education: Percent of population age 25 and over with: High school diploma (including GED) or higher: 88.8% (2007); Bachelor's degree or higher: 26.7% (2007); Master's degree or higher: 10.8% (2007).

School District(s)

Bourbonnais SD 53 (PK-08)
2005-06 Enrollment: 2,497 . . . . (815) 939-2574
Kankakee Area Career Center
2005-06 Enrollment: n/a . . . . (815) 939-4971
St George CCSD 258 (PK-08)
2005-06 Enrollment: 331 . . . . (815) 933-1503

Four-year College(s)

Olivet Nazarene University (Private, Not-for-profit, Church of the Nazarene)
Fall 2007 Enrollment: 4,636. . . . . (815) 939-5011
2007-08 Tuition: In-state $19,590; Out-of-state $19,590

Housing: Homeownership rate: 63.3% (2007); Median home value: $155,997 (2007); Median rent: $526 per month (2000); Median age of housing: 24 years (2000).
Safety: Violent crime rate: 10.7 per 10,000 population; Property crime rate: 225.2 per 10,000 population (2006).
Newspapers: Daily Journal - Bourbonnais Bureau (Local news; Circulation 0)
Transportation: Commute to work: 91.0% car, 1.0% public transportation, 4.9% walk, 2.9% work from home (2000); Travel time to work: 52.8% less than 15 minutes, 25.4% 15 to 30 minutes, 8.0% 30 to 45 minutes, 4.6% 45 to 60 minutes, 9.2% 60 minutes or more (2000)

Additional Information Contacts

Bradley-Bourbonnais Regional Chamber of Commerce . . . (815) 932-2222
http://www.bbchamber.com
Village of Bourbonnais. . . . . (815) 937-3570
http://www.villageofbourbonnais.com

BRADLEY (village). Covers a land area of 3.781 square miles and a water area of 0.005 square miles. Located at 41.14° N. Lat.; 87.85° W. Long. Elevation is 636 feet.
History: Bradley was known as North Kankakee when it was organized in 1892, but soon was renamed for resident and factory-owner David Bradley.
Population: 11,287 (1990); 12,784 (2000); 13,823 (2007); 14,445 (2012 projected); Race: 94.2% White, 1.7% Black, 0.9% Asian, 5.2% Hispanic of any race (2007); Density: 3,656.1 persons per square mile (2007); Average household size: 2.50 (2007); Median age: 34.5 (2007); Males per 100 females: 94.8 (2007); Marriage status: 23.6% never married, 54.9% now married, 8.1% widowed, 13.4% divorced (2000); Foreign born: 1.8% (2000); Ancestry (includes multiple ancestries): 27.0% German, 16.4% Irish, 13.5% French (except Basque), 9.2% English, 8.9% Other groups (2000).
Economy: Single-family building permits issued: 119 (2007); Multi-family building permits issued: 0 (2007); Employment by occupation: 9.2% management, 13.5% professional, 14.2% services, 31.6% sales, 0.3% farming, 12.2% construction, 19.1% production (2000).
Income: Per capita income: $22,808 (2007); Median household income: $48,150 (2007); Average household income: $56,460 (2007); Percent of households with income of $100,000 or more: 11.3% (2007); Poverty rate: 6.8% (2000).
Education: Percent of population age 25 and over with: High school diploma (including GED) or higher: 83.8% (2007); Bachelor's degree or higher: 12.9% (2007); Master's degree or higher: 4.7% (2007).

School District(s)

Bradley Bourbonnais CHSD 307 (09-12)
2005-06 Enrollment: 1,947 . . . . (815) 937-3707
Bradley SD 61 (PK-08)
2005-06 Enrollment: 1,506 . . . . (815) 933-3371

Vocational/Technical School(s)

Trend Setters College of Cosmetology (Private, For-profit)
Fall 2007 Enrollment: 52 . . . . (815) 932-5049
2007-08 Tuition: $17,900

Housing: Homeownership rate: 66.9% (2007); Median home value: $117,930 (2007); Median rent: $487 per month (2000); Median age of housing: 38 years (2000).
Safety: Violent crime rate: 48.2 per 10,000 population; Property crime rate: 544.6 per 10,000 population (2006).
Transportation: Commute to work: 95.3% car, 1.0% public transportation, 1.7% walk, 1.1% work from home (2000); Travel time to work: 55.8% less than 15 minutes, 26.0% 15 to 30 minutes, 7.0% 30 to 45 minutes, 5.1% 45 to 60 minutes, 6.2% 60 minutes or more (2000)

Additional Information Contacts

Village of Bradley. . . . . (815) 932-2125
http://www.bradleyil.org

BUCKINGHAM (village). Covers a land area of 0.276 square miles and a water area of 0 square miles. Located at 41.04° N. Lat.; 88.17° W. Long. Elevation is 656 feet.
Population: 340 (1990); 237 (2000); 199 (2007); 201 (2012 projected); Race: 100.0% White, 0.0% Black, 0.0% Asian, 0.5% Hispanic of any race (2007); Density: 721.6 persons per square mile (2007); Average household size: 2.88 (2007); Median age: 33.0 (2007); Males per 100 females: 99.0 (2007); Marriage status: 24.3% never married, 64.4% now married, 4.0% widowed, 7.3% divorced (2000); Foreign born: 0.0% (2000); Ancestry (includes multiple ancestries): 27.2% German, 17.2% Irish, 17.2% Other groups, 14.2% French (except Basque), 9.5% United States or American (2000).
Economy: Single-family building permits issued: 2 (2007); Multi-family building permits issued: 0 (2007); Employment by occupation: 1.7% management, 12.6% professional, 21.0% services, 17.6% sales, 0.0% farming, 13.4% construction, 33.6% production (2000).
Income: Per capita income: $24,020 (2007); Median household income: $65,833 (2007); Average household income: $69,275 (2007); Percent of households with income of $100,000 or more: 18.8% (2007); Poverty rate: 8.3% (2000).
Education: Percent of population age 25 and over with: High school diploma (including GED) or higher: 82.6% (2007); Bachelor's degree or higher: 10.7% (2007); Master's degree or higher: 1.7% (2007).
Housing: Homeownership rate: 92.8% (2007); Median home value: $109,091 (2007); Median rent: $363 per month (2000); Median age of housing: 42 years (2000).
Transportation: Commute to work: 95.3% car, 0.0% public transportation, 0.0% walk, 4.7% work from home (2000); Travel time to work: 14.7% less than 15 minutes, 33.3% 15 to 30 minutes, 39.2% 30 to 45 minutes, 7.8% 45 to 60 minutes, 4.9% 60 minutes or more (2000)

ESSEX (village). Covers a land area of 2.030 square miles and a water area of 0.024 square miles. Located at 41.17° N. Lat.; 88.19° W. Long. Elevation is 591 feet.
Population: 503 (1990); 554 (2000); 697 (2007); 767 (2012 projected); Race: 97.8% White, 0.0% Black, 0.0% Asian, 0.0% Hispanic of any race (2007); Density: 343.4 persons per square mile (2007); Average household size: 2.73 (2007); Median age: 37.3 (2007); Males per 100 females: 106.8 (2007); Marriage status: 21.2% never married, 67.1% now married, 5.5% widowed, 6.2% divorced (2000); Foreign born: 0.5% (2000); Ancestry (includes multiple ancestries): 26.9% German, 17.4% Irish, 11.1% Italian, 9.5% English, 8.0% Polish (2000).
Economy: Single-family building permits issued: 0 (2007); Multi-family building permits issued: 0 (2007); Employment by occupation: 5.1% management, 14.9% professional, 19.9% services, 18.8% sales, 0.0% farming, 19.2% construction, 22.1% production (2000).
Income: Per capita income: $22,852 (2007); Median household income: $60,136 (2007); Average household income: $62,461 (2007); Percent of households with income of $100,000 or more: 12.9% (2007); Poverty rate: 5.8% (2000).
Education: Percent of population age 25 and over with: High school diploma (including GED) or higher: 87.3% (2007); Bachelor's degree or higher: 6.7% (2007); Master's degree or higher: 0.2% (2007).
Housing: Homeownership rate: 90.2% (2007); Median home value: $145,536 (2007); Median rent: $500 per month (2000); Median age of housing: 29 years (2000).
Safety: Violent crime rate: 0.0 per 10,000 population; Property crime rate: 162.0 per 10,000 population (2006).

Transportation: Commute to work: 98.1% car, 0.0% public transportation, 0.0% walk, 1.1% work from home (2000); Travel time to work: 21.9% less than 15 minutes, 23.5% 15 to 30 minutes, 26.5% 30 to 45 minutes, 13.1% 45 to 60 minutes, 15.0% 60 minutes or more (2000)

GRANT PARK (village).

Covers a land area of 0.618 square miles and a water area of 0.026 square miles. Located at 41.24° N. Lat.; 87.64° W. Long. Elevation is 699 feet.

Population: 1,141 (1990); 1,358 (2000); 1,385 (2007); 1,393 (2012 projected); Race: 97.5% White, 0.1% Black, 0.4% Asian, 2.1% Hispanic of any race (2007); Density: 2,239.8 persons per square mile (2007); Average household size: 2.68 (2007); Median age: 37.1 (2007); Males per 100 females: 94.2 (2007); Marriage status: 20.7% never married, 65.3% now married, 7.6% widowed, 6.5% divorced (2000); Foreign born: 1.7% (2000); Ancestry (includes multiple ancestries): 37.7% German, 19.4% Irish, 13.5% Polish, 8.2% Italian, 8.1% Other groups (2000).

Economy: Single-family building permits issued: 2 (2007); Multi-family building permits issued: 10 (2007); Employment by occupation: 12.1% management, 9.6% professional, 9.7% services, 27.5% sales, 0.6% farming, 14.6% construction, 25.8% production (2000).

Income: Per capita income: $26,682 (2007); Median household income: $62,143 (2007); Average household income: $71,618 (2007); Percent of households with income of $100,000 or more: 21.5% (2007); Poverty rate: 4.4% (2000).

Education: Percent of population age 25 and over with: High school diploma (including GED) or higher: 85.0% (2007); Bachelor's degree or higher: 9.4% (2007); Master's degree or higher: 2.1% (2007).

School District(s)

Grant Park CUSD 6 (KG-12)
2005-06 Enrollment: 581 . . . . (815) 465-6013

Housing: Homeownership rate: 71.7% (2007); Median home value: $162,132 (2007); Median rent: $460 per month (2000); Median age of housing: 37 years (2000).

Safety: Violent crime rate: 77.1 per 10,000 population; Property crime rate: 186.3 per 10,000 population (2006).

Transportation: Commute to work: 90.3% car, 1.2% public transportation, 5.0% walk, 2.7% work from home (2000); Travel time to work: 25.5% less than 15 minutes, 23.1% 15 to 30 minutes, 23.4% 30 to 45 minutes, 13.8% 45 to 60 minutes, 14.1% 60 minutes or more (2000)

Additional Information Contacts

Grant Park Chamber of Commerce . . . . (815) 465-0604
http://www.grantparkchamber.com

HERSCHER (village).

Covers a land area of 1.725 square miles and a water area of 0 square miles. Located at 41.05° N. Lat.; 88.09° W. Long. Elevation is 659 feet.

Population: 1,286 (1990); 1,523 (2000); 1,586 (2007); 1,637 (2012 projected); Race: 97.5% White, 0.3% Black, 0.3% Asian, 0.6% Hispanic of any race (2007); Density: 919.6 persons per square mile (2007); Average household size: 2.80 (2007); Median age: 32.1 (2007); Males per 100 females: 98.7 (2007); Marriage status: 26.2% never married, 60.8% now married, 6.0% widowed, 7.0% divorced (2000); Foreign born: 0.7% (2000); Ancestry (includes multiple ancestries): 36.6% German, 18.2% Irish, 13.5% English, 10.9% French (except Basque), 9.4% United States or American (2000).

Economy: Single-family building permits issued: 3 (2007); Multi-family building permits issued: 0 (2007); Employment by occupation: 13.2% management, 25.2% professional, 11.7% services, 24.5% sales, 0.3% farming, 8.2% construction, 16.7% production (2000).

Income: Per capita income: $23,487 (2007); Median household income: $57,255 (2007); Average household income: $65,813 (2007); Percent of households with income of $100,000 or more: 17.8% (2007); Poverty rate: 7.7% (2000).

Education: Percent of population age 25 and over with: High school diploma (including GED) or higher: 92.4% (2007); Bachelor's degree or higher: 26.6% (2007); Master's degree or higher: 9.3% (2007).

School District(s)

Herscher CUSD 2 (PK-12)
2005-06 Enrollment: 2,160 . . . . (815) 426-2162

Housing: Homeownership rate: 76.1% (2007); Median home value: $149,093 (2007); Median rent: $431 per month (2000); Median age of housing: 34 years (2000).

Safety: Violent crime rate: 6.4 per 10,000 population; Property crime rate: 103.0 per 10,000 population (2006).

Newspapers: Herscher Pilot (Local news; Circulation 2,200)

Transportation: Commute to work: 92.7% car, 0.0% public transportation, 4.4% walk, 3.0% work from home (2000); Travel time to work: 28.2% less than 15 minutes, 35.0% 15 to 30 minutes, 21.9% 30 to 45 minutes, 5.7% 45 to 60 minutes, 9.2% 60 minutes or more (2000)

Additional Information Contacts

Herscher Chamber of Commerce . . . . (815) 426-2131
http://www.herscher.net

HOPKINS PARK (village).

Aka Pembroke. Covers a land area of 3.661 square miles and a water area of 0 square miles. Located at 41.07° N. Lat.; 87.60° W. Long. Elevation is 679 feet.

Population: 696 (1990); 711 (2000); 804 (2007); 856 (2012 projected); Race: 3.7% White, 90.8% Black, 0.1% Asian, 3.7% Hispanic of any race (2007); Density: 219.6 persons per square mile (2007); Average household size: 2.99 (2007); Median age: 27.0 (2007); Males per 100 females: 89.2 (2007); Marriage status: 42.6% never married, 30.8% now married, 13.1% widowed, 13.5% divorced (2000); Foreign born: 0.3% (2000); Ancestry (includes multiple ancestries): 68.5% Other groups, 2.0% United States or American, 1.9% African, 0.5% English, 0.4% Polish (2000).

Economy: Single-family building permits issued: 0 (2007); Multi-family building permits issued: 0 (2007); Employment by occupation: 4.6% management, 29.1% professional, 22.9% services, 14.9% sales, 0.0% farming, 0.6% construction, 28.0% production (2000).

Income: Per capita income: $9,512 (2007); Median household income: $20,761 (2007); Average household income: $28,429 (2007); Percent of households with income of $100,000 or more: 3.3% (2007); Poverty rate: 44.2% (2000).

Education: Percent of population age 25 and over with: High school diploma (including GED) or higher: 52.8% (2007); Bachelor's degree or higher: 3.1% (2007); Master's degree or higher: 0.9% (2007).

School District(s)

Pembroke CCSD 259 (PK-08)
2005-06 Enrollment: 317 . . . . (815) 944-8168

Housing: Homeownership rate: 68.4% (2007); Median home value: $61,250 (2007); Median rent: $350 per month (2000); Median age of housing: 28 years (2000).

Safety: Violent crime rate: 0.0 per 10,000 population; Property crime rate: 0.0 per 10,000 population (2006).

Transportation: Commute to work: 93.4% car, 2.4% public transportation, 0.0% walk, 4.2% work from home (2000); Travel time to work: 18.1% less than 15 minutes, 28.7% 15 to 30 minutes, 35.6% 30 to 45 minutes, 12.5% 45 to 60 minutes, 5.0% 60 minutes or more (2000)

IRWIN (village).

Covers a land area of 0.068 square miles and a water area of 0 square miles. Located at 41.05° N. Lat.; 87.98° W. Long. Elevation is 659 feet.

Population: 50 (1990); 92 (2000); 96 (2007); 97 (2012 projected); Race: 89.6% White, 0.0% Black, 2.1% Asian, 3.1% Hispanic of any race (2007); Density: 1,414.0 persons per square mile (2007); Average household size: 2.67 (2007); Median age: 33.8 (2007); Males per 100 females: 88.2 (2007); Marriage status: 25.4% never married, 46.0% now married, 17.5% widowed, 11.1% divorced (2000); Foreign born: 0.0% (2000); Ancestry (includes multiple ancestries): 38.1% German, 20.6% Irish, 19.0% French (except Basque), 11.1% English, 6.3% Scotch-Irish (2000).

Economy: Single-family building permits issued: 0 (2007); Multi-family building permits issued: 0 (2007); Employment by occupation: 0.0% management, 16.7% professional, 50.0% services, 8.3% sales, 12.5% farming, 12.5% construction, 0.0% production (2000).

Income: Per capita income: $16,771 (2007); Median household income: $42,500 (2007); Average household income: $44,722 (2007); Percent of households with income of $100,000 or more: 2.8% (2007); Poverty rate: 0.0% (2000).

Education: Percent of population age 25 and over with: High school diploma (including GED) or higher: 73.2% (2007); Bachelor's degree or higher: 25.0% (2007); Master's degree or higher: 7.1% (2007).

Housing: Homeownership rate: 77.8% (2007); Median home value: $110,714 (2007); Median rent: $325 per month (2000); Median age of housing: 42 years (2000).

Transportation: Commute to work: 83.3% car, 0.0% public transportation, 16.7% walk, 0.0% work from home (2000); Travel time to work: 50.0% less than 15 minutes, 41.7% 15 to 30 minutes, 8.3% 30 to 45 minutes, 0.0% 45 to 60 minutes, 0.0% 60 minutes or more (2000)

KANKAKEE (city). County seat. Covers a land area of 12.274 square miles and a water area of 0.476 square miles. Located at 41.11° N. Lat.; 87.86° W. Long. Elevation is 656 feet.
History: Kankakee developed around the Illinois Central Railroad depot, and was incorporated in 1855.
Population: 27,822 (1990); 27,491 (2000); 26,255 (2007); 25,545 (2012 projected); Race: 46.4% White, 41.8% Black, 0.4% Asian, 14.7% Hispanic of any race (2007); Density: 2,139.1 persons per square mile (2007); Average household size: 2.77 (2007); Median age: 33.0 (2007); Males per 100 females: 92.6 (2007); Marriage status: 33.8% never married, 44.6% now married, 9.4% widowed, 12.2% divorced (2000); Foreign born: 6.7% (2000); Ancestry (includes multiple ancestries): 45.3% Other groups, 14.0% German, 7.7% Irish, 6.5% French (except Basque), 4.2% English (2000).
Economy: Unemployment rate: 9.1% (4/2008); Total civilian labor force: 11,936 (4/2008); Single-family building permits issued: 24 (2007); Multi-family building permits issued: 6 (2007); Employment by occupation: 6.9% management, 15.6% professional, 21.5% services, 22.1% sales, 0.8% farming, 7.8% construction, 25.4% production (2000).
Income: Per capita income: $17,223 (2007); Median household income: $34,002 (2007); Average household income: $45,623 (2007); Percent of households with income of $100,000 or more: 7.5% (2007); Poverty rate: 21.4% (2000).
Education: Percent of population age 25 and over with: High school diploma (including GED) or higher: 68.1% (2007); Bachelor's degree or higher: 13.2% (2007); Master's degree or higher: 5.0% (2007).

School District(s)

Herscher CUSD 2 (PK-12)
2005-06 Enrollment: 2,160 . . . . (815) 426-2162
Iroquois/Kankakee Roe (07-11)
2005-06 Enrollment: 43 . . . . (815) 937-2950
Kankakee Area Spec Educ Coop (01-12)
2005-06 Enrollment: 60 . . . . (815) 939-3651
Kankakee SD 111 (PK-12)
2005-06 Enrollment: 5,971 . . . . (815) 933-0700

Two-year College(s)

Kankakee Community College (Public)
Fall 2007 Enrollment: 3,591. . . . . (815) 802-8500
2007-08 Tuition: In-state $5,485; Out-of-state $9,894
Housing: Homeownership rate: 53.5% (2007); Median home value: $94,111 (2007); Median rent: $401 per month (2000); Median age of housing: 48 years (2000).
Hospitals: Riverside Medical Center (336 beds); St. Mary's Hospital of Kankakee (186 beds)
Safety: Violent crime rate: 98.0 per 10,000 population; Property crime rate: 548.0 per 10,000 population (2006).
Newspapers: The Daily Journal (Community news; Circulation 9,000)
Transportation: Commute to work: 90.9% car, 1.4% public transportation, 3.0% walk, 2.0% work from home (2000); Travel time to work: 45.3% less than 15 minutes, 30.9% 15 to 30 minutes, 11.1% 30 to 45 minutes, 3.8% 45 to 60 minutes, 8.9% 60 minutes or more (2000); Amtrak: Service available.
Airports: Greater Kankakee (general aviation)
Additional Information Contacts
City of Kankakee . . . . (815) 933-0480
http://www.ci.kankakee.il.us
Kankakee River Valley Chamber. . . . . (815) 933-7721

MANTENO (village). Covers a land area of 2.993 square miles and a water area of 0.032 square miles. Located at 41.25° N. Lat.; 87.83° W. Long. Elevation is 686 feet.
History: Incorporated 1878.
Population: 4,304 (1990); 6,414 (2000); 8,097 (2007); 9,186 (2012 projected); Race: 97.1% White, 0.2% Black, 0.2% Asian, 4.5% Hispanic of any race (2007); Density: 2,705.3 persons per square mile (2007); Average household size: 2.46 (2007); Median age: 37.1 (2007); Males per 100 females: 96.2 (2007); Marriage status: 19.5% never married, 64.2% now married, 7.6% widowed, 8.7% divorced (2000); Foreign born: 2.0% (2000); Ancestry (includes multiple ancestries): 32.6% German, 19.8% Irish, 9.6% English, 9.0% French (except Basque), 8.5% Polish (2000).
Economy: Single-family building permits issued: 29 (2007); Multi-family building permits issued: 8 (2007); Employment by occupation: 12.3% management, 14.2% professional, 15.9% services, 27.2% sales, 0.2% farming, 9.7% construction, 20.5% production (2000).
Income: Per capita income: $28,060 (2007); Median household income: $57,996 (2007); Average household income: $68,853 (2007); Percent of households with income of $100,000 or more: 20.8% (2007); Poverty rate: 5.3% (2000).
Education: Percent of population age 25 and over with: High school diploma (including GED) or higher: 85.9% (2007); Bachelor's degree or higher: 17.0% (2007); Master's degree or higher: 6.0% (2007).

School District(s)

Dept of Corrections Sch Dist 428 (08-12)
2005-06 Enrollment: 2,271 . . . . (217) 522-2666
Manteno CUSD 5 (PK-12)
2005-06 Enrollment: 2,130 . . . . (815) 928-7001
Housing: Homeownership rate: 69.7% (2007); Median home value: $154,464 (2007); Median rent: $526 per month (2000); Median age of housing: 16 years (2000).
Safety: Violent crime rate: 13.8 per 10,000 population; Property crime rate: 299.2 per 10,000 population (2006).
Transportation: Commute to work: 94.1% car, 1.9% public transportation, 1.1% walk, 2.8% work from home (2000); Travel time to work: 29.1% less than 15 minutes, 29.8% 15 to 30 minutes, 18.8% 30 to 45 minutes, 10.2% 45 to 60 minutes, 12.2% 60 minutes or more (2000)
Additional Information Contacts
Manteno Chamber of Commerce. . . . . (815) 468-6226
http://www.mantenochamber.com
Village of Manteno . . . . (815) 929-4800
http://manteno.govoffice.com

MOMENCE (city). Covers a land area of 1.369 square miles and a water area of 0.077 square miles. Located at 41.16° N. Lat.; 87.66° W. Long. Elevation is 627 feet.
History: Momence, named for Isadore Momence, was laid out in 1844 on the Kankakee River. This was a camping place for travelers on the Hubbard Trail, who forded the Kankakee here.
Population: 2,975 (1990); 3,171 (2000); 3,186 (2007); 3,199 (2012 projected); Race: 86.5% White, 4.5% Black, 0.1% Asian, 17.3% Hispanic of any race (2007); Density: 2,327.2 persons per square mile (2007); Average household size: 2.71 (2007); Median age: 37.8 (2007); Males per 100 females: 92.3 (2007); Marriage status: 22.7% never married, 55.9% now married, 11.9% widowed, 9.5% divorced (2000); Foreign born: 6.4% (2000); Ancestry (includes multiple ancestries): 26.7% German, 15.4% Other groups, 14.2% Irish, 11.1% English, 10.1% French (except Basque) (2000).
Economy: Single-family building permits issued: 2 (2007); Multi-family building permits issued: 0 (2007); Employment by occupation: 7.0% management, 14.6% professional, 10.9% services, 24.8% sales, 2.2% farming, 12.7% construction, 27.7% production (2000).
Income: Per capita income: $21,281 (2007); Median household income: $45,221 (2007); Average household income: $56,550 (2007); Percent of households with income of $100,000 or more: 11.8% (2007); Poverty rate: 9.2% (2000).
Education: Percent of population age 25 and over with: High school diploma (including GED) or higher: 73.0% (2007); Bachelor's degree or higher: 11.6% (2007); Master's degree or higher: 5.2% (2007).

School District(s)

Momence CUSD 1 (PK-12)
2005-06 Enrollment: 1,309 . . . . (815) 472-3500
Housing: Homeownership rate: 65.6% (2007); Median home value: $128,322 (2007); Median rent: $399 per month (2000); Median age of housing: 59 years (2000).
Safety: Violent crime rate: 48.9 per 10,000 population; Property crime rate: 179.4 per 10,000 population (2006).
Newspapers: Momence Progress-Reporter (Local news; Circulation 2,200)
Transportation: Commute to work: 87.7% car, 0.6% public transportation, 8.7% walk, 1.6% work from home (2000); Travel time to work: 48.0% less than 15 minutes, 31.2% 15 to 30 minutes, 8.5% 30 to 45 minutes, 3.8% 45 to 60 minutes, 8.4% 60 minutes or more (2000)
Additional Information Contacts
Momence Chamber of Commerce. (815) 472-4620
http://www.momence.net

REDDICK (village). Covers a land area of 0.234 square miles and a water area of 0 square miles. Located at 41.09° N. Lat.; 88.24° W. Long. Elevation is 610 feet.

Population: 208 (1990); 219 (2000); 184 (2007); 186 (2012 projected); Race: 96.2% White, 0.0% Black, 0.0% Asian, 0.5% Hispanic of any race (2007); Density: 786.6 persons per square mile (2007); Average household size: 2.71 (2007); Median age: 37.5 (2007); Males per 100 females: 89.7 (2007); Marriage status: 34.8% never married, 58.0% now married, 4.8% widowed, 2.4% divorced (2000); Foreign born: 0.8% (2000); Ancestry (includes multiple ancestries): 40.2% German, 16.0% Irish, 14.5% French (except Basque), 10.5% Italian, 5.9% English (2000).
Economy: Employment by occupation: 8.1% management, 18.4% professional, 16.2% services, 20.6% sales, 0.0% farming, 14.0% construction, 22.8% production (2000).
Income: Per capita income: $28,750 (2007); Median household income: $75,000 (2007); Average household income: $77,794 (2007); Percent of households with income of $100,000 or more: 22.1% (2007); Poverty rate: 8.7% (2000).
Education: Percent of population age 25 and over with: High school diploma (including GED) or higher: 93.5% (2007); Bachelor's degree or higher: 12.2% (2007); Master's degree or higher: 6.5% (2007).

School District(s)

Herscher CUSD 2 (PK-12)
2005-06 Enrollment: 2,160 . . . . (815) 426-2162

Housing: Homeownership rate: 91.2% (2007); Median home value: $127,083 (2007); Median rent: $675 per month (2000); Median age of housing: 46 years (2000).
Transportation: Commute to work: 94.0% car, 2.2% public transportation, 0.0% walk, 2.2% work from home (2000); Travel time to work: 10.7% less than 15 minutes, 35.1% 15 to 30 minutes, 27.5% 30 to 45 minutes, 17.6% 45 to 60 minutes, 9.2% 60 minutes or more (2000)

SAINT ANNE (village). Covers a land area of 0.508 square miles and a water area of 0.007 square miles. Located at 41.02° N. Lat.; 87.71° W. Long. Elevation is 666 feet.
History: In 1852 Father Charles Chiniquy and many of his French-Canadian parishioners immigrated here from Bourbonnais and founded the town of St. Anne.
Population: 1,153 (1990); 1,212 (2000); 1,165 (2007); 1,152 (2012 projected); Race: 86.2% White, 0.9% Black, 0.1% Asian, 14.5% Hispanic of any race (2007); Density: 2,292.8 persons per square mile (2007); Average household size: 2.55 (2007); Median age: 33.3 (2007); Males per 100 females: 95.1 (2007); Marriage status: 23.9% never married, 59.7% now married, 5.2% widowed, 11.2% divorced (2000); Foreign born: 4.7% (2000); Ancestry (includes multiple ancestries): 23.7% German, 19.8% French (except Basque), 17.3% Other groups, 10.0% Irish, 9.5% United States or American (2000).
Economy: Single-family building permits issued: 4 (2007); Multi-family building permits issued: 0 (2007); Employment by occupation: 7.0% management, 12.4% professional, 15.2% services, 26.1% sales, 2.3% farming, 10.9% construction, 26.1% production (2000).
Income: Per capita income: $20,594 (2007); Median household income: $45,645 (2007); Average household income: $52,615 (2007); Percent of households with income of $100,000 or more: 7.2% (2007); Poverty rate: 13.4% (2000).
Education: Percent of population age 25 and over with: High school diploma (including GED) or higher: 80.7% (2007); Bachelor's degree or higher: 11.9% (2007); Master's degree or higher: 3.7% (2007).

School District(s)

St Anne CCSD 256 (PK-08)
2005-06 Enrollment: 392 . . . . (815) 427-8190
St Anne CHSD 302 (09-12)
2005-06 Enrollment: 319 . . . . (815) 427-8141

Housing: Homeownership rate: 69.1% (2007); Median home value: $102,549 (2007); Median rent: $347 per month (2000); Median age of housing: 56 years (2000).
Safety: Violent crime rate: 41.2 per 10,000 population; Property crime rate: 461.3 per 10,000 population (2006).
Newspapers: Record (Community news; Circulation 620)
Transportation: Commute to work: 92.0% car, 0.0% public transportation, 4.5% walk, 2.9% work from home (2000); Travel time to work: 25.5% less than 15 minutes, 43.5% 15 to 30 minutes, 18.9% 30 to 45 minutes, 3.7% 45 to 60 minutes, 8.4% 60 minutes or more (2000)

SUN RIVER TERRACE (village). Covers a land area of 0.454 square miles and a water area of 0.025 square miles. Located at 41.12° N. Lat.; 87.73° W. Long. Elevation is 614 feet.
Population: 532 (1990); 383 (2000); 372 (2007); 369 (2012 projected); Race: 10.5% White, 88.2% Black, 0.0% Asian, 2.7% Hispanic of any race (2007); Density: 819.0 persons per square mile (2007); Average household size: 2.70 (2007); Median age: 29.6 (2007); Males per 100 females: 86.9 (2007); Marriage status: 31.6% never married, 46.4% now married, 10.5% widowed, 11.5% divorced (2000); Foreign born: 1.2% (2000); Ancestry (includes multiple ancestries): 80.1% Other groups, 1.0% United States or American, 0.7% African, 0.5% Jamaican, 0.5% Italian (2000).
Economy: Single-family building permits issued: 1 (2007); Multi-family building permits issued: 0 (2007); Employment by occupation: 0.0% management, 17.3% professional, 25.2% services, 26.8% sales, 0.0% farming, 3.9% construction, 26.8% production (2000).
Income: Per capita income: $12,849 (2007); Median household income: $32,273 (2007); Average household income: $34,638 (2007); Percent of households with income of $100,000 or more: 3.6% (2007); Poverty rate: 17.5% (2000).
Education: Percent of population age 25 and over with: High school diploma (including GED) or higher: 59.4% (2007); Bachelor's degree or higher: 5.2% (2007); Master's degree or higher: 2.4% (2007).
Housing: Homeownership rate: 66.7% (2007); Median home value: $91,111 (2007); Median rent: $194 per month (2000); Median age of housing: 33 years (2000).
Transportation: Commute to work: 99.2% car, 0.0% public transportation, 0.8% walk, 0.0% work from home (2000); Travel time to work: 13.1% less than 15 minutes, 70.5% 15 to 30 minutes, 6.6% 30 to 45 minutes, 4.1% 45 to 60 minutes, 5.7% 60 minutes or more (2000)

UNION HILL (village). Covers a land area of 0.047 square miles and a water area of 0 square miles. Located at 41.10° N. Lat.; 88.14° W. Long. Elevation is 617 feet.
Population: 37 (1990); 66 (2000); 56 (2007); 56 (2012 projected); Race: 96.4% White, 0.0% Black, 0.0% Asian, 0.0% Hispanic of any race (2007); Density: 1,203.0 persons per square mile (2007); Average household size: 2.24 (2007); Median age: 35.0 (2007); Males per 100 females: 93.1 (2007); Marriage status: 38.1% never married, 38.1% now married, 9.5% widowed, 14.3% divorced (2000); Foreign born: 0.0% (2000); Ancestry (includes multiple ancestries): 62.5% German, 8.3% French (except Basque), 8.3% Polish, 8.3% Irish (2000).
Economy: Single-family building permits issued: 0 (2007); Multi-family building permits issued: 0 (2007); Employment by occupation: 0.0% management, 0.0% professional, 12.5% services, 31.3% sales, 0.0% farming, 0.0% construction, 56.3% production (2000).
Income: Per capita income: $24,911 (2007); Median household income: $38,125 (2007); Average household income: $55,800 (2007); Percent of households with income of $100,000 or more: 16.0% (2007); Poverty rate: 0.0% (2000).
Education: Percent of population age 25 and over with: High school diploma (including GED) or higher: 100.0% (2007); Bachelor's degree or higher: 0.0% (2007); Master's degree or higher: 0.0% (2007).
Housing: Homeownership rate: 84.0% (2007); Median home value: $114,583 (2007); Median rent: $n/a per month (2000); Median age of housing: 60+ years (2000).
Transportation: Commute to work: 81.3% car, 0.0% public transportation, 18.8% walk, 0.0% work from home (2000); Travel time to work: 18.8% less than 15 minutes, 43.8% 15 to 30 minutes, 37.5% 30 to 45 minutes, 0.0% 45 to 60 minutes, 0.0% 60 minutes or more (2000)

Kendall County

Located in northeastern Illinois; drained by the Fox River. Covers a land area of 320.58 square miles, a water area of 2.09 square miles, and is located in the Central Time Zone. The county was founded in 1841. County seat is Yorkville.

Kendall County is part of the Chicago-Naperville-Joliet, IL-IN-WI Metropolitan Statistical Area. The entire metro area includes: Chicago-Naperville-Joliet, IL Metropolitan Division (Cook County, IL; DeKalb County, IL; DuPage County, IL; Grundy County, IL; Kane County, IL; Kendall County, IL; McHenry County, IL; Will County, IL); Gary, IN Metropolitan Division (Jasper County, IN; Lake County, IN; Newton County, IN; Porter County, IN); Lake County-Kenosha County, IL-WI Metropolitan Division (Lake County, IL; Kenosha County, WI)

Population: 39,413 (1990); 54,544 (2000); 87,832 (2007); 111,924 (2012 projected); Race: 86.0% White, 3.3% Black, 1.9% Asian, 13.9% Hispanic of any race (2007); Density: 274.0 persons per square mile (2007); Average

household size: 2.87 (2007); Median age: 32.7 (2007); Males per 100 females: 100.3 (2007).
Religion: Five largest groups: 17.9% Catholic Church, 4.3% The United Methodist Church, 3.6% Lutheran Church—Missouri Synod, 3.0% The Association of Free Lutheran Congregations, 2.3% Evangelical Lutheran Church in America (2000).
Economy: Unemployment rate: 5.9% (4/2008); Total civilian labor force: 52,533 (4/2008); Leading industries: 20.9% retail trade; 14.0% manufacturing; 12.4% accommodation & food services (2005); Farms: 412 totaling 168,082 acres (2002); Companies that employ 500 or more persons: 1 (2006); Companies that employ 100 to 499 persons: 22 (2006); Companies that employ less than 100 persons: 1,542 (2006); Black-owned businesses: n/a (2002); Hispanic-owned businesses: n/a (2002); Asian-owned businesses: n/a (2002); Women-owned businesses: 1,169 (2002); Retail sales per capita: $10,317 (2008). Single-family building permits issued: 1,048 (2007); Multi-family building permits issued: 107 (2007).
Income: Per capita income: $29,622 (2007); Median household income: $74,008 (2007); Average household income: $84,984 (2007); Percent of households with income of $100,000 or more: 28.5% (2007); Poverty rate: 3.1% (2005); Bankruptcy rate: 2.93% (2007).
Taxes: Total county taxes per capita: $151 (2006); County property taxes per capita: $135 (2006).
Education: Percent of population age 25 and over with: High school diploma (including GED) or higher: 90.1% (2007); Bachelor's degree or higher: 25.7% (2007); Master's degree or higher: 7.3% (2007).
Housing: Homeownership rate: 84.6% (2007); Median home value: $231,544 (2007); Median rent: $638 per month (2000); Median age of housing: 24 years (2000).
Health: Birth rate: 200.9 per 10,000 population (2007); Death rate: 39.9 per 10,000 population (2007); Age-adjusted cancer mortality rate: 188.4 deaths per 100,000 population (2005); Number of physicians: 6.2 per 10,000 population (2005); Hospital beds: 0.0 per 10,000 population (2004); Hospital admissions: 0.0 per 10,000 population (2004).
Elections: 2004 Presidential election results: 60.8% Bush, 38.4% Kerry, 0.0% Nader, 0.8% Badnarik
National and State Parks: Silver Springs State Park
Additional Information Contacts
Kendall County Government . . . . (630) 553-4143
http://www.co.kendall.il.us
City of Plano. . . . . (630) 552-8275
http://www.cityofplanoil.com
Oswego Chamber of Commerce . . . . (630) 554-3505
http://www.oswegochamber.org
Plano Area Chamber of Commerce. . . . . (630) 552-7272
http://www.planocommerce.org
United City of Yorkville. . . . . (630) 553-4350
http://www.yorkville.il.us
Village of Oswego . . . . (630) 554-3618
http://www.oswegoil.org
Yorkville Area Chamber of Commerce . . . . (630) 553-6853
http://www.yorkvillechamber.org

Kendall County Communities

BOULDER HILL (CDP). Covers a land area of 1.458 square miles and a water area of 0.009 square miles. Located at 41.71° N. Lat.; 88.33° W. Long. Elevation is 669 feet.
Population: 8,894 (1990); 8,169 (2000); 9,247 (2007); 10,202 (2012 projected); Race: 80.5% White, 4.1% Black, 0.9% Asian, 22.1% Hispanic of any race (2007); Density: 6,343.9 persons per square mile (2007); Average household size: 2.84 (2007); Median age: 32.0 (2007); Males per 100 females: 100.1 (2007); Marriage status: 22.6% never married, 63.6% now married, 4.7% widowed, 9.0% divorced (2000); Foreign born: 4.1% (2000); Ancestry (includes multiple ancestries): 34.5% German, 15.7% Irish, 15.6% Other groups, 10.4% English, 6.0% Italian (2000).
Economy: Employment by occupation: 9.4% management, 17.3% professional, 13.5% services, 34.5% sales, 0.2% farming, 10.1% construction, 15.0% production (2000).
Income: Per capita income: $24,869 (2007); Median household income: $66,033 (2007); Average household income: $70,715 (2007); Percent of households with income of $100,000 or more: 18.8% (2007); Poverty rate: 1.8% (2000).
Education: Percent of population age 25 and over with: High school diploma (including GED) or higher: 90.1% (2007); Bachelor's degree or higher: 21.4% (2007); Master's degree or higher: 5.4% (2007).
Housing: Homeownership rate: 87.1% (2007); Median home value: $169,401 (2007); Median rent: $765 per month (2000); Median age of housing: 29 years (2000).
Transportation: Commute to work: 94.4% car, 1.4% public transportation, 1.3% walk, 2.9% work from home (2000); Travel time to work: 28.6% less than 15 minutes, 35.4% 15 to 30 minutes, 20.9% 30 to 45 minutes, 7.4% 45 to 60 minutes, 7.7% 60 minutes or more (2000)

BRISTOL (unincorporated postal area, zip code 60512). Aka Bristol Station. Covers a land area of 10.460 square miles and a water area of 0 square miles. Located at 41.70° N. Lat.; 88.41° W. Long. Elevation is 640 feet.
Population: 892 (2000); Race: 94.0% White, 0.0% Black, 4.5% Asian, 2.5% Hispanic of any race (2000); Density: 85.3 persons per square mile (2000); Age: 16.8% under 18, 17.5% over 64 (2000); Marriage status: 22.3% never married, 68.9% now married, 4.1% widowed, 4.7% divorced (2000); Foreign born: 9.2% (2000); Ancestry (includes multiple ancestries): 37.9% German, 18.3% Irish, 9.8% English, 8.4% Other groups, 6.2% Swedish (2000).
Economy: Employment by occupation: 12.0% management, 22.3% professional, 5.6% services, 26.3% sales, 0.0% farming, 18.2% construction, 15.6% production (2000).
Income: Per capita income: $28,669 (2000); Median household income: $65,625 (2000); Poverty rate: 1.5% (2000).
Education: Percent of population age 25 and over with: High school diploma (including GED) or higher: 88.0% (2000); Bachelor's degree or higher: 20.7% (2000).

School District(s)

Yorkville CUSD 115 (PK-12)
2005-06 Enrollment: 3,607 . . . . (630) 553-4382
Housing: Homeownership rate: 92.9% (2000); Median home value: $176,700 (2000); Median rent: $442 per month (2000); Median age of housing: 30 years (2000).
Transportation: Commute to work: 93.9% car, 2.6% public transportation, 2.3% walk, 1.3% work from home (2000); Travel time to work: 12.2% less than 15 minutes, 46.1% 15 to 30 minutes, 10.6% 30 to 45 minutes, 4.4% 45 to 60 minutes, 26.7% 60 minutes or more (2000)

LISBON (village). Covers a land area of 0.310 square miles and a water area of 0 square miles. Located at 41.48° N. Lat.; 88.48° W. Long. Elevation is 669 feet.
Population: 216 (1990); 248 (2000); 404 (2007); 513 (2012 projected); Race: 99.5% White, 0.0% Black, 0.0% Asian, 3.0% Hispanic of any race (2007); Density: 1,304.9 persons per square mile (2007); Average household size: 2.66 (2007); Median age: 33.1 (2007); Males per 100 females: 105.1 (2007); Marriage status: 22.4% never married, 58.2% now married, 10.7% widowed, 8.7% divorced (2000); Foreign born: 0.8% (2000); Ancestry (includes multiple ancestries): 35.4% German, 26.8% Norwegian, 17.5% Irish, 10.6% Other groups, 10.2% Italian (2000).
Economy: Single-family building permits issued: 2 (2007); Multi-family building permits issued: 0 (2007); Employment by occupation: 6.1% management, 19.1% professional, 16.8% services, 16.0% sales, 0.0% farming, 17.6% construction, 24.4% production (2000).
Income: Per capita income: $24,220 (2007); Median household income: $57,857 (2007); Average household income: $64,375 (2007); Percent of households with income of $100,000 or more: 19.1% (2007); Poverty rate: 0.8% (2000).
Education: Percent of population age 25 and over with: High school diploma (including GED) or higher: 82.5% (2007); Bachelor's degree or higher: 11.0% (2007); Master's degree or higher: 4.2% (2007).
Housing: Homeownership rate: 86.8% (2007); Median home value: $153,846 (2007); Median rent: $430 per month (2000); Median age of housing: 49 years (2000).
Transportation: Commute to work: 94.6% car, 0.0% public transportation, 0.0% walk, 5.4% work from home (2000); Travel time to work: 13.9% less than 15 minutes, 23.0% 15 to 30 minutes, 37.7% 30 to 45 minutes, 13.9% 45 to 60 minutes, 11.5% 60 minutes or more (2000)

MILLINGTON (village). Covers a land area of 0.557 square miles and a water area of 0.052 square miles. Located at 41.56° N. Lat.; 88.60° W. Long. Elevation is 564 feet.

Population: 533 (1990); 458 (2000); 469 (2007); 505 (2012 projected); Race: 95.5% White, 2.3% Black, 1.5% Asian, 5.3% Hispanic of any race (2007); Density: 842.6 persons per square mile (2007); Average household size: 3.05 (2007); Median age: 30.0 (2007); Males per 100 females: 117.1 (2007); Marriage status: 20.7% never married, 70.3% now married, 3.6% widowed, 5.4% divorced (2000); Foreign born: 0.6% (2000); Ancestry (includes multiple ancestries): 38.1% German, 15.2% Irish, 9.7% English, 8.7% Norwegian, 8.0% Swedish (2000).
Economy: Employment by occupation: 10.4% management, 5.2% professional, 19.0% services, 32.0% sales, 0.4% farming, 12.1% construction, 20.8% production (2000).
Income: Per capita income: $18,854 (2007); Median household income: $49,545 (2007); Average household income: $57,419 (2007); Percent of households with income of $100,000 or more: 13.6% (2007); Poverty rate: 10.4% (2000).
Education: Percent of population age 25 and over with: High school diploma (including GED) or higher: 74.0% (2007); Bachelor's degree or higher: 3.1% (2007); Master's degree or higher: 1.4% (2007).
Housing: Homeownership rate: 83.8% (2007); Median home value: $148,611 (2007); Median rent: $525 per month (2000); Median age of housing: 42 years (2000).
Transportation: Commute to work: 98.7% car, 0.0% public transportation, 1.3% walk, 0.0% work from home (2000); Travel time to work: 18.9% less than 15 minutes, 23.7% 15 to 30 minutes, 26.3% 30 to 45 minutes, 14.5% 45 to 60 minutes, 16.7% 60 minutes or more (2000)

NEWARK (village). Covers a land area of 1.133 square miles and a water area of <.001 square miles. Located at 41.53° N. Lat.; 88.58° W. Long. Elevation is 673 feet.
Population: 870 (1990); 887 (2000); 1,420 (2007); 1,790 (2012 projected); Race: 96.9% White, 0.0% Black, 0.6% Asian, 3.7% Hispanic of any race (2007); Density: 1,253.1 persons per square mile (2007); Average household size: 2.77 (2007); Median age: 32.5 (2007); Males per 100 females: 110.7 (2007); Marriage status: 25.5% never married, 63.0% now married, 8.0% widowed, 3.4% divorced (2000); Foreign born: 2.3% (2000); Ancestry (includes multiple ancestries): 34.1% Norwegian, 27.3% German, 12.3% Irish, 11.9% English, 7.8% Italian (2000).
Economy: Single-family building permits issued: 3 (2007); Multi-family building permits issued: 0 (2007); Employment by occupation: 10.8% management, 14.9% professional, 18.5% services, 23.2% sales, 0.8% farming, 14.1% construction, 17.7% production (2000).
Income: Per capita income: $28,123 (2007); Median household income: $69,583 (2007); Average household income: $77,846 (2007); Percent of households with income of $100,000 or more: 22.6% (2007); Poverty rate: 3.7% (2000).
Education: Percent of population age 25 and over with: High school diploma (including GED) or higher: 91.5% (2007); Bachelor's degree or higher: 15.6% (2007); Master's degree or higher: 3.3% (2007).

School District(s)

Lisbon CCSD 90 (PK-08)
2005-06 Enrollment: 126 . . . . (815) 736-6324
Newark CCSD 66 (KG-08)
2005-06 Enrollment: 285 . . . . (815) 695-5143
Newark CHSD 18 (09-12)
2005-06 Enrollment: 186 . . . . (815) 695-5164

Housing: Homeownership rate: 79.9% (2007); Median home value: $184,836 (2007); Median rent: $525 per month (2000); Median age of housing: 44 years (2000).
Transportation: Commute to work: 89.5% car, 1.2% public transportation, 2.7% walk, 6.6% work from home (2000); Travel time to work: 20.5% less than 15 minutes, 31.1% 15 to 30 minutes, 20.7% 30 to 45 minutes, 12.6% 45 to 60 minutes, 15.2% 60 minutes or more (2000)

OSWEGO (village). Covers a land area of 6.582 square miles and a water area of 0.097 square miles. Located at 41.69° N. Lat.; 88.34° W. Long. Elevation is 640 feet.
Population: 5,970 (1990); 13,326 (2000); 22,770 (2007); 29,478 (2012 projected); Race: 85.0% White, 4.9% Black, 3.0% Asian, 11.3% Hispanic of any race (2007); Density: 3,459.3 persons per square mile (2007); Average household size: 2.94 (2007); Median age: 32.4 (2007); Males per 100 females: 97.4 (2007); Marriage status: 18.0% never married, 71.3% now married, 5.1% widowed, 5.7% divorced (2000); Foreign born: 4.7% (2000); Ancestry (includes multiple ancestries): 33.9% German, 20.0% Irish, 13.2% Other groups, 11.3% Polish, 11.3% English (2000).
Economy: Unemployment rate: 4.9% (4/2008); Total civilian labor force: 15,153 (4/2008); Single-family building permits issued: 421 (2007); Multi-family building permits issued: 11 (2007); Employment by occupation: 17.2% management, 24.6% professional, 8.9% services, 31.9% sales, 0.2% farming, 7.5% construction, 9.7% production (2000).
Income: Per capita income: $31,228 (2007); Median household income: $82,483 (2007); Average household income: $91,576 (2007); Percent of households with income of $100,000 or more: 33.6% (2007); Poverty rate: 2.8% (2000).
Education: Percent of population age 25 and over with: High school diploma (including GED) or higher: 93.4% (2007); Bachelor's degree or higher: 32.3% (2007); Master's degree or higher: 10.0% (2007).

School District(s)

Grundy/Kendall Roe (09-12)
2005-06 Enrollment: 119 . . . . (815) 941-3247
Kendall Co Spec Educ Coop (02-12)
2005-06 Enrollment: 61 . . . . (630) 553-5833
Oswego CUSD 308 (PK-12)
2005-06 Enrollment: 12,599 . . . . (630) 636-3080

Vocational/Technical School(s)

Hair Professionals School of Cosmetology (Private, For-profit)
Fall 2007 Enrollment: 142 . . . . (630) 554-2266
2007-08 Tuition: $16,400

Housing: Homeownership rate: 92.2% (2007); Median home value: $241,127 (2007); Median rent: $657 per month (2000); Median age of housing: 5 years (2000).
Safety: Violent crime rate: 11.7 per 10,000 population; Property crime rate: 209.6 per 10,000 population (2006).
Newspapers: Oswego Ledger Sentinel (Community news; Circulation 5,100)
Transportation: Commute to work: 89.7% car, 3.7% public transportation, 0.5% walk, 5.7% work from home (2000); Travel time to work: 19.3% less than 15 minutes, 29.0% 15 to 30 minutes, 22.4% 30 to 45 minutes, 13.7% 45 to 60 minutes, 15.6% 60 minutes or more (2000)

Additional Information Contacts

Oswego Chamber of Commerce . . . . (630) 554-3505
http://www.oswegochamber.org
Village of Oswego . . . . (630) 554-3618
http://www.oswegoil.org

PLANO (city). Covers a land area of 3.513 square miles and a water area of 0.042 square miles. Located at 41.66° N. Lat.; 88.53° W. Long. Elevation is 650 feet.
History: Plano was settled by a group of Norwegian Quakers led by Kleng Peerson in 1835.
Population: 5,192 (1990); 5,633 (2000); 7,582 (2007); 9,076 (2012 projected); Race: 68.8% White, 0.8% Black, 0.4% Asian, 47.6% Hispanic of any race (2007); Density: 2,158.0 persons per square mile (2007); Average household size: 2.98 (2007); Median age: 30.3 (2007); Males per 100 females: 98.7 (2007); Marriage status: 25.5% never married, 56.4% now married, 6.1% widowed, 12.0% divorced (2000); Foreign born: 17.0% (2000); Ancestry (includes multiple ancestries): 32.5% Other groups, 21.5% German, 10.7% Irish, 7.2% English, 5.0% Norwegian (2000).
Economy: Single-family building permits issued: 167 (2007); Multi-family building permits issued: 0 (2007); Employment by occupation: 10.1% management, 7.6% professional, 11.1% services, 24.6% sales, 0.0% farming, 9.7% construction, 36.8% production (2000).
Income: Per capita income: $19,343 (2007); Median household income: $52,727 (2007); Average household income: $57,693 (2007); Percent of households with income of $100,000 or more: 10.1% (2007); Poverty rate: 5.4% (2000).
Education: Percent of population age 25 and over with: High school diploma (including GED) or higher: 75.9% (2007); Bachelor's degree or higher: 10.7% (2007); Master's degree or higher: 2.1% (2007).

School District(s)

Grundy/Kendall Roe (09-12)
2005-06 Enrollment: 119 . . . . (815) 941-3247
Plano CUSD 88 (PK-12)
2005-06 Enrollment: 1,619 . . . . (630) 552-8978

Housing: Homeownership rate: 70.6% (2007); Median home value: $168,267 (2007); Median rent: $527 per month (2000); Median age of housing: 37 years (2000).
Safety: Violent crime rate: 24.5 per 10,000 population; Property crime rate: 313.4 per 10,000 population (2006).

Transportation: Commute to work: 92.0% car, 0.0% public transportation, 3.4% walk, 4.3% work from home (2000); Travel time to work: 38.2% less than 15 minutes, 26.5% 15 to 30 minutes, 21.2% 30 to 45 minutes, 7.7% 45 to 60 minutes, 6.5% 60 minutes or more (2000); Amtrak: Service available.

Additional Information Contacts

City of Plano. . . . . (630) 552-8275
http://www.cityofplanoil.com

Plano Area Chamber of Commerce. . . . . (630) 552-7272
http://www.planocommerce.org

YORKVILLE (city). County seat. Covers a land area of 7.043 square miles and a water area of 0.111 square miles. Located at 41.64° N. Lat.; 88.44° W. Long. Elevation is 607 feet.

Population: 4,716 (1990); 6,189 (2000); 9,868 (2007); 12,530 (2012 projected); Race: 94.0% White, 1.0% Black, 0.8% Asian, 6.4% Hispanic of any race (2007); Density: 1,401.1 persons per square mile (2007); Average household size: 2.72 (2007); Median age: 31.8 (2007); Males per 100 females: 99.6 (2007); Marriage status: 18.9% never married, 66.9% now married, 6.5% widowed, 7.7% divorced (2000); Foreign born: 3.6% (2000); Ancestry (includes multiple ancestries): 34.0% German, 15.5% Irish, 8.8% English, 8.4% Polish, 6.7% Other groups (2000).

Economy: Single-family building permits issued: 413 (2007); Multi-family building permits issued: 96 (2007); Employment by occupation: 18.2% management, 16.9% professional, 12.8% services, 26.4% sales, 0.0% farming, 9.2% construction, 16.4% production (2000).

Income: Per capita income: $28,316 (2007); Median household income: $66,386 (2007); Average household income: $76,529 (2007); Percent of households with income of $100,000 or more: 21.1% (2007); Poverty rate: 1.4% (2000).

Education: Percent of population age 25 and over with: High school diploma (including GED) or higher: 90.7% (2007); Bachelor's degree or higher: 24.6% (2007); Master's degree or higher: 6.7% (2007).

School District(s)

Grundy/Kendall Roe (09-12)
2005-06 Enrollment: 119 . . . . (815) 941-3247

Yorkville CUSD 115 (PK-12)
2005-06 Enrollment: 3,607 . . . . (630) 553-4382

Housing: Homeownership rate: 73.7% (2007); Median home value: $226,066 (2007); Median rent: $652 per month (2000); Median age of housing: 21 years (2000).

Safety: Violent crime rate: 18.7 per 10,000 population; Property crime rate: 264.2 per 10,000 population (2006).

Newspapers: Fox Valley Shopping News (Local news; Circulation 35,000); Kendall County Record (Community news; Circulation 4,650); Plano Record (Community news; Circulation 1,400); Sandwich Record (Community news; Circulation 4,950)

Transportation: Commute to work: 95.3% car, 1.6% public transportation, 0.6% walk, 2.6% work from home (2000); Travel time to work: 22.3% less than 15 minutes, 31.3% 15 to 30 minutes, 23.5% 30 to 45 minutes, 12.6% 45 to 60 minutes, 10.3% 60 minutes or more (2000)

Additional Information Contacts

United City of Yorkville. . . . . (630) 553-4350
http://www.yorkville.il.us

Yorkville Area Chamber of Commerce . . . . (630) 553-6853
http://www.yorkvillechamber.org

Knox County

Located in northwest central Illinois; drained by the Spoon River and Pope and Henderson Creeks. Covers a land area of 716.28 square miles, a water area of 3.42 square miles, and is located in the Central Time Zone. The county was founded in 1825. County seat is Galesburg.

Knox County is part of the Galesburg, IL Micropolitan Statistical Area. The entire metro area includes: Knox County, IL; Warren County, IL

Weather Station: Galesburg — Elevation: 770 feet

	Jan	Feb	Mar	Apr	May	Jun	Jul	Aug	Sep	Oct	Nov	Dec
High	29	35	48	61	72	82	85	82	75	63	48	35
Low	13	19	29	40	51	61	65	63	55	43	31	20
Precip	1.4	1.5	2.8	3.9	4.0	4.2	4.4	4.2	3.7	2.5	2.7	2.3
Snow	8.2	5.4	3.0	1.8	tr	0.0	0.0	0.0	0.0	tr	1.8	5.1

High and Low temperatures in degrees Fahrenheit; Precipitation and Snow in inches

Population: 56,393 (1990); 55,836 (2000); 52,601 (2007); 50,190 (2012 projected); Race: 88.4% White, 7.2% Black, 0.8% Asian, 3.9% Hispanic of any race (2007); Density: 73.4 persons per square mile (2007); Average household size: 2.50 (2007); Median age: 40.4 (2007); Males per 100 females: 100.3 (2007).

Religion: Five largest groups: 10.4% Catholic Church, 7.0% The United Methodist Church, 5.6% Evangelical Lutheran Church in America, 3.0% Christian Church (Disciples of Christ), 2.5% Presbyterian Church (U.S.A.) (2000).

Economy: Unemployment rate: 5.6% (4/2008); Total civilian labor force: 26,137 (4/2008); Leading industries: 29.9% health care and social assistance; 20.5% retail trade; 10.3% accommodation & food services (2005); Farms: 921 totaling 393,976 acres (2002); Companies that employ 500 or more persons: 4 (2006); Companies that employ 100 to 499 persons: 23 (2006); Companies that employ less than 100 persons: 1,133 (2006); Black-owned businesses: n/a (2002); Hispanic-owned businesses: n/a (2002); Asian-owned businesses: n/a (2002); Women-owned businesses: 994 (2002); Retail sales per capita: $14,683 (2008). Single-family building permits issued: 61 (2007); Multi-family building permits issued: 0 (2007).

Income: Per capita income: $20,831 (2007); Median household income: $40,187 (2007); Average household income: $50,344 (2007); Percent of households with income of $100,000 or more: 8.4% (2007); Poverty rate: 14.7% (2005); Bankruptcy rate: 4.05% (2007).

Taxes: Total county taxes per capita: $135 (2006); County property taxes per capita: $119 (2006).

Education: Percent of population age 25 and over with: High school diploma (including GED) or higher: 81.5% (2007); Bachelor's degree or higher: 14.7% (2007); Master's degree or higher: 5.0% (2007).

Housing: Homeownership rate: 71.9% (2007); Median home value: $93,596 (2007); Median rent: $315 per month (2000); Median age of housing: 48 years (2000).

Health: Birth rate: 114.9 per 10,000 population (2007); Death rate: 129.2 per 10,000 population (2007); Age-adjusted cancer mortality rate: 194.3 deaths per 100,000 population (2005); Number of physicians: 19.7 per 10,000 population (2005); Hospital beds: 51.9 per 10,000 population (2004); Hospital admissions: 1,857.8 per 10,000 population (2004).

Elections: 2004 Presidential election results: 45.0% Bush, 54.2% Kerry, 0.0% Nader, 0.7% Badnarik

National and State Parks: Snakeden Hollow State Fish and Wildlife Area

Additional Information Contacts

Knox County Government . . . . (309) 343-3121
http://www.knoxclerk.org

City of Galesburg . . . . (309) 343-4181
http://www.ci.galesburg.il.us

Galesburg Chamber of Commerce . . . . (309) 343-1194
http://www.galesburg.org

Knox County Communities

ABINGDON (city). Covers a land area of 1.459 square miles and a water area of 0 square miles. Located at 40.80° N. Lat.; 90.40° W. Long. Elevation is 751 feet.

History: Incorporated 1857.

Population: 3,685 (1990); 3,612 (2000); 3,297 (2007); 3,061 (2012 projected); Race: 97.9% White, 0.6% Black, 0.1% Asian, 1.3% Hispanic of any race (2007); Density: 2,259.3 persons per square mile (2007); Average household size: 2.48 (2007); Median age: 39.4 (2007); Males per 100 females: 91.8 (2007); Marriage status: 20.5% never married, 57.4% now married, 9.4% widowed, 12.8% divorced (2000); Foreign born: 0.3% (2000); Ancestry (includes multiple ancestries): 18.2% German, 14.6% Irish, 11.9% Other groups, 9.8% English, 9.3% United States or American (2000).

Economy: Single-family building permits issued: 2 (2007); Multi-family building permits issued: 0 (2007); Employment by occupation: 7.1% management, 13.3% professional, 17.4% services, 21.1% sales, 0.6% farming, 9.0% construction, 31.5% production (2000).

Income: Per capita income: $19,106 (2007); Median household income: $41,429 (2007); Average household income: $46,653 (2007); Percent of households with income of $100,000 or more: 5.6% (2007); Poverty rate: 9.9% (2000).

Education: Percent of population age 25 and over with: High school diploma (including GED) or higher: 81.3% (2007); Bachelor's degree or higher: 8.2% (2007); Master's degree or higher: 2.7% (2007).

School District(s)

Abingdon CUSD 217 (PK-12)
2005-06 Enrollment: 786 . . . . (309) 462-2301

Housing: Homeownership rate: 79.5% (2007); Median home value: $75,310 (2007); Median rent: $279 per month (2000); Median age of housing: 44 years (2000).

Safety: Violent crime rate: 20.7 per 10,000 population; Property crime rate: 251.6 per 10,000 population (2006).

Newspapers: Abingdon Argus (Community news; Circulation 2,050); Avon Sentinel (Community news; Circulation 850)

Transportation: Commute to work: 95.1% car, 0.0% public transportation, 2.4% walk, 1.7% work from home (2000); Travel time to work: 28.5% less than 15 minutes, 47.9% 15 to 30 minutes, 12.9% 30 to 45 minutes, 1.2% 45 to 60 minutes, 9.6% 60 minutes or more (2000)

ALTONA (village). Covers a land area of 1.016 square miles and a water area of 0 square miles. Located at 41.11° N. Lat.; 90.16° W. Long. Elevation is 761 feet.

Population: 559 (1990); 570 (2000); 531 (2007); 506 (2012 projected); Race: 99.2% White, 0.0% Black, 0.4% Asian, 1.1% Hispanic of any race (2007); Density: 522.4 persons per square mile (2007); Average household size: 2.63 (2007); Median age: 37.8 (2007); Males per 100 females: 95.2 (2007); Marriage status: 18.1% never married, 68.8% now married, 7.0% widowed, 6.1% divorced (2000); Foreign born: 0.0% (2000); Ancestry (includes multiple ancestries): 31.9% Swedish, 22.3% German, 12.7% English, 11.8% Irish, 6.3% Other groups (2000).

Economy: Employment by occupation: 8.3% management, 9.3% professional, 18.0% services, 22.5% sales, 6.6% farming, 10.7% construction, 24.6% production (2000).

Income: Per capita income: $17,100 (2007); Median household income: $38,333 (2007); Average household income: $44,950 (2007); Percent of households with income of $100,000 or more: 5.9% (2007); Poverty rate: 6.2% (2000).

Education: Percent of population age 25 and over with: High school diploma (including GED) or higher: 86.9% (2007); Bachelor's degree or higher: 10.2% (2007); Master's degree or higher: 1.7% (2007).

School District(s)

R O W V A CUSD 208 (PK-12)
2005-06 Enrollment: 773 . . . . (309) 483-3711

Housing: Homeownership rate: 88.1% (2007); Median home value: $72,381 (2007); Median rent: $269 per month (2000); Median age of housing: 49 years (2000).

Transportation: Commute to work: 97.2% car, 0.0% public transportation, 0.0% walk, 2.8% work from home (2000); Travel time to work: 30.2% less than 15 minutes, 43.2% 15 to 30 minutes, 18.7% 30 to 45 minutes, 1.8% 45 to 60 minutes, 6.1% 60 minutes or more (2000)

DAHINDA (unincorporated postal area, zip code 61428). Covers a land area of 33.362 square miles and a water area of 0.953 square miles. Located at 40.95° N. Lat.; 90.12° W. Long. Elevation is 584 feet.

Population: 954 (2000); Race: 97.2% White, 0.0% Black, 0.0% Asian, 1.8% Hispanic of any race (2000); Density: 28.6 persons per square mile (2000); Age: 17.1% under 18, 21.7% over 64 (2000); Marriage status: 15.6% never married, 75.3% now married, 3.8% widowed, 5.3% divorced (2000); Foreign born: 2.2% (2000); Ancestry (includes multiple ancestries): 24.4% English, 19.5% German, 16.9% Irish, 13.5% United States or American, 7.1% Swedish (2000).

Economy: Employment by occupation: 12.1% management, 17.5% professional, 8.8% services, 26.5% sales, 0.0% farming, 16.3% construction, 18.8% production (2000).

Income: Per capita income: $23,532 (2000); Median household income: $46,188 (2000); Poverty rate: 5.2% (2000).

Education: Percent of population age 25 and over with: High school diploma (including GED) or higher: 89.8% (2000); Bachelor's degree or higher: 17.8% (2000).

Housing: Homeownership rate: 89.8% (2000); Median home value: $92,900 (2000); Median rent: $355 per month (2000); Median age of housing: 22 years (2000).

Transportation: Commute to work: 96.7% car, 0.0% public transportation, 1.5% walk, 1.9% work from home (2000); Travel time to work: 12.8% less than 15 minutes, 36.6% 15 to 30 minutes, 31.1% 30 to 45 minutes, 8.9% 45 to 60 minutes, 10.6% 60 minutes or more (2000)

EAST GALESBURG (village). Covers a land area of 1.460 square miles and a water area of 0.051 square miles. Located at 40.94° N. Lat.; 90.31° W. Long. Elevation is 774 feet.

Population: 887 (1990); 839 (2000); 762 (2007); 735 (2012 projected); Race: 97.1% White, 0.3% Black, 1.0% Asian, 1.7% Hispanic of any race (2007); Density: 521.9 persons per square mile (2007); Average household size: 2.37 (2007); Median age: 42.9 (2007); Males per 100 females: 97.4 (2007); Marriage status: 15.9% never married, 66.2% now married, 5.7% widowed, 12.2% divorced (2000); Foreign born: 1.1% (2000); Ancestry (includes multiple ancestries): 19.6% German, 13.4% Irish, 13.2% English, 9.4% United States or American, 7.6% Swedish (2000).

Economy: Single-family building permits issued: 1 (2007); Multi-family building permits issued: 0 (2007); Employment by occupation: 9.9% management, 23.1% professional, 12.0% services, 20.5% sales, 0.5% farming, 8.5% construction, 25.5% production (2000).

Income: Per capita income: $25,702 (2007); Median household income: $46,389 (2007); Average household income: $60,823 (2007); Percent of households with income of $100,000 or more: 12.1% (2007); Poverty rate: 6.3% (2000).

Education: Percent of population age 25 and over with: High school diploma (including GED) or higher: 81.3% (2007); Bachelor's degree or higher: 20.7% (2007); Master's degree or higher: 9.3% (2007).

Housing: Homeownership rate: 83.2% (2007); Median home value: $93,000 (2007); Median rent: $378 per month (2000); Median age of housing: 33 years (2000).

Safety: Violent crime rate: 12.5 per 10,000 population; Property crime rate: 225.3 per 10,000 population (2006).

Transportation: Commute to work: 97.6% car, 0.2% public transportation, 0.0% walk, 1.7% work from home (2000); Travel time to work: 50.4% less than 15 minutes, 36.0% 15 to 30 minutes, 4.1% 30 to 45 minutes, 4.1% 45 to 60 minutes, 5.4% 60 minutes or more (2000)

GALESBURG (city). County seat. Covers a land area of 16.896 square miles and a water area of 0.178 square miles. Located at 40.95° N. Lat.; 90.36° W. Long. Elevation is 771 feet.

History: Galesburg was settled in 1836 on a site selected by an advance guard sent by Reverend George Washington Gale, a Presbyterian minister from New York who planned a town where morality and industry would rule. Among the early residents was the Ferris family, one of whom invented the ferris wheel, first shown at the Columbian Exposition in Chicago in 1893. Formerly Randall.

Population: 33,637 (1990); 33,706 (2000); 31,505 (2007); 29,906 (2012 projected); Race: 81.8% White, 11.8% Black, 1.2% Asian, 5.7% Hispanic of any race (2007); Density: 1,864.6 persons per square mile (2007); Average household size: 2.54 (2007); Median age: 38.6 (2007); Males per 100 females: 102.0 (2007); Marriage status: 24.2% never married, 51.6% now married, 9.3% widowed, 14.9% divorced (2000); Foreign born: 2.2% (2000); Ancestry (includes multiple ancestries): 18.0% German, 14.2% Other groups, 12.3% Irish, 10.0% English, 10.0% Swedish (2000).

Economy: Unemployment rate: 5.9% (4/2008); Total civilian labor force: 14,962 (4/2008); Single-family building permits issued: 4 (2007); Multi-family building permits issued: 0 (2007); Employment by occupation: 8.2% management, 18.5% professional, 19.8% services, 23.0% sales, 0.5% farming, 8.0% construction, 22.0% production (2000).

Income: Per capita income: $19,328 (2007); Median household income: $35,639 (2007); Average household income: $46,302 (2007); Percent of households with income of $100,000 or more: 7.3% (2007); Poverty rate: 14.7% (2000).

Education: Percent of population age 25 and over with: High school diploma (including GED) or higher: 78.8% (2007); Bachelor's degree or higher: 14.9% (2007); Master's degree or higher: 5.6% (2007).

School District(s)

Dept of Corrections Sch Dist 428 (08-12)
2005-06 Enrollment: 2,271 . . . . (217) 522-2666

Galesburg Area Voc Ctr
2005-06 Enrollment: n/a . . . . (309) 343-3733

Galesburg CUSD 205 (PK-12)
2005-06 Enrollment: 4,877 . . . . (309) 343-1151

Knox Roe (07-12)
2005-06 Enrollment: 39 . . . . (309) 345-3832

Knox-Warren Spec Educ District (06-12)
2005-06 Enrollment: 18 . . . . (309) 343-2143

Four-year College(s)

Knox College (Private, Not-for-profit)
Fall 2007 Enrollment: 1,371. . . . . (309) 341-7000
2007-08 Tuition: In-state $29,178; Out-of-state $29,178

Two-year College(s)

Carl Sandburg College (Public)
Fall 2007 Enrollment: 2,693. . . . . (309) 344-2518
2007-08 Tuition: In-state $3,855; Out-of-state $4,560

Housing: Homeownership rate: 64.5% (2007); Median home value: $86,207 (2007); Median rent: $322 per month (2000); Median age of housing: 51 years (2000).

Hospitals: Galesburg Cottage Hospital (170 beds); OSF St Mary Medical Center (156 beds)

Safety: Violent crime rate: 53.7 per 10,000 population; Property crime rate: 514.4 per 10,000 population (2006).

Newspapers: Extra (Community news; Circulation 16,000); Galesburg Register-Mail (Local news; Circulation 17,948); Knoxville Journal - Galesburg Bureau (Local news; Circulation 0); The Zephyr (Community news; Circulation 2,000)

Transportation: Commute to work: 89.4% car, 1.6% public transportation, 5.8% walk, 1.8% work from home (2000); Travel time to work: 69.2% less than 15 minutes, 20.7% 15 to 30 minutes, 3.4% 30 to 45 minutes, 2.8% 45 to 60 minutes, 3.8% 60 minutes or more (2000); Amtrak: Service available.

Airports: Galesburg Municipal (general aviation)

Additional Information Contacts

City of Galesburg . . . . (309) 343-4181
http://www.ci.galesburg.il.us
Galesburg Chamber of Commerce . . . . (309) 343-1194
http://www.galesburg.org

GILSON (unincorporated postal area, zip code 61436). Covers a land area of 64.363 square miles and a water area of 0.015 square miles. Located at 40.86° N. Lat.; 90.22° W. Long. Elevation is 679 feet.

Population: 1,021 (2000); Race: 99.2% White, 0.0% Black, 0.8% Asian, 0.0% Hispanic of any race (2000); Density: 15.9 persons per square mile (2000); Age: 23.4% under 18, 12.6% over 64 (2000); Marriage status: 14.5% never married, 74.9% now married, 3.8% widowed, 6.8% divorced (2000); Foreign born: 0.8% (2000); Ancestry (includes multiple ancestries): 27.4% German, 17.5% United States or American, 17.3% English, 15.6% Swedish, 9.3% Irish (2000).

Economy: Employment by occupation: 12.9% management, 5.1% professional, 11.6% services, 21.3% sales, 5.3% farming, 5.1% construction, 38.7% production (2000).

Income: Per capita income: $19,092 (2000); Median household income: $44,000 (2000); Poverty rate: 1.5% (2000).

Education: Percent of population age 25 and over with: High school diploma (including GED) or higher: 88.3% (2000); Bachelor's degree or higher: 8.7% (2000).

Housing: Homeownership rate: 87.1% (2000); Median home value: $68,400 (2000); Median rent: $211 per month (2000); Median age of housing: 60+ years (2000).

Transportation: Commute to work: 89.2% car, 0.0% public transportation, 0.0% walk, 9.7% work from home (2000); Travel time to work: 19.1% less than 15 minutes, 57.1% 15 to 30 minutes, 15.1% 30 to 45 minutes, 4.0% 45 to 60 minutes, 4.6% 60 minutes or more (2000)

HENDERSON (village). Aka Soperville. Covers a land area of 0.272 square miles and a water area of 0 square miles. Located at 41.02° N. Lat.; 90.35° W. Long. Elevation is 817 feet.

Population: 290 (1990); 319 (2000); 297 (2007); 281 (2012 projected); Race: 96.3% White, 1.0% Black, 0.0% Asian, 2.4% Hispanic of any race (2007); Density: 1,091.5 persons per square mile (2007); Average household size: 2.28 (2007); Median age: 48.7 (2007); Males per 100 females: 98.0 (2007); Marriage status: 17.0% never married, 68.6% now married, 2.5% widowed, 11.9% divorced (2000); Foreign born: 3.4% (2000); Ancestry (includes multiple ancestries): 19.5% Irish, 19.5% German, 13.6% Swedish, 6.8% Other groups, 6.5% United States or American (2000).

Economy: Employment by occupation: 6.4% management, 24.0% professional, 15.2% services, 20.5% sales, 0.0% farming, 14.6% construction, 19.3% production (2000).

Income: Per capita income: $22,677 (2007); Median household income: $40,714 (2007); Average household income: $51,808 (2007); Percent of households with income of $100,000 or more: 10.0% (2007); Poverty rate: 7.9% (2000).

Education: Percent of population age 25 and over with: High school diploma (including GED) or higher: 82.6% (2007); Bachelor's degree or higher: 11.1% (2007); Master's degree or higher: 3.4% (2007).

Housing: Homeownership rate: 90.0% (2007); Median home value: $92,083 (2007); Median rent: $221 per month (2000); Median age of housing: 38 years (2000).

Transportation: Commute to work: 97.1% car, 0.0% public transportation, 0.0% walk, 2.9% work from home (2000); Travel time to work: 52.4% less than 15 minutes, 39.2% 15 to 30 minutes, 3.0% 30 to 45 minutes, 1.2% 45 to 60 minutes, 4.2% 60 minutes or more (2000)

KNOXVILLE (city). Covers a land area of 2.198 square miles and a water area of 0 square miles. Located at 40.90° N. Lat.; 90.28° W. Long. Elevation is 781 feet.

History: Incorporated 1832. Formerly the county seat.

Population: 3,244 (1990); 3,183 (2000); 2,948 (2007); 2,771 (2012 projected); Race: 98.4% White, 0.4% Black, 0.1% Asian, 0.6% Hispanic of any race (2007); Density: 1,341.0 persons per square mile (2007); Average household size: 2.58 (2007); Median age: 43.8 (2007); Males per 100 females: 86.7 (2007); Marriage status: 16.4% never married, 68.3% now married, 6.5% widowed, 8.7% divorced (2000); Foreign born: 0.6% (2000); Ancestry (includes multiple ancestries): 19.1% German, 17.9% English, 11.3% Swedish, 9.5% United States or American, 8.9% Irish (2000).

Economy: Single-family building permits issued: 1 (2007); Multi-family building permits issued: 0 (2007); Employment by occupation: 11.0% management, 17.6% professional, 16.6% services, 24.9% sales, 0.0% farming, 6.5% construction, 23.4% production (2000).

Income: Per capita income: $21,984 (2007); Median household income: $49,685 (2007); Average household income: $54,367 (2007); Percent of households with income of $100,000 or more: 8.2% (2007); Poverty rate: 3.1% (2000).

Education: Percent of population age 25 and over with: High school diploma (including GED) or higher: 80.9% (2007); Bachelor's degree or higher: 14.2% (2007); Master's degree or higher: 4.3% (2007).

School District(s)

Knoxville CUSD 202 (PK-12)
2005-06 Enrollment: 1,093 . . . . (309) 289-2328

Housing: Homeownership rate: 80.4% (2007); Median home value: $111,117 (2007); Median rent: $253 per month (2000); Median age of housing: 47 years (2000).

Safety: Violent crime rate: 13.3 per 10,000 population; Property crime rate: 282.9 per 10,000 population (2006).

Transportation: Commute to work: 93.4% car, 0.0% public transportation, 2.1% walk, 4.0% work from home (2000); Travel time to work: 44.9% less than 15 minutes, 43.8% 15 to 30 minutes, 4.2% 30 to 45 minutes, 3.1% 45 to 60 minutes, 3.9% 60 minutes or more (2000)

MAQUON (village). Covers a land area of 0.161 square miles and a water area of 0 square miles. Located at 40.79° N. Lat.; 90.16° W. Long. Elevation is 633 feet.

Population: 331 (1990); 318 (2000); 296 (2007); 286 (2012 projected); Race: 97.6% White, 0.0% Black, 0.7% Asian, 4.1% Hispanic of any race (2007); Density: 1,835.0 persons per square mile (2007); Average household size: 2.23 (2007); Median age: 37.0 (2007); Males per 100 females: 85.0 (2007); Marriage status: 21.3% never married, 55.3% now married, 9.9% widowed, 13.4% divorced (2000); Foreign born: 0.0% (2000); Ancestry (includes multiple ancestries): 34.6% United States or American, 10.1% English, 9.5% Irish, 8.9% Swedish, 7.0% German (2000).

Economy: Single-family building permits issued: 0 (2007); Multi-family building permits issued: 0 (2007); Employment by occupation: 7.2% management, 9.2% professional, 19.0% services, 15.7% sales, 3.3% farming, 11.1% construction, 34.6% production (2000).

Income: Per capita income: $19,840 (2007); Median household income: $37,763 (2007); Average household income: $44,154 (2007); Percent of households with income of $100,000 or more: 3.8% (2007); Poverty rate: 10.3% (2000).

Education: Percent of population age 25 and over with: High school diploma (including GED) or higher: 81.2% (2007); Bachelor's degree or higher: 6.3% (2007); Master's degree or higher: 2.1% (2007).

Housing: Homeownership rate: 82.0% (2007); Median home value: $68,750 (2007); Median rent: $319 per month (2000); Median age of housing: 60+ years (2000).

Transportation: Commute to work: 89.6% car, 0.0% public transportation, 6.5% walk, 1.3% work from home (2000); Travel time to work: 11.8% less

than 15 minutes, 33.6% 15 to 30 minutes, 25.7% 30 to 45 minutes, 11.2% 45 to 60 minutes, 17.8% 60 minutes or more (2000)

ONEIDA (city). Covers a land area of 0.726 square miles and a water area of 0 square miles. Located at 41.07° N. Lat.; 90.22° W. Long. Elevation is 814 feet.

Population: 723 (1990); 752 (2000); 734 (2007); 689 (2012 projected); Race: 97.7% White, 0.0% Black, 1.1% Asian, 2.0% Hispanic of any race (2007); Density: 1,011.1 persons per square mile (2007); Average household size: 2.45 (2007); Median age: 39.4 (2007); Males per 100 females: 97.3 (2007); Marriage status: 20.0% never married, 61.8% now married, 8.8% widowed, 9.3% divorced (2000); Foreign born: 0.0% (2000); Ancestry (includes multiple ancestries): 22.6% Swedish, 20.1% German, 18.0% Irish, 15.2% English, 6.7% Other groups (2000).

Economy: Employment by occupation: 12.4% management, 14.7% professional, 7.9% services, 23.2% sales, 0.8% farming, 15.8% construction, 25.1% production (2000).

Income: Per capita income: $20,828 (2007); Median household income: $44,868 (2007); Average household income: $51,129 (2007); Percent of households with income of $100,000 or more: 6.7% (2007); Poverty rate: 5.3% (2000).

Education: Percent of population age 25 and over with: High school diploma (including GED) or higher: 90.9% (2007); Bachelor's degree or higher: 15.6% (2007); Master's degree or higher: 5.3% (2007).

School District(s)

R O W V A CUSD 208 (PK-12)
2005-06 Enrollment: 773 . . . . (309) 483-3711

Housing: Homeownership rate: 78.3% (2007); Median home value: $93,043 (2007); Median rent: $353 per month (2000); Median age of housing: 60 years (2000).

Transportation: Commute to work: 94.6% car, 0.0% public transportation, 2.3% walk, 3.1% work from home (2000); Travel time to work: 22.4% less than 15 minutes, 54.6% 15 to 30 minutes, 9.1% 30 to 45 minutes, 3.8% 45 to 60 minutes, 10.0% 60 minutes or more (2000)

RIO (village). Covers a land area of 0.325 square miles and a water area of 0 square miles. Located at 41.11° N. Lat.; 90.39° W. Long. Elevation is 778 feet.

Population: 260 (1990); 240 (2000); 226 (2007); 215 (2012 projected); Race: 99.1% White, 0.0% Black, 0.0% Asian, 3.1% Hispanic of any race (2007); Density: 694.6 persons per square mile (2007); Average household size: 2.54 (2007); Median age: 39.5 (2007); Males per 100 females: 105.5 (2007); Marriage status: 19.7% never married, 67.2% now married, 7.6% widowed, 5.6% divorced (2000); Foreign born: 0.4% (2000); Ancestry (includes multiple ancestries): 40.4% Swedish, 20.4% German, 12.0% Irish, 6.0% United States or American, 5.2% Italian (2000).

Economy: Employment by occupation: 6.0% management, 13.7% professional, 17.9% services, 18.8% sales, 5.1% farming, 11.1% construction, 27.4% production (2000).

Income: Per capita income: $20,918 (2007); Median household income: $43,750 (2007); Average household income: $53,118 (2007); Percent of households with income of $100,000 or more: 5.6% (2007); Poverty rate: 2.0% (2000).

Education: Percent of population age 25 and over with: High school diploma (including GED) or higher: 85.2% (2007); Bachelor's degree or higher: 11.6% (2007); Master's degree or higher: 2.6% (2007).

Housing: Homeownership rate: 89.9% (2007); Median home value: $101,923 (2007); Median rent: $313 per month (2000); Median age of housing: 42 years (2000).

Transportation: Commute to work: 86.0% car, 0.0% public transportation, 5.6% walk, 8.4% work from home (2000); Travel time to work: 22.4% less than 15 minutes, 52.0% 15 to 30 minutes, 18.4% 30 to 45 minutes, 4.1% 45 to 60 minutes, 3.1% 60 minutes or more (2000)

SAINT AUGUSTINE (village). Covers a land area of 0.615 square miles and a water area of 0 square miles. Located at 40.72° N. Lat.; 90.41° W. Long. Elevation is 643 feet.

Population: 151 (1990); 152 (2000); 140 (2007); 130 (2012 projected); Race: 100.0% White, 0.0% Black, 0.0% Asian, 0.0% Hispanic of any race (2007); Density: 227.7 persons per square mile (2007); Average household size: 2.19 (2007); Median age: 50.4 (2007); Males per 100 females: 72.8 (2007); Marriage status: 23.4% never married, 54.5% now married, 8.3% widowed, 13.8% divorced (2000); Foreign born: 0.6% (2000); Ancestry (includes multiple ancestries): 20.6% German, 13.1% Irish, 11.9% United States or American, 5.6% Swedish, 3.1% English (2000).

Economy: Single-family building permits issued: 0 (2007); Multi-family building permits issued: 0 (2007); Employment by occupation: 4.8% management, 7.2% professional, 34.9% services, 19.3% sales, 0.0% farming, 2.4% construction, 31.3% production (2000).

Income: Per capita income: $19,018 (2007); Median household income: $40,000 (2007); Average household income: $41,602 (2007); Percent of households with income of $100,000 or more: 0.0% (2007); Poverty rate: 5.6% (2000).

Education: Percent of population age 25 and over with: High school diploma (including GED) or higher: 82.7% (2007); Bachelor's degree or higher: 7.7% (2007); Master's degree or higher: 0.0% (2007).

Housing: Homeownership rate: 92.2% (2007); Median home value: $62,143 (2007); Median rent: $238 per month (2000); Median age of housing: 52 years (2000).

Transportation: Commute to work: 87.5% car, 0.0% public transportation, 10.0% walk, 2.5% work from home (2000); Travel time to work: 30.8% less than 15 minutes, 43.6% 15 to 30 minutes, 17.9% 30 to 45 minutes, 2.6% 45 to 60 minutes, 5.1% 60 minutes or more (2000)

VICTORIA (village). Covers a land area of 0.663 square miles and a water area of 0 square miles. Located at 41.03° N. Lat.; 90.09° W. Long. Elevation is 833 feet.

Population: 315 (1990); 323 (2000); 294 (2007); 281 (2012 projected); Race: 99.0% White, 0.0% Black, 0.0% Asian, 0.7% Hispanic of any race (2007); Density: 443.2 persons per square mile (2007); Average household size: 2.75 (2007); Median age: 34.7 (2007); Males per 100 females: 104.2 (2007); Marriage status: 20.0% never married, 61.7% now married, 12.3% widowed, 6.0% divorced (2000); Foreign born: 0.0% (2000); Ancestry (includes multiple ancestries): 20.7% German, 15.7% English, 14.7% United States or American, 12.0% Swedish, 11.0% Irish (2000).

Economy: Single-family building permits issued: 0 (2007); Multi-family building permits issued: 0 (2007); Employment by occupation: 9.8% management, 9.8% professional, 14.3% services, 24.1% sales, 0.0% farming, 8.0% construction, 33.9% production (2000).

Income: Per capita income: $13,444 (2007); Median household income: $32,500 (2007); Average household income: $36,939 (2007); Percent of households with income of $100,000 or more: 3.7% (2007); Poverty rate: 7.3% (2000).

Education: Percent of population age 25 and over with: High school diploma (including GED) or higher: 80.8% (2007); Bachelor's degree or higher: 2.8% (2007); Master's degree or higher: 0.6% (2007).

Housing: Homeownership rate: 84.1% (2007); Median home value: $55,455 (2007); Median rent: $179 per month (2000); Median age of housing: 60+ years (2000).

Transportation: Commute to work: 91.1% car, 0.0% public transportation, 8.0% walk, 0.0% work from home (2000); Travel time to work: 9.8% less than 15 minutes, 56.3% 15 to 30 minutes, 26.8% 30 to 45 minutes, 6.3% 45 to 60 minutes, 0.9% 60 minutes or more (2000)

WATAGA (village). Covers a land area of 0.866 square miles and a water area of 0 square miles. Located at 41.02° N. Lat.; 90.27° W. Long. Elevation is 830 feet.

Population: 888 (1990); 857 (2000); 752 (2007); 725 (2012 projected); Race: 97.6% White, 0.4% Black, 0.1% Asian, 1.7% Hispanic of any race (2007); Density: 868.3 persons per square mile (2007); Average household size: 2.50 (2007); Median age: 36.0 (2007); Males per 100 females: 86.1 (2007); Marriage status: 21.4% never married, 61.2% now married, 4.0% widowed, 13.4% divorced (2000); Foreign born: 0.2% (2000); Ancestry (includes multiple ancestries): 24.5% German, 13.3% Swedish, 12.1% Irish, 11.3% United States or American, 10.6% English (2000).

Economy: Single-family building permits issued: 2 (2007); Multi-family building permits issued: 0 (2007); Employment by occupation: 8.8% management, 14.1% professional, 14.5% services, 25.6% sales, 1.2% farming, 12.9% construction, 22.9% production (2000).

Income: Per capita income: $20,695 (2007); Median household income: $47,083 (2007); Average household income: $51,703 (2007); Percent of households with income of $100,000 or more: 6.6% (2007); Poverty rate: 11.2% (2000).

Education: Percent of population age 25 and over with: High school diploma (including GED) or higher: 82.9% (2007); Bachelor's degree or higher: 10.4% (2007); Master's degree or higher: 2.0% (2007).

School District(s)

R O W V A CUSD 208 (PK-12)
2005-06 Enrollment: 773 . . . . (309) 483-3711

Housing: Homeownership rate: 80.7% (2007); Median home value: $84,792 (2007); Median rent: $328 per month (2000); Median age of housing: 37 years (2000).
Transportation: Commute to work: 94.5% car, 0.0% public transportation, 0.7% walk, 1.9% work from home (2000); Travel time to work: 30.0% less than 15 minutes, 52.2% 15 to 30 minutes, 6.8% 30 to 45 minutes, 5.3% 45 to 60 minutes, 5.8% 60 minutes or more (2000)

WILLIAMSFIELD (village). Covers a land area of 1.271 square miles and a water area of 0 square miles. Located at 40.92° N. Lat.; 90.01° W. Long. Elevation is 705 feet.
Population: 621 (1990); 620 (2000); 588 (2007); 561 (2012 projected); Race: 99.5% White, 0.0% Black, 0.0% Asian, 0.0% Hispanic of any race (2007); Density: 462.8 persons per square mile (2007); Average household size: 2.53 (2007); Median age: 36.4 (2007); Males per 100 females: 98.0 (2007); Marriage status: 24.5% never married, 56.7% now married, 11.4% widowed, 7.3% divorced (2000); Foreign born: 0.3% (2000); Ancestry (includes multiple ancestries): 21.9% German, 19.3% English, 14.7% Irish, 12.8% Swedish, 10.1% United States or American (2000).
Economy: Employment by occupation: 7.6% management, 13.7% professional, 18.2% services, 24.2% sales, 0.0% farming, 8.0% construction, 28.3% production (2000).
Income: Per capita income: $20,695 (2007); Median household income: $43,235 (2007); Average household income: $51,756 (2007); Percent of households with income of $100,000 or more: 6.0% (2007); Poverty rate: 5.3% (2000).
Education: Percent of population age 25 and over with: High school diploma (including GED) or higher: 89.5% (2007); Bachelor's degree or higher: 15.6% (2007); Master's degree or higher: 3.3% (2007).

School District(s)

Williamsfield CUSD 210 (PK-12)
2005-06 Enrollment: 272 . . . . (309) 639-2219
Housing: Homeownership rate: 83.6% (2007); Median home value: $91,250 (2007); Median rent: $275 per month (2000); Median age of housing: 45 years (2000).
Safety: Violent crime rate: 50.6 per 10,000 population; Property crime rate: 84.3 per 10,000 population (2006).
Transportation: Commute to work: 94.9% car, 0.0% public transportation, 1.6% walk, 2.9% work from home (2000); Travel time to work: 22.0% less than 15 minutes, 22.4% 15 to 30 minutes, 45.1% 30 to 45 minutes, 10.2% 45 to 60 minutes, 0.3% 60 minutes or more (2000)

YATES CITY (village). Covers a land area of 0.587 square miles and a water area of 0 square miles. Located at 40.77° N. Lat.; 90.01° W. Long. Elevation is 669 feet.
Population: 789 (1990); 725 (2000); 647 (2007); 632 (2012 projected); Race: 98.5% White, 0.8% Black, 0.0% Asian, 0.0% Hispanic of any race (2007); Density: 1,102.3 persons per square mile (2007); Average household size: 2.37 (2007); Median age: 38.7 (2007); Males per 100 females: 103.5 (2007); Marriage status: 14.9% never married, 65.4% now married, 10.8% widowed, 8.9% divorced (2000); Foreign born: 0.0% (2000); Ancestry (includes multiple ancestries): 21.9% German, 17.7% English, 13.3% United States or American, 12.1% Irish, 9.2% Other groups (2000).
Economy: Employment by occupation: 4.5% management, 11.9% professional, 15.0% services, 26.9% sales, 2.5% farming, 11.0% construction, 28.0% production (2000).
Income: Per capita income: $21,338 (2007); Median household income: $42,283 (2007); Average household income: $50,110 (2007); Percent of households with income of $100,000 or more: 7.7% (2007); Poverty rate: 8.5% (2000).
Education: Percent of population age 25 and over with: High school diploma (including GED) or higher: 88.0% (2007); Bachelor's degree or higher: 10.0% (2007); Master's degree or higher: 2.5% (2007).
Housing: Homeownership rate: 86.4% (2007); Median home value: $107,759 (2007); Median rent: $316 per month (2000); Median age of housing: 55 years (2000).
Safety: Violent crime rate: 14.5 per 10,000 population; Property crime rate: 72.4 per 10,000 population (2006).
Transportation: Commute to work: 96.5% car, 0.0% public transportation, 0.6% walk, 2.0% work from home (2000); Travel time to work: 16.2% less than 15 minutes, 12.1% 15 to 30 minutes, 52.4% 30 to 45 minutes, 15.6% 45 to 60 minutes, 3.8% 60 minutes or more (2000)

La Salle County

Located in northern Illinois; drained by the Illinois, Fox, Vermilion, and Little Vermilion Rivers. Covers a land area of 1,134.92 square miles, a water area of 13.12 square miles, and is located in the Central Time Zone. The county was founded in 1831. County seat is Ottawa.

La Salle County is part of the Ottawa-Streator, IL Micropolitan Statistical Area. The entire metro area includes: Bureau County, IL; La Salle County, IL; Putnam County, IL

Weather Station: Ottawa 5 SW Elevation: 524 feet

	Jan	Feb	Mar	Apr	May	Jun	Jul	Aug	Sep	Oct	Nov	Dec
High	31	37	49	63	74	82	85	84	77	66	50	37
Low	14	19	30	40	51	60	65	62	54	42	32	21
Precip	1.5	1.3	2.6	3.5	4.1	4.2	3.7	3.8	3.7	2.6	2.9	2.3
Snow	8.6	5.0	3.2	0.8	0.0	0.0	0.0	0.0	0.0	tr	1.0	5.4

High and Low temperatures in degrees Fahrenheit; Precipitation and Snow in inches

Weather Station: Peru Elevation: 620 feet

	Jan	Feb	Mar	Apr	May	Jun	Jul	Aug	Sep	Oct	Nov	Dec
High	29	35	47	61	73	83	86	84	77	65	49	36
Low	12	18	28	38	49	59	63	61	52	41	31	20
Precip	1.4	1.4	2.8	3.8	4.8	4.2	4.1	4.3	3.8	3.1	2.8	2.3
Snow	8.0	4.5	3.6	0.6	tr	0.0	0.0	0.0	0.0	0.1	1.3	5.6

High and Low temperatures in degrees Fahrenheit; Precipitation and Snow in inches

Population: 106,913 (1990); 111,509 (2000); 113,010 (2007); 113,796 (2012 projected); Race: 94.1% White, 1.6% Black, 0.7% Asian, 6.7% Hispanic of any race (2007); Density: 99.6 persons per square mile (2007); Average household size: 2.53 (2007); Median age: 39.3 (2007); Males per 100 females: 97.0 (2007).
Religion: Five largest groups: 40.1% Catholic Church, 6.1% The United Methodist Church, 5.0% Evangelical Lutheran Church in America, 1.4% Presbyterian Church (U.S.A.), 1.3% Church of the Nazarene (2000).
Economy: Unemployment rate: 6.8% (4/2008); Total civilian labor force: 59,806 (4/2008); Leading industries: 19.2% retail trade; 16.2% manufacturing; 14.2% health care and social assistance (2005); Farms: 1,478 totaling 579,141 acres (2002); Companies that employ 500 or more persons: 4 (2006); Companies that employ 100 to 499 persons: 64 (2006); Companies that employ less than 100 persons: 2,885 (2006); Black-owned businesses: n/a (2002); Hispanic-owned businesses: n/a (2002); Asian-owned businesses: n/a (2002); Women-owned businesses: n/a (2002); Retail sales per capita: $16,850 (2008). Single-family building permits issued: 250 (2007); Multi-family building permits issued: 59 (2007).
Income: Per capita income: $22,474 (2007); Median household income: $45,728 (2007); Average household income: $55,793 (2007); Percent of households with income of $100,000 or more: 11.5% (2007); Poverty rate: 11.7% (2005); Bankruptcy rate: 3.94% (2007).
Taxes: Total county taxes per capita: $181 (2006); County property taxes per capita: $129 (2006).
Education: Percent of population age 25 and over with: High school diploma (including GED) or higher: 81.6% (2007); Bachelor's degree or higher: 13.4% (2007); Master's degree or higher: 4.4% (2007).
Housing: Homeownership rate: 75.3% (2007); Median home value: $118,934 (2007); Median rent: $379 per month (2000); Median age of housing: 47 years (2000).
Health: Birth rate: 132.4 per 10,000 population (2007); Death rate: 110.6 per 10,000 population (2007); Age-adjusted cancer mortality rate: 236.8 deaths per 100,000 population (2005); Air Quality Index: 71.5% good, 28.2% moderate, 0.3% unhealthy for sensitive individuals, 0.0% unhealthy (percent of days in 2007); Number of physicians: 10.6 per 10,000 population (2005); Hospital beds: 30.4 per 10,000 population (2004); Hospital admissions: 1,225.6 per 10,000 population (2004).
Elections: 2004 Presidential election results: 51.5% Bush, 47.8% Kerry, 0.0% Nader, 0.7% Badnarik
National and State Parks: Buffalo Rock State Park; Illini State Park; La Salle Lake State Fish and Wildlife Area; Marseilles State Fish and Wildlife Area; Matthiessen State Park; Norwegian Settlers State Memorial; Starved Rock State Park
Additional Information Contacts
La Salle County Government. . . . . (815) 434-8200
http://www.lasallecounty.org
City of La Salle. . . . . (815) 223-3755
http://www.lasalle-il.gov
City of Mendota . . . . (815) 539-7459
http://www.mendota.il.us

City of Ottawa . . . . (815) 433-0161
http://www.cityofottawa.org
City of Peru . . . . (815) 223-0061
http://www.peru.il.us
City of Streator. . . . . (815) 672-2517
http://www.ci.streator.il.us/cms
Illinois River Area Chamber of Commerce. . . . . (815) 795-2323
http://www.marseillesil.org
Illinois Valley Area Chamber of Commerce & Economic Developm . . (815) 223-0227
http://www.ivaced.org
Mendota Chamber of Commerce. . . . . (815) 539-6507
http://www.mendotachamber.com
Ottawa Area Chamber of Commerce. . . . . (815) 433-0084
http://www.ottawachamberillinois.com
Streator Area Chamber of Commerce & Industry . . . . (815) 672-2921
http://www.streatorchamber.com

La Salle County Communities

CEDAR POINT (village). Covers a land area of 1.022 square miles and a water area of 0 square miles. Located at 41.26° N. Lat.; 89.12° W. Long. Elevation is 659 feet.
Population: 275 (1990); 262 (2000); 248 (2007); 234 (2012 projected); Race: 97.6% White, 1.6% Black, 0.0% Asian, 1.2% Hispanic of any race (2007); Density: 242.6 persons per square mile (2007); Average household size: 2.19 (2007); Median age: 40.9 (2007); Males per 100 females: 90.8 (2007); Marriage status: 21.8% never married, 55.1% now married, 10.6% widowed, 12.5% divorced (2000); Foreign born: 0.7% (2000); Ancestry (includes multiple ancestries): 33.9% Italian, 15.9% German, 14.4% Irish, 10.0% Other groups, 10.0% English (2000).
Economy: Single-family building permits issued: 0 (2007); Multi-family building permits issued: 0 (2007); Employment by occupation: 4.7% management, 7.1% professional, 15.0% services, 31.5% sales, 0.0% farming, 11.0% construction, 30.7% production (2000).
Income: Per capita income: $26,027 (2007); Median household income: $46,500 (2007); Average household income: $48,473 (2007); Percent of households with income of $100,000 or more: 4.4% (2007); Poverty rate: 3.0% (2000).
Education: Percent of population age 25 and over with: High school diploma (including GED) or higher: 83.8% (2007); Bachelor's degree or higher: 3.2% (2007); Master's degree or higher: 0.0% (2007).
Housing: Homeownership rate: 81.4% (2007); Median home value: $92,000 (2007); Median rent: $331 per month (2000); Median age of housing: 60+ years (2000).
Transportation: Commute to work: 96.8% car, 0.0% public transportation, 1.6% walk, 1.6% work from home (2000); Travel time to work: 40.7% less than 15 minutes, 39.8% 15 to 30 minutes, 9.8% 30 to 45 minutes, 0.8% 45 to 60 minutes, 8.9% 60 minutes or more (2000)

DANA (village). Covers a land area of 0.220 square miles and a water area of 0 square miles. Located at 40.95° N. Lat.; 88.95° W. Long. Elevation is 669 feet.
Population: 165 (1990); 171 (2000); 153 (2007); 150 (2012 projected); Race: 98.7% White, 0.0% Black, 1.3% Asian, 4.6% Hispanic of any race (2007); Density: 696.5 persons per square mile (2007); Average household size: 2.89 (2007); Median age: 31.1 (2007); Males per 100 females: 96.2 (2007); Marriage status: 20.1% never married, 59.0% now married, 8.2% widowed, 12.7% divorced (2000); Foreign born: 1.1% (2000); Ancestry (includes multiple ancestries): 22.7% German, 14.8% English, 13.1% Other groups, 11.9% Irish, 8.5% United States or American (2000).
Economy: Employment by occupation: 6.9% management, 3.4% professional, 27.6% services, 22.4% sales, 0.0% farming, 8.6% construction, 31.0% production (2000).
Income: Per capita income: $14,690 (2007); Median household income: $35,417 (2007); Average household income: $42,406 (2007); Percent of households with income of $100,000 or more: 9.4% (2007); Poverty rate: 26.7% (2000).
Education: Percent of population age 25 and over with: High school diploma (including GED) or higher: 75.9% (2007); Bachelor's degree or higher: 0.0% (2007); Master's degree or higher: 0.0% (2007).
Housing: Homeownership rate: 79.2% (2007); Median home value: $45,556 (2007); Median rent: $225 per month (2000); Median age of housing: 54 years (2000).
Transportation: Commute to work: 100.0% car, 0.0% public transportation, 0.0% walk, 0.0% work from home (2000); Travel time to work: 6.9% less than 15 minutes, 34.5% 15 to 30 minutes, 31.0% 30 to 45 minutes, 19.0% 45 to 60 minutes, 8.6% 60 minutes or more (2000)

EARLVILLE (city). Covers a land area of 1.164 square miles and a water area of 0 square miles. Located at 41.58° N. Lat.; 88.92° W. Long. Elevation is 705 feet.
History: Founded c.1854, incorporated 1869.
Population: 1,570 (1990); 1,778 (2000); 1,759 (2007); 1,793 (2012 projected); Race: 97.4% White, 0.1% Black, 0.1% Asian, 2.8% Hispanic of any race (2007); Density: 1,511.1 persons per square mile (2007); Average household size: 2.57 (2007); Median age: 35.9 (2007); Males per 100 females: 97.6 (2007); Marriage status: 17.6% never married, 64.3% now married, 7.3% widowed, 10.7% divorced (2000); Foreign born: 0.8% (2000); Ancestry (includes multiple ancestries): 30.2% German, 17.0% Irish, 11.2% English, 8.6% Other groups, 7.5% Norwegian (2000).
Economy: Single-family building permits issued: 2 (2007); Multi-family building permits issued: 0 (2007); Employment by occupation: 7.3% management, 11.0% professional, 17.3% services, 24.0% sales, 0.5% farming, 13.8% construction, 26.2% production (2000).
Income: Per capita income: $18,699 (2007); Median household income: $43,514 (2007); Average household income: $47,935 (2007); Percent of households with income of $100,000 or more: 6.7% (2007); Poverty rate: 7.5% (2000).
Education: Percent of population age 25 and over with: High school diploma (including GED) or higher: 81.8% (2007); Bachelor's degree or higher: 10.4% (2007); Master's degree or higher: 4.4% (2007).

School District(s)

Earlville CUSD 9 (PK-12)
2005-06 Enrollment: 442 . . . . (815) 246-8361
Serena CUSD 2 (KG-12)
2005-06 Enrollment: 853 . . . . (815) 496-2850

Housing: Homeownership rate: 72.4% (2007); Median home value: $125,781 (2007); Median rent: $339 per month (2000); Median age of housing: 52 years (2000).
Safety: Violent crime rate: 38.4 per 10,000 population; Property crime rate: 302.0 per 10,000 population (2006).
Newspapers: Somonauk Reporter (Local news; Circulation 1,000)
Transportation: Commute to work: 91.8% car, 0.0% public transportation, 3.3% walk, 3.5% work from home (2000); Travel time to work: 23.5% less than 15 minutes, 25.0% 15 to 30 minutes, 19.1% 30 to 45 minutes, 15.4% 45 to 60 minutes, 16.9% 60 minutes or more (2000)

GRAND RIDGE (village). Covers a land area of 0.474 square miles and a water area of 0 square miles. Located at 41.23° N. Lat.; 88.83° W. Long. Elevation is 643 feet.
Population: 560 (1990); 546 (2000); 507 (2007); 505 (2012 projected); Race: 100.0% White, 0.0% Black, 0.0% Asian, 4.1% Hispanic of any race (2007); Density: 1,070.1 persons per square mile (2007); Average household size: 2.64 (2007); Median age: 37.0 (2007); Males per 100 females: 84.4 (2007); Marriage status: 19.3% never married, 68.5% now married, 7.2% widowed, 4.9% divorced (2000); Foreign born: 11.1% (2000); Ancestry (includes multiple ancestries): 24.6% German, 16.6% Irish, 12.8% English, 9.5% Other groups, 6.1% United States or American (2000).
Economy: Single-family building permits issued: 0 (2007); Multi-family building permits issued: 0 (2007); Employment by occupation: 10.2% management, 20.1% professional, 15.7% services, 17.3% sales, 2.0% farming, 15.7% construction, 18.9% production (2000).
Income: Per capita income: $21,425 (2007); Median household income: $50,000 (2007); Average household income: $56,576 (2007); Percent of households with income of $100,000 or more: 12.0% (2007); Poverty rate: 5.6% (2000).
Education: Percent of population age 25 and over with: High school diploma (including GED) or higher: 86.3% (2007); Bachelor's degree or higher: 12.4% (2007); Master's degree or higher: 5.9% (2007).

School District(s)

Grand Ridge CCSD 95 (KG-08)
2005-06 Enrollment: 346 . . . . (815) 249-6225

Housing: Homeownership rate: 83.3% (2007); Median home value: $102,564 (2007); Median rent: $392 per month (2000); Median age of housing: 60 years (2000).
Safety: Violent crime rate: 0.0 per 10,000 population; Property crime rate: 19.1 per 10,000 population (2006).

Transportation: Commute to work: 88.3% car, 0.8% public transportation, 7.7% walk, 1.2% work from home (2000); Travel time to work: 30.6% less than 15 minutes, 50.2% 15 to 30 minutes, 7.8% 30 to 45 minutes, 3.3% 45 to 60 minutes, 8.2% 60 minutes or more (2000)

KANGLEY (village). Covers a land area of 0.338 square miles and a water area of 0 square miles. Located at 41.14° N. Lat.; 88.87° W. Long. Elevation is 627 feet.
Population: 258 (1990); 287 (2000); 318 (2007); 332 (2012 projected); Race: 98.4% White, 0.0% Black, 0.0% Asian, 2.8% Hispanic of any race (2007); Density: 941.2 persons per square mile (2007); Average household size: 2.43 (2007); Median age: 39.6 (2007); Males per 100 females: 101.3 (2007); Marriage status: 29.9% never married, 52.8% now married, 5.2% widowed, 12.1% divorced (2000); Foreign born: 2.0% (2000); Ancestry (includes multiple ancestries): 14.1% Irish, 13.8% German, 13.1% English, 6.4% Other groups, 6.0% Polish (2000).
Economy: Single-family building permits issued: 1 (2007); Multi-family building permits issued: 0 (2007); Employment by occupation: 4.0% management, 8.0% professional, 18.4% services, 23.2% sales, 0.0% farming, 17.6% construction, 28.8% production (2000).
Income: Per capita income: $18,192 (2007); Median household income: $35,625 (2007); Average household income: $44,160 (2007); Percent of households with income of $100,000 or more: 3.1% (2007); Poverty rate: 14.8% (2000).
Education: Percent of population age 25 and over with: High school diploma (including GED) or higher: 78.0% (2007); Bachelor's degree or higher: 6.4% (2007); Master's degree or higher: 2.3% (2007).
Housing: Homeownership rate: 88.5% (2007); Median home value: $69,000 (2007); Median rent: $292 per month (2000); Median age of housing: 54 years (2000).
Transportation: Commute to work: 96.7% car, 0.0% public transportation, 2.4% walk, 0.8% work from home (2000); Travel time to work: 39.3% less than 15 minutes, 16.4% 15 to 30 minutes, 16.4% 30 to 45 minutes, 12.3% 45 to 60 minutes, 15.6% 60 minutes or more (2000)

LA SALLE (city). Aka La Salle-Peru. Covers a land area of 6.346 square miles and a water area of 0.093 square miles. Located at 41.34° N. Lat.; 89.09° W. Long. Elevation is 571 feet.
History: La Salle was organized in 1827, and prospered with the opening of the Illinois & Michigan Canal in 1848. When the railroads replaced canal traffic, mining became an important industry for La Salle. The Matthiessen & Hegeler Zinc Company plant was established here in 1858. The town was named for La Salle, the French explorer of North America, who crossed this area in 1679.
Population: 10,091 (1990); 9,796 (2000); 9,425 (2007); 9,175 (2012 projected); Race: 91.8% White, 1.6% Black, 0.6% Asian, 10.9% Hispanic of any race (2007); Density: 1,485.1 persons per square mile (2007); Average household size: 2.34 (2007); Median age: 38.9 (2007); Males per 100 females: 98.0 (2007); Marriage status: 28.5% never married, 50.9% now married, 9.0% widowed, 11.7% divorced (2000); Foreign born: 3.3% (2000); Ancestry (includes multiple ancestries): 27.9% German, 19.6% Polish, 15.4% Irish, 11.8% Italian, 10.8% Other groups (2000).
Economy: Single-family building permits issued: 9 (2007); Multi-family building permits issued: 0 (2007); Employment by occupation: 7.4% management, 13.6% professional, 16.1% services, 27.6% sales, 0.9% farming, 13.5% construction, 21.0% production (2000).
Income: Per capita income: $22,043 (2007); Median household income: $36,878 (2007); Average household income: $49,788 (2007); Percent of households with income of $100,000 or more: 8.5% (2007); Poverty rate: 15.7% (2000).
Taxes: Total city taxes per capita: $479 (2006); City property taxes per capita: $273 (2006).
Education: Percent of population age 25 and over with: High school diploma (including GED) or higher: 79.4% (2007); Bachelor's degree or higher: 12.2% (2007); Master's degree or higher: 3.9% (2007).

School District(s)

Dimmick CCSD 175 (KG-08)
2005-06 Enrollment: 104 . . . . (815) 223-2933
La Salle ESD 122 (PK-08)
2005-06 Enrollment: 904 . . . . (815) 223-0786
La Salle-Peru Twp HSD 120 (09-12)
2005-06 Enrollment: 1,279 . . . . (815) 223-1721
Lasalle-Peru Area Career Ctr
2005-06 Enrollment: n/a . . . . (815) 223-2454

Vocational/Technical School(s)

Educators of Beauty (Private, For-profit)
Fall 2007 Enrollment: 5 . . . . (815) 223-7326
2007-08 Tuition: $11,775
Housing: Homeownership rate: 65.3% (2007); Median home value: $100,115 (2007); Median rent: $339 per month (2000); Median age of housing: 58 years (2000).
Safety: Violent crime rate: 51.5 per 10,000 population; Property crime rate: 443.7 per 10,000 population (2006).
Newspapers: Daily News Tribune (Local news; Circulation 19,525); NewsTribune (Local news; Circulation 19,447)
Transportation: Commute to work: 91.6% car, 0.4% public transportation, 4.9% walk, 1.9% work from home (2000); Travel time to work: 60.6% less than 15 minutes, 23.4% 15 to 30 minutes, 6.4% 30 to 45 minutes, 3.0% 45 to 60 minutes, 6.6% 60 minutes or more (2000)
Additional Information Contacts
City of La Salle. . . . . (815) 223-3755
http://www.lasalle-il.gov
Illinois Valley Area Chamber of Commerce & Economic Developm . . (815) 223-0227
http://www.ivaced.org

LELAND (village). Covers a land area of 0.542 square miles and a water area of 0 square miles. Located at 41.61° N. Lat.; 88.79° W. Long. Elevation is 696 feet.
Population: 895 (1990); 970 (2000); 866 (2007); 874 (2012 projected); Race: 96.4% White, 0.0% Black, 0.0% Asian, 5.3% Hispanic of any race (2007); Density: 1,596.4 persons per square mile (2007); Average household size: 2.70 (2007); Median age: 35.5 (2007); Males per 100 females: 99.5 (2007); Marriage status: 21.3% never married, 62.0% now married, 7.7% widowed, 9.0% divorced (2000); Foreign born: 1.6% (2000); Ancestry (includes multiple ancestries): 29.7% German, 18.2% Irish, 13.6% Norwegian, 10.1% Other groups, 7.7% English (2000).
Economy: Single-family building permits issued: 2 (2007); Multi-family building permits issued: 0 (2007); Employment by occupation: 6.4% management, 12.2% professional, 15.7% services, 26.4% sales, 0.9% farming, 14.6% construction, 23.7% production (2000).
Income: Per capita income: $20,165 (2007); Median household income: $50,294 (2007); Average household income: $54,400 (2007); Percent of households with income of $100,000 or more: 7.2% (2007); Poverty rate: 6.4% (2000).
Education: Percent of population age 25 and over with: High school diploma (including GED) or higher: 85.6% (2007); Bachelor's degree or higher: 15.0% (2007); Master's degree or higher: 3.0% (2007).

School District(s)

Leland CUSD 1 (KG-12)
2005-06 Enrollment: 313 . . . . (815) 495-3821
Housing: Homeownership rate: 75.4% (2007); Median home value: $141,935 (2007); Median rent: $464 per month (2000); Median age of housing: 52 years (2000).
Safety: Violent crime rate: 21.2 per 10,000 population; Property crime rate: 159.2 per 10,000 population (2006).
Transportation: Commute to work: 93.9% car, 0.0% public transportation, 5.6% walk, 0.4% work from home (2000); Travel time to work: 15.8% less than 15 minutes, 26.4% 15 to 30 minutes, 18.9% 30 to 45 minutes, 19.8% 45 to 60 minutes, 19.1% 60 minutes or more (2000)

LEONORE (village). Covers a land area of 0.086 square miles and a water area of 0 square miles. Located at 41.18° N. Lat.; 88.98° W. Long. Elevation is 679 feet.
Population: 134 (1990); 110 (2000); 108 (2007); 105 (2012 projected); Race: 98.1% White, 0.0% Black, 0.0% Asian, 0.9% Hispanic of any race (2007); Density: 1,256.5 persons per square mile (2007); Average household size: 2.08 (2007); Median age: 43.1 (2007); Males per 100 females: 77.0 (2007); Marriage status: 14.0% never married, 61.3% now married, 10.8% widowed, 14.0% divorced (2000); Foreign born: 1.8% (2000); Ancestry (includes multiple ancestries): 48.2% German, 14.5% Irish, 10.9% Italian, 8.2% United States or American, 8.2% English (2000).
Economy: Employment by occupation: 12.0% management, 2.0% professional, 10.0% services, 24.0% sales, 0.0% farming, 8.0% construction, 44.0% production (2000).
Income: Per capita income: $21,157 (2007); Median household income: $38,333 (2007); Average household income: $43,942 (2007); Percent of households with income of $100,000 or more: 1.9% (2007); Poverty rate: 1.8% (2000).

Education: Percent of population age 25 and over with: High school diploma (including GED) or higher: 70.7% (2007); Bachelor's degree or higher: 6.1% (2007); Master's degree or higher: 0.0% (2007).
Housing: Homeownership rate: 90.4% (2007); Median home value: $75,833 (2007); Median rent: $300 per month (2000); Median age of housing: 60+ years (2000).
Transportation: Commute to work: 84.0% car, 0.0% public transportation, 16.0% walk, 0.0% work from home (2000); Travel time to work: 26.0% less than 15 minutes, 58.0% 15 to 30 minutes, 0.0% 30 to 45 minutes, 14.0% 45 to 60 minutes, 2.0% 60 minutes or more (2000)

LOSTANT (village). Covers a land area of 0.386 square miles and a water area of 0 square miles. Located at 41.14° N. Lat.; 89.06° W. Long. Elevation is 696 feet.
Population: 510 (1990); 486 (2000); 449 (2007); 440 (2012 projected); Race: 98.7% White, 0.2% Black, 0.0% Asian, 0.4% Hispanic of any race (2007); Density: 1,163.8 persons per square mile (2007); Average household size: 2.39 (2007); Median age: 38.8 (2007); Males per 100 females: 95.2 (2007); Marriage status: 22.7% never married, 62.0% now married, 8.3% widowed, 7.0% divorced (2000); Foreign born: 1.4% (2000); Ancestry (includes multiple ancestries): 44.5% German, 10.0% Italian, 9.1% Polish, 8.3% Irish, 6.7% English (2000).
Economy: Single-family building permits issued: 2 (2007); Multi-family building permits issued: 0 (2007); Employment by occupation: 13.5% management, 13.9% professional, 14.7% services, 19.5% sales, 0.0% farming, 7.1% construction, 31.2% production (2000).
Income: Per capita income: $22,055 (2007); Median household income: $45,000 (2007); Average household income: $52,673 (2007); Percent of households with income of $100,000 or more: 10.1% (2007); Poverty rate: 4.3% (2000).
Education: Percent of population age 25 and over with: High school diploma (including GED) or higher: 87.5% (2007); Bachelor's degree or higher: 14.1% (2007); Master's degree or higher: 3.3% (2007).

School District(s)

Lostant CUSD 425 (KG-08)
2005-06 Enrollment: 92 . . . . (815) 368-3392
Housing: Homeownership rate: 85.6% (2007); Median home value: $94,688 (2007); Median rent: $283 per month (2000); Median age of housing: 50 years (2000).
Transportation: Commute to work: 92.4% car, 0.0% public transportation, 5.3% walk, 2.3% work from home (2000); Travel time to work: 37.4% less than 15 minutes, 31.5% 15 to 30 minutes, 17.1% 30 to 45 minutes, 7.4% 45 to 60 minutes, 6.6% 60 minutes or more (2000)

MARSEILLES (city). Covers a land area of 8.311 square miles and a water area of 0.387 square miles. Located at 41.32° N. Lat.; 88.70° W. Long. Elevation is 518 feet.
History: Marseilles developed along a stretch of rapids on the Illinois River, providing water power for its early industries which included a paper mill.
Population: 4,834 (1990); 4,655 (2000); 4,706 (2007); 4,748 (2012 projected); Race: 97.6% White, 0.1% Black, 0.2% Asian, 2.7% Hispanic of any race (2007); Density: 566.2 persons per square mile (2007); Average household size: 2.44 (2007); Median age: 38.9 (2007); Males per 100 females: 94.3 (2007); Marriage status: 18.2% never married, 58.2% now married, 10.9% widowed, 12.7% divorced (2000); Foreign born: 1.2% (2000); Ancestry (includes multiple ancestries): 24.0% German, 20.3% Irish, 12.5% English, 11.2% Italian, 8.5% Norwegian (2000).
Economy: Single-family building permits issued: 19 (2007); Multi-family building permits issued: 0 (2007); Employment by occupation: 7.3% management, 12.7% professional, 19.1% services, 26.1% sales, 0.7% farming, 14.4% construction, 19.7% production (2000).
Income: Per capita income: $20,557 (2007); Median household income: $42,067 (2007); Average household income: $49,385 (2007); Percent of households with income of $100,000 or more: 6.7% (2007); Poverty rate: 8.7% (2000).
Education: Percent of population age 25 and over with: High school diploma (including GED) or higher: 81.8% (2007); Bachelor's degree or higher: 8.1% (2007); Master's degree or higher: 2.5% (2007).

School District(s)

Marseilles ESD 150 (PK-08)
2005-06 Enrollment: 594 . . . . (815) 795-2162
Miller Twp CCSD 210 (KG-08)
2005-06 Enrollment: 237 . . . . (815) 357-8151
Housing: Homeownership rate: 74.7% (2007); Median home value: $104,559 (2007); Median rent: $370 per month (2000); Median age of housing: 50 years (2000).
Safety: Violent crime rate: 90.5 per 10,000 population; Property crime rate: 185.2 per 10,000 population (2006).
Transportation: Commute to work: 91.9% car, 0.8% public transportation, 2.4% walk, 3.7% work from home (2000); Travel time to work: 34.6% less than 15 minutes, 32.8% 15 to 30 minutes, 12.9% 30 to 45 minutes, 10.4% 45 to 60 minutes, 9.4% 60 minutes or more (2000)
Additional Information Contacts
Illinois River Area Chamber of Commerce. . . . . (815) 795-2323
http://www.marseillesil.org

MENDOTA (city). Covers a land area of 3.779 square miles and a water area of 0.096 square miles. Located at 41.54° N. Lat.; 89.11° W. Long. Elevation is 741 feet.
History: Mendota developed as a trading and processing center for the produce of an agricultural area.
Population: 7,114 (1990); 7,272 (2000); 7,033 (2007); 6,865 (2012 projected); Race: 86.5% White, 0.5% Black, 0.5% Asian, 24.7% Hispanic of any race (2007); Density: 1,861.0 persons per square mile (2007); Average household size: 2.64 (2007); Median age: 37.6 (2007); Males per 100 females: 90.4 (2007); Marriage status: 21.2% never married, 59.9% now married, 10.0% widowed, 8.9% divorced (2000); Foreign born: 8.7% (2000); Ancestry (includes multiple ancestries): 31.2% German, 20.4% Other groups, 14.2% Irish, 7.8% English, 6.0% United States or American (2000).
Economy: Single-family building permits issued: 3 (2007); Multi-family building permits issued: 0 (2007); Employment by occupation: 9.5% management, 13.8% professional, 17.4% services, 18.4% sales, 1.4% farming, 9.3% construction, 30.2% production (2000).
Income: Per capita income: $20,564 (2007); Median household income: $43,756 (2007); Average household income: $52,071 (2007); Percent of households with income of $100,000 or more: 9.7% (2007); Poverty rate: 11.2% (2000).
Education: Percent of population age 25 and over with: High school diploma (including GED) or higher: 76.4% (2007); Bachelor's degree or higher: 13.2% (2007); Master's degree or higher: 6.0% (2007).

School District(s)

Mendota CCSD 289 (PK-08)
2005-06 Enrollment: 1,284 . . . . (815) 539-7631
Mendota Twp HSD 280 (09-12)
2005-06 Enrollment: 635 . . . . (815) 539-7446
Housing: Homeownership rate: 73.8% (2007); Median home value: $117,043 (2007); Median rent: $368 per month (2000); Median age of housing: 50 years (2000).
Hospitals: Mendota Community Hospital (68 beds)
Safety: Violent crime rate: 80.5 per 10,000 population; Property crime rate: 288.3 per 10,000 population (2006).
Newspapers: Mendota Reporter (Local news; Circulation 5,000)
Transportation: Commute to work: 90.7% car, 0.2% public transportation, 5.0% walk, 2.7% work from home (2000); Travel time to work: 64.3% less than 15 minutes, 14.0% 15 to 30 minutes, 12.2% 30 to 45 minutes, 5.0% 45 to 60 minutes, 4.4% 60 minutes or more (2000); Amtrak: Service available.
Additional Information Contacts
City of Mendota . . . . (815) 539-7459
http://www.mendota.il.us
Mendota Chamber of Commerce. . . . . (815) 539-6507
http://www.mendotachamber.com

NAPLATE (village). Covers a land area of 0.112 square miles and a water area of 0 square miles. Located at 41.33° N. Lat.; 88.87° W. Long. Elevation is 463 feet.
Population: 609 (1990); 523 (2000); 546 (2007); 547 (2012 projected); Race: 97.3% White, 0.0% Black, 0.2% Asian, 2.7% Hispanic of any race (2007); Density: 4,877.1 persons per square mile (2007); Average household size: 2.20 (2007); Median age: 42.7 (2007); Males per 100 females: 83.2 (2007); Marriage status: 25.0% never married, 49.8% now married, 10.6% widowed, 14.7% divorced (2000); Foreign born: 3.2% (2000); Ancestry (includes multiple ancestries): 18.8% Irish, 17.1% German, 15.2% Italian, 11.6% Polish, 9.7% Other groups (2000).
Economy: Employment by occupation: 5.2% management, 10.9% professional, 22.6% services, 23.9% sales, 0.0% farming, 14.3% construction, 23.0% production (2000).

Income: Per capita income: $19,479 (2007); Median household income: $34,667 (2007); Average household income: $41,956 (2007); Percent of households with income of $100,000 or more: 5.6% (2007); Poverty rate: 9.7% (2000).
Education: Percent of population age 25 and over with: High school diploma (including GED) or higher: 73.2% (2007); Bachelor's degree or higher: 7.1% (2007); Master's degree or higher: 2.0% (2007).
Housing: Homeownership rate: 75.0% (2007); Median home value: $96,071 (2007); Median rent: $386 per month (2000); Median age of housing: 60+ years (2000).
Transportation: Commute to work: 94.2% car, 0.0% public transportation, 2.2% walk, 3.5% work from home (2000); Travel time to work: 61.9% less than 15 minutes, 24.8% 15 to 30 minutes, 6.9% 30 to 45 minutes, 0.9% 45 to 60 minutes, 5.5% 60 minutes or more (2000)

NORTH UTICA (village). Aka Utica. Covers a land area of 1.506 square miles and a water area of 0 square miles. Located at 41.34° N. Lat.; 89.01° W. Long. Elevation is 476 feet.
Population: 907 (1990); 977 (2000); 1,044 (2007); 1,125 (2012 projected); Race: 96.8% White, 0.4% Black, 0.3% Asian, 2.5% Hispanic of any race (2007); Density: 693.1 persons per square mile (2007); Average household size: 2.32 (2007); Median age: 41.2 (2007); Males per 100 females: 89.8 (2007); Marriage status: 18.5% never married, 62.0% now married, 8.1% widowed, 11.5% divorced (2000); Foreign born: 1.2% (2000); Ancestry (includes multiple ancestries): 31.2% German, 15.5% Irish, 14.8% English, 14.0% Polish, 13.3% Italian (2000).
Economy: Single-family building permits issued: 11 (2007); Multi-family building permits issued: 4 (2007); Employment by occupation: 10.7% management, 10.1% professional, 18.2% services, 32.4% sales, 0.0% farming, 12.8% construction, 15.8% production (2000).
Income: Per capita income: $26,181 (2007); Median household income: $51,579 (2007); Average household income: $60,678 (2007); Percent of households with income of $100,000 or more: 11.1% (2007); Poverty rate: 7.2% (2000).
Education: Percent of population age 25 and over with: High school diploma (including GED) or higher: 87.3% (2007); Bachelor's degree or higher: 12.3% (2007); Master's degree or higher: 1.9% (2007).
Housing: Homeownership rate: 82.7% (2007); Median home value: $116,848 (2007); Median rent: $461 per month (2000); Median age of housing: 40 years (2000).
Transportation: Commute to work: 95.8% car, 0.8% public transportation, 1.5% walk, 1.5% work from home (2000); Travel time to work: 39.4% less than 15 minutes, 41.9% 15 to 30 minutes, 7.0% 30 to 45 minutes, 1.7% 45 to 60 minutes, 10.0% 60 minutes or more (2000)

OGLESBY (city). Covers a land area of 4.001 square miles and a water area of 0 square miles. Located at 41.29° N. Lat.; 89.06° W. Long. Elevation is 630 feet.
History: Oglesby developed as an industrial town, producing cement from the nearby limestone deposits. The town was named for Governor Richard J. Oglesby.
Population: 3,648 (1990); 3,647 (2000); 3,632 (2007); 3,622 (2012 projected); Race: 97.8% White, 0.4% Black, 0.4% Asian, 3.4% Hispanic of any race (2007); Density: 907.9 persons per square mile (2007); Average household size: 2.25 (2007); Median age: 41.3 (2007); Males per 100 females: 91.6 (2007); Marriage status: 21.4% never married, 59.2% now married, 9.4% widowed, 9.9% divorced (2000); Foreign born: 1.8% (2000); Ancestry (includes multiple ancestries): 29.6% German, 25.2% Italian, 18.3% Polish, 11.5% Irish, 10.0% English (2000).
Economy: Single-family building permits issued: 17 (2007); Multi-family building permits issued: 0 (2007); Employment by occupation: 13.1% management, 15.2% professional, 18.4% services, 21.7% sales, 0.1% farming, 10.4% construction, 21.1% production (2000).
Income: Per capita income: $21,602 (2007); Median household income: $39,519 (2007); Average household income: $48,309 (2007); Percent of households with income of $100,000 or more: 8.9% (2007); Poverty rate: 10.1% (2000).
Education: Percent of population age 25 and over with: High school diploma (including GED) or higher: 80.0% (2007); Bachelor's degree or higher: 10.8% (2007); Master's degree or higher: 3.0% (2007).

School District(s)

Oglesby ESD 125 (PK-08)
2005-06 Enrollment: 497 . . . . (815) 883-9297

Two-year College(s)

Illinois Valley Community College (Public)
Fall 2007 Enrollment: 4,103. . . . . (815) 224-2720
2007-08 Tuition: In-state $7,042; Out-of-state $8,054
Housing: Homeownership rate: 79.0% (2007); Median home value: $103,526 (2007); Median rent: $329 per month (2000); Median age of housing: 52 years (2000).
Safety: Violent crime rate: 5.5 per 10,000 population; Property crime rate: 154.7 per 10,000 population (2006).
Transportation: Commute to work: 94.2% car, 0.5% public transportation, 0.8% walk, 1.9% work from home (2000); Travel time to work: 52.8% less than 15 minutes, 32.4% 15 to 30 minutes, 7.6% 30 to 45 minutes, 2.9% 45 to 60 minutes, 4.3% 60 minutes or more (2000)

OTTAWA (city). County seat. Covers a land area of 7.329 square miles and a water area of 0.334 square miles. Located at 41.34° N. Lat.; 88.84° W. Long. Elevation is 482 feet.
History: Ottawa was laid out in 1830 by the Illinois & Michigan Canal commissioners. A settlement soon grew as the town was on the travel route between Chicago and the Illinois Valley. In 1858 Abraham Lincoln and Stephen Douglas held their first, highly-publicized debate in Ottawa.
Population: 17,954 (1990); 18,307 (2000); 18,485 (2007); 18,631 (2012 projected); Race: 94.5% White, 1.6% Black, 1.0% Asian, 6.3% Hispanic of any race (2007); Density: 2,522.2 persons per square mile (2007); Average household size: 2.40 (2007); Median age: 39.2 (2007); Males per 100 females: 91.1 (2007); Marriage status: 24.2% never married, 54.7% now married, 10.2% widowed, 10.9% divorced (2000); Foreign born: 2.0% (2000); Ancestry (includes multiple ancestries): 27.4% German, 20.8% Irish, 9.7% Other groups, 9.0% English, 8.4% Italian (2000).
Economy: Single-family building permits issued: 39 (2007); Multi-family building permits issued: 0 (2007); Employment by occupation: 8.3% management, 18.1% professional, 17.1% services, 27.1% sales, 0.3% farming, 9.9% construction, 19.2% production (2000).
Income: Per capita income: $22,392 (2007); Median household income: $40,772 (2007); Average household income: $52,969 (2007); Percent of households with income of $100,000 or more: 11.4% (2007); Poverty rate: 11.3% (2000).
Education: Percent of population age 25 and over with: High school diploma (including GED) or higher: 82.6% (2007); Bachelor's degree or higher: 16.5% (2007); Master's degree or higher: 5.2% (2007).

School District(s)

Deer Park CCSD 82 (PK-08)
2005-06 Enrollment: 71 . . . . (815) 434-6930
Lasalle Roe (07-12)
2005-06 Enrollment: 65 . . . . (815) 434-0780
Ottawa ESD 141 (PK-08)
2005-06 Enrollment: 2,023 . . . . (815) 433-1133
Ottawa Twp HSD 140 (09-12)
2005-06 Enrollment: 1,646 . . . . (815) 433-1323
Rutland CCSD 230 (KG-08)
2005-06 Enrollment: 113 . . . . (815) 433-2949
Wallace CCSD 195 (KG-08)
2005-06 Enrollment: 300 . . . . (815) 433-2986
Housing: Homeownership rate: 67.6% (2007); Median home value: $118,641 (2007); Median rent: $413 per month (2000); Median age of housing: 49 years (2000).
Hospitals: Community Hospital of Ottawa (124 beds)
Safety: Violent crime rate: 21.8 per 10,000 population; Property crime rate: 308.1 per 10,000 population (2006).
Newspapers: Illinois Valley Thrif-T-Nikel (Community news; Circulation 19,000); Joy in Our Town - WWTO-TV (Regional news; Circulation 0); Ottawa Daily Times (Local news; Circulation 13,879); The Times (Circulation 20,000); Town & Country (Local news; Circulation 19,500)
Transportation: Commute to work: 93.6% car, 0.9% public transportation, 2.2% walk, 2.1% work from home (2000); Travel time to work: 53.5% less than 15 minutes, 24.2% 15 to 30 minutes, 9.4% 30 to 45 minutes, 4.5% 45 to 60 minutes, 8.3% 60 minutes or more (2000)
Airports: Skydive Chicago (general aviation)

Additional Information Contacts

City of Ottawa . . . . (815) 433-0161
http://www.cityofottawa.org
Ottawa Area Chamber of Commerce. . . . . (815) 433-0084
http://www.ottawachamberillinois.com

PERU (city). Covers a land area of 5.941 square miles and a water area of 0.108 square miles. Located at 41.33° N. Lat.; 89.12° W. Long. Elevation is 600 feet.

History: Peru's name is of Indian origin, meaning "plenty of everything." The town was founded in 1835 on the Illinois River, and became the terminus of the Illinois & Michigan Canal. River traffic influenced the development of Peru's early industries, which included the Peru Wheel Company and the Star Union Products Company.

Population: 9,318 (1990); 9,835 (2000); 9,801 (2007); 9,740 (2012 projected); Race: 95.4% White, 0.3% Black, 1.6% Asian, 5.6% Hispanic of any race (2007); Density: 1,649.8 persons per square mile (2007); Average household size: 2.31 (2007); Median age: 42.5 (2007); Males per 100 females: 89.8 (2007); Marriage status: 21.7% never married, 60.0% now married, 9.4% widowed, 8.9% divorced (2000); Foreign born: 3.4% (2000); Ancestry (includes multiple ancestries): 31.1% German, 21.5% Polish, 17.4% Italian, 15.4% Irish, 9.5% English (2000).

Economy: Single-family building permits issued: 17 (2007); Multi-family building permits issued: 0 (2007); Employment by occupation: 8.6% management, 19.1% professional, 17.0% services, 28.2% sales, 0.5% farming, 8.6% construction, 18.0% production (2000).

Income: Per capita income: $23,867 (2007); Median household income: $42,156 (2007); Average household income: $53,946 (2007); Percent of households with income of $100,000 or more: 9.8% (2007); Poverty rate: 7.5% (2000).

Taxes: Total city taxes per capita: $179 (2006); City property taxes per capita: $62 (2006).

Education: Percent of population age 25 and over with: High school diploma (including GED) or higher: 81.4% (2007); Bachelor's degree or higher: 17.3% (2007); Master's degree or higher: 6.2% (2007).

School District(s)

Peru ESD 124 (PK-08)
2005-06 Enrollment: 939 . . . . (815) 223-0486

Housing: Homeownership rate: 74.9% (2007); Median home value: $118,497 (2007); Median rent: $410 per month (2000); Median age of housing: 49 years (2000).

Hospitals: Illinois Valley Community Hospital

Safety: Violent crime rate: 16.3 per 10,000 population; Property crime rate: 350.5 per 10,000 population (2006).

Transportation: Commute to work: 94.8% car, 0.5% public transportation, 1.3% walk, 2.8% work from home (2000); Travel time to work: 62.4% less than 15 minutes, 22.7% 15 to 30 minutes, 7.0% 30 to 45 minutes, 1.8% 45 to 60 minutes, 6.1% 60 minutes or more (2000)

Airports: Illinois Valley Regional-Walter A Duncan Field (general aviation)

Additional Information Contacts

City of Peru . . . . (815) 223-0061
http://www.peru.il.us

RANSOM (village). Covers a land area of 0.991 square miles and a water area of 0 square miles. Located at 41.15° N. Lat.; 88.65° W. Long. Elevation is 705 feet.

Population: 438 (1990); 409 (2000); 384 (2007); 382 (2012 projected); Race: 97.9% White, 0.0% Black, 0.0% Asian, 3.9% Hispanic of any race (2007); Density: 387.3 persons per square mile (2007); Average household size: 2.70 (2007); Median age: 35.0 (2007); Males per 100 females: 99.0 (2007); Marriage status: 18.9% never married, 64.6% now married, 8.7% widowed, 7.8% divorced (2000); Foreign born: 0.0% (2000); Ancestry (includes multiple ancestries): 39.8% German, 26.2% Irish, 8.9% United States or American, 6.3% Other groups, 4.8% Norwegian (2000).

Economy: Single-family building permits issued: 0 (2007); Multi-family building permits issued: 0 (2007); Employment by occupation: 7.9% management, 9.7% professional, 23.8% services, 25.1% sales, 0.0% farming, 9.7% construction, 23.8% production (2000).

Income: Per capita income: $22,070 (2007); Median household income: $56,923 (2007); Average household income: $59,683 (2007); Percent of households with income of $100,000 or more: 9.2% (2007); Poverty rate: 1.9% (2000).

Education: Percent of population age 25 and over with: High school diploma (including GED) or higher: 88.0% (2007); Bachelor's degree or higher: 9.1% (2007); Master's degree or higher: 1.2% (2007).

School District(s)

Allen-Otter Creek CCSD 65 (KG-08)
2005-06 Enrollment: 122 . . . . (815) 586-4611

Housing: Homeownership rate: 81.7% (2007); Median home value: $96,364 (2007); Median rent: $438 per month (2000); Median age of housing: 58 years (2000).

Transportation: Commute to work: 96.8% car, 0.0% public transportation, 0.9% walk, 0.9% work from home (2000); Travel time to work: 32.7% less than 15 minutes, 38.6% 15 to 30 minutes, 16.4% 30 to 45 minutes, 4.1% 45 to 60 minutes, 8.2% 60 minutes or more (2000)

RUTLAND (village). Covers a land area of 0.820 square miles and a water area of 0 square miles. Located at 40.98° N. Lat.; 89.04° W. Long. Elevation is 702 feet.

Population: 391 (1990); 354 (2000); 315 (2007); 311 (2012 projected); Race: 99.0% White, 0.3% Black, 0.0% Asian, 0.3% Hispanic of any race (2007); Density: 383.9 persons per square mile (2007); Average household size: 2.35 (2007); Median age: 42.4 (2007); Males per 100 females: 98.1 (2007); Marriage status: 17.8% never married, 61.6% now married, 8.2% widowed, 12.3% divorced (2000); Foreign born: 0.9% (2000); Ancestry (includes multiple ancestries): 31.3% German, 13.3% Irish, 9.6% Polish, 7.8% United States or American, 7.5% Italian (2000).

Economy: Employment by occupation: 7.4% management, 7.4% professional, 25.3% services, 14.8% sales, 0.0% farming, 11.7% construction, 33.3% production (2000).

Income: Per capita income: $17,405 (2007); Median household income: $33,125 (2007); Average household income: $40,914 (2007); Percent of households with income of $100,000 or more: 4.5% (2007); Poverty rate: 4.3% (2000).

Education: Percent of population age 25 and over with: High school diploma (including GED) or higher: 77.5% (2007); Bachelor's degree or higher: 5.3% (2007); Master's degree or higher: 2.2% (2007).

Housing: Homeownership rate: 87.3% (2007); Median home value: $54,167 (2007); Median rent: $267 per month (2000); Median age of housing: 43 years (2000).

Transportation: Commute to work: 98.8% car, 0.0% public transportation, 0.0% walk, 0.0% work from home (2000); Travel time to work: 48.8% less than 15 minutes, 14.2% 15 to 30 minutes, 23.5% 30 to 45 minutes, 11.1% 45 to 60 minutes, 2.5% 60 minutes or more (2000)

SENECA (village). Aka Crotty. Covers a land area of 3.307 square miles and a water area of 0.258 square miles. Located at 41.30° N. Lat.; 88.60° W. Long. Elevation is 509 feet.

History: Seneca was built along the Illinois & Michigan Canal, and developed as a sawmill town.

Population: 1,966 (1990); 2,053 (2000); 2,127 (2007); 2,160 (2012 projected); Race: 97.9% White, 0.0% Black, 0.0% Asian, 2.4% Hispanic of any race (2007); Density: 643.1 persons per square mile (2007); Average household size: 2.70 (2007); Median age: 36.9 (2007); Males per 100 females: 95.3 (2007); Marriage status: 22.2% never married, 63.9% now married, 6.3% widowed, 7.5% divorced (2000); Foreign born: 1.2% (2000); Ancestry (includes multiple ancestries): 27.4% German, 23.6% Irish, 14.5% English, 11.4% Norwegian, 8.1% Italian (2000).

Economy: Single-family building permits issued: 10 (2007); Multi-family building permits issued: 0 (2007); Employment by occupation: 8.5% management, 18.1% professional, 14.9% services, 26.4% sales, 0.2% farming, 14.5% construction, 17.5% production (2000).

Income: Per capita income: $24,181 (2007); Median household income: $58,827 (2007); Average household income: $65,343 (2007); Percent of households with income of $100,000 or more: 16.5% (2007); Poverty rate: 7.3% (2000).

Education: Percent of population age 25 and over with: High school diploma (including GED) or higher: 86.4% (2007); Bachelor's degree or higher: 13.2% (2007); Master's degree or higher: 4.5% (2007).

School District(s)

Lasalle Putnam Alliance (04-12)
2005-06 Enrollment: 37 . . . . (815) 433-6433

Seneca CCSD 170 (PK-08)
2005-06 Enrollment: 614 . . . . (815) 357-8744

Seneca Twp HSD 160 (09-12)
2005-06 Enrollment: 498 . . . . (815) 357-5000

Housing: Homeownership rate: 81.6% (2007); Median home value: $142,557 (2007); Median rent: $391 per month (2000); Median age of housing: 41 years (2000).

Safety: Violent crime rate: 43.8 per 10,000 population; Property crime rate: 379.2 per 10,000 population (2006).

Transportation: Commute to work: 92.5% car, 0.0% public transportation, 3.3% walk, 3.0% work from home (2000); Travel time to work: 36.2% less

than 15 minutes, 28.3% 15 to 30 minutes, 16.8% 30 to 45 minutes, 7.9% 45 to 60 minutes, 10.8% 60 minutes or more (2000)

SERENA (unincorporated postal area, zip code 60549). Covers a land area of 24.144 square miles and a water area of 0 square miles. Located at 41.49° N. Lat.; 88.75° W. Long. Elevation is 633 feet.
Population: 594 (2000); Race: 100.0% White, 0.0% Black, 0.0% Asian, 5.2% Hispanic of any race (2000); Density: 24.6 persons per square mile (2000); Age: 23.0% under 18, 10.6% over 64 (2000); Marriage status: 15.7% never married, 70.6% now married, 1.1% widowed, 12.5% divorced (2000); Foreign born: 0.0% (2000); Ancestry (includes multiple ancestries): 30.3% Norwegian, 22.8% Irish, 21.7% German, 18.5% English, 9.9% Italian (2000).
Economy: Employment by occupation: 25.0% management, 22.7% professional, 10.5% services, 18.4% sales, 0.0% farming, 16.1% construction, 7.2% production (2000).
Income: Per capita income: $20,022 (2000); Median household income: $52,000 (2000); Poverty rate: 6.5% (2000).
Education: Percent of population age 25 and over with: High school diploma (including GED) or higher: 93.7% (2000); Bachelor's degree or higher: 13.2% (2000).

School District(s)

Serena CUSD 2 (KG-12)
2005-06 Enrollment: 853 . . . . (815) 496-2850

Housing: Homeownership rate: 79.5% (2000); Median home value: $126,400 (2000); Median rent: $443 per month (2000); Median age of housing: 38 years (2000).
Transportation: Commute to work: 95.1% car, 0.0% public transportation, 0.0% walk, 4.9% work from home (2000); Travel time to work: 15.6% less than 15 minutes, 49.8% 15 to 30 minutes, 23.9% 30 to 45 minutes, 10.7% 45 to 60 minutes, 0.0% 60 minutes or more (2000)

SHERIDAN (village). Covers a land area of 1.405 square miles and a water area of 0.040 square miles. Located at 41.52° N. Lat.; 88.68° W. Long. Elevation is 594 feet.
Population: 1,517 (1990); 2,411 (2000); 2,229 (2007); 2,153 (2012 projected); Race: 47.6% White, 39.8% Black, 0.7% Asian, 13.1% Hispanic of any race (2007); Density: 1,586.0 persons per square mile (2007); Average household size: 7.79 (2007); Median age: 30.6 (2007); Males per 100 females: 449.0 (2007); Marriage status: 6.7% never married, 76.1% now married, 8.1% widowed, 9.1% divorced (2000); Foreign born: 2.9% (2000); Ancestry (includes multiple ancestries): 10.4% German, 6.8% Irish, 6.1% English, 4.0% Norwegian, 2.4% Other groups (2000).
Economy: Single-family building permits issued: 5 (2007); Multi-family building permits issued: 0 (2007); Employment by occupation: 5.0% management, 9.4% professional, 17.0% services, 26.6% sales, 0.0% farming, 20.6% construction, 21.3% production (2000).
Income: Per capita income: $11,971 (2007); Median household income: $48,929 (2007); Average household income: $52,177 (2007); Percent of households with income of $100,000 or more: 5.9% (2007); Poverty rate: 3.3% (2000).
Education: Percent of population age 25 and over with: High school diploma (including GED) or higher: 50.5% (2007); Bachelor's degree or higher: 3.5% (2007); Master's degree or higher: 0.6% (2007).

School District(s)

Dept of Corrections Sch Dist 428 (08-12)
2005-06 Enrollment: 2,271 . . . . (217) 522-2666
Serena CUSD 2 (KG-12)
2005-06 Enrollment: 853 . . . . (815) 496-2850

Housing: Homeownership rate: 74.5% (2007); Median home value: $138,068 (2007); Median rent: $473 per month (2000); Median age of housing: 54 years (2000).
Safety: Violent crime rate: 0.0 per 10,000 population; Property crime rate: 18.0 per 10,000 population (2006).
Transportation: Commute to work: 96.1% car, 0.0% public transportation, 3.2% walk, 0.7% work from home (2000); Travel time to work: 17.6% less than 15 minutes, 29.7% 15 to 30 minutes, 23.0% 30 to 45 minutes, 17.6% 45 to 60 minutes, 12.1% 60 minutes or more (2000)

STREATOR (city). Covers a land area of 5.767 square miles and a water area of 0.013 square miles. Located at 41.12° N. Lat.; 88.83° W. Long. Elevation is 620 feet.
History: Coal mining began in Streator in 1872, and the name of the town was changed from Unionville to Streator to honor the president of the coal company. Streator was sited near deposits of shale, clay, and sand which led to the manufacturing of glass.
Population: 14,861 (1990); 14,190 (2000); 13,923 (2007); 13,727 (2012 projected); Race: 93.8% White, 2.0% Black, 0.6% Asian, 8.6% Hispanic of any race (2007); Density: 2,414.3 persons per square mile (2007); Average household size: 2.43 (2007); Median age: 38.9 (2007); Males per 100 females: 92.1 (2007); Marriage status: 23.6% never married, 53.0% now married, 11.9% widowed, 11.5% divorced (2000); Foreign born: 3.2% (2000); Ancestry (includes multiple ancestries): 22.0% German, 14.8% Irish, 11.7% Slovak, 10.8% Other groups, 10.2% United States or American (2000).
Economy: Single-family building permits issued: 10 (2007); Multi-family building permits issued: 7 (2007); Employment by occupation: 7.1% management, 12.8% professional, 18.9% services, 21.7% sales, 0.7% farming, 7.7% construction, 31.3% production (2000).
Income: Per capita income: $20,002 (2007); Median household income: $39,156 (2007); Average household income: $47,775 (2007); Percent of households with income of $100,000 or more: 7.6% (2007); Poverty rate: 11.3% (2000).
Education: Percent of population age 25 and over with: High school diploma (including GED) or higher: 74.2% (2007); Bachelor's degree or higher: 9.2% (2007); Master's degree or higher: 3.4% (2007).

School District(s)

Streator ESD 44 (PK-08)
2005-06 Enrollment: 1,903 . . . . (815) 672-2926
Streator Twp HSD 40 (09-12)
2005-06 Enrollment: 1,054 . . . . (815) 672-0545
Woodland CUSD 5 (PK-12)
2005-06 Enrollment: 498 . . . . (815) 672-5974

Housing: Homeownership rate: 71.0% (2007); Median home value: $76,062 (2007); Median rent: $359 per month (2000); Median age of housing: 55 years (2000).
Hospitals: St. Mary's Hospital (251 beds)
Safety: Violent crime rate: 24.5 per 10,000 population; Property crime rate: 368.4 per 10,000 population (2006).
Newspapers: The Times-Press (Local news; Circulation 8,621)
Transportation: Commute to work: 94.0% car, 0.1% public transportation, 3.4% walk, 1.0% work from home (2000); Travel time to work: 58.4% less than 15 minutes, 15.9% 15 to 30 minutes, 15.0% 30 to 45 minutes, 4.8% 45 to 60 minutes, 6.0% 60 minutes or more (2000)

Additional Information Contacts

City of Streator . . . . (815) 672-2517
http://www.ci.streator.il.us/cms
Streator Area Chamber of Commerce & Industry . . . . (815) 672-2921
http://www.streatorchamber.com

TONICA (village). Covers a land area of 1.355 square miles and a water area of 0 square miles. Located at 41.21° N. Lat.; 89.06° W. Long. Elevation is 659 feet.
Population: 794 (1990); 685 (2000); 659 (2007); 638 (2012 projected); Race: 98.6% White, 0.0% Black, 0.2% Asian, 5.9% Hispanic of any race (2007); Density: 486.3 persons per square mile (2007); Average household size: 2.29 (2007); Median age: 42.7 (2007); Males per 100 females: 100.3 (2007); Marriage status: 15.7% never married, 61.7% now married, 10.4% widowed, 12.2% divorced (2000); Foreign born: 3.7% (2000); Ancestry (includes multiple ancestries): 40.6% German, 15.1% Irish, 11.6% English, 11.3% Polish, 8.5% Italian (2000).
Economy: Single-family building permits issued: 1 (2007); Multi-family building permits issued: 0 (2007); Employment by occupation: 6.6% management, 13.2% professional, 14.1% services, 25.8% sales, 1.8% farming, 15.6% construction, 22.8% production (2000).
Income: Per capita income: $23,547 (2007); Median household income: $42,143 (2007); Average household income: $53,880 (2007); Percent of households with income of $100,000 or more: 9.0% (2007); Poverty rate: 5.3% (2000).
Education: Percent of population age 25 and over with: High school diploma (including GED) or higher: 81.8% (2007); Bachelor's degree or higher: 11.8% (2007); Master's degree or higher: 4.8% (2007).

School District(s)

Tonica CCSD 79 (PK-08)
2005-06 Enrollment: 215 . . . . (815) 442-3420

Housing: Homeownership rate: 78.1% (2007); Median home value: $107,366 (2007); Median rent: $297 per month (2000); Median age of housing: 60+ years (2000).

Safety: Violent crime rate: 14.3 per 10,000 population; Property crime rate: 28.7 per 10,000 population (2006).
Newspapers: Tonica News (Local news; Circulation 1,150)
Transportation: Commute to work: 90.5% car, 0.0% public transportation, 5.4% walk, 3.2% work from home (2000); Travel time to work: 36.1% less than 15 minutes, 38.4% 15 to 30 minutes, 16.7% 30 to 45 minutes, 4.3% 45 to 60 minutes, 4.6% 60 minutes or more (2000)

TROY GROVE (village). Covers a land area of 0.687 square miles and a water area of 0 square miles. Located at 41.46° N. Lat.; 89.08° W. Long. Elevation is 673 feet.
History: Troy Grove is the birthplace and boyhood home of James Butler "Wild Bill" Hickok (1837-1876), who toured with Buffalo Bill Cody in 1872-1873.
Population: 259 (1990); 305 (2000); 303 (2007); 297 (2012 projected); Race: 92.7% White, 0.0% Black, 3.3% Asian, 7.3% Hispanic of any race (2007); Density: 441.3 persons per square mile (2007); Average household size: 2.89 (2007); Median age: 32.8 (2007); Males per 100 females: 88.2 (2007); Marriage status: 26.1% never married, 60.6% now married, 4.0% widowed, 9.3% divorced (2000); Foreign born: 1.6% (2000); Ancestry (includes multiple ancestries): 32.6% German, 15.8% Irish, 10.6% Other groups, 10.3% United States or American, 8.7% Polish (2000).
Economy: Employment by occupation: 7.7% management, 12.3% professional, 14.2% services, 34.8% sales, 0.0% farming, 12.9% construction, 18.1% production (2000).
Income: Per capita income: $22,054 (2007); Median household income: $61,705 (2007); Average household income: $63,643 (2007); Percent of households with income of $100,000 or more: 10.5% (2007); Poverty rate: 4.5% (2000).
Education: Percent of population age 25 and over with: High school diploma (including GED) or higher: 84.4% (2007); Bachelor's degree or higher: 11.3% (2007); Master's degree or higher: 1.1% (2007).
Housing: Homeownership rate: 78.1% (2007); Median home value: $123,913 (2007); Median rent: $300 per month (2000); Median age of housing: 43 years (2000).
Transportation: Commute to work: 88.7% car, 3.3% public transportation, 4.0% walk, 4.0% work from home (2000); Travel time to work: 45.1% less than 15 minutes, 34.7% 15 to 30 minutes, 4.9% 30 to 45 minutes, 4.2% 45 to 60 minutes, 11.1% 60 minutes or more (2000)

UTICA (unincorporated postal area, zip code 61373). Aka North Utica. Covers a land area of 48.603 square miles and a water area of 0.177 square miles. Located at 41.41° N. Lat.; 89.00° W. Long. Elevation is 476 feet.
Population: 1,998 (2000); Race: 97.5% White, 0.1% Black, 0.6% Asian, 1.1% Hispanic of any race (2000); Density: 41.1 persons per square mile (2000); Age: 26.8% under 18, 11.3% over 64 (2000); Marriage status: 19.6% never married, 66.9% now married, 5.8% widowed, 7.6% divorced (2000); Foreign born: 1.1% (2000); Ancestry (includes multiple ancestries): 32.8% German, 19.0% Irish, 12.5% English, 11.6% Polish, 10.9% Italian (2000).
Economy: Employment by occupation: 15.0% management, 14.4% professional, 13.0% services, 30.3% sales, 0.6% farming, 12.7% construction, 14.0% production (2000).
Income: Per capita income: $22,970 (2000); Median household income: $49,688 (2000); Poverty rate: 4.9% (2000).
Education: Percent of population age 25 and over with: High school diploma (including GED) or higher: 89.5% (2000); Bachelor's degree or higher: 16.5% (2000).

School District(s)

Waltham CCSD 185 (KG-08)
2005-06 Enrollment: 228 . . . . (815) 667-4417
Housing: Homeownership rate: 82.0% (2000); Median home value: $120,900 (2000); Median rent: $448 per month (2000); Median age of housing: 32 years (2000).
Transportation: Commute to work: 92.0% car, 0.4% public transportation, 2.1% walk, 5.0% work from home (2000); Travel time to work: 37.3% less than 15 minutes, 43.6% 15 to 30 minutes, 7.9% 30 to 45 minutes, 2.2% 45 to 60 minutes, 9.0% 60 minutes or more (2000)

Lake County

Located in northeastern Illinois; bounded on the east by Lake Michigan, and on the north by Wisconsin; drained by the Fox and Des Plaines Rivers; includes many lakes. Covers a land area of 447.56 square miles, a water area of 920.39 square miles, and is located in the Central Time Zone. The county was founded in 1839. County seat is Waukegan.

Lake County is part of the Chicago-Naperville-Joliet, IL-IN-WI Metropolitan Statistical Area. The entire metro area includes: Chicago-Naperville-Joliet, IL Metropolitan Division (Cook County, IL; DeKalb County, IL; DuPage County, IL; Grundy County, IL; Kane County, IL; Kendall County, IL; McHenry County, IL; Will County, IL); Gary, IN Metropolitan Division (Jasper County, IN; Lake County, IN; Newton County, IN; Porter County, IN); Lake County-Kenosha County, IL-WI Metropolitan Division (Lake County, IL; Kenosha County, WI)

Weather Station: Waukegan Elevation: 698 feet

	Jan	Feb	Mar	Apr	May	Jun	Jul	Aug	Sep	Oct	Nov	Dec
High	28	33	42	54	67	77	81	80	72	61	47	34
Low	12	16	26	36	46	55	61	60	52	41	30	19
Precip	1.6	1.3	2.2	3.7	3.4	3.6	3.4	4.2	3.5	2.5	2.7	2.1
Snow	12.0	9.2	5.7	1.7	tr	0.0	0.0	0.0	0.0	0.1	1.9	7.3

High and Low temperatures in degrees Fahrenheit; Precipitation and Snow in inches

Population: 516,418 (1990); 644,356 (2000); 717,278 (2007); 764,585 (2012 projected); Race: 76.1% White, 6.4% Black, 5.7% Asian, 19.0% Hispanic of any race (2007); Density: 1,602.6 persons per square mile (2007); Average household size: 2.97 (2007); Median age: 34.9 (2007); Males per 100 females: 100.5 (2007).
Religion: Five largest groups: 39.3% Catholic Church, 3.9% Jewish Estimate, 2.8% Independent, Non-Charismatic Churches, 2.5% Evangelical Lutheran Church in America, 1.6% Presbyterian Church (U.S.A.) (2000).
Economy: Unemployment rate: 5.2% (4/2008); Total civilian labor force: 379,199 (4/2008); Leading industries: 14.4% manufacturing; 14.0% retail trade; 9.8% wholesale trade (2005); Farms: 337 totaling 38,860 acres (2002); Companies that employ 500 or more persons: 66 (2006); Companies that employ 100 to 499 persons: 407 (2006); Companies that employ less than 100 persons: 19,066 (2006); Black-owned businesses: 1,384 (2002); Hispanic-owned businesses: 2,339 (2002); Asian-owned businesses: 2,845 (2002); Women-owned businesses: 15,534 (2002); Retail sales per capita: $25,208 (2008). Single-family building permits issued: 1,859 (2007); Multi-family building permits issued: 366 (2007).
Income: Per capita income: $35,411 (2007); Median household income: $74,705 (2007); Average household income: $104,109 (2007); Percent of households with income of $100,000 or more: 34.9% (2007); Poverty rate: 7.0% (2005); Bankruptcy rate: 2.32% (2007).
Taxes: Total county taxes per capita: $302 (2006); County property taxes per capita: $296 (2006).
Education: Percent of population age 25 and over with: High school diploma (including GED) or higher: 86.3% (2007); Bachelor's degree or higher: 37.8% (2007); Master's degree or higher: 14.1% (2007).
Housing: Homeownership rate: 78.6% (2007); Median home value: $271,045 (2007); Median rent: $669 per month (2000); Median age of housing: 25 years (2000).
Health: Birth rate: 150.0 per 10,000 population (2007); Death rate: 56.5 per 10,000 population (2007); Age-adjusted cancer mortality rate: 184.6 deaths per 100,000 population (2005); Air Quality Index: 86.3% good, 11.8% moderate, 1.9% unhealthy for sensitive individuals, 0.0% unhealthy (percent of days in 2007); Number of physicians: 32.1 per 10,000 population (2005); Hospital beds: 20.5 per 10,000 population (2004); Hospital admissions: 827.2 per 10,000 population (2004).
Elections: 2004 Presidential election results: 50.5% Bush, 48.8% Kerry, 0.1% Nader, 0.6% Badnarik
National and State Parks: Chain O'Lakes State Park; Illinois Beach State Park; Volo Bog State Nature Preserve
Additional Information Contacts
Lake County Government . . . . (847) 377-2000
http://www.co.lake.il.us
Antioch Chamber of Commerce. . . . . (847) 395-2233
http://www.antiochchamber.org
Buffalo Grove Area Chamber of Commerce . . . . (847) 541-7799
http://www.buffalogrovechamber.org
City of Highland Park . . . . (847) 432-0800
http://www.ci.highland-park.il.us
City of Lake Forest. . . . . (847) 234-2600
http://www.cityoflakeforest.com
City of North Chicago. . . . . (847) 596-8600
http://www.northchicago.org
City of Waukegan. . . . . (847) 599-2500
http://www.waukeganweb.net

City of Zion . . . . . (847) 746-4000
http://www.cityofzion.com
DBR Chamber of Commerce . . . . . (847) 945-4660
http://www.dbrchamber.com
Fox Lake Area Chamber of Commerce . . . . . (847) 587-7474
http://www.discoverfoxlake.com
GLMV Area Chamber of Commerce . . . . . (847) 680-0750
http://www.glmvchamber.org
Grayslake Area Chamber of Commerce & Industry . . . . . (847) 223-6888
http://www.grayslakechamber.com
Greater Lincolnshire Chamber of Commerce . . . . . (847) 793-2409
http://www.lincolnshirechamber.org
Highland Park Chamber of Commerce . . . . . (847) 432-0284
http://www.ehighlandpark.com
Highwood Chamber of Commerce . . . . . (847) 433-2100
http://www.highwoodchamberofcommerce.com
Illinois Women's Chamber of Commerce . . . . . (847) 269-6395
http://www.illinoiswomenschamber.com
Lake County Chamber of Commerce . . . . . (847) 249-3800
http://www.lakecountychamber.com
Lake Forest/Lake Bluff Chamber of Commerce . . . . . (847) 234-4282
http://www.lakeforestonline.com
Lake Zurich Area Chamber of Commerce . . . . . (847) 438-5572
http://www.lzacc.com
Lindenhurst Lake Villa Chamber . . . . . (847) 356-2146
http://www.llvchamber.com
Round Lake Area Chamber of Commerce & Industry . . . . . (847) 546-2002
http://www.rlchamber.org
Round Lake Chamber of Commerce . . . . . (847) 546-2002
Village of Antioch . . . . . (847) 395-1000
http://www.antioch.il.gov
Village of Beach Park . . . . . (847) 746-1770
http://www.villageofbeachpark.com
Village of Buffalo Grove . . . . . (847) 459-2500
http://www.vbg.org
Village of Deerfield . . . . . (847) 945-5000
http://www.deerfield-il.org
Village of Fox Lake . . . . . (847) 587-2151
http://www.foxlake.org
Village of Grayslake . . . . . (847) 223-8515
http://www.villageofgrayslake.com
Village of Gurnee . . . . . (847) 599-7500
http://www.gurnee.il.us
Village of Hawthorn Woods . . . . . (847) 438-5500
http://www.vhw.org
Village of Lake Bluff . . . . . (847) 234-0774
http://www.lakebluff.org
Village of Lake Villa . . . . . (847) 356-6100
http://www.lake-villa.org
Village of Lake Zurich . . . . . (847) 438-5141
http://www.volz.org
Village of Libertyville . . . . . (847) 362-2430
http://www.libertyville.com/index.htm
Village of Lincolnshire . . . . . (847) 883-8600
http://www.village.lincolnshire.il.us
Village of Lindenhurst . . . . . (847) 356-8252
http://lindenhurstil.org
Village of Long Grove . . . . . (847) 634-9440
http://www.longgrove.net
Village of Mundelein . . . . . (847) 949-3200
http://www.mundelein.org
Village of Round Lake . . . . . (847) 546-5400
http://www.eroundlake.com
Village of Round Lake Beach . . . . . (847) 546-2351
http://www.villageofroundlakebeach.com
Village of Round Lake Park . . . . . (847) 546-2790
http://www.roundlakepark.us
Village of Vernon Hills . . . . . (847) 367-3700
http://www.vernonhills.org
Village of Wauconda . . . . . (847) 526-9600
http://www.wauconda-il.gov
Wauconda Chamber of Commerce . . . . . (847) 526-5580
http://www.waucondachamber.org
Winthrop Harbor Chamber of Commerce . . . . . (847) 872-7723
http://www.winthropharborchamberofcommerce.com
Zion Chamber of Commerce . . . . . (847) 872-5405
http://www.zionchamber.com

Lake County Communities

ANTIOCH (village). Covers a land area of 7.383 square miles and a water area of 0.262 square miles. Located at 42.47° N. Lat.; 88.09° W. Long. Elevation is 784 feet.
History: Settled 1836, incorporated 1857.
Population: 6,395 (1990); 8,788 (2000); 12,588 (2007); 14,918 (2012 projected); Race: 93.1% White, 1.6% Black, 1.8% Asian, 7.0% Hispanic of any race (2007); Density: 1,705.1 persons per square mile (2007); Average household size: 2.72 (2007); Median age: 34.5 (2007); Males per 100 females: 96.2 (2007); Marriage status: 25.6% never married, 59.6% now married, 5.4% widowed, 9.3% divorced (2000); Foreign born: 3.3% (2000); Ancestry (includes multiple ancestries): 33.4% German, 20.3% Irish, 12.2% Polish, 10.3% Italian, 9.2% English (2000).
Economy: Single-family building permits issued: 90 (2007); Multi-family building permits issued: 0 (2007); Employment by occupation: 15.8% management, 21.1% professional, 10.0% services, 31.4% sales, 0.2% farming, 10.1% construction, 11.4% production (2000).
Income: Per capita income: $29,628 (2007); Median household income: $63,896 (2007); Average household income: $80,387 (2007); Percent of households with income of $100,000 or more: 25.0% (2007); Poverty rate: 3.9% (2000).
Education: Percent of population age 25 and over with: High school diploma (including GED) or higher: 89.3% (2007); Bachelor's degree or higher: 26.5% (2007); Master's degree or higher: 8.4% (2007).

School District(s)

Antioch CCSD 34 (PK-08)
2005-06 Enrollment: 2,934 . . . . . (847) 838-8400
CHSD 117 (03-12)
2005-06 Enrollment: 2,629 . . . . . (847) 838-7170
Emmons SD 33 (KG-08)
2005-06 Enrollment: 393 . . . . . (847) 395-1105
Grass Lake SD 36 (PK-08)
2005-06 Enrollment: 221 . . . . . (847) 395-1550

Housing: Homeownership rate: 67.2% (2007); Median home value: $240,762 (2007); Median rent: $631 per month (2000); Median age of housing: 21 years (2000).
Safety: Violent crime rate: 8.7 per 10,000 population; Property crime rate: 221.5 per 10,000 population (2006).
Transportation: Commute to work: 92.3% car, 1.6% public transportation, 3.1% walk, 2.4% work from home (2000); Travel time to work: 23.9% less than 15 minutes, 21.0% 15 to 30 minutes, 27.9% 30 to 45 minutes, 15.5% 45 to 60 minutes, 11.6% 60 minutes or more (2000)

Additional Information Contacts

Antioch Chamber of Commerce . . . . . (847) 395-2233
http://www.antiochchamber.org
Village of Antioch . . . . . (847) 395-1000
http://www.antioch.il.gov

BANNOCKBURN (village). Covers a land area of 2.024 square miles and a water area of 0.008 square miles. Located at 42.19° N. Lat.; 87.86° W. Long. Elevation is 686 feet.
Population: 1,388 (1990); 1,429 (2000); 1,480 (2007); 1,471 (2012 projected); Race: 88.8% White, 2.0% Black, 4.2% Asian, 5.5% Hispanic of any race (2007); Density: 731.3 persons per square mile (2007); Average household size: 5.38 (2007); Median age: 22.2 (2007); Males per 100 females: 102.2 (2007); Marriage status: 62.2% never married, 34.9% now married, 1.7% widowed, 1.2% divorced (2000); Foreign born: 13.0% (2000); Ancestry (includes multiple ancestries): 21.2% German, 12.1% Other groups, 7.3% Swedish, 7.0% Italian, 6.7% Irish (2000).
Economy: Single-family building permits issued: 4 (2007); Multi-family building permits issued: 0 (2007); Employment by occupation: 12.4% management, 31.7% professional, 17.6% services, 35.7% sales, 0.0% farming, 2.2% construction, 0.6% production (2000).
Income: Per capita income: $44,821 (2007); Median household income: $166,346 (2007); Average household income: $223,391 (2007); Percent of households with income of $100,000 or more: 62.9% (2007); Poverty rate: 3.0% (2000).
Education: Percent of population age 25 and over with: High school diploma (including GED) or higher: 97.8% (2007); Bachelor's degree or higher: 76.6% (2007); Master's degree or higher: 30.0% (2007).

School District(s)

Bannockburn SD 106 (KG-08)
2005-06 Enrollment: 166 . . . . (847) 945-5900

Housing: Homeownership rate: 81.5% (2007); Median home value: $1 million+ (2007); Median rent: $634 per month (2000); Median age of housing: 28 years (2000).

Safety: Violent crime rate: 6.2 per 10,000 population; Property crime rate: 217.5 per 10,000 population (2006).

Transportation: Commute to work: 79.8% car, 4.1% public transportation, 7.1% walk, 3.6% work from home (2000); Travel time to work: 56.1% less than 15 minutes, 20.5% 15 to 30 minutes, 13.7% 30 to 45 minutes, 4.1% 45 to 60 minutes, 5.6% 60 minutes or more (2000)

BEACH PARK (village). Covers a land area of 6.419 square miles and a water area of 0 square miles. Located at 42.42° N. Lat.; 87.84° W. Long. Elevation is 699 feet.

Population: 9,540 (1990); 10,072 (2000); 12,087 (2007); 13,344 (2012 projected); Race: 79.9% White, 5.3% Black, 2.0% Asian, 20.9% Hispanic of any race (2007); Density: 1,882.9 persons per square mile (2007); Average household size: 2.75 (2007); Median age: 38.1 (2007); Males per 100 females: 98.0 (2007); Marriage status: 22.1% never married, 60.7% now married, 6.6% widowed, 10.6% divorced (2000); Foreign born: 7.5% (2000); Ancestry (includes multiple ancestries): 27.4% German, 20.0% Other groups, 16.1% Irish, 9.4% English, 8.7% Polish (2000).

Economy: Single-family building permits issued: 59 (2007); Multi-family building permits issued: 0 (2007); Employment by occupation: 10.1% management, 16.0% professional, 12.7% services, 29.3% sales, 0.2% farming, 16.7% construction, 15.1% production (2000).

Income: Per capita income: $27,059 (2007); Median household income: $63,463 (2007); Average household income: $74,047 (2007); Percent of households with income of $100,000 or more: 20.4% (2007); Poverty rate: 3.7% (2000).

Education: Percent of population age 25 and over with: High school diploma (including GED) or higher: 84.2% (2007); Bachelor's degree or higher: 14.9% (2007); Master's degree or higher: 5.0% (2007).

School District(s)

Beach Park CCSD 3 (PK-08)
2005-06 Enrollment: 2,507 . . . . (847) 599-5005

Housing: Homeownership rate: 87.9% (2007); Median home value: $191,741 (2007); Median rent: $623 per month (2000); Median age of housing: 25 years (2000).

Transportation: Commute to work: 94.8% car, 1.6% public transportation, 0.2% walk, 2.4% work from home (2000); Travel time to work: 24.4% less than 15 minutes, 34.0% 15 to 30 minutes, 21.3% 30 to 45 minutes, 9.8% 45 to 60 minutes, 10.5% 60 minutes or more (2000)

Additional Information Contacts

Village of Beach Park. . . . . (847) 746-1770
http://www.villageofbeachpark.com

BUFFALO GROVE (village). Covers a land area of 9.194 square miles and a water area of 0.020 square miles. Located at 42.16° N. Lat.; 87.96° W. Long.

Population: 37,883 (1990); 42,909 (2000); 43,140 (2007); 43,126 (2012 projected); Race: 83.9% White, 0.7% Black, 12.6% Asian, 4.3% Hispanic of any race (2007); Density: 4,692.0 persons per square mile (2007); Average household size: 2.73 (2007); Median age: 39.2 (2007); Males per 100 females: 93.5 (2007); Marriage status: 20.7% never married, 67.7% now married, 4.4% widowed, 7.2% divorced (2000); Foreign born: 20.4% (2000); Ancestry (includes multiple ancestries): 19.1% Other groups, 16.1% German, 15.4% Russian, 12.7% Polish, 9.7% Irish (2000).

Economy: Unemployment rate: 3.7% (4/2008); Total civilian labor force: 25,119 (4/2008); Single-family building permits issued: 18 (2007); Multi-family building permits issued: 0 (2007); Employment by occupation: 24.7% management, 30.2% professional, 6.2% services, 29.3% sales, 0.0% farming, 4.0% construction, 5.6% production (2000).

Income: Per capita income: $41,524 (2007); Median household income: $90,009 (2007); Average household income: $113,193 (2007); Percent of households with income of $100,000 or more: 43.5% (2007); Poverty rate: 2.3% (2000).

Education: Percent of population age 25 and over with: High school diploma (including GED) or higher: 95.4% (2007); Bachelor's degree or higher: 56.2% (2007); Master's degree or higher: 20.8% (2007).

School District(s)

Aptakisic-Tripp CCSD 102 (PK-08)
2005-06 Enrollment: 2,166 . . . . (847) 353-5660

Kildeer Countryside CCSD 96 (PK-08)
2005-06 Enrollment: 3,432 . . . . (847) 459-4260

Township HSD 214 (09-12)
2005-06 Enrollment: 12,542 . . . . (847) 718-7600

Wheeling CCSD 21 (PK-08)
2005-06 Enrollment: 6,725 . . . . (847) 537-8270

Housing: Homeownership rate: 87.0% (2007); Median home value: $309,959 (2007); Median rent: $994 per month (2000); Median age of housing: 18 years (2000).

Safety: Violent crime rate: 2.8 per 10,000 population; Property crime rate: 118.8 per 10,000 population (2006).

Transportation: Commute to work: 89.0% car, 5.5% public transportation, 0.9% walk, 4.1% work from home (2000); Travel time to work: 20.5% less than 15 minutes, 30.7% 15 to 30 minutes, 27.0% 30 to 45 minutes, 10.5% 45 to 60 minutes, 11.2% 60 minutes or more (2000)

Additional Information Contacts

Buffalo Grove Area Chamber of Commerce . . . . (847) 541-7799
http://www.buffalogrovechamber.org

Village of Buffalo Grove . . . . (847) 459-2500
http://www.vbg.org

CHANNEL LAKE (CDP). Covers a land area of 1.949 square miles and a water area of 0.338 square miles. Located at 42.47° N. Lat.; 88.14° W. Long. Elevation is 745 feet.

Population: 1,677 (1990); 1,785 (2000); 1,743 (2007); 1,713 (2012 projected); Race: 94.7% White, 0.2% Black, 1.0% Asian, 2.1% Hispanic of any race (2007); Density: 894.5 persons per square mile (2007); Average household size: 2.53 (2007); Median age: 40.1 (2007); Males per 100 females: 111.0 (2007); Marriage status: 25.6% never married, 54.7% now married, 5.4% widowed, 14.3% divorced (2000); Foreign born: 3.9% (2000); Ancestry (includes multiple ancestries): 35.0% German, 16.9% Polish, 14.7% Irish, 8.6% English, 5.7% Italian (2000).

Economy: Employment by occupation: 7.3% management, 16.9% professional, 9.9% services, 26.2% sales, 1.9% farming, 20.5% construction, 17.4% production (2000).

Income: Per capita income: $29,105 (2007); Median household income: $58,284 (2007); Average household income: $73,628 (2007); Percent of households with income of $100,000 or more: 18.6% (2007); Poverty rate: 9.9% (2000).

Education: Percent of population age 25 and over with: High school diploma (including GED) or higher: 82.5% (2007); Bachelor's degree or higher: 18.6% (2007); Master's degree or higher: 3.4% (2007).

Housing: Homeownership rate: 81.1% (2007); Median home value: $209,831 (2007); Median rent: $599 per month (2000); Median age of housing: 44 years (2000).

Transportation: Commute to work: 88.4% car, 0.9% public transportation, 0.9% walk, 7.7% work from home (2000); Travel time to work: 6.5% less than 15 minutes, 18.9% 15 to 30 minutes, 27.5% 30 to 45 minutes, 19.9% 45 to 60 minutes, 27.2% 60 minutes or more (2000)

DEER PARK (village). Covers a land area of 3.646 square miles and a water area of 0.061 square miles. Located at 42.16° N. Lat.; 88.08° W. Long. Elevation is 850 feet.

Population: 2,817 (1990); 3,102 (2000); 3,236 (2007); 3,336 (2012 projected); Race: 94.9% White, 0.5% Black, 3.1% Asian, 2.1% Hispanic of any race (2007); Density: 887.5 persons per square mile (2007); Average household size: 3.15 (2007); Median age: 41.6 (2007); Males per 100 females: 98.8 (2007); Marriage status: 17.8% never married, 76.4% now married, 2.5% widowed, 3.3% divorced (2000); Foreign born: 8.4% (2000); Ancestry (includes multiple ancestries): 29.1% German, 19.0% Irish, 14.6% Italian, 14.2% Polish, 8.0% English (2000).

Economy: Single-family building permits issued: 39 (2007); Multi-family building permits issued: 0 (2007); Employment by occupation: 40.2% management, 21.0% professional, 5.3% services, 26.8% sales, 0.0% farming, 2.3% construction, 4.5% production (2000).

Income: Per capita income: $80,005 (2007); Median household income: $181,637 (2007); Average household income: $252,089 (2007); Percent of households with income of $100,000 or more: 75.6% (2007); Poverty rate: 0.6% (2000).

Education: Percent of population age 25 and over with: High school diploma (including GED) or higher: 97.1% (2007); Bachelor's degree or higher: 61.7% (2007); Master's degree or higher: 24.1% (2007).

Housing: Homeownership rate: 97.1% (2007); Median home value: $634,530 (2007); Median rent: $642 per month (2000); Median age of housing: 16 years (2000).

Safety: Violent crime rate: 0.0 per 10,000 population; Property crime rate: 193.7 per 10,000 population (2006).
Transportation: Commute to work: 85.3% car, 7.0% public transportation, 0.0% walk, 6.9% work from home (2000); Travel time to work: 12.6% less than 15 minutes, 35.9% 15 to 30 minutes, 31.6% 30 to 45 minutes, 8.2% 45 to 60 minutes, 11.7% 60 minutes or more (2000)

DEERFIELD (village). Covers a land area of 5.483 square miles and a water area of 0.035 square miles. Located at 42.16° N. Lat.; 87.85° W. Long. Elevation is 686 feet.
History: Named for the abundance of deer in the area. Incorporated 1903.
Population: 17,341 (1990); 18,420 (2000); 19,664 (2007); 20,503 (2012 projected); Race: 94.6% White, 0.3% Black, 3.4% Asian, 2.2% Hispanic of any race (2007); Density: 3,586.3 persons per square mile (2007); Average household size: 2.86 (2007); Median age: 41.0 (2007); Males per 100 females: 93.5 (2007); Marriage status: 15.4% never married, 72.4% now married, 5.5% widowed, 6.6% divorced (2000); Foreign born: 8.8% (2000); Ancestry (includes multiple ancestries): 17.6% German, 13.4% Russian, 11.2% Irish, 10.4% Other groups, 9.0% Polish (2000).
Economy: Single-family building permits issued: 67 (2007); Multi-family building permits issued: 0 (2007); Employment by occupation: 25.2% management, 34.3% professional, 5.2% services, 29.2% sales, 0.0% farming, 2.1% construction, 4.0% production (2000).
Income: Per capita income: $56,669 (2007); Median household income: $119,545 (2007); Average household income: $161,012 (2007); Percent of households with income of $100,000 or more: 59.6% (2007); Poverty rate: 1.6% (2000).
Education: Percent of population age 25 and over with: High school diploma (including GED) or higher: 95.8% (2007); Bachelor's degree or higher: 68.4% (2007); Master's degree or higher: 32.2% (2007).

School District(s)

Deerfield SD 109 (PK-08)
2005-06 Enrollment: 3,111 . . . . (847) 945-1844
Twp HSD 113 (09-12)
2005-06 Enrollment: 3,681 . . . . (224) 765-1000

Four-year College(s)

Trinity International University (Private, Not-for-profit, Evangelical Free Church of America)
Fall 2007 Enrollment: 2,783. . . . . (847) 945-8800
2007-08 Tuition: In-state $21,080; Out-of-state $21,080
Housing: Homeownership rate: 90.0% (2007); Median home value: $481,652 (2007); Median rent: $963 per month (2000); Median age of housing: 37 years (2000).
Safety: Violent crime rate: 3.4 per 10,000 population; Property crime rate: 144.2 per 10,000 population (2006).
Transportation: Commute to work: 79.2% car, 11.3% public transportation, 0.9% walk, 7.9% work from home (2000); Travel time to work: 25.4% less than 15 minutes, 31.2% 15 to 30 minutes, 17.3% 30 to 45 minutes, 10.6% 45 to 60 minutes, 15.4% 60 minutes or more (2000)

Additional Information Contacts

DBR Chamber of Commerce . . . . (847) 945-4660
http://www.dbrchamber.com
Village of Deerfield. . . . . (847) 945-5000
http://www.deerfield-il.org

FOREST LAKE (CDP). Covers a land area of 0.632 square miles and a water area of 0.062 square miles. Located at 42.20° N. Lat.; 88.05° W. Long. Elevation is 814 feet.
Population: 997 (1990); 1,530 (2000); 2,005 (2007); 2,321 (2012 projected); Race: 94.2% White, 0.7% Black, 1.6% Asian, 6.2% Hispanic of any race (2007); Density: 3,173.4 persons per square mile (2007); Average household size: 2.87 (2007); Median age: 39.0 (2007); Males per 100 females: 100.7 (2007); Marriage status: 24.8% never married, 63.2% now married, 3.7% widowed, 8.4% divorced (2000); Foreign born: 10.1% (2000); Ancestry (includes multiple ancestries): 28.8% Irish, 24.6% German, 18.4% Polish, 11.0% English, 8.7% Other groups (2000).
Economy: Employment by occupation: 13.8% management, 20.7% professional, 8.4% services, 30.3% sales, 1.4% farming, 13.2% construction, 12.2% production (2000).
Income: Per capita income: $37,228 (2007); Median household income: $92,198 (2007); Average household income: $106,785 (2007); Percent of households with income of $100,000 or more: 43.3% (2007); Poverty rate: 3.0% (2000).
Education: Percent of population age 25 and over with: High school diploma (including GED) or higher: 94.2% (2007); Bachelor's degree or higher: 39.8% (2007); Master's degree or higher: 7.3% (2007).
Housing: Homeownership rate: 90.4% (2007); Median home value: $280,890 (2007); Median rent: $984 per month (2000); Median age of housing: 30 years (2000).
Transportation: Commute to work: 84.7% car, 1.7% public transportation, 0.0% walk, 7.8% work from home (2000); Travel time to work: 15.0% less than 15 minutes, 32.3% 15 to 30 minutes, 30.0% 30 to 45 minutes, 15.1% 45 to 60 minutes, 7.6% 60 minutes or more (2000)

FORT SHERIDAN (unincorporated postal area, zip code 60037). Covers a land area of 0.450 square miles and a water area of 0 square miles. Located at 42.25° N. Lat.; 87.81° W. Long.
Population: 901 (2000); Race: 82.5% White, 14.7% Black, 0.0% Asian, 3.8% Hispanic of any race (2000); Density: 2,002.2 persons per square mile (2000); Age: 47.0% under 18, 0.0% over 64 (2000); Marriage status: 7.1% never married, 89.8% now married, 0.0% widowed, 3.1% divorced (2000); Foreign born: 1.7% (2000); Ancestry (includes multiple ancestries): 26.1% German, 24.3% Other groups, 10.0% United States or American, 9.8% Irish, 9.5% English (2000).
Economy: Employment by occupation: 9.2% management, 34.1% professional, 9.6% services, 36.0% sales, 0.0% farming, 5.4% construction, 5.7% production (2000).
Income: Per capita income: $16,727 (2000); Median household income: $46,750 (2000); Poverty rate: 0.0% (2000).
Education: Percent of population age 25 and over with: High school diploma (including GED) or higher: 98.7% (2000); Bachelor's degree or higher: 36.8% (2000).
Housing: Homeownership rate: 4.6% (2000); Median home value: $700,000 (2000); Median rent: $779 per month (2000); Median age of housing: 39 years (2000).
Transportation: Commute to work: 92.8% car, 0.0% public transportation, 1.9% walk, 3.9% work from home (2000); Travel time to work: 21.8% less than 15 minutes, 55.1% 15 to 30 minutes, 17.8% 30 to 45 minutes, 1.5% 45 to 60 minutes, 3.8% 60 minutes or more (2000)

FOX LAKE (village). Covers a land area of 7.348 square miles and a water area of 1.632 square miles. Located at 42.40° N. Lat.; 88.17° W. Long. Elevation is 748 feet.
History: Fox Lake developed as a resort community for vacationers who enjoyed the numerous lakes in the area.
Population: 8,117 (1990); 9,178 (2000); 10,141 (2007); 10,721 (2012 projected); Race: 93.7% White, 1.0% Black, 1.0% Asian, 8.6% Hispanic of any race (2007); Density: 1,380.1 persons per square mile (2007); Average household size: 2.26 (2007); Median age: 38.5 (2007); Males per 100 females: 101.7 (2007); Marriage status: 24.9% never married, 53.9% now married, 7.2% widowed, 13.9% divorced (2000); Foreign born: 6.7% (2000); Ancestry (includes multiple ancestries): 29.7% German, 17.5% Irish, 12.5% Polish, 10.3% Other groups, 10.0% Italian (2000).
Economy: Single-family building permits issued: 30 (2007); Multi-family building permits issued: 0 (2007); Employment by occupation: 11.9% management, 14.2% professional, 11.5% services, 34.4% sales, 0.5% farming, 12.8% construction, 14.7% production (2000).
Income: Per capita income: $27,375 (2007); Median household income: $52,262 (2007); Average household income: $61,786 (2007); Percent of households with income of $100,000 or more: 15.5% (2007); Poverty rate: 6.4% (2000).
Education: Percent of population age 25 and over with: High school diploma (including GED) or higher: 84.5% (2007); Bachelor's degree or higher: 15.5% (2007); Master's degree or higher: 4.9% (2007).

School District(s)

Fox Lake GSD 114 (PK-08)
2005-06 Enrollment: 918 . . . . (847) 973-4100
Grant CHSD 124 (09-12)
2005-06 Enrollment: 1,578 . . . . (847) 587-2561
Housing: Homeownership rate: 66.2% (2007); Median home value: $181,844 (2007); Median rent: $631 per month (2000); Median age of housing: 28 years (2000).
Safety: Violent crime rate: 25.1 per 10,000 population; Property crime rate: 321.3 per 10,000 population (2006).
Transportation: Commute to work: 92.1% car, 3.8% public transportation, 2.4% walk, 1.6% work from home (2000); Travel time to work: 19.0% less than 15 minutes, 24.7% 15 to 30 minutes, 16.0% 30 to 45 minutes, 16.7% 45 to 60 minutes, 23.5% 60 minutes or more (2000)

Additional Information Contacts
Fox Lake Area Chamber of Commerce . . . . (847) 587-7474
http://www.discoverfoxlake.com
Village of Fox Lake . . . . (847) 587-2151
http://www.foxlake.org

FOX LAKE HILLS (CDP). Covers a land area of 1.328 square miles and a water area of 0.456 square miles. Located at 42.40° N. Lat.; 88.12° W. Long. Elevation is 751 feet.
Population: 2,612 (1990); 2,561 (2000); 2,598 (2007); 2,610 (2012 projected); Race: 94.7% White, 1.8% Black, 0.8% Asian, 4.3% Hispanic of any race (2007); Density: 1,956.5 persons per square mile (2007); Average household size: 2.81 (2007); Median age: 39.3 (2007); Males per 100 females: 98.2 (2007); Marriage status: 16.3% never married, 69.4% now married, 5.5% widowed, 8.8% divorced (2000); Foreign born: 2.9% (2000); Ancestry (includes multiple ancestries): 27.2% German, 18.4% Irish, 13.8% Polish, 9.4% Other groups, 9.2% English (2000).
Economy: Employment by occupation: 14.2% management, 22.4% professional, 8.8% services, 27.8% sales, 0.0% farming, 11.2% construction, 15.6% production (2000).
Income: Per capita income: $30,309 (2007); Median household income: $75,957 (2007); Average household income: $85,311 (2007); Percent of households with income of $100,000 or more: 26.9% (2007); Poverty rate: 3.0% (2000).
Education: Percent of population age 25 and over with: High school diploma (including GED) or higher: 88.2% (2007); Bachelor's degree or higher: 24.0% (2007); Master's degree or higher: 6.0% (2007).
Housing: Homeownership rate: 92.2% (2007); Median home value: $191,286 (2007); Median rent: $733 per month (2000); Median age of housing: 29 years (2000).
Transportation: Commute to work: 93.9% car, 2.5% public transportation, 0.0% walk, 3.5% work from home (2000); Travel time to work: 12.7% less than 15 minutes, 23.1% 15 to 30 minutes, 24.7% 30 to 45 minutes, 17.9% 45 to 60 minutes, 21.7% 60 minutes or more (2000)

GAGES LAKE (CDP). Covers a land area of 3.087 square miles and a water area of 0.219 square miles. Located at 42.35° N. Lat.; 87.98° W. Long. Elevation is 768 feet.
Population: 8,138 (1990); 10,415 (2000); 10,477 (2007); 10,436 (2012 projected); Race: 87.8% White, 2.6% Black, 5.3% Asian, 5.8% Hispanic of any race (2007); Density: 3,394.1 persons per square mile (2007); Average household size: 2.80 (2007); Median age: 36.8 (2007); Males per 100 females: 98.1 (2007); Marriage status: 21.7% never married, 65.0% now married, 3.8% widowed, 9.5% divorced (2000); Foreign born: 8.3% (2000); Ancestry (includes multiple ancestries): 35.1% German, 17.4% Irish, 12.1% Other groups, 11.4% Polish, 10.0% English (2000).
Economy: Employment by occupation: 20.1% management, 21.9% professional, 11.4% services, 31.3% sales, 0.0% farming, 6.8% construction, 8.4% production (2000).
Income: Per capita income: $34,583 (2007); Median household income: $82,934 (2007); Average household income: $96,913 (2007); Percent of households with income of $100,000 or more: 37.6% (2007); Poverty rate: 3.0% (2000).
Education: Percent of population age 25 and over with: High school diploma (including GED) or higher: 92.9% (2007); Bachelor's degree or higher: 38.4% (2007); Master's degree or higher: 12.1% (2007).

School District(s)

Lake Roe (06-12)
2005-06 Enrollment: 48 . . . . (847) 543-7833
Spec Educ Dist Lake County/Sedol (PK-12)
2005-06 Enrollment: 518 . . . . (847) 548-8470
Woodland CCSD 50 (PK-08)
2005-06 Enrollment: 7,084 . . . . (847) 856-3590

Housing: Homeownership rate: 87.2% (2007); Median home value: $231,515 (2007); Median rent: $778 per month (2000); Median age of housing: 20 years (2000).
Transportation: Commute to work: 93.8% car, 2.2% public transportation, 0.5% walk, 3.4% work from home (2000); Travel time to work: 21.7% less than 15 minutes, 33.3% 15 to 30 minutes, 22.4% 30 to 45 minutes, 11.8% 45 to 60 minutes, 10.8% 60 minutes or more (2000)

GRANDWOOD PARK (CDP). Covers a land area of 1.616 square miles and a water area of 0.015 square miles. Located at 42.39° N. Lat.; 87.98° W. Long. Elevation is 745 feet.
Population: 2,439 (1990); 4,521 (2000); 5,419 (2007); 5,982 (2012 projected); Race: 80.6% White, 5.8% Black, 7.0% Asian, 8.5% Hispanic of any race (2007); Density: 3,354.2 persons per square mile (2007); Average household size: 2.87 (2007); Median age: 35.2 (2007); Males per 100 females: 96.8 (2007); Marriage status: 19.7% never married, 65.7% now married, 4.2% widowed, 10.4% divorced (2000); Foreign born: 9.2% (2000); Ancestry (includes multiple ancestries): 26.7% German, 17.8% Other groups, 17.4% Irish, 11.6% Polish, 8.5% Italian (2000).
Economy: Employment by occupation: 25.2% management, 17.9% professional, 11.0% services, 26.0% sales, 0.0% farming, 8.5% construction, 11.4% production (2000).
Income: Per capita income: $37,740 (2007); Median household income: $83,697 (2007); Average household income: $108,152 (2007); Percent of households with income of $100,000 or more: 37.8% (2007); Poverty rate: 3.2% (2000).
Education: Percent of population age 25 and over with: High school diploma (including GED) or higher: 91.8% (2007); Bachelor's degree or higher: 44.6% (2007); Master's degree or higher: 13.5% (2007).
Housing: Homeownership rate: 85.6% (2007); Median home value: $245,746 (2007); Median rent: $938 per month (2000); Median age of housing: 10 years (2000).
Transportation: Commute to work: 92.9% car, 2.1% public transportation, 0.7% walk, 3.2% work from home (2000); Travel time to work: 17.3% less than 15 minutes, 30.4% 15 to 30 minutes, 27.9% 30 to 45 minutes, 12.0% 45 to 60 minutes, 12.4% 60 minutes or more (2000)

GRAYSLAKE (village). Aka Grays Lake. Covers a land area of 9.398 square miles and a water area of 0.157 square miles. Located at 42.34° N. Lat.; 88.03° W. Long. Elevation is 784 feet.
History: Named for William Gray, an early settler. College of Lake County here. Incorporated 1895.
Population: 8,307 (1990); 18,506 (2000); 22,201 (2007); 24,529 (2012 projected); Race: 86.2% White, 2.1% Black, 7.2% Asian, 7.1% Hispanic of any race (2007); Density: 2,362.4 persons per square mile (2007); Average household size: 2.94 (2007); Median age: 33.7 (2007); Males per 100 females: 96.4 (2007); Marriage status: 18.9% never married, 70.4% now married, 2.7% widowed, 7.9% divorced (2000); Foreign born: 8.4% (2000); Ancestry (includes multiple ancestries): 31.4% German, 16.9% Irish, 13.9% Other groups, 10.8% Polish, 10.2% Italian (2000).
Economy: Single-family building permits issued: 44 (2007); Multi-family building permits issued: 0 (2007); Employment by occupation: 24.8% management, 27.2% professional, 7.7% services, 26.9% sales, 0.1% farming, 7.0% construction, 6.4% production (2000).
Income: Per capita income: $34,039 (2007); Median household income: $87,451 (2007); Average household income: $99,956 (2007); Percent of households with income of $100,000 or more: 39.7% (2007); Poverty rate: 3.0% (2000).
Education: Percent of population age 25 and over with: High school diploma (including GED) or higher: 94.4% (2007); Bachelor's degree or higher: 51.1% (2007); Master's degree or higher: 17.9% (2007).

School District(s)

Grayslake CCSD 46 (PK-08)
2005-06 Enrollment: 4,108 . . . . (847) 223-3650
Grayslake CHSD 127 (09-12)
2005-06 Enrollment: 2,475 . . . . (847) 986-3400
Lake Co High Schools Tech Campus
2005-06 Enrollment: n/a . . . . (847) 543-6001
Prairie Crossing Charter School (KG-08)
2005-06 Enrollment: 339 . . . . (847) 543-9722
Spec Educ Dist Lake County/Sedol (PK-12)
2005-06 Enrollment: 518 . . . . (847) 548-8470

Two-year College(s)

College of Lake County (Public)
Fall 2007 Enrollment: 16,010. . . . . (847) 543-2000
2007-08 Tuition: In-state $6,020; Out-of-state $8,008

Housing: Homeownership rate: 80.1% (2007); Median home value: $267,297 (2007); Median rent: $754 per month (2000); Median age of housing: 9 years (2000).
Safety: Violent crime rate: 9.5 per 10,000 population; Property crime rate: 209.5 per 10,000 population (2006).
Newspapers: Antioch News Reporter (Regional news; Circulation 4,881); Fox Lake Press (Regional news; Circulation 5,579); Grayslake Times (Regional news; Circulation 4,326); Great Lakes Bulletin (Regional news; Circulation 0); Gurnee Press (Regional news; Circulation 4,842); Lake Villa Record (Regional news; Circulation 2,742); Lake Zurich Enterprise (Local

news; Circulation 3,721); Libertyville News (Regional news; Circulation 3,200); Lindenhurst News (Regional news; Circulation 2,711); Market/Journal (Community news; Circulation 90,162); Market/Journal II (Community news; Circulation 14,171); Market/Journal III (Community news; Circulation 10,338); Market/Journal V (Community news; Circulation 19,012); Market/Journal VI (Community news; Circulation 11,117); Market/Journal VII (Community news; Circulation 11,141); Market/Journal VIII (Community news; Circulation 11,141); Mundelein News (Regional news; Circulation 3,107); Vernon Hills News (Local news; Circulation 2,820); Wadsworth News (Regional news; Circulation 2,361)
Transportation: Commute to work: 88.9% car, 6.2% public transportation, 0.8% walk, 3.8% work from home (2000); Travel time to work: 16.7% less than 15 minutes, 24.0% 15 to 30 minutes, 25.2% 30 to 45 minutes, 17.4% 45 to 60 minutes, 16.7% 60 minutes or more (2000)
Additional Information Contacts
Grayslake Area Chamber of Commerce & Industry....... (847) 223-6888
http://www.grayslakechamber.com
Village of Grayslake............................... (847) 223-8515
http://www.villageofgrayslake.com

GREAT LAKES (unincorporated postal area, zip code 60088).

Covers a land area of 2.362 square miles and a water area of 0 square miles. Located at 42.30° N. Lat.; 87.85° W. Long. Elevation is 659 feet.
Population: 13,319 (2000); Race: 63.7% White, 20.7% Black, 5.0% Asian, 10.6% Hispanic of any race (2000); Density: 5,638.9 persons per square mile (2000); Age: 23.9% under 18, 0.1% over 64 (2000); Marriage status: 53.9% never married, 42.8% now married, 0.1% widowed, 3.3% divorced (2000); Foreign born: 6.8% (2000); Ancestry (includes multiple ancestries): 40.1% Other groups, 15.5% German, 12.2% Irish, 6.2% English, 6.1% United States or American (2000).
Economy: Employment by occupation: 14.3% management, 24.0% professional, 22.2% services, 29.0% sales, 0.0% farming, 1.9% construction, 8.6% production (2000).
Income: Per capita income: $12,340 (2000); Median household income: $39,299 (2000); Poverty rate: 6.5% (2000).
Education: Percent of population age 25 and over with: High school diploma (including GED) or higher: 95.0% (2000); Bachelor's degree or higher: 17.6% (2000).

School District(s)

North Chicago SD 187 (PK-12)
2005-06 Enrollment: 4,323 .... (847) 689-8150
Housing: Homeownership rate: 4.6% (2000); Median home value: $112,500 (2000); Median rent: $818 per month (2000); Median age of housing: 32 years (2000).
Hospitals: Naval Health Clinic: Great Lakes (186 beds)
Transportation: Commute to work: 39.6% car, 0.5% public transportation, 55.9% walk, 1.7% work from home (2000); Travel time to work: 76.1% less than 15 minutes, 16.0% 15 to 30 minutes, 3.2% 30 to 45 minutes, 2.4% 45 to 60 minutes, 2.2% 60 minutes or more (2000)

GREEN OAKS (village).

Aka Oak Grove. Covers a land area of 4.004 square miles and a water area of 0.056 square miles. Located at 42.28° N. Lat.; 87.91° W. Long. Elevation is 689 feet.
Population: 2,357 (1990); 3,572 (2000); 4,015 (2007); 4,292 (2012 projected); Race: 86.5% White, 2.6% Black, 8.4% Asian, 4.5% Hispanic of any race (2007); Density: 1,002.7 persons per square mile (2007); Average household size: 3.29 (2007); Median age: 37.1 (2007); Males per 100 females: 100.0 (2007); Marriage status: 14.9% never married, 80.2% now married, 2.3% widowed, 2.6% divorced (2000); Foreign born: 9.6% (2000); Ancestry (includes multiple ancestries): 30.9% German, 16.3% Irish, 10.8% Other groups, 10.5% Italian, 9.3% Polish (2000).
Economy: Single-family building permits issued: 3 (2007); Multi-family building permits issued: 0 (2007); Employment by occupation: 36.7% management, 26.5% professional, 5.3% services, 23.4% sales, 0.0% farming, 3.3% construction, 4.8% production (2000).
Income: Per capita income: $57,052 (2007); Median household income: $140,870 (2007); Average household income: $186,969 (2007); Percent of households with income of $100,000 or more: 67.3% (2007); Poverty rate: 1.7% (2000).
Education: Percent of population age 25 and over with: High school diploma (including GED) or higher: 94.9% (2007); Bachelor's degree or higher: 59.1% (2007); Master's degree or higher: 27.4% (2007).

School District(s)

Oak Grove SD 68 (KG-08)
2005-06 Enrollment: 1,052 .... (847) 367-4120
Housing: Homeownership rate: 97.5% (2007); Median home value: $560,105 (2007); Median rent: $1,222 per month (2000); Median age of housing: 15 years (2000).
Transportation: Commute to work: 87.6% car, 6.1% public transportation, 0.7% walk, 5.6% work from home (2000); Travel time to work: 27.3% less than 15 minutes, 28.1% 15 to 30 minutes, 25.1% 30 to 45 minutes, 8.8% 45 to 60 minutes, 10.8% 60 minutes or more (2000)

GURNEE (village).

Covers a land area of 13.401 square miles and a water area of 0.014 square miles. Located at 42.37° N. Lat.; 87.93° W. Long. Elevation is 679 feet.
Population: 14,698 (1990); 28,834 (2000); 30,912 (2007); 32,315 (2012 projected); Race: 72.8% White, 6.5% Black, 13.7% Asian, 9.2% Hispanic of any race (2007); Density: 2,306.6 persons per square mile (2007); Average household size: 2.76 (2007); Median age: 35.7 (2007); Males per 100 females: 94.5 (2007); Marriage status: 20.9% never married, 67.0% now married, 3.8% widowed, 8.3% divorced (2000); Foreign born: 11.7% (2000); Ancestry (includes multiple ancestries): 27.3% German, 20.9% Other groups, 14.5% Irish, 9.2% Polish, 8.6% Italian (2000).
Economy: Unemployment rate: 4.3% (4/2008); Total civilian labor force: 17,637 (4/2008); Single-family building permits issued: 59 (2007); Multi-family building permits issued: 0 (2007); Employment by occupation: 24.0% management, 26.4% professional, 7.6% services, 28.6% sales, 0.1% farming, 5.6% construction, 7.6% production (2000).
Income: Per capita income: $36,586 (2007); Median household income: $86,083 (2007); Average household income: $100,989 (2007); Percent of households with income of $100,000 or more: 41.6% (2007); Poverty rate: 3.0% (2000).
Education: Percent of population age 25 and over with: High school diploma (including GED) or higher: 94.3% (2007); Bachelor's degree or higher: 48.4% (2007); Master's degree or higher: 17.3% (2007).

School District(s)

Gurnee SD 56 (PK-08)
2005-06 Enrollment: 2,071 .... (847) 336-0800
Warren Twp HSD 121 (09-12)
2005-06 Enrollment: 3,828 .... (847) 662-1400
Woodland CCSD 50 (PK-08)
2005-06 Enrollment: 7,084 .... (847) 856-3590
Housing: Homeownership rate: 78.6% (2007); Median home value: $276,971 (2007); Median rent: $733 per month (2000); Median age of housing: 10 years (2000).
Safety: Violent crime rate: 13.2 per 10,000 population; Property crime rate: 500.5 per 10,000 population (2006).
Transportation: Commute to work: 93.4% car, 2.7% public transportation, 0.6% walk, 3.0% work from home (2000); Travel time to work: 20.1% less than 15 minutes, 34.0% 15 to 30 minutes, 21.5% 30 to 45 minutes, 11.9% 45 to 60 minutes, 12.4% 60 minutes or more (2000)
Additional Information Contacts
Lake County Chamber of Commerce .... (847) 249-3800
http://www.lakecountychamber.com
Village of Gurnee................................. (847) 599-7500
http://www.gurnee.il.us

HAINESVILLE (village).

Covers a land area of 1.743 square miles and a water area of 0.034 square miles. Located at 42.34° N. Lat.; 88.06° W. Long. Elevation is 801 feet.
Population: 282 (1990); 2,129 (2000); 2,756 (2007); 3,151 (2012 projected); Race: 76.3% White, 3.0% Black, 9.4% Asian, 14.8% Hispanic of any race (2007); Density: 1,580.8 persons per square mile (2007); Average household size: 3.10 (2007); Median age: 31.4 (2007); Males per 100 females: 102.9 (2007); Marriage status: 12.2% never married, 81.0% now married, 1.5% widowed, 5.4% divorced (2000); Foreign born: 13.9% (2000); Ancestry (includes multiple ancestries): 27.0% German, 21.8% Polish, 21.5% Other groups, 14.5% Irish, 8.9% Italian (2000).
Economy: Single-family building permits issued: 0 (2007); Multi-family building permits issued: 0 (2007); Employment by occupation: 22.5% management, 24.0% professional, 11.5% services, 22.2% sales, 0.0% farming, 8.0% construction, 11.9% production (2000).
Income: Per capita income: $27,886 (2007); Median household income: $84,783 (2007); Average household income: $86,546 (2007); Percent of households with income of $100,000 or more: 32.7% (2007); Poverty rate: 3.9% (2000).
Education: Percent of population age 25 and over with: High school diploma (including GED) or higher: 89.5% (2007); Bachelor's degree or higher: 36.4% (2007); Master's degree or higher: 9.7% (2007).

School District(s)

Grayslake CCSD 46 (PK-08)
2005-06 Enrollment: 4,108 . . . . (847) 223-3650

Housing: Homeownership rate: 91.2% (2007); Median home value: $250,195 (2007); Median rent: $665 per month (2000); Median age of housing: 3 years (2000).

Safety: Violent crime rate: 2.7 per 10,000 population; Property crime rate: 326.7 per 10,000 population (2006).

Transportation: Commute to work: 90.5% car, 5.8% public transportation, 0.0% walk, 3.7% work from home (2000); Travel time to work: 11.3% less than 15 minutes, 20.4% 15 to 30 minutes, 26.7% 30 to 45 minutes, 20.3% 45 to 60 minutes, 21.4% 60 minutes or more (2000)

HAWTHORN WOODS (village). Covers a land area of 5.359 square miles and a water area of 0.056 square miles. Located at 42.22° N. Lat.; 88.05° W. Long. Elevation is 801 feet.

Population: 4,540 (1990); 6,002 (2000); 7,036 (2007); 7,672 (2012 projected); Race: 92.6% White, 0.5% Black, 4.6% Asian, 3.1% Hispanic of any race (2007); Density: 1,312.9 persons per square mile (2007); Average household size: 3.31 (2007); Median age: 38.1 (2007); Males per 100 females: 99.7 (2007); Marriage status: 16.0% never married, 79.8% now married, 1.3% widowed, 2.8% divorced (2000); Foreign born: 7.1% (2000); Ancestry (includes multiple ancestries): 31.3% German, 16.1% Irish, 13.2% Italian, 10.6% Polish, 7.5% Other groups (2000).

Economy: Single-family building permits issued: 52 (2007); Multi-family building permits issued: 0 (2007); Employment by occupation: 34.3% management, 25.6% professional, 5.4% services, 28.1% sales, 0.0% farming, 2.7% construction, 3.9% production (2000).

Income: Per capita income: $59,545 (2007); Median household income: $156,467 (2007); Average household income: $194,245 (2007); Percent of households with income of $100,000 or more: 74.3% (2007); Poverty rate: 1.9% (2000).

Education: Percent of population age 25 and over with: High school diploma (including GED) or higher: 97.3% (2007); Bachelor's degree or higher: 59.7% (2007); Master's degree or higher: 22.4% (2007).

School District(s)

Lake Zurich CUSD 95 (PK-12)
2005-06 Enrollment: 6,557 . . . . (847) 438-2831

Housing: Homeownership rate: 98.6% (2007); Median home value: $578,752 (2007); Median rent: $2,000+ per month (2000); Median age of housing: 14 years (2000).

Safety: Violent crime rate: 1.4 per 10,000 population; Property crime rate: 50.2 per 10,000 population (2006).

Transportation: Commute to work: 87.4% car, 5.9% public transportation, 0.0% walk, 6.0% work from home (2000); Travel time to work: 14.7% less than 15 minutes, 28.7% 15 to 30 minutes, 28.7% 30 to 45 minutes, 14.2% 45 to 60 minutes, 13.6% 60 minutes or more (2000)

Additional Information Contacts

Village of Hawthorn Woods . . . . (847) 438-5500
http://www.vhw.org

HIGHLAND PARK (city). Covers a land area of 12.360 square miles and a water area of 0.006 square miles. Located at 42.18° N. Lat.; 87.80° W. Long. Elevation is 696 feet.

History: Named for its train station, by the railroad company. The Green Bay House tavern was opened in 1834 on the Chicago-Milwaukee post road, where the city of Highland Park later developed. The name was given by the railroad company to their station here, and the town was incorporated under that name in 1867.

Population: 30,761 (1990); 31,365 (2000); 32,808 (2007); 33,781 (2012 projected); Race: 88.3% White, 1.8% Black, 2.7% Asian, 13.3% Hispanic of any race (2007); Density: 2,654.3 persons per square mile (2007); Average household size: 2.73 (2007); Median age: 41.1 (2007); Males per 100 females: 96.1 (2007); Marriage status: 17.1% never married, 71.9% now married, 5.6% widowed, 5.3% divorced (2000); Foreign born: 15.3% (2000); Ancestry (includes multiple ancestries): 17.5% Other groups, 16.4% Russian, 12.6% German, 8.8% United States or American, 8.7% Polish (2000).

Economy: Unemployment rate: 3.3% (4/2008); Total civilian labor force: 17,014 (4/2008); Single-family building permits issued: 31 (2007); Multi-family building permits issued: 37 (2007); Employment by occupation: 25.0% management, 30.6% professional, 10.4% services, 27.3% sales, 0.0% farming, 3.2% construction, 3.5% production (2000).

Income: Per capita income: $57,128 (2007); Median household income: $105,109 (2007); Average household income: $155,238 (2007); Percent of households with income of $100,000 or more: 52.3% (2007); Poverty rate: 3.8% (2000).

Education: Percent of population age 25 and over with: High school diploma (including GED) or higher: 91.4% (2007); Bachelor's degree or higher: 61.1% (2007); Master's degree or higher: 28.1% (2007).

School District(s)

North Shore SD 112 (PK-08)
2005-06 Enrollment: 4,321 . . . . (847) 681-6700
Northern Suburban Spec Ed Dist (KG-12)
2005-06 Enrollment: 127 . . . . (847) 831-5100
Twp HSD 113 (09-12)
2005-06 Enrollment: 3,681 . . . . (224) 765-1000

Housing: Homeownership rate: 81.9% (2007); Median home value: $545,317 (2007); Median rent: $852 per month (2000); Median age of housing: 41 years (2000).

Hospitals: Highland Park Hospital (239 beds)

Safety: Violent crime rate: 8.0 per 10,000 population; Property crime rate: 161.9 per 10,000 population (2006).

Transportation: Commute to work: 78.2% car, 12.3% public transportation, 2.2% walk, 6.3% work from home (2000); Travel time to work: 26.1% less than 15 minutes, 27.6% 15 to 30 minutes, 20.3% 30 to 45 minutes, 10.8% 45 to 60 minutes, 15.1% 60 minutes or more (2000)

Additional Information Contacts

City of Highland Park . . . . (847) 432-0800
http://www.ci.highland-park.il.us
Highland Park Chamber of Commerce . . . . (847) 432-0284
http://www.ehighlandpark.com

HIGHWOOD (city). Covers a land area of 0.632 square miles and a water area of 0 square miles. Located at 42.20° N. Lat.; 87.81° W. Long. Elevation is 676 feet.

History: Fort Sheridan decommissioned in 1990s. Incorporated 1886.

Population: 4,854 (1990); 4,143 (2000); 4,115 (2007); 4,113 (2012 projected); Race: 64.7% White, 1.7% Black, 2.9% Asian, 48.6% Hispanic of any race (2007); Density: 6,507.8 persons per square mile (2007); Average household size: 2.72 (2007); Median age: 35.0 (2007); Males per 100 females: 100.7 (2007); Marriage status: 32.8% never married, 50.6% now married, 7.2% widowed, 9.3% divorced (2000); Foreign born: 38.6% (2000); Ancestry (includes multiple ancestries): 37.9% Other groups, 22.6% Italian, 10.0% Irish, 9.3% German, 3.5% English (2000).

Economy: Single-family building permits issued: 2 (2007); Multi-family building permits issued: 0 (2007); Employment by occupation: 12.4% management, 16.3% professional, 26.6% services, 26.2% sales, 0.0% farming, 9.6% construction, 8.9% production (2000).

Income: Per capita income: $27,351 (2007); Median household income: $47,861 (2007); Average household income: $73,099 (2007); Percent of households with income of $100,000 or more: 16.1% (2007); Poverty rate: 7.0% (2000).

Education: Percent of population age 25 and over with: High school diploma (including GED) or higher: 70.2% (2007); Bachelor's degree or higher: 27.4% (2007); Master's degree or higher: 12.1% (2007).

School District(s)

North Shore SD 112 (PK-08)
2005-06 Enrollment: 4,321 . . . . (847) 681-6700

Housing: Homeownership rate: 42.0% (2007); Median home value: $349,032 (2007); Median rent: $723 per month (2000); Median age of housing: 48 years (2000).

Safety: Violent crime rate: 32.9 per 10,000 population; Property crime rate: 106.1 per 10,000 population (2006).

Transportation: Commute to work: 83.4% car, 7.8% public transportation, 5.3% walk, 3.3% work from home (2000); Travel time to work: 36.0% less than 15 minutes, 38.8% 15 to 30 minutes, 11.2% 30 to 45 minutes, 4.4% 45 to 60 minutes, 9.5% 60 minutes or more (2000)

Additional Information Contacts

Highwood Chamber of Commerce. (847) 433-2100
http://www.highwoodchamberofcommerce.com

INDIAN CREEK (village). Covers a land area of 0.267 square miles and a water area of 0 square miles. Located at 42.22° N. Lat.; 87.97° W. Long. Elevation is 741 feet.

Population: 188 (1990); 194 (2000); 265 (2007); 309 (2012 projected); Race: 95.8% White, 0.0% Black, 1.1% Asian, 6.8% Hispanic of any race (2007); Density: 992.3 persons per square mile (2007); Average household size: 3.01 (2007); Median age: 42.6 (2007); Males per 100 females: 103.8 (2007); Marriage status: 15.5% never married, 76.8% now married, 6.5%

widowed, 1.3% divorced (2000); Foreign born: 2.4% (2000); Ancestry (includes multiple ancestries): 42.2% German, 12.8% Polish, 10.9% Norwegian, 9.5% Irish, 8.5% English (2000).
Economy: Single-family building permits issued: 1 (2007); Multi-family building permits issued: 0 (2007); Employment by occupation: 34.5% management, 28.3% professional, 4.4% services, 27.4% sales, 0.0% farming, 4.4% construction, 0.9% production (2000).
Income: Per capita income: $39,801 (2007); Median household income: $94,118 (2007); Average household income: $119,063 (2007); Percent of households with income of $100,000 or more: 45.5% (2007); Poverty rate: 0.9% (2000).
Education: Percent of population age 25 and over with: High school diploma (including GED) or higher: 93.7% (2007); Bachelor's degree or higher: 50.3% (2007); Master's degree or higher: 20.6% (2007).
Housing: Homeownership rate: 96.6% (2007); Median home value: $338,372 (2007); Median rent: $n/a per month (2000); Median age of housing: 34 years (2000).
Transportation: Commute to work: 87.6% car, 0.0% public transportation, 2.7% walk, 9.7% work from home (2000); Travel time to work: 33.3% less than 15 minutes, 30.4% 15 to 30 minutes, 19.6% 30 to 45 minutes, 10.8% 45 to 60 minutes, 5.9% 60 minutes or more (2000)

INGLESIDE (unincorporated postal area, zip code 60041). Part of the Village of Fox Lake. Covers a land area of 11.437 square miles and a water area of 0.538 square miles. Located at 42.37° N. Lat.; 88.15° W. Long. Elevation is 764 feet.

Population: 9,286 (2000); Race: 96.8% White, 0.9% Black, 0.3% Asian, 1.7% Hispanic of any race (2000); Density: 811.9 persons per square mile (2000); Age: 26.5% under 18, 8.0% over 64 (2000); Marriage status: 23.8% never married, 62.3% now married, 4.8% widowed, 9.1% divorced (2000); Foreign born: 4.0% (2000); Ancestry (includes multiple ancestries): 36.1% German, 15.9% Polish, 15.1% Irish, 8.2% Italian, 7.6% Other groups (2000).
Economy: Employment by occupation: 10.9% management, 15.9% professional, 13.4% services, 30.8% sales, 0.0% farming, 14.7% construction, 14.2% production (2000).
Income: Per capita income: $24,726 (2000); Median household income: $59,874 (2000); Poverty rate: 3.8% (2000).
Education: Percent of population age 25 and over with: High school diploma (including GED) or higher: 88.8% (2000); Bachelor's degree or higher: 18.6% (2000).

School District(s)

Big Hollow SD 38 (PK-08)
2005-06 Enrollment: 1,235 . . . . (847) 587-2632
Gavin SD 37 (PK-08)
2005-06 Enrollment: 905 . . . . (847) 546-2916
Housing: Homeownership rate: 82.0% (2000); Median home value: $153,800 (2000); Median rent: $692 per month (2000); Median age of housing: 39 years (2000).
Transportation: Commute to work: 92.9% car, 2.0% public transportation, 0.9% walk, 4.1% work from home (2000); Travel time to work: 21.2% less than 15 minutes, 24.5% 15 to 30 minutes, 21.9% 30 to 45 minutes, 17.8% 45 to 60 minutes, 14.6% 60 minutes or more (2000)

KILDEER (village). Covers a land area of 3.472 square miles and a water area of 0.046 square miles. Located at 42.18° N. Lat.; 88.05° W. Long. Elevation is 778 feet.

Population: 2,748 (1990); 3,460 (2000); 4,246 (2007); 4,760 (2012 projected); Race: 90.7% White, 1.2% Black, 6.6% Asian, 3.2% Hispanic of any race (2007); Density: 1,223.1 persons per square mile (2007); Average household size: 3.22 (2007); Median age: 40.4 (2007); Males per 100 females: 97.0 (2007); Marriage status: 15.5% never married, 79.4% now married, 1.7% widowed, 3.4% divorced (2000); Foreign born: 8.3% (2000); Ancestry (includes multiple ancestries): 27.4% German, 19.3% Irish, 15.1% Polish, 14.2% Italian, 12.7% English (2000).
Economy: Single-family building permits issued: 5 (2007); Multi-family building permits issued: 0 (2007); Employment by occupation: 36.1% management, 21.0% professional, 6.4% services, 31.6% sales, 0.2% farming, 2.1% construction, 2.4% production (2000).
Income: Per capita income: $60,682 (2007); Median household income: $151,609 (2007); Average household income: $195,343 (2007); Percent of households with income of $100,000 or more: 70.1% (2007); Poverty rate: 0.5% (2000).
Education: Percent of population age 25 and over with: High school diploma (including GED) or higher: 97.3% (2007); Bachelor's degree or higher: 65.0% (2007); Master's degree or higher: 25.3% (2007).
Housing: Homeownership rate: 98.3% (2007); Median home value: $640,671 (2007); Median rent: $575 per month (2000); Median age of housing: 18 years (2000).
Safety: Violent crime rate: 10.1 per 10,000 population; Property crime rate: 133.7 per 10,000 population (2006).
Transportation: Commute to work: 81.3% car, 6.5% public transportation, 0.2% walk, 11.4% work from home (2000); Travel time to work: 14.2% less than 15 minutes, 29.8% 15 to 30 minutes, 28.0% 30 to 45 minutes, 12.3% 45 to 60 minutes, 15.7% 60 minutes or more (2000)

LAKE BARRINGTON (village). Covers a land area of 5.336 square miles and a water area of 0.232 square miles. Located at 42.21° N. Lat.; 88.16° W. Long. Elevation is 804 feet.

Population: 4,349 (1990); 4,757 (2000); 5,216 (2007); 5,528 (2012 projected); Race: 96.7% White, 0.4% Black, 1.4% Asian, 1.4% Hispanic of any race (2007); Density: 977.6 persons per square mile (2007); Average household size: 2.32 (2007); Median age: 51.6 (2007); Males per 100 females: 93.4 (2007); Marriage status: 17.4% never married, 68.7% now married, 5.9% widowed, 8.0% divorced (2000); Foreign born: 5.1% (2000); Ancestry (includes multiple ancestries): 29.7% German, 18.7% Irish, 14.0% English, 11.6% Italian, 11.4% Polish (2000).
Economy: Single-family building permits issued: 9 (2007); Multi-family building permits issued: 0 (2007); Employment by occupation: 41.0% management, 18.8% professional, 5.8% services, 28.3% sales, 0.0% farming, 2.5% construction, 3.7% production (2000).
Income: Per capita income: $67,068 (2007); Median household income: $111,859 (2007); Average household income: $155,756 (2007); Percent of households with income of $100,000 or more: 56.6% (2007); Poverty rate: 2.0% (2000).
Education: Percent of population age 25 and over with: High school diploma (including GED) or higher: 97.8% (2007); Bachelor's degree or higher: 57.0% (2007); Master's degree or higher: 24.2% (2007).
Housing: Homeownership rate: 96.4% (2007); Median home value: $427,119 (2007); Median rent: $1,406 per month (2000); Median age of housing: 18 years (2000).
Transportation: Commute to work: 82.8% car, 7.6% public transportation, 0.3% walk, 8.1% work from home (2000); Travel time to work: 15.4% less than 15 minutes, 19.1% 15 to 30 minutes, 20.7% 30 to 45 minutes, 20.6% 45 to 60 minutes, 24.1% 60 minutes or more (2000)

LAKE BLUFF (village). Covers a land area of 4.059 square miles and a water area of 0.003 square miles. Located at 42.28° N. Lat.; 87.84° W. Long. Elevation is 659 feet.

History: Lake Bluff began in 1874 as a Methodist camp-meeting ground.
Population: 5,650 (1990); 6,056 (2000); 6,325 (2007); 6,494 (2012 projected); Race: 92.9% White, 0.4% Black, 5.6% Asian, 1.5% Hispanic of any race (2007); Density: 1,558.3 persons per square mile (2007); Average household size: 2.92 (2007); Median age: 39.1 (2007); Males per 100 females: 92.8 (2007); Marriage status: 14.9% never married, 74.3% now married, 4.6% widowed, 6.1% divorced (2000); Foreign born: 7.4% (2000); Ancestry (includes multiple ancestries): 28.4% German, 22.7% Irish, 18.2% English, 7.0% Other groups, 6.7% Italian (2000).
Economy: Single-family building permits issued: 10 (2007); Multi-family building permits issued: 0 (2007); Employment by occupation: 31.2% management, 29.5% professional, 5.8% services, 28.9% sales, 0.0% farming, 1.8% construction, 2.6% production (2000).
Income: Per capita income: $59,077 (2007); Median household income: $124,620 (2007); Average household income: $172,512 (2007); Percent of households with income of $100,000 or more: 62.0% (2007); Poverty rate: 1.1% (2000).
Education: Percent of population age 25 and over with: High school diploma (including GED) or higher: 98.7% (2007); Bachelor's degree or higher: 73.3% (2007); Master's degree or higher: 30.8% (2007).

School District(s)

Lake Bluff ESD 65 (KG-08)
2005-06 Enrollment: 1,054 . . . . (847) 234-9400
Housing: Homeownership rate: 90.6% (2007); Median home value: $661,694 (2007); Median rent: $782 per month (2000); Median age of housing: 34 years (2000).
Safety: Violent crime rate: 3.2 per 10,000 population; Property crime rate: 120.0 per 10,000 population (2006).

Transportation: Commute to work: 79.5% car, 9.6% public transportation, 1.1% walk, 9.8% work from home (2000); Travel time to work: 29.4% less than 15 minutes, 23.5% 15 to 30 minutes, 20.2% 30 to 45 minutes, 7.1% 45 to 60 minutes, 19.9% 60 minutes or more (2000)

Additional Information Contacts

Village of Lake Bluff . . . . (847) 234-0774
http://www.lakebluff.org

LAKE CATHERINE (CDP). Covers a land area of 1.064 square miles and a water area of 0.484 square miles. Located at 42.48° N. Lat.; 88.12° W. Long. Elevation is 748 feet.

Population: 1,432 (1990); 1,490 (2000); 2,119 (2007); 2,526 (2012 projected); Race: 96.8% White, 1.2% Black, 0.0% Asian, 4.2% Hispanic of any race (2007); Density: 1,991.4 persons per square mile (2007); Average household size: 2.53 (2007); Median age: 40.8 (2007); Males per 100 females: 105.1 (2007); Marriage status: 20.4% never married, 64.3% now married, 6.3% widowed, 9.0% divorced (2000); Foreign born: 7.4% (2000); Ancestry (includes multiple ancestries): 28.1% German, 20.8% Irish, 10.9% English, 7.8% Other groups, 6.0% Italian (2000).

Economy: Employment by occupation: 15.5% management, 12.3% professional, 15.2% services, 27.6% sales, 0.0% farming, 17.3% construction, 12.1% production (2000).

Income: Per capita income: $28,531 (2007); Median household income: $66,621 (2007); Average household income: $72,059 (2007); Percent of households with income of $100,000 or more: 23.8% (2007); Poverty rate: 8.5% (2000).

Education: Percent of population age 25 and over with: High school diploma (including GED) or higher: 86.4% (2007); Bachelor's degree or higher: 14.6% (2007); Master's degree or higher: 3.2% (2007).

Housing: Homeownership rate: 85.9% (2007); Median home value: $206,076 (2007); Median rent: $744 per month (2000); Median age of housing: 45 years (2000).

Transportation: Commute to work: 90.5% car, 3.5% public transportation, 0.0% walk, 5.9% work from home (2000); Travel time to work: 22.6% less than 15 minutes, 21.4% 15 to 30 minutes, 19.7% 30 to 45 minutes, 12.9% 45 to 60 minutes, 23.4% 60 minutes or more (2000)

LAKE FOREST (city). Covers a land area of 16.865 square miles and a water area of 0.048 square miles. Located at 42.23° N. Lat.; 87.85° W. Long. Elevation is 689 feet.

History: Named for Lake Michigan and for the forests in the area. Lake Forest was laid out in 1856 by David Hotchkiss, a St. Louis landscape architect, for a company of Chicago businessmen who had purchased land here. The town grew around Lake Forest College, opened in 1857.

Population: 17,966 (1990); 20,059 (2000); 21,289 (2007); 22,109 (2012 projected); Race: 91.8% White, 1.4% Black, 4.8% Asian, 2.5% Hispanic of any race (2007); Density: 1,262.3 persons per square mile (2007); Average household size: 2.96 (2007); Median age: 41.5 (2007); Males per 100 females: 91.2 (2007); Marriage status: 20.6% never married, 69.4% now married, 5.1% widowed, 5.0% divorced (2000); Foreign born: 6.5% (2000); Ancestry (includes multiple ancestries): 22.3% German, 20.0% Irish, 16.4% English, 8.4% Italian, 8.0% Other groups (2000).

Economy: Single-family building permits issued: 30 (2007); Multi-family building permits issued: 45 (2007); Employment by occupation: 35.8% management, 25.5% professional, 6.2% services, 28.8% sales, 0.1% farming, 2.0% construction, 1.5% production (2000).

Income: Per capita income: $73,439 (2007); Median household income: $150,795 (2007); Average household income: $215,976 (2007); Percent of households with income of $100,000 or more: 65.0% (2007); Poverty rate: 2.1% (2000).

Taxes: Total city taxes per capita: $1,440 (2006); City property taxes per capita: $1,105 (2006).

Education: Percent of population age 25 and over with: High school diploma (including GED) or higher: 97.3% (2007); Bachelor's degree or higher: 74.0% (2007); Master's degree or higher: 34.1% (2007).

School District(s)

Lake Forest CHSD 115 (09-12)
2005-06 Enrollment: 1,738 . . . . (847) 234-3600
Lake Forest SD 67 (PK-08)
2005-06 Enrollment: 2,304 . . . . (847) 234-6010
Rondout SD 72 (KG-08)
2005-06 Enrollment: 139 . . . . (847) 362-2021

Four-year College(s)

Lake Forest College (Private, Not-for-profit)
Fall 2007 Enrollment: 1,456 . . . . (847) 234-3100
2007-08 Tuition: In-state $30,964; Out-of-state $30,964
Lake Forest Graduate School of Management (Private, Not-for-profit)
Fall 2007 Enrollment: 750 . . . . (847) 234-5005

Housing: Homeownership rate: 87.3% (2007); Median home value: $839,521 (2007); Median rent: $908 per month (2000); Median age of housing: 32 years (2000).

Hospitals: Lake Forest Hospital (261 beds)

Safety: Violent crime rate: 0.9 per 10,000 population; Property crime rate: 73.9 per 10,000 population (2006).

Transportation: Commute to work: 72.4% car, 12.0% public transportation, 4.9% walk, 9.9% work from home (2000); Travel time to work: 25.2% less than 15 minutes, 30.8% 15 to 30 minutes, 17.2% 30 to 45 minutes, 9.7% 45 to 60 minutes, 17.1% 60 minutes or more (2000)

Additional Information Contacts

City of Lake Forest . . . . (847) 234-2600
http://www.cityoflakeforest.com
Lake Forest/Lake Bluff Chamber of Commerce . . . . (847) 234-4282
http://www.lakeforestonline.com

LAKE VILLA (village). Covers a land area of 5.724 square miles and a water area of 0.754 square miles. Located at 42.41° N. Lat.; 88.08° W. Long. Elevation is 791 feet.

History: Lake Villa grew around a railroad station and the resort trade. It was the site of the Allendale Farm School, an experimental community founded in 1897 as a home for neglected boys.

Population: 3,273 (1990); 5,864 (2000); 7,426 (2007); 8,405 (2012 projected); Race: 89.7% White, 3.4% Black, 2.7% Asian, 4.5% Hispanic of any race (2007); Density: 1,297.3 persons per square mile (2007); Average household size: 2.86 (2007); Median age: 33.8 (2007); Males per 100 females: 100.1 (2007); Marriage status: 23.4% never married, 65.8% now married, 5.1% widowed, 5.7% divorced (2000); Foreign born: 4.6% (2000); Ancestry (includes multiple ancestries): 32.6% German, 17.9% Irish, 11.4% Polish, 10.8% Italian, 10.1% Other groups (2000).

Economy: Single-family building permits issued: 31 (2007); Multi-family building permits issued: 0 (2007); Employment by occupation: 24.5% management, 21.6% professional, 11.1% services, 26.7% sales, 0.0% farming, 8.7% construction, 7.4% production (2000).

Income: Per capita income: $30,953 (2007); Median household income: $73,947 (2007); Average household income: $88,320 (2007); Percent of households with income of $100,000 or more: 31.8% (2007); Poverty rate: 3.7% (2000).

Education: Percent of population age 25 and over with: High school diploma (including GED) or higher: 92.8% (2007); Bachelor's degree or higher: 36.6% (2007); Master's degree or higher: 9.6% (2007).

School District(s)

CHSD 117 (03-12)
2005-06 Enrollment: 2,629 . . . . (847) 838-7170
Lake Villa CCSD 41 (PK-08)
2005-06 Enrollment: 3,362 . . . . (847) 356-2385

Housing: Homeownership rate: 77.3% (2007); Median home value: $288,995 (2007); Median rent: $750 per month (2000); Median age of housing: 10 years (2000).

Safety: Violent crime rate: 83.6 per 10,000 population; Property crime rate: 149.6 per 10,000 population (2006).

Transportation: Commute to work: 94.0% car, 2.2% public transportation, 1.6% walk, 2.2% work from home (2000); Travel time to work: 16.4% less than 15 minutes, 24.2% 15 to 30 minutes, 27.5% 30 to 45 minutes, 15.9% 45 to 60 minutes, 16.0% 60 minutes or more (2000)

Additional Information Contacts

Illinois Women's Chamber of Commerce . . . . (847) 269-6395
http://www.illinoiswomenschamber.com
Village of Lake Villa . . . . (847) 356-6100
http://www.lake-villa.org

LAKE ZURICH (village). Covers a land area of 6.484 square miles and a water area of 0.359 square miles. Located at 42.19° N. Lat.; 88.08° W. Long. Elevation is 876 feet.

Population: 15,857 (1990); 18,104 (2000); 20,274 (2007); 21,643 (2012 projected); Race: 89.1% White, 0.8% Black, 5.6% Asian, 7.6% Hispanic of any race (2007); Density: 3,127.0 persons per square mile (2007); Average household size: 3.16 (2007); Median age: 35.3 (2007); Males per 100 females: 100.2 (2007); Marriage status: 19.9% never married, 71.1% now

married, 2.4% widowed, 6.6% divorced (2000); Foreign born: 8.8% (2000); Ancestry (includes multiple ancestries): 31.0% German, 16.5% Polish, 16.5% Irish, 12.8% Other groups, 10.6% Italian (2000).
Economy: Single-family building permits issued: 28 (2007); Multi-family building permits issued: 0 (2007); Employment by occupation: 23.9% management, 21.2% professional, 9.3% services, 31.8% sales, 0.1% farming, 6.3% construction, 7.3% production (2000).
Income: Per capita income: $35,800 (2007); Median household income: $96,015 (2007); Average household income: $112,990 (2007); Percent of households with income of $100,000 or more: 47.1% (2007); Poverty rate: 2.5% (2000).
Education: Percent of population age 25 and over with: High school diploma (including GED) or higher: 94.0% (2007); Bachelor's degree or higher: 44.2% (2007); Master's degree or higher: 13.6% (2007).

School District(s)

Lake Zurich CUSD 95 (PK-12)
2005-06 Enrollment: 6,557 . . . . (847) 438-2831
Housing: Homeownership rate: 91.4% (2007); Median home value: $317,769 (2007); Median rent: $725 per month (2000); Median age of housing: 19 years (2000).
Safety: Violent crime rate: 4.5 per 10,000 population; Property crime rate: 166.6 per 10,000 population (2006).
Transportation: Commute to work: 90.7% car, 3.1% public transportation, 1.5% walk, 4.4% work from home (2000); Travel time to work: 18.9% less than 15 minutes, 25.6% 15 to 30 minutes, 30.9% 30 to 45 minutes, 13.8% 45 to 60 minutes, 10.8% 60 minutes or more (2000)
Additional Information Contacts
Lake Zurich Area Chamber of Commerce . . . . (847) 438-5572
http://www.lzacc.com
Village of Lake Zurich . . . . (847) 438-5141
http://www.volz.org

LIBERTYVILLE (village). Covers a land area of 8.772 square miles and a water area of 0.291 square miles. Located at 42.28° N. Lat.; 87.96° W. Long. Elevation is 699 feet.
History: Named for the community's patriotism. Daniel Webster (1782-1852) was one of the first purchasers of land in Independence Grove, which changed its name to Libertyville in 1837 when the post office was established. Settlers and vacationists were attracted by the mineral springs in the area.
Population: 20,114 (1990); 20,742 (2000); 22,166 (2007); 23,115 (2012 projected); Race: 89.7% White, 1.2% Black, 6.1% Asian, 3.4% Hispanic of any race (2007); Density: 2,526.9 persons per square mile (2007); Average household size: 2.81 (2007); Median age: 40.5 (2007); Males per 100 females: 94.2 (2007); Marriage status: 21.4% never married, 65.6% now married, 5.8% widowed, 7.2% divorced (2000); Foreign born: 10.3% (2000); Ancestry (includes multiple ancestries): 27.1% German, 18.3% Irish, 12.5% English, 10.0% Other groups, 9.5% Italian (2000).
Economy: Single-family building permits issued: 48 (2007); Multi-family building permits issued: 0 (2007); Employment by occupation: 25.7% management, 29.3% professional, 7.7% services, 27.5% sales, 0.0% farming, 3.5% construction, 6.3% production (2000).
Income: Per capita income: $45,938 (2007); Median household income: $98,885 (2007); Average household income: $127,238 (2007); Percent of households with income of $100,000 or more: 49.4% (2007); Poverty rate: 3.5% (2000).
Education: Percent of population age 25 and over with: High school diploma (including GED) or higher: 94.1% (2007); Bachelor's degree or higher: 56.2% (2007); Master's degree or higher: 23.5% (2007).

School District(s)

CHSD 128 (09-12)
2005-06 Enrollment: 3,214 . . . . (847) 367-3159
Libertyville SD 70 (PK-08)
2005-06 Enrollment: 2,641 . . . . (847) 362-9695
Spec Educ Dist Lake County/Sedol (PK-12)
2005-06 Enrollment: 518 . . . . (847) 548-8470
Housing: Homeownership rate: 81.8% (2007); Median home value: $365,904 (2007); Median rent: $771 per month (2000); Median age of housing: 27 years (2000).
Hospitals: Condell Medical Center (305 beds)
Safety: Violent crime rate: 4.1 per 10,000 population; Property crime rate: 164.1 per 10,000 population (2006).
Transportation: Commute to work: 87.7% car, 5.7% public transportation, 1.7% walk, 4.4% work from home (2000); Travel time to work: 29.0% less than 15 minutes, 34.8% 15 to 30 minutes, 16.7% 30 to 45 minutes, 8.6% 45 to 60 minutes, 10.8% 60 minutes or more (2000)
Additional Information Contacts
GLMV Area Chamber of Commerce . . . . (847) 680-0750
http://www.glmvchamber.org
Village of Libertyville . . . . (847) 362-2430
http://www.libertyville.com/index.htm

LINCOLNSHIRE (village). Covers a land area of 4.406 square miles and a water area of 0.029 square miles. Located at 42.19° N. Lat.; 87.91° W. Long. Elevation is 659 feet.
Population: 5,497 (1990); 6,108 (2000); 6,975 (2007); 7,529 (2012 projected); Race: 91.8% White, 0.6% Black, 5.5% Asian, 3.2% Hispanic of any race (2007); Density: 1,583.0 persons per square mile (2007); Average household size: 2.80 (2007); Median age: 46.6 (2007); Males per 100 females: 94.6 (2007); Marriage status: 14.7% never married, 77.7% now married, 4.8% widowed, 2.9% divorced (2000); Foreign born: 10.6% (2000); Ancestry (includes multiple ancestries): 21.4% German, 13.5% Irish, 10.3% Polish, 8.8% Other groups, 8.7% English (2000).
Economy: Single-family building permits issued: 10 (2007); Multi-family building permits issued: 134 (2007); Employment by occupation: 36.4% management, 22.5% professional, 3.7% services, 32.6% sales, 0.1% farming, 1.0% construction, 3.8% production (2000).
Income: Per capita income: $67,969 (2007); Median household income: $146,540 (2007); Average household income: $187,839 (2007); Percent of households with income of $100,000 or more: 67.1% (2007); Poverty rate: 1.6% (2000).
Education: Percent of population age 25 and over with: High school diploma (including GED) or higher: 96.2% (2007); Bachelor's degree or higher: 64.3% (2007); Master's degree or higher: 26.8% (2007).

School District(s)

Adlai E Stevenson HSD 125 (09-12)
2005-06 Enrollment: 4,510 . . . . (847) 634-4000
Lincolnshire-Prairieview SD 103 (KG-08)
2005-06 Enrollment: 1,688 . . . . (847) 295-4030
Housing: Homeownership rate: 96.0% (2007); Median home value: $595,558 (2007); Median rent: $1,058 per month (2000); Median age of housing: 23 years (2000).
Safety: Violent crime rate: 5.8 per 10,000 population; Property crime rate: 254.3 per 10,000 population (2006).
Transportation: Commute to work: 85.7% car, 7.9% public transportation, 1.0% walk, 4.9% work from home (2000); Travel time to work: 20.7% less than 15 minutes, 34.1% 15 to 30 minutes, 22.5% 30 to 45 minutes, 10.8% 45 to 60 minutes, 12.0% 60 minutes or more (2000)
Additional Information Contacts
Greater Lincolnshire Chamber of Commerce . . . . (847) 793-2409
http://www.lincolnshirechamber.org
Village of Lincolnshire . . . . (847) 883-8600
http://www.village.lincolnshire.il.us

LINDENHURST (village). Covers a land area of 3.721 square miles and a water area of 0.361 square miles. Located at 42.41° N. Lat.; 88.02° W. Long. Elevation is 797 feet.
Population: 8,799 (1990); 12,539 (2000); 14,559 (2007); 15,827 (2012 projected); Race: 88.9% White, 2.0% Black, 5.0% Asian, 6.2% Hispanic of any race (2007); Density: 3,912.3 persons per square mile (2007); Average household size: 2.93 (2007); Median age: 35.1 (2007); Males per 100 females: 97.5 (2007); Marriage status: 19.4% never married, 71.7% now married, 3.1% widowed, 5.8% divorced (2000); Foreign born: 5.3% (2000); Ancestry (includes multiple ancestries): 30.4% German, 18.0% Irish, 13.7% Polish, 9.5% Other groups, 9.1% English (2000).
Economy: Single-family building permits issued: 44 (2007); Multi-family building permits issued: 0 (2007); Employment by occupation: 20.2% management, 22.6% professional, 8.3% services, 31.0% sales, 0.0% farming, 8.4% construction, 9.5% production (2000).
Income: Per capita income: $32,053 (2007); Median household income: $84,127 (2007); Average household income: $93,507 (2007); Percent of households with income of $100,000 or more: 35.8% (2007); Poverty rate: 1.6% (2000).
Education: Percent of population age 25 and over with: High school diploma (including GED) or higher: 93.9% (2007); Bachelor's degree or higher: 38.7% (2007); Master's degree or higher: 9.9% (2007).

School District(s)

Lake Villa CCSD 41 (PK-08)
2005-06 Enrollment: 3,362 . . . . (847) 356-2385

Millburn CCSD 24 (PK-08)
2005-06 Enrollment: 1,537 . . . . (847) 356-8331
Housing: Homeownership rate: 89.9% (2007); Median home value: $234,766 (2007); Median rent: $862 per month (2000); Median age of housing: 16 years (2000).
Safety: Violent crime rate: 3.5 per 10,000 population; Property crime rate: 95.1 per 10,000 population (2006).
Transportation: Commute to work: 94.0% car, 1.1% public transportation, 0.5% walk, 3.9% work from home (2000); Travel time to work: 14.5% less than 15 minutes, 27.2% 15 to 30 minutes, 27.6% 30 to 45 minutes, 15.4% 45 to 60 minutes, 15.4% 60 minutes or more (2000)
Additional Information Contacts
Lindenhurst Lake Villa Chamber . . . . (847) 356-2146
http://www.llvchamber.com
Village of Lindenhurst . . . . (847) 356-8252
http://lindenhurstil.org

LONG GROVE (village). Aka Longgrove. Covers a land area of 12.275 square miles and a water area of 0.155 square miles. Located at 42.20° N. Lat.; 88.00° W. Long. Elevation is 732 feet.
Population: 4,541 (1990); 6,735 (2000); 7,684 (2007); 8,237 (2012 projected); Race: 86.6% White, 1.0% Black, 10.6% Asian, 3.6% Hispanic of any race (2007); Density: 626.0 persons per square mile (2007); Average household size: 3.42 (2007); Median age: 42.3 (2007); Males per 100 females: 99.6 (2007); Marriage status: 19.6% never married, 75.1% now married, 2.7% widowed, 2.5% divorced (2000); Foreign born: 8.3% (2000); Ancestry (includes multiple ancestries): 21.8% German, 13.3% Irish, 11.8% Other groups, 10.5% Polish, 9.6% Italian (2000).
Economy: Single-family building permits issued: 13 (2007); Multi-family building permits issued: 0 (2007); Employment by occupation: 34.2% management, 23.6% professional, 4.4% services, 30.5% sales, 0.0% farming, 3.1% construction, 4.1% production (2000).
Income: Per capita income: $68,087 (2007); Median household income: $174,399 (2007); Average household income: $229,827 (2007); Percent of households with income of $100,000 or more: 72.2% (2007); Poverty rate: 2.6% (2000).
Education: Percent of population age 25 and over with: High school diploma (including GED) or higher: 97.2% (2007); Bachelor's degree or higher: 57.3% (2007); Master's degree or higher: 23.6% (2007).

School District(s)

Kildeer Countryside CCSD 96 (PK-08)
2005-06 Enrollment: 3,432 . . . . (847) 459-4260
Housing: Homeownership rate: 96.5% (2007); Median home value: $739,874 (2007); Median rent: $635 per month (2000); Median age of housing: 15 years (2000).
Transportation: Commute to work: 85.9% car, 5.8% public transportation, 0.0% walk, 8.0% work from home (2000); Travel time to work: 13.4% less than 15 minutes, 33.4% 15 to 30 minutes, 27.9% 30 to 45 minutes, 10.3% 45 to 60 minutes, 15.0% 60 minutes or more (2000)
Additional Information Contacts
Village of Long Grove . . . . (847) 634-9440
http://www.longgrove.net

LONG LAKE (CDP). Covers a land area of 1.051 square miles and a water area of 0.606 square miles. Located at 42.37° N. Lat.; 88.12° W. Long. Elevation is 751 feet.
Population: 2,743 (1990); 3,356 (2000); 4,051 (2007); 4,493 (2012 projected); Race: 89.1% White, 0.3% Black, 1.2% Asian, 19.7% Hispanic of any race (2007); Density: 3,854.6 persons per square mile (2007); Average household size: 2.93 (2007); Median age: 34.2 (2007); Males per 100 females: 108.5 (2007); Marriage status: 25.7% never married, 59.4% now married, 4.4% widowed, 10.5% divorced (2000); Foreign born: 6.4% (2000); Ancestry (includes multiple ancestries): 34.1% German, 15.8% Irish, 14.8% Polish, 14.3% Other groups, 9.4% United States or American (2000).
Economy: Employment by occupation: 11.7% management, 14.8% professional, 11.5% services, 22.1% sales, 0.0% farming, 21.2% construction, 18.7% production (2000).
Income: Per capita income: $24,332 (2007); Median household income: $65,308 (2007); Average household income: $71,374 (2007); Percent of households with income of $100,000 or more: 19.0% (2007); Poverty rate: 3.8% (2000).
Education: Percent of population age 25 and over with: High school diploma (including GED) or higher: 77.4% (2007); Bachelor's degree or higher: 11.2% (2007); Master's degree or higher: 2.2% (2007).
Housing: Homeownership rate: 80.3% (2007); Median home value: $174,544 (2007); Median rent: $698 per month (2000); Median age of housing: 47 years (2000).
Transportation: Commute to work: 96.2% car, 1.5% public transportation, 0.0% walk, 2.2% work from home (2000); Travel time to work: 16.3% less than 15 minutes, 22.8% 15 to 30 minutes, 24.1% 30 to 45 minutes, 20.0% 45 to 60 minutes, 16.8% 60 minutes or more (2000)

METTAWA (village). Covers a land area of 5.467 square miles and a water area of 0.026 square miles. Located at 42.24° N. Lat.; 87.91° W. Long. Elevation is 682 feet.
Population: 379 (1990); 367 (2000); 431 (2007); 475 (2012 projected); Race: 95.6% White, 0.0% Black, 2.8% Asian, 6.0% Hispanic of any race (2007); Density: 78.8 persons per square mile (2007); Average household size: 2.68 (2007); Median age: 47.1 (2007); Males per 100 females: 100.5 (2007); Marriage status: 19.2% never married, 70.3% now married, 4.9% widowed, 5.6% divorced (2000); Foreign born: 20.7% (2000); Ancestry (includes multiple ancestries): 27.2% German, 16.0% Other groups, 13.6% Irish, 7.7% Italian, 7.7% Scottish (2000).
Economy: Single-family building permits issued: 6 (2007); Multi-family building permits issued: 0 (2007); Employment by occupation: 28.8% management, 25.4% professional, 13.0% services, 22.0% sales, 0.0% farming, 0.6% construction, 10.2% production (2000).
Income: Per capita income: $71,731 (2007); Median household income: $131,944 (2007); Average household income: $190,342 (2007); Percent of households with income of $100,000 or more: 59.0% (2007); Poverty rate: 4.6% (2000).
Education: Percent of population age 25 and over with: High school diploma (including GED) or higher: 93.7% (2007); Bachelor's degree or higher: 55.5% (2007); Master's degree or higher: 22.9% (2007).
Housing: Homeownership rate: 90.1% (2007); Median home value: $1 million+ (2007); Median rent: $925 per month (2000); Median age of housing: 20 years (2000).
Transportation: Commute to work: 75.1% car, 9.2% public transportation, 6.4% walk, 8.7% work from home (2000); Travel time to work: 25.3% less than 15 minutes, 37.3% 15 to 30 minutes, 19.6% 30 to 45 minutes, 6.3% 45 to 60 minutes, 11.4% 60 minutes or more (2000)

MUNDELEIN (village). Covers a land area of 8.623 square miles and a water area of 0.323 square miles. Located at 42.26° N. Lat.; 88.00° W. Long. Elevation is 735 feet.
History: Named for Cardinal George William Mundelein (1872-1939), Archbishop of Chicago. The community here developed around the Sheldon School of Business Administration and was called Area, a reflection of the school's motto of "Ability, Reliability, Endurance, and Action." When this school was replaced by a Catholic seminary, the town name was changed to Mundelein for George Cardinal Mundelein, Archbishop of Chicago.
Population: 22,023 (1990); 30,935 (2000); 33,805 (2007); 35,652 (2012 projected); Race: 70.7% White, 1.9% Black, 10.3% Asian, 32.5% Hispanic of any race (2007); Density: 3,920.3 persons per square mile (2007); Average household size: 3.20 (2007); Median age: 32.7 (2007); Males per 100 females: 104.0 (2007); Marriage status: 25.3% never married, 64.9% now married, 3.1% widowed, 6.7% divorced (2000); Foreign born: 23.8% (2000); Ancestry (includes multiple ancestries): 31.6% Other groups, 22.8% German, 13.9% Irish, 10.7% Polish, 7.5% Italian (2000).
Economy: Unemployment rate: 5.1% (4/2008); Total civilian labor force: 18,194 (4/2008); Single-family building permits issued: 406 (2007); Multi-family building permits issued: 0 (2007); Employment by occupation: 18.8% management, 22.4% professional, 12.8% services, 25.0% sales, 0.3% farming, 7.9% construction, 12.8% production (2000).
Income: Per capita income: $29,283 (2007); Median household income: $78,113 (2007); Average household income: $93,311 (2007); Percent of households with income of $100,000 or more: 33.2% (2007); Poverty rate: 4.6% (2000).
Education: Percent of population age 25 and over with: High school diploma (including GED) or higher: 82.5% (2007); Bachelor's degree or higher: 39.2% (2007); Master's degree or higher: 13.3% (2007).

School District(s)

Diamond Lake SD 76 (PK-08)
2005-06 Enrollment: 1,241 . . . . (847) 566-9221
Fremont SD 79 (PK-08)
2005-06 Enrollment: 1,877 . . . . (847) 566-0169
Mundelein Cons HSD 120 (09-12)
2005-06 Enrollment: 2,269 . . . . (847) 949-2200

Mundelein ESD 75 (PK-08)
2005-06 Enrollment: 2,175 . . . . (847) 949-2700
Spec Educ Dist Lake County/Sedol (PK-12)
2005-06 Enrollment: 518 . . . . (847) 548-8470

Four-year College(s)

University of Saint Mary of the Lake (Private, Not-for-profit, Roman Catholic)
Fall 2007 Enrollment: 241 . . . . (847) 566-6401

Housing: Homeownership rate: 79.7% (2007); Median home value: $229,628 (2007); Median rent: $726 per month (2000); Median age of housing: 21 years (2000).
Safety: Violent crime rate: 13.4 per 10,000 population; Property crime rate: 173.0 per 10,000 population (2006).
Transportation: Commute to work: 90.5% car, 4.1% public transportation, 0.8% walk, 3.3% work from home (2000); Travel time to work: 24.6% less than 15 minutes, 31.4% 15 to 30 minutes, 23.0% 30 to 45 minutes, 11.3% 45 to 60 minutes, 9.6% 60 minutes or more (2000)
Additional Information Contacts
Village of Mundelein. . . . . (847) 949-3200
http://www.mundelein.org

NORTH BARRINGTON (village). Covers a land area of 4.389 square miles and a water area of 0.197 square miles. Located at 42.20° N. Lat.; 88.13° W. Long. Elevation is 791 feet.
Population: 2,013 (1990); 2,918 (2000); 3,305 (2007); 3,553 (2012 projected); Race: 95.3% White, 0.3% Black, 2.3% Asian, 3.2% Hispanic of any race (2007); Density: 753.1 persons per square mile (2007); Average household size: 2.89 (2007); Median age: 44.7 (2007); Males per 100 females: 97.5 (2007); Marriage status: 13.8% never married, 81.1% now married, 2.0% widowed, 3.1% divorced (2000); Foreign born: 6.9% (2000); Ancestry (includes multiple ancestries): 26.3% German, 21.7% Irish, 12.3% Italian, 12.0% English, 10.1% Polish (2000).
Economy: Single-family building permits issued: 7 (2007); Multi-family building permits issued: 0 (2007); Employment by occupation: 37.1% management, 26.8% professional, 2.7% services, 27.4% sales, 0.0% farming, 3.0% construction, 2.9% production (2000).
Income: Per capita income: $80,572 (2007); Median household income: $164,552 (2007); Average household income: $233,179 (2007); Percent of households with income of $100,000 or more: 73.4% (2007); Poverty rate: 2.8% (2000).
Education: Percent of population age 25 and over with: High school diploma (including GED) or higher: 98.4% (2007); Bachelor's degree or higher: 61.8% (2007); Master's degree or higher: 22.4% (2007).
Housing: Homeownership rate: 97.5% (2007); Median home value: $730,385 (2007); Median rent: $1,563 per month (2000); Median age of housing: 19 years (2000).
Transportation: Commute to work: 79.0% car, 10.6% public transportation, 0.0% walk, 9.5% work from home (2000); Travel time to work: 15.0% less than 15 minutes, 23.8% 15 to 30 minutes, 26.1% 30 to 45 minutes, 13.3% 45 to 60 minutes, 21.8% 60 minutes or more (2000)

NORTH CHICAGO (city). Covers a land area of 7.832 square miles and a water area of 0.013 square miles. Located at 42.32° N. Lat.; 87.85° W. Long. Elevation is 659 feet.
History: Named for its location north of Chicago. A sit-down strike at a steel plant here in 1937 led to a U.S. Supreme Court decision (1939) ruling sit-down strikes illegal. Incorporated 1895.
Population: 35,785 (1990); 35,918 (2000); 32,137 (2007); 31,004 (2012 projected); Race: 43.4% White, 36.2% Black, 4.6% Asian, 25.8% Hispanic of any race (2007); Density: 4,103.5 persons per square mile (2007); Average household size: 4.44 (2007); Median age: 23.2 (2007); Males per 100 females: 149.4 (2007); Marriage status: 51.3% never married, 39.5% now married, 2.8% widowed, 6.4% divorced (2000); Foreign born: 12.9% (2000); Ancestry (includes multiple ancestries): 51.9% Other groups, 10.0% German, 7.7% Irish, 4.0% English, 3.5% United States or American (2000).
Economy: Unemployment rate: 9.8% (4/2008); Total civilian labor force: 9,784 (4/2008); Single-family building permits issued: 4 (2007); Multi-family building permits issued: 0 (2007); Employment by occupation: 10.9% management, 14.3% professional, 22.3% services, 26.8% sales, 0.4% farming, 5.3% construction, 20.1% production (2000).
Income: Per capita income: $15,224 (2007); Median household income: $40,978 (2007); Average household income: $51,281 (2007); Percent of households with income of $100,000 or more: 8.2% (2007); Poverty rate: 15.1% (2000).
Education: Percent of population age 25 and over with: High school diploma (including GED) or higher: 75.2% (2007); Bachelor's degree or higher: 15.5% (2007); Master's degree or higher: 5.9% (2007).

School District(s)

North Chicago SD 187 (PK-12)
2005-06 Enrollment: 4,323 . . . . (847) 689-8150

Four-year College(s)

Rosalind Franklin University of Medicine and Science (Private, Not-for-profit)
Fall 2007 Enrollment: 1,729. . . . . (847) 578-3000

Housing: Homeownership rate: 39.2% (2007); Median home value: $144,096 (2007); Median rent: $595 per month (2000); Median age of housing: 34 years (2000).
Hospitals: North Chicago Veterans Affairs Medical Center (1101 beds)
Safety: Violent crime rate: 77.6 per 10,000 population; Property crime rate: 213.6 per 10,000 population (2006).
Transportation: Commute to work: 48.6% car, 1.4% public transportation, 27.2% walk, 6.6% work from home (2000); Travel time to work: 61.3% less than 15 minutes, 22.1% 15 to 30 minutes, 9.0% 30 to 45 minutes, 3.9% 45 to 60 minutes, 3.6% 60 minutes or more (2000)
Additional Information Contacts
City of North Chicago. . . . . (847) 596-8600
http://www.northchicago.org

OLD MILL CREEK (village). Aka Mill Creek. Covers a land area of 10.113 square miles and a water area of 0.119 square miles. Located at 42.42° N. Lat.; 87.98° W. Long. Elevation is 705 feet.
Population: 143 (1990); 251 (2000); 333 (2007); 384 (2012 projected); Race: 80.5% White, 3.6% Black, 9.9% Asian, 3.9% Hispanic of any race (2007); Density: 32.9 persons per square mile (2007); Average household size: 2.49 (2007); Median age: 40.4 (2007); Males per 100 females: 101.8 (2007); Marriage status: 30.3% never married, 56.4% now married, 5.1% widowed, 8.1% divorced (2000); Foreign born: 12.2% (2000); Ancestry (includes multiple ancestries): 22.8% Irish, 22.4% German, 16.8% Other groups, 11.6% English, 11.2% French (except Basque) (2000).
Economy: Single-family building permits issued: 0 (2007); Multi-family building permits issued: 0 (2007); Employment by occupation: 25.4% management, 22.5% professional, 13.3% services, 24.3% sales, 4.0% farming, 7.5% construction, 2.9% production (2000).
Income: Per capita income: $55,571 (2007); Median household income: $91,304 (2007); Average household income: $138,097 (2007); Percent of households with income of $100,000 or more: 44.0% (2007); Poverty rate: 2.7% (2000).
Education: Percent of population age 25 and over with: High school diploma (including GED) or higher: 95.0% (2007); Bachelor's degree or higher: 40.8% (2007); Master's degree or higher: 13.9% (2007).
Housing: Homeownership rate: 61.9% (2007); Median home value: $403,125 (2007); Median rent: $933 per month (2000); Median age of housing: 48 years (2000).
Transportation: Commute to work: 85.9% car, 6.5% public transportation, 2.4% walk, 5.3% work from home (2000); Travel time to work: 27.3% less than 15 minutes, 26.7% 15 to 30 minutes, 17.4% 30 to 45 minutes, 5.6% 45 to 60 minutes, 23.0% 60 minutes or more (2000)

PARK CITY (city). Covers a land area of 1.150 square miles and a water area of 0 square miles. Located at 42.35° N. Lat.; 87.88° W. Long. Elevation is 699 feet.
Population: 4,705 (1990); 6,637 (2000); 6,329 (2007); 6,244 (2012 projected); Race: 49.9% White, 7.3% Black, 11.6% Asian, 52.6% Hispanic of any race (2007); Density: 5,505.1 persons per square mile (2007); Average household size: 2.62 (2007); Median age: 31.6 (2007); Males per 100 females: 103.3 (2007); Marriage status: 32.0% never married, 50.1% now married, 3.8% widowed, 14.0% divorced (2000); Foreign born: 30.7% (2000); Ancestry (includes multiple ancestries): 47.4% Other groups, 12.3% German, 7.4% Irish, 5.6% Polish, 3.9% United States or American (2000).
Economy: Single-family building permits issued: 0 (2007); Multi-family building permits issued: 0 (2007); Employment by occupation: 10.2% management, 12.8% professional, 19.4% services, 25.6% sales, 0.2% farming, 9.7% construction, 22.0% production (2000).
Income: Per capita income: $18,862 (2007); Median household income: $40,597 (2007); Average household income: $49,472 (2007); Percent of households with income of $100,000 or more: 6.4% (2007); Poverty rate: 8.0% (2000).

Education: Percent of population age 25 and over with: High school diploma (including GED) or higher: 70.9% (2007); Bachelor's degree or higher: 17.3% (2007); Master's degree or higher: 5.4% (2007).
Housing: Homeownership rate: 59.3% (2007); Median home value: $25,408 (2007); Median rent: $612 per month (2000); Median age of housing: 16 years (2000).
Safety: Violent crime rate: 19.2 per 10,000 population; Property crime rate: 271.6 per 10,000 population (2006).
Transportation: Commute to work: 94.5% car, 1.8% public transportation, 2.8% walk, 0.2% work from home (2000); Travel time to work: 25.8% less than 15 minutes, 37.6% 15 to 30 minutes, 22.0% 30 to 45 minutes, 4.9% 45 to 60 minutes, 9.7% 60 minutes or more (2000)

RIVERWOODS (village). Covers a land area of 3.989 square miles and a water area of 0.011 square miles. Located at 42.17° N. Lat.; 87.89° W. Long. Elevation is 656 feet.
Population: 3,000 (1990); 3,843 (2000); 4,211 (2007); 4,455 (2012 projected); Race: 91.9% White, 0.3% Black, 6.4% Asian, 2.8% Hispanic of any race (2007); Density: 1,055.6 persons per square mile (2007); Average household size: 3.04 (2007); Median age: 45.0 (2007); Males per 100 females: 93.3 (2007); Marriage status: 13.5% never married, 80.6% now married, 3.4% widowed, 2.5% divorced (2000); Foreign born: 13.8% (2000); Ancestry (includes multiple ancestries): 17.4% German, 11.9% Russian, 11.9% Irish, 11.6% Other groups, 10.6% United States or American (2000).
Economy: Single-family building permits issued: 0 (2007); Multi-family building permits issued: 0 (2007); Employment by occupation: 29.1% management, 32.9% professional, 3.6% services, 29.0% sales, 0.0% farming, 2.5% construction, 2.9% production (2000).
Income: Per capita income: $68,536 (2007); Median household income: $168,289 (2007); Average household income: $206,352 (2007); Percent of households with income of $100,000 or more: 70.9% (2007); Poverty rate: 3.2% (2000).
Education: Percent of population age 25 and over with: High school diploma (including GED) or higher: 94.4% (2007); Bachelor's degree or higher: 65.1% (2007); Master's degree or higher: 28.4% (2007).
Housing: Homeownership rate: 97.1% (2007); Median home value: $700,234 (2007); Median rent: $539 per month (2000); Median age of housing: 22 years (2000).
Transportation: Commute to work: 80.5% car, 8.8% public transportation, 0.2% walk, 10.5% work from home (2000); Travel time to work: 15.7% less than 15 minutes, 32.8% 15 to 30 minutes, 24.6% 30 to 45 minutes, 14.2% 45 to 60 minutes, 12.7% 60 minutes or more (2000)

ROUND LAKE (village). Covers a land area of 3.520 square miles and a water area of 0.064 square miles. Located at 42.35° N. Lat.; 88.10° W. Long. Elevation is 797 feet.
Population: 3,764 (1990); 5,842 (2000); 12,591 (2007); 16,700 (2012 projected); Race: 73.5% White, 2.8% Black, 3.6% Asian, 27.7% Hispanic of any race (2007); Density: 3,577.4 persons per square mile (2007); Average household size: 2.92 (2007); Median age: 32.4 (2007); Males per 100 females: 102.0 (2007); Marriage status: 23.2% never married, 60.2% now married, 5.8% widowed, 10.8% divorced (2000); Foreign born: 21.0% (2000); Ancestry (includes multiple ancestries): 32.3% Other groups, 25.6% German, 12.6% Irish, 12.3% Polish, 6.7% English (2000).
Economy: Single-family building permits issued: 33 (2007); Multi-family building permits issued: 0 (2007); Employment by occupation: 14.5% management, 14.3% professional, 14.9% services, 31.3% sales, 0.0% farming, 10.0% construction, 15.0% production (2000).
Income: Per capita income: $25,953 (2007); Median household income: $70,370 (2007); Average household income: $75,692 (2007); Percent of households with income of $100,000 or more: 24.8% (2007); Poverty rate: 6.8% (2000).
Education: Percent of population age 25 and over with: High school diploma (including GED) or higher: 76.2% (2007); Bachelor's degree or higher: 23.9% (2007); Master's degree or higher: 5.4% (2007).

School District(s)

Round Lake CUSD 116 (PK-12)
2005-06 Enrollment: 6,687 . . . . (847) 270-9000
Housing: Homeownership rate: 77.3% (2007); Median home value: $207,155 (2007); Median rent: $531 per month (2000); Median age of housing: 20 years (2000).
Transportation: Commute to work: 90.1% car, 4.7% public transportation, 2.2% walk, 2.7% work from home (2000); Travel time to work: 17.2% less than 15 minutes, 21.8% 15 to 30 minutes, 27.0% 30 to 45 minutes, 17.8% 45 to 60 minutes, 16.2% 60 minutes or more (2000)

Additional Information Contacts

Round Lake Chamber of Commerce . . . . (847) 546-2002
Village of Round Lake . . . . (847) 546-5400
http://www.eroundlake.com

ROUND LAKE BEACH (village). Covers a land area of 4.996 square miles and a water area of 0.100 square miles. Located at 42.37° N. Lat.; 88.08° W. Long. Elevation is 764 feet.
History: Named for a small round lake close to the city. Incorporated 1937.
Population: 17,438 (1990); 25,859 (2000); 29,354 (2007); 31,563 (2012 projected); Race: 63.4% White, 4.2% Black, 3.4% Asian, 43.7% Hispanic of any race (2007); Density: 5,876.0 persons per square mile (2007); Average household size: 3.57 (2007); Median age: 30.6 (2007); Males per 100 females: 101.4 (2007); Marriage status: 24.1% never married, 64.0% now married, 3.5% widowed, 8.4% divorced (2000); Foreign born: 21.5% (2000); Ancestry (includes multiple ancestries): 36.9% Other groups, 23.7% German, 13.8% Irish, 10.2% Polish, 6.2% English (2000).
Economy: Unemployment rate: 8.5% (4/2008); Total civilian labor force: 15,483 (4/2008); Single-family building permits issued: 8 (2007); Multi-family building permits issued: 0 (2007); Employment by occupation: 11.9% management, 11.4% professional, 15.3% services, 30.4% sales, 0.3% farming, 11.4% construction, 19.3% production (2000).
Income: Per capita income: $20,265 (2007); Median household income: $65,559 (2007); Average household income: $72,173 (2007); Percent of households with income of $100,000 or more: 19.8% (2007); Poverty rate: 5.1% (2000).
Taxes: Total city taxes per capita: $269 (2006); City property taxes per capita: $146 (2006).
Education: Percent of population age 25 and over with: High school diploma (including GED) or higher: 75.3% (2007); Bachelor's degree or higher: 16.5% (2007); Master's degree or higher: 4.3% (2007).

School District(s)

Grayslake CCSD 46 (PK-08)
2005-06 Enrollment: 4,108 . . . . (847) 223-3650
Housing: Homeownership rate: 85.3% (2007); Median home value: $172,795 (2007); Median rent: $696 per month (2000); Median age of housing: 20 years (2000).
Safety: Violent crime rate: 18.4 per 10,000 population; Property crime rate: 256.6 per 10,000 population (2006).
Transportation: Commute to work: 92.6% car, 3.0% public transportation, 0.9% walk, 2.4% work from home (2000); Travel time to work: 15.3% less than 15 minutes, 25.1% 15 to 30 minutes, 26.8% 30 to 45 minutes, 16.4% 45 to 60 minutes, 16.4% 60 minutes or more (2000)

Additional Information Contacts

Round Lake Area Chamber of Commerce & Industry . . . . . (847) 546-2002
http://www.rlchamber.org
Village of Round Lake Beach. . . . . (847) 546-2351
http://www.villageofroundlakebeach.com

ROUND LAKE HEIGHTS (village). Aka Indian Hills. Covers a land area of 0.612 square miles and a water area of 0 square miles. Located at 42.38° N. Lat.; 88.10° W. Long. Elevation is 784 feet.
Population: 1,251 (1990); 1,347 (2000); 1,591 (2007); 1,730 (2012 projected); Race: 75.5% White, 3.3% Black, 1.3% Asian, 27.8% Hispanic of any race (2007); Density: 2,599.3 persons per square mile (2007); Average household size: 3.11 (2007); Median age: 31.6 (2007); Males per 100 females: 101.9 (2007); Marriage status: 27.8% never married, 58.8% now married, 4.9% widowed, 8.6% divorced (2000); Foreign born: 11.4% (2000); Ancestry (includes multiple ancestries): 28.0% German, 25.7% Other groups, 17.5% Irish, 10.5% Polish, 7.6% Italian (2000).
Economy: Single-family building permits issued: 0 (2007); Multi-family building permits issued: 0 (2007); Employment by occupation: 8.4% management, 12.3% professional, 13.3% services, 33.3% sales, 0.0% farming, 13.9% construction, 18.7% production (2000).
Income: Per capita income: $21,933 (2007); Median household income: $60,082 (2007); Average household income: $68,288 (2007); Percent of households with income of $100,000 or more: 15.9% (2007); Poverty rate: 5.9% (2000).
Education: Percent of population age 25 and over with: High school diploma (including GED) or higher: 79.1% (2007); Bachelor's degree or higher: 12.8% (2007); Master's degree or higher: 3.4% (2007).

Housing: Homeownership rate: 84.7% (2007); Median home value: $141,272 (2007); Median rent: $709 per month (2000); Median age of housing: 41 years (2000).
Safety: Violent crime rate: 25.2 per 10,000 population; Property crime rate: 183.9 per 10,000 population (2006).
Transportation: Commute to work: 92.8% car, 2.4% public transportation, 1.9% walk, 2.8% work from home (2000); Travel time to work: 22.3% less than 15 minutes, 23.4% 15 to 30 minutes, 22.3% 30 to 45 minutes, 14.9% 45 to 60 minutes, 16.9% 60 minutes or more (2000)

ROUND LAKE PARK (village). Covers a land area of 2.990 square miles and a water area of 0.055 square miles. Located at 42.34° N. Lat.; 88.07° W. Long. Elevation is 791 feet.
History: Incorporated 1947.
Population: 4,034 (1990); 6,038 (2000); 9,518 (2007); 11,672 (2012 projected); Race: 73.7% White, 2.3% Black, 0.9% Asian, 35.9% Hispanic of any race (2007); Density: 3,183.3 persons per square mile (2007); Average household size: 2.78 (2007); Median age: 37.9 (2007); Males per 100 females: 98.3 (2007); Marriage status: 21.8% never married, 61.3% now married, 7.1% widowed, 9.8% divorced (2000); Foreign born: 15.4% (2000); Ancestry (includes multiple ancestries): 25.3% Other groups, 25.1% German, 15.4% Irish, 10.9% Polish, 7.0% English (2000).
Economy: Single-family building permits issued: 9 (2007); Multi-family building permits issued: 0 (2007); Employment by occupation: 7.8% management, 9.5% professional, 15.5% services, 30.2% sales, 0.4% farming, 15.0% construction, 21.6% production (2000).
Income: Per capita income: $20,023 (2007); Median household income: $47,799 (2007); Average household income: $55,611 (2007); Percent of households with income of $100,000 or more: 9.6% (2007); Poverty rate: 10.0% (2000).
Education: Percent of population age 25 and over with: High school diploma (including GED) or higher: 74.9% (2007); Bachelor's degree or higher: 10.7% (2007); Master's degree or higher: 3.0% (2007).
Housing: Homeownership rate: 87.7% (2007); Median home value: $165,031 (2007); Median rent: $677 per month (2000); Median age of housing: 20 years (2000).
Safety: Violent crime rate: 9.6 per 10,000 population; Property crime rate: 221.7 per 10,000 population (2006).
Transportation: Commute to work: 94.9% car, 2.7% public transportation, 0.4% walk, 1.3% work from home (2000); Travel time to work: 21.3% less than 15 minutes, 24.2% 15 to 30 minutes, 31.4% 30 to 45 minutes, 10.9% 45 to 60 minutes, 12.1% 60 minutes or more (2000)
Additional Information Contacts
Village of Round Lake Park . . . . (847) 546-2790
http://www.roundlakepark.us

THIRD LAKE (village). Covers a land area of 0.548 square miles and a water area of 0.252 square miles. Located at 42.36° N. Lat.; 88.00° W. Long. Elevation is 771 feet.
Population: 1,116 (1990); 1,355 (2000); 1,537 (2007); 1,639 (2012 projected); Race: 92.9% White, 0.7% Black, 3.1% Asian, 5.5% Hispanic of any race (2007); Density: 2,807.1 persons per square mile (2007); Average household size: 3.25 (2007); Median age: 37.3 (2007); Males per 100 females: 104.7 (2007); Marriage status: 22.3% never married, 70.1% now married, 3.2% widowed, 4.5% divorced (2000); Foreign born: 5.2% (2000); Ancestry (includes multiple ancestries): 34.7% German, 25.3% Irish, 13.3% Polish, 10.8% English, 5.7% United States or American (2000).
Economy: Single-family building permits issued: 0 (2007); Multi-family building permits issued: 0 (2007); Employment by occupation: 23.2% management, 33.1% professional, 7.4% services, 25.3% sales, 0.3% farming, 4.2% construction, 6.5% production (2000).
Income: Per capita income: $36,573 (2007); Median household income: $110,031 (2007); Average household income: $118,251 (2007); Percent of households with income of $100,000 or more: 56.9% (2007); Poverty rate: 2.7% (2000).
Education: Percent of population age 25 and over with: High school diploma (including GED) or higher: 97.4% (2007); Bachelor's degree or higher: 55.1% (2007); Master's degree or higher: 23.0% (2007).
Housing: Homeownership rate: 96.6% (2007); Median home value: $290,485 (2007); Median rent: $1,054 per month (2000); Median age of housing: 16 years (2000).
Transportation: Commute to work: 87.6% car, 4.0% public transportation, 3.8% walk, 4.0% work from home (2000); Travel time to work: 17.4% less than 15 minutes, 30.9% 15 to 30 minutes, 26.6% 30 to 45 minutes, 13.7% 45 to 60 minutes, 11.4% 60 minutes or more (2000)

TOWER LAKES (village). Covers a land area of 0.947 square miles and a water area of 0.120 square miles. Located at 42.23° N. Lat.; 88.15° W. Long. Elevation is 781 feet.
Population: 1,360 (1990); 1,310 (2000); 1,206 (2007); 1,211 (2012 projected); Race: 96.8% White, 0.3% Black, 0.9% Asian, 1.7% Hispanic of any race (2007); Density: 1,273.4 persons per square mile (2007); Average household size: 2.89 (2007); Median age: 42.4 (2007); Males per 100 females: 92.3 (2007); Marriage status: 18.8% never married, 74.8% now married, 3.2% widowed, 3.3% divorced (2000); Foreign born: 7.5% (2000); Ancestry (includes multiple ancestries): 32.9% German, 18.7% Irish, 14.3% English, 13.7% Italian, 11.3% Polish (2000).
Economy: Single-family building permits issued: 0 (2007); Multi-family building permits issued: 0 (2007); Employment by occupation: 30.8% management, 28.9% professional, 5.6% services, 28.9% sales, 0.0% farming, 2.7% construction, 3.0% production (2000).
Income: Per capita income: $57,678 (2007); Median household income: $141,750 (2007); Average household income: $166,811 (2007); Percent of households with income of $100,000 or more: 66.4% (2007); Poverty rate: 2.1% (2000).
Education: Percent of population age 25 and over with: High school diploma (including GED) or higher: 98.8% (2007); Bachelor's degree or higher: 64.9% (2007); Master's degree or higher: 28.2% (2007).
Housing: Homeownership rate: 98.6% (2007); Median home value: $514,167 (2007); Median rent: $1,125 per month (2000); Median age of housing: 32 years (2000).
Safety: Violent crime rate: 7.5 per 10,000 population; Property crime rate: 105.3 per 10,000 population (2006).
Transportation: Commute to work: 78.8% car, 11.4% public transportation, 1.3% walk, 8.0% work from home (2000); Travel time to work: 13.8% less than 15 minutes, 20.1% 15 to 30 minutes, 22.2% 30 to 45 minutes, 17.6% 45 to 60 minutes, 26.4% 60 minutes or more (2000)

VENETIAN VILLAGE (CDP). Covers a land area of 2.418 square miles and a water area of 0.696 square miles. Located at 42.39° N. Lat.; 88.04° W. Long. Elevation is 797 feet.
Population: 2,516 (1990); 3,082 (2000); 3,795 (2007); 4,247 (2012 projected); Race: 92.1% White, 1.6% Black, 1.2% Asian, 6.1% Hispanic of any race (2007); Density: 1,569.4 persons per square mile (2007); Average household size: 2.76 (2007); Median age: 36.1 (2007); Males per 100 females: 104.9 (2007); Marriage status: 21.9% never married, 66.3% now married, 4.2% widowed, 7.5% divorced (2000); Foreign born: 4.1% (2000); Ancestry (includes multiple ancestries): 37.3% German, 19.0% Irish, 12.9% Polish, 9.8% Swedish, 9.3% English (2000).
Economy: Employment by occupation: 10.6% management, 15.1% professional, 11.9% services, 30.4% sales, 0.0% farming, 17.7% construction, 14.3% production (2000).
Income: Per capita income: $26,799 (2007); Median household income: $68,075 (2007); Average household income: $74,073 (2007); Percent of households with income of $100,000 or more: 19.4% (2007); Poverty rate: 3.0% (2000).
Education: Percent of population age 25 and over with: High school diploma (including GED) or higher: 90.5% (2007); Bachelor's degree or higher: 19.2% (2007); Master's degree or higher: 4.8% (2007).
Housing: Homeownership rate: 91.3% (2007); Median home value: $193,125 (2007); Median rent: $738 per month (2000); Median age of housing: 35 years (2000).
Transportation: Commute to work: 96.0% car, 1.1% public transportation, 0.2% walk, 2.3% work from home (2000); Travel time to work: 23.6% less than 15 minutes, 24.8% 15 to 30 minutes, 22.6% 30 to 45 minutes, 13.9% 45 to 60 minutes, 15.1% 60 minutes or more (2000)

VERNON HILLS (village). Covers a land area of 7.429 square miles and a water area of 0.190 square miles. Located at 42.23° N. Lat.; 87.96° W. Long. Elevation is 735 feet.
Population: 15,529 (1990); 20,120 (2000); 24,208 (2007); 26,782 (2012 projected); Race: 74.5% White, 1.6% Black, 17.6% Asian, 10.1% Hispanic of any race (2007); Density: 3,258.6 persons per square mile (2007); Average household size: 2.69 (2007); Median age: 35.9 (2007); Males per 100 females: 94.3 (2007); Marriage status: 24.8% never married, 62.0% now married, 4.3% widowed, 8.9% divorced (2000); Foreign born: 21.2% (2000); Ancestry (includes multiple ancestries): 24.5% Other groups, 18.8% German, 13.9% Irish, 10.1% Polish, 9.2% Italian (2000).
Economy: Single-family building permits issued: 31 (2007); Multi-family building permits issued: 146 (2007); Employment by occupation: 23.4%

management, 28.1% professional, 7.8% services, 29.7% sales, 0.0% farming, 4.1% construction, 6.9% production (2000).
Income: Per capita income: $37,256 (2007); Median household income: $80,071 (2007); Average household income: $100,166 (2007); Percent of households with income of $100,000 or more: 37.0% (2007); Poverty rate: 2.9% (2000).
Education: Percent of population age 25 and over with: High school diploma (including GED) or higher: 93.8% (2007); Bachelor's degree or higher: 54.5% (2007); Master's degree or higher: 18.7% (2007).

School District(s)

CHSD 128 (09-12)
2005-06 Enrollment: 3,214 . . . . (847) 367-3159
Hawthorn CCSD 73 (PK-08)
2005-06 Enrollment: 3,697 . . . . (847) 990-4210
Spec Educ Dist Lake County/Sedol (PK-12)
2005-06 Enrollment: 518 . . . . (847) 548-8470

Housing: Homeownership rate: 79.9% (2007); Median home value: $284,564 (2007); Median rent: $825 per month (2000); Median age of housing: 17 years (2000).
Safety: Violent crime rate: 8.8 per 10,000 population; Property crime rate: 282.6 per 10,000 population (2006).
Newspapers: Chicago Tribune - Vernon Hills Bureau (Local news; Circulation 0); Daily Herald - Vernon Hills Bureau (Local news; Circulation 0)
Transportation: Commute to work: 91.5% car, 3.8% public transportation, 0.6% walk, 3.5% work from home (2000); Travel time to work: 23.0% less than 15 minutes, 31.2% 15 to 30 minutes, 24.8% 30 to 45 minutes, 10.0% 45 to 60 minutes, 10.9% 60 minutes or more (2000)

Additional Information Contacts

Village of Vernon Hills . . . . (847) 367-3700
http://www.vernonhills.org

VOLO (village). Covers a land area of 2.791 square miles and a water area of 0.012 square miles. Located at 42.33° N. Lat.; 88.16° W. Long. Elevation is 794 feet.
Population: 157 (1990); 180 (2000); 302 (2007); 372 (2012 projected); Race: 90.7% White, 0.0% Black, 2.0% Asian, 39.7% Hispanic of any race (2007); Density: 108.2 persons per square mile (2007); Average household size: 3.25 (2007); Median age: 36.5 (2007); Males per 100 females: 115.7 (2007); Marriage status: 28.6% never married, 52.8% now married, 11.8% widowed, 6.8% divorced (2000); Foreign born: 29.7% (2000); Ancestry (includes multiple ancestries): 30.1% Other groups, 19.6% German, 12.0% Polish, 7.7% English, 3.8% Irish (2000).
Economy: Single-family building permits issued: 232 (2007); Multi-family building permits issued: 0 (2007); Employment by occupation: 12.7% management, 9.5% professional, 20.6% services, 23.8% sales, 0.0% farming, 9.5% construction, 23.8% production (2000).
Income: Per capita income: $21,978 (2007); Median household income: $59,000 (2007); Average household income: $68,414 (2007); Percent of households with income of $100,000 or more: 12.9% (2007); Poverty rate: 33.0% (2000).
Education: Percent of population age 25 and over with: High school diploma (including GED) or higher: 56.6% (2007); Bachelor's degree or higher: 4.7% (2007); Master's degree or higher: 0.0% (2007).
Housing: Homeownership rate: 55.9% (2007); Median home value: $381,818 (2007); Median rent: $642 per month (2000); Median age of housing: 47 years (2000).
Transportation: Commute to work: 58.7% car, 0.0% public transportation, 22.2% walk, 12.7% work from home (2000); Travel time to work: 34.5% less than 15 minutes, 34.5% 15 to 30 minutes, 9.1% 30 to 45 minutes, 3.6% 45 to 60 minutes, 18.2% 60 minutes or more (2000)

WADSWORTH (village). Covers a land area of 8.773 square miles and a water area of 0.037 square miles. Located at 42.43° N. Lat.; 87.92° W. Long. Elevation is 705 feet.
Population: 2,570 (1990); 3,083 (2000); 3,733 (2007); 4,136 (2012 projected); Race: 92.1% White, 2.0% Black, 1.4% Asian, 4.5% Hispanic of any race (2007); Density: 425.5 persons per square mile (2007); Average household size: 2.95 (2007); Median age: 41.7 (2007); Males per 100 females: 99.8 (2007); Marriage status: 18.8% never married, 71.6% now married, 3.9% widowed, 5.7% divorced (2000); Foreign born: 5.1% (2000); Ancestry (includes multiple ancestries): 32.1% German, 15.2% Irish, 14.4% English, 13.0% Polish, 8.7% Italian (2000).
Economy: Single-family building permits issued: 8 (2007); Multi-family building permits issued: 0 (2007); Employment by occupation: 25.3% management, 20.5% professional, 8.3% services, 29.1% sales, 0.0% farming, 7.9% construction, 8.9% production (2000).
Income: Per capita income: $41,163 (2007); Median household income: $96,728 (2007); Average household income: $121,374 (2007); Percent of households with income of $100,000 or more: 48.0% (2007); Poverty rate: 2.2% (2000).
Education: Percent of population age 25 and over with: High school diploma (including GED) or higher: 95.5% (2007); Bachelor's degree or higher: 38.8% (2007); Master's degree or higher: 15.2% (2007).

School District(s)

Beach Park CCSD 3 (PK-08)
2005-06 Enrollment: 2,507 . . . . (847) 599-5005
Millburn CCSD 24 (PK-08)
2005-06 Enrollment: 1,537 . . . . (847) 356-8331

Housing: Homeownership rate: 93.4% (2007); Median home value: $353,207 (2007); Median rent: $640 per month (2000); Median age of housing: 20 years (2000).
Transportation: Commute to work: 94.8% car, 0.8% public transportation, 0.4% walk, 2.8% work from home (2000); Travel time to work: 18.3% less than 15 minutes, 49.5% 15 to 30 minutes, 16.8% 30 to 45 minutes, 6.6% 45 to 60 minutes, 8.8% 60 minutes or more (2000)

WAUCONDA (village). Covers a land area of 3.864 square miles and a water area of 0.419 square miles. Located at 42.26° N. Lat.; 88.14° W. Long. Elevation is 804 feet.
History: Wauconda was settled in 1836 by Justus Bangs. The name he gave the village probably came from a favorite book of his, and was Indian in origin.
Population: 7,481 (1990); 9,448 (2000); 11,629 (2007); 12,999 (2012 projected); Race: 85.1% White, 0.7% Black, 3.1% Asian, 16.9% Hispanic of any race (2007); Density: 3,009.4 persons per square mile (2007); Average household size: 2.61 (2007); Median age: 37.4 (2007); Males per 100 females: 102.7 (2007); Marriage status: 21.4% never married, 61.0% now married, 5.7% widowed, 11.9% divorced (2000); Foreign born: 11.9% (2000); Ancestry (includes multiple ancestries): 28.2% German, 14.5% Other groups, 12.3% Irish, 11.4% Polish, 9.1% Italian (2000).
Economy: Single-family building permits issued: 108 (2007); Multi-family building permits issued: 0 (2007); Employment by occupation: 12.8% management, 16.0% professional, 13.0% services, 31.0% sales, 0.0% farming, 13.3% construction, 13.9% production (2000).
Income: Per capita income: $30,512 (2007); Median household income: $66,430 (2007); Average household income: $78,922 (2007); Percent of households with income of $100,000 or more: 23.6% (2007); Poverty rate: 4.0% (2000).
Education: Percent of population age 25 and over with: High school diploma (including GED) or higher: 87.5% (2007); Bachelor's degree or higher: 24.6% (2007); Master's degree or higher: 6.0% (2007).

School District(s)

Wauconda CUSD 118 (PK-12)
2005-06 Enrollment: 4,198 . . . . (847) 526-7690

Housing: Homeownership rate: 82.0% (2007); Median home value: $219,782 (2007); Median rent: $720 per month (2000); Median age of housing: 24 years (2000).
Safety: Violent crime rate: 13.5 per 10,000 population; Property crime rate: 183.1 per 10,000 population (2006).
Transportation: Commute to work: 93.2% car, 1.3% public transportation, 1.5% walk, 2.6% work from home (2000); Travel time to work: 26.3% less than 15 minutes, 23.7% 15 to 30 minutes, 26.7% 30 to 45 minutes, 11.4% 45 to 60 minutes, 11.9% 60 minutes or more (2000)

Additional Information Contacts

Village of Wauconda . . . . (847) 526-9600
http://www.wauconda-il.gov
Wauconda Chamber of Commerce . . . . (847) 526-5580
http://www.waucondachamber.org

WAUKEGAN (city). County seat. Covers a land area of 23.012 square miles and a water area of 0.079 square miles. Located at 42.37° N. Lat.; 87.86° W. Long. Elevation is 653 feet.
History: Named for the Indian translation of "sheltering place". Waukegan began with the founding of Little Fort by the French in the 1700's, the present name being of Indian origin meaning "fort or trading post." Settlers came to Little Fort in 1835, and in 1846 it was designated as a U.S. port of entry. Waukegan was incorporated as a village in 1849, and as a city in 1859.

Population: 70,309 (1990); 87,901 (2000); 92,366 (2007); 95,245 (2012 projected); Race: 45.9% White, 16.6% Black, 4.5% Asian, 56.0% Hispanic of any race (2007); Density: 4,013.9 persons per square mile (2007); Average household size: 3.21 (2007); Median age: 31.0 (2007); Males per 100 females: 103.4 (2007); Marriage status: 31.6% never married, 55.0% now married, 4.8% widowed, 8.5% divorced (2000); Foreign born: 30.2% (2000); Ancestry (includes multiple ancestries): 59.6% Other groups, 8.6% German, 5.1% Irish, 3.3% English, 3.2% Polish (2000).
Economy: Unemployment rate: 7.2% (4/2008); Total civilian labor force: 45,230 (4/2008); Single-family building permits issued: 51 (2007); Multi-family building permits issued: 0 (2007); Employment by occupation: 9.2% management, 13.5% professional, 17.9% services, 24.6% sales, 0.3% farming, 9.7% construction, 25.0% production (2000).
Income: Per capita income: $18,430 (2007); Median household income: $46,502 (2007); Average household income: $58,154 (2007); Percent of households with income of $100,000 or more: 12.5% (2007); Poverty rate: 13.9% (2000).
Education: Percent of population age 25 and over with: High school diploma (including GED) or higher: 66.7% (2007); Bachelor's degree or higher: 16.2% (2007); Master's degree or higher: 5.5% (2007).

School District(s)

Waukegan CUSD 60 (PK-12)
2005-06 Enrollment: 15,841 . . . . (847) 336-3100
Housing: Homeownership rate: 56.8% (2007); Median home value: $165,116 (2007); Median rent: $586 per month (2000); Median age of housing: 38 years (2000).
Hospitals: Vista Health - Saint Therese Medical Center (388 beds); Vista Medical Center East (299 beds)
Safety: Violent crime rate: 38.1 per 10,000 population; Property crime rate: 232.6 per 10,000 population (2006).
Newspapers: Antioch Review (Community news; Circulation 1,644); Deerfield Review (Community news; Circulation 5,282); Grayslake Review (Community news; Circulation 3,520); Gurnee Review (Community news; Circulation 3,694); Highland Park News (Community news; Circulation 7,392); Lake Forester (Community news; Circulation 6,811); Lake Villa/Lindenhurst Review (Community news; Circulation 2,381); Libertyville Review (Community news; Circulation 4,480); Lincolnshire Review (Community news; Circulation 0); Mundelein Review (Community news; Circulation 2,538); News Sun (Local news; Circulation 21,299); Vernon Hills Review (Community news; Circulation 2,200)
Transportation: Commute to work: 91.3% car, 3.6% public transportation, 2.0% walk, 1.6% work from home (2000); Travel time to work: 23.4% less than 15 minutes, 37.9% 15 to 30 minutes, 21.8% 30 to 45 minutes, 9.5% 45 to 60 minutes, 7.4% 60 minutes or more (2000)
Airports: Waukegan Regional (general aviation)
Additional Information Contacts
City of Waukegan. . . . . (847) 599-2500
http://www.waukeganweb.net

WINTHROP HARBOR (village). Covers a land area of 4.309 square miles and a water area of 0.069 square miles. Located at 42.48° N. Lat.; 87.82° W. Long. Elevation is 636 feet.
History: The Winthrop Harbor and Dock Company purchased land here in 1892, but plans to develop the harbor and town were abandoned. The community that grew here depended on dairying.
Population: 6,397 (1990); 6,670 (2000); 7,079 (2007); 7,358 (2012 projected); Race: 91.5% White, 0.8% Black, 2.3% Asian, 6.9% Hispanic of any race (2007); Density: 1,642.9 persons per square mile (2007); Average household size: 2.79 (2007); Median age: 37.6 (2007); Males per 100 females: 99.7 (2007); Marriage status: 20.7% never married, 67.4% now married, 3.6% widowed, 8.3% divorced (2000); Foreign born: 3.0% (2000); Ancestry (includes multiple ancestries): 25.7% German, 16.0% Irish, 11.5% English, 11.0% Other groups, 7.2% United States or American (2000).
Economy: Single-family building permits issued: 13 (2007); Multi-family building permits issued: 0 (2007); Employment by occupation: 15.8% management, 13.0% professional, 11.0% services, 30.4% sales, 0.5% farming, 11.6% construction, 17.6% production (2000).
Income: Per capita income: $27,165 (2007); Median household income: $67,693 (2007); Average household income: $75,594 (2007); Percent of households with income of $100,000 or more: 24.9% (2007); Poverty rate: 3.1% (2000).
Education: Percent of population age 25 and over with: High school diploma (including GED) or higher: 89.9% (2007); Bachelor's degree or higher: 18.6% (2007); Master's degree or higher: 5.3% (2007).

School District(s)

Winthrop Harbor SD 1 (PK-08)
2005-06 Enrollment: 765 . . . . (847) 731-3085
Housing: Homeownership rate: 84.1% (2007); Median home value: $205,136 (2007); Median rent: $646 per month (2000); Median age of housing: 28 years (2000).
Safety: Violent crime rate: 16.9 per 10,000 population; Property crime rate: 126.9 per 10,000 population (2006).
Transportation: Commute to work: 96.7% car, 0.7% public transportation, 0.7% walk, 1.7% work from home (2000); Travel time to work: 25.4% less than 15 minutes, 34.2% 15 to 30 minutes, 23.3% 30 to 45 minutes, 8.2% 45 to 60 minutes, 8.9% 60 minutes or more (2000)
Additional Information Contacts
Winthrop Harbor Chamber of Commerce . . . . (847) 872-7723
http://www.winthropharborchamberofcommerce.com

ZION (city). Covers a land area of 8.197 square miles and a water area of 0 square miles. Located at 42.45° N. Lat.; 87.84° W. Long. Elevation is 650 feet.
History: Named for Mount Zion in Palestine. Zion began as the dream of John Alexander Dowie (1847-1907), the Scottish founder of the Christian Catholic Apostolic Church, who planned Zion as a city where the tenets of the church would govern. In 1899 Dowie's followers began to settle here. Dowie was succeeded by Wilbur Glenn Voliva, who attempted to industrialize Zion, but the church owned all industries and commercial establishments. In 1939, after several bankruptcies, titles were transferred to individuals.
Population: 20,171 (1990); 22,866 (2000); 24,864 (2007); 26,123 (2012 projected); Race: 49.4% White, 29.7% Black, 2.7% Asian, 23.4% Hispanic of any race (2007); Density: 3,033.2 persons per square mile (2007); Average household size: 3.03 (2007); Median age: 31.5 (2007); Males per 100 females: 95.4 (2007); Marriage status: 28.2% never married, 54.9% now married, 5.0% widowed, 11.9% divorced (2000); Foreign born: 8.8% (2000); Ancestry (includes multiple ancestries): 40.5% Other groups, 16.0% German, 7.9% Irish, 6.7% English, 4.6% United States or American (2000).
Economy: Single-family building permits issued: 60 (2007); Multi-family building permits issued: 4 (2007); Employment by occupation: 8.5% management, 15.1% professional, 16.4% services, 30.4% sales, 0.0% farming, 10.5% construction, 19.1% production (2000).
Income: Per capita income: $20,063 (2007); Median household income: $50,626 (2007); Average household income: $59,591 (2007); Percent of households with income of $100,000 or more: 13.4% (2007); Poverty rate: 11.9% (2000).
Education: Percent of population age 25 and over with: High school diploma (including GED) or higher: 78.5% (2007); Bachelor's degree or higher: 16.0% (2007); Master's degree or higher: 5.7% (2007).

School District(s)

Lake Roe (06-12)
2005-06 Enrollment: 48 . . . . (847) 543-7833
Zion ESD 6 (PK-08)
2005-06 Enrollment: 2,946 . . . . (847) 872-5455
Zion-Benton Twp HSD 126 (09-12)
2005-06 Enrollment: 2,581 . . . . (847) 731-9792
Housing: Homeownership rate: 58.7% (2007); Median home value: $165,093 (2007); Median rent: $595 per month (2000); Median age of housing: 32 years (2000).
Hospitals: Midwestern Regional Medical Center (95 beds)
Safety: Violent crime rate: 63.0 per 10,000 population; Property crime rate: 313.1 per 10,000 population (2006).
Newspapers: Bargaineer (Community news; Circulation 28,000); Zion-Benton News (Community news; Circulation 3,500)
Transportation: Commute to work: 92.4% car, 3.5% public transportation, 1.3% walk, 1.9% work from home (2000); Travel time to work: 17.7% less than 15 minutes, 34.9% 15 to 30 minutes, 24.4% 30 to 45 minutes, 12.2% 45 to 60 minutes, 10.8% 60 minutes or more (2000)
Additional Information Contacts
City of Zion. . . . . (847) 746-4000
http://www.cityofzion.com
Zion Chamber of Commerce . . . . (847) 872-5405
http://www.zionchamber.com

Lawrence County

Located in southeastern Illinois; bounded on the east by the Wabash River and the Indiana border; drained by the Embarrass River. Covers a land area of 371.98 square miles, a water area of 1.96 square miles, and is located in the Central Time Zone. The county was founded in 1821. County seat is Lawrenceville.

Population: 15,972 (1990); 15,452 (2000); 15,966 (2007); 16,200 (2012 projected); Race: 94.0% White, 4.7% Black, 0.2% Asian, 1.5% Hispanic of any race (2007); Density: 42.9 persons per square mile (2007); Average household size: 2.56 (2007); Median age: 42.5 (2007); Males per 100 females: 95.6 (2007).

Religion: Five largest groups: 15.2% The United Methodist Church, 10.2% Christian Churches and Churches of Christ, 5.2% Catholic Church, 5.1% Southern Baptist Convention, 2.5% The Wesleyan Church (2000).

Economy: Unemployment rate: 5.3% (4/2008); Total civilian labor force: 8,345 (4/2008); Leading industries: 22.7% health care and social assistance; 17.6% manufacturing; 11.7% retail trade (2005); Farms: 355 totaling 192,048 acres (2002); Companies that employ 500 or more persons: 1 (2006); Companies that employ 100 to 499 persons: 5 (2006); Companies that employ less than 100 persons: 326 (2006); Black-owned businesses: n/a (2002); Hispanic-owned businesses: n/a (2002); Asian-owned businesses: n/a (2002); Women-owned businesses: 195 (2002); Retail sales per capita: $6,495 (2008). Single-family building permits issued: 0 (2007); Multi-family building permits issued: 0 (2007).

Income: Per capita income: $19,946 (2007); Median household income: $35,974 (2007); Average household income: $46,382 (2007); Percent of households with income of $100,000 or more: 7.2% (2007); Poverty rate: 14.9% (2005); Bankruptcy rate: 3.08% (2007).

Education: Percent of population age 25 and over with: High school diploma (including GED) or higher: 80.7% (2007); Bachelor's degree or higher: 9.4% (2007); Master's degree or higher: 3.4% (2007).

Housing: Homeownership rate: 77.6% (2007); Median home value: $59,757 (2007); Median rent: $253 per month (2000); Median age of housing: 45 years (2000).

Health: Birth rate: 103.3 per 10,000 population (2007); Death rate: 146.3 per 10,000 population (2007); Age-adjusted cancer mortality rate: 205.8 deaths per 100,000 population (2005); Number of physicians: 6.9 per 10,000 population (2005); Hospital beds: 34.0 per 10,000 population (2004); Hospital admissions: 770.9 per 10,000 population (2004).

Elections: 2004 Presidential election results: 61.9% Bush, 37.4% Kerry, 0.1% Nader, 0.7% Badnarik

National and State Parks: Lincoln Trail State Memorial; Red Hills State Park

Additional Information Contacts

Lawrence County Government . . . . (618) 943-2346
http://www.lawrencecountyillinois.com

Lawrence County Chamber of Commerce. . . . . (618) 943-3516
http://www.lawrencecountyillinois.com

Lawrence County Communities

BIRDS (village). Covers a land area of 0.216 square miles and a water area of 0 square miles. Located at 38.83° N. Lat.; 87.66° W. Long. Elevation is 436 feet.

Population: 160 (1990); 51 (2000); 44 (2007); 42 (2012 projected); Race: 100.0% White, 0.0% Black, 0.0% Asian, 4.5% Hispanic of any race (2007); Density: 203.3 persons per square mile (2007); Average household size: 2.32 (2007); Median age: 41.7 (2007); Males per 100 females: 83.3 (2007); Marriage status: 24.3% never married, 35.1% now married, 10.8% widowed, 29.7% divorced (2000); Foreign born: 0.0% (2000); Ancestry (includes multiple ancestries): 12.0% Irish, 8.0% German, 4.0% Scotch-Irish, 4.0% United States or American (2000).

Economy: Employment by occupation: 0.0% management, 5.0% professional, 20.0% services, 20.0% sales, 0.0% farming, 10.0% construction, 45.0% production (2000).

Income: Per capita income: $14,034 (2007); Median household income: $28,750 (2007); Average household income: $32,500 (2007); Percent of households with income of $100,000 or more: 0.0% (2007); Poverty rate: 20.0% (2000).

Education: Percent of population age 25 and over with: High school diploma (including GED) or higher: 100.0% (2007); Bachelor's degree or higher: 10.0% (2007); Master's degree or higher: 3.3% (2007).

Housing: Homeownership rate: 68.4% (2007); Median home value: $38,125 (2007); Median rent: $213 per month (2000); Median age of housing: 35 years (2000).

Transportation: Commute to work: 85.0% car, 0.0% public transportation, 10.0% walk, 5.0% work from home (2000); Travel time to work: 26.3% less than 15 minutes, 42.1% 15 to 30 minutes, 10.5% 30 to 45 minutes, 21.1% 45 to 60 minutes, 0.0% 60 minutes or more (2000)

BRIDGEPORT (city). Covers a land area of 1.071 square miles and a water area of 0.025 square miles. Located at 38.71° N. Lat.; 87.75° W. Long. Elevation is 446 feet.

History: Bridgeport was the center of an early oil boom, when a company built a pumping station and supply yards here.

Population: 2,118 (1990); 2,168 (2000); 2,117 (2007); 2,082 (2012 projected); Race: 95.9% White, 3.1% Black, 0.0% Asian, 0.6% Hispanic of any race (2007); Density: 1,976.4 persons per square mile (2007); Average household size: 2.56 (2007); Median age: 38.0 (2007); Males per 100 females: 94.9 (2007); Marriage status: 23.0% never married, 52.8% now married, 9.8% widowed, 14.4% divorced (2000); Foreign born: 0.0% (2000); Ancestry (includes multiple ancestries): 19.9% United States or American, 13.3% English, 11.6% German, 8.7% Irish, 6.2% Other groups (2000).

Economy: Employment by occupation: 4.8% management, 9.8% professional, 25.4% services, 21.6% sales, 0.0% farming, 12.6% construction, 25.8% production (2000).

Income: Per capita income: $16,011 (2007); Median household income: $32,679 (2007); Average household income: $38,814 (2007); Percent of households with income of $100,000 or more: 3.4% (2007); Poverty rate: 17.3% (2000).

Education: Percent of population age 25 and over with: High school diploma (including GED) or higher: 75.4% (2007); Bachelor's degree or higher: 4.9% (2007); Master's degree or higher: 2.0% (2007).

School District(s)

Red Hill CUSD 10 (PK-12)
2005-06 Enrollment: 1,109 . . . . (618) 945-2061

Housing: Homeownership rate: 73.0% (2007); Median home value: $52,563 (2007); Median rent: $263 per month (2000); Median age of housing: 45 years (2000).

Safety: Violent crime rate: 60.5 per 10,000 population; Property crime rate: 111.7 per 10,000 population (2006).

Newspapers: Bridgeport Leader (Local news; Circulation 6,000)

Transportation: Commute to work: 91.6% car, 0.0% public transportation, 2.9% walk, 4.0% work from home (2000); Travel time to work: 48.2% less than 15 minutes, 27.9% 15 to 30 minutes, 16.6% 30 to 45 minutes, 4.9% 45 to 60 minutes, 2.3% 60 minutes or more (2000)

LAWRENCEVILLE (city). County seat. Covers a land area of 2.022 square miles and a water area of 0 square miles. Located at 38.72° N. Lat.; 87.68° W. Long. Elevation is 469 feet.

History: The first settler here was Captain Toussaint Dubois, veteran of the American Revolution, who came about 1780 and planted an orchard. Jessie K. Dubois, the captain's son, was a friend of Abraham Lincoln and one of the pall bearers at his funeral. Lawrenceville was organized in 1821 and named for Captain James Lawrence, commander of the "Chesapeake" in the War of 1812, who said, "Don't give up the ship." Lawrenceville developed as an oil town in the early 1900's, and as the seat of Lawrence County.

Population: 4,902 (1990); 4,745 (2000); 4,763 (2007); 4,712 (2012 projected); Race: 93.3% White, 5.3% Black, 0.3% Asian, 2.5% Hispanic of any race (2007); Density: 2,355.7 persons per square mile (2007); Average household size: 2.59 (2007); Median age: 47.8 (2007); Males per 100 females: 78.0 (2007); Marriage status: 16.7% never married, 56.5% now married, 15.5% widowed, 11.3% divorced (2000); Foreign born: 1.1% (2000); Ancestry (includes multiple ancestries): 20.4% German, 13.6% United States or American, 13.1% English, 10.7% Irish, 8.5% Other groups (2000).

Economy: Single-family building permits issued: 0 (2007); Multi-family building permits issued: 0 (2007); Employment by occupation: 8.7% management, 18.8% professional, 20.3% services, 25.4% sales, 0.0% farming, 9.6% construction, 17.2% production (2000).

Income: Per capita income: $19,447 (2007); Median household income: $29,503 (2007); Average household income: $42,998 (2007); Percent of households with income of $100,000 or more: 7.4% (2007); Poverty rate: 16.9% (2000).

Education: Percent of population age 25 and over with: High school diploma (including GED) or higher: 80.0% (2007); Bachelor's degree or higher: 13.0% (2007); Master's degree or higher: 4.5% (2007).

School District(s)

Clay/Cwford/Jsper/Lwrnce/Rhland
2005-06 Enrollment: n/a . . . . (618) 392-4631

Lawrence County CUD 20 (PK-12)
2005-06 Enrollment: 1,372 . . . . (618) 943-2326

Housing: Homeownership rate: 67.6% (2007); Median home value: $52,965 (2007); Median rent: $230 per month (2000); Median age of housing: 52 years (2000).

Hospitals: Lawrence County Memorial Hospital (25 beds)

Safety: Violent crime rate: 97.5 per 10,000 population; Property crime rate: 250.4 per 10,000 population (2006).

Newspapers: Daily Record (Local news; Circulation 4,300); Lawrence County News (Community news; Circulation 900)

Transportation: Commute to work: 93.5% car, 0.0% public transportation, 4.7% walk, 1.3% work from home (2000); Travel time to work: 55.7% less than 15 minutes, 25.9% 15 to 30 minutes, 11.0% 30 to 45 minutes, 1.7% 45 to 60 minutes, 5.6% 60 minutes or more (2000)

Airports: Lawrenceville-Vincennes International (general aviation)

Additional Information Contacts

Lawrence County Chamber of Commerce. . . . . (618) 943-3516
http://www.lawrencecountyillinois.com

RUSSELLVILLE (village). Covers a land area of 0.459 square miles and a water area of 0 square miles. Located at 38.82° N. Lat.; 87.53° W. Long. Elevation is 427 feet.

History: Russellville grew around a ferry that crossed the Wabash River here.

Population: 133 (1990); 119 (2000); 113 (2007); 106 (2012 projected); Race: 92.0% White, 0.0% Black, 0.0% Asian, 16.8% Hispanic of any race (2007); Density: 246.5 persons per square mile (2007); Average household size: 2.26 (2007); Median age: 32.5 (2007); Males per 100 females: 113.2 (2007); Marriage status: 11.8% never married, 60.5% now married, 10.5% widowed, 17.1% divorced (2000); Foreign born: 0.0% (2000); Ancestry (includes multiple ancestries): 8.3% Other groups, 5.0% Irish, 3.3% English, 1.7% Polish, 1.7% German (2000).

Economy: Employment by occupation: 0.0% management, 9.8% professional, 14.6% services, 29.3% sales, 0.0% farming, 31.7% construction, 14.6% production (2000).

Income: Per capita income: $17,920 (2007); Median household income: $31,667 (2007); Average household income: $40,500 (2007); Percent of households with income of $100,000 or more: 8.0% (2007); Poverty rate: 42.5% (2000).

Education: Percent of population age 25 and over with: High school diploma (including GED) or higher: 75.0% (2007); Bachelor's degree or higher: 0.0% (2007); Master's degree or higher: 0.0% (2007).

Housing: Homeownership rate: 88.0% (2007); Median home value: $27,000 (2007); Median rent: $317 per month (2000); Median age of housing: 36 years (2000).

Transportation: Commute to work: 89.7% car, 0.0% public transportation, 10.3% walk, 0.0% work from home (2000); Travel time to work: 20.5% less than 15 minutes, 66.7% 15 to 30 minutes, 5.1% 30 to 45 minutes, 7.7% 45 to 60 minutes, 0.0% 60 minutes or more (2000)

SAINT FRANCISVILLE (city). Covers a land area of 0.746 square miles and a water area of 0.034 square miles. Located at 38.59° N. Lat.; 87.64° W. Long. Elevation is 466 feet.

Population: 851 (1990); 759 (2000); 888 (2007); 968 (2012 projected); Race: 98.8% White, 0.7% Black, 0.0% Asian, 0.0% Hispanic of any race (2007); Density: 1,190.2 persons per square mile (2007); Average household size: 2.33 (2007); Median age: 36.6 (2007); Males per 100 females: 97.3 (2007); Marriage status: 28.3% never married, 49.4% now married, 9.9% widowed, 12.4% divorced (2000); Foreign born: 0.1% (2000); Ancestry (includes multiple ancestries): 20.3% German, 12.8% United States or American, 11.3% Irish, 6.8% English, 5.0% French (except Basque) (2000).

Economy: Employment by occupation: 4.5% management, 15.0% professional, 18.4% services, 23.8% sales, 1.1% farming, 16.1% construction, 21.0% production (2000).

Income: Per capita income: $14,032 (2007); Median household income: $28,438 (2007); Average household income: $32,703 (2007); Percent of households with income of $100,000 or more: 2.9% (2007); Poverty rate: 21.1% (2000).

Education: Percent of population age 25 and over with: High school diploma (including GED) or higher: 75.7% (2007); Bachelor's degree or higher: 6.5% (2007); Master's degree or higher: 1.7% (2007).

Housing: Homeownership rate: 78.0% (2007); Median home value: $37,065 (2007); Median rent: $216 per month (2000); Median age of housing: 54 years (2000).

Safety: Violent crime rate: 0.0 per 10,000 population; Property crime rate: 0.0 per 10,000 population (2006).

Transportation: Commute to work: 96.5% car, 0.0% public transportation, 2.0% walk, 0.6% work from home (2000); Travel time to work: 17.4% less than 15 minutes, 53.2% 15 to 30 minutes, 20.0% 30 to 45 minutes, 8.2% 45 to 60 minutes, 1.2% 60 minutes or more (2000)

SUMNER (city). Covers a land area of 1.031 square miles and a water area of 0 square miles. Located at 38.71° N. Lat.; 87.86° W. Long. Elevation is 449 feet.

History: Incorporated 1887.

Population: 1,083 (1990); 1,022 (2000); 1,384 (2007); 1,587 (2012 projected); Race: 84.6% White, 14.3% Black, 0.0% Asian, 1.1% Hispanic of any race (2007); Density: 1,342.0 persons per square mile (2007); Average household size: 3.41 (2007); Median age: 45.2 (2007); Males per 100 females: 95.2 (2007); Marriage status: 27.5% never married, 53.8% now married, 7.5% widowed, 11.2% divorced (2000); Foreign born: 0.5% (2000); Ancestry (includes multiple ancestries): 18.9% German, 18.2% English, 9.8% United States or American, 9.5% Irish, 4.5% Other groups (2000).

Economy: Employment by occupation: 4.7% management, 15.5% professional, 14.3% services, 23.8% sales, 0.4% farming, 13.0% construction, 28.3% production (2000).

Income: Per capita income: $19,067 (2007); Median household income: $28,667 (2007); Average household income: $33,534 (2007); Percent of households with income of $100,000 or more: 1.7% (2007); Poverty rate: 16.9% (2000).

Education: Percent of population age 25 and over with: High school diploma (including GED) or higher: 62.8% (2007); Bachelor's degree or higher: 4.0% (2007); Master's degree or higher: 1.6% (2007).

School District(s)

Dept of Corrections Sch Dist 428 (08-12)
2005-06 Enrollment: 2,271 . . . . (217) 522-2666

Red Hill CUSD 10 (PK-12)
2005-06 Enrollment: 1,109 . . . . (618) 945-2061

Housing: Homeownership rate: 74.6% (2007); Median home value: $43,852 (2007); Median rent: $255 per month (2000); Median age of housing: 56 years (2000).

Safety: Violent crime rate: 22.0 per 10,000 population; Property crime rate: 126.4 per 10,000 population (2006).

Newspapers: Sumner Press (Regional news; Circulation 2,150)

Transportation: Commute to work: 86.8% car, 8.5% public transportation, 2.4% walk, 0.9% work from home (2000); Travel time to work: 33.0% less than 15 minutes, 43.8% 15 to 30 minutes, 13.3% 30 to 45 minutes, 4.8% 45 to 60 minutes, 5.0% 60 minutes or more (2000)

Lee County

Located in northern Illinois; drained by the Rock, Green, and Kyte Rivers. Covers a land area of 725.36 square miles, a water area of 3.92 square miles, and is located in the Central Time Zone. The county was founded in 1839. County seat is Dixon.

Lee County is part of the Dixon, IL Micropolitan Statistical Area. The entire metro area includes: Lee County, IL

Weather Station: Dixon 1 NW — Elevation: 698 feet

	Jan	Feb	Mar	Apr	May	Jun	Jul	Aug	Sep	Oct	Nov	Dec
High	28	33	46	60	72	81	84	82	75	63	47	33
Low	10	15	27	38	49	58	62	60	51	40	29	17
Precip	1.6	1.4	2.6	3.6	4.4	4.8	3.4	4.4	3.5	2.8	2.8	2.1
Snow	11.1	6.8	4.6	1.2	0.0	0.0	0.0	0.0	0.0	tr	2.1	8.4

High and Low temperatures in degrees Fahrenheit; Precipitation and Snow in inches

Weather Station: Paw Paw 2 NW — Elevation: 948 feet

	Jan	Feb	Mar	Apr	May	Jun	Jul	Aug	Sep	Oct	Nov	Dec
High	26	31	43	58	70	80	83	80	74	62	45	32
Low	10	15	25	36	48	57	62	59	51	39	28	17
Precip	1.4	1.2	2.3	3.5	4.3	4.5	3.6	4.2	4.2	2.7	3.0	2.2
Snow	9.0	5.8	4.2	1.0	tr	0.0	0.0	0.0	0.0	0.2	2.6	7.4

High and Low temperatures in degrees Fahrenheit; Precipitation and Snow in inches

Population: 34,392 (1990); 36,062 (2000); 35,652 (2007); 35,340 (2012 projected); Race: 92.7% White, 4.5% Black, 0.8% Asian, 4.2% Hispanic of any race (2007); Density: 49.2 persons per square mile (2007); Average household size: 2.65 (2007); Median age: 39.7 (2007); Males per 100 females: 103.0 (2007).

Religion: Five largest groups: 33.3% Catholic Church, 10.4% Evangelical Lutheran Church in America, 8.5% The United Methodist Church, 1.7% Southern Baptist Convention, 1.5% New Testament Association of Independent Baptist Churches and other Fundame

Economy: Unemployment rate: 6.1% (4/2008); Total civilian labor force: 18,729 (4/2008); Leading industries: 34.8% manufacturing; 17.1% health care and social assistance; 11.4% retail trade (2005); Farms: 842 totaling 389,037 acres (2002); Companies that employ 500 or more persons: 3 (2006); Companies that employ 100 to 499 persons: 22 (2006); Companies that employ less than 100 persons: 746 (2006); Black-owned businesses: n/a (2002); Hispanic-owned businesses: n/a (2002); Asian-owned businesses: n/a (2002); Women-owned businesses: 514 (2002); Retail sales per capita: $9,777 (2008). Single-family building permits issued: 110 (2007); Multi-family building permits issued: 50 (2007).

Income: Per capita income: $22,559 (2007); Median household income: $47,838 (2007); Average household income: $58,156 (2007); Percent of households with income of $100,000 or more: 12.2% (2007); Poverty rate: 9.2% (2005); Bankruptcy rate: 2.31% (2007).

Taxes: Total county taxes per capita: $180 (2006); County property taxes per capita: $106 (2006).

Education: Percent of population age 25 and over with: High school diploma (including GED) or higher: 80.4% (2007); Bachelor's degree or higher: 13.2% (2007); Master's degree or higher: 4.6% (2007).

Housing: Homeownership rate: 74.1% (2007); Median home value: $125,501 (2007); Median rent: $374 per month (2000); Median age of housing: 47 years (2000).

Health: Birth rate: 115.7 per 10,000 population (2007); Death rate: 98.2 per 10,000 population (2007); Age-adjusted cancer mortality rate: 233.2 deaths per 100,000 population (2005); Number of physicians: 14.2 per 10,000 population (2005); Hospital beds: 28.0 per 10,000 population (2004); Hospital admissions: 1,129.2 per 10,000 population (2004).

Elections: 2004 Presidential election results: 58.6% Bush, 40.4% Kerry, 0.0% Nader, 0.9% Badnarik

National and State Parks: Franklin Creek State Park; Green River State Wildlife Management Area; Hennepin Canal Parkway State Park

Additional Information Contacts

Lee County Government . . . . (815) 288-3309
http://www.countyoflee.org

City of Dixon. . . . . (815) 288-1485
http://www.dixonil.com

Dixon Area Chamber of Commerce & Industry . . . . (815) 284-3361
http://www.dixonillinoischamber.com

Lee County Communities

AMBOY (city). Covers a land area of 1.258 square miles and a water area of 0 square miles. Located at 41.71° N. Lat.; 89.33° W. Long. Elevation is 745 feet.

History: In Amboy in 1854, Scotch-Irish immigrants Samuel Carson and John T. Pirie opened a small grocery store which later became the firm of Carson Pirie Scott & Company.

Population: 2,377 (1990); 2,561 (2000); 2,555 (2007); 2,535 (2012 projected); Race: 97.5% White, 1.0% Black, 0.0% Asian, 3.2% Hispanic of any race (2007); Density: 2,030.7 persons per square mile (2007); Average household size: 2.60 (2007); Median age: 37.5 (2007); Males per 100 females: 94.3 (2007); Marriage status: 22.4% never married, 59.1% now married, 7.0% widowed, 11.4% divorced (2000); Foreign born: 1.5% (2000); Ancestry (includes multiple ancestries): 35.8% German, 24.2% Irish, 10.0% English, 6.5% United States or American, 6.2% Other groups (2000).

Economy: Single-family building permits issued: 8 (2007); Multi-family building permits issued: 0 (2007); Employment by occupation: 8.9% management, 12.5% professional, 18.0% services, 20.5% sales, 0.0% farming, 10.7% construction, 29.4% production (2000).

Income: Per capita income: $21,147 (2007); Median household income: $42,404 (2007); Average household income: $53,596 (2007); Percent of households with income of $100,000 or more: 8.3% (2007); Poverty rate: 8.3% (2000).

Education: Percent of population age 25 and over with: High school diploma (including GED) or higher: 79.7% (2007); Bachelor's degree or higher: 8.5% (2007); Master's degree or higher: 2.6% (2007).

School District(s)

Amboy CUSD 272 (PK-12)
2005-06 Enrollment: 1,040 . . . . (815) 857-2164

Housing: Homeownership rate: 70.2% (2007); Median home value: $114,947 (2007); Median rent: $358 per month (2000); Median age of housing: 52 years (2000).

Safety: Violent crime rate: 144.0 per 10,000 population; Property crime rate: 190.7 per 10,000 population (2006).

Newspapers: Amboy News (Local news; Circulation 2,250)

Transportation: Commute to work: 90.9% car, 0.0% public transportation, 4.8% walk, 2.8% work from home (2000); Travel time to work: 31.5% less than 15 minutes, 32.7% 15 to 30 minutes, 23.2% 30 to 45 minutes, 5.0% 45 to 60 minutes, 7.6% 60 minutes or more (2000)

ASHTON (village). Covers a land area of 0.661 square miles and a water area of 0 square miles. Located at 41.86° N. Lat.; 89.22° W. Long. Elevation is 823 feet.

Population: 1,042 (1990); 1,142 (2000); 1,096 (2007); 1,091 (2012 projected); Race: 97.7% White, 1.3% Black, 0.0% Asian, 3.6% Hispanic of any race (2007); Density: 1,658.1 persons per square mile (2007); Average household size: 2.54 (2007); Median age: 37.4 (2007); Males per 100 females: 90.6 (2007); Marriage status: 24.1% never married, 53.1% now married, 7.4% widowed, 15.4% divorced (2000); Foreign born: 1.5% (2000); Ancestry (includes multiple ancestries): 36.0% German, 12.4% Irish, 8.9% United States or American, 7.9% Other groups, 7.6% English (2000).

Economy: Single-family building permits issued: 0 (2007); Multi-family building permits issued: 0 (2007); Employment by occupation: 6.8% management, 14.8% professional, 12.2% services, 20.3% sales, 0.4% farming, 13.2% construction, 32.4% production (2000).

Income: Per capita income: $22,919 (2007); Median household income: $47,566 (2007); Average household income: $57,906 (2007); Percent of households with income of $100,000 or more: 10.4% (2007); Poverty rate: 6.2% (2000).

Education: Percent of population age 25 and over with: High school diploma (including GED) or higher: 81.4% (2007); Bachelor's degree or higher: 11.9% (2007); Master's degree or higher: 3.5% (2007).

School District(s)

Ashton-Franklin Center CUSD 275 (KG-12)
2005-06 Enrollment: 632 . . . . (815) 453-7461

Housing: Homeownership rate: 69.4% (2007); Median home value: $120,471 (2007); Median rent: $330 per month (2000); Median age of housing: 60+ years (2000).

Newspapers: Ashton Gazette (Community news; Circulation 1,050)

Transportation: Commute to work: 89.1% car, 0.0% public transportation, 7.0% walk, 2.5% work from home (2000); Travel time to work: 42.4% less than 15 minutes, 31.1% 15 to 30 minutes, 9.3% 30 to 45 minutes, 11.6% 45 to 60 minutes, 5.6% 60 minutes or more (2000)

COMPTON (village). Covers a land area of 0.166 square miles and a water area of 0 square miles. Located at 41.69° N. Lat.; 89.08° W. Long. Elevation is 968 feet.

Population: 343 (1990); 347 (2000); 396 (2007); 422 (2012 projected); Race: 98.7% White, 0.0% Black, 0.5% Asian, 1.8% Hispanic of any race (2007); Density: 2,387.6 persons per square mile (2007); Average household size: 2.69 (2007); Median age: 34.1 (2007); Males per 100 females: 101.0 (2007); Marriage status: 15.0% never married, 62.4% now married, 6.2% widowed, 16.4% divorced (2000); Foreign born: 1.8% (2000); Ancestry (includes multiple ancestries): 32.0% Irish, 31.7% German, 12.4% English, 8.6% Other groups, 5.0% French (except Basque) (2000).

Economy: Employment by occupation: 6.5% management, 9.4% professional, 17.4% services, 18.1% sales, 0.0% farming, 15.9% construction, 32.6% production (2000).

Income: Per capita income: $17,664 (2007); Median household income: $42,955 (2007); Average household income: $47,585 (2007); Percent of households with income of $100,000 or more: 4.1% (2007); Poverty rate: 4.8% (2000).

Education: Percent of population age 25 and over with: High school diploma (including GED) or higher: 76.4% (2007); Bachelor's degree or higher: 7.9% (2007); Master's degree or higher: 2.5% (2007).

Housing: Homeownership rate: 85.7% (2007); Median home value: $113,889 (2007); Median rent: $388 per month (2000); Median age of housing: 60+ years (2000).
Transportation: Commute to work: 81.9% car, 2.2% public transportation, 4.3% walk, 7.2% work from home (2000); Travel time to work: 14.1% less than 15 minutes, 37.5% 15 to 30 minutes, 12.5% 30 to 45 minutes, 7.8% 45 to 60 minutes, 28.1% 60 minutes or more (2000)

DIXON (city). County seat. Covers a land area of 6.326 square miles and a water area of 0.421 square miles. Located at 41.84° N. Lat.; 89.48° W. Long. Elevation is 682 feet.
History: Dixon was settled in 1830 by John Dixon, who operated a trading post and tavern. Industry soon came to Dixon because of the water power available from the Rock River.
Population: 15,718 (1990); 15,941 (2000); 15,017 (2007); 14,458 (2012 projected); Race: 86.6% White, 9.9% Black, 1.1% Asian, 5.8% Hispanic of any race (2007); Density: 2,373.8 persons per square mile (2007); Average household size: 2.72 (2007); Median age: 38.5 (2007); Males per 100 females: 108.9 (2007); Marriage status: 21.1% never married, 55.4% now married, 8.2% widowed, 15.4% divorced (2000); Foreign born: 2.6% (2000); Ancestry (includes multiple ancestries): 27.3% German, 15.7% Irish, 9.3% Other groups, 8.7% English, 5.8% United States or American (2000).
Economy: Single-family building permits issued: 46 (2007); Multi-family building permits issued: 50 (2007); Employment by occupation: 8.2% management, 15.8% professional, 18.5% services, 22.8% sales, 0.3% farming, 9.2% construction, 25.2% production (2000).
Income: Per capita income: $19,455 (2007); Median household income: $40,677 (2007); Average household income: $49,172 (2007); Percent of households with income of $100,000 or more: 8.3% (2007); Poverty rate: 10.1% (2000).
Education: Percent of population age 25 and over with: High school diploma (including GED) or higher: 73.9% (2007); Bachelor's degree or higher: 12.7% (2007); Master's degree or higher: 4.4% (2007).

School District(s)

Dept of Corrections Sch Dist 428 (08-12)
2005-06 Enrollment: 2,271 . . . . (217) 522-2666
Dixon USD 170 (PK-12)
2005-06 Enrollment: 2,929 . . . . (815) 284-7722

Two-year College(s)

Sauk Valley Community College (Public)
Fall 2007 Enrollment: 2,700. . . . . (815) 288-5511
2007-08 Tuition: In-state $7,808; Out-of-state $8,896

Housing: Homeownership rate: 66.6% (2007); Median home value: $108,314 (2007); Median rent: $371 per month (2000); Median age of housing: 50 years (2000).
Safety: Violent crime rate: 28.0 per 10,000 population; Property crime rate: 358.4 per 10,000 population (2006).
Newspapers: Telegraph (Local news; Circulation 9,448)
Transportation: Commute to work: 91.6% car, 1.4% public transportation, 3.6% walk, 2.3% work from home (2000); Travel time to work: 60.9% less than 15 minutes, 23.9% 15 to 30 minutes, 6.9% 30 to 45 minutes, 2.1% 45 to 60 minutes, 6.1% 60 minutes or more (2000)

Additional Information Contacts

City of Dixon. . . . . (815) 288-1485
http://www.dixonil.com
Dixon Area Chamber of Commerce & Industry . . . . (815) 284-3361
http://www.dixonillinoischamber.com

FRANKLIN GROVE (village). Covers a land area of 0.371 square miles and a water area of 0 square miles. Located at 41.84° N. Lat.; 89.30° W. Long. Elevation is 804 feet.
Population: 968 (1990); 1,052 (2000); 1,016 (2007); 1,010 (2012 projected); Race: 99.2% White, 0.1% Black, 0.1% Asian, 0.7% Hispanic of any race (2007); Density: 2,738.5 persons per square mile (2007); Average household size: 2.75 (2007); Median age: 42.4 (2007); Males per 100 females: 86.8 (2007); Marriage status: 18.5% never married, 61.8% now married, 10.9% widowed, 8.9% divorced (2000); Foreign born: 0.2% (2000); Ancestry (includes multiple ancestries): 27.1% German, 14.2% English, 13.9% Irish, 9.2% United States or American, 5.9% Other groups (2000).
Economy: Single-family building permits issued: 1 (2007); Multi-family building permits issued: 0 (2007); Employment by occupation: 6.7% management, 11.6% professional, 20.8% services, 23.9% sales, 0.0% farming, 10.7% construction, 26.2% production (2000).
Income: Per capita income: $19,880 (2007); Median household income: $49,435 (2007); Average household income: $54,085 (2007); Percent of households with income of $100,000 or more: 10.0% (2007); Poverty rate: 7.7% (2000).
Education: Percent of population age 25 and over with: High school diploma (including GED) or higher: 82.9% (2007); Bachelor's degree or higher: 13.7% (2007); Master's degree or higher: 5.9% (2007).

School District(s)

Ashton-Franklin Center CUSD 275 (KG-12)
2005-06 Enrollment: 632 . . . . (815) 453-7461

Housing: Homeownership rate: 68.3% (2007); Median home value: $121,181 (2007); Median rent: $443 per month (2000); Median age of housing: 58 years (2000).
Transportation: Commute to work: 93.2% car, 0.0% public transportation, 4.3% walk, 1.1% work from home (2000); Travel time to work: 28.5% less than 15 minutes, 46.0% 15 to 30 minutes, 11.3% 30 to 45 minutes, 4.6% 45 to 60 minutes, 9.7% 60 minutes or more (2000)

HARMON (village). Covers a land area of 0.142 square miles and a water area of 0 square miles. Located at 41.72° N. Lat.; 89.55° W. Long. Elevation is 676 feet.
Population: 186 (1990); 149 (2000); 145 (2007); 141 (2012 projected); Race: 100.0% White, 0.0% Black, 0.0% Asian, 2.8% Hispanic of any race (2007); Density: 1,021.6 persons per square mile (2007); Average household size: 2.50 (2007); Median age: 38.6 (2007); Males per 100 females: 116.4 (2007); Marriage status: 40.4% never married, 52.9% now married, 2.9% widowed, 3.7% divorced (2000); Foreign born: 0.0% (2000); Ancestry (includes multiple ancestries): 64.3% German, 46.5% Irish, 8.9% United States or American, 6.4% Swedish, 6.4% French (except Basque) (2000).
Economy: Employment by occupation: 6.7% management, 14.7% professional, 8.0% services, 33.3% sales, 0.0% farming, 8.0% construction, 29.3% production (2000).
Income: Per capita income: $25,931 (2007); Median household income: $62,500 (2007); Average household income: $64,828 (2007); Percent of households with income of $100,000 or more: 15.5% (2007); Poverty rate: 3.2% (2000).
Education: Percent of population age 25 and over with: High school diploma (including GED) or higher: 82.5% (2007); Bachelor's degree or higher: 2.9% (2007); Master's degree or higher: 1.9% (2007).
Housing: Homeownership rate: 81.0% (2007); Median home value: $84,167 (2007); Median rent: $725 per month (2000); Median age of housing: 60+ years (2000).
Transportation: Commute to work: 98.7% car, 0.0% public transportation, 1.3% walk, 0.0% work from home (2000); Travel time to work: 2.7% less than 15 minutes, 80.0% 15 to 30 minutes, 2.7% 30 to 45 minutes, 10.7% 45 to 60 minutes, 4.0% 60 minutes or more (2000)

LEE (village). Covers a land area of 0.223 square miles and a water area of 0 square miles. Located at 41.79° N. Lat.; 88.94° W. Long. Elevation is 938 feet.
Population: 347 (1990); 313 (2000); 345 (2007); 362 (2012 projected); Race: 93.0% White, 0.0% Black, 0.9% Asian, 5.2% Hispanic of any race (2007); Density: 1,547.7 persons per square mile (2007); Average household size: 2.59 (2007); Median age: 32.5 (2007); Males per 100 females: 104.1 (2007); Marriage status: 27.8% never married, 55.5% now married, 9.1% widowed, 7.7% divorced (2000); Foreign born: 0.7% (2000); Ancestry (includes multiple ancestries): 32.4% German, 17.3% Irish, 16.9% English, 16.5% Norwegian, 8.1% Other groups (2000).
Economy: Single-family building permits issued: 0 (2007); Multi-family building permits issued: 0 (2007); Employment by occupation: 8.7% management, 20.3% professional, 16.7% services, 31.2% sales, 1.4% farming, 12.3% construction, 9.4% production (2000).
Income: Per capita income: $22,746 (2007); Median household income: $55,000 (2007); Average household income: $59,004 (2007); Percent of households with income of $100,000 or more: 12.8% (2007); Poverty rate: 11.5% (2000).
Education: Percent of population age 25 and over with: High school diploma (including GED) or higher: 92.5% (2007); Bachelor's degree or higher: 18.2% (2007); Master's degree or higher: 4.7% (2007).
Housing: Homeownership rate: 71.4% (2007); Median home value: $147,596 (2007); Median rent: $503 per month (2000); Median age of housing: 60+ years (2000).
Transportation: Commute to work: 92.6% car, 0.0% public transportation, 3.7% walk, 3.7% work from home (2000); Travel time to work: 11.5% less

than 15 minutes, 16.0% 15 to 30 minutes, 47.3% 30 to 45 minutes, 19.8% 45 to 60 minutes, 5.3% 60 minutes or more (2000)

NELSON (village). Covers a land area of 0.227 square miles and a water area of 0.005 square miles. Located at 41.79° N. Lat.; 89.60° W. Long. Elevation is 653 feet.

Population: 200 (1990); 163 (2000); 179 (2007); 187 (2012 projected); Race: 96.1% White, 0.6% Black, 0.0% Asian, 5.6% Hispanic of any race (2007); Density: 789.6 persons per square mile (2007); Average household size: 2.49 (2007); Median age: 43.5 (2007); Males per 100 females: 103.4 (2007); Marriage status: 22.0% never married, 64.4% now married, 5.1% widowed, 8.5% divorced (2000); Foreign born: 1.3% (2000); Ancestry (includes multiple ancestries): 39.3% German, 8.0% Danish, 7.3% English, 6.0% Irish, 4.0% United States or American (2000).

Economy: Employment by occupation: 5.6% management, 3.7% professional, 11.1% services, 13.0% sales, 0.0% farming, 29.6% construction, 37.0% production (2000).

Income: Per capita income: $20,642 (2007); Median household income: $41,667 (2007); Average household income: $51,319 (2007); Percent of households with income of $100,000 or more: 6.9% (2007); Poverty rate: 30.0% (2000).

Education: Percent of population age 25 and over with: High school diploma (including GED) or higher: 60.0% (2007); Bachelor's degree or higher: 0.0% (2007); Master's degree or higher: 0.0% (2007).

School District(s)

Nelson ESD 8 (KG-08)
2005-06 Enrollment: 38 . . . . (815) 251-4412

Housing: Homeownership rate: 83.3% (2007); Median home value: $80,769 (2007); Median rent: $313 per month (2000); Median age of housing: 60+ years (2000).

Transportation: Commute to work: 90.7% car, 0.0% public transportation, 5.6% walk, 0.0% work from home (2000); Travel time to work: 25.9% less than 15 minutes, 51.9% 15 to 30 minutes, 11.1% 30 to 45 minutes, 1.9% 45 to 60 minutes, 9.3% 60 minutes or more (2000)

PAW PAW (village). Aka Pawpaw. Covers a land area of 0.566 square miles and a water area of 0 square miles. Located at 41.68° N. Lat.; 88.98° W. Long. Elevation is 945 feet.

Population: 833 (1990); 852 (2000); 923 (2007); 953 (2012 projected); Race: 98.8% White, 0.0% Black, 0.3% Asian, 1.6% Hispanic of any race (2007); Density: 1,631.8 persons per square mile (2007); Average household size: 2.45 (2007); Median age: 40.5 (2007); Males per 100 females: 98.9 (2007); Marriage status: 23.0% never married, 59.4% now married, 10.3% widowed, 7.4% divorced (2000); Foreign born: 0.2% (2000); Ancestry (includes multiple ancestries): 30.5% German, 13.5% Irish, 11.8% English, 5.7% Swedish, 5.3% United States or American (2000).

Economy: Single-family building permits issued: 0 (2007); Multi-family building permits issued: 0 (2007); Employment by occupation: 9.1% management, 7.4% professional, 17.5% services, 26.2% sales, 1.7% farming, 14.1% construction, 24.0% production (2000).

Income: Per capita income: $20,428 (2007); Median household income: $43,125 (2007); Average household income: $50,146 (2007); Percent of households with income of $100,000 or more: 6.6% (2007); Poverty rate: 5.9% (2000).

Education: Percent of population age 25 and over with: High school diploma (including GED) or higher: 85.0% (2007); Bachelor's degree or higher: 8.6% (2007); Master's degree or higher: 1.5% (2007).

School District(s)

Paw Paw CUSD 271 (KG-12)
2005-06 Enrollment: 324 . . . . (815) 627-2841

Housing: Homeownership rate: 80.3% (2007); Median home value: $142,000 (2007); Median rent: $439 per month (2000); Median age of housing: 56 years (2000).

Transportation: Commute to work: 91.5% car, 1.3% public transportation, 5.0% walk, 2.3% work from home (2000); Travel time to work: 20.2% less than 15 minutes, 21.2% 15 to 30 minutes, 22.8% 30 to 45 minutes, 16.4% 45 to 60 minutes, 19.4% 60 minutes or more (2000)

STEWARD (village). Covers a land area of 0.124 square miles and a water area of 0 square miles. Located at 41.84° N. Lat.; 89.02° W. Long. Elevation is 820 feet.

Population: 282 (1990); 271 (2000); 306 (2007); 324 (2012 projected); Race: 98.4% White, 0.7% Black, 0.0% Asian, 3.6% Hispanic of any race (2007); Density: 2,462.5 persons per square mile (2007); Average household size: 2.66 (2007); Median age: 37.7 (2007); Males per 100 females: 114.0 (2007); Marriage status: 16.0% never married, 71.6% now married, 3.6% widowed, 8.8% divorced (2000); Foreign born: 0.0% (2000); Ancestry (includes multiple ancestries): 29.9% German, 17.2% Irish, 14.6% English, 12.4% French (except Basque), 11.3% Norwegian (2000).

Economy: Employment by occupation: 8.1% management, 22.6% professional, 12.9% services, 24.2% sales, 0.0% farming, 4.0% construction, 28.2% production (2000).

Income: Per capita income: $20,564 (2007); Median household income: $53,889 (2007); Average household income: $54,717 (2007); Percent of households with income of $100,000 or more: 7.0% (2007); Poverty rate: 4.5% (2000).

Education: Percent of population age 25 and over with: High school diploma (including GED) or higher: 83.5% (2007); Bachelor's degree or higher: 17.5% (2007); Master's degree or higher: 6.0% (2007).

School District(s)

Steward ESD 220 (KG-08)
2005-06 Enrollment: 93 . . . . (815) 396-2413

Housing: Homeownership rate: 85.2% (2007); Median home value: $132,000 (2007); Median rent: $375 per month (2000); Median age of housing: 60+ years (2000).

Transportation: Commute to work: 94.4% car, 0.0% public transportation, 2.4% walk, 3.2% work from home (2000); Travel time to work: 14.2% less than 15 minutes, 41.7% 15 to 30 minutes, 28.3% 30 to 45 minutes, 10.0% 45 to 60 minutes, 5.8% 60 minutes or more (2000)

SUBLETTE (village). Covers a land area of 0.350 square miles and a water area of 0 square miles. Located at 41.64° N. Lat.; 89.23° W. Long. Elevation is 919 feet.

Population: 405 (1990); 456 (2000); 422 (2007); 424 (2012 projected); Race: 97.2% White, 0.7% Black, 0.0% Asian, 7.1% Hispanic of any race (2007); Density: 1,206.3 persons per square mile (2007); Average household size: 2.38 (2007); Median age: 37.6 (2007); Males per 100 females: 100.0 (2007); Marriage status: 25.1% never married, 61.6% now married, 8.1% widowed, 5.3% divorced (2000); Foreign born: 4.9% (2000); Ancestry (includes multiple ancestries): 41.2% German, 20.3% Irish, 10.0% Other groups, 7.8% English, 7.3% Dutch (2000).

Economy: Employment by occupation: 11.3% management, 12.2% professional, 13.5% services, 32.4% sales, 0.0% farming, 8.1% construction, 22.5% production (2000).

Income: Per capita income: $27,921 (2007); Median household income: $54,643 (2007); Average household income: $66,568 (2007); Percent of households with income of $100,000 or more: 14.1% (2007); Poverty rate: 4.0% (2000).

Education: Percent of population age 25 and over with: High school diploma (including GED) or higher: 82.3% (2007); Bachelor's degree or higher: 5.9% (2007); Master's degree or higher: 2.1% (2007).

Housing: Homeownership rate: 75.1% (2007); Median home value: $131,090 (2007); Median rent: $300 per month (2000); Median age of housing: 29 years (2000).

Transportation: Commute to work: 95.9% car, 0.0% public transportation, 3.2% walk, 0.9% work from home (2000); Travel time to work: 45.9% less than 15 minutes, 17.3% 15 to 30 minutes, 25.5% 30 to 45 minutes, 2.7% 45 to 60 minutes, 8.6% 60 minutes or more (2000)

WEST BROOKLYN (village). Covers a land area of 0.107 square miles and a water area of 0 square miles. Located at 41.69° N. Lat.; 89.14° W. Long. Elevation is 945 feet.

Population: 164 (1990); 174 (2000); 174 (2007); 170 (2012 projected); Race: 88.5% White, 0.6% Black, 1.1% Asian, 8.6% Hispanic of any race (2007); Density: 1,629.0 persons per square mile (2007); Average household size: 2.85 (2007); Median age: 33.6 (2007); Males per 100 females: 95.5 (2007); Marriage status: 13.8% never married, 77.6% now married, 4.3% widowed, 4.3% divorced (2000); Foreign born: 1.1% (2000); Ancestry (includes multiple ancestries): 39.7% German, 17.9% French (except Basque), 15.1% Other groups, 12.3% Irish, 7.8% English (2000).

Economy: Employment by occupation: 7.2% management, 12.0% professional, 13.3% services, 30.1% sales, 0.0% farming, 18.1% construction, 19.3% production (2000).

Income: Per capita income: $18,707 (2007); Median household income: $43,750 (2007); Average household income: $53,361 (2007); Percent of households with income of $100,000 or more: 11.5% (2007); Poverty rate: 1.7% (2000).

Education: Percent of population age 25 and over with: High school diploma (including GED) or higher: 84.0% (2007); Bachelor's degree or higher: 6.0% (2007); Master's degree or higher: 2.0% (2007).
Housing: Homeownership rate: 86.9% (2007); Median home value: $114,500 (2007); Median rent: $238 per month (2000); Median age of housing: 60+ years (2000).
Transportation: Commute to work: 95.1% car, 0.0% public transportation, 4.9% walk, 0.0% work from home (2000); Travel time to work: 12.3% less than 15 minutes, 59.3% 15 to 30 minutes, 7.4% 30 to 45 minutes, 12.3% 45 to 60 minutes, 8.6% 60 minutes or more (2000)

Livingston County

Located in east central Illinois; drained by the Vermilion River. Covers a land area of 1,043.76 square miles, a water area of 1.67 square miles, and is located in the Central Time Zone. The county was founded in 1837. County seat is Pontiac.

Livingston County is part of the Pontiac, IL Micropolitan Statistical Area. The entire metro area includes: Livingston County, IL

Weather Station: Pontiac Elevation: 649 feet

	Jan	Feb	Mar	Apr	May	Jun	Jul	Aug	Sep	Oct	Nov	Dec
High	30	36	48	62	73	82	85	83	77	65	49	36
Low	14	19	29	40	51	61	64	62	54	42	32	21
Precip	1.6	1.4	2.8	3.5	4.0	4.1	4.1	3.6	3.2	2.7	2.9	2.5
Snow	8.9	5.7	3.3	1.0	0.0	0.0	0.0	0.0	0.0	tr	1.7	5.2

High and Low temperatures in degrees Fahrenheit; Precipitation and Snow in inches

Population: 39,301 (1990); 39,678 (2000); 39,172 (2007); 38,808 (2012 projected); Race: 92.1% White, 5.4% Black, 0.3% Asian, 2.8% Hispanic of any race (2007); Density: 37.5 persons per square mile (2007); Average household size: 2.69 (2007); Median age: 38.2 (2007); Males per 100 females: 98.4 (2007).
Religion: Five largest groups: 17.7% Catholic Church, 12.7% Evangelical Lutheran Church in America, 11.1% The United Methodist Church, 3.9% American Baptist Churches in the USA, 3.5% Apostolic Christian Church of America, Inc. (2000).
Economy: Unemployment rate: 5.2% (4/2008); Total civilian labor force: 19,634 (4/2008); Leading industries: 33.1% manufacturing; 16.1% retail trade; 14.4% health care and social assistance (2005); Farms: 1,330 totaling 636,406 acres (2002); Companies that employ 500 or more persons: 4 (2006); Companies that employ 100 to 499 persons: 15 (2006); Companies that employ less than 100 persons: 898 (2006); Black-owned businesses: n/a (2002); Hispanic-owned businesses: n/a (2002); Asian-owned businesses: n/a (2002); Women-owned businesses: 547 (2002); Retail sales per capita: $15,000 (2008). Single-family building permits issued: 49 (2007); Multi-family building permits issued: 88 (2007).
Income: Per capita income: $22,248 (2007); Median household income: $48,820 (2007); Average household income: $57,804 (2007); Percent of households with income of $100,000 or more: 12.6% (2007); Poverty rate: 9.7% (2005); Bankruptcy rate: 3.63% (2007).
Taxes: Total county taxes per capita: $156 (2006); County property taxes per capita: $155 (2006).
Education: Percent of population age 25 and over with: High school diploma (including GED) or higher: 78.2% (2007); Bachelor's degree or higher: 12.5% (2007); Master's degree or higher: 3.9% (2007).
Housing: Homeownership rate: 74.1% (2007); Median home value: $115,405 (2007); Median rent: $364 per month (2000); Median age of housing: 45 years (2000).
Health: Birth rate: 139.6 per 10,000 population (2007); Death rate: 109.3 per 10,000 population (2007); Age-adjusted cancer mortality rate: 207.9 deaths per 100,000 population (2005); Number of physicians: 9.0 per 10,000 population (2005); Hospital beds: 10.8 per 10,000 population (2004); Hospital admissions: 469.0 per 10,000 population (2004).
Elections: 2004 Presidential election results: 64.3% Bush, 35.1% Kerry, 0.1% Nader, 0.5% Badnarik

Additional Information Contacts

Livingston County Government . . . . (815) 844-2006
http://www.livingstoncounty-il.org
Dwight Area Chamber of Commerce . . . . (815) 584-2091
http://www.dwightchamber.net
Pontiac Area Chamber of Commerce . . . . (815) 844-5131
http://www.pontiacchamber.org
Village of Dwight . . . . (815) 584-3077
http://www.dwightillinois.org

Livingston County Communities

ANCONA (unincorporated postal area, zip code 61311). Covers a land area of 28.939 square miles and a water area of 0 square miles. Located at 41.04° N. Lat.; 88.86° W. Long. Elevation is 620 feet.
Population: 353 (2000); Race: 96.8% White, 0.0% Black, 0.0% Asian, 7.6% Hispanic of any race (2000); Density: 12.2 persons per square mile (2000); Age: 28.9% under 18, 15.2% over 64 (2000); Marriage status: 20.3% never married, 69.0% now married, 4.6% widowed, 6.1% divorced (2000); Foreign born: 0.0% (2000); Ancestry (includes multiple ancestries): 29.8% German, 9.4% Irish, 8.5% English, 7.0% Norwegian, 6.7% Slovak (2000).
Economy: Employment by occupation: 18.5% management, 22.2% professional, 8.6% services, 11.1% sales, 1.2% farming, 16.7% construction, 21.6% production (2000).
Income: Per capita income: $23,007 (2000); Median household income: $55,500 (2000); Poverty rate: 11.7% (2000).
Education: Percent of population age 25 and over with: High school diploma (including GED) or higher: 80.5% (2000); Bachelor's degree or higher: 20.3% (2000).
Housing: Homeownership rate: 88.4% (2000); Median home value: $90,300 (2000); Median rent: $n/a per month (2000); Median age of housing: 60+ years (2000).
Transportation: Commute to work: 80.9% car, 0.0% public transportation, 0.0% walk, 19.1% work from home (2000); Travel time to work: 35.1% less than 15 minutes, 35.1% 15 to 30 minutes, 22.1% 30 to 45 minutes, 0.0% 45 to 60 minutes, 7.6% 60 minutes or more (2000)

BLACKSTONE (unincorporated postal area, zip code 61313). Covers a land area of 44.936 square miles and a water area of 0 square miles. Located at 41.06° N. Lat.; 88.66° W. Long. Elevation is 738 feet.
Population: 316 (2000); Race: 95.8% White, 4.2% Black, 0.0% Asian, 0.0% Hispanic of any race (2000); Density: 7.0 persons per square mile (2000); Age: 27.6% under 18, 12.0% over 64 (2000); Marriage status: 20.7% never married, 70.0% now married, 2.1% widowed, 7.1% divorced (2000); Foreign born: 0.3% (2000); Ancestry (includes multiple ancestries): 33.4% German, 12.0% United States or American, 10.3% Irish, 8.4% English, 7.8% Other groups (2000).
Economy: Employment by occupation: 20.9% management, 18.6% professional, 21.9% services, 6.0% sales, 0.5% farming, 10.7% construction, 21.4% production (2000).
Income: Per capita income: $22,553 (2000); Median household income: $59,583 (2000); Poverty rate: 3.3% (2000).
Education: Percent of population age 25 and over with: High school diploma (including GED) or higher: 90.9% (2000); Bachelor's degree or higher: 19.0% (2000).
Housing: Homeownership rate: 81.3% (2000); Median home value: $86,300 (2000); Median rent: $392 per month (2000); Median age of housing: 59 years (2000).
Transportation: Commute to work: 88.2% car, 0.0% public transportation, 3.8% walk, 6.6% work from home (2000); Travel time to work: 23.9% less than 15 minutes, 58.9% 15 to 30 minutes, 8.6% 30 to 45 minutes, 2.5% 45 to 60 minutes, 6.1% 60 minutes or more (2000)

CAMPUS (village). Covers a land area of 0.099 square miles and a water area of 0 square miles. Located at 41.02° N. Lat.; 88.30° W. Long. Elevation is 656 feet.
Population: 137 (1990); 145 (2000); 139 (2007); 135 (2012 projected); Race: 100.0% White, 0.0% Black, 0.0% Asian, 2.9% Hispanic of any race (2007); Density: 1,398.8 persons per square mile (2007); Average household size: 3.56 (2007); Median age: 24.1 (2007); Males per 100 females: 110.6 (2007); Marriage status: 29.9% never married, 51.7% now married, 5.7% widowed, 12.6% divorced (2000); Foreign born: 2.5% (2000); Ancestry (includes multiple ancestries): 52.1% United States or American, 20.2% French (except Basque), 17.6% German, 6.7% Irish, 6.7% Polish (2000).
Economy: Employment by occupation: 1.8% management, 10.7% professional, 21.4% services, 19.6% sales, 0.0% farming, 3.6% construction, 42.9% production (2000).
Income: Per capita income: $17,852 (2007); Median household income: $54,375 (2007); Average household income: $63,269 (2007); Percent of households with income of $100,000 or more: 12.8% (2007); Poverty rate: 3.4% (2000).

Education: Percent of population age 25 and over with: High school diploma (including GED) or higher: 82.1% (2007); Bachelor's degree or higher: 4.5% (2007); Master's degree or higher: 4.5% (2007).
Housing: Homeownership rate: 74.4% (2007); Median home value: $82,500 (2007); Median rent: $350 per month (2000); Median age of housing: 60 years (2000).
Transportation: Commute to work: 91.1% car, 0.0% public transportation, 8.9% walk, 0.0% work from home (2000); Travel time to work: 12.5% less than 15 minutes, 33.9% 15 to 30 minutes, 44.6% 30 to 45 minutes, 8.9% 45 to 60 minutes, 0.0% 60 minutes or more (2000)

CHATSWORTH (town). Covers a land area of 0.895 square miles and a water area of 0 square miles. Located at 40.75° N. Lat.; 88.29° W. Long. Elevation is 735 feet.
History: Chatsworth was laid out in 1858, and devloped as a farming community and manufacturer of tiles and bricks from local clay.
Population: 1,206 (1990); 1,265 (2000); 1,292 (2007); 1,285 (2012 projected); Race: 98.9% White, 0.5% Black, 0.1% Asian, 1.8% Hispanic of any race (2007); Density: 1,443.0 persons per square mile (2007); Average household size: 2.33 (2007); Median age: 39.2 (2007); Males per 100 females: 94.9 (2007); Marriage status: 20.7% never married, 53.8% now married, 11.3% widowed, 14.2% divorced (2000); Foreign born: 0.7% (2000); Ancestry (includes multiple ancestries): 39.0% German, 15.7% Irish, 12.4% United States or American, 6.9% Italian, 6.2% Other groups (2000).
Economy: Single-family building permits issued: 0 (2007); Multi-family building permits issued: 0 (2007); Employment by occupation: 5.8% management, 8.0% professional, 16.7% services, 20.6% sales, 2.0% farming, 11.1% construction, 35.7% production (2000).
Income: Per capita income: $19,706 (2007); Median household income: $39,427 (2007); Average household income: $45,874 (2007); Percent of households with income of $100,000 or more: 6.7% (2007); Poverty rate: 14.1% (2000).
Education: Percent of population age 25 and over with: High school diploma (including GED) or higher: 79.9% (2007); Bachelor's degree or higher: 8.7% (2007); Master's degree or higher: 3.2% (2007).

School District(s)

Prairie Central CUSD 8 (PK-12)
2005-06 Enrollment: 2,241 . . . . (815) 692-2504
Housing: Homeownership rate: 68.8% (2007); Median home value: $85,094 (2007); Median rent: $263 per month (2000); Median age of housing: 57 years (2000).
Transportation: Commute to work: 94.1% car, 0.0% public transportation, 2.4% walk, 1.4% work from home (2000); Travel time to work: 49.8% less than 15 minutes, 14.7% 15 to 30 minutes, 16.1% 30 to 45 minutes, 10.8% 45 to 60 minutes, 8.6% 60 minutes or more (2000)

CORNELL (village). Covers a land area of 0.636 square miles and a water area of 0 square miles. Located at 40.99° N. Lat.; 88.73° W. Long. Elevation is 630 feet.
Population: 556 (1990); 511 (2000); 534 (2007); 547 (2012 projected); Race: 98.5% White, 0.7% Black, 0.0% Asian, 1.1% Hispanic of any race (2007); Density: 840.0 persons per square mile (2007); Average household size: 2.43 (2007); Median age: 38.6 (2007); Males per 100 females: 94.2 (2007); Marriage status: 24.5% never married, 60.7% now married, 6.1% widowed, 8.8% divorced (2000); Foreign born: 0.7% (2000); Ancestry (includes multiple ancestries): 38.0% German, 10.4% United States or American, 9.9% English, 9.3% Other groups, 9.1% Irish (2000).
Economy: Single-family building permits issued: 1 (2007); Multi-family building permits issued: 0 (2007); Employment by occupation: 3.4% management, 10.1% professional, 18.5% services, 22.2% sales, 1.7% farming, 10.1% construction, 34.0% production (2000).
Income: Per capita income: $26,063 (2007); Median household income: $60,750 (2007); Average household income: $63,261 (2007); Percent of households with income of $100,000 or more: 14.1% (2007); Poverty rate: 8.8% (2000).
Education: Percent of population age 25 and over with: High school diploma (including GED) or higher: 83.7% (2007); Bachelor's degree or higher: 8.3% (2007); Master's degree or higher: 1.7% (2007).

School District(s)

Cornell CCSD 426 (KG-08)
2005-06 Enrollment: 110 . . . . (815) 358-2214
Housing: Homeownership rate: 75.0% (2007); Median home value: $81,154 (2007); Median rent: $306 per month (2000); Median age of housing: 41 years (2000).
Transportation: Commute to work: 91.0% car, 1.4% public transportation, 6.6% walk, 0.7% work from home (2000); Travel time to work: 21.5% less than 15 minutes, 57.6% 15 to 30 minutes, 4.9% 30 to 45 minutes, 7.3% 45 to 60 minutes, 8.7% 60 minutes or more (2000)

CULLOM (village). Covers a land area of 0.308 square miles and a water area of 0 square miles. Located at 40.87° N. Lat.; 88.26° W. Long. Elevation is 682 feet.
Population: 568 (1990); 563 (2000); 505 (2007); 503 (2012 projected); Race: 98.6% White, 0.6% Black, 0.0% Asian, 0.8% Hispanic of any race (2007); Density: 1,638.8 persons per square mile (2007); Average household size: 2.21 (2007); Median age: 39.6 (2007); Males per 100 females: 89.1 (2007); Marriage status: 18.0% never married, 63.2% now married, 10.0% widowed, 8.7% divorced (2000); Foreign born: 0.4% (2000); Ancestry (includes multiple ancestries): 34.2% German, 13.7% Irish, 13.0% English, 10.7% United States or American, 4.8% Other groups (2000).
Economy: Single-family building permits issued: 2 (2007); Multi-family building permits issued: 0 (2007); Employment by occupation: 6.8% management, 11.0% professional, 18.6% services, 27.0% sales, 1.1% farming, 12.5% construction, 22.8% production (2000).
Income: Per capita income: $18,876 (2007); Median household income: $34,342 (2007); Average household income: $41,627 (2007); Percent of households with income of $100,000 or more: 4.4% (2007); Poverty rate: 5.3% (2000).
Education: Percent of population age 25 and over with: High school diploma (including GED) or higher: 84.9% (2007); Bachelor's degree or higher: 9.4% (2007); Master's degree or higher: 5.1% (2007).

School District(s)

Tri Point CUSD 6-J (PK-12)
2005-06 Enrollment: 583 . . . . (815) 253-6299
Housing: Homeownership rate: 79.9% (2007); Median home value: $101,330 (2007); Median rent: $275 per month (2000); Median age of housing: 55 years (2000).
Transportation: Commute to work: 85.9% car, 0.0% public transportation, 9.4% walk, 3.9% work from home (2000); Travel time to work: 43.5% less than 15 minutes, 17.5% 15 to 30 minutes, 20.3% 30 to 45 minutes, 11.0% 45 to 60 minutes, 7.7% 60 minutes or more (2000)

DWIGHT (village). Covers a land area of 2.574 square miles and a water area of 0.008 square miles. Located at 41.09° N. Lat.; 88.42° W. Long. Elevation is 630 feet.
History: In Dwight, Dr. Leslie Keeley, a Civil War surgeon, established the Keeley Institute for the treatment of alcoholism and drug addiction, and achieved much success and acclaim.
Population: 4,242 (1990); 4,363 (2000); 4,344 (2007); 4,314 (2012 projected); Race: 96.5% White, 0.9% Black, 0.2% Asian, 3.2% Hispanic of any race (2007); Density: 1,687.4 persons per square mile (2007); Average household size: 2.60 (2007); Median age: 37.2 (2007); Males per 100 females: 90.4 (2007); Marriage status: 23.0% never married, 58.8% now married, 7.8% widowed, 10.5% divorced (2000); Foreign born: 1.9% (2000); Ancestry (includes multiple ancestries): 30.8% German, 19.4% Irish, 8.3% United States or American, 7.2% Danish, 6.8% English (2000).
Economy: Single-family building permits issued: 2 (2007); Multi-family building permits issued: 14 (2007); Employment by occupation: 8.1% management, 16.2% professional, 17.5% services, 21.7% sales, 0.0% farming, 12.4% construction, 24.1% production (2000).
Income: Per capita income: $23,278 (2007); Median household income: $46,007 (2007); Average household income: $59,668 (2007); Percent of households with income of $100,000 or more: 15.6% (2007); Poverty rate: 10.8% (2000).
Education: Percent of population age 25 and over with: High school diploma (including GED) or higher: 79.8% (2007); Bachelor's degree or higher: 10.8% (2007); Master's degree or higher: 3.3% (2007).

School District(s)

Dept of Corrections Sch Dist 428 (08-12)
2005-06 Enrollment: 2,271 . . . . (217) 522-2666
Dwight Common SD 232 (PK-08)
2005-06 Enrollment: 713 . . . . (815) 584-6217
Dwight Twp HSD 230 (09-12)
2005-06 Enrollment: 346 . . . . (815) 524-6217
Housing: Homeownership rate: 71.3% (2007); Median home value: $133,317 (2007); Median rent: $409 per month (2000); Median age of housing: 43 years (2000).

Safety: Violent crime rate: 13.8 per 10,000 population; Property crime rate: 192.7 per 10,000 population (2006).
Newspapers: Courier Press (Community news; Circulation 1,500); Dwight Star & Herald (Community news; Circulation 2,409)
Transportation: Commute to work: 93.4% car, 1.1% public transportation, 4.3% walk, 1.3% work from home (2000); Travel time to work: 55.9% less than 15 minutes, 12.7% 15 to 30 minutes, 15.6% 30 to 45 minutes, 6.4% 45 to 60 minutes, 9.4% 60 minutes or more (2000); Amtrak: Service available.

Additional Information Contacts

Dwight Area Chamber of Commerce . . . . (815) 584-2091
http://www.dwightchamber.net
Village of Dwight . . . . (815) 584-3077
http://www.dwightillinois.org

EMINGTON (village). Covers a land area of 0.101 square miles and a water area of 0 square miles. Located at 40.97° N. Lat.; 88.35° W. Long. Elevation is 715 feet.
Population: 135 (1990); 120 (2000); 116 (2007); 114 (2012 projected); Race: 98.3% White, 0.0% Black, 0.9% Asian, 0.0% Hispanic of any race (2007); Density: 1,145.2 persons per square mile (2007); Average household size: 2.37 (2007); Median age: 35.0 (2007); Males per 100 females: 103.5 (2007); Marriage status: 21.6% never married, 56.8% now married, 10.2% widowed, 11.4% divorced (2000); Foreign born: 0.0% (2000); Ancestry (includes multiple ancestries): 43.8% United States or American, 19.5% German, 8.6% Irish, 8.6% Other groups, 6.3% English (2000).
Economy: Single-family building permits issued: 0 (2007); Multi-family building permits issued: 0 (2007); Employment by occupation: 0.0% management, 19.1% professional, 8.5% services, 21.3% sales, 0.0% farming, 25.5% construction, 25.5% production (2000).
Income: Per capita income: $16,293 (2007); Median household income: $29,500 (2007); Average household income: $38,571 (2007); Percent of households with income of $100,000 or more: 0.0% (2007); Poverty rate: 12.5% (2000).
Education: Percent of population age 25 and over with: High school diploma (including GED) or higher: 79.2% (2007); Bachelor's degree or higher: 4.2% (2007); Master's degree or higher: 0.0% (2007).
Housing: Homeownership rate: 75.5% (2007); Median home value: $88,750 (2007); Median rent: $400 per month (2000); Median age of housing: 60+ years (2000).
Transportation: Commute to work: 93.6% car, 0.0% public transportation, 0.0% walk, 6.4% work from home (2000); Travel time to work: 0.0% less than 15 minutes, 34.1% 15 to 30 minutes, 25.0% 30 to 45 minutes, 6.8% 45 to 60 minutes, 34.1% 60 minutes or more (2000)

FAIRBURY (city). Covers a land area of 1.297 square miles and a water area of 0 square miles. Located at 40.74° N. Lat.; 88.51° W. Long. Elevation is 682 feet.
History: Incorporated 1890.
Population: 3,850 (1990); 3,968 (2000); 4,039 (2007); 4,052 (2012 projected); Race: 96.5% White, 0.4% Black, 0.5% Asian, 2.5% Hispanic of any race (2007); Density: 3,114.9 persons per square mile (2007); Average household size: 2.51 (2007); Median age: 38.7 (2007); Males per 100 females: 92.2 (2007); Marriage status: 20.4% never married, 66.3% now married, 7.4% widowed, 6.0% divorced (2000); Foreign born: 1.1% (2000); Ancestry (includes multiple ancestries): 36.4% German, 17.6% United States or American, 14.0% Irish, 9.3% English, 7.8% Other groups (2000).
Economy: Single-family building permits issued: 5 (2007); Multi-family building permits issued: 0 (2007); Employment by occupation: 11.0% management, 17.5% professional, 18.6% services, 18.6% sales, 1.1% farming, 9.2% construction, 23.9% production (2000).
Income: Per capita income: $22,762 (2007); Median household income: $47,458 (2007); Average household income: $55,026 (2007); Percent of households with income of $100,000 or more: 10.9% (2007); Poverty rate: 4.9% (2000).
Education: Percent of population age 25 and over with: High school diploma (including GED) or higher: 78.2% (2007); Bachelor's degree or higher: 15.2% (2007); Master's degree or higher: 6.4% (2007).

School District(s)

Prairie Central CUSD 8 (PK-12)
2005-06 Enrollment: 2,241 . . . . (815) 692-2504
Housing: Homeownership rate: 70.4% (2007); Median home value: $125,152 (2007); Median rent: $383 per month (2000); Median age of housing: 41 years (2000).
Safety: Violent crime rate: 28.1 per 10,000 population; Property crime rate: 165.9 per 10,000 population (2006).
Newspapers: Blade (Community news; Circulation 3,400)
Transportation: Commute to work: 91.2% car, 0.8% public transportation, 4.4% walk, 3.3% work from home (2000); Travel time to work: 46.4% less than 15 minutes, 25.2% 15 to 30 minutes, 11.6% 30 to 45 minutes, 11.8% 45 to 60 minutes, 5.0% 60 minutes or more (2000)

FLANAGAN (village). Covers a land area of 0.534 square miles and a water area of 0 square miles. Located at 40.87° N. Lat.; 88.85° W. Long. Elevation is 673 feet.
Population: 989 (1990); 1,083 (2000); 1,067 (2007); 1,064 (2012 projected); Race: 98.8% White, 0.4% Black, 0.1% Asian, 0.0% Hispanic of any race (2007); Density: 1,998.8 persons per square mile (2007); Average household size: 2.33 (2007); Median age: 45.0 (2007); Males per 100 females: 86.5 (2007); Marriage status: 14.9% never married, 65.0% now married, 12.8% widowed, 7.3% divorced (2000); Foreign born: 1.4% (2000); Ancestry (includes multiple ancestries): 39.9% German, 11.2% English, 10.5% Irish, 9.5% United States or American, 3.8% Dutch (2000).
Economy: Single-family building permits issued: 0 (2007); Multi-family building permits issued: 0 (2007); Employment by occupation: 10.0% management, 17.4% professional, 19.2% services, 26.7% sales, 1.3% farming, 6.4% construction, 19.1% production (2000).
Income: Per capita income: $25,493 (2007); Median household income: $48,295 (2007); Average household income: $58,282 (2007); Percent of households with income of $100,000 or more: 12.5% (2007); Poverty rate: 4.9% (2000).
Education: Percent of population age 25 and over with: High school diploma (including GED) or higher: 87.6% (2007); Bachelor's degree or higher: 19.8% (2007); Master's degree or higher: 6.5% (2007).

School District(s)

Flanagan CUSD 4 (PK-12)
2005-06 Enrollment: 388 . . . . (815) 796-2233
Housing: Homeownership rate: 74.8% (2007); Median home value: $110,345 (2007); Median rent: $406 per month (2000); Median age of housing: 45 years (2000).
Newspapers: Flanagan Home Times (Community news; Circulation 1,200)
Transportation: Commute to work: 91.5% car, 0.6% public transportation, 4.8% walk, 1.9% work from home (2000); Travel time to work: 40.3% less than 15 minutes, 43.1% 15 to 30 minutes, 7.2% 30 to 45 minutes, 6.4% 45 to 60 minutes, 3.0% 60 minutes or more (2000)

FORREST (village). Covers a land area of 0.626 square miles and a water area of 0 square miles. Located at 40.75° N. Lat.; 88.41° W. Long. Elevation is 686 feet.
History: Forrest was settled in 1836, but grew in the 1860's when German-Amish immigrants arrived.
Population: 1,198 (1990); 1,225 (2000); 1,255 (2007); 1,264 (2012 projected); Race: 95.5% White, 1.0% Black, 0.1% Asian, 3.7% Hispanic of any race (2007); Density: 2,004.4 persons per square mile (2007); Average household size: 2.65 (2007); Median age: 36.7 (2007); Males per 100 females: 98.9 (2007); Marriage status: 20.6% never married, 61.7% now married, 8.9% widowed, 8.9% divorced (2000); Foreign born: 2.6% (2000); Ancestry (includes multiple ancestries): 29.7% German, 13.6% Irish, 9.4% English, 8.7% Other groups, 8.3% United States or American (2000).
Economy: Single-family building permits issued: 1 (2007); Multi-family building permits issued: 6 (2007); Employment by occupation: 10.5% management, 16.2% professional, 15.5% services, 22.4% sales, 0.9% farming, 9.8% construction, 24.8% production (2000).
Income: Per capita income: $22,295 (2007); Median household income: $51,667 (2007); Average household income: $59,154 (2007); Percent of households with income of $100,000 or more: 11.2% (2007); Poverty rate: 8.9% (2000).
Education: Percent of population age 25 and over with: High school diploma (including GED) or higher: 78.7% (2007); Bachelor's degree or higher: 14.8% (2007); Master's degree or higher: 5.1% (2007).

School District(s)

Prairie Central CUSD 8 (PK-12)
2005-06 Enrollment: 2,241 . . . . (815) 692-2504
Housing: Homeownership rate: 73.2% (2007); Median home value: $111,215 (2007); Median rent: $344 per month (2000); Median age of housing: 52 years (2000).
Transportation: Commute to work: 95.1% car, 0.0% public transportation, 2.3% walk, 1.4% work from home (2000); Travel time to work: 51.8% less

than 15 minutes, 19.0% 15 to 30 minutes, 11.2% 30 to 45 minutes, 10.0% 45 to 60 minutes, 8.0% 60 minutes or more (2000)

GRAYMONT (unincorporated postal area, zip code 61743). Covers a land area of 15.916 square miles and a water area of 0 square miles. Located at 40.87° N. Lat.; 88.77° W. Long. Elevation is 653 feet.

Population: 270 (2000); Race: 100.0% White, 0.0% Black, 0.0% Asian, 0.0% Hispanic of any race (2000); Density: 17.0 persons per square mile (2000); Age: 32.2% under 18, 11.4% over 64 (2000); Marriage status: 21.7% never married, 59.3% now married, 5.8% widowed, 13.2% divorced (2000); Foreign born: 0.0% (2000); Ancestry (includes multiple ancestries): 44.7% German, 15.7% English, 14.1% United States or American, 9.4% Irish, 3.9% Scotch-Irish (2000).

Economy: Employment by occupation: 13.1% management, 12.4% professional, 25.5% services, 19.0% sales, 0.0% farming, 13.1% construction, 16.8% production (2000).

Income: Per capita income: $16,810 (2000); Median household income: $41,250 (2000); Poverty rate: 9.9% (2000).

Education: Percent of population age 25 and over with: High school diploma (including GED) or higher: 90.0% (2000); Bachelor's degree or higher: 14.7% (2000).

School District(s)

Rooks Creek CCSD 425 (KG-08)
2005-06 Enrollment: 50 . . . . (815) 743-5346

Housing: Homeownership rate: 71.0% (2000); Median home value: $49,200 (2000); Median rent: $332 per month (2000); Median age of housing: 60+ years (2000).

Transportation: Commute to work: 82.8% car, 0.0% public transportation, 6.7% walk, 9.7% work from home (2000); Travel time to work: 50.4% less than 15 minutes, 25.6% 15 to 30 minutes, 9.9% 30 to 45 minutes, 9.1% 45 to 60 minutes, 5.0% 60 minutes or more (2000)

LONG POINT (village). Covers a land area of 0.188 square miles and a water area of 0 square miles. Located at 41.00° N. Lat.; 88.89° W. Long. Elevation is 640 feet.

Population: 208 (1990); 247 (2000); 259 (2007); 267 (2012 projected); Race: 98.1% White, 0.0% Black, 0.4% Asian, 0.0% Hispanic of any race (2007); Density: 1,377.7 persons per square mile (2007); Average household size: 2.64 (2007); Median age: 40.7 (2007); Males per 100 females: 91.9 (2007); Marriage status: 26.9% never married, 59.6% now married, 5.3% widowed, 8.2% divorced (2000); Foreign born: 0.8% (2000); Ancestry (includes multiple ancestries): 39.7% German, 14.4% English, 14.0% Other groups, 8.6% United States or American, 8.2% Irish (2000).

Economy: Employment by occupation: 14.6% management, 7.7% professional, 20.0% services, 17.7% sales, 0.0% farming, 16.9% construction, 23.1% production (2000).

Income: Per capita income: $24,662 (2007); Median household income: $60,000 (2007); Average household income: $65,179 (2007); Percent of households with income of $100,000 or more: 17.3% (2007); Poverty rate: 6.6% (2000).

Education: Percent of population age 25 and over with: High school diploma (including GED) or higher: 82.0% (2007); Bachelor's degree or higher: 5.8% (2007); Master's degree or higher: 1.2% (2007).

Housing: Homeownership rate: 88.8% (2007); Median home value: $71,500 (2007); Median rent: $263 per month (2000); Median age of housing: 60+ years (2000).

Transportation: Commute to work: 91.8% car, 0.0% public transportation, 2.5% walk, 5.7% work from home (2000); Travel time to work: 16.5% less than 15 minutes, 67.0% 15 to 30 minutes, 7.0% 30 to 45 minutes, 1.7% 45 to 60 minutes, 7.8% 60 minutes or more (2000)

ODELL (village). Covers a land area of 1.115 square miles and a water area of 0.014 square miles. Located at 41.00° N. Lat.; 88.52° W. Long. Elevation is 719 feet.

Population: 1,030 (1990); 1,014 (2000); 1,025 (2007); 996 (2012 projected); Race: 98.0% White, 0.2% Black, 0.3% Asian, 2.6% Hispanic of any race (2007); Density: 918.9 persons per square mile (2007); Average household size: 2.42 (2007); Median age: 38.5 (2007); Males per 100 females: 94.5 (2007); Marriage status: 21.0% never married, 61.3% now married, 5.1% widowed, 12.6% divorced (2000); Foreign born: 0.9% (2000); Ancestry (includes multiple ancestries): 36.2% German, 24.3% Irish, 12.2% English, 7.7% United States or American, 6.3% French (except Basque) (2000).

Economy: Single-family building permits issued: 3 (2007); Multi-family building permits issued: 0 (2007); Employment by occupation: 7.6% management, 18.0% professional, 17.3% services, 22.0% sales, 1.0% farming, 11.6% construction, 22.4% production (2000).

Income: Per capita income: $21,378 (2007); Median household income: $45,400 (2007); Average household income: $51,680 (2007); Percent of households with income of $100,000 or more: 7.3% (2007); Poverty rate: 8.9% (2000).

Education: Percent of population age 25 and over with: High school diploma (including GED) or higher: 86.4% (2007); Bachelor's degree or higher: 12.0% (2007); Master's degree or higher: 3.1% (2007).

School District(s)

Odell CCSD 435 (PK-08)
2005-06 Enrollment: 175 . . . . (815) 998-2272

Housing: Homeownership rate: 79.0% (2007); Median home value: $115,091 (2007); Median rent: $402 per month (2000); Median age of housing: 49 years (2000).

Transportation: Commute to work: 97.1% car, 0.0% public transportation, 1.3% walk, 1.3% work from home (2000); Travel time to work: 31.8% less than 15 minutes, 45.6% 15 to 30 minutes, 5.7% 30 to 45 minutes, 8.9% 45 to 60 minutes, 8.1% 60 minutes or more (2000)

PONTIAC (city). County seat. Covers a land area of 5.243 square miles and a water area of 0.010 square miles. Located at 40.88° N. Lat.; 88.63° W. Long. Elevation is 646 feet.

History: Pontiac was founded in 1837 and named for the Ottawa Chief Pontiac. Jesse W. Fell was a leader in the development of Pontiac, and chose the name for the town. Pontiac developed as the seat of Livingston County.

Population: 11,752 (1990); 11,864 (2000); 11,329 (2007); 10,966 (2012 projected); Race: 86.6% White, 10.1% Black, 0.4% Asian, 4.3% Hispanic of any race (2007); Density: 2,160.9 persons per square mile (2007); Average household size: 2.80 (2007); Median age: 35.5 (2007); Males per 100 females: 119.6 (2007); Marriage status: 18.3% never married, 60.5% now married, 6.8% widowed, 14.4% divorced (2000); Foreign born: 2.3% (2000); Ancestry (includes multiple ancestries): 26.1% German, 14.7% Irish, 10.1% United States or American, 9.7% English, 7.0% Other groups (2000).

Economy: Single-family building permits issued: 13 (2007); Multi-family building permits issued: 68 (2007); Employment by occupation: 7.6% management, 14.9% professional, 21.5% services, 23.3% sales, 0.3% farming, 7.7% construction, 24.7% production (2000).

Income: Per capita income: $20,046 (2007); Median household income: $43,460 (2007); Average household income: $51,474 (2007); Percent of households with income of $100,000 or more: 10.2% (2007); Poverty rate: 11.7% (2000).

Education: Percent of population age 25 and over with: High school diploma (including GED) or higher: 74.4% (2007); Bachelor's degree or higher: 13.4% (2007); Master's degree or higher: 4.2% (2007).

School District(s)

Dept of Corrections Sch Dist 428 (08-12)
2005-06 Enrollment: 2,271 . . . . (217) 522-2666
Livingston Area Voc Ctr
2005-06 Enrollment: n/a . . . . (815) 842-2557
Livingston Co Spec Services Unit
2005-06 Enrollment: n/a . . . . (815) 844-7115
Pontiac CCSD 429 (PK-08)
2005-06 Enrollment: 1,319 . . . . (815) 844-5632
Pontiac Twp HSD 90 (09-12)
2005-06 Enrollment: 905 . . . . (815) 844-6113

Housing: Homeownership rate: 66.6% (2007); Median home value: $107,159 (2007); Median rent: $360 per month (2000); Median age of housing: 40 years (2000).

Hospitals: OSF Saint James-John W Albrecht Medical Center

Safety: Violent crime rate: 30.5 per 10,000 population; Property crime rate: 259.2 per 10,000 population (2006).

Newspapers: Pontiac Daily Leader (Local news; Circulation 6,200)

Transportation: Commute to work: 89.4% car, 1.7% public transportation, 4.7% walk, 3.4% work from home (2000); Travel time to work: 71.4% less than 15 minutes, 12.6% 15 to 30 minutes, 7.8% 30 to 45 minutes, 4.1% 45 to 60 minutes, 4.1% 60 minutes or more (2000); Amtrak: Service available.

Airports: Pontiac Municipal (general aviation)

Additional Information Contacts

Pontiac Area Chamber of Commerce . . . . (815) 844-5131
http://www.pontiacchamber.org

SAUNEMIN (village). Covers a land area of 0.223 square miles and a water area of 0 square miles. Located at 40.89° N. Lat.; 88.40° W. Long. Elevation is 689 feet.

Population: 399 (1990); 456 (2000); 441 (2007); 436 (2012 projected); Race: 99.5% White, 0.2% Black, 0.0% Asian, 2.5% Hispanic of any race (2007); Density: 1,978.6 persons per square mile (2007); Average household size: 3.00 (2007); Median age: 32.8 (2007); Males per 100 females: 112.0 (2007); Marriage status: 27.5% never married, 55.6% now married, 3.8% widowed, 13.0% divorced (2000); Foreign born: 0.2% (2000); Ancestry (includes multiple ancestries): 32.9% German, 14.5% English, 12.7% United States or American, 12.3% Irish, 4.6% French (except Basque) (2000).

Economy: Employment by occupation: 8.5% management, 4.0% professional, 23.6% services, 19.6% sales, 0.0% farming, 10.1% construction, 34.2% production (2000).

Income: Per capita income: $20,561 (2007); Median household income: $57,750 (2007); Average household income: $61,684 (2007); Percent of households with income of $100,000 or more: 10.9% (2007); Poverty rate: 6.5% (2000).

Education: Percent of population age 25 and over with: High school diploma (including GED) or higher: 86.3% (2007); Bachelor's degree or higher: 8.0% (2007); Master's degree or higher: 0.8% (2007).

School District(s)

Saunemin CCSD 438 (PK-08)
2005-06 Enrollment: 160 . . . . (815) 832-4421

Housing: Homeownership rate: 81.6% (2007); Median home value: $98,462 (2007); Median rent: $315 per month (2000); Median age of housing: 60+ years (2000).

Transportation: Commute to work: 95.9% car, 0.0% public transportation, 1.0% walk, 3.1% work from home (2000); Travel time to work: 9.5% less than 15 minutes, 67.4% 15 to 30 minutes, 5.3% 30 to 45 minutes, 6.8% 45 to 60 minutes, 11.1% 60 minutes or more (2000)

STRAWN (village). Covers a land area of 0.142 square miles and a water area of 0 square miles. Located at 40.65° N. Lat.; 88.39° W. Long. Elevation is 771 feet.

Population: 130 (1990); 104 (2000); 98 (2007); 99 (2012 projected); Race: 82.7% White, 12.2% Black, 1.0% Asian, 0.0% Hispanic of any race (2007); Density: 690.3 persons per square mile (2007); Average household size: 2.39 (2007); Median age: 30.0 (2007); Males per 100 females: 92.2 (2007); Marriage status: 19.5% never married, 61.0% now married, 8.5% widowed, 11.0% divorced (2000); Foreign born: 0.0% (2000); Ancestry (includes multiple ancestries): 32.2% United States or American, 21.7% Irish, 13.0% German, 13.0% Dutch, 2.6% English (2000).

Economy: Employment by occupation: 1.6% management, 6.6% professional, 26.2% services, 19.7% sales, 3.3% farming, 14.8% construction, 27.9% production (2000).

Income: Per capita income: $24,770 (2007); Median household income: $53,182 (2007); Average household income: $59,207 (2007); Percent of households with income of $100,000 or more: 17.1% (2007); Poverty rate: 2.6% (2000).

Education: Percent of population age 25 and over with: High school diploma (including GED) or higher: 83.9% (2007); Bachelor's degree or higher: 3.6% (2007); Master's degree or higher: 0.0% (2007).

Housing: Homeownership rate: 85.4% (2007); Median home value: $53,182 (2007); Median rent: $275 per month (2000); Median age of housing: 60+ years (2000).

Transportation: Commute to work: 83.3% car, 0.0% public transportation, 0.0% walk, 13.3% work from home (2000); Travel time to work: 0.0% less than 15 minutes, 53.8% 15 to 30 minutes, 23.1% 30 to 45 minutes, 23.1% 45 to 60 minutes, 0.0% 60 minutes or more (2000)

Logan County

Located in central Illinois; drained by Salt and Kickapoo Creeks. Covers a land area of 618.14 square miles, a water area of 0.87 square miles, and is located in the Central Time Zone. The county was founded in 1839. County seat is Lincoln.

Logan County is part of the Lincoln, IL Micropolitan Statistical Area. The entire metro area includes: Logan County, IL

Weather Station: Lincoln — Elevation: 580 feet

	Jan	Feb	Mar	Apr	May	Jun	Jul	Aug	Sep	Oct	Nov	Dec
High	32	39	51	64	75	83	86	84	78	67	51	39
Low	15	21	31	41	52	61	65	63	54	42	32	22
Precip	1.7	1.5	3.1	3.8	4.6	4.0	4.2	4.0	3.2	2.9	3.0	2.6
Snow	6.6	4.8	2.1	0.6	0.0	0.0	0.0	0.0	0.0	tr	1.2	4.6

High and Low temperatures in degrees Fahrenheit; Precipitation and Snow in inches

Population: 30,798 (1990); 31,183 (2000); 30,489 (2007); 29,956 (2012 projected); Race: 91.1% White, 6.9% Black, 0.9% Asian, 1.9% Hispanic of any race (2007); Density: 49.3 persons per square mile (2007); Average household size: 2.80 (2007); Median age: 37.5 (2007); Males per 100 females: 100.8 (2007).

Religion: Five largest groups: 15.4% Christian Churches and Churches of Christ, 12.4% Catholic Church, 7.6% The United Methodist Church, 7.1% Lutheran Church—Missouri Synod, 6.1% Evangelical Lutheran Church in America (2000).

Economy: Unemployment rate: 5.7% (4/2008); Total civilian labor force: 13,609 (4/2008); Leading industries: 18.5% health care and social assistance; 18.5% manufacturing; 15.6% retail trade (2005); Farms: 692 totaling 358,767 acres (2002); Companies that employ 500 or more persons: 1 (2006); Companies that employ 100 to 499 persons: 9 (2006); Companies that employ less than 100 persons: 666 (2006); Black-owned businesses: n/a (2002); Hispanic-owned businesses: n/a (2002); Asian-owned businesses: n/a (2002); Women-owned businesses: 582 (2002); Retail sales per capita: $12,528 (2008). Single-family building permits issued: 28 (2007); Multi-family building permits issued: 46 (2007).

Income: Per capita income: $20,709 (2007); Median household income: $44,920 (2007); Average household income: $53,882 (2007); Percent of households with income of $100,000 or more: 10.5% (2007); Poverty rate: 11.3% (2005); Bankruptcy rate: 3.60% (2007).

Education: Percent of population age 25 and over with: High school diploma (including GED) or higher: 80.0% (2007); Bachelor's degree or higher: 14.1% (2007); Master's degree or higher: 4.2% (2007).

Housing: Homeownership rate: 71.7% (2007); Median home value: $105,857 (2007); Median rent: $345 per month (2000); Median age of housing: 45 years (2000).

Health: Birth rate: 115.5 per 10,000 population (2007); Death rate: 105.8 per 10,000 population (2007); Age-adjusted cancer mortality rate: 220.8 deaths per 100,000 population (2005); Number of physicians: 4.9 per 10,000 population (2005); Hospital beds: 8.2 per 10,000 population (2004); Hospital admissions: 452.3 per 10,000 population (2004).

Elections: 2004 Presidential election results: 67.7% Bush, 31.7% Kerry, 0.1% Nader, 0.5% Badnarik

National and State Parks: Railsplitter State Park

Additional Information Contacts

Logan County Government . . . . (217) 732-4148
http://www.co.logan.il.us

Lincoln/Logan County Chamber of Commerce . . . . (217) 735-2385
http://www.lincolnillinois.com

Logan County Communities

ATLANTA (city). Covers a land area of 1.258 square miles and a water area of 0.008 square miles. Located at 40.26° N. Lat.; 89.23° W. Long. Elevation is 709 feet.

History: Atlanta came into existence when the Chicago & Mississippi Railroad placed its tracks a mile away from the village of Newcastle, and the village moved to the railroad. The railroad station had been named Zenia, but town and railroad adopted the name of Atlanta in 1855.

Population: 1,622 (1990); 1,649 (2000); 1,567 (2007); 1,561 (2012 projected); Race: 99.7% White, 0.0% Black, 0.0% Asian, 0.4% Hispanic of any race (2007); Density: 1,245.3 persons per square mile (2007); Average household size: 2.32 (2007); Median age: 39.5 (2007); Males per 100 females: 91.3 (2007); Marriage status: 20.5% never married, 62.1% now married, 7.6% widowed, 9.9% divorced (2000); Foreign born: 0.1% (2000); Ancestry (includes multiple ancestries): 28.9% German, 12.3% Irish, 12.3% United States or American, 11.2% English, 5.6% Other groups (2000).

Economy: Single-family building permits issued: 5 (2007); Multi-family building permits issued: 0 (2007); Employment by occupation: 9.7% management, 12.6% professional, 15.5% services, 25.1% sales, 1.2% farming, 12.6% construction, 23.4% production (2000).

Income: Per capita income: $25,268 (2007); Median household income: $49,500 (2007); Average household income: $58,572 (2007); Percent of households with income of $100,000 or more: 11.4% (2007); Poverty rate: 4.4% (2000).

Education: Percent of population age 25 and over with: High school diploma (including GED) or higher: 84.5% (2007); Bachelor's degree or higher: 14.6% (2007); Master's degree or higher: 4.3% (2007).

School District(s)

Olympia CUSD 16 (PK-12)
2005-06 Enrollment: 2,084 . . . . (309) 379-6011

Housing: Homeownership rate: 79.0% (2007); Median home value: $112,230 (2007); Median rent: $371 per month (2000); Median age of housing: 43 years (2000).

Safety: Violent crime rate: 47.9 per 10,000 population; Property crime rate: 155.6 per 10,000 population (2006).

Transportation: Commute to work: 96.0% car, 0.4% public transportation, 0.5% walk, 2.7% work from home (2000); Travel time to work: 24.0% less than 15 minutes, 33.1% 15 to 30 minutes, 30.0% 30 to 45 minutes, 6.2% 45 to 60 minutes, 6.7% 60 minutes or more (2000)

BEASON (unincorporated postal area, zip code 62512). Covers a land area of 43.004 square miles and a water area of 0.004 square miles. Located at 40.13° N. Lat.; 89.20° W. Long. Elevation is 640 feet.

Population: 552 (2000); Race: 100.0% White, 0.0% Black, 0.0% Asian, 0.9% Hispanic of any race (2000); Density: 12.8 persons per square mile (2000); Age: 28.7% under 18, 13.0% over 64 (2000); Marriage status: 18.6% never married, 71.6% now married, 4.4% widowed, 5.3% divorced (2000); Foreign born: 0.0% (2000); Ancestry (includes multiple ancestries): 37.8% German, 21.8% Irish, 17.3% United States or American, 13.4% Other groups, 10.6% English (2000).

Economy: Employment by occupation: 2.8% management, 21.2% professional, 14.2% services, 12.2% sales, 7.6% farming, 2.4% construction, 39.6% production (2000).

Income: Per capita income: $19,329 (2000); Median household income: $57,875 (2000); Poverty rate: 1.7% (2000).

Education: Percent of population age 25 and over with: High school diploma (including GED) or higher: 91.6% (2000); Bachelor's degree or higher: 12.8% (2000).

Housing: Homeownership rate: 83.5% (2000); Median home value: $77,100 (2000); Median rent: $198 per month (2000); Median age of housing: 59 years (2000).

Transportation: Commute to work: 98.6% car, 0.0% public transportation, 0.0% walk, 1.4% work from home (2000); Travel time to work: 11.3% less than 15 minutes, 38.7% 15 to 30 minutes, 12.7% 30 to 45 minutes, 16.1% 45 to 60 minutes, 21.2% 60 minutes or more (2000)

BROADWELL (village). Covers a land area of 0.191 square miles and a water area of 0 square miles. Located at 40.06° N. Lat.; 89.44° W. Long. Elevation is 591 feet.

Population: 146 (1990); 169 (2000); 198 (2007); 212 (2012 projected); Race: 100.0% White, 0.0% Black, 0.0% Asian, 0.0% Hispanic of any race (2007); Density: 1,036.0 persons per square mile (2007); Average household size: 2.39 (2007); Median age: 41.5 (2007); Males per 100 females: 98.0 (2007); Marriage status: 27.8% never married, 58.7% now married, 8.7% widowed, 4.8% divorced (2000); Foreign born: 0.0% (2000); Ancestry (includes multiple ancestries): 33.3% German, 30.4% United States or American, 10.7% Irish, 8.9% French (except Basque), 4.8% Other groups (2000).

Economy: Single-family building permits issued: 0 (2007); Multi-family building permits issued: 0 (2007); Employment by occupation: 6.8% management, 19.3% professional, 30.7% services, 17.0% sales, 0.0% farming, 8.0% construction, 18.2% production (2000).

Income: Per capita income: $26,881 (2007); Median household income: $47,500 (2007); Average household income: $64,127 (2007); Percent of households with income of $100,000 or more: 10.8% (2007); Poverty rate: 8.5% (2000).

Education: Percent of population age 25 and over with: High school diploma (including GED) or higher: 93.5% (2007); Bachelor's degree or higher: 13.8% (2007); Master's degree or higher: 5.1% (2007).

Housing: Homeownership rate: 72.3% (2007); Median home value: $87,500 (2007); Median rent: $318 per month (2000); Median age of housing: 60+ years (2000).

Transportation: Commute to work: 92.0% car, 0.0% public transportation, 1.1% walk, 6.8% work from home (2000); Travel time to work: 47.6% less than 15 minutes, 26.8% 15 to 30 minutes, 17.1% 30 to 45 minutes, 4.9% 45 to 60 minutes, 3.7% 60 minutes or more (2000)

CHESTNUT (unincorporated postal area, zip code 62518). Covers a land area of 24.895 square miles and a water area of 0.025 square miles. Located at 40.05° N. Lat.; 89.18° W. Long. Elevation is 617 feet.

Population: 468 (2000); Race: 100.0% White, 0.0% Black, 0.0% Asian, 0.0% Hispanic of any race (2000); Density: 18.8 persons per square mile (2000); Age: 21.2% under 18, 14.5% over 64 (2000); Marriage status: 21.5% never married, 71.0% now married, 3.5% widowed, 4.0% divorced (2000); Foreign born: 1.1% (2000); Ancestry (includes multiple ancestries): 37.8% German, 22.5% Irish, 12.3% Other groups, 7.6% English, 6.0% Dutch (2000).

Economy: Employment by occupation: 13.8% management, 16.3% professional, 21.1% services, 27.6% sales, 5.3% farming, 8.5% construction, 7.3% production (2000).

Income: Per capita income: $17,836 (2000); Median household income: $45,288 (2000); Poverty rate: 0.0% (2000).

Education: Percent of population age 25 and over with: High school diploma (including GED) or higher: 87.8% (2000); Bachelor's degree or higher: 23.1% (2000).

Housing: Homeownership rate: 85.6% (2000); Median home value: $62,500 (2000); Median rent: $359 per month (2000); Median age of housing: 60+ years (2000).

Transportation: Commute to work: 100.0% car, 0.0% public transportation, 0.0% walk, 0.0% work from home (2000); Travel time to work: 23.2% less than 15 minutes, 29.9% 15 to 30 minutes, 24.5% 30 to 45 minutes, 12.4% 45 to 60 minutes, 10.0% 60 minutes or more (2000)

ELKHART (village). Aka Elk Hart City. Covers a land area of 1.458 square miles and a water area of 0.008 square miles. Located at 40.02° N. Lat.; 89.48° W. Long. Elevation is 594 feet.

History: Elkhart was the home of Richard J. Oglesby (1824-1899), a man of many occupations (farmer, carpenter, ropemaker, lawyer, miner, soldier) who served three times as the governor of Illinois, and as a U.S. senator.

Population: 475 (1990); 443 (2000); 410 (2007); 406 (2012 projected); Race: 99.3% White, 0.2% Black, 0.5% Asian, 0.0% Hispanic of any race (2007); Density: 281.2 persons per square mile (2007); Average household size: 2.36 (2007); Median age: 40.2 (2007); Males per 100 females: 95.2 (2007); Marriage status: 26.6% never married, 58.4% now married, 6.8% widowed, 8.2% divorced (2000); Foreign born: 0.0% (2000); Ancestry (includes multiple ancestries): 37.0% German, 14.9% English, 12.9% Irish, 9.8% United States or American, 5.3% Swedish (2000).

Economy: Single-family building permits issued: 0 (2007); Multi-family building permits issued: 0 (2007); Employment by occupation: 12.8% management, 16.2% professional, 20.0% services, 31.9% sales, 3.0% farming, 6.8% construction, 9.4% production (2000).

Income: Per capita income: $27,037 (2007); Median household income: $57,500 (2007); Average household income: $63,707 (2007); Percent of households with income of $100,000 or more: 14.9% (2007); Poverty rate: 4.2% (2000).

Education: Percent of population age 25 and over with: High school diploma (including GED) or higher: 90.2% (2007); Bachelor's degree or higher: 23.8% (2007); Master's degree or higher: 4.5% (2007).

School District(s)

Mt Pulaski CUSD 23 (PK-12)
2005-06 Enrollment: 633 . . . . (217) 792-7222

Housing: Homeownership rate: 83.3% (2007); Median home value: $99,118 (2007); Median rent: $350 per month (2000); Median age of housing: 51 years (2000).

Transportation: Commute to work: 97.0% car, 0.0% public transportation, 0.0% walk, 3.0% work from home (2000); Travel time to work: 30.5% less than 15 minutes, 44.7% 15 to 30 minutes, 17.7% 30 to 45 minutes, 4.0% 45 to 60 minutes, 3.1% 60 minutes or more (2000)

EMDEN (village). Covers a land area of 0.226 square miles and a water area of 0 square miles. Located at 40.29° N. Lat.; 89.48° W. Long. Elevation is 591 feet.

Population: 488 (1990); 515 (2000); 495 (2007); 466 (2012 projected); Race: 99.4% White, 0.0% Black, 0.0% Asian, 0.0% Hispanic of any race (2007); Density: 2,190.4 persons per square mile (2007); Average household size: 2.40 (2007); Median age: 41.9 (2007); Males per 100 females: 86.8 (2007); Marriage status: 19.9% never married, 65.2% now married, 9.1% widowed, 5.8% divorced (2000); Foreign born: 0.6% (2000); Ancestry (includes multiple ancestries): 54.7% German, 13.7% Irish, 11.8% United States or American, 7.8% English, 7.4% Other groups (2000).

Economy: Single-family building permits issued: 1 (2007); Multi-family building permits issued: 0 (2007); Employment by occupation: 11.2% management, 11.5% professional, 18.2% services, 28.2% sales, 0.0% farming, 14.8% construction, 16.1% production (2000).
Income: Per capita income: $21,621 (2007); Median household income: $43,750 (2007); Average household income: $51,954 (2007); Percent of households with income of $100,000 or more: 12.1% (2007); Poverty rate: 6.1% (2000).
Education: Percent of population age 25 and over with: High school diploma (including GED) or higher: 91.7% (2007); Bachelor's degree or higher: 14.6% (2007); Master's degree or higher: 1.8% (2007).

School District(s)

Hartsburg Emden CUSD 21 (PK-12)
2005-06 Enrollment: 251 . . . . (217) 642-5244
Housing: Homeownership rate: 82.5% (2007); Median home value: $94,211 (2007); Median rent: $375 per month (2000); Median age of housing: 56 years (2000).
Transportation: Commute to work: 92.6% car, 0.0% public transportation, 3.8% walk, 2.6% work from home (2000); Travel time to work: 36.5% less than 15 minutes, 35.9% 15 to 30 minutes, 20.1% 30 to 45 minutes, 4.9% 45 to 60 minutes, 2.6% 60 minutes or more (2000)

HARTSBURG (village). Covers a land area of 0.145 square miles and a water area of 0 square miles. Located at 40.25° N. Lat.; 89.44° W. Long. Elevation is 604 feet.
Population: 306 (1990); 358 (2000); 398 (2007); 397 (2012 projected); Race: 99.7% White, 0.0% Black, 0.0% Asian, 0.0% Hispanic of any race (2007); Density: 2,741.1 persons per square mile (2007); Average household size: 2.71 (2007); Median age: 35.2 (2007); Males per 100 females: 105.2 (2007); Marriage status: 26.1% never married, 58.0% now married, 7.1% widowed, 8.8% divorced (2000); Foreign born: 0.0% (2000); Ancestry (includes multiple ancestries): 37.3% German, 9.5% Irish, 7.4% Other groups, 5.3% English, 2.6% French (except Basque) (2000).
Economy: Single-family building permits issued: 0 (2007); Multi-family building permits issued: 0 (2007); Employment by occupation: 7.1% management, 11.2% professional, 27.0% services, 24.5% sales, 4.1% farming, 7.1% construction, 18.9% production (2000).
Income: Per capita income: $21,193 (2007); Median household income: $47,679 (2007); Average household income: $57,381 (2007); Percent of households with income of $100,000 or more: 8.8% (2007); Poverty rate: 8.5% (2000).
Education: Percent of population age 25 and over with: High school diploma (including GED) or higher: 86.3% (2007); Bachelor's degree or higher: 12.1% (2007); Master's degree or higher: 3.1% (2007).

School District(s)

Hartsburg Emden CUSD 21 (PK-12)
2005-06 Enrollment: 251 . . . . (217) 642-5244
Housing: Homeownership rate: 78.2% (2007); Median home value: $83,235 (2007); Median rent: $335 per month (2000); Median age of housing: 59 years (2000).
Transportation: Commute to work: 93.9% car, 0.0% public transportation, 6.1% walk, 0.0% work from home (2000); Travel time to work: 46.9% less than 15 minutes, 30.6% 15 to 30 minutes, 10.2% 30 to 45 minutes, 9.7% 45 to 60 minutes, 2.6% 60 minutes or more (2000)

LATHAM (village). Covers a land area of 0.278 square miles and a water area of 0 square miles. Located at 39.96° N. Lat.; 89.16° W. Long. Elevation is 614 feet.
Population: 482 (1990); 371 (2000); 309 (2007); 303 (2012 projected); Race: 99.7% White, 0.0% Black, 0.0% Asian, 0.0% Hispanic of any race (2007); Density: 1,110.8 persons per square mile (2007); Average household size: 2.34 (2007); Median age: 38.1 (2007); Males per 100 females: 98.1 (2007); Marriage status: 17.7% never married, 63.3% now married, 4.6% widowed, 14.5% divorced (2000); Foreign born: 1.0% (2000); Ancestry (includes multiple ancestries): 25.1% German, 19.9% United States or American, 16.1% Irish, 12.5% English, 3.1% Other groups (2000).
Economy: Single-family building permits issued: 0 (2007); Multi-family building permits issued: 0 (2007); Employment by occupation: 7.2% management, 18.6% professional, 10.8% services, 18.6% sales, 1.5% farming, 8.8% construction, 34.5% production (2000).
Income: Per capita income: $23,883 (2007); Median household income: $54,118 (2007); Average household income: $55,909 (2007); Percent of households with income of $100,000 or more: 9.8% (2007); Poverty rate: 12.9% (2000).
Education: Percent of population age 25 and over with: High school diploma (including GED) or higher: 93.2% (2007); Bachelor's degree or higher: 12.1% (2007); Master's degree or higher: 5.3% (2007).
Housing: Homeownership rate: 77.3% (2007); Median home value: $87,000 (2007); Median rent: $259 per month (2000); Median age of housing: 57 years (2000).
Transportation: Commute to work: 92.2% car, 0.0% public transportation, 2.6% walk, 3.6% work from home (2000); Travel time to work: 15.7% less than 15 minutes, 48.1% 15 to 30 minutes, 27.6% 30 to 45 minutes, 2.7% 45 to 60 minutes, 5.9% 60 minutes or more (2000)

LINCOLN (city). County seat. Covers a land area of 5.919 square miles and a water area of 0 square miles. Located at 40.15° N. Lat.; 89.36° W. Long. Elevation is 581 feet.
History: Lincoln was settled in 1853 on land owned by promoter Colonel Latham, who hired Springfield lawyer Abraham Lincoln to draw up the documents for the town lots and decided to name the town Lincoln. The seat of Logan County was changed from Mount Pulaski to Lincoln, which is the only town named for Lincoln with his knowledge and consent.
Population: 15,288 (1990); 15,369 (2000); 14,762 (2007); 14,306 (2012 projected); Race: 94.6% White, 2.6% Black, 1.4% Asian, 1.4% Hispanic of any race (2007); Density: 2,494.1 persons per square mile (2007); Average household size: 2.57 (2007); Median age: 37.4 (2007); Males per 100 females: 91.5 (2007); Marriage status: 23.0% never married, 56.5% now married, 7.7% widowed, 12.7% divorced (2000); Foreign born: 1.5% (2000); Ancestry (includes multiple ancestries): 28.6% German, 12.4% United States or American, 11.8% Irish, 10.0% English, 7.8% Other groups (2000).
Economy: Single-family building permits issued: 5 (2007); Multi-family building permits issued: 46 (2007); Employment by occupation: 8.7% management, 14.7% professional, 24.6% services, 24.1% sales, 0.3% farming, 9.2% construction, 18.4% production (2000).
Income: Per capita income: $19,201 (2007); Median household income: $38,203 (2007); Average household income: $45,760 (2007); Percent of households with income of $100,000 or more: 6.6% (2007); Poverty rate: 10.7% (2000).
Taxes: Total city taxes per capita: $139 (2006); City property taxes per capita: $103 (2006).
Education: Percent of population age 25 and over with: High school diploma (including GED) or higher: 82.3% (2007); Bachelor's degree or higher: 13.6% (2007); Master's degree or higher: 4.4% (2007).

School District(s)

Chester-East Lincoln CCSD 61 (PK-08)
2005-06 Enrollment: 316 . . . . (217) 732-4136
Dept of Corrections Sch Dist 428 (08-12)
2005-06 Enrollment: 2,271 . . . . (217) 522-2666
Lincoln CHSD 404 (09-12)
2005-06 Enrollment: 912 . . . . (217) 732-4131
Lincoln ESD 27 (PK-08)
2005-06 Enrollment: 1,300 . . . . (217) 732-2522
Lincolnland Technical Ed Ctr
2005-06 Enrollment: n/a . . . . (217) 732-4131
West Lincoln-Broadwell ESD 92 (KG-08)
2005-06 Enrollment: 195 . . . . (217) 732-2630

Four-year College(s)

Lincoln Christian College and Seminary (Private, Not-for-profit, Christian Churches and Churches of Christ)
Fall 2007 Enrollment: 1,055. . . . . (217) 732-3168
2007-08 Tuition: In-state $11,400; Out-of-state $11,400
Lincoln College (Private, Not-for-profit)
Fall 2007 Enrollment: 1,266. . . . . (217) 732-3155
2007-08 Tuition: In-state $18,000; Out-of-state $18,000
Housing: Homeownership rate: 65.1% (2007); Median home value: $99,986 (2007); Median rent: $351 per month (2000); Median age of housing: 43 years (2000).
Hospitals: Abraham Lincoln Memorial Hospital (66 beds)
Safety: Violent crime rate: 77.5 per 10,000 population; Property crime rate: 474.9 per 10,000 population (2006).
Newspapers: Lincoln Courier (Local news; Circulation 7,000); Lincoln Daily News (Local news; Circulation 16,000); Logan County Shopper (Community news; Circulation 5,800)
Transportation: Commute to work: 92.3% car, 1.0% public transportation, 2.8% walk, 2.3% work from home (2000); Travel time to work: 64.3% less than 15 minutes, 13.6% 15 to 30 minutes, 10.2% 30 to 45 minutes, 8.9%

45 to 60 minutes, 3.1% 60 minutes or more (2000); Amtrak: Service available.

Additional Information Contacts

Lincoln/Logan County Chamber of Commerce . . . . (217) 735-2385
http://www.lincolnillinois.com

MIDDLETOWN (village). Covers a land area of 0.240 square miles and a water area of 0 square miles. Located at 40.10° N. Lat.; 89.59° W. Long. Elevation is 584 feet.

Population: 436 (1990); 434 (2000); 421 (2007); 408 (2012 projected); Race: 97.1% White, 0.5% Black, 0.0% Asian, 1.4% Hispanic of any race (2007); Density: 1,755.3 persons per square mile (2007); Average household size: 2.61 (2007); Median age: 34.8 (2007); Males per 100 females: 91.4 (2007); Marriage status: 26.1% never married, 55.7% now married, 6.7% widowed, 11.5% divorced (2000); Foreign born: 0.0% (2000); Ancestry (includes multiple ancestries): 25.2% German, 17.6% Irish, 11.0% United States or American, 9.3% Other groups, 9.0% English (2000).

Economy: Employment by occupation: 7.7% management, 12.0% professional, 16.4% services, 26.2% sales, 0.0% farming, 16.9% construction, 20.8% production (2000).

Income: Per capita income: $18,913 (2007); Median household income: $40,357 (2007); Average household income: $49,457 (2007); Percent of households with income of $100,000 or more: 6.8% (2007); Poverty rate: 16.1% (2000).

Education: Percent of population age 25 and over with: High school diploma (including GED) or higher: 79.2% (2007); Bachelor's degree or higher: 9.8% (2007); Master's degree or higher: 2.4% (2007).

School District(s)

New Holland-Middletown Ed 88 (KG-08)
2005-06 Enrollment: 87 . . . . (217) 445-2421

Housing: Homeownership rate: 77.6% (2007); Median home value: $69,643 (2007); Median rent: $263 per month (2000); Median age of housing: 55 years (2000).

Transportation: Commute to work: 97.8% car, 0.0% public transportation, 0.0% walk, 1.1% work from home (2000); Travel time to work: 10.6% less than 15 minutes, 47.2% 15 to 30 minutes, 22.2% 30 to 45 minutes, 11.7% 45 to 60 minutes, 8.3% 60 minutes or more (2000)

MOUNT PULASKI (city). Covers a land area of 1.139 square miles and a water area of 0 square miles. Located at 40.01° N. Lat.; 89.28° W. Long. Elevation is 663 feet.

History: Mount Pulaski served as the seat of Logan County from 1847 to 1853.

Population: 1,635 (1990); 1,701 (2000); 1,768 (2007); 1,694 (2012 projected); Race: 99.6% White, 0.0% Black, 0.0% Asian, 0.4% Hispanic of any race (2007); Density: 1,552.9 persons per square mile (2007); Average household size: 2.42 (2007); Median age: 43.3 (2007); Males per 100 females: 89.5 (2007); Marriage status: 17.4% never married, 64.0% now married, 11.0% widowed, 7.6% divorced (2000); Foreign born: 0.4% (2000); Ancestry (includes multiple ancestries): 30.2% German, 15.4% United States or American, 13.6% Irish, 11.4% English, 3.6% French (except Basque) (2000).

Economy: Single-family building permits issued: 1 (2007); Multi-family building permits issued: 0 (2007); Employment by occupation: 13.7% management, 17.0% professional, 19.7% services, 20.7% sales, 0.8% farming, 10.5% construction, 17.7% production (2000).

Income: Per capita income: $21,922 (2007); Median household income: $44,875 (2007); Average household income: $51,575 (2007); Percent of households with income of $100,000 or more: 7.9% (2007); Poverty rate: 5.6% (2000).

Taxes: Total city taxes per capita: $143 (2006); City property taxes per capita: $103 (2006).

Education: Percent of population age 25 and over with: High school diploma (including GED) or higher: 82.8% (2007); Bachelor's degree or higher: 15.9% (2007); Master's degree or higher: 5.6% (2007).

School District(s)

Mt Pulaski CUSD 23 (PK-12)
2005-06 Enrollment: 633 . . . . (217) 792-7222

Housing: Homeownership rate: 77.5% (2007); Median home value: $102,158 (2007); Median rent: $317 per month (2000); Median age of housing: 53 years (2000).

Safety: Violent crime rate: 6.1 per 10,000 population; Property crime rate: 24.5 per 10,000 population (2006).

Newspapers: Mount Pulaski Weekly News (Community news; Circulation 1,650)

Transportation: Commute to work: 95.4% car, 0.0% public transportation, 0.9% walk, 2.8% work from home (2000); Travel time to work: 35.7% less than 15 minutes, 30.3% 15 to 30 minutes, 23.7% 30 to 45 minutes, 6.9% 45 to 60 minutes, 3.5% 60 minutes or more (2000)

NEW HOLLAND (village). Covers a land area of 0.287 square miles and a water area of 0 square miles. Located at 40.18° N. Lat.; 89.58° W. Long. Elevation is 554 feet.

Population: 330 (1990); 318 (2000); 267 (2007); 261 (2012 projected); Race: 99.3% White, 0.0% Black, 0.0% Asian, 0.0% Hispanic of any race (2007); Density: 930.1 persons per square mile (2007); Average household size: 2.54 (2007); Median age: 35.5 (2007); Males per 100 females: 100.8 (2007); Marriage status: 18.5% never married, 65.0% now married, 10.2% widowed, 6.3% divorced (2000); Foreign born: 0.0% (2000); Ancestry (includes multiple ancestries): 39.2% German, 19.3% United States or American, 13.6% Irish, 9.8% English, 3.5% Dutch (2000).

Economy: Employment by occupation: 11.7% management, 17.9% professional, 19.3% services, 26.2% sales, 0.0% farming, 13.1% construction, 11.7% production (2000).

Income: Per capita income: $21,283 (2007); Median household income: $49,722 (2007); Average household income: $54,119 (2007); Percent of households with income of $100,000 or more: 7.6% (2007); Poverty rate: 10.8% (2000).

Education: Percent of population age 25 and over with: High school diploma (including GED) or higher: 85.2% (2007); Bachelor's degree or higher: 15.4% (2007); Master's degree or higher: 5.9% (2007).

Housing: Homeownership rate: 85.7% (2007); Median home value: $78,000 (2007); Median rent: $300 per month (2000); Median age of housing: 60+ years (2000).

Transportation: Commute to work: 89.2% car, 0.0% public transportation, 0.0% walk, 10.8% work from home (2000); Travel time to work: 7.6% less than 15 minutes, 55.3% 15 to 30 minutes, 15.2% 30 to 45 minutes, 14.4% 45 to 60 minutes, 7.6% 60 minutes or more (2000)

Macon County

Located in central Illinois; drained by the Sangamon River. Covers a land area of 580.52 square miles, a water area of 4.86 square miles, and is located in the Central Time Zone. The county was founded in 1829. County seat is Decatur.

Macon County is part of the Decatur, IL Metropolitan Statistical Area. The entire metro area includes: Macon County, IL

Weather Station: Decatur Elevation: 620 feet

	Jan	Feb	Mar	Apr	May	Jun	Jul	Aug	Sep	Oct	Nov	Dec
High	34	40	52	65	76	85	88	86	80	68	52	40
Low	17	22	32	42	51	60	64	63	55	44	33	23
Precip	2.1	1.9	3.3	3.8	4.6	3.9	4.4	4.0	3.0	2.8	3.1	2.8
Snow	7.8	5.1	2.7	0.4	tr	0.0	0.0	0.0	0.0	tr	1.1	5.4

High and Low temperatures in degrees Fahrenheit; Precipitation and Snow in inches

Population: 117,206 (1990); 114,706 (2000); 109,282 (2007); 105,499 (2012 projected); Race: 82.0% White, 14.5% Black, 1.0% Asian, 1.2% Hispanic of any race (2007); Density: 188.2 persons per square mile (2007); Average household size: 2.40 (2007); Median age: 39.3 (2007); Males per 100 females: 91.4 (2007).

Religion: Five largest groups: 9.3% Catholic Church, 6.8% The United Methodist Church, 5.7% Lutheran Church—Missouri Synod, 4.8% Southern Baptist Convention, 4.2% Christian Church (Disciples of Christ) (2000).

Economy: Unemployment rate: 5.7% (4/2008); Total civilian labor force: 55,514 (4/2008); Leading industries: 17.1% manufacturing; 15.9% health care and social assistance; 13.7% retail trade (2005); Farms: 646 totaling 320,646 acres (2002); Companies that employ 500 or more persons: 6 (2006); Companies that employ 100 to 499 persons: 65 (2006); Companies that employ less than 100 persons: 2,570 (2006); Black-owned businesses: 600 (2002); Hispanic-owned businesses: n/a (2002); Asian-owned businesses: n/a (2002); Women-owned businesses: 1,900 (2002); Retail sales per capita: $17,182 (2008). Single-family building permits issued: 134 (2007); Multi-family building permits issued: 12 (2007).

Income: Per capita income: $22,980 (2007); Median household income: $42,026 (2007); Average household income: $54,582 (2007); Percent of

households with income of $100,000 or more: 11.3% (2007); Poverty rate: 15.2% (2005); Bankruptcy rate: 4.41% (2007).
Taxes: Total county taxes per capita: $153 (2006); County property taxes per capita: $150 (2006).
Education: Percent of population age 25 and over with: High school diploma (including GED) or higher: 83.3% (2007); Bachelor's degree or higher: 17.0% (2007); Master's degree or higher: 5.6% (2007).
Housing: Homeownership rate: 72.1% (2007); Median home value: $86,517 (2007); Median rent: $349 per month (2000); Median age of housing: 41 years (2000).
Health: Birth rate: 129.4 per 10,000 population (2007); Death rate: 108.6 per 10,000 population (2007); Age-adjusted cancer mortality rate: 237.4 deaths per 100,000 population (2005); Air Quality Index: 68.5% good, 30.1% moderate, 1.4% unhealthy for sensitive individuals, 0.0% unhealthy (percent of days in 2007); Number of physicians: 21.9 per 10,000 population (2005); Hospital beds: 44.9 per 10,000 population (2004); Hospital admissions: 1,911.6 per 10,000 population (2004).
Elections: 2004 Presidential election results: 54.3% Bush, 45.1% Kerry, 0.1% Nader, 0.5% Badnarik
National and State Parks: Lincoln Trail Homestead State Park; Spitler Woods State Park
Additional Information Contacts
Macon County Government . . . . (217) 424-1470
http://www.maconcounty-il.gov
City of Decatur . . . . (217) 424-2700
http://www.ci.decatur.il.us
Mount Zion Chamber of Commerce. . . . . (217) 864-2526
http://www.mtzionchamberofcommerce.com

Macon County Communities

ARGENTA (village). Covers a land area of 0.560 square miles and a water area of 0 square miles. Located at 39.98° N. Lat.; 88.82° W. Long. Elevation is 686 feet.
Population: 984 (1990); 921 (2000); 779 (2007); 762 (2012 projected); Race: 99.1% White, 0.1% Black, 0.0% Asian, 0.1% Hispanic of any race (2007); Density: 1,390.4 persons per square mile (2007); Average household size: 2.37 (2007); Median age: 39.9 (2007); Males per 100 females: 105.0 (2007); Marriage status: 18.8% never married, 62.9% now married, 7.8% widowed, 10.4% divorced (2000); Foreign born: 0.6% (2000); Ancestry (includes multiple ancestries): 24.1% German, 11.1% United States or American, 10.5% English, 9.5% Irish, 6.8% Other groups (2000).
Economy: Single-family building permits issued: 2 (2007); Multi-family building permits issued: 0 (2007); Employment by occupation: 8.2% management, 11.4% professional, 12.8% services, 26.9% sales, 0.9% farming, 14.1% construction, 25.7% production (2000).
Income: Per capita income: $23,479 (2007); Median household income: $52,547 (2007); Average household income: $55,593 (2007); Percent of households with income of $100,000 or more: 8.8% (2007); Poverty rate: 3.7% (2000).
Education: Percent of population age 25 and over with: High school diploma (including GED) or higher: 89.7% (2007); Bachelor's degree or higher: 7.6% (2007); Master's degree or higher: 2.5% (2007).

School District(s)

Argenta-Oreana CUSD 1 (PK-12)
2005-06 Enrollment: 994 . . . . (217) 795-2313
Housing: Homeownership rate: 84.2% (2007); Median home value: $86,574 (2007); Median rent: $300 per month (2000); Median age of housing: 47 years (2000).
Safety: Violent crime rate: 82.2 per 10,000 population; Property crime rate: 176.1 per 10,000 population (2006).
Transportation: Commute to work: 94.8% car, 0.0% public transportation, 2.5% walk, 1.8% work from home (2000); Travel time to work: 26.7% less than 15 minutes, 47.8% 15 to 30 minutes, 16.2% 30 to 45 minutes, 4.2% 45 to 60 minutes, 5.1% 60 minutes or more (2000)

BLUE MOUND (village). Covers a land area of 0.595 square miles and a water area of 0 square miles. Located at 39.70° N. Lat.; 89.12° W. Long. Elevation is 623 feet.
Population: 1,226 (1990); 1,129 (2000); 1,027 (2007); 993 (2012 projected); Race: 99.6% White, 0.0% Black, 0.0% Asian, 0.3% Hispanic of any race (2007); Density: 1,727.3 persons per square mile (2007); Average household size: 2.37 (2007); Median age: 37.4 (2007); Males per 100 females: 91.6 (2007); Marriage status: 20.4% never married, 58.5% now married, 9.5% widowed, 11.6% divorced (2000); Foreign born: 0.4% (2000); Ancestry (includes multiple ancestries): 23.3% United States or American, 21.4% German, 11.2% Irish, 9.0% English, 6.3% Other groups (2000).
Economy: Single-family building permits issued: 0 (2007); Multi-family building permits issued: 0 (2007); Employment by occupation: 4.9% management, 14.5% professional, 13.1% services, 32.8% sales, 1.0% farming, 9.4% construction, 24.2% production (2000).
Income: Per capita income: $22,644 (2007); Median household income: $48,750 (2007); Average household income: $53,707 (2007); Percent of households with income of $100,000 or more: 8.8% (2007); Poverty rate: 4.2% (2000).
Education: Percent of population age 25 and over with: High school diploma (including GED) or higher: 88.0% (2007); Bachelor's degree or higher: 11.6% (2007); Master's degree or higher: 3.8% (2007).

School District(s)

Meridian CUSD 15 (PK-12)
2005-06 Enrollment: 1,102 . . . . (217) 692-2599
Housing: Homeownership rate: 80.8% (2007); Median home value: $80,508 (2007); Median rent: $312 per month (2000); Median age of housing: 46 years (2000).
Safety: Violent crime rate: 85.2 per 10,000 population; Property crime rate: 104.2 per 10,000 population (2006).
Newspapers: Blue Mound Leader (Community news; Circulation 800)
Transportation: Commute to work: 96.6% car, 0.0% public transportation, 1.9% walk, 0.3% work from home (2000); Travel time to work: 24.8% less than 15 minutes, 26.7% 15 to 30 minutes, 39.1% 30 to 45 minutes, 6.5% 45 to 60 minutes, 2.9% 60 minutes or more (2000)

BOODY (unincorporated postal area, zip code 62514). Covers a land area of 4.047 square miles and a water area of 0 square miles. Located at 39.76° N. Lat.; 89.05° W. Long. Elevation is 682 feet.
Population: 340 (2000); Race: 100.0% White, 0.0% Black, 0.0% Asian, 0.0% Hispanic of any race (2000); Density: 84.0 persons per square mile (2000); Age: 19.8% under 18, 9.7% over 64 (2000); Marriage status: 21.8% never married, 64.3% now married, 4.8% widowed, 9.1% divorced (2000); Foreign born: 0.0% (2000); Ancestry (includes multiple ancestries): 28.5% German, 28.2% English, 19.5% Irish, 19.1% United States or American, 8.1% French (except Basque) (2000).
Economy: Employment by occupation: 3.8% management, 18.9% professional, 29.6% services, 18.9% sales, 0.0% farming, 25.8% construction, 3.1% production (2000).
Income: Per capita income: $17,957 (2000); Median household income: $39,875 (2000); Poverty rate: 2.0% (2000).
Education: Percent of population age 25 and over with: High school diploma (including GED) or higher: 96.3% (2000); Bachelor's degree or higher: 2.3% (2000).
Housing: Homeownership rate: 85.0% (2000); Median home value: $36,500 (2000); Median rent: <$100 per month (2000); Median age of housing: 60+ years (2000).
Transportation: Commute to work: 91.2% car, 0.0% public transportation, 1.9% walk, 6.9% work from home (2000); Travel time to work: 2.0% less than 15 minutes, 75.0% 15 to 30 minutes, 18.9% 30 to 45 minutes, 4.1% 45 to 60 minutes, 0.0% 60 minutes or more (2000)

DECATUR (city). County seat. Covers a land area of 41.560 square miles and a water area of 4.317 square miles. Located at 39.85° N. Lat.; 88.94° W. Long. Elevation is 673 feet.
History: Decatur was named and designated the seat of Macon County in 1829, though there was no settlement here at the time. In 1830 Abraham Lincoln and his family settled nearby, and in 1836 Richard J. Oglesby, who was to become a senator, three times governor of the state, and a friend of Lincoln's. First an agricultural center, manufacturing began in Decatur with the arrival of the railroad in 1854. Coal was discovered under the city in 1874.
Population: 85,750 (1990); 81,860 (2000); 76,719 (2007); 73,244 (2012 projected); Race: 75.5% White, 20.5% Black, 1.1% Asian, 1.5% Hispanic of any race (2007); Density: 1,846.0 persons per square mile (2007); Average household size: 2.35 (2007); Median age: 37.9 (2007); Males per 100 females: 88.3 (2007); Marriage status: 26.3% never married, 52.1% now married, 8.2% widowed, 13.3% divorced (2000); Foreign born: 1.6% (2000); Ancestry (includes multiple ancestries): 22.2% Other groups, 19.3% German, 11.2% Irish, 10.3% United States or American, 9.3% English (2000).

Economy: Unemployment rate: 6.1% (4/2008); Total civilian labor force: 37,450 (4/2008); Single-family building permits issued: 22 (2007); Multi-family building permits issued: 0 (2007); Employment by occupation: 9.9% management, 17.5% professional, 16.9% services, 26.5% sales, 0.3% farming, 8.9% construction, 20.1% production (2000).
Income: Per capita income: $21,107 (2007); Median household income: $36,475 (2007); Average household income: $48,768 (2007); Percent of households with income of $100,000 or more: 9.0% (2007); Poverty rate: 16.5% (2000).
Taxes: Total city taxes per capita: $393 (2006); City property taxes per capita: $149 (2006).
Education: Percent of population age 25 and over with: High school diploma (including GED) or higher: 80.8% (2007); Bachelor's degree or higher: 17.0% (2007); Master's degree or higher: 5.7% (2007).

School District(s)

Decatur Area Technical Academy
2005-06 Enrollment: n/a . . . . (217) 424-3070
Decatur SD 61 (PK-12)
2005-06 Enrollment: 9,822 . . . . (217) 424-3011
Dept of Corrections Sch Dist 428 (08-12)
2005-06 Enrollment: 2,271 . . . . (217) 522-2666
Heartland Region
2005-06 Enrollment: n/a . . . . (217) 424-3438
Macon/Piatt Roe (06-12)
2005-06 Enrollment: 116 . . . . (217) 872-3721

Four-year College(s)

Millikin University (Private, Not-for-profit, Presbyterian Church (USA))
Fall 2007 Enrollment: 2,376 . . . . (217) 424-6211
2007-08 Tuition: In-state $23,945; Out-of-state $23,945

Two-year College(s)

Mr John's School of Cosmetology Esthetics & Nails (Private, For-profit)
Fall 2007 Enrollment: 68 . . . . (217) 423-8173
Richland Community College (Public)
Fall 2007 Enrollment: 3,274 . . . . (217) 875-7200
2007-08 Tuition: In-state $10,679; Out-of-state $11,795

Housing: Homeownership rate: 66.6% (2007); Median home value: $74,075 (2007); Median rent: $350 per month (2000); Median age of housing: 43 years (2000).
Hospitals: Decatur Memorial Hospital (314 beds); St. Mary's Hospital (371 beds)
Safety: Violent crime rate: 82.6 per 10,000 population; Property crime rate: 503.6 per 10,000 population (2006).
Newspapers: Decatur Tribune (Community news; Circulation 8,000); Herald & Review (Local news; Circulation 35,799); Prairie Shopper (Local news; Circulation 0)
Transportation: Commute to work: 93.1% car, 1.3% public transportation, 2.7% walk, 2.0% work from home (2000); Travel time to work: 53.3% less than 15 minutes, 34.9% 15 to 30 minutes, 4.5% 30 to 45 minutes, 3.8% 45 to 60 minutes, 3.5% 60 minutes or more (2000)
Airports: Decatur (commercial service)

Additional Information Contacts

City of Decatur . . . . (217) 424-2700
http://www.ci.decatur.il.us

FORSYTH (village). Covers a land area of 2.104 square miles and a water area of 0 square miles. Located at 39.92° N. Lat.; 88.95° W. Long. Elevation is 679 feet.
Population: 1,766 (1990); 2,434 (2000); 2,851 (2007); 3,108 (2012 projected); Race: 96.4% White, 1.5% Black, 1.6% Asian, 0.4% Hispanic of any race (2007); Density: 1,354.7 persons per square mile (2007); Average household size: 2.60 (2007); Median age: 43.0 (2007); Males per 100 females: 96.1 (2007); Marriage status: 15.0% never married, 75.4% now married, 5.6% widowed, 4.0% divorced (2000); Foreign born: 2.3% (2000); Ancestry (includes multiple ancestries): 26.0% German, 16.5% English, 13.9% Irish, 8.4% United States or American, 6.7% Other groups (2000).
Economy: Single-family building permits issued: 24 (2007); Multi-family building permits issued: 12 (2007); Employment by occupation: 25.6% management, 23.3% professional, 6.1% services, 28.8% sales, 0.0% farming, 5.6% construction, 10.7% production (2000).
Income: Per capita income: $41,957 (2007); Median household income: $82,982 (2007); Average household income: $108,056 (2007); Percent of households with income of $100,000 or more: 39.7% (2007); Poverty rate: 1.9% (2000).
Taxes: Total city taxes per capita: $223 (2006); City property taxes per capita: $142 (2006).
Education: Percent of population age 25 and over with: High school diploma (including GED) or higher: 94.2% (2007); Bachelor's degree or higher: 36.5% (2007); Master's degree or higher: 11.1% (2007).

School District(s)

Maroa Forsyth CUSD 2 (PK-12)
2005-06 Enrollment: 1,112 . . . . (217) 794-3488

Housing: Homeownership rate: 94.4% (2007); Median home value: $186,925 (2007); Median rent: $383 per month (2000); Median age of housing: 21 years (2000).
Transportation: Commute to work: 95.6% car, 0.0% public transportation, 1.0% walk, 3.2% work from home (2000); Travel time to work: 36.0% less than 15 minutes, 52.1% 15 to 30 minutes, 5.2% 30 to 45 minutes, 3.9% 45 to 60 minutes, 2.9% 60 minutes or more (2000)

HARRISTOWN (village). Covers a land area of 1.856 square miles and a water area of 0 square miles. Located at 39.84° N. Lat.; 89.06° W. Long. Elevation is 689 feet.
Population: 1,364 (1990); 1,338 (2000); 1,437 (2007); 1,399 (2012 projected); Race: 98.4% White, 0.3% Black, 0.2% Asian, 0.4% Hispanic of any race (2007); Density: 774.2 persons per square mile (2007); Average household size: 2.53 (2007); Median age: 40.5 (2007); Males per 100 females: 98.8 (2007); Marriage status: 16.0% never married, 69.1% now married, 5.1% widowed, 9.8% divorced (2000); Foreign born: 0.5% (2000); Ancestry (includes multiple ancestries): 20.4% German, 16.7% United States or American, 14.4% Irish, 13.8% English, 6.8% Other groups (2000).
Economy: Single-family building permits issued: 2 (2007); Multi-family building permits issued: 0 (2007); Employment by occupation: 8.4% management, 12.0% professional, 14.3% services, 26.7% sales, 0.0% farming, 16.5% construction, 22.1% production (2000).
Income: Per capita income: $22,373 (2007); Median household income: $49,934 (2007); Average household income: $56,702 (2007); Percent of households with income of $100,000 or more: 9.3% (2007); Poverty rate: 5.0% (2000).
Education: Percent of population age 25 and over with: High school diploma (including GED) or higher: 84.5% (2007); Bachelor's degree or higher: 10.5% (2007); Master's degree or higher: 3.9% (2007).

School District(s)

Sangamon Valley CUSD 9 (PK-12)
2005-06 Enrollment: 822 . . . . (217) 668-2338

Housing: Homeownership rate: 88.4% (2007); Median home value: $90,738 (2007); Median rent: $328 per month (2000); Median age of housing: 43 years (2000).
Transportation: Commute to work: 95.3% car, 0.0% public transportation, 1.0% walk, 3.3% work from home (2000); Travel time to work: 19.2% less than 15 minutes, 58.7% 15 to 30 minutes, 12.9% 30 to 45 minutes, 4.0% 45 to 60 minutes, 5.2% 60 minutes or more (2000)

LONG CREEK (village). Covers a land area of 2.658 square miles and a water area of 0 square miles. Located at 39.80° N. Lat.; 88.85° W. Long. Elevation is 669 feet.
Population: 1,330 (1990); 1,364 (2000); 1,372 (2007); 1,372 (2012 projected); Race: 98.0% White, 0.6% Black, 0.6% Asian, 0.9% Hispanic of any race (2007); Density: 516.2 persons per square mile (2007); Average household size: 2.71 (2007); Median age: 41.4 (2007); Males per 100 females: 97.7 (2007); Marriage status: 17.2% never married, 72.4% now married, 3.0% widowed, 7.5% divorced (2000); Foreign born: 0.7% (2000); Ancestry (includes multiple ancestries): 26.9% German, 12.6% English, 11.5% United States or American, 11.3% Irish, 3.6% Other groups (2000).
Economy: Single-family building permits issued: 4 (2007); Multi-family building permits issued: 0 (2007); Employment by occupation: 10.0% management, 12.1% professional, 10.8% services, 29.2% sales, 0.0% farming, 15.1% construction, 22.8% production (2000).
Income: Per capita income: $29,679 (2007); Median household income: $68,250 (2007); Average household income: $80,316 (2007); Percent of households with income of $100,000 or more: 23.1% (2007); Poverty rate: 5.1% (2000).
Education: Percent of population age 25 and over with: High school diploma (including GED) or higher: 87.2% (2007); Bachelor's degree or higher: 14.8% (2007); Master's degree or higher: 3.6% (2007).
Housing: Homeownership rate: 92.7% (2007); Median home value: $115,152 (2007); Median rent: $450 per month (2000); Median age of housing: 31 years (2000).
Transportation: Commute to work: 97.5% car, 0.0% public transportation, 0.0% walk, 2.1% work from home (2000); Travel time to work: 24.6% less

than 15 minutes, 59.5% 15 to 30 minutes, 7.4% 30 to 45 minutes, 3.1% 45 to 60 minutes, 5.4% 60 minutes or more (2000)

MACON (city). Covers a land area of 0.881 square miles and a water area of 0 square miles. Located at 39.70° N. Lat.; 89.00° W. Long. Elevation is 715 feet.

Population: 1,376 (1990); 1,213 (2000); 1,106 (2007); 1,063 (2012 projected); Race: 98.6% White, 0.1% Black, 0.5% Asian, 0.8% Hispanic of any race (2007); Density: 1,254.8 persons per square mile (2007); Average household size: 2.51 (2007); Median age: 41.4 (2007); Males per 100 females: 88.4 (2007); Marriage status: 16.7% never married, 59.5% now married, 11.6% widowed, 12.1% divorced (2000); Foreign born: 0.2% (2000); Ancestry (includes multiple ancestries): 21.9% German, 11.8% United States or American, 11.8% English, 9.0% Irish, 7.6% Other groups (2000).

Economy: Single-family building permits issued: 1 (2007); Multi-family building permits issued: 0 (2007); Employment by occupation: 7.3% management, 12.5% professional, 16.0% services, 26.3% sales, 0.0% farming, 14.2% construction, 23.7% production (2000).

Income: Per capita income: $21,058 (2007); Median household income: $44,857 (2007); Average household income: $52,205 (2007); Percent of households with income of $100,000 or more: 6.6% (2007); Poverty rate: 5.8% (2000).

Education: Percent of population age 25 and over with: High school diploma (including GED) or higher: 90.3% (2007); Bachelor's degree or higher: 7.8% (2007); Master's degree or higher: 2.2% (2007).

School District(s)

Meridian CUSD 15 (PK-12)
2005-06 Enrollment: 1,102 . . . . (217) 692-2599

Housing: Homeownership rate: 79.3% (2007); Median home value: $80,490 (2007); Median rent: $343 per month (2000); Median age of housing: 47 years (2000).

Transportation: Commute to work: 96.9% car, 0.0% public transportation, 1.6% walk, 1.6% work from home (2000); Travel time to work: 24.9% less than 15 minutes, 49.6% 15 to 30 minutes, 15.8% 30 to 45 minutes, 5.1% 45 to 60 minutes, 4.7% 60 minutes or more (2000)

MAROA (city). Covers a land area of 0.673 square miles and a water area of 0 square miles. Located at 40.03° N. Lat.; 88.95° W. Long. Elevation is 725 feet.

Population: 1,621 (1990); 1,654 (2000); 1,606 (2007); 1,545 (2012 projected); Race: 99.1% White, 0.2% Black, 0.1% Asian, 1.1% Hispanic of any race (2007); Density: 2,384.9 persons per square mile (2007); Average household size: 2.45 (2007); Median age: 37.4 (2007); Males per 100 females: 98.8 (2007); Marriage status: 19.7% never married, 59.4% now married, 7.5% widowed, 13.4% divorced (2000); Foreign born: 1.0% (2000); Ancestry (includes multiple ancestries): 26.7% German, 13.9% Irish, 13.8% English, 9.9% United States or American, 6.7% Other groups (2000).

Economy: Single-family building permits issued: 5 (2007); Multi-family building permits issued: 0 (2007); Employment by occupation: 6.7% management, 9.6% professional, 17.8% services, 28.5% sales, 0.4% farming, 12.0% construction, 25.2% production (2000).

Income: Per capita income: $22,279 (2007); Median household income: $49,611 (2007); Average household income: $54,626 (2007); Percent of households with income of $100,000 or more: 8.4% (2007); Poverty rate: 4.4% (2000).

Education: Percent of population age 25 and over with: High school diploma (including GED) or higher: 86.7% (2007); Bachelor's degree or higher: 10.6% (2007); Master's degree or higher: 2.2% (2007).

School District(s)

Maroa Forsyth CUSD 2 (PK-12)
2005-06 Enrollment: 1,112 . . . . (217) 794-3488

Housing: Homeownership rate: 79.1% (2007); Median home value: $77,778 (2007); Median rent: $332 per month (2000); Median age of housing: 43 years (2000).

Safety: Violent crime rate: 19.2 per 10,000 population; Property crime rate: 128.0 per 10,000 population (2006).

Transportation: Commute to work: 96.4% car, 0.0% public transportation, 1.9% walk, 1.6% work from home (2000); Travel time to work: 21.3% less than 15 minutes, 51.4% 15 to 30 minutes, 15.0% 30 to 45 minutes, 9.4% 45 to 60 minutes, 3.0% 60 minutes or more (2000)

MOUNT ZION (village). Covers a land area of 3.768 square miles and a water area of <.001 square miles. Located at 39.77° N. Lat.; 88.87° W. Long. Elevation is 696 feet.

Population: 4,857 (1990); 4,845 (2000); 4,909 (2007); 4,946 (2012 projected); Race: 97.2% White, 0.1% Black, 1.4% Asian, 0.3% Hispanic of any race (2007); Density: 1,302.7 persons per square mile (2007); Average household size: 2.57 (2007); Median age: 39.6 (2007); Males per 100 females: 98.7 (2007); Marriage status: 20.4% never married, 70.0% now married, 4.0% widowed, 5.5% divorced (2000); Foreign born: 0.7% (2000); Ancestry (includes multiple ancestries): 27.1% German, 13.7% United States or American, 13.4% Irish, 13.3% English, 5.2% Other groups (2000).

Economy: Single-family building permits issued: 36 (2007); Multi-family building permits issued: 0 (2007); Employment by occupation: 14.9% management, 23.9% professional, 12.9% services, 24.6% sales, 0.0% farming, 6.4% construction, 17.2% production (2000).

Income: Per capita income: $26,719 (2007); Median household income: $59,938 (2007); Average household income: $68,558 (2007); Percent of households with income of $100,000 or more: 17.6% (2007); Poverty rate: 5.0% (2000).

Education: Percent of population age 25 and over with: High school diploma (including GED) or higher: 90.3% (2007); Bachelor's degree or higher: 23.8% (2007); Master's degree or higher: 7.4% (2007).

School District(s)

Mt Zion CUSD 3 (PK-12)
2005-06 Enrollment: 2,450 . . . . (217) 864-2366

Housing: Homeownership rate: 77.1% (2007); Median home value: $116,174 (2007); Median rent: $353 per month (2000); Median age of housing: 27 years (2000).

Safety: Violent crime rate: 17.9 per 10,000 population; Property crime rate: 218.6 per 10,000 population (2006).

Newspapers: Mount Zion Region News (Local news; Circulation 1,800)

Transportation: Commute to work: 96.7% car, 0.0% public transportation, 0.7% walk, 2.3% work from home (2000); Travel time to work: 27.3% less than 15 minutes, 60.8% 15 to 30 minutes, 4.9% 30 to 45 minutes, 2.5% 45 to 60 minutes, 4.6% 60 minutes or more (2000)

Additional Information Contacts

Mount Zion Chamber of Commerce. (217) 864-2526
http://www.mtzionchamberofcommerce.com

NIANTIC (village). Covers a land area of 1.075 square miles and a water area of 0 square miles. Located at 39.85° N. Lat.; 89.16° W. Long. Elevation is 604 feet.

Population: 699 (1990); 738 (2000); 643 (2007); 620 (2012 projected); Race: 99.5% White, 0.0% Black, 0.0% Asian, 1.1% Hispanic of any race (2007); Density: 598.3 persons per square mile (2007); Average household size: 2.65 (2007); Median age: 34.0 (2007); Males per 100 females: 96.6 (2007); Marriage status: 20.3% never married, 67.9% now married, 6.0% widowed, 5.8% divorced (2000); Foreign born: 0.3% (2000); Ancestry (includes multiple ancestries): 21.9% German, 17.3% United States or American, 15.5% English, 13.7% Irish, 6.9% Other groups (2000).

Economy: Single-family building permits issued: 0 (2007); Multi-family building permits issued: 0 (2007); Employment by occupation: 6.7% management, 11.6% professional, 15.2% services, 25.8% sales, 3.0% farming, 15.2% construction, 22.5% production (2000).

Income: Per capita income: $21,120 (2007); Median household income: $47,614 (2007); Average household income: $55,885 (2007); Percent of households with income of $100,000 or more: 8.2% (2007); Poverty rate: 7.8% (2000).

Education: Percent of population age 25 and over with: High school diploma (including GED) or higher: 90.4% (2007); Bachelor's degree or higher: 12.0% (2007); Master's degree or higher: 2.3% (2007).

School District(s)

Sangamon Valley CUSD 9 (PK-12)
2005-06 Enrollment: 822 . . . . (217) 668-2338

Housing: Homeownership rate: 86.8% (2007); Median home value: $93,393 (2007); Median rent: $305 per month (2000); Median age of housing: 47 years (2000).

Transportation: Commute to work: 94.4% car, 0.9% public transportation, 1.2% walk, 1.6% work from home (2000); Travel time to work: 14.6% less than 15 minutes, 44.6% 15 to 30 minutes, 26.6% 30 to 45 minutes, 7.9% 45 to 60 minutes, 6.3% 60 minutes or more (2000)

OAKLEY (unincorporated postal area, zip code 62552). Covers a land area of 38.230 square miles and a water area of 0.004 square miles. Located at 39.87° N. Lat.; 88.81° W. Long. Elevation is 689 feet.
Population: 1,063 (2000); Race: 100.0% White, 0.0% Black, 0.0% Asian, 0.0% Hispanic of any race (2000); Density: 27.8 persons per square mile (2000); Age: 19.7% under 18, 13.8% over 64 (2000); Marriage status: 13.9% never married, 75.1% now married, 2.7% widowed, 8.3% divorced (2000); Foreign born: 0.0% (2000); Ancestry (includes multiple ancestries): 22.4% German, 16.9% English, 10.9% United States or American, 5.1% Irish, 4.3% Other groups (2000).
Economy: Employment by occupation: 7.5% management, 15.7% professional, 16.1% services, 25.7% sales, 1.4% farming, 17.3% construction, 16.3% production (2000).
Income: Per capita income: $19,102 (2000); Median household income: $49,228 (2000); Poverty rate: 3.3% (2000).
Education: Percent of population age 25 and over with: High school diploma (including GED) or higher: 82.6% (2000); Bachelor's degree or higher: 5.3% (2000).
Housing: Homeownership rate: 85.2% (2000); Median home value: $80,600 (2000); Median rent: $373 per month (2000); Median age of housing: 35 years (2000).
Transportation: Commute to work: 96.9% car, 0.0% public transportation, 1.2% walk, 2.0% work from home (2000); Travel time to work: 16.8% less than 15 minutes, 59.1% 15 to 30 minutes, 11.2% 30 to 45 minutes, 3.2% 45 to 60 minutes, 9.6% 60 minutes or more (2000)

OREANA (village). Covers a land area of 0.500 square miles and a water area of 0 square miles. Located at 39.93° N. Lat.; 88.86° W. Long. Elevation is 689 feet.
Population: 847 (1990); 892 (2000); 843 (2007); 829 (2012 projected); Race: 98.6% White, 0.0% Black, 0.1% Asian, 0.7% Hispanic of any race (2007); Density: 1,687.2 persons per square mile (2007); Average household size: 2.49 (2007); Median age: 40.6 (2007); Males per 100 females: 103.1 (2007); Marriage status: 17.8% never married, 68.7% now married, 6.2% widowed, 7.3% divorced (2000); Foreign born: 0.2% (2000); Ancestry (includes multiple ancestries): 23.5% German, 15.4% Irish, 13.6% English, 11.2% United States or American, 3.2% Other groups (2000).
Economy: Single-family building permits issued: 0 (2007); Multi-family building permits issued: 0 (2007); Employment by occupation: 5.2% management, 13.4% professional, 18.3% services, 26.1% sales, 0.4% farming, 14.0% construction, 22.6% production (2000).
Income: Per capita income: $24,508 (2007); Median household income: $58,182 (2007); Average household income: $61,124 (2007); Percent of households with income of $100,000 or more: 13.0% (2007); Poverty rate: 2.8% (2000).
Education: Percent of population age 25 and over with: High school diploma (including GED) or higher: 91.3% (2007); Bachelor's degree or higher: 11.1% (2007); Master's degree or higher: 3.0% (2007).

School District(s)

Argenta-Oreana CUSD 1 (PK-12)
2005-06 Enrollment: 994 . . . . (217) 795-2313
Housing: Homeownership rate: 88.8% (2007); Median home value: $94,643 (2007); Median rent: $280 per month (2000); Median age of housing: 36 years (2000).
Transportation: Commute to work: 96.3% car, 0.0% public transportation, 0.9% walk, 2.4% work from home (2000); Travel time to work: 29.8% less than 15 minutes, 56.4% 15 to 30 minutes, 7.0% 30 to 45 minutes, 2.3% 45 to 60 minutes, 4.5% 60 minutes or more (2000)

WARRENSBURG (village). Covers a land area of 0.678 square miles and a water area of 0 square miles. Located at 39.93° N. Lat.; 89.06° W. Long. Elevation is 705 feet.
Population: 1,293 (1990); 1,289 (2000); 1,139 (2007); 1,098 (2012 projected); Race: 97.0% White, 0.9% Black, 0.1% Asian, 0.6% Hispanic of any race (2007); Density: 1,679.4 persons per square mile (2007); Average household size: 2.49 (2007); Median age: 36.8 (2007); Males per 100 females: 95.7 (2007); Marriage status: 22.7% never married, 59.8% now married, 5.1% widowed, 12.5% divorced (2000); Foreign born: 0.9% (2000); Ancestry (includes multiple ancestries): 29.5% German, 17.2% Irish, 15.1% English, 9.0% Other groups, 6.5% United States or American (2000).
Economy: Single-family building permits issued: 0 (2007); Multi-family building permits issued: 0 (2007); Employment by occupation: 9.3% management, 19.3% professional, 17.1% services, 24.0% sales, 0.0% farming, 10.5% construction, 19.8% production (2000).
Income: Per capita income: $24,079 (2007); Median household income: $52,836 (2007); Average household income: $58,062 (2007); Percent of households with income of $100,000 or more: 9.8% (2007); Poverty rate: 3.7% (2000).
Education: Percent of population age 25 and over with: High school diploma (including GED) or higher: 88.6% (2007); Bachelor's degree or higher: 15.4% (2007); Master's degree or higher: 3.4% (2007).

School District(s)

Warrensburg-Latham CUSD 11 (PK-12)
2005-06 Enrollment: 1,115 . . . . (217) 672-3514
Housing: Homeownership rate: 74.2% (2007); Median home value: $99,444 (2007); Median rent: $323 per month (2000); Median age of housing: 30 years (2000).
Safety: Violent crime rate: 49.6 per 10,000 population; Property crime rate: 157.2 per 10,000 population (2006).
Transportation: Commute to work: 96.1% car, 0.0% public transportation, 1.0% walk, 2.5% work from home (2000); Travel time to work: 27.6% less than 15 minutes, 56.2% 15 to 30 minutes, 8.0% 30 to 45 minutes, 4.3% 45 to 60 minutes, 3.9% 60 minutes or more (2000)

Macoupin County

Located in southwest central Illinois; drained by Macoupin, Cahokia, and Otter Creeks. Covers a land area of 863.57 square miles, a water area of 4.04 square miles, and is located in the Central Time Zone. The county was founded in 1829. County seat is Carlinville.

Macoupin County is part of the St. Louis, MO-IL Metropolitan Statistical Area. The entire metro area includes: Bond County, IL; Calhoun County, IL; Clinton County, IL; Jersey County, IL; Macoupin County, IL; Madison County, IL; Monroe County, IL; St. Clair County, IL; Crawford County, MO (pt.)*; Franklin County, MO; Jefferson County, MO; Lincoln County, MO; St. Charles County, MO; St. Louis County, MO; Warren County, MO; Washington County, MO; St. Louis city, MO

Weather Station: Carlinville — Elevation: 629 feet

	Jan	Feb	Mar	Apr	May	Jun	Jul	Aug	Sep	Oct	Nov	Dec
High	35	42	53	66	76	84	88	86	80	68	53	41
Low	18	24	33	43	53	62	66	64	56	45	35	25
Precip	2.0	1.9	3.5	4.2	4.3	3.8	3.6	3.4	3.1	2.7	3.6	2.9
Snow	6.8	4.4	3.3	0.7	tr	0.0	0.0	0.0	0.0	tr	1.4	3.6

High and Low temperatures in degrees Fahrenheit; Precipitation and Snow in inches

Weather Station: Virden — Elevation: 672 feet

	Jan	Feb	Mar	Apr	May	Jun	Jul	Aug	Sep	Oct	Nov	Dec
High	35	40	52	66	76	84	88	86	80	68	52	40
Low	18	23	33	44	54	62	66	63	56	45	34	24
Precip	1.8	2.0	3.3	3.8	4.4	3.9	3.5	3.1	3.0	2.5	3.3	2.5
Snow	6.5	6.5	3.9	0.7	0.0	0.0	0.0	0.0	0.0	tr	1.5	4.7

High and Low temperatures in degrees Fahrenheit; Precipitation and Snow in inches

Population: 47,679 (1990); 49,019 (2000); 49,170 (2007); 49,163 (2012 projected); Race: 97.7% White, 1.1% Black, 0.3% Asian, 0.7% Hispanic of any race (2007); Density: 56.9 persons per square mile (2007); Average household size: 2.52 (2007); Median age: 40.3 (2007); Males per 100 females: 95.4 (2007).
Religion: Five largest groups: 14.4% Catholic Church, 9.3% Southern Baptist Convention, 6.4% Lutheran Church—Missouri Synod, 6.2% The United Methodist Church, 2.5% United Church of Christ (2000).
Economy: Unemployment rate: 6.1% (4/2008); Total civilian labor force: 25,707 (4/2008); Leading industries: 14.7% health care and social assistance; 14.7% retail trade; 8.4% accommodation & food services (2005); Farms: 1,214 totaling 427,173 acres (2002); Companies that employ 500 or more persons: 0 (2006); Companies that employ 100 to 499 persons: 11 (2006); Companies that employ less than 100 persons: 1,039 (2006); Black-owned businesses: n/a (2002); Hispanic-owned businesses: n/a (2002); Asian-owned businesses: n/a (2002); Women-owned businesses: 1,146 (2002); Retail sales per capita: $10,020 (2008). Single-family building permits issued: 69 (2007); Multi-family building permits issued: 4 (2007).
Income: Per capita income: $21,035 (2007); Median household income: $43,172 (2007); Average household income: $52,389 (2007); Percent of households with income of $100,000 or more: 9.7% (2007); Poverty rate: 10.4% (2005); Bankruptcy rate: 2.24% (2007).

Education: Percent of population age 25 and over with: High school diploma (including GED) or higher: 82.0% (2007); Bachelor's degree or higher: 11.8% (2007); Master's degree or higher: 3.8% (2007).
Housing: Homeownership rate: 79.1% (2007); Median home value: $95,723 (2007); Median rent: $299 per month (2000); Median age of housing: 42 years (2000).
Health: Birth rate: 123.6 per 10,000 population (2007); Death rate: 120.0 per 10,000 population (2007); Age-adjusted cancer mortality rate: 193.7 deaths per 100,000 population (2005); Air Quality Index: 92.3% good, 7.4% moderate, 0.3% unhealthy for sensitive individuals, 0.0% unhealthy (percent of days in 2007); Number of physicians: 6.0 per 10,000 population (2005); Hospital beds: 11.9 per 10,000 population (2004); Hospital admissions: 344.4 per 10,000 population (2004).
Elections: 2004 Presidential election results: 50.1% Bush, 49.1% Kerry, 0.1% Nader, 0.7% Badnarik
National and State Parks: Beaver Dam State Park
Additional Information Contacts
Macoupin County Government . . . . (217) 854-3214
http://www.macoupincountyil.gov
Carlinville Chamber of Commerce . . . . (217) 854-2141
http://carlinvillechamber.com
City of Carlinville . . . . (217) 854-4076
City of Staunton . . . . (618) 635-2233
http://www.stauntonil.com/government.html
Coal Country Chamber of Commerce . . . . (217) 839-4888
Staunton Chamber of Commerce . . . . (618) 635-8356
http://www.stauntonil.com/chamber.html
Virden Area Association of Commerce . . . . (217) 965-3321

Macoupin County Communities

ATWATER (unincorporated postal area, zip code 62511). Covers a land area of 12.205 square miles and a water area of 0 square miles. Located at 39.34° N. Lat.; 89.73° W. Long. Elevation is 633 feet.
Population: 176 (2000); Race: 100.0% White, 0.0% Black, 0.0% Asian, 0.0% Hispanic of any race (2000); Density: 14.4 persons per square mile (2000); Age: 16.9% under 18, 13.6% over 64 (2000); Marriage status: 14.2% never married, 66.5% now married, 11.6% widowed, 7.7% divorced (2000); Foreign born: 0.0% (2000); Ancestry (includes multiple ancestries): 37.3% German, 19.8% Irish, 14.1% Scotch-Irish, 9.6% English, 7.9% United States or American (2000).
Economy: Employment by occupation: 16.5% management, 3.5% professional, 10.4% services, 37.4% sales, 0.0% farming, 10.4% construction, 21.7% production (2000).
Income: Per capita income: $19,332 (2000); Median household income: $33,958 (2000); Poverty rate: 0.0% (2000).
Education: Percent of population age 25 and over with: High school diploma (including GED) or higher: 82.1% (2000); Bachelor's degree or higher: 3.7% (2000).
Housing: Homeownership rate: 80.7% (2000); Median home value: $125,000 (2000); Median rent: $n/a per month (2000); Median age of housing: 27 years (2000).
Transportation: Commute to work: 88.7% car, 0.0% public transportation, 0.0% walk, 11.3% work from home (2000); Travel time to work: 18.6% less than 15 minutes, 49.0% 15 to 30 minutes, 18.6% 30 to 45 minutes, 9.8% 45 to 60 minutes, 3.9% 60 minutes or more (2000)

BENLD (city). Covers a land area of 1.058 square miles and a water area of 0 square miles. Located at 39.09° N. Lat.; 89.80° W. Long. Elevation is 633 feet.
History: Incorporated 1904; reincorporated 1930 as city.
Population: 1,604 (1990); 1,541 (2000); 1,476 (2007); 1,463 (2012 projected); Race: 97.6% White, 0.9% Black, 0.0% Asian, 1.2% Hispanic of any race (2007); Density: 1,394.5 persons per square mile (2007); Average household size: 2.23 (2007); Median age: 38.3 (2007); Males per 100 females: 91.4 (2007); Marriage status: 21.1% never married, 53.7% now married, 11.1% widowed, 14.2% divorced (2000); Foreign born: 0.5% (2000); Ancestry (includes multiple ancestries): 22.2% German, 19.2% Italian, 13.3% Irish, 11.3% United States or American, 6.5% Other groups (2000).
Economy: Single-family building permits issued: 1 (2007); Multi-family building permits issued: 0 (2007); Employment by occupation: 8.4% management, 16.9% professional, 20.6% services, 22.8% sales, 0.3% farming, 11.2% construction, 19.6% production (2000).
Income: Per capita income: $19,180 (2007); Median household income: $35,817 (2007); Average household income: $42,829 (2007); Percent of households with income of $100,000 or more: 6.1% (2007); Poverty rate: 14.3% (2000).
Education: Percent of population age 25 and over with: High school diploma (including GED) or higher: 77.1% (2007); Bachelor's degree or higher: 9.9% (2007); Master's degree or higher: 2.6% (2007).

School District(s)

Gillespie CUSD 7 (PK-12)
2005-06 Enrollment: 1,312 . . . . (217) 839-2464
Housing: Homeownership rate: 79.4% (2007); Median home value: $65,486 (2007); Median rent: $315 per month (2000); Median age of housing: 60+ years (2000).
Safety: Violent crime rate: 0.0 per 10,000 population; Property crime rate: 60.4 per 10,000 population (2006).
Transportation: Commute to work: 96.6% car, 0.3% public transportation, 0.3% walk, 2.0% work from home (2000); Travel time to work: 37.4% less than 15 minutes, 25.4% 15 to 30 minutes, 11.3% 30 to 45 minutes, 11.1% 45 to 60 minutes, 14.8% 60 minutes or more (2000)

BRIGHTON (village). Covers a land area of 1.610 square miles and a water area of 0.030 square miles. Located at 39.03° N. Lat.; 90.14° W. Long. Elevation is 663 feet.
Population: 2,315 (1990); 2,196 (2000); 2,315 (2007); 2,349 (2012 projected); Race: 98.2% White, 0.1% Black, 0.6% Asian, 1.3% Hispanic of any race (2007); Density: 1,438.2 persons per square mile (2007); Average household size: 2.63 (2007); Median age: 38.0 (2007); Males per 100 females: 95.5 (2007); Marriage status: 19.6% never married, 60.7% now married, 9.3% widowed, 10.5% divorced (2000); Foreign born: 0.6% (2000); Ancestry (includes multiple ancestries): 26.5% German, 13.9% English, 11.4% Irish, 10.9% Other groups, 9.5% United States or American (2000).
Economy: Single-family building permits issued: 11 (2007); Multi-family building permits issued: 0 (2007); Employment by occupation: 8.2% management, 13.9% professional, 19.1% services, 26.7% sales, 0.3% farming, 11.8% construction, 19.9% production (2000).
Income: Per capita income: $19,405 (2007); Median household income: $43,731 (2007); Average household income: $50,338 (2007); Percent of households with income of $100,000 or more: 8.1% (2007); Poverty rate: 6.5% (2000).
Education: Percent of population age 25 and over with: High school diploma (including GED) or higher: 85.5% (2007); Bachelor's degree or higher: 12.3% (2007); Master's degree or higher: 3.2% (2007).

School District(s)

Southwestern CUSD 9 (PK-12)
2005-06 Enrollment: 1,789 . . . . (618) 729-3221
Housing: Homeownership rate: 81.7% (2007); Median home value: $106,158 (2007); Median rent: $341 per month (2000); Median age of housing: 34 years (2000).
Safety: Violent crime rate: 21.5 per 10,000 population; Property crime rate: 86.1 per 10,000 population (2006).
Newspapers: Southwestern Journal (Local news; Circulation 1,550); Southwestern Shoppers Guide (Community news; Circulation 8,600)
Transportation: Commute to work: 98.2% car, 0.2% public transportation, 0.7% walk, 0.7% work from home (2000); Travel time to work: 16.7% less than 15 minutes, 35.6% 15 to 30 minutes, 18.6% 30 to 45 minutes, 10.9% 45 to 60 minutes, 18.2% 60 minutes or more (2000)

BUNKER HILL (city). Covers a land area of 1.180 square miles and a water area of 0.023 square miles. Located at 39.04° N. Lat.; 89.95° W. Long. Elevation is 663 feet.
History: Incorporated 1857.
Population: 1,737 (1990); 1,801 (2000); 1,681 (2007); 1,658 (2012 projected); Race: 97.3% White, 1.4% Black, 0.2% Asian, 0.5% Hispanic of any race (2007); Density: 1,425.2 persons per square mile (2007); Average household size: 2.53 (2007); Median age: 37.8 (2007); Males per 100 females: 89.7 (2007); Marriage status: 19.6% never married, 62.8% now married, 9.3% widowed, 8.3% divorced (2000); Foreign born: 0.4% (2000); Ancestry (includes multiple ancestries): 31.3% German, 14.1% English, 13.6% Irish, 8.4% Other groups, 7.5% United States or American (2000).
Economy: Employment by occupation: 7.5% management, 14.8% professional, 14.4% services, 26.3% sales, 0.5% farming, 16.1% construction, 20.4% production (2000).
Income: Per capita income: $21,478 (2007); Median household income: $46,923 (2007); Average household income: $53,780 (2007); Percent of

households with income of $100,000 or more: 10.1% (2007); Poverty rate: 10.3% (2000).
Education: Percent of population age 25 and over with: High school diploma (including GED) or higher: 80.8% (2007); Bachelor's degree or higher: 11.7% (2007); Master's degree or higher: 2.1% (2007).

School District(s)

Bunker Hill CUSD 8 (PK-12)
2005-06 Enrollment: 727 . . . . (618) 585-3116
Housing: Homeownership rate: 72.1% (2007); Median home value: $88,214 (2007); Median rent: $288 per month (2000); Median age of housing: 41 years (2000).
Safety: Violent crime rate: 128.1 per 10,000 population; Property crime rate: 334.3 per 10,000 population (2006).
Newspapers: Bunker Hill Gazette-News (Local news; Circulation 1,550); Southwest Advertiser (Local news; Circulation 7,700)
Transportation: Commute to work: 94.9% car, 0.0% public transportation, 3.2% walk, 1.5% work from home (2000); Travel time to work: 26.2% less than 15 minutes, 20.7% 15 to 30 minutes, 30.3% 30 to 45 minutes, 8.6% 45 to 60 minutes, 14.1% 60 minutes or more (2000)

CARLINVILLE (city). County seat. Covers a land area of 2.379 square miles and a water area of 0 square miles. Located at 39.28° N. Lat.; 89.88° W. Long. Elevation is 620 feet.
History: Carlinville was the site of the "million-dollar courthouse" of Macoupin County, completed in 1870 at a cost of $1,380,500, and opposed by the taxpayers. Built of limestone, the courthouse was designed as two rectangles crossing at the center under a dome that rose 191 feet.
Population: 5,511 (1990); 5,685 (2000); 5,566 (2007); 5,470 (2012 projected); Race: 96.5% White, 2.2% Black, 0.2% Asian, 0.8% Hispanic of any race (2007); Density: 2,339.8 persons per square mile (2007); Average household size: 2.71 (2007); Median age: 36.8 (2007); Males per 100 females: 90.4 (2007); Marriage status: 24.8% never married, 56.6% now married, 7.3% widowed, 11.3% divorced (2000); Foreign born: 0.1% (2000); Ancestry (includes multiple ancestries): 34.8% German, 15.4% English, 12.4% Irish, 7.9% Other groups, 7.1% United States or American (2000).
Economy: Employment by occupation: 10.9% management, 18.2% professional, 21.0% services, 25.6% sales, 0.0% farming, 10.7% construction, 13.7% production (2000).
Income: Per capita income: $19,600 (2007); Median household income: $40,220 (2007); Average household income: $50,664 (2007); Percent of households with income of $100,000 or more: 10.0% (2007); Poverty rate: 12.5% (2000).
Education: Percent of population age 25 and over with: High school diploma (including GED) or higher: 79.6% (2007); Bachelor's degree or higher: 16.5% (2007); Master's degree or higher: 7.2% (2007).

School District(s)

Calhoun/Greene/Jersey/Macoupn Roe (06-12)
2005-06 Enrollment: 73 . . . . (217) 854-4016
Carlinville CUSD 1 (PK-12)
2005-06 Enrollment: 1,511 . . . . (217) 854-9823

Four-year College(s)

Blackburn College (Private, Not-for-profit, Presbyterian Church (USA))
Fall 2007 Enrollment: 617 . . . . (217) 854-3231
2007-08 Tuition: In-state $15,770; Out-of-state $15,770
Housing: Homeownership rate: 69.3% (2007); Median home value: $91,076 (2007); Median rent: $305 per month (2000); Median age of housing: 54 years (2000).
Hospitals: Carlinville Area Hospital (33 beds)
Safety: Violent crime rate: 29.5 per 10,000 population; Property crime rate: 154.3 per 10,000 population (2006).
Newspapers: Macoupin County Enquirer (Regional news; Circulation 4,900); Macoutin County Inquirer-Democrat (Community news; Circulation 2,500)
Transportation: Commute to work: 86.6% car, 0.4% public transportation, 8.3% walk, 4.2% work from home (2000); Travel time to work: 63.1% less than 15 minutes, 14.2% 15 to 30 minutes, 3.7% 30 to 45 minutes, 7.1% 45 to 60 minutes, 11.9% 60 minutes or more (2000); Amtrak: Service available.

Additional Information Contacts

Carlinville Chamber of Commerce . . . . (217) 854-2141
http://carlinvillechamber.com
City of Carlinville . . . . (217) 854-4076

CHESTERFIELD (village). Covers a land area of 0.541 square miles and a water area of 0 square miles. Located at 39.25° N. Lat.; 90.06° W. Long. Elevation is 587 feet.
Population: 230 (1990); 223 (2000); 193 (2007); 185 (2012 projected); Race: 97.9% White, 0.0% Black, 0.0% Asian, 0.0% Hispanic of any race (2007); Density: 356.8 persons per square mile (2007); Average household size: 2.54 (2007); Median age: 39.2 (2007); Males per 100 females: 87.4 (2007); Marriage status: 30.1% never married, 56.6% now married, 7.7% widowed, 5.6% divorced (2000); Foreign born: 1.2% (2000); Ancestry (includes multiple ancestries): 19.0% English, 14.0% German, 13.6% Irish, 13.2% Italian, 8.7% French (except Basque) (2000).
Economy: Employment by occupation: 5.9% management, 12.6% professional, 16.8% services, 16.0% sales, 1.7% farming, 12.6% construction, 34.5% production (2000).
Income: Per capita income: $21,619 (2007); Median household income: $41,667 (2007); Average household income: $54,901 (2007); Percent of households with income of $100,000 or more: 10.5% (2007); Poverty rate: 12.1% (2000).
Education: Percent of population age 25 and over with: High school diploma (including GED) or higher: 79.1% (2007); Bachelor's degree or higher: 7.8% (2007); Master's degree or higher: 0.0% (2007).
Housing: Homeownership rate: 85.5% (2007); Median home value: $64,583 (2007); Median rent: $308 per month (2000); Median age of housing: 48 years (2000).
Transportation: Commute to work: 93.0% car, 0.0% public transportation, 1.8% walk, 5.3% work from home (2000); Travel time to work: 14.8% less than 15 minutes, 41.7% 15 to 30 minutes, 18.5% 30 to 45 minutes, 13.0% 45 to 60 minutes, 12.0% 60 minutes or more (2000)

DORCHESTER (village). Covers a land area of 0.715 square miles and a water area of 0 square miles. Located at 39.08° N. Lat.; 89.88° W. Long. Elevation is 656 feet.
Population: 145 (1990); 142 (2000); 161 (2007); 168 (2012 projected); Race: 98.8% White, 0.0% Black, 0.0% Asian, 0.0% Hispanic of any race (2007); Density: 225.0 persons per square mile (2007); Average household size: 2.44 (2007); Median age: 41.5 (2007); Males per 100 females: 111.8 (2007); Marriage status: 22.1% never married, 58.8% now married, 7.4% widowed, 11.8% divorced (2000); Foreign born: 0.0% (2000); Ancestry (includes multiple ancestries): 36.6% German, 16.1% United States or American, 15.5% Italian, 9.9% Scottish, 8.7% Irish (2000).
Economy: Single-family building permits issued: 0 (2007); Multi-family building permits issued: 0 (2007); Employment by occupation: 18.4% management, 8.2% professional, 25.5% services, 15.3% sales, 3.1% farming, 15.3% construction, 14.3% production (2000).
Income: Per capita income: $24,270 (2007); Median household income: $50,000 (2007); Average household income: $59,205 (2007); Percent of households with income of $100,000 or more: 15.2% (2007); Poverty rate: 5.6% (2000).
Education: Percent of population age 25 and over with: High school diploma (including GED) or higher: 87.2% (2007); Bachelor's degree or higher: 2.8% (2007); Master's degree or higher: 0.0% (2007).
Housing: Homeownership rate: 92.4% (2007); Median home value: $65,000 (2007); Median rent: $275 per month (2000); Median age of housing: 51 years (2000).
Transportation: Commute to work: 95.9% car, 0.0% public transportation, 0.0% walk, 4.1% work from home (2000); Travel time to work: 8.5% less than 15 minutes, 44.7% 15 to 30 minutes, 30.9% 30 to 45 minutes, 11.7% 45 to 60 minutes, 4.3% 60 minutes or more (2000)

EAGARVILLE (village). Aka Eagerville. Covers a land area of 0.931 square miles and a water area of 0.002 square miles. Located at 39.11° N. Lat.; 89.78° W. Long. Elevation is 643 feet.
Population: 121 (1990); 128 (2000); 133 (2007); 131 (2012 projected); Race: 100.0% White, 0.0% Black, 0.0% Asian, 0.0% Hispanic of any race (2007); Density: 142.9 persons per square mile (2007); Average household size: 2.83 (2007); Median age: 33.3 (2007); Males per 100 females: 125.4 (2007); Marriage status: 14.3% never married, 73.6% now married, 6.6% widowed, 5.5% divorced (2000); Foreign born: 0.0% (2000); Ancestry (includes multiple ancestries): 20.0% Italian, 18.3% German, 12.5% Other groups, 10.8% Irish, 10.0% United States or American (2000).
Economy: Employment by occupation: 5.5% management, 10.9% professional, 25.5% services, 30.9% sales, 0.0% farming, 9.1% construction, 18.2% production (2000).

Income: Per capita income: $21,861 (2007); Median household income: $41,875 (2007); Average household income: $61,862 (2007); Percent of households with income of $100,000 or more: 8.5% (2007); Poverty rate: 4.2% (2000).
Education: Percent of population age 25 and over with: High school diploma (including GED) or higher: 84.1% (2007); Bachelor's degree or higher: 13.4% (2007); Master's degree or higher: 7.3% (2007).
Housing: Homeownership rate: 85.1% (2007); Median home value: $68,000 (2007); Median rent: $425 per month (2000); Median age of housing: 44 years (2000).
Transportation: Commute to work: 85.5% car, 7.3% public transportation, 0.0% walk, 0.0% work from home (2000); Travel time to work: 20.0% less than 15 minutes, 18.2% 15 to 30 minutes, 32.7% 30 to 45 minutes, 5.5% 45 to 60 minutes, 23.6% 60 minutes or more (2000)

EAST GILLESPIE (village). Covers a land area of 0.318 square miles and a water area of 0 square miles. Located at 39.13° N. Lat.; 89.81° W. Long. Elevation is 659 feet.
Population: 205 (1990); 234 (2000); 225 (2007); 214 (2012 projected); Race: 98.2% White, 0.9% Black, 0.0% Asian, 0.9% Hispanic of any race (2007); Density: 707.6 persons per square mile (2007); Average household size: 2.50 (2007); Median age: 42.0 (2007); Males per 100 females: 112.3 (2007); Marriage status: 29.8% never married, 55.5% now married, 7.9% widowed, 6.8% divorced (2000); Foreign born: 0.9% (2000); Ancestry (includes multiple ancestries): 31.3% German, 13.7% Italian, 13.7% Other groups, 8.4% English, 7.5% Irish (2000).
Economy: Single-family building permits issued: 3 (2007); Multi-family building permits issued: 0 (2007); Employment by occupation: 8.0% management, 4.0% professional, 20.0% services, 10.0% sales, 0.0% farming, 6.0% construction, 52.0% production (2000).
Income: Per capita income: $21,444 (2007); Median household income: $42,222 (2007); Average household income: $53,611 (2007); Percent of households with income of $100,000 or more: 7.8% (2007); Poverty rate: 5.3% (2000).
Education: Percent of population age 25 and over with: High school diploma (including GED) or higher: 81.6% (2007); Bachelor's degree or higher: 5.5% (2007); Master's degree or higher: 3.1% (2007).
Housing: Homeownership rate: 84.4% (2007); Median home value: $68,235 (2007); Median rent: $300 per month (2000); Median age of housing: 53 years (2000).
Transportation: Commute to work: 82.7% car, 0.0% public transportation, 4.1% walk, 5.1% work from home (2000); Travel time to work: 36.6% less than 15 minutes, 26.9% 15 to 30 minutes, 10.8% 30 to 45 minutes, 4.3% 45 to 60 minutes, 21.5% 60 minutes or more (2000)

GILLESPIE (city). Covers a land area of 1.452 square miles and a water area of 0 square miles. Located at 39.12° N. Lat.; 89.81° W. Long. Elevation is 659 feet.
Population: 3,628 (1990); 3,412 (2000); 3,205 (2007); 3,062 (2012 projected); Race: 98.2% White, 0.6% Black, 0.2% Asian, 0.9% Hispanic of any race (2007); Density: 2,206.7 persons per square mile (2007); Average household size: 2.30 (2007); Median age: 39.8 (2007); Males per 100 females: 89.2 (2007); Marriage status: 21.9% never married, 56.7% now married, 10.1% widowed, 11.3% divorced (2000); Foreign born: 0.7% (2000); Ancestry (includes multiple ancestries): 28.9% German, 16.3% Italian, 12.1% Irish, 10.0% English, 7.1% Scottish (2000).
Economy: Single-family building permits issued: 4 (2007); Multi-family building permits issued: 0 (2007); Employment by occupation: 7.8% management, 12.3% professional, 18.6% services, 26.1% sales, 1.1% farming, 10.4% construction, 23.7% production (2000).
Income: Per capita income: $21,955 (2007); Median household income: $39,023 (2007); Average household income: $50,513 (2007); Percent of households with income of $100,000 or more: 10.2% (2007); Poverty rate: 12.4% (2000).
Education: Percent of population age 25 and over with: High school diploma (including GED) or higher: 83.9% (2007); Bachelor's degree or higher: 7.6% (2007); Master's degree or higher: 3.6% (2007).

School District(s)

Gillespie CUSD 7 (PK-12)
2005-06 Enrollment: 1,312 . . . . (217) 839-2464
Housing: Homeownership rate: 76.6% (2007); Median home value: $78,894 (2007); Median rent: $316 per month (2000); Median age of housing: 55 years (2000).
Safety: Violent crime rate: 21.4 per 10,000 population; Property crime rate: 302.0 per 10,000 population (2006).
Newspapers: Gillespie Area News (Community news; Circulation 2,700)
Transportation: Commute to work: 95.0% car, 0.8% public transportation, 1.2% walk, 2.3% work from home (2000); Travel time to work: 37.6% less than 15 minutes, 23.0% 15 to 30 minutes, 10.3% 30 to 45 minutes, 10.1% 45 to 60 minutes, 19.0% 60 minutes or more (2000)

Additional Information Contacts

Coal Country Chamber of Commerce . . . . (217) 839-4888

GIRARD (city). Covers a land area of 0.936 square miles and a water area of 0 square miles. Located at 39.44° N. Lat.; 89.78° W. Long. Elevation is 669 feet.
History: Incorporated 1855.
Population: 2,164 (1990); 2,245 (2000); 2,284 (2007); 2,271 (2012 projected); Race: 98.9% White, 0.2% Black, 0.0% Asian, 1.5% Hispanic of any race (2007); Density: 2,440.5 persons per square mile (2007); Average household size: 2.55 (2007); Median age: 38.2 (2007); Males per 100 females: 96.7 (2007); Marriage status: 23.2% never married, 53.9% now married, 10.9% widowed, 12.0% divorced (2000); Foreign born: 0.5% (2000); Ancestry (includes multiple ancestries): 22.6% German, 15.1% English, 13.8% Irish, 13.0% United States or American, 9.6% Other groups (2000).
Economy: Employment by occupation: 11.4% management, 14.5% professional, 19.0% services, 21.8% sales, 0.8% farming, 11.4% construction, 21.1% production (2000).
Income: Per capita income: $17,074 (2007); Median household income: $37,077 (2007); Average household income: $42,679 (2007); Percent of households with income of $100,000 or more: 5.3% (2007); Poverty rate: 13.2% (2000).
Taxes: Total city taxes per capita: $60 (2006); City property taxes per capita: $32 (2006).
Education: Percent of population age 25 and over with: High school diploma (including GED) or higher: 79.4% (2007); Bachelor's degree or higher: 9.9% (2007); Master's degree or higher: 3.5% (2007).

School District(s)

Girard CUSD 3 (PK-12)
2005-06 Enrollment: 722 . . . . (217) 627-2915
Housing: Homeownership rate: 69.6% (2007); Median home value: $82,857 (2007); Median rent: $282 per month (2000); Median age of housing: 47 years (2000).
Safety: Violent crime rate: 53.6 per 10,000 population; Property crime rate: 205.6 per 10,000 population (2006).
Newspapers: Girard Gazette (Local news; Circulation 1,400)
Transportation: Commute to work: 92.1% car, 0.0% public transportation, 3.9% walk, 2.6% work from home (2000); Travel time to work: 37.7% less than 15 minutes, 22.6% 15 to 30 minutes, 21.3% 30 to 45 minutes, 12.9% 45 to 60 minutes, 5.5% 60 minutes or more (2000)

HETTICK (village). Covers a land area of 0.332 square miles and a water area of 0 square miles. Located at 39.35° N. Lat.; 90.03° W. Long. Elevation is 597 feet.
Population: 211 (1990); 182 (2000); 179 (2007); 177 (2012 projected); Race: 100.0% White, 0.0% Black, 0.0% Asian, 0.0% Hispanic of any race (2007); Density: 539.9 persons per square mile (2007); Average household size: 2.16 (2007); Median age: 39.1 (2007); Males per 100 females: 92.5 (2007); Marriage status: 14.4% never married, 66.4% now married, 7.5% widowed, 11.6% divorced (2000); Foreign born: 0.0% (2000); Ancestry (includes multiple ancestries): 21.6% German, 12.1% Irish, 11.1% English, 5.3% United States or American, 2.6% Italian (2000).
Economy: Employment by occupation: 5.1% management, 16.7% professional, 6.4% services, 24.4% sales, 6.4% farming, 17.9% construction, 23.1% production (2000).
Income: Per capita income: $21,522 (2007); Median household income: $40,500 (2007); Average household income: $46,416 (2007); Percent of households with income of $100,000 or more: 3.6% (2007); Poverty rate: 10.5% (2000).
Education: Percent of population age 25 and over with: High school diploma (including GED) or higher: 69.0% (2007); Bachelor's degree or higher: 7.8% (2007); Master's degree or higher: 2.3% (2007).
Housing: Homeownership rate: 80.7% (2007); Median home value: $63,571 (2007); Median rent: $188 per month (2000); Median age of housing: 48 years (2000).
Transportation: Commute to work: 100.0% car, 0.0% public transportation, 0.0% walk, 0.0% work from home (2000); Travel time to work: 32.1% less than 15 minutes, 39.7% 15 to 30 minutes, 7.7% 30 to 45 minutes, 15.4% 45 to 60 minutes, 5.1% 60 minutes or more (2000)

MEDORA (village). Covers a land area of 0.313 square miles and a water area of 0 square miles. Located at 39.17° N. Lat.; 90.14° W. Long. Elevation is 610 feet.
Population: 420 (1990); 501 (2000); 436 (2007); 417 (2012 projected); Race: 96.3% White, 0.0% Black, 0.0% Asian, 2.8% Hispanic of any race (2007); Density: 1,391.3 persons per square mile (2007); Average household size: 2.83 (2007); Median age: 32.2 (2007); Males per 100 females: 86.3 (2007); Marriage status: 29.3% never married, 55.9% now married, 6.8% widowed, 7.9% divorced (2000); Foreign born: 0.0% (2000); Ancestry (includes multiple ancestries): 24.1% German, 13.6% English, 11.7% United States or American, 10.9% Irish, 8.5% Other groups (2000).
Economy: Employment by occupation: 5.9% management, 7.0% professional, 18.3% services, 19.9% sales, 1.6% farming, 17.2% construction, 30.1% production (2000).
Income: Per capita income: $13,303 (2007); Median household income: $31,667 (2007); Average household income: $37,662 (2007); Percent of households with income of $100,000 or more: 3.9% (2007); Poverty rate: 12.4% (2000).
Education: Percent of population age 25 and over with: High school diploma (including GED) or higher: 78.1% (2007); Bachelor's degree or higher: 2.7% (2007); Master's degree or higher: 0.8% (2007).

School District(s)

Southwestern CUSD 9 (PK-12)
2005-06 Enrollment: 1,789 . . . . (618) 729-3221
Housing: Homeownership rate: 82.5% (2007); Median home value: $62,143 (2007); Median rent: $250 per month (2000); Median age of housing: 56 years (2000).
Safety: Violent crime rate: 0.0 per 10,000 population; Property crime rate: 140.6 per 10,000 population (2006).
Transportation: Commute to work: 95.1% car, 0.0% public transportation, 2.7% walk, 2.2% work from home (2000); Travel time to work: 23.9% less than 15 minutes, 25.0% 15 to 30 minutes, 28.9% 30 to 45 minutes, 8.9% 45 to 60 minutes, 13.3% 60 minutes or more (2000)

MODESTO (village). Covers a land area of 0.561 square miles and a water area of 0 square miles. Located at 39.47° N. Lat.; 89.98° W. Long. Elevation is 679 feet.
Population: 240 (1990); 252 (2000); 245 (2007); 244 (2012 projected); Race: 100.0% White, 0.0% Black, 0.0% Asian, 0.0% Hispanic of any race (2007); Density: 436.7 persons per square mile (2007); Average household size: 2.40 (2007); Median age: 40.7 (2007); Males per 100 females: 99.2 (2007); Marriage status: 23.7% never married, 58.8% now married, 10.4% widowed, 7.1% divorced (2000); Foreign born: 0.0% (2000); Ancestry (includes multiple ancestries): 15.1% United States or American, 13.6% German, 12.4% English, 5.8% Irish, 2.3% Other groups (2000).
Economy: Employment by occupation: 20.3% management, 6.3% professional, 16.4% services, 23.4% sales, 2.3% farming, 8.6% construction, 22.7% production (2000).
Income: Per capita income: $17,806 (2007); Median household income: $43,750 (2007); Average household income: $42,770 (2007); Percent of households with income of $100,000 or more: 1.0% (2007); Poverty rate: 12.4% (2000).
Education: Percent of population age 25 and over with: High school diploma (including GED) or higher: 81.4% (2007); Bachelor's degree or higher: 10.2% (2007); Master's degree or higher: 1.2% (2007).
Housing: Homeownership rate: 71.6% (2007); Median home value: $63,000 (2007); Median rent: $250 per month (2000); Median age of housing: 47 years (2000).
Transportation: Commute to work: 89.1% car, 0.0% public transportation, 7.0% walk, 0.0% work from home (2000); Travel time to work: 39.1% less than 15 minutes, 15.6% 15 to 30 minutes, 21.1% 30 to 45 minutes, 10.9% 45 to 60 minutes, 13.3% 60 minutes or more (2000)

MOUNT CLARE (village). Covers a land area of 1.516 square miles and a water area of 0.036 square miles. Located at 39.10° N. Lat.; 89.82° W. Long. Elevation is 643 feet.
Population: 297 (1990); 433 (2000); 416 (2007); 416 (2012 projected); Race: 96.4% White, 2.2% Black, 0.0% Asian, 0.2% Hispanic of any race (2007); Density: 274.3 persons per square mile (2007); Average household size: 3.28 (2007); Median age: 62.7 (2007); Males per 100 females: 62.5 (2007); Marriage status: 17.9% never married, 40.8% now married, 33.7% widowed, 7.6% divorced (2000); Foreign born: 0.2% (2000); Ancestry (includes multiple ancestries): 27.6% Italian, 26.7% German, 13.0% Irish, 9.5% Scottish, 7.8% United States or American (2000).
Economy: Employment by occupation: 11.8% management, 11.8% professional, 17.4% services, 18.6% sales, 0.0% farming, 13.7% construction, 26.7% production (2000).
Income: Per capita income: $17,440 (2007); Median household income: $45,250 (2007); Average household income: $50,630 (2007); Percent of households with income of $100,000 or more: 7.1% (2007); Poverty rate: 6.0% (2000).
Education: Percent of population age 25 and over with: High school diploma (including GED) or higher: 60.4% (2007); Bachelor's degree or higher: 5.6% (2007); Master's degree or higher: 4.4% (2007).
Housing: Homeownership rate: 81.9% (2007); Median home value: $67,500 (2007); Median rent: $296 per month (2000); Median age of housing: 48 years (2000).
Transportation: Commute to work: 92.5% car, 1.9% public transportation, 1.3% walk, 4.4% work from home (2000); Travel time to work: 28.3% less than 15 minutes, 32.2% 15 to 30 minutes, 13.8% 30 to 45 minutes, 13.8% 45 to 60 minutes, 11.8% 60 minutes or more (2000)

MOUNT OLIVE (city). Covers a land area of 1.104 square miles and a water area of 0 square miles. Located at 39.07° N. Lat.; 89.72° W. Long. Elevation is 686 feet.
History: Mount Olive, an early coal-mining town, was connected with two labor organizers. Alexander Bradley (1866-1918) was a leader in union organization. "Mother" Jones (1830-1930), born Mary Harris in Ireland, was buried in Mount Olive.
Population: 2,126 (1990); 2,150 (2000); 2,040 (2007); 1,956 (2012 projected); Race: 98.6% White, 0.0% Black, 0.1% Asian, 1.0% Hispanic of any race (2007); Density: 1,848.6 persons per square mile (2007); Average household size: 2.37 (2007); Median age: 39.9 (2007); Males per 100 females: 96.3 (2007); Marriage status: 21.1% never married, 59.6% now married, 10.2% widowed, 9.1% divorced (2000); Foreign born: 1.1% (2000); Ancestry (includes multiple ancestries): 36.8% German, 14.9% United States or American, 6.9% Irish, 5.7% English, 5.5% Other groups (2000).
Economy: Single-family building permits issued: 1 (2007); Multi-family building permits issued: 0 (2007); Employment by occupation: 8.3% management, 16.9% professional, 13.5% services, 23.0% sales, 0.2% farming, 9.7% construction, 28.4% production (2000).
Income: Per capita income: $21,520 (2007); Median household income: $42,222 (2007); Average household income: $51,047 (2007); Percent of households with income of $100,000 or more: 8.3% (2007); Poverty rate: 6.1% (2000).
Education: Percent of population age 25 and over with: High school diploma (including GED) or higher: 80.1% (2007); Bachelor's degree or higher: 8.4% (2007); Master's degree or higher: 4.6% (2007).

School District(s)

Mount Olive CUSD 5 (PK-12)
2005-06 Enrollment: 600 . . . . (217) 999-7831
Housing: Homeownership rate: 82.3% (2007); Median home value: $63,918 (2007); Median rent: $257 per month (2000); Median age of housing: 60+ years (2000).
Safety: Violent crime rate: 4.8 per 10,000 population; Property crime rate: 90.5 per 10,000 population (2006).
Newspapers: Mount Olive Herald (Regional news; Circulation 1,550)
Transportation: Commute to work: 95.4% car, 0.0% public transportation, 1.9% walk, 1.5% work from home (2000); Travel time to work: 39.8% less than 15 minutes, 22.4% 15 to 30 minutes, 12.1% 30 to 45 minutes, 6.7% 45 to 60 minutes, 19.0% 60 minutes or more (2000)

NILWOOD (town). Covers a land area of 0.465 square miles and a water area of 0 square miles. Located at 39.39° N. Lat.; 89.80° W. Long. Elevation is 669 feet.
Population: 238 (1990); 284 (2000); 364 (2007); 413 (2012 projected); Race: 100.0% White, 0.0% Black, 0.0% Asian, 1.4% Hispanic of any race (2007); Density: 782.3 persons per square mile (2007); Average household size: 2.58 (2007); Median age: 39.2 (2007); Males per 100 females: 102.2 (2007); Marriage status: 19.5% never married, 64.9% now married, 6.3% widowed, 9.3% divorced (2000); Foreign born: 0.0% (2000); Ancestry (includes multiple ancestries): 23.0% German, 15.2% Irish, 14.1% English, 10.6% Other groups, 9.5% United States or American (2000).
Economy: Employment by occupation: 6.9% management, 2.6% professional, 17.2% services, 28.4% sales, 0.0% farming, 21.6% construction, 23.3% production (2000).
Income: Per capita income: $15,192 (2007); Median household income: $35,500 (2007); Average household income: $39,220 (2007); Percent of

households with income of $100,000 or more: 2.1% (2007); Poverty rate: 16.7% (2000).
Education: Percent of population age 25 and over with: High school diploma (including GED) or higher: 69.2% (2007); Bachelor's degree or higher: 4.8% (2007); Master's degree or higher: 1.2% (2007).
Housing: Homeownership rate: 91.5% (2007); Median home value: $68,214 (2007); Median rent: $225 per month (2000); Median age of housing: 47 years (2000).
Transportation: Commute to work: 96.5% car, 0.0% public transportation, 0.0% walk, 3.5% work from home (2000); Travel time to work: 20.9% less than 15 minutes, 35.5% 15 to 30 minutes, 18.2% 30 to 45 minutes, 12.7% 45 to 60 minutes, 12.7% 60 minutes or more (2000)

PALMYRA (village). Covers a land area of 1.000 square miles and a water area of 0 square miles. Located at 39.43° N. Lat.; 89.99° W. Long. Elevation is 673 feet.
Population: 727 (1990); 733 (2000); 729 (2007); 713 (2012 projected); Race: 98.6% White, 1.0% Black, 0.0% Asian, 0.1% Hispanic of any race (2007); Density: 728.9 persons per square mile (2007); Average household size: 2.15 (2007); Median age: 44.1 (2007); Males per 100 females: 96.0 (2007); Marriage status: 21.9% never married, 54.9% now married, 12.2% widowed, 11.0% divorced (2000); Foreign born: 0.0% (2000); Ancestry (includes multiple ancestries): 20.0% German, 15.0% Irish, 14.6% English, 8.5% United States or American, 6.3% Other groups (2000).
Economy: Employment by occupation: 8.3% management, 8.0% professional, 17.7% services, 31.0% sales, 0.6% farming, 17.7% construction, 16.8% production (2000).
Income: Per capita income: $18,697 (2007); Median household income: $33,375 (2007); Average household income: $40,206 (2007); Percent of households with income of $100,000 or more: 4.4% (2007); Poverty rate: 14.7% (2000).
Education: Percent of population age 25 and over with: High school diploma (including GED) or higher: 73.4% (2007); Bachelor's degree or higher: 6.0% (2007); Master's degree or higher: 0.6% (2007).

School District(s)

Northwestern CUSD 2 (PK-12)
2005-06 Enrollment: 397 . . . . (217) 436-2210

Housing: Homeownership rate: 72.6% (2007); Median home value: $60,000 (2007); Median rent: $264 per month (2000); Median age of housing: 52 years (2000).
Safety: Violent crime rate: 13.7 per 10,000 population; Property crime rate: 27.4 per 10,000 population (2006).
Transportation: Commute to work: 94.0% car, 0.0% public transportation, 3.6% walk, 1.5% work from home (2000); Travel time to work: 24.8% less than 15 minutes, 26.4% 15 to 30 minutes, 23.0% 30 to 45 minutes, 10.1% 45 to 60 minutes, 15.6% 60 minutes or more (2000)

PIASA (unincorporated postal area, zip code 62079). Covers a land area of 6.456 square miles and a water area of 0.031 square miles. Located at 39.11° N. Lat.; 90.13° W. Long. Elevation is 594 feet.
Population: 180 (2000); Race: 100.0% White, 0.0% Black, 0.0% Asian, 0.0% Hispanic of any race (2000); Density: 27.9 persons per square mile (2000); Age: 27.5% under 18, 11.3% over 64 (2000); Marriage status: 12.0% never married, 75.2% now married, 4.8% widowed, 8.0% divorced (2000); Foreign born: 0.0% (2000); Ancestry (includes multiple ancestries): 42.5% German, 20.6% United States or American, 8.8% English, 3.8% Irish, 3.8% Other groups (2000).
Economy: Employment by occupation: 27.6% management, 5.3% professional, 11.8% services, 39.5% sales, 0.0% farming, 0.0% construction, 15.8% production (2000).
Income: Per capita income: $25,089 (2000); Median household income: $66,000 (2000); Poverty rate: 3.8% (2000).
Education: Percent of population age 25 and over with: High school diploma (including GED) or higher: 79.3% (2000); Bachelor's degree or higher: 23.3% (2000).

School District(s)

Southwestern CUSD 9 (PK-12)
2005-06 Enrollment: 1,789 . . . . (618) 729-3221

Housing: Homeownership rate: 73.0% (2000); Median home value: $98,600 (2000); Median rent: $225 per month (2000); Median age of housing: 24 years (2000).
Transportation: Commute to work: 100.0% car, 0.0% public transportation, 0.0% walk, 0.0% work from home (2000); Travel time to work: 35.5% less than 15 minutes, 40.8% 15 to 30 minutes, 6.6% 30 to 45 minutes, 17.1% 45 to 60 minutes, 0.0% 60 minutes or more (2000)

ROYAL LAKES (village). Aka Royal Lake. Covers a land area of 0.466 square miles and a water area of 0.046 square miles. Located at 39.11° N. Lat.; 89.96° W. Long. Elevation is 623 feet.
Population: 272 (1990); 190 (2000); 211 (2007); 218 (2012 projected); Race: 30.3% White, 64.9% Black, 0.0% Asian, 1.4% Hispanic of any race (2007); Density: 453.3 persons per square mile (2007); Average household size: 2.29 (2007); Median age: 39.5 (2007); Males per 100 females: 95.4 (2007); Marriage status: 22.7% never married, 53.8% now married, 13.6% widowed, 9.8% divorced (2000); Foreign born: 0.0% (2000); Ancestry (includes multiple ancestries): 39.2% Other groups, 4.5% German, 1.1% West Indian, 1.1% African (2000).
Economy: Employment by occupation: 0.0% management, 3.4% professional, 33.9% services, 8.5% sales, 0.0% farming, 16.9% construction, 37.3% production (2000).
Income: Per capita income: $12,559 (2007); Median household income: $20,417 (2007); Average household income: $28,804 (2007); Percent of households with income of $100,000 or more: 3.3% (2007); Poverty rate: 27.3% (2000).
Education: Percent of population age 25 and over with: High school diploma (including GED) or higher: 53.2% (2007); Bachelor's degree or higher: 2.1% (2007); Master's degree or higher: 0.0% (2007).
Housing: Homeownership rate: 77.2% (2007); Median home value: $60,833 (2007); Median rent: $255 per month (2000); Median age of housing: 32 years (2000).
Transportation: Commute to work: 90.9% car, 0.0% public transportation, 9.1% walk, 0.0% work from home (2000); Travel time to work: 23.6% less than 15 minutes, 21.8% 15 to 30 minutes, 21.8% 30 to 45 minutes, 14.5% 45 to 60 minutes, 18.2% 60 minutes or more (2000)

SAWYERVILLE (village). Covers a land area of 1.013 square miles and a water area of 0 square miles. Located at 39.07° N. Lat.; 89.80° W. Long. Elevation is 630 feet.
Population: 312 (1990); 295 (2000); 290 (2007); 286 (2012 projected); Race: 96.9% White, 1.4% Black, 0.0% Asian, 0.0% Hispanic of any race (2007); Density: 286.2 persons per square mile (2007); Average household size: 2.48 (2007); Median age: 40.0 (2007); Males per 100 females: 93.3 (2007); Marriage status: 26.7% never married, 55.3% now married, 8.0% widowed, 9.9% divorced (2000); Foreign born: 0.0% (2000); Ancestry (includes multiple ancestries): 25.2% German, 12.6% Italian, 10.1% Irish, 8.8% English, 8.2% United States or American (2000).
Economy: Employment by occupation: 9.0% management, 9.0% professional, 26.9% services, 20.9% sales, 0.7% farming, 9.0% construction, 24.6% production (2000).
Income: Per capita income: $17,284 (2007); Median household income: $32,500 (2007); Average household income: $42,842 (2007); Percent of households with income of $100,000 or more: 9.4% (2007); Poverty rate: 15.4% (2000).
Education: Percent of population age 25 and over with: High school diploma (including GED) or higher: 69.6% (2007); Bachelor's degree or higher: 10.3% (2007); Master's degree or higher: 4.4% (2007).
Housing: Homeownership rate: 85.5% (2007); Median home value: $73,077 (2007); Median rent: $217 per month (2000); Median age of housing: 53 years (2000).
Transportation: Commute to work: 94.7% car, 0.0% public transportation, 0.0% walk, 5.3% work from home (2000); Travel time to work: 35.2% less than 15 minutes, 28.8% 15 to 30 minutes, 16.8% 30 to 45 minutes, 8.8% 45 to 60 minutes, 10.4% 60 minutes or more (2000)

SCOTTVILLE (village). Aka Scottsville. Covers a land area of 1.001 square miles and a water area of 0 square miles. Located at 39.47° N. Lat.; 90.10° W. Long. Elevation is 659 feet.
Population: 165 (1990); 140 (2000); 130 (2007); 130 (2012 projected); Race: 100.0% White, 0.0% Black, 0.0% Asian, 0.0% Hispanic of any race (2007); Density: 129.9 persons per square mile (2007); Average household size: 2.36 (2007); Median age: 46.4 (2007); Males per 100 females: 97.0 (2007); Marriage status: 21.7% never married, 57.4% now married, 6.1% widowed, 14.8% divorced (2000); Foreign born: 0.0% (2000); Ancestry (includes multiple ancestries): 15.4% United States or American, 15.4% Irish, 14.0% Other groups, 9.8% English, 8.4% German (2000).
Economy: Employment by occupation: 12.0% management, 13.3% professional, 9.3% services, 16.0% sales, 5.3% farming, 8.0% construction, 36.0% production (2000).
Income: Per capita income: $20,096 (2007); Median household income: $42,500 (2007); Average household income: $47,500 (2007); Percent of

households with income of $100,000 or more: 3.6% (2007); Poverty rate: 17.5% (2000).
Education: Percent of population age 25 and over with: High school diploma (including GED) or higher: 76.3% (2007); Bachelor's degree or higher: 4.1% (2007); Master's degree or higher: 4.1% (2007).
Housing: Homeownership rate: 92.7% (2007); Median home value: $62,500 (2007); Median rent: $142 per month (2000); Median age of housing: 60+ years (2000).
Transportation: Commute to work: 88.4% car, 0.0% public transportation, 2.9% walk, 5.8% work from home (2000); Travel time to work: 15.4% less than 15 minutes, 16.9% 15 to 30 minutes, 29.2% 30 to 45 minutes, 12.3% 45 to 60 minutes, 26.2% 60 minutes or more (2000)

SHIPMAN (town). Covers a land area of 1.321 square miles and a water area of 0.013 square miles. Located at 39.11° N. Lat.; 90.04° W. Long. Elevation is 636 feet.
Population: 624 (1990); 655 (2000); 574 (2007); 574 (2012 projected); Race: 96.7% White, 1.6% Black, 0.5% Asian, 1.0% Hispanic of any race (2007); Density: 434.5 persons per square mile (2007); Average household size: 2.59 (2007); Median age: 35.2 (2007); Males per 100 females: 105.7 (2007); Marriage status: 20.5% never married, 64.4% now married, 5.6% widowed, 9.5% divorced (2000); Foreign born: 0.3% (2000); Ancestry (includes multiple ancestries): 20.2% German, 16.7% Irish, 14.9% United States or American, 10.8% English, 7.5% Other groups (2000).
Economy: Employment by occupation: 7.2% management, 12.1% professional, 14.1% services, 23.8% sales, 2.1% farming, 15.2% construction, 25.5% production (2000).
Income: Per capita income: $18,780 (2007); Median household income: $41,071 (2007); Average household income: $48,559 (2007); Percent of households with income of $100,000 or more: 7.7% (2007); Poverty rate: 14.6% (2000).
Education: Percent of population age 25 and over with: High school diploma (including GED) or higher: 83.4% (2007); Bachelor's degree or higher: 6.8% (2007); Master's degree or higher: 3.8% (2007).

School District(s)

Southwestern CUSD 9 (PK-12)
2005-06 Enrollment: 1,789 . . . . (618) 729-3221
Housing: Homeownership rate: 77.5% (2007); Median home value: $75,455 (2007); Median rent: $273 per month (2000); Median age of housing: 32 years (2000).
Transportation: Commute to work: 90.0% car, 0.0% public transportation, 5.9% walk, 3.1% work from home (2000); Travel time to work: 22.1% less than 15 minutes, 25.4% 15 to 30 minutes, 33.9% 30 to 45 minutes, 6.8% 45 to 60 minutes, 11.8% 60 minutes or more (2000)

STANDARD CITY (village). Aka South Standard. Covers a land area of 0.637 square miles and a water area of 0.003 square miles. Located at 39.35° N. Lat.; 89.78° W. Long. Elevation is 640 feet.
Population: 128 (1990); 138 (2000); 174 (2007); 198 (2012 projected); Race: 98.9% White, 0.0% Black, 1.1% Asian, 0.0% Hispanic of any race (2007); Density: 273.3 persons per square mile (2007); Average household size: 2.32 (2007); Median age: 36.5 (2007); Males per 100 females: 97.7 (2007); Marriage status: 26.3% never married, 48.2% now married, 9.6% widowed, 15.8% divorced (2000); Foreign born: 0.0% (2000); Ancestry (includes multiple ancestries): 29.0% German, 15.9% United States or American, 13.8% English, 12.3% Italian, 10.9% Other groups (2000).
Economy: Employment by occupation: 2.8% management, 8.3% professional, 33.3% services, 19.4% sales, 6.9% farming, 9.7% construction, 19.4% production (2000).
Income: Per capita income: $17,256 (2007); Median household income: $24,500 (2007); Average household income: $40,033 (2007); Percent of households with income of $100,000 or more: 5.3% (2007); Poverty rate: 22.5% (2000).
Education: Percent of population age 25 and over with: High school diploma (including GED) or higher: 73.7% (2007); Bachelor's degree or higher: 2.5% (2007); Master's degree or higher: 2.5% (2007).
Housing: Homeownership rate: 89.3% (2007); Median home value: $46,429 (2007); Median rent: $275 per month (2000); Median age of housing: 40 years (2000).
Transportation: Commute to work: 84.3% car, 0.0% public transportation, 2.9% walk, 2.9% work from home (2000); Travel time to work: 11.8% less than 15 minutes, 45.6% 15 to 30 minutes, 20.6% 30 to 45 minutes, 22.1% 45 to 60 minutes, 0.0% 60 minutes or more (2000)

STAUNTON (city). Covers a land area of 2.282 square miles and a water area of 0.027 square miles. Located at 39.01° N. Lat.; 89.78° W. Long. Elevation is 620 feet.
History: Staunton was settled in 1817 by John Wood of Virginia, and a village was laid out in 1835. Staunton was named for one of its founders, and operated as a trading point for settlers. Later, coal mining was an important industry.
Population: 4,849 (1990); 5,030 (2000); 5,102 (2007); 5,149 (2012 projected); Race: 98.6% White, 0.1% Black, 0.5% Asian, 1.0% Hispanic of any race (2007); Density: 2,236.2 persons per square mile (2007); Average household size: 2.48 (2007); Median age: 39.0 (2007); Males per 100 females: 92.2 (2007); Marriage status: 18.9% never married, 62.8% now married, 7.9% widowed, 10.3% divorced (2000); Foreign born: 0.6% (2000); Ancestry (includes multiple ancestries): 36.2% German, 13.6% Irish, 12.8% Italian, 7.9% English, 7.8% Other groups (2000).
Economy: Single-family building permits issued: 8 (2007); Multi-family building permits issued: 4 (2007); Employment by occupation: 8.5% management, 15.1% professional, 14.8% services, 29.9% sales, 0.0% farming, 14.6% construction, 17.2% production (2000).
Income: Per capita income: $19,861 (2007); Median household income: $41,328 (2007); Average household income: $48,849 (2007); Percent of households with income of $100,000 or more: 6.7% (2007); Poverty rate: 6.6% (2000).
Education: Percent of population age 25 and over with: High school diploma (including GED) or higher: 82.8% (2007); Bachelor's degree or higher: 12.9% (2007); Master's degree or higher: 4.1% (2007).

School District(s)

Staunton CUSD 6 (PK-12)
2005-06 Enrollment: 1,344 . . . . (618) 635-2962
Housing: Homeownership rate: 75.4% (2007); Median home value: $97,047 (2007); Median rent: $315 per month (2000); Median age of housing: 51 years (2000).
Hospitals: Community Memorial Hospital (49 beds)
Safety: Violent crime rate: 7.8 per 10,000 population; Property crime rate: 78.3 per 10,000 population (2006).
Newspapers: Staunton Star-Times (Local news; Circulation 3,995)
Transportation: Commute to work: 95.3% car, 0.0% public transportation, 1.6% walk, 2.0% work from home (2000); Travel time to work: 40.1% less than 15 minutes, 16.7% 15 to 30 minutes, 21.6% 30 to 45 minutes, 14.3% 45 to 60 minutes, 7.3% 60 minutes or more (2000)
Additional Information Contacts
City of Staunton . . . . (618) 635-2233
http://www.stauntonil.com/government.html
Staunton Chamber of Commerce . . . . (618) 635-8356
http://www.stauntonil.com/chamber.html

VIRDEN (city). Covers a land area of 1.716 square miles and a water area of 0 square miles. Located at 39.50° N. Lat.; 89.76° W. Long. Elevation is 686 feet.
History: Virden was a coal mining town and the location of the Virden riot in 1898 when mine operators refused to pay the rates established by the Illinois Coal Operators Association.
Population: 3,652 (1990); 3,488 (2000); 3,497 (2007); 3,486 (2012 projected); Race: 98.5% White, 0.6% Black, 0.1% Asian, 0.6% Hispanic of any race (2007); Density: 2,037.8 persons per square mile (2007); Average household size: 2.36 (2007); Median age: 40.0 (2007); Males per 100 females: 88.4 (2007); Marriage status: 17.8% never married, 61.4% now married, 9.5% widowed, 11.2% divorced (2000); Foreign born: 0.3% (2000); Ancestry (includes multiple ancestries): 22.9% German, 16.8% English, 13.5% Irish, 11.5% United States or American, 5.4% Other groups (2000).
Economy: Employment by occupation: 9.1% management, 20.3% professional, 13.9% services, 27.7% sales, 0.7% farming, 10.2% construction, 18.2% production (2000).
Income: Per capita income: $20,486 (2007); Median household income: $39,268 (2007); Average household income: $47,355 (2007); Percent of households with income of $100,000 or more: 7.4% (2007); Poverty rate: 10.7% (2000).
Education: Percent of population age 25 and over with: High school diploma (including GED) or higher: 82.1% (2007); Bachelor's degree or higher: 9.7% (2007); Master's degree or higher: 2.2% (2007).

School District(s)

Virden CUSD 4 (PK-12)
2005-06 Enrollment: 975 . . . . (217) 965-4226

Housing: Homeownership rate: 73.1% (2007); Median home value: $88,655 (2007); Median rent: $299 per month (2000); Median age of housing: 48 years (2000).
Safety: Violent crime rate: 23.0 per 10,000 population; Property crime rate: 167.1 per 10,000 population (2006).
Newspapers: Northwestern News (Community news; Circulation 1,100); Panhandle Press (Community news; Circulation 1,200); Virden Recorder (Community news; Circulation 2,400)
Transportation: Commute to work: 93.8% car, 0.0% public transportation, 1.5% walk, 4.3% work from home (2000); Travel time to work: 33.0% less than 15 minutes, 18.8% 15 to 30 minutes, 33.0% 30 to 45 minutes, 11.5% 45 to 60 minutes, 3.7% 60 minutes or more (2000)
Additional Information Contacts
Virden Area Association of Commerce .... (217) 965-3321

WHITE CITY (village). Covers a land area of 1.215 square miles and a water area of 0 square miles. Located at 39.07° N. Lat.; 89.76° W. Long. Elevation is 653 feet.
Population: 229 (1990); 221 (2000); 234 (2007); 242 (2012 projected); Race: 98.7% White, 0.0% Black, 0.0% Asian, 0.4% Hispanic of any race (2007); Density: 192.6 persons per square mile (2007); Average household size: 2.41 (2007); Median age: 40.8 (2007); Males per 100 females: 100.0 (2007); Marriage status: 20.6% never married, 42.6% now married, 12.9% widowed, 23.9% divorced (2000); Foreign born: 0.0% (2000); Ancestry (includes multiple ancestries): 43.7% German, 12.7% Other groups, 12.7% English, 12.2% Irish, 11.7% United States or American (2000).
Economy: Single-family building permits issued: 0 (2007); Multi-family building permits issued: 0 (2007); Employment by occupation: 9.7% management, 6.9% professional, 20.8% services, 27.8% sales, 0.0% farming, 16.7% construction, 18.1% production (2000).
Income: Per capita income: $18,771 (2007); Median household income: $33,750 (2007); Average household income: $45,284 (2007); Percent of households with income of $100,000 or more: 7.2% (2007); Poverty rate: 19.3% (2000).
Education: Percent of population age 25 and over with: High school diploma (including GED) or higher: 82.8% (2007); Bachelor's degree or higher: 3.2% (2007); Master's degree or higher: 0.0% (2007).
Housing: Homeownership rate: 88.7% (2007); Median home value: $86,000 (2007); Median rent: $225 per month (2000); Median age of housing: 32 years (2000).
Transportation: Commute to work: 97.1% car, 0.0% public transportation, 0.0% walk, 2.9% work from home (2000); Travel time to work: 25.8% less than 15 minutes, 33.3% 15 to 30 minutes, 18.2% 30 to 45 minutes, 13.6% 45 to 60 minutes, 9.1% 60 minutes or more (2000)

WILSONVILLE (village). Covers a land area of 0.954 square miles and a water area of 0.024 square miles. Located at 39.07° N. Lat.; 89.85° W. Long. Elevation is 643 feet.
Population: 609 (1990); 604 (2000); 564 (2007); 558 (2012 projected); Race: 98.8% White, 0.0% Black, 0.0% Asian, 0.5% Hispanic of any race (2007); Density: 591.4 persons per square mile (2007); Average household size: 2.35 (2007); Median age: 38.1 (2007); Males per 100 females: 88.0 (2007); Marriage status: 25.2% never married, 55.7% now married, 10.4% widowed, 8.7% divorced (2000); Foreign born: 1.0% (2000); Ancestry (includes multiple ancestries): 20.8% Italian, 16.9% United States or American, 15.1% Other groups, 14.7% German, 9.8% English (2000).
Economy: Employment by occupation: 5.7% management, 11.7% professional, 10.0% services, 21.3% sales, 0.0% farming, 13.5% construction, 37.8% production (2000).
Income: Per capita income: $21,432 (2007); Median household income: $36,333 (2007); Average household income: $50,365 (2007); Percent of households with income of $100,000 or more: 10.8% (2007); Poverty rate: 9.8% (2000).
Education: Percent of population age 25 and over with: High school diploma (including GED) or higher: 74.8% (2007); Bachelor's degree or higher: 4.9% (2007); Master's degree or higher: 0.8% (2007).
Housing: Homeownership rate: 84.6% (2007); Median home value: $58,167 (2007); Median rent: $336 per month (2000); Median age of housing: 60+ years (2000).
Transportation: Commute to work: 93.7% car, 0.0% public transportation, 0.0% walk, 3.2% work from home (2000); Travel time to work: 12.6% less than 15 minutes, 23.7% 15 to 30 minutes, 20.0% 30 to 45 minutes, 18.6% 45 to 60 minutes, 25.1% 60 minutes or more (2000)

Madison County

Located in southwestern Illinois; bounded on the west by the Mississippi River and the Missouri border; drained by Cahokia and Silver Creeks. Covers a land area of 725.02 square miles, a water area of 15.33 square miles, and is located in the Central Time Zone. The county was founded in 1812. County seat is Edwardsville.

Madison County is part of the St. Louis, MO-IL Metropolitan Statistical Area. The entire metro area includes: Bond County, IL; Calhoun County, IL; Clinton County, IL; Jersey County, IL; Macoupin County, IL; Madison County, IL; Monroe County, IL; St. Clair County, IL; Crawford County, MO (pt.)*; Franklin County, MO; Jefferson County, MO; Lincoln County, MO; St. Charles County, MO; St. Louis County, MO; Warren County, MO; Washington County, MO; St. Louis city, MO

Weather Station: Alton Melvin Price Lock & Dam Elevation: 429 feet

	Jan	Feb	Mar	Apr	May	Jun	Jul	Aug	Sep	Oct	Nov	Dec
High	35	41	52	64	75	84	88	86	79	67	53	41
Low	19	23	33	45	55	64	69	66	58	46	35	25
Precip	2.0	2.1	3.5	4.4	4.3	3.2	3.5	3.1	3.1	2.7	3.8	3.0
Snow	na	na	2.1	0.4	0.0	0.0	0.0	0.0	0.0	tr	0.3	0.4

High and Low temperatures in degrees Fahrenheit; Precipitation and Snow in inches

Population: 249,238 (1990); 258,941 (2000); 265,704 (2007); 269,571 (2012 projected); Race: 89.2% White, 7.9% Black, 0.7% Asian, 2.0% Hispanic of any race (2007); Density: 366.5 persons per square mile (2007); Average household size: 2.49 (2007); Median age: 37.5 (2007); Males per 100 females: 93.6 (2007).
Religion: Five largest groups: 16.4% Catholic Church, 8.5% Southern Baptist Convention, 5.3% Lutheran Church—Missouri Synod, 4.3% United Church of Christ, 3.6% The United Methodist Church (2000).
Economy: Unemployment rate: 5.0% (4/2008); Total civilian labor force: 142,171 (4/2008); Leading industries: 16.5% manufacturing; 15.5% health care and social assistance; 14.1% retail trade (2005); Farms: 1,152 totaling 295,677 acres (2002); Companies that employ 500 or more persons: 11 (2006); Companies that employ 100 to 499 persons: 114 (2006); Companies that employ less than 100 persons: 6,005 (2006); Black-owned businesses: n/a (2002); Hispanic-owned businesses: 186 (2002); Asian-owned businesses: 222 (2002); Women-owned businesses: 5,964 (2002); Retail sales per capita: $15,290 (2008). Single-family building permits issued: 778 (2007); Multi-family building permits issued: 115 (2007).
Income: Per capita income: $24,903 (2007); Median household income: $49,341 (2007); Average household income: $61,459 (2007); Percent of households with income of $100,000 or more: 15.2% (2007); Poverty rate: 11.0% (2005); Bankruptcy rate: 4.23% (2007).
Taxes: Total county taxes per capita: $95 (2006); County property taxes per capita: $93 (2006).
Education: Percent of population age 25 and over with: High school diploma (including GED) or higher: 84.6% (2007); Bachelor's degree or higher: 19.9% (2007); Master's degree or higher: 7.1% (2007).
Housing: Homeownership rate: 74.3% (2007); Median home value: $107,691 (2007); Median rent: $383 per month (2000); Median age of housing: 38 years (2000).
Health: Birth rate: 132.7 per 10,000 population (2007); Death rate: 97.5 per 10,000 population (2007); Age-adjusted cancer mortality rate: 195.4 deaths per 100,000 population (2005); Air Quality Index: 63.3% good, 31.5% moderate, 4.9% unhealthy for sensitive individuals, 0.3% unhealthy (percent of days in 2007); Number of physicians: 11.6 per 10,000 population (2005); Hospital beds: 38.3 per 10,000 population (2004); Hospital admissions: 1,087.1 per 10,000 population (2004).
Elections: 2004 Presidential election results: 48.0% Bush, 51.3% Kerry, 0.1% Nader, 0.6% Badnarik
National and State Parks: Horseshoe Lake State Park; Lovejoy State Memorial
Additional Information Contacts
Madison County Government .... (618) 692-6200
http://www.co.madison.il.us
City of Alton .... (618) 463-3500
http://www.alton-il.com
City of Collinsville................................ (618) 344-5252
http://www.ci.collinsville.il.us
City of Edwardsville .... (618) 692-7520
http://www.cityofedwardsville.com

City of Granite City . . . . (618) 452-6200
http://www.granitecity.illinois.gov
City of Highland . . . . (618) 654-9891
http://www.ci.highland.il.us
City of Troy. . . . . (618) 667-6741
http://www.ci.troy.il.us
City of Wood River . . . . (618) 251-3100
http://www.woodriver.org
Collinsville Chamber of Commerce . . . . (618) 344-2884
http://www.discovercollinsville.com
Edwardsville & Glen Carbon Chamber of Commerce . . . . . (618) 656-7600
http://www.edglenchamber.com
Highland Chamber of Commerce . . . . (618) 654-3721
http://www.highlandillinois.com
River Bend Growth Association . . . . (618) 467-2280
http://www.growthassociation.com
The Chamber of Commerce of Southwestern Madison County. . . . . . (618) 876-6400
http://www.chamberswmadisoncounty.com
Troy/Maryville Area Chamber of Commerce . . . . (618) 667-8769
http://www.troycoc.com
Village of Bethalto . . . . (618) 377-8051
http://www.bethalto.com
Village of East Alton. . . . . (618) 259-7714
http://www.eastaltonvillage.org
Village of Glen Carbon. . . . . (618) 288-1200
http://www.glen-carbon.il.us
Village of Godfrey . . . . (618) 466-3324
http://www.godfreyil.org
Village of Pontoon Beach. . . . . (618) 931-6100
http://www.pontoonbeach.org

Madison County Communities

ALHAMBRA (village). Covers a land area of 0.755 square miles and a water area of 0.006 square miles. Located at 38.88° N. Lat.; 89.73° W. Long. Elevation is 564 feet.

Population: 709 (1990); 630 (2000); 727 (2007); 761 (2012 projected); Race: 98.3% White, 0.0% Black, 0.0% Asian, 0.0% Hispanic of any race (2007); Density: 962.8 persons per square mile (2007); Average household size: 2.94 (2007); Median age: 54.9 (2007); Males per 100 females: 78.2 (2007); Marriage status: 15.5% never married, 62.8% now married, 14.9% widowed, 6.9% divorced (2000); Foreign born: 0.0% (2000); Ancestry (includes multiple ancestries): 46.9% German, 13.2% Irish, 9.6% English, 7.6% United States or American, 7.5% Other groups (2000).

Economy: Single-family building permits issued: 0 (2007); Multi-family building permits issued: 0 (2007); Employment by occupation: 10.3% management, 6.5% professional, 14.5% services, 29.4% sales, 0.0% farming, 17.6% construction, 21.8% production (2000).

Income: Per capita income: $21,127 (2007); Median household income: $45,962 (2007); Average household income: $54,767 (2007); Percent of households with income of $100,000 or more: 12.1% (2007); Poverty rate: 4.7% (2000).

Education: Percent of population age 25 and over with: High school diploma (including GED) or higher: 69.6% (2007); Bachelor's degree or higher: 8.5% (2007); Master's degree or higher: 2.6% (2007).

School District(s)

Highland CUSD 5 (PK-12)
2005-06 Enrollment: 3,093 . . . . (618) 654-2106

Housing: Homeownership rate: 78.1% (2007); Median home value: $98,043 (2007); Median rent: $317 per month (2000); Median age of housing: 39 years (2000).

Transportation: Commute to work: 85.7% car, 0.0% public transportation, 5.8% walk, 7.7% work from home (2000); Travel time to work: 24.3% less than 15 minutes, 32.2% 15 to 30 minutes, 24.3% 30 to 45 minutes, 10.0% 45 to 60 minutes, 9.2% 60 minutes or more (2000)

ALTON (city). Covers a land area of 15.645 square miles and a water area of 0.961 square miles. Located at 38.90° N. Lat.; 90.16° W. Long. Elevation is 499 feet.

History: Alton's first known settler arrived about 1783, but significant settlement began between 1816 and 1818, when three towns were founded at this advantageous river location. One of these, planned by Colonel Rufus Easton and named for one of his sons, Alton, absorbed the other towns and was incorporated as a city in 1837. Alton was the site of the Lincoln-Shields duel in 1842, and the last Lincoln-Douglas debate in 1858.

Population: 32,996 (1990); 30,496 (2000); 29,131 (2007); 28,130 (2012 projected); Race: 70.6% White, 26.0% Black, 0.4% Asian, 1.9% Hispanic of any race (2007); Density: 1,862.0 persons per square mile (2007); Average household size: 2.38 (2007); Median age: 35.6 (2007); Males per 100 females: 89.9 (2007); Marriage status: 29.0% never married, 47.9% now married, 9.7% widowed, 13.4% divorced (2000); Foreign born: 0.9% (2000); Ancestry (includes multiple ancestries): 27.4% Other groups, 22.1% German, 12.2% Irish, 8.2% United States or American, 7.9% English (2000).

Economy: Unemployment rate: 6.2% (4/2008); Total civilian labor force: 14,239 (4/2008); Single-family building permits issued: 16 (2007); Multi-family building permits issued: 28 (2007); Employment by occupation: 7.4% management, 18.1% professional, 22.3% services, 26.2% sales, 0.2% farming, 7.5% construction, 18.4% production (2000).

Income: Per capita income: $19,294 (2007); Median household income: $36,222 (2007); Average household income: $44,680 (2007); Percent of households with income of $100,000 or more: 7.0% (2007); Poverty rate: 18.7% (2000).

Education: Percent of population age 25 and over with: High school diploma (including GED) or higher: 81.4% (2007); Bachelor's degree or higher: 16.2% (2007); Master's degree or higher: 5.3% (2007).

School District(s)

Alton CUSD 11 (PK-12)
2005-06 Enrollment: 6,798 . . . . (618) 474-2600
Madison Co Educ Therapy Ctr (05-12)
2005-06 Enrollment: 40 . . . . (618) 692-6200
Madison Roe (07-12)
2005-06 Enrollment: 34 . . . . (618) 692-6200

Vocational/Technical School(s)

CALC Institute of Technology (Private, For-profit)
Fall 2007 Enrollment: 117 . . . . (618) 474-0616
2007-08 Tuition: $10,036

Housing: Homeownership rate: 65.7% (2007); Median home value: $77,301 (2007); Median rent: $330 per month (2000); Median age of housing: 51 years (2000).

Hospitals: Alton Memorial Hospital (222 beds); Saint Anthony's Health Center (292 beds)

Safety: Violent crime rate: 113.8 per 10,000 population; Property crime rate: 547.3 per 10,000 population (2006).

Newspapers: Alton Telegraph (Local news; Circulation 27,600); The Telegraph (Regional news; Circulation 20,000)

Transportation: Commute to work: 92.9% car, 2.6% public transportation, 2.1% walk, 1.5% work from home (2000); Travel time to work: 39.5% less than 15 minutes, 26.7% 15 to 30 minutes, 17.5% 30 to 45 minutes, 11.6% 45 to 60 minutes, 4.6% 60 minutes or more (2000); Amtrak: Service available.

Airports: St Louis Regional (general aviation)

Additional Information Contacts

City of Alton . . . . (618) 463-3500
http://www.alton-il.com

BETHALTO (village). Covers a land area of 6.578 square miles and a water area of 0 square miles. Located at 38.90° N. Lat.; 90.04° W. Long. Elevation is 525 feet.

History: Incorporated 1869.

Population: 9,646 (1990); 9,454 (2000); 9,537 (2007); 9,578 (2012 projected); Race: 97.6% White, 0.8% Black, 0.4% Asian, 1.6% Hispanic of any race (2007); Density: 1,449.9 persons per square mile (2007); Average household size: 2.43 (2007); Median age: 38.4 (2007); Males per 100 females: 91.4 (2007); Marriage status: 22.4% never married, 58.7% now married, 8.1% widowed, 10.9% divorced (2000); Foreign born: 1.2% (2000); Ancestry (includes multiple ancestries): 25.4% German, 14.8% Irish, 13.1% United States or American, 12.4% English, 7.3% Other groups (2000).

Economy: Single-family building permits issued: 31 (2007); Multi-family building permits issued: 0 (2007); Employment by occupation: 8.0% management, 17.8% professional, 18.2% services, 24.7% sales, 0.0% farming, 12.3% construction, 18.9% production (2000).

Income: Per capita income: $23,196 (2007); Median household income: $49,069 (2007); Average household income: $56,133 (2007); Percent of households with income of $100,000 or more: 12.8% (2007); Poverty rate: 9.2% (2000).

Education: Percent of population age 25 and over with: High school diploma (including GED) or higher: 85.9% (2007); Bachelor's degree or higher: 13.8% (2007); Master's degree or higher: 5.5% (2007).

School District(s)

Bethalto CUSD 8 (PK-12)
2005-06 Enrollment: 2,738 . . . . (618) 377-7200

Housing: Homeownership rate: 71.7% (2007); Median home value: $109,193 (2007); Median rent: $422 per month (2000); Median age of housing: 31 years (2000).
Safety: Violent crime rate: 80.7 per 10,000 population; Property crime rate: 202.9 per 10,000 population (2006).
Transportation: Commute to work: 96.3% car, 0.2% public transportation, 1.7% walk, 1.2% work from home (2000); Travel time to work: 35.6% less than 15 minutes, 37.8% 15 to 30 minutes, 14.2% 30 to 45 minutes, 8.9% 45 to 60 minutes, 3.5% 60 minutes or more (2000)

Additional Information Contacts

Village of Bethalto . . . . (618) 377-8051
http://www.bethalto.com

COLLINSVILLE (city). Covers a land area of 13.594 square miles and a water area of 0.014 square miles. Located at 38.67° N. Lat.; 89.99° W. Long. Elevation is 561 feet.
History: Named for William Collins and his family, founders of the town. Collinsville was settled in 1817 by William Collins and his brothers from Connecticut. Between the five brothers they operated a store, blacksmith shop, shoe shop, wagon shop, sawmill, tannery, distillery, and a church. Collinsville was incorporated as a village in 1856, and as a city in 1859. The arrival of the railroad in 1869 led to mining of a coal seam and building of an ore-smelting furnace.
Population: 23,754 (1990); 24,707 (2000); 25,380 (2007); 25,819 (2012 projected); Race: 89.6% White, 7.2% Black, 0.6% Asian, 2.8% Hispanic of any race (2007); Density: 1,867.0 persons per square mile (2007); Average household size: 2.32 (2007); Median age: 37.4 (2007); Males per 100 females: 94.3 (2007); Marriage status: 25.1% never married, 54.1% now married, 8.8% widowed, 12.0% divorced (2000); Foreign born: 1.7% (2000); Ancestry (includes multiple ancestries): 32.5% German, 16.3% Irish, 12.8% Other groups, 12.1% English, 9.3% Italian (2000).
Economy: Unemployment rate: 5.0% (4/2008); Total civilian labor force: 14,697 (4/2008); Single-family building permits issued: 28 (2007); Multi-family building permits issued: 27 (2007); Employment by occupation: 12.6% management, 20.3% professional, 13.8% services, 30.0% sales, 0.3% farming, 9.2% construction, 13.7% production (2000).
Income: Per capita income: $25,467 (2007); Median household income: $49,860 (2007); Average household income: $58,823 (2007); Percent of households with income of $100,000 or more: 14.4% (2007); Poverty rate: 7.2% (2000).
Taxes: Total city taxes per capita: $221 (2006); City property taxes per capita: $127 (2006).
Education: Percent of population age 25 and over with: High school diploma (including GED) or higher: 85.5% (2007); Bachelor's degree or higher: 21.3% (2007); Master's degree or higher: 6.8% (2007).

School District(s)

Collinsville Area Career Ctr
2005-06 Enrollment: n/a . . . . (618) 346-6320
Collinsville CUSD 10 (PK-12)
2005-06 Enrollment: 6,342 . . . . (618) 346-6350
Madison Roe (07-12)
2005-06 Enrollment: 34 . . . . (618) 692-6200

Vocational/Technical School(s)

Sanford-Brown College (Private, For-profit)
Fall 2007 Enrollment: 501 . . . . (618) 344-5600
2007-08 Tuition: $18,519

Housing: Homeownership rate: 67.5% (2007); Median home value: $111,545 (2007); Median rent: $415 per month (2000); Median age of housing: 35 years (2000).
Safety: Violent crime rate: 25.9 per 10,000 population; Property crime rate: 244.0 per 10,000 population (2006).
Newspapers: Collinsville Herald (Community news; Circulation 20,200); Collinsville Journal (Community news; Circulation 0); Edwardsville Journal (Community news; Circulation 0); Granite City Press Record Journal (Community news; Circulation 22,140); Granite City Press-Record (Community news; Circulation 0)
Transportation: Commute to work: 95.1% car, 1.5% public transportation, 1.1% walk, 1.6% work from home (2000); Travel time to work: 27.0% less than 15 minutes, 35.5% 15 to 30 minutes, 25.0% 30 to 45 minutes, 8.4% 45 to 60 minutes, 4.3% 60 minutes or more (2000)

Additional Information Contacts

City of Collinsville . . . . (618) 344-5252
http://www.ci.collinsville.il.us
Collinsville Chamber of Commerce . . . . (618) 344-2884
http://www.discovercollinsville.com

COTTAGE HILLS (unincorporated postal area, zip code 62018). Covers a land area of 3.618 square miles and a water area of 0 square miles. Located at 38.90° N. Lat.; 90.08° W. Long. Elevation is 512 feet.
Population: 4,387 (2000); Race: 94.4% White, 2.5% Black, 0.0% Asian, 0.6% Hispanic of any race (2000); Density: 1,212.5 persons per square mile (2000); Age: 27.2% under 18, 10.8% over 64 (2000); Marriage status: 28.0% never married, 52.3% now married, 6.1% widowed, 13.6% divorced (2000); Foreign born: 0.6% (2000); Ancestry (includes multiple ancestries): 23.9% German, 23.4% United States or American, 12.5% Other groups, 8.0% Irish, 4.4% French (except Basque) (2000).
Economy: Employment by occupation: 5.3% management, 9.5% professional, 24.8% services, 25.8% sales, 0.0% farming, 14.9% construction, 19.7% production (2000).
Income: Per capita income: $13,242 (2000); Median household income: $29,898 (2000); Poverty rate: 17.3% (2000).
Education: Percent of population age 25 and over with: High school diploma (including GED) or higher: 75.0% (2000); Bachelor's degree or higher: 3.2% (2000).
Housing: Homeownership rate: 73.3% (2000); Median home value: $52,300 (2000); Median rent: $326 per month (2000); Median age of housing: 38 years (2000).
Transportation: Commute to work: 96.8% car, 0.0% public transportation, 2.1% walk, 0.7% work from home (2000); Travel time to work: 32.0% less than 15 minutes, 35.8% 15 to 30 minutes, 17.0% 30 to 45 minutes, 9.9% 45 to 60 minutes, 5.4% 60 minutes or more (2000)

DORSEY (unincorporated postal area, zip code 62021). Aka Dorsey's. Covers a land area of 20.799 square miles and a water area of 0.041 square miles. Located at 38.97° N. Lat.; 89.97° W. Long. Elevation is 587 feet.
Population: 965 (2000); Race: 100.0% White, 0.0% Black, 0.0% Asian, 0.0% Hispanic of any race (2000); Density: 46.4 persons per square mile (2000); Age: 24.5% under 18, 10.4% over 64 (2000); Marriage status: 17.6% never married, 70.9% now married, 3.7% widowed, 7.8% divorced (2000); Foreign born: 0.5% (2000); Ancestry (includes multiple ancestries): 41.5% German, 14.2% United States or American, 12.1% Irish, 7.4% English, 5.7% Italian (2000).
Economy: Employment by occupation: 13.6% management, 14.5% professional, 10.9% services, 26.4% sales, 0.9% farming, 14.5% construction, 19.2% production (2000).
Income: Per capita income: $21,055 (2000); Median household income: $40,000 (2000); Poverty rate: 0.0% (2000).
Education: Percent of population age 25 and over with: High school diploma (including GED) or higher: 89.7% (2000); Bachelor's degree or higher: 17.5% (2000).
Housing: Homeownership rate: 95.1% (2000); Median home value: $85,700 (2000); Median rent: $375 per month (2000); Median age of housing: 32 years (2000).
Transportation: Commute to work: 96.8% car, 0.0% public transportation, 0.0% walk, 3.2% work from home (2000); Travel time to work: 20.0% less than 15 minutes, 46.5% 15 to 30 minutes, 22.7% 30 to 45 minutes, 9.3% 45 to 60 minutes, 1.5% 60 minutes or more (2000)

EAST ALTON (village). Covers a land area of 5.502 square miles and a water area of 0.131 square miles. Located at 38.88° N. Lat.; 90.10° W. Long. Elevation is 436 feet.
History: In 1893 the Western Cartridge Company established a powder mill in East Alton and began the manufacture of ammunition.
Population: 7,222 (1990); 6,830 (2000); 6,585 (2007); 6,372 (2012 projected); Race: 95.5% White, 1.4% Black, 0.5% Asian, 1.5% Hispanic of any race (2007); Density: 1,196.8 persons per square mile (2007); Average household size: 2.25 (2007); Median age: 36.5 (2007); Males per 100 females: 93.2 (2007); Marriage status: 22.2% never married, 51.4% now married, 10.8% widowed, 15.7% divorced (2000); Foreign born: 0.5% (2000); Ancestry (includes multiple ancestries): 23.6% German, 13.4% Irish, 12.0% Other groups, 11.9% English, 10.7% United States or American (2000).

Economy: Single-family building permits issued: 7 (2007); Multi-family building permits issued: 0 (2007); Employment by occupation: 6.6% management, 11.3% professional, 19.9% services, 31.0% sales, 0.3% farming, 12.1% construction, 18.9% production (2000).
Income: Per capita income: $18,358 (2007); Median household income: $30,936 (2007); Average household income: $41,273 (2007); Percent of households with income of $100,000 or more: 4.7% (2007); Poverty rate: 13.3% (2000).
Education: Percent of population age 25 and over with: High school diploma (including GED) or higher: 73.2% (2007); Bachelor's degree or higher: 7.5% (2007); Master's degree or higher: 1.2% (2007).

School District(s)

East Alton SD 13 (PK-08)
2005-06 Enrollment: 961 . . . . (618) 433-2051

Housing: Homeownership rate: 58.8% (2007); Median home value: $77,645 (2007); Median rent: $317 per month (2000); Median age of housing: 51 years (2000).
Safety: Violent crime rate: 48.4 per 10,000 population; Property crime rate: 458.5 per 10,000 population (2006).
Transportation: Commute to work: 94.8% car, 0.8% public transportation, 1.6% walk, 1.8% work from home (2000); Travel time to work: 40.5% less than 15 minutes, 26.6% 15 to 30 minutes, 18.7% 30 to 45 minutes, 9.1% 45 to 60 minutes, 5.1% 60 minutes or more (2000)

Additional Information Contacts

Village of East Alton. . . . . (618) 259-7714
http://www.eastaltonvillage.org

EDWARDSVILLE (city). County seat. Covers a land area of 13.872 square miles and a water area of 0.218 square miles. Located at 38.80° N. Lat.; 89.95° W. Long. Elevation is 541 feet.
History: Edwardsville was settled by James Gillham of Kentucky in 1800. Some of his friends followed and a town was platted in 1813, named for Ninian Edwards, governor of Illinois Territory from 1809-1818. Edwardsville was incorporated in 1837.
Population: 17,105 (1990); 21,491 (2000); 23,091 (2007); 24,090 (2012 projected); Race: 86.6% White, 9.4% Black, 1.7% Asian, 1.3% Hispanic of any race (2007); Density: 1,664.6 persons per square mile (2007); Average household size: 2.65 (2007); Median age: 34.4 (2007); Males per 100 females: 88.6 (2007); Marriage status: 28.8% never married, 56.0% now married, 5.7% widowed, 9.4% divorced (2000); Foreign born: 3.1% (2000); Ancestry (includes multiple ancestries): 33.9% German, 15.8% Other groups, 12.9% Irish, 11.6% English, 5.3% Italian (2000).
Economy: Single-family building permits issued: 55 (2007); Multi-family building permits issued: 18 (2007); Employment by occupation: 16.5% management, 30.4% professional, 14.4% services, 24.5% sales, 0.1% farming, 5.3% construction, 8.7% production (2000).
Income: Per capita income: $31,574 (2007); Median household income: $62,468 (2007); Average household income: $82,018 (2007); Percent of households with income of $100,000 or more: 26.6% (2007); Poverty rate: 8.6% (2000).
Education: Percent of population age 25 and over with: High school diploma (including GED) or higher: 92.8% (2007); Bachelor's degree or higher: 42.9% (2007); Master's degree or higher: 17.0% (2007).

School District(s)

Edwardsville CUSD 7 (PK-12)
2005-06 Enrollment: 7,365 . . . . (618) 656-1182

Four-year College(s)

Southern Illinois University Edwardsville (Public)
Fall 2007 Enrollment: 13,398. . . . . (618) 650-2000
2007-08 Tuition: In-state $7,033; Out-of-state $14,874

Vocational/Technical School(s)

Alvareitas College of Cosmetology (Private, For-profit)
Fall 2007 Enrollment: 31 . . . . (618) 656-2593
2007-08 Tuition: $9,700

Housing: Homeownership rate: 71.0% (2007); Median home value: $141,660 (2007); Median rent: $473 per month (2000); Median age of housing: 33 years (2000).
Safety: Violent crime rate: 7.9 per 10,000 population; Property crime rate: 152.2 per 10,000 population (2006).
Newspapers: Edwardsville Intelligencer (Local news; Circulation 5,406); The Record (Regional news; Circulation 0); St. Louis Post-Dispatch - Edwardsville Bureau (Local news; Circulation 490,000)
Transportation: Commute to work: 91.9% car, 2.0% public transportation, 2.8% walk, 2.5% work from home (2000); Travel time to work: 35.4% less than 15 minutes, 25.6% 15 to 30 minutes, 23.1% 30 to 45 minutes, 11.3% 45 to 60 minutes, 4.7% 60 minutes or more (2000)

Additional Information Contacts

City of Edwardsville . . . . (618) 692-7520
http://www.cityofedwardsville.com
Edwardsville & Glen Carbon Chamber of Commerce . . . . . (618) 656-7600
http://www.edglenchamber.com

GLEN CARBON (village). Covers a land area of 7.417 square miles and a water area of 0.043 square miles. Located at 38.76° N. Lat.; 89.96° W. Long. Elevation is 466 feet.
History: Incorporated 1892.
Population: 8,151 (1990); 10,425 (2000); 12,189 (2007); 13,268 (2012 projected); Race: 88.6% White, 7.2% Black, 2.3% Asian, 2.0% Hispanic of any race (2007); Density: 1,643.4 persons per square mile (2007); Average household size: 2.55 (2007); Median age: 36.2 (2007); Males per 100 females: 94.4 (2007); Marriage status: 24.3% never married, 64.0% now married, 5.6% widowed, 6.1% divorced (2000); Foreign born: 2.4% (2000); Ancestry (includes multiple ancestries): 32.7% German, 15.1% Irish, 13.7% Other groups, 12.0% English, 4.9% United States or American (2000).
Economy: Single-family building permits issued: 38 (2007); Multi-family building permits issued: 0 (2007); Employment by occupation: 19.5% management, 30.0% professional, 10.1% services, 24.9% sales, 0.0% farming, 5.0% construction, 10.5% production (2000).
Income: Per capita income: $32,752 (2007); Median household income: $68,152 (2007); Average household income: $83,066 (2007); Percent of households with income of $100,000 or more: 30.6% (2007); Poverty rate: 5.8% (2000).
Education: Percent of population age 25 and over with: High school diploma (including GED) or higher: 90.6% (2007); Bachelor's degree or higher: 44.0% (2007); Master's degree or higher: 17.2% (2007).

School District(s)

Edwardsville CUSD 7 (PK-12)
2005-06 Enrollment: 7,365 . . . . (618) 656-1182

Housing: Homeownership rate: 73.3% (2007); Median home value: $168,359 (2007); Median rent: $494 per month (2000); Median age of housing: 16 years (2000).
Safety: Violent crime rate: 7.5 per 10,000 population; Property crime rate: 124.0 per 10,000 population (2006).
Transportation: Commute to work: 94.4% car, 1.2% public transportation, 0.7% walk, 3.5% work from home (2000); Travel time to work: 25.3% less than 15 minutes, 30.9% 15 to 30 minutes, 29.4% 30 to 45 minutes, 10.4% 45 to 60 minutes, 4.1% 60 minutes or more (2000)

Additional Information Contacts

Village of Glen Carbon. . . . . (618) 288-1200
http://www.glen-carbon.il.us

GODFREY (village). Covers a land area of 34.481 square miles and a water area of 1.686 square miles. Located at 38.94° N. Lat.; 90.20° W. Long. Elevation is 610 feet.
History: Godfrey grew around the Monticello College and Preparatory School for Girls, founded in 1835 by a retired Cape Cod sea captain, Benjamin Godfrey.
Population: 15,785 (1990); 16,286 (2000); 16,821 (2007); 17,196 (2012 projected); Race: 93.5% White, 4.4% Black, 0.6% Asian, 1.3% Hispanic of any race (2007); Density: 487.8 persons per square mile (2007); Average household size: 2.47 (2007); Median age: 42.7 (2007); Males per 100 females: 95.9 (2007); Marriage status: 20.4% never married, 63.3% now married, 8.1% widowed, 8.2% divorced (2000); Foreign born: 1.8% (2000); Ancestry (includes multiple ancestries): 34.2% German, 14.2% Irish, 13.6% English, 9.9% Other groups, 8.4% United States or American (2000).
Economy: Single-family building permits issued: 73 (2007); Multi-family building permits issued: 0 (2007); Employment by occupation: 13.2% management, 24.4% professional, 13.2% services, 25.6% sales, 0.2% farming, 8.7% construction, 14.8% production (2000).
Income: Per capita income: $29,337 (2007); Median household income: $58,162 (2007); Average household income: $71,915 (2007); Percent of households with income of $100,000 or more: 18.8% (2007); Poverty rate: 5.9% (2000).
Education: Percent of population age 25 and over with: High school diploma (including GED) or higher: 88.0% (2007); Bachelor's degree or higher: 25.3% (2007); Master's degree or higher: 9.8% (2007).

School District(s)

Alton CUSD 11 (PK-12)
2005-06 Enrollment: 6,798 . . . . (618) 474-2600

Two-year College(s)

Lewis and Clark Community College (Public)
Fall 2007 Enrollment: 7,875. . . . . (618) 468-3411
2007-08 Tuition: In-state $6,660; Out-of-state $8,790

Vocational/Technical School(s)

Alvareitas College of Cosmetology (Private, For-profit)
Fall 2007 Enrollment: 41 . . . . (618) 466-9723
2007-08 Tuition: $9,700

Housing: Homeownership rate: 85.5% (2007); Median home value: $125,171 (2007); Median rent: $436 per month (2000); Median age of housing: 32 years (2000).
Transportation: Commute to work: 96.0% car, 0.7% public transportation, 0.6% walk, 2.1% work from home (2000); Travel time to work: 31.7% less than 15 minutes, 35.1% 15 to 30 minutes, 14.2% 30 to 45 minutes, 11.5% 45 to 60 minutes, 7.6% 60 minutes or more (2000)

Additional Information Contacts

River Bend Growth Association . . . . (618) 467-2280
http://www.growthassociation.com
Village of Godfrey . . . . (618) 466-3324
http://www.godfreyil.org

GRANITE CITY (city). Covers a land area of 16.683 square miles and a water area of 0.487 square miles. Located at 38.71° N. Lat.; 90.13° W. Long. Elevation is 423 feet.
History: Farmers settled here in the early 1800's, but Granite City began when William F. Niedringhaus purchased land here for his National Enameling and Stamping Company plant. The American Steel Foundry followed, and in 1896 Granite City was incorporated, named for the granite ware produced there.
Population: 34,236 (1990); 31,301 (2000); 29,697 (2007); 28,568 (2012 projected); Race: 93.4% White, 2.6% Black, 0.5% Asian, 3.9% Hispanic of any race (2007); Density: 1,780.1 persons per square mile (2007); Average household size: 2.40 (2007); Median age: 38.6 (2007); Males per 100 females: 93.2 (2007); Marriage status: 25.2% never married, 51.7% now married, 9.6% widowed, 13.6% divorced (2000); Foreign born: 1.1% (2000); Ancestry (includes multiple ancestries): 20.6% German, 16.8% Irish, 14.0% Other groups, 10.3% United States or American, 9.7% English (2000).
Economy: Unemployment rate: 5.6% (4/2008); Total civilian labor force: 15,491 (4/2008); Single-family building permits issued: 80 (2007); Multi-family building permits issued: 0 (2007); Employment by occupation: 9.0% management, 12.9% professional, 17.2% services, 27.5% sales, 0.2% farming, 9.3% construction, 24.0% production (2000).
Income: Per capita income: $20,605 (2007); Median household income: $40,446 (2007); Average household income: $49,097 (2007); Percent of households with income of $100,000 or more: 7.4% (2007); Poverty rate: 11.3% (2000).
Education: Percent of population age 25 and over with: High school diploma (including GED) or higher: 78.0% (2007); Bachelor's degree or higher: 9.9% (2007); Master's degree or higher: 3.0% (2007).

School District(s)

Granite City CUSD 9 (PK-12)
2005-06 Enrollment: 7,352 . . . . (618) 451-5800

Housing: Homeownership rate: 70.8% (2007); Median home value: $74,937 (2007); Median rent: $341 per month (2000); Median age of housing: 46 years (2000).
Hospitals: Gateway Regional Medical Center (393 beds)
Safety: Violent crime rate: 52.3 per 10,000 population; Property crime rate: 441.0 per 10,000 population (2006).
Transportation: Commute to work: 93.8% car, 2.1% public transportation, 1.9% walk, 1.2% work from home (2000); Travel time to work: 38.4% less than 15 minutes, 31.2% 15 to 30 minutes, 18.6% 30 to 45 minutes, 8.2% 45 to 60 minutes, 3.6% 60 minutes or more (2000)

Additional Information Contacts

City of Granite City. . . . . (618) 452-6200
http://www.granitecity.illinois.gov
The Chamber of Commerce of Southwestern Madison County. . . . . . (618) 876-6400
http://www.chamberswmadisoncounty.com

GRANTFORK (village). Covers a land area of 0.228 square miles and a water area of 0 square miles. Located at 38.83° N. Lat.; 89.66° W. Long. Elevation is 535 feet.
Population: 276 (1990); 254 (2000); 287 (2007); 303 (2012 projected); Race: 98.6% White, 0.0% Black, 0.0% Asian, 0.3% Hispanic of any race (2007); Density: 1,256.5 persons per square mile (2007); Average household size: 2.41 (2007); Median age: 33.8 (2007); Males per 100 females: 95.2 (2007); Marriage status: 29.6% never married, 50.5% now married, 11.2% widowed, 8.7% divorced (2000); Foreign born: 0.0% (2000); Ancestry (includes multiple ancestries): 41.5% German, 10.7% English, 8.7% United States or American, 8.3% Other groups, 5.1% Irish (2000).
Economy: Single-family building permits issued: 9 (2007); Multi-family building permits issued: 0 (2007); Employment by occupation: 11.0% management, 5.1% professional, 30.1% services, 21.3% sales, 0.0% farming, 12.5% construction, 19.9% production (2000).
Income: Per capita income: $22,770 (2007); Median household income: $50,417 (2007); Average household income: $54,916 (2007); Percent of households with income of $100,000 or more: 8.4% (2007); Poverty rate: 4.4% (2000).
Education: Percent of population age 25 and over with: High school diploma (including GED) or higher: 82.3% (2007); Bachelor's degree or higher: 9.1% (2007); Master's degree or higher: 4.0% (2007).
Housing: Homeownership rate: 84.9% (2007); Median home value: $78,214 (2007); Median rent: $368 per month (2000); Median age of housing: 28 years (2000).
Safety: Violent crime rate: 0.0 per 10,000 population; Property crime rate: 36.8 per 10,000 population (2006).
Transportation: Commute to work: 93.4% car, 0.0% public transportation, 2.2% walk, 4.4% work from home (2000); Travel time to work: 41.5% less than 15 minutes, 26.9% 15 to 30 minutes, 15.4% 30 to 45 minutes, 10.0% 45 to 60 minutes, 6.2% 60 minutes or more (2000)

HAMEL (village). Covers a land area of 1.160 square miles and a water area of 0 square miles. Located at 38.88° N. Lat.; 89.84° W. Long. Elevation is 545 feet.
Population: 530 (1990); 570 (2000); 729 (2007); 830 (2012 projected); Race: 98.2% White, 0.0% Black, 0.0% Asian, 1.1% Hispanic of any race (2007); Density: 628.3 persons per square mile (2007); Average household size: 2.39 (2007); Median age: 38.5 (2007); Males per 100 females: 93.9 (2007); Marriage status: 16.2% never married, 72.1% now married, 5.6% widowed, 6.1% divorced (2000); Foreign born: 0.7% (2000); Ancestry (includes multiple ancestries): 48.6% German, 12.5% Other groups, 10.6% English, 6.9% Irish, 6.7% United States or American (2000).
Economy: Single-family building permits issued: 0 (2007); Multi-family building permits issued: 0 (2007); Employment by occupation: 12.2% management, 14.2% professional, 19.8% services, 25.0% sales, 0.3% farming, 9.4% construction, 19.1% production (2000).
Income: Per capita income: $24,952 (2007); Median household income: $53,676 (2007); Average household income: $59,639 (2007); Percent of households with income of $100,000 or more: 14.4% (2007); Poverty rate: 3.6% (2000).
Education: Percent of population age 25 and over with: High school diploma (including GED) or higher: 85.4% (2007); Bachelor's degree or higher: 14.2% (2007); Master's degree or higher: 3.0% (2007).

School District(s)

Edwardsville CUSD 7 (PK-12)
2005-06 Enrollment: 7,365 . . . . (618) 656-1182

Housing: Homeownership rate: 75.1% (2007); Median home value: $118,958 (2007); Median rent: $419 per month (2000); Median age of housing: 29 years (2000).
Transportation: Commute to work: 92.7% car, 0.7% public transportation, 4.2% walk, 2.4% work from home (2000); Travel time to work: 26.3% less than 15 minutes, 32.4% 15 to 30 minutes, 21.4% 30 to 45 minutes, 13.2% 45 to 60 minutes, 6.8% 60 minutes or more (2000)

HARTFORD (village). Covers a land area of 3.898 square miles and a water area of 0.014 square miles. Located at 38.82° N. Lat.; 90.09° W. Long. Elevation is 430 feet.
History: In 1915 the International Shoe Company established a tannery in Hartford, and the town developed around it.
Population: 1,690 (1990); 1,545 (2000); 1,464 (2007); 1,419 (2012 projected); Race: 98.0% White, 0.1% Black, 0.4% Asian, 0.9% Hispanic of any race (2007); Density: 375.6 persons per square mile (2007); Average household size: 2.32 (2007); Median age: 39.6 (2007); Males per 100 females: 100.5 (2007); Marriage status: 18.4% never married, 59.2% now married, 9.0% widowed, 13.4% divorced (2000); Foreign born: 1.0% (2000); Ancestry (includes multiple ancestries): 20.5% German, 14.2% United States or American, 12.9% Irish, 10.7% English, 10.5% Other groups (2000).

Economy: Single-family building permits issued: 0 (2007); Multi-family building permits issued: 0 (2007); Employment by occupation: 7.6% management, 8.0% professional, 21.9% services, 24.2% sales, 0.0% farming, 16.5% construction, 21.9% production (2000).
Income: Per capita income: $18,911 (2007); Median household income: $38,071 (2007); Average household income: $43,875 (2007); Percent of households with income of $100,000 or more: 5.5% (2007); Poverty rate: 13.0% (2000).
Education: Percent of population age 25 and over with: High school diploma (including GED) or higher: 77.1% (2007); Bachelor's degree or higher: 3.1% (2007); Master's degree or higher: 0.5% (2007).

School District(s)

Wood River-Hartford ESD 15 (PK-08)
2005-06 Enrollment: 833 . . . . (618) 254-0607
Housing: Homeownership rate: 78.0% (2007); Median home value: $61,111 (2007); Median rent: $318 per month (2000); Median age of housing: 52 years (2000).
Safety: Violent crime rate: 6.7 per 10,000 population; Property crime rate: 241.3 per 10,000 population (2006).
Transportation: Commute to work: 95.6% car, 0.4% public transportation, 1.0% walk, 1.6% work from home (2000); Travel time to work: 39.5% less than 15 minutes, 33.8% 15 to 30 minutes, 13.4% 30 to 45 minutes, 6.8% 45 to 60 minutes, 6.6% 60 minutes or more (2000)

HIGHLAND (city). Covers a land area of 5.405 square miles and a water area of 1.018 square miles. Located at 38.74° N. Lat.; 89.67° W. Long. Elevation is 525 feet.
History: Highland was settled about 1804 by families from Kentucky and North Carolina. In 1831 a group of Swiss colonists led by Dr. Caspar Koepfli located in Highland, and the community became a dairy producer. A leading firm here in the early 1900's was the Wicks Organ Company.
Population: 7,847 (1990); 8,438 (2000); 9,088 (2007); 9,506 (2012 projected); Race: 98.3% White, 0.1% Black, 0.6% Asian, 2.0% Hispanic of any race (2007); Density: 1,681.4 persons per square mile (2007); Average household size: 2.38 (2007); Median age: 37.9 (2007); Males per 100 females: 89.2 (2007); Marriage status: 20.9% never married, 58.0% now married, 10.9% widowed, 10.2% divorced (2000); Foreign born: 1.0% (2000); Ancestry (includes multiple ancestries): 48.2% German, 9.0% United States or American, 9.0% Irish, 7.5% English, 6.5% Swiss (2000).
Economy: Single-family building permits issued: 50 (2007); Multi-family building permits issued: 42 (2007); Employment by occupation: 10.8% management, 18.3% professional, 15.3% services, 30.9% sales, 0.0% farming, 8.0% construction, 16.8% production (2000).
Income: Per capita income: $25,004 (2007); Median household income: $46,109 (2007); Average household income: $59,190 (2007); Percent of households with income of $100,000 or more: 14.3% (2007); Poverty rate: 6.8% (2000).
Taxes: Total city taxes per capita: $316 (2006); City property taxes per capita: $289 (2006).
Education: Percent of population age 25 and over with: High school diploma (including GED) or higher: 85.5% (2007); Bachelor's degree or higher: 22.0% (2007); Master's degree or higher: 7.1% (2007).

School District(s)

Highland CUSD 5 (PK-12)
2005-06 Enrollment: 3,093 . . . . (618) 654-2106
Housing: Homeownership rate: 69.8% (2007); Median home value: $122,496 (2007); Median rent: $386 per month (2000); Median age of housing: 31 years (2000).
Hospitals: St. Joseph's Hospital (106 beds)
Safety: Violent crime rate: 16.3 per 10,000 population; Property crime rate: 209.8 per 10,000 population (2006).
Newspapers: Highland News Leader (Local news; Circulation 15,000)
Transportation: Commute to work: 94.1% car, 1.3% public transportation, 2.9% walk, 1.6% work from home (2000); Travel time to work: 49.4% less than 15 minutes, 15.6% 15 to 30 minutes, 14.0% 30 to 45 minutes, 14.5% 45 to 60 minutes, 6.5% 60 minutes or more (2000)

Additional Information Contacts

City of Highland . . . . (618) 654-9891
http://www.ci.highland.il.us
Highland Chamber of Commerce . . . . (618) 654-3721
http://www.highlandillinois.com

LIVINGSTON (village). Covers a land area of 1.061 square miles and a water area of 0.008 square miles. Located at 38.96° N. Lat.; 89.76° W. Long. Elevation is 591 feet.
History: Incorporated 1905.
Population: 928 (1990); 825 (2000); 677 (2007); 692 (2012 projected); Race: 98.7% White, 0.0% Black, 0.1% Asian, 0.4% Hispanic of any race (2007); Density: 638.0 persons per square mile (2007); Average household size: 2.18 (2007); Median age: 39.0 (2007); Males per 100 females: 100.3 (2007); Marriage status: 25.8% never married, 53.0% now married, 9.9% widowed, 11.4% divorced (2000); Foreign born: 2.2% (2000); Ancestry (includes multiple ancestries): 42.5% German, 12.7% Italian, 10.8% Other groups, 8.8% Irish, 7.8% United States or American (2000).
Economy: Single-family building permits issued: 0 (2007); Multi-family building permits issued: 0 (2007); Employment by occupation: 4.8% management, 14.5% professional, 21.3% services, 17.8% sales, 0.0% farming, 15.5% construction, 26.1% production (2000).
Income: Per capita income: $22,980 (2007); Median household income: $47,130 (2007); Average household income: $50,024 (2007); Percent of households with income of $100,000 or more: 4.8% (2007); Poverty rate: 9.1% (2000).
Education: Percent of population age 25 and over with: High school diploma (including GED) or higher: 78.6% (2007); Bachelor's degree or higher: 5.6% (2007); Master's degree or higher: 1.3% (2007).

School District(s)

Staunton CUSD 6 (PK-12)
2005-06 Enrollment: 1,344 . . . . (618) 635-2962
Housing: Homeownership rate: 79.1% (2007); Median home value: $69,688 (2007); Median rent: $283 per month (2000); Median age of housing: 48 years (2000).
Safety: Violent crime rate: 50.2 per 10,000 population; Property crime rate: 112.9 per 10,000 population (2006).
Transportation: Commute to work: 96.1% car, 0.0% public transportation, 1.8% walk, 1.3% work from home (2000); Travel time to work: 19.5% less than 15 minutes, 32.0% 15 to 30 minutes, 25.6% 30 to 45 minutes, 10.7% 45 to 60 minutes, 12.3% 60 minutes or more (2000)

MADISON (city). Covers a land area of 7.011 square miles and a water area of 0.266 square miles. Located at 38.68° N. Lat.; 90.15° W. Long. Elevation is 413 feet.
History: The Madison Land Syndicate was formed in 1887 by a group of St. Louis businessmen who promoted the construction of Merchants Bridge over the Mississippi River. An American Car and Foundry plant was built near the new bridge, and the town of Madison was incorporated in 1891 by the Land Syndicate.
Population: 5,215 (1990); 4,545 (2000); 4,449 (2007); 4,415 (2012 projected); Race: 44.8% White, 52.2% Black, 0.1% Asian, 2.4% Hispanic of any race (2007); Density: 634.6 persons per square mile (2007); Average household size: 2.44 (2007); Median age: 33.3 (2007); Males per 100 females: 96.4 (2007); Marriage status: 33.0% never married, 37.4% now married, 10.3% widowed, 19.3% divorced (2000); Foreign born: 0.7% (2000); Ancestry (includes multiple ancestries): 36.8% Other groups, 11.9% German, 6.7% Irish, 5.1% Polish, 4.4% English (2000).
Economy: Single-family building permits issued: 2 (2007); Multi-family building permits issued: 0 (2007); Employment by occupation: 9.3% management, 9.6% professional, 25.6% services, 20.0% sales, 0.0% farming, 10.5% construction, 25.0% production (2000).
Income: Per capita income: $15,384 (2007); Median household income: $28,687 (2007); Average household income: $37,427 (2007); Percent of households with income of $100,000 or more: 4.8% (2007); Poverty rate: 24.0% (2000).
Education: Percent of population age 25 and over with: High school diploma (including GED) or higher: 66.8% (2007); Bachelor's degree or higher: 5.1% (2007); Master's degree or higher: 2.5% (2007).

School District(s)

Madison CUSD 12 (PK-12)
2005-06 Enrollment: 1,056 . . . . (618) 877-1712
Housing: Homeownership rate: 59.8% (2007); Median home value: $50,842 (2007); Median rent: $295 per month (2000); Median age of housing: 50 years (2000).
Safety: Violent crime rate: 149.2 per 10,000 population; Property crime rate: 673.5 per 10,000 population (2006).
Transportation: Commute to work: 88.2% car, 6.4% public transportation, 2.9% walk, 2.5% work from home (2000); Travel time to work: 31.6% less than 15 minutes, 38.2% 15 to 30 minutes, 19.7% 30 to 45 minutes, 3.4% 45 to 60 minutes, 7.2% 60 minutes or more (2000)

MARINE (village). Covers a land area of 0.761 square miles and a water area of 0.019 square miles. Located at 38.78° N. Lat.; 89.77° W. Long. Elevation is 522 feet.

Population: 972 (1990); 910 (2000); 828 (2007); 840 (2012 projected); Race: 97.8% White, 0.0% Black, 0.1% Asian, 0.8% Hispanic of any race (2007); Density: 1,088.5 persons per square mile (2007); Average household size: 2.44 (2007); Median age: 35.3 (2007); Males per 100 females: 96.2 (2007); Marriage status: 23.0% never married, 59.9% now married, 7.2% widowed, 9.8% divorced (2000); Foreign born: 0.0% (2000); Ancestry (includes multiple ancestries): 38.4% German, 13.7% Irish, 12.9% English, 8.3% United States or American, 4.8% Other groups (2000).
Economy: Single-family building permits issued: 3 (2007); Multi-family building permits issued: 0 (2007); Employment by occupation: 14.6% management, 13.5% professional, 17.8% services, 27.5% sales, 0.0% farming, 12.6% construction, 14.0% production (2000).
Income: Per capita income: $22,998 (2007); Median household income: $44,853 (2007); Average household income: $56,173 (2007); Percent of households with income of $100,000 or more: 13.6% (2007); Poverty rate: 6.2% (2000).
Education: Percent of population age 25 and over with: High school diploma (including GED) or higher: 83.5% (2007); Bachelor's degree or higher: 12.1% (2007); Master's degree or higher: 4.8% (2007).

School District(s)

Triad CUSD 2 (PK-12)
2005-06 Enrollment: 3,873 . . . . (618) 667-8851

Housing: Homeownership rate: 72.0% (2007); Median home value: $114,402 (2007); Median rent: $354 per month (2000); Median age of housing: 44 years (2000).
Safety: Violent crime rate: 0.0 per 10,000 population; Property crime rate: 10.6 per 10,000 population (2006).
Transportation: Commute to work: 92.8% car, 0.2% public transportation, 2.7% walk, 4.1% work from home (2000); Travel time to work: 19.3% less than 15 minutes, 44.0% 15 to 30 minutes, 19.8% 30 to 45 minutes, 11.6% 45 to 60 minutes, 5.3% 60 minutes or more (2000)

MARYVILLE (village). Covers a land area of 4.667 square miles and a water area of 0.032 square miles. Located at 38.72° N. Lat.; 89.95° W. Long. Elevation is 577 feet.

Population: 3,477 (1990); 4,651 (2000); 5,951 (2007); 6,722 (2012 projected); Race: 92.4% White, 4.4% Black, 0.6% Asian, 2.4% Hispanic of any race (2007); Density: 1,275.0 persons per square mile (2007); Average household size: 2.59 (2007); Median age: 37.6 (2007); Males per 100 females: 91.8 (2007); Marriage status: 20.3% never married, 66.6% now married, 4.1% widowed, 9.0% divorced (2000); Foreign born: 1.5% (2000); Ancestry (includes multiple ancestries): 31.6% German, 12.4% Irish, 12.1% English, 8.4% Other groups, 7.8% Italian (2000).
Economy: Single-family building permits issued: 106 (2007); Multi-family building permits issued: 0 (2007); Employment by occupation: 12.5% management, 28.2% professional, 9.9% services, 32.7% sales, 0.0% farming, 6.1% construction, 10.5% production (2000).
Income: Per capita income: $32,840 (2007); Median household income: $72,298 (2007); Average household income: $83,690 (2007); Percent of households with income of $100,000 or more: 25.8% (2007); Poverty rate: 4.1% (2000).
Education: Percent of population age 25 and over with: High school diploma (including GED) or higher: 87.8% (2007); Bachelor's degree or higher: 28.0% (2007); Master's degree or higher: 8.2% (2007).

School District(s)

Collinsville CUSD 10 (PK-12)
2005-06 Enrollment: 6,342 . . . . (618) 346-6350

Housing: Homeownership rate: 78.5% (2007); Median home value: $159,375 (2007); Median rent: $369 per month (2000); Median age of housing: 16 years (2000).
Hospitals: Anderson Hospital (130 beds)
Safety: Violent crime rate: 12.1 per 10,000 population; Property crime rate: 117.7 per 10,000 population (2006).
Transportation: Commute to work: 94.6% car, 0.3% public transportation, 0.0% walk, 5.1% work from home (2000); Travel time to work: 19.5% less than 15 minutes, 37.2% 15 to 30 minutes, 30.3% 30 to 45 minutes, 9.1% 45 to 60 minutes, 4.0% 60 minutes or more (2000)

MORO (unincorporated postal area, zip code 62067). Covers a land area of 16.810 square miles and a water area of 0.046 square miles. Located at 38.92° N. Lat.; 90.01° W. Long. Elevation is 531 feet.
Population: 2,089 (2000); Race: 98.9% White, 0.0% Black, 0.0% Asian, 0.3% Hispanic of any race (2000); Density: 124.3 persons per square mile (2000); Age: 23.6% under 18, 15.6% over 64 (2000); Marriage status: 21.5% never married, 66.0% now married, 6.1% widowed, 6.4% divorced (2000); Foreign born: 1.0% (2000); Ancestry (includes multiple ancestries): 36.8% German, 14.2% English, 13.9% United States or American, 6.3% Irish, 5.4% French (except Basque) (2000).
Economy: Employment by occupation: 17.8% management, 11.8% professional, 16.7% services, 21.2% sales, 0.8% farming, 13.3% construction, 18.3% production (2000).
Income: Per capita income: $18,510 (2000); Median household income: $38,491 (2000); Poverty rate: 9.3% (2000).
Education: Percent of population age 25 and over with: High school diploma (including GED) or higher: 81.3% (2000); Bachelor's degree or higher: 15.5% (2000).

School District(s)

Bethalto CUSD 8 (PK-12)
2005-06 Enrollment: 2,738 . . . . (618) 377-7200
Edwardsville CUSD 7 (PK-12)
2005-06 Enrollment: 7,365 . . . . (618) 656-1182

Housing: Homeownership rate: 85.4% (2000); Median home value: $78,200 (2000); Median rent: $334 per month (2000); Median age of housing: 30 years (2000).
Transportation: Commute to work: 91.1% car, 0.7% public transportation, 0.8% walk, 7.4% work from home (2000); Travel time to work: 21.1% less than 15 minutes, 47.6% 15 to 30 minutes, 20.8% 30 to 45 minutes, 5.1% 45 to 60 minutes, 5.4% 60 minutes or more (2000)

NEW DOUGLAS (village). Covers a land area of 1.068 square miles and a water area of 0 square miles. Located at 38.97° N. Lat.; 89.66° W. Long. Elevation is 620 feet.

Population: 387 (1990); 369 (2000); 404 (2007); 415 (2012 projected); Race: 97.3% White, 0.0% Black, 0.5% Asian, 5.2% Hispanic of any race (2007); Density: 378.3 persons per square mile (2007); Average household size: 2.43 (2007); Median age: 38.8 (2007); Males per 100 females: 103.0 (2007); Marriage status: 23.7% never married, 62.3% now married, 6.7% widowed, 7.3% divorced (2000); Foreign born: 2.1% (2000); Ancestry (includes multiple ancestries): 33.0% German, 16.4% Other groups, 14.8% Irish, 11.9% United States or American, 5.5% English (2000).
Economy: Single-family building permits issued: 5 (2007); Multi-family building permits issued: 0 (2007); Employment by occupation: 8.7% management, 11.2% professional, 12.4% services, 26.1% sales, 1.2% farming, 23.6% construction, 16.8% production (2000).
Income: Per capita income: $19,524 (2007); Median household income: $36,667 (2007); Average household income: $47,515 (2007); Percent of households with income of $100,000 or more: 9.6% (2007); Poverty rate: 9.7% (2000).
Education: Percent of population age 25 and over with: High school diploma (including GED) or higher: 77.9% (2007); Bachelor's degree or higher: 10.3% (2007); Master's degree or higher: 6.6% (2007).

School District(s)

Highland CUSD 5 (PK-12)
2005-06 Enrollment: 3,093 . . . . (618) 654-2106

Housing: Homeownership rate: 76.5% (2007); Median home value: $75,000 (2007); Median rent: $260 per month (2000); Median age of housing: 52 years (2000).
Transportation: Commute to work: 85.7% car, 0.0% public transportation, 1.9% walk, 12.4% work from home (2000); Travel time to work: 17.0% less than 15 minutes, 23.4% 15 to 30 minutes, 20.6% 30 to 45 minutes, 14.9% 45 to 60 minutes, 24.1% 60 minutes or more (2000)

PONTOON BEACH (village). Covers a land area of 8.182 square miles and a water area of 0.279 square miles. Located at 38.72° N. Lat.; 90.06° W. Long. Elevation is 417 feet.

Population: 5,045 (1990); 5,620 (2000); 5,881 (2007); 6,019 (2012 projected); Race: 82.7% White, 13.2% Black, 0.9% Asian, 2.4% Hispanic of any race (2007); Density: 718.8 persons per square mile (2007); Average household size: 2.59 (2007); Median age: 33.3 (2007); Males per 100 females: 97.0 (2007); Marriage status: 26.3% never married, 56.6% now married, 5.7% widowed, 11.5% divorced (2000); Foreign born: 1.5% (2000); Ancestry (includes multiple ancestries): 19.6% Other groups, 18.3% German, 12.2% United States or American, 11.8% Irish, 6.2% English (2000).
Economy: Single-family building permits issued: 16 (2007); Multi-family building permits issued: 0 (2007); Employment by occupation: 10.3%

management, 12.0% professional, 15.0% services, 32.9% sales, 0.7% farming, 9.2% construction, 19.8% production (2000).
Income: Per capita income: $20,169 (2007); Median household income: $44,963 (2007); Average household income: $51,981 (2007); Percent of households with income of $100,000 or more: 7.9% (2007); Poverty rate: 10.6% (2000).
Education: Percent of population age 25 and over with: High school diploma (including GED) or higher: 82.8% (2007); Bachelor's degree or higher: 10.0% (2007); Master's degree or higher: 4.7% (2007).
Housing: Homeownership rate: 68.6% (2007); Median home value: $80,093 (2007); Median rent: $428 per month (2000); Median age of housing: 22 years (2000).
Safety: Violent crime rate: 24.8 per 10,000 population; Property crime rate: 315.9 per 10,000 population (2006).
Transportation: Commute to work: 93.7% car, 2.4% public transportation, 2.3% walk, 1.3% work from home (2000); Travel time to work: 25.5% less than 15 minutes, 41.9% 15 to 30 minutes, 19.7% 30 to 45 minutes, 9.1% 45 to 60 minutes, 3.8% 60 minutes or more (2000)
Additional Information Contacts
Village of Pontoon Beach. . . . . (618) 931-6100
http://www.pontoonbeach.org

ROSEWOOD HEIGHTS (CDP). Covers a land area of 2.144 square miles and a water area of 0 square miles. Located at 38.89° N. Lat.; 90.07° W. Long. Elevation is 548 feet.
Population: 4,596 (1990); 4,262 (2000); 3,956 (2007); 3,776 (2012 projected); Race: 98.6% White, 0.2% Black, 0.2% Asian, 0.9% Hispanic of any race (2007); Density: 1,845.3 persons per square mile (2007); Average household size: 2.46 (2007); Median age: 42.5 (2007); Males per 100 females: 90.4 (2007); Marriage status: 19.5% never married, 62.0% now married, 7.8% widowed, 10.8% divorced (2000); Foreign born: 0.2% (2000); Ancestry (includes multiple ancestries): 26.6% German, 13.5% United States or American, 12.3% English, 9.4% Irish, 6.8% Other groups (2000).
Economy: Employment by occupation: 8.1% management, 22.4% professional, 12.6% services, 25.2% sales, 0.0% farming, 14.2% construction, 17.4% production (2000).
Income: Per capita income: $24,656 (2007); Median household income: $55,028 (2007); Average household income: $60,735 (2007); Percent of households with income of $100,000 or more: 12.5% (2007); Poverty rate: 7.8% (2000).
Education: Percent of population age 25 and over with: High school diploma (including GED) or higher: 89.4% (2007); Bachelor's degree or higher: 15.3% (2007); Master's degree or higher: 3.6% (2007).
Housing: Homeownership rate: 88.7% (2007); Median home value: $105,029 (2007); Median rent: $293 per month (2000); Median age of housing: 42 years (2000).
Transportation: Commute to work: 97.6% car, 0.0% public transportation, 0.4% walk, 1.6% work from home (2000); Travel time to work: 42.6% less than 15 minutes, 27.5% 15 to 30 minutes, 16.2% 30 to 45 minutes, 8.0% 45 to 60 minutes, 5.8% 60 minutes or more (2000)

ROXANA (village). Covers a land area of 6.801 square miles and a water area of 0.022 square miles. Located at 38.83° N. Lat.; 90.06° W. Long. Elevation is 446 feet.
History: Incorporated 1921.
Population: 1,639 (1990); 1,547 (2000); 1,550 (2007); 1,498 (2012 projected); Race: 98.6% White, 0.1% Black, 0.1% Asian, 0.8% Hispanic of any race (2007); Density: 227.9 persons per square mile (2007); Average household size: 2.31 (2007); Median age: 37.6 (2007); Males per 100 females: 92.3 (2007); Marriage status: 19.0% never married, 62.3% now married, 8.6% widowed, 10.2% divorced (2000); Foreign born: 0.0% (2000); Ancestry (includes multiple ancestries): 23.4% German, 14.4% Other groups, 12.2% English, 10.6% Irish, 9.6% United States or American (2000).
Economy: Single-family building permits issued: 0 (2007); Multi-family building permits issued: 0 (2007); Employment by occupation: 14.3% management, 10.4% professional, 18.3% services, 22.2% sales, 0.1% farming, 10.4% construction, 24.3% production (2000).
Income: Per capita income: $23,835 (2007); Median household income: $45,370 (2007); Average household income: $54,978 (2007); Percent of households with income of $100,000 or more: 12.8% (2007); Poverty rate: 3.8% (2000).
Education: Percent of population age 25 and over with: High school diploma (including GED) or higher: 86.0% (2007); Bachelor's degree or higher: 10.2% (2007); Master's degree or higher: 5.0% (2007).

School District(s)

Roxana CUSD 1 (PK-12)
2005-06 Enrollment: 2,029 . . . . (618) 254-7544
Housing: Homeownership rate: 71.4% (2007); Median home value: $72,667 (2007); Median rent: $401 per month (2000); Median age of housing: 51 years (2000).
Safety: Violent crime rate: 26.6 per 10,000 population; Property crime rate: 432.2 per 10,000 population (2006).
Transportation: Commute to work: 94.6% car, 1.1% public transportation, 2.3% walk, 2.0% work from home (2000); Travel time to work: 31.6% less than 15 minutes, 26.4% 15 to 30 minutes, 20.0% 30 to 45 minutes, 15.7% 45 to 60 minutes, 6.4% 60 minutes or more (2000)

SAINT JACOB (village). Covers a land area of 0.559 square miles and a water area of 0 square miles. Located at 38.71° N. Lat.; 89.76° W. Long. Elevation is 512 feet.
History: St. Jacob was built near the site of Fort Chilton, established in 1812.
Population: 776 (1990); 801 (2000); 870 (2007); 904 (2012 projected); Race: 98.2% White, 0.0% Black, 0.1% Asian, 2.6% Hispanic of any race (2007); Density: 1,556.6 persons per square mile (2007); Average household size: 2.58 (2007); Median age: 35.4 (2007); Males per 100 females: 98.6 (2007); Marriage status: 22.7% never married, 61.1% now married, 3.6% widowed, 12.5% divorced (2000); Foreign born: 0.4% (2000); Ancestry (includes multiple ancestries): 48.5% German, 11.0% Other groups, 10.2% Irish, 7.0% United States or American, 6.1% French (except Basque) (2000).
Economy: Single-family building permits issued: 2 (2007); Multi-family building permits issued: 0 (2007); Employment by occupation: 13.8% management, 8.0% professional, 12.8% services, 26.6% sales, 0.0% farming, 15.3% construction, 23.5% production (2000).
Income: Per capita income: $25,951 (2007); Median household income: $57,206 (2007); Average household income: $66,996 (2007); Percent of households with income of $100,000 or more: 16.3% (2007); Poverty rate: 9.7% (2000).
Education: Percent of population age 25 and over with: High school diploma (including GED) or higher: 83.7% (2007); Bachelor's degree or higher: 11.2% (2007); Master's degree or higher: 2.5% (2007).

School District(s)

Triad CUSD 2 (PK-12)
2005-06 Enrollment: 3,873 . . . . (618) 667-8851
Housing: Homeownership rate: 81.0% (2007); Median home value: $109,491 (2007); Median rent: $309 per month (2000); Median age of housing: 38 years (2000).
Transportation: Commute to work: 89.6% car, 2.0% public transportation, 5.2% walk, 3.2% work from home (2000); Travel time to work: 31.1% less than 15 minutes, 23.1% 15 to 30 minutes, 28.0% 30 to 45 minutes, 12.6% 45 to 60 minutes, 5.1% 60 minutes or more (2000)

SOUTH ROXANA (village). Covers a land area of 1.587 square miles and a water area of 0 square miles. Located at 38.82° N. Lat.; 90.05° W. Long. Elevation is 440 feet.
Population: 1,961 (1990); 1,888 (2000); 2,051 (2007); 2,137 (2012 projected); Race: 97.3% White, 0.5% Black, 0.3% Asian, 0.9% Hispanic of any race (2007); Density: 1,292.7 persons per square mile (2007); Average household size: 2.60 (2007); Median age: 34.9 (2007); Males per 100 females: 96.6 (2007); Marriage status: 23.0% never married, 56.4% now married, 6.9% widowed, 13.7% divorced (2000); Foreign born: 1.0% (2000); Ancestry (includes multiple ancestries): 20.3% German, 18.1% Irish, 13.2% Other groups, 12.9% United States or American, 11.8% English (2000).
Economy: Single-family building permits issued: 0 (2007); Multi-family building permits issued: 0 (2007); Employment by occupation: 7.2% management, 8.5% professional, 19.9% services, 20.2% sales, 0.2% farming, 14.8% construction, 29.1% production (2000).
Income: Per capita income: $16,910 (2007); Median household income: $37,065 (2007); Average household income: $44,013 (2007); Percent of households with income of $100,000 or more: 3.8% (2007); Poverty rate: 19.8% (2000).
Education: Percent of population age 25 and over with: High school diploma (including GED) or higher: 73.3% (2007); Bachelor's degree or higher: 3.4% (2007); Master's degree or higher: 1.3% (2007).

School District(s)

Roxana CUSD 1 (PK-12)
2005-06 Enrollment: 2,029 . . . . (618) 254-7544

Housing: Homeownership rate: 74.5% (2007); Median home value: $62,344 (2007); Median rent: $351 per month (2000); Median age of housing: 40 years (2000).
Safety: Violent crime rate: 21.9 per 10,000 population; Property crime rate: 164.3 per 10,000 population (2006).
Transportation: Commute to work: 91.6% car, 0.5% public transportation, 2.0% walk, 3.2% work from home (2000); Travel time to work: 28.2% less than 15 minutes, 38.9% 15 to 30 minutes, 16.8% 30 to 45 minutes, 8.9% 45 to 60 minutes, 7.1% 60 minutes or more (2000)

TROY (city). Covers a land area of 4.183 square miles and a water area of 0 square miles. Located at 38.72° N. Lat.; 89.89° W. Long. Elevation is 561 feet.
History: Troy began as the community of Columbia, with a grist mill and tavern built by John G. Jarvis about 1814. When the property was purchased in 1819 by land speculators, it was renamed Troy, for the New York town. In 1857 Mechanicsburg, which had been platted in 1836, merged with Troy, and in 1891 Brookside did the same. Troy was incorporated as a city in 1892.
Population: 6,879 (1990); 8,524 (2000); 9,312 (2007); 9,801 (2012 projected); Race: 94.0% White, 2.1% Black, 1.0% Asian, 2.1% Hispanic of any race (2007); Density: 2,225.9 persons per square mile (2007); Average household size: 2.71 (2007); Median age: 34.0 (2007); Males per 100 females: 96.6 (2007); Marriage status: 22.4% never married, 62.3% now married, 5.6% widowed, 9.7% divorced (2000); Foreign born: 0.6% (2000); Ancestry (includes multiple ancestries): 36.0% German, 16.4% Irish, 11.9% Other groups, 10.2% English, 8.2% United States or American (2000).
Economy: Single-family building permits issued: 64 (2007); Multi-family building permits issued: 0 (2007); Employment by occupation: 13.8% management, 18.5% professional, 16.8% services, 26.8% sales, 0.0% farming, 8.4% construction, 15.8% production (2000).
Income: Per capita income: $27,177 (2007); Median household income: $65,577 (2007); Average household income: $73,186 (2007); Percent of households with income of $100,000 or more: 21.8% (2007); Poverty rate: 3.4% (2000).
Education: Percent of population age 25 and over with: High school diploma (including GED) or higher: 90.2% (2007); Bachelor's degree or higher: 24.6% (2007); Master's degree or higher: 8.5% (2007).

School District(s)

Triad CUSD 2 (PK-12)
2005-06 Enrollment: 3,873 . . . . (618) 667-8851

Housing: Homeownership rate: 74.0% (2007); Median home value: $138,072 (2007); Median rent: $459 per month (2000); Median age of housing: 17 years (2000).
Safety: Violent crime rate: 8.5 per 10,000 population; Property crime rate: 150.4 per 10,000 population (2006).
Newspapers: Times Tribune (Local news; Circulation 3,850)
Transportation: Commute to work: 93.3% car, 1.5% public transportation, 0.9% walk, 3.1% work from home (2000); Travel time to work: 25.2% less than 15 minutes, 36.2% 15 to 30 minutes, 27.6% 30 to 45 minutes, 6.0% 45 to 60 minutes, 5.0% 60 minutes or more (2000)

Additional Information Contacts

City of Troy. . . . . (618) 667-6741
http://www.ci.troy.il.us
Troy/Maryville Area Chamber of Commerce . . . . (618) 667-8769
http://www.troycoc.com

VENICE (city). Covers a land area of 1.875 square miles and a water area of 0 square miles. Located at 38.67° N. Lat.; 90.16° W. Long. Elevation is 410 feet.
History: Before the construction of levees, Venice experienced frequent flooding of its streets, which led to its being named after the Italian city of waterways. A ferry landing was established here in 1804. The town was platted in 1841 and incorporated in 1873.
Population: 3,571 (1990); 2,528 (2000); 2,425 (2007); 2,348 (2012 projected); Race: 4.2% White, 94.6% Black, 0.0% Asian, 0.8% Hispanic of any race (2007); Density: 1,293.6 persons per square mile (2007); Average household size: 2.60 (2007); Median age: 30.3 (2007); Males per 100 females: 81.9 (2007); Marriage status: 49.7% never married, 31.0% now married, 8.6% widowed, 10.7% divorced (2000); Foreign born: 0.2% (2000); Ancestry (includes multiple ancestries): 75.7% Other groups, 1.5% African, 1.4% German, 0.9% Irish, 0.8% United States or American (2000).
Economy: Single-family building permits issued: 0 (2007); Multi-family building permits issued: 0 (2007); Employment by occupation: 6.7% management, 10.5% professional, 24.1% services, 29.8% sales, 0.4% farming, 8.6% construction, 20.0% production (2000).
Income: Per capita income: $13,422 (2007); Median household income: $22,917 (2007); Average household income: $34,847 (2007); Percent of households with income of $100,000 or more: 7.0% (2007); Poverty rate: 39.6% (2000).
Education: Percent of population age 25 and over with: High school diploma (including GED) or higher: 67.1% (2007); Bachelor's degree or higher: 5.3% (2007); Master's degree or higher: 0.8% (2007).

School District(s)

Venice CUSD 3 (KG-12)
2005-06 Enrollment: 142 . . . . (618) 451-7953

Housing: Homeownership rate: 45.9% (2007); Median home value: $40,730 (2007); Median rent: $277 per month (2000); Median age of housing: 47 years (2000).
Safety: Violent crime rate: 200.2 per 10,000 population; Property crime rate: 179.7 per 10,000 population (2006).
Transportation: Commute to work: 81.9% car, 9.3% public transportation, 4.5% walk, 3.0% work from home (2000); Travel time to work: 30.8% less than 15 minutes, 40.6% 15 to 30 minutes, 18.3% 30 to 45 minutes, 4.1% 45 to 60 minutes, 6.2% 60 minutes or more (2000)

WILLIAMSON (village). Covers a land area of 1.518 square miles and a water area of 0.043 square miles. Located at 38.98° N. Lat.; 89.76° W. Long. Elevation is 604 feet.
Population: 278 (1990); 251 (2000); 292 (2007); 310 (2012 projected); Race: 97.6% White, 0.0% Black, 0.0% Asian, 0.0% Hispanic of any race (2007); Density: 192.4 persons per square mile (2007); Average household size: 2.43 (2007); Median age: 36.7 (2007); Males per 100 females: 111.6 (2007); Marriage status: 21.1% never married, 53.8% now married, 11.7% widowed, 13.5% divorced (2000); Foreign born: 0.0% (2000); Ancestry (includes multiple ancestries): 18.1% German, 14.9% Italian, 12.1% Irish, 11.6% English, 9.3% United States or American (2000).
Economy: Single-family building permits issued: 0 (2007); Multi-family building permits issued: 0 (2007); Employment by occupation: 3.0% management, 13.0% professional, 30.0% services, 17.0% sales, 0.0% farming, 17.0% construction, 20.0% production (2000).
Income: Per capita income: $15,231 (2007); Median household income: $29,286 (2007); Average household income: $37,063 (2007); Percent of households with income of $100,000 or more: 4.2% (2007); Poverty rate: 14.4% (2000).
Education: Percent of population age 25 and over with: High school diploma (including GED) or higher: 79.9% (2007); Bachelor's degree or higher: 7.7% (2007); Master's degree or higher: 1.5% (2007).
Housing: Homeownership rate: 86.7% (2007); Median home value: $49,091 (2007); Median rent: $317 per month (2000); Median age of housing: 59 years (2000).
Safety: Violent crime rate: 40.7 per 10,000 population; Property crime rate: 406.5 per 10,000 population (2006).
Transportation: Commute to work: 98.0% car, 0.0% public transportation, 2.0% walk, 0.0% work from home (2000); Travel time to work: 20.4% less than 15 minutes, 27.6% 15 to 30 minutes, 28.6% 30 to 45 minutes, 17.3% 45 to 60 minutes, 6.1% 60 minutes or more (2000)

WOOD RIVER (city). Covers a land area of 6.056 square miles and a water area of 0.025 square miles. Located at 38.86° N. Lat.; 90.08° W. Long. Elevation is 436 feet.
History: Named for a small stream that used to be in the city. Wood River was selected by the Standard Oil Company in 1907 as the site of its refinery because of the rail and river transportation available here.
Population: 11,628 (1990); 11,296 (2000); 10,895 (2007); 10,665 (2012 projected); Race: 96.9% White, 0.9% Black, 0.6% Asian, 1.8% Hispanic of any race (2007); Density: 1,799.0 persons per square mile (2007); Average household size: 2.33 (2007); Median age: 36.7 (2007); Males per 100 females: 91.6 (2007); Marriage status: 21.8% never married, 55.5% now married, 9.1% widowed, 13.6% divorced (2000); Foreign born: 0.6% (2000); Ancestry (includes multiple ancestries): 21.5% German, 13.5% Irish, 12.7% United States or American, 10.3% English, 9.7% Other groups (2000).
Economy: Single-family building permits issued: 7 (2007); Multi-family building permits issued: 0 (2007); Employment by occupation: 10.5% management, 14.5% professional, 19.4% services, 27.9% sales, 0.0% farming, 8.3% construction, 19.4% production (2000).

Income: Per capita income: $20,451 (2007); Median household income: $38,467 (2007); Average household income: $47,014 (2007); Percent of households with income of $100,000 or more: 7.9% (2007); Poverty rate: 14.8% (2000).
Education: Percent of population age 25 and over with: High school diploma (including GED) or higher: 83.9% (2007); Bachelor's degree or higher: 11.0% (2007); Master's degree or higher: 3.3% (2007).

School District(s)

East Alton-Wood River CHSD 14 (09-12)
2005-06 Enrollment: 771 . . . . (618) 254-3151
Wood River-Hartford ESD 15 (PK-08)
2005-06 Enrollment: 833 . . . . (618) 254-0607

Housing: Homeownership rate: 66.8% (2007); Median home value: $81,088 (2007); Median rent: $375 per month (2000); Median age of housing: 47 years (2000).
Safety: Violent crime rate: 45.5 per 10,000 population; Property crime rate: 505.2 per 10,000 population (2006).
Transportation: Commute to work: 93.8% car, 1.2% public transportation, 1.6% walk, 2.7% work from home (2000); Travel time to work: 34.6% less than 15 minutes, 31.5% 15 to 30 minutes, 21.1% 30 to 45 minutes, 9.5% 45 to 60 minutes, 3.2% 60 minutes or more (2000)

Additional Information Contacts

City of Wood River . . . . (618) 251-3100
http://www.woodriver.org

WORDEN (village). Covers a land area of 0.660 square miles and a water area of 0 square miles. Located at 38.93° N. Lat.; 89.84° W. Long. Elevation is 568 feet.
History: Incorporated 1877.
Population: 900 (1990); 905 (2000); 883 (2007); 877 (2012 projected); Race: 99.5% White, 0.0% Black, 0.0% Asian, 2.3% Hispanic of any race (2007); Density: 1,337.0 persons per square mile (2007); Average household size: 2.33 (2007); Median age: 36.6 (2007); Males per 100 females: 90.3 (2007); Marriage status: 21.3% never married, 58.9% now married, 10.4% widowed, 9.4% divorced (2000); Foreign born: 0.2% (2000); Ancestry (includes multiple ancestries): 41.8% German, 16.8% Irish, 9.8% English, 7.2% Other groups, 5.1% United States or American (2000).
Economy: Single-family building permits issued: 5 (2007); Multi-family building permits issued: 0 (2007); Employment by occupation: 6.6% management, 14.9% professional, 15.9% services, 21.6% sales, 0.9% farming, 14.5% construction, 25.6% production (2000).
Income: Per capita income: $22,528 (2007); Median household income: $43,583 (2007); Average household income: $52,487 (2007); Percent of households with income of $100,000 or more: 8.2% (2007); Poverty rate: 12.0% (2000).
Education: Percent of population age 25 and over with: High school diploma (including GED) or higher: 80.2% (2007); Bachelor's degree or higher: 8.1% (2007); Master's degree or higher: 2.9% (2007).

School District(s)

Edwardsville CUSD 7 (PK-12)
2005-06 Enrollment: 7,365 . . . . (618) 656-1182

Housing: Homeownership rate: 78.9% (2007); Median home value: $73,966 (2007); Median rent: $263 per month (2000); Median age of housing: 55 years (2000).
Safety: Violent crime rate: 0.0 per 10,000 population; Property crime rate: 80.2 per 10,000 population (2006).
Newspapers: Madison County Chronicle (Local news; Circulation 1,225)
Transportation: Commute to work: 93.5% car, 0.0% public transportation, 4.1% walk, 1.9% work from home (2000); Travel time to work: 21.8% less than 15 minutes, 22.8% 15 to 30 minutes, 33.3% 30 to 45 minutes, 13.0% 45 to 60 minutes, 9.1% 60 minutes or more (2000)

Marion County

Located in south central Illinois; drained by Skillet Fork, Crooked Creek, and a headstream of Kaskaskia River. Covers a land area of 572.26 square miles, a water area of 3.44 square miles, and is located in the Central Time Zone. The county was founded in 1823. County seat is Salem.

Marion County is part of the Centralia, IL Micropolitan Statistical Area. The entire metro area includes: Marion County, IL

Weather Station: Salem Leckrone Airport Elevation: 567 feet

	Jan	Feb	Mar	Apr	May	Jun	Jul	Aug	Sep	Oct	Nov	Dec
High	38	44	55	67	77	85	89	87	81	69	55	43
Low	21	25	34	44	54	63	67	65	57	45	36	26
Precip	2.4	2.5	4.0	4.2	4.3	4.2	3.8	3.3	3.2	3.1	4.0	3.2
Snow	5.4	3.5	1.1	0.3	0.0	0.0	0.0	0.0	0.0	tr	0.7	2.7

High and Low temperatures in degrees Fahrenheit; Precipitation and Snow in inches

Population: 41,561 (1990); 41,691 (2000); 39,714 (2007); 38,224 (2012 projected); Race: 93.6% White, 4.0% Black, 0.7% Asian, 1.0% Hispanic of any race (2007); Density: 69.4 persons per square mile (2007); Average household size: 2.49 (2007); Median age: 40.2 (2007); Males per 100 females: 93.2 (2007).
Religion: Five largest groups: 17.2% Southern Baptist Convention, 10.9% Christian Churches and Churches of Christ, 8.5% Catholic Church, 6.5% The United Methodist Church, 5.3% Lutheran Church—Missouri Synod (2000).
Economy: Unemployment rate: 6.6% (4/2008); Total civilian labor force: 18,956 (4/2008); Leading industries: 25.2% manufacturing; 22.2% health care and social assistance; 12.7% retail trade (2005); Farms: 1,095 totaling 261,899 acres (2002); Companies that employ 500 or more persons: 2 (2006); Companies that employ 100 to 499 persons: 19 (2006); Companies that employ less than 100 persons: 1,025 (2006); Black-owned businesses: n/a (2002); Hispanic-owned businesses: n/a (2002); Asian-owned businesses: n/a (2002); Women-owned businesses: 547 (2002); Retail sales per capita: $11,969 (2008). Single-family building permits issued: 12 (2007); Multi-family building permits issued: 0 (2007).
Income: Per capita income: $20,409 (2007); Median household income: $40,346 (2007); Average household income: $50,100 (2007); Percent of households with income of $100,000 or more: 8.3% (2007); Poverty rate: 16.1% (2005); Bankruptcy rate: 4.04% (2007).
Taxes: Total county taxes per capita: $93 (2006); County property taxes per capita: $70 (2006).
Education: Percent of population age 25 and over with: High school diploma (including GED) or higher: 79.5% (2007); Bachelor's degree or higher: 12.2% (2007); Master's degree or higher: 4.1% (2007).
Housing: Homeownership rate: 77.0% (2007); Median home value: $73,902 (2007); Median rent: $266 per month (2000); Median age of housing: 37 years (2000).
Health: Birth rate: 127.6 per 10,000 population (2007); Death rate: 125.8 per 10,000 population (2007); Age-adjusted cancer mortality rate: 250.4 deaths per 100,000 population (2005); Number of physicians: 17.1 per 10,000 population (2005); Hospital beds: 38.9 per 10,000 population (2004); Hospital admissions: 2,179.6 per 10,000 population (2004).
Elections: 2004 Presidential election results: 54.7% Bush, 44.7% Kerry, 0.1% Nader, 0.6% Badnarik
National and State Parks: Stephen A Forbes State Park

Additional Information Contacts

Marion County Government . . . . (618) 548-3400

City of Centralia . . . . (618) 533-7623
http://www.city.centralia.il.us
City of Salem . . . . (618) 548-2222
http://www.salemil.us
Greater Salem Chamber of Commerce . . . . (618) 548-3010
http://www.salemilchamber.com
The Greater Centralia Chamber of Commerce . . . . (618) 532-6789
http://www.centraliail.com

Marion County Communities

ALMA (village). Covers a land area of 1.080 square miles and a water area of 0 square miles. Located at 38.72° N. Lat.; 88.91° W. Long. Elevation is 623 feet.
Population: 419 (1990); 386 (2000); 338 (2007); 318 (2012 projected); Race: 98.8% White, 0.6% Black, 0.0% Asian, 0.0% Hispanic of any race (2007); Density: 313.0 persons per square mile (2007); Average household size: 2.25 (2007); Median age: 38.1 (2007); Males per 100 females: 96.5 (2007); Marriage status: 27.9% never married, 44.9% now married, 8.2% widowed, 19.0% divorced (2000); Foreign born: 0.8% (2000); Ancestry (includes multiple ancestries): 39.8% United States or American, 15.6% German, 9.1% Irish, 7.8% English, 3.0% Other groups (2000).
Economy: Employment by occupation: 4.9% management, 9.8% professional, 24.5% services, 15.3% sales, 0.0% farming, 14.7% construction, 30.7% production (2000).

Income: Per capita income: $17,389 (2007); Median household income: $32,500 (2007); Average household income: $39,183 (2007); Percent of households with income of $100,000 or more: 8.0% (2007); Poverty rate: 24.9% (2000).
Education: Percent of population age 25 and over with: High school diploma (including GED) or higher: 73.7% (2007); Bachelor's degree or higher: 5.8% (2007); Master's degree or higher: 0.9% (2007).
Housing: Homeownership rate: 79.3% (2007); Median home value: $43,667 (2007); Median rent: $125 per month (2000); Median age of housing: 39 years (2000).
Transportation: Commute to work: 95.8% car, 0.0% public transportation, 4.2% walk, 0.0% work from home (2000); Travel time to work: 28.1% less than 15 minutes, 52.1% 15 to 30 minutes, 14.4% 30 to 45 minutes, 2.4% 45 to 60 minutes, 3.0% 60 minutes or more (2000)

CENTRAL CITY (village). Covers a land area of 0.580 square miles and a water area of 0 square miles. Located at 38.54° N. Lat.; 89.12° W. Long. Elevation is 486 feet.
History: Central City was settled by German immigrants, and incorporated in 1857.
Population: 1,414 (1990); 1,371 (2000); 1,343 (2007); 1,271 (2012 projected); Race: 93.2% White, 2.6% Black, 0.3% Asian, 2.9% Hispanic of any race (2007); Density: 2,317.1 persons per square mile (2007); Average household size: 2.54 (2007); Median age: 34.3 (2007); Males per 100 females: 94.9 (2007); Marriage status: 28.2% never married, 53.8% now married, 6.1% widowed, 11.9% divorced (2000); Foreign born: 0.5% (2000); Ancestry (includes multiple ancestries): 26.8% German, 13.5% Other groups, 13.4% Irish, 12.2% United States or American, 10.0% English (2000).
Economy: Employment by occupation: 7.1% management, 13.8% professional, 19.7% services, 17.4% sales, 0.0% farming, 13.6% construction, 28.4% production (2000).
Income: Per capita income: $15,977 (2007); Median household income: $34,946 (2007); Average household income: $40,562 (2007); Percent of households with income of $100,000 or more: 3.2% (2007); Poverty rate: 15.1% (2000).
Education: Percent of population age 25 and over with: High school diploma (including GED) or higher: 76.1% (2007); Bachelor's degree or higher: 6.3% (2007); Master's degree or higher: 1.3% (2007).
Housing: Homeownership rate: 74.1% (2007); Median home value: $45,217 (2007); Median rent: $281 per month (2000); Median age of housing: 32 years (2000).
Safety: Violent crime rate: 22.4 per 10,000 population; Property crime rate: 394.9 per 10,000 population (2006).
Transportation: Commute to work: 92.7% car, 0.0% public transportation, 2.6% walk, 3.9% work from home (2000); Travel time to work: 58.8% less than 15 minutes, 26.4% 15 to 30 minutes, 7.1% 30 to 45 minutes, 3.4% 45 to 60 minutes, 4.4% 60 minutes or more (2000)

CENTRALIA (city). Covers a land area of 7.502 square miles and a water area of 0.137 square miles. Located at 38.52° N. Lat.; 89.13° W. Long. Elevation is 492 feet.
History: Centralia was laid out by the Illinois Central Railroad in 1853, and named for the company. Many early residents were of German descent. Since Centralia was located in a fruit-producing area, the railroad company was interested in refrigerated cars for shipping the fruit, and in 1868 the first such train began operation between Centralia and Chicago.
Population: 14,585 (1990); 14,136 (2000); 13,354 (2007); 12,762 (2012 projected); Race: 86.1% White, 10.4% Black, 0.9% Asian, 1.3% Hispanic of any race (2007); Density: 1,780.2 persons per square mile (2007); Average household size: 2.43 (2007); Median age: 41.1 (2007); Males per 100 females: 86.3 (2007); Marriage status: 21.4% never married, 53.4% now married, 10.9% widowed, 14.2% divorced (2000); Foreign born: 1.3% (2000); Ancestry (includes multiple ancestries): 23.4% German, 14.6% Other groups, 11.1% United States or American, 10.0% Irish, 9.9% English (2000).
Economy: Single-family building permits issued: 6 (2007); Multi-family building permits issued: 0 (2007); Employment by occupation: 7.0% management, 16.8% professional, 20.2% services, 20.7% sales, 0.6% farming, 6.3% construction, 28.5% production (2000).
Income: Per capita income: $19,768 (2007); Median household income: $35,575 (2007); Average household income: $46,699 (2007); Percent of households with income of $100,000 or more: 7.1% (2007); Poverty rate: 14.6% (2000).
Education: Percent of population age 25 and over with: High school diploma (including GED) or higher: 75.4% (2007); Bachelor's degree or higher: 14.4% (2007); Master's degree or higher: 5.4% (2007).

School District(s)

Central City SD 133 (PK-08)
2005-06 Enrollment: 264 . . . . (618) 532-9521
Centralia HSD 200 (09-12)
2005-06 Enrollment: 1,087 . . . . (618) 532-7391
Centralia SD 135 (PK-08)
2005-06 Enrollment: 1,407 . . . . (618) 532-1907
Clinton/Marion/Washington Roe (PK-12)
2005-06 Enrollment: 276 . . . . (618) 594-2432
Dept of Corrections Sch Dist 428 (08-12)
2005-06 Enrollment: 2,271 . . . . (217) 522-2666
Grand Prairie CCSD 6 (KG-08)
2005-06 Enrollment: 96 . . . . (618) 249-6289
Kaskaskia Spec Educ District (03-12)
2005-06 Enrollment: 139 . . . . (618) 532-4721
North Wamac SD 186 (PK-08)
2005-06 Enrollment: 87 . . . . (618) 532-1826
Raccoon Cons SD 1 (KG-08)
2005-06 Enrollment: 276 . . . . (618) 532-7329
Willow Grove SD 46 (PK-08)
2005-06 Enrollment: 210 . . . . (618) 532-3313

Two-year College(s)

Kaskaskia College (Public)
Fall 2007 Enrollment: 5,041 . . . . (618) 545-3000
2007-08 Tuition: In-state $3,968; Out-of-state $8,977

Housing: Homeownership rate: 69.5% (2007); Median home value: $65,062 (2007); Median rent: $277 per month (2000); Median age of housing: 45 years (2000).
Hospitals: St. Mary's Good Samaritan (276 beds)
Safety: Violent crime rate: 104.4 per 10,000 population; Property crime rate: 602.2 per 10,000 population (2006).
Newspapers: The Morning Sentinel (Local news; Circulation 0)
Transportation: Commute to work: 92.7% car, 0.7% public transportation, 3.4% walk, 2.5% work from home (2000); Travel time to work: 65.6% less than 15 minutes, 19.4% 15 to 30 minutes, 8.4% 30 to 45 minutes, 2.3% 45 to 60 minutes, 4.3% 60 minutes or more (2000); Amtrak: Service available.

Additional Information Contacts

City of Centralia . . . . (618) 533-7623
http://www.city.centralia.il.us
The Greater Centralia Chamber of Commerce . . . . (618) 532-6789
http://www.centraliail.com

IUKA (village). Covers a land area of 0.792 square miles and a water area of 0.002 square miles. Located at 38.61° N. Lat.; 88.78° W. Long. Elevation is 518 feet.
Population: 494 (1990); 598 (2000); 558 (2007); 541 (2012 projected); Race: 98.9% White, 0.0% Black, 0.2% Asian, 1.1% Hispanic of any race (2007); Density: 704.2 persons per square mile (2007); Average household size: 2.70 (2007); Median age: 34.8 (2007); Males per 100 females: 90.4 (2007); Marriage status: 15.5% never married, 62.8% now married, 9.2% widowed, 12.5% divorced (2000); Foreign born: 0.3% (2000); Ancestry (includes multiple ancestries): 15.7% German, 12.6% Irish, 11.7% United States or American, 9.3% Other groups, 8.9% English (2000).
Economy: Employment by occupation: 2.4% management, 15.9% professional, 16.7% services, 15.5% sales, 0.0% farming, 8.6% construction, 40.8% production (2000).
Income: Per capita income: $13,239 (2007); Median household income: $30,109 (2007); Average household income: $35,688 (2007); Percent of households with income of $100,000 or more: 2.9% (2007); Poverty rate: 16.7% (2000).
Education: Percent of population age 25 and over with: High school diploma (including GED) or higher: 72.9% (2007); Bachelor's degree or higher: 5.5% (2007); Master's degree or higher: 2.3% (2007).

School District(s)

Iuka CCSD 7 (PK-08)
2005-06 Enrollment: 300 . . . . (618) 323-6233

Housing: Homeownership rate: 81.6% (2007); Median home value: $51,842 (2007); Median rent: $217 per month (2000); Median age of housing: 40 years (2000).
Transportation: Commute to work: 96.5% car, 0.0% public transportation, 0.9% walk, 0.0% work from home (2000); Travel time to work: 19.9% less

than 15 minutes, 41.2% 15 to 30 minutes, 14.2% 30 to 45 minutes, 9.3% 45 to 60 minutes, 15.5% 60 minutes or more (2000)

JUNCTION CITY (village). Aka Glenridge. Covers a land area of 0.675 square miles and a water area of 0.018 square miles. Located at 38.58° N. Lat.; 89.12° W. Long. Elevation is 492 feet.

Population: 539 (1990); 559 (2000); 562 (2007); 533 (2012 projected); Race: 98.2% White, 0.0% Black, 0.4% Asian, 0.4% Hispanic of any race (2007); Density: 832.3 persons per square mile (2007); Average household size: 2.68 (2007); Median age: 33.9 (2007); Males per 100 females: 94.5 (2007); Marriage status: 16.3% never married, 67.4% now married, 7.3% widowed, 9.0% divorced (2000); Foreign born: 0.6% (2000); Ancestry (includes multiple ancestries): 18.7% German, 18.5% United States or American, 13.1% Irish, 10.8% Other groups, 5.8% English (2000).

Economy: Employment by occupation: 0.0% management, 7.2% professional, 19.6% services, 11.9% sales, 0.0% farming, 11.5% construction, 49.8% production (2000).

Income: Per capita income: $15,876 (2007); Median household income: $41,136 (2007); Average household income: $42,488 (2007); Percent of households with income of $100,000 or more: 1.0% (2007); Poverty rate: 9.9% (2000).

Education: Percent of population age 25 and over with: High school diploma (including GED) or higher: 58.1% (2007); Bachelor's degree or higher: 4.0% (2007); Master's degree or higher: 1.7% (2007).

Housing: Homeownership rate: 86.7% (2007); Median home value: $46,129 (2007); Median rent: $219 per month (2000); Median age of housing: 24 years (2000).

Safety: Violent crime rate: 0.0 per 10,000 population; Property crime rate: 36.4 per 10,000 population (2006).

Transportation: Commute to work: 91.6% car, 1.3% public transportation, 0.0% walk, 3.6% work from home (2000); Travel time to work: 20.7% less than 15 minutes, 56.2% 15 to 30 minutes, 8.3% 30 to 45 minutes, 4.1% 45 to 60 minutes, 10.6% 60 minutes or more (2000)

KELL (village). Covers a land area of 1.010 square miles and a water area of 0 square miles. Located at 38.49° N. Lat.; 88.90° W. Long. Elevation is 610 feet.

Population: 213 (1990); 231 (2000); 204 (2007); 200 (2012 projected); Race: 100.0% White, 0.0% Black, 0.0% Asian, 0.0% Hispanic of any race (2007); Density: 202.0 persons per square mile (2007); Average household size: 2.68 (2007); Median age: 40.9 (2007); Males per 100 females: 96.2 (2007); Marriage status: 15.9% never married, 72.8% now married, 6.0% widowed, 5.3% divorced (2000); Foreign born: 0.0% (2000); Ancestry (includes multiple ancestries): 24.9% United States or American, 19.7% German, 14.5% Irish, 8.1% English, 5.8% Other groups (2000).

Economy: Employment by occupation: 6.3% management, 22.9% professional, 8.3% services, 20.8% sales, 0.0% farming, 15.6% construction, 26.0% production (2000).

Income: Per capita income: $18,113 (2007); Median household income: $46,667 (2007); Average household income: $48,618 (2007); Percent of households with income of $100,000 or more: 7.9% (2007); Poverty rate: 0.0% (2000).

Taxes: Total city taxes per capita: $27 (2006); City property taxes per capita: $27 (2006).

Education: Percent of population age 25 and over with: High school diploma (including GED) or higher: 76.3% (2007); Bachelor's degree or higher: 11.9% (2007); Master's degree or higher: 5.9% (2007).

School District(s)

Kell Cons SD 2 (KG-08)
2005-06 Enrollment: 108 . . . . (618) 822-6234

Housing: Homeownership rate: 92.1% (2007); Median home value: $52,000 (2007); Median rent: $175 per month (2000); Median age of housing: 49 years (2000).

Transportation: Commute to work: 95.8% car, 0.0% public transportation, 4.2% walk, 0.0% work from home (2000); Travel time to work: 13.5% less than 15 minutes, 53.1% 15 to 30 minutes, 18.8% 30 to 45 minutes, 3.1% 45 to 60 minutes, 11.5% 60 minutes or more (2000)

KINMUNDY (city). Covers a land area of 1.031 square miles and a water area of 0 square miles. Located at 38.77° N. Lat.; 88.85° W. Long. Elevation is 604 feet.

Population: 879 (1990); 892 (2000); 703 (2007); 681 (2012 projected); Race: 97.9% White, 0.4% Black, 0.0% Asian, 0.3% Hispanic of any race (2007); Density: 681.9 persons per square mile (2007); Average household size: 2.38 (2007); Median age: 38.5 (2007); Males per 100 females: 91.6 (2007); Marriage status: 19.6% never married, 56.7% now married, 12.1% widowed, 11.5% divorced (2000); Foreign born: 0.2% (2000); Ancestry (includes multiple ancestries): 22.7% United States or American, 12.5% German, 8.2% Irish, 6.9% Other groups, 5.2% English (2000).

Economy: Employment by occupation: 9.3% management, 16.6% professional, 18.5% services, 18.0% sales, 3.0% farming, 9.3% construction, 25.3% production (2000).

Income: Per capita income: $18,090 (2007); Median household income: $33,796 (2007); Average household income: $43,110 (2007); Percent of households with income of $100,000 or more: 6.8% (2007); Poverty rate: 12.8% (2000).

Education: Percent of population age 25 and over with: High school diploma (including GED) or higher: 75.6% (2007); Bachelor's degree or higher: 8.5% (2007); Master's degree or higher: 1.1% (2007).

School District(s)

South Central Cud 401 (PK-12)
2005-06 Enrollment: 731 . . . . (618) 547-3414

Housing: Homeownership rate: 76.6% (2007); Median home value: $52,308 (2007); Median rent: $206 per month (2000); Median age of housing: 37 years (2000).

Newspapers: Kinmundy Express (Community news; Circulation 900)

Transportation: Commute to work: 90.7% car, 0.0% public transportation, 3.6% walk, 3.3% work from home (2000); Travel time to work: 24.4% less than 15 minutes, 47.6% 15 to 30 minutes, 13.9% 30 to 45 minutes, 8.8% 45 to 60 minutes, 5.4% 60 minutes or more (2000)

ODIN (village). Covers a land area of 1.010 square miles and a water area of 0 square miles. Located at 38.61° N. Lat.; 89.05° W. Long. Elevation is 528 feet.

History: Odin developed as a mining and agricultural center along the Illinois Central Railroad.

Population: 1,150 (1990); 1,122 (2000); 1,083 (2007); 1,051 (2012 projected); Race: 98.5% White, 0.6% Black, 0.1% Asian, 0.7% Hispanic of any race (2007); Density: 1,072.2 persons per square mile (2007); Average household size: 2.50 (2007); Median age: 40.0 (2007); Males per 100 females: 84.2 (2007); Marriage status: 17.5% never married, 60.7% now married, 5.5% widowed, 16.2% divorced (2000); Foreign born: 0.3% (2000); Ancestry (includes multiple ancestries): 22.5% United States or American, 16.8% German, 15.8% Irish, 7.1% Other groups, 6.5% English (2000).

Economy: Single-family building permits issued: 0 (2007); Multi-family building permits issued: 0 (2007); Employment by occupation: 6.3% management, 16.0% professional, 18.1% services, 21.9% sales, 0.0% farming, 8.7% construction, 29.0% production (2000).

Income: Per capita income: $17,812 (2007); Median household income: $38,661 (2007); Average household income: $43,025 (2007); Percent of households with income of $100,000 or more: 4.6% (2007); Poverty rate: 11.7% (2000).

Education: Percent of population age 25 and over with: High school diploma (including GED) or higher: 77.0% (2007); Bachelor's degree or higher: 7.0% (2007); Master's degree or higher: 0.1% (2007).

School District(s)

Odin CHSD 700 (09-12)
2005-06 Enrollment: 111 . . . . (618) 775-8266
Odin SD 122 (PK-08)
2005-06 Enrollment: 263 . . . . (618) 775-8266

Housing: Homeownership rate: 76.9% (2007); Median home value: $51,900 (2007); Median rent: $265 per month (2000); Median age of housing: 35 years (2000).

Transportation: Commute to work: 95.4% car, 0.0% public transportation, 2.2% walk, 1.6% work from home (2000); Travel time to work: 47.3% less than 15 minutes, 32.0% 15 to 30 minutes, 11.7% 30 to 45 minutes, 2.9% 45 to 60 minutes, 6.1% 60 minutes or more (2000)

PATOKA (village). Covers a land area of 1.100 square miles and a water area of 0 square miles. Located at 38.75° N. Lat.; 89.09° W. Long. Elevation is 505 feet.

History: Patoka was named for an Indian chief. Oil was discovered in Patoka in 1937, bringing new growth to the town.

Population: 656 (1990); 633 (2000); 595 (2007); 596 (2012 projected); Race: 98.5% White, 0.0% Black, 0.3% Asian, 1.8% Hispanic of any race (2007); Density: 540.9 persons per square mile (2007); Average household size: 2.23 (2007); Median age: 41.1 (2007); Males per 100 females: 95.1 (2007); Marriage status: 20.5% never married, 55.5% now married, 12.4% widowed, 11.6% divorced (2000); Foreign born: 0.0% (2000); Ancestry

(includes multiple ancestries): 24.3% German, 12.5% Irish, 11.8% English, 10.7% United States or American, 7.8% Other groups (2000).
Economy: Employment by occupation: 6.9% management, 14.5% professional, 23.3% services, 16.7% sales, 0.7% farming, 9.1% construction, 28.7% production (2000).
Income: Per capita income: $18,382 (2007); Median household income: $33,611 (2007); Average household income: $40,964 (2007); Percent of households with income of $100,000 or more: 4.1% (2007); Poverty rate: 13.3% (2000).
Education: Percent of population age 25 and over with: High school diploma (including GED) or higher: 74.9% (2007); Bachelor's degree or higher: 4.9% (2007); Master's degree or higher: 1.7% (2007).

School District(s)

Patoka CUSD 100 (KG-12)
2005-06 Enrollment: 270 . . . . (618) 432-5440
Housing: Homeownership rate: 79.8% (2007); Median home value: $60,263 (2007); Median rent: $188 per month (2000); Median age of housing: 41 years (2000).
Transportation: Commute to work: 93.0% car, 0.4% public transportation, 5.2% walk, 1.1% work from home (2000); Travel time to work: 25.8% less than 15 minutes, 38.2% 15 to 30 minutes, 26.6% 30 to 45 minutes, 2.2% 45 to 60 minutes, 7.1% 60 minutes or more (2000)

SALEM (city). County seat. Covers a land area of 6.100 square miles and a water area of 0.157 square miles. Located at 38.62° N. Lat.; 88.94° W. Long. Elevation is 538 feet.
History: Salem was laid out in 1813 on the St. Louis-Vincennes stagecoach route, and incorporated in 1837. William Jennings Bryan (1860-1925) was born and grew up in Salem. Oil was discovered in Salem in 1939.
Population: 7,795 (1990); 7,909 (2000); 7,452 (2007); 7,099 (2012 projected); Race: 96.8% White, 1.0% Black, 1.2% Asian, 0.8% Hispanic of any race (2007); Density: 1,221.5 persons per square mile (2007); Average household size: 2.40 (2007); Median age: 40.9 (2007); Males per 100 females: 88.3 (2007); Marriage status: 21.6% never married, 56.7% now married, 9.4% widowed, 12.2% divorced (2000); Foreign born: 0.8% (2000); Ancestry (includes multiple ancestries): 18.8% German, 10.6% English, 10.5% Irish, 10.2% United States or American, 7.7% Other groups (2000).
Economy: Single-family building permits issued: 6 (2007); Multi-family building permits issued: 0 (2007); Employment by occupation: 9.0% management, 19.9% professional, 15.8% services, 21.5% sales, 0.0% farming, 5.5% construction, 28.4% production (2000).
Income: Per capita income: $19,331 (2007); Median household income: $36,816 (2007); Average household income: $45,193 (2007); Percent of households with income of $100,000 or more: 6.8% (2007); Poverty rate: 9.2% (2000).
Education: Percent of population age 25 and over with: High school diploma (including GED) or higher: 77.5% (2007); Bachelor's degree or higher: 13.4% (2007); Master's degree or higher: 3.8% (2007).

School District(s)

Clinton/Marion/Washington Roe (PK-12)
2005-06 Enrollment: 276 . . . . (618) 594-2432
Marion/Clinton/Wash Co Rds
2005-06 Enrollment: n/a . . . . (618) 548-6385
Salem CHSD 600 (09-12)
2005-06 Enrollment: 814 . . . . (618) 548-0727
Salem SD 111 (PK-08)
2005-06 Enrollment: 993 . . . . (618) 548-7702
Selmaville CCSD 10 (KG-08)
2005-06 Enrollment: 235 . . . . (618) 548-2416
Housing: Homeownership rate: 69.9% (2007); Median home value: $78,381 (2007); Median rent: $277 per month (2000); Median age of housing: 35 years (2000).
Hospitals: Salem Township Hospital (46 beds)
Safety: Violent crime rate: 19.8 per 10,000 population; Property crime rate: 470.0 per 10,000 population (2006).
Newspapers: Salem Times-Commoner (Local news; Circulation 4,350); Town & County Crier (Local news; Circulation 15,000)
Transportation: Commute to work: 94.6% car, 0.0% public transportation, 2.9% walk, 1.9% work from home (2000); Travel time to work: 63.2% less than 15 minutes, 17.8% 15 to 30 minutes, 11.4% 30 to 45 minutes, 3.7% 45 to 60 minutes, 3.9% 60 minutes or more (2000)
Additional Information Contacts
City of Salem . . . . (618) 548-2222
http://www.salemil.us
Greater Salem Chamber of Commerce . . . . (618) 548-3010
http://www.salemilchamber.com

SANDOVAL (village). Covers a land area of 0.960 square miles and a water area of 0 square miles. Located at 38.61° N. Lat.; 89.12° W. Long. Elevation is 509 feet.
History: Incorporated 1859.
Population: 1,535 (1990); 1,434 (2000); 1,308 (2007); 1,271 (2012 projected); Race: 97.5% White, 0.6% Black, 0.2% Asian, 1.4% Hispanic of any race (2007); Density: 1,362.7 persons per square mile (2007); Average household size: 2.53 (2007); Median age: 35.4 (2007); Males per 100 females: 94.4 (2007); Marriage status: 22.2% never married, 58.1% now married, 4.0% widowed, 15.7% divorced (2000); Foreign born: 0.7% (2000); Ancestry (includes multiple ancestries): 22.5% United States or American, 16.2% German, 11.9% Other groups, 8.0% Irish, 6.5% English (2000).
Economy: Single-family building permits issued: 0 (2007); Multi-family building permits issued: 0 (2007); Employment by occupation: 3.8% management, 11.0% professional, 21.8% services, 18.2% sales, 1.4% farming, 11.5% construction, 32.2% production (2000).
Income: Per capita income: $18,444 (2007); Median household income: $37,273 (2007); Average household income: $46,573 (2007); Percent of households with income of $100,000 or more: 5.2% (2007); Poverty rate: 21.1% (2000).
Education: Percent of population age 25 and over with: High school diploma (including GED) or higher: 73.2% (2007); Bachelor's degree or higher: 5.7% (2007); Master's degree or higher: 1.5% (2007).

School District(s)

Sandoval CUSD 501 (PK-12)
2005-06 Enrollment: 604 . . . . (618) 247-3233
Housing: Homeownership rate: 68.5% (2007); Median home value: $47,031 (2007); Median rent: $219 per month (2000); Median age of housing: 32 years (2000).
Transportation: Commute to work: 94.0% car, 0.0% public transportation, 0.8% walk, 3.7% work from home (2000); Travel time to work: 30.4% less than 15 minutes, 49.2% 15 to 30 minutes, 9.6% 30 to 45 minutes, 3.4% 45 to 60 minutes, 7.6% 60 minutes or more (2000)

VERNON (village). Covers a land area of 0.911 square miles and a water area of 0 square miles. Located at 38.80° N. Lat.; 89.08° W. Long. Elevation is 515 feet.
History: Vernon developed as the center of a peach and pear growing area.
Population: 207 (1990); 178 (2000); 183 (2007); 184 (2012 projected); Race: 98.9% White, 0.0% Black, 0.0% Asian, 2.7% Hispanic of any race (2007); Density: 200.9 persons per square mile (2007); Average household size: 2.29 (2007); Median age: 46.8 (2007); Males per 100 females: 103.3 (2007); Marriage status: 19.5% never married, 58.5% now married, 10.7% widowed, 11.3% divorced (2000); Foreign born: 0.0% (2000); Ancestry (includes multiple ancestries): 26.4% United States or American, 18.9% Other groups, 15.9% Irish, 15.9% German, 7.5% English (2000).
Economy: Employment by occupation: 5.1% management, 3.8% professional, 23.1% services, 12.8% sales, 2.6% farming, 16.7% construction, 35.9% production (2000).
Income: Per capita income: $12,514 (2007); Median household income: $25,000 (2007); Average household income: $28,625 (2007); Percent of households with income of $100,000 or more: 0.0% (2007); Poverty rate: 27.4% (2000).
Education: Percent of population age 25 and over with: High school diploma (including GED) or higher: 70.3% (2007); Bachelor's degree or higher: 2.2% (2007); Master's degree or higher: 2.2% (2007).
Housing: Homeownership rate: 87.5% (2007); Median home value: $43,333 (2007); Median rent: $188 per month (2000); Median age of housing: 43 years (2000).
Transportation: Commute to work: 89.7% car, 0.0% public transportation, 0.0% walk, 3.8% work from home (2000); Travel time to work: 26.7% less than 15 minutes, 57.3% 15 to 30 minutes, 8.0% 30 to 45 minutes, 0.0% 45 to 60 minutes, 8.0% 60 minutes or more (2000)

WALNUT HILL (village). Covers a land area of 0.371 square miles and a water area of 0 square miles. Located at 38.47° N. Lat.; 89.04° W. Long. Elevation is 568 feet.

Population: 133 (1990); 109 (2000); 99 (2007); 97 (2012 projected); Race: 99.0% White, 1.0% Black, 0.0% Asian, 0.0% Hispanic of any race (2007); Density: 267.2 persons per square mile (2007); Average household size: 2.41 (2007); Median age: 32.1 (2007); Males per 100 females: 76.8 (2007); Marriage status: 14.7% never married, 60.3% now married, 17.6% widowed, 7.4% divorced (2000); Foreign born: 0.0% (2000); Ancestry (includes multiple ancestries): 15.7% Other groups, 13.7% United States or American, 9.8% Irish, 8.8% German, 6.9% Italian (2000).
Economy: Employment by occupation: 0.0% management, 10.0% professional, 18.0% services, 18.0% sales, 0.0% farming, 0.0% construction, 54.0% production (2000).
Income: Per capita income: $12,500 (2007); Median household income: $27,500 (2007); Average household income: $30,183 (2007); Percent of households with income of $100,000 or more: 0.0% (2007); Poverty rate: 3.9% (2000).
Education: Percent of population age 25 and over with: High school diploma (including GED) or higher: 73.2% (2007); Bachelor's degree or higher: 0.0% (2007); Master's degree or higher: 0.0% (2007).
Housing: Homeownership rate: 85.4% (2007); Median home value: $59,286 (2007); Median rent: $225 per month (2000); Median age of housing: 35 years (2000).
Transportation: Commute to work: 100.0% car, 0.0% public transportation, 0.0% walk, 0.0% work from home (2000); Travel time to work: 19.1% less than 15 minutes, 44.7% 15 to 30 minutes, 23.4% 30 to 45 minutes, 0.0% 45 to 60 minutes, 12.8% 60 minutes or more (2000)

WAMAC (city). Covers a land area of 1.508 square miles and a water area of 0 square miles. Located at 38.50° N. Lat.; 89.14° W. Long.
History: Wamac was incorporated as a city in 1913. Its name was made from the first letters of the counties in which the town was situated—Washington, Marion, and Clinton.
Population: 1,501 (1990); 1,378 (2000); 1,244 (2007); 1,179 (2012 projected); Race: 96.7% White, 2.0% Black, 0.1% Asian, 1.9% Hispanic of any race (2007); Density: 824.8 persons per square mile (2007); Average household size: 2.37 (2007); Median age: 34.7 (2007); Males per 100 females: 90.5 (2007); Marriage status: 22.6% never married, 51.1% now married, 8.2% widowed, 18.1% divorced (2000); Foreign born: 0.4% (2000); Ancestry (includes multiple ancestries): 19.0% German, 17.6% United States or American, 9.7% Irish, 8.8% Other groups, 7.6% English (2000).
Economy: Single-family building permits issued: 0 (2007); Multi-family building permits issued: 0 (2007); Employment by occupation: 2.6% management, 7.5% professional, 24.3% services, 16.1% sales, 0.3% farming, 10.6% construction, 38.5% production (2000).
Income: Per capita income: $16,383 (2007); Median household income: $31,250 (2007); Average household income: $38,745 (2007); Percent of households with income of $100,000 or more: 3.2% (2007); Poverty rate: 27.3% (2000).
Education: Percent of population age 25 and over with: High school diploma (including GED) or higher: 69.9% (2007); Bachelor's degree or higher: 2.5% (2007); Master's degree or higher: 0.9% (2007).
Housing: Homeownership rate: 67.3% (2007); Median home value: $33,103 (2007); Median rent: $261 per month (2000); Median age of housing: 36 years (2000).
Safety: Violent crime rate: 23.1 per 10,000 population; Property crime rate: 208.2 per 10,000 population (2006).
Transportation: Commute to work: 88.7% car, 0.0% public transportation, 7.4% walk, 1.6% work from home (2000); Travel time to work: 66.5% less than 15 minutes, 18.4% 15 to 30 minutes, 9.1% 30 to 45 minutes, 2.7% 45 to 60 minutes, 3.2% 60 minutes or more (2000)

Marshall County

Located in north central Illinois; drained by the Illinois River and Sandy Creek. Covers a land area of 386.06 square miles, a water area of 12.45 square miles, and is located in the Central Time Zone. The county was founded in 1839. County seat is Lacon.

Marshall County is part of the Peoria, IL Metropolitan Statistical Area. The entire metro area includes: Marshall County, IL; Peoria County, IL; Stark County, IL; Tazewell County, IL; Woodford County, IL

Weather Station: Lacon 1 N Elevation: 459 feet

	Jan	Feb	Mar	Apr	May	Jun	Jul	Aug	Sep	Oct	Nov	Dec
High	31	38	50	64	75	84	87	85	78	66	51	38
Low	15	20	30	41	51	60	64	62	54	43	32	22
Precip	1.6	1.6	3.2	4.1	4.4	4.3	4.2	3.7	3.7	3.1	3.0	2.3
Snow	7.3	4.6	2.8	0.8	tr	0.0	0.0	0.0	0.0	tr	1.7	5.4

High and Low temperatures in degrees Fahrenheit; Precipitation and Snow in inches

Population: 12,846 (1990); 13,180 (2000); 13,291 (2007); 13,395 (2012 projected); Race: 97.7% White, 0.5% Black, 0.4% Asian, 2.0% Hispanic of any race (2007); Density: 34.4 persons per square mile (2007); Average household size: 2.48 (2007); Median age: 42.0 (2007); Males per 100 females: 98.9 (2007).
Religion: Five largest groups: 26.7% Catholic Church, 7.0% Evangelical Lutheran Church in America, 6.9% The United Methodist Church, 4.9% Christian Church (Disciples of Christ), 3.9% Lutheran Church—Missouri Synod (2000).
Economy: Unemployment rate: 4.7% (4/2008); Total civilian labor force: 7,611 (4/2008); Leading industries: 35.5% manufacturing; 16.5% health care and social assistance; 11.7% retail trade (2005); Farms: 454 totaling 191,323 acres (2002); Companies that employ 500 or more persons: 0 (2006); Companies that employ 100 to 499 persons: 4 (2006); Companies that employ less than 100 persons: 266 (2006); Black-owned businesses: n/a (2002); Hispanic-owned businesses: n/a (2002); Asian-owned businesses: n/a (2002); Women-owned businesses: n/a (2002); Retail sales per capita: $7,540 (2008). Single-family building permits issued: 20 (2007); Multi-family building permits issued: 0 (2007).
Income: Per capita income: $23,224 (2007); Median household income: $49,050 (2007); Average household income: $56,940 (2007); Percent of households with income of $100,000 or more: 11.1% (2007); Poverty rate: 8.0% (2005); Bankruptcy rate: 3.35% (2007).
Education: Percent of population age 25 and over with: High school diploma (including GED) or higher: 85.1% (2007); Bachelor's degree or higher: 14.9% (2007); Master's degree or higher: 4.2% (2007).
Housing: Homeownership rate: 79.9% (2007); Median home value: $104,797 (2007); Median rent: $303 per month (2000); Median age of housing: 46 years (2000).
Health: Birth rate: 121.4 per 10,000 population (2007); Death rate: 137.7 per 10,000 population (2007); Age-adjusted cancer mortality rate: 250.9 deaths per 100,000 population (2005); Number of physicians: 5.4 per 10,000 population (2005); Hospital beds: 0.0 per 10,000 population (2004); Hospital admissions: 0.0 per 10,000 population (2004).
Elections: 2004 Presidential election results: 56.7% Bush, 42.6% Kerry, 0.1% Nader, 0.6% Badnarik
National and State Parks: Cameron National Wildlife Refuge; Marshall County State Conservation Areas; Sparland State Conservation Area
Additional Information Contacts
Marshall County Government . . . . (309) 246-6325

Henry Area Chamber of Commerce . . . . (309) 364-3261
http://www.henryil.com
Lacon Chamber of Commerce. . . . . (309) 246-5222
http://www.laconchamber.com

Marshall County Communities

HENRY (city). Covers a land area of 1.395 square miles and a water area of 0.069 square miles. Located at 41.11° N. Lat.; 89.36° W. Long. Elevation is 492 feet.
History: Founded in early 1840s; incorporated 1854.
Population: 2,662 (1990); 2,540 (2000); 2,532 (2007); 2,535 (2012 projected); Race: 97.4% White, 0.8% Black, 0.4% Asian, 1.1% Hispanic of any race (2007); Density: 1,815.6 persons per square mile (2007); Average household size: 2.46 (2007); Median age: 42.3 (2007); Males per 100 females: 91.2 (2007); Marriage status: 18.2% never married, 65.2% now married, 8.2% widowed, 8.3% divorced (2000); Foreign born: 1.6% (2000); Ancestry (includes multiple ancestries): 34.5% German, 16.5% Irish, 13.3% English, 6.7% Other groups, 6.0% Swedish (2000).
Economy: Single-family building permits issued: 0 (2007); Multi-family building permits issued: 0 (2007); Employment by occupation: 6.0% management, 16.7% professional, 21.3% services, 21.3% sales, 0.2% farming, 10.3% construction, 24.1% production (2000).
Income: Per capita income: $22,911 (2007); Median household income: $47,313 (2007); Average household income: $55,760 (2007); Percent of households with income of $100,000 or more: 9.5% (2007); Poverty rate: 5.6% (2000).

Education: Percent of population age 25 and over with: High school diploma (including GED) or higher: 81.6% (2007); Bachelor's degree or higher: 17.1% (2007); Master's degree or higher: 6.0% (2007).

School District(s)

Henry-Senachwine CUSD 5 (PK-12)
2005-06 Enrollment: 623 . . . . (309) 364-3614

Housing: Homeownership rate: 77.9% (2007); Median home value: $92,174 (2007); Median rent: $350 per month (2000); Median age of housing: 53 years (2000).
Safety: Violent crime rate: 27.7 per 10,000 population; Property crime rate: 253.0 per 10,000 population (2006).
Newspapers: Henry News Republican (Local news; Circulation 2,850); Wenona Index (Community news; Circulation 900)
Transportation: Commute to work: 94.2% car, 0.3% public transportation, 2.4% walk, 2.0% work from home (2000); Travel time to work: 46.9% less than 15 minutes, 19.2% 15 to 30 minutes, 17.6% 30 to 45 minutes, 10.1% 45 to 60 minutes, 6.2% 60 minutes or more (2000)

Additional Information Contacts

Henry Area Chamber of Commerce . . . . (309) 364-3261
http://www.henryil.com

HOPEWELL (village). Covers a land area of 1.125 square miles and a water area of 0 square miles. Located at 40.98° N. Lat.; 89.45° W. Long. Elevation is 633 feet.
Population: 343 (1990); 396 (2000); 420 (2007); 433 (2012 projected); Race: 99.0% White, 0.5% Black, 0.5% Asian, 1.7% Hispanic of any race (2007); Density: 373.3 persons per square mile (2007); Average household size: 2.78 (2007); Median age: 43.8 (2007); Males per 100 females: 98.1 (2007); Marriage status: 14.3% never married, 73.5% now married, 0.0% widowed, 12.2% divorced (2000); Foreign born: 1.1% (2000); Ancestry (includes multiple ancestries): 30.8% German, 14.3% English, 11.8% Irish, 5.5% Swedish, 4.7% Italian (2000).
Economy: Single-family building permits issued: 4 (2007); Multi-family building permits issued: 0 (2007); Employment by occupation: 9.5% management, 36.7% professional, 7.7% services, 24.9% sales, 0.9% farming, 7.7% construction, 12.7% production (2000).
Income: Per capita income: $25,429 (2007); Median household income: $70,658 (2007); Average household income: $70,728 (2007); Percent of households with income of $100,000 or more: 22.5% (2007); Poverty rate: 0.0% (2000).
Education: Percent of population age 25 and over with: High school diploma (including GED) or higher: 97.6% (2007); Bachelor's degree or higher: 24.3% (2007); Master's degree or higher: 8.3% (2007).
Housing: Homeownership rate: 99.3% (2007); Median home value: $160,833 (2007); Median rent: $175 per month (2000); Median age of housing: 21 years (2000).
Transportation: Commute to work: 100.0% car, 0.0% public transportation, 0.0% walk, 0.0% work from home (2000); Travel time to work: 23.0% less than 15 minutes, 35.9% 15 to 30 minutes, 30.4% 30 to 45 minutes, 6.5% 45 to 60 minutes, 4.1% 60 minutes or more (2000)

LA ROSE (village). Covers a land area of 0.220 square miles and a water area of 0 square miles. Located at 40.98° N. Lat.; 89.23° W. Long. Elevation is 682 feet.
Population: 130 (1990); 159 (2000); 151 (2007); 148 (2012 projected); Race: 96.7% White, 0.0% Black, 0.0% Asian, 2.6% Hispanic of any race (2007); Density: 686.1 persons per square mile (2007); Average household size: 2.52 (2007); Median age: 35.6 (2007); Males per 100 females: 88.8 (2007); Marriage status: 24.0% never married, 63.3% now married, 5.3% widowed, 7.3% divorced (2000); Foreign born: 1.1% (2000); Ancestry (includes multiple ancestries): 42.9% German, 13.8% English, 11.6% Swedish, 10.1% United States or American, 10.1% Irish (2000).
Economy: Single-family building permits issued: 0 (2007); Multi-family building permits issued: 0 (2007); Employment by occupation: 8.8% management, 5.9% professional, 21.6% services, 23.5% sales, 0.0% farming, 6.9% construction, 33.3% production (2000).
Income: Per capita income: $23,311 (2007); Median household income: $56,364 (2007); Average household income: $58,667 (2007); Percent of households with income of $100,000 or more: 6.7% (2007); Poverty rate: 10.1% (2000).
Education: Percent of population age 25 and over with: High school diploma (including GED) or higher: 85.0% (2007); Bachelor's degree or higher: 7.0% (2007); Master's degree or higher: 2.0% (2007).
Housing: Homeownership rate: 85.0% (2007); Median home value: $65,833 (2007); Median rent: $231 per month (2000); Median age of housing: 60+ years (2000).
Transportation: Commute to work: 97.0% car, 0.0% public transportation, 3.0% walk, 0.0% work from home (2000); Travel time to work: 34.3% less than 15 minutes, 29.3% 15 to 30 minutes, 22.2% 30 to 45 minutes, 7.1% 45 to 60 minutes, 7.1% 60 minutes or more (2000)

LACON (city). County seat. Covers a land area of 1.604 square miles and a water area of 0.044 square miles. Located at 41.02° N. Lat.; 89.40° W. Long. Elevation is 476 feet.
History: Laid out as Columbia in 1826; incorporated 1839.
Population: 1,989 (1990); 1,979 (2000); 1,956 (2007); 1,890 (2012 projected); Race: 99.0% White, 0.1% Black, 0.2% Asian, 1.9% Hispanic of any race (2007); Density: 1,219.5 persons per square mile (2007); Average household size: 2.43 (2007); Median age: 43.7 (2007); Males per 100 females: 92.0 (2007); Marriage status: 20.2% never married, 57.4% now married, 12.4% widowed, 10.0% divorced (2000); Foreign born: 0.5% (2000); Ancestry (includes multiple ancestries): 28.8% German, 15.1% Irish, 12.0% English, 7.3% Swedish, 6.3% United States or American (2000).
Economy: Single-family building permits issued: 1 (2007); Multi-family building permits issued: 0 (2007); Employment by occupation: 7.0% management, 15.6% professional, 19.9% services, 22.2% sales, 0.0% farming, 10.5% construction, 24.8% production (2000).
Income: Per capita income: $23,677 (2007); Median household income: $50,217 (2007); Average household income: $55,457 (2007); Percent of households with income of $100,000 or more: 10.0% (2007); Poverty rate: 5.0% (2000).
Education: Percent of population age 25 and over with: High school diploma (including GED) or higher: 82.1% (2007); Bachelor's degree or higher: 12.7% (2007); Master's degree or higher: 3.3% (2007).

School District(s)

Midland CUSD 7 (PK-12)
2005-06 Enrollment: 874 . . . . (309) 246-2310

Housing: Homeownership rate: 77.0% (2007); Median home value: $99,911 (2007); Median rent: $306 per month (2000); Median age of housing: 52 years (2000).
Safety: Violent crime rate: 10.4 per 10,000 population; Property crime rate: 156.0 per 10,000 population (2006).
Newspapers: Illinois Valley Peach (Community news; Circulation 9,800); Lacon Home Journal (Community news; Circulation 2,400)
Transportation: Commute to work: 89.5% car, 2.2% public transportation, 5.5% walk, 1.6% work from home (2000); Travel time to work: 36.7% less than 15 minutes, 19.6% 15 to 30 minutes, 26.2% 30 to 45 minutes, 12.0% 45 to 60 minutes, 5.5% 60 minutes or more (2000)

Additional Information Contacts

Lacon Chamber of Commerce. . . . . (309) 246-5222
http://www.laconchamber.com

SPARLAND (village). Covers a land area of 0.582 square miles and a water area of 0 square miles. Located at 41.03° N. Lat.; 89.43° W. Long. Elevation is 472 feet.
Population: 412 (1990); 504 (2000); 535 (2007); 556 (2012 projected); Race: 98.7% White, 0.0% Black, 0.0% Asian, 3.6% Hispanic of any race (2007); Density: 918.5 persons per square mile (2007); Average household size: 2.68 (2007); Median age: 36.5 (2007); Males per 100 females: 110.6 (2007); Marriage status: 16.6% never married, 69.6% now married, 5.3% widowed, 8.4% divorced (2000); Foreign born: 1.2% (2000); Ancestry (includes multiple ancestries): 24.4% German, 16.3% Irish, 14.9% United States or American, 10.9% English, 10.7% Other groups (2000).
Economy: Employment by occupation: 3.8% management, 8.0% professional, 17.6% services, 24.4% sales, 0.0% farming, 17.6% construction, 28.6% production (2000).
Income: Per capita income: $16,276 (2007); Median household income: $37,308 (2007); Average household income: $43,538 (2007); Percent of households with income of $100,000 or more: 5.0% (2007); Poverty rate: 5.8% (2000).
Education: Percent of population age 25 and over with: High school diploma (including GED) or higher: 74.5% (2007); Bachelor's degree or higher: 3.0% (2007); Master's degree or higher: 0.0% (2007).

School District(s)

Midland CUSD 7 (PK-12)
2005-06 Enrollment: 874 . . . . (309) 246-2310

Housing: Homeownership rate: 78.5% (2007); Median home value: $88,409 (2007); Median rent: $248 per month (2000); Median age of housing: 59 years (2000).
Transportation: Commute to work: 97.3% car, 0.0% public transportation, 1.5% walk, 1.2% work from home (2000); Travel time to work: 34.4% less than 15 minutes, 16.0% 15 to 30 minutes, 37.9% 30 to 45 minutes, 5.9% 45 to 60 minutes, 5.9% 60 minutes or more (2000)

TOLUCA (city). Covers a land area of 1.062 square miles and a water area of 0 square miles. Located at 41.00° N. Lat.; 89.13° W. Long. Elevation is 692 feet.
History: Incorporated 1894.
Population: 1,315 (1990); 1,339 (2000); 1,284 (2007); 1,247 (2012 projected); Race: 97.1% White, 0.0% Black, 0.7% Asian, 2.3% Hispanic of any race (2007); Density: 1,209.1 persons per square mile (2007); Average household size: 2.27 (2007); Median age: 44.8 (2007); Males per 100 females: 85.8 (2007); Marriage status: 17.9% never married, 59.3% now married, 11.9% widowed, 11.0% divorced (2000); Foreign born: 1.9% (2000); Ancestry (includes multiple ancestries): 42.5% German, 16.0% Italian, 8.7% Irish, 7.8% English, 7.4% Polish (2000).
Economy: Single-family building permits issued: 0 (2007); Multi-family building permits issued: 0 (2007); Employment by occupation: 12.2% management, 12.4% professional, 16.0% services, 18.9% sales, 0.5% farming, 7.7% construction, 32.3% production (2000).
Income: Per capita income: $24,226 (2007); Median household income: $43,830 (2007); Average household income: $53,874 (2007); Percent of households with income of $100,000 or more: 7.8% (2007); Poverty rate: 6.5% (2000).
Education: Percent of population age 25 and over with: High school diploma (including GED) or higher: 80.2% (2007); Bachelor's degree or higher: 12.4% (2007); Master's degree or higher: 3.1% (2007).

School District(s)

Fieldcrest CUSD 6 (PK-12)
2005-06 Enrollment: 1,276 . . . . (309) 432-2177

Housing: Homeownership rate: 77.4% (2007); Median home value: $84,324 (2007); Median rent: $265 per month (2000); Median age of housing: 51 years (2000).
Transportation: Commute to work: 88.4% car, 0.0% public transportation, 8.2% walk, 2.8% work from home (2000); Travel time to work: 62.1% less than 15 minutes, 11.7% 15 to 30 minutes, 13.2% 30 to 45 minutes, 10.3% 45 to 60 minutes, 2.7% 60 minutes or more (2000)

VARNA (village). Covers a land area of 0.293 square miles and a water area of 0 square miles. Located at 41.03° N. Lat.; 89.22° W. Long. Elevation is 728 feet.
Population: 408 (1990); 436 (2000); 450 (2007); 462 (2012 projected); Race: 98.9% White, 0.4% Black, 0.0% Asian, 2.4% Hispanic of any race (2007); Density: 1,536.0 persons per square mile (2007); Average household size: 2.41 (2007); Median age: 40.9 (2007); Males per 100 females: 98.2 (2007); Marriage status: 16.5% never married, 69.1% now married, 7.2% widowed, 7.2% divorced (2000); Foreign born: 1.2% (2000); Ancestry (includes multiple ancestries): 45.0% German, 14.2% Irish, 12.3% English, 10.0% Other groups, 7.6% Italian (2000).
Economy: Employment by occupation: 5.2% management, 7.3% professional, 27.1% services, 20.3% sales, 0.0% farming, 5.7% construction, 34.4% production (2000).
Income: Per capita income: $20,014 (2007); Median household income: $40,500 (2007); Average household income: $46,230 (2007); Percent of households with income of $100,000 or more: 3.7% (2007); Poverty rate: 8.1% (2000).
Education: Percent of population age 25 and over with: High school diploma (including GED) or higher: 84.7% (2007); Bachelor's degree or higher: 4.5% (2007); Master's degree or higher: 0.0% (2007).

School District(s)

Midland CUSD 7 (PK-12)
2005-06 Enrollment: 874 . . . . (309) 246-2310

Housing: Homeownership rate: 88.2% (2007); Median home value: $83,400 (2007); Median rent: $314 per month (2000); Median age of housing: 60+ years (2000).
Newspapers: Lake Wildwood Sunbeam (Community news; Circulation 1,450)
Transportation: Commute to work: 85.9% car, 0.0% public transportation, 4.7% walk, 6.3% work from home (2000); Travel time to work: 34.4% less than 15 minutes, 30.6% 15 to 30 minutes, 17.8% 30 to 45 minutes, 7.2% 45 to 60 minutes, 10.0% 60 minutes or more (2000)

WENONA (city). Covers a land area of 0.672 square miles and a water area of 0 square miles. Located at 41.05° N. Lat.; 89.05° W. Long. Elevation is 699 feet.
History: Wenona's early economy was based on soy beans and corn.
Population: 981 (1990); 1,065 (2000); 1,096 (2007); 1,124 (2012 projected); Race: 97.6% White, 0.5% Black, 0.1% Asian, 2.7% Hispanic of any race (2007); Density: 1,630.0 persons per square mile (2007); Average household size: 2.30 (2007); Median age: 39.0 (2007); Males per 100 females: 96.8 (2007); Marriage status: 24.3% never married, 57.0% now married, 10.1% widowed, 8.6% divorced (2000); Foreign born: 0.7% (2000); Ancestry (includes multiple ancestries): 41.4% German, 17.6% Irish, 12.2% Italian, 9.5% Swedish, 8.0% English (2000).
Economy: Single-family building permits issued: 1 (2007); Multi-family building permits issued: 0 (2007); Employment by occupation: 8.3% management, 15.4% professional, 22.4% services, 23.9% sales, 0.4% farming, 9.6% construction, 20.0% production (2000).
Income: Per capita income: $20,265 (2007); Median household income: $40,806 (2007); Average household income: $46,660 (2007); Percent of households with income of $100,000 or more: 5.9% (2007); Poverty rate: 7.8% (2000).
Education: Percent of population age 25 and over with: High school diploma (including GED) or higher: 86.0% (2007); Bachelor's degree or higher: 12.3% (2007); Master's degree or higher: 3.2% (2007).

School District(s)

Fieldcrest CUSD 6 (PK-12)
2005-06 Enrollment: 1,276 . . . . (309) 432-2177

Housing: Homeownership rate: 77.5% (2007); Median home value: $87,019 (2007); Median rent: $258 per month (2000); Median age of housing: 58 years (2000).
Safety: Violent crime rate: 250.7 per 10,000 population; Property crime rate: 204.3 per 10,000 population (2006).
Transportation: Commute to work: 93.5% car, 0.4% public transportation, 2.9% walk, 2.5% work from home (2000); Travel time to work: 39.1% less than 15 minutes, 28.2% 15 to 30 minutes, 11.2% 30 to 45 minutes, 15.9% 45 to 60 minutes, 5.7% 60 minutes or more (2000)

Mason County

Located in central Illinois; bounded on the west by the Illinois River, and on the south by the Sangamon River and Salt Creek. Covers a land area of 538.94 square miles, a water area of 24.43 square miles, and is located in the Central Time Zone. The county was founded in 1841. County seat is Havana.

Weather Station: Havana 4 NNE Elevation: 459 feet

	Jan	Feb	Mar	Apr	May	Jun	Jul	Aug	Sep	Oct	Nov	Dec
High	32	38	51	64	74	84	88	86	79	67	51	38
Low	15	20	30	41	51	61	65	62	54	42	32	21
Precip	1.8	1.9	3.0	3.5	4.5	3.7	3.8	3.6	3.5	2.9	3.2	2.6
Snow	9.9	7.7	3.8	1.1	0.0	0.0	0.0	0.0	0.0	tr	1.5	6.1

High and Low temperatures in degrees Fahrenheit; Precipitation and Snow in inches

Weather Station: Mason City 1 W Elevation: 583 feet

	Jan	Feb	Mar	Apr	May	Jun	Jul	Aug	Sep	Oct	Nov	Dec
High	33	39	51	65	75	84	87	85	79	67	51	38
Low	16	21	31	42	52	61	65	63	55	44	33	22
Precip	1.5	1.5	2.8	3.5	4.3	3.6	3.9	3.5	3.2	2.8	2.9	2.4
Snow	6.0	4.9	2.4	0.6	tr	0.0	0.0	0.0	0.0	tr	1.3	4.6

High and Low temperatures in degrees Fahrenheit; Precipitation and Snow in inches

Population: 16,269 (1990); 16,038 (2000); 15,622 (2007); 15,258 (2012 projected); Race: 98.6% White, 0.3% Black, 0.3% Asian, 0.6% Hispanic of any race (2007); Density: 29.0 persons per square mile (2007); Average household size: 2.48 (2007); Median age: 40.9 (2007); Males per 100 females: 96.1 (2007).
Religion: Five largest groups: 13.9% Lutheran Church—Missouri Synod, 9.1% The United Methodist Church, 6.6% Catholic Church, 4.7% American Baptist Churches in the USA, 4.1% Christian Churches and Churches of Christ (2000).
Economy: Unemployment rate: 6.7% (4/2008); Total civilian labor force: 7,312 (4/2008); Leading industries: 20.7% health care and social assistance; 18.0% retail trade; 8.6% transportation & warehousing (2005); Farms: 443 totaling 285,097 acres (2002); Companies that employ 500 or more persons: 0 (2006); Companies that employ 100 to 499 persons: 1 (2006); Companies that employ less than 100 persons: 311 (2006);

Black-owned businesses: n/a (2002); Hispanic-owned businesses: n/a (2002); Asian-owned businesses: n/a (2002); Women-owned businesses: n/a (2002); Retail sales per capita: $9,785 (2008). Single-family building permits issued: 12 (2007); Multi-family building permits issued: 0 (2007).
Income: Per capita income: $20,868 (2007); Median household income: $42,382 (2007); Average household income: $51,228 (2007); Percent of households with income of $100,000 or more: 8.3% (2007); Poverty rate: 14.2% (2005); Bankruptcy rate: 3.63% (2007).
Taxes: Total county taxes per capita: $208 (2006); County property taxes per capita: $166 (2006).
Education: Percent of population age 25 and over with: High school diploma (including GED) or higher: 79.4% (2007); Bachelor's degree or higher: 11.2% (2007); Master's degree or higher: 3.5% (2007).
Housing: Homeownership rate: 76.8% (2007); Median home value: $88,016 (2007); Median rent: $289 per month (2000); Median age of housing: 46 years (2000).
Health: Birth rate: 122.1 per 10,000 population (2007); Death rate: 130.7 per 10,000 population (2007); Age-adjusted cancer mortality rate: 245.6 deaths per 100,000 population (2005); Number of physicians: 5.2 per 10,000 population (2005); Hospital beds: 16.0 per 10,000 population (2004); Hospital admissions: 299.9 per 10,000 population (2004).
Elections: 2004 Presidential election results: 54.4% Bush, 44.8% Kerry, 0.0% Nader, 0.8% Badnarik
National and State Parks: Chautaugua National Wildlife Refuge; Chautauqua National Migratory Waterfowl Refuge; Mason County State Wildlife Refuge and Recreation; Sand Ridge State Forest
Additional Information Contacts
Mason County Government . . . . (309) 543-6661
http://www.masoncountyil.org
Havana Area Chamber of Commerce . . . . (309) 543-3528
http://www.scenichavana.com
The Manito Chamber of Commerce. . . . . (309) 968-6585

Mason County Communities

BATH (village). Covers a land area of 0.365 square miles and a water area of <.001 square miles. Located at 40.19° N. Lat.; 90.14° W. Long. Elevation is 463 feet.
History: Bath was surveyed in 1836 by Abraham Lincoln, who was then the Deputy Surveyor of Sangamon County. Bath served as the county seat from 1843 to 1851.
Population: 388 (1990); 310 (2000); 312 (2007); 312 (2012 projected); Race: 97.1% White, 1.0% Black, 0.0% Asian, 0.6% Hispanic of any race (2007); Density: 854.3 persons per square mile (2007); Average household size: 2.33 (2007); Median age: 35.2 (2007); Males per 100 females: 95.0 (2007); Marriage status: 22.7% never married, 63.2% now married, 5.9% widowed, 8.2% divorced (2000); Foreign born: 0.6% (2000); Ancestry (includes multiple ancestries): 18.3% United States or American, 17.4% German, 11.4% Irish, 6.9% English, 5.0% Other groups (2000).
Economy: Single-family building permits issued: 1 (2007); Multi-family building permits issued: 0 (2007); Employment by occupation: 6.0% management, 3.4% professional, 16.4% services, 23.3% sales, 4.3% farming, 19.8% construction, 26.7% production (2000).
Income: Per capita income: $16,370 (2007); Median household income: $35,556 (2007); Average household income: $38,116 (2007); Percent of households with income of $100,000 or more: 0.0% (2007); Poverty rate: 24.7% (2000).
Education: Percent of population age 25 and over with: High school diploma (including GED) or higher: 81.6% (2007); Bachelor's degree or higher: 2.0% (2007); Master's degree or higher: 1.0% (2007).
Housing: Homeownership rate: 82.8% (2007); Median home value: $54,500 (2007); Median rent: $288 per month (2000); Median age of housing: 37 years (2000).
Transportation: Commute to work: 94.0% car, 0.0% public transportation, 1.7% walk, 2.6% work from home (2000); Travel time to work: 26.5% less than 15 minutes, 31.0% 15 to 30 minutes, 21.2% 30 to 45 minutes, 7.1% 45 to 60 minutes, 14.2% 60 minutes or more (2000)

EASTON (village). Covers a land area of 0.233 square miles and a water area of 0 square miles. Located at 40.23° N. Lat.; 89.84° W. Long. Elevation is 512 feet.
Population: 375 (1990); 373 (2000); 358 (2007); 356 (2012 projected); Race: 99.4% White, 0.0% Black, 0.0% Asian, 0.6% Hispanic of any race (2007); Density: 1,535.2 persons per square mile (2007); Average household size: 2.45 (2007); Median age: 43.6 (2007); Males per 100 females: 94.6 (2007); Marriage status: 21.7% never married, 68.0% now married, 7.0% widowed, 3.3% divorced (2000); Foreign born: 0.0% (2000); Ancestry (includes multiple ancestries): 36.2% German, 20.6% English, 13.5% Irish, 4.7% Other groups, 3.1% French (except Basque) (2000).
Economy: Single-family building permits issued: 0 (2007); Multi-family building permits issued: 0 (2007); Employment by occupation: 8.2% management, 9.9% professional, 25.7% services, 14.0% sales, 9.9% farming, 13.5% construction, 18.7% production (2000).
Income: Per capita income: $19,693 (2007); Median household income: $37,500 (2007); Average household income: $48,288 (2007); Percent of households with income of $100,000 or more: 4.8% (2007); Poverty rate: 1.0% (2000).
Education: Percent of population age 25 and over with: High school diploma (including GED) or higher: 86.2% (2007); Bachelor's degree or higher: 16.5% (2007); Master's degree or higher: 3.9% (2007).
School District(s)
Illini Central CUSD 189 (PK-12)
2005-06 Enrollment: 916 . . . . (217) 482-5180
Housing: Homeownership rate: 86.3% (2007); Median home value: $72,143 (2007); Median rent: $320 per month (2000); Median age of housing: 54 years (2000).
Safety: Violent crime rate: 0.0 per 10,000 population; Property crime rate: 135.1 per 10,000 population (2006).
Transportation: Commute to work: 95.3% car, 0.0% public transportation, 3.0% walk, 0.0% work from home (2000); Travel time to work: 29.0% less than 15 minutes, 26.6% 15 to 30 minutes, 10.7% 30 to 45 minutes, 20.7% 45 to 60 minutes, 13.0% 60 minutes or more (2000)

FOREST CITY (village). Covers a land area of 0.524 square miles and a water area of 0 square miles. Located at 40.37° N. Lat.; 89.82° W. Long. Elevation is 492 feet.
Population: 321 (1990); 287 (2000); 256 (2007); 250 (2012 projected); Race: 98.0% White, 0.0% Black, 0.0% Asian, 0.0% Hispanic of any race (2007); Density: 488.7 persons per square mile (2007); Average household size: 2.78 (2007); Median age: 35.8 (2007); Males per 100 females: 111.6 (2007); Marriage status: 17.3% never married, 67.1% now married, 2.4% widowed, 13.3% divorced (2000); Foreign born: 0.0% (2000); Ancestry (includes multiple ancestries): 17.7% United States or American, 15.3% German, 11.8% Other groups, 9.7% Irish, 4.7% Scottish (2000).
Economy: Employment by occupation: 10.3% management, 0.0% professional, 19.0% services, 24.6% sales, 4.8% farming, 11.9% construction, 29.4% production (2000).
Income: Per capita income: $19,072 (2007); Median household income: $43,214 (2007); Average household income: $53,071 (2007); Percent of households with income of $100,000 or more: 7.6% (2007); Poverty rate: 8.0% (2000).
Education: Percent of population age 25 and over with: High school diploma (including GED) or higher: 71.6% (2007); Bachelor's degree or higher: 4.3% (2007); Master's degree or higher: 1.2% (2007).
Housing: Homeownership rate: 82.6% (2007); Median home value: $58,667 (2007); Median rent: $363 per month (2000); Median age of housing: 54 years (2000).
Safety: Violent crime rate: 107.1 per 10,000 population; Property crime rate: 250.0 per 10,000 population (2006).
Transportation: Commute to work: 96.8% car, 0.0% public transportation, 1.6% walk, 1.6% work from home (2000); Travel time to work: 16.9% less than 15 minutes, 17.7% 15 to 30 minutes, 37.1% 30 to 45 minutes, 16.1% 45 to 60 minutes, 12.1% 60 minutes or more (2000)

HAVANA (city). County seat. Covers a land area of 2.628 square miles and a water area of 0.151 square miles. Located at 40.29° N. Lat.; 90.06° W. Long. Elevation is 476 feet.
History: Havana grew up around the ferry across the Spoon River, established in 1824 by Major Ossian M. Ross. Havana shared in the prosperity brought by steamboat travel on the Illinois River, shipping grain and produce to market. Commercial fishing was important here in the early 1900's.
Population: 3,672 (1990); 3,577 (2000); 3,444 (2007); 3,332 (2012 projected); Race: 98.1% White, 0.3% Black, 0.8% Asian, 0.7% Hispanic of any race (2007); Density: 1,310.4 persons per square mile (2007); Average household size: 2.44 (2007); Median age: 40.2 (2007); Males per 100 females: 88.9 (2007); Marriage status: 21.4% never married, 57.2% now married, 11.2% widowed, 10.3% divorced (2000); Foreign born: 0.9% (2000); Ancestry (includes multiple ancestries): 23.1% German, 14.0%

English, 11.8% United States or American, 10.1% Irish, 6.3% French (except Basque) (2000).
Economy: Single-family building permits issued: 1 (2007); Multi-family building permits issued: 0 (2007); Employment by occupation: 9.7% management, 10.6% professional, 25.1% services, 30.6% sales, 2.6% farming, 7.6% construction, 13.7% production (2000).
Income: Per capita income: $19,458 (2007); Median household income: $34,939 (2007); Average household income: $45,677 (2007); Percent of households with income of $100,000 or more: 7.0% (2007); Poverty rate: 12.0% (2000).
Education: Percent of population age 25 and over with: High school diploma (including GED) or higher: 77.4% (2007); Bachelor's degree or higher: 11.9% (2007); Master's degree or higher: 4.1% (2007).

School District(s)

Havana CUSD 126 (PK-12)
2005-06 Enrollment: 1,174 . . . . (309) 543-3384
Housing: Homeownership rate: 67.9% (2007); Median home value: $74,720 (2007); Median rent: $291 per month (2000); Median age of housing: 57 years (2000).
Hospitals: Mason District Hospital (48 beds)
Safety: Violent crime rate: 57.5 per 10,000 population; Property crime rate: 310.7 per 10,000 population (2006).
Newspapers: Market Place (Community news; Circulation 6,300); Mason County Democrat (Community news; Circulation 6,300)
Transportation: Commute to work: 90.7% car, 0.7% public transportation, 3.4% walk, 3.1% work from home (2000); Travel time to work: 56.7% less than 15 minutes, 8.3% 15 to 30 minutes, 13.0% 30 to 45 minutes, 8.9% 45 to 60 minutes, 13.1% 60 minutes or more (2000)
Additional Information Contacts
Havana Area Chamber of Commerce . . . . (309) 543-3528
http://www.scenichavana.com

KILBOURNE (village). Covers a land area of 1.062 square miles and a water area of 0 square miles. Located at 40.15° N. Lat.; 90.01° W. Long. Elevation is 495 feet.
Population: 358 (1990); 375 (2000); 384 (2007); 390 (2012 projected); Race: 95.8% White, 0.8% Black, 0.3% Asian, 1.0% Hispanic of any race (2007); Density: 361.6 persons per square mile (2007); Average household size: 2.49 (2007); Median age: 36.5 (2007); Males per 100 females: 104.3 (2007); Marriage status: 15.8% never married, 63.8% now married, 6.8% widowed, 13.6% divorced (2000); Foreign born: 0.0% (2000); Ancestry (includes multiple ancestries): 18.2% English, 16.9% German, 8.5% Other groups, 6.4% Irish, 4.4% United States or American (2000).
Economy: Employment by occupation: 4.9% management, 7.3% professional, 28.5% services, 27.6% sales, 4.9% farming, 12.2% construction, 14.6% production (2000).
Income: Per capita income: $15,033 (2007); Median household income: $30,000 (2007); Average household income: $37,484 (2007); Percent of households with income of $100,000 or more: 5.8% (2007); Poverty rate: 22.1% (2000).
Education: Percent of population age 25 and over with: High school diploma (including GED) or higher: 76.9% (2007); Bachelor's degree or higher: 3.7% (2007); Master's degree or higher: 0.0% (2007).
Housing: Homeownership rate: 79.9% (2007); Median home value: $55,476 (2007); Median rent: $267 per month (2000); Median age of housing: 47 years (2000).
Transportation: Commute to work: 93.5% car, 0.0% public transportation, 0.0% walk, 6.5% work from home (2000); Travel time to work: 29.6% less than 15 minutes, 32.2% 15 to 30 minutes, 7.0% 30 to 45 minutes, 19.1% 45 to 60 minutes, 12.2% 60 minutes or more (2000)

MANITO (village). Covers a land area of 1.539 square miles and a water area of 0 square miles. Located at 40.42° N. Lat.; 89.78° W. Long. Elevation is 495 feet.
Population: 1,743 (1990); 1,733 (2000); 1,811 (2007); 1,776 (2012 projected); Race: 98.5% White, 0.8% Black, 0.2% Asian, 0.4% Hispanic of any race (2007); Density: 1,176.7 persons per square mile (2007); Average household size: 2.48 (2007); Median age: 38.6 (2007); Males per 100 females: 101.7 (2007); Marriage status: 19.2% never married, 65.3% now married, 5.8% widowed, 9.6% divorced (2000); Foreign born: 0.0% (2000); Ancestry (includes multiple ancestries): 30.0% German, 14.6% Irish, 10.5% English, 9.8% Other groups, 8.4% United States or American (2000).
Economy: Single-family building permits issued: 0 (2007); Multi-family building permits issued: 0 (2007); Employment by occupation: 5.2% management, 16.1% professional, 13.2% services, 23.3% sales, 2.3% farming, 14.6% construction, 25.4% production (2000).
Income: Per capita income: $20,780 (2007); Median household income: $46,324 (2007); Average household income: $51,526 (2007); Percent of households with income of $100,000 or more: 7.7% (2007); Poverty rate: 8.2% (2000).
Education: Percent of population age 25 and over with: High school diploma (including GED) or higher: 82.3% (2007); Bachelor's degree or higher: 10.5% (2007); Master's degree or higher: 3.0% (2007).

School District(s)

Midwest Central CUSD 191 (PK-12)
2005-06 Enrollment: 1,165 . . . . (309) 968-6868
Spring Lake CCSD 606 (KG-06)
2005-06 Enrollment: 66 . . . . (309) 545-2241
Housing: Homeownership rate: 76.5% (2007); Median home value: $113,462 (2007); Median rent: $282 per month (2000); Median age of housing: 37 years (2000).
Safety: Violent crime rate: 70.5 per 10,000 population; Property crime rate: 182.1 per 10,000 population (2006).
Transportation: Commute to work: 96.8% car, 0.4% public transportation, 1.1% walk, 1.6% work from home (2000); Travel time to work: 28.4% less than 15 minutes, 22.6% 15 to 30 minutes, 24.8% 30 to 45 minutes, 15.9% 45 to 60 minutes, 8.4% 60 minutes or more (2000)
Additional Information Contacts
The Manito Chamber of Commerce. . . . . (309) 968-6585

MASON CITY (city). Covers a land area of 0.984 square miles and a water area of 0 square miles. Located at 40.20° N. Lat.; 89.69° W. Long. Elevation is 581 feet.
History: Incorporated 1869.
Population: 2,378 (1990); 2,558 (2000); 2,446 (2007); 2,353 (2012 projected); Race: 98.8% White, 0.0% Black, 0.3% Asian, 0.7% Hispanic of any race (2007); Density: 2,485.3 persons per square mile (2007); Average household size: 2.46 (2007); Median age: 41.5 (2007); Males per 100 females: 87.3 (2007); Marriage status: 22.3% never married, 56.8% now married, 12.6% widowed, 8.3% divorced (2000); Foreign born: 0.5% (2000); Ancestry (includes multiple ancestries): 30.8% German, 13.5% United States or American, 12.4% English, 11.1% Irish, 9.1% Other groups (2000).
Economy: Single-family building permits issued: 0 (2007); Multi-family building permits issued: 0 (2007); Employment by occupation: 8.8% management, 15.1% professional, 15.8% services, 29.2% sales, 0.6% farming, 8.9% construction, 21.6% production (2000).
Income: Per capita income: $21,331 (2007); Median household income: $41,231 (2007); Average household income: $51,231 (2007); Percent of households with income of $100,000 or more: 6.9% (2007); Poverty rate: 9.3% (2000).
Education: Percent of population age 25 and over with: High school diploma (including GED) or higher: 80.8% (2007); Bachelor's degree or higher: 11.3% (2007); Master's degree or higher: 4.0% (2007).

School District(s)

Illini Central CUSD 189 (PK-12)
2005-06 Enrollment: 916 . . . . (217) 482-5180
Housing: Homeownership rate: 76.9% (2007); Median home value: $82,083 (2007); Median rent: $259 per month (2000); Median age of housing: 47 years (2000).
Safety: Violent crime rate: 125.4 per 10,000 population; Property crime rate: 177.9 per 10,000 population (2006).
Newspapers: Mason City Banner Times (Local news; Circulation 20,000)
Transportation: Commute to work: 96.5% car, 0.0% public transportation, 1.1% walk, 2.4% work from home (2000); Travel time to work: 32.8% less than 15 minutes, 18.2% 15 to 30 minutes, 21.2% 30 to 45 minutes, 18.9% 45 to 60 minutes, 9.0% 60 minutes or more (2000)

SAN JOSE (village). Covers a land area of 0.511 square miles and a water area of 0 square miles. Located at 40.30° N. Lat.; 89.60° W. Long.
Population: 573 (1990); 696 (2000); 654 (2007); 643 (2012 projected); Race: 98.8% White, 0.5% Black, 0.0% Asian, 1.2% Hispanic of any race (2007); Density: 1,279.2 persons per square mile (2007); Average household size: 2.63 (2007); Median age: 36.8 (2007); Males per 100 females: 87.9 (2007); Marriage status: 22.5% never married, 63.7% now married, 4.3% widowed, 9.5% divorced (2000); Foreign born: 0.3% (2000); Ancestry (includes multiple ancestries): 36.3% German, 10.9% Other groups, 10.3% English, 9.5% United States or American, 7.3% Irish (2000).

Economy: Single-family building permits issued: 1 (2007); Multi-family building permits issued: 0 (2007); Employment by occupation: 10.2% management, 11.1% professional, 12.7% services, 29.8% sales, 1.3% farming, 11.1% construction, 23.8% production (2000).
Income: Per capita income: $22,882 (2007); Median household income: $48,833 (2007); Average household income: $60,100 (2007); Percent of households with income of $100,000 or more: 16.9% (2007); Poverty rate: 2.9% (2000).
Education: Percent of population age 25 and over with: High school diploma (including GED) or higher: 87.7% (2007); Bachelor's degree or higher: 10.9% (2007); Master's degree or higher: 1.2% (2007).
Housing: Homeownership rate: 77.1% (2007); Median home value: $74,000 (2007); Median rent: $305 per month (2000); Median age of housing: 52 years (2000).
Safety: Violent crime rate: 0.0 per 10,000 population; Property crime rate: 149.0 per 10,000 population (2006).
Transportation: Commute to work: 94.0% car, 0.0% public transportation, 0.9% walk, 3.4% work from home (2000); Travel time to work: 19.2% less than 15 minutes, 24.0% 15 to 30 minutes, 26.0% 30 to 45 minutes, 18.2% 45 to 60 minutes, 12.7% 60 minutes or more (2000)

TOPEKA (village). Covers a land area of 0.139 square miles and a water area of 0 square miles. Located at 40.33° N. Lat.; 89.93° W. Long. Elevation is 472 feet.
Population: 93 (1990); 90 (2000); 83 (2007); 80 (2012 projected); Race: 97.6% White, 0.0% Black, 0.0% Asian, 0.0% Hispanic of any race (2007); Density: 597.6 persons per square mile (2007); Average household size: 2.44 (2007); Median age: 36.5 (2007); Males per 100 females: 97.6 (2007); Marriage status: 8.2% never married, 73.5% now married, 0.0% widowed, 18.4% divorced (2000); Foreign born: 0.0% (2000); Ancestry (includes multiple ancestries): 42.5% German, 26.0% Irish, 13.7% Portuguese, 9.6% Other groups, 6.8% Dutch (2000).
Economy: Employment by occupation: 0.0% management, 48.6% professional, 8.1% services, 10.8% sales, 8.1% farming, 0.0% construction, 24.3% production (2000).
Income: Per capita income: $40,633 (2007); Median household income: $54,545 (2007); Average household income: $99,191 (2007); Percent of households with income of $100,000 or more: 17.6% (2007); Poverty rate: 0.0% (2000).
Education: Percent of population age 25 and over with: High school diploma (including GED) or higher: 87.7% (2007); Bachelor's degree or higher: 0.0% (2007); Master's degree or higher: 0.0% (2007).
Housing: Homeownership rate: 76.5% (2007); Median home value: $68,000 (2007); Median rent: $n/a per month (2000); Median age of housing: 29 years (2000).
Transportation: Commute to work: 100.0% car, 0.0% public transportation, 0.0% walk, 0.0% work from home (2000); Travel time to work: 35.1% less than 15 minutes, 35.1% 15 to 30 minutes, 29.7% 30 to 45 minutes, 0.0% 45 to 60 minutes, 0.0% 60 minutes or more (2000)

Massac County

Located in southern Illinois; bounded on the south and east by the Ohio River and the Kentucky border, and on the northwest by the Cache River; includes part of Shawnee National Forest. Covers a land area of 239.05 square miles, a water area of 3.06 square miles, and is located in the Central Time Zone. The county was founded in 1843. County seat is Metropolis.

Massac County is part of the Paducah, KY-IL Micropolitan Statistical Area. The entire metro area includes: Massac County, IL; Ballard County, KY; Livingston County, KY; McCracken County, KY

Weather Station: Brookport Dam 52 Elevation: 328 feet

	Jan	Feb	Mar	Apr	May	Jun	Jul	Aug	Sep	Oct	Nov	Dec
High	42	48	58	69	78	86	90	88	82	71	58	47
Low	25	29	37	47	56	64	68	66	59	47	38	29
Precip	3.4	3.8	4.5	4.9	4.7	4.1	4.2	3.0	3.2	3.4	4.4	4.5
Snow	3.3	3.0	1.3	tr	0.0	0.0	0.0	0.0	0.0	0.0	tr	1.0

High and Low temperatures in degrees Fahrenheit; Precipitation and Snow in inches

Population: 14,752 (1990); 15,161 (2000); 15,447 (2007); 15,640 (2012 projected); Race: 92.1% White, 6.1% Black, 0.2% Asian, 1.2% Hispanic of any race (2007); Density: 64.6 persons per square mile (2007); Average household size: 2.39 (2007); Median age: 39.9 (2007); Males per 100 females: 92.7 (2007).
Religion: Five largest groups: 37.9% Southern Baptist Convention, 5.9% The United Methodist Church, 5.2% Evangelical Lutheran Church in America, 3.6% Churches of Christ, 2.5% United Church of Christ (2000).
Economy: Unemployment rate: 5.4% (4/2008); Total civilian labor force: 7,731 (4/2008); Leading industries: 15.0% health care and social assistance; 14.6% manufacturing; 13.1% transportation & warehousing (2005); Farms: 434 totaling 124,597 acres (2002); Companies that employ 500 or more persons: 1 (2006); Companies that employ 100 to 499 persons: 8 (2006); Companies that employ less than 100 persons: 242 (2006); Black-owned businesses: n/a (2002); Hispanic-owned businesses: n/a (2002); Asian-owned businesses: n/a (2002); Women-owned businesses: n/a (2002); Retail sales per capita: $9,287 (2008). Single-family building permits issued: 7 (2007); Multi-family building permits issued: 0 (2007).
Income: Per capita income: $19,948 (2007); Median household income: $37,830 (2007); Average household income: $46,767 (2007); Percent of households with income of $100,000 or more: 8.7% (2007); Poverty rate: 16.4% (2005); Bankruptcy rate: 4.37% (2007).
Education: Percent of population age 25 and over with: High school diploma (including GED) or higher: 76.8% (2007); Bachelor's degree or higher: 10.9% (2007); Master's degree or higher: 3.4% (2007).
Housing: Homeownership rate: 79.1% (2007); Median home value: $90,949 (2007); Median rent: $263 per month (2000); Median age of housing: 35 years (2000).
Health: Birth rate: 138.3 per 10,000 population (2007); Death rate: 138.3 per 10,000 population (2007); Age-adjusted cancer mortality rate: 155.7 deaths per 100,000 population (2005); Number of physicians: 5.3 per 10,000 population (2005); Hospital beds: 16.4 per 10,000 population (2004); Hospital admissions: 674.8 per 10,000 population (2004).
Elections: 2004 Presidential election results: 61.7% Bush, 37.8% Kerry, 0.0% Nader, 0.4% Badnarik
National and State Parks: Fort Massac State Park; Mermet Lake State Conservation Area
Additional Information Contacts
Massac County Government . . . . (618) 524-5213

Metropolis Chamber of Commerce . . . . (618) 524-2714
http://www.metropolischamber.com

Massac County Communities

BROOKPORT (city). Covers a land area of 0.797 square miles and a water area of 0 square miles. Located at 37.12° N. Lat.; 88.62° W. Long. Elevation is 338 feet.
History: Brookport developed as an agricultural trading center on the Ohio River. The flooding of the river in 1937 damaged much of Brookport.
Population: 1,090 (1990); 1,054 (2000); 1,002 (2007); 990 (2012 projected); Race: 91.1% White, 6.7% Black, 0.3% Asian, 2.8% Hispanic of any race (2007); Density: 1,256.6 persons per square mile (2007); Average household size: 2.29 (2007); Median age: 34.8 (2007); Males per 100 females: 95.7 (2007); Marriage status: 21.7% never married, 54.2% now married, 7.8% widowed, 16.4% divorced (2000); Foreign born: 0.3% (2000); Ancestry (includes multiple ancestries): 25.7% Other groups, 15.3% German, 12.9% United States or American, 11.8% Irish, 7.4% English (2000).
Economy: Single-family building permits issued: 0 (2007); Multi-family building permits issued: 0 (2007); Employment by occupation: 6.9% management, 7.6% professional, 27.5% services, 25.9% sales, 0.7% farming, 9.2% construction, 22.3% production (2000).
Income: Per capita income: $15,729 (2007); Median household income: $29,236 (2007); Average household income: $36,064 (2007); Percent of households with income of $100,000 or more: 1.6% (2007); Poverty rate: 19.8% (2000).
Education: Percent of population age 25 and over with: High school diploma (including GED) or higher: 66.5% (2007); Bachelor's degree or higher: 3.8% (2007); Master's degree or higher: 0.6% (2007).

School District(s)

Massac UD 1 (PK-12)
2005-06 Enrollment: 2,387 . . . . (618) 524-9376
Housing: Homeownership rate: 73.5% (2007); Median home value: $56,064 (2007); Median rent: $216 per month (2000); Median age of housing: 32 years (2000).
Safety: Violent crime rate: 188.5 per 10,000 population; Property crime rate: 169.7 per 10,000 population (2006).

Transportation: Commute to work: 98.6% car, 0.0% public transportation, 1.2% walk, 0.0% work from home (2000); Travel time to work: 28.8% less than 15 minutes, 53.1% 15 to 30 minutes, 7.9% 30 to 45 minutes, 5.6% 45 to 60 minutes, 4.6% 60 minutes or more (2000)

JOPPA (village). Covers a land area of 0.488 square miles and a water area of 0.008 square miles. Located at 37.20° N. Lat.; 88.84° W. Long. Elevation is 354 feet.

Population: 492 (1990); 409 (2000); 352 (2007); 357 (2012 projected); Race: 91.2% White, 5.4% Black, 0.0% Asian, 4.0% Hispanic of any race (2007); Density: 721.4 persons per square mile (2007); Average household size: 2.43 (2007); Median age: 34.3 (2007); Males per 100 females: 109.5 (2007); Marriage status: 20.1% never married, 52.0% now married, 10.9% widowed, 17.0% divorced (2000); Foreign born: 0.0% (2000); Ancestry (includes multiple ancestries): 17.2% Other groups, 11.0% United States or American, 8.1% Irish, 7.6% German, 2.6% English (2000).
Economy: Employment by occupation: 4.2% management, 10.1% professional, 28.6% services, 16.0% sales, 0.0% farming, 16.0% construction, 25.2% production (2000).
Income: Per capita income: $11,314 (2007); Median household income: $21,042 (2007); Average household income: $27,466 (2007); Percent of households with income of $100,000 or more: 0.7% (2007); Poverty rate: 44.6% (2000).
Education: Percent of population age 25 and over with: High school diploma (including GED) or higher: 60.6% (2007); Bachelor's degree or higher: 6.8% (2007); Master's degree or higher: 3.6% (2007).

School District(s)

Five County Reg Voc System
2005-06 Enrollment: n/a . . . . (618) 747-2703
Joppa-Maple Grove UD 38 (PK-12)
2005-06 Enrollment: 314 . . . . (618) 543-9023

Housing: Homeownership rate: 69.0% (2007); Median home value: $39,286 (2007); Median rent: $169 per month (2000); Median age of housing: 47 years (2000).
Transportation: Commute to work: 92.1% car, 3.5% public transportation, 0.0% walk, 3.5% work from home (2000); Travel time to work: 23.6% less than 15 minutes, 41.8% 15 to 30 minutes, 21.8% 30 to 45 minutes, 3.6% 45 to 60 minutes, 9.1% 60 minutes or more (2000)

METROPOLIS (city). County seat. Covers a land area of 5.005 square miles and a water area of 0.064 square miles. Located at 37.15° N. Lat.; 88.72° W. Long. Elevation is 361 feet.

History: The first settlement in Metropolis was in 1796. This was platted in 1836 as the City of Massac. Metropolis City was platted in 1839 by William A. McBane and James H.G. Wilcox, who dreamed that their community would be a metropolis. Metropolis City was incorporated in 1845, and in 1892 the two communities united.
Population: 6,921 (1990); 6,482 (2000); 6,412 (2007); 6,371 (2012 projected); Race: 89.3% White, 9.0% Black, 0.2% Asian, 1.0% Hispanic of any race (2007); Density: 1,281.1 persons per square mile (2007); Average household size: 2.21 (2007); Median age: 42.9 (2007); Males per 100 females: 82.0 (2007); Marriage status: 17.5% never married, 54.9% now married, 13.0% widowed, 14.6% divorced (2000); Foreign born: 0.1% (2000); Ancestry (includes multiple ancestries): 18.3% Other groups, 18.1% German, 13.4% English, 10.9% Irish, 10.2% United States or American (2000).
Economy: Single-family building permits issued: 7 (2007); Multi-family building permits issued: 0 (2007); Employment by occupation: 7.5% management, 14.2% professional, 23.9% services, 26.3% sales, 0.0% farming, 9.5% construction, 18.5% production (2000).
Income: Per capita income: $18,161 (2007); Median household income: $29,321 (2007); Average household income: $38,320 (2007); Percent of households with income of $100,000 or more: 4.9% (2007); Poverty rate: 17.2% (2000).
Education: Percent of population age 25 and over with: High school diploma (including GED) or higher: 73.9% (2007); Bachelor's degree or higher: 9.8% (2007); Master's degree or higher: 3.8% (2007).

School District(s)

Five County Reg Voc System
2005-06 Enrollment: n/a . . . . (618) 747-2703
Joppa-Maple Grove UD 38 (PK-12)
2005-06 Enrollment: 314 . . . . (618) 543-9023
Massac UD 1 (PK-12)
2005-06 Enrollment: 2,387 . . . . (618) 524-9376

Housing: Homeownership rate: 69.2% (2007); Median home value: $75,455 (2007); Median rent: $279 per month (2000); Median age of housing: 45 years (2000).
Hospitals: Massac Memorial Hospital (57 beds)
Safety: Violent crime rate: 89.7 per 10,000 population; Property crime rate: 426.7 per 10,000 population (2006).
Newspapers: Metropolis Planet (Community news; Circulation 5,533); Southern Scene (Community news; Circulation 13,000)
Transportation: Commute to work: 93.9% car, 0.3% public transportation, 3.4% walk, 1.3% work from home (2000); Travel time to work: 53.8% less than 15 minutes, 26.7% 15 to 30 minutes, 12.4% 30 to 45 minutes, 2.6% 45 to 60 minutes, 4.5% 60 minutes or more (2000)
Additional Information Contacts
Metropolis Chamber of Commerce . . . . (618) 524-2714
http://www.metropolischamber.com

McDonough County

Located in western Illinois; drained by the La Moine River. Covers a land area of 589.27 square miles, a water area of 0.75 square miles, and is located in the Central Time Zone. The county was founded in 1826. County seat is Macomb.

McDonough County is part of the Macomb, IL Micropolitan Statistical Area. The entire metro area includes: McDonough County, IL

Population: 35,244 (1990); 32,913 (2000); 31,588 (2007); 30,480 (2012 projected); Race: 90.8% White, 4.5% Black, 2.9% Asian, 1.9% Hispanic of any race (2007); Density: 53.6 persons per square mile (2007); Average household size: 2.68 (2007); Median age: 30.4 (2007); Males per 100 females: 95.5 (2007).
Religion: Five largest groups: 7.8% The United Methodist Church, 6.8% Catholic Church, 3.8% Presbyterian Church (U.S.A.), 3.6% Christian Churches and Churches of Christ, 2.8% Assemblies of God (2000).
Economy: Unemployment rate: 3.8% (4/2008); Total civilian labor force: 17,829 (4/2008); Leading industries: 18.9% retail trade; 18.5% accommodation & food services; 16.7% health care and social assistance (2005); Farms: 752 totaling 324,724 acres (2002); Companies that employ 500 or more persons: 1 (2006); Companies that employ 100 to 499 persons: 11 (2006); Companies that employ less than 100 persons: 743 (2006); Black-owned businesses: n/a (2002); Hispanic-owned businesses: n/a (2002); Asian-owned businesses: n/a (2002); Women-owned businesses: n/a (2002); Retail sales per capita: $9,945 (2008). Single-family building permits issued: 14 (2007); Multi-family building permits issued: 86 (2007).
Income: Per capita income: $18,193 (2007); Median household income: $37,156 (2007); Average household income: $46,600 (2007); Percent of households with income of $100,000 or more: 8.4% (2007); Poverty rate: 20.9% (2005); Bankruptcy rate: 2.19% (2007).
Taxes: Total county taxes per capita: $114 (2006); County property taxes per capita: $114 (2006).
Education: Percent of population age 25 and over with: High school diploma (including GED) or higher: 87.0% (2007); Bachelor's degree or higher: 27.6% (2007); Master's degree or higher: 13.7% (2007).
Housing: Homeownership rate: 62.3% (2007); Median home value: $89,391 (2007); Median rent: $321 per month (2000); Median age of housing: 40 years (2000).
Health: Birth rate: 91.6 per 10,000 population (2007); Death rate: 86.3 per 10,000 population (2007); Age-adjusted cancer mortality rate: 186.6 deaths per 100,000 population (2005); Number of physicians: 13.4 per 10,000 population (2005); Hospital beds: 28.2 per 10,000 population (2004); Hospital admissions: 1,112.5 per 10,000 population (2004).
Elections: 2004 Presidential election results: 51.3% Bush, 47.7% Kerry, 0.3% Nader, 0.7% Badnarik
National and State Parks: Argyle Lake State Park
Additional Information Contacts
McDonough County Government . . . . (309) 837-2308

City of Macomb . . . . (309) 833-2575
http://www.cityofmacomb.com
Macomb Area Chamber of Commerce & Downtown Development Corpo
(309) 837-4855
http://www.macombareachamber.com
Macomb Area Convention & Visitors Bureau. . . . . (309) 833-1315
http://www.makeitmacomb.com

McDonough County Communities

ADAIR (unincorporated postal area, zip code 61411). Covers a land area of 38.024 square miles and a water area of 0.016 square miles. Located at 40.40° N. Lat.; 90.50° W. Long. Elevation is 646 feet.
Population: 419 (2000); Race: 100.0% White, 0.0% Black, 0.0% Asian, 0.0% Hispanic of any race (2000); Density: 11.0 persons per square mile (2000); Age: 14.4% under 18, 22.2% over 64 (2000); Marriage status: 22.0% never married, 58.8% now married, 10.4% widowed, 8.8% divorced (2000); Foreign born: 0.0% (2000); Ancestry (includes multiple ancestries): 21.0% English, 17.4% United States or American, 15.4% German, 5.6% Other groups, 4.5% Swedish (2000).
Economy: Employment by occupation: 19.4% management, 21.0% professional, 9.7% services, 20.6% sales, 5.6% farming, 5.6% construction, 18.1% production (2000).
Income: Per capita income: $20,915 (2000); Median household income: $40,893 (2000); Poverty rate: 3.8% (2000).
Education: Percent of population age 25 and over with: High school diploma (including GED) or higher: 84.5% (2000); Bachelor's degree or higher: 13.8% (2000).
Housing: Homeownership rate: 72.2% (2000); Median home value: $49,700 (2000); Median rent: $218 per month (2000); Median age of housing: 57 years (2000).
Transportation: Commute to work: 91.1% car, 0.0% public transportation, 0.0% walk, 0.8% work from home (2000); Travel time to work: 26.8% less than 15 minutes, 53.3% 15 to 30 minutes, 12.2% 30 to 45 minutes, 7.7% 45 to 60 minutes, 0.0% 60 minutes or more (2000)

BARDOLPH (village). Covers a land area of 0.595 square miles and a water area of 0 square miles. Located at 40.49° N. Lat.; 90.56° W. Long. Elevation is 673 feet.
Population: 301 (1990); 253 (2000); 212 (2007); 189 (2012 projected); Race: 100.0% White, 0.0% Black, 0.0% Asian, 0.0% Hispanic of any race (2007); Density: 356.5 persons per square mile (2007); Average household size: 2.86 (2007); Median age: 28.2 (2007); Males per 100 females: 92.7 (2007); Marriage status: 24.3% never married, 60.5% now married, 4.6% widowed, 10.5% divorced (2000); Foreign born: 0.0% (2000); Ancestry (includes multiple ancestries): 21.2% United States or American, 11.9% German, 10.2% Other groups, 8.4% Irish, 6.6% English (2000).
Economy: Employment by occupation: 4.2% management, 16.8% professional, 21.1% services, 21.1% sales, 0.0% farming, 12.6% construction, 24.2% production (2000).
Income: Per capita income: $12,729 (2007); Median household income: $30,000 (2007); Average household income: $36,216 (2007); Percent of households with income of $100,000 or more: 4.1% (2007); Poverty rate: 28.8% (2000).
Education: Percent of population age 25 and over with: High school diploma (including GED) or higher: 72.9% (2007); Bachelor's degree or higher: 13.6% (2007); Master's degree or higher: 8.5% (2007).
Housing: Homeownership rate: 58.1% (2007); Median home value: $37,500 (2007); Median rent: $316 per month (2000); Median age of housing: 35 years (2000).
Transportation: Commute to work: 95.7% car, 2.2% public transportation, 0.0% walk, 0.0% work from home (2000); Travel time to work: 33.3% less than 15 minutes, 41.9% 15 to 30 minutes, 12.9% 30 to 45 minutes, 4.3% 45 to 60 minutes, 7.5% 60 minutes or more (2000)

BLANDINSVILLE (village). Covers a land area of 0.885 square miles and a water area of 0 square miles. Located at 40.55° N. Lat.; 90.86° W. Long. Elevation is 728 feet.
Population: 762 (1990); 777 (2000); 606 (2007); 577 (2012 projected); Race: 98.3% White, 0.0% Black, 0.2% Asian, 0.7% Hispanic of any race (2007); Density: 684.9 persons per square mile (2007); Average household size: 2.29 (2007); Median age: 42.1 (2007); Males per 100 females: 100.7 (2007); Marriage status: 21.9% never married, 57.5% now married, 12.3% widowed, 8.4% divorced (2000); Foreign born: 0.3% (2000); Ancestry (includes multiple ancestries): 21.3% German, 14.0% English, 12.8% United States or American, 8.0% Other groups, 6.0% Irish (2000).
Economy: Employment by occupation: 12.0% management, 11.5% professional, 15.8% services, 31.2% sales, 1.0% farming, 6.0% construction, 22.5% production (2000).
Income: Per capita income: $19,769 (2007); Median household income: $36,125 (2007); Average household income: $45,208 (2007); Percent of households with income of $100,000 or more: 3.4% (2007); Poverty rate: 8.8% (2000).
Education: Percent of population age 25 and over with: High school diploma (including GED) or higher: 84.9% (2007); Bachelor's degree or higher: 11.2% (2007); Master's degree or higher: 1.6% (2007).
Housing: Homeownership rate: 80.8% (2007); Median home value: $71,818 (2007); Median rent: $264 per month (2000); Median age of housing: 60+ years (2000).
Safety: Violent crime rate: 27.8 per 10,000 population; Property crime rate: 153.0 per 10,000 population (2006).
Transportation: Commute to work: 95.4% car, 1.2% public transportation, 2.4% walk, 1.0% work from home (2000); Travel time to work: 24.2% less than 15 minutes, 48.9% 15 to 30 minutes, 13.4% 30 to 45 minutes, 7.3% 45 to 60 minutes, 6.1% 60 minutes or more (2000)

BUSHNELL (city). Covers a land area of 2.047 square miles and a water area of 0.008 square miles. Located at 40.55° N. Lat.; 90.50° W. Long. Elevation is 653 feet.
History: Incorporated 1865.
Population: 3,290 (1990); 3,221 (2000); 2,913 (2007); 2,668 (2012 projected); Race: 98.4% White, 0.2% Black, 0.1% Asian, 0.8% Hispanic of any race (2007); Density: 1,423.4 persons per square mile (2007); Average household size: 2.44 (2007); Median age: 38.0 (2007); Males per 100 females: 93.2 (2007); Marriage status: 21.8% never married, 58.5% now married, 9.5% widowed, 10.1% divorced (2000); Foreign born: 0.2% (2000); Ancestry (includes multiple ancestries): 15.7% United States or American, 15.2% German, 13.3% Irish, 10.4% English, 4.7% Other groups (2000).
Economy: Employment by occupation: 5.1% management, 13.7% professional, 19.5% services, 23.7% sales, 0.4% farming, 13.0% construction, 24.5% production (2000).
Income: Per capita income: $17,657 (2007); Median household income: $34,900 (2007); Average household income: $43,150 (2007); Percent of households with income of $100,000 or more: 4.9% (2007); Poverty rate: 17.0% (2000).
Education: Percent of population age 25 and over with: High school diploma (including GED) or higher: 82.6% (2007); Bachelor's degree or higher: 10.0% (2007); Master's degree or higher: 4.1% (2007).

School District(s)

Bushnell Prairie City CUSD 170 (PK-12)
2005-06 Enrollment: 821 . . . . (309) 772-9461

Housing: Homeownership rate: 74.7% (2007); Median home value: $59,115 (2007); Median rent: $247 per month (2000); Median age of housing: 48 years (2000).
Newspapers: McDonough Democrat (Community news; Circulation 5,000)
Transportation: Commute to work: 86.4% car, 0.0% public transportation, 7.9% walk, 3.4% work from home (2000); Travel time to work: 51.4% less than 15 minutes, 30.6% 15 to 30 minutes, 9.8% 30 to 45 minutes, 3.0% 45 to 60 minutes, 5.2% 60 minutes or more (2000)

COLCHESTER (city). Covers a land area of 0.995 square miles and a water area of 0 square miles. Located at 40.42° N. Lat.; 90.79° W. Long. Elevation is 692 feet.
History: Incorporated 1867.
Population: 1,658 (1990); 1,493 (2000); 1,255 (2007); 1,202 (2012 projected); Race: 99.4% White, 0.0% Black, 0.1% Asian, 0.6% Hispanic of any race (2007); Density: 1,261.5 persons per square mile (2007); Average household size: 2.32 (2007); Median age: 40.5 (2007); Males per 100 females: 87.6 (2007); Marriage status: 19.0% never married, 58.8% now married, 11.1% widowed, 11.1% divorced (2000); Foreign born: 0.8% (2000); Ancestry (includes multiple ancestries): 21.2% English, 19.6% German, 9.2% Irish, 9.1% United States or American, 6.9% Other groups (2000).
Economy: Employment by occupation: 5.9% management, 14.8% professional, 23.9% services, 23.0% sales, 1.0% farming, 9.6% construction, 21.8% production (2000).
Income: Per capita income: $19,338 (2007); Median household income: $36,221 (2007); Average household income: $43,965 (2007); Percent of households with income of $100,000 or more: 5.0% (2007); Poverty rate: 7.3% (2000).
Education: Percent of population age 25 and over with: High school diploma (including GED) or higher: 84.3% (2007); Bachelor's degree or higher: 10.4% (2007); Master's degree or higher: 2.4% (2007).

School District(s)

West Prairie CUSD 103 (PK-12)
2005-06 Enrollment: 775 . . . . (309) 776-3180

Housing: Homeownership rate: 74.5% (2007); Median home value: $59,894 (2007); Median rent: $256 per month (2000); Median age of housing: 46 years (2000).
Transportation: Commute to work: 91.4% car, 0.3% public transportation, 3.5% walk, 2.7% work from home (2000); Travel time to work: 33.7% less than 15 minutes, 51.0% 15 to 30 minutes, 6.9% 30 to 45 minutes, 1.9% 45 to 60 minutes, 6.6% 60 minutes or more (2000)

GOOD HOPE (village). Covers a land area of 0.295 square miles and a water area of 0 square miles. Located at 40.55° N. Lat.; 90.67° W. Long. Elevation is 709 feet.
History: When Good Hope was platted in 1866, it was called Sheridan by its founder, J.E. Morris. The town of Milan was laid out next to Sheridan the following year. Since both were served by the post office which was called Good Hope, that is the name that survived.
Population: 447 (1990); 415 (2000); 388 (2007); 352 (2012 projected); Race: 99.0% White, 0.0% Black, 0.0% Asian, 0.8% Hispanic of any race (2007); Density: 1,316.4 persons per square mile (2007); Average household size: 2.35 (2007); Median age: 41.3 (2007); Males per 100 females: 103.1 (2007); Marriage status: 20.2% never married, 65.7% now married, 7.1% widowed, 7.1% divorced (2000); Foreign born: 1.2% (2000); Ancestry (includes multiple ancestries): 25.1% German, 23.8% English, 8.1% United States or American, 8.1% Irish, 6.9% Scottish (2000).
Economy: Employment by occupation: 8.9% management, 15.6% professional, 25.0% services, 21.4% sales, 3.1% farming, 16.1% construction, 9.9% production (2000).
Income: Per capita income: $19,259 (2007); Median household income: $45,921 (2007); Average household income: $45,288 (2007); Percent of households with income of $100,000 or more: 1.8% (2007); Poverty rate: 9.8% (2000).
Education: Percent of population age 25 and over with: High school diploma (including GED) or higher: 90.6% (2007); Bachelor's degree or higher: 18.4% (2007); Master's degree or higher: 5.2% (2007).

School District(s)

West Prairie CUSD 103 (PK-12)
2005-06 Enrollment: 775 . . . . (309) 776-3180
Housing: Homeownership rate: 79.4% (2007); Median home value: $87,308 (2007); Median rent: $275 per month (2000); Median age of housing: 52 years (2000).
Transportation: Commute to work: 96.9% car, 0.0% public transportation, 1.6% walk, 1.6% work from home (2000); Travel time to work: 41.8% less than 15 minutes, 46.6% 15 to 30 minutes, 5.3% 30 to 45 minutes, 3.2% 45 to 60 minutes, 3.2% 60 minutes or more (2000)

INDUSTRY (village). Covers a land area of 0.471 square miles and a water area of <.001 square miles. Located at 40.32° N. Lat.; 90.60° W. Long. Elevation is 659 feet.
History: The first settler in Industry was William Carter who came in 1826. The village was organized in the 1840's.
Population: 571 (1990); 540 (2000); 469 (2007); 420 (2012 projected); Race: 96.6% White, 0.2% Black, 1.3% Asian, 1.3% Hispanic of any race (2007); Density: 995.5 persons per square mile (2007); Average household size: 2.54 (2007); Median age: 34.5 (2007); Males per 100 females: 96.2 (2007); Marriage status: 18.9% never married, 67.4% now married, 7.2% widowed, 6.5% divorced (2000); Foreign born: 0.0% (2000); Ancestry (includes multiple ancestries): 18.6% German, 12.3% English, 11.5% United States or American, 6.7% Dutch, 4.5% Other groups (2000).
Economy: Employment by occupation: 8.8% management, 19.2% professional, 16.0% services, 23.6% sales, 1.2% farming, 13.6% construction, 17.6% production (2000).
Income: Per capita income: $17,916 (2007); Median household income: $41,731 (2007); Average household income: $45,419 (2007); Percent of households with income of $100,000 or more: 4.3% (2007); Poverty rate: 13.8% (2000).
Education: Percent of population age 25 and over with: High school diploma (including GED) or higher: 83.8% (2007); Bachelor's degree or higher: 18.2% (2007); Master's degree or higher: 3.8% (2007).

School District(s)

Schuyler-Industry CUSD 5 (PK-12)
2005-06 Enrollment: 1,339 . . . . (217) 322-4311
Housing: Homeownership rate: 84.3% (2007); Median home value: $69,000 (2007); Median rent: $208 per month (2000); Median age of housing: 50 years (2000).
Transportation: Commute to work: 89.8% car, 0.0% public transportation, 6.9% walk, 2.8% work from home (2000); Travel time to work: 33.5% less than 15 minutes, 54.8% 15 to 30 minutes, 6.7% 30 to 45 minutes, 3.8% 45 to 60 minutes, 1.3% 60 minutes or more (2000)

MACOMB (city). County seat. Covers a land area of 9.849 square miles and a water area of 0.401 square miles. Located at 40.46° N. Lat.; 90.67° W. Long. Elevation is 705 feet.
History: Macomb was settled in 1830, incorporated as a village in 1841, and as a city in 1856. Many of the early settlers were from New England, and they named the town for Alexander Macomb, Commander-in-Chief of the U.S. Army from 1828 to 1841.
Population: 20,205 (1990); 18,558 (2000); 18,616 (2007); 18,537 (2012 projected); Race: 86.1% White, 7.3% Black, 4.2% Asian, 2.6% Hispanic of any race (2007); Density: 1,890.1 persons per square mile (2007); Average household size: 2.86 (2007); Median age: 24.5 (2007); Males per 100 females: 94.9 (2007); Marriage status: 49.3% never married, 39.2% now married, 5.6% widowed, 5.9% divorced (2000); Foreign born: 4.1% (2000); Ancestry (includes multiple ancestries): 26.5% German, 15.7% Irish, 12.8% Other groups, 11.7% English, 6.5% United States or American (2000).
Economy: Single-family building permits issued: 14 (2007); Multi-family building permits issued: 86 (2007); Employment by occupation: 7.0% management, 27.4% professional, 23.4% services, 26.4% sales, 1.3% farming, 5.3% construction, 9.2% production (2000).
Income: Per capita income: $15,330 (2007); Median household income: $29,793 (2007); Average household income: $40,034 (2007); Percent of households with income of $100,000 or more: 7.0% (2007); Poverty rate: 29.1% (2000).
Taxes: Total city taxes per capita: $77 (2006); City property taxes per capita: $31 (2006).
Education: Percent of population age 25 and over with: High school diploma (including GED) or higher: 88.3% (2007); Bachelor's degree or higher: 36.3% (2007); Master's degree or higher: 19.3% (2007).

School District(s)

Hancock/Mc Donough Roe (08-12)
2005-06 Enrollment: 40 . . . . (309) 837-4821
Macomb CUSD 185 (PK-12)
2005-06 Enrollment: 1,876 . . . . (309) 833-4161
West Central Ill Spec Educ Coop (07-12)
2005-06 Enrollment: 80 . . . . (309) 837-3911
Western Area Career System 265
2005-06 Enrollment: n/a . . . . (309) 837-4821

Four-year College(s)

Western Illinois University (Public)
Fall 2007 Enrollment: 13,331 . . . . (309) 295-1414
2007-08 Tuition: In-state $8,079; Out-of-state $11,027
Housing: Homeownership rate: 48.2% (2007); Median home value: $97,077 (2007); Median rent: $340 per month (2000); Median age of housing: 37 years (2000).
Hospitals: McDonough District Hospital (113 beds)
Safety: Violent crime rate: 39.3 per 10,000 population; Property crime rate: 212.0 per 10,000 population (2006).
Newspapers: Macomb Eagle (Community news; Circulation 2,500); Macomb Journal (Local news; Circulation 7,000)
Transportation: Commute to work: 77.3% car, 2.3% public transportation, 15.5% walk, 2.9% work from home (2000); Travel time to work: 76.8% less than 15 minutes, 14.1% 15 to 30 minutes, 4.6% 30 to 45 minutes, 1.2% 45 to 60 minutes, 3.4% 60 minutes or more (2000); Amtrak: Service available.
Airports: Macomb Municipal (general aviation)

Additional Information Contacts

City of Macomb . . . . (309) 833-2575
http://www.cityofmacomb.com
Macomb Area Chamber of Commerce & Downtown Development Corpo
(309) 837-4855
http://www.macombareachamber.com
Macomb Area Convention & Visitors Bureau . . . . (309) 833-1315
http://www.makeitmacomb.com

PRAIRIE CITY (village). Covers a land area of 1.013 square miles and a water area of 0 square miles. Located at 40.62° N. Lat.; 90.46° W. Long. Elevation is 669 feet.
Population: 497 (1990); 461 (2000); 410 (2007); 381 (2012 projected); Race: 96.3% White, 0.0% Black, 2.2% Asian, 1.2% Hispanic of any race (2007); Density: 404.8 persons per square mile (2007); Average household size: 3.01 (2007); Median age: 39.8 (2007); Males per 100 females: 94.3 (2007); Marriage status: 26.0% never married, 52.8% now married, 14.1% widowed, 7.1% divorced (2000); Foreign born: 0.2% (2000); Ancestry

(includes multiple ancestries): 14.8% German, 12.2% United States or American, 5.8% English, 5.6% Welsh, 5.2% Irish (2000).
Economy: Employment by occupation: 8.9% management, 8.4% professional, 14.0% services, 21.2% sales, 0.0% farming, 8.9% construction, 38.5% production (2000).
Income: Per capita income: $17,061 (2007); Median household income: $44,286 (2007); Average household income: $49,908 (2007); Percent of households with income of $100,000 or more: 5.1% (2007); Poverty rate: 22.6% (2000).
Education: Percent of population age 25 and over with: High school diploma (including GED) or higher: 81.9% (2007); Bachelor's degree or higher: 6.5% (2007); Master's degree or higher: 4.0% (2007).
Housing: Homeownership rate: 90.4% (2007); Median home value: $39,643 (2007); Median rent: $219 per month (2000); Median age of housing: 60+ years (2000).
Transportation: Commute to work: 93.4% car, 0.0% public transportation, 3.8% walk, 0.0% work from home (2000); Travel time to work: 44.5% less than 15 minutes, 21.4% 15 to 30 minutes, 22.0% 30 to 45 minutes, 2.7% 45 to 60 minutes, 9.3% 60 minutes or more (2000)

SCIOTA (village). Covers a land area of 0.317 square miles and a water area of 0 square miles. Located at 40.56° N. Lat.; 90.75° W. Long. Elevation is 758 feet.
Population: 68 (1990); 58 (2000); 60 (2007); 54 (2012 projected); Race: 100.0% White, 0.0% Black, 0.0% Asian, 0.0% Hispanic of any race (2007); Density: 189.0 persons per square mile (2007); Average household size: 2.07 (2007); Median age: 36.2 (2007); Males per 100 females: 81.8 (2007); Marriage status: 19.4% never married, 44.4% now married, 16.7% widowed, 19.4% divorced (2000); Foreign born: 0.0% (2000); Ancestry (includes multiple ancestries): 11.1% Swedish, 11.1% English, 6.7% United States or American, 6.7% German, 6.7% Danish (2000).
Economy: Employment by occupation: 22.7% management, 9.1% professional, 18.2% services, 13.6% sales, 0.0% farming, 27.3% construction, 9.1% production (2000).
Income: Per capita income: $20,667 (2007); Median household income: $40,833 (2007); Average household income: $42,759 (2007); Percent of households with income of $100,000 or more: 3.4% (2007); Poverty rate: 4.4% (2000).
Taxes: Total city taxes per capita: $38 (2006); City property taxes per capita: $38 (2006).
Education: Percent of population age 25 and over with: High school diploma (including GED) or higher: 94.9% (2007); Bachelor's degree or higher: 15.4% (2007); Master's degree or higher: 0.0% (2007).

School District(s)

West Prairie CUSD 103 (PK-12)
2005-06 Enrollment: 775 . . . . (309) 776-3180
Housing: Homeownership rate: 72.4% (2007); Median home value: $23,125 (2007); Median rent: $225 per month (2000); Median age of housing: 60+ years (2000).
Transportation: Commute to work: 90.9% car, 0.0% public transportation, 9.1% walk, 0.0% work from home (2000); Travel time to work: 27.3% less than 15 minutes, 59.1% 15 to 30 minutes, 13.6% 30 to 45 minutes, 0.0% 45 to 60 minutes, 0.0% 60 minutes or more (2000)

TENNESSEE (village). Covers a land area of 0.425 square miles and a water area of 0 square miles. Located at 40.41° N. Lat.; 90.83° W. Long. Elevation is 686 feet.
Population: 127 (1990); 144 (2000); 147 (2007); 135 (2012 projected); Race: 98.6% White, 0.0% Black, 0.0% Asian, 0.0% Hispanic of any race (2007); Density: 346.3 persons per square mile (2007); Average household size: 2.23 (2007); Median age: 41.1 (2007); Males per 100 females: 93.4 (2007); Marriage status: 10.3% never married, 65.0% now married, 14.5% widowed, 10.3% divorced (2000); Foreign born: 0.0% (2000); Ancestry (includes multiple ancestries): 22.3% German, 12.9% Other groups, 11.5% United States or American, 7.2% English, 5.0% Irish (2000).
Economy: Employment by occupation: 5.9% management, 5.9% professional, 17.6% services, 17.6% sales, 2.0% farming, 13.7% construction, 37.3% production (2000).
Income: Per capita income: $14,558 (2007); Median household income: $29,286 (2007); Average household income: $32,424 (2007); Percent of households with income of $100,000 or more: 1.5% (2007); Poverty rate: 22.3% (2000).
Education: Percent of population age 25 and over with: High school diploma (including GED) or higher: 74.5% (2007); Bachelor's degree or higher: 2.0% (2007); Master's degree or higher: 2.0% (2007).
Housing: Homeownership rate: 89.4% (2007); Median home value: $48,750 (2007); Median rent: $275 per month (2000); Median age of housing: 41 years (2000).
Transportation: Commute to work: 91.8% car, 0.0% public transportation, 0.0% walk, 8.2% work from home (2000); Travel time to work: 37.8% less than 15 minutes, 57.8% 15 to 30 minutes, 0.0% 30 to 45 minutes, 0.0% 45 to 60 minutes, 4.4% 60 minutes or more (2000)

McHenry County

Located in northeastern Illinois; bounded on the north by Wisconsin; drained by the Fox and Kishwaukee Rivers; includes many lakes. Covers a land area of 603.51 square miles, a water area of 7.62 square miles, and is located in the Central Time Zone. The county was founded in 1836. County seat is Woodstock.

McHenry County is part of the Chicago-Naperville-Joliet, IL-IN-WI Metropolitan Statistical Area. The entire metro area includes: Chicago-Naperville-Joliet, IL Metropolitan Division (Cook County, IL; DeKalb County, IL; DuPage County, IL; Grundy County, IL; Kane County, IL; Kendall County, IL; McHenry County, IL; Will County, IL); Gary, IN Metropolitan Division (Jasper County, IN; Lake County, IN; Newton County, IN; Porter County, IN); Lake County-Kenosha County, IL-WI Metropolitan Division (Lake County, IL; Kenosha County, WI)

Weather Station: Marengo Elevation: 816 feet

	Jan	Feb	Mar	Apr	May	Jun	Jul	Aug	Sep	Oct	Nov	Dec
High	28	33	45	59	72	82	85	82	75	63	47	33
Low	10	14	25	36	46	56	61	59	50	38	28	16
Precip	1.4	1.2	2.4	3.6	3.9	4.4	3.9	4.4	3.6	2.7	2.7	2.0
Snow	11.7	7.7	4.8	1.7	0.1	0.0	0.0	0.0	0.0	tr	2.5	8.4

High and Low temperatures in degrees Fahrenheit; Precipitation and Snow in inches

Population: 183,241 (1990); 260,077 (2000); 315,673 (2007); 353,088 (2012 projected); Race: 90.7% White, 1.0% Black, 2.6% Asian, 10.7% Hispanic of any race (2007); Density: 523.1 persons per square mile (2007); Average household size: 2.91 (2007); Median age: 35.5 (2007); Males per 100 females: 100.7 (2007).
Religion: Five largest groups: 29.4% Catholic Church, 4.9% Evangelical Lutheran Church in America, 4.0% Lutheran Church—Missouri Synod, 2.6% The United Methodist Church, 2.1% United Church of Christ (2000).
Economy: Unemployment rate: 5.3% (4/2008); Total civilian labor force: 181,940 (4/2008); Leading industries: 21.5% manufacturing; 14.7% retail trade; 11.6% wholesale trade (2005); Farms: 870 totaling 233,458 acres (2002); Companies that employ 500 or more persons: 9 (2006); Companies that employ 100 to 499 persons: 135 (2006); Companies that employ less than 100 persons: 7,853 (2006); Black-owned businesses: 143 (2002); Hispanic-owned businesses: 611 (2002); Asian-owned businesses: 635 (2002); Women-owned businesses: 6,402 (2002); Retail sales per capita: $14,853 (2008). Single-family building permits issued: 1,536 (2007); Multi-family building permits issued: 122 (2007).
Income: Per capita income: $31,001 (2007); Median household income: $74,826 (2007); Average household income: $89,787 (2007); Percent of households with income of $100,000 or more: 31.2% (2007); Poverty rate: 4.6% (2005); Bankruptcy rate: 2.47% (2007).
Taxes: Total county taxes per capita: $195 (2006); County property taxes per capita: $166 (2006).
Education: Percent of population age 25 and over with: High school diploma (including GED) or higher: 89.4% (2007); Bachelor's degree or higher: 28.0% (2007); Master's degree or higher: 8.1% (2007).
Housing: Homeownership rate: 83.5% (2007); Median home value: $242,915 (2007); Median rent: $677 per month (2000); Median age of housing: 22 years (2000).
Health: Birth rate: 148.4 per 10,000 population (2007); Death rate: 58.9 per 10,000 population (2007); Age-adjusted cancer mortality rate: 186.1 deaths per 100,000 population (2005); Air Quality Index: 76.4% good, 22.7% moderate, 0.8% unhealthy for sensitive individuals, 0.0% unhealthy (percent of days in 2007); Number of physicians: 12.3 per 10,000 population (2005); Hospital beds: 13.0 per 10,000 population (2004); Hospital admissions: 709.1 per 10,000 population (2004).
Elections: 2004 Presidential election results: 59.7% Bush, 39.3% Kerry, 0.2% Nader, 0.8% Badnarik
National and State Parks: Moraine Hills State Park
Additional Information Contacts
McHenry County Government . . . . (815) 334-4000
http://www.co.mchenry.il.us

Algonquin/Lake in the Hills Chamber of Commerce . . . . . . (847) 658-5300
http://www.algonquin-lith-chamber.com
Cary Grove Area Chamber of Commerce . . . . (847) 639-2800
http://www.carygrovechamber.com
City of Crystal Lake . . . . (815) 459-2020
http://www.crystallake.org
City of Harvard . . . . (815) 943-6468
http://www.cityofharvard.org
City of Marengo . . . . (815) 568-7112
http://www.cityofmarengo.com
City of McHenry . . . . (815) 363-2100
http://www.ci.mchenry.il.us
City of Woodstock . . . . (815) 338-4300
http://www.woodstock-il.com
Crystal Lake Chamber of Commerce. . . . . (815) 459-1300
http://www.clchamber.com
Harvard Chamber of Commerce . . . . (815) 943-4404
http://www.harvcc.net
Huntley Area Chamber of Commerce & Industry. . . . . (847) 669-0166
http://www.huntleychamber.org
Island Lake Area Chamber of Commerce . . . . (847) 604-4522
http://www.islandlakechamber.org
Marengo Union Chamber of Commerce . . . . (815) 568-6680
http://www.marengo-union.com
McHenry Area Chamber of Commerce . . . . (815) 385-4300
http://www.mchenrychamber.com
Richmond/Spring Grove Chamber of Commerce . . . . (815) 678-7742
http://www.rsgchamber.com
Village of Algonquin . . . . (847) 658-2700
http://www.algonquin.org
Village of Cary . . . . (847) 639-0003
http://www.caryillinois.com
Village of Huntley . . . . (847) 669-9600
http://www.huntley.il.us
Village of Island Lake. . . . . (847) 526-8764
http://www.villageofislandlake.com
Village of Johnsburg . . . . (815) 385-6023
http://www.johnsburg.org
Village of Lake in the Hills . . . . (847) 960-7400
http://www.lith.org
Wonder Lake Chamber of Commerce . . . . (815) 728-0682
http://www.wonderlake.org
Woodstock Chamber of Commerce & Industry . . . . (815) 338-2436
http://www.woodstockilchamber.com

McHenry County Communities

ALGONQUIN (village). Covers a land area of 9.832 square miles and a water area of 0.164 square miles. Located at 42.16° N. Lat.; 88.30° W. Long. Elevation is 741 feet.
Population: 12,745 (1990); 23,276 (2000); 32,031 (2007); 37,732 (2012 projected); Race: 90.6% White, 1.5% Black, 4.2% Asian, 6.2% Hispanic of any race (2007); Density: 3,257.8 persons per square mile (2007); Average household size: 3.06 (2007); Median age: 35.2 (2007); Males per 100 females: 98.8 (2007); Marriage status: 18.5% never married, 71.4% now married, 3.3% widowed, 6.7% divorced (2000); Foreign born: 6.3% (2000); Ancestry (includes multiple ancestries): 33.1% German, 18.6% Polish, 17.0% Irish, 12.1% Italian, 9.1% English (2000).
Economy: Unemployment rate: 4.5% (4/2008); Total civilian labor force: 17,048 (4/2008); Single-family building permits issued: 33 (2007); Multi-family building permits issued: 0 (2007); Employment by occupation: 20.9% management, 22.1% professional, 8.6% services, 30.9% sales, 0.0% farming, 7.4% construction, 10.0% production (2000).
Income: Per capita income: $35,210 (2007); Median household income: $93,317 (2007); Average household income: $107,553 (2007); Percent of households with income of $100,000 or more: 45.1% (2007); Poverty rate: 1.7% (2000).
Education: Percent of population age 25 and over with: High school diploma (including GED) or higher: 94.9% (2007); Bachelor's degree or higher: 39.0% (2007); Master's degree or higher: 11.1% (2007).

School District(s)

CUSD 300 (PK-12)
2005-06 Enrollment: 18,670 . . . . (847) 426-1300
Cons SD 158 (PK-12)
2005-06 Enrollment: 6,929 . . . . (847) 659-6158

Housing: Homeownership rate: 94.2% (2007); Median home value: $279,515 (2007); Median rent: $711 per month (2000); Median age of housing: 10 years (2000).
Safety: Violent crime rate: 10.3 per 10,000 population; Property crime rate: 186.4 per 10,000 population (2006).
Newspapers: Algonquin Countryside (Community news; Circulation 2,243); Cary-Grove Countryside (Community news; Circulation 2,442); Lake Zurich Courier (Local news; Circulation 4,279); Pioneer Press - Northwest/Barrington Bureau (Community news; Circulation 0); Wauconda Leader (Regional news; Circulation 4,309)
Transportation: Commute to work: 91.5% car, 2.5% public transportation, 1.0% walk, 4.1% work from home (2000); Travel time to work: 16.2% less than 15 minutes, 24.9% 15 to 30 minutes, 27.7% 30 to 45 minutes, 16.2% 45 to 60 minutes, 15.0% 60 minutes or more (2000)

Additional Information Contacts

Algonquin/Lake in the Hills Chamber of Commerce . . . . . . (847) 658-5300
http://www.algonquin-lith-chamber.com
Village of Algonquin . . . . (847) 658-2700
http://www.algonquin.org

BULL VALLEY (village). Covers a land area of 5.609 square miles and a water area of 0 square miles. Located at 42.31° N. Lat.; 88.36° W. Long. Elevation is 922 feet.
Population: 699 (1990); 726 (2000); 922 (2007); 1,061 (2012 projected); Race: 94.8% White, 1.0% Black, 2.2% Asian, 3.7% Hispanic of any race (2007); Density: 164.4 persons per square mile (2007); Average household size: 2.70 (2007); Median age: 47.5 (2007); Males per 100 females: 87.8 (2007); Marriage status: 14.5% never married, 76.7% now married, 5.7% widowed, 3.1% divorced (2000); Foreign born: 4.2% (2000); Ancestry (includes multiple ancestries): 34.6% German, 18.0% Irish, 13.3% English, 9.7% Italian, 8.1% Other groups (2000).
Economy: Single-family building permits issued: 6 (2007); Multi-family building permits issued: 0 (2007); Employment by occupation: 33.5% management, 26.9% professional, 2.5% services, 28.8% sales, 0.3% farming, 3.5% construction, 4.4% production (2000).
Income: Per capita income: $62,322 (2007); Median household income: $104,167 (2007); Average household income: $168,380 (2007); Percent of households with income of $100,000 or more: 51.3% (2007); Poverty rate: 2.3% (2000).
Education: Percent of population age 25 and over with: High school diploma (including GED) or higher: 95.8% (2007); Bachelor's degree or higher: 50.8% (2007); Master's degree or higher: 21.9% (2007).
Housing: Homeownership rate: 95.6% (2007); Median home value: $557,522 (2007); Median rent: $1,542 per month (2000); Median age of housing: 26 years (2000).
Safety: Violent crime rate: 0.0 per 10,000 population; Property crime rate: 116.7 per 10,000 population (2006).
Transportation: Commute to work: 78.8% car, 9.1% public transportation, 1.6% walk, 9.8% work from home (2000); Travel time to work: 29.6% less than 15 minutes, 26.0% 15 to 30 minutes, 14.8% 30 to 45 minutes, 5.1% 45 to 60 minutes, 24.5% 60 minutes or more (2000)

CARY (village). Covers a land area of 5.253 square miles and a water area of 0.058 square miles. Located at 42.21° N. Lat.; 88.24° W. Long. Elevation is 823 feet.
Population: 10,305 (1990); 15,531 (2000); 18,842 (2007); 21,062 (2012 projected); Race: 93.4% White, 0.5% Black, 2.4% Asian, 7.7% Hispanic of any race (2007); Density: 3,586.6 persons per square mile (2007); Average household size: 3.20 (2007); Median age: 34.5 (2007); Males per 100 females: 98.3 (2007); Marriage status: 20.2% never married, 69.8% now married, 2.9% widowed, 7.0% divorced (2000); Foreign born: 4.4% (2000); Ancestry (includes multiple ancestries): 33.9% German, 24.0% Irish, 13.7% Polish, 12.2% Italian, 10.3% English (2000).
Economy: Single-family building permits issued: 8 (2007); Multi-family building permits issued: 0 (2007); Employment by occupation: 20.3% management, 22.0% professional, 10.3% services, 31.1% sales, 0.0% farming, 6.6% construction, 9.7% production (2000).
Income: Per capita income: $30,963 (2007); Median household income: $87,924 (2007); Average household income: $99,212 (2007); Percent of households with income of $100,000 or more: 40.1% (2007); Poverty rate: 1.3% (2000).
Education: Percent of population age 25 and over with: High school diploma (including GED) or higher: 94.4% (2007); Bachelor's degree or higher: 42.5% (2007); Master's degree or higher: 13.6% (2007).

School District(s)

CHSD 155 (09-12)
2005-06 Enrollment: 6,939 . . . . (815) 455-8500
Cary CCSD 26 (PK-08)
2005-06 Enrollment: 3,632 . . . . (847) 639-7788

Housing: Homeownership rate: 91.5% (2007); Median home value: $265,088 (2007); Median rent: $746 per month (2000); Median age of housing: 17 years (2000).
Safety: Violent crime rate: 11.5 per 10,000 population; Property crime rate: 161.1 per 10,000 population (2006).
Transportation: Commute to work: 87.6% car, 6.6% public transportation, 0.4% walk, 4.2% work from home (2000); Travel time to work: 24.3% less than 15 minutes, 18.0% 15 to 30 minutes, 20.2% 30 to 45 minutes, 16.4% 45 to 60 minutes, 21.1% 60 minutes or more (2000)
Additional Information Contacts
Cary Grove Area Chamber of Commerce . . . . (847) 639-2800
http://www.carygrovechamber.com
Village of Cary . . . . (847) 639-0003
http://www.caryillinois.com

CRYSTAL LAKE (city). Covers a land area of 16.243 square miles and a water area of 0.560 square miles. Located at 42.22° N. Lat.; 88.33° W. Long. Elevation is 915 feet.
History: Named for the small lake around which the town developed. Crystal Lake was settled in 1825 when the Erie Canal opened, and grew when the Chicago & North Western Railroad arrived.
Population: 25,852 (1990); 38,000 (2000); 41,572 (2007); 44,163 (2012 projected); Race: 91.0% White, 0.9% Black, 3.2% Asian, 10.2% Hispanic of any race (2007); Density: 2,559.4 persons per square mile (2007); Average household size: 2.89 (2007); Median age: 35.4 (2007); Males per 100 females: 98.3 (2007); Marriage status: 21.3% never married, 65.2% now married, 5.4% widowed, 8.1% divorced (2000); Foreign born: 7.4% (2000); Ancestry (includes multiple ancestries): 34.5% German, 21.1% Irish, 11.9% Polish, 10.0% English, 9.3% Other groups (2000).
Economy: Unemployment rate: 4.9% (4/2008); Total civilian labor force: 22,847 (4/2008); Single-family building permits issued: 107 (2007); Multi-family building permits issued: 0 (2007); Employment by occupation: 19.5% management, 21.2% professional, 10.4% services, 29.7% sales, 0.1% farming, 7.2% construction, 11.9% production (2000).
Income: Per capita income: $30,658 (2007); Median household income: $76,073 (2007); Average household income: $88,494 (2007); Percent of households with income of $100,000 or more: 31.5% (2007); Poverty rate: 3.5% (2000).
Education: Percent of population age 25 and over with: High school diploma (including GED) or higher: 91.6% (2007); Bachelor's degree or higher: 36.8% (2007); Master's degree or higher: 10.9% (2007).

School District(s)

CHSD 155 (09-12)
2005-06 Enrollment: 6,939 . . . . (815) 455-8500
Crystal Lake CCSD 47 (PK-08)
2005-06 Enrollment: 9,266 . . . . (815) 459-6070
Prairie Grove Csd 46 (KG-08)
2005-06 Enrollment: 1,053 . . . . (815) 459-3023

Two-year College(s)

McHenry County College (Public)
Fall 2007 Enrollment: 5,274. . . . . (815) 455-3700
2007-08 Tuition: In-state $8,041; Out-of-state $9,678

Vocational/Technical School(s)

Cosmetology & Spa Institute (Private, For-profit)
Fall 2007 Enrollment: 73 . . . . (815) 455-5900
2007-08 Tuition: $14,000
First Institute Inc (Private, For-profit)
Fall 2007 Enrollment: 79 . . . . (815) 459-3500
2007-08 Tuition: $10,000

Housing: Homeownership rate: 79.4% (2007); Median home value: $233,988 (2007); Median rent: $773 per month (2000); Median age of housing: 19 years (2000).
Safety: Violent crime rate: 17.6 per 10,000 population; Property crime rate: 281.5 per 10,000 population (2006).
Newspapers: Northwest Herald (Local news; Circulation 33,800)
Transportation: Commute to work: 90.3% car, 4.3% public transportation, 1.3% walk, 3.3% work from home (2000); Travel time to work: 29.6% less than 15 minutes, 23.9% 15 to 30 minutes, 16.9% 30 to 45 minutes, 12.5% 45 to 60 minutes, 17.1% 60 minutes or more (2000)
Additional Information Contacts
City of Crystal Lake . . . . (815) 459-2020
http://www.crystallake.org
Crystal Lake Chamber of Commerce. . . . . (815) 459-1300
http://www.clchamber.com

FOX RIVER GROVE (village). Covers a land area of 1.660 square miles and a water area of 0.104 square miles. Located at 42.19° N. Lat.; 88.21° W. Long. Elevation is 817 feet.
History: Fox River Grove developed as a summer resort town.
Population: 3,900 (1990); 4,862 (2000); 5,095 (2007); 5,286 (2012 projected); Race: 93.9% White, 1.0% Black, 1.9% Asian, 4.9% Hispanic of any race (2007); Density: 3,070.0 persons per square mile (2007); Average household size: 2.91 (2007); Median age: 36.3 (2007); Males per 100 females: 104.5 (2007); Marriage status: 20.8% never married, 66.9% now married, 1.8% widowed, 10.4% divorced (2000); Foreign born: 4.4% (2000); Ancestry (includes multiple ancestries): 32.3% German, 22.4% Irish, 13.9% Polish, 11.5% Italian, 7.9% English (2000).
Economy: Single-family building permits issued: 4 (2007); Multi-family building permits issued: 0 (2007); Employment by occupation: 16.4% management, 18.9% professional, 10.1% services, 31.8% sales, 0.0% farming, 11.0% construction, 11.8% production (2000).
Income: Per capita income: $32,627 (2007); Median household income: $75,896 (2007); Average household income: $94,990 (2007); Percent of households with income of $100,000 or more: 31.5% (2007); Poverty rate: 7.1% (2000).
Education: Percent of population age 25 and over with: High school diploma (including GED) or higher: 92.3% (2007); Bachelor's degree or higher: 32.7% (2007); Master's degree or higher: 7.3% (2007).

School District(s)

Fox River Grove Cons SD 3 (PK-08)
2005-06 Enrollment: 588 . . . . (847) 516-5100

Housing: Homeownership rate: 83.9% (2007); Median home value: $265,283 (2007); Median rent: $720 per month (2000); Median age of housing: 24 years (2000).
Safety: Violent crime rate: 13.8 per 10,000 population; Property crime rate: 157.4 per 10,000 population (2006).
Transportation: Commute to work: 86.0% car, 6.5% public transportation, 1.2% walk, 6.0% work from home (2000); Travel time to work: 21.2% less than 15 minutes, 21.7% 15 to 30 minutes, 20.6% 30 to 45 minutes, 13.4% 45 to 60 minutes, 23.0% 60 minutes or more (2000)

FOX RIVER VALLEY GARDENS (village). Covers a land area of 0.979 square miles and a water area of 0.096 square miles. Located at 42.24° N. Lat.; 88.19° W. Long. Elevation is 738 feet.
Population: 637 (1990); 788 (2000); 965 (2007); 1,079 (2012 projected); Race: 95.8% White, 0.6% Black, 1.9% Asian, 4.5% Hispanic of any race (2007); Density: 985.9 persons per square mile (2007); Average household size: 2.68 (2007); Median age: 37.3 (2007); Males per 100 females: 95.3 (2007); Marriage status: 16.5% never married, 73.5% now married, 3.1% widowed, 6.9% divorced (2000); Foreign born: 8.6% (2000); Ancestry (includes multiple ancestries): 37.6% German, 25.0% Irish, 12.9% Other groups, 12.4% Italian, 8.8% English (2000).
Economy: Employment by occupation: 23.1% management, 16.4% professional, 8.6% services, 30.5% sales, 0.0% farming, 10.8% construction, 10.6% production (2000).
Income: Per capita income: $48,698 (2007); Median household income: $93,868 (2007); Average household income: $129,563 (2007); Percent of households with income of $100,000 or more: 46.4% (2007); Poverty rate: 2.5% (2000).
Education: Percent of population age 25 and over with: High school diploma (including GED) or higher: 91.5% (2007); Bachelor's degree or higher: 30.0% (2007); Master's degree or higher: 7.4% (2007).
Housing: Homeownership rate: 95.6% (2007); Median home value: $284,884 (2007); Median rent: $756 per month (2000); Median age of housing: 19 years (2000).
Transportation: Commute to work: 90.2% car, 3.9% public transportation, 0.0% walk, 5.0% work from home (2000); Travel time to work: 7.9% less than 15 minutes, 17.3% 15 to 30 minutes, 22.6% 30 to 45 minutes, 20.2% 45 to 60 minutes, 32.0% 60 minutes or more (2000)

GREENWOOD (village). Covers a land area of 1.559 square miles and a water area of 0 square miles. Located at 42.39° N. Lat.; 88.38° W. Long. Elevation is 856 feet.
Population: 214 (1990); 244 (2000); 276 (2007); 298 (2012 projected); Race: 89.1% White, 0.0% Black, 4.0% Asian, 9.4% Hispanic of any race

(2007); Density: 177.1 persons per square mile (2007); Average household size: 2.82 (2007); Median age: 41.6 (2007); Males per 100 females: 107.5 (2007); Marriage status: 20.9% never married, 67.0% now married, 3.3% widowed, 8.8% divorced (2000); Foreign born: 0.0% (2000); Ancestry (includes multiple ancestries): 46.4% German, 15.1% English, 14.0% United States or American, 12.8% Polish, 10.6% Irish (2000).
Economy: Employment by occupation: 14.8% management, 24.2% professional, 17.2% services, 13.3% sales, 0.0% farming, 18.0% construction, 12.5% production (2000).
Income: Per capita income: $28,868 (2007); Median household income: $63,529 (2007); Average household income: $81,301 (2007); Percent of households with income of $100,000 or more: 17.3% (2007); Poverty rate: 7.2% (2000).
Education: Percent of population age 25 and over with: High school diploma (including GED) or higher: 93.1% (2007); Bachelor's degree or higher: 22.9% (2007); Master's degree or higher: 7.4% (2007).
Housing: Homeownership rate: 81.6% (2007); Median home value: $263,333 (2007); Median rent: $850 per month (2000); Median age of housing: 60+ years (2000).
Transportation: Commute to work: 96.0% car, 0.8% public transportation, 0.0% walk, 3.2% work from home (2000); Travel time to work: 18.0% less than 15 minutes, 50.8% 15 to 30 minutes, 16.4% 30 to 45 minutes, 9.0% 45 to 60 minutes, 5.7% 60 minutes or more (2000)
Airports: Galt Field (general aviation)

HARVARD (city). Covers a land area of 5.337 square miles and a water area of 0 square miles. Located at 42.42° N. Lat.; 88.61° W. Long. Elevation is 958 feet.
History: Incorporated 1867.
Population: 6,401 (1990); 7,996 (2000); 8,818 (2007); 9,405 (2012 projected); Race: 66.5% White, 1.2% Black, 2.5% Asian, 54.7% Hispanic of any race (2007); Density: 1,652.2 persons per square mile (2007); Average household size: 3.11 (2007); Median age: 30.9 (2007); Males per 100 females: 108.2 (2007); Marriage status: 28.0% never married, 59.4% now married, 6.2% widowed, 6.4% divorced (2000); Foreign born: 26.8% (2000); Ancestry (includes multiple ancestries): 37.4% Other groups, 23.1% German, 10.5% Irish, 6.1% English, 3.2% Norwegian (2000).
Economy: Single-family building permits issued: 17 (2007); Multi-family building permits issued: 2 (2007); Employment by occupation: 6.0% management, 13.6% professional, 16.4% services, 19.5% sales, 1.7% farming, 11.8% construction, 31.0% production (2000).
Income: Per capita income: $18,686 (2007); Median household income: $49,094 (2007); Average household income: $57,619 (2007); Percent of households with income of $100,000 or more: 8.5% (2007); Poverty rate: 9.1% (2000).
Education: Percent of population age 25 and over with: High school diploma (including GED) or higher: 69.3% (2007); Bachelor's degree or higher: 14.7% (2007); Master's degree or higher: 5.5% (2007).

School District(s)

Harvard CUSD 50 (PK-12)
2005-06 Enrollment: 2,334 . . . . (815) 943-4022
Housing: Homeownership rate: 53.7% (2007); Median home value: $160,277 (2007); Median rent: $582 per month (2000); Median age of housing: 37 years (2000).
Hospitals: Mercy Harvard Hospital (46 beds)
Safety: Violent crime rate: 20.9 per 10,000 population; Property crime rate: 209.8 per 10,000 population (2006).
Transportation: Commute to work: 90.1% car, 1.5% public transportation, 5.2% walk, 2.1% work from home (2000); Travel time to work: 35.7% less than 15 minutes, 30.6% 15 to 30 minutes, 20.7% 30 to 45 minutes, 3.7% 45 to 60 minutes, 9.2% 60 minutes or more (2000)
Additional Information Contacts
City of Harvard . . . . (815) 943-6468
http://www.cityofharvard.org
Harvard Chamber of Commerce . . . . (815) 943-4404
http://www.harvcc.net

HEBRON (village). Covers a land area of 0.685 square miles and a water area of 0 square miles. Located at 42.47° N. Lat.; 88.43° W. Long. Elevation is 928 feet.
Population: 895 (1990); 1,038 (2000); 1,418 (2007); 1,663 (2012 projected); Race: 97.0% White, 0.2% Black, 0.3% Asian, 7.5% Hispanic of any race (2007); Density: 2,070.9 persons per square mile (2007); Average household size: 2.61 (2007); Median age: 34.1 (2007); Males per 100 females: 103.2 (2007); Marriage status: 26.8% never married, 54.6% now married, 5.2% widowed, 13.4% divorced (2000); Foreign born: 1.4% (2000); Ancestry (includes multiple ancestries): 43.7% German, 19.9% Irish, 9.7% English, 9.1% Polish, 7.6% Italian (2000).
Economy: Single-family building permits issued: 19 (2007); Multi-family building permits issued: 2 (2007); Employment by occupation: 2.2% management, 10.4% professional, 10.7% services, 31.4% sales, 0.9% farming, 21.8% construction, 22.6% production (2000).
Income: Per capita income: $21,594 (2007); Median household income: $52,547 (2007); Average household income: $56,390 (2007); Percent of households with income of $100,000 or more: 10.3% (2007); Poverty rate: 5.1% (2000).
Education: Percent of population age 25 and over with: High school diploma (including GED) or higher: 87.4% (2007); Bachelor's degree or higher: 9.1% (2007); Master's degree or higher: 4.2% (2007).

School District(s)

Alden Hebron SD 19 (PK-12)
2005-06 Enrollment: 495 . . . . (815) 648-2886
Housing: Homeownership rate: 65.4% (2007); Median home value: $190,036 (2007); Median rent: $507 per month (2000); Median age of housing: 60+ years (2000).
Safety: Violent crime rate: 35.1 per 10,000 population; Property crime rate: 236.6 per 10,000 population (2006).
Transportation: Commute to work: 93.7% car, 0.7% public transportation, 3.5% walk, 1.3% work from home (2000); Travel time to work: 24.4% less than 15 minutes, 39.5% 15 to 30 minutes, 20.5% 30 to 45 minutes, 7.7% 45 to 60 minutes, 7.9% 60 minutes or more (2000)

HOLIDAY HILLS (village). Covers a land area of 0.947 square miles and a water area of 0.037 square miles. Located at 42.29° N. Lat.; 88.22° W. Long. Elevation is 741 feet.
Population: 855 (1990); 831 (2000); 830 (2007); 837 (2012 projected); Race: 91.4% White, 2.2% Black, 0.5% Asian, 7.1% Hispanic of any race (2007); Density: 876.6 persons per square mile (2007); Average household size: 2.91 (2007); Median age: 36.6 (2007); Males per 100 females: 103.4 (2007); Marriage status: 25.6% never married, 63.7% now married, 3.1% widowed, 7.6% divorced (2000); Foreign born: 3.3% (2000); Ancestry (includes multiple ancestries): 33.9% German, 17.4% Polish, 17.1% Irish, 12.1% Italian, 10.2% Other groups (2000).
Economy: Single-family building permits issued: 1 (2007); Multi-family building permits issued: 0 (2007); Employment by occupation: 11.0% management, 11.9% professional, 12.6% services, 34.0% sales, 0.0% farming, 14.5% construction, 16.0% production (2000).
Income: Per capita income: $25,569 (2007); Median household income: $67,621 (2007); Average household income: $74,465 (2007); Percent of households with income of $100,000 or more: 17.2% (2007); Poverty rate: 0.0% (2000).
Education: Percent of population age 25 and over with: High school diploma (including GED) or higher: 84.9% (2007); Bachelor's degree or higher: 14.4% (2007); Master's degree or higher: 2.5% (2007).
Housing: Homeownership rate: 93.7% (2007); Median home value: $186,213 (2007); Median rent: $775 per month (2000); Median age of housing: 38 years (2000).
Safety: Violent crime rate: 0.0 per 10,000 population; Property crime rate: 135.3 per 10,000 population (2006).
Transportation: Commute to work: 96.0% car, 0.4% public transportation, 0.0% walk, 3.1% work from home (2000); Travel time to work: 15.1% less than 15 minutes, 33.9% 15 to 30 minutes, 23.8% 30 to 45 minutes, 11.7% 45 to 60 minutes, 15.6% 60 minutes or more (2000)

HUNTLEY (village). Covers a land area of 11.716 square miles and a water area of 0.032 square miles. Located at 42.16° N. Lat.; 88.42° W. Long. Elevation is 889 feet.
Population: 2,695 (1990); 5,730 (2000); 13,472 (2007); 18,328 (2012 projected); Race: 92.1% White, 0.7% Black, 3.2% Asian, 6.1% Hispanic of any race (2007); Density: 1,149.9 persons per square mile (2007); Average household size: 2.43 (2007); Median age: 41.5 (2007); Males per 100 females: 94.0 (2007); Marriage status: 13.9% never married, 71.7% now married, 6.2% widowed, 8.2% divorced (2000); Foreign born: 5.6% (2000); Ancestry (includes multiple ancestries): 40.3% German, 14.9% Irish, 13.7% Polish, 10.9% Italian, 10.5% English (2000).
Economy: Single-family building permits issued: 465 (2007); Multi-family building permits issued: 0 (2007); Employment by occupation: 14.2% management, 17.3% professional, 11.9% services, 33.7% sales, 0.7% farming, 8.3% construction, 13.8% production (2000).

Income: Per capita income: $33,906 (2007); Median household income: $68,370 (2007); Average household income: $82,288 (2007); Percent of households with income of $100,000 or more: 24.7% (2007); Poverty rate: 2.8% (2000).
Education: Percent of population age 25 and over with: High school diploma (including GED) or higher: 89.3% (2007); Bachelor's degree or higher: 22.2% (2007); Master's degree or higher: 6.2% (2007).

School District(s)

Cons SD 158 (PK-12)
2005-06 Enrollment: 6,929 . . . . (847) 659-6158
Housing: Homeownership rate: 77.5% (2007); Median home value: $279,145 (2007); Median rent: $714 per month (2000); Median age of housing: 4 years (2000).
Transportation: Commute to work: 90.7% car, 2.5% public transportation, 3.3% walk, 2.6% work from home (2000); Travel time to work: 28.0% less than 15 minutes, 27.1% 15 to 30 minutes, 19.0% 30 to 45 minutes, 9.1% 45 to 60 minutes, 16.7% 60 minutes or more (2000)
Additional Information Contacts
Huntley Area Chamber of Commerce & Industry. . . . . (847) 669-0166
http://www.huntleychamber.org
Village of Huntley . . . . (847) 669-9600
http://www.huntley.il.us

ISLAND LAKE (village). Covers a land area of 2.854 square miles and a water area of 0.208 square miles. Located at 42.27° N. Lat.; 88.20° W. Long.
Population: 4,839 (1990); 8,153 (2000); 8,493 (2007); 8,759 (2012 projected); Race: 90.5% White, 0.7% Black, 2.6% Asian, 11.9% Hispanic of any race (2007); Density: 2,975.4 persons per square mile (2007); Average household size: 2.88 (2007); Median age: 33.9 (2007); Males per 100 females: 98.9 (2007); Marriage status: 20.2% never married, 65.9% now married, 4.2% widowed, 9.7% divorced (2000); Foreign born: 5.7% (2000); Ancestry (includes multiple ancestries): 34.9% German, 17.3% Irish, 14.9% Polish, 12.0% Other groups, 11.3% Italian (2000).
Economy: Single-family building permits issued: 39 (2007); Multi-family building permits issued: 0 (2007); Employment by occupation: 14.4% management, 17.9% professional, 8.8% services, 30.7% sales, 0.0% farming, 15.0% construction, 13.2% production (2000).
Income: Per capita income: $28,612 (2007); Median household income: $72,464 (2007); Average household income: $82,458 (2007); Percent of households with income of $100,000 or more: 27.0% (2007); Poverty rate: 2.6% (2000).
Education: Percent of population age 25 and over with: High school diploma (including GED) or higher: 89.6% (2007); Bachelor's degree or higher: 23.5% (2007); Master's degree or higher: 5.2% (2007).

School District(s)

Wauconda CUSD 118 (PK-12)
2005-06 Enrollment: 4,198 . . . . (847) 526-7690
Housing: Homeownership rate: 91.3% (2007); Median home value: $209,618 (2007); Median rent: $839 per month (2000); Median age of housing: 12 years (2000).
Safety: Violent crime rate: 27.3 per 10,000 population; Property crime rate: 92.6 per 10,000 population (2006).
Transportation: Commute to work: 93.7% car, 0.9% public transportation, 0.5% walk, 4.4% work from home (2000); Travel time to work: 14.2% less than 15 minutes, 24.2% 15 to 30 minutes, 22.9% 30 to 45 minutes, 22.1% 45 to 60 minutes, 16.7% 60 minutes or more (2000)
Additional Information Contacts
Island Lake Area Chamber of Commerce . . . . (847) 604-4522
http://www.islandlakechamber.org
Village of Island Lake. . . . . (847) 526-8764
http://www.villageofislandlake.com

JOHNSBURG (village). Aka Sunnyside. Covers a land area of 5.537 square miles and a water area of 0.576 square miles. Located at 42.38° N. Lat.; 88.23° W. Long. Elevation is 751 feet.
Population: 4,589 (1990); 5,391 (2000); 6,330 (2007); 6,973 (2012 projected); Race: 98.2% White, 0.2% Black, 0.3% Asian, 2.1% Hispanic of any race (2007); Density: 1,143.3 persons per square mile (2007); Average household size: 2.99 (2007); Median age: 39.1 (2007); Males per 100 females: 101.0 (2007); Marriage status: 23.1% never married, 64.3% now married, 3.5% widowed, 9.1% divorced (2000); Foreign born: 0.8% (2000); Ancestry (includes multiple ancestries): 40.9% German, 19.7% Irish, 13.7% Polish, 8.8% Italian, 7.6% English (2000).
Economy: Single-family building permits issued: 39 (2007); Multi-family building permits issued: 0 (2007); Employment by occupation: 18.5% management, 16.3% professional, 10.3% services, 26.9% sales, 0.2% farming, 16.7% construction, 11.1% production (2000).
Income: Per capita income: $32,602 (2007); Median household income: $79,747 (2007); Average household income: $97,276 (2007); Percent of households with income of $100,000 or more: 31.9% (2007); Poverty rate: 1.3% (2000).
Education: Percent of population age 25 and over with: High school diploma (including GED) or higher: 91.6% (2007); Bachelor's degree or higher: 27.6% (2007); Master's degree or higher: 7.2% (2007).

School District(s)

Johnsburg CUSD 12 (PK-12)
2005-06 Enrollment: 2,639 . . . . (815) 385-6916
Housing: Homeownership rate: 91.0% (2007); Median home value: $282,740 (2007); Median rent: $807 per month (2000); Median age of housing: 28 years (2000).
Safety: Violent crime rate: 6.4 per 10,000 population; Property crime rate: 148.2 per 10,000 population (2006).
Transportation: Commute to work: 91.4% car, 2.9% public transportation, 0.6% walk, 3.6% work from home (2000); Travel time to work: 29.3% less than 15 minutes, 27.3% 15 to 30 minutes, 13.1% 30 to 45 minutes, 12.9% 45 to 60 minutes, 17.5% 60 minutes or more (2000)
Additional Information Contacts
Village of Johnsburg . . . . (815) 385-6023
http://www.johnsburg.org

LAKE IN THE HILLS (village). Covers a land area of 9.404 square miles and a water area of 0.232 square miles. Located at 42.18° N. Lat.; 88.34° W. Long. Elevation is 866 feet.
Population: 7,263 (1990); 23,152 (2000); 33,862 (2007); 40,792 (2012 projected); Race: 85.4% White, 2.9% Black, 6.6% Asian, 8.8% Hispanic of any race (2007); Density: 3,600.8 persons per square mile (2007); Average household size: 3.07 (2007); Median age: 32.2 (2007); Males per 100 females: 101.0 (2007); Marriage status: 17.6% never married, 74.0% now married, 2.1% widowed, 6.3% divorced (2000); Foreign born: 8.5% (2000); Ancestry (includes multiple ancestries): 30.8% German, 18.3% Irish, 17.8% Italian, 16.6% Polish, 13.1% Other groups (2000).
Economy: Unemployment rate: 4.9% (4/2008); Total civilian labor force: 17,445 (4/2008); Single-family building permits issued: 36 (2007); Multi-family building permits issued: 0 (2007); Employment by occupation: 20.6% management, 21.4% professional, 9.4% services, 28.3% sales, 0.1% farming, 8.7% construction, 11.6% production (2000).
Income: Per capita income: $32,613 (2007); Median household income: $87,509 (2007); Average household income: $100,005 (2007); Percent of households with income of $100,000 or more: 37.7% (2007); Poverty rate: 2.1% (2000).
Education: Percent of population age 25 and over with: High school diploma (including GED) or higher: 93.5% (2007); Bachelor's degree or higher: 33.2% (2007); Master's degree or higher: 6.6% (2007).

School District(s)

CUSD 300 (PK-12)
2005-06 Enrollment: 18,670 . . . . (847) 426-1300
Cons SD 158 (PK-12)
2005-06 Enrollment: 6,929 . . . . (847) 659-6158
Housing: Homeownership rate: 94.1% (2007); Median home value: $238,969 (2007); Median rent: $872 per month (2000); Median age of housing: 5 years (2000).
Safety: Violent crime rate: 8.7 per 10,000 population; Property crime rate: 80.2 per 10,000 population (2006).
Transportation: Commute to work: 94.2% car, 2.3% public transportation, 0.2% walk, 3.1% work from home (2000); Travel time to work: 14.3% less than 15 minutes, 25.2% 15 to 30 minutes, 23.1% 30 to 45 minutes, 18.7% 45 to 60 minutes, 18.7% 60 minutes or more (2000)
Airports: Lake in the Hills (general aviation)
Additional Information Contacts
Village of Lake in the Hills . . . . (847) 960-7400
http://www.lith.org

LAKEMOOR (village). Covers a land area of 4.280 square miles and a water area of 0.221 square miles. Located at 42.33° N. Lat.; 88.20° W. Long. Elevation is 761 feet.
Population: 1,638 (1990); 2,788 (2000); 3,780 (2007); 4,434 (2012 projected); Race: 88.5% White, 0.9% Black, 3.3% Asian, 10.2% Hispanic of any race (2007); Density: 883.1 persons per square mile (2007); Average

household size: 2.64 (2007); Median age: 32.4 (2007); Males per 100 females: 107.8 (2007); Marriage status: 19.7% never married, 66.3% now married, 2.5% widowed, 11.6% divorced (2000); Foreign born: 4.0% (2000); Ancestry (includes multiple ancestries): 37.7% German, 15.4% Irish, 14.2% Polish, 8.1% Other groups, 7.1% Italian (2000).
Economy: Single-family building permits issued: 93 (2007); Multi-family building permits issued: 0 (2007); Employment by occupation: 12.4% management, 17.3% professional, 13.0% services, 29.6% sales, 0.0% farming, 16.1% construction, 11.6% production (2000).
Income: Per capita income: $26,901 (2007); Median household income: $64,173 (2007); Average household income: $71,110 (2007); Percent of households with income of $100,000 or more: 18.7% (2007); Poverty rate: 8.7% (2000).
Education: Percent of population age 25 and over with: High school diploma (including GED) or higher: 84.7% (2007); Bachelor's degree or higher: 16.9% (2007); Master's degree or higher: 2.7% (2007).
Housing: Homeownership rate: 74.3% (2007); Median home value: $208,960 (2007); Median rent: $846 per month (2000); Median age of housing: 7 years (2000).
Safety: Violent crime rate: 21.6 per 10,000 population; Property crime rate: 153.4 per 10,000 population (2006).
Transportation: Commute to work: 95.3% car, 2.3% public transportation, 0.6% walk, 1.2% work from home (2000); Travel time to work: 17.4% less than 15 minutes, 23.0% 15 to 30 minutes, 27.0% 30 to 45 minutes, 17.0% 45 to 60 minutes, 15.6% 60 minutes or more (2000)

LAKEWOOD (village). Covers a land area of 3.091 square miles and a water area of 0.294 square miles. Located at 42.22° N. Lat.; 88.37° W. Long. Elevation is 889 feet.
Population: 1,711 (1990); 2,337 (2000); 2,649 (2007); 2,896 (2012 projected); Race: 93.7% White, 1.2% Black, 2.8% Asian, 2.8% Hispanic of any race (2007); Density: 856.9 persons per square mile (2007); Average household size: 2.81 (2007); Median age: 42.8 (2007); Males per 100 females: 96.2 (2007); Marriage status: 16.2% never married, 76.1% now married, 3.1% widowed, 4.6% divorced (2000); Foreign born: 4.9% (2000); Ancestry (includes multiple ancestries): 32.0% German, 24.8% Irish, 11.4% English, 9.9% Italian, 9.8% Polish (2000).
Economy: Single-family building permits issued: 25 (2007); Multi-family building permits issued: 12 (2007); Employment by occupation: 29.9% management, 25.3% professional, 5.6% services, 28.0% sales, 0.3% farming, 5.6% construction, 5.3% production (2000).
Income: Per capita income: $58,771 (2007); Median household income: $130,894 (2007); Average household income: $165,157 (2007); Percent of households with income of $100,000 or more: 64.9% (2007); Poverty rate: 1.7% (2000).
Education: Percent of population age 25 and over with: High school diploma (including GED) or higher: 95.5% (2007); Bachelor's degree or higher: 56.1% (2007); Master's degree or higher: 18.8% (2007).
Housing: Homeownership rate: 97.6% (2007); Median home value: $438,851 (2007); Median rent: $775 per month (2000); Median age of housing: 16 years (2000).
Safety: Violent crime rate: 0.0 per 10,000 population; Property crime rate: 37.1 per 10,000 population (2006).
Transportation: Commute to work: 86.7% car, 6.3% public transportation, 0.0% walk, 6.6% work from home (2000); Travel time to work: 19.1% less than 15 minutes, 31.7% 15 to 30 minutes, 14.2% 30 to 45 minutes, 11.8% 45 to 60 minutes, 23.2% 60 minutes or more (2000)

MARENGO (city). Covers a land area of 3.975 square miles and a water area of 0 square miles. Located at 42.25° N. Lat.; 88.60° W. Long. Elevation is 833 feet.
History: Marengo was the birthplace of Egbert Van Alstyne who composed the songs "In the Shade of the Old Apple Tree," and "Pony Boy." An early industry here was the McGill Metal Products Plant, a manufacturer of mousetraps.
Population: 4,872 (1990); 6,355 (2000); 7,640 (2007); 8,522 (2012 projected); Race: 89.2% White, 0.4% Black, 0.4% Asian, 17.2% Hispanic of any race (2007); Density: 1,921.8 persons per square mile (2007); Average household size: 2.69 (2007); Median age: 34.6 (2007); Males per 100 females: 97.1 (2007); Marriage status: 19.7% never married, 63.2% now married, 6.2% widowed, 11.0% divorced (2000); Foreign born: 7.1% (2000); Ancestry (includes multiple ancestries): 38.6% German, 14.4% Other groups, 12.7% Irish, 12.1% Polish, 9.0% Italian (2000).
Economy: Single-family building permits issued: 11 (2007); Multi-family building permits issued: 0 (2007); Employment by occupation: 9.3% management, 14.5% professional, 12.2% services, 26.4% sales, 0.2% farming, 14.6% construction, 22.8% production (2000).
Income: Per capita income: $25,192 (2007); Median household income: $57,844 (2007); Average household income: $67,121 (2007); Percent of households with income of $100,000 or more: 17.3% (2007); Poverty rate: 4.4% (2000).
Education: Percent of population age 25 and over with: High school diploma (including GED) or higher: 85.8% (2007); Bachelor's degree or higher: 13.7% (2007); Master's degree or higher: 3.9% (2007).

School District(s)

Marengo CHSD 154 (09-12)
2005-06 Enrollment: 840 . . . . (815) 568-6511
Marengo-Union E Cons D 165 (PK-08)
2005-06 Enrollment: 1,228 . . . . (815) 568-8323
Riley CCSD 18 (KG-08)
2005-06 Enrollment: 299 . . . . (815) 568-8637

Housing: Homeownership rate: 66.3% (2007); Median home value: $201,402 (2007); Median rent: $551 per month (2000); Median age of housing: 35 years (2000).
Safety: Violent crime rate: 6.8 per 10,000 population; Property crime rate: 142.3 per 10,000 population (2006).
Transportation: Commute to work: 90.9% car, 2.2% public transportation, 3.2% walk, 2.6% work from home (2000); Travel time to work: 36.5% less than 15 minutes, 23.1% 15 to 30 minutes, 19.6% 30 to 45 minutes, 5.9% 45 to 60 minutes, 14.9% 60 minutes or more (2000)

Additional Information Contacts

City of Marengo . . . . (815) 568-7112
http://www.cityofmarengo.com
Marengo Union Chamber of Commerce . . . . (815) 568-6680
http://www.marengo-union.com

MCCULLOM LAKE (village). Covers a land area of 0.280 square miles and a water area of 0 square miles. Located at 42.37° N. Lat.; 88.29° W. Long. Elevation is 787 feet.
Population: 1,099 (1990); 1,038 (2000); 1,174 (2007); 1,277 (2012 projected); Race: 94.9% White, 1.5% Black, 0.4% Asian, 4.7% Hispanic of any race (2007); Density: 4,194.1 persons per square mile (2007); Average household size: 2.67 (2007); Median age: 35.9 (2007); Males per 100 females: 101.0 (2007); Marriage status: 25.8% never married, 62.2% now married, 6.1% widowed, 6.0% divorced (2000); Foreign born: 2.6% (2000); Ancestry (includes multiple ancestries): 37.3% German, 20.6% Irish, 13.9% Polish, 10.4% Italian, 9.4% Other groups (2000).
Economy: Single-family building permits issued: 7 (2007); Multi-family building permits issued: 0 (2007); Employment by occupation: 8.6% management, 11.4% professional, 17.2% services, 24.9% sales, 0.4% farming, 18.7% construction, 18.9% production (2000).
Income: Per capita income: $23,147 (2007); Median household income: $56,400 (2007); Average household income: $61,761 (2007); Percent of households with income of $100,000 or more: 10.0% (2007); Poverty rate: 5.5% (2000).
Education: Percent of population age 25 and over with: High school diploma (including GED) or higher: 81.4% (2007); Bachelor's degree or higher: 6.4% (2007); Master's degree or higher: 1.1% (2007).
Housing: Homeownership rate: 78.6% (2007); Median home value: $170,000 (2007); Median rent: $703 per month (2000); Median age of housing: 50 years (2000).
Safety: Violent crime rate: 28.9 per 10,000 population; Property crime rate: 96.4 per 10,000 population (2006).
Transportation: Commute to work: 94.6% car, 0.9% public transportation, 0.8% walk, 3.2% work from home (2000); Travel time to work: 33.5% less than 15 minutes, 31.2% 15 to 30 minutes, 15.3% 30 to 45 minutes, 6.2% 45 to 60 minutes, 13.8% 60 minutes or more (2000)

MCHENRY (city). Covers a land area of 11.621 square miles and a water area of 0.491 square miles. Located at 42.33° N. Lat.; 88.28° W. Long. Elevation is 797 feet.
History: Named for William McHenry (1774-1839), who fought in the Black Hawk War of 1832. McHenry began in 1836 when Dr. Christy C. Wheeler became the first postmaster and storekeeper. McHenry was located on the Chicago Pike route and entertained many travelers. Later the economy depended on butter, cheese, and pickle production.
Population: 17,677 (1990); 21,501 (2000); 25,682 (2007); 28,532 (2012 projected); Race: 90.9% White, 0.5% Black, 1.3% Asian, 10.9% Hispanic of any race (2007); Density: 2,210.0 persons per square mile (2007); Average household size: 2.71 (2007); Median age: 35.8 (2007); Males per 100

females: 96.1 (2007); Marriage status: 22.3% never married, 61.0% now married, 6.6% widowed, 10.1% divorced (2000); Foreign born: 6.2% (2000); Ancestry (includes multiple ancestries): 36.6% German, 20.9% Irish, 13.1% Polish, 9.4% Other groups, 8.7% Italian (2000).
Economy: Unemployment rate: 5.6% (4/2008); Total civilian labor force: 15,045 (4/2008); Single-family building permits issued: 124 (2007); Multi-family building permits issued: 62 (2007); Employment by occupation: 14.0% management, 17.4% professional, 11.9% services, 29.4% sales, 0.1% farming, 11.3% construction, 16.0% production (2000).
Income: Per capita income: $26,969 (2007); Median household income: $62,898 (2007); Average household income: $72,208 (2007); Percent of households with income of $100,000 or more: 21.6% (2007); Poverty rate: 4.6% (2000).
Education: Percent of population age 25 and over with: High school diploma (including GED) or higher: 87.2% (2007); Bachelor's degree or higher: 22.2% (2007); Master's degree or higher: 5.9% (2007).

School District(s)

Mc Henry CHSD 156 (09-12)
2005-06 Enrollment: 2,409 . . . . (815) 385-7900
Mchenry CCSD 15 (PK-08)
2005-06 Enrollment: 4,846 . . . . (815) 385-7210

Housing: Homeownership rate: 77.1% (2007); Median home value: $214,484 (2007); Median rent: $645 per month (2000); Median age of housing: 22 years (2000).
Hospitals: Centegra Northern Illinois Medical Center (196 beds)
Safety: Violent crime rate: 22.1 per 10,000 population; Property crime rate: 233.3 per 10,000 population (2006).
Transportation: Commute to work: 94.2% car, 1.7% public transportation, 1.4% walk, 2.0% work from home (2000); Travel time to work: 30.8% less than 15 minutes, 29.5% 15 to 30 minutes, 14.0% 30 to 45 minutes, 11.4% 45 to 60 minutes, 14.4% 60 minutes or more (2000)

Additional Information Contacts

City of McHenry . . . . (815) 363-2100
http://www.ci.mchenry.il.us
McHenry Area Chamber of Commerce . . . . (815) 385-4300
http://www.mchenrychamber.com

OAKWOOD HILLS (village). Covers a land area of 1.129 square miles and a water area of 0.079 square miles. Located at 42.24° N. Lat.; 88.24° W. Long. Elevation is 827 feet.
Population: 1,699 (1990); 2,194 (2000); 2,393 (2007); 2,534 (2012 projected); Race: 97.2% White, 0.5% Black, 0.5% Asian, 4.4% Hispanic of any race (2007); Density: 2,120.2 persons per square mile (2007); Average household size: 3.03 (2007); Median age: 34.9 (2007); Males per 100 females: 101.3 (2007); Marriage status: 21.6% never married, 67.6% now married, 2.3% widowed, 8.5% divorced (2000); Foreign born: 5.4% (2000); Ancestry (includes multiple ancestries): 38.6% German, 22.4% Irish, 16.0% Polish, 11.8% Italian, 9.9% English (2000).
Economy: Single-family building permits issued: 4 (2007); Multi-family building permits issued: 0 (2007); Employment by occupation: 15.3% management, 17.8% professional, 10.3% services, 31.5% sales, 0.3% farming, 11.3% construction, 13.5% production (2000).
Income: Per capita income: $29,366 (2007); Median household income: $73,558 (2007); Average household income: $89,065 (2007); Percent of households with income of $100,000 or more: 29.0% (2007); Poverty rate: 5.0% (2000).
Education: Percent of population age 25 and over with: High school diploma (including GED) or higher: 92.3% (2007); Bachelor's degree or higher: 29.9% (2007); Master's degree or higher: 7.7% (2007).
Housing: Homeownership rate: 95.2% (2007); Median home value: $244,977 (2007); Median rent: $850 per month (2000); Median age of housing: 21 years (2000).
Safety: Violent crime rate: 0.0 per 10,000 population; Property crime rate: 119.3 per 10,000 population (2006).
Transportation: Commute to work: 90.4% car, 5.1% public transportation, 0.0% walk, 4.5% work from home (2000); Travel time to work: 20.7% less than 15 minutes, 26.7% 15 to 30 minutes, 20.7% 30 to 45 minutes, 14.8% 45 to 60 minutes, 17.1% 60 minutes or more (2000)

PISTAKEE HIGHLANDS (CDP). Aka Pistakee. Covers a land area of 1.437 square miles and a water area of 0.329 square miles. Located at 42.40° N. Lat.; 88.21° W. Long. Elevation is 758 feet.
Population: 3,785 (1990); 3,812 (2000); 3,912 (2007); 4,023 (2012 projected); Race: 97.4% White, 0.2% Black, 0.1% Asian, 4.9% Hispanic of any race (2007); Density: 2,722.6 persons per square mile (2007); Average household size: 2.78 (2007); Median age: 37.4 (2007); Males per 100 females: 103.9 (2007); Marriage status: 25.2% never married, 62.8% now married, 3.4% widowed, 8.5% divorced (2000); Foreign born: 2.1% (2000); Ancestry (includes multiple ancestries): 36.7% German, 14.4% Polish, 14.0% Irish, 6.0% Other groups, 5.3% English (2000).
Economy: Employment by occupation: 11.0% management, 16.3% professional, 10.4% services, 26.6% sales, 0.5% farming, 12.9% construction, 22.3% production (2000).
Income: Per capita income: $26,681 (2007); Median household income: $66,682 (2007); Average household income: $74,184 (2007); Percent of households with income of $100,000 or more: 24.5% (2007); Poverty rate: 4.4% (2000).
Education: Percent of population age 25 and over with: High school diploma (including GED) or higher: 85.0% (2007); Bachelor's degree or higher: 11.9% (2007); Master's degree or higher: 2.7% (2007).
Housing: Homeownership rate: 92.4% (2007); Median home value: $182,971 (2007); Median rent: $820 per month (2000); Median age of housing: 30 years (2000).
Transportation: Commute to work: 92.7% car, 5.5% public transportation, 0.0% walk, 1.8% work from home (2000); Travel time to work: 25.4% less than 15 minutes, 19.8% 15 to 30 minutes, 20.7% 30 to 45 minutes, 15.4% 45 to 60 minutes, 18.7% 60 minutes or more (2000)

PRAIRIE GROVE (village). Covers a land area of 4.633 square miles and a water area of 0.139 square miles. Located at 42.27° N. Lat.; 88.26° W. Long. Elevation is 758 feet.
Population: 801 (1990); 960 (2000); 1,121 (2007); 1,234 (2012 projected); Race: 94.8% White, 0.9% Black, 1.9% Asian, 1.7% Hispanic of any race (2007); Density: 242.0 persons per square mile (2007); Average household size: 3.12 (2007); Median age: 39.0 (2007); Males per 100 females: 99.1 (2007); Marriage status: 22.3% never married, 65.4% now married, 4.2% widowed, 8.1% divorced (2000); Foreign born: 3.7% (2000); Ancestry (includes multiple ancestries): 30.7% German, 17.0% Irish, 11.4% Polish, 8.2% Italian, 7.5% English (2000).
Economy: Single-family building permits issued: 9 (2007); Multi-family building permits issued: 0 (2007); Employment by occupation: 22.3% management, 21.2% professional, 14.0% services, 21.1% sales, 0.4% farming, 10.9% construction, 10.2% production (2000).
Income: Per capita income: $41,488 (2007); Median household income: $105,819 (2007); Average household income: $129,547 (2007); Percent of households with income of $100,000 or more: 53.8% (2007); Poverty rate: 1.3% (2000).
Education: Percent of population age 25 and over with: High school diploma (including GED) or higher: 90.5% (2007); Bachelor's degree or higher: 38.4% (2007); Master's degree or higher: 12.0% (2007).
Housing: Homeownership rate: 91.6% (2007); Median home value: $435,606 (2007); Median rent: $675 per month (2000); Median age of housing: 22 years (2000).
Safety: Violent crime rate: 11.0 per 10,000 population; Property crime rate: 165.4 per 10,000 population (2006).
Transportation: Commute to work: 94.7% car, 2.0% public transportation, 0.0% walk, 3.3% work from home (2000); Travel time to work: 25.2% less than 15 minutes, 25.8% 15 to 30 minutes, 21.8% 30 to 45 minutes, 10.7% 45 to 60 minutes, 16.5% 60 minutes or more (2000)

RICHMOND (village). Covers a land area of 1.360 square miles and a water area of 0 square miles. Located at 42.47° N. Lat.; 88.30° W. Long. Elevation is 820 feet.
History: Richmond was settled in 1837, and developed around a grist mill.
Population: 1,083 (1990); 1,091 (2000); 1,544 (2007); 1,840 (2012 projected); Race: 96.7% White, 0.3% Black, 1.2% Asian, 6.0% Hispanic of any race (2007); Density: 1,135.4 persons per square mile (2007); Average household size: 2.57 (2007); Median age: 38.4 (2007); Males per 100 females: 99.5 (2007); Marriage status: 27.8% never married, 56.1% now married, 6.3% widowed, 9.8% divorced (2000); Foreign born: 3.4% (2000); Ancestry (includes multiple ancestries): 36.9% German, 20.5% Irish, 11.3% Polish, 9.6% English, 9.1% Italian (2000).
Economy: Single-family building permits issued: 11 (2007); Multi-family building permits issued: 0 (2007); Employment by occupation: 12.2% management, 14.9% professional, 15.1% services, 20.7% sales, 0.0% farming, 14.9% construction, 22.3% production (2000).
Income: Per capita income: $27,757 (2007); Median household income: $58,113 (2007); Average household income: $71,429 (2007); Percent of households with income of $100,000 or more: 18.5% (2007); Poverty rate: 6.5% (2000).

Education: Percent of population age 25 and over with: High school diploma (including GED) or higher: 88.7% (2007); Bachelor's degree or higher: 20.5% (2007); Master's degree or higher: 6.0% (2007).

School District(s)

Nippersink SD 2 (PK-08)
2005-06 Enrollment: 1,617 . . . . (815) 678-4242
Richmond-Burton CHSD 157 (09-12)
2005-06 Enrollment: 755 . . . . (815) 678-4525

Housing: Homeownership rate: 69.8% (2007); Median home value: $214,962 (2007); Median rent: $581 per month (2000); Median age of housing: 45 years (2000).

Safety: Violent crime rate: 9.0 per 10,000 population; Property crime rate: 189.6 per 10,000 population (2006).

Transportation: Commute to work: 84.2% car, 1.8% public transportation, 9.0% walk, 4.6% work from home (2000); Travel time to work: 42.2% less than 15 minutes, 22.5% 15 to 30 minutes, 17.1% 30 to 45 minutes, 7.9% 45 to 60 minutes, 10.2% 60 minutes or more (2000)

Additional Information Contacts

Richmond/Spring Grove Chamber of Commerce . . . . (815) 678-7742
http://www.rsgchamber.com

RINGWOOD (village). Covers a land area of 2.338 square miles and a water area of 0 square miles. Located at 42.39° N. Lat.; 88.30° W. Long. Elevation is 856 feet.

Population: 371 (1990); 471 (2000); 567 (2007); 632 (2012 projected); Race: 97.9% White, 0.4% Black, 1.2% Asian, 0.5% Hispanic of any race (2007); Density: 242.6 persons per square mile (2007); Average household size: 2.74 (2007); Median age: 45.3 (2007); Males per 100 females: 103.2 (2007); Marriage status: 19.5% never married, 70.1% now married, 5.7% widowed, 4.7% divorced (2000); Foreign born: 7.0% (2000); Ancestry (includes multiple ancestries): 42.1% German, 14.9% Irish, 11.3% English, 9.2% Polish, 7.2% Italian (2000).

Economy: Employment by occupation: 14.8% management, 16.9% professional, 7.8% services, 28.0% sales, 1.6% farming, 16.9% construction, 14.0% production (2000).

Income: Per capita income: $32,619 (2007); Median household income: $85,372 (2007); Average household income: $89,348 (2007); Percent of households with income of $100,000 or more: 36.7% (2007); Poverty rate: 0.9% (2000).

Education: Percent of population age 25 and over with: High school diploma (including GED) or higher: 86.4% (2007); Bachelor's degree or higher: 21.3% (2007); Master's degree or higher: 10.4% (2007).

School District(s)

Johnsburg CUSD 12 (PK-12)
2005-06 Enrollment: 2,639 . . . . (815) 385-6916

Housing: Homeownership rate: 83.1% (2007); Median home value: $292,045 (2007); Median rent: $566 per month (2000); Median age of housing: 29 years (2000).

Transportation: Commute to work: 86.3% car, 2.9% public transportation, 5.4% walk, 5.4% work from home (2000); Travel time to work: 34.4% less than 15 minutes, 27.3% 15 to 30 minutes, 16.7% 30 to 45 minutes, 5.3% 45 to 60 minutes, 16.3% 60 minutes or more (2000)

SPRING GROVE (village). Covers a land area of 6.211 square miles and a water area of 0.025 square miles. Located at 42.45° N. Lat.; 88.24° W. Long. Elevation is 764 feet.

Population: 1,725 (1990); 3,880 (2000); 5,484 (2007); 6,534 (2012 projected); Race: 95.7% White, 0.2% Black, 1.6% Asian, 2.2% Hispanic of any race (2007); Density: 882.9 persons per square mile (2007); Average household size: 3.37 (2007); Median age: 35.4 (2007); Males per 100 females: 99.5 (2007); Marriage status: 18.1% never married, 76.1% now married, 2.4% widowed, 3.4% divorced (2000); Foreign born: 2.1% (2000); Ancestry (includes multiple ancestries): 37.7% German, 18.9% Irish, 18.6% Polish, 7.7% Italian, 7.6% English (2000).

Economy: Single-family building permits issued: 29 (2007); Multi-family building permits issued: 0 (2007); Employment by occupation: 19.8% management, 19.3% professional, 10.2% services, 26.1% sales, 0.2% farming, 12.7% construction, 11.7% production (2000).

Income: Per capita income: $30,249 (2007); Median household income: $91,750 (2007); Average household income: $102,085 (2007); Percent of households with income of $100,000 or more: 42.9% (2007); Poverty rate: 2.4% (2000).

Education: Percent of population age 25 and over with: High school diploma (including GED) or higher: 94.2% (2007); Bachelor's degree or higher: 28.7% (2007); Master's degree or higher: 8.3% (2007).

School District(s)

Fox Lake GSD 114 (PK-08)
2005-06 Enrollment: 918 . . . . (847) 973-4100
Nippersink SD 2 (PK-08)
2005-06 Enrollment: 1,617 . . . . (815) 678-4242

Housing: Homeownership rate: 95.9% (2007); Median home value: $365,559 (2007); Median rent: $538 per month (2000); Median age of housing: 7 years (2000).

Safety: Violent crime rate: 3.8 per 10,000 population; Property crime rate: 109.4 per 10,000 population (2006).

Transportation: Commute to work: 90.6% car, 3.7% public transportation, 1.9% walk, 3.8% work from home (2000); Travel time to work: 19.4% less than 15 minutes, 23.9% 15 to 30 minutes, 17.6% 30 to 45 minutes, 16.4% 45 to 60 minutes, 22.8% 60 minutes or more (2000)

TROUT VALLEY (village). Covers a land area of 0.428 square miles and a water area of <.001 square miles. Located at 42.19° N. Lat.; 88.25° W. Long. Elevation is 794 feet.

Population: 599 (1990); 599 (2000); 671 (2007); 723 (2012 projected); Race: 91.7% White, 0.7% Black, 1.8% Asian, 6.4% Hispanic of any race (2007); Density: 1,567.9 persons per square mile (2007); Average household size: 2.98 (2007); Median age: 42.4 (2007); Males per 100 females: 98.5 (2007); Marriage status: 16.4% never married, 75.1% now married, 2.8% widowed, 5.8% divorced (2000); Foreign born: 4.2% (2000); Ancestry (includes multiple ancestries): 28.5% German, 24.6% Irish, 17.0% Italian, 10.6% English, 7.9% Polish (2000).

Economy: Employment by occupation: 30.8% management, 23.7% professional, 2.3% services, 33.5% sales, 0.0% farming, 4.5% construction, 5.3% production (2000).

Income: Per capita income: $56,237 (2007); Median household income: $117,083 (2007); Average household income: $167,711 (2007); Percent of households with income of $100,000 or more: 59.1% (2007); Poverty rate: 3.4% (2000).

Education: Percent of population age 25 and over with: High school diploma (including GED) or higher: 96.5% (2007); Bachelor's degree or higher: 60.7% (2007); Master's degree or higher: 21.4% (2007).

Housing: Homeownership rate: 97.8% (2007); Median home value: $433,846 (2007); Median rent: $850 per month (2000); Median age of housing: 35 years (2000).

Transportation: Commute to work: 77.8% car, 13.5% public transportation, 1.9% walk, 6.0% work from home (2000); Travel time to work: 24.8% less than 15 minutes, 14.0% 15 to 30 minutes, 14.8% 30 to 45 minutes, 16.8% 45 to 60 minutes, 29.6% 60 minutes or more (2000)

UNION (village). Covers a land area of 0.606 square miles and a water area of 0 square miles. Located at 42.23° N. Lat.; 88.54° W. Long. Elevation is 840 feet.

History: Illinois Railroad Museum here.

Population: 552 (1990); 576 (2000); 556 (2007); 561 (2012 projected); Race: 97.5% White, 0.0% Black, 0.0% Asian, 5.2% Hispanic of any race (2007); Density: 917.4 persons per square mile (2007); Average household size: 2.75 (2007); Median age: 36.9 (2007); Males per 100 females: 92.4 (2007); Marriage status: 25.5% never married, 62.3% now married, 4.0% widowed, 8.1% divorced (2000); Foreign born: 2.1% (2000); Ancestry (includes multiple ancestries): 53.8% German, 11.9% Irish, 6.7% Polish, 5.9% English, 4.7% Other groups (2000).

Economy: Single-family building permits issued: 4 (2007); Multi-family building permits issued: 0 (2007); Employment by occupation: 11.0% management, 14.6% professional, 14.0% services, 23.0% sales, 0.6% farming, 15.7% construction, 21.1% production (2000).

Income: Per capita income: $25,454 (2007); Median household income: $65,417 (2007); Average household income: $70,062 (2007); Percent of households with income of $100,000 or more: 22.8% (2007); Poverty rate: 5.2% (2000).

Education: Percent of population age 25 and over with: High school diploma (including GED) or higher: 84.3% (2007); Bachelor's degree or higher: 14.0% (2007); Master's degree or higher: 4.4% (2007).

School District(s)

Spec Ed Dist of Mchenry Co-Sedom (PK-12)
2005-06 Enrollment: 139 . . . . (815) 338-3622

Housing: Homeownership rate: 84.2% (2007); Median home value: $200,000 (2007); Median rent: $571 per month (2000); Median age of housing: 53 years (2000).

Transportation: Commute to work: 92.6% car, 1.5% public transportation, 1.8% walk, 4.2% work from home (2000); Travel time to work: 31.4% less

than 15 minutes, 36.0% 15 to 30 minutes, 13.0% 30 to 45 minutes, 11.2% 45 to 60 minutes, 8.4% 60 minutes or more (2000)

WONDER LAKE (CDP). Aka Wonder Center. Covers a land area of 6.247 square miles and a water area of 0.965 square miles. Located at 42.38° N. Lat.; 88.35° W. Long. Elevation is 837 feet.
Population: 6,505 (1990); 7,463 (2000); 7,939 (2007); 8,360 (2012 projected); Race: 94.7% White, 0.4% Black, 0.8% Asian, 7.4% Hispanic of any race (2007); Density: 1,270.8 persons per square mile (2007); Average household size: 2.77 (2007); Median age: 35.5 (2007); Males per 100 females: 105.7 (2007); Marriage status: 22.3% never married, 64.1% now married, 5.4% widowed, 8.3% divorced (2000); Foreign born: 4.5% (2000); Ancestry (includes multiple ancestries): 35.1% German, 18.4% Irish, 13.6% Polish, 13.3% Italian, 8.2% English (2000).
Economy: Employment by occupation: 7.6% management, 11.2% professional, 13.1% services, 26.8% sales, 0.1% farming, 16.8% construction, 24.4% production (2000).
Income: Per capita income: $24,624 (2007); Median household income: $59,585 (2007); Average household income: $68,038 (2007); Percent of households with income of $100,000 or more: 17.4% (2007); Poverty rate: 3.4% (2000).
Education: Percent of population age 25 and over with: High school diploma (including GED) or higher: 85.1% (2007); Bachelor's degree or higher: 10.1% (2007); Master's degree or higher: 3.2% (2007).

School District(s)

Harrison SD 36 (PK-08)
2005-06 Enrollment: 461 . . . . (815) 653-2311

Housing: Homeownership rate: 86.9% (2007); Median home value: $176,656 (2007); Median rent: $763 per month (2000); Median age of housing: 40 years (2000).
Transportation: Commute to work: 96.2% car, 1.1% public transportation, 1.1% walk, 1.4% work from home (2000); Travel time to work: 18.5% less than 15 minutes, 37.1% 15 to 30 minutes, 21.3% 30 to 45 minutes, 9.2% 45 to 60 minutes, 14.0% 60 minutes or more (2000)

Additional Information Contacts

Wonder Lake Chamber of Commerce . . . . (815) 728-0682
http://www.wonderlake.org

WONDER LAKE (village). Aka Wonder Center. Covers a land area of 0.811 square miles and a water area of 0.005 square miles. Located at 42.38° N. Lat.; 88.36° W. Long. Elevation is 837 feet.
Population: 1,057 (1990); 1,345 (2000); 1,534 (2007); 1,665 (2012 projected); Race: 95.8% White, 0.5% Black, 0.4% Asian, 6.7% Hispanic of any race (2007); Density: 1,890.3 persons per square mile (2007); Average household size: 2.96 (2007); Median age: 35.5 (2007); Males per 100 females: 104.8 (2007); Marriage status: 21.2% never married, 66.0% now married, 3.7% widowed, 9.1% divorced (2000); Foreign born: 2.1% (2000); Ancestry (includes multiple ancestries): 37.0% German, 20.0% Irish, 14.8% Polish, 10.6% Italian, 8.3% Other groups (2000).
Economy: Single-family building permits issued: 27 (2007); Multi-family building permits issued: 0 (2007); Employment by occupation: 12.8% management, 13.0% professional, 14.1% services, 27.9% sales, 0.0% farming, 19.1% construction, 13.1% production (2000).
Income: Per capita income: $25,799 (2007); Median household income: $67,500 (2007); Average household income: $76,400 (2007); Percent of households with income of $100,000 or more: 23.2% (2007); Poverty rate: 2.7% (2000).
Education: Percent of population age 25 and over with: High school diploma (including GED) or higher: 89.9% (2007); Bachelor's degree or higher: 15.5% (2007); Master's degree or higher: 4.2% (2007).

School District(s)

Harrison SD 36 (PK-08)
2005-06 Enrollment: 461 . . . . (815) 653-2311

Housing: Homeownership rate: 93.8% (2007); Median home value: $217,014 (2007); Median rent: $821 per month (2000); Median age of housing: 23 years (2000).
Safety: Violent crime rate: 65.4 per 10,000 population; Property crime rate: 341.7 per 10,000 population (2006).
Transportation: Commute to work: 95.8% car, 2.1% public transportation, 0.0% walk, 1.7% work from home (2000); Travel time to work: 13.0% less than 15 minutes, 35.9% 15 to 30 minutes, 20.5% 30 to 45 minutes, 10.0% 45 to 60 minutes, 20.5% 60 minutes or more (2000)

WOODSTOCK (city). County seat. Covers a land area of 10.656 square miles and a water area of 0 square miles. Located at 42.31° N. Lat.; 88.44° W. Long. Elevation is 945 feet.
History: Woodstock was settled in the 1830's and 1840's by people from Vermont, who named it for the Vermont town. After 1844, Woodstock grew as the seat of McHenry County.
Population: 15,150 (1990); 20,151 (2000); 22,381 (2007); 23,982 (2012 projected); Race: 82.5% White, 1.5% Black, 2.9% Asian, 27.3% Hispanic of any race (2007); Density: 2,100.4 persons per square mile (2007); Average household size: 2.77 (2007); Median age: 33.6 (2007); Males per 100 females: 101.4 (2007); Marriage status: 24.4% never married, 58.4% now married, 6.1% widowed, 11.1% divorced (2000); Foreign born: 16.8% (2000); Ancestry (includes multiple ancestries): 31.3% German, 22.9% Other groups, 13.7% Irish, 8.4% English, 6.7% Polish (2000).
Economy: Single-family building permits issued: 276 (2007); Multi-family building permits issued: 44 (2007); Employment by occupation: 12.5% management, 16.8% professional, 13.1% services, 24.1% sales, 0.7% farming, 9.7% construction, 23.0% production (2000).
Income: Per capita income: $25,873 (2007); Median household income: $55,264 (2007); Average household income: $69,056 (2007); Percent of households with income of $100,000 or more: 18.2% (2007); Poverty rate: 7.2% (2000).
Taxes: Total city taxes per capita: $393 (2006); City property taxes per capita: $306 (2006).
Education: Percent of population age 25 and over with: High school diploma (including GED) or higher: 80.5% (2007); Bachelor's degree or higher: 23.2% (2007); Master's degree or higher: 7.2% (2007).

School District(s)

Mchenry Roe (07-12)
2005-06 Enrollment: 13 . . . . (815) 334-4475
Spec Ed Dist of Mchenry Co-Sedom (PK-12)
2005-06 Enrollment: 139 . . . . (815) 338-3622
Woodstock CUSD 200 (PK-12)
2005-06 Enrollment: 6,258 . . . . (815) 337-5406

Housing: Homeownership rate: 61.7% (2007); Median home value: $209,077 (2007); Median rent: $633 per month (2000); Median age of housing: 27 years (2000).
Hospitals: Centegra Memorial Medical Center (154 beds)
Safety: Violent crime rate: 19.6 per 10,000 population; Property crime rate: 343.4 per 10,000 population (2006).
Newspapers: Independent Plus (Community news; Circulation 22,000); Woodstock Independent (Community news; Circulation 2,800)
Transportation: Commute to work: 91.2% car, 3.7% public transportation, 1.9% walk, 2.1% work from home (2000); Travel time to work: 35.8% less than 15 minutes, 31.0% 15 to 30 minutes, 15.1% 30 to 45 minutes, 5.9% 45 to 60 minutes, 12.1% 60 minutes or more (2000)

Additional Information Contacts

City of Woodstock . . . . (815) 338-4300
http://www.woodstock-il.com
Woodstock Chamber of Commerce & Industry . . . . (815) 338-2436
http://www.woodstockilchamber.com

McLean County

Located in central Illinois; drained by the Sangamon and Mackinaw Rivers; includes Lake Bloomington. Covers a land area of 1,183.53 square miles, a water area of 2.76 square miles, and is located in the Central Time Zone. The county was founded in 1830. County seat is Bloomington.

McLean County is part of the Bloomington-Normal, IL Metropolitan Statistical Area. The entire metro area includes: McLean County, IL

Weather Station: Chenoa — Elevation: 711 feet

	Jan	Feb	Mar	Apr	May	Jun	Jul	Aug	Sep	Oct	Nov	Dec
High	31	37	49	63	74	83	86	84	78	65	50	37
Low	15	20	30	40	50	60	64	61	54	43	32	21
Precip	1.6	1.4	3.0	3.4	3.9	4.1	3.4	3.3	3.1	2.7	2.6	2.5
Snow	7.0	5.4	2.8	1.1	tr	0.0	0.0	0.0	0.0	tr	1.6	4.8

High and Low temperatures in degrees Fahrenheit; Precipitation and Snow in inches

Population: 129,180 (1990); 150,433 (2000); 161,014 (2007); 167,611 (2012 projected); Race: 87.4% White, 6.5% Black, 2.8% Asian, 3.2% Hispanic of any race (2007); Density: 136.0 persons per square mile (2007); Average household size: 2.66 (2007); Median age: 30.7 (2007); Males per 100 females: 93.8 (2007).

Religion: Five largest groups: 12.7% Catholic Church, 6.5% The United Methodist Church, 3.7% Lutheran Church—Missouri Synod, 3.7% Christian Churches and Churches of Christ, 2.9% Evangelical Lutheran Church in America (2000).
Economy: Unemployment rate: 4.0% (4/2008); Total civilian labor force: 92,900 (4/2008); Leading industries: 28.6% finance & insurance; 13.4% retail trade; 10.7% health care and social assistance (2005); Farms: 1,442 totaling 688,063 acres (2002); Companies that employ 500 or more persons: 10 (2006); Companies that employ 100 to 499 persons: 88 (2006); Companies that employ less than 100 persons: 3,661 (2006); Black-owned businesses: 272 (2002); Hispanic-owned businesses: n/a (2002); Asian-owned businesses: 278 (2002); Women-owned businesses: 2,993 (2002); Retail sales per capita: $18,516 (2008). Single-family building permits issued: 425 (2007); Multi-family building permits issued: 228 (2007).
Income: Per capita income: $26,431 (2007); Median household income: $54,855 (2007); Average household income: $69,137 (2007); Percent of households with income of $100,000 or more: 19.9% (2007); Poverty rate: 11.4% (2005); Bankruptcy rate: 2.79% (2007).
Taxes: Total county taxes per capita: $208 (2006); County property taxes per capita: $162 (2006).
Education: Percent of population age 25 and over with: High school diploma (including GED) or higher: 91.2% (2007); Bachelor's degree or higher: 37.6% (2007); Master's degree or higher: 11.3% (2007).
Housing: Homeownership rate: 67.3% (2007); Median home value: $142,475 (2007); Median rent: $461 per month (2000); Median age of housing: 27 years (2000).
Health: Birth rate: 140.2 per 10,000 population (2007); Death rate: 64.2 per 10,000 population (2007); Age-adjusted cancer mortality rate: 169.8 deaths per 100,000 population (2005); Air Quality Index: 82.7% good, 16.4% moderate, 0.8% unhealthy for sensitive individuals, 0.0% unhealthy (percent of days in 2007); Number of physicians: 21.2 per 10,000 population (2005); Hospital beds: 24.9 per 10,000 population (2004); Hospital admissions: 1,015.4 per 10,000 population (2004).
Elections: 2004 Presidential election results: 57.6% Bush, 41.7% Kerry, 0.1% Nader, 0.5% Badnarik
National and State Parks: Moraine View State Park
Additional Information Contacts
McLean County Government . . . . (309) 888-5110
http://www.co.mclean.il.us
Bloomington-Normal Convention & Visitors Bureau . . . . . . (309) 665-0033
http://www.bloomingtonnormalcvb.org/
City of Bloomington . . . . (309) 434-2509
http://www.cityblm.org/
LeRoy Business Development Group . . . . (309) 962-5751
http://www.leroybiz.org
McLean County Chamber of Commerce . . . . (309) 829-6344
http://www.mcleancochamber.org/
Town of Normal . . . . (309) 454-2444
http://www.normal.org

McLean County Communities

ANCHOR (village). Covers a land area of 0.193 square miles and a water area of 0 square miles. Located at 40.56° N. Lat.; 88.53° W. Long. Elevation is 778 feet.
Population: 178 (1990); 175 (2000); 181 (2007); 184 (2012 projected); Race: 96.1% White, 0.0% Black, 0.0% Asian, 0.0% Hispanic of any race (2007); Density: 935.6 persons per square mile (2007); Average household size: 2.70 (2007); Median age: 38.9 (2007); Males per 100 females: 92.6 (2007); Marriage status: 16.0% never married, 66.4% now married, 8.8% widowed, 8.8% divorced (2000); Foreign born: 0.0% (2000); Ancestry (includes multiple ancestries): 38.7% German, 32.5% Irish, 12.9% English, 11.7% Other groups, 6.1% Norwegian (2000).
Economy: Single-family building permits issued: 0 (2007); Multi-family building permits issued: 0 (2007); Employment by occupation: 1.4% management, 13.7% professional, 11.0% services, 37.0% sales, 0.0% farming, 17.8% construction, 19.2% production (2000).
Income: Per capita income: $22,017 (2007); Median household income: $60,577 (2007); Average household income: $59,478 (2007); Percent of households with income of $100,000 or more: 14.9% (2007); Poverty rate: 1.9% (2000).
Education: Percent of population age 25 and over with: High school diploma (including GED) or higher: 86.6% (2007); Bachelor's degree or higher: 10.7% (2007); Master's degree or higher: 0.0% (2007).
Housing: Homeownership rate: 91.0% (2007); Median home value: $76,875 (2007); Median rent: $342 per month (2000); Median age of housing: 50 years (2000).
Transportation: Commute to work: 97.3% car, 0.0% public transportation, 0.0% walk, 2.7% work from home (2000); Travel time to work: 21.1% less than 15 minutes, 14.1% 15 to 30 minutes, 50.7% 30 to 45 minutes, 7.0% 45 to 60 minutes, 7.0% 60 minutes or more (2000)

ARROWSMITH (village). Covers a land area of 0.203 square miles and a water area of 0 square miles. Located at 40.44° N. Lat.; 88.63° W. Long. Elevation is 883 feet.
Population: 313 (1990); 298 (2000); 264 (2007); 255 (2012 projected); Race: 98.5% White, 0.0% Black, 0.0% Asian, 0.8% Hispanic of any race (2007); Density: 1,297.4 persons per square mile (2007); Average household size: 2.75 (2007); Median age: 32.8 (2007); Males per 100 females: 85.9 (2007); Marriage status: 15.1% never married, 72.7% now married, 4.2% widowed, 8.0% divorced (2000); Foreign born: 1.0% (2000); Ancestry (includes multiple ancestries): 24.7% German, 11.0% Irish, 9.7% Other groups, 7.5% United States or American, 6.8% English (2000).
Economy: Single-family building permits issued: 0 (2007); Multi-family building permits issued: 0 (2007); Employment by occupation: 8.7% management, 17.4% professional, 14.0% services, 27.3% sales, 1.7% farming, 15.7% construction, 15.1% production (2000).
Income: Per capita income: $25,180 (2007); Median household income: $66,000 (2007); Average household income: $69,245 (2007); Percent of households with income of $100,000 or more: 19.8% (2007); Poverty rate: 3.3% (2000).
Education: Percent of population age 25 and over with: High school diploma (including GED) or higher: 94.0% (2007); Bachelor's degree or higher: 16.8% (2007); Master's degree or higher: 3.0% (2007).
Housing: Homeownership rate: 91.7% (2007); Median home value: $112,097 (2007); Median rent: $517 per month (2000); Median age of housing: 56 years (2000).
Transportation: Commute to work: 94.7% car, 0.0% public transportation, 4.1% walk, 1.2% work from home (2000); Travel time to work: 11.4% less than 15 minutes, 40.7% 15 to 30 minutes, 37.7% 30 to 45 minutes, 6.6% 45 to 60 minutes, 3.6% 60 minutes or more (2000)

BELLFLOWER (village). Covers a land area of 0.365 square miles and a water area of 0 square miles. Located at 40.34° N. Lat.; 88.52° W. Long. Elevation is 784 feet.
Population: 405 (1990); 408 (2000); 342 (2007); 346 (2012 projected); Race: 100.0% White, 0.0% Black, 0.0% Asian, 0.0% Hispanic of any race (2007); Density: 937.2 persons per square mile (2007); Average household size: 2.50 (2007); Median age: 38.6 (2007); Males per 100 females: 97.7 (2007); Marriage status: 19.6% never married, 61.5% now married, 8.2% widowed, 10.7% divorced (2000); Foreign born: 0.0% (2000); Ancestry (includes multiple ancestries): 25.8% German, 13.3% English, 8.6% Other groups, 8.4% Irish, 5.4% United States or American (2000).
Economy: Single-family building permits issued: 0 (2007); Multi-family building permits issued: 0 (2007); Employment by occupation: 11.3% management, 9.9% professional, 13.7% services, 31.1% sales, 1.4% farming, 10.8% construction, 21.7% production (2000).
Income: Per capita income: $22,412 (2007); Median household income: $49,265 (2007); Average household income: $55,949 (2007); Percent of households with income of $100,000 or more: 9.5% (2007); Poverty rate: 0.5% (2000).
Education: Percent of population age 25 and over with: High school diploma (including GED) or higher: 85.8% (2007); Bachelor's degree or higher: 12.0% (2007); Master's degree or higher: 3.9% (2007).
Housing: Homeownership rate: 84.7% (2007); Median home value: $86,429 (2007); Median rent: $315 per month (2000); Median age of housing: 60 years (2000).
Transportation: Commute to work: 92.8% car, 0.0% public transportation, 1.4% walk, 3.4% work from home (2000); Travel time to work: 14.9% less than 15 minutes, 23.9% 15 to 30 minutes, 52.2% 30 to 45 minutes, 5.0% 45 to 60 minutes, 4.0% 60 minutes or more (2000)

BLOOMINGTON (city). County seat. Covers a land area of 22.500 square miles and a water area of 0 square miles. Located at 40.47° N. Lat.; 88.98° W. Long. Elevation is 797 feet.
History: Bloomington was laid out in 1831 on land belonging to James Allin, adjoining the settlement called Blooming Grove. Allin also donated land for the county courthouse. Bloomington's growth was given impetus by the founding in 1853 of Illinois Wesleyan University, and the arrival in

1854 of both the Illinois Central and the Chicago & Mississippi Railroads. Adlai Stevenson (1835-1914) practiced law in Bloomington before serving in Congress and as vice-president, and returned to Bloomington in 1900.
Population: 53,588 (1990); 64,808 (2000); 70,395 (2007); 73,707 (2012 projected); Race: 82.9% White, 8.5% Black, 4.4% Asian, 4.1% Hispanic of any race (2007); Density: 3,128.6 persons per square mile (2007); Average household size: 2.47 (2007); Median age: 33.0 (2007); Males per 100 females: 95.0 (2007); Marriage status: 29.7% never married, 54.1% now married, 5.3% widowed, 10.9% divorced (2000); Foreign born: 4.5% (2000); Ancestry (includes multiple ancestries): 28.0% German, 17.0% Other groups, 14.1% Irish, 10.8% English, 7.1% United States or American (2000).
Economy: Unemployment rate: 3.9% (4/2008); Total civilian labor force: 42,125 (4/2008); Single-family building permits issued: 200 (2007); Multi-family building permits issued: 101 (2007); Employment by occupation: 16.9% management, 23.9% professional, 13.9% services, 28.1% sales, 0.2% farming, 6.7% construction, 10.4% production (2000).
Income: Per capita income: $29,631 (2007); Median household income: $54,971 (2007); Average household income: $72,513 (2007); Percent of households with income of $100,000 or more: 21.6% (2007); Poverty rate: 7.8% (2000).
Education: Percent of population age 25 and over with: High school diploma (including GED) or higher: 90.6% (2007); Bachelor's degree or higher: 41.7% (2007); Master's degree or higher: 12.3% (2007).

School District(s)

Bloomington Area Voc Ctr
2005-06 Enrollment: n/a . . . . (309) 829-8671
Bloomington SD 87 (PK-12)
2005-06 Enrollment: 5,515 . . . . (309) 827-6031
De Witt Livingston Mclean Roe (07-12)
2005-06 Enrollment: 258 . . . . (309) 888-5120
Mclean County USD 5 (PK-12)
2005-06 Enrollment: 11,760 . . . . (309) 452-4476

Four-year College(s)

Illinois Wesleyan University (Private, Not-for-profit)
Fall 2007 Enrollment: 2,094. . . . . (309) 556-1000
2007-08 Tuition: In-state $30,750; Out-of-state $30,750

Vocational/Technical School(s)

Hairmasters Institute of Cosmetology (Private, For-profit)
Fall 2007 Enrollment: 152 . . . . (309) 828-1884
2007-08 Tuition: $9,750

Housing: Homeownership rate: 65.6% (2007); Median home value: $145,773 (2007); Median rent: $461 per month (2000); Median age of housing: 27 years (2000).
Hospitals: BroMenn Regional Medical Center (224 beds); St. Joseph Medical Center (157 beds)
Safety: Violent crime rate: 56.4 per 10,000 population; Property crime rate: 298.9 per 10,000 population (2006).
Newspapers: The Pantagraph (Local news; Circulation 49,659)
Transportation: Commute to work: 91.6% car, 1.4% public transportation, 3.5% walk, 2.7% work from home (2000); Travel time to work: 58.8% less than 15 minutes, 31.1% 15 to 30 minutes, 4.0% 30 to 45 minutes, 2.9% 45 to 60 minutes, 3.0% 60 minutes or more (2000); Amtrak: Service available.
Airports: Central IL Regional Airport at Bloomington-Normal (primary service)

Additional Information Contacts

Bloomington-Normal Convention & Visitors Bureau . . . . . . (309) 665-0033
http://www.bloomingtonnormalcvb.org/
City of Bloomington . . . . (309) 434-2509
http://www.cityblm.org/
McLean County Chamber of Commerce . . . . (309) 829-6344
http://www.mcleancochamber.org/

CARLOCK (village). Covers a land area of 0.244 square miles and a water area of 0 square miles. Located at 40.58° N. Lat.; 89.13° W. Long. Elevation is 771 feet.
Population: 442 (1990); 456 (2000); 502 (2007); 507 (2012 projected); Race: 96.8% White, 0.2% Black, 1.4% Asian, 0.6% Hispanic of any race (2007); Density: 2,060.7 persons per square mile (2007); Average household size: 2.51 (2007); Median age: 34.7 (2007); Males per 100 females: 99.2 (2007); Marriage status: 22.3% never married, 68.8% now married, 1.9% widowed, 7.1% divorced (2000); Foreign born: 1.5% (2000); Ancestry (includes multiple ancestries): 44.2% German, 13.5% Irish, 9.9% Other groups, 7.7% English, 5.7% French (except Basque) (2000).
Economy: Single-family building permits issued: 6 (2007); Multi-family building permits issued: 0 (2007); Employment by occupation: 12.2% management, 16.8% professional, 20.2% services, 22.3% sales, 0.0% farming, 12.2% construction, 16.4% production (2000).
Income: Per capita income: $25,533 (2007); Median household income: $61,277 (2007); Average household income: $64,088 (2007); Percent of households with income of $100,000 or more: 13.0% (2007); Poverty rate: 5.3% (2000).
Education: Percent of population age 25 and over with: High school diploma (including GED) or higher: 86.7% (2007); Bachelor's degree or higher: 22.3% (2007); Master's degree or higher: 3.4% (2007).

School District(s)

Mclean County USD 5 (PK-12)
2005-06 Enrollment: 11,760 . . . . (309) 452-4476

Housing: Homeownership rate: 78.0% (2007); Median home value: $113,776 (2007); Median rent: $413 per month (2000); Median age of housing: 52 years (2000).
Transportation: Commute to work: 98.7% car, 0.0% public transportation, 0.8% walk, 0.4% work from home (2000); Travel time to work: 23.3% less than 15 minutes, 60.2% 15 to 30 minutes, 11.9% 30 to 45 minutes, 2.5% 45 to 60 minutes, 2.1% 60 minutes or more (2000)

CHENOA (city). Covers a land area of 1.253 square miles and a water area of 0.037 square miles. Located at 40.74° N. Lat.; 88.72° W. Long. Elevation is 719 feet.
History: Chenoa was laid out in 1856 by Matthew T. Scott, and grew up around the junction of the Peoria & Oquawka and the Chicago & Mississippi Railroads. Chenoa is of Indian origin and means "white dove."
Population: 1,740 (1990); 1,845 (2000); 1,875 (2007); 1,848 (2012 projected); Race: 97.3% White, 0.2% Black, 0.5% Asian, 2.5% Hispanic of any race (2007); Density: 1,496.1 persons per square mile (2007); Average household size: 2.57 (2007); Median age: 34.9 (2007); Males per 100 females: 98.6 (2007); Marriage status: 14.6% never married, 68.8% now married, 7.3% widowed, 9.3% divorced (2000); Foreign born: 1.1% (2000); Ancestry (includes multiple ancestries): 31.5% German, 12.8% Irish, 12.8% English, 11.1% United States or American, 9.0% Other groups (2000).
Economy: Single-family building permits issued: 1 (2007); Multi-family building permits issued: 0 (2007); Employment by occupation: 8.2% management, 10.6% professional, 20.3% services, 25.9% sales, 0.4% farming, 10.3% construction, 24.3% production (2000).
Income: Per capita income: $21,565 (2007); Median household income: $49,423 (2007); Average household income: $55,390 (2007); Percent of households with income of $100,000 or more: 8.6% (2007); Poverty rate: 5.7% (2000).
Education: Percent of population age 25 and over with: High school diploma (including GED) or higher: 83.1% (2007); Bachelor's degree or higher: 15.1% (2007); Master's degree or higher: 4.3% (2007).

School District(s)

Prairie Central CUSD 8 (PK-12)
2005-06 Enrollment: 2,241 . . . . (815) 692-2504

Housing: Homeownership rate: 82.1% (2007); Median home value: $98,214 (2007); Median rent: $369 per month (2000); Median age of housing: 45 years (2000).
Safety: Violent crime rate: 22.2 per 10,000 population; Property crime rate: 166.2 per 10,000 population (2006).
Transportation: Commute to work: 92.2% car, 0.0% public transportation, 3.7% walk, 3.5% work from home (2000); Travel time to work: 38.6% less than 15 minutes, 31.0% 15 to 30 minutes, 24.7% 30 to 45 minutes, 2.8% 45 to 60 minutes, 2.9% 60 minutes or more (2000)

COLFAX (village). Covers a land area of 0.541 square miles and a water area of 0 square miles. Located at 40.56° N. Lat.; 88.61° W. Long. Elevation is 755 feet.
History: Site of defunct coal mine.
Population: 908 (1990); 989 (2000); 967 (2007); 968 (2012 projected); Race: 99.3% White, 0.0% Black, 0.0% Asian, 1.9% Hispanic of any race (2007); Density: 1,788.7 persons per square mile (2007); Average household size: 2.51 (2007); Median age: 40.8 (2007); Males per 100 females: 95.0 (2007); Marriage status: 15.1% never married, 64.4% now married, 10.1% widowed, 10.4% divorced (2000); Foreign born: 0.3% (2000); Ancestry (includes multiple ancestries): 37.7% German, 15.6% English, 11.7% United States or American, 11.5% Irish, 5.1% Other groups (2000).
Economy: Single-family building permits issued: 1 (2007); Multi-family building permits issued: 0 (2007); Employment by occupation: 9.8%

management, 15.9% professional, 14.8% services, 29.4% sales, 0.8% farming, 11.1% construction, 18.2% production (2000).
Income: Per capita income: $23,020 (2007); Median household income: $54,744 (2007); Average household income: $56,760 (2007); Percent of households with income of $100,000 or more: 9.9% (2007); Poverty rate: 3.1% (2000).
Education: Percent of population age 25 and over with: High school diploma (including GED) or higher: 81.3% (2007); Bachelor's degree or higher: 15.3% (2007); Master's degree or higher: 4.2% (2007).

School District(s)

Ridgeview CUSD 19 (PK-12)
2005-06 Enrollment: 661 . . . . (309) 723-5111
Housing: Homeownership rate: 83.1% (2007); Median home value: $97,500 (2007); Median rent: $299 per month (2000); Median age of housing: 52 years (2000).
Safety: Violent crime rate: 10.1 per 10,000 population; Property crime rate: 191.7 per 10,000 population (2006).
Transportation: Commute to work: 90.6% car, 0.8% public transportation, 4.2% walk, 3.4% work from home (2000); Travel time to work: 30.6% less than 15 minutes, 14.1% 15 to 30 minutes, 44.3% 30 to 45 minutes, 3.9% 45 to 60 minutes, 7.2% 60 minutes or more (2000)

COOKSVILLE (village). Covers a land area of 0.232 square miles and a water area of 0 square miles. Located at 40.54° N. Lat.; 88.71° W. Long. Elevation is 768 feet.
Population: 211 (1990); 213 (2000); 218 (2007); 219 (2012 projected); Race: 99.1% White, 0.0% Black, 0.0% Asian, 0.9% Hispanic of any race (2007); Density: 939.5 persons per square mile (2007); Average household size: 2.32 (2007); Median age: 36.3 (2007); Males per 100 females: 86.3 (2007); Marriage status: 13.1% never married, 72.6% now married, 4.6% widowed, 9.7% divorced (2000); Foreign born: 0.0% (2000); Ancestry (includes multiple ancestries): 23.1% German, 16.8% Irish, 8.0% Polish, 7.1% United States or American, 5.5% Scottish (2000).
Economy: Single-family building permits issued: 0 (2007); Multi-family building permits issued: 0 (2007); Employment by occupation: 11.6% management, 6.2% professional, 12.4% services, 34.9% sales, 1.6% farming, 11.6% construction, 21.7% production (2000).
Income: Per capita income: $27,339 (2007); Median household income: $54,615 (2007); Average household income: $63,404 (2007); Percent of households with income of $100,000 or more: 10.6% (2007); Poverty rate: 0.8% (2000).
Education: Percent of population age 25 and over with: High school diploma (including GED) or higher: 95.9% (2007); Bachelor's degree or higher: 10.2% (2007); Master's degree or higher: 0.0% (2007).
Housing: Homeownership rate: 88.3% (2007); Median home value: $103,906 (2007); Median rent: $508 per month (2000); Median age of housing: 60+ years (2000).
Transportation: Commute to work: 96.9% car, 0.0% public transportation, 0.0% walk, 3.1% work from home (2000); Travel time to work: 16.8% less than 15 minutes, 63.2% 15 to 30 minutes, 14.4% 30 to 45 minutes, 4.0% 45 to 60 minutes, 1.6% 60 minutes or more (2000)

CROPSEY (unincorporated postal area, zip code 61731). Covers a land area of 19.941 square miles and a water area of 0 square miles. Located at 40.60° N. Lat.; 88.49° W. Long. Elevation is 801 feet.
Population: 254 (2000); Race: 100.0% White, 0.0% Black, 0.0% Asian, 0.0% Hispanic of any race (2000); Density: 12.7 persons per square mile (2000); Age: 37.1% under 18, 12.9% over 64 (2000); Marriage status: 20.8% never married, 66.9% now married, 12.3% widowed, 0.0% divorced (2000); Foreign born: 0.0% (2000); Ancestry (includes multiple ancestries): 48.7% German, 8.5% English, 7.1% European, 6.3% Irish, 5.8% Other groups (2000).
Economy: Employment by occupation: 18.9% management, 6.6% professional, 0.0% services, 0.0% sales, 11.3% farming, 19.8% construction, 43.4% production (2000).
Income: Per capita income: $14,385 (2000); Median household income: $42,625 (2000); Poverty rate: 37.9% (2000).
Education: Percent of population age 25 and over with: High school diploma (including GED) or higher: 72.4% (2000); Bachelor's degree or higher: 8.2% (2000).
Housing: Homeownership rate: 72.2% (2000); Median home value: $62,400 (2000); Median rent: $325 per month (2000); Median age of housing: 60+ years (2000).
Transportation: Commute to work: 86.8% car, 0.0% public transportation, 0.0% walk, 13.2% work from home (2000); Travel time to work: 18.5% less than 15 minutes, 35.9% 15 to 30 minutes, 9.8% 30 to 45 minutes, 35.9% 45 to 60 minutes, 0.0% 60 minutes or more (2000)

DANVERS (village). Covers a land area of 0.864 square miles and a water area of 0 square miles. Located at 40.52° N. Lat.; 89.17° W. Long. Elevation is 814 feet.
Population: 1,041 (1990); 1,183 (2000); 1,093 (2007); 1,056 (2012 projected); Race: 97.3% White, 1.3% Black, 0.0% Asian, 0.7% Hispanic of any race (2007); Density: 1,264.5 persons per square mile (2007); Average household size: 2.75 (2007); Median age: 32.7 (2007); Males per 100 females: 93.1 (2007); Marriage status: 21.6% never married, 63.7% now married, 5.1% widowed, 9.7% divorced (2000); Foreign born: 1.5% (2000); Ancestry (includes multiple ancestries): 35.5% German, 10.4% Irish, 8.0% English, 5.0% Other groups, 5.0% United States or American (2000).
Economy: Single-family building permits issued: 0 (2007); Multi-family building permits issued: 0 (2007); Employment by occupation: 13.3% management, 14.0% professional, 11.2% services, 26.8% sales, 0.3% farming, 13.8% construction, 20.5% production (2000).
Income: Per capita income: $26,479 (2007); Median household income: $69,107 (2007); Average household income: $72,859 (2007); Percent of households with income of $100,000 or more: 21.7% (2007); Poverty rate: 6.5% (2000).
Education: Percent of population age 25 and over with: High school diploma (including GED) or higher: 94.0% (2007); Bachelor's degree or higher: 22.0% (2007); Master's degree or higher: 5.4% (2007).

School District(s)

Olympia CUSD 16 (PK-12)
2005-06 Enrollment: 2,084 . . . . (309) 379-6011
Housing: Homeownership rate: 85.1% (2007); Median home value: $125,725 (2007); Median rent: $377 per month (2000); Median age of housing: 42 years (2000).
Safety: Violent crime rate: 0.0 per 10,000 population; Property crime rate: 35.3 per 10,000 population (2006).
Transportation: Commute to work: 95.1% car, 0.0% public transportation, 1.8% walk, 3.1% work from home (2000); Travel time to work: 15.3% less than 15 minutes, 64.1% 15 to 30 minutes, 18.6% 30 to 45 minutes, 0.7% 45 to 60 minutes, 1.4% 60 minutes or more (2000)

DOWNS (village). Covers a land area of 2.706 square miles and a water area of 0 square miles. Located at 40.39° N. Lat.; 88.88° W. Long. Elevation is 804 feet.
Population: 692 (1990); 776 (2000); 687 (2007); 672 (2012 projected); Race: 96.8% White, 1.2% Black, 0.1% Asian, 1.5% Hispanic of any race (2007); Density: 253.9 persons per square mile (2007); Average household size: 2.72 (2007); Median age: 35.3 (2007); Males per 100 females: 103.3 (2007); Marriage status: 19.8% never married, 64.8% now married, 4.6% widowed, 10.9% divorced (2000); Foreign born: 0.9% (2000); Ancestry (includes multiple ancestries): 33.5% German, 13.5% United States or American, 11.4% Irish, 11.3% English, 6.0% Other groups (2000).
Economy: Single-family building permits issued: 0 (2007); Multi-family building permits issued: 0 (2007); Employment by occupation: 12.9% management, 12.9% professional, 11.2% services, 33.3% sales, 0.9% farming, 8.7% construction, 20.1% production (2000).
Income: Per capita income: $25,950 (2007); Median household income: $62,679 (2007); Average household income: $70,464 (2007); Percent of households with income of $100,000 or more: 17.4% (2007); Poverty rate: 4.3% (2000).
Education: Percent of population age 25 and over with: High school diploma (including GED) or higher: 87.7% (2007); Bachelor's degree or higher: 20.0% (2007); Master's degree or higher: 3.6% (2007).

School District(s)

Tri Valley CUSD 3 (PK-12)
2005-06 Enrollment: 1,098 . . . . (309) 378-2351
Housing: Homeownership rate: 85.4% (2007); Median home value: $116,935 (2007); Median rent: $430 per month (2000); Median age of housing: 37 years (2000).
Transportation: Commute to work: 94.3% car, 0.0% public transportation, 1.0% walk, 3.8% work from home (2000); Travel time to work: 32.9% less than 15 minutes, 57.4% 15 to 30 minutes, 5.4% 30 to 45 minutes, 3.5% 45 to 60 minutes, 0.7% 60 minutes or more (2000)

ELLSWORTH (village). Covers a land area of 0.237 square miles and a water area of 0 square miles. Located at 40.44° N. Lat.; 88.71° W. Long. Elevation is 866 feet.

Population: 224 (1990); 271 (2000); 242 (2007); 233 (2012 projected); Race: 93.8% White, 0.4% Black, 0.0% Asian, 1.7% Hispanic of any race (2007); Density: 1,023.1 persons per square mile (2007); Average household size: 2.92 (2007); Median age: 31.0 (2007); Males per 100 females: 92.1 (2007); Marriage status: 21.6% never married, 69.8% now married, 3.5% widowed, 5.0% divorced (2000); Foreign born: 0.0% (2000); Ancestry (includes multiple ancestries): 39.3% German, 16.3% Irish, 13.7% Other groups, 11.9% United States or American, 8.5% English (2000).
Economy: Single-family building permits issued: 0 (2007); Multi-family building permits issued: 0 (2007); Employment by occupation: 11.7% management, 12.4% professional, 13.1% services, 32.4% sales, 0.7% farming, 9.7% construction, 20.0% production (2000).
Income: Per capita income: $23,533 (2007); Median household income: $57,727 (2007); Average household income: $68,614 (2007); Percent of households with income of $100,000 or more: 13.3% (2007); Poverty rate: 1.5% (2000).
Education: Percent of population age 25 and over with: High school diploma (including GED) or higher: 88.7% (2007); Bachelor's degree or higher: 16.9% (2007); Master's degree or higher: 3.5% (2007).
Housing: Homeownership rate: 81.9% (2007); Median home value: $112,069 (2007); Median rent: $375 per month (2000); Median age of housing: 60+ years (2000).
Safety: Violent crime rate: 0.0 per 10,000 population; Property crime rate: 0.0 per 10,000 population (2006).
Transportation: Commute to work: 90.8% car, 0.0% public transportation, 1.4% walk, 4.3% work from home (2000); Travel time to work: 11.9% less than 15 minutes, 40.0% 15 to 30 minutes, 40.7% 30 to 45 minutes, 5.9% 45 to 60 minutes, 1.5% 60 minutes or more (2000)

GRIDLEY (village). Covers a land area of 1.161 square miles and a water area of 0 square miles. Located at 40.74° N. Lat.; 88.88° W. Long. Elevation is 755 feet.
History: Gridley was named for Asahel Gridley (1810-1881), a New Yorker who came to Illinois in 1831 and served in the Civil War as a brigadier general.
Population: 1,353 (1990); 1,411 (2000); 1,297 (2007); 1,277 (2012 projected); Race: 97.8% White, 0.4% Black, 0.5% Asian, 0.7% Hispanic of any race (2007); Density: 1,117.4 persons per square mile (2007); Average household size: 2.53 (2007); Median age: 35.2 (2007); Males per 100 females: 98.6 (2007); Marriage status: 23.8% never married, 59.8% now married, 9.0% widowed, 7.3% divorced (2000); Foreign born: 0.6% (2000); Ancestry (includes multiple ancestries): 43.4% German, 10.1% Irish, 9.4% English, 7.8% United States or American, 6.7% Swiss (2000).
Economy: Single-family building permits issued: 2 (2007); Multi-family building permits issued: 2 (2007); Employment by occupation: 11.0% management, 18.4% professional, 15.5% services, 26.3% sales, 0.6% farming, 13.1% construction, 15.2% production (2000).
Income: Per capita income: $23,994 (2007); Median household income: $54,789 (2007); Average household income: $60,781 (2007); Percent of households with income of $100,000 or more: 14.5% (2007); Poverty rate: 6.4% (2000).
Education: Percent of population age 25 and over with: High school diploma (including GED) or higher: 87.2% (2007); Bachelor's degree or higher: 21.8% (2007); Master's degree or higher: 6.3% (2007).

School District(s)

El Paso-Gridley CUSD 11 (PK-12)
2005-06 Enrollment: 1,341 . . . . (309) 527-4410
Housing: Homeownership rate: 79.7% (2007); Median home value: $108,553 (2007); Median rent: $408 per month (2000); Median age of housing: 37 years (2000).
Newspapers: Gridley Village Times (Local news; Circulation 0)
Transportation: Commute to work: 93.4% car, 0.5% public transportation, 2.6% walk, 3.3% work from home (2000); Travel time to work: 30.6% less than 15 minutes, 28.1% 15 to 30 minutes, 33.1% 30 to 45 minutes, 5.8% 45 to 60 minutes, 2.5% 60 minutes or more (2000)

HEYWORTH (village). Covers a land area of 1.545 square miles and a water area of 0 square miles. Located at 40.31° N. Lat.; 88.97° W. Long. Elevation is 755 feet.
Population: 1,703 (1990); 2,431 (2000); 2,150 (2007); 2,102 (2012 projected); Race: 97.0% White, 0.2% Black, 0.6% Asian, 1.1% Hispanic of any race (2007); Density: 1,391.7 persons per square mile (2007); Average household size: 2.69 (2007); Median age: 32.8 (2007); Males per 100 females: 96.0 (2007); Marriage status: 17.1% never married, 67.8% now married, 5.6% widowed, 9.5% divorced (2000); Foreign born: 0.9% (2000); Ancestry (includes multiple ancestries): 25.3% German, 12.0% Irish, 11.8% United States or American, 9.3% Other groups, 8.9% English (2000).
Economy: Single-family building permits issued: 17 (2007); Multi-family building permits issued: 0 (2007); Employment by occupation: 10.5% management, 15.7% professional, 12.4% services, 32.5% sales, 0.5% farming, 12.1% construction, 16.3% production (2000).
Income: Per capita income: $25,135 (2007); Median household income: $61,486 (2007); Average household income: $67,719 (2007); Percent of households with income of $100,000 or more: 17.7% (2007); Poverty rate: 3.1% (2000).
Education: Percent of population age 25 and over with: High school diploma (including GED) or higher: 86.8% (2007); Bachelor's degree or higher: 18.8% (2007); Master's degree or higher: 3.2% (2007).

School District(s)

Heyworth CUSD 4 (PK-12)
2005-06 Enrollment: 940 . . . . (309) 473-3727
Housing: Homeownership rate: 83.1% (2007); Median home value: $122,153 (2007); Median rent: $388 per month (2000); Median age of housing: 28 years (2000).
Safety: Violent crime rate: 24.3 per 10,000 population; Property crime rate: 113.4 per 10,000 population (2006).
Newspapers: Heyworth Star (Community news; Circulation 1,150)
Transportation: Commute to work: 94.6% car, 0.2% public transportation, 0.8% walk, 3.8% work from home (2000); Travel time to work: 15.4% less than 15 minutes, 61.6% 15 to 30 minutes, 17.5% 30 to 45 minutes, 1.5% 45 to 60 minutes, 4.0% 60 minutes or more (2000)

HUDSON (village). Covers a land area of 0.665 square miles and a water area of 0 square miles. Located at 40.60° N. Lat.; 88.98° W. Long. Elevation is 768 feet.
History: Hudson was settled in 1836 by a group of New Yorkers called the Hudson Colony.
Population: 1,097 (1990); 1,510 (2000); 1,441 (2007); 1,397 (2012 projected); Race: 98.0% White, 0.0% Black, 0.5% Asian, 1.4% Hispanic of any race (2007); Density: 2,168.2 persons per square mile (2007); Average household size: 2.99 (2007); Median age: 32.8 (2007); Males per 100 females: 95.3 (2007); Marriage status: 16.7% never married, 74.8% now married, 2.8% widowed, 5.8% divorced (2000); Foreign born: 1.1% (2000); Ancestry (includes multiple ancestries): 38.8% German, 16.3% Irish, 10.9% English, 6.6% Other groups, 6.2% United States or American (2000).
Economy: Single-family building permits issued: 6 (2007); Multi-family building permits issued: 0 (2007); Employment by occupation: 11.9% management, 22.1% professional, 16.2% services, 27.4% sales, 0.6% farming, 8.6% construction, 13.3% production (2000).
Income: Per capita income: $27,635 (2007); Median household income: $75,234 (2007); Average household income: $82,619 (2007); Percent of households with income of $100,000 or more: 28.0% (2007); Poverty rate: 1.2% (2000).
Education: Percent of population age 25 and over with: High school diploma (including GED) or higher: 92.5% (2007); Bachelor's degree or higher: 30.5% (2007); Master's degree or higher: 6.9% (2007).

School District(s)

Mclean County USD 5 (PK-12)
2005-06 Enrollment: 11,760 . . . . (309) 452-4476
Housing: Homeownership rate: 93.2% (2007); Median home value: $147,066 (2007); Median rent: $505 per month (2000); Median age of housing: 24 years (2000).
Transportation: Commute to work: 96.4% car, 0.0% public transportation, 0.4% walk, 3.0% work from home (2000); Travel time to work: 21.7% less than 15 minutes, 67.3% 15 to 30 minutes, 7.0% 30 to 45 minutes, 2.7% 45 to 60 minutes, 1.2% 60 minutes or more (2000)

LE ROY (city). Aka Leroy. Covers a land area of 2.221 square miles and a water area of 0.016 square miles. Located at 40.34° N. Lat.; 88.76° W. Long. Elevation is 791 feet.
History: Incorporated 1857.
Population: 2,980 (1990); 3,332 (2000); 3,435 (2007); 3,467 (2012 projected); Race: 99.1% White, 0.1% Black, 0.1% Asian, 1.6% Hispanic of any race (2007); Density: 1,546.7 persons per square mile (2007); Average household size: 2.57 (2007); Median age: 36.4 (2007); Males per 100 females: 91.7 (2007); Marriage status: 19.6% never married, 64.4% now married, 7.4% widowed, 8.6% divorced (2000); Foreign born: 0.4% (2000); Ancestry (includes multiple ancestries): 23.9% German, 14.7% United States or American, 13.4% English, 12.4% Irish, 5.3% Other groups (2000).

Economy: Single-family building permits issued: 13 (2007); Multi-family building permits issued: 0 (2007); Employment by occupation: 9.9% management, 15.0% professional, 18.0% services, 28.2% sales, 0.9% farming, 10.6% construction, 17.4% production (2000).
Income: Per capita income: $24,569 (2007); Median household income: $53,283 (2007); Average household income: $62,537 (2007); Percent of households with income of $100,000 or more: 14.0% (2007); Poverty rate: 1.9% (2000).
Education: Percent of population age 25 and over with: High school diploma (including GED) or higher: 87.4% (2007); Bachelor's degree or higher: 16.9% (2007); Master's degree or higher: 4.0% (2007).

School District(s)

Leroy CUSD 2 (PK-12)
2005-06 Enrollment: 792 . . . . (309) 962-4211

Housing: Homeownership rate: 78.8% (2007); Median home value: $125,266 (2007); Median rent: $401 per month (2000); Median age of housing: 36 years (2000).
Safety: Violent crime rate: 17.7 per 10,000 population; Property crime rate: 212.3 per 10,000 population (2006).
Newspapers: Le Roy Journal (Local news; Circulation 3,050)
Transportation: Commute to work: 93.3% car, 0.0% public transportation, 2.9% walk, 3.8% work from home (2000); Travel time to work: 24.9% less than 15 minutes, 48.3% 15 to 30 minutes, 20.7% 30 to 45 minutes, 3.6% 45 to 60 minutes, 2.5% 60 minutes or more (2000)
Additional Information Contacts
LeRoy Business Development Group . . . . (309) 962-5751
http://www.leroybiz.org

LEXINGTON (city). Covers a land area of 1.050 square miles and a water area of 0 square miles. Located at 40.64° N. Lat.; 88.78° W. Long. Elevation is 751 feet.
History: Lexington was settled in 1828 and named for the battlefield in Massachusetts. The town developed along the Chicago & Mississippi Railroad as a produce center.
Population: 1,900 (1990); 1,912 (2000); 1,882 (2007); 1,851 (2012 projected); Race: 98.8% White, 0.1% Black, 0.0% Asian, 0.6% Hispanic of any race (2007); Density: 1,791.7 persons per square mile (2007); Average household size: 2.50 (2007); Median age: 36.5 (2007); Males per 100 females: 95.8 (2007); Marriage status: 23.1% never married, 61.4% now married, 8.1% widowed, 7.4% divorced (2000); Foreign born: 0.5% (2000); Ancestry (includes multiple ancestries): 34.3% German, 16.6% Irish, 13.8% United States or American, 13.2% English, 5.4% Other groups (2000).
Economy: Single-family building permits issued: 3 (2007); Multi-family building permits issued: 0 (2007); Employment by occupation: 12.0% management, 18.4% professional, 13.1% services, 24.7% sales, 0.3% farming, 12.8% construction, 18.6% production (2000).
Income: Per capita income: $23,479 (2007); Median household income: $51,149 (2007); Average household income: $58,604 (2007); Percent of households with income of $100,000 or more: 13.0% (2007); Poverty rate: 4.4% (2000).
Education: Percent of population age 25 and over with: High school diploma (including GED) or higher: 89.2% (2007); Bachelor's degree or higher: 19.4% (2007); Master's degree or higher: 5.3% (2007).

School District(s)

Lexington CUSD 7 (PK-12)
2005-06 Enrollment: 569 . . . . (309) 365-4141

Housing: Homeownership rate: 82.6% (2007); Median home value: $121,830 (2007); Median rent: $358 per month (2000); Median age of housing: 41 years (2000).
Safety: Violent crime rate: 0.0 per 10,000 population; Property crime rate: 53.6 per 10,000 population (2006).
Newspapers: Lexingtonian (Local news; Circulation 700)
Transportation: Commute to work: 91.5% car, 0.2% public transportation, 3.0% walk, 4.9% work from home (2000); Travel time to work: 29.4% less than 15 minutes, 42.8% 15 to 30 minutes, 20.9% 30 to 45 minutes, 2.8% 45 to 60 minutes, 4.1% 60 minutes or more (2000)

MCLEAN (village). Covers a land area of 0.431 square miles and a water area of 0 square miles. Located at 40.31° N. Lat.; 89.17° W. Long. Elevation is 709 feet.
Population: 797 (1990); 808 (2000); 774 (2007); 748 (2012 projected); Race: 97.2% White, 0.9% Black, 0.9% Asian, 0.0% Hispanic of any race (2007); Density: 1,795.2 persons per square mile (2007); Average household size: 2.54 (2007); Median age: 38.1 (2007); Males per 100 females: 91.1 (2007); Marriage status: 15.3% never married, 70.0% now married, 4.7% widowed, 10.1% divorced (2000); Foreign born: 1.5% (2000); Ancestry (includes multiple ancestries): 26.7% German, 17.6% United States or American, 12.0% Irish, 8.1% English, 8.0% Other groups (2000).
Economy: Single-family building permits issued: 0 (2007); Multi-family building permits issued: 0 (2007); Employment by occupation: 13.4% management, 13.2% professional, 14.5% services, 28.6% sales, 0.4% farming, 12.3% construction, 17.6% production (2000).
Income: Per capita income: $22,103 (2007); Median household income: $53,500 (2007); Average household income: $56,090 (2007); Percent of households with income of $100,000 or more: 6.9% (2007); Poverty rate: 0.7% (2000).
Education: Percent of population age 25 and over with: High school diploma (including GED) or higher: 84.3% (2007); Bachelor's degree or higher: 10.0% (2007); Master's degree or higher: 2.6% (2007).
Housing: Homeownership rate: 88.9% (2007); Median home value: $100,463 (2007); Median rent: $416 per month (2000); Median age of housing: 48 years (2000).
Safety: Violent crime rate: 0.0 per 10,000 population; Property crime rate: 89.4 per 10,000 population (2006).
Transportation: Commute to work: 95.0% car, 0.0% public transportation, 1.6% walk, 2.3% work from home (2000); Travel time to work: 13.6% less than 15 minutes, 45.5% 15 to 30 minutes, 33.5% 30 to 45 minutes, 3.5% 45 to 60 minutes, 3.9% 60 minutes or more (2000)

NORMAL (town). Covers a land area of 13.619 square miles and a water area of 0.062 square miles. Located at 40.51° N. Lat.; 88.98° W. Long. Elevation is 801 feet.
History: Normal began as North Bloomington, but soon changed its name to Normal when the Illinois State Normal University was founded here in 1857.
Population: 40,139 (1990); 45,386 (2000); 50,687 (2007); 54,048 (2012 projected); Race: 85.9% White, 8.3% Black, 2.6% Asian, 3.2% Hispanic of any race (2007); Density: 3,721.8 persons per square mile (2007); Average household size: 2.96 (2007); Median age: 24.4 (2007); Males per 100 females: 88.8 (2007); Marriage status: 47.9% never married, 42.9% now married, 3.4% widowed, 5.9% divorced (2000); Foreign born: 3.6% (2000); Ancestry (includes multiple ancestries): 31.3% German, 15.1% Irish, 12.6% Other groups, 9.9% English, 5.1% Italian (2000).
Economy: Unemployment rate: 3.8% (4/2008); Total civilian labor force: 28,456 (4/2008); Single-family building permits issued: 129 (2007); Multi-family building permits issued: 125 (2007); Employment by occupation: 13.3% management, 22.2% professional, 19.5% services, 32.4% sales, 0.1% farming, 4.8% construction, 7.6% production (2000).
Income: Per capita income: $20,390 (2007); Median household income: $45,641 (2007); Average household income: $57,423 (2007); Percent of households with income of $100,000 or more: 14.3% (2007); Poverty rate: 19.3% (2000).
Education: Percent of population age 25 and over with: High school diploma (including GED) or higher: 93.9% (2007); Bachelor's degree or higher: 42.3% (2007); Master's degree or higher: 13.9% (2007).

School District(s)

ISU Laboratory Schools (PK-12)
2005-06 Enrollment: 1,050 . . . . (309) 438-8542
Mclean County USD 5 (PK-12)
2005-06 Enrollment: 11,760 . . . . (309) 452-4476

Four-year College(s)

Illinois State University (Public)
Fall 2007 Enrollment: 20,274. . . . . (309) 438-2111
2007-08 Tuition: In-state $9,019; Out-of-state $16,339

Two-year College(s)

Heartland Community College (Public)
Fall 2007 Enrollment: 4,827. . . . . (309) 268-8000
2007-08 Tuition: In-state $4,470; Out-of-state $6,630

Housing: Homeownership rate: 55.6% (2007); Median home value: $145,472 (2007); Median rent: $480 per month (2000); Median age of housing: 23 years (2000).
Safety: Violent crime rate: 45.1 per 10,000 population; Property crime rate: 291.8 per 10,000 population (2006).
Newspapers: Normalite (Community news; Circulation 12,500)
Transportation: Commute to work: 83.8% car, 1.5% public transportation, 11.0% walk, 2.5% work from home (2000); Travel time to work: 55.9% less than 15 minutes, 35.4% 15 to 30 minutes, 4.3% 30 to 45 minutes, 2.2% 45 to 60 minutes, 2.3% 60 minutes or more (2000); Amtrak: Service available.

Airports: Central IL Regional Airport at Bloomington-Normal (primary service)

Additional Information Contacts

Town of Normal .... (309) 454-2444
http://www.normal.org

SAYBROOK (village). Covers a land area of 0.792 square miles and a water area of 0.027 square miles. Located at 40.42° N. Lat.; 88.52° W. Long. Elevation is 801 feet.

Population: 767 (1990); 764 (2000); 814 (2007); 797 (2012 projected); Race: 98.5% White, 0.1% Black, 0.2% Asian, 0.2% Hispanic of any race (2007); Density: 1,027.4 persons per square mile (2007); Average household size: 2.33 (2007); Median age: 38.2 (2007); Males per 100 females: 90.6 (2007); Marriage status: 22.4% never married, 59.9% now married, 6.4% widowed, 11.3% divorced (2000); Foreign born: 0.7% (2000); Ancestry (includes multiple ancestries): 24.9% German, 8.9% United States or American, 8.9% Irish, 8.6% English, 4.3% Other groups (2000).

Economy: Single-family building permits issued: 1 (2007); Multi-family building permits issued: 0 (2007); Employment by occupation: 8.0% management, 7.6% professional, 21.0% services, 25.1% sales, 0.7% farming, 8.0% construction, 29.5% production (2000).

Income: Per capita income: $22,092 (2007); Median household income: $48,375 (2007); Average household income: $51,526 (2007); Percent of households with income of $100,000 or more: 6.3% (2007); Poverty rate: 8.6% (2000).

Education: Percent of population age 25 and over with: High school diploma (including GED) or higher: 87.7% (2007); Bachelor's degree or higher: 7.0% (2007); Master's degree or higher: 1.7% (2007).

Housing: Homeownership rate: 76.8% (2007); Median home value: $89,259 (2007); Median rent: $280 per month (2000); Median age of housing: 60+ years (2000).

Transportation: Commute to work: 93.7% car, 0.0% public transportation, 2.7% walk, 3.2% work from home (2000); Travel time to work: 16.6% less than 15 minutes, 21.7% 15 to 30 minutes, 36.8% 30 to 45 minutes, 19.6% 45 to 60 minutes, 5.3% 60 minutes or more (2000)

SHIRLEY (unincorporated postal area, zip code 61772). Covers a land area of 24.352 square miles and a water area of 0 square miles. Located at 40.40° N. Lat.; 89.06° W. Long. Elevation is 764 feet.

Population: 388 (2000); Race: 94.9% White, 0.0% Black, 2.0% Asian, 3.1% Hispanic of any race (2000); Density: 15.9 persons per square mile (2000); Age: 14.8% under 18, 14.5% over 64 (2000); Marriage status: 18.4% never married, 60.5% now married, 8.2% widowed, 12.8% divorced (2000); Foreign born: 2.0% (2000); Ancestry (includes multiple ancestries): 30.7% German, 23.6% United States or American, 11.1% English, 8.0% Other groups, 6.3% Italian (2000).

Economy: Employment by occupation: 4.7% management, 16.8% professional, 23.7% services, 16.8% sales, 0.0% farming, 13.2% construction, 24.7% production (2000).

Income: Per capita income: $28,002 (2000); Median household income: $67,917 (2000); Poverty rate: 4.8% (2000).

Education: Percent of population age 25 and over with: High school diploma (including GED) or higher: 93.0% (2000); Bachelor's degree or higher: 22.4% (2000).

Housing: Homeownership rate: 85.2% (2000); Median home value: $80,800 (2000); Median rent: $425 per month (2000); Median age of housing: 39 years (2000).

Transportation: Commute to work: 97.4% car, 0.0% public transportation, 2.6% walk, 0.0% work from home (2000); Travel time to work: 11.1% less than 15 minutes, 75.8% 15 to 30 minutes, 3.2% 30 to 45 minutes, 10.0% 45 to 60 minutes, 0.0% 60 minutes or more (2000)

STANFORD (village). Covers a land area of 0.383 square miles and a water area of 0 square miles. Located at 40.43° N. Lat.; 89.22° W. Long. Elevation is 679 feet.

Population: 615 (1990); 670 (2000); 555 (2007); 539 (2012 projected); Race: 97.3% White, 0.0% Black, 0.2% Asian, 0.9% Hispanic of any race (2007); Density: 1,449.5 persons per square mile (2007); Average household size: 2.80 (2007); Median age: 30.6 (2007); Males per 100 females: 96.1 (2007); Marriage status: 27.5% never married, 58.2% now married, 6.8% widowed, 7.6% divorced (2000); Foreign born: 0.0% (2000); Ancestry (includes multiple ancestries): 25.9% German, 15.9% Irish, 10.7% United States or American, 9.7% Other groups, 6.4% Dutch (2000).

Economy: Single-family building permits issued: 0 (2007); Multi-family building permits issued: 0 (2007); Employment by occupation: 8.0% management, 17.3% professional, 16.9% services, 24.0% sales, 0.0% farming, 11.2% construction, 22.7% production (2000).

Income: Per capita income: $23,613 (2007); Median household income: $62,250 (2007); Average household income: $66,187 (2007); Percent of households with income of $100,000 or more: 16.2% (2007); Poverty rate: 3.7% (2000).

Education: Percent of population age 25 and over with: High school diploma (including GED) or higher: 85.4% (2007); Bachelor's degree or higher: 12.2% (2007); Master's degree or higher: 2.7% (2007).

School District(s)

Olympia CUSD 16 (PK-12)
2005-06 Enrollment: 2,084 .... (309) 379-6011

Housing: Homeownership rate: 81.3% (2007); Median home value: $94,531 (2007); Median rent: $334 per month (2000); Median age of housing: 52 years (2000).

Safety: Violent crime rate: 0.0 per 10,000 population; Property crime rate: 93.2 per 10,000 population (2006).

Transportation: Commute to work: 92.6% car, 0.0% public transportation, 2.6% walk, 2.9% work from home (2000); Travel time to work: 15.0% less than 15 minutes, 37.7% 15 to 30 minutes, 37.0% 30 to 45 minutes, 7.0% 45 to 60 minutes, 3.3% 60 minutes or more (2000)

TOWANDA (village). Covers a land area of 0.695 square miles and a water area of 0 square miles. Located at 40.56° N. Lat.; 88.89° W. Long. Elevation is 781 feet.

History: The first settler in Towanda was John Smith, who built a home in 1826 at Smith's Grove. The town of Towanda was laid out in 1854 when the railroad reached the community. The name is of Indian origin and means "where we bury our dead."

Population: 858 (1990); 493 (2000); 453 (2007); 445 (2012 projected); Race: 98.2% White, 0.2% Black, 0.0% Asian, 0.9% Hispanic of any race (2007); Density: 651.4 persons per square mile (2007); Average household size: 2.46 (2007); Median age: 37.4 (2007); Males per 100 females: 93.6 (2007); Marriage status: 18.0% never married, 66.8% now married, 7.0% widowed, 8.3% divorced (2000); Foreign born: 0.4% (2000); Ancestry (includes multiple ancestries): 33.3% German, 14.7% Irish, 14.5% English, 8.9% United States or American, 5.7% Italian (2000).

Economy: Single-family building permits issued: 0 (2007); Multi-family building permits issued: 0 (2007); Employment by occupation: 11.1% management, 12.8% professional, 12.8% services, 30.2% sales, 0.0% farming, 13.9% construction, 19.1% production (2000).

Income: Per capita income: $23,262 (2007); Median household income: $49,643 (2007); Average household income: $57,269 (2007); Percent of households with income of $100,000 or more: 10.3% (2007); Poverty rate: 5.3% (2000).

Education: Percent of population age 25 and over with: High school diploma (including GED) or higher: 89.2% (2007); Bachelor's degree or higher: 18.3% (2007); Master's degree or higher: 2.3% (2007).

School District(s)

Mclean County USD 5 (PK-12)
2005-06 Enrollment: 11,760 .... (309) 452-4476

Housing: Homeownership rate: 81.5% (2007); Median home value: $108,491 (2007); Median rent: $433 per month (2000); Median age of housing: 41 years (2000).

Transportation: Commute to work: 98.3% car, 0.0% public transportation, 0.0% walk, 1.7% work from home (2000); Travel time to work: 32.9% less than 15 minutes, 50.2% 15 to 30 minutes, 10.2% 30 to 45 minutes, 2.5% 45 to 60 minutes, 4.2% 60 minutes or more (2000)

Menard County

Located in central Illinois; drained by the Sangamon River and Salt Creek. Covers a land area of 314.25 square miles, a water area of 1.13 square miles, and is located in the Central Time Zone. The county was founded in 1839. County seat is Petersburg.

Menard County is part of the Springfield, IL Metropolitan Statistical Area. The entire metro area includes: Menard County, IL; Sangamon County, IL

Population: 11,164 (1990); 12,486 (2000); 12,791 (2007); 12,954 (2012 projected); Race: 98.5% White, 0.6% Black, 0.2% Asian, 1.0% Hispanic of any race (2007); Density: 40.7 persons per square mile (2007); Average

household size: 2.52 (2007); Median age: 41.0 (2007); Males per 100 females: 96.9 (2007).
Religion: Five largest groups: 11.4% Catholic Church, 10.7% Christian Churches and Churches of Christ, 8.4% Southern Baptist Convention, 6.2% Presbyterian Church (U.S.A.), 6.2% The United Methodist Church (2000).
Economy: Unemployment rate: 4.5% (4/2008); Total civilian labor force: 7,164 (4/2008); Leading industries: 20.8% retail trade; 11.9% construction; 11.2% accommodation & food services (2005); Farms: 329 totaling 155,024 acres (2002); Companies that employ 500 or more persons: 0 (2006); Companies that employ 100 to 499 persons: 1 (2006); Companies that employ less than 100 persons: 248 (2006); Black-owned businesses: n/a (2002); Hispanic-owned businesses: n/a (2002); Asian-owned businesses: n/a (2002); Women-owned businesses: 338 (2002); Retail sales per capita: $5,695 (2008). Single-family building permits issued: 47 (2007); Multi-family building permits issued: 0 (2007).
Income: Per capita income: $26,294 (2007); Median household income: $55,009 (2007); Average household income: $65,837 (2007); Percent of households with income of $100,000 or more: 16.0% (2007); Poverty rate: 9.3% (2005); Bankruptcy rate: 2.49% (2007).
Taxes: Total county taxes per capita: $227 (2006); County property taxes per capita: $225 (2006).
Education: Percent of population age 25 and over with: High school diploma (including GED) or higher: 88.6% (2007); Bachelor's degree or higher: 20.3% (2007); Master's degree or higher: 5.7% (2007).
Housing: Homeownership rate: 79.1% (2007); Median home value: $122,145 (2007); Median rent: $335 per month (2000); Median age of housing: 31 years (2000).
Health: Birth rate: 110.7 per 10,000 population (2007); Death rate: 107.5 per 10,000 population (2007); Age-adjusted cancer mortality rate: 271.0 deaths per 100,000 population (2005); Number of physicians: 6.4 per 10,000 population (2005); Hospital beds: 0.0 per 10,000 population (2004); Hospital admissions: 0.0 per 10,000 population (2004).
Elections: 2004 Presidential election results: 67.1% Bush, 32.5% Kerry, 0.0% Nader, 0.4% Badnarik
National and State Parks: Lincolns New Salem State Park
Additional Information Contacts
Menard County Government . . . . (217) 632-2415

The Petersburg Chamber of Commerce . . . . (217) 632-7363
http://www.petersburgil.com

Menard County Communities

ATHENS (city). Covers a land area of 1.468 square miles and a water area of 0 square miles. Located at 39.96° N. Lat.; 89.72° W. Long. Elevation is 600 feet.
History: Incorporated 1892.
Population: 1,570 (1990); 1,726 (2000); 1,883 (2007); 1,964 (2012 projected); Race: 98.2% White, 0.6% Black, 0.2% Asian, 1.7% Hispanic of any race (2007); Density: 1,282.3 persons per square mile (2007); Average household size: 2.44 (2007); Median age: 37.2 (2007); Males per 100 females: 85.0 (2007); Marriage status: 24.2% never married, 54.1% now married, 8.9% widowed, 12.8% divorced (2000); Foreign born: 0.6% (2000); Ancestry (includes multiple ancestries): 29.1% German, 13.2% Irish, 10.0% United States or American, 9.9% English, 7.0% Other groups (2000).
Economy: Single-family building permits issued: 5 (2007); Multi-family building permits issued: 0 (2007); Employment by occupation: 10.5% management, 15.5% professional, 14.1% services, 34.7% sales, 1.3% farming, 11.1% construction, 12.8% production (2000).
Income: Per capita income: $23,611 (2007); Median household income: $48,958 (2007); Average household income: $57,665 (2007); Percent of households with income of $100,000 or more: 13.0% (2007); Poverty rate: 6.9% (2000).
Education: Percent of population age 25 and over with: High school diploma (including GED) or higher: 86.7% (2007); Bachelor's degree or higher: 16.8% (2007); Master's degree or higher: 5.9% (2007).

School District(s)

Athens CUSD 213 (PK-12)
2005-06 Enrollment: 1,061 . . . . (217) 636-8761
Logan/Mason/Menard Roe (07-12)
2005-06 Enrollment: 29 . . . . (217) 732-8388

Housing: Homeownership rate: 77.3% (2007); Median home value: $108,640 (2007); Median rent: $369 per month (2000); Median age of housing: 30 years (2000).
Safety: Violent crime rate: 5.6 per 10,000 population; Property crime rate: 116.7 per 10,000 population (2006).
Transportation: Commute to work: 95.7% car, 0.1% public transportation, 1.3% walk, 2.8% work from home (2000); Travel time to work: 11.5% less than 15 minutes, 46.1% 15 to 30 minutes, 34.9% 30 to 45 minutes, 4.2% 45 to 60 minutes, 3.2% 60 minutes or more (2000)

GREENVIEW (village). Covers a land area of 0.850 square miles and a water area of 0 square miles. Located at 40.08° N. Lat.; 89.74° W. Long. Elevation is 541 feet.
Population: 861 (1990); 862 (2000); 830 (2007); 818 (2012 projected); Race: 99.5% White, 0.2% Black, 0.1% Asian, 0.1% Hispanic of any race (2007); Density: 976.5 persons per square mile (2007); Average household size: 2.30 (2007); Median age: 38.6 (2007); Males per 100 females: 96.7 (2007); Marriage status: 22.9% never married, 57.9% now married, 8.5% widowed, 10.7% divorced (2000); Foreign born: 0.5% (2000); Ancestry (includes multiple ancestries): 33.2% German, 17.0% United States or American, 10.8% English, 9.3% Irish, 4.8% Other groups (2000).
Economy: Single-family building permits issued: 1 (2007); Multi-family building permits issued: 0 (2007); Employment by occupation: 10.4% management, 13.9% professional, 19.8% services, 26.3% sales, 2.4% farming, 13.9% construction, 13.3% production (2000).
Income: Per capita income: $24,482 (2007); Median household income: $46,875 (2007); Average household income: $56,288 (2007); Percent of households with income of $100,000 or more: 10.2% (2007); Poverty rate: 7.5% (2000).
Education: Percent of population age 25 and over with: High school diploma (including GED) or higher: 82.5% (2007); Bachelor's degree or higher: 17.1% (2007); Master's degree or higher: 3.3% (2007).

School District(s)

Greenview CUSD 200 (KG-12)
2005-06 Enrollment: 261 . . . . (217) 968-2295
Housing: Homeownership rate: 76.7% (2007); Median home value: $85,893 (2007); Median rent: $293 per month (2000); Median age of housing: 60+ years (2000).
Transportation: Commute to work: 88.6% car, 0.0% public transportation, 5.0% walk, 6.4% work from home (2000); Travel time to work: 27.6% less than 15 minutes, 22.0% 15 to 30 minutes, 39.1% 30 to 45 minutes, 8.2% 45 to 60 minutes, 3.0% 60 minutes or more (2000)

OAKFORD (village). Covers a land area of 0.247 square miles and a water area of 0 square miles. Located at 40.10° N. Lat.; 89.96° W. Long. Elevation is 495 feet.
Population: 246 (1990); 309 (2000); 296 (2007); 291 (2012 projected); Race: 98.3% White, 0.7% Black, 0.3% Asian, 0.0% Hispanic of any race (2007); Density: 1,196.7 persons per square mile (2007); Average household size: 2.31 (2007); Median age: 37.6 (2007); Males per 100 females: 98.7 (2007); Marriage status: 21.8% never married, 59.3% now married, 9.5% widowed, 9.5% divorced (2000); Foreign born: 0.0% (2000); Ancestry (includes multiple ancestries): 15.5% German, 13.7% United States or American, 12.8% English, 6.4% Irish, 4.9% Other groups (2000).
Economy: Employment by occupation: 13.2% management, 10.3% professional, 16.9% services, 25.0% sales, 6.6% farming, 5.1% construction, 22.8% production (2000).
Income: Per capita income: $22,103 (2007); Median household income: $44,000 (2007); Average household income: $51,113 (2007); Percent of households with income of $100,000 or more: 6.3% (2007); Poverty rate: 13.7% (2000).
Education: Percent of population age 25 and over with: High school diploma (including GED) or higher: 90.9% (2007); Bachelor's degree or higher: 14.2% (2007); Master's degree or higher: 4.1% (2007).
Housing: Homeownership rate: 78.1% (2007); Median home value: $58,095 (2007); Median rent: $185 per month (2000); Median age of housing: 45 years (2000).
Transportation: Commute to work: 97.0% car, 0.0% public transportation, 3.0% walk, 0.0% work from home (2000); Travel time to work: 26.1% less than 15 minutes, 20.1% 15 to 30 minutes, 17.2% 30 to 45 minutes, 29.1% 45 to 60 minutes, 7.5% 60 minutes or more (2000)

PETERSBURG (city). County seat. Covers a land area of 1.348 square miles and a water area of 0 square miles. Located at 40.01° N. Lat.; 89.85° W. Long. Elevation is 512 feet.

History: Founded c.1836, incorporated 1841. Ann Rutledge's grave is here. Lincoln's New Salem (State Historic Site) is South.
Population: 2,354 (1990); 2,299 (2000); 2,325 (2007); 2,317 (2012 projected); Race: 97.2% White, 1.5% Black, 0.2% Asian, 1.2% Hispanic of any race (2007); Density: 1,724.9 persons per square mile (2007); Average household size: 2.29 (2007); Median age: 40.0 (2007); Males per 100 females: 84.8 (2007); Marriage status: 23.9% never married, 50.9% now married, 12.9% widowed, 12.3% divorced (2000); Foreign born: 0.5% (2000); Ancestry (includes multiple ancestries): 25.8% German, 13.2% English, 11.5% United States or American, 10.9% Irish, 7.1% Other groups (2000).
Economy: Single-family building permits issued: 1 (2007); Multi-family building permits issued: 0 (2007); Employment by occupation: 12.2% management, 25.7% professional, 23.8% services, 22.9% sales, 0.1% farming, 6.7% construction, 8.5% production (2000).
Income: Per capita income: $22,728 (2007); Median household income: $42,366 (2007); Average household income: $51,153 (2007); Percent of households with income of $100,000 or more: 8.6% (2007); Poverty rate: 16.0% (2000).
Education: Percent of population age 25 and over with: High school diploma (including GED) or higher: 84.4% (2007); Bachelor's degree or higher: 18.8% (2007); Master's degree or higher: 3.8% (2007).

School District(s)

Porta CUSD 202 (PK-12)
2005-06 Enrollment: 1,323 . . . . (217) 632-3803

Housing: Homeownership rate: 62.0% (2007); Median home value: $106,337 (2007); Median rent: $303 per month (2000); Median age of housing: 43 years (2000).
Safety: Violent crime rate: 13.4 per 10,000 population; Property crime rate: 125.0 per 10,000 population (2006).
Newspapers: Menard County Review (Community news; Circulation 1,600); Petersburg Observer (Local news; Circulation 3,200)
Transportation: Commute to work: 94.8% car, 0.0% public transportation, 2.3% walk, 2.9% work from home (2000); Travel time to work: 36.8% less than 15 minutes, 9.2% 15 to 30 minutes, 40.6% 30 to 45 minutes, 11.2% 45 to 60 minutes, 2.1% 60 minutes or more (2000)

Additional Information Contacts

The Petersburg Chamber of Commerce . . . . (217) 632-7363
http://www.petersburgil.com

TALLULA (village). Covers a land area of 0.528 square miles and a water area of 0 square miles. Located at 39.94° N. Lat.; 89.93° W. Long. Elevation is 623 feet.
Population: 598 (1990); 638 (2000); 614 (2007); 609 (2012 projected); Race: 99.3% White, 0.0% Black, 0.0% Asian, 0.7% Hispanic of any race (2007); Density: 1,162.0 persons per square mile (2007); Average household size: 2.64 (2007); Median age: 38.3 (2007); Males per 100 females: 104.0 (2007); Marriage status: 22.0% never married, 66.1% now married, 6.1% widowed, 5.7% divorced (2000); Foreign born: 0.0% (2000); Ancestry (includes multiple ancestries): 18.4% German, 14.9% United States or American, 13.4% English, 12.7% Irish, 8.6% Other groups (2000).
Economy: Employment by occupation: 8.1% management, 12.1% professional, 18.9% services, 18.9% sales, 2.7% farming, 21.9% construction, 17.5% production (2000).
Income: Per capita income: $19,776 (2007); Median household income: $43,625 (2007); Average household income: $52,114 (2007); Percent of households with income of $100,000 or more: 9.0% (2007); Poverty rate: 18.9% (2000).
Education: Percent of population age 25 and over with: High school diploma (including GED) or higher: 73.3% (2007); Bachelor's degree or higher: 7.4% (2007); Master's degree or higher: 1.7% (2007).

School District(s)

Porta CUSD 202 (PK-12)
2005-06 Enrollment: 1,323 . . . . (217) 632-3803

Housing: Homeownership rate: 77.7% (2007); Median home value: $59,167 (2007); Median rent: $354 per month (2000); Median age of housing: 57 years (2000).
Transportation: Commute to work: 96.6% car, 0.0% public transportation, 0.7% walk, 2.7% work from home (2000); Travel time to work: 11.4% less than 15 minutes, 25.9% 15 to 30 minutes, 33.4% 30 to 45 minutes, 23.8% 45 to 60 minutes, 5.5% 60 minutes or more (2000)

Mercer County

Located in northwestern Illinois; bounded on the west by the Mississippi River and the Iowa border; drained by the Edwards River. Covers a land area of 561.02 square miles, a water area of 7.86 square miles, and is located in the Central Time Zone. The county was founded in 1825. County seat is Aledo.

Mercer County is part of the Davenport-Moline-Rock Island, IA-IL Metropolitan Statistical Area. The entire metro area includes: Henry County, IL; Mercer County, IL; Rock Island County, IL; Scott County, IA

Weather Station: Aledo Elevation: 718 feet

	Jan	Feb	Mar	Apr	May	Jun	Jul	Aug	Sep	Oct	Nov	Dec
High	30	36	48	62	74	82	86	84	76	64	48	35
Low	13	19	29	40	51	60	64	62	53	42	31	19
Precip	1.3	1.3	2.5	3.6	4.0	4.4	4.1	4.4	3.4	2.8	2.5	2.0
Snow	8.7	6.1	4.0	1.1	tr	0.0	0.0	0.0	0.0	0.2	2.2	5.8

High and Low temperatures in degrees Fahrenheit; Precipitation and Snow in inches

Population: 17,290 (1990); 16,957 (2000); 16,880 (2007); 16,761 (2012 projected); Race: 98.2% White, 0.5% Black, 0.2% Asian, 1.5% Hispanic of any race (2007); Density: 30.1 persons per square mile (2007); Average household size: 2.53 (2007); Median age: 41.9 (2007); Males per 100 females: 98.4 (2007).
Religion: Five largest groups: 15.3% Catholic Church, 9.6% The United Methodist Church, 8.4% Evangelical Lutheran Church in America, 6.9% Presbyterian Church (U.S.A.), 3.4% American Baptist Churches in the USA (2000).
Economy: Unemployment rate: 5.9% (4/2008); Total civilian labor force: 9,258 (4/2008); Leading industries: 19.9% retail trade; 19.6% manufacturing; 15.0% health care and social assistance (2005); Farms: 746 totaling 292,719 acres (2002); Companies that employ 500 or more persons: 0 (2006); Companies that employ 100 to 499 persons: 2 (2006); Companies that employ less than 100 persons: 306 (2006); Black-owned businesses: n/a (2002); Hispanic-owned businesses: n/a (2002); Asian-owned businesses: n/a (2002); Women-owned businesses: 356 (2002); Retail sales per capita: $7,515 (2008). Single-family building permits issued: 20 (2007); Multi-family building permits issued: 0 (2007).
Income: Per capita income: $22,612 (2007); Median household income: $48,666 (2007); Average household income: $56,792 (2007); Percent of households with income of $100,000 or more: 10.9% (2007); Poverty rate: 8.1% (2005); Bankruptcy rate: 3.40% (2007).
Education: Percent of population age 25 and over with: High school diploma (including GED) or higher: 84.3% (2007); Bachelor's degree or higher: 12.7% (2007); Master's degree or higher: 3.4% (2007).
Housing: Homeownership rate: 79.8% (2007); Median home value: $98,984 (2007); Median rent: $292 per month (2000); Median age of housing: 48 years (2000).
Health: Birth rate: 113.4 per 10,000 population (2007); Death rate: 114.6 per 10,000 population (2007); Age-adjusted cancer mortality rate: 186.3 deaths per 100,000 population (2005); Number of physicians: 4.8 per 10,000 population (2005); Hospital beds: 23.3 per 10,000 population (2004); Hospital admissions: 236.9 per 10,000 population (2004).
Elections: 2004 Presidential election results: 49.1% Bush, 50.3% Kerry, 0.0% Nader, 0.6% Badnarik
National and State Parks: Mark Twain National Wildlife Refuge

Additional Information Contacts

Mercer County Government. . . . . (309) 582-7021
http://www.co.mclean.il.us
City of Aledo. . . . . (309) 582-7241
http://www.aledo-il.org
Viola Area Chamber of Commerce . . . . (309) 596-2188

Mercer County Communities

ALEDO (city). County seat. Covers a land area of 2.242 square miles and a water area of 0.014 square miles. Located at 41.20° N. Lat.; 90.75° W. Long. Elevation is 735 feet.
History: Aledo developed as a trading center, and as the seat of Mercer County.
Population: 3,695 (1990); 3,613 (2000); 3,512 (2007); 3,425 (2012 projected); Race: 98.1% White, 0.8% Black, 0.3% Asian, 0.8% Hispanic of any race (2007); Density: 1,566.1 persons per square mile (2007); Average household size: 2.36 (2007); Median age: 43.5 (2007); Males per 100 females: 90.0 (2007); Marriage status: 18.6% never married, 59.7% now

married, 11.0% widowed, 10.8% divorced (2000); Foreign born: 0.0% (2000); Ancestry (includes multiple ancestries): 22.2% German, 14.1% English, 12.5% Irish, 12.3% United States or American, 9.3% Swedish (2000).
Economy: Single-family building permits issued: 2 (2007); Multi-family building permits issued: 0 (2007); Employment by occupation: 8.8% management, 19.8% professional, 18.5% services, 24.5% sales, 0.4% farming, 11.4% construction, 16.6% production (2000).
Income: Per capita income: $20,845 (2007); Median household income: $38,381 (2007); Average household income: $48,343 (2007); Percent of households with income of $100,000 or more: 7.1% (2007); Poverty rate: 8.1% (2000).
Education: Percent of population age 25 and over with: High school diploma (including GED) or higher: 81.6% (2007); Bachelor's degree or higher: 17.8% (2007); Master's degree or higher: 3.8% (2007).

School District(s)

Aledo CUSD 201 (PK-12)
2005-06 Enrollment: 963 . . . . (309) 582-2238
Housing: Homeownership rate: 72.5% (2007); Median home value: $95,183 (2007); Median rent: $322 per month (2000); Median age of housing: 49 years (2000).
Safety: Violent crime rate: 14.1 per 10,000 population; Property crime rate: 121.6 per 10,000 population (2006).
Newspapers: Times Record (Regional news; Circulation 3,200)
Transportation: Commute to work: 94.8% car, 0.0% public transportation, 2.3% walk, 1.3% work from home (2000); Travel time to work: 50.9% less than 15 minutes, 7.8% 15 to 30 minutes, 21.9% 30 to 45 minutes, 12.5% 45 to 60 minutes, 6.9% 60 minutes or more (2000)

Additional Information Contacts

City of Aledo. . . . . (309) 582-7241
http://www.aledo-il.org

JOY (village). Covers a land area of 0.420 square miles and a water area of 0 square miles. Located at 41.19° N. Lat.; 90.88° W. Long. Elevation is 686 feet.
Population: 452 (1990); 373 (2000); 344 (2007); 338 (2012 projected); Race: 99.7% White, 0.0% Black, 0.0% Asian, 0.9% Hispanic of any race (2007); Density: 819.3 persons per square mile (2007); Average household size: 2.36 (2007); Median age: 36.3 (2007); Males per 100 females: 95.5 (2007); Marriage status: 17.6% never married, 64.0% now married, 7.6% widowed, 10.7% divorced (2000); Foreign born: 0.0% (2000); Ancestry (includes multiple ancestries): 28.3% German, 19.5% United States or American, 12.6% Irish, 10.2% English, 10.0% Swedish (2000).
Economy: Single-family building permits issued: 0 (2007); Multi-family building permits issued: 0 (2007); Employment by occupation: 3.6% management, 10.7% professional, 20.8% services, 15.5% sales, 0.6% farming, 17.9% construction, 31.0% production (2000).
Income: Per capita income: $20,531 (2007); Median household income: $44,231 (2007); Average household income: $48,373 (2007); Percent of households with income of $100,000 or more: 4.8% (2007); Poverty rate: 18.6% (2000).
Education: Percent of population age 25 and over with: High school diploma (including GED) or higher: 84.0% (2007); Bachelor's degree or higher: 4.3% (2007); Master's degree or higher: 1.7% (2007).

School District(s)

Westmer CUSD 203 (PK-12)
2005-06 Enrollment: 559 . . . . (309) 584-4173
Housing: Homeownership rate: 85.6% (2007); Median home value: $57,667 (2007); Median rent: $363 per month (2000); Median age of housing: 60+ years (2000).
Transportation: Commute to work: 91.5% car, 0.0% public transportation, 1.2% walk, 6.7% work from home (2000); Travel time to work: 41.8% less than 15 minutes, 13.1% 15 to 30 minutes, 19.0% 30 to 45 minutes, 18.3% 45 to 60 minutes, 7.8% 60 minutes or more (2000)

KEITHSBURG (city). Covers a land area of 2.579 square miles and a water area of 0.599 square miles. Located at 41.10° N. Lat.; 90.93° W. Long. Elevation is 545 feet.
History: Incorporated 1857.
Population: 747 (1990); 714 (2000); 736 (2007); 729 (2012 projected); Race: 98.6% White, 0.0% Black, 0.0% Asian, 0.5% Hispanic of any race (2007); Density: 285.4 persons per square mile (2007); Average household size: 2.54 (2007); Median age: 37.4 (2007); Males per 100 females: 92.2 (2007); Marriage status: 21.1% never married, 62.2% now married, 7.0% widowed, 9.7% divorced (2000); Foreign born: 0.0% (2000); Ancestry (includes multiple ancestries): 22.5% German, 9.7% Other groups, 9.7% Irish, 8.0% United States or American, 5.9% Swedish (2000).
Economy: Single-family building permits issued: 1 (2007); Multi-family building permits issued: 0 (2007); Employment by occupation: 4.7% management, 9.0% professional, 20.1% services, 15.8% sales, 1.8% farming, 14.0% construction, 34.8% production (2000).
Income: Per capita income: $18,166 (2007); Median household income: $39,074 (2007); Average household income: $46,103 (2007); Percent of households with income of $100,000 or more: 2.4% (2007); Poverty rate: 14.0% (2000).
Education: Percent of population age 25 and over with: High school diploma (including GED) or higher: 71.9% (2007); Bachelor's degree or higher: 7.3% (2007); Master's degree or higher: 3.7% (2007).
Housing: Homeownership rate: 82.4% (2007); Median home value: $56,094 (2007); Median rent: $272 per month (2000); Median age of housing: 30 years (2000).
Transportation: Commute to work: 96.4% car, 0.0% public transportation, 2.2% walk, 1.4% work from home (2000); Travel time to work: 24.5% less than 15 minutes, 23.1% 15 to 30 minutes, 15.4% 30 to 45 minutes, 17.2% 45 to 60 minutes, 19.8% 60 minutes or more (2000)

MATHERVILLE (village). Covers a land area of 0.392 square miles and a water area of 0.007 square miles. Located at 41.26° N. Lat.; 90.60° W. Long. Elevation is 748 feet.
Population: 708 (1990); 772 (2000); 652 (2007); 650 (2012 projected); Race: 98.0% White, 0.0% Black, 0.3% Asian, 1.7% Hispanic of any race (2007); Density: 1,662.7 persons per square mile (2007); Average household size: 2.62 (2007); Median age: 32.9 (2007); Males per 100 females: 92.9 (2007); Marriage status: 21.4% never married, 55.6% now married, 6.7% widowed, 16.3% divorced (2000); Foreign born: 0.6% (2000); Ancestry (includes multiple ancestries): 17.8% Irish, 16.7% German, 14.1% United States or American, 10.6% English, 5.7% Dutch (2000).
Economy: Single-family building permits issued: 0 (2007); Multi-family building permits issued: 0 (2007); Employment by occupation: 9.8% management, 5.0% professional, 17.7% services, 27.8% sales, 0.0% farming, 13.2% construction, 26.5% production (2000).
Income: Per capita income: $18,815 (2007); Median household income: $43,816 (2007); Average household income: $49,267 (2007); Percent of households with income of $100,000 or more: 8.0% (2007); Poverty rate: 15.8% (2000).
Education: Percent of population age 25 and over with: High school diploma (including GED) or higher: 85.6% (2007); Bachelor's degree or higher: 4.1% (2007); Master's degree or higher: 1.3% (2007).

School District(s)

Sherrard CUSD 200 (PK-12)
2005-06 Enrollment: 1,770 . . . . (309) 593-4075
Housing: Homeownership rate: 74.7% (2007); Median home value: $71,538 (2007); Median rent: $156 per month (2000); Median age of housing: 55 years (2000).
Transportation: Commute to work: 95.8% car, 0.0% public transportation, 0.0% walk, 2.9% work from home (2000); Travel time to work: 14.9% less than 15 minutes, 34.4% 15 to 30 minutes, 36.4% 30 to 45 minutes, 9.9% 45 to 60 minutes, 4.3% 60 minutes or more (2000)

NEW BOSTON (city). Covers a land area of 0.940 square miles and a water area of 0.453 square miles. Located at 41.17° N. Lat.; 90.99° W. Long. Elevation is 568 feet.
Population: 620 (1990); 632 (2000); 669 (2007); 668 (2012 projected); Race: 99.3% White, 0.6% Black, 0.0% Asian, 0.0% Hispanic of any race (2007); Density: 712.0 persons per square mile (2007); Average household size: 2.33 (2007); Median age: 42.3 (2007); Males per 100 females: 104.0 (2007); Marriage status: 16.7% never married, 61.5% now married, 8.8% widowed, 13.0% divorced (2000); Foreign born: 0.3% (2000); Ancestry (includes multiple ancestries): 17.8% German, 10.4% United States or American, 10.3% English, 6.6% Other groups, 6.4% Irish (2000).
Economy: Employment by occupation: 5.2% management, 2.4% professional, 26.3% services, 22.3% sales, 2.0% farming, 15.9% construction, 25.9% production (2000).
Income: Per capita income: $18,475 (2007); Median household income: $35,125 (2007); Average household income: $43,066 (2007); Percent of households with income of $100,000 or more: 4.5% (2007); Poverty rate: 11.2% (2000).

Education: Percent of population age 25 and over with: High school diploma (including GED) or higher: 70.1% (2007); Bachelor's degree or higher: 2.3% (2007); Master's degree or higher: 1.3% (2007).

School District(s)

Westmer CUSD 203 (PK-12)
2005-06 Enrollment: 559 . . . . (309) 584-4173

Housing: Homeownership rate: 81.9% (2007); Median home value: $67,750 (2007); Median rent: $225 per month (2000); Median age of housing: 47 years (2000).

Transportation: Commute to work: 89.5% car, 0.0% public transportation, 6.1% walk, 4.0% work from home (2000); Travel time to work: 26.6% less than 15 minutes, 26.2% 15 to 30 minutes, 21.5% 30 to 45 minutes, 12.2% 45 to 60 minutes, 13.5% 60 minutes or more (2000)

NEW WINDSOR (unincorporated postal area, zip code 61465). Aka Windsor. Covers a land area of 36.425 square miles and a water area of 0.017 square miles. Located at 41.17° N. Lat.; 90.68° W. Long. Elevation is 804 feet.

Population: 1,144 (2000); Race: 97.9% White, 0.0% Black, 0.5% Asian, 2.0% Hispanic of any race (2000); Density: 31.4 persons per square mile (2000); Age: 23.0% under 18, 19.9% over 64 (2000); Marriage status: 16.2% never married, 63.7% now married, 10.2% widowed, 10.0% divorced (2000); Foreign born: 0.5% (2000); Ancestry (includes multiple ancestries): 20.0% German, 18.0% Swedish, 14.9% Irish, 10.6% English, 9.3% Other groups (2000).

Economy: Employment by occupation: 10.2% management, 13.3% professional, 14.5% services, 22.7% sales, 2.8% farming, 11.4% construction, 25.1% production (2000).

Income: Per capita income: $19,286 (2000); Median household income: $40,069 (2000); Poverty rate: 12.0% (2000).

Education: Percent of population age 25 and over with: High school diploma (including GED) or higher: 86.8% (2000); Bachelor's degree or higher: 11.1% (2000).

Housing: Homeownership rate: 80.9% (2000); Median home value: $64,200 (2000); Median rent: $228 per month (2000); Median age of housing: 52 years (2000).

Transportation: Commute to work: 94.4% car, 0.0% public transportation, 0.6% walk, 2.8% work from home (2000); Travel time to work: 26.1% less than 15 minutes, 20.6% 15 to 30 minutes, 23.0% 30 to 45 minutes, 24.1% 45 to 60 minutes, 6.2% 60 minutes or more (2000)

NORTH HENDERSON (village). Covers a land area of 0.225 square miles and a water area of 0 square miles. Located at 41.09° N. Lat.; 90.47° W. Long. Elevation is 774 feet.

Population: 184 (1990); 187 (2000); 167 (2007); 162 (2012 projected); Race: 100.0% White, 0.0% Black, 0.0% Asian, 1.8% Hispanic of any race (2007); Density: 743.3 persons per square mile (2007); Average household size: 2.53 (2007); Median age: 38.7 (2007); Males per 100 females: 131.9 (2007); Marriage status: 22.8% never married, 64.6% now married, 7.6% widowed, 5.1% divorced (2000); Foreign born: 0.0% (2000); Ancestry (includes multiple ancestries): 29.8% Irish, 20.2% English, 19.2% German, 15.2% Swedish, 3.0% Swiss (2000).

Economy: Employment by occupation: 8.2% management, 9.3% professional, 10.3% services, 32.0% sales, 0.0% farming, 7.2% construction, 33.0% production (2000).

Income: Per capita income: $22,395 (2007); Median household income: $47,500 (2007); Average household income: $56,667 (2007); Percent of households with income of $100,000 or more: 13.6% (2007); Poverty rate: 8.7% (2000).

Education: Percent of population age 25 and over with: High school diploma (including GED) or higher: 87.4% (2007); Bachelor's degree or higher: 6.7% (2007); Master's degree or higher: 3.4% (2007).

Housing: Homeownership rate: 92.4% (2007); Median home value: $53,462 (2007); Median rent: $250 per month (2000); Median age of housing: 60+ years (2000).

Transportation: Commute to work: 91.6% car, 0.0% public transportation, 0.0% walk, 4.2% work from home (2000); Travel time to work: 14.3% less than 15 minutes, 52.7% 15 to 30 minutes, 19.8% 30 to 45 minutes, 0.0% 45 to 60 minutes, 13.2% 60 minutes or more (2000)

SEATON (village). Covers a land area of 1.568 square miles and a water area of 0 square miles. Located at 41.10° N. Lat.; 90.80° W. Long. Elevation is 614 feet.

Population: 221 (1990); 242 (2000); 213 (2007); 212 (2012 projected); Race: 92.0% White, 8.0% Black, 0.0% Asian, 0.0% Hispanic of any race (2007); Density: 135.8 persons per square mile (2007); Average household size: 2.73 (2007); Median age: 38.3 (2007); Males per 100 females: 90.2 (2007); Marriage status: 20.2% never married, 66.1% now married, 4.4% widowed, 9.3% divorced (2000); Foreign born: 0.0% (2000); Ancestry (includes multiple ancestries): 15.9% English, 15.5% United States or American, 14.2% Irish, 11.1% Other groups, 9.3% German (2000).

Economy: Single-family building permits issued: 0 (2007); Multi-family building permits issued: 0 (2007); Employment by occupation: 15.8% management, 15.8% professional, 28.4% services, 11.6% sales, 3.2% farming, 2.1% construction, 23.2% production (2000).

Income: Per capita income: $24,531 (2007); Median household income: $50,769 (2007); Average household income: $66,987 (2007); Percent of households with income of $100,000 or more: 12.8% (2007); Poverty rate: 2.7% (2000).

Education: Percent of population age 25 and over with: High school diploma (including GED) or higher: 87.5% (2007); Bachelor's degree or higher: 11.8% (2007); Master's degree or higher: 5.1% (2007).

Housing: Homeownership rate: 89.7% (2007); Median home value: $67,778 (2007); Median rent: $294 per month (2000); Median age of housing: 60+ years (2000).

Transportation: Commute to work: 89.5% car, 0.0% public transportation, 2.1% walk, 0.0% work from home (2000); Travel time to work: 43.2% less than 15 minutes, 36.8% 15 to 30 minutes, 7.4% 30 to 45 minutes, 3.2% 45 to 60 minutes, 9.5% 60 minutes or more (2000)

SHERRARD (village). Covers a land area of 0.419 square miles and a water area of 0 square miles. Located at 41.31° N. Lat.; 90.50° W. Long. Elevation is 801 feet.

Population: 697 (1990); 694 (2000); 593 (2007); 589 (2012 projected); Race: 98.1% White, 0.0% Black, 0.2% Asian, 1.7% Hispanic of any race (2007); Density: 1,416.9 persons per square mile (2007); Average household size: 2.52 (2007); Median age: 38.4 (2007); Males per 100 females: 95.7 (2007); Marriage status: 20.4% never married, 62.7% now married, 6.9% widowed, 10.0% divorced (2000); Foreign born: 0.0% (2000); Ancestry (includes multiple ancestries): 26.3% German, 19.0% Swedish, 10.2% Irish, 9.4% Belgian, 9.4% English (2000).

Economy: Single-family building permits issued: 0 (2007); Multi-family building permits issued: 0 (2007); Employment by occupation: 7.6% management, 15.7% professional, 13.7% services, 27.9% sales, 0.0% farming, 15.5% construction, 19.5% production (2000).

Income: Per capita income: $27,567 (2007); Median household income: $62,063 (2007); Average household income: $69,564 (2007); Percent of households with income of $100,000 or more: 13.2% (2007); Poverty rate: 5.0% (2000).

Education: Percent of population age 25 and over with: High school diploma (including GED) or higher: 91.2% (2007); Bachelor's degree or higher: 10.3% (2007); Master's degree or higher: 2.8% (2007).

School District(s)

Sherrard CUSD 200 (PK-12)
2005-06 Enrollment: 1,770 . . . . (309) 593-4075

Housing: Homeownership rate: 82.6% (2007); Median home value: $93,333 (2007); Median rent: $319 per month (2000); Median age of housing: 44 years (2000).

Transportation: Commute to work: 97.4% car, 0.0% public transportation, 1.5% walk, 0.8% work from home (2000); Travel time to work: 12.6% less than 15 minutes, 42.0% 15 to 30 minutes, 36.9% 30 to 45 minutes, 4.4% 45 to 60 minutes, 4.1% 60 minutes or more (2000)

VIOLA (village). Covers a land area of 0.827 square miles and a water area of 0 square miles. Located at 41.20° N. Lat.; 90.58° W. Long. Elevation is 791 feet.

History: Viola developed as a coal mining town.

Population: 964 (1990); 956 (2000); 906 (2007); 887 (2012 projected); Race: 98.5% White, 0.0% Black, 0.0% Asian, 2.1% Hispanic of any race (2007); Density: 1,095.4 persons per square mile (2007); Average household size: 2.46 (2007); Median age: 40.6 (2007); Males per 100 females: 89.5 (2007); Marriage status: 17.5% never married, 66.7% now married, 7.1% widowed, 8.7% divorced (2000); Foreign born: 1.3% (2000); Ancestry (includes multiple ancestries): 22.5% German, 15.8% Irish, 15.0% Swedish, 13.2% United States or American, 10.3% English (2000).

Economy: Single-family building permits issued: 4 (2007); Multi-family building permits issued: 0 (2007); Employment by occupation: 7.6% management, 13.2% professional, 17.9% services, 27.5% sales, 1.6% farming, 10.1% construction, 22.1% production (2000).

Income: Per capita income: $22,961 (2007); Median household income: $51,020 (2007); Average household income: $56,529 (2007); Percent of households with income of $100,000 or more: 10.3% (2007); Poverty rate: 8.5% (2000).
Education: Percent of population age 25 and over with: High school diploma (including GED) or higher: 83.1% (2007); Bachelor's degree or higher: 11.5% (2007); Master's degree or higher: 3.2% (2007).

School District(s)

Sherrard CUSD 200 (PK-12)
2005-06 Enrollment: 1,770 . . . . (309) 593-4075
Housing: Homeownership rate: 82.6% (2007); Median home value: $89,615 (2007); Median rent: $323 per month (2000); Median age of housing: 47 years (2000).
Transportation: Commute to work: 91.1% car, 0.0% public transportation, 3.0% walk, 4.3% work from home (2000); Travel time to work: 26.2% less than 15 minutes, 23.1% 15 to 30 minutes, 35.5% 30 to 45 minutes, 12.1% 45 to 60 minutes, 3.1% 60 minutes or more (2000)
Additional Information Contacts
Viola Area Chamber of Commerce . . . . (309) 596-2188

WINDSOR (village). Aka New Windsor. Covers a land area of 0.442 square miles and a water area of 0 square miles. Located at 41.20° N. Lat.; 90.44° W. Long. Elevation is 804 feet.
Population: 774 (1990); 720 (2000); 633 (2007); 616 (2012 projected); Race: 98.7% White, 0.0% Black, 0.5% Asian, 3.0% Hispanic of any race (2007); Density: 1,431.7 persons per square mile (2007); Average household size: 2.32 (2007); Median age: 43.1 (2007); Males per 100 females: 102.9 (2007); Marriage status: 16.0% never married, 63.9% now married, 8.5% widowed, 11.6% divorced (2000); Foreign born: 0.8% (2000); Ancestry (includes multiple ancestries): 20.8% German, 20.0% Swedish, 14.0% Irish, 13.1% English, 12.8% Other groups (2000).
Economy: Single-family building permits issued: 0 (2007); Multi-family building permits issued: 0 (2007); Employment by occupation: 6.1% management, 17.7% professional, 15.3% services, 24.5% sales, 0.9% farming, 11.9% construction, 23.5% production (2000).
Income: Per capita income: $23,851 (2007); Median household income: $46,528 (2007); Average household income: $55,302 (2007); Percent of households with income of $100,000 or more: 7.7% (2007); Poverty rate: 7.8% (2000).
Education: Percent of population age 25 and over with: High school diploma (including GED) or higher: 87.7% (2007); Bachelor's degree or higher: 9.2% (2007); Master's degree or higher: 3.3% (2007).
Housing: Homeownership rate: 79.1% (2007); Median home value: $85,556 (2007); Median rent: $225 per month (2000); Median age of housing: 48 years (2000).
Transportation: Commute to work: 91.4% car, 0.0% public transportation, 0.9% walk, 4.3% work from home (2000); Travel time to work: 25.1% less than 15 minutes, 19.0% 15 to 30 minutes, 26.4% 30 to 45 minutes, 22.2% 45 to 60 minutes, 7.4% 60 minutes or more (2000)

Monroe County

Located in southwestern Illinois; bounded on the west by the Mississippi River and the Missouri border; drained by the Kaskaskia River. Covers a land area of 388.29 square miles, a water area of 9.42 square miles, and is located in the Central Time Zone. The county was founded in 1816. County seat is Waterloo.

Monroe County is part of the St. Louis, MO-IL Metropolitan Statistical Area. The entire metro area includes: Bond County, IL; Calhoun County, IL; Clinton County, IL; Jersey County, IL; Macoupin County, IL; Madison County, IL; Monroe County, IL; St. Clair County, IL; Crawford County, MO (pt.)*; Franklin County, MO; Jefferson County, MO; Lincoln County, MO; St. Charles County, MO; St. Louis County, MO; Warren County, MO; Washington County, MO; St. Louis city, MO

Weather Station: Waterloo Elevation: 649 feet

	Jan	Feb	Mar	Apr	May	Jun	Jul	Aug	Sep	Oct	Nov	Dec
High	38	44	55	67	76	85	89	87	80	69	55	43
Low	21	26	35	45	55	64	68	66	58	47	37	26
Precip	2.3	2.4	3.8	4.2	4.0	3.8	4.0	3.1	3.3	3.1	4.0	3.4
Snow	4.5	3.2	2.0	0.7	0.0	0.0	0.0	0.0	0.0	0.0	1.2	3.0

High and Low temperatures in degrees Fahrenheit; Precipitation and Snow in inches

Population: 22,422 (1990); 27,619 (2000); 31,961 (2007); 34,872 (2012 projected); Race: 98.5% White, 0.2% Black, 0.3% Asian, 1.4% Hispanic of any race (2007); Density: 82.3 persons per square mile (2007); Average household size: 2.66 (2007); Median age: 38.2 (2007); Males per 100 females: 98.8 (2007).
Religion: Five largest groups: 35.4% Catholic Church, 18.3% United Church of Christ, 8.4% Lutheran Church—Missouri Synod, 6.2% Southern Baptist Convention, 0.7% The United Methodist Church (2000).
Economy: Unemployment rate: 4.1% (4/2008); Total civilian labor force: 18,682 (4/2008); Leading industries: 17.8% retail trade; 12.1% construction; 11.7% accommodation & food services (2005); Farms: 531 totaling 177,430 acres (2002); Companies that employ 500 or more persons: 0 (2006); Companies that employ 100 to 499 persons: 11 (2006); Companies that employ less than 100 persons: 774 (2006); Black-owned businesses: n/a (2002); Hispanic-owned businesses: n/a (2002); Asian-owned businesses: n/a (2002); Women-owned businesses: 679 (2002); Retail sales per capita: $12,772 (2008). Single-family building permits issued: 168 (2007); Multi-family building permits issued: 8 (2007).
Income: Per capita income: $28,310 (2007); Median household income: $66,187 (2007); Average household income: $74,814 (2007); Percent of households with income of $100,000 or more: 22.6% (2007); Poverty rate: 3.8% (2005); Bankruptcy rate: 3.18% (2007).
Taxes: Total county taxes per capita: $200 (2006); County property taxes per capita: $200 (2006).
Education: Percent of population age 25 and over with: High school diploma (including GED) or higher: 87.1% (2007); Bachelor's degree or higher: 20.2% (2007); Master's degree or higher: 6.9% (2007).
Housing: Homeownership rate: 80.4% (2007); Median home value: $179,580 (2007); Median rent: $449 per month (2000); Median age of housing: 26 years (2000).
Health: Birth rate: 127.9 per 10,000 population (2007); Death rate: 83.1 per 10,000 population (2007); Age-adjusted cancer mortality rate: 186.5 deaths per 100,000 population (2005); Number of physicians: 8.0 per 10,000 population (2005); Hospital beds: 0.0 per 10,000 population (2004); Hospital admissions: 0.0 per 10,000 population (2004).
Elections: 2004 Presidential election results: 57.8% Bush, 41.5% Kerry, 0.0% Nader, 0.7% Badnarik
National and State Parks: Illinois Caverns State Natural Area
Additional Information Contacts
Monroe County Government . . . . (618) 939-8681

City of Columbia. . . . . (618) 281-7144
http://www.columbiaillinois.com
City of Waterloo . . . . (618) 939-8600
http://www.waterloo.il.us
Waterloo Chamber of Commerce . . . . (618) 939-5300
http://www.enjoywaterloo.com

Monroe County Communities

COLUMBIA (city). Covers a land area of 9.414 square miles and a water area of 0.021 square miles. Located at 38.44° N. Lat.; 90.20° W. Long. Elevation is 502 feet.
History: Columbia was established as a stop on the Kaskaskia-Cahokia trail. Many early residents were of German descent. The quarrying of Keokuk limestone began here in 1840.
Population: 6,110 (1990); 7,922 (2000); 8,765 (2007); 9,318 (2012 projected); Race: 98.0% White, 0.5% Black, 0.3% Asian, 1.9% Hispanic of any race (2007); Density: 931.1 persons per square mile (2007); Average household size: 2.51 (2007); Median age: 38.7 (2007); Males per 100 females: 96.3 (2007); Marriage status: 18.1% never married, 66.3% now married, 6.4% widowed, 9.2% divorced (2000); Foreign born: 1.0% (2000); Ancestry (includes multiple ancestries): 49.7% German, 16.0% Irish, 10.0% English, 6.9% French (except Basque), 5.6% Other groups (2000).
Economy: Single-family building permits issued: 44 (2007); Multi-family building permits issued: 0 (2007); Employment by occupation: 17.1% management, 26.5% professional, 8.7% services, 26.3% sales, 0.6% farming, 9.8% construction, 11.0% production (2000).
Income: Per capita income: $31,658 (2007); Median household income: $69,781 (2007); Average household income: $78,728 (2007); Percent of households with income of $100,000 or more: 25.6% (2007); Poverty rate: 2.5% (2000).
Education: Percent of population age 25 and over with: High school diploma (including GED) or higher: 89.7% (2007); Bachelor's degree or higher: 28.3% (2007); Master's degree or higher: 9.7% (2007).

School District(s)

Columbia CUSD 4 (PK-12)
2005-06 Enrollment: 1,781 . . . . (618) 281-4772

Housing: Homeownership rate: 76.6% (2007); Median home value: $175,623 (2007); Median rent: $520 per month (2000); Median age of housing: 27 years (2000).
Safety: Violent crime rate: 19.1 per 10,000 population; Property crime rate: 139.3 per 10,000 population (2006).
Newspapers: Enterprise Journal (Community news; Circulation 3,900); Monroe County Clarion-Journal (Local news; Circulation 13,986)
Transportation: Commute to work: 94.4% car, 0.3% public transportation, 1.0% walk, 3.4% work from home (2000); Travel time to work: 25.2% less than 15 minutes, 31.9% 15 to 30 minutes, 29.7% 30 to 45 minutes, 11.0% 45 to 60 minutes, 2.1% 60 minutes or more (2000)

Additional Information Contacts

City of Columbia. . . . . (618) 281-7144
http://www.columbiaillinois.com

FULTS (village). Covers a land area of 0.068 square miles and a water area of 0 square miles. Located at 38.16° N. Lat.; 90.21° W. Long. Elevation is 394 feet.
History: Heavily damaged in floods of 1993.
Population: 43 (1990); 28 (2000); 28 (2007); 28 (2012 projected); Race: 100.0% White, 0.0% Black, 0.0% Asian, 0.0% Hispanic of any race (2007); Density: 411.2 persons per square mile (2007); Average household size: 3.11 (2007); Median age: 30.0 (2007); Males per 100 females: 47.4 (2007); Marriage status: 27.3% never married, 72.7% now married, 0.0% widowed, 0.0% divorced (2000); Foreign born: 0.0% (2000); Ancestry (includes multiple ancestries): 100.0% German, 5.3% Italian (2000).
Economy: Employment by occupation: 25.0% management, 12.5% professional, 12.5% services, 0.0% sales, 0.0% farming, 37.5% construction, 12.5% production (2000).
Income: Per capita income: $17,946 (2007); Median household income: $56,250 (2007); Average household income: $55,833 (2007); Percent of households with income of $100,000 or more: 0.0% (2007); Poverty rate: 0.0% (2000).
Education: Percent of population age 25 and over with: High school diploma (including GED) or higher: 100.0% (2007); Bachelor's degree or higher: 0.0% (2007); Master's degree or higher: 0.0% (2007).
Housing: Homeownership rate: 100.0% (2007); Median home value: $75,000 (2007); Median rent: $n/a per month (2000); Median age of housing: 60+ years (2000).
Transportation: Commute to work: 87.5% car, 0.0% public transportation, 12.5% walk, 0.0% work from home (2000); Travel time to work: 25.0% less than 15 minutes, 37.5% 15 to 30 minutes, 0.0% 30 to 45 minutes, 0.0% 45 to 60 minutes, 37.5% 60 minutes or more (2000)

HECKER (village). Covers a land area of 0.238 square miles and a water area of 0 square miles. Located at 38.30° N. Lat.; 89.99° W. Long. Elevation is 472 feet.
Population: 534 (1990); 475 (2000); 482 (2007); 483 (2012 projected); Race: 99.2% White, 0.4% Black, 0.0% Asian, 1.0% Hispanic of any race (2007); Density: 2,023.2 persons per square mile (2007); Average household size: 2.48 (2007); Median age: 35.8 (2007); Males per 100 females: 109.6 (2007); Marriage status: 21.9% never married, 62.8% now married, 6.8% widowed, 8.5% divorced (2000); Foreign born: 0.6% (2000); Ancestry (includes multiple ancestries): 46.9% German, 10.8% French (except Basque), 9.1% Irish, 8.9% English, 8.9% United States or American (2000).
Economy: Single-family building permits issued: 0 (2007); Multi-family building permits issued: 0 (2007); Employment by occupation: 10.5% management, 10.1% professional, 15.6% services, 31.1% sales, 1.2% farming, 13.6% construction, 17.9% production (2000).
Income: Per capita income: $26,323 (2007); Median household income: $56,923 (2007); Average household income: $65,399 (2007); Percent of households with income of $100,000 or more: 18.0% (2007); Poverty rate: 4.7% (2000).
Education: Percent of population age 25 and over with: High school diploma (including GED) or higher: 82.6% (2007); Bachelor's degree or higher: 6.1% (2007); Master's degree or higher: 1.2% (2007).
Housing: Homeownership rate: 80.4% (2007); Median home value: $136,719 (2007); Median rent: $352 per month (2000); Median age of housing: 30 years (2000).
Transportation: Commute to work: 92.5% car, 0.4% public transportation, 0.4% walk, 5.6% work from home (2000); Travel time to work: 14.3% less than 15 minutes, 37.4% 15 to 30 minutes, 21.4% 30 to 45 minutes, 16.4% 45 to 60 minutes, 10.5% 60 minutes or more (2000)

MAEYSTOWN (village). Covers a land area of 0.304 square miles and a water area of 0 square miles. Located at 38.22° N. Lat.; 90.23° W. Long. Elevation is 469 feet.
Population: 143 (1990); 148 (2000); 156 (2007); 161 (2012 projected); Race: 97.4% White, 0.0% Black, 1.3% Asian, 1.3% Hispanic of any race (2007); Density: 513.6 persons per square mile (2007); Average household size: 2.69 (2007); Median age: 36.7 (2007); Males per 100 females: 119.7 (2007); Marriage status: 21.4% never married, 73.8% now married, 4.9% widowed, 0.0% divorced (2000); Foreign born: 1.4% (2000); Ancestry (includes multiple ancestries): 49.0% German, 8.3% Irish, 7.6% United States or American, 7.6% English, 6.9% Other groups (2000).
Economy: Employment by occupation: 5.8% management, 13.0% professional, 13.0% services, 23.2% sales, 0.0% farming, 30.4% construction, 14.5% production (2000).
Income: Per capita income: $17,901 (2007); Median household income: $46,667 (2007); Average household income: $48,147 (2007); Percent of households with income of $100,000 or more: 1.7% (2007); Poverty rate: 4.1% (2000).
Education: Percent of population age 25 and over with: High school diploma (including GED) or higher: 89.7% (2007); Bachelor's degree or higher: 14.0% (2007); Master's degree or higher: 2.8% (2007).
Housing: Homeownership rate: 89.7% (2007); Median home value: $90,000 (2007); Median rent: $425 per month (2000); Median age of housing: 60+ years (2000).
Transportation: Commute to work: 86.4% car, 0.0% public transportation, 3.0% walk, 9.1% work from home (2000); Travel time to work: 15.0% less than 15 minutes, 53.3% 15 to 30 minutes, 10.0% 30 to 45 minutes, 10.0% 45 to 60 minutes, 11.7% 60 minutes or more (2000)

VALMEYER (village). Aka Maeys. Covers a land area of 3.328 square miles and a water area of 0.026 square miles. Located at 38.30° N. Lat.; 90.30° W. Long. Elevation is 735 feet.
History: Town established by Swiss farmers at the end of the 19th century on rich Mississippi bottom land. Town flooded twice in September and October of 1993, with 90% of the homes beyond repair. A new town was constructed two miles east of the old Valmeyer on 500 acres of former dairy lands.
Population: 1,117 (1990); 608 (2000); 904 (2007); 1,113 (2012 projected); Race: 98.3% White, 0.7% Black, 0.4% Asian, 1.0% Hispanic of any race (2007); Density: 271.6 persons per square mile (2007); Average household size: 2.73 (2007); Median age: 33.9 (2007); Males per 100 females: 91.9 (2007); Marriage status: 20.8% never married, 65.2% now married, 8.3% widowed, 5.7% divorced (2000); Foreign born: 0.8% (2000); Ancestry (includes multiple ancestries): 46.4% German, 11.9% United States or American, 11.2% English, 9.9% Irish, 6.2% Other groups (2000).
Economy: Single-family building permits issued: 10 (2007); Multi-family building permits issued: 0 (2007); Employment by occupation: 8.7% management, 16.3% professional, 21.3% services, 23.6% sales, 0.0% farming, 8.2% construction, 21.9% production (2000).
Income: Per capita income: $24,624 (2007); Median household income: $63,029 (2007); Average household income: $67,251 (2007); Percent of households with income of $100,000 or more: 21.1% (2007); Poverty rate: 3.0% (2000).
Education: Percent of population age 25 and over with: High school diploma (including GED) or higher: 79.6% (2007); Bachelor's degree or higher: 12.6% (2007); Master's degree or higher: 2.4% (2007).

School District(s)

Valmeyer CUSD 3 (PK-12)
2005-06 Enrollment: 504 . . . . (618) 935-2100

Housing: Homeownership rate: 84.3% (2007); Median home value: $173,311 (2007); Median rent: $164 per month (2000); Median age of housing: 3 years (2000).
Safety: Violent crime rate: 25.7 per 10,000 population; Property crime rate: 179.9 per 10,000 population (2006).
Transportation: Commute to work: 99.1% car, 0.0% public transportation, 0.0% walk, 0.9% work from home (2000); Travel time to work: 20.8% less than 15 minutes, 25.8% 15 to 30 minutes, 29.4% 30 to 45 minutes, 18.4% 45 to 60 minutes, 5.6% 60 minutes or more (2000)

WATERLOO (city). County seat. Covers a land area of 5.567 square miles and a water area of 0.051 square miles. Located at 38.33° N. Lat.; 90.15° W. Long. Elevation is 709 feet.

History: Waterloo was established on the trail from Fort Chartresto Cahokia, and developed as the seat of Monroe County. For a time it had a reputation as a place for quick marriages.
Population: 5,885 (1990); 7,614 (2000); 8,754 (2007); 9,473 (2012 projected); Race: 98.6% White, 0.0% Black, 0.3% Asian, 1.4% Hispanic of any race (2007); Density: 1,572.6 persons per square mile (2007); Average household size: 2.59 (2007); Median age: 37.0 (2007); Males per 100 females: 92.1 (2007); Marriage status: 20.2% never married, 63.0% now married, 8.3% widowed, 8.6% divorced (2000); Foreign born: 0.9% (2000); Ancestry (includes multiple ancestries): 56.9% German, 15.2% Irish, 7.4% French (except Basque), 7.3% English, 5.2% Other groups (2000).
Economy: Single-family building permits issued: 62 (2007); Multi-family building permits issued: 8 (2007); Employment by occupation: 13.3% management, 16.9% professional, 16.8% services, 32.6% sales, 0.0% farming, 10.1% construction, 10.3% production (2000).
Income: Per capita income: $25,045 (2007); Median household income: $55,434 (2007); Average household income: $63,530 (2007); Percent of households with income of $100,000 or more: 17.1% (2007); Poverty rate: 3.8% (2000).
Education: Percent of population age 25 and over with: High school diploma (including GED) or higher: 85.0% (2007); Bachelor's degree or higher: 19.4% (2007); Master's degree or higher: 6.3% (2007).

School District(s)

Waterloo CUSD 5 (PK-12)
2005-06 Enrollment: 2,694 . . . . (618) 939-3453

Housing: Homeownership rate: 70.9% (2007); Median home value: $171,731 (2007); Median rent: $424 per month (2000); Median age of housing: 29 years (2000).
Safety: Violent crime rate: 10.8 per 10,000 population; Property crime rate: 85.6 per 10,000 population (2006).
Newspapers: Cahokia-Dupo Herald (Local news; Circulation 14,000); Herald (Local news; Circulation 14,000); Waterloo Republic-Times (Local news; Circulation 4,000); Waterloo Republic-Times Shopper (Community news; Circulation 13,000)
Transportation: Commute to work: 94.9% car, 2.0% public transportation, 0.7% walk, 1.9% work from home (2000); Travel time to work: 33.9% less than 15 minutes, 15.0% 15 to 30 minutes, 28.2% 30 to 45 minutes, 16.0% 45 to 60 minutes, 7.0% 60 minutes or more (2000)

Additional Information Contacts

City of Waterloo . . . . (618) 939-8600
http://www.waterloo.il.us
Waterloo Chamber of Commerce . . . . (618) 939-5300
http://www.enjoywaterloo.com

Montgomery County

Located in south central Illinois; drained by Shoal and Macoupin Creeks. Covers a land area of 703.80 square miles, a water area of 5.96 square miles, and is located in the Central Time Zone. The county was founded in 1821. County seat is Hillsboro.

Weather Station: Hillsboro Elevation: 629 feet

	Jan	Feb	Mar	Apr	May	Jun	Jul	Aug	Sep	Oct	Nov	Dec
High	36	43	55	67	77	86	90	87	81	69	54	42
Low	19	24	33	44	53	62	66	64	56	45	35	25
Precip	2.1	2.0	3.5	4.4	4.3	4.0	3.5	3.4	3.2	2.9	3.7	3.0
Snow	5.8	4.2	3.2	0.5	tr	0.0	0.0	0.0	0.0	tr	1.0	3.9

High and Low temperatures in degrees Fahrenheit; Precipitation and Snow in inches

Population: 30,728 (1990); 30,652 (2000); 30,351 (2007); 30,076 (2012 projected); Race: 94.7% White, 3.9% Black, 0.3% Asian, 1.2% Hispanic of any race (2007); Density: 43.1 persons per square mile (2007); Average household size: 2.63 (2007); Median age: 39.6 (2007); Males per 100 females: 106.5 (2007).
Religion: Five largest groups: 12.6% Southern Baptist Convention, 10.9% Catholic Church, 6.8% Lutheran Church—Missouri Synod, 5.0% The United Methodist Church, 4.4% Evangelical Lutheran Church in America (2000).
Economy: Unemployment rate: 6.9% (4/2008); Total civilian labor force: 13,642 (4/2008); Leading industries: 20.5% health care and social assistance; 19.3% retail trade; 15.4% manufacturing (2005); Farms: 1,001 totaling 362,300 acres (2002); Companies that employ 500 or more persons: 0 (2006); Companies that employ 100 to 499 persons: 8 (2006); Companies that employ less than 100 persons: 739 (2006); Black-owned businesses: n/a (2002); Hispanic-owned businesses: n/a (2002); Asian-owned businesses: n/a (2002); Women-owned businesses: 674 (2002); Retail sales per capita: $14,014 (2008). Single-family building permits issued: 35 (2007); Multi-family building permits issued: 0 (2007).
Income: Per capita income: $19,099 (2007); Median household income: $38,167 (2007); Average household income: $47,471 (2007); Percent of households with income of $100,000 or more: 7.5% (2007); Poverty rate: 15.4% (2005); Bankruptcy rate: 3.46% (2007).
Education: Percent of population age 25 and over with: High school diploma (including GED) or higher: 77.1% (2007); Bachelor's degree or higher: 11.1% (2007); Master's degree or higher: 3.5% (2007).
Housing: Homeownership rate: 78.5% (2007); Median home value: $77,843 (2007); Median rent: $275 per month (2000); Median age of housing: 48 years (2000).
Health: Birth rate: 114.4 per 10,000 population (2007); Death rate: 119.4 per 10,000 population (2007); Age-adjusted cancer mortality rate: 199.6 deaths per 100,000 population (2005); Number of physicians: 6.7 per 10,000 population (2005); Hospital beds: 54.1 per 10,000 population (2004); Hospital admissions: 1,245.4 per 10,000 population (2004).
Elections: 2004 Presidential election results: 53.0% Bush, 46.2% Kerry, 0.0% Nader, 0.7% Badnarik
National and State Parks: Coffeen Lake State Fish and Wildlife Area

Additional Information Contacts

Montgomery County Government . . . . (217) 532-9530
http://www.montgomeryco.com
Hillsboro Chamber of Commerce. . . . . (217) 532-3711
http://www.hillsborochamber.net
Litchfield Chamber of Commerce . . . . (217) 324-2533
http://www.litchfieldil.com/chamber
Nokomis Chamber of Commerce. . . . . (217) 563-8311
http://www.nokomisonline.com/coc

Montgomery County Communities

BUTLER (village). Covers a land area of 0.570 square miles and a water area of 0 square miles. Located at 39.19° N. Lat.; 89.53° W. Long. Elevation is 630 feet.
Population: 165 (1990); 197 (2000); 196 (2007); 189 (2012 projected); Race: 100.0% White, 0.0% Black, 0.0% Asian, 0.0% Hispanic of any race (2007); Density: 344.0 persons per square mile (2007); Average household size: 2.51 (2007); Median age: 37.5 (2007); Males per 100 females: 84.9 (2007); Marriage status: 15.7% never married, 65.1% now married, 10.5% widowed, 8.7% divorced (2000); Foreign born: 0.9% (2000); Ancestry (includes multiple ancestries): 29.6% German, 19.0% United States or American, 12.5% English, 9.7% Irish, 3.7% Italian (2000).
Economy: Employment by occupation: 4.8% management, 0.0% professional, 22.6% services, 27.4% sales, 0.0% farming, 19.0% construction, 26.2% production (2000).
Income: Per capita income: $13,699 (2007); Median household income: $37,188 (2007); Average household income: $34,423 (2007); Percent of households with income of $100,000 or more: 0.0% (2007); Poverty rate: 17.5% (2000).
Education: Percent of population age 25 and over with: High school diploma (including GED) or higher: 76.2% (2007); Bachelor's degree or higher: 0.0% (2007); Master's degree or higher: 0.0% (2007).
Housing: Homeownership rate: 92.3% (2007); Median home value: $48,889 (2007); Median rent: $n/a per month (2000); Median age of housing: 60+ years (2000).
Transportation: Commute to work: 86.9% car, 0.0% public transportation, 8.3% walk, 4.8% work from home (2000); Travel time to work: 12.5% less than 15 minutes, 56.3% 15 to 30 minutes, 8.8% 30 to 45 minutes, 5.0% 45 to 60 minutes, 17.5% 60 minutes or more (2000)

COALTON (village). Covers a land area of 0.519 square miles and a water area of 0 square miles. Located at 39.28° N. Lat.; 89.30° W. Long. Elevation is 676 feet.
Population: 359 (1990); 307 (2000); 278 (2007); 279 (2012 projected); Race: 96.4% White, 0.0% Black, 0.7% Asian, 1.4% Hispanic of any race (2007); Density: 536.1 persons per square mile (2007); Average household size: 2.44 (2007); Median age: 39.1 (2007); Males per 100 females: 87.8 (2007); Marriage status: 18.6% never married, 66.2% now married, 7.6% widowed, 7.6% divorced (2000); Foreign born: 2.7% (2000); Ancestry (includes multiple ancestries): 19.5% German, 9.4% Other groups, 8.1% Irish, 7.0% United States or American, 5.4% English (2000).
Economy: Employment by occupation: 9.9% management, 17.4% professional, 12.4% services, 21.5% sales, 0.0% farming, 18.2% construction, 20.7% production (2000).

Income: Per capita income: $22,509 (2007); Median household income: $42,500 (2007); Average household income: $54,890 (2007); Percent of households with income of $100,000 or more: 10.5% (2007); Poverty rate: 22.6% (2000).
Education: Percent of population age 25 and over with: High school diploma (including GED) or higher: 80.0% (2007); Bachelor's degree or higher: 10.0% (2007); Master's degree or higher: 1.7% (2007).
Housing: Homeownership rate: 93.0% (2007); Median home value: $51,111 (2007); Median rent: $413 per month (2000); Median age of housing: 60+ years (2000).
Transportation: Commute to work: 87.6% car, 0.0% public transportation, 0.0% walk, 9.9% work from home (2000); Travel time to work: 43.1% less than 15 minutes, 18.3% 15 to 30 minutes, 20.2% 30 to 45 minutes, 7.3% 45 to 60 minutes, 11.0% 60 minutes or more (2000)

COFFEEN (city). Covers a land area of 1.032 square miles and a water area of 0 square miles. Located at 39.09° N. Lat.; 89.39° W. Long. Elevation is 630 feet.
Population: 741 (1990); 709 (2000); 712 (2007); 686 (2012 projected); Race: 98.9% White, 0.0% Black, 0.6% Asian, 0.0% Hispanic of any race (2007); Density: 690.1 persons per square mile (2007); Average household size: 2.38 (2007); Median age: 40.8 (2007); Males per 100 females: 97.2 (2007); Marriage status: 18.5% never married, 60.6% now married, 10.7% widowed, 10.2% divorced (2000); Foreign born: 0.8% (2000); Ancestry (includes multiple ancestries): 25.4% United States or American, 18.4% German, 9.4% Irish, 7.3% English, 5.0% Other groups (2000).
Economy: Employment by occupation: 7.6% management, 10.9% professional, 33.7% services, 22.5% sales, 0.0% farming, 12.3% construction, 13.0% production (2000).
Income: Per capita income: $17,219 (2007); Median household income: $37,500 (2007); Average household income: $41,003 (2007); Percent of households with income of $100,000 or more: 2.7% (2007); Poverty rate: 20.6% (2000).
Education: Percent of population age 25 and over with: High school diploma (including GED) or higher: 78.0% (2007); Bachelor's degree or higher: 5.5% (2007); Master's degree or higher: 0.8% (2007).

School District(s)

Hillsboro CUSD 3 (PK-12)
2005-06 Enrollment: 2,025 . . . . (217) 532-2942
Housing: Homeownership rate: 77.3% (2007); Median home value: $43,036 (2007); Median rent: $217 per month (2000); Median age of housing: 37 years (2000).
Transportation: Commute to work: 94.4% car, 0.0% public transportation, 2.2% walk, 3.4% work from home (2000); Travel time to work: 31.4% less than 15 minutes, 44.6% 15 to 30 minutes, 9.7% 30 to 45 minutes, 4.7% 45 to 60 minutes, 9.7% 60 minutes or more (2000)

DONNELLSON (village). Covers a land area of 0.238 square miles and a water area of 0 square miles. Located at 39.03° N. Lat.; 89.47° W. Long. Elevation is 614 feet.
Population: 167 (1990); 243 (2000); 239 (2007); 250 (2012 projected); Race: 98.3% White, 0.4% Black, 0.0% Asian, 0.0% Hispanic of any race (2007); Density: 1,004.4 persons per square mile (2007); Average household size: 2.60 (2007); Median age: 34.1 (2007); Males per 100 females: 123.4 (2007); Marriage status: 23.7% never married, 58.8% now married, 8.5% widowed, 9.0% divorced (2000); Foreign born: 0.0% (2000); Ancestry (includes multiple ancestries): 32.1% German, 22.8% Irish, 17.0% English, 12.9% Other groups, 10.7% United States or American (2000).
Economy: Employment by occupation: 7.1% management, 9.4% professional, 22.4% services, 22.4% sales, 0.0% farming, 16.5% construction, 22.4% production (2000).
Income: Per capita income: $16,297 (2007); Median household income: $34,063 (2007); Average household income: $42,337 (2007); Percent of households with income of $100,000 or more: 6.5% (2007); Poverty rate: 13.4% (2000).
Education: Percent of population age 25 and over with: High school diploma (including GED) or higher: 65.1% (2007); Bachelor's degree or higher: 5.3% (2007); Master's degree or higher: 3.3% (2007).
Housing: Homeownership rate: 85.9% (2007); Median home value: $53,889 (2007); Median rent: $192 per month (2000); Median age of housing: 45 years (2000).
Transportation: Commute to work: 91.0% car, 0.0% public transportation, 2.6% walk, 3.8% work from home (2000); Travel time to work: 14.7% less than 15 minutes, 44.0% 15 to 30 minutes, 25.3% 30 to 45 minutes, 5.3% 45 to 60 minutes, 10.7% 60 minutes or more (2000)

FARMERSVILLE (village). Covers a land area of 0.988 square miles and a water area of 0.008 square miles. Located at 39.44° N. Lat.; 89.65° W. Long. Elevation is 643 feet.
Population: 698 (1990); 768 (2000); 802 (2007); 810 (2012 projected); Race: 98.0% White, 0.0% Black, 1.5% Asian, 0.2% Hispanic of any race (2007); Density: 812.1 persons per square mile (2007); Average household size: 2.42 (2007); Median age: 36.2 (2007); Males per 100 females: 86.1 (2007); Marriage status: 23.3% never married, 59.3% now married, 6.8% widowed, 10.6% divorced (2000); Foreign born: 0.0% (2000); Ancestry (includes multiple ancestries): 28.0% German, 18.0% Irish, 8.8% Other groups, 8.1% United States or American, 6.1% English (2000).
Economy: Employment by occupation: 6.4% management, 15.7% professional, 25.3% services, 24.0% sales, 0.0% farming, 14.2% construction, 14.4% production (2000).
Income: Per capita income: $20,854 (2007); Median household income: $43,056 (2007); Average household income: $50,377 (2007); Percent of households with income of $100,000 or more: 8.4% (2007); Poverty rate: 8.2% (2000).
Education: Percent of population age 25 and over with: High school diploma (including GED) or higher: 82.5% (2007); Bachelor's degree or higher: 11.6% (2007); Master's degree or higher: 2.1% (2007).

School District(s)

Panhandle CUSD 2 (PK-12)
2005-06 Enrollment: 553 . . . . (217) 229-4215
Housing: Homeownership rate: 78.3% (2007); Median home value: $89,677 (2007); Median rent: $293 per month (2000); Median age of housing: 29 years (2000).
Transportation: Commute to work: 88.8% car, 0.0% public transportation, 1.8% walk, 4.7% work from home (2000); Travel time to work: 26.0% less than 15 minutes, 27.0% 15 to 30 minutes, 33.1% 30 to 45 minutes, 8.5% 45 to 60 minutes, 5.5% 60 minutes or more (2000)

FILLMORE (village). Covers a land area of 0.774 square miles and a water area of 0 square miles. Located at 39.11° N. Lat.; 89.27° W. Long. Elevation is 633 feet.
Population: 326 (1990); 362 (2000); 386 (2007); 386 (2012 projected); Race: 98.7% White, 0.0% Black, 0.0% Asian, 1.3% Hispanic of any race (2007); Density: 498.5 persons per square mile (2007); Average household size: 2.46 (2007); Median age: 37.8 (2007); Males per 100 females: 97.9 (2007); Marriage status: 19.3% never married, 62.2% now married, 11.3% widowed, 7.3% divorced (2000); Foreign born: 0.0% (2000); Ancestry (includes multiple ancestries): 23.8% German, 12.7% Irish, 10.5% United States or American, 8.9% Other groups, 4.7% English (2000).
Economy: Employment by occupation: 5.8% management, 3.2% professional, 33.1% services, 25.3% sales, 1.3% farming, 13.0% construction, 18.2% production (2000).
Income: Per capita income: $17,448 (2007); Median household income: $35,500 (2007); Average household income: $42,898 (2007); Percent of households with income of $100,000 or more: 4.5% (2007); Poverty rate: 21.6% (2000).
Education: Percent of population age 25 and over with: High school diploma (including GED) or higher: 76.0% (2007); Bachelor's degree or higher: 3.5% (2007); Master's degree or higher: 0.0% (2007).
Housing: Homeownership rate: 83.4% (2007); Median home value: $52,045 (2007); Median rent: $242 per month (2000); Median age of housing: 48 years (2000).
Transportation: Commute to work: 89.4% car, 0.0% public transportation, 5.3% walk, 4.0% work from home (2000); Travel time to work: 22.1% less than 15 minutes, 51.7% 15 to 30 minutes, 8.3% 30 to 45 minutes, 0.0% 45 to 60 minutes, 17.9% 60 minutes or more (2000)

HARVEL (village). Covers a land area of 0.727 square miles and a water area of 0 square miles. Located at 39.35° N. Lat.; 89.53° W. Long. Elevation is 636 feet.
Population: 213 (1990); 235 (2000); 215 (2007); 214 (2012 projected); Race: 95.3% White, 0.9% Black, 2.8% Asian, 0.0% Hispanic of any race (2007); Density: 295.7 persons per square mile (2007); Average household size: 2.34 (2007); Median age: 41.9 (2007); Males per 100 females: 93.7 (2007); Marriage status: 20.4% never married, 57.1% now married, 9.9% widowed, 12.6% divorced (2000); Foreign born: 1.7% (2000); Ancestry (includes multiple ancestries): 27.2% German, 23.0% United States or American, 6.8% Irish, 6.8% Other groups, 5.1% French (except Basque) (2000).

Economy: Employment by occupation: 14.3% management, 14.3% professional, 21.4% services, 21.4% sales, 1.8% farming, 12.5% construction, 14.3% production (2000).
Income: Per capita income: $16,616 (2007); Median household income: $33,667 (2007); Average household income: $38,832 (2007); Percent of households with income of $100,000 or more: 3.3% (2007); Poverty rate: 14.9% (2000).
Education: Percent of population age 25 and over with: High school diploma (including GED) or higher: 80.4% (2007); Bachelor's degree or higher: 5.7% (2007); Master's degree or higher: 1.3% (2007).
Housing: Homeownership rate: 85.9% (2007); Median home value: $52,500 (2007); Median rent: $269 per month (2000); Median age of housing: 55 years (2000).
Transportation: Commute to work: 86.1% car, 0.0% public transportation, 0.9% walk, 10.2% work from home (2000); Travel time to work: 18.6% less than 15 minutes, 13.4% 15 to 30 minutes, 47.4% 30 to 45 minutes, 14.4% 45 to 60 minutes, 6.2% 60 minutes or more (2000)

HILLSBORO (city). County seat. Covers a land area of 3.588 square miles and a water area of 1.742 square miles. Located at 39.16° N. Lat.; 89.48° W. Long. Elevation is 633 feet.
History: Incorporated 1855.
Population: 4,445 (1990); 4,359 (2000); 4,186 (2007); 4,072 (2012 projected); Race: 97.8% White, 0.7% Black, 0.5% Asian, 0.8% Hispanic of any race (2007); Density: 1,166.7 persons per square mile (2007); Average household size: 2.39 (2007); Median age: 38.6 (2007); Males per 100 females: 86.0 (2007); Marriage status: 20.9% never married, 57.3% now married, 10.0% widowed, 11.8% divorced (2000); Foreign born: 1.0% (2000); Ancestry (includes multiple ancestries): 26.8% German, 11.6% English, 10.6% Irish, 7.7% Other groups, 6.3% United States or American (2000).
Economy: Employment by occupation: 13.2% management, 16.5% professional, 22.1% services, 26.1% sales, 0.5% farming, 10.2% construction, 11.4% production (2000).
Income: Per capita income: $19,495 (2007); Median household income: $36,136 (2007); Average household income: $46,124 (2007); Percent of households with income of $100,000 or more: 6.4% (2007); Poverty rate: 17.2% (2000).
Education: Percent of population age 25 and over with: High school diploma (including GED) or higher: 83.0% (2007); Bachelor's degree or higher: 14.9% (2007); Master's degree or higher: 5.2% (2007).

School District(s)

Dept of Corrections Sch Dist 428 (08-12)
2005-06 Enrollment: 2,271 . . . . (217) 522-2666
Hillsboro CUSD 3 (PK-12)
2005-06 Enrollment: 2,025 . . . . (217) 532-2942

Housing: Homeownership rate: 68.7% (2007); Median home value: $86,716 (2007); Median rent: $293 per month (2000); Median age of housing: 49 years (2000).
Hospitals: Hillsboro Area Hospital (100 beds)
Safety: Violent crime rate: 32.8 per 10,000 population; Property crime rate: 180.2 per 10,000 population (2006).
Newspapers: Hillsboro Journal (Local news; Circulation 6,566); M & M Journal (Local news; Circulation 21,945); Montgomery County News (Community news; Circulation 4,000); Raymond News (Local news; Circulation 655); Sorento News (Community news; Circulation 500)
Transportation: Commute to work: 95.9% car, 0.0% public transportation, 2.1% walk, 2.0% work from home (2000); Travel time to work: 50.6% less than 15 minutes, 25.0% 15 to 30 minutes, 7.6% 30 to 45 minutes, 5.1% 45 to 60 minutes, 11.7% 60 minutes or more (2000)

Additional Information Contacts

Hillsboro Chamber of Commerce. . . . . (217) 532-3711
http://www.hillsborochamber.net

IRVING (village). Covers a land area of 0.818 square miles and a water area of 0 square miles. Located at 39.20° N. Lat.; 89.40° W. Long. Elevation is 656 feet.
Population: 516 (1990); 2,484 (2000); 2,513 (2007); 2,552 (2012 projected); Race: 49.4% White, 45.1% Black, 0.0% Asian, 7.5% Hispanic of any race (2007); Density: 3,073.6 persons per square mile (2007); Average household size: 12.69 (2007); Median age: 32.1 (2007); Males per 100 females: 897.2 (2007); Marriage status: 29.1% never married, 43.3% now married, 2.6% widowed, 25.1% divorced (2000); Foreign born: 2.6% (2000); Ancestry (includes multiple ancestries): 4.3% United States or American, 3.2% German, 1.9% English, 1.6% Other groups, 1.0% Irish (2000).
Economy: Employment by occupation: 9.4% management, 6.7% professional, 21.1% services, 23.9% sales, 2.8% farming, 12.8% construction, 23.3% production (2000).
Income: Per capita income: $12,757 (2007); Median household income: $30,000 (2007); Average household income: $37,513 (2007); Percent of households with income of $100,000 or more: 1.5% (2007); Poverty rate: 29.2% (2000).
Education: Percent of population age 25 and over with: High school diploma (including GED) or higher: 45.7% (2007); Bachelor's degree or higher: 0.3% (2007); Master's degree or higher: 0.0% (2007).
Housing: Homeownership rate: 77.8% (2007); Median home value: $44,762 (2007); Median rent: $257 per month (2000); Median age of housing: 57 years (2000).
Safety: Violent crime rate: 203.3 per 10,000 population; Property crime rate: 264.2 per 10,000 population (2006).
Transportation: Commute to work: 88.8% car, 0.0% public transportation, 7.3% walk, 2.2% work from home (2000); Travel time to work: 27.6% less than 15 minutes, 38.5% 15 to 30 minutes, 14.9% 30 to 45 minutes, 10.9% 45 to 60 minutes, 8.0% 60 minutes or more (2000)

LITCHFIELD (city). Covers a land area of 5.091 square miles and a water area of 0.003 square miles. Located at 39.17° N. Lat.; 89.65° W. Long. Elevation is 689 feet.
History: Litchfield was incorporated in 1859 and developed around a coal field. An early employer was the International Stove Company.
Population: 7,105 (1990); 6,815 (2000); 6,630 (2007); 6,464 (2012 projected); Race: 98.6% White, 0.2% Black, 0.3% Asian, 0.9% Hispanic of any race (2007); Density: 1,302.2 persons per square mile (2007); Average household size: 2.45 (2007); Median age: 40.1 (2007); Males per 100 females: 86.7 (2007); Marriage status: 20.1% never married, 54.2% now married, 11.4% widowed, 14.2% divorced (2000); Foreign born: 1.0% (2000); Ancestry (includes multiple ancestries): 26.5% German, 13.0% United States or American, 12.4% English, 10.4% Irish, 8.8% Other groups (2000).
Economy: Employment by occupation: 8.5% management, 13.1% professional, 20.7% services, 28.2% sales, 0.4% farming, 9.4% construction, 19.8% production (2000).
Income: Per capita income: $17,069 (2007); Median household income: $31,525 (2007); Average household income: $40,283 (2007); Percent of households with income of $100,000 or more: 4.4% (2007); Poverty rate: 16.6% (2000).
Education: Percent of population age 25 and over with: High school diploma (including GED) or higher: 73.5% (2007); Bachelor's degree or higher: 10.6% (2007); Master's degree or higher: 3.2% (2007).

School District(s)

Litchfield CUSD 12 (PK-12)
2005-06 Enrollment: 1,623 . . . . (217) 324-2157

Vocational/Technical School(s)

Tri-County Beauty Academy (Private, For-profit)
Fall 2007 Enrollment: 30 . . . . (217) 324-9062
2007-08 Tuition: $8,775

Housing: Homeownership rate: 72.7% (2007); Median home value: $70,357 (2007); Median rent: $267 per month (2000); Median age of housing: 50 years (2000).
Hospitals: St. Francis Hospital (138 beds)
Safety: Violent crime rate: 56.1 per 10,000 population; Property crime rate: 413.5 per 10,000 population (2006).
Newspapers: News-Herald (Local news; Circulation 5,800)
Transportation: Commute to work: 93.3% car, 0.6% public transportation, 2.7% walk, 1.7% work from home (2000); Travel time to work: 65.3% less than 15 minutes, 12.6% 15 to 30 minutes, 6.2% 30 to 45 minutes, 6.8% 45 to 60 minutes, 9.1% 60 minutes or more (2000)

Additional Information Contacts

Litchfield Chamber of Commerce . . . . (217) 324-2533
http://www.litchfieldil.com/chamber

NOKOMIS (city). Covers a land area of 1.300 square miles and a water area of 0 square miles. Located at 39.30° N. Lat.; 89.28° W. Long. Elevation is 673 feet.
History: Incorporated 1867.
Population: 2,574 (1990); 2,389 (2000); 2,361 (2007); 2,317 (2012 projected); Race: 99.5% White, 0.0% Black, 0.1% Asian, 0.1% Hispanic of any race (2007); Density: 1,815.8 persons per square mile (2007); Average

household size: 2.28 (2007); Median age: 43.8 (2007); Males per 100 females: 88.4 (2007); Marriage status: 21.9% never married, 58.2% now married, 8.9% widowed, 10.9% divorced (2000); Foreign born: 1.0% (2000); Ancestry (includes multiple ancestries): 27.6% German, 11.1% United States or American, 10.4% Irish, 10.0% English, 5.9% Italian (2000).
Economy: Employment by occupation: 9.6% management, 15.2% professional, 19.2% services, 21.2% sales, 1.9% farming, 11.7% construction, 21.1% production (2000).
Income: Per capita income: $19,556 (2007); Median household income: $34,505 (2007); Average household income: $42,812 (2007); Percent of households with income of $100,000 or more: 5.8% (2007); Poverty rate: 14.3% (2000).
Education: Percent of population age 25 and over with: High school diploma (including GED) or higher: 79.4% (2007); Bachelor's degree or higher: 10.5% (2007); Master's degree or higher: 4.6% (2007).

School District(s)

Nokomis CUSD 22 (PK-12)
2005-06 Enrollment: 747 . . . . (217) 563-7311
Housing: Homeownership rate: 80.6% (2007); Median home value: $64,615 (2007); Median rent: $262 per month (2000); Median age of housing: 59 years (2000).
Safety: Violent crime rate: 64.7 per 10,000 population; Property crime rate: 151.1 per 10,000 population (2006).
Newspapers: Free Press-Progress (Local news; Circulation 3,000)
Transportation: Commute to work: 87.3% car, 0.0% public transportation, 2.1% walk, 6.3% work from home (2000); Travel time to work: 34.8% less than 15 minutes, 19.4% 15 to 30 minutes, 17.8% 30 to 45 minutes, 5.9% 45 to 60 minutes, 22.1% 60 minutes or more (2000)
Additional Information Contacts
Nokomis Chamber of Commerce. . . . . (217) 563-8311
http://www.nokomisonline.com/coc

PANAMA (village). Covers a land area of 0.337 square miles and a water area of <.001 square miles. Located at 39.03° N. Lat.; 89.52° W. Long. Elevation is 591 feet.
Population: 297 (1990); 323 (2000); 289 (2007); 289 (2012 projected); Race: 98.6% White, 0.0% Black, 0.0% Asian, 0.0% Hispanic of any race (2007); Density: 857.4 persons per square mile (2007); Average household size: 2.05 (2007); Median age: 45.6 (2007); Males per 100 females: 86.5 (2007); Marriage status: 21.3% never married, 56.3% now married, 8.2% widowed, 14.2% divorced (2000); Foreign born: 0.6% (2000); Ancestry (includes multiple ancestries): 29.7% German, 20.3% Irish, 16.1% English, 8.2% Other groups, 6.7% Italian (2000).
Economy: Employment by occupation: 1.4% management, 8.0% professional, 20.3% services, 26.8% sales, 0.0% farming, 10.9% construction, 32.6% production (2000).
Income: Per capita income: $23,322 (2007); Median household income: $35,313 (2007); Average household income: $47,801 (2007); Percent of households with income of $100,000 or more: 7.1% (2007); Poverty rate: 14.0% (2000).
Education: Percent of population age 25 and over with: High school diploma (including GED) or higher: 72.8% (2007); Bachelor's degree or higher: 1.4% (2007); Master's degree or higher: 0.5% (2007).
Housing: Homeownership rate: 90.8% (2007); Median home value: $36,818 (2007); Median rent: $238 per month (2000); Median age of housing: 60+ years (2000).
Safety: Violent crime rate: 0.0 per 10,000 population; Property crime rate: 0.0 per 10,000 population (2006).
Transportation: Commute to work: 95.6% car, 0.0% public transportation, 0.0% walk, 4.4% work from home (2000); Travel time to work: 4.6% less than 15 minutes, 47.3% 15 to 30 minutes, 22.9% 30 to 45 minutes, 8.4% 45 to 60 minutes, 16.8% 60 minutes or more (2000)

RAYMOND (village). Covers a land area of 1.255 square miles and a water area of 0 square miles. Located at 39.32° N. Lat.; 89.57° W. Long. Elevation is 643 feet.
Population: 851 (1990); 927 (2000); 907 (2007); 894 (2012 projected); Race: 99.7% White, 0.1% Black, 0.0% Asian, 0.1% Hispanic of any race (2007); Density: 722.7 persons per square mile (2007); Average household size: 2.33 (2007); Median age: 41.4 (2007); Males per 100 females: 89.0 (2007); Marriage status: 17.2% never married, 65.3% now married, 8.2% widowed, 9.4% divorced (2000); Foreign born: 0.2% (2000); Ancestry (includes multiple ancestries): 41.5% German, 11.9% Irish, 10.7% English, 8.3% United States or American, 5.2% Other groups (2000).
Economy: Employment by occupation: 13.7% management, 15.6% professional, 12.7% services, 30.8% sales, 0.6% farming, 12.7% construction, 13.9% production (2000).
Income: Per capita income: $21,301 (2007); Median household income: $43,700 (2007); Average household income: $49,666 (2007); Percent of households with income of $100,000 or more: 8.5% (2007); Poverty rate: 8.4% (2000).
Education: Percent of population age 25 and over with: High school diploma (including GED) or higher: 81.5% (2007); Bachelor's degree or higher: 15.3% (2007); Master's degree or higher: 5.9% (2007).

School District(s)

Panhandle CUSD 2 (PK-12)
2005-06 Enrollment: 553 . . . . (217) 229-4215
Housing: Homeownership rate: 76.6% (2007); Median home value: $85,217 (2007); Median rent: $309 per month (2000); Median age of housing: 43 years (2000).
Safety: Violent crime rate: 10.8 per 10,000 population; Property crime rate: 75.9 per 10,000 population (2006).
Transportation: Commute to work: 94.0% car, 0.6% public transportation, 1.9% walk, 2.6% work from home (2000); Travel time to work: 34.7% less than 15 minutes, 24.5% 15 to 30 minutes, 17.9% 30 to 45 minutes, 15.9% 45 to 60 minutes, 7.0% 60 minutes or more (2000)

SCHRAM CITY (village). Covers a land area of 0.733 square miles and a water area of 0 square miles. Located at 39.16° N. Lat.; 89.46° W. Long. Elevation is 607 feet.
Population: 682 (1990); 653 (2000); 635 (2007); 607 (2012 projected); Race: 99.4% White, 0.3% Black, 0.2% Asian, 0.5% Hispanic of any race (2007); Density: 866.6 persons per square mile (2007); Average household size: 2.43 (2007); Median age: 41.4 (2007); Males per 100 females: 97.8 (2007); Marriage status: 24.0% never married, 51.3% now married, 12.5% widowed, 12.2% divorced (2000); Foreign born: 0.6% (2000); Ancestry (includes multiple ancestries): 21.1% United States or American, 20.8% German, 12.4% Irish, 9.2% Italian, 8.2% English (2000).
Economy: Employment by occupation: 8.4% management, 8.1% professional, 17.6% services, 24.0% sales, 0.7% farming, 11.1% construction, 30.1% production (2000).
Income: Per capita income: $20,388 (2007); Median household income: $39,167 (2007); Average household income: $48,898 (2007); Percent of households with income of $100,000 or more: 6.9% (2007); Poverty rate: 7.9% (2000).
Education: Percent of population age 25 and over with: High school diploma (including GED) or higher: 74.3% (2007); Bachelor's degree or higher: 4.7% (2007); Master's degree or higher: 1.6% (2007).
Housing: Homeownership rate: 83.9% (2007); Median home value: $66,379 (2007); Median rent: $298 per month (2000); Median age of housing: 57 years (2000).
Transportation: Commute to work: 95.5% car, 0.0% public transportation, 1.7% walk, 1.7% work from home (2000); Travel time to work: 35.1% less than 15 minutes, 36.1% 15 to 30 minutes, 6.0% 30 to 45 minutes, 3.5% 45 to 60 minutes, 19.3% 60 minutes or more (2000)

TAYLOR SPRINGS (village). Covers a land area of 0.861 square miles and a water area of 0.033 square miles. Located at 39.13° N. Lat.; 89.49° W. Long. Elevation is 627 feet.
Population: 672 (1990); 583 (2000); 538 (2007); 529 (2012 projected); Race: 99.4% White, 0.0% Black, 0.0% Asian, 0.6% Hispanic of any race (2007); Density: 624.9 persons per square mile (2007); Average household size: 2.28 (2007); Median age: 40.3 (2007); Males per 100 females: 106.9 (2007); Marriage status: 23.7% never married, 55.8% now married, 7.8% widowed, 12.8% divorced (2000); Foreign born: 1.2% (2000); Ancestry (includes multiple ancestries): 20.7% German, 15.5% Irish, 15.3% United States or American, 12.7% Other groups, 8.9% English (2000).
Economy: Employment by occupation: 6.7% management, 12.8% professional, 25.9% services, 17.7% sales, 0.0% farming, 16.0% construction, 20.9% production (2000).
Income: Per capita income: $17,816 (2007); Median household income: $34,750 (2007); Average household income: $40,614 (2007); Percent of households with income of $100,000 or more: 4.2% (2007); Poverty rate: 9.1% (2000).
Education: Percent of population age 25 and over with: High school diploma (including GED) or higher: 76.7% (2007); Bachelor's degree or higher: 5.4% (2007); Master's degree or higher: 0.8% (2007).

Housing: Homeownership rate: 80.1% (2007); Median home value: $55,833 (2007); Median rent: $280 per month (2000); Median age of housing: 45 years (2000).
Transportation: Commute to work: 96.4% car, 0.0% public transportation, 0.0% walk, 2.9% work from home (2000); Travel time to work: 53.1% less than 15 minutes, 26.6% 15 to 30 minutes, 7.0% 30 to 45 minutes, 1.8% 45 to 60 minutes, 11.4% 60 minutes or more (2000)

WAGGONER (village). Covers a land area of 0.264 square miles and a water area of 0 square miles. Located at 39.37° N. Lat.; 89.65° W. Long. Elevation is 640 feet.
Population: 221 (1990); 245 (2000); 239 (2007); 236 (2012 projected); Race: 99.2% White, 0.0% Black, 0.0% Asian, 0.0% Hispanic of any race (2007); Density: 907.0 persons per square mile (2007); Average household size: 2.60 (2007); Median age: 32.7 (2007); Males per 100 females: 102.5 (2007); Marriage status: 22.6% never married, 54.8% now married, 11.8% widowed, 10.9% divorced (2000); Foreign born: 0.0% (2000); Ancestry (includes multiple ancestries): 24.7% English, 18.7% German, 9.3% Irish, 7.0% United States or American, 4.3% French (except Basque) (2000).
Economy: Employment by occupation: 8.3% management, 5.3% professional, 30.3% services, 20.5% sales, 0.0% farming, 12.1% construction, 23.5% production (2000).
Income: Per capita income: $15,199 (2007); Median household income: $32,857 (2007); Average household income: $39,484 (2007); Percent of households with income of $100,000 or more: 1.1% (2007); Poverty rate: 12.3% (2000).
Education: Percent of population age 25 and over with: High school diploma (including GED) or higher: 68.0% (2007); Bachelor's degree or higher: 4.0% (2007); Master's degree or higher: 1.3% (2007).
Housing: Homeownership rate: 80.4% (2007); Median home value: $44,167 (2007); Median rent: $308 per month (2000); Median age of housing: 32 years (2000).
Transportation: Commute to work: 86.2% car, 0.0% public transportation, 0.0% walk, 13.8% work from home (2000); Travel time to work: 10.4% less than 15 minutes, 20.8% 15 to 30 minutes, 65.1% 30 to 45 minutes, 3.8% 45 to 60 minutes, 0.0% 60 minutes or more (2000)

WALSHVILLE (village). Covers a land area of 0.256 square miles and a water area of 0 square miles. Located at 39.07° N. Lat.; 89.61° W. Long. Elevation is 617 feet.
Population: 44 (1990); 89 (2000); 80 (2007); 79 (2012 projected); Race: 100.0% White, 0.0% Black, 0.0% Asian, 0.0% Hispanic of any race (2007); Density: 312.9 persons per square mile (2007); Average household size: 3.08 (2007); Median age: 37.0 (2007); Males per 100 females: 122.2 (2007); Marriage status: 19.0% never married, 52.4% now married, 6.3% widowed, 22.2% divorced (2000); Foreign born: 0.0% (2000); Ancestry (includes multiple ancestries): 32.9% United States or American, 12.9% English, 9.4% German, 4.7% Scotch-Irish, 4.7% British (2000).
Economy: Employment by occupation: 6.5% management, 6.5% professional, 12.9% services, 29.0% sales, 0.0% farming, 22.6% construction, 22.6% production (2000).
Income: Per capita income: $11,969 (2007); Median household income: $20,000 (2007); Average household income: $36,827 (2007); Percent of households with income of $100,000 or more: 15.4% (2007); Poverty rate: 40.0% (2000).
Education: Percent of population age 25 and over with: High school diploma (including GED) or higher: 62.7% (2007); Bachelor's degree or higher: 7.8% (2007); Master's degree or higher: 0.0% (2007).
Housing: Homeownership rate: 80.8% (2007); Median home value: $75,000 (2007); Median rent: $325 per month (2000); Median age of housing: 30 years (2000).
Transportation: Commute to work: 93.5% car, 0.0% public transportation, 0.0% walk, 6.5% work from home (2000); Travel time to work: 20.7% less than 15 minutes, 48.3% 15 to 30 minutes, 10.3% 30 to 45 minutes, 20.7% 45 to 60 minutes, 0.0% 60 minutes or more (2000)

WENONAH (village). Covers a land area of 1.509 square miles and a water area of 0 square miles. Located at 39.32° N. Lat.; 89.28° W. Long. Elevation is 673 feet.
Population: 40 (1990); 44 (2000); 47 (2007); 49 (2012 projected); Race: 100.0% White, 0.0% Black, 0.0% Asian, 0.0% Hispanic of any race (2007); Density: 31.1 persons per square mile (2007); Average household size: 2.61 (2007); Median age: 46.5 (2007); Males per 100 females: 80.8 (2007); Marriage status: 10.3% never married, 79.3% now married, 0.0% widowed, 10.3% divorced (2000); Foreign born: 0.0% (2000); Ancestry (includes multiple ancestries): 35.5% German, 19.4% Irish, 16.1% Scotch-Irish, 9.7% Italian, 6.5% English (2000).
Economy: Employment by occupation: 0.0% management, 0.0% professional, 54.5% services, 0.0% sales, 0.0% farming, 0.0% construction, 45.5% production (2000).
Income: Per capita income: $17,766 (2007); Median household income: $40,000 (2007); Average household income: $46,389 (2007); Percent of households with income of $100,000 or more: 0.0% (2007); Poverty rate: 0.0% (2000).
Education: Percent of population age 25 and over with: High school diploma (including GED) or higher: 74.3% (2007); Bachelor's degree or higher: 0.0% (2007); Master's degree or higher: 0.0% (2007).
Housing: Homeownership rate: 100.0% (2007); Median home value: $67,143 (2007); Median rent: $n/a per month (2000); Median age of housing: 47 years (2000).
Transportation: Commute to work: 100.0% car, 0.0% public transportation, 0.0% walk, 0.0% work from home (2000); Travel time to work: 20.0% less than 15 minutes, 10.0% 15 to 30 minutes, 40.0% 30 to 45 minutes, 0.0% 45 to 60 minutes, 30.0% 60 minutes or more (2000)

WITT (city). Covers a land area of 1.394 square miles and a water area of 0 square miles. Located at 39.25° N. Lat.; 89.35° W. Long. Elevation is 663 feet.
Population: 866 (1990); 991 (2000); 1,028 (2007); 1,066 (2012 projected); Race: 99.5% White, 0.2% Black, 0.2% Asian, 0.4% Hispanic of any race (2007); Density: 737.4 persons per square mile (2007); Average household size: 2.23 (2007); Median age: 40.1 (2007); Males per 100 females: 85.9 (2007); Marriage status: 19.7% never married, 53.6% now married, 11.1% widowed, 15.5% divorced (2000); Foreign born: 0.0% (2000); Ancestry (includes multiple ancestries): 23.7% German, 18.7% United States or American, 13.4% English, 10.3% Other groups, 9.5% Irish (2000).
Economy: Employment by occupation: 6.0% management, 10.2% professional, 21.4% services, 24.2% sales, 0.5% farming, 7.7% construction, 29.9% production (2000).
Income: Per capita income: $18,256 (2007); Median household income: $29,375 (2007); Average household income: $40,622 (2007); Percent of households with income of $100,000 or more: 5.4% (2007); Poverty rate: 21.4% (2000).
Education: Percent of population age 25 and over with: High school diploma (including GED) or higher: 73.7% (2007); Bachelor's degree or higher: 7.2% (2007); Master's degree or higher: 2.5% (2007).

School District(s)

Hillsboro CUSD 3 (PK-12)
2005-06 Enrollment: 2,025 . . . . (217) 532-2942

Housing: Homeownership rate: 81.0% (2007); Median home value: $52,973 (2007); Median rent: $192 per month (2000); Median age of housing: 55 years (2000).
Safety: Violent crime rate: 0.0 per 10,000 population; Property crime rate: 10.1 per 10,000 population (2006).
Transportation: Commute to work: 91.9% car, 0.5% public transportation, 4.3% walk, 1.5% work from home (2000); Travel time to work: 22.8% less than 15 minutes, 30.8% 15 to 30 minutes, 18.5% 30 to 45 minutes, 11.5% 45 to 60 minutes, 16.4% 60 minutes or more (2000)

Morgan County

Located in west central Illinois; bounded on the west by the Illinois River; includes part of Lake Meredosia. Covers a land area of 568.76 square miles, a water area of 3.51 square miles, and is located in the Central Time Zone. The county was founded in 1823. County seat is Jacksonville.

Morgan County is part of the Jacksonville, IL Micropolitan Statistical Area. The entire metro area includes: Morgan County, IL; Scott County, IL

Weather Station: Jacksonville 2 E Elevation: 606 feet

	Jan	Feb	Mar	Apr	May	Jun	Jul	Aug	Sep	Oct	Nov	Dec
High	33	39	51	63	74	83	86	84	79	67	52	39
Low	15	20	29	40	50	60	64	61	53	42	32	21
Precip	1.4	1.7	3.2	3.9	5.0	4.3	3.8	3.4	3.6	2.7	3.4	2.6
Snow	7.3	5.6	3.1	0.5	0.0	0.0	0.0	0.0	0.0	tr	1.4	5.0

High and Low temperatures in degrees Fahrenheit; Precipitation and Snow in inches

Population: 36,397 (1990); 36,616 (2000); 35,498 (2007); 34,636 (2012 projected); Race: 92.1% White, 5.5% Black, 0.6% Asian, 1.6% Hispanic of any race (2007); Density: 62.4 persons per square mile (2007); Average

household size: 2.58 (2007); Median age: 39.2 (2007); Males per 100 females: 99.0 (2007).
Religion: Five largest groups: 11.2% Catholic Church, 7.3% The United Methodist Church, 6.3% Christian Church (Disciples of Christ), 5.4% Southern Baptist Convention, 5.3% Lutheran Church—Missouri Synod (2000).
Economy: Unemployment rate: 5.0% (4/2008); Total civilian labor force: 18,122 (4/2008); Leading industries: 18.8% health care and social assistance; 16.1% manufacturing; 13.7% retail trade (2005); Farms: 682 totaling 292,740 acres (2002); Companies that employ 500 or more persons: 3 (2006); Companies that employ 100 to 499 persons: 23 (2006); Companies that employ less than 100 persons: 880 (2006); Black-owned businesses: n/a (2002); Hispanic-owned businesses: n/a (2002); Asian-owned businesses: n/a (2002); Women-owned businesses: 547 (2002); Retail sales per capita: $15,218 (2008). Single-family building permits issued: 19 (2007); Multi-family building permits issued: 22 (2007).
Income: Per capita income: $21,826 (2007); Median household income: $42,884 (2007); Average household income: $53,964 (2007); Percent of households with income of $100,000 or more: 10.2% (2007); Poverty rate: 13.6% (2005); Bankruptcy rate: 3.26% (2007).
Taxes: Total county taxes per capita: $158 (2006); County property taxes per capita: $135 (2006).
Education: Percent of population age 25 and over with: High school diploma (including GED) or higher: 80.1% (2007); Bachelor's degree or higher: 20.4% (2007); Master's degree or higher: 6.6% (2007).
Housing: Homeownership rate: 70.6% (2007); Median home value: $104,668 (2007); Median rent: $322 per month (2000); Median age of housing: 40 years (2000).
Health: Birth rate: 118.8 per 10,000 population (2007); Death rate: 115.4 per 10,000 population (2007); Age-adjusted cancer mortality rate: 161.0 deaths per 100,000 population (2005); Number of physicians: 13.2 per 10,000 population (2005); Hospital beds: 31.2 per 10,000 population (2004); Hospital admissions: 1,150.3 per 10,000 population (2004).
Elections: 2004 Presidential election results: 61.9% Bush, 37.2% Kerry, 0.0% Nader, 0.8% Badnarik

Additional Information Contacts

Morgan County Government . . . . (217) 245-4619
http://www.morgancounty-il.com
City of Jacksonville . . . . (217) 479-4600
http://www.jacksonvilleil.com
Jacksonville Area Chamber of Commerce. . . . . (217) 245-2174
http://www.jacksonvilleareachamber.org

Morgan County Communities

ALEXANDER (unincorporated postal area, zip code 62601). Covers a land area of 55.344 square miles and a water area of 0 square miles. Located at 39.75° N. Lat.; 90.02° W. Long. Elevation is 659 feet.
Population: 512 (2000); Race: 97.7% White, 1.3% Black, 0.0% Asian, 0.0% Hispanic of any race (2000); Density: 9.3 persons per square mile (2000); Age: 25.0% under 18, 11.4% over 64 (2000); Marriage status: 20.1% never married, 63.8% now married, 4.6% widowed, 11.4% divorced (2000); Foreign born: 0.0% (2000); Ancestry (includes multiple ancestries): 23.3% German, 20.3% English, 10.9% Irish, 7.7% United States or American, 3.8% Swedish (2000).
Economy: Employment by occupation: 22.6% management, 7.7% professional, 13.1% services, 26.2% sales, 4.5% farming, 12.8% construction, 13.1% production (2000).
Income: Per capita income: $19,414 (2000); Median household income: $46,932 (2000); Poverty rate: 6.2% (2000).
Education: Percent of population age 25 and over with: High school diploma (including GED) or higher: 86.3% (2000); Bachelor's degree or higher: 12.9% (2000).

School District(s)

Franklin CUSD 1 (PK-12)
2005-06 Enrollment: 353 . . . . (217) 478-3011
Housing: Homeownership rate: 73.1% (2000); Median home value: $75,700 (2000); Median rent: $352 per month (2000); Median age of housing: 55 years (2000).
Transportation: Commute to work: 90.1% car, 0.0% public transportation, 1.8% walk, 8.1% work from home (2000); Travel time to work: 29.3% less than 15 minutes, 40.1% 15 to 30 minutes, 20.2% 30 to 45 minutes, 8.8% 45 to 60 minutes, 1.6% 60 minutes or more (2000)

CHAPIN (village). Covers a land area of 0.975 square miles and a water area of 0 square miles. Located at 39.76° N. Lat.; 90.40° W. Long. Elevation is 620 feet.
Population: 632 (1990); 592 (2000); 476 (2007); 445 (2012 projected); Race: 99.2% White, 0.0% Black, 0.0% Asian, 0.0% Hispanic of any race (2007); Density: 488.1 persons per square mile (2007); Average household size: 2.53 (2007); Median age: 36.4 (2007); Males per 100 females: 106.1 (2007); Marriage status: 16.7% never married, 65.2% now married, 6.9% widowed, 11.2% divorced (2000); Foreign born: 0.0% (2000); Ancestry (includes multiple ancestries): 28.7% German, 14.5% Irish, 11.3% English, 10.1% Other groups, 8.9% United States or American (2000).
Economy: Employment by occupation: 9.0% management, 10.9% professional, 13.2% services, 28.9% sales, 0.0% farming, 9.0% construction, 28.9% production (2000).
Income: Per capita income: $23,246 (2007); Median household income: $52,632 (2007); Average household income: $58,856 (2007); Percent of households with income of $100,000 or more: 6.4% (2007); Poverty rate: 8.9% (2000).
Education: Percent of population age 25 and over with: High school diploma (including GED) or higher: 86.1% (2007); Bachelor's degree or higher: 9.1% (2007); Master's degree or higher: 1.4% (2007).
Housing: Homeownership rate: 89.4% (2007); Median home value: $78,333 (2007); Median rent: $271 per month (2000); Median age of housing: 58 years (2000).
Safety: Violent crime rate: 0.0 per 10,000 population; Property crime rate: 34.2 per 10,000 population (2006).
Transportation: Commute to work: 98.5% car, 0.0% public transportation, 1.5% walk, 0.0% work from home (2000); Travel time to work: 32.3% less than 15 minutes, 54.1% 15 to 30 minutes, 4.9% 30 to 45 minutes, 1.9% 45 to 60 minutes, 6.8% 60 minutes or more (2000)

CONCORD (village). Covers a land area of 0.263 square miles and a water area of 0 square miles. Located at 39.81° N. Lat.; 90.37° W. Long. Elevation is 594 feet.
Population: 172 (1990); 176 (2000); 189 (2007); 174 (2012 projected); Race: 99.5% White, 0.0% Black, 0.0% Asian, 0.0% Hispanic of any race (2007); Density: 719.7 persons per square mile (2007); Average household size: 2.49 (2007); Median age: 39.5 (2007); Males per 100 females: 127.7 (2007); Marriage status: 13.5% never married, 70.3% now married, 3.4% widowed, 12.8% divorced (2000); Foreign born: 1.1% (2000); Ancestry (includes multiple ancestries): 25.1% German, 21.3% Irish, 19.1% English, 14.2% United States or American, 12.0% Other groups (2000).
Economy: Employment by occupation: 0.0% management, 15.3% professional, 17.6% services, 23.5% sales, 0.0% farming, 15.3% construction, 28.2% production (2000).
Income: Per capita income: $15,648 (2007); Median household income: $36,250 (2007); Average household income: $38,914 (2007); Percent of households with income of $100,000 or more: 1.3% (2007); Poverty rate: 18.6% (2000).
Education: Percent of population age 25 and over with: High school diploma (including GED) or higher: 72.8% (2007); Bachelor's degree or higher: 7.2% (2007); Master's degree or higher: 4.8% (2007).

School District(s)

Triopia CUSD 27 (PK-12)
2005-06 Enrollment: 457 . . . . (217) 457-2283
Housing: Homeownership rate: 89.5% (2007); Median home value: $60,000 (2007); Median rent: $250 per month (2000); Median age of housing: 60+ years (2000).
Transportation: Commute to work: 98.8% car, 0.0% public transportation, 0.0% walk, 1.2% work from home (2000); Travel time to work: 15.5% less than 15 minutes, 58.3% 15 to 30 minutes, 9.5% 30 to 45 minutes, 11.9% 45 to 60 minutes, 4.8% 60 minutes or more (2000)

FRANKLIN (village). Covers a land area of 0.731 square miles and a water area of 0 square miles. Located at 39.62° N. Lat.; 90.04° W. Long. Elevation is 682 feet.
Population: 681 (1990); 586 (2000); 501 (2007); 466 (2012 projected); Race: 99.2% White, 0.0% Black, 0.0% Asian, 1.2% Hispanic of any race (2007); Density: 685.0 persons per square mile (2007); Average household size: 2.53 (2007); Median age: 36.1 (2007); Males per 100 females: 97.2 (2007); Marriage status: 15.9% never married, 69.1% now married, 5.2% widowed, 9.9% divorced (2000); Foreign born: 0.3% (2000); Ancestry (includes multiple ancestries): 19.3% Irish, 16.4% German, 13.5% Other groups, 12.6% English, 9.1% United States or American (2000).

Economy: Employment by occupation: 8.8% management, 17.8% professional, 18.5% services, 20.5% sales, 1.0% farming, 11.8% construction, 21.5% production (2000).
Income: Per capita income: $21,502 (2007); Median household income: $45,000 (2007); Average household income: $54,407 (2007); Percent of households with income of $100,000 or more: 13.1% (2007); Poverty rate: 8.6% (2000).
Education: Percent of population age 25 and over with: High school diploma (including GED) or higher: 89.1% (2007); Bachelor's degree or higher: 14.6% (2007); Master's degree or higher: 5.0% (2007).

School District(s)

Franklin CUSD 1 (PK-12)
2005-06 Enrollment: 353 . . . . (217) 478-3011

Housing: Homeownership rate: 78.3% (2007); Median home value: $89,444 (2007); Median rent: $371 per month (2000); Median age of housing: 39 years (2000).
Safety: Violent crime rate: 0.0 per 10,000 population; Property crime rate: 0.0 per 10,000 population (2006).
Newspapers: Franklin Times (Community news; Circulation 800); Murrayville Gazette (Local news; Circulation 800)
Transportation: Commute to work: 87.3% car, 0.0% public transportation, 7.2% walk, 3.1% work from home (2000); Travel time to work: 25.1% less than 15 minutes, 42.4% 15 to 30 minutes, 15.5% 30 to 45 minutes, 13.4% 45 to 60 minutes, 3.5% 60 minutes or more (2000)

JACKSONVILLE (city). County seat. Covers a land area of 10.133 square miles and a water area of 0.193 square miles. Located at 39.73° N. Lat.; 90.23° W. Long. Elevation is 610 feet.
History: Jacksonville was founded in 1825, and named for Andrew Jackson. The first settlers were southerners, but they were followed by people from New England. Abolitionist sentiment was strong, and Jacksonville served as a station on the Underground Railroad. Both William Jennings Bryan (1883) and Stephen A. Douglas (1834) began their law practices in Jacksonville, and Abraham Lincoln was a frequent speaker here.
Population: 19,613 (1990); 18,940 (2000); 18,294 (2007); 17,776 (2012 projected); Race: 90.8% White, 6.1% Black, 0.9% Asian, 1.8% Hispanic of any race (2007); Density: 1,805.4 persons per square mile (2007); Average household size: 2.58 (2007); Median age: 38.0 (2007); Males per 100 females: 92.0 (2007); Marriage status: 25.0% never married, 56.2% now married, 8.1% widowed, 10.8% divorced (2000); Foreign born: 1.4% (2000); Ancestry (includes multiple ancestries): 19.6% German, 13.8% English, 11.2% Other groups, 10.5% United States or American, 10.0% Irish (2000).
Economy: Single-family building permits issued: 17 (2007); Multi-family building permits issued: 22 (2007); Employment by occupation: 9.3% management, 21.2% professional, 19.8% services, 24.0% sales, 0.8% farming, 6.6% construction, 18.2% production (2000).
Income: Per capita income: $20,364 (2007); Median household income: $37,528 (2007); Average household income: $50,146 (2007); Percent of households with income of $100,000 or more: 9.4% (2007); Poverty rate: 12.4% (2000).
Taxes: Total city taxes per capita: $236 (2006); City property taxes per capita: $194 (2006).
Education: Percent of population age 25 and over with: High school diploma (including GED) or higher: 79.9% (2007); Bachelor's degree or higher: 23.9% (2007); Master's degree or higher: 8.0% (2007).

School District(s)

Brown/Cass/Morgan/Scott Roe (07-12)
2005-06 Enrollment: 99 . . . . (217) 243-1804
Dept of Corrections Sch Dist 428 (08-12)
2005-06 Enrollment: 2,271 . . . . (217) 522-2666
Dept of Human Services (PK-12)
2005-06 Enrollment: 298 . . . . (217) 524-1379
Four Rivers Spec Educ Dist (03-12)
2005-06 Enrollment: 78 . . . . (217) 245-7174
Jacksonville SD 117 (PK-12)
2005-06 Enrollment: 3,713 . . . . (217) 243-9411

Four-year College(s)

Illinois College (Private, Not-for-profit, Presbyterian Church (USA))
Fall 2007 Enrollment: 1,014. . . . . (217) 245-3000
2007-08 Tuition: In-state $18,800; Out-of-state $18,800
MacMurray College (Private, Not-for-profit, United Methodist)
Fall 2007 Enrollment: 648 . . . . (217) 479-7000
2007-08 Tuition: In-state $16,850; Out-of-state $16,850

Vocational/Technical School(s)

Mr John's School of Cosmetology & Nails (Private, For-profit)
Fall 2007 Enrollment: 34 . . . . (217) 243-1744
2007-08 Tuition: $10,545

Housing: Homeownership rate: 61.8% (2007); Median home value: $101,758 (2007); Median rent: $324 per month (2000); Median age of housing: 43 years (2000).
Hospitals: Passavant Memorial Area Hospital (99 beds)
Safety: Violent crime rate: 44.7 per 10,000 population; Property crime rate: 298.4 per 10,000 population (2006).
Newspapers: Jacksonville Journal Courier (Local news; Circulation 14,969); Shoppers Guide (Local news; Circulation 14,000)
Transportation: Commute to work: 88.0% car, 0.9% public transportation, 6.4% walk, 2.7% work from home (2000); Travel time to work: 68.9% less than 15 minutes, 14.9% 15 to 30 minutes, 6.3% 30 to 45 minutes, 6.2% 45 to 60 minutes, 3.6% 60 minutes or more (2000)
Airports: Jacksonville Municipal (general aviation)

Additional Information Contacts

City of Jacksonville . . . . (217) 479-4600
http://www.jacksonvilleil.com
Jacksonville Area Chamber of Commerce. . . . . (217) 245-2174
http://www.jacksonvilleareachamber.org

LYNNVILLE (village). Covers a land area of 0.079 square miles and a water area of 0 square miles. Located at 39.68° N. Lat.; 90.34° W. Long. Elevation is 620 feet.
Population: 125 (1990); 137 (2000); 151 (2007); 159 (2012 projected); Race: 99.3% White, 0.0% Black, 0.0% Asian, 1.3% Hispanic of any race (2007); Density: 1,914.7 persons per square mile (2007); Average household size: 2.44 (2007); Median age: 37.3 (2007); Males per 100 females: 115.7 (2007); Marriage status: 20.5% never married, 65.2% now married, 6.3% widowed, 8.0% divorced (2000); Foreign born: 0.0% (2000); Ancestry (includes multiple ancestries): 22.1% United States or American, 13.1% English, 10.3% German, 6.9% Irish, 6.2% Dutch (2000).
Economy: Employment by occupation: 2.8% management, 9.9% professional, 22.5% services, 21.1% sales, 2.8% farming, 14.1% construction, 26.8% production (2000).
Income: Per capita income: $20,596 (2007); Median household income: $46,364 (2007); Average household income: $50,161 (2007); Percent of households with income of $100,000 or more: 6.5% (2007); Poverty rate: 1.4% (2000).
Education: Percent of population age 25 and over with: High school diploma (including GED) or higher: 71.2% (2007); Bachelor's degree or higher: 9.6% (2007); Master's degree or higher: 3.8% (2007).
Housing: Homeownership rate: 82.3% (2007); Median home value: $72,143 (2007); Median rent: $363 per month (2000); Median age of housing: 20 years (2000).
Transportation: Commute to work: 95.8% car, 0.0% public transportation, 0.0% walk, 4.2% work from home (2000); Travel time to work: 33.8% less than 15 minutes, 63.2% 15 to 30 minutes, 0.0% 30 to 45 minutes, 0.0% 45 to 60 minutes, 2.9% 60 minutes or more (2000)

MEREDOSIA (village). Covers a land area of 0.921 square miles and a water area of 0.078 square miles. Located at 39.83° N. Lat.; 90.55° W. Long. Elevation is 446 feet.
History: The name of Meredosia is from the French "marais d'osier" meaning "swamp of the basket reeds." The town was located at the mouth of Meredosia Lake. The railroad connecting with the Illinois & Michigan Canal was constructed here in 1838, but the Canal continued to hold supremacy over the railroad until 1878.
Population: 1,166 (1990); 1,041 (2000); 908 (2007); 833 (2012 projected); Race: 99.9% White, 0.0% Black, 0.0% Asian, 0.1% Hispanic of any race (2007); Density: 985.9 persons per square mile (2007); Average household size: 2.26 (2007); Median age: 42.5 (2007); Males per 100 females: 99.6 (2007); Marriage status: 17.0% never married, 61.6% now married, 10.9% widowed, 10.5% divorced (2000); Foreign born: 0.2% (2000); Ancestry (includes multiple ancestries): 22.8% German, 12.6% English, 8.7% United States or American, 8.7% Irish, 5.0% Other groups (2000).
Economy: Single-family building permits issued: 0 (2007); Multi-family building permits issued: 0 (2007); Employment by occupation: 4.9% management, 10.8% professional, 18.1% services, 21.6% sales, 0.0% farming, 7.9% construction, 36.6% production (2000).
Income: Per capita income: $20,435 (2007); Median household income: $37,667 (2007); Average household income: $46,157 (2007); Percent of households with income of $100,000 or more: 3.7% (2007); Poverty rate: 9.2% (2000).

Education: Percent of population age 25 and over with: High school diploma (including GED) or higher: 75.9% (2007); Bachelor's degree or higher: 5.3% (2007); Master's degree or higher: 2.9% (2007).

School District(s)

Meredosia-Chambersburg CUSD 11 (PK-12)
2005-06 Enrollment: 322 . . . . (217) 584-1744

Housing: Homeownership rate: 82.3% (2007); Median home value: $63,723 (2007); Median rent: $279 per month (2000); Median age of housing: 37 years (2000).

Safety: Violent crime rate: 60.2 per 10,000 population; Property crime rate: 351.4 per 10,000 population (2006).

Transportation: Commute to work: 94.0% car, 0.0% public transportation, 3.1% walk, 0.9% work from home (2000); Travel time to work: 38.7% less than 15 minutes, 28.6% 15 to 30 minutes, 20.7% 30 to 45 minutes, 4.7% 45 to 60 minutes, 7.2% 60 minutes or more (2000)

MURRAYVILLE (village). Covers a land area of 0.498 square miles and a water area of 0 square miles. Located at 39.58° N. Lat.; 90.25° W. Long. Elevation is 692 feet.

Population: 673 (1990); 644 (2000); 664 (2007); 661 (2012 projected); Race: 99.4% White, 0.0% Black, 0.0% Asian, 0.0% Hispanic of any race (2007); Density: 1,332.6 persons per square mile (2007); Average household size: 2.57 (2007); Median age: 37.8 (2007); Males per 100 females: 93.6 (2007); Marriage status: 21.0% never married, 64.2% now married, 7.3% widowed, 7.5% divorced (2000); Foreign born: 0.0% (2000); Ancestry (includes multiple ancestries): 25.5% German, 20.4% United States or American, 16.0% English, 11.6% Irish, 3.9% Other groups (2000).

Economy: Employment by occupation: 4.8% management, 8.4% professional, 13.6% services, 30.1% sales, 0.6% farming, 15.1% construction, 27.4% production (2000).

Income: Per capita income: $21,438 (2007); Median household income: $53,333 (2007); Average household income: $55,174 (2007); Percent of households with income of $100,000 or more: 4.3% (2007); Poverty rate: 11.2% (2000).

Education: Percent of population age 25 and over with: High school diploma (including GED) or higher: 83.1% (2007); Bachelor's degree or higher: 9.0% (2007); Master's degree or higher: 3.8% (2007).

School District(s)

Jacksonville SD 117 (PK-12)
2005-06 Enrollment: 3,713 . . . . (217) 243-9411

Housing: Homeownership rate: 82.2% (2007); Median home value: $91,154 (2007); Median rent: $321 per month (2000); Median age of housing: 49 years (2000).

Transportation: Commute to work: 95.2% car, 0.0% public transportation, 2.4% walk, 2.4% work from home (2000); Travel time to work: 16.0% less than 15 minutes, 58.6% 15 to 30 minutes, 14.5% 30 to 45 minutes, 6.5% 45 to 60 minutes, 4.3% 60 minutes or more (2000)

SOUTH JACKSONVILLE (village). Covers a land area of 1.653 square miles and a water area of 0.058 square miles. Located at 39.71° N. Lat.; 90.23° W. Long. Elevation is 620 feet.

Population: 3,292 (1990); 3,475 (2000); 3,208 (2007); 3,015 (2012 projected); Race: 96.3% White, 1.8% Black, 0.8% Asian, 1.2% Hispanic of any race (2007); Density: 1,940.7 persons per square mile (2007); Average household size: 2.14 (2007); Median age: 45.2 (2007); Males per 100 females: 83.0 (2007); Marriage status: 21.0% never married, 57.6% now married, 10.4% widowed, 11.1% divorced (2000); Foreign born: 1.1% (2000); Ancestry (includes multiple ancestries): 26.1% German, 16.2% English, 12.3% United States or American, 11.3% Irish, 6.3% Other groups (2000).

Economy: Single-family building permits issued: 2 (2007); Multi-family building permits issued: 0 (2007); Employment by occupation: 13.1% management, 23.6% professional, 16.8% services, 27.6% sales, 0.0% farming, 5.8% construction, 13.0% production (2000).

Income: Per capita income: $25,839 (2007); Median household income: $44,418 (2007); Average household income: $54,425 (2007); Percent of households with income of $100,000 or more: 11.0% (2007); Poverty rate: 6.5% (2000).

Education: Percent of population age 25 and over with: High school diploma (including GED) or higher: 83.9% (2007); Bachelor's degree or higher: 26.5% (2007); Master's degree or higher: 7.8% (2007).

Housing: Homeownership rate: 69.6% (2007); Median home value: $113,132 (2007); Median rent: $309 per month (2000); Median age of housing: 38 years (2000).

Safety: Violent crime rate: 18.0 per 10,000 population; Property crime rate: 153.2 per 10,000 population (2006).

Transportation: Commute to work: 94.7% car, 0.0% public transportation, 0.2% walk, 3.7% work from home (2000); Travel time to work: 59.5% less than 15 minutes, 19.1% 15 to 30 minutes, 12.6% 30 to 45 minutes, 6.5% 45 to 60 minutes, 2.4% 60 minutes or more (2000)

WAVERLY (city). Covers a land area of 1.032 square miles and a water area of 0 square miles. Located at 39.59° N. Lat.; 89.95° W. Long. Elevation is 682 feet.

History: Incorporated 1867.

Population: 1,402 (1990); 1,346 (2000); 1,250 (2007); 1,138 (2012 projected); Race: 99.5% White, 0.0% Black, 0.0% Asian, 0.3% Hispanic of any race (2007); Density: 1,210.9 persons per square mile (2007); Average household size: 2.28 (2007); Median age: 40.9 (2007); Males per 100 females: 89.7 (2007); Marriage status: 21.5% never married, 58.7% now married, 10.6% widowed, 9.2% divorced (2000); Foreign born: 0.7% (2000); Ancestry (includes multiple ancestries): 20.9% German, 18.2% English, 12.9% Irish, 12.8% United States or American, 7.8% Other groups (2000).

Economy: Single-family building permits issued: 0 (2007); Multi-family building permits issued: 0 (2007); Employment by occupation: 13.3% management, 9.8% professional, 12.3% services, 32.1% sales, 0.3% farming, 9.5% construction, 22.6% production (2000).

Income: Per capita income: $23,598 (2007); Median household income: $43,857 (2007); Average household income: $53,828 (2007); Percent of households with income of $100,000 or more: 10.2% (2007); Poverty rate: 8.0% (2000).

Education: Percent of population age 25 and over with: High school diploma (including GED) or higher: 82.7% (2007); Bachelor's degree or higher: 12.8% (2007); Master's degree or higher: 4.3% (2007).

School District(s)

Waverly CUSD 6 (PK-12)
2005-06 Enrollment: 401 . . . . (217) 435-8121

Housing: Homeownership rate: 81.4% (2007); Median home value: $80,526 (2007); Median rent: $308 per month (2000); Median age of housing: 56 years (2000).

Safety: Violent crime rate: 55.0 per 10,000 population; Property crime rate: 110.1 per 10,000 population (2006).

Newspapers: Waverly Journal (Community news; Circulation 1,561)

Transportation: Commute to work: 90.8% car, 0.3% public transportation, 2.5% walk, 4.9% work from home (2000); Travel time to work: 23.4% less than 15 minutes, 21.2% 15 to 30 minutes, 34.6% 30 to 45 minutes, 16.9% 45 to 60 minutes, 3.8% 60 minutes or more (2000)

WOODSON (village). Covers a land area of 0.387 square miles and a water area of 0 square miles. Located at 39.62° N. Lat.; 90.22° W. Long. Elevation is 679 feet.

Population: 509 (1990); 559 (2000); 524 (2007); 523 (2012 projected); Race: 97.3% White, 0.8% Black, 0.4% Asian, 0.6% Hispanic of any race (2007); Density: 1,352.3 persons per square mile (2007); Average household size: 2.61 (2007); Median age: 36.0 (2007); Males per 100 females: 97.7 (2007); Marriage status: 24.2% never married, 60.8% now married, 6.2% widowed, 8.9% divorced (2000); Foreign born: 0.4% (2000); Ancestry (includes multiple ancestries): 22.3% German, 16.2% United States or American, 12.1% English, 12.0% Irish, 5.8% Other groups (2000).

Economy: Employment by occupation: 12.1% management, 15.7% professional, 20.3% services, 23.6% sales, 0.0% farming, 11.5% construction, 16.7% production (2000).

Income: Per capita income: $20,353 (2007); Median household income: $48,125 (2007); Average household income: $53,060 (2007); Percent of households with income of $100,000 or more: 7.0% (2007); Poverty rate: 6.2% (2000).

Education: Percent of population age 25 and over with: High school diploma (including GED) or higher: 82.9% (2007); Bachelor's degree or higher: 14.7% (2007); Master's degree or higher: 3.2% (2007).

Housing: Homeownership rate: 90.5% (2007); Median home value: $97,857 (2007); Median rent: $369 per month (2000); Median age of housing: 26 years (2000).

Transportation: Commute to work: 97.3% car, 0.0% public transportation, 0.0% walk, 1.0% work from home (2000); Travel time to work: 26.6% less than 15 minutes, 51.2% 15 to 30 minutes, 9.4% 30 to 45 minutes, 7.4% 45 to 60 minutes, 5.4% 60 minutes or more (2000)

Moultrie County

Located in central Illinois; drained by the Kaskaskia River. Covers a land area of 335.60 square miles, a water area of 8.87 square miles, and is located in the Central Time Zone. The county was founded in 1843. County seat is Sullivan.

Population: 13,930 (1990); 14,287 (2000); 14,594 (2007); 14,784 (2012 projected); Race: 98.9% White, 0.3% Black, 0.1% Asian, 0.7% Hispanic of any race (2007); Density: 43.5 persons per square mile (2007); Average household size: 2.62 (2007); Median age: 39.9 (2007); Males per 100 females: 94.6 (2007).

Religion: Five largest groups: 10.0% Christian Church (Disciples of Christ), 7.4% The United Methodist Church, 6.0% Southern Baptist Convention, 4.2% Catholic Church, 3.1% Lutheran Church—Missouri Synod (2000).

Economy: Unemployment rate: 4.2% (4/2008); Total civilian labor force: 8,132 (4/2008); Leading industries: 42.6% manufacturing; 16.2% health care and social assistance; 12.4% retail trade (2005); Farms: 441 totaling 186,478 acres (2002); Companies that employ 500 or more persons: 1 (2006); Companies that employ 100 to 499 persons: 5 (2006); Companies that employ less than 100 persons: 286 (2006); Black-owned businesses: n/a (2002); Hispanic-owned businesses: n/a (2002); Asian-owned businesses: n/a (2002); Women-owned businesses: n/a (2002); Retail sales per capita: $4,824 (2008). Single-family building permits issued: 45 (2007); Multi-family building permits issued: 0 (2007).

Income: Per capita income: $22,044 (2007); Median household income: $46,070 (2007); Average household income: $55,485 (2007); Percent of households with income of $100,000 or more: 10.7% (2007); Poverty rate: 9.5% (2005); Bankruptcy rate: 2.51% (2007).

Education: Percent of population age 25 and over with: High school diploma (including GED) or higher: 79.2% (2007); Bachelor's degree or higher: 15.1% (2007); Master's degree or higher: 4.1% (2007).

Housing: Homeownership rate: 78.6% (2007); Median home value: $110,639 (2007); Median rent: $331 per month (2000); Median age of housing: 41 years (2000).

Health: Birth rate: 129.2 per 10,000 population (2007); Death rate: 132.6 per 10,000 population (2007); Age-adjusted cancer mortality rate: 253.0 deaths per 100,000 population (2005); Number of physicians: 3.5 per 10,000 population (2005); Hospital beds: 0.0 per 10,000 population (2004); Hospital admissions: 0.0 per 10,000 population (2004).

Elections: 2004 Presidential election results: 62.3% Bush, 36.9% Kerry, 0.1% Nader, 0.7% Badnarik

National and State Parks: Kaskaskia River State Fish and Wildlife Management; West Okaw River State Fish and Wildlife Management

Additional Information Contacts

Moultrie County Government . . . . (217) 728-4389

Sullivan Chamber of Commerce . . . . (217) 728-4223
http://www.sullivanchamber.com

Moultrie County Communities

ALLENVILLE (village). Covers a land area of 0.582 square miles and a water area of 0 square miles. Located at 39.55° N. Lat.; 88.53° W. Long. Elevation is 650 feet.

Population: 166 (1990); 154 (2000); 156 (2007); 155 (2012 projected); Race: 100.0% White, 0.0% Black, 0.0% Asian, 0.0% Hispanic of any race (2007); Density: 267.8 persons per square mile (2007); Average household size: 2.56 (2007); Median age: 46.1 (2007); Males per 100 females: 113.7 (2007); Marriage status: 27.6% never married, 59.2% now married, 4.6% widowed, 8.6% divorced (2000); Foreign born: 1.2% (2000); Ancestry (includes multiple ancestries): 31.4% United States or American, 18.3% German, 10.7% Irish, 10.1% Other groups, 4.1% English (2000).

Economy: Single-family building permits issued: 0 (2007); Multi-family building permits issued: 0 (2007); Employment by occupation: 12.1% management, 3.7% professional, 15.9% services, 26.2% sales, 0.0% farming, 6.5% construction, 35.5% production (2000).

Income: Per capita income: $20,224 (2007); Median household income: $52,333 (2007); Average household income: $51,721 (2007); Percent of households with income of $100,000 or more: 6.6% (2007); Poverty rate: 7.7% (2000).

Education: Percent of population age 25 and over with: High school diploma (including GED) or higher: 77.1% (2007); Bachelor's degree or higher: 5.9% (2007); Master's degree or higher: 0.0% (2007).

Housing: Homeownership rate: 95.1% (2007); Median home value: $70,000 (2007); Median rent: $275 per month (2000); Median age of housing: 29 years (2000).

Transportation: Commute to work: 95.1% car, 0.0% public transportation, 2.0% walk, 2.9% work from home (2000); Travel time to work: 17.2% less than 15 minutes, 59.6% 15 to 30 minutes, 12.1% 30 to 45 minutes, 6.1% 45 to 60 minutes, 5.1% 60 minutes or more (2000)

BETHANY (village). Covers a land area of 0.972 square miles and a water area of 0.004 square miles. Located at 39.64° N. Lat.; 88.73° W. Long. Elevation is 650 feet.

Population: 1,438 (1990); 1,287 (2000); 1,312 (2007); 1,330 (2012 projected); Race: 98.9% White, 0.2% Black, 0.0% Asian, 0.3% Hispanic of any race (2007); Density: 1,349.3 persons per square mile (2007); Average household size: 2.32 (2007); Median age: 41.4 (2007); Males per 100 females: 97.6 (2007); Marriage status: 16.8% never married, 63.8% now married, 12.1% widowed, 7.3% divorced (2000); Foreign born: 1.1% (2000); Ancestry (includes multiple ancestries): 23.0% German, 17.8% United States or American, 12.0% English, 12.0% Irish, 6.4% Other groups (2000).

Economy: Single-family building permits issued: 0 (2007); Multi-family building permits issued: 0 (2007); Employment by occupation: 9.9% management, 9.6% professional, 13.8% services, 21.9% sales, 0.8% farming, 9.4% construction, 34.5% production (2000).

Income: Per capita income: $19,823 (2007); Median household income: $39,490 (2007); Average household income: $45,950 (2007); Percent of households with income of $100,000 or more: 3.5% (2007); Poverty rate: 7.4% (2000).

Education: Percent of population age 25 and over with: High school diploma (including GED) or higher: 85.3% (2007); Bachelor's degree or higher: 7.5% (2007); Master's degree or higher: 2.4% (2007).

School District(s)

Okaw Valley CUSD 302 (PK-12)
2005-06 Enrollment: 573 . . . . (217) 665-3232

Housing: Homeownership rate: 83.0% (2007); Median home value: $93,000 (2007); Median rent: $256 per month (2000); Median age of housing: 43 years (2000).

Safety: Violent crime rate: 0.0 per 10,000 population; Property crime rate: 0.0 per 10,000 population (2006).

Transportation: Commute to work: 91.8% car, 0.0% public transportation, 6.1% walk, 1.4% work from home (2000); Travel time to work: 33.6% less than 15 minutes, 30.2% 15 to 30 minutes, 26.5% 30 to 45 minutes, 5.3% 45 to 60 minutes, 4.4% 60 minutes or more (2000)

DALTON CITY (village). Covers a land area of 0.617 square miles and a water area of 0.003 square miles. Located at 39.71° N. Lat.; 88.80° W. Long. Elevation is 689 feet.

Population: 600 (1990); 581 (2000); 586 (2007); 584 (2012 projected); Race: 98.6% White, 0.7% Black, 0.0% Asian, 2.6% Hispanic of any race (2007); Density: 949.8 persons per square mile (2007); Average household size: 2.68 (2007); Median age: 35.0 (2007); Males per 100 females: 93.4 (2007); Marriage status: 18.0% never married, 72.9% now married, 3.6% widowed, 5.6% divorced (2000); Foreign born: 0.8% (2000); Ancestry (includes multiple ancestries): 26.8% German, 17.8% Irish, 12.4% English, 8.5% United States or American, 6.5% Other groups (2000).

Economy: Single-family building permits issued: 0 (2007); Multi-family building permits issued: 0 (2007); Employment by occupation: 6.9% management, 11.6% professional, 14.8% services, 25.5% sales, 1.3% farming, 18.6% construction, 21.4% production (2000).

Income: Per capita income: $21,020 (2007); Median household income: $55,000 (2007); Average household income: $56,244 (2007); Percent of households with income of $100,000 or more: 6.4% (2007); Poverty rate: 4.1% (2000).

Education: Percent of population age 25 and over with: High school diploma (including GED) or higher: 88.9% (2007); Bachelor's degree or higher: 8.1% (2007); Master's degree or higher: 1.3% (2007).

Housing: Homeownership rate: 80.8% (2007); Median home value: $100,708 (2007); Median rent: $360 per month (2000); Median age of housing: 40 years (2000).

Transportation: Commute to work: 95.8% car, 0.0% public transportation, 1.6% walk, 1.3% work from home (2000); Travel time to work: 17.9% less than 15 minutes, 56.0% 15 to 30 minutes, 17.5% 30 to 45 minutes, 0.7% 45 to 60 minutes, 7.9% 60 minutes or more (2000)

GAYS (village). Covers a land area of 0.409 square miles and a water area of 0 square miles. Located at 39.45° N. Lat.; 88.49° W. Long. Elevation is 755 feet.
Population: 265 (1990); 259 (2000); 334 (2007); 382 (2012 projected); Race: 98.8% White, 0.0% Black, 0.0% Asian, 0.0% Hispanic of any race (2007); Density: 816.9 persons per square mile (2007); Average household size: 2.69 (2007); Median age: 34.4 (2007); Males per 100 females: 108.7 (2007); Marriage status: 17.4% never married, 72.6% now married, 1.1% widowed, 8.9% divorced (2000); Foreign born: 0.4% (2000); Ancestry (includes multiple ancestries): 22.5% United States or American, 14.6% German, 7.9% Other groups, 5.1% English, 4.7% Irish (2000).
Economy: Single-family building permits issued: 0 (2007); Multi-family building permits issued: 0 (2007); Employment by occupation: 7.8% management, 15.7% professional, 15.7% services, 26.1% sales, 0.0% farming, 7.8% construction, 27.0% production (2000).
Income: Per capita income: $21,377 (2007); Median household income: $46,250 (2007); Average household income: $57,581 (2007); Percent of households with income of $100,000 or more: 7.3% (2007); Poverty rate: 3.6% (2000).
Education: Percent of population age 25 and over with: High school diploma (including GED) or higher: 92.7% (2007); Bachelor's degree or higher: 12.7% (2007); Master's degree or higher: 4.4% (2007).
Housing: Homeownership rate: 87.1% (2007); Median home value: $83,077 (2007); Median rent: $425 per month (2000); Median age of housing: 55 years (2000).
Transportation: Commute to work: 97.5% car, 0.0% public transportation, 0.0% walk, 2.5% work from home (2000); Travel time to work: 19.0% less than 15 minutes, 57.8% 15 to 30 minutes, 14.7% 30 to 45 minutes, 1.7% 45 to 60 minutes, 6.9% 60 minutes or more (2000)

LOVINGTON (village). Covers a land area of 0.805 square miles and a water area of 0 square miles. Located at 39.71° N. Lat.; 88.63° W. Long. Elevation is 679 feet.
History: Incorporated 1873.
Population: 1,143 (1990); 1,222 (2000); 1,240 (2007); 1,257 (2012 projected); Race: 98.8% White, 0.3% Black, 0.2% Asian, 0.4% Hispanic of any race (2007); Density: 1,540.8 persons per square mile (2007); Average household size: 2.37 (2007); Median age: 37.9 (2007); Males per 100 females: 92.2 (2007); Marriage status: 23.7% never married, 59.0% now married, 9.2% widowed, 8.1% divorced (2000); Foreign born: 0.2% (2000); Ancestry (includes multiple ancestries): 21.1% German, 17.3% United States or American, 12.9% Irish, 12.3% English, 7.2% Other groups (2000).
Economy: Single-family building permits issued: 2 (2007); Multi-family building permits issued: 0 (2007); Employment by occupation: 12.1% management, 10.2% professional, 17.3% services, 18.8% sales, 0.5% farming, 8.3% construction, 32.8% production (2000).
Income: Per capita income: $21,205 (2007); Median household income: $39,950 (2007); Average household income: $49,369 (2007); Percent of households with income of $100,000 or more: 7.5% (2007); Poverty rate: 8.7% (2000).
Education: Percent of population age 25 and over with: High school diploma (including GED) or higher: 82.1% (2007); Bachelor's degree or higher: 8.5% (2007); Master's degree or higher: 2.1% (2007).

School District(s)

Lovington CUSD 303 (PK-12)
2005-06 Enrollment: 320 . . . . (217) 873-4310
Housing: Homeownership rate: 74.2% (2007); Median home value: $78,710 (2007); Median rent: $288 per month (2000); Median age of housing: 50 years (2000).
Safety: Violent crime rate: 117.1 per 10,000 population; Property crime rate: 100.3 per 10,000 population (2006).
Transportation: Commute to work: 93.9% car, 0.9% public transportation, 0.9% walk, 2.8% work from home (2000); Travel time to work: 27.2% less than 15 minutes, 36.9% 15 to 30 minutes, 29.1% 30 to 45 minutes, 4.0% 45 to 60 minutes, 2.9% 60 minutes or more (2000)

SULLIVAN (city). County seat. Covers a land area of 2.039 square miles and a water area of 0.004 square miles. Located at 39.59° N. Lat.; 88.61° W. Long. Elevation is 673 feet.
History: Incorporated 1869.
Population: 4,410 (1990); 4,326 (2000); 4,332 (2007); 4,337 (2012 projected); Race: 98.5% White, 0.6% Black, 0.2% Asian, 0.6% Hispanic of any race (2007); Density: 2,124.4 persons per square mile (2007); Average household size: 2.32 (2007); Median age: 41.0 (2007); Males per 100 females: 86.6 (2007); Marriage status: 17.3% never married, 57.9% now married, 13.3% widowed, 11.5% divorced (2000); Foreign born: 0.5% (2000); Ancestry (includes multiple ancestries): 23.9% United States or American, 18.5% German, 10.8% Irish, 7.9% English, 4.7% Other groups (2000).
Economy: Single-family building permits issued: 12 (2007); Multi-family building permits issued: 0 (2007); Employment by occupation: 9.1% management, 16.6% professional, 18.0% services, 20.1% sales, 0.4% farming, 7.9% construction, 28.0% production (2000).
Income: Per capita income: $21,183 (2007); Median household income: $37,938 (2007); Average household income: $46,884 (2007); Percent of households with income of $100,000 or more: 7.2% (2007); Poverty rate: 8.8% (2000).
Education: Percent of population age 25 and over with: High school diploma (including GED) or higher: 78.6% (2007); Bachelor's degree or higher: 16.6% (2007); Master's degree or higher: 5.2% (2007).

School District(s)

Eastern Ill Area of Spec Educ (PK-12)
2005-06 Enrollment: 577 . . . . (217) 348-7700
Sullivan CUSD 300 (PK-12)
2005-06 Enrollment: 1,148 . . . . (217) 728-8341
Housing: Homeownership rate: 72.2% (2007); Median home value: $102,213 (2007); Median rent: $355 per month (2000); Median age of housing: 42 years (2000).
Safety: Violent crime rate: 16.2 per 10,000 population; Property crime rate: 108.7 per 10,000 population (2006).
Newspapers: News-Progress (Regional news; Circulation 3,800)
Transportation: Commute to work: 95.2% car, 0.2% public transportation, 2.7% walk, 1.3% work from home (2000); Travel time to work: 53.0% less than 15 minutes, 20.5% 15 to 30 minutes, 16.1% 30 to 45 minutes, 5.5% 45 to 60 minutes, 4.8% 60 minutes or more (2000)
Additional Information Contacts
Sullivan Chamber of Commerce . . . . (217) 728-4223
http://www.sullivanchamber.com

Ogle County

Located in northern Illinois; drained by the Rock, Leaf, and Kyte Rivers. Covers a land area of 758.83 square miles, a water area of 4.43 square miles, and is located in the Central Time Zone. The county was founded in 1836. County seat is Oregon.

Ogle County is part of the Rochelle, IL Micropolitan Statistical Area. The entire metro area includes: Ogle County, IL

Population: 45,957 (1990); 51,032 (2000); 55,275 (2007); 58,138 (2012 projected); Race: 93.7% White, 0.8% Black, 0.5% Asian, 8.0% Hispanic of any race (2007); Density: 72.8 persons per square mile (2007); Average household size: 2.63 (2007); Median age: 38.8 (2007); Males per 100 females: 97.4 (2007).
Religion: Five largest groups: 16.4% Catholic Church, 7.8% Evangelical Lutheran Church in America, 7.5% The United Methodist Church, 3.2% Presbyterian Church (U.S.A.), 2.6% Lutheran Church—Missouri Synod (2000).
Economy: Unemployment rate: 7.0% (4/2008); Total civilian labor force: 28,151 (4/2008); Leading industries: 32.0% manufacturing; 10.9% retail trade; 9.3% health care and social assistance (2005); Farms: 1,129 totaling 372,285 acres (2002); Companies that employ 500 or more persons: 6 (2006); Companies that employ 100 to 499 persons: 20 (2006); Companies that employ less than 100 persons: 1,079 (2006); Black-owned businesses: n/a (2002); Hispanic-owned businesses: n/a (2002); Asian-owned businesses: n/a (2002); Women-owned businesses: 952 (2002); Retail sales per capita: $8,932 (2008). Single-family building permits issued: 198 (2007); Multi-family building permits issued: 17 (2007).
Income: Per capita income: $24,042 (2007); Median household income: $51,788 (2007); Average household income: $62,804 (2007); Percent of households with income of $100,000 or more: 15.5% (2007); Poverty rate: 8.4% (2005); Bankruptcy rate: 2.91% (2007).
Taxes: Total county taxes per capita: $161 (2006); County property taxes per capita: $155 (2006).
Education: Percent of population age 25 and over with: High school diploma (including GED) or higher: 83.1% (2007); Bachelor's degree or higher: 17.0% (2007); Master's degree or higher: 5.8% (2007).

Housing: Homeownership rate: 74.9% (2007); Median home value: $157,126 (2007); Median rent: $401 per month (2000); Median age of housing: 39 years (2000).
Health: Birth rate: 120.9 per 10,000 population (2007); Death rate: 88.2 per 10,000 population (2007); Age-adjusted cancer mortality rate: 184.4 deaths per 100,000 population (2005); Number of physicians: 7.8 per 10,000 population (2005); Hospital beds: 10.1 per 10,000 population (2004); Hospital admissions: 164.1 per 10,000 population (2004).
Elections: 2004 Presidential election results: 61.9% Bush, 37.4% Kerry, 0.1% Nader, 0.5% Badnarik
National and State Parks: Lowden State Park; White Pines Forest State Park
Additional Information Contacts
Ogle County Government .... (815) 732-3201
http://www.oglecounty.org
Byron Area Chamber of Commerce.................. (815) 234-5500
http://www.byronchamber.org
City of Byron .... (815) 234-2762
http://byron.govoffice.com
City of Rochelle .... (815) 562-6161
http://www.cityofrochelle.net
Mt Morris Chamber of Commerce .... (815) 734-7423
Oregon Area Chamber of Commerce .... (815) 732-2100
http://www.oregonil.com
Polo Chamber of Commerce .... (815) 946-3131
http://www.poloil.net
Rochelle Area Chamber of Commerce .... (815) 562-4189
http://www.rochellechamber.org

Ogle County Communities

ADELINE (village). Covers a land area of 0.269 square miles and a water area of 0 square miles. Located at 42.14° N. Lat.; 89.49° W. Long. Elevation is 797 feet.
Population: 156 (1990); 139 (2000); 168 (2007); 186 (2012 projected); Race: 97.0% White, 0.0% Black, 0.0% Asian, 3.0% Hispanic of any race (2007); Density: 625.0 persons per square mile (2007); Average household size: 2.75 (2007); Median age: 42.2 (2007); Males per 100 females: 86.7 (2007); Marriage status: 21.4% never married, 64.1% now married, 9.7% widowed, 4.9% divorced (2000); Foreign born: 0.0% (2000); Ancestry (includes multiple ancestries): 35.5% German, 12.1% Dutch, 7.1% Other groups, 6.4% English, 5.0% Scotch-Irish (2000).
Economy: Employment by occupation: 11.9% management, 3.4% professional, 5.1% services, 5.1% sales, 0.0% farming, 18.6% construction, 55.9% production (2000).
Income: Per capita income: $24,717 (2007); Median household income: $69,500 (2007); Average household income: $68,074 (2007); Percent of households with income of $100,000 or more: 19.7% (2007); Poverty rate: 2.8% (2000).
Education: Percent of population age 25 and over with: High school diploma (including GED) or higher: 82.2% (2007); Bachelor's degree or higher: 5.9% (2007); Master's degree or higher: 2.5% (2007).
Housing: Homeownership rate: 90.2% (2007); Median home value: $117,045 (2007); Median rent: $375 per month (2000); Median age of housing: 60+ years (2000).
Transportation: Commute to work: 96.6% car, 0.0% public transportation, 0.0% walk, 0.0% work from home (2000); Travel time to work: 11.9% less than 15 minutes, 45.8% 15 to 30 minutes, 27.1% 30 to 45 minutes, 0.0% 45 to 60 minutes, 15.3% 60 minutes or more (2000)

BAILEYVILLE (unincorporated postal area, zip code 61007). Covers a land area of 24.962 square miles and a water area of 0 square miles. Located at 42.19° N. Lat.; 89.59° W. Long. Elevation is 925 feet.
Population: 548 (2000); Race: 100.0% White, 0.0% Black, 0.0% Asian, 0.0% Hispanic of any race (2000); Density: 22.0 persons per square mile (2000); Age: 22.0% under 18, 13.1% over 64 (2000); Marriage status: 12.9% never married, 79.6% now married, 2.4% widowed, 5.2% divorced (2000); Foreign born: 0.0% (2000); Ancestry (includes multiple ancestries): 52.1% German, 10.7% United States or American, 7.5% Irish, 6.3% Polish, 5.9% Norwegian (2000).
Economy: Employment by occupation: 15.5% management, 12.6% professional, 9.1% services, 14.2% sales, 4.5% farming, 14.9% construction, 29.1% production (2000).
Income: Per capita income: $17,301 (2000); Median household income: $49,375 (2000); Poverty rate: 3.7% (2000).
Education: Percent of population age 25 and over with: High school diploma (including GED) or higher: 79.6% (2000); Bachelor's degree or higher: 11.9% (2000).
Housing: Homeownership rate: 84.7% (2000); Median home value: $96,300 (2000); Median rent: $419 per month (2000); Median age of housing: 60+ years (2000).
Transportation: Commute to work: 84.0% car, 0.0% public transportation, 0.0% walk, 16.0% work from home (2000); Travel time to work: 50.0% less than 15 minutes, 33.5% 15 to 30 minutes, 7.0% 30 to 45 minutes, 1.7% 45 to 60 minutes, 7.9% 60 minutes or more (2000)

BYRON (city). Covers a land area of 2.474 square miles and a water area of <.001 square miles. Located at 42.12° N. Lat.; 89.26° W. Long. Elevation is 728 feet.
History: Byron was founded in 1835 by settlers from New England, and named for the English poet Lord Byron. Many houses in Byron were stations on the Underground Railroad, offering escape for slaves from the south.
Population: 2,381 (1990); 2,917 (2000); 3,523 (2007); 3,899 (2012 projected); Race: 97.0% White, 0.8% Black, 0.3% Asian, 2.1% Hispanic of any race (2007); Density: 1,424.2 persons per square mile (2007); Average household size: 2.61 (2007); Median age: 35.2 (2007); Males per 100 females: 88.9 (2007); Marriage status: 22.4% never married, 58.0% now married, 7.0% widowed, 12.6% divorced (2000); Foreign born: 2.0% (2000); Ancestry (includes multiple ancestries): 29.8% German, 18.7% Irish, 10.0% English, 6.7% Other groups, 6.2% Italian (2000).
Economy: Single-family building permits issued: 16 (2007); Multi-family building permits issued: 17 (2007); Employment by occupation: 10.0% management, 17.8% professional, 17.8% services, 24.3% sales, 0.2% farming, 11.4% construction, 18.4% production (2000).
Income: Per capita income: $20,663 (2007); Median household income: $42,917 (2007); Average household income: $53,144 (2007); Percent of households with income of $100,000 or more: 10.6% (2007); Poverty rate: 7.8% (2000).
Education: Percent of population age 25 and over with: High school diploma (including GED) or higher: 86.7% (2007); Bachelor's degree or higher: 13.2% (2007); Master's degree or higher: 3.5% (2007).

School District(s)

Byron CUSD 226 (PK-12)
2005-06 Enrollment: 1,793 .... (815) 234-5491
Housing: Homeownership rate: 61.8% (2007); Median home value: $151,983 (2007); Median rent: $461 per month (2000); Median age of housing: 28 years (2000).
Safety: Violent crime rate: 5.3 per 10,000 population; Property crime rate: 222.3 per 10,000 population (2006).
Transportation: Commute to work: 92.6% car, 0.3% public transportation, 2.8% walk, 3.8% work from home (2000); Travel time to work: 30.3% less than 15 minutes, 40.5% 15 to 30 minutes, 21.9% 30 to 45 minutes, 3.0% 45 to 60 minutes, 4.3% 60 minutes or more (2000)
Additional Information Contacts
Byron Area Chamber of Commerce.................. (815) 234-5500
http://www.byronchamber.org
City of Byron .... (815) 234-2762
http://byron.govoffice.com

CHANA (unincorporated postal area, zip code 61015). Covers a land area of 40.799 square miles and a water area of 0.057 square miles. Located at 41.98° N. Lat.; 89.21° W. Long. Elevation is 781 feet.
Population: 993 (2000); Race: 99.0% White, 0.3% Black, 0.0% Asian, 1.8% Hispanic of any race (2000); Density: 24.3 persons per square mile (2000); Age: 21.5% under 18, 11.2% over 64 (2000); Marriage status: 21.4% never married, 66.5% now married, 5.5% widowed, 6.6% divorced (2000); Foreign born: 0.2% (2000); Ancestry (includes multiple ancestries): 39.5% German, 12.1% English, 7.6% Irish, 5.6% Polish, 5.1% Norwegian (2000).
Economy: Employment by occupation: 12.4% management, 7.4% professional, 12.7% services, 23.3% sales, 0.0% farming, 20.5% construction, 23.7% production (2000).
Income: Per capita income: $20,508 (2000); Median household income: $49,000 (2000); Poverty rate: 0.7% (2000).
Education: Percent of population age 25 and over with: High school diploma (including GED) or higher: 86.7% (2000); Bachelor's degree or higher: 15.9% (2000).

School District(s)

Lee/Ogle Roe (07-12)
2005-06 Enrollment: 38 . . . . (815) 652-2054
Ogle Co Education Cooperative
2005-06 Enrollment: n/a . . . . (815) 234-2722

Housing: Homeownership rate: 80.3% (2000); Median home value: $114,400 (2000); Median rent: $342 per month (2000); Median age of housing: 47 years (2000).

Transportation: Commute to work: 97.8% car, 0.0% public transportation, 1.8% walk, 0.4% work from home (2000); Travel time to work: 8.5% less than 15 minutes, 40.0% 15 to 30 minutes, 28.9% 30 to 45 minutes, 11.4% 45 to 60 minutes, 11.2% 60 minutes or more (2000)

CRESTON (village). Covers a land area of 0.418 square miles and a water area of 0 square miles. Located at 41.93° N. Lat.; 88.96° W. Long. Elevation is 906 feet.

Population: 581 (1990); 543 (2000); 574 (2007); 595 (2012 projected); Race: 93.4% White, 1.9% Black, 0.5% Asian, 8.5% Hispanic of any race (2007); Density: 1,373.5 persons per square mile (2007); Average household size: 2.83 (2007); Median age: 35.0 (2007); Males per 100 females: 93.3 (2007); Marriage status: 22.4% never married, 58.4% now married, 9.3% widowed, 9.8% divorced (2000); Foreign born: 0.4% (2000); Ancestry (includes multiple ancestries): 26.2% German, 12.0% English, 10.7% United States or American, 9.6% Irish, 7.2% Norwegian (2000).

Economy: Single-family building permits issued: 12 (2007); Multi-family building permits issued: 0 (2007); Employment by occupation: 8.2% management, 15.7% professional, 9.3% services, 23.6% sales, 2.1% farming, 9.6% construction, 31.4% production (2000).

Income: Per capita income: $19,107 (2007); Median household income: $43,393 (2007); Average household income: $54,027 (2007); Percent of households with income of $100,000 or more: 14.8% (2007); Poverty rate: 5.2% (2000).

Education: Percent of population age 25 and over with: High school diploma (including GED) or higher: 81.0% (2007); Bachelor's degree or higher: 14.3% (2007); Master's degree or higher: 1.1% (2007).

School District(s)

Creston CCSD 161 (KG-08)
2005-06 Enrollment: 107 . . . . (815) 384-3920

Housing: Homeownership rate: 71.4% (2007); Median home value: $137,500 (2007); Median rent: $481 per month (2000); Median age of housing: 40 years (2000).

Transportation: Commute to work: 94.3% car, 0.0% public transportation, 3.9% walk, 1.8% work from home (2000); Travel time to work: 27.6% less than 15 minutes, 42.2% 15 to 30 minutes, 16.0% 30 to 45 minutes, 5.1% 45 to 60 minutes, 9.1% 60 minutes or more (2000)

DAVIS JUNCTION (village). Covers a land area of 3.790 square miles and a water area of 0 square miles. Located at 42.10° N. Lat.; 89.09° W. Long. Elevation is 791 feet.

Population: 356 (1990); 491 (2000); 657 (2007); 770 (2012 projected); Race: 98.0% White, 0.0% Black, 0.8% Asian, 0.6% Hispanic of any race (2007); Density: 173.4 persons per square mile (2007); Average household size: 2.93 (2007); Median age: 33.2 (2007); Males per 100 females: 104.0 (2007); Marriage status: 13.8% never married, 63.3% now married, 11.9% widowed, 11.0% divorced (2000); Foreign born: 2.4% (2000); Ancestry (includes multiple ancestries): 29.0% German, 13.4% United States or American, 12.7% Other groups, 12.1% Irish, 6.8% Swedish (2000).

Economy: Single-family building permits issued: 51 (2007); Multi-family building permits issued: 0 (2007); Employment by occupation: 9.6% management, 11.8% professional, 8.0% services, 35.8% sales, 0.0% farming, 11.8% construction, 23.0% production (2000).

Income: Per capita income: $18,950 (2007); Median household income: $54,474 (2007); Average household income: $55,580 (2007); Percent of households with income of $100,000 or more: 9.4% (2007); Poverty rate: 2.6% (2000).

Education: Percent of population age 25 and over with: High school diploma (including GED) or higher: 81.8% (2007); Bachelor's degree or higher: 9.6% (2007); Master's degree or higher: 3.3% (2007).

Housing: Homeownership rate: 87.9% (2007); Median home value: $169,415 (2007); Median rent: $838 per month (2000); Median age of housing: 7 years (2000).

Transportation: Commute to work: 97.3% car, 0.0% public transportation, 0.5% walk, 2.2% work from home (2000); Travel time to work: 8.2% less than 15 minutes, 61.5% 15 to 30 minutes, 20.9% 30 to 45 minutes, 6.0% 45 to 60 minutes, 3.3% 60 minutes or more (2000)

FORRESTON (village). Covers a land area of 0.831 square miles and a water area of 0 square miles. Located at 42.12° N. Lat.; 89.58° W. Long. Elevation is 938 feet.

History: The first sauerkraut festival was held in Forreston in 1913.

Population: 1,372 (1990); 1,469 (2000); 1,580 (2007); 1,651 (2012 projected); Race: 99.2% White, 0.0% Black, 0.4% Asian, 1.5% Hispanic of any race (2007); Density: 1,900.9 persons per square mile (2007); Average household size: 2.45 (2007); Median age: 38.0 (2007); Males per 100 females: 91.1 (2007); Marriage status: 17.8% never married, 62.7% now married, 10.8% widowed, 8.7% divorced (2000); Foreign born: 1.4% (2000); Ancestry (includes multiple ancestries): 46.3% German, 12.9% Irish, 8.6% English, 7.6% United States or American, 3.7% Other groups (2000).

Economy: Single-family building permits issued: 2 (2007); Multi-family building permits issued: 0 (2007); Employment by occupation: 8.6% management, 13.8% professional, 12.4% services, 22.5% sales, 1.5% farming, 8.8% construction, 32.4% production (2000).

Income: Per capita income: $19,563 (2007); Median household income: $41,889 (2007); Average household income: $47,848 (2007); Percent of households with income of $100,000 or more: 6.5% (2007); Poverty rate: 9.6% (2000).

Education: Percent of population age 25 and over with: High school diploma (including GED) or higher: 81.2% (2007); Bachelor's degree or higher: 16.0% (2007); Master's degree or higher: 5.7% (2007).

School District(s)

Forrestville Valley CUSD 221 (PK-12)
2005-06 Enrollment: 1,039 . . . . (815) 938-2036

Housing: Homeownership rate: 76.9% (2007); Median home value: $118,079 (2007); Median rent: $312 per month (2000); Median age of housing: 47 years (2000).

Newspapers: Forreston Journal (Community news; Circulation 800)

Transportation: Commute to work: 88.2% car, 0.0% public transportation, 7.5% walk, 3.2% work from home (2000); Travel time to work: 32.9% less than 15 minutes, 45.6% 15 to 30 minutes, 11.1% 30 to 45 minutes, 5.9% 45 to 60 minutes, 4.5% 60 minutes or more (2000)

HILLCREST (village). Covers a land area of 0.557 square miles and a water area of 0 square miles. Located at 41.95° N. Lat.; 89.06° W. Long. Elevation is 830 feet.

Population: 843 (1990); 1,158 (2000); 1,220 (2007); 1,262 (2012 projected); Race: 82.6% White, 0.6% Black, 0.3% Asian, 28.4% Hispanic of any race (2007); Density: 2,192.2 persons per square mile (2007); Average household size: 3.47 (2007); Median age: 31.2 (2007); Males per 100 females: 104.7 (2007); Marriage status: 23.4% never married, 66.5% now married, 3.4% widowed, 6.6% divorced (2000); Foreign born: 9.4% (2000); Ancestry (includes multiple ancestries): 27.4% Other groups, 23.8% German, 12.1% Irish, 8.4% United States or American, 5.6% English (2000).

Economy: Single-family building permits issued: 1 (2007); Multi-family building permits issued: 0 (2007); Employment by occupation: 7.8% management, 8.9% professional, 16.1% services, 21.5% sales, 1.1% farming, 8.7% construction, 36.0% production (2000).

Income: Per capita income: $17,482 (2007); Median household income: $54,706 (2007); Average household income: $60,589 (2007); Percent of households with income of $100,000 or more: 11.6% (2007); Poverty rate: 6.1% (2000).

Education: Percent of population age 25 and over with: High school diploma (including GED) or higher: 71.8% (2007); Bachelor's degree or higher: 7.6% (2007); Master's degree or higher: 2.3% (2007).

Housing: Homeownership rate: 88.9% (2007); Median home value: $141,454 (2007); Median rent: $493 per month (2000); Median age of housing: 25 years (2000).

Transportation: Commute to work: 95.8% car, 0.4% public transportation, 0.6% walk, 2.4% work from home (2000); Travel time to work: 48.1% less than 15 minutes, 21.5% 15 to 30 minutes, 17.7% 30 to 45 minutes, 4.9% 45 to 60 minutes, 7.7% 60 minutes or more (2000)

LEAF RIVER (village). Covers a land area of 0.857 square miles and a water area of 0 square miles. Located at 42.12° N. Lat.; 89.40° W. Long. Elevation is 725 feet.

Population: 546 (1990); 555 (2000); 485 (2007); 491 (2012 projected); Race: 95.9% White, 4.1% Black, 0.0% Asian, 0.8% Hispanic of any race (2007); Density: 565.9 persons per square mile (2007); Average household size: 2.59 (2007); Median age: 36.6 (2007); Males per 100 females: 90.2

(2007); Marriage status: 20.1% never married, 61.6% now married, 5.9% widowed, 12.4% divorced (2000); Foreign born: 0.5% (2000); Ancestry (includes multiple ancestries): 36.8% German, 12.9% English, 11.6% Irish, 7.0% United States or American, 5.9% Swedish (2000).
Economy: Single-family building permits issued: 0 (2007); Multi-family building permits issued: 0 (2007); Employment by occupation: 2.0% management, 11.4% professional, 11.8% services, 31.7% sales, 0.4% farming, 8.9% construction, 33.7% production (2000).
Income: Per capita income: $16,742 (2007); Median household income: $39,265 (2007); Average household income: $43,422 (2007); Percent of households with income of $100,000 or more: 3.7% (2007); Poverty rate: 5.7% (2000).
Taxes: Total city taxes per capita: $92 (2006); City property taxes per capita: $27 (2006).
Education: Percent of population age 25 and over with: High school diploma (including GED) or higher: 81.6% (2007); Bachelor's degree or higher: 7.2% (2007); Master's degree or higher: 2.7% (2007).
Housing: Homeownership rate: 70.1% (2007); Median home value: $112,500 (2007); Median rent: $353 per month (2000); Median age of housing: 60+ years (2000).
Transportation: Commute to work: 93.3% car, 0.0% public transportation, 2.9% walk, 2.5% work from home (2000); Travel time to work: 33.3% less than 15 minutes, 28.6% 15 to 30 minutes, 19.2% 30 to 45 minutes, 12.8% 45 to 60 minutes, 6.0% 60 minutes or more (2000)

LINDENWOOD (unincorporated postal area, zip code 61049). Covers a land area of 17.773 square miles and a water area of 0 square miles. Located at 42.05° N. Lat.; 89.02° W. Long. Elevation is 771 feet.
Population: 505 (2000); Race: 96.6% White, 0.4% Black, 0.2% Asian, 1.9% Hispanic of any race (2000); Density: 28.4 persons per square mile (2000); Age: 24.5% under 18, 14.8% over 64 (2000); Marriage status: 21.0% never married, 65.3% now married, 4.0% widowed, 9.7% divorced (2000); Foreign born: 1.9% (2000); Ancestry (includes multiple ancestries): 40.1% German, 11.0% Norwegian, 10.5% Irish, 10.3% English, 8.6% United States or American (2000).
Economy: Employment by occupation: 9.4% management, 13.5% professional, 8.8% services, 31.6% sales, 3.0% farming, 12.1% construction, 21.5% production (2000).
Income: Per capita income: $22,639 (2000); Median household income: $47,625 (2000); Poverty rate: 3.6% (2000).
Education: Percent of population age 25 and over with: High school diploma (including GED) or higher: 88.1% (2000); Bachelor's degree or higher: 14.6% (2000).

School District(s)

Eswood CCSD 269 (KG-08)
2005-06 Enrollment: 106 . . . . (815) 393-4477
Housing: Homeownership rate: 79.7% (2000); Median home value: $108,200 (2000); Median rent: $439 per month (2000); Median age of housing: 60+ years (2000).
Transportation: Commute to work: 84.2% car, 4.1% public transportation, 3.8% walk, 7.2% work from home (2000); Travel time to work: 18.1% less than 15 minutes, 37.0% 15 to 30 minutes, 28.9% 30 to 45 minutes, 5.9% 45 to 60 minutes, 10.0% 60 minutes or more (2000)

MONROE CENTER (unincorporated postal area, zip code 61052). Covers a land area of 26.156 square miles and a water area of 0 square miles. Located at 42.11° N. Lat.; 89.00° W. Long. Elevation is 853 feet.
Population: 1,238 (2000); Race: 98.9% White, 0.0% Black, 0.0% Asian, 3.0% Hispanic of any race (2000); Density: 47.3 persons per square mile (2000); Age: 30.8% under 18, 6.9% over 64 (2000); Marriage status: 25.1% never married, 61.6% now married, 4.0% widowed, 9.3% divorced (2000); Foreign born: 1.5% (2000); Ancestry (includes multiple ancestries): 37.1% German, 12.3% English, 10.2% Irish, 8.0% Norwegian, 7.1% Swedish (2000).
Economy: Employment by occupation: 7.8% management, 17.4% professional, 9.5% services, 34.6% sales, 2.4% farming, 12.3% construction, 16.1% production (2000).
Income: Per capita income: $23,232 (2000); Median household income: $59,309 (2000); Poverty rate: 3.9% (2000).
Education: Percent of population age 25 and over with: High school diploma (including GED) or higher: 90.3% (2000); Bachelor's degree or higher: 17.8% (2000).

School District(s)

Meridian CUSD 223 (PK-12)
2005-06 Enrollment: 1,895 . . . . (815) 645-2606
Housing: Homeownership rate: 82.5% (2000); Median home value: $127,900 (2000); Median rent: $475 per month (2000); Median age of housing: 35 years (2000).
Transportation: Commute to work: 95.2% car, 0.0% public transportation, 0.0% walk, 3.5% work from home (2000); Travel time to work: 12.6% less than 15 minutes, 58.9% 15 to 30 minutes, 17.6% 30 to 45 minutes, 1.1% 45 to 60 minutes, 9.8% 60 minutes or more (2000)

MOUNT MORRIS (village). Covers a land area of 1.166 square miles and a water area of 0 square miles. Located at 42.04° N. Lat.; 89.43° W. Long. Elevation is 909 feet.
History: Mount Morris was settled in 1838 by a group from Maryland. The railroad bypassed Mount Morris, but the town continued to grow. An early industry was the Kable Brothers printing company founded in 1898.
Population: 2,934 (1990); 3,013 (2000); 3,043 (2007); 3,083 (2012 projected); Race: 96.1% White, 0.2% Black, 0.6% Asian, 4.1% Hispanic of any race (2007); Density: 2,610.8 persons per square mile (2007); Average household size: 2.34 (2007); Median age: 40.6 (2007); Males per 100 females: 91.3 (2007); Marriage status: 21.3% never married, 56.7% now married, 10.3% widowed, 11.7% divorced (2000); Foreign born: 1.9% (2000); Ancestry (includes multiple ancestries): 32.2% German, 15.3% Irish, 11.6% English, 11.3% United States or American, 6.9% Other groups (2000).
Economy: Single-family building permits issued: 6 (2007); Multi-family building permits issued: 0 (2007); Employment by occupation: 6.0% management, 16.9% professional, 12.3% services, 26.7% sales, 0.0% farming, 10.6% construction, 27.5% production (2000).
Income: Per capita income: $24,666 (2007); Median household income: $46,753 (2007); Average household income: $56,150 (2007); Percent of households with income of $100,000 or more: 10.9% (2007); Poverty rate: 6.9% (2000).
Education: Percent of population age 25 and over with: High school diploma (including GED) or higher: 85.8% (2007); Bachelor's degree or higher: 17.4% (2007); Master's degree or higher: 6.0% (2007).

School District(s)

Oregon CUSD 220 (PK-12)
2005-06 Enrollment: 1,814 . . . . (815) 732-2186
Housing: Homeownership rate: 68.6% (2007); Median home value: $123,837 (2007); Median rent: $318 per month (2000); Median age of housing: 49 years (2000).
Safety: Violent crime rate: 13.0 per 10,000 population; Property crime rate: 208.7 per 10,000 population (2006).
Transportation: Commute to work: 92.1% car, 0.8% public transportation, 6.4% walk, 0.4% work from home (2000); Travel time to work: 54.2% less than 15 minutes, 24.1% 15 to 30 minutes, 9.8% 30 to 45 minutes, 6.3% 45 to 60 minutes, 5.5% 60 minutes or more (2000)

Additional Information Contacts

Mt Morris Chamber of Commerce . . . . (815) 734-7423

OREGON (city). County seat. Covers a land area of 2.031 square miles and a water area of 0.079 square miles. Located at 42.01° N. Lat.; 89.33° W. Long. Elevation is 709 feet.
History: Oregon developed as a trading center and industrial town, and as the seat of Ogle County. It was also known as an artistic community, with the Eagle's Nest Art Colony established nearby in 1898.
Population: 4,110 (1990); 4,060 (2000); 4,135 (2007); 4,202 (2012 projected); Race: 94.1% White, 2.2% Black, 0.6% Asian, 3.2% Hispanic of any race (2007); Density: 2,035.4 persons per square mile (2007); Average household size: 2.40 (2007); Median age: 40.0 (2007); Males per 100 females: 92.7 (2007); Marriage status: 25.4% never married, 55.6% now married, 8.8% widowed, 10.2% divorced (2000); Foreign born: 4.2% (2000); Ancestry (includes multiple ancestries): 32.1% German, 14.2% Irish, 12.4% English, 8.2% United States or American, 7.8% Other groups (2000).
Economy: Single-family building permits issued: 3 (2007); Multi-family building permits issued: 0 (2007); Employment by occupation: 10.1% management, 21.0% professional, 20.8% services, 21.6% sales, 0.4% farming, 6.3% construction, 19.7% production (2000).
Income: Per capita income: $21,343 (2007); Median household income: $37,981 (2007); Average household income: $50,025 (2007); Percent of households with income of $100,000 or more: 12.1% (2007); Poverty rate: 15.9% (2000).
Education: Percent of population age 25 and over with: High school diploma (including GED) or higher: 79.2% (2007); Bachelor's degree or higher: 16.8% (2007); Master's degree or higher: 9.0% (2007).

School District(s)

Oregon CUSD 220 (PK-12)
2005-06 Enrollment: 1,814 . . . . (815) 732-2186

Housing: Homeownership rate: 65.2% (2007); Median home value: $135,033 (2007); Median rent: $381 per month (2000); Median age of housing: 49 years (2000).

Safety: Violent crime rate: 21.6 per 10,000 population; Property crime rate: 345.9 per 10,000 population (2006).

Newspapers: Mount Morris Times (Community news; Circulation 2,000); Ogle County Life (Community news; Circulation 12,000); Ogle County News (Community news; Circulation 1,000); Oregon Republican Reporter (Community news; Circulation 1,000); Tri-County Press (Community news; Circulation 17,000)

Transportation: Commute to work: 88.2% car, 0.0% public transportation, 7.7% walk, 3.7% work from home (2000); Travel time to work: 53.8% less than 15 minutes, 21.8% 15 to 30 minutes, 11.4% 30 to 45 minutes, 6.8% 45 to 60 minutes, 6.2% 60 minutes or more (2000)

Additional Information Contacts

Oregon Area Chamber of Commerce . . . . (815) 732-2100
http://www.oregonil.com

POLO (city). Covers a land area of 1.313 square miles and a water area of 0 square miles. Located at 41.98° N. Lat.; 89.57° W. Long. Elevation is 863 feet.

History: The city of Polo was named for Venetian traveler Marco Polo, and developed as a trading center for a stock raising area.

Population: 2,531 (1990); 2,477 (2000); 2,736 (2007); 2,872 (2012 projected); Race: 98.2% White, 0.1% Black, 0.4% Asian, 2.0% Hispanic of any race (2007); Density: 2,083.4 persons per square mile (2007); Average household size: 2.42 (2007); Median age: 41.7 (2007); Males per 100 females: 92.8 (2007); Marriage status: 21.2% never married, 55.9% now married, 9.8% widowed, 13.1% divorced (2000); Foreign born: 0.8% (2000); Ancestry (includes multiple ancestries): 40.9% German, 18.2% Irish, 12.4% English, 6.5% Other groups, 5.0% Dutch (2000).

Economy: Single-family building permits issued: 4 (2007); Multi-family building permits issued: 0 (2007); Employment by occupation: 9.8% management, 19.2% professional, 11.0% services, 23.8% sales, 0.7% farming, 10.4% construction, 25.1% production (2000).

Income: Per capita income: $21,683 (2007); Median household income: $43,789 (2007); Average household income: $51,256 (2007); Percent of households with income of $100,000 or more: 9.5% (2007); Poverty rate: 9.2% (2000).

Education: Percent of population age 25 and over with: High school diploma (including GED) or higher: 82.6% (2007); Bachelor's degree or higher: 12.8% (2007); Master's degree or higher: 5.0% (2007).

School District(s)

Polo CUSD 222 (PK-12)
2005-06 Enrollment: 765 . . . . (815) 946-3815

Housing: Homeownership rate: 71.7% (2007); Median home value: $119,508 (2007); Median rent: $331 per month (2000); Median age of housing: 56 years (2000).

Safety: Violent crime rate: 0.0 per 10,000 population; Property crime rate: 119.7 per 10,000 population (2006).

Transportation: Commute to work: 92.1% car, 1.0% public transportation, 4.9% walk, 1.6% work from home (2000); Travel time to work: 33.4% less than 15 minutes, 41.5% 15 to 30 minutes, 12.7% 30 to 45 minutes, 5.9% 45 to 60 minutes, 6.6% 60 minutes or more (2000)

Additional Information Contacts

Polo Chamber of Commerce . . . . (815) 946-3131
http://www.poloil.net

ROCHELLE (city). Covers a land area of 7.474 square miles and a water area of 0.023 square miles. Located at 41.92° N. Lat.; 89.06° W. Long. Elevation is 823 feet.

History: Rochelle developed as an agricultural center and the home of the Del Monte cannery. Charles Butterfield, composer of "When You and I Were Young, Maggie," and Francis Rose, who wrote "Just Before the Battle, Mother," both lived in Rochelle.

Population: 8,944 (1990); 9,424 (2000); 10,035 (2007); 10,466 (2012 projected); Race: 82.8% White, 2.0% Black, 1.1% Asian, 25.1% Hispanic of any race (2007); Density: 1,342.6 persons per square mile (2007); Average household size: 2.54 (2007); Median age: 35.2 (2007); Males per 100 females: 96.5 (2007); Marriage status: 23.7% never married, 56.8% now married, 7.5% widowed, 12.0% divorced (2000); Foreign born: 13.1% (2000); Ancestry (includes multiple ancestries): 21.9% German, 20.7% Other groups, 10.6% Irish, 9.5% United States or American, 7.9% English (2000).

Economy: Single-family building permits issued: 15 (2007); Multi-family building permits issued: 0 (2007); Employment by occupation: 8.7% management, 14.1% professional, 17.1% services, 22.5% sales, 0.3% farming, 10.1% construction, 27.2% production (2000).

Income: Per capita income: $20,756 (2007); Median household income: $43,439 (2007); Average household income: $52,238 (2007); Percent of households with income of $100,000 or more: 9.7% (2007); Poverty rate: 10.4% (2000).

Education: Percent of population age 25 and over with: High school diploma (including GED) or higher: 73.3% (2007); Bachelor's degree or higher: 16.1% (2007); Master's degree or higher: 5.5% (2007).

School District(s)

Rochelle CCSD 231 (PK-08)
2005-06 Enrollment: 1,735 . . . . (815) 562-6363

Rochelle Twp HSD 212 (09-12)
2005-06 Enrollment: 1,151 . . . . (815) 562-4161

Housing: Homeownership rate: 57.8% (2007); Median home value: $146,462 (2007); Median rent: $403 per month (2000); Median age of housing: 38 years (2000).

Safety: Violent crime rate: 22.7 per 10,000 population; Property crime rate: 300.7 per 10,000 population (2006).

Newspapers: Rochelle News Leader (Local news; Circulation 5,500)

Transportation: Commute to work: 90.0% car, 0.5% public transportation, 5.0% walk, 2.2% work from home (2000); Travel time to work: 59.8% less than 15 minutes, 13.4% 15 to 30 minutes, 16.5% 30 to 45 minutes, 5.3% 45 to 60 minutes, 5.0% 60 minutes or more (2000)

Airports: Rochelle Municipal Airport-Koritz Field (general aviation)

Additional Information Contacts

City of Rochelle . . . . (815) 562-6161
http://www.cityofrochelle.net

Rochelle Area Chamber of Commerce . . . . (815) 562-4189
http://www.rochellechamber.org

STILLMAN VALLEY (village). Covers a land area of 0.548 square miles and a water area of 0 square miles. Located at 42.10° N. Lat.; 89.18° W. Long. Elevation is 712 feet.

History: The Battle of Stillman's Run took place here in 1832, where a monument was placed to mark the dead.

Population: 874 (1990); 1,048 (2000); 1,070 (2007); 1,078 (2012 projected); Race: 96.1% White, 0.5% Black, 0.3% Asian, 2.3% Hispanic of any race (2007); Density: 1,952.9 persons per square mile (2007); Average household size: 2.62 (2007); Median age: 37.0 (2007); Males per 100 females: 91.1 (2007); Marriage status: 22.9% never married, 63.3% now married, 3.6% widowed, 10.2% divorced (2000); Foreign born: 0.8% (2000); Ancestry (includes multiple ancestries): 45.4% German, 14.1% Swedish, 10.5% Irish, 9.1% English, 7.1% Other groups (2000).

Economy: Single-family building permits issued: 3 (2007); Multi-family building permits issued: 0 (2007); Employment by occupation: 12.2% management, 17.5% professional, 13.3% services, 18.6% sales, 0.4% farming, 9.8% construction, 28.2% production (2000).

Income: Per capita income: $24,853 (2007); Median household income: $51,875 (2007); Average household income: $65,178 (2007); Percent of households with income of $100,000 or more: 13.7% (2007); Poverty rate: 4.6% (2000).

Education: Percent of population age 25 and over with: High school diploma (including GED) or higher: 87.5% (2007); Bachelor's degree or higher: 17.2% (2007); Master's degree or higher: 6.0% (2007).

School District(s)

Meridian CUSD 223 (PK-12)
2005-06 Enrollment: 1,895 . . . . (815) 645-2606

Housing: Homeownership rate: 73.3% (2007); Median home value: $164,258 (2007); Median rent: $479 per month (2000); Median age of housing: 36 years (2000).

Transportation: Commute to work: 95.0% car, 0.0% public transportation, 2.6% walk, 2.4% work from home (2000); Travel time to work: 27.5% less than 15 minutes, 42.8% 15 to 30 minutes, 20.1% 30 to 45 minutes, 7.1% 45 to 60 minutes, 2.5% 60 minutes or more (2000)

Peoria County

Located in central Illinois; bounded on the east and south by the Illinois River and Lake Peorio; drained by the Spoon River and Kickapoo Creek. Covers a land area of 619.52 square miles, a water area of 11.36 square miles, and is located in the Central Time Zone. The county was founded in 1825. County seat is Peoria.

Peoria County is part of the Peoria, IL Metropolitan Statistical Area. The entire metro area includes: Marshall County, IL; Peoria County, IL; Stark County, IL; Tazewell County, IL; Woodford County, IL

Weather Station: Greater Peoria Airport Elevation: 649 feet

	Jan	Feb	Mar	Apr	May	Jun	Jul	Aug	Sep	Oct	Nov	Dec
High	30	36	49	62	73	82	86	83	77	64	49	36
Low	14	20	30	41	51	60	65	63	55	43	32	21
Precip	1.5	1.6	2.8	3.7	4.2	3.8	4.1	3.2	3.4	2.9	2.9	2.4
Snow	8.0	5.8	3.5	1.1	tr	0.0	tr	0.0	tr	tr	2.1	6.3

High and Low temperatures in degrees Fahrenheit; Precipitation and Snow in inches

Weather Station: Princeville Elevation: 734 feet

	Jan	Feb	Mar	Apr	May	Jun	Jul	Aug	Sep	Oct	Nov	Dec
High	30	36	49	62	73	81	85	83	76	65	49	36
Low	11	17	27	37	48	57	61	59	51	40	29	18
Precip	1.7	1.7	3.1	3.9	4.7	3.9	4.0	3.7	3.7	2.9	3.0	2.5
Snow	6.4	5.6	2.9	0.7	tr	0.0	0.0	0.0	0.0	0.1	2.1	5.5

High and Low temperatures in degrees Fahrenheit; Precipitation and Snow in inches

Population: 182,827 (1990); 183,433 (2000); 182,401 (2007); 181,472 (2012 projected); Race: 77.0% White, 16.9% Black, 2.3% Asian, 2.7% Hispanic of any race (2007); Density: 294.4 persons per square mile (2007); Average household size: 2.49 (2007); Median age: 36.2 (2007); Males per 100 females: 93.2 (2007).
Religion: Five largest groups: 19.3% Catholic Church, 5.4% The United Methodist Church, 3.5% Evangelical Lutheran Church in America, 3.1% Lutheran Church—Missouri Synod, 2.0% Southern Baptist Convention (2000).
Economy: Unemployment rate: 4.8% (4/2008); Total civilian labor force: 99,734 (4/2008); Leading industries: 19.5% health care and social assistance; 11.5% retail trade; 10.8% manufacturing (2005); Farms: 892 totaling 266,280 acres (2002); Companies that employ 500 or more persons: 19 (2006); Companies that employ 100 to 499 persons: 141 (2006); Companies that employ less than 100 persons: 4,707 (2006); Black-owned businesses: 591 (2002); Hispanic-owned businesses: 279 (2002); Asian-owned businesses: 431 (2002); Women-owned businesses: 3,797 (2002); Retail sales per capita: $15,197 (2008). Single-family building permits issued: 529 (2007); Multi-family building permits issued: 125 (2007).
Income: Per capita income: $25,069 (2007); Median household income: $46,446 (2007); Average household income: $61,182 (2007); Percent of households with income of $100,000 or more: 15.2% (2007); Poverty rate: 12.8% (2005); Bankruptcy rate: 4.57% (2007).
Taxes: Total county taxes per capita: $138 (2006); County property taxes per capita: $107 (2006).
Education: Percent of population age 25 and over with: High school diploma (including GED) or higher: 84.1% (2007); Bachelor's degree or higher: 23.9% (2007); Master's degree or higher: 8.4% (2007).
Housing: Homeownership rate: 68.3% (2007); Median home value: $112,860 (2007); Median rent: $400 per month (2000); Median age of housing: 41 years (2000).
Health: Birth rate: 146.9 per 10,000 population (2007); Death rate: 95.7 per 10,000 population (2007); Age-adjusted cancer mortality rate: 208.1 deaths per 100,000 population (2005); Air Quality Index: 63.8% good, 34.2% moderate, 1.9% unhealthy for sensitive individuals, 0.0% unhealthy (percent of days in 2007); Number of physicians: 47.7 per 10,000 population (2005); Hospital beds: 58.4 per 10,000 population (2004); Hospital admissions: 2,613.9 per 10,000 population (2004).
Elections: 2004 Presidential election results: 49.6% Bush, 49.7% Kerry, 0.1% Nader, 0.5% Badnarik
National and State Parks: Jubilee College State Park; Spring Branch State Conservation Area; Spring Lake State Park
Additional Information Contacts
Peoria County Government . . . . (309) 672-6059
http://www.peoriacounty.org
Bartonville-Limestone Chamber of Commerce . . . . (309) 697-1031
http://limestonechamber.com
Chillicothe Chamber of Commerce . . . . (309) 274-4556
http://www.chillicothechamber.com
City of Chillicothe . . . . (309) 274-5056
http://www.ci.chillicothe.il.us
City of Peoria . . . . (309) 494-2273
http://www.ci.peoria.il.us
Peoria Area Chamber of Commerce . . . . (309) 676-0755
http://www.peoriachamber.org
Peoria Heights Chamber of Commerce . . . . (309) 685-4812
http://www.peoriaheights.org

Peoria County Communities

BARTONVILLE (village). Covers a land area of 8.026 square miles and a water area of 0.424 square miles. Located at 40.64° N. Lat.; 89.66° W. Long. Elevation is 505 feet.
History: Bartonville developed as a coal mining community, with factories that manufactured steel wire and fence.
Population: 6,555 (1990); 6,310 (2000); 6,051 (2007); 5,857 (2012 projected); Race: 97.6% White, 0.3% Black, 0.5% Asian, 1.2% Hispanic of any race (2007); Density: 753.9 persons per square mile (2007); Average household size: 2.36 (2007); Median age: 39.9 (2007); Males per 100 females: 94.1 (2007); Marriage status: 20.8% never married, 60.5% now married, 5.8% widowed, 12.9% divorced (2000); Foreign born: 0.9% (2000); Ancestry (includes multiple ancestries): 31.2% German, 11.9% Irish, 11.5% English, 10.5% United States or American, 7.2% Other groups (2000).
Economy: Single-family building permits issued: 10 (2007); Multi-family building permits issued: 0 (2007); Employment by occupation: 9.4% management, 14.3% professional, 14.5% services, 31.6% sales, 0.4% farming, 11.2% construction, 18.6% production (2000).
Income: Per capita income: $24,503 (2007); Median household income: $47,917 (2007); Average household income: $57,895 (2007); Percent of households with income of $100,000 or more: 10.7% (2007); Poverty rate: 7.0% (2000).
Education: Percent of population age 25 and over with: High school diploma (including GED) or higher: 81.4% (2007); Bachelor's degree or higher: 10.1% (2007); Master's degree or higher: 2.3% (2007).

School District(s)

Bartonville SD 66 (PK-08)
2005-06 Enrollment: 337 . . . . (309) 697-3253
Limestone CHSD 310 (09-12)
2005-06 Enrollment: 1,112 . . . . (309) 697-6271
Monroe SD 70 (KG-08)
2005-06 Enrollment: 291 . . . . (309) 697-3120
Oak Grove SD 68 (KG-08)
2005-06 Enrollment: 472 . . . . (309) 697-3367
Housing: Homeownership rate: 80.4% (2007); Median home value: $96,803 (2007); Median rent: $396 per month (2000); Median age of housing: 46 years (2000).
Safety: Violent crime rate: 112.3 per 10,000 population; Property crime rate: 454.0 per 10,000 population (2006).
Newspapers: Limestone Independent News (Local news; Circulation 2,000)
Transportation: Commute to work: 95.0% car, 0.3% public transportation, 1.6% walk, 2.2% work from home (2000); Travel time to work: 29.8% less than 15 minutes, 55.0% 15 to 30 minutes, 9.2% 30 to 45 minutes, 2.9% 45 to 60 minutes, 3.1% 60 minutes or more (2000)
Additional Information Contacts
Bartonville-Limestone Chamber of Commerce . . . . (309) 697-1031
http://limestonechamber.com

BELLEVUE (village). Covers a land area of 1.678 square miles and a water area of 0 square miles. Located at 40.68° N. Lat.; 89.66° W. Long. Elevation is 676 feet.
History: Incorporated 1941.
Population: 1,675 (1990); 1,887 (2000); 1,741 (2007); 1,685 (2012 projected); Race: 93.7% White, 1.4% Black, 1.1% Asian, 2.2% Hispanic of any race (2007); Density: 1,037.3 persons per square mile (2007); Average household size: 2.47 (2007); Median age: 33.9 (2007); Males per 100 females: 96.1 (2007); Marriage status: 21.2% never married, 60.8% now married, 5.5% widowed, 12.5% divorced (2000); Foreign born: 0.2% (2000); Ancestry (includes multiple ancestries): 24.1% German, 15.1% United States or American, 11.4% Irish, 9.6% English, 9.0% Other groups (2000).
Economy: Single-family building permits issued: 0 (2007); Multi-family building permits issued: 0 (2007); Employment by occupation: 3.6% management, 11.8% professional, 20.9% services, 26.0% sales, 0.0% farming, 14.2% construction, 23.6% production (2000).
Income: Per capita income: $16,558 (2007); Median household income: $34,753 (2007); Average household income: $40,890 (2007); Percent of

households with income of $100,000 or more: 2.3% (2007); Poverty rate: 10.9% (2000).
Education: Percent of population age 25 and over with: High school diploma (including GED) or higher: 69.7% (2007); Bachelor's degree or higher: 6.1% (2007); Master's degree or higher: 1.4% (2007).
Housing: Homeownership rate: 78.7% (2007); Median home value: $69,868 (2007); Median rent: $386 per month (2000); Median age of housing: 35 years (2000).
Transportation: Commute to work: 97.9% car, 0.5% public transportation, 1.0% walk, 0.6% work from home (2000); Travel time to work: 32.5% less than 15 minutes, 54.1% 15 to 30 minutes, 7.9% 30 to 45 minutes, 1.4% 45 to 60 minutes, 4.0% 60 minutes or more (2000)

BRIMFIELD (village). Covers a land area of 0.753 square miles and a water area of 0.005 square miles. Located at 40.83° N. Lat.; 89.88° W. Long. Elevation is 702 feet.
Population: 811 (1990); 933 (2000); 862 (2007); 851 (2012 projected); Race: 97.7% White, 0.0% Black, 0.0% Asian, 1.0% Hispanic of any race (2007); Density: 1,144.4 persons per square mile (2007); Average household size: 2.49 (2007); Median age: 34.3 (2007); Males per 100 females: 100.0 (2007); Marriage status: 25.0% never married, 58.5% now married, 6.7% widowed, 9.8% divorced (2000); Foreign born: 0.1% (2000); Ancestry (includes multiple ancestries): 32.8% German, 18.4% English, 16.1% Irish, 9.1% United States or American, 6.6% Other groups (2000).
Economy: Single-family building permits issued: 2 (2007); Multi-family building permits issued: 0 (2007); Employment by occupation: 10.7% management, 17.9% professional, 19.4% services, 22.0% sales, 0.0% farming, 11.7% construction, 18.3% production (2000).
Income: Per capita income: $21,770 (2007); Median household income: $46,207 (2007); Average household income: $53,309 (2007); Percent of households with income of $100,000 or more: 9.8% (2007); Poverty rate: 8.5% (2000).
Education: Percent of population age 25 and over with: High school diploma (including GED) or higher: 87.5% (2007); Bachelor's degree or higher: 13.4% (2007); Master's degree or higher: 3.2% (2007).

School District(s)

Brimfield CUSD 309 (PK-12)
2005-06 Enrollment: 693 .... (309) 446-3378

Housing: Homeownership rate: 82.1% (2007); Median home value: $101,736 (2007); Median rent: $314 per month (2000); Median age of housing: 39 years (2000).
Transportation: Commute to work: 92.5% car, 0.4% public transportation, 2.4% walk, 3.0% work from home (2000); Travel time to work: 21.1% less than 15 minutes, 44.2% 15 to 30 minutes, 29.6% 30 to 45 minutes, 1.6% 45 to 60 minutes, 3.6% 60 minutes or more (2000)

CHILLICOTHE (city). Covers a land area of 4.940 square miles and a water area of 0.283 square miles. Located at 40.92° N. Lat.; 89.49° W. Long. Elevation is 499 feet.
History: Incorporated 1861.
Population: 6,054 (1990); 5,996 (2000); 5,732 (2007); 5,533 (2012 projected); Race: 97.1% White, 0.2% Black, 0.2% Asian, 3.6% Hispanic of any race (2007); Density: 1,160.3 persons per square mile (2007); Average household size: 2.41 (2007); Median age: 38.2 (2007); Males per 100 females: 90.7 (2007); Marriage status: 21.3% never married, 60.5% now married, 9.6% widowed, 8.5% divorced (2000); Foreign born: 1.2% (2000); Ancestry (includes multiple ancestries): 30.1% German, 17.9% Irish, 12.5% English, 7.8% United States or American, 7.4% Other groups (2000).
Economy: Single-family building permits issued: 29 (2007); Multi-family building permits issued: 0 (2007); Employment by occupation: 7.1% management, 19.7% professional, 16.8% services, 28.8% sales, 0.0% farming, 10.6% construction, 17.0% production (2000).
Income: Per capita income: $24,071 (2007); Median household income: $47,220 (2007); Average household income: $57,437 (2007); Percent of households with income of $100,000 or more: 12.6% (2007); Poverty rate: 6.2% (2000).
Education: Percent of population age 25 and over with: High school diploma (including GED) or higher: 86.6% (2007); Bachelor's degree or higher: 12.7% (2007); Master's degree or higher: 3.8% (2007).

School District(s)

Illinois Valley Central USD 321 (PK-12)
2005-06 Enrollment: 2,166 .... (309) 274-5418

Housing: Homeownership rate: 75.0% (2007); Median home value: $104,183 (2007); Median rent: $347 per month (2000); Median age of housing: 42 years (2000).
Safety: Violent crime rate: 34.6 per 10,000 population; Property crime rate: 226.6 per 10,000 population (2006).
Transportation: Commute to work: 94.5% car, 0.6% public transportation, 1.5% walk, 2.2% work from home (2000); Travel time to work: 39.5% less than 15 minutes, 31.4% 15 to 30 minutes, 24.3% 30 to 45 minutes, 3.2% 45 to 60 minutes, 1.7% 60 minutes or more (2000)

Additional Information Contacts

Chillicothe Chamber of Commerce .... (309) 274-4556
http://www.chillicothechamber.com
City of Chillicothe .... (309) 274-5056
http://www.ci.chillicothe.il.us

DUNLAP (village). Covers a land area of 0.373 square miles and a water area of 0 square miles. Located at 40.86° N. Lat.; 89.67° W. Long. Elevation is 735 feet.
Population: 985 (1990); 926 (2000); 907 (2007); 925 (2012 projected); Race: 97.1% White, 0.6% Black, 1.8% Asian, 2.0% Hispanic of any race (2007); Density: 2,431.4 persons per square mile (2007); Average household size: 2.69 (2007); Median age: 35.4 (2007); Males per 100 females: 99.3 (2007); Marriage status: 25.8% never married, 62.4% now married, 4.7% widowed, 7.1% divorced (2000); Foreign born: 4.5% (2000); Ancestry (includes multiple ancestries): 30.0% German, 12.4% Irish, 10.0% English, 8.1% Other groups, 7.1% United States or American (2000).
Economy: Employment by occupation: 12.7% management, 24.0% professional, 15.3% services, 28.2% sales, 0.0% farming, 7.9% construction, 12.0% production (2000).
Income: Per capita income: $27,624 (2007); Median household income: $66,768 (2007); Average household income: $74,347 (2007); Percent of households with income of $100,000 or more: 26.4% (2007); Poverty rate: 6.3% (2000).
Education: Percent of population age 25 and over with: High school diploma (including GED) or higher: 90.6% (2007); Bachelor's degree or higher: 32.7% (2007); Master's degree or higher: 8.3% (2007).

School District(s)

Dunlap CUSD 323 (PK-12)
2005-06 Enrollment: 2,798 .... (309) 243-7716

Housing: Homeownership rate: 78.0% (2007); Median home value: $149,013 (2007); Median rent: $396 per month (2000); Median age of housing: 30 years (2000).
Hospitals: Greenview Regional Hospital (211 beds)
Transportation: Commute to work: 96.0% car, 0.7% public transportation, 0.4% walk, 1.1% work from home (2000); Travel time to work: 28.9% less than 15 minutes, 50.4% 15 to 30 minutes, 15.9% 30 to 45 minutes, 1.3% 45 to 60 minutes, 3.4% 60 minutes or more (2000)

EDELSTEIN (unincorporated postal area, zip code 61526). Covers a land area of 33.664 square miles and a water area of 0.009 square miles. Located at 40.93° N. Lat.; 89.62° W. Long. Elevation is 814 feet.
Population: 1,173 (2000); Race: 97.9% White, 0.0% Black, 0.0% Asian, 0.0% Hispanic of any race (2000); Density: 34.8 persons per square mile (2000); Age: 28.2% under 18, 12.1% over 64 (2000); Marriage status: 14.6% never married, 77.3% now married, 4.1% widowed, 4.0% divorced (2000); Foreign born: 0.5% (2000); Ancestry (includes multiple ancestries): 41.3% German, 18.8% English, 12.6% Irish, 5.7% United States or American, 3.8% Swedish (2000).
Economy: Employment by occupation: 11.7% management, 20.8% professional, 9.2% services, 29.2% sales, 0.0% farming, 14.1% construction, 15.1% production (2000).
Income: Per capita income: $24,575 (2000); Median household income: $65,217 (2000); Poverty rate: 0.8% (2000).
Education: Percent of population age 25 and over with: High school diploma (including GED) or higher: 84.1% (2000); Bachelor's degree or higher: 17.0% (2000).
Housing: Homeownership rate: 96.1% (2000); Median home value: $123,600 (2000); Median rent: $275 per month (2000); Median age of housing: 28 years (2000).
Transportation: Commute to work: 94.8% car, 0.0% public transportation, 1.0% walk, 4.2% work from home (2000); Travel time to work: 24.7% less than 15 minutes, 46.6% 15 to 30 minutes, 19.8% 30 to 45 minutes, 5.2% 45 to 60 minutes, 3.7% 60 minutes or more (2000)

EDWARDS (unincorporated postal area, zip code 61528). Covers a land area of 17.631 square miles and a water area of 0 square miles. Located at 40.77° N. Lat.; 89.74° W. Long. Elevation is 525 feet.

Population: 1,608 (2000); Race: 97.8% White, 0.2% Black, 0.4% Asian, 1.3% Hispanic of any race (2000); Density: 91.2 persons per square mile (2000); Age: 25.7% under 18, 12.3% over 64 (2000); Marriage status: 21.0% never married, 67.6% now married, 5.2% widowed, 6.2% divorced (2000); Foreign born: 1.3% (2000); Ancestry (includes multiple ancestries): 35.3% German, 17.4% Irish, 17.1% English, 10.0% United States or American, 6.0% French (except Basque) (2000).
Economy: Employment by occupation: 16.6% management, 21.9% professional, 15.4% services, 23.2% sales, 0.0% farming, 8.4% construction, 14.5% production (2000).
Income: Per capita income: $28,248 (2000); Median household income: $63,867 (2000); Poverty rate: 3.6% (2000).
Education: Percent of population age 25 and over with: High school diploma (including GED) or higher: 85.8% (2000); Bachelor's degree or higher: 29.5% (2000).
Housing: Homeownership rate: 92.4% (2000); Median home value: $136,800 (2000); Median rent: $328 per month (2000); Median age of housing: 28 years (2000).
Transportation: Commute to work: 95.2% car, 0.0% public transportation, 0.9% walk, 3.9% work from home (2000); Travel time to work: 18.3% less than 15 minutes, 63.8% 15 to 30 minutes, 13.0% 30 to 45 minutes, 2.6% 45 to 60 minutes, 2.3% 60 minutes or more (2000)

ELMWOOD (city). Covers a land area of 1.233 square miles and a water area of 0 square miles. Located at 40.77° N. Lat.; 89.96° W. Long. Elevation is 643 feet.
History: Incorporated 1867. Lorado Taft born here; his statue PIONEERS OF THE PRAIRIESITAL (1928) IS IN CITY PARK.
Population: 1,892 (1990); 1,945 (2000); 1,915 (2007); 1,921 (2012 projected); Race: 98.4% White, 0.3% Black, 0.2% Asian, 1.1% Hispanic of any race (2007); Density: 1,552.8 persons per square mile (2007); Average household size: 2.45 (2007); Median age: 37.9 (2007); Males per 100 females: 90.5 (2007); Marriage status: 18.0% never married, 67.6% now married, 7.3% widowed, 7.1% divorced (2000); Foreign born: 1.0% (2000); Ancestry (includes multiple ancestries): 32.3% German, 21.1% English, 11.0% Irish, 8.4% United States or American, 4.8% Other groups (2000).
Economy: Employment by occupation: 11.0% management, 22.6% professional, 11.2% services, 28.1% sales, 0.2% farming, 9.7% construction, 17.3% production (2000).
Income: Per capita income: $26,467 (2007); Median household income: $56,712 (2007); Average household income: $64,118 (2007); Percent of households with income of $100,000 or more: 15.3% (2007); Poverty rate: 2.8% (2000).
Education: Percent of population age 25 and over with: High school diploma (including GED) or higher: 88.1% (2007); Bachelor's degree or higher: 16.5% (2007); Master's degree or higher: 3.7% (2007).

School District(s)

Elmwood CUSD 322 (PK-12)
2005-06 Enrollment: 727 . . . . (309) 742-8464
Housing: Homeownership rate: 82.2% (2007); Median home value: $105,743 (2007); Median rent: $364 per month (2000); Median age of housing: 51 years (2000).
Safety: Violent crime rate: 79.2 per 10,000 population; Property crime rate: 179.6 per 10,000 population (2006).
Newspapers: Advertiser (Local news; Circulation 6,980); Home Shopper (Community news; Circulation 7,995); Tri County News-Elmwood Gazette Edition (Local news; Circulation 400); Tri County News-Yates City Banner Edition (Local news; Circulation 100); Tri-County News Princeville Telephone (Community news; Circulation 450); Tri-County News-Farmington Bugle Edition (Local news; Circulation 150); Tri-County News-Williamsfield Times Edition (Local news; Circulation 500)
Transportation: Commute to work: 94.2% car, 0.0% public transportation, 4.0% walk, 1.0% work from home (2000); Travel time to work: 32.4% less than 15 minutes, 15.0% 15 to 30 minutes, 39.2% 30 to 45 minutes, 8.1% 45 to 60 minutes, 5.3% 60 minutes or more (2000)

GLASFORD (village). Covers a land area of 0.883 square miles and a water area of 0 square miles. Located at 40.57° N. Lat.; 89.81° W. Long. Elevation is 614 feet.
Population: 1,234 (1990); 1,076 (2000); 971 (2007); 962 (2012 projected); Race: 99.3% White, 0.0% Black, 0.0% Asian, 1.9% Hispanic of any race (2007); Density: 1,099.5 persons per square mile (2007); Average household size: 2.45 (2007); Median age: 36.3 (2007); Males per 100 females: 91.9 (2007); Marriage status: 23.4% never married, 61.7% now married, 6.3% widowed, 8.6% divorced (2000); Foreign born: 0.5% (2000); Ancestry (includes multiple ancestries): 28.7% German, 14.9% United States or American, 13.4% English, 11.0% Irish, 6.0% Other groups (2000).
Economy: Single-family building permits issued: 0 (2007); Multi-family building permits issued: 0 (2007); Employment by occupation: 6.6% management, 13.8% professional, 16.5% services, 28.7% sales, 0.0% farming, 10.2% construction, 24.1% production (2000).
Income: Per capita income: $22,191 (2007); Median household income: $44,028 (2007); Average household income: $54,276 (2007); Percent of households with income of $100,000 or more: 11.8% (2007); Poverty rate: 7.1% (2000).
Education: Percent of population age 25 and over with: High school diploma (including GED) or higher: 86.7% (2007); Bachelor's degree or higher: 11.5% (2007); Master's degree or higher: 3.2% (2007).

School District(s)

Illini Bluffs CUSD 327 (PK-12)
2005-06 Enrollment: 993 . . . . (309) 389-2231
Housing: Homeownership rate: 80.1% (2007); Median home value: $90,857 (2007); Median rent: $323 per month (2000); Median age of housing: 46 years (2000).
Safety: Violent crime rate: 48.2 per 10,000 population; Property crime rate: 57.8 per 10,000 population (2006).
Newspapers: Glasford Gazette (Local news; Circulation 1,300)
Transportation: Commute to work: 93.7% car, 0.0% public transportation, 4.3% walk, 0.6% work from home (2000); Travel time to work: 25.4% less than 15 minutes, 30.8% 15 to 30 minutes, 35.0% 30 to 45 minutes, 4.7% 45 to 60 minutes, 4.1% 60 minutes or more (2000)

HANNA CITY (village). Aka Hanna. Covers a land area of 0.477 square miles and a water area of 0 square miles. Located at 40.69° N. Lat.; 89.79° W. Long. Elevation is 728 feet.
Population: 1,248 (1990); 1,013 (2000); 1,010 (2007); 993 (2012 projected); Race: 96.2% White, 0.3% Black, 1.8% Asian, 1.5% Hispanic of any race (2007); Density: 2,117.5 persons per square mile (2007); Average household size: 2.48 (2007); Median age: 37.3 (2007); Males per 100 females: 94.2 (2007); Marriage status: 22.1% never married, 62.1% now married, 7.9% widowed, 7.9% divorced (2000); Foreign born: 1.5% (2000); Ancestry (includes multiple ancestries): 26.1% German, 11.6% English, 10.7% Irish, 8.7% United States or American, 5.9% Other groups (2000).
Economy: Employment by occupation: 10.5% management, 12.5% professional, 16.6% services, 32.9% sales, 0.0% farming, 10.5% construction, 17.0% production (2000).
Income: Per capita income: $24,090 (2007); Median household income: $52,424 (2007); Average household income: $58,248 (2007); Percent of households with income of $100,000 or more: 11.3% (2007); Poverty rate: 7.2% (2000).
Education: Percent of population age 25 and over with: High school diploma (including GED) or higher: 83.3% (2007); Bachelor's degree or higher: 9.2% (2007); Master's degree or higher: 0.9% (2007).
Housing: Homeownership rate: 82.4% (2007); Median home value: $104,167 (2007); Median rent: $398 per month (2000); Median age of housing: 41 years (2000).
Transportation: Commute to work: 93.2% car, 1.4% public transportation, 4.0% walk, 1.4% work from home (2000); Travel time to work: 17.9% less than 15 minutes, 52.1% 15 to 30 minutes, 20.8% 30 to 45 minutes, 4.1% 45 to 60 minutes, 5.1% 60 minutes or more (2000)

KINGSTON MINES (village). Covers a land area of 1.340 square miles and a water area of 0.103 square miles. Located at 40.55° N. Lat.; 89.77° W. Long. Elevation is 463 feet.
Population: 293 (1990); 259 (2000); 228 (2007); 227 (2012 projected); Race: 93.9% White, 0.0% Black, 0.0% Asian, 4.4% Hispanic of any race (2007); Density: 170.1 persons per square mile (2007); Average household size: 2.53 (2007); Median age: 35.8 (2007); Males per 100 females: 100.0 (2007); Marriage status: 29.6% never married, 49.3% now married, 11.3% widowed, 9.9% divorced (2000); Foreign born: 0.0% (2000); Ancestry (includes multiple ancestries): 24.2% United States or American, 18.1% German, 14.5% Irish, 9.3% Other groups, 7.7% English (2000).
Economy: Single-family building permits issued: 1 (2007); Multi-family building permits issued: 0 (2007); Employment by occupation: 1.8% management, 8.3% professional, 17.4% services, 22.0% sales, 0.0% farming, 11.0% construction, 39.4% production (2000).
Income: Per capita income: $18,410 (2007); Median household income: $36,667 (2007); Average household income: $46,639 (2007); Percent of

households with income of $100,000 or more: 8.9% (2007); Poverty rate: 5.2% (2000).
Education: Percent of population age 25 and over with: High school diploma (including GED) or higher: 76.5% (2007); Bachelor's degree or higher: 2.6% (2007); Master's degree or higher: 0.7% (2007).
Housing: Homeownership rate: 83.3% (2007); Median home value: $73,462 (2007); Median rent: $275 per month (2000); Median age of housing: 55 years (2000).
Transportation: Commute to work: 98.1% car, 0.0% public transportation, 0.0% walk, 1.9% work from home (2000); Travel time to work: 21.2% less than 15 minutes, 32.7% 15 to 30 minutes, 32.7% 30 to 45 minutes, 3.8% 45 to 60 minutes, 9.6% 60 minutes or more (2000)

LAURA (unincorporated postal area, zip code 61451). Covers a land area of 22.326 square miles and a water area of 0.106 square miles. Located at 40.95° N. Lat.; 89.94° W. Long. Elevation is 728 feet.
Population: 383 (2000); Race: 98.9% White, 0.0% Black, 0.0% Asian, 0.0% Hispanic of any race (2000); Density: 17.2 persons per square mile (2000); Age: 23.9% under 18, 8.8% over 64 (2000); Marriage status: 17.8% never married, 60.1% now married, 8.7% widowed, 13.4% divorced (2000); Foreign born: 0.0% (2000); Ancestry (includes multiple ancestries): 22.1% German, 15.2% English, 10.9% Irish, 7.7% French (except Basque), 7.7% Swedish (2000).
Economy: Employment by occupation: 9.7% management, 2.2% professional, 14.0% services, 15.6% sales, 1.6% farming, 23.1% construction, 33.9% production (2000).
Income: Per capita income: $18,145 (2000); Median household income: $45,000 (2000); Poverty rate: 0.0% (2000).
Education: Percent of population age 25 and over with: High school diploma (including GED) or higher: 92.0% (2000); Bachelor's degree or higher: 12.5% (2000).
Housing: Homeownership rate: 82.2% (2000); Median home value: $49,200 (2000); Median rent: $200 per month (2000); Median age of housing: 58 years (2000).
Transportation: Commute to work: 93.0% car, 0.0% public transportation, 0.0% walk, 7.0% work from home (2000); Travel time to work: 14.5% less than 15 minutes, 26.6% 15 to 30 minutes, 46.2% 30 to 45 minutes, 8.7% 45 to 60 minutes, 4.0% 60 minutes or more (2000)

MAPLETON (village). Covers a land area of 0.718 square miles and a water area of 0 square miles. Located at 40.57° N. Lat.; 89.72° W. Long. Elevation is 469 feet.
Population: 270 (1990); 227 (2000); 243 (2007); 246 (2012 projected); Race: 96.7% White, 0.0% Black, 0.0% Asian, 0.0% Hispanic of any race (2007); Density: 338.4 persons per square mile (2007); Average household size: 2.19 (2007); Median age: 41.5 (2007); Males per 100 females: 117.0 (2007); Marriage status: 13.4% never married, 54.1% now married, 10.3% widowed, 22.2% divorced (2000); Foreign born: 5.3% (2000); Ancestry (includes multiple ancestries): 35.4% United States or American, 14.6% German, 9.7% Other groups, 8.8% Irish, 4.9% English (2000).
Economy: Single-family building permits issued: 0 (2007); Multi-family building permits issued: 0 (2007); Employment by occupation: 4.1% management, 21.5% professional, 10.7% services, 23.1% sales, 0.0% farming, 9.9% construction, 30.6% production (2000).
Income: Per capita income: $29,763 (2007); Median household income: $60,417 (2007); Average household income: $65,158 (2007); Percent of households with income of $100,000 or more: 16.2% (2007); Poverty rate: 6.6% (2000).
Education: Percent of population age 25 and over with: High school diploma (including GED) or higher: 74.4% (2007); Bachelor's degree or higher: 12.8% (2007); Master's degree or higher: 2.8% (2007).
Housing: Homeownership rate: 78.4% (2007); Median home value: $89,375 (2007); Median rent: $248 per month (2000); Median age of housing: 43 years (2000).
Transportation: Commute to work: 98.3% car, 0.0% public transportation, 1.7% walk, 0.0% work from home (2000); Travel time to work: 24.0% less than 15 minutes, 33.9% 15 to 30 minutes, 32.2% 30 to 45 minutes, 3.3% 45 to 60 minutes, 6.6% 60 minutes or more (2000)

NORWOOD (village). Aka Norwood Park. Covers a land area of 0.264 square miles and a water area of 0 square miles. Located at 40.70° N. Lat.; 89.70° W. Long. Elevation is 696 feet.
Population: 517 (1990); 473 (2000); 473 (2007); 455 (2012 projected); Race: 98.5% White, 0.0% Black, 0.4% Asian, 0.4% Hispanic of any race (2007); Density: 1,788.9 persons per square mile (2007); Average household size: 2.63 (2007); Median age: 41.6 (2007); Males per 100 females: 91.5 (2007); Marriage status: 20.3% never married, 61.8% now married, 4.8% widowed, 13.1% divorced (2000); Foreign born: 0.0% (2000); Ancestry (includes multiple ancestries): 27.9% German, 10.3% Other groups, 7.6% English, 7.1% Italian, 6.3% Irish (2000).
Economy: Employment by occupation: 9.8% management, 16.4% professional, 10.4% services, 31.7% sales, 0.0% farming, 14.2% construction, 17.5% production (2000).
Income: Per capita income: $19,440 (2007); Median household income: $45,769 (2007); Average household income: $51,083 (2007); Percent of households with income of $100,000 or more: 7.2% (2007); Poverty rate: 7.5% (2000).
Taxes: Total city taxes per capita: $50 (2006); City property taxes per capita: $48 (2006).
Education: Percent of population age 25 and over with: High school diploma (including GED) or higher: 77.7% (2007); Bachelor's degree or higher: 5.6% (2007); Master's degree or higher: 2.8% (2007).
Housing: Homeownership rate: 93.3% (2007); Median home value: $88,000 (2007); Median rent: $525 per month (2000); Median age of housing: 43 years (2000).
Safety: Violent crime rate: 21.7 per 10,000 population; Property crime rate: 21.7 per 10,000 population (2006).
Transportation: Commute to work: 95.0% car, 0.0% public transportation, 0.0% walk, 2.2% work from home (2000); Travel time to work: 16.0% less than 15 minutes, 68.6% 15 to 30 minutes, 10.9% 30 to 45 minutes, 1.1% 45 to 60 minutes, 3.4% 60 minutes or more (2000)

PEORIA (city). County seat. Covers a land area of 44.404 square miles and a water area of 2.230 square miles. Located at 40.72° N. Lat.; 89.60° W. Long. Elevation is 502 feet.
History: Peoria began with the establishment by the French of Fort Pimiteoui on Lake Peoria in 1691. This trading post thrived for over a century, and the village which grew around it was at times called Au Pe, Le Pe, Opa, Au Pay, and Piorias. The American Fort Clark was erected here in 1813 and settlers from New England moved in. When Peoria County was created in 1825, the French-Indian name of Peoria was given to the community at Fort Clark, which became the county seat. Peoria was incorporated as a town in 1835, and received a city charter in 1845. In a speech in Peoria in 1854, following a talk by Stephen Douglas that lasted all afternoon, Abraham Lincoln first publicly denounced slavery.
Population: 114,341 (1990); 112,936 (2000); 112,354 (2007); 111,782 (2012 projected); Race: 66.0% White, 26.0% Black, 3.3% Asian, 3.4% Hispanic of any race (2007); Density: 2,530.3 persons per square mile (2007); Average household size: 2.47 (2007); Median age: 34.3 (2007); Males per 100 females: 91.0 (2007); Marriage status: 32.3% never married, 49.1% now married, 7.6% widowed, 11.0% divorced (2000); Foreign born: 4.4% (2000); Ancestry (includes multiple ancestries): 29.4% Other groups, 21.9% German, 12.2% Irish, 8.8% English, 5.6% United States or American (2000).
Economy: Unemployment rate: 5.0% (4/2008); Total civilian labor force: 58,870 (4/2008); Single-family building permits issued: 306 (2007); Multi-family building permits issued: 125 (2007); Employment by occupation: 11.6% management, 26.8% professional, 17.7% services, 26.4% sales, 0.1% farming, 5.7% construction, 11.8% production (2000).
Income: Per capita income: $23,968 (2007); Median household income: $41,409 (2007); Average household income: $57,978 (2007); Percent of households with income of $100,000 or more: 14.0% (2007); Poverty rate: 18.8% (2000).
Taxes: Total city taxes per capita: $575 (2006); City property taxes per capita: $218 (2006).
Education: Percent of population age 25 and over with: High school diploma (including GED) or higher: 83.2% (2007); Bachelor's degree or higher: 28.8% (2007); Master's degree or higher: 10.8% (2007).

School District(s)

Dunlap CUSD 323 (PK-12)
2005-06 Enrollment: 2,798 . . . . (309) 243-7716
Hollis Cons SD 328 (KG-08)
2005-06 Enrollment: 134 . . . . (309) 697-1325
Limestone Walters CCSD 316 (KG-08)
2005-06 Enrollment: 201 . . . . (309) 697-3035
Norwood ESD 63 (PK-08)
2005-06 Enrollment: 514 . . . . (309) 676-3523
Peoria Educ Reg for Emp Training
2005-06 Enrollment: n/a . . . . (309) 693-7373

Peoria Roe
2005-06 Enrollment: n/a . . . . (309) 672-6906
Peoria SD 150 (PK-12)
2005-06 Enrollment: 15,203 . . . . (309) 672-6768
Pleasant Hill SD 69 (PK-08)
2005-06 Enrollment: 235 . . . . (309) 637-6829
Pleasant Valley SD 62 (PK-08)
2005-06 Enrollment: 505 . . . . (309) 673-6750

Four-year College(s)

Bradley University (Private, Not-for-profit)
Fall 2007 Enrollment: 6,053 . . . . (309) 676-7611
2007-08 Tuition: In-state $21,378; Out-of-state $21,378
Methodist College of Nursing (Private, Not-for-profit)
Fall 2007 Enrollment: 118 . . . . (309) 672-5512
Midstate College (Private, For-profit)
Fall 2007 Enrollment: 641 . . . . (309) 692-4092
2007-08 Tuition: In-state $11,250; Out-of-state $11,250
Saint Francis Medical Center College of Nursing (Private, Not-for-profit, Roman Catholic)
Fall 2007 Enrollment: 434 . . . . (309) 655-2201

Vocational/Technical School(s)

Regency Beauty Institute (Private, For-profit)
Fall 2007 Enrollment: 57 . . . . (800) 787-6456
2007-08 Tuition: $14,200

Housing: Homeownership rate: 60.3% (2007); Median home value: $109,724 (2007); Median rent: $406 per month (2000); Median age of housing: 41 years (2000).
Hospitals: Methodist Medical Center of Illinois (330 beds); OSF Saint Francis Medical Center (616 beds); Proctor Hospital (175 beds)
Safety: Violent crime rate: 91.8 per 10,000 population; Property crime rate: 581.0 per 10,000 population (2006).
Newspapers: Catholic Post (Regional news; Circulation 27,089); Chillicothe Times-Bulletin (Local news; Circulation 2,000); East Peoria Courier (Local news; Circulation 8,250); Journal Star (Regional news; Circulation 75,500); Morton Times-News (Local news; Circulation 2,700); Peoria Times-Observer (Local news; Circulation 18,320); Tazewell Times Extra (Community news; Circulation 3,150); Washington Reporter (Local news; Circulation 8,445); Washington Times Reporter (Local news; Circulation 2,700)
Transportation: Commute to work: 90.5% car, 3.2% public transportation, 3.8% walk, 2.0% work from home (2000); Travel time to work: 45.2% less than 15 minutes, 42.9% 15 to 30 minutes, 7.1% 30 to 45 minutes, 2.1% 45 to 60 minutes, 2.7% 60 minutes or more (2000)
Airports: Greater Peoria Regional (primary service); Mount Hawley Auxiliary (general aviation)
Additional Information Contacts
City of Peoria . . . . (309) 494-2273
http://www.ci.peoria.il.us
Peoria Area Chamber of Commerce . . . . (309) 676-0755
http://www.peoriachamber.org

PEORIA HEIGHTS (village). Covers a land area of 2.644 square miles and a water area of 4.268 square miles. Located at 40.74° N. Lat.; 89.57° W. Long. Elevation is 784 feet.
History: Incorporated 1898.
Population: 6,948 (1990); 6,635 (2000); 6,237 (2007); 5,964 (2012 projected); Race: 91.9% White, 3.1% Black, 1.4% Asian, 2.4% Hispanic of any race (2007); Density: 2,358.5 persons per square mile (2007); Average household size: 2.09 (2007); Median age: 39.3 (2007); Males per 100 females: 94.5 (2007); Marriage status: 28.2% never married, 47.8% now married, 8.6% widowed, 15.4% divorced (2000); Foreign born: 2.1% (2000); Ancestry (includes multiple ancestries): 25.9% German, 18.7% Irish, 13.4% Other groups, 13.2% English, 10.3% United States or American (2000).
Economy: Single-family building permits issued: 2 (2007); Multi-family building permits issued: 0 (2007); Employment by occupation: 11.4% management, 20.0% professional, 17.6% services, 28.2% sales, 0.0% farming, 9.5% construction, 13.3% production (2000).
Income: Per capita income: $25,920 (2007); Median household income: $40,265 (2007); Average household income: $53,528 (2007); Percent of households with income of $100,000 or more: 8.6% (2007); Poverty rate: 8.8% (2000).
Education: Percent of population age 25 and over with: High school diploma (including GED) or higher: 85.0% (2007); Bachelor's degree or higher: 15.6% (2007); Master's degree or higher: 4.4% (2007).

School District(s)

Peoria Heights CUSD 325 (PK-12)
2005-06 Enrollment: 849 . . . . (309) 686-8800
Housing: Homeownership rate: 60.0% (2007); Median home value: $79,847 (2007); Median rent: $393 per month (2000); Median age of housing: 46 years (2000).
Safety: Violent crime rate: 66.7 per 10,000 population; Property crime rate: 295.3 per 10,000 population (2006).
Transportation: Commute to work: 97.0% car, 0.5% public transportation, 0.6% walk, 1.5% work from home (2000); Travel time to work: 43.3% less than 15 minutes, 44.1% 15 to 30 minutes, 7.6% 30 to 45 minutes, 2.0% 45 to 60 minutes, 3.1% 60 minutes or more (2000)
Additional Information Contacts
Peoria Heights Chamber of Commerce . . . . (309) 685-4812
http://www.peoriaheights.org

PRINCEVILLE (village). Covers a land area of 1.308 square miles and a water area of 0 square miles. Located at 40.93° N. Lat.; 89.75° W. Long. Elevation is 738 feet.
Population: 1,522 (1990); 1,621 (2000); 1,718 (2007); 1,782 (2012 projected); Race: 97.0% White, 0.0% Black, 0.2% Asian, 3.4% Hispanic of any race (2007); Density: 1,313.6 persons per square mile (2007); Average household size: 2.40 (2007); Median age: 36.5 (2007); Males per 100 females: 94.1 (2007); Marriage status: 24.3% never married, 59.1% now married, 8.4% widowed, 8.2% divorced (2000); Foreign born: 1.5% (2000); Ancestry (includes multiple ancestries): 32.9% German, 15.7% English, 12.9% Irish, 9.9% Other groups, 8.4% United States or American (2000).
Economy: Single-family building permits issued: 3 (2007); Multi-family building permits issued: 0 (2007); Employment by occupation: 10.8% management, 15.8% professional, 12.7% services, 27.1% sales, 1.3% farming, 8.5% construction, 23.7% production (2000).
Income: Per capita income: $23,352 (2007); Median household income: $46,802 (2007); Average household income: $55,336 (2007); Percent of households with income of $100,000 or more: 11.5% (2007); Poverty rate: 6.7% (2000).
Education: Percent of population age 25 and over with: High school diploma (including GED) or higher: 87.0% (2007); Bachelor's degree or higher: 14.0% (2007); Master's degree or higher: 3.3% (2007).

School District(s)

Princeville CUSD 326 (PK-12)
2005-06 Enrollment: 706 . . . . (309) 385-2213
Housing: Homeownership rate: 76.1% (2007); Median home value: $108,784 (2007); Median rent: $364 per month (2000); Median age of housing: 39 years (2000).
Transportation: Commute to work: 91.2% car, 0.0% public transportation, 6.1% walk, 2.1% work from home (2000); Travel time to work: 38.9% less than 15 minutes, 28.1% 15 to 30 minutes, 24.1% 30 to 45 minutes, 4.2% 45 to 60 minutes, 4.6% 60 minutes or more (2000)

ROME (CDP). Covers a land area of 1.905 square miles and a water area of 0 square miles. Located at 40.87° N. Lat.; 89.50° W. Long. Elevation is 463 feet.
Population: 1,860 (1990); 1,776 (2000); 1,691 (2007); 1,647 (2012 projected); Race: 97.8% White, 0.3% Black, 0.4% Asian, 1.5% Hispanic of any race (2007); Density: 887.8 persons per square mile (2007); Average household size: 2.46 (2007); Median age: 39.8 (2007); Males per 100 females: 104.0 (2007); Marriage status: 20.3% never married, 62.3% now married, 5.6% widowed, 11.8% divorced (2000); Foreign born: 1.8% (2000); Ancestry (includes multiple ancestries): 24.5% German, 20.1% Irish, 15.9% English, 6.3% United States or American, 5.9% Italian (2000).
Economy: Employment by occupation: 4.8% management, 18.9% professional, 19.3% services, 26.5% sales, 0.0% farming, 11.0% construction, 19.5% production (2000).
Income: Per capita income: $22,484 (2007); Median household income: $47,300 (2007); Average household income: $54,589 (2007); Percent of households with income of $100,000 or more: 10.3% (2007); Poverty rate: 4.4% (2000).
Education: Percent of population age 25 and over with: High school diploma (including GED) or higher: 85.7% (2007); Bachelor's degree or higher: 16.4% (2007); Master's degree or higher: 6.0% (2007).
Housing: Homeownership rate: 85.2% (2007); Median home value: $110,714 (2007); Median rent: $388 per month (2000); Median age of housing: 38 years (2000).
Transportation: Commute to work: 97.4% car, 0.0% public transportation, 0.0% walk, 1.8% work from home (2000); Travel time to work: 34.1% less

than 15 minutes, 44.6% 15 to 30 minutes, 15.4% 30 to 45 minutes, 1.2% 45 to 60 minutes, 4.8% 60 minutes or more (2000)

TRIVOLI (unincorporated postal area, zip code 61569). Covers a land area of 38.577 square miles and a water area of 0.317 square miles. Located at 40.69° N. Lat.; 89.89° W. Long. Elevation is 751 feet.
Population: 1,215 (2000); Race: 100.0% White, 0.0% Black, 0.0% Asian, 0.0% Hispanic of any race (2000); Density: 31.5 persons per square mile (2000); Age: 18.9% under 18, 21.2% over 64 (2000); Marriage status: 15.1% never married, 75.4% now married, 4.6% widowed, 4.8% divorced (2000); Foreign born: 0.0% (2000); Ancestry (includes multiple ancestries): 29.2% German, 16.9% English, 16.9% Irish, 7.8% United States or American, 7.4% French (except Basque) (2000).
Economy: Employment by occupation: 16.6% management, 10.9% professional, 16.1% services, 26.0% sales, 0.0% farming, 14.9% construction, 15.6% production (2000).
Income: Per capita income: $24,636 (2000); Median household income: $53,542 (2000); Poverty rate: 3.9% (2000).
Education: Percent of population age 25 and over with: High school diploma (including GED) or higher: 92.5% (2000); Bachelor's degree or higher: 16.4% (2000).
Housing: Homeownership rate: 93.4% (2000); Median home value: $102,700 (2000); Median rent: $415 per month (2000); Median age of housing: 37 years (2000).
Transportation: Commute to work: 93.7% car, 0.0% public transportation, 1.9% walk, 4.4% work from home (2000); Travel time to work: 21.6% less than 15 minutes, 39.5% 15 to 30 minutes, 29.2% 30 to 45 minutes, 6.4% 45 to 60 minutes, 3.4% 60 minutes or more (2000)

WEST PEORIA (city). Covers a land area of 1.286 square miles and a water area of 0 square miles. Located at 40.69° N. Lat.; 89.63° W. Long. Elevation is 594 feet.
History: Bradley University to East.
Population: 5,315 (1990); 4,762 (2000); 4,640 (2007); 4,582 (2012 projected); Race: 85.2% White, 10.5% Black, 0.9% Asian, 1.7% Hispanic of any race (2007); Density: 3,608.8 persons per square mile (2007); Average household size: 2.35 (2007); Median age: 39.0 (2007); Males per 100 females: 86.6 (2007); Marriage status: 26.2% never married, 52.4% now married, 9.4% widowed, 11.9% divorced (2000); Foreign born: 0.6% (2000); Ancestry (includes multiple ancestries): 35.2% German, 17.7% Irish, 11.9% Other groups, 11.1% United States or American, 10.1% English (2000).
Economy: Employment by occupation: 13.4% management, 18.4% professional, 15.2% services, 31.8% sales, 0.3% farming, 7.1% construction, 13.9% production (2000).
Income: Per capita income: $26,873 (2007); Median household income: $49,139 (2007); Average household income: $60,837 (2007); Percent of households with income of $100,000 or more: 14.0% (2007); Poverty rate: 8.1% (2000).
Education: Percent of population age 25 and over with: High school diploma (including GED) or higher: 83.6% (2007); Bachelor's degree or higher: 21.5% (2007); Master's degree or higher: 5.3% (2007).
Housing: Homeownership rate: 80.0% (2007); Median home value: $96,061 (2007); Median rent: $388 per month (2000); Median age of housing: 53 years (2000).
Transportation: Commute to work: 95.9% car, 0.9% public transportation, 1.0% walk, 2.2% work from home (2000); Travel time to work: 43.5% less than 15 minutes, 45.5% 15 to 30 minutes, 3.8% 30 to 45 minutes, 4.5% 45 to 60 minutes, 2.8% 60 minutes or more (2000)

Perry County

Located in southwestern Illinois; bounded partly on the east by the Little Muddy River; drained by Beaucoup and Galum Creeks. Covers a land area of 440.96 square miles, a water area of 5.85 square miles, and is located in the Central Time Zone. The county was founded in 1827. County seat is Pinckneyville.

Weather Station: Du Quoin 4 SE — Elevation: 419 feet

	Jan	Feb	Mar	Apr	May	Jun	Jul	Aug	Sep	Oct	Nov	Dec
High	39	46	56	68	77	85	90	88	81	70	56	44
Low	21	26	35	45	55	63	67	64	57	45	36	27
Precip	2.7	2.6	4.3	4.3	4.8	4.1	3.5	3.2	3.3	3.3	4.4	3.4
Snow	5.1	3.4	1.2	0.5	0.0	0.0	0.0	0.0	0.0	0.2	0.8	2.5

High and Low temperatures in degrees Fahrenheit; Precipitation and Snow in inches

Population: 21,412 (1990); 23,094 (2000); 22,841 (2007); 22,684 (2012 projected); Race: 88.9% White, 8.4% Black, 0.4% Asian, 2.1% Hispanic of any race (2007); Density: 51.8 persons per square mile (2007); Average household size: 2.68 (2007); Median age: 38.3 (2007); Males per 100 females: 116.9 (2007).
Religion: Five largest groups: 26.2% Southern Baptist Convention, 14.7% Catholic Church, 4.3% The United Methodist Church, 3.1% United Church of Christ, 2.5% Christian Church (Disciples of Christ) (2000).
Economy: Unemployment rate: 8.2% (4/2008); Total civilian labor force: 9,837 (4/2008); Leading industries: 27.2% manufacturing; 19.4% health care and social assistance; 15.1% retail trade (2005); Farms: 549 totaling 193,989 acres (2002); Companies that employ 500 or more persons: 1 (2006); Companies that employ 100 to 499 persons: 5 (2006); Companies that employ less than 100 persons: 419 (2006); Black-owned businesses: n/a (2002); Hispanic-owned businesses: n/a (2002); Asian-owned businesses: n/a (2002); Women-owned businesses: n/a (2002); Retail sales per capita: $8,521 (2008). Single-family building permits issued: 0 (2007); Multi-family building permits issued: 0 (2007).
Income: Per capita income: $19,432 (2007); Median household income: $39,799 (2007); Average household income: $48,208 (2007); Percent of households with income of $100,000 or more: 7.5% (2007); Poverty rate: 16.2% (2005); Bankruptcy rate: 3.58% (2007).
Taxes: Total county taxes per capita: $107 (2006); County property taxes per capita: $92 (2006).
Education: Percent of population age 25 and over with: High school diploma (including GED) or higher: 72.2% (2007); Bachelor's degree or higher: 10.3% (2007); Master's degree or higher: 2.8% (2007).
Housing: Homeownership rate: 79.0% (2007); Median home value: $71,208 (2007); Median rent: $257 per month (2000); Median age of housing: 39 years (2000).
Health: Birth rate: 118.2 per 10,000 population (2007); Death rate: 111.5 per 10,000 population (2007); Age-adjusted cancer mortality rate: 198.9 deaths per 100,000 population (2005); Number of physicians: 7.9 per 10,000 population (2005); Hospital beds: 47.8 per 10,000 population (2004); Hospital admissions: 1,045.2 per 10,000 population (2004).
Elections: 2004 Presidential election results: 53.6% Bush, 45.8% Kerry, 0.0% Nader, 0.6% Badnarik
National and State Parks: Pyramid State Park
Additional Information Contacts
Perry County Government . . . . (618) 357-5116
http://www.perrycountyil.org
City of Du Quoin . . . . (618) 542-3841
http://www.duquoin.org
City of Pinckneyville . . . . (618) 357-6916
http://www.ci.pinckneyville.il.us
Du Quoin Chamber of Commerce . . . . (618) 542-9570
Pinckneyville Chamber of Commerce . . . . (618) 357-3243
http://www.pinckneyville.com

Perry County Communities

CUTLER (village). Covers a land area of 0.474 square miles and a water area of 0 square miles. Located at 38.03° N. Lat.; 89.56° W. Long. Elevation is 499 feet.
Population: 523 (1990); 543 (2000); 516 (2007); 508 (2012 projected); Race: 99.4% White, 0.2% Black, 0.0% Asian, 0.2% Hispanic of any race (2007); Density: 1,089.4 persons per square mile (2007); Average household size: 2.69 (2007); Median age: 32.6 (2007); Males per 100 females: 95.5 (2007); Marriage status: 24.0% never married, 53.2% now married, 8.6% widowed, 14.2% divorced (2000); Foreign born: 0.0% (2000); Ancestry (includes multiple ancestries): 23.4% German, 18.6% United States or American, 15.4% Other groups, 11.1% Irish, 3.5% Dutch (2000).
Economy: Employment by occupation: 3.1% management, 7.3% professional, 28.1% services, 16.7% sales, 0.0% farming, 9.4% construction, 35.4% production (2000).
Income: Per capita income: $17,282 (2007); Median household income: $39,615 (2007); Average household income: $46,445 (2007); Percent of households with income of $100,000 or more: 7.3% (2007); Poverty rate: 29.2% (2000).
Education: Percent of population age 25 and over with: High school diploma (including GED) or higher: 58.0% (2007); Bachelor's degree or higher: 3.8% (2007); Master's degree or higher: 0.0% (2007).

Housing: Homeownership rate: 77.6% (2007); Median home value: $43,281 (2007); Median rent: $228 per month (2000); Median age of housing: 40 years (2000).
Transportation: Commute to work: 92.5% car, 0.0% public transportation, 1.6% walk, 3.7% work from home (2000); Travel time to work: 18.9% less than 15 minutes, 29.4% 15 to 30 minutes, 21.1% 30 to 45 minutes, 16.1% 45 to 60 minutes, 14.4% 60 minutes or more (2000)

DU QUOIN (city). Covers a land area of 6.865 square miles and a water area of 0.067 square miles. Located at 38.00° N. Lat.; 89.23° W. Long. Elevation is 459 feet.
History: Du Quoin developed as a coal mining town. It was named for Jean Baptiste Du Quoigne, chief of the Kaskaskia tribe.
Population: 6,773 (1990); 6,448 (2000); 6,265 (2007); 6,138 (2012 projected); Race: 91.7% White, 5.9% Black, 0.3% Asian, 1.7% Hispanic of any race (2007); Density: 912.7 persons per square mile (2007); Average household size: 2.33 (2007); Median age: 38.8 (2007); Males per 100 females: 92.6 (2007); Marriage status: 18.0% never married, 56.2% now married, 12.7% widowed, 13.1% divorced (2000); Foreign born: 0.6% (2000); Ancestry (includes multiple ancestries): 20.7% German, 11.9% Other groups, 10.0% Irish, 10.0% English, 9.0% United States or American (2000).
Economy: Employment by occupation: 8.2% management, 14.8% professional, 17.1% services, 27.9% sales, 0.4% farming, 8.3% construction, 23.2% production (2000).
Income: Per capita income: $18,521 (2007); Median household income: $34,043 (2007); Average household income: $42,431 (2007); Percent of households with income of $100,000 or more: 6.3% (2007); Poverty rate: 18.1% (2000).
Education: Percent of population age 25 and over with: High school diploma (including GED) or higher: 74.1% (2007); Bachelor's degree or higher: 13.8% (2007); Master's degree or higher: 4.1% (2007).

School District(s)

Duquoin CUSD 300 (PK-12)
2005-06 Enrollment: 1,467 . . . . (618) 542-3856
Tri-County Sp Ed Jnt Agreement (PK-12)
2005-06 Enrollment: 149 . . . . (618) 684-2109

Housing: Homeownership rate: 71.0% (2007); Median home value: $61,615 (2007); Median rent: $261 per month (2000); Median age of housing: 50 years (2000).
Hospitals: Marshall Browning Hospital (25 beds)
Safety: Violent crime rate: 25.0 per 10,000 population; Property crime rate: 138.8 per 10,000 population (2006).
Newspapers: Ashley News (Local news; Circulation 4,000); Du Quoin Evening Call (Local news; Circulation 4,350)
Transportation: Commute to work: 92.0% car, 0.3% public transportation, 4.5% walk, 1.9% work from home (2000); Travel time to work: 52.0% less than 15 minutes, 18.8% 15 to 30 minutes, 15.3% 30 to 45 minutes, 8.7% 45 to 60 minutes, 5.2% 60 minutes or more (2000); Amtrak: Service available.

Additional Information Contacts

City of Du Quoin. . . . . (618) 542-3841
http://www.duquoin.org
Du Quoin Chamber of Commerce . . . . (618) 542-9570

PINCKNEYVILLE (city). County seat. Covers a land area of 3.161 square miles and a water area of 0.002 square miles. Located at 38.07° N. Lat.; 89.38° W. Long. Elevation is 433 feet.
History: Pyramid State Park to South, created from reclaimed coal strip mines. Incorporated 1861.
Population: 4,021 (1990); 5,464 (2000); 5,367 (2007); 5,264 (2012 projected); Race: 66.6% White, 28.0% Black, 0.3% Asian, 5.5% Hispanic of any race (2007); Density: 1,697.8 persons per square mile (2007); Average household size: 3.70 (2007); Median age: 34.5 (2007); Males per 100 females: 205.1 (2007); Marriage status: 15.5% never married, 64.7% now married, 5.0% widowed, 14.8% divorced (2000); Foreign born: 1.3% (2000); Ancestry (includes multiple ancestries): 14.1% German, 10.7% United States or American, 9.0% Irish, 8.7% Other groups, 4.2% English (2000).
Economy: Employment by occupation: 9.9% management, 15.6% professional, 22.2% services, 18.3% sales, 0.8% farming, 8.3% construction, 24.9% production (2000).
Income: Per capita income: $17,857 (2007); Median household income: $34,712 (2007); Average household income: $45,102 (2007); Percent of households with income of $100,000 or more: 5.5% (2007); Poverty rate: 11.0% (2000).
Education: Percent of population age 25 and over with: High school diploma (including GED) or higher: 57.9% (2007); Bachelor's degree or higher: 7.2% (2007); Master's degree or higher: 3.0% (2007).

School District(s)

CCSD 204 (KG-08)
2005-06 Enrollment: 193 . . . . (618) 357-2419
Dept of Corrections Sch Dist 428 (08-12)
2005-06 Enrollment: 2,271 . . . . (217) 522-2666
Pinckneyville CHSD 101 (09-12)
2005-06 Enrollment: 507 . . . . (618) 357-5013
Pinckneyville SD 50 (PK-08)
2005-06 Enrollment: 606 . . . . (618) 357-5161

Housing: Homeownership rate: 72.0% (2007); Median home value: $69,717 (2007); Median rent: $261 per month (2000); Median age of housing: 46 years (2000).
Hospitals: Pinckneyville Community Hospital (85 beds)
Safety: Violent crime rate: 5.5 per 10,000 population; Property crime rate: 82.5 per 10,000 population (2006).
Newspapers: Pinckneyville Democrat (Community news; Circulation 2,800)
Transportation: Commute to work: 90.1% car, 0.7% public transportation, 3.1% walk, 5.4% work from home (2000); Travel time to work: 49.3% less than 15 minutes, 17.8% 15 to 30 minutes, 17.4% 30 to 45 minutes, 11.7% 45 to 60 minutes, 3.8% 60 minutes or more (2000)

Additional Information Contacts

City of Pinckneyville . . . . (618) 357-6916
http://www.ci.pinckneyville.il.us
Pinckneyville Chamber of Commerce . . . . (618) 357-3243
http://www.pinckneyville.com

SAINT JOHNS (village). Covers a land area of 0.703 square miles and a water area of 0.045 square miles. Located at 38.03° N. Lat.; 89.24° W. Long. Elevation is 463 feet.
Population: 261 (1990); 218 (2000); 218 (2007); 217 (2012 projected); Race: 92.7% White, 3.2% Black, 1.4% Asian, 0.5% Hispanic of any race (2007); Density: 310.0 persons per square mile (2007); Average household size: 2.20 (2007); Median age: 42.6 (2007); Males per 100 females: 134.4 (2007); Marriage status: 30.7% never married, 46.3% now married, 9.8% widowed, 13.2% divorced (2000); Foreign born: 1.7% (2000); Ancestry (includes multiple ancestries): 36.4% German, 22.5% Other groups, 13.0% Irish, 10.4% English, 5.6% Swedish (2000).
Economy: Employment by occupation: 5.9% management, 11.0% professional, 18.4% services, 17.6% sales, 0.0% farming, 11.0% construction, 36.0% production (2000).
Income: Per capita income: $17,856 (2007); Median household income: $34,167 (2007); Average household income: $39,318 (2007); Percent of households with income of $100,000 or more: 1.0% (2007); Poverty rate: 11.4% (2000).
Education: Percent of population age 25 and over with: High school diploma (including GED) or higher: 80.3% (2007); Bachelor's degree or higher: 9.9% (2007); Master's degree or higher: 3.3% (2007).
Housing: Homeownership rate: 71.7% (2007); Median home value: $49,444 (2007); Median rent: $246 per month (2000); Median age of housing: 29 years (2000).
Transportation: Commute to work: 97.0% car, 0.0% public transportation, 1.5% walk, 1.5% work from home (2000); Travel time to work: 43.9% less than 15 minutes, 13.6% 15 to 30 minutes, 19.7% 30 to 45 minutes, 10.6% 45 to 60 minutes, 12.1% 60 minutes or more (2000)

TAMAROA (village). Covers a land area of 0.983 square miles and a water area of 0 square miles. Located at 38.13° N. Lat.; 89.22° W. Long. Elevation is 509 feet.
History: Tamaroa was named for the Tamaroa Indians that lived in this area.
Population: 786 (1990); 740 (2000); 742 (2007); 751 (2012 projected); Race: 96.9% White, 0.1% Black, 0.3% Asian, 0.5% Hispanic of any race (2007); Density: 755.1 persons per square mile (2007); Average household size: 2.40 (2007); Median age: 37.2 (2007); Males per 100 females: 96.8 (2007); Marriage status: 27.0% never married, 50.8% now married, 10.0% widowed, 12.3% divorced (2000); Foreign born: 0.8% (2000); Ancestry (includes multiple ancestries): 23.7% German, 15.2% Irish, 10.3% Other groups, 9.5% Polish, 6.5% English (2000).

Economy: Employment by occupation: 1.9% management, 14.6% professional, 23.2% services, 17.5% sales, 0.6% farming, 6.7% construction, 35.4% production (2000).
Income: Per capita income: $16,910 (2007); Median household income: $31,324 (2007); Average household income: $40,607 (2007); Percent of households with income of $100,000 or more: 3.9% (2007); Poverty rate: 17.3% (2000).
Education: Percent of population age 25 and over with: High school diploma (including GED) or higher: 68.0% (2007); Bachelor's degree or higher: 4.8% (2007); Master's degree or higher: 2.6% (2007).

School District(s)

Tamaroa School Dist 5 (KG-08)
2005-06 Enrollment: 120 . . . . (618) 496-5513
Housing: Homeownership rate: 80.6% (2007); Median home value: $47,821 (2007); Median rent: $219 per month (2000); Median age of housing: 47 years (2000).
Transportation: Commute to work: 93.5% car, 0.0% public transportation, 3.6% walk, 2.3% work from home (2000); Travel time to work: 20.9% less than 15 minutes, 38.5% 15 to 30 minutes, 19.3% 30 to 45 minutes, 7.6% 45 to 60 minutes, 13.6% 60 minutes or more (2000)

WILLISVILLE (village). Covers a land area of 0.377 square miles and a water area of 0 square miles. Located at 37.98° N. Lat.; 89.59° W. Long. Elevation is 495 feet.
Population: 577 (1990); 694 (2000); 706 (2007); 694 (2012 projected); Race: 99.4% White, 0.0% Black, 0.0% Asian, 0.8% Hispanic of any race (2007); Density: 1,872.2 persons per square mile (2007); Average household size: 2.54 (2007); Median age: 34.4 (2007); Males per 100 females: 98.9 (2007); Marriage status: 21.2% never married, 59.1% now married, 7.9% widowed, 11.8% divorced (2000); Foreign born: 0.3% (2000); Ancestry (includes multiple ancestries): 33.6% German, 14.4% Irish, 13.0% United States or American, 11.9% Other groups, 6.9% French (except Basque) (2000).
Economy: Employment by occupation: 2.6% management, 9.0% professional, 20.6% services, 13.9% sales, 1.0% farming, 14.8% construction, 38.1% production (2000).
Income: Per capita income: $17,280 (2007); Median household income: $40,294 (2007); Average household income: $43,885 (2007); Percent of households with income of $100,000 or more: 4.0% (2007); Poverty rate: 17.8% (2000).
Education: Percent of population age 25 and over with: High school diploma (including GED) or higher: 67.1% (2007); Bachelor's degree or higher: 2.3% (2007); Master's degree or higher: 1.4% (2007).
Housing: Homeownership rate: 77.7% (2007); Median home value: $47,619 (2007); Median rent: $250 per month (2000); Median age of housing: 41 years (2000).
Transportation: Commute to work: 92.9% car, 0.0% public transportation, 2.4% walk, 4.1% work from home (2000); Travel time to work: 32.3% less than 15 minutes, 30.5% 15 to 30 minutes, 19.5% 30 to 45 minutes, 7.4% 45 to 60 minutes, 10.3% 60 minutes or more (2000)

Piatt County

Located in central Illinois; drained by the Sangamon River. Covers a land area of 440.02 square miles, a water area of 0.31 square miles, and is located in the Central Time Zone. The county was founded in 1841. County seat is Monticello.

Piatt County is part of the Champaign-Urbana, IL Metropolitan Statistical Area. The entire metro area includes: Champaign County, IL; Ford County, IL; Piatt County, IL

Population: 15,548 (1990); 16,365 (2000); 16,856 (2007); 17,220 (2012 projected); Race: 98.3% White, 0.4% Black, 0.6% Asian, 0.8% Hispanic of any race (2007); Density: 38.3 persons per square mile (2007); Average household size: 2.49 (2007); Median age: 41.5 (2007); Males per 100 females: 96.6 (2007).
Religion: Five largest groups: 17.2% The United Methodist Church, 6.0% Southern Baptist Convention, 5.8% Christian Churches and Churches of Christ, 5.8% Catholic Church, 4.0% United Church of Christ (2000).
Economy: Unemployment rate: 3.7% (4/2008); Total civilian labor force: 9,601 (4/2008); Leading industries: 20.2% retail trade; 12.9% health care and social assistance; 11.3% manufacturing (2005); Farms: 442 totaling 257,869 acres (2002); Companies that employ 500 or more persons: 0 (2006); Companies that employ 100 to 499 persons: 2 (2006); Companies that employ less than 100 persons: 353 (2006); Black-owned businesses: n/a (2002); Hispanic-owned businesses: n/a (2002); Asian-owned businesses: n/a (2002); Women-owned businesses: 338 (2002); Retail sales per capita: $7,722 (2008). Single-family building permits issued: 60 (2007); Multi-family building permits issued: 0 (2007).
Income: Per capita income: $25,526 (2007); Median household income: $53,276 (2007); Average household income: $63,331 (2007); Percent of households with income of $100,000 or more: 14.0% (2007); Poverty rate: 6.2% (2005); Bankruptcy rate: 3.64% (2007).
Taxes: Total county taxes per capita: $196 (2006); County property taxes per capita: $179 (2006).
Education: Percent of population age 25 and over with: High school diploma (including GED) or higher: 88.7% (2007); Bachelor's degree or higher: 21.0% (2007); Master's degree or higher: 7.6% (2007).
Housing: Homeownership rate: 80.3% (2007); Median home value: $114,587 (2007); Median rent: $346 per month (2000); Median age of housing: 40 years (2000).
Health: Birth rate: 127.9 per 10,000 population (2007); Death rate: 96.4 per 10,000 population (2007); Age-adjusted cancer mortality rate: 197.5 deaths per 100,000 population (2005); Number of physicians: 6.7 per 10,000 population (2005); Hospital beds: 9.8 per 10,000 population (2004); Hospital admissions: 206.0 per 10,000 population (2004).
Elections: 2004 Presidential election results: 62.8% Bush, 36.4% Kerry, 0.0% Nader, 0.8% Badnarik

Additional Information Contacts

Piatt County Government. . . . . (217) 762-9487
http://www.piattcounty.org
City of Monticello . . . . (217) 762-2583
http://www.monticelloillinois.net
Mansfield Chamber of Commerce . . . . (217) 489-3351
Monticello Chamber of Commerce . . . . (217) 762-7921
http://www.monticellochamber.org

Piatt County Communities

ATWOOD (village). Covers a land area of 0.569 square miles and a water area of 0 square miles. Located at 39.80° N. Lat.; 88.46° W. Long. Elevation is 669 feet.
Population: 1,314 (1990); 1,290 (2000); 1,094 (2007); 1,102 (2012 projected); Race: 98.4% White, 0.5% Black, 0.2% Asian, 0.9% Hispanic of any race (2007); Density: 1,921.6 persons per square mile (2007); Average household size: 2.39 (2007); Median age: 40.5 (2007); Males per 100 females: 90.9 (2007); Marriage status: 17.7% never married, 61.7% now married, 9.6% widowed, 11.0% divorced (2000); Foreign born: 1.3% (2000); Ancestry (includes multiple ancestries): 20.7% German, 18.8% United States or American, 9.5% English, 8.1% Irish, 5.3% Other groups (2000).
Economy: Single-family building permits issued: 0 (2007); Multi-family building permits issued: 0 (2007); Employment by occupation: 10.1% management, 10.3% professional, 13.9% services, 24.3% sales, 1.2% farming, 13.6% construction, 26.7% production (2000).
Income: Per capita income: $21,467 (2007); Median household income: $42,417 (2007); Average household income: $51,389 (2007); Percent of households with income of $100,000 or more: 7.4% (2007); Poverty rate: 12.0% (2000).
Education: Percent of population age 25 and over with: High school diploma (including GED) or higher: 83.7% (2007); Bachelor's degree or higher: 9.4% (2007); Master's degree or higher: 3.1% (2007).

School District(s)

Atwood Hammond CUSD 39 (PK-12)
2005-06 Enrollment: 447 . . . . (217) 578-3111
Housing: Homeownership rate: 80.1% (2007); Median home value: $86,744 (2007); Median rent: $300 per month (2000); Median age of housing: 39 years (2000).
Safety: Violent crime rate: 32.0 per 10,000 population; Property crime rate: 136.0 per 10,000 population (2006).
Newspapers: Atwood Herald (Local news; Circulation 1,000)
Transportation: Commute to work: 91.8% car, 0.0% public transportation, 3.6% walk, 3.3% work from home (2000); Travel time to work: 39.8% less than 15 minutes, 25.6% 15 to 30 minutes, 15.6% 30 to 45 minutes, 14.6% 45 to 60 minutes, 4.4% 60 minutes or more (2000)

BEMENT (village). Covers a land area of 0.812 square miles and a water area of 0 square miles. Located at 39.92° N. Lat.; 88.57° W. Long. Elevation is 689 feet.
History: Incorporated 1874. Bryant Cottage State Historical Site.

Population: 1,676 (1990); 1,784 (2000); 1,937 (2007); 1,959 (2012 projected); Race: 97.0% White, 1.4% Black, 1.1% Asian, 0.4% Hispanic of any race (2007); Density: 2,385.5 persons per square mile (2007); Average household size: 2.54 (2007); Median age: 39.9 (2007); Males per 100 females: 97.7 (2007); Marriage status: 23.5% never married, 55.3% now married, 9.6% widowed, 11.6% divorced (2000); Foreign born: 0.7% (2000); Ancestry (includes multiple ancestries): 21.0% German, 15.2% United States or American, 10.1% English, 9.6% Irish, 5.2% Other groups (2000).
Economy: Single-family building permits issued: 0 (2007); Multi-family building permits issued: 0 (2007); Employment by occupation: 9.2% management, 11.2% professional, 19.9% services, 22.4% sales, 0.0% farming, 9.6% construction, 27.8% production (2000).
Income: Per capita income: $22,405 (2007); Median household income: $46,310 (2007); Average household income: $55,669 (2007); Percent of households with income of $100,000 or more: 7.3% (2007); Poverty rate: 6.2% (2000).
Education: Percent of population age 25 and over with: High school diploma (including GED) or higher: 84.4% (2007); Bachelor's degree or higher: 11.9% (2007); Master's degree or higher: 4.1% (2007).

School District(s)

Bement CUSD 5 (PK-12)
2005-06 Enrollment: 402 . . . . (217) 678-4200
Housing: Homeownership rate: 82.0% (2007); Median home value: $86,791 (2007); Median rent: $330 per month (2000); Median age of housing: 46 years (2000).
Newspapers: News Record (Local news; Circulation 1,500)
Transportation: Commute to work: 89.4% car, 0.8% public transportation, 5.9% walk, 3.2% work from home (2000); Travel time to work: 33.9% less than 15 minutes, 18.8% 15 to 30 minutes, 30.6% 30 to 45 minutes, 13.3% 45 to 60 minutes, 3.4% 60 minutes or more (2000)

CERRO GORDO (village). Covers a land area of 0.741 square miles and a water area of 0 square miles. Located at 39.89° N. Lat.; 88.73° W. Long. Elevation is 745 feet.
History: Incorporated 1873.
Population: 1,436 (1990); 1,436 (2000); 1,494 (2007); 1,535 (2012 projected); Race: 99.4% White, 0.1% Black, 0.4% Asian, 0.1% Hispanic of any race (2007); Density: 2,016.3 persons per square mile (2007); Average household size: 2.52 (2007); Median age: 38.9 (2007); Males per 100 females: 93.8 (2007); Marriage status: 19.7% never married, 60.1% now married, 8.0% widowed, 12.2% divorced (2000); Foreign born: 0.0% (2000); Ancestry (includes multiple ancestries): 28.4% German, 12.4% English, 10.2% Irish, 7.3% United States or American, 5.6% Other groups (2000).
Economy: Single-family building permits issued: 0 (2007); Multi-family building permits issued: 0 (2007); Employment by occupation: 6.4% management, 15.6% professional, 15.0% services, 27.0% sales, 1.4% farming, 9.9% construction, 24.7% production (2000).
Income: Per capita income: $20,201 (2007); Median household income: $46,364 (2007); Average household income: $50,980 (2007); Percent of households with income of $100,000 or more: 7.8% (2007); Poverty rate: 7.1% (2000).
Education: Percent of population age 25 and over with: High school diploma (including GED) or higher: 88.9% (2007); Bachelor's degree or higher: 10.4% (2007); Master's degree or higher: 2.6% (2007).

School District(s)

Cerro Gordo CUSD 100 (PK-12)
2005-06 Enrollment: 617 . . . . (217) 763-5221
Housing: Homeownership rate: 81.9% (2007); Median home value: $99,700 (2007); Median rent: $324 per month (2000); Median age of housing: 43 years (2000).
Transportation: Commute to work: 94.8% car, 0.0% public transportation, 2.4% walk, 2.0% work from home (2000); Travel time to work: 19.3% less than 15 minutes, 51.8% 15 to 30 minutes, 19.7% 30 to 45 minutes, 3.3% 45 to 60 minutes, 5.9% 60 minutes or more (2000)

CISCO (village). Covers a land area of 0.381 square miles and a water area of 0 square miles. Located at 40.01° N. Lat.; 88.72° W. Long. Elevation is 689 feet.
Population: 280 (1990); 264 (2000); 264 (2007); 265 (2012 projected); Race: 98.9% White, 0.0% Black, 0.0% Asian, 0.0% Hispanic of any race (2007); Density: 692.7 persons per square mile (2007); Average household size: 2.38 (2007); Median age: 37.5 (2007); Males per 100 females: 98.5 (2007); Marriage status: 15.7% never married, 69.4% now married, 10.2% widowed, 4.7% divorced (2000); Foreign born: 1.1% (2000); Ancestry (includes multiple ancestries): 16.3% German, 13.0% Irish, 11.2% Other groups, 8.3% English, 5.8% Dutch (2000).
Economy: Single-family building permits issued: 0 (2007); Multi-family building permits issued: 0 (2007); Employment by occupation: 11.1% management, 17.0% professional, 22.9% services, 15.0% sales, 1.3% farming, 17.0% construction, 15.7% production (2000).
Income: Per capita income: $19,725 (2007); Median household income: $45,536 (2007); Average household income: $46,914 (2007); Percent of households with income of $100,000 or more: 3.6% (2007); Poverty rate: 8.3% (2000).
Taxes: Total city taxes per capita: $102 (2006); City property taxes per capita: $53 (2006).
Education: Percent of population age 25 and over with: High school diploma (including GED) or higher: 90.9% (2007); Bachelor's degree or higher: 8.6% (2007); Master's degree or higher: 4.8% (2007).
Housing: Homeownership rate: 82.0% (2007); Median home value: $99,167 (2007); Median rent: $375 per month (2000); Median age of housing: 60+ years (2000).
Transportation: Commute to work: 92.0% car, 0.0% public transportation, 4.0% walk, 4.0% work from home (2000); Travel time to work: 21.5% less than 15 minutes, 38.2% 15 to 30 minutes, 28.5% 30 to 45 minutes, 4.9% 45 to 60 minutes, 6.9% 60 minutes or more (2000)

DE LAND (village). Aka Deland. Covers a land area of 0.396 square miles and a water area of 0 square miles. Located at 40.12° N. Lat.; 88.64° W. Long. Elevation is 702 feet.
Population: 458 (1990); 475 (2000); 482 (2007); 486 (2012 projected); Race: 98.8% White, 0.2% Black, 0.4% Asian, 1.5% Hispanic of any race (2007); Density: 1,215.7 persons per square mile (2007); Average household size: 2.46 (2007); Median age: 40.6 (2007); Males per 100 females: 96.7 (2007); Marriage status: 21.5% never married, 63.7% now married, 7.3% widowed, 7.5% divorced (2000); Foreign born: 0.8% (2000); Ancestry (includes multiple ancestries): 18.9% German, 16.4% English, 13.0% Irish, 12.2% United States or American, 9.7% Other groups (2000).
Economy: Single-family building permits issued: 1 (2007); Multi-family building permits issued: 0 (2007); Employment by occupation: 9.1% management, 11.6% professional, 21.1% services, 22.4% sales, 2.6% farming, 11.6% construction, 21.6% production (2000).
Income: Per capita income: $23,869 (2007); Median household income: $52,000 (2007); Average household income: $58,699 (2007); Percent of households with income of $100,000 or more: 9.2% (2007); Poverty rate: 4.6% (2000).
Education: Percent of population age 25 and over with: High school diploma (including GED) or higher: 82.9% (2007); Bachelor's degree or higher: 7.2% (2007); Master's degree or higher: 1.2% (2007).

School District(s)

Deland-Weldon CUSD 57 (PK-12)
2005-06 Enrollment: 194 . . . . (217) 736-2311
Housing: Homeownership rate: 75.0% (2007); Median home value: $89,318 (2007); Median rent: $267 per month (2000); Median age of housing: 47 years (2000).
Transportation: Commute to work: 90.9% car, 0.9% public transportation, 1.7% walk, 4.3% work from home (2000); Travel time to work: 27.1% less than 15 minutes, 28.5% 15 to 30 minutes, 38.0% 30 to 45 minutes, 4.5% 45 to 60 minutes, 1.8% 60 minutes or more (2000)

HAMMOND (village). Covers a land area of 0.762 square miles and a water area of 0.006 square miles. Located at 39.79° N. Lat.; 88.59° W. Long. Elevation is 673 feet.
Population: 527 (1990); 518 (2000); 478 (2007); 469 (2012 projected); Race: 97.3% White, 1.0% Black, 1.0% Asian, 0.2% Hispanic of any race (2007); Density: 627.3 persons per square mile (2007); Average household size: 2.27 (2007); Median age: 41.7 (2007); Males per 100 females: 113.4 (2007); Marriage status: 17.3% never married, 62.4% now married, 7.7% widowed, 12.5% divorced (2000); Foreign born: 1.2% (2000); Ancestry (includes multiple ancestries): 28.3% German, 15.4% English, 14.5% United States or American, 12.7% Irish, 8.5% Other groups (2000).
Economy: Single-family building permits issued: 0 (2007); Multi-family building permits issued: 0 (2007); Employment by occupation: 7.5% management, 8.3% professional, 8.3% services, 18.1% sales, 0.8% farming, 17.7% construction, 39.4% production (2000).
Income: Per capita income: $24,446 (2007); Median household income: $52,969 (2007); Average household income: $55,379 (2007); Percent of

households with income of $100,000 or more: 8.5% (2007); Poverty rate: 7.1% (2000).
Education: Percent of population age 25 and over with: High school diploma (including GED) or higher: 85.4% (2007); Bachelor's degree or higher: 7.3% (2007); Master's degree or higher: 1.2% (2007).
Housing: Homeownership rate: 76.3% (2007); Median home value: $92,500 (2007); Median rent: $231 per month (2000); Median age of housing: 40 years (2000).
Transportation: Commute to work: 96.7% car, 0.4% public transportation, 2.0% walk, 0.8% work from home (2000); Travel time to work: 16.4% less than 15 minutes, 29.5% 15 to 30 minutes, 39.3% 30 to 45 minutes, 6.1% 45 to 60 minutes, 8.6% 60 minutes or more (2000)

MANSFIELD (village). Covers a land area of 0.511 square miles and a water area of 0.025 square miles. Located at 40.21° N. Lat.; 88.50° W. Long. Elevation is 728 feet.
Population: 940 (1990); 949 (2000); 946 (2007); 952 (2012 projected); Race: 97.6% White, 0.0% Black, 2.0% Asian, 1.0% Hispanic of any race (2007); Density: 1,850.4 persons per square mile (2007); Average household size: 2.35 (2007); Median age: 41.3 (2007); Males per 100 females: 96.3 (2007); Marriage status: 17.2% never married, 68.8% now married, 6.1% widowed, 7.8% divorced (2000); Foreign born: 0.2% (2000); Ancestry (includes multiple ancestries): 29.9% German, 15.4% United States or American, 13.1% Irish, 11.0% English, 4.6% Other groups (2000).
Economy: Single-family building permits issued: 0 (2007); Multi-family building permits issued: 0 (2007); Employment by occupation: 9.1% management, 14.3% professional, 15.8% services, 31.6% sales, 0.4% farming, 13.5% construction, 15.4% production (2000).
Income: Per capita income: $25,515 (2007); Median household income: $52,857 (2007); Average household income: $60,044 (2007); Percent of households with income of $100,000 or more: 9.2% (2007); Poverty rate: 3.9% (2000).
Education: Percent of population age 25 and over with: High school diploma (including GED) or higher: 87.9% (2007); Bachelor's degree or higher: 14.7% (2007); Master's degree or higher: 5.4% (2007).

School District(s)

Blue Ridge CUSD 18 (PK-12)
2005-06 Enrollment: 943 . . . . (309) 928-9141
Housing: Homeownership rate: 79.1% (2007); Median home value: $103,763 (2007); Median rent: $384 per month (2000); Median age of housing: 44 years (2000).
Transportation: Commute to work: 95.5% car, 0.0% public transportation, 2.7% walk, 1.4% work from home (2000); Travel time to work: 26.2% less than 15 minutes, 50.1% 15 to 30 minutes, 16.5% 30 to 45 minutes, 5.2% 45 to 60 minutes, 2.0% 60 minutes or more (2000)
Additional Information Contacts
Mansfield Chamber of Commerce . . . . (217) 489-3351

MILMINE (unincorporated postal area, zip code 61855). Covers a land area of 5.535 square miles and a water area of 0 square miles. Located at 39.92° N. Lat.; 88.67° W. Long. Elevation is 712 feet.
Population: 74 (2000); Race: 100.0% White, 0.0% Black, 0.0% Asian, 0.0% Hispanic of any race (2000); Density: 13.4 persons per square mile (2000); Age: 19.6% under 18, 16.1% over 64 (2000); Marriage status: 6.7% never married, 86.7% now married, 6.7% widowed, 0.0% divorced (2000); Foreign born: 0.0% (2000); Ancestry (includes multiple ancestries): 10.7% English, 10.7% United States or American, 8.9% Other groups, 7.1% Norwegian, 7.1% French (except Basque) (2000).
Economy: Employment by occupation: 0.0% management, 13.0% professional, 17.4% services, 13.0% sales, 0.0% farming, 21.7% construction, 34.8% production (2000).
Income: Per capita income: $18,811 (2000); Median household income: $34,531 (2000); Poverty rate: 0.0% (2000).
Education: Percent of population age 25 and over with: High school diploma (including GED) or higher: 70.7% (2000); Bachelor's degree or higher: 0.0% (2000).
Housing: Homeownership rate: 77.8% (2000); Median home value: $58,100 (2000); Median rent: $225 per month (2000); Median age of housing: 60+ years (2000).
Transportation: Commute to work: 100.0% car, 0.0% public transportation, 0.0% walk, 0.0% work from home (2000); Travel time to work: 0.0% less than 15 minutes, 47.8% 15 to 30 minutes, 30.4% 30 to 45 minutes, 21.7% 45 to 60 minutes, 0.0% 60 minutes or more (2000)

MONTICELLO (city). County seat. Covers a land area of 2.979 square miles and a water area of 0 square miles. Located at 40.02° N. Lat.; 88.57° W. Long. Elevation is 659 feet.
History: Incorporated 1841.
Population: 4,919 (1990); 5,138 (2000); 5,278 (2007); 5,385 (2012 projected); Race: 98.7% White, 0.1% Black, 0.6% Asian, 1.0% Hispanic of any race (2007); Density: 1,771.7 persons per square mile (2007); Average household size: 2.36 (2007); Median age: 43.4 (2007); Males per 100 females: 90.5 (2007); Marriage status: 18.5% never married, 62.1% now married, 8.0% widowed, 11.3% divorced (2000); Foreign born: 1.2% (2000); Ancestry (includes multiple ancestries): 26.2% German, 13.5% Irish, 12.4% English, 6.9% Other groups, 6.1% United States or American (2000).
Economy: Single-family building permits issued: 34 (2007); Multi-family building permits issued: 0 (2007); Employment by occupation: 15.5% management, 26.4% professional, 14.1% services, 24.9% sales, 0.5% farming, 6.3% construction, 12.3% production (2000).
Income: Per capita income: $27,952 (2007); Median household income: $52,150 (2007); Average household income: $65,676 (2007); Percent of households with income of $100,000 or more: 16.6% (2007); Poverty rate: 3.8% (2000).
Education: Percent of population age 25 and over with: High school diploma (including GED) or higher: 88.5% (2007); Bachelor's degree or higher: 30.9% (2007); Master's degree or higher: 12.2% (2007).

School District(s)

Monticello CUSD 25 (PK-12)
2005-06 Enrollment: 1,682 . . . . (217) 762-8511
Housing: Homeownership rate: 79.1% (2007); Median home value: $131,398 (2007); Median rent: $404 per month (2000); Median age of housing: 37 years (2000).
Hospitals: John & Mary Kirby Hospital (17 beds)
Safety: Violent crime rate: 9.5 per 10,000 population; Property crime rate: 102.4 per 10,000 population (2006).
Newspapers: Piatt County Journal-Republican (Community news; Circulation 3,800)
Transportation: Commute to work: 90.2% car, 0.3% public transportation, 5.0% walk, 3.3% work from home (2000); Travel time to work: 43.9% less than 15 minutes, 22.2% 15 to 30 minutes, 28.9% 30 to 45 minutes, 2.3% 45 to 60 minutes, 2.8% 60 minutes or more (2000)
Additional Information Contacts
City of Monticello . . . . (217) 762-2583
http://www.monticelloillinois.net
Monticello Chamber of Commerce . . . . (217) 762-7921
http://www.monticellochamber.org

WHITE HEATH (unincorporated postal area, zip code 61884). Covers a land area of 25.358 square miles and a water area of 0.081 square miles. Located at 40.10° N. Lat.; 88.49° W. Long. Elevation is 722 feet.
Population: 1,172 (2000); Race: 100.0% White, 0.0% Black, 0.0% Asian, 0.0% Hispanic of any race (2000); Density: 46.2 persons per square mile (2000); Age: 32.7% under 18, 10.6% over 64 (2000); Marriage status: 23.3% never married, 70.5% now married, 2.4% widowed, 3.9% divorced (2000); Foreign born: 0.0% (2000); Ancestry (includes multiple ancestries): 18.5% German, 17.9% Irish, 15.5% United States or American, 12.0% English, 3.7% Italian (2000).
Economy: Employment by occupation: 8.9% management, 19.7% professional, 12.2% services, 27.4% sales, 3.5% farming, 8.2% construction, 20.1% production (2000).
Income: Per capita income: $23,131 (2000); Median household income: $53,819 (2000); Poverty rate: 0.5% (2000).
Education: Percent of population age 25 and over with: High school diploma (including GED) or higher: 92.4% (2000); Bachelor's degree or higher: 28.1% (2000).

School District(s)

Monticello CUSD 25 (PK-12)
2005-06 Enrollment: 1,682 . . . . (217) 762-8511
Housing: Homeownership rate: 87.7% (2000); Median home value: $128,800 (2000); Median rent: $360 per month (2000); Median age of housing: 27 years (2000).
Transportation: Commute to work: 93.8% car, 0.0% public transportation, 0.0% walk, 5.1% work from home (2000); Travel time to work: 18.4% less than 15 minutes, 47.8% 15 to 30 minutes, 19.5% 30 to 45 minutes, 3.3% 45 to 60 minutes, 11.0% 60 minutes or more (2000)

Pike County

Located in western Illinois; bounded on the west and southwest by the Mississippi River and the Missouri border, and on the east by the Illinois River. Covers a land area of 830.30 square miles, a water area of 18.57 square miles, and is located in the Central Time Zone. The county was founded in 1821. County seat is Pittsfield.

Population: 17,577 (1990); 17,384 (2000); 17,094 (2007); 16,907 (2012 projected); Race: 97.4% White, 1.5% Black, 0.3% Asian, 0.6% Hispanic of any race (2007); Density: 20.6 persons per square mile (2007); Average household size: 2.51 (2007); Median age: 41.2 (2007); Males per 100 females: 98.1 (2007).

Religion: Five largest groups: 11.8% The United Methodist Church, 9.2% Christian Churches and Churches of Christ, 7.1% Southern Baptist Convention, 5.3% Christian Church (Disciples of Christ), 3.5% Assemblies of God (2000).

Economy: Unemployment rate: 5.2% (4/2008); Total civilian labor force: 8,579 (4/2008); Leading industries: 18.3% health care and social assistance; 17.9% retail trade; 12.7% accommodation & food services (2005); Farms: 1,041 totaling 425,817 acres (2002); Companies that employ 500 or more persons: 0 (2006); Companies that employ 100 to 499 persons: 5 (2006); Companies that employ less than 100 persons: 372 (2006); Black-owned businesses: n/a (2002); Hispanic-owned businesses: n/a (2002); Asian-owned businesses: n/a (2002); Women-owned businesses: 362 (2002); Retail sales per capita: $10,836 (2008). Single-family building permits issued: 23 (2007); Multi-family building permits issued: 2 (2007).

Income: Per capita income: $19,511 (2007); Median household income: $38,422 (2007); Average household income: $47,406 (2007); Percent of households with income of $100,000 or more: 6.5% (2007); Poverty rate: 14.3% (2005); Bankruptcy rate: 2.21% (2007).

Education: Percent of population age 25 and over with: High school diploma (including GED) or higher: 79.7% (2007); Bachelor's degree or higher: 10.0% (2007); Master's degree or higher: 2.9% (2007).

Housing: Homeownership rate: 77.2% (2007); Median home value: $84,296 (2007); Median rent: $235 per month (2000); Median age of housing: 47 years (2000).

Health: Birth rate: 116.1 per 10,000 population (2007); Death rate: 128.7 per 10,000 population (2007); Age-adjusted cancer mortality rate: 215.8 deaths per 100,000 population (2005); Number of physicians: 7.1 per 10,000 population (2005); Hospital beds: 14.8 per 10,000 population (2004); Hospital admissions: 537.2 per 10,000 population (2004).

Elections: 2004 Presidential election results: 63.1% Bush, 35.7% Kerry, 0.0% Nader, 1.2% Badnarik

Additional Information Contacts

Pike County Government. . . . . (217) 285-6812

Pike County Chamber of Commerce . . . . (217) 285-2971
http://www.pikeil.org

Pike County Communities

BARRY (city). Covers a land area of 1.142 square miles and a water area of 0 square miles. Located at 39.69° N. Lat.; 91.04° W. Long. Elevation is 712 feet.

History: Barry developed as a trading center for a dairying and agricultural area.

Population: 1,440 (1990); 1,368 (2000); 1,361 (2007); 1,329 (2012 projected); Race: 99.0% White, 0.0% Black, 0.9% Asian, 0.9% Hispanic of any race (2007); Density: 1,191.9 persons per square mile (2007); Average household size: 2.43 (2007); Median age: 43.1 (2007); Males per 100 females: 86.7 (2007); Marriage status: 17.4% never married, 58.5% now married, 15.0% widowed, 9.1% divorced (2000); Foreign born: 0.7% (2000); Ancestry (includes multiple ancestries): 24.2% United States or American, 14.7% German, 10.2% English, 9.8% Irish, 7.6% Other groups (2000).

Economy: Single-family building permits issued: 2 (2007); Multi-family building permits issued: 0 (2007); Employment by occupation: 6.8% management, 14.9% professional, 22.2% services, 23.0% sales, 2.0% farming, 8.1% construction, 23.0% production (2000).

Income: Per capita income: $18,756 (2007); Median household income: $29,911 (2007); Average household income: $43,857 (2007); Percent of households with income of $100,000 or more: 5.9% (2007); Poverty rate: 11.5% (2000).

Education: Percent of population age 25 and over with: High school diploma (including GED) or higher: 73.4% (2007); Bachelor's degree or higher: 8.2% (2007); Master's degree or higher: 2.7% (2007).

School District(s)

Barry CUSD 1 (PK-12)
2005-06 Enrollment: 440 . . . . (217) 335-2323

Housing: Homeownership rate: 75.5% (2007); Median home value: $76,379 (2007); Median rent: $216 per month (2000); Median age of housing: 60+ years (2000).

Safety: Violent crime rate: 30.1 per 10,000 population; Property crime rate: 15.0 per 10,000 population (2006).

Transportation: Commute to work: 93.0% car, 0.0% public transportation, 3.9% walk, 2.2% work from home (2000); Travel time to work: 47.6% less than 15 minutes, 14.5% 15 to 30 minutes, 21.9% 30 to 45 minutes, 11.6% 45 to 60 minutes, 4.4% 60 minutes or more (2000)

BAYLIS (village). Covers a land area of 0.479 square miles and a water area of 0 square miles. Located at 39.72° N. Lat.; 90.90° W. Long. Elevation is 863 feet.

Population: 257 (1990); 265 (2000); 259 (2007); 254 (2012 projected); Race: 98.1% White, 0.0% Black, 1.2% Asian, 0.0% Hispanic of any race (2007); Density: 540.2 persons per square mile (2007); Average household size: 2.94 (2007); Median age: 34.5 (2007); Males per 100 females: 99.2 (2007); Marriage status: 20.2% never married, 63.1% now married, 5.9% widowed, 10.8% divorced (2000); Foreign born: 0.0% (2000); Ancestry (includes multiple ancestries): 10.0% United States or American, 8.0% English, 5.5% Irish, 5.1% German, 5.1% Other groups (2000).

Economy: Employment by occupation: 7.0% management, 11.4% professional, 8.8% services, 12.3% sales, 0.0% farming, 7.9% construction, 52.6% production (2000).

Income: Per capita income: $16,757 (2007); Median household income: $43,824 (2007); Average household income: $49,318 (2007); Percent of households with income of $100,000 or more: 8.0% (2007); Poverty rate: 15.8% (2000).

Education: Percent of population age 25 and over with: High school diploma (including GED) or higher: 74.5% (2007); Bachelor's degree or higher: 3.8% (2007); Master's degree or higher: 0.6% (2007).

Housing: Homeownership rate: 77.3% (2007); Median home value: $40,000 (2007); Median rent: $258 per month (2000); Median age of housing: 60+ years (2000).

Transportation: Commute to work: 100.0% car, 0.0% public transportation, 0.0% walk, 0.0% work from home (2000); Travel time to work: 1.9% less than 15 minutes, 39.8% 15 to 30 minutes, 4.9% 30 to 45 minutes, 37.9% 45 to 60 minutes, 15.5% 60 minutes or more (2000)

CHAMBERSBURG (unincorporated postal area, zip code 62323). Covers a land area of 42.802 square miles and a water area of 0.058 square miles. Located at 39.81° N. Lat.; 90.66° W. Long. Elevation is 466 feet.

Population: 294 (2000); Race: 99.1% White, 0.0% Black, 0.0% Asian, 0.0% Hispanic of any race (2000); Density: 6.9 persons per square mile (2000); Age: 23.5% under 18, 17.4% over 64 (2000); Marriage status: 18.0% never married, 73.9% now married, 3.2% widowed, 4.9% divorced (2000); Foreign born: 0.0% (2000); Ancestry (includes multiple ancestries): 47.7% German, 16.9% English, 14.0% Irish, 12.8% Other groups, 7.8% United States or American (2000).

Economy: Employment by occupation: 19.2% management, 16.8% professional, 11.4% services, 13.8% sales, 1.8% farming, 9.6% construction, 27.5% production (2000).

Income: Per capita income: $18,810 (2000); Median household income: $31,875 (2000); Poverty rate: 3.8% (2000).

Education: Percent of population age 25 and over with: High school diploma (including GED) or higher: 91.1% (2000); Bachelor's degree or higher: 12.2% (2000).

Housing: Homeownership rate: 75.2% (2000); Median home value: $57,500 (2000); Median rent: $265 per month (2000); Median age of housing: 49 years (2000).

Transportation: Commute to work: 96.2% car, 0.0% public transportation, 1.3% walk, 2.5% work from home (2000); Travel time to work: 43.2% less than 15 minutes, 20.0% 15 to 30 minutes, 17.4% 30 to 45 minutes, 10.3% 45 to 60 minutes, 9.0% 60 minutes or more (2000)

DETROIT (village). Covers a land area of 0.239 square miles and a water area of 0 square miles. Located at 39.62° N. Lat.; 90.67° W. Long. Elevation is 640 feet.

Population: 126 (1990); 93 (2000); 95 (2007); 94 (2012 projected); Race: 98.9% White, 0.0% Black, 0.0% Asian, 8.4% Hispanic of any race (2007); Density: 397.1 persons per square mile (2007); Average household size: 2.50 (2007); Median age: 34.6 (2007); Males per 100 females: 102.1 (2007); Marriage status: 15.0% never married, 62.5% now married, 10.0% widowed, 12.5% divorced (2000); Foreign born: 0.0% (2000); Ancestry (includes multiple ancestries): 8.8% Irish, 7.1% Other groups, 6.2% United States or American, 5.3% English, 4.4% Dutch (2000).
Economy: Employment by occupation: 5.4% management, 8.1% professional, 35.1% services, 10.8% sales, 8.1% farming, 5.4% construction, 27.0% production (2000).
Income: Per capita income: $18,500 (2007); Median household income: $35,000 (2007); Average household income: $46,250 (2007); Percent of households with income of $100,000 or more: 7.9% (2007); Poverty rate: 13.1% (2000).
Education: Percent of population age 25 and over with: High school diploma (including GED) or higher: 83.1% (2007); Bachelor's degree or higher: 5.1% (2007); Master's degree or higher: 0.0% (2007).
Housing: Homeownership rate: 76.3% (2007); Median home value: $45,000 (2007); Median rent: $185 per month (2000); Median age of housing: 43 years (2000).
Transportation: Commute to work: 91.4% car, 0.0% public transportation, 0.0% walk, 2.9% work from home (2000); Travel time to work: 41.2% less than 15 minutes, 35.3% 15 to 30 minutes, 8.8% 30 to 45 minutes, 0.0% 45 to 60 minutes, 14.7% 60 minutes or more (2000)

EL DARA (village). Covers a land area of 0.967 square miles and a water area of 0 square miles. Located at 39.62° N. Lat.; 90.99° W. Long. Elevation is 735 feet.
Population: 94 (1990); 89 (2000); 91 (2007); 91 (2012 projected); Race: 100.0% White, 0.0% Black, 0.0% Asian, 0.0% Hispanic of any race (2007); Density: 94.1 persons per square mile (2007); Average household size: 2.76 (2007); Median age: 36.6 (2007); Males per 100 females: 68.5 (2007); Marriage status: 18.7% never married, 66.7% now married, 10.7% widowed, 4.0% divorced (2000); Foreign born: 1.8% (2000); Ancestry (includes multiple ancestries): 21.1% United States or American, 15.8% German, 2.6% Irish, 1.8% French (except Basque), 1.8% Welsh (2000).
Economy: Employment by occupation: 11.4% management, 20.5% professional, 25.0% services, 15.9% sales, 4.5% farming, 0.0% construction, 22.7% production (2000).
Income: Per capita income: $15,962 (2007); Median household income: $39,167 (2007); Average household income: $44,015 (2007); Percent of households with income of $100,000 or more: 3.0% (2007); Poverty rate: 9.6% (2000).
Education: Percent of population age 25 and over with: High school diploma (including GED) or higher: 85.7% (2007); Bachelor's degree or higher: 1.8% (2007); Master's degree or higher: 1.8% (2007).
Housing: Homeownership rate: 93.9% (2007); Median home value: $52,500 (2007); Median rent: $n/a per month (2000); Median age of housing: 60+ years (2000).
Transportation: Commute to work: 100.0% car, 0.0% public transportation, 0.0% walk, 0.0% work from home (2000); Travel time to work: 22.7% less than 15 minutes, 34.1% 15 to 30 minutes, 22.7% 30 to 45 minutes, 4.5% 45 to 60 minutes, 15.9% 60 minutes or more (2000)

FLORENCE (village). Covers a land area of 0.203 square miles and a water area of 0 square miles. Located at 39.62° N. Lat.; 90.61° W. Long. Elevation is 453 feet.
Population: 45 (1990); 71 (2000); 73 (2007); 73 (2012 projected); Race: 100.0% White, 0.0% Black, 0.0% Asian, 0.0% Hispanic of any race (2007); Density: 360.2 persons per square mile (2007); Average household size: 2.35 (2007); Median age: 46.9 (2007); Males per 100 females: 135.5 (2007); Marriage status: 18.0% never married, 56.0% now married, 16.0% widowed, 10.0% divorced (2000); Foreign born: 0.0% (2000); Ancestry (includes multiple ancestries): 30.5% English, 8.5% German, 3.4% Dutch, 3.4% Irish, 3.4% Other groups (2000).
Economy: Employment by occupation: 0.0% management, 0.0% professional, 77.8% services, 11.1% sales, 0.0% farming, 11.1% construction, 0.0% production (2000).
Income: Per capita income: $12,226 (2007); Median household income: $27,813 (2007); Average household income: $28,790 (2007); Percent of households with income of $100,000 or more: 0.0% (2007); Poverty rate: 15.1% (2000).
Education: Percent of population age 25 and over with: High school diploma (including GED) or higher: 44.2% (2007); Bachelor's degree or higher: 0.0% (2007); Master's degree or higher: 0.0% (2007).
Housing: Homeownership rate: 71.0% (2007); Median home value: $29,444 (2007); Median rent: $225 per month (2000); Median age of housing: 45 years (2000).
Transportation: Commute to work: 77.8% car, 0.0% public transportation, 11.1% walk, 0.0% work from home (2000); Travel time to work: 33.3% less than 15 minutes, 22.2% 15 to 30 minutes, 22.2% 30 to 45 minutes, 0.0% 45 to 60 minutes, 22.2% 60 minutes or more (2000)

GRIGGSVILLE (city). Covers a land area of 1.035 square miles and a water area of 0 square miles. Located at 39.70° N. Lat.; 90.72° W. Long. Elevation is 705 feet.
History: Incorporated 1878.
Population: 1,218 (1990); 1,258 (2000); 1,244 (2007); 1,215 (2012 projected); Race: 99.4% White, 0.1% Black, 0.1% Asian, 0.2% Hispanic of any race (2007); Density: 1,201.5 persons per square mile (2007); Average household size: 2.53 (2007); Median age: 38.0 (2007); Males per 100 females: 92.6 (2007); Marriage status: 17.6% never married, 63.3% now married, 8.7% widowed, 10.4% divorced (2000); Foreign born: 0.3% (2000); Ancestry (includes multiple ancestries): 21.7% German, 14.9% United States or American, 14.5% English, 10.2% Irish, 3.3% Other groups (2000).
Economy: Single-family building permits issued: 2 (2007); Multi-family building permits issued: 0 (2007); Employment by occupation: 12.9% management, 11.5% professional, 19.1% services, 18.4% sales, 2.7% farming, 11.2% construction, 24.1% production (2000).
Income: Per capita income: $19,159 (2007); Median household income: $41,711 (2007); Average household income: $47,942 (2007); Percent of households with income of $100,000 or more: 5.5% (2007); Poverty rate: 12.3% (2000).
Education: Percent of population age 25 and over with: High school diploma (including GED) or higher: 82.3% (2007); Bachelor's degree or higher: 9.3% (2007); Master's degree or higher: 2.4% (2007).

School District(s)

Griggsville-Perry CUSD 4 (PK-12)
2005-06 Enrollment: 466 . . . . (217) 833-2352

Housing: Homeownership rate: 76.0% (2007); Median home value: $74,615 (2007); Median rent: $258 per month (2000); Median age of housing: 45 years (2000).
Transportation: Commute to work: 91.5% car, 0.4% public transportation, 3.1% walk, 3.1% work from home (2000); Travel time to work: 41.0% less than 15 minutes, 26.7% 15 to 30 minutes, 17.7% 30 to 45 minutes, 11.9% 45 to 60 minutes, 2.6% 60 minutes or more (2000)

HULL (village). Aka Hulls. Covers a land area of 1.836 square miles and a water area of 0.010 square miles. Located at 39.70° N. Lat.; 91.20° W. Long. Elevation is 469 feet.
Population: 514 (1990); 474 (2000); 433 (2007); 423 (2012 projected); Race: 99.3% White, 0.0% Black, 0.0% Asian, 0.0% Hispanic of any race (2007); Density: 235.9 persons per square mile (2007); Average household size: 2.43 (2007); Median age: 38.1 (2007); Males per 100 females: 96.8 (2007); Marriage status: 21.1% never married, 58.0% now married, 7.8% widowed, 13.1% divorced (2000); Foreign born: 0.0% (2000); Ancestry (includes multiple ancestries): 29.5% German, 18.5% United States or American, 15.5% Irish, 14.5% English, 6.4% Dutch (2000).
Economy: Single-family building permits issued: 0 (2007); Multi-family building permits issued: 0 (2007); Employment by occupation: 11.0% management, 9.0% professional, 14.5% services, 27.8% sales, 2.4% farming, 13.3% construction, 22.0% production (2000).
Income: Per capita income: $16,149 (2007); Median household income: $32,083 (2007); Average household income: $39,284 (2007); Percent of households with income of $100,000 or more: 3.9% (2007); Poverty rate: 16.4% (2000).
Education: Percent of population age 25 and over with: High school diploma (including GED) or higher: 73.6% (2007); Bachelor's degree or higher: 15.2% (2007); Master's degree or higher: 3.7% (2007).

School District(s)

West Pike CUSD 2 (PK-12)
2005-06 Enrollment: 269 . . . . (217) 432-8324

Housing: Homeownership rate: 80.3% (2007); Median home value: $71,250 (2007); Median rent: $291 per month (2000); Median age of housing: 48 years (2000).

Transportation: Commute to work: 92.4% car, 0.8% public transportation, 4.0% walk, 1.2% work from home (2000); Travel time to work: 20.6% less than 15 minutes, 36.7% 15 to 30 minutes, 31.0% 30 to 45 minutes, 6.0% 45 to 60 minutes, 5.6% 60 minutes or more (2000)

KINDERHOOK (village). Covers a land area of 0.884 square miles and a water area of 0 square miles. Located at 39.70° N. Lat.; 91.15° W. Long. Elevation is 486 feet.
Population: 269 (1990); 249 (2000); 258 (2007); 250 (2012 projected); Race: 98.4% White, 0.8% Black, 0.0% Asian, 1.9% Hispanic of any race (2007); Density: 291.8 persons per square mile (2007); Average household size: 2.43 (2007); Median age: 39.0 (2007); Males per 100 females: 103.1 (2007); Marriage status: 19.5% never married, 65.4% now married, 4.9% widowed, 10.2% divorced (2000); Foreign born: 0.8% (2000); Ancestry (includes multiple ancestries): 29.5% United States or American, 16.7% German, 16.7% English, 7.4% Irish, 5.4% Other groups (2000).
Economy: Employment by occupation: 5.4% management, 16.2% professional, 17.6% services, 20.9% sales, 0.0% farming, 9.5% construction, 30.4% production (2000).
Income: Per capita income: $20,552 (2007); Median household income: $46,667 (2007); Average household income: $50,024 (2007); Percent of households with income of $100,000 or more: 6.6% (2007); Poverty rate: 6.3% (2000).
Education: Percent of population age 25 and over with: High school diploma (including GED) or higher: 85.5% (2007); Bachelor's degree or higher: 5.8% (2007); Master's degree or higher: 2.9% (2007).

School District(s)

West Pike CUSD 2 (PK-12)
2005-06 Enrollment: 269 . . . . (217) 432-8324
Housing: Homeownership rate: 85.8% (2007); Median home value: $59,545 (2007); Median rent: $254 per month (2000); Median age of housing: 46 years (2000).
Transportation: Commute to work: 95.9% car, 0.0% public transportation, 2.7% walk, 1.4% work from home (2000); Travel time to work: 15.1% less than 15 minutes, 19.9% 15 to 30 minutes, 50.7% 30 to 45 minutes, 5.5% 45 to 60 minutes, 8.9% 60 minutes or more (2000)

MILTON (village). Covers a land area of 0.375 square miles and a water area of 0 square miles. Located at 39.56° N. Lat.; 90.64° W. Long. Elevation is 666 feet.
Population: 270 (1990); 274 (2000); 280 (2007); 279 (2012 projected); Race: 100.0% White, 0.0% Black, 0.0% Asian, 0.7% Hispanic of any race (2007); Density: 747.0 persons per square mile (2007); Average household size: 2.57 (2007); Median age: 35.7 (2007); Males per 100 females: 77.2 (2007); Marriage status: 17.9% never married, 57.2% now married, 19.4% widowed, 5.5% divorced (2000); Foreign born: 0.0% (2000); Ancestry (includes multiple ancestries): 16.2% United States or American, 15.5% English, 10.0% French (except Basque), 9.2% Irish, 6.6% German (2000).
Economy: Employment by occupation: 2.9% management, 11.8% professional, 17.6% services, 19.6% sales, 2.9% farming, 17.6% construction, 27.5% production (2000).
Income: Per capita income: $16,019 (2007); Median household income: $35,156 (2007); Average household income: $40,757 (2007); Percent of households with income of $100,000 or more: 1.8% (2007); Poverty rate: 10.0% (2000).
Education: Percent of population age 25 and over with: High school diploma (including GED) or higher: 72.6% (2007); Bachelor's degree or higher: 4.3% (2007); Master's degree or higher: 0.0% (2007).
Housing: Homeownership rate: 87.2% (2007); Median home value: $50,625 (2007); Median rent: $142 per month (2000); Median age of housing: 45 years (2000).
Transportation: Commute to work: 86.7% car, 0.0% public transportation, 3.1% walk, 7.1% work from home (2000); Travel time to work: 20.9% less than 15 minutes, 36.3% 15 to 30 minutes, 7.7% 30 to 45 minutes, 15.4% 45 to 60 minutes, 19.8% 60 minutes or more (2000)

NEBO (village). Covers a land area of 0.423 square miles and a water area of 0.006 square miles. Located at 39.44° N. Lat.; 90.78° W. Long. Elevation is 482 feet.
Population: 400 (1990); 408 (2000); 392 (2007); 389 (2012 projected); Race: 97.7% White, 0.0% Black, 0.0% Asian, 3.1% Hispanic of any race (2007); Density: 927.0 persons per square mile (2007); Average household size: 2.58 (2007); Median age: 34.4 (2007); Males per 100 females: 106.3 (2007); Marriage status: 23.4% never married, 50.5% now married, 10.0% widowed, 16.1% divorced (2000); Foreign born: 1.3% (2000); Ancestry (includes multiple ancestries): 18.8% United States or American, 18.3% German, 12.2% Other groups, 9.7% Irish, 6.1% Dutch (2000).
Economy: Employment by occupation: 1.9% management, 8.1% professional, 18.1% services, 12.5% sales, 3.8% farming, 22.5% construction, 33.1% production (2000).
Income: Per capita income: $17,188 (2007); Median household income: $40,833 (2007); Average household income: $44,326 (2007); Percent of households with income of $100,000 or more: 4.6% (2007); Poverty rate: 20.1% (2000).
Education: Percent of population age 25 and over with: High school diploma (including GED) or higher: 71.4% (2007); Bachelor's degree or higher: 5.3% (2007); Master's degree or higher: 0.8% (2007).
Housing: Homeownership rate: 88.8% (2007); Median home value: $48,810 (2007); Median rent: $144 per month (2000); Median age of housing: 49 years (2000).
Transportation: Commute to work: 93.1% car, 1.3% public transportation, 1.9% walk, 1.9% work from home (2000); Travel time to work: 10.2% less than 15 minutes, 35.7% 15 to 30 minutes, 20.4% 30 to 45 minutes, 10.2% 45 to 60 minutes, 23.6% 60 minutes or more (2000)

NEW CANTON (town). Covers a land area of 0.778 square miles and a water area of 0 square miles. Located at 39.63° N. Lat.; 91.09° W. Long. Elevation is 476 feet.
Population: 405 (1990); 417 (2000); 414 (2007); 408 (2012 projected); Race: 100.0% White, 0.0% Black, 0.0% Asian, 0.0% Hispanic of any race (2007); Density: 532.0 persons per square mile (2007); Average household size: 2.34 (2007); Median age: 40.4 (2007); Males per 100 females: 84.0 (2007); Marriage status: 16.2% never married, 58.6% now married, 11.4% widowed, 13.8% divorced (2000); Foreign born: 0.7% (2000); Ancestry (includes multiple ancestries): 22.4% German, 14.3% United States or American, 12.3% Irish, 10.7% English, 8.5% Other groups (2000).
Economy: Employment by occupation: 5.9% management, 10.7% professional, 17.2% services, 18.3% sales, 3.6% farming, 16.6% construction, 27.8% production (2000).
Income: Per capita income: $15,761 (2007); Median household income: $31,250 (2007); Average household income: $36,864 (2007); Percent of households with income of $100,000 or more: 2.3% (2007); Poverty rate: 19.9% (2000).
Education: Percent of population age 25 and over with: High school diploma (including GED) or higher: 79.1% (2007); Bachelor's degree or higher: 5.9% (2007); Master's degree or higher: 2.8% (2007).
Housing: Homeownership rate: 78.0% (2007); Median home value: $51,176 (2007); Median rent: $218 per month (2000); Median age of housing: 56 years (2000).
Transportation: Commute to work: 97.0% car, 0.0% public transportation, 0.6% walk, 2.4% work from home (2000); Travel time to work: 23.9% less than 15 minutes, 21.5% 15 to 30 minutes, 34.4% 30 to 45 minutes, 15.3% 45 to 60 minutes, 4.9% 60 minutes or more (2000)

NEW SALEM (village). Covers a land area of 1.043 square miles and a water area of 0 square miles. Located at 39.70° N. Lat.; 90.84° W. Long. Elevation is 784 feet.
Population: 147 (1990); 136 (2000); 131 (2007); 127 (2012 projected); Race: 99.2% White, 0.0% Black, 0.0% Asian, 0.0% Hispanic of any race (2007); Density: 125.7 persons per square mile (2007); Average household size: 2.52 (2007); Median age: 40.6 (2007); Males per 100 females: 79.5 (2007); Marriage status: 18.0% never married, 70.0% now married, 9.0% widowed, 3.0% divorced (2000); Foreign born: 0.0% (2000); Ancestry (includes multiple ancestries): 24.0% United States or American, 23.3% German, 18.7% Irish, 11.3% English, 6.0% British (2000).
Economy: Employment by occupation: 22.7% management, 15.9% professional, 31.8% services, 9.1% sales, 0.0% farming, 6.8% construction, 13.6% production (2000).
Income: Per capita income: $24,365 (2007); Median household income: $36,111 (2007); Average household income: $58,606 (2007); Percent of households with income of $100,000 or more: 5.8% (2007); Poverty rate: 24.7% (2000).
Education: Percent of population age 25 and over with: High school diploma (including GED) or higher: 72.7% (2007); Bachelor's degree or higher: 13.6% (2007); Master's degree or higher: 2.3% (2007).
Housing: Homeownership rate: 73.1% (2007); Median home value: $67,500 (2007); Median rent: $288 per month (2000); Median age of housing: 60+ years (2000).
Transportation: Commute to work: 81.8% car, 0.0% public transportation, 4.5% walk, 13.6% work from home (2000); Travel time to work: 26.3% less

than 15 minutes, 34.2% 15 to 30 minutes, 5.3% 30 to 45 minutes, 23.7% 45 to 60 minutes, 10.5% 60 minutes or more (2000)

PEARL (village). Covers a land area of 1.507 square miles and a water area of 0.087 square miles. Located at 39.45° N. Lat.; 90.62° W. Long. Elevation is 459 feet.
Population: 177 (1990); 187 (2000); 177 (2007); 177 (2012 projected); Race: 99.4% White, 0.0% Black, 0.0% Asian, 0.0% Hispanic of any race (2007); Density: 117.5 persons per square mile (2007); Average household size: 2.49 (2007); Median age: 30.6 (2007); Males per 100 females: 101.1 (2007); Marriage status: 20.0% never married, 49.2% now married, 15.4% widowed, 15.4% divorced (2000); Foreign born: 0.0% (2000); Ancestry (includes multiple ancestries): 26.1% Irish, 21.8% German, 17.0% United States or American, 11.7% English, 3.7% Italian (2000).
Economy: Employment by occupation: 5.4% management, 7.1% professional, 25.0% services, 28.6% sales, 0.0% farming, 19.6% construction, 14.3% production (2000).
Income: Per capita income: $14,251 (2007); Median household income: $22,500 (2007); Average household income: $35,528 (2007); Percent of households with income of $100,000 or more: 2.8% (2007); Poverty rate: 29.8% (2000).
Education: Percent of population age 25 and over with: High school diploma (including GED) or higher: 65.0% (2007); Bachelor's degree or higher: 0.0% (2007); Master's degree or higher: 0.0% (2007).
Housing: Homeownership rate: 85.9% (2007); Median home value: $23,500 (2007); Median rent: $133 per month (2000); Median age of housing: 60+ years (2000).
Transportation: Commute to work: 80.4% car, 0.0% public transportation, 7.1% walk, 12.5% work from home (2000); Travel time to work: 22.4% less than 15 minutes, 16.3% 15 to 30 minutes, 28.6% 30 to 45 minutes, 14.3% 45 to 60 minutes, 18.4% 60 minutes or more (2000)

PERRY (village). Covers a land area of 0.382 square miles and a water area of 0 square miles. Located at 39.78° N. Lat.; 90.74° W. Long. Elevation is 591 feet.
Population: 491 (1990); 437 (2000); 417 (2007); 411 (2012 projected); Race: 98.8% White, 0.0% Black, 0.5% Asian, 0.0% Hispanic of any race (2007); Density: 1,091.2 persons per square mile (2007); Average household size: 2.22 (2007); Median age: 39.9 (2007); Males per 100 females: 81.3 (2007); Marriage status: 14.7% never married, 59.1% now married, 16.9% widowed, 9.3% divorced (2000); Foreign born: 0.0% (2000); Ancestry (includes multiple ancestries): 23.3% German, 19.2% English, 11.7% United States or American, 6.0% Irish, 5.7% Other groups (2000).
Economy: Single-family building permits issued: 0 (2007); Multi-family building permits issued: 0 (2007); Employment by occupation: 13.1% management, 11.0% professional, 25.5% services, 19.3% sales, 4.8% farming, 10.3% construction, 15.9% production (2000).
Income: Per capita income: $19,718 (2007); Median household income: $32,500 (2007); Average household income: $43,737 (2007); Percent of households with income of $100,000 or more: 8.0% (2007); Poverty rate: 24.4% (2000).
Education: Percent of population age 25 and over with: High school diploma (including GED) or higher: 81.1% (2007); Bachelor's degree or higher: 7.5% (2007); Master's degree or higher: 2.5% (2007).

School District(s)

Griggsville-Perry CUSD 4 (PK-12)
2005-06 Enrollment: 466 . . . . (217) 833-2352
Housing: Homeownership rate: 77.1% (2007); Median home value: $53,750 (2007); Median rent: $137 per month (2000); Median age of housing: 37 years (2000).
Transportation: Commute to work: 84.1% car, 0.0% public transportation, 6.2% walk, 6.9% work from home (2000); Travel time to work: 35.6% less than 15 minutes, 33.3% 15 to 30 minutes, 20.0% 30 to 45 minutes, 7.4% 45 to 60 minutes, 3.7% 60 minutes or more (2000)

PITTSFIELD (city). County seat. Covers a land area of 3.574 square miles and a water area of 0.045 square miles. Located at 39.61° N. Lat.; 90.80° W. Long. Elevation is 732 feet.
History: Pittsfield was founded in 1833 by settlers from Pittsfield, Massachusetts. The town developed as the seat of Pike County, and as a pork-packing center, using barrels made of white oak that grew around the town. John Hay (1838-1905), Secretary of State under Presidents McKinley and Theodore Roosevelt, was a resident of Pittsfield for several years.
Population: 4,193 (1990); 4,211 (2000); 4,197 (2007); 4,202 (2012 projected); Race: 98.5% White, 0.2% Black, 0.4% Asian, 0.5% Hispanic of any race (2007); Density: 1,174.3 persons per square mile (2007); Average household size: 2.31 (2007); Median age: 46.2 (2007); Males per 100 females: 83.6 (2007); Marriage status: 19.2% never married, 56.1% now married, 13.5% widowed, 11.2% divorced (2000); Foreign born: 2.0% (2000); Ancestry (includes multiple ancestries): 20.1% German, 16.3% United States or American, 15.8% English, 10.6% Irish, 9.2% Other groups (2000).
Economy: Single-family building permits issued: 2 (2007); Multi-family building permits issued: 2 (2007); Employment by occupation: 6.8% management, 19.2% professional, 20.5% services, 26.2% sales, 2.3% farming, 8.0% construction, 17.0% production (2000).
Income: Per capita income: $20,083 (2007); Median household income: $34,295 (2007); Average household income: $43,440 (2007); Percent of households with income of $100,000 or more: 4.6% (2007); Poverty rate: 12.3% (2000).
Education: Percent of population age 25 and over with: High school diploma (including GED) or higher: 82.5% (2007); Bachelor's degree or higher: 14.0% (2007); Master's degree or higher: 3.8% (2007).

School District(s)

Dept of Corrections Sch Dist 428 (08-12)
2005-06 Enrollment: 2,271 . . . . (217) 522-2666
Pikeland CUSD 10 (PK-12)
2005-06 Enrollment: 1,375 . . . . (217) 285-2147
Housing: Homeownership rate: 72.8% (2007); Median home value: $97,217 (2007); Median rent: $280 per month (2000); Median age of housing: 44 years (2000).
Hospitals: Illinois Community Hospital (37 beds)
Safety: Violent crime rate: 6.5 per 10,000 population; Property crime rate: 87.0 per 10,000 population (2006).
Newspapers: Pike County Express (Local news; Circulation 4,100); Pike Press (Community news; Circulation 7,850)
Transportation: Commute to work: 92.2% car, 0.2% public transportation, 4.6% walk, 2.9% work from home (2000); Travel time to work: 68.4% less than 15 minutes, 9.5% 15 to 30 minutes, 7.4% 30 to 45 minutes, 9.8% 45 to 60 minutes, 4.9% 60 minutes or more (2000)
Airports: Pittsfield Penstone Municipal (general aviation)
Additional Information Contacts
Pike County Chamber of Commerce . . . . (217) 285-2971
http://www.pikeil.org

PLEASANT HILL (village). Covers a land area of 0.763 square miles and a water area of 0.023 square miles. Located at 39.44° N. Lat.; 90.87° W. Long. Elevation is 469 feet.
Population: 1,124 (1990); 1,047 (2000); 1,011 (2007); 1,007 (2012 projected); Race: 98.3% White, 0.0% Black, 0.0% Asian, 0.8% Hispanic of any race (2007); Density: 1,325.6 persons per square mile (2007); Average household size: 2.33 (2007); Median age: 40.0 (2007); Males per 100 females: 99.4 (2007); Marriage status: 16.6% never married, 61.4% now married, 14.1% widowed, 7.9% divorced (2000); Foreign born: 1.3% (2000); Ancestry (includes multiple ancestries): 18.0% United States or American, 15.2% German, 10.0% English, 9.6% Irish, 5.4% Other groups (2000).
Economy: Employment by occupation: 9.8% management, 13.8% professional, 17.6% services, 26.9% sales, 5.2% farming, 8.6% construction, 18.1% production (2000).
Income: Per capita income: $16,004 (2007); Median household income: $29,595 (2007); Average household income: $34,937 (2007); Percent of households with income of $100,000 or more: 2.3% (2007); Poverty rate: 17.0% (2000).
Education: Percent of population age 25 and over with: High school diploma (including GED) or higher: 72.3% (2007); Bachelor's degree or higher: 9.5% (2007); Master's degree or higher: 3.9% (2007).

School District(s)

Pleasant Hill CUSD 3 (PK-12)
2005-06 Enrollment: 336 . . . . (217) 734-2311
Housing: Homeownership rate: 79.0% (2007); Median home value: $70,500 (2007); Median rent: $207 per month (2000); Median age of housing: 45 years (2000).
Safety: Violent crime rate: 49.4 per 10,000 population; Property crime rate: 39.5 per 10,000 population (2006).
Newspapers: Weekly Messenger (Local news; Circulation 1,500)
Transportation: Commute to work: 93.9% car, 0.0% public transportation, 1.7% walk, 3.6% work from home (2000); Travel time to work: 38.1% less

than 15 minutes, 37.9% 15 to 30 minutes, 15.7% 30 to 45 minutes, 2.0% 45 to 60 minutes, 6.3% 60 minutes or more (2000)

ROCKPORT (unincorporated postal area, zip code 62370). Covers a land area of 55.630 square miles and a water area of 0.377 square miles. Located at 39.51° N. Lat.; 90.99° W. Long. Elevation is 489 feet.
Population: 641 (2000); Race: 100.0% White, 0.0% Black, 0.0% Asian, 0.0% Hispanic of any race (2000); Density: 11.5 persons per square mile (2000); Age: 29.7% under 18, 8.3% over 64 (2000); Marriage status: 25.4% never married, 60.1% now married, 5.4% widowed, 9.1% divorced (2000); Foreign born: 0.9% (2000); Ancestry (includes multiple ancestries): 28.6% United States or American, 16.3% German, 7.1% English, 6.9% Other groups, 6.3% Irish (2000).
Economy: Employment by occupation: 13.7% management, 8.5% professional, 18.6% services, 22.9% sales, 7.3% farming, 7.6% construction, 21.3% production (2000).
Income: Per capita income: $14,348 (2000); Median household income: $33,036 (2000); Poverty rate: 10.4% (2000).
Education: Percent of population age 25 and over with: High school diploma (including GED) or higher: 83.3% (2000); Bachelor's degree or higher: 2.5% (2000).
Housing: Homeownership rate: 81.7% (2000); Median home value: $51,700 (2000); Median rent: $225 per month (2000); Median age of housing: 46 years (2000).
Transportation: Commute to work: 95.0% car, 0.0% public transportation, 0.0% walk, 4.3% work from home (2000); Travel time to work: 18.2% less than 15 minutes, 41.6% 15 to 30 minutes, 14.9% 30 to 45 minutes, 9.1% 45 to 60 minutes, 16.2% 60 minutes or more (2000)

TIME (village). Covers a land area of 0.436 square miles and a water area of 0 square miles. Located at 39.56° N. Lat.; 90.72° W. Long. Elevation is 692 feet.
Population: 36 (1990); 29 (2000); 27 (2007); 27 (2012 projected); Race: 100.0% White, 0.0% Black, 0.0% Asian, 0.0% Hispanic of any race (2007); Density: 61.9 persons per square mile (2007); Average household size: 2.25 (2007); Median age: 52.5 (2007); Males per 100 females: 170.0 (2007); Marriage status: 22.2% never married, 22.2% now married, 38.9% widowed, 16.7% divorced (2000); Foreign born: 0.0% (2000); Ancestry (includes multiple ancestries): 52.6% German, 21.1% Irish, 5.3% English (2000).
Economy: Employment by occupation: 0.0% management, 0.0% professional, 0.0% services, 0.0% sales, 0.0% farming, 100.0% construction, 0.0% production (2000).
Income: Per capita income: $11,574 (2007); Median household income: $17,500 (2007); Average household income: $26,042 (2007); Percent of households with income of $100,000 or more: 0.0% (2007); Poverty rate: 5.3% (2000).
Education: Percent of population age 25 and over with: High school diploma (including GED) or higher: 17.4% (2007); Bachelor's degree or higher: 0.0% (2007); Master's degree or higher: 0.0% (2007).
Housing: Homeownership rate: 66.7% (2007); Median home value: $22,500 (2007); Median rent: $225 per month (2000); Median age of housing: 55 years (2000).
Transportation: Commute to work: 100.0% car, 0.0% public transportation, 0.0% walk, 0.0% work from home (2000); Travel time to work: 0.0% less than 15 minutes, 0.0% 15 to 30 minutes, 0.0% 30 to 45 minutes, 100.0% 45 to 60 minutes, 0.0% 60 minutes or more (2000)

VALLEY CITY (village). Covers a land area of 0.196 square miles and a water area of 0.013 square miles. Located at 39.70° N. Lat.; 90.65° W. Long. Elevation is 486 feet.
Population: 23 (1990); 14 (2000); 14 (2007); 14 (2012 projected); Race: 100.0% White, 0.0% Black, 0.0% Asian, 0.0% Hispanic of any race (2007); Density: 71.5 persons per square mile (2007); Average household size: 3.50 (2007); Median age: 47.5 (2007); Males per 100 females: 100.0 (2007); Marriage status: 40.0% never married, 40.0% now married, 0.0% widowed, 20.0% divorced (2000); Foreign born: 0.0% (2000); Ancestry (includes multiple ancestries): 100.0% United States or American (2000).
Economy: Employment by occupation: 0.0% management, 0.0% professional, 0.0% services, 0.0% sales, 0.0% farming, 0.0% construction, 100.0% production (2000).
Income: Per capita income: $17,500 (2007); Median household income: $60,000 (2007); Average household income: $61,250 (2007); Percent of households with income of $100,000 or more: 0.0% (2007); Poverty rate: 0.0% (2000).
Education: Percent of population age 25 and over with: High school diploma (including GED) or higher: 0.0% (2007); Bachelor's degree or higher: 0.0% (2007); Master's degree or higher: 0.0% (2007).
Housing: Homeownership rate: 100.0% (2007); Median home value: $45,000 (2007); Median rent: $n/a per month (2000); Median age of housing: 35 years (2000).
Transportation: Commute to work: 100.0% car, 0.0% public transportation, 0.0% walk, 0.0% work from home (2000); Travel time to work: 0.0% less than 15 minutes, 0.0% 15 to 30 minutes, 0.0% 30 to 45 minutes, 0.0% 45 to 60 minutes, 100.0% 60 minutes or more (2000)

Pope County

Located in southeastern Illinois, partly in the Ozarks; bounded on the east by the Ohio River and the Kentucky border; drained by tributaries of the Ohio River; includes part of Shawnee National Forest. Covers a land area of 370.86 square miles, a water area of 3.77 square miles, and is located in the Central Time Zone. The county was founded in 1816. County seat is Golconda.

Weather Station: Dixon Springs Agr. Center Elevation: 538 feet

	Jan	Feb	Mar	Apr	May	Jun	Jul	Aug	Sep	Oct	Nov	Dec
High	42	48	59	69	78	85	89	88	82	72	58	47
Low	24	28	38	47	55	63	67	65	58	47	39	30
Precip	3.2	3.3	4.7	4.9	5.2	4.1	3.7	3.6	3.2	3.3	4.6	4.3
Snow	3.8	3.3	1.5	0.1	0.0	0.0	0.0	0.0	0.0	0.2	tr	0.8

High and Low temperatures in degrees Fahrenheit; Precipitation and Snow in inches

Population: 4,373 (1990); 4,413 (2000); 4,143 (2007); 3,933 (2012 projected); Race: 92.5% White, 4.9% Black, 0.3% Asian, 1.2% Hispanic of any race (2007); Density: 11.2 persons per square mile (2007); Average household size: 2.49 (2007); Median age: 43.1 (2007); Males per 100 females: 104.6 (2007).
Religion: Five largest groups: 33.7% Southern Baptist Convention, 4.5% The United Methodist Church, 2.7% Lutheran Church—Missouri Synod, 2.6% Church of God (Cleveland, Tennessee), 0.9% Presbyterian Church (U.S.A.) (2000).
Economy: Unemployment rate: 6.5% (4/2008); Total civilian labor force: 1,966 (4/2008); Leading industries: 37.2% health care and social assistance; 11.3% retail trade; 7.4% construction (2005); Farms: 341 totaling 76,935 acres (2002); Companies that employ 500 or more persons: 0 (2006); Companies that employ 100 to 499 persons: 0 (2006); Companies that employ less than 100 persons: 65 (2006); Black-owned businesses: n/a (2002); Hispanic-owned businesses: n/a (2002); Asian-owned businesses: n/a (2002); Women-owned businesses: n/a (2002); Retail sales per capita: $2,043 (2008). Single-family building permits issued: 0 (2007); Multi-family building permits issued: 0 (2007).
Income: Per capita income: $18,533 (2007); Median household income: $34,742 (2007); Average household income: $44,252 (2007); Percent of households with income of $100,000 or more: 5.9% (2007); Poverty rate: 17.9% (2005); Bankruptcy rate: 3.83% (2007).
Education: Percent of population age 25 and over with: High school diploma (including GED) or higher: 76.1% (2007); Bachelor's degree or higher: 10.4% (2007); Master's degree or higher: 4.7% (2007).
Housing: Homeownership rate: 82.8% (2007); Median home value: $88,333 (2007); Median rent: $169 per month (2000); Median age of housing: 29 years (2000).
Health: Birth rate: 93.3 per 10,000 population (2007); Death rate: 95.6 per 10,000 population (2007); Age-adjusted cancer mortality rate: 277.4 (Unreliable) deaths per 100,000 population (2005); Number of physicians: 4.8 per 10,000 population (2005); Hospital beds: 0.0 per 10,000 population (2004); Hospital admissions: 0.0 per 10,000 population (2004).
Elections: 2004 Presidential election results: 61.6% Bush, 37.7% Kerry, 0.0% Nader, 0.7% Badnarik
National and State Parks: Dixon Springs State Park; Dog Island State Wetlands; Millstone Bluff National Register Site; Shawnee National Forest
Additional Information Contacts
Pope County Government . . . . (618) 683-4466

Golconda Pope County Chamber . . . . (618) 683-9702

Pope County Communities

EDDYVILLE (village). Covers a land area of 0.287 square miles and a water area of 0 square miles. Located at 37.50° N. Lat.; 88.58° W. Long. Elevation is 699 feet.

Population: 151 (1990); 153 (2000); 146 (2007); 142 (2012 projected); Race: 93.8% White, 0.0% Black, 1.4% Asian, 1.4% Hispanic of any race (2007); Density: 508.7 persons per square mile (2007); Average household size: 2.28 (2007); Median age: 36.1 (2007); Males per 100 females: 108.6 (2007); Marriage status: 16.8% never married, 58.9% now married, 16.8% widowed, 7.4% divorced (2000); Foreign born: 0.0% (2000); Ancestry (includes multiple ancestries): 24.4% German, 20.2% Irish, 8.4% United States or American, 7.6% English, 5.0% Other groups (2000).
Economy: Employment by occupation: 4.9% management, 9.8% professional, 24.4% services, 22.0% sales, 0.0% farming, 14.6% construction, 24.4% production (2000).
Income: Per capita income: $15,223 (2007); Median household income: $29,375 (2007); Average household income: $34,727 (2007); Percent of households with income of $100,000 or more: 0.0% (2007); Poverty rate: 16.8% (2000).
Education: Percent of population age 25 and over with: High school diploma (including GED) or higher: 67.7% (2007); Bachelor's degree or higher: 1.0% (2007); Master's degree or higher: 0.0% (2007).
Housing: Homeownership rate: 67.2% (2007); Median home value: $67,857 (2007); Median rent: $142 per month (2000); Median age of housing: 34 years (2000).
Transportation: Commute to work: 97.4% car, 0.0% public transportation, 0.0% walk, 0.0% work from home (2000); Travel time to work: 0.0% less than 15 minutes, 48.7% 15 to 30 minutes, 33.3% 30 to 45 minutes, 5.1% 45 to 60 minutes, 12.8% 60 minutes or more (2000)

GOLCONDA (city). County seat. Covers a land area of 0.564 square miles and a water area of 0.026 square miles. Located at 37.36° N. Lat.; 88.48° W. Long. Elevation is 354 feet.
History: Incorporated 1845.
Population: 877 (1990); 726 (2000); 629 (2007); 596 (2012 projected); Race: 94.4% White, 2.7% Black, 0.3% Asian, 0.5% Hispanic of any race (2007); Density: 1,115.1 persons per square mile (2007); Average household size: 2.24 (2007); Median age: 48.9 (2007); Males per 100 females: 78.2 (2007); Marriage status: 21.9% never married, 43.2% now married, 21.2% widowed, 13.7% divorced (2000); Foreign born: 0.5% (2000); Ancestry (includes multiple ancestries): 25.6% German, 13.7% Irish, 13.3% English, 7.7% Other groups, 7.4% United States or American (2000).
Economy: Single-family building permits issued: 0 (2007); Multi-family building permits issued: 0 (2007); Employment by occupation: 6.3% management, 11.4% professional, 24.8% services, 29.5% sales, 0.0% farming, 8.3% construction, 19.7% production (2000).
Income: Per capita income: $18,130 (2007); Median household income: $22,500 (2007); Average household income: $34,297 (2007); Percent of households with income of $100,000 or more: 3.6% (2007); Poverty rate: 25.0% (2000).
Education: Percent of population age 25 and over with: High school diploma (including GED) or higher: 65.9% (2007); Bachelor's degree or higher: 9.4% (2007); Master's degree or higher: 4.4% (2007).

School District(s)

Pope Co Cud 1 (PK-12)
2005-06 Enrollment: 570 . . . . (618) 683-2301
Housing: Homeownership rate: 55.2% (2007); Median home value: $57,000 (2007); Median rent: $153 per month (2000); Median age of housing: 40 years (2000).
Newspapers: Herald-Enterprise (Local news; Circulation 2,000)
Transportation: Commute to work: 78.9% car, 1.2% public transportation, 11.8% walk, 6.9% work from home (2000); Travel time to work: 48.9% less than 15 minutes, 9.2% 15 to 30 minutes, 15.3% 30 to 45 minutes, 16.6% 45 to 60 minutes, 10.0% 60 minutes or more (2000)
Additional Information Contacts
Golconda Pope County Chamber . . . . (618) 683-9702

HEROD (unincorporated postal area, zip code 62947). Covers a land area of 68.806 square miles and a water area of 0.144 square miles. Located at 37.56° N. Lat.; 88.39° W. Long. Elevation is 423 feet.
Population: 597 (2000); Race: 98.8% White, 0.0% Black, 0.0% Asian, 0.0% Hispanic of any race (2000); Density: 8.7 persons per square mile (2000); Age: 23.2% under 18, 6.6% over 64 (2000); Marriage status: 28.7% never married, 54.9% now married, 2.8% widowed, 13.6% divorced (2000); Foreign born: 8.1% (2000); Ancestry (includes multiple ancestries): 14.0% United States or American, 10.7% German, 10.5% Irish, 8.1% Swiss, 7.6% Other groups (2000).
Economy: Employment by occupation: 13.1% management, 13.1% professional, 12.7% services, 15.0% sales, 0.0% farming, 28.1% construction, 18.0% production (2000).
Income: Per capita income: $18,727 (2000); Median household income: $35,769 (2000); Poverty rate: 7.4% (2000).
Education: Percent of population age 25 and over with: High school diploma (including GED) or higher: 91.0% (2000); Bachelor's degree or higher: 19.3% (2000).
Housing: Homeownership rate: 90.2% (2000); Median home value: $36,400 (2000); Median rent: $275 per month (2000); Median age of housing: 29 years (2000).
Transportation: Commute to work: 95.7% car, 0.0% public transportation, 0.0% walk, 2.3% work from home (2000); Travel time to work: 7.9% less than 15 minutes, 54.5% 15 to 30 minutes, 15.4% 30 to 45 minutes, 13.7% 45 to 60 minutes, 8.6% 60 minutes or more (2000)

Pulaski County

Located in southern Illinois; bounded on the south by the Ohio River and the Kentucky border; drained by the Cache River. Covers a land area of 200.79 square miles, a water area of 2.55 square miles, and is located in the Central Time Zone. The county was founded in 1843. County seat is Mound City.
Population: 7,523 (1990); 7,348 (2000); 6,617 (2007); 6,070 (2012 projected); Race: 67.2% White, 30.4% Black, 1.0% Asian, 1.6% Hispanic of any race (2007); Density: 33.0 persons per square mile (2007); Average household size: 2.52 (2007); Median age: 37.5 (2007); Males per 100 females: 91.3 (2007).
Religion: Five largest groups: 30.5% Southern Baptist Convention, 8.4% Catholic Church, 6.8% The United Methodist Church, 3.0% Conservative Congregational Christian Conference, 2.8% Churches of Christ (2000).
Economy: Unemployment rate: 7.2% (4/2008); Total civilian labor force: 3,054 (4/2008); Leading industries: 22.0% health care and social assistance; 13.7% retail trade; 10.0% administration, support, waste management, remediation services (2005); Farms: 253 totaling 86,289 acres (2002); Companies that employ 500 or more persons: 0 (2006); Companies that employ 100 to 499 persons: 0 (2006); Companies that employ less than 100 persons: 112 (2006); Black-owned businesses: n/a (2002); Hispanic-owned businesses: n/a (2002); Asian-owned businesses: n/a (2002); Women-owned businesses: n/a (2002); Retail sales per capita: $3,601 (2008). Single-family building permits issued: 5 (2007); Multi-family building permits issued: 4 (2007).
Income: Per capita income: $16,535 (2007); Median household income: $30,688 (2007); Average household income: $39,526 (2007); Percent of households with income of $100,000 or more: 6.1% (2007); Poverty rate: 28.7% (2005); Bankruptcy rate: 6.63% (2007).
Education: Percent of population age 25 and over with: High school diploma (including GED) or higher: 71.0% (2007); Bachelor's degree or higher: 7.1% (2007); Master's degree or higher: 2.1% (2007).
Housing: Homeownership rate: 75.6% (2007); Median home value: $45,718 (2007); Median rent: $201 per month (2000); Median age of housing: 36 years (2000).
Health: Birth rate: 140.2 per 10,000 population (2007); Death rate: 124.8 per 10,000 population (2007); Age-adjusted cancer mortality rate: 325.7 deaths per 100,000 population (2005); Number of physicians: 0.0 per 10,000 population (2005); Hospital beds: 0.0 per 10,000 population (2004); Hospital admissions: 0.0 per 10,000 population (2004).
Elections: 2004 Presidential election results: 55.3% Bush, 44.1% Kerry, 0.0% Nader, 0.5% Badnarik
Additional Information Contacts
Pulaski County Government . . . . (618) 748-9360

Pulaski County Communities

GRAND CHAIN (unincorporated postal area, zip code 62941). Aka New Grand Chain. Covers a land area of 35.579 square miles and a water area of 0.817 square miles. Located at 37.24° N. Lat.; 88.99° W. Long. Elevation is 394 feet.
Population: 890 (2000); Race: 90.7% White, 6.0% Black, 0.0% Asian, 0.0% Hispanic of any race (2000); Density: 25.0 persons per square mile (2000); Age: 24.1% under 18, 16.9% over 64 (2000); Marriage status: 13.9% never married, 66.7% now married, 8.7% widowed, 10.7% divorced (2000); Foreign born: 0.4% (2000); Ancestry (includes multiple ancestries):

27.6% German, 18.3% Other groups, 16.6% Irish, 14.6% English, 6.3% United States or American (2000).
Economy: Employment by occupation: 10.9% management, 15.6% professional, 20.3% services, 17.4% sales, 1.0% farming, 16.6% construction, 18.1% production (2000).
Income: Per capita income: $19,028 (2000); Median household income: $38,173 (2000); Poverty rate: 14.6% (2000).
Education: Percent of population age 25 and over with: High school diploma (including GED) or higher: 82.8% (2000); Bachelor's degree or higher: 8.1% (2000).

School District(s)

Jamp Spec Educ Services (04-12)
2005-06 Enrollment: 34 . . . . (618) 742-6231
Housing: Homeownership rate: 84.7% (2000); Median home value: $51,500 (2000); Median rent: $244 per month (2000); Median age of housing: 32 years (2000).
Transportation: Commute to work: 91.6% car, 1.5% public transportation, 1.3% walk, 4.3% work from home (2000); Travel time to work: 23.8% less than 15 minutes, 29.1% 15 to 30 minutes, 24.1% 30 to 45 minutes, 13.1% 45 to 60 minutes, 9.9% 60 minutes or more (2000)

KARNAK (village). Covers a land area of 1.813 square miles and a water area of 0 square miles. Located at 37.29° N. Lat.; 88.97° W. Long. Elevation is 341 feet.
History: Karnak was established as a company town for a logging and milling industry.
Population: 581 (1990); 619 (2000); 587 (2007); 536 (2012 projected); Race: 91.7% White, 7.5% Black, 0.0% Asian, 4.3% Hispanic of any race (2007); Density: 323.7 persons per square mile (2007); Average household size: 2.35 (2007); Median age: 35.4 (2007); Males per 100 females: 82.3 (2007); Marriage status: 19.6% never married, 60.0% now married, 11.7% widowed, 8.7% divorced (2000); Foreign born: 2.4% (2000); Ancestry (includes multiple ancestries): 19.7% United States or American, 14.4% Other groups, 13.2% German, 6.2% English, 6.0% Irish (2000).
Economy: Employment by occupation: 6.7% management, 12.2% professional, 29.8% services, 13.0% sales, 0.0% farming, 14.7% construction, 23.5% production (2000).
Income: Per capita income: $18,369 (2007); Median household income: $35,263 (2007); Average household income: $43,130 (2007); Percent of households with income of $100,000 or more: 6.4% (2007); Poverty rate: 20.0% (2000).
Education: Percent of population age 25 and over with: High school diploma (including GED) or higher: 74.3% (2007); Bachelor's degree or higher: 6.7% (2007); Master's degree or higher: 2.0% (2007).
Housing: Homeownership rate: 76.0% (2007); Median home value: $44,815 (2007); Median rent: $248 per month (2000); Median age of housing: 37 years (2000).
Transportation: Commute to work: 91.5% car, 0.0% public transportation, 2.6% walk, 3.8% work from home (2000); Travel time to work: 34.7% less than 15 minutes, 27.6% 15 to 30 minutes, 23.1% 30 to 45 minutes, 8.0% 45 to 60 minutes, 6.7% 60 minutes or more (2000)

MOUND CITY (city). County seat. Covers a land area of 0.711 square miles and a water area of 0.050 square miles. Located at 37.08° N. Lat.; 89.16° W. Long. Elevation is 318 feet.
History: Important Union naval base in Civil War. National cemetery is nearby. City severely damaged in 1937 flood. Incorporated 1857.
Population: 765 (1990); 692 (2000); 572 (2007); 542 (2012 projected); Race: 50.7% White, 48.8% Black, 0.0% Asian, 1.2% Hispanic of any race (2007); Density: 804.7 persons per square mile (2007); Average household size: 2.47 (2007); Median age: 30.2 (2007); Males per 100 females: 72.8 (2007); Marriage status: 32.6% never married, 43.3% now married, 11.1% widowed, 13.0% divorced (2000); Foreign born: 0.3% (2000); Ancestry (includes multiple ancestries): 38.9% Other groups, 25.0% United States or American, 6.3% German, 2.1% Irish, 1.5% English (2000).
Economy: Single-family building permits issued: 0 (2007); Multi-family building permits issued: 0 (2007); Employment by occupation: 3.2% management, 9.9% professional, 30.2% services, 26.1% sales, 0.0% farming, 8.6% construction, 22.1% production (2000).
Income: Per capita income: $13,844 (2007); Median household income: $21,000 (2007); Average household income: $34,052 (2007); Percent of households with income of $100,000 or more: 7.3% (2007); Poverty rate: 39.3% (2000).
Education: Percent of population age 25 and over with: High school diploma (including GED) or higher: 66.0% (2007); Bachelor's degree or higher: 5.8% (2007); Master's degree or higher: 0.6% (2007).
Housing: Homeownership rate: 56.9% (2007); Median home value: $38,000 (2007); Median rent: $138 per month (2000); Median age of housing: 30 years (2000).
Safety: Violent crime rate: 63.2 per 10,000 population; Property crime rate: 158.0 per 10,000 population (2006).
Transportation: Commute to work: 91.2% car, 0.9% public transportation, 3.2% walk, 2.3% work from home (2000); Travel time to work: 43.1% less than 15 minutes, 40.3% 15 to 30 minutes, 1.4% 30 to 45 minutes, 7.6% 45 to 60 minutes, 7.6% 60 minutes or more (2000)

MOUNDS (city). Covers a land area of 1.216 square miles and a water area of 0 square miles. Located at 37.11° N. Lat.; 89.19° W. Long. Elevation is 325 feet.
History: Incorporated 1904.
Population: 1,407 (1990); 1,117 (2000); 1,055 (2007); 955 (2012 projected); Race: 33.6% White, 64.0% Black, 0.1% Asian, 0.7% Hispanic of any race (2007); Density: 867.9 persons per square mile (2007); Average household size: 2.70 (2007); Median age: 31.6 (2007); Males per 100 females: 83.2 (2007); Marriage status: 30.2% never married, 41.2% now married, 15.1% widowed, 13.5% divorced (2000); Foreign born: 0.0% (2000); Ancestry (includes multiple ancestries): 41.7% Other groups, 20.2% United States or American, 6.5% English, 5.5% German, 4.1% Irish (2000).
Economy: Single-family building permits issued: 1 (2007); Multi-family building permits issued: 4 (2007); Employment by occupation: 5.2% management, 11.3% professional, 32.6% services, 14.5% sales, 0.0% farming, 9.0% construction, 27.3% production (2000).
Income: Per capita income: $12,696 (2007); Median household income: $21,643 (2007); Average household income: $29,821 (2007); Percent of households with income of $100,000 or more: 1.3% (2007); Poverty rate: 42.8% (2000).
Education: Percent of population age 25 and over with: High school diploma (including GED) or higher: 65.5% (2007); Bachelor's degree or higher: 6.1% (2007); Master's degree or higher: 3.3% (2007).

School District(s)

Meridian CUSD 101 (PK-12)
2005-06 Enrollment: 702 . . . . (618) 342-6776
Housing: Homeownership rate: 62.9% (2007); Median home value: $26,818 (2007); Median rent: $188 per month (2000); Median age of housing: 53 years (2000).
Newspapers: Pulaski Enterprise (Community news; Circulation 4,789)
Transportation: Commute to work: 81.2% car, 3.8% public transportation, 9.1% walk, 2.4% work from home (2000); Travel time to work: 39.5% less than 15 minutes, 36.7% 15 to 30 minutes, 4.2% 30 to 45 minutes, 11.1% 45 to 60 minutes, 8.4% 60 minutes or more (2000)

NEW GRAND CHAIN (village). Aka Grand Chain. Covers a land area of 1.058 square miles and a water area of 0 square miles. Located at 37.25° N. Lat.; 89.02° W. Long. Elevation is 410 feet.
History: New Grand Chain was named for a row of rocks in the Ohio River, where the town was first located. It was moved in 1872 to be on the new railroad line.
Population: 273 (1990); 233 (2000); 213 (2007); 197 (2012 projected); Race: 91.5% White, 8.5% Black, 0.0% Asian, 0.0% Hispanic of any race (2007); Density: 201.3 persons per square mile (2007); Average household size: 2.37 (2007); Median age: 37.8 (2007); Males per 100 females: 97.2 (2007); Marriage status: 19.0% never married, 57.7% now married, 7.1% widowed, 16.1% divorced (2000); Foreign born: 0.0% (2000); Ancestry (includes multiple ancestries): 16.2% German, 15.4% Other groups, 12.3% Irish, 7.9% English, 7.9% United States or American (2000).
Economy: Employment by occupation: 7.8% management, 16.7% professional, 22.5% services, 16.7% sales, 3.9% farming, 14.7% construction, 17.6% production (2000).
Income: Per capita income: $19,941 (2007); Median household income: $36,667 (2007); Average household income: $47,194 (2007); Percent of households with income of $100,000 or more: 12.2% (2007); Poverty rate: 21.5% (2000).
Education: Percent of population age 25 and over with: High school diploma (including GED) or higher: 85.2% (2007); Bachelor's degree or higher: 11.1% (2007); Master's degree or higher: 3.7% (2007).

Housing: Homeownership rate: 71.1% (2007); Median home value: $58,333 (2007); Median rent: $250 per month (2000); Median age of housing: 49 years (2000).
Transportation: Commute to work: 93.9% car, 2.0% public transportation, 3.1% walk, 1.0% work from home (2000); Travel time to work: 33.0% less than 15 minutes, 24.7% 15 to 30 minutes, 17.5% 30 to 45 minutes, 9.3% 45 to 60 minutes, 15.5% 60 minutes or more (2000)

OLMSTED (village). Covers a land area of 1.680 square miles and a water area of 0.045 square miles. Located at 37.18° N. Lat.; 89.08° W. Long. Elevation is 358 feet.
Population: 358 (1990); 299 (2000); 274 (2007); 253 (2012 projected); Race: 82.8% White, 15.0% Black, 0.0% Asian, 0.7% Hispanic of any race (2007); Density: 163.1 persons per square mile (2007); Average household size: 2.14 (2007); Median age: 43.7 (2007); Males per 100 females: 79.1 (2007); Marriage status: 18.3% never married, 54.8% now married, 19.4% widowed, 7.5% divorced (2000); Foreign born: 0.0% (2000); Ancestry (includes multiple ancestries): 33.3% Other groups, 20.3% United States or American, 17.3% German, 10.7% Irish, 6.3% Dutch (2000).
Economy: Employment by occupation: 11.8% management, 11.8% professional, 22.7% services, 18.2% sales, 1.8% farming, 11.8% construction, 21.8% production (2000).
Income: Per capita income: $15,721 (2007); Median household income: $25,000 (2007); Average household income: $33,652 (2007); Percent of households with income of $100,000 or more: 3.9% (2007); Poverty rate: 21.7% (2000).
Education: Percent of population age 25 and over with: High school diploma (including GED) or higher: 64.8% (2007); Bachelor's degree or higher: 4.1% (2007); Master's degree or higher: 0.0% (2007).

School District(s)

Jamp Spec Educ Services (04-12)
2005-06 Enrollment: 34 . . . . (618) 742-6231

Housing: Homeownership rate: 71.1% (2007); Median home value: $49,063 (2007); Median rent: $196 per month (2000); Median age of housing: 36 years (2000).
Transportation: Commute to work: 95.5% car, 0.0% public transportation, 0.0% walk, 4.5% work from home (2000); Travel time to work: 32.4% less than 15 minutes, 29.5% 15 to 30 minutes, 30.5% 30 to 45 minutes, 4.8% 45 to 60 minutes, 2.9% 60 minutes or more (2000)

PULASKI (village). Covers a land area of 1.275 square miles and a water area of 0 square miles. Located at 37.21° N. Lat.; 89.20° W. Long. Elevation is 344 feet.
Population: 361 (1990); 274 (2000); 213 (2007); 198 (2012 projected); Race: 28.6% White, 70.4% Black, 0.0% Asian, 0.0% Hispanic of any race (2007); Density: 167.1 persons per square mile (2007); Average household size: 2.32 (2007); Median age: 36.9 (2007); Males per 100 females: 91.9 (2007); Marriage status: 31.1% never married, 43.3% now married, 18.1% widowed, 7.6% divorced (2000); Foreign born: 0.0% (2000); Ancestry (includes multiple ancestries): 41.1% United States or American, 34.6% Other groups, 5.1% African, 2.1% Irish, 1.0% English (2000).
Economy: Single-family building permits issued: 0 (2007); Multi-family building permits issued: 0 (2007); Employment by occupation: 6.0% management, 9.5% professional, 28.6% services, 17.9% sales, 0.0% farming, 7.1% construction, 31.0% production (2000).
Income: Per capita income: $16,808 (2007); Median household income: $21,111 (2007); Average household income: $38,913 (2007); Percent of households with income of $100,000 or more: 6.5% (2007); Poverty rate: 32.9% (2000).
Education: Percent of population age 25 and over with: High school diploma (including GED) or higher: 61.5% (2007); Bachelor's degree or higher: 5.9% (2007); Master's degree or higher: 0.0% (2007).
Housing: Homeownership rate: 80.4% (2007); Median home value: $26,250 (2007); Median rent: $190 per month (2000); Median age of housing: 28 years (2000).
Transportation: Commute to work: 92.9% car, 0.0% public transportation, 6.0% walk, 1.2% work from home (2000); Travel time to work: 36.1% less than 15 minutes, 27.7% 15 to 30 minutes, 8.4% 30 to 45 minutes, 18.1% 45 to 60 minutes, 9.6% 60 minutes or more (2000)

ULLIN (village). Covers a land area of 2.863 square miles and a water area of 0 square miles. Located at 37.27° N. Lat.; 89.18° W. Long. Elevation is 341 feet.
Population: 602 (1990); 779 (2000); 696 (2007); 653 (2012 projected); Race: 60.1% White, 28.2% Black, 9.1% Asian, 6.6% Hispanic of any race (2007); Density: 243.1 persons per square mile (2007); Average household size: 3.25 (2007); Median age: 35.5 (2007); Males per 100 females: 138.4 (2007); Marriage status: 21.8% never married, 56.0% now married, 11.9% widowed, 10.3% divorced (2000); Foreign born: 0.3% (2000); Ancestry (includes multiple ancestries): 24.9% Other groups, 13.9% United States or American, 8.7% German, 6.3% Irish, 2.9% English (2000).
Economy: Single-family building permits issued: 0 (2007); Multi-family building permits issued: 0 (2007); Employment by occupation: 5.6% management, 20.6% professional, 34.6% services, 14.5% sales, 2.3% farming, 7.0% construction, 15.4% production (2000).
Income: Per capita income: $14,724 (2007); Median household income: $23,824 (2007); Average household income: $31,285 (2007); Percent of households with income of $100,000 or more: 1.4% (2007); Poverty rate: 16.8% (2000).
Education: Percent of population age 25 and over with: High school diploma (including GED) or higher: 75.1% (2007); Bachelor's degree or higher: 6.4% (2007); Master's degree or higher: 1.1% (2007).

School District(s)

Alxndr/John/Masc/Pulski/Union Roe (06-12)
2005-06 Enrollment: 191 . . . . (618) 634-2292
Century CUSD 100 (PK-12)
2005-06 Enrollment: 438 . . . . (618) 845-3447

Two-year College(s)

Shawnee Community College (Public)
Fall 2007 Enrollment: 2,176. . . . . (618) 634-3200
2007-08 Tuition: In-state $3,206; Out-of-state $3,206

Housing: Homeownership rate: 65.4% (2007); Median home value: $40,400 (2007); Median rent: $292 per month (2000); Median age of housing: 26 years (2000).
Safety: Violent crime rate: 13.8 per 10,000 population; Property crime rate: 27.7 per 10,000 population (2006).
Transportation: Commute to work: 88.6% car, 2.8% public transportation, 3.8% walk, 2.8% work from home (2000); Travel time to work: 27.3% less than 15 minutes, 30.2% 15 to 30 minutes, 19.5% 30 to 45 minutes, 7.8% 45 to 60 minutes, 15.1% 60 minutes or more (2000)

VILLA RIDGE (unincorporated postal area, zip code 62996). Covers a land area of 26.870 square miles and a water area of 0.031 square miles. Located at 37.15° N. Lat.; 89.16° W. Long. Elevation is 387 feet.
Population: 759 (2000); Race: 70.9% White, 25.7% Black, 1.1% Asian, 0.9% Hispanic of any race (2000); Density: 28.2 persons per square mile (2000); Age: 26.0% under 18, 9.3% over 64 (2000); Marriage status: 17.3% never married, 71.5% now married, 3.9% widowed, 7.3% divorced (2000); Foreign born: 2.0% (2000); Ancestry (includes multiple ancestries): 26.7% Other groups, 24.5% United States or American, 12.8% Irish, 10.9% German, 8.6% English (2000).
Economy: Employment by occupation: 13.7% management, 8.1% professional, 16.3% services, 32.8% sales, 1.5% farming, 10.7% construction, 16.8% production (2000).
Income: Per capita income: $13,995 (2000); Median household income: $26,513 (2000); Poverty rate: 12.9% (2000).
Education: Percent of population age 25 and over with: High school diploma (including GED) or higher: 70.3% (2000); Bachelor's degree or higher: 3.7% (2000).
Housing: Homeownership rate: 89.1% (2000); Median home value: $48,000 (2000); Median rent: $232 per month (2000); Median age of housing: 30 years (2000).
Transportation: Commute to work: 93.5% car, 0.0% public transportation, 0.0% walk, 6.5% work from home (2000); Travel time to work: 31.5% less than 15 minutes, 41.6% 15 to 30 minutes, 18.2% 30 to 45 minutes, 6.4% 45 to 60 minutes, 2.3% 60 minutes or more (2000)

Putnam County

Located in north central Illinois; bounded on the north and west by the Illinois River. Covers a land area of 159.80 square miles, a water area of 12.45 square miles, and is located in the Central Time Zone. The county was founded in 1825. County seat is Hennepin.

Putnam County is part of the Ottawa-Streator, IL Micropolitan Statistical Area. The entire metro area includes: Bureau County, IL; La Salle County, IL; Putnam County, IL

Weather Station: Hennepin Power Plant Elevation: 459 feet

	Jan	Feb	Mar	Apr	May	Jun	Jul	Aug	Sep	Oct	Nov	Dec
High	30	36	48	62	74	83	86	84	78	65	49	36
Low	11	16	28	38	48	58	62	60	52	40	29	18
Precip	1.1	1.1	2.2	3.3	3.8	4.3	3.9	4.5	3.9	2.7	2.5	2.2
Snow	na	na	na	0.4	0.0	0.0	0.0	0.0	0.0	tr	0.8	na

High and Low temperatures in degrees Fahrenheit; Precipitation and Snow in inches

Population: 5,730 (1990); 6,086 (2000); 6,092 (2007); 6,074 (2012 projected); Race: 97.2% White, 0.8% Black, 0.4% Asian, 4.0% Hispanic of any race (2007); Density: 38.1 persons per square mile (2007); Average household size: 2.48 (2007); Median age: 42.5 (2007); Males per 100 females: 99.1 (2007).
Religion: Five largest groups: 27.1% Catholic Church, 6.7% United Church of Christ, 5.3% The United Methodist Church, 4.6% Evangelical Lutheran Church in America, 1.1% Friends (Quakers) (2000).
Economy: Unemployment rate: 6.1% (4/2008); Total civilian labor force: 3,231 (4/2008); Leading industries: 45.1% manufacturing; 13.9% construction; 7.4% retail trade (2005); Farms: 175 totaling 71,265 acres (2002); Companies that employ 500 or more persons: 0 (2006); Companies that employ 100 to 499 persons: 2 (2006); Companies that employ less than 100 persons: 149 (2006); Black-owned businesses: n/a (2002); Hispanic-owned businesses: n/a (2002); Asian-owned businesses: n/a (2002); Women-owned businesses: 110 (2002); Retail sales per capita: $4,671 (2008). Single-family building permits issued: 28 (2007); Multi-family building permits issued: 0 (2007).
Income: Per capita income: $24,336 (2007); Median household income: $53,510 (2007); Average household income: $60,296 (2007); Percent of households with income of $100,000 or more: 13.0% (2007); Poverty rate: 6.6% (2005); Bankruptcy rate: 2.66% (2007).
Education: Percent of population age 25 and over with: High school diploma (including GED) or higher: 83.8% (2007); Bachelor's degree or higher: 12.2% (2007); Master's degree or higher: 4.2% (2007).
Housing: Homeownership rate: 82.7% (2007); Median home value: $134,948 (2007); Median rent: $340 per month (2000); Median age of housing: 33 years (2000).
Health: Birth rate: 93.1 per 10,000 population (2007); Death rate: 103.1 per 10,000 population (2007); Age-adjusted cancer mortality rate: 278.0 deaths per 100,000 population (2005); Number of physicians: 1.7 per 10,000 population (2005); Hospital beds: 0.0 per 10,000 population (2004); Hospital admissions: 0.0 per 10,000 population (2004).
Elections: 2004 Presidential election results: 48.4% Bush, 50.8% Kerry, 0.0% Nader, 0.7% Badnarik
National and State Parks: Donnelley State Fish and Wildlife Area; Fox Run State Conservation Area
Additional Information Contacts
Putnam County Government . . . . (815) 925-7129

Putnam County Communities

GRANVILLE (village). Covers a land area of 0.957 square miles and a water area of 0 square miles. Located at 41.26° N. Lat.; 89.22° W. Long. Elevation is 686 feet.
History: Incorporated 1861.
Population: 1,407 (1990); 1,414 (2000); 1,420 (2007); 1,413 (2012 projected); Race: 98.0% White, 0.4% Black, 0.6% Asian, 4.4% Hispanic of any race (2007); Density: 1,483.0 persons per square mile (2007); Average household size: 2.38 (2007); Median age: 42.2 (2007); Males per 100 females: 88.8 (2007); Marriage status: 17.6% never married, 62.3% now married, 9.6% widowed, 10.5% divorced (2000); Foreign born: 3.5% (2000); Ancestry (includes multiple ancestries): 35.2% German, 19.3% Italian, 11.3% Irish, 11.0% English, 8.6% Polish (2000).
Economy: Single-family building permits issued: 1 (2007); Multi-family building permits issued: 0 (2007); Employment by occupation: 6.9% management, 13.2% professional, 12.5% services, 29.5% sales, 0.4% farming, 15.3% construction, 22.2% production (2000).
Income: Per capita income: $24,127 (2007); Median household income: $48,929 (2007); Average household income: $57,483 (2007); Percent of households with income of $100,000 or more: 13.9% (2007); Poverty rate: 4.1% (2000).
Education: Percent of population age 25 and over with: High school diploma (including GED) or higher: 83.4% (2007); Bachelor's degree or higher: 10.6% (2007); Master's degree or higher: 4.1% (2007).

School District(s)
Putnam County CUSD 535 (PK-12)
2005-06 Enrollment: 968 . . . . (815) 339-2238
Housing: Homeownership rate: 80.7% (2007); Median home value: $131,865 (2007); Median rent: $330 per month (2000); Median age of housing: 39 years (2000).
Safety: Violent crime rate: 0.0 per 10,000 population; Property crime rate: 36.0 per 10,000 population (2006).
Newspapers: Putnam County Record (Community news; Circulation 3,200)
Transportation: Commute to work: 94.9% car, 0.0% public transportation, 2.6% walk, 1.8% work from home (2000); Travel time to work: 45.0% less than 15 minutes, 36.2% 15 to 30 minutes, 9.5% 30 to 45 minutes, 1.9% 45 to 60 minutes, 7.3% 60 minutes or more (2000)

HENNEPIN (village). County seat. Covers a land area of 5.223 square miles and a water area of 0.360 square miles. Located at 41.25° N. Lat.; 89.33° W. Long. Elevation is 502 feet.
History: Hennepin was named for Father Louis Hennepin, an early missionary pilot who guided explorers on the waterways.
Population: 669 (1990); 707 (2000); 667 (2007); 663 (2012 projected); Race: 97.0% White, 1.2% Black, 1.2% Asian, 5.1% Hispanic of any race (2007); Density: 127.7 persons per square mile (2007); Average household size: 2.28 (2007); Median age: 44.6 (2007); Males per 100 females: 99.1 (2007); Marriage status: 18.0% never married, 59.4% now married, 10.0% widowed, 12.6% divorced (2000); Foreign born: 2.7% (2000); Ancestry (includes multiple ancestries): 34.7% German, 16.6% Irish, 13.8% Italian, 13.5% English, 8.8% Other groups (2000).
Economy: Single-family building permits issued: 2 (2007); Multi-family building permits issued: 0 (2007); Employment by occupation: 14.3% management, 12.8% professional, 16.2% services, 23.8% sales, 0.9% farming, 11.0% construction, 21.0% production (2000).
Income: Per capita income: $27,825 (2007); Median household income: $52,576 (2007); Average household income: $63,089 (2007); Percent of households with income of $100,000 or more: 15.0% (2007); Poverty rate: 2.9% (2000).
Education: Percent of population age 25 and over with: High school diploma (including GED) or higher: 81.4% (2007); Bachelor's degree or higher: 12.3% (2007); Master's degree or higher: 4.5% (2007).

School District(s)
Putnam County CUSD 535 (PK-12)
2005-06 Enrollment: 968 . . . . (815) 339-2238
Housing: Homeownership rate: 81.2% (2007); Median home value: $140,341 (2007); Median rent: $351 per month (2000); Median age of housing: 32 years (2000).
Transportation: Commute to work: 89.0% car, 0.6% public transportation, 5.0% walk, 4.7% work from home (2000); Travel time to work: 57.1% less than 15 minutes, 26.7% 15 to 30 minutes, 9.2% 30 to 45 minutes, 2.3% 45 to 60 minutes, 4.6% 60 minutes or more (2000)

MAGNOLIA (village). Covers a land area of 0.298 square miles and a water area of 0 square miles. Located at 41.11° N. Lat.; 89.19° W. Long. Elevation is 663 feet.
Population: 262 (1990); 279 (2000); 302 (2007); 311 (2012 projected); Race: 94.0% White, 3.6% Black, 1.7% Asian, 0.7% Hispanic of any race (2007); Density: 1,014.1 persons per square mile (2007); Average household size: 2.63 (2007); Median age: 38.6 (2007); Males per 100 females: 89.9 (2007); Marriage status: 23.3% never married, 54.7% now married, 9.4% widowed, 12.6% divorced (2000); Foreign born: 2.5% (2000); Ancestry (includes multiple ancestries): 33.9% German, 14.7% Other groups, 14.4% Swedish, 9.4% English, 8.8% French (except Basque) (2000).
Economy: Single-family building permits issued: 0 (2007); Multi-family building permits issued: 0 (2007); Employment by occupation: 4.7% management, 6.1% professional, 20.3% services, 25.0% sales, 5.4% farming, 7.4% construction, 31.1% production (2000).
Income: Per capita income: $20,687 (2007); Median household income: $47,250 (2007); Average household income: $54,326 (2007); Percent of households with income of $100,000 or more: 10.4% (2007); Poverty rate: 11.1% (2000).
Education: Percent of population age 25 and over with: High school diploma (including GED) or higher: 73.2% (2007); Bachelor's degree or higher: 7.3% (2007); Master's degree or higher: 3.4% (2007).

Housing: Homeownership rate: 85.2% (2007); Median home value: $85,000 (2007); Median rent: $320 per month (2000); Median age of housing: 60+ years (2000).
Transportation: Commute to work: 97.9% car, 0.0% public transportation, 2.1% walk, 0.0% work from home (2000); Travel time to work: 15.8% less than 15 minutes, 46.6% 15 to 30 minutes, 24.0% 30 to 45 minutes, 8.9% 45 to 60 minutes, 4.8% 60 minutes or more (2000)

MARK (village). Covers a land area of 0.812 square miles and a water area of 0 square miles. Located at 41.26° N. Lat.; 89.24° W. Long. Elevation is 689 feet.
Population: 399 (1990); 491 (2000); 505 (2007); 504 (2012 projected); Race: 98.0% White, 0.0% Black, 0.0% Asian, 6.9% Hispanic of any race (2007); Density: 622.1 persons per square mile (2007); Average household size: 2.55 (2007); Median age: 39.5 (2007); Males per 100 females: 90.6 (2007); Marriage status: 24.6% never married, 59.1% now married, 7.7% widowed, 8.7% divorced (2000); Foreign born: 0.8% (2000); Ancestry (includes multiple ancestries): 27.6% Italian, 27.4% German, 13.9% Polish, 12.5% Irish, 10.6% Other groups (2000).
Economy: Single-family building permits issued: 5 (2007); Multi-family building permits issued: 0 (2007); Employment by occupation: 7.9% management, 16.5% professional, 14.3% services, 27.4% sales, 0.4% farming, 10.9% construction, 22.6% production (2000).
Income: Per capita income: $23,173 (2007); Median household income: $53,929 (2007); Average household income: $59,104 (2007); Percent of households with income of $100,000 or more: 12.1% (2007); Poverty rate: 10.3% (2000).
Education: Percent of population age 25 and over with: High school diploma (including GED) or higher: 83.2% (2007); Bachelor's degree or higher: 10.9% (2007); Master's degree or higher: 1.5% (2007).
Housing: Homeownership rate: 86.4% (2007); Median home value: $118,750 (2007); Median rent: $375 per month (2000); Median age of housing: 47 years (2000).
Transportation: Commute to work: 93.2% car, 0.0% public transportation, 2.6% walk, 4.1% work from home (2000); Travel time to work: 31.8% less than 15 minutes, 48.6% 15 to 30 minutes, 8.6% 30 to 45 minutes, 3.1% 45 to 60 minutes, 7.8% 60 minutes or more (2000)

MCNABB (village). Covers a land area of 0.199 square miles and a water area of 0 square miles. Located at 41.17° N. Lat.; 89.20° W. Long. Elevation is 686 feet.
Population: 310 (1990); 310 (2000); 335 (2007); 346 (2012 projected); Race: 100.0% White, 0.0% Black, 0.0% Asian, 0.0% Hispanic of any race (2007); Density: 1,680.8 persons per square mile (2007); Average household size: 2.41 (2007); Median age: 39.9 (2007); Males per 100 females: 105.5 (2007); Marriage status: 18.3% never married, 67.8% now married, 5.7% widowed, 8.3% divorced (2000); Foreign born: 0.0% (2000); Ancestry (includes multiple ancestries): 40.8% German, 17.8% English, 11.5% Irish, 10.1% Italian, 8.7% Swedish (2000).
Economy: Single-family building permits issued: 1 (2007); Multi-family building permits issued: 0 (2007); Employment by occupation: 5.1% management, 17.7% professional, 19.0% services, 19.6% sales, 0.0% farming, 11.4% construction, 27.2% production (2000).
Income: Per capita income: $25,410 (2007); Median household income: $62,109 (2007); Average household income: $61,241 (2007); Percent of households with income of $100,000 or more: 12.9% (2007); Poverty rate: 5.6% (2000).
Education: Percent of population age 25 and over with: High school diploma (including GED) or higher: 89.3% (2007); Bachelor's degree or higher: 18.5% (2007); Master's degree or higher: 7.3% (2007).

School District(s)

Putnam County CUSD 535 (PK-12)
2005-06 Enrollment: 968 . . . . (815) 339-2238

Housing: Homeownership rate: 79.9% (2007); Median home value: $127,841 (2007); Median rent: $307 per month (2000); Median age of housing: 43 years (2000).
Transportation: Commute to work: 95.4% car, 0.0% public transportation, 0.0% walk, 4.6% work from home (2000); Travel time to work: 18.6% less than 15 minutes, 51.0% 15 to 30 minutes, 13.8% 30 to 45 minutes, 4.1% 45 to 60 minutes, 12.4% 60 minutes or more (2000)

PUTNAM (unincorporated postal area, zip code 61560). Covers a land area of 33.771 square miles and a water area of 0.505 square miles. Located at 41.19° N. Lat.; 89.43° W. Long. Elevation is 518 feet.
Population: 705 (2000); Race: 98.9% White, 0.3% Black, 0.0% Asian, 1.6% Hispanic of any race (2000); Density: 20.9 persons per square mile (2000); Age: 15.9% under 18, 19.8% over 64 (2000); Marriage status: 19.6% never married, 71.3% now married, 5.6% widowed, 3.6% divorced (2000); Foreign born: 0.5% (2000); Ancestry (includes multiple ancestries): 36.0% German, 15.6% Irish, 12.4% Polish, 12.0% English, 7.1% Swedish (2000).
Economy: Employment by occupation: 16.0% management, 15.7% professional, 7.1% services, 16.3% sales, 1.3% farming, 15.7% construction, 27.9% production (2000).
Income: Per capita income: $21,515 (2000); Median household income: $46,917 (2000); Poverty rate: 5.0% (2000).
Education: Percent of population age 25 and over with: High school diploma (including GED) or higher: 93.3% (2000); Bachelor's degree or higher: 20.3% (2000).
Housing: Homeownership rate: 90.3% (2000); Median home value: $118,200 (2000); Median rent: $275 per month (2000); Median age of housing: 18 years (2000).
Transportation: Commute to work: 88.3% car, 2.0% public transportation, 4.0% walk, 5.7% work from home (2000); Travel time to work: 24.2% less than 15 minutes, 40.9% 15 to 30 minutes, 7.5% 30 to 45 minutes, 12.1% 45 to 60 minutes, 15.3% 60 minutes or more (2000)

STANDARD (village). Covers a land area of 0.565 square miles and a water area of 0 square miles. Located at 41.25° N. Lat.; 89.17° W. Long. Elevation is 679 feet.
Population: 260 (1990); 256 (2000); 242 (2007); 241 (2012 projected); Race: 98.8% White, 0.0% Black, 0.0% Asian, 2.9% Hispanic of any race (2007); Density: 428.4 persons per square mile (2007); Average household size: 2.20 (2007); Median age: 42.5 (2007); Males per 100 females: 106.8 (2007); Marriage status: 26.9% never married, 50.0% now married, 14.6% widowed, 8.5% divorced (2000); Foreign born: 3.9% (2000); Ancestry (includes multiple ancestries): 44.2% Italian, 25.6% German, 13.6% Irish, 8.9% English, 7.4% Other groups (2000).
Economy: Single-family building permits issued: 0 (2007); Multi-family building permits issued: 0 (2007); Employment by occupation: 11.5% management, 17.2% professional, 12.3% services, 22.1% sales, 1.6% farming, 11.5% construction, 23.8% production (2000).
Income: Per capita income: $22,066 (2007); Median household income: $45,556 (2007); Average household income: $48,545 (2007); Percent of households with income of $100,000 or more: 0.9% (2007); Poverty rate: 5.8% (2000).
Education: Percent of population age 25 and over with: High school diploma (including GED) or higher: 77.9% (2007); Bachelor's degree or higher: 9.3% (2007); Master's degree or higher: 2.9% (2007).
Housing: Homeownership rate: 80.9% (2007); Median home value: $94,091 (2007); Median rent: $269 per month (2000); Median age of housing: 60+ years (2000).
Transportation: Commute to work: 97.5% car, 0.0% public transportation, 1.6% walk, 0.8% work from home (2000); Travel time to work: 21.5% less than 15 minutes, 65.3% 15 to 30 minutes, 7.4% 30 to 45 minutes, 0.0% 45 to 60 minutes, 5.8% 60 minutes or more (2000)

Randolph County

Located in southwestern Illinois; bounded on the west and south by the Mississippi River and the Missouri border; drained by the Kaskaskia River. Covers a land area of 578.42 square miles, a water area of 18.84 square miles, and is located in the Central Time Zone. The county was founded in 1795. County seat is Chester.

Weather Station: Sparta 1 W Elevation: 534 feet

	Jan	Feb	Mar	Apr	May	Jun	Jul	Aug	Sep	Oct	Nov	Dec
High	39	46	57	68	77	86	90	88	81	70	56	44
Low	22	27	36	45	54	64	67	65	58	46	37	27
Precip	2.4	2.5	4.2	4.1	4.5	3.7	3.9	3.3	2.9	3.4	4.1	3.3
Snow	5.1	3.5	2.0	0.5	0.0	0.0	0.0	0.0	0.0	tr	1.0	2.7

High and Low temperatures in degrees Fahrenheit; Precipitation and Snow in inches

Population: 34,583 (1990); 33,893 (2000); 32,964 (2007); 32,268 (2012 projected); Race: 89.0% White, 9.0% Black, 0.3% Asian, 1.7% Hispanic of any race (2007); Density: 57.0 persons per square mile (2007); Average household size: 2.72 (2007); Median age: 38.4 (2007); Males per 100 females: 113.0 (2007).
Religion: Five largest groups: 18.8% Catholic Church, 18.5% Lutheran Church—Missouri Synod, 7.9% Southern Baptist Convention, 5.5%

Evangelical Lutheran Church in America, 4.1% The United Methodist Church (2000).
Economy: Unemployment rate: 5.3% (4/2008); Total civilian labor force: 15,928 (4/2008); Leading industries: 23.4% manufacturing; 21.4% health care and social assistance; 13.3% retail trade (2005); Farms: 823 totaling 253,863 acres (2002); Companies that employ 500 or more persons: 2 (2006); Companies that employ 100 to 499 persons: 17 (2006); Companies that employ less than 100 persons: 713 (2006); Black-owned businesses: n/a (2002); Hispanic-owned businesses: n/a (2002); Asian-owned businesses: n/a (2002); Women-owned businesses: n/a (2002); Retail sales per capita: $12,800 (2008). Single-family building permits issued: 62 (2007); Multi-family building permits issued: 2 (2007).
Income: Per capita income: $20,489 (2007); Median household income: $43,274 (2007); Average household income: $52,333 (2007); Percent of households with income of $100,000 or more: 8.6% (2007); Poverty rate: 12.8% (2005); Bankruptcy rate: 3.42% (2007).
Taxes: Total county taxes per capita: $124 (2006); County property taxes per capita: $123 (2006).
Education: Percent of population age 25 and over with: High school diploma (including GED) or higher: 71.7% (2007); Bachelor's degree or higher: 9.0% (2007); Master's degree or higher: 2.9% (2007).
Housing: Homeownership rate: 79.6% (2007); Median home value: $87,362 (2007); Median rent: $286 per month (2000); Median age of housing: 38 years (2000).
Health: Birth rate: 119.0 per 10,000 population (2007); Death rate: 107.4 per 10,000 population (2007); Age-adjusted cancer mortality rate: 171.6 deaths per 100,000 population (2005); Air Quality Index: 81.4% good, 16.4% moderate, 2.2% unhealthy for sensitive individuals, 0.0% unhealthy (percent of days in 2007); Number of physicians: 9.4 per 10,000 population (2005); Hospital beds: 174.5 per 10,000 population (2004); Hospital admissions: 1,473.1 per 10,000 population (2004).
Elections: 2004 Presidential election results: 54.0% Bush, 45.3% Kerry, 0.0% Nader, 0.7% Badnarik
National and State Parks: Baldwin Lake State Fish and Wildlife Area; Fort Chartres State Park; Fort Kaskaskia State Park; Modoc Rock Shelter National Historic Site; Randolph County State Conservation Area
Additional Information Contacts
Randolph County Government . . . . (618) 826-5000
http://www.randolphco.org/gov
Chester Chamber of Commerce . . . . (618) 826-2721
http://www.chesterill.com/chamber
City of Chester . . . . (618) 826-5114
http://www.chesterill.com
Red Bud Chamber of Commerce. . . . . (618) 282-3505
http://www.redbudchamber.com
Sparta Area Chamber of Commerce . . . . (618) 443-6908
http://www.spartaillinois.us
Steeleville Chamber of Commerce Inc. . . . . (618) 965-9568
http://www.steeleville.org

Randolph County Communities

BALDWIN (village). Covers a land area of 0.669 square miles and a water area of 0 square miles. Located at 38.18° N. Lat.; 89.84° W. Long. Elevation is 459 feet.
Population: 426 (1990); 3,627 (2000); 3,283 (2007); 3,127 (2012 projected); Race: 22.3% White, 69.3% Black, 0.2% Asian, 9.7% Hispanic of any race (2007); Density: 4,907.5 persons per square mile (2007); Average household size: 20.65 (2007); Median age: 30.5 (2007); Males per 100 females: ***.* (2007); Marriage status: 2.3% never married, 91.3% now married, 1.5% widowed, 4.9% divorced (2000); Foreign born: 2.2% (2000); Ancestry (includes multiple ancestries): 5.8% German, 1.6% Irish, 1.5% Other groups, 1.3% English, 0.6% French (except Basque) (2000).
Economy: Single-family building permits issued: 0 (2007); Multi-family building permits issued: 0 (2007); Employment by occupation: 2.7% management, 15.1% professional, 12.4% services, 23.2% sales, 0.0% farming, 9.2% construction, 37.3% production (2000).
Income: Per capita income: $13,366 (2007); Median household income: $37,361 (2007); Average household income: $46,855 (2007); Percent of households with income of $100,000 or more: 4.4% (2007); Poverty rate: 9.3% (2000).
Education: Percent of population age 25 and over with: High school diploma (including GED) or higher: 28.3% (2007); Bachelor's degree or higher: 1.0% (2007); Master's degree or higher: 0.1% (2007).
Housing: Homeownership rate: 83.0% (2007); Median home value: $49,231 (2007); Median rent: $263 per month (2000); Median age of housing: 46 years (2000).
Transportation: Commute to work: 96.7% car, 0.0% public transportation, 2.2% walk, 1.1% work from home (2000); Travel time to work: 30.7% less than 15 minutes, 27.4% 15 to 30 minutes, 20.7% 30 to 45 minutes, 16.2% 45 to 60 minutes, 5.0% 60 minutes or more (2000)

CHESTER (city). County seat. Covers a land area of 5.893 square miles and a water area of 0.012 square miles. Located at 37.91° N. Lat.; 89.82° W. Long. Elevation is 669 feet.
History: Chester was established in 1819 as a commercial rival for Kaskaskia by a land company from Cincinnati.
Population: 8,185 (1990); 5,185 (2000); 4,862 (2007); 4,639 (2012 projected); Race: 97.0% White, 1.8% Black, 0.3% Asian, 0.6% Hispanic of any race (2007); Density: 825.1 persons per square mile (2007); Average household size: 2.54 (2007); Median age: 40.8 (2007); Males per 100 females: 104.4 (2007); Marriage status: 24.8% never married, 53.1% now married, 9.2% widowed, 12.9% divorced (2000); Foreign born: 0.7% (2000); Ancestry (includes multiple ancestries): 33.8% German, 12.3% Irish, 8.7% United States or American, 8.7% Other groups, 7.2% English (2000).
Economy: Single-family building permits issued: 1 (2007); Multi-family building permits issued: 0 (2007); Employment by occupation: 11.1% management, 17.8% professional, 21.1% services, 19.7% sales, 0.5% farming, 8.4% construction, 21.4% production (2000).
Income: Per capita income: $23,890 (2007); Median household income: $45,424 (2007); Average household income: $59,748 (2007); Percent of households with income of $100,000 or more: 11.3% (2007); Poverty rate: 9.7% (2000).
Education: Percent of population age 25 and over with: High school diploma (including GED) or higher: 72.0% (2007); Bachelor's degree or higher: 11.2% (2007); Master's degree or higher: 3.6% (2007).

School District(s)

Chester CUSD 139 (PK-12)
2005-06 Enrollment: 1,031 . . . . (618) 826-4509
Housing: Homeownership rate: 74.5% (2007); Median home value: $80,116 (2007); Median rent: $284 per month (2000); Median age of housing: 46 years (2000).
Hospitals: Memorial Hospital (25 beds)
Safety: Violent crime rate: 33.0 per 10,000 population; Property crime rate: 152.4 per 10,000 population (2006).
Newspapers: Randolph Herald Tribune (Local news; Circulation 3,500)
Transportation: Commute to work: 94.9% car, 0.0% public transportation, 3.1% walk, 1.7% work from home (2000); Travel time to work: 66.8% less than 15 minutes, 18.0% 15 to 30 minutes, 8.3% 30 to 45 minutes, 2.0% 45 to 60 minutes, 4.9% 60 minutes or more (2000)
Additional Information Contacts
Chester Chamber of Commerce . . . . (618) 826-2721
http://www.chesterill.com/chamber
City of Chester . . . . (618) 826-5114
http://www.chesterill.com

COULTERVILLE (village). Covers a land area of 0.566 square miles and a water area of 0 square miles. Located at 38.18° N. Lat.; 89.60° W. Long. Elevation is 551 feet.
History: Incorporated 1874.
Population: 986 (1990); 1,230 (2000); 1,079 (2007); 1,029 (2012 projected); Race: 97.2% White, 1.0% Black, 0.4% Asian, 0.1% Hispanic of any race (2007); Density: 1,907.5 persons per square mile (2007); Average household size: 2.33 (2007); Median age: 36.1 (2007); Males per 100 females: 90.6 (2007); Marriage status: 21.4% never married, 55.6% now married, 8.3% widowed, 14.6% divorced (2000); Foreign born: 0.4% (2000); Ancestry (includes multiple ancestries): 25.7% German, 15.7% United States or American, 12.5% Irish, 9.7% English, 8.0% Other groups (2000).
Economy: Employment by occupation: 7.0% management, 6.8% professional, 19.9% services, 17.5% sales, 0.0% farming, 15.0% construction, 33.7% production (2000).
Income: Per capita income: $17,579 (2007); Median household income: $29,936 (2007); Average household income: $40,967 (2007); Percent of households with income of $100,000 or more: 6.0% (2007); Poverty rate: 18.6% (2000).

Education: Percent of population age 25 and over with: High school diploma (including GED) or higher: 72.3% (2007); Bachelor's degree or higher: 5.2% (2007); Master's degree or higher: 2.2% (2007).

School District(s)

Coulterville USD 1 (KG-12)
2005-06 Enrollment: 213 . . . . (618) 758-2881

Housing: Homeownership rate: 78.4% (2007); Median home value: $52,561 (2007); Median rent: $264 per month (2000); Median age of housing: 44 years (2000).
Safety: Violent crime rate: 8.4 per 10,000 population; Property crime rate: 109.3 per 10,000 population (2006).
Transportation: Commute to work: 95.3% car, 0.0% public transportation, 1.5% walk, 0.8% work from home (2000); Travel time to work: 32.5% less than 15 minutes, 39.8% 15 to 30 minutes, 15.4% 30 to 45 minutes, 2.3% 45 to 60 minutes, 10.1% 60 minutes or more (2000)

ELLIS GROVE (village). Aka Ellisgrove. Covers a land area of 0.465 square miles and a water area of 0 square miles. Located at 38.01° N. Lat.; 89.90° W. Long. Elevation is 548 feet.
History: Fort Kaskaskia State Historical Site nearby.
Population: 372 (1990); 381 (2000); 342 (2007); 339 (2012 projected); Race: 99.7% White, 0.0% Black, 0.0% Asian, 0.0% Hispanic of any race (2007); Density: 735.5 persons per square mile (2007); Average household size: 2.55 (2007); Median age: 35.8 (2007); Males per 100 females: 95.4 (2007); Marriage status: 17.4% never married, 62.1% now married, 8.4% widowed, 12.1% divorced (2000); Foreign born: 0.0% (2000); Ancestry (includes multiple ancestries): 38.8% German, 16.5% Irish, 14.0% United States or American, 12.9% French (except Basque), 12.1% Other groups (2000).
Economy: Employment by occupation: 3.7% management, 11.2% professional, 29.2% services, 21.1% sales, 3.7% farming, 8.7% construction, 22.4% production (2000).
Income: Per capita income: $19,123 (2007); Median household income: $40,833 (2007); Average household income: $48,806 (2007); Percent of households with income of $100,000 or more: 6.7% (2007); Poverty rate: 8.3% (2000).
Education: Percent of population age 25 and over with: High school diploma (including GED) or higher: 63.1% (2007); Bachelor's degree or higher: 5.1% (2007); Master's degree or higher: 1.4% (2007).
Housing: Homeownership rate: 77.6% (2007); Median home value: $70,000 (2007); Median rent: $288 per month (2000); Median age of housing: 33 years (2000).
Transportation: Commute to work: 98.7% car, 0.0% public transportation, 1.3% walk, 0.0% work from home (2000); Travel time to work: 30.2% less than 15 minutes, 26.4% 15 to 30 minutes, 20.8% 30 to 45 minutes, 5.7% 45 to 60 minutes, 17.0% 60 minutes or more (2000)

EVANSVILLE (village). Covers a land area of 0.741 square miles and a water area of 0.018 square miles. Located at 38.09° N. Lat.; 89.93° W. Long. Elevation is 390 feet.
Population: 861 (1990); 724 (2000); 637 (2007); 644 (2012 projected); Race: 99.1% White, 0.5% Black, 0.2% Asian, 0.5% Hispanic of any race (2007); Density: 859.5 persons per square mile (2007); Average household size: 2.37 (2007); Median age: 37.8 (2007); Males per 100 females: 93.6 (2007); Marriage status: 21.6% never married, 57.6% now married, 10.2% widowed, 10.6% divorced (2000); Foreign born: 0.0% (2000); Ancestry (includes multiple ancestries): 43.3% German, 10.1% French (except Basque), 5.8% Other groups, 5.7% Irish, 5.5% United States or American (2000).
Economy: Single-family building permits issued: 0 (2007); Multi-family building permits issued: 0 (2007); Employment by occupation: 6.2% management, 11.1% professional, 18.6% services, 15.5% sales, 0.0% farming, 17.6% construction, 31.0% production (2000).
Income: Per capita income: $19,902 (2007); Median household income: $36,250 (2007); Average household income: $47,119 (2007); Percent of households with income of $100,000 or more: 3.7% (2007); Poverty rate: 14.0% (2000).
Education: Percent of population age 25 and over with: High school diploma (including GED) or higher: 75.4% (2007); Bachelor's degree or higher: 3.8% (2007); Master's degree or higher: 1.9% (2007).

School District(s)

Perandoe Spec Educ District
2005-06 Enrollment: n/a . . . . (618) 282-6251
Sparta CUSD 140 (PK-12)
2005-06 Enrollment: 1,529 . . . . (618) 443-5331

Housing: Homeownership rate: 80.7% (2007); Median home value: $70,625 (2007); Median rent: $263 per month (2000); Median age of housing: 49 years (2000).
Transportation: Commute to work: 93.4% car, 2.5% public transportation, 0.9% walk, 0.0% work from home (2000); Travel time to work: 19.1% less than 15 minutes, 32.2% 15 to 30 minutes, 16.6% 30 to 45 minutes, 5.9% 45 to 60 minutes, 26.3% 60 minutes or more (2000)

MODOC (unincorporated postal area, zip code 62261). Covers a land area of 31.259 square miles and a water area of 0.032 square miles. Located at 37.98° N. Lat.; 90.00° W. Long. Elevation is 397 feet.
Population: 221 (2000); Race: 100.0% White, 0.0% Black, 0.0% Asian, 0.0% Hispanic of any race (2000); Density: 7.1 persons per square mile (2000); Age: 32.8% under 18, 11.2% over 64 (2000); Marriage status: 20.8% never married, 58.9% now married, 7.1% widowed, 13.1% divorced (2000); Foreign born: 0.0% (2000); Ancestry (includes multiple ancestries): 37.6% German, 24.0% United States or American, 11.6% French (except Basque), 3.6% Scottish, 3.2% Other groups (2000).
Economy: Employment by occupation: 7.3% management, 16.5% professional, 14.7% services, 14.7% sales, 0.0% farming, 14.7% construction, 32.1% production (2000).
Income: Per capita income: $15,081 (2000); Median household income: $34,286 (2000); Poverty rate: 2.9% (2000).
Education: Percent of population age 25 and over with: High school diploma (including GED) or higher: 77.6% (2000); Bachelor's degree or higher: 12.2% (2000).
Housing: Homeownership rate: 91.6% (2000); Median home value: $43,300 (2000); Median rent: $2,000+ per month (2000); Median age of housing: 33 years (2000).
Transportation: Commute to work: 93.6% car, 0.0% public transportation, 0.0% walk, 6.4% work from home (2000); Travel time to work: 25.5% less than 15 minutes, 30.4% 15 to 30 minutes, 31.4% 30 to 45 minutes, 0.0% 45 to 60 minutes, 12.7% 60 minutes or more (2000)

PERCY (village). Covers a land area of 0.880 square miles and a water area of 0 square miles. Located at 38.01° N. Lat.; 89.61° W. Long. Elevation is 472 feet.
Population: 966 (1990); 942 (2000); 897 (2007); 880 (2012 projected); Race: 98.9% White, 0.1% Black, 0.0% Asian, 2.3% Hispanic of any race (2007); Density: 1,019.4 persons per square mile (2007); Average household size: 2.39 (2007); Median age: 39.2 (2007); Males per 100 females: 86.9 (2007); Marriage status: 17.2% never married, 63.5% now married, 9.3% widowed, 10.0% divorced (2000); Foreign born: 2.1% (2000); Ancestry (includes multiple ancestries): 34.2% German, 13.6% Irish, 9.9% Other groups, 8.3% United States or American, 6.2% English (2000).
Economy: Employment by occupation: 3.3% management, 11.5% professional, 18.4% services, 17.2% sales, 1.2% farming, 12.0% construction, 36.5% production (2000).
Income: Per capita income: $18,244 (2007); Median household income: $35,758 (2007); Average household income: $42,733 (2007); Percent of households with income of $100,000 or more: 3.5% (2007); Poverty rate: 11.3% (2000).
Education: Percent of population age 25 and over with: High school diploma (including GED) or higher: 71.0% (2007); Bachelor's degree or higher: 6.0% (2007); Master's degree or higher: 1.1% (2007).
Housing: Homeownership rate: 74.5% (2007); Median home value: $59,189 (2007); Median rent: $246 per month (2000); Median age of housing: 42 years (2000).
Newspapers: County Journal (Local news; Circulation 7,100)
Transportation: Commute to work: 91.3% car, 0.0% public transportation, 2.2% walk, 3.4% work from home (2000); Travel time to work: 41.1% less than 15 minutes, 27.4% 15 to 30 minutes, 13.5% 30 to 45 minutes, 9.2% 45 to 60 minutes, 8.7% 60 minutes or more (2000)

PRAIRIE DU ROCHER (village). Aka Prairie Du Rocher. Covers a land area of 0.570 square miles and a water area of 0 square miles. Located at 38.08° N. Lat.; 90.09° W. Long. Elevation is 394 feet.
History: Prairie du Rocher was founded in the early 1700's by people brought to the area by John Law, a Scotch promoter who organized a company and was granted a charter for the Louisiana Territory.
Population: 540 (1990); 613 (2000); 679 (2007); 706 (2012 projected); Race: 99.3% White, 0.0% Black, 0.0% Asian, 0.0% Hispanic of any race (2007); Density: 1,192.0 persons per square mile (2007); Average household size: 2.49 (2007); Median age: 32.7 (2007); Males per 100

females: 81.6 (2007); Marriage status: 22.8% never married, 58.5% now married, 7.3% widowed, 11.4% divorced (2000); Foreign born: 0.0% (2000); Ancestry (includes multiple ancestries): 36.0% German, 31.0% French (except Basque), 13.3% Irish, 11.8% Other groups, 7.0% United States or American (2000).
Economy: Single-family building permits issued: 0 (2007); Multi-family building permits issued: 0 (2007); Employment by occupation: 7.5% management, 10.4% professional, 20.4% services, 21.4% sales, 0.7% farming, 13.2% construction, 26.4% production (2000).
Income: Per capita income: $19,856 (2007); Median household income: $44,405 (2007); Average household income: $49,386 (2007); Percent of households with income of $100,000 or more: 4.8% (2007); Poverty rate: 8.3% (2000).
Education: Percent of population age 25 and over with: High school diploma (including GED) or higher: 73.4% (2007); Bachelor's degree or higher: 8.3% (2007); Master's degree or higher: 2.9% (2007).

School District(s)

Prairie Du Rocher CCSD 134 (PK-08)
2005-06 Enrollment: 180 . . . . (618) 284-3530
Housing: Homeownership rate: 75.5% (2007); Median home value: $81,379 (2007); Median rent: $325 per month (2000); Median age of housing: 42 years (2000).
Transportation: Commute to work: 90.9% car, 1.5% public transportation, 5.1% walk, 2.2% work from home (2000); Travel time to work: 20.1% less than 15 minutes, 23.5% 15 to 30 minutes, 22.8% 30 to 45 minutes, 9.3% 45 to 60 minutes, 24.3% 60 minutes or more (2000)

RED BUD (city). Covers a land area of 2.104 square miles and a water area of 0.007 square miles. Located at 38.21° N. Lat.; 89.99° W. Long. Elevation is 472 feet.
History: Red Bud was named for the red-bud trees that once covered the town site.
Population: 3,329 (1990); 3,422 (2000); 3,520 (2007); 3,572 (2012 projected); Race: 99.0% White, 0.0% Black, 0.2% Asian, 0.9% Hispanic of any race (2007); Density: 1,672.9 persons per square mile (2007); Average household size: 2.44 (2007); Median age: 40.9 (2007); Males per 100 females: 87.1 (2007); Marriage status: 20.6% never married, 63.5% now married, 9.2% widowed, 6.7% divorced (2000); Foreign born: 1.8% (2000); Ancestry (includes multiple ancestries): 45.6% German, 11.6% French (except Basque), 8.4% Irish, 7.7% English, 6.6% Other groups (2000).
Economy: Single-family building permits issued: 24 (2007); Multi-family building permits issued: 0 (2007); Employment by occupation: 10.0% management, 21.3% professional, 16.5% services, 23.1% sales, 0.4% farming, 12.9% construction, 15.7% production (2000).
Income: Per capita income: $22,975 (2007); Median household income: $47,722 (2007); Average household income: $55,367 (2007); Percent of households with income of $100,000 or more: 10.3% (2007); Poverty rate: 9.4% (2000).
Education: Percent of population age 25 and over with: High school diploma (including GED) or higher: 77.7% (2007); Bachelor's degree or higher: 14.7% (2007); Master's degree or higher: 3.9% (2007).

School District(s)

Beck Area Career Center
2005-06 Enrollment: n/a . . . . (618) 473-2222
Monroe/Randolph Roe (06-12)
2005-06 Enrollment: 141 . . . . (618) 939-5650
Red Bud CUSD 132 (PK-12)
2005-06 Enrollment: 1,052 . . . . (618) 282-3507

Vocational/Technical School(s)

Beck Area Career Center-Red Bud (Public)
Fall 2007 Enrollment: 94 . . . . (618) 473-2222
2007-08 Tuition: $9,500
Housing: Homeownership rate: 77.8% (2007); Median home value: $122,423 (2007); Median rent: $311 per month (2000); Median age of housing: 32 years (2000).
Hospitals: Red Bud Regional Hospital (202 beds)
Safety: Violent crime rate: 96.5 per 10,000 population; Property crime rate: 238.5 per 10,000 population (2006).
Newspapers: North County News (Local news; Circulation 4,000)
Transportation: Commute to work: 88.7% car, 0.4% public transportation, 4.2% walk, 4.3% work from home (2000); Travel time to work: 43.1% less than 15 minutes, 21.3% 15 to 30 minutes, 14.6% 30 to 45 minutes, 14.7% 45 to 60 minutes, 6.3% 60 minutes or more (2000)
Additional Information Contacts
Red Bud Chamber of Commerce. . . . . (618) 282-3505
http://www.redbudchamber.com

ROCKWOOD (village). Covers a land area of 0.211 square miles and a water area of 0 square miles. Located at 37.83° N. Lat.; 89.69° W. Long. Elevation is 381 feet.
History: Early settlers in Rockwood provided river steamers with wood for fuel, and built flatboats for transporting cargo.
Population: 55 (1990); 41 (2000); 43 (2007); 42 (2012 projected); Race: 100.0% White, 0.0% Black, 0.0% Asian, 0.0% Hispanic of any race (2007); Density: 203.3 persons per square mile (2007); Average household size: 3.91 (2007); Median age: 33.1 (2007); Males per 100 females: 95.5 (2007); Marriage status: 45.2% never married, 48.4% now married, 0.0% widowed, 6.5% divorced (2000); Foreign born: 0.0% (2000); Ancestry (includes multiple ancestries): 80.9% United States or American, 10.6% German, 4.3% French (except Basque) (2000).
Economy: Employment by occupation: 18.8% management, 0.0% professional, 43.8% services, 0.0% sales, 0.0% farming, 12.5% construction, 25.0% production (2000).
Income: Per capita income: $19,593 (2007); Median household income: $84,722 (2007); Average household income: $76,591 (2007); Percent of households with income of $100,000 or more: 0.0% (2007); Poverty rate: 0.0% (2000).
Education: Percent of population age 25 and over with: High school diploma (including GED) or higher: 50.0% (2007); Bachelor's degree or higher: 11.5% (2007); Master's degree or higher: 0.0% (2007).
Housing: Homeownership rate: 72.7% (2007); Median home value: $47,500 (2007); Median rent: $225 per month (2000); Median age of housing: 32 years (2000).
Transportation: Commute to work: 100.0% car, 0.0% public transportation, 0.0% walk, 0.0% work from home (2000); Travel time to work: 0.0% less than 15 minutes, 100.0% 15 to 30 minutes, 0.0% 30 to 45 minutes, 0.0% 45 to 60 minutes, 0.0% 60 minutes or more (2000)

RUMA (village). Covers a land area of 0.410 square miles and a water area of 0 square miles. Located at 38.13° N. Lat.; 89.99° W. Long. Elevation is 443 feet.
Population: 272 (1990); 260 (2000); 280 (2007); 286 (2012 projected); Race: 98.2% White, 0.0% Black, 1.8% Asian, 0.0% Hispanic of any race (2007); Density: 682.8 persons per square mile (2007); Average household size: 2.55 (2007); Median age: 31.8 (2007); Males per 100 females: 104.4 (2007); Marriage status: 20.6% never married, 60.3% now married, 4.8% widowed, 14.4% divorced (2000); Foreign born: 3.0% (2000); Ancestry (includes multiple ancestries): 47.7% German, 16.3% French (except Basque), 14.0% Irish, 9.8% Other groups, 8.3% English (2000).
Economy: Single-family building permits issued: 4 (2007); Multi-family building permits issued: 0 (2007); Employment by occupation: 4.0% management, 10.4% professional, 20.8% services, 23.2% sales, 0.0% farming, 13.6% construction, 28.0% production (2000).
Income: Per capita income: $19,420 (2007); Median household income: $42,222 (2007); Average household income: $49,432 (2007); Percent of households with income of $100,000 or more: 8.2% (2007); Poverty rate: 13.6% (2000).
Education: Percent of population age 25 and over with: High school diploma (including GED) or higher: 79.8% (2007); Bachelor's degree or higher: 7.4% (2007); Master's degree or higher: 4.3% (2007).
Housing: Homeownership rate: 81.8% (2007); Median home value: $85,714 (2007); Median rent: $363 per month (2000); Median age of housing: 23 years (2000).
Safety: Violent crime rate: 0.0 per 10,000 population; Property crime rate: 39.1 per 10,000 population (2006).
Transportation: Commute to work: 96.7% car, 0.0% public transportation, 3.3% walk, 0.0% work from home (2000); Travel time to work: 29.5% less than 15 minutes, 25.4% 15 to 30 minutes, 27.9% 30 to 45 minutes, 4.9% 45 to 60 minutes, 12.3% 60 minutes or more (2000)

SPARTA (city). Covers a land area of 9.033 square miles and a water area of 0.150 square miles. Located at 38.12° N. Lat.; 89.70° W. Long. Elevation is 528 feet.
History: Incorporated 1847.
Population: 4,942 (1990); 4,486 (2000); 4,332 (2007); 4,188 (2012 projected); Race: 85.9% White, 11.6% Black, 0.6% Asian, 1.7% Hispanic of any race (2007); Density: 479.6 persons per square mile (2007); Average household size: 2.46 (2007); Median age: 39.9 (2007); Males per 100 females: 82.9 (2007); Marriage status: 23.1% never married, 57.8% now

married, 9.5% widowed, 9.6% divorced (2000); Foreign born: 0.7% (2000); Ancestry (includes multiple ancestries): 26.2% German, 16.1% Other groups, 12.2% Irish, 9.0% English, 6.3% United States or American (2000).
Economy: Single-family building permits issued: 2 (2007); Multi-family building permits issued: 2 (2007); Employment by occupation: 6.8% management, 18.1% professional, 16.3% services, 25.7% sales, 0.3% farming, 9.8% construction, 23.1% production (2000).
Income: Per capita income: $18,825 (2007); Median household income: $38,070 (2007); Average household income: $45,034 (2007); Percent of households with income of $100,000 or more: 6.8% (2007); Poverty rate: 16.0% (2000).
Education: Percent of population age 25 and over with: High school diploma (including GED) or higher: 82.9% (2007); Bachelor's degree or higher: 12.7% (2007); Master's degree or higher: 5.0% (2007).

School District(s)

Sparta CUSD 140 (PK-12)
2005-06 Enrollment: 1,529 . . . . (618) 443-5331

Housing: Homeownership rate: 72.7% (2007); Median home value: $71,272 (2007); Median rent: $306 per month (2000); Median age of housing: 40 years (2000).
Hospitals: Sparta Community Hospital (39 beds)
Safety: Violent crime rate: 29.6 per 10,000 population; Property crime rate: 218.4 per 10,000 population (2006).
Newspapers: Sparta News-Plaindealer (Community news; Circulation 5,000)
Transportation: Commute to work: 93.2% car, 1.3% public transportation, 1.7% walk, 3.0% work from home (2000); Travel time to work: 62.2% less than 15 minutes, 16.0% 15 to 30 minutes, 9.4% 30 to 45 minutes, 5.4% 45 to 60 minutes, 7.0% 60 minutes or more (2000)

Additional Information Contacts

Sparta Area Chamber of Commerce . . . . (618) 443-6908
http://www.spartaillinois.us

STEELEVILLE (village). Covers a land area of 1.304 square miles and a water area of 0.008 square miles. Located at 38.00° N. Lat.; 89.65° W. Long. Elevation is 413 feet.
History: Incorporated 1851.
Population: 2,113 (1990); 2,077 (2000); 2,065 (2007); 2,027 (2012 projected); Race: 98.7% White, 0.0% Black, 0.6% Asian, 0.7% Hispanic of any race (2007); Density: 1,583.8 persons per square mile (2007); Average household size: 2.24 (2007); Median age: 40.5 (2007); Males per 100 females: 86.9 (2007); Marriage status: 19.6% never married, 57.2% now married, 11.8% widowed, 11.4% divorced (2000); Foreign born: 0.9% (2000); Ancestry (includes multiple ancestries): 45.9% German, 10.9% Irish, 7.1% Other groups, 6.8% English, 6.8% United States or American (2000).
Economy: Single-family building permits issued: 0 (2007); Multi-family building permits issued: 0 (2007); Employment by occupation: 8.1% management, 18.2% professional, 18.9% services, 22.5% sales, 0.5% farming, 9.4% construction, 22.4% production (2000).
Income: Per capita income: $22,074 (2007); Median household income: $39,141 (2007); Average household income: $49,439 (2007); Percent of households with income of $100,000 or more: 9.0% (2007); Poverty rate: 7.9% (2000).
Education: Percent of population age 25 and over with: High school diploma (including GED) or higher: 76.9% (2007); Bachelor's degree or higher: 9.9% (2007); Master's degree or higher: 2.1% (2007).

School District(s)

Steeleville CUSD 138 (KG-12)
2005-06 Enrollment: 414 . . . . (618) 965-3432

Housing: Homeownership rate: 79.2% (2007); Median home value: $91,233 (2007); Median rent: $304 per month (2000); Median age of housing: 41 years (2000).
Newspapers: Steeleville Ledger (Local news; Circulation 1,350)
Transportation: Commute to work: 89.0% car, 0.0% public transportation, 8.6% walk, 2.4% work from home (2000); Travel time to work: 50.7% less than 15 minutes, 30.9% 15 to 30 minutes, 7.4% 30 to 45 minutes, 2.7% 45 to 60 minutes, 8.2% 60 minutes or more (2000)

Additional Information Contacts

Steeleville Chamber of Commerce Inc. . . . . (618) 965-9568
http://www.steeleville.org

TILDEN (village). Covers a land area of 0.965 square miles and a water area of 0.010 square miles. Located at 38.21° N. Lat.; 89.68° W. Long. Elevation is 525 feet.
Population: 919 (1990); 922 (2000); 761 (2007); 756 (2012 projected); Race: 99.3% White, 0.0% Black, 0.0% Asian, 2.0% Hispanic of any race (2007); Density: 788.4 persons per square mile (2007); Average household size: 2.49 (2007); Median age: 35.5 (2007); Males per 100 females: 95.6 (2007); Marriage status: 22.5% never married, 53.8% now married, 9.2% widowed, 14.5% divorced (2000); Foreign born: 0.0% (2000); Ancestry (includes multiple ancestries): 27.9% German, 19.4% Irish, 18.9% Other groups, 10.4% United States or American, 6.0% French (except Basque) (2000).
Economy: Employment by occupation: 4.1% management, 13.4% professional, 20.5% services, 12.9% sales, 1.1% farming, 14.0% construction, 34.0% production (2000).
Income: Per capita income: $18,262 (2007); Median household income: $40,833 (2007); Average household income: $45,417 (2007); Percent of households with income of $100,000 or more: 3.9% (2007); Poverty rate: 14.7% (2000).
Education: Percent of population age 25 and over with: High school diploma (including GED) or higher: 75.4% (2007); Bachelor's degree or higher: 4.2% (2007); Master's degree or higher: 1.5% (2007).

School District(s)

Sparta CUSD 140 (PK-12)
2005-06 Enrollment: 1,529 . . . . (618) 443-5331

Housing: Homeownership rate: 73.5% (2007); Median home value: $50,714 (2007); Median rent: $255 per month (2000); Median age of housing: 28 years (2000).
Transportation: Commute to work: 98.0% car, 0.0% public transportation, 2.0% walk, 0.0% work from home (2000); Travel time to work: 28.1% less than 15 minutes, 26.4% 15 to 30 minutes, 18.1% 30 to 45 minutes, 12.9% 45 to 60 minutes, 14.6% 60 minutes or more (2000)

WALSH (unincorporated postal area, zip code 62297). Covers a land area of 22.664 square miles and a water area of 0.064 square miles. Located at 38.05° N. Lat.; 89.80° W. Long. Elevation is 479 feet.
Population: 411 (2000); Race: 100.0% White, 0.0% Black, 0.0% Asian, 0.0% Hispanic of any race (2000); Density: 18.1 persons per square mile (2000); Age: 21.0% under 18, 20.5% over 64 (2000); Marriage status: 18.8% never married, 76.1% now married, 5.2% widowed, 0.0% divorced (2000); Foreign born: 0.0% (2000); Ancestry (includes multiple ancestries): 51.7% German, 13.8% Irish, 8.8% Italian, 7.5% United States or American, 7.0% Scotch-Irish (2000).
Economy: Employment by occupation: 2.5% management, 8.7% professional, 10.6% services, 23.0% sales, 0.0% farming, 20.5% construction, 34.8% production (2000).
Income: Per capita income: $17,737 (2000); Median household income: $50,197 (2000); Poverty rate: 2.8% (2000).
Education: Percent of population age 25 and over with: High school diploma (including GED) or higher: 77.8% (2000); Bachelor's degree or higher: 6.6% (2000).
Housing: Homeownership rate: 96.2% (2000); Median home value: $68,600 (2000); Median rent: $n/a per month (2000); Median age of housing: 53 years (2000).
Transportation: Commute to work: 94.4% car, 0.0% public transportation, 5.6% walk, 0.0% work from home (2000); Travel time to work: 8.1% less than 15 minutes, 47.8% 15 to 30 minutes, 21.1% 30 to 45 minutes, 4.3% 45 to 60 minutes, 18.6% 60 minutes or more (2000)

Richland County

Located in southeastern Illinois; bounded partly on the west by the Little Wabash River; drained by the Fox River and Bonpas Creek. Covers a land area of 360.14 square miles, a water area of 1.87 square miles, and is located in the Central Time Zone. The county was founded in 1841. County seat is Olney.

Weather Station: Olney 2 S — Elevation: 479 feet

	Jan	Feb	Mar	Apr	May	Jun	Jul	Aug	Sep	Oct	Nov	Dec
High	37	43	54	66	76	85	88	87	81	69	55	43
Low	21	25	35	44	53	62	66	64	57	45	36	26
Precip	2.8	2.6	4.3	4.6	4.6	4.0	3.9	3.3	3.1	3.3	4.4	3.6
Snow	4.2	3.3	1.9	0.2	0.0	0.0	0.0	0.0	0.0	tr	0.8	2.9

High and Low temperatures in degrees Fahrenheit; Precipitation and Snow in inches

Population: 16,545 (1990); 16,149 (2000); 15,709 (2007); 15,365 (2012 projected); Race: 98.0% White, 0.6% Black, 0.6% Asian, 0.9% Hispanic of any race (2007); Density: 43.6 persons per square mile (2007); Average

household size: 2.38 (2007); Median age: 41.1 (2007); Males per 100 females: 95.1 (2007).
Religion: Five largest groups: 14.8% Catholic Church, 13.6% Christian Churches and Churches of Christ, 10.1% The United Methodist Church, 4.7% Southern Baptist Convention, 3.9% Evangelical Lutheran Church in America (2000).
Economy: Unemployment rate: 5.2% (4/2008); Total civilian labor force: 7,621 (4/2008); Leading industries: 17.0% health care and social assistance; 15.1% transportation & warehousing; 15.1% retail trade (2005); Farms: 506 totaling 209,273 acres (2002); Companies that employ 500 or more persons: 1 (2006); Companies that employ 100 to 499 persons: 5 (2006); Companies that employ less than 100 persons: 476 (2006); Black-owned businesses: n/a (2002); Hispanic-owned businesses: n/a (2002); Asian-owned businesses: n/a (2002); Women-owned businesses: 469 (2002); Retail sales per capita: $13,222 (2008). Single-family building permits issued: 11 (2007); Multi-family building permits issued: 0 (2007).
Income: Per capita income: $19,736 (2007); Median household income: $36,390 (2007); Average household income: $46,882 (2007); Percent of households with income of $100,000 or more: 7.8% (2007); Poverty rate: 15.2% (2005); Bankruptcy rate: 3.28% (2007).
Education: Percent of population age 25 and over with: High school diploma (including GED) or higher: 83.2% (2007); Bachelor's degree or higher: 15.2% (2007); Master's degree or higher: 4.6% (2007).
Housing: Homeownership rate: 76.6% (2007); Median home value: $92,536 (2007); Median rent: $288 per month (2000); Median age of housing: 38 years (2000).
Health: Birth rate: 124.1 per 10,000 population (2007); Death rate: 128.0 per 10,000 population (2007); Age-adjusted cancer mortality rate: 220.2 deaths per 100,000 population (2005); Number of physicians: 22.9 per 10,000 population (2005); Hospital beds: 56.9 per 10,000 population (2004); Hospital admissions: 1,814.3 per 10,000 population (2004).
Elections: 2004 Presidential election results: 66.5% Bush, 32.6% Kerry, 0.0% Nader, 0.8% Badnarik

Additional Information Contacts

Richland County Government . . . . (618) 392-3111

City of Olney . . . . (618) 395-7302
http://www.ci.olney.il.us

Olney and the Greater Richland County Chamber of Commerce . . . . (618) 392-2241
http://www.olneychamber.com

Richland County Communities

CALHOUN (village). Covers a land area of 1.047 square miles and a water area of 0 square miles. Located at 38.65° N. Lat.; 88.04° W. Long. Elevation is 541 feet.
Population: 232 (1990); 222 (2000); 182 (2007); 180 (2012 projected); Race: 92.9% White, 0.0% Black, 4.9% Asian, 0.0% Hispanic of any race (2007); Density: 173.8 persons per square mile (2007); Average household size: 2.53 (2007); Median age: 36.0 (2007); Males per 100 females: 91.6 (2007); Marriage status: 21.2% never married, 51.3% now married, 9.5% widowed, 18.0% divorced (2000); Foreign born: 0.0% (2000); Ancestry (includes multiple ancestries): 23.4% German, 20.0% English, 9.4% Other groups, 8.5% Irish, 6.8% United States or American (2000).
Economy: Employment by occupation: 6.9% management, 8.0% professional, 25.3% services, 11.5% sales, 0.0% farming, 12.6% construction, 35.6% production (2000).
Income: Per capita income: $15,014 (2007); Median household income: $31,071 (2007); Average household income: $37,951 (2007); Percent of households with income of $100,000 or more: 4.2% (2007); Poverty rate: 27.2% (2000).
Education: Percent of population age 25 and over with: High school diploma (including GED) or higher: 76.7% (2007); Bachelor's degree or higher: 9.5% (2007); Master's degree or higher: 3.4% (2007).
Housing: Homeownership rate: 80.6% (2007); Median home value: $60,000 (2007); Median rent: $188 per month (2000); Median age of housing: 34 years (2000).
Transportation: Commute to work: 96.5% car, 0.0% public transportation, 0.0% walk, 3.5% work from home (2000); Travel time to work: 11.0% less than 15 minutes, 67.1% 15 to 30 minutes, 18.3% 30 to 45 minutes, 0.0% 45 to 60 minutes, 3.7% 60 minutes or more (2000)

CLAREMONT (village). Covers a land area of 1.135 square miles and a water area of 0 square miles. Located at 38.72° N. Lat.; 87.97° W. Long. Elevation is 509 feet.
Population: 256 (1990); 212 (2000); 201 (2007); 192 (2012 projected); Race: 100.0% White, 0.0% Black, 0.0% Asian, 0.0% Hispanic of any race (2007); Density: 177.1 persons per square mile (2007); Average household size: 2.28 (2007); Median age: 43.8 (2007); Males per 100 females: 118.5 (2007); Marriage status: 10.8% never married, 77.2% now married, 4.2% widowed, 7.8% divorced (2000); Foreign born: 1.5% (2000); Ancestry (includes multiple ancestries): 22.3% United States or American, 16.0% German, 12.1% Irish, 8.7% Other groups, 6.3% English (2000).
Economy: Employment by occupation: 16.9% management, 19.1% professional, 5.6% services, 15.7% sales, 0.0% farming, 16.9% construction, 25.8% production (2000).
Income: Per capita income: $18,321 (2007); Median household income: $37,143 (2007); Average household income: $41,847 (2007); Percent of households with income of $100,000 or more: 4.5% (2007); Poverty rate: 2.5% (2000).
Education: Percent of population age 25 and over with: High school diploma (including GED) or higher: 73.6% (2007); Bachelor's degree or higher: 11.5% (2007); Master's degree or higher: 5.4% (2007).
Housing: Homeownership rate: 84.1% (2007); Median home value: $56,364 (2007); Median rent: $296 per month (2000); Median age of housing: 44 years (2000).
Transportation: Commute to work: 100.0% car, 0.0% public transportation, 0.0% walk, 0.0% work from home (2000); Travel time to work: 31.5% less than 15 minutes, 37.1% 15 to 30 minutes, 25.8% 30 to 45 minutes, 4.5% 45 to 60 minutes, 1.1% 60 minutes or more (2000)

DUNDAS (unincorporated postal area, zip code 62425). Covers a land area of 43.742 square miles and a water area of 0.009 square miles. Located at 38.83° N. Lat.; 88.09° W. Long. Elevation is 472 feet.
Population: 716 (2000); Race: 100.0% White, 0.0% Black, 0.0% Asian, 2.0% Hispanic of any race (2000); Density: 16.4 persons per square mile (2000); Age: 32.8% under 18, 24.4% over 64 (2000); Marriage status: 17.0% never married, 69.7% now married, 9.8% widowed, 3.4% divorced (2000); Foreign born: 0.0% (2000); Ancestry (includes multiple ancestries): 36.3% German, 16.0% United States or American, 13.6% English, 10.3% Irish, 3.0% Other groups (2000).
Economy: Employment by occupation: 15.1% management, 18.3% professional, 12.3% services, 25.4% sales, 4.6% farming, 10.9% construction, 13.4% production (2000).
Income: Per capita income: $14,419 (2000); Median household income: $32,222 (2000); Poverty rate: 6.0% (2000).
Education: Percent of population age 25 and over with: High school diploma (including GED) or higher: 80.6% (2000); Bachelor's degree or higher: 9.3% (2000).
Housing: Homeownership rate: 91.2% (2000); Median home value: $55,700 (2000); Median rent: $253 per month (2000); Median age of housing: 37 years (2000).
Transportation: Commute to work: 90.1% car, 0.0% public transportation, 0.0% walk, 9.9% work from home (2000); Travel time to work: 43.8% less than 15 minutes, 35.2% 15 to 30 minutes, 14.8% 30 to 45 minutes, 3.1% 45 to 60 minutes, 3.1% 60 minutes or more (2000)

NOBLE (village). Covers a land area of 1.024 square miles and a water area of 0.005 square miles. Located at 38.69° N. Lat.; 88.22° W. Long. Elevation is 476 feet.
Population: 757 (1990); 746 (2000); 596 (2007); 593 (2012 projected); Race: 99.3% White, 0.0% Black, 0.0% Asian, 1.2% Hispanic of any race (2007); Density: 582.2 persons per square mile (2007); Average household size: 2.29 (2007); Median age: 36.7 (2007); Males per 100 females: 100.0 (2007); Marriage status: 16.2% never married, 58.9% now married, 9.1% widowed, 15.8% divorced (2000); Foreign born: 0.4% (2000); Ancestry (includes multiple ancestries): 17.5% German, 13.3% United States or American, 8.2% English, 8.0% Irish, 6.6% Other groups (2000).
Economy: Single-family building permits issued: 0 (2007); Multi-family building permits issued: 0 (2007); Employment by occupation: 7.1% management, 9.2% professional, 16.4% services, 24.1% sales, 0.6% farming, 5.7% construction, 36.9% production (2000).
Income: Per capita income: $18,238 (2007); Median household income: $36,500 (2007); Average household income: $41,808 (2007); Percent of households with income of $100,000 or more: 5.4% (2007); Poverty rate: 18.6% (2000).

Education: Percent of population age 25 and over with: High school diploma (including GED) or higher: 80.2% (2007); Bachelor's degree or higher: 12.3% (2007); Master's degree or higher: 3.3% (2007).

School District(s)

West Richland CUSD 2 (PK-12)
2005-06 Enrollment: 442 . . . . (618) 723-2334

Housing: Homeownership rate: 73.8% (2007); Median home value: $67,222 (2007); Median rent: $269 per month (2000); Median age of housing: 41 years (2000).
Newspapers: County Commoner (Local news; Circulation 1,300)
Transportation: Commute to work: 91.0% car, 0.0% public transportation, 3.1% walk, 2.8% work from home (2000); Travel time to work: 36.9% less than 15 minutes, 40.8% 15 to 30 minutes, 16.6% 30 to 45 minutes, 1.6% 45 to 60 minutes, 4.1% 60 minutes or more (2000)

OLNEY (city). County seat. Covers a land area of 5.760 square miles and a water area of <.001 square miles. Located at 38.73° N. Lat.; 88.08° W. Long. Elevation is 479 feet.
History: Olney was named for John Olney, lawyer and officer in the Civil War. It developed as a shipping and trading center, and as the seat of Richland County. In 1902 a naturalist brought a pair of albino squirrels to Olney and set them loose. Soon Olney became known as "the home of white squirrels," as thousands of these squirrels took up residence in the parks and gardens.
Population: 9,096 (1990); 8,631 (2000); 8,358 (2007); 8,145 (2012 projected); Race: 97.4% White, 0.9% Black, 0.7% Asian, 1.1% Hispanic of any race (2007); Density: 1,451.0 persons per square mile (2007); Average household size: 2.26 (2007); Median age: 40.7 (2007); Males per 100 females: 89.2 (2007); Marriage status: 23.1% never married, 51.6% now married, 11.3% widowed, 14.0% divorced (2000); Foreign born: 0.9% (2000); Ancestry (includes multiple ancestries): 24.9% German, 19.1% United States or American, 9.2% English, 7.7% Irish, 6.8% Other groups (2000).
Economy: Single-family building permits issued: 11 (2007); Multi-family building permits issued: 0 (2007); Employment by occupation: 13.0% management, 17.5% professional, 21.0% services, 24.2% sales, 0.2% farming, 8.4% construction, 15.6% production (2000).
Income: Per capita income: $18,705 (2007); Median household income: $31,794 (2007); Average household income: $42,111 (2007); Percent of households with income of $100,000 or more: 6.5% (2007); Poverty rate: 17.0% (2000).
Education: Percent of population age 25 and over with: High school diploma (including GED) or higher: 83.1% (2007); Bachelor's degree or higher: 16.2% (2007); Master's degree or higher: 5.5% (2007).

School District(s)

Clay/Cwford/Jsper/Lwrnce/Rhland
2005-06 Enrollment: n/a . . . . (618) 392-4631
East Richland CUSD 1 (PK-12)
2005-06 Enrollment: 2,139 . . . . (618) 395-2324

Two-year College(s)

Illinois Eastern Community Colleges-Olney Central College (Public)
Fall 2007 Enrollment: 1,610. . . . . (618) 393-2982
2007-08 Tuition: In-state $6,117; Out-of-state $7,615

Housing: Homeownership rate: 69.0% (2007); Median home value: $79,874 (2007); Median rent: $295 per month (2000); Median age of housing: 42 years (2000).
Hospitals: Richland Memorial Hospital (135 beds)
Safety: Violent crime rate: 27.2 per 10,000 population; Property crime rate: 364.8 per 10,000 population (2006).
Newspapers: Olney Daily Mail (Regional news; Circulation 5,000)
Transportation: Commute to work: 94.3% car, 0.2% public transportation, 2.2% walk, 2.6% work from home (2000); Travel time to work: 71.8% less than 15 minutes, 14.8% 15 to 30 minutes, 8.0% 30 to 45 minutes, 2.9% 45 to 60 minutes, 2.5% 60 minutes or more (2000)
Airports: Olney-Noble (general aviation)
Additional Information Contacts
City of Olney . . . . (618) 395-7302
http://www.ci.olney.il.us
Olney and the Greater Richland County Chamber of Commerce . . . . (618) 392-2241
http://www.olneychamber.com

PARKERSBURG (village). Covers a land area of 0.746 square miles and a water area of 0 square miles. Located at 38.59° N. Lat.; 88.05° W. Long. Elevation is 479 feet.
Population: 223 (1990); 234 (2000); 189 (2007); 188 (2012 projected); Race: 100.0% White, 0.0% Black, 0.0% Asian, 0.0% Hispanic of any race (2007); Density: 253.3 persons per square mile (2007); Average household size: 2.36 (2007); Median age: 37.3 (2007); Males per 100 females: 107.7 (2007); Marriage status: 17.6% never married, 58.0% now married, 10.8% widowed, 13.6% divorced (2000); Foreign born: 0.0% (2000); Ancestry (includes multiple ancestries): 15.7% United States or American, 13.2% German, 6.4% English, 4.9% Irish, 4.9% Dutch (2000).
Economy: Employment by occupation: 4.5% management, 7.9% professional, 4.5% services, 22.5% sales, 0.0% farming, 9.0% construction, 51.7% production (2000).
Income: Per capita income: $14,392 (2007); Median household income: $26,111 (2007); Average household income: $34,000 (2007); Percent of households with income of $100,000 or more: 2.5% (2007); Poverty rate: 18.6% (2000).
Education: Percent of population age 25 and over with: High school diploma (including GED) or higher: 70.1% (2007); Bachelor's degree or higher: 0.0% (2007); Master's degree or higher: 0.0% (2007).
Housing: Homeownership rate: 90.0% (2007); Median home value: $50,833 (2007); Median rent: $186 per month (2000); Median age of housing: 46 years (2000).
Transportation: Commute to work: 95.4% car, 0.0% public transportation, 2.3% walk, 2.3% work from home (2000); Travel time to work: 43.5% less than 15 minutes, 48.2% 15 to 30 minutes, 5.9% 30 to 45 minutes, 2.4% 45 to 60 minutes, 0.0% 60 minutes or more (2000)

Rock Island County

Located in northwestern Illinois; bounded on the north and west by the Mississippi River and the Iowa border, and partly on the east by the Rock River. Covers a land area of 426.75 square miles, a water area of 24.40 square miles, and is located in the Central Time Zone. The county was founded in 1831. County seat is Rock Island.

Rock Island County is part of the Davenport-Moline-Rock Island, IA-IL Metropolitan Statistical Area. The entire metro area includes: Henry County, IL; Mercer County, IL; Rock Island County, IL; Scott County, IA

Weather Station: Moline Quad City Airport — Elevation: 590 feet

	Jan	Feb	Mar	Apr	May	Jun	Jul	Aug	Sep	Oct	Nov	Dec
High	29	35	48	61	73	83	86	84	76	64	48	35
Low	12	18	29	39	50	60	65	62	53	41	30	19
Precip	1.6	1.4	3.0	3.8	4.5	4.5	4.1	4.5	3.5	2.8	2.7	2.2
Snow	9.8	6.7	5.2	1.6	tr	tr	tr	0.0	tr	0.2	3.0	7.3

High and Low temperatures in degrees Fahrenheit; Precipitation and Snow in inches

Population: 148,723 (1990); 149,374 (2000); 147,716 (2007); 146,414 (2012 projected); Race: 83.9% White, 7.6% Black, 1.2% Asian, 10.5% Hispanic of any race (2007); Density: 346.1 persons per square mile (2007); Average household size: 2.44 (2007); Median age: 38.6 (2007); Males per 100 females: 94.6 (2007).
Religion: Five largest groups: 18.7% Catholic Church, 4.5% Evangelical Lutheran Church in America, 3.9% The United Methodist Church, 3.5% Lutheran Church—Missouri Synod, 2.4% International Church of the Foursquare Gospel (2000).
Economy: Unemployment rate: 4.6% (4/2008); Total civilian labor force: 81,028 (4/2008); Leading industries: 14.5% health care and social assistance; 13.0% retail trade; 12.8% manufacturing (2005); Farms: 659 totaling 169,612 acres (2002); Companies that employ 500 or more persons: 8 (2006); Companies that employ 100 to 499 persons: 95 (2006); Companies that employ less than 100 persons: 3,406 (2006); Black-owned businesses: 228 (2002); Hispanic-owned businesses: 200 (2002); Asian-owned businesses: 123 (2002); Women-owned businesses: 2,732 (2002); Retail sales per capita: $14,876 (2008). Single-family building permits issued: 185 (2007); Multi-family building permits issued: 194 (2007).
Income: Per capita income: $23,701 (2007); Median household income: $44,716 (2007); Average household income: $56,875 (2007); Percent of households with income of $100,000 or more: 12.8% (2007); Poverty rate: 13.4% (2005); Bankruptcy rate: 3.24% (2007).
Taxes: Total county taxes per capita: $134 (2006); County property taxes per capita: $117 (2006).
Education: Percent of population age 25 and over with: High school diploma (including GED) or higher: 82.6% (2007); Bachelor's degree or higher: 17.0% (2007); Master's degree or higher: 5.6% (2007).

Housing: Homeownership rate: 70.0% (2007); Median home value: $100,907 (2007); Median rent: $376 per month (2000); Median age of housing: 43 years (2000).
Health: Birth rate: 136.8 per 10,000 population (2007); Death rate: 98.2 per 10,000 population (2007); Age-adjusted cancer mortality rate: 180.3 deaths per 100,000 population (2005); Air Quality Index: 90.4% good, 9.0% moderate, 0.5% unhealthy for sensitive individuals, 0.0% unhealthy (percent of days in 2007); Number of physicians: 18.5 per 10,000 population (2005); Hospital beds: 30.0 per 10,000 population (2004); Hospital admissions: 1,582.2 per 10,000 population (2004).
Elections: 2004 Presidential election results: 42.4% Bush, 57.0% Kerry, 0.1% Nader, 0.5% Badnarik
National and State Parks: Black Hawk State Historical Site; Campbells Island State Park
Additional Information Contacts
Rock Island County Government . . . . (309) 558-3605
http://www.co.rock-island.il.us
City of East Moline . . . . (309) 752-1599
http://www.eastmoline.com
City of Moline . . . . (309) 764-3558
http://www.moline.il.us
City of Rock Island . . . . (309) 732-2000
http://www.rigov.org
City of Silvis . . . . (309) 792-9181
http://www.silvisil.org
Illinois Quad City Chamber of Commerce . . . . (309) 757-5416
http://www.quadcitychamber.com
Milan Chamber of Commerce . . . . (309) 787-3144
http://www.milanilchamber.org
Village of Milan . . . . (309) 787-8500
http://www.milanil.org

Rock Island County Communities

ANDALUSIA (village). Covers a land area of 0.717 square miles and a water area of 0.004 square miles. Located at 41.44° N. Lat.; 90.72° W. Long. Elevation is 574 feet.
History: Andalusia was the location on the Mississippi River of Clark's Ferry which gave passage to Buffalo, Iowa, to thousands of settlers in the 1830's.
Population: 967 (1990); 1,050 (2000); 884 (2007); 888 (2012 projected); Race: 95.9% White, 0.8% Black, 0.0% Asian, 3.4% Hispanic of any race (2007); Density: 1,232.1 persons per square mile (2007); Average household size: 2.55 (2007); Median age: 40.6 (2007); Males per 100 females: 93.0 (2007); Marriage status: 21.8% never married, 60.2% now married, 6.9% widowed, 11.1% divorced (2000); Foreign born: 1.4% (2000); Ancestry (includes multiple ancestries): 32.8% German, 16.4% Irish, 12.4% United States or American, 11.0% English, 5.5% Swedish (2000).
Economy: Single-family building permits issued: 5 (2007); Multi-family building permits issued: 0 (2007); Employment by occupation: 11.2% management, 14.2% professional, 13.4% services, 29.0% sales, 0.5% farming, 9.5% construction, 22.2% production (2000).
Income: Per capita income: $25,631 (2007); Median household income: $55,957 (2007); Average household income: $65,484 (2007); Percent of households with income of $100,000 or more: 16.8% (2007); Poverty rate: 2.9% (2000).
Education: Percent of population age 25 and over with: High school diploma (including GED) or higher: 90.2% (2007); Bachelor's degree or higher: 12.9% (2007); Master's degree or higher: 5.1% (2007).
School District(s)
Rockridge CUSD 300 (PK-12)
2005-06 Enrollment: 1,369 . . . . (309) 795-1167
Housing: Homeownership rate: 86.4% (2007); Median home value: $111,483 (2007); Median rent: $383 per month (2000); Median age of housing: 33 years (2000).
Transportation: Commute to work: 96.2% car, 0.2% public transportation, 0.7% walk, 2.0% work from home (2000); Travel time to work: 16.6% less than 15 minutes, 48.6% 15 to 30 minutes, 28.7% 30 to 45 minutes, 3.9% 45 to 60 minutes, 2.2% 60 minutes or more (2000)

CARBON CLIFF (village). Covers a land area of 2.041 square miles and a water area of 0 square miles. Located at 41.49° N. Lat.; 90.39° W. Long. Elevation is 604 feet.
Population: 1,674 (1990); 1,689 (2000); 1,743 (2007); 1,747 (2012 projected); Race: 88.0% White, 5.9% Black, 0.3% Asian, 6.6% Hispanic of any race (2007); Density: 853.8 persons per square mile (2007); Average household size: 2.42 (2007); Median age: 35.4 (2007); Males per 100 females: 94.3 (2007); Marriage status: 24.4% never married, 56.0% now married, 4.3% widowed, 15.3% divorced (2000); Foreign born: 2.1% (2000); Ancestry (includes multiple ancestries): 24.7% German, 14.4% Other groups, 14.1% Irish, 13.4% United States or American, 8.6% Swedish (2000).
Economy: Single-family building permits issued: 1 (2007); Multi-family building permits issued: 0 (2007); Employment by occupation: 8.9% management, 11.1% professional, 18.7% services, 28.9% sales, 0.0% farming, 10.7% construction, 21.6% production (2000).
Income: Per capita income: $20,639 (2007); Median household income: $41,429 (2007); Average household income: $49,785 (2007); Percent of households with income of $100,000 or more: 6.7% (2007); Poverty rate: 12.0% (2000).
Education: Percent of population age 25 and over with: High school diploma (including GED) or higher: 81.1% (2007); Bachelor's degree or higher: 11.1% (2007); Master's degree or higher: 3.4% (2007).
School District(s)
Black Hawk Area Sp Ed District (07-12)
2005-06 Enrollment: 46 . . . . (309) 796-2500
Housing: Homeownership rate: 68.1% (2007); Median home value: $90,192 (2007); Median rent: $462 per month (2000); Median age of housing: 38 years (2000).
Transportation: Commute to work: 93.4% car, 0.6% public transportation, 2.2% walk, 2.1% work from home (2000); Travel time to work: 36.3% less than 15 minutes, 41.6% 15 to 30 minutes, 16.3% 30 to 45 minutes, 1.3% 45 to 60 minutes, 4.6% 60 minutes or more (2000)

COAL VALLEY (village). Covers a land area of 2.861 square miles and a water area of 0 square miles. Located at 41.44° N. Lat.; 90.45° W. Long. Elevation is 623 feet.
Population: 3,548 (1990); 3,606 (2000); 3,912 (2007); 4,099 (2012 projected); Race: 96.5% White, 1.0% Black, 0.3% Asian, 3.8% Hispanic of any race (2007); Density: 1,367.4 persons per square mile (2007); Average household size: 2.57 (2007); Median age: 38.9 (2007); Males per 100 females: 98.5 (2007); Marriage status: 20.8% never married, 62.7% now married, 3.6% widowed, 12.9% divorced (2000); Foreign born: 1.5% (2000); Ancestry (includes multiple ancestries): 26.1% German, 14.4% Irish, 11.6% English, 9.6% Swedish, 9.5% United States or American (2000).
Economy: Single-family building permits issued: 16 (2007); Multi-family building permits issued: 0 (2007); Employment by occupation: 9.1% management, 18.6% professional, 15.0% services, 29.9% sales, 0.0% farming, 12.2% construction, 15.1% production (2000).
Income: Per capita income: $25,704 (2007); Median household income: $58,204 (2007); Average household income: $66,111 (2007); Percent of households with income of $100,000 or more: 19.5% (2007); Poverty rate: 7.4% (2000).
Education: Percent of population age 25 and over with: High school diploma (including GED) or higher: 85.1% (2007); Bachelor's degree or higher: 17.6% (2007); Master's degree or higher: 6.2% (2007).
School District(s)
Moline USD 40 (PK-12)
2005-06 Enrollment: 7,606 . . . . (309) 743-1600
Housing: Homeownership rate: 92.6% (2007); Median home value: $118,140 (2007); Median rent: $379 per month (2000); Median age of housing: 28 years (2000).
Safety: Violent crime rate: 10.2 per 10,000 population; Property crime rate: 125.5 per 10,000 population (2006).
Transportation: Commute to work: 96.2% car, 0.3% public transportation, 0.8% walk, 2.4% work from home (2000); Travel time to work: 24.9% less than 15 minutes, 62.0% 15 to 30 minutes, 9.8% 30 to 45 minutes, 1.3% 45 to 60 minutes, 2.1% 60 minutes or more (2000)

CORDOVA (village). Covers a land area of 0.562 square miles and a water area of 0.005 square miles. Located at 41.67° N. Lat.; 90.32° W. Long. Elevation is 591 feet.
Population: 678 (1990); 633 (2000); 654 (2007); 667 (2012 projected); Race: 95.4% White, 0.3% Black, 0.2% Asian, 3.4% Hispanic of any race (2007); Density: 1,163.3 persons per square mile (2007); Average household size: 2.52 (2007); Median age: 42.0 (2007); Males per 100 females: 106.3 (2007); Marriage status: 19.4% never married, 57.9% now

married, 8.4% widowed, 14.4% divorced (2000); Foreign born: 1.0% (2000); Ancestry (includes multiple ancestries): 23.8% German, 19.2% Irish, 14.5% English, 7.3% Other groups, 6.2% Belgian (2000).
Economy: Single-family building permits issued: 0 (2007); Multi-family building permits issued: 0 (2007); Employment by occupation: 10.3% management, 12.2% professional, 19.1% services, 21.0% sales, 0.6% farming, 21.3% construction, 15.4% production (2000).
Income: Per capita income: $26,582 (2007); Median household income: $58,889 (2007); Average household income: $65,913 (2007); Percent of households with income of $100,000 or more: 18.8% (2007); Poverty rate: 6.2% (2000).
Education: Percent of population age 25 and over with: High school diploma (including GED) or higher: 86.5% (2007); Bachelor's degree or higher: 13.5% (2007); Master's degree or higher: 4.6% (2007).
Housing: Homeownership rate: 82.7% (2007); Median home value: $112,772 (2007); Median rent: $315 per month (2000); Median age of housing: 40 years (2000).
Safety: Violent crime rate: 87.1 per 10,000 population; Property crime rate: 203.2 per 10,000 population (2006).
Transportation: Commute to work: 94.6% car, 0.6% public transportation, 3.2% walk, 1.6% work from home (2000); Travel time to work: 23.4% less than 15 minutes, 31.4% 15 to 30 minutes, 30.4% 30 to 45 minutes, 8.7% 45 to 60 minutes, 6.1% 60 minutes or more (2000)

COYNE CENTER (CDP). Covers a land area of 1.793 square miles and a water area of 0 square miles. Located at 41.40° N. Lat.; 90.56° W. Long. Elevation is 748 feet.
Population: 1,137 (1990); 906 (2000); 927 (2007); 941 (2012 projected); Race: 98.7% White, 0.9% Black, 0.0% Asian, 0.3% Hispanic of any race (2007); Density: 517.1 persons per square mile (2007); Average household size: 2.51 (2007); Median age: 47.2 (2007); Males per 100 females: 99.4 (2007); Marriage status: 15.4% never married, 66.2% now married, 8.2% widowed, 10.2% divorced (2000); Foreign born: 1.7% (2000); Ancestry (includes multiple ancestries): 30.4% German, 16.6% Irish, 13.0% English, 11.0% United States or American, 7.7% Other groups (2000).
Economy: Employment by occupation: 10.3% management, 13.0% professional, 10.1% services, 26.2% sales, 0.0% farming, 18.8% construction, 21.6% production (2000).
Income: Per capita income: $24,210 (2007); Median household income: $58,289 (2007); Average household income: $60,820 (2007); Percent of households with income of $100,000 or more: 11.4% (2007); Poverty rate: 4.3% (2000).
Education: Percent of population age 25 and over with: High school diploma (including GED) or higher: 85.4% (2007); Bachelor's degree or higher: 9.7% (2007); Master's degree or higher: 1.2% (2007).
Housing: Homeownership rate: 96.2% (2007); Median home value: $108,500 (2007); Median rent: $375 per month (2000); Median age of housing: 39 years (2000).
Transportation: Commute to work: 96.4% car, 0.0% public transportation, 0.6% walk, 2.9% work from home (2000); Travel time to work: 17.1% less than 15 minutes, 63.0% 15 to 30 minutes, 15.6% 30 to 45 minutes, 0.0% 45 to 60 minutes, 4.3% 60 minutes or more (2000)

EAST MOLINE (city). Covers a land area of 9.017 square miles and a water area of 0 square miles. Located at 41.51° N. Lat.; 90.43° W. Long. Elevation is 702 feet.
History: East Moline was incorporated as a city in 1907, and developed as an industrial center for nearby Moline and Rock Island. An International Harvester plant was a major employer.
Population: 20,575 (1990); 20,333 (2000); 19,974 (2007); 19,766 (2012 projected); Race: 78.0% White, 6.5% Black, 3.0% Asian, 19.0% Hispanic of any race (2007); Density: 2,215.1 persons per square mile (2007); Average household size: 2.38 (2007); Median age: 37.6 (2007); Males per 100 females: 91.8 (2007); Marriage status: 25.1% never married, 52.8% now married, 9.4% widowed, 12.7% divorced (2000); Foreign born: 8.2% (2000); Ancestry (includes multiple ancestries): 24.9% Other groups, 22.3% German, 11.0% Irish, 9.0% English, 7.3% Belgian (2000).
Economy: Single-family building permits issued: 8 (2007); Multi-family building permits issued: 0 (2007); Employment by occupation: 10.3% management, 17.7% professional, 19.0% services, 24.2% sales, 0.0% farming, 8.4% construction, 20.4% production (2000).
Income: Per capita income: $21,209 (2007); Median household income: $41,055 (2007); Average household income: $49,931 (2007); Percent of households with income of $100,000 or more: 9.5% (2007); Poverty rate: 13.9% (2000).
Education: Percent of population age 25 and over with: High school diploma (including GED) or higher: 80.9% (2007); Bachelor's degree or higher: 15.5% (2007); Master's degree or higher: 5.0% (2007).

School District(s)

Dept of Corrections Sch Dist 428 (08-12)
2005-06 Enrollment: 2,271 . . . . (217) 522-2666
East Moline SD 37 (PK-08)
2005-06 Enrollment: 2,436 . . . . (309) 755-4533
Moline USD 40 (PK-12)
2005-06 Enrollment: 7,606 . . . . (309) 743-1600
United Twp Area Career Ctr
2005-06 Enrollment: n/a . . . . (309) 752-1691
United Twp HSD 30 (09-12)
2005-06 Enrollment: 1,842 . . . . (309) 752-1611

Vocational/Technical School(s)

La James International College (Private, For-profit)
Fall 2007 Enrollment: 34 . . . . (309) 755-1313
2007-08 Tuition: $14,490

Housing: Homeownership rate: 64.4% (2007); Median home value: $100,060 (2007); Median rent: $353 per month (2000); Median age of housing: 37 years (2000).
Safety: Violent crime rate: 57.9 per 10,000 population; Property crime rate: 407.1 per 10,000 population (2006).
Transportation: Commute to work: 94.6% car, 1.1% public transportation, 1.4% walk, 2.0% work from home (2000); Travel time to work: 39.5% less than 15 minutes, 47.1% 15 to 30 minutes, 10.5% 30 to 45 minutes, 1.0% 45 to 60 minutes, 1.9% 60 minutes or more (2000)

Additional Information Contacts

City of East Moline . . . . (309) 752-1599
http://www.eastmoline.com

HAMPTON (village). Covers a land area of 1.580 square miles and a water area of 0 square miles. Located at 41.55° N. Lat.; 90.40° W. Long. Elevation is 587 feet.
Population: 1,626 (1990); 1,626 (2000); 1,717 (2007); 1,779 (2012 projected); Race: 95.1% White, 0.1% Black, 0.1% Asian, 5.4% Hispanic of any race (2007); Density: 1,086.4 persons per square mile (2007); Average household size: 2.52 (2007); Median age: 41.3 (2007); Males per 100 females: 91.8 (2007); Marriage status: 19.5% never married, 62.2% now married, 6.7% widowed, 11.5% divorced (2000); Foreign born: 5.1% (2000); Ancestry (includes multiple ancestries): 28.3% German, 15.1% Irish, 13.3% English, 10.9% Swedish, 10.5% Other groups (2000).
Economy: Single-family building permits issued: 6 (2007); Multi-family building permits issued: 0 (2007); Employment by occupation: 11.7% management, 15.7% professional, 14.6% services, 32.0% sales, 0.0% farming, 7.8% construction, 18.1% production (2000).
Income: Per capita income: $27,709 (2007); Median household income: $58,188 (2007); Average household income: $69,420 (2007); Percent of households with income of $100,000 or more: 19.8% (2007); Poverty rate: 7.3% (2000).
Education: Percent of population age 25 and over with: High school diploma (including GED) or higher: 85.1% (2007); Bachelor's degree or higher: 14.6% (2007); Master's degree or higher: 7.2% (2007).

School District(s)

Hampton SD 29 (KG-08)
2005-06 Enrollment: 219 . . . . (309) 755-0693

Housing: Homeownership rate: 86.5% (2007); Median home value: $110,651 (2007); Median rent: $456 per month (2000); Median age of housing: 34 years (2000).
Safety: Violent crime rate: 5.7 per 10,000 population; Property crime rate: 280.6 per 10,000 population (2006).
Transportation: Commute to work: 95.9% car, 1.6% public transportation, 0.7% walk, 1.8% work from home (2000); Travel time to work: 24.2% less than 15 minutes, 51.2% 15 to 30 minutes, 18.0% 30 to 45 minutes, 0.6% 45 to 60 minutes, 6.0% 60 minutes or more (2000)

HILLSDALE (village). Covers a land area of 0.754 square miles and a water area of 0.025 square miles. Located at 41.61° N. Lat.; 90.17° W. Long. Elevation is 581 feet.
Population: 557 (1990); 588 (2000); 597 (2007); 602 (2012 projected); Race: 94.3% White, 0.7% Black, 0.0% Asian, 3.9% Hispanic of any race (2007); Density: 792.1 persons per square mile (2007); Average household size: 2.63 (2007); Median age: 35.6 (2007); Males per 100 females: 90.7 (2007); Marriage status: 22.1% never married, 51.4% now married, 6.5% widowed, 20.0% divorced (2000); Foreign born: 0.0% (2000); Ancestry

(includes multiple ancestries): 30.2% German, 12.0% Irish, 8.9% English, 7.9% Other groups, 7.5% Dutch (2000).
Economy: Employment by occupation: 6.0% management, 9.7% professional, 23.3% services, 18.2% sales, 0.0% farming, 11.6% construction, 31.1% production (2000).
Income: Per capita income: $22,240 (2007); Median household income: $54,032 (2007); Average household income: $58,491 (2007); Percent of households with income of $100,000 or more: 9.7% (2007); Poverty rate: 11.0% (2000).
Education: Percent of population age 25 and over with: High school diploma (including GED) or higher: 81.3% (2007); Bachelor's degree or higher: 5.3% (2007); Master's degree or higher: 2.1% (2007).
Housing: Homeownership rate: 75.8% (2007); Median home value: $90,000 (2007); Median rent: $371 per month (2000); Median age of housing: 39 years (2000).
Safety: Violent crime rate: 278.3 per 10,000 population; Property crime rate: 52.2 per 10,000 population (2006).
Transportation: Commute to work: 91.8% car, 0.0% public transportation, 3.2% walk, 3.2% work from home (2000); Travel time to work: 20.3% less than 15 minutes, 35.6% 15 to 30 minutes, 30.7% 30 to 45 minutes, 8.8% 45 to 60 minutes, 4.6% 60 minutes or more (2000)

ILLINOIS CITY (unincorporated postal area, zip code 61259). Covers a land area of 61.147 square miles and a water area of 0.376 square miles. Located at 41.36° N. Lat.; 90.92° W. Long. Elevation is 764 feet.
Population: 1,209 (2000); Race: 95.5% White, 0.0% Black, 0.5% Asian, 3.1% Hispanic of any race (2000); Density: 19.8 persons per square mile (2000); Age: 21.0% under 18, 15.1% over 64 (2000); Marriage status: 18.7% never married, 74.0% now married, 3.4% widowed, 4.0% divorced (2000); Foreign born: 0.9% (2000); Ancestry (includes multiple ancestries): 26.9% German, 12.9% English, 9.8% Irish, 7.0% Swedish, 6.0% Other groups (2000).
Economy: Employment by occupation: 10.1% management, 15.3% professional, 11.5% services, 26.8% sales, 1.9% farming, 11.2% construction, 23.3% production (2000).
Income: Per capita income: $21,311 (2000); Median household income: $46,741 (2000); Poverty rate: 3.8% (2000).
Education: Percent of population age 25 and over with: High school diploma (including GED) or higher: 78.3% (2000); Bachelor's degree or higher: 15.7% (2000).

School District(s)

Rockridge CUSD 300 (PK-12)
2005-06 Enrollment: 1,369 . . . . (309) 795-1167
Housing: Homeownership rate: 83.4% (2000); Median home value: $107,400 (2000); Median rent: $438 per month (2000); Median age of housing: 45 years (2000).
Transportation: Commute to work: 95.9% car, 0.0% public transportation, 0.6% walk, 3.5% work from home (2000); Travel time to work: 9.5% less than 15 minutes, 56.6% 15 to 30 minutes, 26.1% 30 to 45 minutes, 5.9% 45 to 60 minutes, 2.0% 60 minutes or more (2000)

MILAN (village). Covers a land area of 5.537 square miles and a water area of 0.514 square miles. Located at 41.44° N. Lat.; 90.56° W. Long. Elevation is 568 feet.
History: Incorporated 1865.
Population: 6,077 (1990); 5,348 (2000); 5,134 (2007); 5,012 (2012 projected); Race: 90.0% White, 6.1% Black, 0.4% Asian, 3.6% Hispanic of any race (2007); Density: 927.2 persons per square mile (2007); Average household size: 2.28 (2007); Median age: 37.4 (2007); Males per 100 females: 94.0 (2007); Marriage status: 22.7% never married, 52.9% now married, 9.4% widowed, 15.1% divorced (2000); Foreign born: 1.1% (2000); Ancestry (includes multiple ancestries): 25.1% German, 14.2% Irish, 14.0% Other groups, 9.4% United States or American, 8.5% English (2000).
Economy: Single-family building permits issued: 15 (2007); Multi-family building permits issued: 0 (2007); Employment by occupation: 8.6% management, 12.1% professional, 21.1% services, 30.5% sales, 0.4% farming, 8.9% construction, 18.5% production (2000).
Income: Per capita income: $21,437 (2007); Median household income: $39,921 (2007); Average household income: $48,559 (2007); Percent of households with income of $100,000 or more: 9.0% (2007); Poverty rate: 10.7% (2000).
Education: Percent of population age 25 and over with: High school diploma (including GED) or higher: 80.1% (2007); Bachelor's degree or higher: 8.3% (2007); Master's degree or higher: 2.2% (2007).

School District(s)

Rock Island SD 41 (PK-12)
2005-06 Enrollment: 6,299 . . . . (309) 793-5900
Sherrard CUSD 200 (PK-12)
2005-06 Enrollment: 1,770 . . . . (309) 593-4075
Housing: Homeownership rate: 67.6% (2007); Median home value: $86,815 (2007); Median rent: $287 per month (2000); Median age of housing: 34 years (2000).
Safety: Violent crime rate: 34.4 per 10,000 population; Property crime rate: 372.4 per 10,000 population (2006).
Transportation: Commute to work: 95.0% car, 0.2% public transportation, 3.0% walk, 1.5% work from home (2000); Travel time to work: 35.7% less than 15 minutes, 49.2% 15 to 30 minutes, 11.8% 30 to 45 minutes, 1.6% 45 to 60 minutes, 1.7% 60 minutes or more (2000)

Additional Information Contacts

Milan Chamber of Commerce . . . . (309) 787-3144
http://www.milanilchamber.org
Village of Milan. . . . . (309) 787-8500
http://www.milanil.org

MOLINE (city). Covers a land area of 15.599 square miles and a water area of 0.222 square miles. Located at 41.49° N. Lat.; 90.50° W. Long. Elevation is 577 feet.
History: Moline was laid out in 1843. An early resident was John Deere, who had been producing plows in Grand Detour, but moved to Moline for the availability of steel for his machinery. The John Deere plants founded here soon became a major employer. Moline was incorporated as a town in 1848, and as a city in 1872.
Population: 43,798 (1990); 43,768 (2000); 42,670 (2007); 41,847 (2012 projected); Race: 85.9% White, 3.6% Black, 1.7% Asian, 14.8% Hispanic of any race (2007); Density: 2,735.4 persons per square mile (2007); Average household size: 2.36 (2007); Median age: 38.7 (2007); Males per 100 females: 91.8 (2007); Marriage status: 24.8% never married, 55.2% now married, 7.6% widowed, 12.4% divorced (2000); Foreign born: 7.1% (2000); Ancestry (includes multiple ancestries): 24.1% German, 18.2% Other groups, 13.9% Irish, 10.0% English, 9.3% Swedish (2000).
Economy: Unemployment rate: 4.5% (4/2008); Total civilian labor force: 24,208 (4/2008); Single-family building permits issued: 46 (2007); Multi-family building permits issued: 192 (2007); Employment by occupation: 11.0% management, 18.2% professional, 17.5% services, 27.3% sales, 0.1% farming, 7.4% construction, 18.4% production (2000).
Income: Per capita income: $24,735 (2007); Median household income: $44,716 (2007); Average household income: $57,992 (2007); Percent of households with income of $100,000 or more: 12.8% (2007); Poverty rate: 9.5% (2000).
Education: Percent of population age 25 and over with: High school diploma (including GED) or higher: 84.0% (2007); Bachelor's degree or higher: 20.7% (2007); Master's degree or higher: 6.8% (2007).

School District(s)

Black Hawk Area Sp Ed District (07-12)
2005-06 Enrollment: 46 . . . . (309) 796-2500
Moline USD 40 (PK-12)
2005-06 Enrollment: 7,606 . . . . (309) 743-1600
Rock Island Roe
2005-06 Enrollment: n/a . . . . (309) 736-1111
Rock Island SD 41 (PK-12)
2005-06 Enrollment: 6,299 . . . . (309) 793-5900

Two-year College(s)

Black Hawk College (Public)
Fall 2007 Enrollment: 6,311. . . . . (309) 796-5000
2007-08 Tuition: In-state $4,650; Out-of-state $8,220

Vocational/Technical School(s)

Brown Mackie College-Moline (Private, For-profit)
Fall 2007 Enrollment: 152 . . . . (309) 762-2100
2007-08 Tuition: In-state $8,028; Out-of-state $8,028
Housing: Homeownership rate: 67.4% (2007); Median home value: $101,770 (2007); Median rent: $405 per month (2000); Median age of housing: 48 years (2000).
Safety: Violent crime rate: 49.4 per 10,000 population; Property crime rate: 504.3 per 10,000 population (2006).
Newspapers: Dispatch (Community news; Circulation 31,716)
Transportation: Commute to work: 93.6% car, 1.9% public transportation, 1.6% walk, 2.1% work from home (2000); Travel time to work: 43.5% less than 15 minutes, 45.6% 15 to 30 minutes, 6.2% 30 to 45 minutes, 1.7% 45 to 60 minutes, 2.9% 60 minutes or more (2000); Amtrak: Service available.

Airports: Quad City International (primary service/small hub)
Additional Information Contacts
City of Moline . . . . (309) 764-3558
http://www.moline.il.us
Illinois Quad City Chamber of Commerce . . . . (309) 757-5416
http://www.quadcitychamber.com

OAK GROVE (village). Aka Oak Grove Park. Covers a land area of 0.631 square miles and a water area of 0 square miles. Located at 41.41° N. Lat.; 90.57° W. Long. Elevation is 722 feet.
Population: 201 (1990); 1,318 (2000); 1,315 (2007); 1,322 (2012 projected); Race: 18.6% White, 70.7% Black, 0.3% Asian, 11.3% Hispanic of any race (2007); Density: 2,083.4 persons per square mile (2007); Average household size: 11.74 (2007); Median age: 33.1 (2007); Males per 100 females: ***.* (2007); Marriage status: 22.5% never married, 43.4% now married, 0.5% widowed, 33.5% divorced (2000); Foreign born: 1.2% (2000); Ancestry (includes multiple ancestries): 3.9% German, 2.1% Irish, 1.7% Other groups, 1.0% Swedish, 0.7% English (2000).
Economy: Single-family building permits issued: 0 (2007); Multi-family building permits issued: 0 (2007); Employment by occupation: 7.8% management, 7.0% professional, 21.7% services, 21.7% sales, 0.0% farming, 14.0% construction, 27.9% production (2000).
Income: Per capita income: $15,729 (2007); Median household income: $38,529 (2007); Average household income: $44,308 (2007); Percent of households with income of $100,000 or more: 6.3% (2007); Poverty rate: 13.3% (2000).
Education: Percent of population age 25 and over with: High school diploma (including GED) or higher: 34.4% (2007); Bachelor's degree or higher: 1.0% (2007); Master's degree or higher: 0.2% (2007).
Housing: Homeownership rate: 40.2% (2007); Median home value: $88,750 (2007); Median rent: $263 per month (2000); Median age of housing: 34 years (2000).
Transportation: Commute to work: 96.1% car, 0.8% public transportation, 0.0% walk, 1.6% work from home (2000); Travel time to work: 18.9% less than 15 minutes, 67.7% 15 to 30 minutes, 4.7% 30 to 45 minutes, 4.7% 45 to 60 minutes, 3.9% 60 minutes or more (2000)

PORT BYRON (village). Covers a land area of 2.311 square miles and a water area of 0 square miles. Located at 41.61° N. Lat.; 90.33° W. Long. Elevation is 600 feet.
Population: 1,098 (1990); 1,535 (2000); 1,597 (2007); 1,640 (2012 projected); Race: 98.7% White, 0.1% Black, 0.0% Asian, 2.0% Hispanic of any race (2007); Density: 691.2 persons per square mile (2007); Average household size: 2.42 (2007); Median age: 41.9 (2007); Males per 100 females: 102.4 (2007); Marriage status: 20.0% never married, 63.2% now married, 6.7% widowed, 10.1% divorced (2000); Foreign born: 1.4% (2000); Ancestry (includes multiple ancestries): 32.1% German, 15.7% Irish, 12.1% English, 8.2% Swedish, 5.6% Belgian (2000).
Economy: Single-family building permits issued: 5 (2007); Multi-family building permits issued: 2 (2007); Employment by occupation: 15.2% management, 15.1% professional, 11.0% services, 27.1% sales, 0.5% farming, 14.3% construction, 16.8% production (2000).
Income: Per capita income: $29,035 (2007); Median household income: $56,204 (2007); Average household income: $70,095 (2007); Percent of households with income of $100,000 or more: 19.2% (2007); Poverty rate: 4.0% (2000).
Education: Percent of population age 25 and over with: High school diploma (including GED) or higher: 91.7% (2007); Bachelor's degree or higher: 19.1% (2007); Master's degree or higher: 7.0% (2007).

School District(s)

Riverdale CUSD 100 (PK-12)
2005-06 Enrollment: 1,190 . . . . (309) 523-3184
Housing: Homeownership rate: 74.6% (2007); Median home value: $141,071 (2007); Median rent: $289 per month (2000); Median age of housing: 35 years (2000).
Safety: Violent crime rate: 6.2 per 10,000 population; Property crime rate: 80.1 per 10,000 population (2006).
Transportation: Commute to work: 95.0% car, 0.0% public transportation, 2.1% walk, 2.6% work from home (2000); Travel time to work: 23.6% less than 15 minutes, 44.5% 15 to 30 minutes, 25.5% 30 to 45 minutes, 2.8% 45 to 60 minutes, 3.5% 60 minutes or more (2000)

RAPIDS CITY (village). Covers a land area of 1.530 square miles and a water area of 0 square miles. Located at 41.58° N. Lat.; 90.34° W. Long. Elevation is 581 feet.
Population: 934 (1990); 953 (2000); 991 (2007); 1,018 (2012 projected); Race: 98.2% White, 0.0% Black, 0.1% Asian, 3.1% Hispanic of any race (2007); Density: 647.9 persons per square mile (2007); Average household size: 2.65 (2007); Median age: 39.5 (2007); Males per 100 females: 99.4 (2007); Marriage status: 18.1% never married, 65.0% now married, 6.0% widowed, 10.9% divorced (2000); Foreign born: 0.0% (2000); Ancestry (includes multiple ancestries): 27.2% German, 11.1% Irish, 9.7% English, 7.4% Belgian, 6.8% United States or American (2000).
Economy: Single-family building permits issued: 4 (2007); Multi-family building permits issued: 0 (2007); Employment by occupation: 15.8% management, 19.1% professional, 11.0% services, 21.6% sales, 0.0% farming, 12.2% construction, 20.3% production (2000).
Income: Per capita income: $28,562 (2007); Median household income: $54,390 (2007); Average household income: $75,682 (2007); Percent of households with income of $100,000 or more: 17.6% (2007); Poverty rate: 3.0% (2000).
Education: Percent of population age 25 and over with: High school diploma (including GED) or higher: 87.8% (2007); Bachelor's degree or higher: 18.2% (2007); Master's degree or higher: 9.0% (2007).
Housing: Homeownership rate: 91.2% (2007); Median home value: $119,643 (2007); Median rent: $393 per month (2000); Median age of housing: 33 years (2000).
Transportation: Commute to work: 96.4% car, 0.7% public transportation, 1.4% walk, 1.6% work from home (2000); Travel time to work: 15.2% less than 15 minutes, 56.6% 15 to 30 minutes, 26.2% 30 to 45 minutes, 0.7% 45 to 60 minutes, 1.4% 60 minutes or more (2000)

REYNOLDS (village). Covers a land area of 0.369 square miles and a water area of 0 square miles. Located at 41.33° N. Lat.; 90.67° W. Long. Elevation is 810 feet.
Population: 600 (1990); 508 (2000); 454 (2007); 453 (2012 projected); Race: 99.6% White, 0.0% Black, 0.0% Asian, 0.9% Hispanic of any race (2007); Density: 1,231.2 persons per square mile (2007); Average household size: 2.41 (2007); Median age: 38.6 (2007); Males per 100 females: 90.8 (2007); Marriage status: 16.5% never married, 60.7% now married, 6.2% widowed, 16.5% divorced (2000); Foreign born: 0.0% (2000); Ancestry (includes multiple ancestries): 24.2% German, 22.2% Irish, 18.6% English, 9.4% Other groups, 8.2% Swedish (2000).
Economy: Single-family building permits issued: 0 (2007); Multi-family building permits issued: 0 (2007); Employment by occupation: 7.3% management, 12.2% professional, 12.2% services, 35.0% sales, 0.8% farming, 11.8% construction, 20.7% production (2000).
Income: Per capita income: $25,198 (2007); Median household income: $51,923 (2007); Average household income: $60,851 (2007); Percent of households with income of $100,000 or more: 13.8% (2007); Poverty rate: 10.2% (2000).
Education: Percent of population age 25 and over with: High school diploma (including GED) or higher: 91.9% (2007); Bachelor's degree or higher: 15.0% (2007); Master's degree or higher: 2.3% (2007).

School District(s)

Rockridge CUSD 300 (PK-12)
2005-06 Enrollment: 1,369 . . . . (309) 795-1167
Housing: Homeownership rate: 78.7% (2007); Median home value: $105,769 (2007); Median rent: $346 per month (2000); Median age of housing: 57 years (2000).
Transportation: Commute to work: 92.2% car, 0.0% public transportation, 2.9% walk, 4.9% work from home (2000); Travel time to work: 14.7% less than 15 minutes, 35.1% 15 to 30 minutes, 39.8% 30 to 45 minutes, 7.4% 45 to 60 minutes, 3.0% 60 minutes or more (2000)

ROCK ISLAND (city). Aka Quad Cities. County seat. Covers a land area of 15.924 square miles and a water area of 1.223 square miles. Located at 41.48° N. Lat.; 90.57° W. Long. Elevation is 561 feet.
History: Rock Island developed from a community called Stephenson, whose name was changed in 1841. Rock Island was a steamboat port until the Rock Island Railroad Company completed a bridge across the Mississippi in 1855 and rail began to replace water as the means of transportation of goods. The Farmall Works of the International Harvester Company was established in Rock Island. The limestone island that became the location of the Rock Island Arsenal first served as a prison for Confederate soldiers, with more than 12,000 at a time confined here.
Population: 40,511 (1990); 39,684 (2000); 38,626 (2007); 37,721 (2012 projected); Race: 76.1% White, 16.8% Black, 0.9% Asian, 7.3% Hispanic of any race (2007); Density: 2,425.6 persons per square mile (2007); Average household size: 2.44 (2007); Median age: 37.1 (2007); Males per 100

females: 89.8 (2007); Marriage status: 30.9% never married, 48.4% now married, 9.2% widowed, 11.5% divorced (2000); Foreign born: 3.2% (2000); Ancestry (includes multiple ancestries): 24.0% Other groups, 23.4% German, 13.2% Irish, 8.2% English, 6.8% United States or American (2000).
Economy: Unemployment rate: 5.0% (4/2008); Total civilian labor force: 20,376 (4/2008); Single-family building permits issued: 10 (2007); Multi-family building permits issued: 0 (2007); Employment by occupation: 9.0% management, 18.4% professional, 18.5% services, 28.5% sales, 0.4% farming, 7.6% construction, 17.8% production (2000).
Income: Per capita income: $22,186 (2007); Median household income: $40,071 (2007); Average household income: $52,698 (2007); Percent of households with income of $100,000 or more: 10.3% (2007); Poverty rate: 14.5% (2000).
Education: Percent of population age 25 and over with: High school diploma (including GED) or higher: 83.0% (2007); Bachelor's degree or higher: 18.6% (2007); Master's degree or higher: 6.3% (2007).

School District(s)

Rock Island SD 41 (PK-12)
2005-06 Enrollment: 6,299 . . . . (309) 793-5900

Four-year College(s)

Augustana College (Private, Not-for-profit, Evangelical Lutheran Church)
Fall 2007 Enrollment: 2,537. . . . . (309) 794-7000
2007-08 Tuition: In-state $26,484; Out-of-state $26,484
Trinity College of Nursing and Health Sciences (Private, Not-for-profit)
Fall 2007 Enrollment: 210 . . . . (309) 779-7700
2007-08 Tuition: In-state $10,214; Out-of-state $10,214
Housing: Homeownership rate: 65.6% (2007); Median home value: $89,167 (2007); Median rent: $361 per month (2000); Median age of housing: 51 years (2000).
Hospitals: Trinity Medical Center (349 beds)
Safety: Violent crime rate: 97.9 per 10,000 population; Property crime rate: 503.3 per 10,000 population (2006).
Newspapers: Leader (Local news; Circulation 53,000); Rock Island Argus (Community news; Circulation 12,729)
Transportation: Commute to work: 89.2% car, 2.3% public transportation, 5.7% walk, 1.7% work from home (2000); Travel time to work: 46.8% less than 15 minutes, 40.5% 15 to 30 minutes, 6.9% 30 to 45 minutes, 2.4% 45 to 60 minutes, 3.4% 60 minutes or more (2000)
Additional Information Contacts
City of Rock Island. . . . . (309) 732-2000
http://www.rigov.org

ROCK ISLAND ARSENAL (CDP). Covers a land area of 1.595 square miles and a water area of 0.968 square miles. Located at 41.51° N. Lat.; 90.53° W. Long.
Population: 212 (1990); 145 (2000); 145 (2007); 145 (2012 projected); Race: 69.7% White, 18.6% Black, 0.0% Asian, 1.4% Hispanic of any race (2007); Density: 90.9 persons per square mile (2007); Average household size: 3.30 (2007); Median age: 29.0 (2007); Males per 100 females: 107.1 (2007); Marriage status: 26.1% never married, 73.9% now married, 0.0% widowed, 0.0% divorced (2000); Foreign born: 8.3% (2000); Ancestry (includes multiple ancestries): 28.6% Other groups, 18.0% German, 7.5% Scottish, 4.5% English, 3.0% Irish (2000).
Economy: Employment by occupation: 10.9% management, 0.0% professional, 18.2% services, 49.1% sales, 0.0% farming, 10.9% construction, 10.9% production (2000).
Income: Per capita income: $15,621 (2007); Median household income: $45,000 (2007); Average household income: $51,477 (2007); Percent of households with income of $100,000 or more: 13.6% (2007); Poverty rate: 0.0% (2000).
Education: Percent of population age 25 and over with: High school diploma (including GED) or higher: 72.3% (2007); Bachelor's degree or higher: 7.2% (2007); Master's degree or higher: 0.0% (2007).
Housing: Homeownership rate: 0.0% (2007); Median home value: $n/a (2007); Median rent: $350 per month (2000); Median age of housing: 36 years (2000).
Transportation: Commute to work: 93.0% car, 0.0% public transportation, 0.0% walk, 7.0% work from home (2000); Travel time to work: 83.3% less than 15 minutes, 16.7% 15 to 30 minutes, 0.0% 30 to 45 minutes, 0.0% 45 to 60 minutes, 0.0% 60 minutes or more (2000)

SILVIS (city). Covers a land area of 3.646 square miles and a water area of 0 square miles. Located at 41.50° N. Lat.; 90.41° W. Long. Elevation is 594 feet.
History: Incorporated 1906.
Population: 7,048 (1990); 7,269 (2000); 7,555 (2007); 7,709 (2012 projected); Race: 84.6% White, 3.7% Black, 0.9% Asian, 15.2% Hispanic of any race (2007); Density: 2,072.3 persons per square mile (2007); Average household size: 2.38 (2007); Median age: 37.4 (2007); Males per 100 females: 92.4 (2007); Marriage status: 18.7% never married, 57.2% now married, 9.6% widowed, 14.5% divorced (2000); Foreign born: 4.1% (2000); Ancestry (includes multiple ancestries): 20.9% Other groups, 19.4% German, 13.4% Irish, 6.8% United States or American, 6.5% Belgian (2000).
Economy: Single-family building permits issued: 10 (2007); Multi-family building permits issued: 0 (2007); Employment by occupation: 9.6% management, 9.1% professional, 19.1% services, 26.9% sales, 0.2% farming, 10.4% construction, 24.6% production (2000).
Income: Per capita income: $20,367 (2007); Median household income: $40,679 (2007); Average household income: $48,035 (2007); Percent of households with income of $100,000 or more: 9.3% (2007); Poverty rate: 9.5% (2000).
Education: Percent of population age 25 and over with: High school diploma (including GED) or higher: 75.5% (2007); Bachelor's degree or higher: 9.0% (2007); Master's degree or higher: 3.0% (2007).

School District(s)

Carbon Cliff-Barstow SD 36 (KG-08)
2005-06 Enrollment: 283 . . . . (309) 792-2002
East Moline SD 37 (PK-08)
2005-06 Enrollment: 2,436 . . . . (309) 755-4533
Silvis SD 34 (PK-08)
2005-06 Enrollment: 659 . . . . (309) 792-9325
Housing: Homeownership rate: 61.3% (2007); Median home value: $96,215 (2007); Median rent: $381 per month (2000); Median age of housing: 37 years (2000).
Hospitals: Genesis Medical Center-Illini Campus (150 beds)
Safety: Violent crime rate: 45.4 per 10,000 population; Property crime rate: 405.9 per 10,000 population (2006).
Newspapers: Hola America (Community news; Circulation 10,000)
Transportation: Commute to work: 92.1% car, 0.6% public transportation, 2.5% walk, 2.4% work from home (2000); Travel time to work: 37.9% less than 15 minutes, 42.9% 15 to 30 minutes, 15.3% 30 to 45 minutes, 0.9% 45 to 60 minutes, 3.0% 60 minutes or more (2000)
Additional Information Contacts
City of Silvis . . . . (309) 792-9181
http://www.silvisil.org

TAYLOR RIDGE (unincorporated postal area, zip code 61284). Covers a land area of 56.358 square miles and a water area of 0.198 square miles. Located at 41.40° N. Lat.; 90.73° W. Long. Elevation is 771 feet.
Population: 3,439 (2000); Race: 98.6% White, 0.9% Black, 0.0% Asian, 0.7% Hispanic of any race (2000); Density: 61.0 persons per square mile (2000); Age: 26.9% under 18, 10.6% over 64 (2000); Marriage status: 18.4% never married, 69.0% now married, 5.9% widowed, 6.7% divorced (2000); Foreign born: 0.1% (2000); Ancestry (includes multiple ancestries): 34.4% German, 12.5% Irish, 9.3% English, 7.5% United States or American, 6.1% Belgian (2000).
Economy: Employment by occupation: 16.2% management, 19.3% professional, 8.8% services, 28.1% sales, 0.2% farming, 8.6% construction, 18.8% production (2000).
Income: Per capita income: $26,077 (2000); Median household income: $62,882 (2000); Poverty rate: 5.0% (2000).
Education: Percent of population age 25 and over with: High school diploma (including GED) or higher: 88.9% (2000); Bachelor's degree or higher: 19.1% (2000).

School District(s)

Rockridge CUSD 300 (PK-12)
2005-06 Enrollment: 1,369 . . . . (309) 795-1167
Housing: Homeownership rate: 91.8% (2000); Median home value: $109,800 (2000); Median rent: $378 per month (2000); Median age of housing: 31 years (2000).
Transportation: Commute to work: 94.8% car, 0.1% public transportation, 0.8% walk, 4.1% work from home (2000); Travel time to work: 12.8% less than 15 minutes, 54.4% 15 to 30 minutes, 26.8% 30 to 45 minutes, 2.7% 45 to 60 minutes, 3.3% 60 minutes or more (2000)

Saline County

Located in southeastern Illinois, partly in the Ozarks; drained by the Saline River; includes part of Shawnee National Forest. Covers a land area of 383.31 square miles, a water area of 3.67 square miles, and is located in the Central Time Zone. The county was founded in 1847. County seat is Harrisburg.

Saline County is part of the Harrisburg, IL Micropolitan Statistical Area. The entire metro area includes: Saline County, IL

Weather Station: Harrisburg Elevation: 364 feet

	Jan	Feb	Mar	Apr	May	Jun	Jul	Aug	Sep	Oct	Nov	Dec
High	40	47	57	69	78	86	90	89	82	71	57	46
Low	23	27	36	46	55	64	67	65	58	45	37	29
Precip	3.0	2.7	4.5	4.8	4.8	4.4	4.0	3.2	3.1	3.1	4.1	4.0
Snow	4.8	3.8	2.3	0.4	0.0	0.0	0.0	0.0	0.0	tr	0.6	1.7

High and Low temperatures in degrees Fahrenheit; Precipitation and Snow in inches

Population: 26,551 (1990); 26,733 (2000); 25,962 (2007); 25,410 (2012 projected); Race: 93.6% White, 4.5% Black, 0.2% Asian, 1.1% Hispanic of any race (2007); Density: 67.7 persons per square mile (2007); Average household size: 2.42 (2007); Median age: 40.7 (2007); Males per 100 females: 94.6 (2007).
Religion: Five largest groups: 41.1% Southern Baptist Convention, 4.3% The United Methodist Church, 4.3% Catholic Church, 1.6% Church of God (Cleveland, Tennessee), 1.4% Christian Churches and Churches of Christ (2000).
Economy: Unemployment rate: 6.6% (4/2008); Total civilian labor force: 12,879 (4/2008); Leading industries: 27.3% health care and social assistance; 16.9% retail trade; 8.9% accommodation & food services (2005); Farms: 446 totaling 129,943 acres (2002); Companies that employ 500 or more persons: 1 (2006); Companies that employ 100 to 499 persons: 8 (2006); Companies that employ less than 100 persons: 602 (2006); Black-owned businesses: n/a (2002); Hispanic-owned businesses: n/a (2002); Asian-owned businesses: n/a (2002); Women-owned businesses: 477 (2002); Retail sales per capita: $14,162 (2008). Single-family building permits issued: 0 (2007); Multi-family building permits issued: 0 (2007).
Income: Per capita income: $18,908 (2007); Median household income: $34,539 (2007); Average household income: $44,913 (2007); Percent of households with income of $100,000 or more: 7.2% (2007); Poverty rate: 20.6% (2005); Bankruptcy rate: 3.29% (2007).
Education: Percent of population age 25 and over with: High school diploma (including GED) or higher: 76.1% (2007); Bachelor's degree or higher: 12.1% (2007); Master's degree or higher: 4.5% (2007).
Housing: Homeownership rate: 76.8% (2007); Median home value: $63,438 (2007); Median rent: $226 per month (2000); Median age of housing: 39 years (2000).
Health: Birth rate: 128.0 per 10,000 population (2007); Death rate: 150.6 per 10,000 population (2007); Age-adjusted cancer mortality rate: 256.8 deaths per 100,000 population (2005); Number of physicians: 10.8 per 10,000 population (2005); Hospital beds: 44.4 per 10,000 population (2004); Hospital admissions: 1,580.7 per 10,000 population (2004).
Elections: 2004 Presidential election results: 59.7% Bush, 39.8% Kerry, 0.1% Nader, 0.4% Badnarik
National and State Parks: Saline County State Conservation Area
Additional Information Contacts
Saline County Government . . . . (618) 252-6905

Eldorado Chamber of Commerce . . . . (618) 273-3119
Saline County Chamber of Commerce . . . . (618) 252-4192
http://www.salinecountychamber.org

Saline County Communities

CARRIER MILLS (village). Aka Carriers Mills. Covers a land area of 1.238 square miles and a water area of 0.005 square miles. Located at 37.68° N. Lat.; 88.62° W. Long. Elevation is 387 feet.
History: Carriers (or Carrier) Mills was named for William H. Carrier who built a sawmill here in 1870. The town developed around the mining industry.
Population: 1,991 (1990); 1,886 (2000); 1,676 (2007); 1,616 (2012 projected); Race: 83.5% White, 14.3% Black, 0.2% Asian, 1.1% Hispanic of any race (2007); Density: 1,353.3 persons per square mile (2007); Average household size: 2.34 (2007); Median age: 41.6 (2007); Males per 100 females: 87.9 (2007); Marriage status: 11.7% never married, 65.6% now married, 12.5% widowed, 10.1% divorced (2000); Foreign born: 0.0% (2000); Ancestry (includes multiple ancestries): 16.6% United States or American, 15.6% Other groups, 11.2% English, 10.2% Irish, 9.0% German (2000).
Economy: Employment by occupation: 8.5% management, 17.4% professional, 14.9% services, 25.1% sales, 0.6% farming, 19.0% construction, 14.6% production (2000).
Income: Per capita income: $17,493 (2007); Median household income: $30,577 (2007); Average household income: $39,245 (2007); Percent of households with income of $100,000 or more: 5.2% (2007); Poverty rate: 17.7% (2000).
Education: Percent of population age 25 and over with: High school diploma (including GED) or higher: 72.5% (2007); Bachelor's degree or higher: 8.7% (2007); Master's degree or higher: 3.4% (2007).

School District(s)

Carrier Mills-Stonefort CUSD 2 (PK-12)
2005-06 Enrollment: 516 . . . . (618) 994-2392
Housing: Homeownership rate: 74.7% (2007); Median home value: $51,571 (2007); Median rent: $224 per month (2000); Median age of housing: 36 years (2000).
Safety: Violent crime rate: 119.5 per 10,000 population; Property crime rate: 179.3 per 10,000 population (2006).
Transportation: Commute to work: 92.1% car, 0.6% public transportation, 2.8% walk, 0.7% work from home (2000); Travel time to work: 33.8% less than 15 minutes, 29.9% 15 to 30 minutes, 17.6% 30 to 45 minutes, 7.5% 45 to 60 minutes, 11.2% 60 minutes or more (2000)

ELDORADO (city). Covers a land area of 2.304 square miles and a water area of 0.032 square miles. Located at 37.81° N. Lat.; 88.44° W. Long. Elevation is 394 feet.
History: Incorporated 1873.
Population: 4,645 (1990); 4,534 (2000); 4,366 (2007); 4,223 (2012 projected); Race: 98.0% White, 0.5% Black, 0.0% Asian, 1.6% Hispanic of any race (2007); Density: 1,894.9 persons per square mile (2007); Average household size: 2.33 (2007); Median age: 42.4 (2007); Males per 100 females: 86.3 (2007); Marriage status: 20.3% never married, 53.6% now married, 13.9% widowed, 12.2% divorced (2000); Foreign born: 0.1% (2000); Ancestry (includes multiple ancestries): 15.6% Irish, 14.0% United States or American, 13.8% German, 8.8% English, 7.7% Other groups (2000).
Economy: Employment by occupation: 5.3% management, 14.7% professional, 27.9% services, 18.8% sales, 1.1% farming, 16.3% construction, 15.9% production (2000).
Income: Per capita income: $14,931 (2007); Median household income: $26,547 (2007); Average household income: $33,786 (2007); Percent of households with income of $100,000 or more: 2.3% (2007); Poverty rate: 23.1% (2000).
Education: Percent of population age 25 and over with: High school diploma (including GED) or higher: 66.6% (2007); Bachelor's degree or higher: 8.5% (2007); Master's degree or higher: 3.2% (2007).

School District(s)

Eldorado CUSD 4 (PK-12)
2005-06 Enrollment: 1,192 . . . . (618) 273-6394
Housing: Homeownership rate: 71.2% (2007); Median home value: $44,273 (2007); Median rent: $203 per month (2000); Median age of housing: 48 years (2000).
Hospitals: Ferrell Hospital (25 beds)
Safety: Violent crime rate: 34.0 per 10,000 population; Property crime rate: 224.2 per 10,000 population (2006).
Newspapers: Eldorado Daily Journal (Local news; Circulation 18,000)
Transportation: Commute to work: 93.7% car, 0.5% public transportation, 3.1% walk, 2.0% work from home (2000); Travel time to work: 46.3% less than 15 minutes, 25.2% 15 to 30 minutes, 12.1% 30 to 45 minutes, 9.9% 45 to 60 minutes, 6.5% 60 minutes or more (2000)
Additional Information Contacts
Eldorado Chamber of Commerce . . . . (618) 273-3119

GALATIA (village). Covers a land area of 1.961 square miles and a water area of 0.016 square miles. Located at 37.84° N. Lat.; 88.61° W. Long. Elevation is 420 feet.
Population: 983 (1990); 1,013 (2000); 921 (2007); 917 (2012 projected); Race: 97.9% White, 0.2% Black, 0.0% Asian, 0.7% Hispanic of any race (2007); Density: 469.6 persons per square mile (2007); Average household size: 2.36 (2007); Median age: 40.8 (2007); Males per 100 females: 76.8

(2007); Marriage status: 20.9% never married, 53.9% now married, 14.8% widowed, 10.4% divorced (2000); Foreign born: 0.3% (2000); Ancestry (includes multiple ancestries): 19.0% Irish, 18.0% German, 16.0% United States or American, 11.8% English, 4.8% French (except Basque) (2000).
Economy: Employment by occupation: 3.7% management, 18.6% professional, 24.6% services, 25.7% sales, 0.6% farming, 11.7% construction, 15.1% production (2000).
Income: Per capita income: $16,842 (2007); Median household income: $30,391 (2007); Average household income: $36,803 (2007); Percent of households with income of $100,000 or more: 3.6% (2007); Poverty rate: 16.7% (2000).
Education: Percent of population age 25 and over with: High school diploma (including GED) or higher: 71.8% (2007); Bachelor's degree or higher: 6.5% (2007); Master's degree or higher: 2.5% (2007).

School District(s)

Galatia CUSD 1 (PK-12)
2005-06 Enrollment: 406 . . . . (618) 268-6371
Housing: Homeownership rate: 72.4% (2007); Median home value: $63,085 (2007); Median rent: $192 per month (2000); Median age of housing: 39 years (2000).
Transportation: Commute to work: 87.9% car, 0.0% public transportation, 5.9% walk, 5.9% work from home (2000); Travel time to work: 35.7% less than 15 minutes, 41.4% 15 to 30 minutes, 7.5% 30 to 45 minutes, 6.6% 45 to 60 minutes, 8.8% 60 minutes or more (2000)

HARRISBURG (city). County seat. Covers a land area of 6.239 square miles and a water area of 0.141 square miles. Located at 37.73° N. Lat.; 88.54° W. Long. Elevation is 397 feet.
History: Harrisburg was platted in 1853 and developed as an industrial center with planing, flour, and woolen mills founded in the late 1800's. Coal mining began in 1905.
Population: 9,592 (1990); 9,860 (2000); 9,490 (2007); 9,210 (2012 projected); Race: 89.4% White, 8.1% Black, 0.4% Asian, 1.7% Hispanic of any race (2007); Density: 1,521.0 persons per square mile (2007); Average household size: 2.41 (2007); Median age: 38.7 (2007); Males per 100 females: 96.4 (2007); Marriage status: 23.0% never married, 50.2% now married, 12.0% widowed, 14.8% divorced (2000); Foreign born: 1.4% (2000); Ancestry (includes multiple ancestries): 14.8% United States or American, 12.7% German, 12.0% Irish, 11.0% English, 10.0% Other groups (2000).
Economy: Employment by occupation: 8.9% management, 18.7% professional, 21.7% services, 24.9% sales, 0.0% farming, 11.8% construction, 14.0% production (2000).
Income: Per capita income: $18,228 (2007); Median household income: $31,704 (2007); Average household income: $42,778 (2007); Percent of households with income of $100,000 or more: 6.1% (2007); Poverty rate: 13.2% (2000).
Education: Percent of population age 25 and over with: High school diploma (including GED) or higher: 75.2% (2007); Bachelor's degree or higher: 12.8% (2007); Master's degree or higher: 4.7% (2007).

School District(s)

Dept of Corrections Sch Dist 428 (08-12)
2005-06 Enrollment: 2,271 . . . . (217) 522-2666
Edwd/Gltn/Hdin/Pop/Slne/Wbh/Wn/Wh (07-12)
2005-06 Enrollment: 47 . . . . (618) 253-5581
Harrisburg CUSD 3 (PK-12)
2005-06 Enrollment: 2,144 . . . . (618) 253-7637

Two-year College(s)

Southeastern Illinois College (Public)
Fall 2007 Enrollment: 2,606. . . . . (618) 252-5400
2007-08 Tuition: In-state $3,392; Out-of-state $3,488
Housing: Homeownership rate: 69.8% (2007); Median home value: $55,103 (2007); Median rent: $253 per month (2000); Median age of housing: 44 years (2000).
Hospitals: Harrisburg Medical Center (86 beds)
Safety: Violent crime rate: 17.7 per 10,000 population; Property crime rate: 193.2 per 10,000 population (2006).
Newspapers: American Weekend - Daily Register (Community news; Circulation 0); Daily Register (Regional news; Circulation 6,100); The Daily Register (Local news; Circulation 3,500)
Transportation: Commute to work: 91.1% car, 1.6% public transportation, 2.9% walk, 3.6% work from home (2000); Travel time to work: 57.7% less than 15 minutes, 21.1% 15 to 30 minutes, 9.7% 30 to 45 minutes, 4.7% 45 to 60 minutes, 6.8% 60 minutes or more (2000)
Airports: Harrisburg-Raleigh (general aviation)

Additional Information Contacts

Saline County Chamber of Commerce . . . . (618) 252-4192
http://www.salinecountychamber.org

MUDDY (village). Covers a land area of 0.263 square miles and a water area of 0 square miles. Located at 37.76° N. Lat.; 88.51° W. Long. Elevation is 371 feet.
Population: 108 (1990); 78 (2000); 73 (2007); 74 (2012 projected); Race: 87.7% White, 8.2% Black, 0.0% Asian, 2.7% Hispanic of any race (2007); Density: 277.9 persons per square mile (2007); Average household size: 2.28 (2007); Median age: 31.3 (2007); Males per 100 females: 97.3 (2007); Marriage status: 13.0% never married, 66.2% now married, 0.0% widowed, 20.8% divorced (2000); Foreign born: 0.0% (2000); Ancestry (includes multiple ancestries): 27.5% German, 15.4% Italian, 14.3% United States or American, 12.1% Irish, 9.9% Dutch (2000).
Economy: Single-family building permits issued: 0 (2007); Multi-family building permits issued: 0 (2007); Employment by occupation: 16.7% management, 9.5% professional, 19.0% services, 11.9% sales, 0.0% farming, 7.1% construction, 35.7% production (2000).
Income: Per capita income: $17,705 (2007); Median household income: $32,000 (2007); Average household income: $40,391 (2007); Percent of households with income of $100,000 or more: 6.3% (2007); Poverty rate: 7.7% (2000).
Education: Percent of population age 25 and over with: High school diploma (including GED) or higher: 77.3% (2007); Bachelor's degree or higher: 6.8% (2007); Master's degree or higher: 0.0% (2007).
Housing: Homeownership rate: 37.5% (2007); Median home value: $80,000 (2007); Median rent: $180 per month (2000); Median age of housing: 54 years (2000).
Transportation: Commute to work: 95.2% car, 0.0% public transportation, 0.0% walk, 4.8% work from home (2000); Travel time to work: 67.5% less than 15 minutes, 17.5% 15 to 30 minutes, 0.0% 30 to 45 minutes, 5.0% 45 to 60 minutes, 10.0% 60 minutes or more (2000)

RALEIGH (village). Covers a land area of 1.974 square miles and a water area of 0 square miles. Located at 37.82° N. Lat.; 88.53° W. Long. Elevation is 410 feet.
Population: 305 (1990); 330 (2000); 300 (2007); 297 (2012 projected); Race: 99.0% White, 0.0% Black, 0.0% Asian, 0.3% Hispanic of any race (2007); Density: 151.9 persons per square mile (2007); Average household size: 2.26 (2007); Median age: 35.8 (2007); Males per 100 females: 104.1 (2007); Marriage status: 15.1% never married, 65.3% now married, 6.3% widowed, 13.3% divorced (2000); Foreign born: 1.1% (2000); Ancestry (includes multiple ancestries): 25.1% United States or American, 12.4% Irish, 6.2% German, 5.9% Other groups, 5.1% English (2000).
Economy: Employment by occupation: 6.2% management, 18.6% professional, 15.9% services, 17.9% sales, 0.0% farming, 18.6% construction, 22.8% production (2000).
Income: Per capita income: $16,142 (2007); Median household income: $37,500 (2007); Average household income: $36,410 (2007); Percent of households with income of $100,000 or more: 2.3% (2007); Poverty rate: 29.4% (2000).
Education: Percent of population age 25 and over with: High school diploma (including GED) or higher: 81.4% (2007); Bachelor's degree or higher: 11.3% (2007); Master's degree or higher: 2.6% (2007).
Housing: Homeownership rate: 82.0% (2007); Median home value: $66,053 (2007); Median rent: $197 per month (2000); Median age of housing: 39 years (2000).
Transportation: Commute to work: 93.7% car, 0.0% public transportation, 0.0% walk, 4.2% work from home (2000); Travel time to work: 30.7% less than 15 minutes, 33.6% 15 to 30 minutes, 9.5% 30 to 45 minutes, 8.8% 45 to 60 minutes, 17.5% 60 minutes or more (2000)

Sangamon County

Located in central Illinois; drained by the Sangamon River and its South Fork; includes Lake Springfield. Covers a land area of 868.18 square miles, a water area of 8.82 square miles, and is located in the Central Time Zone. The county was founded in 1821. County seat is Springfield.

Sangamon County is part of the Springfield, IL Metropolitan Statistical Area. The entire metro area includes: Menard County, IL; Sangamon County, IL

Weather Station: Springfield Capital Airport Elevation: 583 feet

	Jan	Feb	Mar	Apr	May	Jun	Jul	Aug	Sep	Oct	Nov	Dec
High	33	39	51	64	75	84	87	85	79	67	51	39
Low	17	22	32	42	53	62	66	64	56	44	34	23
Precip	1.6	1.8	3.1	3.6	4.1	3.7	3.5	3.4	3.0	2.6	2.8	2.6
Snow	7.4	5.9	3.4	0.8	tr	0.0	tr	0.0	0.0	tr	1.6	5.0

High and Low temperatures in degrees Fahrenheit; Precipitation and Snow in inches

Population: 178,386 (1990); 188,951 (2000); 193,603 (2007); 196,081 (2012 projected); Race: 86.0% White, 10.4% Black, 1.3% Asian, 1.3% Hispanic of any race (2007); Density: 223.0 persons per square mile (2007); Average household size: 2.37 (2007); Median age: 38.7 (2007); Males per 100 females: 91.5 (2007).
Religion: Five largest groups: 19.5% Catholic Church, 7.9% Assemblies of God, 6.0% The United Methodist Church, 4.3% Lutheran Church—Missouri Synod, 3.9% Christian Churches and Churches of Christ (2000).
Economy: Unemployment rate: 4.5% (4/2008); Total civilian labor force: 109,504 (4/2008); Leading industries: 22.0% health care and social assistance; 15.2% retail trade; 10.9% accommodation & food services (2005); Farms: 970 totaling 468,314 acres (2002); Companies that employ 500 or more persons: 12 (2006); Companies that employ 100 to 499 persons: 103 (2006); Companies that employ less than 100 persons: 5,232 (2006); Black-owned businesses: 563 (2002); Hispanic-owned businesses: n/a (2002); Asian-owned businesses: 383 (2002); Women-owned businesses: 5,355 (2002); Retail sales per capita: $15,321 (2008). Single-family building permits issued: 412 (2007); Multi-family building permits issued: 149 (2007).
Income: Per capita income: $27,197 (2007); Median household income: $49,382 (2007); Average household income: $63,889 (2007); Percent of households with income of $100,000 or more: 16.0% (2007); Poverty rate: 11.2% (2005); Bankruptcy rate: 3.24% (2007).
Taxes: Total county taxes per capita: $119 (2006); County property taxes per capita: $118 (2006).
Education: Percent of population age 25 and over with: High school diploma (including GED) or higher: 88.4% (2007); Bachelor's degree or higher: 29.4% (2007); Master's degree or higher: 10.6% (2007).
Housing: Homeownership rate: 70.8% (2007); Median home value: $110,739 (2007); Median rent: $424 per month (2000); Median age of housing: 32 years (2000).
Health: Birth rate: 135.2 per 10,000 population (2007); Death rate: 93.4 per 10,000 population (2007); Age-adjusted cancer mortality rate: 217.3 deaths per 100,000 population (2005); Air Quality Index: 89.0% good, 10.4% moderate, 0.5% unhealthy for sensitive individuals, 0.0% unhealthy (percent of days in 2007); Number of physicians: 49.2 per 10,000 population (2005); Hospital beds: 83.0 per 10,000 population (2004); Hospital admissions: 2,317.9 per 10,000 population (2004).
Elections: 2004 Presidential election results: 58.6% Bush, 40.5% Kerry, 0.1% Nader, 0.8% Badnarik
National and State Parks: Lincoln Home National Historic Site; Lincolns Tomb State Historic Site; Sangchris Lake State Park
Additional Information Contacts
Sangamon County Government . . . . (217) 753-6600
http://www.co.sangamon.il.us
Chatham Area Chamber of Commerce . . . . (217) 483-6450
http://www.chatham-il-chamber.com
City of Springfield. . . . . (217) 789-2000
http://www.springfield.il.us
Illinois Chamber of Commerce. . . . . (217) 522-5512
http://www.ilchamber.org
Pawnee Chamber of Commerce . . . . (217) 625-7779
http://www.pawneechamber.org
Springfield Convention & Visitors Bureau . . . . (217) 789-2360
http://www.visit-springfieldillinois.com
The Greater Springfield Chamber of Commerce . . . . (217) 525-1173
http://www.gscc.org
Village of Chatham. . . . . (217) 483-2451
http://www.chathamil.net

Sangamon County Communities

AUBURN (city). Covers a land area of 3.156 square miles and a water area of 0 square miles. Located at 39.58° N. Lat.; 89.74° W. Long. Elevation is 627 feet.
History: Incorporated 1865.
Population: 3,865 (1990); 4,317 (2000); 4,179 (2007); 4,081 (2012 projected); Race: 98.0% White, 0.4% Black, 0.3% Asian, 0.8% Hispanic of any race (2007); Density: 1,324.3 persons per square mile (2007); Average household size: 2.60 (2007); Median age: 34.0 (2007); Males per 100 females: 88.5 (2007); Marriage status: 16.7% never married, 66.1% now married, 5.7% widowed, 11.5% divorced (2000); Foreign born: 1.0% (2000); Ancestry (includes multiple ancestries): 32.3% German, 15.6% Irish, 12.0% English, 7.3% United States or American, 6.9% Italian (2000).
Economy: Single-family building permits issued: 11 (2007); Multi-family building permits issued: 10 (2007); Employment by occupation: 12.5% management, 22.1% professional, 17.4% services, 26.9% sales, 1.2% farming, 11.4% construction, 8.5% production (2000).
Income: Per capita income: $23,643 (2007); Median household income: $53,107 (2007); Average household income: $60,827 (2007); Percent of households with income of $100,000 or more: 11.5% (2007); Poverty rate: 5.5% (2000).
Education: Percent of population age 25 and over with: High school diploma (including GED) or higher: 88.0% (2007); Bachelor's degree or higher: 19.6% (2007); Master's degree or higher: 4.1% (2007).

School District(s)

Auburn CUSD 10 (PK-12)
2005-06 Enrollment: 1,270 . . . . (217) 438-6164
Housing: Homeownership rate: 75.3% (2007); Median home value: $108,322 (2007); Median rent: $357 per month (2000); Median age of housing: 33 years (2000).
Safety: Violent crime rate: 9.4 per 10,000 population; Property crime rate: 133.4 per 10,000 population (2006).
Newspapers: Auburn Citizen (Local news; Circulation 0); Divernon News (Local news; Circulation 0); Pawnee Post (Local news; Circulation 800); Rochester Times (Local news; Circulation 925)
Transportation: Commute to work: 94.1% car, 0.5% public transportation, 2.0% walk, 2.5% work from home (2000); Travel time to work: 24.1% less than 15 minutes, 26.2% 15 to 30 minutes, 39.9% 30 to 45 minutes, 3.6% 45 to 60 minutes, 6.2% 60 minutes or more (2000)

BERLIN (village). Covers a land area of 0.996 square miles and a water area of 0 square miles. Located at 39.75° N. Lat.; 89.90° W. Long. Elevation is 636 feet.
Population: 180 (1990); 140 (2000); 145 (2007); 138 (2012 projected); Race: 98.6% White, 1.4% Black, 0.0% Asian, 0.0% Hispanic of any race (2007); Density: 145.6 persons per square mile (2007); Average household size: 2.23 (2007); Median age: 47.3 (2007); Males per 100 females: 95.9 (2007); Marriage status: 13.7% never married, 54.9% now married, 7.8% widowed, 23.5% divorced (2000); Foreign born: 0.0% (2000); Ancestry (includes multiple ancestries): 15.3% German, 13.7% United States or American, 11.5% Other groups, 4.6% Scottish, 3.8% Irish (2000).
Economy: Employment by occupation: 5.2% management, 5.2% professional, 13.8% services, 39.7% sales, 0.0% farming, 19.0% construction, 17.2% production (2000).
Income: Per capita income: $21,586 (2007); Median household income: $48,750 (2007); Average household income: $48,154 (2007); Percent of households with income of $100,000 or more: 3.1% (2007); Poverty rate: 21.1% (2000).
Education: Percent of population age 25 and over with: High school diploma (including GED) or higher: 78.6% (2007); Bachelor's degree or higher: 3.6% (2007); Master's degree or higher: 3.6% (2007).
Housing: Homeownership rate: 81.5% (2007); Median home value: $83,000 (2007); Median rent: $425 per month (2000); Median age of housing: 32 years (2000).
Transportation: Commute to work: 87.9% car, 0.0% public transportation, 1.7% walk, 6.9% work from home (2000); Travel time to work: 22.2% less than 15 minutes, 44.4% 15 to 30 minutes, 33.3% 30 to 45 minutes, 0.0% 45 to 60 minutes, 0.0% 60 minutes or more (2000)

BUFFALO (village). Covers a land area of 0.369 square miles and a water area of 0 square miles. Located at 39.85° N. Lat.; 89.40° W. Long. Elevation is 614 feet.
Population: 503 (1990); 491 (2000); 494 (2007); 457 (2012 projected); Race: 97.0% White, 0.0% Black, 0.2% Asian, 1.2% Hispanic of any race (2007); Density: 1,340.3 persons per square mile (2007); Average household size: 2.41 (2007); Median age: 36.5 (2007); Males per 100 females: 101.6 (2007); Marriage status: 24.3% never married, 52.8% now married, 11.1% widowed, 11.9% divorced (2000); Foreign born: 2.4% (2000); Ancestry (includes multiple ancestries): 16.9% German, 13.9% English, 12.6% Irish, 7.3% Other groups, 4.9% United States or American (2000).

Economy: Single-family building permits issued: 0 (2007); Multi-family building permits issued: 0 (2007); Employment by occupation: 11.8% management, 11.8% professional, 15.3% services, 34.5% sales, 0.0% farming, 12.5% construction, 14.1% production (2000).
Income: Per capita income: $22,100 (2007); Median household income: $42,045 (2007); Average household income: $53,256 (2007); Percent of households with income of $100,000 or more: 12.7% (2007); Poverty rate: 10.8% (2000).
Education: Percent of population age 25 and over with: High school diploma (including GED) or higher: 86.0% (2007); Bachelor's degree or higher: 12.1% (2007); Master's degree or higher: 5.0% (2007).

School District(s)

Tri City CUSD 1 (PK-12)
2005-06 Enrollment: 632 . . . . (217) 364-4811
Housing: Homeownership rate: 74.1% (2007); Median home value: $83,077 (2007); Median rent: $216 per month (2000); Median age of housing: 40 years (2000).
Safety: Violent crime rate: 21.6 per 10,000 population; Property crime rate: 324.0 per 10,000 population (2006).
Transportation: Commute to work: 90.8% car, 0.0% public transportation, 6.0% walk, 3.2% work from home (2000); Travel time to work: 13.6% less than 15 minutes, 43.8% 15 to 30 minutes, 33.9% 30 to 45 minutes, 3.3% 45 to 60 minutes, 5.4% 60 minutes or more (2000)

CANTRALL (village). Covers a land area of 0.255 square miles and a water area of 0 square miles. Located at 39.93° N. Lat.; 89.67° W. Long. Elevation is 594 feet.
Population: 123 (1990); 139 (2000); 139 (2007); 138 (2012 projected); Race: 98.6% White, 0.0% Black, 1.4% Asian, 0.0% Hispanic of any race (2007); Density: 545.3 persons per square mile (2007); Average household size: 2.57 (2007); Median age: 41.7 (2007); Males per 100 females: 104.4 (2007); Marriage status: 15.7% never married, 73.0% now married, 6.1% widowed, 5.2% divorced (2000); Foreign born: 0.0% (2000); Ancestry (includes multiple ancestries): 40.6% German, 21.0% English, 8.7% Italian, 8.7% Dutch, 5.1% Irish (2000).
Economy: Employment by occupation: 8.3% management, 16.7% professional, 33.3% services, 19.4% sales, 0.0% farming, 16.7% construction, 5.6% production (2000).
Income: Per capita income: $26,133 (2007); Median household income: $54,286 (2007); Average household income: $67,269 (2007); Percent of households with income of $100,000 or more: 13.0% (2007); Poverty rate: 1.4% (2000).
Education: Percent of population age 25 and over with: High school diploma (including GED) or higher: 91.7% (2007); Bachelor's degree or higher: 20.8% (2007); Master's degree or higher: 8.3% (2007).

School District(s)

Athens CUSD 213 (PK-12)
2005-06 Enrollment: 1,061 . . . . (217) 636-8761
Housing: Homeownership rate: 92.6% (2007); Median home value: $100,000 (2007); Median rent: $358 per month (2000); Median age of housing: 43 years (2000).
Transportation: Commute to work: 100.0% car, 0.0% public transportation, 0.0% walk, 0.0% work from home (2000); Travel time to work: 19.4% less than 15 minutes, 70.8% 15 to 30 minutes, 5.6% 30 to 45 minutes, 1.4% 45 to 60 minutes, 2.8% 60 minutes or more (2000)

CHATHAM (village). Covers a land area of 4.965 square miles and a water area of 0.003 square miles. Located at 39.67° N. Lat.; 89.69° W. Long. Elevation is 600 feet.
Population: 6,443 (1990); 8,583 (2000); 9,898 (2007); 10,710 (2012 projected); Race: 96.9% White, 1.0% Black, 1.1% Asian, 0.7% Hispanic of any race (2007); Density: 1,993.5 persons per square mile (2007); Average household size: 2.72 (2007); Median age: 36.2 (2007); Males per 100 females: 95.5 (2007); Marriage status: 19.8% never married, 65.6% now married, 3.6% widowed, 11.0% divorced (2000); Foreign born: 1.2% (2000); Ancestry (includes multiple ancestries): 35.7% German, 19.1% Irish, 14.5% English, 6.4% Italian, 6.2% United States or American (2000).
Economy: Single-family building permits issued: 110 (2007); Multi-family building permits issued: 15 (2007); Employment by occupation: 20.2% management, 26.9% professional, 12.2% services, 29.1% sales, 0.0% farming, 6.5% construction, 5.1% production (2000).
Income: Per capita income: $28,030 (2007); Median household income: $69,382 (2007); Average household income: $76,315 (2007); Percent of households with income of $100,000 or more: 22.9% (2007); Poverty rate: 4.7% (2000).
Education: Percent of population age 25 and over with: High school diploma (including GED) or higher: 94.6% (2007); Bachelor's degree or higher: 36.9% (2007); Master's degree or higher: 10.3% (2007).

School District(s)

Ball Chatham CUSD 5 (PK-12)
2005-06 Enrollment: 4,127 . . . . (217) 483-2416
Housing: Homeownership rate: 84.9% (2007); Median home value: $130,719 (2007); Median rent: $493 per month (2000); Median age of housing: 21 years (2000).
Safety: Violent crime rate: 9.2 per 10,000 population; Property crime rate: 132.8 per 10,000 population (2006).
Newspapers: Chatham Clarion (Community news; Circulation 1,900)
Transportation: Commute to work: 93.7% car, 0.2% public transportation, 1.4% walk, 4.7% work from home (2000); Travel time to work: 21.5% less than 15 minutes, 56.6% 15 to 30 minutes, 17.9% 30 to 45 minutes, 1.5% 45 to 60 minutes, 2.4% 60 minutes or more (2000)

Additional Information Contacts

Chatham Area Chamber of Commerce . . . . (217) 483-6450
http://www.chatham-il-chamber.com
Village of Chatham. . . . . (217) 483-2451
http://www.chathamil.net

CLEAR LAKE (village). Covers a land area of 0.093 square miles and a water area of 0 square miles. Located at 39.81° N. Lat.; 89.56° W. Long. Elevation is 574 feet.
Population: 231 (1990); 267 (2000); 225 (2007); 218 (2012 projected); Race: 94.7% White, 1.3% Black, 1.8% Asian, 2.2% Hispanic of any race (2007); Density: 2,420.1 persons per square mile (2007); Average household size: 2.56 (2007); Median age: 40.9 (2007); Males per 100 females: 90.7 (2007); Marriage status: 25.6% never married, 42.0% now married, 7.6% widowed, 24.8% divorced (2000); Foreign born: 0.0% (2000); Ancestry (includes multiple ancestries): 13.9% United States or American, 7.5% English, 7.5% German, 6.8% Irish, 6.4% Italian (2000).
Economy: Employment by occupation: 10.0% management, 12.5% professional, 4.2% services, 22.5% sales, 0.0% farming, 8.3% construction, 42.5% production (2000).
Income: Per capita income: $16,233 (2007); Median household income: $38,846 (2007); Average household income: $41,506 (2007); Percent of households with income of $100,000 or more: 2.3% (2007); Poverty rate: 14.1% (2000).
Education: Percent of population age 25 and over with: High school diploma (including GED) or higher: 67.5% (2007); Bachelor's degree or higher: 8.6% (2007); Master's degree or higher: 2.0% (2007).
Housing: Homeownership rate: 85.2% (2007); Median home value: $71,071 (2007); Median rent: $325 per month (2000); Median age of housing: 32 years (2000).
Transportation: Commute to work: 100.0% car, 0.0% public transportation, 0.0% walk, 0.0% work from home (2000); Travel time to work: 28.6% less than 15 minutes, 43.8% 15 to 30 minutes, 21.4% 30 to 45 minutes, 4.5% 45 to 60 minutes, 1.8% 60 minutes or more (2000)

DAWSON (village). Covers a land area of 0.871 square miles and a water area of 0 square miles. Located at 39.85° N. Lat.; 89.46° W. Long. Elevation is 600 feet.
Population: 536 (1990); 466 (2000); 396 (2007); 370 (2012 projected); Race: 98.7% White, 0.0% Black, 0.0% Asian, 0.5% Hispanic of any race (2007); Density: 454.7 persons per square mile (2007); Average household size: 2.44 (2007); Median age: 39.7 (2007); Males per 100 females: 98.0 (2007); Marriage status: 25.9% never married, 56.7% now married, 5.7% widowed, 11.8% divorced (2000); Foreign born: 0.0% (2000); Ancestry (includes multiple ancestries): 22.0% English, 22.0% German, 11.0% United States or American, 9.1% Irish, 3.4% Other groups (2000).
Economy: Single-family building permits issued: 0 (2007); Multi-family building permits issued: 0 (2007); Employment by occupation: 8.7% management, 17.4% professional, 10.1% services, 35.8% sales, 0.0% farming, 15.6% construction, 12.5% production (2000).
Income: Per capita income: $26,540 (2007); Median household income: $63,571 (2007); Average household income: $64,722 (2007); Percent of households with income of $100,000 or more: 11.1% (2007); Poverty rate: 5.9% (2000).
Education: Percent of population age 25 and over with: High school diploma (including GED) or higher: 88.9% (2007); Bachelor's degree or higher: 13.9% (2007); Master's degree or higher: 3.9% (2007).

Housing: Homeownership rate: 82.1% (2007); Median home value: $92,083 (2007); Median rent: $378 per month (2000); Median age of housing: 34 years (2000).
Transportation: Commute to work: 96.9% car, 0.0% public transportation, 2.1% walk, 1.0% work from home (2000); Travel time to work: 18.9% less than 15 minutes, 55.8% 15 to 30 minutes, 23.9% 30 to 45 minutes, 1.4% 45 to 60 minutes, 0.0% 60 minutes or more (2000)

DIVERNON (village). Covers a land area of 0.797 square miles and a water area of 0.002 square miles. Located at 39.56° N. Lat.; 89.65° W. Long. Elevation is 614 feet.
History: Incorporated 1900.
Population: 1,230 (1990); 1,201 (2000); 1,148 (2007); 1,092 (2012 projected); Race: 98.4% White, 0.4% Black, 0.3% Asian, 1.6% Hispanic of any race (2007); Density: 1,440.8 persons per square mile (2007); Average household size: 2.44 (2007); Median age: 36.9 (2007); Males per 100 females: 92.0 (2007); Marriage status: 26.1% never married, 57.9% now married, 5.3% widowed, 10.7% divorced (2000); Foreign born: 0.4% (2000); Ancestry (includes multiple ancestries): 28.0% German, 13.1% English, 10.5% Irish, 8.9% Italian, 6.5% United States or American (2000).
Economy: Single-family building permits issued: 0 (2007); Multi-family building permits issued: 0 (2007); Employment by occupation: 13.2% management, 12.2% professional, 13.8% services, 37.4% sales, 0.0% farming, 11.0% construction, 12.4% production (2000).
Income: Per capita income: $25,856 (2007); Median household income: $55,556 (2007); Average household income: $63,154 (2007); Percent of households with income of $100,000 or more: 14.0% (2007); Poverty rate: 7.2% (2000).
Education: Percent of population age 25 and over with: High school diploma (including GED) or higher: 91.3% (2007); Bachelor's degree or higher: 14.7% (2007); Master's degree or higher: 2.8% (2007).

School District(s)

Divernon CUSD 13 (PK-12)
2005-06 Enrollment: 270 . . . . (217) 628-3414
Housing: Homeownership rate: 77.4% (2007); Median home value: $98,864 (2007); Median rent: $413 per month (2000); Median age of housing: 37 years (2000).
Safety: Violent crime rate: 17.5 per 10,000 population; Property crime rate: 69.9 per 10,000 population (2006).
Transportation: Commute to work: 93.9% car, 0.0% public transportation, 2.2% walk, 2.9% work from home (2000); Travel time to work: 15.5% less than 15 minutes, 44.6% 15 to 30 minutes, 33.3% 30 to 45 minutes, 3.6% 45 to 60 minutes, 2.9% 60 minutes or more (2000)

GLENARM (unincorporated postal area, zip code 62536). Covers a land area of 7.817 square miles and a water area of 0.066 square miles. Located at 39.64° N. Lat.; 89.65° W. Long. Elevation is 600 feet.
Population: 942 (2000); Race: 100.0% White, 0.0% Black, 0.0% Asian, 0.0% Hispanic of any race (2000); Density: 120.5 persons per square mile (2000); Age: 22.2% under 18, 7.5% over 64 (2000); Marriage status: 13.4% never married, 76.0% now married, 3.3% widowed, 7.3% divorced (2000); Foreign born: 1.1% (2000); Ancestry (includes multiple ancestries): 35.2% German, 24.4% Irish, 19.7% English, 8.0% United States or American, 7.7% Dutch (2000).
Economy: Employment by occupation: 16.6% management, 31.0% professional, 4.9% services, 27.9% sales, 1.9% farming, 12.7% construction, 5.0% production (2000).
Income: Per capita income: $27,618 (2000); Median household income: $62,382 (2000); Poverty rate: 0.8% (2000).
Education: Percent of population age 25 and over with: High school diploma (including GED) or higher: 94.0% (2000); Bachelor's degree or higher: 32.4% (2000).
Housing: Homeownership rate: 89.0% (2000); Median home value: $118,500 (2000); Median rent: $668 per month (2000); Median age of housing: 18 years (2000).
Transportation: Commute to work: 93.2% car, 0.0% public transportation, 0.0% walk, 6.8% work from home (2000); Travel time to work: 16.2% less than 15 minutes, 59.5% 15 to 30 minutes, 18.0% 30 to 45 minutes, 6.3% 45 to 60 minutes, 0.0% 60 minutes or more (2000)

GRANDVIEW (village). Covers a land area of 0.341 square miles and a water area of 0 square miles. Located at 39.81° N. Lat.; 89.62° W. Long. Elevation is 597 feet.
History: Incorporated 1939.
Population: 1,640 (1990); 1,537 (2000); 1,505 (2007); 1,476 (2012 projected); Race: 91.8% White, 6.1% Black, 0.1% Asian, 0.7% Hispanic of any race (2007); Density: 4,407.7 persons per square mile (2007); Average household size: 2.33 (2007); Median age: 39.2 (2007); Males per 100 females: 94.4 (2007); Marriage status: 26.2% never married, 52.1% now married, 7.7% widowed, 14.0% divorced (2000); Foreign born: 1.2% (2000); Ancestry (includes multiple ancestries): 21.6% German, 14.4% United States or American, 13.9% Irish, 11.9% English, 11.3% Other groups (2000).
Economy: Single-family building permits issued: 0 (2007); Multi-family building permits issued: 0 (2007); Employment by occupation: 6.6% management, 12.5% professional, 18.3% services, 36.7% sales, 0.5% farming, 13.6% construction, 11.8% production (2000).
Income: Per capita income: $18,650 (2007); Median household income: $38,698 (2007); Average household income: $43,516 (2007); Percent of households with income of $100,000 or more: 3.3% (2007); Poverty rate: 12.3% (2000).
Education: Percent of population age 25 and over with: High school diploma (including GED) or higher: 77.9% (2007); Bachelor's degree or higher: 8.4% (2007); Master's degree or higher: 1.9% (2007).
Housing: Homeownership rate: 77.2% (2007); Median home value: $74,875 (2007); Median rent: $455 per month (2000); Median age of housing: 47 years (2000).
Safety: Violent crime rate: 76.1 per 10,000 population; Property crime rate: 311.4 per 10,000 population (2006).
Transportation: Commute to work: 94.8% car, 1.2% public transportation, 0.3% walk, 2.4% work from home (2000); Travel time to work: 32.6% less than 15 minutes, 52.8% 15 to 30 minutes, 10.6% 30 to 45 minutes, 2.6% 45 to 60 minutes, 1.5% 60 minutes or more (2000)

ILLIOPOLIS (village). Covers a land area of 0.452 square miles and a water area of 0 square miles. Located at 39.85° N. Lat.; 89.24° W. Long. Elevation is 604 feet.
Population: 947 (1990); 916 (2000); 803 (2007); 775 (2012 projected); Race: 98.5% White, 0.0% Black, 0.0% Asian, 0.1% Hispanic of any race (2007); Density: 1,776.9 persons per square mile (2007); Average household size: 2.46 (2007); Median age: 38.5 (2007); Males per 100 females: 94.9 (2007); Marriage status: 23.4% never married, 62.4% now married, 5.9% widowed, 8.3% divorced (2000); Foreign born: 0.3% (2000); Ancestry (includes multiple ancestries): 26.8% German, 13.0% English, 12.9% Irish, 11.6% United States or American, 4.6% Other groups (2000).
Economy: Single-family building permits issued: 2 (2007); Multi-family building permits issued: 0 (2007); Employment by occupation: 11.2% management, 15.0% professional, 13.3% services, 23.9% sales, 2.1% farming, 11.4% construction, 23.0% production (2000).
Income: Per capita income: $25,118 (2007); Median household income: $57,200 (2007); Average household income: $61,871 (2007); Percent of households with income of $100,000 or more: 12.6% (2007); Poverty rate: 3.0% (2000).
Education: Percent of population age 25 and over with: High school diploma (including GED) or higher: 88.8% (2007); Bachelor's degree or higher: 13.1% (2007); Master's degree or higher: 4.3% (2007).

School District(s)

Sangamon Valley CUSD 9 (PK-12)
2005-06 Enrollment: 822 . . . . (217) 668-2338
Housing: Homeownership rate: 78.8% (2007); Median home value: $85,870 (2007); Median rent: $325 per month (2000); Median age of housing: 49 years (2000).
Safety: Violent crime rate: 34.6 per 10,000 population; Property crime rate: 69.2 per 10,000 population (2006).
Newspapers: County Line Observer (Community news; Circulation 700)
Transportation: Commute to work: 95.7% car, 0.0% public transportation, 2.6% walk, 1.3% work from home (2000); Travel time to work: 34.0% less than 15 minutes, 20.6% 15 to 30 minutes, 32.0% 30 to 45 minutes, 9.1% 45 to 60 minutes, 4.3% 60 minutes or more (2000)

JEROME (village). Covers a land area of 0.371 square miles and a water area of 0 square miles. Located at 39.76° N. Lat.; 89.67° W. Long. Elevation is 600 feet.
Population: 1,530 (1990); 1,414 (2000); 1,406 (2007); 1,360 (2012 projected); Race: 90.5% White, 3.3% Black, 3.0% Asian, 2.5% Hispanic of any race (2007); Density: 3,785.2 persons per square mile (2007); Average household size: 1.98 (2007); Median age: 44.1 (2007); Males per 100 females: 89.2 (2007); Marriage status: 21.0% never married, 53.6% now married, 10.0% widowed, 15.4% divorced (2000); Foreign born: 1.5%

(2000); Ancestry (includes multiple ancestries): 31.8% German, 16.4% Irish, 16.1% English, 8.7% United States or American, 8.4% Other groups (2000).
Economy: Single-family building permits issued: 0 (2007); Multi-family building permits issued: 0 (2007); Employment by occupation: 18.5% management, 20.5% professional, 12.5% services, 34.7% sales, 0.3% farming, 6.5% construction, 7.0% production (2000).
Income: Per capita income: $26,783 (2007); Median household income: $46,974 (2007); Average household income: $52,964 (2007); Percent of households with income of $100,000 or more: 7.0% (2007); Poverty rate: 3.5% (2000).
Education: Percent of population age 25 and over with: High school diploma (including GED) or higher: 92.6% (2007); Bachelor's degree or higher: 25.9% (2007); Master's degree or higher: 7.5% (2007).
Housing: Homeownership rate: 83.0% (2007); Median home value: $96,983 (2007); Median rent: $498 per month (2000); Median age of housing: 46 years (2000).
Safety: Violent crime rate: 52.8 per 10,000 population; Property crime rate: 339.1 per 10,000 population (2006).
Transportation: Commute to work: 94.0% car, 1.7% public transportation, 1.0% walk, 2.4% work from home (2000); Travel time to work: 40.4% less than 15 minutes, 49.0% 15 to 30 minutes, 6.2% 30 to 45 minutes, 1.0% 45 to 60 minutes, 3.4% 60 minutes or more (2000)

LELAND GROVE (city). Covers a land area of 0.627 square miles and a water area of 0 square miles. Located at 39.77° N. Lat.; 89.68° W. Long. Elevation is 600 feet.
Population: 1,644 (1990); 1,592 (2000); 1,561 (2007); 1,519 (2012 projected); Race: 96.3% White, 0.8% Black, 1.0% Asian, 1.3% Hispanic of any race (2007); Density: 2,490.9 persons per square mile (2007); Average household size: 2.24 (2007); Median age: 49.6 (2007); Males per 100 females: 85.6 (2007); Marriage status: 17.5% never married, 66.4% now married, 7.6% widowed, 8.5% divorced (2000); Foreign born: 2.3% (2000); Ancestry (includes multiple ancestries): 31.1% German, 20.8% English, 18.0% Irish, 6.1% Italian, 4.7% Scottish (2000).
Economy: Single-family building permits issued: 0 (2007); Multi-family building permits issued: 0 (2007); Employment by occupation: 28.6% management, 44.5% professional, 4.4% services, 18.6% sales, 0.0% farming, 2.3% construction, 1.6% production (2000).
Income: Per capita income: $52,047 (2007); Median household income: $80,000 (2007); Average household income: $116,397 (2007); Percent of households with income of $100,000 or more: 38.5% (2007); Poverty rate: 2.7% (2000).
Education: Percent of population age 25 and over with: High school diploma (including GED) or higher: 98.1% (2007); Bachelor's degree or higher: 65.6% (2007); Master's degree or higher: 34.8% (2007).
Housing: Homeownership rate: 93.3% (2007); Median home value: $197,860 (2007); Median rent: $488 per month (2000); Median age of housing: 49 years (2000).
Safety: Violent crime rate: 13.5 per 10,000 population; Property crime rate: 108.0 per 10,000 population (2006).
Transportation: Commute to work: 93.3% car, 0.7% public transportation, 0.6% walk, 5.4% work from home (2000); Travel time to work: 60.8% less than 15 minutes, 30.3% 15 to 30 minutes, 4.1% 30 to 45 minutes, 1.2% 45 to 60 minutes, 3.5% 60 minutes or more (2000)

LOAMI (village). Covers a land area of 0.977 square miles and a water area of 0.004 square miles. Located at 39.67° N. Lat.; 89.84° W. Long. Elevation is 633 feet.
Population: 826 (1990); 804 (2000); 659 (2007); 652 (2012 projected); Race: 97.4% White, 0.3% Black, 0.8% Asian, 2.4% Hispanic of any race (2007); Density: 674.2 persons per square mile (2007); Average household size: 2.64 (2007); Median age: 35.3 (2007); Males per 100 females: 92.7 (2007); Marriage status: 30.2% never married, 56.8% now married, 2.7% widowed, 10.2% divorced (2000); Foreign born: 0.0% (2000); Ancestry (includes multiple ancestries): 31.1% German, 13.7% Irish, 13.5% English, 12.1% Other groups, 8.8% United States or American (2000).
Economy: Single-family building permits issued: 1 (2007); Multi-family building permits issued: 0 (2007); Employment by occupation: 11.6% management, 15.6% professional, 16.3% services, 35.3% sales, 0.2% farming, 10.5% construction, 10.5% production (2000).
Income: Per capita income: $23,945 (2007); Median household income: $54,634 (2007); Average household income: $63,120 (2007); Percent of households with income of $100,000 or more: 15.2% (2007); Poverty rate: 10.0% (2000).
Education: Percent of population age 25 and over with: High school diploma (including GED) or higher: 87.4% (2007); Bachelor's degree or higher: 13.5% (2007); Master's degree or higher: 2.1% (2007).

School District(s)

New Berlin CUSD 16 (PK-12)
2005-06 Enrollment: 745 . . . . (217) 488-6111

Housing: Homeownership rate: 88.4% (2007); Median home value: $76,538 (2007); Median rent: $410 per month (2000); Median age of housing: 29 years (2000).
Safety: Violent crime rate: 77.0 per 10,000 population; Property crime rate: 192.6 per 10,000 population (2006).
Transportation: Commute to work: 95.2% car, 0.0% public transportation, 1.1% walk, 3.2% work from home (2000); Travel time to work: 4.5% less than 15 minutes, 54.1% 15 to 30 minutes, 35.7% 30 to 45 minutes, 4.5% 45 to 60 minutes, 1.2% 60 minutes or more (2000)

MECHANICSBURG (village). Covers a land area of 0.379 square miles and a water area of 0 square miles. Located at 39.80° N. Lat.; 89.39° W. Long. Elevation is 591 feet.
Population: 538 (1990); 456 (2000); 367 (2007); 349 (2012 projected); Race: 97.3% White, 0.5% Black, 0.8% Asian, 0.3% Hispanic of any race (2007); Density: 968.3 persons per square mile (2007); Average household size: 2.57 (2007); Median age: 35.1 (2007); Males per 100 females: 106.2 (2007); Marriage status: 25.2% never married, 53.6% now married, 8.0% widowed, 13.2% divorced (2000); Foreign born: 0.0% (2000); Ancestry (includes multiple ancestries): 32.9% German, 18.8% Irish, 12.3% United States or American, 8.9% English, 5.6% French (except Basque) (2000).
Economy: Single-family building permits issued: 1 (2007); Multi-family building permits issued: 0 (2007); Employment by occupation: 10.1% management, 10.9% professional, 26.5% services, 22.3% sales, 0.0% farming, 16.8% construction, 13.4% production (2000).
Income: Per capita income: $19,748 (2007); Median household income: $42,813 (2007); Average household income: $50,682 (2007); Percent of households with income of $100,000 or more: 8.4% (2007); Poverty rate: 3.2% (2000).
Education: Percent of population age 25 and over with: High school diploma (including GED) or higher: 71.0% (2007); Bachelor's degree or higher: 2.6% (2007); Master's degree or higher: 0.0% (2007).
Housing: Homeownership rate: 83.2% (2007); Median home value: $72,059 (2007); Median rent: $391 per month (2000); Median age of housing: 39 years (2000).
Safety: Violent crime rate: 158.7 per 10,000 population; Property crime rate: 294.8 per 10,000 population (2006).
Transportation: Commute to work: 92.0% car, 1.7% public transportation, 0.8% walk, 2.5% work from home (2000); Travel time to work: 9.1% less than 15 minutes, 41.8% 15 to 30 minutes, 38.4% 30 to 45 minutes, 6.0% 45 to 60 minutes, 4.7% 60 minutes or more (2000)

NEW BERLIN (village). Covers a land area of 1.108 square miles and a water area of 0 square miles. Located at 39.72° N. Lat.; 89.91° W. Long. Elevation is 650 feet.
Population: 810 (1990); 1,030 (2000); 1,225 (2007); 1,274 (2012 projected); Race: 97.9% White, 0.7% Black, 0.0% Asian, 0.7% Hispanic of any race (2007); Density: 1,105.3 persons per square mile (2007); Average household size: 2.37 (2007); Median age: 36.9 (2007); Males per 100 females: 91.4 (2007); Marriage status: 18.6% never married, 65.7% now married, 6.6% widowed, 9.2% divorced (2000); Foreign born: 1.1% (2000); Ancestry (includes multiple ancestries): 33.3% German, 18.8% Irish, 14.1% English, 8.9% United States or American, 4.3% Other groups (2000).
Economy: Single-family building permits issued: 3 (2007); Multi-family building permits issued: 0 (2007); Employment by occupation: 15.1% management, 21.4% professional, 12.2% services, 33.6% sales, 1.8% farming, 8.2% construction, 7.7% production (2000).
Income: Per capita income: $23,778 (2007); Median household income: $49,318 (2007); Average household income: $56,339 (2007); Percent of households with income of $100,000 or more: 8.9% (2007); Poverty rate: 5.8% (2000).
Education: Percent of population age 25 and over with: High school diploma (including GED) or higher: 87.3% (2007); Bachelor's degree or higher: 21.9% (2007); Master's degree or higher: 7.6% (2007).

School District(s)

New Berlin CUSD 16 (PK-12)
2005-06 Enrollment: 745 . . . . (217) 488-6111

Housing: Homeownership rate: 81.8% (2007); Median home value: $107,482 (2007); Median rent: $414 per month (2000); Median age of housing: 29 years (2000).
Transportation: Commute to work: 94.0% car, 0.0% public transportation, 1.9% walk, 4.1% work from home (2000); Travel time to work: 24.8% less than 15 minutes, 40.5% 15 to 30 minutes, 30.0% 30 to 45 minutes, 1.2% 45 to 60 minutes, 3.5% 60 minutes or more (2000)

PAWNEE (village). Covers a land area of 1.192 square miles and a water area of 0 square miles. Located at 39.59° N. Lat.; 89.58° W. Long. Elevation is 604 feet.
History: Incorporated 1891.
Population: 2,430 (1990); 2,647 (2000); 2,449 (2007); 2,346 (2012 projected); Race: 98.7% White, 0.2% Black, 0.1% Asian, 0.4% Hispanic of any race (2007); Density: 2,054.9 persons per square mile (2007); Average household size: 2.51 (2007); Median age: 36.4 (2007); Males per 100 females: 92.8 (2007); Marriage status: 18.8% never married, 63.5% now married, 7.6% widowed, 10.1% divorced (2000); Foreign born: 0.1% (2000); Ancestry (includes multiple ancestries): 31.7% German, 13.9% Irish, 12.8% English, 6.9% United States or American, 5.2% Italian (2000).
Economy: Single-family building permits issued: 3 (2007); Multi-family building permits issued: 2 (2007); Employment by occupation: 13.3% management, 21.1% professional, 16.2% services, 29.5% sales, 0.0% farming, 10.7% construction, 9.1% production (2000).
Income: Per capita income: $27,317 (2007); Median household income: $61,119 (2007); Average household income: $68,615 (2007); Percent of households with income of $100,000 or more: 17.9% (2007); Poverty rate: 6.3% (2000).
Education: Percent of population age 25 and over with: High school diploma (including GED) or higher: 88.8% (2007); Bachelor's degree or higher: 19.5% (2007); Master's degree or higher: 5.9% (2007).

School District(s)

Pawnee CUSD 11 (PK-12)
2005-06 Enrollment: 714 . . . . (217) 625-2471
Housing: Homeownership rate: 84.7% (2007); Median home value: $101,046 (2007); Median rent: $417 per month (2000); Median age of housing: 34 years (2000).
Safety: Violent crime rate: 7.8 per 10,000 population; Property crime rate: 27.2 per 10,000 population (2006).
Transportation: Commute to work: 95.0% car, 0.0% public transportation, 2.0% walk, 2.2% work from home (2000); Travel time to work: 20.3% less than 15 minutes, 33.2% 15 to 30 minutes, 41.3% 30 to 45 minutes, 3.3% 45 to 60 minutes, 1.9% 60 minutes or more (2000)

Additional Information Contacts

Pawnee Chamber of Commerce . . . . (217) 625-7779
http://www.pawneechamber.org

PLEASANT PLAINS (village). Covers a land area of 1.241 square miles and a water area of 0 square miles. Located at 39.87° N. Lat.; 89.92° W. Long. Elevation is 610 feet.
Population: 751 (1990); 777 (2000); 684 (2007); 662 (2012 projected); Race: 98.1% White, 0.4% Black, 0.4% Asian, 0.9% Hispanic of any race (2007); Density: 551.0 persons per square mile (2007); Average household size: 2.57 (2007); Median age: 36.9 (2007); Males per 100 females: 89.5 (2007); Marriage status: 22.7% never married, 63.8% now married, 3.2% widowed, 10.4% divorced (2000); Foreign born: 0.0% (2000); Ancestry (includes multiple ancestries): 37.6% German, 14.0% English, 11.3% Irish, 7.7% United States or American, 2.7% Polish (2000).
Economy: Single-family building permits issued: 1 (2007); Multi-family building permits issued: 0 (2007); Employment by occupation: 11.7% management, 15.9% professional, 15.6% services, 33.6% sales, 0.8% farming, 9.6% construction, 12.8% production (2000).
Income: Per capita income: $24,569 (2007); Median household income: $53,611 (2007); Average household income: $63,177 (2007); Percent of households with income of $100,000 or more: 13.2% (2007); Poverty rate: 2.9% (2000).
Education: Percent of population age 25 and over with: High school diploma (including GED) or higher: 88.0% (2007); Bachelor's degree or higher: 15.2% (2007); Master's degree or higher: 4.8% (2007).

School District(s)

Pleasant Plains CUSD 8 (PK-12)
2005-06 Enrollment: 1,328 . . . . (217) 626-1041
Housing: Homeownership rate: 87.2% (2007); Median home value: $107,787 (2007); Median rent: $404 per month (2000); Median age of housing: 33 years (2000).
Safety: Violent crime rate: 13.6 per 10,000 population; Property crime rate: 135.5 per 10,000 population (2006).
Transportation: Commute to work: 97.6% car, 0.0% public transportation, 0.5% walk, 1.9% work from home (2000); Travel time to work: 20.7% less than 15 minutes, 41.6% 15 to 30 minutes, 33.9% 30 to 45 minutes, 0.6% 45 to 60 minutes, 3.3% 60 minutes or more (2000)

RIVERTON (village). Covers a land area of 2.036 square miles and a water area of 0.035 square miles. Located at 39.84° N. Lat.; 89.54° W. Long. Elevation is 571 feet.
History: Incorporated 1873.
Population: 2,981 (1990); 3,048 (2000); 2,876 (2007); 2,854 (2012 projected); Race: 98.7% White, 0.1% Black, 0.1% Asian, 1.3% Hispanic of any race (2007); Density: 1,412.9 persons per square mile (2007); Average household size: 2.39 (2007); Median age: 36.4 (2007); Males per 100 females: 95.1 (2007); Marriage status: 24.3% never married, 58.6% now married, 6.9% widowed, 10.2% divorced (2000); Foreign born: 0.2% (2000); Ancestry (includes multiple ancestries): 26.1% German, 15.0% Irish, 14.3% English, 13.3% Italian, 6.4% United States or American (2000).
Economy: Single-family building permits issued: 5 (2007); Multi-family building permits issued: 0 (2007); Employment by occupation: 9.7% management, 19.2% professional, 13.6% services, 31.7% sales, 0.0% farming, 13.1% construction, 12.7% production (2000).
Income: Per capita income: $25,765 (2007); Median household income: $52,015 (2007); Average household income: $61,550 (2007); Percent of households with income of $100,000 or more: 16.1% (2007); Poverty rate: 6.8% (2000).
Education: Percent of population age 25 and over with: High school diploma (including GED) or higher: 89.8% (2007); Bachelor's degree or higher: 19.7% (2007); Master's degree or higher: 4.3% (2007).

School District(s)

Riverton CUSD 14 (PK-12)
2005-06 Enrollment: 1,531 . . . . (217) 629-6009
Housing: Homeownership rate: 74.5% (2007); Median home value: $101,894 (2007); Median rent: $381 per month (2000); Median age of housing: 26 years (2000).
Safety: Violent crime rate: 42.7 per 10,000 population; Property crime rate: 463.4 per 10,000 population (2006).
Newspapers: Tri-City Register (Community news; Circulation 600); Williamsville Sun (Community news; Circulation 400)
Transportation: Commute to work: 97.5% car, 0.2% public transportation, 1.2% walk, 0.6% work from home (2000); Travel time to work: 20.6% less than 15 minutes, 64.9% 15 to 30 minutes, 9.4% 30 to 45 minutes, 4.6% 45 to 60 minutes, 0.5% 60 minutes or more (2000)

ROCHESTER (village). Covers a land area of 2.107 square miles and a water area of 0.011 square miles. Located at 39.75° N. Lat.; 89.54° W. Long. Elevation is 558 feet.
Population: 2,894 (1990); 2,893 (2000); 2,772 (2007); 2,712 (2012 projected); Race: 98.4% White, 0.3% Black, 0.4% Asian, 0.9% Hispanic of any race (2007); Density: 1,315.5 persons per square mile (2007); Average household size: 2.64 (2007); Median age: 42.2 (2007); Males per 100 females: 93.7 (2007); Marriage status: 20.3% never married, 67.2% now married, 4.8% widowed, 7.8% divorced (2000); Foreign born: 0.7% (2000); Ancestry (includes multiple ancestries): 33.9% German, 17.5% English, 17.4% Irish, 7.5% Italian, 4.9% Other groups (2000).
Economy: Single-family building permits issued: 16 (2007); Multi-family building permits issued: 10 (2007); Employment by occupation: 17.0% management, 32.7% professional, 9.8% services, 31.8% sales, 0.0% farming, 4.0% construction, 4.7% production (2000).
Income: Per capita income: $32,964 (2007); Median household income: $74,679 (2007); Average household income: $86,943 (2007); Percent of households with income of $100,000 or more: 32.4% (2007); Poverty rate: 1.2% (2000).
Education: Percent of population age 25 and over with: High school diploma (including GED) or higher: 93.1% (2007); Bachelor's degree or higher: 45.2% (2007); Master's degree or higher: 16.2% (2007).

School District(s)

Rochester CUSD 3a (PK-12)
2005-06 Enrollment: 2,065 . . . . (217) 498-6210
Housing: Homeownership rate: 91.0% (2007); Median home value: $143,199 (2007); Median rent: $422 per month (2000); Median age of housing: 26 years (2000).

Safety: Violent crime rate: 3.3 per 10,000 population; Property crime rate: 159.8 per 10,000 population (2006).
Transportation: Commute to work: 94.8% car, 0.2% public transportation, 1.1% walk, 3.5% work from home (2000); Travel time to work: 20.3% less than 15 minutes, 65.6% 15 to 30 minutes, 11.0% 30 to 45 minutes, 2.0% 45 to 60 minutes, 1.2% 60 minutes or more (2000)

SHERMAN (village). Covers a land area of 3.076 square miles and a water area of 0.050 square miles. Located at 39.89° N. Lat.; 89.60° W. Long. Elevation is 581 feet.
Population: 2,169 (1990); 2,871 (2000); 3,267 (2007); 3,510 (2012 projected); Race: 97.3% White, 0.3% Black, 1.3% Asian, 0.4% Hispanic of any race (2007); Density: 1,062.2 persons per square mile (2007); Average household size: 2.88 (2007); Median age: 41.3 (2007); Males per 100 females: 91.3 (2007); Marriage status: 21.2% never married, 59.4% now married, 10.3% widowed, 9.1% divorced (2000); Foreign born: 1.5% (2000); Ancestry (includes multiple ancestries): 31.9% German, 18.9% Irish, 13.1% English, 8.7% Italian, 4.5% Other groups (2000).
Economy: Single-family building permits issued: 39 (2007); Multi-family building permits issued: 2 (2007); Employment by occupation: 19.4% management, 30.5% professional, 9.4% services, 29.3% sales, 0.0% farming, 6.2% construction, 5.2% production (2000).
Income: Per capita income: $32,806 (2007); Median household income: $79,167 (2007); Average household income: $92,665 (2007); Percent of households with income of $100,000 or more: 32.1% (2007); Poverty rate: 3.0% (2000).
Education: Percent of population age 25 and over with: High school diploma (including GED) or higher: 90.5% (2007); Bachelor's degree or higher: 34.1% (2007); Master's degree or higher: 12.5% (2007).

School District(s)

Williamsville CUSD 15 (PK-12)
2005-06 Enrollment: 1,406 . . . . (217) 566-2014

Housing: Homeownership rate: 84.5% (2007); Median home value: $158,264 (2007); Median rent: $497 per month (2000); Median age of housing: 20 years (2000).
Safety: Violent crime rate: 2.9 per 10,000 population; Property crime rate: 69.3 per 10,000 population (2006).
Transportation: Commute to work: 97.8% car, 0.2% public transportation, 0.0% walk, 2.0% work from home (2000); Travel time to work: 16.4% less than 15 minutes, 65.3% 15 to 30 minutes, 11.1% 30 to 45 minutes, 2.3% 45 to 60 minutes, 5.0% 60 minutes or more (2000)

SOUTHERN VIEW (village). Covers a land area of 0.527 square miles and a water area of 0 square miles. Located at 39.75° N. Lat.; 89.65° W. Long. Elevation is 610 feet.
Population: 1,896 (1990); 1,695 (2000); 1,594 (2007); 1,471 (2012 projected); Race: 95.5% White, 0.8% Black, 1.1% Asian, 2.1% Hispanic of any race (2007); Density: 3,026.6 persons per square mile (2007); Average household size: 2.07 (2007); Median age: 41.6 (2007); Males per 100 females: 86.4 (2007); Marriage status: 24.2% never married, 52.7% now married, 9.1% widowed, 14.0% divorced (2000); Foreign born: 1.3% (2000); Ancestry (includes multiple ancestries): 27.6% German, 18.9% Irish, 11.1% English, 7.3% United States or American, 6.9% Other groups (2000).
Economy: Single-family building permits issued: 0 (2007); Multi-family building permits issued: 0 (2007); Employment by occupation: 11.5% management, 16.5% professional, 16.0% services, 38.9% sales, 0.0% farming, 8.9% construction, 8.2% production (2000).
Income: Per capita income: $22,040 (2007); Median household income: $40,500 (2007); Average household income: $45,627 (2007); Percent of households with income of $100,000 or more: 3.6% (2007); Poverty rate: 7.6% (2000).
Education: Percent of population age 25 and over with: High school diploma (including GED) or higher: 87.1% (2007); Bachelor's degree or higher: 14.2% (2007); Master's degree or higher: 4.0% (2007).
Housing: Homeownership rate: 76.2% (2007); Median home value: $82,839 (2007); Median rent: $476 per month (2000); Median age of housing: 47 years (2000).
Safety: Violent crime rate: 83.2 per 10,000 population; Property crime rate: 416.2 per 10,000 population (2006).
Transportation: Commute to work: 96.3% car, 0.5% public transportation, 2.0% walk, 1.3% work from home (2000); Travel time to work: 41.5% less than 15 minutes, 47.5% 15 to 30 minutes, 6.1% 30 to 45 minutes, 2.4% 45 to 60 minutes, 2.6% 60 minutes or more (2000)

SPAULDING (village). Covers a land area of 0.777 square miles and a water area of 0.002 square miles. Located at 39.86° N. Lat.; 89.54° W. Long. Elevation is 581 feet.
Population: 477 (1990); 559 (2000); 637 (2007); 665 (2012 projected); Race: 98.4% White, 0.0% Black, 0.0% Asian, 0.9% Hispanic of any race (2007); Density: 819.8 persons per square mile (2007); Average household size: 2.87 (2007); Median age: 38.8 (2007); Males per 100 females: 99.7 (2007); Marriage status: 20.8% never married, 69.4% now married, 1.8% widowed, 8.1% divorced (2000); Foreign born: 0.0% (2000); Ancestry (includes multiple ancestries): 25.3% German, 16.7% Irish, 16.5% English, 12.0% Other groups, 9.3% Italian (2000).
Economy: Single-family building permits issued: 3 (2007); Multi-family building permits issued: 0 (2007); Employment by occupation: 22.4% management, 19.7% professional, 9.9% services, 28.9% sales, 0.0% farming, 13.2% construction, 5.9% production (2000).
Income: Per capita income: $27,206 (2007); Median household income: $78,750 (2007); Average household income: $78,063 (2007); Percent of households with income of $100,000 or more: 27.0% (2007); Poverty rate: 5.1% (2000).
Education: Percent of population age 25 and over with: High school diploma (including GED) or higher: 92.4% (2007); Bachelor's degree or higher: 16.6% (2007); Master's degree or higher: 5.2% (2007).
Housing: Homeownership rate: 85.6% (2007); Median home value: $138,542 (2007); Median rent: $525 per month (2000); Median age of housing: 20 years (2000).
Safety: Violent crime rate: 0.0 per 10,000 population; Property crime rate: 12.8 per 10,000 population (2006).
Transportation: Commute to work: 96.7% car, 1.3% public transportation, 0.0% walk, 2.0% work from home (2000); Travel time to work: 21.7% less than 15 minutes, 51.5% 15 to 30 minutes, 19.0% 30 to 45 minutes, 2.7% 45 to 60 minutes, 5.1% 60 minutes or more (2000)

SPRINGFIELD (city). Aka Southlawn. County seat. Covers a land area of 54.001 square miles and a water area of 6.307 square miles. Located at 39.78° N. Lat.; 89.65° W. Long. Elevation is 597 feet.
History: Springfield's history is closely linked with Abraham Lincoln, who practiced law here from 1837 to 1861. The first settlers here were Elisha Kelly and his brothers, and in 1821 Springfield received its name, from nearby Spring Creek, and became the seat of the new Sangamon County, with the courthouse built in John Kelly's field. Due to Lincoln's leadership, Springfield was chosen for the state capital in 1837, and was incorporated as a city in 1840. Coal mining became an important industry after 1867.
Population: 108,997 (1990); 111,454 (2000); 114,894 (2007); 116,931 (2012 projected); Race: 79.3% White, 16.3% Black, 1.8% Asian, 1.4% Hispanic of any race (2007); Density: 2,127.6 persons per square mile (2007); Average household size: 2.27 (2007); Median age: 38.3 (2007); Males per 100 females: 89.2 (2007); Marriage status: 29.1% never married, 49.8% now married, 8.0% widowed, 13.1% divorced (2000); Foreign born: 2.3% (2000); Ancestry (includes multiple ancestries): 24.4% German, 17.0% Other groups, 15.6% Irish, 11.8% English, 7.1% United States or American (2000).
Economy: Unemployment rate: 4.5% (4/2008); Total civilian labor force: 64,978 (4/2008); Single-family building permits issued: 179 (2007); Multi-family building permits issued: 110 (2007); Employment by occupation: 16.0% management, 24.3% professional, 15.6% services, 29.9% sales, 0.1% farming, 6.4% construction, 7.7% production (2000).
Income: Per capita income: $26,982 (2007); Median household income: $44,652 (2007); Average household income: $60,633 (2007); Percent of households with income of $100,000 or more: 14.4% (2007); Poverty rate: 11.7% (2000).
Taxes: Total city taxes per capita: $455 (2006); City property taxes per capita: $185 (2006).
Education: Percent of population age 25 and over with: High school diploma (including GED) or higher: 87.9% (2007); Bachelor's degree or higher: 31.8% (2007); Master's degree or higher: 12.1% (2007).

School District(s)

Capital Area Career Center
2005-06 Enrollment: n/a . . . . (217) 529-5431
Sangamon Area Spec Ed Dist (01-12)
2005-06 Enrollment: 69 . . . . (217) 786-3250
Sangamon Roe (07-12)
2005-06 Enrollment: 73 . . . . (217) 753-6620
Springfield SD 186 (PK-12)
2005-06 Enrollment: 15,097 . . . . (217) 525-3002

Four-year College(s)

St Johns College (Private, Not-for-profit, Roman Catholic)
Fall 2007 Enrollment: 69 . . . . (217) 525-5628

University of Illinois at Springfield (Public)
Fall 2007 Enrollment: 4,855. . . . . (217) 206-6600
2007-08 Tuition: In-state $6,348; Out-of-state $13,668

Two-year College(s)

Lincoln Land Community College (Public)
Fall 2007 Enrollment: 6,655. . . . . (217) 786-2200
2007-08 Tuition: In-state $4,620; Out-of-state $6,780

Springfield College in Illinois (Private, Not-for-profit, Roman Catholic)
Fall 2007 Enrollment: 608 . . . . (217) 525-1420
2007-08 Tuition: In-state $7,744; Out-of-state $7,744

Vocational/Technical School(s)

Capital Area School of Practical Nursing (Public)
Fall 2007 Enrollment: 54 . . . . (217) 585-2160
2007-08 Tuition: $6,544

Midwest Technical Institute (Private, For-profit)
Fall 2007 Enrollment: 706 . . . . (217) 527-8324
2007-08 Tuition: $8,170

St Johns Hospital School of Clinical Lab Science (Private, Not-for-profit, Roman Catholic)
Fall 2007 Enrollment: 5 . . . . (217) 757-6788

University of Spa & Cosmetology Arts (Private, For-profit)
Fall 2007 Enrollment: 214 . . . . (217) 753-8990
2007-08 Tuition: $10,300

Housing: Homeownership rate: 63.9% (2007); Median home value: $105,900 (2007); Median rent: $427 per month (2000); Median age of housing: 33 years (2000).

Hospitals: Andrew McFarland Mental Health Center (118 beds); Memorial Medical Center (444 beds); St. John's Hospital (742 beds)

Safety: Violent crime rate: 156.1 per 10,000 population; Property crime rate: 669.8 per 10,000 population (2006).

Newspapers: Catholic Times (Regional news; Circulation 49,700); Chicago Sun-Times - Springfield Bureau (Regional news; Circulation 0); Chicago Tribune - Springfield Bureau (Local news; Circulation 0); Herald & Review - Springfield Bureau (Local news; Circulation 0); Pure News USA (Regional news; Circulation 50,000); Small Newspaper Group - Springfield Bureau (Local news; Circulation 100,000); St. Louis Post-Dispatch - Springfield Bureau (Local news; Circulation 0); State Journal-Register (Community news; Circulation 63,674)

Transportation: Commute to work: 91.8% car, 2.5% public transportation, 2.6% walk, 2.1% work from home (2000); Travel time to work: 41.6% less than 15 minutes, 47.6% 15 to 30 minutes, 6.1% 30 to 45 minutes, 1.7% 45 to 60 minutes, 3.0% 60 minutes or more (2000); Amtrak: Service available.

Airports: Abraham Lincoln Capital (primary service)

Additional Information Contacts

City of Springfield. . . . . (217) 789-2000
http://www.springfield.il.us

Illinois Chamber of Commerce. . . . . (217) 522-5512
http://www.ilchamber.org

Springfield Convention & Visitors Bureau . . . . (217) 789-2360
http://www.visit-springfieldillinois.com

The Greater Springfield Chamber of Commerce . . . . (217) 525-1173
http://www.gscc.org

THAYER (village). Covers a land area of 0.601 square miles and a water area of 0 square miles. Located at 39.53° N. Lat.; 89.76° W. Long. Elevation is 643 feet.

Population: 730 (1990); 750 (2000); 718 (2007); 700 (2012 projected); Race: 98.9% White, 0.1% Black, 0.0% Asian, 0.8% Hispanic of any race (2007); Density: 1,195.1 persons per square mile (2007); Average household size: 2.67 (2007); Median age: 32.5 (2007); Males per 100 females: 104.0 (2007); Marriage status: 18.7% never married, 62.7% now married, 7.4% widowed, 11.2% divorced (2000); Foreign born: 0.6% (2000); Ancestry (includes multiple ancestries): 17.7% German, 16.8% English, 13.7% United States or American, 9.7% Irish, 8.8% Italian (2000).

Economy: Single-family building permits issued: 0 (2007); Multi-family building permits issued: 0 (2007); Employment by occupation: 16.5% management, 18.4% professional, 10.8% services, 26.3% sales, 0.0% farming, 14.1% construction, 13.8% production (2000).

Income: Per capita income: $24,645 (2007); Median household income: $52,321 (2007); Average household income: $65,781 (2007); Percent of households with income of $100,000 or more: 16.7% (2007); Poverty rate: 5.1% (2000).

Education: Percent of population age 25 and over with: High school diploma (including GED) or higher: 80.2% (2007); Bachelor's degree or higher: 11.3% (2007); Master's degree or higher: 2.5% (2007).

Housing: Homeownership rate: 88.5% (2007); Median home value: $79,630 (2007); Median rent: $404 per month (2000); Median age of housing: 48 years (2000).

Safety: Violent crime rate: 42.6 per 10,000 population; Property crime rate: 56.7 per 10,000 population (2006).

Transportation: Commute to work: 96.0% car, 0.0% public transportation, 0.8% walk, 3.2% work from home (2000); Travel time to work: 23.4% less than 15 minutes, 18.4% 15 to 30 minutes, 44.8% 30 to 45 minutes, 9.5% 45 to 60 minutes, 3.9% 60 minutes or more (2000)

WILLIAMSVILLE (village). Covers a land area of 1.242 square miles and a water area of 0 square miles. Located at 39.95° N. Lat.; 89.55° W. Long. Elevation is 600 feet.

Population: 1,280 (1990); 1,439 (2000); 1,410 (2007); 1,409 (2012 projected); Race: 97.9% White, 0.6% Black, 0.2% Asian, 0.9% Hispanic of any race (2007); Density: 1,135.7 persons per square mile (2007); Average household size: 2.64 (2007); Median age: 36.6 (2007); Males per 100 females: 89.8 (2007); Marriage status: 19.1% never married, 69.7% now married, 5.6% widowed, 5.7% divorced (2000); Foreign born: 1.3% (2000); Ancestry (includes multiple ancestries): 29.1% German, 16.3% English, 16.0% Irish, 8.2% Italian, 7.9% United States or American (2000).

Economy: Single-family building permits issued: 4 (2007); Multi-family building permits issued: 0 (2007); Employment by occupation: 15.7% management, 22.4% professional, 11.7% services, 30.5% sales, 0.6% farming, 11.0% construction, 8.1% production (2000).

Income: Per capita income: $22,619 (2007); Median household income: $54,000 (2007); Average household income: $59,724 (2007); Percent of households with income of $100,000 or more: 13.1% (2007); Poverty rate: 3.1% (2000).

Education: Percent of population age 25 and over with: High school diploma (including GED) or higher: 87.9% (2007); Bachelor's degree or higher: 23.7% (2007); Master's degree or higher: 5.2% (2007).

School District(s)

Williamsville CUSD 15 (PK-12)
2005-06 Enrollment: 1,406 . . . . (217) 566-2014

Housing: Homeownership rate: 82.2% (2007); Median home value: $122,875 (2007); Median rent: $394 per month (2000); Median age of housing: 28 years (2000).

Safety: Violent crime rate: 7.2 per 10,000 population; Property crime rate: 28.7 per 10,000 population (2006).

Transportation: Commute to work: 94.7% car, 0.0% public transportation, 2.2% walk, 2.4% work from home (2000); Travel time to work: 19.8% less than 15 minutes, 56.0% 15 to 30 minutes, 18.2% 30 to 45 minutes, 3.0% 45 to 60 minutes, 3.0% 60 minutes or more (2000)

Schuyler County

Located in western Illinois; bounded on the southeast by the Illinois River; drained by the La Moine River. Covers a land area of 437.31 square miles, a water area of 4.07 square miles, and is located in the Central Time Zone. The county was founded in 1825. County seat is Rushville.

Weather Station: Rushville — Elevation: 659 feet

	Jan	Feb	Mar	Apr	May	Jun	Jul	Aug	Sep	Oct	Nov	Dec
High	33	39	51	64	74	83	87	85	78	66	51	38
Low	15	21	31	42	52	61	65	63	55	43	32	22
Precip	1.5	1.8	3.1	4.0	5.2	4.0	3.8	3.7	4.0	3.3	3.1	2.5
Snow	5.6	4.6	2.3	0.7	0.0	0.0	0.0	0.0	0.0	tr	1.0	3.7

High and Low temperatures in degrees Fahrenheit; Precipitation and Snow in inches

Population: 7,498 (1990); 7,189 (2000); 7,098 (2007); 7,061 (2012 projected); Race: 97.8% White, 1.0% Black, 0.2% Asian, 1.0% Hispanic of any race (2007); Density: 16.2 persons per square mile (2007); Average household size: 2.38 (2007); Median age: 42.1 (2007); Males per 100 females: 99.2 (2007).

Religion: Five largest groups: 15.9% The United Methodist Church, 8.9% Christian Churches and Churches of Christ, 6.6% Christian Church (Disciples of Christ), 5.8% Southern Baptist Convention, 4.1% Catholic Church (2000).

Economy: Unemployment rate: 4.3% (4/2008); Total civilian labor force: 4,241 (4/2008); Leading industries: 27.3% health care and social assistance; 15.8% retail trade; 9.9% accommodation & food services (2005); Farms: 538 totaling 207,446 acres (2002); Companies that employ

500 or more persons: 0 (2006); Companies that employ 100 to 499 persons: 2 (2006); Companies that employ less than 100 persons: 160 (2006); Black-owned businesses: n/a (2002); Hispanic-owned businesses: n/a (2002); Asian-owned businesses: n/a (2002); Women-owned businesses: n/a (2002); Retail sales per capita: $8,916 (2008). Single-family building permits issued: n/a (2007); Multi-family building permits issued: n/a (2007).
Income: Per capita income: $21,561 (2007); Median household income: $43,253 (2007); Average household income: $51,132 (2007); Percent of households with income of $100,000 or more: 8.2% (2007); Poverty rate: 11.2% (2005); Bankruptcy rate: 2.72% (2007).
Education: Percent of population age 25 and over with: High school diploma (including GED) or higher: 84.1% (2007); Bachelor's degree or higher: 11.5% (2007); Master's degree or higher: 3.2% (2007).
Housing: Homeownership rate: 78.8% (2007); Median home value: $74,692 (2007); Median rent: $253 per month (2000); Median age of housing: 41 years (2000).
Health: Birth rate: 114.4 per 10,000 population (2007); Death rate: 135.9 per 10,000 population (2007); Age-adjusted cancer mortality rate: 207.0 deaths per 100,000 population (2005); Number of physicians: 5.7 per 10,000 population (2005); Hospital beds: 82.5 per 10,000 population (2004); Hospital admissions: 1,138.0 per 10,000 population (2004).
Elections: 2004 Presidential election results: 59.6% Bush, 39.5% Kerry, 0.1% Nader, 0.8% Badnarik
National and State Parks: Weinborg-King State Park
Additional Information Contacts
Schuyler County Government . . . . (217) 322-4734

Rushville Area Chamber of Commerce & Main Street. . . . . (217) 322-3689
http://www.rushville.org

Schuyler County Communities

BROWNING (village). Covers a land area of 0.310 square miles and a water area of 0 square miles. Located at 40.12° N. Lat.; 90.37° W. Long. Elevation is 449 feet.
Population: 193 (1990); 130 (2000); 113 (2007); 114 (2012 projected); Race: 99.1% White, 0.0% Black, 0.0% Asian, 2.7% Hispanic of any race (2007); Density: 364.2 persons per square mile (2007); Average household size: 2.22 (2007); Median age: 48.1 (2007); Males per 100 females: 105.5 (2007); Marriage status: 8.8% never married, 64.8% now married, 6.4% widowed, 20.0% divorced (2000); Foreign born: 0.0% (2000); Ancestry (includes multiple ancestries): 27.9% United States or American, 19.9% German, 13.2% Irish, 6.6% English, 3.7% Other groups (2000).
Economy: Employment by occupation: 10.4% management, 0.0% professional, 23.9% services, 26.9% sales, 0.0% farming, 22.4% construction, 16.4% production (2000).
Income: Per capita income: $21,394 (2007); Median household income: $51,875 (2007); Average household income: $47,402 (2007); Percent of households with income of $100,000 or more: 0.0% (2007); Poverty rate: 3.7% (2000).
Education: Percent of population age 25 and over with: High school diploma (including GED) or higher: 73.6% (2007); Bachelor's degree or higher: 0.0% (2007); Master's degree or higher: 0.0% (2007).
Housing: Homeownership rate: 90.2% (2007); Median home value: $40,000 (2007); Median rent: $n/a per month (2000); Median age of housing: 55 years (2000).
Transportation: Commute to work: 100.0% car, 0.0% public transportation, 0.0% walk, 0.0% work from home (2000); Travel time to work: 40.3% less than 15 minutes, 19.4% 15 to 30 minutes, 25.4% 30 to 45 minutes, 14.9% 45 to 60 minutes, 0.0% 60 minutes or more (2000)

CAMDEN (village). Covers a land area of 0.762 square miles and a water area of 0 square miles. Located at 40.15° N. Lat.; 90.77° W. Long. Elevation is 600 feet.
Population: 115 (1990); 97 (2000); 94 (2007); 95 (2012 projected); Race: 100.0% White, 0.0% Black, 0.0% Asian, 0.0% Hispanic of any race (2007); Density: 123.3 persons per square mile (2007); Average household size: 2.47 (2007); Median age: 32.5 (2007); Males per 100 females: 123.8 (2007); Marriage status: 11.1% never married, 75.0% now married, 8.3% widowed, 5.6% divorced (2000); Foreign born: 0.0% (2000); Ancestry (includes multiple ancestries): 21.9% German, 14.6% United States or American, 11.5% Irish, 6.3% Scottish, 4.2% Scotch-Irish (2000).
Economy: Employment by occupation: 13.5% management, 0.0% professional, 2.7% services, 35.1% sales, 0.0% farming, 8.1% construction, 40.5% production (2000).
Income: Per capita income: $14,388 (2007); Median household income: $40,000 (2007); Average household income: $35,592 (2007); Percent of households with income of $100,000 or more: 0.0% (2007); Poverty rate: 33.3% (2000).
Education: Percent of population age 25 and over with: High school diploma (including GED) or higher: 72.9% (2007); Bachelor's degree or higher: 0.0% (2007); Master's degree or higher: 0.0% (2007).
Housing: Homeownership rate: 92.1% (2007); Median home value: $38,750 (2007); Median rent: <$100 per month (2000); Median age of housing: 32 years (2000).
Transportation: Commute to work: 89.2% car, 0.0% public transportation, 8.1% walk, 2.7% work from home (2000); Travel time to work: 13.9% less than 15 minutes, 30.6% 15 to 30 minutes, 50.0% 30 to 45 minutes, 5.6% 45 to 60 minutes, 0.0% 60 minutes or more (2000)

FREDERICK (unincorporated postal area, zip code 62639). Covers a land area of 34.538 square miles and a water area of 1.058 square miles. Located at 40.04° N. Lat.; 90.46° W. Long. Elevation is 446 feet.
Population: 341 (2000); Race: 97.4% White, 0.0% Black, 0.0% Asian, 2.6% Hispanic of any race (2000); Density: 9.9 persons per square mile (2000); Age: 24.9% under 18, 14.9% over 64 (2000); Marriage status: 27.4% never married, 61.4% now married, 3.2% widowed, 8.1% divorced (2000); Foreign born: 0.0% (2000); Ancestry (includes multiple ancestries): 24.1% German, 10.6% English, 9.7% Irish, 8.3% Italian, 6.6% British (2000).
Economy: Employment by occupation: 11.6% management, 16.3% professional, 21.8% services, 25.2% sales, 0.0% farming, 3.4% construction, 21.8% production (2000).
Income: Per capita income: $16,011 (2000); Median household income: $38,125 (2000); Poverty rate: 20.3% (2000).
Education: Percent of population age 25 and over with: High school diploma (including GED) or higher: 90.1% (2000); Bachelor's degree or higher: 8.3% (2000).
Housing: Homeownership rate: 92.6% (2000); Median home value: $43,700 (2000); Median rent: $n/a per month (2000); Median age of housing: 49 years (2000).
Transportation: Commute to work: 95.0% car, 0.0% public transportation, 0.0% walk, 0.0% work from home (2000); Travel time to work: 37.1% less than 15 minutes, 42.1% 15 to 30 minutes, 5.0% 30 to 45 minutes, 0.0% 45 to 60 minutes, 15.7% 60 minutes or more (2000)

HUNTSVILLE (unincorporated postal area, zip code 62344). Covers a land area of 37.078 square miles and a water area of 0 square miles. Located at 40.18° N. Lat.; 90.81° W. Long. Elevation is 659 feet.
Population: 185 (2000); Race: 100.0% White, 0.0% Black, 0.0% Asian, 0.0% Hispanic of any race (2000); Density: 5.0 persons per square mile (2000); Age: 29.3% under 18, 2.4% over 64 (2000); Marriage status: 23.6% never married, 61.5% now married, 3.1% widowed, 11.8% divorced (2000); Foreign born: 0.0% (2000); Ancestry (includes multiple ancestries): 39.9% English, 32.2% German, 21.2% United States or American, 10.6% Irish, 5.3% Dutch (2000).
Economy: Employment by occupation: 26.4% management, 21.8% professional, 16.4% services, 14.5% sales, 4.5% farming, 4.5% construction, 11.8% production (2000).
Income: Per capita income: $10,976 (2000); Median household income: $38,542 (2000); Poverty rate: 4.8% (2000).
Education: Percent of population age 25 and over with: High school diploma (including GED) or higher: 79.3% (2000); Bachelor's degree or higher: 12.4% (2000).
Housing: Homeownership rate: 69.1% (2000); Median home value: $58,000 (2000); Median rent: $125 per month (2000); Median age of housing: 52 years (2000).
Transportation: Commute to work: 100.0% car, 0.0% public transportation, 0.0% walk, 0.0% work from home (2000); Travel time to work: 20.0% less than 15 minutes, 25.5% 15 to 30 minutes, 20.0% 30 to 45 minutes, 6.4% 45 to 60 minutes, 28.2% 60 minutes or more (2000)

LITTLETON (village). Covers a land area of 1.163 square miles and a water area of 0 square miles. Located at 40.23° N. Lat.; 90.61° W. Long. Elevation is 679 feet.
Population: 181 (1990); 197 (2000); 199 (2007); 201 (2012 projected); Race: 95.0% White, 5.0% Black, 0.0% Asian, 6.5% Hispanic of any race

(2007); Density: 171.1 persons per square mile (2007); Average household size: 2.80 (2007); Median age: 33.9 (2007); Males per 100 females: 101.0 (2007); Marriage status: 25.5% never married, 61.4% now married, 5.5% widowed, 7.6% divorced (2000); Foreign born: 0.0% (2000); Ancestry (includes multiple ancestries): 20.4% German, 15.9% Other groups, 12.4% United States or American, 9.5% English, 7.5% Irish (2000).
Economy: Employment by occupation: 5.8% management, 13.6% professional, 24.3% services, 14.6% sales, 0.0% farming, 6.8% construction, 35.0% production (2000).
Income: Per capita income: $20,503 (2007); Median household income: $51,875 (2007); Average household income: $57,465 (2007); Percent of households with income of $100,000 or more: 8.5% (2007); Poverty rate: 0.5% (2000).
Education: Percent of population age 25 and over with: High school diploma (including GED) or higher: 85.7% (2007); Bachelor's degree or higher: 8.4% (2007); Master's degree or higher: 0.0% (2007).
Housing: Homeownership rate: 83.1% (2007); Median home value: $50,500 (2007); Median rent: $163 per month (2000); Median age of housing: 60+ years (2000).
Transportation: Commute to work: 90.3% car, 0.0% public transportation, 5.8% walk, 0.0% work from home (2000); Travel time to work: 16.5% less than 15 minutes, 31.1% 15 to 30 minutes, 41.7% 30 to 45 minutes, 1.9% 45 to 60 minutes, 8.7% 60 minutes or more (2000)

RUSHVILLE (city). County seat. Covers a land area of 1.572 square miles and a water area of 0 square miles. Located at 40.12° N. Lat.; 90.56° W. Long. Elevation is 676 feet.
History: Rushville was founded in 1825 as Rushton. Both names honor Dr. William Rush, a Philadelphia physician.
Population: 3,342 (1990); 3,212 (2000); 3,200 (2007); 3,199 (2012 projected); Race: 98.8% White, 0.2% Black, 0.1% Asian, 0.8% Hispanic of any race (2007); Density: 2,036.0 persons per square mile (2007); Average household size: 2.28 (2007); Median age: 42.9 (2007); Males per 100 females: 90.7 (2007); Marriage status: 14.5% never married, 63.1% now married, 13.8% widowed, 8.6% divorced (2000); Foreign born: 0.7% (2000); Ancestry (includes multiple ancestries): 21.1% United States or American, 15.3% German, 12.4% Irish, 10.8% English, 3.8% Dutch (2000).
Economy: Employment by occupation: 6.7% management, 15.2% professional, 24.0% services, 22.1% sales, 0.5% farming, 7.7% construction, 23.9% production (2000).
Income: Per capita income: $20,269 (2007); Median household income: $38,265 (2007); Average household income: $45,791 (2007); Percent of households with income of $100,000 or more: 7.2% (2007); Poverty rate: 10.8% (2000).
Education: Percent of population age 25 and over with: High school diploma (including GED) or higher: 83.6% (2007); Bachelor's degree or higher: 12.7% (2007); Master's degree or higher: 3.6% (2007).

School District(s)

Schuyler-Industry CUSD 5 (PK-12)
2005-06 Enrollment: 1,339 . . . . (217) 322-4311
Housing: Homeownership rate: 73.5% (2007); Median home value: $67,933 (2007); Median rent: $264 per month (2000); Median age of housing: 46 years (2000).
Hospitals: Sarah D Culbertson Memorial Hospital (55 beds)
Safety: Violent crime rate: 6.3 per 10,000 population; Property crime rate: 230.9 per 10,000 population (2006).
Newspapers: Rushville Times (Community news; Circulation 3,669)
Transportation: Commute to work: 89.8% car, 0.0% public transportation, 3.5% walk, 4.8% work from home (2000); Travel time to work: 53.9% less than 15 minutes, 26.4% 15 to 30 minutes, 9.8% 30 to 45 minutes, 3.8% 45 to 60 minutes, 6.0% 60 minutes or more (2000)

Additional Information Contacts

Rushville Area Chamber of Commerce & Main Street. . . . . (217) 322-3689
http://www.rushville.org

Scott County

Located in west central Illinois; bounded on the west by the Illinois River; drained by Sandy and Mauvaise Terre Creeks. Covers a land area of 250.92 square miles, a water area of 1.85 square miles, and is located in the Central Time Zone. The county was founded in 1839. County seat is Winchester.

Scott County is part of the Jacksonville, IL Micropolitan Statistical Area. The entire metro area includes: Morgan County, IL; Scott County, IL

Population: 5,644 (1990); 5,537 (2000); 5,375 (2007); 5,245 (2012 projected); Race: 99.4% White, 0.0% Black, 0.2% Asian, 0.2% Hispanic of any race (2007); Density: 21.4 persons per square mile (2007); Average household size: 2.46 (2007); Median age: 41.7 (2007); Males per 100 females: 94.5 (2007).
Religion: Five largest groups: 17.9% American Baptist Churches in the USA, 17.2% Southern Baptist Convention, 9.5% Lutheran Church—Missouri Synod, 8.7% Catholic Church, 8.1% The United Methodist Church (2000).
Economy: Unemployment rate: 5.0% (4/2008); Total civilian labor force: 2,838 (4/2008); Leading industries: 18.2% retail trade; 15.3% finance & insurance; 13.8% manufacturing (2005); Farms: 291 totaling 115,923 acres (2002); Companies that employ 500 or more persons: 0 (2006); Companies that employ 100 to 499 persons: 0 (2006); Companies that employ less than 100 persons: 88 (2006); Black-owned businesses: n/a (2002); Hispanic-owned businesses: n/a (2002); Asian-owned businesses: n/a (2002); Women-owned businesses: n/a (2002); Retail sales per capita: $6,133 (2008). Single-family building permits issued: n/a (2007); Multi-family building permits issued: n/a (2007).
Income: Per capita income: $20,698 (2007); Median household income: $43,925 (2007); Average household income: $50,495 (2007); Percent of households with income of $100,000 or more: 8.1% (2007); Poverty rate: 10.6% (2005); Bankruptcy rate: 2.30% (2007).
Taxes: Total county taxes per capita: $268 (2006); County property taxes per capita: $257 (2006).
Education: Percent of population age 25 and over with: High school diploma (including GED) or higher: 83.2% (2007); Bachelor's degree or higher: 11.9% (2007); Master's degree or higher: 2.2% (2007).
Housing: Homeownership rate: 77.2% (2007); Median home value: $85,041 (2007); Median rent: $221 per month (2000); Median age of housing: 46 years (2000).
Health: Birth rate: 117.0 per 10,000 population (2007); Death rate: 120.8 per 10,000 population (2007); Age-adjusted cancer mortality rate: 236.2 (Unreliable) deaths per 100,000 population (2005); Number of physicians: 3.7 per 10,000 population (2005); Hospital beds: 0.0 per 10,000 population (2004); Hospital admissions: 0.0 per 10,000 population (2004).
Elections: 2004 Presidential election results: 64.3% Bush, 35.2% Kerry, 0.0% Nader, 0.5% Badnarik

Additional Information Contacts

Scott County Government . . . . (217) 742-3178

Winchester Chamber of Commerce. . . . . (217) 742-3219
http://www.wincoinet.com/chamber/cofc.htm

Scott County Communities

ALSEY (village). Covers a land area of 0.557 square miles and a water area of 0.010 square miles. Located at 39.56° N. Lat.; 90.43° W. Long. Elevation is 630 feet.
Population: 253 (1990); 246 (2000); 220 (2007); 218 (2012 projected); Race: 98.2% White, 0.0% Black, 0.0% Asian, 0.0% Hispanic of any race (2007); Density: 395.0 persons per square mile (2007); Average household size: 2.50 (2007); Median age: 39.1 (2007); Males per 100 females: 101.8 (2007); Marriage status: 15.1% never married, 60.3% now married, 16.6% widowed, 8.0% divorced (2000); Foreign born: 0.8% (2000); Ancestry (includes multiple ancestries): 16.7% United States or American, 16.3% Other groups, 12.2% English, 11.8% German, 6.5% Irish (2000).
Economy: Employment by occupation: 5.2% management, 8.7% professional, 13.9% services, 28.7% sales, 0.0% farming, 9.6% construction, 33.9% production (2000).
Income: Per capita income: $19,125 (2007); Median household income: $45,000 (2007); Average household income: $47,813 (2007); Percent of households with income of $100,000 or more: 3.4% (2007); Poverty rate: 8.1% (2000).
Education: Percent of population age 25 and over with: High school diploma (including GED) or higher: 71.6% (2007); Bachelor's degree or higher: 4.1% (2007); Master's degree or higher: 1.4% (2007).
Housing: Homeownership rate: 86.4% (2007); Median home value: $50,000 (2007); Median rent: $238 per month (2000); Median age of housing: 48 years (2000).
Transportation: Commute to work: 96.5% car, 0.0% public transportation, 3.5% walk, 0.0% work from home (2000); Travel time to work: 11.3% less than 15 minutes, 20.9% 15 to 30 minutes, 53.0% 30 to 45 minutes, 7.8% 45 to 60 minutes, 7.0% 60 minutes or more (2000)

BLUFFS (village). Covers a land area of 1.015 square miles and a water area of 0 square miles. Located at 39.74° N. Lat.; 90.53° W. Long. Elevation is 469 feet.
Population: 774 (1990); 748 (2000); 698 (2007); 673 (2012 projected); Race: 99.7% White, 0.0% Black, 0.3% Asian, 0.0% Hispanic of any race (2007); Density: 687.7 persons per square mile (2007); Average household size: 2.40 (2007); Median age: 37.2 (2007); Males per 100 females: 94.4 (2007); Marriage status: 23.7% never married, 57.0% now married, 9.9% widowed, 9.4% divorced (2000); Foreign born: 0.5% (2000); Ancestry (includes multiple ancestries): 32.4% German, 17.4% English, 10.2% United States or American, 8.8% Other groups, 7.1% Irish (2000).
Economy: Employment by occupation: 10.9% management, 17.9% professional, 11.7% services, 29.3% sales, 2.0% farming, 11.5% construction, 16.8% production (2000).
Income: Per capita income: $21,762 (2007); Median household income: $40,682 (2007); Average household income: $52,199 (2007); Percent of households with income of $100,000 or more: 11.3% (2007); Poverty rate: 11.8% (2000).
Education: Percent of population age 25 and over with: High school diploma (including GED) or higher: 82.6% (2007); Bachelor's degree or higher: 13.3% (2007); Master's degree or higher: 2.2% (2007).

School District(s)

Scott-Morgan CUSD 2 (PK-12)
2005-06 Enrollment: 266 . . . . (217) 754-3351
Housing: Homeownership rate: 78.4% (2007); Median home value: $69,091 (2007); Median rent: $115 per month (2000); Median age of housing: 60 years (2000).
Newspapers: Bluffs Times (Community news; Circulation 2,850); Meredosia Budget (Community news; Circulation 2,850)
Transportation: Commute to work: 97.5% car, 0.0% public transportation, 1.4% walk, 0.6% work from home (2000); Travel time to work: 33.3% less than 15 minutes, 32.5% 15 to 30 minutes, 25.1% 30 to 45 minutes, 2.3% 45 to 60 minutes, 6.8% 60 minutes or more (2000)

EXETER (village). Covers a land area of 0.690 square miles and a water area of 0 square miles. Located at 39.71° N. Lat.; 90.49° W. Long. Elevation is 554 feet.
Population: 59 (1990); 70 (2000); 69 (2007); 65 (2012 projected); Race: 97.1% White, 0.0% Black, 0.0% Asian, 0.0% Hispanic of any race (2007); Density: 100.1 persons per square mile (2007); Average household size: 2.46 (2007); Median age: 45.5 (2007); Males per 100 females: 86.5 (2007); Marriage status: 42.0% never married, 42.0% now married, 10.1% widowed, 5.8% divorced (2000); Foreign born: 0.0% (2000); Ancestry (includes multiple ancestries): 23.8% English, 13.8% Irish, 12.5% United States or American, 7.5% German, 3.8% Swiss (2000).
Economy: Employment by occupation: 22.0% management, 14.0% professional, 20.0% services, 6.0% sales, 4.0% farming, 8.0% construction, 26.0% production (2000).
Income: Per capita income: $33,913 (2007); Median household income: $60,000 (2007); Average household income: $83,571 (2007); Percent of households with income of $100,000 or more: 10.7% (2007); Poverty rate: 0.0% (2000).
Education: Percent of population age 25 and over with: High school diploma (including GED) or higher: 70.6% (2007); Bachelor's degree or higher: 13.7% (2007); Master's degree or higher: 13.7% (2007).
Housing: Homeownership rate: 92.9% (2007); Median home value: $103,125 (2007); Median rent: $275 per month (2000); Median age of housing: 60+ years (2000).
Transportation: Commute to work: 86.0% car, 0.0% public transportation, 14.0% walk, 0.0% work from home (2000); Travel time to work: 24.0% less than 15 minutes, 60.0% 15 to 30 minutes, 16.0% 30 to 45 minutes, 0.0% 45 to 60 minutes, 0.0% 60 minutes or more (2000)

GLASGOW (village). Covers a land area of 1.011 square miles and a water area of 0 square miles. Located at 39.55° N. Lat.; 90.48° W. Long. Elevation is 584 feet.
Population: 163 (1990); 170 (2000); 179 (2007); 179 (2012 projected); Race: 100.0% White, 0.0% Black, 0.0% Asian, 0.0% Hispanic of any race (2007); Density: 177.0 persons per square mile (2007); Average household size: 2.56 (2007); Median age: 43.0 (2007); Males per 100 females: 108.1 (2007); Marriage status: 7.7% never married, 82.1% now married, 3.4% widowed, 6.8% divorced (2000); Foreign born: 1.2% (2000); Ancestry (includes multiple ancestries): 13.5% United States or American, 11.0% English, 10.4% German, 9.2% Irish, 9.2% Other groups (2000).
Economy: Employment by occupation: 4.8% management, 4.8% professional, 31.7% services, 17.5% sales, 3.2% farming, 23.8% construction, 14.3% production (2000).
Income: Per capita income: $13,198 (2007); Median household income: $29,500 (2007); Average household income: $33,750 (2007); Percent of households with income of $100,000 or more: 2.9% (2007); Poverty rate: 20.2% (2000).
Education: Percent of population age 25 and over with: High school diploma (including GED) or higher: 87.2% (2007); Bachelor's degree or higher: 2.4% (2007); Master's degree or higher: 0.0% (2007).
Housing: Homeownership rate: 87.1% (2007); Median home value: $36,250 (2007); Median rent: $250 per month (2000); Median age of housing: 31 years (2000).
Transportation: Commute to work: 93.3% car, 0.0% public transportation, 3.3% walk, 3.3% work from home (2000); Travel time to work: 34.5% less than 15 minutes, 13.8% 15 to 30 minutes, 31.0% 30 to 45 minutes, 8.6% 45 to 60 minutes, 12.1% 60 minutes or more (2000)

MANCHESTER (village). Covers a land area of 1.036 square miles and a water area of 0 square miles. Located at 39.54° N. Lat.; 90.32° W. Long. Elevation is 686 feet.
Population: 347 (1990); 354 (2000); 313 (2007); 310 (2012 projected); Race: 100.0% White, 0.0% Black, 0.0% Asian, 0.0% Hispanic of any race (2007); Density: 302.2 persons per square mile (2007); Average household size: 2.54 (2007); Median age: 37.7 (2007); Males per 100 females: 101.9 (2007); Marriage status: 16.4% never married, 68.2% now married, 2.6% widowed, 12.8% divorced (2000); Foreign born: 0.0% (2000); Ancestry (includes multiple ancestries): 26.5% English, 20.4% German, 14.2% Irish, 7.0% United States or American, 6.7% Other groups (2000).
Economy: Employment by occupation: 7.0% management, 12.9% professional, 15.1% services, 30.1% sales, 1.1% farming, 9.1% construction, 24.7% production (2000).
Income: Per capita income: $16,502 (2007); Median household income: $36,875 (2007); Average household income: $41,992 (2007); Percent of households with income of $100,000 or more: 0.0% (2007); Poverty rate: 10.7% (2000).
Education: Percent of population age 25 and over with: High school diploma (including GED) or higher: 84.4% (2007); Bachelor's degree or higher: 10.8% (2007); Master's degree or higher: 0.0% (2007).
Housing: Homeownership rate: 86.2% (2007); Median home value: $72,143 (2007); Median rent: $256 per month (2000); Median age of housing: 40 years (2000).
Transportation: Commute to work: 89.4% car, 0.0% public transportation, 3.9% walk, 5.6% work from home (2000); Travel time to work: 13.6% less than 15 minutes, 49.7% 15 to 30 minutes, 27.2% 30 to 45 minutes, 4.1% 45 to 60 minutes, 5.3% 60 minutes or more (2000)

NAPLES (town). Covers a land area of 0.605 square miles and a water area of 0 square miles. Located at 39.75° N. Lat.; 90.60° W. Long. Elevation is 440 feet.
History: It was in Naples that the steamboat "Olitippa" was built on the Illinois River, before regular steamboat service began.
Population: 130 (1990); 134 (2000); 129 (2007); 124 (2012 projected); Race: 98.4% White, 0.0% Black, 0.0% Asian, 5.4% Hispanic of any race (2007); Density: 213.3 persons per square mile (2007); Average household size: 2.93 (2007); Median age: 35.3 (2007); Males per 100 females: 89.7 (2007); Marriage status: 27.6% never married, 44.8% now married, 9.2% widowed, 18.4% divorced (2000); Foreign born: 9.5% (2000); Ancestry (includes multiple ancestries): 24.1% German, 15.5% United States or American, 12.9% Other groups, 12.9% Irish, 12.9% Polish (2000).
Economy: Employment by occupation: 0.0% management, 0.0% professional, 30.9% services, 30.9% sales, 0.0% farming, 7.3% construction, 30.9% production (2000).
Income: Per capita income: $13,488 (2007); Median household income: $33,750 (2007); Average household income: $39,545 (2007); Percent of households with income of $100,000 or more: 6.8% (2007); Poverty rate: 29.3% (2000).
Education: Percent of population age 25 and over with: High school diploma (including GED) or higher: 66.7% (2007); Bachelor's degree or higher: 3.7% (2007); Master's degree or higher: 3.7% (2007).
Housing: Homeownership rate: 65.9% (2007); Median home value: $38,750 (2007); Median rent: $217 per month (2000); Median age of housing: 31 years (2000).
Transportation: Commute to work: 100.0% car, 0.0% public transportation, 0.0% walk, 0.0% work from home (2000); Travel time to

work: 21.8% less than 15 minutes, 9.1% 15 to 30 minutes, 61.8% 30 to 45 minutes, 0.0% 45 to 60 minutes, 7.3% 60 minutes or more (2000)

WINCHESTER (city). County seat. Covers a land area of 1.064 square miles and a water area of 0 square miles. Located at 39.63° N. Lat.; 90.45° W. Long. Elevation is 541 feet.
History: A grist mill was operating in Winchester in 1824. When the town was platted in 1830, so the story is told, the surveyor allowed a resident from Kentucky to name the townsite in exchange for a jug of whiskey. Stephen A. Douglas taught school and began his legal career here in 1833. Winchester developed as the seat of Scott County.
Population: 1,770 (1990); 1,650 (2000); 1,710 (2007); 1,680 (2012 projected); Race: 99.8% White, 0.0% Black, 0.0% Asian, 0.2% Hispanic of any race (2007); Density: 1,607.8 persons per square mile (2007); Average household size: 2.25 (2007); Median age: 42.9 (2007); Males per 100 females: 87.5 (2007); Marriage status: 20.0% never married, 56.7% now married, 12.7% widowed, 10.7% divorced (2000); Foreign born: 0.2% (2000); Ancestry (includes multiple ancestries): 19.6% German, 18.0% English, 13.9% United States or American, 11.1% Irish, 4.5% Other groups (2000).
Economy: Employment by occupation: 10.3% management, 16.5% professional, 18.2% services, 26.1% sales, 0.8% farming, 8.6% construction, 19.5% production (2000).
Income: Per capita income: $20,256 (2007); Median household income: $37,222 (2007); Average household income: $45,576 (2007); Percent of households with income of $100,000 or more: 6.2% (2007); Poverty rate: 10.4% (2000).
Education: Percent of population age 25 and over with: High school diploma (including GED) or higher: 82.0% (2007); Bachelor's degree or higher: 14.1% (2007); Master's degree or higher: 3.5% (2007).

School District(s)

Winchester CUSD 1 (PK-12)
2005-06 Enrollment: 722 . . . . (217) 742-3175

Housing: Homeownership rate: 71.8% (2007); Median home value: $87,755 (2007); Median rent: $199 per month (2000); Median age of housing: 55 years (2000).
Safety: Violent crime rate: 37.3 per 10,000 population; Property crime rate: 74.6 per 10,000 population (2006).
Newspapers: Scott County Times (Community news; Circulation 1,800)
Transportation: Commute to work: 90.9% car, 0.0% public transportation, 4.3% walk, 4.3% work from home (2000); Travel time to work: 35.9% less than 15 minutes, 33.6% 15 to 30 minutes, 20.1% 30 to 45 minutes, 3.0% 45 to 60 minutes, 7.5% 60 minutes or more (2000)

Additional Information Contacts

Winchester Chamber of Commerce. . . . . (217) 742-3219
http://www.wincoinet.com/chamber/cofc.htm

Shelby County

Located in central Illinois; drained by the South Fork of the Sangamon River, and by the Kaskaskia and Little Wabash Rivers. Covers a land area of 758.51 square miles, a water area of 9.54 square miles, and is located in the Central Time Zone. The county was founded in 1827. County seat is Shelbyville.

Weather Station: Moweaqua Elevation: 613 feet

	Jan	Feb	Mar	Apr	May	Jun	Jul	Aug	Sep	Oct	Nov	Dec
High	34	40	52	65	75	84	87	85	80	68	52	40
Low	17	21	31	41	52	61	64	62	54	43	33	23
Precip	1.7	1.9	2.9	3.9	4.2	4.2	4.0	3.3	3.0	2.8	3.6	2.2
Snow	na	na	0.9	0.2	tr	0.0	0.0	0.0	0.0	tr	0.5	na

High and Low temperatures in degrees Fahrenheit; Precipitation and Snow in inches

Weather Station: Windsor Elevation: 688 feet

	Jan	Feb	Mar	Apr	May	Jun	Jul	Aug	Sep	Oct	Nov	Dec
High	35	41	52	65	75	84	87	85	80	68	52	40
Low	19	23	33	43	53	62	66	63	56	45	35	25
Precip	2.0	1.9	3.3	3.9	4.0	3.9	4.0	3.1	3.0	3.0	3.7	3.0
Snow	7.9	4.3	3.0	0.3	0.0	0.0	0.0	0.0	0.0	tr	1.3	5.0

High and Low temperatures in degrees Fahrenheit; Precipitation and Snow in inches

Population: 22,261 (1990); 22,893 (2000); 22,211 (2007); 21,711 (2012 projected); Race: 98.9% White, 0.3% Black, 0.2% Asian, 0.5% Hispanic of any race (2007); Density: 29.3 persons per square mile (2007); Average household size: 2.49 (2007); Median age: 41.7 (2007); Males per 100 females: 98.5 (2007).
Religion: Five largest groups: 13.3% Christian Churches and Churches of Christ, 11.7% The United Methodist Church, 7.7% Lutheran Church—Missouri Synod, 7.6% Catholic Church, 3.9% Southern Baptist Convention (2000).
Economy: Unemployment rate: 5.3% (4/2008); Total civilian labor force: 11,277 (4/2008); Leading industries: 26.4% manufacturing; 16.7% health care and social assistance; 10.6% retail trade (2005); Farms: 1,228 totaling 419,814 acres (2002); Companies that employ 500 or more persons: 1 (2006); Companies that employ 100 to 499 persons: 4 (2006); Companies that employ less than 100 persons: 457 (2006); Black-owned businesses: n/a (2002); Hispanic-owned businesses: n/a (2002); Asian-owned businesses: n/a (2002); Women-owned businesses: 144 (2002); Retail sales per capita: $6,907 (2008). Single-family building permits issued: 125 (2007); Multi-family building permits issued: 10 (2007).
Income: Per capita income: $20,753 (2007); Median household income: $43,377 (2007); Average household income: $51,275 (2007); Percent of households with income of $100,000 or more: 8.5% (2007); Poverty rate: 10.5% (2005); Bankruptcy rate: 2.25% (2007).
Education: Percent of population age 25 and over with: High school diploma (including GED) or higher: 82.6% (2007); Bachelor's degree or higher: 11.4% (2007); Master's degree or higher: 3.9% (2007).
Housing: Homeownership rate: 81.2% (2007); Median home value: $99,171 (2007); Median rent: $301 per month (2000); Median age of housing: 39 years (2000).
Health: Birth rate: 123.6 per 10,000 population (2007); Death rate: 111.7 per 10,000 population (2007); Age-adjusted cancer mortality rate: 168.2 deaths per 100,000 population (2005); Number of physicians: 4.5 per 10,000 population (2005); Hospital beds: 20.3 per 10,000 population (2004); Hospital admissions: 801.9 per 10,000 population (2004).
Elections: 2004 Presidential election results: 63.8% Bush, 35.4% Kerry, 0.0% Nader, 0.6% Badnarik
National and State Parks: Eagle Creek State Park; Hidden Springs State Forest; Wolf Creek State Park

Additional Information Contacts

Shelby County Government. . . . . (217) 774-4421

Greater Shelbyville Area Chamber of Commerce . . . . (217) 774-2221
http://www.shelbyvillechamberofcommerce.com

Shelby County Communities

COWDEN (village). Covers a land area of 0.401 square miles and a water area of 0 square miles. Located at 39.24° N. Lat.; 88.86° W. Long. Elevation is 597 feet.
Population: 599 (1990); 612 (2000); 568 (2007); 565 (2012 projected); Race: 97.7% White, 0.9% Black, 0.0% Asian, 0.0% Hispanic of any race (2007); Density: 1,416.6 persons per square mile (2007); Average household size: 2.52 (2007); Median age: 32.8 (2007); Males per 100 females: 90.6 (2007); Marriage status: 20.8% never married, 59.4% now married, 8.3% widowed, 11.4% divorced (2000); Foreign born: 0.0% (2000); Ancestry (includes multiple ancestries): 20.9% German, 17.8% Irish, 17.0% United States or American, 13.3% Other groups, 5.5% English (2000).
Economy: Single-family building permits issued: 0 (2007); Multi-family building permits issued: 0 (2007); Employment by occupation: 5.0% management, 10.4% professional, 11.8% services, 21.3% sales, 0.0% farming, 10.9% construction, 40.7% production (2000).
Income: Per capita income: $15,911 (2007); Median household income: $31,324 (2007); Average household income: $40,167 (2007); Percent of households with income of $100,000 or more: 4.4% (2007); Poverty rate: 19.8% (2000).
Education: Percent of population age 25 and over with: High school diploma (including GED) or higher: 77.5% (2007); Bachelor's degree or higher: 6.5% (2007); Master's degree or higher: 0.9% (2007).

School District(s)

Cowden-Herrick CUSD 3a (PK-12)
2005-06 Enrollment: 479 . . . . (217) 783-2126

Housing: Homeownership rate: 77.8% (2007); Median home value: $49,464 (2007); Median rent: $294 per month (2000); Median age of housing: 35 years (2000).
Transportation: Commute to work: 99.5% car, 0.0% public transportation, 0.5% walk, 0.0% work from home (2000); Travel time to work: 18.1% less than 15 minutes, 40.3% 15 to 30 minutes, 21.8% 30 to 45 minutes, 4.6% 45 to 60 minutes, 15.3% 60 minutes or more (2000)

FINDLAY (village). Covers a land area of 0.919 square miles and a water area of 0 square miles. Located at 39.52° N. Lat.; 88.75° W. Long. Elevation is 679 feet.

Population: 787 (1990); 723 (2000); 715 (2007); 704 (2012 projected); Race: 97.9% White, 1.4% Black, 0.1% Asian, 1.1% Hispanic of any race (2007); Density: 777.9 persons per square mile (2007); Average household size: 2.28 (2007); Median age: 40.1 (2007); Males per 100 females: 90.2 (2007); Marriage status: 19.7% never married, 63.6% now married, 10.0% widowed, 6.6% divorced (2000); Foreign born: 0.0% (2000); Ancestry (includes multiple ancestries): 19.7% German, 10.1% United States or American, 9.9% Irish, 9.2% English, 5.0% Other groups (2000).
Economy: Single-family building permits issued: 3 (2007); Multi-family building permits issued: 0 (2007); Employment by occupation: 8.2% management, 20.7% professional, 16.4% services, 16.7% sales, 0.8% farming, 8.8% construction, 28.3% production (2000).
Income: Per capita income: $18,077 (2007); Median household income: $32,708 (2007); Average household income: $41,162 (2007); Percent of households with income of $100,000 or more: 5.7% (2007); Poverty rate: 12.6% (2000).
Education: Percent of population age 25 and over with: High school diploma (including GED) or higher: 82.9% (2007); Bachelor's degree or higher: 12.4% (2007); Master's degree or higher: 4.5% (2007).

School District(s)

Okaw Valley CUSD 302 (PK-12)
2005-06 Enrollment: 573 . . . . (217) 665-3232
Housing: Homeownership rate: 73.6% (2007); Median home value: $75,000 (2007); Median rent: $293 per month (2000); Median age of housing: 52 years (2000).
Safety: Violent crime rate: 0.0 per 10,000 population; Property crime rate: 29.2 per 10,000 population (2006).
Transportation: Commute to work: 91.4% car, 0.6% public transportation, 3.2% walk, 2.0% work from home (2000); Travel time to work: 24.0% less than 15 minutes, 35.1% 15 to 30 minutes, 22.2% 30 to 45 minutes, 13.7% 45 to 60 minutes, 5.0% 60 minutes or more (2000)

HERRICK (village). Covers a land area of 0.363 square miles and a water area of 0 square miles. Located at 39.21° N. Lat.; 88.98° W. Long. Elevation is 600 feet.

Population: 466 (1990); 524 (2000); 521 (2007); 509 (2012 projected); Race: 99.6% White, 0.0% Black, 0.0% Asian, 0.4% Hispanic of any race (2007); Density: 1,434.6 persons per square mile (2007); Average household size: 2.62 (2007); Median age: 33.7 (2007); Males per 100 females: 105.9 (2007); Marriage status: 20.5% never married, 59.8% now married, 11.6% widowed, 8.1% divorced (2000); Foreign born: 0.0% (2000); Ancestry (includes multiple ancestries): 20.9% German, 15.7% United States or American, 10.6% Other groups, 7.4% Irish, 5.0% English (2000).
Economy: Employment by occupation: 8.9% management, 8.3% professional, 17.3% services, 24.4% sales, 1.8% farming, 14.9% construction, 24.4% production (2000).
Income: Per capita income: $13,983 (2007); Median household income: $31,618 (2007); Average household income: $36,608 (2007); Percent of households with income of $100,000 or more: 3.5% (2007); Poverty rate: 22.0% (2000).
Education: Percent of population age 25 and over with: High school diploma (including GED) or higher: 53.7% (2007); Bachelor's degree or higher: 1.6% (2007); Master's degree or higher: 1.0% (2007).

School District(s)

Cowden-Herrick CUSD 3a (PK-12)
2005-06 Enrollment: 479 . . . . (217) 783-2126
Housing: Homeownership rate: 81.9% (2007); Median home value: $48,158 (2007); Median rent: $238 per month (2000); Median age of housing: 28 years (2000).
Transportation: Commute to work: 94.0% car, 2.4% public transportation, 3.0% walk, 0.0% work from home (2000); Travel time to work: 21.1% less than 15 minutes, 4.8% 15 to 30 minutes, 36.7% 30 to 45 minutes, 15.7% 45 to 60 minutes, 21.7% 60 minutes or more (2000)

LAKEWOOD (unincorporated postal area, zip code 62438). Covers a land area of 26.118 square miles and a water area of 0 square miles. Located at 39.31° N. Lat.; 88.87° W. Long. Elevation is 627 feet.
Population: 404 (2000); Race: 100.0% White, 0.0% Black, 0.0% Asian, 1.1% Hispanic of any race (2000); Density: 15.5 persons per square mile (2000); Age: 28.9% under 18, 12.8% over 64 (2000); Marriage status: 20.5% never married, 71.8% now married, 0.0% widowed, 7.8% divorced (2000); Foreign born: 0.0% (2000); Ancestry (includes multiple ancestries): 12.6% United States or American, 10.5% German, 8.5% English, 3.6% Irish, 2.9% European (2000).
Economy: Employment by occupation: 17.0% management, 4.8% professional, 6.1% services, 15.7% sales, 4.3% farming, 13.0% construction, 39.1% production (2000).
Income: Per capita income: $16,951 (2000); Median household income: $38,750 (2000); Poverty rate: 7.6% (2000).
Education: Percent of population age 25 and over with: High school diploma (including GED) or higher: 90.3% (2000); Bachelor's degree or higher: 5.9% (2000).
Housing: Homeownership rate: 82.5% (2000); Median home value: $46,000 (2000); Median rent: $320 per month (2000); Median age of housing: 45 years (2000).
Transportation: Commute to work: 93.0% car, 0.0% public transportation, 0.0% walk, 7.0% work from home (2000); Travel time to work: 16.6% less than 15 minutes, 49.3% 15 to 30 minutes, 13.3% 30 to 45 minutes, 10.0% 45 to 60 minutes, 10.9% 60 minutes or more (2000)

MODE (unincorporated postal area, zip code 62444). Covers a land area of 20.301 square miles and a water area of 0 square miles. Located at 39.43° N. Lat.; 88.80° W. Long. Elevation is 627 feet.
Population: 339 (2000); Race: 100.0% White, 0.0% Black, 0.0% Asian, 0.0% Hispanic of any race (2000); Density: 16.7 persons per square mile (2000); Age: 15.8% under 18, 16.1% over 64 (2000); Marriage status: 8.2% never married, 66.3% now married, 5.8% widowed, 19.6% divorced (2000); Foreign born: 0.0% (2000); Ancestry (includes multiple ancestries): 21.4% United States or American, 16.7% German, 12.0% Irish, 11.4% English, 5.6% Other groups (2000).
Economy: Employment by occupation: 9.6% management, 9.0% professional, 15.4% services, 9.6% sales, 10.3% farming, 9.0% construction, 37.2% production (2000).
Income: Per capita income: $18,500 (2000); Median household income: $32,083 (2000); Poverty rate: 16.1% (2000).
Education: Percent of population age 25 and over with: High school diploma (including GED) or higher: 61.8% (2000); Bachelor's degree or higher: 8.1% (2000).
Housing: Homeownership rate: 86.6% (2000); Median home value: $56,700 (2000); Median rent: $205 per month (2000); Median age of housing: 36 years (2000).
Transportation: Commute to work: 100.0% car, 0.0% public transportation, 0.0% walk, 0.0% work from home (2000); Travel time to work: 11.5% less than 15 minutes, 20.5% 15 to 30 minutes, 48.7% 30 to 45 minutes, 4.5% 45 to 60 minutes, 14.7% 60 minutes or more (2000)

MOWEAQUA (village). Covers a land area of 1.118 square miles and a water area of 0 square miles. Located at 39.62° N. Lat.; 89.01° W. Long. Elevation is 633 feet.
History: Incorporated 1877.
Population: 1,840 (1990); 1,923 (2000); 1,897 (2007); 1,893 (2012 projected); Race: 99.2% White, 0.0% Black, 0.3% Asian, 0.6% Hispanic of any race (2007); Density: 1,696.8 persons per square mile (2007); Average household size: 2.44 (2007); Median age: 42.7 (2007); Males per 100 females: 82.4 (2007); Marriage status: 14.8% never married, 65.7% now married, 11.2% widowed, 8.3% divorced (2000); Foreign born: 0.9% (2000); Ancestry (includes multiple ancestries): 25.7% German, 14.3% English, 13.6% Irish, 12.0% United States or American, 8.8% Other groups (2000).
Economy: Single-family building permits issued: 6 (2007); Multi-family building permits issued: 0 (2007); Employment by occupation: 11.2% management, 20.8% professional, 13.2% services, 21.4% sales, 0.8% farming, 8.4% construction, 24.2% production (2000).
Income: Per capita income: $21,146 (2007); Median household income: $44,615 (2007); Average household income: $50,883 (2007); Percent of households with income of $100,000 or more: 8.2% (2007); Poverty rate: 11.9% (2000).
Education: Percent of population age 25 and over with: High school diploma (including GED) or higher: 80.4% (2007); Bachelor's degree or higher: 15.0% (2007); Master's degree or higher: 7.0% (2007).

School District(s)

Central A & M Cud 21 (PK-12)
2005-06 Enrollment: 965 . . . . (217) 226-4042

Housing: Homeownership rate: 79.3% (2007); Median home value: $101,476 (2007); Median rent: $334 per month (2000); Median age of housing: 47 years (2000).
Safety: Violent crime rate: 5.4 per 10,000 population; Property crime rate: 0.0 per 10,000 population (2006).
Transportation: Commute to work: 94.8% car, 0.6% public transportation, 1.0% walk, 3.2% work from home (2000); Travel time to work: 27.4% less than 15 minutes, 31.6% 15 to 30 minutes, 33.2% 30 to 45 minutes, 5.4% 45 to 60 minutes, 2.4% 60 minutes or more (2000)

OCONEE (village). Covers a land area of 0.360 square miles and a water area of 0 square miles. Located at 39.28° N. Lat.; 89.10° W. Long. Elevation is 669 feet.
Population: 201 (1990); 202 (2000); 203 (2007); 200 (2012 projected); Race: 100.0% White, 0.0% Black, 0.0% Asian, 1.0% Hispanic of any race (2007); Density: 563.6 persons per square mile (2007); Average household size: 2.57 (2007); Median age: 35.2 (2007); Males per 100 females: 99.0 (2007); Marriage status: 12.9% never married, 79.1% now married, 6.7% widowed, 1.2% divorced (2000); Foreign born: 0.0% (2000); Ancestry (includes multiple ancestries): 25.6% United States or American, 12.8% German, 11.3% Irish, 6.7% Other groups, 4.1% French (except Basque) (2000).
Economy: Single-family building permits issued: 0 (2007); Multi-family building permits issued: 0 (2007); Employment by occupation: 8.0% management, 12.5% professional, 19.3% services, 20.5% sales, 2.3% farming, 18.2% construction, 19.3% production (2000).
Income: Per capita income: $17,438 (2007); Median household income: $41,250 (2007); Average household income: $44,810 (2007); Percent of households with income of $100,000 or more: 0.0% (2007); Poverty rate: 3.6% (2000).
Education: Percent of population age 25 and over with: High school diploma (including GED) or higher: 76.5% (2007); Bachelor's degree or higher: 2.9% (2007); Master's degree or higher: 1.5% (2007).
Housing: Homeownership rate: 88.6% (2007); Median home value: $48,182 (2007); Median rent: $300 per month (2000); Median age of housing: 51 years (2000).
Transportation: Commute to work: 100.0% car, 0.0% public transportation, 0.0% walk, 0.0% work from home (2000); Travel time to work: 37.6% less than 15 minutes, 24.7% 15 to 30 minutes, 25.9% 30 to 45 minutes, 5.9% 45 to 60 minutes, 5.9% 60 minutes or more (2000)

SHELBYVILLE (city). County seat. Covers a land area of 3.696 square miles and a water area of 0.185 square miles. Located at 39.40° N. Lat.; 88.80° W. Long. Elevation is 640 feet.
History: Incorporated 1839.
Population: 4,990 (1990); 4,971 (2000); 4,697 (2007); 4,488 (2012 projected); Race: 98.6% White, 0.2% Black, 0.3% Asian, 0.9% Hispanic of any race (2007); Density: 1,270.9 persons per square mile (2007); Average household size: 2.30 (2007); Median age: 42.3 (2007); Males per 100 females: 93.1 (2007); Marriage status: 21.1% never married, 53.6% now married, 14.3% widowed, 11.0% divorced (2000); Foreign born: 0.1% (2000); Ancestry (includes multiple ancestries): 21.3% German, 14.4% United States or American, 9.1% English, 8.7% Irish, 5.0% Other groups (2000).
Economy: Single-family building permits issued: 15 (2007); Multi-family building permits issued: 2 (2007); Employment by occupation: 9.7% management, 13.0% professional, 19.2% services, 21.8% sales, 0.7% farming, 10.4% construction, 25.2% production (2000).
Income: Per capita income: $20,432 (2007); Median household income: $37,278 (2007); Average household income: $46,142 (2007); Percent of households with income of $100,000 or more: 7.0% (2007); Poverty rate: 9.9% (2000).
Education: Percent of population age 25 and over with: High school diploma (including GED) or higher: 82.0% (2007); Bachelor's degree or higher: 13.0% (2007); Master's degree or higher: 5.5% (2007).

School District(s)

Clk Cls Cmbn Dglas Edgr Mltr Shlb (06-12)
2005-06 Enrollment: 103 . . . . (217) 348-0151
Eastern Ill Area of Spec Educ (PK-12)
2005-06 Enrollment: 577 . . . . (217) 348-7700
Shelbyville CUSD 4 (PK-12)
2005-06 Enrollment: 1,294 . . . . (217) 774-4626

Two-year College(s)

Sparks College (Private, For-profit)
Fall 2007 Enrollment: 25 . . . . (217) 774-5112
2007-08 Tuition: In-state $4,990; Out-of-state $4,990
Housing: Homeownership rate: 71.6% (2007); Median home value: $94,762 (2007); Median rent: $303 per month (2000); Median age of housing: 48 years (2000).
Hospitals: Shelby Memorial Hospital (54 beds)
Safety: Violent crime rate: 14.8 per 10,000 population; Property crime rate: 78.1 per 10,000 population (2006).
Newspapers: Shelbyville Daily Union (Local news; Circulation 12,000)
Transportation: Commute to work: 89.5% car, 0.0% public transportation, 3.4% walk, 6.3% work from home (2000); Travel time to work: 61.9% less than 15 minutes, 6.4% 15 to 30 minutes, 11.8% 30 to 45 minutes, 9.7% 45 to 60 minutes, 10.2% 60 minutes or more (2000)
Additional Information Contacts
Greater Shelbyville Area Chamber of Commerce . . . . (217) 774-2221
http://www.shelbyvillechamberofcommerce.com

SIGEL (town). Covers a land area of 0.273 square miles and a water area of 0.008 square miles. Located at 39.22° N. Lat.; 88.49° W. Long. Elevation is 636 feet.
Population: 364 (1990); 386 (2000); 379 (2007); 375 (2012 projected); Race: 99.5% White, 0.0% Black, 0.0% Asian, 1.8% Hispanic of any race (2007); Density: 1,386.0 persons per square mile (2007); Average household size: 2.67 (2007); Median age: 34.9 (2007); Males per 100 females: 103.8 (2007); Marriage status: 35.8% never married, 47.5% now married, 9.0% widowed, 7.7% divorced (2000); Foreign born: 0.0% (2000); Ancestry (includes multiple ancestries): 69.8% German, 12.4% Irish, 11.4% United States or American, 5.4% English, 1.3% Other groups (2000).
Economy: Single-family building permits issued: 0 (2007); Multi-family building permits issued: 0 (2007); Employment by occupation: 11.8% management, 9.6% professional, 14.6% services, 24.7% sales, 5.1% farming, 12.9% construction, 21.3% production (2000).
Income: Per capita income: $21,916 (2007); Median household income: $43,750 (2007); Average household income: $56,268 (2007); Percent of households with income of $100,000 or more: 14.1% (2007); Poverty rate: 3.9% (2000).
Education: Percent of population age 25 and over with: High school diploma (including GED) or higher: 85.9% (2007); Bachelor's degree or higher: 10.3% (2007); Master's degree or higher: 5.1% (2007).

School District(s)

Teutopolis CUSD 50 (PK-12)
2005-06 Enrollment: 1,377 . . . . (217) 857-3535
Housing: Homeownership rate: 76.8% (2007); Median home value: $108,854 (2007); Median rent: $314 per month (2000); Median age of housing: 42 years (2000).
Transportation: Commute to work: 92.4% car, 0.0% public transportation, 5.3% walk, 1.2% work from home (2000); Travel time to work: 37.3% less than 15 minutes, 44.4% 15 to 30 minutes, 10.7% 30 to 45 minutes, 3.6% 45 to 60 minutes, 4.1% 60 minutes or more (2000)

STEWARDSON (village). Covers a land area of 0.605 square miles and a water area of 0 square miles. Located at 39.26° N. Lat.; 88.62° W. Long. Elevation is 643 feet.
Population: 672 (1990); 747 (2000); 725 (2007); 722 (2012 projected); Race: 99.4% White, 0.0% Black, 0.3% Asian, 0.0% Hispanic of any race (2007); Density: 1,198.6 persons per square mile (2007); Average household size: 2.40 (2007); Median age: 38.4 (2007); Males per 100 females: 99.2 (2007); Marriage status: 25.2% never married, 55.8% now married, 10.8% widowed, 8.1% divorced (2000); Foreign born: 1.5% (2000); Ancestry (includes multiple ancestries): 28.7% German, 13.9% United States or American, 6.4% Irish, 5.7% Other groups, 3.2% English (2000).
Economy: Single-family building permits issued: 3 (2007); Multi-family building permits issued: 0 (2007); Employment by occupation: 10.3% management, 9.0% professional, 22.0% services, 21.2% sales, 1.0% farming, 8.5% construction, 27.9% production (2000).
Income: Per capita income: $18,514 (2007); Median household income: $37,857 (2007); Average household income: $44,445 (2007); Percent of households with income of $100,000 or more: 5.3% (2007); Poverty rate: 11.6% (2000).
Education: Percent of population age 25 and over with: High school diploma (including GED) or higher: 83.0% (2007); Bachelor's degree or higher: 8.2% (2007); Master's degree or higher: 3.5% (2007).

Housing: Homeownership rate: 76.8% (2007); Median home value: $81,600 (2007); Median rent: $279 per month (2000); Median age of housing: 38 years (2000).
Transportation: Commute to work: 86.1% car, 2.7% public transportation, 3.3% walk, 3.0% work from home (2000); Travel time to work: 23.9% less than 15 minutes, 48.9% 15 to 30 minutes, 17.7% 30 to 45 minutes, 6.5% 45 to 60 minutes, 3.1% 60 minutes or more (2000)

STRASBURG (village). Covers a land area of 0.528 square miles and a water area of 0 square miles. Located at 39.35° N. Lat.; 88.61° W. Long. Elevation is 636 feet.
Population: 478 (1990); 603 (2000); 598 (2007); 581 (2012 projected); Race: 100.0% White, 0.0% Black, 0.0% Asian, 0.2% Hispanic of any race (2007); Density: 1,132.4 persons per square mile (2007); Average household size: 2.90 (2007); Median age: 55.5 (2007); Males per 100 females: 82.9 (2007); Marriage status: 11.2% never married, 64.4% now married, 16.3% widowed, 8.1% divorced (2000); Foreign born: 0.0% (2000); Ancestry (includes multiple ancestries): 30.9% German, 16.2% United States or American, 7.8% Irish, 6.2% English, 2.1% Dutch (2000).
Economy: Single-family building permits issued: 0 (2007); Multi-family building permits issued: 0 (2007); Employment by occupation: 6.1% management, 16.8% professional, 12.3% services, 23.8% sales, 2.0% farming, 10.7% construction, 28.3% production (2000).
Income: Per capita income: $19,529 (2007); Median household income: $45,435 (2007); Average household income: $49,612 (2007); Percent of households with income of $100,000 or more: 4.9% (2007); Poverty rate: 6.0% (2000).
Education: Percent of population age 25 and over with: High school diploma (including GED) or higher: 84.6% (2007); Bachelor's degree or higher: 14.2% (2007); Master's degree or higher: 4.2% (2007).

School District(s)

Stewardson-Strasburg CUD 5a (PK-12)
2005-06 Enrollment: 460 . . . . (217) 682-3355

Housing: Homeownership rate: 92.2% (2007); Median home value: $92,143 (2007); Median rent: $313 per month (2000); Median age of housing: 45 years (2000).
Transportation: Commute to work: 98.0% car, 0.0% public transportation, 1.2% walk, 0.8% work from home (2000); Travel time to work: 24.0% less than 15 minutes, 27.7% 15 to 30 minutes, 33.1% 30 to 45 minutes, 6.2% 45 to 60 minutes, 9.1% 60 minutes or more (2000)

TOWER HILL (village). Covers a land area of 1.003 square miles and a water area of 0 square miles. Located at 39.38° N. Lat.; 88.96° W. Long. Elevation is 659 feet.
Population: 601 (1990); 609 (2000); 581 (2007); 567 (2012 projected); Race: 99.0% White, 0.0% Black, 0.0% Asian, 0.3% Hispanic of any race (2007); Density: 579.2 persons per square mile (2007); Average household size: 2.56 (2007); Median age: 36.3 (2007); Males per 100 females: 92.4 (2007); Marriage status: 24.8% never married, 51.5% now married, 8.1% widowed, 15.7% divorced (2000); Foreign born: 0.3% (2000); Ancestry (includes multiple ancestries): 16.4% German, 13.3% United States or American, 11.0% Irish, 6.2% English, 3.9% Dutch (2000).
Economy: Employment by occupation: 2.5% management, 8.3% professional, 20.2% services, 20.9% sales, 3.2% farming, 10.8% construction, 33.9% production (2000).
Income: Per capita income: $15,977 (2007); Median household income: $34,881 (2007); Average household income: $40,892 (2007); Percent of households with income of $100,000 or more: 3.1% (2007); Poverty rate: 16.7% (2000).
Education: Percent of population age 25 and over with: High school diploma (including GED) or higher: 78.3% (2007); Bachelor's degree or higher: 7.5% (2007); Master's degree or higher: 3.5% (2007).

School District(s)

Pana CUSD 8 (PK-12)
2005-06 Enrollment: 1,565 . . . . (217) 562-1500

Housing: Homeownership rate: 78.4% (2007); Median home value: $48,929 (2007); Median rent: $296 per month (2000); Median age of housing: 60+ years (2000).
Transportation: Commute to work: 92.8% car, 0.0% public transportation, 2.2% walk, 4.3% work from home (2000); Travel time to work: 26.0% less than 15 minutes, 38.5% 15 to 30 minutes, 9.4% 30 to 45 minutes, 12.1% 45 to 60 minutes, 14.0% 60 minutes or more (2000)

WINDSOR (city). Covers a land area of 0.618 square miles and a water area of 0 square miles. Located at 39.43° N. Lat.; 88.59° W. Long. Elevation is 702 feet.
History: Incorporated 1869.
Population: 1,143 (1990); 1,125 (2000); 1,044 (2007); 1,025 (2012 projected); Race: 99.1% White, 0.0% Black, 0.0% Asian, 0.4% Hispanic of any race (2007); Density: 1,689.2 persons per square mile (2007); Average household size: 2.41 (2007); Median age: 38.1 (2007); Males per 100 females: 89.8 (2007); Marriage status: 15.3% never married, 62.3% now married, 8.7% widowed, 13.7% divorced (2000); Foreign born: 0.6% (2000); Ancestry (includes multiple ancestries): 22.6% German, 14.3% United States or American, 10.3% Irish, 7.0% Other groups, 6.7% English (2000).
Economy: Single-family building permits issued: 0 (2007); Multi-family building permits issued: 0 (2007); Employment by occupation: 6.6% management, 9.2% professional, 15.9% services, 24.7% sales, 0.8% farming, 9.4% construction, 33.5% production (2000).
Income: Per capita income: $19,116 (2007); Median household income: $38,516 (2007); Average household income: $46,091 (2007); Percent of households with income of $100,000 or more: 6.7% (2007); Poverty rate: 8.4% (2000).
Education: Percent of population age 25 and over with: High school diploma (including GED) or higher: 79.8% (2007); Bachelor's degree or higher: 7.8% (2007); Master's degree or higher: 2.0% (2007).

School District(s)

Windsor CUSD 1 (PK-12)
2005-06 Enrollment: 436 . . . . (217) 459-2636

Housing: Homeownership rate: 80.6% (2007); Median home value: $73,710 (2007); Median rent: $320 per month (2000); Median age of housing: 40 years (2000).
Transportation: Commute to work: 95.1% car, 0.4% public transportation, 2.3% walk, 2.3% work from home (2000); Travel time to work: 24.2% less than 15 minutes, 45.7% 15 to 30 minutes, 22.5% 30 to 45 minutes, 1.7% 45 to 60 minutes, 5.9% 60 minutes or more (2000)

Saint Clair County

Located in southwestern Illinois; bounded on the northwest by the Mississippi River and the Missouri border; also drained by the Kaskaskia River and Silver Creek. Covers a land area of 663.81 square miles, a water area of 10.15 square miles, and is located in the Central Time Zone. The county was founded in 1790. County seat is Belleville.

Saint Clair County is part of the St. Louis, MO-IL Metropolitan Statistical Area. The entire metro area includes: Bond County, IL; Calhoun County, IL; Clinton County, IL; Jersey County, IL; Macoupin County, IL; Madison County, IL; Monroe County, IL; St. Clair County, IL; Crawford County, MO (pt.)*; Franklin County, MO; Jefferson County, MO; Lincoln County, MO; St. Charles County, MO; St. Louis County, MO; Warren County, MO; Washington County, MO; St. Louis city, MO

Weather Station: Belleville Scott AFB Elevation: 442 feet

	Jan	Feb	Mar	Apr	May	Jun	Jul	Aug	Sep	Oct	Nov	Dec
High	39	46	57	68	77	86	90	88	82	71	56	44
Low	22	26	35	45	54	62	66	63	56	45	36	27
Precip	2.0	2.2	3.6	4.0	4.2	3.8	3.3	3.3	3.1	2.9	3.8	3.0
Snow	6.5	3.2	2.1	0.8	0.0	0.0	0.0	0.0	0.0	0.0	0.9	2.6

High and Low temperatures in degrees Fahrenheit; Precipitation and Snow in inches

Population: 262,852 (1990); 256,082 (2000); 261,401 (2007); 264,551 (2012 projected); Race: 66.4% White, 29.5% Black, 1.1% Asian, 2.7% Hispanic of any race (2007); Density: 393.8 persons per square mile (2007); Average household size: 2.58 (2007); Median age: 35.8 (2007); Males per 100 females: 91.9 (2007).
Religion: Five largest groups: 20.6% Catholic Church, 6.6% Southern Baptist Convention, 4.3% United Church of Christ, 2.7% The United Methodist Church, 1.9% Lutheran Church—Missouri Synod (2000).
Economy: Unemployment rate: 5.8% (4/2008); Total civilian labor force: 127,610 (4/2008); Leading industries: 17.4% retail trade; 17.2% health care and social assistance; 13.4% accommodation & food services (2005); Farms: 811 totaling 269,820 acres (2002); Companies that employ 500 or more persons: 8 (2006); Companies that employ 100 to 499 persons: 115 (2006); Companies that employ less than 100 persons: 5,421 (2006); Black-owned businesses: 1,657 (2002); Hispanic-owned businesses: 145 (2002); Asian-owned businesses: 493 (2002); Women-owned businesses:

5,394 (2002); Retail sales per capita: $13,407 (2008). Single-family building permits issued: 1,094 (2007); Multi-family building permits issued: 150 (2007).
Income: Per capita income: $23,268 (2007); Median household income: $46,478 (2007); Average household income: $59,406 (2007); Percent of households with income of $100,000 or more: 14.5% (2007); Poverty rate: 13.0% (2005); Bankruptcy rate: 4.94% (2007).
Taxes: Total county taxes per capita: $105 (2006); County property taxes per capita: $100 (2006).
Education: Percent of population age 25 and over with: High school diploma (including GED) or higher: 81.4% (2007); Bachelor's degree or higher: 19.9% (2007); Master's degree or higher: 7.5% (2007).
Housing: Homeownership rate: 67.6% (2007); Median home value: $101,817 (2007); Median rent: $379 per month (2000); Median age of housing: 36 years (2000).
Health: Birth rate: 149.7 per 10,000 population (2007); Death rate: 97.2 per 10,000 population (2007); Age-adjusted cancer mortality rate: 211.1 deaths per 100,000 population (2005); Air Quality Index: 60.5% good, 38.1% moderate, 1.4% unhealthy for sensitive individuals, 0.0% unhealthy (percent of days in 2007); Number of physicians: 17.1 per 10,000 population (2005); Hospital beds: 37.5 per 10,000 population (2004); Hospital admissions: 1,378.5 per 10,000 population (2004).
Elections: 2004 Presidential election results: 44.4% Bush, 55.1% Kerry, 0.1% Nader, 0.4% Badnarik
National and State Parks: Cahokia Mounds State Park; Holten State Park
Additional Information Contacts
Saint Clair County Government . . . . (618) 277-6600
http://www.co.st-clair.il.us
Belleville Chamber of Commerce . . . . (618) 233-6810
http://www.bellevillechamber.org
Cahokia Chamber of Commerce . . . . (618) 332-4258
http://www.cahokiachamber.com
City of East Saint Louis . . . . (618) 482-6601
http://www.cesl.us
City of Fairview Heights . . . . (618) 489-2000
http://www.fairviewheightscity.com
City of Mascoutah . . . . (618) 566-2964
http://www.mascoutah.com
City of O'Fallon . . . . (618) 624-4500
http://www.ofallon.org
Fairview Heights Chamber of Commerce . . . . (618) 397-3127
http://www.fairviewheightschamber.org/
Greater East St. Louis Chamber of Commerce . . . . (618) 271-2855
Lebanon Chamber of Commerce. . . . . (618) 537-8420
http://www.lebanonil.org/chamber.htm
O'Fallon Chamber of Commerce . . . . (618) 632-3377
http://www.ofallonchamber.com
Shiloh Chamber of Commerce. . . . . (618) 632-1022
http://www.shilohchamber.org
Smithton Chamber of Commerce . . . . (618) 239-3366
http://www.smithtonchamber.org
Swansea Chamber of Commerce . . . . (618) 233-3938
http://www.swanseachamber.org
Village of Cahokia . . . . (618) 337-9500
http://www.norcom2000.com/users/cahokia
Village of Shiloh . . . . (618) 632-1022
http://www.shilohil.org
Village of Swansea . . . . (618) 234-0044
http://www.swanseail.org

Saint Clair County Communities

ALORTON (village). Covers a land area of 1.779 square miles and a water area of 0 square miles. Located at 38.58° N. Lat.; 90.11° W. Long. Elevation is 417 feet.
History: Incorporated 1944.
Population: 2,960 (1990); 2,749 (2000); 2,606 (2007); 2,508 (2012 projected); Race: 1.3% White, 96.9% Black, 0.0% Asian, 1.1% Hispanic of any race (2007); Density: 1,464.9 persons per square mile (2007); Average household size: 3.00 (2007); Median age: 26.9 (2007); Males per 100 females: 88.6 (2007); Marriage status: 45.7% never married, 35.8% now married, 7.7% widowed, 10.7% divorced (2000); Foreign born: 1.1% (2000); Ancestry (includes multiple ancestries): 76.3% Other groups, 1.1% African, 0.4% Belizean, 0.2% United States or American, 0.1% Jordanian (2000).
Economy: Employment by occupation: 2.3% management, 8.2% professional, 37.5% services, 26.7% sales, 0.0% farming, 6.8% construction, 18.6% production (2000).
Income: Per capita income: $10,495 (2007); Median household income: $20,135 (2007); Average household income: $31,227 (2007); Percent of households with income of $100,000 or more: 4.6% (2007); Poverty rate: 47.3% (2000).
Education: Percent of population age 25 and over with: High school diploma (including GED) or higher: 58.2% (2007); Bachelor's degree or higher: 2.9% (2007); Master's degree or higher: 0.4% (2007).

School District(s)

East St Louis SD 189 (PK-12)
2005-06 Enrollment: 9,873 . . . . (618) 646-3009
Housing: Homeownership rate: 44.9% (2007); Median home value: $46,500 (2007); Median rent: $274 per month (2000); Median age of housing: 35 years (2000).
Safety: Violent crime rate: 435.1 per 10,000 population; Property crime rate: 480.9 per 10,000 population (2006).
Transportation: Commute to work: 75.9% car, 15.6% public transportation, 4.4% walk, 4.1% work from home (2000); Travel time to work: 16.4% less than 15 minutes, 44.1% 15 to 30 minutes, 26.0% 30 to 45 minutes, 9.3% 45 to 60 minutes, 4.1% 60 minutes or more (2000)

BELLEVILLE (city). County seat. Covers a land area of 18.854 square miles and a water area of 0.128 square miles. Located at 38.52° N. Lat.; 89.99° W. Long. Elevation is 515 feet.
History: Named for the French translation of "beautiful city," by George Blair. Settlers came to Belleville early in the 1800's, and in 1814 the settlement became the seat of St. Clair County, succeeding Cahokia. The town was incorporated in 1819. The discovery of coal in 1828 brought many German immigrants to Belleville, which came to be known as Dutch Town.
Population: 43,445 (1990); 41,410 (2000); 39,461 (2007); 38,226 (2012 projected); Race: 77.2% White, 19.3% Black, 1.0% Asian, 1.9% Hispanic of any race (2007); Density: 2,093.0 persons per square mile (2007); Average household size: 2.30 (2007); Median age: 38.2 (2007); Males per 100 females: 89.2 (2007); Marriage status: 26.3% never married, 50.9% now married, 9.4% widowed, 13.5% divorced (2000); Foreign born: 1.9% (2000); Ancestry (includes multiple ancestries): 33.2% German, 19.7% Other groups, 11.5% Irish, 8.4% English, 6.0% United States or American (2000).
Economy: Unemployment rate: 5.8% (4/2008); Total civilian labor force: 22,162 (4/2008); Single-family building permits issued: 198 (2007); Multi-family building permits issued: 17 (2007); Employment by occupation: 9.8% management, 18.9% professional, 19.3% services, 29.7% sales, 0.0% farming, 8.3% construction, 14.0% production (2000).
Income: Per capita income: $22,738 (2007); Median household income: $40,810 (2007); Average household income: $51,182 (2007); Percent of households with income of $100,000 or more: 9.4% (2007); Poverty rate: 11.7% (2000).
Education: Percent of population age 25 and over with: High school diploma (including GED) or higher: 83.8% (2007); Bachelor's degree or higher: 18.0% (2007); Master's degree or higher: 6.1% (2007).

School District(s)

Belle Valley SD 119 (PK-08)
2005-06 Enrollment: 918 . . . . (618) 234-3445
Belleville Area Special Services (02-12)
2005-06 Enrollment: 91 . . . . (618) 355-4700
Belleville SD 118 (PK-08)
2005-06 Enrollment: 3,722 . . . . (618) 233-2830
Belleville Twp HSD 201 (09-12)
2005-06 Enrollment: 5,075 . . . . (618) 222-8241
East St Louis SD 189 (PK-12)
2005-06 Enrollment: 9,873 . . . . (618) 646-3009
Harmony Emge SD 175 (PK-08)
2005-06 Enrollment: 854 . . . . (618) 397-8444
Signal Hill SD 181 (PK-08)
2005-06 Enrollment: 439 . . . . (618) 397-0325
St Clair Roe (06-12)
2005-06 Enrollment: 25 . . . . (618) 397-8930
Whiteside SD 115 (PK-08)
2005-06 Enrollment: 1,320 . . . . (618) 239-0000

Two-year College(s)

Southwestern Illinois College (Public)
Fall 2007 Enrollment: 13,713. . . . . (618) 235-2700
2007-08 Tuition: In-state $4,928; Out-of-state $7,700

Vocational/Technical School(s)

Alvareitas College of Cosmetology (Private, For-profit)
Fall 2007 Enrollment: 20 . . . . (618) 257-9193
2007-08 Tuition: $9,700
Midwest Institute of Massage Therapy (Private, For-profit)
Fall 2007 Enrollment: n/a. . . . . (618) 239-6468
2007-08 Tuition: $5,156

Housing: Homeownership rate: 60.7% (2007); Median home value: $90,120 (2007); Median rent: $380 per month (2000); Median age of housing: 44 years (2000).
Hospitals: Memorial Hospital (313 beds); St. Elizabeth's Hospital (498 beds)
Safety: Violent crime rate: 52.3 per 10,000 population; Property crime rate: 488.5 per 10,000 population (2006).
Newspapers: Belleville News-Democrat (Local news; Circulation 53,365); Cahokia Journal (Local news; Circulation 13,000); Cahokia-Dupo Journal (Local news; Circulation 13,700); East St. Louis Journal (Local news; Circulation 20,990); The Messenger (Regional news; Circulation 14,000); O'Fallon Journal (Community news; Circulation 7,912); St. Louis Post-Dispatch - Belleville Bureau (Local news; Circulation 0)
Transportation: Commute to work: 92.4% car, 2.8% public transportation, 2.1% walk, 2.2% work from home (2000); Travel time to work: 34.7% less than 15 minutes, 32.5% 15 to 30 minutes, 18.4% 30 to 45 minutes, 9.2% 45 to 60 minutes, 5.3% 60 minutes or more (2000)
Airports: Scott AFB/Midamerica (primary service)

Additional Information Contacts

Belleville Chamber of Commerce . . . . (618) 233-6810
http://www.bellevillechamber.org

BROOKLYN (village). Aka Lovejoy. Covers a land area of 0.843 square miles and a water area of 0 square miles. Located at 38.65° N. Lat.; 90.16° W. Long. Elevation is 413 feet.
History: When it was incorporated in 1874 Brooklyn was called Lovejoy, in honor of Abolitionist editor Elijah P. Lovejoy.
Population: 1,144 (1990); 676 (2000); 467 (2007); 478 (2012 projected); Race: 0.4% White, 98.5% Black, 0.0% Asian, 0.6% Hispanic of any race (2007); Density: 554.0 persons per square mile (2007); Average household size: 2.46 (2007); Median age: 30.7 (2007); Males per 100 females: 72.3 (2007); Marriage status: 43.2% never married, 18.4% now married, 14.8% widowed, 23.7% divorced (2000); Foreign born: 0.0% (2000); Ancestry (includes multiple ancestries): 59.3% Other groups, 4.6% English, 4.6% Lithuanian (2000).
Economy: Employment by occupation: 7.0% management, 37.3% professional, 19.6% services, 20.9% sales, 0.0% farming, 0.0% construction, 15.2% production (2000).
Income: Per capita income: $11,317 (2007); Median household income: $18,200 (2007); Average household income: $27,816 (2007); Percent of households with income of $100,000 or more: 1.1% (2007); Poverty rate: 48.5% (2000).
Education: Percent of population age 25 and over with: High school diploma (including GED) or higher: 55.8% (2007); Bachelor's degree or higher: 3.6% (2007); Master's degree or higher: 0.4% (2007).

School District(s)

Brooklyn UD 188 (KG-12)
2005-06 Enrollment: 202 . . . . (618) 271-1028

Housing: Homeownership rate: 52.1% (2007); Median home value: $56,429 (2007); Median rent: $193 per month (2000); Median age of housing: 29 years (2000).
Safety: Violent crime rate: 264.4 per 10,000 population; Property crime rate: 326.6 per 10,000 population (2006).
Transportation: Commute to work: 50.3% car, 23.4% public transportation, 21.8% walk, 4.4% work from home (2000); Travel time to work: 38.4% less than 15 minutes, 12.6% 15 to 30 minutes, 19.2% 30 to 45 minutes, 25.8% 45 to 60 minutes, 4.0% 60 minutes or more (2000)

CAHOKIA (village). Aka Maplewood Park. Covers a land area of 9.609 square miles and a water area of 0.367 square miles. Located at 38.56° N. Lat.; 90.17° W. Long. Elevation is 407 feet.
History: Named for an Indian tribe of the Illinois Confederacy. Cahokia began with a mission established in 1699 by Jean Francois Buisson de St. Cosme of the Seminary of Foreign Missions, and a trading post developed around the mission. In 1809 county lines were redrawn so that Cahokia served as the seat of a territory that later was divided into 80 northern counties.
Population: 17,550 (1990); 16,391 (2000); 15,556 (2007); 14,767 (2012 projected); Race: 45.0% White, 51.6% Black, 0.3% Asian, 2.6% Hispanic of any race (2007); Density: 1,618.9 persons per square mile (2007); Average household size: 2.86 (2007); Median age: 31.1 (2007); Males per 100 females: 88.7 (2007); Marriage status: 32.0% never married, 48.3% now married, 8.3% widowed, 11.4% divorced (2000); Foreign born: 0.7% (2000); Ancestry (includes multiple ancestries): 35.7% Other groups, 14.0% German, 9.0% Irish, 7.8% United States or American, 5.2% English (2000).
Economy: Single-family building permits issued: 5 (2007); Multi-family building permits issued: 0 (2007); Employment by occupation: 6.9% management, 10.1% professional, 21.2% services, 28.2% sales, 0.2% farming, 10.6% construction, 23.0% production (2000).
Income: Per capita income: $14,311 (2007); Median household income: $32,845 (2007); Average household income: $40,438 (2007); Percent of households with income of $100,000 or more: 3.8% (2007); Poverty rate: 24.9% (2000).
Education: Percent of population age 25 and over with: High school diploma (including GED) or higher: 71.0% (2007); Bachelor's degree or higher: 5.7% (2007); Master's degree or higher: 2.1% (2007).

School District(s)

Cahokia CUSD 187 (PK-12)
2005-06 Enrollment: 5,046 . . . . (618) 332-3700

Housing: Homeownership rate: 67.1% (2007); Median home value: $48,850 (2007); Median rent: $419 per month (2000); Median age of housing: 40 years (2000).
Safety: Violent crime rate: 30.1 per 10,000 population; Property crime rate: 399.8 per 10,000 population (2006).
Transportation: Commute to work: 93.0% car, 2.3% public transportation, 1.5% walk, 1.8% work from home (2000); Travel time to work: 25.7% less than 15 minutes, 41.4% 15 to 30 minutes, 21.5% 30 to 45 minutes, 4.6% 45 to 60 minutes, 6.8% 60 minutes or more (2000)
Airports: St Louis Downtown (general aviation)

Additional Information Contacts

Cahokia Chamber of Commerce . . . . (618) 332-4258
http://www.cahokiachamber.com
Village of Cahokia . . . . (618) 337-9500
http://www.norcom2000.com/users/cahokia

CASEYVILLE (village). Covers a land area of 6.211 square miles and a water area of 0 square miles. Located at 38.63° N. Lat.; 90.03° W. Long. Elevation is 453 feet.
Population: 5,001 (1990); 4,310 (2000); 4,337 (2007); 4,390 (2012 projected); Race: 87.3% White, 9.1% Black, 0.2% Asian, 4.7% Hispanic of any race (2007); Density: 698.3 persons per square mile (2007); Average household size: 2.47 (2007); Median age: 40.0 (2007); Males per 100 females: 92.7 (2007); Marriage status: 24.1% never married, 53.2% now married, 10.8% widowed, 11.9% divorced (2000); Foreign born: 1.4% (2000); Ancestry (includes multiple ancestries): 25.4% German, 15.4% Other groups, 14.5% Irish, 7.0% English, 5.8% United States or American (2000).
Economy: Single-family building permits issued: 0 (2007); Multi-family building permits issued: 0 (2007); Employment by occupation: 4.8% management, 11.8% professional, 19.8% services, 31.1% sales, 1.2% farming, 15.7% construction, 15.6% production (2000).
Income: Per capita income: $17,705 (2007); Median household income: $35,599 (2007); Average household income: $42,981 (2007); Percent of households with income of $100,000 or more: 4.2% (2007); Poverty rate: 9.8% (2000).
Education: Percent of population age 25 and over with: High school diploma (including GED) or higher: 71.2% (2007); Bachelor's degree or higher: 8.1% (2007); Master's degree or higher: 2.7% (2007).

School District(s)

Collinsville CUSD 10 (PK-12)
2005-06 Enrollment: 6,342 . . . . (618) 346-6350

Housing: Homeownership rate: 79.1% (2007); Median home value: $80,549 (2007); Median rent: $384 per month (2000); Median age of housing: 42 years (2000).
Safety: Violent crime rate: 32.6 per 10,000 population; Property crime rate: 218.8 per 10,000 population (2006).
Transportation: Commute to work: 96.2% car, 0.0% public transportation, 0.8% walk, 1.6% work from home (2000); Travel time to work: 19.0% less

than 15 minutes, 53.7% 15 to 30 minutes, 18.4% 30 to 45 minutes, 6.2% 45 to 60 minutes, 2.8% 60 minutes or more (2000)

CENTREVILLE (city). Covers a land area of 4.333 square miles and a water area of 0 square miles. Located at 38.58° N. Lat.; 90.10° W. Long. Elevation is 413 feet.
Population: 7,413 (1990); 5,951 (2000); 5,747 (2007); 5,608 (2012 projected); Race: 3.3% White, 95.2% Black, 0.0% Asian, 0.7% Hispanic of any race (2007); Density: 1,326.3 persons per square mile (2007); Average household size: 2.70 (2007); Median age: 30.3 (2007); Males per 100 females: 86.5 (2007); Marriage status: 41.1% never married, 35.7% now married, 12.5% widowed, 10.8% divorced (2000); Foreign born: 0.4% (2000); Ancestry (includes multiple ancestries): 77.0% Other groups, 1.8% African, 0.8% United States or American, 0.7% Irish, 0.5% Greek (2000).
Economy: Single-family building permits issued: 2 (2007); Multi-family building permits issued: 0 (2007); Employment by occupation: 4.3% management, 12.5% professional, 30.0% services, 26.3% sales, 0.0% farming, 6.0% construction, 20.9% production (2000).
Income: Per capita income: $13,937 (2007); Median household income: $28,214 (2007); Average household income: $37,693 (2007); Percent of households with income of $100,000 or more: 5.0% (2007); Poverty rate: 34.4% (2000).
Education: Percent of population age 25 and over with: High school diploma (including GED) or higher: 67.3% (2007); Bachelor's degree or higher: 9.7% (2007); Master's degree or higher: 4.0% (2007).

School District(s)

Cahokia CUSD 187 (PK-12)
2005-06 Enrollment: 5,046 . . . . (618) 332-3700
Housing: Homeownership rate: 59.1% (2007); Median home value: $58,387 (2007); Median rent: $246 per month (2000); Median age of housing: 38 years (2000).
Hospitals: Touchette Regional Hospital (114 beds)
Safety: Violent crime rate: 334.1 per 10,000 population; Property crime rate: 306.7 per 10,000 population (2006).
Transportation: Commute to work: 85.1% car, 11.5% public transportation, 0.5% walk, 2.7% work from home (2000); Travel time to work: 23.0% less than 15 minutes, 44.6% 15 to 30 minutes, 15.9% 30 to 45 minutes, 7.4% 45 to 60 minutes, 9.0% 60 minutes or more (2000)

DUPO (village). Aka Sugar Loaf Heights. Covers a land area of 4.426 square miles and a water area of 0 square miles. Located at 38.51° N. Lat.; 90.20° W. Long. Elevation is 417 feet.
History: The name of Dupo is a shortened form of Prairie du Pont, which is a French term meaning "meadow of the bridge." Oil was discovered near Dupo in 1928 and a brief period of fast growth ensued.
Population: 3,634 (1990); 3,933 (2000); 4,049 (2007); 4,136 (2012 projected); Race: 97.1% White, 1.0% Black, 0.3% Asian, 0.7% Hispanic of any race (2007); Density: 914.8 persons per square mile (2007); Average household size: 2.46 (2007); Median age: 35.7 (2007); Males per 100 females: 95.3 (2007); Marriage status: 21.3% never married, 60.2% now married, 8.1% widowed, 10.3% divorced (2000); Foreign born: 0.9% (2000); Ancestry (includes multiple ancestries): 25.4% German, 11.6% Other groups, 11.5% Irish, 10.6% United States or American, 9.0% French (except Basque) (2000).
Economy: Single-family building permits issued: 23 (2007); Multi-family building permits issued: 9 (2007); Employment by occupation: 8.1% management, 14.3% professional, 17.3% services, 33.7% sales, 0.0% farming, 8.9% construction, 17.8% production (2000).
Income: Per capita income: $23,971 (2007); Median household income: $52,511 (2007); Average household income: $58,931 (2007); Percent of households with income of $100,000 or more: 11.0% (2007); Poverty rate: 4.3% (2000).
Education: Percent of population age 25 and over with: High school diploma (including GED) or higher: 75.3% (2007); Bachelor's degree or higher: 10.6% (2007); Master's degree or higher: 3.6% (2007).

School District(s)

Dupo CUSD 196 (PK-12)
2005-06 Enrollment: 1,294 . . . . (618) 286-3812
Housing: Homeownership rate: 72.7% (2007); Median home value: $89,828 (2007); Median rent: $374 per month (2000); Median age of housing: 43 years (2000).
Safety: Violent crime rate: 15.2 per 10,000 population; Property crime rate: 197.1 per 10,000 population (2006).
Transportation: Commute to work: 98.0% car, 0.0% public transportation, 0.0% walk, 2.0% work from home (2000); Travel time to work: 18.9% less than 15 minutes, 42.1% 15 to 30 minutes, 30.4% 30 to 45 minutes, 6.3% 45 to 60 minutes, 2.3% 60 minutes or more (2000)

EAST CARONDELET (village). Covers a land area of 1.251 square miles and a water area of 0.412 square miles. Located at 38.54° N. Lat.; 90.23° W. Long. Elevation is 410 feet.
History: Damaged in floods of 1993.
Population: 644 (1990); 267 (2000); 238 (2007); 242 (2012 projected); Race: 94.5% White, 1.3% Black, 0.0% Asian, 0.0% Hispanic of any race (2007); Density: 190.3 persons per square mile (2007); Average household size: 2.77 (2007); Median age: 35.3 (2007); Males per 100 females: 91.9 (2007); Marriage status: 32.5% never married, 54.6% now married, 2.5% widowed, 10.4% divorced (2000); Foreign born: 0.0% (2000); Ancestry (includes multiple ancestries): 18.8% German, 15.0% Irish, 10.1% United States or American, 7.2% Other groups, 6.3% Italian (2000).
Economy: Single-family building permits issued: 0 (2007); Multi-family building permits issued: 0 (2007); Employment by occupation: 6.9% management, 2.3% professional, 17.2% services, 19.5% sales, 0.0% farming, 19.5% construction, 34.5% production (2000).
Income: Per capita income: $18,718 (2007); Median household income: $45,000 (2007); Average household income: $51,802 (2007); Percent of households with income of $100,000 or more: 10.5% (2007); Poverty rate: 2.9% (2000).
Education: Percent of population age 25 and over with: High school diploma (including GED) or higher: 67.3% (2007); Bachelor's degree or higher: 0.0% (2007); Master's degree or higher: 0.0% (2007).
Housing: Homeownership rate: 76.7% (2007); Median home value: $72,727 (2007); Median rent: $313 per month (2000); Median age of housing: 41 years (2000).
Safety: Violent crime rate: 243.1 per 10,000 population; Property crime rate: 208.3 per 10,000 population (2006).
Transportation: Commute to work: 95.5% car, 2.2% public transportation, 2.2% walk, 0.0% work from home (2000); Travel time to work: 22.5% less than 15 minutes, 40.4% 15 to 30 minutes, 32.6% 30 to 45 minutes, 2.2% 45 to 60 minutes, 2.2% 60 minutes or more (2000)

EAST SAINT LOUIS (city). Covers a land area of 14.063 square miles and a water area of 0.367 square miles. Located at 38.61° N. Lat.; 90.12° W. Long. Elevation is 417 feet.
History: Settlement across the Mississippi River from St. Louis, Missouri, was achieved by Captain James Piggott who established ferry service here in 1795. A village called Illinoistown was platted near the ferry dock in 1816. When Illinoistown was incorporated in 1859, a town called East St. Louis had been established nearby. In 1861 the charter of Illinoistown was extended to include the new town, and the name was changed to East St. Louis. Near the end of the 19th century, East St. Louis changed from a river town to an industrial center.
Population: 40,944 (1990); 31,542 (2000); 29,388 (2007); 27,818 (2012 projected); Race: 1.2% White, 97.3% Black, 0.1% Asian, 1.0% Hispanic of any race (2007); Density: 2,089.8 persons per square mile (2007); Average household size: 2.73 (2007); Median age: 30.8 (2007); Males per 100 females: 82.9 (2007); Marriage status: 45.3% never married, 30.7% now married, 10.9% widowed, 13.2% divorced (2000); Foreign born: 0.3% (2000); Ancestry (includes multiple ancestries): 77.5% Other groups, 1.1% African, 0.6% United States or American, 0.4% German, 0.4% Irish (2000).
Economy: Unemployment rate: 9.5% (4/2008); Total civilian labor force: 10,211 (4/2008); Single-family building permits issued: 6 (2007); Multi-family building permits issued: 0 (2007); Employment by occupation: 5.5% management, 16.4% professional, 30.8% services, 23.6% sales, 0.1% farming, 5.2% construction, 18.4% production (2000).
Income: Per capita income: $12,713 (2007); Median household income: $23,695 (2007); Average household income: $34,474 (2007); Percent of households with income of $100,000 or more: 5.1% (2007); Poverty rate: 35.1% (2000).
Education: Percent of population age 25 and over with: High school diploma (including GED) or higher: 66.5% (2007); Bachelor's degree or higher: 8.9% (2007); Master's degree or higher: 2.7% (2007).

School District(s)

Dept of Corrections Sch Dist 428 (08-12)
2005-06 Enrollment: 2,271 . . . . (217) 522-2666
East St Louis SD 189 (PK-12)
2005-06 Enrollment: 9,873 . . . . (618) 646-3009

Vocational/Technical School(s)

Vees School of Beauty Culture (Private, For-profit)
Fall 2007 Enrollment: 36 . . . . (618) 274-1751
2007-08 Tuition: In-state $8,350; Out-of-state $8,350

Housing: Homeownership rate: 52.6% (2007); Median home value: $55,448 (2007); Median rent: $265 per month (2000); Median age of housing: 47 years (2000).

Hospitals: Kenneth Hall Regional Hospital (169 beds)

Safety: Violent crime rate: 752.9 per 10,000 population; Property crime rate: 735.9 per 10,000 population (2006).

Newspapers: East Saint Louis Monitor (Local news; Circulation 5,400)

Transportation: Commute to work: 79.6% car, 14.6% public transportation, 2.4% walk, 2.6% work from home (2000); Travel time to work: 23.0% less than 15 minutes, 40.0% 15 to 30 minutes, 21.4% 30 to 45 minutes, 6.6% 45 to 60 minutes, 9.0% 60 minutes or more (2000)

Additional Information Contacts

City of East Saint Louis . . . . (618) 482-6601
http://www.cesl.us

Greater East St. Louis Chamber of Commerce . . . . (618) 271-2855

FAIRMONT CITY (village). Covers a land area of 2.405 square miles and a water area of 0 square miles. Located at 38.65° N. Lat.; 90.10° W. Long. Elevation is 420 feet.

History: Fairmont City came into being in 1910 when the Pennsylvania Railroad built a roundhouse here. First called Willow Town, the name was changed to Fairmont City when it was incorporated in 1914.

Population: 2,140 (1990); 2,436 (2000); 2,282 (2007); 2,175 (2012 projected); Race: 59.5% White, 1.2% Black, 0.0% Asian, 67.8% Hispanic of any race (2007); Density: 949.0 persons per square mile (2007); Average household size: 2.81 (2007); Median age: 32.3 (2007); Males per 100 females: 114.1 (2007); Marriage status: 25.7% never married, 56.3% now married, 9.0% widowed, 9.0% divorced (2000); Foreign born: 34.9% (2000); Ancestry (includes multiple ancestries): 55.3% Other groups, 9.6% German, 5.6% Polish, 5.5% Irish, 3.1% United States or American (2000).

Economy: Employment by occupation: 7.5% management, 5.9% professional, 21.0% services, 21.3% sales, 5.3% farming, 15.5% construction, 23.4% production (2000).

Income: Per capita income: $13,834 (2007); Median household income: $31,205 (2007); Average household income: $38,879 (2007); Percent of households with income of $100,000 or more: 3.2% (2007); Poverty rate: 18.4% (2000).

Education: Percent of population age 25 and over with: High school diploma (including GED) or higher: 46.8% (2007); Bachelor's degree or higher: 5.1% (2007); Master's degree or higher: 1.5% (2007).

Housing: Homeownership rate: 73.5% (2007); Median home value: $55,440 (2007); Median rent: $295 per month (2000); Median age of housing: 41 years (2000).

Safety: Violent crime rate: 17.2 per 10,000 population; Property crime rate: 249.6 per 10,000 population (2006).

Transportation: Commute to work: 93.8% car, 0.8% public transportation, 2.8% walk, 0.0% work from home (2000); Travel time to work: 27.8% less than 15 minutes, 36.2% 15 to 30 minutes, 23.1% 30 to 45 minutes, 4.6% 45 to 60 minutes, 8.4% 60 minutes or more (2000)

FAIRVIEW HEIGHTS (city). Aka Fairview. Covers a land area of 11.148 square miles and a water area of 0.065 square miles. Located at 38.59° N. Lat.; 89.99° W. Long. Elevation is 584 feet.

History: Named to promote the town as a good place to live. Also known as Fairview. Formerly called Lincoln Heights.

Population: 15,019 (1990); 15,034 (2000); 16,558 (2007); 17,468 (2012 projected); Race: 72.9% White, 21.6% Black, 2.6% Asian, 2.3% Hispanic of any race (2007); Density: 1,485.3 persons per square mile (2007); Average household size: 2.41 (2007); Median age: 40.5 (2007); Males per 100 females: 92.6 (2007); Marriage status: 22.6% never married, 59.4% now married, 7.1% widowed, 11.0% divorced (2000); Foreign born: 3.3% (2000); Ancestry (includes multiple ancestries): 28.7% German, 21.8% Other groups, 14.3% Irish, 9.7% English, 5.3% French (except Basque) (2000).

Economy: Single-family building permits issued: 107 (2007); Multi-family building permits issued: 23 (2007); Employment by occupation: 13.2% management, 23.3% professional, 13.7% services, 27.9% sales, 0.0% farming, 8.4% construction, 13.6% production (2000).

Income: Per capita income: $28,046 (2007); Median household income: $56,877 (2007); Average household income: $66,985 (2007); Percent of households with income of $100,000 or more: 17.7% (2007); Poverty rate: 5.9% (2000).

Education: Percent of population age 25 and over with: High school diploma (including GED) or higher: 84.6% (2007); Bachelor's degree or higher: 26.5% (2007); Master's degree or higher: 10.2% (2007).

School District(s)

Grant CCSD 110 (PK-08)
2005-06 Enrollment: 775 . . . . (618) 398-5577

Pontiac-W Holliday SD 105 (PK-08)
2005-06 Enrollment: 703 . . . . (618) 233-2320

Vocational/Technical School(s)

Regency Beauty Institute (Private, For-profit)
Fall 2007 Enrollment: 61 . . . . (800) 787-6456
2007-08 Tuition: $14,200

Housing: Homeownership rate: 76.8% (2007); Median home value: $112,705 (2007); Median rent: $503 per month (2000); Median age of housing: 33 years (2000).

Safety: Violent crime rate: 36.4 per 10,000 population; Property crime rate: 385.5 per 10,000 population (2006).

Transportation: Commute to work: 94.0% car, 1.0% public transportation, 1.6% walk, 2.8% work from home (2000); Travel time to work: 23.5% less than 15 minutes, 38.5% 15 to 30 minutes, 25.4% 30 to 45 minutes, 8.4% 45 to 60 minutes, 4.3% 60 minutes or more (2000)

Additional Information Contacts

City of Fairview Heights . . . . (618) 489-2000
http://www.fairviewheightscity.com

Fairview Heights Chamber of Commerce . . . . (618) 397-3127
http://www.fairviewheightschamber.org/

FAYETTEVILLE (village). Covers a land area of 0.255 square miles and a water area of 0 square miles. Located at 38.37° N. Lat.; 89.79° W. Long. Elevation is 413 feet.

Population: 402 (1990); 384 (2000); 427 (2007); 446 (2012 projected); Race: 99.1% White, 0.0% Black, 0.5% Asian, 1.4% Hispanic of any race (2007); Density: 1,672.1 persons per square mile (2007); Average household size: 2.69 (2007); Median age: 36.6 (2007); Males per 100 females: 110.3 (2007); Marriage status: 25.2% never married, 59.4% now married, 3.5% widowed, 11.8% divorced (2000); Foreign born: 1.8% (2000); Ancestry (includes multiple ancestries): 53.9% German, 11.7% Other groups, 9.6% Polish, 9.6% Irish, 8.9% English (2000).

Economy: Single-family building permits issued: 0 (2007); Multi-family building permits issued: 0 (2007); Employment by occupation: 1.8% management, 9.6% professional, 13.8% services, 25.1% sales, 1.2% farming, 17.4% construction, 31.1% production (2000).

Income: Per capita income: $20,474 (2007); Median household income: $46,458 (2007); Average household income: $54,984 (2007); Percent of households with income of $100,000 or more: 12.6% (2007); Poverty rate: 21.0% (2000).

Education: Percent of population age 25 and over with: High school diploma (including GED) or higher: 84.5% (2007); Bachelor's degree or higher: 3.5% (2007); Master's degree or higher: 0.7% (2007).

Housing: Homeownership rate: 77.4% (2007); Median home value: $68,438 (2007); Median rent: $392 per month (2000); Median age of housing: 38 years (2000).

Transportation: Commute to work: 94.6% car, 0.0% public transportation, 3.6% walk, 1.8% work from home (2000); Travel time to work: 26.7% less than 15 minutes, 28.5% 15 to 30 minutes, 23.0% 30 to 45 minutes, 12.1% 45 to 60 minutes, 9.7% 60 minutes or more (2000)

FREEBURG (village). Covers a land area of 3.187 square miles and a water area of 0.051 square miles. Located at 38.42° N. Lat.; 89.91° W. Long. Elevation is 509 feet.

History: Incorporated 1859.

Population: 3,490 (1990); 3,872 (2000); 4,135 (2007); 4,296 (2012 projected); Race: 98.5% White, 0.2% Black, 0.2% Asian, 1.2% Hispanic of any race (2007); Density: 1,297.6 persons per square mile (2007); Average household size: 2.64 (2007); Median age: 39.8 (2007); Males per 100 females: 92.5 (2007); Marriage status: 20.2% never married, 60.3% now married, 8.9% widowed, 10.5% divorced (2000); Foreign born: 0.9% (2000); Ancestry (includes multiple ancestries): 51.9% German, 16.2% Irish, 13.5% English, 5.4% French (except Basque), 5.4% Other groups (2000).

Economy: Single-family building permits issued: 23 (2007); Multi-family building permits issued: 8 (2007); Employment by occupation: 13.1% management, 24.2% professional, 11.4% services, 25.2% sales, 0.0% farming, 13.8% construction, 12.3% production (2000).

Income: Per capita income: $25,253 (2007); Median household income: $61,902 (2007); Average household income: $65,918 (2007); Percent of households with income of $100,000 or more: 17.3% (2007); Poverty rate: 5.7% (2000).
Education: Percent of population age 25 and over with: High school diploma (including GED) or higher: 88.1% (2007); Bachelor's degree or higher: 17.5% (2007); Master's degree or higher: 6.5% (2007).

School District(s)

Freeburg CCSD 70 (PK-08)
2005-06 Enrollment: 745 . . . . (618) 539-3188
Freeburg CHSD 77 (09-12)
2005-06 Enrollment: 744 . . . . (618) 539-5533

Housing: Homeownership rate: 80.7% (2007); Median home value: $135,760 (2007); Median rent: $460 per month (2000); Median age of housing: 29 years (2000).
Safety: Violent crime rate: 4.9 per 10,000 population; Property crime rate: 122.2 per 10,000 population (2006).
Newspapers: Freeburg Tribune (Local news; Circulation 2,800)
Transportation: Commute to work: 94.9% car, 0.0% public transportation, 2.8% walk, 2.1% work from home (2000); Travel time to work: 26.4% less than 15 minutes, 41.1% 15 to 30 minutes, 20.9% 30 to 45 minutes, 6.1% 45 to 60 minutes, 5.5% 60 minutes or more (2000)

LEBANON (city). Covers a land area of 2.146 square miles and a water area of 0.002 square miles. Located at 38.60° N. Lat.; 89.81° W. Long. Elevation is 512 feet.
History: Lebanon was platted in the early 1800's. It grew as the site of McKendree College, organized in 1818 by the Methodist Church. Both Abraham Lincoln and Charles Dickens were guests at the Mermaid Inn, built in 1830 in Lebanon.
Population: 3,839 (1990); 3,523 (2000); 3,552 (2007); 3,587 (2012 projected); Race: 79.9% White, 17.0% Black, 0.3% Asian, 1.6% Hispanic of any race (2007); Density: 1,654.9 persons per square mile (2007); Average household size: 2.68 (2007); Median age: 34.2 (2007); Males per 100 females: 84.8 (2007); Marriage status: 31.5% never married, 49.3% now married, 11.2% widowed, 7.9% divorced (2000); Foreign born: 3.3% (2000); Ancestry (includes multiple ancestries): 36.3% German, 24.4% Other groups, 9.3% English, 8.4% Irish, 4.7% French (except Basque) (2000).
Economy: Single-family building permits issued: 15 (2007); Multi-family building permits issued: 21 (2007); Employment by occupation: 11.3% management, 24.7% professional, 19.0% services, 27.6% sales, 0.0% farming, 7.6% construction, 9.8% production (2000).
Income: Per capita income: $21,538 (2007); Median household income: $44,330 (2007); Average household income: $53,725 (2007); Percent of households with income of $100,000 or more: 11.4% (2007); Poverty rate: 13.4% (2000).
Education: Percent of population age 25 and over with: High school diploma (including GED) or higher: 80.8% (2007); Bachelor's degree or higher: 26.2% (2007); Master's degree or higher: 12.9% (2007).

School District(s)

Lebanon CUSD 9 (PK-12)
2005-06 Enrollment: 694 . . . . (618) 537-4611

Four-year College(s)

McKendree University (Private, Not-for-profit, United Methodist)
Fall 2007 Enrollment: 3,312. . . . . (618) 537-4481
2007-08 Tuition: In-state $20,150; Out-of-state $20,150

Housing: Homeownership rate: 60.5% (2007); Median home value: $111,085 (2007); Median rent: $345 per month (2000); Median age of housing: 41 years (2000).
Safety: Violent crime rate: 17.4 per 10,000 population; Property crime rate: 218.2 per 10,000 population (2006).
Newspapers: Lebanon Advertiser (International news; Circulation 1,542)
Transportation: Commute to work: 86.8% car, 0.6% public transportation, 10.3% walk, 1.7% work from home (2000); Travel time to work: 36.6% less than 15 minutes, 37.0% 15 to 30 minutes, 13.5% 30 to 45 minutes, 7.7% 45 to 60 minutes, 5.2% 60 minutes or more (2000)
Additional Information Contacts
Lebanon Chamber of Commerce. . . . . (618) 537-8420
http://www.lebanonil.org/chamber.htm

LENZBURG (village). Covers a land area of 1.235 square miles and a water area of 0.059 square miles. Located at 38.28° N. Lat.; 89.81° W. Long. Elevation is 443 feet.
Population: 510 (1990); 577 (2000); 614 (2007); 623 (2012 projected); Race: 99.3% White, 0.0% Black, 0.0% Asian, 0.8% Hispanic of any race (2007); Density: 497.1 persons per square mile (2007); Average household size: 2.55 (2007); Median age: 34.5 (2007); Males per 100 females: 96.8 (2007); Marriage status: 19.4% never married, 57.0% now married, 7.1% widowed, 16.5% divorced (2000); Foreign born: 0.7% (2000); Ancestry (includes multiple ancestries): 43.7% German, 16.5% Other groups, 14.6% Irish, 8.8% French (except Basque), 7.5% United States or American (2000).
Economy: Employment by occupation: 12.9% management, 6.2% professional, 19.5% services, 17.6% sales, 0.0% farming, 14.8% construction, 29.0% production (2000).
Income: Per capita income: $18,270 (2007); Median household income: $38,250 (2007); Average household income: $46,546 (2007); Percent of households with income of $100,000 or more: 9.1% (2007); Poverty rate: 12.7% (2000).
Education: Percent of population age 25 and over with: High school diploma (including GED) or higher: 75.0% (2007); Bachelor's degree or higher: 5.9% (2007); Master's degree or higher: 1.6% (2007).
Housing: Homeownership rate: 72.6% (2007); Median home value: $74,333 (2007); Median rent: $225 per month (2000); Median age of housing: 38 years (2000).
Safety: Violent crime rate: 0.0 per 10,000 population; Property crime rate: 0.0 per 10,000 population (2006).
Transportation: Commute to work: 95.8% car, 0.0% public transportation, 0.9% walk, 3.3% work from home (2000); Travel time to work: 21.0% less than 15 minutes, 16.6% 15 to 30 minutes, 37.1% 30 to 45 minutes, 17.1% 45 to 60 minutes, 8.3% 60 minutes or more (2000)

MARISSA (village). Covers a land area of 3.717 square miles and a water area of 0.195 square miles. Located at 38.24° N. Lat.; 89.75° W. Long. Elevation is 453 feet.
History: Incorporated 1882.
Population: 2,441 (1990); 2,141 (2000); 2,068 (2007); 2,038 (2012 projected); Race: 98.8% White, 0.3% Black, 0.2% Asian, 1.1% Hispanic of any race (2007); Density: 556.4 persons per square mile (2007); Average household size: 2.36 (2007); Median age: 37.0 (2007); Males per 100 females: 92.9 (2007); Marriage status: 21.4% never married, 58.2% now married, 8.2% widowed, 12.2% divorced (2000); Foreign born: 0.9% (2000); Ancestry (includes multiple ancestries): 30.8% German, 15.0% Irish, 12.2% United States or American, 10.7% English, 5.2% Other groups (2000).
Economy: Single-family building permits issued: 1 (2007); Multi-family building permits issued: 0 (2007); Employment by occupation: 7.9% management, 16.6% professional, 16.0% services, 20.6% sales, 0.7% farming, 13.1% construction, 25.2% production (2000).
Income: Per capita income: $20,907 (2007); Median household income: $40,889 (2007); Average household income: $49,243 (2007); Percent of households with income of $100,000 or more: 8.9% (2007); Poverty rate: 9.5% (2000).
Education: Percent of population age 25 and over with: High school diploma (including GED) or higher: 77.5% (2007); Bachelor's degree or higher: 10.5% (2007); Master's degree or higher: 2.3% (2007).

School District(s)

Marissa CUSD 40 (PK-12)
2005-06 Enrollment: 614 . . . . (618) 295-2313

Housing: Homeownership rate: 76.1% (2007); Median home value: $65,068 (2007); Median rent: $275 per month (2000); Median age of housing: 44 years (2000).
Safety: Violent crime rate: 9.8 per 10,000 population; Property crime rate: 171.2 per 10,000 population (2006).
Newspapers: This Week in Marissa (Community news; Circulation 780)
Transportation: Commute to work: 92.2% car, 0.8% public transportation, 3.9% walk, 2.5% work from home (2000); Travel time to work: 32.0% less than 15 minutes, 18.8% 15 to 30 minutes, 27.5% 30 to 45 minutes, 10.5% 45 to 60 minutes, 11.3% 60 minutes or more (2000)

MASCOUTAH (city). Covers a land area of 8.638 square miles and a water area of 0.061 square miles. Located at 38.49° N. Lat.; 89.80° W. Long. Elevation is 430 feet.
History: Incorporated 1839.
Population: 5,770 (1990); 5,659 (2000); 5,914 (2007); 6,090 (2012 projected); Race: 92.0% White, 3.3% Black, 1.1% Asian, 2.1% Hispanic of any race (2007); Density: 684.7 persons per square mile (2007); Average household size: 2.53 (2007); Median age: 38.2 (2007); Males per 100

females: 92.6 (2007); Marriage status: 24.0% never married, 60.8% now married, 6.2% widowed, 9.0% divorced (2000); Foreign born: 2.0% (2000); Ancestry (includes multiple ancestries): 46.3% German, 12.2% Other groups, 8.9% Irish, 8.6% English, 5.5% United States or American (2000).
Economy: Single-family building permits issued: 125 (2007); Multi-family building permits issued: 0 (2007); Employment by occupation: 10.1% management, 18.7% professional, 21.9% services, 28.2% sales, 0.0% farming, 8.4% construction, 12.6% production (2000).
Income: Per capita income: $26,207 (2007); Median household income: $55,743 (2007); Average household income: $65,627 (2007); Percent of households with income of $100,000 or more: 14.2% (2007); Poverty rate: 7.8% (2000).
Education: Percent of population age 25 and over with: High school diploma (including GED) or higher: 87.1% (2007); Bachelor's degree or higher: 19.3% (2007); Master's degree or higher: 8.2% (2007).

School District(s)

Mascoutah CUD 19 (PK-12)
2005-06 Enrollment: 2,757 . . . . (618) 566-7414
Housing: Homeownership rate: 71.9% (2007); Median home value: $107,592 (2007); Median rent: $406 per month (2000); Median age of housing: 36 years (2000).
Safety: Violent crime rate: 5.2 per 10,000 population; Property crime rate: 128.8 per 10,000 population (2006).
Newspapers: Clinton County News (Community news; Circulation 1,800); Fairview Heights Tribune (Community news; Circulation 1,200); Herald Publications (Local news; Circulation 2,400); Herald Scott Flier (Community news; Circulation 5,000)
Transportation: Commute to work: 93.7% car, 0.3% public transportation, 2.5% walk, 3.3% work from home (2000); Travel time to work: 34.8% less than 15 minutes, 37.9% 15 to 30 minutes, 13.9% 30 to 45 minutes, 6.5% 45 to 60 minutes, 6.9% 60 minutes or more (2000)

Additional Information Contacts

City of Mascoutah . . . . (618) 566-2964
http://www.mascoutah.com

MILLSTADT (village). Covers a land area of 1.112 square miles and a water area of 0 square miles. Located at 38.45° N. Lat.; 90.09° W. Long. Elevation is 617 feet.
History: Incorporated 1878.
Population: 2,774 (1990); 2,794 (2000); 2,897 (2007); 2,965 (2012 projected); Race: 98.5% White, 0.0% Black, 0.2% Asian, 0.7% Hispanic of any race (2007); Density: 2,604.5 persons per square mile (2007); Average household size: 2.36 (2007); Median age: 38.8 (2007); Males per 100 females: 92.4 (2007); Marriage status: 20.2% never married, 64.4% now married, 7.0% widowed, 8.4% divorced (2000); Foreign born: 0.8% (2000); Ancestry (includes multiple ancestries): 50.0% German, 16.9% Irish, 9.4% French (except Basque), 8.4% English, 6.4% Other groups (2000).
Economy: Single-family building permits issued: 26 (2007); Multi-family building permits issued: 2 (2007); Employment by occupation: 13.5% management, 19.6% professional, 13.3% services, 26.1% sales, 0.0% farming, 10.3% construction, 17.2% production (2000).
Income: Per capita income: $27,528 (2007); Median household income: $56,059 (2007); Average household income: $65,102 (2007); Percent of households with income of $100,000 or more: 17.2% (2007); Poverty rate: 4.0% (2000).
Education: Percent of population age 25 and over with: High school diploma (including GED) or higher: 84.2% (2007); Bachelor's degree or higher: 18.7% (2007); Master's degree or higher: 5.8% (2007).

School District(s)

Millstadt CCSD 160 (PK-08)
2005-06 Enrollment: 828 . . . . (618) 476-1803
Housing: Homeownership rate: 74.8% (2007); Median home value: $141,578 (2007); Median rent: $411 per month (2000); Median age of housing: 32 years (2000).
Safety: Violent crime rate: 13.0 per 10,000 population; Property crime rate: 136.9 per 10,000 population (2006).
Transportation: Commute to work: 96.2% car, 0.0% public transportation, 2.3% walk, 0.9% work from home (2000); Travel time to work: 22.9% less than 15 minutes, 40.2% 15 to 30 minutes, 21.0% 30 to 45 minutes, 12.6% 45 to 60 minutes, 3.2% 60 minutes or more (2000)

NEW ATHENS (village). Covers a land area of 1.725 square miles and a water area of 0.111 square miles. Located at 38.32° N. Lat.; 89.87° W. Long. Elevation is 397 feet.
History: Incorporated 1869.
Population: 2,010 (1990); 1,981 (2000); 2,060 (2007); 2,106 (2012 projected); Race: 97.8% White, 0.8% Black, 0.3% Asian, 0.9% Hispanic of any race (2007); Density: 1,194.1 persons per square mile (2007); Average household size: 2.48 (2007); Median age: 38.6 (2007); Males per 100 females: 89.0 (2007); Marriage status: 21.5% never married, 59.2% now married, 10.2% widowed, 9.0% divorced (2000); Foreign born: 0.5% (2000); Ancestry (includes multiple ancestries): 49.5% German, 13.0% Irish, 8.9% English, 8.9% United States or American, 4.6% French (except Basque) (2000).
Economy: Single-family building permits issued: 6 (2007); Multi-family building permits issued: 0 (2007); Employment by occupation: 8.8% management, 15.0% professional, 15.2% services, 24.2% sales, 0.2% farming, 14.4% construction, 22.1% production (2000).
Income: Per capita income: $23,317 (2007); Median household income: $48,707 (2007); Average household income: $57,320 (2007); Percent of households with income of $100,000 or more: 10.6% (2007); Poverty rate: 8.4% (2000).
Education: Percent of population age 25 and over with: High school diploma (including GED) or higher: 79.8% (2007); Bachelor's degree or higher: 11.7% (2007); Master's degree or higher: 3.2% (2007).

School District(s)

New Athens CUSD 60 (PK-12)
2005-06 Enrollment: 611 . . . . (618) 475-2174
Housing: Homeownership rate: 80.0% (2007); Median home value: $103,636 (2007); Median rent: $292 per month (2000); Median age of housing: 50 years (2000).
Safety: Violent crime rate: 9.9 per 10,000 population; Property crime rate: 119.3 per 10,000 population (2006).
Newspapers: Journal-Messenger (Community news; Circulation 2,800)
Transportation: Commute to work: 93.0% car, 0.0% public transportation, 2.8% walk, 3.5% work from home (2000); Travel time to work: 29.4% less than 15 minutes, 19.4% 15 to 30 minutes, 26.4% 30 to 45 minutes, 13.8% 45 to 60 minutes, 11.0% 60 minutes or more (2000)

O'FALLON (city). Covers a land area of 10.913 square miles and a water area of 0.012 square miles. Located at 38.59° N. Lat.; 89.91° W. Long. Elevation is 548 feet.
History: O'Fallon developed in 1854 along the railroad route. Named for the owner of the land on which the town was sited, it grew as a residential community.
Population: 17,169 (1990); 21,910 (2000); 25,755 (2007); 28,180 (2012 projected); Race: 80.2% White, 13.3% Black, 3.0% Asian, 2.7% Hispanic of any race (2007); Density: 2,360.0 persons per square mile (2007); Average household size: 2.61 (2007); Median age: 36.4 (2007); Males per 100 females: 93.7 (2007); Marriage status: 23.3% never married, 63.5% now married, 4.0% widowed, 9.2% divorced (2000); Foreign born: 3.7% (2000); Ancestry (includes multiple ancestries): 30.8% German, 19.2% Other groups, 12.6% Irish, 11.1% English, 6.1% United States or American (2000).
Economy: Unemployment rate: 4.3% (4/2008); Total civilian labor force: 13,740 (4/2008); Single-family building permits issued: 203 (2007); Multi-family building permits issued: 2 (2007); Employment by occupation: 16.3% management, 26.1% professional, 13.4% services, 27.6% sales, 0.3% farming, 6.2% construction, 10.1% production (2000).
Income: Per capita income: $30,335 (2007); Median household income: $66,321 (2007); Average household income: $78,863 (2007); Percent of households with income of $100,000 or more: 26.8% (2007); Poverty rate: 5.0% (2000).
Taxes: Total city taxes per capita: $274 (2006); City property taxes per capita: $169 (2006).
Education: Percent of population age 25 and over with: High school diploma (including GED) or higher: 92.3% (2007); Bachelor's degree or higher: 38.7% (2007); Master's degree or higher: 16.8% (2007).

School District(s)

Central SD 104 (PK-08)
2005-06 Enrollment: 433 . . . . (618) 632-6336
O'Fallon CCSD 90 (PK-08)
2005-06 Enrollment: 3,351 . . . . (618) 632-3666
O'Fallon Twp HSD 203 (09-12)
2005-06 Enrollment: 2,345 . . . . (618) 632-3507
Housing: Homeownership rate: 69.4% (2007); Median home value: $146,042 (2007); Median rent: $541 per month (2000); Median age of housing: 17 years (2000).
Safety: Violent crime rate: 14.3 per 10,000 population; Property crime rate: 267.9 per 10,000 population (2006).

Newspapers: O'Fallon Progress (Community news; Circulation 6,000)
Transportation: Commute to work: 95.2% car, 0.9% public transportation, 1.2% walk, 2.2% work from home (2000); Travel time to work: 29.5% less than 15 minutes, 41.1% 15 to 30 minutes, 16.5% 30 to 45 minutes, 8.2% 45 to 60 minutes, 4.7% 60 minutes or more (2000)

Additional Information Contacts

City of O'Fallon . . . . (618) 624-4500
http://www.ofallon.org
O'Fallon Chamber of Commerce . . . . (618) 632-3377
http://www.ofallonchamber.com

SAINT LIBORY (village). Covers a land area of 0.943 square miles and a water area of 0 square miles. Located at 38.36° N. Lat.; 89.71° W. Long. Elevation is 407 feet.
Population: 590 (1990); 583 (2000); 537 (2007); 535 (2012 projected); Race: 97.4% White, 0.0% Black, 0.0% Asian, 0.2% Hispanic of any race (2007); Density: 569.3 persons per square mile (2007); Average household size: 2.63 (2007); Median age: 36.0 (2007); Males per 100 females: 85.8 (2007); Marriage status: 19.3% never married, 60.0% now married, 8.7% widowed, 12.0% divorced (2000); Foreign born: 0.5% (2000); Ancestry (includes multiple ancestries): 67.2% German, 10.2% Irish, 7.7% Polish, 5.3% United States or American, 4.8% French (except Basque) (2000).
Economy: Single-family building permits issued: 2 (2007); Multi-family building permits issued: 0 (2007); Employment by occupation: 17.5% management, 8.0% professional, 14.0% services, 26.8% sales, 0.6% farming, 10.8% construction, 22.3% production (2000).
Income: Per capita income: $25,107 (2007); Median household income: $63,500 (2007); Average household income: $66,091 (2007); Percent of households with income of $100,000 or more: 16.7% (2007); Poverty rate: 6.0% (2000).
Education: Percent of population age 25 and over with: High school diploma (including GED) or higher: 78.4% (2007); Bachelor's degree or higher: 7.9% (2007); Master's degree or higher: 2.6% (2007).

School District(s)

St Libory Cons SD 30 (PK-08)
2005-06 Enrollment: 102 . . . . (618) 768-4923
Housing: Homeownership rate: 79.4% (2007); Median home value: $117,647 (2007); Median rent: $269 per month (2000); Median age of housing: 29 years (2000).
Transportation: Commute to work: 93.6% car, 0.7% public transportation, 1.3% walk, 4.3% work from home (2000); Travel time to work: 17.5% less than 15 minutes, 25.2% 15 to 30 minutes, 26.6% 30 to 45 minutes, 17.8% 45 to 60 minutes, 12.9% 60 minutes or more (2000)

SAUGET (village). Aka Monsanto. Covers a land area of 4.130 square miles and a water area of 0.319 square miles. Located at 38.58° N. Lat.; 90.16° W. Long. Elevation is 410 feet.
History: Formerly called Monsanto.
Population: 273 (1990); 249 (2000); 282 (2007); 288 (2012 projected); Race: 69.5% White, 29.1% Black, 0.7% Asian, 0.4% Hispanic of any race (2007); Density: 68.3 persons per square mile (2007); Average household size: 2.41 (2007); Median age: 37.7 (2007); Males per 100 females: 86.8 (2007); Marriage status: 23.4% never married, 51.3% now married, 13.3% widowed, 12.0% divorced (2000); Foreign born: 0.0% (2000); Ancestry (includes multiple ancestries): 24.2% German, 17.2% Irish, 10.2% Other groups, 9.1% United States or American, 9.1% English (2000).
Economy: Employment by occupation: 11.9% management, 7.1% professional, 28.6% services, 20.2% sales, 0.0% farming, 13.1% construction, 19.0% production (2000).
Income: Per capita income: $19,113 (2007); Median household income: $35,278 (2007); Average household income: $46,068 (2007); Percent of households with income of $100,000 or more: 8.5% (2007); Poverty rate: 17.3% (2000).
Education: Percent of population age 25 and over with: High school diploma (including GED) or higher: 83.2% (2007); Bachelor's degree or higher: 6.8% (2007); Master's degree or higher: 2.6% (2007).
Housing: Homeownership rate: 57.3% (2007); Median home value: $53,000 (2007); Median rent: $333 per month (2000); Median age of housing: 40 years (2000).
Transportation: Commute to work: 100.0% car, 0.0% public transportation, 0.0% walk, 0.0% work from home (2000); Travel time to work: 58.8% less than 15 minutes, 31.3% 15 to 30 minutes, 6.3% 30 to 45 minutes, 0.0% 45 to 60 minutes, 3.8% 60 minutes or more (2000)

SCOTT AFB (CDP). Covers a land area of 3.755 square miles and a water area of 0 square miles. Located at 38.54° N. Lat.; 89.85° W. Long.
Population: 7,245 (1990); 2,707 (2000); 2,097 (2007); 1,772 (2012 projected); Race: 81.7% White, 11.2% Black, 2.3% Asian, 4.1% Hispanic of any race (2007); Density: 558.5 persons per square mile (2007); Average household size: 4.03 (2007); Median age: 23.4 (2007); Males per 100 females: 100.1 (2007); Marriage status: 19.1% never married, 75.4% now married, 0.8% widowed, 4.8% divorced (2000); Foreign born: 4.3% (2000); Ancestry (includes multiple ancestries): 20.7% Other groups, 17.6% German, 12.0% United States or American, 6.3% Irish, 5.9% English (2000).
Economy: Employment by occupation: 11.8% management, 21.9% professional, 17.8% services, 39.9% sales, 0.0% farming, 0.9% construction, 7.7% production (2000).
Income: Per capita income: $18,492 (2007); Median household income: $64,065 (2007); Average household income: $71,870 (2007); Percent of households with income of $100,000 or more: 16.9% (2007); Poverty rate: 1.5% (2000).
Education: Percent of population age 25 and over with: High school diploma (including GED) or higher: 98.9% (2007); Bachelor's degree or higher: 44.9% (2007); Master's degree or higher: 17.7% (2007).

School District(s)

Mascoutah CUD 19 (PK-12)
2005-06 Enrollment: 2,757 . . . . (618) 566-7414
Housing: Homeownership rate: 11.7% (2007); Median home value: $36,389 (2007); Median rent: $742 per month (2000); Median age of housing: 34 years (2000).
Newspapers: Command Post (Local news; Circulation 14,300)
Transportation: Commute to work: 87.3% car, 0.8% public transportation, 9.7% walk, 1.5% work from home (2000); Travel time to work: 73.8% less than 15 minutes, 16.5% 15 to 30 minutes, 5.0% 30 to 45 minutes, 4.1% 45 to 60 minutes, 0.7% 60 minutes or more (2000)

SHILOH (village). Covers a land area of 10.054 square miles and a water area of 0.033 square miles. Located at 38.55° N. Lat.; 89.91° W. Long. Elevation is 663 feet.
Population: 4,935 (1990); 7,643 (2000); 9,199 (2007); 10,151 (2012 projected); Race: 80.2% White, 14.8% Black, 1.9% Asian, 3.1% Hispanic of any race (2007); Density: 914.9 persons per square mile (2007); Average household size: 2.69 (2007); Median age: 34.0 (2007); Males per 100 females: 100.4 (2007); Marriage status: 23.5% never married, 64.2% now married, 4.1% widowed, 8.2% divorced (2000); Foreign born: 2.3% (2000); Ancestry (includes multiple ancestries): 28.3% German, 23.5% Other groups, 15.8% Irish, 7.0% United States or American, 6.7% English (2000).
Economy: Single-family building permits issued: 88 (2007); Multi-family building permits issued: 68 (2007); Employment by occupation: 14.9% management, 23.3% professional, 12.0% services, 29.5% sales, 0.0% farming, 7.6% construction, 12.7% production (2000).
Income: Per capita income: $33,446 (2007); Median household income: $71,063 (2007); Average household income: $89,048 (2007); Percent of households with income of $100,000 or more: 32.1% (2007); Poverty rate: 7.7% (2000).
Education: Percent of population age 25 and over with: High school diploma (including GED) or higher: 91.5% (2007); Bachelor's degree or higher: 33.5% (2007); Master's degree or higher: 14.6% (2007).

School District(s)

Shiloh Village SD 85 (PK-08)
2005-06 Enrollment: 621 . . . . (618) 632-7434
Housing: Homeownership rate: 70.7% (2007); Median home value: $171,037 (2007); Median rent: $431 per month (2000); Median age of housing: 11 years (2000).
Safety: Violent crime rate: 27.0 per 10,000 population; Property crime rate: 154.3 per 10,000 population (2006).
Transportation: Commute to work: 94.3% car, 0.7% public transportation, 2.2% walk, 2.5% work from home (2000); Travel time to work: 29.2% less than 15 minutes, 34.9% 15 to 30 minutes, 21.0% 30 to 45 minutes, 10.2% 45 to 60 minutes, 4.7% 60 minutes or more (2000)

Additional Information Contacts

Shiloh Chamber of Commerce. . . . . (618) 632-1022
http://www.shilohchamber.org
Village of Shiloh . . . . (618) 632-1022
http://www.shilohil.org

SMITHTON (village). Covers a land area of 1.672 square miles and a water area of 0.006 square miles. Located at 38.40° N. Lat.; 89.99° W. Long. Elevation is 476 feet.

Population: 1,796 (1990); 2,248 (2000); 2,614 (2007); 2,855 (2012 projected); Race: 97.5% White, 0.5% Black, 0.5% Asian, 0.1% Hispanic of any race (2007); Density: 1,563.4 persons per square mile (2007); Average household size: 2.76 (2007); Median age: 37.3 (2007); Males per 100 females: 94.6 (2007); Marriage status: 22.1% never married, 59.6% now married, 6.1% widowed, 12.1% divorced (2000); Foreign born: 0.6% (2000); Ancestry (includes multiple ancestries): 42.4% German, 11.4% Irish, 9.1% United States or American, 7.0% Other groups, 5.1% English (2000).

Economy: Single-family building permits issued: 37 (2007); Multi-family building permits issued: 0 (2007); Employment by occupation: 10.6% management, 17.0% professional, 12.9% services, 32.8% sales, 0.0% farming, 10.8% construction, 15.9% production (2000).

Income: Per capita income: $25,064 (2007); Median household income: $63,264 (2007); Average household income: $67,455 (2007); Percent of households with income of $100,000 or more: 19.6% (2007); Poverty rate: 9.3% (2000).

Education: Percent of population age 25 and over with: High school diploma (including GED) or higher: 85.2% (2007); Bachelor's degree or higher: 16.6% (2007); Master's degree or higher: 3.6% (2007).

School District(s)

Smithton CCSD 130 (PK-08)
2005-06 Enrollment: 374 . . . . (618) 233-6863

Housing: Homeownership rate: 88.0% (2007); Median home value: $137,089 (2007); Median rent: $369 per month (2000); Median age of housing: 17 years (2000).

Safety: Violent crime rate: 7.0 per 10,000 population; Property crime rate: 27.9 per 10,000 population (2006).

Transportation: Commute to work: 94.4% car, 0.0% public transportation, 1.3% walk, 3.6% work from home (2000); Travel time to work: 14.1% less than 15 minutes, 37.7% 15 to 30 minutes, 30.7% 30 to 45 minutes, 12.6% 45 to 60 minutes, 4.8% 60 minutes or more (2000)

Additional Information Contacts

Smithton Chamber of Commerce . . . . (618) 239-3366
http://www.smithtonchamber.org

SUMMERFIELD (village). Covers a land area of 0.420 square miles and a water area of 0 square miles. Located at 38.59° N. Lat.; 89.75° W. Long. Elevation is 479 feet.

Population: 509 (1990); 472 (2000); 467 (2007); 463 (2012 projected); Race: 97.0% White, 0.6% Black, 0.2% Asian, 2.6% Hispanic of any race (2007); Density: 1,110.7 persons per square mile (2007); Average household size: 2.81 (2007); Median age: 34.7 (2007); Males per 100 females: 109.4 (2007); Marriage status: 24.0% never married, 60.0% now married, 6.3% widowed, 9.7% divorced (2000); Foreign born: 1.0% (2000); Ancestry (includes multiple ancestries): 21.9% Other groups, 20.5% Irish, 14.5% German, 13.7% French (except Basque), 7.2% English (2000).

Economy: Single-family building permits issued: 0 (2007); Multi-family building permits issued: 0 (2007); Employment by occupation: 7.6% management, 12.1% professional, 21.5% services, 13.9% sales, 0.9% farming, 21.5% construction, 22.4% production (2000).

Income: Per capita income: $17,971 (2007); Median household income: $50,000 (2007); Average household income: $50,557 (2007); Percent of households with income of $100,000 or more: 3.6% (2007); Poverty rate: 6.7% (2000).

Education: Percent of population age 25 and over with: High school diploma (including GED) or higher: 66.7% (2007); Bachelor's degree or higher: 11.7% (2007); Master's degree or higher: 3.1% (2007).

School District(s)

Lebanon CUSD 9 (PK-12)
2005-06 Enrollment: 694 . . . . (618) 537-4611

Housing: Homeownership rate: 80.1% (2007); Median home value: $81,750 (2007); Median rent: $327 per month (2000); Median age of housing: 39 years (2000).

Safety: Violent crime rate: 162.6 per 10,000 population; Property crime rate: 122.0 per 10,000 population (2006).

Transportation: Commute to work: 93.8% car, 0.0% public transportation, 5.7% walk, 0.5% work from home (2000); Travel time to work: 21.9% less than 15 minutes, 44.3% 15 to 30 minutes, 18.1% 30 to 45 minutes, 11.9% 45 to 60 minutes, 3.8% 60 minutes or more (2000)

SWANSEA (village). Covers a land area of 5.073 square miles and a water area of 0.020 square miles. Located at 38.54° N. Lat.; 89.98° W. Long. Elevation is 545 feet.

History: Incorporated 1895.

Population: 9,325 (1990); 10,579 (2000); 11,485 (2007); 12,029 (2012 projected); Race: 85.8% White, 10.3% Black, 1.9% Asian, 1.8% Hispanic of any race (2007); Density: 2,264.2 persons per square mile (2007); Average household size: 2.66 (2007); Median age: 39.0 (2007); Males per 100 females: 90.9 (2007); Marriage status: 23.0% never married, 58.7% now married, 6.8% widowed, 11.4% divorced (2000); Foreign born: 1.4% (2000); Ancestry (includes multiple ancestries): 39.3% German, 14.1% Irish, 13.3% Other groups, 10.5% English, 6.4% United States or American (2000).

Economy: Single-family building permits issued: 112 (2007); Multi-family building permits issued: 0 (2007); Employment by occupation: 13.7% management, 22.4% professional, 13.2% services, 31.9% sales, 0.2% farming, 9.0% construction, 9.6% production (2000).

Income: Per capita income: $29,669 (2007); Median household income: $57,867 (2007); Average household income: $77,428 (2007); Percent of households with income of $100,000 or more: 22.6% (2007); Poverty rate: 6.7% (2000).

Education: Percent of population age 25 and over with: High school diploma (including GED) or higher: 84.7% (2007); Bachelor's degree or higher: 27.8% (2007); Master's degree or higher: 11.3% (2007).

School District(s)

High Mount SD 116 (PK-08)
2005-06 Enrollment: 442 . . . . (618) 233-1054

Wolf Branch SD 113 (KG-08)
2005-06 Enrollment: 920 . . . . (618) 277-2100

Housing: Homeownership rate: 78.1% (2007); Median home value: $141,723 (2007); Median rent: $408 per month (2000); Median age of housing: 22 years (2000).

Safety: Violent crime rate: 35.8 per 10,000 population; Property crime rate: 338.1 per 10,000 population (2006).

Newspapers: Belleville Journal (Local news; Circulation 34,009); East St. Louis News Journal (Community news; Circulation 20,990)

Transportation: Commute to work: 95.2% car, 1.7% public transportation, 0.6% walk, 2.4% work from home (2000); Travel time to work: 35.6% less than 15 minutes, 32.8% 15 to 30 minutes, 15.9% 30 to 45 minutes, 11.5% 45 to 60 minutes, 4.2% 60 minutes or more (2000)

Additional Information Contacts

Swansea Chamber of Commerce . . . . (618) 233-3938
http://www.swanseachamber.org

Village of Swansea . . . . (618) 234-0044
http://www.swanseail.org

WASHINGTON PARK (village). Covers a land area of 2.451 square miles and a water area of 0 square miles. Located at 38.63° N. Lat.; 90.09° W. Long. Elevation is 410 feet.

History: Incorporated 1917.

Population: 7,431 (1990); 5,345 (2000); 5,107 (2007); 4,941 (2012 projected); Race: 5.2% White, 92.5% Black, 0.1% Asian, 2.2% Hispanic of any race (2007); Density: 2,083.3 persons per square mile (2007); Average household size: 3.05 (2007); Median age: 27.7 (2007); Males per 100 females: 84.2 (2007); Marriage status: 45.5% never married, 38.1% now married, 6.3% widowed, 10.2% divorced (2000); Foreign born: 1.0% (2000); Ancestry (includes multiple ancestries): 74.0% Other groups, 1.7% African, 1.3% United States or American, 1.2% Polish, 0.6% German (2000).

Economy: Single-family building permits issued: 0 (2007); Multi-family building permits issued: 0 (2007); Employment by occupation: 5.3% management, 7.4% professional, 34.0% services, 19.4% sales, 0.0% farming, 6.3% construction, 27.6% production (2000).

Income: Per capita income: $10,452 (2007); Median household income: $24,381 (2007); Average household income: $31,284 (2007); Percent of households with income of $100,000 or more: 2.6% (2007); Poverty rate: 44.8% (2000).

Education: Percent of population age 25 and over with: High school diploma (including GED) or higher: 63.1% (2007); Bachelor's degree or higher: 3.7% (2007); Master's degree or higher: 1.0% (2007).

Housing: Homeownership rate: 56.7% (2007); Median home value: $45,725 (2007); Median rent: $337 per month (2000); Median age of housing: 43 years (2000).

Safety: Violent crime rate: 327.5 per 10,000 population; Property crime rate: 494.8 per 10,000 population (2006).
Transportation: Commute to work: 81.7% car, 14.5% public transportation, 0.5% walk, 2.0% work from home (2000); Travel time to work: 15.8% less than 15 minutes, 39.5% 15 to 30 minutes, 28.2% 30 to 45 minutes, 4.8% 45 to 60 minutes, 11.7% 60 minutes or more (2000)

Stark County

Located in north central Illinois; drained by the Spoon River and Indian Creek. Covers a land area of 287.94 square miles, a water area of 0.28 square miles, and is located in the Central Time Zone. The county was founded in 1839. County seat is Toulon.

Stark County is part of the Peoria, IL Metropolitan Statistical Area. The entire metro area includes: Marshall County, IL; Peoria County, IL; Stark County, IL; Tazewell County, IL; Woodford County, IL

Population: 6,534 (1990); 6,332 (2000); 6,135 (2007); 5,989 (2012 projected); Race: 98.6% White, 0.1% Black, 0.2% Asian, 1.1% Hispanic of any race (2007); Density: 21.3 persons per square mile (2007); Average household size: 2.47 (2007); Median age: 42.1 (2007); Males per 100 females: 91.5 (2007).
Religion: Five largest groups: 14.6% Apostolic Christian Church of America, Inc., 14.3% The United Methodist Church, 13.6% Catholic Church, 4.4% New Testament Association of Independent Baptist Churches and other Fundamental Baptist Associations, 3
Economy: Unemployment rate: 5.6% (4/2008); Total civilian labor force: 3,103 (4/2008); Leading industries: 23.8% manufacturing; 16.5% retail trade; 7.4% professional, scientific & technical services (2005); Farms: 335 totaling 174,311 acres (2002); Companies that employ 500 or more persons: 0 (2006); Companies that employ 100 to 499 persons: 1 (2006); Companies that employ less than 100 persons: 127 (2006); Black-owned businesses: n/a (2002); Hispanic-owned businesses: n/a (2002); Asian-owned businesses: n/a (2002); Women-owned businesses: n/a (2002); Retail sales per capita: $6,549 (2008). Single-family building permits issued: 5 (2007); Multi-family building permits issued: 0 (2007).
Income: Per capita income: $20,282 (2007); Median household income: $41,472 (2007); Average household income: $49,240 (2007); Percent of households with income of $100,000 or more: 7.5% (2007); Poverty rate: 10.4% (2005); Bankruptcy rate: 3.72% (2007).
Education: Percent of population age 25 and over with: High school diploma (including GED) or higher: 83.5% (2007); Bachelor's degree or higher: 13.3% (2007); Master's degree or higher: 3.1% (2007).
Housing: Homeownership rate: 77.3% (2007); Median home value: $87,640 (2007); Median rent: $280 per month (2000); Median age of housing: n/a years (2000).
Health: Birth rate: 132.5 per 10,000 population (2007); Death rate: 132.5 per 10,000 population (2007); Age-adjusted cancer mortality rate: 207.8 (Unreliable) deaths per 100,000 population (2005); Number of physicians: 1.6 per 10,000 population (2005); Hospital beds: 0.0 per 10,000 population (2004); Hospital admissions: 0.0 per 10,000 population (2004).
Elections: 2004 Presidential election results: 60.1% Bush, 38.8% Kerry, 0.0% Nader, 1.0% Badnarik
Additional Information Contacts
Stark County Government . . . . (309) 286-5911

Wyoming Chamber of Commerce . . . . (309) 695-2055
http://www.wyoming-chamber.org

Stark County Communities

BRADFORD (village). Covers a land area of 0.397 square miles and a water area of 0 square miles. Located at 41.17° N. Lat.; 89.65° W. Long. Elevation is 807 feet.
Population: 836 (1990); 787 (2000); 749 (2007); 735 (2012 projected); Race: 98.5% White, 0.0% Black, 0.5% Asian, 0.9% Hispanic of any race (2007); Density: 1,889.0 persons per square mile (2007); Average household size: 2.43 (2007); Median age: 38.4 (2007); Males per 100 females: 87.7 (2007); Marriage status: 14.3% never married, 64.6% now married, 11.4% widowed, 9.6% divorced (2000); Foreign born: 0.7% (2000); Ancestry (includes multiple ancestries): 23.9% German, 18.3% Irish, 17.1% English, 6.5% United States or American, 5.1% Other groups (2000).
Economy: Employment by occupation: 5.8% management, 17.1% professional, 18.7% services, 20.0% sales, 1.9% farming, 11.0% construction, 25.5% production (2000).
Income: Per capita income: $18,261 (2007); Median household income: $38,889 (2007); Average household income: $44,407 (2007); Percent of households with income of $100,000 or more: 4.2% (2007); Poverty rate: 9.8% (2000).
Education: Percent of population age 25 and over with: High school diploma (including GED) or higher: 78.8% (2007); Bachelor's degree or higher: 8.9% (2007); Master's degree or higher: 1.5% (2007).

School District(s)

Bradford CUSD 1 (PK-08)
2005-06 Enrollment: 235 . . . . (309) 897-2801
Housing: Homeownership rate: 84.1% (2007); Median home value: $70,484 (2007); Median rent: $275 per month (2000); Median age of housing: 60+ years (2000).
Transportation: Commute to work: 92.2% car, 0.0% public transportation, 2.6% walk, 4.2% work from home (2000); Travel time to work: 23.1% less than 15 minutes, 23.7% 15 to 30 minutes, 35.3% 30 to 45 minutes, 14.2% 45 to 60 minutes, 3.7% 60 minutes or more (2000)

LA FAYETTE (village). Aka Lafayette. Covers a land area of 0.184 square miles and a water area of 0 square miles. Located at 41.11° N. Lat.; 89.97° W. Long. Elevation is 797 feet.
Population: 231 (1990); 227 (2000); 218 (2007); 213 (2012 projected); Race: 96.3% White, 0.0% Black, 0.0% Asian, 2.8% Hispanic of any race (2007); Density: 1,186.2 persons per square mile (2007); Average household size: 2.45 (2007); Median age: 41.2 (2007); Males per 100 females: 81.7 (2007); Marriage status: 17.4% never married, 64.2% now married, 3.7% widowed, 14.7% divorced (2000); Foreign born: 0.9% (2000); Ancestry (includes multiple ancestries): 18.9% English, 11.9% Irish, 8.4% German, 7.0% Other groups, 4.8% Scottish (2000).
Economy: Employment by occupation: 26.0% management, 2.7% professional, 13.7% services, 32.9% sales, 0.0% farming, 9.6% construction, 15.1% production (2000).
Income: Per capita income: $17,489 (2007); Median household income: $31,563 (2007); Average household income: $42,837 (2007); Percent of households with income of $100,000 or more: 6.7% (2007); Poverty rate: 13.2% (2000).
Education: Percent of population age 25 and over with: High school diploma (including GED) or higher: 78.9% (2007); Bachelor's degree or higher: 5.9% (2007); Master's degree or higher: 2.0% (2007).
Housing: Homeownership rate: 77.5% (2007); Median home value: $55,909 (2007); Median rent: $236 per month (2000); Median age of housing: 60+ years (2000).
Newspapers: Prairie Shopper (Community news; Circulation 5,851)
Transportation: Commute to work: 87.7% car, 0.0% public transportation, 2.7% walk, 9.6% work from home (2000); Travel time to work: 36.4% less than 15 minutes, 33.3% 15 to 30 minutes, 12.1% 30 to 45 minutes, 6.1% 45 to 60 minutes, 12.1% 60 minutes or more (2000)

SPEER (unincorporated postal area, zip code 61479). Covers a land area of 13.178 square miles and a water area of 0 square miles. Located at 40.99° N. Lat.; 89.65° W. Long. Elevation is 741 feet.
Population: 169 (2000); Race: 100.0% White, 0.0% Black, 0.0% Asian, 0.0% Hispanic of any race (2000); Density: 12.8 persons per square mile (2000); Age: 16.5% under 18, 12.0% over 64 (2000); Marriage status: 12.5% never married, 79.2% now married, 8.3% widowed, 0.0% divorced (2000); Foreign born: 0.0% (2000); Ancestry (includes multiple ancestries): 42.4% German, 19.6% French (except Basque), 19.6% Irish, 13.3% Scottish, 12.0% English (2000).
Economy: Employment by occupation: 7.2% management, 7.2% professional, 15.9% services, 34.8% sales, 0.0% farming, 0.0% construction, 34.8% production (2000).
Income: Per capita income: $19,389 (2000); Median household income: $35,455 (2000); Poverty rate: 0.0% (2000).
Education: Percent of population age 25 and over with: High school diploma (including GED) or higher: 85.7% (2000); Bachelor's degree or higher: 4.0% (2000).
Housing: Homeownership rate: 78.9% (2000); Median home value: $70,800 (2000); Median rent: $397 per month (2000); Median age of housing: 60+ years (2000).
Transportation: Commute to work: 89.9% car, 0.0% public transportation, 10.1% walk, 0.0% work from home (2000); Travel time to work: 33.3% less

than 15 minutes, 58.0% 15 to 30 minutes, 8.7% 30 to 45 minutes, 0.0% 45 to 60 minutes, 0.0% 60 minutes or more (2000)

TOULON (city). County seat. Covers a land area of 0.889 square miles and a water area of 0 square miles. Located at 41.09° N. Lat.; 89.86° W. Long. Elevation is 728 feet.
History: Incorporated 1859.
Population: 1,341 (1990); 1,400 (2000); 1,377 (2007); 1,337 (2012 projected); Race: 98.6% White, 0.5% Black, 0.1% Asian, 0.3% Hispanic of any race (2007); Density: 1,549.6 persons per square mile (2007); Average household size: 2.49 (2007); Median age: 45.0 (2007); Males per 100 females: 78.6 (2007); Marriage status: 17.7% never married, 64.9% now married, 8.9% widowed, 8.5% divorced (2000); Foreign born: 0.3% (2000); Ancestry (includes multiple ancestries): 19.4% German, 16.5% English, 13.1% Irish, 9.1% Other groups, 5.7% United States or American (2000).
Economy: Employment by occupation: 9.5% management, 17.2% professional, 14.4% services, 25.4% sales, 1.8% farming, 9.7% construction, 22.1% production (2000).
Income: Per capita income: $19,603 (2007); Median household income: $37,361 (2007); Average household income: $45,679 (2007); Percent of households with income of $100,000 or more: 6.2% (2007); Poverty rate: 7.4% (2000).
Education: Percent of population age 25 and over with: High school diploma (including GED) or higher: 81.9% (2007); Bachelor's degree or higher: 13.3% (2007); Master's degree or higher: 5.4% (2007).

School District(s)

Stark County CUSD 100 (PK-12)
2005-06 Enrollment: 904 . . . . (309) 695-6123

Housing: Homeownership rate: 74.1% (2007); Median home value: $77,500 (2007); Median rent: $270 per month (2000); Median age of housing: 57 years (2000).
Transportation: Commute to work: 91.2% car, 0.0% public transportation, 6.0% walk, 2.0% work from home (2000); Travel time to work: 37.4% less than 15 minutes, 24.5% 15 to 30 minutes, 12.9% 30 to 45 minutes, 20.7% 45 to 60 minutes, 4.5% 60 minutes or more (2000)

WYOMING (city). Covers a land area of 0.742 square miles and a water area of 0 square miles. Located at 41.06° N. Lat.; 89.77° W. Long. Elevation is 699 feet.
History: Incorporated 1865.
Population: 1,462 (1990); 1,424 (2000); 1,487 (2007); 1,459 (2012 projected); Race: 99.3% White, 0.0% Black, 0.2% Asian, 0.1% Hispanic of any race (2007); Density: 2,003.0 persons per square mile (2007); Average household size: 2.23 (2007); Median age: 43.2 (2007); Males per 100 females: 86.3 (2007); Marriage status: 21.7% never married, 57.8% now married, 10.9% widowed, 9.7% divorced (2000); Foreign born: 0.4% (2000); Ancestry (includes multiple ancestries): 19.9% German, 15.1% Irish, 14.4% English, 11.6% United States or American, 6.4% Other groups (2000).
Economy: Employment by occupation: 7.6% management, 14.5% professional, 15.9% services, 26.7% sales, 0.9% farming, 9.2% construction, 25.3% production (2000).
Income: Per capita income: $18,971 (2007); Median household income: $34,833 (2007); Average household income: $42,231 (2007); Percent of households with income of $100,000 or more: 5.2% (2007); Poverty rate: 10.6% (2000).
Education: Percent of population age 25 and over with: High school diploma (including GED) or higher: 81.8% (2007); Bachelor's degree or higher: 12.8% (2007); Master's degree or higher: 4.7% (2007).

School District(s)

Stark County CUSD 100 (PK-12)
2005-06 Enrollment: 904 . . . . (309) 695-6123

Housing: Homeownership rate: 77.7% (2007); Median home value: $87,881 (2007); Median rent: $292 per month (2000); Median age of housing: 49 years (2000).
Transportation: Commute to work: 90.4% car, 0.3% public transportation, 3.7% walk, 4.0% work from home (2000); Travel time to work: 40.8% less than 15 minutes, 14.0% 15 to 30 minutes, 28.1% 30 to 45 minutes, 13.8% 45 to 60 minutes, 3.2% 60 minutes or more (2000)

Additional Information Contacts

Wyoming Chamber of Commerce . . . . (309) 695-2055
http://www.wyoming-chamber.org

Stephenson County

Located in northern Illinois; bounded on the north by Wisconsin; drained by the Pecatonica River. Covers a land area of 564.18 square miles, a water area of 0.54 square miles, and is located in the Central Time Zone. The county was founded in 1837. County seat is Freeport.

Stephenson County is part of the Freeport, IL Micropolitan Statistical Area. The entire metro area includes: Stephenson County, IL

Weather Station: Freeport Waste Water Plant — Elevation: 748 feet

	Jan	Feb	Mar	Apr	May	Jun	Jul	Aug	Sep	Oct	Nov	Dec
High	26	32	44	58	71	80	84	81	74	62	46	32
Low	9	14	25	36	48	57	62	59	50	38	28	16
Precip	1.3	1.3	2.2	3.2	4.0	4.3	3.6	4.1	3.7	2.6	2.7	1.7
Snow	9.6	6.5	4.4	1.7	tr	0.0	0.0	0.0	0.0	tr	2.5	7.3

High and Low temperatures in degrees Fahrenheit; Precipitation and Snow in inches

Population: 48,052 (1990); 48,979 (2000); 47,785 (2007); 46,900 (2012 projected); Race: 88.3% White, 7.9% Black, 0.8% Asian, 2.2% Hispanic of any race (2007); Density: 84.7 persons per square mile (2007); Average household size: 2.45 (2007); Median age: 40.7 (2007); Males per 100 females: 93.6 (2007).
Religion: Five largest groups: 17.1% Catholic Church, 11.6% The United Methodist Church, 5.2% Evangelical Lutheran Church in America, 4.7% United Church of Christ, 4.0% Lutheran Church—Missouri Synod (2000).
Economy: Unemployment rate: 6.1% (4/2008); Total civilian labor force: 25,350 (4/2008); Leading industries: 23.9% manufacturing; 15.7% health care and social assistance; 12.8% retail trade (2005); Farms: 1,075 totaling 324,118 acres (2002); Companies that employ 500 or more persons: 5 (2006); Companies that employ 100 to 499 persons: 23 (2006); Companies that employ less than 100 persons: 1,105 (2006); Black-owned businesses: n/a (2002); Hispanic-owned businesses: n/a (2002); Asian-owned businesses: n/a (2002); Women-owned businesses: 869 (2002); Retail sales per capita: $13,546 (2008). Single-family building permits issued: 59 (2007); Multi-family building permits issued: 10 (2007).
Income: Per capita income: $22,571 (2007); Median household income: $45,207 (2007); Average household income: $54,597 (2007); Percent of households with income of $100,000 or more: 10.6% (2007); Poverty rate: 10.7% (2005); Bankruptcy rate: 3.95% (2007).
Taxes: Total county taxes per capita: $158 (2006); County property taxes per capita: $123 (2006).
Education: Percent of population age 25 and over with: High school diploma (including GED) or higher: 84.1% (2007); Bachelor's degree or higher: 15.8% (2007); Master's degree or higher: 5.1% (2007).
Housing: Homeownership rate: 75.3% (2007); Median home value: $115,502 (2007); Median rent: $331 per month (2000); Median age of housing: 46 years (2000).
Health: Birth rate: 123.0 per 10,000 population (2007); Death rate: 111.7 per 10,000 population (2007); Age-adjusted cancer mortality rate: 214.1 deaths per 100,000 population (2005); Number of physicians: 14.1 per 10,000 population (2005); Hospital beds: 39.5 per 10,000 population (2004); Hospital admissions: 1,411.6 per 10,000 population (2004).
Elections: 2004 Presidential election results: 57.3% Bush, 41.8% Kerry, 0.1% Nader, 0.8% Badnarik
National and State Parks: Lake Le-Aqua-Na State Park

Additional Information Contacts

Stephenson County Government. . . . . (815) 235-8277
http://www.co.stephenson.il.us
City of Freeport . . . . (815) 235-8200
http://www.ci.freeport.il.us
Freeport Area Chamber of Commerce . . . . (815) 233-1350
http://www.freeportilchamber.com

Stephenson County Communities

CEDARVILLE (village). Covers a land area of 0.449 square miles and a water area of 0 square miles. Located at 42.37° N. Lat.; 89.63° W. Long. Elevation is 866 feet.
History: Cedarville was the birthplace and burial place of Jane Addams (1860-1935), whose parents built a house here in 1850 and raised their family on the homestead. John Addams operated a mill.
Population: 753 (1990); 719 (2000); 647 (2007); 642 (2012 projected); Race: 98.6% White, 0.0% Black, 1.2% Asian, 0.2% Hispanic of any race (2007); Density: 1,439.6 persons per square mile (2007); Average household size: 2.41 (2007); Median age: 41.0 (2007); Males per 100

females: 100.9 (2007); Marriage status: 17.2% never married, 71.9% now married, 5.2% widowed, 5.7% divorced (2000); Foreign born: 0.6% (2000); Ancestry (includes multiple ancestries): 45.1% German, 12.4% Irish, 11.8% English, 6.4% United States or American, 4.0% Swiss (2000).
Economy: Single-family building permits issued: 0 (2007); Multi-family building permits issued: 0 (2007); Employment by occupation: 6.9% management, 17.3% professional, 9.6% services, 26.9% sales, 0.5% farming, 14.9% construction, 23.9% production (2000).
Income: Per capita income: $23,887 (2007); Median household income: $51,250 (2007); Average household income: $57,454 (2007); Percent of households with income of $100,000 or more: 9.7% (2007); Poverty rate: 2.6% (2000).
Education: Percent of population age 25 and over with: High school diploma (including GED) or higher: 89.3% (2007); Bachelor's degree or higher: 17.9% (2007); Master's degree or higher: 3.9% (2007).
Housing: Homeownership rate: 91.1% (2007); Median home value: $110,129 (2007); Median rent: $500 per month (2000); Median age of housing: 39 years (2000).
Transportation: Commute to work: 95.1% car, 0.0% public transportation, 1.4% walk, 3.5% work from home (2000); Travel time to work: 36.1% less than 15 minutes, 43.9% 15 to 30 minutes, 8.7% 30 to 45 minutes, 5.1% 45 to 60 minutes, 6.2% 60 minutes or more (2000)

DAKOTA (village). Covers a land area of 0.288 square miles and a water area of 0 square miles. Located at 42.38° N. Lat.; 89.52° W. Long. Elevation is 945 feet.
Population: 560 (1990); 499 (2000); 442 (2007); 440 (2012 projected); Race: 97.7% White, 0.9% Black, 0.7% Asian, 0.5% Hispanic of any race (2007); Density: 1,534.1 persons per square mile (2007); Average household size: 2.48 (2007); Median age: 38.6 (2007); Males per 100 females: 95.6 (2007); Marriage status: 25.5% never married, 56.9% now married, 8.2% widowed, 9.4% divorced (2000); Foreign born: 0.8% (2000); Ancestry (includes multiple ancestries): 46.8% German, 9.1% Irish, 8.3% English, 7.9% United States or American, 5.3% Swiss (2000).
Economy: Single-family building permits issued: 0 (2007); Multi-family building permits issued: 0 (2007); Employment by occupation: 5.7% management, 13.4% professional, 16.4% services, 19.1% sales, 1.7% farming, 9.4% construction, 34.2% production (2000).
Income: Per capita income: $22,381 (2007); Median household income: $51,200 (2007); Average household income: $55,576 (2007); Percent of households with income of $100,000 or more: 8.4% (2007); Poverty rate: 3.9% (2000).
Education: Percent of population age 25 and over with: High school diploma (including GED) or higher: 87.2% (2007); Bachelor's degree or higher: 6.7% (2007); Master's degree or higher: 1.3% (2007).

School District(s)

Dakota CUSD 201 (PK-12)
2005-06 Enrollment: 907 . . . . (815) 449-2832
Housing: Homeownership rate: 77.5% (2007); Median home value: $116,667 (2007); Median rent: $321 per month (2000); Median age of housing: 57 years (2000).
Transportation: Commute to work: 91.2% car, 0.7% public transportation, 4.7% walk, 3.0% work from home (2000); Travel time to work: 28.5% less than 15 minutes, 50.3% 15 to 30 minutes, 10.8% 30 to 45 minutes, 5.9% 45 to 60 minutes, 4.5% 60 minutes or more (2000)

DAVIS (village). Covers a land area of 0.428 square miles and a water area of 0 square miles. Located at 42.42° N. Lat.; 89.41° W. Long. Elevation is 889 feet.
Population: 608 (1990); 662 (2000); 703 (2007); 705 (2012 projected); Race: 98.6% White, 0.3% Black, 0.1% Asian, 2.1% Hispanic of any race (2007); Density: 1,642.5 persons per square mile (2007); Average household size: 2.56 (2007); Median age: 35.2 (2007); Males per 100 females: 99.7 (2007); Marriage status: 18.4% never married, 65.5% now married, 7.1% widowed, 8.9% divorced (2000); Foreign born: 0.3% (2000); Ancestry (includes multiple ancestries): 42.0% German, 8.9% Irish, 6.8% Swiss, 6.3% United States or American, 4.9% Norwegian (2000).
Economy: Single-family building permits issued: 1 (2007); Multi-family building permits issued: 0 (2007); Employment by occupation: 10.8% management, 10.5% professional, 12.0% services, 27.9% sales, 2.6% farming, 17.1% construction, 19.1% production (2000).
Income: Per capita income: $22,550 (2007); Median household income: $55,139 (2007); Average household income: $57,645 (2007); Percent of households with income of $100,000 or more: 9.5% (2007); Poverty rate: 7.1% (2000).
Education: Percent of population age 25 and over with: High school diploma (including GED) or higher: 80.9% (2007); Bachelor's degree or higher: 11.4% (2007); Master's degree or higher: 2.1% (2007).
Housing: Homeownership rate: 85.5% (2007); Median home value: $129,953 (2007); Median rent: $288 per month (2000); Median age of housing: 50 years (2000).
Transportation: Commute to work: 94.0% car, 0.6% public transportation, 1.1% walk, 4.3% work from home (2000); Travel time to work: 22.8% less than 15 minutes, 26.6% 15 to 30 minutes, 31.4% 30 to 45 minutes, 11.4% 45 to 60 minutes, 7.8% 60 minutes or more (2000)

FREEPORT (city). County seat. Covers a land area of 11.413 square miles and a water area of 0.010 square miles. Located at 42.29° N. Lat.; 89.63° W. Long. Elevation is 778 feet.
History: Freeport was settled in 1835 by William "Tutty" Baker and his wife. The name reportedly came from Baker's generosity in sharing his food with anyone who came along. Miners returning from the Galena lead mines joined the Bakers, and Freeport became the seat of Stephenson County. It was here that the second Lincoln-Douglas debate took place in 1858.
Population: 26,316 (1990); 26,443 (2000); 25,421 (2007); 24,677 (2012 projected); Race: 80.1% White, 14.3% Black, 1.2% Asian, 3.1% Hispanic of any race (2007); Density: 2,227.3 persons per square mile (2007); Average household size: 2.34 (2007); Median age: 39.7 (2007); Males per 100 females: 88.4 (2007); Marriage status: 26.2% never married, 53.2% now married, 8.9% widowed, 11.6% divorced (2000); Foreign born: 2.7% (2000); Ancestry (includes multiple ancestries): 36.3% German, 18.8% Other groups, 11.0% Irish, 8.1% English, 5.2% United States or American (2000).
Economy: Unemployment rate: 6.4% (4/2008); Total civilian labor force: 12,788 (4/2008); Single-family building permits issued: 6 (2007); Multi-family building permits issued: 10 (2007); Employment by occupation: 10.3% management, 17.8% professional, 14.7% services, 26.1% sales, 0.1% farming, 7.8% construction, 23.2% production (2000).
Income: Per capita income: $20,658 (2007); Median household income: $38,685 (2007); Average household income: $47,426 (2007); Percent of households with income of $100,000 or more: 7.3% (2007); Poverty rate: 13.1% (2000).
Education: Percent of population age 25 and over with: High school diploma (including GED) or higher: 82.6% (2007); Bachelor's degree or higher: 17.7% (2007); Master's degree or higher: 5.5% (2007).

School District(s)

Career & Tech Educ Consortium
2005-06 Enrollment: n/a . . . . (815) 232-0709
Carroll/Jo Daviess/Stephenson Roe (06-12)
2005-06 Enrollment: 80 . . . . (815) 947-3810
Freeport SD 145 (PK-12)
2005-06 Enrollment: 4,435 . . . . (815) 232-0300

Two-year College(s)

Highland Community College (Public)
Fall 2007 Enrollment: 2,049. . . . . (815) 235-6121
2007-08 Tuition: In-state $3,870; Out-of-state $3,870
Housing: Homeownership rate: 68.7% (2007); Median home value: $94,938 (2007); Median rent: $328 per month (2000); Median age of housing: 48 years (2000).
Hospitals: FHN Memorial Hospital (194 beds)
Safety: Violent crime rate: 46.1 per 10,000 population; Property crime rate: 558.7 per 10,000 population (2006).
Newspapers: Advertizer Shopping News (Local news; Circulation 22,800); The Journal-Standard (Local news; Circulation 36,000)
Transportation: Commute to work: 94.0% car, 1.2% public transportation, 2.7% walk, 1.8% work from home (2000); Travel time to work: 66.2% less than 15 minutes, 17.2% 15 to 30 minutes, 8.3% 30 to 45 minutes, 4.5% 45 to 60 minutes, 3.9% 60 minutes or more (2000)
Airports: Albertus (general aviation)

Additional Information Contacts

City of Freeport . . . . (815) 235-8200
http://www.ci.freeport.il.us
Freeport Area Chamber of Commerce . . . . (815) 233-1350
http://www.freeportilchamber.com

GERMAN VALLEY (village). Covers a land area of 0.487 square miles and a water area of 0 square miles. Located at 42.21° N. Lat.; 89.47° W. Long. Elevation is 823 feet.

Population: 507 (1990); 481 (2000); 446 (2007); 442 (2012 projected); Race: 99.1% White, 0.0% Black, 0.2% Asian, 3.6% Hispanic of any race (2007); Density: 916.0 persons per square mile (2007); Average household size: 2.62 (2007); Median age: 37.5 (2007); Males per 100 females: 98.2 (2007); Marriage status: 21.1% never married, 60.8% now married, 6.8% widowed, 11.3% divorced (2000); Foreign born: 1.4% (2000); Ancestry (includes multiple ancestries): 59.5% German, 10.0% Irish, 8.0% Norwegian, 7.0% English, 5.5% Other groups (2000).
Economy: Single-family building permits issued: 0 (2007); Multi-family building permits issued: 0 (2007); Employment by occupation: 9.8% management, 20.1% professional, 16.3% services, 23.5% sales, 0.0% farming, 9.8% construction, 20.5% production (2000).
Income: Per capita income: $21,934 (2007); Median household income: $47,000 (2007); Average household income: $57,544 (2007); Percent of households with income of $100,000 or more: 12.9% (2007); Poverty rate: 6.2% (2000).
Education: Percent of population age 25 and over with: High school diploma (including GED) or higher: 91.8% (2007); Bachelor's degree or higher: 12.2% (2007); Master's degree or higher: 3.4% (2007).

School District(s)

Forrestville Valley CUSD 221 (PK-12)
2005-06 Enrollment: 1,039 . . . . (815) 938-2036
Housing: Homeownership rate: 83.5% (2007); Median home value: $115,476 (2007); Median rent: $375 per month (2000); Median age of housing: 44 years (2000).
Transportation: Commute to work: 91.5% car, 0.8% public transportation, 3.5% walk, 3.5% work from home (2000); Travel time to work: 15.5% less than 15 minutes, 51.0% 15 to 30 minutes, 24.7% 30 to 45 minutes, 7.2% 45 to 60 minutes, 1.6% 60 minutes or more (2000)

KENT (unincorporated postal area, zip code 61044). Covers a land area of 14.493 square miles and a water area of 0 square miles. Located at 42.32° N. Lat.; 89.91° W. Long. Elevation is 899 feet.
Population: 234 (2000); Race: 100.0% White, 0.0% Black, 0.0% Asian, 0.0% Hispanic of any race (2000); Density: 16.1 persons per square mile (2000); Age: 19.2% under 18, 5.3% over 64 (2000); Marriage status: 17.3% never married, 77.2% now married, 3.1% widowed, 2.4% divorced (2000); Foreign born: 0.0% (2000); Ancestry (includes multiple ancestries): 76.8% German, 16.6% Dutch, 15.9% English, 10.6% Irish, 4.6% Swedish (2000).
Economy: Employment by occupation: 28.7% management, 4.3% professional, 7.0% services, 24.3% sales, 0.0% farming, 8.7% construction, 27.0% production (2000).
Income: Per capita income: $24,019 (2000); Median household income: $44,000 (2000); Poverty rate: 0.0% (2000).
Education: Percent of population age 25 and over with: High school diploma (including GED) or higher: 90.9% (2000); Bachelor's degree or higher: 6.4% (2000).
Housing: Homeownership rate: 89.8% (2000); Median home value: $65,000 (2000); Median rent: $n/a per month (2000); Median age of housing: 60+ years (2000).
Transportation: Commute to work: 82.7% car, 0.0% public transportation, 4.5% walk, 12.7% work from home (2000); Travel time to work: 38.5% less than 15 minutes, 28.1% 15 to 30 minutes, 30.2% 30 to 45 minutes, 0.0% 45 to 60 minutes, 3.1% 60 minutes or more (2000)

LENA (village). Covers a land area of 2.139 square miles and a water area of 0 square miles. Located at 42.37° N. Lat.; 89.82° W. Long. Elevation is 948 feet.
History: Lena was known as one of the first places in the United States where Camembert and Brie cheeses were made.
Population: 2,794 (1990); 2,887 (2000); 2,799 (2007); 2,779 (2012 projected); Race: 98.0% White, 0.3% Black, 0.1% Asian, 1.6% Hispanic of any race (2007); Density: 1,308.8 persons per square mile (2007); Average household size: 2.43 (2007); Median age: 42.9 (2007); Males per 100 females: 89.4 (2007); Marriage status: 17.5% never married, 64.9% now married, 10.3% widowed, 7.3% divorced (2000); Foreign born: 1.1% (2000); Ancestry (includes multiple ancestries): 46.0% German, 12.4% Irish, 11.2% English, 7.0% United States or American, 6.7% Dutch (2000).
Economy: Single-family building permits issued: 7 (2007); Multi-family building permits issued: 0 (2007); Employment by occupation: 8.1% management, 18.2% professional, 11.6% services, 28.5% sales, 2.9% farming, 8.4% construction, 22.3% production (2000).
Income: Per capita income: $21,900 (2007); Median household income: $44,722 (2007); Average household income: $52,168 (2007); Percent of households with income of $100,000 or more: 9.2% (2007); Poverty rate: 4.7% (2000).
Education: Percent of population age 25 and over with: High school diploma (including GED) or higher: 84.0% (2007); Bachelor's degree or higher: 14.2% (2007); Master's degree or higher: 5.8% (2007).

School District(s)

Lena Winslow CUSD 202 (PK-12)
2005-06 Enrollment: 1,056 . . . . (815) 369-3100
Housing: Homeownership rate: 77.3% (2007); Median home value: $132,581 (2007); Median rent: $336 per month (2000); Median age of housing: 32 years (2000).
Safety: Violent crime rate: 49.1 per 10,000 population; Property crime rate: 157.7 per 10,000 population (2006).
Transportation: Commute to work: 95.7% car, 0.0% public transportation, 1.1% walk, 2.9% work from home (2000); Travel time to work: 37.8% less than 15 minutes, 39.5% 15 to 30 minutes, 13.3% 30 to 45 minutes, 3.2% 45 to 60 minutes, 6.1% 60 minutes or more (2000)

MCCONNELL (unincorporated postal area, zip code 61050). Covers a land area of 13.223 square miles and a water area of 0 square miles. Located at 42.44° N. Lat.; 89.72° W. Long. Elevation is 778 feet.
Population: 447 (2000); Race: 100.0% White, 0.0% Black, 0.0% Asian, 0.0% Hispanic of any race (2000); Density: 33.8 persons per square mile (2000); Age: 20.2% under 18, 18.0% over 64 (2000); Marriage status: 16.1% never married, 67.4% now married, 4.9% widowed, 11.7% divorced (2000); Foreign born: 2.8% (2000); Ancestry (includes multiple ancestries): 50.6% German, 13.7% Irish, 10.7% English, 9.9% Swiss, 9.4% United States or American (2000).
Economy: Employment by occupation: 23.5% management, 11.3% professional, 9.0% services, 21.3% sales, 1.8% farming, 12.2% construction, 20.8% production (2000).
Income: Per capita income: $16,634 (2000); Median household income: $32,143 (2000); Poverty rate: 11.8% (2000).
Education: Percent of population age 25 and over with: High school diploma (including GED) or higher: 85.0% (2000); Bachelor's degree or higher: 2.2% (2000).
Housing: Homeownership rate: 83.5% (2000); Median home value: $65,000 (2000); Median rent: $325 per month (2000); Median age of housing: 60+ years (2000).
Transportation: Commute to work: 84.7% car, 0.0% public transportation, 0.0% walk, 15.3% work from home (2000); Travel time to work: 26.9% less than 15 minutes, 34.6% 15 to 30 minutes, 25.3% 30 to 45 minutes, 7.1% 45 to 60 minutes, 6.0% 60 minutes or more (2000)

ORANGEVILLE (village). Covers a land area of 0.642 square miles and a water area of 0 square miles. Located at 42.46° N. Lat.; 89.64° W. Long. Elevation is 820 feet.
Population: 637 (1990); 751 (2000); 738 (2007); 723 (2012 projected); Race: 99.5% White, 0.1% Black, 0.0% Asian, 0.9% Hispanic of any race (2007); Density: 1,148.7 persons per square mile (2007); Average household size: 2.48 (2007); Median age: 36.9 (2007); Males per 100 females: 102.2 (2007); Marriage status: 18.4% never married, 66.4% now married, 6.3% widowed, 8.8% divorced (2000); Foreign born: 1.1% (2000); Ancestry (includes multiple ancestries): 55.0% German, 13.2% Irish, 9.1% Swiss, 5.8% English, 5.0% United States or American (2000).
Economy: Single-family building permits issued: 3 (2007); Multi-family building permits issued: 0 (2007); Employment by occupation: 4.4% management, 10.9% professional, 11.1% services, 23.8% sales, 3.1% farming, 7.8% construction, 38.9% production (2000).
Income: Per capita income: $20,152 (2007); Median household income: $45,161 (2007); Average household income: $49,908 (2007); Percent of households with income of $100,000 or more: 5.0% (2007); Poverty rate: 3.3% (2000).
Education: Percent of population age 25 and over with: High school diploma (including GED) or higher: 87.9% (2007); Bachelor's degree or higher: 11.0% (2007); Master's degree or higher: 3.8% (2007).

School District(s)

Orangeville CUSD 203 (PK-12)
2005-06 Enrollment: 484 . . . . (815) 789-4450
Housing: Homeownership rate: 75.8% (2007); Median home value: $116,810 (2007); Median rent: $308 per month (2000); Median age of housing: 46 years (2000).
Transportation: Commute to work: 89.3% car, 0.0% public transportation, 5.2% walk, 4.7% work from home (2000); Travel time to work: 21.9% less

than 15 minutes, 56.6% 15 to 30 minutes, 12.0% 30 to 45 minutes, 4.9% 45 to 60 minutes, 4.6% 60 minutes or more (2000)

PEARL CITY (village). Covers a land area of 0.567 square miles and a water area of 0.009 square miles. Located at 42.26° N. Lat.; 89.82° W. Long. Elevation is 833 feet.
Population: 700 (1990); 780 (2000); 814 (2007); 831 (2012 projected); Race: 98.6% White, 0.4% Black, 0.1% Asian, 1.0% Hispanic of any race (2007); Density: 1,436.7 persons per square mile (2007); Average household size: 2.62 (2007); Median age: 34.6 (2007); Males per 100 females: 92.0 (2007); Marriage status: 24.0% never married, 59.6% now married, 8.1% widowed, 8.4% divorced (2000); Foreign born: 0.9% (2000); Ancestry (includes multiple ancestries): 58.0% German, 10.3% English, 10.2% Irish, 5.3% United States or American, 4.5% Norwegian (2000).
Economy: Single-family building permits issued: 1 (2007); Multi-family building permits issued: 0 (2007); Employment by occupation: 10.6% management, 14.2% professional, 17.7% services, 24.1% sales, 3.4% farming, 11.7% construction, 18.3% production (2000).
Income: Per capita income: $21,873 (2007); Median household income: $49,028 (2007); Average household income: $57,251 (2007); Percent of households with income of $100,000 or more: 10.3% (2007); Poverty rate: 4.6% (2000).
Education: Percent of population age 25 and over with: High school diploma (including GED) or higher: 90.4% (2007); Bachelor's degree or higher: 14.5% (2007); Master's degree or higher: 1.6% (2007).

School District(s)

Pearl City CUSD 200 (PK-12)
2005-06 Enrollment: 551 . . . . (815) 443-2715

Housing: Homeownership rate: 82.3% (2007); Median home value: $121,382 (2007); Median rent: $331 per month (2000); Median age of housing: 46 years (2000).
Transportation: Commute to work: 91.5% car, 0.0% public transportation, 4.6% walk, 3.0% work from home (2000); Travel time to work: 28.1% less than 15 minutes, 54.1% 15 to 30 minutes, 10.6% 30 to 45 minutes, 1.2% 45 to 60 minutes, 5.9% 60 minutes or more (2000)

RIDOTT (village). Covers a land area of 0.105 square miles and a water area of 0 square miles. Located at 42.29° N. Lat.; 89.47° W. Long. Elevation is 758 feet.
Population: 156 (1990); 159 (2000); 160 (2007); 156 (2012 projected); Race: 100.0% White, 0.0% Black, 0.0% Asian, 0.0% Hispanic of any race (2007); Density: 1,528.5 persons per square mile (2007); Average household size: 2.50 (2007); Median age: 42.3 (2007); Males per 100 females: 119.2 (2007); Marriage status: 10.0% never married, 82.5% now married, 5.0% widowed, 2.5% divorced (2000); Foreign born: 2.2% (2000); Ancestry (includes multiple ancestries): 25.0% German, 11.8% Swedish, 7.4% Irish, 6.6% Other groups, 6.6% Swiss (2000).
Economy: Employment by occupation: 2.6% management, 6.6% professional, 18.4% services, 32.9% sales, 2.6% farming, 14.5% construction, 22.4% production (2000).
Income: Per capita income: $18,781 (2007); Median household income: $50,588 (2007); Average household income: $46,953 (2007); Percent of households with income of $100,000 or more: 3.1% (2007); Poverty rate: 2.9% (2000).
Education: Percent of population age 25 and over with: High school diploma (including GED) or higher: 69.3% (2007); Bachelor's degree or higher: 1.8% (2007); Master's degree or higher: 1.8% (2007).
Housing: Homeownership rate: 89.1% (2007); Median home value: $82,500 (2007); Median rent: $342 per month (2000); Median age of housing: 60+ years (2000).
Transportation: Commute to work: 97.1% car, 0.0% public transportation, 0.0% walk, 2.9% work from home (2000); Travel time to work: 3.0% less than 15 minutes, 69.7% 15 to 30 minutes, 16.7% 30 to 45 minutes, 6.1% 45 to 60 minutes, 4.5% 60 minutes or more (2000)

ROCK CITY (village). Covers a land area of 0.143 square miles and a water area of 0 square miles. Located at 42.41° N. Lat.; 89.46° W. Long. Elevation is 909 feet.
Population: 331 (1990); 313 (2000); 305 (2007); 294 (2012 projected); Race: 99.7% White, 0.0% Black, 0.0% Asian, 0.0% Hispanic of any race (2007); Density: 2,139.6 persons per square mile (2007); Average household size: 2.54 (2007); Median age: 35.7 (2007); Males per 100 females: 100.7 (2007); Marriage status: 18.3% never married, 55.7% now married, 16.0% widowed, 9.9% divorced (2000); Foreign born: 0.0% (2000); Ancestry (includes multiple ancestries): 41.5% German, 11.9% Swedish, 7.7% Irish, 6.8% Swiss, 5.9% United States or American (2000).
Economy: Single-family building permits issued: 3 (2007); Multi-family building permits issued: 0 (2007); Employment by occupation: 7.5% management, 16.3% professional, 10.2% services, 25.2% sales, 1.4% farming, 6.1% construction, 33.3% production (2000).
Income: Per capita income: $24,230 (2007); Median household income: $54,737 (2007); Average household income: $61,583 (2007); Percent of households with income of $100,000 or more: 9.2% (2007); Poverty rate: 4.7% (2000).
Education: Percent of population age 25 and over with: High school diploma (including GED) or higher: 80.6% (2007); Bachelor's degree or higher: 6.3% (2007); Master's degree or higher: 3.1% (2007).
Housing: Homeownership rate: 83.3% (2007); Median home value: $116,379 (2007); Median rent: $200 per month (2000); Median age of housing: 47 years (2000).
Transportation: Commute to work: 81.8% car, 0.0% public transportation, 2.1% walk, 14.7% work from home (2000); Travel time to work: 32.8% less than 15 minutes, 29.5% 15 to 30 minutes, 24.6% 30 to 45 minutes, 11.5% 45 to 60 minutes, 1.6% 60 minutes or more (2000)

WINSLOW (village). Covers a land area of 0.446 square miles and a water area of 0 square miles. Located at 42.49° N. Lat.; 89.79° W. Long. Elevation is 774 feet.
Population: 317 (1990); 345 (2000); 366 (2007); 369 (2012 projected); Race: 95.4% White, 0.0% Black, 0.0% Asian, 3.8% Hispanic of any race (2007); Density: 820.1 persons per square mile (2007); Average household size: 2.51 (2007); Median age: 38.5 (2007); Males per 100 females: 98.9 (2007); Marriage status: 35.2% never married, 53.0% now married, 5.9% widowed, 5.9% divorced (2000); Foreign born: 0.0% (2000); Ancestry (includes multiple ancestries): 50.3% German, 16.1% Irish, 7.5% English, 6.9% Swiss, 6.9% Other groups (2000).
Economy: Single-family building permits issued: 1 (2007); Multi-family building permits issued: 0 (2007); Employment by occupation: 3.8% management, 7.6% professional, 15.2% services, 22.3% sales, 10.3% farming, 9.8% construction, 31.0% production (2000).
Income: Per capita income: $21,257 (2007); Median household income: $50,690 (2007); Average household income: $53,288 (2007); Percent of households with income of $100,000 or more: 10.3% (2007); Poverty rate: 5.5% (2000).
Education: Percent of population age 25 and over with: High school diploma (including GED) or higher: 82.4% (2007); Bachelor's degree or higher: 7.0% (2007); Master's degree or higher: 0.8% (2007).

School District(s)

Lena Winslow CUSD 202 (PK-12)
2005-06 Enrollment: 1,056 . . . . (815) 369-3100

Housing: Homeownership rate: 76.7% (2007); Median home value: $94,167 (2007); Median rent: $285 per month (2000); Median age of housing: 60+ years (2000).
Transportation: Commute to work: 90.8% car, 0.0% public transportation, 3.3% walk, 3.8% work from home (2000); Travel time to work: 27.1% less than 15 minutes, 40.1% 15 to 30 minutes, 18.6% 30 to 45 minutes, 8.5% 45 to 60 minutes, 5.6% 60 minutes or more (2000)

Tazewell County

Located in central Illinois; bounded on the northwest by the Illinois River; drained by the Mackinaw River. Covers a land area of 648.86 square miles, a water area of 9.03 square miles, and is located in the Central Time Zone. The county was founded in 1827. County seat is Pekin.

Tazewell County is part of the Peoria, IL Metropolitan Statistical Area. The entire metro area includes: Marshall County, IL; Peoria County, IL; Stark County, IL; Tazewell County, IL; Woodford County, IL

Population: 123,692 (1990); 128,485 (2000); 130,935 (2007); 132,692 (2012 projected); Race: 96.9% White, 1.1% Black, 0.6% Asian, 1.4% Hispanic of any race (2007); Density: 201.8 persons per square mile (2007); Average household size: 2.50 (2007); Median age: 39.6 (2007); Males per 100 females: 96.9 (2007).
Religion: Five largest groups: 11.0% Catholic Church, 5.8% The United Methodist Church, 5.2% Lutheran Church—Missouri Synod, 3.0% Southern Baptist Convention, 2.2% Christian Churches and Churches of Christ (2000).
Economy: Unemployment rate: 4.3% (4/2008); Total civilian labor force: 74,890 (4/2008); Leading industries: 19.9% manufacturing; 15.1% retail

trade; 12.6% accommodation & food services (2005); Farms: 918 totaling 327,236 acres (2002); Companies that employ 500 or more persons: 6 (2006); Companies that employ 100 to 499 persons: 62 (2006); Companies that employ less than 100 persons: 2,784 (2006); Black-owned businesses: n/a (2002); Hispanic-owned businesses: n/a (2002); Asian-owned businesses: n/a (2002); Women-owned businesses: 2,532 (2002); Retail sales per capita: $19,234 (2008). Single-family building permits issued: 410 (2007); Multi-family building permits issued: 110 (2007).
Income: Per capita income: $25,580 (2007); Median household income: $52,104 (2007); Average household income: $62,823 (2007); Percent of households with income of $100,000 or more: 15.2% (2007); Poverty rate: 8.7% (2005); Bankruptcy rate: 3.90% (2007).
Taxes: Total county taxes per capita: $106 (2006); County property taxes per capita: $59 (2006).
Education: Percent of population age 25 and over with: High school diploma (including GED) or higher: 85.2% (2007); Bachelor's degree or higher: 18.5% (2007); Master's degree or higher: 5.8% (2007).
Housing: Homeownership rate: 76.3% (2007); Median home value: $119,725 (2007); Median rent: $378 per month (2000); Median age of housing: 37 years (2000).
Health: Birth rate: 133.6 per 10,000 population (2007); Death rate: 100.9 per 10,000 population (2007); Age-adjusted cancer mortality rate: 219.4 deaths per 100,000 population (2005); Air Quality Index: 98.1% good, 1.6% moderate, 0.3% unhealthy for sensitive individuals, 0.0% unhealthy (percent of days in 2007); Number of physicians: 11.8 per 10,000 population (2005); Hospital beds: 20.9 per 10,000 population (2004); Hospital admissions: 369.1 per 10,000 population (2004).
Elections: 2004 Presidential election results: 57.8% Bush, 41.4% Kerry, 0.0% Nader, 0.7% Badnarik
National and State Parks: Fort Creve Coeur State Park
Additional Information Contacts
Tazewell County Government . . . . (309) 477-2272
http://www.tazewell.com
City of East Peoria . . . . (309) 698-4715
http://www.cityofeastpeoria.com
City of Pekin . . . . (309) 477-2300
http://www.ci.pekin.il.us
City of Washington . . . . (309) 444-3196
http://ci.washington.il.us
East Peoria Chamber of Commerce . . . . (309) 699-6212
http://www.epcc.org
Morton Chamber of Commerce . . . . (309) 263-2491
http://www.mortonchamber.org
Pekin Area Chamber of Commerce . . . . (309) 346-2106
http://www.pekin.net
Village of Morton . . . . (309) 266-5361
http://www.morton-il.gov
Washington Chamber of Commerce . . . . (309) 444-9921
http://www.washingtoncoc.com

Tazewell County Communities

ARMINGTON (village). Covers a land area of 0.287 square miles and a water area of 0 square miles. Located at 40.33° N. Lat.; 89.31° W. Long. Elevation is 630 feet.
Population: 344 (1990); 368 (2000); 355 (2007); 356 (2012 projected); Race: 99.4% White, 0.0% Black, 0.0% Asian, 4.8% Hispanic of any race (2007); Density: 1,238.3 persons per square mile (2007); Average household size: 2.69 (2007); Median age: 32.2 (2007); Males per 100 females: 102.9 (2007); Marriage status: 12.9% never married, 72.2% now married, 5.5% widowed, 9.4% divorced (2000); Foreign born: 1.2% (2000); Ancestry (includes multiple ancestries): 31.5% German, 14.7% English, 10.3% Irish, 8.2% United States or American, 7.9% Other groups (2000).
Economy: Single-family building permits issued: 0 (2007); Multi-family building permits issued: 0 (2007); Employment by occupation: 7.7% management, 18.7% professional, 12.3% services, 23.9% sales, 1.3% farming, 15.5% construction, 20.6% production (2000).
Income: Per capita income: $19,345 (2007); Median household income: $44,545 (2007); Average household income: $52,027 (2007); Percent of households with income of $100,000 or more: 9.8% (2007); Poverty rate: 8.0% (2000).
Education: Percent of population age 25 and over with: High school diploma (including GED) or higher: 84.2% (2007); Bachelor's degree or higher: 15.3% (2007); Master's degree or higher: 5.4% (2007).
Housing: Homeownership rate: 87.1% (2007); Median home value: $81,500 (2007); Median rent: $263 per month (2000); Median age of housing: 60+ years (2000).
Safety: Violent crime rate: 28.1 per 10,000 population; Property crime rate: 449.4 per 10,000 population (2006).
Transportation: Commute to work: 88.9% car, 1.3% public transportation, 2.0% walk, 3.9% work from home (2000); Travel time to work: 25.9% less than 15 minutes, 9.5% 15 to 30 minutes, 47.6% 30 to 45 minutes, 12.9% 45 to 60 minutes, 4.1% 60 minutes or more (2000)

CREVE COEUR (village). Covers a land area of 4.059 square miles and a water area of 0.376 square miles. Located at 40.64° N. Lat.; 89.59° W. Long. Elevation is 686 feet.
History: Incorporated 1921. Nearby is site of old Fort Creve Coeur, built 1680 by La Salle.
Population: 5,935 (1990); 5,448 (2000); 5,230 (2007); 5,081 (2012 projected); Race: 96.8% White, 0.4% Black, 0.1% Asian, 2.4% Hispanic of any race (2007); Density: 1,288.5 persons per square mile (2007); Average household size: 2.39 (2007); Median age: 37.9 (2007); Males per 100 females: 98.4 (2007); Marriage status: 21.8% never married, 56.8% now married, 8.5% widowed, 12.9% divorced (2000); Foreign born: 1.2% (2000); Ancestry (includes multiple ancestries): 22.9% German, 16.1% United States or American, 10.7% Irish, 9.4% Other groups, 8.5% English (2000).
Economy: Single-family building permits issued: 7 (2007); Multi-family building permits issued: 0 (2007); Employment by occupation: 5.7% management, 8.6% professional, 20.0% services, 30.4% sales, 0.3% farming, 9.2% construction, 25.9% production (2000).
Income: Per capita income: $18,375 (2007); Median household income: $38,693 (2007); Average household income: $43,921 (2007); Percent of households with income of $100,000 or more: 3.2% (2007); Poverty rate: 7.3% (2000).
Education: Percent of population age 25 and over with: High school diploma (including GED) or higher: 79.9% (2007); Bachelor's degree or higher: 5.4% (2007); Master's degree or higher: 1.7% (2007).
School District(s)
Creve Coeur SD 76 (PK-08)
2005-06 Enrollment: 704 . . . . (309) 698-3600
Tazewell Roe (08-12)
2005-06 Enrollment: 79 . . . . (309) 477-2290
Housing: Homeownership rate: 75.0% (2007); Median home value: $79,082 (2007); Median rent: $345 per month (2000); Median age of housing: 45 years (2000).
Safety: Violent crime rate: 174.9 per 10,000 population; Property crime rate: 378.3 per 10,000 population (2006).
Transportation: Commute to work: 94.2% car, 0.9% public transportation, 1.6% walk, 2.1% work from home (2000); Travel time to work: 32.1% less than 15 minutes, 53.8% 15 to 30 minutes, 9.2% 30 to 45 minutes, 1.5% 45 to 60 minutes, 3.4% 60 minutes or more (2000)

DEER CREEK (village). Covers a land area of 0.314 square miles and a water area of 0 square miles. Located at 40.62° N. Lat.; 89.33° W. Long. Elevation is 761 feet.
Population: 630 (1990); 605 (2000); 718 (2007); 780 (2012 projected); Race: 98.5% White, 0.0% Black, 0.8% Asian, 0.1% Hispanic of any race (2007); Density: 2,283.5 persons per square mile (2007); Average household size: 2.58 (2007); Median age: 36.9 (2007); Males per 100 females: 103.4 (2007); Marriage status: 23.6% never married, 60.3% now married, 4.4% widowed, 11.7% divorced (2000); Foreign born: 2.1% (2000); Ancestry (includes multiple ancestries): 45.9% German, 19.2% Irish, 12.8% Other groups, 9.3% English, 8.1% United States or American (2000).
Economy: Single-family building permits issued: 0 (2007); Multi-family building permits issued: 6 (2007); Employment by occupation: 6.4% management, 13.4% professional, 17.3% services, 21.2% sales, 0.7% farming, 17.0% construction, 24.0% production (2000).
Income: Per capita income: $21,783 (2007); Median household income: $45,333 (2007); Average household income: $56,259 (2007); Percent of households with income of $100,000 or more: 12.2% (2007); Poverty rate: 5.5% (2000).
Education: Percent of population age 25 and over with: High school diploma (including GED) or higher: 87.4% (2007); Bachelor's degree or higher: 8.8% (2007); Master's degree or higher: 1.5% (2007).

School District(s)

Deer Creek-Mackinaw CUSD 701 (PK-12)
2005-06 Enrollment: 994 . . . . (309) 359-8965

Housing: Homeownership rate: 78.4% (2007); Median home value: $113,988 (2007); Median rent: $402 per month (2000); Median age of housing: 44 years (2000).

Transportation: Commute to work: 95.3% car, 0.0% public transportation, 1.4% walk, 3.2% work from home (2000); Travel time to work: 34.8% less than 15 minutes, 33.7% 15 to 30 minutes, 17.0% 30 to 45 minutes, 6.3% 45 to 60 minutes, 8.1% 60 minutes or more (2000)

DELAVAN (city). Covers a land area of 0.711 square miles and a water area of 0 square miles. Located at 40.37° N. Lat.; 89.54° W. Long. Elevation is 617 feet.

History: Founded 1837, incorporated 1888.

Population: 1,670 (1990); 1,825 (2000); 1,753 (2007); 1,744 (2012 projected); Race: 98.2% White, 0.5% Black, 0.1% Asian, 0.7% Hispanic of any race (2007); Density: 2,466.1 persons per square mile (2007); Average household size: 2.54 (2007); Median age: 37.5 (2007); Males per 100 females: 95.2 (2007); Marriage status: 20.0% never married, 63.5% now married, 8.6% widowed, 7.9% divorced (2000); Foreign born: 0.5% (2000); Ancestry (includes multiple ancestries): 34.4% German, 15.8% Irish, 11.0% United States or American, 7.5% English, 6.3% Other groups (2000).

Economy: Single-family building permits issued: 1 (2007); Multi-family building permits issued: 0 (2007); Employment by occupation: 6.0% management, 13.5% professional, 17.4% services, 27.3% sales, 1.3% farming, 14.1% construction, 20.4% production (2000).

Income: Per capita income: $21,921 (2007); Median household income: $44,847 (2007); Average household income: $55,611 (2007); Percent of households with income of $100,000 or more: 9.3% (2007); Poverty rate: 5.7% (2000).

Education: Percent of population age 25 and over with: High school diploma (including GED) or higher: 86.6% (2007); Bachelor's degree or higher: 11.9% (2007); Master's degree or higher: 2.8% (2007).

School District(s)

Delavan CUSD 703 (PK-12)
2005-06 Enrollment: 487 . . . . (309) 244-8283

Housing: Homeownership rate: 79.0% (2007); Median home value: $97,538 (2007); Median rent: $291 per month (2000); Median age of housing: 48 years (2000).

Newspapers: Delavan Times (National news; Circulation 1,400)

Transportation: Commute to work: 93.2% car, 0.0% public transportation, 4.7% walk, 1.8% work from home (2000); Travel time to work: 24.1% less than 15 minutes, 25.9% 15 to 30 minutes, 31.1% 30 to 45 minutes, 13.2% 45 to 60 minutes, 5.7% 60 minutes or more (2000)

EAST PEORIA (city). Covers a land area of 18.812 square miles and a water area of 2.215 square miles. Located at 40.66° N. Lat.; 89.54° W. Long. Elevation is 463 feet.

History: East Peoria developed as an industrial and residential neighbor of Peoria. The Caterpillar Tractor Company plant was a major industry.

Population: 22,946 (1990); 22,638 (2000); 22,583 (2007); 22,582 (2012 projected); Race: 96.9% White, 0.5% Black, 0.8% Asian, 1.6% Hispanic of any race (2007); Density: 1,200.4 persons per square mile (2007); Average household size: 2.33 (2007); Median age: 41.7 (2007); Males per 100 females: 93.7 (2007); Marriage status: 20.7% never married, 59.7% now married, 7.4% widowed, 12.3% divorced (2000); Foreign born: 1.2% (2000); Ancestry (includes multiple ancestries): 29.8% German, 14.2% Irish, 13.2% English, 12.2% United States or American, 7.8% Other groups (2000).

Economy: Single-family building permits issued: 70 (2007); Multi-family building permits issued: 5 (2007); Employment by occupation: 9.9% management, 16.0% professional, 15.6% services, 31.0% sales, 0.1% farming, 10.0% construction, 17.4% production (2000).

Income: Per capita income: $24,351 (2007); Median household income: $47,510 (2007); Average household income: $56,288 (2007); Percent of households with income of $100,000 or more: 11.6% (2007); Poverty rate: 7.2% (2000).

Education: Percent of population age 25 and over with: High school diploma (including GED) or higher: 82.0% (2007); Bachelor's degree or higher: 15.0% (2007); Master's degree or higher: 3.9% (2007).

School District(s)

East Peoria CHSD 309 (09-12)
2005-06 Enrollment: 1,204 . . . . (309) 694-8300

East Peoria SD 86 (PK-08)
2005-06 Enrollment: 1,887 . . . . (309) 427-5100

Riverview CCSD 2 (PK-08)
2005-06 Enrollment: 311 . . . . (309) 822-8550

Robein SD 85 (KG-08)
2005-06 Enrollment: 208 . . . . (309) 694-1409

Tazewell Roe (08-12)
2005-06 Enrollment: 79 . . . . (309) 477-2290

Two-year College(s)

Illinois Central College (Public)
Fall 2007 Enrollment: 11,804 . . . . (309) 694-5011
2007-08 Tuition: In-state $4,950; Out-of-state $4,950

Vocational/Technical School(s)

Oehrlein School of Cosmetology (Private, For-profit)
Fall 2007 Enrollment: 69 . . . . (309) 699-1561
2007-08 Tuition: $9,994

Housing: Homeownership rate: 73.4% (2007); Median home value: $120,292 (2007); Median rent: $364 per month (2000); Median age of housing: 38 years (2000).

Safety: Violent crime rate: 71.4 per 10,000 population; Property crime rate: 339.5 per 10,000 population (2006).

Transportation: Commute to work: 95.1% car, 1.0% public transportation, 0.9% walk, 1.9% work from home (2000); Travel time to work: 36.8% less than 15 minutes, 49.6% 15 to 30 minutes, 9.0% 30 to 45 minutes, 2.0% 45 to 60 minutes, 2.5% 60 minutes or more (2000)

Additional Information Contacts

City of East Peoria . . . . (309) 698-4715
http://www.cityofeastpeoria.com

East Peoria Chamber of Commerce . . . . (309) 699-6212
http://www.epcc.org

GREEN VALLEY (village). Covers a land area of 0.308 square miles and a water area of 0 square miles. Located at 40.40° N. Lat.; 89.64° W. Long. Elevation is 538 feet.

Population: 770 (1990); 728 (2000); 625 (2007); 626 (2012 projected); Race: 98.9% White, 0.2% Black, 0.5% Asian, 0.6% Hispanic of any race (2007); Density: 2,026.6 persons per square mile (2007); Average household size: 2.74 (2007); Median age: 34.5 (2007); Males per 100 females: 82.7 (2007); Marriage status: 17.4% never married, 66.3% now married, 8.2% widowed, 8.1% divorced (2000); Foreign born: 0.0% (2000); Ancestry (includes multiple ancestries): 28.8% German, 12.6% Irish, 11.5% United States or American, 7.4% Other groups, 6.5% English (2000).

Economy: Single-family building permits issued: 1 (2007); Multi-family building permits issued: 0 (2007); Employment by occupation: 7.0% management, 9.8% professional, 17.4% services, 26.8% sales, 1.5% farming, 10.7% construction, 26.8% production (2000).

Income: Per capita income: $20,374 (2007); Median household income: $46,429 (2007); Average household income: $53,015 (2007); Percent of households with income of $100,000 or more: 9.2% (2007); Poverty rate: 7.5% (2000).

Education: Percent of population age 25 and over with: High school diploma (including GED) or higher: 82.8% (2007); Bachelor's degree or higher: 9.7% (2007); Master's degree or higher: 1.5% (2007).

School District(s)

Midwest Central CUSD 191 (PK-12)
2005-06 Enrollment: 1,165 . . . . (309) 968-6868

Housing: Homeownership rate: 82.0% (2007); Median home value: $98,750 (2007); Median rent: $320 per month (2000); Median age of housing: 45 years (2000).

Safety: Violent crime rate: 42.7 per 10,000 population; Property crime rate: 57.0 per 10,000 population (2006).

Transportation: Commute to work: 95.4% car, 0.6% public transportation, 0.0% walk, 2.2% work from home (2000); Travel time to work: 16.8% less than 15 minutes, 43.0% 15 to 30 minutes, 21.5% 30 to 45 minutes, 13.9% 45 to 60 minutes, 4.7% 60 minutes or more (2000)

GROVELAND (unincorporated postal area, zip code 61535). Covers a land area of 8.063 square miles and a water area of 0.077 square miles. Located at 40.60° N. Lat.; 89.55° W. Long. Elevation is 771 feet.

Population: 1,398 (2000); Race: 97.9% White, 0.0% Black, 0.0% Asian, 0.0% Hispanic of any race (2000); Density: 173.4 persons per square mile (2000); Age: 29.1% under 18, 7.0% over 64 (2000); Marriage status: 16.9% never married, 74.7% now married, 4.4% widowed, 4.0% divorced (2000); Foreign born: 0.0% (2000); Ancestry (includes multiple ancestries): 45.9%

German, 13.3% Irish, 12.8% English, 6.8% Italian, 4.5% United States or American (2000).
Economy: Employment by occupation: 14.1% management, 38.7% professional, 10.1% services, 27.2% sales, 0.0% farming, 4.7% construction, 5.3% production (2000).
Income: Per capita income: $28,588 (2000); Median household income: $61,359 (2000); Poverty rate: 2.1% (2000).
Education: Percent of population age 25 and over with: High school diploma (including GED) or higher: 96.2% (2000); Bachelor's degree or higher: 32.3% (2000).
Housing: Homeownership rate: 92.5% (2000); Median home value: $141,100 (2000); Median rent: $478 per month (2000); Median age of housing: 27 years (2000).
Transportation: Commute to work: 95.6% car, 1.8% public transportation, 1.7% walk, 0.9% work from home (2000); Travel time to work: 29.1% less than 15 minutes, 54.2% 15 to 30 minutes, 8.5% 30 to 45 minutes, 5.8% 45 to 60 minutes, 2.4% 60 minutes or more (2000)

HOPEDALE (village). Covers a land area of 0.537 square miles and a water area of 0.004 square miles. Located at 40.42° N. Lat.; 89.41° W. Long. Elevation is 643 feet.
Population: 814 (1990); 929 (2000); 970 (2007); 990 (2012 projected); Race: 99.8% White, 0.0% Black, 0.0% Asian, 0.2% Hispanic of any race (2007); Density: 1,806.1 persons per square mile (2007); Average household size: 2.83 (2007); Median age: 44.2 (2007); Males per 100 females: 88.7 (2007); Marriage status: 19.5% never married, 62.2% now married, 10.8% widowed, 7.5% divorced (2000); Foreign born: 4.2% (2000); Ancestry (includes multiple ancestries): 38.2% German, 15.4% Irish, 12.9% United States or American, 12.8% English, 5.6% Other groups (2000).
Economy: Single-family building permits issued: 4 (2007); Multi-family building permits issued: 0 (2007); Employment by occupation: 9.0% management, 16.4% professional, 17.6% services, 21.2% sales, 3.6% farming, 13.0% construction, 19.2% production (2000).
Income: Per capita income: $21,107 (2007); Median household income: $42,685 (2007); Average household income: $53,768 (2007); Percent of households with income of $100,000 or more: 11.1% (2007); Poverty rate: 6.4% (2000).
Education: Percent of population age 25 and over with: High school diploma (including GED) or higher: 79.7% (2007); Bachelor's degree or higher: 12.6% (2007); Master's degree or higher: 3.0% (2007).
Housing: Homeownership rate: 70.0% (2007); Median home value: $107,083 (2007); Median rent: $334 per month (2000); Median age of housing: 42 years (2000).
Safety: Violent crime rate: 11.0 per 10,000 population; Property crime rate: 120.5 per 10,000 population (2006).
Transportation: Commute to work: 91.6% car, 0.0% public transportation, 4.2% walk, 3.7% work from home (2000); Travel time to work: 37.0% less than 15 minutes, 20.1% 15 to 30 minutes, 28.8% 30 to 45 minutes, 6.0% 45 to 60 minutes, 8.2% 60 minutes or more (2000)

MACKINAW (village). Covers a land area of 1.255 square miles and a water area of 0.030 square miles. Located at 40.53° N. Lat.; 89.35° W. Long. Elevation is 682 feet.
Population: 1,345 (1990); 1,452 (2000); 1,363 (2007); 1,372 (2012 projected); Race: 97.3% White, 0.4% Black, 0.3% Asian, 2.0% Hispanic of any race (2007); Density: 1,086.3 persons per square mile (2007); Average household size: 2.43 (2007); Median age: 36.5 (2007); Males per 100 females: 94.2 (2007); Marriage status: 20.8% never married, 60.9% now married, 10.0% widowed, 8.3% divorced (2000); Foreign born: 1.3% (2000); Ancestry (includes multiple ancestries): 23.6% German, 12.8% Irish, 10.8% United States or American, 9.6% English, 6.6% Other groups (2000).
Economy: Single-family building permits issued: 18 (2007); Multi-family building permits issued: 0 (2007); Employment by occupation: 9.4% management, 13.9% professional, 18.5% services, 26.6% sales, 0.3% farming, 11.7% construction, 19.6% production (2000).
Income: Per capita income: $23,474 (2007); Median household income: $47,432 (2007); Average household income: $57,134 (2007); Percent of households with income of $100,000 or more: 11.3% (2007); Poverty rate: 3.1% (2000).
Education: Percent of population age 25 and over with: High school diploma (including GED) or higher: 85.0% (2007); Bachelor's degree or higher: 12.0% (2007); Master's degree or higher: 2.3% (2007).

School District(s)

Deer Creek-Mackinaw CUSD 701 (PK-12)
2005-06 Enrollment: 994 . . . . (309) 359-8965

Housing: Homeownership rate: 75.4% (2007); Median home value: $108,523 (2007); Median rent: $399 per month (2000); Median age of housing: 44 years (2000).
Safety: Violent crime rate: 12.4 per 10,000 population; Property crime rate: 130.1 per 10,000 population (2006).
Transportation: Commute to work: 90.9% car, 0.0% public transportation, 5.4% walk, 3.7% work from home (2000); Travel time to work: 29.1% less than 15 minutes, 38.8% 15 to 30 minutes, 23.1% 30 to 45 minutes, 5.3% 45 to 60 minutes, 3.7% 60 minutes or more (2000)

MARQUETTE HEIGHTS (city). Covers a land area of 1.641 square miles and a water area of 0 square miles. Located at 40.61° N. Lat.; 89.60° W. Long. Elevation is 620 feet.
Population: 3,080 (1990); 2,794 (2000); 2,898 (2007); 2,975 (2012 projected); Race: 98.0% White, 0.4% Black, 0.3% Asian, 1.7% Hispanic of any race (2007); Density: 1,766.1 persons per square mile (2007); Average household size: 2.77 (2007); Median age: 36.8 (2007); Males per 100 females: 100.4 (2007); Marriage status: 22.5% never married, 64.7% now married, 5.2% widowed, 7.6% divorced (2000); Foreign born: 1.4% (2000); Ancestry (includes multiple ancestries): 33.8% German, 16.9% Irish, 12.9% English, 8.7% United States or American, 6.2% Other groups (2000).
Economy: Single-family building permits issued: 7 (2007); Multi-family building permits issued: 0 (2007); Employment by occupation: 7.4% management, 11.5% professional, 16.2% services, 31.2% sales, 0.2% farming, 12.0% construction, 21.5% production (2000).
Income: Per capita income: $21,002 (2007); Median household income: $52,308 (2007); Average household income: $58,186 (2007); Percent of households with income of $100,000 or more: 9.3% (2007); Poverty rate: 2.9% (2000).
Education: Percent of population age 25 and over with: High school diploma (including GED) or higher: 87.2% (2007); Bachelor's degree or higher: 9.5% (2007); Master's degree or higher: 3.6% (2007).

School District(s)

North Pekin & Marquette Hght SD 102 (PK-08)
2005-06 Enrollment: 690 . . . . (309) 382-2172

Housing: Homeownership rate: 91.3% (2007); Median home value: $98,648 (2007); Median rent: $470 per month (2000); Median age of housing: 42 years (2000).
Safety: Violent crime rate: 14.2 per 10,000 population; Property crime rate: 99.1 per 10,000 population (2006).
Transportation: Commute to work: 96.6% car, 0.0% public transportation, 0.6% walk, 2.0% work from home (2000); Travel time to work: 20.5% less than 15 minutes, 63.7% 15 to 30 minutes, 10.8% 30 to 45 minutes, 2.8% 45 to 60 minutes, 2.2% 60 minutes or more (2000)

MINIER (village). Covers a land area of 0.625 square miles and a water area of 0 square miles. Located at 40.43° N. Lat.; 89.31° W. Long. Elevation is 636 feet.
Population: 1,179 (1990); 1,244 (2000); 1,312 (2007); 1,355 (2012 projected); Race: 98.6% White, 0.2% Black, 0.2% Asian, 1.8% Hispanic of any race (2007); Density: 2,100.1 persons per square mile (2007); Average household size: 2.43 (2007); Median age: 38.8 (2007); Males per 100 females: 91.0 (2007); Marriage status: 18.9% never married, 62.5% now married, 8.5% widowed, 10.1% divorced (2000); Foreign born: 1.1% (2000); Ancestry (includes multiple ancestries): 33.0% German, 13.6% Irish, 11.7% United States or American, 11.3% English, 8.3% Other groups (2000).
Economy: Single-family building permits issued: 2 (2007); Multi-family building permits issued: 2 (2007); Employment by occupation: 7.9% management, 13.4% professional, 13.6% services, 32.6% sales, 1.1% farming, 7.9% construction, 23.6% production (2000).
Income: Per capita income: $23,436 (2007); Median household income: $49,934 (2007); Average household income: $56,835 (2007); Percent of households with income of $100,000 or more: 10.2% (2007); Poverty rate: 7.9% (2000).
Education: Percent of population age 25 and over with: High school diploma (including GED) or higher: 85.9% (2007); Bachelor's degree or higher: 14.1% (2007); Master's degree or higher: 2.8% (2007).

School District(s)

Olympia CUSD 16 (PK-12)
2005-06 Enrollment: 2,084 . . . . (309) 379-6011

Housing: Homeownership rate: 76.7% (2007); Median home value: $112,146 (2007); Median rent: $402 per month (2000); Median age of housing: 39 years (2000).
Safety: Violent crime rate: 23.9 per 10,000 population; Property crime rate: 127.5 per 10,000 population (2006).
Newspapers: Olympia Review (Local news; Circulation 7,000)
Transportation: Commute to work: 96.2% car, 0.3% public transportation, 1.3% walk, 1.5% work from home (2000); Travel time to work: 35.1% less than 15 minutes, 21.8% 15 to 30 minutes, 38.0% 30 to 45 minutes, 3.2% 45 to 60 minutes, 1.8% 60 minutes or more (2000)

MORTON (village). Covers a land area of 12.182 square miles and a water area of 0.044 square miles. Located at 40.61° N. Lat.; 89.46° W. Long. Elevation is 715 feet.
History: Incorporated 1877.
Population: 14,148 (1990); 15,198 (2000); 15,751 (2007); 16,121 (2012 projected); Race: 97.3% White, 0.1% Black, 1.6% Asian, 1.0% Hispanic of any race (2007); Density: 1,293.0 persons per square mile (2007); Average household size: 2.47 (2007); Median age: 42.2 (2007); Males per 100 females: 93.0 (2007); Marriage status: 21.5% never married, 64.6% now married, 7.2% widowed, 6.7% divorced (2000); Foreign born: 2.1% (2000); Ancestry (includes multiple ancestries): 40.2% German, 13.4% Irish, 13.2% English, 5.8% United States or American, 4.0% Other groups (2000).
Economy: Single-family building permits issued: 27 (2007); Multi-family building permits issued: 19 (2007); Employment by occupation: 18.0% management, 25.8% professional, 11.2% services, 26.6% sales, 0.1% farming, 7.2% construction, 11.1% production (2000).
Income: Per capita income: $30,899 (2007); Median household income: $61,765 (2007); Average household income: $75,134 (2007); Percent of households with income of $100,000 or more: 23.0% (2007); Poverty rate: 5.0% (2000).
Education: Percent of population age 25 and over with: High school diploma (including GED) or higher: 89.9% (2007); Bachelor's degree or higher: 34.3% (2007); Master's degree or higher: 10.6% (2007).

School District(s)

Morton CUSD 709 (PK-12)
2005-06 Enrollment: 2,655 . . . . (309) 263-2581
Housing: Homeownership rate: 77.2% (2007); Median home value: $164,288 (2007); Median rent: $475 per month (2000); Median age of housing: 30 years (2000).
Safety: Violent crime rate: 6.6 per 10,000 population; Property crime rate: 127.8 per 10,000 population (2006).
Newspapers: Morton Courier (Community news; Circulation 8,700)
Transportation: Commute to work: 95.1% car, 0.5% public transportation, 1.2% walk, 2.5% work from home (2000); Travel time to work: 40.6% less than 15 minutes, 44.0% 15 to 30 minutes, 11.6% 30 to 45 minutes, 2.0% 45 to 60 minutes, 1.7% 60 minutes or more (2000)

Additional Information Contacts

Morton Chamber of Commerce . . . . (309) 263-2491
http://www.mortonchamber.org
Village of Morton . . . . (309) 266-5361
http://www.morton-il.gov

NORTH PEKIN (village). Covers a land area of 1.157 square miles and a water area of 0.028 square miles. Located at 40.61° N. Lat.; 89.62° W. Long. Elevation is 482 feet.
Population: 1,582 (1990); 1,574 (2000); 1,618 (2007); 1,650 (2012 projected); Race: 97.4% White, 0.0% Black, 0.8% Asian, 0.4% Hispanic of any race (2007); Density: 1,397.9 persons per square mile (2007); Average household size: 2.55 (2007); Median age: 38.0 (2007); Males per 100 females: 98.8 (2007); Marriage status: 17.3% never married, 66.2% now married, 5.0% widowed, 11.5% divorced (2000); Foreign born: 1.3% (2000); Ancestry (includes multiple ancestries): 30.9% German, 17.2% United States or American, 12.9% Irish, 11.1% Other groups, 7.1% English (2000).
Economy: Single-family building permits issued: 13 (2007); Multi-family building permits issued: 0 (2007); Employment by occupation: 3.6% management, 7.9% professional, 22.0% services, 29.2% sales, 0.0% farming, 17.1% construction, 20.2% production (2000).
Income: Per capita income: $20,068 (2007); Median household income: $45,091 (2007); Average household income: $51,215 (2007); Percent of households with income of $100,000 or more: 6.9% (2007); Poverty rate: 8.4% (2000).
Education: Percent of population age 25 and over with: High school diploma (including GED) or higher: 82.2% (2007); Bachelor's degree or higher: 2.6% (2007); Master's degree or higher: 1.0% (2007).
Housing: Homeownership rate: 83.4% (2007); Median home value: $88,239 (2007); Median rent: $381 per month (2000); Median age of housing: 45 years (2000).
Safety: Violent crime rate: 102.9 per 10,000 population; Property crime rate: 167.2 per 10,000 population (2006).
Transportation: Commute to work: 95.4% car, 0.0% public transportation, 0.7% walk, 3.0% work from home (2000); Travel time to work: 29.9% less than 15 minutes, 48.8% 15 to 30 minutes, 12.0% 30 to 45 minutes, 6.5% 45 to 60 minutes, 2.8% 60 minutes or more (2000)

PEKIN (city). County seat. Covers a land area of 13.150 square miles and a water area of 0.596 square miles. Located at 40.56° N. Lat.; 89.63° W. Long. Elevation is 502 feet.
History: Pekin was settled by pioneers of English descent who came from Virginia, Kentucky, and Tennessee. Abraham Lincoln argued many of his legal cases in the courthouse at Pekin. Incorporated 1948.
Population: 33,227 (1990); 33,857 (2000); 33,470 (2007); 33,211 (2012 projected); Race: 94.8% White, 3.4% Black, 0.4% Asian, 1.8% Hispanic of any race (2007); Density: 2,545.3 persons per square mile (2007); Average household size: 2.48 (2007); Median age: 38.0 (2007); Males per 100 females: 97.2 (2007); Marriage status: 20.5% never married, 59.3% now married, 8.2% widowed, 12.0% divorced (2000); Foreign born: 0.8% (2000); Ancestry (includes multiple ancestries): 28.4% German, 11.5% Irish, 11.3% English, 10.2% United States or American, 7.8% Other groups (2000).
Economy: Unemployment rate: 5.2% (4/2008); Total civilian labor force: 18,057 (4/2008); Single-family building permits issued: 56 (2007); Multi-family building permits issued: 78 (2007); Employment by occupation: 9.5% management, 15.3% professional, 17.4% services, 29.7% sales, 0.1% farming, 8.1% construction, 20.0% production (2000).
Income: Per capita income: $22,901 (2007); Median household income: $43,256 (2007); Average household income: $53,912 (2007); Percent of households with income of $100,000 or more: 10.8% (2007); Poverty rate: 9.4% (2000).
Taxes: Total city taxes per capita: $296 (2006); City property taxes per capita: $158 (2006).
Education: Percent of population age 25 and over with: High school diploma (including GED) or higher: 81.8% (2007); Bachelor's degree or higher: 13.7% (2007); Master's degree or higher: 5.2% (2007).

School District(s)

Pekin Csd 303 (09-12)
2005-06 Enrollment: 2,168 . . . . (309) 477-4222
Pekin Psd 108 (PK-08)
2005-06 Enrollment: 3,767 . . . . (309) 477-4740
Rankin Csd 98 (KG-08)
2005-06 Enrollment: 202 . . . . (309) 346-3182
Tazewell Co Area Efe Rds
2005-06 Enrollment: n/a . . . . (309) 353-5011
Tazewell-Mason Cntys Sp Ed Assoc (PK-12)
2005-06 Enrollment: 51 . . . . (309) 347-5164
Housing: Homeownership rate: 67.1% (2007); Median home value: $100,174 (2007); Median rent: $349 per month (2000); Median age of housing: 41 years (2000).
Hospitals: Pekin Hospital (125 beds)
Safety: Violent crime rate: 37.8 per 10,000 population; Property crime rate: 281.4 per 10,000 population (2006).
Newspapers: Pekin Daily Times (Local news; Circulation 9,000)
Transportation: Commute to work: 95.7% car, 0.6% public transportation, 1.5% walk, 1.6% work from home (2000); Travel time to work: 43.4% less than 15 minutes, 35.1% 15 to 30 minutes, 14.5% 30 to 45 minutes, 3.5% 45 to 60 minutes, 3.5% 60 minutes or more (2000)

Additional Information Contacts

City of Pekin. . . . . (309) 477-2300
http://www.ci.pekin.il.us
Pekin Area Chamber of Commerce. . . . . (309) 346-2106
http://www.pekin.net

SOUTH PEKIN (village). Covers a land area of 0.429 square miles and a water area of 0 square miles. Located at 40.49° N. Lat.; 89.65° W. Long. Elevation is 515 feet.
History: Incorporated 1917.

Population: 1,185 (1990); 1,162 (2000); 920 (2007); 921 (2012 projected); Race: 99.0% White, 0.3% Black, 0.2% Asian, 2.3% Hispanic of any race (2007); Density: 2,144.2 persons per square mile (2007); Average household size: 2.73 (2007); Median age: 32.1 (2007); Males per 100 females: 98.7 (2007); Marriage status: 23.2% never married, 62.4% now married, 5.6% widowed, 8.8% divorced (2000); Foreign born: 0.7% (2000); Ancestry (includes multiple ancestries): 26.8% German, 12.4% Irish, 11.7% English, 9.9% Other groups, 6.3% United States or American (2000).
Economy: Single-family building permits issued: 1 (2007); Multi-family building permits issued: 0 (2007); Employment by occupation: 4.3% management, 9.0% professional, 23.4% services, 25.6% sales, 0.0% farming, 13.9% construction, 23.7% production (2000).
Income: Per capita income: $20,033 (2007); Median household income: $51,170 (2007); Average household income: $54,407 (2007); Percent of households with income of $100,000 or more: 9.2% (2007); Poverty rate: 7.1% (2000).
Education: Percent of population age 25 and over with: High school diploma (including GED) or higher: 77.3% (2007); Bachelor's degree or higher: 2.5% (2007); Master's degree or higher: 0.2% (2007).

School District(s)

South Pekin SD 137 (PK-08)
2005-06 Enrollment: 256 . . . . (309) 348-3695
Housing: Homeownership rate: 78.0% (2007); Median home value: $76,250 (2007); Median rent: $363 per month (2000); Median age of housing: 44 years (2000).
Safety: Violent crime rate: 74.2 per 10,000 population; Property crime rate: 123.7 per 10,000 population (2006).
Transportation: Commute to work: 94.9% car, 0.7% public transportation, 0.9% walk, 1.2% work from home (2000); Travel time to work: 29.5% less than 15 minutes, 42.5% 15 to 30 minutes, 20.5% 30 to 45 minutes, 5.0% 45 to 60 minutes, 2.5% 60 minutes or more (2000)

TREMONT (village). Covers a land area of 0.953 square miles and a water area of 0 square miles. Located at 40.52° N. Lat.; 89.49° W. Long. Elevation is 643 feet.
Population: 2,088 (1990); 2,029 (2000); 1,922 (2007); 1,931 (2012 projected); Race: 99.5% White, 0.1% Black, 0.2% Asian, 0.6% Hispanic of any race (2007); Density: 2,016.5 persons per square mile (2007); Average household size: 2.44 (2007); Median age: 37.7 (2007); Males per 100 females: 93.2 (2007); Marriage status: 18.0% never married, 68.7% now married, 5.9% widowed, 7.4% divorced (2000); Foreign born: 0.5% (2000); Ancestry (includes multiple ancestries): 41.6% German, 11.3% English, 10.7% Irish, 7.5% United States or American, 3.9% Other groups (2000).
Economy: Single-family building permits issued: 3 (2007); Multi-family building permits issued: 0 (2007); Employment by occupation: 12.6% management, 19.7% professional, 12.7% services, 24.8% sales, 0.2% farming, 11.5% construction, 18.4% production (2000).
Income: Per capita income: $27,339 (2007); Median household income: $57,554 (2007); Average household income: $66,597 (2007); Percent of households with income of $100,000 or more: 18.0% (2007); Poverty rate: 2.5% (2000).
Education: Percent of population age 25 and over with: High school diploma (including GED) or higher: 91.1% (2007); Bachelor's degree or higher: 20.5% (2007); Master's degree or higher: 6.0% (2007).

School District(s)

Tremont CUSD 702 (PK-12)
2005-06 Enrollment: 986 . . . . (309) 925-3461
Housing: Homeownership rate: 74.1% (2007); Median home value: $125,931 (2007); Median rent: $380 per month (2000); Median age of housing: 40 years (2000).
Safety: Violent crime rate: 29.1 per 10,000 population; Property crime rate: 106.5 per 10,000 population (2006).
Transportation: Commute to work: 94.3% car, 0.0% public transportation, 2.0% walk, 3.3% work from home (2000); Travel time to work: 35.6% less than 15 minutes, 36.6% 15 to 30 minutes, 19.4% 30 to 45 minutes, 5.2% 45 to 60 minutes, 3.2% 60 minutes or more (2000)

WASHINGTON (city). Covers a land area of 7.476 square miles and a water area of 0.012 square miles. Located at 40.70° N. Lat.; 89.42° W. Long. Elevation is 761 feet.
History: Incorporated 1857.
Population: 10,778 (1990); 10,841 (2000); 11,803 (2007); 12,420 (2012 projected); Race: 98.2% White, 0.2% Black, 0.5% Asian, 0.9% Hispanic of any race (2007); Density: 1,578.7 persons per square mile (2007); Average household size: 2.52 (2007); Median age: 38.2 (2007); Males per 100 females: 95.7 (2007); Marriage status: 18.1% never married, 66.3% now married, 6.9% widowed, 8.7% divorced (2000); Foreign born: 1.1% (2000); Ancestry (includes multiple ancestries): 39.8% German, 15.7% English, 14.8% Irish, 7.2% United States or American, 5.8% Other groups (2000).
Economy: Single-family building permits issued: 104 (2007); Multi-family building permits issued: 0 (2007); Employment by occupation: 11.6% management, 26.6% professional, 13.3% services, 27.5% sales, 0.1% farming, 8.1% construction, 12.8% production (2000).
Income: Per capita income: $28,273 (2007); Median household income: $61,182 (2007); Average household income: $70,985 (2007); Percent of households with income of $100,000 or more: 19.5% (2007); Poverty rate: 4.1% (2000).
Education: Percent of population age 25 and over with: High school diploma (including GED) or higher: 91.7% (2007); Bachelor's degree or higher: 30.6% (2007); Master's degree or higher: 9.3% (2007).

School District(s)

Central SD 51 (PK-08)
2005-06 Enrollment: 750 . . . . (309) 444-3943
District 50 Schools (PK-08)
2005-06 Enrollment: 793 . . . . (309) 745-8914
Washington CHSD 308 (09-12)
2005-06 Enrollment: 1,079 . . . . (309) 444-7704
Washington SD 52 (KG-08)
2005-06 Enrollment: 807 . . . . (309) 444-4182
Housing: Homeownership rate: 78.4% (2007); Median home value: $132,793 (2007); Median rent: $460 per month (2000); Median age of housing: 37 years (2000).
Safety: Violent crime rate: 37.6 per 10,000 population; Property crime rate: 123.8 per 10,000 population (2006).
Newspapers: Washington Courier (Community news; Circulation 0); Woodford Courier (Community news; Circulation 0)
Transportation: Commute to work: 94.6% car, 0.0% public transportation, 1.5% walk, 3.5% work from home (2000); Travel time to work: 28.5% less than 15 minutes, 49.4% 15 to 30 minutes, 16.4% 30 to 45 minutes, 2.6% 45 to 60 minutes, 3.1% 60 minutes or more (2000)
Additional Information Contacts
City of Washington. . . . . (309) 444-3196
http://ci.washington.il.us
Washington Chamber of Commerce . . . . (309) 444-9921
http://www.washingtoncoc.com

Union County

Located in southern Illinois; bounded on the west by the Mississippi River and the Missouri border; drained by the Cache River; includes part of Shawnee National Forest. Covers a land area of 416.16 square miles, a water area of 5.97 square miles, and is located in the Central Time Zone. The county was founded in 1818. County seat is Jonesboro.

Weather Station: Anna 2 NNE Elevation: 597 feet

	Jan	Feb	Mar	Apr	May	Jun	Jul	Aug	Sep	Oct	Nov	Dec
High	41	47	58	68	77	85	89	88	81	70	57	46
Low	23	28	36	46	55	63	68	66	58	47	37	28
Precip	3.5	3.3	4.8	4.9	5.2	4.3	3.2	3.6	3.1	3.5	4.6	4.3
Snow	4.9	4.5	2.3	0.1	0.0	0.0	0.0	0.0	0.0	0.1	0.5	2.3

High and Low temperatures in degrees Fahrenheit; Precipitation and Snow in inches

Population: 17,619 (1990); 18,293 (2000); 18,207 (2007); 18,121 (2012 projected); Race: 95.4% White, 1.0% Black, 0.4% Asian, 3.7% Hispanic of any race (2007); Density: 43.7 persons per square mile (2007); Average household size: 2.49 (2007); Median age: 41.0 (2007); Males per 100 females: 94.5 (2007).
Religion: Five largest groups: 43.8% Southern Baptist Convention, 7.7% Catholic Church, 5.1% Evangelical Lutheran Church in America, 2.0% Christian Churches and Churches of Christ, 2.0% The United Methodist Church (2000).
Economy: Unemployment rate: 7.6% (4/2008); Total civilian labor force: 8,599 (4/2008); Leading industries: 25.6% health care and social assistance; 18.7% retail trade; 16.6% manufacturing (2005); Farms: 666 totaling 152,288 acres (2002); Companies that employ 500 or more persons: 0 (2006); Companies that employ 100 to 499 persons: 7 (2006); Companies that employ less than 100 persons: 344 (2006); Black-owned businesses: n/a (2002); Hispanic-owned businesses: n/a (2002); Asian-owned businesses: n/a (2002); Women-owned businesses: 413 (2002); Retail sales per capita: $10,561 (2008). Single-family building permits issued: 51 (2007); Multi-family building permits issued: 0 (2007).

Income: Per capita income: $19,565 (2007); Median household income: $36,748 (2007); Average household income: $47,018 (2007); Percent of households with income of $100,000 or more: 8.4% (2007); Poverty rate: 16.7% (2005); Bankruptcy rate: 2.85% (2007).
Education: Percent of population age 25 and over with: High school diploma (including GED) or higher: 74.9% (2007); Bachelor's degree or higher: 15.9% (2007); Master's degree or higher: 6.4% (2007).
Housing: Homeownership rate: 75.8% (2007); Median home value: $87,013 (2007); Median rent: $257 per month (2000); Median age of housing: 37 years (2000).
Health: Birth rate: 131.5 per 10,000 population (2007); Death rate: 129.3 per 10,000 population (2007); Age-adjusted cancer mortality rate: 204.8 deaths per 100,000 population (2005); Number of physicians: 13.8 per 10,000 population (2005); Hospital beds: 301.6 per 10,000 population (2004); Hospital admissions: 860.5 per 10,000 population (2004).
Elections: 2004 Presidential election results: 58.5% Bush, 41.0% Kerry, 0.1% Nader, 0.5% Badnarik
National and State Parks: Larue-Pine Hills National Natural Landmark; Trail of Tears State Forest; Union County State Conservation Area; Union County State Forest
Additional Information Contacts
Union County Government . . . . (618) 833-5711

City of Anna . . . . (618) 833-8528
http://www.cityofanna.org

Union County Communities

ALTO PASS (village). Covers a land area of 2.150 square miles and a water area of 0.025 square miles. Located at 37.57° N. Lat.; 89.31° W. Long. Elevation is 748 feet.
Population: 417 (1990); 388 (2000); 388 (2007); 387 (2012 projected); Race: 83.0% White, 0.0% Black, 0.0% Asian, 21.1% Hispanic of any race (2007); Density: 180.5 persons per square mile (2007); Average household size: 2.40 (2007); Median age: 40.0 (2007); Males per 100 females: 101.0 (2007); Marriage status: 14.5% never married, 69.3% now married, 9.1% widowed, 7.1% divorced (2000); Foreign born: 17.1% (2000); Ancestry (includes multiple ancestries): 25.9% Other groups, 17.6% United States or American, 10.1% German, 9.0% English, 3.0% Irish (2000).
Economy: Employment by occupation: 5.8% management, 25.4% professional, 15.0% services, 9.2% sales, 9.8% farming, 9.8% construction, 24.9% production (2000).
Income: Per capita income: $20,773 (2007); Median household income: $39,375 (2007); Average household income: $49,753 (2007); Percent of households with income of $100,000 or more: 10.5% (2007); Poverty rate: 15.3% (2000).
Education: Percent of population age 25 and over with: High school diploma (including GED) or higher: 70.4% (2007); Bachelor's degree or higher: 14.4% (2007); Master's degree or higher: 4.0% (2007).
Housing: Homeownership rate: 88.9% (2007); Median home value: $48,077 (2007); Median rent: $219 per month (2000); Median age of housing: 30 years (2000).
Transportation: Commute to work: 89.2% car, 0.0% public transportation, 2.4% walk, 6.6% work from home (2000); Travel time to work: 14.8% less than 15 minutes, 49.0% 15 to 30 minutes, 9.7% 30 to 45 minutes, 16.1% 45 to 60 minutes, 10.3% 60 minutes or more (2000)

ANNA (city). Covers a land area of 3.380 square miles and a water area of 0.009 square miles. Located at 37.46° N. Lat.; 89.24° W. Long. Elevation is 630 feet.
History: Incorporated 1865.
Population: 4,854 (1990); 5,136 (2000); 4,947 (2007); 4,791 (2012 projected); Race: 95.7% White, 2.2% Black, 0.3% Asian, 2.0% Hispanic of any race (2007); Density: 1,463.4 persons per square mile (2007); Average household size: 2.38 (2007); Median age: 43.1 (2007); Males per 100 females: 88.3 (2007); Marriage status: 21.5% never married, 51.4% now married, 14.0% widowed, 13.2% divorced (2000); Foreign born: 0.0% (2000); Ancestry (includes multiple ancestries): 16.8% German, 13.1% Irish, 11.5% Other groups, 11.2% United States or American, 8.4% English (2000).
Economy: Single-family building permits issued: 0 (2007); Multi-family building permits issued: 0 (2007); Employment by occupation: 8.1% management, 23.8% professional, 23.6% services, 25.0% sales, 0.5% farming, 8.3% construction, 10.7% production (2000).
Income: Per capita income: $17,658 (2007); Median household income: $28,322 (2007); Average household income: $38,006 (2007); Percent of households with income of $100,000 or more: 5.6% (2007); Poverty rate: 23.6% (2000).
Education: Percent of population age 25 and over with: High school diploma (including GED) or higher: 67.6% (2007); Bachelor's degree or higher: 14.7% (2007); Master's degree or higher: 7.5% (2007).

School District(s)

Anna CCSD 37 (PK-08)
2005-06 Enrollment: 739 . . . . (618) 833-6812
Anna Jonesboro CHSD 81 (09-12)
2005-06 Enrollment: 567 . . . . (618) 833-8421
Five County Reg Voc System
2005-06 Enrollment: n/a . . . . (618) 747-2703
Tri-County Sp Ed Jnt Agreement (PK-12)
2005-06 Enrollment: 149 . . . . (618) 684-2109
Housing: Homeownership rate: 57.9% (2007); Median home value: $77,526 (2007); Median rent: $261 per month (2000); Median age of housing: 45 years (2000).
Hospitals: Union County Hospital (47 beds)
Safety: Violent crime rate: 19.7 per 10,000 population; Property crime rate: 108.5 per 10,000 population (2006).
Newspapers: Gazette-Democrat (Local news; Circulation 4,400); Monday's Pub (Community news; Circulation 19,500)
Transportation: Commute to work: 88.3% car, 3.2% public transportation, 3.7% walk, 3.7% work from home (2000); Travel time to work: 60.6% less than 15 minutes, 13.2% 15 to 30 minutes, 19.4% 30 to 45 minutes, 4.0% 45 to 60 minutes, 2.8% 60 minutes or more (2000)
Additional Information Contacts
City of Anna . . . . (618) 833-8528
http://www.cityofanna.org

COBDEN (village). Covers a land area of 1.228 square miles and a water area of 0 square miles. Located at 37.53° N. Lat.; 89.25° W. Long. Elevation is 587 feet.
History: Cobden was named for an English director of the railroad. The town grew as a fruit shipping station on the Illinois Central Railroad.
Population: 1,092 (1990); 1,116 (2000); 1,039 (2007); 1,053 (2012 projected); Race: 87.5% White, 1.3% Black, 0.0% Asian, 20.3% Hispanic of any race (2007); Density: 845.9 persons per square mile (2007); Average household size: 2.57 (2007); Median age: 39.9 (2007); Males per 100 females: 85.2 (2007); Marriage status: 29.3% never married, 47.3% now married, 12.5% widowed, 10.8% divorced (2000); Foreign born: 11.5% (2000); Ancestry (includes multiple ancestries): 19.1% German, 18.4% Other groups, 9.5% United States or American, 9.1% Irish, 4.9% English (2000).
Economy: Single-family building permits issued: 0 (2007); Multi-family building permits issued: 0 (2007); Employment by occupation: 8.9% management, 17.4% professional, 26.6% services, 20.7% sales, 3.1% farming, 9.6% construction, 13.6% production (2000).
Income: Per capita income: $15,996 (2007); Median household income: $30,000 (2007); Average household income: $39,059 (2007); Percent of households with income of $100,000 or more: 5.4% (2007); Poverty rate: 22.1% (2000).
Education: Percent of population age 25 and over with: High school diploma (including GED) or higher: 67.1% (2007); Bachelor's degree or higher: 17.1% (2007); Master's degree or higher: 5.3% (2007).

School District(s)

Cobden Sud 17 (PK-12)
2005-06 Enrollment: 655 . . . . (618) 893-2313
Five County Reg Voc System
2005-06 Enrollment: n/a . . . . (618) 747-2703
Housing: Homeownership rate: 73.0% (2007); Median home value: $72,031 (2007); Median rent: $243 per month (2000); Median age of housing: 42 years (2000).
Safety: Violent crime rate: 36.3 per 10,000 population; Property crime rate: 136.1 per 10,000 population (2006).
Transportation: Commute to work: 95.5% car, 0.0% public transportation, 1.2% walk, 3.3% work from home (2000); Travel time to work: 37.6% less than 15 minutes, 34.4% 15 to 30 minutes, 15.8% 30 to 45 minutes, 4.2% 45 to 60 minutes, 7.9% 60 minutes or more (2000)

DONGOLA (village). Covers a land area of 1.106 square miles and a water area of 0.030 square miles. Located at 37.36° N. Lat.; 89.16° W. Long. Elevation is 394 feet.

Population: 728 (1990); 806 (2000); 850 (2007); 878 (2012 projected); Race: 95.9% White, 0.2% Black, 0.8% Asian, 0.2% Hispanic of any race (2007); Density: 768.6 persons per square mile (2007); Average household size: 2.40 (2007); Median age: 34.8 (2007); Males per 100 females: 88.9 (2007); Marriage status: 24.1% never married, 55.1% now married, 8.7% widowed, 12.1% divorced (2000); Foreign born: 0.2% (2000); Ancestry (includes multiple ancestries): 18.1% German, 11.6% Other groups, 10.8% United States or American, 10.5% English, 9.9% Irish (2000).
Economy: Employment by occupation: 3.3% management, 22.3% professional, 23.3% services, 19.3% sales, 0.0% farming, 12.1% construction, 19.7% production (2000).
Income: Per capita income: $14,816 (2007); Median household income: $28,871 (2007); Average household income: $35,523 (2007); Percent of households with income of $100,000 or more: 3.1% (2007); Poverty rate: 21.5% (2000).
Education: Percent of population age 25 and over with: High school diploma (including GED) or higher: 71.7% (2007); Bachelor's degree or higher: 8.5% (2007); Master's degree or higher: 3.5% (2007).

School District(s)

Dongola Sud 66 (PK-12)
2005-06 Enrollment: 323 . . . . (618) 827-3841
Housing: Homeownership rate: 73.2% (2007); Median home value: $58,721 (2007); Median rent: $205 per month (2000); Median age of housing: 45 years (2000).
Newspapers: Dongola Tri-County Record (Regional news; Circulation 0)
Transportation: Commute to work: 97.0% car, 0.0% public transportation, 0.0% walk, 3.0% work from home (2000); Travel time to work: 25.0% less than 15 minutes, 42.4% 15 to 30 minutes, 14.2% 30 to 45 minutes, 10.8% 45 to 60 minutes, 7.6% 60 minutes or more (2000)

JONESBORO (city). County seat. Covers a land area of 1.914 square miles and a water area of 0 square miles. Located at 37.45° N. Lat.; 89.26° W. Long. Elevation is 564 feet.
History: Jonesboro was platted in 1816 and named for a physician who was a resident there.
Population: 1,810 (1990); 1,853 (2000); 1,793 (2007); 1,755 (2012 projected); Race: 95.5% White, 1.1% Black, 1.0% Asian, 1.8% Hispanic of any race (2007); Density: 936.7 persons per square mile (2007); Average household size: 2.52 (2007); Median age: 40.9 (2007); Males per 100 females: 89.9 (2007); Marriage status: 20.6% never married, 56.4% now married, 11.7% widowed, 11.3% divorced (2000); Foreign born: 1.4% (2000); Ancestry (includes multiple ancestries): 17.1% German, 10.9% United States or American, 9.8% Irish, 9.6% Other groups, 9.2% English (2000).
Economy: Single-family building permits issued: 3 (2007); Multi-family building permits issued: 0 (2007); Employment by occupation: 9.4% management, 21.3% professional, 21.7% services, 24.8% sales, 0.5% farming, 7.9% construction, 14.4% production (2000).
Income: Per capita income: $18,644 (2007); Median household income: $35,855 (2007); Average household income: $45,186 (2007); Percent of households with income of $100,000 or more: 5.9% (2007); Poverty rate: 17.1% (2000).
Education: Percent of population age 25 and over with: High school diploma (including GED) or higher: 76.8% (2007); Bachelor's degree or higher: 13.8% (2007); Master's degree or higher: 4.1% (2007).

School District(s)

Jonesboro CCSD 43 (PK-08)
2005-06 Enrollment: 477 . . . . (618) 833-6651
Housing: Homeownership rate: 74.3% (2007); Median home value: $67,727 (2007); Median rent: $221 per month (2000); Median age of housing: 42 years (2000).
Safety: Violent crime rate: 10.9 per 10,000 population; Property crime rate: 10.9 per 10,000 population (2006).
Transportation: Commute to work: 94.0% car, 0.0% public transportation, 1.2% walk, 3.6% work from home (2000); Travel time to work: 50.6% less than 15 minutes, 21.1% 15 to 30 minutes, 18.6% 30 to 45 minutes, 7.2% 45 to 60 minutes, 2.5% 60 minutes or more (2000)

MILL CREEK (village). Aka Millcreek. Covers a land area of 0.366 square miles and a water area of 0.009 square miles. Located at 37.34° N. Lat.; 89.25° W. Long. Elevation is 381 feet.
Population: 87 (1990); 76 (2000); 79 (2007); 81 (2012 projected); Race: 100.0% White, 0.0% Black, 0.0% Asian, 0.0% Hispanic of any race (2007); Density: 215.9 persons per square mile (2007); Average household size: 2.55 (2007); Median age: 32.5 (2007); Males per 100 females: 119.4 (2007); Marriage status: 21.3% never married, 67.2% now married, 6.6% widowed, 4.9% divorced (2000); Foreign born: 0.0% (2000); Ancestry (includes multiple ancestries): 20.2% German, 13.1% United States or American, 13.1% Other groups, 2.4% Scottish, 2.4% Scotch-Irish (2000).
Economy: Employment by occupation: 0.0% management, 12.0% professional, 32.0% services, 12.0% sales, 0.0% farming, 16.0% construction, 28.0% production (2000).
Income: Per capita income: $12,057 (2007); Median household income: $21,250 (2007); Average household income: $30,726 (2007); Percent of households with income of $100,000 or more: 6.5% (2007); Poverty rate: 36.9% (2000).
Education: Percent of population age 25 and over with: High school diploma (including GED) or higher: 62.5% (2007); Bachelor's degree or higher: 6.3% (2007); Master's degree or higher: 0.0% (2007).
Housing: Homeownership rate: 93.5% (2007); Median home value: $33,125 (2007); Median rent: $n/a per month (2000); Median age of housing: 55 years (2000).
Transportation: Commute to work: 91.3% car, 0.0% public transportation, 0.0% walk, 8.7% work from home (2000); Travel time to work: 0.0% less than 15 minutes, 52.4% 15 to 30 minutes, 23.8% 30 to 45 minutes, 23.8% 45 to 60 minutes, 0.0% 60 minutes or more (2000)

WOLF LAKE (unincorporated postal area, zip code 62998). Covers a land area of 41.246 square miles and a water area of 0.528 square miles. Located at 37.50° N. Lat.; 89.44° W. Long. Elevation is 354 feet.
Population: 491 (2000); Race: 100.0% White, 0.0% Black, 0.0% Asian, 0.0% Hispanic of any race (2000); Density: 11.9 persons per square mile (2000); Age: 23.6% under 18, 8.1% over 64 (2000); Marriage status: 30.6% never married, 51.7% now married, 6.6% widowed, 11.0% divorced (2000); Foreign born: 0.0% (2000); Ancestry (includes multiple ancestries): 21.0% United States or American, 16.9% German, 7.9% English, 7.2% Irish, 4.2% Scotch-Irish (2000).
Economy: Employment by occupation: 4.9% management, 3.3% professional, 24.6% services, 20.2% sales, 3.8% farming, 18.0% construction, 25.1% production (2000).
Income: Per capita income: $17,343 (2000); Median household income: $32,833 (2000); Poverty rate: 19.4% (2000).
Education: Percent of population age 25 and over with: High school diploma (including GED) or higher: 78.4% (2000); Bachelor's degree or higher: 17.3% (2000).

School District(s)

Shawnee CUSD 84 (KG-12)
2005-06 Enrollment: 481 . . . . (618) 833-5709
Housing: Homeownership rate: 80.4% (2000); Median home value: $50,000 (2000); Median rent: $250 per month (2000); Median age of housing: 37 years (2000).
Transportation: Commute to work: 100.0% car, 0.0% public transportation, 0.0% walk, 0.0% work from home (2000); Travel time to work: 37.6% less than 15 minutes, 34.4% 15 to 30 minutes, 0.0% 30 to 45 minutes, 8.9% 45 to 60 minutes, 19.1% 60 minutes or more (2000)

Vermilion County

Located in eastern Illinois; bounded on the east by Indiana; drained by the Vermilion and Little Vermilion Rivers; includes Lake Vermilion. Covers a land area of 899.08 square miles, a water area of 3.06 square miles, and is located in the Central Time Zone. The county was founded in 1826. County seat is Danville.

Vermilion County is part of the Danville, IL Metropolitan Statistical Area. The entire metro area includes: Vermilion County, IL

Weather Station: Danville Elevation: 557 feet

	Jan	Feb	Mar	Apr	May	Jun	Jul	Aug	Sep	Oct	Nov	Dec
High	34	40	51	65	75	84	86	84	78	67	52	39
Low	17	22	31	41	51	60	64	63	55	43	34	24
Precip	2.0	1.9	3.2	4.1	4.5	4.5	4.5	4.0	3.0	3.1	3.5	2.8
Snow	6.2	4.1	3.1	0.3	tr	0.0	0.0	0.0	0.0	0.2	1.2	4.7

High and Low temperatures in degrees Fahrenheit; Precipitation and Snow in inches

Weather Station: Hoopeston 1 NE Elevation: 708 feet

	Jan	Feb	Mar	Apr	May	Jun	Jul	Aug	Sep	Oct	Nov	Dec
High	32	37	49	62	74	83	85	83	77	65	50	37
Low	17	21	31	41	51	61	65	62	55	44	34	23
Precip	1.5	1.6	3.0	3.7	4.2	4.0	4.1	3.8	2.9	3.1	2.9	2.4
Snow	5.4	4.1	2.2	0.6	tr	0.0	0.0	0.0	0.0	0.1	1.2	4.2

High and Low temperatures in degrees Fahrenheit; Precipitation and Snow in inches

Population: 88,257 (1990); 83,919 (2000); 81,960 (2007); 80,402 (2012 projected); Race: 85.0% White, 11.1% Black, 0.5% Asian, 3.5% Hispanic of any race (2007); Density: 91.2 persons per square mile (2007); Average household size: 2.47 (2007); Median age: 38.6 (2007); Males per 100 females: 96.1 (2007).
Religion: Five largest groups: 7.6% Christian Churches and Churches of Christ, 7.0% Catholic Church, 6.1% The United Methodist Church, 2.7% Church of the Nazarene, 2.6% Lutheran Church—Missouri Synod (2000).
Economy: Unemployment rate: 6.3% (4/2008); Total civilian labor force: 38,466 (4/2008); Leading industries: 18.7% manufacturing; 16.8% health care and social assistance; 15.0% retail trade (2005); Farms: 909 totaling 449,964 acres (2002); Companies that employ 500 or more persons: 6 (2006); Companies that employ 100 to 499 persons: 35 (2006); Companies that employ less than 100 persons: 1,593 (2006); Black-owned businesses: 223 (2002); Hispanic-owned businesses: n/a (2002); Asian-owned businesses: 101 (2002); Women-owned businesses: n/a (2002); Retail sales per capita: $11,183 (2008). Single-family building permits issued: 23 (2007); Multi-family building permits issued: 24 (2007).
Income: Per capita income: $19,747 (2007); Median household income: $38,951 (2007); Average household income: $48,084 (2007); Percent of households with income of $100,000 or more: 7.9% (2007); Poverty rate: 18.3% (2005); Bankruptcy rate: 4.42% (2007).
Taxes: Total county taxes per capita: $122 (2006); County property taxes per capita: $101 (2006).
Education: Percent of population age 25 and over with: High school diploma (including GED) or higher: 78.7% (2007); Bachelor's degree or higher: 12.4% (2007); Master's degree or higher: 4.1% (2007).
Housing: Homeownership rate: 71.9% (2007); Median home value: $68,887 (2007); Median rent: $312 per month (2000); Median age of housing: 45 years (2000).
Health: Birth rate: 136.8 per 10,000 population (2007); Death rate: 117.7 per 10,000 population (2007); Age-adjusted cancer mortality rate: 178.0 deaths per 100,000 population (2005); Number of physicians: 14.5 per 10,000 population (2005); Hospital beds: 80.1 per 10,000 population (2004); Hospital admissions: 1,606.8 per 10,000 population (2004).
Elections: 2004 Presidential election results: 55.6% Bush, 43.7% Kerry, 0.1% Nader, 0.7% Badnarik
National and State Parks: Kickapoo State Park; Middle Fork State Fish and Wildlife Areas

Additional Information Contacts

Vermilion County Government. . . . . (217) 554-6000
http://www.co.vermilion.il.us
City of Danville. . . . . (217) 431-2400
http://www.cityofdanville.org
City of Hoopeston . . . . (217) 283-5833
http://www.hoopeston-il.gov
Danville Area Convention & Visitors' Bureau. . . . . (217) 442-2096
http://www.danvillecvb.com
Hoopeston Chamber of Commerce . . . . (217) 283-7873
http://www.hoopestonchamber.com

Vermilion County Communities

ALLERTON (village). Covers a land area of 0.645 square miles and a water area of 0 square miles. Located at 39.91° N. Lat.; 87.93° W. Long. Elevation is 702 feet.
Population: 274 (1990); 293 (2000); 325 (2007); 334 (2012 projected); Race: 97.5% White, 0.0% Black, 0.0% Asian, 3.4% Hispanic of any race (2007); Density: 504.0 persons per square mile (2007); Average household size: 2.58 (2007); Median age: 38.3 (2007); Males per 100 females: 94.6 (2007); Marriage status: 19.1% never married, 58.6% now married, 10.9% widowed, 11.4% divorced (2000); Foreign born: 3.3% (2000); Ancestry (includes multiple ancestries): 30.2% United States or American, 22.2% German, 14.9% Other groups, 12.0% English, 10.9% Irish (2000).
Economy: Single-family building permits issued: 0 (2007); Multi-family building permits issued: 0 (2007); Employment by occupation: 7.0% management, 10.6% professional, 19.0% services, 33.8% sales, 2.1% farming, 12.0% construction, 15.5% production (2000).
Income: Per capita income: $22,308 (2007); Median household income: $55,714 (2007); Average household income: $57,540 (2007); Percent of households with income of $100,000 or more: 13.5% (2007); Poverty rate: 4.5% (2000).
Education: Percent of population age 25 and over with: High school diploma (including GED) or higher: 85.3% (2007); Bachelor's degree or higher: 7.6% (2007); Master's degree or higher: 3.8% (2007).
Housing: Homeownership rate: 83.3% (2007); Median home value: $61,364 (2007); Median rent: $240 per month (2000); Median age of housing: 60+ years (2000).
Transportation: Commute to work: 100.0% car, 0.0% public transportation, 0.0% walk, 0.0% work from home (2000); Travel time to work: 32.4% less than 15 minutes, 7.2% 15 to 30 minutes, 46.0% 30 to 45 minutes, 12.9% 45 to 60 minutes, 1.4% 60 minutes or more (2000)

ALVIN (village). Aka Alvan. Covers a land area of 0.795 square miles and a water area of 0 square miles. Located at 40.30° N. Lat.; 87.60° W. Long. Elevation is 653 feet.
History: Alvin was platted in 1876. The village developed around a grain elevator.
Population: 339 (1990); 316 (2000); 309 (2007); 298 (2012 projected); Race: 97.7% White, 0.0% Black, 0.3% Asian, 0.3% Hispanic of any race (2007); Density: 388.4 persons per square mile (2007); Average household size: 2.92 (2007); Median age: 31.0 (2007); Males per 100 females: 93.1 (2007); Marriage status: 21.2% never married, 63.1% now married, 5.5% widowed, 10.1% divorced (2000); Foreign born: 0.0% (2000); Ancestry (includes multiple ancestries): 17.5% English, 13.4% Other groups, 13.0% German, 10.3% Irish, 7.9% United States or American (2000).
Economy: Employment by occupation: 6.8% management, 6.8% professional, 11.9% services, 24.6% sales, 1.7% farming, 11.0% construction, 37.3% production (2000).
Income: Per capita income: $17,209 (2007); Median household income: $43,571 (2007); Average household income: $50,165 (2007); Percent of households with income of $100,000 or more: 5.7% (2007); Poverty rate: 8.2% (2000).
Education: Percent of population age 25 and over with: High school diploma (including GED) or higher: 77.4% (2007); Bachelor's degree or higher: 4.5% (2007); Master's degree or higher: 0.0% (2007).
Housing: Homeownership rate: 83.0% (2007); Median home value: $55,000 (2007); Median rent: $350 per month (2000); Median age of housing: 39 years (2000).
Transportation: Commute to work: 87.0% car, 0.0% public transportation, 8.7% walk, 4.3% work from home (2000); Travel time to work: 13.6% less than 15 minutes, 55.5% 15 to 30 minutes, 18.2% 30 to 45 minutes, 7.3% 45 to 60 minutes, 5.5% 60 minutes or more (2000)

ARMSTRONG (unincorporated postal area, zip code 61812). Covers a land area of 27.238 square miles and a water area of 0 square miles. Located at 40.27° N. Lat.; 87.88° W. Long. Elevation is 696 feet.
Population: 420 (2000); Race: 96.8% White, 3.0% Black, 0.0% Asian, 0.7% Hispanic of any race (2000); Density: 15.4 persons per square mile (2000); Age: 25.3% under 18, 16.4% over 64 (2000); Marriage status: 17.3% never married, 63.0% now married, 9.9% widowed, 9.9% divorced (2000); Foreign born: 1.0% (2000); Ancestry (includes multiple ancestries): 20.6% German, 11.2% English, 6.9% Other groups, 6.7% United States or American, 4.2% Irish (2000).
Economy: Employment by occupation: 14.4% management, 14.4% professional, 10.8% services, 14.9% sales, 2.1% farming, 13.9% construction, 29.4% production (2000).
Income: Per capita income: $17,395 (2000); Median household income: $34,091 (2000); Poverty rate: 4.0% (2000).
Education: Percent of population age 25 and over with: High school diploma (including GED) or higher: 90.7% (2000); Bachelor's degree or higher: 11.7% (2000).

School District(s)

Armstrong Twp HSD 225 (09-12)
2005-06 Enrollment: 193 . . . . (217) 569-2122
Armstrong-Ellis Cons SD 61 (KG-08)
2005-06 Enrollment: 103 . . . . (217) 569-2115

Housing: Homeownership rate: 82.4% (2000); Median home value: $55,400 (2000); Median rent: $313 per month (2000); Median age of housing: 43 years (2000).
Transportation: Commute to work: 86.8% car, 0.0% public transportation, 0.5% walk, 11.6% work from home (2000); Travel time to work: 11.9% less than 15 minutes, 26.2% 15 to 30 minutes, 40.5% 30 to 45 minutes, 14.3% 45 to 60 minutes, 7.1% 60 minutes or more (2000)

BELGIUM (village). Covers a land area of 0.423 square miles and a water area of 0 square miles. Located at 40.06° N. Lat.; 87.63° W. Long. Elevation is 653 feet.

History: Many of the early residents of Belgium were from the country of Belgium. The village was incorporated in 1909, with coal mining as the major industry.

Population: 511 (1990); 466 (2000); 454 (2007); 440 (2012 projected); Race: 98.5% White, 0.0% Black, 0.0% Asian, 3.3% Hispanic of any race (2007); Density: 1,072.8 persons per square mile (2007); Average household size: 2.47 (2007); Median age: 35.0 (2007); Males per 100 females: 92.4 (2007); Marriage status: 27.9% never married, 50.0% now married, 6.2% widowed, 15.9% divorced (2000); Foreign born: 0.9% (2000); Ancestry (includes multiple ancestries): 29.2% United States or American, 9.9% English, 7.5% French (except Basque), 6.4% German, 4.7% Irish (2000).

Economy: Single-family building permits issued: 0 (2007); Multi-family building permits issued: 0 (2007); Employment by occupation: 4.9% management, 10.3% professional, 17.4% services, 31.5% sales, 0.0% farming, 9.8% construction, 26.1% production (2000).

Income: Per capita income: $17,434 (2007); Median household income: $38,000 (2007); Average household income: $43,016 (2007); Percent of households with income of $100,000 or more: 3.3% (2007); Poverty rate: 13.1% (2000).

Education: Percent of population age 25 and over with: High school diploma (including GED) or higher: 72.6% (2007); Bachelor's degree or higher: 4.8% (2007); Master's degree or higher: 0.0% (2007).

Housing: Homeownership rate: 75.0% (2007); Median home value: $53,636 (2007); Median rent: $310 per month (2000); Median age of housing: 40 years (2000).

Safety: Violent crime rate: 21.2 per 10,000 population; Property crime rate: 0.0 per 10,000 population (2006).

Transportation: Commute to work: 98.9% car, 0.0% public transportation, 0.0% walk, 1.1% work from home (2000); Travel time to work: 28.3% less than 15 minutes, 53.3% 15 to 30 minutes, 7.8% 30 to 45 minutes, 6.1% 45 to 60 minutes, 4.4% 60 minutes or more (2000)

BISMARCK (village). Covers a land area of 0.679 square miles and a water area of 0 square miles. Located at 40.26° N. Lat.; 87.61° W. Long. Elevation is 646 feet.

Population: 542 (1990); 542 (2000); 559 (2007); 568 (2012 projected); Race: 99.8% White, 0.0% Black, 0.0% Asian, 0.0% Hispanic of any race (2007); Density: 822.8 persons per square mile (2007); Average household size: 2.59 (2007); Median age: 39.1 (2007); Males per 100 females: 95.5 (2007); Marriage status: 22.7% never married, 63.2% now married, 5.5% widowed, 8.6% divorced (2000); Foreign born: 0.0% (2000); Ancestry (includes multiple ancestries): 27.5% German, 14.0% English, 11.0% Irish, 8.1% United States or American, 6.0% Other groups (2000).

Economy: Single-family building permits issued: 0 (2007); Multi-family building permits issued: 0 (2007); Employment by occupation: 11.2% management, 10.9% professional, 13.2% services, 32.6% sales, 0.0% farming, 9.3% construction, 22.9% production (2000).

Income: Per capita income: $19,835 (2007); Median household income: $47,647 (2007); Average household income: $51,331 (2007); Percent of households with income of $100,000 or more: 5.1% (2007); Poverty rate: 4.2% (2000).

Education: Percent of population age 25 and over with: High school diploma (including GED) or higher: 84.3% (2007); Bachelor's degree or higher: 15.4% (2007); Master's degree or higher: 6.0% (2007).

School District(s)

Bismarck Henning CUSD (KG-12)
2005-06 Enrollment: 979 . . . . (217) 759-7261

Housing: Homeownership rate: 80.6% (2007); Median home value: $78,846 (2007); Median rent: $381 per month (2000); Median age of housing: 45 years (2000).

Transportation: Commute to work: 96.0% car, 0.0% public transportation, 1.2% walk, 2.8% work from home (2000); Travel time to work: 23.8% less than 15 minutes, 60.2% 15 to 30 minutes, 9.0% 30 to 45 minutes, 4.1% 45 to 60 minutes, 2.9% 60 minutes or more (2000)

CATLIN (village). Covers a land area of 0.785 square miles and a water area of 0.004 square miles. Located at 40.06° N. Lat.; 87.70° W. Long. Elevation is 659 feet.

Population: 2,203 (1990); 2,087 (2000); 2,049 (2007); 2,021 (2012 projected); Race: 99.0% White, 0.0% Black, 0.0% Asian, 0.5% Hispanic of any race (2007); Density: 2,608.8 persons per square mile (2007); Average household size: 2.47 (2007); Median age: 38.7 (2007); Males per 100 females: 88.7 (2007); Marriage status: 17.8% never married, 66.4% now married, 5.9% widowed, 9.9% divorced (2000); Foreign born: 0.2% (2000); Ancestry (includes multiple ancestries): 22.5% German, 16.6% United States or American, 13.1% English, 13.1% Irish, 5.2% Other groups (2000).

Economy: Single-family building permits issued: 0 (2007); Multi-family building permits issued: 24 (2007); Employment by occupation: 9.6% management, 20.1% professional, 14.8% services, 29.3% sales, 0.0% farming, 8.1% construction, 18.1% production (2000).

Income: Per capita income: $22,011 (2007); Median household income: $49,818 (2007); Average household income: $54,245 (2007); Percent of households with income of $100,000 or more: 8.0% (2007); Poverty rate: 4.0% (2000).

Education: Percent of population age 25 and over with: High school diploma (including GED) or higher: 89.4% (2007); Bachelor's degree or higher: 18.4% (2007); Master's degree or higher: 6.5% (2007).

School District(s)

Catlin CUSD 5 (PK-12)
2005-06 Enrollment: 557 . . . . (217) 427-2116

Housing: Homeownership rate: 79.8% (2007); Median home value: $86,717 (2007); Median rent: $382 per month (2000); Median age of housing: 37 years (2000).

Safety: Violent crime rate: 9.8 per 10,000 population; Property crime rate: 19.5 per 10,000 population (2006).

Transportation: Commute to work: 96.2% car, 0.5% public transportation, 0.5% walk, 1.9% work from home (2000); Travel time to work: 29.2% less than 15 minutes, 54.5% 15 to 30 minutes, 8.6% 30 to 45 minutes, 4.8% 45 to 60 minutes, 3.0% 60 minutes or more (2000)

COLLISON (unincorporated postal area, zip code 61831). Covers a land area of 11.691 square miles and a water area of 0 square miles. Located at 40.21° N. Lat.; 87.78° W. Long. Elevation is 692 feet.

Population: 180 (2000); Race: 100.0% White, 0.0% Black, 0.0% Asian, 0.0% Hispanic of any race (2000); Density: 15.4 persons per square mile (2000); Age: 24.5% under 18, 10.9% over 64 (2000); Marriage status: 15.8% never married, 65.0% now married, 7.5% widowed, 11.7% divorced (2000); Foreign born: 0.0% (2000); Ancestry (includes multiple ancestries): 19.7% United States or American, 17.7% Irish, 17.0% German, 12.2% Other groups, 8.2% English (2000).

Economy: Employment by occupation: 5.1% management, 10.3% professional, 7.7% services, 41.0% sales, 2.6% farming, 9.0% construction, 24.4% production (2000).

Income: Per capita income: $16,937 (2000); Median household income: $42,750 (2000); Poverty rate: 8.8% (2000).

Education: Percent of population age 25 and over with: High school diploma (including GED) or higher: 82.7% (2000); Bachelor's degree or higher: 11.5% (2000).

Housing: Homeownership rate: 87.9% (2000); Median home value: $63,000 (2000); Median rent: $263 per month (2000); Median age of housing: 50 years (2000).

Transportation: Commute to work: 96.2% car, 0.0% public transportation, 0.0% walk, 3.8% work from home (2000); Travel time to work: 12.0% less than 15 minutes, 36.0% 15 to 30 minutes, 44.0% 30 to 45 minutes, 5.3% 45 to 60 minutes, 2.7% 60 minutes or more (2000)

DANVILLE (city). County seat. Covers a land area of 17.003 square miles and a water area of 0.095 square miles. Located at 40.13° N. Lat.; 87.62° W. Long. Elevation is 600 feet.

History: Danville had its beginning when a salt works was established in 1824. The town was laid out nearby in 1827 by Dan Beckwith, on land donated by him and Guy W. Smith, and the town was named for Beckwith.

Population: 35,622 (1990); 33,904 (2000); 32,664 (2007); 31,758 (2012 projected); Race: 68.2% White, 26.0% Black, 1.1% Asian, 5.5% Hispanic of any race (2007); Density: 1,921.1 persons per square mile (2007); Average household size: 2.52 (2007); Median age: 36.5 (2007); Males per 100 females: 99.1 (2007); Marriage status: 25.8% never married, 52.7% now married, 8.6% widowed, 12.9% divorced (2000); Foreign born: 2.9% (2000); Ancestry (includes multiple ancestries): 26.0% Other groups, 15.7% German, 9.6% Irish, 8.9% United States or American, 7.8% English (2000).

Economy: Unemployment rate: 6.8% (4/2008); Total civilian labor force: 13,738 (4/2008); Single-family building permits issued: 10 (2007); Multi-family building permits issued: 0 (2007); Employment by occupation:

8.6% management, 18.5% professional, 18.3% services, 24.8% sales, 0.4% farming, 7.5% construction, 21.8% production (2000).
Income: Per capita income: $18,484 (2007); Median household income: $33,506 (2007); Average household income: $45,032 (2007); Percent of households with income of $100,000 or more: 7.8% (2007); Poverty rate: 18.1% (2000).
Taxes: Total city taxes per capita: $430 (2006); City property taxes per capita: $188 (2006).
Education: Percent of population age 25 and over with: High school diploma (including GED) or higher: 75.0% (2007); Bachelor's degree or higher: 15.5% (2007); Master's degree or higher: 5.2% (2007).

School District(s)

Danville CCSD 118 (PK-12)
2005-06 Enrollment: 6,470 . . . . (217) 444-1004
Dept of Corrections Sch Dist 428 (08-12)
2005-06 Enrollment: 2,271 . . . . (217) 522-2666
Oakwood CUSD 76 (PK-12)
2005-06 Enrollment: 1,173 . . . . (217) 354-4355
Vermilion Assoc for Spec Educ
2005-06 Enrollment: n/a . . . . (217) 443-8273
Vermilion Voc Ed Deliver System
2005-06 Enrollment: n/a . . . . (217) 442-0461
Vermillion Roe (KG-11)
2005-06 Enrollment: 48 . . . . (217) 431-2668

Four-year College(s)

Lakeview College of Nursing (Private, Not-for-profit)
Fall 2007 Enrollment: 246 . . . . (217) 443-5238

Two-year College(s)

Danville Area Community College (Public)
Fall 2007 Enrollment: 2,832. . . . . (217) 443-3222
2007-08 Tuition: In-state $4,800; Out-of-state $4,800

Vocational/Technical School(s)

Concept College of Cosmetology (Private, For-profit)
Fall 2007 Enrollment: 99 . . . . (217) 442-9329
2007-08 Tuition: $8,950

Housing: Homeownership rate: 62.4% (2007); Median home value: $62,009 (2007); Median rent: $317 per month (2000); Median age of housing: 49 years (2000).
Hospitals: Provena United Samaritans Medical Center (210 beds); VA Illiana Health Care System (422 beds)
Safety: Violent crime rate: 133.7 per 10,000 population; Property crime rate: 747.9 per 10,000 population (2006).
Newspapers: Commercial-News (Community news; Circulation 0); News-Gazette - Danville Bureau (Regional news; Circulation 0)
Transportation: Commute to work: 93.1% car, 1.2% public transportation, 2.4% walk, 2.4% work from home (2000); Travel time to work: 60.0% less than 15 minutes, 27.9% 15 to 30 minutes, 5.3% 30 to 45 minutes, 4.0% 45 to 60 minutes, 2.8% 60 minutes or more (2000); Amtrak: Service available.
Airports: Vermilion County (general aviation)
Additional Information Contacts
City of Danville. . . . . (217) 431-2400
http://www.cityofdanville.org
Danville Area Convention & Visitors' Bureau. . . . . (217) 442-2096
http://www.danvillecvb.com

FAIRMOUNT (village). Covers a land area of 0.311 square miles and a water area of 0 square miles. Located at 40.04° N. Lat.; 87.83° W. Long. Elevation is 666 feet.
Population: 716 (1990); 640 (2000); 623 (2007); 607 (2012 projected); Race: 98.6% White, 0.5% Black, 0.0% Asian, 0.8% Hispanic of any race (2007); Density: 2,000.8 persons per square mile (2007); Average household size: 2.41 (2007); Median age: 39.1 (2007); Males per 100 females: 94.1 (2007); Marriage status: 19.0% never married, 62.3% now married, 11.0% widowed, 7.6% divorced (2000); Foreign born: 0.5% (2000); Ancestry (includes multiple ancestries): 32.3% United States or American, 14.9% German, 9.2% English, 9.1% Irish, 8.2% Other groups (2000).
Economy: Employment by occupation: 5.7% management, 8.7% professional, 15.3% services, 29.0% sales, 1.3% farming, 18.7% construction, 21.3% production (2000).
Income: Per capita income: $21,878 (2007); Median household income: $49,405 (2007); Average household income: $52,625 (2007); Percent of households with income of $100,000 or more: 6.9% (2007); Poverty rate: 9.5% (2000).
Education: Percent of population age 25 and over with: High school diploma (including GED) or higher: 77.2% (2007); Bachelor's degree or higher: 4.9% (2007); Master's degree or higher: 1.9% (2007).
Housing: Homeownership rate: 83.8% (2007); Median home value: $71,000 (2007); Median rent: $308 per month (2000); Median age of housing: 47 years (2000).
Safety: Violent crime rate: 0.0 per 10,000 population; Property crime rate: 0.0 per 10,000 population (2006).
Transportation: Commute to work: 89.1% car, 0.0% public transportation, 5.4% walk, 4.4% work from home (2000); Travel time to work: 22.8% less than 15 minutes, 34.2% 15 to 30 minutes, 30.2% 30 to 45 minutes, 7.5% 45 to 60 minutes, 5.3% 60 minutes or more (2000)

FITHIAN (village). Covers a land area of 0.387 square miles and a water area of 0 square miles. Located at 40.11° N. Lat.; 87.87° W. Long. Elevation is 663 feet.
Population: 512 (1990); 506 (2000); 461 (2007); 464 (2012 projected); Race: 98.9% White, 0.7% Black, 0.0% Asian, 1.1% Hispanic of any race (2007); Density: 1,192.5 persons per square mile (2007); Average household size: 2.45 (2007); Median age: 37.6 (2007); Males per 100 females: 114.4 (2007); Marriage status: 16.5% never married, 71.5% now married, 6.1% widowed, 5.9% divorced (2000); Foreign born: 0.0% (2000); Ancestry (includes multiple ancestries): 23.1% German, 14.6% English, 12.0% United States or American, 9.1% Irish, 8.9% Other groups (2000).
Economy: Single-family building permits issued: 1 (2007); Multi-family building permits issued: 0 (2007); Employment by occupation: 3.8% management, 13.2% professional, 11.7% services, 30.9% sales, 1.5% farming, 10.2% construction, 28.7% production (2000).
Income: Per capita income: $24,555 (2007); Median household income: $59,286 (2007); Average household income: $60,213 (2007); Percent of households with income of $100,000 or more: 11.7% (2007); Poverty rate: 4.9% (2000).
Education: Percent of population age 25 and over with: High school diploma (including GED) or higher: 89.2% (2007); Bachelor's degree or higher: 8.2% (2007); Master's degree or higher: 3.0% (2007).

School District(s)

Oakwood CUSD 76 (PK-12)
2005-06 Enrollment: 1,173 . . . . (217) 354-4355

Housing: Homeownership rate: 80.3% (2007); Median home value: $77,308 (2007); Median rent: $408 per month (2000); Median age of housing: 45 years (2000).
Safety: Violent crime rate: 0.0 per 10,000 population; Property crime rate: 36.2 per 10,000 population (2006).
Transportation: Commute to work: 94.0% car, 0.0% public transportation, 0.8% walk, 4.5% work from home (2000); Travel time to work: 9.5% less than 15 minutes, 48.6% 15 to 30 minutes, 34.8% 30 to 45 minutes, 3.6% 45 to 60 minutes, 3.6% 60 minutes or more (2000)

GEORGETOWN (city). Covers a land area of 1.612 square miles and a water area of 0 square miles. Located at 39.97° N. Lat.; 87.63° W. Long. Elevation is 669 feet.
History: Georgetown was settled by Quakers from Tennessee and North Carolina. The town was laid out in 1827.
Population: 3,684 (1990); 3,628 (2000); 3,553 (2007); 3,459 (2012 projected); Race: 96.6% White, 1.7% Black, 0.0% Asian, 1.4% Hispanic of any race (2007); Density: 2,204.1 persons per square mile (2007); Average household size: 2.41 (2007); Median age: 36.4 (2007); Males per 100 females: 90.1 (2007); Marriage status: 22.6% never married, 53.9% now married, 8.2% widowed, 15.3% divorced (2000); Foreign born: 0.5% (2000); Ancestry (includes multiple ancestries): 23.6% United States or American, 17.8% German, 9.0% English, 8.7% Irish, 7.9% Other groups (2000).
Economy: Single-family building permits issued: 1 (2007); Multi-family building permits issued: 0 (2007); Employment by occupation: 8.1% management, 12.8% professional, 16.3% services, 25.5% sales, 1.0% farming, 13.4% construction, 23.0% production (2000).
Income: Per capita income: $18,501 (2007); Median household income: $40,018 (2007); Average household income: $44,625 (2007); Percent of households with income of $100,000 or more: 5.0% (2007); Poverty rate: 13.9% (2000).
Education: Percent of population age 25 and over with: High school diploma (including GED) or higher: 76.1% (2007); Bachelor's degree or higher: 6.4% (2007); Master's degree or higher: 2.0% (2007).

School District(s)

Georgetown-Ridge Farm CUD 4 (PK-12)
2005-06 Enrollment: 1,285 . . . . (217) 662-8488

Housing: Homeownership rate: 73.4% (2007); Median home value: $57,919 (2007); Median rent: $283 per month (2000); Median age of housing: 41 years (2000).

Safety: Violent crime rate: 42.7 per 10,000 population; Property crime rate: 267.3 per 10,000 population (2006).

Newspapers: Independent News (Local news; Circulation 17,253)

Transportation: Commute to work: 95.8% car, 0.3% public transportation, 1.9% walk, 1.1% work from home (2000); Travel time to work: 17.3% less than 15 minutes, 44.2% 15 to 30 minutes, 26.3% 30 to 45 minutes, 7.0% 45 to 60 minutes, 5.2% 60 minutes or more (2000)

HENNING (village). Covers a land area of 1.524 square miles and a water area of 0 square miles. Located at 40.30° N. Lat.; 87.70° W. Long. Elevation is 686 feet.

Population: 273 (1990); 241 (2000); 236 (2007); 227 (2012 projected); Race: 100.0% White, 0.0% Black, 0.0% Asian, 0.0% Hispanic of any race (2007); Density: 154.9 persons per square mile (2007); Average household size: 2.46 (2007); Median age: 35.0 (2007); Males per 100 females: 101.7 (2007); Marriage status: 23.2% never married, 53.6% now married, 16.5% widowed, 6.7% divorced (2000); Foreign born: 0.0% (2000); Ancestry (includes multiple ancestries): 18.4% German, 16.8% United States or American, 16.8% Irish, 16.8% Other groups, 11.1% English (2000).

Economy: Single-family building permits issued: 0 (2007); Multi-family building permits issued: 0 (2007); Employment by occupation: 6.1% management, 3.8% professional, 13.0% services, 20.6% sales, 0.0% farming, 13.7% construction, 42.7% production (2000).

Income: Per capita income: $20,487 (2007); Median household income: $45,833 (2007); Average household income: $50,365 (2007); Percent of households with income of $100,000 or more: 6.3% (2007); Poverty rate: 4.5% (2000).

Education: Percent of population age 25 and over with: High school diploma (including GED) or higher: 80.8% (2007); Bachelor's degree or higher: 5.3% (2007); Master's degree or higher: 2.6% (2007).

Housing: Homeownership rate: 83.3% (2007); Median home value: $45,000 (2007); Median rent: $229 per month (2000); Median age of housing: 46 years (2000).

Safety: Violent crime rate: 0.0 per 10,000 population; Property crime rate: 42.6 per 10,000 population (2006).

Transportation: Commute to work: 93.8% car, 0.0% public transportation, 3.1% walk, 2.3% work from home (2000); Travel time to work: 11.2% less than 15 minutes, 52.8% 15 to 30 minutes, 23.2% 30 to 45 minutes, 7.2% 45 to 60 minutes, 5.6% 60 minutes or more (2000)

HOOPESTON (city). Covers a land area of 3.117 square miles and a water area of 0 square miles. Located at 40.46° N. Lat.; 87.67° W. Long. Elevation is 725 feet.

History: Townsites were laid out on the Hoope farm, near the intersection of two railway lines, in 1871. Hoopeston grew rapidly as a canning center.

Population: 5,891 (1990); 5,965 (2000); 5,720 (2007); 5,523 (2012 projected); Race: 90.0% White, 1.0% Black, 0.1% Asian, 9.5% Hispanic of any race (2007); Density: 1,835.2 persons per square mile (2007); Average household size: 2.55 (2007); Median age: 40.4 (2007); Males per 100 females: 99.0 (2007); Marriage status: 22.7% never married, 60.7% now married, 7.3% widowed, 9.2% divorced (2000); Foreign born: 2.0% (2000); Ancestry (includes multiple ancestries): 16.3% Other groups, 14.2% German, 13.9% United States or American, 12.3% English, 7.4% Irish (2000).

Economy: Single-family building permits issued: 1 (2007); Multi-family building permits issued: 0 (2007); Employment by occupation: 7.1% management, 13.2% professional, 17.0% services, 23.6% sales, 1.9% farming, 8.8% construction, 28.4% production (2000).

Income: Per capita income: $17,415 (2007); Median household income: $35,725 (2007); Average household income: $43,467 (2007); Percent of households with income of $100,000 or more: 6.0% (2007); Poverty rate: 13.8% (2000).

Education: Percent of population age 25 and over with: High school diploma (including GED) or higher: 76.0% (2007); Bachelor's degree or higher: 7.9% (2007); Master's degree or higher: 3.3% (2007).

School District(s)

Hoopeston Area CUSD 11 (PK-12)
2005-06 Enrollment: 1,361 . . . . (217) 283-6668

Housing: Homeownership rate: 68.2% (2007); Median home value: $63,256 (2007); Median rent: $299 per month (2000); Median age of housing: 50 years (2000).

Hospitals: Hoopeston Community Memorial Hospital (25 beds)

Safety: Violent crime rate: 50.4 per 10,000 population; Property crime rate: 328.5 per 10,000 population (2006).

Newspapers: Chronicle (Community news; Circulation 2,205)

Transportation: Commute to work: 93.6% car, 0.0% public transportation, 3.3% walk, 2.8% work from home (2000); Travel time to work: 54.2% less than 15 minutes, 10.5% 15 to 30 minutes, 17.4% 30 to 45 minutes, 8.8% 45 to 60 minutes, 9.1% 60 minutes or more (2000)

Additional Information Contacts

City of Hoopeston . . . . (217) 283-5833
http://www.hoopeston-il.gov

Hoopeston Chamber of Commerce . . . . (217) 283-7873
http://www.hoopestonchamber.com

INDIANOLA (village). Covers a land area of 0.386 square miles and a water area of 0 square miles. Located at 39.92° N. Lat.; 87.74° W. Long. Elevation is 673 feet.

Population: 336 (1990); 207 (2000); 166 (2007); 171 (2012 projected); Race: 98.8% White, 0.0% Black, 1.2% Asian, 0.0% Hispanic of any race (2007); Density: 429.6 persons per square mile (2007); Average household size: 2.59 (2007); Median age: 36.7 (2007); Males per 100 females: 95.3 (2007); Marriage status: 19.7% never married, 62.8% now married, 9.6% widowed, 8.0% divorced (2000); Foreign born: 1.3% (2000); Ancestry (includes multiple ancestries): 27.4% United States or American, 14.1% German, 9.0% Other groups, 8.5% English, 8.1% Irish (2000).

Economy: Employment by occupation: 0.9% management, 9.5% professional, 20.7% services, 25.0% sales, 0.0% farming, 12.9% construction, 31.0% production (2000).

Income: Per capita income: $21,596 (2007); Median household income: $52,308 (2007); Average household income: $56,016 (2007); Percent of households with income of $100,000 or more: 10.9% (2007); Poverty rate: 6.0% (2000).

Education: Percent of population age 25 and over with: High school diploma (including GED) or higher: 81.3% (2007); Bachelor's degree or higher: 6.5% (2007); Master's degree or higher: 2.8% (2007).

Housing: Homeownership rate: 87.5% (2007); Median home value: $46,667 (2007); Median rent: $333 per month (2000); Median age of housing: 37 years (2000).

Safety: Violent crime rate: 0.0 per 10,000 population; Property crime rate: 0.0 per 10,000 population (2006).

Transportation: Commute to work: 100.0% car, 0.0% public transportation, 0.0% walk, 0.0% work from home (2000); Travel time to work: 10.1% less than 15 minutes, 34.9% 15 to 30 minutes, 36.7% 30 to 45 minutes, 12.8% 45 to 60 minutes, 5.5% 60 minutes or more (2000)

MUNCIE (village). Covers a land area of 0.180 square miles and a water area of 0 square miles. Located at 40.11° N. Lat.; 87.84° W. Long. Elevation is 646 feet.

Population: 182 (1990); 155 (2000); 164 (2007); 167 (2012 projected); Race: 100.0% White, 0.0% Black, 0.0% Asian, 0.0% Hispanic of any race (2007); Density: 909.4 persons per square mile (2007); Average household size: 2.22 (2007); Median age: 39.4 (2007); Males per 100 females: 90.7 (2007); Marriage status: 26.1% never married, 59.7% now married, 5.0% widowed, 9.2% divorced (2000); Foreign born: 0.0% (2000); Ancestry (includes multiple ancestries): 19.8% United States or American, 19.8% English, 11.1% German, 6.2% Irish, 4.3% Other groups (2000).

Economy: Single-family building permits issued: 0 (2007); Multi-family building permits issued: 0 (2007); Employment by occupation: 2.5% management, 31.6% professional, 15.2% services, 16.5% sales, 1.3% farming, 17.7% construction, 15.2% production (2000).

Income: Per capita income: $19,604 (2007); Median household income: $43,125 (2007); Average household income: $43,446 (2007); Percent of households with income of $100,000 or more: 1.4% (2007); Poverty rate: 8.0% (2000).

Education: Percent of population age 25 and over with: High school diploma (including GED) or higher: 76.1% (2007); Bachelor's degree or higher: 16.2% (2007); Master's degree or higher: 7.7% (2007).

Housing: Homeownership rate: 83.8% (2007); Median home value: $65,000 (2007); Median rent: $367 per month (2000); Median age of housing: 56 years (2000).

Transportation: Commute to work: 87.3% car, 0.0% public transportation, 6.3% walk, 6.3% work from home (2000); Travel time to work: 23.0% less

than 15 minutes, 45.9% 15 to 30 minutes, 31.1% 30 to 45 minutes, 0.0% 45 to 60 minutes, 0.0% 60 minutes or more (2000)

OAKWOOD (village). Covers a land area of 0.899 square miles and a water area of 0 square miles. Located at 40.11° N. Lat.; 87.77° W. Long. Elevation is 646 feet.

Population: 1,535 (1990); 1,502 (2000); 1,517 (2007); 1,501 (2012 projected); Race: 99.3% White, 0.2% Black, 0.0% Asian, 0.5% Hispanic of any race (2007); Density: 1,686.5 persons per square mile (2007); Average household size: 2.36 (2007); Median age: 37.4 (2007); Males per 100 females: 91.5 (2007); Marriage status: 21.8% never married, 54.5% now married, 9.4% widowed, 14.3% divorced (2000); Foreign born: 0.4% (2000); Ancestry (includes multiple ancestries): 17.0% German, 16.0% United States or American, 14.2% Irish, 11.4% English, 10.0% Other groups (2000).

Economy: Single-family building permits issued: 0 (2007); Multi-family building permits issued: 0 (2007); Employment by occupation: 7.5% management, 9.5% professional, 16.6% services, 27.8% sales, 0.3% farming, 12.3% construction, 26.1% production (2000).

Income: Per capita income: $22,625 (2007); Median household income: $47,692 (2007); Average household income: $53,462 (2007); Percent of households with income of $100,000 or more: 8.4% (2007); Poverty rate: 8.1% (2000).

Education: Percent of population age 25 and over with: High school diploma (including GED) or higher: 86.1% (2007); Bachelor's degree or higher: 10.5% (2007); Master's degree or higher: 3.4% (2007).

School District(s)

Oakwood CUSD 76 (PK-12)
2005-06 Enrollment: 1,173 . . . . (217) 354-4355
Vermillion Roe (KG-11)
2005-06 Enrollment: 48 . . . . (217) 431-2668

Housing: Homeownership rate: 81.6% (2007); Median home value: $68,824 (2007); Median rent: $307 per month (2000); Median age of housing: 28 years (2000).

Safety: Violent crime rate: 34.1 per 10,000 population; Property crime rate: 81.9 per 10,000 population (2006).

Transportation: Commute to work: 96.1% car, 0.0% public transportation, 1.6% walk, 2.1% work from home (2000); Travel time to work: 22.7% less than 15 minutes, 50.8% 15 to 30 minutes, 19.4% 30 to 45 minutes, 4.0% 45 to 60 minutes, 3.1% 60 minutes or more (2000)

POTOMAC (village). Covers a land area of 0.483 square miles and a water area of 0 square miles. Located at 40.30° N. Lat.; 87.80° W. Long. Elevation is 669 feet.

Population: 753 (1990); 681 (2000); 558 (2007); 565 (2012 projected); Race: 97.1% White, 0.0% Black, 0.0% Asian, 2.5% Hispanic of any race (2007); Density: 1,154.1 persons per square mile (2007); Average household size: 2.64 (2007); Median age: 35.9 (2007); Males per 100 females: 97.2 (2007); Marriage status: 22.4% never married, 59.2% now married, 8.4% widowed, 10.0% divorced (2000); Foreign born: 0.0% (2000); Ancestry (includes multiple ancestries): 27.1% German, 18.1% English, 15.0% Irish, 12.2% United States or American, 7.1% Other groups (2000).

Economy: Single-family building permits issued: 2 (2007); Multi-family building permits issued: 0 (2007); Employment by occupation: 8.5% management, 9.8% professional, 18.6% services, 24.1% sales, 0.6% farming, 7.3% construction, 31.1% production (2000).

Income: Per capita income: $19,247 (2007); Median household income: $47,125 (2007); Average household income: $50,900 (2007); Percent of households with income of $100,000 or more: 7.1% (2007); Poverty rate: 9.1% (2000).

Education: Percent of population age 25 and over with: High school diploma (including GED) or higher: 83.9% (2007); Bachelor's degree or higher: 10.2% (2007); Master's degree or higher: 5.4% (2007).

School District(s)

Potomac CUSD 10 (PK-08)
2005-06 Enrollment: 183 . . . . (217) 987-6155

Housing: Homeownership rate: 81.5% (2007); Median home value: $55,417 (2007); Median rent: $320 per month (2000); Median age of housing: 54 years (2000).

Safety: Violent crime rate: 15.0 per 10,000 population; Property crime rate: 30.0 per 10,000 population (2006).

Transportation: Commute to work: 91.1% car, 0.0% public transportation, 3.1% walk, 3.7% work from home (2000); Travel time to work: 21.1% less than 15 minutes, 25.2% 15 to 30 minutes, 34.8% 30 to 45 minutes, 13.7% 45 to 60 minutes, 5.1% 60 minutes or more (2000)

RANKIN (village). Covers a land area of 0.572 square miles and a water area of 0 square miles. Located at 40.46° N. Lat.; 87.89° W. Long. Elevation is 722 feet.

Population: 619 (1990); 617 (2000); 511 (2007); 515 (2012 projected); Race: 91.2% White, 0.2% Black, 0.4% Asian, 8.2% Hispanic of any race (2007); Density: 893.0 persons per square mile (2007); Average household size: 2.43 (2007); Median age: 37.6 (2007); Males per 100 females: 99.6 (2007); Marriage status: 22.2% never married, 56.8% now married, 10.9% widowed, 10.0% divorced (2000); Foreign born: 7.7% (2000); Ancestry (includes multiple ancestries): 14.7% German, 13.7% Other groups, 9.8% United States or American, 9.3% Irish, 6.7% English (2000).

Economy: Single-family building permits issued: 0 (2007); Multi-family building permits issued: 0 (2007); Employment by occupation: 8.4% management, 8.8% professional, 20.3% services, 17.6% sales, 0.0% farming, 11.0% construction, 33.9% production (2000).

Income: Per capita income: $16,468 (2007); Median household income: $33,333 (2007); Average household income: $40,071 (2007); Percent of households with income of $100,000 or more: 2.9% (2007); Poverty rate: 13.6% (2000).

Education: Percent of population age 25 and over with: High school diploma (including GED) or higher: 74.2% (2007); Bachelor's degree or higher: 7.1% (2007); Master's degree or higher: 3.4% (2007).

Housing: Homeownership rate: 80.5% (2007); Median home value: $47,381 (2007); Median rent: $268 per month (2000); Median age of housing: 60 years (2000).

Safety: Violent crime rate: 0.0 per 10,000 population; Property crime rate: 0.0 per 10,000 population (2006).

Transportation: Commute to work: 96.9% car, 0.4% public transportation, 1.3% walk, 1.3% work from home (2000); Travel time to work: 20.9% less than 15 minutes, 28.9% 15 to 30 minutes, 28.4% 30 to 45 minutes, 10.7% 45 to 60 minutes, 11.1% 60 minutes or more (2000)

RIDGE FARM (village). Covers a land area of 3.127 square miles and a water area of 0 square miles. Located at 39.89° N. Lat.; 87.65° W. Long. Elevation is 702 feet.

History: Ridge Farm was platted in 1853 and incorporated as a village in 1874. It developed as a trading center.

Population: 939 (1990); 912 (2000); 789 (2007); 781 (2012 projected); Race: 99.5% White, 0.0% Black, 0.0% Asian, 0.6% Hispanic of any race (2007); Density: 252.3 persons per square mile (2007); Average household size: 2.44 (2007); Median age: 38.1 (2007); Males per 100 females: 94.8 (2007); Marriage status: 15.6% never married, 63.7% now married, 10.1% widowed, 10.6% divorced (2000); Foreign born: 0.2% (2000); Ancestry (includes multiple ancestries): 22.3% United States or American, 17.6% German, 11.9% Irish, 7.8% English, 6.7% Other groups (2000).

Economy: Single-family building permits issued: 1 (2007); Multi-family building permits issued: 0 (2007); Employment by occupation: 6.1% management, 10.8% professional, 19.7% services, 20.6% sales, 0.0% farming, 16.4% construction, 26.4% production (2000).

Income: Per capita income: $18,676 (2007); Median household income: $37,391 (2007); Average household income: $45,478 (2007); Percent of households with income of $100,000 or more: 7.7% (2007); Poverty rate: 10.5% (2000).

Education: Percent of population age 25 and over with: High school diploma (including GED) or higher: 80.3% (2007); Bachelor's degree or higher: 10.4% (2007); Master's degree or higher: 3.3% (2007).

School District(s)

Georgetown-Ridge Farm CUD 4 (PK-12)
2005-06 Enrollment: 1,285 . . . . (217) 662-8488

Housing: Homeownership rate: 79.6% (2007); Median home value: $58,750 (2007); Median rent: $245 per month (2000); Median age of housing: 47 years (2000).

Safety: Violent crime rate: 0.0 per 10,000 population; Property crime rate: 57.0 per 10,000 population (2006).

Transportation: Commute to work: 94.9% car, 0.0% public transportation, 1.1% walk, 1.7% work from home (2000); Travel time to work: 17.1% less than 15 minutes, 22.9% 15 to 30 minutes, 46.9% 30 to 45 minutes, 7.7% 45 to 60 minutes, 5.4% 60 minutes or more (2000)

ROSSVILLE (village). Covers a land area of 1.345 square miles and a water area of 0 square miles. Located at 40.38° N. Lat.; 87.66° W. Long. Elevation is 689 feet.

History: Rossville was laid out in 1857 and named for early settler Jacob Ross. The site at the intersection of two roads had previously been called Henpeck.
Population: 1,334 (1990); 1,217 (2000); 1,240 (2007); 1,207 (2012 projected); Race: 97.3% White, 0.3% Black, 0.1% Asian, 2.4% Hispanic of any race (2007); Density: 922.2 persons per square mile (2007); Average household size: 2.23 (2007); Median age: 41.3 (2007); Males per 100 females: 88.7 (2007); Marriage status: 21.9% never married, 56.9% now married, 10.1% widowed, 11.1% divorced (2000); Foreign born: 1.0% (2000); Ancestry (includes multiple ancestries): 20.5% German, 17.0% English, 11.6% United States or American, 10.9% Irish, 8.3% Other groups (2000).
Economy: Single-family building permits issued: 0 (2007); Multi-family building permits issued: 0 (2007); Employment by occupation: 8.8% management, 12.6% professional, 14.2% services, 28.1% sales, 1.1% farming, 8.2% construction, 27.0% production (2000).
Income: Per capita income: $20,809 (2007); Median household income: $41,719 (2007); Average household income: $46,394 (2007); Percent of households with income of $100,000 or more: 6.1% (2007); Poverty rate: 9.8% (2000).
Education: Percent of population age 25 and over with: High school diploma (including GED) or higher: 81.3% (2007); Bachelor's degree or higher: 12.6% (2007); Master's degree or higher: 2.6% (2007).

School District(s)

Rossville-Alvin CUSD 7 (PK-08)
2005-06 Enrollment: 346 . . . . (217) 748-6666

Housing: Homeownership rate: 77.0% (2007); Median home value: $74,000 (2007); Median rent: $285 per month (2000); Median age of housing: 60+ years (2000).
Safety: Violent crime rate: 0.0 per 10,000 population; Property crime rate: 42.3 per 10,000 population (2006).
Transportation: Commute to work: 93.3% car, 0.2% public transportation, 3.9% walk, 1.7% work from home (2000); Travel time to work: 38.0% less than 15 minutes, 23.6% 15 to 30 minutes, 31.6% 30 to 45 minutes, 2.5% 45 to 60 minutes, 4.4% 60 minutes or more (2000)

SIDELL (village). Covers a land area of 0.928 square miles and a water area of 0 square miles. Located at 39.91° N. Lat.; 87.82° W. Long. Elevation is 682 feet.
Population: 584 (1990); 626 (2000); 633 (2007); 614 (2012 projected); Race: 99.5% White, 0.3% Black, 0.0% Asian, 0.6% Hispanic of any race (2007); Density: 682.3 persons per square mile (2007); Average household size: 2.62 (2007); Median age: 37.1 (2007); Males per 100 females: 99.1 (2007); Marriage status: 18.4% never married, 63.9% now married, 6.1% widowed, 11.7% divorced (2000); Foreign born: 0.3% (2000); Ancestry (includes multiple ancestries): 33.5% United States or American, 12.5% German, 11.8% Irish, 11.3% English, 8.7% Other groups (2000).
Economy: Single-family building permits issued: 2 (2007); Multi-family building permits issued: 0 (2007); Employment by occupation: 4.2% management, 14.6% professional, 13.5% services, 26.9% sales, 1.5% farming, 5.0% construction, 34.2% production (2000).
Income: Per capita income: $18,092 (2007); Median household income: $39,722 (2007); Average household income: $47,324 (2007); Percent of households with income of $100,000 or more: 5.4% (2007); Poverty rate: 9.6% (2000).
Education: Percent of population age 25 and over with: High school diploma (including GED) or higher: 76.8% (2007); Bachelor's degree or higher: 6.5% (2007); Master's degree or higher: 1.8% (2007).

School District(s)

Jamaica CUSD 12 (PK-12)
2005-06 Enrollment: 465 . . . . (217) 288-9306

Housing: Homeownership rate: 81.8% (2007); Median home value: $57,619 (2007); Median rent: $296 per month (2000); Median age of housing: 56 years (2000).
Safety: Violent crime rate: 0.0 per 10,000 population; Property crime rate: 16.6 per 10,000 population (2006).
Newspapers: Sidell Reporter (Community news; Circulation 900)
Transportation: Commute to work: 91.5% car, 1.2% public transportation, 1.9% walk, 4.7% work from home (2000); Travel time to work: 29.7% less than 15 minutes, 18.7% 15 to 30 minutes, 33.3% 30 to 45 minutes, 17.5% 45 to 60 minutes, 0.8% 60 minutes or more (2000)

TILTON (village). Covers a land area of 3.098 square miles and a water area of 0.028 square miles. Located at 40.09° N. Lat.; 87.64° W. Long. Elevation is 643 feet.
History: Incorporated 1884.
Population: 3,263 (1990); 2,976 (2000); 2,838 (2007); 2,733 (2012 projected); Race: 98.0% White, 0.2% Black, 0.1% Asian, 1.1% Hispanic of any race (2007); Density: 916.0 persons per square mile (2007); Average household size: 2.20 (2007); Median age: 41.4 (2007); Males per 100 females: 88.9 (2007); Marriage status: 18.5% never married, 55.1% now married, 8.5% widowed, 17.9% divorced (2000); Foreign born: 0.9% (2000); Ancestry (includes multiple ancestries): 18.6% German, 16.5% United States or American, 13.1% Irish, 10.6% English, 9.5% Other groups (2000).
Economy: Single-family building permits issued: 0 (2007); Multi-family building permits issued: 0 (2007); Employment by occupation: 9.1% management, 10.0% professional, 23.7% services, 23.9% sales, 0.3% farming, 12.4% construction, 20.6% production (2000).
Income: Per capita income: $19,490 (2007); Median household income: $37,083 (2007); Average household income: $42,911 (2007); Percent of households with income of $100,000 or more: 5.5% (2007); Poverty rate: 8.6% (2000).
Education: Percent of population age 25 and over with: High school diploma (including GED) or higher: 77.6% (2007); Bachelor's degree or higher: 5.3% (2007); Master's degree or higher: 0.6% (2007).
Housing: Homeownership rate: 76.4% (2007); Median home value: $61,680 (2007); Median rent: $290 per month (2000); Median age of housing: 48 years (2000).
Safety: Violent crime rate: 24.6 per 10,000 population; Property crime rate: 172.1 per 10,000 population (2006).
Transportation: Commute to work: 96.4% car, 0.4% public transportation, 0.0% walk, 2.4% work from home (2000); Travel time to work: 45.0% less than 15 minutes, 40.9% 15 to 30 minutes, 9.6% 30 to 45 minutes, 2.9% 45 to 60 minutes, 1.7% 60 minutes or more (2000)

WESTVILLE (village). Covers a land area of 1.595 square miles and a water area of 0 square miles. Located at 40.04° N. Lat.; 87.63° W. Long. Elevation is 669 feet.
History: Westville was named for W.P. and E.A. West, who laid out the town in 1873. Coal mining was the first major industry.
Population: 3,387 (1990); 3,175 (2000); 3,063 (2007); 2,992 (2012 projected); Race: 97.7% White, 0.3% Black, 0.0% Asian, 1.0% Hispanic of any race (2007); Density: 1,920.3 persons per square mile (2007); Average household size: 2.19 (2007); Median age: 42.0 (2007); Males per 100 females: 90.1 (2007); Marriage status: 21.7% never married, 58.1% now married, 9.3% widowed, 10.9% divorced (2000); Foreign born: 0.7% (2000); Ancestry (includes multiple ancestries): 13.6% German, 12.4% United States or American, 11.5% Irish, 10.3% English, 10.2% Other groups (2000).
Economy: Single-family building permits issued: 2 (2007); Multi-family building permits issued: 0 (2007); Employment by occupation: 7.7% management, 11.1% professional, 18.1% services, 27.8% sales, 0.0% farming, 9.6% construction, 25.6% production (2000).
Income: Per capita income: $22,086 (2007); Median household income: $41,294 (2007); Average household income: $48,321 (2007); Percent of households with income of $100,000 or more: 6.4% (2007); Poverty rate: 7.4% (2000).
Education: Percent of population age 25 and over with: High school diploma (including GED) or higher: 79.6% (2007); Bachelor's degree or higher: 8.6% (2007); Master's degree or higher: 2.8% (2007).

School District(s)

Westville CUSD 2 (PK-12)
2005-06 Enrollment: 1,249 . . . . (217) 267-3141

Housing: Homeownership rate: 79.4% (2007); Median home value: $71,312 (2007); Median rent: $312 per month (2000); Median age of housing: 46 years (2000).
Safety: Violent crime rate: 52.3 per 10,000 population; Property crime rate: 300.9 per 10,000 population (2006).
Transportation: Commute to work: 97.0% car, 0.5% public transportation, 0.9% walk, 1.6% work from home (2000); Travel time to work: 26.8% less than 15 minutes, 52.1% 15 to 30 minutes, 12.4% 30 to 45 minutes, 4.9% 45 to 60 minutes, 3.9% 60 minutes or more (2000)

Wabash County

Located in southeastern Illinois; bounded on the east and south by the Wabash River, and the Indiana border. Covers a land area of 223.47 square miles, a water area of 4.29 square miles, and is located in the

Central Time Zone. The county was founded in 1824. County seat is Mount Carmel.
Population: 13,111 (1990); 12,937 (2000); 12,498 (2007); 12,181 (2012 projected); Race: 97.7% White, 0.6% Black, 0.6% Asian, 1.0% Hispanic of any race (2007); Density: 55.9 persons per square mile (2007); Average household size: 2.45 (2007); Median age: 41.0 (2007); Males per 100 females: 95.7 (2007).
Religion: Five largest groups: 12.7% Catholic Church, 9.9% The United Methodist Church, 9.6% Christian Churches and Churches of Christ, 5.2% Christian Church (Disciples of Christ), 4.3% Southern Baptist Convention (2000).
Economy: Unemployment rate: 5.2% (4/2008); Total civilian labor force: 6,266 (4/2008); Leading industries: 22.9% health care and social assistance; 15.7% retail trade; 13.6% mining (2005); Farms: 199 totaling 110,560 acres (2002); Companies that employ 500 or more persons: 0 (2006); Companies that employ 100 to 499 persons: 6 (2006); Companies that employ less than 100 persons: 270 (2006); Black-owned businesses: n/a (2002); Hispanic-owned businesses: n/a (2002); Asian-owned businesses: n/a (2002); Women-owned businesses: 130 (2002); Retail sales per capita: $9,108 (2008). Single-family building permits issued: 4 (2007); Multi-family building permits issued: 0 (2007).
Income: Per capita income: $21,039 (2007); Median household income: $41,799 (2007); Average household income: $50,909 (2007); Percent of households with income of $100,000 or more: 9.0% (2007); Poverty rate: 14.8% (2005); Bankruptcy rate: 2.22% (2007).
Education: Percent of population age 25 and over with: High school diploma (including GED) or higher: 82.1% (2007); Bachelor's degree or higher: 12.7% (2007); Master's degree or higher: 4.3% (2007).
Housing: Homeownership rate: 75.7% (2007); Median home value: $65,809 (2007); Median rent: $241 per month (2000); Median age of housing: 42 years (2000).
Health: Birth rate: 128.2 per 10,000 population (2007); Death rate: 122.5 per 10,000 population (2007); Age-adjusted cancer mortality rate: 217.4 deaths per 100,000 population (2005); Air Quality Index: 100.0% good, 0.0% moderate, 0.0% unhealthy for sensitive individuals, 0.0% unhealthy (percent of days in 2007); Number of physicians: 8.0 per 10,000 population (2005); Hospital beds: 20.0 per 10,000 population (2004); Hospital admissions: 629.4 per 10,000 population (2004).
Elections: 2004 Presidential election results: 70.1% Bush, 29.2% Kerry, 0.0% Nader, 0.7% Badnarik
National and State Parks: Beall Woods State Conservation and Natural Area

Additional Information Contacts

Wabash County Government. . . . . (618) 262-4561

City of Mount Carmel . . . . (618) 262-4003
http://www.cityofmtcarmel.com
Wabash County Chamber of Commerce . . . . (618) 262-5116
http://www.wabashcountychamber.com

Wabash County Communities

ALLENDALE (village). Aka Orio. Covers a land area of 0.301 square miles and a water area of 0 square miles. Located at 38.52° N. Lat.; 87.71° W. Long. Elevation is 492 feet.
Population: 476 (1990); 528 (2000); 450 (2007); 452 (2012 projected); Race: 96.9% White, 1.6% Black, 0.0% Asian, 1.1% Hispanic of any race (2007); Density: 1,496.2 persons per square mile (2007); Average household size: 2.69 (2007); Median age: 38.4 (2007); Males per 100 females: 98.2 (2007); Marriage status: 25.4% never married, 62.1% now married, 7.7% widowed, 4.9% divorced (2000); Foreign born: 2.0% (2000); Ancestry (includes multiple ancestries): 20.1% German, 16.1% United States or American, 13.3% Other groups, 11.8% Irish, 11.3% English (2000).
Economy: Single-family building permits issued: 0 (2007); Multi-family building permits issued: 0 (2007); Employment by occupation: 5.8% management, 20.3% professional, 15.4% services, 22.0% sales, 0.0% farming, 12.9% construction, 23.7% production (2000).
Income: Per capita income: $17,258 (2007); Median household income: $41,731 (2007); Average household income: $45,434 (2007); Percent of households with income of $100,000 or more: 4.2% (2007); Poverty rate: 16.6% (2000).
Education: Percent of population age 25 and over with: High school diploma (including GED) or higher: 89.3% (2007); Bachelor's degree or higher: 13.0% (2007); Master's degree or higher: 4.7% (2007).

School District(s)

Allendale CCSD 17 (PK-08)
2005-06 Enrollment: 125 . . . . (618) 299-3161
Housing: Homeownership rate: 85.0% (2007); Median home value: $64,167 (2007); Median rent: $296 per month (2000); Median age of housing: 27 years (2000).
Transportation: Commute to work: 96.2% car, 0.0% public transportation, 0.9% walk, 2.1% work from home (2000); Travel time to work: 29.6% less than 15 minutes, 44.3% 15 to 30 minutes, 16.1% 30 to 45 minutes, 7.8% 45 to 60 minutes, 2.2% 60 minutes or more (2000)

BELLMONT (village). Covers a land area of 0.365 square miles and a water area of 0 square miles. Located at 38.38° N. Lat.; 87.90° W. Long. Elevation is 446 feet.
Population: 271 (1990); 297 (2000); 308 (2007); 303 (2012 projected); Race: 97.4% White, 1.0% Black, 0.6% Asian, 0.3% Hispanic of any race (2007); Density: 844.1 persons per square mile (2007); Average household size: 2.37 (2007); Median age: 36.7 (2007); Males per 100 females: 109.5 (2007); Marriage status: 17.3% never married, 66.7% now married, 6.1% widowed, 10.0% divorced (2000); Foreign born: 1.0% (2000); Ancestry (includes multiple ancestries): 30.0% German, 18.2% English, 9.6% Irish, 9.6% United States or American, 8.3% Other groups (2000).
Economy: Employment by occupation: 4.4% management, 8.1% professional, 9.6% services, 25.9% sales, 0.0% farming, 12.6% construction, 39.3% production (2000).
Income: Per capita income: $16,282 (2007); Median household income: $35,833 (2007); Average household income: $38,577 (2007); Percent of households with income of $100,000 or more: 6.2% (2007); Poverty rate: 11.9% (2000).
Education: Percent of population age 25 and over with: High school diploma (including GED) or higher: 90.5% (2007); Bachelor's degree or higher: 6.5% (2007); Master's degree or higher: 1.0% (2007).
Housing: Homeownership rate: 81.5% (2007); Median home value: $47,083 (2007); Median rent: $195 per month (2000); Median age of housing: 42 years (2000).
Transportation: Commute to work: 93.3% car, 0.0% public transportation, 4.4% walk, 2.2% work from home (2000); Travel time to work: 35.6% less than 15 minutes, 33.3% 15 to 30 minutes, 15.9% 30 to 45 minutes, 6.8% 45 to 60 minutes, 8.3% 60 minutes or more (2000)

KEENSBURG (village). Covers a land area of 0.258 square miles and a water area of 0 square miles. Located at 38.35° N. Lat.; 87.86° W. Long. Elevation is 436 feet.
Population: 238 (1990); 252 (2000); 226 (2007); 223 (2012 projected); Race: 99.6% White, 0.0% Black, 0.0% Asian, 0.0% Hispanic of any race (2007); Density: 877.6 persons per square mile (2007); Average household size: 2.43 (2007); Median age: 41.5 (2007); Males per 100 females: 107.3 (2007); Marriage status: 25.0% never married, 61.2% now married, 6.1% widowed, 7.7% divorced (2000); Foreign born: 0.0% (2000); Ancestry (includes multiple ancestries): 24.9% German, 16.5% United States or American, 14.3% Other groups, 8.9% Scottish, 8.9% Irish (2000).
Economy: Employment by occupation: 2.9% management, 7.2% professional, 11.6% services, 21.7% sales, 2.2% farming, 10.1% construction, 44.2% production (2000).
Income: Per capita income: $18,396 (2007); Median household income: $39,688 (2007); Average household income: $44,704 (2007); Percent of households with income of $100,000 or more: 3.2% (2007); Poverty rate: 5.6% (2000).
Education: Percent of population age 25 and over with: High school diploma (including GED) or higher: 78.0% (2007); Bachelor's degree or higher: 6.5% (2007); Master's degree or higher: 1.8% (2007).
Housing: Homeownership rate: 83.9% (2007); Median home value: $20,000 (2007); Median rent: $275 per month (2000); Median age of housing: 38 years (2000).
Transportation: Commute to work: 96.3% car, 0.0% public transportation, 0.0% walk, 0.0% work from home (2000); Travel time to work: 30.9% less than 15 minutes, 40.4% 15 to 30 minutes, 13.2% 30 to 45 minutes, 6.6% 45 to 60 minutes, 8.8% 60 minutes or more (2000)

MOUNT CARMEL (city). Aka Sugar Creek. County seat. Covers a land area of 4.617 square miles and a water area of 0.153 square miles. Located at 38.41° N. Lat.; 87.76° W. Long. Elevation is 449 feet.
History: Mount Carmel was founded in 1818 by Rev. Thomas S. Hinde of Ohio, who hoped for a "moral, temperate, and industrious village." A mussel and pearl industry began here in 1900.

Population: 8,353 (1990); 7,982 (2000); 7,517 (2007); 7,197 (2012 projected); Race: 97.6% White, 0.7% Black, 0.6% Asian, 1.2% Hispanic of any race (2007); Density: 1,628.0 persons per square mile (2007); Average household size: 2.38 (2007); Median age: 40.8 (2007); Males per 100 females: 91.2 (2007); Marriage status: 22.1% never married, 56.5% now married, 9.3% widowed, 12.1% divorced (2000); Foreign born: 0.6% (2000); Ancestry (includes multiple ancestries): 24.5% German, 17.4% United States or American, 10.8% Irish, 9.3% English, 9.2% Other groups (2000).
Economy: Single-family building permits issued: 4 (2007); Multi-family building permits issued: 0 (2007); Employment by occupation: 6.1% management, 13.8% professional, 21.6% services, 22.7% sales, 0.3% farming, 12.2% construction, 23.3% production (2000).
Income: Per capita income: $20,182 (2007); Median household income: $37,989 (2007); Average household income: $47,133 (2007); Percent of households with income of $100,000 or more: 8.3% (2007); Poverty rate: 15.8% (2000).
Education: Percent of population age 25 and over with: High school diploma (including GED) or higher: 79.9% (2007); Bachelor's degree or higher: 13.1% (2007); Master's degree or higher: 4.6% (2007).

School District(s)

Wabash CUSD 348 (PK-12)
2005-06 Enrollment: 1,873 . . . . (618) 262-4181

Two-year College(s)

Illinois Eastern Community Colleges-Wabash Valley College (Public)
Fall 2007 Enrollment: 4,206. . . . . (618) 393-2982
2007-08 Tuition: In-state $6,117; Out-of-state $7,615

Housing: Homeownership rate: 69.2% (2007); Median home value: $61,071 (2007); Median rent: $241 per month (2000); Median age of housing: 46 years (2000).
Hospitals: Wabash General Hospital (56 beds)
Safety: Violent crime rate: 19.5 per 10,000 population; Property crime rate: 308.2 per 10,000 population (2006).
Newspapers: Daily Republican Register (Local news; Circulation 4,300)
Transportation: Commute to work: 91.4% car, 0.0% public transportation, 5.1% walk, 2.7% work from home (2000); Travel time to work: 54.8% less than 15 minutes, 21.7% 15 to 30 minutes, 7.1% 30 to 45 minutes, 8.7% 45 to 60 minutes, 7.7% 60 minutes or more (2000)

Additional Information Contacts

City of Mount Carmel . . . . (618) 262-4003
http://www.cityofmtcarmel.com
Wabash County Chamber of Commerce . . . . (618) 262-5116
http://www.wabashcountychamber.com

Warren County

Located in western Illinois; drained by Henderson Creek. Covers a land area of 542.52 square miles, a water area of 0.65 square miles, and is located in the Central Time Zone. The county was founded in 1825. County seat is Monmouth.

Warren County is part of the Galesburg, IL Micropolitan Statistical Area. The entire metro area includes: Knox County, IL; Warren County, IL

Weather Station: Monmouth Elevation: 744 feet

	Jan	Feb	Mar	Apr	May	Jun	Jul	Aug	Sep	Oct	Nov	Dec
High	31	38	50	64	75	83	87	84	78	65	49	36
Low	14	20	30	40	51	60	64	62	54	43	31	21
Precip	1.6	1.7	2.9	3.8	4.3	4.1	4.4	4.2	3.7	3.0	2.7	2.3
Snow	8.6	5.8	3.5	1.6	0.0	0.0	0.0	0.0	0.0	tr	2.3	6.4

High and Low temperatures in degrees Fahrenheit; Precipitation and Snow in inches

Population: 19,181 (1990); 18,735 (2000); 17,214 (2007); 16,090 (2012 projected); Race: 93.9% White, 2.1% Black, 0.7% Asian, 4.9% Hispanic of any race (2007); Density: 31.7 persons per square mile (2007); Average household size: 2.62 (2007); Median age: 39.4 (2007); Males per 100 females: 94.5 (2007).
Religion: Five largest groups: 11.0% Catholic Church, 9.7% The United Methodist Church, 7.2% Presbyterian Church (U.S.A.), 5.1% Christian Churches and Churches of Christ, 4.6% Christian Church (Disciples of Christ) (2000).
Economy: Unemployment rate: 4.5% (4/2008); Total civilian labor force: 9,203 (4/2008); Leading industries: 27.4% manufacturing; 17.1% health care and social assistance; 11.9% retail trade (2005); Farms: 633 totaling 326,912 acres (2002); Companies that employ 500 or more persons: 2 (2006); Companies that employ 100 to 499 persons: 1 (2006); Companies that employ less than 100 persons: 377 (2006); Black-owned businesses: n/a (2002); Hispanic-owned businesses: n/a (2002); Asian-owned businesses: n/a (2002); Women-owned businesses: 264 (2002); Retail sales per capita: $9,146 (2008). Single-family building permits issued: 13 (2007); Multi-family building permits issued: 9 (2007).
Income: Per capita income: $20,753 (2007); Median household income: $44,325 (2007); Average household income: $53,125 (2007); Percent of households with income of $100,000 or more: 10.3% (2007); Poverty rate: 13.3% (2005); Bankruptcy rate: 3.91% (2007).
Taxes: Total county taxes per capita: $112 (2006); County property taxes per capita: $112 (2006).
Education: Percent of population age 25 and over with: High school diploma (including GED) or higher: 82.2% (2007); Bachelor's degree or higher: 15.4% (2007); Master's degree or higher: 4.6% (2007).
Housing: Homeownership rate: 74.5% (2007); Median home value: $88,220 (2007); Median rent: $276 per month (2000); Median age of housing: 54 years (2000).
Health: Birth rate: 123.5 per 10,000 population (2007); Death rate: 112.6 per 10,000 population (2007); Age-adjusted cancer mortality rate: 260.0 deaths per 100,000 population (2005); Number of physicians: 8.0 per 10,000 population (2005); Hospital beds: 38.5 per 10,000 population (2004); Hospital admissions: 526.9 per 10,000 population (2004).
Elections: 2004 Presidential election results: 52.9% Bush, 46.6% Kerry, 0.0% Nader, 0.5% Badnarik

Additional Information Contacts

Warren County Government . . . . (309) 734-8592
http://www.warrencountyil.com
City of Monmouth. . . . . (309) 734-2141
http://www.ci.monmouth.il.us
Monmouth Area Chamber of Commerce. . . . . (309) 734-3181
http://www.ci.monmouth.il.us/coc
Roseville Chamber of Commerce . . . . (309) 426-2351

Warren County Communities

ALEXIS (village). Covers a land area of 0.485 square miles and a water area of 0 square miles. Located at 41.06° N. Lat.; 90.55° W. Long. Elevation is 699 feet.
Population: 921 (1990); 863 (2000); 735 (2007); 711 (2012 projected); Race: 99.6% White, 0.0% Black, 0.0% Asian, 3.1% Hispanic of any race (2007); Density: 1,514.8 persons per square mile (2007); Average household size: 2.35 (2007); Median age: 42.6 (2007); Males per 100 females: 87.0 (2007); Marriage status: 17.9% never married, 61.4% now married, 11.7% widowed, 9.0% divorced (2000); Foreign born: 0.0% (2000); Ancestry (includes multiple ancestries): 23.0% Irish, 20.6% German, 15.4% Swedish, 12.1% English, 9.4% United States or American (2000).
Economy: Single-family building permits issued: 0 (2007); Multi-family building permits issued: 0 (2007); Employment by occupation: 6.1% management, 13.3% professional, 12.6% services, 24.5% sales, 1.9% farming, 11.2% construction, 30.3% production (2000).
Income: Per capita income: $20,721 (2007); Median household income: $44,063 (2007); Average household income: $48,658 (2007); Percent of households with income of $100,000 or more: 4.2% (2007); Poverty rate: 5.9% (2000).
Education: Percent of population age 25 and over with: High school diploma (including GED) or higher: 87.8% (2007); Bachelor's degree or higher: 9.8% (2007); Master's degree or higher: 3.1% (2007).

School District(s)

United CUSD 304 (KG-12)
2005-06 Enrollment: 605 . . . . (309) 482-3344

Housing: Homeownership rate: 84.3% (2007); Median home value: $76,207 (2007); Median rent: $283 per month (2000); Median age of housing: 60+ years (2000).
Safety: Violent crime rate: 0.0 per 10,000 population; Property crime rate: 24.3 per 10,000 population (2006).
Transportation: Commute to work: 95.3% car, 0.0% public transportation, 3.0% walk, 1.7% work from home (2000); Travel time to work: 22.6% less than 15 minutes, 46.1% 15 to 30 minutes, 20.3% 30 to 45 minutes, 5.3% 45 to 60 minutes, 5.8% 60 minutes or more (2000)

BERWICK (unincorporated postal area, zip code 61417). Covers a land area of 28.943 square miles and a water area of 0 square miles. Located at 40.78° N. Lat.; 90.52° W. Long. Elevation is 709 feet.

Population: 324 (2000); Race: 100.0% White, 0.0% Black, 0.0% Asian, 0.0% Hispanic of any race (2000); Density: 11.2 persons per square mile (2000); Age: 14.0% under 18, 12.2% over 64 (2000); Marriage status: 17.6% never married, 69.3% now married, 3.0% widowed, 10.1% divorced (2000); Foreign born: 0.0% (2000); Ancestry (includes multiple ancestries): 31.3% United States or American, 11.9% English, 8.8% Swedish, 6.1% Irish, 4.9% German (2000).
Economy: Employment by occupation: 23.2% management, 6.2% professional, 10.0% services, 19.9% sales, 1.4% farming, 8.5% construction, 30.8% production (2000).
Income: Per capita income: $19,834 (2000); Median household income: $40,268 (2000); Poverty rate: 3.1% (2000).
Education: Percent of population age 25 and over with: High school diploma (including GED) or higher: 91.6% (2000); Bachelor's degree or higher: 10.4% (2000).
Housing: Homeownership rate: 72.1% (2000); Median home value: $48,300 (2000); Median rent: $269 per month (2000); Median age of housing: 60+ years (2000).
Transportation: Commute to work: 86.4% car, 0.0% public transportation, 2.4% walk, 11.2% work from home (2000); Travel time to work: 31.7% less than 15 minutes, 13.1% 15 to 30 minutes, 43.7% 30 to 45 minutes, 6.0% 45 to 60 minutes, 5.5% 60 minutes or more (2000)

CAMERON (unincorporated postal area, zip code 61423). Covers a land area of 53.529 square miles and a water area of 0 square miles. Located at 40.88° N. Lat.; 90.50° W. Long. Elevation is 771 feet.
Population: 779 (2000); Race: 100.0% White, 0.0% Black, 0.0% Asian, 2.9% Hispanic of any race (2000); Density: 14.6 persons per square mile (2000); Age: 26.1% under 18, 11.9% over 64 (2000); Marriage status: 19.0% never married, 74.4% now married, 2.2% widowed, 4.3% divorced (2000); Foreign born: 0.0% (2000); Ancestry (includes multiple ancestries): 23.9% United States or American, 17.7% German, 16.9% Irish, 13.9% English, 12.0% Swedish (2000).
Economy: Employment by occupation: 11.3% management, 16.9% professional, 17.3% services, 14.9% sales, 2.9% farming, 5.6% construction, 31.1% production (2000).
Income: Per capita income: $19,469 (2000); Median household income: $47,596 (2000); Poverty rate: 6.0% (2000).
Education: Percent of population age 25 and over with: High school diploma (including GED) or higher: 85.8% (2000); Bachelor's degree or higher: 10.7% (2000).
Housing: Homeownership rate: 89.0% (2000); Median home value: $75,000 (2000); Median rent: $304 per month (2000); Median age of housing: 48 years (2000).
Transportation: Commute to work: 95.8% car, 0.0% public transportation, 0.7% walk, 2.8% work from home (2000); Travel time to work: 15.3% less than 15 minutes, 59.6% 15 to 30 minutes, 7.2% 30 to 45 minutes, 0.7% 45 to 60 minutes, 17.2% 60 minutes or more (2000)

GERLAW (unincorporated postal area, zip code 61435). Covers a land area of 9.520 square miles and a water area of 0 square miles. Located at 40.97° N. Lat.; 90.54° W. Long. Elevation is 735 feet.
Population: 85 (2000); Race: 100.0% White, 0.0% Black, 0.0% Asian, 0.0% Hispanic of any race (2000); Density: 8.9 persons per square mile (2000); Age: 31.6% under 18, 14.0% over 64 (2000); Marriage status: 27.9% never married, 62.8% now married, 0.0% widowed, 9.3% divorced (2000); Foreign born: 0.0% (2000); Ancestry (includes multiple ancestries): 29.8% United States or American, 26.3% English, 19.3% German, 14.0% Swedish, 5.3% Scandinavian (2000).
Economy: Employment by occupation: 33.3% management, 12.5% professional, 0.0% services, 41.7% sales, 0.0% farming, 0.0% construction, 12.5% production (2000).
Income: Per capita income: $14,618 (2000); Median household income: $29,063 (2000); Poverty rate: 7.0% (2000).
Education: Percent of population age 25 and over with: High school diploma (including GED) or higher: 91.7% (2000); Bachelor's degree or higher: 8.3% (2000).
Housing: Homeownership rate: 63.6% (2000); Median home value: $105,000 (2000); Median rent: $n/a per month (2000); Median age of housing: 60+ years (2000).
Transportation: Commute to work: 66.7% car, 0.0% public transportation, 12.5% walk, 20.8% work from home (2000); Travel time to work: 31.6% less than 15 minutes, 68.4% 15 to 30 minutes, 0.0% 30 to 45 minutes, 0.0% 45 to 60 minutes, 0.0% 60 minutes or more (2000)

KIRKWOOD (village). Covers a land area of 0.909 square miles and a water area of 0 square miles. Located at 40.86° N. Lat.; 90.75° W. Long. Elevation is 741 feet.
Population: 902 (1990); 794 (2000); 647 (2007); 610 (2012 projected); Race: 98.6% White, 0.0% Black, 0.5% Asian, 2.0% Hispanic of any race (2007); Density: 712.0 persons per square mile (2007); Average household size: 2.53 (2007); Median age: 40.1 (2007); Males per 100 females: 95.5 (2007); Marriage status: 20.2% never married, 63.7% now married, 7.9% widowed, 8.2% divorced (2000); Foreign born: 0.5% (2000); Ancestry (includes multiple ancestries): 23.5% United States or American, 14.7% German, 11.3% Irish, 9.9% English, 5.9% Swedish (2000).
Economy: Single-family building permits issued: 0 (2007); Multi-family building permits issued: 0 (2007); Employment by occupation: 6.1% management, 13.0% professional, 12.5% services, 22.4% sales, 3.8% farming, 11.5% construction, 30.8% production (2000).
Income: Per capita income: $16,974 (2007); Median household income: $39,423 (2007); Average household income: $42,900 (2007); Percent of households with income of $100,000 or more: 2.3% (2007); Poverty rate: 3.4% (2000).
Education: Percent of population age 25 and over with: High school diploma (including GED) or higher: 85.0% (2007); Bachelor's degree or higher: 7.9% (2007); Master's degree or higher: 2.3% (2007).
Housing: Homeownership rate: 83.2% (2007); Median home value: $66,538 (2007); Median rent: $264 per month (2000); Median age of housing: 60+ years (2000).
Transportation: Commute to work: 93.1% car, 0.0% public transportation, 0.5% walk, 1.6% work from home (2000); Travel time to work: 24.4% less than 15 minutes, 31.6% 15 to 30 minutes, 26.5% 30 to 45 minutes, 6.7% 45 to 60 minutes, 10.7% 60 minutes or more (2000)

LITTLE YORK (village). Covers a land area of 0.258 square miles and a water area of 0 square miles. Located at 41.01° N. Lat.; 90.74° W. Long. Elevation is 614 feet.
Population: 349 (1990); 269 (2000); 247 (2007); 225 (2012 projected); Race: 99.2% White, 0.0% Black, 0.0% Asian, 2.8% Hispanic of any race (2007); Density: 958.0 persons per square mile (2007); Average household size: 2.42 (2007); Median age: 40.5 (2007); Males per 100 females: 96.0 (2007); Marriage status: 21.9% never married, 51.9% now married, 11.4% widowed, 14.8% divorced (2000); Foreign born: 0.0% (2000); Ancestry (includes multiple ancestries): 17.3% German, 15.2% Swedish, 14.1% English, 11.9% United States or American, 10.5% Irish (2000).
Economy: Single-family building permits issued: 0 (2007); Multi-family building permits issued: 0 (2007); Employment by occupation: 8.1% management, 12.1% professional, 14.8% services, 20.8% sales, 1.3% farming, 10.1% construction, 32.9% production (2000).
Income: Per capita income: $20,192 (2007); Median household income: $37,000 (2007); Average household income: $48,897 (2007); Percent of households with income of $100,000 or more: 10.8% (2007); Poverty rate: 14.8% (2000).
Education: Percent of population age 25 and over with: High school diploma (including GED) or higher: 80.6% (2007); Bachelor's degree or higher: 5.3% (2007); Master's degree or higher: 0.6% (2007).
Housing: Homeownership rate: 86.3% (2007); Median home value: $60,000 (2007); Median rent: $150 per month (2000); Median age of housing: 60+ years (2000).
Transportation: Commute to work: 91.7% car, 0.0% public transportation, 1.4% walk, 6.9% work from home (2000); Travel time to work: 24.6% less than 15 minutes, 34.3% 15 to 30 minutes, 15.7% 30 to 45 minutes, 9.7% 45 to 60 minutes, 15.7% 60 minutes or more (2000)

MONMOUTH (city). County seat. Covers a land area of 4.029 square miles and a water area of 0.021 square miles. Located at 40.91° N. Lat.; 90.64° W. Long. Elevation is 761 feet.
History: Monmouth was named in remembrance of the Revolutionary War battle that took place at Monmouth, New Jersey. Monmouth was established in 1831, and grew as the seat of Warren County.
Population: 9,495 (1990); 9,841 (2000); 9,024 (2007); 8,405 (2012 projected); Race: 90.0% White, 3.6% Black, 0.9% Asian, 7.9% Hispanic of any race (2007); Density: 2,239.5 persons per square mile (2007); Average household size: 2.73 (2007); Median age: 34.2 (2007); Males per 100 females: 89.7 (2007); Marriage status: 27.1% never married, 52.3% now married, 9.4% widowed, 11.2% divorced (2000); Foreign born: 2.2% (2000); Ancestry (includes multiple ancestries): 16.5% German, 14.2%

English, 13.0% Other groups, 11.2% United States or American, 10.7% Irish (2000).
Economy: Single-family building permits issued: 0 (2007); Multi-family building permits issued: 9 (2007); Employment by occupation: 9.6% management, 15.2% professional, 20.3% services, 25.6% sales, 0.3% farming, 6.7% construction, 22.3% production (2000).
Income: Per capita income: $19,278 (2007); Median household income: $41,940 (2007); Average household income: $50,584 (2007); Percent of households with income of $100,000 or more: 9.8% (2007); Poverty rate: 11.1% (2000).
Education: Percent of population age 25 and over with: High school diploma (including GED) or higher: 77.8% (2007); Bachelor's degree or higher: 16.7% (2007); Master's degree or higher: 5.4% (2007).

School District(s)

Henderson/Mercer/Warren Roe (08-12)
2005-06 Enrollment: 59 . . . . (309) 734-6822
Monmouth-Roseville CUSD 238 (PK-12)
2005-06 Enrollment: 1,761 . . . . (309) 734-4712
United CUSD 304 (KG-12)
2005-06 Enrollment: 605 . . . . (309) 482-3344
Yorkwood CUSD 225 (PK-12)
2005-06 Enrollment: 354 . . . . (309) 734-8514

Four-year College(s)

Monmouth College (Private, Not-for-profit)
Fall 2007 Enrollment: 1,343. . . . . (309) 457-2311
2007-08 Tuition: In-state $22,000; Out-of-state $22,000

Housing: Homeownership rate: 69.8% (2007); Median home value: $74,624 (2007); Median rent: $280 per month (2000); Median age of housing: 54 years (2000).
Hospitals: Community Medical Center (68 beds)
Safety: Violent crime rate: 50.0 per 10,000 population; Property crime rate: 476.2 per 10,000 population (2006).
Newspapers: Daily Review Atlas (Local news; Circulation 3,750); The Register-Mail - Monmouth Bureau (Local news; Circulation 0)
Transportation: Commute to work: 88.0% car, 0.1% public transportation, 7.4% walk, 3.5% work from home (2000); Travel time to work: 63.4% less than 15 minutes, 22.3% 15 to 30 minutes, 9.6% 30 to 45 minutes, 1.4% 45 to 60 minutes, 3.3% 60 minutes or more (2000)

Additional Information Contacts

City of Monmouth. . . . . (309) 734-2141
http://www.ci.monmouth.il.us
Monmouth Area Chamber of Commerce. . . . . (309) 734-3181
http://www.ci.monmouth.il.us/coc

ROSEVILLE (village). Covers a land area of 0.812 square miles and a water area of 0 square miles. Located at 40.73° N. Lat.; 90.66° W. Long. Elevation is 745 feet.
History: Roseville grew as a trading center and shipping point for oats and soy beans. The town was first called Hat Grove, referring to the shape of a particular grove of trees.
Population: 1,151 (1990); 1,083 (2000); 921 (2007); 875 (2012 projected); Race: 99.2% White, 0.4% Black, 0.2% Asian, 0.9% Hispanic of any race (2007); Density: 1,133.9 persons per square mile (2007); Average household size: 2.42 (2007); Median age: 45.2 (2007); Males per 100 females: 82.7 (2007); Marriage status: 16.5% never married, 58.2% now married, 15.7% widowed, 9.6% divorced (2000); Foreign born: 0.2% (2000); Ancestry (includes multiple ancestries): 22.6% German, 16.5% United States or American, 14.0% Irish, 13.8% English, 5.6% Swedish (2000).
Economy: Single-family building permits issued: 0 (2007); Multi-family building permits issued: 0 (2007); Employment by occupation: 11.0% management, 19.2% professional, 17.8% services, 21.6% sales, 1.4% farming, 8.6% construction, 20.4% production (2000).
Income: Per capita income: $20,651 (2007); Median household income: $37,941 (2007); Average household income: $47,257 (2007); Percent of households with income of $100,000 or more: 8.4% (2007); Poverty rate: 10.8% (2000).
Education: Percent of population age 25 and over with: High school diploma (including GED) or higher: 78.2% (2007); Bachelor's degree or higher: 14.3% (2007); Master's degree or higher: 3.5% (2007).

School District(s)

Monmouth-Roseville CUSD 238 (PK-12)
2005-06 Enrollment: 1,761 . . . . (309) 734-4712

Housing: Homeownership rate: 80.5% (2007); Median home value: $75,714 (2007); Median rent: $238 per month (2000); Median age of housing: 58 years (2000).
Newspapers: Roseville Independent (Community news; Circulation 950)
Transportation: Commute to work: 94.2% car, 0.0% public transportation, 3.3% walk, 2.5% work from home (2000); Travel time to work: 38.6% less than 15 minutes, 34.3% 15 to 30 minutes, 19.0% 30 to 45 minutes, 5.5% 45 to 60 minutes, 2.6% 60 minutes or more (2000)

Additional Information Contacts

Roseville Chamber of Commerce . . . . (309) 426-2351

SMITHSHIRE (unincorporated postal area, zip code 61478). Covers a land area of 36.926 square miles and a water area of 0 square miles. Located at 40.77° N. Lat.; 90.76° W. Long. Elevation is 735 feet.
Population: 337 (2000); Race: 100.0% White, 0.0% Black, 0.0% Asian, 0.7% Hispanic of any race (2000); Density: 9.1 persons per square mile (2000); Age: 22.2% under 18, 18.5% over 64 (2000); Marriage status: 11.6% never married, 72.6% now married, 11.2% widowed, 4.6% divorced (2000); Foreign born: 0.7% (2000); Ancestry (includes multiple ancestries): 19.9% German, 13.2% United States or American, 12.3% English, 8.3% Irish, 6.0% Other groups (2000).
Economy: Employment by occupation: 6.9% management, 13.8% professional, 19.2% services, 27.7% sales, 3.1% farming, 6.9% construction, 22.3% production (2000).
Income: Per capita income: $19,660 (2000); Median household income: $36,250 (2000); Poverty rate: 8.9% (2000).
Education: Percent of population age 25 and over with: High school diploma (including GED) or higher: 74.5% (2000); Bachelor's degree or higher: 6.9% (2000).
Housing: Homeownership rate: 82.5% (2000); Median home value: $38,600 (2000); Median rent: $186 per month (2000); Median age of housing: 53 years (2000).
Transportation: Commute to work: 83.8% car, 0.0% public transportation, 2.3% walk, 13.8% work from home (2000); Travel time to work: 20.5% less than 15 minutes, 35.7% 15 to 30 minutes, 35.7% 30 to 45 minutes, 8.0% 45 to 60 minutes, 0.0% 60 minutes or more (2000)

Washington County

Located in southwestern Illinois; bounded on the north by the Kaskaskia River; drained by the Little Muddy River. Covers a land area of 562.61 square miles, a water area of 1.51 square miles, and is located in the Central Time Zone. The county was founded in 1818. County seat is Nashville.

Weather Station: Nashville 4 NE Elevation: 515 feet

	Jan	Feb	Mar	Apr	May	Jun	Jul	Aug	Sep	Oct	Nov	Dec
High	38	44	55	67	76	85	88	87	80	69	54	43
Low	21	26	35	45	55	64	68	65	58	47	37	27
Precip	2.2	2.3	3.5	3.9	4.1	3.6	3.4	2.7	3.2	3.1	3.7	3.0
Snow	5.8	4.3	1.5	0.6	0.0	0.0	0.0	0.0	0.0	tr	0.9	3.2

High and Low temperatures in degrees Fahrenheit; Precipitation and Snow in inches

Population: 14,965 (1990); 15,148 (2000); 14,780 (2007); 14,415 (2012 projected); Race: 98.4% White, 0.5% Black, 0.3% Asian, 1.1% Hispanic of any race (2007); Density: 26.3 persons per square mile (2007); Average household size: 2.57 (2007); Median age: 40.4 (2007); Males per 100 females: 98.5 (2007).
Religion: Five largest groups: 30.0% Catholic Church, 18.3% Lutheran Church—Missouri Synod, 15.5% United Church of Christ, 6.8% Southern Baptist Convention, 4.9% The United Methodist Church (2000).
Economy: Unemployment rate: 5.2% (4/2008); Total civilian labor force: 8,522 (4/2008); Leading industries: 36.6% manufacturing; 13.5% retail trade; 9.2% transportation & warehousing (2005); Farms: 756 totaling 332,286 acres (2002); Companies that employ 500 or more persons: 1 (2006); Companies that employ 100 to 499 persons: 4 (2006); Companies that employ less than 100 persons: 412 (2006); Black-owned businesses: n/a (2002); Hispanic-owned businesses: n/a (2002); Asian-owned businesses: n/a (2002); Women-owned businesses: n/a (2002); Retail sales per capita: $17,877 (2008). Single-family building permits issued: 7 (2007); Multi-family building permits issued: 6 (2007).
Income: Per capita income: $23,130 (2007); Median household income: $48,556 (2007); Average household income: $58,688 (2007); Percent of households with income of $100,000 or more: 11.7% (2007); Poverty rate: 7.8% (2005); Bankruptcy rate: 2.57% (2007).

Education: Percent of population age 25 and over with: High school diploma (including GED) or higher: 79.2% (2007); Bachelor's degree or higher: 13.3% (2007); Master's degree or higher: 4.8% (2007).
Housing: Homeownership rate: 81.3% (2007); Median home value: $105,787 (2007); Median rent: $300 per month (2000); Median age of housing: 39 years (2000).
Health: Birth rate: 130.7 per 10,000 population (2007); Death rate: 112.4 per 10,000 population (2007); Age-adjusted cancer mortality rate: 202.3 deaths per 100,000 population (2005); Number of physicians: 7.4 per 10,000 population (2005); Hospital beds: 38.6 per 10,000 population (2004); Hospital admissions: 335.6 per 10,000 population (2004).
Elections: 2004 Presidential election results: 62.6% Bush, 36.8% Kerry, 0.0% Nader, 0.5% Badnarik
National and State Parks: Washington County State Conservation Area
Additional Information Contacts
Washington County Government. . . . . (618) 327-4800

Nashville Chamber of Commerce . . . . (618) 327-3700
http://www.nashville-il.com
Okawville Chamber of Commerce . . . . (618) 243-5428
http://www.okawvillecc.com

Washington County Communities

ADDIEVILLE (village). Covers a land area of 1.053 square miles and a water area of 0 square miles. Located at 38.39° N. Lat.; 89.48° W. Long. Elevation is 469 feet.
Population: 257 (1990); 267 (2000); 241 (2007); 238 (2012 projected); Race: 98.3% White, 0.0% Black, 0.0% Asian, 0.8% Hispanic of any race (2007); Density: 228.9 persons per square mile (2007); Average household size: 2.43 (2007); Median age: 38.0 (2007); Males per 100 females: 97.5 (2007); Marriage status: 21.8% never married, 67.8% now married, 2.5% widowed, 7.9% divorced (2000); Foreign born: 0.0% (2000); Ancestry (includes multiple ancestries): 61.4% German, 11.2% United States or American, 6.4% Other groups, 5.2% Irish, 4.9% Polish (2000).
Economy: Employment by occupation: 5.7% management, 14.9% professional, 13.5% services, 22.0% sales, 2.8% farming, 15.6% construction, 25.5% production (2000).
Income: Per capita income: $22,386 (2007); Median household income: $52,917 (2007); Average household income: $54,495 (2007); Percent of households with income of $100,000 or more: 6.1% (2007); Poverty rate: 2.7% (2000).
Education: Percent of population age 25 and over with: High school diploma (including GED) or higher: 83.0% (2007); Bachelor's degree or higher: 11.3% (2007); Master's degree or higher: 0.0% (2007).
Housing: Homeownership rate: 86.9% (2007); Median home value: $97,692 (2007); Median rent: $175 per month (2000); Median age of housing: 60+ years (2000).
Transportation: Commute to work: 95.8% car, 0.0% public transportation, 1.4% walk, 0.0% work from home (2000); Travel time to work: 19.6% less than 15 minutes, 27.3% 15 to 30 minutes, 14.7% 30 to 45 minutes, 20.3% 45 to 60 minutes, 18.2% 60 minutes or more (2000)

ASHLEY (city). Covers a land area of 1.107 square miles and a water area of 0.022 square miles. Located at 38.32° N. Lat.; 89.18° W. Long. Elevation is 548 feet.
History: Ashley was named for early settler John Ashley.
Population: 583 (1990); 613 (2000); 497 (2007); 497 (2012 projected); Race: 98.0% White, 0.2% Black, 0.0% Asian, 0.6% Hispanic of any race (2007); Density: 448.9 persons per square mile (2007); Average household size: 2.47 (2007); Median age: 37.9 (2007); Males per 100 females: 98.8 (2007); Marriage status: 21.7% never married, 47.7% now married, 14.8% widowed, 15.8% divorced (2000); Foreign born: 1.0% (2000); Ancestry (includes multiple ancestries): 31.1% German, 16.7% Polish, 13.9% Irish, 11.2% United States or American, 9.1% English (2000).
Economy: Single-family building permits issued: 1 (2007); Multi-family building permits issued: 0 (2007); Employment by occupation: 2.8% management, 8.0% professional, 22.3% services, 10.0% sales, 0.0% farming, 20.3% construction, 36.7% production (2000).
Income: Per capita income: $17,088 (2007); Median household income: $36,719 (2007); Average household income: $42,251 (2007); Percent of households with income of $100,000 or more: 5.0% (2007); Poverty rate: 17.0% (2000).
Education: Percent of population age 25 and over with: High school diploma (including GED) or higher: 73.9% (2007); Bachelor's degree or higher: 4.0% (2007); Master's degree or higher: 0.6% (2007).

School District(s)

Ashley CCSD 15 (KG-08)
2005-06 Enrollment: 166 . . . . (618) 485-6611
Housing: Homeownership rate: 79.1% (2007); Median home value: $48,913 (2007); Median rent: $271 per month (2000); Median age of housing: 55 years (2000).
Transportation: Commute to work: 93.5% car, 0.0% public transportation, 0.8% walk, 4.9% work from home (2000); Travel time to work: 14.2% less than 15 minutes, 48.5% 15 to 30 minutes, 17.6% 30 to 45 minutes, 4.7% 45 to 60 minutes, 15.0% 60 minutes or more (2000)

DU BOIS (village). Covers a land area of 1.068 square miles and a water area of 0 square miles. Located at 38.22° N. Lat.; 89.21° W. Long. Elevation is 522 feet.
Population: 216 (1990); 222 (2000); 204 (2007); 198 (2012 projected); Race: 97.5% White, 0.0% Black, 0.0% Asian, 3.4% Hispanic of any race (2007); Density: 191.0 persons per square mile (2007); Average household size: 2.29 (2007); Median age: 36.2 (2007); Males per 100 females: 117.0 (2007); Marriage status: 19.0% never married, 49.0% now married, 15.6% widowed, 16.3% divorced (2000); Foreign born: 0.0% (2000); Ancestry (includes multiple ancestries): 51.0% Polish, 15.2% German, 5.7% Other groups, 4.3% Italian, 2.9% United States or American (2000).
Economy: Single-family building permits issued: 0 (2007); Multi-family building permits issued: 0 (2007); Employment by occupation: 8.3% management, 4.8% professional, 21.4% services, 21.4% sales, 3.6% farming, 10.7% construction, 29.8% production (2000).
Income: Per capita income: $13,676 (2007); Median household income: $32,083 (2007); Average household income: $31,348 (2007); Percent of households with income of $100,000 or more: 0.0% (2007); Poverty rate: 15.7% (2000).
Education: Percent of population age 25 and over with: High school diploma (including GED) or higher: 69.0% (2007); Bachelor's degree or higher: 1.6% (2007); Master's degree or higher: 0.0% (2007).
Housing: Homeownership rate: 80.9% (2007); Median home value: $61,111 (2007); Median rent: $260 per month (2000); Median age of housing: 46 years (2000).
Transportation: Commute to work: 75.6% car, 0.0% public transportation, 12.2% walk, 7.3% work from home (2000); Travel time to work: 22.4% less than 15 minutes, 38.2% 15 to 30 minutes, 25.0% 30 to 45 minutes, 0.0% 45 to 60 minutes, 14.5% 60 minutes or more (2000)

HOYLETON (village). Covers a land area of 0.750 square miles and a water area of 0 square miles. Located at 38.44° N. Lat.; 89.27° W. Long. Elevation is 518 feet.
Population: 508 (1990); 520 (2000); 505 (2007); 478 (2012 projected); Race: 93.7% White, 4.6% Black, 1.0% Asian, 0.0% Hispanic of any race (2007); Density: 672.9 persons per square mile (2007); Average household size: 2.77 (2007); Median age: 33.9 (2007); Males per 100 females: 100.4 (2007); Marriage status: 26.1% never married, 54.7% now married, 10.9% widowed, 8.2% divorced (2000); Foreign born: 0.4% (2000); Ancestry (includes multiple ancestries): 53.6% German, 9.8% Other groups, 8.5% Irish, 6.6% United States or American, 4.0% Polish (2000).
Economy: Single-family building permits issued: 0 (2007); Multi-family building permits issued: 0 (2007); Employment by occupation: 8.6% management, 13.9% professional, 16.4% services, 16.0% sales, 2.5% farming, 12.3% construction, 30.3% production (2000).
Income: Per capita income: $20,985 (2007); Median household income: $50,526 (2007); Average household income: $56,690 (2007); Percent of households with income of $100,000 or more: 8.8% (2007); Poverty rate: 6.5% (2000).
Education: Percent of population age 25 and over with: High school diploma (including GED) or higher: 75.2% (2007); Bachelor's degree or higher: 14.9% (2007); Master's degree or higher: 3.6% (2007).

School District(s)

Hoyleton Cons SD 29 (KG-08)
2005-06 Enrollment: 99 . . . . (618) 493-7787
Kaskaskia Spec Educ District (03-12)
2005-06 Enrollment: 139 . . . . (618) 532-4721
Housing: Homeownership rate: 75.8% (2007); Median home value: $77,097 (2007); Median rent: $364 per month (2000); Median age of housing: 56 years (2000).

Transportation: Commute to work: 78.8% car, 6.6% public transportation, 8.7% walk, 3.7% work from home (2000); Travel time to work: 34.9% less than 15 minutes, 44.8% 15 to 30 minutes, 15.5% 30 to 45 minutes, 1.3% 45 to 60 minutes, 3.4% 60 minutes or more (2000)

IRVINGTON (village). Covers a land area of 0.838 square miles and a water area of 0 square miles. Located at 38.43° N. Lat.; 89.16° W. Long. Elevation is 531 feet.
History: Irvington was a major strawberry-producing center in the 1890's, when special trains took the produce to Chicago.
Population: 857 (1990); 736 (2000); 588 (2007); 587 (2012 projected); Race: 97.4% White, 0.2% Black, 0.7% Asian, 0.9% Hispanic of any race (2007); Density: 701.9 persons per square mile (2007); Average household size: 2.58 (2007); Median age: 34.6 (2007); Males per 100 females: 102.1 (2007); Marriage status: 21.3% never married, 59.1% now married, 6.6% widowed, 13.0% divorced (2000); Foreign born: 0.1% (2000); Ancestry (includes multiple ancestries): 39.6% German, 13.7% Irish, 10.5% Other groups, 7.2% English, 5.9% United States or American (2000).
Economy: Single-family building permits issued: 1 (2007); Multi-family building permits issued: 6 (2007); Employment by occupation: 10.3% management, 16.8% professional, 14.5% services, 20.4% sales, 0.0% farming, 10.9% construction, 27.1% production (2000).
Income: Per capita income: $21,407 (2007); Median household income: $51,481 (2007); Average household income: $55,208 (2007); Percent of households with income of $100,000 or more: 8.8% (2007); Poverty rate: 9.0% (2000).
Education: Percent of population age 25 and over with: High school diploma (including GED) or higher: 82.7% (2007); Bachelor's degree or higher: 11.9% (2007); Master's degree or higher: 2.4% (2007).

School District(s)

Irvington CCSD 11 (PK-08)
2005-06 Enrollment: 106 . . . . (618) 249-6439
Housing: Homeownership rate: 72.8% (2007); Median home value: $85,000 (2007); Median rent: $296 per month (2000); Median age of housing: 30 years (2000).
Transportation: Commute to work: 91.5% car, 0.0% public transportation, 2.8% walk, 4.3% work from home (2000); Travel time to work: 44.5% less than 15 minutes, 36.5% 15 to 30 minutes, 14.2% 30 to 45 minutes, 0.9% 45 to 60 minutes, 3.9% 60 minutes or more (2000)

NASHVILLE (city). County seat. Covers a land area of 2.681 square miles and a water area of 0.089 square miles. Located at 38.34° N. Lat.; 89.38° W. Long. Elevation is 518 feet.
History: Incorporated 1853.
Population: 3,280 (1990); 3,147 (2000); 3,020 (2007); 2,904 (2012 projected); Race: 98.7% White, 0.2% Black, 0.5% Asian, 1.3% Hispanic of any race (2007); Density: 1,126.6 persons per square mile (2007); Average household size: 2.39 (2007); Median age: 40.4 (2007); Males per 100 females: 88.9 (2007); Marriage status: 21.0% never married, 60.6% now married, 10.3% widowed, 8.1% divorced (2000); Foreign born: 0.3% (2000); Ancestry (includes multiple ancestries): 49.0% German, 15.2% Polish, 12.6% United States or American, 9.1% Irish, 8.7% English (2000).
Economy: Single-family building permits issued: 0 (2007); Multi-family building permits issued: 0 (2007); Employment by occupation: 10.4% management, 22.4% professional, 19.0% services, 23.9% sales, 0.7% farming, 7.1% construction, 16.5% production (2000).
Income: Per capita income: $25,945 (2007); Median household income: $49,509 (2007); Average household income: $60,715 (2007); Percent of households with income of $100,000 or more: 14.2% (2007); Poverty rate: 4.4% (2000).
Education: Percent of population age 25 and over with: High school diploma (including GED) or higher: 84.7% (2007); Bachelor's degree or higher: 21.7% (2007); Master's degree or higher: 9.4% (2007).

School District(s)

Nashville CCSD 49 (PK-08)
2005-06 Enrollment: 576 . . . . (618) 327-4304
Nashville CHSD 99 (09-12)
2005-06 Enrollment: 527 . . . . (618) 327-8286
Housing: Homeownership rate: 72.4% (2007); Median home value: $112,958 (2007); Median rent: $337 per month (2000); Median age of housing: 44 years (2000).
Hospitals: Washington County Hospital (61 beds)
Safety: Violent crime rate: 22.7 per 10,000 population; Property crime rate: 278.9 per 10,000 population (2006).
Newspapers: Nashville News (Local news; Circulation 5,400)
Transportation: Commute to work: 91.1% car, 1.3% public transportation, 2.6% walk, 3.3% work from home (2000); Travel time to work: 63.5% less than 15 minutes, 13.0% 15 to 30 minutes, 12.3% 30 to 45 minutes, 3.4% 45 to 60 minutes, 7.9% 60 minutes or more (2000)
Additional Information Contacts
Nashville Chamber of Commerce . . . . (618) 327-3700
http://www.nashville-il.com

NEW MINDEN (village). Covers a land area of 0.275 square miles and a water area of 0 square miles. Located at 38.43° N. Lat.; 89.36° W. Long. Elevation is 453 feet.
Population: 219 (1990); 204 (2000); 202 (2007); 189 (2012 projected); Race: 99.5% White, 0.0% Black, 0.0% Asian, 2.0% Hispanic of any race (2007); Density: 734.5 persons per square mile (2007); Average household size: 2.30 (2007); Median age: 38.9 (2007); Males per 100 females: 82.0 (2007); Marriage status: 16.6% never married, 62.6% now married, 13.5% widowed, 7.4% divorced (2000); Foreign born: 0.0% (2000); Ancestry (includes multiple ancestries): 50.0% German, 7.8% Polish, 5.9% Dutch, 5.9% Other groups, 4.9% English (2000).
Economy: Employment by occupation: 12.9% management, 8.6% professional, 19.0% services, 25.9% sales, 9.5% farming, 10.3% construction, 13.8% production (2000).
Income: Per capita income: $24,740 (2007); Median household income: $52,500 (2007); Average household income: $56,790 (2007); Percent of households with income of $100,000 or more: 9.1% (2007); Poverty rate: 2.5% (2000).
Education: Percent of population age 25 and over with: High school diploma (including GED) or higher: 76.6% (2007); Bachelor's degree or higher: 13.9% (2007); Master's degree or higher: 2.9% (2007).
Housing: Homeownership rate: 88.6% (2007); Median home value: $71,818 (2007); Median rent: $283 per month (2000); Median age of housing: 44 years (2000).
Transportation: Commute to work: 93.8% car, 0.0% public transportation, 3.5% walk, 1.8% work from home (2000); Travel time to work: 33.3% less than 15 minutes, 23.4% 15 to 30 minutes, 23.4% 30 to 45 minutes, 8.1% 45 to 60 minutes, 11.7% 60 minutes or more (2000)

OAKDALE (village). Covers a land area of 1.660 square miles and a water area of 0 square miles. Located at 38.26° N. Lat.; 89.50° W. Long. Elevation is 518 feet.
Population: 206 (1990); 213 (2000); 230 (2007); 227 (2012 projected); Race: 97.8% White, 0.0% Black, 0.0% Asian, 0.0% Hispanic of any race (2007); Density: 138.5 persons per square mile (2007); Average household size: 2.50 (2007); Median age: 36.9 (2007); Males per 100 females: 94.9 (2007); Marriage status: 20.0% never married, 68.1% now married, 6.9% widowed, 5.0% divorced (2000); Foreign born: 0.0% (2000); Ancestry (includes multiple ancestries): 46.3% German, 14.9% Irish, 12.4% English, 5.5% United States or American, 5.0% French (except Basque) (2000).
Economy: Employment by occupation: 8.8% management, 17.6% professional, 14.3% services, 13.2% sales, 2.2% farming, 9.9% construction, 34.1% production (2000).
Income: Per capita income: $21,641 (2007); Median household income: $50,000 (2007); Average household income: $54,103 (2007); Percent of households with income of $100,000 or more: 9.8% (2007); Poverty rate: 3.0% (2000).
Education: Percent of population age 25 and over with: High school diploma (including GED) or higher: 87.0% (2007); Bachelor's degree or higher: 11.0% (2007); Master's degree or higher: 8.2% (2007).

School District(s)

Oakdale CCSD 1 (KG-08)
2005-06 Enrollment: 85 . . . . (618) 329-5292
Housing: Homeownership rate: 89.1% (2007); Median home value: $75,000 (2007); Median rent: $270 per month (2000); Median age of housing: 47 years (2000).
Transportation: Commute to work: 86.8% car, 0.0% public transportation, 5.5% walk, 7.7% work from home (2000); Travel time to work: 29.8% less than 15 minutes, 38.1% 15 to 30 minutes, 7.1% 30 to 45 minutes, 9.5% 45 to 60 minutes, 15.5% 60 minutes or more (2000)

OKAWVILLE (village). Covers a land area of 2.027 square miles and a water area of 0 square miles. Located at 38.43° N. Lat.; 89.54° W. Long. Elevation is 440 feet.
Population: 1,304 (1990); 1,355 (2000); 1,293 (2007); 1,249 (2012 projected); Race: 98.1% White, 0.7% Black, 0.2% Asian, 0.5% Hispanic of any race (2007); Density: 638.0 persons per square mile (2007); Average

household size: 2.33 (2007); Median age: 38.6 (2007); Males per 100 females: 98.9 (2007); Marriage status: 20.8% never married, 59.8% now married, 9.6% widowed, 9.8% divorced (2000); Foreign born: 1.3% (2000); Ancestry (includes multiple ancestries): 52.5% German, 9.8% Irish, 9.1% United States or American, 7.1% Other groups, 4.7% English (2000).
Economy: Single-family building permits issued: 5 (2007); Multi-family building permits issued: 0 (2007); Employment by occupation: 11.3% management, 18.4% professional, 19.1% services, 21.4% sales, 0.8% farming, 13.1% construction, 15.9% production (2000).
Income: Per capita income: $24,424 (2007); Median household income: $46,339 (2007); Average household income: $56,901 (2007); Percent of households with income of $100,000 or more: 9.0% (2007); Poverty rate: 6.5% (2000).
Education: Percent of population age 25 and over with: High school diploma (including GED) or higher: 80.0% (2007); Bachelor's degree or higher: 17.1% (2007); Master's degree or higher: 6.2% (2007).

School District(s)

West Washington Co Cud 10 (KG-12)
2005-06 Enrollment: 594 . . . . (618) 243-6454
Housing: Homeownership rate: 77.7% (2007); Median home value: $106,439 (2007); Median rent: $322 per month (2000); Median age of housing: 43 years (2000).
Safety: Violent crime rate: 15.0 per 10,000 population; Property crime rate: 367.6 per 10,000 population (2006).
Newspapers: Okawville Times (Regional news; Circulation 2,200)
Transportation: Commute to work: 94.5% car, 0.4% public transportation, 2.2% walk, 1.7% work from home (2000); Travel time to work: 36.9% less than 15 minutes, 18.4% 15 to 30 minutes, 24.0% 30 to 45 minutes, 12.0% 45 to 60 minutes, 8.7% 60 minutes or more (2000)

Additional Information Contacts

Okawville Chamber of Commerce . . . . (618) 243-5428
http://www.okawvillecc.com

RADOM (village). Covers a land area of 1.037 square miles and a water area of 0 square miles. Located at 38.28° N. Lat.; 89.19° W. Long. Elevation is 535 feet.
Population: 174 (1990); 395 (2000); 373 (2007); 358 (2012 projected); Race: 94.9% White, 4.6% Black, 0.0% Asian, 1.3% Hispanic of any race (2007); Density: 359.7 persons per square mile (2007); Average household size: 4.55 (2007); Median age: 76.0 (2007); Males per 100 females: 75.9 (2007); Marriage status: 25.1% never married, 41.7% now married, 32.1% widowed, 1.1% divorced (2000); Foreign born: 0.0% (2000); Ancestry (includes multiple ancestries): 38.8% Polish, 24.7% German, 12.7% Irish, 10.6% United States or American, 3.4% English (2000).
Economy: Employment by occupation: 3.8% management, 4.8% professional, 13.5% services, 26.0% sales, 2.9% farming, 9.6% construction, 39.4% production (2000).
Income: Per capita income: $15,530 (2007); Median household income: $35,000 (2007); Average household income: $42,988 (2007); Percent of households with income of $100,000 or more: 4.9% (2007); Poverty rate: 8.3% (2000).
Education: Percent of population age 25 and over with: High school diploma (including GED) or higher: 43.9% (2007); Bachelor's degree or higher: 3.1% (2007); Master's degree or higher: 2.5% (2007).
Housing: Homeownership rate: 97.6% (2007); Median home value: $65,000 (2007); Median rent: $n/a per month (2000); Median age of housing: 35 years (2000).
Transportation: Commute to work: 96.1% car, 0.0% public transportation, 1.9% walk, 0.0% work from home (2000); Travel time to work: 18.4% less than 15 minutes, 45.6% 15 to 30 minutes, 27.2% 30 to 45 minutes, 3.9% 45 to 60 minutes, 4.9% 60 minutes or more (2000)

RICHVIEW (village). Covers a land area of 1.112 square miles and a water area of 0 square miles. Located at 38.37° N. Lat.; 89.18° W. Long. Elevation is 541 feet.
Population: 325 (1990); 308 (2000); 311 (2007); 293 (2012 projected); Race: 96.5% White, 1.3% Black, 1.3% Asian, 3.2% Hispanic of any race (2007); Density: 279.6 persons per square mile (2007); Average household size: 2.64 (2007); Median age: 34.5 (2007); Males per 100 females: 110.1 (2007); Marriage status: 26.8% never married, 55.8% now married, 4.9% widowed, 12.5% divorced (2000); Foreign born: 0.0% (2000); Ancestry (includes multiple ancestries): 30.0% German, 14.8% United States or American, 12.3% Irish, 11.0% Polish, 9.4% English (2000).
Economy: Single-family building permits issued: 0 (2007); Multi-family building permits issued: 0 (2007); Employment by occupation: 2.1% management, 15.4% professional, 22.4% services, 12.6% sales, 0.0% farming, 6.3% construction, 41.3% production (2000).
Income: Per capita income: $20,892 (2007); Median household income: $46,538 (2007); Average household income: $55,064 (2007); Percent of households with income of $100,000 or more: 7.6% (2007); Poverty rate: 8.8% (2000).
Education: Percent of population age 25 and over with: High school diploma (including GED) or higher: 77.9% (2007); Bachelor's degree or higher: 7.5% (2007); Master's degree or higher: 1.0% (2007).
Housing: Homeownership rate: 79.7% (2007); Median home value: $70,000 (2007); Median rent: $258 per month (2000); Median age of housing: 27 years (2000).
Transportation: Commute to work: 92.4% car, 0.0% public transportation, 2.1% walk, 3.5% work from home (2000); Travel time to work: 23.7% less than 15 minutes, 48.2% 15 to 30 minutes, 15.1% 30 to 45 minutes, 4.3% 45 to 60 minutes, 8.6% 60 minutes or more (2000)

VENEDY (village). Covers a land area of 0.286 square miles and a water area of 0 square miles. Located at 38.39° N. Lat.; 89.64° W. Long. Elevation is 453 feet.
Population: 158 (1990); 137 (2000); 142 (2007); 139 (2012 projected); Race: 99.3% White, 0.0% Black, 0.0% Asian, 4.2% Hispanic of any race (2007); Density: 496.6 persons per square mile (2007); Average household size: 2.49 (2007); Median age: 45.6 (2007); Males per 100 females: 108.8 (2007); Marriage status: 18.7% never married, 68.2% now married, 6.5% widowed, 6.5% divorced (2000); Foreign born: 0.0% (2000); Ancestry (includes multiple ancestries): 53.0% German, 20.5% Irish, 12.1% English, 6.8% United States or American, 6.8% Italian (2000).
Economy: Employment by occupation: 8.1% management, 17.6% professional, 18.9% services, 18.9% sales, 0.0% farming, 10.8% construction, 25.7% production (2000).
Income: Per capita income: $23,081 (2007); Median household income: $55,000 (2007); Average household income: $57,500 (2007); Percent of households with income of $100,000 or more: 10.5% (2007); Poverty rate: 4.5% (2000).
Education: Percent of population age 25 and over with: High school diploma (including GED) or higher: 71.2% (2007); Bachelor's degree or higher: 7.7% (2007); Master's degree or higher: 1.0% (2007).

School District(s)

West Washington Co Cud 10 (KG-12)
2005-06 Enrollment: 594 . . . . (618) 243-6454
Housing: Homeownership rate: 87.7% (2007); Median home value: $78,000 (2007); Median rent: $300 per month (2000); Median age of housing: 46 years (2000).
Transportation: Commute to work: 89.7% car, 7.4% public transportation, 0.0% walk, 2.9% work from home (2000); Travel time to work: 24.2% less than 15 minutes, 34.8% 15 to 30 minutes, 9.1% 30 to 45 minutes, 24.2% 45 to 60 minutes, 7.6% 60 minutes or more (2000)

Wayne County

Located in southeastern Illinois; drained by the Little Wabash River. Covers a land area of 713.90 square miles, a water area of 1.66 square miles, and is located in the Central Time Zone. The county was founded in 1819. County seat is Fairfield.

Weather Station: Fairfield Radio WFIW — Elevation: 429 feet

	Jan	Feb	Mar	Apr	May	Jun	Jul	Aug	Sep	Oct	Nov	Dec
High	38	44	55	67	76	85	88	87	80	69	54	43
Low	21	25	34	44	53	62	66	63	56	45	36	26
Precip	2.8	2.6	4.6	4.9	4.7	4.0	3.8	3.2	2.9	3.4	4.3	3.5
Snow	5.2	3.7	2.4	0.3	0.0	0.0	0.0	0.0	0.0	tr	0.7	2.9

High and Low temperatures in degrees Fahrenheit; Precipitation and Snow in inches

Population: 17,241 (1990); 17,151 (2000); 16,716 (2007); 16,381 (2012 projected); Race: 98.4% White, 0.5% Black, 0.4% Asian, 0.7% Hispanic of any race (2007); Density: 23.4 persons per square mile (2007); Average household size: 2.36 (2007); Median age: 41.4 (2007); Males per 100 females: 95.5 (2007).
Religion: Five largest groups: 23.5% Southern Baptist Convention, 12.6% Christian Churches and Churches of Christ, 8.4% The United Methodist Church, 3.6% Cumberland Presbyterian Church, 1.8% National Association of Free Will Baptists (2000).
Economy: Unemployment rate: 5.5% (4/2008); Total civilian labor force: 8,441 (4/2008); Leading industries: 26.4% manufacturing; 19.4% health care and social assistance; 17.1% retail trade (2005); Farms: 1,092 totaling

356,268 acres (2002); Companies that employ 500 or more persons: 1 (2006); Companies that employ 100 to 499 persons: 3 (2006); Companies that employ less than 100 persons: 359 (2006); Black-owned businesses: n/a (2002); Hispanic-owned businesses: n/a (2002); Asian-owned businesses: n/a (2002); Women-owned businesses: n/a (2002); Retail sales per capita: $8,845 (2008). Single-family building permits issued: 2 (2007); Multi-family building permits issued: 0 (2007).

Income: Per capita income: $19,253 (2007); Median household income: $36,505 (2007); Average household income: $45,048 (2007); Percent of households with income of $100,000 or more: 6.0% (2007); Poverty rate: 14.9% (2005); Bankruptcy rate: 2.11% (2007).

Education: Percent of population age 25 and over with: High school diploma (including GED) or higher: 75.0% (2007); Bachelor's degree or higher: 10.0% (2007); Master's degree or higher: 3.3% (2007).

Housing: Homeownership rate: 79.4% (2007); Median home value: $62,981 (2007); Median rent: $218 per month (2000); Median age of housing: 38 years (2000).

Health: Birth rate: 115.3 per 10,000 population (2007); Death rate: 123.1 per 10,000 population (2007); Age-adjusted cancer mortality rate: 204.8 deaths per 100,000 population (2005); Number of physicians: 7.2 per 10,000 population (2005); Hospital beds: 97.7 per 10,000 population (2004); Hospital admissions: 796.2 per 10,000 population (2004).

Elections: 2004 Presidential election results: 73.6% Bush, 25.8% Kerry, 0.0% Nader, 0.6% Badnarik

National and State Parks: Sam Dale Lake State Conservation Area

Additional Information Contacts

Wayne County Government. . . . . (618) 842-5182

City of Fairfield . . . . (618) 842-3871
http://www.fairfield-il.com
Fairfield Chamber of Commerce . . . . (618) 842-6116

Wayne County Communities

BARNHILL (unincorporated postal area, zip code 62809). Aka Barn Hill. Covers a land area of 14.526 square miles and a water area of 0.026 square miles. Located at 38.26° N. Lat.; 88.34° W. Long. Elevation is 397 feet.

Population: 239 (2000); Race: 98.6% White, 0.0% Black, 0.0% Asian, 2.7% Hispanic of any race (2000); Density: 16.5 persons per square mile (2000); Age: 22.8% under 18, 13.7% over 64 (2000); Marriage status: 11.1% never married, 72.2% now married, 4.4% widowed, 12.2% divorced (2000); Foreign born: 0.0% (2000); Ancestry (includes multiple ancestries): 27.9% United States or American, 13.2% English, 10.0% Other groups, 9.6% German, 5.5% Irish (2000).

Economy: Employment by occupation: 14.0% management, 11.4% professional, 5.3% services, 25.4% sales, 0.0% farming, 9.6% construction, 34.2% production (2000).

Income: Per capita income: $16,212 (2000); Median household income: $31,250 (2000); Poverty rate: 6.4% (2000).

Education: Percent of population age 25 and over with: High school diploma (including GED) or higher: 80.1% (2000); Bachelor's degree or higher: 8.7% (2000).

Housing: Homeownership rate: 83.7% (2000); Median home value: $33,100 (2000); Median rent: $267 per month (2000); Median age of housing: 32 years (2000).

Transportation: Commute to work: 89.1% car, 1.8% public transportation, 5.5% walk, 1.8% work from home (2000); Travel time to work: 51.9% less than 15 minutes, 26.9% 15 to 30 minutes, 5.6% 30 to 45 minutes, 10.2% 45 to 60 minutes, 5.6% 60 minutes or more (2000)

CISNE (village). Covers a land area of 0.638 square miles and a water area of 0 square miles. Located at 38.51° N. Lat.; 88.43° W. Long. Elevation is 459 feet.

Population: 645 (1990); 673 (2000); 660 (2007); 657 (2012 projected); Race: 97.9% White, 1.4% Black, 0.3% Asian, 0.6% Hispanic of any race (2007); Density: 1,034.4 persons per square mile (2007); Average household size: 2.27 (2007); Median age: 43.2 (2007); Males per 100 females: 88.0 (2007); Marriage status: 17.8% never married, 60.8% now married, 10.7% widowed, 10.7% divorced (2000); Foreign born: 0.6% (2000); Ancestry (includes multiple ancestries): 15.4% English, 13.8% United States or American, 12.9% German, 11.5% Other groups, 6.4% Irish (2000).

Economy: Employment by occupation: 7.7% management, 17.9% professional, 19.0% services, 20.4% sales, 1.8% farming, 9.5% construction, 23.7% production (2000).

Income: Per capita income: $17,486 (2007); Median household income: $31,563 (2007); Average household income: $37,216 (2007); Percent of households with income of $100,000 or more: 2.4% (2007); Poverty rate: 15.5% (2000).

Education: Percent of population age 25 and over with: High school diploma (including GED) or higher: 69.7% (2007); Bachelor's degree or higher: 11.5% (2007); Master's degree or higher: 2.7% (2007).

School District(s)

North Wayne CUSD 200 (PK-12)
2005-06 Enrollment: 452 . . . . (618) 673-2151
Wayne City CUSD 100 (PK-12)
2005-06 Enrollment: 606 . . . . (618) 895-3103

Housing: Homeownership rate: 78.7% (2007); Median home value: $51,286 (2007); Median rent: $211 per month (2000); Median age of housing: 44 years (2000).

Transportation: Commute to work: 95.6% car, 0.4% public transportation, 1.8% walk, 1.8% work from home (2000); Travel time to work: 27.3% less than 15 minutes, 45.3% 15 to 30 minutes, 17.2% 30 to 45 minutes, 4.1% 45 to 60 minutes, 6.0% 60 minutes or more (2000)

FAIRFIELD (city). Aka Thomas Prairie. County seat. Covers a land area of 3.616 square miles and a water area of 0.034 square miles. Located at 38.38° N. Lat.; 88.36° W. Long. Elevation is 440 feet.

History: Fairfield was established in 1819, and developed as the seat of Wayne County. Clothing and automobile parts manufacturing were early industries.

Population: 5,573 (1990); 5,421 (2000); 5,233 (2007); 5,042 (2012 projected); Race: 98.2% White, 0.3% Black, 0.8% Asian, 0.5% Hispanic of any race (2007); Density: 1,447.0 persons per square mile (2007); Average household size: 2.13 (2007); Median age: 44.0 (2007); Males per 100 females: 84.1 (2007); Marriage status: 15.4% never married, 57.4% now married, 14.2% widowed, 13.0% divorced (2000); Foreign born: 2.3% (2000); Ancestry (includes multiple ancestries): 20.2% United States or American, 14.6% German, 14.3% English, 10.3% Other groups, 8.2% Irish (2000).

Economy: Single-family building permits issued: 2 (2007); Multi-family building permits issued: 0 (2007); Employment by occupation: 6.3% management, 16.4% professional, 15.4% services, 26.3% sales, 0.6% farming, 8.1% construction, 27.0% production (2000).

Income: Per capita income: $20,287 (2007); Median household income: $30,411 (2007); Average household income: $42,546 (2007); Percent of households with income of $100,000 or more: 5.9% (2007); Poverty rate: 13.1% (2000).

Education: Percent of population age 25 and over with: High school diploma (including GED) or higher: 73.6% (2007); Bachelor's degree or higher: 11.7% (2007); Master's degree or higher: 4.3% (2007).

School District(s)

Fairfield Comm H S Dist 225 (09-12)
2005-06 Enrollment: 497 . . . . (618) 842-2649
Fairfield Psd 112 (PK-08)
2005-06 Enrollment: 710 . . . . (618) 842-6501
Jasper CCSD 17 (KG-08)
2005-06 Enrollment: 178 . . . . (618) 842-3048
New Hope CCSD 6 (KG-08)
2005-06 Enrollment: 190 . . . . (618) 842-3296

Two-year College(s)

Illinois Eastern Community Colleges-Frontier Community College (Public)
Fall 2007 Enrollment: 2,102. . . . . (618) 393-2982
2007-08 Tuition: In-state $6,117; Out-of-state $7,615

Housing: Homeownership rate: 68.6% (2007); Median home value: $58,880 (2007); Median rent: $217 per month (2000); Median age of housing: 47 years (2000).

Hospitals: Fairfield Memorial Hospital (80 beds)

Safety: Violent crime rate: 32.5 per 10,000 population; Property crime rate: 153.0 per 10,000 population (2006).

Newspapers: Wayne County Press (Local news; Circulation 8,125)

Transportation: Commute to work: 93.3% car, 0.6% public transportation, 4.1% walk, 1.3% work from home (2000); Travel time to work: 71.2% less than 15 minutes, 10.2% 15 to 30 minutes, 12.3% 30 to 45 minutes, 3.4% 45 to 60 minutes, 2.8% 60 minutes or more (2000)

Airports: Fairfield Municipal (general aviation)

Additional Information Contacts

City of Fairfield . . . . (618) 842-3871
http://www.fairfield-il.com
Fairfield Chamber of Commerce . . . . (618) 842-6116

GEFF (unincorporated postal area, zip code 62842). Aka Jeffersonville. Covers a land area of 41.983 square miles and a water area of 0.010 square miles. Located at 38.44° N. Lat.; 88.41° W. Long. Elevation is 459 feet.
Population: 840 (2000); Race: 97.6% White, 0.0% Black, 0.0% Asian, 2.3% Hispanic of any race (2000); Density: 20.0 persons per square mile (2000); Age: 25.7% under 18, 18.4% over 64 (2000); Marriage status: 18.2% never married, 65.1% now married, 9.0% widowed, 7.6% divorced (2000); Foreign born: 0.2% (2000); Ancestry (includes multiple ancestries): 16.4% Other groups, 16.0% United States or American, 12.6% German, 10.3% English, 7.4% Irish (2000).
Economy: Employment by occupation: 15.8% management, 7.0% professional, 16.8% services, 14.2% sales, 4.8% farming, 8.6% construction, 32.9% production (2000).
Income: Per capita income: $14,504 (2000); Median household income: $30,040 (2000); Poverty rate: 10.9% (2000).
Education: Percent of population age 25 and over with: High school diploma (including GED) or higher: 74.5% (2000); Bachelor's degree or higher: 8.2% (2000).

School District(s)

Geff CCSD 14 (KG-08)
2005-06 Enrollment: 99 . . . . (618) 897-2465
Housing: Homeownership rate: 85.3% (2000); Median home value: $39,800 (2000); Median rent: $252 per month (2000); Median age of housing: 34 years (2000).
Transportation: Commute to work: 93.0% car, 0.0% public transportation, 0.0% walk, 6.5% work from home (2000); Travel time to work: 35.9% less than 15 minutes, 35.7% 15 to 30 minutes, 19.4% 30 to 45 minutes, 4.9% 45 to 60 minutes, 4.1% 60 minutes or more (2000)

GOLDEN GATE (village). Aka Goldengate. Covers a land area of 0.077 square miles and a water area of 0 square miles. Located at 38.35° N. Lat.; 88.20° W. Long. Elevation is 397 feet.
Population: 90 (1990); 100 (2000); 97 (2007); 96 (2012 projected); Race: 100.0% White, 0.0% Black, 0.0% Asian, 5.2% Hispanic of any race (2007); Density: 1,267.4 persons per square mile (2007); Average household size: 2.49 (2007); Median age: 38.9 (2007); Males per 100 females: 102.1 (2007); Marriage status: 20.0% never married, 63.2% now married, 4.2% widowed, 12.6% divorced (2000); Foreign born: 0.0% (2000); Ancestry (includes multiple ancestries): 16.8% United States or American, 13.6% Other groups, 12.8% German, 11.2% Irish, 7.2% English (2000).
Economy: Employment by occupation: 13.2% management, 5.7% professional, 7.5% services, 15.1% sales, 7.5% farming, 5.7% construction, 45.3% production (2000).
Income: Per capita income: $11,418 (2007); Median household income: $21,875 (2007); Average household income: $28,397 (2007); Percent of households with income of $100,000 or more: 0.0% (2007); Poverty rate: 19.2% (2000).
Education: Percent of population age 25 and over with: High school diploma (including GED) or higher: 79.4% (2007); Bachelor's degree or higher: 3.2% (2007); Master's degree or higher: 0.0% (2007).
Housing: Homeownership rate: 87.2% (2007); Median home value: $21,667 (2007); Median rent: $225 per month (2000); Median age of housing: 29 years (2000).
Transportation: Commute to work: 94.3% car, 0.0% public transportation, 5.7% walk, 0.0% work from home (2000); Travel time to work: 3.8% less than 15 minutes, 60.4% 15 to 30 minutes, 15.1% 30 to 45 minutes, 17.0% 45 to 60 minutes, 3.8% 60 minutes or more (2000)

JEFFERSONVILLE (village). Aka Geff. Covers a land area of 1.020 square miles and a water area of 0 square miles. Located at 38.44° N. Lat.; 88.40° W. Long. Elevation is 459 feet.
History: Also known as Geff.
Population: 311 (1990); 366 (2000); 364 (2007); 361 (2012 projected); Race: 98.4% White, 1.4% Black, 0.0% Asian, 2.2% Hispanic of any race (2007); Density: 356.8 persons per square mile (2007); Average household size: 2.30 (2007); Median age: 34.8 (2007); Males per 100 females: 98.9 (2007); Marriage status: 19.4% never married, 56.1% now married, 12.5% widowed, 12.1% divorced (2000); Foreign born: 0.0% (2000); Ancestry (includes multiple ancestries): 19.4% German, 17.6% United States or American, 17.4% Other groups, 9.0% Irish, 8.2% English (2000).
Economy: Employment by occupation: 6.3% management, 12.0% professional, 22.2% services, 22.8% sales, 0.0% farming, 6.3% construction, 30.4% production (2000).
Income: Per capita income: $14,876 (2007); Median household income: $30,625 (2007); Average household income: $34,272 (2007); Percent of households with income of $100,000 or more: 1.9% (2007); Poverty rate: 19.7% (2000).
Education: Percent of population age 25 and over with: High school diploma (including GED) or higher: 77.9% (2007); Bachelor's degree or higher: 6.5% (2007); Master's degree or higher: 0.9% (2007).
Housing: Homeownership rate: 79.1% (2007); Median home value: $33,370 (2007); Median rent: $238 per month (2000); Median age of housing: 32 years (2000).
Transportation: Commute to work: 95.6% car, 0.0% public transportation, 0.0% walk, 4.4% work from home (2000); Travel time to work: 43.0% less than 15 minutes, 35.1% 15 to 30 minutes, 15.9% 30 to 45 minutes, 0.0% 45 to 60 minutes, 6.0% 60 minutes or more (2000)

JOHNSONVILLE (village). Covers a land area of 0.212 square miles and a water area of 0 square miles. Located at 38.52° N. Lat.; 88.53° W. Long. Elevation is 541 feet.
Population: 68 (1990); 69 (2000); 67 (2007); 66 (2012 projected); Race: 100.0% White, 0.0% Black, 0.0% Asian, 0.0% Hispanic of any race (2007); Density: 316.4 persons per square mile (2007); Average household size: 2.68 (2007); Median age: 39.5 (2007); Males per 100 females: 63.4 (2007); Marriage status: 24.6% never married, 59.0% now married, 4.9% widowed, 11.5% divorced (2000); Foreign born: 0.0% (2000); Ancestry (includes multiple ancestries): 26.3% German, 23.7% Other groups, 18.4% Irish, 10.5% English, 6.6% United States or American (2000).
Economy: Employment by occupation: 4.2% management, 14.6% professional, 6.3% services, 18.8% sales, 6.3% farming, 2.1% construction, 47.9% production (2000).
Income: Per capita income: $18,769 (2007); Median household income: $51,250 (2007); Average household income: $50,300 (2007); Percent of households with income of $100,000 or more: 0.0% (2007); Poverty rate: 0.0% (2000).
Education: Percent of population age 25 and over with: High school diploma (including GED) or higher: 82.2% (2007); Bachelor's degree or higher: 11.1% (2007); Master's degree or higher: 0.0% (2007).

School District(s)

North Wayne CUSD 200 (PK-12)
2005-06 Enrollment: 452 . . . . (618) 673-2151
Housing: Homeownership rate: 92.0% (2007); Median home value: $34,167 (2007); Median rent: $175 per month (2000); Median age of housing: 52 years (2000).
Transportation: Commute to work: 93.3% car, 0.0% public transportation, 0.0% walk, 0.0% work from home (2000); Travel time to work: 6.7% less than 15 minutes, 48.9% 15 to 30 minutes, 33.3% 30 to 45 minutes, 0.0% 45 to 60 minutes, 11.1% 60 minutes or more (2000)

KEENES (village). Covers a land area of 0.130 square miles and a water area of 0 square miles. Located at 38.33° N. Lat.; 88.64° W. Long. Elevation is 449 feet.
Population: 62 (1990); 99 (2000); 100 (2007); 98 (2012 projected); Race: 100.0% White, 0.0% Black, 0.0% Asian, 0.0% Hispanic of any race (2007); Density: 769.9 persons per square mile (2007); Average household size: 2.56 (2007); Median age: 32.2 (2007); Males per 100 females: 81.8 (2007); Marriage status: 13.2% never married, 63.2% now married, 4.4% widowed, 19.1% divorced (2000); Foreign born: 0.0% (2000); Ancestry (includes multiple ancestries): 16.0% United States or American, 14.9% English, 4.3% French (except Basque), 4.3% Other groups, 2.1% Scottish (2000).
Economy: Employment by occupation: 0.0% management, 0.0% professional, 36.6% services, 19.5% sales, 4.9% farming, 4.9% construction, 34.1% production (2000).
Income: Per capita income: $12,500 (2007); Median household income: $24,375 (2007); Average household income: $32,051 (2007); Percent of households with income of $100,000 or more: 0.0% (2007); Poverty rate: 40.4% (2000).
Education: Percent of population age 25 and over with: High school diploma (including GED) or higher: 67.7% (2007); Bachelor's degree or higher: 1.6% (2007); Master's degree or higher: 0.0% (2007).
Housing: Homeownership rate: 87.2% (2007); Median home value: $35,000 (2007); Median rent: $n/a per month (2000); Median age of housing: 34 years (2000).

Transportation: Commute to work: 82.9% car, 4.9% public transportation, 0.0% walk, 0.0% work from home (2000); Travel time to work: 48.8% less than 15 minutes, 17.1% 15 to 30 minutes, 12.2% 30 to 45 minutes, 17.1% 45 to 60 minutes, 4.9% 60 minutes or more (2000)

MOUNT ERIE (village). Covers a land area of 0.389 square miles and a water area of 0 square miles. Located at 38.51° N. Lat.; 88.23° W. Long. Elevation is 499 feet.
Population: 155 (1990); 105 (2000); 96 (2007); 95 (2012 projected); Race: 99.0% White, 0.0% Black, 0.0% Asian, 3.1% Hispanic of any race (2007); Density: 246.6 persons per square mile (2007); Average household size: 2.18 (2007); Median age: 38.3 (2007); Males per 100 females: 123.3 (2007); Marriage status: 5.6% never married, 77.8% now married, 12.5% widowed, 4.2% divorced (2000); Foreign born: 2.0% (2000); Ancestry (includes multiple ancestries): 20.2% United States or American, 10.1% English, 7.1% Irish, 6.1% German, 2.0% Norwegian (2000).
Economy: Employment by occupation: 12.5% management, 9.4% professional, 15.6% services, 21.9% sales, 0.0% farming, 0.0% construction, 40.6% production (2000).
Income: Per capita income: $14,115 (2007); Median household income: $27,500 (2007); Average household income: $30,795 (2007); Percent of households with income of $100,000 or more: 0.0% (2007); Poverty rate: 19.2% (2000).
Education: Percent of population age 25 and over with: High school diploma (including GED) or higher: 63.6% (2007); Bachelor's degree or higher: 6.1% (2007); Master's degree or higher: 1.5% (2007).

School District(s)

North Wayne CUSD 200 (PK-12)
2005-06 Enrollment: 452 . . . . (618) 673-2151

Housing: Homeownership rate: 77.3% (2007); Median home value: $28,750 (2007); Median rent: $210 per month (2000); Median age of housing: 37 years (2000).
Transportation: Commute to work: 96.6% car, 0.0% public transportation, 0.0% walk, 3.4% work from home (2000); Travel time to work: 7.1% less than 15 minutes, 28.6% 15 to 30 minutes, 32.1% 30 to 45 minutes, 10.7% 45 to 60 minutes, 21.4% 60 minutes or more (2000)

RINARD (unincorporated postal area, zip code 62878). Covers a land area of 44.117 square miles and a water area of 0.011 square miles. Located at 38.57° N. Lat.; 88.49° W. Long. Elevation is 459 feet.
Population: 463 (2000); Race: 100.0% White, 0.0% Black, 0.0% Asian, 0.0% Hispanic of any race (2000); Density: 10.5 persons per square mile (2000); Age: 21.2% under 18, 20.8% over 64 (2000); Marriage status: 12.5% never married, 63.7% now married, 11.0% widowed, 12.8% divorced (2000); Foreign born: 0.0% (2000); Ancestry (includes multiple ancestries): 18.6% United States or American, 14.1% German, 4.3% English, 4.1% Other groups, 3.8% Irish (2000).
Economy: Employment by occupation: 14.1% management, 22.4% professional, 13.5% services, 5.7% sales, 0.0% farming, 10.4% construction, 33.9% production (2000).
Income: Per capita income: $16,474 (2000); Median household income: $33,000 (2000); Poverty rate: 7.4% (2000).
Education: Percent of population age 25 and over with: High school diploma (including GED) or higher: 65.6% (2000); Bachelor's degree or higher: 11.8% (2000).
Housing: Homeownership rate: 85.1% (2000); Median home value: $36,100 (2000); Median rent: $196 per month (2000); Median age of housing: 42 years (2000).
Transportation: Commute to work: 92.0% car, 2.1% public transportation, 0.0% walk, 5.9% work from home (2000); Travel time to work: 14.2% less than 15 minutes, 45.5% 15 to 30 minutes, 27.3% 30 to 45 minutes, 5.1% 45 to 60 minutes, 8.0% 60 minutes or more (2000)

SIMS (village). Covers a land area of 1.200 square miles and a water area of 0 square miles. Located at 38.36° N. Lat.; 88.53° W. Long. Elevation is 410 feet.
Population: 338 (1990); 273 (2000); 258 (2007); 257 (2012 projected); Race: 92.6% White, 7.0% Black, 0.4% Asian, 0.0% Hispanic of any race (2007); Density: 215.0 persons per square mile (2007); Average household size: 2.69 (2007); Median age: 36.3 (2007); Males per 100 females: 98.5 (2007); Marriage status: 24.7% never married, 51.0% now married, 8.6% widowed, 15.7% divorced (2000); Foreign born: 0.8% (2000); Ancestry (includes multiple ancestries): 19.5% United States or American, 10.0% Irish, 8.8% German, 7.7% English, 5.0% Canadian (2000).
Economy: Employment by occupation: 1.0% management, 3.8% professional, 21.2% services, 13.5% sales, 0.0% farming, 20.2% construction, 40.4% production (2000).
Income: Per capita income: $14,079 (2007); Median household income: $28,611 (2007); Average household income: $37,839 (2007); Percent of households with income of $100,000 or more: 4.2% (2007); Poverty rate: 31.0% (2000).
Education: Percent of population age 25 and over with: High school diploma (including GED) or higher: 69.1% (2007); Bachelor's degree or higher: 1.1% (2007); Master's degree or higher: 1.1% (2007).
Housing: Homeownership rate: 84.4% (2007); Median home value: $35,227 (2007); Median rent: $244 per month (2000); Median age of housing: 46 years (2000).
Transportation: Commute to work: 96.1% car, 0.0% public transportation, 0.0% walk, 2.0% work from home (2000); Travel time to work: 18.0% less than 15 minutes, 36.0% 15 to 30 minutes, 30.0% 30 to 45 minutes, 15.0% 45 to 60 minutes, 1.0% 60 minutes or more (2000)

WAYNE CITY (village). Covers a land area of 1.677 square miles and a water area of 0 square miles. Located at 38.34° N. Lat.; 88.59° W. Long. Elevation is 433 feet.
Population: 1,186 (1990); 1,089 (2000); 1,053 (2007); 1,038 (2012 projected); Race: 99.5% White, 0.0% Black, 0.0% Asian, 0.5% Hispanic of any race (2007); Density: 627.8 persons per square mile (2007); Average household size: 2.26 (2007); Median age: 37.6 (2007); Males per 100 females: 91.1 (2007); Marriage status: 18.3% never married, 56.8% now married, 13.0% widowed, 11.8% divorced (2000); Foreign born: 0.3% (2000); Ancestry (includes multiple ancestries): 26.8% United States or American, 11.5% English, 9.7% German, 4.9% Other groups, 4.5% Irish (2000).
Economy: Employment by occupation: 8.7% management, 18.7% professional, 11.4% services, 16.4% sales, 0.7% farming, 10.7% construction, 33.5% production (2000).
Income: Per capita income: $18,780 (2007); Median household income: $35,900 (2007); Average household income: $42,527 (2007); Percent of households with income of $100,000 or more: 6.0% (2007); Poverty rate: 18.4% (2000).
Education: Percent of population age 25 and over with: High school diploma (including GED) or higher: 69.2% (2007); Bachelor's degree or higher: 9.3% (2007); Master's degree or higher: 2.0% (2007).

School District(s)

Wayne City CUSD 100 (PK-12)
2005-06 Enrollment: 606 . . . . (618) 895-3103

Housing: Homeownership rate: 73.3% (2007); Median home value: $56,481 (2007); Median rent: $229 per month (2000); Median age of housing: 28 years (2000).
Transportation: Commute to work: 95.4% car, 0.0% public transportation, 2.1% walk, 2.1% work from home (2000); Travel time to work: 30.0% less than 15 minutes, 37.8% 15 to 30 minutes, 24.4% 30 to 45 minutes, 3.3% 45 to 60 minutes, 4.5% 60 minutes or more (2000)

White County

Located in southeastern Illinois; bounded on the east by the Wabash River and the Indiana border; drained by the Little Wabash River. Covers a land area of 494.87 square miles, a water area of 6.83 square miles, and is located in the Central Time Zone. The county was founded in 1815. County seat is Carmi.

Weather Station: Fulton Lock & Dam 13 — Elevation: 590 feet

	Jan	Feb	Mar	Apr	May	Jun	Jul	Aug	Sep	Oct	Nov	Dec
High	28	33	45	59	71	80	84	82	74	63	47	33
Low	11	16	27	39	51	60	64	62	54	42	30	18
Precip	1.3	1.2	2.4	3.4	3.9	4.2	3.4	4.5	3.3	2.7	2.7	1.8
Snow	6.4	3.8	2.0	0.8	0.0	0.0	0.0	0.0	0.0	tr	0.9	3.8

High and Low temperatures in degrees Fahrenheit; Precipitation and Snow in inches

Weather Station: Morrison — Elevation: 600 feet

	Jan	Feb	Mar	Apr	May	Jun	Jul	Aug	Sep	Oct	Nov	Dec
High	29	34	47	61	73	82	85	83	76	64	48	34
Low	10	15	27	38	49	58	62	60	51	39	29	17
Precip	1.5	1.4	2.8	3.7	4.7	4.2	3.8	4.8	3.1	2.9	2.9	2.1
Snow	10.7	6.8	4.6	1.4	0.0	0.0	0.0	0.0	0.0	tr	2.2	8.3

High and Low temperatures in degrees Fahrenheit; Precipitation and Snow in inches

Population: 16,522 (1990); 15,371 (2000); 15,328 (2007); 15,310 (2012 projected); Race: 98.3% White, 0.5% Black, 0.1% Asian, 0.7% Hispanic of any race (2007); Density: 31.0 persons per square mile (2007); Average household size: 2.32 (2007); Median age: 43.3 (2007); Males per 100 females: 91.1 (2007).
Religion: Five largest groups: 17.7% Southern Baptist Convention, 13.0% Christian Churches and Churches of Christ, 10.7% The United Methodist Church, 5.4% Catholic Church, 2.9% Independent, Charismatic Churches (2000).
Economy: Unemployment rate: 5.4% (4/2008); Total civilian labor force: 8,050 (4/2008); Leading industries: 15.3% health care and social assistance; 15.2% retail trade; 12.1% mining (2005); Farms: 482 totaling 280,827 acres (2002); Companies that employ 500 or more persons: 0 (2006); Companies that employ 100 to 499 persons: 5 (2006); Companies that employ less than 100 persons: 392 (2006); Black-owned businesses: n/a (2002); Hispanic-owned businesses: n/a (2002); Asian-owned businesses: n/a (2002); Women-owned businesses: 301 (2002); Retail sales per capita: $11,453 (2008). Single-family building permits issued: 0 (2007); Multi-family building permits issued: 0 (2007).
Income: Per capita income: $19,711 (2007); Median household income: $34,865 (2007); Average household income: $44,674 (2007); Percent of households with income of $100,000 or more: 6.8% (2007); Poverty rate: 14.1% (2005); Bankruptcy rate: 2.93% (2007).
Education: Percent of population age 25 and over with: High school diploma (including GED) or higher: 74.8% (2007); Bachelor's degree or higher: 10.5% (2007); Master's degree or higher: 3.4% (2007).
Housing: Homeownership rate: 78.2% (2007); Median home value: $53,161 (2007); Median rent: $210 per month (2000); Median age of housing: 42 years (2000).
Health: Birth rate: 126.2 per 10,000 population (2007); Death rate: 159.7 per 10,000 population (2007); Age-adjusted cancer mortality rate: 324.1 deaths per 100,000 population (2005); Number of physicians: 5.3 per 10,000 population (2005); Hospital beds: 55.9 per 10,000 population (2004); Hospital admissions: 286.2 per 10,000 population (2004).
Elections: 2004 Presidential election results: 62.4% Bush, 37.0% Kerry, 0.1% Nader, 0.5% Badnarik

Additional Information Contacts

White County Government. . . . . (618) 382-7211
http://www.whitecounty-il.gov
City of Carmi . . . . (618) 382-8118
http://www.cityofcarmi.com
Grayville Chamber of Commerce. . . . . (618) 375-7518
http://www.cityofgrayville.com

White County Communities

BURNT PRAIRIE (village). Aka Liberty. Covers a land area of 0.080 square miles and a water area of 0 square miles. Located at 38.25° N. Lat.; 88.25° W. Long. Elevation is 446 feet.
Population: 71 (1990); 58 (2000); 54 (2007); 53 (2012 projected); Race: 100.0% White, 0.0% Black, 0.0% Asian, 1.9% Hispanic of any race (2007); Density: 678.1 persons per square mile (2007); Average household size: 1.86 (2007); Median age: 48.8 (2007); Males per 100 females: 92.9 (2007); Marriage status: 25.0% never married, 52.3% now married, 13.6% widowed, 9.1% divorced (2000); Foreign born: 0.0% (2000); Ancestry (includes multiple ancestries): 21.7% German, 19.6% United States or American, 17.4% English, 4.3% Austrian, 4.3% Scotch-Irish (2000).
Economy: Employment by occupation: 0.0% management, 9.1% professional, 27.3% services, 18.2% sales, 0.0% farming, 18.2% construction, 27.3% production (2000).
Income: Per capita income: $18,472 (2007); Median household income: $22,500 (2007); Average household income: $34,397 (2007); Percent of households with income of $100,000 or more: 0.0% (2007); Poverty rate: 28.3% (2000).
Education: Percent of population age 25 and over with: High school diploma (including GED) or higher: 65.9% (2007); Bachelor's degree or higher: 6.8% (2007); Master's degree or higher: 6.8% (2007).
Housing: Homeownership rate: 79.3% (2007); Median home value: $35,625 (2007); Median rent: $142 per month (2000); Median age of housing: 55 years (2000).
Transportation: Commute to work: 75.0% car, 0.0% public transportation, 10.0% walk, 0.0% work from home (2000); Travel time to work: 30.0% less than 15 minutes, 30.0% 15 to 30 minutes, 25.0% 30 to 45 minutes, 0.0% 45 to 60 minutes, 15.0% 60 minutes or more (2000)

CARMI (city). County seat. Covers a land area of 2.478 square miles and a water area of 0.034 square miles. Located at 38.08° N. Lat.; 88.16° W. Long. Elevation is 394 feet.
History: Carmi, platted in 1816, developed as the seat of White County.
Population: 5,684 (1990); 5,422 (2000); 5,359 (2007); 5,318 (2012 projected); Race: 98.2% White, 0.9% Black, 0.2% Asian, 0.7% Hispanic of any race (2007); Density: 2,162.3 persons per square mile (2007); Average household size: 2.26 (2007); Median age: 43.9 (2007); Males per 100 females: 84.5 (2007); Marriage status: 16.2% never married, 59.2% now married, 12.2% widowed, 12.4% divorced (2000); Foreign born: 0.2% (2000); Ancestry (includes multiple ancestries): 16.7% German, 12.0% English, 11.6% United States or American, 11.6% Irish, 7.9% Other groups (2000).
Economy: Employment by occupation: 6.5% management, 14.0% professional, 23.9% services, 22.4% sales, 1.4% farming, 12.5% construction, 19.3% production (2000).
Income: Per capita income: $18,405 (2007); Median household income: $29,254 (2007); Average household income: $39,344 (2007); Percent of households with income of $100,000 or more: 5.4% (2007); Poverty rate: 15.1% (2000).
Education: Percent of population age 25 and over with: High school diploma (including GED) or higher: 71.5% (2007); Bachelor's degree or higher: 10.6% (2007); Master's degree or higher: 3.8% (2007).

School District(s)

Carmi-White County CUSD 5 (PK-12)
2005-06 Enrollment: 1,450 . . . . (618) 382-2341
Housing: Homeownership rate: 70.3% (2007); Median home value: $49,576 (2007); Median rent: $233 per month (2000); Median age of housing: 44 years (2000).
Hospitals: White County Medical Center (49 beds)
Safety: Violent crime rate: 40.6 per 10,000 population; Property crime rate: 288.1 per 10,000 population (2006).
Newspapers: Carmi Times & Weekly Times (Local news; Circulation 3,900); Weekly Times (National news; Circulation 500); White County Shopper News (National news; Circulation 500)
Transportation: Commute to work: 93.7% car, 1.0% public transportation, 2.4% walk, 1.9% work from home (2000); Travel time to work: 57.0% less than 15 minutes, 17.4% 15 to 30 minutes, 8.5% 30 to 45 minutes, 6.2% 45 to 60 minutes, 10.9% 60 minutes or more (2000)

Additional Information Contacts

City of Carmi . . . . (618) 382-8118
http://www.cityofcarmi.com

CROSSVILLE (village). Covers a land area of 0.642 square miles and a water area of 0 square miles. Located at 38.16° N. Lat.; 88.06° W. Long. Elevation is 410 feet.
Population: 805 (1990); 782 (2000); 716 (2007); 702 (2012 projected); Race: 98.0% White, 0.0% Black, 0.0% Asian, 1.1% Hispanic of any race (2007); Density: 1,114.4 persons per square mile (2007); Average household size: 2.25 (2007); Median age: 40.8 (2007); Males per 100 females: 96.2 (2007); Marriage status: 14.9% never married, 65.7% now married, 12.3% widowed, 7.1% divorced (2000); Foreign born: 0.7% (2000); Ancestry (includes multiple ancestries): 17.4% United States or American, 16.9% German, 11.4% English, 9.7% Irish, 8.7% Other groups (2000).
Economy: Single-family building permits issued: 0 (2007); Multi-family building permits issued: 0 (2007); Employment by occupation: 7.0% management, 15.2% professional, 21.6% services, 13.1% sales, 1.5% farming, 11.6% construction, 30.1% production (2000).
Income: Per capita income: $20,192 (2007); Median household income: $39,583 (2007); Average household income: $45,464 (2007); Percent of households with income of $100,000 or more: 4.4% (2007); Poverty rate: 16.4% (2000).
Education: Percent of population age 25 and over with: High school diploma (including GED) or higher: 69.2% (2007); Bachelor's degree or higher: 6.1% (2007); Master's degree or higher: 1.6% (2007).

School District(s)

Carmi-White County CUSD 5 (PK-12)
2005-06 Enrollment: 1,450 . . . . (618) 382-2341
Housing: Homeownership rate: 76.4% (2007); Median home value: $44,259 (2007); Median rent: $219 per month (2000); Median age of housing: 43 years (2000).
Safety: Violent crime rate: 0.0 per 10,000 population; Property crime rate: 13.4 per 10,000 population (2006).

Transportation: Commute to work: 93.6% car, 0.0% public transportation, 3.0% walk, 2.1% work from home (2000); Travel time to work: 33.5% less than 15 minutes, 32.0% 15 to 30 minutes, 16.5% 30 to 45 minutes, 10.2% 45 to 60 minutes, 7.8% 60 minutes or more (2000)

ENFIELD (village). Covers a land area of 1.160 square miles and a water area of 0 square miles. Located at 38.09° N. Lat.; 88.34° W. Long. Elevation is 486 feet.

History: Enfield was settled in 1813.

Population: 683 (1990); 625 (2000); 595 (2007); 584 (2012 projected); Race: 99.0% White, 0.2% Black, 0.0% Asian, 0.0% Hispanic of any race (2007); Density: 512.9 persons per square mile (2007); Average household size: 2.31 (2007); Median age: 47.0 (2007); Males per 100 females: 77.6 (2007); Marriage status: 22.2% never married, 52.2% now married, 14.7% widowed, 10.8% divorced (2000); Foreign born: 0.0% (2000); Ancestry (includes multiple ancestries): 14.2% United States or American, 10.3% German, 4.6% English, 4.2% Irish, 3.2% Other groups (2000).

Economy: Employment by occupation: 5.1% management, 13.9% professional, 17.7% services, 13.9% sales, 0.8% farming, 18.6% construction, 30.0% production (2000).

Income: Per capita income: $16,534 (2007); Median household income: $28,810 (2007); Average household income: $34,903 (2007); Percent of households with income of $100,000 or more: 3.5% (2007); Poverty rate: 24.7% (2000).

Education: Percent of population age 25 and over with: High school diploma (including GED) or higher: 62.6% (2007); Bachelor's degree or higher: 6.8% (2007); Master's degree or higher: 3.0% (2007).

School District(s)

Norris City-Omaha-Enfield CUSD 3 (PK-12)
2005-06 Enrollment: 738 . . . . (618) 378-3222

Housing: Homeownership rate: 82.6% (2007); Median home value: $37,969 (2007); Median rent: $155 per month (2000); Median age of housing: 42 years (2000).

Safety: Violent crime rate: 0.0 per 10,000 population; Property crime rate: 0.0 per 10,000 population (2006).

Transportation: Commute to work: 95.4% car, 0.8% public transportation, 2.1% walk, 1.7% work from home (2000); Travel time to work: 38.6% less than 15 minutes, 28.8% 15 to 30 minutes, 5.2% 30 to 45 minutes, 13.3% 45 to 60 minutes, 14.2% 60 minutes or more (2000)

GRAYVILLE (city). Covers a land area of 1.489 square miles and a water area of 0.043 square miles. Located at 38.25° N. Lat.; 87.99° W. Long.

Population: 2,044 (1990); 1,725 (2000); 1,739 (2007); 1,712 (2012 projected); Race: 99.0% White, 0.1% Black, 0.1% Asian, 0.4% Hispanic of any race (2007); Density: 1,167.6 persons per square mile (2007); Average household size: 2.24 (2007); Median age: 46.1 (2007); Males per 100 females: 87.2 (2007); Marriage status: 21.2% never married, 55.6% now married, 11.2% widowed, 12.0% divorced (2000); Foreign born: 0.4% (2000); Ancestry (includes multiple ancestries): 20.8% United States or American, 13.9% English, 12.6% German, 10.4% Other groups, 8.7% Irish (2000).

Economy: Single-family building permits issued: 0 (2007); Multi-family building permits issued: 0 (2007); Employment by occupation: 7.1% management, 10.1% professional, 19.6% services, 23.9% sales, 0.4% farming, 12.5% construction, 26.3% production (2000).

Income: Per capita income: $20,218 (2007); Median household income: $38,784 (2007); Average household income: $44,640 (2007); Percent of households with income of $100,000 or more: 4.8% (2007); Poverty rate: 13.3% (2000).

Education: Percent of population age 25 and over with: High school diploma (including GED) or higher: 77.1% (2007); Bachelor's degree or higher: 6.0% (2007); Master's degree or higher: 1.6% (2007).

School District(s)

Grayville CUSD 1 (PK-12)
2005-06 Enrollment: 354 . . . . (618) 375-7114

Housing: Homeownership rate: 75.8% (2007); Median home value: $45,946 (2007); Median rent: $185 per month (2000); Median age of housing: 48 years (2000).

Safety: Violent crime rate: 18.3 per 10,000 population; Property crime rate: 170.9 per 10,000 population (2006).

Transportation: Commute to work: 92.9% car, 0.0% public transportation, 3.4% walk, 2.4% work from home (2000); Travel time to work: 47.1% less than 15 minutes, 21.0% 15 to 30 minutes, 16.1% 30 to 45 minutes, 9.7% 45 to 60 minutes, 6.1% 60 minutes or more (2000)

Additional Information Contacts

Grayville Chamber of Commerce. . . . . (618) 375-7518
http://www.cityofgrayville.com

MAUNIE (village). Covers a land area of 0.161 square miles and a water area of 0 square miles. Located at 38.03° N. Lat.; 88.04° W. Long. Elevation is 371 feet.

Population: 119 (1990); 177 (2000); 165 (2007); 160 (2012 projected); Race: 95.2% White, 1.8% Black, 0.6% Asian, 0.0% Hispanic of any race (2007); Density: 1,021.9 persons per square mile (2007); Average household size: 2.26 (2007); Median age: 43.1 (2007); Males per 100 females: 114.3 (2007); Marriage status: 19.4% never married, 49.0% now married, 9.7% widowed, 21.9% divorced (2000); Foreign born: 1.1% (2000); Ancestry (includes multiple ancestries): 25.9% German, 14.6% Irish, 13.0% Other groups, 10.8% French (except Basque), 10.3% United States or American (2000).

Economy: Employment by occupation: 0.0% management, 16.0% professional, 25.3% services, 10.7% sales, 9.3% farming, 5.3% construction, 33.3% production (2000).

Income: Per capita income: $11,212 (2007); Median household income: $18,864 (2007); Average household income: $25,342 (2007); Percent of households with income of $100,000 or more: 0.0% (2007); Poverty rate: 26.0% (2000).

Taxes: Total city taxes per capita: $17 (2006); City property taxes per capita: $11 (2006).

Education: Percent of population age 25 and over with: High school diploma (including GED) or higher: 49.6% (2007); Bachelor's degree or higher: 0.0% (2007); Master's degree or higher: 0.0% (2007).

Housing: Homeownership rate: 86.3% (2007); Median home value: $22,321 (2007); Median rent: $200 per month (2000); Median age of housing: 40 years (2000).

Transportation: Commute to work: 92.6% car, 0.0% public transportation, 0.0% walk, 0.0% work from home (2000); Travel time to work: 20.6% less than 15 minutes, 32.4% 15 to 30 minutes, 19.1% 30 to 45 minutes, 5.9% 45 to 60 minutes, 22.1% 60 minutes or more (2000)

MILL SHOALS (village). Covers a land area of 0.783 square miles and a water area of 0 square miles. Located at 38.24° N. Lat.; 88.34° W. Long. Elevation is 381 feet.

Population: 300 (1990); 235 (2000); 219 (2007); 217 (2012 projected); Race: 100.0% White, 0.0% Black, 0.0% Asian, 0.0% Hispanic of any race (2007); Density: 279.5 persons per square mile (2007); Average household size: 2.09 (2007); Median age: 47.3 (2007); Males per 100 females: 85.6 (2007); Marriage status: 12.0% never married, 71.0% now married, 7.1% widowed, 9.8% divorced (2000); Foreign born: 0.0% (2000); Ancestry (includes multiple ancestries): 17.0% United States or American, 15.2% German, 12.1% English, 11.7% Irish, 7.2% Other groups (2000).

Economy: Employment by occupation: 14.1% management, 4.0% professional, 18.2% services, 23.2% sales, 0.0% farming, 6.1% construction, 34.3% production (2000).

Income: Per capita income: $19,521 (2007); Median household income: $34,063 (2007); Average household income: $40,714 (2007); Percent of households with income of $100,000 or more: 2.9% (2007); Poverty rate: 9.9% (2000).

Education: Percent of population age 25 and over with: High school diploma (including GED) or higher: 67.5% (2007); Bachelor's degree or higher: 6.0% (2007); Master's degree or higher: 1.8% (2007).

School District(s)

Edwd/Gltn/Hdin/Pop/Slne/Wbh/Wn/Wh (07-12)
2005-06 Enrollment: 47 . . . . (618) 253-5581

Housing: Homeownership rate: 82.9% (2007); Median home value: $29,063 (2007); Median rent: $175 per month (2000); Median age of housing: 38 years (2000).

Transportation: Commute to work: 94.9% car, 0.0% public transportation, 2.0% walk, 3.0% work from home (2000); Travel time to work: 22.9% less than 15 minutes, 58.3% 15 to 30 minutes, 6.3% 30 to 45 minutes, 2.1% 45 to 60 minutes, 10.4% 60 minutes or more (2000)

NORRIS CITY (village). Covers a land area of 1.159 square miles and a water area of 0 square miles. Located at 37.98° N. Lat.; 88.32° W. Long. Elevation is 420 feet.

History: Norris City was named for pioneer settler William Norris. It developed as an agricultural and coal mining trading area.

Population: 1,341 (1990); 1,057 (2000); 902 (2007); 896 (2012 projected); Race: 98.4% White, 0.0% Black, 0.4% Asian, 0.2% Hispanic of any race

(2007); Density: 777.9 persons per square mile (2007); Average household size: 2.09 (2007); Median age: 42.0 (2007); Males per 100 females: 87.5 (2007); Marriage status: 15.8% never married, 61.3% now married, 11.3% widowed, 11.6% divorced (2000); Foreign born: 0.2% (2000); Ancestry (includes multiple ancestries): 17.5% German, 14.5% Irish, 8.7% English, 8.4% United States or American, 8.3% Other groups (2000).
Economy: Employment by occupation: 4.0% management, 14.0% professional, 19.0% services, 20.5% sales, 0.5% farming, 13.3% construction, 28.6% production (2000).
Income: Per capita income: $15,951 (2007); Median household income: $25,204 (2007); Average household income: $33,304 (2007); Percent of households with income of $100,000 or more: 2.1% (2007); Poverty rate: 14.4% (2000).
Education: Percent of population age 25 and over with: High school diploma (including GED) or higher: 77.3% (2007); Bachelor's degree or higher: 7.6% (2007); Master's degree or higher: 2.5% (2007).

School District(s)

Norris City-Omaha-Enfield CUSD 3 (PK-12)
2005-06 Enrollment: 738 . . . . (618) 378-3222
Wabash & Ohio Valley Sp Ed Dist
2005-06 Enrollment: n/a . . . . (618) 378-2131

Housing: Homeownership rate: 76.9% (2007); Median home value: $42,419 (2007); Median rent: $171 per month (2000); Median age of housing: 45 years (2000).
Safety: Violent crime rate: 0.0 per 10,000 population; Property crime rate: 0.0 per 10,000 population (2006).
Newspapers: Norris City Banner (Community news; Circulation 1,304)
Transportation: Commute to work: 94.2% car, 0.0% public transportation, 3.9% walk, 1.5% work from home (2000); Travel time to work: 34.3% less than 15 minutes, 23.5% 15 to 30 minutes, 21.0% 30 to 45 minutes, 9.1% 45 to 60 minutes, 12.1% 60 minutes or more (2000)

PHILLIPSTOWN (village). Covers a land area of 0.271 square miles and a water area of 0 square miles. Located at 38.14° N. Lat.; 88.02° W. Long. Elevation is 545 feet.
Population: 48 (1990); 28 (2000); 27 (2007); 27 (2012 projected); Race: 100.0% White, 0.0% Black, 0.0% Asian, 0.0% Hispanic of any race (2007); Density: 99.6 persons per square mile (2007); Average household size: 2.08 (2007); Median age: 47.5 (2007); Males per 100 females: 107.7 (2007); Marriage status: 0.0% never married, 71.4% now married, 9.5% widowed, 19.0% divorced (2000); Foreign born: 0.0% (2000); Ancestry (includes multiple ancestries): 32.0% United States or American, 8.0% Other groups, 8.0% German, 4.0% Irish, 4.0% Norwegian (2000).
Economy: Employment by occupation: 0.0% management, 40.0% professional, 13.3% services, 20.0% sales, 0.0% farming, 20.0% construction, 6.7% production (2000).
Income: Per capita income: $21,296 (2007); Median household income: $32,500 (2007); Average household income: $44,231 (2007); Percent of households with income of $100,000 or more: 7.7% (2007); Poverty rate: 4.0% (2000).
Education: Percent of population age 25 and over with: High school diploma (including GED) or higher: 100.0% (2007); Bachelor's degree or higher: 25.0% (2007); Master's degree or higher: 15.0% (2007).
Housing: Homeownership rate: 84.6% (2007); Median home value: $75,000 (2007); Median rent: $n/a per month (2000); Median age of housing: 17 years (2000).
Transportation: Commute to work: 86.7% car, 0.0% public transportation, 0.0% walk, 13.3% work from home (2000); Travel time to work: 23.1% less than 15 minutes, 7.7% 15 to 30 minutes, 38.5% 30 to 45 minutes, 15.4% 45 to 60 minutes, 15.4% 60 minutes or more (2000)

SPRINGERTON (village). Aka Springer. Covers a land area of 0.125 square miles and a water area of 0 square miles. Located at 38.17° N. Lat.; 88.35° W. Long. Elevation is 394 feet.
Population: 164 (1990); 134 (2000); 135 (2007); 132 (2012 projected); Race: 97.8% White, 0.0% Black, 0.0% Asian, 0.0% Hispanic of any race (2007); Density: 1,076.7 persons per square mile (2007); Average household size: 2.37 (2007); Median age: 38.3 (2007); Males per 100 females: 92.9 (2007); Marriage status: 12.5% never married, 74.0% now married, 9.6% widowed, 3.8% divorced (2000); Foreign born: 0.0% (2000); Ancestry (includes multiple ancestries): 18.4% German, 14.9% Other groups, 9.9% United States or American, 9.2% Irish, 7.1% French (except Basque) (2000).
Economy: Employment by occupation: 10.3% management, 22.4% professional, 13.8% services, 15.5% sales, 8.6% farming, 5.2% construction, 24.1% production (2000).
Income: Per capita income: $14,889 (2007); Median household income: $30,313 (2007); Average household income: $35,263 (2007); Percent of households with income of $100,000 or more: 3.5% (2007); Poverty rate: 10.6% (2000).
Education: Percent of population age 25 and over with: High school diploma (including GED) or higher: 62.1% (2007); Bachelor's degree or higher: 3.4% (2007); Master's degree or higher: 0.0% (2007).
Housing: Homeownership rate: 89.5% (2007); Median home value: $34,167 (2007); Median rent: $n/a per month (2000); Median age of housing: 47 years (2000).
Transportation: Commute to work: 100.0% car, 0.0% public transportation, 0.0% walk, 0.0% work from home (2000); Travel time to work: 28.6% less than 15 minutes, 44.6% 15 to 30 minutes, 3.6% 30 to 45 minutes, 10.7% 45 to 60 minutes, 12.5% 60 minutes or more (2000)

Whiteside County

Located in northwestern Illinois; bounded on the northwest by the Mississippi River and the Iowa border; drained by the Rock River. Covers a land area of 684.77 square miles, a water area of 12.24 square miles, and is located in the Central Time Zone. The county was founded in 1836. County seat is Morrison.

Whiteside County is part of the Sterling, IL Micropolitan Statistical Area. The entire metro area includes: Whiteside County, IL

Weather Station: Fulton Lock & Dam 13 Elevation: 590 feet

	Jan	Feb	Mar	Apr	May	Jun	Jul	Aug	Sep	Oct	Nov	Dec
High	28	33	45	59	71	80	84	82	74	63	47	33
Low	11	16	27	39	51	60	64	62	54	42	30	18
Precip	1.3	1.2	2.4	3.4	3.9	4.2	3.4	4.5	3.3	2.7	2.7	1.8
Snow	6.4	3.8	2.0	0.8	0.0	0.0	0.0	0.0	0.0	tr	0.9	3.8

High and Low temperatures in degrees Fahrenheit; Precipitation and Snow in inches

Weather Station: Morrison Elevation: 600 feet

	Jan	Feb	Mar	Apr	May	Jun	Jul	Aug	Sep	Oct	Nov	Dec
High	29	34	47	61	73	82	85	83	76	64	48	34
Low	10	15	27	38	49	58	62	60	51	39	29	17
Precip	1.5	1.4	2.8	3.7	4.7	4.2	3.8	4.8	3.1	2.9	2.9	2.1
Snow	10.7	6.8	4.6	1.4	0.0	0.0	0.0	0.0	0.0	tr	2.2	8.3

High and Low temperatures in degrees Fahrenheit; Precipitation and Snow in inches

Population: 60,186 (1990); 60,653 (2000); 59,707 (2007); 58,931 (2012 projected); Race: 91.9% White, 1.2% Black, 0.5% Asian, 9.6% Hispanic of any race (2007); Density: 87.2 persons per square mile (2007); Average household size: 2.52 (2007); Median age: 40.2 (2007); Males per 100 females: 95.0 (2007).
Religion: Five largest groups: 22.7% Catholic Church, 8.4% The United Methodist Church, 6.6% Evangelical Lutheran Church in America, 5.6% Reformed Church in America, 3.2% Lutheran Church—Missouri Synod (2000).
Economy: Unemployment rate: 5.6% (4/2008); Total civilian labor force: 31,168 (4/2008); Leading industries: 24.3% manufacturing; 20.7% health care and social assistance; 17.8% retail trade (2005); Farms: 1,001 totaling 379,366 acres (2002); Companies that employ 500 or more persons: 3 (2006); Companies that employ 100 to 499 persons: 25 (2006); Companies that employ less than 100 persons: 1,327 (2006); Black-owned businesses: n/a (2002); Hispanic-owned businesses: n/a (2002); Asian-owned businesses: n/a (2002); Women-owned businesses: 844 (2002); Retail sales per capita: $13,617 (2008). Single-family building permits issued: 85 (2007); Multi-family building permits issued: 6 (2007).
Income: Per capita income: $22,020 (2007); Median household income: $45,007 (2007); Average household income: $54,658 (2007); Percent of households with income of $100,000 or more: 9.6% (2007); Poverty rate: 10.9% (2005); Bankruptcy rate: 2.03% (2007).
Taxes: Total county taxes per capita: $118 (2006); County property taxes per capita: $113 (2006).
Education: Percent of population age 25 and over with: High school diploma (including GED) or higher: 79.9% (2007); Bachelor's degree or higher: 11.4% (2007); Master's degree or higher: 3.5% (2007).
Housing: Homeownership rate: 74.5% (2007); Median home value: $112,281 (2007); Median rent: $367 per month (2000); Median age of housing: 44 years (2000).

Health: Birth rate: 130.4 per 10,000 population (2007); Death rate: 110.1 per 10,000 population (2007); Age-adjusted cancer mortality rate: 217.4 deaths per 100,000 population (2005); Number of physicians: 11.5 per 10,000 population (2005); Hospital beds: 36.8 per 10,000 population (2004); Hospital admissions: 1,440.2 per 10,000 population (2004).
Elections: 2004 Presidential election results: 48.2% Bush, 51.1% Kerry, 0.0% Nader, 0.7% Badnarik
National and State Parks: Big Bend State Conservation Area; Morrison-Rockwood State Park; Prophetstown State Park
Additional Information Contacts
Whiteside County Government . . . . (815) 772-5100
http://www.whiteside.org
City of Rock Falls . . . . (815) 622-1100
http://www.rockfalls61071.com
City of Sterling . . . . (815) 632-6621
http://ci.sterling.il.us/main
Fulton Chamber of Commerce . . . . (815) 589-4545
Morrison Chamber of Commerce . . . . (815) 772-3757
http://www.thecity1.com/biz/morrisoncc
Prophetstown Main Street . . . . (815) 537-5139
http://www.prophetstown.net
Rock Falls Chamber of Commerce . . . . (815) 625-4500
http://www.rockfallschamber.com
Sauk Valley Area Chamber of Commerce . . . . (815) 625-2400
http://www.saukvalleyareachamber.com

Whiteside County Communities

ALBANY (village). Covers a land area of 1.000 square miles and a water area of 0 square miles. Located at 41.78° N. Lat.; 90.21° W. Long. Elevation is 614 feet.
Population: 835 (1990); 895 (2000); 848 (2007); 847 (2012 projected); Race: 98.2% White, 0.9% Black, 0.0% Asian, 0.4% Hispanic of any race (2007); Density: 847.8 persons per square mile (2007); Average household size: 2.51 (2007); Median age: 39.9 (2007); Males per 100 females: 92.7 (2007); Marriage status: 17.8% never married, 65.0% now married, 8.5% widowed, 8.8% divorced (2000); Foreign born: 0.5% (2000); Ancestry (includes multiple ancestries): 31.0% German, 15.4% United States or American, 15.0% Irish, 12.9% Dutch, 12.0% English (2000).
Economy: Single-family building permits issued: 1 (2007); Multi-family building permits issued: 2 (2007); Employment by occupation: 9.9% management, 17.8% professional, 14.2% services, 22.4% sales, 0.0% farming, 9.9% construction, 25.8% production (2000).
Income: Per capita income: $23,160 (2007); Median household income: $52,105 (2007); Average household income: $58,107 (2007); Percent of households with income of $100,000 or more: 11.8% (2007); Poverty rate: 5.3% (2000).
Education: Percent of population age 25 and over with: High school diploma (including GED) or higher: 86.5% (2007); Bachelor's degree or higher: 12.8% (2007); Master's degree or higher: 2.3% (2007).
Housing: Homeownership rate: 88.8% (2007); Median home value: $119,196 (2007); Median rent: $359 per month (2000); Median age of housing: 38 years (2000).
Safety: Violent crime rate: 0.0 per 10,000 population; Property crime rate: 77.4 per 10,000 population (2006).
Transportation: Commute to work: 94.6% car, 0.0% public transportation, 3.2% walk, 1.2% work from home (2000); Travel time to work: 30.8% less than 15 minutes, 41.3% 15 to 30 minutes, 12.8% 30 to 45 minutes, 11.3% 45 to 60 minutes, 4.0% 60 minutes or more (2000)

COLETA (village). Covers a land area of 0.455 square miles and a water area of 0 square miles. Located at 41.90° N. Lat.; 89.80° W. Long. Elevation is 817 feet.
Population: 154 (1990); 155 (2000); 159 (2007); 157 (2012 projected); Race: 95.6% White, 2.5% Black, 0.0% Asian, 4.4% Hispanic of any race (2007); Density: 349.8 persons per square mile (2007); Average household size: 2.52 (2007); Median age: 42.8 (2007); Males per 100 females: 93.9 (2007); Marriage status: 25.4% never married, 57.2% now married, 4.3% widowed, 13.0% divorced (2000); Foreign born: 7.5% (2000); Ancestry (includes multiple ancestries): 24.4% German, 11.9% Irish, 9.4% United States or American, 7.5% French (except Basque), 6.9% English (2000).
Economy: Employment by occupation: 23.9% management, 1.5% professional, 6.0% services, 31.3% sales, 0.0% farming, 10.4% construction, 26.9% production (2000).
Income: Per capita income: $23,459 (2007); Median household income: $39,500 (2007); Average household income: $59,206 (2007); Percent of households with income of $100,000 or more: 17.5% (2007); Poverty rate: 8.8% (2000).
Education: Percent of population age 25 and over with: High school diploma (including GED) or higher: 82.6% (2007); Bachelor's degree or higher: 2.8% (2007); Master's degree or higher: 0.0% (2007).
Housing: Homeownership rate: 93.7% (2007); Median home value: $90,833 (2007); Median rent: $n/a per month (2000); Median age of housing: 60+ years (2000).
Transportation: Commute to work: 92.4% car, 0.0% public transportation, 4.5% walk, 3.0% work from home (2000); Travel time to work: 31.3% less than 15 minutes, 50.0% 15 to 30 minutes, 9.4% 30 to 45 minutes, 7.8% 45 to 60 minutes, 1.6% 60 minutes or more (2000)

DEER GROVE (village). Covers a land area of 0.456 square miles and a water area of 0 square miles. Located at 41.60° N. Lat.; 89.69° W. Long. Elevation is 646 feet.
Population: 44 (1990); 48 (2000); 50 (2007); 49 (2012 projected); Race: 86.0% White, 4.0% Black, 0.0% Asian, 12.0% Hispanic of any race (2007); Density: 109.7 persons per square mile (2007); Average household size: 2.17 (2007); Median age: 41.3 (2007); Males per 100 females: 61.3 (2007); Marriage status: 40.5% never married, 45.2% now married, 9.5% widowed, 4.8% divorced (2000); Foreign born: 0.0% (2000); Ancestry (includes multiple ancestries): 37.7% Irish, 37.7% German, 11.3% Swedish, 11.3% Belgian, 9.4% Other groups (2000).
Economy: Employment by occupation: 3.1% management, 0.0% professional, 28.1% services, 25.0% sales, 0.0% farming, 12.5% construction, 31.3% production (2000).
Income: Per capita income: $26,650 (2007); Median household income: $52,500 (2007); Average household income: $57,935 (2007); Percent of households with income of $100,000 or more: 0.0% (2007); Poverty rate: 5.7% (2000).
Education: Percent of population age 25 and over with: High school diploma (including GED) or higher: 79.4% (2007); Bachelor's degree or higher: 5.9% (2007); Master's degree or higher: 5.9% (2007).
Housing: Homeownership rate: 82.6% (2007); Median home value: $75,000 (2007); Median rent: $225 per month (2000); Median age of housing: 60+ years (2000).
Transportation: Commute to work: 71.9% car, 0.0% public transportation, 0.0% walk, 28.1% work from home (2000); Travel time to work: 17.4% less than 15 minutes, 52.2% 15 to 30 minutes, 21.7% 30 to 45 minutes, 8.7% 45 to 60 minutes, 0.0% 60 minutes or more (2000)

ERIE (village). Covers a land area of 1.403 square miles and a water area of 0.009 square miles. Located at 41.65° N. Lat.; 90.07° W. Long. Elevation is 591 feet.
History: Incorporated 1872.
Population: 1,580 (1990); 1,589 (2000); 1,625 (2007); 1,637 (2012 projected); Race: 98.3% White, 0.3% Black, 0.0% Asian, 0.9% Hispanic of any race (2007); Density: 1,158.4 persons per square mile (2007); Average household size: 2.47 (2007); Median age: 40.2 (2007); Males per 100 females: 88.5 (2007); Marriage status: 21.3% never married, 60.6% now married, 8.3% widowed, 9.8% divorced (2000); Foreign born: 1.1% (2000); Ancestry (includes multiple ancestries): 30.1% German, 14.0% Irish, 11.1% English, 9.5% Dutch, 7.1% Swedish (2000).
Economy: Single-family building permits issued: 2 (2007); Multi-family building permits issued: 0 (2007); Employment by occupation: 10.4% management, 12.0% professional, 15.0% services, 21.2% sales, 1.3% farming, 11.2% construction, 28.9% production (2000).
Income: Per capita income: $22,218 (2007); Median household income: $47,634 (2007); Average household income: $54,788 (2007); Percent of households with income of $100,000 or more: 10.0% (2007); Poverty rate: 5.1% (2000).
Education: Percent of population age 25 and over with: High school diploma (including GED) or higher: 84.7% (2007); Bachelor's degree or higher: 12.4% (2007); Master's degree or higher: 3.8% (2007).

School District(s)

Erie CUSD 1 (PK-12)
2005-06 Enrollment: 714 . . . . (309) 659-2239
Housing: Homeownership rate: 80.3% (2007); Median home value: $121,445 (2007); Median rent: $290 per month (2000); Median age of housing: 41 years (2000).
Safety: Violent crime rate: 0.0 per 10,000 population; Property crime rate: 0.0 per 10,000 population (2006).

Newspapers: Review (Regional news; Circulation 1,700)
Transportation: Commute to work: 95.5% car, 0.4% public transportation, 2.7% walk, 1.1% work from home (2000); Travel time to work: 32.9% less than 15 minutes, 31.0% 15 to 30 minutes, 24.6% 30 to 45 minutes, 6.5% 45 to 60 minutes, 5.0% 60 minutes or more (2000)

FENTON (unincorporated postal area, zip code 61251). Covers a land area of 17.109 square miles and a water area of 0 square miles. Located at 41.73° N. Lat.; 90.06° W. Long. Elevation is 620 feet.
Population: 317 (2000); Race: 100.0% White, 0.0% Black, 0.0% Asian, 0.0% Hispanic of any race (2000); Density: 18.5 persons per square mile (2000); Age: 29.2% under 18, 9.4% over 64 (2000); Marriage status: 24.2% never married, 70.3% now married, 3.7% widowed, 1.9% divorced (2000); Foreign born: 0.0% (2000); Ancestry (includes multiple ancestries): 23.1% English, 21.3% Irish, 14.6% German, 13.7% Scotch-Irish, 12.9% Dutch (2000).
Economy: Employment by occupation: 13.4% management, 12.7% professional, 15.9% services, 8.9% sales, 5.1% farming, 10.8% construction, 33.1% production (2000).
Income: Per capita income: $15,537 (2000); Median household income: $47,813 (2000); Poverty rate: 0.0% (2000).
Education: Percent of population age 25 and over with: High school diploma (including GED) or higher: 90.7% (2000); Bachelor's degree or higher: 11.8% (2000).
Housing: Homeownership rate: 85.7% (2000); Median home value: $66,200 (2000); Median rent: $225 per month (2000); Median age of housing: 60+ years (2000).
Transportation: Commute to work: 100.0% car, 0.0% public transportation, 0.0% walk, 0.0% work from home (2000); Travel time to work: 19.7% less than 15 minutes, 40.1% 15 to 30 minutes, 26.1% 30 to 45 minutes, 10.8% 45 to 60 minutes, 3.2% 60 minutes or more (2000)

FULTON (city). Covers a land area of 2.272 square miles and a water area of 0.071 square miles. Located at 41.86° N. Lat.; 90.15° W. Long. Elevation is 650 feet.
History: The name of Fulton honors the inventor of the steamboat, and the city itself owes its early development to river commerce. Later it became the center of an agricultural area, producing tomatoes and cucumbers.
Population: 3,708 (1990); 3,881 (2000); 3,839 (2007); 3,808 (2012 projected); Race: 97.3% White, 0.9% Black, 0.5% Asian, 1.6% Hispanic of any race (2007); Density: 1,689.5 persons per square mile (2007); Average household size: 2.40 (2007); Median age: 42.5 (2007); Males per 100 females: 96.6 (2007); Marriage status: 22.0% never married, 62.1% now married, 8.3% widowed, 7.6% divorced (2000); Foreign born: 2.0% (2000); Ancestry (includes multiple ancestries): 37.3% Dutch, 30.4% German, 11.8% Irish, 9.0% English, 5.5% United States or American (2000).
Economy: Single-family building permits issued: 6 (2007); Multi-family building permits issued: 0 (2007); Employment by occupation: 8.1% management, 19.2% professional, 11.9% services, 19.8% sales, 0.0% farming, 10.2% construction, 30.9% production (2000).
Income: Per capita income: $22,214 (2007); Median household income: $40,966 (2007); Average household income: $51,977 (2007); Percent of households with income of $100,000 or more: 7.2% (2007); Poverty rate: 5.8% (2000).
Education: Percent of population age 25 and over with: High school diploma (including GED) or higher: 79.2% (2007); Bachelor's degree or higher: 12.5% (2007); Master's degree or higher: 3.4% (2007).

School District(s)

Bi-County Special Educ Coop
2005-06 Enrollment: n/a . . . . (815) 622-0858
River Bend CUSD 2 (PK-12)
2005-06 Enrollment: 1,093 . . . . (815) 589-2711

Housing: Homeownership rate: 76.3% (2007); Median home value: $118,218 (2007); Median rent: $348 per month (2000); Median age of housing: 50 years (2000).
Safety: Violent crime rate: 20.8 per 10,000 population; Property crime rate: 168.7 per 10,000 population (2006).
Newspapers: Fulton Journal (Local news; Circulation 2,300); Whiteside Shopper (Local news; Circulation 3,400)
Transportation: Commute to work: 93.5% car, 0.0% public transportation, 3.3% walk, 1.5% work from home (2000); Travel time to work: 53.4% less than 15 minutes, 34.0% 15 to 30 minutes, 5.7% 30 to 45 minutes, 4.2% 45 to 60 minutes, 2.8% 60 minutes or more (2000)

Additional Information Contacts

Fulton Chamber of Commerce. . . . . (815) 589-4545

LYNDON (village). Covers a land area of 0.821 square miles and a water area of 0 square miles. Located at 41.71° N. Lat.; 89.92° W. Long. Elevation is 614 feet.
Population: 615 (1990); 566 (2000); 522 (2007); 518 (2012 projected); Race: 95.8% White, 0.2% Black, 0.0% Asian, 1.7% Hispanic of any race (2007); Density: 636.0 persons per square mile (2007); Average household size: 2.34 (2007); Median age: 43.7 (2007); Males per 100 females: 101.5 (2007); Marriage status: 26.3% never married, 56.6% now married, 5.7% widowed, 11.5% divorced (2000); Foreign born: 0.7% (2000); Ancestry (includes multiple ancestries): 25.4% German, 11.2% Irish, 9.8% United States or American, 9.3% English, 8.8% Dutch (2000).
Economy: Single-family building permits issued: 3 (2007); Multi-family building permits issued: 0 (2007); Employment by occupation: 6.9% management, 10.2% professional, 18.8% services, 15.1% sales, 0.0% farming, 13.8% construction, 35.2% production (2000).
Income: Per capita income: $19,459 (2007); Median household income: $40,921 (2007); Average household income: $45,549 (2007); Percent of households with income of $100,000 or more: 4.0% (2007); Poverty rate: 6.8% (2000).
Education: Percent of population age 25 and over with: High school diploma (including GED) or higher: 75.8% (2007); Bachelor's degree or higher: 5.3% (2007); Master's degree or higher: 2.4% (2007).
Housing: Homeownership rate: 87.9% (2007); Median home value: $94,231 (2007); Median rent: $270 per month (2000); Median age of housing: 47 years (2000).
Safety: Violent crime rate: 18.3 per 10,000 population; Property crime rate: 0.0 per 10,000 population (2006).
Transportation: Commute to work: 92.3% car, 1.0% public transportation, 3.3% walk, 1.7% work from home (2000); Travel time to work: 35.7% less than 15 minutes, 38.4% 15 to 30 minutes, 16.3% 30 to 45 minutes, 5.4% 45 to 60 minutes, 4.1% 60 minutes or more (2000)

MORRISON (city). County seat. Covers a land area of 2.141 square miles and a water area of 0 square miles. Located at 41.80° N. Lat.; 89.96° W. Long. Elevation is 679 feet.
History: Morrison developed when the Chicago & North Western Railway built its station here. It was in Morrison in 1874 that James Sargent installed the first time lock in the First National Bank of Morrison.
Population: 4,534 (1990); 4,447 (2000); 4,334 (2007); 4,252 (2012 projected); Race: 97.1% White, 0.9% Black, 0.2% Asian, 2.6% Hispanic of any race (2007); Density: 2,024.8 persons per square mile (2007); Average household size: 2.45 (2007); Median age: 42.8 (2007); Males per 100 females: 92.7 (2007); Marriage status: 20.5% never married, 59.2% now married, 11.3% widowed, 9.0% divorced (2000); Foreign born: 0.5% (2000); Ancestry (includes multiple ancestries): 29.9% German, 23.2% Dutch, 10.9% English, 10.1% Irish, 5.3% United States or American (2000).
Economy: Single-family building permits issued: 3 (2007); Multi-family building permits issued: 2 (2007); Employment by occupation: 7.9% management, 19.1% professional, 15.5% services, 21.1% sales, 0.9% farming, 10.6% construction, 24.9% production (2000).
Income: Per capita income: $22,929 (2007); Median household income: $44,917 (2007); Average household income: $54,047 (2007); Percent of households with income of $100,000 or more: 8.9% (2007); Poverty rate: 6.1% (2000).
Education: Percent of population age 25 and over with: High school diploma (including GED) or higher: 84.3% (2007); Bachelor's degree or higher: 15.1% (2007); Master's degree or higher: 4.8% (2007).

School District(s)

Morrison CUSD 6 (PK-12)
2005-06 Enrollment: 1,206 . . . . (815) 772-2064

Two-year College(s)

Morrison Institute of Technology (Private, Not-for-profit)
Fall 2007 Enrollment: 143 . . . . (815) 772-7218
2007-08 Tuition: In-state $12,980; Out-of-state $12,980

Housing: Homeownership rate: 77.0% (2007); Median home value: $113,244 (2007); Median rent: $352 per month (2000); Median age of housing: 51 years (2000).
Hospitals: Morrison Community Hospital
Safety: Violent crime rate: 25.5 per 10,000 population; Property crime rate: 101.9 per 10,000 population (2006).
Newspapers: Whiteside News Sentinel (Local news; Circulation 3,000)
Transportation: Commute to work: 90.4% car, 0.3% public transportation, 7.1% walk, 0.8% work from home (2000); Travel time to work: 47.2% less

than 15 minutes, 30.5% 15 to 30 minutes, 15.3% 30 to 45 minutes, 3.5% 45 to 60 minutes, 3.5% 60 minutes or more (2000)

Additional Information Contacts

Morrison Chamber of Commerce. . . . . (815) 772-3757
http://www.thecity1.com/biz/morrisoncc

PROPHETSTOWN (city). Covers a land area of 1.363 square miles and a water area of 0.021 square miles. Located at 41.67° N. Lat.; 89.93° W. Long. Elevation is 620 feet.

History: The name of Prophetstown refers to the Indian prophet White Cloud, who warned his people about the loss of their lands. The town was founded on the Rock River, where White Cloud had lived.

Population: 1,924 (1990); 2,023 (2000); 2,045 (2007); 2,027 (2012 projected); Race: 97.3% White, 1.3% Black, 0.0% Asian, 0.8% Hispanic of any race (2007); Density: 1,500.6 persons per square mile (2007); Average household size: 2.48 (2007); Median age: 44.1 (2007); Males per 100 females: 92.4 (2007); Marriage status: 18.6% never married, 64.1% now married, 9.3% widowed, 8.0% divorced (2000); Foreign born: 1.2% (2000); Ancestry (includes multiple ancestries): 34.8% German, 15.9% Irish, 11.7% English, 8.7% Swedish, 6.9% Other groups (2000).

Economy: Single-family building permits issued: 2 (2007); Multi-family building permits issued: 0 (2007); Employment by occupation: 13.3% management, 13.1% professional, 15.5% services, 20.0% sales, 1.6% farming, 7.0% construction, 29.5% production (2000).

Income: Per capita income: $23,140 (2007); Median household income: $41,684 (2007); Average household income: $55,082 (2007); Percent of households with income of $100,000 or more: 9.9% (2007); Poverty rate: 9.5% (2000).

Education: Percent of population age 25 and over with: High school diploma (including GED) or higher: 86.6% (2007); Bachelor's degree or higher: 13.8% (2007); Master's degree or higher: 4.1% (2007).

School District(s)

Prophetstown-Lyndon-Tampico CUSD3 (PK-12)
2005-06 Enrollment: 1,071 . . . . (815) 537-5101

Housing: Homeownership rate: 77.3% (2007); Median home value: $110,227 (2007); Median rent: $307 per month (2000); Median age of housing: 52 years (2000).

Safety: Violent crime rate: 0.0 per 10,000 population; Property crime rate: 5.1 per 10,000 population (2006).

Transportation: Commute to work: 91.1% car, 0.3% public transportation, 4.7% walk, 3.3% work from home (2000); Travel time to work: 54.6% less than 15 minutes, 24.2% 15 to 30 minutes, 11.4% 30 to 45 minutes, 6.3% 45 to 60 minutes, 3.5% 60 minutes or more (2000)

Additional Information Contacts

Prophetstown Main Street . . . . (815) 537-5139
http://www.prophetstown.net

ROCK FALLS (city). Covers a land area of 3.317 square miles and a water area of 0.114 square miles. Located at 41.77° N. Lat.; 89.69° W. Long. Elevation is 646 feet.

History: Rock Falls was platted in 1837. Development came when a dam was built across the river, and later when a feeder canal connected Rock Falls and the Rock River with the Illinois & Mississippi Canal.

Population: 9,950 (1990); 9,580 (2000); 9,439 (2007); 9,272 (2012 projected); Race: 91.2% White, 1.0% Black, 0.2% Asian, 12.6% Hispanic of any race (2007); Density: 2,845.5 persons per square mile (2007); Average household size: 2.41 (2007); Median age: 37.5 (2007); Males per 100 females: 90.6 (2007); Marriage status: 22.9% never married, 53.5% now married, 8.4% widowed, 15.2% divorced (2000); Foreign born: 3.3% (2000); Ancestry (includes multiple ancestries): 27.9% German, 15.9% Other groups, 15.3% Irish, 9.0% English, 7.6% United States or American (2000).

Economy: Single-family building permits issued: 3 (2007); Multi-family building permits issued: 2 (2007); Employment by occupation: 6.0% management, 11.7% professional, 19.0% services, 22.2% sales, 0.4% farming, 7.9% construction, 33.0% production (2000).

Income: Per capita income: $19,351 (2007); Median household income: $38,833 (2007); Average household income: $46,170 (2007); Percent of households with income of $100,000 or more: 5.8% (2007); Poverty rate: 11.5% (2000).

Education: Percent of population age 25 and over with: High school diploma (including GED) or higher: 72.4% (2007); Bachelor's degree or higher: 5.9% (2007); Master's degree or higher: 2.2% (2007).

School District(s)

Bi-County Special Educ Coop
2005-06 Enrollment: n/a . . . . (815) 622-0858
East Coloma SD 12 (KG-08)
2005-06 Enrollment: 262 . . . . (815) 625-4400
Montmorency CCSD 145 (KG-08)
2005-06 Enrollment: 298 . . . . (815) 625-6616
Riverdale SD 14 (KG-08)
2005-06 Enrollment: 96 . . . . (815) 625-5280
Rock Falls ESD 13 (PK-08)
2005-06 Enrollment: 1,040 . . . . (815) 626-2604
Rock Falls Twp HSD 301 (09-12)
2005-06 Enrollment: 748 . . . . (815) 625-3886

Housing: Homeownership rate: 63.9% (2007); Median home value: $91,416 (2007); Median rent: $362 per month (2000); Median age of housing: 45 years (2000).

Safety: Violent crime rate: 49.6 per 10,000 population; Property crime rate: 303.1 per 10,000 population (2006).

Transportation: Commute to work: 92.9% car, 0.5% public transportation, 3.5% walk, 1.4% work from home (2000); Travel time to work: 60.3% less than 15 minutes, 24.2% 15 to 30 minutes, 6.2% 30 to 45 minutes, 3.7% 45 to 60 minutes, 5.6% 60 minutes or more (2000)

Additional Information Contacts

City of Rock Falls . . . . (815) 622-1100
http://www.rockfalls61071.com
Rock Falls Chamber of Commerce . . . . (815) 625-4500
http://www.rockfallschamber.com

STERLING (city). Covers a land area of 4.672 square miles and a water area of 0.188 square miles. Located at 41.79° N. Lat.; 89.69° W. Long. Elevation is 659 feet.

History: Sterling originated in 1839 from the union of Chatham and Harrisburg in the hopes that the new town would become the seat of Whiteside County. Though Sterling was chosen, it soon lost the honor to Morrison.

Population: 15,602 (1990); 15,451 (2000); 14,891 (2007); 14,478 (2012 projected); Race: 82.1% White, 2.7% Black, 1.0% Asian, 21.3% Hispanic of any race (2007); Density: 3,187.2 persons per square mile (2007); Average household size: 2.46 (2007); Median age: 37.4 (2007); Males per 100 females: 90.5 (2007); Marriage status: 24.0% never married, 54.8% now married, 8.5% widowed, 12.6% divorced (2000); Foreign born: 5.4% (2000); Ancestry (includes multiple ancestries): 25.8% German, 24.6% Other groups, 14.7% Irish, 7.7% English, 6.5% United States or American (2000).

Economy: Single-family building permits issued: 3 (2007); Multi-family building permits issued: 0 (2007); Employment by occupation: 9.7% management, 15.0% professional, 17.8% services, 22.5% sales, 0.4% farming, 8.1% construction, 26.5% production (2000).

Income: Per capita income: $20,612 (2007); Median household income: $41,020 (2007); Average household income: $49,345 (2007); Percent of households with income of $100,000 or more: 7.0% (2007); Poverty rate: 10.8% (2000).

Taxes: Total city taxes per capita: $230 (2006); City property taxes per capita: $188 (2006).

Education: Percent of population age 25 and over with: High school diploma (including GED) or higher: 78.3% (2007); Bachelor's degree or higher: 12.2% (2007); Master's degree or higher: 3.6% (2007).

School District(s)

Bi-County Special Educ Coop
2005-06 Enrollment: n/a . . . . (815) 622-0858
Sterling CUSD 5 (PK-12)
2005-06 Enrollment: 3,612 . . . . (815) 626-5050
Whiteside Area Career
2005-06 Enrollment: n/a . . . . (815) 626-5810
Whiteside Roe (07-08)
2005-06 Enrollment: 6 . . . . (815) 625-1495

Vocational/Technical School(s)

Educators of Beauty (Private, For-profit)
Fall 2007 Enrollment: 80 . . . . (815) 625-0247
2007-08 Tuition: $11,775

Housing: Homeownership rate: 62.7% (2007); Median home value: $101,633 (2007); Median rent: $391 per month (2000); Median age of housing: 47 years (2000).

Hospitals: CGH Medical Center (139 beds)

Safety: Violent crime rate: 36.4 per 10,000 population; Property crime rate: 594.2 per 10,000 population (2006).
Newspapers: Daily Gazette (Local news; Circulation 12,206); Sauk Valley Sunday (Community news; Circulation 15,000); The Telegraph (Local news; Circulation 8,972)
Transportation: Commute to work: 92.1% car, 1.7% public transportation, 2.3% walk, 2.3% work from home (2000); Travel time to work: 61.0% less than 15 minutes, 23.5% 15 to 30 minutes, 8.5% 30 to 45 minutes, 4.0% 45 to 60 minutes, 3.0% 60 minutes or more (2000)
Airports: Whiteside County-Jos H Bittorf Field (general aviation)
Additional Information Contacts
City of Sterling . . . . (815) 632-6621
http://ci.sterling.il.us/main
Sauk Valley Area Chamber of Commerce . . . . (815) 625-2400
http://www.saukvalleyareachamber.com

TAMPICO (village). Covers a land area of 0.398 square miles and a water area of 0 square miles. Located at 41.63° N. Lat.; 89.78° W. Long. Elevation is 640 feet.
History: Birthplace of Ronald Reagan.
Population: 815 (1990); 772 (2000); 688 (2007); 680 (2012 projected); Race: 100.0% White, 0.0% Black, 0.0% Asian, 2.0% Hispanic of any race (2007); Density: 1,730.0 persons per square mile (2007); Average household size: 2.58 (2007); Median age: 36.7 (2007); Males per 100 females: 101.2 (2007); Marriage status: 18.7% never married, 63.9% now married, 8.7% widowed, 8.7% divorced (2000); Foreign born: 0.8% (2000); Ancestry (includes multiple ancestries): 34.9% German, 14.9% Irish, 12.8% English, 10.4% United States or American, 6.5% Belgian (2000).
Economy: Single-family building permits issued: 0 (2007); Multi-family building permits issued: 0 (2007); Employment by occupation: 6.6% management, 8.3% professional, 19.3% services, 19.8% sales, 1.4% farming, 12.1% construction, 32.5% production (2000).
Income: Per capita income: $18,906 (2007); Median household income: $46,447 (2007); Average household income: $48,717 (2007); Percent of households with income of $100,000 or more: 6.7% (2007); Poverty rate: 8.5% (2000).
Education: Percent of population age 25 and over with: High school diploma (including GED) or higher: 79.8% (2007); Bachelor's degree or higher: 9.0% (2007); Master's degree or higher: 0.9% (2007).

School District(s)

Prophetstown-Lyndon-Tampico CUSD3 (PK-12)
2005-06 Enrollment: 1,071 . . . . (815) 537-5101
Housing: Homeownership rate: 78.7% (2007); Median home value: $101,953 (2007); Median rent: $317 per month (2000); Median age of housing: 60+ years (2000).
Safety: Violent crime rate: 80.5 per 10,000 population; Property crime rate: 40.3 per 10,000 population (2006).
Transportation: Commute to work: 92.7% car, 0.0% public transportation, 3.7% walk, 2.8% work from home (2000); Travel time to work: 19.8% less than 15 minutes, 39.8% 15 to 30 minutes, 26.5% 30 to 45 minutes, 7.8% 45 to 60 minutes, 6.1% 60 minutes or more (2000)

Will County

Located in northeastern Illinois; bounded on the east by Indiana; drained by the Des Plaines, Du Page, and Kankakee Rivers. Covers a land area of 836.94 square miles, a water area of 12.45 square miles, and is located in the Central Time Zone. The county was founded in 1836. County seat is Joliet.

Will County is part of the Chicago-Naperville-Joliet, IL-IN-WI Metropolitan Statistical Area. The entire metro area includes: Chicago-Naperville-Joliet, IL Metropolitan Division (Cook County, IL; DeKalb County, IL; DuPage County, IL; Grundy County, IL; Kane County, IL; Kendall County, IL; McHenry County, IL; Will County, IL); Gary, IN Metropolitan Division (Jasper County, IN; Lake County, IN; Newton County, IN; Porter County, IN); Lake County-Kenosha County, IL-WI Metropolitan Division (Lake County, IL; Kenosha County, WI)

Weather Station: Marion 4 NNE Elevation: 475 feet

	Jan	Feb	Mar	Apr	May	Jun	Jul	Aug	Sep	Oct	Nov	Dec
High	38	44	55	66	75	83	87	86	79	68	55	43
Low	20	24	34	43	53	62	66	64	56	44	35	25
Precip	3.0	3.0	4.6	4.7	5.0	4.1	3.8	3.8	3.3	3.1	4.9	3.7
Snow	5.9	5.4	2.5	0.5	0.0	0.0	0.0	0.0	0.0	0.2	0.8	2.9

High and Low temperatures in degrees Fahrenheit; Precipitation and Snow in inches

Population: 357,313 (1990); 502,266 (2000); 681,781 (2007); 804,842 (2012 projected); Race: 77.6% White, 10.5% Black, 3.6% Asian, 13.7% Hispanic of any race (2007); Density: 814.6 persons per square mile (2007); Average household size: 2.96 (2007); Median age: 33.4 (2007); Males per 100 females: 99.5 (2007).
Religion: Five largest groups: 38.9% Catholic Church, 2.3% Evangelical Lutheran Church in America, 2.0% The United Methodist Church, 1.9% Lutheran Church—Missouri Synod, 1.3% United Church of Christ (2000).
Economy: Unemployment rate: 5.5% (4/2008); Total civilian labor force: 367,867 (4/2008); Leading industries: 14.1% retail trade; 12.0% manufacturing; 11.5% construction (2005); Farms: 830 totaling 265,490 acres (2002); Companies that employ 500 or more persons: 25 (2006); Companies that employ 100 to 499 persons: 267 (2006); Companies that employ less than 100 persons: 12,906 (2006); Black-owned businesses: 2,169 (2002); Hispanic-owned businesses: 1,325 (2002); Asian-owned businesses: 1,083 (2002); Women-owned businesses: 11,204 (2002); Retail sales per capita: $11,252 (2008). Single-family building permits issued: 2,782 (2007); Multi-family building permits issued: 53 (2007).
Income: Per capita income: $28,896 (2007); Median household income: $71,383 (2007); Average household income: $84,997 (2007); Percent of households with income of $100,000 or more: 29.1% (2007); Poverty rate: 5.4% (2005); Bankruptcy rate: 3.36% (2007).
Taxes: Total county taxes per capita: $155 (2006); County property taxes per capita: $150 (2006).
Education: Percent of population age 25 and over with: High school diploma (including GED) or higher: 87.5% (2007); Bachelor's degree or higher: 25.9% (2007); Master's degree or higher: 7.7% (2007).
Housing: Homeownership rate: 83.8% (2007); Median home value: $227,998 (2007); Median rent: $554 per month (2000); Median age of housing: 23 years (2000).
Health: Birth rate: 171.2 per 10,000 population (2007); Death rate: 53.6 per 10,000 population (2007); Age-adjusted cancer mortality rate: 197.0 deaths per 100,000 population (2005); Air Quality Index: 87.1% good, 12.6% moderate, 0.3% unhealthy for sensitive individuals, 0.0% unhealthy (percent of days in 2007); Number of physicians: 11.4 per 10,000 population (2005); Hospital beds: 11.7 per 10,000 population (2004); Hospital admissions: 627.4 per 10,000 population (2004).
Elections: 2004 Presidential election results: 52.4% Bush, 46.9% Kerry, 0.1% Nader, 0.6% Badnarik
National and State Parks: Channahon Parkway State Park; Des Plaines State Conservation Area; Kankakee River State Park; Midewin National Tallgrass Prairie
Additional Information Contacts
Will County Government . . . . (815) 740-4602
http://www.willcountyillinois.com
Bolingbrook Area Chamber of Commerce . . . . (630) 226-8420
http://www.bolingbrookchamber.org
City of Braidwood . . . . (815) 458-2333
http://www.braidwood.us
City of Crest Hill . . . . (815) 741-5100
http://www.cityofcresthill.com
City of Joliet . . . . (815) 724-3780
http://www.ci.joliet.il.us
City of Lockport . . . . (815) 838-0549
http://www.lockport.org
City of Wilmington . . . . (815) 476-2175
http://www.wilmington-il.com
Crete Chamber of Commerce . . . . (708) 672-9216
http://www.cretechamber.com
Frankfort Chamber of Commerce . . . . (815) 469-3356
http://www.frankfortchamber.com
Homer Township Chamber of Commerce . . . . (708) 301-8111
http://www.homerchamber.com
Joliet Region Chamber of Commerce & Industry . . . . (815) 727-5371
http://www.jolietchamber.com
Lockport Chamber of Commerce . . . . (815) 838-3357
http://www.lockportchamber.com
Manhattan Chamber of Commerce . . . . (815) 478-3811
http://www.manhattan-il.com
Mokena Chamber of Commerce . . . . (708) 479-2468
http://www.mokena.com
Monee Chamber of Commerce . . . . (708) 534-5332
http://www.moneechamber.com
New Lenox Chamber of Commerce . . . . (815) 485-4241
http://www.newlenoxchamber.com

Peotone Chamber of Commerce . . . . (708) 258-9450
http://www.peotonechamber.com
Plainfield Area Chamber of Commerce . . . . (815) 436-4431
http://www.plainfieldchamber.com
Romeoville Chamber of Commerce. . . . . (815) 886-2076
http://www.romeovillechamber.org
Shorewood Area Chamber of Commerce . . . . (815) 725-2900
http://www.shorewoodchamber.com
Village of Bolingbrook . . . . (630) 226-8400
http://www.bolingbrook.com
Village of Channahon. . . . . (815) 467-6644
http://www.channahon.org
Village of Crete . . . . (708) 672-5431
http://www.villageofcrete.org
Village of Frankfort. . . . . (815) 469-2177
http://www.villageoffrankfort.com
Village of Mokena . . . . (708) 479-3900
http://www.mokena.org
Village of New Lenox . . . . (815) 485-6431
http://www.newlenox.net
Village of Plainfield. . . . . (815) 436-7093
http://www.plainfield-il.org
Village of Romeoville . . . . (815) 866-7200
http://www.romeoville.org
Village of Shorewood . . . . (815) 725-2150
http://www.vil.shorewood.il.us
Village of Steger. . . . . (708) 754-3395
http://www.villageofsteger.com
Village of University Park . . . . (708) 534-6451
http://www.university-park-il.com
Will County Center for Economic Development. . . . . (815) 723-1800
http://www.c-e-d.org
Wilmington Chamber of Commerce. . . . . (815) 476-5991
http://www.wilmingtonchamberofcommerce.org

Will County Communities

BEECHER (village). Covers a land area of 2.108 square miles and a water area of 0 square miles. Located at 41.34° N. Lat.; 87.62° W. Long. Elevation is 735 feet.

History: Beecher was platted in 1870 when the Chicago & Eastern Illinois Railway was being built here. The village was named for Henry Ward Beecher.

Population: 2,105 (1990); 2,033 (2000); 2,247 (2007); 2,417 (2012 projected); Race: 96.5% White, 0.0% Black, 0.9% Asian, 3.3% Hispanic of any race (2007); Density: 1,065.9 persons per square mile (2007); Average household size: 2.37 (2007); Median age: 42.2 (2007); Males per 100 females: 90.9 (2007); Marriage status: 21.7% never married, 62.4% now married, 8.7% widowed, 7.2% divorced (2000); Foreign born: 2.5% (2000); Ancestry (includes multiple ancestries): 44.2% German, 12.7% Irish, 10.1% Polish, 8.6% Italian, 7.9% English (2000).

Economy: Single-family building permits issued: 29 (2007); Multi-family building permits issued: 0 (2007); Employment by occupation: 16.3% management, 11.6% professional, 12.9% services, 30.8% sales, 0.3% farming, 12.3% construction, 15.8% production (2000).

Income: Per capita income: $23,845 (2007); Median household income: $51,023 (2007); Average household income: $56,519 (2007); Percent of households with income of $100,000 or more: 11.8% (2007); Poverty rate: 4.0% (2000).

Education: Percent of population age 25 and over with: High school diploma (including GED) or higher: 86.7% (2007); Bachelor's degree or higher: 16.2% (2007); Master's degree or higher: 5.5% (2007).

School District(s)

Beecher CUSD 200u (KG-12)
2005-06 Enrollment: 1,008 . . . . (708) 946-2266

Housing: Homeownership rate: 78.3% (2007); Median home value: $215,927 (2007); Median rent: $489 per month (2000); Median age of housing: 39 years (2000).

Safety: Violent crime rate: 10.8 per 10,000 population; Property crime rate: 205.9 per 10,000 population (2006).

Transportation: Commute to work: 92.5% car, 1.3% public transportation, 3.5% walk, 2.4% work from home (2000); Travel time to work: 29.1% less than 15 minutes, 28.8% 15 to 30 minutes, 22.5% 30 to 45 minutes, 9.3% 45 to 60 minutes, 10.3% 60 minutes or more (2000)

BOLINGBROOK (village). Covers a land area of 20.506 square miles and a water area of 0.237 square miles. Located at 41.69° N. Lat.; 88.08° W. Long. Elevation is 702 feet.

Population: 41,386 (1990); 56,321 (2000); 70,689 (2007); 80,794 (2012 projected); Race: 54.0% White, 22.8% Black, 9.2% Asian, 21.8% Hispanic of any race (2007); Density: 3,447.2 persons per square mile (2007); Average household size: 3.21 (2007); Median age: 32.0 (2007); Males per 100 females: 99.8 (2007); Marriage status: 25.8% never married, 62.9% now married, 3.7% widowed, 7.6% divorced (2000); Foreign born: 14.4% (2000); Ancestry (includes multiple ancestries): 38.0% Other groups, 19.6% German, 12.8% Irish, 9.8% Polish, 7.7% Italian (2000).

Economy: Unemployment rate: 4.9% (4/2008); Total civilian labor force: 40,427 (4/2008); Single-family building permits issued: 125 (2007); Multi-family building permits issued: 0 (2007); Employment by occupation: 15.8% management, 21.0% professional, 11.5% services, 28.8% sales, 0.1% farming, 9.2% construction, 13.7% production (2000).

Income: Per capita income: $27,639 (2007); Median household income: $78,877 (2007); Average household income: $88,486 (2007); Percent of households with income of $100,000 or more: 33.0% (2007); Poverty rate: 4.1% (2000).

Taxes: Total city taxes per capita: $435 (2006); City property taxes per capita: $233 (2006).

Education: Percent of population age 25 and over with: High school diploma (including GED) or higher: 87.9% (2007); Bachelor's degree or higher: 30.4% (2007); Master's degree or higher: 7.6% (2007).

School District(s)

Indian Prairie CUSD 204 (PK-12)
2005-06 Enrollment: 28,510 . . . . (630) 375-3000
Plainfield SD 202 (PK-12)
2005-06 Enrollment: 24,371 . . . . (815) 577-4000
Valley View CUSD 365u (PK-12)
2005-06 Enrollment: 17,510 . . . . (815) 886-2700
Will Roe (07-12)
2005-06 Enrollment: 274 . . . . (815) 740-8360

Housing: Homeownership rate: 87.1% (2007); Median home value: $212,639 (2007); Median rent: $712 per month (2000); Median age of housing: 22 years (2000).

Safety: Violent crime rate: 34.2 per 10,000 population; Property crime rate: 177.4 per 10,000 population (2006).

Newspapers: Chicago China News Digest (Circulation 10,000)

Transportation: Commute to work: 91.3% car, 4.1% public transportation, 1.0% walk, 3.0% work from home (2000); Travel time to work: 19.5% less than 15 minutes, 28.4% 15 to 30 minutes, 24.6% 30 to 45 minutes, 12.5% 45 to 60 minutes, 15.0% 60 minutes or more (2000)

Airports: Bolingbrook's Clow International (general aviation)

Additional Information Contacts

Bolingbrook Area Chamber of Commerce . . . . (630) 226-8420
http://www.bolingbrookchamber.org
Village of Bolingbrook . . . . (630) 226-8400
http://www.bolingbrook.com

BRAIDWOOD (city). Covers a land area of 4.629 square miles and a water area of 0.126 square miles. Located at 41.27° N. Lat.; 88.21° W. Long. Elevation is 574 feet.

History: Braidwood was a crowded coal-mining town in the 1880's, with many mining syndicates operating. The first coal vein was discovered in 1865 by settler William Henneberry. By 1873 Braidwood was incorporated as a city.

Population: 3,658 (1990); 5,203 (2000); 6,789 (2007); 7,888 (2012 projected); Race: 96.0% White, 0.4% Black, 0.6% Asian, 5.2% Hispanic of any race (2007); Density: 1,466.6 persons per square mile (2007); Average household size: 2.77 (2007); Median age: 33.8 (2007); Males per 100 females: 101.8 (2007); Marriage status: 23.1% never married, 60.3% now married, 5.3% widowed, 11.3% divorced (2000); Foreign born: 1.5% (2000); Ancestry (includes multiple ancestries): 27.4% German, 14.9% Irish, 14.7% Italian, 9.8% Other groups, 8.9% Polish (2000).

Economy: Single-family building permits issued: 35 (2007); Multi-family building permits issued: 0 (2007); Employment by occupation: 8.8% management, 12.0% professional, 17.3% services, 19.1% sales, 0.0% farming, 18.2% construction, 24.5% production (2000).

Income: Per capita income: $25,899 (2007); Median household income: $62,834 (2007); Average household income: $71,574 (2007); Percent of households with income of $100,000 or more: 22.0% (2007); Poverty rate: 5.5% (2000).

Education: Percent of population age 25 and over with: High school diploma (including GED) or higher: 84.8% (2007); Bachelor's degree or higher: 8.9% (2007); Master's degree or higher: 2.1% (2007).

School District(s)

Reed Custer CUSD 255u (PK-12)
2005-06 Enrollment: 1,891 . . . . (815) 458-2307

Housing: Homeownership rate: 85.0% (2007); Median home value: $168,352 (2007); Median rent: $474 per month (2000); Median age of housing: 18 years (2000).

Safety: Violent crime rate: 11.1 per 10,000 population; Property crime rate: 344.9 per 10,000 population (2006).

Transportation: Commute to work: 97.1% car, 0.3% public transportation, 0.8% walk, 1.3% work from home (2000); Travel time to work: 29.1% less than 15 minutes, 24.9% 15 to 30 minutes, 24.6% 30 to 45 minutes, 6.9% 45 to 60 minutes, 14.4% 60 minutes or more (2000)

Additional Information Contacts

City of Braidwood. . . . . (815) 458-2333
http://www.braidwood.us

CHANNAHON (village). Covers a land area of 7.207 square miles and a water area of 0.669 square miles. Located at 41.43° N. Lat.; 88.21° W. Long. Elevation is 528 feet.

History: Channahon was settled in 1832 and developed when the Illinois & Michigan Canal was built. Early industries included grain shipping, quarrying, and the manufacture of farm equipment.

Population: 5,088 (1990); 7,344 (2000); 12,460 (2007); 15,844 (2012 projected); Race: 95.5% White, 0.4% Black, 0.5% Asian, 6.3% Hispanic of any race (2007); Density: 1,728.8 persons per square mile (2007); Average household size: 3.20 (2007); Median age: 33.1 (2007); Males per 100 females: 104.3 (2007); Marriage status: 19.3% never married, 73.0% now married, 2.5% widowed, 5.2% divorced (2000); Foreign born: 1.3% (2000); Ancestry (includes multiple ancestries): 29.2% German, 21.2% Irish, 14.0% Italian, 8.4% Polish, 7.3% English (2000).

Economy: Single-family building permits issued: 52 (2007); Multi-family building permits issued: 15 (2007); Employment by occupation: 11.7% management, 18.4% professional, 12.6% services, 25.0% sales, 0.2% farming, 14.1% construction, 17.9% production (2000).

Income: Per capita income: $27,804 (2007); Median household income: $82,382 (2007); Average household income: $88,900 (2007); Percent of households with income of $100,000 or more: 32.3% (2007); Poverty rate: 1.7% (2000).

Education: Percent of population age 25 and over with: High school diploma (including GED) or higher: 94.0% (2007); Bachelor's degree or higher: 18.6% (2007); Master's degree or higher: 3.9% (2007).

School District(s)

Channahon SD 17 (PK-08)
2005-06 Enrollment: 1,621 . . . . (815) 467-4315

Housing: Homeownership rate: 92.6% (2007); Median home value: $240,533 (2007); Median rent: $663 per month (2000); Median age of housing: 14 years (2000).

Safety: Violent crime rate: 15.6 per 10,000 population; Property crime rate: 117.0 per 10,000 population (2006).

Transportation: Commute to work: 96.6% car, 0.5% public transportation, 0.5% walk, 2.4% work from home (2000); Travel time to work: 21.0% less than 15 minutes, 40.5% 15 to 30 minutes, 16.2% 30 to 45 minutes, 11.3% 45 to 60 minutes, 11.0% 60 minutes or more (2000)

Additional Information Contacts

Village of Channahon. . . . . (815) 467-6644
http://www.channahon.org

CREST HILL (city). Covers a land area of 7.161 square miles and a water area of 0.106 square miles. Located at 41.56° N. Lat.; 88.10° W. Long. Elevation is 643 feet.

Population: 10,628 (1990); 13,329 (2000); 18,869 (2007); 22,417 (2012 projected); Race: 73.2% White, 16.5% Black, 2.1% Asian, 14.4% Hispanic of any race (2007); Density: 2,634.8 persons per square mile (2007); Average household size: 2.70 (2007); Median age: 33.2 (2007); Males per 100 females: 131.0 (2007); Marriage status: 22.8% never married, 55.5% now married, 6.0% widowed, 15.7% divorced (2000); Foreign born: 4.4% (2000); Ancestry (includes multiple ancestries): 21.1% German, 13.9% Other groups, 12.3% Irish, 9.3% Polish, 9.1% Italian (2000).

Economy: Single-family building permits issued: 19 (2007); Multi-family building permits issued: 0 (2007); Employment by occupation: 10.3% management, 17.7% professional, 17.5% services, 29.7% sales, 0.0% farming, 11.4% construction, 13.4% production (2000).

Income: Per capita income: $25,428 (2007); Median household income: $50,213 (2007); Average household income: $61,683 (2007); Percent of households with income of $100,000 or more: 11.6% (2007); Poverty rate: 4.8% (2000).

Taxes: Total city taxes per capita: $181 (2006); City property taxes per capita: $63 (2006).

Education: Percent of population age 25 and over with: High school diploma (including GED) or higher: 76.5% (2007); Bachelor's degree or higher: 12.6% (2007); Master's degree or higher: 2.8% (2007).

School District(s)

Chaney-Monge SD 88 (PK-08)
2005-06 Enrollment: 460 . . . . (815) 722-6673
Richland GSD 88a (PK-08)
2005-06 Enrollment: 779 . . . . (815) 744-7288

Housing: Homeownership rate: 65.2% (2007); Median home value: $159,013 (2007); Median rent: $593 per month (2000); Median age of housing: 27 years (2000).

Safety: Violent crime rate: 15.9 per 10,000 population; Property crime rate: 283.0 per 10,000 population (2006).

Transportation: Commute to work: 96.8% car, 0.9% public transportation, 1.4% walk, 0.8% work from home (2000); Travel time to work: 29.0% less than 15 minutes, 32.9% 15 to 30 minutes, 17.2% 30 to 45 minutes, 12.0% 45 to 60 minutes, 8.8% 60 minutes or more (2000)

Additional Information Contacts

City of Crest Hill . . . . (815) 741-5100
http://www.cityofcresthill.com

CRETE (village). Covers a land area of 6.378 square miles and a water area of 0.025 square miles. Located at 41.45° N. Lat.; 87.61° W. Long. Elevation is 728 feet.

History: Crete was laid out in 1849 by William Wood, operator of a tavern for travelers on the Chicago-Vincennes Road.

Population: 6,952 (1990); 7,346 (2000); 8,390 (2007); 9,197 (2012 projected); Race: 81.5% White, 14.0% Black, 1.0% Asian, 5.7% Hispanic of any race (2007); Density: 1,315.5 persons per square mile (2007); Average household size: 2.66 (2007); Median age: 40.7 (2007); Males per 100 females: 96.6 (2007); Marriage status: 19.6% never married, 67.2% now married, 6.0% widowed, 7.2% divorced (2000); Foreign born: 1.6% (2000); Ancestry (includes multiple ancestries): 36.7% German, 16.6% Irish, 12.8% Other groups, 10.2% Polish, 9.9% English (2000).

Economy: Single-family building permits issued: 13 (2007); Multi-family building permits issued: 0 (2007); Employment by occupation: 16.9% management, 20.5% professional, 12.3% services, 26.5% sales, 0.1% farming, 11.8% construction, 11.9% production (2000).

Income: Per capita income: $34,470 (2007); Median household income: $76,114 (2007); Average household income: $91,013 (2007); Percent of households with income of $100,000 or more: 33.0% (2007); Poverty rate: 1.6% (2000).

Education: Percent of population age 25 and over with: High school diploma (including GED) or higher: 93.5% (2007); Bachelor's degree or higher: 28.5% (2007); Master's degree or higher: 9.6% (2007).

School District(s)

Crete Monee CUSD 201u (PK-12)
2005-06 Enrollment: 4,774 . . . . (708) 367-8300
Will Roe (07-12)
2005-06 Enrollment: 274 . . . . (815) 740-8360

Housing: Homeownership rate: 88.9% (2007); Median home value: $222,682 (2007); Median rent: $573 per month (2000); Median age of housing: 26 years (2000).

Safety: Violent crime rate: 23.9 per 10,000 population; Property crime rate: 232.6 per 10,000 population (2006).

Transportation: Commute to work: 92.5% car, 3.4% public transportation, 0.2% walk, 3.9% work from home (2000); Travel time to work: 23.4% less than 15 minutes, 33.3% 15 to 30 minutes, 18.6% 30 to 45 minutes, 8.2% 45 to 60 minutes, 16.5% 60 minutes or more (2000)

Additional Information Contacts

Crete Chamber of Commerce . . . . (708) 672-9216
http://www.cretechamber.com
Village of Crete . . . . (708) 672-5431
http://www.villageofcrete.org

CRYSTAL LAWNS (CDP). Covers a land area of 0.993 square miles and a water area of 0 square miles. Located at 41.57° N. Lat.; 88.15° W. Long. Elevation is 604 feet.

Population: 2,925 (1990); 2,933 (2000); 3,864 (2007); 4,527 (2012 projected); Race: 92.1% White, 1.1% Black, 0.9% Asian, 9.5% Hispanic of any race (2007); Density: 3,892.3 persons per square mile (2007); Average household size: 2.91 (2007); Median age: 35.4 (2007); Males per 100 females: 103.3 (2007); Marriage status: 22.8% never married, 61.7% now married, 5.1% widowed, 10.4% divorced (2000); Foreign born: 2.9% (2000); Ancestry (includes multiple ancestries): 28.1% German, 13.9% Irish, 12.6% English, 8.7% Other groups, 8.1% Polish (2000).
Economy: Employment by occupation: 10.5% management, 21.4% professional, 12.8% services, 27.2% sales, 0.0% farming, 16.8% construction, 11.4% production (2000).
Income: Per capita income: $23,247 (2007); Median household income: $61,796 (2007); Average household income: $67,641 (2007); Percent of households with income of $100,000 or more: 18.6% (2007); Poverty rate: 6.2% (2000).
Education: Percent of population age 25 and over with: High school diploma (including GED) or higher: 88.8% (2007); Bachelor's degree or higher: 15.7% (2007); Master's degree or higher: 5.5% (2007).
Housing: Homeownership rate: 92.4% (2007); Median home value: $174,954 (2007); Median rent: $911 per month (2000); Median age of housing: 36 years (2000).
Transportation: Commute to work: 94.7% car, 3.2% public transportation, 0.0% walk, 1.0% work from home (2000); Travel time to work: 24.3% less than 15 minutes, 34.3% 15 to 30 minutes, 18.1% 30 to 45 minutes, 12.2% 45 to 60 minutes, 11.0% 60 minutes or more (2000)

ELWOOD (village). Covers a land area of 2.711 square miles and a water area of 0 square miles. Located at 41.41° N. Lat.; 88.11° W. Long. Elevation is 646 feet.
Population: 1,022 (1990); 1,620 (2000); 2,653 (2007); 3,347 (2012 projected); Race: 96.3% White, 0.0% Black, 0.6% Asian, 6.7% Hispanic of any race (2007); Density: 978.6 persons per square mile (2007); Average household size: 2.51 (2007); Median age: 35.5 (2007); Males per 100 females: 92.9 (2007); Marriage status: 18.1% never married, 63.9% now married, 9.1% widowed, 9.0% divorced (2000); Foreign born: 2.0% (2000); Ancestry (includes multiple ancestries): 31.2% German, 19.7% Irish, 13.6% Italian, 9.7% Other groups, 9.4% Polish (2000).
Economy: Single-family building permits issued: 6 (2007); Multi-family building permits issued: 0 (2007); Employment by occupation: 8.3% management, 13.4% professional, 12.6% services, 27.9% sales, 0.3% farming, 18.3% construction, 19.2% production (2000).
Income: Per capita income: $26,825 (2007); Median household income: $61,521 (2007); Average household income: $67,203 (2007); Percent of households with income of $100,000 or more: 18.8% (2007); Poverty rate: 4.6% (2000).
Taxes: Total city taxes per capita: $2,213 (2006); City property taxes per capita: $1,777 (2006).
Education: Percent of population age 25 and over with: High school diploma (including GED) or higher: 88.6% (2007); Bachelor's degree or higher: 10.6% (2007); Master's degree or higher: 2.6% (2007).

School District(s)

Elwood CCSD 203 (KG-08)
2005-06 Enrollment: 438 . . . . (815) 423-5588

Housing: Homeownership rate: 83.2% (2007); Median home value: $187,031 (2007); Median rent: $391 per month (2000); Median age of housing: 9 years (2000).
Safety: Violent crime rate: 26.8 per 10,000 population; Property crime rate: 165.4 per 10,000 population (2006).
Transportation: Commute to work: 95.5% car, 0.7% public transportation, 0.7% walk, 2.4% work from home (2000); Travel time to work: 10.9% less than 15 minutes, 47.0% 15 to 30 minutes, 19.3% 30 to 45 minutes, 10.7% 45 to 60 minutes, 12.0% 60 minutes or more (2000)

FAIRMONT (CDP). Covers a land area of 1.648 square miles and a water area of 0 square miles. Located at 41.56° N. Lat.; 88.06° W. Long. Elevation is 633 feet.
Population: 2,774 (1990); 2,563 (2000); 2,962 (2007); 3,244 (2012 projected); Race: 34.3% White, 49.6% Black, 0.6% Asian, 17.3% Hispanic of any race (2007); Density: 1,797.8 persons per square mile (2007); Average household size: 2.94 (2007); Median age: 33.1 (2007); Males per 100 females: 102.6 (2007); Marriage status: 35.4% never married, 45.1% now married, 9.0% widowed, 10.5% divorced (2000); Foreign born: 4.7% (2000); Ancestry (includes multiple ancestries): 56.9% Other groups, 10.1% Irish, 9.5% German, 4.2% English, 2.6% Polish (2000).
Economy: Employment by occupation: 8.6% management, 8.6% professional, 19.9% services, 33.0% sales, 0.0% farming, 6.8% construction, 23.1% production (2000).
Income: Per capita income: $19,391 (2007); Median household income: $45,580 (2007); Average household income: $56,675 (2007); Percent of households with income of $100,000 or more: 15.5% (2007); Poverty rate: 14.0% (2000).
Education: Percent of population age 25 and over with: High school diploma (including GED) or higher: 73.2% (2007); Bachelor's degree or higher: 4.7% (2007); Master's degree or higher: 1.8% (2007).
Housing: Homeownership rate: 74.8% (2007); Median home value: $119,355 (2007); Median rent: $460 per month (2000); Median age of housing: 45 years (2000).
Transportation: Commute to work: 93.4% car, 2.6% public transportation, 0.5% walk, 0.4% work from home (2000); Travel time to work: 17.3% less than 15 minutes, 43.3% 15 to 30 minutes, 20.3% 30 to 45 minutes, 12.3% 45 to 60 minutes, 6.8% 60 minutes or more (2000)

FRANKFORT (village). Covers a land area of 10.907 square miles and a water area of 0 square miles. Located at 41.49° N. Lat.; 87.85° W. Long. Elevation is 761 feet.
Population: 7,827 (1990); 10,391 (2000); 15,709 (2007); 19,248 (2012 projected); Race: 90.5% White, 3.6% Black, 3.3% Asian, 4.1% Hispanic of any race (2007); Density: 1,440.3 persons per square mile (2007); Average household size: 2.98 (2007); Median age: 39.4 (2007); Males per 100 females: 94.7 (2007); Marriage status: 18.7% never married, 72.2% now married, 3.9% widowed, 5.1% divorced (2000); Foreign born: 4.3% (2000); Ancestry (includes multiple ancestries): 26.5% German, 21.8% Irish, 14.2% Polish, 12.7% Italian, 7.8% English (2000).
Economy: Single-family building permits issued: 189 (2007); Multi-family building permits issued: 0 (2007); Employment by occupation: 21.6% management, 27.2% professional, 7.0% services, 27.2% sales, 0.0% farming, 8.2% construction, 8.8% production (2000).
Income: Per capita income: $40,542 (2007); Median household income: $97,516 (2007); Average household income: $120,336 (2007); Percent of households with income of $100,000 or more: 48.2% (2007); Poverty rate: 2.3% (2000).
Education: Percent of population age 25 and over with: High school diploma (including GED) or higher: 95.0% (2007); Bachelor's degree or higher: 41.4% (2007); Master's degree or higher: 16.6% (2007).

School District(s)

Frankfort CCSD 157c (PK-08)
2005-06 Enrollment: 2,247 . . . . (815) 469-5922
Lincoln Way CHSD 210 (09-12)
2005-06 Enrollment: 6,632 . . . . (815) 462-2100
Peotone CUSD 207u (PK-12)
2005-06 Enrollment: 1,999 . . . . (708) 258-0991
Summit Hill SD 161 (PK-08)
2005-06 Enrollment: 3,583 . . . . (815) 469-9103

Housing: Homeownership rate: 92.3% (2007); Median home value: $368,178 (2007); Median rent: $638 per month (2000); Median age of housing: 16 years (2000).
Safety: Violent crime rate: 11.4 per 10,000 population; Property crime rate: 209.9 per 10,000 population (2006).
Transportation: Commute to work: 86.3% car, 6.9% public transportation, 1.2% walk, 5.2% work from home (2000); Travel time to work: 23.9% less than 15 minutes, 26.8% 15 to 30 minutes, 21.6% 30 to 45 minutes, 10.3% 45 to 60 minutes, 17.3% 60 minutes or more (2000)

Additional Information Contacts

Frankfort Chamber of Commerce . . . . (815) 469-3356
http://www.frankfortchamber.com
Village of Frankfort. . . . . (815) 469-2177
http://www.villageoffrankfort.com

FRANKFORT SQUARE (CDP). Covers a land area of 2.096 square miles and a water area of 0 square miles. Located at 41.51° N. Lat.; 87.80° W. Long. Elevation is 709 feet.
Population: 6,317 (1990); 7,766 (2000); 9,279 (2007); 10,349 (2012 projected); Race: 92.6% White, 1.3% Black, 2.3% Asian, 6.8% Hispanic of any race (2007); Density: 4,427.3 persons per square mile (2007); Average household size: 3.26 (2007); Median age: 30.5 (2007); Males per 100 females: 97.2 (2007); Marriage status: 23.6% never married, 64.4% now married, 2.3% widowed, 9.7% divorced (2000); Foreign born: 3.3% (2000); Ancestry (includes multiple ancestries): 27.8% Irish, 27.6% German, 20.7% Polish, 11.0% Italian, 9.4% Other groups (2000).

Economy: Employment by occupation: 14.1% management, 17.5% professional, 9.1% services, 31.1% sales, 0.0% farming, 13.0% construction, 15.2% production (2000).
Income: Per capita income: $26,307 (2007); Median household income: $82,417 (2007); Average household income: $85,832 (2007); Percent of households with income of $100,000 or more: 32.9% (2007); Poverty rate: 2.4% (2000).
Education: Percent of population age 25 and over with: High school diploma (including GED) or higher: 94.2% (2007); Bachelor's degree or higher: 22.2% (2007); Master's degree or higher: 4.9% (2007).
Housing: Homeownership rate: 95.6% (2007); Median home value: $231,599 (2007); Median rent: $726 per month (2000); Median age of housing: 20 years (2000).
Transportation: Commute to work: 85.3% car, 10.9% public transportation, 0.5% walk, 2.5% work from home (2000); Travel time to work: 20.7% less than 15 minutes, 27.5% 15 to 30 minutes, 19.1% 30 to 45 minutes, 9.1% 45 to 60 minutes, 23.6% 60 minutes or more (2000)

GODLEY (village). Covers a land area of 1.086 square miles and a water area of 0 square miles. Located at 41.23° N. Lat.; 88.24° W. Long. Elevation is 587 feet.
History: Godley began as a coal town settled by Scotch, Irish, and Welsh miners in the 1880's. The population declined when the mines closed in the early 1900's.
Population: 322 (1990); 594 (2000); 826 (2007); 985 (2012 projected); Race: 93.1% White, 0.4% Black, 0.0% Asian, 11.1% Hispanic of any race (2007); Density: 760.6 persons per square mile (2007); Average household size: 2.92 (2007); Median age: 28.4 (2007); Males per 100 females: 99.0 (2007); Marriage status: 18.6% never married, 63.6% now married, 4.1% widowed, 13.7% divorced (2000); Foreign born: 1.9% (2000); Ancestry (includes multiple ancestries): 22.3% Other groups, 16.4% German, 15.9% Irish, 11.3% English, 8.9% Italian (2000).
Economy: Single-family building permits issued: 0 (2007); Multi-family building permits issued: 0 (2007); Employment by occupation: 6.5% management, 7.8% professional, 21.2% services, 19.0% sales, 0.0% farming, 20.3% construction, 25.1% production (2000).
Income: Per capita income: $19,110 (2007); Median household income: $49,688 (2007); Average household income: $55,777 (2007); Percent of households with income of $100,000 or more: 11.0% (2007); Poverty rate: 14.2% (2000).
Education: Percent of population age 25 and over with: High school diploma (including GED) or higher: 78.5% (2007); Bachelor's degree or higher: 3.7% (2007); Master's degree or higher: 1.5% (2007).
Housing: Homeownership rate: 77.7% (2007); Median home value: $123,276 (2007); Median rent: $475 per month (2000); Median age of housing: 12 years (2000).
Transportation: Commute to work: 91.5% car, 0.4% public transportation, 0.4% walk, 0.4% work from home (2000); Travel time to work: 28.7% less than 15 minutes, 28.3% 15 to 30 minutes, 17.0% 30 to 45 minutes, 11.2% 45 to 60 minutes, 14.8% 60 minutes or more (2000)

GOODINGS GROVE (CDP). Aka Now known as Homer Glen (incorp. April 7, 2001). Covers a land area of 9.420 square miles and a water area of 0.009 square miles. Located at 41.62° N. Lat.; 87.94° W. Long. Elevation is 758 feet.
Population: 14,054 (1990); 17,084 (2000); 18,583 (2007); 19,798 (2012 projected); Race: 94.8% White, 0.4% Black, 2.4% Asian, 5.7% Hispanic of any race (2007); Density: 1,972.7 persons per square mile (2007); Average household size: 3.29 (2007); Median age: 34.9 (2007); Males per 100 females: 99.8 (2007); Marriage status: 23.3% never married, 69.7% now married, 3.2% widowed, 3.8% divorced (2000); Foreign born: 8.0% (2000); Ancestry (includes multiple ancestries): 28.2% Polish, 24.7% Irish, 23.5% German, 15.7% Italian, 5.7% Other groups (2000).
Economy: Employment by occupation: 18.0% management, 18.0% professional, 10.2% services, 31.6% sales, 0.0% farming, 11.4% construction, 10.7% production (2000).
Income: Per capita income: $34,590 (2007); Median household income: $99,197 (2007); Average household income: $113,875 (2007); Percent of households with income of $100,000 or more: 49.4% (2007); Poverty rate: 1.8% (2000).
Education: Percent of population age 25 and over with: High school diploma (including GED) or higher: 92.3% (2007); Bachelor's degree or higher: 30.2% (2007); Master's degree or higher: 9.4% (2007).

School District(s)

Homer CCSD 33c (KG-08)
2005-06 Enrollment: 3,401 . . . . (708) 226-7600
Will County SD 92 (PK-08)
2005-06 Enrollment: 2,037 . . . . (815) 838-8031
Housing: Homeownership rate: 97.9% (2007); Median home value: $307,628 (2007); Median rent: $830 per month (2000); Median age of housing: 16 years (2000).
Transportation: Commute to work: 93.8% car, 2.7% public transportation, 0.3% walk, 2.6% work from home (2000); Travel time to work: 13.9% less than 15 minutes, 24.1% 15 to 30 minutes, 26.7% 30 to 45 minutes, 18.2% 45 to 60 minutes, 17.1% 60 minutes or more (2000)
Additional Information Contacts
Homer Township Chamber of Commerce . . . . (708) 301-8111
http://www.homerchamber.com

INGALLS PARK (CDP). Covers a land area of 1.081 square miles and a water area of 0 square miles. Located at 41.52° N. Lat.; 88.03° W. Long. Elevation is 610 feet.
Population: 3,189 (1990); 3,082 (2000); 3,393 (2007); 3,653 (2012 projected); Race: 83.6% White, 4.3% Black, 0.3% Asian, 23.4% Hispanic of any race (2007); Density: 3,137.9 persons per square mile (2007); Average household size: 2.45 (2007); Median age: 33.8 (2007); Males per 100 females: 103.5 (2007); Marriage status: 24.4% never married, 58.3% now married, 5.0% widowed, 12.3% divorced (2000); Foreign born: 4.0% (2000); Ancestry (includes multiple ancestries): 31.5% German, 22.9% Irish, 20.5% Other groups, 11.4% Italian, 10.0% English (2000).
Economy: Employment by occupation: 8.0% management, 8.7% professional, 12.4% services, 29.8% sales, 0.0% farming, 14.9% construction, 26.2% production (2000).
Income: Per capita income: $22,182 (2007); Median household income: $48,787 (2007); Average household income: $54,420 (2007); Percent of households with income of $100,000 or more: 8.0% (2007); Poverty rate: 5.1% (2000).
Education: Percent of population age 25 and over with: High school diploma (including GED) or higher: 82.9% (2007); Bachelor's degree or higher: 5.9% (2007); Master's degree or higher: 2.0% (2007).
Housing: Homeownership rate: 76.6% (2007); Median home value: $122,419 (2007); Median rent: $502 per month (2000); Median age of housing: 52 years (2000).
Transportation: Commute to work: 95.3% car, 1.4% public transportation, 0.6% walk, 1.9% work from home (2000); Travel time to work: 33.1% less than 15 minutes, 36.5% 15 to 30 minutes, 15.3% 30 to 45 minutes, 8.0% 45 to 60 minutes, 7.2% 60 minutes or more (2000)

JOLIET (city). County seat. Covers a land area of 38.059 square miles and a water area of 0.286 square miles. Located at 41.53° N. Lat.; 88.10° W. Long. Elevation is 541 feet.
History: Named for Louis Joliet (1645-1700), French-Canadian explorer. The town of Joliet was laid out in 1834 with the name of Juliet (a neighboring village was Romeo) and incorporated in 1837 as the seat of Will County. Industry bloomed in Joliet when the Illinois & Michigan Canal was completed here in 1848. Limestone from the Joliet quarries was shipped across the country. Steel manufacturing in the late 1800's was replaced by the production of wallpaper as a leading industry.
Population: 82,008 (1990); 106,221 (2000); 140,691 (2007); 164,614 (2012 projected); Race: 65.0% White, 17.1% Black, 1.8% Asian, 26.9% Hispanic of any race (2007); Density: 3,696.6 persons per square mile (2007); Average household size: 2.91 (2007); Median age: 31.8 (2007); Males per 100 females: 98.5 (2007); Marriage status: 27.9% never married, 56.0% now married, 7.0% widowed, 9.1% divorced (2000); Foreign born: 10.9% (2000); Ancestry (includes multiple ancestries): 34.4% Other groups, 18.0% German, 13.8% Irish, 8.7% Italian, 7.7% Polish (2000).
Economy: Unemployment rate: 7.2% (4/2008); Total civilian labor force: 71,917 (4/2008); Single-family building permits issued: 769 (2007); Multi-family building permits issued: 16 (2007); Employment by occupation: 10.0% management, 17.7% professional, 16.2% services, 27.4% sales, 0.2% farming, 10.4% construction, 18.3% production (2000).
Income: Per capita income: $21,823 (2007); Median household income: $54,016 (2007); Average household income: $62,888 (2007); Percent of households with income of $100,000 or more: 16.0% (2007); Poverty rate: 10.8% (2000).
Taxes: Total city taxes per capita: $435 (2006); City property taxes per capita: $185 (2006).

Education: Percent of population age 25 and over with: High school diploma (including GED) or higher: 79.8% (2007); Bachelor's degree or higher: 19.3% (2007); Master's degree or higher: 5.7% (2007).

School District(s)

Dept of Corrections Sch Dist 428 (08-12)
2005-06 Enrollment: 2,271 . . . . (217) 522-2666
Grundy/Kendall Roe (09-12)
2005-06 Enrollment: 119 . . . . (815) 941-3247
Joliet PSD 86 (PK-08)
2005-06 Enrollment: 10,111 . . . . (815) 740-3196
Joliet Twp HSD 204 (09-12)
2005-06 Enrollment: 5,208 . . . . (815) 727-6970
Laraway CCSD 70c (KG-08)
2005-06 Enrollment: 395 . . . . (815) 727-5115
Plainfield SD 202 (PK-12)
2005-06 Enrollment: 24,371 . . . . (815) 577-4000
Rockdale SD 84 (KG-08)
2005-06 Enrollment: 243 . . . . (815) 725-5321
South Will Co Coop for Spec Ed (KG-12)
2005-06 Enrollment: 56 . . . . (815) 741-7777
Troy CCSD 30c (PK-08)
2005-06 Enrollment: 3,709 . . . . (815) 577-6760
Union SD 81 (KG-08)
2005-06 Enrollment: 128 . . . . (815) 726-5218
Will Roe (07-12)
2005-06 Enrollment: 274 . . . . (815) 740-8360

Four-year College(s)

University of St Francis (Private, Not-for-profit, Roman Catholic)
Fall 2007 Enrollment: 3,503 . . . . (815) 740-3360
2007-08 Tuition: In-state $20,830; Out-of-state $20,830

Two-year College(s)

Joliet Junior College (Public)
Fall 2007 Enrollment: 13,149 . . . . (815) 729-9020
2007-08 Tuition: In-state $6,983; Out-of-state $7,855

Vocational/Technical School(s)

Professionals Choice Hair Design Academy (Private, For-profit)
Fall 2007 Enrollment: 15 . . . . (815) 741-8224
2007-08 Tuition: $13,700
Regency Beauty Institute (Private, For-profit)
Fall 2007 Enrollment: 62 . . . . (815) 254-2793
2007-08 Tuition: $14,200

Housing: Homeownership rate: 71.9% (2007); Median home value: $175,036 (2007); Median rent: $487 per month (2000); Median age of housing: 36 years (2000).
Hospitals: Silver Cross Hospital (297 beds); St. Joseph Medical Center (452 beds); Stateville Correctional Center Hospital (32 beds)
Safety: Violent crime rate: 43.6 per 10,000 population; Property crime rate: 277.7 per 10,000 population (2006).
Newspapers: The Herald News (Local news; Circulation 44,344); KSKJ Boyce - Amerikanski Slovenec (National news; Circulation 11,000); Times Weekly Newspaper (Local news; Circulation 30,000)
Transportation: Commute to work: 92.8% car, 2.6% public transportation, 1.6% walk, 1.8% work from home (2000); Travel time to work: 28.9% less than 15 minutes, 29.9% 15 to 30 minutes, 18.1% 30 to 45 minutes, 10.8% 45 to 60 minutes, 12.4% 60 minutes or more (2000); Amtrak: Service available.

Additional Information Contacts

City of Joliet . . . . (815) 724-3780
http://www.ci.joliet.il.us
Joliet Region Chamber of Commerce & Industry . . . . (815) 727-5371
http://www.jolietchamber.com
Will County Center for Economic Development . . . . (815) 723-1800
http://www.c-e-d.org

LAKEWOOD SHORES (CDP). Covers a land area of 2.321 square miles and a water area of 0.423 square miles. Located at 41.26° N. Lat.; 88.13° W. Long. Elevation is 564 feet.
Population: 1,606 (1990); 1,487 (2000); 1,731 (2007); 1,921 (2012 projected); Race: 96.1% White, 0.0% Black, 0.6% Asian, 4.2% Hispanic of any race (2007); Density: 745.8 persons per square mile (2007); Average household size: 2.81 (2007); Median age: 35.3 (2007); Males per 100 females: 110.3 (2007); Marriage status: 22.1% never married, 62.2% now married, 2.5% widowed, 13.2% divorced (2000); Foreign born: 1.3% (2000); Ancestry (includes multiple ancestries): 22.5% Irish, 16.7% German, 13.7% Polish, 11.0% English, 10.7% United States or American (2000).
Economy: Employment by occupation: 6.2% management, 8.0% professional, 11.7% services, 21.8% sales, 0.0% farming, 25.1% construction, 27.2% production (2000).
Income: Per capita income: $22,155 (2007); Median household income: $58,750 (2007); Average household income: $62,358 (2007); Percent of households with income of $100,000 or more: 12.0% (2007); Poverty rate: 2.6% (2000).
Education: Percent of population age 25 and over with: High school diploma (including GED) or higher: 81.6% (2007); Bachelor's degree or higher: 5.6% (2007); Master's degree or higher: 2.0% (2007).
Housing: Homeownership rate: 90.4% (2007); Median home value: $164,935 (2007); Median rent: $623 per month (2000); Median age of housing: 39 years (2000).
Transportation: Commute to work: 92.1% car, 0.0% public transportation, 0.9% walk, 7.1% work from home (2000); Travel time to work: 18.8% less than 15 minutes, 36.5% 15 to 30 minutes, 25.2% 30 to 45 minutes, 9.0% 45 to 60 minutes, 10.5% 60 minutes or more (2000)

LOCKPORT (city). Covers a land area of 7.084 square miles and a water area of 0.011 square miles. Located at 41.58° N. Lat.; 88.04° W. Long. Elevation is 594 feet.
History: Named for the locks on the Illinois and Michigan Canal. Lockport developed as a shipping and transfer point on the Illinois & Michigan Canal. This was the location of the lock that controlled the volume of water from Lake Michigan. The canal company offices were located here also.
Population: 11,341 (1990); 15,191 (2000); 22,022 (2007); 26,680 (2012 projected); Race: 93.8% White, 1.3% Black, 1.2% Asian, 7.2% Hispanic of any race (2007); Density: 3,108.6 persons per square mile (2007); Average household size: 2.67 (2007); Median age: 34.0 (2007); Males per 100 females: 97.4 (2007); Marriage status: 22.9% never married, 63.6% now married, 5.5% widowed, 8.0% divorced (2000); Foreign born: 4.0% (2000); Ancestry (includes multiple ancestries): 31.0% German, 24.5% Irish, 20.5% Polish, 16.2% Italian, 8.1% Other groups (2000).
Economy: Single-family building permits issued: 152 (2007); Multi-family building permits issued: 0 (2007); Employment by occupation: 12.3% management, 19.6% professional, 11.4% services, 28.8% sales, 0.0% farming, 12.8% construction, 15.0% production (2000).
Income: Per capita income: $27,573 (2007); Median household income: $65,574 (2007); Average household income: $73,575 (2007); Percent of households with income of $100,000 or more: 20.3% (2007); Poverty rate: 3.5% (2000).
Education: Percent of population age 25 and over with: High school diploma (including GED) or higher: 90.1% (2007); Bachelor's degree or higher: 23.4% (2007); Master's degree or higher: 6.7% (2007).

School District(s)

Fairmont SD 89 (PK-08)
2005-06 Enrollment: 334 . . . . (815) 726-6318
Homer CCSD 33c (KG-08)
2005-06 Enrollment: 3,401 . . . . (708) 226-7600
Lockport SD 91 (PK-08)
2005-06 Enrollment: 669 . . . . (815) 838-0737
Lockport Twp HSD 205 (09-12)
2005-06 Enrollment: 3,728 . . . . (815) 588-8100
Taft SD 90 (KG-08)
2005-06 Enrollment: 343 . . . . (815) 838-0408
Will County SD 92 (PK-08)
2005-06 Enrollment: 2,037 . . . . (815) 838-8031

Housing: Homeownership rate: 79.7% (2007); Median home value: $224,153 (2007); Median rent: $576 per month (2000); Median age of housing: 28 years (2000).
Safety: Violent crime rate: 9.3 per 10,000 population; Property crime rate: 169.6 per 10,000 population (2006).
Transportation: Commute to work: 93.2% car, 3.7% public transportation, 0.7% walk, 1.8% work from home (2000); Travel time to work: 19.3% less than 15 minutes, 28.7% 15 to 30 minutes, 23.1% 30 to 45 minutes, 11.7% 45 to 60 minutes, 17.1% 60 minutes or more (2000)

Additional Information Contacts

City of Lockport . . . . (815) 838-0549
http://www.lockport.org
Lockport Chamber of Commerce . . . . (815) 838-3357
http://www.lockportchamber.com

MANHATTAN (village). Covers a land area of 3.366 square miles and a water area of 0 square miles. Located at 41.42° N. Lat.; 87.98° W. Long. Elevation is 682 feet.

Population: 2,149 (1990); 3,330 (2000); 5,172 (2007); 6,402 (2012 projected); Race: 95.0% White, 0.3% Black, 0.3% Asian, 5.4% Hispanic of any race (2007); Density: 1,536.5 persons per square mile (2007); Average household size: 2.88 (2007); Median age: 31.5 (2007); Males per 100 females: 104.7 (2007); Marriage status: 23.6% never married, 61.9% now married, 5.3% widowed, 9.2% divorced (2000); Foreign born: 2.5% (2000); Ancestry (includes multiple ancestries): 34.0% German, 31.3% Irish, 11.8% Polish, 10.1% English, 9.9% Italian (2000).

Economy: Single-family building permits issued: 164 (2007); Multi-family building permits issued: 0 (2007); Employment by occupation: 13.0% management, 18.7% professional, 12.8% services, 25.9% sales, 0.2% farming, 15.5% construction, 13.9% production (2000).

Income: Per capita income: $25,670 (2007); Median household income: $65,722 (2007); Average household income: $74,048 (2007); Percent of households with income of $100,000 or more: 25.2% (2007); Poverty rate: 3.6% (2000).

Education: Percent of population age 25 and over with: High school diploma (including GED) or higher: 92.9% (2007); Bachelor's degree or higher: 18.7% (2007); Master's degree or higher: 3.8% (2007).

School District(s)

Manhattan SD 114 (PK-08)
2005-06 Enrollment: 1,076 . . . . (815) 478-6090
Peotone CUSD 207u (PK-12)
2005-06 Enrollment: 1,999 . . . . (708) 258-0991

Housing: Homeownership rate: 77.6% (2007); Median home value: $238,018 (2007); Median rent: $574 per month (2000); Median age of housing: 23 years (2000).

Safety: Violent crime rate: 7.7 per 10,000 population; Property crime rate: 65.8 per 10,000 population (2006).

Transportation: Commute to work: 92.5% car, 2.5% public transportation, 2.0% walk, 2.7% work from home (2000); Travel time to work: 22.2% less than 15 minutes, 35.8% 15 to 30 minutes, 20.7% 30 to 45 minutes, 9.1% 45 to 60 minutes, 12.2% 60 minutes or more (2000)

Additional Information Contacts

Manhattan Chamber of Commerce . . . . (815) 478-3811
http://www.manhattan-il.com

MOKENA (village). Covers a land area of 5.995 square miles and a water area of 0.004 square miles. Located at 41.53° N. Lat.; 87.87° W. Long. Elevation is 705 feet.

Population: 7,878 (1990); 14,583 (2000); 18,739 (2007); 21,669 (2012 projected); Race: 94.5% White, 0.8% Black, 2.4% Asian, 5.1% Hispanic of any race (2007); Density: 3,125.6 persons per square mile (2007); Average household size: 3.14 (2007); Median age: 33.3 (2007); Males per 100 females: 100.9 (2007); Marriage status: 23.7% never married, 68.5% now married, 2.6% widowed, 5.2% divorced (2000); Foreign born: 4.1% (2000); Ancestry (includes multiple ancestries): 29.4% Irish, 29.1% German, 18.5% Polish, 14.5% Italian, 6.3% Other groups (2000).

Economy: Single-family building permits issued: 110 (2007); Multi-family building permits issued: 0 (2007); Employment by occupation: 19.1% management, 22.6% professional, 9.0% services, 30.5% sales, 0.0% farming, 10.9% construction, 7.9% production (2000).

Income: Per capita income: $32,957 (2007); Median household income: $92,060 (2007); Average household income: $103,351 (2007); Percent of households with income of $100,000 or more: 43.9% (2007); Poverty rate: 1.0% (2000).

Education: Percent of population age 25 and over with: High school diploma (including GED) or higher: 94.6% (2007); Bachelor's degree or higher: 34.7% (2007); Master's degree or higher: 11.4% (2007).

School District(s)

Mokena SD 159 (PK-08)
2005-06 Enrollment: 2,396 . . . . (708) 342-4900
Summit Hill SD 161 (PK-08)
2005-06 Enrollment: 3,583 . . . . (815) 469-9103

Housing: Homeownership rate: 88.5% (2007); Median home value: $319,042 (2007); Median rent: $613 per month (2000); Median age of housing: 9 years (2000).

Safety: Violent crime rate: 7.5 per 10,000 population; Property crime rate: 136.8 per 10,000 population (2006).

Transportation: Commute to work: 86.5% car, 9.9% public transportation, 1.0% walk, 2.4% work from home (2000); Travel time to work: 18.9% less than 15 minutes, 28.7% 15 to 30 minutes, 20.9% 30 to 45 minutes, 11.3% 45 to 60 minutes, 20.1% 60 minutes or more (2000)

Additional Information Contacts

Mokena Chamber of Commerce . . . . (708) 479-2468
http://www.mokena.com
Village of Mokena . . . . (708) 479-3900
http://www.mokena.org

MONEE (village). Covers a land area of 3.100 square miles and a water area of 0 square miles. Located at 41.41° N. Lat.; 87.74° W. Long. Elevation is 797 feet.

Population: 1,458 (1990); 2,924 (2000); 4,593 (2007); 5,707 (2012 projected); Race: 90.2% White, 3.1% Black, 0.8% Asian, 5.3% Hispanic of any race (2007); Density: 1,481.7 persons per square mile (2007); Average household size: 2.38 (2007); Median age: 37.6 (2007); Males per 100 females: 101.4 (2007); Marriage status: 13.3% never married, 71.3% now married, 5.5% widowed, 9.9% divorced (2000); Foreign born: 1.7% (2000); Ancestry (includes multiple ancestries): 30.4% German, 24.5% Irish, 13.6% Polish, 12.5% Italian, 8.5% Other groups (2000).

Economy: Single-family building permits issued: 20 (2007); Multi-family building permits issued: 0 (2007); Employment by occupation: 14.1% management, 16.8% professional, 11.5% services, 28.8% sales, 0.3% farming, 13.0% construction, 15.6% production (2000).

Income: Per capita income: $34,180 (2007); Median household income: $68,250 (2007); Average household income: $81,066 (2007); Percent of households with income of $100,000 or more: 25.5% (2007); Poverty rate: 3.4% (2000).

Education: Percent of population age 25 and over with: High school diploma (including GED) or higher: 86.4% (2007); Bachelor's degree or higher: 16.8% (2007); Master's degree or higher: 4.3% (2007).

School District(s)

Crete Monee CUSD 201u (PK-12)
2005-06 Enrollment: 4,774 . . . . (708) 367-8300

Housing: Homeownership rate: 87.1% (2007); Median home value: $206,237 (2007); Median rent: $545 per month (2000); Median age of housing: 5 years (2000).

Safety: Violent crime rate: 15.1 per 10,000 population; Property crime rate: 235.5 per 10,000 population (2006).

Transportation: Commute to work: 88.5% car, 3.9% public transportation, 1.6% walk, 4.7% work from home (2000); Travel time to work: 19.8% less than 15 minutes, 35.2% 15 to 30 minutes, 20.1% 30 to 45 minutes, 9.0% 45 to 60 minutes, 15.9% 60 minutes or more (2000)

Additional Information Contacts

Monee Chamber of Commerce . . . . (708) 534-5332
http://www.moneechamber.com

NEW LENOX (village). Covers a land area of 10.094 square miles and a water area of 0.018 square miles. Located at 41.50° N. Lat.; 87.97° W. Long. Elevation is 669 feet.

History: New Lenox was first settled in the 1820's along Hickory Creek.

Population: 11,574 (1990); 17,771 (2000); 23,834 (2007); 28,046 (2012 projected); Race: 96.1% White, 0.4% Black, 0.6% Asian, 5.2% Hispanic of any race (2007); Density: 2,361.2 persons per square mile (2007); Average household size: 3.04 (2007); Median age: 33.2 (2007); Males per 100 females: 95.2 (2007); Marriage status: 21.2% never married, 67.8% now married, 4.4% widowed, 6.6% divorced (2000); Foreign born: 1.3% (2000); Ancestry (includes multiple ancestries): 31.5% German, 27.9% Irish, 16.8% Polish, 13.4% Italian, 7.9% English (2000).

Economy: Single-family building permits issued: 135 (2007); Multi-family building permits issued: 0 (2007); Employment by occupation: 15.0% management, 20.2% professional, 8.8% services, 30.8% sales, 0.1% farming, 13.0% construction, 12.1% production (2000).

Income: Per capita income: $30,599 (2007); Median household income: $82,162 (2007); Average household income: $92,880 (2007); Percent of households with income of $100,000 or more: 34.9% (2007); Poverty rate: 2.4% (2000).

Taxes: Total city taxes per capita: $136 (2006); City property taxes per capita: $86 (2006).

Education: Percent of population age 25 and over with: High school diploma (including GED) or higher: 92.4% (2007); Bachelor's degree or higher: 26.2% (2007); Master's degree or higher: 7.3% (2007).

School District(s)

Lincoln Way CHSD 210 (09-12)
2005-06 Enrollment: 6,632 . . . . (815) 462-2100

Lincoln-Way Area Spec Ed Ja Dist (05-12)
2005-06 Enrollment: 54 . . . . (815) 806-4600
New Lenox SD 122 (PK-08)
2005-06 Enrollment: 5,457 . . . . (815) 485-2169
Housing: Homeownership rate: 89.7% (2007); Median home value: $265,477 (2007); Median rent: $631 per month (2000); Median age of housing: 13 years (2000).
Safety: Violent crime rate: 8.2 per 10,000 population; Property crime rate: 156.1 per 10,000 population (2006).
Transportation: Commute to work: 89.4% car, 6.1% public transportation, 0.5% walk, 3.1% work from home (2000); Travel time to work: 21.2% less than 15 minutes, 27.3% 15 to 30 minutes, 21.1% 30 to 45 minutes, 11.6% 45 to 60 minutes, 18.9% 60 minutes or more (2000)
Additional Information Contacts
New Lenox Chamber of Commerce. . . . . (815) 485-4241
http://www.newlenoxchamber.com
Village of New Lenox . . . . (815) 485-6431
http://www.newlenox.net

PEOTONE (village). Covers a land area of 1.516 square miles and a water area of 0.003 square miles. Located at 41.32° N. Lat.; 87.79° W. Long. Elevation is 705 feet.
History: Incorporated 1869.
Population: 3,094 (1990); 3,385 (2000); 4,206 (2007); 4,781 (2012 projected); Race: 96.3% White, 0.4% Black, 0.7% Asian, 2.6% Hispanic of any race (2007); Density: 2,773.8 persons per square mile (2007); Average household size: 2.64 (2007); Median age: 35.9 (2007); Males per 100 females: 93.4 (2007); Marriage status: 21.9% never married, 60.6% now married, 7.1% widowed, 10.4% divorced (2000); Foreign born: 1.0% (2000); Ancestry (includes multiple ancestries): 39.7% German, 23.9% Irish, 14.7% English, 11.7% Polish, 9.9% Italian (2000).
Economy: Single-family building permits issued: 23 (2007); Multi-family building permits issued: 0 (2007); Employment by occupation: 10.0% management, 19.0% professional, 10.9% services, 28.5% sales, 2.2% farming, 17.4% construction, 12.0% production (2000).
Income: Per capita income: $28,003 (2007); Median household income: $64,261 (2007); Average household income: $73,891 (2007); Percent of households with income of $100,000 or more: 19.2% (2007); Poverty rate: 0.8% (2000).
Education: Percent of population age 25 and over with: High school diploma (including GED) or higher: 90.7% (2007); Bachelor's degree or higher: 21.3% (2007); Master's degree or higher: 5.2% (2007).
School District(s)
Peotone CUSD 207u (PK-12)
2005-06 Enrollment: 1,999 . . . . (708) 258-0991
Housing: Homeownership rate: 73.6% (2007); Median home value: $220,319 (2007); Median rent: $514 per month (2000); Median age of housing: 36 years (2000).
Safety: Violent crime rate: 10.0 per 10,000 population; Property crime rate: 168.3 per 10,000 population (2006).
Newspapers: Crete Record (Community news; Circulation 5,000); Daily Journal - Peotone Bureau (Local news; Circulation 0); Grant Park Gazette (Community news; Circulation 20,000); Manhattan American (Community news; Circulation 8,500); Manteno News (Community news; Circulation 0)
Transportation: Commute to work: 92.9% car, 3.0% public transportation, 2.8% walk, 0.8% work from home (2000); Travel time to work: 32.0% less than 15 minutes, 26.5% 15 to 30 minutes, 20.2% 30 to 45 minutes, 6.7% 45 to 60 minutes, 14.6% 60 minutes or more (2000)
Additional Information Contacts
Peotone Chamber of Commerce . . . . (708) 258-9450
http://www.peotonechamber.com

PLAINFIELD (village). Covers a land area of 11.612 square miles and a water area of 0.835 square miles. Located at 41.61° N. Lat.; 88.20° W. Long. Elevation is 617 feet.
History: Plainfield began as a trading post founded by the Frenchman Du Pazhe about 1790, and later operated by Vetel Vermette for the American Fur Trading Company. The town grew around a cabin built by Captain James Walker in 1829, and was first known as Walker's Grove. The name of Plainfield refers to the flat prairie setting.
Population: 6,409 (1990); 13,038 (2000); 24,320 (2007); 31,713 (2012 projected); Race: 92.8% White, 1.4% Black, 2.3% Asian, 7.1% Hispanic of any race (2007); Density: 2,094.4 persons per square mile (2007); Average household size: 3.07 (2007); Median age: 33.6 (2007); Males per 100 females: 99.8 (2007); Marriage status: 19.4% never married, 71.3% now married, 4.0% widowed, 5.3% divorced (2000); Foreign born: 3.9% (2000); Ancestry (includes multiple ancestries): 31.1% German, 20.2% Irish, 16.0% Italian, 15.4% Polish, 9.2% English (2000).
Economy: Unemployment rate: 5.0% (4/2008); Total civilian labor force: 18,405 (4/2008); Single-family building permits issued: 400 (2007); Multi-family building permits issued: 4 (2007); Employment by occupation: 18.9% management, 23.5% professional, 8.1% services, 29.4% sales, 0.0% farming, 10.3% construction, 9.8% production (2000).
Income: Per capita income: $33,907 (2007); Median household income: $94,285 (2007); Average household income: $103,767 (2007); Percent of households with income of $100,000 or more: 44.6% (2007); Poverty rate: 1.8% (2000).
Taxes: Total city taxes per capita: $412 (2006); City property taxes per capita: $109 (2006).
Education: Percent of population age 25 and over with: High school diploma (including GED) or higher: 94.9% (2007); Bachelor's degree or higher: 35.1% (2007); Master's degree or higher: 8.4% (2007).
School District(s)
Plainfield SD 202 (PK-12)
2005-06 Enrollment: 24,371 . . . . (815) 577-4000
Troy CCSD 30c (PK-08)
2005-06 Enrollment: 3,709 . . . . (815) 577-6760
Housing: Homeownership rate: 87.2% (2007); Median home value: $290,618 (2007); Median rent: $631 per month (2000); Median age of housing: 6 years (2000).
Safety: Violent crime rate: 14.9 per 10,000 population; Property crime rate: 170.4 per 10,000 population (2006).
Newspapers: Enterprise (Local news; Circulation 6,000); Plainfield Sun (Local news; Circulation 15,000)
Transportation: Commute to work: 92.5% car, 2.2% public transportation, 1.0% walk, 3.8% work from home (2000); Travel time to work: 18.3% less than 15 minutes, 27.1% 15 to 30 minutes, 24.6% 30 to 45 minutes, 14.9% 45 to 60 minutes, 15.1% 60 minutes or more (2000)
Additional Information Contacts
Plainfield Area Chamber of Commerce . . . . (815) 436-4431
http://www.plainfieldchamber.com
Village of Plainfield. . . . . (815) 436-7093
http://www.plainfield-il.org

PRESTON HEIGHTS (CDP). Covers a land area of 1.494 square miles and a water area of 0 square miles. Located at 41.49° N. Lat.; 88.07° W. Long. Elevation is 630 feet.
Population: 2,563 (1990); 2,527 (2000); 2,897 (2007); 3,183 (2012 projected); Race: 21.1% White, 70.1% Black, 0.1% Asian, 9.1% Hispanic of any race (2007); Density: 1,939.0 persons per square mile (2007); Average household size: 2.84 (2007); Median age: 30.9 (2007); Males per 100 females: 91.9 (2007); Marriage status: 32.2% never married, 51.7% now married, 6.5% widowed, 9.5% divorced (2000); Foreign born: 3.5% (2000); Ancestry (includes multiple ancestries): 62.2% Other groups, 8.6% German, 6.2% Irish, 4.0% Italian, 3.8% United States or American (2000).
Economy: Employment by occupation: 7.1% management, 9.0% professional, 20.8% services, 30.9% sales, 0.0% farming, 7.7% construction, 24.5% production (2000).
Income: Per capita income: $20,261 (2007); Median household income: $44,469 (2007); Average household income: $57,490 (2007); Percent of households with income of $100,000 or more: 13.4% (2007); Poverty rate: 9.7% (2000).
Education: Percent of population age 25 and over with: High school diploma (including GED) or higher: 77.4% (2007); Bachelor's degree or higher: 9.9% (2007); Master's degree or higher: 2.3% (2007).
Housing: Homeownership rate: 65.8% (2007); Median home value: $134,155 (2007); Median rent: $504 per month (2000); Median age of housing: 36 years (2000).
Transportation: Commute to work: 93.1% car, 4.2% public transportation, 0.7% walk, 1.6% work from home (2000); Travel time to work: 28.3% less than 15 minutes, 38.2% 15 to 30 minutes, 13.5% 30 to 45 minutes, 9.9% 45 to 60 minutes, 10.1% 60 minutes or more (2000)

ROCKDALE (village). Covers a land area of 0.794 square miles and a water area of 0 square miles. Located at 41.50° N. Lat.; 88.11° W. Long. Elevation is 551 feet.
History: Incorporated 1903.
Population: 1,725 (1990); 1,888 (2000); 2,144 (2007); 2,345 (2012 projected); Race: 73.6% White, 1.2% Black, 0.7% Asian, 35.0% Hispanic of any race (2007); Density: 2,699.8 persons per square mile (2007); Average

household size: 2.49 (2007); Median age: 34.4 (2007); Males per 100 females: 103.4 (2007); Marriage status: 26.7% never married, 51.8% now married, 8.7% widowed, 12.8% divorced (2000); Foreign born: 9.1% (2000); Ancestry (includes multiple ancestries): 27.6% Other groups, 18.7% German, 14.8% Irish, 12.7% Italian, 9.2% Polish (2000).
Economy: Single-family building permits issued: 3 (2007); Multi-family building permits issued: 0 (2007); Employment by occupation: 7.4% management, 7.7% professional, 15.0% services, 27.3% sales, 0.0% farming, 16.9% construction, 25.7% production (2000).
Income: Per capita income: $19,400 (2007); Median household income: $40,560 (2007); Average household income: $48,281 (2007); Percent of households with income of $100,000 or more: 7.9% (2007); Poverty rate: 9.3% (2000).
Education: Percent of population age 25 and over with: High school diploma (including GED) or higher: 77.0% (2007); Bachelor's degree or higher: 7.6% (2007); Master's degree or higher: 1.5% (2007).
Housing: Homeownership rate: 57.6% (2007); Median home value: $138,715 (2007); Median rent: $499 per month (2000); Median age of housing: 52 years (2000).
Safety: Violent crime rate: 39.6 per 10,000 population; Property crime rate: 411.3 per 10,000 population (2006).
Transportation: Commute to work: 92.1% car, 1.1% public transportation, 3.5% walk, 0.7% work from home (2000); Travel time to work: 42.4% less than 15 minutes, 25.9% 15 to 30 minutes, 15.6% 30 to 45 minutes, 6.6% 45 to 60 minutes, 9.5% 60 minutes or more (2000)

ROMEOVILLE (village). Aka Romeo. Covers a land area of 14.514 square miles and a water area of 0.381 square miles. Located at 41.64° N. Lat.; 88.10° W. Long. Elevation is 617 feet.
History: Named for the hero of Shakespeare's "Romeo and Juliet". Romeoville developed along the Illinois & Michigan Canal. An early industry was the Globe Oil Refinery.
Population: 15,337 (1990); 21,153 (2000); 36,301 (2007); 46,221 (2012 projected); Race: 78.1% White, 6.8% Black, 4.3% Asian, 19.9% Hispanic of any race (2007); Density: 2,501.1 persons per square mile (2007); Average household size: 2.99 (2007); Median age: 31.0 (2007); Males per 100 females: 101.0 (2007); Marriage status: 28.2% never married, 62.1% now married, 3.4% widowed, 6.3% divorced (2000); Foreign born: 9.4% (2000); Ancestry (includes multiple ancestries): 22.8% German, 22.5% Other groups, 19.3% Irish, 15.7% Polish, 9.8% Italian (2000).
Economy: Unemployment rate: 5.4% (4/2008); Total civilian labor force: 22,144 (4/2008); Single-family building permits issued: 57 (2007); Multi-family building permits issued: 0 (2007); Employment by occupation: 12.2% management, 16.3% professional, 10.9% services, 31.5% sales, 0.0% farming, 10.9% construction, 18.1% production (2000).
Income: Per capita income: $24,117 (2007); Median household income: $65,645 (2007); Average household income: $71,744 (2007); Percent of households with income of $100,000 or more: 17.5% (2007); Poverty rate: 1.9% (2000).
Taxes: Total city taxes per capita: $616 (2006); City property taxes per capita: $286 (2006).
Education: Percent of population age 25 and over with: High school diploma (including GED) or higher: 85.7% (2007); Bachelor's degree or higher: 21.6% (2007); Master's degree or higher: 4.6% (2007).

School District(s)

Valley View CUSD 365u (PK-12)
2005-06 Enrollment: 17,510 . . . . (815) 886-2700
Wilco Area Career Center
2005-06 Enrollment: n/a . . . . (815) 838-6941

Four-year College(s)

Lewis University (Private, Not-for-profit, Roman Catholic)
Fall 2007 Enrollment: 5,347. . . . . (815) 838-0500
2007-08 Tuition: In-state $20,450; Out-of-state $20,450
Housing: Homeownership rate: 83.2% (2007); Median home value: $177,257 (2007); Median rent: $808 per month (2000); Median age of housing: 21 years (2000).
Safety: Violent crime rate: 21.4 per 10,000 population; Property crime rate: 191.8 per 10,000 population (2006).
Newspapers: Catholic Explorer (Regional news; Circulation 25,000)
Transportation: Commute to work: 92.4% car, 2.6% public transportation, 3.0% walk, 1.4% work from home (2000); Travel time to work: 23.0% less than 15 minutes, 23.4% 15 to 30 minutes, 24.2% 30 to 45 minutes, 14.6% 45 to 60 minutes, 14.7% 60 minutes or more (2000)
Airports: Lewis University (general aviation)
Additional Information Contacts
Romeoville Chamber of Commerce. . . . . (815) 886-2076
http://www.romeovillechamber.org
Village of Romeoville . . . . (815) 866-7200
http://www.romeoville.org

SHOREWOOD (village). Covers a land area of 3.887 square miles and a water area of 0.065 square miles. Located at 41.51° N. Lat.; 88.20° W. Long. Elevation is 577 feet.
Population: 6,415 (1990); 7,686 (2000); 12,275 (2007); 15,270 (2012 projected); Race: 88.6% White, 2.7% Black, 1.8% Asian, 9.0% Hispanic of any race (2007); Density: 3,157.6 persons per square mile (2007); Average household size: 2.95 (2007); Median age: 35.9 (2007); Males per 100 females: 98.9 (2007); Marriage status: 22.5% never married, 65.8% now married, 3.7% widowed, 7.9% divorced (2000); Foreign born: 4.3% (2000); Ancestry (includes multiple ancestries): 29.6% German, 18.3% Irish, 13.5% Italian, 13.4% Polish, 10.8% Other groups (2000).
Economy: Single-family building permits issued: 256 (2007); Multi-family building permits issued: 0 (2007); Employment by occupation: 16.2% management, 22.5% professional, 8.9% services, 27.8% sales, 0.0% farming, 10.1% construction, 14.5% production (2000).
Income: Per capita income: $35,885 (2007); Median household income: $89,024 (2007); Average household income: $105,834 (2007); Percent of households with income of $100,000 or more: 41.5% (2007); Poverty rate: 2.0% (2000).
Education: Percent of population age 25 and over with: High school diploma (including GED) or higher: 93.6% (2007); Bachelor's degree or higher: 34.7% (2007); Master's degree or higher: 8.9% (2007).

School District(s)

Minooka CCSD 201 (PK-08)
2005-06 Enrollment: 2,784 . . . . (815) 467-6121
Troy CCSD 30c (PK-08)
2005-06 Enrollment: 3,709 . . . . (815) 577-6760
Housing: Homeownership rate: 96.0% (2007); Median home value: $229,097 (2007); Median rent: $894 per month (2000); Median age of housing: 18 years (2000).
Safety: Violent crime rate: 15.7 per 10,000 population; Property crime rate: 222.1 per 10,000 population (2006).
Transportation: Commute to work: 95.0% car, 0.6% public transportation, 1.0% walk, 2.9% work from home (2000); Travel time to work: 25.9% less than 15 minutes, 37.2% 15 to 30 minutes, 15.2% 30 to 45 minutes, 11.3% 45 to 60 minutes, 10.4% 60 minutes or more (2000)
Additional Information Contacts
Shorewood Area Chamber of Commerce . . . . (815) 725-2900
http://www.shorewoodchamber.com
Village of Shorewood. . . . . (815) 725-2150
http://www.vil.shorewood.il.us

STEGER (village). Covers a land area of 3.524 square miles and a water area of 0 square miles. Located at 41.47° N. Lat.; 87.63° W. Long.
History: Steger grew up around the piano factory founded by John V. Steger.
Population: 9,386 (1990); 9,682 (2000); 10,778 (2007); 11,508 (2012 projected); Race: 81.5% White, 10.5% Black, 0.7% Asian, 10.1% Hispanic of any race (2007); Density: 3,058.3 persons per square mile (2007); Average household size: 2.48 (2007); Median age: 34.9 (2007); Males per 100 females: 100.6 (2007); Marriage status: 27.5% never married, 54.1% now married, 6.6% widowed, 11.8% divorced (2000); Foreign born: 4.6% (2000); Ancestry (includes multiple ancestries): 25.1% German, 17.0% Irish, 16.4% Other groups, 15.5% Italian, 11.0% Polish (2000).
Economy: Single-family building permits issued: 7 (2007); Multi-family building permits issued: 0 (2007); Employment by occupation: 10.6% management, 12.9% professional, 13.5% services, 28.1% sales, 0.1% farming, 13.8% construction, 21.0% production (2000).
Income: Per capita income: $21,813 (2007); Median household income: $45,930 (2007); Average household income: $53,945 (2007); Percent of households with income of $100,000 or more: 11.3% (2007); Poverty rate: 8.5% (2000).
Education: Percent of population age 25 and over with: High school diploma (including GED) or higher: 81.7% (2007); Bachelor's degree or higher: 10.5% (2007); Master's degree or higher: 3.3% (2007).

School District(s)

Steger SD 194 (PK-08)
2005-06 Enrollment: 1,613 . . . . (708) 755-0022

Housing: Homeownership rate: 64.8% (2007); Median home value: $147,346 (2007); Median rent: $563 per month (2000); Median age of housing: 36 years (2000).
Safety: Violent crime rate: 23.1 per 10,000 population; Property crime rate: 392.9 per 10,000 population (2006).
Transportation: Commute to work: 89.8% car, 4.6% public transportation, 2.3% walk, 2.0% work from home (2000); Travel time to work: 29.9% less than 15 minutes, 33.4% 15 to 30 minutes, 17.6% 30 to 45 minutes, 5.9% 45 to 60 minutes, 13.2% 60 minutes or more (2000)
Additional Information Contacts
Village of Steger. . . . . (708) 754-3395
http://www.villageofsteger.com

SYMERTON (village). Covers a land area of 0.051 square miles and a water area of 0 square miles. Located at 41.32° N. Lat.; 88.05° W. Long. Elevation is 640 feet.
Population: 110 (1990); 106 (2000); 174 (2007); 220 (2012 projected); Race: 98.3% White, 1.7% Black, 0.0% Asian, 0.0% Hispanic of any race (2007); Density: 3,388.2 persons per square mile (2007); Average household size: 3.05 (2007); Median age: 32.8 (2007); Males per 100 females: 104.7 (2007); Marriage status: 13.0% never married, 66.7% now married, 11.6% widowed, 8.7% divorced (2000); Foreign born: 0.0% (2000); Ancestry (includes multiple ancestries): 37.0% German, 32.0% Irish, 22.0% Italian, 16.0% English, 8.0% Other groups (2000).
Economy: Single-family building permits issued: 0 (2007); Multi-family building permits issued: 0 (2007); Employment by occupation: 23.8% management, 0.0% professional, 33.3% services, 11.9% sales, 0.0% farming, 7.1% construction, 23.8% production (2000).
Income: Per capita income: $22,960 (2007); Median household income: $72,500 (2007); Average household income: $70,088 (2007); Percent of households with income of $100,000 or more: 14.0% (2007); Poverty rate: 0.0% (2000).
Education: Percent of population age 25 and over with: High school diploma (including GED) or higher: 86.7% (2007); Bachelor's degree or higher: 5.3% (2007); Master's degree or higher: 0.0% (2007).
Housing: Homeownership rate: 93.0% (2007); Median home value: $139,167 (2007); Median rent: $950 per month (2000); Median age of housing: 60+ years (2000).
Transportation: Commute to work: 100.0% car, 0.0% public transportation, 0.0% walk, 0.0% work from home (2000); Travel time to work: 23.8% less than 15 minutes, 26.2% 15 to 30 minutes, 38.1% 30 to 45 minutes, 11.9% 45 to 60 minutes, 0.0% 60 minutes or more (2000)

UNIVERSITY PARK (village). Aka Park Forest South. Covers a land area of 9.758 square miles and a water area of 0.008 square miles. Located at 41.43° N. Lat.; 87.69° W. Long. Elevation is 771 feet.
History: Seat of Governors State University.
Population: 6,225 (1990); 6,662 (2000); 8,070 (2007); 9,080 (2012 projected); Race: 9.3% White, 85.7% Black, 0.4% Asian, 2.7% Hispanic of any race (2007); Density: 827.0 persons per square mile (2007); Average household size: 2.90 (2007); Median age: 30.4 (2007); Males per 100 females: 86.2 (2007); Marriage status: 36.2% never married, 47.4% now married, 5.3% widowed, 11.2% divorced (2000); Foreign born: 3.7% (2000); Ancestry (includes multiple ancestries): 80.7% Other groups, 3.2% German, 3.0% United States or American, 1.1% Guyanese, 1.0% Jamaican (2000).
Economy: Single-family building permits issued: 16 (2007); Multi-family building permits issued: 0 (2007); Employment by occupation: 12.2% management, 20.0% professional, 14.2% services, 34.6% sales, 0.0% farming, 6.5% construction, 12.5% production (2000).
Income: Per capita income: $22,953 (2007); Median household income: $57,245 (2007); Average household income: $66,553 (2007); Percent of households with income of $100,000 or more: 18.4% (2007); Poverty rate: 9.1% (2000).
Education: Percent of population age 25 and over with: High school diploma (including GED) or higher: 91.8% (2007); Bachelor's degree or higher: 25.4% (2007); Master's degree or higher: 9.6% (2007).

School District(s)

Crete Monee CUSD 201u (PK-12)
2005-06 Enrollment: 4,774 . . . . (708) 367-8300

Four-year College(s)

Governors State University (Public)
Fall 2007 Enrollment: 5,692. . . . . (708) 534-5000

Housing: Homeownership rate: 58.7% (2007); Median home value: $136,827 (2007); Median rent: $630 per month (2000); Median age of housing: 26 years (2000).
Transportation: Commute to work: 84.4% car, 12.5% public transportation, 1.1% walk, 1.6% work from home (2000); Travel time to work: 15.0% less than 15 minutes, 29.1% 15 to 30 minutes, 13.8% 30 to 45 minutes, 14.4% 45 to 60 minutes, 27.7% 60 minutes or more (2000)
Additional Information Contacts
Village of University Park. . . . . (708) 534-6451
http://www.university-park-il.com

WILLOWBROOK (CDP). Covers a land area of 3.376 square miles and a water area of 0.016 square miles. Located at 41.45° N. Lat.; 87.54° W. Long. Elevation is 715 feet.
Population: 1,837 (1990); 2,130 (2000); 2,493 (2007); 2,768 (2012 projected); Race: 58.7% White, 35.7% Black, 1.8% Asian, 7.6% Hispanic of any race (2007); Density: 738.5 persons per square mile (2007); Average household size: 2.89 (2007); Median age: 45.0 (2007); Males per 100 females: 99.6 (2007); Marriage status: 18.2% never married, 71.1% now married, 6.8% widowed, 4.0% divorced (2000); Foreign born: 3.7% (2000); Ancestry (includes multiple ancestries): 27.4% Other groups, 20.1% German, 16.4% Irish, 15.2% Polish, 10.8% Italian (2000).
Economy: Employment by occupation: 21.8% management, 24.8% professional, 8.3% services, 26.5% sales, 0.0% farming, 9.8% construction, 8.8% production (2000).
Income: Per capita income: $43,497 (2007); Median household income: $106,977 (2007); Average household income: $125,506 (2007); Percent of households with income of $100,000 or more: 55.6% (2007); Poverty rate: 2.9% (2000).
Education: Percent of population age 25 and over with: High school diploma (including GED) or higher: 94.2% (2007); Bachelor's degree or higher: 33.2% (2007); Master's degree or higher: 14.0% (2007).
Housing: Homeownership rate: 98.7% (2007); Median home value: $360,549 (2007); Median rent: $534 per month (2000); Median age of housing: 16 years (2000).
Transportation: Commute to work: 92.1% car, 2.8% public transportation, 0.0% walk, 5.1% work from home (2000); Travel time to work: 11.5% less than 15 minutes, 27.0% 15 to 30 minutes, 25.4% 30 to 45 minutes, 10.4% 45 to 60 minutes, 25.7% 60 minutes or more (2000)

WILMINGTON (city). Covers a land area of 4.214 square miles and a water area of 0.310 square miles. Located at 41.30° N. Lat.; 88.14° W. Long. Elevation is 545 feet.
History: Wilmington was laid out in the 1840's by Thomas Fox, who called it Winchester. In 1854 it was incorporated as a village with the name of Wilmington. The village grew around grist, saw, and carding mills operated by Fox.
Population: 4,872 (1990); 5,134 (2000); 6,181 (2007); 6,932 (2012 projected); Race: 95.5% White, 1.1% Black, 0.5% Asian, 3.5% Hispanic of any race (2007); Density: 1,466.7 persons per square mile (2007); Average household size: 2.52 (2007); Median age: 35.5 (2007); Males per 100 females: 95.2 (2007); Marriage status: 23.4% never married, 59.3% now married, 8.6% widowed, 8.7% divorced (2000); Foreign born: 1.4% (2000); Ancestry (includes multiple ancestries): 26.4% German, 22.6% Irish, 13.0% English, 8.5% Italian, 7.5% Polish (2000).
Economy: Single-family building permits issued: 16 (2007); Multi-family building permits issued: 0 (2007); Employment by occupation: 6.6% management, 14.4% professional, 13.7% services, 27.7% sales, 0.0% farming, 14.8% construction, 22.8% production (2000).
Income: Per capita income: $25,552 (2007); Median household income: $50,954 (2007); Average household income: $62,192 (2007); Percent of households with income of $100,000 or more: 17.7% (2007); Poverty rate: 5.2% (2000).
Education: Percent of population age 25 and over with: High school diploma (including GED) or higher: 86.1% (2007); Bachelor's degree or higher: 10.4% (2007); Master's degree or higher: 3.5% (2007).

School District(s)

Wilmington CUSD 209u (PK-12)
2005-06 Enrollment: 1,528 . . . . (815) 476-2594

Housing: Homeownership rate: 68.3% (2007); Median home value: $156,250 (2007); Median rent: $423 per month (2000); Median age of housing: 38 years (2000).
Newspapers: Braidwood Journal (Local news; Circulation 2,000); Braidwood Journal - Wilmington Bureau (Community news; Circulation 2,000); Free Press Advocate (Local news; Circulation 21,000); Outdoor

Times (Regional news; Circulation 150,000); Prairie Shopper (Local news; Circulation 2,000)
Transportation: Commute to work: 96.3% car, 0.3% public transportation, 0.4% walk, 3.0% work from home (2000); Travel time to work: 26.6% less than 15 minutes, 26.2% 15 to 30 minutes, 26.1% 30 to 45 minutes, 8.6% 45 to 60 minutes, 12.6% 60 minutes or more (2000)
Additional Information Contacts
City of Wilmington . . . . (815) 476-2175
http://www.wilmington-il.com
Wilmington Chamber of Commerce. . . . . (815) 476-5991
http://www.wilmingtonchamberofcommerce.org

Williamson County

Located in southern Illinois; drained by the Big Muddy and South Fork of the Saline River; includes Crab Orchard Lake. Covers a land area of 423.41 square miles, a water area of 20.96 square miles, and is located in the Central Time Zone. The county was founded in 1839. County seat is Marion.

Williamson County is part of the Marion-Herrin, IL Micropolitan Statistical Area. The entire metro area includes: Williamson County, IL

Weather Station: Marion 4 NNE Elevation: 475 feet

	Jan	Feb	Mar	Apr	May	Jun	Jul	Aug	Sep	Oct	Nov	Dec
High	38	44	55	66	75	83	87	86	79	68	55	43
Low	20	24	34	43	53	62	66	64	56	44	35	25
Precip	3.0	3.0	4.6	4.7	5.0	4.1	3.8	3.8	3.3	3.1	4.9	3.7
Snow	5.9	5.4	2.5	0.5	0.0	0.0	0.0	0.0	0.0	0.2	0.8	2.9

High and Low temperatures in degrees Fahrenheit; Precipitation and Snow in inches

Population: 57,733 (1990); 61,296 (2000); 64,340 (2007); 66,340 (2012 projected); Race: 94.1% White, 3.2% Black, 0.7% Asian, 1.7% Hispanic of any race (2007); Density: 152.0 persons per square mile (2007); Average household size: 2.39 (2007); Median age: 39.1 (2007); Males per 100 females: 94.9 (2007).
Religion: Five largest groups: 24.4% Southern Baptist Convention, 7.6% Catholic Church, 5.3% The United Methodist Church, 2.9% Christian Churches and Churches of Christ, 2.5% American Baptist Churches in the USA (2000).
Economy: Unemployment rate: 5.7% (4/2008); Total civilian labor force: 36,847 (4/2008); Leading industries: 20.9% manufacturing; 19.9% health care and social assistance; 14.6% retail trade (2005); Farms: 631 totaling 105,325 acres (2002); Companies that employ 500 or more persons: 6 (2006); Companies that employ 100 to 499 persons: 31 (2006); Companies that employ less than 100 persons: 1,606 (2006); Black-owned businesses: n/a (2002); Hispanic-owned businesses: n/a (2002); Asian-owned businesses: n/a (2002); Women-owned businesses: 1,194 (2002); Retail sales per capita: $16,829 (2008). Single-family building permits issued: 225 (2007); Multi-family building permits issued: 55 (2007).
Income: Per capita income: $21,497 (2007); Median household income: $38,361 (2007); Average household income: $50,338 (2007); Percent of households with income of $100,000 or more: 9.7% (2007); Poverty rate: 13.0% (2005); Bankruptcy rate: 5.38% (2007).
Taxes: Total county taxes per capita: $102 (2006); County property taxes per capita: $101 (2006).
Education: Percent of population age 25 and over with: High school diploma (including GED) or higher: 79.8% (2007); Bachelor's degree or higher: 17.5% (2007); Master's degree or higher: 6.2% (2007).
Housing: Homeownership rate: 73.7% (2007); Median home value: $86,369 (2007); Median rent: $311 per month (2000); Median age of housing: 32 years (2000).
Health: Birth rate: 126.9 per 10,000 population (2007); Death rate: 113.4 per 10,000 population (2007); Age-adjusted cancer mortality rate: 220.8 deaths per 100,000 population (2005); Number of physicians: 18.7 per 10,000 population (2005); Hospital beds: 47.4 per 10,000 population (2004); Hospital admissions: 1,889.3 per 10,000 population (2004).
Elections: 2004 Presidential election results: 60.4% Bush, 39.0% Kerry, 0.1% Nader, 0.6% Badnarik
National and State Parks: Crab Orchard National Wildlife Refuge
Additional Information Contacts
Williamson County Government . . . . (618) 997-1301

Carterville Chamber of Commerce . . . . (618) 985-6942
http://www.cartervillechamber.com
City of Herrin . . . . (618) 942-3175
http://www.herrinillinois.com/pages/comm_gov.php
City of Marion. . . . . (618) 997-6281
http://www.cityofmarionil.gov
Herrin Chamber of Commerce. . . . . (618) 942-5163
http://www.herrinillinois.com
Marion Area Chamber of Commerce . . . . (618) 997-6311
http://www.marionillinois.com

Williamson County Communities

BUSH (village). Covers a land area of 0.461 square miles and a water area of 0.006 square miles. Located at 37.84° N. Lat.; 89.13° W. Long. Elevation is 410 feet.
Population: 351 (1990); 257 (2000); 228 (2007); 224 (2012 projected); Race: 98.2% White, 0.0% Black, 0.9% Asian, 0.0% Hispanic of any race (2007); Density: 495.0 persons per square mile (2007); Average household size: 2.30 (2007); Median age: 40.5 (2007); Males per 100 females: 96.6 (2007); Marriage status: 22.2% never married, 53.4% now married, 9.5% widowed, 14.8% divorced (2000); Foreign born: 0.4% (2000); Ancestry (includes multiple ancestries): 30.1% United States or American, 8.9% Irish, 8.5% German, 7.2% English, 4.2% Polish (2000).
Economy: Employment by occupation: 2.3% management, 15.1% professional, 14.0% services, 19.8% sales, 1.2% farming, 18.6% construction, 29.1% production (2000).
Income: Per capita income: $14,221 (2007); Median household income: $18,906 (2007); Average household income: $32,753 (2007); Percent of households with income of $100,000 or more: 4.0% (2007); Poverty rate: 38.1% (2000).
Education: Percent of population age 25 and over with: High school diploma (including GED) or higher: 56.5% (2007); Bachelor's degree or higher: 2.5% (2007); Master's degree or higher: 0.0% (2007).
Housing: Homeownership rate: 81.8% (2007); Median home value: $31,563 (2007); Median rent: $175 per month (2000); Median age of housing: 44 years (2000).
Transportation: Commute to work: 95.1% car, 0.0% public transportation, 0.0% walk, 4.9% work from home (2000); Travel time to work: 6.4% less than 15 minutes, 44.9% 15 to 30 minutes, 28.2% 30 to 45 minutes, 5.1% 45 to 60 minutes, 15.4% 60 minutes or more (2000)

CAMBRIA (village). Covers a land area of 1.365 square miles and a water area of 0.010 square miles. Located at 37.78° N. Lat.; 89.11° W. Long. Elevation is 423 feet.
Population: 1,358 (1990); 1,330 (2000); 1,315 (2007); 1,294 (2012 projected); Race: 93.7% White, 3.0% Black, 0.0% Asian, 2.2% Hispanic of any race (2007); Density: 963.3 persons per square mile (2007); Average household size: 2.32 (2007); Median age: 31.9 (2007); Males per 100 females: 94.5 (2007); Marriage status: 24.8% never married, 55.1% now married, 7.7% widowed, 12.4% divorced (2000); Foreign born: 0.9% (2000); Ancestry (includes multiple ancestries): 15.3% German, 14.4% Irish, 12.4% Other groups, 10.6% United States or American, 9.4% English (2000).
Economy: Single-family building permits issued: 3 (2007); Multi-family building permits issued: 0 (2007); Employment by occupation: 7.3% management, 13.3% professional, 18.5% services, 31.0% sales, 0.0% farming, 11.0% construction, 18.8% production (2000).
Income: Per capita income: $17,245 (2007); Median household income: $32,174 (2007); Average household income: $40,066 (2007); Percent of households with income of $100,000 or more: 3.4% (2007); Poverty rate: 23.2% (2000).
Education: Percent of population age 25 and over with: High school diploma (including GED) or higher: 73.8% (2007); Bachelor's degree or higher: 12.8% (2007); Master's degree or higher: 2.2% (2007).
Housing: Homeownership rate: 62.9% (2007); Median home value: $52,903 (2007); Median rent: $309 per month (2000); Median age of housing: 25 years (2000).
Transportation: Commute to work: 96.4% car, 0.3% public transportation, 1.6% walk, 1.0% work from home (2000); Travel time to work: 27.4% less than 15 minutes, 57.5% 15 to 30 minutes, 10.7% 30 to 45 minutes, 1.5% 45 to 60 minutes, 3.0% 60 minutes or more (2000)

CARTERVILLE (city). Covers a land area of 4.347 square miles and a water area of 0.010 square miles. Located at 37.76° N. Lat.; 89.08° W. Long. Elevation is 449 feet.
History: Incorporated 1892.

Population: 4,293 (1990); 4,616 (2000); 4,792 (2007); 4,908 (2012 projected); Race: 95.1% White, 1.9% Black, 1.1% Asian, 1.2% Hispanic of any race (2007); Density: 1,102.3 persons per square mile (2007); Average household size: 2.35 (2007); Median age: 35.8 (2007); Males per 100 females: 94.7 (2007); Marriage status: 24.8% never married, 57.1% now married, 5.3% widowed, 12.7% divorced (2000); Foreign born: 1.7% (2000); Ancestry (includes multiple ancestries): 25.5% German, 15.0% Irish, 13.6% English, 12.5% Other groups, 7.9% United States or American (2000).
Economy: Single-family building permits issued: 46 (2007); Multi-family building permits issued: 6 (2007); Employment by occupation: 10.8% management, 29.0% professional, 14.2% services, 27.8% sales, 0.3% farming, 6.2% construction, 11.7% production (2000).
Income: Per capita income: $23,281 (2007); Median household income: $43,262 (2007); Average household income: $54,768 (2007); Percent of households with income of $100,000 or more: 12.9% (2007); Poverty rate: 14.6% (2000).
Education: Percent of population age 25 and over with: High school diploma (including GED) or higher: 85.1% (2007); Bachelor's degree or higher: 31.5% (2007); Master's degree or higher: 11.5% (2007).

School District(s)

Carterville CUSD 5 (PK-12)
2005-06 Enrollment: 1,727 . . . . (618) 985-4826

Two-year College(s)

John A Logan College (Public)
Fall 2007 Enrollment: 7,559. . . . . (618) 985-3741
2007-08 Tuition: In-state $5,030; Out-of-state $6,984

Housing: Homeownership rate: 69.4% (2007); Median home value: $101,815 (2007); Median rent: $389 per month (2000); Median age of housing: 28 years (2000).
Safety: Violent crime rate: 25.5 per 10,000 population; Property crime rate: 258.9 per 10,000 population (2006).
Transportation: Commute to work: 95.4% car, 0.0% public transportation, 0.7% walk, 3.5% work from home (2000); Travel time to work: 37.2% less than 15 minutes, 48.0% 15 to 30 minutes, 7.8% 30 to 45 minutes, 1.8% 45 to 60 minutes, 5.2% 60 minutes or more (2000)

Additional Information Contacts

Carterville Chamber of Commerce . . . . (618) 985-6942
http://www.cartervillechamber.com

COLP (village). Covers a land area of 0.142 square miles and a water area of 0 square miles. Located at 37.80° N. Lat.; 89.07° W. Long. Elevation is 400 feet.
Population: 235 (1990); 224 (2000); 244 (2007); 245 (2012 projected); Race: 81.1% White, 16.8% Black, 0.0% Asian, 0.0% Hispanic of any race (2007); Density: 1,717.2 persons per square mile (2007); Average household size: 2.14 (2007); Median age: 39.5 (2007); Males per 100 females: 87.7 (2007); Marriage status: 26.9% never married, 39.2% now married, 19.4% widowed, 14.5% divorced (2000); Foreign born: 2.2% (2000); Ancestry (includes multiple ancestries): 26.5% Other groups, 10.6% German, 9.7% Irish, 9.3% Polish, 8.8% Dutch (2000).
Economy: Employment by occupation: 13.4% management, 2.4% professional, 24.4% services, 14.6% sales, 0.0% farming, 4.9% construction, 40.2% production (2000).
Income: Per capita income: $13,975 (2007); Median household income: $18,462 (2007); Average household income: $29,912 (2007); Percent of households with income of $100,000 or more: 1.8% (2007); Poverty rate: 37.6% (2000).
Education: Percent of population age 25 and over with: High school diploma (including GED) or higher: 80.2% (2007); Bachelor's degree or higher: 4.1% (2007); Master's degree or higher: 2.9% (2007).
Housing: Homeownership rate: 84.2% (2007); Median home value: $46,316 (2007); Median rent: $263 per month (2000); Median age of housing: 45 years (2000).
Transportation: Commute to work: 97.5% car, 0.0% public transportation, 0.0% walk, 2.5% work from home (2000); Travel time to work: 48.1% less than 15 minutes, 27.3% 15 to 30 minutes, 15.6% 30 to 45 minutes, 3.9% 45 to 60 minutes, 5.2% 60 minutes or more (2000)

CRAINVILLE (village). Covers a land area of 1.397 square miles and a water area of 0 square miles. Located at 37.74° N. Lat.; 89.06° W. Long. Elevation is 469 feet.
Population: 1,030 (1990); 992 (2000); 1,108 (2007); 1,174 (2012 projected); Race: 97.1% White, 1.2% Black, 0.4% Asian, 0.5% Hispanic of any race (2007); Density: 793.0 persons per square mile (2007); Average household size: 2.33 (2007); Median age: 38.2 (2007); Males per 100 females: 85.0 (2007); Marriage status: 21.9% never married, 54.8% now married, 7.9% widowed, 15.4% divorced (2000); Foreign born: 0.0% (2000); Ancestry (includes multiple ancestries): 18.5% German, 16.9% English, 16.5% United States or American, 11.3% Irish, 6.3% Other groups (2000).
Economy: Single-family building permits issued: 14 (2007); Multi-family building permits issued: 10 (2007); Employment by occupation: 7.5% management, 21.5% professional, 20.5% services, 28.9% sales, 0.0% farming, 8.1% construction, 13.6% production (2000).
Income: Per capita income: $21,907 (2007); Median household income: $40,833 (2007); Average household income: $50,993 (2007); Percent of households with income of $100,000 or more: 9.9% (2007); Poverty rate: 8.8% (2000).
Taxes: Total city taxes per capita: $146 (2006); City property taxes per capita: $33 (2006).
Education: Percent of population age 25 and over with: High school diploma (including GED) or higher: 89.4% (2007); Bachelor's degree or higher: 26.8% (2007); Master's degree or higher: 8.4% (2007).
Housing: Homeownership rate: 71.2% (2007); Median home value: $87,738 (2007); Median rent: $323 per month (2000); Median age of housing: 27 years (2000).
Transportation: Commute to work: 97.0% car, 0.0% public transportation, 1.6% walk, 1.0% work from home (2000); Travel time to work: 47.6% less than 15 minutes, 37.6% 15 to 30 minutes, 8.7% 30 to 45 minutes, 1.6% 45 to 60 minutes, 4.5% 60 minutes or more (2000)

CREAL SPRINGS (city). Covers a land area of 0.990 square miles and a water area of 0.007 square miles. Located at 37.62° N. Lat.; 88.83° W. Long. Elevation is 509 feet.
Population: 851 (1990); 702 (2000); 660 (2007); 662 (2012 projected); Race: 96.7% White, 0.0% Black, 0.2% Asian, 2.9% Hispanic of any race (2007); Density: 666.6 persons per square mile (2007); Average household size: 2.38 (2007); Median age: 41.5 (2007); Males per 100 females: 97.0 (2007); Marriage status: 17.4% never married, 58.4% now married, 14.6% widowed, 9.6% divorced (2000); Foreign born: 0.2% (2000); Ancestry (includes multiple ancestries): 24.0% United States or American, 17.6% Irish, 15.9% Other groups, 9.6% German, 6.6% English (2000).
Economy: Employment by occupation: 4.8% management, 3.5% professional, 34.1% services, 17.9% sales, 1.7% farming, 15.7% construction, 22.3% production (2000).
Income: Per capita income: $17,761 (2007); Median household income: $29,306 (2007); Average household income: $40,217 (2007); Percent of households with income of $100,000 or more: 5.1% (2007); Poverty rate: 23.7% (2000).
Education: Percent of population age 25 and over with: High school diploma (including GED) or higher: 60.2% (2007); Bachelor's degree or higher: 7.3% (2007); Master's degree or higher: 1.3% (2007).

School District(s)

Marion CUSD 2 (PK-12)
2005-06 Enrollment: 4,025 . . . . (618) 993-2321

Housing: Homeownership rate: 79.4% (2007); Median home value: $42,381 (2007); Median rent: $230 per month (2000); Median age of housing: 42 years (2000).
Transportation: Commute to work: 92.9% car, 0.9% public transportation, 1.3% walk, 4.0% work from home (2000); Travel time to work: 24.0% less than 15 minutes, 35.0% 15 to 30 minutes, 26.3% 30 to 45 minutes, 6.0% 45 to 60 minutes, 8.8% 60 minutes or more (2000)

ENERGY (village). Covers a land area of 1.186 square miles and a water area of 0.009 square miles. Located at 37.77° N. Lat.; 89.02° W. Long. Elevation is 459 feet.
Population: 1,105 (1990); 1,175 (2000); 1,371 (2007); 1,495 (2012 projected); Race: 97.2% White, 1.1% Black, 0.7% Asian, 0.7% Hispanic of any race (2007); Density: 1,156.2 persons per square mile (2007); Average household size: 2.38 (2007); Median age: 45.6 (2007); Males per 100 females: 86.3 (2007); Marriage status: 19.3% never married, 58.7% now married, 9.1% widowed, 12.9% divorced (2000); Foreign born: 0.9% (2000); Ancestry (includes multiple ancestries): 15.4% German, 15.0% Irish, 10.8% United States or American, 10.8% English, 8.7% Other groups (2000).
Economy: Single-family building permits issued: 0 (2007); Multi-family building permits issued: 0 (2007); Employment by occupation: 10.8% management, 13.3% professional, 16.0% services, 32.9% sales, 0.0% farming, 8.4% construction, 18.6% production (2000).

Income: Per capita income: $17,571 (2007); Median household income: $35,068 (2007); Average household income: $41,778 (2007); Percent of households with income of $100,000 or more: 4.9% (2007); Poverty rate: 12.1% (2000).
Education: Percent of population age 25 and over with: High school diploma (including GED) or higher: 75.6% (2007); Bachelor's degree or higher: 15.1% (2007); Master's degree or higher: 3.2% (2007).
Housing: Homeownership rate: 58.4% (2007); Median home value: $102,885 (2007); Median rent: $331 per month (2000); Median age of housing: 25 years (2000).
Safety: Violent crime rate: 8.5 per 10,000 population; Property crime rate: 178.4 per 10,000 population (2006).
Transportation: Commute to work: 95.4% car, 0.0% public transportation, 2.0% walk, 2.6% work from home (2000); Travel time to work: 40.5% less than 15 minutes, 36.7% 15 to 30 minutes, 12.2% 30 to 45 minutes, 5.3% 45 to 60 minutes, 5.1% 60 minutes or more (2000)

FREEMAN SPUR (village). Aka Freemanspur. Covers a land area of 0.404 square miles and a water area of 0 square miles. Located at 37.86° N. Lat.; 89.00° W. Long. Elevation is 397 feet.
Population: 290 (1990); 273 (2000); 286 (2007); 291 (2012 projected); Race: 89.9% White, 5.2% Black, 0.0% Asian, 3.1% Hispanic of any race (2007); Density: 708.2 persons per square mile (2007); Average household size: 2.44 (2007); Median age: 36.2 (2007); Males per 100 females: 105.8 (2007); Marriage status: 26.3% never married, 46.0% now married, 10.1% widowed, 17.7% divorced (2000); Foreign born: 0.0% (2000); Ancestry (includes multiple ancestries): 21.8% Other groups, 18.7% Irish, 12.2% German, 10.3% Italian, 8.4% United States or American (2000).
Economy: Employment by occupation: 0.0% management, 7.1% professional, 29.3% services, 20.2% sales, 2.0% farming, 14.1% construction, 27.3% production (2000).
Income: Per capita income: $14,755 (2007); Median household income: $27,656 (2007); Average household income: $36,068 (2007); Percent of households with income of $100,000 or more: 4.3% (2007); Poverty rate: 22.1% (2000).
Education: Percent of population age 25 and over with: High school diploma (including GED) or higher: 67.7% (2007); Bachelor's degree or higher: 5.3% (2007); Master's degree or higher: 0.0% (2007).
Housing: Homeownership rate: 81.2% (2007); Median home value: $45,000 (2007); Median rent: $289 per month (2000); Median age of housing: 53 years (2000).
Transportation: Commute to work: 94.9% car, 0.0% public transportation, 0.0% walk, 5.1% work from home (2000); Travel time to work: 22.3% less than 15 minutes, 38.3% 15 to 30 minutes, 30.9% 30 to 45 minutes, 3.2% 45 to 60 minutes, 5.3% 60 minutes or more (2000)

HERRIN (city). Covers a land area of 8.202 square miles and a water area of 0.174 square miles. Located at 37.80° N. Lat.; 89.02° W. Long. Elevation is 420 feet.
History: Coal mining began in Herrin in 1895. It was incorporated as a village in 1898 and as a city in 1900.
Population: 11,097 (1990); 11,298 (2000); 11,604 (2007); 11,822 (2012 projected); Race: 95.6% White, 1.3% Black, 0.9% Asian, 1.5% Hispanic of any race (2007); Density: 1,414.8 persons per square mile (2007); Average household size: 2.32 (2007); Median age: 40.1 (2007); Males per 100 females: 86.0 (2007); Marriage status: 19.0% never married, 56.6% now married, 11.7% widowed, 12.7% divorced (2000); Foreign born: 1.6% (2000); Ancestry (includes multiple ancestries): 14.6% German, 13.2% Irish, 13.1% United States or American, 11.7% English, 11.5% Other groups (2000).
Economy: Single-family building permits issued: 118 (2007); Multi-family building permits issued: 0 (2007); Employment by occupation: 9.5% management, 17.0% professional, 18.5% services, 27.7% sales, 0.2% farming, 8.8% construction, 18.3% production (2000).
Income: Per capita income: $19,439 (2007); Median household income: $32,876 (2007); Average household income: $43,975 (2007); Percent of households with income of $100,000 or more: 8.1% (2007); Poverty rate: 16.0% (2000).
Education: Percent of population age 25 and over with: High school diploma (including GED) or higher: 79.0% (2007); Bachelor's degree or higher: 17.3% (2007); Master's degree or higher: 5.8% (2007).

School District(s)

Herrin CUSD 4 (PK-12)
2005-06 Enrollment: 2,262 . . . . (618) 988-8024
Williamson Co Spec Educ Dist (07-12)
2005-06 Enrollment: 24 . . . . (618) 993-2138
Housing: Homeownership rate: 71.6% (2007); Median home value: $67,089 (2007); Median rent: $296 per month (2000); Median age of housing: 46 years (2000).
Hospitals: Herrin Hospital (92 beds)
Safety: Violent crime rate: 31.7 per 10,000 population; Property crime rate: 332.0 per 10,000 population (2006).
Newspapers: Spokesman (Community news; Circulation 2,100); Spokesman Sunday (Community news; Circulation 10,200)
Transportation: Commute to work: 93.3% car, 0.0% public transportation, 4.1% walk, 1.6% work from home (2000); Travel time to work: 44.4% less than 15 minutes, 31.5% 15 to 30 minutes, 14.4% 30 to 45 minutes, 4.5% 45 to 60 minutes, 5.2% 60 minutes or more (2000)
Additional Information Contacts
City of Herrin . . . . (618) 942-3175
http://www.herrinillinois.com/pages/comm_gov.php
Herrin Chamber of Commerce. . . . . (618) 942-5163
http://www.herrinillinois.com

HURST (city). Covers a land area of 0.861 square miles and a water area of 0 square miles. Located at 37.83° N. Lat.; 89.14° W. Long. Elevation is 390 feet.
Population: 843 (1990); 805 (2000); 713 (2007); 705 (2012 projected); Race: 95.9% White, 1.7% Black, 0.0% Asian, 1.7% Hispanic of any race (2007); Density: 828.2 persons per square mile (2007); Average household size: 2.19 (2007); Median age: 36.0 (2007); Males per 100 females: 92.2 (2007); Marriage status: 26.0% never married, 47.6% now married, 12.9% widowed, 13.5% divorced (2000); Foreign born: 1.7% (2000); Ancestry (includes multiple ancestries): 16.3% Irish, 12.7% Other groups, 12.6% German, 10.2% English, 6.0% United States or American (2000).
Economy: Single-family building permits issued: 0 (2007); Multi-family building permits issued: 0 (2007); Employment by occupation: 7.3% management, 8.5% professional, 20.3% services, 28.8% sales, 0.6% farming, 13.6% construction, 20.9% production (2000).
Income: Per capita income: $15,056 (2007); Median household income: $25,870 (2007); Average household income: $32,929 (2007); Percent of households with income of $100,000 or more: 3.1% (2007); Poverty rate: 24.8% (2000).
Education: Percent of population age 25 and over with: High school diploma (including GED) or higher: 66.7% (2007); Bachelor's degree or higher: 7.3% (2007); Master's degree or higher: 1.9% (2007).
Housing: Homeownership rate: 70.2% (2007); Median home value: $41,700 (2007); Median rent: $199 per month (2000); Median age of housing: 48 years (2000).
Transportation: Commute to work: 95.1% car, 0.7% public transportation, 0.7% walk, 3.6% work from home (2000); Travel time to work: 13.6% less than 15 minutes, 56.8% 15 to 30 minutes, 17.0% 30 to 45 minutes, 8.8% 45 to 60 minutes, 3.7% 60 minutes or more (2000)

JOHNSTON CITY (city). Covers a land area of 1.953 square miles and a water area of 0.058 square miles. Located at 37.82° N. Lat.; 88.92° W. Long. Elevation is 430 feet.
History: Incorporated 1896.
Population: 3,770 (1990); 3,557 (2000); 3,414 (2007); 3,309 (2012 projected); Race: 98.9% White, 0.1% Black, 0.1% Asian, 1.4% Hispanic of any race (2007); Density: 1,747.7 persons per square mile (2007); Average household size: 2.24 (2007); Median age: 39.2 (2007); Males per 100 females: 87.2 (2007); Marriage status: 22.1% never married, 56.8% now married, 11.6% widowed, 9.5% divorced (2000); Foreign born: 1.3% (2000); Ancestry (includes multiple ancestries): 17.5% German, 14.9% Irish, 11.7% United States or American, 10.4% Other groups, 8.7% English (2000).
Economy: Single-family building permits issued: 7 (2007); Multi-family building permits issued: 0 (2007); Employment by occupation: 6.4% management, 11.9% professional, 25.7% services, 23.7% sales, 0.0% farming, 10.6% construction, 21.7% production (2000).
Income: Per capita income: $15,809 (2007); Median household income: $30,104 (2007); Average household income: $35,345 (2007); Percent of households with income of $100,000 or more: 1.7% (2007); Poverty rate: 22.5% (2000).
Taxes: Total city taxes per capita: $144 (2006); City property taxes per capita: $63 (2006).

Education: Percent of population age 25 and over with: High school diploma (including GED) or higher: 71.1% (2007); Bachelor's degree or higher: 7.3% (2007); Master's degree or higher: 3.3% (2007).

School District(s)

Franklin/Williamson Roe (06-12)
2005-06 Enrollment: 166 . . . . (618) 438-9711
Johnston City CUSD 1 (PK-12)
2005-06 Enrollment: 1,255 . . . . (618) 983-8021

Housing: Homeownership rate: 75.1% (2007); Median home value: $49,673 (2007); Median rent: $264 per month (2000); Median age of housing: 60+ years (2000).

Safety: Violent crime rate: 46.0 per 10,000 population; Property crime rate: 316.5 per 10,000 population (2006).

Transportation: Commute to work: 93.0% car, 0.0% public transportation, 5.5% walk, 1.6% work from home (2000); Travel time to work: 36.3% less than 15 minutes, 38.5% 15 to 30 minutes, 13.1% 30 to 45 minutes, 8.7% 45 to 60 minutes, 3.5% 60 minutes or more (2000)

MARION (city). County seat. Covers a land area of 12.826 square miles and a water area of 0.697 square miles. Located at 37.73° N. Lat.; 88.93° W. Long. Elevation is 423 feet.

History: Marion was established in the mid-1800's. Early residents were Robert G. Ingersoll and John A. Logan, both of whom became colonels serving in the Civil War.

Population: 14,971 (1990); 16,035 (2000); 17,052 (2007); 17,704 (2012 projected); Race: 90.9% White, 5.7% Black, 1.1% Asian, 2.2% Hispanic of any race (2007); Density: 1,329.5 persons per square mile (2007); Average household size: 2.30 (2007); Median age: 39.5 (2007); Males per 100 females: 89.2 (2007); Marriage status: 19.0% never married, 55.9% now married, 10.6% widowed, 14.5% divorced (2000); Foreign born: 0.9% (2000); Ancestry (includes multiple ancestries): 15.5% German, 13.2% English, 12.0% Other groups, 11.2% United States or American, 11.1% Irish (2000).

Economy: Single-family building permits issued: 37 (2007); Multi-family building permits issued: 39 (2007); Employment by occupation: 12.8% management, 18.0% professional, 19.3% services, 28.7% sales, 0.0% farming, 6.7% construction, 14.5% production (2000).

Income: Per capita income: $23,025 (2007); Median household income: $35,809 (2007); Average household income: $52,147 (2007); Percent of households with income of $100,000 or more: 10.9% (2007); Poverty rate: 14.9% (2000).

Education: Percent of population age 25 and over with: High school diploma (including GED) or higher: 79.5% (2007); Bachelor's degree or higher: 17.1% (2007); Master's degree or higher: 6.6% (2007).

School District(s)

Crab Orchard CUSD 3 (PK-12)
2005-06 Enrollment: 411 . . . . (618) 982-2181
Marion CUSD 2 (PK-12)
2005-06 Enrollment: 4,025 . . . . (618) 993-2321
Williamson Co Spec Educ Dist (07-12)
2005-06 Enrollment: 24 . . . . (618) 993-2138

Housing: Homeownership rate: 65.3% (2007); Median home value: $90,967 (2007); Median rent: $338 per month (2000); Median age of housing: 33 years (2000).

Hospitals: US Penitentiary Infirmary; Veterans Affairs Medical Center (39 beds)

Safety: Violent crime rate: 156.1 per 10,000 population; Property crime rate: 457.2 per 10,000 population (2006).

Newspapers: Marion Daily Republican (Community news; Circulation 3,500); Williamson County Extra (Community news; Circulation 20,000)

Transportation: Commute to work: 96.4% car, 0.1% public transportation, 0.9% walk, 2.0% work from home (2000); Travel time to work: 52.2% less than 15 minutes, 28.5% 15 to 30 minutes, 11.8% 30 to 45 minutes, 2.7% 45 to 60 minutes, 4.7% 60 minutes or more (2000)

Airports: Williamson County Regional (commercial service)

Additional Information Contacts

City of Marion . . . . (618) 997-6281
http://www.cityofmarionil.gov
Marion Area Chamber of Commerce . . . . (618) 997-6311
http://www.marionillinois.com

PITTSBURG (village). Covers a land area of 2.085 square miles and a water area of 0.027 square miles. Located at 37.77° N. Lat.; 88.85° W. Long. Elevation is 466 feet.

Population: 602 (1990); 575 (2000); 570 (2007); 560 (2012 projected); Race: 97.0% White, 1.9% Black, 0.4% Asian, 0.4% Hispanic of any race (2007); Density: 273.4 persons per square mile (2007); Average household size: 2.47 (2007); Median age: 37.2 (2007); Males per 100 females: 111.9 (2007); Marriage status: 23.9% never married, 61.3% now married, 6.9% widowed, 8.0% divorced (2000); Foreign born: 0.4% (2000); Ancestry (includes multiple ancestries): 19.0% German, 13.2% Irish, 12.1% Other groups, 11.7% United States or American, 7.1% English (2000).

Economy: Employment by occupation: 1.6% management, 12.7% professional, 39.6% services, 22.0% sales, 0.0% farming, 12.7% construction, 11.4% production (2000).

Income: Per capita income: $15,807 (2007); Median household income: $34,239 (2007); Average household income: $39,004 (2007); Percent of households with income of $100,000 or more: 3.0% (2007); Poverty rate: 11.3% (2000).

Education: Percent of population age 25 and over with: High school diploma (including GED) or higher: 76.5% (2007); Bachelor's degree or higher: 6.5% (2007); Master's degree or higher: 0.5% (2007).

School District(s)

Johnston City CUSD 1 (PK-12)
2005-06 Enrollment: 1,255 . . . . (618) 983-8021

Housing: Homeownership rate: 86.6% (2007); Median home value: $57,931 (2007); Median rent: $244 per month (2000); Median age of housing: 57 years (2000).

Transportation: Commute to work: 99.2% car, 0.0% public transportation, 0.8% walk, 0.0% work from home (2000); Travel time to work: 19.4% less than 15 minutes, 42.6% 15 to 30 minutes, 16.1% 30 to 45 minutes, 14.0% 45 to 60 minutes, 7.9% 60 minutes or more (2000)

SPILLERTOWN (village). Covers a land area of 0.311 square miles and a water area of 0 square miles. Located at 37.76° N. Lat.; 88.91° W. Long. Elevation is 482 feet.

Population: 249 (1990); 220 (2000); 219 (2007); 215 (2012 projected); Race: 95.9% White, 2.7% Black, 0.5% Asian, 6.4% Hispanic of any race (2007); Density: 704.3 persons per square mile (2007); Average household size: 2.58 (2007); Median age: 31.3 (2007); Males per 100 females: 104.7 (2007); Marriage status: 26.8% never married, 51.4% now married, 12.6% widowed, 9.3% divorced (2000); Foreign born: 0.9% (2000); Ancestry (includes multiple ancestries): 16.8% Other groups, 10.5% United States or American, 10.0% Irish, 9.1% English, 8.2% German (2000).

Economy: Employment by occupation: 12.0% management, 8.0% professional, 17.0% services, 30.0% sales, 0.0% farming, 16.0% construction, 17.0% production (2000).

Income: Per capita income: $20,331 (2007); Median household income: $36,875 (2007); Average household income: $52,382 (2007); Percent of households with income of $100,000 or more: 10.6% (2007); Poverty rate: 6.4% (2000).

Education: Percent of population age 25 and over with: High school diploma (including GED) or higher: 71.7% (2007); Bachelor's degree or higher: 3.6% (2007); Master's degree or higher: 2.2% (2007).

Housing: Homeownership rate: 75.3% (2007); Median home value: $72,000 (2007); Median rent: $300 per month (2000); Median age of housing: 44 years (2000).

Transportation: Commute to work: 91.0% car, 0.0% public transportation, 0.0% walk, 2.0% work from home (2000); Travel time to work: 40.8% less than 15 minutes, 39.8% 15 to 30 minutes, 16.3% 30 to 45 minutes, 0.0% 45 to 60 minutes, 3.1% 60 minutes or more (2000)

STONEFORT (village). Covers a land area of 1.461 square miles and a water area of 0.003 square miles. Located at 37.61° N. Lat.; 88.70° W. Long. Elevation is 410 feet.

History: Stonefort was built on the ruins of an old stone fort, a prehistoric structure on a cliff with a stone barricade on the approachable side. In 1872 the town was moved to take advantage of the arrival of the railroad.

Population: 301 (1990); 292 (2000); 281 (2007); 278 (2012 projected); Race: 96.1% White, 1.4% Black, 0.0% Asian, 3.2% Hispanic of any race (2007); Density: 192.4 persons per square mile (2007); Average household size: 2.20 (2007); Median age: 48.8 (2007); Males per 100 females: 81.3 (2007); Marriage status: 14.1% never married, 62.7% now married, 8.7% widowed, 14.5% divorced (2000); Foreign born: 0.0% (2000); Ancestry (includes multiple ancestries): 14.4% United States or American, 12.6% German, 11.1% English, 10.7% Irish, 6.3% Other groups (2000).

Economy: Employment by occupation: 9.7% management, 11.1% professional, 34.7% services, 13.9% sales, 0.0% farming, 15.3% construction, 15.3% production (2000).

Income: Per capita income: $17,500 (2007); Median household income: $33,846 (2007); Average household income: $38,418 (2007); Percent of households with income of $100,000 or more: 4.7% (2007); Poverty rate: 16.9% (2000).
Education: Percent of population age 25 and over with: High school diploma (including GED) or higher: 68.9% (2007); Bachelor's degree or higher: 7.2% (2007); Master's degree or higher: 1.4% (2007).
Housing: Homeownership rate: 85.9% (2007); Median home value: $45,714 (2007); Median rent: $181 per month (2000); Median age of housing: 44 years (2000).
Transportation: Commute to work: 98.5% car, 0.0% public transportation, 0.0% walk, 1.5% work from home (2000); Travel time to work: 11.9% less than 15 minutes, 31.3% 15 to 30 minutes, 38.8% 30 to 45 minutes, 4.5% 45 to 60 minutes, 13.4% 60 minutes or more (2000)

WHITEASH (village). Covers a land area of 0.870 square miles and a water area of 0.024 square miles. Located at 37.78° N. Lat.; 88.92° W. Long.
Population: 249 (1990); 268 (2000); 266 (2007); 265 (2012 projected); Race: 96.2% White, 1.1% Black, 0.0% Asian, 1.9% Hispanic of any race (2007); Density: 305.8 persons per square mile (2007); Average household size: 2.29 (2007); Median age: 41.9 (2007); Males per 100 females: 95.6 (2007); Marriage status: 14.9% never married, 63.1% now married, 13.1% widowed, 9.0% divorced (2000); Foreign born: 1.1% (2000); Ancestry (includes multiple ancestries): 16.1% German, 16.1% English, 15.0% United States or American, 11.8% Irish, 8.2% Other groups (2000).
Economy: Employment by occupation: 3.7% management, 13.8% professional, 19.3% services, 33.0% sales, 2.8% farming, 11.0% construction, 16.5% production (2000).
Income: Per capita income: $16,400 (2007); Median household income: $29,231 (2007); Average household income: $37,608 (2007); Percent of households with income of $100,000 or more: 5.2% (2007); Poverty rate: 23.3% (2000).
Education: Percent of population age 25 and over with: High school diploma (including GED) or higher: 74.5% (2007); Bachelor's degree or higher: 2.1% (2007); Master's degree or higher: 0.0% (2007).
Housing: Homeownership rate: 69.8% (2007); Median home value: $66,250 (2007); Median rent: $238 per month (2000); Median age of housing: 32 years (2000).
Transportation: Commute to work: 95.3% car, 0.0% public transportation, 0.9% walk, 1.9% work from home (2000); Travel time to work: 22.9% less than 15 minutes, 51.4% 15 to 30 minutes, 20.0% 30 to 45 minutes, 1.9% 45 to 60 minutes, 3.8% 60 minutes or more (2000)

Winnebago County

Located in northern Illinois; bounded on the north by Wisconsin; drained by the Rock, Pecatonica, and Kishwaukee Rivers. Covers a land area of 513.74 square miles, a water area of 5.54 square miles, and is located in the Central Time Zone. The county was founded in 1836. County seat is Rockford.

Winnebago County is part of the Rockford, IL Metropolitan Statistical Area. The entire metro area includes: Boone County, IL; Winnebago County, IL

Weather Station: Rockford Greater Rockford Arpt. Elevation: 679 feet

	Jan	Feb	Mar	Apr	May	Jun	Jul	Aug	Sep	Oct	Nov	Dec
High	27	32	45	59	71	81	84	82	74	62	46	33
Low	10	16	26	37	48	58	63	61	52	40	29	17
Precip	1.4	1.3	2.4	3.6	4.0	4.7	4.1	4.1	3.6	2.7	2.6	2.0
Snow	10.1	7.6	5.7	1.6	tr	tr	tr	tr	0.0	tr	2.6	9.8

High and Low temperatures in degrees Fahrenheit; Precipitation and Snow in inches

Population: 252,913 (1990); 278,418 (2000); 291,868 (2007); 300,665 (2012 projected); Race: 79.6% White, 11.0% Black, 2.0% Asian, 10.2% Hispanic of any race (2007); Density: 568.1 persons per square mile (2007); Average household size: 2.56 (2007); Median age: 36.7 (2007); Males per 100 females: 96.9 (2007).
Religion: Five largest groups: 22.2% Catholic Church, 7.1% Evangelical Lutheran Church in America, 3.6% The United Methodist Church, 2.4% Assemblies of God, 2.0% Lutheran Church—Missouri Synod (2000).
Economy: Unemployment rate: 7.0% (4/2008); Total civilian labor force: 152,318 (4/2008); Leading industries: 21.4% manufacturing; 15.2% health care and social assistance; 13.5% retail trade (2005); Farms: 695 totaling 191,455 acres (2002); Companies that employ 500 or more persons: 17 (2006); Companies that employ 100 to 499 persons: 194 (2006); Companies that employ less than 100 persons: 6,815 (2006); Black-owned businesses: 1,016 (2002); Hispanic-owned businesses: n/a (2002); Asian-owned businesses: 394 (2002); Women-owned businesses: 5,911 (2002); Retail sales per capita: $15,865 (2008). Single-family building permits issued: 877 (2007); Multi-family building permits issued: 174 (2007).
Income: Per capita income: $23,609 (2007); Median household income: $47,791 (2007); Average household income: $59,831 (2007); Percent of households with income of $100,000 or more: 13.4% (2007); Poverty rate: 11.9% (2005); Bankruptcy rate: 4.64% (2007).
Taxes: Total county taxes per capita: $211 (2006); County property taxes per capita: $111 (2006).
Education: Percent of population age 25 and over with: High school diploma (including GED) or higher: 81.8% (2007); Bachelor's degree or higher: 19.6% (2007); Master's degree or higher: 6.7% (2007).
Housing: Homeownership rate: 70.5% (2007); Median home value: $119,045 (2007); Median rent: $436 per month (2000); Median age of housing: 35 years (2000).
Health: Birth rate: 143.2 per 10,000 population (2007); Death rate: 85.9 per 10,000 population (2007); Age-adjusted cancer mortality rate: 210.3 deaths per 100,000 population (2005); Air Quality Index: 85.5% good, 14.0% moderate, 0.5% unhealthy for sensitive individuals, 0.0% unhealthy (percent of days in 2007); Number of physicians: 24.9 per 10,000 population (2005); Hospital beds: 35.3 per 10,000 population (2004); Hospital admissions: 1,518.4 per 10,000 population (2004).
Elections: 2004 Presidential election results: 50.1% Bush, 49.2% Kerry, 0.1% Nader, 0.6% Badnarik
National and State Parks: Rock Cut State Park
Additional Information Contacts
Winnebago County Government . . . . (815) 987-2590
http://www.co.winnebago.il.us
City of Loves Park . . . . (815) 654-5030
http://www.loves-park.il.us
City of Rockford . . . . (815) 987-5590
http://www.cityofrockford.net
City of South Beloit . . . . (815) 389-3023
http://www.southbeloit.org
Rockford Chamber of Commerce . . . . (815) 987-8100
http://www.rockfordchamber.com
Rockton Chamber of Commerce . . . . (815) 624-7625
http://www.rocktonchamber.com
Roscoe Area Chamber of Commerce . . . . (815) 623-9065
http://www.roscoechamber.com
The Parks Chamber of Commerce . . . . (815) 633-3999
http://www.parkschamber.com
Village of Machesney Park . . . . (815) 877-5432
http://www.machesney-park.il.us
Village of Rockton . . . . (815) 624-7600
http://www.rockton.ws
Village of Roscoe . . . . (815) 623-2829
http://www.villageofroscoe.com

Winnebago County Communities

CHERRY VALLEY (village). Covers a land area of 3.757 square miles and a water area of 0.049 square miles. Located at 42.23° N. Lat.; 88.96° W. Long. Elevation is 728 feet.
Population: 1,819 (1990); 2,191 (2000); 2,260 (2007); 2,322 (2012 projected); Race: 91.7% White, 2.3% Black, 3.5% Asian, 3.5% Hispanic of any race (2007); Density: 601.6 persons per square mile (2007); Average household size: 2.49 (2007); Median age: 38.4 (2007); Males per 100 females: 101.1 (2007); Marriage status: 22.7% never married, 64.7% now married, 2.9% widowed, 9.7% divorced (2000); Foreign born: 5.1% (2000); Ancestry (includes multiple ancestries): 28.8% German, 18.1% Irish, 14.0% Other groups, 10.9% English, 10.6% Swedish (2000).
Economy: Employment by occupation: 12.4% management, 15.1% professional, 8.0% services, 35.9% sales, 0.0% farming, 10.3% construction, 18.3% production (2000).
Income: Per capita income: $31,503 (2007); Median household income: $67,768 (2007); Average household income: $78,190 (2007); Percent of households with income of $100,000 or more: 23.2% (2007); Poverty rate: 6.3% (2000).
Education: Percent of population age 25 and over with: High school diploma (including GED) or higher: 90.0% (2007); Bachelor's degree or higher: 23.7% (2007); Master's degree or higher: 5.3% (2007).

School District(s)

Rockford SD 205 (PK-12)
2005-06 Enrollment: 29,145 . . . . (815) 966-3101

Housing: Homeownership rate: 75.1% (2007); Median home value: $170,536 (2007); Median rent: $473 per month (2000); Median age of housing: 18 years (2000).

Safety: Violent crime rate: 53.9 per 10,000 population; Property crime rate: 2,351.9 per 10,000 population (2006).

Transportation: Commute to work: 98.3% car, 0.0% public transportation, 0.0% walk, 1.3% work from home (2000); Travel time to work: 35.1% less than 15 minutes, 39.6% 15 to 30 minutes, 11.4% 30 to 45 minutes, 4.6% 45 to 60 minutes, 9.3% 60 minutes or more (2000)

DURAND (village). Covers a land area of 0.900 square miles and a water area of 0 square miles. Located at 42.43° N. Lat.; 89.32° W. Long. Elevation is 771 feet.

Population: 1,156 (1990); 1,081 (2000); 1,242 (2007); 1,339 (2012 projected); Race: 95.9% White, 0.8% Black, 0.0% Asian, 1.4% Hispanic of any race (2007); Density: 1,379.8 persons per square mile (2007); Average household size: 2.39 (2007); Median age: 36.0 (2007); Males per 100 females: 95.0 (2007); Marriage status: 23.0% never married, 57.6% now married, 6.4% widowed, 12.9% divorced (2000); Foreign born: 0.2% (2000); Ancestry (includes multiple ancestries): 36.2% German, 22.7% Irish, 11.0% English, 11.0% United States or American, 7.5% Norwegian (2000).

Economy: Employment by occupation: 7.5% management, 18.4% professional, 15.2% services, 24.4% sales, 0.8% farming, 10.4% construction, 23.4% production (2000).

Income: Per capita income: $24,114 (2007); Median household income: $50,299 (2007); Average household income: $57,582 (2007); Percent of households with income of $100,000 or more: 12.1% (2007); Poverty rate: 5.6% (2000).

Education: Percent of population age 25 and over with: High school diploma (including GED) or higher: 88.3% (2007); Bachelor's degree or higher: 16.3% (2007); Master's degree or higher: 4.1% (2007).

School District(s)

Durand CUSD 322 (PK-12)
2005-06 Enrollment: 725 . . . . (815) 248-2171

Housing: Homeownership rate: 71.7% (2007); Median home value: $116,805 (2007); Median rent: $381 per month (2000); Median age of housing: 40 years (2000).

Safety: Violent crime rate: 9.3 per 10,000 population; Property crime rate: 204.3 per 10,000 population (2006).

Newspapers: Durand Volunteer (Community news; Circulation 2,000)

Transportation: Commute to work: 91.8% car, 0.0% public transportation, 3.7% walk, 3.3% work from home (2000); Travel time to work: 24.0% less than 15 minutes, 20.2% 15 to 30 minutes, 42.6% 30 to 45 minutes, 6.7% 45 to 60 minutes, 6.5% 60 minutes or more (2000)

LAKE SUMMERSET (CDP). Covers a land area of 2.071 square miles and a water area of 0.425 square miles. Located at 42.44° N. Lat.; 89.39° W. Long. Elevation is 860 feet.

Population: 1,296 (1990); 2,061 (2000); 2,539 (2007); 2,809 (2012 projected); Race: 98.5% White, 0.4% Black, 0.2% Asian, 0.9% Hispanic of any race (2007); Density: 1,226.1 persons per square mile (2007); Average household size: 2.48 (2007); Median age: 48.5 (2007); Males per 100 females: 92.9 (2007); Marriage status: 12.5% never married, 74.6% now married, 3.6% widowed, 9.3% divorced (2000); Foreign born: 1.9% (2000); Ancestry (includes multiple ancestries): 34.0% German, 21.4% Irish, 14.3% English, 8.8% Swedish, 7.0% Norwegian (2000).

Economy: Employment by occupation: 16.4% management, 23.9% professional, 7.3% services, 26.7% sales, 0.0% farming, 9.5% construction, 16.2% production (2000).

Income: Per capita income: $33,289 (2007); Median household income: $70,088 (2007); Average household income: $82,701 (2007); Percent of households with income of $100,000 or more: 26.1% (2007); Poverty rate: 0.8% (2000).

Education: Percent of population age 25 and over with: High school diploma (including GED) or higher: 94.7% (2007); Bachelor's degree or higher: 30.5% (2007); Master's degree or higher: 9.1% (2007).

Housing: Homeownership rate: 96.5% (2007); Median home value: $169,828 (2007); Median rent: $648 per month (2000); Median age of housing: 15 years (2000).

Transportation: Commute to work: 95.5% car, 0.0% public transportation, 0.0% walk, 3.2% work from home (2000); Travel time to work: 13.1% less than 15 minutes, 14.3% 15 to 30 minutes, 48.7% 30 to 45 minutes, 13.4% 45 to 60 minutes, 10.6% 60 minutes or more (2000)

LOVES PARK (city). Covers a land area of 14.450 square miles and a water area of 0.368 square miles. Located at 42.32° N. Lat.; 89.02° W. Long. Elevation is 728 feet.

History: Incorporated 1947.

Population: 16,327 (1990); 20,044 (2000); 23,377 (2007); 25,465 (2012 projected); Race: 90.1% White, 3.2% Black, 2.5% Asian, 4.6% Hispanic of any race (2007); Density: 1,617.8 persons per square mile (2007); Average household size: 2.44 (2007); Median age: 36.0 (2007); Males per 100 females: 97.4 (2007); Marriage status: 23.7% never married, 57.2% now married, 6.7% widowed, 12.3% divorced (2000); Foreign born: 4.2% (2000); Ancestry (includes multiple ancestries): 29.1% German, 14.7% Irish, 11.1% Other groups, 10.8% Swedish, 10.0% English (2000).

Economy: Single-family building permits issued: 102 (2007); Multi-family building permits issued: 0 (2007); Employment by occupation: 11.1% management, 18.3% professional, 10.4% services, 28.6% sales, 0.1% farming, 8.4% construction, 23.1% production (2000).

Income: Per capita income: $22,782 (2007); Median household income: $48,858 (2007); Average household income: $55,531 (2007); Percent of households with income of $100,000 or more: 8.9% (2007); Poverty rate: 5.0% (2000).

Education: Percent of population age 25 and over with: High school diploma (including GED) or higher: 86.9% (2007); Bachelor's degree or higher: 18.5% (2007); Master's degree or higher: 5.9% (2007).

School District(s)

Boone/Winnebago Roe (06-12)
2005-06 Enrollment: 267 . . . . (815) 636-3060

Harlem UD 122 (PK-12)
2005-06 Enrollment: 7,838 . . . . (815) 654-4500

Housing: Homeownership rate: 69.7% (2007); Median home value: $115,756 (2007); Median rent: $533 per month (2000); Median age of housing: 26 years (2000).

Safety: Violent crime rate: 40.5 per 10,000 population; Property crime rate: 559.1 per 10,000 population (2006).

Transportation: Commute to work: 95.7% car, 0.6% public transportation, 0.5% walk, 2.6% work from home (2000); Travel time to work: 34.1% less than 15 minutes, 49.0% 15 to 30 minutes, 8.8% 30 to 45 minutes, 3.1% 45 to 60 minutes, 5.0% 60 minutes or more (2000)

Additional Information Contacts

City of Loves Park . . . . (815) 654-5030
http://www.loves-park.il.us

The Parks Chamber of Commerce . . . . (815) 633-3999
http://www.parkschamber.com

MACHESNEY PARK (village). Covers a land area of 12.008 square miles and a water area of 0.381 square miles. Located at 42.35° N. Lat.; 89.04° W. Long. Elevation is 741 feet.

Population: 19,112 (1990); 20,759 (2000); 21,756 (2007); 22,423 (2012 projected); Race: 94.2% White, 1.7% Black, 1.1% Asian, 3.8% Hispanic of any race (2007); Density: 1,811.8 persons per square mile (2007); Average household size: 2.62 (2007); Median age: 37.1 (2007); Males per 100 females: 99.0 (2007); Marriage status: 22.5% never married, 60.7% now married, 5.1% widowed, 11.8% divorced (2000); Foreign born: 2.0% (2000); Ancestry (includes multiple ancestries): 29.0% German, 14.8% Irish, 10.8% Other groups, 9.4% English, 8.9% Swedish (2000).

Economy: Single-family building permits issued: 0 (2007); Multi-family building permits issued: 0 (2007); Employment by occupation: 9.9% management, 14.1% professional, 11.6% services, 27.8% sales, 0.1% farming, 9.9% construction, 26.6% production (2000).

Income: Per capita income: $21,846 (2007); Median household income: $51,462 (2007); Average household income: $57,339 (2007); Percent of households with income of $100,000 or more: 9.2% (2007); Poverty rate: 5.3% (2000).

Education: Percent of population age 25 and over with: High school diploma (including GED) or higher: 81.1% (2007); Bachelor's degree or higher: 11.5% (2007); Master's degree or higher: 2.8% (2007).

School District(s)

Harlem UD 122 (PK-12)
2005-06 Enrollment: 7,838 . . . . (815) 654-4500

Housing: Homeownership rate: 83.8% (2007); Median home value: $119,208 (2007); Median rent: $501 per month (2000); Median age of housing: 30 years (2000).

Safety: Violent crime rate: 28.8 per 10,000 population; Property crime rate: 473.8 per 10,000 population (2006).
Newspapers: Channooka Weekly Trading Post (Community news; Circulation 4,000); Chanooka Weekly (Local news; Circulation 1,500); Durand/Stephenson Gazette (Community news; Circulation 4,416); Gazette (Community news; Circulation 8,730); North Suburban Herald (Community news; Circulation 1,568); Northern Ogle County Tempo (Local news; Circulation 4,800); Parks Journal (Community news; Circulation 20,600); Pecatonica/Winnebago Gazette (Local news; Circulation 7,141); Post Journal (Community news; Circulation 14,550); Rockford Journal (Community news; Circulation 5,500); Senior Courier (Local news; Circulation 10,000)
Transportation: Commute to work: 96.4% car, 0.1% public transportation, 0.4% walk, 1.7% work from home (2000); Travel time to work: 32.1% less than 15 minutes, 51.3% 15 to 30 minutes, 10.9% 30 to 45 minutes, 1.5% 45 to 60 minutes, 4.2% 60 minutes or more (2000)
Additional Information Contacts
Village of Machesney Park . . . . (815) 877-5432
http://www.machesney-park.il.us

NEW MILLFORD (village). Covers a land area of 1.089 square miles and a water area of 0.025 square miles. Located at 42.18° N. Lat.; 89.07° W. Long.
Population: 662 (1990); 541 (2000); 507 (2007); 507 (2012 projected); Race: 90.7% White, 2.8% Black, 2.2% Asian, 4.5% Hispanic of any race (2007); Density: 465.4 persons per square mile (2007); Average household size: 2.22 (2007); Median age: 40.3 (2007); Males per 100 females: 121.4 (2007); Marriage status: 20.0% never married, 61.2% now married, 5.3% widowed, 13.5% divorced (2000); Foreign born: 1.1% (2000); Ancestry (includes multiple ancestries): 24.4% German, 18.4% Other groups, 16.8% Irish, 14.2% Swedish, 8.4% English (2000).
Economy: Employment by occupation: 8.0% management, 12.1% professional, 15.5% services, 24.5% sales, 0.0% farming, 12.4% construction, 27.6% production (2000).
Income: Per capita income: $33,757 (2007); Median household income: $47,857 (2007); Average household income: $75,066 (2007); Percent of households with income of $100,000 or more: 15.4% (2007); Poverty rate: 9.9% (2000).
Education: Percent of population age 25 and over with: High school diploma (including GED) or higher: 77.8% (2007); Bachelor's degree or higher: 8.1% (2007); Master's degree or higher: 2.7% (2007).
Housing: Homeownership rate: 84.6% (2007); Median home value: $55,833 (2007); Median rent: $375 per month (2000); Median age of housing: 22 years (2000).
Transportation: Commute to work: 95.0% car, 0.0% public transportation, 0.6% walk, 4.4% work from home (2000); Travel time to work: 34.6% less than 15 minutes, 44.1% 15 to 30 minutes, 12.1% 30 to 45 minutes, 2.9% 45 to 60 minutes, 6.2% 60 minutes or more (2000)

PECATONICA (village). Covers a land area of 1.243 square miles and a water area of 0.018 square miles. Located at 42.31° N. Lat.; 89.35° W. Long. Elevation is 771 feet.
History: Incorporated 1869.
Population: 1,838 (1990); 1,997 (2000); 2,318 (2007); 2,500 (2012 projected); Race: 97.6% White, 0.4% Black, 0.1% Asian, 0.9% Hispanic of any race (2007); Density: 1,865.6 persons per square mile (2007); Average household size: 2.46 (2007); Median age: 37.5 (2007); Males per 100 females: 92.7 (2007); Marriage status: 20.7% never married, 61.7% now married, 7.3% widowed, 10.3% divorced (2000); Foreign born: 0.7% (2000); Ancestry (includes multiple ancestries): 42.4% German, 13.7% Irish, 11.3% English, 11.2% Swedish, 5.6% United States or American (2000).
Economy: Single-family building permits issued: 2 (2007); Multi-family building permits issued: 0 (2007); Employment by occupation: 8.4% management, 14.6% professional, 14.8% services, 26.6% sales, 1.3% farming, 11.3% construction, 23.0% production (2000).
Income: Per capita income: $23,779 (2007); Median household income: $53,333 (2007); Average household income: $58,439 (2007); Percent of households with income of $100,000 or more: 10.4% (2007); Poverty rate: 4.7% (2000).
Education: Percent of population age 25 and over with: High school diploma (including GED) or higher: 88.6% (2007); Bachelor's degree or higher: 13.5% (2007); Master's degree or higher: 4.8% (2007).

School District(s)
Pecatonica CUSD 321 (PK-12)
2005-06 Enrollment: 945 . . . . (815) 239-1639
Housing: Homeownership rate: 80.9% (2007); Median home value: $124,645 (2007); Median rent: $383 per month (2000); Median age of housing: 47 years (2000).
Safety: Violent crime rate: 97.2 per 10,000 population; Property crime rate: 212.9 per 10,000 population (2006).
Transportation: Commute to work: 92.2% car, 0.2% public transportation, 4.3% walk, 2.3% work from home (2000); Travel time to work: 29.5% less than 15 minutes, 38.7% 15 to 30 minutes, 26.5% 30 to 45 minutes, 2.9% 45 to 60 minutes, 2.5% 60 minutes or more (2000)

ROCKFORD (city). County seat. Covers a land area of 56.005 square miles and a water area of 0.713 square miles. Located at 42.27° N. Lat.; 89.07° W. Long. Elevation is 715 feet.
History: Rockford was named for the ford across the Rock River where the stagecoach crossed before the town was built. Rockford was settled by New Englanders after Germanicus Kent and Thatcher Blake of Galena laid out the town and opened a sawmill. The availability of water power accounted for Rockford's growth, and it was incorporated in 1839 along with a village that had grown up on the other side of the river. In the 1850's both the Rockford Water Power Company and the Manny Company, producer of reaper-mower machines, were founded. After 1852, when the Chicago & Galena Union Railroad arrived, many people of Swedish descent settled here.
Population: 146,309 (1990); 150,115 (2000); 152,549 (2007); 154,370 (2012 projected); Race: 68.1% White, 18.4% Black, 2.5% Asian, 15.5% Hispanic of any race (2007); Density: 2,723.8 persons per square mile (2007); Average household size: 2.53 (2007); Median age: 35.2 (2007); Males per 100 females: 94.9 (2007); Marriage status: 28.2% never married, 51.8% now married, 7.3% widowed, 12.7% divorced (2000); Foreign born: 8.7% (2000); Ancestry (includes multiple ancestries): 28.2% Other groups, 19.7% German, 11.2% Irish, 9.8% Swedish, 7.9% English (2000).
Economy: Unemployment rate: 7.8% (4/2008); Total civilian labor force: 75,079 (4/2008); Single-family building permits issued: 157 (2007); Multi-family building permits issued: 170 (2007); Employment by occupation: 10.9% management, 18.3% professional, 14.8% services, 26.0% sales, 0.2% farming, 7.3% construction, 22.6% production (2000).
Income: Per capita income: $21,571 (2007); Median household income: $39,937 (2007); Average household income: $53,534 (2007); Percent of households with income of $100,000 or more: 10.5% (2007); Poverty rate: 14.0% (2000).
Taxes: Total city taxes per capita: $400 (2006); City property taxes per capita: $303 (2006).
Education: Percent of population age 25 and over with: High school diploma (including GED) or higher: 77.7% (2007); Bachelor's degree or higher: 19.9% (2007); Master's degree or higher: 7.2% (2007).

School District(s)
Boone/Winnebago Roe (06-12)
2005-06 Enrollment: 267 . . . . (815) 636-3060
Career Educ Assoc of N Central IL
2005-06 Enrollment: n/a . . . . (815) 921-1651
Rockford SD 205 (PK-12)
2005-06 Enrollment: 29,145 . . . . (815) 966-3101

Four-year College(s)
Rockford College (Private, Not-for-profit)
Fall 2007 Enrollment: 1,566. . . . . (815) 226-4000
2007-08 Tuition: In-state $22,950; Out-of-state $22,950
Saint Anthony College of Nursing (Private, Not-for-profit, Roman Catholic)
Fall 2007 Enrollment: 182 . . . . (815) 395-5091

Two-year College(s)
Rasmussen College-Rockford (Private, For-profit)
Fall 2007 Enrollment: 321 . . . . (815) 316-4800
2007-08 Tuition: In-state $13,560; Out-of-state $13,560
Rock Valley College (Public)
Fall 2007 Enrollment: 7,923. . . . . (815) 921-7821
2007-08 Tuition: In-state $7,594; Out-of-state $12,274
Rockford Business College (Private, For-profit)
Fall 2007 Enrollment: 560 . . . . (815) 965-8616
2007-08 Tuition: In-state $8,840; Out-of-state $8,840

Vocational/Technical School(s)
Educators of Beauty (Private, For-profit)
Fall 2007 Enrollment: 24 . . . . (815) 969-7030
2007-08 Tuition: $11,775

Regency Beauty Institute (Private, For-profit)
Fall 2007 Enrollment: 39 . . . . (815) 209-2423
2007-08 Tuition: $14,200

Housing: Homeownership rate: 61.3% (2007); Median home value: $101,456 (2007); Median rent: $423 per month (2000); Median age of housing: 42 years (2000).

Hospitals: H. Douglas Singer Mental Health & Development Center (80 beds); Rockford Memorial Hospital (396 beds); Saint Anthony Medical Center (254 beds); Swedish American Hospital (357 beds)

Safety: Violent crime rate: 112.1 per 10,000 population; Property crime rate: 697.2 per 10,000 population (2006).

Newspapers: The Observer (Regional news; Circulation 32,500); Rock River Times (Regional news; Circulation 19,000); Rockford Labor News (National news; Circulation 20,000); Rockford Register Star (Local news; Circulation 86,000)

Transportation: Commute to work: 93.1% car, 1.8% public transportation, 1.9% walk, 2.3% work from home (2000); Travel time to work: 39.6% less than 15 minutes, 44.0% 15 to 30 minutes, 8.2% 30 to 45 minutes, 2.8% 45 to 60 minutes, 5.5% 60 minutes or more (2000); Amtrak: Service available.

Airports: Chicago/Rockford International (primary service)

Additional Information Contacts

City of Rockford . . . . (815) 987-5590
http://www.cityofrockford.net
Rockford Chamber of Commerce . . . . (815) 987-8100
http://www.rockfordchamber.com

ROCKTON (village). Covers a land area of 3.518 square miles and a water area of 0.182 square miles. Located at 42.45° N. Lat.; 89.06° W. Long. Elevation is 738 feet.

History: Incorporated 1847.

Population: 3,530 (1990); 5,296 (2000); 5,445 (2007); 5,563 (2012 projected); Race: 97.1% White, 0.7% Black, 0.9% Asian, 1.9% Hispanic of any race (2007); Density: 1,547.8 persons per square mile (2007); Average household size: 2.78 (2007); Median age: 35.5 (2007); Males per 100 females: 98.2 (2007); Marriage status: 15.3% never married, 73.0% now married, 4.3% widowed, 7.3% divorced (2000); Foreign born: 1.8% (2000); Ancestry (includes multiple ancestries): 36.6% German, 14.2% English, 14.0% Irish, 8.9% Norwegian, 7.4% Swedish (2000).

Economy: Employment by occupation: 15.4% management, 24.9% professional, 11.7% services, 24.5% sales, 0.0% farming, 8.7% construction, 14.9% production (2000).

Income: Per capita income: $26,399 (2007); Median household income: $63,447 (2007); Average household income: $73,137 (2007); Percent of households with income of $100,000 or more: 21.1% (2007); Poverty rate: 1.3% (2000).

Education: Percent of population age 25 and over with: High school diploma (including GED) or higher: 93.0% (2007); Bachelor's degree or higher: 29.2% (2007); Master's degree or higher: 10.3% (2007).

School District(s)

Hononegah Chd 207 (09-12)
2005-06 Enrollment: 1,951 . . . . (815) 624-5010
Rockton SD 140 (PK-08)
2005-06 Enrollment: 1,442 . . . . (815) 624-7143

Housing: Homeownership rate: 80.1% (2007); Median home value: $160,861 (2007); Median rent: $504 per month (2000); Median age of housing: 16 years (2000).

Safety: Violent crime rate: 21.5 per 10,000 population; Property crime rate: 184.1 per 10,000 population (2006).

Transportation: Commute to work: 94.9% car, 0.3% public transportation, 2.2% walk, 2.4% work from home (2000); Travel time to work: 34.4% less than 15 minutes, 35.1% 15 to 30 minutes, 23.9% 30 to 45 minutes, 2.2% 45 to 60 minutes, 4.5% 60 minutes or more (2000)

Additional Information Contacts

Rockton Chamber of Commerce . . . . (815) 624-7625
http://www.rocktonchamber.com
Village of Rockton . . . . (815) 624-7600
http://www.rockton.ws

ROSCOE (village). Covers a land area of 9.249 square miles and a water area of 0.072 square miles. Located at 42.41° N. Lat.; 89.01° W. Long. Elevation is 738 feet.

Population: 2,632 (1990); 6,244 (2000); 7,082 (2007); 7,565 (2012 projected); Race: 93.7% White, 2.5% Black, 0.8% Asian, 3.9% Hispanic of any race (2007); Density: 765.7 persons per square mile (2007); Average household size: 2.78 (2007); Median age: 34.2 (2007); Males per 100 females: 99.7 (2007); Marriage status: 18.6% never married, 71.2% now married, 2.9% widowed, 7.3% divorced (2000); Foreign born: 3.1% (2000); Ancestry (includes multiple ancestries): 25.6% German, 17.7% Irish, 10.7% Other groups, 9.0% English, 7.9% United States or American (2000).

Economy: Employment by occupation: 18.4% management, 18.0% professional, 10.9% services, 22.9% sales, 0.2% farming, 9.3% construction, 20.4% production (2000).

Income: Per capita income: $27,529 (2007); Median household income: $65,122 (2007); Average household income: $76,665 (2007); Percent of households with income of $100,000 or more: 19.7% (2007); Poverty rate: 2.9% (2000).

Education: Percent of population age 25 and over with: High school diploma (including GED) or higher: 90.5% (2007); Bachelor's degree or higher: 21.8% (2007); Master's degree or higher: 5.5% (2007).

School District(s)

Kinnikinnick CCSD 131 (PK-08)
2005-06 Enrollment: 2,052 . . . . (815) 623-2837

Housing: Homeownership rate: 73.8% (2007); Median home value: $155,066 (2007); Median rent: $621 per month (2000); Median age of housing: 7 years (2000).

Safety: Violent crime rate: 18.2 per 10,000 population; Property crime rate: 435.1 per 10,000 population (2006).

Transportation: Commute to work: 97.6% car, 0.3% public transportation, 0.3% walk, 1.8% work from home (2000); Travel time to work: 22.0% less than 15 minutes, 50.3% 15 to 30 minutes, 19.2% 30 to 45 minutes, 2.4% 45 to 60 minutes, 6.0% 60 minutes or more (2000)

Additional Information Contacts

Roscoe Area Chamber of Commerce . . . . (815) 623-9065
http://www.roscoechamber.com
Village of Roscoe . . . . (815) 623-2829
http://www.villageofroscoe.com

SOUTH BELOIT (city). Covers a land area of 3.960 square miles and a water area of 0.125 square miles. Located at 42.48° N. Lat.; 89.03° W. Long. Elevation is 738 feet.

History: Incorporated 1917.

Population: 4,376 (1990); 5,397 (2000); 5,118 (2007); 4,993 (2012 projected); Race: 87.6% White, 3.8% Black, 1.1% Asian, 9.5% Hispanic of any race (2007); Density: 1,292.4 persons per square mile (2007); Average household size: 2.50 (2007); Median age: 34.4 (2007); Males per 100 females: 98.4 (2007); Marriage status: 25.0% never married, 55.2% now married, 7.2% widowed, 12.6% divorced (2000); Foreign born: 2.2% (2000); Ancestry (includes multiple ancestries): 28.1% German, 17.0% Other groups, 11.0% Irish, 9.9% English, 7.3% Norwegian (2000).

Economy: Employment by occupation: 8.0% management, 13.4% professional, 12.5% services, 21.2% sales, 0.3% farming, 10.1% construction, 34.6% production (2000).

Income: Per capita income: $20,003 (2007); Median household income: $41,857 (2007); Average household income: $49,276 (2007); Percent of households with income of $100,000 or more: 7.4% (2007); Poverty rate: 10.0% (2000).

Education: Percent of population age 25 and over with: High school diploma (including GED) or higher: 74.6% (2007); Bachelor's degree or higher: 7.9% (2007); Master's degree or higher: 1.8% (2007).

School District(s)

Prairie Hill CCSD 133 (KG-08)
2005-06 Enrollment: 599 . . . . (815) 389-4694
South Beloit CUSD 320 (PK-12)
2005-06 Enrollment: 1,152 . . . . (815) 389-3478

Housing: Homeownership rate: 69.8% (2007); Median home value: $110,322 (2007); Median rent: $438 per month (2000); Median age of housing: 35 years (2000).

Safety: Violent crime rate: 49.8 per 10,000 population; Property crime rate: 636.4 per 10,000 population (2006).

Transportation: Commute to work: 95.0% car, 0.2% public transportation, 2.0% walk, 1.4% work from home (2000); Travel time to work: 40.5% less than 15 minutes, 37.4% 15 to 30 minutes, 17.0% 30 to 45 minutes, 2.4% 45 to 60 minutes, 2.7% 60 minutes or more (2000); Amtrak: Service available.

Additional Information Contacts

City of South Beloit . . . . (815) 389-3023
http://www.southbeloit.org

WINNEBAGO (village). Covers a land area of 1.392 square miles and a water area of 0 square miles. Located at 42.26° N. Lat.; 89.24° W. Long. Elevation is 869 feet.
Population: 2,172 (1990); 2,958 (2000); 3,195 (2007); 3,322 (2012 projected); Race: 97.5% White, 1.7% Black, 0.2% Asian, 1.6% Hispanic of any race (2007); Density: 2,295.6 persons per square mile (2007); Average household size: 2.95 (2007); Median age: 33.4 (2007); Males per 100 females: 95.1 (2007); Marriage status: 20.3% never married, 68.1% now married, 4.9% widowed, 6.7% divorced (2000); Foreign born: 0.6% (2000); Ancestry (includes multiple ancestries): 36.1% German, 13.5% Irish, 10.2% Swedish, 9.9% English, 7.3% Italian (2000).
Economy: Single-family building permits issued: 13 (2007); Multi-family building permits issued: 0 (2007); Employment by occupation: 12.2% management, 17.5% professional, 12.6% services, 25.6% sales, 0.5% farming, 11.4% construction, 20.2% production (2000).
Income: Per capita income: $24,628 (2007); Median household income: $69,055 (2007); Average household income: $72,724 (2007); Percent of households with income of $100,000 or more: 22.6% (2007); Poverty rate: 1.1% (2000).
Education: Percent of population age 25 and over with: High school diploma (including GED) or higher: 90.8% (2007); Bachelor's degree or higher: 20.0% (2007); Master's degree or higher: 6.8% (2007).

School District(s)

Winnebago CUSD 323 (PK-12)
2005-06 Enrollment: 1,681 . . . . (815) 335-2456
Housing: Homeownership rate: 87.8% (2007); Median home value: $147,133 (2007); Median rent: $353 per month (2000); Median age of housing: 24 years (2000).
Safety: Violent crime rate: 26.1 per 10,000 population; Property crime rate: 371.9 per 10,000 population (2006).
Transportation: Commute to work: 96.2% car, 0.0% public transportation, 1.5% walk, 2.3% work from home (2000); Travel time to work: 26.4% less than 15 minutes, 55.2% 15 to 30 minutes, 15.4% 30 to 45 minutes, 1.1% 45 to 60 minutes, 1.8% 60 minutes or more (2000)

Woodford County

Located in central Illinois; bounded on the west by the Illinois River; drained by the Mackinaw River. Covers a land area of 527.95 square miles, a water area of 14.79 square miles, and is located in the Central Time Zone. The county was founded in 1841. County seat is Eureka.

Woodford County is part of the Peoria, IL Metropolitan Statistical Area. The entire metro area includes: Marshall County, IL; Peoria County, IL; Stark County, IL; Tazewell County, IL; Woodford County, IL

Weather Station: Minonk Elevation: 748 feet

	Jan	Feb	Mar	Apr	May	Jun	Jul	Aug	Sep	Oct	Nov	Dec
High	30	36	48	62	74	83	86	84	78	66	49	36
Low	13	18	28	38	49	59	63	60	52	41	30	19
Precip	1.8	1.9	3.2	3.7	4.4	3.7	3.8	3.4	3.3	2.9	3.3	2.4
Snow	9.0	6.8	3.6	0.9	tr	0.0	0.0	0.0	0.0	tr	1.6	6.2

High and Low temperatures in degrees Fahrenheit; Precipitation and Snow in inches

Population: 32,653 (1990); 35,469 (2000); 38,125 (2007); 39,972 (2012 projected); Race: 97.7% White, 0.6% Black, 0.5% Asian, 1.1% Hispanic of any race (2007); Density: 72.2 persons per square mile (2007); Average household size: 2.73 (2007); Median age: 38.6 (2007); Males per 100 females: 96.6 (2007).
Religion: Five largest groups: 15.9% Catholic Church, 7.4% The United Methodist Church, 7.3% Apostolic Christian Church of America, Inc., 4.3% United Church of Christ, 4.0% Lutheran Church—Missouri Synod (2000).
Economy: Unemployment rate: 3.5% (4/2008); Total civilian labor force: 21,911 (4/2008); Leading industries: 22.7% manufacturing; 15.0% retail trade; 14.1% health care and social assistance (2005); Farms: 919 totaling 309,591 acres (2002); Companies that employ 500 or more persons: 0 (2006); Companies that employ 100 to 499 persons: 15 (2006); Companies that employ less than 100 persons: 770 (2006); Black-owned businesses: n/a (2002); Hispanic-owned businesses: n/a (2002); Asian-owned businesses: n/a (2002); Women-owned businesses: 790 (2002); Retail sales per capita: $11,594 (2008). Single-family building permits issued: 129 (2007); Multi-family building permits issued: 24 (2007).
Income: Per capita income: $26,259 (2007); Median household income: $60,374 (2007); Average household income: $71,053 (2007); Percent of households with income of $100,000 or more: 19.6% (2007); Poverty rate: 5.5% (2005); Bankruptcy rate: 2.55% (2007).
Education: Percent of population age 25 and over with: High school diploma (including GED) or higher: 88.0% (2007); Bachelor's degree or higher: 21.7% (2007); Master's degree or higher: 6.1% (2007).
Housing: Homeownership rate: 83.0% (2007); Median home value: $142,045 (2007); Median rent: $396 per month (2000); Median age of housing: 35 years (2000).
Health: Birth rate: 135.7 per 10,000 population (2007); Death rate: 91.5 per 10,000 population (2007); Age-adjusted cancer mortality rate: 191.4 deaths per 100,000 population (2005); Number of physicians: 8.4 per 10,000 population (2005); Hospital beds: 0.0 per 10,000 population (2004); Hospital admissions: 0.0 per 10,000 population (2004).
Elections: 2004 Presidential election results: 67.5% Bush, 31.9% Kerry, 0.1% Nader, 0.5% Badnarik
National and State Parks: Woodford County State Conservation Area
Additional Information Contacts
Woodford County Government . . . . (309) 467-2822

Woodford County Communities

BAY VIEW GARDENS (village). Covers a land area of 0.178 square miles and a water area of 0 square miles. Located at 40.81° N. Lat.; 89.51° W. Long. Elevation is 525 feet.
Population: 418 (1990); 366 (2000); 365 (2007); 366 (2012 projected); Race: 99.7% White, 0.3% Black, 0.0% Asian, 1.1% Hispanic of any race (2007); Density: 2,051.3 persons per square mile (2007); Average household size: 2.53 (2007); Median age: 40.1 (2007); Males per 100 females: 108.6 (2007); Marriage status: 23.6% never married, 63.0% now married, 6.9% widowed, 6.5% divorced (2000); Foreign born: 0.0% (2000); Ancestry (includes multiple ancestries): 26.0% German, 14.4% Other groups, 13.8% English, 9.4% Irish, 7.2% United States or American (2000).
Economy: Single-family building permits issued: 0 (2007); Multi-family building permits issued: 0 (2007); Employment by occupation: 4.5% management, 11.8% professional, 17.4% services, 29.8% sales, 0.0% farming, 14.0% construction, 22.5% production (2000).
Income: Per capita income: $16,692 (2007); Median household income: $36,786 (2007); Average household income: $42,309 (2007); Percent of households with income of $100,000 or more: 5.6% (2007); Poverty rate: 5.3% (2000).
Education: Percent of population age 25 and over with: High school diploma (including GED) or higher: 73.7% (2007); Bachelor's degree or higher: 6.6% (2007); Master's degree or higher: 4.1% (2007).
Housing: Homeownership rate: 80.6% (2007); Median home value: $94,211 (2007); Median rent: $465 per month (2000); Median age of housing: 39 years (2000).
Transportation: Commute to work: 94.9% car, 0.0% public transportation, 2.8% walk, 1.7% work from home (2000); Travel time to work: 27.2% less than 15 minutes, 43.4% 15 to 30 minutes, 19.7% 30 to 45 minutes, 6.4% 45 to 60 minutes, 3.5% 60 minutes or more (2000)

BENSON (village). Covers a land area of 0.174 square miles and a water area of 0 square miles. Located at 40.85° N. Lat.; 89.12° W. Long. Elevation is 764 feet.
Population: 415 (1990); 408 (2000); 373 (2007); 376 (2012 projected); Race: 99.7% White, 0.0% Black, 0.0% Asian, 0.8% Hispanic of any race (2007); Density: 2,138.0 persons per square mile (2007); Average household size: 2.38 (2007); Median age: 39.1 (2007); Males per 100 females: 100.5 (2007); Marriage status: 17.8% never married, 64.2% now married, 10.1% widowed, 8.0% divorced (2000); Foreign born: 1.2% (2000); Ancestry (includes multiple ancestries): 59.0% German, 10.2% Irish, 7.6% English, 4.4% United States or American, 3.7% Italian (2000).
Economy: Single-family building permits issued: 0 (2007); Multi-family building permits issued: 0 (2007); Employment by occupation: 11.0% management, 6.8% professional, 19.4% services, 23.6% sales, 0.0% farming, 18.8% construction, 20.4% production (2000).
Income: Per capita income: $21,119 (2007); Median household income: $45,417 (2007); Average household income: $50,175 (2007); Percent of households with income of $100,000 or more: 6.4% (2007); Poverty rate: 4.1% (2000).
Education: Percent of population age 25 and over with: High school diploma (including GED) or higher: 86.3% (2007); Bachelor's degree or higher: 5.2% (2007); Master's degree or higher: 1.2% (2007).

School District(s)

Roanoke Benson CUSD 60 (PK-12)
2005-06 Enrollment: 621 . . . . (309) 923-8921

Housing: Homeownership rate: 84.1% (2007); Median home value: $85,625 (2007); Median rent: $344 per month (2000); Median age of housing: 52 years (2000).

Transportation: Commute to work: 93.2% car, 0.0% public transportation, 4.2% walk, 2.6% work from home (2000); Travel time to work: 39.0% less than 15 minutes, 22.5% 15 to 30 minutes, 22.5% 30 to 45 minutes, 10.7% 45 to 60 minutes, 5.3% 60 minutes or more (2000)

CONGERVILLE (village). Covers a land area of 0.757 square miles and a water area of 0.004 square miles. Located at 40.61° N. Lat.; 89.20° W. Long. Elevation is 748 feet.

Population: 452 (1990); 466 (2000); 491 (2007); 509 (2012 projected); Race: 99.6% White, 0.0% Black, 0.2% Asian, 0.0% Hispanic of any race (2007); Density: 648.3 persons per square mile (2007); Average household size: 2.79 (2007); Median age: 32.0 (2007); Males per 100 females: 103.7 (2007); Marriage status: 24.1% never married, 66.0% now married, 6.3% widowed, 3.6% divorced (2000); Foreign born: 0.7% (2000); Ancestry (includes multiple ancestries): 50.0% German, 12.3% United States or American, 11.6% Swiss, 6.5% Irish, 4.5% English (2000).

Economy: Single-family building permits issued: 2 (2007); Multi-family building permits issued: 0 (2007); Employment by occupation: 8.8% management, 9.6% professional, 24.9% services, 22.1% sales, 0.8% farming, 11.6% construction, 22.1% production (2000).

Income: Per capita income: $28,065 (2007); Median household income: $61,500 (2007); Average household income: $78,295 (2007); Percent of households with income of $100,000 or more: 17.0% (2007); Poverty rate: 0.7% (2000).

Education: Percent of population age 25 and over with: High school diploma (including GED) or higher: 91.9% (2007); Bachelor's degree or higher: 14.8% (2007); Master's degree or higher: 2.6% (2007).

School District(s)

Eureka CUD 140 (PK-12)
2005-06 Enrollment: 1,610 . . . . (309) 467-3737

Housing: Homeownership rate: 75.6% (2007); Median home value: $125,625 (2007); Median rent: $405 per month (2000); Median age of housing: 29 years (2000).

Transportation: Commute to work: 94.8% car, 0.0% public transportation, 1.6% walk, 3.6% work from home (2000); Travel time to work: 24.7% less than 15 minutes, 45.6% 15 to 30 minutes, 23.0% 30 to 45 minutes, 2.1% 45 to 60 minutes, 4.6% 60 minutes or more (2000)

EL PASO (city). Covers a land area of 1.545 square miles and a water area of 0 square miles. Located at 40.73° N. Lat.; 89.01° W. Long. Elevation is 751 feet.

History: El Paso was the home of Lester Pfister who developed a hybrid corn that gave a high yield.

Population: 2,547 (1990); 2,695 (2000); 2,884 (2007); 2,987 (2012 projected); Race: 98.8% White, 0.3% Black, 0.2% Asian, 1.1% Hispanic of any race (2007); Density: 1,866.2 persons per square mile (2007); Average household size: 2.71 (2007); Median age: 36.9 (2007); Males per 100 females: 94.6 (2007); Marriage status: 19.9% never married, 60.2% now married, 9.0% widowed, 10.8% divorced (2000); Foreign born: 1.0% (2000); Ancestry (includes multiple ancestries): 35.4% German, 16.6% Irish, 12.2% English, 9.7% United States or American, 3.9% French (except Basque) (2000).

Economy: Single-family building permits issued: 7 (2007); Multi-family building permits issued: 4 (2007); Employment by occupation: 11.6% management, 17.9% professional, 17.1% services, 27.6% sales, 0.6% farming, 6.7% construction, 18.5% production (2000).

Income: Per capita income: $24,042 (2007); Median household income: $54,803 (2007); Average household income: $63,501 (2007); Percent of households with income of $100,000 or more: 12.5% (2007); Poverty rate: 3.2% (2000).

Education: Percent of population age 25 and over with: High school diploma (including GED) or higher: 82.9% (2007); Bachelor's degree or higher: 18.7% (2007); Master's degree or higher: 4.7% (2007).

School District(s)

El Paso-Gridley CUSD 11 (PK-12)
2005-06 Enrollment: 1,341 . . . . (309) 527-4410

Housing: Homeownership rate: 74.5% (2007); Median home value: $116,979 (2007); Median rent: $415 per month (2000); Median age of housing: 46 years (2000).

Safety: Violent crime rate: 14.6 per 10,000 population; Property crime rate: 272.9 per 10,000 population (2006).

Newspapers: El Paso Journal (Regional news; Circulation 1,175)

Transportation: Commute to work: 92.2% car, 0.0% public transportation, 2.3% walk, 3.6% work from home (2000); Travel time to work: 48.2% less than 15 minutes, 18.5% 15 to 30 minutes, 27.5% 30 to 45 minutes, 4.1% 45 to 60 minutes, 1.7% 60 minutes or more (2000)

EUREKA (city). County seat. Covers a land area of 2.690 square miles and a water area of 0.048 square miles. Located at 40.71° N. Lat.; 89.27° W. Long. Elevation is 768 feet.

History: Eureka was settled in the 1830's, and developed around Eureka College, which began in 1848 as a seminary founded by the Disciples of Christ. Eureka was named the seat of Woodford County in 1896.

Population: 4,724 (1990); 4,871 (2000); 5,065 (2007); 5,202 (2012 projected); Race: 96.8% White, 1.5% Black, 0.5% Asian, 1.6% Hispanic of any race (2007); Density: 1,882.6 persons per square mile (2007); Average household size: 2.72 (2007); Median age: 34.1 (2007); Males per 100 females: 88.2 (2007); Marriage status: 26.5% never married, 56.0% now married, 12.3% widowed, 5.3% divorced (2000); Foreign born: 1.8% (2000); Ancestry (includes multiple ancestries): 36.1% German, 11.3% Irish, 9.3% English, 6.3% United States or American, 5.3% Other groups (2000).

Economy: Single-family building permits issued: 13 (2007); Multi-family building permits issued: 0 (2007); Employment by occupation: 10.3% management, 21.9% professional, 16.7% services, 26.3% sales, 0.8% farming, 8.0% construction, 16.0% production (2000).

Income: Per capita income: $25,622 (2007); Median household income: $53,365 (2007); Average household income: $68,117 (2007); Percent of households with income of $100,000 or more: 17.1% (2007); Poverty rate: 2.4% (2000).

Education: Percent of population age 25 and over with: High school diploma (including GED) or higher: 82.3% (2007); Bachelor's degree or higher: 22.2% (2007); Master's degree or higher: 6.3% (2007).

School District(s)

Eureka CUD 140 (PK-12)
2005-06 Enrollment: 1,610 . . . . (309) 467-3737

Four-year College(s)

Eureka College (Private, Not-for-profit, Christian Church (Disciples of Christ))
Fall 2007 Enrollment: 672 . . . . (309) 467-3721
2007-08 Tuition: In-state $15,360; Out-of-state $15,360

Housing: Homeownership rate: 71.1% (2007); Median home value: $126,236 (2007); Median rent: $394 per month (2000); Median age of housing: 35 years (2000).

Hospitals: Eureka Community Hospital (25 beds)

Safety: Violent crime rate: 9.8 per 10,000 population; Property crime rate: 102.3 per 10,000 population (2006).

Newspapers: Woodford County Journal (Local news; Circulation 1,810); Woodford Star (Local news; Circulation 14,000)

Transportation: Commute to work: 89.5% car, 0.0% public transportation, 7.7% walk, 1.7% work from home (2000); Travel time to work: 52.3% less than 15 minutes, 21.1% 15 to 30 minutes, 22.8% 30 to 45 minutes, 2.0% 45 to 60 minutes, 1.9% 60 minutes or more (2000)

GERMANTOWN HILLS (village). Aka Oak Grove Park. Covers a land area of 1.285 square miles and a water area of 0.043 square miles. Located at 40.76° N. Lat.; 89.46° W. Long. Elevation is 804 feet.

Population: 1,293 (1990); 2,111 (2000); 2,774 (2007); 3,193 (2012 projected); Race: 97.0% White, 0.2% Black, 1.4% Asian, 1.3% Hispanic of any race (2007); Density: 2,159.3 persons per square mile (2007); Average household size: 2.95 (2007); Median age: 36.4 (2007); Males per 100 females: 98.6 (2007); Marriage status: 19.1% never married, 71.0% now married, 4.4% widowed, 5.5% divorced (2000); Foreign born: 1.0% (2000); Ancestry (includes multiple ancestries): 41.4% German, 13.3% Irish, 11.6% English, 6.9% United States or American, 4.2% Swedish (2000).

Economy: Single-family building permits issued: 16 (2007); Multi-family building permits issued: 12 (2007); Employment by occupation: 19.2% management, 31.4% professional, 9.7% services, 24.6% sales, 0.0% farming, 5.7% construction, 9.4% production (2000).

Income: Per capita income: $32,573 (2007); Median household income: $86,513 (2007); Average household income: $96,227 (2007); Percent of households with income of $100,000 or more: 39.1% (2007); Poverty rate: 2.5% (2000).

Education: Percent of population age 25 and over with: High school diploma (including GED) or higher: 94.8% (2007); Bachelor's degree or higher: 41.9% (2007); Master's degree or higher: 15.1% (2007).
Housing: Homeownership rate: 92.2% (2007); Median home value: $203,481 (2007); Median rent: $367 per month (2000); Median age of housing: 11 years (2000).
Transportation: Commute to work: 96.4% car, 0.0% public transportation, 0.6% walk, 2.6% work from home (2000); Travel time to work: 18.3% less than 15 minutes, 64.0% 15 to 30 minutes, 12.2% 30 to 45 minutes, 1.8% 45 to 60 minutes, 3.7% 60 minutes or more (2000)

GOODFIELD (village). Covers a land area of 1.447 square miles and a water area of 0.007 square miles. Located at 40.62° N. Lat.; 89.27° W. Long. Elevation is 741 feet.
Population: 588 (1990); 686 (2000); 752 (2007); 795 (2012 projected); Race: 99.1% White, 0.1% Black, 0.0% Asian, 0.0% Hispanic of any race (2007); Density: 519.8 persons per square mile (2007); Average household size: 2.93 (2007); Median age: 33.0 (2007); Males per 100 females: 98.4 (2007); Marriage status: 20.0% never married, 73.5% now married, 3.3% widowed, 3.3% divorced (2000); Foreign born: 0.9% (2000); Ancestry (includes multiple ancestries): 51.4% German, 14.4% Irish, 10.0% United States or American, 7.2% English, 7.2% Swiss (2000).
Economy: Single-family building permits issued: 6 (2007); Multi-family building permits issued: 0 (2007); Employment by occupation: 10.1% management, 22.8% professional, 15.4% services, 22.8% sales, 0.6% farming, 11.0% construction, 17.2% production (2000).
Income: Per capita income: $27,334 (2007); Median household income: $73,836 (2007); Average household income: $79,981 (2007); Percent of households with income of $100,000 or more: 21.8% (2007); Poverty rate: 3.2% (2000).
Education: Percent of population age 25 and over with: High school diploma (including GED) or higher: 89.4% (2007); Bachelor's degree or higher: 28.8% (2007); Master's degree or higher: 6.7% (2007).

School District(s)

Eureka CUD 140 (PK-12)
2005-06 Enrollment: 1,610 . . . . (309) 467-3737
Housing: Homeownership rate: 89.1% (2007); Median home value: $150,481 (2007); Median rent: $381 per month (2000); Median age of housing: 30 years (2000).
Transportation: Commute to work: 95.8% car, 0.0% public transportation, 0.6% walk, 3.6% work from home (2000); Travel time to work: 32.4% less than 15 minutes, 44.2% 15 to 30 minutes, 16.8% 30 to 45 minutes, 4.0% 45 to 60 minutes, 2.5% 60 minutes or more (2000)

KAPPA (village). Covers a land area of 0.228 square miles and a water area of 0 square miles. Located at 40.67° N. Lat.; 89.00° W. Long. Elevation is 738 feet.
Population: 134 (1990); 170 (2000); 177 (2007); 179 (2012 projected); Race: 95.5% White, 0.0% Black, 0.0% Asian, 4.5% Hispanic of any race (2007); Density: 777.9 persons per square mile (2007); Average household size: 2.68 (2007); Median age: 35.9 (2007); Males per 100 females: 98.9 (2007); Marriage status: 18.4% never married, 69.6% now married, 4.8% widowed, 7.2% divorced (2000); Foreign born: 0.0% (2000); Ancestry (includes multiple ancestries): 40.7% German, 25.6% Irish, 18.6% United States or American, 10.5% English, 5.8% Swiss (2000).
Economy: Single-family building permits issued: 4 (2007); Multi-family building permits issued: 0 (2007); Employment by occupation: 8.4% management, 15.8% professional, 22.1% services, 28.4% sales, 0.0% farming, 14.7% construction, 10.5% production (2000).
Income: Per capita income: $23,333 (2007); Median household income: $62,500 (2007); Average household income: $62,576 (2007); Percent of households with income of $100,000 or more: 18.2% (2007); Poverty rate: 9.6% (2000).
Education: Percent of population age 25 and over with: High school diploma (including GED) or higher: 89.7% (2007); Bachelor's degree or higher: 13.1% (2007); Master's degree or higher: 0.0% (2007).
Housing: Homeownership rate: 74.2% (2007); Median home value: $106,618 (2007); Median rent: $288 per month (2000); Median age of housing: 28 years (2000).
Transportation: Commute to work: 90.1% car, 0.0% public transportation, 0.0% walk, 9.9% work from home (2000); Travel time to work: 32.9% less than 15 minutes, 41.5% 15 to 30 minutes, 19.5% 30 to 45 minutes, 2.4% 45 to 60 minutes, 3.7% 60 minutes or more (2000)

LOWPOINT (unincorporated postal area, zip code 61545). Aka Low Point. Covers a land area of 31.763 square miles and a water area of 0.031 square miles. Located at 40.87° N. Lat.; 89.37° W. Long.
Population: 651 (2000); Race: 100.0% White, 0.0% Black, 0.0% Asian, 0.0% Hispanic of any race (2000); Density: 20.5 persons per square mile (2000); Age: 29.6% under 18, 12.6% over 64 (2000); Marriage status: 19.7% never married, 66.8% now married, 8.5% widowed, 5.0% divorced (2000); Foreign born: 0.0% (2000); Ancestry (includes multiple ancestries): 48.5% German, 15.5% English, 8.4% Irish, 7.5% Other groups, 5.3% Swiss (2000).
Economy: Employment by occupation: 13.2% management, 16.5% professional, 15.9% services, 14.7% sales, 2.4% farming, 13.2% construction, 24.3% production (2000).
Income: Per capita income: $16,658 (2000); Median household income: $44,167 (2000); Poverty rate: 8.2% (2000).
Education: Percent of population age 25 and over with: High school diploma (including GED) or higher: 82.0% (2000); Bachelor's degree or higher: 9.9% (2000).
Housing: Homeownership rate: 86.2% (2000); Median home value: $69,000 (2000); Median rent: $444 per month (2000); Median age of housing: 59 years (2000).
Transportation: Commute to work: 94.3% car, 0.0% public transportation, 2.1% walk, 1.8% work from home (2000); Travel time to work: 24.4% less than 15 minutes, 36.0% 15 to 30 minutes, 17.4% 30 to 45 minutes, 12.8% 45 to 60 minutes, 9.5% 60 minutes or more (2000)

METAMORA (village). Covers a land area of 1.389 square miles and a water area of 0.002 square miles. Located at 40.79° N. Lat.; 89.36° W. Long. Elevation is 817 feet.
History: Former capital of Woodford county. Old courthouse is now state memorial to Lincoln, who often argued cases here. Incorporated 1845.
Population: 2,597 (1990); 2,700 (2000); 2,885 (2007); 3,015 (2012 projected); Race: 98.4% White, 0.9% Black, 0.1% Asian, 1.2% Hispanic of any race (2007); Density: 2,077.7 persons per square mile (2007); Average household size: 2.52 (2007); Median age: 43.3 (2007); Males per 100 females: 89.3 (2007); Marriage status: 15.9% never married, 65.8% now married, 12.0% widowed, 6.2% divorced (2000); Foreign born: 1.2% (2000); Ancestry (includes multiple ancestries): 46.4% German, 14.3% English, 12.5% Irish, 6.5% French (except Basque), 4.6% United States or American (2000).
Economy: Single-family building permits issued: 19 (2007); Multi-family building permits issued: 8 (2007); Employment by occupation: 11.3% management, 24.9% professional, 14.4% services, 22.3% sales, 0.0% farming, 11.4% construction, 15.7% production (2000).
Income: Per capita income: $22,839 (2007); Median household income: $51,429 (2007); Average household income: $56,353 (2007); Percent of households with income of $100,000 or more: 9.9% (2007); Poverty rate: 2.9% (2000).
Education: Percent of population age 25 and over with: High school diploma (including GED) or higher: 87.4% (2007); Bachelor's degree or higher: 21.9% (2007); Master's degree or higher: 4.1% (2007).

School District(s)

Central Illinois Voc Ed Coop
2005-06 Enrollment: n/a . . . . (309) 367-2783
Germantown Hills SD 69 (PK-08)
2005-06 Enrollment: 890 . . . . (309) 383-2121
Metamora CCSD 1 (PK-08)
2005-06 Enrollment: 776 . . . . (309) 367-2361
Metamora Twp HSD 122 (09-12)
2005-06 Enrollment: 933 . . . . (309) 367-4151
Housing: Homeownership rate: 78.0% (2007); Median home value: $132,105 (2007); Median rent: $396 per month (2000); Median age of housing: 37 years (2000).
Safety: Violent crime rate: 13.0 per 10,000 population; Property crime rate: 267.4 per 10,000 population (2006).
Newspapers: Metamora Herald (Community news; Circulation 3,300); Washburn Leader (Community news; Circulation 3,600); Woodford County Shopper (Community news; Circulation 7,500)
Transportation: Commute to work: 90.5% car, 0.0% public transportation, 5.3% walk, 3.4% work from home (2000); Travel time to work: 39.8% less than 15 minutes, 33.2% 15 to 30 minutes, 17.0% 30 to 45 minutes, 6.2% 45 to 60 minutes, 3.7% 60 minutes or more (2000)

MINONK (city). Covers a land area of 1.366 square miles and a water area of 0 square miles. Located at 40.90° N. Lat.; 89.03° W. Long. Elevation is 741 feet.
History: Incorporated 1867.
Population: 2,008 (1990); 2,168 (2000); 2,289 (2007); 2,345 (2012 projected); Race: 98.2% White, 0.1% Black, 0.1% Asian, 2.2% Hispanic of any race (2007); Density: 1,676.2 persons per square mile (2007); Average household size: 2.57 (2007); Median age: 40.0 (2007); Males per 100 females: 94.0 (2007); Marriage status: 18.6% never married, 59.3% now married, 11.3% widowed, 10.8% divorced (2000); Foreign born: 0.7% (2000); Ancestry (includes multiple ancestries): 39.8% German, 15.1% Irish, 7.6% United States or American, 7.4% Polish, 7.1% English (2000).
Economy: Single-family building permits issued: 1 (2007); Multi-family building permits issued: 0 (2007); Employment by occupation: 9.0% management, 15.6% professional, 17.6% services, 26.7% sales, 0.9% farming, 9.0% construction, 21.3% production (2000).
Income: Per capita income: $21,220 (2007); Median household income: $50,354 (2007); Average household income: $54,181 (2007); Percent of households with income of $100,000 or more: 9.2% (2007); Poverty rate: 8.6% (2000).
Education: Percent of population age 25 and over with: High school diploma (including GED) or higher: 83.8% (2007); Bachelor's degree or higher: 14.1% (2007); Master's degree or higher: 5.4% (2007).

School District(s)

Fieldcrest CUSD 6 (PK-12)
2005-06 Enrollment: 1,276 . . . . (309) 432-2177
Housing: Homeownership rate: 78.6% (2007); Median home value: $95,625 (2007); Median rent: $351 per month (2000); Median age of housing: 47 years (2000).
Safety: Violent crime rate: 27.8 per 10,000 population; Property crime rate: 296.6 per 10,000 population (2006).
Newspapers: Minonk News-Dispatch (Local news; Circulation 750)
Transportation: Commute to work: 92.4% car, 0.3% public transportation, 3.7% walk, 3.1% work from home (2000); Travel time to work: 39.2% less than 15 minutes, 18.7% 15 to 30 minutes, 26.7% 30 to 45 minutes, 10.8% 45 to 60 minutes, 4.6% 60 minutes or more (2000)

PANOLA (village). Covers a land area of 0.202 square miles and a water area of 0 square miles. Located at 40.78° N. Lat.; 89.02° W. Long. Elevation is 735 feet.
Population: 43 (1990); 33 (2000); 32 (2007); 32 (2012 projected); Race: 90.6% White, 0.0% Black, 9.4% Asian, 0.0% Hispanic of any race (2007); Density: 158.6 persons per square mile (2007); Average household size: 2.46 (2007); Median age: 50.0 (2007); Males per 100 females: 100.0 (2007); Marriage status: 28.1% never married, 46.9% now married, 0.0% widowed, 25.0% divorced (2000); Foreign born: 0.0% (2000); Ancestry (includes multiple ancestries): 59.4% German, 12.5% Welsh, 12.5% French (except Basque), 6.3% English, 3.1% United States or American (2000).
Economy: Employment by occupation: 0.0% management, 25.0% professional, 10.0% services, 20.0% sales, 0.0% farming, 20.0% construction, 25.0% production (2000).
Income: Per capita income: $25,625 (2007); Median household income: $48,750 (2007); Average household income: $63,077 (2007); Percent of households with income of $100,000 or more: 23.1% (2007); Poverty rate: 0.0% (2000).
Education: Percent of population age 25 and over with: High school diploma (including GED) or higher: 93.1% (2007); Bachelor's degree or higher: 10.3% (2007); Master's degree or higher: 0.0% (2007).
Housing: Homeownership rate: 100.0% (2007); Median home value: $98,750 (2007); Median rent: $n/a per month (2000); Median age of housing: 60+ years (2000).
Transportation: Commute to work: 90.0% car, 0.0% public transportation, 0.0% walk, 10.0% work from home (2000); Travel time to work: 22.2% less than 15 minutes, 33.3% 15 to 30 minutes, 44.4% 30 to 45 minutes, 0.0% 45 to 60 minutes, 0.0% 60 minutes or more (2000)

ROANOKE (village). Covers a land area of 0.910 square miles and a water area of 0.037 square miles. Located at 40.79° N. Lat.; 89.20° W. Long. Elevation is 732 feet.
History: Incorporated 1874.
Population: 1,932 (1990); 1,994 (2000); 1,997 (2007); 2,022 (2012 projected); Race: 98.8% White, 0.2% Black, 0.1% Asian, 0.1% Hispanic of any race (2007); Density: 2,195.3 persons per square mile (2007); Average household size: 2.56 (2007); Median age: 39.0 (2007); Males per 100 females: 97.1 (2007); Marriage status: 20.0% never married, 66.3% now married, 7.4% widowed, 6.3% divorced (2000); Foreign born: 0.4% (2000); Ancestry (includes multiple ancestries): 56.3% German, 8.8% Irish, 8.0% Swiss, 8.0% Italian, 7.7% English (2000).
Economy: Single-family building permits issued: 8 (2007); Multi-family building permits issued: 0 (2007); Employment by occupation: 10.7% management, 16.7% professional, 16.5% services, 27.3% sales, 1.9% farming, 9.7% construction, 17.3% production (2000).
Income: Per capita income: $25,965 (2007); Median household income: $49,000 (2007); Average household income: $65,407 (2007); Percent of households with income of $100,000 or more: 15.1% (2007); Poverty rate: 4.9% (2000).
Education: Percent of population age 25 and over with: High school diploma (including GED) or higher: 87.9% (2007); Bachelor's degree or higher: 15.6% (2007); Master's degree or higher: 4.2% (2007).

School District(s)

Roanoke Benson CUSD 60 (PK-12)
2005-06 Enrollment: 621 . . . . (309) 923-8921
Housing: Homeownership rate: 82.7% (2007); Median home value: $113,598 (2007); Median rent: $416 per month (2000); Median age of housing: 43 years (2000).
Newspapers: Roanoke Review (Community news; Circulation 1,025)
Transportation: Commute to work: 94.4% car, 0.0% public transportation, 3.0% walk, 2.6% work from home (2000); Travel time to work: 46.0% less than 15 minutes, 21.4% 15 to 30 minutes, 25.3% 30 to 45 minutes, 5.3% 45 to 60 minutes, 2.0% 60 minutes or more (2000)

SECOR (village). Covers a land area of 0.355 square miles and a water area of 0 square miles. Located at 40.74° N. Lat.; 89.13° W. Long. Elevation is 732 feet.
Population: 391 (1990); 379 (2000); 346 (2007); 350 (2012 projected); Race: 99.4% White, 0.6% Black, 0.0% Asian, 0.0% Hispanic of any race (2007); Density: 975.6 persons per square mile (2007); Average household size: 2.60 (2007); Median age: 37.3 (2007); Males per 100 females: 96.6 (2007); Marriage status: 18.4% never married, 63.5% now married, 5.8% widowed, 12.3% divorced (2000); Foreign born: 0.0% (2000); Ancestry (includes multiple ancestries): 40.4% German, 10.8% Other groups, 10.2% Irish, 7.9% English, 5.8% Dutch (2000).
Economy: Single-family building permits issued: 0 (2007); Multi-family building permits issued: 0 (2007); Employment by occupation: 5.1% management, 12.5% professional, 23.3% services, 19.3% sales, 1.1% farming, 9.7% construction, 29.0% production (2000).
Income: Per capita income: $27,240 (2007); Median household income: $51,786 (2007); Average household income: $70,865 (2007); Percent of households with income of $100,000 or more: 15.8% (2007); Poverty rate: 8.2% (2000).
Education: Percent of population age 25 and over with: High school diploma (including GED) or higher: 74.9% (2007); Bachelor's degree or higher: 5.4% (2007); Master's degree or higher: 2.2% (2007).
Housing: Homeownership rate: 80.5% (2007); Median home value: $85,909 (2007); Median rent: $311 per month (2000); Median age of housing: 53 years (2000).
Transportation: Commute to work: 93.7% car, 0.0% public transportation, 0.6% walk, 5.2% work from home (2000); Travel time to work: 35.2% less than 15 minutes, 20.0% 15 to 30 minutes, 33.9% 30 to 45 minutes, 7.3% 45 to 60 minutes, 3.6% 60 minutes or more (2000)

SPRING BAY (village). Covers a land area of 0.806 square miles and a water area of 0.331 square miles. Located at 40.82° N. Lat.; 89.52° W. Long. Elevation is 469 feet.
Population: 469 (1990); 436 (2000); 427 (2007); 429 (2012 projected); Race: 98.1% White, 1.2% Black, 0.0% Asian, 0.7% Hispanic of any race (2007); Density: 529.8 persons per square mile (2007); Average household size: 2.47 (2007); Median age: 38.7 (2007); Males per 100 females: 95.0 (2007); Marriage status: 22.6% never married, 61.2% now married, 6.6% widowed, 9.7% divorced (2000); Foreign born: 0.0% (2000); Ancestry (includes multiple ancestries): 30.7% German, 11.5% United States or American, 10.2% Other groups, 10.2% Irish, 9.8% English (2000).
Economy: Single-family building permits issued: 2 (2007); Multi-family building permits issued: 0 (2007); Employment by occupation: 3.9% management, 11.2% professional, 14.7% services, 24.7% sales, 1.2% farming, 14.7% construction, 29.7% production (2000).
Income: Per capita income: $20,995 (2007); Median household income: $47,361 (2007); Average household income: $51,821 (2007); Percent of

households with income of $100,000 or more: 7.5% (2007); Poverty rate: 4.8% (2000).
Education: Percent of population age 25 and over with: High school diploma (including GED) or higher: 85.2% (2007); Bachelor's degree or higher: 8.4% (2007); Master's degree or higher: 2.0% (2007).
Housing: Homeownership rate: 83.8% (2007); Median home value: $102,917 (2007); Median rent: $339 per month (2000); Median age of housing: 32 years (2000).
Transportation: Commute to work: 98.4% car, 0.0% public transportation, 0.8% walk, 0.0% work from home (2000); Travel time to work: 26.5% less than 15 minutes, 46.2% 15 to 30 minutes, 17.8% 30 to 45 minutes, 3.6% 45 to 60 minutes, 5.9% 60 minutes or more (2000)

WASHBURN (village). Covers a land area of 0.727 square miles and a water area of 0 square miles. Located at 40.92° N. Lat.; 89.29° W. Long. Elevation is 686 feet.
Population: 1,154 (1990); 1,147 (2000); 1,171 (2007); 1,187 (2012 projected); Race: 95.9% White, 0.3% Black, 0.3% Asian, 1.4% Hispanic of any race (2007); Density: 1,609.6 persons per square mile (2007); Average household size: 2.57 (2007); Median age: 35.7 (2007); Males per 100 females: 100.9 (2007); Marriage status: 26.9% never married, 61.0% now married, 6.1% widowed, 6.0% divorced (2000); Foreign born: 1.0% (2000); Ancestry (includes multiple ancestries): 37.4% German, 10.5% Irish, 9.6% English, 9.2% United States or American, 7.0% Other groups (2000).
Economy: Single-family building permits issued: 0 (2007); Multi-family building permits issued: 0 (2007); Employment by occupation: 8.2% management, 13.7% professional, 15.4% services, 25.3% sales, 2.4% farming, 11.5% construction, 23.4% production (2000).
Income: Per capita income: $25,583 (2007); Median household income: $56,017 (2007); Average household income: $65,841 (2007); Percent of households with income of $100,000 or more: 17.4% (2007); Poverty rate: 8.4% (2000).
Education: Percent of population age 25 and over with: High school diploma (including GED) or higher: 85.4% (2007); Bachelor's degree or higher: 11.7% (2007); Master's degree or higher: 4.7% (2007).

School District(s)

Lowpoint-Washburn CUSD 21 (PK-12)
2005-06 Enrollment: 412 . . . . (309) 248-7522
Housing: Homeownership rate: 80.2% (2007); Median home value: $94,868 (2007); Median rent: $304 per month (2000); Median age of housing: 57 years (2000).
Safety: Violent crime rate: 180.7 per 10,000 population; Property crime rate: 370.4 per 10,000 population (2006).
Transportation: Commute to work: 95.7% car, 0.0% public transportation, 2.2% walk, 1.7% work from home (2000); Travel time to work: 25.2% less than 15 minutes, 23.9% 15 to 30 minutes, 31.1% 30 to 45 minutes, 16.4% 45 to 60 minutes, 3.4% 60 minutes or more (2000);

A

B

C

D

E

CDP = Census Designated Place

F

G

H

CDP = Census Designated Place

CDP = Census Designated Place

CDP = Census Designated Place

CDP = Census Designated Place

S

T

CDP = Census Designated Place

Comparative Statistics

Population

Place	1990	2000	2007 Estimate	2012 Projection
Addison village *Du Page Co.*	33,723	35,914	36,750	37,213
Algonquin village *McHenry Co.*	12,745	23,276	32,031	37,732
Alton city *Madison Co.*	32,996	30,496	29,131	28,130
Arlington Heights village *Cook Co.*	75,201	76,031	73,135	70,926
Aurora city *Kane Co.*	102,513	142,990	176,446	198,088
Bartlett village *Du Page Co.*	19,814	36,706	39,234	40,643
Batavia city *Kane Co.*	17,818	23,866	27,044	29,193
Belleville city *Saint Clair Co.*	43,445	41,410	39,461	38,226
Belvidere city *Boone Co.*	16,801	20,820	25,776	29,322
Berwyn city *Cook Co.*	45,426	54,016	50,557	47,963
Bloomington city *McLean Co.*	53,588	64,808	70,395	73,707
Bolingbrook village *Will Co.*	41,386	56,321	70,689	80,794
Buffalo Grove village *Lake Co.*	37,883	42,909	43,140	43,126
Burbank city *Cook Co.*	27,600	27,902	27,478	27,015
Calumet City city *Cook Co.*	37,803	39,071	37,397	36,047
Carol Stream village *Du Page Co.*	32,079	40,438	40,037	39,694
Carpentersville village *Kane Co.*	23,869	30,586	37,732	42,348
Champaign city *Champaign Co.*	65,449	67,518	69,618	70,939
Chicago city *Cook Co.*	2,783,726	2,896,016	2,823,257	2,761,878
Chicago Heights city *Cook Co.*	33,156	32,776	30,934	29,641
Cicero town *Cook Co.*	67,436	85,616	82,072	79,277
Collinsville city *Madison Co.*	23,754	24,707	25,380	25,819
Crystal Lake city *McHenry Co.*	25,852	38,000	41,572	44,163
Danville city *Vermilion Co.*	35,622	33,904	32,664	31,758
De Kalb city *De Kalb Co.*	36,443	39,018	42,793	45,506
Decatur city *Macon Co.*	85,750	81,860	76,719	73,244
Des Plaines city *Cook Co.*	54,783	58,720	58,126	57,352
Dolton village *Cook Co.*	24,035	25,614	24,145	23,080
Downers Grove village *Du Page Co.*	48,477	48,724	48,433	47,958
East Saint Louis city *Saint Clair Co.*	40,944	31,542	29,388	27,818
Edwardsville city *Madison Co.*	17,105	21,491	23,091	24,090
Elgin city *Kane Co.*	78,650	94,487	99,739	103,587
Elk Grove Village village *Cook Co.*	33,624	34,727	33,526	32,690
Elmhurst city *Du Page Co.*	42,108	42,762	45,584	47,237
Elmwood Park village *Cook Co.*	23,206	25,405	24,254	23,427
Evanston city *Cook Co.*	73,233	74,239	76,344	77,360
Freeport city *Stephenson Co.*	26,316	26,443	25,421	24,677
Galesburg city *Knox Co.*	33,637	33,706	31,505	29,906
Geneva city *Kane Co.*	13,292	19,515	24,072	27,090
Glen Ellyn village *Du Page Co.*	26,153	26,999	26,767	26,514
Glendale Heights village *Du Page Co.*	28,241	31,765	32,433	32,656
Glenview village *Cook Co.*	40,177	41,847	44,617	46,149
Granite City city *Madison Co.*	34,236	31,301	29,697	28,568
Gurnee village *Lake Co.*	14,698	28,834	30,912	32,315
Hanover Park village *Cook Co.*	32,993	38,278	37,563	37,096
Harvey city *Cook Co.*	29,771	30,000	28,493	27,347
Highland Park city *Lake Co.*	30,761	31,365	32,808	33,781
Hoffman Estates village *Cook Co.*	46,320	49,495	48,855	49,104
Joliet city *Will Co.*	82,008	106,221	140,691	164,614
Kankakee city *Kankakee Co.*	27,822	27,491	26,255	25,545

Place	1990	2000	2007 Estimate	2012 Projection
Lake in the Hills village *McHenry Co.*	7,263	23,152	33,862	40,792
Lansing village *Cook Co.*	28,446	28,332	26,962	25,969
Lombard village *Du Page Co.*	40,229	42,322	42,350	42,094
Loves Park city *Winnebago Co.*	16,327	20,044	23,377	25,465
Maywood village *Cook Co.*	27,139	26,987	25,378	24,198
McHenry city *McHenry Co.*	17,677	21,501	25,682	28,532
Moline city *Rock Island Co.*	43,798	43,768	42,670	41,847
Mount Prospect village *Cook Co.*	53,114	56,265	54,082	52,523
Mundelein village *Lake Co.*	22,023	30,935	33,805	35,652
Naperville city *Du Page Co.*	90,506	128,358	143,591	153,513
New Lenox village *Will Co.*	11,574	17,771	23,834	28,046
Niles village *Cook Co.*	28,533	30,068	29,151	28,382
Normal town *McLean Co.*	40,139	45,386	50,687	54,048
North Chicago city *Lake Co.*	35,785	35,918	32,137	31,004
Northbrook village *Cook Co.*	33,020	33,435	34,279	34,626
O'Fallon city *Saint Clair Co.*	17,169	21,910	25,755	28,180
Oak Forest city *Cook Co.*	26,662	28,051	28,382	28,500
Oak Lawn village *Cook Co.*	56,325	55,245	53,463	52,051
Oak Park village *Cook Co.*	53,648	52,524	50,355	48,665
Orland Park village *Cook Co.*	38,946	51,077	57,385	61,118
Oswego village *Kendall Co.*	5,970	13,326	22,770	29,478
Palatine village *Cook Co.*	58,182	65,479	66,680	67,391
Park Forest village *Cook Co.*	24,770	23,462	22,909	22,523
Park Ridge city *Cook Co.*	37,075	37,775	36,376	35,280
Pekin city *Tazewell Co.*	33,227	33,857	33,470	33,211
Peoria city *Peoria Co.*	114,341	112,936	112,354	111,782
Plainfield village *Will Co.*	6,409	13,038	24,320	31,713
Quincy city *Adams Co.*	41,151	40,366	39,073	38,094
Rock Island city *Rock Island Co.*	40,511	39,684	38,626	37,721
Rockford city *Winnebago Co.*	146,309	150,115	152,549	154,370
Rolling Meadows city *Cook Co.*	23,056	24,604	23,873	23,249
Romeoville village *Will Co.*	15,337	21,153	36,301	46,221
Roselle village *Du Page Co.*	21,424	23,115	23,122	22,972
Round Lake Beach village *Lake Co.*	17,438	25,859	29,354	31,563
Saint Charles city *Kane Co.*	24,173	27,896	32,053	34,834
Schaumburg village *Cook Co.*	68,706	75,386	74,400	72,641
Skokie village *Cook Co.*	59,432	63,348	65,302	66,332
Springfield city *Sangamon Co.*	108,997	111,454	114,894	116,931
Streamwood village *Cook Co.*	31,724	36,407	36,151	35,833
Tinley Park village *Cook Co.*	38,640	48,401	56,060	60,560
Urbana city *Champaign Co.*	37,214	36,395	37,654	38,297
Vernon Hills village *Lake Co.*	15,529	20,120	24,208	26,782
Waukegan city *Lake Co.*	70,309	87,901	92,366	95,245
West Chicago city *Du Page Co.*	15,874	23,469	26,258	27,875
Westmont village *Du Page Co.*	22,443	24,554	24,666	24,563
Wheaton city *Du Page Co.*	52,280	55,416	54,541	53,881
Wheeling village *Cook Co.*	30,008	34,496	34,696	34,559
Wilmette village *Cook Co.*	26,685	27,651	26,704	25,966
Woodridge village *Du Page Co.*	27,524	30,934	34,123	36,006
Zion city *Lake Co.*	20,171	22,866	24,864	26,123

Physical Characteristics

Place	Density (persons per square mile)	Land Area (square miles)	Water Area (square miles)	Elevation (feet)
Addison village *Du Page Co.*	3,896.2	9.43	0.05	689
Algonquin village *McHenry Co.*	3,257.8	9.83	0.16	741
Alton city *Madison Co.*	1,862.0	15.64	0.96	499
Arlington Heights village *Cook Co.*	4,456.9	16.41	0.03	702
Aurora city *Kane Co.*	4,579.9	38.53	0.89	679
Bartlett village *Du Page Co.*	2,648.5	14.81	0.14	n/a
Batavia city *Kane Co.*	2,989.7	9.05	0.14	715
Belleville city *Saint Clair Co.*	2,093.0	18.85	0.13	515
Belvidere city *Boone Co.*	2,841.6	9.07	0.05	781
Berwyn city *Cook Co.*	12,987.6	3.89	0.00	617
Bloomington city *McLean Co.*	3,128.6	22.50	0.00	797
Bolingbrook village *Will Co.*	3,447.2	20.51	0.24	702
Buffalo Grove village *Lake Co.*	4,692.0	9.19	0.02	n/a
Burbank city *Cook Co.*	6,585.0	4.17	0.00	620
Calumet City city *Cook Co.*	5,147.6	7.26	0.12	591
Carol Stream village *Du Page Co.*	4,500.7	8.90	0.03	758
Carpentersville village *Kane Co.*	5,064.6	7.45	0.15	889
Champaign city *Champaign Co.*	4,098.3	16.99	0.02	738
Chicago city *Cook Co.*	12,430.0	227.13	6.87	587
Chicago Heights city *Cook Co.*	3,232.0	9.57	0.01	659
Cicero town *Cook Co.*	14,039.0	5.85	0.00	604
Collinsville city *Madison Co.*	1,867.0	13.59	0.01	561
Crystal Lake city *McHenry Co.*	2,559.4	16.24	0.56	915
Danville city *Vermilion Co.*	1,921.1	17.00	0.10	600
De Kalb city *De Kalb Co.*	3,393.3	12.61	0.01	880
Decatur city *Macon Co.*	1,846.0	41.56	4.32	673
Des Plaines city *Cook Co.*	4,030.0	14.42	0.11	633
Dolton village *Cook Co.*	5,304.9	4.55	0.12	604
Downers Grove village *Du Page Co.*	3,399.8	14.25	0.01	741
East Saint Louis city *Saint Clair Co.*	2,089.8	14.06	0.37	417
Edwardsville city *Madison Co.*	1,664.6	13.87	0.22	541
Elgin city *Kane Co.*	3,989.1	25.00	0.39	745
Elk Grove Village village *Cook Co.*	3,037.0	11.04	0.06	686
Elmhurst city *Du Page Co.*	4,440.9	10.26	0.00	686
Elmwood Park village *Cook Co.*	12,724.6	1.91	0.00	643
Evanston city *Cook Co.*	9,855.8	7.75	0.02	614
Freeport city *Stephenson Co.*	2,227.3	11.41	0.01	778
Galesburg city *Knox Co.*	1,864.6	16.90	0.18	771
Geneva city *Kane Co.*	2,863.5	8.41	0.18	712
Glen Ellyn village *Du Page Co.*	4,045.6	6.62	0.02	741
Glendale Heights village *Du Page Co.*	6,001.4	5.40	0.00	761
Glenview village *Cook Co.*	3,317.2	13.45	0.04	653
Granite City city *Madison Co.*	1,780.1	16.68	0.49	423
Gurnee village *Lake Co.*	2,306.6	13.40	0.01	679
Hanover Park village *Cook Co.*	5,529.1	6.79	0.00	n/a
Harvey city *Cook Co.*	4,598.9	6.20	0.00	604
Highland Park city *Lake Co.*	2,654.3	12.36	0.01	696
Hoffman Estates village *Cook Co.*	2,478.7	19.71	0.16	784
Joliet city *Will Co.*	3,696.6	38.06	0.29	541
Kankakee city *Kankakee Co.*	2,139.1	12.27	0.48	656

Place	Density (persons per square mile)	Land Area (square miles)	Water Area (square miles)	Elevation (feet)
Lake in the Hills village *McHenry Co.*	3,600.8	9.40	0.23	866
Lansing village *Cook Co.*	3,986.2	6.76	0.06	630
Lombard village *Du Page Co.*	4,372.7	9.69	0.01	719
Loves Park city *Winnebago Co.*	1,617.8	14.45	0.37	728
Maywood village *Cook Co.*	9,371.5	2.71	0.00	627
McHenry city *McHenry Co.*	2,210.0	11.62	0.49	797
Moline city *Rock Island Co.*	2,735.4	15.60	0.22	577
Mount Prospect village *Cook Co.*	5,299.2	10.21	0.04	669
Mundelein village *Lake Co.*	3,920.3	8.62	0.32	735
Naperville city *Du Page Co.*	4,058.9	35.38	0.14	709
New Lenox village *Will Co.*	2,361.2	10.09	0.02	669
Niles village *Cook Co.*	4,961.8	5.88	0.00	636
Normal town *McLean Co.*	3,721.8	13.62	0.06	801
North Chicago city *Lake Co.*	4,103.5	7.83	0.01	659
Northbrook village *Cook Co.*	2,653.5	12.92	0.05	646
O'Fallon city *Saint Clair Co.*	2,360.0	10.91	0.01	548
Oak Forest city *Cook Co.*	5,024.0	5.65	0.05	673
Oak Lawn village *Cook Co.*	6,219.9	8.60	0.00	597
Oak Park village *Cook Co.*	10,712.0	4.70	0.00	620
Orland Park village *Cook Co.*	2,998.0	19.14	0.29	705
Oswego village *Kendall Co.*	3,459.3	6.58	0.10	640
Palatine village *Cook Co.*	5,139.8	12.97	0.13	741
Park Forest village *Cook Co.*	4,651.3	4.93	0.00	712
Park Ridge city *Cook Co.*	5,175.5	7.03	0.04	643
Pekin city *Tazewell Co.*	2,545.3	13.15	0.60	502
Peoria city *Peoria Co.*	2,530.3	44.40	2.23	502
Plainfield village *Will Co.*	2,094.4	11.61	0.83	617
Quincy city *Adams Co.*	2,672.8	14.62	0.03	568
Rock Island city *Rock Island Co.*	2,425.6	15.92	1.22	561
Rockford city *Winnebago Co.*	2,723.8	56.01	0.71	715
Rolling Meadows city *Cook Co.*	4,376.4	5.45	0.00	719
Romeoville village *Will Co.*	2,501.1	14.51	0.38	617
Roselle village *Du Page Co.*	4,302.4	5.37	0.02	771
Round Lake Beach village *Lake Co.*	5,876.0	5.00	0.10	764
Saint Charles city *Kane Co.*	2,291.1	13.99	0.16	732
Schaumburg village *Cook Co.*	3,915.2	19.00	0.12	794
Skokie village *Cook Co.*	6,503.3	10.04	0.00	607
Springfield city *Sangamon Co.*	2,127.6	54.00	6.31	597
Streamwood village *Cook Co.*	4,954.0	7.30	0.03	807
Tinley Park village *Cook Co.*	3,749.1	14.95	0.04	699
Urbana city *Champaign Co.*	3,588.3	10.49	0.01	728
Vernon Hills village *Lake Co.*	3,258.6	7.43	0.19	735
Waukegan city *Lake Co.*	4,013.9	23.01	0.08	653
West Chicago city *Du Page Co.*	1,897.4	13.84	0.00	784
Westmont village *Du Page Co.*	5,037.2	4.90	0.01	748
Wheaton city *Du Page Co.*	4,860.6	11.22	0.04	758
Wheeling village *Cook Co.*	4,130.3	8.40	0.04	650
Wilmette village *Cook Co.*	4,959.9	5.38	0.01	636
Woodridge village *Du Page Co.*	4,099.9	8.32	0.02	732
Zion city *Lake Co.*	3,033.2	8.20	0.00	650

NOTE: Population Density figures as of 2007; Land Area and Water Area figures as of 2000.

Population by Race/Hispanic Origin

Place	White Alone[1] (%)	Black Alone[1] (%)	Asian Alone[1] (%)	Hispanic[2] (%)
Addison village *Du Page Co.*	68.3	3.4	9.4	37.8
Algonquin village *McHenry Co.*	90.6	1.5	4.2	6.2
Alton city *Madison Co.*	70.6	26.0	0.4	1.9
Arlington Heights village *Cook Co.*	89.0	1.1	7.0	5.3
Aurora city *Kane Co.*	63.0	11.2	4.6	38.5
Bartlett village *Du Page Co.*	82.7	2.6	10.9	7.4
Batavia city *Kane Co.*	91.9	2.4	1.9	7.1
Belleville city *Saint Clair Co.*	77.2	19.3	1.0	1.9
Belvidere city *Boone Co.*	77.1	2.0	0.9	28.5
Berwyn city *Cook Co.*	63.3	1.7	2.8	52.8
Bloomington city *McLean Co.*	82.9	8.5	4.4	4.1
Bolingbrook village *Will Co.*	54.0	22.8	9.2	21.8
Buffalo Grove village *Lake Co.*	83.9	0.7	12.6	4.3
Burbank city *Cook Co.*	87.7	0.4	2.0	15.0
Calumet City city *Cook Co.*	29.6	59.9	0.6	13.3
Carol Stream village *Du Page Co.*	72.6	5.2	14.6	12.7
Carpentersville village *Kane Co.*	60.8	4.0	3.3	51.0
Champaign city *Champaign Co.*	69.7	15.3	9.1	5.8
Chicago city *Cook Co.*	40.8	36.0	4.6	28.9
Chicago Heights city *Cook Co.*	40.9	38.8	0.5	28.4
Cicero town *Cook Co.*	43.3	1.3	0.6	85.4
Collinsville city *Madison Co.*	89.6	7.2	0.6	2.8
Crystal Lake city *McHenry Co.*	91.0	0.9	3.2	10.2
Danville city *Vermilion Co.*	68.2	26.0	1.1	5.5
De Kalb city *De Kalb Co.*	75.3	10.2	5.3	12.6
Decatur city *Macon Co.*	75.5	20.5	1.1	1.5
Des Plaines city *Cook Co.*	80.6	1.3	9.1	18.5
Dolton village *Cook Co.*	11.3	85.7	0.5	2.9
Downers Grove village *Du Page Co.*	87.5	2.4	7.3	4.5
East Saint Louis city *Saint Clair Co.*	1.2	97.3	0.1	1.0
Edwardsville city *Madison Co.*	86.6	9.4	1.7	1.3
Elgin city *Kane Co.*	65.1	6.2	5.3	43.5
Elk Grove Village village *Cook Co.*	83.6	1.7	9.7	8.0
Elmhurst city *Du Page Co.*	91.6	1.4	4.4	4.9
Elmwood Park village *Cook Co.*	88.6	0.7	2.6	15.3
Evanston city *Cook Co.*	64.2	21.2	7.1	7.9
Freeport city *Stephenson Co.*	80.1	14.3	1.2	3.1
Galesburg city *Knox Co.*	81.8	11.8	1.2	5.7
Geneva city *Kane Co.*	95.6	1.0	1.9	3.4
Glen Ellyn village *Du Page Co.*	86.8	2.5	5.8	6.1
Glendale Heights village *Du Page Co.*	52.7	6.9	24.6	25.8
Glenview village *Cook Co.*	81.8	3.6	10.8	5.5
Granite City city *Madison Co.*	93.4	2.6	0.5	3.9
Gurnee village *Lake Co.*	72.8	6.5	13.7	9.2
Hanover Park village *Cook Co.*	60.0	7.6	14.3	33.9
Harvey city *Cook Co.*	9.7	76.8	0.5	17.1
Highland Park city *Lake Co.*	88.3	1.8	2.7	13.3
Hoffman Estates village *Cook Co.*	68.5	5.0	18.5	13.8
Joliet city *Will Co.*	65.0	17.1	1.8	26.9
Kankakee city *Kankakee Co.*	46.4	41.8	0.4	14.7

Place	White Alone[1] (%)	Black Alone[1] (%)	Asian Alone[1] (%)	Hispanic[2] (%)
Lake in the Hills village *McHenry Co.*	85.4	2.9	6.6	8.8
Lansing village *Cook Co.*	80.5	14.8	0.9	7.6
Lombard village *Du Page Co.*	82.6	4.0	9.0	6.2
Loves Park city *Winnebago Co.*	90.1	3.2	2.5	4.6
Maywood village *Cook Co.*	9.7	80.9	0.3	13.4
McHenry city *McHenry Co.*	90.9	0.5	1.3	10.9
Moline city *Rock Island Co.*	85.9	3.6	1.7	14.8
Mount Prospect village *Cook Co.*	76.6	2.1	13.2	14.8
Mundelein village *Lake Co.*	70.7	1.9	10.3	32.5
Naperville city *Du Page Co.*	78.2	4.3	14.6	4.6
New Lenox village *Will Co.*	96.1	0.4	0.6	5.2
Niles village *Cook Co.*	79.4	0.5	15.5	6.0
Normal town *McLean Co.*	85.9	8.3	2.6	3.2
North Chicago city *Lake Co.*	43.4	36.2	4.6	25.8
Northbrook village *Cook Co.*	87.9	0.7	9.8	2.1
O'Fallon city *Saint Clair Co.*	80.2	13.3	3.0	2.7
Oak Forest city *Cook Co.*	87.6	4.8	3.3	7.9
Oak Lawn village *Cook Co.*	91.2	1.8	2.1	7.2
Oak Park village *Cook Co.*	65.9	24.2	4.6	5.3
Orland Park village *Cook Co.*	92.9	0.9	3.6	4.3
Oswego village *Kendall Co.*	85.0	4.9	3.0	11.3
Palatine village *Cook Co.*	80.4	2.1	9.0	17.5
Park Forest village *Cook Co.*	46.5	47.4	0.8	6.6
Park Ridge city *Cook Co.*	94.6	0.3	2.9	3.9
Pekin city *Tazewell Co.*	94.8	3.4	0.4	1.8
Peoria city *Peoria Co.*	66.0	26.0	3.3	3.4
Plainfield village *Will Co.*	92.8	1.4	2.3	7.1
Quincy city *Adams Co.*	92.4	4.9	0.6	1.2
Rock Island city *Rock Island Co.*	76.1	16.8	0.9	7.3
Rockford city *Winnebago Co.*	68.1	18.4	2.5	15.5
Rolling Meadows city *Cook Co.*	77.6	3.3	8.1	23.1
Romeoville village *Will Co.*	78.1	6.8	4.3	19.9
Roselle village *Du Page Co.*	85.1	2.2	8.5	6.8
Round Lake Beach village *Lake Co.*	63.4	4.2	3.4	43.7
Saint Charles city *Kane Co.*	90.5	2.0	3.1	8.5
Schaumburg village *Cook Co.*	73.3	3.9	18.0	7.1
Skokie village *Cook Co.*	63.7	5.7	24.1	6.9
Springfield city *Sangamon Co.*	79.3	16.3	1.8	1.4
Streamwood village *Cook Co.*	69.9	4.8	11.4	22.7
Tinley Park village *Cook Co.*	91.7	2.2	2.9	5.2
Urbana city *Champaign Co.*	63.8	14.1	16.4	4.6
Vernon Hills village *Lake Co.*	74.5	1.6	17.6	10.1
Waukegan city *Lake Co.*	45.9	16.6	4.5	56.0
West Chicago city *Du Page Co.*	75.4	1.7	2.4	59.7
Westmont village *Du Page Co.*	71.7	7.5	14.7	9.1
Wheaton city *Du Page Co.*	87.6	3.5	5.7	4.7
Wheeling village *Cook Co.*	69.3	2.7	11.3	29.1
Wilmette village *Cook Co.*	88.8	0.6	8.7	2.4
Woodridge village *Du Page Co.*	67.7	10.4	14.8	12.2
Zion city *Lake Co.*	49.4	29.7	2.7	23.4

NOTE: Data as of 2007; (1) Figures are not in combination with any other race; (2) Persons of Hispanic Origin may be of any race

Avg. Household Size, Median Age, Male/Female Ratio & Foreign Born

Place	Average Household Size (persons)	Median Age (years)	Male/Female Ratio (males per 100 females)	Foreign Born (%)
Addison village *Du Page Co.*	3.09	34.8	103.6	34.3
Algonquin village *McHenry Co.*	3.06	35.2	98.8	6.3
Alton city *Madison Co.*	2.38	35.6	89.9	0.9
Arlington Heights village *Cook Co.*	2.45	41.8	92.8	13.9
Aurora city *Kane Co.*	3.11	30.8	102.4	21.5
Bartlett village *Du Page Co.*	3.01	35.3	97.8	10.9
Batavia city *Kane Co.*	2.87	34.8	97.0	5.2
Belleville city *Saint Clair Co.*	2.30	38.2	89.2	1.9
Belvidere city *Boone Co.*	2.81	32.9	99.6	11.9
Berwyn city *Cook Co.*	2.81	35.4	96.1	25.1
Bloomington city *McLean Co.*	2.47	33.0	95.0	4.5
Bolingbrook village *Will Co.*	3.21	32.0	99.8	14.4
Buffalo Grove village *Lake Co.*	2.73	39.2	93.5	20.4
Burbank city *Cook Co.*	3.01	38.1	96.0	21.8
Calumet City city *Cook Co.*	2.63	35.0	87.9	7.3
Carol Stream village *Du Page Co.*	2.95	33.7	98.2	16.8
Carpentersville village *Kane Co.*	3.46	30.1	106.9	26.4
Champaign city *Champaign Co.*	2.46	26.6	104.0	9.4
Chicago city *Cook Co.*	2.73	33.8	95.3	21.7
Chicago Heights city *Cook Co.*	3.09	31.9	95.6	11.2
Cicero town *Cook Co.*	3.80	28.0	105.5	43.6
Collinsville city *Madison Co.*	2.32	37.4	94.3	1.7
Crystal Lake city *McHenry Co.*	2.89	35.4	98.3	7.4
Danville city *Vermilion Co.*	2.52	36.5	99.1	2.9
De Kalb city *De Kalb Co.*	2.98	24.5	98.4	9.1
Decatur city *Macon Co.*	2.35	37.9	88.3	1.6
Des Plaines city *Cook Co.*	2.64	41.4	94.0	23.9
Dolton village *Cook Co.*	3.06	34.3	87.9	3.7
Downers Grove village *Du Page Co.*	2.55	41.3	93.6	9.8
East Saint Louis city *Saint Clair Co.*	2.73	30.8	82.9	0.3
Edwardsville city *Madison Co.*	2.65	34.4	88.6	3.1
Elgin city *Kane Co.*	3.03	32.0	101.3	23.7
Elk Grove Village village *Cook Co.*	2.58	40.2	95.0	14.3
Elmhurst city *Du Page Co.*	2.71	40.9	93.8	8.0
Elmwood Park village *Cook Co.*	2.62	40.6	91.7	24.3
Evanston city *Cook Co.*	2.49	34.7	90.1	15.4
Freeport city *Stephenson Co.*	2.34	39.7	88.4	2.7
Galesburg city *Knox Co.*	2.54	38.6	102.0	2.2
Geneva city *Kane Co.*	2.98	35.2	101.3	4.5
Glen Ellyn village *Du Page Co.*	2.65	38.9	96.3	10.7
Glendale Heights village *Du Page Co.*	2.93	33.7	104.2	30.3
Glenview village *Cook Co.*	2.71	41.8	92.7	19.5
Granite City city *Madison Co.*	2.40	38.6	93.2	1.1
Gurnee village *Lake Co.*	2.76	35.7	94.5	11.7
Hanover Park village *Cook Co.*	3.44	32.1	105.3	28.4
Harvey city *Cook Co.*	3.36	29.1	93.1	8.2
Highland Park city *Lake Co.*	2.73	41.1	96.1	15.3
Hoffman Estates village *Cook Co.*	2.92	35.8	98.7	23.1
Joliet city *Will Co.*	2.91	31.8	98.5	10.9
Kankakee city *Kankakee Co.*	2.77	33.0	92.6	6.7

Place	Average Household Size (persons)	Median Age (years)	Male/Female Ratio (males per 100 females)	Foreign Born (%)
Lake in the Hills village *McHenry Co.*	3.07	32.2	101.0	8.5
Lansing village *Cook Co.*	2.46	39.6	91.1	5.6
Lombard village *Du Page Co.*	2.52	39.5	95.5	11.6
Loves Park city *Winnebago Co.*	2.44	36.0	97.4	4.2
Maywood village *Cook Co.*	3.42	32.1	88.8	7.2
McHenry city *McHenry Co.*	2.71	35.8	96.1	6.2
Moline city *Rock Island Co.*	2.36	38.7	91.8	7.1
Mount Prospect village *Cook Co.*	2.62	38.9	99.0	26.7
Mundelein village *Lake Co.*	3.20	32.7	104.0	23.8
Naperville city *Du Page Co.*	2.94	35.4	96.3	11.7
New Lenox village *Will Co.*	3.04	33.2	95.2	1.3
Niles village *Cook Co.*	2.50	49.1	87.1	33.7
Normal town *McLean Co.*	2.96	24.4	88.8	3.6
North Chicago city *Lake Co.*	4.44	23.2	149.4	12.9
Northbrook village *Cook Co.*	2.73	46.0	93.4	15.2
O'Fallon city *Saint Clair Co.*	2.61	36.4	93.7	3.7
Oak Forest city *Cook Co.*	2.84	37.5	99.0	5.8
Oak Lawn village *Cook Co.*	2.45	43.1	89.2	11.5
Oak Park village *Cook Co.*	2.24	38.5	88.1	9.8
Orland Park village *Cook Co.*	2.70	42.9	91.9	9.4
Oswego village *Kendall Co.*	2.94	32.4	97.4	4.7
Palatine village *Cook Co.*	2.56	36.7	98.9	21.9
Park Forest village *Cook Co.*	2.53	36.5	88.0	3.1
Park Ridge city *Cook Co.*	2.65	44.4	90.4	12.7
Pekin city *Tazewell Co.*	2.48	38.0	97.2	0.8
Peoria city *Peoria Co.*	2.47	34.3	91.0	4.4
Plainfield village *Will Co.*	3.07	33.6	99.8	3.9
Quincy city *Adams Co.*	2.41	39.6	89.3	1.0
Rock Island city *Rock Island Co.*	2.44	37.1	89.8	3.2
Rockford city *Winnebago Co.*	2.53	35.2	94.9	8.7
Rolling Meadows city *Cook Co.*	2.77	36.5	102.0	21.3
Romeoville village *Will Co.*	2.99	31.0	101.0	9.4
Roselle village *Du Page Co.*	2.70	38.1	96.4	15.1
Round Lake Beach village *Lake Co.*	3.57	30.6	101.4	21.5
Saint Charles city *Kane Co.*	2.67	36.3	101.1	6.6
Schaumburg village *Cook Co.*	2.37	38.2	95.3	19.1
Skokie village *Cook Co.*	2.78	43.6	90.4	37.0
Springfield city *Sangamon Co.*	2.27	38.3	89.2	2.3
Streamwood village *Cook Co.*	3.00	34.9	99.9	19.9
Tinley Park village *Cook Co.*	2.74	38.3	94.4	5.8
Urbana city *Champaign Co.*	2.51	26.0	113.3	15.8
Vernon Hills village *Lake Co.*	2.69	35.9	94.3	21.2
Waukegan city *Lake Co.*	3.21	31.0	103.4	30.2
West Chicago city *Du Page Co.*	3.75	30.6	112.6	34.1
Westmont village *Du Page Co.*	2.45	39.1	89.7	19.7
Wheaton city *Du Page Co.*	2.84	37.8	95.5	9.5
Wheeling village *Cook Co.*	2.64	37.1	97.3	31.4
Wilmette village *Cook Co.*	2.78	43.6	92.1	13.2
Woodridge village *Du Page Co.*	2.68	35.8	99.7	17.3
Zion city *Lake Co.*	3.03	31.5	95.4	8.8

NOTE: Average Household Size, Median Age, and Male/Female Ratio figures as of 2007. Foreign Born figures as of 2000.

Five Largest Ancestry Groups

Place	Group 1	Group 2	Group 3	Group 4	Group 5
Addison village *Du Page Co.*	Other (36.9%)	Italian (16.3%)	German (14.3%)	Polish (13.0%)	Irish (8.8%)
Algonquin village *McHenry Co.*	German (33.1%)	Polish (18.6%)	Irish (17.0%)	Italian (12.1%)	English (9.1%)
Alton city *Madison Co.*	Other (27.4%)	German (22.1%)	Irish (12.2%)	American (8.2%)	English (7.9%)
Arlington Heights village *Cook Co.*	German (27.5%)	Irish (19.2%)	Polish (14.5%)	Other (12.0%)	Italian (11.1%)
Aurora city *Kane Co.*	Other (44.4%)	German (17.5%)	Irish (9.7%)	English (5.6%)	Italian (4.7%)
Bartlett village *Du Page Co.*	German (28.5%)	Italian (17.2%)	Other (16.4%)	Irish (16.3%)	Polish (15.3%)
Batavia city *Kane Co.*	German (31.6%)	Irish (18.1%)	English (11.5%)	Other (10.8%)	Italian (8.8%)
Belleville city *Saint Clair Co.*	German (33.2%)	Other (19.7%)	Irish (11.5%)	English (8.4%)	American (6.0%)
Belvidere city *Boone Co.*	German (30.6%)	Other (23.3%)	Irish (13.2%)	English (9.0%)	Swedish (6.9%)
Berwyn city *Cook Co.*	Other (39.4%)	Polish (12.0%)	German (11.8%)	Irish (11.1%)	Italian (10.4%)
Bloomington city *McLean Co.*	German (28.0%)	Other (17.0%)	Irish (14.1%)	English (10.8%)	American (7.1%)
Bolingbrook village *Will Co.*	Other (38.0%)	German (19.6%)	Irish (12.8%)	Polish (9.8%)	Italian (7.7%)
Buffalo Grove village *Lake Co.*	Other (19.1%)	German (16.1%)	Russian (15.4%)	Polish (12.7%)	Irish (9.7%)
Burbank city *Cook Co.*	Polish (30.3%)	Irish (18.7%)	German (16.1%)	Other (13.4%)	Italian (9.3%)
Calumet City city *Cook Co.*	Other (58.6%)	Polish (12.7%)	German (6.5%)	Irish (5.1%)	Italian (3.8%)
Carol Stream village *Du Page Co.*	Other (24.5%)	German (24.3%)	Irish (14.3%)	Italian (14.2%)	Polish (12.7%)
Carpentersville village *Kane Co.*	Other (43.0%)	German (17.9%)	Irish (9.6%)	Polish (7.7%)	Italian (5.2%)
Champaign city *Champaign Co.*	Other (26.1%)	German (24.2%)	Irish (13.4%)	English (10.5%)	Polish (4.6%)
Chicago city *Cook Co.*	Other (56.8%)	Polish (7.3%)	Irish (6.6%)	German (6.5%)	Italian (3.5%)
Chicago Heights city *Cook Co.*	Other (55.9%)	Italian (11.4%)	German (10.2%)	Irish (6.6%)	Polish (6.2%)
Cicero town *Cook Co.*	Other (72.6%)	Polish (4.7%)	Irish (3.7%)	German (3.7%)	Italian (3.0%)
Collinsville city *Madison Co.*	German (32.5%)	Irish (16.3%)	Other (12.8%)	English (12.1%)	Italian (9.3%)
Crystal Lake city *McHenry Co.*	German (34.5%)	Irish (21.1%)	Polish (11.9%)	English (10.0%)	Other (9.3%)
Danville city *Vermilion Co.*	Other (26.0%)	German (15.7%)	Irish (9.6%)	American (8.9%)	English (7.8%)
De Kalb city *De Kalb Co.*	German (24.5%)	Other (21.9%)	Irish (14.5%)	English (7.5%)	Polish (6.1%)
Decatur city *Macon Co.*	Other (22.2%)	German (19.3%)	Irish (11.2%)	American (10.3%)	English (9.3%)
Des Plaines city *Cook Co.*	Other (22.7%)	German (21.5%)	Polish (18.2%)	Irish (13.8%)	Italian (10.6%)
Dolton village *Cook Co.*	Other (74.3%)	German (3.6%)	Polish (2.6%)	Irish (2.4%)	African (1.6%)
Downers Grove village *Du Page Co.*	German (25.5%)	Irish (20.3%)	Polish (14.9%)	Other (12.4%)	Italian (10.8%)
East Saint Louis city *Saint Clair Co.*	Other (77.5%)	African (1.1%)	American (0.6%)	German (0.4%)	Irish (0.4%)
Edwardsville city *Madison Co.*	German (33.9%)	Other (15.8%)	Irish (12.9%)	English (11.6%)	Italian (5.3%)
Elgin city *Kane Co.*	Other (41.2%)	German (22.0%)	Irish (9.8%)	Polish (6.3%)	English (5.6%)
Elk Grove Village village *Cook Co.*	German (25.5%)	Polish (19.3%)	Other (17.3%)	Irish (17.1%)	Italian (14.7%)
Elmhurst city *Du Page Co.*	German (26.5%)	Irish (21.5%)	Italian (14.2%)	Polish (13.2%)	Other (9.5%)
Elmwood Park village *Cook Co.*	Italian (28.7%)	Polish (24.7%)	Other (13.5%)	Irish (12.3%)	German (12.0%)
Evanston city *Cook Co.*	Other (29.7%)	German (16.2%)	Irish (12.5%)	English (9.0%)	Polish (5.6%)
Freeport city *Stephenson Co.*	German (36.3%)	Other (18.8%)	Irish (11.0%)	English (8.1%)	American (5.2%)
Galesburg city *Knox Co.*	German (18.0%)	Other (14.2%)	Irish (12.3%)	English (10.0%)	Swedish (10.0%)
Geneva city *Kane Co.*	German (29.7%)	Irish (23.9%)	Polish (11.0%)	English (10.3%)	Italian (9.8%)
Glen Ellyn village *Du Page Co.*	German (27.8%)	Irish (22.5%)	English (13.3%)	Other (13.0%)	Italian (10.3%)
Glendale Heights village *Du Page Co.*	Other (40.0%)	German (16.8%)	Polish (11.4%)	Italian (10.1%)	Irish (9.5%)
Glenview village *Cook Co.*	German (20.6%)	Other (18.6%)	Irish (17.0%)	Polish (9.3%)	English (7.5%)
Granite City city *Madison Co.*	German (20.6%)	Irish (16.8%)	Other (14.0%)	American (10.3%)	English (9.7%)
Gurnee village *Lake Co.*	German (27.3%)	Other (20.9%)	Irish (14.5%)	Polish (9.2%)	Italian (8.6%)
Hanover Park village *Cook Co.*	Other (40.7%)	German (15.5%)	Irish (12.6%)	Polish (11.0%)	Italian (8.7%)
Harvey city *Cook Co.*	Other (77.7%)	African (2.5%)	Polish (1.6%)	German (1.2%)	American (1.1%)
Highland Park city *Lake Co.*	Other (17.5%)	Russian (16.4%)	German (12.6%)	American (8.8%)	Polish (8.7%)
Hoffman Estates village *Cook Co.*	Other (29.4%)	German (21.9%)	Irish (14.7%)	Polish (13.3%)	Italian (10.8%)
Joliet city *Will Co.*	Other (34.4%)	German (18.0%)	Irish (13.8%)	Italian (8.7%)	Polish (7.7%)
Kankakee city *Kankakee Co.*	Other (45.3%)	German (14.0%)	Irish (7.7%)	French (6.5%)	English (4.2%)

Place	Group 1	Group 2	Group 3	Group 4	Group 5
Lake in the Hills village *McHenry Co.*	German (30.8%)	Irish (18.3%)	Italian (17.8%)	Polish (16.6%)	Other (13.1%)
Lansing village *Cook Co.*	German (20.4%)	Other (17.2%)	Polish (15.7%)	Irish (15.5%)	Dutch (13.7%)
Lombard village *Du Page Co.*	German (27.1%)	Irish (19.7%)	Other (15.3%)	Italian (14.4%)	Polish (11.0%)
Loves Park city *Winnebago Co.*	German (29.1%)	Irish (14.7%)	Other (11.1%)	Swedish (10.8%)	English (10.0%)
Maywood village *Cook Co.*	Other (79.1%)	German (1.4%)	Irish (1.1%)	African (1.1%)	Italian (0.8%)
McHenry city *McHenry Co.*	German (36.6%)	Irish (20.9%)	Polish (13.1%)	Other (9.4%)	Italian (8.7%)
Moline city *Rock Island Co.*	German (24.1%)	Other (18.2%)	Irish (13.9%)	English (10.0%)	Swedish (9.3%)
Mount Prospect village *Cook Co.*	Other (25.0%)	German (21.1%)	Polish (16.3%)	Irish (13.4%)	Italian (10.9%)
Mundelein village *Lake Co.*	Other (31.6%)	German (22.8%)	Irish (13.9%)	Polish (10.7%)	Italian (7.5%)
Naperville city *Du Page Co.*	German (27.0%)	Irish (18.5%)	Other (16.8%)	Polish (10.9%)	Italian (10.6%)
New Lenox village *Will Co.*	German (31.5%)	Irish (27.9%)	Polish (16.8%)	Italian (13.4%)	English (7.9%)
Niles village *Cook Co.*	Polish (22.8%)	Other (19.3%)	German (14.2%)	Irish (9.8%)	Italian (8.9%)
Normal town *McLean Co.*	German (31.3%)	Irish (15.1%)	Other (12.6%)	English (9.9%)	Italian (5.1%)
North Chicago city *Lake Co.*	Other (51.9%)	German (10.0%)	Irish (7.7%)	English (4.0%)	American (3.5%)
Northbrook village *Cook Co.*	German (18.3%)	Other (15.6%)	Russian (12.3%)	Irish (12.1%)	Polish (10.0%)
O'Fallon city *Saint Clair Co.*	German (30.8%)	Other (19.2%)	Irish (12.6%)	English (11.1%)	American (6.1%)
Oak Forest city *Cook Co.*	Irish (26.3%)	German (25.1%)	Polish (18.3%)	Italian (13.0%)	Other (11.2%)
Oak Lawn village *Cook Co.*	Irish (30.4%)	German (19.5%)	Polish (19.3%)	Italian (9.7%)	Other (8.9%)
Oak Park village *Cook Co.*	Other (29.3%)	German (18.0%)	Irish (17.4%)	English (8.7%)	Italian (7.5%)
Orland Park village *Cook Co.*	Irish (26.5%)	German (19.5%)	Polish (18.5%)	Italian (14.8%)	Other (9.3%)
Oswego village *Kendall Co.*	German (33.9%)	Irish (20.0%)	Other (13.2%)	Polish (11.3%)	English (11.3%)
Palatine village *Cook Co.*	Other (25.2%)	German (25.1%)	Irish (14.8%)	Polish (12.0%)	Italian (9.1%)
Park Forest village *Cook Co.*	Other (42.0%)	German (19.4%)	Irish (11.9%)	English (8.2%)	Italian (6.7%)
Park Ridge city *Cook Co.*	German (24.1%)	Irish (22.4%)	Polish (20.8%)	Italian (16.3%)	Other (7.1%)
Pekin city *Tazewell Co.*	German (28.4%)	Irish (11.5%)	English (11.3%)	American (10.2%)	Other (7.8%)
Peoria city *Peoria Co.*	Other (29.4%)	German (21.9%)	Irish (12.2%)	English (8.8%)	American (5.6%)
Plainfield village *Will Co.*	German (31.1%)	Irish (20.2%)	Italian (16.0%)	Polish (15.4%)	English (9.2%)
Quincy city *Adams Co.*	German (36.6%)	Irish (12.1%)	American (9.0%)	Other (8.8%)	English (8.5%)
Rock Island city *Rock Island Co.*	Other (24.0%)	German (23.4%)	Irish (13.2%)	English (8.2%)	American (6.8%)
Rockford city *Winnebago Co.*	Other (28.2%)	German (19.7%)	Irish (11.2%)	Swedish (9.8%)	English (7.9%)
Rolling Meadows city *Cook Co.*	Other (27.7%)	German (26.5%)	Irish (14.9%)	Polish (11.7%)	Italian (9.4%)
Romeoville village *Will Co.*	German (22.8%)	Other (22.5%)	Irish (19.3%)	Polish (15.7%)	Italian (9.8%)
Roselle village *Du Page Co.*	German (28.3%)	Polish (17.1%)	Irish (17.0%)	Other (16.1%)	Italian (16.0%)
Round Lake Beach village *Lake Co.*	Other (36.9%)	German (23.7%)	Irish (13.8%)	Polish (10.2%)	English (6.2%)
Saint Charles city *Kane Co.*	German (29.7%)	Irish (17.9%)	English (12.2%)	Polish (10.6%)	Italian (9.6%)
Schaumburg village *Cook Co.*	German (24.8%)	Other (23.2%)	Irish (15.0%)	Polish (14.9%)	Italian (12.6%)
Skokie village *Cook Co.*	Other (35.9%)	German (9.3%)	Russian (8.9%)	Polish (6.7%)	Irish (6.1%)
Springfield city *Sangamon Co.*	German (24.4%)	Other (17.0%)	Irish (15.6%)	English (11.8%)	American (7.1%)
Streamwood village *Cook Co.*	Other (30.3%)	German (21.2%)	Polish (14.6%)	Irish (13.7%)	Italian (10.5%)
Tinley Park village *Cook Co.*	Irish (25.4%)	German (23.1%)	Polish (19.7%)	Italian (14.3%)	Other (8.6%)
Urbana city *Champaign Co.*	Other (32.6%)	German (20.5%)	Irish (10.9%)	English (9.8%)	Polish (4.1%)
Vernon Hills village *Lake Co.*	Other (24.5%)	German (18.8%)	Irish (13.9%)	Polish (10.1%)	Italian (9.2%)
Waukegan city *Lake Co.*	Other (59.6%)	German (8.6%)	Irish (5.1%)	English (3.3%)	Polish (3.2%)
West Chicago city *Du Page Co.*	Other (45.3%)	German (17.2%)	Irish (9.7%)	Italian (6.4%)	Polish (6.4%)
Westmont village *Du Page Co.*	Other (25.3%)	German (17.6%)	Irish (15.3%)	Polish (13.7%)	Italian (8.7%)
Wheaton city *Du Page Co.*	German (28.1%)	Irish (18.4%)	English (12.9%)	Other (12.0%)	Italian (9.4%)
Wheeling village *Cook Co.*	Other (33.6%)	German (16.7%)	Polish (10.8%)	Irish (9.7%)	Russian (6.8%)
Wilmette village *Cook Co.*	German (20.2%)	Irish (19.4%)	Other (15.1%)	English (11.5%)	Polish (7.2%)
Woodridge village *Du Page Co.*	Other (27.4%)	German (21.6%)	Irish (17.4%)	Polish (12.0%)	Italian (10.0%)
Zion city *Lake Co.*	Other (40.5%)	German (16.0%)	Irish (7.9%)	English (6.7%)	American (4.6%)

NOTE: Data as of 2000; "Other" includes Hispanic and race groups; "French" excludes Basque; Please refer to the Explanation of Data for more information.

Marriage Status

Place	Never Married (%)	Now Married (%)	Widowed (%)	Divorced (%)
Addison village *Du Page Co.*	28.1	60.0	4.8	7.2
Algonquin village *McHenry Co.*	18.5	71.4	3.3	6.7
Alton city *Madison Co.*	29.0	47.9	9.7	13.4
Arlington Heights village *Cook Co.*	22.0	62.6	7.6	7.8
Aurora city *Kane Co.*	29.0	58.9	4.0	8.2
Bartlett village *Du Page Co.*	19.5	70.3	3.2	7.1
Batavia city *Kane Co.*	21.4	64.8	5.7	8.0
Belleville city *Saint Clair Co.*	26.3	50.9	9.4	13.5
Belvidere city *Boone Co.*	23.9	58.6	6.8	10.7
Berwyn city *Cook Co.*	31.1	51.4	8.1	9.4
Bloomington city *McLean Co.*	29.7	54.1	5.3	10.9
Bolingbrook village *Will Co.*	25.8	62.9	3.7	7.6
Buffalo Grove village *Lake Co.*	20.7	67.7	4.4	7.2
Burbank city *Cook Co.*	28.4	55.1	9.1	7.5
Calumet City city *Cook Co.*	31.7	47.6	9.0	11.7
Carol Stream village *Du Page Co.*	25.7	61.8	4.9	7.5
Carpentersville village *Kane Co.*	28.2	60.4	3.8	7.5
Champaign city *Champaign Co.*	50.5	38.4	3.9	7.2
Chicago city *Cook Co.*	40.9	43.3	7.0	8.8
Chicago Heights city *Cook Co.*	35.2	48.7	7.8	8.2
Cicero town *Cook Co.*	32.5	56.1	5.3	6.1
Collinsville city *Madison Co.*	25.1	54.1	8.8	12.0
Crystal Lake city *McHenry Co.*	21.3	65.2	5.4	8.1
Danville city *Vermilion Co.*	25.8	52.7	8.6	12.9
De Kalb city *De Kalb Co.*	52.5	38.2	3.6	5.7
Decatur city *Macon Co.*	26.3	52.1	8.2	13.3
Des Plaines city *Cook Co.*	24.9	58.0	9.2	8.0
Dolton village *Cook Co.*	33.4	49.0	6.4	11.2
Downers Grove village *Du Page Co.*	23.1	62.0	8.1	6.9
East Saint Louis city *Saint Clair Co.*	45.3	30.7	10.9	13.2
Edwardsville city *Madison Co.*	28.8	56.0	5.7	9.4
Elgin city *Kane Co.*	28.6	57.5	5.0	8.9
Elk Grove Village village *Cook Co.*	23.6	61.2	6.3	8.9
Elmhurst city *Du Page Co.*	22.8	63.2	7.6	6.4
Elmwood Park village *Cook Co.*	27.2	52.8	10.1	10.0
Evanston city *Cook Co.*	39.2	47.2	5.4	8.2
Freeport city *Stephenson Co.*	26.2	53.2	8.9	11.6
Galesburg city *Knox Co.*	24.2	51.6	9.3	14.9
Geneva city *Kane Co.*	20.4	67.0	5.2	7.4
Glen Ellyn village *Du Page Co.*	22.0	65.7	5.6	6.8
Glendale Heights village *Du Page Co.*	31.0	56.8	3.6	8.6
Glenview village *Cook Co.*	19.2	67.8	6.3	6.8
Granite City city *Madison Co.*	25.2	51.7	9.6	13.6
Gurnee village *Lake Co.*	20.9	67.0	3.8	8.3
Hanover Park village *Cook Co.*	29.7	58.9	3.2	8.2
Harvey city *Cook Co.*	38.8	44.5	7.6	9.1
Highland Park city *Lake Co.*	17.1	71.9	5.6	5.3
Hoffman Estates village *Cook Co.*	27.6	59.9	4.5	8.0
Joliet city *Will Co.*	27.9	56.0	7.0	9.1
Kankakee city *Kankakee Co.*	33.8	44.6	9.4	12.2

Place	Never Married (%)	Now Married (%)	Widowed (%)	Divorced (%)
Lake in the Hills village *McHenry Co.*	17.6	74.0	2.1	6.3
Lansing village *Cook Co.*	25.7	56.7	8.5	9.1
Lombard village *Du Page Co.*	26.1	58.0	7.5	8.5
Loves Park city *Winnebago Co.*	23.7	57.2	6.7	12.3
Maywood village *Cook Co.*	42.0	41.4	7.2	9.5
McHenry city *McHenry Co.*	22.3	61.0	6.6	10.1
Moline city *Rock Island Co.*	24.8	55.2	7.6	12.4
Mount Prospect village *Cook Co.*	25.4	61.8	6.1	6.7
Mundelein village *Lake Co.*	25.3	64.9	3.1	6.7
Naperville city *Du Page Co.*	22.2	68.4	3.5	6.0
New Lenox village *Will Co.*	21.2	67.8	4.4	6.6
Niles village *Cook Co.*	24.3	55.5	13.0	7.2
Normal town *McLean Co.*	47.9	42.9	3.4	5.9
North Chicago city *Lake Co.*	51.3	39.5	2.8	6.4
Northbrook village *Cook Co.*	17.5	70.1	6.7	5.6
O'Fallon city *Saint Clair Co.*	23.3	63.5	4.0	9.2
Oak Forest city *Cook Co.*	26.7	60.0	5.6	7.6
Oak Lawn village *Cook Co.*	24.7	55.9	11.6	7.8
Oak Park village *Cook Co.*	33.5	51.1	5.3	10.0
Orland Park village *Cook Co.*	22.8	63.6	7.6	6.1
Oswego village *Kendall Co.*	18.0	71.3	5.1	5.7
Palatine village *Cook Co.*	27.4	59.2	5.0	8.5
Park Forest village *Cook Co.*	30.3	49.7	7.3	12.7
Park Ridge city *Cook Co.*	21.9	63.5	8.8	5.8
Pekin city *Tazewell Co.*	20.5	59.3	8.2	12.0
Peoria city *Peoria Co.*	32.3	49.1	7.6	11.0
Plainfield village *Will Co.*	19.4	71.3	4.0	5.3
Quincy city *Adams Co.*	24.0	54.2	10.6	11.2
Rock Island city *Rock Island Co.*	30.9	48.4	9.2	11.5
Rockford city *Winnebago Co.*	28.2	51.8	7.3	12.7
Rolling Meadows city *Cook Co.*	27.2	60.3	4.8	7.7
Romeoville village *Will Co.*	28.2	62.1	3.4	6.3
Roselle village *Du Page Co.*	24.9	62.2	4.7	8.2
Round Lake Beach village *Lake Co.*	24.1	64.0	3.5	8.4
Saint Charles city *Kane Co.*	24.3	61.6	5.4	8.8
Schaumburg village *Cook Co.*	29.5	54.9	6.0	9.6
Skokie village *Cook Co.*	24.2	59.6	9.7	6.5
Springfield city *Sangamon Co.*	29.1	49.8	8.0	13.1
Streamwood village *Cook Co.*	24.8	61.6	4.5	9.1
Tinley Park village *Cook Co.*	25.2	60.3	7.1	7.4
Urbana city *Champaign Co.*	53.6	35.6	4.1	6.7
Vernon Hills village *Lake Co.*	24.8	62.0	4.3	8.9
Waukegan city *Lake Co.*	31.6	55.0	4.8	8.5
West Chicago city *Du Page Co.*	29.7	61.8	2.8	5.8
Westmont village *Du Page Co.*	26.0	55.9	8.2	9.9
Wheaton city *Du Page Co.*	26.9	61.3	4.9	6.8
Wheeling village *Cook Co.*	27.6	57.8	5.5	9.1
Wilmette village *Cook Co.*	18.4	69.5	6.4	5.7
Woodridge village *Du Page Co.*	28.2	59.3	3.6	8.8
Zion city *Lake Co.*	28.2	54.9	5.0	11.9

NOTE: Data as of 2000

Employment and Building Permits Issued

Place	Unemployment Rate (%)	Total Civilian Labor Force	Single-Family Building Permits	Multi-Family Building Permits
Addison village *Du Page Co.*	6.3	20,489	29	5
Algonquin village *McHenry Co.*	4.5	17,048	33	0
Alton city *Madison Co.*	6.2	14,239	16	28
Arlington Heights village *Cook Co.*	3.6	42,699	109	0
Aurora city *Kane Co.*	5.9	92,411	338	0
Bartlett village *Du Page Co.*	4.4	23,752	252	144
Batavia city *Kane Co.*	4.3	15,427	25	48
Belleville city *Saint Clair Co.*	5.8	22,162	198	17
Belvidere city *Boone Co.*	9.3	13,255	106	32
Berwyn city *Cook Co.*	5.8	26,230	1	12
Bloomington city *McLean Co.*	3.9	42,125	200	101
Bolingbrook village *Will Co.*	4.9	40,427	125	0
Buffalo Grove village *Lake Co.*	3.7	25,119	18	0
Burbank city *Cook Co.*	5.2	14,753	56	0
Calumet City city *Cook Co.*	7.3	18,565	12	0
Carol Stream village *Du Page Co.*	4.5	23,708	148	0
Carpentersville village *Kane Co.*	7.8	19,009	54	0
Champaign city *Champaign Co.*	4.0	42,496	206	593
Chicago city *Cook Co.*	5.9	1,343,803	870	12,591
Chicago Heights city *Cook Co.*	9.4	13,761	5	2
Cicero town *Cook Co.*	7.4	33,398	0	0
Collinsville city *Madison Co.*	5.0	14,697	28	27
Crystal Lake city *McHenry Co.*	4.9	22,847	107	0
Danville city *Vermilion Co.*	6.8	13,738	10	0
De Kalb city *De Kalb Co.*	4.7	23,628	111	15
Decatur city *Macon Co.*	6.1	37,450	22	0
Des Plaines city *Cook Co.*	5.2	31,067	32	180
Dolton village *Cook Co.*	7.2	12,497	16	0
Downers Grove village *Du Page Co.*	3.6	28,041	86	4
East Saint Louis city *Saint Clair Co.*	9.5	10,211	6	0
Edwardsville city *Madison Co.*	n/a	n/a	55	18
Elgin city *Kane Co.*	7.5	57,058	756	10
Elk Grove Village village *Cook Co.*	4.0	20,783	3	0
Elmhurst city *Du Page Co.*	3.5	25,227	108	32
Elmwood Park village *Cook Co.*	4.8	13,542	11	38
Evanston city *Cook Co.*	3.9	42,846	16	402
Freeport city *Stephenson Co.*	6.4	12,788	6	10
Galesburg city *Knox Co.*	5.9	14,962	4	0
Geneva city *Kane Co.*	n/a	n/a	31	0
Glen Ellyn village *Du Page Co.*	3.6	15,057	41	4
Glendale Heights village *Du Page Co.*	5.4	19,724	5	0
Glenview village *Cook Co.*	3.4	24,906	82	0
Granite City city *Madison Co.*	5.6	15,491	80	0
Gurnee village *Lake Co.*	4.3	17,637	59	0
Hanover Park village *Cook Co.*	6.1	21,564	19	0
Harvey city *Cook Co.*	9.0	11,288	13	4
Highland Park city *Lake Co.*	3.3	17,014	31	37
Hoffman Estates village *Cook Co.*	4.1	31,315	198	0
Joliet city *Will Co.*	7.2	71,917	769	16
Kankakee city *Kankakee Co.*	9.1	11,936	24	6

Place	Unemployment Rate (%)	Total Civilian Labor Force	Single-Family Building Permits	Multi-Family Building Permits
Lake in the Hills village *McHenry Co.*	4.9	17,445	36	0
Lansing village *Cook Co.*	6.2	14,803	11	0
Lombard village *Du Page Co.*	4.6	25,065	33	80
Loves Park city *Winnebago Co.*	n/a	n/a	102	0
Maywood village *Cook Co.*	8.2	11,916	0	0
McHenry city *McHenry Co.*	5.6	15,045	124	62
Moline city *Rock Island Co.*	4.5	24,208	46	192
Mount Prospect village *Cook Co.*	3.7	31,335	12	0
Mundelein village *Lake Co.*	5.1	18,194	406	0
Naperville city *Du Page Co.*	3.6	78,872	281	62
New Lenox village *Will Co.*	n/a	n/a	135	0
Niles village *Cook Co.*	4.5	14,720	13	0
Normal town *McLean Co.*	3.8	28,456	129	125
North Chicago city *Lake Co.*	9.8	9,784	4	0
Northbrook village *Cook Co.*	3.4	17,850	59	0
O'Fallon city *Saint Clair Co.*	4.3	13,740	203	2
Oak Forest city *Cook Co.*	5.1	16,335	4	12
Oak Lawn village *Cook Co.*	5.6	27,345	30	80
Oak Park village *Cook Co.*	3.6	31,517	35	32
Orland Park village *Cook Co.*	4.2	29,786	45	24
Oswego village *Kendall Co.*	4.9	15,153	421	11
Palatine village *Cook Co.*	4.2	42,021	40	56
Park Forest village *Cook Co.*	6.1	12,731	24	0
Park Ridge city *Cook Co.*	3.5	19,705	48	114
Pekin city *Tazewell Co.*	5.2	18,057	56	78
Peoria city *Peoria Co.*	5.0	58,870	306	125
Plainfield village *Will Co.*	5.0	18,405	400	4
Quincy city *Adams Co.*	4.1	22,632	62	51
Rock Island city *Rock Island Co.*	5.0	20,376	10	0
Rockford city *Winnebago Co.*	7.8	75,079	157	170
Rolling Meadows city *Cook Co.*	n/a	n/a	3	0
Romeoville village *Will Co.*	5.4	22,144	57	0
Roselle village *Du Page Co.*	n/a	n/a	18	0
Round Lake Beach village *Lake Co.*	8.5	15,483	8	0
Saint Charles city *Kane Co.*	4.3	19,467	30	0
Schaumburg village *Cook Co.*	4.1	46,859	25	0
Skokie village *Cook Co.*	4.1	34,960	38	0
Springfield city *Sangamon Co.*	4.5	64,978	179	110
Streamwood village *Cook Co.*	5.4	22,864	26	0
Tinley Park village *Cook Co.*	4.0	33,403	94	0
Urbana city *Champaign Co.*	4.4	21,369	83	328
Vernon Hills village *Lake Co.*	n/a	n/a	31	146
Waukegan city *Lake Co.*	7.2	45,230	51	0
West Chicago city *Du Page Co.*	5.9	14,978	9	0
Westmont village *Du Page Co.*	4.3	13,969	35	0
Wheaton city *Du Page Co.*	3.4	30,324	68	0
Wheeling village *Cook Co.*	4.3	22,596	14	72
Wilmette village *Cook Co.*	3.2	13,268	30	0
Woodridge village *Du Page Co.*	4.2	20,836	38	0
Zion city *Lake Co.*	n/a	n/a	60	4

NOTE: Unemployment Rate and Civilian Labor Force as of April 2008; Building permit data covers 2007; n/a not available.

Employment by Occupation

Place	Sales	Prof.	Mgmt	Services	Production	Constr.
Addison village *Du Page Co.*	29.6	14.4	12.5	11.5	21.7	10.2
Algonquin village *McHenry Co.*	30.9	22.1	20.9	8.6	10.0	7.4
Alton city *Madison Co.*	26.2	18.1	7.4	22.3	18.4	7.5
Arlington Heights village *Cook Co.*	29.8	27.0	23.5	7.5	7.3	4.8
Aurora city *Kane Co.*	25.9	18.3	15.0	12.4	20.5	7.6
Bartlett village *Du Page Co.*	31.9	19.9	23.3	7.9	9.8	7.2
Batavia city *Kane Co.*	28.0	23.8	20.5	10.8	9.7	7.1
Belleville city *Saint Clair Co.*	29.7	18.9	9.8	19.3	14.0	8.3
Belvidere city *Boone Co.*	24.7	10.6	7.9	14.9	31.0	10.1
Berwyn city *Cook Co.*	30.0	15.9	10.3	14.1	20.1	9.6
Bloomington city *McLean Co.*	28.1	23.9	16.9	13.9	10.4	6.7
Bolingbrook village *Will Co.*	28.8	21.0	15.8	11.5	13.7	9.2
Buffalo Grove village *Lake Co.*	29.3	30.2	24.7	6.2	5.6	4.0
Burbank city *Cook Co.*	30.5	8.3	8.5	15.1	25.4	12.2
Calumet City city *Cook Co.*	32.7	15.1	9.5	14.0	19.7	8.9
Carol Stream village *Du Page Co.*	33.4	19.9	17.8	9.0	13.1	6.8
Carpentersville village *Kane Co.*	29.4	10.5	9.2	14.6	24.7	11.1
Champaign city *Champaign Co.*	25.7	33.9	11.2	16.3	8.7	4.0
Chicago city *Cook Co.*	27.0	20.2	13.3	16.6	16.2	6.6
Chicago Heights city *Cook Co.*	26.4	15.9	8.1	20.0	21.9	7.6
Cicero town *Cook Co.*	24.2	6.3	4.9	16.6	35.5	12.0
Collinsville city *Madison Co.*	30.0	20.3	12.6	13.8	13.7	9.2
Crystal Lake city *McHenry Co.*	29.7	21.2	19.5	10.4	11.9	7.2
Danville city *Vermilion Co.*	24.8	18.5	8.6	18.3	21.8	7.5
De Kalb city *De Kalb Co.*	27.5	26.7	10.3	18.1	11.7	5.5
Decatur city *Macon Co.*	26.5	17.5	9.9	16.9	20.1	8.9
Des Plaines city *Cook Co.*	31.5	17.9	14.3	12.3	14.7	9.1
Dolton village *Cook Co.*	33.5	16.2	11.0	14.4	18.6	6.2
Downers Grove village *Du Page Co.*	30.2	27.5	21.5	8.1	7.7	5.0
East Saint Louis city *Saint Clair Co.*	23.6	16.4	5.5	30.8	18.4	5.2
Edwardsville city *Madison Co.*	24.5	30.4	16.5	14.4	8.7	5.3
Elgin city *Kane Co.*	25.5	15.6	12.3	15.0	22.6	8.6
Elk Grove Village village *Cook Co.*	34.9	19.3	17.4	9.2	11.8	7.4
Elmhurst city *Du Page Co.*	31.6	26.5	20.9	7.8	7.5	5.7
Elmwood Park village *Cook Co.*	33.3	13.4	13.7	12.9	16.4	10.0
Evanston city *Cook Co.*	22.3	40.9	19.8	9.1	5.1	2.8
Freeport city *Stephenson Co.*	26.1	17.8	10.3	14.7	23.2	7.8
Galesburg city *Knox Co.*	23.0	18.5	8.2	19.8	22.0	8.0
Geneva city *Kane Co.*	27.7	27.4	24.5	8.8	6.8	4.5
Glen Ellyn village *Du Page Co.*	29.2	29.1	24.3	8.0	6.2	3.3
Glendale Heights village *Du Page Co.*	31.8	17.4	13.3	10.1	19.3	8.0
Glenview village *Cook Co.*	28.1	28.8	24.8	8.0	6.1	4.0
Granite City city *Madison Co.*	27.5	12.9	9.0	17.2	24.0	9.3
Gurnee village *Lake Co.*	28.6	26.4	24.0	7.6	7.6	5.6
Hanover Park village *Cook Co.*	31.5	14.1	12.2	13.4	19.9	8.8
Harvey city *Cook Co.*	28.5	14.1	5.9	21.9	22.0	7.3
Highland Park city *Lake Co.*	27.3	30.6	25.0	10.4	3.5	3.2
Hoffman Estates village *Cook Co.*	31.2	22.8	18.3	9.6	11.9	6.1
Joliet city *Will Co.*	27.4	17.7	10.0	16.2	18.3	10.4
Kankakee city *Kankakee Co.*	22.1	15.6	6.9	21.5	25.4	7.8

Place	Sales	Prof.	Mgmt	Services	Production	Constr.
Lake in the Hills village *McHenry Co.*	28.3	21.4	20.6	9.4	11.6	8.7
Lansing village *Cook Co.*	29.2	17.5	12.4	13.3	15.0	12.6
Lombard village *Du Page Co.*	35.4	22.9	17.0	8.0	9.2	7.4
Loves Park city *Winnebago Co.*	28.6	18.3	11.1	10.4	23.1	8.4
Maywood village *Cook Co.*	33.2	12.8	7.9	17.9	23.3	4.7
McHenry city *McHenry Co.*	29.4	17.4	14.0	11.9	16.0	11.3
Moline city *Rock Island Co.*	27.3	18.2	11.0	17.5	18.4	7.4
Mount Prospect village *Cook Co.*	31.3	21.9	17.5	10.4	12.9	5.9
Mundelein village *Lake Co.*	25.0	22.4	18.8	12.8	12.8	7.9
Naperville city *Du Page Co.*	28.2	29.1	26.9	7.5	4.7	3.6
New Lenox village *Will Co.*	30.8	20.2	15.0	8.8	12.1	13.0
Niles village *Cook Co.*	32.4	18.7	12.6	13.2	14.9	8.2
Normal town *McLean Co.*	32.4	22.2	13.3	19.5	7.6	4.8
North Chicago city *Lake Co.*	26.8	14.3	10.9	22.3	20.1	5.3
Northbrook village *Cook Co.*	31.6	31.3	26.4	4.7	3.3	2.6
O'Fallon city *Saint Clair Co.*	27.6	26.1	16.3	13.4	10.1	6.2
Oak Forest city *Cook Co.*	31.6	19.6	12.6	11.4	12.8	12.0
Oak Lawn village *Cook Co.*	31.2	18.9	13.0	10.7	14.1	12.0
Oak Park village *Cook Co.*	23.8	40.9	19.6	7.9	5.1	2.8
Orland Park village *Cook Co.*	32.1	21.8	18.7	9.4	9.9	8.1
Oswego village *Kendall Co.*	31.9	24.6	17.2	8.9	9.7	7.5
Palatine village *Cook Co.*	30.0	24.4	19.4	10.5	10.0	5.7
Park Forest village *Cook Co.*	28.8	24.1	12.0	14.9	13.1	7.0
Park Ridge city *Cook Co.*	29.5	27.3	23.0	8.3	6.7	5.2
Pekin city *Tazewell Co.*	29.7	15.3	9.5	17.4	20.0	8.1
Peoria city *Peoria Co.*	26.4	26.8	11.6	17.7	11.8	5.7
Plainfield village *Will Co.*	29.4	23.5	18.9	8.1	9.8	10.3
Quincy city *Adams Co.*	28.4	17.3	9.9	18.4	18.4	7.5
Rock Island city *Rock Island Co.*	28.5	18.4	9.0	18.5	17.8	7.6
Rockford city *Winnebago Co.*	26.0	18.3	10.9	14.8	22.6	7.3
Rolling Meadows city *Cook Co.*	29.9	18.2	17.5	14.7	12.8	6.9
Romeoville village *Will Co.*	31.5	16.3	12.2	10.9	18.1	10.9
Roselle village *Du Page Co.*	33.9	20.2	19.4	9.8	10.5	6.2
Round Lake Beach village *Lake Co.*	30.4	11.4	11.9	15.3	19.3	11.4
Saint Charles city *Kane Co.*	31.8	22.7	20.1	9.8	8.9	6.5
Schaumburg village *Cook Co.*	32.2	25.0	19.3	8.6	9.6	5.3
Skokie village *Cook Co.*	29.1	30.2	16.1	10.5	9.7	4.3
Springfield city *Sangamon Co.*	29.9	24.3	16.0	15.6	7.7	6.4
Streamwood village *Cook Co.*	32.1	18.3	14.7	11.3	14.1	9.3
Tinley Park village *Cook Co.*	30.2	20.4	15.8	11.0	11.3	11.4
Urbana city *Champaign Co.*	21.7	45.6	7.3	14.8	6.7	3.6
Vernon Hills village *Lake Co.*	29.7	28.1	23.4	7.8	6.9	4.1
Waukegan city *Lake Co.*	24.6	13.5	9.2	17.9	25.0	9.7
West Chicago city *Du Page Co.*	23.3	14.4	11.3	17.6	22.5	10.5
Westmont village *Du Page Co.*	30.7	22.4	15.9	13.7	10.2	7.0
Wheaton city *Du Page Co.*	28.0	31.1	22.7	8.8	5.2	4.2
Wheeling village *Cook Co.*	31.3	21.7	13.4	12.4	14.8	6.2
Wilmette village *Cook Co.*	24.6	39.5	27.4	4.5	2.1	1.8
Woodridge village *Du Page Co.*	29.6	24.8	18.4	10.3	10.0	6.9
Zion city *Lake Co.*	30.4	15.1	8.5	16.4	19.1	10.5

NOTE: Data as of 2000

Educational Attainment

Place	Percent of Population 25 Years and Over with: High School Diploma including Equivalency	Bachelor's Degree or Higher	Masters's Degree or Higher
Addison village *Du Page Co.*	73.0	19.3	5.1
Algonquin village *McHenry Co.*	94.9	39.0	11.1
Alton city *Madison Co.*	81.4	16.2	5.3
Arlington Heights village *Cook Co.*	92.5	46.3	16.2
Aurora city *Kane Co.*	76.1	30.5	9.4
Bartlett village *Du Page Co.*	92.3	38.8	10.9
Batavia city *Kane Co.*	93.8	43.4	15.2
Belleville city *Saint Clair Co.*	83.8	18.0	6.1
Belvidere city *Boone Co.*	74.1	8.8	2.0
Berwyn city *Cook Co.*	74.6	17.2	6.0
Bloomington city *McLean Co.*	90.6	41.7	12.3
Bolingbrook village *Will Co.*	87.9	30.4	7.6
Buffalo Grove village *Lake Co.*	95.4	56.2	20.8
Burbank city *Cook Co.*	73.7	9.5	3.1
Calumet City city *Cook Co.*	80.8	14.1	3.8
Carol Stream village *Du Page Co.*	89.7	31.9	8.4
Carpentersville village *Kane Co.*	68.2	13.6	3.1
Champaign city *Champaign Co.*	91.4	44.5	22.4
Chicago city *Cook Co.*	71.7	25.9	10.2
Chicago Heights city *Cook Co.*	71.6	12.2	3.9
Cicero town *Cook Co.*	48.0	6.1	2.2
Collinsville city *Madison Co.*	85.5	21.3	6.8
Crystal Lake city *McHenry Co.*	91.6	36.8	10.9
Danville city *Vermilion Co.*	75.0	15.5	5.2
De Kalb city *De Kalb Co.*	87.9	38.7	18.2
Decatur city *Macon Co.*	80.8	17.0	5.7
Des Plaines city *Cook Co.*	82.0	24.7	8.1
Dolton village *Cook Co.*	82.7	15.3	3.2
Downers Grove village *Du Page Co.*	93.0	46.3	18.0
East Saint Louis city *Saint Clair Co.*	66.5	8.9	2.7
Edwardsville city *Madison Co.*	92.8	42.9	17.0
Elgin city *Kane Co.*	73.8	20.6	6.0
Elk Grove Village village *Cook Co.*	90.3	31.9	8.8
Elmhurst city *Du Page Co.*	91.2	44.6	17.0
Elmwood Park village *Cook Co.*	79.7	19.2	6.3
Evanston city *Cook Co.*	91.4	62.6	33.2
Freeport city *Stephenson Co.*	82.6	17.7	5.5
Galesburg city *Knox Co.*	78.8	14.9	5.6
Geneva city *Kane Co.*	95.7	53.6	19.7
Glen Ellyn village *Du Page Co.*	94.3	58.5	22.5
Glendale Heights village *Du Page Co.*	81.7	26.9	6.8
Glenview village *Cook Co.*	94.0	54.2	23.3
Granite City city *Madison Co.*	78.0	9.9	3.0
Gurnee village *Lake Co.*	94.3	48.4	17.3
Hanover Park village *Cook Co.*	78.7	20.0	3.9
Harvey city *Cook Co.*	69.5	8.2	2.4
Highland Park city *Lake Co.*	91.4	61.1	28.1
Hoffman Estates village *Cook Co.*	89.6	36.0	11.7
Joliet city *Will Co.*	79.8	19.3	5.7
Kankakee city *Kankakee Co.*	68.1	13.2	5.0

Place	Percent of Population 25 Years and Over with: High School Diploma including Equivalency	Bachelor's Degree or Higher	Masters's Degree or Higher
Lake in the Hills village *McHenry Co.*	93.5	33.2	6.6
Lansing village *Cook Co.*	86.7	18.4	5.2
Lombard village *Du Page Co.*	90.4	36.3	10.9
Loves Park city *Winnebago Co.*	86.9	18.5	5.9
Maywood village *Cook Co.*	74.5	10.6	3.8
McHenry city *McHenry Co.*	87.2	22.2	5.9
Moline city *Rock Island Co.*	84.0	20.7	6.8
Mount Prospect village *Cook Co.*	85.4	35.3	11.9
Mundelein village *Lake Co.*	82.5	39.2	13.3
Naperville city *Du Page Co.*	96.4	61.0	23.7
New Lenox village *Will Co.*	92.4	26.2	7.3
Niles village *Cook Co.*	81.4	25.0	8.9
Normal town *McLean Co.*	93.9	42.3	13.9
North Chicago city *Lake Co.*	75.2	15.5	5.9
Northbrook village *Cook Co.*	95.5	62.2	27.7
O'Fallon city *Saint Clair Co.*	92.3	38.7	16.8
Oak Forest city *Cook Co.*	89.2	22.5	6.7
Oak Lawn village *Cook Co.*	83.4	21.0	6.9
Oak Park village *Cook Co.*	94.3	61.8	30.6
Orland Park village *Cook Co.*	90.0	31.5	11.9
Oswego village *Kendall Co.*	93.4	32.3	10.0
Palatine village *Cook Co.*	88.8	41.2	13.9
Park Forest village *Cook Co.*	88.1	27.0	10.3
Park Ridge city *Cook Co.*	92.3	46.2	18.2
Pekin city *Tazewell Co.*	81.8	13.7	5.2
Peoria city *Peoria Co.*	83.2	28.8	10.8
Plainfield village *Will Co.*	94.9	35.1	8.4
Quincy city *Adams Co.*	82.9	19.7	6.9
Rock Island city *Rock Island Co.*	83.0	18.6	6.3
Rockford city *Winnebago Co.*	77.7	19.9	7.2
Rolling Meadows city *Cook Co.*	83.3	31.6	9.6
Romeoville village *Will Co.*	85.7	21.6	4.6
Roselle village *Du Page Co.*	90.8	33.9	9.6
Round Lake Beach village *Lake Co.*	75.3	16.5	4.3
Saint Charles city *Kane Co.*	91.6	43.0	14.6
Schaumburg village *Cook Co.*	91.9	39.4	12.6
Skokie village *Cook Co.*	87.3	42.3	17.4
Springfield city *Sangamon Co.*	87.9	31.8	12.1
Streamwood village *Cook Co.*	85.6	27.1	6.8
Tinley Park village *Cook Co.*	89.4	25.0	7.5
Urbana city *Champaign Co.*	91.2	54.3	33.1
Vernon Hills village *Lake Co.*	93.8	54.5	18.7
Waukegan city *Lake Co.*	66.7	16.2	5.5
West Chicago city *Du Page Co.*	66.9	21.8	5.1
Westmont village *Du Page Co.*	86.5	35.2	12.2
Wheaton city *Du Page Co.*	94.1	57.2	22.0
Wheeling village *Cook Co.*	82.5	32.3	10.5
Wilmette village *Cook Co.*	96.8	72.4	38.2
Woodridge village *Du Page Co.*	90.0	39.4	12.5
Zion city *Lake Co.*	78.5	16.0	5.7

NOTE: Data as of 2007

Income and Poverty

Place	Average Household Income ($)	Median Household Income ($)	Per Capita Income ($)	Households w/$100,000+ Income (%)	Poverty Rate[1] (%)
Addison village *Du Page Co.*	72,241	58,071	23,443	20.9	9.6
Algonquin village *McHenry Co.*	107,553	93,317	35,210	45.1	1.7
Alton city *Madison Co.*	44,680	36,222	19,294	7.0	18.7
Arlington Heights village *Cook Co.*	94,470	76,227	38,916	35.5	2.5
Aurora city *Kane Co.*	77,525	61,987	25,141	24.1	8.5
Bartlett village *Du Page Co.*	105,128	92,120	34,982	43.7	1.9
Batavia city *Kane Co.*	91,494	80,155	32,049	36.4	3.6
Belleville city *Saint Clair Co.*	51,182	40,810	22,738	9.4	11.7
Belvidere city *Boone Co.*	53,453	46,983	19,166	9.0	10.0
Berwyn city *Cook Co.*	58,902	48,723	21,008	13.6	7.9
Bloomington city *McLean Co.*	72,513	54,971	29,631	21.6	7.8
Bolingbrook village *Will Co.*	88,486	78,877	27,639	33.0	4.1
Buffalo Grove village *Lake Co.*	113,193	90,009	41,524	43.5	2.3
Burbank city *Cook Co.*	61,395	53,130	20,638	14.5	5.1
Calumet City city *Cook Co.*	51,109	42,569	19,446	9.3	12.2
Carol Stream village *Du Page Co.*	83,163	73,572	28,369	30.7	3.4
Carpentersville village *Kane Co.*	69,854	60,330	20,197	18.5	8.5
Champaign city *Champaign Co.*	53,335	37,953	22,234	12.0	22.1
Chicago city *Cook Co.*	62,748	44,461	23,243	16.3	19.6
Chicago Heights city *Cook Co.*	50,859	40,904	16,677	10.7	17.5
Cicero town *Cook Co.*	51,025	42,640	13,475	8.4	15.5
Collinsville city *Madison Co.*	58,823	49,860	25,467	14.4	7.2
Crystal Lake city *McHenry Co.*	88,494	76,073	30,658	31.5	3.5
Danville city *Vermilion Co.*	45,032	33,506	18,484	7.8	18.1
De Kalb city *De Kalb Co.*	48,556	38,061	17,428	9.6	21.3
Decatur city *Macon Co.*	48,768	36,475	21,107	9.0	16.5
Des Plaines city *Cook Co.*	72,137	60,467	27,574	20.7	4.6
Dolton village *Cook Co.*	58,958	51,589	19,360	12.1	8.4
Downers Grove village *Du Page Co.*	90,201	72,555	35,674	32.7	2.3
East Saint Louis city *Saint Clair Co.*	34,474	23,695	12,713	5.1	35.1
Edwardsville city *Madison Co.*	82,018	62,468	31,574	26.6	8.6
Elgin city *Kane Co.*	69,048	58,569	23,049	19.1	8.1
Elk Grove Village village *Cook Co.*	83,332	69,932	32,641	27.4	2.0
Elmhurst city *Du Page Co.*	100,114	78,865	37,477	36.4	2.5
Elmwood Park village *Cook Co.*	65,756	53,828	25,202	17.8	5.2
Evanston city *Cook Co.*	93,085	63,251	37,924	30.8	11.1
Freeport city *Stephenson Co.*	47,426	38,685	20,658	7.3	13.1
Galesburg city *Knox Co.*	46,302	35,639	19,328	7.3	14.7
Geneva city *Kane Co.*	111,162	90,279	37,599	43.8	2.2
Glen Ellyn village *Du Page Co.*	111,474	82,487	42,271	40.8	2.8
Glendale Heights village *Du Page Co.*	69,619	60,776	23,763	17.6	6.1
Glenview village *Cook Co.*	128,117	89,312	47,455	44.2	2.0
Granite City city *Madison Co.*	49,097	40,446	20,605	7.4	11.3
Gurnee village *Lake Co.*	100,989	86,083	36,586	41.6	3.0
Hanover Park village *Cook Co.*	82,959	73,312	24,129	27.3	6.1
Harvey city *Cook Co.*	43,140	34,210	13,107	6.4	21.7
Highland Park city *Lake Co.*	155,238	105,109	57,128	52.3	3.8
Hoffman Estates village *Cook Co.*	91,156	76,350	31,420	33.8	4.4
Joliet city *Will Co.*	62,888	54,016	21,823	16.0	10.8
Kankakee city *Kankakee Co.*	45,623	34,002	17,223	7.5	21.4

Place	Average Household Income ($)	Median Household Income ($)	Per Capita Income ($)	Households w/$100,000+ Income (%)	Poverty Rate[1] (%)
Lake in the Hills village *McHenry Co.*	100,005	87,509	32,613	37.7	2.1
Lansing village *Cook Co.*	62,099	52,669	25,225	14.0	5.4
Lombard village *Du Page Co.*	77,507	65,375	31,104	23.8	3.8
Loves Park city *Winnebago Co.*	55,531	48,858	22,782	8.9	5.0
Maywood village *Cook Co.*	57,063	46,833	16,816	13.2	13.4
McHenry city *McHenry Co.*	72,208	62,898	26,969	21.6	4.6
Moline city *Rock Island Co.*	57,992	44,716	24,735	12.8	9.5
Mount Prospect village *Cook Co.*	79,018	64,474	30,277	25.5	4.6
Mundelein village *Lake Co.*	93,311	78,113	29,283	33.2	4.6
Naperville city *Du Page Co.*	119,817	99,200	40,965	49.5	2.2
New Lenox village *Will Co.*	92,880	82,162	30,599	34.9	2.4
Niles village *Cook Co.*	66,624	55,153	27,415	18.6	5.4
Normal town *McLean Co.*	57,423	45,641	20,390	14.3	19.3
North Chicago city *Lake Co.*	51,281	40,978	15,224	8.2	15.1
Northbrook village *Cook Co.*	142,153	101,455	52,489	50.7	2.3
O'Fallon city *Saint Clair Co.*	78,863	66,321	30,335	26.8	5.0
Oak Forest city *Cook Co.*	77,505	68,813	27,426	25.1	3.6
Oak Lawn village *Cook Co.*	66,748	53,414	27,423	18.8	5.4
Oak Park village *Cook Co.*	97,457	68,371	43,709	32.5	5.6
Orland Park village *Cook Co.*	97,954	80,413	36,347	36.6	3.1
Oswego village *Kendall Co.*	91,576	82,483	31,228	33.6	2.8
Palatine village *Cook Co.*	92,274	73,750	36,125	32.2	4.8
Park Forest village *Cook Co.*	60,179	52,079	24,105	12.4	6.7
Park Ridge city *Cook Co.*	106,882	82,842	40,699	39.0	2.4
Pekin city *Tazewell Co.*	53,912	43,256	22,901	10.8	9.4
Peoria city *Peoria Co.*	57,978	41,409	23,968	14.0	18.8
Plainfield village *Will Co.*	103,767	94,285	33,907	44.6	1.8
Quincy city *Adams Co.*	47,997	36,676	20,626	7.4	12.2
Rock Island city *Rock Island Co.*	52,698	40,071	22,186	10.3	14.5
Rockford city *Winnebago Co.*	53,534	39,937	21,571	10.5	14.0
Rolling Meadows city *Cook Co.*	81,906	66,630	29,829	26.3	5.1
Romeoville village *Will Co.*	71,744	65,645	24,117	17.5	1.9
Roselle village *Du Page Co.*	86,608	72,271	32,095	28.8	2.0
Round Lake Beach village *Lake Co.*	72,173	65,559	20,265	19.8	5.1
Saint Charles city *Kane Co.*	103,198	79,060	38,950	36.7	3.4
Schaumburg village *Cook Co.*	82,609	68,798	35,119	26.8	3.0
Skokie village *Cook Co.*	83,480	64,977	30,254	27.5	5.4
Springfield city *Sangamon Co.*	60,633	44,652	26,982	14.4	11.7
Streamwood village *Cook Co.*	84,688	74,099	28,337	27.4	3.0
Tinley Park village *Cook Co.*	83,701	73,656	30,845	29.9	2.5
Urbana city *Champaign Co.*	44,979	31,331	18,796	8.7	27.3
Vernon Hills village *Lake Co.*	100,166	80,071	37,256	37.0	2.9
Waukegan city *Lake Co.*	58,154	46,502	18,430	12.5	13.9
West Chicago city *Du Page Co.*	81,536	70,449	21,848	27.7	9.3
Westmont village *Du Page Co.*	72,935	57,560	30,456	21.0	5.8
Wheaton city *Du Page Co.*	108,565	80,083	39,052	37.9	3.6
Wheeling village *Cook Co.*	75,240	62,720	28,656	21.5	5.3
Wilmette village *Cook Co.*	166,273	117,848	59,894	57.7	2.3
Woodridge village *Du Page Co.*	85,206	69,903	31,809	28.7	3.8
Zion city *Lake Co.*	59,591	50,626	20,063	13.4	11.9

NOTE: Data as of 2007 except for Poverty Rate which is from 2000; (1) Percentage of population with income below the poverty level

Taxes

Place	Total City Taxes Per Capita ($)	City Property Taxes Per Capita ($)
Addison village *Du Page Co.*	485	237
Algonquin village *McHenry Co.*	n/a	n/a
Alton city *Madison Co.*	n/a	n/a
Arlington Heights village *Cook Co.*	762	483
Aurora city *Kane Co.*	619	373
Bartlett village *Du Page Co.*	n/a	n/a
Batavia city *Kane Co.*	317	193
Belleville city *Saint Clair Co.*	n/a	n/a
Belvidere city *Boone Co.*	n/a	n/a
Berwyn city *Cook Co.*	727	440
Bloomington city *McLean Co.*	n/a	n/a
Bolingbrook village *Will Co.*	435	233
Buffalo Grove village *Lake Co.*	n/a	n/a
Burbank city *Cook Co.*	n/a	n/a
Calumet City city *Cook Co.*	n/a	n/a
Carol Stream village *Du Page Co.*	n/a	n/a
Carpentersville village *Kane Co.*	n/a	n/a
Champaign city *Champaign Co.*	563	223
Chicago city *Cook Co.*	769	151
Chicago Heights city *Cook Co.*	n/a	n/a
Cicero town *Cook Co.*	n/a	n/a
Collinsville city *Madison Co.*	221	127
Crystal Lake city *McHenry Co.*	n/a	n/a
Danville city *Vermilion Co.*	430	188
De Kalb city *De Kalb Co.*	n/a	n/a
Decatur city *Macon Co.*	393	149
Des Plaines city *Cook Co.*	751	440
Dolton village *Cook Co.*	n/a	n/a
Downers Grove village *Du Page Co.*	567	292
East Saint Louis city *Saint Clair Co.*	n/a	n/a
Edwardsville city *Madison Co.*	n/a	n/a
Elgin city *Kane Co.*	458	369
Elk Grove Village village *Cook Co.*	n/a	n/a
Elmhurst city *Du Page Co.*	n/a	n/a
Elmwood Park village *Cook Co.*	n/a	n/a
Evanston city *Cook Co.*	990	527
Freeport city *Stephenson Co.*	n/a	n/a
Galesburg city *Knox Co.*	n/a	n/a
Geneva city *Kane Co.*	413	287
Glen Ellyn village *Du Page Co.*	n/a	n/a
Glendale Heights village *Du Page Co.*	n/a	n/a
Glenview village *Cook Co.*	978	694
Granite City city *Madison Co.*	n/a	n/a
Gurnee village *Lake Co.*	n/a	n/a
Hanover Park village *Cook Co.*	n/a	n/a
Harvey city *Cook Co.*	n/a	n/a
Highland Park city *Lake Co.*	n/a	n/a
Hoffman Estates village *Cook Co.*	603	334
Joliet city *Will Co.*	435	185
Kankakee city *Kankakee Co.*	n/a	n/a

Place	Total City Taxes Per Capita ($)	City Property Taxes Per Capita ($)
Lake in the Hills village *McHenry Co.*	n/a	n/a
Lansing village *Cook Co.*	735	587
Lombard village *Du Page Co.*	409	156
Loves Park city *Winnebago Co.*	n/a	n/a
Maywood village *Cook Co.*	821	672
McHenry city *McHenry Co.*	n/a	n/a
Moline city *Rock Island Co.*	n/a	n/a
Mount Prospect village *Cook Co.*	699	435
Mundelein village *Lake Co.*	n/a	n/a
Naperville city *Du Page Co.*	469	280
New Lenox village *Will Co.*	136	86
Niles village *Cook Co.*	863	303
Normal town *McLean Co.*	n/a	n/a
North Chicago city *Lake Co.*	n/a	n/a
Northbrook village *Cook Co.*	721	396
O'Fallon city *Saint Clair Co.*	274	169
Oak Forest city *Cook Co.*	n/a	n/a
Oak Lawn village *Cook Co.*	451	315
Oak Park village *Cook Co.*	904	586
Orland Park village *Cook Co.*	n/a	n/a
Oswego village *Kendall Co.*	n/a	n/a
Palatine village *Cook Co.*	537	373
Park Forest village *Cook Co.*	n/a	n/a
Park Ridge city *Cook Co.*	n/a	n/a
Pekin city *Tazewell Co.*	296	158
Peoria city *Peoria Co.*	575	218
Plainfield village *Will Co.*	412	109
Quincy city *Adams Co.*	287	71
Rock Island city *Rock Island Co.*	n/a	n/a
Rockford city *Winnebago Co.*	400	303
Rolling Meadows city *Cook Co.*	n/a	n/a
Romeoville village *Will Co.*	616	286
Roselle village *Du Page Co.*	n/a	n/a
Round Lake Beach village *Lake Co.*	269	146
Saint Charles city *Kane Co.*	714	316
Schaumburg village *Cook Co.*	698	31
Skokie village *Cook Co.*	647	390
Springfield city *Sangamon Co.*	455	185
Streamwood village *Cook Co.*	n/a	n/a
Tinley Park village *Cook Co.*	n/a	n/a
Urbana city *Champaign Co.*	n/a	n/a
Vernon Hills village *Lake Co.*	n/a	n/a
Waukegan city *Lake Co.*	n/a	n/a
West Chicago city *Du Page Co.*	256	127
Westmont village *Du Page Co.*	n/a	n/a
Wheaton city *Du Page Co.*	n/a	n/a
Wheeling village *Cook Co.*	n/a	n/a
Wilmette village *Cook Co.*	n/a	n/a
Woodridge village *Du Page Co.*	n/a	n/a
Zion city *Lake Co.*	n/a	n/a

NOTE: Data as of 2006.

Housing

Place	Homeownership Rate (%)	Median Home Value ($)	Median Age of Housing (years)	Median Rent ($/month)
Addison village *Du Page Co.*	68.0	270,821	29	644
Algonquin village *McHenry Co.*	94.2	279,515	10	711
Alton city *Madison Co.*	65.7	77,301	51	330
Arlington Heights village *Cook Co.*	76.5	340,158	30	876
Aurora city *Kane Co.*	70.4	199,854	25	609
Bartlett village *Du Page Co.*	93.6	302,478	11	691
Batavia city *Kane Co.*	78.7	286,919	22	702
Belleville city *Saint Clair Co.*	60.7	90,120	44	380
Belvidere city *Boone Co.*	68.2	135,076	37	451
Berwyn city *Cook Co.*	61.4	217,773	60	545
Bloomington city *McLean Co.*	65.6	145,773	27	461
Bolingbrook village *Will Co.*	87.1	212,639	22	712
Buffalo Grove village *Lake Co.*	87.0	309,959	18	994
Burbank city *Cook Co.*	83.3	215,268	38	629
Calumet City city *Cook Co.*	63.5	134,992	35	552
Carol Stream village *Du Page Co.*	70.5	246,507	17	750
Carpentersville village *Kane Co.*	81.5	170,189	34	618
Champaign city *Champaign Co.*	48.2	119,318	31	467
Chicago city *Cook Co.*	43.6	234,398	52	543
Chicago Heights city *Cook Co.*	63.5	141,540	44	500
Cicero town *Cook Co.*	55.2	188,039	55	498
Collinsville city *Madison Co.*	67.5	111,545	35	415
Crystal Lake city *McHenry Co.*	79.4	233,988	19	773
Danville city *Vermilion Co.*	62.4	62,009	49	317
De Kalb city *De Kalb Co.*	42.4	173,225	29	499
Decatur city *Macon Co.*	66.6	74,075	43	350
Des Plaines city *Cook Co.*	78.8	266,338	37	710
Dolton village *Cook Co.*	81.1	140,423	37	623
Downers Grove village *Du Page Co.*	79.2	311,347	32	718
East Saint Louis city *Saint Clair Co.*	52.6	55,448	47	265
Edwardsville city *Madison Co.*	71.0	141,660	33	473
Elgin city *Kane Co.*	70.9	199,837	31	611
Elk Grove Village village *Cook Co.*	75.7	273,541	27	776
Elmhurst city *Du Page Co.*	82.7	343,811	44	780
Elmwood Park village *Cook Co.*	64.8	271,791	46	625
Evanston city *Cook Co.*	51.8	358,144	57	813
Freeport city *Stephenson Co.*	68.7	94,938	48	328
Galesburg city *Knox Co.*	64.5	86,207	51	322
Geneva city *Kane Co.*	84.7	319,495	20	810
Glen Ellyn village *Du Page Co.*	77.5	410,936	35	687
Glendale Heights village *Du Page Co.*	69.7	217,033	23	764
Glenview village *Cook Co.*	85.0	464,460	33	783
Granite City city *Madison Co.*	70.8	74,937	46	341
Gurnee village *Lake Co.*	78.6	276,971	10	733
Hanover Park village *Cook Co.*	82.7	210,018	25	696
Harvey city *Cook Co.*	56.8	102,823	41	490
Highland Park city *Lake Co.*	81.9	545,317	41	852
Hoffman Estates village *Cook Co.*	78.0	262,113	25	845
Joliet city *Will Co.*	71.9	175,036	36	487
Kankakee city *Kankakee Co.*	53.5	94,111	48	401

Place	Homeownership Rate (%)	Median Home Value ($)	Median Age of Housing (years)	Median Rent ($/month)
Lake in the Hills village *McHenry Co.*	94.1	238,969	5	872
Lansing village *Cook Co.*	75.2	173,999	36	612
Lombard village *Du Page Co.*	74.5	255,701	33	845
Loves Park city *Winnebago Co.*	69.7	115,756	26	533
Maywood village *Cook Co.*	62.9	166,627	54	543
McHenry city *McHenry Co.*	77.1	214,484	22	645
Moline city *Rock Island Co.*	67.4	101,770	48	405
Mount Prospect village *Cook Co.*	71.7	311,959	32	738
Mundelein village *Lake Co.*	79.7	229,628	21	726
Naperville city *Du Page Co.*	80.4	383,602	14	865
New Lenox village *Will Co.*	89.7	265,477	13	631
Niles village *Cook Co.*	76.2	309,676	37	707
Normal town *McLean Co.*	55.6	145,472	23	480
North Chicago city *Lake Co.*	39.2	144,096	34	595
Northbrook village *Cook Co.*	91.6	531,141	31	1,215
O'Fallon city *Saint Clair Co.*	69.4	146,042	17	541
Oak Forest city *Cook Co.*	81.5	216,553	28	629
Oak Lawn village *Cook Co.*	82.8	222,650	35	639
Oak Park village *Cook Co.*	55.9	332,968	60+	674
Orland Park village *Cook Co.*	91.6	291,438	15	710
Oswego village *Kendall Co.*	92.2	241,127	5	657
Palatine village *Cook Co.*	68.8	276,121	24	817
Park Forest village *Cook Co.*	73.0	121,677	44	606
Park Ridge city *Cook Co.*	87.1	459,543	44	797
Pekin city *Tazewell Co.*	67.1	100,174	41	349
Peoria city *Peoria Co.*	60.3	109,724	41	406
Plainfield village *Will Co.*	87.2	290,618	6	631
Quincy city *Adams Co.*	67.3	87,283	50	323
Rock Island city *Rock Island Co.*	65.6	89,167	51	361
Rockford city *Winnebago Co.*	61.3	101,456	42	423
Rolling Meadows city *Cook Co.*	76.3	245,515	31	822
Romeoville village *Will Co.*	83.2	177,257	21	808
Roselle village *Du Page Co.*	81.3	258,338	23	842
Round Lake Beach village *Lake Co.*	85.3	172,795	20	696
Saint Charles city *Kane Co.*	73.5	280,006	22	748
Schaumburg village *Cook Co.*	69.3	238,449	22	918
Skokie village *Cook Co.*	74.7	328,708	42	748
Springfield city *Sangamon Co.*	63.9	105,900	33	427
Streamwood village *Cook Co.*	89.6	214,880	20	970
Tinley Park village *Cook Co.*	85.1	239,889	18	661
Urbana city *Champaign Co.*	37.5	121,474	31	463
Vernon Hills village *Lake Co.*	79.9	284,564	17	825
Waukegan city *Lake Co.*	56.8	165,116	38	586
West Chicago city *Du Page Co.*	69.2	250,494	27	715
Westmont village *Du Page Co.*	54.2	276,709	26	711
Wheaton city *Du Page Co.*	73.9	333,929	27	834
Wheeling village *Cook Co.*	65.9	226,132	24	824
Wilmette village *Cook Co.*	86.7	654,021	48	958
Woodridge village *Du Page Co.*	66.2	243,967	24	719
Zion city *Lake Co.*	58.7	165,093	32	595

NOTE: Homeownership Rate and Median Home Value as of 2007; Median Rent and Median Age of Housing as of 2000.

Commute to Work

Place	Automobile (%)	Public Transportation (%)	Walk (%)	Work from Home (%)
Addison village *Du Page Co.*	92.2	2.6	2.4	1.7
Algonquin village *McHenry Co.*	91.5	2.5	1.0	4.1
Alton city *Madison Co.*	92.9	2.6	2.1	1.5
Arlington Heights village *Cook Co.*	86.3	7.8	1.7	3.7
Aurora city *Kane Co.*	88.9	5.5	1.6	2.7
Bartlett village *Du Page Co.*	90.1	5.4	0.3	3.4
Batavia city *Kane Co.*	90.2	2.3	1.6	4.4
Belleville city *Saint Clair Co.*	92.4	2.8	2.1	2.2
Belvidere city *Boone Co.*	95.3	0.4	1.9	1.9
Berwyn city *Cook Co.*	83.7	10.8	3.2	1.6
Bloomington city *McLean Co.*	91.6	1.4	3.5	2.7
Bolingbrook village *Will Co.*	91.3	4.1	1.0	3.0
Buffalo Grove village *Lake Co.*	89.0	5.5	0.9	4.1
Burbank city *Cook Co.*	90.4	5.6	2.0	0.9
Calumet City city *Cook Co.*	85.1	10.9	2.3	0.8
Carol Stream village *Du Page Co.*	91.9	3.7	0.9	2.9
Carpentersville village *Kane Co.*	94.6	1.1	1.1	1.4
Champaign city *Champaign Co.*	75.3	6.2	12.3	3.4
Chicago city *Cook Co.*	64.6	26.1	5.7	2.4
Chicago Heights city *Cook Co.*	87.8	6.5	2.7	1.4
Cicero town *Cook Co.*	83.9	9.7	3.7	1.1
Collinsville city *Madison Co.*	95.1	1.5	1.1	1.6
Crystal Lake city *McHenry Co.*	90.3	4.3	1.3	3.3
Danville city *Vermilion Co.*	93.1	1.2	2.4	2.4
De Kalb city *De Kalb Co.*	80.0	2.5	12.8	2.4
Decatur city *Macon Co.*	93.1	1.3	2.7	2.0
Des Plaines city *Cook Co.*	88.8	6.7	1.5	2.5
Dolton village *Cook Co.*	81.8	13.0	1.4	2.6
Downers Grove village *Du Page Co.*	82.8	10.7	1.6	4.3
East Saint Louis city *Saint Clair Co.*	79.6	14.6	2.4	2.6
Edwardsville city *Madison Co.*	91.9	2.0	2.8	2.5
Elgin city *Kane Co.*	92.6	2.7	1.9	2.1
Elk Grove Village village *Cook Co.*	93.0	3.5	0.9	2.4
Elmhurst city *Du Page Co.*	85.3	7.5	3.1	3.2
Elmwood Park village *Cook Co.*	86.6	8.8	2.3	1.5
Evanston city *Cook Co.*	61.7	18.4	11.7	6.1
Freeport city *Stephenson Co.*	94.0	1.2	2.7	1.8
Galesburg city *Knox Co.*	89.4	1.6	5.8	1.8
Geneva city *Kane Co.*	87.9	5.8	2.0	4.0
Glen Ellyn village *Du Page Co.*	78.6	11.7	2.8	5.7
Glendale Heights village *Du Page Co.*	93.9	2.6	1.1	1.5
Glenview village *Cook Co.*	84.7	8.1	1.5	5.0
Granite City city *Madison Co.*	93.8	2.1	1.9	1.2
Gurnee village *Lake Co.*	93.4	2.7	0.6	3.0
Hanover Park village *Cook Co.*	92.0	3.7	1.8	1.5
Harvey city *Cook Co.*	80.6	13.1	3.6	2.2
Highland Park city *Lake Co.*	78.2	12.3	2.2	6.3
Hoffman Estates village *Cook Co.*	91.8	3.3	1.3	2.7
Joliet city *Will Co.*	92.8	2.6	1.6	1.8
Kankakee city *Kankakee Co.*	90.9	1.4	3.0	2.0

Place	Automobile (%)	Public Transportation (%)	Walk (%)	Work from Home (%)
Lake in the Hills village *McHenry Co.*	94.2	2.3	0.2	3.1
Lansing village *Cook Co.*	89.2	6.1	2.3	2.1
Lombard village *Du Page Co.*	88.7	6.4	1.6	2.7
Loves Park city *Winnebago Co.*	95.7	0.6	0.5	2.6
Maywood village *Cook Co.*	83.9	9.4	3.2	1.7
McHenry city *McHenry Co.*	94.2	1.7	1.4	2.0
Moline city *Rock Island Co.*	93.6	1.9	1.6	2.1
Mount Prospect village *Cook Co.*	88.6	6.0	2.1	2.2
Mundelein village *Lake Co.*	90.5	4.1	0.8	3.3
Naperville city *Du Page Co.*	83.4	9.0	1.4	5.6
New Lenox village *Will Co.*	89.4	6.1	0.5	3.1
Niles village *Cook Co.*	88.9	6.1	2.0	2.0
Normal town *McLean Co.*	83.8	1.5	11.0	2.5
North Chicago city *Lake Co.*	48.6	1.4	27.2	6.6
Northbrook village *Cook Co.*	81.5	9.9	1.3	6.6
O'Fallon city *Saint Clair Co.*	95.2	0.9	1.2	2.2
Oak Forest city *Cook Co.*	87.2	8.8	1.0	2.4
Oak Lawn village *Cook Co.*	87.5	8.2	1.8	2.1
Oak Park village *Cook Co.*	68.4	21.8	4.0	5.1
Orland Park village *Cook Co.*	89.7	6.5	1.1	2.1
Oswego village *Kendall Co.*	89.7	3.7	0.5	5.7
Palatine village *Cook Co.*	90.3	4.7	1.4	2.5
Park Forest village *Cook Co.*	86.8	10.1	0.8	1.7
Park Ridge city *Cook Co.*	83.6	10.1	1.8	4.0
Pekin city *Tazewell Co.*	95.7	0.6	1.5	1.6
Peoria city *Peoria Co.*	90.5	3.2	3.8	2.0
Plainfield village *Will Co.*	92.5	2.2	1.0	3.8
Quincy city *Adams Co.*	92.3	0.9	3.6	2.3
Rock Island city *Rock Island Co.*	89.2	2.3	5.7	1.7
Rockford city *Winnebago Co.*	93.1	1.8	1.9	2.3
Rolling Meadows city *Cook Co.*	87.5	4.4	2.7	3.0
Romeoville village *Will Co.*	92.4	2.6	3.0	1.4
Roselle village *Du Page Co.*	89.0	6.1	1.1	3.4
Round Lake Beach village *Lake Co.*	92.6	3.0	0.9	2.4
Saint Charles city *Kane Co.*	90.9	3.2	1.6	3.8
Schaumburg village *Cook Co.*	91.9	4.1	0.9	2.7
Skokie village *Cook Co.*	85.3	8.1	2.2	3.5
Springfield city *Sangamon Co.*	91.8	2.5	2.6	2.1
Streamwood village *Cook Co.*	93.0	3.3	0.7	2.3
Tinley Park village *Cook Co.*	86.9	10.2	0.8	1.7
Urbana city *Champaign Co.*	63.8	10.9	17.0	3.2
Vernon Hills village *Lake Co.*	91.5	3.8	0.6	3.5
Waukegan city *Lake Co.*	91.3	3.6	2.0	1.6
West Chicago city *Du Page Co.*	89.7	3.1	3.0	2.0
Westmont village *Du Page Co.*	86.2	7.6	1.9	2.7
Wheaton city *Du Page Co.*	81.7	8.5	4.2	4.5
Wheeling village *Cook Co.*	92.3	3.3	1.8	1.9
Wilmette village *Cook Co.*	72.1	18.7	1.3	7.1
Woodridge village *Du Page Co.*	88.2	7.0	1.4	2.7
Zion city *Lake Co.*	92.4	3.5	1.3	1.9

NOTE: Data as of 2000

Travel Time to Work

Place	Less than 15 Minutes (%)	15 to 30 Minutes (%)	30 to 45 Minutes (%)	45 to 60 Minutes (%)	60 Minutes or More (%)
Addison village *Du Page Co.*	27.4	38.2	20.5	6.5	7.4
Algonquin village *McHenry Co.*	16.2	24.9	27.7	16.2	15.0
Alton city *Madison Co.*	39.5	26.7	17.5	11.6	4.6
Arlington Heights village *Cook Co.*	22.5	34.1	22.3	9.4	11.7
Aurora city *Kane Co.*	23.5	35.6	19.5	9.3	12.1
Bartlett village *Du Page Co.*	15.3	29.3	27.8	12.6	15.0
Batavia city *Kane Co.*	31.9	31.3	18.1	7.9	10.8
Belleville city *Saint Clair Co.*	34.7	32.5	18.4	9.2	5.3
Belvidere city *Boone Co.*	37.8	27.0	17.7	7.8	9.7
Berwyn city *Cook Co.*	17.8	28.8	27.5	15.3	10.6
Bloomington city *McLean Co.*	58.8	31.1	4.0	2.9	3.0
Bolingbrook village *Will Co.*	19.5	28.4	24.6	12.5	15.0
Buffalo Grove village *Lake Co.*	20.5	30.7	27.0	10.5	11.2
Burbank city *Cook Co.*	22.2	30.4	23.4	11.2	12.8
Calumet City city *Cook Co.*	18.3	25.4	23.1	11.8	21.4
Carol Stream village *Du Page Co.*	24.1	29.1	25.5	10.0	11.3
Carpentersville village *Kane Co.*	20.6	31.2	23.1	13.6	11.5
Champaign city *Champaign Co.*	57.1	34.0	5.1	1.7	2.1
Chicago city *Cook Co.*	13.2	27.9	28.3	14.7	16.0
Chicago Heights city *Cook Co.*	33.9	33.5	12.9	7.9	11.8
Cicero town *Cook Co.*	14.7	30.7	27.6	13.5	13.5
Collinsville city *Madison Co.*	27.0	35.5	25.0	8.4	4.3
Crystal Lake city *McHenry Co.*	29.6	23.9	16.9	12.5	17.1
Danville city *Vermilion Co.*	60.0	27.9	5.3	4.0	2.8
De Kalb city *De Kalb Co.*	55.9	18.7	10.5	7.2	7.7
Decatur city *Macon Co.*	53.3	34.9	4.5	3.8	3.5
Des Plaines city *Cook Co.*	24.3	34.9	23.3	8.5	9.0
Dolton village *Cook Co.*	16.9	21.0	21.6	16.1	24.4
Downers Grove village *Du Page Co.*	23.4	31.6	20.6	11.9	12.5
East Saint Louis city *Saint Clair Co.*	23.0	40.0	21.4	6.6	9.0
Edwardsville city *Madison Co.*	35.4	25.6	23.1	11.3	4.7
Elgin city *Kane Co.*	29.5	32.7	19.8	9.3	8.6
Elk Grove Village village *Cook Co.*	28.2	36.7	18.8	8.0	8.3
Elmhurst city *Du Page Co.*	27.9	32.4	21.7	9.2	8.8
Elmwood Park village *Cook Co.*	19.3	27.8	31.7	12.3	8.9
Evanston city *Cook Co.*	26.4	23.6	22.5	15.6	11.9
Freeport city *Stephenson Co.*	66.2	17.2	8.3	4.5	3.9
Galesburg city *Knox Co.*	69.2	20.7	3.4	2.8	3.8
Geneva city *Kane Co.*	32.7	26.7	16.4	9.1	15.1
Glen Ellyn village *Du Page Co.*	25.3	31.3	17.0	10.3	16.2
Glendale Heights village *Du Page Co.*	23.0	33.9	25.7	8.4	9.0
Glenview village *Cook Co.*	19.9	33.0	25.6	11.5	10.0
Granite City city *Madison Co.*	38.4	31.2	18.6	8.2	3.6
Gurnee village *Lake Co.*	20.1	34.0	21.5	11.9	12.4
Hanover Park village *Cook Co.*	19.6	34.5	24.8	11.0	10.1
Harvey city *Cook Co.*	19.4	31.4	20.3	10.8	18.2
Highland Park city *Lake Co.*	26.1	27.6	20.3	10.8	15.1
Hoffman Estates village *Cook Co.*	18.5	37.8	24.9	9.8	9.0
Joliet city *Will Co.*	28.9	29.9	18.1	10.8	12.4
Kankakee city *Kankakee Co.*	45.3	30.9	11.1	3.8	8.9

Place	Less than 15 Minutes (%)	15 to 30 Minutes (%)	30 to 45 Minutes (%)	45 to 60 Minutes (%)	60 Minutes or More (%)
Lake in the Hills village *McHenry Co.*	14.3	25.2	23.1	18.7	18.7
Lansing village *Cook Co.*	29.1	29.9	16.6	9.7	14.8
Lombard village *Du Page Co.*	24.4	32.5	23.4	9.3	10.4
Loves Park city *Winnebago Co.*	34.1	49.0	8.8	3.1	5.0
Maywood village *Cook Co.*	22.7	30.9	25.5	9.6	11.3
McHenry city *McHenry Co.*	30.8	29.5	14.0	11.4	14.4
Moline city *Rock Island Co.*	43.5	45.6	6.2	1.7	2.9
Mount Prospect village *Cook Co.*	23.4	35.6	23.6	8.4	8.9
Mundelein village *Lake Co.*	24.6	31.4	23.0	11.3	9.6
Naperville city *Du Page Co.*	21.3	29.8	19.0	11.8	17.9
New Lenox village *Will Co.*	21.2	27.3	21.1	11.6	18.9
Niles village *Cook Co.*	20.6	32.0	26.7	10.5	10.2
Normal town *McLean Co.*	55.9	35.4	4.3	2.2	2.3
North Chicago city *Lake Co.*	61.3	22.1	9.0	3.9	3.6
Northbrook village *Cook Co.*	24.2	29.8	21.9	12.1	12.0
O'Fallon city *Saint Clair Co.*	29.5	41.1	16.5	8.2	4.7
Oak Forest city *Cook Co.*	22.5	29.2	19.8	11.8	16.7
Oak Lawn village *Cook Co.*	24.5	26.1	21.5	13.9	14.0
Oak Park village *Cook Co.*	16.9	26.4	34.6	14.2	7.8
Orland Park village *Cook Co.*	19.5	26.0	21.7	12.5	20.3
Oswego village *Kendall Co.*	19.3	29.0	22.4	13.7	15.6
Palatine village *Cook Co.*	21.8	36.4	24.4	8.5	8.9
Park Forest village *Cook Co.*	25.2	29.2	16.4	10.7	18.6
Park Ridge city *Cook Co.*	26.3	29.3	26.6	9.3	8.5
Pekin city *Tazewell Co.*	43.4	35.1	14.5	3.5	3.5
Peoria city *Peoria Co.*	45.2	42.9	7.1	2.1	2.7
Plainfield village *Will Co.*	18.3	27.1	24.6	14.9	15.1
Quincy city *Adams Co.*	68.6	23.5	4.0	1.8	2.0
Rock Island city *Rock Island Co.*	46.8	40.5	6.9	2.4	3.4
Rockford city *Winnebago Co.*	39.6	44.0	8.2	2.8	5.5
Rolling Meadows city *Cook Co.*	28.8	37.0	19.8	6.5	7.9
Romeoville village *Will Co.*	23.0	23.4	24.2	14.6	14.7
Roselle village *Du Page Co.*	18.5	33.9	25.0	11.4	11.1
Round Lake Beach village *Lake Co.*	15.3	25.1	26.8	16.4	16.4
Saint Charles city *Kane Co.*	37.2	26.1	19.2	8.2	9.4
Schaumburg village *Cook Co.*	22.1	33.7	24.0	9.9	10.3
Skokie village *Cook Co.*	22.8	30.9	23.3	13.2	9.9
Springfield city *Sangamon Co.*	41.6	47.6	6.1	1.7	3.0
Streamwood village *Cook Co.*	14.9	34.3	26.8	12.6	11.3
Tinley Park village *Cook Co.*	20.3	27.7	19.4	14.0	18.5
Urbana city *Champaign Co.*	57.3	34.0	5.1	1.7	2.0
Vernon Hills village *Lake Co.*	23.0	31.2	24.8	10.0	10.9
Waukegan city *Lake Co.*	23.4	37.9	21.8	9.5	7.4
West Chicago city *Du Page Co.*	30.0	37.8	17.0	7.1	8.1
Westmont village *Du Page Co.*	24.8	31.6	21.2	9.9	12.6
Wheaton city *Du Page Co.*	32.6	28.1	17.2	8.5	13.7
Wheeling village *Cook Co.*	24.6	38.5	22.4	6.9	7.5
Wilmette village *Cook Co.*	21.1	23.6	21.7	19.9	13.7
Woodridge village *Du Page Co.*	18.5	35.2	23.1	10.1	13.0
Zion city *Lake Co.*	17.7	34.9	24.4	12.2	10.8

NOTE: Data as of 2000

Crime

Place	Violent Crime Rate (crimes per 10,000 population)	Property Crime Rate (crimes per 10,000 population)
Addison village *Du Page Co.*	23.4	236.1
Algonquin village *McHenry Co.*	10.3	186.4
Alton city *Madison Co.*	113.8	547.3
Arlington Heights village *Cook Co.*	6.1	185.8
Aurora city *Kane Co.*	47.0	293.5
Bartlett village *Du Page Co.*	3.9	124.2
Batavia city *Kane Co.*	8.8	223.4
Belleville city *Saint Clair Co.*	52.3	488.5
Belvidere city *Boone Co.*	20.7	276.9
Berwyn city *Cook Co.*	23.1	277.6
Bloomington city *McLean Co.*	56.4	298.9
Bolingbrook village *Will Co.*	34.2	177.4
Buffalo Grove village *Lake Co.*	2.8	118.8
Burbank city *Cook Co.*	34.4	301.4
Calumet City city *Cook Co.*	82.8	607.2
Carol Stream village *Du Page Co.*	20.0	179.3
Carpentersville village *Kane Co.*	21.8	274.4
Champaign city *Champaign Co.*	93.6	357.6
Chicago city *Cook Co.*	124.2	455.5
Chicago Heights city *Cook Co.*	131.6	498.8
Cicero town *Cook Co.*	43.5	281.8
Collinsville city *Madison Co.*	25.9	244.0
Crystal Lake city *McHenry Co.*	17.6	281.5
Danville city *Vermilion Co.*	133.7	747.9
De Kalb city *De Kalb Co.*	45.6	302.7
Decatur city *Macon Co.*	82.6	503.6
Des Plaines city *Cook Co.*	11.1	199.1
Dolton village *Cook Co.*	28.2	481.6
Downers Grove village *Du Page Co.*	14.1	225.5
East Saint Louis city *Saint Clair Co.*	752.9	735.9
Edwardsville city *Madison Co.*	7.9	152.2
Elgin city *Kane Co.*	31.0	275.0
Elk Grove Village village *Cook Co.*	11.8	286.0
Elmhurst city *Du Page Co.*	6.4	197.2
Elmwood Park village *Cook Co.*	11.8	142.9
Evanston city *Cook Co.*	32.4	389.3
Freeport city *Stephenson Co.*	46.1	558.7
Galesburg city *Knox Co.*	53.7	514.4
Geneva city *Kane Co.*	9.8	123.4
Glen Ellyn village *Du Page Co.*	14.0	180.9
Glendale Heights village *Du Page Co.*	16.0	194.7
Glenview village *Cook Co.*	6.3	182.7
Granite City city *Madison Co.*	52.3	441.0
Gurnee village *Lake Co.*	13.2	500.5
Hanover Park village *Cook Co.*	21.0	156.9
Harvey city *Cook Co.*	199.9	719.8
Highland Park city *Lake Co.*	8.0	161.9
Hoffman Estates village *Cook Co.*	9.2	173.1
Joliet city *Will Co.*	43.6	277.7
Kankakee city *Kankakee Co.*	98.0	548.0

Place	Violent Crime Rate (crimes per 10,000 population)	Property Crime Rate (crimes per 10,000 population)
Lake in the Hills village *McHenry Co.*	8.7	80.2
Lansing village *Cook Co.*	20.5	425.6
Lombard village *Du Page Co.*	9.1	271.9
Loves Park city *Winnebago Co.*	40.5	559.1
Maywood village *Cook Co.*	133.8	554.8
McHenry city *McHenry Co.*	22.1	233.3
Moline city *Rock Island Co.*	49.4	504.3
Mount Prospect village *Cook Co.*	7.9	153.1
Mundelein village *Lake Co.*	13.4	173.0
Naperville city *Du Page Co.*	6.7	167.1
New Lenox village *Will Co.*	8.2	156.1
Niles village *Cook Co.*	18.1	276.8
Normal town *McLean Co.*	45.1	291.8
North Chicago city *Lake Co.*	77.6	213.6
Northbrook village *Cook Co.*	4.7	193.6
O'Fallon city *Saint Clair Co.*	14.3	267.9
Oak Forest city *Cook Co.*	22.1	220.9
Oak Lawn village *Cook Co.*	10.4	208.7
Oak Park village *Cook Co.*	40.6	357.4
Orland Park village *Cook Co.*	2.8	196.5
Oswego village *Kendall Co.*	11.7	209.6
Palatine village *Cook Co.*	8.6	192.3
Park Forest village *Cook Co.*	41.7	257.4
Park Ridge city *Cook Co.*	4.9	167.6
Pekin city *Tazewell Co.*	37.8	281.4
Peoria city *Peoria Co.*	91.8	581.0
Plainfield village *Will Co.*	14.9	170.4
Quincy city *Adams Co.*	75.8	397.8
Rock Island city *Rock Island Co.*	97.9	503.3
Rockford city *Winnebago Co.*	112.1	697.2
Rolling Meadows city *Cook Co.*	18.0	220.0
Romeoville village *Will Co.*	21.4	191.8
Roselle village *Du Page Co.*	5.6	148.9
Round Lake Beach village *Lake Co.*	18.4	256.6
Saint Charles city *Kane Co.*	19.5	268.2
Schaumburg village *Cook Co.*	12.1	432.1
Skokie village *Cook Co.*	17.0	299.2
Springfield city *Sangamon Co.*	156.1	669.8
Streamwood village *Cook Co.*	12.9	223.3
Tinley Park village *Cook Co.*	12.0	214.3
Urbana city *Champaign Co.*	84.0	395.4
Vernon Hills village *Lake Co.*	8.8	282.6
Waukegan city *Lake Co.*	38.1	232.6
West Chicago city *Du Page Co.*	18.8	221.4
Westmont village *Du Page Co.*	16.1	222.4
Wheaton city *Du Page Co.*	12.1	153.0
Wheeling village *Cook Co.*	12.3	184.5
Wilmette village *Cook Co.*	1.9	140.0
Woodridge village *Du Page Co.*	14.1	176.5
Zion city *Lake Co.*	63.0	313.1

NOTE: Data as of 2006.

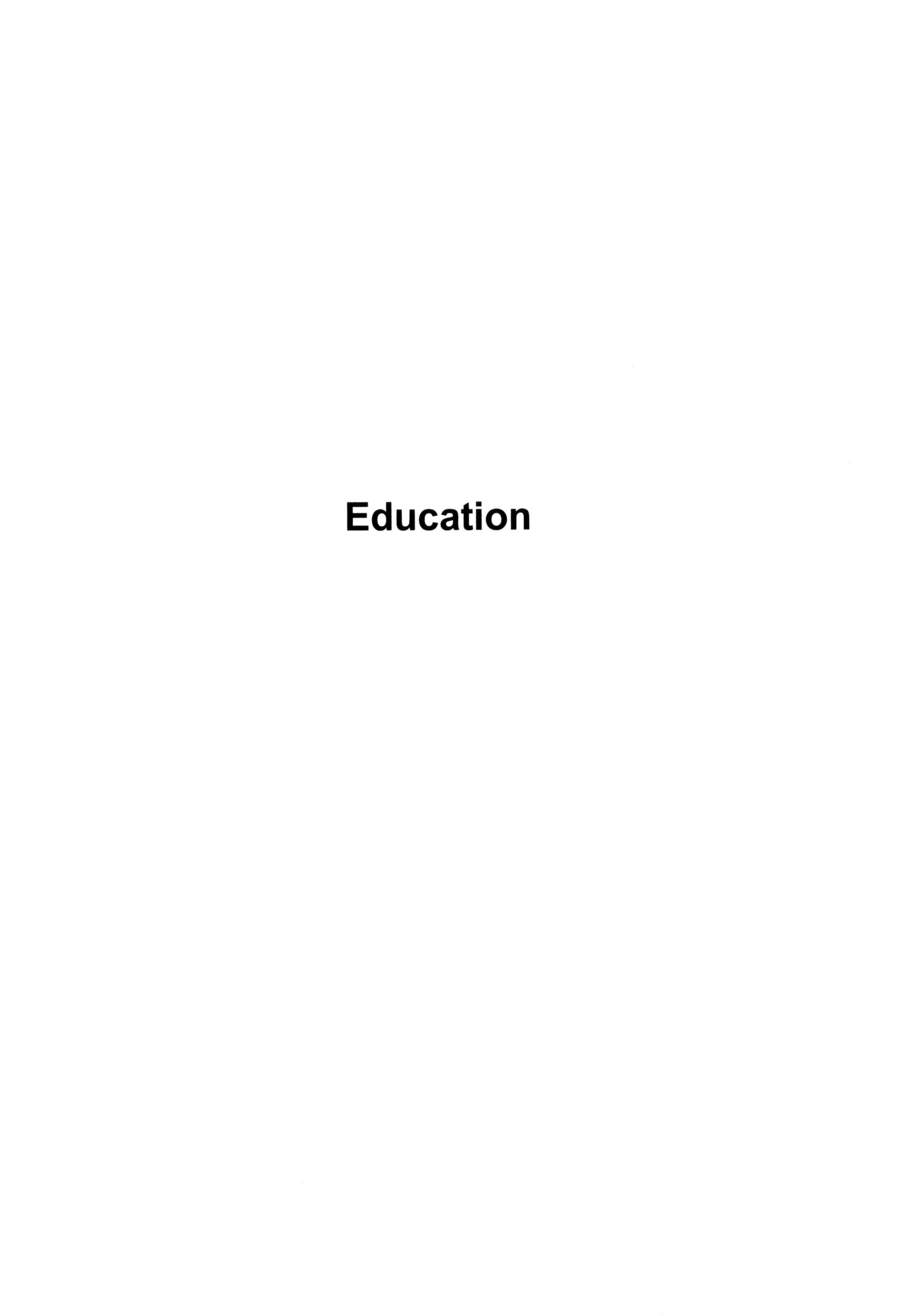

Education

Illinois Public School Educational Profile

Category	Value	Category	Value
Schools *(2005-2006)*	4,434	**Diploma Recipients** *(2004-2005)*	123,615
Instructional Level		White, Non-Hispanic	83,613
Primary	2,564	Black, Non-Hispanic	18,771
Middle	747	Asian/Pacific Islander	5,514
High	755	American Indian/Alaskan Native	363
Other Level	335	Hispanic	14,926
Curriculum		**High School Drop-out Rate** (%) *(2001-2002)*	6.3
Regular	3,909	White, Non-Hispanic	3.6
Special Education	275	Black, Non-Hispanic	13.6
Vocational	50	Asian/Pacific Islander	2.6
Alternative	167	American Indian/Alaskan Native	5.2
Type		Hispanic	10.4
Magnet	347	**Staff** *(2005-2006)*	
Charter	29	Teachers	133,856.8
Title I Eligible	2,312	Average Salary[1] ($)	56,494
School-wide Title I	943	Librarians/Media Specialists	2,193.1
Students *(2005-2006)*	2,111,706	Guidance Counselors	3,172.0
Gender (%)		**Ratios** *(2005-2006)*	
Male	51.4	Student/Teacher Ratio	15.8 to 1
Female	48.6	Student/Librarian Ratio	962.9 to 1
Race/Ethnicity (%)		Student/Counselor Ratio	665.7 to 1
White, Non-Hispanic	55.4	**College Entrance Exam Scores** *(2006)*	
Black, Non-Hispanic	20.3	SAT Reasoning Test™	
Asian/Pacific Islander	3.8	Participation Rate (%)	9
American Indian/Alaskan Native	0.2	Mean SAT Critical Reading Score	591
Hispanic	18.6	Mean SAT Writing Score	586
Classification (%)		Mean SAT Math Score	609
Individual Education Program (IEP)	15.3	American College Testing Program (ACT)	
Migrant *(2004-2005)*	0.0	Participation Rate (%)	100
English Language Learner (ELL)	n/a	Average Composite Score	20.5
Eligible for Free Lunch Program	31.5	Average English Score	20.2
Eligible for Reduced-Price Lunch Program	5.7	Average Math Score	20.3
Current Spending *($ per student in FY 2005)*	8,617	Average Reading Score	20.6
Instruction	5,157	Average Science Score	20.4
Support Services	3,162		

Note: *For an explanation of data, please refer to the User's Guide in the front of the book; (1) Includes extra-duty pay and employer pick-up of employee pension contributions where applicable*

Number of Schools

Rank	Number	District Name	City
1	633	City of Chicago SD 299	Chicago
2	56	School District U-46	Elgin
3	52	Rockford SD 205	Rockford
4	43	Peoria SD 150	Peoria
5	39	Corrections SD 428 Dept of	Springfield
6	35	Springfield SD 186	Springfield
7	32	East St Louis SD 189	E Saint Louis
8	31	Indian Prairie CUSD 204	Aurora
9	27	Schaumburg CCSD 54	Schaumburg
10	25	Decatur SD 61	Decatur
10	25	Plainfield SD 202	Plainfield
12	24	CUSD 300	Carpentersville
12	24	Waukegan CUSD 60	Waukegan
14	21	Joliet Psd 86	Joliet
14	21	Naperville CUSD 203	Naperville
16	20	CUSD 200	Wheaton
16	20	Mclean County USD 5	Normal
16	20	Moline USD 40	Moline
16	20	Palatine CCSD 15	Palatine
16	20	Valley View CUSD 365u	Romeoville
21	18	Aurora West USD 129	Aurora
21	18	Champaign CUSD 4	Champaign
23	17	Aurora East USD 131	Aurora
23	17	Cicero SD 99	Cicero
23	17	Evanston CCSD 65	Evanston
23	17	Oswego CUSD 308	Oswego
23	17	Rock Island SD 41	Rock Island
23	17	Saint Charles CUSD 303	Saint Charles
29	16	Alton CUSD 11	Alton
29	16	Quincy SD 172	Quincy
31	14	Community CSD 59	Arlington Hgts
32	13	Downers Grove Gsd 58	Downers Grove
32	13	Elmhurst SD 205	Elmhurst
32	13	Kankakee SD 111	Kankakee
35	12	Barrington CUSD 220	Barrington
35	12	Chicago Heights SD 170	Chicago Heights
35	12	Collinsville CUSD 10	Collinsville
35	12	Crystal Lake CCSD 47	Crystal Lake
35	12	Dekalb CUSD 428	De Kalb
35	12	Edwardsville CUSD 7	Edwardsville
35	12	New Lenox SD 122	New Lenox
35	12	Wheeling CCSD 21	Wheeling
43	11	Belleville SD 118	Belleville
43	11	CCSD 62	Des Plaines
43	11	Cahokia CUSD 187	Cahokia
43	11	Cook County SD 130	Blue Island
43	11	Danville CCSD 118	Danville
43	11	Galesburg CUSD 205	Galesburg
43	11	Harlem Ud 122	Loves Park
43	11	Jacksonville SD 117	Jacksonville
43	11	Maywood-Melrose Park-Broadview 89	Melrose Park
43	11	North Shore SD 112	Highland Park
43	11	Pekin PSD 108	Pekin
43	11	Township HSD 214	Arlington Hgts
55	10	Belvidere CUSD 100	Belvidere
55	10	Dolton SD 148	Riverdale
55	10	Freeport SD 145	Freeport
55	10	Granite City CUSD 9	Granite City
55	10	North Chicago SD 187	North Chicago
55	10	Oak Park ESD 97	Oak Park
55	10	Orland SD 135	Orland Park
62	9	Arlington Hgts SD 25	Arlington Hgts
62	9	Bloomington SD 87	Bloomington
62	9	Crete Monee CUSD 201u	Crete
62	9	Geneva CUSD 304	Geneva
62	9	Hinsdale CCSD 181	Westmont
62	9	Lake Zurich CUSD 95	Lake Zurich
62	9	Massac UD 1	Metropolis
62	9	Taylorville CUSD 3	Taylorville
62	9	Urbana SD 116	Urbana
62	9	Woodstock CUSD 200	Woodstock
72	8	Addison SD 4	Addison
72	8	Batavia USD 101	Batavia
72	8	Berwyn South SD 100	Berwyn
72	8	CCSD 93	Bloomingdale
72	8	CSD 158	Algonquin
72	8	Effingham CUSD 40	Effingham
72	8	Glenview CCSD 34	Glenview
72	8	Harvey SD 152	Harvey
72	8	Highland CUSD 5	Highland
72	8	Jersey CUSD 100	Jerseyville
72	8	Kirby SD 140	Tinley Park
72	8	Mchenry CCSD 15	Mchenry
72	8	Park Ridge CCSD 64	Park Ridge
72	8	Prairie-Hills ESD 144	Markham
72	8	Round Lake CUSD 116	Round Lake
72	8	School District 45 Dupage County	Villa Park
72	8	Township HSD 211	Palatine
72	8	West Chicago ESD 33	West Chicago
90	7	Bellwood SD 88	Bellwood
90	7	Burbank SD 111	Burbank
90	7	East Maine SD 63	Des Plaines
90	7	East Peoria SD 86	East Peoria
90	7	Geneseo CUSD 228	Geneseo
90	7	Kildeer Countryside CCSD 96	Buffalo Grove
90	7	Lombard SD 44	Lombard
90	7	Marion CUSD 2	Marion
90	7	Matteson ESD 162	Matteson
90	7	Monmouth-Roseville CUSD 238	Monmouth
90	7	Oak Lawn-Hometown SD 123	Oak Lawn
90	7	Prairie Central CUSD 8	Fairbury
90	7	Triad CUSD 2	Troy
90	7	Woodridge SD 68	Woodridge
90	7	Yorkville CUSD 115	Yorkville
90	7	Zion ESD 6	Zion
106	6	Berkeley SD 87	Berkeley
106	6	Bethalto CUSD 8	Bethalto
106	6	Bourbonnais SD 53	Bourbonnais
106	6	Cary CCSD 26	Cary
106	6	Charleston CUSD 1	Charleston
106	6	Clinton CUSD 15	Clinton
106	6	Deerfield SD 109	Deerfield
106	6	Dolton SD 149	Calumet City
106	6	Dunlap CUSD 323	Dunlap
106	6	Flora CUSD 35	Flora
106	6	Grayslake CCSD 46	Grayslake
106	6	Hawthorn CCSD 73	Vernon Hills
106	6	Indian Springs SD 109	Justice
106	6	Kaneland CUSD 302	Maple Park
106	6	Kewanee CUSD 229	Kewanee
106	6	Litchfield CUSD 12	Litchfield
106	6	Lyons SD 103	Lyons
106	6	Morton CUSD 709	Morton
106	6	North Boone CUSD 200	Poplar Grove
106	6	O Fallon CCSD 90	Ofallon
106	6	Park Forest SD 163	Park Forest
106	6	Peotone CUSD 207u	Peotone
106	6	Posen-Robbins ESD 143-5	Posen
106	6	Sandwich CUSD 430	Sandwich
106	6	Sherrard CUSD 200	Sherrard
106	6	Southwestern CUSD 9	Piasa
106	6	Sterling CUSD 5	Sterling
106	6	Summit Hill SD 161	Frankfort
106	6	Sycamore CUSD 427	Sycamore
106	6	Tinley Park CCSD 146	Tinley Park
106	6	Troy CCSD 30c	Plainfield
106	6	Wilmette SD 39	Wilmette
138	5	Antioch CCSD 34	Antioch
138	5	Ball Chatham CUSD 5	Chatham
138	5	Beach Park CCSD 3	Beach Park
138	5	Bensenville SD 2	Bensenville
138	5	Bond County CUSD 2	Greenville
138	5	CCSD 89	Glen Ellyn
138	5	CUSD 201	Westmont
138	5	Canton Union SD 66	Canton
138	5	Carlinville CUSD 1	Carlinville
138	5	Central CUSD 301	Burlington
138	5	Dixon USD 170	Dixon
138	5	ESD 159	Matteson
138	5	East Moline SD 37	East Moline
138	5	Elmwood Park CUSD 401	Elmwood Park
138	5	Eureka CUD 140	Eureka
138	5	Evergreen Park ESD 124	Evergreen Park
138	5	Flossmoor SD 161	Chicago Heights
138	5	Genoa Kingston CUSD 424	Genoa
138	5	Glen Ellyn SD 41	Glen Ellyn
138	5	Harvard CUSD 50	Harvard
138	5	Herscher CUSD 2	Herscher
138	5	Hillsboro CUSD 3	Hillsboro
138	5	Homer CCSD 33c	Homer Glen
138	5	La Grange SD 102	La Grange Park
138	5	Lake Forest SD 67	Lake Forest
138	5	Lake Villa CCSD 41	Lake Villa
138	5	Lansing SD 158	Lansing
138	5	Libertyville SD 70	Libertyville
138	5	Macomb CUSD 185	Macomb
138	5	Mahomet-Seymour CUSD 3	Mahomet
138	5	Maine Township HSD 207	Park Ridge
138	5	Mannheim SD 83	Franklin Park
138	5	Manteno CUSD 5	Manteno
138	5	Marquardt SD 15	Glendale Hgts
138	5	Mattoon CUSD 2	Mattoon
138	5	Minooka CCSD 201	Minooka
138	5	Monticello CUSD 25	Monticello
138	5	Mount Zion CUSD 3	Mount Zion
138	5	Mundelein ESD 75	Mundelein
138	5	North Palos SD 117	Palos Hills
138	5	Olympia CUSD 16	Stanford
138	5	Ottawa ESD 141	Ottawa
138	5	Pana CUSD 8	Pana
138	5	Paris-Union SD 95	Paris
138	5	Rantoul City SD 137	Rantoul
138	5	Ridgeland SD 122	Oak Lawn
138	5	Rochelle CCSD 231	Rochelle
138	5	Sparta CUSD 140	Sparta
138	5	Streator ESD 44	Streator
138	5	Summit SD 104	Summit
138	5	Wauconda CUSD 118	Wauconda
138	5	West Harvey-Dixmoor PSD 147	Harvey
138	5	Winnebago CUSD 323	Winnebago
138	5	Winnetka SD 36	Winnetka
192	4	Alsip-Hazlgrn-Oaklwn SD 126	Alsip
192	4	Aptakisic-Tripp CCSD 102	Buffalo Grove
192	4	Arbor Park SD 145	Oak Forest
192	4	Beardstown CUSD 15	Beardstown
192	4	Berwyn North SD 98	Berwyn
192	4	Bremen CHSD 228	Midlothian
192	4	Byron CUSD 226	Byron
192	4	CHSD 117	Lake Villa
192	4	CHSD 155	Crystal Lake
192	4	CHSD 218	Oak Lawn
192	4	Channahon SD 17	Channahon
192	4	Coal City CUSD 1	Coal City
192	4	Darien SD 61	Darien
192	4	Forest Ridge SD 142	Oak Forest
192	4	Frankfort CUSD 168	West Frankfort
192	4	Glenbard Twp HSD 87	Glen Ellyn
192	4	Gurnee SD 56	Gurnee
192	4	Harrisburg CUSD 3	Harrisburg
192	4	Herrin CUSD 4	Herrin
192	4	Homewood SD 153	Homewood
192	4	IL Valley Central USD 321	Chillicothe
192	4	J S Morton HSD 201	Cicero
192	4	Johnsburg CUSD 12	Johnsburg
192	4	Kinnikinnick CCSD 131	Roscoe
192	4	Lemont-Bromberek CSD 113a	Lemont
192	4	Lisle CUSD 202	Lisle
192	4	Mascoutah CUD 19	Mascoutah
192	4	Meridian CUSD 223	Stillman Valley
192	4	Midlothian SD 143	Midlothian
192	4	Mount Prospect SD 57	Mount Prospect
192	4	Mount Vernon SD 80	Mount Vernon
192	4	Murphysboro CUSD 186	Murphysboro
192	4	Northbrook SD 28	Northbrook
192	4	Northfield Twp HSD 225	Glenview
192	4	Oregon CUSD 220	Oregon
192	4	Paxton-Buckley-Loda CUD 10	Paxton
192	4	Plano CUSD 88	Plano
192	4	Reed Custer CUSD 255u	Braidwood
192	4	Rich Twp HSD 227	Olympia Fields
192	4	Robinson CUSD 2	Robinson
192	4	Rochester CUSD 3a	Rochester
192	4	Roxana CUSD 1	Roxana
192	4	Skokie SD 68	Skokie
192	4	South Holland SD 151	South Holland
192	4	Steger SD 194	Steger
192	4	Tolono CUSD 7	Tolono
192	4	Vandalia CUSD 203	Vandalia
192	4	Wabash CUSD 348	Mount Carmel
192	4	Waterloo CUSD 5	Waterloo
192	4	West Carroll CUSD 314	Thomson
192	4	Will County SD 92	Lockport
192	4	Wilmington CUSD 209u	Wilmington
192	4	Woodland CCSD 50	Gurnee
245	3	Belleville Twp HSD 201	Belleville
245	3	Bloom Twp HSD 206	Chicago Heights
245	3	Bradley SD 61	Bradley
245	3	CCSD 168	Sauk Village
245	3	Carterville CUSD 5	Carterville
245	3	Columbia CUSD 4	Columbia
245	3	Cons HSD 230	Orland Park
245	3	Country Club Hls SD 160	Country Club Hls
245	3	East Richland CUSD 1	Olney
245	3	Frankfort CCSD 157c	Frankfort
245	3	Joliet Twp HSD 204	Joliet
245	3	Keeneyville SD 20	Hanover Park
245	3	Lincolnshire-Prairieview SD 103	Lincolnshire
245	3	Mokena SD 159	Mokena

Rank	Number	District Name	City
245	3	Niles Twp CHSD 219	Skokie
245	3	Nippersink SD 2	Richmond
245	3	Palos CCSD 118	Palos Park
245	3	Proviso Twp HSD 209	Forest Park
245	3	Queen Bee SD 16	Glendale Hgts
245	3	River Trails SD 26	Mount Prospect
245	3	Riverton CUSD 14	Riverton
245	3	Skokie SD 69	Skokie
245	3	Thornton Twp HSD 205	South Holland
268	2	CHSD 128	Libertyville
268	2	CHSD 99	Downers Grove
268	2	Du Page HSD 88	Villa Park
268	2	Fremont SD 79	Mundelein
268	2	Grayslake CHSD 127	Grayslake
268	2	Hinsdale Twp HSD 86	Hinsdale
268	2	Leyden CHSD 212	Franklin Park
268	2	Lincoln Way CHSD 210	New Lenox
268	2	Mc Henry CHSD 156	Mchenry
268	2	Millburn CCSD 24	Wadsworth
268	2	New Trier Twp HSD 203	Northfield
268	2	Thornton Fractional Twp HSD 215	Calumet City
268	2	Twp HSD 113	Highland Park
281	1	Adlai E Stevenson HSD 125	Lincolnshire
281	1	Argo CHSD 217	Summit
281	1	Bradley Bourbonnais CHSD 307	Bradley
281	1	CHSD 94	West Chicago
281	1	Evanston Twp HSD 202	Evanston
281	1	Fenton CHSD 100	Bensenville
281	1	Grant CHSD 124	Fox Lake
281	1	Homewood Flossmoor CHSD 233	Flossmoor
281	1	Hononegah Chd 207	Rockton
281	1	Lake Forest CHSD 115	Lake Forest
281	1	Lake Park CHSD 108	Roselle
281	1	Lockport Twp HSD 205	Lockport
281	1	Lyons Twp HSD 204	La Grange
281	1	Minooka CHSD 111	Minooka
281	1	Mundelein Cons HSD 120	Mundelein
281	1	O Fallon Twp HSD 203	Ofallon
281	1	Oak Lawn CHSD 229	Oak Lawn
281	1	Oak Park-River Forest SD 200	Oak Park
281	1	Ottawa Twp HSD 140	Ottawa
281	1	Pekin CSD 303	Pekin
281	1	Reavis Twp HSD 220	Burbank
281	1	United Twp HSD 30	East Moline
281	1	Warren Twp HSD 121	Gages Lake
281	1	Zion-Benton Twp HSD 126	Zion

Number of Teachers

Rank	Number	District Name	City
1	27,038	City of Chicago SD 299	Chicago
2	2,136	School District U-46	Elgin
3	1,665	Rockford SD 205	Rockford
4	1,646	Indian Prairie CUSD 204	Aurora
5	1,382	Plainfield SD 202	Plainfield
6	1,083	Naperville CUSD 203	Naperville
7	1,044	Peoria SD 150	Peoria
8	971	Valley View CUSD 365u	Romeoville
9	967	CUSD 300	Carpentersville
10	939	Schaumburg CCSD 54	Schaumburg
11	935	Springfield SD 186	Springfield
12	915	Waukegan CUSD 60	Waukegan
13	863	CUSD 200	Wheaton
14	784	Saint Charles CUSD 303	Saint Charles
15	783	Township HSD 211	Palatine
16	775	Cicero SD 99	Cicero
17	755	Township HSD 214	Arlington Hgts
18	722	Mclean County USD 5	Normal
19	712	Aurora West USD 129	Aurora
20	700	Aurora East USD 131	Aurora
21	670	Champaign CUSD 4	Champaign
22	659	Oswego CUSD 308	Oswego
23	655	Palatine CCSD 15	Palatine
24	603	East St Louis SD 189	E Saint Louis
25	563	Joliet Psd 86	Joliet
26	553	Barrington CUSD 220	Barrington
27	529	Crystal Lake CCSD 47	Crystal Lake
28	511	Evanston CCSD 65	Evanston
29	510	Maine Township HSD 207	Park Ridge
30	498	Cons HSD 230	Orland Park
31	476	Wheeling CCSD 21	Wheeling
32	475	Decatur SD 61	Decatur
33	472	Elmhurst SD 205	Elmhurst
34	463	Harlem Ud 122	Loves Park
35	453	Woodland CCSD 50	Gurnee
36	452	Moline USD 40	Moline
37	448	Edwardsville CUSD 7	Edwardsville
38	441	J S Morton HSD 201	Cicero
39	432	Lake Zurich CUSD 95	Lake Zurich
40	431	Quincy SD 172	Quincy
41	430	Glenbard Twp HSD 87	Glen Ellyn
42	422	Alton CUSD 11	Alton
43	416	Community CSD 59	Arlington Hgts
44	413	Belvidere CUSD 100	Belvidere
45	404	CSD 158	Algonquin
46	384	CHSD 155	Crystal Lake
47	383	Danville CCSD 118	Danville
48	379	Rock Island SD 41	Rock Island
49	355	Collinsville CUSD 10	Collinsville
50	352	Granite City CUSD 9	Granite City
51	352	Bloomington SD 87	Bloomington
52	351	Batavia USD 101	Batavia
53	346	Orland SD 135	Orland Park
54	345	Lincoln Way CHSD 210	New Lenox
55	343	Oak Park ESD 97	Oak Park
56	342	Thornton Twp HSD 205	South Holland
57	340	Northfield Twp HSD 225	Glenview
58	339	Woodstock CUSD 200	Woodstock
59	339	Dekalb CUSD 428	De Kalb
60	337	Maywood-Melrose Park-Broadview 89	Melrose Park
61	332	Niles Twp CHSD 219	Skokie
61	332	Round Lake CUSD 116	Round Lake
63	331	New Trier Twp HSD 203	Northfield
64	331	Geneva CUSD 304	Geneva
65	328	Arlington Hgts SD 25	Arlington Hgts
66	328	Urbana SD 116	Urbana
67	328	Bremen CHSD 228	Midlothian
68	325	North Shore SD 112	Highland Park
69	323	Kankakee SD 111	Kankakee
70	322	CHSD 99	Downers Grove
71	322	Joliet Twp HSD 204	Joliet
72	316	CCSD 62	Des Plaines
73	301	Hinsdale Twp HSD 86	Hinsdale
74	300	Park Ridge CCSD 64	Park Ridge
75	299	CHSD 218	Oak Lawn
76	298	CCSD 93	Bloomingdale
77	295	Glenview CCSD 34	Glenview
78	293	Freeport SD 145	Freeport
79	288	Galesburg CUSD 205	Galesburg
80	282	Downers Grove Gsd 58	Downers Grove
81	281	New Lenox SD 122	New Lenox
82	275	Proviso Twp HSD 209	Forest Park
82	275	Wilmette SD 39	Wilmette
84	273	Cahokia CUSD 187	Cahokia
85	268	Adlai E Stevenson HSD 125	Lincolnshire
86	263	Hinsdale CCSD 181	Westmont
86	263	Kirby SD 140	Tinley Park
88	254	Belleville Twp HSD 201	Belleville
89	252	Jacksonville SD 117	Jacksonville
90	251	Mchenry CCSD 15	Mchenry
91	251	Rich Twp HSD 227	Olympia Fields
92	246	Du Page HSD 88	Villa Park
93	246	Twp HSD 113	Highland Park
94	243	Crete Monee CUSD 201u	Crete
95	242	Corrections SD 428 Dept of	Springfield
96	240	Kaneland CUSD 302	Maple Park
97	239	Glen Ellyn SD 41	Glen Ellyn
98	239	Cook County SD 130	Blue Island
99	239	Pekin PSD 108	Pekin
100	239	Wauconda CUSD 118	Wauconda
101	238	Mattoon CUSD 2	Mattoon
102	236	Addison SD 4	Addison
103	235	School District 45 Dupage County	Villa Park
104	234	North Chicago SD 187	North Chicago
105	233	Lyons Twp HSD 204	La Grange
106	232	Hawthorn CCSD 73	Vernon Hills
107	231	West Chicago ESD 33	West Chicago
108	230	Ball Chatham CUSD 5	Chatham
109	229	Warren Twp HSD 121	Gages Lake
110	228	Berwyn South SD 100	Berwyn
111	225	Triad CUSD 2	Troy
112	224	Evanston Twp HSD 202	Evanston
113	224	Deerfield SD 109	Deerfield
114	224	Oak Lawn-Hometown SD 123	Oak Lawn
115	223	Leyden CHSD 212	Franklin Park
116	220	East Maine SD 63	Des Plaines
117	219	Grayslake CCSD 46	Grayslake
118	217	Chicago Heights SD 170	Chicago Heights
119	214	Dolton SD 148	Riverdale
120	213	Kildeer Countryside CCSD 96	Buffalo Grove
121	208	Marion CUSD 2	Marion
122	206	Lombard SD 44	Lombard
123	205	Matteson ESD 162	Matteson
124	201	Sycamore CUSD 427	Sycamore
125	199	CHSD 128	Libertyville
126	198	Sterling CUSD 5	Sterling
127	197	Summit Hill SD 161	Frankfort
128	196	Lake Villa CCSD 41	Lake Villa
129	196	Highland CUSD 5	Highland
130	196	Troy CCSD 30c	Plainfield
131	195	Thornton Fractional Twp HSD 215	Calumet City
132	193	Lockport Twp HSD 205	Lockport
133	192	Oak Park-River Forest SD 200	Oak Park
134	191	Cary CCSD 26	Cary
135	187	Belleville SD 118	Belleville
135	187	La Grange SD 102	La Grange Park
137	187	Homer CCSD 33c	Homer Glen
138	181	Indian Springs SD 109	Justice
139	181	Burbank SD 111	Burbank
139	181	Jersey CUSD 100	Jerseyville
141	180	Antioch CCSD 34	Antioch
142	180	Woodridge SD 68	Woodridge
143	180	Mannheim SD 83	Franklin Park
144	179	Lyons SD 103	Lyons
145	179	CHSD 117	Lake Villa
145	179	Mascoutah CUD 19	Mascoutah
147	178	O Fallon CCSD 90	Ofallon
148	178	Dolton SD 149	Calumet City
149	177	Effingham CUSD 40	Effingham
149	177	Yorkville CUSD 115	Yorkville
151	175	Homewood Flossmoor CHSD 233	Flossmoor
152	173	Canton Union SD 66	Canton
153	173	Berkeley SD 87	Berkeley
154	171	Morton CUSD 709	Morton
155	171	Lake Forest SD 67	Lake Forest
156	171	Central CUSD 301	Burlington
156	171	Winnetka SD 36	Winnetka
158	171	Charleston CUSD 1	Charleston
159	170	Flossmoor SD 161	Chicago Heights
160	169	Bethalto CUSD 8	Bethalto
161	169	Dixon USD 170	Dixon
162	168	Taylorville CUSD 3	Taylorville
163	167	Bloom Twp HSD 206	Chicago Heights
164	166	Libertyville SD 70	Libertyville
165	165	Tinley Park CCSD 146	Tinley Park
166	165	Zion ESD 6	Zion
167	161	Berwyn North SD 98	Berwyn
168	161	Marquardt SD 15	Glendale Hgts
169	160	Waterloo CUSD 5	Waterloo
170	160	Prairie Central CUSD 8	Fairbury
171	155	Sandwich CUSD 430	Sandwich
172	155	Geneseo CUSD 228	Geneseo
173	154	Grayslake CHSD 127	Grayslake
174	154	North Palos SD 117	Palos Hills
175	154	Harvey SD 152	Harvey
176	153	Lake Park CHSD 108	Roselle
177	153	Mahomet-Seymour CUSD 3	Mahomet
178	152	East Moline SD 37	East Moline
178	152	Prairie-Hills ESD 144	Markham
180	152	Northbrook SD 28	Northbrook
181	151	Homewood SD 153	Homewood
182	150	Beach Park CCSD 3	Beach Park
183	149	Mundelein ESD 75	Mundelein
184	149	Aptakisic-Tripp CCSD 102	Buffalo Grove
185	147	Johnsburg CUSD 12	Johnsburg
186	146	CCSD 89	Glen Ellyn
187	146	Bellwood SD 88	Bellwood
188	145	Bensenville SD 2	Bensenville
189	144	Elmwood Park CUSD 401	Elmwood Park
190	144	Lemont-Bromberek CSD 113a	Lemont
191	143	Dunlap CUSD 323	Dunlap
192	142	Queen Bee SD 16	Glendale Hgts
193	140	Massac UD 1	Metropolis
194	139	Evergreen Park ESD 124	Evergreen Park
195	137	Manteno CUSD 5	Manteno
196	135	East Richland CUSD 1	Olney
197	134	Gurnee SD 56	Gurnee
198	133	Bourbonnais SD 53	Bourbonnais
199	133	Harvard CUSD 50	Harvard
199	133	Lansing SD 158	Lansing
201	132	Ottawa ESD 141	Ottawa
202	132	Herscher CUSD 2	Herscher
203	131	Zion-Benton Twp HSD 126	Zion
204	130	Mc Henry CHSD 156	Mchenry
205	130	CHSD 94	West Chicago
206	129	IL Valley Central USD 321	Chillicothe
207	128	Murphysboro CUSD 186	Murphysboro
208	128	Clinton CUSD 15	Clinton
209	128	Frankfort CCSD 157c	Frankfort
210	128	Mount Zion CUSD 3	Mount Zion

211	127	Macomb CUSD 185	Macomb
212	126	Peotone CUSD 207u	Peotone
213	126	Harrisburg CUSD 3	Harrisburg
214	125	Ridgeland SD 122	Oak Lawn
215	125	Minooka CCSD 201	Minooka
216	125	Streator ESD 44	Streator
217	125	Lake Forest CHSD 115	Lake Forest
218	125	Sherrard CUSD 200	Sherrard
219	123	Herrin CUSD 4	Herrin
220	122	Darien SD 61	Darien
220	122	Skokie SD 68	Skokie
222	121	East Peoria SD 86	East Peoria
222	121	Mount Prospect SD 57	Mount Prospect
224	121	Genoa Kingston CUSD 424	Genoa
225	120	Rochelle CCSD 231	Rochelle
226	120	Olympia CUSD 16	Stanford
227	120	Roxana CUSD 1	Roxana
228	119	Monmouth-Roseville CUSD 238	Monmouth
229	119	Palos CCSD 118	Palos Park
230	119	O Fallon Twp HSD 203	Ofallon
231	118	Park Forest SD 163	Park Forest
232	118	Mokena SD 159	Mokena
233	117	Lincolnshire-Prairieview SD 103	Lincolnshire
234	117	Millburn CCSD 24	Wadsworth
235	117	Reed Custer CUSD 255u	Braidwood
236	116	Steger SD 194	Steger
237	115	ESD 159	Matteson
238	114	CUSD 201	Westmont
239	114	Forest Ridge SD 142	Oak Forest
240	114	Pekin CSD 303	Pekin
241	114	Mount Vernon SD 80	Mount Vernon
242	113	Will County SD 92	Lockport
243	113	Lisle CUSD 202	Lisle
244	113	Kinnikinnick CCSD 131	Roscoe
245	113	Paris-Union SD 95	Paris
246	112	Summit SD 104	Summit
247	112	Midlothian SD 143	Midlothian
247	112	Wabash CUSD 348	Mount Carmel
249	111	Rochester CUSD 3a	Rochester
250	111	Columbia CUSD 4	Columbia
251	111	Southwestern CUSD 9	Piasa
252	110	Hillsboro CUSD 3	Hillsboro
253	109	Keeneyville SD 20	Hanover Park
254	109	Bond County CUSD 2	Greenville
255	108	West Carroll CUSD 314	Thomson
255	108	Winnebago CUSD 323	Winnebago
257	108	Coal City CUSD 1	Coal City
258	107	River Trails SD 26	Mount Prospect
258	107	Robinson CUSD 2	Robinson
260	106	Oak Lawn CHSD 229	Oak Lawn
261	104	Plano CUSD 88	Plano
262	104	Byron CUSD 226	Byron
263	104	Alsip-Hazlgrn-Oaklwn SD 126	Alsip
264	103	Fremont SD 79	Mundelein
265	103	Mundelein Cons HSD 120	Mundelein
265	103	Tolono CUSD 7	Tolono
267	101	Frankfort CUSD 168	West Frankfort
268	101	Monticello CUSD 25	Monticello
269	101	Kewanee CUSD 229	Kewanee
270	100	Vandalia CUSD 203	Vandalia
271	100	Hononegah Chd 207	Rockton
272	99	Oregon CUSD 220	Oregon
273	99	Eureka CUD 140	Eureka
274	99	Flora CUSD 35	Flora
275	99	CCSD 168	Sauk Village
276	98	Argo CHSD 217	Summit
277	98	Sparta CUSD 140	Sparta
278	97	Meridian CUSD 223	Stillman Valley
278	97	Paxton-Buckley-Loda CUD 10	Paxton
280	97	Ottawa Twp HSD 140	Ottawa
281	96	Beardstown CUSD 15	Beardstown
282	96	Fenton CHSD 100	Bensenville
283	96	Bradley Bourbonnais CHSD 307	Bradley
284	95	Minooka CHSD 111	Minooka
285	95	Pana CUSD 8	Pana
286	93	Reavis Twp HSD 220	Burbank
287	92	Rantoul City SD 137	Rantoul
288	89	South Holland SD 151	South Holland
289	89	Nippersink SD 2	Richmond
290	89	Litchfield CUSD 12	Litchfield
290	89	Posen-Robbins ESD 143-5	Posen
292	87	Wilmington CUSD 209u	Wilmington
293	86	United Twp HSD 30	East Moline
294	86	Skokie SD 69	Skokie
295	85	Grant CHSD 124	Fox Lake
296	85	North Boone CUSD 200	Poplar Grove
297	85	Arbor Park SD 145	Oak Forest
298	84	Carlinville CUSD 1	Carlinville
299	80	West Harvey-Dixmoor PSD 147	Harvey
300	79	Bradley SD 61	Bradley
301	77	Riverton CUSD 14	Riverton
302	76	Carterville CUSD 5	Carterville
303	74	Country Club Hls SD 160	Country Club Hls
304	63	Channahon SD 17	Channahon

Number of Students

Rank	Number	District Name	City
1	420,982	City of Chicago SD 299	Chicago
2	39,656	School District U-46	Elgin
3	29,145	Rockford SD 205	Rockford
4	28,510	Indian Prairie CUSD 204	Aurora
5	24,371	Plainfield SD 202	Plainfield
6	18,697	Naperville CUSD 203	Naperville
7	18,670	CUSD 300	Carpentersville
8	17,510	Valley View CUSD 365u	Romeoville
9	15,841	Waukegan CUSD 60	Waukegan
10	15,203	Peoria SD 150	Peoria
11	15,097	Springfield SD 186	Springfield
12	14,471	Schaumburg CCSD 54	Schaumburg
13	14,076	CUSD 200	Wheaton
14	13,528	Cicero SD 99	Cicero
15	13,443	Saint Charles CUSD 303	Saint Charles
16	13,026	Township HSD 211	Palatine
17	12,794	Palatine CCSD 15	Palatine
18	12,599	Oswego CUSD 308	Oswego
19	12,542	Township HSD 214	Arlington Hgts
20	12,491	Aurora West USD 129	Aurora
21	12,316	Aurora East USD 131	Aurora
22	11,760	Mclean County USD 5	Normal
23	10,111	Joliet Psd 86	Joliet
24	9,873	East St Louis SD 189	E Saint Louis
25	9,822	Decatur SD 61	Decatur
26	9,266	Crystal Lake CCSD 47	Crystal Lake
27	9,248	Champaign CUSD 4	Champaign
28	9,135	Barrington CUSD 220	Barrington
29	8,998	Glenbard Twp HSD 87	Glen Ellyn
30	8,805	Cons HSD 230	Orland Park
31	8,405	Belvidere CUSD 100	Belvidere
32	8,203	J S Morton HSD 201	Cicero
33	7,838	Harlem Ud 122	Loves Park
34	7,648	Elmhurst SD 205	Elmhurst
35	7,606	Moline USD 40	Moline
36	7,365	Edwardsville CUSD 7	Edwardsville
37	7,352	Granite City CUSD 9	Granite City
38	7,238	Quincy SD 172	Quincy
39	7,084	Woodland CCSD 50	Gurnee
40	6,993	Maine Township HSD 207	Park Ridge
41	6,939	CHSD 155	Crystal Lake
42	6,929	CSD 158	Algonquin
43	6,798	Alton CUSD 11	Alton
44	6,725	Wheeling CCSD 21	Wheeling
45	6,687	Round Lake CUSD 116	Round Lake
46	6,632	Lincoln Way CHSD 210	New Lenox
47	6,557	Lake Zurich CUSD 95	Lake Zurich
48	6,554	Thornton Twp HSD 205	South Holland
49	6,470	Danville CCSD 118	Danville
50	6,468	Evanston CCSD 65	Evanston
51	6,342	Collinsville CUSD 10	Collinsville
52	6,299	Rock Island SD 41	Rock Island
53	6,258	Woodstock CUSD 200	Woodstock
54	6,235	Batavia USD 101	Batavia
55	6,065	Community CSD 59	Arlington Hgts
56	5,971	Kankakee SD 111	Kankakee
57	5,933	Orland SD 135	Orland Park
58	5,814	Geneva CUSD 304	Geneva
59	5,694	Dekalb CUSD 428	De Kalb
60	5,586	Maywood-Melrose Park-Broadview 89	Melrose Park
61	5,559	CHSD 99	Downers Grove
62	5,515	Bloomington SD 87	Bloomington
63	5,457	New Lenox SD 122	New Lenox
64	5,329	CHSD 218	Oak Lawn
65	5,208	Joliet Twp HSD 204	Joliet
66	5,194	Bremen CHSD 228	Midlothian
67	5,075	Belleville Twp HSD 201	Belleville
68	5,046	Cahokia CUSD 187	Cahokia
69	5,023	Downers Grove Gsd 58	Downers Grove
70	4,973	Oak Park ESD 97	Oak Park
71	4,970	Arlington Hgts SD 25	Arlington Hgts
72	4,877	Galesburg CUSD 205	Galesburg
73	4,873	Proviso Twp HSD 209	Forest Park
74	4,868	Northfield Twp HSD 225	Glenview
75	4,846	Mchenry CCSD 15	Mchenry
76	4,774	Crete Monee CUSD 201u	Crete
77	4,772	Niles Twp CHSD 219	Skokie
78	4,771	CCSD 62	Des Plaines
79	4,517	CCSD 93	Bloomingdale
80	4,510	Adlai E Stevenson HSD 125	Lincolnshire
81	4,485	Kirby SD 140	Tinley Park
82	4,480	Hinsdale Twp HSD 86	Hinsdale
83	4,435	Freeport SD 145	Freeport
84	4,370	Urbana SD 116	Urbana
85	4,323	North Chicago SD 187	North Chicago
86	4,321	North Shore SD 112	Highland Park
87	4,307	Park Ridge CCSD 64	Park Ridge
88	4,253	Glenview CCSD 34	Glenview
89	4,198	Wauconda CUSD 118	Wauconda
90	4,127	Ball Chatham CUSD 5	Chatham
91	4,108	Grayslake CCSD 46	Grayslake
92	4,059	Hinsdale CCSD 181	Westmont
93	4,057	Du Page HSD 88	Villa Park
94	4,044	New Trier Twp HSD 203	Northfield
95	4,025	Marion CUSD 2	Marion
96	3,994	Kaneland CUSD 302	Maple Park
97	3,968	Addison SD 4	Addison
98	3,962	Rich Twp HSD 227	Olympia Fields
99	3,948	Cook County SD 130	Blue Island
100	3,944	West Chicago ESD 33	West Chicago
101	3,873	Triad CUSD 2	Troy
102	3,828	Warren Twp HSD 121	Gages Lake
103	3,826	Lyons Twp HSD 204	La Grange
104	3,767	Pekin PSD 108	Pekin
105	3,732	Dolton SD 149	Calumet City
106	3,728	Lockport Twp HSD 205	Lockport
107	3,722	Belleville SD 118	Belleville
108	3,713	Jacksonville SD 117	Jacksonville
109	3,709	Troy CCSD 30c	Plainfield
110	3,697	Hawthorn CCSD 73	Vernon Hills
111	3,681	Twp HSD 113	Highland Park
112	3,632	Cary CCSD 26	Cary
113	3,615	Wilmette SD 39	Wilmette
114	3,612	Sterling CUSD 5	Sterling
115	3,607	Yorkville CUSD 115	Yorkville
116	3,595	School District 45 Dupage County	Villa Park
117	3,583	Summit Hill SD 161	Frankfort
118	3,558	Bloom Twp HSD 206	Chicago Heights
119	3,549	Glen Ellyn SD 41	Glen Ellyn
120	3,537	Leyden CHSD 212	Franklin Park
121	3,517	Chicago Heights SD 170	Chicago Heights
122	3,506	Berwyn South SD 100	Berwyn
123	3,498	East Maine SD 63	Des Plaines
124	3,441	Sycamore CUSD 427	Sycamore
125	3,432	Kildeer Countryside CCSD 96	Buffalo Grove
126	3,402	Thornton Fractional Twp HSD 215	Calumet City
127	3,401	Homer CCSD 33c	Homer Glen
128	3,399	Matteson ESD 162	Matteson
129	3,362	Lake Villa CCSD 41	Lake Villa
130	3,361	Mattoon CUSD 2	Mattoon
131	3,351	O Fallon CCSD 90	Ofallon
132	3,272	Berwyn North SD 98	Berwyn
133	3,240	Burbank SD 111	Burbank
134	3,239	Bellwood SD 88	Bellwood
135	3,214	CHSD 128	Libertyville
136	3,194	Dolton SD 148	Riverdale
137	3,164	Evanston Twp HSD 202	Evanston
138	3,144	Lombard SD 44	Lombard
139	3,111	Deerfield SD 109	Deerfield
140	3,095	Taylorville CUSD 3	Taylorville
141	3,093	Highland CUSD 5	Highland
142	3,076	Oak Park-River Forest SD 200	Oak Park
143	3,026	Lake Park CHSD 108	Roselle
144	3,005	Effingham CUSD 40	Effingham
145	2,955	Prairie-Hills ESD 144	Markham
146	2,946	Zion ESD 6	Zion
147	2,944	Jersey CUSD 100	Jerseyville
148	2,934	Antioch CCSD 34	Antioch
149	2,929	Dixon USD 170	Dixon
150	2,924	Harvey SD 152	Harvey
151	2,920	Homewood Flossmoor CHSD 233	Flossmoor
152	2,902	Charleston CUSD 1	Charleston
153	2,895	Indian Springs SD 109	Justice
154	2,886	Berkeley SD 87	Berkeley
155	2,885	Oak Lawn-Hometown SD 123	Oak Lawn
156	2,854	Woodridge SD 68	Woodridge
157	2,826	Geneseo CUSD 228	Geneseo
158	2,798	Dunlap CUSD 323	Dunlap
159	2,790	North Palos SD 117	Palos Hills
160	2,784	Minooka CCSD 201	Minooka
161	2,776	Mahomet-Seymour CUSD 3	Mahomet
162	2,766	Elmwood Park CUSD 401	Elmwood Park

163	2,757	Mannheim SD 83	Franklin Park
163	2,757	Mascoutah CUD 19	Mascoutah
165	2,738	Bethalto CUSD 8	Bethalto
166	2,694	Waterloo CUSD 5	Waterloo
167	2,685	Canton Union SD 66	Canton
168	2,681	La Grange SD 102	La Grange Park
169	2,655	Morton CUSD 709	Morton
170	2,641	Libertyville SD 70	Libertyville
171	2,639	Johnsburg CUSD 12	Johnsburg
172	2,629	CHSD 117	Lake Villa
173	2,622	Marquardt SD 15	Glendale Hgts
174	2,616	Flossmoor SD 161	Chicago Heights
175	2,594	Central CUSD 301	Burlington
176	2,591	Lemont-Bromberek CSD 113a	Lemont
177	2,581	Zion-Benton Twp HSD 126	Zion
178	2,566	Sandwich CUSD 430	Sandwich
179	2,507	Beach Park CCSD 3	Beach Park
180	2,497	Bourbonnais SD 53	Bourbonnais
181	2,475	Grayslake CHSD 127	Grayslake
182	2,450	Mount Zion CUSD 3	Mount Zion
183	2,436	East Moline SD 37	East Moline
184	2,409	Mc Henry CHSD 156	Mchenry
185	2,407	Tinley Park CCSD 146	Tinley Park
186	2,403	Bensenville SD 2	Bensenville
187	2,396	Mokena SD 159	Mokena
188	2,387	Massac UD 1	Metropolis
189	2,345	O Fallon Twp HSD 203	Ofallon
190	2,334	Harvard CUSD 50	Harvard
191	2,317	Lyons SD 103	Lyons
192	2,313	Lansing SD 158	Lansing
193	2,304	Lake Forest SD 67	Lake Forest
194	2,271	Corrections SD 428 Dept of	Springfield
195	2,269	Mundelein Cons HSD 120	Mundelein
196	2,262	Herrin CUSD 4	Herrin
197	2,250	CCSD 89	Glen Ellyn
198	2,247	Frankfort CCSD 157c	Frankfort
199	2,241	Prairie Central CUSD 8	Fairbury
200	2,202	Park Forest SD 163	Park Forest
201	2,175	Mundelein ESD 75	Mundelein
202	2,168	Pekin CSD 303	Pekin
203	2,166	Aptakisic-Tripp CCSD 102	Buffalo Grove
203	2,166	IL Valley Central USD 321	Chillicothe
205	2,161	Clinton CUSD 15	Clinton
206	2,160	Herscher CUSD 2	Herscher
207	2,144	Harrisburg CUSD 3	Harrisburg
207	2,144	Ridgeland SD 122	Oak Lawn
209	2,139	East Richland CUSD 1	Olney
210	2,132	CHSD 94	West Chicago
211	2,130	Manteno CUSD 5	Manteno
212	2,105	Winnetka SD 36	Winnetka
213	2,084	Olympia CUSD 16	Stanford
214	2,071	Gurnee SD 56	Gurnee
215	2,066	Homewood SD 153	Homewood
216	2,065	Rochester CUSD 3a	Rochester
217	2,064	Mount Prospect SD 57	Mount Prospect
218	2,053	Queen Bee SD 16	Glendale Hgts
219	2,052	Kinnikinnick CCSD 131	Roscoe
220	2,046	Murphysboro CUSD 186	Murphysboro
221	2,037	Will County SD 92	Lockport
222	2,029	Roxana CUSD 1	Roxana
223	2,025	ESD 159	Matteson
223	2,025	Hillsboro CUSD 3	Hillsboro
225	2,023	Ottawa ESD 141	Ottawa
226	2,018	Coal City CUSD 1	Coal City
227	2,004	Evergreen Park ESD 124	Evergreen Park
228	1,999	Peotone CUSD 207u	Peotone
229	1,986	Palos CCSD 118	Palos Park
230	1,951	Hononegah Chd 207	Rockton
231	1,947	Bradley Bourbonnais CHSD 307	Bradley
232	1,940	Genoa Kingston CUSD 424	Genoa
233	1,903	Streator ESD 44	Streator
234	1,895	Bond County CUSD 2	Greenville
234	1,895	Meridian CUSD 223	Stillman Valley
236	1,891	Reed Custer CUSD 255u	Braidwood
237	1,887	East Peoria SD 86	East Peoria
238	1,881	Midlothian SD 143	Midlothian
239	1,877	Fremont SD 79	Mundelein
240	1,876	Macomb CUSD 185	Macomb
241	1,873	Wabash CUSD 348	Mount Carmel
242	1,847	Minooka CHSD 111	Minooka
243	1,845	Frankfort CUSD 168	West Frankfort
244	1,842	United Twp HSD 30	East Moline
245	1,841	Kewanee CUSD 229	Kewanee
246	1,814	Mount Vernon SD 80	Mount Vernon
246	1,814	Oregon CUSD 220	Oregon
248	1,797	CCSD 168	Sauk Village
249	1,793	Byron CUSD 226	Byron
250	1,789	Southwestern CUSD 9	Piasa
251	1,781	Columbia CUSD 4	Columbia
252	1,780	Reavis Twp HSD 220	Burbank
253	1,773	Vandalia CUSD 203	Vandalia
254	1,770	Sherrard CUSD 200	Sherrard
255	1,769	Oak Lawn CHSD 229	Oak Lawn
256	1,761	Monmouth-Roseville CUSD 238	Monmouth
257	1,751	Robinson CUSD 2	Robinson
258	1,744	Argo CHSD 217	Summit
259	1,738	Lake Forest CHSD 115	Lake Forest
260	1,736	Northbrook SD 28	Northbrook
261	1,735	Rochelle CCSD 231	Rochelle
262	1,727	Carterville CUSD 5	Carterville
263	1,713	Lisle CUSD 202	Lisle
263	1,713	Rantoul City SD 137	Rantoul
265	1,708	Keeneyville SD 20	Hanover Park
266	1,705	CUSD 201	Westmont
267	1,698	Forest Ridge SD 142	Oak Forest
268	1,697	Posen-Robbins ESD 143-5	Posen
268	1,697	Summit SD 104	Summit
270	1,688	Lincolnshire-Prairieview SD 103	Lincolnshire
271	1,682	Monticello CUSD 25	Monticello
272	1,681	Winnebago CUSD 323	Winnebago
273	1,667	West Harvey-Dixmoor PSD 147	Harvey
274	1,664	Paris-Union SD 95	Paris
275	1,653	Alsip-Hazlgrn-Oaklwn SD 126	Alsip
276	1,651	Darien SD 61	Darien
277	1,646	Ottawa Twp HSD 140	Ottawa
278	1,639	Country Club Hls SD 160	Country Club Hls
279	1,636	River Trails SD 26	Mount Prospect
280	1,623	Litchfield CUSD 12	Litchfield
281	1,621	Channahon SD 17	Channahon
282	1,619	Plano CUSD 88	Plano
283	1,617	Nippersink SD 2	Richmond
284	1,616	Skokie SD 68	Skokie
285	1,613	Steger SD 194	Steger
286	1,610	Eureka CUD 140	Eureka
287	1,594	South Holland SD 151	South Holland
288	1,587	North Boone CUSD 200	Poplar Grove
289	1,578	Grant CHSD 124	Fox Lake
290	1,565	Pana CUSD 8	Pana
291	1,563	Fenton CHSD 100	Bensenville
292	1,541	West Carroll CUSD 314	Thomson
293	1,539	Flora CUSD 35	Flora
294	1,537	Millburn CCSD 24	Wadsworth
295	1,531	Riverton CUSD 14	Riverton
296	1,529	Sparta CUSD 140	Sparta
297	1,528	Wilmington CUSD 209u	Wilmington
298	1,514	Tolono CUSD 7	Tolono
299	1,511	Carlinville CUSD 1	Carlinville
300	1,506	Bradley SD 61	Bradley
301	1,503	Arbor Park SD 145	Oak Forest
301	1,503	Beardstown CUSD 15	Beardstown
303	1,501	Skokie SD 69	Skokie
304	1,500	Paxton-Buckley-Loda CUD 10	Paxton

Male Students

Rank	Percent	District Name	City
1	91.3	Corrections SD 428 Dept of	Springfield
2	53.9	Herscher CUSD 2	Herscher
3	53.9	Will County SD 92	Lockport
4	53.7	Hinsdale CCSD 181	Westmont
5	53.6	Carlinville CUSD 1	Carlinville
6	53.5	Winnebago CUSD 323	Winnebago
7	53.5	Waterloo CUSD 5	Waterloo
8	53.4	IL Valley Central USD 321	Chillicothe
9	53.4	Grayslake CHSD 127	Grayslake
10	53.4	Bond County CUSD 2	Greenville
11	53.4	Mannheim SD 83	Franklin Park
12	53.4	CHSD 94	West Chicago
13	53.2	Bourbonnais SD 53	Bourbonnais
14	53.1	Keeneyville SD 20	Hanover Park
15	53.1	Tolono CUSD 7	Tolono
16	53.0	Twp HSD 113	Highland Park
17	53.0	Effingham CUSD 40	Effingham
18	53.0	East Richland CUSD 1	Olney
19	53.0	Channahon SD 17	Channahon
20	52.9	Galesburg CUSD 205	Galesburg
21	52.9	Oak Lawn-Hometown SD 123	Oak Lawn
22	52.9	Winnetka SD 36	Winnetka
23	52.9	Taylorville CUSD 3	Taylorville
24	52.8	River Trails SD 26	Mount Prospect
25	52.8	Oregon CUSD 220	Oregon
26	52.8	Gurnee SD 56	Gurnee
27	52.7	Darien SD 61	Darien
28	52.7	Mchenry CCSD 15	Mchenry
29	52.7	Bloom Twp HSD 206	Chicago Heights
30	52.7	Dolton SD 148	Riverdale
31	52.7	Robinson CUSD 2	Robinson
32	52.7	Antioch CCSD 34	Antioch
33	52.7	Canton Union SD 66	Canton
34	52.6	Bethalto CUSD 8	Bethalto
35	52.6	Cook County SD 130	Blue Island
36	52.6	Mount Prospect SD 57	Mount Prospect
37	52.6	New Trier Twp HSD 203	Northfield
38	52.6	Orland SD 135	Orland Park
39	52.6	Belleville SD 118	Belleville
40	52.5	Oswego CUSD 308	Oswego
41	52.5	Collinsville CUSD 10	Collinsville
42	52.5	Lake Villa CCSD 41	Lake Villa
43	52.5	East Moline SD 37	East Moline
44	52.5	Indian Springs SD 109	Justice
45	52.5	Geneseo CUSD 228	Geneseo
46	52.5	Woodland CCSD 50	Gurnee
47	52.5	Woodstock CUSD 200	Woodstock
48	52.5	Homer CCSD 33c	Homer Glen
49	52.5	Frankfort CCSD 157c	Frankfort
50	52.5	East Peoria SD 86	East Peoria
51	52.5	Summit SD 104	Summit
52	52.4	Downers Grove Gsd 58	Downers Grove
53	52.4	Paxton-Buckley-Loda CUD 10	Paxton
54	52.4	Deerfield SD 109	Deerfield
55	52.4	Monticello CUSD 25	Monticello
56	52.4	Litchfield CUSD 12	Litchfield
57	52.3	Wilmington CUSD 209u	Wilmington
58	52.3	Mundelein Cons HSD 120	Mundelein
59	52.3	Park Ridge CCSD 64	Park Ridge
60	52.3	Harvard CUSD 50	Harvard
61	52.3	Lake Forest SD 67	Lake Forest
62	52.3	Peotone CUSD 207u	Peotone
63	52.3	Ridgeland SD 122	Oak Lawn
64	52.3	Southwestern CUSD 9	Piasa
65	52.3	Vandalia CUSD 203	Vandalia
66	52.2	Community CSD 59	Arlington Hgts
67	52.2	Berwyn South SD 100	Berwyn
68	52.2	Mokena SD 159	Mokena
69	52.2	Central CUSD 301	Burlington
70	52.2	School District 45 Dupage County	Villa Park
71	52.2	Cicero SD 99	Cicero
72	52.1	Columbia CUSD 4	Columbia
73	52.1	Nippersink SD 2	Richmond
74	52.1	Yorkville CUSD 115	Yorkville
75	52.1	Lockport Twp HSD 205	Lockport
76	52.1	Ottawa Twp HSD 140	Ottawa
77	52.1	Lemont-Bromberek CSD 113a	Lemont
78	52.1	CUSD 201	Westmont
79	52.1	La Grange SD 102	La Grange Park
80	52.1	CUSD 200	Wheaton
81	52.1	Thornton Fractional Twp HSD 215	Calumet City
82	52.1	New Lenox SD 122	New Lenox
83	52.1	Fremont SD 79	Mundelein
84	52.1	Cary CCSD 26	Cary
85	52.1	Kirby SD 140	Tinley Park
86	52.0	West Carroll CUSD 314	Thomson
87	52.0	CHSD 117	Lake Villa
88	52.0	Mc Henry CHSD 156	Mchenry
89	52.0	Chicago Heights SD 170	Chicago Heights
90	52.0	Bloomington SD 87	Bloomington
91	52.0	Fenton CHSD 100	Bensenville
92	52.0	Bremen CHSD 228	Midlothian
93	51.9	Mundelein ESD 75	Mundelein
94	51.9	Elmhurst SD 205	Elmhurst
95	51.9	Leyden CHSD 212	Franklin Park
96	51.9	United Twp HSD 30	East Moline
97	51.9	Sycamore CUSD 427	Sycamore
98	51.9	Grayslake CCSD 46	Grayslake
99	51.9	CHSD 155	Crystal Lake
100	51.9	CHSD 218	Oak Lawn
101	51.9	Olympia CUSD 16	Stanford
102	51.9	Sandwich CUSD 430	Sandwich
103	51.9	CCSD 93	Bloomingdale
104	51.8	Kaneland CUSD 302	Maple Park
105	51.8	Ball Chatham CUSD 5	Chatham
106	51.8	Champaign CUSD 4	Champaign
107	51.8	Rochelle CCSD 231	Rochelle
108	51.8	Schaumburg CCSD 54	Schaumburg
109	51.8	Wauconda CUSD 118	Wauconda
110	51.8	North Chicago SD 187	North Chicago
111	51.8	Northbrook SD 28	Northbrook
112	51.8	Plainfield SD 202	Plainfield
113	51.8	Triad CUSD 2	Troy
114	51.8	Crete Monee CUSD 201u	Crete

115	51.8	Streator ESD 44	Streator
116	51.7	Eureka CUD 140	Eureka
117	51.7	Lisle CUSD 202	Lisle
118	51.7	Harvey SD 152	Harvey
119	51.7	Naperville CUSD 203	Naperville
120	51.7	North Shore SD 112	Highland Park
121	51.7	Kildeer Countryside CCSD 96	Buffalo Grove
122	51.7	South Holland SD 151	South Holland
123	51.7	North Boone CUSD 200	Poplar Grove
124	51.7	Lake Zurich CUSD 95	Lake Zurich
125	51.7	Bellwood SD 88	Bellwood
126	51.7	Harlem Ud 122	Loves Park
127	51.6	Lake Forest CHSD 115	Lake Forest
128	51.6	Country Club Hls SD 160	Country Club Hls
129	51.6	Oak Park ESD 97	Oak Park
130	51.6	J S Morton HSD 201	Cicero
131	51.6	Du Page HSD 88	Villa Park
132	51.6	Berwyn North SD 98	Berwyn
133	51.6	Tinley Park CCSD 146	Tinley Park
134	51.6	Skokie SD 68	Skokie
135	51.5	Glenview CCSD 34	Glenview
136	51.5	Lyons Twp HSD 204	La Grange
137	51.5	Midlothian SD 143	Midlothian
138	51.5	Bradley Bourbonnais CHSD 307	Bradley
139	51.5	Highland CUSD 5	Highland
140	51.5	Geneva CUSD 304	Geneva
141	51.5	Marquardt SD 15	Glendale Hgts
142	51.5	Massac UD 1	Metropolis
143	51.5	Edwardsville CUSD 7	Edwardsville
144	51.5	Batavia USD 101	Batavia
145	51.5	School District U-46	Elgin
146	51.5	Lyons SD 103	Lyons
147	51.5	Maywood-Melrose Park-Broadview 89	Melrose Park
148	51.5	Round Lake CUSD 116	Round Lake
149	51.5	O Fallon Twp HSD 203	Ofallon
150	51.4	Genoa Kingston CUSD 424	Genoa
151	51.4	Indian Prairie CUSD 204	Aurora
152	51.4	Millburn CCSD 24	Wadsworth
153	51.4	Palatine CCSD 15	Palatine
154	51.4	Rantoul City SD 137	Rantoul
155	51.4	Harrisburg CUSD 3	Harrisburg
156	51.4	Quincy SD 172	Quincy
157	51.4	Lansing SD 158	Lansing
158	51.4	Township HSD 211	Palatine
159	51.4	Jersey CUSD 100	Jerseyville
160	51.4	Beach Park CCSD 3	Beach Park
161	51.4	Waukegan CUSD 60	Waukegan
162	51.4	Morton CUSD 709	Morton
163	51.4	Skokie SD 69	Skokie
164	51.4	O Fallon CCSD 90	Ofallon
165	51.4	Kinnikinnick CCSD 131	Roscoe
166	51.4	Glenbard Twp HSD 87	Glen Ellyn
167	51.4	Kankakee SD 111	Kankakee
168	51.4	Northfield Twp HSD 225	Glenview
169	51.3	Flossmoor SD 161	Chicago Heights
170	51.3	Springfield SD 186	Springfield
171	51.3	Mclean County USD 5	Normal
172	51.3	Saint Charles CUSD 303	Saint Charles
173	51.3	Marion CUSD 2	Marion
174	51.3	Joliet Psd 86	Joliet
175	51.3	Monmouth-Roseville CUSD 238	Monmouth
176	51.3	Berkeley SD 87	Berkeley
177	51.3	Valley View CUSD 365u	Romeoville
178	51.3	Alton CUSD 11	Alton
179	51.3	Moline USD 40	Moline
180	51.3	CCSD 62	Des Plaines
181	51.3	Mount Vernon SD 80	Mount Vernon
182	51.3	CUSD 300	Carpentersville
183	51.2	Belvidere CUSD 100	Belvidere
184	51.2	Maine Township HSD 207	Park Ridge
185	51.2	Bensenville SD 2	Bensenville
186	51.2	Minooka CCSD 201	Minooka
187	51.2	CSD 158	Algonquin
188	51.2	Urbana SD 116	Urbana
189	51.2	Posen-Robbins ESD 143-5	Posen
190	51.2	Wheeling CCSD 21	Wheeling
191	51.2	Roxana CUSD 1	Roxana
192	51.2	Township HSD 214	Arlington Hgts
193	51.2	Argo CHSD 217	Summit
194	51.2	Sherrard CUSD 200	Sherrard
195	51.2	Mattoon CUSD 2	Mattoon
196	51.2	Sterling CUSD 5	Sterling
197	51.2	Woodridge SD 68	Woodridge
198	51.2	Johnsburg CUSD 12	Johnsburg
199	51.1	Charleston CUSD 1	Charleston
200	51.1	Aurora West USD 129	Aurora
201	51.1	Granite City CUSD 9	Granite City
202	51.1	Jacksonville SD 117	Jacksonville
203	51.1	Mascoutah CUD 19	Mascoutah
204	51.1	Dunlap CUSD 323	Dunlap
205	51.1	Rockford SD 205	Rockford
206	51.1	North Palos SD 117	Palos Hills
207	51.0	Frankfort CUSD 168	West Frankfort
208	51.0	Hinsdale Twp HSD 86	Hinsdale
209	51.0	Dolton SD 149	Calumet City
210	51.0	Lombard SD 44	Lombard
211	51.0	Manteno CUSD 5	Manteno
212	51.0	Homewood SD 153	Homewood
213	51.0	Evergreen Park ESD 124	Evergreen Park
214	51.0	Wilmette SD 39	Wilmette
215	51.0	West Chicago ESD 33	West Chicago
216	51.0	CHSD 128	Libertyville
217	51.0	Plano CUSD 88	Plano
218	51.0	Mount Zion CUSD 3	Mount Zion
219	51.0	CCSD 168	Sauk Village
220	50.9	Hillsboro CUSD 3	Hillsboro
221	50.9	Prairie-Hills ESD 144	Markham
222	50.9	Pekin PSD 108	Pekin
223	50.9	East Maine SD 63	Des Plaines
224	50.9	Arbor Park SD 145	Oak Forest
225	50.9	Zion ESD 6	Zion
226	50.9	West Harvey-Dixmoor PSD 147	Harvey
227	50.8	Libertyville SD 70	Libertyville
228	50.8	Lake Park CHSD 108	Roselle
229	50.8	Barrington CUSD 220	Barrington
230	50.8	Matteson ESD 162	Matteson
231	50.8	Prairie Central CUSD 8	Fairbury
232	50.8	Crystal Lake CCSD 47	Crystal Lake
233	50.8	Troy CCSD 30c	Plainfield
234	50.8	Niles Twp CHSD 219	Skokie
235	50.8	Murphysboro CUSD 186	Murphysboro
236	50.8	Aptakisic-Tripp CCSD 102	Buffalo Grove
237	50.7	Evanston CCSD 65	Evanston
238	50.7	Arlington Hgts SD 25	Arlington Hgts
239	50.7	Cons HSD 230	Orland Park
240	50.7	Aurora East USD 131	Aurora
241	50.7	ESD 159	Matteson
242	50.7	Rochester CUSD 3a	Rochester
243	50.7	Palos CCSD 118	Palos Park
244	50.7	Wabash CUSD 348	Mount Carmel
245	50.7	Glen Ellyn SD 41	Glen Ellyn
246	50.6	Evanston Twp HSD 202	Evanston
247	50.6	Forest Ridge SD 142	Oak Forest
248	50.6	Hawthorn CCSD 73	Vernon Hills
249	50.6	Cahokia CUSD 187	Cahokia
250	50.6	Lincolnshire-Prairieview SD 103	Lincolnshire
251	50.6	Macomb CUSD 185	Macomb
252	50.6	Peoria SD 150	Peoria
253	50.5	Alsip-Hazlgrn-Oaklwn SD 126	Alsip
254	50.5	Dixon USD 170	Dixon
255	50.5	Kewanee CUSD 229	Kewanee
256	50.5	Steger SD 194	Steger
257	50.5	Dekalb CUSD 428	De Kalb
258	50.4	Decatur SD 61	Decatur
259	50.4	Ottawa ESD 141	Ottawa
260	50.4	Belleville Twp HSD 201	Belleville
261	50.3	City of Chicago SD 299	Chicago
262	50.3	Freeport SD 145	Freeport
263	50.3	Oak Park-River Forest SD 200	Oak Park
264	50.3	Addison SD 4	Addison
265	50.3	Clinton CUSD 15	Clinton
266	50.3	Flora CUSD 35	Flora
267	50.3	Reed Custer CUSD 255u	Braidwood
268	50.2	Rich Twp HSD 227	Olympia Fields
269	50.2	Danville CCSD 118	Danville
270	50.2	Oak Lawn CHSD 229	Oak Lawn
271	50.2	CCSD 89	Glen Ellyn
272	50.2	Adlai E Stevenson HSD 125	Lincolnshire
273	50.2	Rock Island SD 41	Rock Island
274	50.2	Lincoln Way CHSD 210	New Lenox
275	50.1	Homewood Flossmoor CHSD 233	Flossmoor
276	50.1	Elmwood Park CUSD 401	Elmwood Park
277	50.1	Byron CUSD 226	Byron
278	50.1	Minooka CHSD 111	Minooka
279	50.1	Meridian CUSD 223	Stillman Valley
280	50.0	Park Forest SD 163	Park Forest
281	50.0	Queen Bee SD 16	Glendale Hgts
282	50.0	CHSD 99	Downers Grove
283	49.9	Hononegah Chd 207	Rockton
284	49.8	Summit Hill SD 161	Frankfort
285	49.8	Reavis Twp HSD 220	Burbank
286	49.8	Grant CHSD 124	Fox Lake
287	49.7	Mahomet-Seymour CUSD 3	Mahomet
288	49.7	Warren Twp HSD 121	Gages Lake
289	49.7	Zion-Benton Twp HSD 126	Zion
290	49.7	Carterville CUSD 5	Carterville
291	49.7	Burbank SD 111	Burbank
292	49.6	East St Louis SD 189	E Saint Louis
293	49.5	Coal City CUSD 1	Coal City
294	49.5	Bradley SD 61	Bradley
295	49.3	Pana CUSD 8	Pana
296	49.2	Pekin CSD 303	Pekin
297	49.2	Beardstown CUSD 15	Beardstown
298	49.2	Joliet Twp HSD 204	Joliet
299	49.1	Thornton Twp HSD 205	South Holland
300	49.0	Riverton CUSD 14	Riverton
301	48.8	Sparta CUSD 140	Sparta
302	48.7	Proviso Twp HSD 209	Forest Park
303	48.3	Herrin CUSD 4	Herrin
304	47.3	Paris-Union SD 95	Paris

Female Students

Rank	Percent	District Name	City
1	52.6	Paris-Union SD 95	Paris
2	51.6	Herrin CUSD 4	Herrin
3	51.2	Proviso Twp HSD 209	Forest Park
4	51.1	Sparta CUSD 140	Sparta
5	50.9	Riverton CUSD 14	Riverton
6	50.8	Thornton Twp HSD 205	South Holland
7	50.7	Joliet Twp HSD 204	Joliet
8	50.7	Beardstown CUSD 15	Beardstown
9	50.7	Pekin CSD 303	Pekin
10	50.6	Pana CUSD 8	Pana
11	50.4	Bradley SD 61	Bradley
12	50.4	Coal City CUSD 1	Coal City
13	50.3	East St Louis SD 189	E Saint Louis
14	50.2	Burbank SD 111	Burbank
15	50.2	Carterville CUSD 5	Carterville
16	50.2	Zion-Benton Twp HSD 126	Zion
17	50.2	Warren Twp HSD 121	Gages Lake
18	50.2	Mahomet-Seymour CUSD 3	Mahomet
19	50.1	Grant CHSD 124	Fox Lake
20	50.1	Reavis Twp HSD 220	Burbank
21	50.1	Summit Hill SD 161	Frankfort
22	50.0	Hononegah Chd 207	Rockton
23	49.9	CHSD 99	Downers Grove
24	49.9	Queen Bee SD 16	Glendale Hgts
25	49.9	Park Forest SD 163	Park Forest
26	49.8	Meridian CUSD 223	Stillman Valley
27	49.8	Minooka CHSD 111	Minooka
28	49.8	Byron CUSD 226	Byron
29	49.8	Elmwood Park CUSD 401	Elmwood Park
30	49.8	Homewood Flossmoor CHSD 233	Flossmoor
31	49.7	Lincoln Way CHSD 210	New Lenox
32	49.7	Rock Island SD 41	Rock Island
33	49.7	Adlai E Stevenson HSD 125	Lincolnshire
34	49.7	CCSD 89	Glen Ellyn
35	49.7	Oak Lawn CHSD 229	Oak Lawn
36	49.7	Danville CCSD 118	Danville
37	49.7	Rich Twp HSD 227	Olympia Fields
38	49.6	Reed Custer CUSD 255u	Braidwood
39	49.6	Flora CUSD 35	Flora
40	49.6	Clinton CUSD 15	Clinton
41	49.6	Addison SD 4	Addison
42	49.6	Oak Park-River Forest SD 200	Oak Park
43	49.6	Freeport SD 145	Freeport
44	49.6	City of Chicago SD 299	Chicago
45	49.5	Belleville Twp HSD 201	Belleville
46	49.5	Ottawa ESD 141	Ottawa
47	49.5	Decatur SD 61	Decatur
48	49.4	Dekalb CUSD 428	De Kalb
49	49.4	Steger SD 194	Steger
50	49.4	Kewanee CUSD 229	Kewanee
51	49.4	Dixon USD 170	Dixon
52	49.4	Alsip-Hazlgrn-Oaklwn SD 126	Alsip
53	49.3	Peoria SD 150	Peoria
54	49.3	Macomb CUSD 185	Macomb
55	49.3	Lincolnshire-Prairieview SD 103	Lincolnshire
56	49.3	Cahokia CUSD 187	Cahokia
57	49.3	Hawthorn CCSD 73	Vernon Hills
58	49.3	Forest Ridge SD 142	Oak Forest
59	49.3	Evanston Twp HSD 202	Evanston
60	49.2	Glen Ellyn SD 41	Glen Ellyn
61	49.2	Wabash CUSD 348	Mount Carmel
62	49.2	Palos CCSD 118	Palos Park
63	49.2	Rochester CUSD 3a	Rochester
64	49.2	ESD 159	Matteson
65	49.2	Aurora East USD 131	Aurora
66	49.2	Cons HSD 230	Orland Park

Rank	Percent	District Name	City
67	49.2	Arlington Hgts SD 25	Arlington Hgts
68	49.2	Evanston CCSD 65	Evanston
69	49.1	Aptakisic-Tripp CCSD 102	Buffalo Grove
70	49.1	Murphysboro CUSD 186	Murphysboro
71	49.1	Niles Twp CHSD 219	Skokie
72	49.1	Troy CCSD 30c	Plainfield
73	49.1	Crystal Lake CCSD 47	Crystal Lake
74	49.1	Prairie Central CUSD 8	Fairbury
75	49.1	Matteson ESD 162	Matteson
76	49.1	Barrington CUSD 220	Barrington
77	49.1	Lake Park CHSD 108	Roselle
78	49.1	Libertyville SD 70	Libertyville
79	49.0	West Harvey-Dixmoor PSD 147	Harvey
80	49.0	Zion ESD 6	Zion
81	49.0	Arbor Park SD 145	Oak Forest
82	49.0	East Maine SD 63	Des Plaines
83	49.0	Pekin PSD 108	Pekin
84	49.0	Prairie-Hills ESD 144	Markham
85	49.0	Hillsboro CUSD 3	Hillsboro
86	48.9	CCSD 168	Sauk Village
87	48.9	Mount Zion CUSD 3	Mount Zion
88	48.9	Plano CUSD 88	Plano
89	48.9	CHSD 128	Libertyville
90	48.9	West Chicago ESD 33	West Chicago
91	48.9	Wilmette SD 39	Wilmette
92	48.9	Evergreen Park ESD 124	Evergreen Park
93	48.9	Homewood SD 153	Homewood
94	48.9	Manteno CUSD 5	Manteno
95	48.9	Lombard SD 44	Lombard
96	48.9	Dolton SD 149	Calumet City
97	48.9	Hinsdale Twp HSD 86	Hinsdale
98	48.9	Frankfort CUSD 168	West Frankfort
99	48.8	North Palos SD 117	Palos Hills
100	48.8	Rockford SD 205	Rockford
101	48.8	Dunlap CUSD 323	Dunlap
102	48.8	Mascoutah CUD 19	Mascoutah
103	48.8	Jacksonville SD 117	Jacksonville
104	48.8	Granite City CUSD 9	Granite City
105	48.8	Aurora West USD 129	Aurora
106	48.8	Charleston CUSD 1	Charleston
107	48.8	Johnsburg CUSD 12	Johnsburg
108	48.7	Woodridge SD 68	Woodridge
109	48.7	Sterling CUSD 5	Sterling
110	48.7	Mattoon CUSD 2	Mattoon
111	48.7	Sherrard CUSD 200	Sherrard
112	48.7	Argo CHSD 217	Summit
113	48.7	Township HSD 214	Arlington Hgts
114	48.7	Roxana CUSD 1	Roxana
115	48.7	Wheeling CCSD 21	Wheeling
116	48.7	Posen-Robbins ESD 143-5	Posen
117	48.7	Urbana SD 116	Urbana
118	48.7	CSD 158	Algonquin
119	48.7	Minooka CCSD 201	Minooka
120	48.7	Bensenville SD 2	Bensenville
121	48.7	Maine Township HSD 207	Park Ridge
122	48.7	Belvidere CUSD 100	Belvidere
123	48.6	CUSD 300	Carpentersville
124	48.6	Mount Vernon SD 80	Mount Vernon
125	48.6	CCSD 62	Des Plaines
126	48.6	Moline USD 40	Moline
127	48.6	Alton CUSD 11	Alton
128	48.6	Valley View CUSD 365u	Romeoville
129	48.6	Berkeley SD 87	Berkeley
130	48.6	Monmouth-Roseville CUSD 238	Monmouth
131	48.6	Joliet Psd 86	Joliet
132	48.6	Marion CUSD 2	Marion
133	48.6	Saint Charles CUSD 303	Saint Charles
134	48.6	Mclean County USD 5	Normal
135	48.6	Springfield SD 186	Springfield
136	48.6	Flossmoor SD 161	Chicago Heights
137	48.5	Northfield Twp HSD 225	Glenview
138	48.5	Kankakee SD 111	Kankakee
139	48.5	Glenbard Twp HSD 87	Glen Ellyn
140	48.5	Kinnikinnick CCSD 131	Roscoe
141	48.5	O Fallon CCSD 90	Ofallon
142	48.5	Skokie SD 69	Skokie
143	48.5	Morton CUSD 709	Morton
144	48.5	Waukegan CUSD 60	Waukegan
145	48.5	Beach Park CCSD 3	Beach Park
146	48.5	Jersey CUSD 100	Jerseyville
147	48.5	Township HSD 211	Palatine
148	48.5	Lansing SD 158	Lansing
149	48.5	Quincy SD 172	Quincy
150	48.5	Harrisburg CUSD 3	Harrisburg
151	48.5	Rantoul City SD 137	Rantoul
152	48.5	Palatine CCSD 15	Palatine
153	48.5	Millburn CCSD 24	Wadsworth
154	48.5	Indian Prairie CUSD 204	Aurora
155	48.5	Genoa Kingston CUSD 424	Genoa
156	48.4	O Fallon Twp HSD 203	Ofallon
157	48.4	Round Lake CUSD 116	Round Lake
158	48.4	Maywood-Melrose Park-Broadview 89	Melrose Park
159	48.4	Lyons SD 103	Lyons
160	48.4	School District U-46	Elgin
161	48.4	Batavia USD 101	Batavia
162	48.4	Edwardsville CUSD 7	Edwardsville
163	48.4	Massac UD 1	Metropolis
164	48.4	Marquardt SD 15	Glendale Hgts
165	48.4	Geneva CUSD 304	Geneva
166	48.4	Highland CUSD 5	Highland
167	48.4	Bradley Bourbonnais CHSD 307	Bradley
168	48.4	Midlothian SD 143	Midlothian
169	48.4	Lyons Twp HSD 204	La Grange
170	48.4	Glenview CCSD 34	Glenview
171	48.3	Skokie SD 68	Skokie
172	48.3	Tinley Park CCSD 146	Tinley Park
173	48.3	Berwyn North SD 98	Berwyn
174	48.3	Du Page HSD 88	Villa Park
175	48.3	J S Morton HSD 201	Cicero
176	48.3	Oak Park ESD 97	Oak Park
177	48.3	Country Club Hls SD 160	Country Club Hls
178	48.3	Lake Forest CHSD 115	Lake Forest
179	48.2	Harlem Ud 122	Loves Park
180	48.2	Bellwood SD 88	Bellwood
181	48.2	Lake Zurich CUSD 95	Lake Zurich
182	48.2	North Boone CUSD 200	Poplar Grove
183	48.2	South Holland SD 151	South Holland
184	48.2	Kildeer Countryside CCSD 96	Buffalo Grove
185	48.2	North Shore SD 112	Highland Park
186	48.2	Naperville CUSD 203	Naperville
187	48.2	Harvey SD 152	Harvey
188	48.2	Lisle CUSD 202	Lisle
189	48.2	Eureka CUD 140	Eureka
190	48.1	Streator ESD 44	Streator
191	48.1	Crete Monee CUSD 201u	Crete
192	48.1	Triad CUSD 2	Troy
193	48.1	Plainfield SD 202	Plainfield
194	48.1	Northbrook SD 28	Northbrook
195	48.1	North Chicago SD 187	North Chicago
196	48.1	Wauconda CUSD 118	Wauconda
197	48.1	Schaumburg CCSD 54	Schaumburg
198	48.1	Rochelle CCSD 231	Rochelle
199	48.1	Champaign CUSD 4	Champaign
200	48.1	Ball Chatham CUSD 5	Chatham
201	48.1	Kaneland CUSD 302	Maple Park
202	48.0	CCSD 93	Bloomingdale
203	48.0	Sandwich CUSD 430	Sandwich
204	48.0	Olympia CUSD 16	Stanford
205	48.0	CHSD 218	Oak Lawn
206	48.0	CHSD 155	Crystal Lake
207	48.0	Grayslake CCSD 46	Grayslake
208	48.0	Sycamore CUSD 427	Sycamore
209	48.0	United Twp HSD 30	East Moline
210	48.0	Leyden CHSD 212	Franklin Park
211	48.0	Elmhurst SD 205	Elmhurst
212	48.0	Mundelein ESD 75	Mundelein
213	47.9	Bremen CHSD 228	Midlothian
214	47.9	Fenton CHSD 100	Bensenville
215	47.9	Bloomington SD 87	Bloomington
216	47.9	Chicago Heights SD 170	Chicago Heights
217	47.9	Mc Henry CHSD 156	Mchenry
218	47.9	CHSD 117	Lake Villa
219	47.9	West Carroll CUSD 314	Thomson
220	47.8	Kirby SD 140	Tinley Park
221	47.8	Cary CCSD 26	Cary
222	47.8	Fremont SD 79	Mundelein
223	47.8	New Lenox SD 122	New Lenox
224	47.8	Thornton Fractional Twp HSD 215	Calumet City
225	47.8	CUSD 200	Wheaton
226	47.8	La Grange SD 102	La Grange Park
227	47.8	CUSD 201	Westmont
228	47.8	Lemont-Bromberek CSD 113a	Lemont
229	47.8	Ottawa Twp HSD 140	Ottawa
230	47.8	Lockport Twp HSD 205	Lockport
231	47.8	Yorkville CUSD 115	Yorkville
232	47.8	Nippersink SD 2	Richmond
233	47.8	Columbia CUSD 4	Columbia
234	47.7	Cicero SD 99	Cicero
235	47.7	School District 45 Dupage County	Villa Park
236	47.7	Central CUSD 301	Burlington
237	47.7	Mokena SD 159	Mokena
238	47.7	Berwyn South SD 100	Berwyn
239	47.7	Community CSD 59	Arlington Hgts
240	47.6	Vandalia CUSD 203	Vandalia
241	47.6	Southwestern CUSD 9	Piasa
242	47.6	Ridgeland SD 122	Oak Lawn
243	47.6	Peotone CUSD 207u	Peotone
244	47.6	Lake Forest SD 67	Lake Forest
245	47.6	Harvard CUSD 50	Harvard
246	47.6	Park Ridge CCSD 64	Park Ridge
247	47.6	Mundelein Cons HSD 120	Mundelein
248	47.6	Wilmington CUSD 209u	Wilmington
249	47.5	Litchfield CUSD 12	Litchfield
250	47.5	Monticello CUSD 25	Monticello
251	47.5	Deerfield SD 109	Deerfield
252	47.5	Paxton-Buckley-Loda CUD 10	Paxton
253	47.5	Downers Grove Gsd 58	Downers Grove
254	47.5	Summit SD 104	Summit
255	47.4	East Peoria SD 86	East Peoria
256	47.4	Frankfort CCSD 157c	Frankfort
257	47.4	Homer CCSD 33c	Homer Glen
258	47.4	Woodstock CUSD 200	Woodstock
259	47.4	Woodland CCSD 50	Gurnee
260	47.4	Geneseo CUSD 228	Geneseo
261	47.4	Indian Springs SD 109	Justice
262	47.4	East Moline SD 37	East Moline
263	47.4	Lake Villa CCSD 41	Lake Villa
264	47.4	Collinsville CUSD 10	Collinsville
265	47.4	Oswego CUSD 308	Oswego
266	47.3	Belleville SD 118	Belleville
267	47.3	Orland SD 135	Orland Park
268	47.3	New Trier Twp HSD 203	Northfield
269	47.3	Mount Prospect SD 57	Mount Prospect
270	47.3	Cook County SD 130	Blue Island
271	47.3	Bethalto CUSD 8	Bethalto
272	47.2	Canton Union SD 66	Canton
273	47.2	Antioch CCSD 34	Antioch
274	47.2	Robinson CUSD 2	Robinson
275	47.2	Dolton SD 148	Riverdale
276	47.2	Bloom Twp HSD 206	Chicago Heights
277	47.2	Mchenry CCSD 15	Mchenry
278	47.2	Darien SD 61	Darien
279	47.1	Gurnee SD 56	Gurnee
280	47.1	Oregon CUSD 220	Oregon
281	47.1	River Trails SD 26	Mount Prospect
282	47.0	Taylorville CUSD 3	Taylorville
283	47.0	Winnetka SD 36	Winnetka
284	47.0	Oak Lawn-Hometown SD 123	Oak Lawn
285	47.0	Galesburg CUSD 205	Galesburg
286	46.9	Channahon SD 17	Channahon
287	46.9	East Richland CUSD 1	Olney
288	46.9	Effingham CUSD 40	Effingham
289	46.9	Twp HSD 113	Highland Park
290	46.8	Tolono CUSD 7	Tolono
291	46.8	Keeneyville SD 20	Hanover Park
292	46.7	Bourbonnais SD 53	Bourbonnais
293	46.5	CHSD 94	West Chicago
294	46.5	Mannheim SD 83	Franklin Park
295	46.5	Bond County CUSD 2	Greenville
296	46.5	Grayslake CHSD 127	Grayslake
297	46.5	IL Valley Central USD 321	Chillicothe
298	46.4	Waterloo CUSD 5	Waterloo
299	46.4	Winnebago CUSD 323	Winnebago
300	46.3	Carlinville CUSD 1	Carlinville
301	46.2	Hinsdale CCSD 181	Westmont
302	46.0	Will County SD 92	Lockport
303	46.0	Herscher CUSD 2	Herscher
304	8.6	Corrections SD 428 Dept of	Springfield

Individual Education Program Students

Rank	Percent	District Name	City
1	27.7	Mount Vernon SD 80	Mount Vernon
2	25.6	Charleston CUSD 1	Charleston
2	25.6	Evergreen Park ESD 124	Evergreen Park
4	24.7	Corrections SD 428 Dept of	Springfield
5	24.3	Murphysboro CUSD 186	Murphysboro
6	23.8	Peoria SD 150	Peoria
7	23.5	Frankfort CUSD 168	West Frankfort
8	23.1	Streator ESD 44	Streator
9	23.0	Belleville SD 118	Belleville
10	22.7	Crete Monee CUSD 201u	Crete
11	22.6	Robinson CUSD 2	Robinson
12	22.5	Jacksonville SD 117	Jacksonville
13	22.2	Flora CUSD 35	Flora
14	22.0	Roxana CUSD 1	Roxana
14	22.0	Urbana SD 116	Urbana
16	21.9	Alton CUSD 11	Alton
17	21.8	Lake Villa CCSD 41	Lake Villa
18	21.7	Pekin PSD 108	Pekin

Rank	Value	District	City
19	21.4	Riverton CUSD 14	Riverton
20	21.3	Reed Custer CUSD 255u	Braidwood
21	21.1	Cahokia CUSD 187	Cahokia
21	21.1	Mattoon CUSD 2	Mattoon
23	20.9	Olympia CUSD 16	Stanford
23	20.9	Paris-Union SD 95	Paris
25	20.8	Mchenry CCSD 15	Mchenry
26	20.5	Bethalto CUSD 8	Bethalto
26	20.5	Bradley SD 61	Bradley
28	20.2	Northbrook SD 28	Northbrook
28	20.2	Zion ESD 6	Zion
30	20.1	Harrisburg CUSD 3	Harrisburg
30	20.1	Tolono CUSD 7	Tolono
32	19.9	Cary CCSD 26	Cary
32	19.9	Deerfield SD 109	Deerfield
32	19.9	Elmwood Park CUSD 401	Elmwood Park
32	19.9	Prairie Central CUSD 8	Fairbury
36	19.8	Arlington Hgts SD 25	Arlington Hgts
37	19.6	Ridgeland SD 122	Oak Lawn
38	19.5	East Peoria SD 86	East Peoria
38	19.5	Plano CUSD 88	Plano
38	19.5	Skokie SD 68	Skokie
38	19.5	West Carroll CUSD 314	Thomson
42	19.4	Beardstown CUSD 15	Beardstown
42	19.4	Channahon SD 17	Channahon
42	19.4	Marion CUSD 2	Marion
42	19.4	Springfield SD 186	Springfield
42	19.4	Wilmington CUSD 209u	Wilmington
47	19.3	Lincolnshire-Prairieview SD 103	Lincolnshire
47	19.3	Proviso Twp HSD 209	Forest Park
47	19.3	Winnetka SD 36	Winnetka
50	19.2	Antioch CCSD 34	Antioch
50	19.2	Rock Island SD 41	Rock Island
52	18.9	Herrin CUSD 4	Herrin
52	18.9	Keeneyville SD 20	Hanover Park
52	18.9	Macomb CUSD 185	Macomb
52	18.9	Midlothian SD 143	Midlothian
56	18.8	Kewanee CUSD 229	Kewanee
57	18.7	Bond County CUSD 2	Greenville
57	18.7	Champaign CUSD 4	Champaign
57	18.7	Joliet Twp HSD 204	Joliet
57	18.7	Ottawa Twp HSD 140	Ottawa
61	18.6	Cook County SD 130	Blue Island
61	18.6	Fremont SD 79	Mundelein
61	18.6	La Grange SD 102	La Grange Park
61	18.6	Lombard SD 44	Lombard
61	18.6	Park Ridge CCSD 64	Park Ridge
61	18.6	Tinley Park CCSD 146	Tinley Park
67	18.5	Evanston CCSD 65	Evanston
68	18.4	CCSD 62	Des Plaines
69	18.3	Carterville CUSD 5	Carterville
69	18.3	Clinton CUSD 15	Clinton
69	18.3	East Moline SD 37	East Moline
69	18.3	IL Valley Central USD 321	Chillicothe
69	18.3	Pana CUSD 8	Pana
69	18.3	Sparta CUSD 140	Sparta
69	18.3	Taylorville CUSD 3	Taylorville
76	18.2	Grant CHSD 124	Fox Lake
76	18.2	Ottawa ESD 141	Ottawa
76	18.2	Wabash CUSD 348	Mount Carmel
79	18.1	Granite City CUSD 9	Granite City
80	18.0	Harvard CUSD 50	Harvard
80	18.0	Mc Henry CHSD 156	Mchenry
80	18.0	Steger SD 194	Steger
83	17.9	Homewood SD 153	Homewood
83	17.9	Kankakee SD 111	Kankakee
83	17.9	Oak Park ESD 97	Oak Park
83	17.9	Paxton-Buckley-Loda CUD 10	Paxton
87	17.8	Alsip-Hazlgrn-Oaklwn SD 126	Alsip
87	17.8	Summit SD 104	Summit
87	17.8	United Twp HSD 30	East Moline
90	17.7	Aptakisic-Tripp CCSD 102	Buffalo Grove
90	17.7	Sterling CUSD 5	Sterling
92	17.6	Rochelle CCSD 231	Rochelle
93	17.5	Canton Union SD 66	Canton
93	17.5	Effingham CUSD 40	Effingham
93	17.5	River Trails SD 26	Mount Prospect
96	17.4	Mundelein ESD 75	Mundelein
97	17.3	Bloomington SD 87	Bloomington
97	17.3	Massac UD 1	Metropolis
97	17.3	Park Forest SD 163	Park Forest
97	17.3	Prairie-Hills ESD 144	Markham
97	17.3	Southwestern CUSD 9	Piasa
102	17.2	Collinsville CUSD 10	Collinsville
102	17.2	Lisle CUSD 202	Lisle
102	17.2	Mount Prospect SD 57	Mount Prospect
105	17.1	Kildeer Countryside CCSD 96	Buffalo Grove
105	17.1	Manteno CUSD 5	Manteno
105	17.1	Rich Twp HSD 227	Olympia Fields
108	17.0	Belleville Twp HSD 201	Belleville
108	17.0	Decatur SD 61	Decatur
108	17.0	Lake Forest SD 67	Lake Forest
108	17.0	Monmouth-Roseville CUSD 238	Monmouth
108	17.0	Palos CCSD 118	Palos Park
113	16.9	Mannheim SD 83	Franklin Park
113	16.9	Quincy SD 172	Quincy
113	16.9	West Harvey-Dixmoor PSD 147	Harvey
116	16.8	East St Louis SD 189	E Saint Louis
116	16.8	North Chicago SD 187	North Chicago
116	16.8	Wheeling CCSD 21	Wheeling
119	16.7	CHSD 218	Oak Lawn
119	16.7	Chicago Heights SD 170	Chicago Heights
119	16.7	Danville CCSD 118	Danville
119	16.7	Triad CUSD 2	Troy
119	16.7	Winnebago CUSD 323	Winnebago
124	16.6	CUSD 300	Carpentersville
124	16.6	Highland CUSD 5	Highland
124	16.6	Litchfield CUSD 12	Litchfield
124	16.6	Nippersink SD 2	Richmond
128	16.5	CUSD 201	Westmont
128	16.5	Pekin CSD 303	Pekin
130	16.4	Beach Park CCSD 3	Beach Park
130	16.4	Homer CCSD 33c	Homer Glen
130	16.4	Johnsburg CUSD 12	Johnsburg
130	16.4	Joliet Psd 86	Joliet
130	16.4	Twp HSD 113	Highland Park
130	16.4	West Chicago ESD 33	West Chicago
130	16.4	Woodridge SD 68	Woodridge
130	16.4	Zion-Benton Twp HSD 126	Zion
138	16.3	CUSD 200	Wheaton
138	16.3	Fenton CHSD 100	Bensenville
138	16.3	Forest Ridge SD 142	Oak Forest
138	16.3	Troy CCSD 30c	Plainfield
142	16.2	Byron CUSD 226	Byron
142	16.2	CCSD 93	Bloomingdale
142	16.2	O Fallon CCSD 90	Ofallon
142	16.2	Woodland CCSD 50	Gurnee
146	16.1	Addison SD 4	Addison
146	16.1	Arbor Park SD 145	Oak Forest
146	16.1	Downers Grove Gsd 58	Downers Grove
146	16.1	Galesburg CUSD 205	Galesburg
146	16.1	Grayslake CCSD 46	Grayslake
146	16.1	Wauconda CUSD 118	Wauconda
152	16.0	Oak Lawn-Hometown SD 123	Oak Lawn
152	16.0	Oak Park-River Forest SD 200	Oak Park
154	15.9	School District 45 Dupage County	Villa Park
155	15.8	Berkeley SD 87	Berkeley
155	15.8	Edwardsville CUSD 7	Edwardsville
155	15.8	Jersey CUSD 100	Jerseyville
155	15.8	Lake Forest CHSD 115	Lake Forest
155	15.8	Matteson ESD 162	Matteson
155	15.8	Moline USD 40	Moline
155	15.8	Orland SD 135	Orland Park
155	15.8	Schaumburg CCSD 54	Schaumburg
155	15.8	Yorkville CUSD 115	Yorkville
164	15.7	Hillsboro CUSD 3	Hillsboro
164	15.7	Sandwich CUSD 430	Sandwich
166	15.6	Evanston Twp HSD 202	Evanston
166	15.6	New Trier Twp HSD 203	Northfield
168	15.5	Bourbonnais SD 53	Bourbonnais
168	15.5	Carlinville CUSD 1	Carlinville
168	15.5	Mascoutah CUD 19	Mascoutah
168	15.5	Will County SD 92	Lockport
172	15.4	Berwyn South SD 100	Berwyn
172	15.4	Lyons SD 103	Lyons
172	15.4	Mclean County USD 5	Normal
172	15.4	Niles Twp CHSD 219	Skokie
172	15.4	North Shore SD 112	Highland Park
172	15.4	Rantoul City SD 137	Rantoul
172	15.4	Rochester CUSD 3a	Rochester
172	15.4	Round Lake CUSD 116	Round Lake
180	15.3	Bellwood SD 88	Bellwood
180	15.3	ESD 159	Matteson
180	15.3	Glenview CCSD 34	Glenview
180	15.3	Harlem Ud 122	Loves Park
180	15.3	Maine Township HSD 207	Park Ridge
180	15.3	Morton CUSD 709	Morton
180	15.3	Vandalia CUSD 203	Vandalia
187	15.2	Bloom Twp HSD 206	Chicago Heights
188	15.1	CHSD 117	Lake Villa
188	15.1	Dixon USD 170	Dixon
188	15.1	East Richland CUSD 1	Olney
188	15.1	Lansing SD 158	Lansing
188	15.1	Woodstock CUSD 200	Woodstock
193	15.0	Barrington CUSD 220	Barrington
193	15.0	Darien SD 61	Darien
193	15.0	Leyden CHSD 212	Franklin Park
193	15.0	Minooka CCSD 201	Minooka
193	15.0	Oregon CUSD 220	Oregon
198	14.8	Kinnikinnick CCSD 131	Roscoe
199	14.6	East Maine SD 63	Des Plaines
199	14.6	New Lenox SD 122	New Lenox
199	14.6	Wilmette SD 39	Wilmette
202	14.5	Central CUSD 301	Burlington
202	14.5	Elmhurst SD 205	Elmhurst
202	14.5	Kirby SD 140	Tinley Park
205	14.4	Bradley Bourbonnais CHSD 307	Bradley
205	14.4	CCSD 89	Glen Ellyn
205	14.4	Coal City CUSD 1	Coal City
205	14.4	Mundelein Cons HSD 120	Mundelein
205	14.4	Summit Hill SD 161	Frankfort
210	14.3	Aurora West USD 129	Aurora
210	14.3	Eureka CUD 140	Eureka
210	14.3	Waterloo CUSD 5	Waterloo
210	14.3	Waukegan CUSD 60	Waukegan
214	14.2	Burbank SD 111	Burbank
214	14.2	CCSD 168	Sauk Village
214	14.2	Country Club Hls SD 160	Country Club Hls
214	14.2	Lake Zurich CUSD 95	Lake Zurich
214	14.2	Rockford SD 205	Rockford
214	14.2	Sherrard CUSD 200	Sherrard
214	14.2	Thornton Fractional Twp HSD 215	Calumet City
221	14.1	Bensenville SD 2	Bensenville
221	14.1	Harvey SD 152	Harvey
221	14.1	Valley View CUSD 365u	Romeoville
224	14.0	Freeport SD 145	Freeport
225	13.9	Frankfort CCSD 157c	Frankfort
225	13.9	Gurnee SD 56	Gurnee
225	13.9	Hinsdale CCSD 181	Westmont
225	13.9	Millburn CCSD 24	Wadsworth
229	13.8	Adlai E Stevenson HSD 125	Lincolnshire
229	13.8	Du Page HSD 88	Villa Park
229	13.8	Hawthorn CCSD 73	Vernon Hills
229	13.8	North Boone CUSD 200	Poplar Grove
229	13.8	Oswego CUSD 308	Oswego
234	13.7	Skokie SD 69	Skokie
235	13.6	Aurora East USD 131	Aurora
235	13.6	CHSD 99	Downers Grove
235	13.6	Crystal Lake CCSD 47	Crystal Lake
235	13.6	Glen Ellyn SD 41	Glen Ellyn
235	13.6	South Holland SD 151	South Holland
240	13.4	Ball Chatham CUSD 5	Chatham
240	13.4	CHSD 155	Crystal Lake
240	13.4	Geneva CUSD 304	Geneva
240	13.4	Mokena SD 159	Mokena
244	13.3	Bremen CHSD 228	Midlothian
245	13.2	Mahomet-Seymour CUSD 3	Mahomet
245	13.2	Monticello CUSD 25	Monticello
245	13.2	Palatine CCSD 15	Palatine
245	13.2	Plainfield SD 202	Plainfield
249	13.1	Kaneland CUSD 302	Maple Park
249	13.1	Saint Charles CUSD 303	Saint Charles
251	13.0	Cicero SD 99	Cicero
251	13.0	Community CSD 59	Arlington Hgts
251	13.0	North Palos SD 117	Palos Hills
254	12.9	Township HSD 214	Arlington Hgts
255	12.8	Belvidere CUSD 100	Belvidere
255	12.8	CHSD 128	Libertyville
255	12.8	City of Chicago SD 299	Chicago
255	12.8	Grayslake CHSD 127	Grayslake
255	12.8	Queen Bee SD 16	Glendale Hgts
260	12.7	Dekalb CUSD 428	De Kalb
260	12.7	School District U-46	Elgin
262	12.6	Berwyn North SD 98	Berwyn
262	12.6	Glenbard Twp HSD 87	Glen Ellyn
262	12.6	Lake Park CHSD 108	Roselle
262	12.6	Thornton Twp HSD 205	South Holland
262	12.6	Warren Twp HSD 121	Gages Lake
267	12.5	Naperville CUSD 203	Naperville
267	12.5	Peotone CUSD 207u	Peotone
269	12.4	CSD 158	Algonquin
269	12.4	Maywood-Melrose Park-Broadview 89	Melrose Park
271	12.3	Argo CHSD 217	Summit
271	12.3	Dolton SD 149	Calumet City
271	12.3	Hononegah Chd 207	Rockton
271	12.3	Indian Prairie CUSD 204	Aurora
271	12.3	Lockport Twp HSD 205	Lockport
271	12.3	Meridian CUSD 223	Stillman Valley
277	12.2	Geneseo CUSD 228	Geneseo
277	12.2	Township HSD 211	Palatine
279	11.9	Batavia USD 101	Batavia

279	11.9	Dolton SD 148	Riverdale
279	11.9	Genoa Kingston CUSD 424	Genoa
279	11.9	Homewood Flossmoor CHSD 233	Flossmoor
283	11.8	Columbia CUSD 4	Columbia
283	11.8	Herscher CUSD 2	Herscher
283	11.8	Northfield Twp HSD 225	Glenview
286	11.6	Lyons Twp HSD 204	La Grange
287	11.5	Sycamore CUSD 427	Sycamore
288	11.4	J S Morton HSD 201	Cicero
288	11.4	Minooka CHSD 111	Minooka
290	11.1	Cons HSD 230	Orland Park
290	11.1	Posen-Robbins ESD 143-5	Posen
292	11.0	Flossmoor SD 161	Chicago Heights
292	11.0	Indian Springs SD 109	Justice
292	11.0	Oak Lawn CHSD 229	Oak Lawn
295	10.9	CHSD 94	West Chicago
296	10.4	Lincoln Way CHSD 210	New Lenox
296	10.4	Marquardt SD 15	Glendale Hgts
298	10.3	Hinsdale Twp HSD 86	Hinsdale
299	10.0	Dunlap CUSD 323	Dunlap
300	9.7	Mount Zion CUSD 3	Mount Zion
301	9.1	Lemont-Bromberek CSD 113a	Lemont
302	9.0	Libertyville SD 70	Libertyville
302	9.0	Reavis Twp HSD 220	Burbank
304	8.8	O Fallon Twp HSD 203	Ofallon

English Language Learner Students

Rank	Percent	District Name	City
1	n/a	Addison SD 4	Addison
1	n/a	Adlai E Stevenson HSD 125	Lincolnshire
1	n/a	Alsip-Hazlgrn-Oaklwn SD 126	Alsip
1	n/a	Alton CUSD 11	Alton
1	n/a	Antioch CCSD 34	Antioch
1	n/a	Aptakisic-Tripp CCSD 102	Buffalo Grove
1	n/a	Arbor Park SD 145	Oak Forest
1	n/a	Argo CHSD 217	Summit
1	n/a	Arlington Hgts SD 25	Arlington Hgts
1	n/a	Aurora East USD 131	Aurora
1	n/a	Aurora West USD 129	Aurora
1	n/a	Ball Chatham CUSD 5	Chatham
1	n/a	Barrington CUSD 220	Barrington
1	n/a	Batavia USD 101	Batavia
1	n/a	Beach Park CCSD 3	Beach Park
1	n/a	Beardstown CUSD 15	Beardstown
1	n/a	Belleville SD 118	Belleville
1	n/a	Belleville Twp HSD 201	Belleville
1	n/a	Bellwood SD 88	Bellwood
1	n/a	Belvidere CUSD 100	Belvidere
1	n/a	Bensenville SD 2	Bensenville
1	n/a	Berkeley SD 87	Berkeley
1	n/a	Berwyn North SD 98	Berwyn
1	n/a	Berwyn South SD 100	Berwyn
1	n/a	Bethalto CUSD 8	Bethalto
1	n/a	Bloom Twp HSD 206	Chicago Heights
1	n/a	Bloomington SD 87	Bloomington
1	n/a	Bond County CUSD 2	Greenville
1	n/a	Bourbonnais SD 53	Bourbonnais
1	n/a	Bradley Bourbonnais CHSD 307	Bradley
1	n/a	Bradley SD 61	Bradley
1	n/a	Bremen CHSD 228	Midlothian
1	n/a	Burbank SD 111	Burbank
1	n/a	Byron CUSD 226	Byron
1	n/a	CCSD 168	Sauk Village
1	n/a	CCSD 62	Des Plaines
1	n/a	CCSD 89	Glen Ellyn
1	n/a	CCSD 93	Bloomingdale
1	n/a	CHSD 117	Lake Villa
1	n/a	CHSD 128	Libertyville
1	n/a	CHSD 155	Crystal Lake
1	n/a	CHSD 218	Oak Lawn
1	n/a	CHSD 94	West Chicago
1	n/a	CHSD 99	Downers Grove
1	n/a	CSD 158	Algonquin
1	n/a	CUSD 200	Wheaton
1	n/a	CUSD 201	Westmont
1	n/a	CUSD 300	Carpentersville
1	n/a	Cahokia CUSD 187	Cahokia
1	n/a	Canton Union SD 66	Canton
1	n/a	Carlinville CUSD 1	Carlinville
1	n/a	Carterville CUSD 5	Carterville
1	n/a	Cary CCSD 26	Cary
1	n/a	Central CUSD 301	Burlington
1	n/a	Champaign CUSD 4	Champaign
1	n/a	Channahon SD 17	Channahon
1	n/a	Charleston CUSD 1	Charleston
1	n/a	Chicago Heights SD 170	Chicago Heights
1	n/a	Cicero SD 99	Cicero
1	n/a	City of Chicago SD 299	Chicago
1	n/a	Clinton CUSD 15	Clinton
1	n/a	Coal City CUSD 1	Coal City
1	n/a	Collinsville CUSD 10	Collinsville
1	n/a	Columbia CUSD 4	Columbia
1	n/a	Community CSD 59	Arlington Hgts
1	n/a	Cons HSD 230	Orland Park
1	n/a	Cook County SD 130	Blue Island
1	n/a	Corrections SD 428 Dept of	Springfield
1	n/a	Country Club Hls SD 160	Country Club Hls
1	n/a	Crete Monee CUSD 201u	Crete
1	n/a	Crystal Lake CCSD 47	Crystal Lake
1	n/a	Danville CCSD 118	Danville
1	n/a	Darien SD 61	Darien
1	n/a	Decatur SD 61	Decatur
1	n/a	Deerfield SD 109	Deerfield
1	n/a	Dekalb CUSD 428	De Kalb
1	n/a	Dixon USD 170	Dixon
1	n/a	Dolton SD 148	Riverdale
1	n/a	Dolton SD 149	Calumet City
1	n/a	Downers Grove Gsd 58	Downers Grove
1	n/a	Du Page HSD 88	Villa Park
1	n/a	Dunlap CUSD 323	Dunlap
1	n/a	ESD 159	Matteson
1	n/a	East Maine SD 63	Des Plaines
1	n/a	East Moline SD 37	East Moline
1	n/a	East Peoria SD 86	East Peoria
1	n/a	East Richland CUSD 1	Olney
1	n/a	East St Louis SD 189	E Saint Louis
1	n/a	Edwardsville CUSD 7	Edwardsville
1	n/a	Effingham CUSD 40	Effingham
1	n/a	Elmhurst SD 205	Elmhurst
1	n/a	Elmwood Park CUSD 401	Elmwood Park
1	n/a	Eureka CUD 140	Eureka
1	n/a	Evanston CCSD 65	Evanston
1	n/a	Evanston Twp HSD 202	Evanston
1	n/a	Evergreen Park ESD 124	Evergreen Park
1	n/a	Fenton CHSD 100	Bensenville
1	n/a	Flora CUSD 35	Flora
1	n/a	Flossmoor SD 161	Chicago Heights
1	n/a	Forest Ridge SD 142	Oak Forest
1	n/a	Frankfort CCSD 157c	Frankfort
1	n/a	Frankfort CUSD 168	West Frankfort
1	n/a	Freeport SD 145	Freeport
1	n/a	Fremont SD 79	Mundelein
1	n/a	Galesburg CUSD 205	Galesburg
1	n/a	Geneseo CUSD 228	Geneseo
1	n/a	Geneva CUSD 304	Geneva
1	n/a	Genoa Kingston CUSD 424	Genoa
1	n/a	Glen Ellyn SD 41	Glen Ellyn
1	n/a	Glenbard Twp HSD 87	Glen Ellyn
1	n/a	Glenview CCSD 34	Glenview
1	n/a	Granite City CUSD 9	Granite City
1	n/a	Grant CHSD 124	Fox Lake
1	n/a	Grayslake CCSD 46	Grayslake
1	n/a	Grayslake CHSD 127	Grayslake
1	n/a	Gurnee SD 56	Gurnee
1	n/a	Harlem Ud 122	Loves Park
1	n/a	Harrisburg CUSD 3	Harrisburg
1	n/a	Harvard CUSD 50	Harvard
1	n/a	Harvey SD 152	Harvey
1	n/a	Hawthorn CCSD 73	Vernon Hills
1	n/a	Herrin CUSD 4	Herrin
1	n/a	Herscher CUSD 2	Herscher
1	n/a	Highland CUSD 5	Highland
1	n/a	Hillsboro CUSD 3	Hillsboro
1	n/a	Hinsdale CCSD 181	Westmont
1	n/a	Hinsdale Twp HSD 86	Hinsdale
1	n/a	Homer CCSD 33c	Homer Glen
1	n/a	Homewood Flossmoor CHSD 233	Flossmoor
1	n/a	Homewood SD 153	Homewood
1	n/a	Hononegah Chd 207	Rockton
1	n/a	IL Valley Central USD 321	Chillicothe
1	n/a	Indian Prairie CUSD 204	Aurora
1	n/a	Indian Springs SD 109	Justice
1	n/a	J S Morton HSD 201	Cicero
1	n/a	Jacksonville SD 117	Jacksonville
1	n/a	Jersey CUSD 100	Jerseyville
1	n/a	Johnsburg CUSD 12	Johnsburg
1	n/a	Joliet Psd 86	Joliet
1	n/a	Joliet Twp HSD 204	Joliet
1	n/a	Kaneland CUSD 302	Maple Park
1	n/a	Kankakee SD 111	Kankakee
1	n/a	Keeneyville SD 20	Hanover Park
1	n/a	Kewanee CUSD 229	Kewanee
1	n/a	Kildeer Countryside CCSD 96	Buffalo Grove
1	n/a	Kinnikinnick CCSD 131	Roscoe
1	n/a	Kirby SD 140	Tinley Park
1	n/a	La Grange SD 102	La Grange Park
1	n/a	Lake Forest CHSD 115	Lake Forest
1	n/a	Lake Forest SD 67	Lake Forest
1	n/a	Lake Park CHSD 108	Roselle
1	n/a	Lake Villa CCSD 41	Lake Villa
1	n/a	Lake Zurich CUSD 95	Lake Zurich
1	n/a	Lansing SD 158	Lansing
1	n/a	Lemont-Bromberek CSD 113a	Lemont
1	n/a	Leyden CHSD 212	Franklin Park
1	n/a	Libertyville SD 70	Libertyville
1	n/a	Lincoln Way CHSD 210	New Lenox
1	n/a	Lincolnshire-Prairieview SD 103	Lincolnshire
1	n/a	Lisle CUSD 202	Lisle
1	n/a	Litchfield CUSD 12	Litchfield
1	n/a	Lockport Twp HSD 205	Lockport
1	n/a	Lombard SD 44	Lombard
1	n/a	Lyons SD 103	Lyons
1	n/a	Lyons Twp HSD 204	La Grange
1	n/a	Macomb CUSD 185	Macomb
1	n/a	Mahomet-Seymour CUSD 3	Mahomet
1	n/a	Maine Township HSD 207	Park Ridge
1	n/a	Mannheim SD 83	Franklin Park
1	n/a	Manteno CUSD 5	Manteno
1	n/a	Marion CUSD 2	Marion
1	n/a	Marquardt SD 15	Glendale Hgts
1	n/a	Mascoutah CUD 19	Mascoutah
1	n/a	Massac UD 1	Metropolis
1	n/a	Matteson ESD 162	Matteson
1	n/a	Mattoon CUSD 2	Mattoon
1	n/a	Maywood-Melrose Park-Broadview 89	Melrose Park
1	n/a	Mc Henry CHSD 156	Mchenry
1	n/a	Mchenry CCSD 15	Mchenry
1	n/a	Mclean County USD 5	Normal
1	n/a	Meridian CUSD 223	Stillman Valley
1	n/a	Midlothian SD 143	Midlothian
1	n/a	Millburn CCSD 24	Wadsworth
1	n/a	Minooka CCSD 201	Minooka
1	n/a	Minooka CHSD 111	Minooka
1	n/a	Mokena SD 159	Mokena
1	n/a	Moline USD 40	Moline
1	n/a	Monmouth-Roseville CUSD 238	Monmouth
1	n/a	Monticello CUSD 25	Monticello
1	n/a	Morton CUSD 709	Morton
1	n/a	Mount Prospect SD 57	Mount Prospect
1	n/a	Mount Vernon SD 80	Mount Vernon
1	n/a	Mount Zion CUSD 3	Mount Zion
1	n/a	Mundelein Cons HSD 120	Mundelein
1	n/a	Mundelein ESD 75	Mundelein
1	n/a	Murphysboro CUSD 186	Murphysboro
1	n/a	Naperville CUSD 203	Naperville
1	n/a	New Lenox SD 122	New Lenox
1	n/a	New Trier Twp HSD 203	Northfield
1	n/a	Niles Twp CHSD 219	Skokie
1	n/a	Nippersink SD 2	Richmond
1	n/a	North Boone CUSD 200	Poplar Grove
1	n/a	North Chicago SD 187	North Chicago
1	n/a	North Palos SD 117	Palos Hills
1	n/a	North Shore SD 112	Highland Park
1	n/a	Northbrook SD 28	Northbrook
1	n/a	Northfield Twp HSD 225	Glenview
1	n/a	O Fallon CCSD 90	Ofallon
1	n/a	O Fallon Twp HSD 203	Ofallon
1	n/a	Oak Lawn CHSD 229	Oak Lawn
1	n/a	Oak Lawn-Hometown SD 123	Oak Lawn
1	n/a	Oak Park ESD 97	Oak Park
1	n/a	Oak Park-River Forest SD 200	Oak Park
1	n/a	Olympia CUSD 16	Stanford
1	n/a	Oregon CUSD 220	Oregon
1	n/a	Orland SD 135	Orland Park
1	n/a	Oswego CUSD 308	Oswego
1	n/a	Ottawa ESD 141	Ottawa
1	n/a	Ottawa Twp HSD 140	Ottawa
1	n/a	Palatine CCSD 15	Palatine
1	n/a	Palos CCSD 118	Palos Park
1	n/a	Pana CUSD 8	Pana
1	n/a	Paris-Union SD 95	Paris
1	n/a	Park Forest SD 163	Park Forest
1	n/a	Park Ridge CCSD 64	Park Ridge
1	n/a	Paxton-Buckley-Loda CUD 10	Paxton
1	n/a	Pekin CSD 303	Pekin
1	n/a	Pekin PSD 108	Pekin
1	n/a	Peoria SD 150	Peoria
1	n/a	Peotone CUSD 207u	Peotone
1	n/a	Plainfield SD 202	Plainfield

1	n/a	Plano CUSD 88	Plano
1	n/a	Posen-Robbins ESD 143-5	Posen
1	n/a	Prairie Central CUSD 8	Fairbury
1	n/a	Prairie-Hills ESD 144	Markham
1	n/a	Proviso Twp HSD 209	Forest Park
1	n/a	Queen Bee SD 16	Glendale Hgts
1	n/a	Quincy SD 172	Quincy
1	n/a	Rantoul City SD 137	Rantoul
1	n/a	Reavis Twp HSD 220	Burbank
1	n/a	Reed Custer CUSD 255u	Braidwood
1	n/a	Rich Twp HSD 227	Olympia Fields
1	n/a	Ridgeland SD 122	Oak Lawn
1	n/a	River Trails SD 26	Mount Prospect
1	n/a	Riverton CUSD 14	Riverton
1	n/a	Robinson CUSD 2	Robinson
1	n/a	Rochelle CCSD 231	Rochelle
1	n/a	Rochester CUSD 3a	Rochester
1	n/a	Rock Island SD 41	Rock Island
1	n/a	Rockford SD 205	Rockford
1	n/a	Round Lake CUSD 116	Round Lake
1	n/a	Roxana CUSD 1	Roxana
1	n/a	Saint Charles CUSD 303	Saint Charles
1	n/a	Sandwich CUSD 430	Sandwich
1	n/a	Schaumburg CCSD 54	Schaumburg
1	n/a	School District 45 Dupage County	Villa Park
1	n/a	School District U-46	Elgin
1	n/a	Sherrard CUSD 200	Sherrard
1	n/a	Skokie SD 68	Skokie
1	n/a	Skokie SD 69	Skokie
1	n/a	South Holland SD 151	South Holland
1	n/a	Southwestern CUSD 9	Piasa
1	n/a	Sparta CUSD 140	Sparta
1	n/a	Springfield SD 186	Springfield
1	n/a	Steger SD 194	Steger
1	n/a	Sterling CUSD 5	Sterling
1	n/a	Streator ESD 44	Streator
1	n/a	Summit Hill SD 161	Frankfort
1	n/a	Summit SD 104	Summit
1	n/a	Sycamore CUSD 427	Sycamore
1	n/a	Taylorville CUSD 3	Taylorville
1	n/a	Thornton Fractional Twp HSD 215	Calumet City
1	n/a	Thornton Twp HSD 205	South Holland
1	n/a	Tinley Park CCSD 146	Tinley Park
1	n/a	Tolono CUSD 7	Tolono
1	n/a	Township HSD 211	Palatine
1	n/a	Township HSD 214	Arlington Hgts
1	n/a	Triad CUSD 2	Troy
1	n/a	Troy CCSD 30c	Plainfield
1	n/a	Twp HSD 113	Highland Park
1	n/a	United Twp HSD 30	East Moline
1	n/a	Urbana SD 116	Urbana
1	n/a	Valley View CUSD 365u	Romeoville
1	n/a	Vandalia CUSD 203	Vandalia
1	n/a	Wabash CUSD 348	Mount Carmel
1	n/a	Warren Twp HSD 121	Gages Lake
1	n/a	Waterloo CUSD 5	Waterloo
1	n/a	Wauconda CUSD 118	Wauconda
1	n/a	Waukegan CUSD 60	Waukegan
1	n/a	West Carroll CUSD 314	Thomson
1	n/a	West Chicago ESD 33	West Chicago
1	n/a	West Harvey-Dixmoor PSD 147	Harvey
1	n/a	Wheeling CCSD 21	Wheeling
1	n/a	Will County SD 92	Lockport
1	n/a	Wilmette SD 39	Wilmette
1	n/a	Wilmington CUSD 209u	Wilmington
1	n/a	Winnebago CUSD 323	Winnebago
1	n/a	Winnetka SD 36	Winnetka
1	n/a	Woodland CCSD 50	Gurnee
1	n/a	Woodridge SD 68	Woodridge
1	n/a	Woodstock CUSD 200	Woodstock
1	n/a	Yorkville CUSD 115	Yorkville
1	n/a	Zion ESD 6	Zion
1	n/a	Zion-Benton Twp HSD 126	Zion

Migrant Students

Rank	Percent	District Name	City
1	4.1	Beardstown CUSD 15	Beardstown
2	0.4	Aurora East USD 131	Aurora
2	0.4	Kewanee CUSD 229	Kewanee
4	0.1	Glen Ellyn SD 41	Glen Ellyn
4	0.1	Moline USD 40	Moline
4	0.1	Rochelle CCSD 231	Rochelle
7	0.0	Batavia USD 101	Batavia
7	0.0	Grayslake CHSD 127	Grayslake
7	0.0	Oak Lawn-Hometown SD 123	Oak Lawn
7	0.0	Proviso Twp HSD 209	Forest Park
7	0.0	School District U-46	Elgin
7	0.0	Woodstock CUSD 200	Woodstock
13	0.0	Addison SD 4	Addison
13	0.0	Adlai E Stevenson HSD 125	Lincolnshire
13	0.0	Alsip-Hazlgrn-Oaklwn SD 126	Alsip
13	0.0	Alton CUSD 11	Alton
13	0.0	Antioch CCSD 34	Antioch
13	0.0	Aptakisic-Tripp CCSD 102	Buffalo Grove
13	0.0	Arbor Park SD 145	Oak Forest
13	0.0	Argo CHSD 217	Summit
13	0.0	Arlington Hgts SD 25	Arlington Hgts
13	0.0	Aurora West USD 129	Aurora
13	0.0	Ball Chatham CUSD 5	Chatham
13	0.0	Barrington CUSD 220	Barrington
13	0.0	Beach Park CCSD 3	Beach Park
13	0.0	Belleville SD 118	Belleville
13	0.0	Belleville Twp HSD 201	Belleville
13	0.0	Bellwood SD 88	Bellwood
13	0.0	Belvidere CUSD 100	Belvidere
13	0.0	Bensenville SD 2	Bensenville
13	0.0	Berkeley SD 87	Berkeley
13	0.0	Berwyn North SD 98	Berwyn
13	0.0	Berwyn South SD 100	Berwyn
13	0.0	Bethalto CUSD 8	Bethalto
13	0.0	Bloom Twp HSD 206	Chicago Heights
13	0.0	Bloomington SD 87	Bloomington
13	0.0	Bond County CUSD 2	Greenville
13	0.0	Bourbonnais SD 53	Bourbonnais
13	0.0	Bradley Bourbonnais CHSD 307	Bradley
13	0.0	Bradley SD 61	Bradley
13	0.0	Bremen CHSD 228	Midlothian
13	0.0	Burbank SD 111	Burbank
13	0.0	Byron CUSD 226	Byron
13	0.0	CCSD 168	Sauk Village
13	0.0	CCSD 62	Des Plaines
13	0.0	CCSD 89	Glen Ellyn
13	0.0	CCSD 93	Bloomingdale
13	0.0	CHSD 117	Lake Villa
13	0.0	CHSD 128	Libertyville
13	0.0	CHSD 155	Crystal Lake
13	0.0	CHSD 218	Oak Lawn
13	0.0	CHSD 94	West Chicago
13	0.0	CHSD 99	Downers Grove
13	0.0	CSD 158	Algonquin
13	0.0	CUSD 200	Wheaton
13	0.0	CUSD 201	Westmont
13	0.0	CUSD 300	Carpentersville
13	0.0	Cahokia CUSD 187	Cahokia
13	0.0	Canton Union SD 66	Canton
13	0.0	Carlinville CUSD 1	Carlinville
13	0.0	Carterville CUSD 5	Carterville
13	0.0	Cary CCSD 26	Cary
13	0.0	Central CUSD 301	Burlington
13	0.0	Champaign CUSD 4	Champaign
13	0.0	Channahon SD 17	Channahon
13	0.0	Charleston CUSD 1	Charleston
13	0.0	Chicago Heights SD 170	Chicago Heights
13	0.0	Cicero SD 99	Cicero
13	0.0	City of Chicago SD 299	Chicago
13	0.0	Clinton CUSD 15	Clinton
13	0.0	Coal City CUSD 1	Coal City
13	0.0	Collinsville CUSD 10	Collinsville
13	0.0	Columbia CUSD 4	Columbia
13	0.0	Community CSD 59	Arlington Hgts
13	0.0	Cons HSD 230	Orland Park
13	0.0	Cook County SD 130	Blue Island
13	0.0	Corrections SD 428 Dept of	Springfield
13	0.0	Country Club Hls SD 160	Country Club Hls
13	0.0	Crete Monee CUSD 201u	Crete
13	0.0	Crystal Lake CCSD 47	Crystal Lake
13	0.0	Danville CCSD 118	Danville
13	0.0	Darien SD 61	Darien
13	0.0	Decatur SD 61	Decatur
13	0.0	Deerfield SD 109	Deerfield
13	0.0	Dekalb CUSD 428	De Kalb
13	0.0	Dixon USD 170	Dixon
13	0.0	Dolton SD 148	Riverdale
13	0.0	Dolton SD 149	Calumet City
13	0.0	Downers Grove Gsd 58	Downers Grove
13	0.0	Du Page HSD 88	Villa Park
13	0.0	Dunlap CUSD 323	Dunlap
13	0.0	ESD 159	Matteson
13	0.0	East Maine SD 63	Des Plaines
13	0.0	East Moline SD 37	East Moline
13	0.0	East Peoria SD 86	East Peoria
13	0.0	East Richland CUSD 1	Olney
13	0.0	East St Louis SD 189	E Saint Louis
13	0.0	Edwardsville CUSD 7	Edwardsville
13	0.0	Effingham CUSD 40	Effingham
13	0.0	Elmhurst SD 205	Elmhurst
13	0.0	Elmwood Park CUSD 401	Elmwood Park
13	0.0	Eureka CUD 140	Eureka
13	0.0	Evanston CCSD 65	Evanston
13	0.0	Evanston Twp HSD 202	Evanston
13	0.0	Evergreen Park ESD 124	Evergreen Park
13	0.0	Fenton CHSD 100	Bensenville
13	0.0	Flora CUSD 35	Flora
13	0.0	Flossmoor SD 161	Chicago Heights
13	0.0	Forest Ridge SD 142	Oak Forest
13	0.0	Frankfort CCSD 157c	Frankfort
13	0.0	Frankfort CUSD 168	West Frankfort
13	0.0	Freeport SD 145	Freeport
13	0.0	Fremont SD 79	Mundelein
13	0.0	Galesburg CUSD 205	Galesburg
13	0.0	Geneseo CUSD 228	Geneseo
13	0.0	Geneva CUSD 304	Geneva
13	0.0	Genoa Kingston CUSD 424	Genoa
13	0.0	Glenbard Twp HSD 87	Glen Ellyn
13	0.0	Glenview CCSD 34	Glenview
13	0.0	Granite City CUSD 9	Granite City
13	0.0	Grant CHSD 124	Fox Lake
13	0.0	Grayslake CCSD 46	Grayslake
13	0.0	Gurnee SD 56	Gurnee
13	0.0	Harlem Ud 122	Loves Park
13	0.0	Harrisburg CUSD 3	Harrisburg
13	0.0	Harvard CUSD 50	Harvard
13	0.0	Harvey SD 152	Harvey
13	0.0	Hawthorn CCSD 73	Vernon Hills
13	0.0	Herrin CUSD 4	Herrin
13	0.0	Herscher CUSD 2	Herscher
13	0.0	Highland CUSD 5	Highland
13	0.0	Hillsboro CUSD 3	Hillsboro
13	0.0	Hinsdale CCSD 181	Westmont
13	0.0	Hinsdale Twp HSD 86	Hinsdale
13	0.0	Homer CCSD 33c	Homer Glen
13	0.0	Homewood Flossmoor CHSD 233	Flossmoor
13	0.0	Homewood SD 153	Homewood
13	0.0	Hononegah Chd 207	Rockton
13	0.0	IL Valley Central USD 321	Chillicothe
13	0.0	Indian Prairie CUSD 204	Aurora
13	0.0	Indian Springs SD 109	Justice
13	0.0	J S Morton HSD 201	Cicero
13	0.0	Jacksonville SD 117	Jacksonville
13	0.0	Jersey CUSD 100	Jerseyville
13	0.0	Johnsburg CUSD 12	Johnsburg
13	0.0	Joliet Psd 86	Joliet
13	0.0	Joliet Twp HSD 204	Joliet
13	0.0	Kaneland CUSD 302	Maple Park
13	0.0	Kankakee SD 111	Kankakee
13	0.0	Keeneyville SD 20	Hanover Park
13	0.0	Kildeer Countryside CCSD 96	Buffalo Grove
13	0.0	Kinnikinnick CCSD 131	Roscoe
13	0.0	Kirby SD 140	Tinley Park
13	0.0	La Grange SD 102	La Grange Park
13	0.0	Lake Forest CHSD 115	Lake Forest
13	0.0	Lake Forest SD 67	Lake Forest
13	0.0	Lake Park CHSD 108	Roselle
13	0.0	Lake Villa CCSD 41	Lake Villa
13	0.0	Lake Zurich CUSD 95	Lake Zurich
13	0.0	Lansing SD 158	Lansing
13	0.0	Lemont-Bromberek CSD 113a	Lemont
13	0.0	Leyden CHSD 212	Franklin Park
13	0.0	Libertyville SD 70	Libertyville
13	0.0	Lincoln Way CHSD 210	New Lenox
13	0.0	Lincolnshire-Prairieview SD 103	Lincolnshire
13	0.0	Lisle CUSD 202	Lisle
13	0.0	Litchfield CUSD 12	Litchfield
13	0.0	Lockport Twp HSD 205	Lockport
13	0.0	Lombard SD 44	Lombard
13	0.0	Lyons SD 103	Lyons
13	0.0	Lyons Twp HSD 204	La Grange
13	0.0	Macomb CUSD 185	Macomb
13	0.0	Mahomet-Seymour CUSD 3	Mahomet
13	0.0	Maine Township HSD 207	Park Ridge
13	0.0	Mannheim SD 83	Franklin Park
13	0.0	Manteno CUSD 5	Manteno
13	0.0	Marion CUSD 2	Marion
13	0.0	Marquardt SD 15	Glendale Hgts
13	0.0	Mascoutah CUD 19	Mascoutah
13	0.0	Massac UD 1	Metropolis
13	0.0	Matteson ESD 162	Matteson
13	0.0	Mattoon CUSD 2	Mattoon
13	0.0	Maywood-Melrose Park-Broadview 89	Melrose Park

13	0.0	Mc Henry CHSD 156	Mchenry
13	0.0	Mchenry CCSD 15	Mchenry
13	0.0	Mclean County USD 5	Normal
13	0.0	Meridian CUSD 223	Stillman Valley
13	0.0	Midlothian SD 143	Midlothian
13	0.0	Millburn CCSD 24	Wadsworth
13	0.0	Minooka CCSD 201	Minooka
13	0.0	Minooka CHSD 111	Minooka
13	0.0	Mokena SD 159	Mokena
13	0.0	Monmouth-Roseville CUSD 238	Monmouth
13	0.0	Monticello CUSD 25	Monticello
13	0.0	Morton CUSD 709	Morton
13	0.0	Mount Prospect SD 57	Mount Prospect
13	0.0	Mount Vernon SD 80	Mount Vernon
13	0.0	Mount Zion CUSD 3	Mount Zion
13	0.0	Mundelein Cons HSD 120	Mundelein
13	0.0	Mundelein ESD 75	Mundelein
13	0.0	Murphysboro CUSD 186	Murphysboro
13	0.0	Naperville CUSD 203	Naperville
13	0.0	New Lenox SD 122	New Lenox
13	0.0	New Trier Twp HSD 203	Northfield
13	0.0	Niles Twp CHSD 219	Skokie
13	0.0	Nippersink SD 2	Richmond
13	0.0	North Boone CUSD 200	Poplar Grove
13	0.0	North Chicago SD 187	North Chicago
13	0.0	North Palos SD 117	Palos Hills
13	0.0	North Shore SD 112	Highland Park
13	0.0	Northbrook SD 28	Northbrook
13	0.0	Northfield Twp HSD 225	Glenview
13	0.0	O Fallon CCSD 90	Ofallon
13	0.0	O Fallon Twp HSD 203	Ofallon
13	0.0	Oak Lawn CHSD 229	Oak Lawn
13	0.0	Oak Park ESD 97	Oak Park
13	0.0	Oak Park-River Forest SD 200	Oak Park
13	0.0	Olympia CUSD 16	Stanford
13	0.0	Oregon CUSD 220	Oregon
13	0.0	Orland SD 135	Orland Park
13	0.0	Oswego CUSD 308	Oswego
13	0.0	Ottawa ESD 141	Ottawa
13	0.0	Ottawa Twp HSD 140	Ottawa
13	0.0	Palatine CCSD 15	Palatine
13	0.0	Palos CCSD 118	Palos Park
13	0.0	Pana CUSD 8	Pana
13	0.0	Paris-Union SD 95	Paris
13	0.0	Park Forest SD 163	Park Forest
13	0.0	Park Ridge CCSD 64	Park Ridge
13	0.0	Paxton-Buckley-Loda CUD 10	Paxton
13	0.0	Pekin CSD 303	Pekin
13	0.0	Pekin PSD 108	Pekin
13	0.0	Peoria SD 150	Peoria
13	0.0	Peotone CUSD 207u	Peotone
13	0.0	Plainfield SD 202	Plainfield
13	0.0	Plano CUSD 88	Plano
13	0.0	Posen-Robbins ESD 143-5	Posen
13	0.0	Prairie Central CUSD 8	Fairbury
13	0.0	Prairie-Hills ESD 144	Markham
13	0.0	Queen Bee SD 16	Glendale Hgts
13	0.0	Quincy SD 172	Quincy
13	0.0	Rantoul City SD 137	Rantoul
13	0.0	Reavis Twp HSD 220	Burbank
13	0.0	Reed Custer CUSD 255u	Braidwood
13	0.0	Rich Twp HSD 227	Olympia Fields
13	0.0	Ridgeland SD 122	Oak Lawn
13	0.0	River Trails SD 26	Mount Prospect
13	0.0	Riverton CUSD 14	Riverton
13	0.0	Robinson CUSD 2	Robinson
13	0.0	Rochester CUSD 3a	Rochester
13	0.0	Rock Island SD 41	Rock Island
13	0.0	Rockford SD 205	Rockford
13	0.0	Round Lake CUSD 116	Round Lake
13	0.0	Roxana CUSD 1	Roxana
13	0.0	Saint Charles CUSD 303	Saint Charles
13	0.0	Sandwich CUSD 430	Sandwich
13	0.0	Schaumburg CCSD 54	Schaumburg
13	0.0	School District 45 Dupage County	Villa Park
13	0.0	Sherrard CUSD 200	Sherrard
13	0.0	Skokie SD 68	Skokie
13	0.0	Skokie SD 69	Skokie
13	0.0	South Holland SD 151	South Holland
13	0.0	Southwestern CUSD 9	Piasa
13	0.0	Sparta CUSD 140	Sparta
13	0.0	Springfield SD 186	Springfield
13	0.0	Steger SD 194	Steger
13	0.0	Sterling CUSD 5	Sterling
13	0.0	Streator ESD 44	Streator
13	0.0	Summit Hill SD 161	Frankfort
13	0.0	Summit SD 104	Summit
13	0.0	Sycamore CUSD 427	Sycamore
13	0.0	Taylorville CUSD 3	Taylorville
13	0.0	Thornton Fractional Twp HSD 215	Calumet City
13	0.0	Thornton Twp HSD 205	South Holland
13	0.0	Tinley Park CCSD 146	Tinley Park
13	0.0	Tolono CUSD 7	Tolono
13	0.0	Township HSD 211	Palatine
13	0.0	Township HSD 214	Arlington Hgts
13	0.0	Triad CUSD 2	Troy
13	0.0	Troy CCSD 30c	Plainfield
13	0.0	Twp HSD 113	Highland Park
13	0.0	United Twp HSD 30	East Moline
13	0.0	Urbana SD 116	Urbana
13	0.0	Valley View CUSD 365u	Romeoville
13	0.0	Vandalia CUSD 203	Vandalia
13	0.0	Wabash CUSD 348	Mount Carmel
13	0.0	Warren Twp HSD 121	Gages Lake
13	0.0	Waterloo CUSD 5	Waterloo
13	0.0	Wauconda CUSD 118	Wauconda
13	0.0	Waukegan CUSD 60	Waukegan
13	0.0	West Carroll CUSD 314	Thomson
13	0.0	West Chicago ESD 33	West Chicago
13	0.0	West Harvey-Dixmoor PSD 147	Harvey
13	0.0	Wheeling CCSD 21	Wheeling
13	0.0	Will County SD 92	Lockport
13	0.0	Wilmette SD 39	Wilmette
13	0.0	Wilmington CUSD 209u	Wilmington
13	0.0	Winnebago CUSD 323	Winnebago
13	0.0	Winnetka SD 36	Winnetka
13	0.0	Woodland CCSD 50	Gurnee
13	0.0	Woodridge SD 68	Woodridge
13	0.0	Yorkville CUSD 115	Yorkville
13	0.0	Zion ESD 6	Zion
13	0.0	Zion-Benton Twp HSD 126	Zion

Students Eligible for Free Lunch

Rank	Percent	District Name	City
1	94.5	West Harvey-Dixmoor PSD 147	Harvey
2	87.0	Posen-Robbins ESD 143-5	Posen
3	82.9	Prairie-Hills ESD 144	Markham
4	80.2	Chicago Heights SD 170	Chicago Heights
5	78.9	Harvey SD 152	Harvey
6	75.9	Maywood-Melrose Park-Broadview 89	Melrose Park
7	72.9	Park Forest SD 163	Park Forest
8	70.5	Kankakee SD 111	Kankakee
9	68.3	Cahokia CUSD 187	Cahokia
10	68.2	Mount Vernon SD 80	Mount Vernon
11	68.0	Dolton SD 148	Riverdale
12	66.1	City of Chicago SD 299	Chicago
13	65.0	East St Louis SD 189	E Saint Louis
14	63.9	Corrections SD 428 Dept of	Springfield
15	63.2	Aurora East USD 131	Aurora
15	63.2	Cook County SD 130	Blue Island
17	62.4	Joliet Psd 86	Joliet
18	62.3	Cicero SD 99	Cicero
19	62.2	Zion ESD 6	Zion
20	61.8	South Holland SD 151	South Holland
21	60.4	Bellwood SD 88	Bellwood
22	60.1	Berwyn North SD 98	Berwyn
23	59.7	Danville CCSD 118	Danville
24	57.9	CCSD 168	Sauk Village
24	57.9	Rockford SD 205	Rockford
26	57.3	Dolton SD 149	Calumet City
27	57.1	Decatur SD 61	Decatur
28	53.2	Peoria SD 150	Peoria
29	52.3	Rock Island SD 41	Rock Island
30	51.6	Rantoul City SD 137	Rantoul
31	51.0	East Moline SD 37	East Moline
32	50.1	Springfield SD 186	Springfield
33	49.9	Summit SD 104	Summit
34	49.4	Rich Twp HSD 227	Olympia Fields
35	48.9	Kewanee CUSD 229	Kewanee
36	48.7	North Chicago SD 187	North Chicago
37	47.3	Streator ESD 44	Streator
38	46.9	Murphysboro CUSD 186	Murphysboro
39	46.7	Bloom Twp HSD 206	Chicago Heights
40	46.2	Beardstown CUSD 15	Beardstown
41	45.8	Berwyn South SD 100	Berwyn
42	45.4	J S Morton HSD 201	Cicero
43	45.3	Waukegan CUSD 60	Waukegan
44	44.8	Freeport SD 145	Freeport
45	44.7	Urbana SD 116	Urbana
46	43.6	Galesburg CUSD 205	Galesburg
47	43.4	Round Lake CUSD 116	Round Lake
48	42.9	Alton CUSD 11	Alton
49	42.3	Berkeley SD 87	Berkeley
50	40.7	Sparta CUSD 140	Sparta
51	40.5	Herrin CUSD 4	Herrin
52	39.4	Country Club Hls SD 160	Country Club Hls
53	38.7	Massac UD 1	Metropolis
54	38.6	Pekin PSD 108	Pekin
55	38.3	Pana CUSD 8	Pana
56	38.0	Crete Monee CUSD 201u	Crete
57	37.8	Granite City CUSD 9	Granite City
57	37.8	Jacksonville SD 117	Jacksonville
59	37.3	Frankfort CUSD 168	West Frankfort
60	37.1	Monmouth-Roseville CUSD 238	Monmouth
61	36.5	Thornton Fractional Twp HSD 215	Calumet City
62	36.2	Bloomington SD 87	Bloomington
63	35.8	Matteson ESD 162	Matteson
64	35.7	Champaign CUSD 4	Champaign
65	35.6	Mannheim SD 83	Franklin Park
65	35.6	Quincy SD 172	Quincy
67	35.5	Vandalia CUSD 203	Vandalia
68	34.9	Canton Union SD 66	Canton
69	34.8	East Richland CUSD 1	Olney
70	34.5	Argo CHSD 217	Summit
70	34.5	Steger SD 194	Steger
72	34.4	West Chicago ESD 33	West Chicago
73	33.7	Harvard CUSD 50	Harvard
73	33.7	Paris-Union SD 95	Paris
75	33.5	Belleville SD 118	Belleville
75	33.5	School District U-46	Elgin
77	33.4	Collinsville CUSD 10	Collinsville
78	33.3	Beach Park CCSD 3	Beach Park
79	33.0	Flora CUSD 35	Flora
80	32.8	Lyons SD 103	Lyons
81	32.7	Marion CUSD 2	Marion
82	32.6	Moline USD 40	Moline
83	32.5	Indian Springs SD 109	Justice
84	32.1	Roxana CUSD 1	Roxana
85	32.0	Hillsboro CUSD 3	Hillsboro
86	31.8	Macomb CUSD 185	Macomb
87	31.4	CHSD 218	Oak Lawn
87	31.4	Mattoon CUSD 2	Mattoon
89	30.9	Aurora West USD 129	Aurora
89	30.9	East Peoria SD 86	East Peoria
89	30.9	West Carroll CUSD 314	Thomson
92	30.8	Harrisburg CUSD 3	Harrisburg
93	30.7	Rochelle CCSD 231	Rochelle
94	30.0	Ottawa ESD 141	Ottawa
95	29.9	United Twp HSD 30	East Moline
96	29.8	Evanston CCSD 65	Evanston
96	29.8	Robinson CUSD 2	Robinson
98	29.0	Lansing SD 158	Lansing
99	28.4	Skokie SD 69	Skokie
100	28.2	Marquardt SD 15	Glendale Hgts
101	28.1	Litchfield CUSD 12	Litchfield
102	27.8	Taylorville CUSD 3	Taylorville
103	27.3	Bond County CUSD 2	Greenville
104	27.1	Proviso Twp HSD 209	Forest Park
105	27.0	Dixon USD 170	Dixon
105	27.0	ESD 159	Matteson
105	27.0	Wheeling CCSD 21	Wheeling
108	26.7	Sterling CUSD 5	Sterling
109	26.2	Addison SD 4	Addison
109	26.2	Jersey CUSD 100	Jerseyville
111	26.1	Clinton CUSD 15	Clinton
112	25.7	Valley View CUSD 365u	Romeoville
113	25.6	Bethalto CUSD 8	Bethalto
114	25.2	Zion-Benton Twp HSD 126	Zion
115	25.1	Carlinville CUSD 1	Carlinville
115	25.1	School District 45 Dupage County	Villa Park
117	25.0	Evanston Twp HSD 202	Evanston
118	24.6	CCSD 62	Des Plaines
119	24.4	Bensenville SD 2	Bensenville
120	24.3	Belvidere CUSD 100	Belvidere
120	24.3	Midlothian SD 143	Midlothian
122	24.2	Dekalb CUSD 428	De Kalb
123	23.7	Community CSD 59	Arlington Hgts
124	23.5	Charleston CUSD 1	Charleston
125	23.4	Wabash CUSD 348	Mount Carmel
126	23.1	Ridgeland SD 122	Oak Lawn
127	22.4	Mundelein ESD 75	Mundelein
128	22.2	Effingham CUSD 40	Effingham
129	22.0	Harlem Ud 122	Loves Park
130	21.9	CUSD 300	Carpentersville
131	21.6	Oregon CUSD 220	Oregon
131	21.6	Riverton CUSD 14	Riverton
133	21.2	East Maine SD 63	Des Plaines
134	21.1	Prairie Central CUSD 8	Fairbury
135	20.9	Paxton-Buckley-Loda CUD 10	Paxton

135	20.9	Pekin CSD 303	Pekin
137	20.5	CUSD 201	Westmont
138	20.4	Joliet Twp HSD 204	Joliet
139	19.8	Belleville Twp HSD 201	Belleville
140	19.6	Burbank SD 111	Burbank
140	19.6	Keeneyville SD 20	Hanover Park
140	19.6	North Boone CUSD 200	Poplar Grove
140	19.6	Palatine CCSD 15	Palatine
144	19.4	Woodstock CUSD 200	Woodstock
145	19.2	North Palos SD 117	Palos Hills
146	19.0	Bradley SD 61	Bradley
147	18.8	Reed Custer CUSD 255u	Braidwood
147	18.8	River Trails SD 26	Mount Prospect
149	18.6	Lombard SD 44	Lombard
150	17.8	Oak Park ESD 97	Oak Park
151	17.5	Alsip-Hazlgrn-Oaklwn SD 126	Alsip
152	17.3	Southwestern CUSD 9	Piasa
153	17.1	Woodridge SD 68	Woodridge
154	16.7	Du Page HSD 88	Villa Park
155	16.5	Evergreen Park ESD 124	Evergreen Park
155	16.5	Skokie SD 68	Skokie
157	16.4	Sherrard CUSD 200	Sherrard
158	16.0	Wilmington CUSD 209u	Wilmington
159	15.4	Leyden CHSD 212	Franklin Park
160	15.3	Mclean County USD 5	Normal
161	15.0	Tinley Park CCSD 146	Tinley Park
162	14.8	Bourbonnais SD 53	Bourbonnais
163	14.7	Mundelein Cons HSD 120	Mundelein
164	14.5	Plano CUSD 88	Plano
165	14.4	Tolono CUSD 7	Tolono
166	14.3	Eureka CUD 140	Eureka
166	14.3	IL Valley Central USD 321	Chillicothe
168	13.8	Carterville CUSD 5	Carterville
168	13.8	Herscher CUSD 2	Herscher
170	13.5	Highland CUSD 5	Highland
170	13.5	Oak Lawn-Hometown SD 123	Oak Lawn
172	13.2	Olympia CUSD 16	Stanford
173	13.1	Bradley Bourbonnais CHSD 307	Bradley
173	13.1	Genoa Kingston CUSD 424	Genoa
175	13.0	O Fallon CCSD 90	Ofallon
176	12.9	Mchenry CCSD 15	Mchenry
177	12.6	Elmwood Park CUSD 401	Elmwood Park
178	12.5	Homewood SD 153	Homewood
178	12.5	Wauconda CUSD 118	Wauconda
180	12.4	Coal City CUSD 1	Coal City
181	12.1	CUSD 200	Wheaton
182	12.0	Geneseo CUSD 228	Geneseo
183	11.8	Sandwich CUSD 430	Sandwich
184	11.7	Glenview CCSD 34	Glenview
185	11.0	Mascoutah CUD 19	Mascoutah
186	10.8	Edwardsville CUSD 7	Edwardsville
187	10.7	Hawthorn CCSD 73	Vernon Hills
187	10.7	Oak Park-River Forest SD 200	Oak Park
189	10.5	Manteno CUSD 5	Manteno
190	10.4	Woodland CCSD 50	Gurnee
191	10.2	Darien SD 61	Darien
192	10.1	Mahomet-Seymour CUSD 3	Mahomet
193	10.0	Waterloo CUSD 5	Waterloo
194	9.9	Township HSD 211	Palatine
195	9.5	North Shore SD 112	Highland Park
196	9.4	Antioch CCSD 34	Antioch
196	9.4	Grant CHSD 124	Fox Lake
198	9.3	Grayslake CCSD 46	Grayslake
198	9.3	Monticello CUSD 25	Monticello
200	9.2	Township HSD 214	Arlington Hgts
200	9.2	Troy CCSD 30c	Plainfield
202	9.1	La Grange SD 102	La Grange Park
202	9.1	Meridian CUSD 223	Stillman Valley
204	9.0	Lisle CUSD 202	Lisle
205	8.7	Sycamore CUSD 427	Sycamore
206	8.3	Minooka CCSD 201	Minooka
207	8.1	Winnebago CUSD 323	Winnebago
208	8.0	Barrington CUSD 220	Barrington
209	7.9	Glenbard Twp HSD 87	Glen Ellyn
210	7.8	Triad CUSD 2	Troy
211	7.7	Mount Zion CUSD 3	Mount Zion
212	7.5	Lake Villa CCSD 41	Lake Villa
212	7.5	Palos CCSD 118	Palos Park
214	7.2	CHSD 99	Downers Grove
214	7.2	Hononegah Chd 207	Rockton
216	6.6	O Fallon Twp HSD 203	Ofallon
217	6.4	Cary CCSD 26	Cary
217	6.4	Channahon SD 17	Channahon
217	6.4	Crystal Lake CCSD 47	Crystal Lake
220	6.3	Ball Chatham CUSD 5	Chatham
220	6.3	Kinnikinnick CCSD 131	Roscoe
222	5.8	Oswego CUSD 308	Oswego
223	5.3	Columbia CUSD 4	Columbia
223	5.3	Peotone CUSD 207u	Peotone
225	4.9	Nippersink SD 2	Richmond
226	4.7	Johnsburg CUSD 12	Johnsburg
226	4.7	Morton CUSD 709	Morton
228	4.4	CHSD 155	Crystal Lake
228	4.4	Dunlap CUSD 323	Dunlap
228	4.4	Mokena SD 159	Mokena
228	4.4	Will County SD 92	Lockport
232	4.2	Arlington Hgts SD 25	Arlington Hgts
233	4.1	Plainfield SD 202	Plainfield
234	3.7	Lake Zurich CUSD 95	Lake Zurich
235	3.6	Kildeer Countryside CCSD 96	Buffalo Grove
236	3.3	CSD 158	Algonquin
237	3.2	New Lenox SD 122	New Lenox
238	3.0	Lemont-Bromberek CSD 113a	Lemont
239	2.8	Saint Charles CUSD 303	Saint Charles
240	2.6	Aptakisic-Tripp CCSD 102	Buffalo Grove
240	2.6	Summit Hill SD 161	Frankfort
242	2.5	Lincoln Way CHSD 210	New Lenox
243	2.4	Batavia USD 101	Batavia
244	2.2	Byron CUSD 226	Byron
245	2.1	Millburn CCSD 24	Wadsworth
245	2.1	Rochester CUSD 3a	Rochester
247	2.0	Central CUSD 301	Burlington
247	2.0	Kaneland CUSD 302	Maple Park
249	1.8	Downers Grove Gsd 58	Downers Grove
249	1.8	Libertyville SD 70	Libertyville
251	1.7	Mount Prospect SD 57	Mount Prospect
252	1.6	Naperville CUSD 203	Naperville
253	0.0	Arbor Park SD 145	Oak Forest
253	0.0	Bremen CHSD 228	Midlothian
253	0.0	CCSD 89	Glen Ellyn
253	0.0	CCSD 93	Bloomingdale
253	0.0	CHSD 117	Lake Villa
253	0.0	CHSD 94	West Chicago
253	0.0	Cons HSD 230	Orland Park
253	0.0	Deerfield SD 109	Deerfield
253	0.0	Elmhurst SD 205	Elmhurst
253	0.0	Fenton CHSD 100	Bensenville
253	0.0	Flossmoor SD 161	Chicago Heights
253	0.0	Forest Ridge SD 142	Oak Forest
253	0.0	Frankfort CCSD 157c	Frankfort
253	0.0	Fremont SD 79	Mundelein
253	0.0	Geneva CUSD 304	Geneva
253	0.0	Glen Ellyn SD 41	Glen Ellyn
253	0.0	Grayslake CHSD 127	Grayslake
253	0.0	Gurnee SD 56	Gurnee
253	0.0	Hinsdale Twp HSD 86	Hinsdale
253	0.0	Homer CCSD 33c	Homer Glen
253	0.0	Indian Prairie CUSD 204	Aurora
253	0.0	Kirby SD 140	Tinley Park
253	0.0	Lake Forest CHSD 115	Lake Forest
253	0.0	Lake Forest SD 67	Lake Forest
253	0.0	Lake Park CHSD 108	Roselle
253	0.0	Lincolnshire-Prairieview SD 103	Lincolnshire
253	0.0	Lyons Twp HSD 204	La Grange
253	0.0	Minooka CHSD 111	Minooka
253	0.0	Niles Twp CHSD 219	Skokie
253	0.0	Northbrook SD 28	Northbrook
253	0.0	Orland SD 135	Orland Park
253	0.0	Ottawa Twp HSD 140	Ottawa
253	0.0	Park Ridge CCSD 64	Park Ridge
253	0.0	Queen Bee SD 16	Glendale Hgts
253	0.0	Schaumburg CCSD 54	Schaumburg
253	0.0	Warren Twp HSD 121	Gages Lake
253	0.0	Wilmette SD 39	Wilmette
253	0.0	Winnetka SD 36	Winnetka
253	0.0	Yorkville CUSD 115	Yorkville
292	n/a	Adlai E Stevenson HSD 125	Lincolnshire
292	n/a	CHSD 128	Libertyville
292	n/a	Hinsdale CCSD 181	Westmont
292	n/a	Homewood Flossmoor CHSD 233	Flossmoor
292	n/a	Lockport Twp HSD 205	Lockport
292	n/a	Maine Township HSD 207	Park Ridge
292	n/a	Mc Henry CHSD 156	Mchenry
292	n/a	New Trier Twp HSD 203	Northfield
292	n/a	Northfield Twp HSD 225	Glenview
292	n/a	Oak Lawn CHSD 229	Oak Lawn
292	n/a	Reavis Twp HSD 220	Burbank
292	n/a	Thornton Twp HSD 205	South Holland
292	n/a	Twp HSD 113	Highland Park

Students Eligible for Reduced-Price Lunch

Rank	Percent	District Name	City
1	43.2	North Chicago SD 187	North Chicago
2	17.2	Berwyn South SD 100	Berwyn
3	16.1	Berkeley SD 87	Berkeley
4	15.3	Bellwood SD 88	Bellwood
5	14.9	Berwyn North SD 98	Berwyn
6	14.8	Cicero SD 99	Cicero
6	14.8	Summit SD 104	Summit
8	13.6	Steger SD 194	Steger
9	13.4	Waukegan CUSD 60	Waukegan
10	13.2	Belleville SD 118	Belleville
11	13.1	South Holland SD 151	South Holland
12	12.2	Beardstown CUSD 15	Beardstown
12	12.2	Mannheim SD 83	Franklin Park
14	12.1	J S Morton HSD 201	Cicero
15	11.3	Rantoul City SD 137	Rantoul
15	11.3	Round Lake CUSD 116	Round Lake
17	11.0	Mascoutah CUD 19	Mascoutah
18	10.8	West Chicago ESD 33	West Chicago
19	10.4	Aurora East USD 131	Aurora
19	10.4	Dolton SD 149	Calumet City
21	10.0	CCSD 62	Des Plaines
21	10.0	Galesburg CUSD 205	Galesburg
21	10.0	Joliet Psd 86	Joliet
21	10.0	Paxton-Buckley-Loda CUD 10	Paxton
21	10.0	Pekin PSD 108	Pekin
21	10.0	West Carroll CUSD 314	Thomson
27	9.9	Argo CHSD 217	Summit
27	9.9	Taylorville CUSD 3	Taylorville
27	9.9	Thornton Fractional Twp HSD 215	Calumet City
30	9.8	Pana CUSD 8	Pana
30	9.8	Rich Twp HSD 227	Olympia Fields
32	9.5	Collinsville CUSD 10	Collinsville
33	9.4	Crete Monee CUSD 201u	Crete
34	9.2	Bloom Twp HSD 206	Chicago Heights
34	9.2	Rockford SD 205	Rockford
34	9.2	Roxana CUSD 1	Roxana
37	9.0	CCSD 168	Sauk Village
37	9.0	Flora CUSD 35	Flora
39	8.9	Quincy SD 172	Quincy
40	8.7	Carlinville CUSD 1	Carlinville
40	8.7	Granite City CUSD 9	Granite City
40	8.7	Kewanee CUSD 229	Kewanee
40	8.7	Zion ESD 6	Zion
44	8.6	Sterling CUSD 5	Sterling
45	8.5	Harvard CUSD 50	Harvard
45	8.5	Maywood-Melrose Park-Broadview 89	Melrose Park
47	8.4	Bloomington SD 87	Bloomington
47	8.4	North Boone CUSD 200	Poplar Grove
47	8.4	Streator ESD 44	Streator
50	8.3	Park Forest SD 163	Park Forest
50	8.3	Skokie SD 69	Skokie
52	8.1	City of Chicago SD 299	Chicago
52	8.1	Evanston CCSD 65	Evanston
54	8.0	Bensenville SD 2	Bensenville
54	8.0	Canton Union SD 66	Canton
54	8.0	Matteson ESD 162	Matteson
54	8.0	Paris-Union SD 95	Paris
54	8.0	Southwestern CUSD 9	Piasa
59	7.9	Cook County SD 130	Blue Island
59	7.9	Valley View CUSD 365u	Romeoville
59	7.9	Wheeling CCSD 21	Wheeling
62	7.8	Charleston CUSD 1	Charleston
62	7.8	Dixon USD 170	Dixon
62	7.8	Jersey CUSD 100	Jerseyville
62	7.8	Prairie Central CUSD 8	Fairbury
62	7.8	Rock Island SD 41	Rock Island
67	7.7	Evanston Twp HSD 202	Evanston
68	7.6	Mount Vernon SD 80	Mount Vernon
68	7.6	United Twp HSD 30	East Moline
70	7.5	Jacksonville SD 117	Jacksonville
70	7.5	Vandalia CUSD 203	Vandalia
72	7.4	CHSD 218	Oak Lawn
72	7.4	East Moline SD 37	East Moline
72	7.4	East Richland CUSD 1	Olney
72	7.4	Harlem Ud 122	Loves Park
72	7.4	Pekin CSD 303	Pekin
72	7.4	Skokie SD 68	Skokie
72	7.4	Sparta CUSD 140	Sparta
79	7.3	Danville CCSD 118	Danville
79	7.3	Dolton SD 148	Riverdale
79	7.3	Herrin CUSD 4	Herrin
79	7.3	Lyons SD 103	Lyons
79	7.3	Robinson CUSD 2	Robinson

79	7.3	Urbana SD 116	Urbana
85	7.2	Belvidere CUSD 100	Belvidere
85	7.2	Freeport SD 145	Freeport
87	7.1	Beach Park CCSD 3	Beach Park
87	7.1	Macomb CUSD 185	Macomb
89	7.0	School District U-46	Elgin
90	6.9	Alsip-Hazlgrn-Oaklwn SD 126	Alsip
90	6.9	Decatur SD 61	Decatur
90	6.9	Frankfort CUSD 168	West Frankfort
90	6.9	Olympia CUSD 16	Stanford
94	6.8	Chicago Heights SD 170	Chicago Heights
94	6.8	Mundelein ESD 75	Mundelein
94	6.8	River Trails SD 26	Mount Prospect
97	6.7	CUSD 201	Westmont
97	6.7	Murphysboro CUSD 186	Murphysboro
99	6.6	Belleville Twp HSD 201	Belleville
99	6.6	Evergreen Park ESD 124	Evergreen Park
99	6.6	Litchfield CUSD 12	Litchfield
102	6.5	Posen-Robbins ESD 143-5	Posen
102	6.5	Sherrard CUSD 200	Sherrard
102	6.5	Woodstock CUSD 200	Woodstock
105	6.4	Leyden CHSD 212	Franklin Park
105	6.4	Marion CUSD 2	Marion
105	6.4	Springfield SD 186	Springfield
108	6.3	Alton CUSD 11	Alton
108	6.3	Clinton CUSD 15	Clinton
108	6.3	Peoria SD 150	Peoria
108	6.3	Prairie-Hills ESD 144	Markham
112	6.2	Community CSD 59	Arlington Hgts
113	6.1	Cahokia CUSD 187	Cahokia
113	6.1	Rochelle CCSD 231	Rochelle
115	6.0	Aurora West USD 129	Aurora
115	6.0	Bradley SD 61	Bradley
115	6.0	Zion-Benton Twp HSD 126	Zion
118	5.9	East Maine SD 63	Des Plaines
118	5.9	Moline USD 40	Moline
118	5.9	Wabash CUSD 348	Mount Carmel
121	5.8	ESD 159	Matteson
121	5.8	East Peoria SD 86	East Peoria
121	5.8	Kankakee SD 111	Kankakee
124	5.7	Harrisburg CUSD 3	Harrisburg
124	5.7	Massac UD 1	Metropolis
124	5.7	Ottawa ESD 141	Ottawa
127	5.6	CUSD 300	Carpentersville
127	5.6	Riverton CUSD 14	Riverton
129	5.5	Indian Springs SD 109	Justice
129	5.5	Tolono CUSD 7	Tolono
131	5.4	Effingham CUSD 40	Effingham
131	5.4	Genoa Kingston CUSD 424	Genoa
131	5.4	Marquardt SD 15	Glendale Hgts
131	5.4	Wilmington CUSD 209u	Wilmington
135	5.3	Joliet Twp HSD 204	Joliet
135	5.3	Reed Custer CUSD 255u	Braidwood
137	5.2	Country Club Hls SD 160	Country Club Hls
137	5.2	Geneseo CUSD 228	Geneseo
137	5.2	Lombard SD 44	Lombard
137	5.2	Palatine CCSD 15	Palatine
141	5.0	Bethalto CUSD 8	Bethalto
142	4.9	Champaign CUSD 4	Champaign
142	4.9	Ridgeland SD 122	Oak Lawn
144	4.8	Monmouth-Roseville CUSD 238	Monmouth
144	4.8	Mundelein Cons HSD 120	Mundelein
144	4.8	Tinley Park CCSD 146	Tinley Park
147	4.7	Highland CUSD 5	Highland
147	4.7	Woodridge SD 68	Woodridge
149	4.6	Addison SD 4	Addison
149	4.6	Harvey SD 152	Harvey
149	4.6	Hillsboro CUSD 3	Hillsboro
149	4.6	School District 45 Dupage County	Villa Park
153	4.4	Bond County CUSD 2	Greenville
153	4.4	Herscher CUSD 2	Herscher
153	4.4	Homewood SD 153	Homewood
153	4.4	Woodland CCSD 50	Gurnee
157	4.3	Elmwood Park CUSD 401	Elmwood Park
157	4.3	Eureka CUD 140	Eureka
159	4.2	Mattoon CUSD 2	Mattoon
160	4.1	Oak Park ESD 97	Oak Park
160	4.1	Triad CUSD 2	Troy
160	4.1	Waterloo CUSD 5	Waterloo
163	3.9	Glenview CCSD 34	Glenview
163	3.9	Mchenry CCSD 15	Mchenry
165	3.8	East St Louis SD 189	E Saint Louis
165	3.8	Grayslake CCSD 46	Grayslake
165	3.8	Oregon CUSD 220	Oregon
168	3.7	Monticello CUSD 25	Monticello
169	3.6	Edwardsville CUSD 7	Edwardsville
169	3.6	O Fallon CCSD 90	Ofallon
171	3.5	Dekalb CUSD 428	De Kalb
171	3.5	Lake Villa CCSD 41	Lake Villa
171	3.5	Lisle CUSD 202	Lisle
171	3.5	Township HSD 211	Palatine
175	3.4	Du Page HSD 88	Villa Park
175	3.4	IL Valley Central USD 321	Chillicothe
175	3.4	Sandwich CUSD 430	Sandwich
178	3.3	Lansing SD 158	Lansing
179	3.2	Oswego CUSD 308	Oswego
179	3.2	Township HSD 214	Arlington Hgts
181	3.1	Proviso Twp HSD 209	Forest Park
182	3.0	CUSD 200	Wheaton
182	3.0	O Fallon Twp HSD 203	Ofallon
184	2.9	Darien SD 61	Darien
184	2.9	Mclean County USD 5	Normal
184	2.9	Mount Zion CUSD 3	Mount Zion
187	2.8	Carterville CUSD 5	Carterville
187	2.8	Winnebago CUSD 323	Winnebago
189	2.7	Hawthorn CCSD 73	Vernon Hills
189	2.7	Wauconda CUSD 118	Wauconda
191	2.6	CHSD 99	Downers Grove
191	2.6	Coal City CUSD 1	Coal City
193	2.5	Bradley Bourbonnais CHSD 307	Bradley
193	2.5	Burbank SD 111	Burbank
193	2.5	Grant CHSD 124	Fox Lake
193	2.5	Meridian CUSD 223	Stillman Valley
193	2.5	Troy CCSD 30c	Plainfield
198	2.4	Antioch CCSD 34	Antioch
198	2.4	Crystal Lake CCSD 47	Crystal Lake
198	2.4	Johnsburg CUSD 12	Johnsburg
201	2.3	Barrington CUSD 220	Barrington
201	2.3	Bourbonnais SD 53	Bourbonnais
203	2.2	Arlington Hgts SD 25	Arlington Hgts
204	2.1	Oak Park-River Forest SD 200	Oak Park
205	2.0	Channahon SD 17	Channahon
205	2.0	Morton CUSD 709	Morton
205	2.0	Sycamore CUSD 427	Sycamore
205	2.0	Will County SD 92	Lockport
209	1.9	Hononegah Chd 207	Rockton
209	1.9	Plainfield SD 202	Plainfield
211	1.8	Cary CCSD 26	Cary
211	1.8	Kinnikinnick CCSD 131	Roscoe
211	1.8	Minooka CCSD 201	Minooka
211	1.8	New Lenox SD 122	New Lenox
211	1.8	Nippersink SD 2	Richmond
211	1.8	Oak Lawn-Hometown SD 123	Oak Lawn
217	1.7	Byron CUSD 226	Byron
217	1.7	Columbia CUSD 4	Columbia
217	1.7	Glenbard Twp HSD 87	Glen Ellyn
217	1.7	Plano CUSD 88	Plano
221	1.6	Dunlap CUSD 323	Dunlap
221	1.6	Lincoln Way CHSD 210	New Lenox
221	1.6	Manteno CUSD 5	Manteno
224	1.5	North Palos SD 117	Palos Hills
225	1.4	CSD 158	Algonquin
226	1.3	Aptakisic-Tripp CCSD 102	Buffalo Grove
226	1.3	Kildeer Countryside CCSD 96	Buffalo Grove
226	1.3	Lake Zurich CUSD 95	Lake Zurich
229	1.2	Ball Chatham CUSD 5	Chatham
229	1.2	La Grange SD 102	La Grange Park
229	1.2	West Harvey-Dixmoor PSD 147	Harvey
232	1.1	Kaneland CUSD 302	Maple Park
232	1.1	Mahomet-Seymour CUSD 3	Mahomet
232	1.1	Mokena SD 159	Mokena
232	1.1	Peotone CUSD 207u	Peotone
236	1.0	Saint Charles CUSD 303	Saint Charles
237	0.9	CHSD 155	Crystal Lake
237	0.9	Midlothian SD 143	Midlothian
237	0.9	Palos CCSD 118	Palos Park
240	0.6	Batavia USD 101	Batavia
240	0.6	North Shore SD 112	Highland Park
240	0.6	Summit Hill SD 161	Frankfort
243	0.5	Lemont-Bromberek CSD 113a	Lemont
243	0.5	Millburn CCSD 24	Wadsworth
245	0.4	Downers Grove Gsd 58	Downers Grove
245	0.4	Mount Prospect SD 57	Mount Prospect
245	0.4	Naperville CUSD 203	Naperville
248	0.3	Rochester CUSD 3a	Rochester
249	0.2	Central CUSD 301	Burlington
250	0.1	Keeneyville SD 20	Hanover Park
251	0.0	Libertyville SD 70	Libertyville
252	0.0	Arbor Park SD 145	Oak Forest
252	0.0	Bremen CHSD 228	Midlothian
252	0.0	CCSD 89	Glen Ellyn
252	0.0	CCSD 93	Bloomingdale
252	0.0	CHSD 117	Lake Villa
252	0.0	CHSD 94	West Chicago
252	0.0	Cons HSD 230	Orland Park
252	0.0	Corrections SD 428 Dept of	Springfield
252	0.0	Deerfield SD 109	Deerfield
252	0.0	Elmhurst SD 205	Elmhurst
252	0.0	Fenton CHSD 100	Bensenville
252	0.0	Flossmoor SD 161	Chicago Heights
252	0.0	Forest Ridge SD 142	Oak Forest
252	0.0	Frankfort CCSD 157c	Frankfort
252	0.0	Fremont SD 79	Mundelein
252	0.0	Geneva CUSD 304	Geneva
252	0.0	Glen Ellyn SD 41	Glen Ellyn
252	0.0	Grayslake CHSD 127	Grayslake
252	0.0	Gurnee SD 56	Gurnee
252	0.0	Hinsdale Twp HSD 86	Hinsdale
252	0.0	Homer CCSD 33c	Homer Glen
252	0.0	Indian Prairie CUSD 204	Aurora
252	0.0	Kirby SD 140	Tinley Park
252	0.0	Lake Forest CHSD 115	Lake Forest
252	0.0	Lake Forest SD 67	Lake Forest
252	0.0	Lake Park CHSD 108	Roselle
252	0.0	Lincolnshire-Prairieview SD 103	Lincolnshire
252	0.0	Lyons Twp HSD 204	La Grange
252	0.0	Minooka CHSD 111	Minooka
252	0.0	Niles Twp CHSD 219	Skokie
252	0.0	Northbrook SD 28	Northbrook
252	0.0	Orland SD 135	Orland Park
252	0.0	Ottawa Twp HSD 140	Ottawa
252	0.0	Park Ridge CCSD 64	Park Ridge
252	0.0	Queen Bee SD 16	Glendale Hgts
252	0.0	Schaumburg CCSD 54	Schaumburg
252	0.0	Warren Twp HSD 121	Gages Lake
252	0.0	Wilmette SD 39	Wilmette
252	0.0	Winnetka SD 36	Winnetka
252	0.0	Yorkville CUSD 115	Yorkville
292	n/a	Adlai E Stevenson HSD 125	Lincolnshire
292	n/a	CHSD 128	Libertyville
292	n/a	Hinsdale CCSD 181	Westmont
292	n/a	Homewood Flossmoor CHSD 233	Flossmoor
292	n/a	Lockport Twp HSD 205	Lockport
292	n/a	Maine Township HSD 207	Park Ridge
292	n/a	Mc Henry CHSD 156	Mchenry
292	n/a	New Trier Twp HSD 203	Northfield
292	n/a	Northfield Twp HSD 225	Glenview
292	n/a	Oak Lawn CHSD 229	Oak Lawn
292	n/a	Reavis Twp HSD 220	Burbank
292	n/a	Thornton Twp HSD 205	South Holland
292	n/a	Twp HSD 113	Highland Park

Student/Teacher Ratio

Rank	Ratio	District Name	City
1	25.4	Channahon SD 17	Channahon
2	22.5	Carterville CUSD 5	Carterville
3	22.2	Bellwood SD 88	Bellwood
3	22.2	Minooka CCSD 201	Minooka
5	22.0	Mundelein Cons HSD 120	Mundelein
6	21.9	Country Club Hls SD 160	Country Club Hls
7	21.3	Bloom Twp HSD 206	Chicago Heights
8	21.2	United Twp HSD 30	East Moline
9	20.9	Dolton SD 149	Calumet City
9	20.9	Glenbard Twp HSD 87	Glen Ellyn
9	20.9	Granite City CUSD 9	Granite City
12	20.8	West Harvey-Dixmoor PSD 147	Harvey
13	20.6	Decatur SD 61	Decatur
14	20.3	Belvidere CUSD 100	Belvidere
14	20.3	Berwyn North SD 98	Berwyn
14	20.3	Bradley Bourbonnais CHSD 307	Bradley
14	20.3	Mokena SD 159	Mokena
14	20.3	Yorkville CUSD 115	Yorkville
19	20.1	Round Lake CUSD 116	Round Lake
20	19.9	Belleville SD 118	Belleville
20	19.9	Belleville Twp HSD 201	Belleville
20	19.9	Riverton CUSD 14	Riverton
23	19.7	Lake Park CHSD 108	Roselle
23	19.7	O Fallon Twp HSD 203	Ofallon
25	19.6	Crete Monee CUSD 201u	Crete
25	19.6	Zion-Benton Twp HSD 126	Zion
27	19.5	Dunlap CUSD 323	Dunlap
27	19.5	Meridian CUSD 223	Stillman Valley
27	19.5	Palatine CCSD 15	Palatine
30	19.4	Hononegah Chd 207	Rockton
30	19.4	Marion CUSD 2	Marion
30	19.4	New Lenox SD 122	New Lenox
33	19.3	CUSD 300	Carpentersville
33	19.3	Lockport Twp HSD 205	Lockport
33	19.3	Mchenry CCSD 15	Mchenry

Rank	Value	District	City
33	19.3	Minooka CHSD 111	Minooka
33	19.3	Prairie-Hills ESD 144	Markham
38	19.2	Lincoln Way CHSD 210	New Lenox
39	19.1	Elmwood Park CUSD 401	Elmwood Park
39	19.1	Mount Zion CUSD 3	Mount Zion
39	19.1	Oswego CUSD 308	Oswego
39	19.1	Reavis Twp HSD 220	Burbank
39	19.1	Thornton Twp HSD 205	South Holland
44	19.0	Cary CCSD 26	Cary
44	19.0	Harvey SD 152	Harvey
44	19.0	Pekin CSD 303	Pekin
44	19.0	Posen-Robbins ESD 143-5	Posen
48	18.9	Troy CCSD 30c	Plainfield
49	18.8	Bradley SD 61	Bradley
50	18.7	Bourbonnais SD 53	Bourbonnais
50	18.7	Coal City CUSD 1	Coal City
50	18.7	Grayslake CCSD 46	Grayslake
50	18.7	O Fallon CCSD 90	Ofallon
54	18.6	J S Morton HSD 201	Cicero
54	18.6	North Boone CUSD 200	Poplar Grove
54	18.6	School District U-46	Elgin
57	18.5	Kankakee SD 111	Kankakee
57	18.5	North Chicago SD 187	North Chicago
57	18.5	Park Forest SD 163	Park Forest
57	18.5	Rantoul City SD 137	Rantoul
57	18.5	Rochester CUSD 3a	Rochester
62	18.4	Cahokia CUSD 187	Cahokia
62	18.4	Grant CHSD 124	Fox Lake
62	18.4	Mc Henry CHSD 156	Mchenry
62	18.4	Taylorville CUSD 3	Taylorville
62	18.4	Woodstock CUSD 200	Woodstock
67	18.3	Herrin CUSD 4	Herrin
67	18.3	Hillsboro CUSD 3	Hillsboro
69	18.2	CCSD 168	Sauk Village
69	18.2	Fremont SD 79	Mundelein
69	18.2	Geneseo CUSD 228	Geneseo
69	18.2	Homer CCSD 33c	Homer Glen
69	18.2	Kewanee CUSD 229	Kewanee
69	18.2	Litchfield CUSD 12	Litchfield
69	18.2	Oregon CUSD 220	Oregon
69	18.2	Sterling CUSD 5	Sterling
69	18.2	Summit Hill SD 161	Frankfort
78	18.1	CHSD 155	Crystal Lake
78	18.1	Frankfort CUSD 168	West Frankfort
78	18.1	Kinnikinnick CCSD 131	Roscoe
78	18.1	Mahomet-Seymour CUSD 3	Mahomet
78	18.1	Nippersink SD 2	Richmond
78	18.1	North Palos SD 117	Palos Hills
84	18.0	Lemont-Bromberek CSD 113a	Lemont
84	18.0	Valley View CUSD 365u	Romeoville
86	17.9	Ball Chatham CUSD 5	Chatham
86	17.9	Burbank SD 111	Burbank
86	17.9	Carlinville CUSD 1	Carlinville
86	17.9	Johnsburg CUSD 12	Johnsburg
86	17.9	Joliet Psd 86	Joliet
86	17.9	Will County SD 92	Lockport
86	17.9	Zion ESD 6	Zion
93	17.8	Batavia USD 101	Batavia
93	17.8	CHSD 218	Oak Lawn
93	17.8	Collinsville CUSD 10	Collinsville
93	17.8	Downers Grove Gsd 58	Downers Grove
97	17.7	Arbor Park SD 145	Oak Forest
97	17.7	Argo CHSD 217	Summit
97	17.7	Cons HSD 230	Orland Park
97	17.7	Proviso Twp HSD 209	Forest Park
97	17.7	South Holland SD 151	South Holland
102	17.6	Aurora East USD 131	Aurora
102	17.6	ESD 159	Matteson
102	17.6	Geneva CUSD 304	Geneva
102	17.6	Plainfield SD 202	Plainfield
102	17.6	Vandalia CUSD 203	Vandalia
102	17.6	Wauconda CUSD 118	Wauconda
102	17.6	Wilmington CUSD 209u	Wilmington
109	17.5	Aurora West USD 129	Aurora
109	17.5	Cicero SD 99	Cicero
109	17.5	Crystal Lake CCSD 47	Crystal Lake
109	17.5	Frankfort CCSD 157c	Frankfort
109	17.5	Harvard CUSD 50	Harvard
109	17.5	Rockford SD 205	Rockford
109	17.5	Skokie SD 69	Skokie
116	17.4	Bond County CUSD 2	Greenville
116	17.4	Lansing SD 158	Lansing
116	17.4	Thornton Fractional Twp HSD 215	Calumet City
119	17.3	Dixon USD 170	Dixon
119	17.3	Indian Prairie CUSD 204	Aurora
119	17.3	Naperville CUSD 203	Naperville
119	17.3	Olympia CUSD 16	Stanford
119	17.3	Waukegan CUSD 60	Waukegan
124	17.2	Byron CUSD 226	Byron
124	17.2	CHSD 99	Downers Grove
124	17.2	Triad CUSD 2	Troy
127	17.1	CSD 158	Algonquin
127	17.1	Lake Villa CCSD 41	Lake Villa
127	17.1	Massac UD 1	Metropolis
127	17.1	Orland SD 135	Orland Park
127	17.1	Saint Charles CUSD 303	Saint Charles
127	17.1	Sycamore CUSD 427	Sycamore
127	17.1	West Chicago ESD 33	West Chicago
134	17.0	Charleston CUSD 1	Charleston
134	17.0	Harrisburg CUSD 3	Harrisburg
134	17.0	Kirby SD 140	Tinley Park
134	17.0	Ottawa Twp HSD 140	Ottawa
134	17.0	Ridgeland SD 122	Oak Lawn
139	16.9	Danville CCSD 118	Danville
139	16.9	Effingham CUSD 40	Effingham
139	16.9	Galesburg CUSD 205	Galesburg
139	16.9	Harlem Ud 122	Loves Park
139	16.9	Mount Prospect SD 57	Mount Prospect
139	16.9	Roxana CUSD 1	Roxana
145	16.8	Addison SD 4	Addison
145	16.8	Adlai E Stevenson HSD 125	Lincolnshire
145	16.8	Clinton CUSD 15	Clinton
145	16.8	Dekalb CUSD 428	De Kalb
145	16.8	Midlothian SD 143	Midlothian
145	16.8	Moline USD 40	Moline
145	16.8	Quincy SD 172	Quincy
152	16.7	IL Valley Central USD 321	Chillicothe
152	16.7	Oak Lawn CHSD 229	Oak Lawn
152	16.7	Wabash CUSD 348	Mount Carmel
152	16.7	Warren Twp HSD 121	Gages Lake
152	16.7	Waterloo CUSD 5	Waterloo
157	16.6	Beach Park CCSD 3	Beach Park
157	16.6	Bensenville SD 2	Bensenville
157	16.6	Berkeley SD 87	Berkeley
157	16.6	Homewood Flossmoor CHSD 233	Flossmoor
157	16.6	Kaneland CUSD 302	Maple Park
157	16.6	Matteson ESD 162	Matteson
157	16.6	Maywood-Melrose Park-Broadview 89	Melrose Park
157	16.6	Monticello CUSD 25	Monticello
157	16.6	Palos CCSD 118	Palos Park
157	16.6	Rock Island SD 41	Rock Island
157	16.6	Township HSD 211	Palatine
157	16.6	Township HSD 214	Arlington Hgts
169	16.5	Barrington CUSD 220	Barrington
169	16.5	Cook County SD 130	Blue Island
169	16.5	Sandwich CUSD 430	Sandwich
172	16.4	CHSD 94	West Chicago
172	16.4	Du Page HSD 88	Villa Park
172	16.4	East St Louis SD 189	E Saint Louis
172	16.4	Edwardsville CUSD 7	Edwardsville
172	16.4	Herscher CUSD 2	Herscher
172	16.4	Lyons Twp HSD 204	La Grange
172	16.4	Pana CUSD 8	Pana
179	16.3	Antioch CCSD 34	Antioch
179	16.3	CUSD 200	Wheaton
179	16.3	Jersey CUSD 100	Jerseyville
179	16.3	Marquardt SD 15	Glendale Hgts
179	16.3	Mclean County USD 5	Normal
179	16.3	Robinson CUSD 2	Robinson
185	16.2	Chicago Heights SD 170	Chicago Heights
185	16.2	Elmhurst SD 205	Elmhurst
185	16.2	Eureka CUD 140	Eureka
185	16.2	Fenton CHSD 100	Bensenville
185	16.2	Joliet Twp HSD 204	Joliet
185	16.2	Reed Custer CUSD 255u	Braidwood
191	16.1	Alton CUSD 11	Alton
191	16.1	Bethalto CUSD 8	Bethalto
191	16.1	CHSD 128	Libertyville
191	16.1	Grayslake CHSD 127	Grayslake
191	16.1	Kildeer Countryside CCSD 96	Buffalo Grove
191	16.1	Southwestern CUSD 9	Piasa
191	16.1	Springfield SD 186	Springfield
198	16.0	Columbia CUSD 4	Columbia
198	16.0	Genoa Kingston CUSD 424	Genoa
198	16.0	Indian Springs SD 109	Justice
198	16.0	Oak Park-River Forest SD 200	Oak Park
202	15.9	Alsip-Hazlgrn-Oaklwn SD 126	Alsip
202	15.9	East Maine SD 63	Des Plaines
202	15.9	East Moline SD 37	East Moline
202	15.9	Hawthorn CCSD 73	Vernon Hills
202	15.9	Mount Vernon SD 80	Mount Vernon
202	15.9	Murphysboro CUSD 186	Murphysboro
208	15.8	Bremen CHSD 228	Midlothian
208	15.8	East Richland CUSD 1	Olney
208	15.8	Highland CUSD 5	Highland
208	15.8	Leyden CHSD 212	Franklin Park
208	15.8	Libertyville SD 70	Libertyville
208	15.8	Peotone CUSD 207u	Peotone
208	15.8	Rich Twp HSD 227	Olympia Fields
208	15.8	Woodridge SD 68	Woodridge
216	15.7	Bloomington SD 87	Bloomington
216	15.7	Pekin PSD 108	Pekin
218	15.6	City of Chicago SD 299	Chicago
218	15.6	Woodland CCSD 50	Gurnee
220	15.5	Beardstown CUSD 15	Beardstown
220	15.5	Canton Union SD 66	Canton
220	15.5	East Peoria SD 86	East Peoria
220	15.5	Flora CUSD 35	Flora
220	15.5	Keeneyville SD 20	Hanover Park
220	15.5	Manteno CUSD 5	Manteno
220	15.5	Plano CUSD 88	Plano
220	15.5	Sparta CUSD 140	Sparta
220	15.5	Winnebago CUSD 323	Winnebago
229	15.4	Flossmoor SD 161	Chicago Heights
229	15.4	Gurnee SD 56	Gurnee
229	15.4	Hinsdale CCSD 181	Westmont
229	15.4	Mascoutah CUD 19	Mascoutah
229	15.4	Morton CUSD 709	Morton
229	15.4	Paxton-Buckley-Loda CUD 10	Paxton
229	15.4	Schaumburg CCSD 54	Schaumburg
236	15.3	Berwyn South SD 100	Berwyn
236	15.3	CCSD 89	Glen Ellyn
236	15.3	Mannheim SD 83	Franklin Park
236	15.3	Ottawa ESD 141	Ottawa
240	15.2	Lake Zurich CUSD 95	Lake Zurich
240	15.2	Lombard SD 44	Lombard
240	15.2	River Trails SD 26	Mount Prospect
240	15.2	School District 45 Dupage County	Villa Park
240	15.2	Streator ESD 44	Streator
245	15.1	Arlington Hgts SD 25	Arlington Hgts
245	15.1	CCSD 62	Des Plaines
245	15.1	CCSD 93	Bloomingdale
245	15.1	Central CUSD 301	Burlington
245	15.1	Freeport SD 145	Freeport
245	15.1	Lisle CUSD 202	Lisle
245	15.1	Summit SD 104	Summit
252	14.9	CUSD 201	Westmont
252	14.9	Dolton SD 148	Riverdale
252	14.9	Forest Ridge SD 142	Oak Forest
252	14.9	Hinsdale Twp HSD 86	Hinsdale
252	14.9	Twp HSD 113	Highland Park
257	14.8	Glen Ellyn SD 41	Glen Ellyn
258	14.7	Jacksonville SD 117	Jacksonville
258	14.7	Macomb CUSD 185	Macomb
258	14.7	Monmouth-Roseville CUSD 238	Monmouth
258	14.7	Paris-Union SD 95	Paris
258	14.7	Tolono CUSD 7	Tolono
263	14.6	CHSD 117	Lake Villa
263	14.6	Community CSD 59	Arlington Hgts
265	14.5	Aptakisic-Tripp CCSD 102	Buffalo Grove
265	14.5	Mundelein ESD 75	Mundelein
265	14.5	Oak Park ESD 97	Oak Park
265	14.5	Peoria SD 150	Peoria
265	14.5	Tinley Park CCSD 146	Tinley Park
270	14.4	Evergreen Park ESD 124	Evergreen Park
270	14.4	Glenview CCSD 34	Glenview
270	14.4	Park Ridge CCSD 64	Park Ridge
270	14.4	Queen Bee SD 16	Glendale Hgts
270	14.4	Rochelle CCSD 231	Rochelle
275	14.3	La Grange SD 102	La Grange Park
275	14.3	Lincolnshire-Prairieview SD 103	Lincolnshire
275	14.3	Niles Twp CHSD 219	Skokie
275	14.3	Northfield Twp HSD 225	Glenview
279	14.2	Sherrard CUSD 200	Sherrard
279	14.2	West Carroll CUSD 314	Thomson
281	14.1	Evanston Twp HSD 202	Evanston
281	14.1	Mattoon CUSD 2	Mattoon
281	14.1	Wheeling CCSD 21	Wheeling
284	14.0	Prairie Central CUSD 8	Fairbury
285	13.9	Deerfield SD 109	Deerfield
285	13.9	Lake Forest CHSD 115	Lake Forest
285	13.9	Steger SD 194	Steger
288	13.8	Champaign CUSD 4	Champaign
289	13.7	Maine Township HSD 207	Park Ridge
290	13.6	Homewood SD 153	Homewood
291	13.5	Darien SD 61	Darien
292	13.4	Lake Forest SD 67	Lake Forest
293	13.3	North Shore SD 112	Highland Park
293	13.3	Urbana SD 116	Urbana
295	13.2	Skokie SD 68	Skokie
296	13.1	Millburn CCSD 24	Wadsworth

Rank	Ratio	District Name	City
296	13.1	Wilmette SD 39	Wilmette
298	12.9	Lyons SD 103	Lyons
298	12.9	Oak Lawn-Hometown SD 123	Oak Lawn
300	12.7	Evanston CCSD 65	Evanston
301	12.3	Winnetka SD 36	Winnetka
302	12.2	New Trier Twp HSD 203	Northfield
303	11.4	Northbrook SD 28	Northbrook
304	9.4	Corrections SD 428 Dept of	Springfield

Student/Librarian Ratio

Rank	Ratio	District Name	City
1	21,615.0	North Chicago SD 187	North Chicago
2	13,830.0	Elmwood Park CUSD 401	Elmwood Park
3	7,352.0	Granite City CUSD 9	Granite City
4	7,238.0	Quincy SD 172	Quincy
5	6,687.0	Round Lake CUSD 116	Round Lake
6	6,554.0	Thornton Twp HSD 205	South Holland
7	6,470.0	Danville CCSD 118	Danville
8	5,694.0	Dekalb CUSD 428	De Kalb
9	5,586.0	Maywood-Melrose Park-Broadview 89	Melrose Park
10	5,055.5	Joliet Psd 86	Joliet
11	5,046.0	Cahokia CUSD 187	Cahokia
12	4,774.0	Crete Monee CUSD 201u	Crete
13	3,968.0	Addison SD 4	Addison
14	3,873.0	Triad CUSD 2	Troy
15	3,767.0	Pekin PSD 108	Pekin
16	3,713.0	Jacksonville SD 117	Jacksonville
17	3,709.0	Troy CCSD 30c	Plainfield
18	3,612.0	Sterling CUSD 5	Sterling
19	3,583.0	Summit Hill SD 161	Frankfort
20	3,506.0	Berwyn South SD 100	Berwyn
21	3,441.0	Sycamore CUSD 427	Sycamore
22	3,362.0	Lake Villa CCSD 41	Lake Villa
23	3,351.0	O Fallon CCSD 90	Ofallon
24	3,239.0	Bellwood SD 88	Bellwood
25	3,171.0	Collinsville CUSD 10	Collinsville
26	3,149.5	Rock Island SD 41	Rock Island
27	2,985.5	Kankakee SD 111	Kankakee
28	2,946.0	Zion ESD 6	Zion
29	2,934.0	Antioch CCSD 34	Antioch
30	2,929.0	Dixon USD 170	Dixon
31	2,924.0	Harvey SD 152	Harvey
32	2,694.0	Waterloo CUSD 5	Waterloo
33	2,622.0	Marquardt SD 15	Glendale Hgts
34	2,616.0	Flossmoor SD 161	Chicago Heights
35	2,581.0	Zion-Benton Twp HSD 126	Zion
36	2,566.0	Sandwich CUSD 430	Sandwich
37	2,516.2	Springfield SD 186	Springfield
38	2,507.0	Beach Park CCSD 3	Beach Park
39	2,485.0	Arlington Hgts SD 25	Arlington Hgts
40	2,463.2	Aurora East USD 131	Aurora
41	2,409.0	Mc Henry CHSD 156	Mchenry
42	2,387.0	Massac UD 1	Metropolis
43	2,345.0	O Fallon Twp HSD 203	Ofallon
44	2,332.7	School District U-46	Elgin
45	2,317.0	Lyons SD 103	Lyons
46	2,313.0	Lansing SD 158	Lansing
47	2,255.0	Adlai E Stevenson HSD 125	Lincolnshire
48	2,210.7	Lincoln Way CHSD 210	New Lenox
49	2,202.0	Park Forest SD 163	Park Forest
50	2,168.0	Pekin CSD 303	Pekin
51	2,166.0	IL Valley Central USD 321	Chillicothe
52	2,130.0	Manteno CUSD 5	Manteno
53	2,084.0	Olympia CUSD 16	Stanford
54	2,046.0	Murphysboro CUSD 186	Murphysboro
55	2,028.5	Du Page HSD 88	Villa Park
56	2,023.0	Ottawa ESD 141	Ottawa
57	2,018.0	Coal City CUSD 1	Coal City
58	2,010.0	Rockford SD 205	Rockford
59	2,004.0	Evergreen Park ESD 124	Evergreen Park
60	1,999.0	Peotone CUSD 207u	Peotone
61	1,974.6	East St Louis SD 189	E Saint Louis
62	1,951.0	Hononegah Chd 207	Rockton
63	1,947.0	Bradley Bourbonnais CHSD 307	Bradley
64	1,940.0	Genoa Kingston CUSD 424	Genoa
65	1,903.0	Streator ESD 44	Streator
66	1,900.4	Peoria SD 150	Peoria
67	1,887.0	East Peoria SD 86	East Peoria
68	1,873.0	Wabash CUSD 348	Mount Carmel
69	1,864.0	Lockport Twp HSD 205	Lockport
70	1,847.0	Minooka CHSD 111	Minooka
71	1,845.0	Frankfort CUSD 168	West Frankfort
72	1,842.0	United Twp HSD 30	East Moline
73	1,841.3	Edwardsville CUSD 7	Edwardsville
74	1,841.0	Kewanee CUSD 229	Kewanee
75	1,793.0	Byron CUSD 226	Byron
76	1,791.7	Township HSD 214	Arlington Hgts
77	1,789.0	Southwestern CUSD 9	Piasa
78	1,781.0	Columbia CUSD 4	Columbia
79	1,780.0	Reavis Twp HSD 220	Burbank
80	1,779.0	Bloom Twp HSD 206	Chicago Heights
81	1,773.0	Vandalia CUSD 203	Vandalia
82	1,770.0	Sherrard CUSD 200	Sherrard
83	1,744.0	Argo CHSD 217	Summit
84	1,735.0	Rochelle CCSD 231	Rochelle
85	1,734.8	CHSD 155	Crystal Lake
86	1,727.0	Carterville CUSD 5	Carterville
87	1,701.0	Thornton Fractional Twp HSD 215	Calumet City
88	1,698.0	Forest Ridge SD 142	Oak Forest
89	1,697.0	Posen-Robbins ESD 143-5	Posen
89	1,697.0	Summit SD 104	Summit
91	1,681.0	Belvidere CUSD 100	Belvidere
91	1,681.0	Winnebago CUSD 323	Winnebago
93	1,664.0	Paris-Union SD 95	Paris
94	1,651.0	Darien SD 61	Darien
95	1,646.0	Ottawa Twp HSD 140	Ottawa
96	1,624.3	Proviso Twp HSD 209	Forest Park
97	1,623.0	Litchfield CUSD 12	Litchfield
98	1,617.0	Nippersink SD 2	Richmond
99	1,613.0	Steger SD 194	Steger
100	1,610.0	Eureka CUD 140	Eureka
101	1,594.0	South Holland SD 151	South Holland
102	1,587.0	North Boone CUSD 200	Poplar Grove
103	1,584.1	Waukegan CUSD 60	Waukegan
104	1,578.0	Grant CHSD 124	Fox Lake
105	1,563.0	Fenton CHSD 100	Bensenville
106	1,529.0	Sparta CUSD 140	Sparta
107	1,519.1	J S Morton HSD 201	Cicero
108	1,513.0	Lake Park CHSD 108	Roselle
109	1,511.1	Decatur SD 61	Decatur
110	1,506.0	Bradley SD 61	Bradley
111	1,503.0	Arbor Park SD 145	Oak Forest
111	1,503.0	Beardstown CUSD 15	Beardstown
113	1,502.5	Effingham CUSD 40	Effingham
114	1,478.3	Freeport SD 145	Freeport
115	1,472.0	Jersey CUSD 100	Jerseyville
116	1,467.5	Cons HSD 230	Orland Park
117	1,416.8	Woodland CCSD 50	Gurnee
118	1,399.0	Dunlap CUSD 323	Dunlap
119	1,369.0	Bethalto CUSD 8	Bethalto
120	1,345.0	Wheeling CCSD 21	Wheeling
121	1,342.5	Canton Union SD 66	Canton
122	1,341.7	Marion CUSD 2	Marion
123	1,320.7	Rich Twp HSD 227	Olympia Fields
124	1,315.5	Schaumburg CCSD 54	Schaumburg
125	1,302.0	Joliet Twp HSD 204	Joliet
126	1,297.0	Central CUSD 301	Burlington
127	1,295.5	Lemont-Bromberek CSD 113a	Lemont
128	1,287.6	CUSD 300	Carpentersville
129	1,276.0	Warren Twp HSD 121	Gages Lake
130	1,275.3	Lyons Twp HSD 204	La Grange
131	1,237.5	Grayslake CHSD 127	Grayslake
132	1,211.5	Mchenry CCSD 15	Mchenry
133	1,202.3	Yorkville CUSD 115	Yorkville
134	1,198.3	School District 45 Dupage County	Villa Park
135	1,167.0	Harvard CUSD 50	Harvard
136	1,166.1	Plainfield SD 202	Plainfield
137	1,165.5	Maine Township HSD 207	Park Ridge
138	1,158.5	CHSD 218	Oak Lawn
139	1,152.0	Lake Forest SD 67	Lake Forest
140	1,134.5	Mundelein Cons HSD 120	Mundelein
141	1,133.8	Oregon CUSD 220	Oregon
142	1,133.0	Alton CUSD 11	Alton
143	1,131.0	Herrin CUSD 4	Herrin
144	1,127.3	Cicero SD 99	Cicero
145	1,124.8	Glenbard Twp HSD 87	Glen Ellyn
146	1,111.8	CHSD 99	Downers Grove
147	1,093.5	Palatine CCSD 15	Palatine
148	1,092.8	Lake Zurich CUSD 95	Lake Zurich
149	1,071.3	CHSD 128	Libertyville
150	1,069.5	East Richland CUSD 1	Olney
151	1,054.7	Evanston Twp HSD 202	Evanston
152	1,046.7	Geneseo CUSD 228	Geneseo
153	1,043.0	Woodstock CUSD 200	Woodstock
154	1,032.5	Rochester CUSD 3a	Rochester
155	1,031.8	Ball Chatham CUSD 5	Chatham
156	1,031.7	Taylorville CUSD 3	Taylorville
157	1,031.0	Highland CUSD 5	Highland
158	1,025.3	Oak Park-River Forest SD 200	Oak Park
159	1,023.9	Wauconda CUSD 118	Wauconda
160	1,015.0	Belleville Twp HSD 201	Belleville
161	1,014.5	Roxana CUSD 1	Roxana
162	1,012.5	Hillsboro CUSD 3	Hillsboro
163	978.2	Valley View CUSD 365u	Romeoville
164	976.7	Oswego CUSD 308	Oswego
165	973.3	Homewood Flossmoor CHSD 233	Flossmoor
166	969.0	Geneva CUSD 304	Geneva
167	954.4	Niles Twp CHSD 219	Skokie
168	947.5	Bond County CUSD 2	Greenville
168	947.5	Meridian CUSD 223	Stillman Valley
170	945.5	Reed Custer CUSD 255u	Braidwood
171	938.5	Fremont SD 79	Mundelein
172	938.0	Macomb CUSD 185	Macomb
173	930.4	Township HSD 211	Palatine
174	890.9	Indian Prairie CUSD 204	Aurora
175	884.5	Oak Lawn CHSD 229	Oak Lawn
176	876.3	CHSD 117	Lake Villa
177	875.5	Robinson CUSD 2	Robinson
178	866.1	CSD 158	Algonquin
179	852.5	CUSD 201	Westmont
180	840.3	Mattoon CUSD 2	Mattoon
181	818.0	Berwyn North SD 98	Berwyn
181	818.0	River Trails SD 26	Mount Prospect
183	810.0	Burbank SD 111	Burbank
184	809.5	Plano CUSD 88	Plano
185	782.5	Pana CUSD 8	Pana
186	779.4	Batavia USD 101	Batavia
187	779.0	Naperville CUSD 203	Naperville
188	772.2	Crystal Lake CCSD 47	Crystal Lake
189	768.5	Millburn CCSD 24	Wadsworth
190	764.0	Wilmington CUSD 209u	Wilmington
191	761.3	Barrington CUSD 220	Barrington
192	760.3	City of Chicago SD 299	Chicago
193	755.5	Carlinville CUSD 1	Carlinville
194	750.5	Skokie SD 69	Skokie
195	746.7	Hinsdale Twp HSD 86	Hinsdale
196	745.1	Mascoutah CUD 19	Mascoutah
197	734.8	Aurora West USD 129	Aurora
198	720.3	Clinton CUSD 15	Clinton
199	720.0	Herscher CUSD 2	Herscher
200	714.7	Harrisburg CUSD 3	Harrisburg
201	712.7	Mclean County USD 5	Normal
202	712.5	Harlem Ud 122	Loves Park
203	710.7	CHSD 94	West Chicago
204	709.8	Glen Ellyn SD 41	Glen Ellyn
205	707.5	Saint Charles CUSD 303	Saint Charles
206	703.8	CUSD 200	Wheaton
207	698.7	Lombard SD 44	Lombard
208	697.5	North Palos SD 117	Palos Hills
209	696.7	Galesburg CUSD 205	Galesburg
210	696.0	Minooka CCSD 201	Minooka
211	695.4	Northfield Twp HSD 225	Glenview
212	694.0	Mahomet-Seymour CUSD 3	Mahomet
213	690.3	Gurnee SD 56	Gurnee
214	689.4	Bloomington SD 87	Bloomington
215	689.3	Mannheim SD 83	Franklin Park
216	688.0	Mount Prospect SD 57	Mount Prospect
217	680.6	Mount Zion CUSD 3	Mount Zion
218	670.3	La Grange SD 102	La Grange Park
219	665.7	Kaneland CUSD 302	Maple Park
220	663.8	Morton CUSD 709	Morton
221	659.8	Johnsburg CUSD 12	Johnsburg
222	658.0	Cook County SD 130	Blue Island
223	655.0	Leyden CHSD 212	Franklin Park
224	649.3	Bremen CHSD 228	Midlothian
225	640.3	Prairie Central CUSD 8	Fairbury
226	633.8	Moline USD 40	Moline
227	624.3	Bourbonnais SD 53	Bourbonnais
227	624.3	Urbana SD 116	Urbana
229	622.2	Deerfield SD 109	Deerfield
230	616.2	Hawthorn CCSD 73	Vernon Hills
231	606.3	New Lenox SD 122	New Lenox
232	605.3	Cary CCSD 26	Cary
233	602.5	Wilmette SD 39	Wilmette
234	596.6	Champaign CUSD 4	Champaign
235	593.3	Orland SD 135	Orland Park
236	590.0	Park Ridge CCSD 64	Park Ridge
237	588.3	Elmhurst SD 205	Elmhurst
238	583.0	East Maine SD 63	Des Plaines
239	580.4	Charleston CUSD 1	Charleston
240	578.6	ESD 159	Matteson
241	577.0	Oak Lawn-Hometown SD 123	Oak Lawn
242	569.3	Keeneyville SD 20	Hanover Park
243	566.5	Matteson ESD 162	Matteson
244	564.6	CCSD 93	Bloomingdale
245	563.4	West Chicago ESD 33	West Chicago
246	562.7	Lincolnshire-Prairieview SD 103	Lincolnshire
247	562.5	CCSD 89	Glen Ellyn
248	560.7	Monticello CUSD 25	Monticello

249	560.6	Kirby SD 140	Tinley Park
250	552.6	Oak Park ESD 97	Oak Park
251	547.7	Grayslake CCSD 46	Grayslake
252	543.8	Mundelein ESD 75	Mundelein
253	541.5	Aptakisic-Tripp CCSD 102	Buffalo Grove
254	536.0	Ridgeland SD 122	Oak Lawn
255	531.6	Glenview CCSD 34	Glenview
256	528.2	Libertyville SD 70	Libertyville
257	525.9	Twp HSD 113	Highland Park
258	522.6	Palos CCSD 118	Palos Park
259	513.7	West Carroll CUSD 314	Thomson
260	513.3	Queen Bee SD 16	Glendale Hgts
261	510.3	Riverton CUSD 14	Riverton
262	507.4	Hinsdale CCSD 181	Westmont
263	504.7	Tolono CUSD 7	Tolono
264	500.0	Paxton-Buckley-Loda CUD 10	Paxton
265	490.3	Kildeer Countryside CCSD 96	Buffalo Grove
266	487.2	East Moline SD 37	East Moline
267	480.6	Bensenville SD 2	Bensenville
268	466.5	Community CSD 59	Arlington Hgts
269	434.0	Northbrook SD 28	Northbrook
270	433.7	CCSD 62	Des Plaines
271	432.1	North Shore SD 112	Highland Park
272	431.2	Evanston CCSD 65	Evanston
273	428.3	Lisle CUSD 202	Lisle
274	421.0	Winnetka SD 36	Winnetka
275	416.8	West Harvey-Dixmoor PSD 147	Harvey
276	413.3	Alsip-Hazlgrn-Oaklwn SD 126	Alsip
277	407.7	Woodridge SD 68	Woodridge
278	404.4	New Trier Twp HSD 203	Northfield
279	404.0	Skokie SD 68	Skokie
280	401.2	Tinley Park CCSD 146	Tinley Park
281	399.3	Dolton SD 148	Riverdale
282	358.8	Downers Grove Gsd 58	Downers Grove
283	352.2	Monmouth-Roseville CUSD 238	Monmouth
284	n/a	Belleville SD 118	Belleville
284	n/a	Berkeley SD 87	Berkeley
284	n/a	CCSD 168	Sauk Village
284	n/a	Channahon SD 17	Channahon
284	n/a	Chicago Heights SD 170	Chicago Heights
284	n/a	Corrections SD 428 Dept of	Springfield
284	n/a	Country Club Hls SD 160	Country Club Hls
284	n/a	Dolton SD 149	Calumet City
284	n/a	Flora CUSD 35	Flora
284	n/a	Frankfort CCSD 157c	Frankfort
284	n/a	Homer CCSD 33c	Homer Glen
284	n/a	Homewood SD 153	Homewood
284	n/a	Indian Springs SD 109	Justice
284	n/a	Kinnikinnick CCSD 131	Roscoe
284	n/a	Lake Forest CHSD 115	Lake Forest
284	n/a	Midlothian SD 143	Midlothian
284	n/a	Mokena SD 159	Mokena
284	n/a	Mount Vernon SD 80	Mount Vernon
284	n/a	Prairie-Hills ESD 144	Markham
284	n/a	Rantoul City SD 137	Rantoul
284	n/a	Will County SD 92	Lockport

Student/Counselor Ratio

Rank	Ratio	District Name	City
1	13,528.0	Cicero SD 99	Cicero
2	4,823.7	Schaumburg CCSD 54	Schaumburg
3	3,968.0	Addison SD 4	Addison
4	3,732.0	Dolton SD 149	Calumet City
5	3,517.0	Chicago Heights SD 170	Chicago Heights
6	3,111.0	Deerfield SD 109	Deerfield
7	2,924.0	Harvey SD 152	Harvey
8	2,641.0	Libertyville SD 70	Libertyville
9	2,266.0	Alton CUSD 11	Alton
10	2,250.0	CCSD 89	Glen Ellyn
11	2,175.0	Mundelein ESD 75	Mundelein
12	2,153.5	Park Ridge CCSD 64	Park Ridge
13	2,071.0	Gurnee SD 56	Gurnee
14	2,053.0	Queen Bee SD 16	Glendale Hgts
15	2,052.0	Kinnikinnick CCSD 131	Roscoe
16	1,977.7	Orland SD 135	Orland Park
17	1,972.0	West Chicago ESD 33	West Chicago
18	1,887.0	East Peoria SD 86	East Peoria
19	1,845.0	Frankfort CUSD 168	West Frankfort
20	1,841.0	Kewanee CUSD 229	Kewanee
21	1,791.5	Summit Hill SD 161	Frankfort
22	1,716.0	Kildeer Countryside CCSD 96	Buffalo Grove
23	1,682.0	Cahokia CUSD 187	Cahokia
24	1,674.3	Downers Grove Gsd 58	Downers Grove
25	1,671.8	Round Lake CUSD 116	Round Lake
26	1,651.0	Darien SD 61	Darien
27	1,639.0	Country Club Hls SD 160	Country Club Hls
28	1,624.7	Plainfield SD 202	Plainfield
29	1,617.0	Nippersink SD 2	Richmond
30	1,587.0	North Boone CUSD 200	Poplar Grove
31	1,585.5	Collinsville CUSD 10	Collinsville
32	1,570.0	Carterville CUSD 5	Carterville
33	1,561.4	Aurora West USD 129	Aurora
34	1,503.0	Beardstown CUSD 15	Beardstown
35	1,500.0	Paxton-Buckley-Loda CUD 10	Paxton
36	1,470.4	Granite City CUSD 9	Granite City
37	1,440.3	North Shore SD 112	Highland Park
38	1,427.0	Woodridge SD 68	Woodridge
39	1,383.0	Elmwood Park CUSD 401	Elmwood Park
40	1,369.0	Bethalto CUSD 8	Bethalto
41	1,355.3	Lake Forest SD 67	Lake Forest
42	1,347.0	Waterloo CUSD 5	Waterloo
43	1,333.6	CUSD 300	Carpentersville
44	1,331.3	Kaneland CUSD 302	Maple Park
45	1,308.0	Flossmoor SD 161	Chicago Heights
46	1,279.2	School District U-46	Elgin
47	1,201.5	Bensenville SD 2	Bensenville
48	1,193.5	Massac UD 1	Metropolis
49	1,187.9	Edwardsville CUSD 7	Edwardsville
50	1,183.0	Glen Ellyn SD 41	Glen Ellyn
51	1,167.0	Harvard CUSD 50	Harvard
52	1,134.2	Galesburg CUSD 205	Galesburg
53	1,133.7	Homer CCSD 33c	Homer Glen
54	1,133.0	Matteson ESD 162	Matteson
55	1,080.0	Herscher CUSD 2	Herscher
56	1,078.3	Danville CCSD 118	Danville
57	1,069.5	East Richland CUSD 1	Olney
58	1,049.5	Wauconda CUSD 118	Wauconda
59	1,048.0	Lombard SD 44	Lombard
60	1,031.7	Taylorville CUSD 3	Taylorville
61	1,017.9	Aurora East USD 131	Aurora
62	999.5	Peotone CUSD 207u	Peotone
63	995.2	Kankakee SD 111	Kankakee
64	992.1	Decatur SD 61	Decatur
65	989.9	CSD 158	Algonquin
66	979.8	Harlem Ud 122	Loves Park
67	968.3	Peoria SD 150	Peoria
67	968.3	Triad CUSD 2	Troy
69	952.4	Plano CUSD 88	Plano
70	947.5	Meridian CUSD 223	Stillman Valley
71	945.5	Reed Custer CUSD 255u	Braidwood
72	941.8	Pekin PSD 108	Pekin
73	933.9	Belvidere CUSD 100	Belvidere
74	925.3	Mahomet-Seymour CUSD 3	Mahomet
75	907.0	Mount Vernon SD 80	Mount Vernon
76	901.8	Yorkville CUSD 115	Yorkville
77	899.9	Rock Island SD 41	Rock Island
78	895.0	Canton Union SD 66	Canton
79	894.5	Southwestern CUSD 9	Piasa
80	894.0	Woodstock CUSD 200	Woodstock
81	890.7	Batavia USD 101	Batavia
82	887.5	Manteno CUSD 5	Manteno
83	884.0	Jacksonville SD 117	Jacksonville
84	879.7	Johnsburg CUSD 12	Johnsburg
85	874.0	Urbana SD 116	Urbana
86	868.0	Crete Monee CUSD 201u	Crete
86	868.0	Northbrook SD 28	Northbrook
88	863.7	Lemont-Bromberek CSD 113a	Lemont
89	857.6	Harrisburg CUSD 3	Harrisburg
90	855.3	Sandwich CUSD 430	Sandwich
91	852.5	CUSD 201	Westmont
92	841.0	Monticello CUSD 25	Monticello
93	811.5	Litchfield CUSD 12	Litchfield
94	805.0	Eureka CUD 140	Eureka
95	792.1	Waukegan CUSD 60	Waukegan
96	787.4	Oswego CUSD 308	Oswego
97	785.2	Sterling CUSD 5	Sterling
98	784.0	Mclean County USD 5	Normal
99	782.5	Pana CUSD 8	Pana
100	773.3	Highland CUSD 5	Highland
101	769.5	Flora CUSD 35	Flora
102	764.5	Sparta CUSD 140	Sparta
103	764.0	Wilmington CUSD 209u	Wilmington
104	759.2	Dekalb CUSD 428	De Kalb
105	757.0	Tolono CUSD 7	Tolono
106	755.5	Carlinville CUSD 1	Carlinville
107	747.0	Prairie Central CUSD 8	Fairbury
108	736.0	Jersey CUSD 100	Jerseyville
109	726.8	Geneva CUSD 304	Geneva
110	721.5	Berkeley SD 87	Berkeley
111	720.5	North Chicago SD 187	North Chicago
112	720.3	Clinton CUSD 15	Clinton
113	694.7	Olympia CUSD 16	Stanford
114	691.5	Moline USD 40	Moline
115	689.3	Mascoutah CUD 19	Mascoutah
116	688.3	Rochester CUSD 3a	Rochester
117	688.2	Sycamore CUSD 427	Sycamore
118	687.8	Ball Chatham CUSD 5	Chatham
119	682.1	New Lenox SD 122	New Lenox
120	682.0	Murphysboro CUSD 186	Murphysboro
121	678.8	Indian Prairie CUSD 204	Aurora
122	676.3	Roxana CUSD 1	Roxana
123	675.0	Hillsboro CUSD 3	Hillsboro
124	672.7	Coal City CUSD 1	Coal City
125	672.2	Mattoon CUSD 2	Mattoon
125	672.2	Saint Charles CUSD 303	Saint Charles
127	663.8	Morton CUSD 709	Morton
128	648.5	Central CUSD 301	Burlington
128	648.5	Valley View CUSD 365u	Romeoville
130	646.7	Genoa Kingston CUSD 424	Genoa
131	633.6	Freeport SD 145	Freeport
132	632.1	Sherrard CUSD 200	Sherrard
133	631.7	Bond County CUSD 2	Greenville
134	624.3	Wabash CUSD 348	Mount Carmel
135	622.6	Winnebago CUSD 323	Winnebago
136	618.2	Troy CCSD 30c	Plainfield
137	617.1	East St Louis SD 189	E Saint Louis
138	612.5	Mount Zion CUSD 3	Mount Zion
139	596.1	Lake Zurich CUSD 95	Lake Zurich
140	593.7	Columbia CUSD 4	Columbia
141	583.7	Robinson CUSD 2	Robinson
142	580.4	Charleston CUSD 1	Charleston
143	574.5	Bloomington SD 87	Bloomington
144	571.0	Lisle CUSD 202	Lisle
145	565.5	Herrin CUSD 4	Herrin
146	565.2	Geneseo CUSD 228	Geneseo
147	560.5	Champaign CUSD 4	Champaign
148	560.3	Byron CUSD 226	Byron
149	559.6	Dunlap CUSD 323	Dunlap
150	554.7	Paris-Union SD 95	Paris
151	541.9	Naperville CUSD 203	Naperville
152	541.7	Rockford SD 205	Rockford
153	541.5	IL Valley Central USD 321	Chillicothe
154	537.4	Barrington CUSD 220	Barrington
155	521.3	CUSD 200	Wheaton
156	518.3	Oregon CUSD 220	Oregon
157	510.3	Riverton CUSD 14	Riverton
158	507.5	Belleville Twp HSD 201	Belleville
159	505.8	Ottawa ESD 141	Ottawa
160	500.8	Effingham CUSD 40	Effingham
161	488.2	Dixon USD 170	Dixon
162	469.0	O Fallon Twp HSD 203	Ofallon
163	449.3	New Trier Twp HSD 203	Northfield
164	433.8	Rochelle CCSD 231	Rochelle
165	426.4	City of Chicago SD 299	Chicago
166	416.8	West Harvey-Dixmoor PSD 147	Harvey
167	405.5	West Carroll CUSD 314	Thomson
168	402.5	Elmhurst SD 205	Elmhurst
168	402.5	Marion CUSD 2	Marion
170	395.3	Bloom Twp HSD 206	Chicago Heights
171	394.0	Vandalia CUSD 203	Vandalia
172	390.2	Hononegah Chd 207	Rockton
173	378.0	Thornton Fractional Twp HSD 215	Calumet City
174	375.2	Macomb CUSD 185	Macomb
175	374.8	Proviso Twp HSD 209	Forest Park
176	371.0	Bremen CHSD 228	Midlothian
177	369.4	Minooka CHSD 111	Minooka
178	368.4	United Twp HSD 30	East Moline
179	365.8	Ottawa Twp HSD 140	Ottawa
180	359.2	Joliet Twp HSD 204	Joliet
181	358.5	Lincoln Way CHSD 210	New Lenox
182	356.0	Reavis Twp HSD 220	Burbank
183	353.8	Oak Lawn CHSD 229	Oak Lawn
184	352.2	Monmouth-Roseville CUSD 238	Monmouth
185	348.0	East Moline SD 37	East Moline
186	346.0	CHSD 218	Oak Lawn
187	344.7	Quincy SD 172	Quincy
188	344.1	Mc Henry CHSD 156	Mchenry
189	341.8	J S Morton HSD 201	Cicero
190	338.9	Lockport Twp HSD 205	Lockport
191	335.7	Township HSD 211	Palatine
192	328.6	CHSD 117	Lake Villa
193	326.1	Cons HSD 230	Orland Park
194	324.5	Bradley Bourbonnais CHSD 307	Bradley
195	324.4	Homewood Flossmoor CHSD 233	Flossmoor
196	315.6	Grant CHSD 124	Fox Lake
197	315.4	CHSD 155	Crystal Lake
198	309.7	Pekin CSD 303	Pekin
199	307.6	Oak Park-River Forest SD 200	Oak Park
200	302.6	Lake Park CHSD 108	Roselle

Rank	Value	District Name	City
201	297.9	Thornton Twp HSD 205	South Holland
202	294.5	Warren Twp HSD 121	Gages Lake
203	290.7	Argo CHSD 217	Summit
204	288.4	Glenbard Twp HSD 87	Glen Ellyn
205	288.1	CHSD 94	West Chicago
206	284.5	Grayslake CHSD 127	Grayslake
207	278.0	CHSD 99	Downers Grove
208	270.5	Du Page HSD 88	Villa Park
209	264.1	Rich Twp HSD 227	Olympia Fields
210	260.5	Fenton CHSD 100	Bensenville
211	258.1	Zion-Benton Twp HSD 126	Zion
212	255.1	Lyons Twp HSD 204	La Grange
213	254.5	Leyden CHSD 212	Franklin Park
214	254.3	Maine Township HSD 207	Park Ridge
215	245.9	Northfield Twp HSD 225	Glenview
216	227.2	Niles Twp CHSD 219	Skokie
217	226.9	Mundelein Cons HSD 120	Mundelein
218	226.8	Township HSD 214	Arlington Hgts
219	225.5	Adlai E Stevenson HSD 125	Lincolnshire
220	224.0	Hinsdale Twp HSD 86	Hinsdale
221	217.3	Lake Forest CHSD 115	Lake Forest
222	216.5	Twp HSD 113	Highland Park
223	210.9	Evanston Twp HSD 202	Evanston
224	173.7	CHSD 128	Libertyville
225	n/a	Alsip-Hazlgrn-Oaklwn SD 126	Alsip
225	n/a	Antioch CCSD 34	Antioch
225	n/a	Aptakisic-Tripp CCSD 102	Buffalo Grove
225	n/a	Arbor Park SD 145	Oak Forest
225	n/a	Arlington Hgts SD 25	Arlington Hgts
225	n/a	Beach Park CCSD 3	Beach Park
225	n/a	Belleville SD 118	Belleville
225	n/a	Bellwood SD 88	Bellwood
225	n/a	Berwyn North SD 98	Berwyn
225	n/a	Berwyn South SD 100	Berwyn
225	n/a	Bourbonnais SD 53	Bourbonnais
225	n/a	Bradley SD 61	Bradley
225	n/a	Burbank SD 111	Burbank
225	n/a	CCSD 168	Sauk Village
225	n/a	CCSD 62	Des Plaines
225	n/a	CCSD 93	Bloomingdale
225	n/a	Cary CCSD 26	Cary
225	n/a	Channahon SD 17	Channahon
225	n/a	Community CSD 59	Arlington Hgts
225	n/a	Cook County SD 130	Blue Island
225	n/a	Corrections SD 428 Dept of	Springfield
225	n/a	Crystal Lake CCSD 47	Crystal Lake
225	n/a	Dolton SD 148	Riverdale
225	n/a	ESD 159	Matteson
225	n/a	East Maine SD 63	Des Plaines
225	n/a	Evanston CCSD 65	Evanston
225	n/a	Evergreen Park ESD 124	Evergreen Park
225	n/a	Forest Ridge SD 142	Oak Forest
225	n/a	Frankfort CCSD 157c	Frankfort
225	n/a	Fremont SD 79	Mundelein
225	n/a	Glenview CCSD 34	Glenview
225	n/a	Grayslake CCSD 46	Grayslake
225	n/a	Hawthorn CCSD 73	Vernon Hills
225	n/a	Hinsdale CCSD 181	Westmont
225	n/a	Homewood SD 153	Homewood
225	n/a	Indian Springs SD 109	Justice
225	n/a	Joliet Psd 86	Joliet
225	n/a	Keeneyville SD 20	Hanover Park
225	n/a	Kirby SD 140	Tinley Park
225	n/a	La Grange SD 102	La Grange Park
225	n/a	Lake Villa CCSD 41	Lake Villa
225	n/a	Lansing SD 158	Lansing
225	n/a	Lincolnshire-Prairieview SD 103	Lincolnshire
225	n/a	Lyons SD 103	Lyons
225	n/a	Mannheim SD 83	Franklin Park
225	n/a	Marquardt SD 15	Glendale Hgts
225	n/a	Maywood-Melrose Park-Broadview 89	Melrose Park
225	n/a	Mchenry CCSD 15	Mchenry
225	n/a	Midlothian SD 143	Midlothian
225	n/a	Millburn CCSD 24	Wadsworth
225	n/a	Minooka CCSD 201	Minooka
225	n/a	Mokena SD 159	Mokena
225	n/a	Mount Prospect SD 57	Mount Prospect
225	n/a	North Palos SD 117	Palos Hills
225	n/a	O Fallon CCSD 90	Ofallon
225	n/a	Oak Lawn-Hometown SD 123	Oak Lawn
225	n/a	Oak Park ESD 97	Oak Park
225	n/a	Palatine CCSD 15	Palatine
225	n/a	Palos CCSD 118	Palos Park
225	n/a	Park Forest SD 163	Park Forest
225	n/a	Posen-Robbins ESD 143-5	Posen
225	n/a	Prairie-Hills ESD 144	Markham
225	n/a	Rantoul City SD 137	Rantoul
225	n/a	Ridgeland SD 122	Oak Lawn
225	n/a	River Trails SD 26	Mount Prospect
225	n/a	School District 45 Dupage County	Villa Park
225	n/a	Skokie SD 68	Skokie
225	n/a	Skokie SD 69	Skokie
225	n/a	South Holland SD 151	South Holland
225	n/a	Springfield SD 186	Springfield
225	n/a	Steger SD 194	Steger
225	n/a	Streator ESD 44	Streator
225	n/a	Summit SD 104	Summit
225	n/a	Tinley Park CCSD 146	Tinley Park
225	n/a	Wheeling CCSD 21	Wheeling
225	n/a	Will County SD 92	Lockport
225	n/a	Wilmette SD 39	Wilmette
225	n/a	Winnetka SD 36	Winnetka
225	n/a	Woodland CCSD 50	Gurnee
225	n/a	Zion ESD 6	Zion

Current Spending per Student in FY2003

Rank	Dollars	District Name	City
1	18,334	Evanston Twp HSD 202	Evanston
2	18,299	Twp HSD 113	Highland Park
3	16,783	New Trier Twp HSD 203	Northfield
4	16,444	Northfield Twp HSD 225	Glenview
5	15,751	Niles Twp CHSD 219	Skokie
6	15,372	Oak Park-River Forest SD 200	Oak Park
7	15,276	Lake Forest CHSD 115	Lake Forest
8	14,945	CHSD 128	Libertyville
9	14,450	Township HSD 214	Arlington Hgts
10	13,930	Maine Township HSD 207	Park Ridge
11	13,797	Fenton CHSD 100	Bensenville
12	13,789	Northbrook SD 28	Northbrook
13	13,698	Hinsdale Twp HSD 86	Hinsdale
14	13,368	Lyons Twp HSD 204	La Grange
15	13,340	Leyden CHSD 212	Franklin Park
16	13,293	Adlai E Stevenson HSD 125	Lincolnshire
17	12,964	Township HSD 211	Palatine
18	12,527	Bremen CHSD 228	Midlothian
19	12,484	Rich Twp HSD 227	Olympia Fields
20	12,354	CHSD 99	Downers Grove
21	12,267	Skokie SD 68	Skokie
22	12,204	Bloom Twp HSD 206	Chicago Heights
23	12,085	Evanston CCSD 65	Evanston
24	12,076	CHSD 117	Lake Villa
25	11,991	CHSD 218	Oak Lawn
26	11,971	Lake Park CHSD 108	Roselle
27	11,960	Lincolnshire-Prairieview SD 103	Lincolnshire
28	11,870	Winnetka SD 36	Winnetka
29	11,796	Homewood Flossmoor CHSD 233	Flossmoor
30	11,776	Du Page HSD 88	Villa Park
31	11,754	Lisle CUSD 202	Lisle
32	11,696	North Shore SD 112	Highland Park
33	11,475	Aptakisic-Tripp CCSD 102	Buffalo Grove
34	11,470	Proviso Twp HSD 209	Forest Park
35	11,366	Oak Park ESD 97	Oak Park
36	11,329	River Trails SD 26	Mount Prospect
37	11,304	Lake Forest SD 67	Lake Forest
38	11,262	CUSD 201	Westmont
39	11,250	Argo CHSD 217	Summit
40	11,043	Byron CUSD 226	Byron
41	11,022	Glenbard Twp HSD 87	Glen Ellyn
42	10,986	Thornton Twp HSD 205	South Holland
43	10,903	Oak Lawn CHSD 229	Oak Lawn
44	10,871	Reavis Twp HSD 220	Burbank
45	10,712	Joliet Twp HSD 204	Joliet
46	10,658	Mundelein Cons HSD 120	Mundelein
47	10,593	Community CSD 59	Arlington Hgts
48	10,579	Cons HSD 230	Orland Park
49	10,551	CHSD 94	West Chicago
50	10,514	ESD 159	Matteson
51	10,500	Glenview CCSD 34	Glenview
52	10,499	Tinley Park CCSD 146	Tinley Park
53	10,439	Thornton Fractional Twp HSD 215	Calumet City
54	10,396	Park Ridge CCSD 64	Park Ridge
55	10,370	Grayslake CHSD 127	Grayslake
56	10,266	Woodridge SD 68	Woodridge
57	10,231	Hinsdale CCSD 181	Westmont
58	10,150	Downers Grove Gsd 58	Downers Grove
59	10,149	Wheeling CCSD 21	Wheeling
60	10,145	Elmhurst SD 205	Elmhurst
61	10,119	Schaumburg CCSD 54	Schaumburg
62	10,013	Reed Custer CUSD 255u	Braidwood
63	9,909	Barrington CUSD 220	Barrington
64	9,878	Wilmette SD 39	Wilmette
65	9,710	Lombard SD 44	Lombard
66	9,680	Mannheim SD 83	Franklin Park
67	9,659	Zion-Benton Twp HSD 126	Zion
68	9,649	CCSD 62	Des Plaines
69	9,607	Urbana SD 116	Urbana
70	9,606	Lockport Twp HSD 205	Lockport
71	9,601	Arlington Hgts SD 25	Arlington Hgts
72	9,546	Naperville CUSD 203	Naperville
73	9,523	J S Morton HSD 201	Cicero
74	9,503	Kildeer Countryside CCSD 96	Buffalo Grove
75	9,495	Country Club Hls SD 160	Country Club Hls
76	9,492	Peoria SD 150	Peoria
77	9,475	Palos CCSD 118	Palos Park
78	9,442	Deerfield SD 109	Deerfield
79	9,426	West Harvey-Dixmoor PSD 147	Harvey
80	9,337	Orland SD 135	Orland Park
81	9,321	Palatine CCSD 15	Palatine
82	9,319	Central CUSD 301	Burlington
83	9,284	Ottawa Twp HSD 140	Ottawa
84	9,233	Lake Zurich CUSD 95	Lake Zurich
85	9,228	CCSD 89	Glen Ellyn
86	9,218	Park Forest SD 163	Park Forest
87	9,181	CUSD 200	Wheaton
88	9,129	Hawthorn CCSD 73	Vernon Hills
89	9,126	School District 45 Dupage County	Villa Park
90	9,119	Darien SD 61	Darien
91	9,082	Rockford SD 205	Rockford
92	9,060	East St Louis SD 189	E Saint Louis
93	9,044	CHSD 155	Crystal Lake
94	9,039	Keeneyville SD 20	Hanover Park
95	9,029	Skokie SD 69	Skokie
96	9,027	Warren Twp HSD 121	Gages Lake
97	8,994	Champaign CUSD 4	Champaign
98	8,980	Cahokia CUSD 187	Cahokia
99	8,963	Mattoon CUSD 2	Mattoon
100	8,928	Glen Ellyn SD 41	Glen Ellyn
101	8,909	Grant CHSD 124	Fox Lake
102	8,863	Libertyville SD 70	Libertyville
103	8,841	Prairie-Hills ESD 144	Markham
104	8,830	Mount Vernon SD 80	Mount Vernon
105	8,822	Elmwood Park CUSD 401	Elmwood Park
106	8,816	Oak Lawn-Hometown SD 123	Oak Lawn
107	8,810	Kankakee SD 111	Kankakee
108	8,800	Hononegah Chd 207	Rockton
109	8,788	Zion ESD 6	Zion
110	8,762	Mc Henry CHSD 156	Mchenry
111	8,722	Ottawa ESD 141	Ottawa
112	8,719	Streator ESD 44	Streator
113	8,695	City of Chicago SD 299	Chicago
114	8,657	Danville CCSD 118	Danville
115	8,656	Summit SD 104	Summit
116	8,655	Macomb CUSD 185	Macomb
117	8,646	CCSD 93	Bloomingdale
118	8,620	La Grange SD 102	La Grange Park
119	8,604	Arbor Park SD 145	Oak Forest
120	8,578	Mascoutah CUD 19	Mascoutah
121	8,507	Bloomington SD 87	Bloomington
122	8,495	Flossmoor SD 161	Chicago Heights
123	8,491	Marquardt SD 15	Glendale Hgts
124	8,483	Geneva CUSD 304	Geneva
125	8,466	Woodland CCSD 50	Gurnee
126	8,461	Gurnee SD 56	Gurnee
127	8,453	Aurora East USD 131	Aurora
128	8,415	Joliet Psd 86	Joliet
129	8,384	Morton CUSD 709	Morton
130	8,375	Springfield SD 186	Springfield
131	8,365	Chicago Heights SD 170	Chicago Heights
132	8,354	Belleville SD 118	Belleville
133	8,338	East Moline SD 37	East Moline
134	8,336	Waukegan CUSD 60	Waukegan
135	8,324	Dekalb CUSD 428	De Kalb
136	8,289	Homewood SD 153	Homewood
137	8,269	Bensenville SD 2	Bensenville
138	8,266	School District U-46	Elgin
139	8,251	West Chicago ESD 33	West Chicago
140	8,224	Woodstock CUSD 200	Woodstock
141	8,212	Lincoln Way CHSD 210	New Lenox
141	8,212	Mount Prospect SD 57	Mount Prospect
143	8,179	Valley View CUSD 365u	Romeoville
144	8,151	Saint Charles CUSD 303	Saint Charles
145	8,144	Rock Island SD 41	Rock Island
146	8,136	Dolton SD 149	Calumet City
147	8,121	Clinton CUSD 15	Clinton
148	8,117	Beach Park CCSD 3	Beach Park
149	8,109	Sycamore CUSD 427	Sycamore
150	8,075	Minooka CHSD 111	Minooka
151	8,072	Alton CUSD 11	Alton
152	8,067	Homer CCSD 33c	Homer Glen

153	8,063	Belleville Twp HSD 201	Belleville
154	8,062	Cook County SD 130	Blue Island
155	8,045	Evergreen Park ESD 124	Evergreen Park
156	8,043	Matteson ESD 162	Matteson
157	8,001	Indian Prairie CUSD 204	Aurora
158	7,971	East Peoria SD 86	East Peoria
159	7,935	Freeport SD 145	Freeport
160	7,931	Alsip-Hazlgrn-Oaklwn SD 126	Alsip
161	7,930	Kaneland CUSD 302	Maple Park
162	7,916	Murphysboro CUSD 186	Murphysboro
163	7,912	Jacksonville SD 117	Jacksonville
164	7,853	Ridgeland SD 122	Oak Lawn
165	7,848	North Palos SD 117	Palos Hills
166	7,835	Crete Monee CUSD 201u	Crete
167	7,830	Johnsburg CUSD 12	Johnsburg
168	7,819	Fremont SD 79	Mundelein
169	7,818	Queen Bee SD 16	Glendale Hgts
170	7,801	Harvey SD 152	Harvey
171	7,783	Bethalto CUSD 8	Bethalto
172	7,766	Coal City CUSD 1	Coal City
173	7,763	Pekin CSD 303	Pekin
174	7,757	Robinson CUSD 2	Robinson
175	7,754	United Twp HSD 30	East Moline
176	7,738	Dolton SD 148	Riverdale
177	7,730	East Maine SD 63	Des Plaines
178	7,728	Moline USD 40	Moline
179	7,702	Jersey CUSD 100	Jerseyville
180	7,673	Granite City CUSD 9	Granite City
181	7,651	CUSD 300	Carpentersville
182	7,628	Mclean County USD 5	Normal
183	7,624	Batavia USD 101	Batavia
184	7,611	Roxana CUSD 1	Roxana
185	7,560	Plano CUSD 88	Plano
186	7,559	Posen-Robbins ESD 143-5	Posen
187	7,535	Wauconda CUSD 118	Wauconda
188	7,518	Maywood-Melrose Park-Broadview 89	Melrose Park
189	7,497	Burbank SD 111	Burbank
190	7,490	Frankfort CUSD 168	West Frankfort
191	7,481	Highland CUSD 5	Highland
192	7,463	Bradley Bourbonnais CHSD 307	Bradley
192	7,463	Olympia CUSD 16	Stanford
194	7,456	Berwyn South SD 100	Berwyn
195	7,439	Charleston CUSD 1	Charleston
195	7,439	Harrisburg CUSD 3	Harrisburg
197	7,436	Kirby SD 140	Tinley Park
198	7,433	Sherrard CUSD 200	Sherrard
199	7,408	O Fallon Twp HSD 203	Ofallon
200	7,399	Beardstown CUSD 15	Beardstown
201	7,398	Wilmington CUSD 209u	Wilmington
202	7,397	Addison SD 4	Addison
203	7,393	Sparta CUSD 140	Sparta
204	7,392	Harlem Ud 122	Loves Park
205	7,388	Lyons SD 103	Lyons
206	7,359	Collinsville CUSD 10	Collinsville
207	7,356	Edwardsville CUSD 7	Edwardsville
208	7,334	Forest Ridge SD 142	Oak Forest
209	7,315	Dixon USD 170	Dixon
210	7,306	Prairie Central CUSD 8	Fairbury
211	7,294	Aurora West USD 129	Aurora
212	7,286	Indian Springs SD 109	Justice
213	7,277	Mundelein ESD 75	Mundelein
213	7,277	South Holland SD 151	South Holland
215	7,242	Bellwood SD 88	Bellwood
216	7,238	Antioch CCSD 34	Antioch
217	7,208	Tolono CUSD 7	Tolono
218	7,206	Southwestern CUSD 9	Piasa
219	7,159	Herscher CUSD 2	Herscher
220	7,152	Winnebago CUSD 323	Winnebago
221	7,122	Lemont-Bromberek CSD 113a	Lemont
222	7,121	Flora CUSD 35	Flora
223	7,117	Geneseo CUSD 228	Geneseo
224	7,114	IL Valley Central USD 321	Chillicothe
225	7,112	Sterling CUSD 5	Sterling
226	7,095	Eureka CUD 140	Eureka
227	7,091	Pekin PSD 108	Pekin
228	7,071	Steger SD 194	Steger
229	7,070	Berkeley SD 87	Berkeley
230	7,069	Columbia CUSD 4	Columbia
231	7,052	Decatur SD 61	Decatur
232	7,049	Grayslake CCSD 46	Grayslake
233	7,044	Pana CUSD 8	Pana
234	7,037	Quincy SD 172	Quincy
235	7,031	Effingham CUSD 40	Effingham
236	7,007	Peotone CUSD 207u	Peotone
237	6,992	Frankfort CCSD 157c	Frankfort
238	6,984	Paxton-Buckley-Loda CUD 10	Paxton
239	6,969	Bond County CUSD 2	Greenville
240	6,954	Cicero SD 99	Cicero
241	6,932	Harvard CUSD 50	Harvard
242	6,924	Cary CCSD 26	Cary
243	6,893	Canton Union SD 66	Canton
244	6,887	East Richland CUSD 1	Olney
245	6,871	Bradley SD 61	Bradley
246	6,863	Hillsboro CUSD 3	Hillsboro
247	6,841	Yorkville CUSD 115	Yorkville
248	6,818	Crystal Lake CCSD 47	Crystal Lake
249	6,805	Oregon CUSD 220	Oregon
250	6,799	Wabash CUSD 348	Mount Carmel
251	6,790	Troy CCSD 30c	Plainfield
252	6,773	Waterloo CUSD 5	Waterloo
253	6,743	Kewanee CUSD 229	Kewanee
254	6,733	Oswego CUSD 308	Oswego
255	6,732	Minooka CCSD 201	Minooka
256	6,720	Mchenry CCSD 15	Mchenry
257	6,713	Millburn CCSD 24	Wadsworth
258	6,711	Vandalia CUSD 203	Vandalia
259	6,656	Mahomet-Seymour CUSD 3	Mahomet
260	6,652	Round Lake CUSD 116	Round Lake
261	6,648	Lake Villa CCSD 41	Lake Villa
262	6,608	Litchfield CUSD 12	Litchfield
263	6,584	Nippersink SD 2	Richmond
264	6,572	Plainfield SD 202	Plainfield
265	6,567	Galesburg CUSD 205	Galesburg
266	6,560	Paris-Union SD 95	Paris
267	6,556	Marion CUSD 2	Marion
268	6,552	Massac UD 1	Metropolis
269	6,549	Triad CUSD 2	Troy
270	6,485	Rochelle CCSD 231	Rochelle
271	6,476	Sandwich CUSD 430	Sandwich
272	6,465	Midlothian SD 143	Midlothian
273	6,423	Bourbonnais SD 53	Bourbonnais
274	6,373	Herrin CUSD 4	Herrin
275	6,349	North Boone CUSD 200	Poplar Grove
276	6,283	Berwyn North SD 98	Berwyn
277	6,276	Manteno CUSD 5	Manteno
278	6,258	Rantoul City SD 137	Rantoul
279	6,246	Ball Chatham CUSD 5	Chatham
280	6,236	Will County SD 92	Lockport
281	6,223	Meridian CUSD 223	Stillman Valley
282	6,214	Lansing SD 158	Lansing
283	6,205	Monticello CUSD 25	Monticello
284	6,158	Genoa Kingston CUSD 424	Genoa
285	6,135	New Lenox SD 122	New Lenox
286	6,017	Carlinville CUSD 1	Carlinville
287	6,015	O Fallon CCSD 90	Ofallon
288	5,934	Mount Zion CUSD 3	Mount Zion
289	5,897	Dunlap CUSD 323	Dunlap
290	5,749	Belvidere CUSD 100	Belvidere
291	5,741	CCSD 168	Sauk Village
292	5,731	Kinnikinnick CCSD 131	Roscoe
292	5,731	Taylorville CUSD 3	Taylorville
294	5,648	Rochester CUSD 3a	Rochester
295	5,644	Carterville CUSD 5	Carterville
296	5,613	Summit Hill SD 161	Frankfort
297	5,571	Riverton CUSD 14	Riverton
298	5,517	Channahon SD 17	Channahon
299	5,482	Mokena SD 159	Mokena
300	n/a	CSD 158	Algonquin
300	n/a	Corrections SD 428 Dept of	Springfield
300	n/a	Monmouth-Roseville CUSD 238	Monmouth
300	n/a	North Chicago SD 187	North Chicago
300	n/a	West Carroll CUSD 314	Thomson

Number of Diploma Recipients

Rank	Number	District Name	City
1	15,653	City of Chicago SD 299	Chicago
2	2,815	Township HSD 214	Arlington Hgts
3	2,725	Township HSD 211	Palatine
4	1,946	Glenbard Twp HSD 87	Glen Ellyn
5	1,914	School District U-46	Elgin
6	1,796	Cons HSD 230	Orland Park
7	1,523	Maine Township HSD 207	Park Ridge
8	1,348	Naperville CUSD 203	Naperville
9	1,282	Indian Prairie CUSD 204	Aurora
10	1,226	CHSD 155	Crystal Lake
11	1,222	J S Morton HSD 201	Cicero
12	1,207	CHSD 99	Downers Grove
13	1,187	Rockford SD 205	Rockford
14	1,136	Thornton Twp HSD 205	South Holland
15	1,127	Northfield Twp HSD 225	Glenview
16	1,070	Lincoln Way CHSD 210	New Lenox
17	1,051	Niles Twp CHSD 219	Skokie
18	1,037	CUSD 300	Carpentersville
19	1,018	CUSD 200	Wheaton
20	1,009	Belleville Twp HSD 201	Belleville
21	993	Hinsdale Twp HSD 86	Hinsdale
22	953	Bremen CHSD 228	Midlothian
23	948	New Trier Twp HSD 203	Northfield
24	931	Adlai E Stevenson HSD 125	Lincolnshire
25	894	CHSD 218	Oak Lawn
26	811	Joliet Twp HSD 204	Joliet
27	803	Springfield SD 186	Springfield
28	780	Du Page HSD 88	Villa Park
29	775	Peoria SD 150	Peoria
30	772	Proviso Twp HSD 209	Forest Park
31	763	Saint Charles CUSD 303	Saint Charles
32	753	Valley View CUSD 365u	Romeoville
33	750	Twp HSD 113	Highland Park
34	748	Plainfield SD 202	Plainfield
35	734	Lyons Twp HSD 204	La Grange
35	734	Rich Twp HSD 227	Olympia Fields
37	732	Leyden CHSD 212	Franklin Park
38	674	Warren Twp HSD 121	Gages Lake
39	667	Evanston Twp HSD 202	Evanston
40	648	Waukegan CUSD 60	Waukegan
41	643	Lockport Twp HSD 205	Lockport
42	640	Champaign CUSD 4	Champaign
43	636	Lake Park CHSD 108	Roselle
44	631	CHSD 128	Libertyville
45	615	Mclean County USD 5	Normal
46	577	Barrington CUSD 220	Barrington
47	576	Thornton Fractional Twp HSD 215	Calumet City
48	573	Aurora West USD 129	Aurora
49	563	Homewood Flossmoor CHSD 233	Flossmoor
50	541	Moline USD 40	Moline
51	521	Decatur SD 61	Decatur
52	504	Elmhurst SD 205	Elmhurst
53	491	Bloom Twp HSD 206	Chicago Heights
53	491	Edwardsville CUSD 7	Edwardsville
55	490	Quincy SD 172	Quincy
56	471	O Fallon Twp HSD 203	Ofallon
57	468	Mundelein Cons HSD 120	Mundelein
58	466	CHSD 117	Lake Villa
59	462	Granite City CUSD 9	Granite City
60	453	Mc Henry CHSD 156	Mchenry
61	438	CHSD 94	West Chicago
62	432	Alton CUSD 11	Alton
63	427	Lake Zurich CUSD 95	Lake Zurich
64	424	Aurora East USD 131	Aurora
65	421	Oswego CUSD 308	Oswego
66	413	Pekin CSD 303	Pekin
67	397	Lake Forest CHSD 115	Lake Forest
68	378	Hononegah Chd 207	Rockton
68	378	Zion-Benton Twp HSD 126	Zion
70	376	Bradley Bourbonnais CHSD 307	Bradley
71	372	Harlem Ud 122	Loves Park
72	370	Batavia USD 101	Batavia
73	360	Collinsville CUSD 10	Collinsville
74	359	Argo CHSD 217	Summit
75	354	Urbana SD 116	Urbana
76	353	Belvidere CUSD 100	Belvidere
77	352	Oak Lawn CHSD 229	Oak Lawn
78	347	United Twp HSD 30	East Moline
79	342	Grayslake CHSD 127	Grayslake
80	330	Ottawa Twp HSD 140	Ottawa
81	329	Fenton CHSD 100	Bensenville
82	328	East St Louis SD 189	E Saint Louis
83	321	Geneva CUSD 304	Geneva
84	310	Reavis Twp HSD 220	Burbank
85	308	Dekalb CUSD 428	De Kalb
86	307	Freeport SD 145	Freeport
87	305	Ball Chatham CUSD 5	Chatham
88	303	Woodstock CUSD 200	Woodstock
89	300	Rock Island SD 41	Rock Island
90	275	Galesburg CUSD 205	Galesburg
91	273	Triad CUSD 2	Troy
92	272	Danville CCSD 118	Danville
93	268	Grant CHSD 124	Fox Lake
94	266	Crete Monee CUSD 201u	Crete
95	264	Bloomington SD 87	Bloomington
96	254	Round Lake CUSD 116	Round Lake
97	249	Jacksonville SD 117	Jacksonville
98	246	Kankakee SD 111	Kankakee
99	238	Jersey CUSD 100	Jerseyville
100	234	Highland CUSD 5	Highland
101	232	Marion CUSD 2	Marion
102	231	Sterling CUSD 5	Sterling
103	230	Morton CUSD 709	Morton
104	224	Charleston CUSD 1	Charleston

105	221	Dixon USD 170	Dixon
106	218	Wauconda CUSD 118	Wauconda
107	217	Bethalto CUSD 8	Bethalto
108	216	Sycamore CUSD 427	Sycamore
109	213	Geneseo CUSD 228	Geneseo
110	212	Taylorville CUSD 3	Taylorville
111	204	Mattoon CUSD 2	Mattoon
112	195	Mount Zion CUSD 3	Mount Zion
113	190	Kaneland CUSD 302	Maple Park
114	189	Cahokia CUSD 187	Cahokia
114	189	Effingham CUSD 40	Effingham
116	188	Mahomet-Seymour CUSD 3	Mahomet
117	187	Elmwood Park CUSD 401	Elmwood Park
118	181	Johnsburg CUSD 12	Johnsburg
119	180	Dunlap CUSD 323	Dunlap
120	179	Canton Union SD 66	Canton
120	179	Waterloo CUSD 5	Waterloo
122	175	Yorkville CUSD 115	Yorkville
123	172	Mascoutah CUD 19	Mascoutah
123	172	Murphysboro CUSD 186	Murphysboro
125	158	Wabash CUSD 348	Mount Carmel
126	154	Prairie Central CUSD 8	Fairbury
126	154	Rochester CUSD 3a	Rochester
128	153	Central CUSD 301	Burlington
128	153	Lisle CUSD 202	Lisle
130	151	Sandwich CUSD 430	Sandwich
131	150	Herscher CUSD 2	Herscher
131	150	Southwestern CUSD 9	Piasa
133	146	Byron CUSD 226	Byron
133	146	East Richland CUSD 1	Olney
133	146	IL Valley Central USD 321	Chillicothe
133	146	Oregon CUSD 220	Oregon
137	144	Clinton CUSD 15	Clinton
138	143	Olympia CUSD 16	Stanford
139	139	Massac UD 1	Metropolis
140	138	North Chicago SD 187	North Chicago
141	134	Carlinville CUSD 1	Carlinville
142	132	Bond County CUSD 2	Greenville
143	130	CSD 158	Algonquin
144	129	Herrin CUSD 4	Herrin
144	129	Hillsboro CUSD 3	Hillsboro
144	129	Roxana CUSD 1	Roxana
147	128	Macomb CUSD 185	Macomb
148	123	Robinson CUSD 2	Robinson
149	122	Peotone CUSD 207u	Peotone
149	122	Wilmington CUSD 209u	Wilmington
151	121	Columbia CUSD 4	Columbia
151	121	Harvard CUSD 50	Harvard
153	120	Coal City CUSD 1	Coal City
153	120	Frankfort CUSD 168	West Frankfort
155	119	Harrisburg CUSD 3	Harrisburg
156	117	Manteno CUSD 5	Manteno
157	115	Paxton-Buckley-Loda CUD 10	Paxton
157	115	Sparta CUSD 140	Sparta
159	114	Monticello CUSD 25	Monticello
160	113	Litchfield CUSD 12	Litchfield
160	113	Reed Custer CUSD 255u	Braidwood
162	108	Tolono CUSD 7	Tolono
162	108	Vandalia CUSD 203	Vandalia
164	107	Eureka CUD 140	Eureka
164	107	Riverton CUSD 14	Riverton
164	107	Winnebago CUSD 323	Winnebago
167	106	Sherrard CUSD 200	Sherrard
168	104	Carterville CUSD 5	Carterville
169	103	Flora CUSD 35	Flora
170	100	Kewanee CUSD 229	Kewanee
171	99	Paris-Union SD 95	Paris
172	94	Meridian CUSD 223	Stillman Valley
173	91	CUSD 201	Westmont
173	91	Genoa Kingston CUSD 424	Genoa
175	84	North Boone CUSD 200	Poplar Grove
176	82	Plano CUSD 88	Plano
177	78	Pana CUSD 8	Pana
178	73	Beardstown CUSD 15	Beardstown
179	53	Maywood-Melrose Park-Broadview 89	Melrose Park
180	1	Mannheim SD 83	Franklin Park
181	0	Corrections SD 428 Dept of	Springfield
181	0	Minooka CHSD 111	Minooka
181	0	Oak Park-River Forest SD 200	Oak Park
181	0	Pekin PSD 108	Pekin
185	n/a	Monmouth-Roseville CUSD 238	Monmouth
185	n/a	West Carroll CUSD 314	Thomson
187	n/a	Addison SD 4	Addison
187	n/a	Alsip-Hazlgrn-Oaklwn SD 126	Alsip
187	n/a	Antioch CCSD 34	Antioch
187	n/a	Aptakisic-Tripp CCSD 102	Buffalo Grove
187	n/a	Arbor Park SD 145	Oak Forest
187	n/a	Arlington Hgts SD 25	Arlington Hgts
187	n/a	Beach Park CCSD 3	Beach Park
187	n/a	Belleville SD 118	Belleville
187	n/a	Bellwood SD 88	Bellwood
187	n/a	Bensenville SD 2	Bensenville
187	n/a	Berkeley SD 87	Berkeley
187	n/a	Berwyn North SD 98	Berwyn
187	n/a	Berwyn South SD 100	Berwyn
187	n/a	Bourbonnais SD 53	Bourbonnais
187	n/a	Bradley SD 61	Bradley
187	n/a	Burbank SD 111	Burbank
187	n/a	CCSD 168	Sauk Village
187	n/a	CCSD 62	Des Plaines
187	n/a	CCSD 89	Glen Ellyn
187	n/a	CCSD 93	Bloomingdale
187	n/a	Cary CCSD 26	Cary
187	n/a	Channahon SD 17	Channahon
187	n/a	Chicago Heights SD 170	Chicago Heights
187	n/a	Cicero SD 99	Cicero
187	n/a	Community CSD 59	Arlington Hgts
187	n/a	Cook County SD 130	Blue Island
187	n/a	Country Club Hls SD 160	Country Club Hls
187	n/a	Crystal Lake CCSD 47	Crystal Lake
187	n/a	Darien SD 61	Darien
187	n/a	Deerfield SD 109	Deerfield
187	n/a	Dolton SD 148	Riverdale
187	n/a	Dolton SD 149	Calumet City
187	n/a	Downers Grove Gsd 58	Downers Grove
187	n/a	ESD 159	Matteson
187	n/a	East Maine SD 63	Des Plaines
187	n/a	East Moline SD 37	East Moline
187	n/a	East Peoria SD 86	East Peoria
187	n/a	Evanston CCSD 65	Evanston
187	n/a	Evergreen Park ESD 124	Evergreen Park
187	n/a	Flossmoor SD 161	Chicago Heights
187	n/a	Forest Ridge SD 142	Oak Forest
187	n/a	Frankfort CCSD 157c	Frankfort
187	n/a	Fremont SD 79	Mundelein
187	n/a	Glen Ellyn SD 41	Glen Ellyn
187	n/a	Glenview CCSD 34	Glenview
187	n/a	Grayslake CCSD 46	Grayslake
187	n/a	Gurnee SD 56	Gurnee
187	n/a	Harvey SD 152	Harvey
187	n/a	Hawthorn CCSD 73	Vernon Hills
187	n/a	Hinsdale CCSD 181	Westmont
187	n/a	Homer CCSD 33c	Homer Glen
187	n/a	Homewood SD 153	Homewood
187	n/a	Indian Springs SD 109	Justice
187	n/a	Joliet Psd 86	Joliet
187	n/a	Keeneyville SD 20	Hanover Park
187	n/a	Kildeer Countryside CCSD 96	Buffalo Grove
187	n/a	Kinnikinnick CCSD 131	Roscoe
187	n/a	Kirby SD 140	Tinley Park
187	n/a	La Grange SD 102	La Grange Park
187	n/a	Lake Forest SD 67	Lake Forest
187	n/a	Lake Villa CCSD 41	Lake Villa
187	n/a	Lansing SD 158	Lansing
187	n/a	Lemont-Bromberek CSD 113a	Lemont
187	n/a	Libertyville SD 70	Libertyville
187	n/a	Lincolnshire-Prairieview SD 103	Lincolnshire
187	n/a	Lombard SD 44	Lombard
187	n/a	Lyons SD 103	Lyons
187	n/a	Marquardt SD 15	Glendale Hgts
187	n/a	Matteson ESD 162	Matteson
187	n/a	Mchenry CCSD 15	Mchenry
187	n/a	Midlothian SD 143	Midlothian
187	n/a	Millburn CCSD 24	Wadsworth
187	n/a	Minooka CCSD 201	Minooka
187	n/a	Mokena SD 159	Mokena
187	n/a	Mount Prospect SD 57	Mount Prospect
187	n/a	Mount Vernon SD 80	Mount Vernon
187	n/a	Mundelein ESD 75	Mundelein
187	n/a	New Lenox SD 122	New Lenox
187	n/a	Nippersink SD 2	Richmond
187	n/a	North Palos SD 117	Palos Hills
187	n/a	North Shore SD 112	Highland Park
187	n/a	Northbrook SD 28	Northbrook
187	n/a	O Fallon CCSD 90	Ofallon
187	n/a	Oak Lawn-Hometown SD 123	Oak Lawn
187	n/a	Oak Park ESD 97	Oak Park
187	n/a	Orland SD 135	Orland Park
187	n/a	Ottawa ESD 141	Ottawa
187	n/a	Palatine CCSD 15	Palatine
187	n/a	Palos CCSD 118	Palos Park
187	n/a	Park Forest SD 163	Park Forest
187	n/a	Park Ridge CCSD 64	Park Ridge
187	n/a	Posen-Robbins ESD 143-5	Posen
187	n/a	Prairie-Hills ESD 144	Markham
187	n/a	Queen Bee SD 16	Glendale Hgts
187	n/a	Rantoul City SD 137	Rantoul
187	n/a	Ridgeland SD 122	Oak Lawn
187	n/a	River Trails SD 26	Mount Prospect
187	n/a	Rochelle CCSD 231	Rochelle
187	n/a	Schaumburg CCSD 54	Schaumburg
187	n/a	School District 45 Dupage County	Villa Park
187	n/a	Skokie SD 68	Skokie
187	n/a	Skokie SD 69	Skokie
187	n/a	South Holland SD 151	South Holland
187	n/a	Steger SD 194	Steger
187	n/a	Streator ESD 44	Streator
187	n/a	Summit Hill SD 161	Frankfort
187	n/a	Summit SD 104	Summit
187	n/a	Tinley Park CCSD 146	Tinley Park
187	n/a	Troy CCSD 30c	Plainfield
187	n/a	West Chicago ESD 33	West Chicago
187	n/a	West Harvey-Dixmoor PSD 147	Harvey
187	n/a	Wheeling CCSD 21	Wheeling
187	n/a	Will County SD 92	Lockport
187	n/a	Wilmette SD 39	Wilmette
187	n/a	Winnetka SD 36	Winnetka
187	n/a	Woodland CCSD 50	Gurnee
187	n/a	Woodridge SD 68	Woodridge
187	n/a	Zion ESD 6	Zion

High School Drop-out Rate

Rank	Percent	District Name	City
1	17.6	City of Chicago SD 299	Chicago
2	12.1	Peoria SD 150	Peoria
3	11.3	Danville CCSD 118	Danville
4	11.2	Waukegan CUSD 60	Waukegan
5	10.7	Decatur SD 61	Decatur
6	10.2	East St Louis SD 189	E Saint Louis
7	8.7	Plano CUSD 88	Plano
8	8.6	Bloom Twp HSD 206	Chicago Heights
9	8.4	Granite City CUSD 9	Granite City
10	8.3	Kankakee SD 111	Kankakee
10	8.3	Proviso Twp HSD 209	Forest Park
12	8.0	Kewanee CUSD 229	Kewanee
13	7.8	Roxana CUSD 1	Roxana
14	7.5	Freeport SD 145	Freeport
15	7.4	Flora CUSD 35	Flora
16	7.1	Aurora East USD 131	Aurora
17	6.9	Zion-Benton Twp HSD 126	Zion
18	6.7	Alton CUSD 11	Alton
18	6.7	Pana CUSD 8	Pana
20	6.6	Cahokia CUSD 187	Cahokia
20	6.6	Thornton Twp HSD 205	South Holland
20	6.6	Vandalia CUSD 203	Vandalia
23	6.5	Clinton CUSD 15	Clinton
23	6.5	Galesburg CUSD 205	Galesburg
25	6.4	Rockford SD 205	Rockford
26	6.3	J S Morton HSD 201	Cicero
27	6.2	Mattoon CUSD 2	Mattoon
27	6.2	Round Lake CUSD 116	Round Lake
29	6.1	Aurora West USD 129	Aurora
29	6.1	United Twp HSD 30	East Moline
29	6.1	Urbana SD 116	Urbana
29	6.1	Wabash CUSD 348	Mount Carmel
33	5.8	Dixon USD 170	Dixon
34	5.6	Elmwood Park CUSD 401	Elmwood Park
34	5.6	Winnebago CUSD 323	Winnebago
34	5.6	Woodstock CUSD 200	Woodstock
37	5.5	Harrisburg CUSD 3	Harrisburg
38	5.4	CHSD 218	Oak Lawn
38	5.4	Mclean County USD 5	Normal
38	5.4	Sterling CUSD 5	Sterling
41	5.2	Leyden CHSD 212	Franklin Park
41	5.2	Taylorville CUSD 3	Taylorville
43	5.1	Mundelein Cons HSD 120	Mundelein
43	5.1	Quincy SD 172	Quincy
45	5.0	Bloomington SD 87	Bloomington
45	5.0	Champaign CUSD 4	Champaign
47	4.9	Ottawa Twp HSD 140	Ottawa
48	4.8	Beardstown CUSD 15	Beardstown
48	4.8	IL Valley Central USD 321	Chillicothe
48	4.8	Marion CUSD 2	Marion
51	4.7	Harvard CUSD 50	Harvard
51	4.7	School District U-46	Elgin
53	4.6	Murphysboro CUSD 186	Murphysboro
53	4.6	Rock Island SD 41	Rock Island
55	4.5	Olympia CUSD 16	Stanford
55	4.5	Paris-Union SD 95	Paris

Rank	Value	District	City
55	4.5	Paxton-Buckley-Loda CUD 10	Paxton
58	4.4	Collinsville CUSD 10	Collinsville
59	4.3	Bethalto CUSD 8	Bethalto
60	4.2	Charleston CUSD 1	Charleston
61	4.0	Canton Union SD 66	Canton
61	4.0	Reavis Twp HSD 220	Burbank
63	3.9	CHSD 117	Lake Villa
63	3.9	Jacksonville SD 117	Jacksonville
65	3.8	Belleville Twp HSD 201	Belleville
65	3.8	Du Page HSD 88	Villa Park
65	3.8	Moline USD 40	Moline
65	3.8	Valley View CUSD 365u	Romeoville
69	3.6	East Richland CUSD 1	Olney
69	3.6	Fenton CHSD 100	Bensenville
69	3.6	Hillsboro CUSD 3	Hillsboro
69	3.6	Sandwich CUSD 430	Sandwich
69	3.6	Springfield SD 186	Springfield
69	3.6	Thornton Fractional Twp HSD 215	Calumet City
75	3.5	Argo CHSD 217	Summit
75	3.5	Geneseo CUSD 228	Geneseo
75	3.5	Harlem Ud 122	Loves Park
75	3.5	Pekin CSD 303	Pekin
79	3.4	Township HSD 214	Arlington Hgts
79	3.4	Wilmington CUSD 209u	Wilmington
81	3.3	CHSD 94	West Chicago
81	3.3	Frankfort CUSD 168	West Frankfort
81	3.3	Joliet Twp HSD 204	Joliet
84	3.2	Bremen CHSD 228	Midlothian
84	3.2	Riverton CUSD 14	Riverton
86	3.1	Edwardsville CUSD 7	Edwardsville
86	3.1	Highland CUSD 5	Highland
88	3.0	CUSD 300	Carpentersville
88	3.0	Dekalb CUSD 428	De Kalb
88	3.0	Genoa Kingston CUSD 424	Genoa
88	3.0	Lockport Twp HSD 205	Lockport
88	3.0	Mc Henry CHSD 156	Mchenry
88	3.0	Oswego CUSD 308	Oswego
88	3.0	Plainfield SD 202	Plainfield
95	2.9	Bradley Bourbonnais CHSD 307	Bradley
95	2.9	Reed Custer CUSD 255u	Braidwood
95	2.9	Southwestern CUSD 9	Piasa
98	2.8	Grant CHSD 124	Fox Lake
98	2.8	Herscher CUSD 2	Herscher
98	2.8	Warren Twp HSD 121	Gages Lake
101	2.7	CUSD 200	Wheaton
101	2.7	North Chicago SD 187	North Chicago
101	2.7	Sherrard CUSD 200	Sherrard
104	2.5	Macomb CUSD 185	Macomb
104	2.5	Oak Lawn CHSD 229	Oak Lawn
106	2.4	Carlinville CUSD 1	Carlinville
106	2.4	Robinson CUSD 2	Robinson
108	2.3	Jersey CUSD 100	Jerseyville
108	2.3	Oregon CUSD 220	Oregon
110	2.2	Hinsdale Twp HSD 86	Hinsdale
110	2.2	Prairie Central CUSD 8	Fairbury
110	2.2	Wauconda CUSD 118	Wauconda
113	2.1	CHSD 155	Crystal Lake
114	2.0	Effingham CUSD 40	Effingham
114	2.0	Kaneland CUSD 302	Maple Park
114	2.0	Meridian CUSD 223	Stillman Valley
114	2.0	O Fallon Twp HSD 203	Ofallon
118	1.9	Carterville CUSD 5	Carterville
118	1.9	Evanston Twp HSD 202	Evanston
118	1.9	Waterloo CUSD 5	Waterloo
121	1.8	Glenbard Twp HSD 87	Glen Ellyn
121	1.8	Johnsburg CUSD 12	Johnsburg
123	1.7	CSD 158	Algonquin
123	1.7	Manteno CUSD 5	Manteno
123	1.7	Sycamore CUSD 427	Sycamore
126	1.6	Coal City CUSD 1	Coal City
126	1.6	Monticello CUSD 25	Monticello
128	1.5	Central CUSD 301	Burlington
128	1.5	Geneva CUSD 304	Geneva
128	1.5	Litchfield CUSD 12	Litchfield
128	1.5	Mount Zion CUSD 3	Mount Zion
128	1.5	Tolono CUSD 7	Tolono
128	1.5	Twp HSD 113	Highland Park
134	1.4	Columbia CUSD 4	Columbia
134	1.4	Crete Monee CUSD 201u	Crete
134	1.4	Grayslake CHSD 127	Grayslake
134	1.4	Hononegah Chd 207	Rockton
134	1.4	Mahomet-Seymour CUSD 3	Mahomet
134	1.4	Morton CUSD 709	Morton
140	1.3	CUSD 201	Westmont
140	1.3	Lake Park CHSD 108	Roselle
140	1.3	Lisle CUSD 202	Lisle
140	1.3	Maine Township HSD 207	Park Ridge
144	1.2	Batavia USD 101	Batavia
144	1.2	Belvidere CUSD 100	Belvidere
144	1.2	Bond County CUSD 2	Greenville
144	1.2	CHSD 99	Downers Grove
144	1.2	Cons HSD 230	Orland Park
144	1.2	Eureka CUD 140	Eureka
144	1.2	Lake Zurich CUSD 95	Lake Zurich
144	1.2	Massac UD 1	Metropolis
144	1.2	Saint Charles CUSD 303	Saint Charles
144	1.2	Yorkville CUSD 115	Yorkville
154	1.1	Dunlap CUSD 323	Dunlap
154	1.1	North Boone CUSD 200	Poplar Grove
154	1.1	Rich Twp HSD 227	Olympia Fields
154	1.1	Township HSD 211	Palatine
158	1.0	Ball Chatham CUSD 5	Chatham
158	1.0	Byron CUSD 226	Byron
158	1.0	Elmhurst SD 205	Elmhurst
158	1.0	Homewood Flossmoor CHSD 233	Flossmoor
158	1.0	Lyons Twp HSD 204	La Grange
158	1.0	Niles Twp CHSD 219	Skokie
158	1.0	Triad CUSD 2	Troy
165	0.9	CHSD 128	Libertyville
165	0.9	Indian Prairie CUSD 204	Aurora
167	0.7	Herrin CUSD 4	Herrin
167	0.7	Mascoutah CUD 19	Mascoutah
167	0.7	Northfield Twp HSD 225	Glenview
167	0.7	Peotone CUSD 207u	Peotone
171	0.6	Lincoln Way CHSD 210	New Lenox
172	0.5	Naperville CUSD 203	Naperville
173	0.4	Adlai E Stevenson HSD 125	Lincolnshire
174	0.3	Barrington CUSD 220	Barrington
174	0.3	Rochester CUSD 3a	Rochester
176	0.2	Lake Forest CHSD 115	Lake Forest
176	0.2	New Trier Twp HSD 203	Northfield
178	0.0	Mannheim SD 83	Franklin Park
178	0.0	Pekin PSD 108	Pekin
178	0.0	Sparta CUSD 140	Sparta
181	n/a	Corrections SD 428 Dept of	Springfield
181	n/a	Minooka CHSD 111	Minooka
181	n/a	Monmouth-Roseville CUSD 238	Monmouth
181	n/a	Oak Park-River Forest SD 200	Oak Park
181	n/a	West Carroll CUSD 314	Thomson
186	n/a	Addison SD 4	Addison
186	n/a	Alsip-Hazlgrn-Oaklwn SD 126	Alsip
186	n/a	Antioch CCSD 34	Antioch
186	n/a	Aptakisic-Tripp CCSD 102	Buffalo Grove
186	n/a	Arbor Park SD 145	Oak Forest
186	n/a	Arlington Hgts SD 25	Arlington Hgts
186	n/a	Beach Park CCSD 3	Beach Park
186	n/a	Belleville SD 118	Belleville
186	n/a	Bellwood SD 88	Bellwood
186	n/a	Bensenville SD 2	Bensenville
186	n/a	Berkeley SD 87	Berkeley
186	n/a	Berwyn North SD 98	Berwyn
186	n/a	Berwyn South SD 100	Berwyn
186	n/a	Bourbonnais SD 53	Bourbonnais
186	n/a	Bradley SD 61	Bradley
186	n/a	Burbank SD 111	Burbank
186	n/a	CCSD 168	Sauk Village
186	n/a	CCSD 62	Des Plaines
186	n/a	CCSD 89	Glen Ellyn
186	n/a	CCSD 93	Bloomingdale
186	n/a	Cary CCSD 26	Cary
186	n/a	Channahon SD 17	Channahon
186	n/a	Chicago Heights SD 170	Chicago Heights
186	n/a	Cicero SD 99	Cicero
186	n/a	Community CSD 59	Arlington Hgts
186	n/a	Cook County SD 130	Blue Island
186	n/a	Country Club Hls SD 160	Country Club Hls
186	n/a	Crystal Lake CCSD 47	Crystal Lake
186	n/a	Darien SD 61	Darien
186	n/a	Deerfield SD 109	Deerfield
186	n/a	Dolton SD 148	Riverdale
186	n/a	Dolton SD 149	Calumet City
186	n/a	Downers Grove Gsd 58	Downers Grove
186	n/a	ESD 159	Matteson
186	n/a	East Maine SD 63	Des Plaines
186	n/a	East Moline SD 37	East Moline
186	n/a	East Peoria SD 86	East Peoria
186	n/a	Evanston CCSD 65	Evanston
186	n/a	Evergreen Park ESD 124	Evergreen Park
186	n/a	Flossmoor SD 161	Chicago Heights
186	n/a	Forest Ridge SD 142	Oak Forest
186	n/a	Frankfort CCSD 157c	Frankfort
186	n/a	Fremont SD 79	Mundelein
186	n/a	Glen Ellyn SD 41	Glen Ellyn
186	n/a	Glenview CCSD 34	Glenview
186	n/a	Grayslake CCSD 46	Grayslake
186	n/a	Gurnee SD 56	Gurnee
186	n/a	Harvey SD 152	Harvey
186	n/a	Hawthorn CCSD 73	Vernon Hills
186	n/a	Hinsdale CCSD 181	Westmont
186	n/a	Homer CCSD 33c	Homer Glen
186	n/a	Homewood SD 153	Homewood
186	n/a	Indian Springs SD 109	Justice
186	n/a	Joliet Psd 86	Joliet
186	n/a	Keeneyville SD 20	Hanover Park
186	n/a	Kildeer Countryside CCSD 96	Buffalo Grove
186	n/a	Kinnikinnick CCSD 131	Roscoe
186	n/a	Kirby SD 140	Tinley Park
186	n/a	La Grange SD 102	La Grange Park
186	n/a	Lake Forest SD 67	Lake Forest
186	n/a	Lake Villa CCSD 41	Lake Villa
186	n/a	Lansing SD 158	Lansing
186	n/a	Lemont-Bromberek CSD 113a	Lemont
186	n/a	Libertyville SD 70	Libertyville
186	n/a	Lincolnshire-Prairieview SD 103	Lincolnshire
186	n/a	Lombard SD 44	Lombard
186	n/a	Lyons SD 103	Lyons
186	n/a	Marquardt SD 15	Glendale Hgts
186	n/a	Matteson ESD 162	Matteson
186	n/a	Maywood-Melrose Park-Broadview 89	Melrose Park
186	n/a	Mchenry CCSD 15	Mchenry
186	n/a	Midlothian SD 143	Midlothian
186	n/a	Millburn CCSD 24	Wadsworth
186	n/a	Minooka CCSD 201	Minooka
186	n/a	Mokena SD 159	Mokena
186	n/a	Mount Prospect SD 57	Mount Prospect
186	n/a	Mount Vernon SD 80	Mount Vernon
186	n/a	Mundelein ESD 75	Mundelein
186	n/a	New Lenox SD 122	New Lenox
186	n/a	Nippersink SD 2	Richmond
186	n/a	North Palos SD 117	Palos Hills
186	n/a	North Shore SD 112	Highland Park
186	n/a	Northbrook SD 28	Northbrook
186	n/a	O Fallon CCSD 90	Ofallon
186	n/a	Oak Lawn-Hometown SD 123	Oak Lawn
186	n/a	Oak Park ESD 97	Oak Park
186	n/a	Orland SD 135	Orland Park
186	n/a	Ottawa ESD 141	Ottawa
186	n/a	Palatine CCSD 15	Palatine
186	n/a	Palos CCSD 118	Palos Park
186	n/a	Park Forest SD 163	Park Forest
186	n/a	Park Ridge CCSD 64	Park Ridge
186	n/a	Posen-Robbins ESD 143-5	Posen
186	n/a	Prairie-Hills ESD 144	Markham
186	n/a	Queen Bee SD 16	Glendale Hgts
186	n/a	Rantoul City SD 137	Rantoul
186	n/a	Ridgeland SD 122	Oak Lawn
186	n/a	River Trails SD 26	Mount Prospect
186	n/a	Rochelle CCSD 231	Rochelle
186	n/a	Schaumburg CCSD 54	Schaumburg
186	n/a	School District 45 Dupage County	Villa Park
186	n/a	Skokie SD 68	Skokie
186	n/a	Skokie SD 69	Skokie
186	n/a	South Holland SD 151	South Holland
186	n/a	Steger SD 194	Steger
186	n/a	Streator ESD 44	Streator
186	n/a	Summit Hill SD 161	Frankfort
186	n/a	Summit SD 104	Summit
186	n/a	Tinley Park CCSD 146	Tinley Park
186	n/a	Troy CCSD 30c	Plainfield
186	n/a	West Chicago ESD 33	West Chicago
186	n/a	West Harvey-Dixmoor PSD 147	Harvey
186	n/a	Wheeling CCSD 21	Wheeling
186	n/a	Will County SD 92	Lockport
186	n/a	Wilmette SD 39	Wilmette
186	n/a	Winnetka SD 36	Winnetka
186	n/a	Woodland CCSD 50	Gurnee
186	n/a	Woodridge SD 68	Woodridge
186	n/a	Zion ESD 6	Zion

The National Assessment of Educational Progress (NAEP) assesses mathematics in five content areas: number properties and operations; measurement; geometry; data analysis and probability; and algebra. The NAEP mathematics scale ranges from 0 to 500.

Overall Mathematics Results for Illinois

- In 2007, the average scale score for fourth-grade students in Illinois was 237. This was higher than their average score in 2005 (233) and was higher than their average score in 2000 (223).[1]
- Illinois' average score (237) in 2007 was not significantly different from that of the nation's public schools (239).
- Of the 52 states and other jurisdictions that participated in the 2007 fourth-grade assessment, students' average scale score in Illinois was higher than those in 10 jurisdictions, not significantly different from those in 14 jurisdictions, and lower than those in 27 jurisdictions.[2]
- The percentage of students in Illinois who performed at or above the NAEP *Proficient* level was 36 percent in 2007. This percentage was greater than that in 2005 (32 percent) and was greater than that in 2000 (20 percent).
- The percentage of students in Illinois who performed at or above the NAEP *Basic* level was 79 percent in 2007. This percentage was greater than that in 2005 (74 percent) and was greater than that in 2000 (63 percent).

Percentages at NAEP Achievement Levels and Average Score

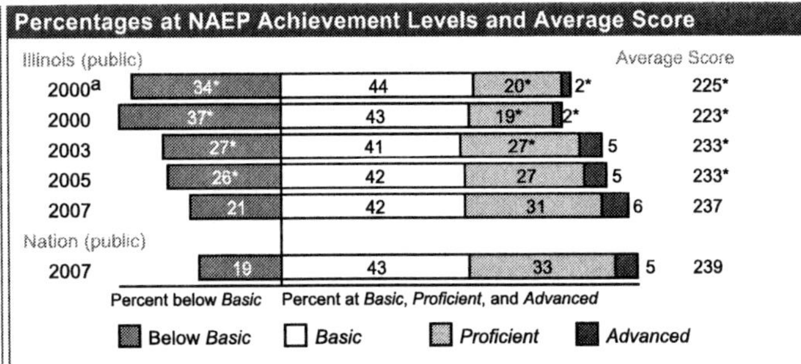

a Accommodations were not permitted for this assessment.

NOTE: The NAEP grade 4 mathematics achievement levels correspond to the following scale points: Below *Basic*, 213 or lower; *Basic*, 214–248; *Proficient*, 249–281; *Advanced*, 282 or above.

Performance of NAEP Reporting Groups in Illinois: 2007

Reporting groups	Percent of students	Average score	Percent below *Basic*	Percent of students at or above *Basic*	Percent of students at or above *Proficient*	Percent *Advanced*
Male	50	239 ↑	21 ↓	79 ↑	40 ↑	7
Female	50	235 ↑	22 ↓	78 ↑	33	4
White	56	248	9	91	50	8
Black	19	216	46	54	9	#
Hispanic	19	223	36	64	19	1
Asian/Pacific Islander	4	257	5	95	62	17
American Indian/Alaska Native	#	‡	‡	‡	‡	‡
Eligible for National School Lunch Program	44	223 ↑	36 ↓	64 ↑	17	1
Not eligible for National School Lunch Program	56	249 ↑	10	90	51	9

Average Score Gaps Between Selected Groups

- In 2007, male students in Illinois had an average score that was higher than that of female students by 4 points. In 2000, there was no significant difference between the average score of male and female students.
- In 2007, Black students had an average score that was lower than that of White students by 32 points. In 2000, the average score for Black students was lower than that of White students by 33 points.
- In 2007, Hispanic students had an average score that was lower than that of White students by 25 points. In 2000, the average score for Hispanic students was lower than that of White students by 24 points.
- In 2007, students who were eligible for free/reduced-price school lunch, a proxy for poverty, had an average score that was lower than that of students who were not eligible for free/reduced-price school lunch by 26 points. In 2000, the average score for students who were eligible for free/reduced-price school lunch was lower than the score of those not eligible by 25 points.
- In 2007, the score gap between students at the 75th percentile and students at the 25th percentile was 40 points. In 2000, the score gap between students at the 75th percentile and students at the 25th percentile was 42 points.

Mathematics Scores at Selected Percentiles

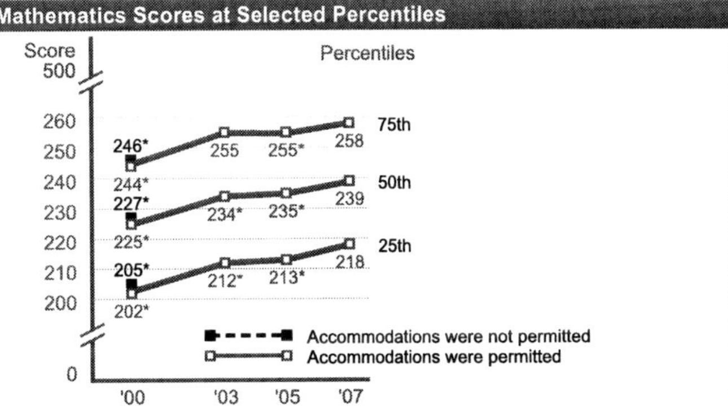

NOTE: Scores at selected percentiles on the NAEP mathematics scale indicate how well students at lower, middle, and higher levels performed.

\# Rounds to zero.
‡ Reporting standards not met.
* Significantly different from 2007.
↑ Significantly higher than 2005. ↓ Significantly lower than 2005.

[1] Comparisons (higher/lower/narrower/wider/not different) are based on statistical tests. The .05 level was used for testing statistical significance. Statistical comparisons are calculated on the basis of unrounded scale scores or percentages. Comparisons across jurisdictions and comparisons with the nation or within a jurisdiction across years may be affected by differences in exclusion rates for students with disabilities (SD) and English language learners (ELL). The exclusion rates for SD and ELL in Illinois were 3 percent and 1 percent in 2007, respectively.For more information on NAEP significance testing see http://nces.ed.gov/nationsreportcard/mathematics/interpret-results.asp#statistical.

[2] "Jurisdictions" refers to states and the District of Columbia and the Department of Defense Education Activity schools.

NOTE: Detail may not sum to totals because of rounding and because the "Information not available" category for the National School Lunch Program, which provides free and reduced-price lunches, and the "Unclassified" category for race/ethnicity are not displayed. Visit http://nces.ed.gov/nationsreportcard/states/ for additional results and detailed information.

SOURCE: U.S. Department of Education, Institute of Education Sciences, National Center for Education Statistics, National Assessment of Educational Progress (NAEP), various years, 2000–2007 Mathematics Assessments.

ies NATIONAL CENTER FOR EDUCATION STATISTICS Institute of Education Sciences

NCES 2007-497IL4

The Nation's Report Card Reading 2007

State Snapshot Report

Illinois
Grade 4
Public Schools

The National Assessment of Educational Progress (NAEP) assesses reading in two content areas in grade 4: reading for literary experience and to gain information. The NAEP reading scale ranges from 0 to 500.

Overall Reading Results for Illinois

- In 2007, the average scale score for fourth-grade students in Illinois was 219. This was not significantly different from their average score in 2005 (216) and was not significantly different from their average score in 2003 (216).[1]
- Illinois' average score (219) in 2007 was not significantly different from that of the nation's public schools (220).
- Of the 52 states and other jurisdictions that participated in the 2007 fourth-grade assessment, students' average scale score in Illinois was higher than those in 12 jurisdictions, not significantly different from those in 14 jurisdictions, and lower than those in 25 jurisdictions.[2]
- The percentage of students in Illinois who performed at or above the NAEP *Proficient* level was 32 percent in 2007. This percentage was not significantly different from that in 2005 (29 percent) and was not significantly different from that in 2003 (31 percent).
- The percentage of students in Illinois who performed at or above the NAEP *Basic* level was 65 percent in 2007. This percentage was not significantly different from that in 2005 (62 percent) and was not significantly different from that in 2003 (61 percent).

Percentages at NAEP Achievement Levels and Average Score

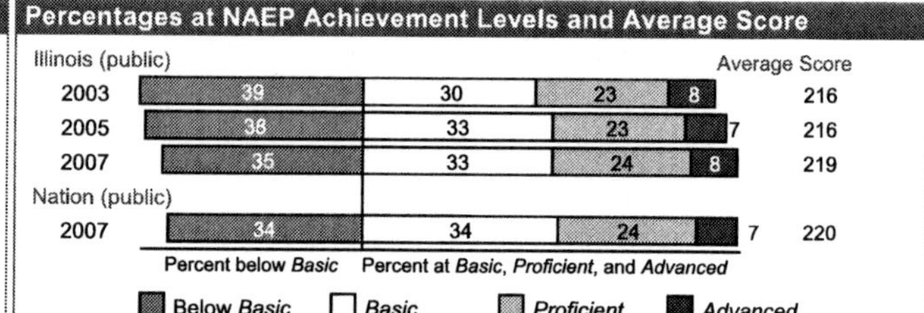

NOTE: The NAEP grade 4 reading achievement levels correspond to the following scale points: Below *Basic*, 207 or lower; *Basic*, 208–237; *Proficient*, 238–267; *Advanced*, 268 or above.

Performance of NAEP Reporting Groups in Illinois: 2007

Reporting groups	Percent of students	Average score	Percent below *Basic*	Percent of students at or above *Basic*	Percent of students at or above *Proficient*	Percent *Advanced*
Male	51	217	37	63	30	7
Female	49	222	33	67	35	9
White	55	230	23	77	42	12
Black	20	201	56	44	14	2
Hispanic	20	205	50	50	18	3
Asian/Pacific Islander	3	240	13	87	54	16
American Indian/Alaska Native	#	‡	‡	‡	‡	‡
Eligible for National School Lunch Program	44	204 ↑	52 ↓	48 ↑	16	2
Not eligible for National School Lunch Program	56	232	21	79	45	12

Average Score Gaps Between Selected Groups

- In 2007, male students in Illinois had an average score that was lower than that of female students by 5 points. In 2003, the average score for male students was lower than that of female students by 5 points.
- In 2007, Black students had an average score that was lower than that of White students by 29 points. In 2003, the average score for Black students was lower than that of White students by 34 points.
- In 2007, Hispanic students had an average score that was lower than that of White students by 24 points. In 2003, the average score for Hispanic students was lower than that of White students by 31 points.
- In 2007, students who were eligible for free/reduced-price school lunch, a proxy for poverty, had an average score that was lower than that of students who were not eligible for free/reduced-price school lunch by 28 points. This performance gap was narrower than that of 2003 (35 points).
- In 2007, the score gap between students at the 75th percentile and students at the 25th percentile was 49 points. In 2003, the score gap between students at the 75th percentile and students at the 25th percentile was 53 points.

Reading Scores at Selected Percentiles

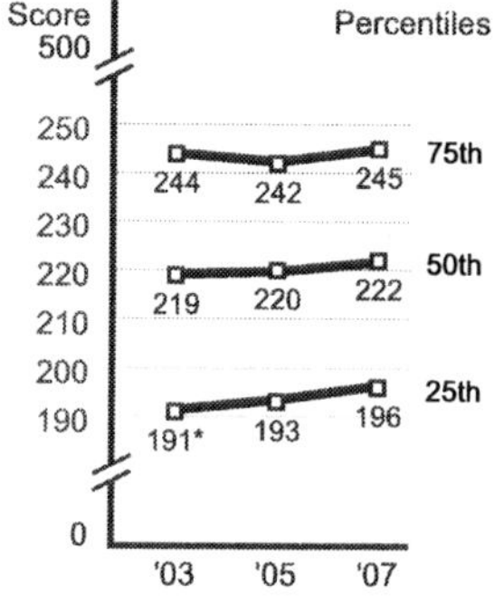

NOTE: Scores at selected percentiles on the NAEP reading scale indicate how well students at lower, middle, and higher levels performed.

Rounds to zero.
‡ Reporting standards not met.
* Significantly different from 2007.
↑ Significantly higher than 2005. ↓ Significantly lower than 2005.

[1] Comparisons (higher/lower/narrower/wider/not different) are based on statistical tests. The .05 level was used for testing statistical significance. Statistical comparisons are calculated on the basis of unrounded scale scores or percentages. Comparisons across jurisdictions and comparisons with the nation or within a jurisdiction across years may be affected by differences in exclusion rates for students with disabilities (SD) and English language learners (ELL). The exclusion rates for SD and ELL in Illinois were 5 percent and 3 percent in 2007, respectively.For more information on NAEP significance testing see http://nces.ed.gov/nationsreportcard/reading/interpret-results.asp#statistical.

[2] "Jurisdictions" refers to states and the District of Columbia and the Department of Defense Education Activity schools.

NOTE: Detail may not sum to totals because of rounding and because the "Information not available" category for the National School Lunch Program, which provides free and reduced-price lunches, and the "Unclassified" category for race/ethnicity are not displayed. Visit http://nces.ed.gov/nationsreportcard/states/ for additional results and detailed information.

SOURCE: U.S. Department of Education, Institute of Education Sciences, National Center for Education Statistics, National Assessment of Educational Progress (NAEP), various years, 2003–2007 Reading Assessments.

The National Assessment of Educational Progress (NAEP) assesses science in two major dimensions: Fields of Science (Earth, Physical, and Life) and Knowing and Doing Science (Conceptual Understanding, Scientific Investigation, and Practical Reasoning). The NAEP science scale ranges from 0 to 300. Scales are created separately for each grade.

Overall Science Results for Illinois

- In 2005, the average scale score for fourth-grade students in Illinois was 148. This was not significantly different from their average score in 2000 (150).[1]
- Illinois' average score (148) in 2005 was not significantly different from that of the nation's public schools (149).
- Of the 44 states and one jurisdiction that participated in the 2005 fourth-grade assessment, students' average scale score in Illinois was higher than those in 8 jurisdictions, not significantly different from those in 11 jurisdictions, and lower than those in 25 jurisdictions.[2]
- The percentage of students in Illinois who performed at or above the NAEP *Proficient* level was 27 percent in 2005. This percentage was not significantly different from that in 2000 (31 percent).
- The percentage of students in Illinois who performed at or above the NAEP *Basic* level was 64 percent in 2005. This percentage was not significantly different from that in 2000 (68 percent).

Student Percentages at NAEP Achievement Levels

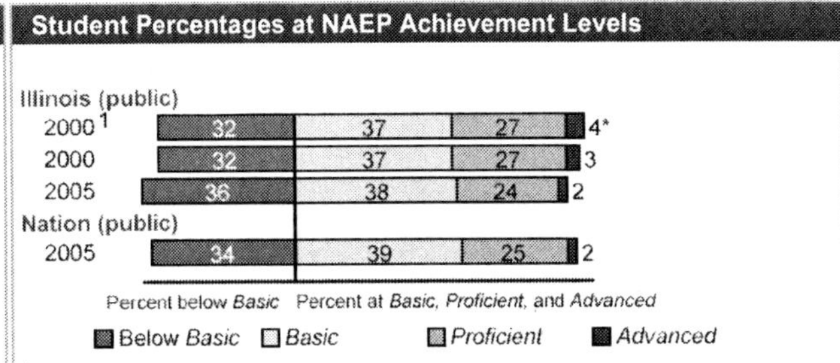

[1] Accommodations were not permitted for this assessment.

NOTE: The NAEP grade 4 science achievement levels correspond to the following scale points: Below *Basic*, 137 or lower; *Basic*, 138–169; *Proficient*, 170–204; *Advanced*, 205 or above.

Performance of NAEP Reporting Groups in Illinois: 2005

Reporting groups	Percent of students	Average score	Percent below *Basic*	Percent of students at or above *Basic*	Percent of students at or above *Proficient*	Percent *Advanced*
Male	50	148	35	65	28	3
Female	50	147	36	64	25	2
White	56	162↓	17	83	39	3
Black	18	122	70	30	5	#
Hispanic	22	130	59	41	9	#
Asian/Pacific Islander	3	168	12	88	49	8
American Indian/Alaska Native	#	‡	‡	‡	‡	‡
Eligible for free/reduced-price school lunch	43	130	58	42	10	1
Not eligible for free/reduced-price school lunch	57	161↓	18↑	82↓	39	3

Average Score Gaps Between Selected Groups

- In 2005, male students in Illinois had an average score that was not significantly different from that of female students. In 2000, there was no significant difference between the average score of male and female students.
- In 2005, Black students had an average score that was lower than that of White students by 39 points. In 2000, the average score for Black students was lower than that of White students by 41 points.
- In 2005, Hispanic students had an average score that was lower than that of White students by 32 points. In 2000, the average score for Hispanic students was lower than that of White students by 41 points.
- In 2005, students who were eligible for free/reduced-price school lunch, an indicator of poverty, had an average score that was lower than that of students who were not eligible for free/reduced-price school lunch by 31 points. In 2000, the average score for students who were eligible for free/reduced-price school lunch was lower than the score of those not eligible by 32 points.
- In 2005, the score gap between students at the 75th percentile and students at the 25th percentile was 45 points. In 2000, the score gap between students at the 75th percentile and students at the 25th percentile was 45 points.

Science Scale Scores at Selected Percentiles

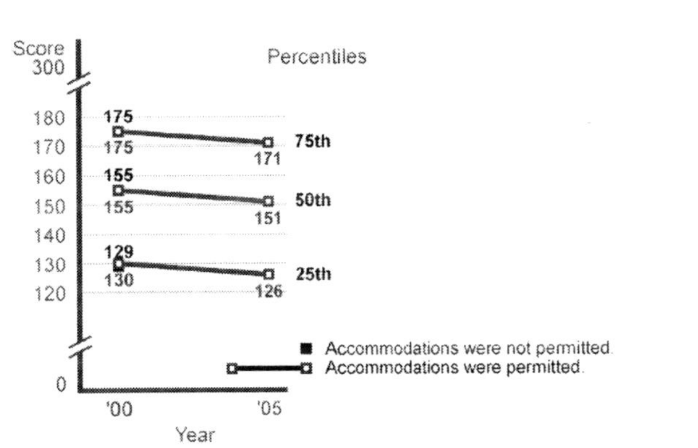

Scores at selected percentiles on the NAEP science scale indicate how well students at lower, middle, and higher levels performed.

The estimate rounds to zero.
‡ Reporting standards not met.
* Significantly different from 2005.
↑ Significantly higher than 2000. ↓ Significantly lower than 2000.

[1] Comparisons (higher/lower/not different) are based on statistical tests. The .05 level was used for testing statistical significance. Comparisons across jurisdictions and comparisons with the nation or within a jurisdiction across years may be affected by differences in exclusion rates for students with disabilities (SD) and English language learners (ELL). The exclusion rates for SD and ELL in Illinois were 2 percent and 1 percent in 2005, respectively. Statistical comparisons are calculated on the basis of unrounded scale scores or percentages.

[2] "Jurisdiction" refers to states and the Department of Defense Education Activity schools.

NOTE: Detail may not sum to totals because of rounding and because the "Information not available" category for free/reduced-price school lunch and the "Unclassifed" category for race/ethnicity are not displayed. Visit http://nces.ed.gov/nationsreportcard/states/ for additional results and detailed information.

SOURCE: U.S. Department of Education, Institute of Education Sciences, National Center for Education Statistics, National Assessment of Educational Progress (NAEP), 2000 and 2005 Science Assessments.

ies NATIONAL CENTER FOR EDUCATION STATISTICS Institute of Education Sciences
NCES 2007-495IL8

The Nation's Report Card Mathematics 2007

State Snapshot Report

Illinois
Grade 8
Public Schools

The National Assessment of Educational Progress (NAEP) assesses mathematics in five content areas: number properties and operations; measurement; geometry; data analysis and probability; and algebra. The NAEP mathematics scale ranges from 0 to 500.

Overall Mathematics Results for Illinois

- In 2007, the average scale score for eighth-grade students in Illinois was 280. This was not significantly different from their average score in 2005 (278) and was higher than their average score in 1990 (261).[1]
- Illinois' average score (280) in 2007 was not significantly different from that of the nation's public schools (280).
- Of the 52 states and other jurisdictions that participated in the 2007 eighth-grade assessment, students' average scale score in Illinois was higher than those in 15 jurisdictions, not significantly different from those in 12 jurisdictions, and lower than those in 24 jurisdictions.[2]
- The percentage of students in Illinois who performed at or above the NAEP *Proficient* level was 31 percent in 2007. This percentage was not significantly different from that in 2005 (29 percent) and was greater than that in 1990 (15 percent).
- The percentage of students in Illinois who performed at or above the NAEP *Basic* level was 70 percent in 2007. This percentage was not significantly different from that in 2005 (68 percent) and was greater than that in 1990 (50 percent).

Percentages at NAEP Achievement Levels and Average Score

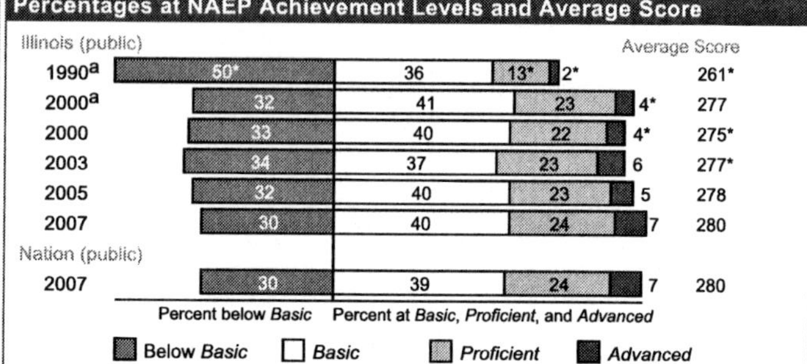

[a] Accommodations were not permitted for this assessment.

NOTE: The NAEP grade 8 mathematics achievement levels correspond to the following scale points: Below *Basic*, 261 or lower; *Basic*, 262–298; *Proficient*, 299–332; *Advanced*, 333 or above.

Performance of NAEP Reporting Groups in Illinois: 2007

Reporting groups	Percent of students	Average score	Percent below *Basic*	Percent of students at or above *Basic*	Percent of students at or above *Proficient*	Percent *Advanced*
Male	50	282	29	71	33	8
Female	50	279	31	69	29	6
White	60	291	19	81	41	9
Black	16	253	59	41	7	#
Hispanic	18	265	45	55	13	1
Asian/Pacific Islander	5	303	13	87	55	23
American Indian/Alaska Native	#	‡	‡	‡	‡	‡
Eligible for National School Lunch Program	39	262	49	51	13	2
Not eligible for National School Lunch Program	61	292	17	83	42	10

Average Score Gaps Between Selected Groups

- In 2007, male students in Illinois had an average score that was not significantly different from that of female students. In 1990, there was no significant difference between the average score of male and female students.
- In 2007, Black students had an average score that was lower than that of White students by 38 points. In 1990, the average score for Black students was lower than that of White students by 38 points.
- In 2007, Hispanic students had an average score that was lower than that of White students by 26 points. In 1990, the average score for Hispanic students was lower than that of White students by 33 points.
- In 2007, students who were eligible for free/reduced-price school lunch, a proxy for poverty, had an average score that was lower than that of students who were not eligible for free/reduced-price school lunch by 30 points. In 2000, the average score for students who were eligible for free/reduced-price school lunch was lower than the score of those not eligible by 30 points.
- In 2007, the score gap between students at the 75th percentile and students at the 25th percentile was 48 points. In 1990, the score gap between students at the 75th percentile and students at the 25th percentile was 49 points.

Mathematics Scores at Selected Percentiles

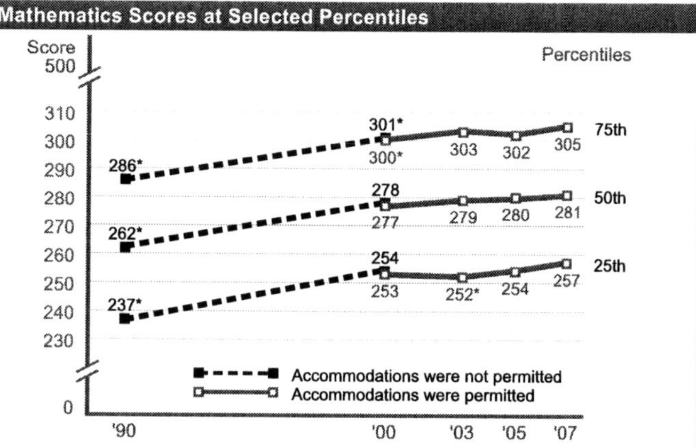

NOTE: Scores at selected percentiles on the NAEP mathematics scale indicate how well students at lower, middle, and higher levels performed.

Rounds to zero.
‡ Reporting standards not met.
* Significantly different from 2007.
↑ Significantly higher than 2005. ↓ Significantly lower than 2005.

[1] Comparisons (higher/lower/narrower/wider/not different) are based on statistical tests. The .05 level was used for testing statistical significance. Statistical comparisons are calculated on the basis of unrounded scale scores or percentages. Comparisons across jurisdictions and comparisons with the nation or within a jurisdiction across years may be affected by differences in exclusion rates for students with disabilities (SD) and English language learners (ELL). The exclusion rates for SD and ELL in Illinois were 5 percent and 1 percent in 2007, respectively.For more information on NAEP significance testing see http://nces.ed.gov/nationsreportcard/mathematics/interpret-results.asp#statistical.

[2] "Jurisdictions" refers to states and the District of Columbia and the Department of Defense Education Activity schools.

NOTE: Detail may not sum to totals because of rounding and because the "Information not available" category for the National School Lunch Program, which provides free and reduced-price lunches, and the "Unclassified" category for race/ethnicity are not displayed. Visit http://nces.ed.gov/nationsreportcard/states/ for additional results and detailed information.

SOURCE: U.S. Department of Education, Institute of Education Sciences, National Center for Education Statistics, National Assessment of Educational Progress (NAEP), various years, 1990–2007 Mathematics Assessments.

Illinois
Grade 8
Public Schools

The National Assessment of Educational Progress (NAEP) assesses reading in three content areas in grade 8: reading for literary experience, to gain information, and to perform a task. The NAEP reading scale ranges from 0 to 500.

Overall Reading Results for Illinois

- In 2007, the average scale score for eighth-grade students in Illinois was 263. This was not significantly different from their average score in 2005 (264) and was lower than their average score in 2003 (266).[1]
- Illinois' average score (263) in 2007 was not significantly different from that of the nation's public schools (261).
- Of the 52 states and other jurisdictions that participated in the 2007 eighth-grade assessment, students' average scale score in Illinois was higher than those in 18 jurisdictions, not significantly different from those in 14 jurisdictions, and lower than those in 19 jurisdictions.[2]
- The percentage of students in Illinois who performed at or above the NAEP *Proficient* level was 30 percent in 2007. This percentage was not significantly different from that in 2005 (31 percent) and was smaller than that in 2003 (35 percent).
- The percentage of students in Illinois who performed at or above the NAEP *Basic* level was 75 percent in 2007. This percentage was not significantly different from that in 2005 (75 percent) and was not significantly different from that in 2003 (77 percent).

Percentages at NAEP Achievement Levels and Average Score

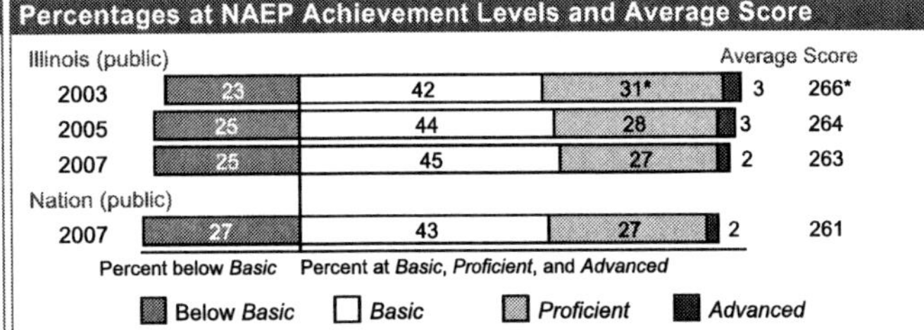

NOTE: The NAEP grade 8 reading achievement levels correspond to the following scale points: Below *Basic*, 242 or lower; *Basic*, 243–280; *Proficient*, 281–322; *Advanced*, 323 or above.

Performance of NAEP Reporting Groups in Illinois: 2007

Reporting groups	Percent of students	Average score	Percent below *Basic*	Percent of students at or above *Basic*	Percent of students at or above *Proficient*	Percent *Advanced*
Male	49	259	30	70	26	2
Female	51	267	21	79	34	3
White	60	271	17	83	38	3
Black	17	244	46	54	10	#
Hispanic	17	250	36	64	16	#
Asian/Pacific Islander	4	277	13	87	46	4
American Indian/Alaska Native	#	‡	‡	‡	‡	‡
Eligible for National School Lunch Program	39	249	39	61	15	1
Not eligible for National School Lunch Program	61	272	16	84	39	3

Average Score Gaps Between Selected Groups

- In 2007, male students in Illinois had an average score that was lower than that of female students by 8 points. In 2003, the average score for male students was lower than that of female students by 6 points.
- In 2007, Black students had an average score that was lower than that of White students by 27 points. In 2003, the average score for Black students was lower than that of White students by 29 points.
- In 2007, Hispanic students had an average score that was lower than that of White students by 21 points. In 2003, the average score for Hispanic students was lower than that of White students by 26 points.
- In 2007, students who were eligible for free/reduced-price school lunch, a proxy for poverty, had an average score that was lower than that of students who were not eligible for free/reduced-price school lunch by 23 points. In 2003, the average score for students who were eligible for free/reduced-price school lunch was lower than the score of those not eligible by 27 points.
- In 2007, the score gap between students at the 75th percentile and students at the 25th percentile was 43 points. In 2003, the score gap between students at the 75th percentile and students at the 25th percentile was 44 points.

Reading Scores at Selected Percentiles

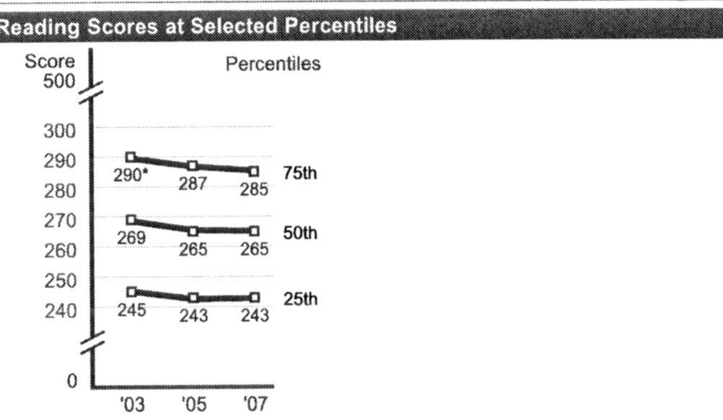

NOTE: Scores at selected percentiles on the NAEP reading scale indicate how well students at lower, middle, and higher levels performed.

Rounds to zero.
‡ Reporting standards not met.
* Significantly different from 2007.
↑ Significantly higher than 2005. ↓ Significantly lower than 2005.

[1] Comparisons (higher/lower/narrower/wider/not different) are based on statistical tests. The .05 level was used for testing statistical significance. Statistical comparisons are calculated on the basis of unrounded scale scores or percentages. Comparisons across jurisdictions and comparisons with the nation or within a jurisdiction across years may be affected by differences in exclusion rates for students with disabilities (SD) and English language learners (ELL). The exclusion rates for SD and ELL in Illinois were 4 percent and 1 percent in 2007, respectively.For more information on NAEP significance testing see http://nces.ed.gov/nationsreportcard/reading/interpret-results.asp#statistical.

[2] "Jurisdictions" refers to states and the District of Columbia and the Department of Defense Education Activity schools.

NOTE: Detail may not sum to totals because of rounding and because the "Information not available" category for the National School Lunch Program, which provides free and reduced-price lunches, and the "Unclassified" category for race/ethnicity are not displayed. Visit http://nces.ed.gov/nationsreportcard/states/ for additional results and detailed information.

SOURCE: U.S. Department of Education, Institute of Education Sciences, National Center for Education Statistics, National Assessment of Educational Progress (NAEP), various years, 2003–2007 Reading Assessments.

The National Assessment of Educational Progress (NAEP) assesses writing for three purposes identified in the NAEP framework: narrative, informative, and persuasive. The NAEP writing scale ranges from 0 to 300.

Overall Writing Results for Illinois

- Illinois' average score (160) in 2007 was higher than that of the nation's public schools (154).[1]
- Of the 45 states and one other jurisdiction that participated in the 2007 eighth-grade assessment, students' average scale score in Illinois was higher than those in 27 jurisdictions, not significantly different from those in 14 jurisdictions, and lower than those in 4 jurisdictions.[2]
- The percentage of students in Illinois who performed at or above the NAEP *Proficient* level was 37 percent in 2007. This percentage was greater than that in the nation (31 percent).
- The percentage of students in Illinois who performed at or above the NAEP *Basic* level was 90 percent in 2007. This percentage was greater than that in the nation (87 percent).

Percentages at NAEP Achievement Levels and Average Score

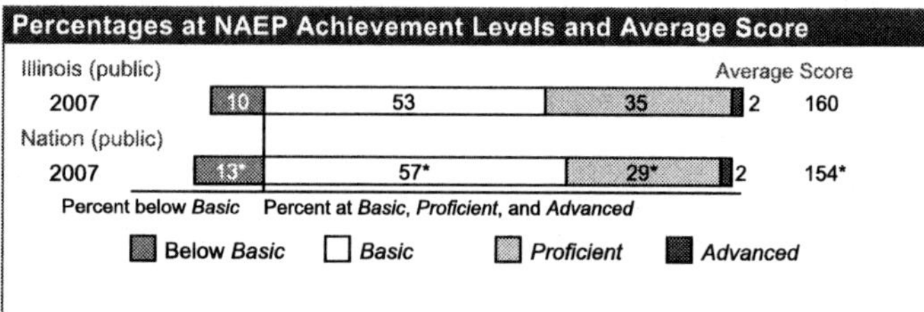

NOTE: The NAEP grade 8 writing achievement levels correspond to the following scale points: Below *Basic*, 113 or lower; *Basic*, 114–172; *Proficient*, 173–223; *Advanced*, 224 or above.

Performance of NAEP Reporting Groups in Illinois: 2007

Reporting groups	Percent of students	Average score	Percent below *Basic*	Percent of students at or above *Basic*	Percent of students at or above *Proficient*	Percent *Advanced*
Male	51	150↑	15↓	85↑	27↑	1
Female	49	170↑	5↓	95↑	48↑	4
White	58	169↑	6↓	94↑	48↑	3
Black	19	142	19	81	18	#
Hispanic	18	143	18	82	17	#
Asian/Pacific Islander	4	180↑	2	98	60↑	8
American Indian/Alaska Native	#↓	‡	‡	‡	‡	‡
Eligible for National School Lunch Program	40	142	19	81	17	#
Not eligible for National School Lunch Program	60	172↑	5↓	95↑	51↑	4

Average Score Gaps Between Selected Groups

- In 2007, male students in Illinois had an average score that was lower than that of female students by 19 points. This performance gap was not significantly different from that of the nation (20 points).
- In 2007, Black students had an average score that was lower than that of White students by 27 points. This performance gap was wider than that of the nation (22 points).
- In 2007, Hispanic students had an average score that was lower than that of White students by 26 points. This performance gap was not significantly different from that of the nation (21 points).
- In 2007, students who were eligible for free/reduced-price school lunch, an indicator of poverty, had an average score that was lower than that of students who were not eligible for free/reduced-price school lunch by 29 points. This performance gap was wider than that of the nation (23 points).
- In 2007, the score gap between students at the 75th percentile and students at the 25th percentile was 47 points. This performance gap was not significantly different from that of the nation (46 points).

Writing Scores at Selected Percentiles: 2007

Jurisdiction	25th Percentile	50th Percentile	75th Percentile
Illinois	138	162	185
Nation (public)	132*	156*	178*

NOTE: Scores at selected percentiles on the NAEP writing scale indicate how well students at lower, middle, and higher levels performed. For example, the data above show that 75 percent of students in public schools nationally scored below 178, while 75 percent of students in Illinois scored below 185.

Rounds to zero. ‡ Reporting standards not met.

* Significantly different from Illinois. ↑ Significantly higher than nation (public). ↓ Significantly lower than nation (public).

[1] Comparisons (higher/lower/narrower/wider/not different) are based on statistical tests. The .05 level with appropriate adjustments for multiple comparisons was used for testing statistical significance. Statistical comparisons are calculated on the basis of unrounded scale scores or percentages. Comparisons across jurisdictions and comparisons with the nation or within a jurisdiction across years may be affected by differences in exclusion rates for students with disabilities (SD) and English language learners (ELL). The exclusion rates for SD and ELL in Illinois were 2 percent and 1 percent in 2007, respectively. For more information on NAEP significance testing, see http://nces.ed.gov/nationsreportcard/writing/interpret-results.asp#statistical.

[2] "Jurisdiction" refers to states, the District of Columbia, and the Department of Defense Education Activity schools.

NOTE: Detail may not sum to totals because of rounding and because the "Information not available" category for the National School Lunch Program, which provides free and reduced-price lunches, and the "Unclassified" category for race/ethnicity are not displayed. Visit http://nces.ed.gov/nationsreportcard/states/ for additional results and detailed information.

SOURCE: U.S. Department of Education, Institute of Education Sciences, National Center for Education Statistics, National Assessment of Educational Progress (NAEP), 2007 Writing Assessment.

The National Assessment of Educational Progress (NAEP) assesses science in two major dimensions: Fields of Science (Earth, Physical, and Life) and Knowing and Doing Science (Conceptual Understanding, Scientific Investigation, and Practical Reasoning). The NAEP science scale ranges from 0 to 300. Scales are created separately for each grade.

Overall Science Results for Illinois

- In 2005, the average scale score for eighth-grade students in Illinois was 148. This was not significantly different from their average score in 2000 (148).[1]
- Illinois' average score (148) in 2005 was not significantly different from that of the nation's public schools (147).
- Of the 44 states and one jurisdiction that participated in the 2005 eighth-grade assessment, students' average scale score in Illinois was higher than those in 13 jurisdictions, not significantly different from those in 7 jurisdictions, and lower than those in 24 jurisdictions.[2]
- The percentage of students in Illinois who performed at or above the NAEP *Proficient* level was 27 percent in 2005. This percentage was not significantly different from that in 2000 (29 percent).
- The percentage of students in Illinois who performed at or above the NAEP *Basic* level was 58 percent in 2005. This percentage was not significantly different from that in 2000 (59 percent).

Student Percentages at NAEP Achievement Levels

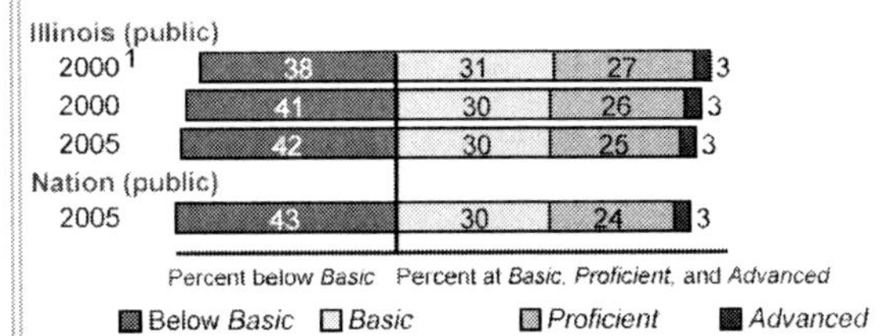

[1] Accommodations were not permitted for this assessment.

NOTE: The NAEP grade 8 science achievement levels correspond to the following scale points: Below *Basic*, 142 or lower; *Basic*, 143–169; *Proficient*, 170–207; *Advanced*, 208 or above.

Performance of NAEP Reporting Groups in Illinois: 2005

Reporting groups	Percent of students	Average score	Percent below *Basic*	Percent of students at or above *Basic*	Percent of students at or above *Proficient*	Percent *Advanced*
Male	50	150	40	60	31	3
Female	50	146	44	56	24	2
White	60	161	26	74	39	4
Black	21	120	78	22	4	#
Hispanic	15	130	65	35	9	#
Asian/Pacific Islander	3	164	22	78	46	7
American Indian/Alaska Native	#	‡	‡	‡	‡	‡
Eligible for free/reduced-price school lunch	40	128	67	33	9	#
Not eligible for free/reduced-price school lunch	60	161	26	74	40	4

Average Score Gaps Between Selected Groups

- In 2005, male students in Illinois had an average score that was higher than that of female students by 4 points. In 2000, there was no significant difference between the average score of male and female students.
- In 2005, Black students had an average score that was lower than that of White students by 41 points. In 2000, the average score for Black students was lower than that of White students by 43 points.
- In 2005, Hispanic students had an average score that was lower than that of White students by 31 points. In 2000, the average score for Hispanic students was lower than that of White students by 36 points.
- In 2005, students who were eligible for free/reduced-price school lunch, an indicator of poverty, had an average score that was lower than that of students who were not eligible for free/reduced-price school lunch by 33 points. In 2000, the average score for students who were eligible for free/reduced-price school lunch was lower than the score of those not eligible by 35 points.
- In 2005, the score gap between students at the 75th percentile and students at the 25th percentile was 48 points. In 2000, the score gap between students at the 75th percentile and students at the 25th percentile was 47 points.

Science Scale Scores at Selected Percentiles

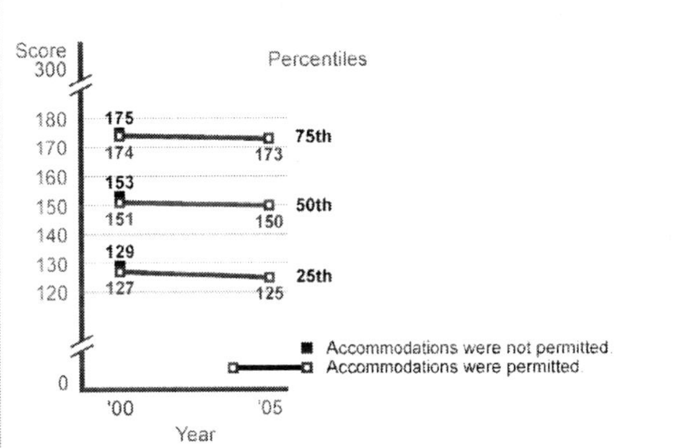

Scores at selected percentiles on the NAEP science scale indicate how well students at lower, middle, and higher levels performed.

The estimate rounds to zero. ‡ Reporting standards not met.

* Significantly different from 2005. ↑ Significantly higher than 2000. ↓ Significantly lower than 2000.

[1] Comparisons (higher/lower/not different) are based on statistical tests. The .05 level was used for testing statistical significance. Comparisons across jurisdictions and comparisons with the nation or within a jurisdiction across years may be affected by differences in exclusion rates for students with disabilities (SD) and English language learners (ELL). The exclusion rates for SD and ELL in Illinois were 2 percent and 1 percent in 2005, respectively. Statistical comparisons are calculated on the basis of unrounded scale scores or percentages.

[2] "Jurisdiction" refers to states and the Department of Defense Education Activity schools.

NOTE: Detail may not sum to totals because of rounding and because the "Information not available" category for free/reduced-price school lunch and the "Unclassifed" category for race/ethnicity are not displayed. Visit http://nces.ed.gov/nationsreportcard/states/ for additional results and detailed information.

SOURCE: U.S. Department of Education, Institute of Education Sciences, National Center for Education Statistics, National Assessment of Educational Progress (NAEP), 2000 and 2005 Science Assessments.

PERFORMANCE ON STATE ASSESSMENTS

Federal law requires that student achievement results for reading, mathematics and science for schools providing Title I services be reported to the general public.

The Illinois Standards Achievement Test (ISAT) is administered to students in grades 3 through 8. The Prairie State Achievement Examination (PSAE) is administered to students in grade 11. The Illinois Measure of Annual Growth in English (IMAGE) is administered to limited-English-proficient students. The Illinois Alternate Assessment (IAA) is administered to students with disabilities whose Individualized Education Programs (IEPs) indicate that participation in the ISAT or PSAE would not be appropriate.

Students with disabilities have an IEP (No Child Left Behind Act). An IEP is a written plan for a child with a disability who is eligible to receive special education services under the Individuals with Disabilities Education Act.

In order to protect students' identities, test data for groups of fewer than ten students are not reported.

PERCENTAGE OF STUDENTS NOT TESTED IN STATE TESTING PROGRAMS

		Gender		Racial/Ethnic Background									
	All	Male	Female	White	Black	Hispanic	Asian/ Pacific Islander	Native American	Multi racial /Ethnic	LEP	Migrant	Students with Disabilities	Economically Disadvantaged
*Enrollment	1,084,882	553,532	530,308	595,977	214,100	206,359	41,730	1,757	23,196	84,125	548	158,457	455,494
Reading	0.2	0.1	0.1	0.1	0.2	0.1	0.1	0.2	0.0	0.2	0.2	0.5	0.1
Mathematics	0.2	0.1	0.1	0.1	0.2	0.1	0.1	0.2	0.0	0.2	0.2	0.5	0.1

* Enrollment as reported during the testing windows.

ILLINOIS STANDARDS ACHIEVEMENT TEST (ISAT)

The following tables show the percentages of student scores in each of four performance levels. These levels were established with the help of Illinois educators who teach the grade levels and learning areas tested. Due to rounding, the sum of the percentages in the four performance levels may not always equal 100.

Level 1 -- Academic Warning - Student work demonstrates limited knowledge and skills in the subject. Because of major gaps in learning, students apply knowledge and skills ineffectively.

Level 2 -- Below Standards - Student work demonstrates basic knowledge and skills in the subject. However, because of gaps in learning, students apply knowledge and skills in limited ways.

Level 3 -- Meets Standards - Student work demonstrates proficient knowledge and skills in the subject. Students effectively apply knowledge and skills to solve problems.

Level 4 -- Exceeds Standards - Student work demonstrates advanced knowledge and skills in the subject. Students creatively apply knowledge and skills to solve problems and evaluate the results.

Grade 3

Grade 3 - All

	Reading				Mathematics			
Levels	1	2	3	4	1	2	3	4
	5.3	21.7	48.8	24.1	3.7	9.5	44.7	42.0

Grade 3 - Gender

	Reading				Mathematics			
Levels	1	2	3	4	1	2	3	4
Male	7.0	24.3	47.5	21.2	4.3	9.4	43.2	43.1
Female	3.6	19.0	50.2	27.2	3.1	9.7	46.4	40.9

Source: 2007 Illinois State Report Card

Grade 3 - Racial/Ethnic Background

	Reading				Mathematics			
Levels	1	2	3	4	1	2	3	4
White	2.7	14.9	50.5	31.9	1.2	4.9	41.6	52.3
Black	12.3	37.2	42.4	8.1	10.8	21.0	49.7	18.4
Hispanic	6.1	28.2	52.2	13.5	3.5	11.7	53.8	31.0
Asian/Pacific Islander	1.1	9.2	48.4	41.4	0.5	2.4	27.8	69.2
Native American	4.7	16.4	56.9	22.0	1.7	7.8	50.2	40.3
Multiracial/Ethnic	4.9	22.3	50.0	22.8	2.8	9.9	47.9	39.5

Grade 3 - Limited-English-Proficient

	Reading				Mathematics			
Levels	1	2	3	4	1	2	3	4
	7.1	26.2	49.7	17.0	4.0	11.3	44.6	40.2

Grade 3 - Migrant

	Reading				Mathematics			
Levels	1	2	3	4	1	2	3	4
	6.3	26.6	55.7	11.4	2.5	8.9	73.4	15.2

Grade 3 - Students with Disabilities

	Reading				Mathematics			
Levels	1	2	3	4	1	2	3	4
IEP	19.9	37.2	32.7	10.2	11.2	18.8	47.0	23.0
Non-IEP	3.0	19.2	51.5	26.4	2.5	8.0	44.4	45.1

Grade 3 - Economically Disadvantaged

	Reading				Mathematics			
Levels	1	2	3	4	1	2	3	4
Free/Reduced Price Lunch	9.8	33.1	46.4	10.8	7.2	16.5	51.6	24.6
Not Eligible	2.2	13.5	50.6	33.8	1.1	4.5	39.8	54.6

Grade 4

Grade 4 - All

	Reading				Mathematics				Science			
Levels	1	2	3	4	1	2	3	4	1	2	3	4
	1.1	25.2	48.3	25.4	1.2	12.5	56.9	29.5	3.5	16.7	61.5	18.2

Grade 4 - Gender

	Reading				Mathematics				Science			
Levels	1	2	3	4	1	2	3	4	1	2	3	4
Male	1.5	27.9	47.2	23.5	1.5	13.1	55.2	30.3	4.0	16.5	59.0	20.5
Female	0.6	22.5	49.5	27.4	0.8	11.9	58.7	28.7	3.0	17.0	64.2	15.8

Grade 4 - Racial/Ethnic Background

	Reading				Mathematics				Science			
Levels	1	2	3	4	1	2	3	4	1	2	3	4
White	0.5	17.0	49.4	33.2	0.5	6.8	55.1	37.6	1.1	8.6	64.4	25.8
Black	2.7	47.1	41.9	8.3	3.4	28.7	58.2	9.8	10.8	37.4	48.5	3.2
Hispanic	1.1	30.5	53.7	14.8	0.9	13.5	66.4	19.1	3.3	21.9	67.8	7.0
Asian/Pacific Islander	0.2	9.2	48.6	42.0	0.2	3.1	40.6	56.1	0.6	6.1	64.5	28.8
Native American	1.7	27.1	47.6	23.6	0.9	14.4	57.6	27.1	3.1	14.9	65.8	16.2
Multiracial/Ethnic	1.0	25.7	49.4	23.9	1.2	12.9	59.8	26.1	3.2	16.3	65.4	15.1

Source: 2007 Illinois State Report Card

Grade 4 - Limited-English-Proficient

	Reading				Mathematics				Science			
Levels	1	2	3	4	1	2	3	4	1	2	3	4
	0.8	21.6	59.9	17.8	1.0	9.0	63.7	26.4	2.7	15.2	74.7	7.4

Grade 4 - Migrant

	Reading				Mathematics				Science			
Levels	1	2	3	4	1	2	3	4	1	2	3	4
	0.0	38.3	45.0	16.7	1.7	6.7	73.3	18.3	3.3	18.3	63.3	15.0

Grade 4 - Students with Disabilities

	Reading				Mathematics				Science			
Levels	1	2	3	4	1	2	3	4	1	2	3	4
IEP	5.1	53.8	31.8	9.3	5.4	30.1	52.5	12.0	9.4	28.9	53.2	8.5
Non-IEP	0.4	20.4	51.2	28.1	0.4	9.5	57.7	32.5	2.5	14.7	63.0	19.9

Grade 4 - Economically Disadvantaged

	Reading				Mathematics				Science			
Levels	1	2	3	4	1	2	3	4	1	2	3	4
Free/Reduced Price Lunch	2.0	40.0	46.6	11.4	2.2	21.4	62.1	14.3	7.0	28.8	57.9	6.3
Not Eligible	0.4	15.0	49.6	35.1	0.4	6.3	53.3	40.0	1.1	8.4	64.1	26.5

Grade 5

Grade 5 - All

	Reading				Mathematics			
Levels	1	2	3	4	1	2	3	4
	0.8	29.6	44.1	25.6	0.5	17.0	62.8	19.7

Grade 5 - Gender

	Reading				Mathematics			
Levels	1	2	3	4	1	2	3	4
Male	1.0	33.0	42.8	23.2	0.7	18.0	60.7	20.7
Female	0.5	26.0	45.5	28.1	0.4	15.9	64.9	18.8

Grade 5 - Racial/Ethnic Background

	Reading				Mathematics			
Levels	1	2	3	4	1	2	3	4
White	0.4	20.5	45.3	33.8	0.2	9.7	64.3	25.8
Black	2.0	53.2	36.6	8.2	1.6	38.2	55.1	5.1
Hispanic	0.7	35.0	49.6	14.7	0.3	18.1	70.5	11.1
Asian/Pacific Islander	0.1	12.2	44.8	42.8	0.1	3.7	49.7	46.5
Native American	0.0	29.6	43.5	26.9	0.4	18.8	67.3	13.5
Multiracial/Ethnic	0.8	28.9	45.7	24.7	0.4	16.6	64.7	18.3

Grade 5 - Limited-English-Proficient

	Reading				Mathematics			
Levels	1	2	3	4	1	2	3	4
	0.7	34.1	52.1	13.0	0.2	18.2	70.4	11.1

Grade 5 - Migrant

	Reading				Mathematics			
Levels	1	2	3	4	1	2	3	4
	0.0	32.8	53.1	14.1	0.0	18.8	70.3	10.9

Source: 2007 Illinois State Report Card

Grade 5 - Students with Disabilities

	Reading				Mathematics			
Levels	1	2	3	4	1	2	3	4
IEP	4.2	62.2	26.1	7.6	2.6	41.5	50.0	5.9
Non-IEP	0.2	24.1	47.1	28.6	0.2	12.9	64.9	22.0

Grade 5 - Economically Disadvantaged

	Reading				Mathematics			
Levels	1	2	3	4	1	2	3	4
Free/Reduced Price Lunch	1.4	45.5	42.1	11.0	1.0	28.4	62.7	7.8
Not Eligible	0.3	18.2	45.6	36.0	0.2	8.8	62.8	28.2

Grade 6

Grade 6 - All

	Reading				Mathematics			
Levels	1	2	3	4	1	2	3	4
	0.2	26.4	54.3	19.1	0.5	18.0	62.2	19.2

Grade 6 - Gender

	Reading				Mathematics			
Levels	1	2	3	4	1	2	3	4
Male	0.3	29.9	53.7	16.2	0.7	19.5	60.1	19.7
Female	0.1	22.8	54.9	22.2	0.3	16.5	64.4	18.7

Grade 6 - Racial/Ethnic Background

	Reading				Mathematics			
Levels	1	2	3	4	1	2	3	4
White	0.1	16.5	57.1	26.2	0.3	10.1	64.2	25.5
Black	0.4	46.2	46.8	6.5	1.4	37.9	54.9	5.9
Hispanic	0.3	37.6	53.8	8.4	0.4	22.1	67.1	10.3
Asian/Pacific Islander	0.1	9.3	53.7	36.9	0.1	3.9	48.2	47.8
Native American	0.0	22.9	62.2	14.9	1.1	16.0	67.9	14.9
Multiracial/Ethnic	0.2	23.7	56.9	19.2	0.4	16.8	65.2	17.6

Grade 6 - Limited-English-Proficient

	Reading				Mathematics			
Levels	1	2	3	4	1	2	3	4
	0.5	62.9	34.7	1.9	0.7	36.3	58.4	4.6

Grade 6 - Migrant

	Reading				Mathematics			
Levels	1	2	3	4	1	2	3	4
	0.0	38.5	53.8	7.7	3.8	30.8	59.0	6.4

Grade 6 - Students with Disabilities

	Reading				Mathematics			
Levels	1	2	3	4	1	2	3	4
IEP	1.2	64.6	30.6	3.6	2.7	48.2	45.1	4.1
Non-IEP	0.0	20.3	58.1	21.6	0.2	13.2	65.0	21.7

Source: 2007 Illinois State Report Card

Grade 6 - Economically Disadvantaged

Levels	Reading 1	Reading 2	Reading 3	Reading 4	Mathematics 1	Mathematics 2	Mathematics 3	Mathematics 4
Free/Reduced Price Lunch	0.4	41.7	50.5	7.4	0.9	29.5	61.6	8.0
Not Eligible	0.1	15.0	57.1	27.9	0.2	9.4	62.6	27.7

Grade 7

Grade 7 - All

Levels	Reading 1	Reading 2	Reading 3	Reading 4	Mathematics 1	Mathematics 2	Mathematics 3	Mathematics 4	Science 1	Science 2	Science 3	Science 4
	0.5	26.1	58.3	15.0	2.3	18.3	54.2	25.2	7.0	13.7	55.2	24.1

Grade 7 - Gender

Levels	Reading 1	Reading 2	Reading 3	Reading 4	Mathematics 1	Mathematics 2	Mathematics 3	Mathematics 4	Science 1	Science 2	Science 3	Science 4
Male	0.7	29.9	56.3	13.1	2.8	18.8	52.0	26.3	7.7	13.3	52.5	26.5
Female	0.3	22.2	60.5	17.1	1.7	17.8	56.5	24.0	6.2	14.3	58.1	21.4

Grade 7 - Racial/Ethnic Background

Levels	Reading 1	Reading 2	Reading 3	Reading 4	Mathematics 1	Mathematics 2	Mathematics 3	Mathematics 4	Science 1	Science 2	Science 3	Science 4
White	0.3	17.4	61.5	20.8	1.1	10.8	53.8	34.3	3.0	7.3	54.7	35.0
Black	1.2	44.2	50.0	4.6	5.5	36.3	51.2	7.0	16.3	26.8	51.9	5.0
Hispanic	0.5	35.1	57.7	6.7	2.3	22.8	61.8	13.1	9.5	20.3	61.2	9.1
Asian/Pacific Islander	0.1	9.3	61.4	29.3	0.5	4.3	39.1	56.0	1.5	4.5	50.9	43.0
Native American	0.4	21.1	69.1	9.3	3.3	19.1	57.3	20.3	5.7	9.0	60.8	24.5
Multiracial/Ethnic	0.5	23.4	61.0	15.1	1.9	17.8	57.1	23.2	5.9	11.6	60.0	22.5

Grade 7 - Limited-English-Proficient

Levels	Reading 1	Reading 2	Reading 3	Reading 4	Mathematics 1	Mathematics 2	Mathematics 3	Mathematics 4	Science 1	Science 2	Science 3	Science 4
	1.1	59.0	38.1	1.7	4.7	37.4	53.0	5.0	19.8	32.4	45.2	2.6

Grade 7 - Migrant

Levels	Reading 1	Reading 2	Reading 3	Reading 4	Mathematics 1	Mathematics 2	Mathematics 3	Mathematics 4	Science 1	Science 2	Science 3	Science 4
	0.0	30.2	68.3	1.6	0.0	26.6	67.2	6.3	3.2	4.8	76.2	15.9

Grade 7 - Students with Disabilities

Levels	Reading 1	Reading 2	Reading 3	Reading 4	Mathematics 1	Mathematics 2	Mathematics 3	Mathematics 4	Science 1	Science 2	Science 3	Science 4
IEP	2.9	65.4	29.6	2.1	11.3	46.8	37.1	4.8	25.3	26.5	41.8	6.4
Non-IEP	0.1	19.6	63.1	17.2	0.8	13.6	57.0	28.6	4.0	11.6	57.4	27.0

Grade 7 - Economically Disadvantaged

Levels	Reading 1	Reading 2	Reading 3	Reading 4	Mathematics 1	Mathematics 2	Mathematics 3	Mathematics 4	Science 1	Science 2	Science 3	Science 4
Free/Reduced Price Lunch	0.9	40.1	53.4	5.6	3.9	29.6	56.2	10.3	12.5	22.6	56.4	8.5
Not Eligible	0.2	15.9	62.0	21.9	1.0	10.1	52.7	36.1	3.0	7.3	54.4	35.4

Source: 2007 Illinois State Report Card

Grade 8

Grade 8 - All

Levels	Reading 1	Reading 2	Reading 3	Reading 4	Mathematics 1	Mathematics 2	Mathematics 3	Mathematics 4
	0.6	17.7	69.9	11.8	1.2	17.5	52.3	29.0

Grade 8 - Gender

Levels	Reading 1	Reading 2	Reading 3	Reading 4	Mathematics 1	Mathematics 2	Mathematics 3	Mathematics 4
Male	0.8	21.6	67.8	9.8	1.5	18.8	50.1	29.6
Female	0.3	13.6	72.2	14.0	0.9	16.2	54.5	28.4

Grade 8 - Racial/Ethnic Background

Levels	Reading 1	Reading 2	Reading 3	Reading 4	Mathematics 1	Mathematics 2	Mathematics 3	Mathematics 4
White	0.3	12.6	71.1	16.0	0.6	10.4	50.8	38.2
Black	1.3	28.9	66.1	3.7	3.0	35.4	52.3	9.2
Hispanic	0.6	23.2	70.8	5.4	1.0	22.2	60.4	16.4
Asian/Pacific Islander	0.2	6.2	70.3	23.4	0.2	4.3	35.5	60.0
Native American	0.0	17.7	73.2	9.1	1.5	20.0	51.3	27.2
Multiracial/Ethnic	0.5	16.5	70.6	12.4	1.2	16.3	54.8	27.7

Grade 8 - Limited-English-Proficient

Levels	Reading 1	Reading 2	Reading 3	Reading 4	Mathematics 1	Mathematics 2	Mathematics 3	Mathematics 4
	2.0	46.0	49.7	2.3	2.7	40.0	48.7	8.6

Grade 8 - Migrant

Levels	Reading 1	Reading 2	Reading 3	Reading 4	Mathematics 1	Mathematics 2	Mathematics 3	Mathematics 4
	0.0	26.3	66.7	7.0	0.0	28.6	62.5	8.9

Grade 8 - Students with Disabilities

Levels	Reading 1	Reading 2	Reading 3	Reading 4	Mathematics 1	Mathematics 2	Mathematics 3	Mathematics 4
IEP	3.4	55.9	39.4	1.3	6.3	51.7	37.2	4.8
Non-IEP	0.1	11.3	75.0	13.6	0.3	11.8	54.8	33.0

Grade 8 - Economically Disadvantaged

Levels	Reading 1	Reading 2	Reading 3	Reading 4	Mathematics 1	Mathematics 2	Mathematics 3	Mathematics 4
Free/Reduced Price Lunch	1.0	27.2	67.4	4.4	2.1	28.9	56.1	13.0
Not Eligible	0.3	11.3	71.6	16.9	0.6	9.9	49.7	39.8

Source: 2007 Illinois State Report Card

PRAIRIE STATE ACHIEVEMENT EXAMINATION (PSAE)

The following tables show the percentages of student scores in each of four performance levels. These levels were established with the help of Illinois educators who teach the grade levels and learning areas tested. Due to rounding, the sum of the percentages in the four performance levels may not always equal 100.

Level 1 -- Academic Warning - Student work demonstrates limited knowledge and skills in the subject. Because of major gaps in learning, students apply knowledge and skills ineffectively.

Level 2 -- Below Standards - Student work demonstrates basic knowledge and skills in the subject. However, because of gaps in learning, students apply knowledge and skills in limited ways.

Level 3 -- Meets Standards - Student work demonstrates proficient knowledge and skills in the subject. Students effectively apply knowledge and skills to solve problems.

Level 4 -- Exceeds Standards - Student work demonstrates advanced knowledge and skills in the subject. Students creatively apply knowledge and skills to solve problems and evaluate the results.

Grade 11

Grade 11 - All

	Reading				Mathematics				Science			
Levels	1	2	3	4	1	2	3	4	1	2	3	4
	8.4	37.5	43.1	10.9	9.8	37.5	42.8	9.9	8.7	40.3	40.3	10.7

Grade 11 - Gender

	Reading				Mathematics				Science			
Levels	1	2	3	4	1	2	3	4	1	2	3	4
Male	10.8	38.1	40.5	10.6	9.4	35.0	43.4	12.1	9.2	36.9	40.1	13.7
Female	6.1	37.0	45.7	11.2	10.1	40.0	42.1	7.8	8.1	43.6	40.5	7.8

Grade 11 - Racial/Ethnic Background

	Reading				Mathematics				Science			
Levels	1	2	3	4	1	2	3	4	1	2	3	4
White	5.7	30.8	49.2	14.4	5.7	31.2	50.4	12.7	5.0	33.1	47.8	14.0
Black	16.2	55.8	26.3	1.6	24.9	55.8	18.6	0.8	20.9	60.2	17.9	1.0
Hispanic	14.3	52.8	30.4	2.6	14.4	52.6	31.1	2.0	14.1	57.7	26.2	2.0
Asian/Pacific Islander	4.0	28.3	50.2	17.5	2.8	21.6	49.2	26.5	3.0	26.4	49.7	20.8
Native American	9.8	34.6	46.6	9.0	8.1	36.3	49.1	6.4	8.2	40.3	42.9	8.6
Multiracial/Ethnic	8.1	39.2	42.8	9.9	11.4	41.6	40.5	6.6	9.2	42.6	39.2	9.0

Grade 11 - Limited-English-Proficient

	Reading				Mathematics				Science			
Levels	1	2	3	4	1	2	3	4	1	2	3	4
	23.5	49.6	22.2	4.7	21.3	46.5	28.5	3.7	21.9	48.8	25.8	3.5

Grade 11 - Migrant

	Reading				Mathematics				Science			
Levels	1	2	3	4	1	2	3	4	1	2	3	4
	22.6	48.4	25.8	3.2	22.6	51.6	25.8	0.0	19.4	51.6	25.8	3.2

Grade 11 - Students with Disabilities

	Reading				Mathematics				Science			
Levels	1	2	3	4	1	2	3	4	1	2	3	4
IEP	36.7	44.0	16.6	2.8	39.7	45.9	13.2	1.3	40.4	45.6	12.2	1.8
Non-IEP	4.8	36.7	46.5	12.0	6.0	36.5	46.5	11.1	4.6	39.7	43.9	11.8

Grade 11 - Economically Disadvantaged

	Reading				Mathematics				Science			
Levels	1	2	3	4	1	2	3	4	1	2	3	4
Free/Reduced Price Lunch	15.8	52.9	28.7	2.6	19.9	52.9	25.6	1.6	18.2	57.1	22.8	2.0
Not Eligible	5.7	31.8	48.5	14.0	6.0	31.8	49.1	13.0	5.1	34.1	46.8	13.9

Source: 2007 Illinois State Report Card

ILLINOIS MEASURE OF ANNUAL GROWTH IN ENGLISH (IMAGE)

The Illinois Measure of Annual Growth in English (IMAGE) is administered to limited-English-proficient students. The table below presents IMAGE results for these students. Due to rounding, the sum of the percentages in the four performance levels may not always equal 100.

Level 1 -- Academic Warning - Students work demonstrates limited knowledge and skills in the subject. Due to major gaps in learning,students apply knowledge and skills ineffectively.

Level 2 --Below Standards - Student work demonstrates basic knowledge and skills in the subject. However, because of gaps in learning, students apply knowledge and skills in limited ways.

Level 3 -- Meets Standards - Student work demonstrates proficient knowledge and skills in the subject. Students effectively apply knowledge and skills to solve problems.

Level 4 -- Exceeds Standards - Student work demonstrates advanced knowledge and skills in the subject. Student creatively apply knowledge and skills to solve probelms and evalaute the results.

Grade 3

Grade 3 - All

	Reading				Mathematics			
Levels	1	2	3	4	1	2	3	4
	8.4	29.0	42.5	20.1	6.2	24.5	52.6	16.7

Grade 3 - Gender

	Reading				Mathematics			
Levels	1	2	3	4	1	2	3	4
Male	9.2	29.2	41.8	19.7	6.8	23.1	51.4	18.7
Female	7.6	28.7	43.2	20.5	5.6	25.9	53.9	14.6

Grade 3 - Racial/Ethnic Background

	Reading				Mathematics			
Levels	1	2	3	4	1	2	3	4
White	4.9	22.1	44.2	28.8	3.8	18.7	54.7	22.8
Black	19.0	28.1	39.2	13.7	19.0	29.1	42.4	9.5
Hispanic	9.0	30.5	42.2	18.3	6.5	25.6	52.6	15.2
Asian/Pacific Islander	3.0	14.7	45.1	37.2	3.1	13.6	50.7	32.6
Native American								
Multiracial/Ethnic	7.2	29.6	44.8	18.4	3.1	23.4	57.0	16.4

Grade 3 - Migrant

	Reading				Mathematics			
Levels	1	2	3	4	1	2	3	4
	12.5	25.0	43.8	18.8	12.5	6.3	75.0	6.3

Grade 3 - Students with Disabilities

	Reading				Mathematics			
Levels	1	2	3	4	1	2	3	4
IEP	26.0	41.5	25.6	7.0	18.3	38.2	37.0	6.5
Non-IEP	6.6	27.7	44.2	21.5	5.0	23.0	54.2	17.8

Grade 3 - Economically Disadvantaged

	Reading				Mathematics			
Levels	1	2	3	4	1	2	3	4
Free/Reduced Price Lunch	9.1	30.2	41.5	19.2	6.5	25.1	52.3	16.1
Not Eligible	5.6	23.8	46.8	23.8	5.0	21.6	53.9	19.5

Source: 2007 Illinois State Report Card

Grade 3 - Economically Disadvantaged

	Reading				Mathematics			
Levels	1	2	3	4	1	2	3	4
Free/Reduced Price Lunch	9.1	30.2	41.5	19.2	6.5	25.1	52.3	16.1
Not Eligible	5.6	23.8	46.8	23.8	5.0	21.6	53.9	19.5

Grade 4

Grade 4 - All

	Reading				Mathematics			
Levels	1	2	3	4	1	2	3	4
	8.3	23.1	46.7	21.9	3.3	27.5	61.6	7.6

Grade 4 - Gender

	Reading				Mathematics			
Levels	1	2	3	4	1	2	3	4
Male	9.3	23.6	47.1	20.0	3.5	26.6	61.6	8.3
Female	7.2	22.5	46.3	24.0	3.2	28.4	61.6	6.9

Grade 4 - Racial/Ethnic Background

	Reading				Mathematics			
Levels	1	2	3	4	1	2	3	4
White	5.5	17.6	45.5	31.4	2.7	20.5	64.4	12.3
Black	15.4	28.5	39.8	16.3	10.4	42.2	43.7	3.7
Hispanic	8.7	24.3	47.0	19.9	3.4	29.0	61.3	6.3
Asian/Pacific Islander	4.8	12.8	44.4	38.0	2.4	13.9	63.8	20.0
Native American	0.0	20.0	80.0	0.0	0.0	30.0	70.0	0.0
Multiracial/Ethnic	5.1	11.4	50.6	32.9	2.5	19.8	67.9	9.9

Grade 4 - Migrant

	Reading				Mathematics			
Levels	1	2	3	4	1	2	3	4
	8.3	29.2	45.8	16.7	4.2	41.7	54.2	0.0

Grade 4 - Students with Disabilities

	Reading				Mathematics			
Levels	1	2	3	4	1	2	3	4
IEP	24.5	36.9	31.0	7.6	10.4	45.0	41.5	3.1
Non-IEP	6.3	21.4	48.7	23.6	2.5	25.3	64.1	8.1

Grade 4 - Economically Disadvantaged

	Reading				Mathematics			
Levels	1	2	3	4	1	2	3	4
Free/Reduced Price Lunch	9.1	24.2	46.4	20.3	3.7	28.8	61.2	6.3
Not Eligible	4.9	18.0	48.1	29.1	1.9	21.7	63.4	13.0

Grade 5

Grade 5 - All

	Reading				Mathematics			
Levels	1	2	3	4	1	2	3	4
	4.4	18.1	42.1	35.4	1.6	45.2	50.7	2.6

Grade 5 - Gender

	Reading				Mathematics			
Levels	1	2	3	4	1	2	3	4
Male	5.0	19.2	41.5	34.3	2.0	44.4	50.9	2.8
Female	3.7	17.0	42.8	36.5	1.1	46.1	50.4	2.3

Source: 2007 Illinois State Report Card

Grade 5 - Racial/Ethnic Background

	Reading				Mathematics			
Levels	1	2	3	4	1	2	3	4
White	3.1	13.3	35.2	48.4	1.0	32.1	61.1	5.8
Black	13.3	19.5	38.9	28.3	5.0	57.1	37.8	0.0
Hispanic	4.4	19.0	43.2	33.4	1.6	47.7	49.0	1.7
Asian/Pacific Islander	3.9	12.4	35.2	48.6	0.6	24.7	63.4	11.3
Native American								
Multiracial/Ethnic	7.5	10.4	44.8	37.3	1.5	43.3	50.7	4.5

Grade 5 - Migrant

	Reading				Mathematics			
Levels	1	2	3	4	1	2	3	4
	0.0	14.3	35.7	50.0	0.0	28.6	71.4	0.0

Grade 5 - Students with Disabilities

	Reading				Mathematics			
Levels	1	2	3	4	1	2	3	4
IEP	12.6	36.0	35.7	15.7	4.2	65.5	29.6	0.7
Non-IEP	3.2	15.5	43.0	38.2	1.2	42.3	53.7	2.8

Grade 5 - Economically Disadvantaged

	Reading				Mathematics			
Levels	1	2	3	4	1	2	3	4
Free/Reduced Price Lunch	4.9	19.5	42.7	32.9	1.8	47.1	49.2	1.9
Not Eligible	2.0	11.9	39.2	46.9	0.7	36.4	57.5	5.4

Grade 6

Grade 6 - All

	Reading				Mathematics			
Levels	1	2	3	4	1	2	3	4
	9.6	20.8	41.7	27.8	4.9	44.5	45.7	4.8

Grade 6 - Gender

	Reading				Mathematics			
Levels	1	2	3	4	1	2	3	4
Male	10.2	20.4	40.6	28.8	5.3	43.6	46.0	5.1
Female	9.0	21.3	43.0	26.8	4.5	45.6	45.4	4.6

Grade 6 - Racial/Ethnic Background

	Reading				Mathematics			
Levels	1	2	3	4	1	2	3	4
White	5.5	15.7	34.3	44.5	3.6	30.3	55.5	10.7
Black	15.9	25.6	40.2	18.3	16.1	51.7	29.9	2.3
Hispanic	10.5	22.2	43.0	24.3	5.2	49.0	43.2	2.6
Asian/Pacific Islander	5.5	14.5	41.7	38.3	2.7	23.1	58.1	16.2
Native American								
Multiracial/Ethnic	6.9	17.2	37.9	37.9	3.4	55.2	31.0	10.3

Grade 6 - Students with Disabilities

	Reading				Mathematics			
Levels	1	2	3	4	1	2	3	4
IEP	18.4	29.3	38.5	13.8	12.1	65.6	22.0	0.2
Non-IEP	8.7	20.0	42.0	29.2	4.2	42.5	48.0	5.3

Source: 2007 Illinois State Report Card

Grade 6 - Economically Disadvantaged

	Reading				Mathematics			
Levels	1	2	3	4	1	2	3	4
Free/Reduced Price Lunch	10.9	23.2	41.8	24.2	5.5	48.0	43.0	3.5
Not Eligible	5.1	13.0	41.6	40.3	3.2	33.0	54.7	9.1

Grade 7

Grade 7 - All

	Reading				Mathematics			
Levels	1	2	3	4	1	2	3	4
	16.2	26.8	41.8	15.2	5.9	38.6	49.2	6.3

Grade 7 - Gender

	Reading				Mathematics			
Levels	1	2	3	4	1	2	3	4
Male	18.2	27.3	39.6	14.9	6.7	37.5	48.7	7.1
Female	13.8	26.3	44.3	15.6	5.0	39.9	49.8	5.3

Grade 7 - Racial/Ethnic Background

	Reading				Mathematics			
Levels	1	2	3	4	1	2	3	4
White	8.6	17.4	47.3	26.6	2.9	22.1	63.8	11.2
Black	24.3	19.4	43.7	12.6	13.1	42.1	41.1	3.7
Hispanic	18.6	29.5	39.8	12.1	6.7	44.3	46.6	2.5
Asian/Pacific Islander	6.4	21.9	48.2	23.5	2.0	19.9	51.8	26.3
Native American								
Multiracial/Ethnic	10.0	15.0	35.0	40.0	15.0	20.0	50.0	15.0

Grade 7 - Migrant

	Reading				Mathematics			
Levels	1	2	3	4	1	2	3	4
	25.0	25.0	35.0	15.0	20.0	30.0	50.0	0.0

Grade 7 - Students with Disabilities

	Reading				Mathematics			
Levels	1	2	3	4	1	2	3	4
IEP	30.8	36.5	28.8	3.8	21.0	56.5	22.1	0.4
Non-IEP	15.2	26.2	42.7	16.0	4.9	37.4	51.0	6.6

Grade 7 - Economically Disadvantaged

	Reading				Mathematics			
Levels	1	2	3	4	1	2	3	4
Free/Reduced Price Lunch	18.9	29.4	39.9	11.9	6.9	42.3	47.0	3.8
Not Eligible	8.7	19.7	47.0	24.5	3.0	28.7	55.4	12.9

Grade 8

Grade 8 - All

	Reading				Mathematics			
Levels	1	2	3	4	1	2	3	4
	21.4	27.4	31.8	19.4	8.5	43.4	41.2	6.9

Grade 8 - Gender

	Reading				Mathematics			
Levels	1	2	3	4	1	2	3	4
Male	24.4	27.4	31.1	17.1	9.5	44.0	40.2	6.3
Female	18.0	27.5	32.6	21.9	7.4	42.7	42.2	7.6

Source: 2007 Illinois State Report Card

Grade 8 - Racial/Ethnic Background

Levels	Reading 1	Reading 2	Reading 3	Reading 4	Mathematics 1	Mathematics 2	Mathematics 3	Mathematics 4
White	10.6	16.7	39.0	33.7	5.5	25.5	53.0	16.0
Black	14.8	32.1	32.1	21.0	17.4	51.2	31.4	0.0
Hispanic	25.0	29.9	29.6	15.5	9.3	49.6	38.3	2.8
Asian/Pacific Islander	11.9	22.5	38.1	27.5	4.4	24.2	47.6	23.8
Native American								
Multiracial/Ethnic	25.0	41.7	33.3	0.0	41.7	41.7	16.7	0.0

Grade 8 - Migrant

Levels	Reading 1	Reading 2	Reading 3	Reading 4	Mathematics 1	Mathematics 2	Mathematics 3	Mathematics 4
	23.5	29.4	41.2	5.9	5.6	61.1	33.3	0.0

Grade 8 - Students with Disabilities

Levels	Reading 1	Reading 2	Reading 3	Reading 4	Mathematics 1	Mathematics 2	Mathematics 3	Mathematics 4
IEP	30.0	34.3	30.5	5.2	25.6	54.5	18.5	1.4
Non-IEP	20.9	27.0	31.9	20.2	7.5	42.7	42.5	7.2

Grade 8 - Economically Disadvantaged

Levels	Reading 1	Reading 2	Reading 3	Reading 4	Mathematics 1	Mathematics 2	Mathematics 3	Mathematics 4
Free/Reduced Price Lunch	23.8	30.3	30.4	15.4	9.3	46.9	39.3	4.5
Not Eligible	13.9	18.3	36.2	31.6	6.1	32.6	46.9	14.4

Grade 11

Grade 11 - All

Levels	Reading 1	Reading 2	Reading 3	Reading 4	Mathematics 1	Mathematics 2	Mathematics 3	Mathematics 4
	11.9	25.2	38.1	24.7	11.8	59.8	25.6	2.8

Grade 11 - Gender

Levels	Reading 1	Reading 2	Reading 3	Reading 4	Mathematics 1	Mathematics 2	Mathematics 3	Mathematics 4
Male	13.2	25.9	38.4	22.5	10.4	59.7	27.2	2.6
Female	10.5	24.5	37.8	27.2	13.4	59.8	23.9	2.9

Grade 11 - Racial/Ethnic Background

Levels	Reading 1	Reading 2	Reading 3	Reading 4	Mathematics 1	Mathematics 2	Mathematics 3	Mathematics 4
White	6.7	17.6	37.8	37.8	5.2	45.6	47.4	1.7
Black	17.2	28.0	43.0	11.8	24.7	63.4	10.8	1.1
Hispanic	15.0	28.5	36.0	20.5	14.9	68.5	16.3	0.2
Asian/Pacific Islander	4.6	20.4	45.7	29.2	4.4	41.5	39.3	14.9
Native American								
Multiracial/Ethnic	16.7	33.3	33.3	16.7	27.8	55.6	16.7	0.0

Grade 11 - Students with Disabilities

Levels	Reading 1	Reading 2	Reading 3	Reading 4	Mathematics 1	Mathematics 2	Mathematics 3	Mathematics 4
IEP	32.1	30.8	29.5	7.7	45.6	51.9	2.5	0.0
Non-IEP	11.3	25.1	38.4	25.3	10.8	60.0	26.3	2.9

Grade 11 - Economically Disadvantaged

Levels	Reading 1	Reading 2	Reading 3	Reading 4	Mathematics 1	Mathematics 2	Mathematics 3	Mathematics 4
Free/Reduced Price Lunch	13.2	27.1	37.5	22.2	13.3	62.4	22.7	1.6
Not Eligible	9.4	21.5	39.3	29.7	9.0	54.7	31.3	5.0

Source: 2007 Illinois State Report Card

ILLINOIS ALTERNATE ASSESSMENT (IAA)

The Illinois Alternate Assessment (IAA) is administered to students with disabilities whose Individualized Education Programs (IEPs) indicate that participation in the ISAT or PSAE would not be appropriate. The table below presents the percentages of student scores in each of four performance levels.

Level 1 -- Attempting - Student work does not demonstrate progress in the knowledge and skills in the subject through connections to the Illinois Learning Standards. Students do not generalize their knowledge and skills.

Level 2 --Emerging - Student work demonstrates limited progress in the knowledge and skills in the subject through minimal connections to the Illinois Learning Standards. Students exhibit an emerging ability to generalize their knowledge and skills.

Level 3 -- Progressing - Student work demonstrates moderate progress in the knowledge and skills in the subject through minimal connections to the Illinois Learning Standards. Students exhibit an emerging ability to generalize their knowledge and skills.

Level 4 -- Attaining - Student work demonstrates extensive progress in the knowledge and skills in the subject through multiple connections to the Illinois Learning Standards. Students exhibit a broad ability to generalize their knowledge and skills.

Grade 3

Grade 3 - All

	Reading				Mathematics			
Levels	1	2	3	4	1	2	3	4
	15.3	16.7	47.0	21.1	12.7	27.3	35.1	24.9

Grade 3 - Gender

	Reading				Mathematics			
Levels	1	2	3	4	1	2	3	4
Male	15.5	16.9	45.5	22.1	13.1	25.6	35.9	25.4
Female	14.9	16.3	49.8	19.0	11.9	30.6	33.6	23.9

Grade 3 - Racial/Ethnic Background

	Reading				Mathematics			
Levels	1	2	3	4	1	2	3	4
White	13.1	16.1	45.3	25.5	10.2	25.0	36.7	28.1
Black	20.7	14.8	52.4	12.1	18.1	31.6	31.9	18.4
Hispanic	15.2	22.6	43.2	19.1	14.3	31.0	33.7	21.0
Asian/Pacific Islander	13.5	9.6	48.1	28.8	7.7	19.2	40.4	32.7
Native American								
Multiracial/Ethnic	11.8	14.7	52.9	20.6	14.7	23.5	29.4	32.4

Grade 3 - Limited-English-Proficient

	Reading				Mathematics			
Levels	1	2	3	4	1	2	3	4
	16.7	28.3	43.3	11.7	20.7	30.2	34.5	14.7

Grade 3 - Economically Disadvantaged

	Reading				Mathematics			
Levels	1	2	3	4	1	2	3	4
Free/Reduced Price Lunch	18.3	19.7	45.9	16.1	16.9	31.1	32.7	19.4
Not Eligible	13.3	14.7	47.7	24.3	10.0	24.9	36.6	28.5

Grade 4

Grade 4 - All

	Reading				Mathematics				Science			
Levels	1	2	3	4	1	2	3	4	1	2	3	4
	18.1	16.2	44.3	21.4	13.5	26.8	37.0	22.8	23.1	35.1	26.9	14.8

Source: 2007 Illinois State Report Card

Grade 4 - Gender

Levels	Reading 1	Reading 2	Reading 3	Reading 4	Mathematics 1	Mathematics 2	Mathematics 3	Mathematics 4	Science 1	Science 2	Science 3	Science 4
Male	18.8	15.3	43.8	22.2	13.5	26.9	35.6	24.0	23.3	34.1	27.0	15.7
Female	16.9	17.9	45.3	19.9	13.3	26.5	39.6	20.6	22.9	37.0	26.8	13.3

Grade 4 - Racial/Ethnic Background

Levels	Reading 1	Reading 2	Reading 3	Reading 4	Mathematics 1	Mathematics 2	Mathematics 3	Mathematics 4	Science 1	Science 2	Science 3	Science 4
White	13.0	14.4	47.8	24.7	8.5	23.1	41.4	27.0	18.2	34.0	29.7	18.1
Black	27.8	17.8	40.2	14.2	19.3	33.6	29.7	17.4	33.3	32.4	25.2	9.2
Hispanic	17.8	18.6	45.5	18.2	18.8	30.8	33.2	17.2	25.4	38.8	24.6	11.3
Asian/Pacific Islander	19.3	19.3	28.1	33.3	14.5	23.6	32.7	29.1	16.4	45.5	18.2	20.0
Native American												
Multiracial/Ethnic	18.4	18.4	34.2	28.9	16.2	18.9	45.9	18.9	20.6	44.1	17.6	17.6

Grade 4 - Limited-English-Proficient

Levels	Reading 1	Reading 2	Reading 3	Reading 4	Mathematics 1	Mathematics 2	Mathematics 3	Mathematics 4	Science 1	Science 2	Science 3	Science 4
	30.7	15.9	38.6	14.8	24.1	30.1	33.7	12.0	27.8	39.2	25.3	7.6

Grade 4 - Economically Disadvantaged

Levels	Reading 1	Reading 2	Reading 3	Reading 4	Mathematics 1	Mathematics 2	Mathematics 3	Mathematics 4	Science 1	Science 2	Science 3	Science 4
Free/Reduced Price Lunch	23.8	17.2	42.2	16.8	19.3	27.5	32.3	20.9	28.8	36.0	23.7	11.6
Not Eligible	14.2	15.5	45.8	24.5	9.5	26.3	40.1	24.1	19.4	34.6	29.0	17.0

Grade 5

Grade 5 - All

Levels	Reading 1	Reading 2	Reading 3	Reading 4	Mathematics 1	Mathematics 2	Mathematics 3	Mathematics 4
	19.4	13.6	46.3	20.8	11.6	27.8	36.9	23.7

Grade 5 - Gender

Levels	Reading 1	Reading 2	Reading 3	Reading 4	Mathematics 1	Mathematics 2	Mathematics 3	Mathematics 4
Male	19.4	12.3	47.2	21.0	11.2	27.0	38.2	23.6
Female	19.3	15.7	44.7	20.4	12.2	29.3	34.7	23.8

Grade 5 - Racial/Ethnic Background

Levels	Reading 1	Reading 2	Reading 3	Reading 4	Mathematics 1	Mathematics 2	Mathematics 3	Mathematics 4
White	16.5	11.8	48.7	23.0	8.6	24.7	39.9	26.8
Black	26.3	16.1	41.8	15.8	17.2	33.2	32.4	17.2
Hispanic	18.5	15.9	46.0	19.6	12.8	30.7	34.7	21.9
Asian/Pacific Islander	20.0	10.0	48.0	22.0	8.0	26.0	38.0	28.0
Native American								
Multiracial/Ethnic	24.1	17.2	34.5	24.1	17.9	21.4	32.1	28.6

Grade 5 - Limited-English-Proficient

Levels	Reading 1	Reading 2	Reading 3	Reading 4	Mathematics 1	Mathematics 2	Mathematics 3	Mathematics 4
	16.8	14.0	49.5	19.6	16.8	33.6	29.0	20.6

Source: 2007 Illinois State Report Card

Grade 5 - Economically Disadvantaged

Levels	Reading 1	Reading 2	Reading 3	Reading 4	Mathematics 1	Mathematics 2	Mathematics 3	Mathematics 4
Free/Reduced Price Lunch	24.0	13.3	43.5	19.2	13.8	31.1	35.5	19.6
Not Eligible	16.2	13.7	48.3	21.9	10.0	25.5	38.0	26.5

Grade 6

Grade 6 - All

Levels	Reading 1	Reading 2	Reading 3	Reading 4	Mathematics 1	Mathematics 2	Mathematics 3	Mathematics 4
	20.7	15.2	43.2	20.9	12.9	30.7	35.4	21.0

Grade 6 - Gender

Levels	Reading 1	Reading 2	Reading 3	Reading 4	Mathematics 1	Mathematics 2	Mathematics 3	Mathematics 4
Male	21.3	15.5	43.2	20.0	14.1	31.9	33.5	20.5
Female	19.6	14.8	43.3	22.3	10.9	28.8	38.5	21.8

Grade 6 - Racial/Ethnic Background

Levels	Reading 1	Reading 2	Reading 3	Reading 4	Mathematics 1	Mathematics 2	Mathematics 3	Mathematics 4
White	17.5	12.5	45.4	24.7	9.3	27.3	38.8	24.7
Black	29.6	16.9	42.9	10.6	21.7	34.7	28.6	15.0
Hispanic	17.8	17.8	39.6	24.7	13.1	34.5	34.8	17.6
Asian/Pacific Islander	18.2	29.1	32.7	20.0	5.5	34.5	32.7	27.3
Native American								
Multiracial/Ethnic	16.7	22.2	44.4	16.7	14.7	26.5	38.2	20.6

Grade 6 - Limited-English-Proficient

Levels	Reading 1	Reading 2	Reading 3	Reading 4	Mathematics 1	Mathematics 2	Mathematics 3	Mathematics 4
	23.8	28.6	31.0	16.7	24.7	31.2	24.7	19.5

Grade 6 - Economically Disadvantaged

Levels	Reading 1	Reading 2	Reading 3	Reading 4	Mathematics 1	Mathematics 2	Mathematics 3	Mathematics 4
Free/Reduced Price Lunch	23.4	16.6	40.3	19.6	15.7	31.1	35.1	18.0
Not Eligible	18.8	14.3	45.2	21.7	11.0	30.5	35.5	23.0

Grade 7

Grade 7 - All

Levels	Reading 1	Reading 2	Reading 3	Reading 4	Mathematics 1	Mathematics 2	Mathematics 3	Mathematics 4	Science 1	Science 2	Science 3	Science 4
	20.6	15.5	43.3	20.6	14.6	27.4	38.3	19.7	21.7	33.3	29.8	15.2

Grade 7 - Gender

Levels	Reading 1	Reading 2	Reading 3	Reading 4	Mathematics 1	Mathematics 2	Mathematics 3	Mathematics 4	Science 1	Science 2	Science 3	Science 4
Male	21.7	15.5	42.6	20.2	14.6	28.1	37.4	19.9	21.8	32.6	30.4	15.2
Female	18.9	15.6	44.4	21.1	14.6	26.3	39.8	19.3	21.7	34.3	28.9	15.1

Source: 2007 Illinois State Report Card

Grade 7 - Racial/Ethnic Background

	Reading				Mathematics				Science			
Levels	1	2	3	4	1	2	3	4	1	2	3	4
White	15.5	14.7	46.1	23.7	9.6	26.8	40.7	22.9	15.4	34.0	33.5	17.1
Black	30.9	15.9	39.0	14.3	23.8	29.7	32.7	13.8	33.7	32.1	22.8	11.4
Hispanic	15.9	17.1	41.6	25.3	14.0	25.8	39.0	21.2	19.9	31.7	32.1	16.3
Asian/Pacific Islander	23.5	17.6	50.0	8.8	12.9	29.0	38.7	19.4	19.4	38.7	25.8	16.1
Native American												
Multiracial/Ethnic	42.1	21.1	34.2	2.6	26.3	34.2	34.2	5.3	45.9	29.7	16.2	8.1

Grade 7- Limited-English-Proficient

	Reading				Mathematics				Science			
Levels	1	2	3	4	1	2	3	4	1	2	3	4
	22.9	19.3	38.6	19.3	17.5	28.8	41.3	12.5	25.7	41.4	25.7	7.1

Grade 7 - Economically Disadvantaged

	Reading				Mathematics				Science			
Levels	1	2	3	4	1	2	3	4	1	2	3	4
Free/Reduced Price Lunch	25.2	16.6	40.8	17.4	17.6	28.9	37.0	16.4	27.6	33.3	26.9	12.2
Not Eligible	17.0	14.7	45.2	23.1	22.2	12.2	26.3	39.3	17.1	33.3	32.2	17.5

Grade 8

Grade 8 - All

	Reading				Mathematics			
Levels	1	2	3	4	1	2	3	4
	21.3	15.4	42.4	21.0	16.0	29.6	34.9	19.5

Grade 8 - Gender

	Reading				Mathematics			
Levels	1	2	3	4	1	2	3	4
Male	22.4	15.3	42.9	19.4	16.7	30.0	35.2	18.1
Female	19.4	15.6	41.4	23.6	14.7	28.9	34.5	21.8

Grade 8 - Racial/Ethnic Background

	Reading				Mathematics			
Levels	1	2	3	4	1	2	3	4
White	17.6	14.0	46.1	22.2	10.3	28.7	38.6	22.4
Black	25.2	19.1	39.9	15.8	21.2	33.5	30.5	14.9
Hispanic	26.6	17.2	34.0	22.3	25.4	28.6	29.8	16.1
Asian/Pacific Islander	18.0	2.0	44.0	36.0	16.0	22.0	34.0	28.0
Native American								
Multiracial/Ethnic	18.8	6.3	56.3	18.8	6.7	33.3	46.7	13.3

Grade 8 - Limited-English-Proficient

	Reading				Mathematics			
Levels	1	2	3	4	1	2	3	4
	30.6	23.5	28.2	17.6	24.7	38.3	25.9	11.1

Grade 8 - Economically Disadvantaged

	Reading				Mathematics			
Levels	1	2	3	4	1	2	3	4
Free/Reduced Price Lunch	23.5	17.9	40.8	17.8	21.9	31.0	30.2	16.9
Not Eligible	19.7	13.7	43.4	23.2	11.8	28.6	38.2	21.4

Source: 2007 Illinois State Report Card

Grade 11

Grade 11 - All

Levels	Reading 1	Reading 2	Reading 3	Reading 4	Mathematics 1	Mathematics 2	Mathematics 3	Mathematics 4	Science 1	Science 2	Science 3	Science 4
	21.8	13.2	39.7	25.3	16.2	26.3	33.1	24.4	19.5	28.3	29.8	22.4

Grade 11 - Gender

Levels	Reading 1	Reading 2	Reading 3	Reading 4	Mathematics 1	Mathematics 2	Mathematics 3	Mathematics 4	Science 1	Science 2	Science 3	Science 4
Male	23.2	14.3	38.6	23.8	17.5	25.4	34.8	22.4	21.9	29.4	29.5	19.1
Female	19.6	11.6	41.3	27.5	14.1	27.8	30.4	27.6	15.7	26.7	30.2	27.4

Grade 11 - Racial/Ethnic Background

Levels	Reading 1	Reading 2	Reading 3	Reading 4	Mathematics 1	Mathematics 2	Mathematics 3	Mathematics 4	Science 1	Science 2	Science 3	Science 4
White	20.3	12.2	41.6	25.8	14.9	26.3	35.8	23.0	20.4	29.6	28.2	21.9
Black	25.7	17.4	37.6	19.3	21.6	25.5	31.4	21.6	22.9	26.6	30.3	20.3
Hispanic	15.1	10.2	41.9	32.8	10.7	22.5	32.6	34.2	10.4	23.5	33.9	32.2
Asian/Pacific Islander	18.4	13.2	21.1	47.4	10.5	39.5	18.4	31.6	13.2	23.7	36.8	26.3
Native American												
Multiracial/Ethnic	26.3	15.8	26.3	31.6	26.3	15.8	21.1	36.8	33.3	16.7	27.8	22.2

Grade 11 - Limited-English-Proficient

Levels	Reading 1	Reading 2	Reading 3	Reading 4	Mathematics 1	Mathematics 2	Mathematics 3	Mathematics 4	Science 1	Science 2	Science 3	Science 4
	33.3	11.8	7.8	47.1	14.6	22.9	16.7	45.8	20.0	17.8	11.1	51.1

Grade 11 - Economically Disadvantaged

Levels	Reading 1	Reading 2	Reading 3	Reading 4	Mathematics 1	Mathematics 2	Mathematics 3	Mathematics 4	Science 1	Science 2	Science 3	Science 4
Free/Reduced Price Lunch	21.5	12.2	35.0	31.3	13.2	21.8	33.2	31.9	16.0	22.5	31.5	30.1
Not Eligible	22.0	13.8	42.0	22.3	17.6	28.6	33.0	20.8	21.2	31.2	29.0	18.6

Source: 2007 Illinois State Report Card

Ancestry

Acadian/Cajun

Top 10 Places Sorted by Number

Based on all places, regardless of population

Place	Number	%
Chicago (city) Cook County	68	0.00
Decatur (city) Macon County	42	0.05
Springfield (city) Sangamon County	41	0.04
North Chicago (city) Lake County	37	0.10
Carbondale (city) Jackson County	31	0.15
Effingham (city) Effingham County	25	0.20
Hanover Park (village) Cook County	20	0.05
Villa Park (village) Du Page County	18	0.08
Rockford (city) Winnebago County	18	0.01
Swansea (village) Saint Clair County	15	0.14

Top 10 Places Sorted by Percent

Based on all places, regardless of population

Place	Number	%
Dunfermline (village) Fulton County	2	0.78
Marine (village) Madison County	4	0.45
Wapella (village) De Witt County	3	0.45
Manito (village) Mason County	7	0.41
North Utica (village) La Salle County	3	0.32
North City (village) Franklin County	2	0.31
Mount Sterling (city) Brown County	6	0.29
Effingham (city) Effingham County	25	0.20
Milledgeville (village) Carroll County	2	0.20
Scott AFB (cdp) Saint Clair County	5	0.18

Top 10 Places Sorted by Percent

Based on places with populations of 10,000 or more

Place	Number	%
Effingham (city) Effingham County	25	0.20
Carbondale (city) Jackson County	31	0.15
Swansea (village) Saint Clair County	15	0.14
North Chicago (city) Lake County	37	0.10
Godfrey (village) Madison County	15	0.09
Villa Park (village) Du Page County	18	0.08
Algonquin (village) McHenry County	14	0.06
Deerfield (village) Lake County	12	0.06
Decatur (city) Macon County	42	0.05
Hanover Park (village) Cook County	20	0.05

Afghan

Top 10 Places Sorted by Number

Based on all places, regardless of population

Place	Number	%
Chicago (city) Cook County	381	0.01
Champaign (city) Champaign County	41	0.06
Naperville (city) Du Page County	31	0.02
Morton Grove (village) Cook County	22	0.10
Wheaton (city) Du Page County	16	0.03
Park City (city) Lake County	14	0.20
Skokie (village) Cook County	14	0.02
Evergreen Park (village) Cook County	11	0.05
Urbana (city) Champaign County	11	0.03
Deer Park (village) Lake County	10	0.31

Top 10 Places Sorted by Percent

Based on all places, regardless of population

Place	Number	%
Deer Park (village) Lake County	10	0.31
Park City (city) Lake County	14	0.20
Morton Grove (village) Cook County	22	0.10
Lincolnwood (village) Cook County	9	0.07
Champaign (city) Champaign County	41	0.06
Evergreen Park (village) Cook County	11	0.05
Wheaton (city) Du Page County	16	0.03
Urbana (city) Champaign County	11	0.03
Lake in the Hills (village) McHenry County	8	0.03
Wilmette (village) Cook County	8	0.03

Top 10 Places Sorted by Percent

Based on places with populations of 10,000 or more

Place	Number	%
Morton Grove (village) Cook County	22	0.10
Lincolnwood (village) Cook County	9	0.07
Champaign (city) Champaign County	41	0.06
Evergreen Park (village) Cook County	11	0.05
Wheaton (city) Du Page County	16	0.03
Urbana (city) Champaign County	11	0.03
Lake in the Hills (village) McHenry County	8	0.03
Wilmette (village) Cook County	8	0.03
Naperville (city) Du Page County	31	0.02
Skokie (village) Cook County	14	0.02

African American/Black

Top 10 Places Sorted by Number

Based on all places, regardless of population

Place	Number	%
Chicago (city) Cook County	1,084,221	37.44
East Saint Louis (city) Saint Clair County	30,983	98.23
Peoria (city) Peoria County	29,553	26.17
Rockford (city) Winnebago County	27,596	18.38
Harvey (city) Cook County	24,232	80.77
Maywood (village) Cook County	22,612	83.79
Dolton (village) Cook County	21,293	83.13
Calumet City (city) Cook County	21,043	53.86
Joliet (city) Will County	20,012	18.84
Springfield (city) Sangamon County	18,072	16.21

Top 10 Places Sorted by Percent

Based on all places, regardless of population

Place	Number	%
Brooklyn (village) Saint Clair County	671	99.26
East Saint Louis (city) Saint Clair County	30,983	98.23
Alorton (village) Saint Clair County	2,692	97.93
Ford Heights (village) Cook County	3,332	96.41
Centreville (city) Saint Clair County	5,723	96.17
Robbins (village) Cook County	6,354	95.76
Phoenix (village) Cook County	2,046	94.85
Venice (city) Madison County	2,377	94.03
Hopkins Park (village) Kankakee County	665	93.53
Washington Park (village) Saint Clair County	4,952	92.65

Top 10 Places Sorted by Percent

Based on places with populations of 10,000 or more

Place	Number	%
East Saint Louis (city) Saint Clair County	30,983	98.23
Riverdale (village) Cook County	13,151	87.35
Maywood (village) Cook County	22,612	83.79
Country Club Hills (city) Cook County	13,468	83.30
Dolton (village) Cook County	21,293	83.13
Bellwood (village) Cook County	16,995	82.76
Harvey (city) Cook County	24,232	80.77
Markham (city) Cook County	10,089	79.94
Hazel Crest (village) Cook County	11,482	77.50
Matteson (village) Cook County	8,284	64.08

African American/Black: Not Hispanic

Top 10 Places Sorted by Number

Based on all places, regardless of population

Place	Number	%
Chicago (city) Cook County	1,068,054	36.88
East Saint Louis (city) Saint Clair County	30,845	97.79
Peoria (city) Peoria County	29,235	25.89
Rockford (city) Winnebago County	27,162	18.09
Harvey (city) Cook County	24,027	80.09
Maywood (village) Cook County	22,485	83.32
Dolton (village) Cook County	21,159	82.61
Calumet City (city) Cook County	20,855	53.38
Joliet (city) Will County	19,763	18.61
Springfield (city) Sangamon County	17,932	16.09

Top 10 Places Sorted by Percent

Based on all places, regardless of population

Place	Number	%
Brooklyn (village) Saint Clair County	668	98.82
East Saint Louis (city) Saint Clair County	30,845	97.79
Alorton (village) Saint Clair County	2,683	97.60
Centreville (city) Saint Clair County	5,695	95.70
Ford Heights (village) Cook County	3,305	95.63
Robbins (village) Cook County	6,317	95.21
Phoenix (village) Cook County	2,031	94.16
Venice (city) Madison County	2,364	93.51
Hopkins Park (village) Kankakee County	664	93.39
Washington Park (village) Saint Clair County	4,929	92.22

Top 10 Places Sorted by Percent

Based on places with populations of 10,000 or more

Place	Number	%
East Saint Louis (city) Saint Clair County	30,845	97.79
Riverdale (village) Cook County	13,066	86.79
Maywood (village) Cook County	22,485	83.32
Country Club Hills (city) Cook County	13,379	82.74
Dolton (village) Cook County	21,159	82.61
Bellwood (village) Cook County	16,848	82.05
Harvey (city) Cook County	24,027	80.09
Markham (city) Cook County	10,030	79.48
Hazel Crest (village) Cook County	11,384	76.84
Matteson (village) Cook County	8,194	63.38

African American/Black: Hispanic

Top 10 Places Sorted by Number

Based on all places, regardless of population

Place	Number	%
Chicago (city) Cook County	16,167	0.56
Waukegan (city) Lake County	822	0.94
Aurora (city) Kane County	715	0.50
Elgin (city) Kane County	487	0.52
Rockford (city) Winnebago County	434	0.29
Evanston (city) Cook County	377	0.51
Cicero (town) Cook County	374	0.44
Peoria (city) Peoria County	318	0.28
North Chicago (city) Lake County	289	0.80
Joliet (city) Will County	249	0.23

Top 10 Places Sorted by Percent

Based on all places, regardless of population

Place	Number	%
Simpson (village) Johnson County	4	7.41
Ullin (village) Pulaski County	14	1.80
Scales Mound (village) Jo Daviess County	6	1.50
Jeffersonville (village) Wayne County	5	1.37
Karnak (village) Pulaski County	8	1.29
Old Mill Creek (village) Lake County	3	1.20
Detroit (village) Pike County	1	1.08
Mound City (city) Pulaski County	7	1.01
Waukegan (city) Lake County	822	0.94
Sauk Village (village) Cook County	94	0.90

Top 10 Places Sorted by Percent

Based on places with populations of 10,000 or more

Place	Number	%
Waukegan (city) Lake County	822	0.94
Sauk Village (village) Cook County	94	0.90
Zion (city) Lake County	198	0.87
North Chicago (city) Lake County	289	0.80
Bellwood (village) Cook County	147	0.72
Matteson (village) Cook County	90	0.70
Forest Park (village) Cook County	108	0.69
Harvey (city) Cook County	205	0.68
Park Forest (village) Cook County	156	0.66
Hazel Crest (village) Cook County	98	0.66

Notes: (cdp) census designated place; Refer to the User's Guide in the front of the book for more detailed information.

African, sub-Saharan

Top 10 Places Sorted by Number
Based on all places, regardless of population

Place	Number	%
Chicago (city) Cook County	36,985	1.28
Rockford (city) Winnebago County	1,481	0.99
Peoria (city) Peoria County	1,264	1.12
Bolingbrook (village) Will County	1,084	1.92
Springfield (city) Sangamon County	996	0.89
Oak Park (village) Cook County	899	1.71
Evanston (city) Cook County	899	1.21
Waukegan (city) Lake County	827	0.94
Champaign (city) Champaign County	798	1.18
Harvey (city) Cook County	757	2.51

Top 10 Places Sorted by Percent
Based on all places, regardless of population

Place	Number	%
Elsah (village) Jersey County	41	6.56
Olympia Fields (village) Cook County	253	5.36
Pulaski (village) Pulaski County	15	5.14
Glenwood (village) Cook County	434	4.80
Makanda (village) Jackson County	18	4.42
Mounds (city) Pulaski County	44	3.93
Justice (village) Cook County	470	3.89
Flossmoor (village) Cook County	324	3.49
Phoenix (village) Cook County	74	3.45
Country Club Hills (city) Cook County	542	3.35

Top 10 Places Sorted by Percent
Based on places with populations of 10,000 or more

Place	Number	%
Justice (village) Cook County	470	3.89
Country Club Hills (city) Cook County	542	3.35
Cahokia (village) Saint Clair County	511	3.10
Riverdale (village) Cook County	406	2.71
Dolton (village) Cook County	655	2.54
Harvey (city) Cook County	757	2.51
South Holland (village) Cook County	543	2.44
Matteson (village) Cook County	303	2.35
Hazel Crest (village) Cook County	330	2.24
Bellwood (village) Cook County	412	2.01

African, Subsaharan: African

Top 10 Places Sorted by Number
Based on all places, regardless of population

Place	Number	%
Chicago (city) Cook County	26,959	0.93
Rockford (city) Winnebago County	1,432	0.96
Peoria (city) Peoria County	1,071	0.95
Harvey (city) Cook County	757	2.51
Evanston (city) Cook County	659	0.89
Springfield (city) Sangamon County	653	0.58
Bolingbrook (village) Will County	614	1.09
Waukegan (city) Lake County	609	0.69
Oak Park (village) Cook County	601	1.14
Champaign (city) Champaign County	545	0.80

Top 10 Places Sorted by Percent
Based on all places, regardless of population

Place	Number	%
Pulaski (village) Pulaski County	15	5.14
Glenwood (village) Cook County	414	4.58
Makanda (village) Jackson County	18	4.42
Mounds (city) Pulaski County	44	3.93
Justice (village) Cook County	431	3.56
Phoenix (village) Cook County	69	3.22
Cahokia (village) Saint Clair County	511	3.10
Country Club Hills (city) Cook County	501	3.09
Hillside (village) Cook County	236	2.86
Harvey (city) Cook County	757	2.51

Top 10 Places Sorted by Percent
Based on places with populations of 10,000 or more

Place	Number	%
Justice (village) Cook County	431	3.56
Cahokia (village) Saint Clair County	511	3.10
Country Club Hills (city) Cook County	501	3.09
Harvey (city) Cook County	757	2.51
Matteson (village) Cook County	268	2.08
South Holland (village) Cook County	420	1.89
Riverdale (village) Cook County	264	1.76
Bellwood (village) Cook County	359	1.75
Dolton (village) Cook County	414	1.61
Hazel Crest (village) Cook County	213	1.45

African, Subsaharan: Cape Verdean

Top 10 Places Sorted by Number
Based on all places, regardless of population

Place	Number	%
Chicago (city) Cook County	66	0.00
Bolingbrook (village) Will County	23	0.04
Beach Park (village) Lake County	13	0.13
Kankakee (city) Kankakee County	11	0.04
Richton Park (village) Cook County	10	0.08
Orland Park (village) Cook County	8	0.02
North Chicago (city) Lake County	6	0.02
Evanston (city) Cook County	6	0.01
Glendale Heights (village) Du Page County	4	0.01

Top 10 Places Sorted by Percent
Based on all places, regardless of population

Place	Number	%
Beach Park (village) Lake County	13	0.13
Richton Park (village) Cook County	10	0.08
Bolingbrook (village) Will County	23	0.04
Kankakee (city) Kankakee County	11	0.04
Orland Park (village) Cook County	8	0.02
North Chicago (city) Lake County	6	0.02
Evanston (city) Cook County	6	0.01
Glendale Heights (village) Du Page County	4	0.01
Chicago (city) Cook County	66	0.00

Top 10 Places Sorted by Percent
Based on places with populations of 10,000 or more

Place	Number	%
Richton Park (village) Cook County	10	0.08
Bolingbrook (village) Will County	23	0.04
Kankakee (city) Kankakee County	11	0.04
Orland Park (village) Cook County	8	0.02
North Chicago (city) Lake County	6	0.02
Evanston (city) Cook County	6	0.01
Glendale Heights (village) Du Page County	4	0.01
Chicago (city) Cook County	66	0.00

African, Subsaharan: Ethiopian

Top 10 Places Sorted by Number
Based on all places, regardless of population

Place	Number	%
Chicago (city) Cook County	1,186	0.04
Springfield (city) Sangamon County	73	0.07
Evanston (city) Cook County	67	0.09
Flossmoor (village) Cook County	55	0.59
Forest Park (village) Cook County	38	0.24
Elgin (city) Kane County	38	0.04
Glen Ellyn (village) Du Page County	37	0.14
Romeoville (village) Will County	33	0.16
Alsip (village) Cook County	27	0.14
Glenview (village) Cook County	21	0.05

Top 10 Places Sorted by Percent
Based on all places, regardless of population

Place	Number	%
Elsah (village) Jersey County	4	0.64
Flossmoor (village) Cook County	55	0.59
Forest Park (village) Cook County	38	0.24
Coulterville (village) Randolph County	2	0.19
Romeoville (village) Will County	33	0.16
Glen Ellyn (village) Du Page County	37	0.14
Alsip (village) Cook County	27	0.14
Evanston (city) Cook County	67	0.09
South Holland (village) Cook County	19	0.09
Springfield (city) Sangamon County	73	0.07

Top 10 Places Sorted by Percent
Based on places with populations of 10,000 or more

Place	Number	%
Forest Park (village) Cook County	38	0.24
Romeoville (village) Will County	33	0.16
Glen Ellyn (village) Du Page County	37	0.14
Alsip (village) Cook County	27	0.14
Evanston (city) Cook County	67	0.09
South Holland (village) Cook County	19	0.09
Springfield (city) Sangamon County	73	0.07
Bellwood (village) Cook County	14	0.07
Glenview (village) Cook County	21	0.05
Glendale Heights (village) Du Page County	15	0.05

African, Subsaharan: Ghanian

Top 10 Places Sorted by Number
Based on all places, regardless of population

Place	Number	%
Chicago (city) Cook County	1,522	0.05
Bolingbrook (village) Will County	301	0.53
Waukegan (city) Lake County	155	0.18
River Forest (village) Cook County	65	0.56
Evanston (city) Cook County	53	0.07
Springfield (city) Sangamon County	48	0.04
Romeoville (village) Will County	46	0.22
Olympia Fields (village) Cook County	42	0.89
Crete (village) Will County	40	0.55
Naperville (city) Du Page County	40	0.03

Top 10 Places Sorted by Percent
Based on all places, regardless of population

Place	Number	%
Olympia Fields (village) Cook County	42	0.89
River Forest (village) Cook County	65	0.56
Crete (village) Will County	40	0.55
Bolingbrook (village) Will County	301	0.53
Sun River Terrace (village) Kankakee County	2	0.48
Romeoville (village) Will County	46	0.22
Effingham (city) Effingham County	26	0.21
Bellwood (village) Cook County	39	0.19
Hazel Crest (village) Cook County	28	0.19
Richton Park (village) Cook County	23	0.19

Top 10 Places Sorted by Percent
Based on places with populations of 10,000 or more

Place	Number	%
River Forest (village) Cook County	65	0.56
Bolingbrook (village) Will County	301	0.53
Romeoville (village) Will County	46	0.22
Effingham (city) Effingham County	26	0.21
Bellwood (village) Cook County	39	0.19
Hazel Crest (village) Cook County	28	0.19
Richton Park (village) Cook County	23	0.19
Waukegan (city) Lake County	155	0.18
Lake in the Hills (village) McHenry County	39	0.17
Forest Park (village) Cook County	17	0.11

Notes: (cdp) census designated place; Refer to the User's Guide in the front of the book for more detailed information.

African, Subsaharan: Kenyan

Top 10 Places Sorted by Number

Based on all places, regardless of population

Place	Number	%
Chicago (city) Cook County	130	0.00
Forest Park (village) Cook County	38	0.24
Urbana (city) Champaign County	32	0.09
Oak Park (village) Cook County	27	0.05
Normal (town) McLean County	26	0.06
Evanston (city) Cook County	25	0.03
Wheaton (city) Du Page County	24	0.04
Macomb (city) McDonough County	19	0.10
Schaumburg (village) Cook County	19	0.03
Dolton (village) Cook County	17	0.07

Top 10 Places Sorted by Percent

Based on all places, regardless of population

Place	Number	%
Elsah (village) Jersey County	4	0.64
Forest Park (village) Cook County	38	0.24
Macomb (city) McDonough County	19	0.10
Urbana (city) Champaign County	32	0.09
Heyworth (village) McLean County	2	0.08
Dolton (village) Cook County	17	0.07
Rolling Meadows (city) Cook County	17	0.07
Murphysboro (city) Jackson County	9	0.07
Normal (town) McLean County	26	0.06
Oak Park (village) Cook County	27	0.05

Top 10 Places Sorted by Percent

Based on places with populations of 10,000 or more

Place	Number	%
Forest Park (village) Cook County	38	0.24
Macomb (city) McDonough County	19	0.10
Urbana (city) Champaign County	32	0.09
Dolton (village) Cook County	17	0.07
Rolling Meadows (city) Cook County	17	0.07
Murphysboro (city) Jackson County	9	0.07
Normal (town) McLean County	26	0.06
Oak Park (village) Cook County	27	0.05
Hinsdale (village) Du Page County	9	0.05
Rantoul (village) Champaign County	7	0.05

African, Subsaharan: Liberian

Top 10 Places Sorted by Number

Based on all places, regardless of population

Place	Number	%
Chicago (city) Cook County	171	0.01
Riverdale (village) Cook County	120	0.80
Champaign (city) Champaign County	95	0.14
Aurora (city) Kane County	74	0.05
Springfield (city) Sangamon County	57	0.05
Decatur (city) Macon County	28	0.03
Gurnee (village) Lake County	21	0.07
Woodridge (village) Du Page County	20	0.06
Kankakee (city) Kankakee County	17	0.06
Rock Island (city) Rock Island County	15	0.04

Top 10 Places Sorted by Percent

Based on all places, regardless of population

Place	Number	%
Riverdale (village) Cook County	120	0.80
Champaign (city) Champaign County	95	0.14
Gurnee (village) Lake County	21	0.07
Woodridge (village) Du Page County	20	0.06
Kankakee (city) Kankakee County	17	0.06
Aurora (city) Kane County	74	0.05
Springfield (city) Sangamon County	57	0.05
Rock Island (city) Rock Island County	15	0.04
Glendale Heights (village) Du Page County	14	0.04
Decatur (city) Macon County	28	0.03

Top 10 Places Sorted by Percent

Based on places with populations of 10,000 or more

Place	Number	%
Riverdale (village) Cook County	120	0.80
Champaign (city) Champaign County	95	0.14
Gurnee (village) Lake County	21	0.07
Woodridge (village) Du Page County	20	0.06
Kankakee (city) Kankakee County	17	0.06
Aurora (city) Kane County	74	0.05
Springfield (city) Sangamon County	57	0.05
Rock Island (city) Rock Island County	15	0.04
Glendale Heights (village) Du Page County	14	0.04
Decatur (city) Macon County	28	0.03

African, Subsaharan: Nigerian

Top 10 Places Sorted by Number

Based on all places, regardless of population

Place	Number	%
Chicago (city) Cook County	5,464	0.19
Dolton (village) Cook County	224	0.87
Oak Park (village) Cook County	185	0.35
Calumet City (city) Cook County	179	0.46
Olympia Fields (village) Cook County	159	3.37
Skokie (village) Cook County	148	0.23
Springfield (city) Sangamon County	137	0.12
Carbondale (city) Jackson County	132	0.64
Urbana (city) Champaign County	119	0.33
Bolingbrook (village) Will County	114	0.20

Top 10 Places Sorted by Percent

Based on all places, regardless of population

Place	Number	%
Olympia Fields (village) Cook County	159	3.37
Elsah (village) Jersey County	14	2.24
Woodland (village) Iroquois County	5	1.54
Flossmoor (village) Cook County	104	1.12
Dolton (village) Cook County	224	0.87
Burnham (village) Cook County	30	0.72
Carbondale (city) Jackson County	132	0.64
Hazel Crest (village) Cook County	79	0.54
Homewood (village) Cook County	98	0.50
Calumet City (city) Cook County	179	0.46

Top 10 Places Sorted by Percent

Based on places with populations of 10,000 or more

Place	Number	%
Dolton (village) Cook County	224	0.87
Carbondale (city) Jackson County	132	0.64
Hazel Crest (village) Cook County	79	0.54
Homewood (village) Cook County	98	0.50
Calumet City (city) Cook County	179	0.46
Oak Park (village) Cook County	185	0.35
Urbana (city) Champaign County	119	0.33
Lansing (village) Cook County	89	0.32
Matteson (village) Cook County	35	0.27
Country Club Hills (city) Cook County	41	0.25

African, Subsaharan: Senegalese

Top 10 Places Sorted by Number

Based on all places, regardless of population

Place	Number	%
Oswego (village) Kendall County	26	0.20
Chicago (city) Cook County	26	0.00
Mount Prospect (village) Cook County	13	0.02
Broadview (village) Cook County	9	0.11

Top 10 Places Sorted by Percent

Based on all places, regardless of population

Place	Number	%
Oswego (village) Kendall County	26	0.20
Broadview (village) Cook County	9	0.11
Mount Prospect (village) Cook County	13	0.02
Chicago (city) Cook County	26	0.00

Top 10 Places Sorted by Percent

Based on places with populations of 10,000 or more

Place	Number	%
Oswego (village) Kendall County	26	0.20
Mount Prospect (village) Cook County	13	0.02
Chicago (city) Cook County	26	0.00

African, Subsaharan: Sierra Leonean

Top 10 Places Sorted by Number

Based on all places, regardless of population

Place	Number	%
Chicago (city) Cook County	55	0.00
South Holland (village) Cook County	30	0.13
Peoria (city) Peoria County	29	0.03
Wheaton (city) Du Page County	20	0.04
Rock Island (city) Rock Island County	16	0.04
Morton (village) Tazewell County	12	0.08

Top 10 Places Sorted by Percent

Based on all places, regardless of population

Place	Number	%
South Holland (village) Cook County	30	0.13
Morton (village) Tazewell County	12	0.08
Wheaton (city) Du Page County	20	0.04
Rock Island (city) Rock Island County	16	0.04
Peoria (city) Peoria County	29	0.03
Chicago (city) Cook County	55	0.00

Top 10 Places Sorted by Percent

Based on places with populations of 10,000 or more

Place	Number	%
South Holland (village) Cook County	30	0.13
Morton (village) Tazewell County	12	0.08
Wheaton (city) Du Page County	20	0.04
Rock Island (city) Rock Island County	16	0.04
Peoria (city) Peoria County	29	0.03
Chicago (city) Cook County	55	0.00

African, Subsaharan: Somalian

Top 10 Places Sorted by Number

Based on all places, regardless of population

Place	Number	%
Chicago (city) Cook County	222	0.01
De Kalb (city) De Kalb County	63	0.16
Bloomington (city) McLean County	20	0.03
Springfield (city) Sangamon County	7	0.01

Top 10 Places Sorted by Percent

Based on all places, regardless of population

Place	Number	%
De Kalb (city) De Kalb County	63	0.16
Bloomington (city) McLean County	20	0.03
Chicago (city) Cook County	222	0.01
Springfield (city) Sangamon County	7	0.01

Top 10 Places Sorted by Percent

Based on places with populations of 10,000 or more

Place	Number	%
De Kalb (city) De Kalb County	63	0.16
Bloomington (city) McLean County	20	0.03
Chicago (city) Cook County	222	0.01
Springfield (city) Sangamon County	7	0.01

Notes: (cdp) census designated place; Refer to the User's Guide in the front of the book for more detailed information.

African, Subsaharan: South African

Top 10 Places Sorted by Number

Based on all places, regardless of population

Place	Number	%
Chicago (city) Cook County	223	0.01
Schaumburg (village) Cook County	84	0.11
Buffalo Grove (village) Lake County	68	0.16
Wheaton (city) Du Page County	65	0.12
Highland Park (city) Lake County	64	0.20
Aurora (city) Kane County	61	0.04
Urbana (city) Champaign County	59	0.16
Palatine (village) Cook County	55	0.08
Skokie (village) Cook County	43	0.07
Decatur (city) Macon County	43	0.05

Top 10 Places Sorted by Percent

Based on all places, regardless of population

Place	Number	%
Burlington (village) Kane County	2	0.43
Riverwoods (village) Lake County	11	0.29
Dongola (village) Union County	2	0.25
Highland Park (city) Lake County	64	0.20
Westmont (village) Du Page County	42	0.17
Buffalo Grove (village) Lake County	68	0.16
Urbana (city) Champaign County	59	0.16
Northfield (village) Cook County	8	0.15
Olympia Fields (village) Cook County	7	0.15
Inverness (village) Cook County	8	0.13

Top 10 Places Sorted by Percent

Based on places with populations of 10,000 or more

Place	Number	%
Highland Park (city) Lake County	64	0.20
Westmont (village) Du Page County	42	0.17
Buffalo Grove (village) Lake County	68	0.16
Urbana (city) Champaign County	59	0.16
Wheaton (city) Du Page County	65	0.12
Lake Forest (city) Lake County	24	0.12
Schaumburg (village) Cook County	84	0.11
Gages Lake (cdp) Lake County	12	0.11
Deerfield (village) Lake County	17	0.09
Palatine (village) Cook County	55	0.08

African, Subsaharan: Sudanese

Top 10 Places Sorted by Number

Based on all places, regardless of population

Place	Number	%
Chicago (city) Cook County	117	0.00
Justice (village) Cook County	30	0.25
Chicago Heights (city) Cook County	9	0.03
Peoria (city) Peoria County	9	0.01
Champaign (city) Champaign County	6	0.01
Macomb (city) McDonough County	4	0.02

Top 10 Places Sorted by Percent

Based on all places, regardless of population

Place	Number	%
Justice (village) Cook County	30	0.25
Chicago Heights (city) Cook County	9	0.03
Macomb (city) McDonough County	4	0.02
Peoria (city) Peoria County	9	0.01
Champaign (city) Champaign County	6	0.01
Chicago (city) Cook County	117	0.00

Top 10 Places Sorted by Percent

Based on places with populations of 10,000 or more

Place	Number	%
Justice (village) Cook County	30	0.25
Chicago Heights (city) Cook County	9	0.03
Macomb (city) McDonough County	4	0.02
Peoria (city) Peoria County	9	0.01
Champaign (city) Champaign County	6	0.01
Chicago (city) Cook County	117	0.00

African, Subsaharan: Ugandan

Top 10 Places Sorted by Number

Based on all places, regardless of population

Place	Number	%
Evanston (city) Cook County	27	0.04
Chicago (city) Cook County	24	0.00
Elmhurst (city) Du Page County	15	0.03
Mount Prospect (village) Cook County	13	0.02
Urbana (city) Champaign County	6	0.02

Top 10 Places Sorted by Percent

Based on all places, regardless of population

Place	Number	%
Evanston (city) Cook County	27	0.04
Elmhurst (city) Du Page County	15	0.03
Mount Prospect (village) Cook County	13	0.02
Urbana (city) Champaign County	6	0.02
Chicago (city) Cook County	24	0.00

Top 10 Places Sorted by Percent

Based on places with populations of 10,000 or more

Place	Number	%
Evanston (city) Cook County	27	0.04
Elmhurst (city) Du Page County	15	0.03
Mount Prospect (village) Cook County	13	0.02
Urbana (city) Champaign County	6	0.02
Chicago (city) Cook County	24	0.00

African, Subsaharan: Zairian

Top 10 Places Sorted by Number

Based on all places, regardless of population

Place	Number	%
Champaign (city) Champaign County	7	0.01

Top 10 Places Sorted by Percent

Based on all places, regardless of population

Place	Number	%
Champaign (city) Champaign County	7	0.01

Top 10 Places Sorted by Percent

Based on places with populations of 10,000 or more

Place	Number	%
Champaign (city) Champaign County	7	0.01

African, Subsaharan: Zimbabwean

Top 10 Places Sorted by Number

Based on all places, regardless of population

Place	Number	%
Chicago (city) Cook County	64	0.00
Glenview (village) Cook County	27	0.06
Forest Park (village) Cook County	15	0.10
Champaign (city) Champaign County	12	0.02
Mount Prospect (village) Cook County	12	0.02
Edwardsville (city) Madison County	10	0.05
Bolingbrook (village) Will County	10	0.02
Aurora (city) Kane County	9	0.01
Woodridge (village) Du Page County	8	0.03
Galesburg (city) Knox County	8	0.02

Top 10 Places Sorted by Percent

Based on all places, regardless of population

Place	Number	%
Coalton (village) Montgomery County	4	1.34
Forest Park (village) Cook County	15	0.10
Peru (city) La Salle County	7	0.07
Glenview (village) Cook County	27	0.06
Edwardsville (city) Madison County	10	0.05
Woodridge (village) Du Page County	8	0.03
Champaign (city) Champaign County	12	0.02
Mount Prospect (village) Cook County	12	0.02
Bolingbrook (village) Will County	10	0.02
Galesburg (city) Knox County	8	0.02

Top 10 Places Sorted by Percent

Based on places with populations of 10,000 or more

Place	Number	%
Forest Park (village) Cook County	15	0.10
Glenview (village) Cook County	27	0.06
Edwardsville (city) Madison County	10	0.05
Woodridge (village) Du Page County	8	0.03
Champaign (city) Champaign County	12	0.02
Mount Prospect (village) Cook County	12	0.02
Bolingbrook (village) Will County	10	0.02
Galesburg (city) Knox County	8	0.02
Kankakee (city) Kankakee County	6	0.02
Aurora (city) Kane County	9	0.01

African, Subsaharan: Other

Top 10 Places Sorted by Number

Based on all places, regardless of population

Place	Number	%
Chicago (city) Cook County	756	0.03
De Kalb (city) De Kalb County	58	0.15
Waukegan (city) Lake County	53	0.06
Aurora (city) Kane County	39	0.03
Zion (city) Lake County	34	0.15
Carbondale (city) Jackson County	30	0.14
Peoria (city) Peoria County	25	0.02
Murphysboro (city) Jackson County	23	0.17
Addison (village) Du Page County	23	0.06
Belleville (city) Saint Clair County	23	0.05

Top 10 Places Sorted by Percent

Based on all places, regardless of population

Place	Number	%
Elsah (village) Jersey County	5	0.80
Lebanon (city) Saint Clair County	9	0.26
Flossmoor (village) Cook County	22	0.24
Shawneetown (city) Gallatin County	3	0.22
Mount Pulaski (city) Logan County	3	0.18
Murphysboro (city) Jackson County	23	0.17
Beardstown (city) Cass County	10	0.17
De Kalb (city) De Kalb County	58	0.15
Zion (city) Lake County	34	0.15
Riverdale (village) Cook County	22	0.15

Top 10 Places Sorted by Percent

Based on places with populations of 10,000 or more

Place	Number	%
Murphysboro (city) Jackson County	23	0.17
De Kalb (city) De Kalb County	58	0.15
Zion (city) Lake County	34	0.15
Riverdale (village) Cook County	22	0.15
Carbondale (city) Jackson County	30	0.14
Lansing (village) Cook County	21	0.07
Forest Park (village) Cook County	11	0.07
Hazel Crest (village) Cook County	10	0.07
Justice (village) Cook County	9	0.07
Waukegan (city) Lake County	53	0.06

Alaska Native tribes, specified

Top 10 Places Sorted by Number

Based on all places, regardless of population

Place	Number	%
Chicago (city) Cook County	68	0.00

Notes: (cdp) census designated place; Refer to the User's Guide in the front of the book for more detailed information.

Place	Number	%
Aurora (city) Kane County	11	0.01
Belleville (city) Saint Clair County	10	0.02
North Chicago (city) Lake County	9	0.03
Naperville (city) Du Page County	7	0.01
Loves Park (city) Winnebago County	6	0.03
Lincoln (city) Logan County	5	0.03
Lansing (village) Cook County	5	0.02
Evanston (city) Cook County	5	0.01
Fairmont (cdp) Will County	4	0.16

Top 10 Places Sorted by Percent

Based on all places, regardless of population

Place	Number	%
Coleta (village) Whiteside County	2	1.29
Saint Johns (village) Perry County	2	0.92
Browning (village) Schuyler County	1	0.77
Kansas (village) Edgar County	3	0.36
Tiskilwa (village) Bureau County	2	0.25
Dawson (village) Sangamon County	1	0.21
Buffalo (village) Sangamon County	1	0.20
McCullom Lake (village) McHenry County	2	0.19
Wilsonville (village) Macoupin County	1	0.17
Fairmont (cdp) Will County	4	0.16

Top 10 Places Sorted by Percent

Based on places with populations of 10,000 or more

Place	Number	%
Beach Park (village) Lake County	4	0.04
North Chicago (city) Lake County	9	0.03
Loves Park (city) Winnebago County	6	0.03
Lincoln (city) Logan County	5	0.03
Rantoul (village) Champaign County	4	0.03
Herrin (city) Williamson County	3	0.03
Belleville (city) Saint Clair County	10	0.02
Lansing (village) Cook County	5	0.02
Batavia (city) Kane County	4	0.02
Country Club Hills (city) Cook County	4	0.02

Alaska Native: Alaska Athabascan

Top 10 Places Sorted by Number

Based on all places, regardless of population

Place	Number	%
Chicago (city) Cook County	9	0.00
Belleville (city) Saint Clair County	7	0.02
Naperville (city) Du Page County	4	0.00
Freeport (city) Stephenson County	3	0.01
Lansing (village) Cook County	3	0.01
Aurora (city) Kane County	3	0.00
Bloomington (city) McLean County	3	0.00
Kildeer (village) Lake County	2	0.06
Bridgeview (village) Cook County	2	0.01
Wilsonville (village) Macoupin County	1	0.17

Top 10 Places Sorted by Percent

Based on all places, regardless of population

Place	Number	%
Wilsonville (village) Macoupin County	1	0.17
Kildeer (village) Lake County	2	0.06
Zeigler (city) Franklin County	1	0.06
Fairmont City (village) Saint Clair County	1	0.04
Belleville (city) Saint Clair County	7	0.02
Fairfield (city) Wayne County	1	0.02
Savoy (village) Champaign County	1	0.02
Freeport (city) Stephenson County	3	0.01
Lansing (village) Cook County	3	0.01
Bridgeview (village) Cook County	2	0.01

Top 10 Places Sorted by Percent

Based on places with populations of 10,000 or more

Place	Number	%
Belleville (city) Saint Clair County	7	0.02
Freeport (city) Stephenson County	3	0.01
Lansing (village) Cook County	3	0.01
Bridgeview (village) Cook County	2	0.01
Hinsdale (village) Du Page County	1	0.01
Lincoln (city) Logan County	1	0.01
New Lenox (village) Will County	1	0.01
Ottawa (city) La Salle County	1	0.01
Warrenville (city) Du Page County	1	0.01
Washington (city) Tazewell County	1	0.01

Alaska Native: Aleut

Top 10 Places Sorted by Number

Based on all places, regardless of population

Place	Number	%
Chicago (city) Cook County	11	0.00
Beach Park (village) Lake County	4	0.04
Downers Grove (village) Du Page County	4	0.01
Herrin (city) Williamson County	3	0.03
Fairmont (cdp) Will County	2	0.08
Marshall (city) Clark County	2	0.05
Bourbonnais (village) Kankakee County	2	0.01
Woodridge (village) Du Page County	2	0.01
Aurora (city) Kane County	2	0.00
Champaign (city) Champaign County	2	0.00

Top 10 Places Sorted by Percent

Based on all places, regardless of population

Place	Number	%
Coleta (village) Whiteside County	1	0.65
Fairmont (cdp) Will County	2	0.08
Channel Lake (cdp) Lake County	1	0.06
Marshall (city) Clark County	2	0.05
Beach Park (village) Lake County	4	0.04
Herrin (city) Williamson County	3	0.03
Carlyle (city) Clinton County	1	0.03
Round Lake Park (village) Lake County	1	0.02
Downers Grove (village) Du Page County	4	0.01
Bourbonnais (village) Kankakee County	2	0.01

Top 10 Places Sorted by Percent

Based on places with populations of 10,000 or more

Place	Number	%
Beach Park (village) Lake County	4	0.04
Herrin (city) Williamson County	3	0.03
Downers Grove (village) Du Page County	4	0.01
Bourbonnais (village) Kankakee County	2	0.01
Woodridge (village) Du Page County	2	0.01
Hinsdale (village) Du Page County	1	0.01
Homewood (village) Cook County	1	0.01
Macomb (city) McDonough County	1	0.01
River Forest (village) Cook County	1	0.01
Chicago (city) Cook County	11	0.00

Alaska Native: Eskimo

Top 10 Places Sorted by Number

Based on all places, regardless of population

Place	Number	%
Chicago (city) Cook County	32	0.00
Loves Park (city) Winnebago County	6	0.03
Rantoul (village) Champaign County	4	0.03
Batavia (city) Kane County	4	0.02
Country Club Hills (city) Cook County	4	0.02
North Chicago (city) Lake County	4	0.01
Aurora (city) Kane County	4	0.00
Kansas (village) Edgar County	3	0.36
Tremont (village) Tazewell County	3	0.15
Oregon (city) Ogle County	3	0.07

Top 10 Places Sorted by Percent

Based on all places, regardless of population

Place	Number	%
Saint Johns (village) Perry County	2	0.92
Browning (village) Schuyler County	1	0.77
Coleta (village) Whiteside County	1	0.65
Kansas (village) Edgar County	3	0.36
Tiskilwa (village) Bureau County	2	0.25
Dawson (village) Sangamon County	1	0.21
Buffalo (village) Sangamon County	1	0.20
Tremont (village) Tazewell County	3	0.15
Wapella (village) De Witt County	1	0.15
Fairmont (cdp) Will County	2	0.08

Top 10 Places Sorted by Percent

Based on places with populations of 10,000 or more

Place	Number	%
Loves Park (city) Winnebago County	6	0.03
Rantoul (village) Champaign County	4	0.03
Batavia (city) Kane County	4	0.02
Country Club Hills (city) Cook County	4	0.02
Grayslake (village) Lake County	3	0.02
North Chicago (city) Lake County	4	0.01
Belleville (city) Saint Clair County	3	0.01
East Peoria (city) Tazewell County	3	0.01
Moline (city) Rock Island County	3	0.01
Lake in the Hills (village) McHenry County	2	0.01

Alaska Native: Tlingit-Haida

Top 10 Places Sorted by Number

Based on all places, regardless of population

Place	Number	%
Chicago (city) Cook County	15	0.00
O'Fallon (city) Saint Clair County	4	0.02
Evanston (city) Cook County	4	0.01
La Grange (village) Cook County	3	0.02
Lincoln (city) Logan County	3	0.02
McCullom Lake (village) McHenry County	2	0.19
Lemont (village) Cook County	2	0.02
Lansing (village) Cook County	2	0.01
Aurora (city) Kane County	2	0.00
Bolingbrook (village) Will County	2	0.00

Top 10 Places Sorted by Percent

Based on all places, regardless of population

Place	Number	%
McCullom Lake (village) McHenry County	2	0.19
Elsah (village) Jersey County	1	0.16
O'Fallon (city) Saint Clair County	4	0.02
La Grange (village) Cook County	3	0.02
Lincoln (city) Logan County	3	0.02
Lemont (village) Cook County	2	0.02
Lake Bluff (village) Lake County	1	0.02
Evanston (city) Cook County	4	0.01
Lansing (village) Cook County	2	0.01
Brookfield (village) Cook County	1	0.01

Top 10 Places Sorted by Percent

Based on places with populations of 10,000 or more

Place	Number	%
O'Fallon (city) Saint Clair County	4	0.02
La Grange (village) Cook County	3	0.02
Lincoln (city) Logan County	3	0.02
Lemont (village) Cook County	2	0.02
Evanston (city) Cook County	4	0.01
Lansing (village) Cook County	2	0.01
Brookfield (village) Cook County	1	0.01
Fairview Heights (city) Saint Clair County	1	0.01
Marion (city) Williamson County	1	0.01
Mattoon (city) Coles County	1	0.01

Alaska Native: All other tribes

Top 10 Places Sorted by Number

Based on all places, regardless of population

Place	Number	%
Pekin (city) Tazewell County	4	0.01

Notes: (cdp) census designated place; Refer to the User's Guide in the front of the book for more detailed information.

Place	Number	%
Harvard (city) McHenry County	3	0.04
North Chicago (city) Lake County	3	0.01
Lombard (village) Du Page County	2	0.00
Carthage (city) Hancock County	1	0.04
Chicago (city) Cook County	1	0.00
Villa Park (village) Du Page County	1	0.00
Wheaton (city) Du Page County	1	0.00

Top 10 Places Sorted by Percent
Based on all places, regardless of population

Place	Number	%
Harvard (city) McHenry County	3	0.04
Carthage (city) Hancock County	1	0.04
Pekin (city) Tazewell County	4	0.01
North Chicago (city) Lake County	3	0.01
Lombard (village) Du Page County	2	0.00
Chicago (city) Cook County	1	0.00
Villa Park (village) Du Page County	1	0.00
Wheaton (city) Du Page County	1	0.00

Top 10 Places Sorted by Percent
Based on places with populations of 10,000 or more

Place	Number	%
Pekin (city) Tazewell County	4	0.01
North Chicago (city) Lake County	3	0.01
Lombard (village) Du Page County	2	0.00
Chicago (city) Cook County	1	0.00
Villa Park (village) Du Page County	1	0.00
Wheaton (city) Du Page County	1	0.00

Alaska Native tribes, not specified

Top 10 Places Sorted by Number
Based on all places, regardless of population

Place	Number	%
Chicago (city) Cook County	8	0.00
Gurnee (village) Lake County	3	0.01
Cicero (town) Cook County	3	0.00
Plymouth (village) Hancock County	1	0.18
Hodgkins (village) Cook County	1	0.05
Fairfield (city) Wayne County	1	0.02
Lincolnshire (village) Lake County	1	0.02
Park City (city) Lake County	1	0.02
Savoy (village) Champaign County	1	0.02
Tuscola (city) Douglas County	1	0.02

Top 10 Places Sorted by Percent
Based on all places, regardless of population

Place	Number	%
Plymouth (village) Hancock County	1	0.18
Hodgkins (village) Cook County	1	0.05
Fairfield (city) Wayne County	1	0.02
Lincolnshire (village) Lake County	1	0.02
Park City (city) Lake County	1	0.02
Savoy (village) Champaign County	1	0.02
Tuscola (city) Douglas County	1	0.02
Gurnee (village) Lake County	3	0.01
Calumet Park (village) Cook County	1	0.01
Herrin (city) Williamson County	1	0.01

Top 10 Places Sorted by Percent
Based on places with populations of 10,000 or more

Place	Number	%
Gurnee (village) Lake County	3	0.01
Herrin (city) Williamson County	1	0.01
Ottawa (city) La Salle County	1	0.01
Chicago (city) Cook County	8	0.00
Cicero (town) Cook County	3	0.00
Aurora (city) Kane County	1	0.00
Belleville (city) Saint Clair County	1	0.00
Belvidere (city) Boone County	1	0.00
Decatur (city) Macon County	1	0.00
East Moline (city) Rock Island County	1	0.00

American Indian or Alaska Native, not specified

Top 10 Places Sorted by Number
Based on all places, regardless of population

Place	Number	%
Chicago (city) Cook County	9,741	0.34
Cicero (town) Cook County	592	0.69
Aurora (city) Kane County	461	0.32
Waukegan (city) Lake County	442	0.50
Rockford (city) Winnebago County	432	0.29
Elgin (city) Kane County	347	0.37
Joliet (city) Will County	324	0.31
Peoria (city) Peoria County	277	0.25
Springfield (city) Sangamon County	268	0.24
Evanston (city) Cook County	206	0.28

Top 10 Places Sorted by Percent
Based on all places, regardless of population

Place	Number	%
Long Point (village) Livingston County	7	2.83
Muddy (village) Saline County	2	2.56
Royal Lakes (village) Macoupin County	4	2.11
Palmer (village) Christian County	5	2.02
Eddyville (village) Pope County	3	1.96
West Brooklyn (village) Lee County	3	1.72
Emington (village) Livingston County	2	1.67
Vergennes (village) Jackson County	8	1.63
Ellsworth (village) McLean County	4	1.48
Winslow (village) Stephenson County	5	1.45

Top 10 Places Sorted by Percent
Based on places with populations of 10,000 or more

Place	Number	%
Cicero (town) Cook County	592	0.69
Round Lake Beach (village) Lake County	146	0.56
North Chicago (city) Lake County	183	0.51
Blue Island (city) Cook County	120	0.51
Waukegan (city) Lake County	442	0.50
Bensenville (village) Du Page County	97	0.47
Mount Vernon (city) Jefferson County	70	0.43
Centralia (city) Marion County	61	0.43
Sauk Village (village) Cook County	45	0.43
Granite City (city) Madison County	130	0.42

Albanian

Top 10 Places Sorted by Number
Based on all places, regardless of population

Place	Number	%
Chicago (city) Cook County	1,368	0.05
Addison (village) Du Page County	267	0.75
Elmwood Park (village) Cook County	202	0.80
Naperville (city) Du Page County	180	0.14
Carol Stream (village) Du Page County	148	0.37
Mount Prospect (village) Cook County	148	0.26
Summit (village) Cook County	144	1.35
Elgin (city) Kane County	116	0.12
Glen Ellyn (village) Du Page County	111	0.41
Joliet (city) Will County	98	0.09

Top 10 Places Sorted by Percent
Based on all places, regardless of population

Place	Number	%
Hindsboro (village) Douglas County	8	2.25
Newark (village) Kendall County	16	1.76
Hampton (village) Rock Island County	27	1.69
Greenup (village) Cumberland County	24	1.57
Summit (village) Cook County	144	1.35
Sandwich (city) De Kalb County	88	1.35
Cordova (village) Rock Island County	8	1.28
Bull Valley (village) McHenry County	8	1.15
Andalusia (village) Rock Island County	12	1.13
Roscoe (village) Winnebago County	69	1.09

Top 10 Places Sorted by Percent
Based on places with populations of 10,000 or more

Place	Number	%
Summit (village) Cook County	144	1.35
Elmwood Park (village) Cook County	202	0.80
Addison (village) Du Page County	267	0.75
Lyons (village) Cook County	74	0.73
Justice (village) Cook County	57	0.47
Bridgeview (village) Cook County	70	0.46
Glen Ellyn (village) Du Page County	111	0.41
Carol Stream (village) Du Page County	148	0.37
Hickory Hills (city) Cook County	52	0.37
Palos Hills (city) Cook County	64	0.36

Alsatian

Top 10 Places Sorted by Number
Based on all places, regardless of population

Place	Number	%
Chicago (city) Cook County	137	0.00
Flossmoor (village) Cook County	55	0.59
Naperville (city) Du Page County	30	0.02
Oak Park (village) Cook County	28	0.05
Niles (village) Cook County	24	0.08
Princeton (city) Bureau County	21	0.28
Lake Forest (city) Lake County	20	0.10
Plainfield (village) Will County	18	0.14
Elmhurst (city) Du Page County	16	0.04
Springfield (city) Sangamon County	16	0.01

Top 10 Places Sorted by Percent
Based on all places, regardless of population

Place	Number	%
Flossmoor (village) Cook County	55	0.59
Princeton (city) Bureau County	21	0.28
Aroma Park (village) Kankakee County	2	0.24
Hopedale (village) Tazewell County	2	0.21
Genoa (city) De Kalb County	8	0.18
Sheldon (village) Iroquois County	2	0.17
Lake Bluff (village) Lake County	9	0.15
Metamora (village) Woodford County	4	0.15
Plainfield (village) Will County	18	0.14
Marengo (city) McHenry County	9	0.14

Top 10 Places Sorted by Percent
Based on places with populations of 10,000 or more

Place	Number	%
Plainfield (village) Will County	18	0.14
Lake Forest (city) Lake County	20	0.10
River Forest (village) Cook County	12	0.10
Niles (village) Cook County	24	0.08
Park Forest (village) Cook County	13	0.06
Lemont (village) Cook County	8	0.06
Oak Park (village) Cook County	28	0.05
Wilmette (village) Cook County	14	0.05
Saint Charles (city) Kane County	13	0.05
Hinsdale (village) Du Page County	8	0.05

American Indian tribes, specified

Top 10 Places Sorted by Number
Based on all places, regardless of population

Place	Number	%
Chicago (city) Cook County	10,059	0.35
Rockford (city) Winnebago County	793	0.53
Aurora (city) Kane County	493	0.34
Cicero (town) Cook County	464	0.54
North Chicago (city) Lake County	410	1.14
Peoria (city) Peoria County	408	0.36
Waukegan (city) Lake County	396	0.45
Springfield (city) Sangamon County	377	0.34
Elgin (city) Kane County	344	0.36
Joliet (city) Will County	329	0.31

Top 10 Places Sorted by Percent

Based on all places, regardless of population

Place	Number	%
Topeka (village) Mason County	4	4.44
Dunfermline (village) Fulton County	8	3.05
Venedy (village) Washington County	4	2.92
Junction (village) Gallatin County	4	2.88
Dongola (village) Union County	22	2.73
Otterville (town) Jersey County	3	2.50
Wilmington (village) Greene County	3	2.50
Alsey (village) Scott County	6	2.44
Shawneetown (city) Gallatin County	32	2.27
Maunie (village) White County	4	2.26

Top 10 Places Sorted by Percent

Based on places with populations of 10,000 or more

Place	Number	%
North Chicago (city) Lake County	410	1.14
Zion (city) Lake County	212	0.93
Rantoul (village) Champaign County	100	0.78
Beach Park (village) Lake County	70	0.69
Carpentersville (village) Kane County	186	0.61
Round Lake Beach (village) Lake County	157	0.61
Sauk Village (village) Cook County	64	0.61
Granite City (city) Madison County	186	0.59
Murphysboro (city) Jackson County	77	0.58
Romeoville (village) Will County	121	0.57

American Indian: Apache

Top 10 Places Sorted by Number

Based on all places, regardless of population

Place	Number	%
Chicago (city) Cook County	278	0.01
Rockford (city) Winnebago County	30	0.02
Peoria (city) Peoria County	20	0.02
North Chicago (city) Lake County	17	0.05
Aurora (city) Kane County	15	0.01
Naperville (city) Du Page County	15	0.01
Burbank (city) Cook County	13	0.05
Chicago Heights (city) Cook County	13	0.04
Springfield (city) Sangamon County	13	0.01
Jacksonville (city) Morgan County	12	0.06

Top 10 Places Sorted by Percent

Based on all places, regardless of population

Place	Number	%
Banner (village) Fulton County	3	2.01
Mapleton (village) Peoria County	2	0.88
Vermont (village) Fulton County	5	0.63
Maunie (village) White County	1	0.56
Elsah (village) Jersey County	3	0.47
Chesterfield (village) Macoupin County	1	0.45
Tonica (village) La Salle County	3	0.44
Owaneco (village) Christian County	1	0.39
Old Shawneetown (village) Gallatin County	1	0.36
Lee (village) Lee County	1	0.32

Top 10 Places Sorted by Percent

Based on places with populations of 10,000 or more

Place	Number	%
Jacksonville (city) Morgan County	12	0.06
Lockport (city) Will County	9	0.06
Chicago Ridge (village) Cook County	8	0.06
Swansea (village) Saint Clair County	6	0.06
North Chicago (city) Lake County	17	0.05
Burbank (city) Cook County	13	0.05
Romeoville (village) Will County	10	0.05
Centralia (city) Marion County	7	0.05
Chicago Heights (city) Cook County	13	0.04
Carpentersville (village) Kane County	11	0.04

American Indian: Blackfeet

Top 10 Places Sorted by Number

Based on all places, regardless of population

Place	Number	%
Chicago (city) Cook County	425	0.01
Rockford (city) Winnebago County	62	0.04
Peoria (city) Peoria County	33	0.03
North Chicago (city) Lake County	29	0.08
Aurora (city) Kane County	28	0.02
Calumet City (city) Cook County	24	0.06
Evanston (city) Cook County	22	0.03
Rock Island (city) Rock Island County	21	0.05
Pekin (city) Tazewell County	19	0.06
Decatur (city) Macon County	19	0.02

Top 10 Places Sorted by Percent

Based on all places, regardless of population

Place	Number	%
Alsey (village) Scott County	3	1.22
Tower Hill (village) Shelby County	5	0.82
New Douglas (village) Madison County	3	0.81
Longview (village) Champaign County	1	0.65
Crossville (village) White County	5	0.64
Ferris (village) Hancock County	1	0.60
Tamms (village) Alexander County	4	0.55
Grafton (city) Jersey County	3	0.49
Patoka (village) Marion County	3	0.47
Greenfield (city) Greene County	5	0.42

Top 10 Places Sorted by Percent

Based on places with populations of 10,000 or more

Place	Number	%
Rantoul (village) Champaign County	11	0.09
North Chicago (city) Lake County	29	0.08
Zion (city) Lake County	18	0.08
Forest Park (village) Cook County	13	0.08
Murphysboro (city) Jackson County	11	0.08
Matteson (village) Cook County	10	0.08
Country Club Hills (city) Cook County	11	0.07
Kewanee (city) Henry County	9	0.07
Richton Park (village) Cook County	9	0.07
Calumet City (city) Cook County	24	0.06

American Indian: Cherokee

Top 10 Places Sorted by Number

Based on all places, regardless of population

Place	Number	%
Chicago (city) Cook County	2,337	0.08
Rockford (city) Winnebago County	346	0.23
Peoria (city) Peoria County	221	0.20
Springfield (city) Sangamon County	207	0.19
North Chicago (city) Lake County	175	0.49
Aurora (city) Kane County	164	0.11
Decatur (city) Macon County	140	0.17
Granite City (city) Madison County	115	0.37
Joliet (city) Will County	115	0.11
Waukegan (city) Lake County	113	0.13

Top 10 Places Sorted by Percent

Based on all places, regardless of population

Place	Number	%
Junction (village) Gallatin County	4	2.88
Otterville (town) Jersey County	3	2.50
Wilmington (village) Greene County	3	2.50
Belknap (village) Johnson County	3	2.26
Panama (village) Montgomery County	7	2.17
Dongola (village) Union County	16	1.99
Alvin (village) Vermilion County	6	1.90
Kilbourne (village) Mason County	7	1.87
Simpson (village) Johnson County	1	1.85
Gorham (village) Jackson County	4	1.56

Top 10 Places Sorted by Percent

Based on places with populations of 10,000 or more

Place	Number	%
North Chicago (city) Lake County	175	0.49
Zion (city) Lake County	89	0.39
Murphysboro (city) Jackson County	52	0.39
Granite City (city) Madison County	115	0.37
Mount Vernon (city) Jefferson County	61	0.37
Carbondale (city) Jackson County	70	0.34
Rantoul (village) Champaign County	42	0.33
O'Fallon (city) Saint Clair County	68	0.31
Beach Park (village) Lake County	31	0.31
Cahokia (village) Saint Clair County	48	0.29

American Indian: Cheyenne

Top 10 Places Sorted by Number

Based on all places, regardless of population

Place	Number	%
Chicago (city) Cook County	44	0.00
University Park (village) Will County	6	0.09
Rockford (city) Winnebago County	6	0.00
Waukegan (city) Lake County	5	0.01
Topeka (village) Mason County	4	4.44
South Beloit (city) Winnebago County	4	0.07
Yorkville (city) Kendall County	4	0.06
Wood River (city) Madison County	4	0.04
Joliet (city) Will County	4	0.00
Peoria (city) Peoria County	4	0.00

Top 10 Places Sorted by Percent

Based on all places, regardless of population

Place	Number	%
Topeka (village) Mason County	4	4.44
Lynnville (village) Morgan County	1	0.73
La Rose (village) Marshall County	1	0.63
Maunie (village) White County	1	0.56
Thawville (village) Iroquois County	1	0.39
Hanover (village) Jo Daviess County	1	0.12
Lakemoor (village) McHenry County	3	0.11
Hardin (village) Calhoun County	1	0.10
University Park (village) Will County	6	0.09
Energy (village) Williamson County	1	0.09

Top 10 Places Sorted by Percent

Based on places with populations of 10,000 or more

Place	Number	%
Wood River (city) Madison County	4	0.04
Pontiac (city) Livingston County	3	0.03
Crest Hill (city) Will County	3	0.02
Goodings Grove (cdp) Will County	3	0.02
Macomb (city) McDonough County	3	0.02
Waukegan (city) Lake County	5	0.01
North Chicago (city) Lake County	3	0.01
Orland Park (village) Cook County	3	0.01
Zion (city) Lake County	3	0.01
Alton (city) Madison County	2	0.01

American Indian: Chickasaw

Top 10 Places Sorted by Number

Based on all places, regardless of population

Place	Number	%
Chicago (city) Cook County	46	0.00
Forest Park (village) Cook County	5	0.03
Ottawa (city) La Salle County	5	0.03
Belleville (city) Saint Clair County	5	0.01
Evanston (city) Cook County	5	0.01
El Paso (city) Woodford County	4	0.15
Caseyville (village) Saint Clair County	4	0.09
Jacksonville (city) Morgan County	4	0.02
Morton Grove (village) Cook County	4	0.02
Bolingbrook (village) Will County	4	0.01

Notes: (cdp) census designated place; Refer to the User's Guide in the front of the book for more detailed information.

Top 10 Places Sorted by Percent

Based on all places, regardless of population

Place	Number	%
Donovan (village) Iroquois County	1	0.28
Mackinaw (village) Tazewell County	3	0.21
Hecker (village) Monroe County	1	0.21
El Paso (city) Woodford County	4	0.15
Colfax (village) McLean County	1	0.10
Elkville (village) Jackson County	1	0.10
Stillman Valley (village) Ogle County	1	0.10
Caseyville (village) Saint Clair County	4	0.09
Hillcrest (village) Ogle County	1	0.09
Ashland (village) Cass County	1	0.07

Top 10 Places Sorted by Percent

Based on places with populations of 10,000 or more

Place	Number	%
Forest Park (village) Cook County	5	0.03
Ottawa (city) La Salle County	5	0.03
Jacksonville (city) Morgan County	4	0.02
Morton Grove (village) Cook County	4	0.02
Bourbonnais (village) Kankakee County	3	0.02
Godfrey (village) Madison County	3	0.02
Glen Carbon (village) Madison County	2	0.02
Murphysboro (city) Jackson County	2	0.02
Belleville (city) Saint Clair County	5	0.01
Evanston (city) Cook County	5	0.01

American Indian: Chippewa

Top 10 Places Sorted by Number

Based on all places, regardless of population

Place	Number	%
Chicago (city) Cook County	636	0.02
Waukegan (city) Lake County	33	0.04
Rockford (city) Winnebago County	31	0.02
Zion (city) Lake County	29	0.13
Round Lake Beach (village) Lake County	29	0.11
Berwyn (city) Cook County	28	0.05
Elgin (city) Kane County	24	0.03
Joliet (city) Will County	23	0.02
Evanston (city) Cook County	22	0.03
Aurora (city) Kane County	22	0.02

Top 10 Places Sorted by Percent

Based on all places, regardless of population

Place	Number	%
Dunfermline (village) Fulton County	4	1.53
Thomson (village) Carroll County	5	0.89
Donovan (village) Iroquois County	2	0.57
Waltonville (village) Jefferson County	2	0.47
Greenwood (village) McHenry County	1	0.41
Round Lake Heights (village) Lake County	5	0.37
Toulon (city) Stark County	5	0.36
Rankin (village) Vermilion County	2	0.32
Andalusia (village) Rock Island County	3	0.29
Stillman Valley (village) Ogle County	3	0.29

Top 10 Places Sorted by Percent

Based on places with populations of 10,000 or more

Place	Number	%
Zion (city) Lake County	29	0.13
Round Lake Beach (village) Lake County	29	0.11
Beach Park (village) Lake County	10	0.10
Lindenhurst (village) Lake County	10	0.08
Sycamore (city) De Kalb County	10	0.08
Gurnee (village) Lake County	19	0.07
Darien (city) Du Page County	16	0.07
Carpentersville (village) Kane County	17	0.06
Worth (village) Cook County	7	0.06
Lyons (village) Cook County	6	0.06

American Indian: Choctaw

Top 10 Places Sorted by Number

Based on all places, regardless of population

Place	Number	%
Chicago (city) Cook County	401	0.01
North Chicago (city) Lake County	20	0.06
Rockford (city) Winnebago County	19	0.01
Elgin (city) Kane County	18	0.02
Springfield (city) Sangamon County	18	0.02
Waukegan (city) Lake County	16	0.02
Aurora (city) Kane County	16	0.01
Berwyn (city) Cook County	14	0.03
Tinley Park (village) Cook County	14	0.03
Burbank (city) Cook County	12	0.04

Top 10 Places Sorted by Percent

Based on all places, regardless of population

Place	Number	%
Venedy (village) Washington County	2	1.46
Whiteash (village) Williamson County	3	1.12
Bath (village) Mason County	2	0.65
Bay View Gardens (village) Woodford County	2	0.55
Alma (village) Marion County	2	0.52
Mill Shoals (village) White County	1	0.43
Donnellson (village) Montgomery County	1	0.41
Morrisonville (village) Christian County	4	0.37
Thompsonville (village) Franklin County	2	0.35
Lakewood Shores (cdp) Will County	5	0.34

Top 10 Places Sorted by Percent

Based on places with populations of 10,000 or more

Place	Number	%
Glen Carbon (village) Madison County	9	0.09
Country Club Hills (city) Cook County	11	0.07
Barrington (village) Cook County	7	0.07
North Chicago (city) Lake County	20	0.06
Rantoul (village) Champaign County	8	0.06
Burbank (city) Cook County	12	0.04
Maywood (village) Cook County	12	0.04
Carpentersville (village) Kane County	11	0.04
O'Fallon (city) Saint Clair County	8	0.04
Ottawa (city) La Salle County	7	0.04

American Indian: Colville

Top 10 Places Sorted by Number

Based on all places, regardless of population

Place	Number	%
Monmouth (city) Warren County	4	0.04
Bloomington (city) McLean County	3	0.00
Chicago (city) Cook County	3	0.00
Jacksonville (city) Morgan County	1	0.01
Lemont (village) Cook County	1	0.01
Cicero (town) Cook County	1	0.00
East Moline (city) Rock Island County	1	0.00
Springfield (city) Sangamon County	1	0.00

Top 10 Places Sorted by Percent

Based on all places, regardless of population

Place	Number	%
Monmouth (city) Warren County	4	0.04
Jacksonville (city) Morgan County	1	0.01
Lemont (village) Cook County	1	0.01
Bloomington (city) McLean County	3	0.00
Chicago (city) Cook County	3	0.00
Cicero (town) Cook County	1	0.00
East Moline (city) Rock Island County	1	0.00
Springfield (city) Sangamon County	1	0.00

Top 10 Places Sorted by Percent

Based on places with populations of 10,000 or more

Place	Number	%
Jacksonville (city) Morgan County	1	0.01
Lemont (village) Cook County	1	0.01
Bloomington (city) McLean County	3	0.00
Chicago (city) Cook County	3	0.00
Cicero (town) Cook County	1	0.00
East Moline (city) Rock Island County	1	0.00
Springfield (city) Sangamon County	1	0.00

American Indian: Comanche

Top 10 Places Sorted by Number

Based on all places, regardless of population

Place	Number	%
Chicago (city) Cook County	53	0.00
Round Lake Beach (village) Lake County	7	0.03
Rockdale (village) Will County	5	0.26
Bourbonnais (village) Kankakee County	5	0.03
East Peoria (city) Tazewell County	5	0.02
Zion (city) Lake County	5	0.02
Belleville (city) Saint Clair County	5	0.01
De Kalb (city) De Kalb County	5	0.01
North Chicago (city) Lake County	5	0.01
Palatine (village) Cook County	5	0.01

Top 10 Places Sorted by Percent

Based on all places, regardless of population

Place	Number	%
Smithfield (village) Fulton County	1	0.47
Rockdale (village) Will County	5	0.26
Ohio (village) Bureau County	1	0.19
Enfield (village) White County	1	0.16
Grand Tower (city) Jackson County	1	0.16
Pierron (village) Bond County	1	0.15
Schram City (village) Montgomery County	1	0.15
Gifford (village) Champaign County	1	0.12
Mansfield (village) Piatt County	1	0.11
Tilton (village) Vermilion County	3	0.10

Top 10 Places Sorted by Percent

Based on places with populations of 10,000 or more

Place	Number	%
Round Lake Beach (village) Lake County	7	0.03
Bourbonnais (village) Kankakee County	5	0.03
East Peoria (city) Tazewell County	5	0.02
Zion (city) Lake County	5	0.02
Forest Park (village) Cook County	3	0.02
Mount Vernon (city) Jefferson County	3	0.02
Norridge (village) Cook County	3	0.02
Belleville (city) Saint Clair County	5	0.01
De Kalb (city) De Kalb County	5	0.01
North Chicago (city) Lake County	5	0.01

American Indian: Cree

Top 10 Places Sorted by Number

Based on all places, regardless of population

Place	Number	%
Chicago (city) Cook County	62	0.00
Evanston (city) Cook County	6	0.01
Schaumburg (village) Cook County	6	0.01
Marion (city) Williamson County	5	0.03
Rockford (city) Winnebago County	5	0.00
Midlothian (village) Cook County	4	0.03
Oak Park (village) Cook County	4	0.01
Wyoming (city) Stark County	3	0.21
Worth (village) Cook County	3	0.03
Brookfield (village) Cook County	3	0.02

Notes: (cdp) census designated place; Refer to the User's Guide in the front of the book for more detailed information.

Top 10 Places Sorted by Percent
Based on all places, regardless of population

Place	Number	%
Wyoming (city) Stark County	3	0.21
Poplar Grove (village) Boone County	2	0.15
Mulberry Grove (village) Bond County	1	0.15
Rockdale (village) Will County	2	0.11
Shabbona (village) De Kalb County	1	0.11
Oakland (city) Coles County	1	0.10
Amboy (city) Lee County	2	0.08
Beecher (village) Will County	1	0.05
Stone Park (village) Cook County	2	0.04
Marion (city) Williamson County	5	0.03

Top 10 Places Sorted by Percent
Based on places with populations of 10,000 or more

Place	Number	%
Marion (city) Williamson County	5	0.03
Midlothian (village) Cook County	4	0.03
Worth (village) Cook County	3	0.03
Brookfield (village) Cook County	3	0.02
Riverdale (village) Cook County	3	0.02
Beach Park (village) Lake County	2	0.02
Plainfield (village) Will County	2	0.02
Evanston (city) Cook County	6	0.01
Schaumburg (village) Cook County	6	0.01
Oak Park (village) Cook County	4	0.01

American Indian: Creek

Top 10 Places Sorted by Number
Based on all places, regardless of population

Place	Number	%
Chicago (city) Cook County	102	0.00
Joliet (city) Will County	12	0.01
Woodridge (village) Du Page County	8	0.03
Cicero (town) Cook County	8	0.01
Springfield (city) Sangamon County	7	0.01
Waukegan (city) Lake County	7	0.01
Rosewood Heights (cdp) Madison County	6	0.14
Zion (city) Lake County	6	0.03
Naperville (city) Du Page County	6	0.00
Channel Lake (cdp) Lake County	5	0.28

Top 10 Places Sorted by Percent
Based on all places, regardless of population

Place	Number	%
Elliott (village) Ford County	4	1.17
Royal Lakes (village) Macoupin County	1	0.53
Arlington (village) Bureau County	1	0.47
Varna (village) Marshall County	2	0.46
Channel Lake (cdp) Lake County	5	0.28
Crossville (village) White County	2	0.26
Ellis Grove (village) Randolph County	1	0.26
Leland Grove (city) Sangamon County	4	0.25
Danvers (village) McLean County	3	0.25
Dakota (village) Stephenson County	1	0.20

Top 10 Places Sorted by Percent
Based on places with populations of 10,000 or more

Place	Number	%
Sauk Village (village) Cook County	4	0.04
Woodridge (village) Du Page County	8	0.03
Zion (city) Lake County	6	0.03
Palos Hills (city) Cook County	5	0.03
Justice (village) Cook County	3	0.02
Matteson (village) Cook County	3	0.02
Sterling (city) Whiteside County	3	0.02
Joliet (city) Will County	12	0.01
Cicero (town) Cook County	8	0.01
Springfield (city) Sangamon County	7	0.01

American Indian: Crow

Top 10 Places Sorted by Number
Based on all places, regardless of population

Place	Number	%
Chicago (city) Cook County	22	0.00
Aurora (city) Kane County	6	0.00
Rockford (city) Winnebago County	5	0.00
Roanoke (village) Woodford County	4	0.20
Gages Lake (cdp) Lake County	4	0.04
Alton (city) Madison County	4	0.01
North Chicago (city) Lake County	4	0.01
Sherman (village) Sangamon County	3	0.10
Metropolis (city) Massac County	3	0.05
Troy (city) Madison County	3	0.04

Top 10 Places Sorted by Percent
Based on all places, regardless of population

Place	Number	%
West Brooklyn (village) Lee County	2	1.15
Roanoke (village) Woodford County	4	0.20
Sherman (village) Sangamon County	3	0.10
Leland (village) La Salle County	1	0.10
Rushville (city) Schuyler County	2	0.06
Maroa (city) Macon County	1	0.06
Metropolis (city) Massac County	3	0.05
Gages Lake (cdp) Lake County	4	0.04
Troy (city) Madison County	3	0.04
Coal City (village) Grundy County	2	0.04

Top 10 Places Sorted by Percent
Based on places with populations of 10,000 or more

Place	Number	%
Gages Lake (cdp) Lake County	4	0.04
Midlothian (village) Cook County	3	0.02
Oswego (village) Kendall County	3	0.02
Herrin (city) Williamson County	2	0.02
Alton (city) Madison County	4	0.01
North Chicago (city) Lake County	4	0.01
Des Plaines (city) Cook County	3	0.01
East Moline (city) Rock Island County	2	0.01
Mount Vernon (city) Jefferson County	2	0.01
Bourbonnais (village) Kankakee County	1	0.01

American Indian: Delaware

Top 10 Places Sorted by Number
Based on all places, regardless of population

Place	Number	%
Chicago (city) Cook County	26	0.00
Romeoville (village) Will County	6	0.03
Watseka (city) Iroquois County	5	0.09
Decatur (city) Macon County	5	0.01
Hoffman Estates (village) Cook County	5	0.01
Bolingbrook (village) Will County	4	0.01
Mount Prospect (village) Cook County	3	0.01
Pekin (city) Tazewell County	3	0.01
Naperville (city) Du Page County	3	0.00
Rockford (city) Winnebago County	3	0.00

Top 10 Places Sorted by Percent
Based on all places, regardless of population

Place	Number	%
Saint Libory (village) Saint Clair County	2	0.34
Atkinson (town) Henry County	2	0.20
Crossville (village) White County	1	0.13
Beckemeyer (village) Clinton County	1	0.10
New Berlin (village) Sangamon County	1	0.10
Watseka (city) Iroquois County	5	0.09
Clifton (village) Iroquois County	1	0.08
Crystal Lawns (cdp) Will County	2	0.07
Winnebago (village) Winnebago County	2	0.07
Cuba (city) Fulton County	1	0.07

Top 10 Places Sorted by Percent
Based on places with populations of 10,000 or more

Place	Number	%
Romeoville (village) Will County	6	0.03
Decatur (city) Macon County	5	0.01
Hoffman Estates (village) Cook County	5	0.01
Bolingbrook (village) Will County	4	0.01
Mount Prospect (village) Cook County	3	0.01
Pekin (city) Tazewell County	3	0.01
Belvidere (city) Boone County	2	0.01
Jacksonville (city) Morgan County	1	0.01
Palos Hills (city) Cook County	1	0.01
Prospect Heights (city) Cook County	1	0.01

American Indian: Houma

Top 10 Places Sorted by Number
Based on all places, regardless of population

Place	Number	%
Chicago (city) Cook County	5	0.00
Wheaton (city) Du Page County	4	0.01
Norris City (village) White County	2	0.19
Peoria (city) Peoria County	2	0.00
Harvard (city) McHenry County	1	0.01
Aurora (city) Kane County	1	0.00
Bensenville (village) Du Page County	1	0.00
Glenview (village) Cook County	1	0.00

Top 10 Places Sorted by Percent
Based on all places, regardless of population

Place	Number	%
Norris City (village) White County	2	0.19
Wheaton (city) Du Page County	4	0.01
Harvard (city) McHenry County	1	0.01
Chicago (city) Cook County	5	0.00
Peoria (city) Peoria County	2	0.00
Aurora (city) Kane County	1	0.00
Bensenville (village) Du Page County	1	0.00
Glenview (village) Cook County	1	0.00

Top 10 Places Sorted by Percent
Based on places with populations of 10,000 or more

Place	Number	%
Wheaton (city) Du Page County	4	0.01
Chicago (city) Cook County	5	0.00
Peoria (city) Peoria County	2	0.00
Aurora (city) Kane County	1	0.00
Bensenville (village) Du Page County	1	0.00
Glenview (village) Cook County	1	0.00

American Indian: Iroquois

Top 10 Places Sorted by Number
Based on all places, regardless of population

Place	Number	%
Chicago (city) Cook County	401	0.01
Rockford (city) Winnebago County	25	0.02
Lansing (village) Cook County	21	0.07
De Kalb (city) De Kalb County	12	0.03
Des Plaines (city) Cook County	12	0.02
Oak Park (village) Cook County	12	0.02
Cicero (town) Cook County	12	0.01
Villa Park (village) Du Page County	11	0.05
Crystal Lake (city) McHenry County	11	0.03
Wheeling (village) Cook County	11	0.03

Top 10 Places Sorted by Percent
Based on all places, regardless of population

Place	Number	%
Whiteash (village) Williamson County	3	1.12
Calhoun (village) Richland County	2	0.90
Mount Auburn (village) Christian County	4	0.78
Magnolia (village) Putnam County	2	0.72

Notes: (cdp) census designated place; Refer to the User's Guide in the front of the book for more detailed information.

Place	Number	%
Hanover (village) Jo Daviess County	5	0.60
Thawville (village) Iroquois County	1	0.39
San Jose (village) Mason County	2	0.29
Pittsburg (village) Williamson County	1	0.17
Hinckley (village) De Kalb County	3	0.15
Genoa (city) De Kalb County	6	0.14

Top 10 Places Sorted by Percent

Based on places with populations of 10,000 or more

Place	Number	%
Lansing (village) Cook County	21	0.07
Villa Park (village) Du Page County	11	0.05
Lockport (city) Will County	7	0.05
Plainfield (village) Will County	6	0.05
Gages Lake (cdp) Lake County	5	0.05
Bloomingdale (village) Du Page County	8	0.04
Evergreen Park (village) Cook County	8	0.04
Lake Zurich (village) Lake County	8	0.04
Ottawa (city) La Salle County	7	0.04
South Elgin (village) Kane County	7	0.04

American Indian: Kiowa

Top 10 Places Sorted by Number

Based on all places, regardless of population

Place	Number	%
Chicago (city) Cook County	18	0.00
Effingham (city) Effingham County	7	0.06
Bloomington (city) McLean County	4	0.01
Mount Morris (village) Ogle County	3	0.10
Litchfield (city) Montgomery County	3	0.04
Marine (village) Madison County	2	0.22
Clay City (village) Clay County	2	0.20
Chicago Heights (city) Cook County	2	0.01
O'Fallon (city) Saint Clair County	2	0.01
Merrionette Park (village) Cook County	1	0.05

Top 10 Places Sorted by Percent

Based on all places, regardless of population

Place	Number	%
Marine (village) Madison County	2	0.22
Clay City (village) Clay County	2	0.20
Mount Morris (village) Ogle County	3	0.10
Effingham (city) Effingham County	7	0.06
Merrionette Park (village) Cook County	1	0.05
Mount Olive (city) Macoupin County	1	0.05
Litchfield (city) Montgomery County	3	0.04
Byron (city) Ogle County	1	0.03
Staunton (city) Macoupin County	1	0.02
Bloomington (city) McLean County	4	0.01

Top 10 Places Sorted by Percent

Based on places with populations of 10,000 or more

Place	Number	%
Effingham (city) Effingham County	7	0.06
Bloomington (city) McLean County	4	0.01
Chicago Heights (city) Cook County	2	0.01
O'Fallon (city) Saint Clair County	2	0.01
Alsip (village) Cook County	1	0.01
Barrington (village) Cook County	1	0.01
Gages Lake (cdp) Lake County	1	0.01
Hickory Hills (city) Cook County	1	0.01
Marion (city) Williamson County	1	0.01
Chicago (city) Cook County	18	0.00

American Indian: Latin American Indians

Top 10 Places Sorted by Number

Based on all places, regardless of population

Place	Number	%
Chicago (city) Cook County	3,250	0.11
Cicero (town) Cook County	249	0.29
Waukegan (city) Lake County	125	0.14
Aurora (city) Kane County	125	0.09
Elgin (city) Kane County	113	0.12
Rockford (city) Winnebago County	107	0.07
Berwyn (city) Cook County	75	0.14
Joliet (city) Will County	67	0.06
Chicago Heights (city) Cook County	53	0.16
Blue Island (city) Cook County	51	0.22

Top 10 Places Sorted by Percent

Based on all places, regardless of population

Place	Number	%
Mark (village) Putnam County	7	1.43
Shawneetown (city) Gallatin County	14	0.99
Trout Valley (village) McHenry County	4	0.67
Tallula (village) Menard County	4	0.63
Nelson (village) Lee County	1	0.61
Allerton (village) Vermilion County	1	0.34
Rochelle (city) Ogle County	31	0.33
Rosemont (village) Cook County	14	0.33
Stone Park (village) Cook County	16	0.31
Cicero (town) Cook County	249	0.29

Top 10 Places Sorted by Percent

Based on places with populations of 10,000 or more

Place	Number	%
Cicero (town) Cook County	249	0.29
Northlake (city) Cook County	27	0.23
Blue Island (city) Cook County	51	0.22
Melrose Park (village) Cook County	45	0.19
Chicago Heights (city) Cook County	53	0.16
Bensenville (village) Du Page County	33	0.16
Franklin Park (village) Cook County	31	0.16
Summit (village) Cook County	17	0.16
Waukegan (city) Lake County	125	0.14
Berwyn (city) Cook County	75	0.14

American Indian: Lumbee

Top 10 Places Sorted by Number

Based on all places, regardless of population

Place	Number	%
Chicago (city) Cook County	26	0.00
Peoria (city) Peoria County	6	0.01
Naperville (city) Du Page County	5	0.00
Orland Hills (village) Cook County	4	0.06
Romeoville (village) Will County	4	0.02
Waukegan (city) Lake County	4	0.00
Worden (village) Madison County	3	0.33
Northlake (city) Cook County	3	0.03
Swansea (village) Saint Clair County	3	0.03
Riverdale (village) Cook County	3	0.02

Top 10 Places Sorted by Percent

Based on all places, regardless of population

Place	Number	%
Worden (village) Madison County	3	0.33
Valmeyer (village) Monroe County	2	0.33
Greenview (village) Menard County	1	0.12
Edinburg (village) Christian County	1	0.09
Orland Hills (village) Cook County	4	0.06
Bellevue (village) Peoria County	1	0.05
Eureka (city) Woodford County	2	0.04
Northlake (city) Cook County	3	0.03
Swansea (village) Saint Clair County	3	0.03
Stickney (village) Cook County	2	0.03

Top 10 Places Sorted by Percent

Based on places with populations of 10,000 or more

Place	Number	%
Northlake (city) Cook County	3	0.03
Swansea (village) Saint Clair County	3	0.03
Romeoville (village) Will County	4	0.02
Riverdale (village) Cook County	3	0.02
Peoria (city) Peoria County	6	0.01
Crystal Lake (city) McHenry County	3	0.01
Collinsville (city) Madison County	2	0.01
Granite City (city) Madison County	2	0.01
North Chicago (city) Lake County	2	0.01
Wilmette (village) Cook County	2	0.01

American Indian: Menominee

Top 10 Places Sorted by Number

Based on all places, regardless of population

Place	Number	%
Chicago (city) Cook County	183	0.01
Springfield (city) Sangamon County	9	0.01
Rock Island (city) Rock Island County	7	0.02
Rockford (city) Winnebago County	7	0.00
Lyons (village) Cook County	6	0.06
Antioch (village) Lake County	5	0.06
Barrington (village) Cook County	5	0.05
Franklin Park (village) Cook County	5	0.03
Berwyn (city) Cook County	5	0.01
Crystal Lake (city) McHenry County	5	0.01

Top 10 Places Sorted by Percent

Based on all places, regardless of population

Place	Number	%
Buffalo (village) Sangamon County	4	0.81
Cave-In-Rock (village) Hardin County	1	0.29
Lyndon (village) Whiteside County	1	0.18
Carlinville (city) Macoupin County	4	0.07
Lyons (village) Cook County	6	0.06
Antioch (village) Lake County	5	0.06
South Beloit (city) Winnebago County	3	0.06
Channel Lake (cdp) Lake County	1	0.06
Hampton (village) Rock Island County	1	0.06
Barrington (village) Cook County	5	0.05

Top 10 Places Sorted by Percent

Based on places with populations of 10,000 or more

Place	Number	%
Lyons (village) Cook County	6	0.06
Barrington (village) Cook County	5	0.05
Franklin Park (village) Cook County	5	0.03
Cary (village) McHenry County	4	0.03
Schiller Park (village) Cook County	4	0.03
Rock Island (city) Rock Island County	7	0.02
Bradley (village) Kankakee County	3	0.02
Cahokia (village) Saint Clair County	3	0.02
Chicago Ridge (village) Cook County	3	0.02
Crestwood (village) Cook County	2	0.02

American Indian: Navajo

Top 10 Places Sorted by Number

Based on all places, regardless of population

Place	Number	%
Chicago (city) Cook County	245	0.01
Rockford (city) Winnebago County	21	0.01
North Chicago (city) Lake County	20	0.06
Aurora (city) Kane County	20	0.01
Boulder Hill (cdp) Kendall County	11	0.13
Carpentersville (village) Kane County	10	0.03
Bridgeview (village) Cook County	9	0.06
Zion (city) Lake County	9	0.04
Schaumburg (village) Cook County	9	0.01
Park Forest (village) Cook County	8	0.03

Top 10 Places Sorted by Percent

Based on all places, regardless of population

Place	Number	%
Galatia (village) Saline County	6	0.59
Redmon (village) Edgar County	1	0.50
Gulf Port (village) Henderson County	1	0.48
White City (village) Macoupin County	1	0.45

Notes: (cdp) census designated place; Refer to the User's Guide in the front of the book for more detailed information.

Place	Number	%
West City (village) Franklin County	3	0.42
Raleigh (village) Saline County	1	0.30
Blue Mound (village) Macon County	2	0.18
Andover (village) Henry County	1	0.17
Stone Park (village) Cook County	7	0.14
Hillsboro (city) Montgomery County	6	0.14

Top 10 Places Sorted by Percent

Based on places with populations of 10,000 or more

Place	Number	%
North Chicago (city) Lake County	20	0.06
Bridgeview (village) Cook County	9	0.06
Zion (city) Lake County	9	0.04
Godfrey (village) Madison County	7	0.04
Carpentersville (village) Kane County	10	0.03
Park Forest (village) Cook County	8	0.03
Homewood (village) Cook County	5	0.03
Crest Hill (city) Will County	4	0.03
Frankfort (village) Will County	3	0.03
Palos Heights (city) Cook County	3	0.03

American Indian: Osage

Top 10 Places Sorted by Number

Based on all places, regardless of population

Place	Number	%
Chicago (city) Cook County	20	0.00
Lombard (village) Du Page County	7	0.02
Midlothian (village) Cook County	4	0.03
Rockford (city) Winnebago County	4	0.00
Itasca (village) Du Page County	3	0.04
Swansea (village) Saint Clair County	3	0.03
Deerfield (village) Lake County	3	0.02
Granite City (city) Madison County	3	0.01
Machesney Park (village) Winnebago County	3	0.01
Aurora (city) Kane County	3	0.00

Top 10 Places Sorted by Percent

Based on all places, regardless of population

Place	Number	%
Media (village) Henderson County	1	0.77
East Cape Girardeau (village) Alexander County	2	0.46
Dunfermline (village) Fulton County	1	0.38
Sawyerville (village) Macoupin County	1	0.34
Mounds (city) Pulaski County	2	0.18
Roseville (village) Warren County	1	0.09
Minier (village) Tazewell County	1	0.08
Poplar Grove (village) Boone County	1	0.07
Grayville (city) White County	1	0.06
Teutopolis (village) Effingham County	1	0.06

Top 10 Places Sorted by Percent

Based on places with populations of 10,000 or more

Place	Number	%
Midlothian (village) Cook County	4	0.03
Swansea (village) Saint Clair County	3	0.03
Lombard (village) Du Page County	7	0.02
Deerfield (village) Lake County	3	0.02
Worth (village) Cook County	2	0.02
Granite City (city) Madison County	3	0.01
Machesney Park (village) Winnebago County	3	0.01
Charleston (city) Coles County	2	0.01
Collinsville (city) Madison County	2	0.01
Mattoon (city) Coles County	2	0.01

American Indian: Ottawa

Top 10 Places Sorted by Number

Based on all places, regardless of population

Place	Number	%
Chicago (city) Cook County	40	0.00
Bloomingdale (village) Du Page County	5	0.02
Round Lake Beach (village) Lake County	5	0.02
Rockford (city) Winnebago County	5	0.00
Lemont (village) Cook County	4	0.03
Schaumburg (village) Cook County	4	0.01
Aurora (city) Kane County	4	0.00
Cicero (town) Cook County	4	0.00
Elburn (village) Kane County	3	0.11
Westchester (village) Cook County	3	0.02

Top 10 Places Sorted by Percent

Based on all places, regardless of population

Place	Number	%
Livingston (village) Madison County	1	0.12
Elburn (village) Kane County	3	0.11
Brimfield (village) Peoria County	1	0.11
Crainville (village) Williamson County	1	0.10
Oakwood Hills (village) McHenry County	2	0.09
Diamond (village) Grundy County	1	0.07
Lake Catherine (cdp) Lake County	1	0.07
Fisher (village) Champaign County	1	0.06
Elmwood (city) Peoria County	1	0.05
South Beloit (city) Winnebago County	2	0.04

Top 10 Places Sorted by Percent

Based on places with populations of 10,000 or more

Place	Number	%
Lemont (village) Cook County	4	0.03
Bloomingdale (village) Du Page County	5	0.02
Round Lake Beach (village) Lake County	5	0.02
Westchester (village) Cook County	3	0.02
Bradley (village) Kankakee County	2	0.02
Washington (city) Tazewell County	2	0.02
Schaumburg (village) Cook County	4	0.01
De Kalb (city) De Kalb County	3	0.01
Orland Park (village) Cook County	3	0.01
Villa Park (village) Du Page County	3	0.01

American Indian: Paiute

Top 10 Places Sorted by Number

Based on all places, regardless of population

Place	Number	%
Chicago (city) Cook County	10	0.00
Rockford (city) Winnebago County	4	0.00
Decatur (city) Macon County	3	0.00
Burbank (city) Cook County	2	0.01
Energy (village) Williamson County	1	0.09
Toluca (city) Marshall County	1	0.07
Brookfield (village) Cook County	1	0.01
Cary (village) McHenry County	1	0.01
Mattoon (city) Coles County	1	0.01
Troy (city) Madison County	1	0.01

Top 10 Places Sorted by Percent

Based on all places, regardless of population

Place	Number	%
Energy (village) Williamson County	1	0.09
Toluca (city) Marshall County	1	0.07
Burbank (city) Cook County	2	0.01
Brookfield (village) Cook County	1	0.01
Cary (village) McHenry County	1	0.01
Mattoon (city) Coles County	1	0.01
Troy (city) Madison County	1	0.01
Chicago (city) Cook County	10	0.00
Rockford (city) Winnebago County	4	0.00
Decatur (city) Macon County	3	0.00

Top 10 Places Sorted by Percent

Based on places with populations of 10,000 or more

Place	Number	%
Burbank (city) Cook County	2	0.01
Brookfield (village) Cook County	1	0.01
Cary (village) McHenry County	1	0.01
Mattoon (city) Coles County	1	0.01
Chicago (city) Cook County	10	0.00
Rockford (city) Winnebago County	4	0.00
Decatur (city) Macon County	3	0.00
Champaign (city) Champaign County	1	0.00
Des Plaines (city) Cook County	1	0.00
Mundelein (village) Lake County	1	0.00

American Indian: Pima

Top 10 Places Sorted by Number

Based on all places, regardless of population

Place	Number	%
Chicago (city) Cook County	21	0.00
Carpentersville (village) Kane County	6	0.02
Lake in the Hills (village) McHenry County	5	0.02
Glen Ellyn (village) Du Page County	4	0.01
Peoria (city) Peoria County	3	0.00
West Frankfort (city) Franklin County	2	0.02
Freeport (city) Stephenson County	2	0.01
McHenry (city) McHenry County	2	0.01
Berwyn (city) Cook County	2	0.00
Des Plaines (city) Cook County	2	0.00

Top 10 Places Sorted by Percent

Based on all places, regardless of population

Place	Number	%
Middletown (village) Logan County	1	0.23
Carpentersville (village) Kane County	6	0.02
Lake in the Hills (village) McHenry County	5	0.02
West Frankfort (city) Franklin County	2	0.02
Park City (city) Lake County	1	0.02
Spring Valley (city) Bureau County	1	0.02
Glen Ellyn (village) Du Page County	4	0.01
Freeport (city) Stephenson County	2	0.01
McHenry (city) McHenry County	2	0.01
Pontiac (city) Livingston County	1	0.01

Top 10 Places Sorted by Percent

Based on places with populations of 10,000 or more

Place	Number	%
Carpentersville (village) Kane County	6	0.02
Lake in the Hills (village) McHenry County	5	0.02
Glen Ellyn (village) Du Page County	4	0.01
Freeport (city) Stephenson County	2	0.01
McHenry (city) McHenry County	2	0.01
Pontiac (city) Livingston County	1	0.01
Chicago (city) Cook County	21	0.00
Peoria (city) Peoria County	3	0.00
Berwyn (city) Cook County	2	0.00
Des Plaines (city) Cook County	2	0.00

American Indian: Potawatomi

Top 10 Places Sorted by Number

Based on all places, regardless of population

Place	Number	%
Chicago (city) Cook County	105	0.00
Bloomington (city) McLean County	20	0.03
Elgin (city) Kane County	12	0.01
Bolingbrook (village) Will County	11	0.02
Woodstock (city) McHenry County	7	0.03
South Elgin (village) Kane County	6	0.04
Rock Island (city) Rock Island County	6	0.02
Belleville (city) Saint Clair County	6	0.01
Chillicothe (city) Peoria County	5	0.08
Lindenhurst (village) Lake County	5	0.04

Top 10 Places Sorted by Percent

Based on all places, regardless of population

Place	Number	%
Kappa (village) Woodford County	2	1.18
Yale (village) Jasper County	1	1.03
Maquon (village) Knox County	2	0.63
Papineau (village) Iroquois County	1	0.51

Notes: (cdp) census designated place; Refer to the User's Guide in the front of the book for more detailed information.

Place	Number	%
Sherrard (village) Mercer County	3	0.43
Okawville (village) Washington County	2	0.15
Thornton (village) Cook County	3	0.12
Crainville (village) Williamson County	1	0.10
Chebanse (village) Iroquois County	1	0.09
Chillicothe (city) Peoria County	5	0.08

Top 10 Places Sorted by Percent
Based on places with populations of 10,000 or more

Place	Number	%
South Elgin (village) Kane County	6	0.04
Lindenhurst (village) Lake County	5	0.04
Bloomington (city) McLean County	20	0.03
Woodstock (city) McHenry County	7	0.03
Northlake (city) Cook County	3	0.03
Bolingbrook (village) Will County	11	0.02
Rock Island (city) Rock Island County	6	0.02
East Peoria (city) Tazewell County	5	0.02
Kankakee (city) Kankakee County	5	0.02
Charleston (city) Coles County	4	0.02

American Indian: Pueblo

Top 10 Places Sorted by Number
Based on all places, regardless of population

Place	Number	%
Chicago (city) Cook County	103	0.00
Hazel Crest (village) Cook County	7	0.05
Lockport (city) Will County	7	0.05
Cicero (town) Cook County	7	0.01
Godfrey (village) Madison County	5	0.03
Lisle (village) Du Page County	5	0.02
Machesney Park (village) Winnebago County	5	0.02
Hoffman Estates (village) Cook County	5	0.01
Wheaton (city) Du Page County	5	0.01
Shawneetown (city) Gallatin County	4	0.28

Top 10 Places Sorted by Percent
Based on all places, regardless of population

Place	Number	%
Rock Island Arsenal (cdp) Rock Island County	2	1.38
Dowell (village) Jackson County	2	0.45
Wyanet (village) Bureau County	3	0.29
Shawneetown (city) Gallatin County	4	0.28
Hillsdale (village) Rock Island County	1	0.17
New Athens (village) Saint Clair County	3	0.15
Millstadt (village) Saint Clair County	4	0.14
Lena (village) Stephenson County	3	0.10
Posen (village) Cook County	4	0.08
Ford Heights (village) Cook County	2	0.06

Top 10 Places Sorted by Percent
Based on places with populations of 10,000 or more

Place	Number	%
Hazel Crest (village) Cook County	7	0.05
Lockport (city) Will County	7	0.05
Sauk Village (village) Cook County	4	0.04
Godfrey (village) Madison County	5	0.03
River Grove (village) Cook County	3	0.03
Lisle (village) Du Page County	5	0.02
Machesney Park (village) Winnebago County	5	0.02
Herrin (city) Williamson County	2	0.02
Cicero (town) Cook County	7	0.01
Hoffman Estates (village) Cook County	5	0.01

American Indian: Puget Sound Salish

Top 10 Places Sorted by Number
Based on all places, regardless of population

Place	Number	%
Peoria (city) Peoria County	4	0.00
Dupo (village) Saint Clair County	3	0.08
Granite City (city) Madison County	3	0.01
Chicago (city) Cook County	3	0.00
Shiloh (village) Saint Clair County	2	0.03
North Chicago (city) Lake County	2	0.01
Evanston (city) Cook County	2	0.00
Warrenville (city) Du Page County	1	0.01
De Kalb (city) De Kalb County	1	0.00
Springfield (city) Sangamon County	1	0.00

Top 10 Places Sorted by Percent
Based on all places, regardless of population

Place	Number	%
Dupo (village) Saint Clair County	3	0.08
Shiloh (village) Saint Clair County	2	0.03
Granite City (city) Madison County	3	0.01
North Chicago (city) Lake County	2	0.01
Warrenville (city) Du Page County	1	0.01
Peoria (city) Peoria County	4	0.00
Chicago (city) Cook County	3	0.00
Evanston (city) Cook County	2	0.00
De Kalb (city) De Kalb County	1	0.00
Springfield (city) Sangamon County	1	0.00

Top 10 Places Sorted by Percent
Based on places with populations of 10,000 or more

Place	Number	%
Granite City (city) Madison County	3	0.01
North Chicago (city) Lake County	2	0.01
Warrenville (city) Du Page County	1	0.01
Peoria (city) Peoria County	4	0.00
Chicago (city) Cook County	3	0.00
Evanston (city) Cook County	2	0.00
De Kalb (city) De Kalb County	1	0.00
Springfield (city) Sangamon County	1	0.00

American Indian: Seminole

Top 10 Places Sorted by Number
Based on all places, regardless of population

Place	Number	%
Chicago (city) Cook County	81	0.00
Evanston (city) Cook County	12	0.02
Jacksonville (city) Morgan County	9	0.05
Rockford (city) Winnebago County	9	0.01
North Chicago (city) Lake County	6	0.02
Oak Park (village) Cook County	6	0.01
Springfield (city) Sangamon County	6	0.01
Mascoutah (city) Saint Clair County	5	0.09
Forest Park (village) Cook County	4	0.03
Round Lake Beach (village) Lake County	4	0.02

Top 10 Places Sorted by Percent
Based on all places, regardless of population

Place	Number	%
Franklin (village) Morgan County	2	0.34
De Land (village) Piatt County	1	0.21
Benld (city) Macoupin County	3	0.19
Princeville (village) Peoria County	3	0.19
Lovington (village) Moultrie County	2	0.16
Hopedale (village) Tazewell County	1	0.11
New Baden (village) Clinton County	3	0.10
Prophetstown (city) Whiteside County	2	0.10
Mascoutah (city) Saint Clair County	5	0.09
Gillespie (city) Macoupin County	3	0.09

Top 10 Places Sorted by Percent
Based on places with populations of 10,000 or more

Place	Number	%
Jacksonville (city) Morgan County	9	0.05
Forest Park (village) Cook County	4	0.03
Sauk Village (village) Cook County	3	0.03
Evanston (city) Cook County	12	0.02
North Chicago (city) Lake County	6	0.02
Round Lake Beach (village) Lake County	4	0.02
Matteson (village) Cook County	3	0.02
Rockford (city) Winnebago County	9	0.01
Oak Park (village) Cook County	6	0.01
Springfield (city) Sangamon County	6	0.01

American Indian: Shoshone

Top 10 Places Sorted by Number
Based on all places, regardless of population

Place	Number	%
Chicago (city) Cook County	15	0.00
Granite City (city) Madison County	7	0.02
Flossmoor (village) Cook County	6	0.06
Round Lake Beach (village) Lake County	4	0.02
Lockport (city) Will County	2	0.01
Rolling Meadows (city) Cook County	2	0.01
Saint Charles (city) Kane County	2	0.01
Berwyn (city) Cook County	2	0.00
Peoria (city) Peoria County	2	0.00
Milledgeville (village) Carroll County	1	0.10

Top 10 Places Sorted by Percent
Based on all places, regardless of population

Place	Number	%
Milledgeville (village) Carroll County	1	0.10
Rosiclare (city) Hardin County	1	0.08
Flossmoor (village) Cook County	6	0.06
Granite City (city) Madison County	7	0.02
Round Lake Beach (village) Lake County	4	0.02
Auburn (city) Sangamon County	1	0.02
Berkeley (village) Cook County	1	0.02
Lockport (city) Will County	2	0.01
Rolling Meadows (city) Cook County	2	0.01
Saint Charles (city) Kane County	2	0.01

Top 10 Places Sorted by Percent
Based on places with populations of 10,000 or more

Place	Number	%
Granite City (city) Madison County	7	0.02
Round Lake Beach (village) Lake County	4	0.02
Lockport (city) Will County	2	0.01
Rolling Meadows (city) Cook County	2	0.01
Saint Charles (city) Kane County	2	0.01
Bradley (village) Kankakee County	1	0.01
Bridgeview (village) Cook County	1	0.01
Dixon (city) Lee County	1	0.01
Streator (city) La Salle County	1	0.01
Westchester (village) Cook County	1	0.01

American Indian: Sioux

Top 10 Places Sorted by Number
Based on all places, regardless of population

Place	Number	%
Chicago (city) Cook County	439	0.02
Rockford (city) Winnebago County	41	0.03
Aurora (city) Kane County	37	0.03
Springfield (city) Sangamon County	33	0.03
Rock Island (city) Rock Island County	32	0.08
Peoria (city) Peoria County	27	0.02
North Chicago (city) Lake County	25	0.07
Moline (city) Rock Island County	22	0.05
Waukegan (city) Lake County	21	0.02
Cicero (town) Cook County	20	0.02

Top 10 Places Sorted by Percent
Based on all places, regardless of population

Place	Number	%
Ellsworth (village) McLean County	4	1.48
West City (village) Franklin County	8	1.12
Malden (village) Bureau County	3	0.87
Dongola (village) Union County	6	0.74
Nebo (village) Pike County	3	0.74
Bartelso (village) Clinton County	4	0.67

Notes: (cdp) census designated place; Refer to the User's Guide in the front of the book for more detailed information.

Place	Number	%
Bath (village) Mason County	2	0.65
Camargo (village) Douglas County	3	0.64
Mount Auburn (village) Christian County	3	0.58
West Point (village) Hancock County	1	0.51

Top 10 Places Sorted by Percent

Based on places with populations of 10,000 or more

Place	Number	%
Godfrey (village) Madison County	14	0.09
Rock Island (city) Rock Island County	32	0.08
North Chicago (city) Lake County	25	0.07
East Moline (city) Rock Island County	15	0.07
Beach Park (village) Lake County	6	0.06
Moline (city) Rock Island County	22	0.05
Belvidere (city) Boone County	11	0.05
Park Forest (village) Cook County	11	0.05
Dixon (city) Lee County	8	0.05
Sterling (city) Whiteside County	7	0.05

American Indian: Tohono O'Odham

Top 10 Places Sorted by Number

Based on all places, regardless of population

Place	Number	%
Chicago (city) Cook County	11	0.00
Mendota (city) La Salle County	4	0.06
Addison (village) Du Page County	4	0.01
East Dundee (village) Kane County	3	0.10
Flora (city) Clay County	2	0.04
McHenry (city) McHenry County	2	0.01
Rolling Meadows (city) Cook County	2	0.01
Des Plaines (city) Cook County	2	0.00
Peoria (city) Peoria County	2	0.00
Long Creek (village) Macon County	1	0.07

Top 10 Places Sorted by Percent

Based on all places, regardless of population

Place	Number	%
East Dundee (village) Kane County	3	0.10
Long Creek (village) Macon County	1	0.07
Mendota (city) La Salle County	4	0.06
Earlville (city) La Salle County	1	0.06
Flora (city) Clay County	2	0.04
Girard (city) Macoupin County	1	0.04
Addison (village) Du Page County	4	0.01
McHenry (city) McHenry County	2	0.01
Rolling Meadows (city) Cook County	2	0.01
Princeton (city) Bureau County	1	0.01

Top 10 Places Sorted by Percent

Based on places with populations of 10,000 or more

Place	Number	%
Addison (village) Du Page County	4	0.01
McHenry (city) McHenry County	2	0.01
Rolling Meadows (city) Cook County	2	0.01
Chicago (city) Cook County	11	0.00
Des Plaines (city) Cook County	2	0.00
Peoria (city) Peoria County	2	0.00
Carpentersville (village) Kane County	1	0.00
Elgin (city) Kane County	1	0.00
Elk Grove Village (village) Cook County	1	0.00
Lansing (village) Cook County	1	0.00

American Indian: Ute

Top 10 Places Sorted by Number

Based on all places, regardless of population

Place	Number	%
Chicago (city) Cook County	12	0.00
Hodgkins (village) Cook County	5	0.23
Hinsdale (village) Du Page County	4	0.02
Rockford (city) Winnebago County	4	0.00
Aurora (city) Kane County	3	0.00
Creve Coeur (village) Tazewell County	1	0.02
Hawthorn Woods (village) Lake County	1	0.02
Forest Park (village) Cook County	1	0.01
Alton (city) Madison County	1	0.00
Evergreen Park (village) Cook County	1	0.00

Top 10 Places Sorted by Percent

Based on all places, regardless of population

Place	Number	%
Hodgkins (village) Cook County	5	0.23
Hinsdale (village) Du Page County	4	0.02
Creve Coeur (village) Tazewell County	1	0.02
Hawthorn Woods (village) Lake County	1	0.02
Forest Park (village) Cook County	1	0.01
Chicago (city) Cook County	12	0.00
Rockford (city) Winnebago County	4	0.00
Aurora (city) Kane County	3	0.00
Alton (city) Madison County	1	0.00
Evergreen Park (village) Cook County	1	0.00

Top 10 Places Sorted by Percent

Based on places with populations of 10,000 or more

Place	Number	%
Hinsdale (village) Du Page County	4	0.02
Forest Park (village) Cook County	1	0.01
Chicago (city) Cook County	12	0.00
Rockford (city) Winnebago County	4	0.00
Aurora (city) Kane County	3	0.00
Alton (city) Madison County	1	0.00
Evergreen Park (village) Cook County	1	0.00
Kankakee (city) Kankakee County	1	0.00
Lisle (village) Du Page County	1	0.00
Villa Park (village) Du Page County	1	0.00

American Indian: Yakama

Top 10 Places Sorted by Number

Based on all places, regardless of population

Place	Number	%
Chicago (city) Cook County	3	0.00
Carol Stream (village) Du Page County	2	0.00
Rockton (village) Winnebago County	1	0.02
Alton (city) Madison County	1	0.00
Aurora (city) Kane County	1	0.00
Evanston (city) Cook County	1	0.00
Niles (village) Cook County	1	0.00

Top 10 Places Sorted by Percent

Based on all places, regardless of population

Place	Number	%
Rockton (village) Winnebago County	1	0.02
Chicago (city) Cook County	3	0.00
Carol Stream (village) Du Page County	2	0.00
Alton (city) Madison County	1	0.00
Aurora (city) Kane County	1	0.00
Evanston (city) Cook County	1	0.00
Niles (village) Cook County	1	0.00

Top 10 Places Sorted by Percent

Based on places with populations of 10,000 or more

Place	Number	%
Chicago (city) Cook County	3	0.00
Carol Stream (village) Du Page County	2	0.00
Alton (city) Madison County	1	0.00
Aurora (city) Kane County	1	0.00
Evanston (city) Cook County	1	0.00
Niles (village) Cook County	1	0.00

American Indian: Yaqui

Top 10 Places Sorted by Number

Based on all places, regardless of population

Place	Number	%
Chicago (city) Cook County	14	0.00
Hoopeston (city) Vermilion County	5	0.08
Willowbrook (village) Du Page County	5	0.06
Fairview Heights (city) Saint Clair County	4	0.03
Warrenville (city) Du Page County	4	0.03
Oak Forest (city) Cook County	4	0.01
Lake of the Woods (cdp) Champaign County	3	0.10
East Moline (city) Rock Island County	3	0.01
Lombard (village) Du Page County	3	0.01
North Chicago (city) Lake County	3	0.01

Top 10 Places Sorted by Percent

Based on all places, regardless of population

Place	Number	%
Lake of the Woods (cdp) Champaign County	3	0.10
Hoopeston (city) Vermilion County	5	0.08
Central City (village) Marion County	1	0.07
Willowbrook (village) Du Page County	5	0.06
Rosewood Heights (cdp) Madison County	2	0.05
Fairview Heights (city) Saint Clair County	4	0.03
Warrenville (city) Du Page County	4	0.03
Crete (village) Will County	2	0.03
Riverside (village) Cook County	2	0.02
Caseyville (village) Saint Clair County	1	0.02

Top 10 Places Sorted by Percent

Based on places with populations of 10,000 or more

Place	Number	%
Fairview Heights (city) Saint Clair County	4	0.03
Warrenville (city) Du Page County	4	0.03
Oak Forest (city) Cook County	4	0.01
East Moline (city) Rock Island County	3	0.01
Lombard (village) Du Page County	3	0.01
North Chicago (city) Lake County	3	0.01
Blue Island (city) Cook County	2	0.01
Cary (village) McHenry County	1	0.01
Morris (city) Grundy County	1	0.01
Richton Park (village) Cook County	1	0.01

American Indian: Yuman

Top 10 Places Sorted by Number

Based on all places, regardless of population

Place	Number	%
Chicago (city) Cook County	7	0.00
North Chicago (city) Lake County	2	0.01
Glenview (village) Cook County	2	0.00
Cortland (town) De Kalb County	1	0.05
Flora (city) Clay County	1	0.02
Chicago Ridge (village) Cook County	1	0.01
Mattoon (city) Coles County	1	0.01
Des Plaines (city) Cook County	1	0.00
Urbana (city) Champaign County	1	0.00

Top 10 Places Sorted by Percent

Based on all places, regardless of population

Place	Number	%
Cortland (town) De Kalb County	1	0.05
Flora (city) Clay County	1	0.02
North Chicago (city) Lake County	2	0.01
Chicago Ridge (village) Cook County	1	0.01
Mattoon (city) Coles County	1	0.01
Chicago (city) Cook County	7	0.00
Glenview (village) Cook County	2	0.00
Des Plaines (city) Cook County	1	0.00
Urbana (city) Champaign County	1	0.00

Top 10 Places Sorted by Percent
Based on places with populations of 10,000 or more

Place	Number	%
North Chicago (city) Lake County	2	0.01
Chicago Ridge (village) Cook County	1	0.01
Mattoon (city) Coles County	1	0.01
Chicago (city) Cook County	7	0.00
Glenview (village) Cook County	2	0.00
Des Plaines (city) Cook County	1	0.00
Urbana (city) Champaign County	1	0.00

American Indian: All other tribes

Top 10 Places Sorted by Number
Based on all places, regardless of population

Place	Number	%
Chicago (city) Cook County	612	0.02
Rockford (city) Winnebago County	40	0.03
North Chicago (city) Lake County	39	0.11
Joliet (city) Will County	36	0.03
Cicero (town) Cook County	31	0.04
Elgin (city) Kane County	31	0.03
Waukegan (city) Lake County	25	0.03
Springfield (city) Sangamon County	21	0.02
Aurora (city) Kane County	21	0.01
Romeoville (village) Will County	20	0.09

Top 10 Places Sorted by Percent
Based on all places, regardless of population

Place	Number	%
Union Hill (village) Kankakee County	1	1.52
Marietta (village) Fulton County	2	1.33
Williamson (village) Madison County	3	1.20
Kane (village) Greene County	5	1.09
Middletown (village) Logan County	4	0.92
Thebes (village) Alexander County	4	0.84
Fillmore (village) Montgomery County	3	0.83
Spaulding (village) Sangamon County	4	0.72
Magnolia (village) Putnam County	2	0.72
Loraine (village) Adams County	2	0.55

Top 10 Places Sorted by Percent
Based on places with populations of 10,000 or more

Place	Number	%
North Chicago (city) Lake County	39	0.11
Romeoville (village) Will County	20	0.09
Zion (city) Lake County	20	0.09
Westmont (village) Du Page County	19	0.08
Kankakee (city) Kankakee County	18	0.07
La Grange (village) Cook County	11	0.07
Lyons (village) Cook County	7	0.07
Sauk Village (village) Cook County	7	0.07
Roselle (village) Du Page County	14	0.06
Brookfield (village) Cook County	11	0.06

American Indian tribes, not specified

Top 10 Places Sorted by Number
Based on all places, regardless of population

Place	Number	%
Chicago (city) Cook County	1,394	0.05
Aurora (city) Kane County	81	0.06
Rockford (city) Winnebago County	75	0.05
Cicero (town) Cook County	65	0.08
Joliet (city) Will County	50	0.05
Peoria (city) Peoria County	46	0.04
Springfield (city) Sangamon County	41	0.04
Waukegan (city) Lake County	38	0.04
Champaign (city) Champaign County	35	0.05
De Kalb (city) De Kalb County	30	0.08

Top 10 Places Sorted by Percent
Based on all places, regardless of population

Place	Number	%
Belknap (village) Johnson County	3	2.26
Oakdale (village) Washington County	3	1.41
Medora (village) Macoupin County	6	1.20
Smithboro (village) Bond County	2	1.00
East Brooklyn (village) Grundy County	1	0.81
Bonnie (village) Jefferson County	3	0.71
Tennessee (village) McDonough County	1	0.69
Coleta (village) Whiteside County	1	0.65
Vernon (village) Marion County	1	0.56
Roberts (village) Ford County	2	0.52

Top 10 Places Sorted by Percent
Based on places with populations of 10,000 or more

Place	Number	%
Centralia (city) Marion County	17	0.12
Blue Island (city) Cook County	25	0.11
Herrin (city) Williamson County	11	0.10
Edwardsville (city) Madison County	20	0.09
Zion (city) Lake County	20	0.09
Wood Dale (city) Du Page County	12	0.09
Cicero (town) Cook County	65	0.08
De Kalb (city) De Kalb County	30	0.08
Matteson (village) Cook County	10	0.08
Richton Park (village) Cook County	10	0.08

Arab

Top 10 Places Sorted by Number
Based on all places, regardless of population

Place	Number	%
Chicago (city) Cook County	14,971	0.52
Oak Lawn (village) Cook County	2,142	3.87
Peoria (city) Peoria County	1,576	1.40
Burbank (city) Cook County	1,273	4.58
Bridgeview (village) Cook County	1,104	7.18
Chicago Ridge (village) Cook County	963	6.94
Orland Park (village) Cook County	960	1.88
Naperville (city) Du Page County	948	0.74
Hickory Hills (city) Cook County	763	5.48
Skokie (village) Cook County	592	0.93

Top 10 Places Sorted by Percent
Based on all places, regardless of population

Place	Number	%
Bridgeview (village) Cook County	1,104	7.18
Chicago Ridge (village) Cook County	963	6.94
Hickory Hills (city) Cook County	763	5.48
Burbank (city) Cook County	1,273	4.58
Oak Brook (village) Du Page County	358	4.24
Justice (village) Cook County	507	4.19
Oak Lawn (village) Cook County	2,142	3.87
Palos Hills (city) Cook County	578	3.26
Hanna City (village) Peoria County	32	3.18
Orland Hills (village) Cook County	179	2.61

Top 10 Places Sorted by Percent
Based on places with populations of 10,000 or more

Place	Number	%
Bridgeview (village) Cook County	1,104	7.18
Chicago Ridge (village) Cook County	963	6.94
Hickory Hills (city) Cook County	763	5.48
Burbank (city) Cook County	1,273	4.58
Justice (village) Cook County	507	4.19
Oak Lawn (village) Cook County	2,142	3.87
Palos Hills (city) Cook County	578	3.26
Worth (village) Cook County	288	2.58
Schiller Park (village) Cook County	234	1.99
Alsip (village) Cook County	388	1.95

Arab: Arab/Arabic

Top 10 Places Sorted by Number
Based on all places, regardless of population

Place	Number	%
Chicago (city) Cook County	5,458	0.19
Oak Lawn (village) Cook County	1,070	1.93
Burbank (city) Cook County	788	2.83
Bridgeview (village) Cook County	743	4.83
Chicago Ridge (village) Cook County	539	3.88
Orland Park (village) Cook County	401	0.78
Hickory Hills (city) Cook County	381	2.73
Alsip (village) Cook County	338	1.70
Tinley Park (village) Cook County	324	0.67
Justice (village) Cook County	290	2.40

Top 10 Places Sorted by Percent
Based on all places, regardless of population

Place	Number	%
Bridgeview (village) Cook County	743	4.83
Chicago Ridge (village) Cook County	539	3.88
Burbank (city) Cook County	788	2.83
Hickory Hills (city) Cook County	381	2.73
Justice (village) Cook County	290	2.40
Orland Hills (village) Cook County	140	2.04
Davis Junction (village) Ogle County	9	1.98
Oak Lawn (village) Cook County	1,070	1.93
Worth (village) Cook County	201	1.80
Alsip (village) Cook County	338	1.70

Top 10 Places Sorted by Percent
Based on places with populations of 10,000 or more

Place	Number	%
Bridgeview (village) Cook County	743	4.83
Chicago Ridge (village) Cook County	539	3.88
Burbank (city) Cook County	788	2.83
Hickory Hills (city) Cook County	381	2.73
Justice (village) Cook County	290	2.40
Oak Lawn (village) Cook County	1,070	1.93
Worth (village) Cook County	201	1.80
Alsip (village) Cook County	338	1.70
Palos Hills (city) Cook County	253	1.42
Orland Park (village) Cook County	401	0.78

Arab: Egyptian

Top 10 Places Sorted by Number
Based on all places, regardless of population

Place	Number	%
Chicago (city) Cook County	556	0.02
Naperville (city) Du Page County	147	0.11
Downers Grove (village) Du Page County	143	0.29
Urbana (city) Champaign County	111	0.31
Oak Brook (village) Du Page County	109	1.29
Aurora (city) Kane County	106	0.07
Evanston (city) Cook County	90	0.12
Arlington Heights (village) Cook County	73	0.10
Palos Hills (city) Cook County	68	0.38
Burr Ridge (village) Du Page County	64	0.62

Top 10 Places Sorted by Percent
Based on all places, regardless of population

Place	Number	%
Oak Brook (village) Du Page County	109	1.29
Willow Springs (village) Cook County	48	0.97
Roscoe (village) Winnebago County	48	0.76
Savoy (village) Champaign County	28	0.65
Manhattan (village) Will County	22	0.65
De Land (village) Piatt County	3	0.63
Burr Ridge (village) Du Page County	64	0.62
Willowbrook (village) Du Page County	56	0.62
Lena (village) Stephenson County	17	0.59
Berkeley (village) Cook County	26	0.50

Notes: (cdp) census designated place; Refer to the User's Guide in the front of the book for more detailed information.

Top 10 Places Sorted by Percent

Based on places with populations of 10,000 or more

Place	Number	%
Burr Ridge (village) Du Page County	64	0.62
River Forest (village) Cook County	52	0.45
Justice (village) Cook County	50	0.41
Palos Hills (city) Cook County	68	0.38
Urbana (city) Champaign County	111	0.31
Norridge (village) Cook County	46	0.31
Downers Grove (village) Du Page County	143	0.29
Bridgeview (village) Cook County	45	0.29
Lisle (village) Du Page County	52	0.25
Hickory Hills (city) Cook County	29	0.21

Arab: Iraqi

Top 10 Places Sorted by Number

Based on all places, regardless of population

Place	Number	%
Chicago (city) Cook County	931	0.03
Skokie (village) Cook County	244	0.39
Springfield (city) Sangamon County	68	0.06
Des Plaines (city) Cook County	58	0.10
Niles (village) Cook County	52	0.17
Arlington Heights (village) Cook County	44	0.06
Morton Grove (village) Cook County	41	0.18
Romeoville (village) Will County	39	0.18
Streamwood (village) Cook County	30	0.08
Naperville (city) Du Page County	27	0.02

Top 10 Places Sorted by Percent

Based on all places, regardless of population

Place	Number	%
Lee (village) Lee County	6	2.21
Skokie (village) Cook County	244	0.39
East Dundee (village) Kane County	6	0.21
Morton Grove (village) Cook County	41	0.18
Romeoville (village) Will County	39	0.18
Niles (village) Cook County	52	0.17
Oglesby (city) La Salle County	6	0.17
Riverdale (village) Cook County	21	0.14
Des Plaines (city) Cook County	58	0.10
Stockton (village) Jo Daviess County	2	0.10

Top 10 Places Sorted by Percent

Based on places with populations of 10,000 or more

Place	Number	%
Skokie (village) Cook County	244	0.39
Morton Grove (village) Cook County	41	0.18
Romeoville (village) Will County	39	0.18
Niles (village) Cook County	52	0.17
Riverdale (village) Cook County	21	0.14
Des Plaines (city) Cook County	58	0.10
Libertyville (village) Lake County	18	0.09
Streamwood (village) Cook County	30	0.08
Springfield (city) Sangamon County	68	0.06
Arlington Heights (village) Cook County	44	0.06

Arab: Jordanian

Top 10 Places Sorted by Number

Based on all places, regardless of population

Place	Number	%
Chicago (city) Cook County	1,078	0.04
Oak Lawn (village) Cook County	194	0.35
Chicago Ridge (village) Cook County	192	1.38
Morton Grove (village) Cook County	189	0.84
Oak Forest (city) Cook County	138	0.49
Des Plaines (city) Cook County	104	0.18
Palos Hills (city) Cook County	102	0.57
Burbank (city) Cook County	96	0.35
Naperville (city) Du Page County	91	0.07
Niles (village) Cook County	89	0.30

Top 10 Places Sorted by Percent

Based on all places, regardless of population

Place	Number	%
Chicago Ridge (village) Cook County	192	1.38
Savanna (city) Carroll County	31	0.88
Morton Grove (village) Cook County	189	0.84
Hickory Hills (city) Cook County	82	0.59
Odell (village) Livingston County	6	0.59
Palos Hills (city) Cook County	102	0.57
Lincolnshire (village) Lake County	31	0.50
Oak Forest (city) Cook County	138	0.49
Bridgeview (village) Cook County	65	0.42
Oak Lawn (village) Cook County	194	0.35

Top 10 Places Sorted by Percent

Based on places with populations of 10,000 or more

Place	Number	%
Chicago Ridge (village) Cook County	192	1.38
Morton Grove (village) Cook County	189	0.84
Hickory Hills (city) Cook County	82	0.59
Palos Hills (city) Cook County	102	0.57
Oak Forest (city) Cook County	138	0.49
Bridgeview (village) Cook County	65	0.42
Oak Lawn (village) Cook County	194	0.35
Burbank (city) Cook County	96	0.35
Niles (village) Cook County	89	0.30
Schiller Park (village) Cook County	33	0.28

Arab: Lebanese

Top 10 Places Sorted by Number

Based on all places, regardless of population

Place	Number	%
Chicago (city) Cook County	2,027	0.07
Peoria (city) Peoria County	1,300	1.15
Naperville (city) Du Page County	374	0.29
East Peoria (city) Tazewell County	187	0.82
Aurora (city) Kane County	169	0.12
Schaumburg (village) Cook County	160	0.21
Wheaton (city) Du Page County	135	0.24
Springfield (city) Sangamon County	115	0.10
Evanston (city) Cook County	107	0.14
Normal (town) McLean County	95	0.21

Top 10 Places Sorted by Percent

Based on all places, regardless of population

Place	Number	%
Hanna City (village) Peoria County	32	3.18
Magnolia (village) Putnam County	7	2.19
Spring Bay (village) Woodford County	7	1.53
Rome (cdp) Peoria County	24	1.38
Yates City (village) Knox County	10	1.38
Mapleton (village) Peoria County	3	1.33
Peoria (city) Peoria County	1,300	1.15
North Riverside (village) Cook County	73	1.08
Oakbrook Terrace (city) Du Page County	24	1.00
West Peoria (city) Peoria County	47	0.98

Top 10 Places Sorted by Percent

Based on places with populations of 10,000 or more

Place	Number	%
Peoria (city) Peoria County	1,300	1.15
East Peoria (city) Tazewell County	187	0.82
Streator (city) La Salle County	78	0.55
Warrenville (city) Du Page County	72	0.55
River Forest (village) Cook County	60	0.52
Western Springs (village) Cook County	57	0.45
Plainfield (village) Will County	51	0.39
Villa Park (village) Du Page County	82	0.37
Morris (city) Grundy County	42	0.35
Westmont (village) Du Page County	78	0.32

Arab: Moroccan

Top 10 Places Sorted by Number

Based on all places, regardless of population

Place	Number	%
Chicago (city) Cook County	733	0.03
Skokie (village) Cook County	67	0.11
Lisle (village) Du Page County	60	0.28
Oak Lawn (village) Cook County	50	0.09
Berwyn (city) Cook County	45	0.08
Aurora (city) Kane County	27	0.02
Carol Stream (village) Du Page County	26	0.07
Buffalo Grove (village) Lake County	25	0.06
De Kalb (city) De Kalb County	24	0.06
Rock Island (city) Rock Island County	24	0.06

Top 10 Places Sorted by Percent

Based on all places, regardless of population

Place	Number	%
Lisle (village) Du Page County	60	0.28
Skokie (village) Cook County	67	0.11
River Grove (village) Cook County	11	0.10
Oak Lawn (village) Cook County	50	0.09
Berwyn (city) Cook County	45	0.08
Carol Stream (village) Du Page County	26	0.07
Glendale Heights (village) Du Page County	22	0.07
Highland Park (city) Lake County	21	0.07
Buffalo Grove (village) Lake County	25	0.06
De Kalb (city) De Kalb County	24	0.06

Top 10 Places Sorted by Percent

Based on places with populations of 10,000 or more

Place	Number	%
Lisle (village) Du Page County	60	0.28
Skokie (village) Cook County	67	0.11
River Grove (village) Cook County	11	0.10
Oak Lawn (village) Cook County	50	0.09
Berwyn (city) Cook County	45	0.08
Carol Stream (village) Du Page County	26	0.07
Glendale Heights (village) Du Page County	22	0.07
Highland Park (city) Lake County	21	0.07
Buffalo Grove (village) Lake County	25	0.06
De Kalb (city) De Kalb County	24	0.06

Arab: Palestinian

Top 10 Places Sorted by Number

Based on all places, regardless of population

Place	Number	%
Chicago (city) Cook County	2,052	0.07
Oak Lawn (village) Cook County	577	1.04
Orland Park (village) Cook County	394	0.77
Burbank (city) Cook County	311	1.12
Hickory Hills (city) Cook County	203	1.46
Chicago Ridge (village) Cook County	183	1.32
Palos Hills (city) Cook County	155	0.87
Bridgeview (village) Cook County	141	0.92
Goodings Grove (cdp) Will County	111	0.65
Summit (village) Cook County	106	1.00

Top 10 Places Sorted by Percent

Based on all places, regardless of population

Place	Number	%
Dunlap (village) Peoria County	19	2.11
Hickory Hills (city) Cook County	203	1.46
Chicago Ridge (village) Cook County	183	1.32
Burbank (city) Cook County	311	1.12
Oak Lawn (village) Cook County	577	1.04
Long Grove (village) Lake County	68	1.03
Summit (village) Cook County	106	1.00
Bridgeview (village) Cook County	141	0.92
Palos Hills (city) Cook County	155	0.87
Justice (village) Cook County	94	0.78

Notes: (cdp) census designated place; Refer to the User's Guide in the front of the book for more detailed information.

Top 10 Places Sorted by Percent
Based on places with populations of 10,000 or more

Place	Number	%
Hickory Hills (city) Cook County	203	1.46
Chicago Ridge (village) Cook County	183	1.32
Burbank (city) Cook County	311	1.12
Oak Lawn (village) Cook County	577	1.04
Summit (village) Cook County	106	1.00
Bridgeview (village) Cook County	141	0.92
Palos Hills (city) Cook County	155	0.87
Justice (village) Cook County	94	0.78
Orland Park (village) Cook County	394	0.77
Goodings Grove (cdp) Will County	111	0.65

Arab: Syrian

Top 10 Places Sorted by Number
Based on all places, regardless of population

Place	Number	%
Chicago (city) Cook County	1,124	0.04
Oak Lawn (village) Cook County	114	0.21
Peoria (city) Peoria County	104	0.09
Schaumburg (village) Cook County	92	0.12
Bridgeview (village) Cook County	91	0.59
Elgin (city) Kane County	89	0.09
Rockford (city) Winnebago County	86	0.06
Naperville (city) Du Page County	78	0.06
Oak Brook (village) Du Page County	74	0.88
Normal (town) McLean County	69	0.15

Top 10 Places Sorted by Percent
Based on all places, regardless of population

Place	Number	%
West Dundee (village) Kane County	50	0.93
Oak Brook (village) Du Page County	74	0.88
Rosemont (village) Cook County	30	0.72
Cairo (city) Alexander County	26	0.71
Kampsville (village) Calhoun County	2	0.68
Westville (village) Vermilion County	20	0.62
Summerfield (village) Saint Clair County	3	0.61
Bridgeview (village) Cook County	91	0.59
Burr Ridge (village) Du Page County	57	0.55
Willowbrook (village) Du Page County	45	0.50

Top 10 Places Sorted by Percent
Based on places with populations of 10,000 or more

Place	Number	%
Bridgeview (village) Cook County	91	0.59
Burr Ridge (village) Du Page County	57	0.55
Schiller Park (village) Cook County	35	0.30
Lake Forest (city) Lake County	51	0.25
Rolling Meadows (city) Cook County	58	0.24
Oak Lawn (village) Cook County	114	0.21
Algonquin (village) McHenry County	47	0.20
Northbrook (village) Cook County	60	0.18
Edwardsville (city) Madison County	37	0.18
Brookfield (village) Cook County	33	0.17

Arab: Other

Top 10 Places Sorted by Number
Based on all places, regardless of population

Place	Number	%
Chicago (city) Cook County	1,012	0.03
Bartlett (village) Du Page County	67	0.18
Schaumburg (village) Cook County	66	0.09
Carbondale (city) Jackson County	65	0.31
Justice (village) Cook County	60	0.50
Macomb (city) McDonough County	57	0.31
Oak Lawn (village) Cook County	45	0.08
Lyons (village) Cook County	44	0.43
Skokie (village) Cook County	44	0.07
Willowbrook (village) Du Page County	40	0.44

Top 10 Places Sorted by Percent
Based on all places, regardless of population

Place	Number	%
Tiskilwa (village) Bureau County	10	1.27
Standard (village) Putnam County	3	1.16
Lerna (village) Coles County	3	0.93
Justice (village) Cook County	60	0.50
Rome (cdp) Peoria County	8	0.46
Willowbrook (village) Du Page County	40	0.44
Lyons (village) Cook County	44	0.43
Grandwood Park (cdp) Lake County	17	0.38
Tilden (village) Randolph County	3	0.32
Carbondale (city) Jackson County	65	0.31

Top 10 Places Sorted by Percent
Based on places with populations of 10,000 or more

Place	Number	%
Justice (village) Cook County	60	0.50
Lyons (village) Cook County	44	0.43
Carbondale (city) Jackson County	65	0.31
Macomb (city) McDonough County	57	0.31
Bartlett (village) Du Page County	67	0.18
Hickory Hills (city) Cook County	25	0.18
Niles (village) Cook County	39	0.13
Chicago Ridge (village) Cook County	18	0.13
Bridgeview (village) Cook County	19	0.12
La Grange Park (village) Cook County	16	0.12

Armenian

Top 10 Places Sorted by Number
Based on all places, regardless of population

Place	Number	%
Chicago (city) Cook County	1,674	0.06
Skokie (village) Cook County	301	0.48
Waukegan (city) Lake County	252	0.29
Lake Forest (city) Lake County	234	1.17
Morton Grove (village) Cook County	169	0.75
Wheeling (village) Cook County	165	0.48
Northbrook (village) Cook County	159	0.48
Hoffman Estates (village) Cook County	137	0.27
Glenview (village) Cook County	136	0.33
Evanston (city) Cook County	136	0.18

Top 10 Places Sorted by Percent
Based on all places, regardless of population

Place	Number	%
Galatia (village) Saline County	36	3.44
Menominee (village) Jo Daviess County	8	3.31
Radom (village) Washington County	10	2.40
Kenilworth (village) Cook County	38	1.52
Trout Valley (village) McHenry County	7	1.18
Lake Forest (city) Lake County	234	1.17
Lakemoor (village) McHenry County	31	1.13
Lily Lake (village) Kane County	9	1.08
Willow Springs (village) Cook County	48	0.97
Enfield (village) White County	6	0.93

Top 10 Places Sorted by Percent
Based on places with populations of 10,000 or more

Place	Number	%
Lake Forest (city) Lake County	234	1.17
Lincolnwood (village) Cook County	98	0.79
Morton Grove (village) Cook County	169	0.75
River Forest (village) Cook County	57	0.49
Skokie (village) Cook County	301	0.48
Wheeling (village) Cook County	165	0.48
Northbrook (village) Cook County	159	0.48
Bloomingdale (village) Du Page County	98	0.45
Gurnee (village) Lake County	121	0.42
Lindenhurst (village) Lake County	50	0.40

Asian

Top 10 Places Sorted by Number
Based on all places, regardless of population

Place	Number	%
Chicago (city) Cook County	143,175	4.94
Skokie (village) Cook County	14,565	22.99
Naperville (city) Du Page County	13,377	10.42
Schaumburg (village) Cook County	11,373	15.09
Hoffman Estates (village) Cook County	8,046	16.26
Glendale Heights (village) Du Page County	6,764	21.29
Mount Prospect (village) Cook County	6,731	11.96
Urbana (city) Champaign County	5,661	15.55
Palatine (village) Cook County	5,439	8.31
Morton Grove (village) Cook County	5,345	23.81

Top 10 Places Sorted by Percent
Based on all places, regardless of population

Place	Number	%
Morton Grove (village) Cook County	5,345	23.81
Skokie (village) Cook County	14,565	22.99
Lincolnwood (village) Cook County	2,822	22.83
Oak Brook (village) Du Page County	1,881	21.62
Glendale Heights (village) Du Page County	6,764	21.29
Hoffman Estates (village) Cook County	8,046	16.26
South Barrington (village) Cook County	594	15.80
Urbana (city) Champaign County	5,661	15.55
Schaumburg (village) Cook County	11,373	15.09
Niles (village) Cook County	4,098	13.63

Top 10 Places Sorted by Percent
Based on places with populations of 10,000 or more

Place	Number	%
Morton Grove (village) Cook County	5,345	23.81
Skokie (village) Cook County	14,565	22.99
Lincolnwood (village) Cook County	2,822	22.83
Glendale Heights (village) Du Page County	6,764	21.29
Hoffman Estates (village) Cook County	8,046	16.26
Urbana (city) Champaign County	5,661	15.55
Schaumburg (village) Cook County	11,373	15.09
Niles (village) Cook County	4,098	13.63
Hanover Park (village) Cook County	4,991	13.04
Vernon Hills (village) Lake County	2,579	12.82

Asian: Bangladeshi

Top 10 Places Sorted by Number
Based on all places, regardless of population

Place	Number	%
Chicago (city) Cook County	376	0.01
Skokie (village) Cook County	32	0.05
Naperville (city) Du Page County	25	0.02
Springfield (city) Sangamon County	25	0.02
Bolingbrook (village) Will County	24	0.04
Palatine (village) Cook County	21	0.03
Carbondale (city) Jackson County	18	0.09
Mount Prospect (village) Cook County	15	0.03
Schaumburg (village) Cook County	13	0.02
O'Fallon (city) Saint Clair County	11	0.05

Top 10 Places Sorted by Percent
Based on all places, regardless of population

Place	Number	%
South Barrington (village) Cook County	7	0.19
Genoa (city) De Kalb County	5	0.12
Carbondale (city) Jackson County	18	0.09
Lake Villa (village) Lake County	5	0.09
Bridgeview (village) Cook County	9	0.06
Skokie (village) Cook County	32	0.05
O'Fallon (city) Saint Clair County	11	0.05
Carlinville (city) Macoupin County	3	0.05
Park City (city) Lake County	3	0.05
Bolingbrook (village) Will County	24	0.04

Notes: (cdp) census designated place; Refer to the User's Guide in the front of the book for more detailed information.

Top 10 Places Sorted by Percent
Based on places with populations of 10,000 or more

Place	Number	%
Carbondale (city) Jackson County	18	0.09
Bridgeview (village) Cook County	9	0.06
Skokie (village) Cook County	32	0.05
O'Fallon (city) Saint Clair County	11	0.05
Bolingbrook (village) Will County	24	0.04
Forest Park (village) Cook County	6	0.04
Lindenhurst (village) Lake County	5	0.04
Palatine (village) Cook County	21	0.03
Mount Prospect (village) Cook County	15	0.03
Roselle (village) Du Page County	8	0.03

Asian: Cambodian

Top 10 Places Sorted by Number
Based on all places, regardless of population

Place	Number	%
Chicago (city) Cook County	1,751	0.06
Joliet (city) Will County	95	0.09
Carol Stream (village) Du Page County	93	0.23
Glendale Heights (village) Du Page County	91	0.29
Mundelein (village) Lake County	83	0.27
Bolingbrook (village) Will County	75	0.13
Skokie (village) Cook County	73	0.12
Wheaton (city) Du Page County	70	0.13
Elgin (city) Kane County	69	0.07
Hanover Park (village) Cook County	68	0.18

Top 10 Places Sorted by Percent
Based on all places, regardless of population

Place	Number	%
Park City (city) Lake County	40	0.60
Cortland (town) De Kalb County	7	0.34
Lee (village) Lee County	1	0.32
Glendale Heights (village) Du Page County	91	0.29
Mundelein (village) Lake County	83	0.27
Warrenville (city) Du Page County	32	0.24
Carol Stream (village) Du Page County	93	0.23
Industry (village) McDonough County	1	0.19
Hanover Park (village) Cook County	68	0.18
Wheeling (village) Cook County	50	0.14

Top 10 Places Sorted by Percent
Based on places with populations of 10,000 or more

Place	Number	%
Glendale Heights (village) Du Page County	91	0.29
Mundelein (village) Lake County	83	0.27
Warrenville (city) Du Page County	32	0.24
Carol Stream (village) Du Page County	93	0.23
Hanover Park (village) Cook County	68	0.18
Wheeling (village) Cook County	50	0.14
Bolingbrook (village) Will County	75	0.13
Wheaton (city) Du Page County	70	0.13
Skokie (village) Cook County	73	0.12
Franklin Park (village) Cook County	21	0.11

Asian: Chinese, except Taiwanese

Top 10 Places Sorted by Number
Based on all places, regardless of population

Place	Number	%
Chicago (city) Cook County	33,701	1.16
Naperville (city) Du Page County	4,072	3.17
Urbana (city) Champaign County	2,034	5.59
Skokie (village) Cook County	1,702	2.69
Evanston (city) Cook County	1,464	1.97
Schaumburg (village) Cook County	1,403	1.86
Champaign (city) Champaign County	1,251	1.85
Hoffman Estates (village) Cook County	907	1.83
Palatine (village) Cook County	882	1.35
Arlington Heights (village) Cook County	818	1.08

Top 10 Places Sorted by Percent
Based on all places, regardless of population

Place	Number	%
Urbana (city) Champaign County	2,034	5.59
Ullin (village) Pulaski County	37	4.75
Oak Brook (village) Du Page County	316	3.63
Calhoun (village) Richland County	8	3.60
Vernon Hills (village) Lake County	649	3.23
Old Mill Creek (village) Lake County	8	3.19
Naperville (city) Du Page County	4,072	3.17
Lisle (village) Du Page County	645	3.05
South Barrington (village) Cook County	110	2.93
Westmont (village) Du Page County	710	2.89

Top 10 Places Sorted by Percent
Based on places with populations of 10,000 or more

Place	Number	%
Urbana (city) Champaign County	2,034	5.59
Vernon Hills (village) Lake County	649	3.23
Naperville (city) Du Page County	4,072	3.17
Lisle (village) Du Page County	645	3.05
Westmont (village) Du Page County	710	2.89
Skokie (village) Cook County	1,702	2.69
Wilmette (village) Cook County	734	2.65
Darien (city) Du Page County	530	2.32
Morton Grove (village) Cook County	511	2.28
Lincolnwood (village) Cook County	268	2.17

Asian: Filipino

Top 10 Places Sorted by Number
Based on all places, regardless of population

Place	Number	%
Chicago (city) Cook County	32,266	1.11
Skokie (village) Cook County	3,594	5.67
Waukegan (city) Lake County	2,008	2.28
Glendale Heights (village) Du Page County	1,926	6.06
Morton Grove (village) Cook County	1,569	6.99
Bolingbrook (village) Will County	1,529	2.71
Hanover Park (village) Cook County	1,274	3.33
Schaumburg (village) Cook County	1,196	1.59
Bartlett (village) Du Page County	1,149	3.13
Carol Stream (village) Du Page County	1,127	2.79

Top 10 Places Sorted by Percent
Based on all places, regardless of population

Place	Number	%
Morton Grove (village) Cook County	1,569	6.99
Glendale Heights (village) Du Page County	1,926	6.06
Skokie (village) Cook County	3,594	5.67
Strawn (village) Livingston County	5	4.81
Old Mill Creek (village) Lake County	12	4.78
Lincolnwood (village) Cook County	575	4.65
Darien (city) Du Page County	930	4.07
Park City (city) Lake County	229	3.45
Gurnee (village) Lake County	977	3.39
Hanover Park (village) Cook County	1,274	3.33

Top 10 Places Sorted by Percent
Based on places with populations of 10,000 or more

Place	Number	%
Morton Grove (village) Cook County	1,569	6.99
Glendale Heights (village) Du Page County	1,926	6.06
Skokie (village) Cook County	3,594	5.67
Lincolnwood (village) Cook County	575	4.65
Darien (city) Du Page County	930	4.07
Gurnee (village) Lake County	977	3.39
Hanover Park (village) Cook County	1,274	3.33
Niles (village) Cook County	958	3.19
Bartlett (village) Du Page County	1,149	3.13
Streamwood (village) Cook County	1,109	3.05

Asian: Hmong

Top 10 Places Sorted by Number
Based on all places, regardless of population

Place	Number	%
Chicago (city) Cook County	173	0.01
Aurora (city) Kane County	95	0.07
Danville (city) Vermilion County	35	0.10
Wheaton (city) Du Page County	20	0.04
Champaign (city) Champaign County	19	0.03
Dixon (city) Lee County	17	0.11
Carpentersville (village) Kane County	15	0.05
Rockford (city) Winnebago County	12	0.01
Plainfield (village) Will County	10	0.08
Goodings Grove (cdp) Will County	10	0.06

Top 10 Places Sorted by Percent
Based on all places, regardless of population

Place	Number	%
Hainesville (village) Lake County	5	0.23
Dixon (city) Lee County	17	0.11
Danville (city) Vermilion County	35	0.10
Plainfield (village) Will County	10	0.08
Aurora (city) Kane County	95	0.07
Goodings Grove (cdp) Will County	10	0.06
Winfield (village) Du Page County	5	0.06
Carpentersville (village) Kane County	15	0.05
Norridge (village) Cook County	8	0.05
Warrenville (city) Du Page County	7	0.05

Top 10 Places Sorted by Percent
Based on places with populations of 10,000 or more

Place	Number	%
Dixon (city) Lee County	17	0.11
Danville (city) Vermilion County	35	0.10
Plainfield (village) Will County	10	0.08
Aurora (city) Kane County	95	0.07
Goodings Grove (cdp) Will County	10	0.06
Carpentersville (village) Kane County	15	0.05
Norridge (village) Cook County	8	0.05
Warrenville (city) Du Page County	7	0.05
Wheaton (city) Du Page County	20	0.04
Rolling Meadows (city) Cook County	10	0.04

Asian: Indian

Top 10 Places Sorted by Number
Based on all places, regardless of population

Place	Number	%
Chicago (city) Cook County	27,889	0.96
Naperville (city) Du Page County	5,261	4.10
Schaumburg (village) Cook County	5,006	6.64
Skokie (village) Cook County	4,142	6.54
Hoffman Estates (village) Cook County	3,371	6.81
Mount Prospect (village) Cook County	3,325	5.91
Glendale Heights (village) Du Page County	2,840	8.94
Des Plaines (city) Cook County	2,339	3.98
Hanover Park (village) Cook County	2,313	6.04
Palatine (village) Cook County	2,229	3.40

Top 10 Places Sorted by Percent
Based on all places, regardless of population

Place	Number	%
Oak Brook (village) Du Page County	949	10.91
Glendale Heights (village) Du Page County	2,840	8.94
South Barrington (village) Cook County	273	7.26
Morton Grove (village) Cook County	1,565	6.97
Hoffman Estates (village) Cook County	3,371	6.81
Schaumburg (village) Cook County	5,006	6.64
Skokie (village) Cook County	4,142	6.54
Lincolnwood (village) Cook County	795	6.43
Burr Ridge (village) Du Page County	664	6.38
Hanover Park (village) Cook County	2,313	6.04

Notes: (cdp) census designated place; Refer to the User's Guide in the front of the book for more detailed information.

Top 10 Places Sorted by Percent
Based on places with populations of 10,000 or more

Place	Number	%
Glendale Heights (village) Du Page County	2,840	8.94
Morton Grove (village) Cook County	1,565	6.97
Hoffman Estates (village) Cook County	3,371	6.81
Schaumburg (village) Cook County	5,006	6.64
Skokie (village) Cook County	4,142	6.54
Lincolnwood (village) Cook County	795	6.43
Burr Ridge (village) Du Page County	664	6.38
Hanover Park (village) Cook County	2,313	6.04
Mount Prospect (village) Cook County	3,325	5.91
Woodridge (village) Du Page County	1,769	5.72

Asian: Indonesian

Top 10 Places Sorted by Number
Based on all places, regardless of population

Place	Number	%
Chicago (city) Cook County	359	0.01
Urbana (city) Champaign County	77	0.21
Skokie (village) Cook County	47	0.07
Schaumburg (village) Cook County	36	0.05
Naperville (city) Du Page County	24	0.02
Carbondale (city) Jackson County	21	0.10
Peoria (city) Peoria County	21	0.02
Arlington Heights (village) Cook County	19	0.02
Champaign (city) Champaign County	18	0.03
Hoffman Estates (village) Cook County	17	0.03

Top 10 Places Sorted by Percent
Based on all places, regardless of population

Place	Number	%
Neponset (village) Bureau County	5	0.96
Saint Libory (village) Saint Clair County	5	0.86
Elsah (village) Jersey County	3	0.47
New Millford (village) Winnebago County	2	0.37
Havana (city) Mason County	8	0.22
Urbana (city) Champaign County	77	0.21
Wayne (village) Kane County	4	0.19
Clarendon Hills (village) Du Page County	10	0.13
Tiskilwa (village) Bureau County	1	0.13
Carbondale (city) Jackson County	21	0.10

Top 10 Places Sorted by Percent
Based on places with populations of 10,000 or more

Place	Number	%
Urbana (city) Champaign County	77	0.21
Carbondale (city) Jackson County	21	0.10
Skokie (village) Cook County	47	0.07
Lincolnwood (village) Cook County	8	0.06
Schaumburg (village) Cook County	36	0.05
De Kalb (city) De Kalb County	14	0.04
Romeoville (village) Will County	9	0.04
La Grange (village) Cook County	6	0.04
Champaign (city) Champaign County	18	0.03
Hoffman Estates (village) Cook County	17	0.03

Asian: Japanese

Top 10 Places Sorted by Number
Based on all places, regardless of population

Place	Number	%
Chicago (city) Cook County	7,114	0.25
Schaumburg (village) Cook County	1,214	1.61
Arlington Heights (village) Cook County	1,108	1.46
Hoffman Estates (village) Cook County	796	1.61
Elk Grove Village (village) Cook County	676	1.95
Buffalo Grove (village) Lake County	600	1.40
Evanston (city) Cook County	597	0.80
Skokie (village) Cook County	494	0.78
Palatine (village) Cook County	490	0.75
Mount Prospect (village) Cook County	408	0.73

Top 10 Places Sorted by Percent
Based on all places, regardless of population

Place	Number	%
Belknap (village) Johnson County	9	6.77
Elk Grove Village (village) Cook County	676	1.95
Schaumburg (village) Cook County	1,214	1.61
Hoffman Estates (village) Cook County	796	1.61
Arlington Heights (village) Cook County	1,108	1.46
Buffalo Grove (village) Lake County	600	1.40
Troy Grove (village) La Salle County	4	1.31
Kempton (village) Ford County	3	1.28
Rose Hill (village) Jasper County	1	1.27
Wilmette (village) Cook County	348	1.26

Top 10 Places Sorted by Percent
Based on places with populations of 10,000 or more

Place	Number	%
Elk Grove Village (village) Cook County	676	1.95
Schaumburg (village) Cook County	1,214	1.61
Hoffman Estates (village) Cook County	796	1.61
Arlington Heights (village) Cook County	1,108	1.46
Buffalo Grove (village) Lake County	600	1.40
Wilmette (village) Cook County	348	1.26
Lincolnwood (village) Cook County	151	1.22
Carbondale (city) Jackson County	229	1.11
Glenview (village) Cook County	406	0.97
Urbana (city) Champaign County	316	0.87

Asian: Korean

Top 10 Places Sorted by Number
Based on all places, regardless of population

Place	Number	%
Chicago (city) Cook County	12,867	0.44
Skokie (village) Cook County	2,557	4.04
Glenview (village) Cook County	1,929	4.61
Schaumburg (village) Cook County	1,641	2.18
Northbrook (village) Cook County	1,520	4.55
Mount Prospect (village) Cook County	1,232	2.19
Naperville (city) Du Page County	1,215	0.95
Hoffman Estates (village) Cook County	1,144	2.31
Urbana (city) Champaign County	1,139	3.13
Buffalo Grove (village) Lake County	1,135	2.65

Top 10 Places Sorted by Percent
Based on all places, regardless of population

Place	Number	%
Belknap (village) Johnson County	9	6.77
Panola (village) Woodford County	2	6.06
Savoy (village) Champaign County	233	5.21
Morton Grove (village) Cook County	1,065	4.74
Lincolnwood (village) Cook County	586	4.74
Glenview (village) Cook County	1,929	4.61
Northbrook (village) Cook County	1,520	4.55
Skokie (village) Cook County	2,557	4.04
Niles (village) Cook County	949	3.16
Urbana (city) Champaign County	1,139	3.13

Top 10 Places Sorted by Percent
Based on places with populations of 10,000 or more

Place	Number	%
Morton Grove (village) Cook County	1,065	4.74
Lincolnwood (village) Cook County	586	4.74
Glenview (village) Cook County	1,929	4.61
Northbrook (village) Cook County	1,520	4.55
Skokie (village) Cook County	2,557	4.04
Niles (village) Cook County	949	3.16
Urbana (city) Champaign County	1,139	3.13
Vernon Hills (village) Lake County	626	3.11
Buffalo Grove (village) Lake County	1,135	2.65
Wilmette (village) Cook County	701	2.54

Asian: Laotian

Top 10 Places Sorted by Number
Based on all places, regardless of population

Place	Number	%
Elgin (city) Kane County	1,507	1.59
Rockford (city) Winnebago County	1,085	0.72
Chicago (city) Cook County	517	0.02
South Elgin (village) Kane County	380	2.36
Joliet (city) Will County	222	0.21
Hanover Park (village) Cook County	147	0.38
Aurora (city) Kane County	125	0.09
Streamwood (village) Cook County	67	0.18
Champaign (city) Champaign County	66	0.10
Carpentersville (village) Kane County	65	0.21

Top 10 Places Sorted by Percent
Based on all places, regardless of population

Place	Number	%
South Elgin (village) Kane County	380	2.36
De Pue (village) Bureau County	36	1.95
Elgin (city) Kane County	1,507	1.59
Ullin (village) Pulaski County	11	1.41
Cherry Valley (village) Winnebago County	23	1.05
Arlington (village) Bureau County	2	0.95
La Fayette (village) Stark County	2	0.88
Rockford (city) Winnebago County	1,085	0.72
North Aurora (village) Kane County	56	0.53
Hanover Park (village) Cook County	147	0.38

Top 10 Places Sorted by Percent
Based on places with populations of 10,000 or more

Place	Number	%
South Elgin (village) Kane County	380	2.36
Elgin (city) Kane County	1,507	1.59
Rockford (city) Winnebago County	1,085	0.72
North Aurora (village) Kane County	56	0.53
Hanover Park (village) Cook County	147	0.38
Loves Park (city) Winnebago County	51	0.25
Joliet (city) Will County	222	0.21
Carpentersville (village) Kane County	65	0.21
Markham (city) Cook County	26	0.21
Streamwood (village) Cook County	67	0.18

Asian: Malaysian

Top 10 Places Sorted by Number
Based on all places, regardless of population

Place	Number	%
Chicago (city) Cook County	186	0.01
Carbondale (city) Jackson County	55	0.27
Urbana (city) Champaign County	33	0.09
Champaign (city) Champaign County	27	0.04
Schaumburg (village) Cook County	20	0.03
De Kalb (city) De Kalb County	18	0.05
Skokie (village) Cook County	17	0.03
Evanston (city) Cook County	17	0.02
Lisle (village) Du Page County	11	0.05
Macomb (city) McDonough County	10	0.05

Top 10 Places Sorted by Percent
Based on all places, regardless of population

Place	Number	%
Davis Junction (village) Ogle County	2	0.41
Kampsville (village) Calhoun County	1	0.33
Carbondale (city) Jackson County	55	0.27
Bluffs (village) Scott County	1	0.13
Green Oaks (village) Lake County	4	0.11
Urbana (city) Champaign County	33	0.09
Savoy (village) Champaign County	3	0.07
De Soto (village) Jackson County	1	0.06
Teutopolis (village) Effingham County	1	0.06
De Kalb (city) De Kalb County	18	0.05

Notes: (cdp) census designated place; Refer to the User's Guide in the front of the book for more detailed information.

Top 10 Places Sorted by Percent

Based on places with populations of 10,000 or more

Place	Number	%
Carbondale (city) Jackson County	55	0.27
Urbana (city) Champaign County	33	0.09
De Kalb (city) De Kalb County	18	0.05
Lisle (village) Du Page County	11	0.05
Macomb (city) McDonough County	10	0.05
Champaign (city) Champaign County	27	0.04
Rolling Meadows (city) Cook County	9	0.04
Forest Park (village) Cook County	6	0.04
Justice (village) Cook County	5	0.04
Gages Lake (cdp) Lake County	4	0.04

Asian: Pakistani

Top 10 Places Sorted by Number

Based on all places, regardless of population

Place	Number	%
Chicago (city) Cook County	7,606	0.26
Skokie (village) Cook County	804	1.27
Naperville (city) Du Page County	403	0.31
Glendale Heights (village) Du Page County	354	1.11
Hanover Park (village) Cook County	351	0.92
Hoffman Estates (village) Cook County	351	0.71
Schaumburg (village) Cook County	326	0.43
Lombard (village) Du Page County	285	0.67
Bolingbrook (village) Will County	256	0.45
Carol Stream (village) Du Page County	245	0.61

Top 10 Places Sorted by Percent

Based on all places, regardless of population

Place	Number	%
Lincolnwood (village) Cook County	203	1.64
Skokie (village) Cook County	804	1.27
Oak Brook (village) Du Page County	107	1.23
Glendale Heights (village) Du Page County	354	1.11
Burr Ridge (village) Du Page County	97	0.93
Hanover Park (village) Cook County	351	0.92
Bensenville (village) Du Page County	187	0.90
Oakbrook Terrace (city) Du Page County	19	0.83
Hoffman Estates (village) Cook County	351	0.71
Lombard (village) Du Page County	285	0.67

Top 10 Places Sorted by Percent

Based on places with populations of 10,000 or more

Place	Number	%
Lincolnwood (village) Cook County	203	1.64
Skokie (village) Cook County	804	1.27
Glendale Heights (village) Du Page County	354	1.11
Burr Ridge (village) Du Page County	97	0.93
Hanover Park (village) Cook County	351	0.92
Bensenville (village) Du Page County	187	0.90
Hoffman Estates (village) Cook County	351	0.71
Lombard (village) Du Page County	285	0.67
Morton Grove (village) Cook County	146	0.65
Glen Ellyn (village) Du Page County	174	0.64

Asian: Sri Lankan

Top 10 Places Sorted by Number

Based on all places, regardless of population

Place	Number	%
Chicago (city) Cook County	144	0.00
Urbana (city) Champaign County	46	0.13
Skokie (village) Cook County	26	0.04
Naperville (city) Du Page County	22	0.02
Tinley Park (village) Cook County	14	0.03
Hoffman Estates (village) Cook County	13	0.03
Normal (town) McLean County	12	0.03
Lisle (village) Du Page County	11	0.05
Wheeling (village) Cook County	11	0.03
Darien (city) Du Page County	10	0.04

Top 10 Places Sorted by Percent

Based on all places, regardless of population

Place	Number	%
Mettawa (village) Lake County	1	0.27
Clifton (village) Iroquois County	2	0.15
Urbana (city) Champaign County	46	0.13
Savoy (village) Champaign County	5	0.11
Oak Brook (village) Du Page County	8	0.09
Willowbrook (village) Du Page County	7	0.08
River Forest (village) Cook County	8	0.07
Long Grove (village) Lake County	4	0.06
Lisle (village) Du Page County	11	0.05
Skokie (village) Cook County	26	0.04

Top 10 Places Sorted by Percent

Based on places with populations of 10,000 or more

Place	Number	%
Urbana (city) Champaign County	46	0.13
River Forest (village) Cook County	8	0.07
Lisle (village) Du Page County	11	0.05
Skokie (village) Cook County	26	0.04
Darien (city) Du Page County	10	0.04
Woodstock (city) McHenry County	8	0.04
Lindenhurst (village) Lake County	5	0.04
Tinley Park (village) Cook County	14	0.03
Hoffman Estates (village) Cook County	13	0.03
Normal (town) McLean County	12	0.03

Asian: Taiwanese

Top 10 Places Sorted by Number

Based on all places, regardless of population

Place	Number	%
Chicago (city) Cook County	669	0.02
Naperville (city) Du Page County	455	0.35
Urbana (city) Champaign County	260	0.71
Evanston (city) Cook County	161	0.22
Schaumburg (village) Cook County	109	0.14
Champaign (city) Champaign County	96	0.14
Skokie (village) Cook County	81	0.13
Hoffman Estates (village) Cook County	79	0.16
Oak Brook (village) Du Page County	77	0.88
Wilmette (village) Cook County	68	0.25

Top 10 Places Sorted by Percent

Based on all places, regardless of population

Place	Number	%
Oak Brook (village) Du Page County	77	0.88
Urbana (city) Champaign County	260	0.71
South Barrington (village) Cook County	26	0.69
Naperville (city) Du Page County	455	0.35
Lisle (village) Du Page County	66	0.31
Savoy (village) Champaign County	14	0.31
Leland Grove (city) Sangamon County	5	0.31
Third Lake (village) Lake County	4	0.30
Willowbrook (village) Du Page County	25	0.28
Wilmette (village) Cook County	68	0.25

Top 10 Places Sorted by Percent

Based on places with populations of 10,000 or more

Place	Number	%
Urbana (city) Champaign County	260	0.71
Naperville (city) Du Page County	455	0.35
Lisle (village) Du Page County	66	0.31
Wilmette (village) Cook County	68	0.25
Darien (city) Du Page County	56	0.24
Evanston (city) Cook County	161	0.22
Westmont (village) Du Page County	54	0.22
Carbondale (city) Jackson County	43	0.21
Vernon Hills (village) Lake County	36	0.18
Northbrook (village) Cook County	57	0.17

Asian: Thai

Top 10 Places Sorted by Number

Based on all places, regardless of population

Place	Number	%
Chicago (city) Cook County	2,385	0.08
Skokie (village) Cook County	243	0.38
Champaign (city) Champaign County	124	0.18
Morton Grove (village) Cook County	97	0.43
Urbana (city) Champaign County	92	0.25
Wilmette (village) Cook County	91	0.33
Evanston (city) Cook County	88	0.12
Elgin (city) Kane County	84	0.09
Glenview (village) Cook County	83	0.20
Darien (city) Du Page County	79	0.35

Top 10 Places Sorted by Percent

Based on all places, regardless of population

Place	Number	%
Damiansville (village) Clinton County	3	0.82
Lincolnwood (village) Cook County	62	0.50
Morton Grove (village) Cook County	97	0.43
Keyesport (village) Clinton County	2	0.42
Ullin (village) Pulaski County	3	0.39
Skokie (village) Cook County	243	0.38
Sims (village) Wayne County	1	0.37
Darien (city) Du Page County	79	0.35
Wilmette (village) Cook County	91	0.33
Bellevue (village) Peoria County	6	0.32

Top 10 Places Sorted by Percent

Based on places with populations of 10,000 or more

Place	Number	%
Lincolnwood (village) Cook County	62	0.50
Morton Grove (village) Cook County	97	0.43
Skokie (village) Cook County	243	0.38
Darien (city) Du Page County	79	0.35
Wilmette (village) Cook County	91	0.33
Forest Park (village) Cook County	43	0.27
Urbana (city) Champaign County	92	0.25
Glenview (village) Cook County	83	0.20
Carbondale (city) Jackson County	41	0.20
Niles (village) Cook County	57	0.19

Asian: Vietnamese

Top 10 Places Sorted by Number

Based on all places, regardless of population

Place	Number	%
Chicago (city) Cook County	8,925	0.31
Glendale Heights (village) Du Page County	805	2.53
Carol Stream (village) Du Page County	605	1.50
Rockford (city) Winnebago County	531	0.35
Wheaton (city) Du Page County	462	0.83
Champaign (city) Champaign County	416	0.62
Peoria (city) Peoria County	382	0.34
Skokie (village) Cook County	326	0.51
Aurora (city) Kane County	243	0.17
Elgin (city) Kane County	221	0.23

Top 10 Places Sorted by Percent

Based on all places, regardless of population

Place	Number	%
Glendale Heights (village) Du Page County	805	2.53
Carol Stream (village) Du Page County	605	1.50
Calhoun (village) Richland County	3	1.35
Volo (village) Lake County	2	1.11
Wheaton (city) Du Page County	462	0.83
Dunlap (village) Peoria County	7	0.76
New Millford (village) Winnebago County	4	0.74
Champaign (city) Champaign County	416	0.62
Lincolnwood (village) Cook County	74	0.60
Northlake (city) Cook County	71	0.60

Notes: (cdp) census designated place; Refer to the User's Guide in the front of the book for more detailed information.

Top 10 Places Sorted by Percent

Based on places with populations of 10,000 or more

Place	Number	%
Glendale Heights (village) Du Page County	805	2.53
Carol Stream (village) Du Page County	605	1.50
Wheaton (city) Du Page County	462	0.83
Champaign (city) Champaign County	416	0.62
Lincolnwood (village) Cook County	74	0.60
Northlake (city) Cook County	71	0.60
Urbana (city) Champaign County	196	0.54
Addison (village) Du Page County	193	0.54
Skokie (village) Cook County	326	0.51
East Moline (city) Rock Island County	98	0.48

Asian: Other Asian, specified

Top 10 Places Sorted by Number

Based on all places, regardless of population

Place	Number	%
Chicago (city) Cook County	404	0.01
Macomb (city) McDonough County	35	0.19
Evanston (city) Cook County	24	0.03
Schaumburg (village) Cook County	23	0.03
Urbana (city) Champaign County	21	0.06
Naperville (city) Du Page County	21	0.02
Niles (village) Cook County	20	0.07
De Kalb (city) De Kalb County	20	0.05
Skokie (village) Cook County	19	0.03
Peoria (city) Peoria County	19	0.02

Top 10 Places Sorted by Percent

Based on all places, regardless of population

Place	Number	%
Minonk (city) Woodford County	9	0.42
Bull Valley (village) McHenry County	2	0.28
Kane (village) Greene County	1	0.22
Macomb (city) McDonough County	35	0.19
Minier (village) Tazewell County	2	0.16
White Hall (city) Greene County	4	0.15
Third Lake (village) Lake County	2	0.15
Oak Brook (village) Du Page County	12	0.14
Mound City (city) Pulaski County	1	0.14
Orangeville (village) Stephenson County	1	0.13

Top 10 Places Sorted by Percent

Based on places with populations of 10,000 or more

Place	Number	%
Macomb (city) McDonough County	35	0.19
Glen Carbon (village) Madison County	8	0.08
Niles (village) Cook County	20	0.07
Urbana (city) Champaign County	21	0.06
Bourbonnais (village) Kankakee County	9	0.06
Markham (city) Cook County	7	0.06
Schiller Park (village) Cook County	7	0.06
De Kalb (city) De Kalb County	20	0.05
Wheeling (village) Cook County	16	0.05
Kewanee (city) Henry County	6	0.05

Asian: Other Asian, not specified

Top 10 Places Sorted by Number

Based on all places, regardless of population

Place	Number	%
Chicago (city) Cook County	5,843	0.20
Skokie (village) Cook County	372	0.59
Elgin (city) Kane County	247	0.26
Aurora (city) Kane County	205	0.14
Rockford (city) Winnebago County	204	0.14
Naperville (city) Du Page County	201	0.16
Schaumburg (village) Cook County	182	0.24
Hoffman Estates (village) Cook County	144	0.29
Evanston (city) Cook County	133	0.18
Champaign (city) Champaign County	119	0.18

Top 10 Places Sorted by Percent

Based on all places, regardless of population

Place	Number	%
Bannockburn (village) Lake County	27	1.89
Springerton (village) White County	2	1.49
Vergennes (village) Jackson County	4	0.81
Mound Station (village) Brown County	1	0.79
Clear Lake (village) Sangamon County	2	0.75
Lincolnwood (village) Cook County	85	0.69
Mechanicsburg (village) Sangamon County	3	0.66
Kampsville (village) Calhoun County	2	0.66
Justice (village) Cook County	77	0.63
Ferris (village) Hancock County	1	0.60

Top 10 Places Sorted by Percent

Based on places with populations of 10,000 or more

Place	Number	%
Lincolnwood (village) Cook County	85	0.69
Justice (village) Cook County	77	0.63
Skokie (village) Cook County	372	0.59
Chicago Ridge (village) Cook County	71	0.50
Niles (village) Cook County	112	0.37
Bridgeview (village) Cook County	57	0.37
Hickory Hills (city) Cook County	52	0.37
Glendale Heights (village) Du Page County	113	0.36
Alsip (village) Cook County	68	0.34
Schiller Park (village) Cook County	39	0.33

Assyrian/Chaldean/Syriac

Top 10 Places Sorted by Number

Based on all places, regardless of population

Place	Number	%
Chicago (city) Cook County	7,121	0.25
Skokie (village) Cook County	2,381	3.76
Morton Grove (village) Cook County	496	2.21
Niles (village) Cook County	458	1.52
Lincolnwood (village) Cook County	438	3.54
Elgin (city) Kane County	334	0.36
Schaumburg (village) Cook County	272	0.37
Mount Prospect (village) Cook County	220	0.39
Glenview (village) Cook County	203	0.49
Elk Grove Village (village) Cook County	169	0.49

Top 10 Places Sorted by Percent

Based on all places, regardless of population

Place	Number	%
Skokie (village) Cook County	2,381	3.76
Lincolnwood (village) Cook County	438	3.54
Golf (village) Cook County	13	2.88
Henderson (village) Knox County	9	2.54
Morton Grove (village) Cook County	496	2.21
Niles (village) Cook County	458	1.52
Mettawa (village) Lake County	3	0.93
Itasca (village) Du Page County	51	0.62
Willow Springs (village) Cook County	29	0.59
Winfield (village) Du Page County	49	0.55

Top 10 Places Sorted by Percent

Based on places with populations of 10,000 or more

Place	Number	%
Skokie (village) Cook County	2,381	3.76
Lincolnwood (village) Cook County	438	3.54
Morton Grove (village) Cook County	496	2.21
Niles (village) Cook County	458	1.52
Glenview (village) Cook County	203	0.49
Elk Grove Village (village) Cook County	169	0.49
Streamwood (village) Cook County	161	0.44
Mount Prospect (village) Cook County	220	0.39
Schaumburg (village) Cook County	272	0.37
Elgin (city) Kane County	334	0.36

Australian

Top 10 Places Sorted by Number

Based on all places, regardless of population

Place	Number	%
Chicago (city) Cook County	486	0.02
Aurora (city) Kane County	59	0.04
Wheaton (city) Du Page County	53	0.10
Elgin (city) Kane County	52	0.06
Washington (city) Tazewell County	50	0.46
Evanston (city) Cook County	49	0.07
Naperville (city) Du Page County	49	0.04
Schaumburg (village) Cook County	48	0.06
Lincolnshire (village) Lake County	41	0.66
Savoy (village) Champaign County	40	0.93

Top 10 Places Sorted by Percent

Based on all places, regardless of population

Place	Number	%
Bannockburn (village) Lake County	37	2.60
Trout Valley (village) McHenry County	6	1.01
Savoy (village) Champaign County	40	0.93
Mettawa (village) Lake County	3	0.93
Lincolnshire (village) Lake County	41	0.66
Saunemin (village) Livingston County	3	0.61
Plano (city) Kendall County	31	0.57
Inverness (village) Cook County	31	0.49
Washington (city) Tazewell County	50	0.46
Wonder Lake (cdp) McHenry County	35	0.46

Top 10 Places Sorted by Percent

Based on places with populations of 10,000 or more

Place	Number	%
Washington (city) Tazewell County	50	0.46
Lockport (city) Will County	40	0.27
Frankfort (village) Will County	16	0.16
River Forest (village) Cook County	17	0.15
Grayslake (village) Lake County	26	0.14
Mokena (village) Will County	20	0.14
Centralia (city) Marion County	19	0.13
Goodings Grove (cdp) Will County	19	0.11
Wheaton (city) Du Page County	53	0.10
Palos Hills (city) Cook County	17	0.10

Austrian

Top 10 Places Sorted by Number

Based on all places, regardless of population

Place	Number	%
Chicago (city) Cook County	8,080	0.28
Naperville (city) Du Page County	806	0.63
Arlington Heights (village) Cook County	712	0.94
Schaumburg (village) Cook County	640	0.86
Orland Park (village) Cook County	628	1.23
Oak Lawn (village) Cook County	619	1.12
Northbrook (village) Cook County	510	1.53
Evanston (city) Cook County	482	0.65
Des Plaines (city) Cook County	462	0.79
Highland Park (city) Lake County	456	1.45

Top 10 Places Sorted by Percent

Based on all places, regardless of population

Place	Number	%
Burnt Prairie (village) White County	2	4.35
Ringwood (village) McHenry County	17	3.83
Liverpool (village) Fulton County	3	3.16
Spaulding (village) Sangamon County	17	3.05
Eagarville (village) Macoupin County	3	2.50
Rockbridge (village) Greene County	4	2.22
Browning (village) Schuyler County	3	2.21
Coffeen (city) Montgomery County	16	2.15
Whiteash (village) Williamson County	6	2.14
New Douglas (village) Madison County	7	1.82

Notes: (cdp) census designated place; Refer to the User's Guide in the front of the book for more detailed information.

Top 10 Places Sorted by Percent

Based on places with populations of 10,000 or more

Place	Number	%
Deerfield (village) Lake County	312	1.69
Palos Heights (city) Cook County	188	1.66
Northbrook (village) Cook County	510	1.53
Highland Park (city) Lake County	456	1.45
Crestwood (village) Cook County	155	1.38
Evergreen Park (village) Cook County	280	1.34
Wood Dale (city) Du Page County	173	1.24
Orland Park (village) Cook County	628	1.23
Oak Forest (city) Cook County	321	1.15
Hickory Hills (city) Cook County	159	1.14

Basque

Top 10 Places Sorted by Number

Based on all places, regardless of population

Place	Number	%
Chicago (city) Cook County	141	0.00
Woodridge (village) Du Page County	89	0.29
Highland Park (city) Lake County	40	0.13
Waukegan (city) Lake County	35	0.04
Oak Park (village) Cook County	27	0.05
Naperville (city) Du Page County	21	0.02
Aurora (city) Kane County	17	0.01
Normal (town) McLean County	16	0.04
Libertyville (village) Lake County	15	0.07
Arlington Heights (village) Cook County	15	0.02

Top 10 Places Sorted by Percent

Based on all places, regardless of population

Place	Number	%
Sauget (village) Saint Clair County	1	0.54
Woodridge (village) Du Page County	89	0.29
Highland Park (city) Lake County	40	0.13
Minooka (village) Grundy County	4	0.10
McCullom Lake (village) McHenry County	1	0.10
Island Lake (village) McHenry County	7	0.09
Libertyville (village) Lake County	15	0.07
Oak Park (village) Cook County	27	0.05
Waukegan (city) Lake County	35	0.04
Normal (town) McLean County	16	0.04

Top 10 Places Sorted by Percent

Based on places with populations of 10,000 or more

Place	Number	%
Woodridge (village) Du Page County	89	0.29
Highland Park (city) Lake County	40	0.13
Libertyville (village) Lake County	15	0.07
Oak Park (village) Cook County	27	0.05
Waukegan (city) Lake County	35	0.04
Normal (town) McLean County	16	0.04
Collinsville (city) Madison County	10	0.04
Lake Zurich (village) Lake County	8	0.04
Chicago Ridge (village) Cook County	6	0.04
Glenview (village) Cook County	13	0.03

Belgian

Top 10 Places Sorted by Number

Based on all places, regardless of population

Place	Number	%
Moline (city) Rock Island County	2,686	6.14
Chicago (city) Cook County	2,366	0.08
East Moline (city) Rock Island County	1,490	7.32
Rock Island (city) Rock Island County	1,480	3.73
Kewanee (city) Henry County	805	6.22
Geneseo (city) Henry County	635	9.68
Silvis (city) Rock Island County	476	6.51
Peoria (city) Peoria County	380	0.34
Atkinson (town) Henry County	340	33.86
Rockford (city) Winnebago County	325	0.22

Top 10 Places Sorted by Percent

Based on all places, regardless of population

Place	Number	%
Atkinson (town) Henry County	340	33.86
Annawan (town) Henry County	290	33.56
Mineral (village) Bureau County	58	21.25
Deer Grove (village) Whiteside County	6	11.32
Geneseo (city) Henry County	635	9.68
Sherrard (village) Mercer County	65	9.45
Hooppole (village) Henry County	15	9.20
Sheffield (village) Bureau County	79	8.49
Apple River (village) Jo Daviess County	33	8.21
Reynolds (village) Rock Island County	40	7.98

Top 10 Places Sorted by Percent

Based on places with populations of 10,000 or more

Place	Number	%
East Moline (city) Rock Island County	1,490	7.32
Kewanee (city) Henry County	805	6.22
Moline (city) Rock Island County	2,686	6.14
Rock Island (city) Rock Island County	1,480	3.73
Geneva (city) Kane County	222	1.14
Saint Charles (city) Kane County	229	0.82
Oswego (village) Kendall County	109	0.82
Winnetka (village) Cook County	92	0.74
Rolling Meadows (city) Cook County	170	0.69
Lake Zurich (village) Lake County	99	0.55

Brazilian

Top 10 Places Sorted by Number

Based on all places, regardless of population

Place	Number	%
Chicago (city) Cook County	833	0.03
Urbana (city) Champaign County	101	0.28
Peoria (city) Peoria County	97	0.09
Libertyville (village) Lake County	79	0.38
Evanston (city) Cook County	76	0.10
Palatine (village) Cook County	73	0.11
Hawthorn Woods (village) Lake County	46	0.72
Oak Park (village) Cook County	42	0.08
Berwyn (city) Cook County	41	0.08
Lake Zurich (village) Lake County	40	0.22

Top 10 Places Sorted by Percent

Based on all places, regardless of population

Place	Number	%
Coleta (village) Whiteside County	9	5.63
Ivesdale (village) Champaign County	4	1.26
Chesterfield (village) Macoupin County	3	1.24
Spillertown (village) Williamson County	2	0.91
Hawthorn Woods (village) Lake County	46	0.72
Kangley (village) La Salle County	2	0.67
Burlington (village) Kane County	3	0.65
Stickney (village) Cook County	37	0.60
Savoy (village) Champaign County	26	0.60
Avon (village) Fulton County	4	0.44

Top 10 Places Sorted by Percent

Based on places with populations of 10,000 or more

Place	Number	%
Libertyville (village) Lake County	79	0.38
Urbana (city) Champaign County	101	0.28
Lake Zurich (village) Lake County	40	0.22
Morton (village) Tazewell County	30	0.20
Hinsdale (village) Du Page County	33	0.19
Bridgeview (village) Cook County	28	0.18
Schiller Park (village) Cook County	21	0.18
Vernon Hills (village) Lake County	29	0.14
Grayslake (village) Lake County	25	0.14
Mundelein (village) Lake County	37	0.12

British

Top 10 Places Sorted by Number

Based on all places, regardless of population

Place	Number	%
Chicago (city) Cook County	4,653	0.16
Naperville (city) Du Page County	711	0.55
Evanston (city) Cook County	596	0.80
Wheaton (city) Du Page County	515	0.93
Rockford (city) Winnebago County	491	0.33
Champaign (city) Champaign County	474	0.70
Aurora (city) Kane County	434	0.30
Peoria (city) Peoria County	347	0.31
Urbana (city) Champaign County	309	0.85
Decatur (city) Macon County	290	0.35

Top 10 Places Sorted by Percent

Based on all places, regardless of population

Place	Number	%
Liverpool (village) Fulton County	10	10.53
New Salem (village) Pike County	9	6.00
Walshville (village) Montgomery County	4	4.71
Parkersburg (village) Richland County	9	4.41
Bannockburn (village) Lake County	51	3.58
Rio (village) Knox County	8	3.20
East Galesburg (village) Knox County	24	2.93
Huey (village) Clinton County	5	2.53
Shabbona (village) De Kalb County	24	2.52
Hettick (village) Macoupin County	4	2.11

Top 10 Places Sorted by Percent

Based on places with populations of 10,000 or more

Place	Number	%
Winnetka (village) Cook County	144	1.16
Wheaton (city) Du Page County	515	0.93
Barrington (village) Cook County	91	0.91
Urbana (city) Champaign County	309	0.85
Evanston (city) Cook County	596	0.80
Rantoul (village) Champaign County	99	0.77
Vernon Hills (village) Lake County	155	0.75
Matteson (village) Cook County	97	0.75
Champaign (city) Champaign County	474	0.70
Batavia (city) Kane County	167	0.70

Bulgarian

Top 10 Places Sorted by Number

Based on all places, regardless of population

Place	Number	%
Chicago (city) Cook County	2,045	0.07
Schiller Park (village) Cook County	244	2.07
Skokie (village) Cook County	208	0.33
Mount Prospect (village) Cook County	164	0.29
Des Plaines (city) Cook County	149	0.25
Rosemont (village) Cook County	119	2.85
Elmwood Park (village) Cook County	106	0.42
Schaumburg (village) Cook County	103	0.14
Roselle (village) Du Page County	89	0.38
Naperville (city) Du Page County	83	0.06

Top 10 Places Sorted by Percent

Based on all places, regardless of population

Place	Number	%
Rosemont (village) Cook County	119	2.85
Schiller Park (village) Cook County	244	2.07
Nelson (village) Lee County	3	2.00
Ogden (village) Champaign County	7	0.95
River Grove (village) Cook County	82	0.77
Hanover (village) Jo Daviess County	6	0.76
Northfield (village) Cook County	38	0.69
Fairmont (cdp) Will County	16	0.61
Kenilworth (village) Cook County	14	0.56
Berkeley (village) Cook County	27	0.51

Notes: (cdp) census designated place; Refer to the User's Guide in the front of the book for more detailed information.

Top 10 Places Sorted by Percent
Based on places with populations of 10,000 or more

Place	Number	%
Schiller Park (village) Cook County	244	2.07
River Grove (village) Cook County	82	0.77
Elmwood Park (village) Cook County	106	0.42
Roselle (village) Du Page County	89	0.38
Grayslake (village) Lake County	64	0.35
Skokie (village) Cook County	208	0.33
Mount Prospect (village) Cook County	164	0.29
Wood Dale (city) Du Page County	39	0.28
Burr Ridge (village) Du Page County	28	0.27
Glen Carbon (village) Madison County	28	0.27

Canadian

Top 10 Places Sorted by Number
Based on all places, regardless of population

Place	Number	%
Chicago (city) Cook County	2,050	0.07
Naperville (city) Du Page County	554	0.43
Arlington Heights (village) Cook County	248	0.33
Wheaton (city) Du Page County	190	0.34
Rockford (city) Winnebago County	181	0.12
Elgin (city) Kane County	173	0.18
Champaign (city) Champaign County	168	0.25
Highland Park (city) Lake County	165	0.53
Aurora (city) Kane County	163	0.11
Bolingbrook (village) Will County	162	0.29

Top 10 Places Sorted by Percent
Based on all places, regardless of population

Place	Number	%
Sims (village) Wayne County	13	4.98
Hebron (village) McHenry County	23	2.28
Raleigh (village) Saline County	8	2.26
Bellmont (village) Wabash County	6	1.98
Mapleton (village) Peoria County	4	1.77
Trout Valley (village) McHenry County	10	1.68
Allendale (village) Wabash County	9	1.66
Joppa (village) Massac County	6	1.57
Pistakee Highlands (cdp) McHenry County	53	1.38
Allenville (village) Moultrie County	2	1.18

Top 10 Places Sorted by Percent
Based on places with populations of 10,000 or more

Place	Number	%
River Forest (village) Cook County	93	0.80
Winnetka (village) Cook County	68	0.55
Highland Park (city) Lake County	165	0.53
Cary (village) McHenry County	75	0.49
Barrington (village) Cook County	48	0.48
Hinsdale (village) Du Page County	82	0.47
Naperville (city) Du Page County	554	0.43
Vernon Hills (village) Lake County	89	0.43
Lansing (village) Cook County	117	0.42
Deerfield (village) Lake County	77	0.42

Carpatho Rusyn

Top 10 Places Sorted by Number
Based on all places, regardless of population

Place	Number	%
Chicago (city) Cook County	37	0.00
Westchester (village) Cook County	15	0.09
Crystal Lake (city) McHenry County	10	0.03
Orland Park (village) Cook County	10	0.02
Sterling (city) Whiteside County	9	0.06
Fairbury (city) Livingston County	7	0.18
Mount Olive (city) Macoupin County	6	0.28
Burnham (village) Cook County	5	0.12
Benld (city) Macoupin County	3	0.19
Leaf River (village) Ogle County	2	0.36

Top 10 Places Sorted by Percent
Based on all places, regardless of population

Place	Number	%
Leaf River (village) Ogle County	2	0.36
Mount Olive (city) Macoupin County	6	0.28
Benld (city) Macoupin County	3	0.19
Fairbury (city) Livingston County	7	0.18
Burnham (village) Cook County	5	0.12
Westchester (village) Cook County	15	0.09
Sterling (city) Whiteside County	9	0.06
Crystal Lake (city) McHenry County	10	0.03
Orland Park (village) Cook County	10	0.02
Chicago (city) Cook County	37	0.00

Top 10 Places Sorted by Percent
Based on places with populations of 10,000 or more

Place	Number	%
Westchester (village) Cook County	15	0.09
Sterling (city) Whiteside County	9	0.06
Crystal Lake (city) McHenry County	10	0.03
Orland Park (village) Cook County	10	0.02
Chicago (city) Cook County	37	0.00

Celtic

Top 10 Places Sorted by Number
Based on all places, regardless of population

Place	Number	%
Chicago (city) Cook County	269	0.01
Cahokia (village) Saint Clair County	59	0.36
Woodstock (city) McHenry County	42	0.21
Champaign (city) Champaign County	42	0.06
Springfield (city) Sangamon County	42	0.04
Arlington Heights (village) Cook County	33	0.04
Rockford (city) Winnebago County	32	0.02
West Chicago (city) Du Page County	31	0.13
Oak Park (village) Cook County	31	0.06
New Lenox (village) Will County	30	0.17

Top 10 Places Sorted by Percent
Based on all places, regardless of population

Place	Number	%
Ellsworth (village) McLean County	3	1.11
Timberlane (village) Boone County	2	1.00
Lerna (village) Coles County	3	0.93
Red Bud (city) Randolph County	27	0.81
Lewistown (city) Fulton County	17	0.68
Ransom (village) La Salle County	3	0.65
Elliott (village) Ford County	2	0.58
Makanda (village) Jackson County	2	0.49
Griggsville (city) Pike County	6	0.47
Tolono (village) Champaign County	11	0.41

Top 10 Places Sorted by Percent
Based on places with populations of 10,000 or more

Place	Number	%
Cahokia (village) Saint Clair County	59	0.36
Woodstock (city) McHenry County	42	0.21
New Lenox (village) Will County	30	0.17
Brookfield (village) Cook County	26	0.14
West Chicago (city) Du Page County	31	0.13
Morton (village) Tazewell County	18	0.12
Charleston (city) Coles County	20	0.10
Zion (city) Lake County	19	0.08
Bellwood (village) Cook County	15	0.07
Champaign (city) Champaign County	42	0.06

Croatian

Top 10 Places Sorted by Number
Based on all places, regardless of population

Place	Number	%
Chicago (city) Cook County	7,819	0.27
Joliet (city) Will County	1,536	1.45
Orland Park (village) Cook County	868	1.70
Oak Lawn (village) Cook County	713	1.29
Naperville (city) Du Page County	680	0.53
Lansing (village) Cook County	564	2.00
Tinley Park (village) Cook County	543	1.12
Downers Grove (village) Du Page County	488	1.00
Crest Hill (city) Will County	437	3.35
Berwyn (city) Cook County	415	0.77

Top 10 Places Sorted by Percent
Based on all places, regardless of population

Place	Number	%
McCook (village) Cook County	37	16.30
Mount Clare (village) Macoupin County	31	7.58
Norris (village) Fulton County	16	7.27
Saint David (village) Fulton County	42	6.94
Sawyerville (village) Macoupin County	21	6.60
Matherville (village) Mercer County	36	4.67
White City (village) Macoupin County	9	4.57
Dunfermline (village) Fulton County	11	4.28
Bryant (village) Fulton County	12	4.08
Mount Olive (city) Macoupin County	83	3.85

Top 10 Places Sorted by Percent
Based on places with populations of 10,000 or more

Place	Number	%
Crest Hill (city) Will County	437	3.35
Lansing (village) Cook County	564	2.00
Palos Hills (city) Cook County	351	1.98
Goodings Grove (cdp) Will County	316	1.85
Canton (city) Fulton County	264	1.73
Crestwood (village) Cook County	193	1.72
Orland Park (village) Cook County	868	1.70
Sauk Village (village) Cook County	175	1.68
Lyons (village) Cook County	157	1.55
Lemont (village) Cook County	202	1.53

Cypriot

Top 10 Places Sorted by Number
Based on all places, regardless of population

Place	Number	%
Chicago (city) Cook County	52	0.00
Carbondale (city) Jackson County	25	0.12
Lincolnwood (village) Cook County	18	0.15
Brookfield (village) Cook County	18	0.09
Des Plaines (city) Cook County	17	0.03
Murphysboro (city) Jackson County	15	0.11
Evanston (city) Cook County	9	0.01
Urbana (city) Champaign County	8	0.02
Naperville (city) Du Page County	8	0.01
Palatine (village) Cook County	8	0.01

Top 10 Places Sorted by Percent
Based on all places, regardless of population

Place	Number	%
East Dundee (village) Kane County	7	0.24
Lincolnwood (village) Cook County	18	0.15
Carbondale (city) Jackson County	25	0.12
Murphysboro (city) Jackson County	15	0.11
Brookfield (village) Cook County	18	0.09
La Grange Park (village) Cook County	6	0.05
Des Plaines (city) Cook County	17	0.03
Norridge (village) Cook County	4	0.03
Urbana (city) Champaign County	8	0.02
Evanston (city) Cook County	9	0.01

Top 10 Places Sorted by Percent
Based on places with populations of 10,000 or more

Place	Number	%
Lincolnwood (village) Cook County	18	0.15
Carbondale (city) Jackson County	25	0.12
Murphysboro (city) Jackson County	15	0.11

Notes: (cdp) census designated place; Refer to the User's Guide in the front of the book for more detailed information.

Place	Number	%
Brookfield (village) Cook County	18	0.09
La Grange Park (village) Cook County	6	0.05
Des Plaines (city) Cook County	17	0.03
Norridge (village) Cook County	4	0.03
Urbana (city) Champaign County	8	0.02
Evanston (city) Cook County	9	0.01
Naperville (city) Du Page County	8	0.01

Czech

Top 10 Places Sorted by Number

Based on all places, regardless of population

Place	Number	%
Chicago (city) Cook County	13,790	0.48
Berwyn (city) Cook County	2,982	5.52
Naperville (city) Du Page County	2,803	2.18
Downers Grove (village) Du Page County	2,563	5.27
Brookfield (village) Cook County	1,802	9.48
Cicero (town) Cook County	1,714	2.00
Bolingbrook (village) Will County	1,532	2.71
Woodridge (village) Du Page County	1,396	4.49
Wheaton (city) Du Page County	1,366	2.46
Schaumburg (village) Cook County	1,356	1.82

Top 10 Places Sorted by Percent

Based on all places, regardless of population

Place	Number	%
Forest View (village) Cook County	130	16.33
Stickney (village) Cook County	792	12.88
North Riverside (village) Cook County	790	11.73
East Brooklyn (village) Grundy County	10	9.80
Lyons (village) Cook County	991	9.78
Brookfield (village) Cook County	1,802	9.48
White City (village) Macoupin County	17	8.63
La Grange Park (village) Cook County	1,072	8.10
Indian Head Park (village) Cook County	285	7.45
Westchester (village) Cook County	1,194	7.17

Top 10 Places Sorted by Percent

Based on places with populations of 10,000 or more

Place	Number	%
Lyons (village) Cook County	991	9.78
Brookfield (village) Cook County	1,802	9.48
La Grange Park (village) Cook County	1,072	8.10
Westchester (village) Cook County	1,194	7.17
Berwyn (city) Cook County	2,982	5.52
La Grange (village) Cook County	853	5.42
Downers Grove (village) Du Page County	2,563	5.27
Darien (city) Du Page County	1,176	5.12
Burr Ridge (village) Du Page County	493	4.77
Woodridge (village) Du Page County	1,396	4.49

Czechoslovakian

Top 10 Places Sorted by Number

Based on all places, regardless of population

Place	Number	%
Chicago (city) Cook County	3,296	0.11
Naperville (city) Du Page County	827	0.64
Berwyn (city) Cook County	717	1.33
Downers Grove (village) Du Page County	374	0.77
Brookfield (village) Cook County	318	1.67
Arlington Heights (village) Cook County	292	0.38
Wheaton (city) Du Page County	288	0.52
Aurora (city) Kane County	282	0.20
Elgin (city) Kane County	265	0.28
Westchester (village) Cook County	260	1.56

Top 10 Places Sorted by Percent

Based on all places, regardless of population

Place	Number	%
Stickney (village) Cook County	203	3.30
Johnsburg (village) McHenry County	149	2.75
North Riverside (village) Cook County	183	2.72
Forest View (village) Cook County	21	2.64
Jeisyville (village) Christian County	2	2.22
Makanda (village) Jackson County	8	1.97
Cherry (village) Bureau County	10	1.95
Dowell (village) Jackson County	9	1.93
La Grange Park (village) Cook County	250	1.89
Donnellson (village) Montgomery County	4	1.79

Top 10 Places Sorted by Percent

Based on places with populations of 10,000 or more

Place	Number	%
La Grange Park (village) Cook County	250	1.89
Brookfield (village) Cook County	318	1.67
Burr Ridge (village) Du Page County	170	1.65
Lyons (village) Cook County	164	1.62
Westchester (village) Cook County	260	1.56
Berwyn (city) Cook County	717	1.33
Western Springs (village) Cook County	131	1.04
La Grange (village) Cook County	159	1.01
Darien (city) Du Page County	225	0.98
Villa Park (village) Du Page County	197	0.88

Danish

Top 10 Places Sorted by Number

Based on all places, regardless of population

Place	Number	%
Chicago (city) Cook County	5,922	0.20
Naperville (city) Du Page County	1,328	1.04
Rockford (city) Winnebago County	847	0.57
Aurora (city) Kane County	757	0.53
Palatine (village) Cook County	728	1.12
Arlington Heights (village) Cook County	667	0.88
Schaumburg (village) Cook County	617	0.83
Downers Grove (village) Du Page County	602	1.24
Crystal Lake (city) McHenry County	568	1.50
Des Plaines (city) Cook County	558	0.95

Top 10 Places Sorted by Percent

Based on all places, regardless of population

Place	Number	%
New Bedford (village) Bureau County	9	9.89
Nelson (village) Lee County	12	8.00
Dwight (village) Livingston County	315	7.19
Sciota (village) McDonough County	3	6.67
Kinsman (village) Grundy County	8	6.56
Prairie Grove (village) McHenry County	66	6.24
Greenwood (village) McHenry County	16	6.04
East Brooklyn (village) Grundy County	6	5.88
Hebron (village) McHenry County	54	5.35
McNabb (village) Putnam County	15	5.23

Top 10 Places Sorted by Percent

Based on places with populations of 10,000 or more

Place	Number	%
Lindenhurst (village) Lake County	230	1.82
Grayslake (village) Lake County	318	1.72
Crystal Lake (city) McHenry County	568	1.50
Oswego (village) Kendall County	198	1.49
Morris (city) Grundy County	170	1.42
Cary (village) McHenry County	208	1.35
Sycamore (city) De Kalb County	152	1.25
Downers Grove (village) Du Page County	602	1.24
Bradley (village) Kankakee County	156	1.23
Warrenville (city) Du Page County	157	1.19

Dutch

Top 10 Places Sorted by Number

Based on all places, regardless of population

Place	Number	%
Chicago (city) Cook County	11,906	0.41
Lansing (village) Cook County	3,857	13.70
Naperville (city) Du Page County	2,808	2.19
South Holland (village) Cook County	2,718	12.20
Tinley Park (village) Cook County	2,566	5.31
Rockford (city) Winnebago County	2,264	1.51
Springfield (city) Sangamon County	2,001	1.78
Aurora (city) Kane County	1,831	1.27
Peoria (city) Peoria County	1,821	1.61
Orland Park (village) Cook County	1,658	3.24

Top 10 Places Sorted by Percent

Based on all places, regardless of population

Place	Number	%
Fulton (city) Whiteside County	1,451	37.29
Wilmington (village) Greene County	26	23.21
Morrison (city) Whiteside County	1,021	23.19
Media (village) Henderson County	16	14.04
Lansing (village) Cook County	3,857	13.70
Strawn (village) Livingston County	15	13.04
Albany (village) Whiteside County	118	12.91
Cypress (village) Johnson County	30	12.61
South Holland (village) Cook County	2,718	12.20
Adeline (village) Ogle County	17	12.06

Top 10 Places Sorted by Percent

Based on places with populations of 10,000 or more

Place	Number	%
Lansing (village) Cook County	3,857	13.70
South Holland (village) Cook County	2,718	12.20
Palos Heights (city) Cook County	1,032	9.12
Tinley Park (village) Cook County	2,566	5.31
Oak Forest (city) Cook County	1,439	5.15
Frankfort (village) Will County	474	4.63
Worth (village) Cook County	500	4.48
Crestwood (village) Cook County	466	4.15
Mokena (village) Will County	563	3.84
Bradley (village) Kankakee County	463	3.64

Eastern European

Top 10 Places Sorted by Number

Based on all places, regardless of population

Place	Number	%
Chicago (city) Cook County	3,388	0.12
Highland Park (city) Lake County	797	2.54
Skokie (village) Cook County	603	0.95
Evanston (city) Cook County	585	0.79
Buffalo Grove (village) Lake County	521	1.22
Deerfield (village) Lake County	444	2.40
Glencoe (village) Cook County	387	4.38
Wilmette (village) Cook County	338	1.22
Northbrook (village) Cook County	331	0.99
Oak Park (village) Cook County	200	0.38

Top 10 Places Sorted by Percent

Based on all places, regardless of population

Place	Number	%
Smithfield (village) Fulton County	15	7.18
Glencoe (village) Cook County	387	4.38
Highland Park (city) Lake County	797	2.54
Deerfield (village) Lake County	444	2.40
Riverwoods (village) Lake County	58	1.54
Mineral (village) Bureau County	4	1.47
Buffalo Grove (village) Lake County	521	1.22
Wilmette (village) Cook County	338	1.22
Lincolnwood (village) Cook County	133	1.08
Northbrook (village) Cook County	331	0.99

Top 10 Places Sorted by Percent

Based on places with populations of 10,000 or more

Place	Number	%
Highland Park (city) Lake County	797	2.54
Deerfield (village) Lake County	444	2.40
Buffalo Grove (village) Lake County	521	1.22

Notes: (cdp) census designated place; Refer to the User's Guide in the front of the book for more detailed information.

Place	Number	%
Wilmette (village) Cook County	338	1.22
Lincolnwood (village) Cook County	133	1.08
Northbrook (village) Cook County	331	0.99
Skokie (village) Cook County	603	0.95
Winnetka (village) Cook County	115	0.93
Evanston (city) Cook County	585	0.79
Vernon Hills (village) Lake County	86	0.42

English

Top 10 Places Sorted by Number

Based on all places, regardless of population

Place	Number	%
Chicago (city) Cook County	57,579	1.99
Springfield (city) Sangamon County	13,288	11.84
Naperville (city) Du Page County	12,672	9.88
Rockford (city) Winnebago County	11,885	7.94
Peoria (city) Peoria County	9,938	8.80
Aurora (city) Kane County	8,014	5.58
Decatur (city) Macon County	7,668	9.34
Wheaton (city) Du Page County	7,150	12.90
Champaign (city) Champaign County	7,102	10.46
Bloomington (city) McLean County	7,025	10.80

Top 10 Places Sorted by Percent

Based on all places, regardless of population

Place	Number	%
Hanaford (village) Franklin County	2	100.00
Simpson (village) Johnson County	22	38.60
Garrett (village) Douglas County	64	31.53
La Prairie (village) Adams County	17	30.91
Neponset (village) Bureau County	154	30.62
Florence (village) Pike County	18	30.51
Manchester (village) Scott County	95	26.54
Albion (city) Edwards County	499	25.01
Waggoner (village) Montgomery County	74	24.67
Golf (village) Cook County	111	24.56

Top 10 Places Sorted by Percent

Based on places with populations of 10,000 or more

Place	Number	%
Winnetka (village) Cook County	2,271	18.33
Lake Forest (city) Lake County	3,288	16.43
Washington (city) Tazewell County	1,713	15.73
Hinsdale (village) Du Page County	2,430	13.90
Jacksonville (city) Morgan County	2,612	13.80
Godfrey (village) Madison County	2,220	13.60
Glen Ellyn (village) Du Page County	3,588	13.27
Morton (village) Tazewell County	1,985	13.19
East Peoria (city) Tazewell County	3,013	13.16
Marion (city) Williamson County	2,104	13.16

Estonian

Top 10 Places Sorted by Number

Based on all places, regardless of population

Place	Number	%
Chicago (city) Cook County	233	0.01
Crestwood (village) Cook County	55	0.49
Arlington Heights (village) Cook County	46	0.06
Naperville (city) Du Page County	45	0.04
Glen Ellyn (village) Du Page County	44	0.16
Grayslake (village) Lake County	35	0.19
Schaumburg (village) Cook County	31	0.04
Evanston (city) Cook County	30	0.04
Springfield (city) Sangamon County	28	0.02
Glencoe (village) Cook County	27	0.31

Top 10 Places Sorted by Percent

Based on all places, regardless of population

Place	Number	%
Third Lake (village) Lake County	7	0.52
Crestwood (village) Cook County	55	0.49
Barrington Hills (village) Cook County	14	0.34
Glencoe (village) Cook County	27	0.31
Riverwoods (village) Lake County	10	0.27
Long Lake (cdp) Lake County	9	0.26
Oakwood Hills (village) McHenry County	5	0.23
Burr Ridge (village) Du Page County	23	0.22
Grayslake (village) Lake County	35	0.19
Fox River Grove (village) McHenry County	9	0.18

Top 10 Places Sorted by Percent

Based on places with populations of 10,000 or more

Place	Number	%
Crestwood (village) Cook County	55	0.49
Burr Ridge (village) Du Page County	23	0.22
Grayslake (village) Lake County	35	0.19
Glen Ellyn (village) Du Page County	44	0.16
La Grange (village) Cook County	25	0.16
Woodstock (city) McHenry County	23	0.11
Canton (city) Fulton County	16	0.10
Mundelein (village) Lake County	26	0.09
Western Springs (village) Cook County	11	0.09
Northbrook (village) Cook County	25	0.07

European

Top 10 Places Sorted by Number

Based on all places, regardless of population

Place	Number	%
Chicago (city) Cook County	7,652	0.26
Evanston (city) Cook County	1,153	1.55
Springfield (city) Sangamon County	1,134	1.01
Naperville (city) Du Page County	962	0.75
Champaign (city) Champaign County	936	1.38
Peoria (city) Peoria County	853	0.76
Wheaton (city) Du Page County	768	1.39
Decatur (city) Macon County	729	0.89
Aurora (city) Kane County	635	0.44
Highland Park (city) Lake County	627	2.00

Top 10 Places Sorted by Percent

Based on all places, regardless of population

Place	Number	%
Cleveland (village) Henry County	24	9.56
Menominee (village) Jo Daviess County	14	5.79
Alhambra (village) Madison County	34	5.28
Havana (city) Mason County	169	4.72
Scott AFB (cdp) Saint Clair County	130	4.67
Cypress (village) Johnson County	11	4.62
Buncombe (village) Johnson County	9	4.43
Lee (village) Lee County	12	4.41
Campus (village) Livingston County	5	4.20
Wilsonville (village) Macoupin County	24	3.91

Top 10 Places Sorted by Percent

Based on places with populations of 10,000 or more

Place	Number	%
Wood River (city) Madison County	299	2.67
Winnetka (village) Cook County	321	2.59
Deerfield (village) Lake County	478	2.58
Godfrey (village) Madison County	415	2.54
Highland Park (city) Lake County	627	2.00
Sycamore (city) De Kalb County	215	1.77
Evanston (city) Cook County	1,153	1.55
O'Fallon (city) Saint Clair County	318	1.45
Carbondale (city) Jackson County	296	1.43
Wheaton (city) Du Page County	768	1.39

Finnish

Top 10 Places Sorted by Number

Based on all places, regardless of population

Place	Number	%
Chicago (city) Cook County	2,163	0.07
Waukegan (city) Lake County	635	0.72
Zion (city) Lake County	423	1.84
Gurnee (village) Lake County	384	1.34
Naperville (city) Du Page County	381	0.30
Rockford (city) Winnebago County	271	0.18
Winthrop Harbor (village) Lake County	266	4.00
Aurora (city) Kane County	253	0.18
Arlington Heights (village) Cook County	218	0.29
Mundelein (village) Lake County	217	0.71

Top 10 Places Sorted by Percent

Based on all places, regardless of population

Place	Number	%
Winthrop Harbor (village) Lake County	266	4.00
Wadsworth (village) Lake County	114	3.78
Kempton (village) Ford County	7	2.64
Lake Catherine (cdp) Lake County	34	2.36
Pingree Grove (village) Kane County	2	2.17
Old Mill Creek (village) Lake County	6	1.98
Beach Park (village) Lake County	187	1.92
Zion (city) Lake County	423	1.84
Vergennes (village) Jackson County	9	1.84
Spring Grove (village) McHenry County	69	1.81

Top 10 Places Sorted by Percent

Based on places with populations of 10,000 or more

Place	Number	%
Zion (city) Lake County	423	1.84
Gurnee (village) Lake County	384	1.34
Gages Lake (cdp) Lake County	114	1.09
McHenry (city) McHenry County	174	0.81
Waukegan (city) Lake County	635	0.72
Mundelein (village) Lake County	217	0.71
Streamwood (village) Cook County	211	0.57
Bloomingdale (village) Du Page County	122	0.57
De Kalb (city) De Kalb County	217	0.56
Grayslake (village) Lake County	104	0.56

French, except Basque

Top 10 Places Sorted by Number

Based on all places, regardless of population

Place	Number	%
Chicago (city) Cook County	24,043	0.83
Naperville (city) Du Page County	3,566	2.78
Rockford (city) Winnebago County	3,501	2.34
Springfield (city) Sangamon County	2,959	2.64
Aurora (city) Kane County	2,482	1.73
Peoria (city) Peoria County	2,428	2.15
Joliet (city) Will County	2,207	2.08
Belleville (city) Saint Clair County	2,141	5.08
Bloomington (city) McLean County	2,019	3.10
Decatur (city) Macon County	1,898	2.31

Top 10 Places Sorted by Percent

Based on all places, regardless of population

Place	Number	%
Prairie du Rocher (village) Randolph County	191	30.96
Ashkum (village) Iroquois County	152	21.35
Beaverville (village) Iroquois County	79	20.63
Campus (village) Livingston County	24	20.17
Saint Anne (village) Kankakee County	238	19.75
Irwin (village) Kankakee County	12	19.05
Donovan (village) Iroquois County	73	18.48
West Brooklyn (village) Lee County	32	17.88
Chebanse (village) Iroquois County	203	17.29
Clifton (village) Iroquois County	228	17.19

Top 10 Places Sorted by Percent

Based on places with populations of 10,000 or more

Place	Number	%
Bradley (village) Kankakee County	1,713	13.46
Bourbonnais (village) Kankakee County	1,854	12.08
Kankakee (city) Kankakee County	1,786	6.48

Notes: (cdp) census designated place; Refer to the User's Guide in the front of the book for more detailed information.

Collinsville (city) Madison County	1,336	5.47
Fairview Heights (city) Saint Clair County	817	5.34
O'Fallon (city) Saint Clair County	1,146	5.24
Ottawa (city) La Salle County	953	5.19
Belleville (city) Saint Clair County	2,141	5.08
Godfrey (village) Madison County	723	4.43
Granite City (city) Madison County	1,310	4.14

French Canadian

Top 10 Places Sorted by Number

Based on all places, regardless of population

Place	Number	%
Chicago (city) Cook County	4,945	0.17
Naperville (city) Du Page County	811	0.63
Aurora (city) Kane County	669	0.47
Bradley (village) Kankakee County	639	5.02
Rockford (city) Winnebago County	546	0.36
Kankakee (city) Kankakee County	496	1.80
Elgin (city) Kane County	454	0.48
Evanston (city) Cook County	376	0.51
Schaumburg (village) Cook County	373	0.50
Peoria (city) Peoria County	368	0.33

Top 10 Places Sorted by Percent

Based on all places, regardless of population

Place	Number	%
Beaverville (village) Iroquois County	46	12.01
Martinton (village) Iroquois County	34	8.72
Irwin (village) Kankakee County	4	6.35
Anchor (village) McLean County	10	6.13
Saint Anne (village) Kankakee County	62	5.15
Bradley (village) Kankakee County	639	5.02
Clifton (village) Iroquois County	65	4.90
Compton (village) Lee County	16	4.73
Buckingham (village) Kankakee County	9	3.88
Papineau (village) Iroquois County	7	3.83

Top 10 Places Sorted by Percent

Based on places with populations of 10,000 or more

Place	Number	%
Bradley (village) Kankakee County	639	5.02
Bourbonnais (village) Kankakee County	337	2.20
Kankakee (city) Kankakee County	496	1.80
Barrington (village) Cook County	131	1.31
Cary (village) McHenry County	194	1.26
Lemont (village) Cook County	132	1.00
Crest Hill (city) Will County	124	0.95
Glen Ellyn (village) Du Page County	244	0.90
Gurnee (village) Lake County	252	0.88
Geneva (city) Kane County	171	0.87

German

Top 10 Places Sorted by Number

Based on all places, regardless of population

Place	Number	%
Chicago (city) Cook County	189,618	6.55
Naperville (city) Du Page County	34,638	27.00
Rockford (city) Winnebago County	29,443	19.67
Springfield (city) Sangamon County	27,385	24.41
Aurora (city) Kane County	25,070	17.46
Peoria (city) Peoria County	24,774	21.94
Arlington Heights (village) Cook County	20,899	27.46
Elgin (city) Kane County	20,620	21.96
Joliet (city) Will County	19,079	17.97
Schaumburg (village) Cook County	18,501	24.83

Top 10 Places Sorted by Percent

Based on all places, regardless of population

Place	Number	%
Fults (village) Monroe County	38	100.00
Hanaford (village) Franklin County	2	100.00
Teutopolis (village) Effingham County	1,106	71.08
Sigel (town) Shelby County	270	69.77
Aviston (village) Clinton County	855	69.12
Germantown (village) Clinton County	769	68.91
Saint Libory (village) Saint Clair County	395	67.18
Bartelso (village) Clinton County	409	65.97
Brussels (village) Calhoun County	91	65.00
Harmon (village) Lee County	101	64.33

Top 10 Places Sorted by Percent

Based on places with populations of 10,000 or more

Place	Number	%
Morton (village) Tazewell County	6,055	40.25
Washington (city) Tazewell County	4,330	39.76
Swansea (village) Saint Clair County	4,089	39.27
Effingham (city) Effingham County	4,633	37.25
McHenry (city) McHenry County	7,904	36.65
Quincy (city) Adams County	14,757	36.64
Freeport (city) Stephenson County	9,600	36.31
Gages Lake (cdp) Lake County	3,676	35.15
Crystal Lake (city) McHenry County	13,035	34.45
Godfrey (village) Madison County	5,575	34.16

German Russian

Top 10 Places Sorted by Number

Based on all places, regardless of population

Place	Number	%
Chicago (city) Cook County	73	0.00
Rockton (village) Winnebago County	25	0.47
Buffalo Grove (village) Lake County	19	0.04
North Chicago (city) Lake County	16	0.04
Bellwood (village) Cook County	11	0.05
Fox River Grove (village) McHenry County	9	0.18
Midlothian (village) Cook County	9	0.06
Park Forest (village) Cook County	9	0.04
Naperville (city) Du Page County	9	0.01
Burr Ridge (village) Du Page County	7	0.07

Top 10 Places Sorted by Percent

Based on all places, regardless of population

Place	Number	%
Rockton (village) Winnebago County	25	0.47
Phoenix (village) Cook County	4	0.19
Fox River Grove (village) McHenry County	9	0.18
Thornton (village) Cook County	4	0.15
Wyoming (city) Stark County	2	0.14
Burr Ridge (village) Du Page County	7	0.07
Midlothian (village) Cook County	9	0.06
Glencoe (village) Cook County	5	0.06
Bellwood (village) Cook County	11	0.05
Herrin (city) Williamson County	5	0.05

Top 10 Places Sorted by Percent

Based on places with populations of 10,000 or more

Place	Number	%
Burr Ridge (village) Du Page County	7	0.07
Midlothian (village) Cook County	9	0.06
Bellwood (village) Cook County	11	0.05
Herrin (city) Williamson County	5	0.05
Buffalo Grove (village) Lake County	19	0.04
North Chicago (city) Lake County	16	0.04
Park Forest (village) Cook County	9	0.04
West Chicago (city) Du Page County	7	0.03
Loves Park (city) Winnebago County	5	0.03
Gages Lake (cdp) Lake County	3	0.03

Greek

Top 10 Places Sorted by Number

Based on all places, regardless of population

Place	Number	%
Chicago (city) Cook County	18,249	0.63
Orland Park (village) Cook County	1,797	3.52
Skokie (village) Cook County	1,706	2.69
Mount Prospect (village) Cook County	1,654	2.92
Naperville (city) Du Page County	1,606	1.25
Arlington Heights (village) Cook County	1,442	1.89
Des Plaines (city) Cook County	1,423	2.42
Glenview (village) Cook County	1,420	3.41
Oak Lawn (village) Cook County	1,378	2.49
Park Ridge (city) Cook County	1,288	3.41

Top 10 Places Sorted by Percent

Based on all places, regardless of population

Place	Number	%
Lincolnwood (village) Cook County	963	7.79
Greenwood (village) McHenry County	20	7.55
South Barrington (village) Cook County	274	7.35
Palos Hills (city) Cook County	1,141	6.43
Palos Park (village) Cook County	276	6.10
Bedford Park (village) Cook County	33	5.87
Cleveland (village) Henry County	12	4.78
Oak Brook (village) Du Page County	383	4.53
Harwood Heights (village) Cook County	357	4.34
Long Grove (village) Lake County	280	4.23

Top 10 Places Sorted by Percent

Based on places with populations of 10,000 or more

Place	Number	%
Lincolnwood (village) Cook County	963	7.79
Palos Hills (city) Cook County	1,141	6.43
Morton Grove (village) Cook County	859	3.83
Norridge (village) Cook County	556	3.78
Orland Park (village) Cook County	1,797	3.52
Glenview (village) Cook County	1,420	3.41
Park Ridge (city) Cook County	1,288	3.41
Niles (village) Cook County	990	3.28
Westchester (village) Cook County	491	2.95
Lake Forest (city) Lake County	586	2.93

Guyanese

Top 10 Places Sorted by Number

Based on all places, regardless of population

Place	Number	%
Chicago (city) Cook County	370	0.01
University Park (village) Will County	74	1.12
Hanover Park (village) Cook County	56	0.15
Rockford (city) Winnebago County	41	0.03
North Chicago (city) Lake County	28	0.08
Freeport (city) Stephenson County	26	0.10
Skokie (village) Cook County	16	0.03
Cortland (town) De Kalb County	15	0.73
Oak Park (village) Cook County	15	0.03
Bolingbrook (village) Will County	13	0.02

Top 10 Places Sorted by Percent

Based on all places, regardless of population

Place	Number	%
University Park (village) Will County	74	1.12
Dalton City (village) Moultrie County	5	0.82
Cortland (town) De Kalb County	15	0.73
Rankin (village) Vermilion County	2	0.33
Hanover Park (village) Cook County	56	0.15
Saint Joseph (village) Champaign County	4	0.14
River Grove (village) Cook County	12	0.11
Freeport (city) Stephenson County	26	0.10
North Chicago (city) Lake County	28	0.08
Bellwood (village) Cook County	12	0.06

Top 10 Places Sorted by Percent

Based on places with populations of 10,000 or more

Place	Number	%
Hanover Park (village) Cook County	56	0.15
River Grove (village) Cook County	12	0.11
Freeport (city) Stephenson County	26	0.10

Notes: (cdp) census designated place; Refer to the User's Guide in the front of the book for more detailed information.

Place	Number	%
North Chicago (city) Lake County	28	0.08
Bellwood (village) Cook County	12	0.06
Prospect Heights (city) Cook County	8	0.05
Matteson (village) Cook County	6	0.05
Rockford (city) Winnebago County	41	0.03
Skokie (village) Cook County	16	0.03
Oak Park (village) Cook County	15	0.03

Hawaii Native/Pacific Islander

Top 10 Places Sorted by Number

Based on all places, regardless of population

Place	Number	%
Chicago (city) Cook County	4,661	0.16
North Chicago (city) Lake County	184	0.51
Evanston (city) Cook County	150	0.20
Elgin (city) Kane County	133	0.14
Rockford (city) Winnebago County	131	0.09
Aurora (city) Kane County	126	0.09
Waukegan (city) Lake County	119	0.14
Peoria (city) Peoria County	107	0.09
Naperville (city) Du Page County	103	0.08
Skokie (village) Cook County	94	0.15

Top 10 Places Sorted by Percent

Based on all places, regardless of population

Place	Number	%
Gulf Port (village) Henderson County	5	2.42
Freeman Spur (village) Franklin County	6	2.20
Bannockburn (village) Lake County	26	1.82
Plymouth (village) Hancock County	10	1.78
Gays (village) Moultrie County	4	1.54
Troy Grove (village) La Salle County	4	1.31
Standard (village) Putnam County	3	1.17
Saint Libory (village) Saint Clair County	5	0.86
Loami (village) Sangamon County	6	0.75
Stronghurst (village) Henderson County	6	0.67

Top 10 Places Sorted by Percent

Based on places with populations of 10,000 or more

Place	Number	%
North Chicago (city) Lake County	184	0.51
Lake Forest (city) Lake County	75	0.37
De Kalb (city) De Kalb County	84	0.22
Evanston (city) Cook County	150	0.20
Crest Hill (city) Will County	26	0.20
O'Fallon (city) Saint Clair County	41	0.19
Urbana (city) Champaign County	67	0.18
Murphysboro (city) Jackson County	23	0.17
Gages Lake (cdp) Lake County	18	0.17
Chicago (city) Cook County	4,661	0.16

Hawaii Native/Pacific Islander: Melanesian

Top 10 Places Sorted by Number

Based on all places, regardless of population

Place	Number	%
Chicago (city) Cook County	23	0.00
Crete (village) Will County	4	0.05
Sauk Village (village) Cook County	4	0.04
Alsip (village) Cook County	4	0.02
Libertyville (village) Lake County	4	0.02
Bloomington (city) McLean County	4	0.01
De Kalb (city) De Kalb County	3	0.01
Glendale Heights (village) Du Page County	3	0.01
Carbon Cliff (village) Rock Island County	2	0.12
Bolingbrook (village) Will County	2	0.00

Top 10 Places Sorted by Percent

Based on all places, regardless of population

Place	Number	%
East Gillespie (village) Macoupin County	1	0.43
Carbon Cliff (village) Rock Island County	2	0.12
Crete (village) Will County	4	0.05
Sauk Village (village) Cook County	4	0.04
Alsip (village) Cook County	4	0.02
Libertyville (village) Lake County	4	0.02
South Beloit (city) Winnebago County	1	0.02
Tuscola (city) Douglas County	1	0.02
Bloomington (city) McLean County	4	0.01
De Kalb (city) De Kalb County	3	0.01

Top 10 Places Sorted by Percent

Based on places with populations of 10,000 or more

Place	Number	%
Sauk Village (village) Cook County	4	0.04
Alsip (village) Cook County	4	0.02
Libertyville (village) Lake County	4	0.02
Bloomington (city) McLean County	4	0.01
De Kalb (city) De Kalb County	3	0.01
Glendale Heights (village) Du Page County	3	0.01
Wood Dale (city) Du Page County	1	0.01
Chicago (city) Cook County	23	0.00
Bolingbrook (village) Will County	2	0.00
Springfield (city) Sangamon County	2	0.00

Hawaii Native/Pacific Islander: Fijian

Top 10 Places Sorted by Number

Based on all places, regardless of population

Place	Number	%
Chicago (city) Cook County	19	0.00
Crete (village) Will County	4	0.05
Sauk Village (village) Cook County	4	0.04
Alsip (village) Cook County	4	0.02
Libertyville (village) Lake County	4	0.02
Bloomington (city) McLean County	4	0.01
Glendale Heights (village) Du Page County	3	0.01
Carbon Cliff (village) Rock Island County	2	0.12
Bolingbrook (village) Will County	2	0.00
Springfield (city) Sangamon County	2	0.00

Top 10 Places Sorted by Percent

Based on all places, regardless of population

Place	Number	%
Carbon Cliff (village) Rock Island County	2	0.12
Crete (village) Will County	4	0.05
Sauk Village (village) Cook County	4	0.04
Alsip (village) Cook County	4	0.02
Libertyville (village) Lake County	4	0.02
South Beloit (city) Winnebago County	1	0.02
Bloomington (city) McLean County	4	0.01
Glendale Heights (village) Du Page County	3	0.01
Wood Dale (city) Du Page County	1	0.01
Chicago (city) Cook County	19	0.00

Top 10 Places Sorted by Percent

Based on places with populations of 10,000 or more

Place	Number	%
Sauk Village (village) Cook County	4	0.04
Alsip (village) Cook County	4	0.02
Libertyville (village) Lake County	4	0.02
Bloomington (city) McLean County	4	0.01
Glendale Heights (village) Du Page County	3	0.01
Wood Dale (city) Du Page County	1	0.01
Chicago (city) Cook County	19	0.00
Bolingbrook (village) Will County	2	0.00
Springfield (city) Sangamon County	2	0.00
Aurora (city) Kane County	1	0.00

Hawaii Native/Pacific Islander: Other Melanesian

Top 10 Places Sorted by Number

Based on all places, regardless of population

Place	Number	%
Chicago (city) Cook County	4	0.00
De Kalb (city) De Kalb County	3	0.01
East Gillespie (village) Macoupin County	1	0.43
Tuscola (city) Douglas County	1	0.02
Berwyn (city) Cook County	1	0.00
Wheaton (city) Du Page County	1	0.00

Top 10 Places Sorted by Percent

Based on all places, regardless of population

Place	Number	%
East Gillespie (village) Macoupin County	1	0.43
Tuscola (city) Douglas County	1	0.02
De Kalb (city) De Kalb County	3	0.01
Chicago (city) Cook County	4	0.00
Berwyn (city) Cook County	1	0.00
Wheaton (city) Du Page County	1	0.00

Top 10 Places Sorted by Percent

Based on places with populations of 10,000 or more

Place	Number	%
De Kalb (city) De Kalb County	3	0.01
Chicago (city) Cook County	4	0.00
Berwyn (city) Cook County	1	0.00
Wheaton (city) Du Page County	1	0.00

Hawaii Native/Pacific Islander: Micronesian

Top 10 Places Sorted by Number

Based on all places, regardless of population

Place	Number	%
Chicago (city) Cook County	663	0.02
North Chicago (city) Lake County	66	0.18
Aurora (city) Kane County	35	0.02
Cicero (town) Cook County	29	0.03
Evanston (city) Cook County	27	0.04
Elgin (city) Kane County	23	0.02
Belleville (city) Saint Clair County	19	0.05
Waukegan (city) Lake County	15	0.02
Woodridge (village) Du Page County	13	0.04
Peoria (city) Peoria County	13	0.01

Top 10 Places Sorted by Percent

Based on all places, regardless of population

Place	Number	%
Gays (village) Moultrie County	4	1.54
Troy Grove (village) La Salle County	4	1.31
Loami (village) Sangamon County	6	0.75
Mulberry Grove (village) Bond County	4	0.60
Makanda (village) Jackson County	2	0.48
Tonica (village) La Salle County	3	0.44
Cordova (village) Rock Island County	2	0.32
Evansville (village) Randolph County	2	0.28
Scott AFB (cdp) Saint Clair County	6	0.22
Sheffield (village) Bureau County	2	0.21

Top 10 Places Sorted by Percent

Based on places with populations of 10,000 or more

Place	Number	%
North Chicago (city) Lake County	66	0.18
Murphysboro (city) Jackson County	9	0.07
Belleville (city) Saint Clair County	19	0.05
Evanston (city) Cook County	27	0.04
Woodridge (village) Du Page County	13	0.04
O'Fallon (city) Saint Clair County	9	0.04
Zion (city) Lake County	9	0.04
Homewood (village) Cook County	7	0.04

Notes: (cdp) census designated place; Refer to the User's Guide in the front of the book for more detailed information.

Place	Number	%
Riverdale (village) Cook County	6	0.04
Wood Dale (city) Du Page County	5	0.04

Hawaii Native/Pacific Islander: Guamanian or Chamorro

Top 10 Places Sorted by Number

Based on all places, regardless of population

Place	Number	%
Chicago (city) Cook County	637	0.02
North Chicago (city) Lake County	55	0.15
Cicero (town) Cook County	29	0.03
Evanston (city) Cook County	26	0.04
Aurora (city) Kane County	23	0.02
Elgin (city) Kane County	23	0.02
Belleville (city) Saint Clair County	18	0.04
Waukegan (city) Lake County	15	0.02
Woodridge (village) Du Page County	12	0.04
Peoria (city) Peoria County	12	0.01

Top 10 Places Sorted by Percent

Based on all places, regardless of population

Place	Number	%
Gays (village) Moultrie County	4	1.54
Troy Grove (village) La Salle County	4	1.31
Loami (village) Sangamon County	6	0.75
Makanda (village) Jackson County	2	0.48
Tonica (village) La Salle County	3	0.44
Cordova (village) Rock Island County	2	0.32
Evansville (village) Randolph County	2	0.28
Scott AFB (cdp) Saint Clair County	6	0.22
Sheffield (village) Bureau County	2	0.21
De Land (village) Piatt County	1	0.21

Top 10 Places Sorted by Percent

Based on places with populations of 10,000 or more

Place	Number	%
North Chicago (city) Lake County	55	0.15
Evanston (city) Cook County	26	0.04
Belleville (city) Saint Clair County	18	0.04
Woodridge (village) Du Page County	12	0.04
O'Fallon (city) Saint Clair County	9	0.04
Zion (city) Lake County	9	0.04
Riverdale (village) Cook County	6	0.04
Murphysboro (city) Jackson County	5	0.04
Wood Dale (city) Du Page County	5	0.04
Swansea (village) Saint Clair County	4	0.04

Hawaii Native/Pacific Islander: Other Micronesian

Top 10 Places Sorted by Number

Based on all places, regardless of population

Place	Number	%
Chicago (city) Cook County	26	0.00
Aurora (city) Kane County	12	0.01
North Chicago (city) Lake County	11	0.03
Park City (city) Lake County	9	0.14
Homewood (village) Cook County	7	0.04
Danville (city) Vermilion County	5	0.01
Mulberry Grove (village) Bond County	4	0.60
Murphysboro (city) Jackson County	4	0.03
Hoffman Estates (village) Cook County	4	0.01
Warrenville (city) Du Page County	3	0.02

Top 10 Places Sorted by Percent

Based on all places, regardless of population

Place	Number	%
Mulberry Grove (village) Bond County	4	0.60
Park City (city) Lake County	9	0.14
Payson (village) Adams County	1	0.09
Clifton (village) Iroquois County	1	0.08
Homewood (village) Cook County	7	0.04
Tolono (village) Champaign County	1	0.04
North Chicago (city) Lake County	11	0.03
Murphysboro (city) Jackson County	4	0.03
Mount Carmel (city) Wabash County	2	0.03
Salem (city) Marion County	2	0.03

Top 10 Places Sorted by Percent

Based on places with populations of 10,000 or more

Place	Number	%
Homewood (village) Cook County	7	0.04
North Chicago (city) Lake County	11	0.03
Murphysboro (city) Jackson County	4	0.03
Warrenville (city) Du Page County	3	0.02
Aurora (city) Kane County	12	0.01
Danville (city) Vermilion County	5	0.01
Hoffman Estates (village) Cook County	4	0.01
Bartlett (village) Du Page County	2	0.01
Charleston (city) Coles County	2	0.01
Darien (city) Du Page County	2	0.01

Hawaii Native/Pacific Islander: Polynesian

Top 10 Places Sorted by Number

Based on all places, regardless of population

Place	Number	%
Chicago (city) Cook County	1,303	0.04
North Chicago (city) Lake County	72	0.20
Rockford (city) Winnebago County	71	0.05
Peoria (city) Peoria County	49	0.04
Waukegan (city) Lake County	47	0.05
Schaumburg (village) Cook County	41	0.05
Elgin (city) Kane County	41	0.04
Springfield (city) Sangamon County	41	0.04
Evanston (city) Cook County	40	0.05
Joliet (city) Will County	39	0.04

Top 10 Places Sorted by Percent

Based on all places, regardless of population

Place	Number	%
Gulf Port (village) Henderson County	5	2.42
Freeman Spur (village) Franklin County	6	2.20
Standard (village) Putnam County	3	1.17
De Witt (village) De Witt County	1	0.53
Alhambra (village) Madison County	3	0.48
Nauvoo (city) Hancock County	5	0.47
Saint Johns (village) Perry County	1	0.46
Colp (village) Williamson County	1	0.45
Watson (village) Effingham County	3	0.41
Lisbon (village) Kendall County	1	0.40

Top 10 Places Sorted by Percent

Based on places with populations of 10,000 or more

Place	Number	%
North Chicago (city) Lake County	72	0.20
Gages Lake (cdp) Lake County	18	0.17
Crest Hill (city) Will County	19	0.14
O'Fallon (city) Saint Clair County	23	0.10
Lyons (village) Cook County	9	0.09
Park Forest (village) Cook County	19	0.08
Rantoul (village) Champaign County	10	0.08
Richton Park (village) Cook County	10	0.08
De Kalb (city) De Kalb County	29	0.07
Edwardsville (city) Madison County	14	0.07

Hawaii Native/Pacific Islander: Native Hawaiian

Top 10 Places Sorted by Number

Based on all places, regardless of population

Place	Number	%
Chicago (city) Cook County	643	0.02
North Chicago (city) Lake County	60	0.17
Waukegan (city) Lake County	34	0.04
Rockford (city) Winnebago County	33	0.02
Peoria (city) Peoria County	30	0.03
Evanston (city) Cook County	27	0.04
Joliet (city) Will County	27	0.03
Des Plaines (city) Cook County	23	0.04
Elgin (city) Kane County	23	0.02
Springfield (city) Sangamon County	23	0.02

Top 10 Places Sorted by Percent

Based on all places, regardless of population

Place	Number	%
Gulf Port (village) Henderson County	5	2.42
Freeman Spur (village) Franklin County	6	2.20
Standard (village) Putnam County	3	1.17
Nauvoo (city) Hancock County	5	0.47
Colp (village) Williamson County	1	0.45
Watson (village) Effingham County	3	0.41
Lisbon (village) Kendall County	1	0.40
Old Mill Creek (village) Lake County	1	0.40
Cullom (village) Livingston County	2	0.36
Forest Lake (cdp) Lake County	5	0.33

Top 10 Places Sorted by Percent

Based on places with populations of 10,000 or more

Place	Number	%
North Chicago (city) Lake County	60	0.17
Crest Hill (city) Will County	13	0.10
Gages Lake (cdp) Lake County	10	0.10
O'Fallon (city) Saint Clair County	18	0.08
Lyons (village) Cook County	8	0.08
Rantoul (village) Champaign County	9	0.07
Fairview Heights (city) Saint Clair County	9	0.06
Effingham (city) Effingham County	7	0.06
Belleville (city) Saint Clair County	20	0.05
Urbana (city) Champaign County	17	0.05

Hawaii Native/Pacific Islander: Samoan

Top 10 Places Sorted by Number

Based on all places, regardless of population

Place	Number	%
Chicago (city) Cook County	618	0.02
Rockford (city) Winnebago County	36	0.02
De Kalb (city) De Kalb County	23	0.06
Peoria (city) Peoria County	19	0.02
Schaumburg (village) Cook County	18	0.02
Elgin (city) Kane County	17	0.02
Springfield (city) Sangamon County	17	0.02
Park Forest (village) Cook County	13	0.06
Waukegan (city) Lake County	13	0.01
Rock Island (city) Rock Island County	12	0.03

Top 10 Places Sorted by Percent

Based on all places, regardless of population

Place	Number	%
De Witt (village) De Witt County	1	0.53
Saint Johns (village) Perry County	1	0.46
Cherry (village) Bureau County	2	0.39
Danforth (village) Iroquois County	2	0.34
Rosiclare (city) Hardin County	3	0.25
East Galesburg (village) Knox County	2	0.24
Smithton (village) Saint Clair County	5	0.22
German Valley (village) Stephenson County	1	0.21
Wilsonville (village) Macoupin County	1	0.17
Alhambra (village) Madison County	1	0.16

Top 10 Places Sorted by Percent

Based on places with populations of 10,000 or more

Place	Number	%
Gages Lake (cdp) Lake County	7	0.07
De Kalb (city) De Kalb County	23	0.06
Park Forest (village) Cook County	13	0.06
Crest Hill (city) Will County	6	0.05
McHenry (city) McHenry County	8	0.04

Notes: (cdp) census designated place; Refer to the User's Guide in the front of the book for more detailed information.

Place	Number	%
Dixon (city) Lee County	7	0.04
Centralia (city) Marion County	5	0.04
Richton Park (village) Cook County	5	0.04
Rock Island (city) Rock Island County	12	0.03
North Chicago (city) Lake County	11	0.03

Hawaii Native/Pacific Islander: Tongan

Top 10 Places Sorted by Number

Based on all places, regardless of population

Place	Number	%
West Chicago (city) Du Page County	7	0.03
Chicago (city) Cook County	7	0.00
Mount Carmel (city) Wabash County	4	0.05
Mount Vernon (city) Jefferson County	4	0.02
Oak Park (village) Cook County	3	0.01
Wheeling (village) Cook County	3	0.01
Alhambra (village) Madison County	2	0.32
Eureka (city) Woodford County	2	0.04
Park Ridge (city) Cook County	2	0.01
Savoy (village) Champaign County	1	0.02

Top 10 Places Sorted by Percent

Based on all places, regardless of population

Place	Number	%
Alhambra (village) Madison County	2	0.32
Mount Carmel (city) Wabash County	4	0.05
Eureka (city) Woodford County	2	0.04
West Chicago (city) Du Page County	7	0.03
Mount Vernon (city) Jefferson County	4	0.02
Savoy (village) Champaign County	1	0.02
Oak Park (village) Cook County	3	0.01
Wheeling (village) Cook County	3	0.01
Park Ridge (city) Cook County	2	0.01
Chicago (city) Cook County	7	0.00

Top 10 Places Sorted by Percent

Based on places with populations of 10,000 or more

Place	Number	%
West Chicago (city) Du Page County	7	0.03
Mount Vernon (city) Jefferson County	4	0.02
Oak Park (village) Cook County	3	0.01
Wheeling (village) Cook County	3	0.01
Park Ridge (city) Cook County	2	0.01
Chicago (city) Cook County	7	0.00
Arlington Heights (village) Cook County	1	0.00
Chicago Heights (city) Cook County	1	0.00
North Chicago (city) Lake County	1	0.00
O'Fallon (city) Saint Clair County	1	0.00

Hawaii Native/Pacific Islander: Other Polynesian

Top 10 Places Sorted by Number

Based on all places, regardless of population

Place	Number	%
Chicago (city) Cook County	35	0.00
Wheaton (city) Du Page County	5	0.01
Mokena (village) Will County	4	0.03
Champaign (city) Champaign County	4	0.01
Evanston (city) Cook County	4	0.01
Mount Olive (city) Macoupin County	3	0.14
Richton Park (village) Cook County	3	0.02
Blue Island (city) Cook County	3	0.01
Schaumburg (village) Cook County	3	0.00
Bartonville (village) Peoria County	2	0.03

Top 10 Places Sorted by Percent

Based on all places, regardless of population

Place	Number	%
Mount Olive (city) Macoupin County	3	0.14
Mokena (village) Will County	4	0.03
Bartonville (village) Peoria County	2	0.03
Stickney (village) Cook County	2	0.03
Casey (city) Clark County	1	0.03
Gibson (city) Ford County	1	0.03
Sleepy Hollow (village) Kane County	1	0.03
Richton Park (village) Cook County	3	0.02
Manteno (village) Kankakee County	1	0.02
Mascoutah (city) Saint Clair County	1	0.02

Top 10 Places Sorted by Percent

Based on places with populations of 10,000 or more

Place	Number	%
Mokena (village) Will County	4	0.03
Richton Park (village) Cook County	3	0.02
Wheaton (city) Du Page County	5	0.01
Champaign (city) Champaign County	4	0.01
Evanston (city) Cook County	4	0.01
Blue Island (city) Cook County	3	0.01
Crystal Lake (city) McHenry County	2	0.01
La Grange (village) Cook County	2	0.01
Wheeling (village) Cook County	2	0.01
Forest Park (village) Cook County	1	0.01

Hawaii Native/Pacific Islander: Other Pacific Islander, specified

Top 10 Places Sorted by Number

Based on all places, regardless of population

Place	Number	%
Chicago (city) Cook County	132	0.00
Minonk (city) Woodford County	9	0.42
Batavia (city) Kane County	8	0.03
Joliet (city) Will County	8	0.01
West Frankfort (city) Franklin County	6	0.07
Kewanee (city) Henry County	6	0.05
Dixon (city) Lee County	6	0.04
Godfrey (village) Madison County	6	0.04
New Lenox (village) Will County	6	0.03
Berwyn (city) Cook County	6	0.01

Top 10 Places Sorted by Percent

Based on all places, regardless of population

Place	Number	%
Minonk (city) Woodford County	9	0.42
White Hall (city) Greene County	4	0.15
Mound City (city) Pulaski County	1	0.14
West Frankfort (city) Franklin County	6	0.07
Harristown (village) Macon County	1	0.07
Kewanee (city) Henry County	6	0.05
Dixon (city) Lee County	6	0.04
Godfrey (village) Madison County	6	0.04
Beach Park (village) Lake County	4	0.04
Lynwood (village) Cook County	3	0.04

Top 10 Places Sorted by Percent

Based on places with populations of 10,000 or more

Place	Number	%
Kewanee (city) Henry County	6	0.05
Dixon (city) Lee County	6	0.04
Godfrey (village) Madison County	6	0.04
Beach Park (village) Lake County	4	0.04
Batavia (city) Kane County	8	0.03
New Lenox (village) Will County	6	0.03
McHenry (city) McHenry County	5	0.02
Ottawa (city) La Salle County	4	0.02
Lake Zurich (village) Lake County	3	0.02
Palos Hills (city) Cook County	3	0.02

Hawaii Native/Pacific Islander: Other Pacific Islander, not specified

Top 10 Places Sorted by Number

Based on all places, regardless of population

Place	Number	%
Chicago (city) Cook County	2,540	0.09
Evanston (city) Cook County	80	0.11
Naperville (city) Du Page County	78	0.06
Lake Forest (city) Lake County	71	0.35
Elgin (city) Kane County	69	0.07
Skokie (village) Cook County	68	0.11
Aurora (city) Kane County	67	0.05
Waukegan (city) Lake County	56	0.06
Rockford (city) Winnebago County	50	0.03
Champaign (city) Champaign County	48	0.07

Top 10 Places Sorted by Percent

Based on all places, regardless of population

Place	Number	%
Bannockburn (village) Lake County	26	1.82
Plymouth (village) Hancock County	10	1.78
Saint Libory (village) Saint Clair County	5	0.86
Sparland (village) Marshall County	3	0.60
Sidney (village) Champaign County	5	0.47
Stronghurst (village) Henderson County	4	0.45
Lanark (city) Carroll County	7	0.44
Warsaw (city) Hancock County	7	0.39
Lake Forest (city) Lake County	71	0.35
South Barrington (village) Cook County	12	0.32

Top 10 Places Sorted by Percent

Based on places with populations of 10,000 or more

Place	Number	%
Lake Forest (city) Lake County	71	0.35
North Chicago (city) Lake County	46	0.13
Evanston (city) Cook County	80	0.11
Skokie (village) Cook County	68	0.11
De Kalb (city) De Kalb County	43	0.11
Streamwood (village) Cook County	40	0.11
Darien (city) Du Page County	26	0.11
Lincolnwood (village) Cook County	13	0.11
Glendale Heights (village) Du Page County	33	0.10
Carpentersville (village) Kane County	30	0.10

Hispanic or Latino

Top 10 Places Sorted by Number

Based on all places, regardless of population

Place	Number	%
Chicago (city) Cook County	753,644	26.02
Cicero (town) Cook County	66,299	77.44
Aurora (city) Kane County	46,557	32.56
Waukegan (city) Lake County	39,396	44.82
Elgin (city) Kane County	32,430	34.32
Berwyn (city) Cook County	20,543	38.03
Joliet (city) Will County	19,552	18.41
Rockford (city) Winnebago County	15,278	10.18
Melrose Park (village) Cook County	12,485	53.88
Carpentersville (village) Kane County	12,410	40.57

Top 10 Places Sorted by Percent

Based on all places, regardless of population

Place	Number	%
Stone Park (village) Cook County	4,057	79.13
Cicero (town) Cook County	66,299	77.44
Fairmont City (village) Saint Clair County	1,349	55.38
Melrose Park (village) Cook County	12,485	53.88
West Chicago (city) Du Page County	11,405	48.60
Summit (village) Cook County	5,156	48.47
De Pue (village) Bureau County	843	45.77
Waukegan (city) Lake County	39,396	44.82
Hodgkins (village) Cook County	933	43.72
Carpentersville (village) Kane County	12,410	40.57

Top 10 Places Sorted by Percent
Based on places with populations of 10,000 or more

Place	Number	%
Cicero (town) Cook County	66,299	77.44
Melrose Park (village) Cook County	12,485	53.88
West Chicago (city) Du Page County	11,405	48.60
Summit (village) Cook County	5,156	48.47
Waukegan (city) Lake County	39,396	44.82
Carpentersville (village) Kane County	12,410	40.57
Franklin Park (village) Cook County	7,399	38.07
Berwyn (city) Cook County	20,543	38.03
Blue Island (city) Cook County	8,899	37.93
Bensenville (village) Du Page County	7,690	37.14

Hispanic: Central American

Top 10 Places Sorted by Number
Based on all places, regardless of population

Place	Number	%
Chicago (city) Cook County	23,339	0.81
Waukegan (city) Lake County	2,082	2.37
Cicero (town) Cook County	879	1.03
Berwyn (city) Cook County	350	0.65
Aurora (city) Kane County	329	0.23
Elgin (city) Kane County	295	0.31
Glendale Heights (village) Du Page County	290	0.91
Carpentersville (village) Kane County	282	0.92
Skokie (village) Cook County	271	0.43
Hanover Park (village) Cook County	270	0.71

Top 10 Places Sorted by Percent
Based on all places, regardless of population

Place	Number	%
Stone Park (village) Cook County	166	3.24
Waukegan (city) Lake County	2,082	2.37
Spillertown (village) Williamson County	3	1.36
Northlake (city) Cook County	146	1.23
Highwood (city) Lake County	50	1.21
Park City (city) Lake County	73	1.10
Bensenville (village) Du Page County	226	1.09
Melrose Park (village) Cook County	243	1.05
Cicero (town) Cook County	879	1.03
Godley (village) Will County	6	1.01

Top 10 Places Sorted by Percent
Based on places with populations of 10,000 or more

Place	Number	%
Waukegan (city) Lake County	2,082	2.37
Northlake (city) Cook County	146	1.23
Bensenville (village) Du Page County	226	1.09
Melrose Park (village) Cook County	243	1.05
Cicero (town) Cook County	879	1.03
Carpentersville (village) Kane County	282	0.92
Glendale Heights (village) Du Page County	290	0.91
Franklin Park (village) Cook County	175	0.90
Rolling Meadows (city) Cook County	214	0.87
Chicago (city) Cook County	23,339	0.81

Hispanic: Costa Rican

Top 10 Places Sorted by Number
Based on all places, regardless of population

Place	Number	%
Chicago (city) Cook County	609	0.02
Rockford (city) Winnebago County	42	0.03
Champaign (city) Champaign County	29	0.04
Des Plaines (city) Cook County	15	0.03
Wheaton (city) Du Page County	15	0.03
Evanston (city) Cook County	13	0.02
Aurora (city) Kane County	12	0.01
Cicero (town) Cook County	12	0.01
Hanover Park (village) Cook County	11	0.03
Lombard (village) Du Page County	11	0.03

Top 10 Places Sorted by Percent
Based on all places, regardless of population

Place	Number	%
Spillertown (village) Williamson County	3	1.36
Godley (village) Will County	6	1.01
Campbell Hill (village) Jackson County	1	0.30
Sidney (village) Champaign County	2	0.19
Findlay (village) Shelby County	1	0.14
Aroma Park (village) Kankakee County	1	0.12
White Hall (city) Greene County	3	0.11
New Berlin (village) Sangamon County	1	0.10
Caseyville (village) Saint Clair County	4	0.09
Lakewood (village) McHenry County	2	0.09

Top 10 Places Sorted by Percent
Based on places with populations of 10,000 or more

Place	Number	%
Lincolnwood (village) Cook County	8	0.06
Midlothian (village) Cook County	7	0.05
Summit (village) Cook County	5	0.05
Champaign (city) Champaign County	29	0.04
Romeoville (village) Will County	8	0.04
Schiller Park (village) Cook County	5	0.04
Lyons (village) Cook County	4	0.04
Rockford (city) Winnebago County	42	0.03
Des Plaines (city) Cook County	15	0.03
Wheaton (city) Du Page County	15	0.03

Hispanic: Guatemalan

Top 10 Places Sorted by Number
Based on all places, regardless of population

Place	Number	%
Chicago (city) Cook County	13,610	0.47
Cicero (town) Cook County	478	0.56
Glendale Heights (village) Du Page County	219	0.69
Addison (village) Du Page County	189	0.53
Waukegan (city) Lake County	189	0.22
Bensenville (village) Du Page County	187	0.90
Melrose Park (village) Cook County	177	0.76
Berwyn (city) Cook County	169	0.31
Stone Park (village) Cook County	129	2.52
Franklin Park (village) Cook County	127	0.65

Top 10 Places Sorted by Percent
Based on all places, regardless of population

Place	Number	%
Stone Park (village) Cook County	129	2.52
Northlake (city) Cook County	112	0.94
Bensenville (village) Du Page County	187	0.90
Coatsburg (village) Adams County	2	0.88
Melrose Park (village) Cook County	177	0.76
Glendale Heights (village) Du Page County	219	0.69
Dalton City (village) Moultrie County	4	0.69
Troy Grove (village) La Salle County	2	0.66
Franklin Park (village) Cook County	127	0.65
Park City (city) Lake County	38	0.57

Top 10 Places Sorted by Percent
Based on places with populations of 10,000 or more

Place	Number	%
Northlake (city) Cook County	112	0.94
Bensenville (village) Du Page County	187	0.90
Melrose Park (village) Cook County	177	0.76
Glendale Heights (village) Du Page County	219	0.69
Franklin Park (village) Cook County	127	0.65
Cicero (town) Cook County	478	0.56
Addison (village) Du Page County	189	0.53
Chicago (city) Cook County	13,610	0.47
Schiller Park (village) Cook County	43	0.36
Hanover Park (village) Cook County	123	0.32

Hispanic: Honduran

Top 10 Places Sorted by Number
Based on all places, regardless of population

Place	Number	%
Chicago (city) Cook County	3,049	0.11
Waukegan (city) Lake County	1,287	1.46
Cicero (town) Cook County	134	0.16
North Chicago (city) Lake County	73	0.20
Aurora (city) Kane County	58	0.04
Zion (city) Lake County	53	0.23
Berwyn (city) Cook County	51	0.09
Skokie (village) Cook County	50	0.08
Rockford (city) Winnebago County	49	0.03
Elgin (city) Kane County	32	0.03

Top 10 Places Sorted by Percent
Based on all places, regardless of population

Place	Number	%
Waukegan (city) Lake County	1,287	1.46
Cobden (village) Union County	5	0.45
Dakota (village) Stephenson County	2	0.40
Park City (city) Lake County	20	0.30
De Pue (village) Bureau County	5	0.27
Hurst (city) Williamson County	2	0.25
Zion (city) Lake County	53	0.23
Highwood (city) Lake County	9	0.22
Chenoa (city) McLean County	4	0.22
North Chicago (city) Lake County	73	0.20

Top 10 Places Sorted by Percent
Based on places with populations of 10,000 or more

Place	Number	%
Waukegan (city) Lake County	1,287	1.46
Zion (city) Lake County	53	0.23
North Chicago (city) Lake County	73	0.20
Cicero (town) Cook County	134	0.16
Beach Park (village) Lake County	12	0.12
Chicago (city) Cook County	3,049	0.11
Northlake (city) Cook County	13	0.11
Franklin Park (village) Cook County	20	0.10
Sauk Village (village) Cook County	10	0.10
Berwyn (city) Cook County	51	0.09

Hispanic: Nicaraguan

Top 10 Places Sorted by Number
Based on all places, regardless of population

Place	Number	%
Chicago (city) Cook County	778	0.03
Cicero (town) Cook County	44	0.05
Aurora (city) Kane County	37	0.03
North Chicago (city) Lake County	27	0.08
Waukegan (city) Lake County	26	0.03
Palatine (village) Cook County	24	0.04
Melrose Park (village) Cook County	22	0.09
Oak Park (village) Cook County	21	0.04
Skokie (village) Cook County	17	0.03
Champaign (city) Champaign County	16	0.02

Top 10 Places Sorted by Percent
Based on all places, regardless of population

Place	Number	%
Jerome (village) Sangamon County	3	0.21
Amboy (city) Lee County	4	0.16
Kenilworth (village) Cook County	3	0.12
Forest Park (village) Cook County	15	0.10
Melrose Park (village) Cook County	22	0.09
North Chicago (city) Lake County	27	0.08
Green Oaks (village) Lake County	3	0.08
Pistakee Highlands (cdp) McHenry County	3	0.08
Lewistown (city) Fulton County	2	0.08
River Forest (village) Cook County	8	0.07

Notes: (cdp) census designated place; Refer to the User's Guide in the front of the book for more detailed information.

Top 10 Places Sorted by Percent

Based on places with populations of 10,000 or more

Place	Number	%
Forest Park (village) Cook County	15	0.10
Melrose Park (village) Cook County	22	0.09
North Chicago (city) Lake County	27	0.08
River Forest (village) Cook County	8	0.07
Cicero (town) Cook County	44	0.05
Murphysboro (city) Jackson County	6	0.05
Lyons (village) Cook County	5	0.05
Palatine (village) Cook County	24	0.04
Oak Park (village) Cook County	21	0.04
Zion (city) Lake County	10	0.04

Hispanic: Panamanian

Top 10 Places Sorted by Number

Based on all places, regardless of population

Place	Number	%
Chicago (city) Cook County	637	0.02
Evanston (city) Cook County	57	0.08
Cicero (town) Cook County	25	0.03
North Chicago (city) Lake County	24	0.07
Waukegan (city) Lake County	24	0.03
Oak Park (village) Cook County	21	0.04
Skokie (village) Cook County	21	0.03
Aurora (city) Kane County	21	0.01
Berwyn (city) Cook County	16	0.03
Wheeling (village) Cook County	14	0.04

Top 10 Places Sorted by Percent

Based on all places, regardless of population

Place	Number	%
Dalzell (village) Bureau County	3	0.42
Hanna City (village) Peoria County	4	0.39
North Barrington (village) Lake County	7	0.24
Glasford (village) Peoria County	2	0.19
Rochester (village) Sangamon County	4	0.14
Creal Springs (city) Williamson County	1	0.14
Broadview (village) Cook County	11	0.13
Pearl City (village) Stephenson County	1	0.13
Gifford (village) Champaign County	1	0.12
Shiloh (village) Saint Clair County	7	0.09

Top 10 Places Sorted by Percent

Based on places with populations of 10,000 or more

Place	Number	%
Evanston (city) Cook County	57	0.08
Sauk Village (village) Cook County	8	0.08
North Chicago (city) Lake County	24	0.07
Fairview Heights (city) Saint Clair County	10	0.07
Oak Park (village) Cook County	21	0.04
Wheeling (village) Cook County	14	0.04
Kankakee (city) Kankakee County	10	0.04
Vernon Hills (village) Lake County	9	0.04
Zion (city) Lake County	9	0.04
Bellwood (village) Cook County	8	0.04

Hispanic: Salvadoran

Top 10 Places Sorted by Number

Based on all places, regardless of population

Place	Number	%
Chicago (city) Cook County	3,468	0.12
Waukegan (city) Lake County	428	0.49
Rolling Meadows (city) Cook County	170	0.69
Carpentersville (village) Kane County	157	0.51
Cicero (town) Cook County	151	0.18
Round Lake Beach (village) Lake County	113	0.44
Mundelein (village) Lake County	107	0.35
Elgin (city) Kane County	107	0.11
Hanover Park (village) Cook County	94	0.25
Wheeling (village) Cook County	86	0.25

Top 10 Places Sorted by Percent

Based on all places, regardless of population

Place	Number	%
Rolling Meadows (city) Cook County	170	0.69
Highwood (city) Lake County	22	0.53
Carpentersville (village) Kane County	157	0.51
Waukegan (city) Lake County	428	0.49
Thomasboro (village) Champaign County	6	0.49
Stone Park (village) Cook County	23	0.45
Round Lake Beach (village) Lake County	113	0.44
Rosemont (village) Cook County	18	0.43
Prospect Heights (city) Cook County	63	0.37
Mundelein (village) Lake County	107	0.35

Top 10 Places Sorted by Percent

Based on places with populations of 10,000 or more

Place	Number	%
Rolling Meadows (city) Cook County	170	0.69
Carpentersville (village) Kane County	157	0.51
Waukegan (city) Lake County	428	0.49
Round Lake Beach (village) Lake County	113	0.44
Prospect Heights (city) Cook County	63	0.37
Mundelein (village) Lake County	107	0.35
Hanover Park (village) Cook County	94	0.25
Wheeling (village) Cook County	86	0.25
Summit (village) Cook County	27	0.25
Cicero (town) Cook County	151	0.18

Hispanic: Other Central American

Top 10 Places Sorted by Number

Based on all places, regardless of population

Place	Number	%
Chicago (city) Cook County	1,188	0.04
Waukegan (city) Lake County	123	0.14
Cicero (town) Cook County	35	0.04
Berwyn (city) Cook County	25	0.05
Skokie (village) Cook County	24	0.04
Elgin (city) Kane County	24	0.03
Des Plaines (city) Cook County	22	0.04
Wheeling (village) Cook County	21	0.06
North Chicago (city) Lake County	20	0.06
Evanston (city) Cook County	20	0.03

Top 10 Places Sorted by Percent

Based on all places, regardless of population

Place	Number	%
Arrowsmith (village) McLean County	1	0.34
Granville (village) Putnam County	3	0.21
Waukegan (city) Lake County	123	0.14
Round Lake Park (village) Lake County	7	0.12
Moweaqua (village) Shelby County	2	0.10
Capron (village) Boone County	1	0.10
Northlake (city) Cook County	11	0.09
Marengo (city) McHenry County	6	0.09
Hainesville (village) Lake County	2	0.09
Park City (city) Lake County	5	0.08

Top 10 Places Sorted by Percent

Based on places with populations of 10,000 or more

Place	Number	%
Waukegan (city) Lake County	123	0.14
Northlake (city) Cook County	11	0.09
East Moline (city) Rock Island County	14	0.07
Summit (village) Cook County	7	0.07
Wheeling (village) Cook County	21	0.06
North Chicago (city) Lake County	20	0.06
Glendale Heights (village) Du Page County	18	0.06
Berwyn (city) Cook County	25	0.05
Mundelein (village) Lake County	16	0.05
Chicago (city) Cook County	1,188	0.04

Hispanic: Cuban

Top 10 Places Sorted by Number

Based on all places, regardless of population

Place	Number	%
Chicago (city) Cook County	8,084	0.28
Skokie (village) Cook County	428	0.68
Melrose Park (village) Cook County	345	1.49
Rockford (city) Winnebago County	310	0.21
Naperville (city) Du Page County	211	0.16
Evanston (city) Cook County	209	0.28
Aurora (city) Kane County	207	0.14
Northlake (city) Cook County	158	1.33
Elmhurst (city) Du Page County	151	0.35
Schaumburg (village) Cook County	142	0.19

Top 10 Places Sorted by Percent

Based on all places, regardless of population

Place	Number	%
Ullin (village) Pulaski County	42	5.39
Venedy (village) Washington County	5	3.65
Birds (village) Lawrence County	1	1.96
Stone Park (village) Cook County	100	1.95
Melrose Park (village) Cook County	345	1.49
Northlake (city) Cook County	158	1.33
Lee (village) Lee County	3	0.96
Rio (village) Knox County	2	0.83
Kangley (village) La Salle County	2	0.70
Skokie (village) Cook County	428	0.68

Top 10 Places Sorted by Percent

Based on places with populations of 10,000 or more

Place	Number	%
Melrose Park (village) Cook County	345	1.49
Northlake (city) Cook County	158	1.33
Skokie (village) Cook County	428	0.68
Lincolnwood (village) Cook County	84	0.68
Franklin Park (village) Cook County	99	0.51
River Grove (village) Cook County	51	0.48
Burr Ridge (village) Du Page County	42	0.40
Wood Dale (city) Du Page County	52	0.38
Elmhurst (city) Du Page County	151	0.35
Glenview (village) Cook County	138	0.33

Hispanic: Dominican Republic

Top 10 Places Sorted by Number

Based on all places, regardless of population

Place	Number	%
Chicago (city) Cook County	1,651	0.06
Cicero (town) Cook County	96	0.11
Waukegan (city) Lake County	69	0.08
North Chicago (city) Lake County	64	0.18
Aurora (city) Kane County	47	0.03
Evanston (city) Cook County	37	0.05
Elgin (city) Kane County	33	0.03
Skokie (village) Cook County	31	0.05
Naperville (city) Du Page County	30	0.02
Rockford (city) Winnebago County	30	0.02

Top 10 Places Sorted by Percent

Based on all places, regardless of population

Place	Number	%
Irwin (village) Kankakee County	2	2.17
Kinmundy (city) Marion County	2	0.22
North Chicago (city) Lake County	64	0.18
Greenville (city) Bond County	8	0.12
Cicero (town) Cook County	96	0.11
Hillside (village) Cook County	8	0.10
River Forest (village) Cook County	10	0.09
Willowbrook (village) Du Page County	8	0.09
Sparta (city) Randolph County	4	0.09
Waukegan (city) Lake County	69	0.08

Notes: (cdp) census designated place; Refer to the User's Guide in the front of the book for more detailed information.

Top 10 Places Sorted by Percent

Based on places with populations of 10,000 or more

Place	Number	%
North Chicago (city) Lake County	64	0.18
Cicero (town) Cook County	96	0.11
River Forest (village) Cook County	10	0.09
Waukegan (city) Lake County	69	0.08
Belvidere (city) Boone County	16	0.08
Chicago (city) Cook County	1,651	0.06
Melrose Park (village) Cook County	15	0.06
Elmwood Park (village) Cook County	14	0.06
Zion (city) Lake County	13	0.06
Lemont (village) Cook County	8	0.06

Hispanic: Mexican

Top 10 Places Sorted by Number

Based on all places, regardless of population

Place	Number	%
Chicago (city) Cook County	530,462	18.32
Cicero (town) Cook County	58,542	68.38
Aurora (city) Kane County	39,351	27.52
Waukegan (city) Lake County	30,717	34.94
Elgin (city) Kane County	27,444	29.05
Joliet (city) Will County	16,939	15.95
Berwyn (city) Cook County	16,745	31.00
Rockford (city) Winnebago County	12,508	8.33
Carpentersville (village) Kane County	10,755	35.16
West Chicago (city) Du Page County	10,550	44.95

Top 10 Places Sorted by Percent

Based on all places, regardless of population

Place	Number	%
Cicero (town) Cook County	58,542	68.38
Stone Park (village) Cook County	3,422	66.74
Fairmont City (village) Saint Clair County	1,204	49.43
Melrose Park (village) Cook County	10,500	45.32
West Chicago (city) Du Page County	10,550	44.95
Summit (village) Cook County	4,717	44.35
Hodgkins (village) Cook County	894	41.89
De Pue (village) Bureau County	718	38.98
Carpentersville (village) Kane County	10,755	35.16
Waukegan (city) Lake County	30,717	34.94

Top 10 Places Sorted by Percent

Based on places with populations of 10,000 or more

Place	Number	%
Cicero (town) Cook County	58,542	68.38
Melrose Park (village) Cook County	10,500	45.32
West Chicago (city) Du Page County	10,550	44.95
Summit (village) Cook County	4,717	44.35
Carpentersville (village) Kane County	10,755	35.16
Waukegan (city) Lake County	30,717	34.94
Blue Island (city) Cook County	7,975	33.99
Bensenville (village) Du Page County	6,524	31.51
Franklin Park (village) Cook County	6,104	31.41
Berwyn (city) Cook County	16,745	31.00

Hispanic: Puerto Rican

Top 10 Places Sorted by Number

Based on all places, regardless of population

Place	Number	%
Chicago (city) Cook County	113,055	3.90
Waukegan (city) Lake County	2,976	3.39
Aurora (city) Kane County	2,611	1.83
Elgin (city) Kane County	2,355	2.49
Cicero (town) Cook County	2,331	2.72
Berwyn (city) Cook County	1,392	2.58
North Chicago (city) Lake County	775	2.16
Elmwood Park (village) Cook County	656	2.58
Bolingbrook (village) Will County	626	1.11
Zion (city) Lake County	616	2.69

Top 10 Places Sorted by Percent

Based on all places, regardless of population

Place	Number	%
Chicago (city) Cook County	113,055	3.90
Muddy (village) Saline County	3	3.85
Waukegan (city) Lake County	2,976	3.39
Wheeler (village) Jasper County	4	3.36
Schiller Park (village) Cook County	330	2.78
Cicero (town) Cook County	2,331	2.72
Zion (city) Lake County	616	2.69
Berwyn (city) Cook County	1,392	2.58
Elmwood Park (village) Cook County	656	2.58
Elgin (city) Kane County	2,355	2.49

Top 10 Places Sorted by Percent

Based on places with populations of 10,000 or more

Place	Number	%
Chicago (city) Cook County	113,055	3.90
Waukegan (city) Lake County	2,976	3.39
Schiller Park (village) Cook County	330	2.78
Cicero (town) Cook County	2,331	2.72
Zion (city) Lake County	616	2.69
Berwyn (city) Cook County	1,392	2.58
Elmwood Park (village) Cook County	656	2.58
Elgin (city) Kane County	2,355	2.49
Franklin Park (village) Cook County	466	2.40
Northlake (city) Cook County	279	2.35

Hispanic: South American

Top 10 Places Sorted by Number

Based on all places, regardless of population

Place	Number	%
Chicago (city) Cook County	20,828	0.72
Skokie (village) Cook County	583	0.92
Cicero (town) Cook County	544	0.64
Berwyn (city) Cook County	445	0.82
Waukegan (city) Lake County	378	0.43
Evanston (city) Cook County	372	0.50
Aurora (city) Kane County	358	0.25
Naperville (city) Du Page County	336	0.26
Schaumburg (village) Cook County	331	0.44
Des Plaines (city) Cook County	304	0.52

Top 10 Places Sorted by Percent

Based on all places, regardless of population

Place	Number	%
Stone Park (village) Cook County	48	0.94
Skokie (village) Cook County	583	0.92
Lincolnwood (village) Cook County	113	0.91
Coatsburg (village) Adams County	2	0.88
Elmwood Park (village) Cook County	216	0.85
Schiller Park (village) Cook County	100	0.84
Berwyn (city) Cook County	445	0.82
Melrose Park (village) Cook County	186	0.80
Morton Grove (village) Cook County	179	0.80
Highwood (city) Lake County	32	0.77

Top 10 Places Sorted by Percent

Based on places with populations of 10,000 or more

Place	Number	%
Skokie (village) Cook County	583	0.92
Lincolnwood (village) Cook County	113	0.91
Elmwood Park (village) Cook County	216	0.85
Schiller Park (village) Cook County	100	0.84
Berwyn (city) Cook County	445	0.82
Melrose Park (village) Cook County	186	0.80
Morton Grove (village) Cook County	179	0.80
Chicago (city) Cook County	20,828	0.72
Streamwood (village) Cook County	236	0.65
Cicero (town) Cook County	544	0.64

Hispanic: Argentinean

Top 10 Places Sorted by Number

Based on all places, regardless of population

Place	Number	%
Chicago (city) Cook County	908	0.03
Evanston (city) Cook County	66	0.09
Elmwood Park (village) Cook County	52	0.20
Urbana (city) Champaign County	48	0.13
Skokie (village) Cook County	43	0.07
Aurora (city) Kane County	43	0.03
Oak Park (village) Cook County	42	0.08
Naperville (city) Du Page County	42	0.03
Wilmette (village) Cook County	33	0.12
Berwyn (city) Cook County	33	0.06

Top 10 Places Sorted by Percent

Based on all places, regardless of population

Place	Number	%
Whiteash (village) Williamson County	2	0.75
Elsah (village) Jersey County	3	0.47
Timberlane (village) Boone County	1	0.43
Buffalo (village) Sangamon County	2	0.41
Wayne (village) Kane County	7	0.33
Port Byron (village) Rock Island County	5	0.33
Elmwood Park (village) Cook County	52	0.20
Lebanon (city) Saint Clair County	6	0.17
Pittsburg (village) Williamson County	1	0.17
Lincolnwood (village) Cook County	18	0.15

Top 10 Places Sorted by Percent

Based on places with populations of 10,000 or more

Place	Number	%
Elmwood Park (village) Cook County	52	0.20
Lincolnwood (village) Cook County	18	0.15
Urbana (city) Champaign County	48	0.13
Wilmette (village) Cook County	33	0.12
Evanston (city) Cook County	66	0.09
Blue Island (city) Cook County	21	0.09
Warrenville (city) Du Page County	12	0.09
Oak Park (village) Cook County	42	0.08
Wheeling (village) Cook County	28	0.08
Schiller Park (village) Cook County	10	0.08

Hispanic: Bolivian

Top 10 Places Sorted by Number

Based on all places, regardless of population

Place	Number	%
Chicago (city) Cook County	414	0.01
Skokie (village) Cook County	69	0.11
Wheaton (city) Du Page County	26	0.05
Oak Lawn (village) Cook County	25	0.05
Des Plaines (city) Cook County	25	0.04
Aurora (city) Kane County	24	0.02
Glen Ellyn (village) Du Page County	20	0.07
Naperville (city) Du Page County	17	0.01
Morton Grove (village) Cook County	14	0.06
River Forest (village) Cook County	13	0.11

Top 10 Places Sorted by Percent

Based on all places, regardless of population

Place	Number	%
Greenfield (city) Greene County	3	0.25
Skokie (village) Cook County	69	0.11
River Forest (village) Cook County	13	0.11
West Peoria (city) Peoria County	5	0.10
Lincolnwood (village) Cook County	11	0.09
Northfield (village) Cook County	5	0.09
Oak Brook (village) Du Page County	7	0.08
Lincolnshire (village) Lake County	5	0.08
Glen Ellyn (village) Du Page County	20	0.07
Lake of the Woods (cdp) Champaign County	2	0.07

Notes: (cdp) census designated place; Refer to the User's Guide in the front of the book for more detailed information.

Top 10 Places Sorted by Percent
Based on places with populations of 10,000 or more

Place	Number	%
Skokie (village) Cook County	69	0.11
River Forest (village) Cook County	13	0.11
Lincolnwood (village) Cook County	11	0.09
Glen Ellyn (village) Du Page County	20	0.07
Morton Grove (village) Cook County	14	0.06
Northlake (city) Cook County	7	0.06
Wheaton (city) Du Page County	26	0.05
Oak Lawn (village) Cook County	25	0.05
Round Lake Beach (village) Lake County	13	0.05
Melrose Park (village) Cook County	12	0.05

Hispanic: Chilean

Top 10 Places Sorted by Number
Based on all places, regardless of population

Place	Number	%
Chicago (city) Cook County	640	0.02
Evanston (city) Cook County	41	0.06
Berwyn (city) Cook County	37	0.07
Oak Park (village) Cook County	31	0.06
Champaign (city) Champaign County	26	0.04
Skokie (village) Cook County	25	0.04
Schaumburg (village) Cook County	25	0.03
Aurora (city) Kane County	24	0.02
Naperville (city) Du Page County	23	0.02
Cicero (town) Cook County	22	0.03

Top 10 Places Sorted by Percent
Based on all places, regardless of population

Place	Number	%
Belgium (village) Vermilion County	2	0.43
Fairmont City (village) Saint Clair County	5	0.21
Ohio (village) Bureau County	1	0.19
Berkeley (village) Cook County	9	0.17
Green Oaks (village) Lake County	6	0.17
Long Lake (cdp) Lake County	5	0.15
Highwood (city) Lake County	6	0.14
Piper City (village) Ford County	1	0.13
Rosemont (village) Cook County	5	0.12
Germantown Hills (village) Woodford County	2	0.09

Top 10 Places Sorted by Percent
Based on places with populations of 10,000 or more

Place	Number	%
North Aurora (village) Kane County	8	0.08
Berwyn (city) Cook County	37	0.07
Evanston (city) Cook County	41	0.06
Oak Park (village) Cook County	31	0.06
Streamwood (village) Cook County	21	0.06
Wilmette (village) Cook County	17	0.06
Loves Park (city) Winnebago County	12	0.06
River Forest (village) Cook County	7	0.06
Barrington (village) Cook County	6	0.06
Zion (city) Lake County	12	0.05

Hispanic: Colombian

Top 10 Places Sorted by Number
Based on all places, regardless of population

Place	Number	%
Chicago (city) Cook County	5,625	0.19
Waukegan (city) Lake County	285	0.32
Rockford (city) Winnebago County	174	0.12
Cicero (town) Cook County	171	0.20
Skokie (village) Cook County	144	0.23
Schaumburg (village) Cook County	127	0.17
Berwyn (city) Cook County	120	0.22
Aurora (city) Kane County	119	0.08
Streamwood (village) Cook County	107	0.29
Hoffman Estates (village) Cook County	104	0.21

Top 10 Places Sorted by Percent
Based on all places, regardless of population

Place	Number	%
Coatsburg (village) Adams County	2	0.88
Stone Park (village) Cook County	33	0.64
Grand Ridge (village) La Salle County	3	0.55
Park City (city) Lake County	27	0.41
Third Lake (village) Lake County	5	0.37
Ohio (village) Bureau County	2	0.37
Andover (village) Henry County	2	0.34
Waukegan (city) Lake County	285	0.32
Highwood (city) Lake County	13	0.31
Streamwood (village) Cook County	107	0.29

Top 10 Places Sorted by Percent
Based on places with populations of 10,000 or more

Place	Number	%
Waukegan (city) Lake County	285	0.32
Streamwood (village) Cook County	107	0.29
Lincolnwood (village) Cook County	36	0.29
Bensenville (village) Du Page County	58	0.28
Elmwood Park (village) Cook County	64	0.25
Morton Grove (village) Cook County	57	0.25
Hanover Park (village) Cook County	90	0.24
Franklin Park (village) Cook County	46	0.24
Skokie (village) Cook County	144	0.23
Carol Stream (village) Du Page County	93	0.23

Hispanic: Ecuadorian

Top 10 Places Sorted by Number
Based on all places, regardless of population

Place	Number	%
Chicago (city) Cook County	8,941	0.31
Cicero (town) Cook County	208	0.24
Berwyn (city) Cook County	141	0.26
Skokie (village) Cook County	127	0.20
Niles (village) Cook County	94	0.31
Des Plaines (city) Cook County	87	0.15
Hoffman Estates (village) Cook County	72	0.15
Mount Prospect (village) Cook County	66	0.12
Elmwood Park (village) Cook County	62	0.24
Arlington Heights (village) Cook County	62	0.08

Top 10 Places Sorted by Percent
Based on all places, regardless of population

Place	Number	%
Warren (village) Jo Daviess County	6	0.40
Chicago (city) Cook County	8,941	0.31
Niles (village) Cook County	94	0.31
Berwyn (city) Cook County	141	0.26
Schiller Park (village) Cook County	31	0.26
Cicero (town) Cook County	208	0.24
Elmwood Park (village) Cook County	62	0.24
Huntley (village) McHenry County	14	0.24
Hainesville (village) Lake County	5	0.23
Skokie (village) Cook County	127	0.20

Top 10 Places Sorted by Percent
Based on places with populations of 10,000 or more

Place	Number	%
Chicago (city) Cook County	8,941	0.31
Niles (village) Cook County	94	0.31
Berwyn (city) Cook County	141	0.26
Schiller Park (village) Cook County	31	0.26
Cicero (town) Cook County	208	0.24
Elmwood Park (village) Cook County	62	0.24
Skokie (village) Cook County	127	0.20
Morton Grove (village) Cook County	43	0.19
Northlake (city) Cook County	23	0.19
Grayslake (village) Lake County	31	0.17

Hispanic: Paraguayan

Top 10 Places Sorted by Number
Based on all places, regardless of population

Place	Number	%
Chicago (city) Cook County	68	0.00
Highland Park (city) Lake County	10	0.03
Oak Park (village) Cook County	10	0.02
Elmhurst (city) Du Page County	8	0.02
Berwyn (city) Cook County	8	0.01
Bloomington (city) McLean County	7	0.01
Brookfield (village) Cook County	6	0.03
Lisle (village) Du Page County	5	0.02
Cicero (town) Cook County	5	0.01
Northbrook (village) Cook County	5	0.01

Top 10 Places Sorted by Percent
Based on all places, regardless of population

Place	Number	%
Forest View (village) Cook County	1	0.13
Wonder Lake (village) McHenry County	1	0.07
Mount Carroll (city) Carroll County	1	0.05
Tolono (village) Champaign County	1	0.04
Highland Park (city) Lake County	10	0.03
Brookfield (village) Cook County	6	0.03
Morris (city) Grundy County	3	0.03
Riverside (village) Cook County	3	0.03
Winfield (village) Du Page County	3	0.03
Clarendon Hills (village) Du Page County	2	0.03

Top 10 Places Sorted by Percent
Based on places with populations of 10,000 or more

Place	Number	%
Highland Park (city) Lake County	10	0.03
Brookfield (village) Cook County	6	0.03
Morris (city) Grundy County	3	0.03
Oak Park (village) Cook County	10	0.02
Elmhurst (city) Du Page County	8	0.02
Lisle (village) Du Page County	5	0.02
Forest Park (village) Cook County	3	0.02
Grayslake (village) Lake County	3	0.02
Lincolnwood (village) Cook County	2	0.02
Berwyn (city) Cook County	8	0.01

Hispanic: Peruvian

Top 10 Places Sorted by Number
Based on all places, regardless of population

Place	Number	%
Chicago (city) Cook County	2,737	0.09
Skokie (village) Cook County	115	0.18
Evanston (city) Cook County	82	0.11
Palatine (village) Cook County	79	0.12
Cicero (town) Cook County	72	0.08
Oak Park (village) Cook County	63	0.12
Berwyn (city) Cook County	58	0.11
Schaumburg (village) Cook County	48	0.06
Aurora (city) Kane County	47	0.03
Naperville (city) Du Page County	40	0.03

Top 10 Places Sorted by Percent
Based on all places, regardless of population

Place	Number	%
Saint Johns (village) Perry County	1	0.46
Fayetteville (village) Saint Clair County	1	0.26
Schiller Park (village) Cook County	22	0.19
Palos Park (village) Cook County	9	0.19
Hainesville (village) Lake County	4	0.19
Oblong (village) Crawford County	3	0.19
Skokie (village) Cook County	115	0.18
Northlake (city) Cook County	20	0.17
Melrose Park (village) Cook County	37	0.16
Lincolnwood (village) Cook County	18	0.15

Notes: (cdp) census designated place; Refer to the User's Guide in the front of the book for more detailed information.

Top 10 Places Sorted by Percent

Based on places with populations of 10,000 or more

Place	Number	%
Schiller Park (village) Cook County	22	0.19
Skokie (village) Cook County	115	0.18
Northlake (city) Cook County	20	0.17
Melrose Park (village) Cook County	37	0.16
Lincolnwood (village) Cook County	18	0.15
River Forest (village) Cook County	18	0.15
Morton Grove (village) Cook County	32	0.14
Forest Park (village) Cook County	21	0.13
Palatine (village) Cook County	79	0.12
Oak Park (village) Cook County	63	0.12

Hispanic: Uruguayan

Top 10 Places Sorted by Number

Based on all places, regardless of population

Place	Number	%
Chicago (city) Cook County	134	0.00
Rockford (city) Winnebago County	19	0.01
Chicago Heights (city) Cook County	14	0.04
Melrose Park (village) Cook County	13	0.06
Berwyn (city) Cook County	13	0.02
Oak Park (village) Cook County	11	0.02
Evergreen Park (village) Cook County	7	0.03
Skokie (village) Cook County	7	0.01
Morton Grove (village) Cook County	6	0.03
Park Ridge (city) Cook County	6	0.02

Top 10 Places Sorted by Percent

Based on all places, regardless of population

Place	Number	%
Elsah (village) Jersey County	1	0.16
Melrose Park (village) Cook County	13	0.06
Chicago Heights (city) Cook County	14	0.04
Evergreen Park (village) Cook County	7	0.03
Morton Grove (village) Cook County	6	0.03
Berwyn (city) Cook County	13	0.02
Oak Park (village) Cook County	11	0.02
Park Ridge (city) Cook County	6	0.02
Roselle (village) Du Page County	5	0.02
Saint Charles (city) Kane County	5	0.02

Top 10 Places Sorted by Percent

Based on places with populations of 10,000 or more

Place	Number	%
Melrose Park (village) Cook County	13	0.06
Chicago Heights (city) Cook County	14	0.04
Evergreen Park (village) Cook County	7	0.03
Morton Grove (village) Cook County	6	0.03
Berwyn (city) Cook County	13	0.02
Oak Park (village) Cook County	11	0.02
Park Ridge (city) Cook County	6	0.02
Roselle (village) Du Page County	5	0.02
Saint Charles (city) Kane County	5	0.02
Deerfield (village) Lake County	3	0.02

Hispanic: Venezuelan

Top 10 Places Sorted by Number

Based on all places, regardless of population

Place	Number	%
Chicago (city) Cook County	600	0.02
Aurora (city) Kane County	52	0.04
Wheeling (village) Cook County	33	0.10
Evanston (city) Cook County	31	0.04
Oak Park (village) Cook County	29	0.06
Lombard (village) Du Page County	24	0.06
Cicero (town) Cook County	24	0.03
Champaign (city) Champaign County	23	0.03
Palatine (village) Cook County	22	0.03
Skokie (village) Cook County	21	0.03

Top 10 Places Sorted by Percent

Based on all places, regardless of population

Place	Number	%
Chenoa (city) McLean County	4	0.22
Golf (village) Cook County	1	0.22
North City (village) Franklin County	1	0.16
Cambria (village) Williamson County	2	0.15
Forest View (village) Cook County	1	0.13
Coal Valley (village) Rock Island County	4	0.11
Wheeling (village) Cook County	33	0.10
Pontiac (city) Livingston County	9	0.08
Breese (city) Clinton County	3	0.07
Oak Park (village) Cook County	29	0.06

Top 10 Places Sorted by Percent

Based on places with populations of 10,000 or more

Place	Number	%
Wheeling (village) Cook County	33	0.10
Pontiac (city) Livingston County	9	0.08
Oak Park (village) Cook County	29	0.06
Lombard (village) Du Page County	24	0.06
Melrose Park (village) Cook County	14	0.06
Wood Dale (city) Du Page County	8	0.06
Addison (village) Du Page County	17	0.05
Urbana (city) Champaign County	17	0.05
Vernon Hills (village) Lake County	10	0.05
Aurora (city) Kane County	52	0.04

Hispanic: Other South American

Top 10 Places Sorted by Number

Based on all places, regardless of population

Place	Number	%
Chicago (city) Cook County	761	0.03
Naperville (city) Du Page County	48	0.04
Des Plaines (city) Cook County	34	0.06
Skokie (village) Cook County	31	0.05
Glenview (village) Cook County	25	0.06
Cicero (town) Cook County	23	0.03
Palatine (village) Cook County	21	0.03
Hoffman Estates (village) Cook County	18	0.04
Champaign (city) Champaign County	17	0.03
Rockford (city) Winnebago County	17	0.01

Top 10 Places Sorted by Percent

Based on all places, regardless of population

Place	Number	%
Round Lake Heights (village) Lake County	5	0.37
Kangley (village) La Salle County	1	0.35
Fairmont (cdp) Will County	5	0.20
Leland Grove (city) Sangamon County	2	0.13
Jerome (village) Sangamon County	1	0.07
Des Plaines (city) Cook County	34	0.06
Glenview (village) Cook County	25	0.06
Morton Grove (village) Cook County	13	0.06
Chicago Ridge (village) Cook County	9	0.06
South Elgin (village) Kane County	9	0.06

Top 10 Places Sorted by Percent

Based on places with populations of 10,000 or more

Place	Number	%
Des Plaines (city) Cook County	34	0.06
Glenview (village) Cook County	25	0.06
Morton Grove (village) Cook County	13	0.06
Chicago Ridge (village) Cook County	9	0.06
South Elgin (village) Kane County	9	0.06
Winnetka (village) Cook County	7	0.06
Skokie (village) Cook County	31	0.05
Melrose Park (village) Cook County	12	0.05
Lincolnwood (village) Cook County	6	0.05
Naperville (city) Du Page County	48	0.04

Hispanic: Other

Top 10 Places Sorted by Number

Based on all places, regardless of population

Place	Number	%
Chicago (city) Cook County	56,225	1.94
Cicero (town) Cook County	3,784	4.42
Aurora (city) Kane County	3,654	2.56
Waukegan (city) Lake County	3,071	3.49
Elgin (city) Kane County	2,009	2.13
Joliet (city) Will County	1,760	1.66
Berwyn (city) Cook County	1,468	2.72
Rockford (city) Winnebago County	1,456	0.97
Carpentersville (village) Kane County	927	3.03
Melrose Park (village) Cook County	748	3.23

Top 10 Places Sorted by Percent

Based on all places, regardless of population

Place	Number	%
Oak Grove (village) Rock Island County	109	8.27
Sheridan (village) La Salle County	195	8.09
Baldwin (village) Randolph County	279	7.69
Detroit (village) Pike County	6	6.45
De Pue (village) Bureau County	117	6.35
Ina (village) Jefferson County	148	6.03
Fairmont City (village) Saint Clair County	131	5.38
Irving (village) Montgomery County	133	5.35
Stone Park (village) Cook County	241	4.70
Naples (town) Scott County	6	4.48

Top 10 Places Sorted by Percent

Based on places with populations of 10,000 or more

Place	Number	%
Cicero (town) Cook County	3,784	4.42
Waukegan (city) Lake County	3,071	3.49
Melrose Park (village) Cook County	748	3.23
Crest Hill (city) Will County	417	3.13
Carpentersville (village) Kane County	927	3.03
Berwyn (city) Cook County	1,468	2.72
Blue Island (city) Cook County	612	2.61
Bensenville (village) Du Page County	539	2.60
Aurora (city) Kane County	3,654	2.56
West Chicago (city) Du Page County	562	2.39

Hungarian

Top 10 Places Sorted by Number

Based on all places, regardless of population

Place	Number	%
Chicago (city) Cook County	9,418	0.33
Naperville (city) Du Page County	1,042	0.81
Aurora (city) Kane County	819	0.57
Skokie (village) Cook County	716	1.13
Evanston (city) Cook County	713	0.96
Arlington Heights (village) Cook County	670	0.88
Joliet (city) Will County	648	0.61
Schaumburg (village) Cook County	597	0.80
Elgin (city) Kane County	553	0.59
Buffalo Grove (village) Lake County	547	1.28

Top 10 Places Sorted by Percent

Based on all places, regardless of population

Place	Number	%
Smithboro (village) Bond County	15	7.69
Kempton (village) Ford County	13	4.91
Nason (city) Jefferson County	9	4.55
Bannockburn (village) Lake County	51	3.58
Christopher (city) Franklin County	79	2.86
Valier (village) Franklin County	18	2.74
Johnsburg (village) McHenry County	142	2.62
Channel Lake (cdp) Lake County	46	2.58
Kildeer (village) Lake County	89	2.49
Fairmont (cdp) Will County	62	2.37

Notes: (cdp) census designated place; Refer to the User's Guide in the front of the book for more detailed information.

Top 10 Places Sorted by Percent
Based on places with populations of 10,000 or more

Place	Number	%
Deerfield (village) Lake County	268	1.45
Lansing (village) Cook County	402	1.43
Highland Park (city) Lake County	439	1.40
Burr Ridge (village) Du Page County	141	1.37
Prospect Heights (city) Cook County	230	1.31
Buffalo Grove (village) Lake County	547	1.28
New Lenox (village) Will County	226	1.28
Plainfield (village) Will County	161	1.24
Lincolnwood (village) Cook County	152	1.23
Granite City (city) Madison County	387	1.22

Icelander

Top 10 Places Sorted by Number
Based on all places, regardless of population

Place	Number	%
Chicago (city) Cook County	176	0.01
Naperville (city) Du Page County	68	0.05
Oak Park (village) Cook County	32	0.06
Batavia (city) Kane County	31	0.13
Urbana (city) Champaign County	31	0.09
Fox Lake (village) Lake County	29	0.31
Bensenville (village) Du Page County	29	0.14
Park Ridge (city) Cook County	28	0.07
Wilmette (village) Cook County	27	0.10
Deerfield (village) Lake County	26	0.14

Top 10 Places Sorted by Percent
Based on all places, regardless of population

Place	Number	%
Matherville (village) Mercer County	5	0.65
Fox River Grove (village) McHenry County	16	0.33
Fox Lake (village) Lake County	29	0.31
Third Lake (village) Lake County	3	0.22
Long Grove (village) Lake County	13	0.20
Richmond (village) McHenry County	2	0.18
Bensenville (village) Du Page County	29	0.14
Deerfield (village) Lake County	26	0.14
Batavia (city) Kane County	31	0.13
Bunker Hill (city) Macoupin County	2	0.11

Top 10 Places Sorted by Percent
Based on places with populations of 10,000 or more

Place	Number	%
Bensenville (village) Du Page County	29	0.14
Deerfield (village) Lake County	26	0.14
Batavia (city) Kane County	31	0.13
Wilmette (village) Cook County	27	0.10
Urbana (city) Champaign County	31	0.09
Sycamore (city) De Kalb County	10	0.08
River Grove (village) Cook County	8	0.08
Park Ridge (city) Cook County	28	0.07
Alton (city) Madison County	21	0.07
Bridgeview (village) Cook County	10	0.07

Iranian

Top 10 Places Sorted by Number
Based on all places, regardless of population

Place	Number	%
Chicago (city) Cook County	1,944	0.07
Naperville (city) Du Page County	479	0.37
Skokie (village) Cook County	307	0.48
Hoffman Estates (village) Cook County	243	0.48
Oak Brook (village) Du Page County	239	2.83
Schaumburg (village) Cook County	175	0.23
Downers Grove (village) Du Page County	154	0.32
Evanston (city) Cook County	145	0.20
Arlington Heights (village) Cook County	121	0.16
Buffalo Grove (village) Lake County	116	0.27

Top 10 Places Sorted by Percent
Based on all places, regardless of population

Place	Number	%
Oak Brook (village) Du Page County	239	2.83
South Barrington (village) Cook County	88	2.36
Parkersburg (village) Richland County	4	1.96
West Dundee (village) Kane County	74	1.38
Wayne (village) Kane County	23	1.10
Elsah (village) Jersey County	5	0.80
Highwood (city) Lake County	31	0.76
Countryside (city) Cook County	43	0.72
Barrington Hills (village) Cook County	30	0.72
Tuscola (city) Douglas County	31	0.69

Top 10 Places Sorted by Percent
Based on places with populations of 10,000 or more

Place	Number	%
Lincolnwood (village) Cook County	66	0.53
Skokie (village) Cook County	307	0.48
Hoffman Estates (village) Cook County	243	0.48
Burr Ridge (village) Du Page County	42	0.41
Naperville (city) Du Page County	479	0.37
Downers Grove (village) Du Page County	154	0.32
Bloomingdale (village) Du Page County	70	0.32
Wheeling (village) Cook County	100	0.29
Glenview (village) Cook County	115	0.28
Wilmette (village) Cook County	77	0.28

Irish

Top 10 Places Sorted by Number
Based on all places, regardless of population

Place	Number	%
Chicago (city) Cook County	191,729	6.62
Naperville (city) Du Page County	23,688	18.46
Springfield (city) Sangamon County	17,457	15.56
Oak Lawn (village) Cook County	16,841	30.40
Rockford (city) Winnebago County	16,786	11.21
Joliet (city) Will County	14,609	13.76
Arlington Heights (village) Cook County	14,592	19.18
Aurora (city) Kane County	13,998	9.75
Peoria (city) Peoria County	13,790	12.22
Orland Park (village) Cook County	13,550	26.52

Top 10 Places Sorted by Percent
Based on all places, regardless of population

Place	Number	%
Harmon (village) Lee County	73	46.50
Evergreen Park (village) Cook County	8,250	39.62
Ivesdale (village) Champaign County	126	39.62
Deer Grove (village) Whiteside County	20	37.74
Merrionette Park (village) Cook County	689	34.47
Hometown (city) Cook County	1,500	33.58
Bentley (town) Hancock County	13	33.33
Golf (village) Cook County	150	33.19
Anchor (village) McLean County	53	32.52
Symerton (village) Will County	32	32.00

Top 10 Places Sorted by Percent
Based on places with populations of 10,000 or more

Place	Number	%
Evergreen Park (village) Cook County	8,250	39.62
River Forest (village) Cook County	3,586	30.82
Oak Lawn (village) Cook County	16,841	30.40
Western Springs (village) Cook County	3,770	29.87
Crestwood (village) Cook County	3,301	29.42
Mokena (village) Will County	4,316	29.41
New Lenox (village) Will County	4,917	27.91
Palos Heights (city) Cook County	3,078	27.19
Midlothian (village) Cook County	3,773	26.53
Orland Park (village) Cook County	13,550	26.52

Israeli

Top 10 Places Sorted by Number
Based on all places, regardless of population

Place	Number	%
Chicago (city) Cook County	1,033	0.04
Highland Park (city) Lake County	251	0.80
Skokie (village) Cook County	251	0.40
Buffalo Grove (village) Lake County	234	0.55
Deerfield (village) Lake County	119	0.64
Wilmette (village) Cook County	118	0.43
Urbana (city) Champaign County	113	0.31
Evanston (city) Cook County	92	0.12
North Chicago (city) Lake County	80	0.22
Waukegan (city) Lake County	76	0.09

Top 10 Places Sorted by Percent
Based on all places, regardless of population

Place	Number	%
Highland Park (city) Lake County	251	0.80
Deerfield (village) Lake County	119	0.64
Buffalo Grove (village) Lake County	234	0.55
Odell (village) Livingston County	5	0.49
Congerville (village) Woodford County	2	0.45
Wilmette (village) Cook County	118	0.43
Skokie (village) Cook County	251	0.40
Urbana (city) Champaign County	113	0.31
Riverwoods (village) Lake County	11	0.29
Flossmoor (village) Cook County	25	0.27

Top 10 Places Sorted by Percent
Based on places with populations of 10,000 or more

Place	Number	%
Highland Park (city) Lake County	251	0.80
Deerfield (village) Lake County	119	0.64
Buffalo Grove (village) Lake County	234	0.55
Wilmette (village) Cook County	118	0.43
Skokie (village) Cook County	251	0.40
Urbana (city) Champaign County	113	0.31
Winnetka (village) Cook County	32	0.26
Vernon Hills (village) Lake County	50	0.24
North Chicago (city) Lake County	80	0.22
Geneva (city) Kane County	40	0.20

Italian

Top 10 Places Sorted by Number
Based on all places, regardless of population

Place	Number	%
Chicago (city) Cook County	101,903	3.52
Naperville (city) Du Page County	13,611	10.61
Rockford (city) Winnebago County	10,571	7.06
Schaumburg (village) Cook County	9,392	12.60
Joliet (city) Will County	9,271	8.73
Arlington Heights (village) Cook County	8,456	11.11
Orland Park (village) Cook County	7,568	14.81
Elmwood Park (village) Cook County	7,293	28.71
Tinley Park (village) Cook County	6,926	14.33
Springfield (city) Sangamon County	6,736	6.00

Top 10 Places Sorted by Percent
Based on all places, regardless of population

Place	Number	%
East Brooklyn (village) Grundy County	56	54.90
Standard (village) Putnam County	114	44.19
South Wilmington (village) Grundy County	247	38.24
Dalzell (village) Bureau County	252	35.69
Cedar Point (village) La Salle County	92	33.95
Hollowayville (village) Bureau County	23	29.11
Elmwood Park (village) Cook County	7,293	28.71
Mount Clare (village) Macoupin County	113	27.63
Mark (village) Putnam County	135	27.61
Ladd (village) Bureau County	341	25.66

Notes: (cdp) census designated place; Refer to the User's Guide in the front of the book for more detailed information.

Top 10 Places Sorted by Percent
Based on places with populations of 10,000 or more

Place	Number	%
Elmwood Park (village) Cook County	7,293	28.71
Norridge (village) Cook County	3,740	25.46
Westchester (village) Cook County	3,483	20.90
Bloomingdale (village) Du Page County	4,471	20.72
Wood Dale (city) Du Page County	2,637	18.85
Melrose Park (village) Cook County	4,368	18.82
Schiller Park (village) Cook County	2,206	18.72
Lake in the Hills (village) McHenry County	4,179	17.81
River Grove (village) Cook County	1,864	17.56
Bartlett (village) Du Page County	6,333	17.19

Latvian

Top 10 Places Sorted by Number
Based on all places, regardless of population

Place	Number	%
Chicago (city) Cook County	1,383	0.05
Palatine (village) Cook County	172	0.26
Oak Park (village) Cook County	146	0.28
Evanston (city) Cook County	124	0.17
Des Plaines (city) Cook County	105	0.18
Mount Prospect (village) Cook County	100	0.18
Buffalo Grove (village) Lake County	97	0.23
Northbrook (village) Cook County	88	0.26
Lombard (village) Du Page County	83	0.20
Highland Park (city) Lake County	76	0.24

Top 10 Places Sorted by Percent
Based on all places, regardless of population

Place	Number	%
Lee (village) Lee County	9	3.31
Hooppole (village) Henry County	5	3.07
Makanda (village) Jackson County	6	1.47
Deer Park (village) Lake County	37	1.15
Glencoe (village) Cook County	48	0.54
Lyons (village) Cook County	54	0.53
Carlinville (city) Macoupin County	30	0.52
Lakewood (village) McHenry County	12	0.50
Kenilworth (village) Cook County	12	0.48
Harwood Heights (village) Cook County	38	0.46

Top 10 Places Sorted by Percent
Based on places with populations of 10,000 or more

Place	Number	%
Lyons (village) Cook County	54	0.53
Deerfield (village) Lake County	69	0.37
Western Springs (village) Cook County	42	0.33
Oak Park (village) Cook County	146	0.28
Winnetka (village) Cook County	34	0.27
Palatine (village) Cook County	172	0.26
Northbrook (village) Cook County	88	0.26
Westchester (village) Cook County	44	0.26
McHenry (city) McHenry County	54	0.25
Highland Park (city) Lake County	76	0.24

Lithuanian

Top 10 Places Sorted by Number
Based on all places, regardless of population

Place	Number	%
Chicago (city) Cook County	15,383	0.53
Oak Lawn (village) Cook County	2,101	3.79
Orland Park (village) Cook County	1,500	2.94
Naperville (city) Du Page County	1,291	1.01
Tinley Park (village) Cook County	1,250	2.59
Springfield (city) Sangamon County	1,091	0.97
Burbank (city) Cook County	960	3.45
Goodings Grove (cdp) Will County	934	5.46
Downers Grove (village) Du Page County	911	1.87
Oak Forest (city) Cook County	869	3.11

Top 10 Places Sorted by Percent
Based on all places, regardless of population

Place	Number	%
Dover (village) Bureau County	10	6.33
Campus (village) Livingston County	7	5.88
Bulpitt (village) Christian County	12	5.85
Westville (village) Vermilion County	180	5.60
Goodings Grove (cdp) Will County	934	5.46
Hickory Hills (city) Cook County	685	4.92
Brooklyn (village) Saint Clair County	30	4.56
Palos Hills (city) Cook County	759	4.27
Lemont (village) Cook County	539	4.09
Worth (village) Cook County	433	3.88

Top 10 Places Sorted by Percent
Based on places with populations of 10,000 or more

Place	Number	%
Goodings Grove (cdp) Will County	934	5.46
Hickory Hills (city) Cook County	685	4.92
Palos Hills (city) Cook County	759	4.27
Lemont (village) Cook County	539	4.09
Worth (village) Cook County	433	3.88
Chicago Ridge (village) Cook County	534	3.85
Oak Lawn (village) Cook County	2,101	3.79
Burbank (city) Cook County	960	3.45
Darien (city) Du Page County	770	3.35
Palos Heights (city) Cook County	360	3.18

Luxemburger

Top 10 Places Sorted by Number
Based on all places, regardless of population

Place	Number	%
Chicago (city) Cook County	756	0.03
Aurora (city) Kane County	597	0.42
Northbrook (village) Cook County	169	0.51
Schaumburg (village) Cook County	154	0.21
Arlington Heights (village) Cook County	141	0.19
Skokie (village) Cook County	138	0.22
Palatine (village) Cook County	131	0.20
Des Plaines (city) Cook County	129	0.22
Glenview (village) Cook County	112	0.27
Naperville (city) Du Page County	108	0.08

Top 10 Places Sorted by Percent
Based on all places, regardless of population

Place	Number	%
Bedford Park (village) Cook County	8	1.42
Creston (village) Ogle County	7	1.29
Montgomery (village) Kane County	62	1.23
Sugar Grove (village) Kane County	34	0.84
Dunlap (village) Peoria County	7	0.78
North Aurora (village) Kane County	81	0.76
Greenwood (village) McHenry County	2	0.75
East Dubuque (city) Jo Daviess County	14	0.73
Jonesboro (city) Union County	14	0.73
Plano (city) Kendall County	35	0.64

Top 10 Places Sorted by Percent
Based on places with populations of 10,000 or more

Place	Number	%
North Aurora (village) Kane County	81	0.76
Northbrook (village) Cook County	169	0.51
Aurora (city) Kane County	597	0.42
Morton Grove (village) Cook County	87	0.39
Gages Lake (cdp) Lake County	38	0.36
Rolling Meadows (city) Cook County	81	0.33
Wilmette (village) Cook County	80	0.29
Batavia (city) Kane County	69	0.29
Glenview (village) Cook County	112	0.27
Cary (village) McHenry County	42	0.27

Macedonian

Top 10 Places Sorted by Number
Based on all places, regardless of population

Place	Number	%
Chicago (city) Cook County	450	0.02
Granite City (city) Madison County	173	0.55
Mount Prospect (village) Cook County	105	0.19
Lemont (village) Cook County	83	0.63
Lansing (village) Cook County	71	0.25
Summit (village) Cook County	60	0.56
Woodstock (city) McHenry County	55	0.27
Countryside (city) Cook County	53	0.89
Waukegan (city) Lake County	50	0.06
Brookfield (village) Cook County	48	0.25

Top 10 Places Sorted by Percent
Based on all places, regardless of population

Place	Number	%
Hindsboro (village) Douglas County	10	2.81
Countryside (city) Cook County	53	0.89
Coal City (village) Grundy County	42	0.87
Prairie Grove (village) McHenry County	7	0.66
Lemont (village) Cook County	83	0.63
Summit (village) Cook County	60	0.56
Granite City (city) Madison County	173	0.55
Pontoon Beach (village) Madison County	31	0.55
Sauget (village) Saint Clair County	1	0.54
Forsyth (village) Macon County	11	0.46

Top 10 Places Sorted by Percent
Based on places with populations of 10,000 or more

Place	Number	%
Lemont (village) Cook County	83	0.63
Summit (village) Cook County	60	0.56
Granite City (city) Madison County	173	0.55
Woodstock (city) McHenry County	55	0.27
Bridgeview (village) Cook County	40	0.26
Chicago Ridge (village) Cook County	36	0.26
Lansing (village) Cook County	71	0.25
Brookfield (village) Cook County	48	0.25
Westchester (village) Cook County	35	0.21
Mount Prospect (village) Cook County	105	0.19

Maltese

Top 10 Places Sorted by Number
Based on all places, regardless of population

Place	Number	%
Chicago (city) Cook County	96	0.00
Lansing (village) Cook County	50	0.18
Edwardsville (city) Madison County	39	0.19
Highland Park (city) Lake County	38	0.12
Evanston (city) Cook County	34	0.05
Hoffman Estates (village) Cook County	21	0.04
Schaumburg (village) Cook County	19	0.03
Libertyville (village) Lake County	17	0.08
Charleston (city) Coles County	15	0.07
Crest Hill (city) Will County	13	0.10

Top 10 Places Sorted by Percent
Based on all places, regardless of population

Place	Number	%
Edwardsville (city) Madison County	39	0.19
Lansing (village) Cook County	50	0.18
Highland Park (city) Lake County	38	0.12
Shannon (village) Carroll County	1	0.12
Crest Hill (city) Will County	13	0.10
Fairfield (city) Wayne County	5	0.09
Libertyville (village) Lake County	17	0.08
Charleston (city) Coles County	15	0.07
Evanston (city) Cook County	34	0.05
Hoffman Estates (village) Cook County	21	0.04

Notes: (cdp) census designated place; Refer to the User's Guide in the front of the book for more detailed information.

Top 10 Places Sorted by Percent

Based on places with populations of 10,000 or more

Place	Number	%
Edwardsville (city) Madison County	39	0.19
Lansing (village) Cook County	50	0.18
Highland Park (city) Lake County	38	0.12
Crest Hill (city) Will County	13	0.10
Libertyville (village) Lake County	17	0.08
Charleston (city) Coles County	15	0.07
Evanston (city) Cook County	34	0.05
Hoffman Estates (village) Cook County	21	0.04
Pekin (city) Tazewell County	12	0.04
Lake Forest (city) Lake County	8	0.04

New Zealander

Top 10 Places Sorted by Number

Based on all places, regardless of population

Place	Number	%
Chicago (city) Cook County	62	0.00
Naperville (city) Du Page County	44	0.03
Streamwood (village) Cook County	30	0.08
Aurora (city) Kane County	30	0.02
Evanston (city) Cook County	23	0.03
Champaign (city) Champaign County	21	0.03
Grayslake (village) Lake County	14	0.08
Bolingbrook (village) Will County	10	0.02
North Chicago (city) Lake County	9	0.02
Springfield (city) Sangamon County	9	0.01

Top 10 Places Sorted by Percent

Based on all places, regardless of population

Place	Number	%
Elsah (village) Jersey County	4	0.64
Lexington (city) McLean County	6	0.31
Farmington (city) Fulton County	7	0.27
Colchester (city) McDonough County	2	0.14
Round Lake Park (village) Lake County	7	0.12
Streamwood (village) Cook County	30	0.08
Grayslake (village) Lake County	14	0.08
Lockport (city) Will County	7	0.05
Westchester (village) Cook County	7	0.04
Naperville (city) Du Page County	44	0.03

Top 10 Places Sorted by Percent

Based on places with populations of 10,000 or more

Place	Number	%
Streamwood (village) Cook County	30	0.08
Grayslake (village) Lake County	14	0.08
Lockport (city) Will County	7	0.05
Westchester (village) Cook County	7	0.04
Naperville (city) Du Page County	44	0.03
Evanston (city) Cook County	23	0.03
Champaign (city) Champaign County	21	0.03
Vernon Hills (village) Lake County	6	0.03
Mount Vernon (city) Jefferson County	5	0.03
Aurora (city) Kane County	30	0.02

Northern European

Top 10 Places Sorted by Number

Based on all places, regardless of population

Place	Number	%
Chicago (city) Cook County	783	0.03
Champaign (city) Champaign County	106	0.16
Evanston (city) Cook County	106	0.14
De Kalb (city) De Kalb County	97	0.25
Palatine (village) Cook County	86	0.13
Wilmette (village) Cook County	81	0.29
Mount Prospect (village) Cook County	81	0.14
Springfield (city) Sangamon County	81	0.07
Winnetka (village) Cook County	77	0.62
Highland Park (city) Lake County	76	0.24

Top 10 Places Sorted by Percent

Based on all places, regardless of population

Place	Number	%
Belle Rive (village) Jefferson County	13	3.46
Iroquois (village) Iroquois County	6	3.23
Union (village) McHenry County	17	2.93
Latham (village) Logan County	7	1.79
Perry (village) Pike County	6	1.55
Carthage (city) Hancock County	36	1.31
Wadsworth (village) Lake County	33	1.09
Deer Park (village) Lake County	22	0.68
Winnetka (village) Cook County	77	0.62
Oregon (city) Ogle County	22	0.54

Top 10 Places Sorted by Percent

Based on places with populations of 10,000 or more

Place	Number	%
Winnetka (village) Cook County	77	0.62
Burr Ridge (village) Du Page County	31	0.30
Barrington (village) Cook County	30	0.30
Wilmette (village) Cook County	81	0.29
Carbondale (city) Jackson County	60	0.29
De Kalb (city) De Kalb County	97	0.25
Highland Park (city) Lake County	76	0.24
North Aurora (village) Kane County	22	0.21
Belvidere (city) Boone County	41	0.20
Washington (city) Tazewell County	22	0.20

Norwegian

Top 10 Places Sorted by Number

Based on all places, regardless of population

Place	Number	%
Chicago (city) Cook County	14,890	0.51
Rockford (city) Winnebago County	5,394	3.60
Naperville (city) Du Page County	2,972	2.32
Aurora (city) Kane County	2,733	1.90
Arlington Heights (village) Cook County	2,053	2.70
Wheaton (city) Du Page County	1,834	3.31
Elgin (city) Kane County	1,822	1.94
Schaumburg (village) Cook County	1,800	2.42
Morris (city) Grundy County	1,595	13.36
Crystal Lake (city) McHenry County	1,475	3.90

Top 10 Places Sorted by Percent

Based on all places, regardless of population

Place	Number	%
Newark (village) Kendall County	310	34.07
Lisbon (village) Kendall County	66	26.83
Lee (village) Lee County	45	16.54
Leland (village) La Salle County	132	13.58
Morris (city) Grundy County	1,595	13.36
Caledonia (village) Boone County	28	12.44
Shabbona (village) De Kalb County	117	12.26
Maple Park (village) Kane County	92	12.03
Seneca (village) La Salle County	239	11.39
Steward (village) Lee County	31	11.31

Top 10 Places Sorted by Percent

Based on places with populations of 10,000 or more

Place	Number	%
Morris (city) Grundy County	1,595	13.36
Ottawa (city) La Salle County	1,455	7.93
Sycamore (city) De Kalb County	701	5.78
Loves Park (city) Winnebago County	1,146	5.76
Machesney Park (village) Winnebago County	1,110	5.37
McHenry (city) McHenry County	939	4.35
Oswego (village) Kendall County	571	4.29
Belvidere (city) Boone County	869	4.20
Algonquin (village) McHenry County	925	3.95
Crystal Lake (city) McHenry County	1,475	3.90

Pennsylvania German

Top 10 Places Sorted by Number

Based on all places, regardless of population

Place	Number	%
Rockford (city) Winnebago County	232	0.15
East Moline (city) Rock Island County	107	0.53
Chicago (city) Cook County	94	0.00
Decatur (city) Macon County	88	0.11
Naperville (city) Du Page County	74	0.06
Quincy (city) Adams County	64	0.16
Peoria (city) Peoria County	63	0.06
Aurora (city) Kane County	55	0.04
Sterling (city) Whiteside County	51	0.33
Freeport (city) Stephenson County	51	0.19

Top 10 Places Sorted by Percent

Based on all places, regardless of population

Place	Number	%
Winslow (village) Stephenson County	15	4.31
La Fayette (village) Stark County	6	2.64
North Henderson (village) Mercer County	4	2.02
Aroma Park (village) Kankakee County	16	1.95
Good Hope (village) McDonough County	7	1.72
Concord (village) Morgan County	3	1.64
Coyne Center (cdp) Rock Island County	15	1.59
Mount Morris (village) Ogle County	43	1.47
Elizabethtown (village) Hardin County	5	1.37
Woodson (village) Morgan County	7	1.23

Top 10 Places Sorted by Percent

Based on places with populations of 10,000 or more

Place	Number	%
East Moline (city) Rock Island County	107	0.53
Oswego (village) Kendall County	46	0.35
Sterling (city) Whiteside County	51	0.33
Freeport (city) Stephenson County	51	0.19
Burr Ridge (village) Du Page County	20	0.19
West Chicago (city) Du Page County	43	0.18
East Peoria (city) Tazewell County	40	0.17
Quincy (city) Adams County	64	0.16
Rockford (city) Winnebago County	232	0.15
Woodridge (village) Du Page County	48	0.15

Polish

Top 10 Places Sorted by Number

Based on all places, regardless of population

Place	Number	%
Chicago (city) Cook County	210,421	7.27
Naperville (city) Du Page County	13,936	10.86
Schaumburg (village) Cook County	11,109	14.91
Arlington Heights (village) Cook County	11,001	14.46
Des Plaines (city) Cook County	10,703	18.23
Oak Lawn (village) Cook County	10,667	19.26
Tinley Park (village) Cook County	9,540	19.74
Orland Park (village) Cook County	9,430	18.45
Mount Prospect (village) Cook County	9,216	16.25
Burbank (city) Cook County	8,427	30.29

Top 10 Places Sorted by Percent

Based on all places, regardless of population

Place	Number	%
Du Bois (village) Washington County	107	50.95
Radom (village) Washington County	162	38.85
Harwood Heights (village) Cook County	3,079	37.43
Lemont (village) Cook County	4,327	32.84
Norridge (village) Cook County	4,673	31.81
River Grove (village) Cook County	3,375	31.79
Burbank (city) Cook County	8,427	30.29
Goodings Grove (cdp) Will County	4,825	28.21
Hickory Hills (city) Cook County	3,750	26.91
Forest View (village) Cook County	206	25.88

Notes: (cdp) census designated place; Refer to the User's Guide in the front of the book for more detailed information.

Top 10 Places Sorted by Percent
Based on places with populations of 10,000 or more

Place	Number	%
Lemont (village) Cook County	4,327	32.84
Norridge (village) Cook County	4,673	31.81
River Grove (village) Cook County	3,375	31.79
Burbank (city) Cook County	8,427	30.29
Goodings Grove (cdp) Will County	4,825	28.21
Hickory Hills (city) Cook County	3,750	26.91
Bridgeview (village) Cook County	3,942	25.65
Elmwood Park (village) Cook County	6,270	24.68
Justice (village) Cook County	2,931	24.24
Niles (village) Cook County	6,880	22.82

Portuguese

Top 10 Places Sorted by Number
Based on all places, regardless of population

Place	Number	%
Chicago (city) Cook County	915	0.03
Springfield (city) Sangamon County	455	0.41
Evanston (city) Cook County	165	0.22
Naperville (city) Du Page County	160	0.12
Jacksonville (city) Morgan County	154	0.81
Peoria (city) Peoria County	135	0.12
Champaign (city) Champaign County	113	0.17
Aurora (city) Kane County	98	0.07
Bloomington (city) McLean County	93	0.14
Mount Prospect (village) Cook County	89	0.16

Top 10 Places Sorted by Percent
Based on all places, regardless of population

Place	Number	%
Topeka (village) Mason County	10	13.70
Clear Lake (village) Sangamon County	15	5.08
Longview (village) Champaign County	6	3.64
Manchester (village) Scott County	11	3.07
Milton (village) Pike County	8	2.95
Millington (village) Kendall County	10	2.11
Scottville (village) Macoupin County	3	2.10
New Burnside (village) Johnson County	5	1.91
Stonefort (village) Williamson County	5	1.85
Berlin (village) Sangamon County	2	1.53

Top 10 Places Sorted by Percent
Based on places with populations of 10,000 or more

Place	Number	%
Jacksonville (city) Morgan County	154	0.81
Washington (city) Tazewell County	56	0.51
Springfield (city) Sangamon County	455	0.41
Swansea (village) Saint Clair County	32	0.31
Barrington (village) Cook County	31	0.31
Carbondale (city) Jackson County	62	0.30
Grayslake (village) Lake County	49	0.27
Frankfort (village) Will County	26	0.25
Evanston (city) Cook County	165	0.22
Urbana (city) Champaign County	72	0.20

Romanian

Top 10 Places Sorted by Number
Based on all places, regardless of population

Place	Number	%
Chicago (city) Cook County	8,227	0.28
Skokie (village) Cook County	822	1.30
Aurora (city) Kane County	711	0.50
Des Plaines (city) Cook County	408	0.70
Lincolnwood (village) Cook County	382	3.09
Morton Grove (village) Cook County	376	1.67
Evanston (city) Cook County	372	0.50
Highland Park (city) Lake County	314	1.00
Buffalo Grove (village) Lake County	302	0.71
Northbrook (village) Cook County	297	0.89

Top 10 Places Sorted by Percent
Based on all places, regardless of population

Place	Number	%
Lincolnwood (village) Cook County	382	3.09
Yorkville (city) Kendall County	150	2.40
Morton Grove (village) Cook County	376	1.67
Mettawa (village) Lake County	5	1.54
Forest Lake (cdp) Lake County	22	1.42
Glencoe (village) Cook County	124	1.40
Round Lake (village) Lake County	79	1.38
Montgomery (village) Kane County	69	1.37
Skokie (village) Cook County	822	1.30
Dover (village) Bureau County	2	1.27

Top 10 Places Sorted by Percent
Based on places with populations of 10,000 or more

Place	Number	%
Lincolnwood (village) Cook County	382	3.09
Morton Grove (village) Cook County	376	1.67
Skokie (village) Cook County	822	1.30
Highland Park (city) Lake County	314	1.00
Vernon Hills (village) Lake County	193	0.94
Northbrook (village) Cook County	297	0.89
Niles (village) Cook County	266	0.88
North Aurora (village) Kane County	84	0.79
Deerfield (village) Lake County	135	0.73
Buffalo Grove (village) Lake County	302	0.71

Russian

Top 10 Places Sorted by Number
Based on all places, regardless of population

Place	Number	%
Chicago (city) Cook County	28,845	1.00
Buffalo Grove (village) Lake County	6,542	15.36
Skokie (village) Cook County	5,609	8.86
Highland Park (city) Lake County	5,157	16.43
Northbrook (village) Cook County	4,101	12.27
Evanston (city) Cook County	2,892	3.90
Glenview (village) Cook County	2,510	6.02
Deerfield (village) Lake County	2,473	13.37
Wheeling (village) Cook County	2,334	6.78
Arlington Heights (village) Cook County	2,046	2.69

Top 10 Places Sorted by Percent
Based on all places, regardless of population

Place	Number	%
Highland Park (city) Lake County	5,157	16.43
Buffalo Grove (village) Lake County	6,542	15.36
Deerfield (village) Lake County	2,473	13.37
Northbrook (village) Cook County	4,101	12.27
Riverwoods (village) Lake County	449	11.90
Glencoe (village) Cook County	1,042	11.80
Skokie (village) Cook County	5,609	8.86
Lincolnwood (village) Cook County	1,078	8.72
Lincolnshire (village) Lake County	528	8.54
Wheeling (village) Cook County	2,334	6.78

Top 10 Places Sorted by Percent
Based on places with populations of 10,000 or more

Place	Number	%
Highland Park (city) Lake County	5,157	16.43
Buffalo Grove (village) Lake County	6,542	15.36
Deerfield (village) Lake County	2,473	13.37
Northbrook (village) Cook County	4,101	12.27
Skokie (village) Cook County	5,609	8.86
Lincolnwood (village) Cook County	1,078	8.72
Wheeling (village) Cook County	2,334	6.78
Glenview (village) Cook County	2,510	6.02
Wilmette (village) Cook County	1,631	5.89
Vernon Hills (village) Lake County	1,214	5.89

Scandinavian

Top 10 Places Sorted by Number
Based on all places, regardless of population

Place	Number	%
Chicago (city) Cook County	1,649	0.06
Naperville (city) Du Page County	347	0.27
Aurora (city) Kane County	295	0.21
Rockford (city) Winnebago County	217	0.14
Des Plaines (city) Cook County	175	0.30
Arlington Heights (village) Cook County	168	0.22
Palatine (village) Cook County	166	0.25
Wheaton (city) Du Page County	159	0.29
Downers Grove (village) Du Page County	158	0.32
Champaign (city) Champaign County	156	0.23

Top 10 Places Sorted by Percent
Based on all places, regardless of population

Place	Number	%
Barrington Hills (village) Cook County	113	2.72
Hecker (village) Monroe County	12	2.37
Channel Lake (cdp) Lake County	34	1.90
Adeline (village) Ogle County	2	1.42
Lake Barrington (village) Lake County	66	1.38
Sherrard (village) Mercer County	9	1.31
Peotone (village) Will County	46	1.30
Ashkum (village) Iroquois County	9	1.26
Mettawa (village) Lake County	4	1.23
Harvard (city) McHenry County	92	1.13

Top 10 Places Sorted by Percent
Based on places with populations of 10,000 or more

Place	Number	%
Barrington (village) Cook County	83	0.83
Sycamore (city) De Kalb County	98	0.81
Cary (village) McHenry County	100	0.65
Lake in the Hills (village) McHenry County	133	0.57
Burr Ridge (village) Du Page County	59	0.57
Machesney Park (village) Winnebago County	109	0.53
Hinsdale (village) Du Page County	82	0.47
Wilmette (village) Cook County	105	0.38
De Kalb (city) De Kalb County	140	0.36
Hanover Park (village) Cook County	140	0.36

Scotch-Irish

Top 10 Places Sorted by Number
Based on all places, regardless of population

Place	Number	%
Chicago (city) Cook County	11,142	0.38
Springfield (city) Sangamon County	1,951	1.74
Naperville (city) Du Page County	1,913	1.49
Rockford (city) Winnebago County	1,614	1.08
Peoria (city) Peoria County	1,547	1.37
Aurora (city) Kane County	1,278	0.89
Decatur (city) Macon County	1,227	1.49
Evanston (city) Cook County	1,201	1.62
Bloomington (city) McLean County	1,117	1.72
Champaign (city) Champaign County	1,033	1.52

Top 10 Places Sorted by Percent
Based on all places, regardless of population

Place	Number	%
Wenonah (village) Montgomery County	5	16.13
Columbus (village) Adams County	10	8.33
Naples (town) Scott County	9	7.76
Huey (village) Clinton County	15	7.58
Verona (village) Grundy County	18	7.17
West Brooklyn (village) Lee County	12	6.70
Biggsville (village) Henderson County	22	6.36
Irwin (village) Kankakee County	4	6.35
Elizabethtown (village) Hardin County	22	6.04
Iroquois (village) Iroquois County	11	5.91

Notes: (cdp) census designated place; Refer to the User's Guide in the front of the book for more detailed information.

Top 10 Places Sorted by Percent
Based on places with populations of 10,000 or more

Place	Number	%
Herrin (city) Williamson County	356	3.21
Libertyville (village) Lake County	514	2.48
Marion (city) Williamson County	388	2.43
Lake Forest (city) Lake County	468	2.34
Loves Park (city) Winnebago County	439	2.21
Winnetka (village) Cook County	271	2.19
Sycamore (city) De Kalb County	264	2.18
Godfrey (village) Madison County	343	2.10
Brookfield (village) Cook County	398	2.09
Galesburg (city) Knox County	704	2.08

Scottish

Top 10 Places Sorted by Number
Based on all places, regardless of population

Place	Number	%
Chicago (city) Cook County	14,285	0.49
Springfield (city) Sangamon County	2,199	1.96
Naperville (city) Du Page County	2,178	1.70
Aurora (city) Kane County	1,947	1.36
Rockford (city) Winnebago County	1,811	1.21
Peoria (city) Peoria County	1,663	1.47
Wheaton (city) Du Page County	1,581	2.85
Evanston (city) Cook County	1,568	2.11
Champaign (city) Champaign County	1,368	2.02
Arlington Heights (village) Cook County	1,296	1.70

Top 10 Places Sorted by Percent
Based on all places, regardless of population

Place	Number	%
Simpson (village) Johnson County	6	10.53
Dorchester (village) Macoupin County	16	9.94
Mount Clare (village) Macoupin County	39	9.54
Standard City (village) Macoupin County	13	9.42
Elsah (village) Jersey County	58	9.28
Keensburg (village) Wabash County	21	8.86
Mettawa (village) Lake County	25	7.72
Rock Island Arsenal (cdp) Rock Island County	10	7.52
Gillespie (city) Macoupin County	237	7.09
Dover (village) Bureau County	11	6.96

Top 10 Places Sorted by Percent
Based on places with populations of 10,000 or more

Place	Number	%
Winnetka (village) Cook County	495	4.00
Glen Ellyn (village) Du Page County	975	3.61
Lake Forest (city) Lake County	720	3.60
Barrington (village) Cook County	343	3.42
Washington (city) Tazewell County	330	3.03
Batavia (city) Kane County	685	2.86
Wheaton (city) Du Page County	1,581	2.85
River Forest (village) Cook County	314	2.70
Hinsdale (village) Du Page County	464	2.65
Warrenville (city) Du Page County	344	2.61

Serbian

Top 10 Places Sorted by Number
Based on all places, regardless of population

Place	Number	%
Chicago (city) Cook County	5,044	0.17
Niles (village) Cook County	439	1.46
Lansing (village) Cook County	385	1.37
Berwyn (city) Cook County	357	0.66
Naperville (city) Du Page County	286	0.22
Elmhurst (city) Du Page County	262	0.61
Lyons (village) Cook County	248	2.45
Carol Stream (village) Du Page County	180	0.45
Countryside (city) Cook County	174	2.91
Westmont (village) Du Page County	167	0.69

Top 10 Places Sorted by Percent
Based on all places, regardless of population

Place	Number	%
East Brooklyn (village) Grundy County	8	7.84
Countryside (city) Cook County	174	2.91
Burlington (village) Kane County	12	2.60
Lyons (village) Cook County	248	2.45
Granville (village) Putnam County	29	2.03
Buckner (village) Franklin County	9	1.88
Willow Springs (village) Cook County	88	1.78
North Barrington (village) Lake County	48	1.66
Niles (village) Cook County	439	1.46
Lansing (village) Cook County	385	1.37

Top 10 Places Sorted by Percent
Based on places with populations of 10,000 or more

Place	Number	%
Lyons (village) Cook County	248	2.45
Niles (village) Cook County	439	1.46
Lansing (village) Cook County	385	1.37
Lincolnwood (village) Cook County	123	1.00
Burr Ridge (village) Du Page County	96	0.93
Norridge (village) Cook County	109	0.74
South Holland (village) Cook County	157	0.70
Westmont (village) Du Page County	167	0.69
Berwyn (city) Cook County	357	0.66
Villa Park (village) Du Page County	147	0.66

Slavic

Top 10 Places Sorted by Number
Based on all places, regardless of population

Place	Number	%
Chicago (city) Cook County	846	0.03
Naperville (city) Du Page County	157	0.12
Joliet (city) Will County	134	0.13
Gurnee (village) Lake County	103	0.36
Rosemont (village) Cook County	78	1.87
Wheaton (city) Du Page County	63	0.11
Belleville (city) Saint Clair County	57	0.14
Villa Park (village) Du Page County	56	0.25
Champaign (city) Champaign County	53	0.08
Waukegan (city) Lake County	52	0.06

Top 10 Places Sorted by Percent
Based on all places, regardless of population

Place	Number	%
Bureau Junction (village) Bureau County	12	3.32
Rosemont (village) Cook County	78	1.87
North Utica (village) La Salle County	17	1.82
McCook (village) Cook County	4	1.76
Maeystown (village) Monroe County	2	1.38
Forest Lake (cdp) Lake County	21	1.35
Coalton (village) Montgomery County	4	1.34
Matherville (village) Mercer County	9	1.17
Ellsworth (village) McLean County	3	1.11
Rockdale (village) Will County	21	1.10

Top 10 Places Sorted by Percent
Based on places with populations of 10,000 or more

Place	Number	%
Gurnee (village) Lake County	103	0.36
Crest Hill (city) Will County	43	0.33
Villa Park (village) Du Page County	56	0.25
La Grange Park (village) Cook County	30	0.23
Wood Dale (city) Du Page County	31	0.22
Plainfield (village) Will County	23	0.18
Kewanee (city) Henry County	21	0.16
Justice (village) Cook County	19	0.16
Edwardsville (city) Madison County	32	0.15
Brookfield (village) Cook County	28	0.15

Slovak

Top 10 Places Sorted by Number
Based on all places, regardless of population

Place	Number	%
Chicago (city) Cook County	6,238	0.22
Streator (city) La Salle County	1,653	11.70
Joliet (city) Will County	1,456	1.37
Naperville (city) Du Page County	809	0.63
Oak Lawn (village) Cook County	533	0.96
Berwyn (city) Cook County	515	0.95
Tinley Park (village) Cook County	454	0.94
Downers Grove (village) Du Page County	448	0.92
Springfield (city) Sangamon County	448	0.40
Burbank (city) Cook County	418	1.50

Top 10 Places Sorted by Percent
Based on all places, regardless of population

Place	Number	%
Streator (city) La Salle County	1,653	11.70
White City (village) Macoupin County	13	6.60
Kangley (village) La Salle County	14	4.70
Mount Olive (city) Macoupin County	101	4.69
Ransom (village) La Salle County	18	3.90
Naplate (village) La Salle County	20	3.80
Williamson (village) Madison County	8	3.72
Shorewood (village) Will County	277	3.56
Sawyerville (village) Macoupin County	11	3.46
Benld (city) Macoupin County	50	3.25

Top 10 Places Sorted by Percent
Based on places with populations of 10,000 or more

Place	Number	%
Streator (city) La Salle County	1,653	11.70
Lockport (city) Will County	232	1.57
Burbank (city) Cook County	418	1.50
Lisle (village) Du Page County	312	1.48
Joliet (city) Will County	1,456	1.37
New Lenox (village) Will County	241	1.37
Westchester (village) Cook County	214	1.28
Crest Hill (city) Will County	162	1.24
Plainfield (village) Will County	152	1.17
Western Springs (village) Cook County	144	1.14

Slovene

Top 10 Places Sorted by Number
Based on all places, regardless of population

Place	Number	%
Joliet (city) Will County	1,770	1.67
Chicago (city) Cook County	1,555	0.05
Waukegan (city) Lake County	444	0.50
Naperville (city) Du Page County	351	0.27
Crest Hill (city) Will County	349	2.68
Shorewood (village) Will County	323	4.15
La Salle (city) La Salle County	258	2.63
Downers Grove (village) Du Page County	206	0.42
Lockport (city) Will County	190	1.28
Channahon (village) Will County	177	2.42

Top 10 Places Sorted by Percent
Based on all places, regardless of population

Place	Number	%
Wayne (village) Kane County	90	4.29
Shorewood (village) Will County	323	4.15
Rockdale (village) Will County	75	3.93
Reddick (village) Kankakee County	10	3.91
Oglesby (city) La Salle County	124	3.44
Crest Hill (city) Will County	349	2.68
La Salle (city) La Salle County	258	2.63
Channahon (village) Will County	177	2.42
Seatonville (village) Bureau County	6	1.88
Peru (city) La Salle County	174	1.77

Notes: (cdp) census designated place; Refer to the User's Guide in the front of the book for more detailed information.

Top 10 Places Sorted by Percent

Based on places with populations of 10,000 or more

Place	Number	%
Crest Hill (city) Will County	349	2.68
Joliet (city) Will County	1,770	1.67
Lockport (city) Will County	190	1.28
Lindenhurst (village) Lake County	131	1.04
New Lenox (village) Will County	137	0.78
Lemont (village) Cook County	94	0.71
Plainfield (village) Will County	71	0.55
Waukegan (city) Lake County	444	0.50
Libertyville (village) Lake County	93	0.45
Downers Grove (village) Du Page County	206	0.42

Soviet Union

Top 10 Places Sorted by Number

Based on all places, regardless of population

Place	Number	%
Chicago (city) Cook County	60	0.00
Northbrook (village) Cook County	34	0.10
Highland Park (city) Lake County	28	0.09
Morton Grove (village) Cook County	15	0.07
Naperville (city) Du Page County	9	0.01
Lincolnwood (village) Cook County	5	0.04
Galatia (village) Saline County	4	0.38

Top 10 Places Sorted by Percent

Based on all places, regardless of population

Place	Number	%
Galatia (village) Saline County	4	0.38
Northbrook (village) Cook County	34	0.10
Highland Park (city) Lake County	28	0.09
Morton Grove (village) Cook County	15	0.07
Lincolnwood (village) Cook County	5	0.04
Naperville (city) Du Page County	9	0.01
Chicago (city) Cook County	60	0.00

Top 10 Places Sorted by Percent

Based on places with populations of 10,000 or more

Place	Number	%
Northbrook (village) Cook County	34	0.10
Highland Park (city) Lake County	28	0.09
Morton Grove (village) Cook County	15	0.07
Lincolnwood (village) Cook County	5	0.04
Naperville (city) Du Page County	9	0.01
Chicago (city) Cook County	60	0.00

Swedish

Top 10 Places Sorted by Number

Based on all places, regardless of population

Place	Number	%
Chicago (city) Cook County	24,882	0.86
Rockford (city) Winnebago County	14,720	9.83
Naperville (city) Du Page County	4,529	3.53
Moline (city) Rock Island County	4,073	9.32
Galesburg (city) Knox County	3,374	9.97
Arlington Heights (village) Cook County	3,307	4.35
Wheaton (city) Du Page County	3,197	5.77
Aurora (city) Kane County	3,129	2.18
Elgin (city) Kane County	2,978	3.17
Joliet (city) Will County	2,645	2.49

Top 10 Places Sorted by Percent

Based on all places, regardless of population

Place	Number	%
Rio (village) Knox County	101	40.40
Altona (village) Knox County	176	31.88
Woodhull (village) Henry County	237	28.69
Bishop Hill (village) Henry County	36	26.28
Oneida (city) Knox County	174	22.57
Orion (village) Henry County	381	22.46
Hooppole (village) Henry County	34	20.86
Cambridge (village) Henry County	455	20.54
Andover (village) Henry County	122	20.54
Windsor (village) Mercer County	145	19.97

Top 10 Places Sorted by Percent

Based on places with populations of 10,000 or more

Place	Number	%
Loves Park (city) Winnebago County	2,149	10.80
Galesburg (city) Knox County	3,374	9.97
Rockford (city) Winnebago County	14,720	9.83
Moline (city) Rock Island County	4,073	9.32
Machesney Park (village) Winnebago County	1,847	8.93
Sycamore (city) De Kalb County	1,030	8.49
Batavia (city) Kane County	1,930	8.07
Kewanee (city) Henry County	987	7.63
Geneva (city) Kane County	1,479	7.56
Libertyville (village) Lake County	1,516	7.33

Swiss

Top 10 Places Sorted by Number

Based on all places, regardless of population

Place	Number	%
Chicago (city) Cook County	3,008	0.10
Naperville (city) Du Page County	681	0.53
Peoria (city) Peoria County	649	0.57
Rockford (city) Winnebago County	642	0.43
Highland (city) Madison County	541	6.46
Elgin (city) Kane County	530	0.56
Freeport (city) Stephenson County	478	1.81
Evanston (city) Cook County	463	0.62
Morton (village) Tazewell County	456	3.03
Champaign (city) Champaign County	370	0.55

Top 10 Places Sorted by Percent

Based on all places, regardless of population

Place	Number	%
Congerville (village) Woodford County	52	11.61
Orangeville (village) Stephenson County	69	9.13
Roanoke (village) Woodford County	159	8.01
Goodfield (village) Woodford County	49	7.22
Winslow (village) Stephenson County	24	6.90
Rock City (village) Stephenson County	23	6.82
Davis (village) Stephenson County	44	6.77
Gridley (village) McLean County	95	6.68
Ridott (village) Stephenson County	9	6.62
Highland (city) Madison County	541	6.46

Top 10 Places Sorted by Percent

Based on places with populations of 10,000 or more

Place	Number	%
Morton (village) Tazewell County	456	3.03
Freeport (city) Stephenson County	478	1.81
River Forest (village) Cook County	120	1.03
Washington (city) Tazewell County	107	0.98
Winnetka (village) Cook County	120	0.97
Plainfield (village) Will County	119	0.91
Lake Forest (city) Lake County	178	0.89
Pontiac (city) Livingston County	102	0.86
Dixon (city) Lee County	120	0.75
Elmhurst (city) Du Page County	286	0.67

Turkish

Top 10 Places Sorted by Number

Based on all places, regardless of population

Place	Number	%
Chicago (city) Cook County	1,178	0.04
Naperville (city) Du Page County	211	0.16
Evanston (city) Cook County	185	0.25
Schaumburg (village) Cook County	141	0.19
Hoffman Estates (village) Cook County	130	0.26
Summit (village) Cook County	112	1.05
Wheeling (village) Cook County	92	0.27
Roselle (village) Du Page County	83	0.36
Champaign (city) Champaign County	70	0.10
Urbana (city) Champaign County	65	0.18

Top 10 Places Sorted by Percent

Based on all places, regardless of population

Place	Number	%
Benson (village) Woodford County	8	1.95
Cedar Point (village) La Salle County	3	1.11
Summit (village) Cook County	112	1.05
Easton (village) Mason County	4	1.04
Barry (city) Pike County	12	0.90
Metamora (village) Woodford County	18	0.67
Cordova (village) Rock Island County	4	0.64
West Dundee (village) Kane County	25	0.46
Richmond (village) McHenry County	5	0.45
Schiller Park (village) Cook County	48	0.41

Top 10 Places Sorted by Percent

Based on places with populations of 10,000 or more

Place	Number	%
Summit (village) Cook County	112	1.05
Schiller Park (village) Cook County	48	0.41
Roselle (village) Du Page County	83	0.36
Lincolnwood (village) Cook County	41	0.33
Wheeling (village) Cook County	92	0.27
Hoffman Estates (village) Cook County	130	0.26
Evanston (city) Cook County	185	0.25
Western Springs (village) Cook County	25	0.20
Schaumburg (village) Cook County	141	0.19
Urbana (city) Champaign County	65	0.18

Ukrainian

Top 10 Places Sorted by Number

Based on all places, regardless of population

Place	Number	%
Chicago (city) Cook County	13,579	0.47
Skokie (village) Cook County	1,206	1.90
Buffalo Grove (village) Lake County	1,017	2.39
Palatine (village) Cook County	785	1.20
Naperville (city) Du Page County	658	0.51
Schaumburg (village) Cook County	626	0.84
Arlington Heights (village) Cook County	617	0.81
Wheeling (village) Cook County	608	1.77
Glenview (village) Cook County	546	1.31
Des Plaines (city) Cook County	532	0.91

Top 10 Places Sorted by Percent

Based on all places, regardless of population

Place	Number	%
McCook (village) Cook County	7	3.08
Peotone (village) Will County	96	2.71
Buffalo Grove (village) Lake County	1,017	2.39
Lake Catherine (cdp) Lake County	32	2.22
Vernon Hills (village) Lake County	437	2.12
Skokie (village) Cook County	1,206	1.90
Naplate (village) La Salle County	10	1.90
Wheeling (village) Cook County	608	1.77
Riverwoods (village) Lake County	66	1.75
Niles (village) Cook County	507	1.68

Top 10 Places Sorted by Percent

Based on places with populations of 10,000 or more

Place	Number	%
Buffalo Grove (village) Lake County	1,017	2.39
Vernon Hills (village) Lake County	437	2.12
Skokie (village) Cook County	1,206	1.90
Wheeling (village) Cook County	608	1.77
Niles (village) Cook County	507	1.68
Elmwood Park (village) Cook County	390	1.54
Highland Park (city) Lake County	465	1.48

Notes: (cdp) census designated place; Refer to the User's Guide in the front of the book for more detailed information.

Place	Number	%
Glenview (village) Cook County	546	1.31
Morton Grove (village) Cook County	294	1.31
Mokena (village) Will County	179	1.22

United States or American

Top 10 Places Sorted by Number
Based on all places, regardless of population

Place	Number	%
Chicago (city) Cook County	38,779	1.34
Decatur (city) Macon County	8,418	10.25
Springfield (city) Sangamon County	7,965	7.10
Peoria (city) Peoria County	6,366	5.64
Rockford (city) Winnebago County	6,352	4.24
Bloomington (city) McLean County	4,589	7.06
Aurora (city) Kane County	4,260	2.97
Quincy (city) Adams County	3,626	9.00
Pekin (city) Tazewell County	3,443	10.17
Naperville (city) Du Page County	3,264	2.54

Top 10 Places Sorted by Percent
Based on all places, regardless of population

Place	Number	%
Valley City (village) Pike County	18	100.00
Rockwood (village) Randolph County	38	80.85
Campus (village) Livingston County	62	52.10
Eldred (village) Greene County	109	49.77
La Prairie (village) Adams County	25	45.45
Emington (village) Livingston County	56	43.75
Pulaski (village) Pulaski County	120	41.10
Humboldt (village) Coles County	197	40.45
Alma (village) Marion County	158	39.80
Coatsburg (village) Adams County	85	39.35

Top 10 Places Sorted by Percent
Based on places with populations of 10,000 or more

Place	Number	%
Mount Vernon (city) Jefferson County	2,594	15.97
Mattoon (city) Coles County	2,907	15.85
Herrin (city) Williamson County	1,449	13.07
Wood River (city) Madison County	1,426	12.73
Lincoln (city) Logan County	1,905	12.39
East Peoria (city) Tazewell County	2,795	12.21
Taylorville (city) Christian County	1,353	11.95
Canton (city) Fulton County	1,732	11.36
Marion (city) Williamson County	1,786	11.17
Centralia (city) Marion County	1,575	11.13

Welsh

Top 10 Places Sorted by Number
Based on all places, regardless of population

Place	Number	%
Chicago (city) Cook County	5,226	0.18
Naperville (city) Du Page County	945	0.74
Springfield (city) Sangamon County	847	0.75
Rockford (city) Winnebago County	693	0.46
Aurora (city) Kane County	568	0.40
Evanston (city) Cook County	523	0.70
Peoria (city) Peoria County	502	0.44
Decatur (city) Macon County	485	0.59
Wheaton (city) Du Page County	453	0.82
Bloomington (city) McLean County	437	0.67

Top 10 Places Sorted by Percent
Based on all places, regardless of population

Place	Number	%
Panola (village) Woodford County	4	12.50
Bishop Hill (village) Henry County	8	5.84
Prairie City (village) McDonough County	26	5.58
Pistakee Highlands (cdp) McHenry County	173	4.50
Nilwood (town) Macoupin County	12	4.24
Mill Shoals (village) White County	9	4.04
Elsah (village) Jersey County	24	3.84
West City (village) Franklin County	26	3.68
La Prairie (village) Adams County	2	3.64
Ludlow (village) Champaign County	10	3.37

Top 10 Places Sorted by Percent
Based on places with populations of 10,000 or more

Place	Number	%
Fairview Heights (city) Saint Clair County	179	1.17
Winnetka (village) Cook County	144	1.16
Barrington (village) Cook County	107	1.07
Batavia (city) Kane County	253	1.06
Glen Carbon (village) Madison County	111	1.06
Granite City (city) Madison County	319	1.01
Glen Ellyn (village) Du Page County	273	1.01
Morton (village) Tazewell County	151	1.00
Frankfort (village) Will County	98	0.96
Crystal Lake (city) McHenry County	358	0.95

West Indian, excluding Hispanic

Top 10 Places Sorted by Number
Based on all places, regardless of population

Place	Number	%
Chicago (city) Cook County	11,698	0.40
Evanston (city) Cook County	3,448	4.64
Waukegan (city) Lake County	722	0.82
Skokie (village) Cook County	640	1.01
North Chicago (city) Lake County	433	1.20
Bolingbrook (village) Will County	355	0.63
Calumet City (city) Cook County	313	0.80
Oak Park (village) Cook County	271	0.52
Country Club Hills (city) Cook County	262	1.62
Dolton (village) Cook County	259	1.01

Top 10 Places Sorted by Percent
Based on all places, regardless of population

Place	Number	%
Evanston (city) Cook County	3,448	4.64
Yale (village) Jasper County	3	3.49
Olympia Fields (village) Cook County	121	2.56
University Park (village) Will County	150	2.26
Country Club Hills (city) Cook County	262	1.62
Flossmoor (village) Cook County	124	1.33
Buckingham (village) Kankakee County	3	1.29
North Chicago (city) Lake County	433	1.20
Royal Lakes (village) Macoupin County	2	1.14
South Holland (village) Cook County	237	1.06

Top 10 Places Sorted by Percent
Based on places with populations of 10,000 or more

Place	Number	%
Evanston (city) Cook County	3,448	4.64
Country Club Hills (city) Cook County	262	1.62
North Chicago (city) Lake County	433	1.20
South Holland (village) Cook County	237	1.06
Skokie (village) Cook County	640	1.01
Dolton (village) Cook County	259	1.01
Bellwood (village) Cook County	187	0.91
Zion (city) Lake County	205	0.89
Richton Park (village) Cook County	111	0.89
Waukegan (city) Lake County	722	0.82

West Indian: Bahamian, excluding Hispanic

Top 10 Places Sorted by Number
Based on all places, regardless of population

Place	Number	%
Chicago (city) Cook County	114	0.00
Evanston (city) Cook County	24	0.03
Loves Park (city) Winnebago County	16	0.08
Westmont (village) Du Page County	12	0.05
Calumet City (city) Cook County	11	0.03
Geneva (city) Kane County	10	0.05
Naperville (city) Du Page County	9	0.01
Broadview (village) Cook County	8	0.10
Carbondale (city) Jackson County	8	0.04
North Chicago (city) Lake County	8	0.02

Top 10 Places Sorted by Percent
Based on all places, regardless of population

Place	Number	%
Braidwood (city) Will County	7	0.13
Broadview (village) Cook County	8	0.10
Loves Park (city) Winnebago County	16	0.08
Westmont (village) Du Page County	12	0.05
Geneva (city) Kane County	10	0.05
Hazel Crest (village) Cook County	7	0.05
Carbondale (city) Jackson County	8	0.04
Evanston (city) Cook County	24	0.03
Calumet City (city) Cook County	11	0.03
North Chicago (city) Lake County	8	0.02

Top 10 Places Sorted by Percent
Based on places with populations of 10,000 or more

Place	Number	%
Loves Park (city) Winnebago County	16	0.08
Westmont (village) Du Page County	12	0.05
Geneva (city) Kane County	10	0.05
Hazel Crest (village) Cook County	7	0.05
Carbondale (city) Jackson County	8	0.04
Evanston (city) Cook County	24	0.03
Calumet City (city) Cook County	11	0.03
North Chicago (city) Lake County	8	0.02
South Holland (village) Cook County	5	0.02
Park Forest (village) Cook County	4	0.02

West Indian: Barbadian, excluding Hispanic

Top 10 Places Sorted by Number
Based on all places, regardless of population

Place	Number	%
Chicago (city) Cook County	144	0.00
Oak Park (village) Cook County	34	0.06
Arlington Heights (village) Cook County	29	0.04
Maywood (village) Cook County	26	0.10
Hanover Park (village) Cook County	24	0.06
North Chicago (city) Lake County	17	0.05
Shiloh (village) Saint Clair County	12	0.15
Broadview (village) Cook County	10	0.12
Bolingbrook (village) Will County	9	0.02
Urbana (city) Champaign County	6	0.02

Top 10 Places Sorted by Percent
Based on all places, regardless of population

Place	Number	%
Shiloh (village) Saint Clair County	12	0.15
Broadview (village) Cook County	10	0.12
Maywood (village) Cook County	26	0.10
Oak Park (village) Cook County	34	0.06
Hanover Park (village) Cook County	24	0.06
North Chicago (city) Lake County	17	0.05
Arlington Heights (village) Cook County	29	0.04
Bolingbrook (village) Will County	9	0.02
Urbana (city) Champaign County	6	0.02
Batavia (city) Kane County	5	0.02

Top 10 Places Sorted by Percent
Based on places with populations of 10,000 or more

Place	Number	%
Maywood (village) Cook County	26	0.10
Oak Park (village) Cook County	34	0.06
Hanover Park (village) Cook County	24	0.06
North Chicago (city) Lake County	17	0.05
Arlington Heights (village) Cook County	29	0.04

Notes: (cdp) census designated place; Refer to the User's Guide in the front of the book for more detailed information.

Place	Number	%
Bolingbrook (village) Will County	9	0.02
Urbana (city) Champaign County	6	0.02
Batavia (city) Kane County	5	0.02
Skokie (village) Cook County	6	0.01
Danville (city) Vermilion County	4	0.01

West Indian: Belizean, excluding Hispanic

Top 10 Places Sorted by Number

Based on all places, regardless of population

Place	Number	%
Chicago (city) Cook County	2,244	0.08
Evanston (city) Cook County	488	0.66
Waukegan (city) Lake County	366	0.42
Zion (city) Lake County	84	0.36
Wheeling (village) Cook County	83	0.24
Skokie (village) Cook County	62	0.10
Berwyn (city) Cook County	60	0.11
North Chicago (city) Lake County	56	0.16
Maywood (village) Cook County	48	0.18
Sauk Village (village) Cook County	46	0.44

Top 10 Places Sorted by Percent

Based on all places, regardless of population

Place	Number	%
Evanston (city) Cook County	488	0.66
Lynwood (village) Cook County	40	0.54
Sauk Village (village) Cook County	46	0.44
Waukegan (city) Lake County	366	0.42
Alorton (village) Saint Clair County	11	0.40
Zion (city) Lake County	84	0.36
Hometown (city) Cook County	13	0.29
Tonica (village) La Salle County	2	0.29
Fairmont (cdp) Will County	7	0.27
Wheeling (village) Cook County	83	0.24

Top 10 Places Sorted by Percent

Based on places with populations of 10,000 or more

Place	Number	%
Evanston (city) Cook County	488	0.66
Sauk Village (village) Cook County	46	0.44
Waukegan (city) Lake County	366	0.42
Zion (city) Lake County	84	0.36
Wheeling (village) Cook County	83	0.24
Country Club Hills (city) Cook County	36	0.22
Markham (city) Cook County	27	0.21
Maywood (village) Cook County	48	0.18
North Chicago (city) Lake County	56	0.16
Evergreen Park (village) Cook County	32	0.15

West Indian: Bermudan, excluding Hispanic

Top 10 Places Sorted by Number

Based on all places, regardless of population

Place	Number	%
Christopher (city) Franklin County	17	0.62
Chicago (city) Cook County	17	0.00
Edwardsville (city) Madison County	10	0.05
Champaign (city) Champaign County	5	0.01

Top 10 Places Sorted by Percent

Based on all places, regardless of population

Place	Number	%
Christopher (city) Franklin County	17	0.62
Edwardsville (city) Madison County	10	0.05
Champaign (city) Champaign County	5	0.01
Chicago (city) Cook County	17	0.00

Top 10 Places Sorted by Percent

Based on places with populations of 10,000 or more

Place	Number	%
Edwardsville (city) Madison County	10	0.05
Champaign (city) Champaign County	5	0.01
Chicago (city) Cook County	17	0.00

West Indian: British West Indian, excluding Hispanic

Top 10 Places Sorted by Number

Based on all places, regardless of population

Place	Number	%
Chicago (city) Cook County	143	0.00
Evanston (city) Cook County	46	0.06
Bensenville (village) Du Page County	41	0.20
North Chicago (city) Lake County	30	0.08
Oak Park (village) Cook County	30	0.06
Bourbonnais (village) Kankakee County	22	0.14
Bolingbrook (village) Will County	20	0.04
Broadview (village) Cook County	19	0.23
Schaumburg (village) Cook County	11	0.01
Blue Island (city) Cook County	9	0.04

Top 10 Places Sorted by Percent

Based on all places, regardless of population

Place	Number	%
Broadview (village) Cook County	19	0.23
Bensenville (village) Du Page County	41	0.20
Bourbonnais (village) Kankakee County	22	0.14
Kildeer (village) Lake County	4	0.11
North Chicago (city) Lake County	30	0.08
Lyons (village) Cook County	7	0.07
Evanston (city) Cook County	46	0.06
Oak Park (village) Cook County	30	0.06
Glenwood (village) Cook County	5	0.06
Bolingbrook (village) Will County	20	0.04

Top 10 Places Sorted by Percent

Based on places with populations of 10,000 or more

Place	Number	%
Bensenville (village) Du Page County	41	0.20
Bourbonnais (village) Kankakee County	22	0.14
North Chicago (city) Lake County	30	0.08
Lyons (village) Cook County	7	0.07
Evanston (city) Cook County	46	0.06
Oak Park (village) Cook County	30	0.06
Bolingbrook (village) Will County	20	0.04
Blue Island (city) Cook County	9	0.04
Zion (city) Lake County	7	0.03
Streamwood (village) Cook County	6	0.02

West Indian: Dutch West Indian, excluding Hispanic

Top 10 Places Sorted by Number

Based on all places, regardless of population

Place	Number	%
Chicago (city) Cook County	32	0.00
Mount Vernon (city) Jefferson County	20	0.12
Roscoe (village) Winnebago County	19	0.30
Bolingbrook (village) Will County	12	0.02
Calumet City (city) Cook County	11	0.03
Evanston (city) Cook County	11	0.01
Jacksonville (city) Morgan County	10	0.05
Decatur (city) Macon County	9	0.01
Lombard (village) Du Page County	8	0.02
Normal (town) McLean County	8	0.02

Top 10 Places Sorted by Percent

Based on all places, regardless of population

Place	Number	%
Yale (village) Jasper County	3	3.49
Old Mill Creek (village) Lake County	2	0.66
New Haven (village) Gallatin County	2	0.46
Tower Hill (village) Shelby County	2	0.33
Roscoe (village) Winnebago County	19	0.30
Shannon (village) Carroll County	2	0.24
Kincaid (village) Christian County	3	0.20
New Baden (village) Clinton County	5	0.16
Ashland (village) Cass County	2	0.15
Roodhouse (city) Greene County	3	0.14

Top 10 Places Sorted by Percent

Based on places with populations of 10,000 or more

Place	Number	%
Mount Vernon (city) Jefferson County	20	0.12
Lyons (village) Cook County	7	0.07
Jacksonville (city) Morgan County	10	0.05
Pontiac (city) Livingston County	5	0.04
Calumet City (city) Cook County	11	0.03
Bolingbrook (village) Will County	12	0.02
Lombard (village) Du Page County	8	0.02
Normal (town) McLean County	8	0.02
Evanston (city) Cook County	11	0.01
Decatur (city) Macon County	9	0.01

West Indian: Haitian, excluding Hispanic

Top 10 Places Sorted by Number

Based on all places, regardless of population

Place	Number	%
Chicago (city) Cook County	3,104	0.11
Evanston (city) Cook County	856	1.15
Skokie (village) Cook County	264	0.42
Calumet City (city) Cook County	133	0.34
Dolton (village) Cook County	108	0.42
Niles (village) Cook County	80	0.27
Olympia Fields (village) Cook County	75	1.59
Waukegan (city) Lake County	75	0.09
Country Club Hills (city) Cook County	70	0.43
Bolingbrook (village) Will County	65	0.12

Top 10 Places Sorted by Percent

Based on all places, regardless of population

Place	Number	%
Olympia Fields (village) Cook County	75	1.59
Evanston (city) Cook County	856	1.15
Bowen (village) Hancock County	3	0.55
Round Lake (village) Lake County	29	0.51
Winthrop Harbor (village) Lake County	33	0.50
University Park (village) Will County	32	0.48
Country Club Hills (city) Cook County	70	0.43
Skokie (village) Cook County	264	0.42
Dolton (village) Cook County	108	0.42
Dupo (village) Saint Clair County	15	0.37

Top 10 Places Sorted by Percent

Based on places with populations of 10,000 or more

Place	Number	%
Evanston (city) Cook County	856	1.15
Country Club Hills (city) Cook County	70	0.43
Skokie (village) Cook County	264	0.42
Dolton (village) Cook County	108	0.42
Calumet City (city) Cook County	133	0.34
Sterling (city) Whiteside County	47	0.31
Niles (village) Cook County	80	0.27
South Holland (village) Cook County	58	0.26
Lincoln (city) Logan County	40	0.26
Murphysboro (city) Jackson County	28	0.21

West Indian: Jamaican, excluding Hispanic

Top 10 Places Sorted by Number

Based on all places, regardless of population

Place	Number	%
Chicago (city) Cook County	4,778	0.16
Evanston (city) Cook County	1,937	2.61
Skokie (village) Cook County	299	0.47

Notes: (cdp) census designated place; Refer to the User's Guide in the front of the book for more detailed information.

Place	Number	%
Waukegan (city) Lake County	241	0.27
North Chicago (city) Lake County	225	0.62
Bolingbrook (village) Will County	220	0.39
South Holland (village) Cook County	159	0.71
Bellwood (village) Cook County	158	0.77
Country Club Hills (city) Cook County	145	0.89
Dolton (village) Cook County	141	0.55

Top 10 Places Sorted by Percent

Based on all places, regardless of population

Place	Number	%
Evanston (city) Cook County	1,937	2.61
Flossmoor (village) Cook County	118	1.27
University Park (village) Will County	67	1.01
Olympia Fields (village) Cook County	46	0.97
Country Club Hills (city) Cook County	145	0.89
Bellwood (village) Cook County	158	0.77
South Holland (village) Cook County	159	0.71
Pulaski (village) Pulaski County	2	0.68
North Chicago (city) Lake County	225	0.62
Richton Park (village) Cook County	75	0.60

Top 10 Places Sorted by Percent

Based on places with populations of 10,000 or more

Place	Number	%
Evanston (city) Cook County	1,937	2.61
Country Club Hills (city) Cook County	145	0.89
Bellwood (village) Cook County	158	0.77
South Holland (village) Cook County	159	0.71
North Chicago (city) Lake County	225	0.62
Richton Park (village) Cook County	75	0.60
Dolton (village) Cook County	141	0.55
Riverdale (village) Cook County	80	0.53
Prospect Heights (city) Cook County	91	0.52
Matteson (village) Cook County	62	0.48

West Indian: Trinidadian and Tobagonian, excluding Hispanic

Top 10 Places Sorted by Number

Based on all places, regardless of population

Place	Number	%
Chicago (city) Cook County	407	0.01
Aurora (city) Kane County	55	0.04
Naperville (city) Du Page County	51	0.04
Mount Prospect (village) Cook County	40	0.07
Joliet (city) Will County	35	0.03
Evanston (city) Cook County	32	0.04
Hanover Park (village) Cook County	30	0.08
Harvey (city) Cook County	29	0.10
De Kalb (city) De Kalb County	27	0.07
Crystal Lake (city) McHenry County	22	0.06

Top 10 Places Sorted by Percent

Based on all places, regardless of population

Place	Number	%
Long Grove (village) Lake County	12	0.18
Warrenville (city) Du Page County	15	0.11
University Park (village) Will County	7	0.11
Mascoutah (city) Saint Clair County	6	0.11
Harvey (city) Cook County	29	0.10
River Forest (village) Cook County	11	0.09
Hanover Park (village) Cook County	30	0.08
Mount Prospect (village) Cook County	40	0.07
De Kalb (city) De Kalb County	27	0.07
Crystal Lake (city) McHenry County	22	0.06

Top 10 Places Sorted by Percent

Based on places with populations of 10,000 or more

Place	Number	%
Warrenville (city) Du Page County	15	0.11
Harvey (city) Cook County	29	0.10
River Forest (village) Cook County	11	0.09
Hanover Park (village) Cook County	30	0.08
Mount Prospect (village) Cook County	40	0.07
De Kalb (city) De Kalb County	27	0.07
Crystal Lake (city) McHenry County	22	0.06
Maywood (village) Cook County	16	0.06
Fairview Heights (city) Saint Clair County	8	0.05
Richton Park (village) Cook County	6	0.05

West Indian: U.S. Virgin Islander, excluding Hispanic

Top 10 Places Sorted by Number

Based on all places, regardless of population

Place	Number	%
Chicago (city) Cook County	154	0.01
University Park (village) Will County	33	0.50
Lisle (village) Du Page County	9	0.04
Country Club Hills (city) Cook County	7	0.04
Decatur (city) Macon County	4	0.00
Phoenix (village) Cook County	2	0.09

Top 10 Places Sorted by Percent

Based on all places, regardless of population

Place	Number	%
University Park (village) Will County	33	0.50
Phoenix (village) Cook County	2	0.09
Lisle (village) Du Page County	9	0.04
Country Club Hills (city) Cook County	7	0.04
Chicago (city) Cook County	154	0.01
Decatur (city) Macon County	4	0.00

Top 10 Places Sorted by Percent

Based on places with populations of 10,000 or more

Place	Number	%
Lisle (village) Du Page County	9	0.04
Country Club Hills (city) Cook County	7	0.04
Chicago (city) Cook County	154	0.01
Decatur (city) Macon County	4	0.00

West Indian: West Indian, excluding Hispanic

Top 10 Places Sorted by Number

Based on all places, regardless of population

Place	Number	%
Chicago (city) Cook County	552	0.02
Evanston (city) Cook County	43	0.06
Oak Park (village) Cook County	36	0.07
North Chicago (city) Lake County	34	0.09
Aurora (city) Kane County	31	0.02
Harvey (city) Cook County	27	0.09
Markham (city) Cook County	26	0.21
Waukegan (city) Lake County	21	0.02
Algonquin (village) McHenry County	19	0.08
Buffalo Grove (village) Lake County	19	0.04

Top 10 Places Sorted by Percent

Based on all places, regardless of population

Place	Number	%
Royal Lakes (village) Macoupin County	2	1.14
Lewistown (city) Fulton County	15	0.60
Scott AFB (cdp) Saint Clair County	9	0.32
Mazon (village) Grundy County	2	0.22
Markham (city) Cook County	26	0.21
Forsyth (village) Macon County	4	0.17
Western Springs (village) Cook County	17	0.13
Willowbrook (village) Du Page County	10	0.11
Forest Park (village) Cook County	15	0.10
Murphysboro (city) Jackson County	14	0.10

Top 10 Places Sorted by Percent

Based on places with populations of 10,000 or more

Place	Number	%
Markham (city) Cook County	26	0.21
Western Springs (village) Cook County	17	0.13
Forest Park (village) Cook County	15	0.10
Murphysboro (city) Jackson County	14	0.10
Glen Carbon (village) Madison County	10	0.10
North Chicago (city) Lake County	34	0.09
Harvey (city) Cook County	27	0.09
Algonquin (village) McHenry County	19	0.08
Oswego (village) Kendall County	10	0.08
Oak Park (village) Cook County	36	0.07

West Indian: Other, excluding Hispanic

Top 10 Places Sorted by Number

Based on all places, regardless of population

Place	Number	%
Evanston (city) Cook County	11	0.01
Bridgeport (city) Lawrence County	9	0.40
Oak Park (village) Cook County	9	0.02
Chicago (city) Cook County	9	0.00
O'Fallon (city) Saint Clair County	8	0.04
Buckingham (village) Kankakee County	3	1.29
Rosiclare (city) Hardin County	3	0.25
Hennepin (village) Putnam County	2	0.29

Top 10 Places Sorted by Percent

Based on all places, regardless of population

Place	Number	%
Buckingham (village) Kankakee County	3	1.29
Bridgeport (city) Lawrence County	9	0.40
Hennepin (village) Putnam County	2	0.29
Rosiclare (city) Hardin County	3	0.25
O'Fallon (city) Saint Clair County	8	0.04
Oak Park (village) Cook County	9	0.02
Evanston (city) Cook County	11	0.01
Chicago (city) Cook County	9	0.00

Top 10 Places Sorted by Percent

Based on places with populations of 10,000 or more

Place	Number	%
O'Fallon (city) Saint Clair County	8	0.04
Oak Park (village) Cook County	9	0.02
Evanston (city) Cook County	11	0.01
Chicago (city) Cook County	9	0.00

White

Top 10 Places Sorted by Number

Based on all places, regardless of population

Place	Number	%
Chicago (city) Cook County	1,282,320	44.28
Rockford (city) Winnebago County	112,487	74.93
Naperville (city) Du Page County	110,648	86.20
Aurora (city) Kane County	100,854	70.53
Springfield (city) Sangamon County	91,715	82.29
Peoria (city) Peoria County	80,323	71.12
Joliet (city) Will County	75,537	71.11
Arlington Heights (village) Cook County	69,645	91.60
Elgin (city) Kane County	68,992	73.02
Decatur (city) Macon County	64,742	79.09

Top 10 Places Sorted by Percent

Based on all places, regardless of population

Place	Number	%
Meredosia (village) Morgan County	1,041	100.00
Stonington (village) Christian County	960	100.00
Hopedale (village) Tazewell County	929	100.00
Annawan (town) Henry County	868	100.00
Augusta (village) Hancock County	657	100.00
Murrayville (village) Morgan County	644	100.00
Alhambra (village) Madison County	630	100.00
Golden (village) Adams County	629	100.00
Williamsfield (village) Knox County	620	100.00
Strasburg (village) Shelby County	603	100.00

Notes: (cdp) census designated place; Refer to the User's Guide in the front of the book for more detailed information.

Top 10 Places Sorted by Percent

Based on places with populations of 10,000 or more

Place	Number	%
Washington (city) Tazewell County	10,728	98.96
Western Springs (village) Cook County	12,345	98.82
Effingham (city) Effingham County	12,185	98.39
New Lenox (village) Will County	17,478	98.35
Morton (village) Tazewell County	14,930	98.24
Wood River (city) Madison County	11,096	98.23
Taylorville (city) Christian County	11,221	98.20
East Peoria (city) Tazewell County	22,216	98.14
Lemont (village) Cook County	12,834	97.98
Herrin (city) Williamson County	11,035	97.67

White: Not Hispanic

Top 10 Places Sorted by Number

Based on all places, regardless of population

Place	Number	%
Chicago (city) Cook County	943,299	32.57
Naperville (city) Du Page County	107,484	83.74
Rockford (city) Winnebago County	104,846	69.84
Springfield (city) Sangamon County	90,850	81.51
Peoria (city) Peoria County	78,976	69.93
Aurora (city) Kane County	76,031	53.17
Arlington Heights (village) Cook County	67,192	88.37
Joliet (city) Will County	65,854	62.00
Decatur (city) Macon County	64,156	78.37
Schaumburg (village) Cook County	57,832	76.71

Top 10 Places Sorted by Percent

Based on all places, regardless of population

Place	Number	%
Murrayville (village) Morgan County	644	100.00
Alhambra (village) Madison County	630	100.00
Williamsfield (village) Knox County	620	100.00
Essex (village) Kankakee County	554	100.00
Camargo (village) Douglas County	469	100.00
Arenzville (village) Cass County	419	100.00
New Canton (town) Pike County	417	100.00
Bellflower (village) McLean County	408	100.00
Loraine (village) Adams County	363	100.00
Manchester (village) Scott County	354	100.00

Top 10 Places Sorted by Percent

Based on places with populations of 10,000 or more

Place	Number	%
Washington (city) Tazewell County	10,678	98.50
Taylorville (city) Christian County	11,178	97.82
Effingham (city) Effingham County	12,110	97.79
Morton (village) Tazewell County	14,853	97.73
Wood River (city) Madison County	10,999	97.37
Western Springs (village) Cook County	12,159	97.33
East Peoria (city) Tazewell County	22,025	97.29
Herrin (city) Williamson County	10,952	96.94
Mattoon (city) Coles County	17,671	96.61
New Lenox (village) Will County	17,074	96.08

White: Hispanic

Top 10 Places Sorted by Number

Based on all places, regardless of population

Place	Number	%
Chicago (city) Cook County	339,021	11.71
Cicero (town) Cook County	26,837	31.35
Aurora (city) Kane County	24,823	17.36
Waukegan (city) Lake County	18,468	21.01
Elgin (city) Kane County	17,098	18.10
Berwyn (city) Cook County	10,181	18.85
Joliet (city) Will County	9,683	9.12
West Chicago (city) Du Page County	7,695	32.79
Melrose Park (village) Cook County	7,662	33.07
Rockford (city) Winnebago County	7,641	5.09

Top 10 Places Sorted by Percent

Based on all places, regardless of population

Place	Number	%
Stone Park (village) Cook County	2,042	39.83
De Pue (village) Bureau County	622	33.77
Melrose Park (village) Cook County	7,662	33.07
West Chicago (city) Du Page County	7,695	32.79
Cicero (town) Cook County	26,837	31.35
Summit (village) Cook County	3,018	28.37
Hodgkins (village) Cook County	575	26.94
Fairmont City (village) Saint Clair County	648	26.60
Franklin Park (village) Cook County	4,452	22.91
Volo (village) Lake County	41	22.78

Top 10 Places Sorted by Percent

Based on places with populations of 10,000 or more

Place	Number	%
Melrose Park (village) Cook County	7,662	33.07
West Chicago (city) Du Page County	7,695	32.79
Cicero (town) Cook County	26,837	31.35
Summit (village) Cook County	3,018	28.37
Franklin Park (village) Cook County	4,452	22.91
Waukegan (city) Lake County	18,468	21.01
Bensenville (village) Du Page County	4,117	19.89
Blue Island (city) Cook County	4,559	19.43
Carpentersville (village) Kane County	5,785	18.91
Berwyn (city) Cook County	10,181	18.85

Yugoslavian

Top 10 Places Sorted by Number

Based on all places, regardless of population

Place	Number	%
Chicago (city) Cook County	10,130	0.35
Rockford (city) Winnebago County	590	0.39
Skokie (village) Cook County	345	0.54
Wheaton (city) Du Page County	305	0.55
Berwyn (city) Cook County	301	0.56
Carol Stream (village) Du Page County	233	0.59
Mount Prospect (village) Cook County	232	0.41
Schaumburg (village) Cook County	228	0.31
Streamwood (village) Cook County	227	0.62
Niles (village) Cook County	214	0.71

Top 10 Places Sorted by Percent

Based on all places, regardless of population

Place	Number	%
East Gillespie (village) Macoupin County	6	2.64
Eagarville (village) Macoupin County	3	2.50
Countryside (city) Cook County	143	2.39
Winthrop Harbor (village) Lake County	128	1.92
Schiller Park (village) Cook County	187	1.59
Lyons (village) Cook County	160	1.58
New Canton (town) Pike County	6	1.34
Wenona (city) Marshall County	14	1.30
Mettawa (village) Lake County	4	1.23
East Dundee (village) Kane County	35	1.21

Top 10 Places Sorted by Percent

Based on places with populations of 10,000 or more

Place	Number	%
Schiller Park (village) Cook County	187	1.59
Lyons (village) Cook County	160	1.58
Loves Park (city) Winnebago County	158	0.79
Brookfield (village) Cook County	151	0.79
Norridge (village) Cook County	106	0.72
Niles (village) Cook County	214	0.71
Lincolnwood (village) Cook County	84	0.68
Summit (village) Cook County	70	0.66
Streamwood (village) Cook County	227	0.62
Carol Stream (village) Du Page County	233	0.59

Hispanic Population

Population

Total Population

Top 10 Places Sorted by Number

Place	Number
Chicago, IL (city) Cook County	2,895,964
Rockford, IL (city) Winnebago County	149,704
Aurora, IL (city) Kane County	143,609
Naperville, IL (city) Du Page County	128,300
Peoria, IL (city) Peoria County	112,892
Springfield, IL (city) Sangamon County	112,201
Joliet, IL (city) Will County	106,157
Elgin, IL (city) Kane County	93,895
Waukegan, IL (city) Lake County	87,969
Cicero, IL (town) Cook County	85,616

Hispanic

Top 10 Places Sorted by Number

Place	Number
Chicago, IL (city) Cook County	753,835
Cicero, IL (town) Cook County	66,188
Aurora, IL (city) Kane County	47,192
Waukegan, IL (city) Lake County	39,706
Elgin, IL (city) Kane County	31,926
Berwyn, IL (city) Cook County	20,543
Joliet, IL (city) Will County	19,328
Rockford, IL (city) Winnebago County	15,301
Carpentersville, IL (village) Kane County	12,510
Melrose Park, IL (village) Cook County	12,508

Hispanic

Top 10 Places Sorted by Percent of Total Population

Place	Percent
Cicero, IL (town) Cook County	77.31
Melrose Park, IL (village) Cook County	53.89
Summit, IL (village) Cook County	48.62
West Chicago, IL (city) Du Page County	47.90
Waukegan, IL (city) Lake County	45.14
Carpentersville, IL (village) Kane County	41.30
Blue Island, IL (city) Cook County	39.66
Berwyn, IL (city) Cook County	38.03
Franklin Park, IL (village) Cook County	37.97
Bensenville, IL (village) Du Page County	36.56

Argentinian

Top 10 Places Sorted by Number

Place	Number
Chicago, IL (city) Cook County	1,064

Argentinian

Top 10 Places Sorted by Percent of Hispanic Population

Place	Percent
Chicago, IL (city) Cook County	0.14

Argentinian

Top 10 Places Sorted by Percent of Total Population

Place	Percent
Chicago, IL (city) Cook County	0.04

Bolivian

Top 10 Places Sorted by Number

Place	Number
Chicago, IL (city) Cook County	477

Bolivian

Top 10 Places Sorted by Percent of Hispanic Population

Place	Percent
Chicago, IL (city) Cook County	0.06

Bolivian

Top 10 Places Sorted by Percent of Total Population

Place	Percent
Chicago, IL (city) Cook County	0.02

Central American

Top 10 Places Sorted by Number

Place	Number
Chicago, IL (city) Cook County	24,160
Waukegan, IL (city) Lake County	2,741
Cicero, IL (town) Cook County	853
Aurora, IL (city) Kane County	494
Skokie, IL (village) Cook County	475

Central American

Top 10 Places Sorted by Percent of Hispanic Population

Place	Percent
Skokie, IL (village) Cook County	13.37
Waukegan, IL (city) Lake County	6.90
Chicago, IL (city) Cook County	3.20
Cicero, IL (town) Cook County	1.29
Aurora, IL (city) Kane County	1.05

Central American

Top 10 Places Sorted by Percent of Total Population

Place	Percent
Waukegan, IL (city) Lake County	3.12
Cicero, IL (town) Cook County	1.00
Chicago, IL (city) Cook County	0.83
Skokie, IL (village) Cook County	0.75
Aurora, IL (city) Kane County	0.34

Chilean

Top 10 Places Sorted by Number

Place	Number
Chicago, IL (city) Cook County	690

Chilean

Top 10 Places Sorted by Percent of Hispanic Population

Place	Percent
Chicago, IL (city) Cook County	0.09

Chilean

Top 10 Places Sorted by Percent of Total Population

Place	Percent
Chicago, IL (city) Cook County	0.02

Colombian

Top 10 Places Sorted by Number

Place	Number
Chicago, IL (city) Cook County	6,091

Colombian

Top 10 Places Sorted by Percent of Hispanic Population

Place	Percent
Chicago, IL (city) Cook County	0.81

Colombian

Top 10 Places Sorted by Percent of Total Population

Place	Percent
Chicago, IL (city) Cook County	0.21

Costa Rican

Top 10 Places Sorted by Number

Place	Number
Chicago, IL (city) Cook County	732

Costa Rican

Top 10 Places Sorted by Percent of Hispanic Population

Place	Percent
Chicago, IL (city) Cook County	0.10

Costa Rican

Top 10 Places Sorted by Percent of Total Population

Place	Percent
Chicago, IL (city) Cook County	0.03

Cuban

Top 10 Places Sorted by Number

Place	Number
Chicago, IL (city) Cook County	8,111
Aurora, IL (city) Kane County	383
Melrose Park, IL (village) Cook County	344

Cuban

Top 10 Places Sorted by Percent of Hispanic Population

Place	Percent
Melrose Park, IL (village) Cook County	2.75
Chicago, IL (city) Cook County	1.08
Aurora, IL (city) Kane County	0.81

Cuban

Top 10 Places Sorted by Percent of Total Population

Place	Percent
Melrose Park, IL (village) Cook County	1.48
Chicago, IL (city) Cook County	0.28
Aurora, IL (city) Kane County	0.27

Dominican

Top 10 Places Sorted by Number

Place	Number
Chicago, IL (city) Cook County	2,066

Dominican

Top 10 Places Sorted by Percent of Hispanic Population

Place	Percent
Chicago, IL (city) Cook County	0.27

Dominican

Top 10 Places Sorted by Percent of Total Population

Place	Percent
Chicago, IL (city) Cook County	0.07

Ecuadorian

Top 10 Places Sorted by Number

Place	Number
Chicago, IL (city) Cook County	9,956

Ecuadorian

Top 10 Places Sorted by Percent of Hispanic Population

Place	Percent
Chicago, IL (city) Cook County	1.32

Ecuadorian

Top 10 Places Sorted by Percent of Total Population

Place	Percent
Chicago, IL (city) Cook County	0.34

Guatelmalan

Top 10 Places Sorted by Number

Place	Number
Chicago, IL (city) Cook County	14,394
Cicero, IL (town) Cook County	446

Notes: Please refer to the User's Guide for an explanation of data; tables include places with populations > 9,999 and reflect only those areas that meet Summary File 4 population thresholds, therefore there may be less than 10 places listed

Guatelmalan
Top 10 Places Sorted by Percent of Hispanic Population

Place	Percent
Chicago, IL (city) Cook County	1.91
Cicero, IL (town) Cook County	0.67

Guatelmalan
Top 10 Places Sorted by Percent of Total Population

Place	Percent
Cicero, IL (town) Cook County	0.52
Chicago, IL (city) Cook County	0.50

Honduran
Top 10 Places Sorted by Number

Place	Number
Chicago, IL (city) Cook County	3,123
Waukegan, IL (city) Lake County	1,544

Honduran
Top 10 Places Sorted by Percent of Hispanic Population

Place	Percent
Waukegan, IL (city) Lake County	3.89
Chicago, IL (city) Cook County	0.41

Honduran
Top 10 Places Sorted by Percent of Total Population

Place	Percent
Waukegan, IL (city) Lake County	1.76
Chicago, IL (city) Cook County	0.11

Mexican
Top 10 Places Sorted by Number

Place	Number
Chicago, IL (city) Cook County	534,045
Cicero, IL (town) Cook County	59,205
Aurora, IL (city) Kane County	40,419
Waukegan, IL (city) Lake County	30,441
Elgin, IL (city) Kane County	27,787
Joliet, IL (city) Will County	17,161
Berwyn, IL (city) Cook County	17,139
Rockford, IL (city) Winnebago County	12,691
Carpentersville, IL (village) Kane County	11,099
West Chicago, IL (city) Du Page County	10,686

Mexican
Top 10 Places Sorted by Percent of Hispanic Population

Place	Percent
Cary, IL (village) McHenry County	97.49
West Chicago, IL (city) Du Page County	93.27
Prospect Heights, IL (city) Cook County	92.62
Summit, IL (village) Cook County	91.99
Woodstock, IL (city) McHenry County	91.58
Dolton, IL (village) Cook County	91.54
Ottawa, IL (city) La Salle County	91.45
Blue Island, IL (city) Cook County	90.92
Chicago Heights, IL (city) Cook County	90.62
Moline, IL (city) Rock Island County	90.46

Mexican
Top 10 Places Sorted by Percent of Total Population

Place	Percent
Cicero, IL (town) Cook County	69.15
Melrose Park, IL (village) Cook County	45.22
Summit, IL (village) Cook County	44.73
West Chicago, IL (city) Du Page County	44.68
Carpentersville, IL (village) Kane County	36.65
Blue Island, IL (city) Cook County	36.06
Waukegan, IL (city) Lake County	34.60
Berwyn, IL (city) Cook County	31.73
Franklin Park, IL (village) Cook County	31.44
Bensenville, IL (village) Du Page County	29.93

Nicaraguan
Top 10 Places Sorted by Number

Place	Number
Chicago, IL (city) Cook County	937

Nicaraguan
Top 10 Places Sorted by Percent of Hispanic Population

Place	Percent
Chicago, IL (city) Cook County	0.12

Nicaraguan
Top 10 Places Sorted by Percent of Total Population

Place	Percent
Chicago, IL (city) Cook County	0.03

Panamanian
Top 10 Places Sorted by Number

Place	Number
Chicago, IL (city) Cook County	844

Panamanian
Top 10 Places Sorted by Percent of Hispanic Population

Place	Percent
Chicago, IL (city) Cook County	0.11

Panamanian
Top 10 Places Sorted by Percent of Total Population

Place	Percent
Chicago, IL (city) Cook County	0.03

Paraguayan
Top 10 Places Sorted by Number

Place	Number
No places met population threshold	

Paraguayan
Top 10 Places Sorted by Percent of Hispanic Population

Place	Percent
No places met population threshold	

Paraguayan
Top 10 Places Sorted by Percent of Total Population

Place	Percent
No places met population threshold	

Peruvian
Top 10 Places Sorted by Number

Place	Number
Chicago, IL (city) Cook County	2,957

Peruvian
Top 10 Places Sorted by Percent of Hispanic Population

Place	Percent
Chicago, IL (city) Cook County	0.39

Peruvian
Top 10 Places Sorted by Percent of Total Population

Place	Percent
Chicago, IL (city) Cook County	0.10

Puerto Rican
Top 10 Places Sorted by Number

Place	Number
Chicago, IL (city) Cook County	111,487
Waukegan, IL (city) Lake County	2,925
Aurora, IL (city) Kane County	2,436
Cicero, IL (town) Cook County	2,370
Elgin, IL (city) Kane County	1,854
Berwyn, IL (city) Cook County	1,274
Elmwood Park, IL (village) Cook County	756
North Chicago, IL (city) Lake County	688
Franklin Park, IL (village) Cook County	590
Joliet, IL (city) Will County	590

Puerto Rican
Top 10 Places Sorted by Percent of Hispanic Population

Place	Percent
Elmwood Park, IL (village) Cook County	27.47
Chicago, IL (city) Cook County	14.79
Schaumburg, IL (village) Cook County	14.05
Naperville, IL (city) Du Page County	11.97
Skokie, IL (village) Cook County	11.54
North Chicago, IL (city) Lake County	10.51
Zion, IL (city) Lake County	9.94
Carol Stream, IL (village) Du Page County	9.77
Streamwood, IL (village) Cook County	8.31
Franklin Park, IL (village) Cook County	7.99

Puerto Rican
Top 10 Places Sorted by Percent of Total Population

Place	Percent
Chicago, IL (city) Cook County	3.85
Waukegan, IL (city) Lake County	3.33
Franklin Park, IL (village) Cook County	3.04
Elmwood Park, IL (village) Cook County	2.98
Cicero, IL (town) Cook County	2.77
Berwyn, IL (city) Cook County	2.36
Melrose Park, IL (village) Cook County	2.32
Elgin, IL (city) Kane County	1.97
North Chicago, IL (city) Lake County	1.91
Aurora, IL (city) Kane County	1.70

Salvadoran
Top 10 Places Sorted by Number

Place	Number
Chicago, IL (city) Cook County	3,363
Waukegan, IL (city) Lake County	547

Salvadoran
Top 10 Places Sorted by Percent of Hispanic Population

Place	Percent
Waukegan, IL (city) Lake County	1.38
Chicago, IL (city) Cook County	0.45

Salvadoran
Top 10 Places Sorted by Percent of Total Population

Place	Percent
Waukegan, IL (city) Lake County	0.62
Chicago, IL (city) Cook County	0.12

South American
Top 10 Places Sorted by Number

Place	Number
Chicago, IL (city) Cook County	23,115
Cicero, IL (town) Cook County	675
Naperville, IL (city) Du Page County	497
Streamwood, IL (village) Cook County	441
Skokie, IL (village) Cook County	437
Berwyn, IL (city) Cook County	430
Aurora, IL (city) Kane County	340

South American
Top 10 Places Sorted by Percent of Hispanic Population

Place	Percent
Skokie, IL (village) Cook County	12.30
Naperville, IL (city) Du Page County	11.06

Notes: Please refer to the User's Guide for an explanation of data; tables include places with populations > 9,999 and reflect only those areas that meet Summary File 4 population thresholds, therefore there may be less than 10 places listed

Place	Percent
Streamwood, IL (village) Cook County	7.31
Chicago, IL (city) Cook County	3.07
Berwyn, IL (city) Cook County	2.09
Cicero, IL (town) Cook County	1.02
Aurora, IL (city) Kane County	0.72

South American

Top 10 Places Sorted by Percent of Total Population

Place	Percent
Streamwood, IL (village) Cook County	1.20
Berwyn, IL (city) Cook County	0.80
Chicago, IL (city) Cook County	0.80
Cicero, IL (town) Cook County	0.79
Skokie, IL (village) Cook County	0.69
Naperville, IL (city) Du Page County	0.39
Aurora, IL (city) Kane County	0.24

Spaniard

Top 10 Places Sorted by Number

Place	Number
Chicago, IL (city) Cook County	844

Spaniard

Top 10 Places Sorted by Percent of Hispanic Population

Place	Percent
Chicago, IL (city) Cook County	0.11

Spaniard

Top 10 Places Sorted by Percent of Total Population

Place	Percent
Chicago, IL (city) Cook County	0.03

Uruguayan

Top 10 Places Sorted by Number

Place	Number
No places met population threshold	

Uruguayan

Top 10 Places Sorted by Percent of Hispanic Population

Place	Percent
No places met population threshold	

Uruguayan

Top 10 Places Sorted by Percent of Total Population

Place	Percent
No places met population threshold	

Venezuelan

Top 10 Places Sorted by Number

Place	Number
Chicago, IL (city) Cook County	782

Venezuelan

Top 10 Places Sorted by Percent of Hispanic Population

Place	Percent
Chicago, IL (city) Cook County	0.10

Venezuelan

Top 10 Places Sorted by Percent of Total Population

Place	Percent
Chicago, IL (city) Cook County	0.03

Other Hispanic

Top 10 Places Sorted by Number

Place	Number
Chicago, IL (city) Cook County	50,007
Waukegan, IL (city) Lake County	3,219
Aurora, IL (city) Kane County	3,083
Cicero, IL (town) Cook County	2,830
Elgin, IL (city) Kane County	1,735
Joliet, IL (city) Will County	1,299
Rockford, IL (city) Winnebago County	1,190
Berwyn, IL (city) Cook County	1,073
Carpentersville, IL (village) Kane County	687
Melrose Park, IL (village) Cook County	638

Other Hispanic

Top 10 Places Sorted by Percent of Hispanic Population

Place	Percent
Dixon, IL (city) Lee County	47.54
Crest Hill, IL (city) Will County	40.67
Danville, IL (city) Vermilion County	26.62
Galesburg, IL (city) Knox County	20.10
Schaumburg, IL (village) Cook County	12.77
Skokie, IL (village) Cook County	11.76
Naperville, IL (city) Du Page County	11.60
Hoffman Estates, IL (village) Cook County	11.32
Burbank, IL (city) Cook County	11.15
Waukegan, IL (city) Lake County	8.11

Other Hispanic

Top 10 Places Sorted by Percent of Total Population

Place	Percent
Waukegan, IL (city) Lake County	3.66
Crest Hill, IL (city) Will County	3.53
Cicero, IL (town) Cook County	3.31
Melrose Park, IL (village) Cook County	2.75
Bensenville, IL (village) Du Page County	2.63
Carpentersville, IL (village) Kane County	2.27
Franklin Park, IL (village) Cook County	2.19
Aurora, IL (city) Kane County	2.15
Dixon, IL (city) Lee County	2.06
Berwyn, IL (city) Cook County	1.99

Median Age

Total Population

Top 10 Places Sorted by Number

Place	Years
Niles, IL (village) Cook County	46.2
Norridge, IL (village) Cook County	46.1
Lincolnwood, IL (village) Cook County	45.4
Morton Grove, IL (village) Cook County	44.6
Westchester, IL (village) Cook County	44.4
Northbrook, IL (village) Cook County	44.2
Park Ridge, IL (city) Cook County	42.5
Wilmette, IL (village) Cook County	42.1
Skokie, IL (village) Cook County	41.9
Oak Lawn, IL (village) Cook County	41.5

Hispanic

Top 10 Places Sorted by Number

Place	Years
Hinsdale, IL (village) Du Page County	35.5
Norridge, IL (village) Cook County	34.1
Morton Grove, IL (village) Cook County	34.0
Wilmette, IL (village) Cook County	33.8
Northbrook, IL (village) Cook County	33.4
Matteson, IL (village) Cook County	32.3
Dixon, IL (city) Lee County	32.2
Lincolnwood, IL (village) Cook County	32.2
Skokie, IL (village) Cook County	30.9
Darien, IL (city) Du Page County	30.8

Argentinian

Top 10 Places Sorted by Number

Place	Years
Chicago, IL (city) Cook County	33.3

Bolivian

Top 10 Places Sorted by Number

Place	Years
Chicago, IL (city) Cook County	29.9

Central American

Top 10 Places Sorted by Number

Place	Years
Chicago, IL (city) Cook County	30.6
Cicero, IL (town) Cook County	30.4
Aurora, IL (city) Kane County	29.9
Skokie, IL (village) Cook County	29.4
Waukegan, IL (city) Lake County	27.7

Chilean

Top 10 Places Sorted by Number

Place	Years
Chicago, IL (city) Cook County	34.6

Colombian

Top 10 Places Sorted by Number

Place	Years
Chicago, IL (city) Cook County	35.3

Costa Rican

Top 10 Places Sorted by Number

Place	Years
Chicago, IL (city) Cook County	30.7

Cuban

Top 10 Places Sorted by Number

Place	Years
Melrose Park, IL (village) Cook County	41.6
Chicago, IL (city) Cook County	39.1
Aurora, IL (city) Kane County	28.2

Dominican

Top 10 Places Sorted by Number

Place	Years
Chicago, IL (city) Cook County	31.1

Ecuadorian

Top 10 Places Sorted by Number

Place	Years
Chicago, IL (city) Cook County	29.9

Guatelmalan

Top 10 Places Sorted by Number

Place	Years
Cicero, IL (town) Cook County	32.3
Chicago, IL (city) Cook County	30.7

Honduran

Top 10 Places Sorted by Number

Place	Years
Chicago, IL (city) Cook County	31.2
Waukegan, IL (city) Lake County	27.1

Mexican

Top 10 Places Sorted by Number

Place	Years
Northbrook, IL (village) Cook County	33.7
Morton Grove, IL (village) Cook County	32.8
Matteson, IL (village) Cook County	32.7
Palos Hills, IL (city) Cook County	32.0
Dixon, IL (city) Lee County	31.7
Darien, IL (city) Du Page County	30.9
Galesburg, IL (city) Knox County	30.6

Notes: Please refer to the User's Guide for an explanation of data; tables include places with populations > 9,999 and reflect only those areas that meet Summary File 4 population thresholds, therefore there may be less than 10 places listed

Place	Years
Libertyville, IL (village) Lake County	30.6
Elk Grove Village, IL (village) Cook County	30.5
Elmwood Park, IL (village) Cook County	30.2

Nicaraguan
Top 10 Places Sorted by Number

Place	Years
Chicago, IL (city) Cook County	26.9

Panamanian
Top 10 Places Sorted by Number

Place	Years
Chicago, IL (city) Cook County	32.0

Paraguayan
Top 10 Places Sorted by Number

Place	Years

No places met population threshold

Peruvian
Top 10 Places Sorted by Number

Place	Years
Chicago, IL (city) Cook County	34.7

Puerto Rican
Top 10 Places Sorted by Number

Place	Years
Carol Stream, IL (village) Du Page County	30.6
Elgin, IL (city) Kane County	30.6
Hanover Park, IL (village) Cook County	30.2
Bolingbrook, IL (village) Will County	29.9
Aurora, IL (city) Kane County	29.5
Chicago, IL (city) Cook County	28.5
Des Plaines, IL (city) Cook County	28.3
Joliet, IL (city) Will County	27.6
Waukegan, IL (city) Lake County	27.6
Evanston, IL (city) Cook County	26.6

Salvadoran
Top 10 Places Sorted by Number

Place	Years
Chicago, IL (city) Cook County	29.1
Waukegan, IL (city) Lake County	26.4

South American
Top 10 Places Sorted by Number

Place	Years
Skokie, IL (village) Cook County	43.2
Naperville, IL (city) Du Page County	35.7
Berwyn, IL (city) Cook County	33.2
Chicago, IL (city) Cook County	31.9
Cicero, IL (town) Cook County	30.3
Streamwood, IL (village) Cook County	30.3
Aurora, IL (city) Kane County	29.2

Spaniard
Top 10 Places Sorted by Number

Place	Years
Chicago, IL (city) Cook County	31.4

Uruguayan
Top 10 Places Sorted by Number

Place	Years

No places met population threshold

Venezuelan
Top 10 Places Sorted by Number

Place	Years
Chicago, IL (city) Cook County	28.7

Other Hispanic
Top 10 Places Sorted by Number

Place	Years
Dixon, IL (city) Lee County	34.1
Blue Island, IL (city) Cook County	32.8
Crest Hill, IL (city) Will County	30.2
Naperville, IL (city) Du Page County	28.9
Galesburg, IL (city) Knox County	28.0
Streamwood, IL (village) Cook County	26.5
Moline, IL (city) Rock Island County	26.3
Skokie, IL (village) Cook County	25.4
Danville, IL (city) Vermilion County	24.8
Wheeling, IL (village) Cook County	24.7

Average Household Size

Total Population
Top 10 Places Sorted by Number

Place	Number
Cicero, IL (town) Cook County	3.69
West Chicago, IL (city) Du Page County	3.65
Carpentersville, IL (village) Kane County	3.49
Round Lake Beach, IL (village) Lake County	3.47
Hanover Park, IL (village) Cook County	3.40
Maywood, IL (village) Cook County	3.38
Goodings Grove, IL (cdp) Will County	3.32
Harvey, IL (city) Cook County	3.30
Bolingbrook, IL (village) Will County	3.23
Bellwood, IL (village) Cook County	3.17

Hispanic
Top 10 Places Sorted by Number

Place	Number
Round Lake Beach, IL (village) Lake County	5.09
Bensenville, IL (village) Du Page County	5.06
Bellwood, IL (village) Cook County	5.04
Carpentersville, IL (village) Kane County	5.03
West Chicago, IL (city) Du Page County	5.03
Maywood, IL (village) Cook County	5.01
Highland Park, IL (city) Lake County	4.79
Cary, IL (village) McHenry County	4.73
Hanover Park, IL (village) Cook County	4.67
Wheeling, IL (village) Cook County	4.65

Argentinian
Top 10 Places Sorted by Number

Place	Number
Chicago, IL (city) Cook County	2.23

Bolivian
Top 10 Places Sorted by Number

Place	Number
Chicago, IL (city) Cook County	2.46

Central American
Top 10 Places Sorted by Number

Place	Number
Cicero, IL (town) Cook County	4.73
Waukegan, IL (city) Lake County	4.08
Aurora, IL (city) Kane County	3.96
Skokie, IL (village) Cook County	3.92
Chicago, IL (city) Cook County	3.70

Chilean
Top 10 Places Sorted by Number

Place	Number
Chicago, IL (city) Cook County	2.83

Colombian
Top 10 Places Sorted by Number

Place	Number
Chicago, IL (city) Cook County	2.92

Costa Rican
Top 10 Places Sorted by Number

Place	Number
Chicago, IL (city) Cook County	3.00

Cuban
Top 10 Places Sorted by Number

Place	Number
Melrose Park, IL (village) Cook County	3.63
Aurora, IL (city) Kane County	2.79
Chicago, IL (city) Cook County	2.55

Dominican
Top 10 Places Sorted by Number

Place	Number
Chicago, IL (city) Cook County	2.98

Ecuadorian
Top 10 Places Sorted by Number

Place	Number
Chicago, IL (city) Cook County	4.04

Guatelmalan
Top 10 Places Sorted by Number

Place	Number
Cicero, IL (town) Cook County	4.92
Chicago, IL (city) Cook County	3.88

Honduran
Top 10 Places Sorted by Number

Place	Number
Waukegan, IL (city) Lake County	4.57
Chicago, IL (city) Cook County	3.27

Mexican
Top 10 Places Sorted by Number

Place	Number
Bensenville, IL (village) Du Page County	5.52
Plainfield, IL (village) Will County	5.32
Round Lake Beach, IL (village) Lake County	5.31
Bellwood, IL (village) Cook County	5.20
Highland Park, IL (city) Lake County	5.20
Carpentersville, IL (village) Kane County	5.18
West Chicago, IL (city) Du Page County	5.16
Maywood, IL (village) Cook County	5.13
Hanover Park, IL (village) Cook County	4.99
Streamwood, IL (village) Cook County	4.94

Nicaraguan
Top 10 Places Sorted by Number

Place	Number
Chicago, IL (city) Cook County	3.76

Panamanian
Top 10 Places Sorted by Number

Place	Number
Chicago, IL (city) Cook County	3.05

Notes: Please refer to the User's Guide for an explanation of data; tables include places with populations > 9,999 and reflect only those areas that meet Summary File 4 population thresholds, therefore there may be less than 10 places listed

Paraguayan
Top 10 Places Sorted by Number

Place	Number
No places met population threshold	

Peruvian
Top 10 Places Sorted by Number

Place	Number
Chicago, IL (city) Cook County	3.20

Puerto Rican
Top 10 Places Sorted by Number

Place	Number
Melrose Park, IL (village) Cook County	3.99
Franklin Park, IL (village) Cook County	3.98
Streamwood, IL (village) Cook County	3.98
North Chicago, IL (city) Lake County	3.88
Bolingbrook, IL (village) Will County	3.80
Carpentersville, IL (village) Kane County	3.64
Cicero, IL (town) Cook County	3.50
Berwyn, IL (city) Cook County	3.33
Aurora, IL (city) Kane County	3.28
Carol Stream, IL (village) Du Page County	3.26

Salvadoran
Top 10 Places Sorted by Number

Place	Number
Waukegan, IL (city) Lake County	3.83
Chicago, IL (city) Cook County	3.80

South American
Top 10 Places Sorted by Number

Place	Number
Streamwood, IL (village) Cook County	4.32
Cicero, IL (town) Cook County	3.99
Aurora, IL (city) Kane County	3.71
Naperville, IL (city) Du Page County	3.40
Chicago, IL (city) Cook County	3.33
Berwyn, IL (city) Cook County	3.19
Skokie, IL (village) Cook County	3.01

Spaniard
Top 10 Places Sorted by Number

Place	Number
Chicago, IL (city) Cook County	2.03

Uruguayan
Top 10 Places Sorted by Number

Place	Number
No places met population threshold	

Venezuelan
Top 10 Places Sorted by Number

Place	Number
Chicago, IL (city) Cook County	2.57

Other Hispanic
Top 10 Places Sorted by Number

Place	Number
Mount Prospect, IL (village) Cook County	5.49
Bensenville, IL (village) Du Page County	4.88
Carpentersville, IL (village) Kane County	4.59
Burbank, IL (city) Cook County	4.58
Chicago Heights, IL (city) Cook County	4.56
Waukegan, IL (city) Lake County	4.56
Cicero, IL (town) Cook County	4.47
Danville, IL (city) Vermilion County	4.45
West Chicago, IL (city) Du Page County	4.36
Addison, IL (village) Du Page County	4.08

Language Spoken at Home: English Only

Total Populations 5 Years and Over Who Speak English-Only at Home
Top 10 Places Sorted by Number

Place	Number
Chicago, IL (city) Cook County	1,726,905
Rockford, IL (city) Winnebago County	119,262
Springfield, IL (city) Sangamon County	100,722
Naperville, IL (city) Du Page County	99,729
Peoria, IL (city) Peoria County	96,641
Aurora, IL (city) Kane County	83,953
Joliet, IL (city) Will County	78,217
Decatur, IL (city) Macon County	73,838
Arlington Heights, IL (village) Cook County	58,797
Evanston, IL (city) Cook County	57,304

Total Populations 5 Years and Over Who Speak English-Only at Home
Top 10 Places Sorted by Percent

Place	Percent
Pekin, IL (city) Tazewell County	97.41
Quincy, IL (city) Adams County	97.25
Alton, IL (city) Madison County	96.78
Granite City, IL (city) Madison County	96.57
New Lenox, IL (village) Will County	96.57
Decatur, IL (city) Macon County	96.38
Collinsville, IL (city) Madison County	96.35
Springfield, IL (city) Sangamon County	95.92
Machesney Park, IL (village) Winnebago County	95.88
Dixon, IL (city) Lee County	95.81

Hispanics 5 Years and Over Who Speak English-Only at Home
Top 10 Places Sorted by Number

Place	Number
Chicago, IL (city) Cook County	81,807
Cicero, IL (town) Cook County	4,561
Aurora, IL (city) Kane County	4,158
Waukegan, IL (city) Lake County	3,613
Joliet, IL (city) Will County	3,245
Rockford, IL (city) Winnebago County	3,011
Berwyn, IL (city) Cook County	2,891
Elgin, IL (city) Kane County	2,706
Naperville, IL (city) Du Page County	1,767
Bolingbrook, IL (village) Will County	1,654

Hispanics 5 Years and Over Who Speak English-Only at Home
Top 10 Places Sorted by Percent

Place	Percent
Alton, IL (city) Madison County	77.52
Mokena, IL (village) Will County	76.49
O'Fallon, IL (city) Saint Clair County	74.00
New Lenox, IL (village) Will County	73.78
Pekin, IL (city) Tazewell County	71.08
Belleville, IL (city) Saint Clair County	67.86
Granite City, IL (city) Madison County	65.94
Collinsville, IL (city) Madison County	64.44
Quincy, IL (city) Adams County	62.46
Machesney Park, IL (village) Winnebago County	59.83

Argentinians 5 Years and Over Who Speak English-Only at Home
Top 10 Places Sorted by Number

Place	Number
Chicago, IL (city) Cook County	97

Argentinians 5 Years and Over Who Speak English-Only at Home
Top 10 Places Sorted by Percent

Place	Percent
Chicago, IL (city) Cook County	9.44

Bolivians 5 Years and Over Who Speak English-Only at Home
Top 10 Places Sorted by Number

Place	Number
Chicago, IL (city) Cook County	84

Bolivians 5 Years and Over Who Speak English-Only at Home
Top 10 Places Sorted by Percent

Place	Percent
Chicago, IL (city) Cook County	19.22

Central Americans 5 Years and Over Who Speak English-Only at Home
Top 10 Places Sorted by Number

Place	Number
Chicago, IL (city) Cook County	1,321
Waukegan, IL (city) Lake County	158
Cicero, IL (town) Cook County	60
Skokie, IL (village) Cook County	29
Aurora, IL (city) Kane County	18

Central Americans 5 Years and Over Who Speak English-Only at Home
Top 10 Places Sorted by Percent

Place	Percent
Cicero, IL (town) Cook County	7.56
Waukegan, IL (city) Lake County	6.32
Skokie, IL (village) Cook County	6.11
Chicago, IL (city) Cook County	5.86
Aurora, IL (city) Kane County	3.78

Chileans 5 Years and Over Who Speak English-Only at Home
Top 10 Places Sorted by Number

Place	Number
Chicago, IL (city) Cook County	68

Chileans 5 Years and Over Who Speak English-Only at Home
Top 10 Places Sorted by Percent

Place	Percent
Chicago, IL (city) Cook County	10.12

Colombians 5 Years and Over Who Speak English-Only at Home
Top 10 Places Sorted by Number

Place	Number
Chicago, IL (city) Cook County	445

Colombians 5 Years and Over Who Speak English-Only at Home
Top 10 Places Sorted by Percent

Place	Percent
Chicago, IL (city) Cook County	7.68

Costa Ricans 5 Years and Over Who Speak English-Only at Home
Top 10 Places Sorted by Number

Place	Number
Chicago, IL (city) Cook County	95

Notes: Please refer to the User's Guide for an explanation of data; tables include places with populations > 9,999 and reflect only those areas that meet Summary File 4 population thresholds, therefore there may be less than 10 places listed

Costa Ricans 5 Years and Over Who Speak English-Only at Home
Top 10 Places Sorted by Percent

Place	Percent
Chicago, IL (city) Cook County	14.37

Cubans 5 Years and Over Who Speak English-Only at Home
Top 10 Places Sorted by Number

Place	Number
Chicago, IL (city) Cook County	1,290
Aurora, IL (city) Kane County	117
Melrose Park, IL (village) Cook County	27

Cubans 5 Years and Over Who Speak English-Only at Home
Top 10 Places Sorted by Percent

Place	Percent
Aurora, IL (city) Kane County	36.22
Chicago, IL (city) Cook County	16.67
Melrose Park, IL (village) Cook County	8.08

Dominicans 5 Years and Over Who Speak English-Only at Home
Top 10 Places Sorted by Number

Place	Number
Chicago, IL (city) Cook County	181

Dominicans 5 Years and Over Who Speak English-Only at Home
Top 10 Places Sorted by Percent

Place	Percent
Chicago, IL (city) Cook County	9.20

Ecuadorians 5 Years and Over Who Speak English-Only at Home
Top 10 Places Sorted by Number

Place	Number
Chicago, IL (city) Cook County	631

Ecuadorians 5 Years and Over Who Speak English-Only at Home
Top 10 Places Sorted by Percent

Place	Percent
Chicago, IL (city) Cook County	6.88

Guatelmalans 5 Years and Over Who Speak English-Only at Home
Top 10 Places Sorted by Number

Place	Number
Chicago, IL (city) Cook County	637
Cicero, IL (town) Cook County	29

Guatelmalans 5 Years and Over Who Speak English-Only at Home
Top 10 Places Sorted by Percent

Place	Percent
Cicero, IL (town) Cook County	7.36
Chicago, IL (city) Cook County	4.76

Hondurans 5 Years and Over Who Speak English-Only at Home
Top 10 Places Sorted by Number

Place	Number
Chicago, IL (city) Cook County	131
Waukegan, IL (city) Lake County	101

Hondurans 5 Years and Over Who Speak English-Only at Home
Top 10 Places Sorted by Percent

Place	Percent
Waukegan, IL (city) Lake County	7.15
Chicago, IL (city) Cook County	4.52

Mexicans 5 Years and Over Who Speak English-Only at Home
Top 10 Places Sorted by Number

Place	Number
Chicago, IL (city) Cook County	52,479
Cicero, IL (town) Cook County	3,672
Aurora, IL (city) Kane County	3,039
Joliet, IL (city) Will County	2,762
Waukegan, IL (city) Lake County	2,486
Berwyn, IL (city) Cook County	2,279
Rockford, IL (city) Winnebago County	2,140
Elgin, IL (city) Kane County	1,965
Bolingbrook, IL (village) Will County	1,203
Moline, IL (city) Rock Island County	1,125

Mexicans 5 Years and Over Who Speak English-Only at Home
Top 10 Places Sorted by Percent

Place	Percent
New Lenox, IL (village) Will County	76.26
Dixon, IL (city) Lee County	73.40
Belleville, IL (city) Saint Clair County	66.07
Granite City, IL (city) Madison County	65.83
Springfield, IL (city) Sangamon County	65.65
Crest Hill, IL (city) Will County	62.74
Normal, IL (town) McLean County	60.61
Machesney Park, IL (village) Winnebago County	59.75
Homewood, IL (village) Cook County	57.45
Ottawa, IL (city) La Salle County	55.51

Nicaraguans 5 Years and Over Who Speak English-Only at Home
Top 10 Places Sorted by Number

Place	Number
Chicago, IL (city) Cook County	46

Nicaraguans 5 Years and Over Who Speak English-Only at Home
Top 10 Places Sorted by Percent

Place	Percent
Chicago, IL (city) Cook County	5.52

Panamanians 5 Years and Over Who Speak English-Only at Home
Top 10 Places Sorted by Number

Place	Number
Chicago, IL (city) Cook County	178

Panamanians 5 Years and Over Who Speak English-Only at Home
Top 10 Places Sorted by Percent

Place	Percent
Chicago, IL (city) Cook County	23.45

Paraguayans 5 Years and Over Who Speak English-Only at Home
Top 10 Places Sorted by Number

Place	Number

No places met population threshold

Paraguayans 5 Years and Over Who Speak English-Only at Home
Top 10 Places Sorted by Percent

Place	Percent

No places met population threshold

Peruvians 5 Years and Over Who Speak English-Only at Home
Top 10 Places Sorted by Number

Place	Number
Chicago, IL (city) Cook County	274

Peruvians 5 Years and Over Who Speak English-Only at Home
Top 10 Places Sorted by Percent

Place	Percent
Chicago, IL (city) Cook County	9.65

Puerto Ricans 5 Years and Over Who Speak English-Only at Home
Top 10 Places Sorted by Number

Place	Number
Chicago, IL (city) Cook County	16,134
Waukegan, IL (city) Lake County	563
Aurora, IL (city) Kane County	438
Cicero, IL (town) Cook County	427
Berwyn, IL (city) Cook County	359
Elgin, IL (city) Kane County	297
Naperville, IL (city) Du Page County	250
Schaumburg, IL (village) Cook County	241
Elmwood Park, IL (village) Cook County	228
North Chicago, IL (city) Lake County	217

Puerto Ricans 5 Years and Over Who Speak English-Only at Home
Top 10 Places Sorted by Percent

Place	Percent
Naperville, IL (city) Du Page County	51.12
Rockford, IL (city) Winnebago County	45.54
Schaumburg, IL (village) Cook County	44.55
Bolingbrook, IL (village) Will County	43.58
Hanover Park, IL (village) Cook County	43.48
Streamwood, IL (village) Cook County	40.10
Carol Stream, IL (village) Du Page County	37.25
Elmwood Park, IL (village) Cook County	33.43
North Chicago, IL (city) Lake County	33.03
Des Plaines, IL (city) Cook County	32.73

Salvadorans 5 Years and Over Who Speak English-Only at Home
Top 10 Places Sorted by Number

Place	Number
Chicago, IL (city) Cook County	187
Waukegan, IL (city) Lake County	23

Salvadorans 5 Years and Over Who Speak English-Only at Home
Top 10 Places Sorted by Percent

Place	Percent
Chicago, IL (city) Cook County	5.75
Waukegan, IL (city) Lake County	4.67

South Americans 5 Years and Over Who Speak English-Only at Home
Top 10 Places Sorted by Number

Place	Number
Chicago, IL (city) Cook County	1,781
Naperville, IL (city) Du Page County	211
Cicero, IL (town) Cook County	54
Skokie, IL (village) Cook County	32

Notes: Please refer to the User's Guide for an explanation of data; tables include places with populations > 9,999 and reflect only those areas that meet Summary File 4 population thresholds, therefore there may be less than 10 places listed

Aurora, IL (city) Kane County	17
Berwyn, IL (city) Cook County	8
Streamwood, IL (village) Cook County	0

South Americans 5 Years and Over Who Speak English-Only at Home
Top 10 Places Sorted by Percent

Place	Percent
Naperville, IL (city) Du Page County	42.45
Cicero, IL (town) Cook County	8.60
Chicago, IL (city) Cook County	8.18
Skokie, IL (village) Cook County	7.53
Aurora, IL (city) Kane County	6.32
Berwyn, IL (city) Cook County	1.91
Streamwood, IL (village) Cook County	0.00

Spaniards 5 Years and Over Who Speak English-Only at Home
Top 10 Places Sorted by Number

Place	Number
Chicago, IL (city) Cook County	207

Spaniards 5 Years and Over Who Speak English-Only at Home
Top 10 Places Sorted by Percent

Place	Percent
Chicago, IL (city) Cook County	27.56

Uruguayans 5 Years and Over Who Speak English-Only at Home
Top 10 Places Sorted by Number

Place	Number
No places met population threshold	

Uruguayans 5 Years and Over Who Speak English-Only at Home
Top 10 Places Sorted by Percent

Place	Percent
No places met population threshold	

Venezuelans 5 Years and Over Who Speak English-Only at Home
Top 10 Places Sorted by Number

Place	Number
Chicago, IL (city) Cook County	86

Venezuelans 5 Years and Over Who Speak English-Only at Home
Top 10 Places Sorted by Percent

Place	Percent
Chicago, IL (city) Cook County	11.15

Other Hispanics 5 Years and Over Who Speak English-Only at Home
Top 10 Places Sorted by Number

Place	Number
Chicago, IL (city) Cook County	8,414
Aurora, IL (city) Kane County	520
Rockford, IL (city) Winnebago County	494
Waukegan, IL (city) Lake County	363
Cicero, IL (town) Cook County	317
Joliet, IL (city) Will County	309
Elgin, IL (city) Kane County	285
Naperville, IL (city) Du Page County	246
Galesburg, IL (city) Knox County	199
Berwyn, IL (city) Cook County	197

Other Hispanics 5 Years and Over Who Speak English-Only at Home
Top 10 Places Sorted by Percent

Place	Percent
Galesburg, IL (city) Knox County	64.82
Naperville, IL (city) Du Page County	57.21
Evanston, IL (city) Cook County	50.76
Rockford, IL (city) Winnebago County	48.53
Dixon, IL (city) Lee County	44.72
Bolingbrook, IL (village) Will County	43.95
North Chicago, IL (city) Lake County	38.34
Schaumburg, IL (village) Cook County	37.00
Burbank, IL (city) Cook County	36.47
Streamwood, IL (village) Cook County	35.19

Language Spoken at Home: Spanish

Total Populations 5 Years and Over Who Speak Spanish at Home
Top 10 Places Sorted by Number

Place	Number
Chicago, IL (city) Cook County	625,240
Cicero, IL (town) Cook County	53,603
Aurora, IL (city) Kane County	38,097
Waukegan, IL (city) Lake County	32,031
Elgin, IL (city) Kane County	26,052
Berwyn, IL (city) Cook County	15,521
Joliet, IL (city) Will County	14,764
Rockford, IL (city) Winnebago County	11,992
Melrose Park, IL (village) Cook County	10,389
Carpentersville, IL (village) Kane County	9,999

Total Populations 5 Years and Over Who Speak Spanish at Home
Top 10 Places Sorted by Percent

Place	Percent
Cicero, IL (town) Cook County	70.21
Melrose Park, IL (village) Cook County	48.95
West Chicago, IL (city) Du Page County	44.28
Summit, IL (village) Cook County	43.88
Waukegan, IL (city) Lake County	40.26
Carpentersville, IL (village) Kane County	36.84
Blue Island, IL (city) Cook County	35.44
Franklin Park, IL (village) Cook County	33.67
Bensenville, IL (village) Du Page County	32.36
Berwyn, IL (city) Cook County	31.21

Hispanics 5 Years and Over Who Speak Spanish at Home
Top 10 Places Sorted by Number

Place	Number
Chicago, IL (city) Cook County	587,594
Cicero, IL (town) Cook County	53,025
Aurora, IL (city) Kane County	36,620
Waukegan, IL (city) Lake County	30,879
Elgin, IL (city) Kane County	25,081
Berwyn, IL (city) Cook County	15,053
Joliet, IL (city) Will County	13,689
Melrose Park, IL (village) Cook County	10,115
Rockford, IL (city) Winnebago County	9,975
Carpentersville, IL (village) Kane County	9,632

Hispanics 5 Years and Over Who Speak Spanish at Home
Top 10 Places Sorted by Percent

Place	Percent
Prospect Heights, IL (city) Cook County	94.07
Northlake, IL (city) Cook County	92.79
Cicero, IL (town) Cook County	91.91
West Chicago, IL (city) Du Page County	91.78
Melrose Park, IL (village) Cook County	91.75
Harvey, IL (city) Cook County	91.30
Franklin Park, IL (village) Cook County	91.02
Addison, IL (village) Du Page County	90.77
Rolling Meadows, IL (city) Cook County	90.60
Summit, IL (village) Cook County	90.60

Argentinians 5 Years and Over Who Speak Spanish at Home
Top 10 Places Sorted by Number

Place	Number
Chicago, IL (city) Cook County	924

Argentinians 5 Years and Over Who Speak Spanish at Home
Top 10 Places Sorted by Percent

Place	Percent
Chicago, IL (city) Cook County	89.88

Bolivians 5 Years and Over Who Speak Spanish at Home
Top 10 Places Sorted by Number

Place	Number
Chicago, IL (city) Cook County	353

Bolivians 5 Years and Over Who Speak Spanish at Home
Top 10 Places Sorted by Percent

Place	Percent
Chicago, IL (city) Cook County	80.78

Central Americans 5 Years and Over Who Speak Spanish at Home
Top 10 Places Sorted by Number

Place	Number
Chicago, IL (city) Cook County	21,147
Waukegan, IL (city) Lake County	2,337
Cicero, IL (town) Cook County	734
Aurora, IL (city) Kane County	458
Skokie, IL (village) Cook County	446

Central Americans 5 Years and Over Who Speak Spanish at Home
Top 10 Places Sorted by Percent

Place	Percent
Aurora, IL (city) Kane County	96.22
Skokie, IL (village) Cook County	93.89
Chicago, IL (city) Cook County	93.81
Waukegan, IL (city) Lake County	93.52
Cicero, IL (town) Cook County	92.44

Chileans 5 Years and Over Who Speak Spanish at Home
Top 10 Places Sorted by Number

Place	Number
Chicago, IL (city) Cook County	598

Chileans 5 Years and Over Who Speak Spanish at Home
Top 10 Places Sorted by Percent

Place	Percent
Chicago, IL (city) Cook County	88.99

Colombians 5 Years and Over Who Speak Spanish at Home
Top 10 Places Sorted by Number

Place	Number
Chicago, IL (city) Cook County	5,273

Notes: Please refer to the User's Guide for an explanation of data; tables include places with populations > 9,999 and reflect only those areas that meet Summary File 4 population thresholds, therefore there may be less than 10 places listed

Colombians 5 Years and Over Who Speak Spanish at Home

Top 10 Places Sorted by Percent

Place	Percent
Chicago, IL (city) Cook County	91.06

Costa Ricans 5 Years and Over Who Speak Spanish at Home

Top 10 Places Sorted by Number

Place	Number
Chicago, IL (city) Cook County	566

Costa Ricans 5 Years and Over Who Speak Spanish at Home

Top 10 Places Sorted by Percent

Place	Percent
Chicago, IL (city) Cook County	85.63

Cubans 5 Years and Over Who Speak Spanish at Home

Top 10 Places Sorted by Number

Place	Number
Chicago, IL (city) Cook County	6,431
Melrose Park, IL (village) Cook County	307
Aurora, IL (city) Kane County	206

Cubans 5 Years and Over Who Speak Spanish at Home

Top 10 Places Sorted by Percent

Place	Percent
Melrose Park, IL (village) Cook County	91.92
Chicago, IL (city) Cook County	83.10
Aurora, IL (city) Kane County	63.78

Dominicans 5 Years and Over Who Speak Spanish at Home

Top 10 Places Sorted by Number

Place	Number
Chicago, IL (city) Cook County	1,787

Dominicans 5 Years and Over Who Speak Spanish at Home

Top 10 Places Sorted by Percent

Place	Percent
Chicago, IL (city) Cook County	90.80

Ecuadorians 5 Years and Over Who Speak Spanish at Home

Top 10 Places Sorted by Number

Place	Number
Chicago, IL (city) Cook County	8,488

Ecuadorians 5 Years and Over Who Speak Spanish at Home

Top 10 Places Sorted by Percent

Place	Percent
Chicago, IL (city) Cook County	92.53

Guatelmalans 5 Years and Over Who Speak Spanish at Home

Top 10 Places Sorted by Number

Place	Number
Chicago, IL (city) Cook County	12,701
Cicero, IL (town) Cook County	365

Guatelmalans 5 Years and Over Who Speak Spanish at Home

Top 10 Places Sorted by Percent

Place	Percent
Chicago, IL (city) Cook County	94.81
Cicero, IL (town) Cook County	92.64

Hondurans 5 Years and Over Who Speak Spanish at Home

Top 10 Places Sorted by Number

Place	Number
Chicago, IL (city) Cook County	2,767
Waukegan, IL (city) Lake County	1,312

Hondurans 5 Years and Over Who Speak Spanish at Home

Top 10 Places Sorted by Percent

Place	Percent
Chicago, IL (city) Cook County	95.48
Waukegan, IL (city) Lake County	92.85

Mexicans 5 Years and Over Who Speak Spanish at Home

Top 10 Places Sorted by Number

Place	Number
Chicago, IL (city) Cook County	419,060
Cicero, IL (town) Cook County	47,780
Aurora, IL (city) Kane County	31,737
Waukegan, IL (city) Lake County	23,885
Elgin, IL (city) Kane County	22,083
Berwyn, IL (city) Cook County	12,702
Joliet, IL (city) Will County	12,341
West Chicago, IL (city) Du Page County	8,824
Carpentersville, IL (village) Kane County	8,733
Melrose Park, IL (village) Cook County	8,628

Mexicans 5 Years and Over Who Speak Spanish at Home

Top 10 Places Sorted by Percent

Place	Percent
Prospect Heights, IL (city) Cook County	96.83
Highland Park, IL (city) Lake County	94.38
Northlake, IL (city) Cook County	94.04
Melrose Park, IL (village) Cook County	93.67
West Chicago, IL (city) Du Page County	93.64
Rolling Meadows, IL (city) Cook County	93.46
Bellwood, IL (village) Cook County	93.25
Franklin Park, IL (village) Cook County	92.84
Cicero, IL (town) Cook County	92.68
Mount Prospect, IL (village) Cook County	92.44

Nicaraguans 5 Years and Over Who Speak Spanish at Home

Top 10 Places Sorted by Number

Place	Number
Chicago, IL (city) Cook County	775

Nicaraguans 5 Years and Over Who Speak Spanish at Home

Top 10 Places Sorted by Percent

Place	Percent
Chicago, IL (city) Cook County	93.04

Panamanians 5 Years and Over Who Speak Spanish at Home

Top 10 Places Sorted by Number

Place	Number
Chicago, IL (city) Cook County	581

Panamanians 5 Years and Over Who Speak Spanish at Home

Top 10 Places Sorted by Percent

Place	Percent
Chicago, IL (city) Cook County	76.55

Paraguayans 5 Years and Over Who Speak Spanish at Home

Top 10 Places Sorted by Number

Place	Number
No places met population threshold	

Paraguayans 5 Years and Over Who Speak Spanish at Home

Top 10 Places Sorted by Percent

Place	Percent
No places met population threshold	

Peruvians 5 Years and Over Who Speak Spanish at Home

Top 10 Places Sorted by Number

Place	Number
Chicago, IL (city) Cook County	2,554

Peruvians 5 Years and Over Who Speak Spanish at Home

Top 10 Places Sorted by Percent

Place	Percent
Chicago, IL (city) Cook County	89.99

Puerto Ricans 5 Years and Over Who Speak Spanish at Home

Top 10 Places Sorted by Number

Place	Number
Chicago, IL (city) Cook County	85,302
Waukegan, IL (city) Lake County	2,088
Aurora, IL (city) Kane County	1,775
Cicero, IL (town) Cook County	1,714
Elgin, IL (city) Kane County	1,373
Berwyn, IL (city) Cook County	815
Elmwood Park, IL (village) Cook County	454
North Chicago, IL (city) Lake County	434
Franklin Park, IL (village) Cook County	403
Joliet, IL (city) Will County	370

Puerto Ricans 5 Years and Over Who Speak Spanish at Home

Top 10 Places Sorted by Percent

Place	Percent
Chicago, IL (city) Cook County	83.83
Elgin, IL (city) Kane County	82.22
Aurora, IL (city) Kane County	80.21
Cicero, IL (town) Cook County	80.06
Waukegan, IL (city) Lake County	78.76
Zion, IL (city) Lake County	75.16
Franklin Park, IL (village) Cook County	74.35
Melrose Park, IL (village) Cook County	72.82
Joliet, IL (city) Will County	71.29
Berwyn, IL (city) Cook County	68.78

Salvadorans 5 Years and Over Who Speak Spanish at Home

Top 10 Places Sorted by Number

Place	Number
Chicago, IL (city) Cook County	3,064
Waukegan, IL (city) Lake County	470

Notes: Please refer to the User's Guide for an explanation of data; tables include places with populations > 9,999 and reflect only those areas that meet Summary File 4 population thresholds, therefore there may be less than 10 places listed

Salvadorans 5 Years and Over Who Speak Spanish at Home
Top 10 Places Sorted by Percent

Place	Percent
Waukegan, IL (city) Lake County	95.33
Chicago, IL (city) Cook County	94.25

South Americans 5 Years and Over Who Speak Spanish at Home
Top 10 Places Sorted by Number

Place	Number
Chicago, IL (city) Cook County	19,782
Cicero, IL (town) Cook County	574
Streamwood, IL (village) Cook County	410
Berwyn, IL (city) Cook County	404
Skokie, IL (village) Cook County	386
Naperville, IL (city) Du Page County	286
Aurora, IL (city) Kane County	252

South Americans 5 Years and Over Who Speak Spanish at Home
Top 10 Places Sorted by Percent

Place	Percent
Streamwood, IL (village) Cook County	100.00
Berwyn, IL (city) Cook County	96.65
Aurora, IL (city) Kane County	93.68
Cicero, IL (town) Cook County	91.40
Chicago, IL (city) Cook County	90.86
Skokie, IL (village) Cook County	90.82
Naperville, IL (city) Du Page County	57.55

Spaniards 5 Years and Over Who Speak Spanish at Home
Top 10 Places Sorted by Number

Place	Number
Chicago, IL (city) Cook County	514

Spaniards 5 Years and Over Who Speak Spanish at Home
Top 10 Places Sorted by Percent

Place	Percent
Chicago, IL (city) Cook County	68.44

Uruguayans 5 Years and Over Who Speak Spanish at Home
Top 10 Places Sorted by Number

Place	Number
No places met population threshold	

Uruguayans 5 Years and Over Who Speak Spanish at Home
Top 10 Places Sorted by Percent

Place	Percent
No places met population threshold	

Venezuelans 5 Years and Over Who Speak Spanish at Home
Top 10 Places Sorted by Number

Place	Number
Chicago, IL (city) Cook County	637

Venezuelans 5 Years and Over Who Speak Spanish at Home
Top 10 Places Sorted by Percent

Place	Percent
Chicago, IL (city) Cook County	82.62

Other Hispanics 5 Years and Over Who Speak Spanish at Home
Top 10 Places Sorted by Number

Place	Number
Chicago, IL (city) Cook County	33,571
Waukegan, IL (city) Lake County	2,247
Aurora, IL (city) Kane County	2,164
Cicero, IL (town) Cook County	2,005
Elgin, IL (city) Kane County	1,266
Joliet, IL (city) Will County	769
Berwyn, IL (city) Cook County	610
Rockford, IL (city) Winnebago County	504
Melrose Park, IL (village) Cook County	444
Carpentersville, IL (village) Kane County	418

Other Hispanics 5 Years and Over Who Speak Spanish at Home
Top 10 Places Sorted by Percent

Place	Percent
Cicero, IL (town) Cook County	86.35
Waukegan, IL (city) Lake County	86.09
Bensenville, IL (village) Du Page County	84.70
Franklin Park, IL (village) Cook County	83.81
Palatine, IL (village) Cook County	83.30
Melrose Park, IL (village) Cook County	82.07
Elgin, IL (city) Kane County	81.62
Aurora, IL (city) Kane County	80.63
Chicago, IL (city) Cook County	78.54
Blue Island, IL (city) Cook County	76.67

Foreign Born

Total Population
Top 10 Places Sorted by Number

Place	Number
Chicago, IL (city) Cook County	628,903
Cicero, IL (town) Cook County	37,343
Aurora, IL (city) Kane County	30,858
Waukegan, IL (city) Lake County	26,556
Skokie, IL (village) Cook County	23,437
Elgin, IL (city) Kane County	22,258
Mount Prospect, IL (village) Cook County	15,159
Naperville, IL (city) Du Page County	14,963
Schaumburg, IL (village) Cook County	14,262
Palatine, IL (village) Cook County	14,249

Total Population
Top 10 Places Sorted by Percent

Place	Percent
Cicero, IL (town) Cook County	43.62
Schiller Park, IL (village) Cook County	39.07
Skokie, IL (village) Cook County	37.01
Prospect Heights, IL (city) Cook County	36.48
Melrose Park, IL (village) Cook County	35.31
Addison, IL (village) Du Page County	34.26
Lincolnwood, IL (village) Cook County	34.11
Summit, IL (village) Cook County	34.09
West Chicago, IL (city) Du Page County	34.07
Niles, IL (village) Cook County	33.65

Hispanic
Top 10 Places Sorted by Number

Place	Number
Chicago, IL (city) Cook County	343,526
Cicero, IL (town) Cook County	34,917
Aurora, IL (city) Kane County	24,647
Waukegan, IL (city) Lake County	22,071
Elgin, IL (city) Kane County	17,777
Joliet, IL (city) Will County	9,034
Berwyn, IL (city) Cook County	8,813
West Chicago, IL (city) Du Page County	7,286
Carpentersville, IL (village) Kane County	7,154
Rockford, IL (city) Winnebago County	7,133

Hispanic
Top 10 Places Sorted by Percent

Place	Percent
Prospect Heights, IL (city) Cook County	70.49
Highland Park, IL (city) Lake County	66.90
Rolling Meadows, IL (city) Cook County	65.06
Woodstock, IL (city) McHenry County	64.18
West Chicago, IL (city) Du Page County	63.59
Mount Prospect, IL (village) Cook County	62.72
Mundelein, IL (village) Lake County	62.29
Palatine, IL (village) Cook County	62.03
Addison, IL (village) Du Page County	61.29
Wheeling, IL (village) Cook County	61.06

Argentinian
Top 10 Places Sorted by Number

Place	Number
Chicago, IL (city) Cook County	859

Argentinian
Top 10 Places Sorted by Percent

Place	Percent
Chicago, IL (city) Cook County	80.73

Bolivian
Top 10 Places Sorted by Number

Place	Number
Chicago, IL (city) Cook County	214

Bolivian
Top 10 Places Sorted by Percent

Place	Percent
Chicago, IL (city) Cook County	44.86

Central American
Top 10 Places Sorted by Number

Place	Number
Chicago, IL (city) Cook County	17,187
Waukegan, IL (city) Lake County	2,202
Cicero, IL (town) Cook County	664
Aurora, IL (city) Kane County	427
Skokie, IL (village) Cook County	361

Central American
Top 10 Places Sorted by Percent

Place	Percent
Aurora, IL (city) Kane County	86.44
Waukegan, IL (city) Lake County	80.34
Cicero, IL (town) Cook County	77.84
Skokie, IL (village) Cook County	76.00
Chicago, IL (city) Cook County	71.14

Chilean
Top 10 Places Sorted by Number

Place	Number
Chicago, IL (city) Cook County	522

Chilean
Top 10 Places Sorted by Percent

Place	Percent
Chicago, IL (city) Cook County	75.65

Colombian
Top 10 Places Sorted by Number

Place	Number
Chicago, IL (city) Cook County	4,365

Notes: Please refer to the User's Guide for an explanation of data; tables include places with populations > 9,999 and reflect only those areas that meet Summary File 4 population thresholds, therefore there may be less than 10 places listed

Colombian
Top 10 Places Sorted by Percent

Place	Percent
Chicago, IL (city) Cook County	71.66

Costa Rican
Top 10 Places Sorted by Number

Place	Number
Chicago, IL (city) Cook County	519

Costa Rican
Top 10 Places Sorted by Percent

Place	Percent
Chicago, IL (city) Cook County	70.90

Cuban
Top 10 Places Sorted by Number

Place	Number
Chicago, IL (city) Cook County	4,962
Melrose Park, IL (village) Cook County	253
Aurora, IL (city) Kane County	120

Cuban
Top 10 Places Sorted by Percent

Place	Percent
Melrose Park, IL (village) Cook County	73.55
Chicago, IL (city) Cook County	61.18
Aurora, IL (city) Kane County	31.33

Dominican
Top 10 Places Sorted by Number

Place	Number
Chicago, IL (city) Cook County	1,236

Dominican
Top 10 Places Sorted by Percent

Place	Percent
Chicago, IL (city) Cook County	59.83

Ecuadorian
Top 10 Places Sorted by Number

Place	Number
Chicago, IL (city) Cook County	7,540

Ecuadorian
Top 10 Places Sorted by Percent

Place	Percent
Chicago, IL (city) Cook County	75.73

Guatelmalan
Top 10 Places Sorted by Number

Place	Number
Chicago, IL (city) Cook County	10,163
Cicero, IL (town) Cook County	306

Guatelmalan
Top 10 Places Sorted by Percent

Place	Percent
Chicago, IL (city) Cook County	70.61
Cicero, IL (town) Cook County	68.61

Honduran
Top 10 Places Sorted by Number

Place	Number
Chicago, IL (city) Cook County	2,327
Waukegan, IL (city) Lake County	1,268

Honduran
Top 10 Places Sorted by Percent

Place	Percent
Waukegan, IL (city) Lake County	82.12
Chicago, IL (city) Cook County	74.51

Mexican
Top 10 Places Sorted by Number

Place	Number
Chicago, IL (city) Cook County	283,531
Cicero, IL (town) Cook County	32,528
Aurora, IL (city) Kane County	22,661
Waukegan, IL (city) Lake County	18,062
Elgin, IL (city) Kane County	16,733
Joliet, IL (city) Will County	8,471
Berwyn, IL (city) Cook County	7,724
West Chicago, IL (city) Du Page County	6,933
Carpentersville, IL (village) Kane County	6,735
Rockford, IL (city) Winnebago County	6,337

Mexican
Top 10 Places Sorted by Percent

Place	Percent
Prospect Heights, IL (city) Cook County	72.57
Highland Park, IL (city) Lake County	71.54
Rolling Meadows, IL (city) Cook County	69.35
Mount Prospect, IL (village) Cook County	68.99
Glen Ellyn, IL (village) Du Page County	65.73
Palatine, IL (village) Cook County	65.67
Woodstock, IL (city) McHenry County	65.45
Mundelein, IL (village) Lake County	65.25
West Chicago, IL (city) Du Page County	64.88
Villa Park, IL (village) Du Page County	63.84

Nicaraguan
Top 10 Places Sorted by Number

Place	Number
Chicago, IL (city) Cook County	622

Nicaraguan
Top 10 Places Sorted by Percent

Place	Percent
Chicago, IL (city) Cook County	66.38

Panamanian
Top 10 Places Sorted by Number

Place	Number
Chicago, IL (city) Cook County	433

Panamanian
Top 10 Places Sorted by Percent

Place	Percent
Chicago, IL (city) Cook County	51.30

Paraguayan
Top 10 Places Sorted by Number

Place	Number
No places met population threshold	

Paraguayan
Top 10 Places Sorted by Percent

Place	Percent
No places met population threshold	

Peruvian
Top 10 Places Sorted by Number

Place	Number
Chicago, IL (city) Cook County	2,250

Peruvian
Top 10 Places Sorted by Percent

Place	Percent
Chicago, IL (city) Cook County	76.09

Puerto Rican
Top 10 Places Sorted by Number

Place	Number
Chicago, IL (city) Cook County	2,330
Aurora, IL (city) Kane County	59
Cicero, IL (town) Cook County	55
Waukegan, IL (city) Lake County	50
North Chicago, IL (city) Lake County	37
Carpentersville, IL (village) Kane County	26
Schaumburg, IL (village) Cook County	18
Bolingbrook, IL (village) Will County	8
Franklin Park, IL (village) Cook County	8
Streamwood, IL (village) Cook County	8

Puerto Rican
Top 10 Places Sorted by Percent

Place	Percent
North Chicago, IL (city) Lake County	5.38
Carpentersville, IL (village) Kane County	5.32
Schaumburg, IL (village) Cook County	3.20
Aurora, IL (city) Kane County	2.42
Cicero, IL (town) Cook County	2.32
Chicago, IL (city) Cook County	2.09
Waukegan, IL (city) Lake County	1.71
Bolingbrook, IL (village) Will County	1.68
Streamwood, IL (village) Cook County	1.60
Evanston, IL (city) Cook County	1.37

Salvadoran
Top 10 Places Sorted by Number

Place	Number
Chicago, IL (city) Cook County	2,531
Waukegan, IL (city) Lake County	399

Salvadoran
Top 10 Places Sorted by Percent

Place	Percent
Chicago, IL (city) Cook County	75.26
Waukegan, IL (city) Lake County	72.94

South American
Top 10 Places Sorted by Number

Place	Number
Chicago, IL (city) Cook County	17,142
Cicero, IL (town) Cook County	501
Berwyn, IL (city) Cook County	335
Naperville, IL (city) Du Page County	334
Skokie, IL (village) Cook County	298
Streamwood, IL (village) Cook County	276
Aurora, IL (city) Kane County	148

South American
Top 10 Places Sorted by Percent

Place	Percent
Berwyn, IL (city) Cook County	77.91
Cicero, IL (town) Cook County	74.22
Chicago, IL (city) Cook County	74.16
Skokie, IL (village) Cook County	68.19
Naperville, IL (city) Du Page County	67.20
Streamwood, IL (village) Cook County	62.59
Aurora, IL (city) Kane County	43.53

Spaniard
Top 10 Places Sorted by Number

Place	Number
Chicago, IL (city) Cook County	380

Notes: Please refer to the User's Guide for an explanation of data; tables include places with populations > 9,999 and reflect only those areas that meet Summary File 4 population thresholds, therefore there may be less than 10 places listed

Spaniard
Top 10 Places Sorted by Percent

Place	Percent
Chicago, IL (city) Cook County	45.02

Uruguayan
Top 10 Places Sorted by Number

Place	Number
No places met population threshold	

Uruguayan
Top 10 Places Sorted by Percent

Place	Percent
No places met population threshold	

Venezuelan
Top 10 Places Sorted by Number

Place	Number
Chicago, IL (city) Cook County	600

Venezuelan
Top 10 Places Sorted by Percent

Place	Percent
Chicago, IL (city) Cook County	76.73

Other Hispanic
Top 10 Places Sorted by Number

Place	Number
Chicago, IL (city) Cook County	16,758
Waukegan, IL (city) Lake County	1,501
Aurora, IL (city) Kane County	1,204
Cicero, IL (town) Cook County	977
Elgin, IL (city) Kane County	740
Joliet, IL (city) Will County	346
Berwyn, IL (city) Cook County	288
Rockford, IL (city) Winnebago County	262
Hoffman Estates, IL (village) Cook County	250
Palatine, IL (village) Cook County	249

Other Hispanic
Top 10 Places Sorted by Percent

Place	Percent
Blue Island, IL (city) Cook County	50.11
Waukegan, IL (city) Lake County	46.63
Wheeling, IL (village) Cook County	45.43
Palatine, IL (village) Cook County	44.78
West Chicago, IL (city) Du Page County	43.60
Bensenville, IL (village) Du Page County	42.86
Elgin, IL (city) Kane County	42.65
Hoffman Estates, IL (village) Cook County	42.16
Addison, IL (village) Du Page County	41.24
Skokie, IL (village) Cook County	41.15

Foreign-Born Naturalized Citizens

Total Population
Top 10 Places Sorted by Number

Place	Number
Chicago, IL (city) Cook County	223,984
Skokie, IL (village) Cook County	13,753
Cicero, IL (town) Cook County	10,076
Aurora, IL (city) Kane County	8,494
Des Plaines, IL (city) Cook County	6,827
Waukegan, IL (city) Lake County	6,422
Niles, IL (village) Cook County	6,401
Naperville, IL (city) Du Page County	6,400
Schaumburg, IL (village) Cook County	6,120
Elgin, IL (city) Kane County	6,059

Total Population
Top 10 Places Sorted by Percent

Place	Percent
Lincolnwood, IL (village) Cook County	26.15
Morton Grove, IL (village) Cook County	23.32
Skokie, IL (village) Cook County	21.72
Niles, IL (village) Cook County	21.23
Norridge, IL (village) Cook County	20.76
Schiller Park, IL (village) Cook County	14.86
Addison, IL (village) Du Page County	12.22
Glenview, IL (village) Cook County	12.06
Glendale Heights, IL (village) Du Page County	12.04
Cicero, IL (town) Cook County	11.77

Hispanic
Top 10 Places Sorted by Number

Place	Number
Chicago, IL (city) Cook County	95,289
Cicero, IL (town) Cook County	8,604
Aurora, IL (city) Kane County	5,561
Waukegan, IL (city) Lake County	4,088
Elgin, IL (city) Kane County	3,575
Berwyn, IL (city) Cook County	3,177
Joliet, IL (city) Will County	1,963
Melrose Park, IL (village) Cook County	1,712
Addison, IL (village) Du Page County	1,494
Blue Island, IL (city) Cook County	1,426

Hispanic
Top 10 Places Sorted by Percent

Place	Percent
Lincolnwood, IL (village) Cook County	36.38
Wilmette, IL (village) Cook County	27.37
Morton Grove, IL (village) Cook County	25.29
Skokie, IL (village) Cook County	25.27
Park Ridge, IL (city) Cook County	24.46
Grayslake, IL (village) Lake County	24.17
Libertyville, IL (village) Lake County	23.46
Norridge, IL (village) Cook County	22.87
Wood Dale, IL (city) Du Page County	22.65
Alsip, IL (village) Cook County	22.34

Argentinian
Top 10 Places Sorted by Number

Place	Number
Chicago, IL (city) Cook County	303

Argentinian
Top 10 Places Sorted by Percent

Place	Percent
Chicago, IL (city) Cook County	28.48

Bolivian
Top 10 Places Sorted by Number

Place	Number
Chicago, IL (city) Cook County	111

Bolivian
Top 10 Places Sorted by Percent

Place	Percent
Chicago, IL (city) Cook County	23.27

Central American
Top 10 Places Sorted by Number

Place	Number
Chicago, IL (city) Cook County	6,188
Waukegan, IL (city) Lake County	501
Cicero, IL (town) Cook County	241
Skokie, IL (village) Cook County	172
Aurora, IL (city) Kane County	124

Central American
Top 10 Places Sorted by Percent

Place	Percent
Skokie, IL (village) Cook County	36.21
Cicero, IL (town) Cook County	28.25
Chicago, IL (city) Cook County	25.61
Aurora, IL (city) Kane County	25.10
Waukegan, IL (city) Lake County	18.28

Chilean
Top 10 Places Sorted by Number

Place	Number
Chicago, IL (city) Cook County	222

Chilean
Top 10 Places Sorted by Percent

Place	Percent
Chicago, IL (city) Cook County	32.17

Colombian
Top 10 Places Sorted by Number

Place	Number
Chicago, IL (city) Cook County	1,989

Colombian
Top 10 Places Sorted by Percent

Place	Percent
Chicago, IL (city) Cook County	32.65

Costa Rican
Top 10 Places Sorted by Number

Place	Number
Chicago, IL (city) Cook County	147

Costa Rican
Top 10 Places Sorted by Percent

Place	Percent
Chicago, IL (city) Cook County	20.08

Cuban
Top 10 Places Sorted by Number

Place	Number
Chicago, IL (city) Cook County	3,085
Melrose Park, IL (village) Cook County	189
Aurora, IL (city) Kane County	114

Cuban
Top 10 Places Sorted by Percent

Place	Percent
Melrose Park, IL (village) Cook County	54.94
Chicago, IL (city) Cook County	38.03
Aurora, IL (city) Kane County	29.77

Dominican
Top 10 Places Sorted by Number

Place	Number
Chicago, IL (city) Cook County	570

Dominican
Top 10 Places Sorted by Percent

Place	Percent
Chicago, IL (city) Cook County	27.59

Notes: Please refer to the User's Guide for an explanation of data; tables include places with populations > 9,999 and reflect only those areas that meet Summary File 4 population thresholds, therefore there may be less than 10 places listed

Ecuadorian
Top 10 Places Sorted by Number

Place	Number
Chicago, IL (city) Cook County	2,446

Ecuadorian
Top 10 Places Sorted by Percent

Place	Percent
Chicago, IL (city) Cook County	24.57

Guatelmalan
Top 10 Places Sorted by Number

Place	Number
Chicago, IL (city) Cook County	3,830
Cicero, IL (town) Cook County	154

Guatelmalan
Top 10 Places Sorted by Percent

Place	Percent
Cicero, IL (town) Cook County	34.53
Chicago, IL (city) Cook County	26.61

Honduran
Top 10 Places Sorted by Number

Place	Number
Chicago, IL (city) Cook County	803
Waukegan, IL (city) Lake County	163

Honduran
Top 10 Places Sorted by Percent

Place	Percent
Chicago, IL (city) Cook County	25.71
Waukegan, IL (city) Lake County	10.56

Mexican
Top 10 Places Sorted by Number

Place	Number
Chicago, IL (city) Cook County	72,337
Cicero, IL (town) Cook County	7,849
Aurora, IL (city) Kane County	4,914
Elgin, IL (city) Kane County	3,266
Waukegan, IL (city) Lake County	3,166
Berwyn, IL (city) Cook County	2,710
Joliet, IL (city) Will County	1,790
Melrose Park, IL (village) Cook County	1,370
Blue Island, IL (city) Cook County	1,259
Carpentersville, IL (village) Kane County	1,203

Mexican
Top 10 Places Sorted by Percent

Place	Percent
Libertyville, IL (village) Lake County	28.23
Alsip, IL (village) Cook County	25.46
Wood Dale, IL (city) Du Page County	23.25
Palos Hills, IL (city) Cook County	22.40
Park Ridge, IL (city) Cook County	22.03
Darien, IL (city) Du Page County	21.99
Morton Grove, IL (village) Cook County	21.69
Elmwood Park, IL (village) Cook County	19.84
Warrenville, IL (city) Du Page County	19.75
Goodings Grove, IL (cdp) Will County	18.64

Nicaraguan
Top 10 Places Sorted by Number

Place	Number
Chicago, IL (city) Cook County	170

Nicaraguan
Top 10 Places Sorted by Percent

Place	Percent
Chicago, IL (city) Cook County	18.14

Panamanian
Top 10 Places Sorted by Number

Place	Number
Chicago, IL (city) Cook County	206

Panamanian
Top 10 Places Sorted by Percent

Place	Percent
Chicago, IL (city) Cook County	24.41

Paraguayan
Top 10 Places Sorted by Number

Place	Number
No places met population threshold	

Paraguayan
Top 10 Places Sorted by Percent

Place	Percent
No places met population threshold	

Peruvian
Top 10 Places Sorted by Number

Place	Number
Chicago, IL (city) Cook County	976

Peruvian
Top 10 Places Sorted by Percent

Place	Percent
Chicago, IL (city) Cook County	33.01

Puerto Rican
Top 10 Places Sorted by Number

Place	Number
Chicago, IL (city) Cook County	1,057
Aurora, IL (city) Kane County	36
North Chicago, IL (city) Lake County	31
Waukegan, IL (city) Lake County	24
Carpentersville, IL (village) Kane County	15
Cicero, IL (town) Cook County	10
Franklin Park, IL (village) Cook County	8
Evanston, IL (city) Cook County	5
Schaumburg, IL (village) Cook County	5
Berwyn, IL (city) Cook County	0

Puerto Rican
Top 10 Places Sorted by Percent

Place	Percent
North Chicago, IL (city) Lake County	4.51
Carpentersville, IL (village) Kane County	3.07
Aurora, IL (city) Kane County	1.48
Evanston, IL (city) Cook County	1.37
Franklin Park, IL (village) Cook County	1.36
Chicago, IL (city) Cook County	0.95
Schaumburg, IL (village) Cook County	0.89
Waukegan, IL (city) Lake County	0.82
Cicero, IL (town) Cook County	0.42
Berwyn, IL (city) Cook County	0.00

Salvadoran
Top 10 Places Sorted by Number

Place	Number
Chicago, IL (city) Cook County	809
Waukegan, IL (city) Lake County	150

Salvadoran
Top 10 Places Sorted by Percent

Place	Percent
Waukegan, IL (city) Lake County	27.42
Chicago, IL (city) Cook County	24.06

South American
Top 10 Places Sorted by Number

Place	Number
Chicago, IL (city) Cook County	6,430
Naperville, IL (city) Du Page County	269
Berwyn, IL (city) Cook County	191
Skokie, IL (village) Cook County	188
Cicero, IL (town) Cook County	168
Streamwood, IL (village) Cook County	60
Aurora, IL (city) Kane County	49

South American
Top 10 Places Sorted by Percent

Place	Percent
Naperville, IL (city) Du Page County	54.12
Berwyn, IL (city) Cook County	44.42
Skokie, IL (village) Cook County	43.02
Chicago, IL (city) Cook County	27.82
Cicero, IL (town) Cook County	24.89
Aurora, IL (city) Kane County	14.41
Streamwood, IL (village) Cook County	13.61

Spaniard
Top 10 Places Sorted by Number

Place	Number
Chicago, IL (city) Cook County	112

Spaniard
Top 10 Places Sorted by Percent

Place	Percent
Chicago, IL (city) Cook County	13.27

Uruguayan
Top 10 Places Sorted by Number

Place	Number
No places met population threshold	

Uruguayan
Top 10 Places Sorted by Percent

Place	Percent
No places met population threshold	

Venezuelan
Top 10 Places Sorted by Number

Place	Number
Chicago, IL (city) Cook County	119

Venezuelan
Top 10 Places Sorted by Percent

Place	Percent
Chicago, IL (city) Cook County	15.22

Other Hispanic
Top 10 Places Sorted by Number

Place	Number
Chicago, IL (city) Cook County	5,510
Aurora, IL (city) Kane County	302
Waukegan, IL (city) Lake County	256
Cicero, IL (town) Cook County	249
Hoffman Estates, IL (village) Cook County	157
Elgin, IL (city) Kane County	154
Berwyn, IL (city) Cook County	121
Skokie, IL (village) Cook County	113

Notes: Please refer to the User's Guide for an explanation of data; tables include places with populations > 9,999 and reflect only those areas that meet Summary File 4 population thresholds, therefore there may be less than 10 places listed

Addison, IL (village) Du Page County	108
Hanover Park, IL (village) Cook County	85

Other Hispanic
Top 10 Places Sorted by Percent

Place	Percent
Skokie, IL (village) Cook County	27.03
Hoffman Estates, IL (village) Cook County	26.48
Addison, IL (village) Du Page County	18.56
Blue Island, IL (city) Cook County	17.49
Franklin Park, IL (village) Cook County	15.26
Hanover Park, IL (village) Cook County	14.66
Moline, IL (city) Rock Island County	13.99
Naperville, IL (city) Du Page County	13.24
Burbank, IL (city) Cook County	12.89
Palatine, IL (village) Cook County	11.51

Educational Attainment: High School Graduates

Total Populations 25 Years and Over Who are High School Graduates
Top 10 Places Sorted by Number

Place	Number
Chicago, IL (city) Cook County	1,304,122
Naperville, IL (city) Du Page County	75,935
Rockford, IL (city) Winnebago County	74,789
Springfield, IL (city) Sangamon County	65,906
Aurora, IL (city) Kane County	63,191
Peoria, IL (city) Peoria County	58,187
Joliet, IL (city) Will County	50,834
Arlington Heights, IL (village) Cook County	50,106
Schaumburg, IL (village) Cook County	47,877
Evanston, IL (city) Cook County	43,244

Total Populations 25 Years and Over Who are High School Graduates
Top 10 Places Sorted by Percent

Place	Percent
Hinsdale, IL (village) Du Page County	97.33
River Forest, IL (village) Cook County	96.79
Wilmette, IL (village) Cook County	96.76
Naperville, IL (city) Du Page County	96.31
Deerfield, IL (village) Lake County	95.91
Northbrook, IL (village) Cook County	95.57
Lisle, IL (village) Du Page County	95.42
Geneva, IL (city) Kane County	95.37
Buffalo Grove, IL (village) Lake County	95.31
Algonquin, IL (village) McHenry County	95.03

Hispanics 25 Years and Over Who are High School Graduates
Top 10 Places Sorted by Number

Place	Number
Chicago, IL (city) Cook County	177,368
Cicero, IL (town) Cook County	11,153
Aurora, IL (city) Kane County	8,071
Waukegan, IL (city) Lake County	6,949
Berwyn, IL (city) Cook County	5,767
Elgin, IL (city) Kane County	5,151
Joliet, IL (city) Will County	4,542
Rockford, IL (city) Winnebago County	2,953
Melrose Park, IL (village) Cook County	2,506
Palatine, IL (village) Cook County	2,225

Hispanics 25 Years and Over Who are High School Graduates
Top 10 Places Sorted by Percent

Place	Percent
Hinsdale, IL (village) Du Page County	96.67
New Lenox, IL (village) Will County	96.15
River Forest, IL (village) Cook County	95.88
Belleville, IL (city) Saint Clair County	92.45
Sycamore, IL (city) De Kalb County	90.17
O'Fallon, IL (city) Saint Clair County	90.03
Mokena, IL (village) Will County	90.00
Pekin, IL (city) Tazewell County	88.76
Oak Park, IL (village) Cook County	87.92
Wilmette, IL (village) Cook County	86.88

Argentinians 25 Years and Over Who are High School Graduates
Top 10 Places Sorted by Number

Place	Number
Chicago, IL (city) Cook County	670

Argentinians 25 Years and Over Who are High School Graduates
Top 10 Places Sorted by Percent

Place	Percent
Chicago, IL (city) Cook County	81.61

Bolivians 25 Years and Over Who are High School Graduates
Top 10 Places Sorted by Number

Place	Number
Chicago, IL (city) Cook County	303

Bolivians 25 Years and Over Who are High School Graduates
Top 10 Places Sorted by Percent

Place	Percent
Chicago, IL (city) Cook County	87.83

Central Americans 25 Years and Over Who are High School Graduates
Top 10 Places Sorted by Number

Place	Number
Chicago, IL (city) Cook County	7,918
Waukegan, IL (city) Lake County	734
Cicero, IL (town) Cook County	189
Aurora, IL (city) Kane County	155
Skokie, IL (village) Cook County	148

Central Americans 25 Years and Over Who are High School Graduates
Top 10 Places Sorted by Percent

Place	Percent
Skokie, IL (village) Cook County	59.92
Chicago, IL (city) Cook County	52.85
Aurora, IL (city) Kane County	52.54
Waukegan, IL (city) Lake County	47.11
Cicero, IL (town) Cook County	37.06

Chileans 25 Years and Over Who are High School Graduates
Top 10 Places Sorted by Number

Place	Number
Chicago, IL (city) Cook County	444

Chileans 25 Years and Over Who are High School Graduates
Top 10 Places Sorted by Percent

Place	Percent
Chicago, IL (city) Cook County	82.22

Colombians 25 Years and Over Who are High School Graduates
Top 10 Places Sorted by Number

Place	Number
Chicago, IL (city) Cook County	3,096

Colombians 25 Years and Over Who are High School Graduates
Top 10 Places Sorted by Percent

Place	Percent
Chicago, IL (city) Cook County	72.57

Costa Ricans 25 Years and Over Who are High School Graduates
Top 10 Places Sorted by Number

Place	Number
Chicago, IL (city) Cook County	349

Costa Ricans 25 Years and Over Who are High School Graduates
Top 10 Places Sorted by Percent

Place	Percent
Chicago, IL (city) Cook County	72.86

Cubans 25 Years and Over Who are High School Graduates
Top 10 Places Sorted by Number

Place	Number
Chicago, IL (city) Cook County	3,958
Aurora, IL (city) Kane County	175
Melrose Park, IL (village) Cook County	112

Cubans 25 Years and Over Who are High School Graduates
Top 10 Places Sorted by Percent

Place	Percent
Aurora, IL (city) Kane County	88.83
Chicago, IL (city) Cook County	65.88
Melrose Park, IL (village) Cook County	40.88

Dominicans 25 Years and Over Who are High School Graduates
Top 10 Places Sorted by Number

Place	Number
Chicago, IL (city) Cook County	846

Dominicans 25 Years and Over Who are High School Graduates
Top 10 Places Sorted by Percent

Place	Percent
Chicago, IL (city) Cook County	62.07

Ecuadorians 25 Years and Over Who are High School Graduates
Top 10 Places Sorted by Number

Place	Number
Chicago, IL (city) Cook County	3,571

Ecuadorians 25 Years and Over Who are High School Graduates
Top 10 Places Sorted by Percent

Place	Percent
Chicago, IL (city) Cook County	57.26

Guatelmalans 25 Years and Over Who are High School Graduates
Top 10 Places Sorted by Number

Place	Number
Chicago, IL (city) Cook County	4,423
Cicero, IL (town) Cook County	131

Notes: Please refer to the User's Guide for an explanation of data; tables include places with populations > 9,999 and reflect only those areas that meet Summary File 4 population thresholds, therefore there may be less than 10 places listed

Guatelmalans 25 Years and Over Who are High School Graduates

Top 10 Places Sorted by Percent

Place	Percent
Chicago, IL (city) Cook County	50.63
Cicero, IL (town) Cook County	46.45

Hondurans 25 Years and Over Who are High School Graduates

Top 10 Places Sorted by Number

Place	Number
Chicago, IL (city) Cook County	1,048
Waukegan, IL (city) Lake County	350

Hondurans 25 Years and Over Who are High School Graduates

Top 10 Places Sorted by Percent

Place	Percent
Chicago, IL (city) Cook County	51.57
Waukegan, IL (city) Lake County	41.32

Mexicans 25 Years and Over Who are High School Graduates

Top 10 Places Sorted by Number

Place	Number
Chicago, IL (city) Cook County	108,150
Cicero, IL (town) Cook County	9,505
Aurora, IL (city) Kane County	6,081
Waukegan, IL (city) Lake County	4,529
Berwyn, IL (city) Cook County	4,518
Elgin, IL (city) Kane County	4,038
Joliet, IL (city) Will County	3,813
Rockford, IL (city) Winnebago County	2,137
Melrose Park, IL (village) Cook County	1,923
Carpentersville, IL (village) Kane County	1,633

Mexicans 25 Years and Over Who are High School Graduates

Top 10 Places Sorted by Percent

Place	Percent
New Lenox, IL (village) Will County	96.81
Darien, IL (city) Du Page County	89.00
Oak Park, IL (village) Cook County	87.89
Belleville, IL (city) Saint Clair County	85.78
Machesney Park, IL (village) Winnebago County	85.54
Westchester, IL (village) Cook County	83.64
Park Forest, IL (village) Cook County	83.25
Crest Hill, IL (city) Will County	82.78
Libertyville, IL (village) Lake County	81.71
Lombard, IL (village) Du Page County	81.01

Nicaraguans 25 Years and Over Who are High School Graduates

Top 10 Places Sorted by Number

Place	Number
Chicago, IL (city) Cook County	266

Nicaraguans 25 Years and Over Who are High School Graduates

Top 10 Places Sorted by Percent

Place	Percent
Chicago, IL (city) Cook County	52.47

Panamanians 25 Years and Over Who are High School Graduates

Top 10 Places Sorted by Number

Place	Number
Chicago, IL (city) Cook County	514

Panamanians 25 Years and Over Who are High School Graduates

Top 10 Places Sorted by Percent

Place	Percent
Chicago, IL (city) Cook County	85.67

Paraguayans 25 Years and Over Who are High School Graduates

Top 10 Places Sorted by Number

Place	Number
No places met population threshold	

Paraguayans 25 Years and Over Who are High School Graduates

Top 10 Places Sorted by Percent

Place	Percent
No places met population threshold	

Peruvians 25 Years and Over Who are High School Graduates

Top 10 Places Sorted by Number

Place	Number
Chicago, IL (city) Cook County	1,775

Peruvians 25 Years and Over Who are High School Graduates

Top 10 Places Sorted by Percent

Place	Percent
Chicago, IL (city) Cook County	83.22

Puerto Ricans 25 Years and Over Who are High School Graduates

Top 10 Places Sorted by Number

Place	Number
Chicago, IL (city) Cook County	34,342
Waukegan, IL (city) Lake County	1,023
Aurora, IL (city) Kane County	869
Cicero, IL (town) Cook County	679
Elgin, IL (city) Kane County	536
Berwyn, IL (city) Cook County	472
Elmwood Park, IL (village) Cook County	303
Joliet, IL (city) Will County	251
Bolingbrook, IL (village) Will County	221
Naperville, IL (city) Du Page County	217

Puerto Ricans 25 Years and Over Who are High School Graduates

Top 10 Places Sorted by Percent

Place	Percent
Naperville, IL (city) Du Page County	93.53
Evanston, IL (city) Cook County	89.55
Skokie, IL (village) Cook County	85.10
Streamwood, IL (village) Cook County	83.98
Hanover Park, IL (village) Cook County	82.43
Carol Stream, IL (village) Du Page County	80.95
Elmwood Park, IL (village) Cook County	79.74
Joliet, IL (city) Will County	78.68
Bolingbrook, IL (village) Will County	78.65
Schaumburg, IL (village) Cook County	75.35

Salvadorans 25 Years and Over Who are High School Graduates

Top 10 Places Sorted by Number

Place	Number
Chicago, IL (city) Cook County	994
Waukegan, IL (city) Lake County	142

Salvadorans 25 Years and Over Who are High School Graduates

Top 10 Places Sorted by Percent

Place	Percent
Chicago, IL (city) Cook County	48.09
Waukegan, IL (city) Lake County	47.33

South Americans 25 Years and Over Who are High School Graduates

Top 10 Places Sorted by Number

Place	Number
Chicago, IL (city) Cook County	10,759
Naperville, IL (city) Du Page County	289
Skokie, IL (village) Cook County	285
Cicero, IL (town) Cook County	281
Berwyn, IL (city) Cook County	261
Streamwood, IL (village) Cook County	184
Aurora, IL (city) Kane County	147

South Americans 25 Years and Over Who are High School Graduates

Top 10 Places Sorted by Percent

Place	Percent
Naperville, IL (city) Du Page County	89.75
Skokie, IL (village) Cook County	85.84
Berwyn, IL (city) Cook County	83.12
Aurora, IL (city) Kane County	78.19
Streamwood, IL (village) Cook County	73.90
Chicago, IL (city) Cook County	68.97
Cicero, IL (town) Cook County	64.01

Spaniards 25 Years and Over Who are High School Graduates

Top 10 Places Sorted by Number

Place	Number
Chicago, IL (city) Cook County	457

Spaniards 25 Years and Over Who are High School Graduates

Top 10 Places Sorted by Percent

Place	Percent
Chicago, IL (city) Cook County	77.59

Uruguayans 25 Years and Over Who are High School Graduates

Top 10 Places Sorted by Number

Place	Number
No places met population threshold	

Uruguayans 25 Years and Over Who are High School Graduates

Top 10 Places Sorted by Percent

Place	Percent
No places met population threshold	

Venezuelans 25 Years and Over Who are High School Graduates

Top 10 Places Sorted by Number

Place	Number
Chicago, IL (city) Cook County	408

Venezuelans 25 Years and Over Who are High School Graduates

Top 10 Places Sorted by Percent

Place	Percent
Chicago, IL (city) Cook County	78.01

Notes: Please refer to the User's Guide for an explanation of data; tables include places with populations > 9,999 and reflect only those areas that meet Summary File 4 population thresholds, therefore there may be less than 10 places listed

Other Hispanics 25 Years and Over Who are High School Graduates

Top 10 Places Sorted by Number

Place	Number
Chicago, IL (city) Cook County	10,938
Aurora, IL (city) Kane County	630
Waukegan, IL (city) Lake County	523
Cicero, IL (town) Cook County	417
Elgin, IL (city) Kane County	342
Joliet, IL (city) Will County	304
Berwyn, IL (city) Cook County	277
Rockford, IL (city) Winnebago County	270
Naperville, IL (city) Du Page County	250
Hoffman Estates, IL (village) Cook County	219

Other Hispanics 25 Years and Over Who are High School Graduates

Top 10 Places Sorted by Percent

Place	Percent
Schaumburg, IL (village) Cook County	90.83
Naperville, IL (city) Du Page County	82.24
Evanston, IL (city) Cook County	82.00
Bolingbrook, IL (village) Will County	79.14
Hoffman Estates, IL (village) Cook County	76.57
Skokie, IL (village) Cook County	76.53
Moline, IL (city) Rock Island County	69.43
Berwyn, IL (city) Cook County	68.23
North Chicago, IL (city) Lake County	64.00
Joliet, IL (city) Will County	60.44

Educational Attainment: Four-Year College Graduates

Total Populations 25 Years and Over Who are Four-Year College Graduates

Top 10 Places Sorted by Number

Place	Number
Chicago, IL (city) Cook County	462,783
Naperville, IL (city) Du Page County	47,805
Evanston, IL (city) Cook County	29,511
Arlington Heights, IL (village) Cook County	25,101
Aurora, IL (city) Kane County	24,991
Springfield, IL (city) Sangamon County	23,061
Oak Park, IL (village) Cook County	22,637
Schaumburg, IL (village) Cook County	20,273
Wheaton, IL (city) Du Page County	20,247
Peoria, IL (city) Peoria County	19,712

Total Populations 25 Years and Over Who are Four-Year College Graduates

Top 10 Places Sorted by Percent

Place	Percent
Wilmette, IL (village) Cook County	72.58
River Forest, IL (village) Cook County	69.70
Hinsdale, IL (village) Du Page County	68.61
Deerfield, IL (village) Lake County	68.53
Evanston, IL (city) Cook County	62.36
Northbrook, IL (village) Cook County	62.20
Oak Park, IL (village) Cook County	62.12
Highland Park, IL (city) Lake County	61.61
Naperville, IL (city) Du Page County	60.63
Glen Ellyn, IL (village) Du Page County	58.84

Hispanics 25 Years and Over Who are Four-Year College Graduates

Top 10 Places Sorted by Number

Place	Number
Chicago, IL (city) Cook County	32,373
Aurora, IL (city) Kane County	1,306
Cicero, IL (town) Cook County	1,172
Berwyn, IL (city) Cook County	886
Naperville, IL (city) Du Page County	812
Evanston, IL (city) Cook County	758
Waukegan, IL (city) Lake County	727
Elgin, IL (city) Kane County	721
Skokie, IL (village) Cook County	546
Oak Park, IL (village) Cook County	545

Hispanics 25 Years and Over Who are Four-Year College Graduates

Top 10 Places Sorted by Percent

Place	Percent
Urbana, IL (city) Champaign County	65.29
River Forest, IL (village) Cook County	65.02
Deerfield, IL (village) Lake County	52.90
Hinsdale, IL (village) Du Page County	49.05
O'Fallon, IL (city) Saint Clair County	44.85
Oak Park, IL (village) Cook County	42.22
Macomb, IL (city) McDonough County	41.79
Quincy, IL (city) Adams County	40.83
Wilmette, IL (village) Cook County	40.05
Naperville, IL (city) Du Page County	35.63

Argentinians 25 Years and Over Who are Four-Year College Graduates

Top 10 Places Sorted by Number

Place	Number
Chicago, IL (city) Cook County	334

Argentinians 25 Years and Over Who are Four-Year College Graduates

Top 10 Places Sorted by Percent

Place	Percent
Chicago, IL (city) Cook County	40.68

Bolivians 25 Years and Over Who are Four-Year College Graduates

Top 10 Places Sorted by Number

Place	Number
Chicago, IL (city) Cook County	221

Bolivians 25 Years and Over Who are Four-Year College Graduates

Top 10 Places Sorted by Percent

Place	Percent
Chicago, IL (city) Cook County	64.06

Central Americans 25 Years and Over Who are Four-Year College Graduates

Top 10 Places Sorted by Number

Place	Number
Chicago, IL (city) Cook County	1,438
Waukegan, IL (city) Lake County	92
Aurora, IL (city) Kane County	69
Cicero, IL (town) Cook County	24
Skokie, IL (village) Cook County	21

Central Americans 25 Years and Over Who are Four-Year College Graduates

Top 10 Places Sorted by Percent

Place	Percent
Aurora, IL (city) Kane County	23.39
Chicago, IL (city) Cook County	9.60
Skokie, IL (village) Cook County	8.50
Waukegan, IL (city) Lake County	5.91
Cicero, IL (town) Cook County	4.71

Chileans 25 Years and Over Who are Four-Year College Graduates

Top 10 Places Sorted by Number

Place	Number
Chicago, IL (city) Cook County	214

Chileans 25 Years and Over Who are Four-Year College Graduates

Top 10 Places Sorted by Percent

Place	Percent
Chicago, IL (city) Cook County	39.63

Colombians 25 Years and Over Who are Four-Year College Graduates

Top 10 Places Sorted by Number

Place	Number
Chicago, IL (city) Cook County	1,301

Colombians 25 Years and Over Who are Four-Year College Graduates

Top 10 Places Sorted by Percent

Place	Percent
Chicago, IL (city) Cook County	30.50

Costa Ricans 25 Years and Over Who are Four-Year College Graduates

Top 10 Places Sorted by Number

Place	Number
Chicago, IL (city) Cook County	150

Costa Ricans 25 Years and Over Who are Four-Year College Graduates

Top 10 Places Sorted by Percent

Place	Percent
Chicago, IL (city) Cook County	31.32

Cubans 25 Years and Over Who are Four-Year College Graduates

Top 10 Places Sorted by Number

Place	Number
Chicago, IL (city) Cook County	1,682
Aurora, IL (city) Kane County	116
Melrose Park, IL (village) Cook County	28

Cubans 25 Years and Over Who are Four-Year College Graduates

Top 10 Places Sorted by Percent

Place	Percent
Aurora, IL (city) Kane County	58.88
Chicago, IL (city) Cook County	28.00
Melrose Park, IL (village) Cook County	10.22

Dominicans 25 Years and Over Who are Four-Year College Graduates

Top 10 Places Sorted by Number

Place	Number
Chicago, IL (city) Cook County	265

Dominicans 25 Years and Over Who are Four-Year College Graduates

Top 10 Places Sorted by Percent

Place	Percent
Chicago, IL (city) Cook County	19.44

Ecuadorians 25 Years and Over Who are Four-Year College Graduates

Top 10 Places Sorted by Number

Place	Number
Chicago, IL (city) Cook County	830

Notes: Please refer to the User's Guide for an explanation of data; tables include places with populations > 9,999 and reflect only those areas that meet Summary File 4 population thresholds, therefore there may be less than 10 places listed

Ecuadorians 25 Years and Over Who are Four-Year College Graduates

Top 10 Places Sorted by Percent

Place	Percent
Chicago, IL (city) Cook County	13.31

Guatelmalans 25 Years and Over Who are Four-Year College Graduates

Top 10 Places Sorted by Number

Place	Number
Chicago, IL (city) Cook County	550
Cicero, IL (town) Cook County	14

Guatelmalans 25 Years and Over Who are Four-Year College Graduates

Top 10 Places Sorted by Percent

Place	Percent
Chicago, IL (city) Cook County	6.30
Cicero, IL (town) Cook County	4.96

Hondurans 25 Years and Over Who are Four-Year College Graduates

Top 10 Places Sorted by Number

Place	Number
Chicago, IL (city) Cook County	208
Waukegan, IL (city) Lake County	38

Hondurans 25 Years and Over Who are Four-Year College Graduates

Top 10 Places Sorted by Percent

Place	Percent
Chicago, IL (city) Cook County	10.24
Waukegan, IL (city) Lake County	4.49

Mexicans 25 Years and Over Who are Four-Year College Graduates

Top 10 Places Sorted by Number

Place	Number
Chicago, IL (city) Cook County	16,235
Cicero, IL (town) Cook County	941
Aurora, IL (city) Kane County	782
Berwyn, IL (city) Cook County	689
Elgin, IL (city) Kane County	559
Waukegan, IL (city) Lake County	428
Joliet, IL (city) Will County	387
Evanston, IL (city) Cook County	314
Rockford, IL (city) Winnebago County	272
Palatine, IL (village) Cook County	259

Mexicans 25 Years and Over Who are Four-Year College Graduates

Top 10 Places Sorted by Percent

Place	Percent
Urbana, IL (city) Champaign County	55.00
Darien, IL (city) Du Page County	37.80
Oak Park, IL (village) Cook County	35.45
Champaign, IL (city) Champaign County	28.40
Machesney Park, IL (village) Winnebago County	27.11
Northbrook, IL (village) Cook County	24.60
Belleville, IL (city) Saint Clair County	24.02
Algonquin, IL (village) McHenry County	23.48
Elmhurst, IL (city) Du Page County	23.08
Orland Park, IL (village) Cook County	22.73

Nicaraguans 25 Years and Over Who are Four-Year College Graduates

Top 10 Places Sorted by Number

Place	Number
Chicago, IL (city) Cook County	66

Nicaraguans 25 Years and Over Who are Four-Year College Graduates

Top 10 Places Sorted by Percent

Place	Percent
Chicago, IL (city) Cook County	13.02

Panamanians 25 Years and Over Who are Four-Year College Graduates

Top 10 Places Sorted by Number

Place	Number
Chicago, IL (city) Cook County	214

Panamanians 25 Years and Over Who are Four-Year College Graduates

Top 10 Places Sorted by Percent

Place	Percent
Chicago, IL (city) Cook County	35.67

Paraguayans 25 Years and Over Who are Four-Year College Graduates

Top 10 Places Sorted by Number

Place	Number
No places met population threshold	

Paraguayans 25 Years and Over Who are Four-Year College Graduates

Top 10 Places Sorted by Percent

Place	Percent
No places met population threshold	

Peruvians 25 Years and Over Who are Four-Year College Graduates

Top 10 Places Sorted by Number

Place	Number
Chicago, IL (city) Cook County	662

Peruvians 25 Years and Over Who are Four-Year College Graduates

Top 10 Places Sorted by Percent

Place	Percent
Chicago, IL (city) Cook County	31.04

Puerto Ricans 25 Years and Over Who are Four-Year College Graduates

Top 10 Places Sorted by Number

Place	Number
Chicago, IL (city) Cook County	5,455
Aurora, IL (city) Kane County	161
Naperville, IL (city) Du Page County	108
Waukegan, IL (city) Lake County	97
Evanston, IL (city) Cook County	74
Schaumburg, IL (village) Cook County	70
Elgin, IL (city) Kane County	55
Rockford, IL (city) Winnebago County	55
Berwyn, IL (city) Cook County	53
Bolingbrook, IL (village) Will County	50

Puerto Ricans 25 Years and Over Who are Four-Year College Graduates

Top 10 Places Sorted by Percent

Place	Percent
Naperville, IL (city) Du Page County	46.55
Evanston, IL (city) Cook County	36.82
Schaumburg, IL (village) Cook County	24.31
Rockford, IL (city) Winnebago County	24.12
Skokie, IL (village) Cook County	19.23
Carpentersville, IL (village) Kane County	19.12
Bolingbrook, IL (village) Will County	17.79
Carol Stream, IL (village) Du Page County	17.75
Des Plaines, IL (city) Cook County	14.68
Melrose Park, IL (village) Cook County	13.94

Salvadorans 25 Years and Over Who are Four-Year College Graduates

Top 10 Places Sorted by Number

Place	Number
Chicago, IL (city) Cook County	193
Waukegan, IL (city) Lake County	0

Salvadorans 25 Years and Over Who are Four-Year College Graduates

Top 10 Places Sorted by Percent

Place	Percent
Chicago, IL (city) Cook County	9.34
Waukegan, IL (city) Lake County	0.00

South Americans 25 Years and Over Who are Four-Year College Graduates

Top 10 Places Sorted by Number

Place	Number
Chicago, IL (city) Cook County	4,081
Naperville, IL (city) Du Page County	175
Skokie, IL (village) Cook County	128
Berwyn, IL (city) Cook County	74
Cicero, IL (town) Cook County	73
Streamwood, IL (village) Cook County	59
Aurora, IL (city) Kane County	47

South Americans 25 Years and Over Who are Four-Year College Graduates

Top 10 Places Sorted by Percent

Place	Percent
Naperville, IL (city) Du Page County	54.35
Skokie, IL (village) Cook County	38.55
Chicago, IL (city) Cook County	26.16
Aurora, IL (city) Kane County	25.00
Streamwood, IL (village) Cook County	23.69
Berwyn, IL (city) Cook County	23.57
Cicero, IL (town) Cook County	16.63

Spaniards 25 Years and Over Who are Four-Year College Graduates

Top 10 Places Sorted by Number

Place	Number
Chicago, IL (city) Cook County	287

Spaniards 25 Years and Over Who are Four-Year College Graduates

Top 10 Places Sorted by Percent

Place	Percent
Chicago, IL (city) Cook County	48.73

Uruguayans 25 Years and Over Who are Four-Year College Graduates

Top 10 Places Sorted by Number

Place	Number
No places met population threshold	

Uruguayans 25 Years and Over Who are Four-Year College Graduates

Top 10 Places Sorted by Percent

Place	Percent
No places met population threshold	

Notes: Please refer to the User's Guide for an explanation of data; tables include places with populations > 9,999 and reflect only those areas that meet Summary File 4 population thresholds, therefore there may be less than 10 places listed

Venezuelans 25 Years and Over Who are Four-Year College Graduates
Top 10 Places Sorted by Number

Place	Number
Chicago, IL (city) Cook County	278

Venezuelans 25 Years and Over Who are Four-Year College Graduates
Top 10 Places Sorted by Percent

Place	Percent
Chicago, IL (city) Cook County	53.15

Other Hispanics 25 Years and Over Who are Four-Year College Graduates
Top 10 Places Sorted by Number

Place	Number
Chicago, IL (city) Cook County	2,930
Aurora, IL (city) Kane County	122
Naperville, IL (city) Du Page County	115
Hoffman Estates, IL (village) Cook County	73
Cicero, IL (town) Cook County	68
Evanston, IL (city) Cook County	62
Waukegan, IL (city) Lake County	61
Skokie, IL (village) Cook County	60
Schaumburg, IL (village) Cook County	58
Berwyn, IL (city) Cook County	52

Other Hispanics 25 Years and Over Who are Four-Year College Graduates
Top 10 Places Sorted by Percent

Place	Percent
Evanston, IL (city) Cook County	41.33
Naperville, IL (city) Du Page County	37.83
Skokie, IL (village) Cook County	28.17
Hoffman Estates, IL (village) Cook County	25.52
Schaumburg, IL (village) Cook County	25.33
North Chicago, IL (city) Lake County	22.67
Streamwood, IL (village) Cook County	16.60
Bolingbrook, IL (village) Will County	15.83
Wheeling, IL (village) Cook County	15.07
Chicago, IL (city) Cook County	14.30

Median Household Income

Total Population
Top 10 Places Sorted by Number

Place	Dollars
Deerfield, IL (village) Lake County	107,194
Wilmette, IL (village) Cook County	106,773
Hinsdale, IL (village) Du Page County	104,551
Highland Park, IL (city) Lake County	100,967
Northbrook, IL (village) Cook County	95,665
River Forest, IL (village) Cook County	89,284
Libertyville, IL (village) Lake County	88,828
Naperville, IL (city) Du Page County	88,771
Goodings Grove, IL (cdp) Will County	84,484
Lake Zurich, IL (village) Lake County	84,125

Hispanic
Top 10 Places Sorted by Number

Place	Dollars
Mokena, IL (village) Will County	152,576
Hinsdale, IL (village) Du Page County	101,611
New Lenox, IL (village) Will County	95,567
Northbrook, IL (village) Cook County	93,181
Lincolnwood, IL (village) Cook County	86,684
O'Fallon, IL (city) Saint Clair County	85,083
Wilmette, IL (village) Cook County	84,399
Goodings Grove, IL (cdp) Will County	82,249
Algonquin, IL (village) McHenry County	82,228
Sycamore, IL (city) De Kalb County	80,625

Argentinian
Top 10 Places Sorted by Number

Place	Dollars
Chicago, IL (city) Cook County	48,095

Bolivian
Top 10 Places Sorted by Number

Place	Dollars
Chicago, IL (city) Cook County	51,964

Central American
Top 10 Places Sorted by Number

Place	Dollars
Aurora, IL (city) Kane County	48,571
Skokie, IL (village) Cook County	45,583
Waukegan, IL (city) Lake County	44,063
Chicago, IL (city) Cook County	39,601
Cicero, IL (town) Cook County	36,719

Chilean
Top 10 Places Sorted by Number

Place	Dollars
Chicago, IL (city) Cook County	58,958

Colombian
Top 10 Places Sorted by Number

Place	Dollars
Chicago, IL (city) Cook County	41,313

Costa Rican
Top 10 Places Sorted by Number

Place	Dollars
Chicago, IL (city) Cook County	39,375

Cuban
Top 10 Places Sorted by Number

Place	Dollars
Aurora, IL (city) Kane County	70,313
Melrose Park, IL (village) Cook County	39,196
Chicago, IL (city) Cook County	33,197

Dominican
Top 10 Places Sorted by Number

Place	Dollars
Chicago, IL (city) Cook County	35,625

Ecuadorian
Top 10 Places Sorted by Number

Place	Dollars
Chicago, IL (city) Cook County	42,017

Guatelmalan
Top 10 Places Sorted by Number

Place	Dollars
Cicero, IL (town) Cook County	42,679
Chicago, IL (city) Cook County	40,470

Honduran
Top 10 Places Sorted by Number

Place	Dollars
Waukegan, IL (city) Lake County	51,293
Chicago, IL (city) Cook County	36,250

Mexican
Top 10 Places Sorted by Number

Place	Dollars
Algonquin, IL (village) McHenry County	101,124
Northbrook, IL (village) Cook County	96,067
Plainfield, IL (village) Will County	92,201
New Lenox, IL (village) Will County	91,984
Darien, IL (city) Du Page County	85,878
Goodings Grove, IL (cdp) Will County	82,912
Libertyville, IL (village) Lake County	80,485
Oswego, IL (village) Kendall County	76,780
Westchester, IL (village) Cook County	75,718
Lake in the Hills, IL (village) McHenry County	75,527

Nicaraguan
Top 10 Places Sorted by Number

Place	Dollars
Chicago, IL (city) Cook County	35,956

Panamanian
Top 10 Places Sorted by Number

Place	Dollars
Chicago, IL (city) Cook County	44,297

Paraguayan
Top 10 Places Sorted by Number

Place	Dollars
No places met population threshold	

Peruvian
Top 10 Places Sorted by Number

Place	Dollars
Chicago, IL (city) Cook County	44,921

Puerto Rican
Top 10 Places Sorted by Number

Place	Dollars
Bolingbrook, IL (village) Will County	87,612
Carol Stream, IL (village) Du Page County	80,701
Skokie, IL (village) Cook County	75,000
Evanston, IL (city) Cook County	70,917
Streamwood, IL (village) Cook County	64,074
Naperville, IL (city) Du Page County	61,667
Franklin Park, IL (village) Cook County	59,737
Schaumburg, IL (village) Cook County	55,625
Des Plaines, IL (city) Cook County	52,250
Elmwood Park, IL (village) Cook County	48,958

Salvadoran
Top 10 Places Sorted by Number

Place	Dollars
Waukegan, IL (city) Lake County	38,958
Chicago, IL (city) Cook County	38,274

South American
Top 10 Places Sorted by Number

Place	Dollars
Naperville, IL (city) Du Page County	86,302
Skokie, IL (village) Cook County	67,750
Streamwood, IL (village) Cook County	60,882
Berwyn, IL (city) Cook County	51,563
Chicago, IL (city) Cook County	43,280
Cicero, IL (town) Cook County	35,350
Aurora, IL (city) Kane County	33,646

Spaniard
Top 10 Places Sorted by Number

Place	Dollars
Chicago, IL (city) Cook County	38,866

Notes: Please refer to the User's Guide for an explanation of data; tables include places with populations > 9,999 and reflect only those areas that meet Summary File 4 population thresholds, therefore there may be less than 10 places listed

Uruguayan
Top 10 Places Sorted by Number

Place	Dollars
No places met population threshold	

Venezuelan
Top 10 Places Sorted by Number

Place	Dollars
Chicago, IL (city) Cook County	36,724

Other Hispanic
Top 10 Places Sorted by Number

Place	Dollars
Burbank, IL (city) Cook County	80,602
Schaumburg, IL (village) Cook County	78,571
Mount Prospect, IL (village) Cook County	63,250
Palatine, IL (village) Cook County	62,679
Streamwood, IL (village) Cook County	62,368
Round Lake Beach, IL (village) Lake County	59,519
Melrose Park, IL (village) Cook County	53,750
Naperville, IL (city) Du Page County	53,281
Franklin Park, IL (village) Cook County	53,125
Skokie, IL (village) Cook County	51,875

Per Capita Income

Total Population
Top 10 Places Sorted by Number

Place	Dollars
Hinsdale, IL (village) Du Page County	63,765
Wilmette, IL (village) Cook County	55,611
Highland Park, IL (city) Lake County	55,331
Northbrook, IL (village) Cook County	50,765
Deerfield, IL (village) Lake County	50,664
River Forest, IL (village) Cook County	46,123
Glenview, IL (village) Cook County	43,384
Libertyville, IL (village) Lake County	40,426
Glen Ellyn, IL (village) Du Page County	39,783
Buffalo Grove, IL (village) Lake County	36,696

Hispanic
Top 10 Places Sorted by Number

Place	Dollars
Hinsdale, IL (village) Du Page County	42,899
River Forest, IL (village) Cook County	35,373
Mokena, IL (village) Will County	28,538
Wilmette, IL (village) Cook County	28,438
Bloomingdale, IL (village) Du Page County	27,478
O'Fallon, IL (city) Saint Clair County	25,539
Roselle, IL (village) Du Page County	24,479
Westchester, IL (village) Cook County	24,173
Buffalo Grove, IL (village) Lake County	23,835
New Lenox, IL (village) Will County	23,575

Argentinian
Top 10 Places Sorted by Number

Place	Dollars
Chicago, IL (city) Cook County	27,553

Bolivian
Top 10 Places Sorted by Number

Place	Dollars
Chicago, IL (city) Cook County	19,579

Central American
Top 10 Places Sorted by Number

Place	Dollars
Aurora, IL (city) Kane County	18,303
Skokie, IL (village) Cook County	14,788
Chicago, IL (city) Cook County	13,654
Waukegan, IL (city) Lake County	13,195
Cicero, IL (town) Cook County	10,176

Chilean
Top 10 Places Sorted by Number

Place	Dollars
Chicago, IL (city) Cook County	24,029

Colombian
Top 10 Places Sorted by Number

Place	Dollars
Chicago, IL (city) Cook County	20,776

Costa Rican
Top 10 Places Sorted by Number

Place	Dollars
Chicago, IL (city) Cook County	13,303

Cuban
Top 10 Places Sorted by Number

Place	Dollars
Aurora, IL (city) Kane County	23,987
Chicago, IL (city) Cook County	22,708
Melrose Park, IL (village) Cook County	22,685

Dominican
Top 10 Places Sorted by Number

Place	Dollars
Chicago, IL (city) Cook County	14,121

Ecuadorian
Top 10 Places Sorted by Number

Place	Dollars
Chicago, IL (city) Cook County	14,688

Guatelmalan
Top 10 Places Sorted by Number

Place	Dollars
Chicago, IL (city) Cook County	13,089
Cicero, IL (town) Cook County	10,154

Honduran
Top 10 Places Sorted by Number

Place	Dollars
Chicago, IL (city) Cook County	13,018
Waukegan, IL (city) Lake County	12,678

Mexican
Top 10 Places Sorted by Number

Place	Dollars
Westchester, IL (village) Cook County	25,119
New Lenox, IL (village) Will County	24,372
Goodings Grove, IL (cdp) Will County	23,977
Northbrook, IL (village) Cook County	23,889
Elmhurst, IL (city) Du Page County	23,147
Palos Hills, IL (city) Cook County	22,935
Crest Hill, IL (city) Will County	22,894
Algonquin, IL (village) McHenry County	22,502
Hazel Crest, IL (village) Cook County	22,293
Bloomingdale, IL (village) Du Page County	22,161

Nicaraguan
Top 10 Places Sorted by Number

Place	Dollars
Chicago, IL (city) Cook County	13,640

Panamanian
Top 10 Places Sorted by Number

Place	Dollars
Chicago, IL (city) Cook County	25,991

Paraguayan
Top 10 Places Sorted by Number

Place	Dollars
No places met population threshold	

Peruvian
Top 10 Places Sorted by Number

Place	Dollars
Chicago, IL (city) Cook County	18,366

Puerto Rican
Top 10 Places Sorted by Number

Place	Dollars
Carol Stream, IL (village) Du Page County	24,906
Evanston, IL (city) Cook County	23,694
Naperville, IL (city) Du Page County	22,113
Bolingbrook, IL (village) Will County	21,023
Des Plaines, IL (city) Cook County	20,789
Skokie, IL (village) Cook County	19,236
Joliet, IL (city) Will County	18,319
Schaumburg, IL (village) Cook County	18,147
Elgin, IL (city) Kane County	17,122
Streamwood, IL (village) Cook County	16,975

Salvadoran
Top 10 Places Sorted by Number

Place	Dollars
Chicago, IL (city) Cook County	13,167
Waukegan, IL (city) Lake County	11,908

South American
Top 10 Places Sorted by Number

Place	Dollars
Naperville, IL (city) Du Page County	30,935
Skokie, IL (village) Cook County	24,899
Berwyn, IL (city) Cook County	22,183
Chicago, IL (city) Cook County	18,092
Streamwood, IL (village) Cook County	13,742
Aurora, IL (city) Kane County	13,338
Cicero, IL (town) Cook County	11,166

Spaniard
Top 10 Places Sorted by Number

Place	Dollars
Chicago, IL (city) Cook County	20,135

Uruguayan
Top 10 Places Sorted by Number

Place	Dollars
No places met population threshold	

Venezuelan
Top 10 Places Sorted by Number

Place	Dollars
Chicago, IL (city) Cook County	21,465

Other Hispanic
Top 10 Places Sorted by Number

Place	Dollars
Naperville, IL (city) Du Page County	22,039
Schaumburg, IL (village) Cook County	19,809
Crest Hill, IL (city) Will County	18,160
Streamwood, IL (village) Cook County	16,475
Bolingbrook, IL (village) Will County	15,480

Notes: Please refer to the User's Guide for an explanation of data; tables include places with populations > 9,999 and reflect only those areas that meet Summary File 4 population thresholds, therefore there may be less than 10 places listed

Burbank, IL (city) Cook County	14,910
Franklin Park, IL (village) Cook County	14,573
Elgin, IL (city) Kane County	13,291
Moline, IL (city) Rock Island County	13,244
Skokie, IL (village) Cook County	13,143

Poverty Status

Total Populations with Income Below Poverty Level
Top 10 Places Sorted by Number

Place	Number
Chicago, IL (city) Cook County	556,791
Rockford, IL (city) Winnebago County	20,351
Peoria, IL (city) Peoria County	20,220
Champaign, IL (city) Champaign County	13,398
Cicero, IL (town) Cook County	13,187
Decatur, IL (city) Macon County	12,999
Springfield, IL (city) Sangamon County	12,847
Waukegan, IL (city) Lake County	12,058
Aurora, IL (city) Kane County	12,034
Joliet, IL (city) Will County	10,946

Total Populations with Income Below Poverty Level
Top 10 Places Sorted by Percent

Place	Percent
Carbondale, IL (city) Jackson County	41.36
Macomb, IL (city) McDonough County	29.08
Urbana, IL (city) Champaign County	27.34
Champaign, IL (city) Champaign County	22.11
Harvey, IL (city) Cook County	21.65
Kankakee, IL (city) Kankakee County	21.36
DeKalb, IL (city) De Kalb County	21.28
Chicago, IL (city) Cook County	19.61
Normal, IL (town) McLean County	19.27
Peoria, IL (city) Peoria County	18.77

Hispanics with Income Below Poverty Level
Top 10 Places Sorted by Number

Place	Number
Chicago, IL (city) Cook County	149,626
Cicero, IL (town) Cook County	10,969
Waukegan, IL (city) Lake County	7,095
Aurora, IL (city) Kane County	5,921
Elgin, IL (city) Kane County	3,917
Joliet, IL (city) Will County	3,091
Rockford, IL (city) Winnebago County	3,085
Berwyn, IL (city) Cook County	2,001
Addison, IL (village) Du Page County	1,905
West Chicago, IL (city) Du Page County	1,687

Hispanics with Income Below Poverty Level
Top 10 Places Sorted by Percent

Place	Percent
Carbondale, IL (city) Jackson County	58.03
Urbana, IL (city) Champaign County	41.97
Macomb, IL (city) McDonough County	38.93
Pontiac, IL (city) Livingston County	30.89
Danville, IL (city) Vermilion County	30.75
Champaign, IL (city) Champaign County	30.33
Kewanee, IL (city) Henry County	28.50
Peoria, IL (city) Peoria County	26.70
East Moline, IL (city) Rock Island County	26.54
DeKalb, IL (city) De Kalb County	26.40

Argentinians with Income Below Poverty Level
Top 10 Places Sorted by Number

Place	Number
Chicago, IL (city) Cook County	291

Argentinians with Income Below Poverty Level
Top 10 Places Sorted by Percent

Place	Percent
Chicago, IL (city) Cook County	27.50

Bolivians with Income Below Poverty Level
Top 10 Places Sorted by Number

Place	Number
Chicago, IL (city) Cook County	72

Bolivians with Income Below Poverty Level
Top 10 Places Sorted by Percent

Place	Percent
Chicago, IL (city) Cook County	15.45

Central Americans with Income Below Poverty Level
Top 10 Places Sorted by Number

Place	Number
Chicago, IL (city) Cook County	3,665
Waukegan, IL (city) Lake County	387
Cicero, IL (town) Cook County	195
Aurora, IL (city) Kane County	36
Skokie, IL (village) Cook County	0

Central Americans with Income Below Poverty Level
Top 10 Places Sorted by Percent

Place	Percent
Cicero, IL (town) Cook County	22.86
Chicago, IL (city) Cook County	15.33
Waukegan, IL (city) Lake County	14.29
Aurora, IL (city) Kane County	7.29
Skokie, IL (village) Cook County	0.00

Chileans with Income Below Poverty Level
Top 10 Places Sorted by Number

Place	Number
Chicago, IL (city) Cook County	56

Chileans with Income Below Poverty Level
Top 10 Places Sorted by Percent

Place	Percent
Chicago, IL (city) Cook County	8.12

Colombians with Income Below Poverty Level
Top 10 Places Sorted by Number

Place	Number
Chicago, IL (city) Cook County	1,066

Colombians with Income Below Poverty Level
Top 10 Places Sorted by Percent

Place	Percent
Chicago, IL (city) Cook County	17.70

Costa Ricans with Income Below Poverty Level
Top 10 Places Sorted by Number

Place	Number
Chicago, IL (city) Cook County	204

Costa Ricans with Income Below Poverty Level
Top 10 Places Sorted by Percent

Place	Percent
Chicago, IL (city) Cook County	27.87

Cubans with Income Below Poverty Level
Top 10 Places Sorted by Number

Place	Number
Chicago, IL (city) Cook County	1,306
Melrose Park, IL (village) Cook County	63
Aurora, IL (city) Kane County	48

Cubans with Income Below Poverty Level
Top 10 Places Sorted by Percent

Place	Percent
Melrose Park, IL (village) Cook County	18.31
Chicago, IL (city) Cook County	16.30
Aurora, IL (city) Kane County	12.53

Dominicans with Income Below Poverty Level
Top 10 Places Sorted by Number

Place	Number
Chicago, IL (city) Cook County	335

Dominicans with Income Below Poverty Level
Top 10 Places Sorted by Percent

Place	Percent
Chicago, IL (city) Cook County	16.41

Ecuadorians with Income Below Poverty Level
Top 10 Places Sorted by Number

Place	Number
Chicago, IL (city) Cook County	912

Ecuadorians with Income Below Poverty Level
Top 10 Places Sorted by Percent

Place	Percent
Chicago, IL (city) Cook County	9.21

Guatelmalans with Income Below Poverty Level
Top 10 Places Sorted by Number

Place	Number
Chicago, IL (city) Cook County	1,989
Cicero, IL (town) Cook County	113

Guatelmalans with Income Below Poverty Level
Top 10 Places Sorted by Percent

Place	Percent
Cicero, IL (town) Cook County	25.34
Chicago, IL (city) Cook County	13.93

Hondurans with Income Below Poverty Level
Top 10 Places Sorted by Number

Place	Number
Chicago, IL (city) Cook County	601
Waukegan, IL (city) Lake County	166

Hondurans with Income Below Poverty Level
Top 10 Places Sorted by Percent

Place	Percent
Chicago, IL (city) Cook County	19.50
Waukegan, IL (city) Lake County	10.98

Mexicans with Income Below Poverty Level
Top 10 Places Sorted by Number

Place	Number
Chicago, IL (city) Cook County	105,715
Cicero, IL (town) Cook County	9,442
Waukegan, IL (city) Lake County	5,545
Aurora, IL (city) Kane County	5,352
Elgin, IL (city) Kane County	3,492
Joliet, IL (city) Will County	2,873
Rockford, IL (city) Winnebago County	2,624

Notes: Please refer to the User's Guide for an explanation of data; tables include places with populations > 9,999 and reflect only those areas that meet Summary File 4 population thresholds, therefore there may be less than 10 places listed

Addison, IL (village) Du Page County	1,755
Berwyn, IL (city) Cook County	1,584
West Chicago, IL (city) Du Page County	1,566

Mexicans with Income Below Poverty Level
Top 10 Places Sorted by Percent

Place	Percent
Urbana, IL (city) Champaign County	49.35
Danville, IL (city) Vermilion County	32.11
Champaign, IL (city) Champaign County	31.96
Peoria, IL (city) Peoria County	29.45
Freeport, IL (city) Stephenson County	29.12
McHenry, IL (city) McHenry County	28.77
Worth, IL (village) Cook County	27.75
Kewanee, IL (city) Henry County	26.73
Niles, IL (village) Cook County	26.67
East Moline, IL (city) Rock Island County	25.95

Nicaraguans with Income Below Poverty Level
Top 10 Places Sorted by Number

Place	Number
Chicago, IL (city) Cook County	144

Nicaraguans with Income Below Poverty Level
Top 10 Places Sorted by Percent

Place	Percent
Chicago, IL (city) Cook County	15.67

Panamanians with Income Below Poverty Level
Top 10 Places Sorted by Number

Place	Number
Chicago, IL (city) Cook County	66

Panamanians with Income Below Poverty Level
Top 10 Places Sorted by Percent

Place	Percent
Chicago, IL (city) Cook County	8.01

Paraguayans with Income Below Poverty Level
Top 10 Places Sorted by Number

Place	Number
No places met population threshold	

Paraguayans with Income Below Poverty Level
Top 10 Places Sorted by Percent

Place	Percent
No places met population threshold	

Peruvians with Income Below Poverty Level
Top 10 Places Sorted by Number

Place	Number
Chicago, IL (city) Cook County	326

Peruvians with Income Below Poverty Level
Top 10 Places Sorted by Percent

Place	Percent
Chicago, IL (city) Cook County	11.25

Puerto Ricans with Income Below Poverty Level
Top 10 Places Sorted by Number

Place	Number
Chicago, IL (city) Cook County	26,263
Cicero, IL (town) Cook County	579
Waukegan, IL (city) Lake County	328
Aurora, IL (city) Kane County	230
Berwyn, IL (city) Cook County	202
North Chicago, IL (city) Lake County	177
Elmwood Park, IL (village) Cook County	156
Elgin, IL (city) Kane County	153
Evanston, IL (city) Cook County	81
Carpentersville, IL (village) Kane County	62

Puerto Ricans with Income Below Poverty Level
Top 10 Places Sorted by Percent

Place	Percent
North Chicago, IL (city) Lake County	36.42
Cicero, IL (town) Cook County	24.72
Chicago, IL (city) Cook County	23.90
Evanston, IL (city) Cook County	23.34
Elmwood Park, IL (village) Cook County	21.17
Berwyn, IL (city) Cook County	15.86
Hanover Park, IL (village) Cook County	14.18
Carpentersville, IL (village) Kane County	12.68
Waukegan, IL (city) Lake County	11.37
Rockford, IL (city) Winnebago County	11.06

Salvadorans with Income Below Poverty Level
Top 10 Places Sorted by Number

Place	Number
Chicago, IL (city) Cook County	557
Waukegan, IL (city) Lake County	102

Salvadorans with Income Below Poverty Level
Top 10 Places Sorted by Percent

Place	Percent
Waukegan, IL (city) Lake County	18.65
Chicago, IL (city) Cook County	16.81

South Americans with Income Below Poverty Level
Top 10 Places Sorted by Number

Place	Number
Chicago, IL (city) Cook County	2,960
Cicero, IL (town) Cook County	139
Streamwood, IL (village) Cook County	54
Berwyn, IL (city) Cook County	52
Skokie, IL (village) Cook County	22
Aurora, IL (city) Kane County	0
Naperville, IL (city) Du Page County	0

South Americans with Income Below Poverty Level
Top 10 Places Sorted by Percent

Place	Percent
Cicero, IL (town) Cook County	20.72
Chicago, IL (city) Cook County	12.95
Streamwood, IL (village) Cook County	12.24
Berwyn, IL (city) Cook County	12.09
Skokie, IL (village) Cook County	5.03
Aurora, IL (city) Kane County	0.00
Naperville, IL (city) Du Page County	0.00

Spaniards with Income Below Poverty Level
Top 10 Places Sorted by Number

Place	Number
Chicago, IL (city) Cook County	33

Spaniards with Income Below Poverty Level
Top 10 Places Sorted by Percent

Place	Percent
Chicago, IL (city) Cook County	4.09

Uruguayans with Income Below Poverty Level
Top 10 Places Sorted by Number

Place	Number
No places met population threshold	

Uruguayans with Income Below Poverty Level
Top 10 Places Sorted by Percent

Place	Percent
No places met population threshold	

Venezuelans with Income Below Poverty Level
Top 10 Places Sorted by Number

Place	Number
Chicago, IL (city) Cook County	116

Venezuelans with Income Below Poverty Level
Top 10 Places Sorted by Percent

Place	Percent
Chicago, IL (city) Cook County	15.65

Other Hispanics with Income Below Poverty Level
Top 10 Places Sorted by Number

Place	Number
Chicago, IL (city) Cook County	9,349
Waukegan, IL (city) Lake County	759
Cicero, IL (town) Cook County	488
Elgin, IL (city) Kane County	258
Aurora, IL (city) Kane County	255
Rockford, IL (city) Winnebago County	211
Joliet, IL (city) Will County	145
Addison, IL (village) Du Page County	108
West Chicago, IL (city) Du Page County	88
Melrose Park, IL (village) Cook County	86

Other Hispanics with Income Below Poverty Level
Top 10 Places Sorted by Percent

Place	Percent
Danville, IL (city) Vermilion County	37.98
Dixon, IL (city) Lee County	33.33
Waukegan, IL (city) Lake County	23.67
Moline, IL (city) Rock Island County	21.28
Evanston, IL (city) Cook County	20.90
Crest Hill, IL (city) Will County	20.51
West Chicago, IL (city) Du Page County	19.78
Chicago, IL (city) Cook County	19.00
Galesburg, IL (city) Knox County	18.90
Addison, IL (village) Du Page County	18.56

Homeownership

Total Populations Who Own Their Own Homes
Top 10 Places Sorted by Number

Place	Number
Chicago, IL (city) Cook County	464,912
Rockford, IL (city) Winnebago County	36,304
Naperville, IL (city) Du Page County	34,952
Aurora, IL (city) Kane County	32,621
Springfield, IL (city) Sangamon County	30,575
Peoria, IL (city) Peoria County	27,041
Joliet, IL (city) Will County	25,465
Arlington Heights, IL (village) Cook County	23,565
Decatur, IL (city) Macon County	22,682
Elgin, IL (city) Kane County	22,167

Total Populations Who Own Their Own Homes
Top 10 Places Sorted by Percent

Place	Percent
Goodings Grove, IL (cdp) Will County	98.23
Morton Grove, IL (village) Cook County	94.54
Westchester, IL (village) Cook County	93.81
Lake in the Hills, IL (village) McHenry County	93.54
Bartlett, IL (village) Du Page County	93.45
Algonquin, IL (village) McHenry County	93.21
South Holland, IL (village) Cook County	93.00
Oswego, IL (village) Kendall County	92.26
Northbrook, IL (village) Cook County	91.63

Notes: Please refer to the User's Guide for an explanation of data; tables include places with populations > 9,999 and reflect only those areas that meet Summary File 4 population thresholds, therefore there may be less than 10 places listed

Lincolnwood, IL (village) Cook County	91.37

Hispanics Who Own Their Own Homes
Top 10 Places Sorted by Number

Place	Number
Chicago, IL (city) Cook County	75,480
Cicero, IL (town) Cook County	7,624
Aurora, IL (city) Kane County	6,564
Waukegan, IL (city) Lake County	4,513
Elgin, IL (city) Kane County	3,828
Berwyn, IL (city) Cook County	3,122
Joliet, IL (city) Will County	2,763
Rockford, IL (city) Winnebago County	2,021
Carpentersville, IL (village) Kane County	1,778
Blue Island, IL (city) Cook County	1,354

Hispanics Who Own Their Own Homes
Top 10 Places Sorted by Percent

Place	Percent
Lincolnwood, IL (village) Cook County	100.00
New Lenox, IL (village) Will County	100.00
Oswego, IL (village) Kendall County	100.00
Algonquin, IL (village) McHenry County	94.58
Goodings Grove, IL (cdp) Will County	94.50
Westchester, IL (village) Cook County	93.87
Northbrook, IL (village) Cook County	93.75
Romeoville, IL (village) Will County	90.90
Lindenhurst, IL (village) Lake County	90.16
Sauk Village, IL (village) Cook County	89.58

Argentinians Who Own Their Own Homes
Top 10 Places Sorted by Number

Place	Number
Chicago, IL (city) Cook County	193

Argentinians Who Own Their Own Homes
Top 10 Places Sorted by Percent

Place	Percent
Chicago, IL (city) Cook County	44.99

Bolivians Who Own Their Own Homes
Top 10 Places Sorted by Number

Place	Number
Chicago, IL (city) Cook County	49

Bolivians Who Own Their Own Homes
Top 10 Places Sorted by Percent

Place	Percent
Chicago, IL (city) Cook County	30.43

Central Americans Who Own Their Own Homes
Top 10 Places Sorted by Number

Place	Number
Chicago, IL (city) Cook County	2,781
Waukegan, IL (city) Lake County	296
Aurora, IL (city) Kane County	118
Cicero, IL (town) Cook County	89
Skokie, IL (village) Cook County	57

Central Americans Who Own Their Own Homes
Top 10 Places Sorted by Percent

Place	Percent
Aurora, IL (city) Kane County	77.63
Cicero, IL (town) Cook County	52.05
Skokie, IL (village) Cook County	51.82
Waukegan, IL (city) Lake County	39.52
Chicago, IL (city) Cook County	38.34

Chileans Who Own Their Own Homes
Top 10 Places Sorted by Number

Place	Number
Chicago, IL (city) Cook County	132

Chileans Who Own Their Own Homes
Top 10 Places Sorted by Percent

Place	Percent
Chicago, IL (city) Cook County	44.75

Colombians Who Own Their Own Homes
Top 10 Places Sorted by Number

Place	Number
Chicago, IL (city) Cook County	825

Colombians Who Own Their Own Homes
Top 10 Places Sorted by Percent

Place	Percent
Chicago, IL (city) Cook County	37.83

Costa Ricans Who Own Their Own Homes
Top 10 Places Sorted by Number

Place	Number
Chicago, IL (city) Cook County	102

Costa Ricans Who Own Their Own Homes
Top 10 Places Sorted by Percent

Place	Percent
Chicago, IL (city) Cook County	41.13

Cubans Who Own Their Own Homes
Top 10 Places Sorted by Number

Place	Number
Chicago, IL (city) Cook County	1,431
Aurora, IL (city) Kane County	101
Melrose Park, IL (village) Cook County	70

Cubans Who Own Their Own Homes
Top 10 Places Sorted by Percent

Place	Percent
Aurora, IL (city) Kane County	82.79
Melrose Park, IL (village) Cook County	57.38
Chicago, IL (city) Cook County	41.77

Dominicans Who Own Their Own Homes
Top 10 Places Sorted by Number

Place	Number
Chicago, IL (city) Cook County	265

Dominicans Who Own Their Own Homes
Top 10 Places Sorted by Percent

Place	Percent
Chicago, IL (city) Cook County	33.89

Ecuadorians Who Own Their Own Homes
Top 10 Places Sorted by Number

Place	Number
Chicago, IL (city) Cook County	1,182

Ecuadorians Who Own Their Own Homes
Top 10 Places Sorted by Percent

Place	Percent
Chicago, IL (city) Cook County	41.27

Guatelmalans Who Own Their Own Homes
Top 10 Places Sorted by Number

Place	Number
Chicago, IL (city) Cook County	1,673
Cicero, IL (town) Cook County	37

Guatelmalans Who Own Their Own Homes
Top 10 Places Sorted by Percent

Place	Percent
Cicero, IL (town) Cook County	46.84
Chicago, IL (city) Cook County	40.63

Hondurans Who Own Their Own Homes
Top 10 Places Sorted by Number

Place	Number
Chicago, IL (city) Cook County	253
Waukegan, IL (city) Lake County	135

Hondurans Who Own Their Own Homes
Top 10 Places Sorted by Percent

Place	Percent
Waukegan, IL (city) Lake County	36.29
Chicago, IL (city) Cook County	25.10

Mexicans Who Own Their Own Homes
Top 10 Places Sorted by Number

Place	Number
Chicago, IL (city) Cook County	52,924
Cicero, IL (town) Cook County	6,881
Aurora, IL (city) Kane County	5,457
Waukegan, IL (city) Lake County	3,470
Elgin, IL (city) Kane County	3,206
Berwyn, IL (city) Cook County	2,598
Joliet, IL (city) Will County	2,395
Rockford, IL (city) Winnebago County	1,627
Carpentersville, IL (village) Kane County	1,549
Blue Island, IL (city) Cook County	1,201

Mexicans Who Own Their Own Homes
Top 10 Places Sorted by Percent

Place	Percent
Algonquin, IL (village) McHenry County	100.00
New Lenox, IL (village) Will County	100.00
Oswego, IL (village) Kendall County	100.00
Homewood, IL (village) Cook County	94.64
Morton Grove, IL (village) Cook County	94.27
Goodings Grove, IL (cdp) Will County	92.41
Westchester, IL (village) Cook County	91.30
Sauk Village, IL (village) Cook County	90.40
Romeoville, IL (village) Will County	90.02
Northbrook, IL (village) Cook County	89.86

Nicaraguans Who Own Their Own Homes
Top 10 Places Sorted by Number

Place	Number
Chicago, IL (city) Cook County	122

Nicaraguans Who Own Their Own Homes
Top 10 Places Sorted by Percent

Place	Percent
Chicago, IL (city) Cook County	46.04

Panamanians Who Own Their Own Homes
Top 10 Places Sorted by Number

Place	Number
Chicago, IL (city) Cook County	124

Notes: Please refer to the User's Guide for an explanation of data; tables include places with populations > 9,999 and reflect only those areas that meet Summary File 4 population thresholds, therefore there may be less than 10 places listed

Panamanians Who Own Their Own Homes
Top 10 Places Sorted by Percent

Place	Percent
Chicago, IL (city) Cook County	35.73

Paraguayans Who Own Their Own Homes
Top 10 Places Sorted by Number

Place	Number

No places met population threshold

Paraguayans Who Own Their Own Homes
Top 10 Places Sorted by Percent

Place	Percent

No places met population threshold

Peruvians Who Own Their Own Homes
Top 10 Places Sorted by Number

Place	Number
Chicago, IL (city) Cook County	493

Peruvians Who Own Their Own Homes
Top 10 Places Sorted by Percent

Place	Percent
Chicago, IL (city) Cook County	45.56

Puerto Ricans Who Own Their Own Homes
Top 10 Places Sorted by Number

Place	Number
Chicago, IL (city) Cook County	11,526
Waukegan, IL (city) Lake County	493
Aurora, IL (city) Kane County	426
Elgin, IL (city) Kane County	340
Cicero, IL (town) Cook County	286
Berwyn, IL (city) Cook County	238
Elmwood Park, IL (village) Cook County	132
Streamwood, IL (village) Cook County	129
Franklin Park, IL (village) Cook County	124
Joliet, IL (city) Will County	124

Puerto Ricans Who Own Their Own Homes
Top 10 Places Sorted by Percent

Place	Percent
Bolingbrook, IL (village) Will County	100.00
Streamwood, IL (village) Cook County	93.48
Hanover Park, IL (village) Cook County	82.40
Carpentersville, IL (village) Kane County	75.00
Franklin Park, IL (village) Cook County	72.09
Joliet, IL (city) Will County	68.51
Des Plaines, IL (city) Cook County	67.80
Skokie, IL (village) Cook County	63.89
Zion, IL (city) Lake County	63.64
Schaumburg, IL (village) Cook County	62.03

Salvadorans Who Own Their Own Homes
Top 10 Places Sorted by Number

Place	Number
Chicago, IL (city) Cook County	395
Waukegan, IL (city) Lake County	98

Salvadorans Who Own Their Own Homes
Top 10 Places Sorted by Percent

Place	Percent
Waukegan, IL (city) Lake County	57.65
Chicago, IL (city) Cook County	38.84

South Americans Who Own Their Own Homes
Top 10 Places Sorted by Number

Place	Number
Chicago, IL (city) Cook County	3,102
Streamwood, IL (village) Cook County	98
Berwyn, IL (city) Cook County	94
Skokie, IL (village) Cook County	92
Naperville, IL (city) Du Page County	84
Cicero, IL (town) Cook County	68
Aurora, IL (city) Kane County	51

South Americans Who Own Their Own Homes
Top 10 Places Sorted by Percent

Place	Percent
Streamwood, IL (village) Cook County	84.48
Berwyn, IL (city) Cook County	66.67
Naperville, IL (city) Du Page County	65.12
Skokie, IL (village) Cook County	61.33
Aurora, IL (city) Kane County	55.43
Chicago, IL (city) Cook County	40.29
Cicero, IL (town) Cook County	34.69

Spaniards Who Own Their Own Homes
Top 10 Places Sorted by Number

Place	Number
Chicago, IL (city) Cook County	81

Spaniards Who Own Their Own Homes
Top 10 Places Sorted by Percent

Place	Percent
Chicago, IL (city) Cook County	25.31

Uruguayans Who Own Their Own Homes
Top 10 Places Sorted by Number

Place	Number

No places met population threshold

Uruguayans Who Own Their Own Homes
Top 10 Places Sorted by Percent

Place	Percent

No places met population threshold

Venezuelans Who Own Their Own Homes
Top 10 Places Sorted by Number

Place	Number
Chicago, IL (city) Cook County	72

Venezuelans Who Own Their Own Homes
Top 10 Places Sorted by Percent

Place	Percent
Chicago, IL (city) Cook County	19.46

Other Hispanics Who Own Their Own Homes
Top 10 Places Sorted by Number

Place	Number
Chicago, IL (city) Cook County	3,370
Aurora, IL (city) Kane County	398
Cicero, IL (town) Cook County	273
Elgin, IL (city) Kane County	214
Waukegan, IL (city) Lake County	202
Joliet, IL (city) Will County	174
Rockford, IL (city) Winnebago County	135
Berwyn, IL (city) Cook County	112
Carpentersville, IL (village) Kane County	103
Streamwood, IL (village) Cook County	87

Other Hispanics Who Own Their Own Homes
Top 10 Places Sorted by Percent

Place	Percent
Burbank, IL (city) Cook County	90.20
Bolingbrook, IL (village) Will County	80.43
Hoffman Estates, IL (village) Cook County	80.37
Carpentersville, IL (village) Kane County	74.64
Skokie, IL (village) Cook County	73.96
Schaumburg, IL (village) Cook County	72.62
Round Lake Beach, IL (village) Lake County	72.22
Joliet, IL (city) Will County	72.20
Streamwood, IL (village) Cook County	71.90
Blue Island, IL (city) Cook County	67.89

Median Gross Rent

All Specified Renter-Occupied Housing Units
Top 10 Places Sorted by Number

Place	Dollars/Month
Lincolnwood, IL (village) Cook County	2,001
Northbrook, IL (village) Cook County	1,279
Streamwood, IL (village) Cook County	1,130
Goodings Grove, IL (cdp) Will County	1,083
Buffalo Grove, IL (village) Lake County	1,079
Wilmette, IL (village) Cook County	1,028
Warrenville, IL (city) Du Page County	1,019
Deerfield, IL (village) Lake County	1,018
Schaumburg, IL (village) Cook County	981
Lake in the Hills, IL (village) McHenry County	963

Specified Housing Units Rented by Hispanics
Top 10 Places Sorted by Number

Place	Dollars/Month
Darien, IL (city) Du Page County	1,288
Mokena, IL (village) Will County	1,125
Streamwood, IL (village) Cook County	1,091
Algonquin, IL (village) McHenry County	950
Roselle, IL (village) Du Page County	950
Hazel Crest, IL (village) Cook County	948
Lisle, IL (village) Du Page County	942
Highland Park, IL (city) Lake County	940
Libertyville, IL (village) Lake County	930
Romeoville, IL (village) Will County	925

Specified Housing Units Rented by Argentinians
Top 10 Places Sorted by Number

Place	Dollars/Month
Chicago, IL (city) Cook County	699

Specified Housing Units Rented by Bolivians
Top 10 Places Sorted by Number

Place	Dollars/Month
Chicago, IL (city) Cook County	882

Specified Housing Units Rented by Central Americans
Top 10 Places Sorted by Number

Place	Dollars/Month
Skokie, IL (village) Cook County	819
Aurora, IL (city) Kane County	767
Waukegan, IL (city) Lake County	691
Cicero, IL (town) Cook County	643
Chicago, IL (city) Cook County	606

Specified Housing Units Rented by Chileans
Top 10 Places Sorted by Number

Place	Dollars/Month
Chicago, IL (city) Cook County	722

Specified Housing Units Rented by Colombians
Top 10 Places Sorted by Number

Place	Dollars/Month
Chicago, IL (city) Cook County	673

Notes: Please refer to the User's Guide for an explanation of data; tables include places with populations > 9,999 and reflect only those areas that meet Summary File 4 population thresholds, therefore there may be less than 10 places listed

Specified Housing Units Rented by Costa Ricans

Top 10 Places Sorted by Number

Place	Dollars/Month
Chicago, IL (city) Cook County	590

Specified Housing Units Rented by Cubans

Top 10 Places Sorted by Number

Place	Dollars/Month
Melrose Park, IL (village) Cook County	625
Chicago, IL (city) Cook County	610
Aurora, IL (city) Kane County	563

Specified Housing Units Rented by Dominicans

Top 10 Places Sorted by Number

Place	Dollars/Month
Chicago, IL (city) Cook County	635

Specified Housing Units Rented by Ecuadorians

Top 10 Places Sorted by Number

Place	Dollars/Month
Chicago, IL (city) Cook County	650

Specified Housing Units Rented by Guatelmalans

Top 10 Places Sorted by Number

Place	Dollars/Month
Cicero, IL (town) Cook County	629
Chicago, IL (city) Cook County	613

Specified Housing Units Rented by Hondurans

Top 10 Places Sorted by Number

Place	Dollars/Month
Waukegan, IL (city) Lake County	678
Chicago, IL (city) Cook County	576

Specified Housing Units Rented by Mexicans

Top 10 Places Sorted by Number

Place	Dollars/Month
Darien, IL (city) Du Page County	1,288
Streamwood, IL (village) Cook County	1,042
Lisle, IL (village) Du Page County	985
Roselle, IL (village) Du Page County	978
Romeoville, IL (village) Will County	950
Hazel Crest, IL (village) Cook County	948
Highland Park, IL (city) Lake County	934
Lombard, IL (village) Du Page County	911
Libertyville, IL (village) Lake County	900
Westchester, IL (village) Cook County	900

Specified Housing Units Rented by Nicaraguans

Top 10 Places Sorted by Number

Place	Dollars/Month
Chicago, IL (city) Cook County	709

Specified Housing Units Rented by Panamanians

Top 10 Places Sorted by Number

Place	Dollars/Month
Chicago, IL (city) Cook County	680

Specified Housing Units Rented by Paraguayans

Top 10 Places Sorted by Number

Place	Dollars/Month

Specified Housing Units Rented by Peruvians

Top 10 Places Sorted by Number

Place	Dollars/Month
Chicago, IL (city) Cook County	638

Specified Housing Units Rented by Puerto Ricans

Top 10 Places Sorted by Number

Place	Dollars/Month
Streamwood, IL (village) Cook County	1,125
Naperville, IL (city) Du Page County	1,039
Skokie, IL (village) Cook County	934
Carol Stream, IL (village) Du Page County	926
Schaumburg, IL (village) Cook County	887
Evanston, IL (city) Cook County	857
Hanover Park, IL (village) Cook County	775
Zion, IL (city) Lake County	735
Des Plaines, IL (city) Cook County	734
Franklin Park, IL (village) Cook County	713

Specified Housing Units Rented by Salvadorans

Top 10 Places Sorted by Number

Place	Dollars/Month
Waukegan, IL (city) Lake County	680
Chicago, IL (city) Cook County	586

Specified Housing Units Rented by South Americans

Top 10 Places Sorted by Number

Place	Dollars/Month
Streamwood, IL (village) Cook County	1,250
Naperville, IL (city) Du Page County	931
Skokie, IL (village) Cook County	766
Aurora, IL (city) Kane County	753
Chicago, IL (city) Cook County	670
Berwyn, IL (city) Cook County	638
Cicero, IL (town) Cook County	578

Specified Housing Units Rented by Spaniards

Top 10 Places Sorted by Number

Place	Dollars/Month
Chicago, IL (city) Cook County	680

Specified Housing Units Rented by Uruguayans

Top 10 Places Sorted by Number

Place	Dollars/Month

Specified Housing Units Rented by Venezuelans

Top 10 Places Sorted by Number

Place	Dollars/Month
Chicago, IL (city) Cook County	764

Specified Housing Units Rented by Other Hispanics

Top 10 Places Sorted by Number

Place	Dollars/Month
West Chicago, IL (city) Du Page County	1,214
Streamwood, IL (village) Cook County	1,202
Blue Island, IL (city) Cook County	1,125
Hoffman Estates, IL (village) Cook County	1,125
Schaumburg, IL (village) Cook County	1,125
Naperville, IL (city) Du Page County	1,079
Round Lake Beach, IL (village) Lake County	956
Bolingbrook, IL (village) Will County	910
Wheeling, IL (village) Cook County	867
Mount Prospect, IL (village) Cook County	845

Median Home Value

All Specified Owner-Occupied Housing Units

Top 10 Places Sorted by Number

Place	Dollars
Hinsdale, IL (village) Du Page County	520,100
Wilmette, IL (village) Cook County	441,600
River Forest, IL (village) Cook County	386,600
Highland Park, IL (city) Lake County	380,000
Northbrook, IL (village) Cook County	370,800
Deerfield, IL (village) Lake County	342,900
Glenview, IL (village) Cook County	336,000
Park Ridge, IL (city) Cook County	295,800
Lincolnwood, IL (village) Cook County	291,400
Evanston, IL (city) Cook County	290,800

Specified Housing Units Owned and Occupied by Hispanics

Top 10 Places Sorted by Number

Place	Dollars
Hinsdale, IL (village) Du Page County	644,700
Deerfield, IL (village) Lake County	450,000
Wilmette, IL (village) Cook County	330,500
River Forest, IL (village) Cook County	326,100
Glen Ellyn, IL (village) Du Page County	292,900
Lisle, IL (village) Du Page County	266,700
Northbrook, IL (village) Cook County	262,500
La Grange, IL (village) Cook County	252,500
Glenview, IL (village) Cook County	234,000
Park Ridge, IL (city) Cook County	231,100

Specified Housing Units Owned and Occupied by Argentinians

Top 10 Places Sorted by Number

Place	Dollars
Chicago, IL (city) Cook County	178,100

Specified Housing Units Owned and Occupied by Bolivians

Top 10 Places Sorted by Number

Place	Dollars
Chicago, IL (city) Cook County	187,500

Specified Housing Units Owned and Occupied by Central Americans

Top 10 Places Sorted by Number

Place	Dollars
Skokie, IL (village) Cook County	210,900
Chicago, IL (city) Cook County	145,900
Aurora, IL (city) Kane County	120,000
Cicero, IL (town) Cook County	112,500
Waukegan, IL (city) Lake County	109,000

Specified Housing Units Owned and Occupied by Chileans

Top 10 Places Sorted by Number

Place	Dollars
Chicago, IL (city) Cook County	179,900

Specified Housing Units Owned and Occupied by Colombians

Top 10 Places Sorted by Number

Place	Dollars
Chicago, IL (city) Cook County	174,500

Specified Housing Units Owned and Occupied by Costa Ricans

Top 10 Places Sorted by Number

Place	Dollars
Chicago, IL (city) Cook County	142,000

Specified Housing Units Owned and Occupied by Cubans

Top 10 Places Sorted by Number

Place	Dollars
Melrose Park, IL (village) Cook County	177,600
Chicago, IL (city) Cook County	167,900
Aurora, IL (city) Kane County	124,700

Notes: Please refer to the User's Guide for an explanation of data; tables include places with populations > 9,999 and reflect only those areas that meet Summary File 4 population thresholds, therefore there may be less than 10 places listed

Specified Housing Units Owned and Occupied by Dominicans

Top 10 Places Sorted by Number

Place	Dollars
Chicago, IL (city) Cook County	176,000

Specified Housing Units Owned and Occupied by Ecuadorians

Top 10 Places Sorted by Number

Place	Dollars
Chicago, IL (city) Cook County	158,000

Specified Housing Units Owned and Occupied by Guatelmalans

Top 10 Places Sorted by Number

Place	Dollars
Chicago, IL (city) Cook County	144,500
Cicero, IL (town) Cook County	88,100

Specified Housing Units Owned and Occupied by Hondurans

Top 10 Places Sorted by Number

Place	Dollars
Chicago, IL (city) Cook County	150,600
Waukegan, IL (city) Lake County	122,100

Specified Housing Units Owned and Occupied by Mexicans

Top 10 Places Sorted by Number

Place	Dollars
Lisle, IL (village) Du Page County	335,300
Glen Ellyn, IL (village) Du Page County	325,000
Decatur, IL (city) Macon County	275,000
Northbrook, IL (village) Cook County	270,500
La Grange, IL (village) Cook County	270,000
Glenview, IL (village) Cook County	260,300
Niles, IL (village) Cook County	237,500
Goodings Grove, IL (cdp) Will County	236,300
Downers Grove, IL (village) Du Page County	228,000
Park Ridge, IL (city) Cook County	222,500

Specified Housing Units Owned and Occupied by Nicaraguans

Top 10 Places Sorted by Number

Place	Dollars
Chicago, IL (city) Cook County	162,500

Specified Housing Units Owned and Occupied by Panamanians

Top 10 Places Sorted by Number

Place	Dollars
Chicago, IL (city) Cook County	135,400

Specified Housing Units Owned and Occupied by Paraguayans

Top 10 Places Sorted by Number

Place	Dollars
No places met population threshold	

Specified Housing Units Owned and Occupied by Peruvians

Top 10 Places Sorted by Number

Place	Dollars
Chicago, IL (city) Cook County	168,900

Specified Housing Units Owned and Occupied by Puerto Ricans

Top 10 Places Sorted by Number

Place	Dollars
Evanston, IL (city) Cook County	270,800
Carol Stream, IL (village) Du Page County	234,600
Naperville, IL (city) Du Page County	227,100
Skokie, IL (village) Cook County	219,700
Bolingbrook, IL (village) Will County	182,800
Elmwood Park, IL (village) Cook County	170,100
Melrose Park, IL (village) Cook County	165,600
Des Plaines, IL (city) Cook County	159,100
Franklin Park, IL (village) Cook County	150,300
Berwyn, IL (city) Cook County	148,100

Specified Housing Units Owned and Occupied by Salvadorans

Top 10 Places Sorted by Number

Place	Dollars
Chicago, IL (city) Cook County	141,400
Waukegan, IL (city) Lake County	98,100

Specified Housing Units Owned and Occupied by South Americans

Top 10 Places Sorted by Number

Place	Dollars
Naperville, IL (city) Du Page County	234,600
Skokie, IL (village) Cook County	177,800
Chicago, IL (city) Cook County	170,700
Berwyn, IL (city) Cook County	132,900
Cicero, IL (town) Cook County	125,000
Aurora, IL (city) Kane County	122,700
Streamwood, IL (village) Cook County	120,800

Specified Housing Units Owned and Occupied by Spaniards

Top 10 Places Sorted by Number

Place	Dollars
Chicago, IL (city) Cook County	185,300

Specified Housing Units Owned and Occupied by Uruguayans

Top 10 Places Sorted by Number

Place	Dollars
No places met population threshold	

Specified Housing Units Owned and Occupied by Venezuelans

Top 10 Places Sorted by Number

Place	Dollars
Chicago, IL (city) Cook County	575,000

Specified Housing Units Owned and Occupied by Other Hispanics

Top 10 Places Sorted by Number

Place	Dollars
Mount Prospect, IL (village) Cook County	275,000
Skokie, IL (village) Cook County	205,900
Evanston, IL (city) Cook County	192,000
Schaumburg, IL (village) Cook County	187,500
Hoffman Estates, IL (village) Cook County	184,100
Naperville, IL (city) Du Page County	182,100
Addison, IL (village) Du Page County	167,900
Wheeling, IL (village) Cook County	167,500
Burbank, IL (city) Cook County	161,100
Franklin Park, IL (village) Cook County	156,500

Notes: Please refer to the User's Guide for an explanation of data; tables include places with populations > 9,999 and reflect only those areas that meet Summary File 4 population thresholds, therefore there may be less than 10 places listed

Asian Population

Population

Total Population
Top 10 Places Sorted by Number

Place	Number
Chicago, IL (city) Cook County	2,895,964
Rockford, IL (city) Winnebago County	149,704
Aurora, IL (city) Kane County	143,609
Naperville, IL (city) Du Page County	128,300
Peoria, IL (city) Peoria County	112,892
Springfield, IL (city) Sangamon County	112,201
Joliet, IL (city) Will County	106,157
Elgin, IL (city) Kane County	93,895
Waukegan, IL (city) Lake County	87,969
Cicero, IL (town) Cook County	85,616

Total Population
Top 10 Places Sorted by Percent of Asian Population

Asian
Top 10 Places Sorted by Number

Place	Number
Chicago, IL (city) Cook County	127,052
Skokie, IL (village) Cook County	13,321
Naperville, IL (city) Du Page County	11,700
Schaumburg, IL (village) Cook County	10,285
Hoffman Estates, IL (village) Cook County	7,480
Mount Prospect, IL (village) Cook County	6,482
Glendale Heights, IL (village) Du Page County	6,298
Urbana, IL (city) Champaign County	5,283
Palatine, IL (village) Cook County	5,225
Morton Grove, IL (village) Cook County	4,931

Asian
Top 10 Places Sorted by Percent of Total Population

Place	Percent
Morton Grove, IL (village) Cook County	21.96
Oak Brook, IL (village) Du Page County	21.94
Lincolnwood, IL (village) Cook County	21.37
Skokie, IL (village) Cook County	21.04
Glendale Heights, IL (village) Du Page County	19.88
South Barrington, IL (village) Cook County	15.82
Hoffman Estates, IL (village) Cook County	14.86
Urbana, IL (city) Champaign County	14.60
Schaumburg, IL (village) Cook County	13.80
Darien, IL (city) Du Page County	12.67

Native Hawaiian and Other Pacific Islander
Top 10 Places Sorted by Number

Place	Number
Chicago, IL (city) Cook County	1,065

Native Hawaiian and Other Pacific Islander
Top 10 Places Sorted by Percent of Asian Population

Place	Percent
Chicago, IL (city) Cook County	100.00

Native Hawaiian and Other Pacific Islander
Top 10 Places Sorted by Percent of Total Population

Place	Percent
Chicago, IL (city) Cook County	0.04

Asian Indian
Top 10 Places Sorted by Number

Place	Number
Chicago, IL (city) Cook County	24,208
Naperville, IL (city) Du Page County	4,674
Schaumburg, IL (village) Cook County	4,529
Skokie, IL (village) Cook County	3,845
Mount Prospect, IL (village) Cook County	3,155
Glendale Heights, IL (village) Du Page County	2,780
Hoffman Estates, IL (village) Cook County	2,740
Palatine, IL (village) Cook County	2,210
Des Plaines, IL (city) Cook County	1,953
Hanover Park, IL (village) Cook County	1,895

Asian Indian
Top 10 Places Sorted by Percent of Asian Population

Place	Percent
Burr Ridge, IL (village) Du Page County	61.72
Bensenville, IL (village) Du Page County	60.79
Elmhurst, IL (city) Du Page County	58.92
Addison, IL (village) Du Page County	55.92
Oak Brook, IL (village) Du Page County	55.42
Darien, IL (city) Du Page County	51.36
Bartlett, IL (village) Du Page County	50.95
Bloomington, IL (city) McLean County	50.65
Mount Prospect, IL (village) Cook County	48.67
Bloomingdale, IL (village) Du Page County	47.41

Asian Indian
Top 10 Places Sorted by Percent of Total Population

Place	Percent
Oak Brook, IL (village) Du Page County	12.16
Glendale Heights, IL (village) Du Page County	8.78
Morton Grove, IL (village) Cook County	6.82
Darien, IL (city) Du Page County	6.51
Lincolnwood, IL (village) Cook County	6.41
Burr Ridge, IL (village) Du Page County	6.17
Schaumburg, IL (village) Cook County	6.08
Skokie, IL (village) Cook County	6.07
South Barrington, IL (village) Cook County	5.95
Mount Prospect, IL (village) Cook County	5.56

Bangladeshi
Top 10 Places Sorted by Number

Place	Number
No places met population threshold.	

Bangladeshi
Top 10 Places Sorted by Percent of Asian Population

Place	Percent
No places met population threshold.	

Bangladeshi
Top 10 Places Sorted by Percent of Total Population

Place	Percent
No places met population threshold.	

Cambodian
Top 10 Places Sorted by Number

Place	Number
Chicago, IL (city) Cook County	1,911

Cambodian
Top 10 Places Sorted by Percent of Asian Population

Place	Percent
Chicago, IL (city) Cook County	1.50

Cambodian
Top 10 Places Sorted by Percent of Total Population

Place	Percent
Chicago, IL (city) Cook County	0.07

Chinese (except Taiwanese)
Top 10 Places Sorted by Number

Place	Number
Chicago, IL (city) Cook County	31,416
Naperville, IL (city) Du Page County	4,044
Urbana, IL (city) Champaign County	1,803
Skokie, IL (village) Cook County	1,657
Schaumburg, IL (village) Cook County	1,336
Evanston, IL (city) Cook County	1,196
Champaign, IL (city) Champaign County	1,063
Hoffman Estates, IL (village) Cook County	821
Peoria, IL (city) Peoria County	809
Glenview, IL (village) Cook County	700

Chinese (except Taiwanese)
Top 10 Places Sorted by Percent of Asian Population

Place	Percent
Naperville, IL (city) Du Page County	34.56
Urbana, IL (city) Champaign County	34.13
Lisle, IL (village) Du Page County	30.62
Peoria, IL (city) Peoria County	29.58
Vernon Hills, IL (village) Lake County	29.32
Evanston, IL (city) Cook County	26.62
Mundelein, IL (village) Lake County	26.39
Chicago, IL (city) Cook County	24.73
Champaign, IL (city) Champaign County	23.10
Oak Park, IL (village) Cook County	21.57

Chinese (except Taiwanese)
Top 10 Places Sorted by Percent of Total Population

Place	Percent
Urbana, IL (city) Champaign County	4.98
Vernon Hills, IL (village) Lake County	3.30
Lisle, IL (village) Du Page County	3.15
Naperville, IL (city) Du Page County	3.15
Skokie, IL (village) Cook County	2.62
Westmont, IL (village) Du Page County	1.97
Schaumburg, IL (village) Cook County	1.79
Mundelein, IL (village) Lake County	1.77
Glenview, IL (village) Cook County	1.68
Hoffman Estates, IL (village) Cook County	1.63

Fijian
Top 10 Places Sorted by Number

Place	Number
No places met population threshold.	

Fijian
Top 10 Places Sorted by Percent of Asian Population

Place	Percent
No places met population threshold.	

Fijian
Top 10 Places Sorted by Percent of Total Population

Place	Percent
No places met population threshold.	

Filipino
Top 10 Places Sorted by Number

Place	Number
Chicago, IL (city) Cook County	27,874
Skokie, IL (village) Cook County	3,090
Morton Grove, IL (village) Cook County	1,786
Glendale Heights, IL (village) Du Page County	1,744
Waukegan, IL (city) Lake County	1,537
Streamwood, IL (village) Cook County	1,183
Bolingbrook, IL (village) Will County	1,166
Hanover Park, IL (village) Cook County	1,163
Woodridge, IL (village) Du Page County	1,162
Carol Stream, IL (village) Du Page County	1,074

Filipino
Top 10 Places Sorted by Percent of Asian Population

Place	Percent
Berwyn, IL (city) Cook County	59.66
North Chicago, IL (city) Lake County	55.14
Park City, IL (city) Lake County	55.14
Waukegan, IL (city) Lake County	50.07
Cicero, IL (town) Cook County	49.06
Morton Grove, IL (village) Cook County	36.22

Notes: Please refer to the User's Guide for an explanation of data; tables reflect only those areas that meet Summary File 4 population thresholds, therefore there may be less than 10 places listed

Place	Percent
Streamwood, IL (village) Cook County	35.70
Tinley Park, IL (village) Cook County	34.67
Woodridge, IL (village) Du Page County	33.17
Gurnee, IL (village) Lake County	32.49

Filipino
Top 10 Places Sorted by Percent of Total Population

Place	Percent
Morton Grove, IL (village) Cook County	7.95
Glendale Heights, IL (village) Du Page County	5.51
Park City, IL (city) Lake County	5.25
Skokie, IL (village) Cook County	4.88
Lincolnwood, IL (village) Cook County	3.99
Woodridge, IL (village) Du Page County	3.74
Darien, IL (city) Du Page County	3.43
Streamwood, IL (village) Cook County	3.22
Hanover Park, IL (village) Cook County	3.03
Carol Stream, IL (village) Du Page County	2.70

Guamanian or Chamorro
Top 10 Places Sorted by Number

Place	Number
No places met population threshold.	

Guamanian or Chamorro
Top 10 Places Sorted by Percent of Asian Population

Place	Percent
No places met population threshold.	

Guamanian or Chamorro
Top 10 Places Sorted by Percent of Total Population

Place	Percent
No places met population threshold.	

Hawaiian, Native
Top 10 Places Sorted by Number

Place	Number
No places met population threshold.	

Hawaiian, Native
Top 10 Places Sorted by Percent of Asian Population

Place	Percent
No places met population threshold.	

Hawaiian, Native
Top 10 Places Sorted by Percent of Total Population

Place	Percent
No places met population threshold.	

Hmong
Top 10 Places Sorted by Number

Place	Number
No places met population threshold.	

Hmong
Top 10 Places Sorted by Percent of Asian Population

Place	Percent
No places met population threshold.	

Hmong
Top 10 Places Sorted by Percent of Total Population

Place	Percent
No places met population threshold.	

Indonesian
Top 10 Places Sorted by Number

Place	Number
No places met population threshold.	

Indonesian
Top 10 Places Sorted by Percent of Asian Population

Place	Percent
No places met population threshold.	

Indonesian
Top 10 Places Sorted by Percent of Total Population

Place	Percent
No places met population threshold.	

Japanese
Top 10 Places Sorted by Number

Place	Number
Chicago, IL (city) Cook County	6,043
Arlington Heights, IL (village) Cook County	994
Schaumburg, IL (village) Cook County	940
Hoffman Estates, IL (village) Cook County	836
Buffalo Grove, IL (village) Lake County	611
Elk Grove Village, IL (village) Cook County	610
Mount Prospect, IL (village) Cook County	445
Evanston, IL (city) Cook County	376
Wilmette, IL (village) Cook County	346
Glenview, IL (village) Cook County	314

Japanese
Top 10 Places Sorted by Percent of Asian Population

Place	Percent
Arlington Heights, IL (village) Cook County	21.28
Elk Grove Village, IL (village) Cook County	18.42
Buffalo Grove, IL (village) Lake County	16.57
Wilmette, IL (village) Cook County	15.63
Hoffman Estates, IL (village) Cook County	11.18
Schaumburg, IL (village) Cook County	9.14
Evanston, IL (city) Cook County	8.37
Glenview, IL (village) Cook County	7.45
Mount Prospect, IL (village) Cook County	6.87
Chicago, IL (city) Cook County	4.76

Japanese
Top 10 Places Sorted by Percent of Total Population

Place	Percent
Elk Grove Village, IL (village) Cook County	1.75
Hoffman Estates, IL (village) Cook County	1.66
Buffalo Grove, IL (village) Lake County	1.43
Arlington Heights, IL (village) Cook County	1.31
Schaumburg, IL (village) Cook County	1.26
Wilmette, IL (village) Cook County	1.25
Mount Prospect, IL (village) Cook County	0.78
Glenview, IL (village) Cook County	0.75
Evanston, IL (city) Cook County	0.51
Chicago, IL (city) Cook County	0.21

Korean
Top 10 Places Sorted by Number

Place	Number
Chicago, IL (city) Cook County	12,576
Skokie, IL (village) Cook County	2,524
Schaumburg, IL (village) Cook County	1,775
Glenview, IL (village) Cook County	1,597
Northbrook, IL (village) Cook County	1,548
Mount Prospect, IL (village) Cook County	1,446
Hoffman Estates, IL (village) Cook County	1,426
Urbana, IL (city) Champaign County	1,157
Buffalo Grove, IL (village) Lake County	1,095
Niles, IL (village) Cook County	1,005

Korean
Top 10 Places Sorted by Percent of Asian Population

Place	Percent
Northbrook, IL (village) Cook County	53.01
Glenview, IL (village) Cook County	37.92
Wilmette, IL (village) Cook County	35.05
Niles, IL (village) Cook County	29.72
Buffalo Grove, IL (village) Lake County	29.70
Vernon Hills, IL (village) Lake County	27.76
Lincolnwood, IL (village) Cook County	24.61
Mount Prospect, IL (village) Cook County	22.31
Urbana, IL (city) Champaign County	21.90
Champaign, IL (city) Champaign County	19.14

Korean
Top 10 Places Sorted by Percent of Total Population

Place	Percent
Lincolnwood, IL (village) Cook County	5.26
Northbrook, IL (village) Cook County	4.63
Skokie, IL (village) Cook County	3.99
Morton Grove, IL (village) Cook County	3.87
Glenview, IL (village) Cook County	3.83
Niles, IL (village) Cook County	3.33
Urbana, IL (city) Champaign County	3.20
Vernon Hills, IL (village) Lake County	3.12
Hoffman Estates, IL (village) Cook County	2.83
Wilmette, IL (village) Cook County	2.80

Laotian
Top 10 Places Sorted by Number

Place	Number
Elgin, IL (city) Kane County	898
Rockford, IL (city) Winnebago County	898

Laotian
Top 10 Places Sorted by Percent of Asian Population

Place	Percent
Rockford, IL (city) Winnebago County	30.28
Elgin, IL (city) Kane County	27.70

Laotian
Top 10 Places Sorted by Percent of Total Population

Place	Percent
Elgin, IL (city) Kane County	0.96
Rockford, IL (city) Winnebago County	0.60

Malaysian
Top 10 Places Sorted by Number

Place	Number
No places met population threshold.	

Malaysian
Top 10 Places Sorted by Percent of Asian Population

Place	Percent
No places met population threshold.	

Malaysian
Top 10 Places Sorted by Percent of Total Population

Place	Percent
No places met population threshold.	

Pakistani
Top 10 Places Sorted by Number

Place	Number
Chicago, IL (city) Cook County	6,437
Skokie, IL (village) Cook County	495

Pakistani
Top 10 Places Sorted by Percent of Asian Population

Place	Percent
Chicago, IL (city) Cook County	5.07
Skokie, IL (village) Cook County	3.72

Notes: Please refer to the User's Guide for an explanation of data; tables reflect only those areas that meet Summary File 4 population thresholds, therefore there may be less than 10 places listed

Pakistani

Top 10 Places Sorted by Percent of Total Population

Place	Percent
Skokie, IL (village) Cook County	0.78
Chicago, IL (city) Cook County	0.22

Samoan

Top 10 Places Sorted by Number

Place	Number

No places met population threshold.

Samoan

Top 10 Places Sorted by Percent of Asian Population

Place	Percent

No places met population threshold.

Samoan

Top 10 Places Sorted by Percent of Total Population

Place	Percent

No places met population threshold.

Sri Lankan

Top 10 Places Sorted by Number

Place	Number

No places met population threshold.

Sri Lankan

Top 10 Places Sorted by Percent of Asian Population

Place	Percent

No places met population threshold.

Sri Lankan

Top 10 Places Sorted by Percent of Total Population

Place	Percent

No places met population threshold.

Taiwanese

Top 10 Places Sorted by Number

Place	Number
Chicago, IL (city) Cook County	776
Naperville, IL (city) Du Page County	431

Taiwanese

Top 10 Places Sorted by Percent of Asian Population

Place	Percent
Naperville, IL (city) Du Page County	3.68
Chicago, IL (city) Cook County	0.61

Taiwanese

Top 10 Places Sorted by Percent of Total Population

Place	Percent
Naperville, IL (city) Du Page County	0.34
Chicago, IL (city) Cook County	0.03

Thai

Top 10 Places Sorted by Number

Place	Number
Chicago, IL (city) Cook County	2,144

Thai

Top 10 Places Sorted by Percent of Asian Population

Place	Percent
Chicago, IL (city) Cook County	1.69

Thai

Top 10 Places Sorted by Percent of Total Population

Place	Percent
Chicago, IL (city) Cook County	0.07

Tongan

Top 10 Places Sorted by Number

Place	Number

No places met population threshold.

Tongan

Top 10 Places Sorted by Percent of Asian Population

Place	Percent

No places met population threshold.

Tongan

Top 10 Places Sorted by Percent of Total Population

Place	Percent

No places met population threshold.

Vietnamese

Top 10 Places Sorted by Number

Place	Number
Chicago, IL (city) Cook County	8,179
Glendale Heights, IL (village) Du Page County	799
Aurora, IL (city) Kane County	490
Carol Stream, IL (village) Du Page County	472
Champaign, IL (city) Champaign County	430
Rockford, IL (city) Winnebago County	403
Wheaton, IL (city) Du Page County	382

Vietnamese

Top 10 Places Sorted by Percent of Asian Population

Place	Percent
Wheaton, IL (city) Du Page County	14.09
Rockford, IL (city) Winnebago County	13.59
Glendale Heights, IL (village) Du Page County	12.69
Carol Stream, IL (village) Du Page County	11.59
Aurora, IL (city) Kane County	11.14
Champaign, IL (city) Champaign County	9.34
Chicago, IL (city) Cook County	6.44

Vietnamese

Top 10 Places Sorted by Percent of Total Population

Place	Percent
Glendale Heights, IL (village) Du Page County	2.52
Carol Stream, IL (village) Du Page County	1.19
Wheaton, IL (city) Du Page County	0.69
Champaign, IL (city) Champaign County	0.63
Aurora, IL (city) Kane County	0.34
Chicago, IL (city) Cook County	0.28
Rockford, IL (city) Winnebago County	0.27

Median Age

Total Population

Top 10 Places Sorted by Number

Place	Years
Oak Brook, IL (village) Du Page County	50.4
Niles, IL (village) Cook County	46.2
Lincolnwood, IL (village) Cook County	45.4
Morton Grove, IL (village) Cook County	44.6
Westchester, IL (village) Cook County	44.4
Lincolnshire, IL (village) Lake County	44.2
Northbrook, IL (village) Cook County	44.2
Willowbrook, IL (village) Du Page County	43.8
Burr Ridge, IL (village) Du Page County	43.1
Harwood Heights, IL (village) Cook County	42.8

Asian

Top 10 Places Sorted by Number

Place	Years
Oak Brook, IL (village) Du Page County	47.9
Flossmoor, IL (village) Cook County	46.5
Long Grove, IL (village) Lake County	45.9
South Barrington, IL (village) Cook County	44.8
Burr Ridge, IL (village) Du Page County	44.0
Northbrook, IL (village) Cook County	41.4
Lincolnshire, IL (village) Lake County	41.3
River Forest, IL (village) Cook County	40.0
Cicero, IL (town) Cook County	39.4
Highland Park, IL (city) Lake County	39.4

Native Hawaiian and Other Pacific Islander

Top 10 Places Sorted by Number

Place	Years
Chicago, IL (city) Cook County	28.3

Asian Indian

Top 10 Places Sorted by Number

Place	Years
Oak Brook, IL (village) Du Page County	47.2
South Barrington, IL (village) Cook County	45.3
Orland Park, IL (village) Cook County	40.7
Glenview, IL (village) Cook County	39.0
Burr Ridge, IL (village) Du Page County	38.0
Rockford, IL (city) Winnebago County	36.8
Lincolnwood, IL (village) Cook County	35.3
Darien, IL (city) Du Page County	35.2
Gurnee, IL (village) Lake County	34.9
Downers Grove, IL (village) Du Page County	34.2

Bangladeshi

Top 10 Places Sorted by Number

Place	Years

No places met population threshold.

Cambodian

Top 10 Places Sorted by Number

Place	Years
Chicago, IL (city) Cook County	27.6

Chinese (except Taiwanese)

Top 10 Places Sorted by Number

Place	Years
Glenview, IL (village) Cook County	44.4
Westmont, IL (village) Du Page County	44.2
Northbrook, IL (village) Cook County	42.3
Elk Grove Village, IL (village) Cook County	40.6
Des Plaines, IL (city) Cook County	38.5
Buffalo Grove, IL (village) Lake County	38.2
Downers Grove, IL (village) Du Page County	37.6
Arlington Heights, IL (village) Cook County	37.0
Skokie, IL (village) Cook County	36.9
Wilmette, IL (village) Cook County	36.6

Fijian

Top 10 Places Sorted by Number

Place	Years

No places met population threshold.

Filipino

Top 10 Places Sorted by Number

Place	Years
Westmont, IL (village) Du Page County	43.1
Lincolnwood, IL (village) Cook County	42.9
Downers Grove, IL (village) Du Page County	41.3
Cicero, IL (town) Cook County	41.0
Addison, IL (village) Du Page County	39.6
Darien, IL (city) Du Page County	39.1
Morton Grove, IL (village) Cook County	37.8

Notes: Please refer to the User's Guide for an explanation of data; tables reflect only those areas that meet Summary File 4 population thresholds, therefore there may be less than 10 places listed

Place	Years
Tinley Park, IL (village) Cook County	37.6
Buffalo Grove, IL (village) Lake County	37.3
Schaumburg, IL (village) Cook County	37.0

Guamanian or Chamorro
Top 10 Places Sorted by Number

Place	Years

No places met population threshold.

Hawaiian, Native
Top 10 Places Sorted by Number

Place	Years

No places met population threshold.

Hmong
Top 10 Places Sorted by Number

Place	Years

No places met population threshold.

Indonesian
Top 10 Places Sorted by Number

Place	Years

No places met population threshold.

Japanese
Top 10 Places Sorted by Number

Place	Years
Chicago, IL (city) Cook County	45.1
Mount Prospect, IL (village) Cook County	40.6
Wilmette, IL (village) Cook County	37.7
Glenview, IL (village) Cook County	36.9
Arlington Heights, IL (village) Cook County	36.4
Buffalo Grove, IL (village) Lake County	36.2
Elk Grove Village, IL (village) Cook County	34.6
Hoffman Estates, IL (village) Cook County	32.9
Evanston, IL (city) Cook County	32.5
Schaumburg, IL (village) Cook County	31.5

Korean
Top 10 Places Sorted by Number

Place	Years
Lincolnwood, IL (village) Cook County	42.3
Niles, IL (village) Cook County	42.0
Northbrook, IL (village) Cook County	41.7
Morton Grove, IL (village) Cook County	40.8
Wilmette, IL (village) Cook County	38.9
Skokie, IL (village) Cook County	37.4
Naperville, IL (city) Du Page County	36.6
Mount Prospect, IL (village) Cook County	35.5
Glenview, IL (village) Cook County	35.1
Vernon Hills, IL (village) Lake County	34.2

Laotian
Top 10 Places Sorted by Number

Place	Years
Elgin, IL (city) Kane County	29.8
Rockford, IL (city) Winnebago County	28.7

Malaysian
Top 10 Places Sorted by Number

Place	Years

No places met population threshold.

Pakistani
Top 10 Places Sorted by Number

Place	Years
Skokie, IL (village) Cook County	30.6
Chicago, IL (city) Cook County	30.5

Samoan
Top 10 Places Sorted by Number

Place	Years

No places met population threshold.

Sri Lankan
Top 10 Places Sorted by Number

Place	Years

No places met population threshold.

Taiwanese
Top 10 Places Sorted by Number

Place	Years
Naperville, IL (city) Du Page County	40.5
Chicago, IL (city) Cook County	26.4

Thai
Top 10 Places Sorted by Number

Place	Years
Chicago, IL (city) Cook County	30.8

Tongan
Top 10 Places Sorted by Number

Place	Years

No places met population threshold.

Vietnamese
Top 10 Places Sorted by Number

Place	Years
Glendale Heights, IL (village) Du Page County	31.4
Champaign, IL (city) Champaign County	28.9
Chicago, IL (city) Cook County	28.8
Rockford, IL (city) Winnebago County	28.8
Carol Stream, IL (village) Du Page County	28.6
Aurora, IL (city) Kane County	27.7
Wheaton, IL (city) Du Page County	27.2

Average Household Size

Total Population
Top 10 Places Sorted by Number

Place	Number
Cicero, IL (town) Cook County	3.69
West Chicago, IL (city) Du Page County	3.65
Carpentersville, IL (village) Kane County	3.49
Round Lake Beach, IL (village) Lake County	3.47
Hanover Park, IL (village) Cook County	3.40
Long Grove, IL (village) Lake County	3.24
South Barrington, IL (village) Cook County	3.24
Bolingbrook, IL (village) Will County	3.23
Lake Zurich, IL (village) Lake County	3.17
Mundelein, IL (village) Lake County	3.11

Asian
Top 10 Places Sorted by Number

Place	Number
South Elgin, IL (village) Kane County	4.77
Villa Park, IL (village) Du Page County	4.24
Lincolnwood, IL (village) Cook County	3.99
Carpentersville, IL (village) Kane County	3.93
Schiller Park, IL (village) Cook County	3.92
Des Plaines, IL (city) Cook County	3.83
Burbank, IL (city) Cook County	3.77
Bolingbrook, IL (village) Will County	3.76
Bartlett, IL (village) Du Page County	3.75
Orland Park, IL (village) Cook County	3.74

Native Hawaiian and Other Pacific Islander
Top 10 Places Sorted by Number

Place	Number
Chicago, IL (city) Cook County	3.32

Asian Indian
Top 10 Places Sorted by Number

Place	Number
Des Plaines, IL (city) Cook County	4.66
Lincolnwood, IL (village) Cook County	4.37
Bloomingdale, IL (village) Du Page County	4.33
Morton Grove, IL (village) Cook County	4.30
Bartlett, IL (village) Du Page County	4.28
Niles, IL (village) Cook County	4.13
Burr Ridge, IL (village) Du Page County	4.10
Orland Park, IL (village) Cook County	4.09
Bolingbrook, IL (village) Will County	4.07
Glendale Heights, IL (village) Du Page County	4.03

Bangladeshi
Top 10 Places Sorted by Number

Place	Number

No places met population threshold.

Cambodian
Top 10 Places Sorted by Number

Place	Number
Chicago, IL (city) Cook County	4.54

Chinese (except Taiwanese)
Top 10 Places Sorted by Number

Place	Number
Mundelein, IL (village) Lake County	3.53
Naperville, IL (city) Du Page County	3.39
Lisle, IL (village) Du Page County	3.22
Vernon Hills, IL (village) Lake County	3.21
Northbrook, IL (village) Cook County	3.18
Wilmette, IL (village) Cook County	3.11
Hoffman Estates, IL (village) Cook County	3.02
Des Plaines, IL (city) Cook County	3.01
Downers Grove, IL (village) Du Page County	2.96
Skokie, IL (village) Cook County	2.92

Fijian
Top 10 Places Sorted by Number

Place	Number

No places met population threshold.

Filipino
Top 10 Places Sorted by Number

Place	Number
North Chicago, IL (city) Lake County	4.48
Park City, IL (city) Lake County	4.43
Gurnee, IL (village) Lake County	4.32
Lincolnwood, IL (village) Cook County	4.14
Addison, IL (village) Du Page County	4.12
Orland Park, IL (village) Cook County	4.12
Carol Stream, IL (village) Du Page County	3.97
Des Plaines, IL (city) Cook County	3.91
Skokie, IL (village) Cook County	3.84
Mundelein, IL (village) Lake County	3.83

Guamanian or Chamorro
Top 10 Places Sorted by Number

Place	Number

No places met population threshold.

Hawaiian, Native
Top 10 Places Sorted by Number

Place	Number

No places met population threshold.

Notes: Please refer to the User's Guide for an explanation of data; tables reflect only those areas that meet Summary File 4 population thresholds, therefore there may be less than 10 places listed

Hmong
Top 10 Places Sorted by Number

Place	Number
No places met population threshold.	

Indonesian
Top 10 Places Sorted by Number

Place	Number
No places met population threshold.	

Japanese
Top 10 Places Sorted by Number

Place	Number
Buffalo Grove, IL (village) Lake County	3.16
Elk Grove Village, IL (village) Cook County	3.13
Hoffman Estates, IL (village) Cook County	3.00
Wilmette, IL (village) Cook County	2.95
Mount Prospect, IL (village) Cook County	2.68
Schaumburg, IL (village) Cook County	2.46
Glenview, IL (village) Cook County	2.41
Evanston, IL (city) Cook County	2.20
Arlington Heights, IL (village) Cook County	2.02
Chicago, IL (city) Cook County	1.85

Korean
Top 10 Places Sorted by Number

Place	Number
Buffalo Grove, IL (village) Lake County	3.73
Lincolnwood, IL (village) Cook County	3.67
Naperville, IL (city) Du Page County	3.55
Glenview, IL (village) Cook County	3.48
Hoffman Estates, IL (village) Cook County	3.47
Morton Grove, IL (village) Cook County	3.39
Northbrook, IL (village) Cook County	3.36
Wilmette, IL (village) Cook County	3.31
Arlington Heights, IL (village) Cook County	3.30
Mount Prospect, IL (village) Cook County	3.29

Laotian
Top 10 Places Sorted by Number

Place	Number
Elgin, IL (city) Kane County	4.50
Rockford, IL (city) Winnebago County	3.75

Malaysian
Top 10 Places Sorted by Number

Place	Number
No places met population threshold.	

Pakistani
Top 10 Places Sorted by Number

Place	Number
Skokie, IL (village) Cook County	4.04
Chicago, IL (city) Cook County	3.57

Samoan
Top 10 Places Sorted by Number

Place	Number
No places met population threshold.	

Sri Lankan
Top 10 Places Sorted by Number

Place	Number
No places met population threshold.	

Taiwanese
Top 10 Places Sorted by Number

Place	Number
Naperville, IL (city) Du Page County	3.36
Chicago, IL (city) Cook County	1.60

Thai
Top 10 Places Sorted by Number

Place	Number
Chicago, IL (city) Cook County	2.30

Tongan
Top 10 Places Sorted by Number

Place	Number
No places met population threshold.	

Vietnamese
Top 10 Places Sorted by Number

Place	Number
Aurora, IL (city) Kane County	4.32
Carol Stream, IL (village) Du Page County	4.22
Wheaton, IL (city) Du Page County	3.73
Chicago, IL (city) Cook County	3.49
Glendale Heights, IL (village) Du Page County	3.47
Champaign, IL (city) Champaign County	3.32
Rockford, IL (city) Winnebago County	3.22

Language Spoken at Home: English Only

Total Populations 5 Years and Over Who Speak English-Only at Home
Top 10 Places Sorted by Number

Place	Number
Chicago, IL (city) Cook County	1,726,905
Rockford, IL (city) Winnebago County	119,262
Springfield, IL (city) Sangamon County	100,722
Naperville, IL (city) Du Page County	99,729
Peoria, IL (city) Peoria County	96,641
Aurora, IL (city) Kane County	83,953
Joliet, IL (city) Will County	78,217
Decatur, IL (city) Macon County	73,838
Arlington Heights, IL (village) Cook County	58,797
Evanston, IL (city) Cook County	57,304

Total Populations 5 Years and Over Who Speak English-Only at Home
Top 10 Places Sorted by Percent

Place	Percent
Decatur, IL (city) Macon County	96.38
Springfield, IL (city) Sangamon County	95.92
Normal, IL (town) McLean County	93.68
Danville, IL (city) Vermilion County	93.62
O'Fallon, IL (city) Saint Clair County	93.36
Winnetka, IL (village) Cook County	93.06
Peoria, IL (city) Peoria County	92.43
Bloomington, IL (city) McLean County	92.04
Macomb, IL (city) McDonough County	91.20
Algonquin, IL (village) McHenry County	90.91

Asians 5 Years and Over Who Speak English-Only at Home
Top 10 Places Sorted by Number

Place	Number
Chicago, IL (city) Cook County	20,070
Skokie, IL (village) Cook County	1,870
Naperville, IL (city) Du Page County	1,570
Evanston, IL (city) Cook County	1,110
Champaign, IL (city) Champaign County	910
Arlington Heights, IL (village) Cook County	880
Schaumburg, IL (village) Cook County	817
Urbana, IL (city) Champaign County	810
Morton Grove, IL (village) Cook County	801
Glenview, IL (village) Cook County	730

Asians 5 Years and Over Who Speak English-Only at Home
Top 10 Places Sorted by Percent

Place	Percent
St. Charles, IL (city) Kane County	44.60
Flossmoor, IL (village) Cook County	43.69
Winnetka, IL (village) Cook County	41.12
Crystal Lake, IL (city) McHenry County	37.90
Lake Forest, IL (city) Lake County	35.48
Willowbrook, IL (village) Du Page County	34.98
Lincolnshire, IL (village) Lake County	33.78
North Chicago, IL (city) Lake County	33.36
DeKalb, IL (city) De Kalb County	32.65
Decatur, IL (city) Macon County	31.88

Native Hawaiian and Other Pacific Islanders 5 Years and Over Who Speak English-Only at Home
Top 10 Places Sorted by Number

Place	Number
Chicago, IL (city) Cook County	293

Native Hawaiian and Other Pacific Islanders 5 Years and Over Who Speak English-Only at Home
Top 10 Places Sorted by Percent

Place	Percent
Chicago, IL (city) Cook County	29.54

Asian Indians 5 Years and Over Who Speak English-Only at Home
Top 10 Places Sorted by Number

Place	Number
Chicago, IL (city) Cook County	3,627
Naperville, IL (city) Du Page County	621
Skokie, IL (village) Cook County	466
Evanston, IL (city) Cook County	408
Schaumburg, IL (village) Cook County	289
Downers Grove, IL (village) Du Page County	267
Hanover Park, IL (village) Cook County	237
Urbana, IL (city) Champaign County	235
Champaign, IL (city) Champaign County	229
Glendale Heights, IL (village) Du Page County	228

Asian Indians 5 Years and Over Who Speak English-Only at Home
Top 10 Places Sorted by Percent

Place	Percent
Elgin, IL (city) Kane County	36.59
Evanston, IL (city) Cook County	35.76
DeKalb, IL (city) De Kalb County	35.19
Orland Park, IL (village) Cook County	25.62
Springfield, IL (city) Sangamon County	24.64
Urbana, IL (city) Champaign County	24.33
Rockford, IL (city) Winnebago County	23.43
Champaign, IL (city) Champaign County	22.39
Oak Brook, IL (village) Du Page County	21.89
Downers Grove, IL (village) Du Page County	21.55

Bangladeshis 5 Years and Over Who Speak English-Only at Home
Top 10 Places Sorted by Number

Place	Number
No places met population threshold.	

Bangladeshis 5 Years and Over Who Speak English-Only at Home
Top 10 Places Sorted by Percent

Place	Percent
No places met population threshold.	

Notes: Please refer to the User's Guide for an explanation of data; tables reflect only those areas that meet Summary File 4 population thresholds, therefore there may be less than 10 places listed

Cambodians 5 Years and Over Who Speak English-Only at Home
Top 10 Places Sorted by Number

Place	Number
Chicago, IL (city) Cook County	175

Cambodians 5 Years and Over Who Speak English-Only at Home
Top 10 Places Sorted by Percent

Place	Percent
Chicago, IL (city) Cook County	9.74

Chinese (except Taiwanese) 5 Years and Over Who Speak English-Only at Home
Top 10 Places Sorted by Number

Place	Number
Chicago, IL (city) Cook County	2,929
Naperville, IL (city) Du Page County	383
Skokie, IL (village) Cook County	220
Champaign, IL (city) Champaign County	170
Evanston, IL (city) Cook County	170
Glenview, IL (village) Cook County	149
Oak Park, IL (village) Cook County	134
Arlington Heights, IL (village) Cook County	117
Urbana, IL (city) Champaign County	113
Buffalo Grove, IL (village) Lake County	105

Chinese (except Taiwanese) 5 Years and Over Who Speak English-Only at Home
Top 10 Places Sorted by Percent

Place	Percent
Oak Park, IL (village) Cook County	34.81
Arlington Heights, IL (village) Cook County	24.02
Glenview, IL (village) Cook County	21.75
Elk Grove Village, IL (village) Cook County	20.77
Buffalo Grove, IL (village) Lake County	19.09
Gurnee, IL (village) Lake County	16.62
Champaign, IL (city) Champaign County	16.54
Des Plaines, IL (city) Cook County	16.45
Northbrook, IL (village) Cook County	15.68
Evanston, IL (city) Cook County	14.96

Fijians 5 Years and Over Who Speak English-Only at Home
Top 10 Places Sorted by Number

Place	Number

No places met population threshold.

Fijians 5 Years and Over Who Speak English-Only at Home
Top 10 Places Sorted by Percent

Place	Percent

No places met population threshold.

Filipinos 5 Years and Over Who Speak English-Only at Home
Top 10 Places Sorted by Number

Place	Number
Chicago, IL (city) Cook County	6,039
Skokie, IL (village) Cook County	627
Morton Grove, IL (village) Cook County	420
Carol Stream, IL (village) Du Page County	354
Glendale Heights, IL (village) Du Page County	352
Woodridge, IL (village) Du Page County	317
Des Plaines, IL (city) Cook County	292
Orland Park, IL (village) Cook County	288
Hanover Park, IL (village) Cook County	278
Waukegan, IL (city) Lake County	251

Filipinos 5 Years and Over Who Speak English-Only at Home
Top 10 Places Sorted by Percent

Place	Percent
Orland Park, IL (village) Cook County	44.72
Buffalo Grove, IL (village) Lake County	40.84
Naperville, IL (city) Du Page County	39.61
Evanston, IL (city) Cook County	34.95
Carol Stream, IL (village) Du Page County	34.20
Downers Grove, IL (village) Du Page County	33.84
Des Plaines, IL (city) Cook County	32.27
Glenview, IL (village) Cook County	31.45
Lombard, IL (village) Du Page County	31.18
North Chicago, IL (city) Lake County	30.74

Guamanian or Chamorros 5 Years and Over Who Speak English-Only at Home
Top 10 Places Sorted by Number

Place	Number

No places met population threshold.

Guamanian or Chamorros 5 Years and Over Who Speak English-Only at Home
Top 10 Places Sorted by Percent

Place	Percent

No places met population threshold.

Hawaiian, Natives 5 Years and Over Who Speak English-Only at Home
Top 10 Places Sorted by Number

Place	Number

No places met population threshold.

Hawaiian, Natives 5 Years and Over Who Speak English-Only at Home
Top 10 Places Sorted by Percent

Place	Percent

No places met population threshold.

Hmongs 5 Years and Over Who Speak English-Only at Home
Top 10 Places Sorted by Number

Place	Number

No places met population threshold.

Hmongs 5 Years and Over Who Speak English-Only at Home
Top 10 Places Sorted by Percent

Place	Percent

No places met population threshold.

Indonesians 5 Years and Over Who Speak English-Only at Home
Top 10 Places Sorted by Number

Place	Number

No places met population threshold.

Indonesians 5 Years and Over Who Speak English-Only at Home
Top 10 Places Sorted by Percent

Place	Percent

No places met population threshold.

Japanese 5 Years and Over Who Speak English-Only at Home
Top 10 Places Sorted by Number

Place	Number
Chicago, IL (city) Cook County	3,129
Arlington Heights, IL (village) Cook County	175
Evanston, IL (city) Cook County	137
Mount Prospect, IL (village) Cook County	112
Schaumburg, IL (village) Cook County	105
Glenview, IL (village) Cook County	102
Wilmette, IL (village) Cook County	99
Buffalo Grove, IL (village) Lake County	73
Elk Grove Village, IL (village) Cook County	49
Hoffman Estates, IL (village) Cook County	36

Japanese 5 Years and Over Who Speak English-Only at Home
Top 10 Places Sorted by Percent

Place	Percent
Chicago, IL (city) Cook County	52.48
Evanston, IL (city) Cook County	38.16
Glenview, IL (village) Cook County	34.00
Wilmette, IL (village) Cook County	29.73
Mount Prospect, IL (village) Cook County	26.73
Arlington Heights, IL (village) Cook County	18.82
Schaumburg, IL (village) Cook County	12.50
Buffalo Grove, IL (village) Lake County	12.46
Elk Grove Village, IL (village) Cook County	9.04
Hoffman Estates, IL (village) Cook County	4.74

Koreans 5 Years and Over Who Speak English-Only at Home
Top 10 Places Sorted by Number

Place	Number
Chicago, IL (city) Cook County	2,166
Champaign, IL (city) Champaign County	176
Skokie, IL (village) Cook County	168
Evanston, IL (city) Cook County	155
Glenview, IL (village) Cook County	155
Naperville, IL (city) Du Page County	144
Urbana, IL (city) Champaign County	120
Arlington Heights, IL (village) Cook County	107
Buffalo Grove, IL (village) Lake County	102
Schaumburg, IL (village) Cook County	102

Koreans 5 Years and Over Who Speak English-Only at Home
Top 10 Places Sorted by Percent

Place	Percent
Evanston, IL (city) Cook County	24.60
Champaign, IL (city) Champaign County	20.71
Chicago, IL (city) Cook County	17.86
Naperville, IL (city) Du Page County	17.50
Arlington Heights, IL (village) Cook County	14.70
Lincolnwood, IL (village) Cook County	11.40
Urbana, IL (city) Champaign County	10.75
Vernon Hills, IL (village) Lake County	10.45
Glenview, IL (village) Cook County	10.29
Buffalo Grove, IL (village) Lake County	9.76

Laotians 5 Years and Over Who Speak English-Only at Home
Top 10 Places Sorted by Number

Place	Number
Rockford, IL (city) Winnebago County	22
Elgin, IL (city) Kane County	8

Laotians 5 Years and Over Who Speak English-Only at Home
Top 10 Places Sorted by Percent

Place	Percent
Rockford, IL (city) Winnebago County	2.62
Elgin, IL (city) Kane County	1.01

Malaysians 5 Years and Over Who Speak English-Only at Home
Top 10 Places Sorted by Number

Place	Number

No places met population threshold.

Notes: Please refer to the User's Guide for an explanation of data; tables reflect only those areas that meet Summary File 4 population thresholds, therefore there may be less than 10 places listed

Malaysians 5 Years and Over Who Speak English-Only at Home

Top 10 Places Sorted by Percent

Place	Percent
No places met population threshold.	

Pakistanis 5 Years and Over Who Speak English-Only at Home

Top 10 Places Sorted by Number

Place	Number
Chicago, IL (city) Cook County	268
Skokie, IL (village) Cook County	52

Pakistanis 5 Years and Over Who Speak English-Only at Home

Top 10 Places Sorted by Percent

Place	Percent
Skokie, IL (village) Cook County	11.61
Chicago, IL (city) Cook County	4.53

Samoans 5 Years and Over Who Speak English-Only at Home

Top 10 Places Sorted by Number

Place	Number
No places met population threshold.	

Samoans 5 Years and Over Who Speak English-Only at Home

Top 10 Places Sorted by Percent

Place	Percent
No places met population threshold.	

Sri Lankans 5 Years and Over Who Speak English-Only at Home

Top 10 Places Sorted by Number

Place	Number
No places met population threshold.	

Sri Lankans 5 Years and Over Who Speak English-Only at Home

Top 10 Places Sorted by Percent

Place	Percent
No places met population threshold.	

Taiwanese 5 Years and Over Who Speak English-Only at Home

Top 10 Places Sorted by Number

Place	Number
Chicago, IL (city) Cook County	162
Naperville, IL (city) Du Page County	28

Taiwanese 5 Years and Over Who Speak English-Only at Home

Top 10 Places Sorted by Percent

Place	Percent
Chicago, IL (city) Cook County	20.88
Naperville, IL (city) Du Page County	6.67

Thais 5 Years and Over Who Speak English-Only at Home

Top 10 Places Sorted by Number

Place	Number
Chicago, IL (city) Cook County	216

Thais 5 Years and Over Who Speak English-Only at Home

Top 10 Places Sorted by Percent

Place	Percent
Chicago, IL (city) Cook County	10.47

Tongans 5 Years and Over Who Speak English-Only at Home

Top 10 Places Sorted by Number

Place	Number
No places met population threshold.	

Tongans 5 Years and Over Who Speak English-Only at Home

Top 10 Places Sorted by Percent

Place	Percent
No places met population threshold.	

Vietnamese 5 Years and Over Who Speak English-Only at Home

Top 10 Places Sorted by Number

Place	Number
Chicago, IL (city) Cook County	467
Carol Stream, IL (village) Du Page County	67
Champaign, IL (city) Champaign County	14
Glendale Heights, IL (village) Du Page County	7
Rockford, IL (city) Winnebago County	7
Wheaton, IL (city) Du Page County	5
Aurora, IL (city) Kane County	4

Vietnamese 5 Years and Over Who Speak English-Only at Home

Top 10 Places Sorted by Percent

Place	Percent
Carol Stream, IL (village) Du Page County	17.49
Chicago, IL (city) Cook County	6.22
Champaign, IL (city) Champaign County	3.43
Rockford, IL (city) Winnebago County	1.76
Wheaton, IL (city) Du Page County	1.48
Glendale Heights, IL (village) Du Page County	0.95
Aurora, IL (city) Kane County	0.88

Foreign Born

Total Population

Top 10 Places Sorted by Number

Place	Number
Chicago, IL (city) Cook County	628,903
Cicero, IL (town) Cook County	37,343
Aurora, IL (city) Kane County	30,858
Waukegan, IL (city) Lake County	26,556
Skokie, IL (village) Cook County	23,437
Elgin, IL (city) Kane County	22,258
Mount Prospect, IL (village) Cook County	15,159
Naperville, IL (city) Du Page County	14,963
Schaumburg, IL (village) Cook County	14,262
Palatine, IL (village) Cook County	14,249

Total Population

Top 10 Places Sorted by Percent

Place	Percent
Cicero, IL (town) Cook County	43.62
Schiller Park, IL (village) Cook County	39.07
Skokie, IL (village) Cook County	37.01
Prospect Heights, IL (city) Cook County	36.48
Melrose Park, IL (village) Cook County	35.31
Addison, IL (village) Du Page County	34.26
Lincolnwood, IL (village) Cook County	34.11
West Chicago, IL (city) Du Page County	34.07
Harwood Heights, IL (village) Cook County	34.05
Niles, IL (village) Cook County	33.65

Asian

Top 10 Places Sorted by Number

Place	Number
Chicago, IL (city) Cook County	93,435
Skokie, IL (village) Cook County	9,557
Naperville, IL (city) Du Page County	8,003
Schaumburg, IL (village) Cook County	7,914
Hoffman Estates, IL (village) Cook County	5,715
Mount Prospect, IL (village) Cook County	4,956
Glendale Heights, IL (village) Du Page County	4,699
Palatine, IL (village) Cook County	3,996
Arlington Heights, IL (village) Cook County	3,641
Urbana, IL (city) Champaign County	3,446

Asian

Top 10 Places Sorted by Percent

Place	Percent
Forest Park, IL (village) Cook County	86.74
Carbondale, IL (city) Jackson County	83.76
Macomb, IL (city) McDonough County	81.78
Harwood Heights, IL (village) Cook County	80.60
Park City, IL (city) Lake County	80.36
Westmont, IL (village) Du Page County	79.34
West Chicago, IL (city) Du Page County	79.17
Bloomington, IL (city) McLean County	78.69
Schiller Park, IL (village) Cook County	78.32
Glen Ellyn, IL (village) Du Page County	78.30

Native Hawaiian and Other Pacific Islander

Top 10 Places Sorted by Number

Place	Number
Chicago, IL (city) Cook County	463

Native Hawaiian and Other Pacific Islander

Top 10 Places Sorted by Percent

Place	Percent
Chicago, IL (city) Cook County	43.47

Asian Indian

Top 10 Places Sorted by Number

Place	Number
Chicago, IL (city) Cook County	18,090
Schaumburg, IL (village) Cook County	3,569
Naperville, IL (city) Du Page County	3,341
Skokie, IL (village) Cook County	2,628
Mount Prospect, IL (village) Cook County	2,558
Hoffman Estates, IL (village) Cook County	2,132
Glendale Heights, IL (village) Du Page County	2,042
Palatine, IL (village) Cook County	1,767
Des Plaines, IL (city) Cook County	1,524
Hanover Park, IL (village) Cook County	1,385

Asian Indian

Top 10 Places Sorted by Percent

Place	Percent
Bloomington, IL (city) McLean County	87.01
Arlington Heights, IL (village) Cook County	85.19
Elgin, IL (city) Kane County	81.36
Mount Prospect, IL (village) Cook County	81.08
Wheaton, IL (city) Du Page County	80.63
Peoria, IL (city) Peoria County	80.57
Westmont, IL (village) Du Page County	80.25
Palatine, IL (village) Cook County	79.95
Glen Ellyn, IL (village) Du Page County	79.80
Addison, IL (village) Du Page County	79.72

Bangladeshi

Top 10 Places Sorted by Number

Place	Number
No places met population threshold.	

Notes: Please refer to the User's Guide for an explanation of data; tables reflect only those areas that meet Summary File 4 population thresholds, therefore there may be less than 10 places listed

Bangladeshi
Top 10 Places Sorted by Percent

Place	Percent

No places met population threshold.

Cambodian
Top 10 Places Sorted by Number

Place	Number
Chicago, IL (city) Cook County	1,379

Cambodian
Top 10 Places Sorted by Percent

Place	Percent
Chicago, IL (city) Cook County	72.16

Chinese (except Taiwanese)
Top 10 Places Sorted by Number

Place	Number
Chicago, IL (city) Cook County	23,501
Naperville, IL (city) Du Page County	2,749
Urbana, IL (city) Champaign County	1,295
Skokie, IL (village) Cook County	1,156
Schaumburg, IL (village) Cook County	1,024
Evanston, IL (city) Cook County	770
Champaign, IL (city) Champaign County	755
Peoria, IL (city) Peoria County	648
Hoffman Estates, IL (village) Cook County	575
Palatine, IL (village) Cook County	552

Chinese (except Taiwanese)
Top 10 Places Sorted by Percent

Place	Percent
Westmont, IL (village) Du Page County	89.56
Palatine, IL (village) Cook County	80.35
Peoria, IL (city) Peoria County	80.10
Gurnee, IL (village) Lake County	77.38
Wilmette, IL (village) Cook County	76.94
Schaumburg, IL (village) Cook County	76.65
Chicago, IL (city) Cook County	74.81
Lisle, IL (village) Du Page County	73.57
Aurora, IL (city) Kane County	72.86
Mount Prospect, IL (village) Cook County	72.57

Fijian
Top 10 Places Sorted by Number

Place	Number

No places met population threshold.

Fijian
Top 10 Places Sorted by Percent

Place	Percent

No places met population threshold.

Filipino
Top 10 Places Sorted by Number

Place	Number
Chicago, IL (city) Cook County	20,755
Skokie, IL (village) Cook County	2,258
Glendale Heights, IL (village) Du Page County	1,294
Morton Grove, IL (village) Cook County	1,271
Waukegan, IL (city) Lake County	1,117
Bolingbrook, IL (village) Will County	966
Streamwood, IL (village) Cook County	929
Hanover Park, IL (village) Cook County	858
Woodridge, IL (village) Du Page County	764
Schaumburg, IL (village) Cook County	721

Filipino
Top 10 Places Sorted by Percent

Place	Percent
Cicero, IL (town) Cook County	83.77
Bolingbrook, IL (village) Will County	82.85
Park City, IL (city) Lake County	81.10
Palatine, IL (village) Cook County	79.44
Arlington Heights, IL (village) Cook County	78.96
Streamwood, IL (village) Cook County	78.53
Schaumburg, IL (village) Cook County	77.86
Berwyn, IL (city) Cook County	77.28
Aurora, IL (city) Kane County	77.04
Addison, IL (village) Du Page County	76.10

Guamanian or Chamorro
Top 10 Places Sorted by Number

Place	Number

No places met population threshold.

Guamanian or Chamorro
Top 10 Places Sorted by Percent

Place	Percent

No places met population threshold.

Hawaiian, Native
Top 10 Places Sorted by Number

Place	Number

No places met population threshold.

Hawaiian, Native
Top 10 Places Sorted by Percent

Place	Percent

No places met population threshold.

Hmong
Top 10 Places Sorted by Number

Place	Number

No places met population threshold.

Hmong
Top 10 Places Sorted by Percent

Place	Percent

No places met population threshold.

Indonesian
Top 10 Places Sorted by Number

Place	Number

No places met population threshold.

Indonesian
Top 10 Places Sorted by Percent

Place	Percent

No places met population threshold.

Japanese
Top 10 Places Sorted by Number

Place	Number
Chicago, IL (city) Cook County	2,120
Schaumburg, IL (village) Cook County	774
Arlington Heights, IL (village) Cook County	764
Hoffman Estates, IL (village) Cook County	737
Buffalo Grove, IL (village) Lake County	536
Elk Grove Village, IL (village) Cook County	505
Mount Prospect, IL (village) Cook County	286
Evanston, IL (city) Cook County	245
Wilmette, IL (village) Cook County	235
Glenview, IL (village) Cook County	200

Japanese
Top 10 Places Sorted by Percent

Place	Percent
Hoffman Estates, IL (village) Cook County	88.16
Buffalo Grove, IL (village) Lake County	87.73
Elk Grove Village, IL (village) Cook County	82.79
Schaumburg, IL (village) Cook County	82.34
Arlington Heights, IL (village) Cook County	76.86
Wilmette, IL (village) Cook County	67.92
Evanston, IL (city) Cook County	65.16
Mount Prospect, IL (village) Cook County	64.27
Glenview, IL (village) Cook County	63.69
Chicago, IL (city) Cook County	35.08

Korean
Top 10 Places Sorted by Number

Place	Number
Chicago, IL (city) Cook County	10,011
Skokie, IL (village) Cook County	2,008
Schaumburg, IL (village) Cook County	1,352
Northbrook, IL (village) Cook County	1,164
Glenview, IL (village) Cook County	1,084
Mount Prospect, IL (village) Cook County	1,084
Hoffman Estates, IL (village) Cook County	1,074
Niles, IL (village) Cook County	861
Urbana, IL (city) Champaign County	800
Buffalo Grove, IL (village) Lake County	742

Korean
Top 10 Places Sorted by Percent

Place	Percent
Niles, IL (village) Cook County	85.67
Chicago, IL (city) Cook County	79.60
Skokie, IL (village) Cook County	79.56
Arlington Heights, IL (village) Cook County	78.77
Schaumburg, IL (village) Cook County	76.17
Hoffman Estates, IL (village) Cook County	75.32
Northbrook, IL (village) Cook County	75.19
Mount Prospect, IL (village) Cook County	74.97
Vernon Hills, IL (village) Lake County	73.41
Naperville, IL (city) Du Page County	73.33

Laotian
Top 10 Places Sorted by Number

Place	Number
Elgin, IL (city) Kane County	675
Rockford, IL (city) Winnebago County	658

Laotian
Top 10 Places Sorted by Percent

Place	Percent
Elgin, IL (city) Kane County	75.17
Rockford, IL (city) Winnebago County	73.27

Malaysian
Top 10 Places Sorted by Number

Place	Number

No places met population threshold.

Malaysian
Top 10 Places Sorted by Percent

Place	Percent

No places met population threshold.

Pakistani
Top 10 Places Sorted by Number

Place	Number
Chicago, IL (city) Cook County	5,404
Skokie, IL (village) Cook County	359

Pakistani
Top 10 Places Sorted by Percent

Place	Percent
Chicago, IL (city) Cook County	83.95
Skokie, IL (village) Cook County	72.53

Notes: Please refer to the User's Guide for an explanation of data; tables reflect only those areas that meet Summary File 4 population thresholds, therefore there may be less than 10 places listed

Samoan
Top 10 Places Sorted by Number

Place	Number

No places met population threshold.

Samoan
Top 10 Places Sorted by Percent

Place	Percent

No places met population threshold.

Sri Lankan
Top 10 Places Sorted by Number

Place	Number

No places met population threshold.

Sri Lankan
Top 10 Places Sorted by Percent

Place	Percent

No places met population threshold.

Taiwanese
Top 10 Places Sorted by Number

Place	Number
Chicago, IL (city) Cook County	536
Naperville, IL (city) Du Page County	285

Taiwanese
Top 10 Places Sorted by Percent

Place	Percent
Chicago, IL (city) Cook County	69.07
Naperville, IL (city) Du Page County	66.13

Thai
Top 10 Places Sorted by Number

Place	Number
Chicago, IL (city) Cook County	1,637

Thai
Top 10 Places Sorted by Percent

Place	Percent
Chicago, IL (city) Cook County	76.35

Tongan
Top 10 Places Sorted by Number

Place	Number

No places met population threshold.

Tongan
Top 10 Places Sorted by Percent

Place	Percent

No places met population threshold.

Vietnamese
Top 10 Places Sorted by Number

Place	Number
Chicago, IL (city) Cook County	6,533
Glendale Heights, IL (village) Du Page County	631
Rockford, IL (city) Winnebago County	370
Carol Stream, IL (village) Du Page County	327
Champaign, IL (city) Champaign County	327
Aurora, IL (city) Kane County	314
Wheaton, IL (city) Du Page County	305

Vietnamese
Top 10 Places Sorted by Percent

Place	Percent
Rockford, IL (city) Winnebago County	91.81
Chicago, IL (city) Cook County	79.88
Wheaton, IL (city) Du Page County	79.84
Glendale Heights, IL (village) Du Page County	78.97
Champaign, IL (city) Champaign County	76.05
Carol Stream, IL (village) Du Page County	69.28
Aurora, IL (city) Kane County	64.08

Foreign-Born Naturalized Citizens

Total Population
Top 10 Places Sorted by Number

Place	Number
Chicago, IL (city) Cook County	223,984
Skokie, IL (village) Cook County	13,753
Cicero, IL (town) Cook County	10,076
Aurora, IL (city) Kane County	8,494
Des Plaines, IL (city) Cook County	6,827
Waukegan, IL (city) Lake County	6,422
Niles, IL (village) Cook County	6,401
Naperville, IL (city) Du Page County	6,400
Schaumburg, IL (village) Cook County	6,120
Elgin, IL (city) Kane County	6,059

Total Population
Top 10 Places Sorted by Percent

Place	Percent
Lincolnwood, IL (village) Cook County	26.15
Morton Grove, IL (village) Cook County	23.32
Skokie, IL (village) Cook County	21.72
Niles, IL (village) Cook County	21.23
Oak Brook, IL (village) Du Page County	20.38
Harwood Heights, IL (village) Cook County	18.13
South Barrington, IL (village) Cook County	15.85
Schiller Park, IL (village) Cook County	14.86
Addison, IL (village) Du Page County	12.22
Glenview, IL (village) Cook County	12.06

Asian
Top 10 Places Sorted by Number

Place	Number
Chicago, IL (city) Cook County	44,502
Skokie, IL (village) Cook County	5,748
Naperville, IL (city) Du Page County	3,709
Schaumburg, IL (village) Cook County	2,972
Hoffman Estates, IL (village) Cook County	2,489
Morton Grove, IL (village) Cook County	2,134
Glendale Heights, IL (village) Du Page County	2,075
Mount Prospect, IL (village) Cook County	1,831
Hanover Park, IL (village) Cook County	1,827
Glenview, IL (village) Cook County	1,798

Asian
Top 10 Places Sorted by Percent

Place	Percent
Oak Brook, IL (village) Du Page County	61.13
Long Grove, IL (village) Lake County	58.31
Burr Ridge, IL (village) Du Page County	56.98
South Barrington, IL (village) Cook County	56.44
Flossmoor, IL (village) Cook County	56.08
Palos Hills, IL (city) Cook County	50.10
Tinley Park, IL (village) Cook County	49.40
Darien, IL (city) Du Page County	48.30
Orland Park, IL (village) Cook County	46.90
Lincolnshire, IL (village) Lake County	46.75

Native Hawaiian and Other Pacific Islander
Top 10 Places Sorted by Number

Place	Number
Chicago, IL (city) Cook County	221

Native Hawaiian and Other Pacific Islander
Top 10 Places Sorted by Percent

Place	Percent
Chicago, IL (city) Cook County	20.75

Asian Indian
Top 10 Places Sorted by Number

Place	Number
Chicago, IL (city) Cook County	6,121
Skokie, IL (village) Cook County	1,693
Naperville, IL (city) Du Page County	1,297
Schaumburg, IL (village) Cook County	1,075
Hoffman Estates, IL (village) Cook County	904
Glendale Heights, IL (village) Du Page County	786
Des Plaines, IL (city) Cook County	776
Hanover Park, IL (village) Cook County	772
Mount Prospect, IL (village) Cook County	735
Carol Stream, IL (village) Du Page County	647

Asian Indian
Top 10 Places Sorted by Percent

Place	Percent
Oak Brook, IL (village) Du Page County	60.60
South Barrington, IL (village) Cook County	57.66
Burr Ridge, IL (village) Du Page County	53.38
Orland Park, IL (village) Cook County	47.45
Skokie, IL (village) Cook County	44.03
Bloomingdale, IL (village) Du Page County	42.90
Darien, IL (city) Du Page County	42.84
Hanover Park, IL (village) Cook County	40.74
Glenview, IL (village) Cook County	40.19
Des Plaines, IL (city) Cook County	39.73

Bangladeshi
Top 10 Places Sorted by Number

Place	Number

No places met population threshold.

Bangladeshi
Top 10 Places Sorted by Percent

Place	Percent

No places met population threshold.

Cambodian
Top 10 Places Sorted by Number

Place	Number
Chicago, IL (city) Cook County	692

Cambodian
Top 10 Places Sorted by Percent

Place	Percent
Chicago, IL (city) Cook County	36.21

Chinese (except Taiwanese)
Top 10 Places Sorted by Number

Place	Number
Chicago, IL (city) Cook County	11,704
Naperville, IL (city) Du Page County	1,280
Skokie, IL (village) Cook County	532
Schaumburg, IL (village) Cook County	509
Glenview, IL (village) Cook County	370
Hoffman Estates, IL (village) Cook County	299
Northbrook, IL (village) Cook County	295
Peoria, IL (city) Peoria County	261
Palatine, IL (village) Cook County	246
Buffalo Grove, IL (village) Lake County	242

Chinese (except Taiwanese)
Top 10 Places Sorted by Percent

Place	Percent
Northbrook, IL (village) Cook County	58.88
Glenview, IL (village) Cook County	52.86
Elk Grove Village, IL (village) Cook County	50.60
Wilmette, IL (village) Cook County	44.90
Buffalo Grove, IL (village) Lake County	39.87
Schaumburg, IL (village) Cook County	38.10
Chicago, IL (city) Cook County	37.25

Notes: Please refer to the User's Guide for an explanation of data; tables reflect only those areas that meet Summary File 4 population thresholds, therefore there may be less than 10 places listed

Hoffman Estates, IL (village) Cook County	36.42
Des Plaines, IL (city) Cook County	36.09
Palatine, IL (village) Cook County	35.81

Fijian
Top 10 Places Sorted by Number

Place	Number

No places met population threshold.

Fijian
Top 10 Places Sorted by Percent

Place	Percent

No places met population threshold.

Filipino
Top 10 Places Sorted by Number

Place	Number
Chicago, IL (city) Cook County	12,744
Skokie, IL (village) Cook County	1,408
Morton Grove, IL (village) Cook County	879
Waukegan, IL (city) Lake County	650
Bolingbrook, IL (village) Will County	527
Glendale Heights, IL (village) Du Page County	523
Woodridge, IL (village) Du Page County	510
Streamwood, IL (village) Cook County	505
Hanover Park, IL (village) Cook County	479
Carol Stream, IL (village) Du Page County	468

Filipino
Top 10 Places Sorted by Percent

Place	Percent
Arlington Heights, IL (village) Cook County	57.33
Darien, IL (city) Du Page County	56.42
Lombard, IL (village) Du Page County	56.22
Lincolnwood, IL (village) Cook County	54.16
Hoffman Estates, IL (village) Cook County	50.98
Palatine, IL (village) Cook County	50.85
Morton Grove, IL (village) Cook County	49.22
Mount Prospect, IL (village) Cook County	48.65
Schaumburg, IL (village) Cook County	48.38
Cicero, IL (town) Cook County	48.21

Guamanian or Chamorro
Top 10 Places Sorted by Number

Place	Number

No places met population threshold.

Guamanian or Chamorro
Top 10 Places Sorted by Percent

Place	Percent

No places met population threshold.

Hawaiian, Native
Top 10 Places Sorted by Number

Place	Number

No places met population threshold.

Hawaiian, Native
Top 10 Places Sorted by Percent

Place	Percent

No places met population threshold.

Hmong
Top 10 Places Sorted by Number

Place	Number

No places met population threshold.

Hmong
Top 10 Places Sorted by Percent

Place	Percent

No places met population threshold.

Indonesian
Top 10 Places Sorted by Number

Place	Number

No places met population threshold.

Indonesian
Top 10 Places Sorted by Percent

Place	Percent

No places met population threshold.

Japanese
Top 10 Places Sorted by Number

Place	Number
Chicago, IL (city) Cook County	463
Evanston, IL (city) Cook County	39
Buffalo Grove, IL (village) Lake County	36
Arlington Heights, IL (village) Cook County	35
Schaumburg, IL (village) Cook County	35
Glenview, IL (village) Cook County	22
Hoffman Estates, IL (village) Cook County	8
Wilmette, IL (village) Cook County	3
Elk Grove Village, IL (village) Cook County	0
Mount Prospect, IL (village) Cook County	0

Japanese
Top 10 Places Sorted by Percent

Place	Percent
Evanston, IL (city) Cook County	10.37
Chicago, IL (city) Cook County	7.66
Glenview, IL (village) Cook County	7.01
Buffalo Grove, IL (village) Lake County	5.89
Schaumburg, IL (village) Cook County	3.72
Arlington Heights, IL (village) Cook County	3.52
Hoffman Estates, IL (village) Cook County	0.96
Wilmette, IL (village) Cook County	0.87
Elk Grove Village, IL (village) Cook County	0.00
Mount Prospect, IL (village) Cook County	0.00

Korean
Top 10 Places Sorted by Number

Place	Number
Chicago, IL (city) Cook County	5,533
Skokie, IL (village) Cook County	1,241
Glenview, IL (village) Cook County	750
Northbrook, IL (village) Cook County	730
Schaumburg, IL (village) Cook County	637
Mount Prospect, IL (village) Cook County	604
Hoffman Estates, IL (village) Cook County	595
Niles, IL (village) Cook County	450
Morton Grove, IL (village) Cook County	431
Buffalo Grove, IL (village) Lake County	352

Korean
Top 10 Places Sorted by Percent

Place	Percent
Lincolnwood, IL (village) Cook County	51.85
Morton Grove, IL (village) Cook County	49.54
Skokie, IL (village) Cook County	49.17
Northbrook, IL (village) Cook County	47.16
Glenview, IL (village) Cook County	46.96
Niles, IL (village) Cook County	44.78
Chicago, IL (city) Cook County	44.00
Arlington Heights, IL (village) Cook County	42.84
Palatine, IL (village) Cook County	42.43
Wilmette, IL (village) Cook County	42.01

Laotian
Top 10 Places Sorted by Number

Place	Number
Elgin, IL (city) Kane County	405
Rockford, IL (city) Winnebago County	309

Laotian
Top 10 Places Sorted by Percent

Place	Percent
Elgin, IL (city) Kane County	45.10
Rockford, IL (city) Winnebago County	34.41

Malaysian
Top 10 Places Sorted by Number

Place	Number

No places met population threshold.

Malaysian
Top 10 Places Sorted by Percent

Place	Percent

No places met population threshold.

Pakistani
Top 10 Places Sorted by Number

Place	Number
Chicago, IL (city) Cook County	1,802
Skokie, IL (village) Cook County	232

Pakistani
Top 10 Places Sorted by Percent

Place	Percent
Skokie, IL (village) Cook County	46.87
Chicago, IL (city) Cook County	27.99

Samoan
Top 10 Places Sorted by Number

Place	Number

No places met population threshold.

Samoan
Top 10 Places Sorted by Percent

Place	Percent

No places met population threshold.

Sri Lankan
Top 10 Places Sorted by Number

Place	Number

No places met population threshold.

Sri Lankan
Top 10 Places Sorted by Percent

Place	Percent

No places met population threshold.

Taiwanese
Top 10 Places Sorted by Number

Place	Number
Chicago, IL (city) Cook County	239
Naperville, IL (city) Du Page County	203

Taiwanese
Top 10 Places Sorted by Percent

Place	Percent
Naperville, IL (city) Du Page County	47.10
Chicago, IL (city) Cook County	30.80

Notes: Please refer to the User's Guide for an explanation of data; tables reflect only those areas that meet Summary File 4 population thresholds, therefore there may be less than 10 places listed

Thai
Top 10 Places Sorted by Number

Place	Number
Chicago, IL (city) Cook County	468

Thai
Top 10 Places Sorted by Percent

Place	Percent
Chicago, IL (city) Cook County	21.83

Tongan
Top 10 Places Sorted by Number

Place	Number

No places met population threshold.

Tongan
Top 10 Places Sorted by Percent

Place	Percent

No places met population threshold.

Vietnamese
Top 10 Places Sorted by Number

Place	Number
Chicago, IL (city) Cook County	3,316
Glendale Heights, IL (village) Du Page County	338
Aurora, IL (city) Kane County	244
Carol Stream, IL (village) Du Page County	188
Champaign, IL (city) Champaign County	131
Wheaton, IL (city) Du Page County	89
Rockford, IL (city) Winnebago County	86

Vietnamese
Top 10 Places Sorted by Percent

Place	Percent
Aurora, IL (city) Kane County	49.80
Glendale Heights, IL (village) Du Page County	42.30
Chicago, IL (city) Cook County	40.54
Carol Stream, IL (village) Du Page County	39.83
Champaign, IL (city) Champaign County	30.47
Wheaton, IL (city) Du Page County	23.30
Rockford, IL (city) Winnebago County	21.34

Educational Attainment: High School Graduates

Total Populations 25 Years and Over Who are High School Graduates
Top 10 Places Sorted by Number

Place	Number
Chicago, IL (city) Cook County	1,304,122
Naperville, IL (city) Du Page County	75,935
Rockford, IL (city) Winnebago County	74,789
Springfield, IL (city) Sangamon County	65,906
Aurora, IL (city) Kane County	63,191
Peoria, IL (city) Peoria County	58,187
Joliet, IL (city) Will County	50,834
Arlington Heights, IL (village) Cook County	50,106
Schaumburg, IL (village) Cook County	47,877
Evanston, IL (city) Cook County	43,244

Total Populations 25 Years and Over Who are High School Graduates
Top 10 Places Sorted by Percent

Place	Percent
Winnetka, IL (village) Cook County	98.99
Hinsdale, IL (village) Du Page County	97.33
Long Grove, IL (village) Lake County	97.24
South Barrington, IL (village) Cook County	97.23
Lake Forest, IL (city) Lake County	97.22
Flossmoor, IL (village) Cook County	96.85
River Forest, IL (village) Cook County	96.79
Wilmette, IL (village) Cook County	96.76
Lincolnshire, IL (village) Lake County	96.44
Naperville, IL (city) Du Page County	96.31

Asians 25 Years and Over Who are High School Graduates
Top 10 Places Sorted by Number

Place	Number
Chicago, IL (city) Cook County	69,751
Skokie, IL (village) Cook County	7,656
Naperville, IL (city) Du Page County	6,863
Schaumburg, IL (village) Cook County	6,663
Hoffman Estates, IL (village) Cook County	4,231
Mount Prospect, IL (village) Cook County	3,746
Palatine, IL (village) Cook County	3,155
Arlington Heights, IL (village) Cook County	3,146
Glendale Heights, IL (village) Du Page County	3,035
Morton Grove, IL (village) Cook County	2,933

Asians 25 Years and Over Who are High School Graduates
Top 10 Places Sorted by Percent

Place	Percent
Algonquin, IL (village) McHenry County	100.00
East Moline, IL (city) Rock Island County	100.00
Long Grove, IL (village) Lake County	100.00
Prospect Heights, IL (city) Cook County	100.00
South Barrington, IL (village) Cook County	99.01
Carbondale, IL (city) Jackson County	98.68
Elmwood Park, IL (village) Cook County	98.57
Flossmoor, IL (village) Cook County	98.48
Urbana, IL (city) Champaign County	98.25
Evanston, IL (city) Cook County	98.09

Native Hawaiian and Other Pacific Islanders 25 Years and Over Who are High School Graduates
Top 10 Places Sorted by Number

Place	Number
Chicago, IL (city) Cook County	348

Native Hawaiian and Other Pacific Islanders 25 Years and Over Who are High School Graduates
Top 10 Places Sorted by Percent

Place	Percent
Chicago, IL (city) Cook County	57.81

Asian Indians 25 Years and Over Who are High School Graduates
Top 10 Places Sorted by Number

Place	Number
Chicago, IL (city) Cook County	12,640
Schaumburg, IL (village) Cook County	2,987
Naperville, IL (city) Du Page County	2,709
Skokie, IL (village) Cook County	1,853
Mount Prospect, IL (village) Cook County	1,719
Hoffman Estates, IL (village) Cook County	1,505
Palatine, IL (village) Cook County	1,240
Glendale Heights, IL (village) Du Page County	1,116
Hanover Park, IL (village) Cook County	1,030
Carol Stream, IL (village) Du Page County	999

Asian Indians 25 Years and Over Who are High School Graduates
Top 10 Places Sorted by Percent

Place	Percent
Bloomington, IL (city) McLean County	100.00
Champaign, IL (city) Champaign County	100.00
Lisle, IL (village) Du Page County	100.00
Peoria, IL (city) Peoria County	100.00
Springfield, IL (city) Sangamon County	100.00
Urbana, IL (city) Champaign County	100.00
Vernon Hills, IL (village) Lake County	100.00
Oak Brook, IL (village) Du Page County	98.89
Evanston, IL (city) Cook County	98.61
Oak Park, IL (village) Cook County	98.05

Bangladeshis 25 Years and Over Who are High School Graduates
Top 10 Places Sorted by Number

Place	Number

No places met population threshold.

Bangladeshis 25 Years and Over Who are High School Graduates
Top 10 Places Sorted by Percent

Place	Percent

No places met population threshold.

Cambodians 25 Years and Over Who are High School Graduates
Top 10 Places Sorted by Number

Place	Number
Chicago, IL (city) Cook County	482

Cambodians 25 Years and Over Who are High School Graduates
Top 10 Places Sorted by Percent

Place	Percent
Chicago, IL (city) Cook County	47.25

Chinese (except Taiwanese) 25 Years and Over Who are High School Graduates
Top 10 Places Sorted by Number

Place	Number
Chicago, IL (city) Cook County	14,871
Naperville, IL (city) Du Page County	2,391
Skokie, IL (village) Cook County	1,046
Urbana, IL (city) Champaign County	909
Schaumburg, IL (village) Cook County	850
Evanston, IL (city) Cook County	542
Peoria, IL (city) Peoria County	527
Champaign, IL (city) Champaign County	526
Hoffman Estates, IL (village) Cook County	501
Glenview, IL (village) Cook County	467

Chinese (except Taiwanese) 25 Years and Over Who are High School Graduates
Top 10 Places Sorted by Percent

Place	Percent
Champaign, IL (city) Champaign County	100.00
Evanston, IL (city) Cook County	100.00
Oak Park, IL (village) Cook County	97.69
Urbana, IL (city) Champaign County	97.64
Buffalo Grove, IL (village) Lake County	96.02
Naperville, IL (city) Du Page County	95.99
Arlington Heights, IL (village) Cook County	95.63
Gurnee, IL (village) Lake County	95.24
Aurora, IL (city) Kane County	95.18
Hoffman Estates, IL (village) Cook County	94.89

Fijians 25 Years and Over Who are High School Graduates
Top 10 Places Sorted by Number

Place	Number

No places met population threshold.

Fijians 25 Years and Over Who are High School Graduates
Top 10 Places Sorted by Percent

Place	Percent

No places met population threshold.

Notes: Please refer to the User's Guide for an explanation of data; tables reflect only those areas that meet Summary File 4 population thresholds, therefore there may be less than 10 places listed

Filipinos 25 Years and Over Who are High School Graduates

Top 10 Places Sorted by Number

Place	Number
Chicago, IL (city) Cook County	18,689
Skokie, IL (village) Cook County	1,848
Morton Grove, IL (village) Cook County	1,122
Glendale Heights, IL (village) Du Page County	1,084
Waukegan, IL (city) Lake County	845
Bolingbrook, IL (village) Will County	790
Streamwood, IL (village) Cook County	775
Schaumburg, IL (village) Cook County	733
Hanover Park, IL (village) Cook County	730
Woodridge, IL (village) Du Page County	671

Filipinos 25 Years and Over Who are High School Graduates

Top 10 Places Sorted by Percent

Place	Percent
Des Plaines, IL (city) Cook County	100.00
Naperville, IL (city) Du Page County	100.00
Tinley Park, IL (village) Cook County	100.00
Orland Park, IL (village) Cook County	98.87
Schaumburg, IL (village) Cook County	98.79
Streamwood, IL (village) Cook County	98.73
Lincolnwood, IL (village) Cook County	98.62
Mount Prospect, IL (village) Cook County	98.06
Gurnee, IL (village) Lake County	98.02
Elgin, IL (city) Kane County	97.98

Guamanian or Chamorros 25 Years and Over Who are High School Graduates

Top 10 Places Sorted by Number

Place	Number
No places met population threshold.	

Guamanian or Chamorros 25 Years and Over Who are High School Graduates

Top 10 Places Sorted by Percent

Place	Percent
No places met population threshold.	

Hawaiian, Natives 25 Years and Over Who are High School Graduates

Top 10 Places Sorted by Number

Place	Number
No places met population threshold.	

Hawaiian, Natives 25 Years and Over Who are High School Graduates

Top 10 Places Sorted by Percent

Place	Percent
No places met population threshold.	

Hmongs 25 Years and Over Who are High School Graduates

Top 10 Places Sorted by Number

Place	Number
No places met population threshold.	

Hmongs 25 Years and Over Who are High School Graduates

Top 10 Places Sorted by Percent

Place	Percent
No places met population threshold.	

Indonesians 25 Years and Over Who are High School Graduates

Top 10 Places Sorted by Number

Place	Number
No places met population threshold.	

Indonesians 25 Years and Over Who are High School Graduates

Top 10 Places Sorted by Percent

Place	Percent
No places met population threshold.	

Japanese 25 Years and Over Who are High School Graduates

Top 10 Places Sorted by Number

Place	Number
Chicago, IL (city) Cook County	4,925
Arlington Heights, IL (village) Cook County	779
Schaumburg, IL (village) Cook County	671
Hoffman Estates, IL (village) Cook County	481
Elk Grove Village, IL (village) Cook County	420
Buffalo Grove, IL (village) Lake County	396
Mount Prospect, IL (village) Cook County	359
Evanston, IL (city) Cook County	284
Glenview, IL (village) Cook County	248
Wilmette, IL (village) Cook County	209

Japanese 25 Years and Over Who are High School Graduates

Top 10 Places Sorted by Percent

Place	Percent
Buffalo Grove, IL (village) Lake County	100.00
Elk Grove Village, IL (village) Cook County	100.00
Glenview, IL (village) Cook County	100.00
Mount Prospect, IL (village) Cook County	100.00
Wilmette, IL (village) Cook County	100.00
Arlington Heights, IL (village) Cook County	99.24
Schaumburg, IL (village) Cook County	99.11
Evanston, IL (city) Cook County	97.59
Chicago, IL (city) Cook County	94.62
Hoffman Estates, IL (village) Cook County	93.58

Koreans 25 Years and Over Who are High School Graduates

Top 10 Places Sorted by Number

Place	Number
Chicago, IL (city) Cook County	7,533
Skokie, IL (village) Cook County	1,650
Schaumburg, IL (village) Cook County	1,042
Northbrook, IL (village) Cook County	974
Glenview, IL (village) Cook County	972
Mount Prospect, IL (village) Cook County	812
Hoffman Estates, IL (village) Cook County	785
Niles, IL (village) Cook County	653
Buffalo Grove, IL (village) Lake County	600
Morton Grove, IL (village) Cook County	533

Koreans 25 Years and Over Who are High School Graduates

Top 10 Places Sorted by Percent

Place	Percent
Evanston, IL (city) Cook County	100.00
Urbana, IL (city) Champaign County	100.00
Wilmette, IL (village) Cook County	98.74
Palatine, IL (village) Cook County	98.24
Glenview, IL (village) Cook County	97.69
Vernon Hills, IL (village) Lake County	97.67
Champaign, IL (city) Champaign County	96.16
Northbrook, IL (village) Cook County	96.06
Buffalo Grove, IL (village) Lake County	95.85
Naperville, IL (city) Du Page County	94.15

Laotians 25 Years and Over Who are High School Graduates

Top 10 Places Sorted by Number

Place	Number
Elgin, IL (city) Kane County	360
Rockford, IL (city) Winnebago County	255

Laotians 25 Years and Over Who are High School Graduates

Top 10 Places Sorted by Percent

Place	Percent
Elgin, IL (city) Kane County	61.43
Rockford, IL (city) Winnebago County	52.04

Malaysians 25 Years and Over Who are High School Graduates

Top 10 Places Sorted by Number

Place	Number
No places met population threshold.	

Malaysians 25 Years and Over Who are High School Graduates

Top 10 Places Sorted by Percent

Place	Percent
No places met population threshold.	

Pakistanis 25 Years and Over Who are High School Graduates

Top 10 Places Sorted by Number

Place	Number
Chicago, IL (city) Cook County	3,088
Skokie, IL (village) Cook County	197

Pakistanis 25 Years and Over Who are High School Graduates

Top 10 Places Sorted by Percent

Place	Percent
Chicago, IL (city) Cook County	79.16
Skokie, IL (village) Cook County	70.61

Samoans 25 Years and Over Who are High School Graduates

Top 10 Places Sorted by Number

Place	Number
No places met population threshold.	

Samoans 25 Years and Over Who are High School Graduates

Top 10 Places Sorted by Percent

Place	Percent
No places met population threshold.	

Sri Lankans 25 Years and Over Who are High School Graduates

Top 10 Places Sorted by Number

Place	Number
No places met population threshold.	

Sri Lankans 25 Years and Over Who are High School Graduates

Top 10 Places Sorted by Percent

Place	Percent
No places met population threshold.	

Notes: Please refer to the User's Guide for an explanation of data; tables reflect only those areas that meet Summary File 4 population thresholds, therefore there may be less than 10 places listed

Taiwanese 25 Years and Over Who are High School Graduates

Top 10 Places Sorted by Number

Place	Number
Chicago, IL (city) Cook County	437
Naperville, IL (city) Du Page County	240

Taiwanese 25 Years and Over Who are High School Graduates

Top 10 Places Sorted by Percent

Place	Percent
Chicago, IL (city) Cook County	95.83
Naperville, IL (city) Du Page County	91.25

Thais 25 Years and Over Who are High School Graduates

Top 10 Places Sorted by Number

Place	Number
Chicago, IL (city) Cook County	1,424

Thais 25 Years and Over Who are High School Graduates

Top 10 Places Sorted by Percent

Place	Percent
Chicago, IL (city) Cook County	93.62

Tongans 25 Years and Over Who are High School Graduates

Top 10 Places Sorted by Number

Place	Number

No places met population threshold.

Tongans 25 Years and Over Who are High School Graduates

Top 10 Places Sorted by Percent

Place	Percent

No places met population threshold.

Vietnamese 25 Years and Over Who are High School Graduates

Top 10 Places Sorted by Number

Place	Number
Chicago, IL (city) Cook County	3,147
Aurora, IL (city) Kane County	261
Glendale Heights, IL (village) Du Page County	254
Carol Stream, IL (village) Du Page County	156
Rockford, IL (city) Winnebago County	131
Champaign, IL (city) Champaign County	98
Wheaton, IL (city) Du Page County	55

Vietnamese 25 Years and Over Who are High School Graduates

Top 10 Places Sorted by Percent

Place	Percent
Aurora, IL (city) Kane County	80.06
Chicago, IL (city) Cook County	62.50
Carol Stream, IL (village) Du Page County	58.65
Glendale Heights, IL (village) Du Page County	50.10
Rockford, IL (city) Winnebago County	47.46
Champaign, IL (city) Champaign County	36.84
Wheaton, IL (city) Du Page County	27.64

Educational Attainment: Four-Year College Graduates

Total Populations 25 Years and Over Who are Four-Year College Graduates

Top 10 Places Sorted by Number

Place	Number
Chicago, IL (city) Cook County	462,783
Naperville, IL (city) Du Page County	47,805
Evanston, IL (city) Cook County	29,511
Arlington Heights, IL (village) Cook County	25,101
Aurora, IL (city) Kane County	24,991
Springfield, IL (city) Sangamon County	23,061
Oak Park, IL (village) Cook County	22,637
Schaumburg, IL (village) Cook County	20,273
Wheaton, IL (city) Du Page County	20,247
Peoria, IL (city) Peoria County	19,712

Total Populations 25 Years and Over Who are Four-Year College Graduates

Top 10 Places Sorted by Percent

Place	Percent
Winnetka, IL (village) Cook County	84.41
Lake Forest, IL (city) Lake County	73.83
Wilmette, IL (village) Cook County	72.58
River Forest, IL (village) Cook County	69.70
Hinsdale, IL (village) Du Page County	68.61
Deerfield, IL (village) Lake County	68.53
Lincolnshire, IL (village) Lake County	66.38
South Barrington, IL (village) Cook County	62.64
Evanston, IL (city) Cook County	62.36
Northbrook, IL (village) Cook County	62.20

Asians 25 Years and Over Who are Four-Year College Graduates

Top 10 Places Sorted by Number

Place	Number
Chicago, IL (city) Cook County	42,187
Naperville, IL (city) Du Page County	5,670
Skokie, IL (village) Cook County	4,839
Schaumburg, IL (village) Cook County	4,675
Hoffman Estates, IL (village) Cook County	2,647
Mount Prospect, IL (village) Cook County	2,466
Arlington Heights, IL (village) Cook County	2,437
Palatine, IL (village) Cook County	2,293
Evanston, IL (city) Cook County	2,028
Urbana, IL (city) Champaign County	2,006

Asians 25 Years and Over Who are Four-Year College Graduates

Top 10 Places Sorted by Percent

Place	Percent
Macomb, IL (city) McDonough County	87.74
Oak Brook, IL (village) Du Page County	87.53
Urbana, IL (city) Champaign County	87.52
Lincolnshire, IL (village) Lake County	87.25
Savoy, IL (village) Champaign County	86.51
Evanston, IL (city) Cook County	86.01
South Barrington, IL (village) Cook County	83.37
Long Grove, IL (village) Lake County	83.15
Lake Forest, IL (city) Lake County	82.51
Burr Ridge, IL (village) Du Page County	82.31

Native Hawaiian and Other Pacific Islanders 25 Years and Over Who are Four-Year College Graduates

Top 10 Places Sorted by Number

Place	Number
Chicago, IL (city) Cook County	86

Native Hawaiian and Other Pacific Islanders 25 Years and Over Who are Four-Year College Graduates

Top 10 Places Sorted by Percent

Place	Percent
Chicago, IL (city) Cook County	14.29

Asian Indians 25 Years and Over Who are Four-Year College Graduates

Top 10 Places Sorted by Number

Place	Number
Chicago, IL (city) Cook County	8,885
Schaumburg, IL (village) Cook County	2,407
Naperville, IL (city) Du Page County	2,367
Mount Prospect, IL (village) Cook County	1,165
Skokie, IL (village) Cook County	1,154
Palatine, IL (village) Cook County	986
Hoffman Estates, IL (village) Cook County	907
Westmont, IL (village) Du Page County	807
Arlington Heights, IL (village) Cook County	781
Woodridge, IL (village) Du Page County	737

Asian Indians 25 Years and Over Who are Four-Year College Graduates

Top 10 Places Sorted by Percent

Place	Percent
Urbana, IL (city) Champaign County	94.95
Vernon Hills, IL (village) Lake County	94.08
Evanston, IL (city) Cook County	93.91
Oak Brook, IL (village) Du Page County	93.16
Lisle, IL (village) Du Page County	91.10
Peoria, IL (city) Peoria County	89.51
Champaign, IL (city) Champaign County	89.19
Bloomington, IL (city) McLean County	88.63
Oak Park, IL (village) Cook County	87.61
Arlington Heights, IL (village) Cook County	87.56

Bangladeshis 25 Years and Over Who are Four-Year College Graduates

Top 10 Places Sorted by Number

Place	Number

No places met population threshold.

Bangladeshis 25 Years and Over Who are Four-Year College Graduates

Top 10 Places Sorted by Percent

Place	Percent

No places met population threshold.

Cambodians 25 Years and Over Who are Four-Year College Graduates

Top 10 Places Sorted by Number

Place	Number
Chicago, IL (city) Cook County	183

Cambodians 25 Years and Over Who are Four-Year College Graduates

Top 10 Places Sorted by Percent

Place	Percent
Chicago, IL (city) Cook County	17.94

Chinese (except Taiwanese) 25 Years and Over Who are Four-Year College Graduates

Top 10 Places Sorted by Number

Place	Number
Chicago, IL (city) Cook County	8,744
Naperville, IL (city) Du Page County	2,002
Urbana, IL (city) Champaign County	795
Skokie, IL (village) Cook County	713
Schaumburg, IL (village) Cook County	613
Evanston, IL (city) Cook County	509
Champaign, IL (city) Champaign County	488
Peoria, IL (city) Peoria County	430
Hoffman Estates, IL (village) Cook County	397
Palatine, IL (village) Cook County	397

Chinese (except Taiwanese) 25 Years and Over Who are Four-Year College Graduates

Top 10 Places Sorted by Percent

Place	Percent
Evanston, IL (city) Cook County	93.91
Champaign, IL (city) Champaign County	92.78
Urbana, IL (city) Champaign County	85.39
Wilmette, IL (village) Cook County	84.59
Aurora, IL (city) Kane County	83.49

Notes: Please refer to the User's Guide for an explanation of data; tables reflect only those areas that meet Summary File 4 population thresholds, therefore there may be less than 10 places listed

Vernon Hills, IL (village) Lake County	81.31
Mundelein, IL (village) Lake County	80.39
Naperville, IL (city) Du Page County	80.37
Lisle, IL (village) Du Page County	80.23
Arlington Heights, IL (village) Cook County	79.23

Fijians 25 Years and Over Who are Four-Year College Graduates

Top 10 Places Sorted by Number

Place	Number

No places met population threshold.

Fijians 25 Years and Over Who are Four-Year College Graduates

Top 10 Places Sorted by Percent

Place	Percent

No places met population threshold.

Filipinos 25 Years and Over Who are Four-Year College Graduates

Top 10 Places Sorted by Number

Place	Number
Chicago, IL (city) Cook County	12,106
Skokie, IL (village) Cook County	1,269
Morton Grove, IL (village) Cook County	794
Glendale Heights, IL (village) Du Page County	660
Schaumburg, IL (village) Cook County	538
Bolingbrook, IL (village) Will County	507
Streamwood, IL (village) Cook County	476
Woodridge, IL (village) Du Page County	473
Aurora, IL (city) Kane County	466
Hanover Park, IL (village) Cook County	452

Filipinos 25 Years and Over Who are Four-Year College Graduates

Top 10 Places Sorted by Percent

Place	Percent
Glenview, IL (village) Cook County	79.71
Lincolnwood, IL (village) Cook County	77.59
Orland Park, IL (village) Cook County	77.38
Mundelein, IL (village) Lake County	77.05
Arlington Heights, IL (village) Cook County	76.70
Lombard, IL (village) Du Page County	76.36
Darien, IL (city) Du Page County	74.55
Gurnee, IL (village) Lake County	74.45
Naperville, IL (city) Du Page County	73.58
Elk Grove Village, IL (village) Cook County	72.52

Guamanian or Chamorros 25 Years and Over Who are Four-Year College Graduates

Top 10 Places Sorted by Number

Place	Number

No places met population threshold.

Guamanian or Chamorros 25 Years and Over Who are Four-Year College Graduates

Top 10 Places Sorted by Percent

Place	Percent

No places met population threshold.

Hawaiian, Natives 25 Years and Over Who are Four-Year College Graduates

Top 10 Places Sorted by Number

Place	Number

No places met population threshold.

Hawaiian, Natives 25 Years and Over Who are Four-Year College Graduates

Top 10 Places Sorted by Percent

Place	Percent

No places met population threshold.

Hmongs 25 Years and Over Who are Four-Year College Graduates

Top 10 Places Sorted by Number

Place	Number

No places met population threshold.

Hmongs 25 Years and Over Who are Four-Year College Graduates

Top 10 Places Sorted by Percent

Place	Percent

No places met population threshold.

Indonesians 25 Years and Over Who are Four-Year College Graduates

Top 10 Places Sorted by Number

Place	Number

No places met population threshold.

Indonesians 25 Years and Over Who are Four-Year College Graduates

Top 10 Places Sorted by Percent

Place	Percent

No places met population threshold.

Japanese 25 Years and Over Who are Four-Year College Graduates

Top 10 Places Sorted by Number

Place	Number
Chicago, IL (city) Cook County	2,470
Arlington Heights, IL (village) Cook County	499
Schaumburg, IL (village) Cook County	286
Hoffman Estates, IL (village) Cook County	268
Elk Grove Village, IL (village) Cook County	249
Buffalo Grove, IL (village) Lake County	234
Evanston, IL (city) Cook County	210
Mount Prospect, IL (village) Cook County	207
Wilmette, IL (village) Cook County	142
Glenview, IL (village) Cook County	126

Japanese 25 Years and Over Who are Four-Year College Graduates

Top 10 Places Sorted by Percent

Place	Percent
Evanston, IL (city) Cook County	72.16
Wilmette, IL (village) Cook County	67.94
Arlington Heights, IL (village) Cook County	63.57
Elk Grove Village, IL (village) Cook County	59.29
Buffalo Grove, IL (village) Lake County	59.09
Mount Prospect, IL (village) Cook County	57.66
Hoffman Estates, IL (village) Cook County	52.14
Glenview, IL (village) Cook County	50.81
Chicago, IL (city) Cook County	47.45
Schaumburg, IL (village) Cook County	42.25

Koreans 25 Years and Over Who are Four-Year College Graduates

Top 10 Places Sorted by Number

Place	Number
Chicago, IL (city) Cook County	4,396
Skokie, IL (village) Cook County	923
Northbrook, IL (village) Cook County	693
Glenview, IL (village) Cook County	620
Schaumburg, IL (village) Cook County	562
Urbana, IL (city) Champaign County	474
Mount Prospect, IL (village) Cook County	434
Hoffman Estates, IL (village) Cook County	415
Buffalo Grove, IL (village) Lake County	409
Niles, IL (village) Cook County	378

Koreans 25 Years and Over Who are Four-Year College Graduates

Top 10 Places Sorted by Percent

Place	Percent
Urbana, IL (city) Champaign County	98.34
Champaign, IL (city) Champaign County	83.45
Evanston, IL (city) Cook County	82.22
Wilmette, IL (village) Cook County	72.80
Northbrook, IL (village) Cook County	68.34
Palatine, IL (village) Cook County	66.75
Buffalo Grove, IL (village) Lake County	65.34
Naperville, IL (city) Du Page County	64.72
Glenview, IL (village) Cook County	62.31
Arlington Heights, IL (village) Cook County	53.55

Laotians 25 Years and Over Who are Four-Year College Graduates

Top 10 Places Sorted by Number

Place	Number
Elgin, IL (city) Kane County	44
Rockford, IL (city) Winnebago County	20

Laotians 25 Years and Over Who are Four-Year College Graduates

Top 10 Places Sorted by Percent

Place	Percent
Elgin, IL (city) Kane County	7.51
Rockford, IL (city) Winnebago County	4.08

Malaysians 25 Years and Over Who are Four-Year College Graduates

Top 10 Places Sorted by Number

Place	Number

No places met population threshold.

Malaysians 25 Years and Over Who are Four-Year College Graduates

Top 10 Places Sorted by Percent

Place	Percent

No places met population threshold.

Pakistanis 25 Years and Over Who are Four-Year College Graduates

Top 10 Places Sorted by Number

Place	Number
Chicago, IL (city) Cook County	1,852
Skokie, IL (village) Cook County	111

Pakistanis 25 Years and Over Who are Four-Year College Graduates

Top 10 Places Sorted by Percent

Place	Percent
Chicago, IL (city) Cook County	47.48
Skokie, IL (village) Cook County	39.78

Samoans 25 Years and Over Who are Four-Year College Graduates

Top 10 Places Sorted by Number

Place	Number

No places met population threshold.

Samoans 25 Years and Over Who are Four-Year College Graduates

Top 10 Places Sorted by Percent

Place	Percent

No places met population threshold.

Notes: Please refer to the User's Guide for an explanation of data; tables reflect only those areas that meet Summary File 4 population thresholds, therefore there may be less than 10 places listed

Sri Lankans 25 Years and Over Who are Four-Year College Graduates
Top 10 Places Sorted by Number

Place	Number

No places met population threshold.

Sri Lankans 25 Years and Over Who are Four-Year College Graduates
Top 10 Places Sorted by Percent

Place	Percent

No places met population threshold.

Taiwanese 25 Years and Over Who are Four-Year College Graduates
Top 10 Places Sorted by Number

Place	Number
Chicago, IL (city) Cook County	380
Naperville, IL (city) Du Page County	213

Taiwanese 25 Years and Over Who are Four-Year College Graduates
Top 10 Places Sorted by Percent

Place	Percent
Chicago, IL (city) Cook County	83.33
Naperville, IL (city) Du Page County	80.99

Thais 25 Years and Over Who are Four-Year College Graduates
Top 10 Places Sorted by Number

Place	Number
Chicago, IL (city) Cook County	829

Thais 25 Years and Over Who are Four-Year College Graduates
Top 10 Places Sorted by Percent

Place	Percent
Chicago, IL (city) Cook County	54.50

Tongans 25 Years and Over Who are Four-Year College Graduates
Top 10 Places Sorted by Number

Place	Number

No places met population threshold.

Tongans 25 Years and Over Who are Four-Year College Graduates
Top 10 Places Sorted by Percent

Place	Percent

No places met population threshold.

Vietnamese 25 Years and Over Who are Four-Year College Graduates
Top 10 Places Sorted by Number

Place	Number
Chicago, IL (city) Cook County	992
Aurora, IL (city) Kane County	107
Glendale Heights, IL (village) Du Page County	50
Rockford, IL (city) Winnebago County	44
Champaign, IL (city) Champaign County	41
Carol Stream, IL (village) Du Page County	15
Wheaton, IL (city) Du Page County	7

Vietnamese 25 Years and Over Who are Four-Year College Graduates
Top 10 Places Sorted by Percent

Place	Percent
Aurora, IL (city) Kane County	32.82
Chicago, IL (city) Cook County	19.70
Rockford, IL (city) Winnebago County	15.94
Champaign, IL (city) Champaign County	15.41
Glendale Heights, IL (village) Du Page County	9.86
Carol Stream, IL (village) Du Page County	5.64
Wheaton, IL (city) Du Page County	3.52

Median Household Income

Total Population
Top 10 Places Sorted by Number

Place	Dollars
South Barrington, IL (village) Cook County	170,755
Winnetka, IL (village) Cook County	167,458
Long Grove, IL (village) Lake County	148,150
Oak Brook, IL (village) Du Page County	146,537
Lake Forest, IL (city) Lake County	136,462
Lincolnshire, IL (village) Lake County	134,259
Burr Ridge, IL (village) Du Page County	129,507
Deerfield, IL (village) Lake County	107,194
Wilmette, IL (village) Cook County	106,773
Hinsdale, IL (village) Du Page County	104,551

Asian
Top 10 Places Sorted by Number

Place	Dollars
Oak Brook, IL (village) Du Page County	200,000+
South Barrington, IL (village) Cook County	200,000+
Lincolnshire, IL (village) Lake County	186,316
Burr Ridge, IL (village) Du Page County	184,734
Lake Forest, IL (city) Lake County	136,461
Danville, IL (city) Vermilion County	129,083
Winnetka, IL (village) Cook County	110,957
Lake Zurich, IL (village) Lake County	109,994
Deerfield, IL (village) Lake County	109,626
Northbrook, IL (village) Cook County	105,894

Native Hawaiian and Other Pacific Islander
Top 10 Places Sorted by Number

Place	Dollars
Chicago, IL (city) Cook County	29,375

Asian Indian
Top 10 Places Sorted by Number

Place	Dollars
Oak Brook, IL (village) Du Page County	200,000+
South Barrington, IL (village) Cook County	200,000+
Burr Ridge, IL (village) Du Page County	161,233
Glenview, IL (village) Cook County	150,000
Orland Park, IL (village) Cook County	115,985
Vernon Hills, IL (village) Lake County	100,883
Darien, IL (city) Du Page County	98,984
Wheaton, IL (city) Du Page County	97,918
Naperville, IL (city) Du Page County	92,686
Bartlett, IL (village) Du Page County	87,227

Bangladeshi
Top 10 Places Sorted by Number

Place	Dollars

No places met population threshold.

Cambodian
Top 10 Places Sorted by Number

Place	Dollars
Chicago, IL (city) Cook County	52,500

Chinese (except Taiwanese)
Top 10 Places Sorted by Number

Place	Dollars
Lisle, IL (village) Du Page County	127,681
Vernon Hills, IL (village) Lake County	113,180
Mundelein, IL (village) Lake County	104,592
Naperville, IL (city) Du Page County	102,958
Northbrook, IL (village) Cook County	95,318
Buffalo Grove, IL (village) Lake County	90,859
Arlington Heights, IL (village) Cook County	89,667
Gurnee, IL (village) Lake County	86,331
Hoffman Estates, IL (village) Cook County	80,921
Wilmette, IL (village) Cook County	77,620

Fijian
Top 10 Places Sorted by Number

Place	Dollars

No places met population threshold.

Filipino
Top 10 Places Sorted by Number

Place	Dollars
Naperville, IL (city) Du Page County	109,761
Mundelein, IL (village) Lake County	98,932
Orland Park, IL (village) Cook County	97,711
Gurnee, IL (village) Lake County	95,181
Morton Grove, IL (village) Cook County	92,310
Glenview, IL (village) Cook County	91,021
Skokie, IL (village) Cook County	90,930
Darien, IL (city) Du Page County	90,728
Downers Grove, IL (village) Du Page County	90,442
Palatine, IL (village) Cook County	90,255

Guamanian or Chamorro
Top 10 Places Sorted by Number

Place	Dollars

No places met population threshold.

Hawaiian, Native
Top 10 Places Sorted by Number

Place	Dollars

No places met population threshold.

Hmong
Top 10 Places Sorted by Number

Place	Dollars

No places met population threshold.

Indonesian
Top 10 Places Sorted by Number

Place	Dollars

No places met population threshold.

Japanese
Top 10 Places Sorted by Number

Place	Dollars
Wilmette, IL (village) Cook County	106,933
Hoffman Estates, IL (village) Cook County	100,146
Glenview, IL (village) Cook County	91,985
Buffalo Grove, IL (village) Lake County	85,598
Elk Grove Village, IL (village) Cook County	79,246
Arlington Heights, IL (village) Cook County	70,625
Schaumburg, IL (village) Cook County	59,345
Chicago, IL (city) Cook County	45,750
Mount Prospect, IL (village) Cook County	41,458
Evanston, IL (city) Cook County	36,250

Korean
Top 10 Places Sorted by Number

Place	Dollars
Buffalo Grove, IL (village) Lake County	83,219
Lincolnwood, IL (village) Cook County	72,604
Northbrook, IL (village) Cook County	72,500
Glenview, IL (village) Cook County	70,987
Arlington Heights, IL (village) Cook County	68,036
Hoffman Estates, IL (village) Cook County	67,500
Vernon Hills, IL (village) Lake County	66,875
Palatine, IL (village) Cook County	62,198
Morton Grove, IL (village) Cook County	61,875

Notes: Please refer to the User's Guide for an explanation of data; tables reflect only those areas that meet Summary File 4 population thresholds, therefore there may be less than 10 places listed

Place	Dollars
Wilmette, IL (village) Cook County	61,012

Laotian
Top 10 Places Sorted by Number

Place	Dollars
Elgin, IL (city) Kane County	85,703
Rockford, IL (city) Winnebago County	53,125

Malaysian
Top 10 Places Sorted by Number

Place	Dollars

No places met population threshold.

Pakistani
Top 10 Places Sorted by Number

Place	Dollars
Skokie, IL (village) Cook County	78,844
Chicago, IL (city) Cook County	28,981

Samoan
Top 10 Places Sorted by Number

Place	Dollars

No places met population threshold.

Sri Lankan
Top 10 Places Sorted by Number

Place	Dollars

No places met population threshold.

Taiwanese
Top 10 Places Sorted by Number

Place	Dollars
Naperville, IL (city) Du Page County	97,763
Chicago, IL (city) Cook County	30,938

Thai
Top 10 Places Sorted by Number

Place	Dollars
Chicago, IL (city) Cook County	39,479

Tongan
Top 10 Places Sorted by Number

Place	Dollars

No places met population threshold.

Vietnamese
Top 10 Places Sorted by Number

Place	Dollars
Glendale Heights, IL (village) Du Page County	68,026
Carol Stream, IL (village) Du Page County	61,250
Aurora, IL (city) Kane County	60,000
Rockford, IL (city) Winnebago County	42,159
Wheaton, IL (city) Du Page County	36,458
Chicago, IL (city) Cook County	35,774
Champaign, IL (city) Champaign County	29,063

Per Capita Income

Total Population
Top 10 Places Sorted by Number

Place	Dollars
Winnetka, IL (village) Cook County	84,134
Lake Forest, IL (city) Lake County	77,092
Oak Brook, IL (village) Du Page County	76,668
South Barrington, IL (village) Cook County	76,078
Hinsdale, IL (village) Du Page County	63,765
Long Grove, IL (village) Lake County	62,185
Lincolnshire, IL (village) Lake County	60,115
Burr Ridge, IL (village) Du Page County	58,518
Wilmette, IL (village) Cook County	55,611
Highland Park, IL (city) Lake County	55,331

Asian
Top 10 Places Sorted by Number

Place	Dollars
Oak Brook, IL (village) Du Page County	84,054
South Barrington, IL (village) Cook County	82,372
Burr Ridge, IL (village) Du Page County	56,585
Lincolnshire, IL (village) Lake County	56,032
Lake Forest, IL (city) Lake County	54,345
Highland Park, IL (city) Lake County	50,311
Long Grove, IL (village) Lake County	47,163
River Forest, IL (village) Cook County	46,961
Moline, IL (city) Rock Island County	44,608
Palos Hills, IL (city) Cook County	43,815

Native Hawaiian and Other Pacific Islander
Top 10 Places Sorted by Number

Place	Dollars
Chicago, IL (city) Cook County	13,017

Asian Indian
Top 10 Places Sorted by Number

Place	Dollars
Oak Brook, IL (village) Du Page County	88,710
South Barrington, IL (village) Cook County	77,731
Orland Park, IL (village) Cook County	58,181
Wheaton, IL (city) Du Page County	49,501
Glenview, IL (village) Cook County	47,032
Burr Ridge, IL (village) Du Page County	40,125
Peoria, IL (city) Peoria County	37,912
Lisle, IL (village) Du Page County	35,708
Arlington Heights, IL (village) Cook County	34,648
Vernon Hills, IL (village) Lake County	33,786

Bangladeshi
Top 10 Places Sorted by Number

Place	Dollars

No places met population threshold.

Cambodian
Top 10 Places Sorted by Number

Place	Dollars
Chicago, IL (city) Cook County	11,594

Chinese (except Taiwanese)
Top 10 Places Sorted by Number

Place	Dollars
Northbrook, IL (village) Cook County	46,018
Lisle, IL (village) Du Page County	45,114
Vernon Hills, IL (village) Lake County	38,354
Glenview, IL (village) Cook County	38,217
Westmont, IL (village) Du Page County	35,526
Mundelein, IL (village) Lake County	33,137
Wilmette, IL (village) Cook County	32,381
Buffalo Grove, IL (village) Lake County	31,647
Naperville, IL (city) Du Page County	31,004
Palatine, IL (village) Cook County	30,817

Fijian
Top 10 Places Sorted by Number

Place	Dollars

No places met population threshold.

Filipino
Top 10 Places Sorted by Number

Place	Dollars
Schaumburg, IL (village) Cook County	37,440
Glenview, IL (village) Cook County	35,960
Palatine, IL (village) Cook County	34,352
Lombard, IL (village) Du Page County	33,356
Lincolnwood, IL (village) Cook County	31,924
Naperville, IL (city) Du Page County	31,584
Darien, IL (city) Du Page County	30,665
Arlington Heights, IL (village) Cook County	30,558
Orland Park, IL (village) Cook County	30,372
Park City, IL (city) Lake County	30,083

Guamanian or Chamorro
Top 10 Places Sorted by Number

Place	Dollars

No places met population threshold.

Hawaiian, Native
Top 10 Places Sorted by Number

Place	Dollars

No places met population threshold.

Hmong
Top 10 Places Sorted by Number

Place	Dollars

No places met population threshold.

Indonesian
Top 10 Places Sorted by Number

Place	Dollars

No places met population threshold.

Japanese
Top 10 Places Sorted by Number

Place	Dollars
Glenview, IL (village) Cook County	70,887
Buffalo Grove, IL (village) Lake County	51,519
Wilmette, IL (village) Cook County	42,897
Arlington Heights, IL (village) Cook County	39,086
Evanston, IL (city) Cook County	34,676
Hoffman Estates, IL (village) Cook County	34,573
Schaumburg, IL (village) Cook County	30,714
Chicago, IL (city) Cook County	30,684
Mount Prospect, IL (village) Cook County	28,904
Elk Grove Village, IL (village) Cook County	26,878

Korean
Top 10 Places Sorted by Number

Place	Dollars
Northbrook, IL (village) Cook County	32,694
Buffalo Grove, IL (village) Lake County	28,119
Glenview, IL (village) Cook County	27,676
Lincolnwood, IL (village) Cook County	26,025
Wilmette, IL (village) Cook County	24,224
Skokie, IL (village) Cook County	23,504
Palatine, IL (village) Cook County	23,000
Morton Grove, IL (village) Cook County	22,730
Vernon Hills, IL (village) Lake County	22,381
Arlington Heights, IL (village) Cook County	21,723

Laotian
Top 10 Places Sorted by Number

Place	Dollars
Elgin, IL (city) Kane County	19,355
Rockford, IL (city) Winnebago County	13,998

Malaysian
Top 10 Places Sorted by Number

Place	Dollars

No places met population threshold.

Notes: Please refer to the User's Guide for an explanation of data; tables reflect only those areas that meet Summary File 4 population thresholds, therefore there may be less than 10 places listed

Pakistani
Top 10 Places Sorted by Number

Place	Dollars
Skokie, IL (village) Cook County	22,213
Chicago, IL (city) Cook County	11,816

Samoan
Top 10 Places Sorted by Number

Place	Dollars

No places met population threshold.

Sri Lankan
Top 10 Places Sorted by Number

Place	Dollars

No places met population threshold.

Taiwanese
Top 10 Places Sorted by Number

Place	Dollars
Naperville, IL (city) Du Page County	35,047
Chicago, IL (city) Cook County	20,133

Thai
Top 10 Places Sorted by Number

Place	Dollars
Chicago, IL (city) Cook County	20,073

Tongan
Top 10 Places Sorted by Number

Place	Dollars

No places met population threshold.

Vietnamese
Top 10 Places Sorted by Number

Place	Dollars
Aurora, IL (city) Kane County	25,551
Glendale Heights, IL (village) Du Page County	20,530
Carol Stream, IL (village) Du Page County	18,204
Rockford, IL (city) Winnebago County	13,769
Chicago, IL (city) Cook County	13,354
Champaign, IL (city) Champaign County	11,643
Wheaton, IL (city) Du Page County	10,257

Poverty Status

Total Populations with Income Below Poverty Level
Top 10 Places Sorted by Number

Place	Number
Chicago, IL (city) Cook County	556,791
Rockford, IL (city) Winnebago County	20,351
Peoria, IL (city) Peoria County	20,220
Champaign, IL (city) Champaign County	13,398
Cicero, IL (town) Cook County	13,187
Decatur, IL (city) Macon County	12,999
Springfield, IL (city) Sangamon County	12,847
Waukegan, IL (city) Lake County	12,058
Aurora, IL (city) Kane County	12,034
Joliet, IL (city) Will County	10,946

Total Populations with Income Below Poverty Level
Top 10 Places Sorted by Percent

Place	Percent
Carbondale, IL (city) Jackson County	41.36
Macomb, IL (city) McDonough County	29.08
Urbana, IL (city) Champaign County	27.34
Champaign, IL (city) Champaign County	22.11
DeKalb, IL (city) De Kalb County	21.28
Chicago, IL (city) Cook County	19.61
Normal, IL (town) McLean County	19.27
Peoria, IL (city) Peoria County	18.77
Danville, IL (city) Vermilion County	18.07
Decatur, IL (city) Macon County	16.53

Asians with Income Below Poverty Level
Top 10 Places Sorted by Number

Place	Number
Chicago, IL (city) Cook County	22,160
Urbana, IL (city) Champaign County	1,847
Champaign, IL (city) Champaign County	1,434
Carbondale, IL (city) Jackson County	776
Evanston, IL (city) Cook County	645
DeKalb, IL (city) De Kalb County	556
Schaumburg, IL (village) Cook County	544
Skokie, IL (village) Cook County	486
Hoffman Estates, IL (village) Cook County	458
Naperville, IL (city) Du Page County	388

Asians with Income Below Poverty Level
Top 10 Places Sorted by Percent

Place	Percent
Carbondale, IL (city) Jackson County	56.64
Macomb, IL (city) McDonough County	54.09
DeKalb, IL (city) De Kalb County	44.95
Urbana, IL (city) Champaign County	44.52
Champaign, IL (city) Champaign County	36.50
Normal, IL (town) McLean County	26.41
Savoy, IL (village) Champaign County	23.68
East Moline, IL (city) Rock Island County	21.15
Evanston, IL (city) Cook County	18.82
Chicago, IL (city) Cook County	17.96

Native Hawaiian and Other Pacific Islanders with Income Below Poverty Level
Top 10 Places Sorted by Number

Place	Number
Chicago, IL (city) Cook County	269

Native Hawaiian and Other Pacific Islanders with Income Below Poverty Level
Top 10 Places Sorted by Percent

Place	Percent
Chicago, IL (city) Cook County	25.64

Asian Indians with Income Below Poverty Level
Top 10 Places Sorted by Number

Place	Number
Chicago, IL (city) Cook County	4,344
Urbana, IL (city) Champaign County	359
Champaign, IL (city) Champaign County	358
Schaumburg, IL (village) Cook County	231
Skokie, IL (village) Cook County	168
DeKalb, IL (city) De Kalb County	165
Evanston, IL (city) Cook County	165
Lombard, IL (village) Du Page County	150
Mount Prospect, IL (village) Cook County	150
Naperville, IL (city) Du Page County	115

Asian Indians with Income Below Poverty Level
Top 10 Places Sorted by Percent

Place	Percent
Urbana, IL (city) Champaign County	47.36
DeKalb, IL (city) De Kalb County	44.12
Champaign, IL (city) Champaign County	35.94
Chicago, IL (city) Cook County	18.77
Evanston, IL (city) Cook County	18.54
Springfield, IL (city) Sangamon County	14.92
Elgin, IL (city) Kane County	14.53
Lombard, IL (village) Du Page County	11.89
Rolling Meadows, IL (city) Cook County	10.50
Bloomington, IL (city) McLean County	7.26

Bangladeshis with Income Below Poverty Level
Top 10 Places Sorted by Number

Place	Number

No places met population threshold.

Bangladeshis with Income Below Poverty Level
Top 10 Places Sorted by Percent

Place	Percent

No places met population threshold.

Cambodians with Income Below Poverty Level
Top 10 Places Sorted by Number

Place	Number
Chicago, IL (city) Cook County	375

Cambodians with Income Below Poverty Level
Top 10 Places Sorted by Percent

Place	Percent
Chicago, IL (city) Cook County	20.34

Chinese (except Taiwanese) with Income Below Poverty Level
Top 10 Places Sorted by Number

Place	Number
Chicago, IL (city) Cook County	5,965
Urbana, IL (city) Champaign County	566
Champaign, IL (city) Champaign County	401
Evanston, IL (city) Cook County	214
Peoria, IL (city) Peoria County	107
Naperville, IL (city) Du Page County	100
Schaumburg, IL (village) Cook County	72
Westmont, IL (village) Du Page County	57
Hoffman Estates, IL (village) Cook County	52
Mundelein, IL (village) Lake County	39

Chinese (except Taiwanese) with Income Below Poverty Level
Top 10 Places Sorted by Percent

Place	Percent
Champaign, IL (city) Champaign County	41.60
Urbana, IL (city) Champaign County	36.63
Evanston, IL (city) Cook County	26.52
Chicago, IL (city) Cook County	19.42
Peoria, IL (city) Peoria County	13.34
Westmont, IL (village) Du Page County	11.90
Mundelein, IL (village) Lake County	7.20
Hoffman Estates, IL (village) Cook County	6.33
Elk Grove Village, IL (village) Cook County	5.97
Palatine, IL (village) Cook County	5.60

Fijians with Income Below Poverty Level
Top 10 Places Sorted by Number

Place	Number

No places met population threshold.

Fijians with Income Below Poverty Level
Top 10 Places Sorted by Percent

Place	Percent

No places met population threshold.

Filipinos with Income Below Poverty Level
Top 10 Places Sorted by Number

Place	Number
Chicago, IL (city) Cook County	1,975
Glendale Heights, IL (village) Du Page County	60
Palatine, IL (village) Cook County	45
Aurora, IL (city) Kane County	38
Skokie, IL (village) Cook County	37
Schaumburg, IL (village) Cook County	30
Elgin, IL (city) Kane County	26
Streamwood, IL (village) Cook County	23

Notes: Please refer to the User's Guide for an explanation of data; tables reflect only those areas that meet Summary File 4 population thresholds, therefore there may be less than 10 places listed

Place	Number
Bolingbrook, IL (village) Will County	18
Arlington Heights, IL (village) Cook County	16

Filipinos with Income Below Poverty Level
Top 10 Places Sorted by Percent

Place	Percent
Chicago, IL (city) Cook County	7.16
Palatine, IL (village) Cook County	6.34
Elgin, IL (city) Kane County	4.31
Aurora, IL (city) Kane County	4.12
Glendale Heights, IL (village) Du Page County	3.44
Schaumburg, IL (village) Cook County	3.24
Addison, IL (village) Du Page County	2.59
Arlington Heights, IL (village) Cook County	2.32
Streamwood, IL (village) Cook County	1.94
Park City, IL (city) Lake County	1.92

Guamanian or Chamorros with Income Below Poverty Level
Top 10 Places Sorted by Number

Place	Number

No places met population threshold.

Guamanian or Chamorros with Income Below Poverty Level
Top 10 Places Sorted by Percent

Place	Percent

No places met population threshold.

Hawaiian, Natives with Income Below Poverty Level
Top 10 Places Sorted by Number

Place	Number

No places met population threshold.

Hawaiian, Natives with Income Below Poverty Level
Top 10 Places Sorted by Percent

Place	Percent

No places met population threshold.

Hmongs with Income Below Poverty Level
Top 10 Places Sorted by Number

Place	Number

No places met population threshold.

Hmongs with Income Below Poverty Level
Top 10 Places Sorted by Percent

Place	Percent

No places met population threshold.

Indonesians with Income Below Poverty Level
Top 10 Places Sorted by Number

Place	Number

No places met population threshold.

Indonesians with Income Below Poverty Level
Top 10 Places Sorted by Percent

Place	Percent

No places met population threshold.

Japanese with Income Below Poverty Level
Top 10 Places Sorted by Number

Place	Number
Chicago, IL (city) Cook County	788
Hoffman Estates, IL (village) Cook County	91
Arlington Heights, IL (village) Cook County	57
Elk Grove Village, IL (village) Cook County	31
Wilmette, IL (village) Cook County	20
Glenview, IL (village) Cook County	18
Evanston, IL (city) Cook County	12
Buffalo Grove, IL (village) Lake County	9
Mount Prospect, IL (village) Cook County	6
Schaumburg, IL (village) Cook County	0

Japanese with Income Below Poverty Level
Top 10 Places Sorted by Percent

Place	Percent
Chicago, IL (city) Cook County	13.53
Hoffman Estates, IL (village) Cook County	10.89
Wilmette, IL (village) Cook County	5.78
Arlington Heights, IL (village) Cook County	5.73
Glenview, IL (village) Cook County	5.73
Elk Grove Village, IL (village) Cook County	5.08
Evanston, IL (city) Cook County	3.70
Buffalo Grove, IL (village) Lake County	1.47
Mount Prospect, IL (village) Cook County	1.35
Schaumburg, IL (village) Cook County	0.00

Koreans with Income Below Poverty Level
Top 10 Places Sorted by Number

Place	Number
Chicago, IL (city) Cook County	3,617
Urbana, IL (city) Champaign County	513
Champaign, IL (city) Champaign County	334
Schaumburg, IL (village) Cook County	200
Evanston, IL (city) Cook County	159
Mount Prospect, IL (village) Cook County	159
Hoffman Estates, IL (village) Cook County	112
Skokie, IL (village) Cook County	96
Niles, IL (village) Cook County	86
Naperville, IL (city) Du Page County	68

Koreans with Income Below Poverty Level
Top 10 Places Sorted by Percent

Place	Percent
Urbana, IL (city) Champaign County	59.58
Champaign, IL (city) Champaign County	46.91
Evanston, IL (city) Cook County	31.80
Chicago, IL (city) Cook County	30.41
Schaumburg, IL (village) Cook County	11.27
Mount Prospect, IL (village) Cook County	11.00
Vernon Hills, IL (village) Lake County	10.33
Niles, IL (village) Cook County	8.56
Hoffman Estates, IL (village) Cook County	7.85
Naperville, IL (city) Du Page County	7.82

Laotians with Income Below Poverty Level
Top 10 Places Sorted by Number

Place	Number
Rockford, IL (city) Winnebago County	65
Elgin, IL (city) Kane County	0

Laotians with Income Below Poverty Level
Top 10 Places Sorted by Percent

Place	Percent
Rockford, IL (city) Winnebago County	7.24
Elgin, IL (city) Kane County	0.00

Malaysians with Income Below Poverty Level
Top 10 Places Sorted by Number

Place	Number

No places met population threshold.

Malaysians with Income Below Poverty Level
Top 10 Places Sorted by Percent

Place	Percent

No places met population threshold.

Pakistanis with Income Below Poverty Level
Top 10 Places Sorted by Number

Place	Number
Chicago, IL (city) Cook County	1,836
Skokie, IL (village) Cook County	0

Pakistanis with Income Below Poverty Level
Top 10 Places Sorted by Percent

Place	Percent
Chicago, IL (city) Cook County	28.69
Skokie, IL (village) Cook County	0.00

Samoans with Income Below Poverty Level
Top 10 Places Sorted by Number

Place	Number

No places met population threshold.

Samoans with Income Below Poverty Level
Top 10 Places Sorted by Percent

Place	Percent

No places met population threshold.

Sri Lankans with Income Below Poverty Level
Top 10 Places Sorted by Number

Place	Number

No places met population threshold.

Sri Lankans with Income Below Poverty Level
Top 10 Places Sorted by Percent

Place	Percent

No places met population threshold.

Taiwanese with Income Below Poverty Level
Top 10 Places Sorted by Number

Place	Number
Chicago, IL (city) Cook County	149
Naperville, IL (city) Du Page County	44

Taiwanese with Income Below Poverty Level
Top 10 Places Sorted by Percent

Place	Percent
Chicago, IL (city) Cook County	24.87
Naperville, IL (city) Du Page County	10.21

Thais with Income Below Poverty Level
Top 10 Places Sorted by Number

Place	Number
Chicago, IL (city) Cook County	399

Thais with Income Below Poverty Level
Top 10 Places Sorted by Percent

Place	Percent
Chicago, IL (city) Cook County	19.49

Tongans with Income Below Poverty Level
Top 10 Places Sorted by Number

Place	Number

No places met population threshold.

Tongans with Income Below Poverty Level
Top 10 Places Sorted by Percent

Place	Percent

No places met population threshold.

Vietnamese with Income Below Poverty Level
Top 10 Places Sorted by Number

Place	Number
Chicago, IL (city) Cook County	1,720
Champaign, IL (city) Champaign County	79
Rockford, IL (city) Winnebago County	42
Aurora, IL (city) Kane County	40
Glendale Heights, IL (village) Du Page County	20

Notes: Please refer to the User's Guide for an explanation of data; tables reflect only those areas that meet Summary File 4 population thresholds, therefore there may be less than 10 places listed

Place	Number
Carol Stream, IL (village) Du Page County	16
Wheaton, IL (city) Du Page County	0

Vietnamese with Income Below Poverty Level
Top 10 Places Sorted by Percent

Place	Percent
Chicago, IL (city) Cook County	21.19
Champaign, IL (city) Champaign County	19.04
Rockford, IL (city) Winnebago County	10.42
Aurora, IL (city) Kane County	8.16
Carol Stream, IL (village) Du Page County	3.39
Glendale Heights, IL (village) Du Page County	2.50
Wheaton, IL (city) Du Page County	0.00

Homeownership

Total Populations Who Own Their Own Homes
Top 10 Places Sorted by Number

Place	Number
Chicago, IL (city) Cook County	464,912
Rockford, IL (city) Winnebago County	36,304
Naperville, IL (city) Du Page County	34,952
Aurora, IL (city) Kane County	32,621
Springfield, IL (city) Sangamon County	30,575
Peoria, IL (city) Peoria County	27,041
Joliet, IL (city) Will County	25,465
Arlington Heights, IL (village) Cook County	23,565
Decatur, IL (city) Macon County	22,682
Elgin, IL (city) Kane County	22,167

Total Populations Who Own Their Own Homes
Top 10 Places Sorted by Percent

Place	Percent
South Barrington, IL (village) Cook County	98.69
Oak Brook, IL (village) Du Page County	97.17
Lincolnshire, IL (village) Lake County	97.11
Long Grove, IL (village) Lake County	97.04
Burr Ridge, IL (village) Du Page County	96.50
Morton Grove, IL (village) Cook County	94.54
Westchester, IL (village) Cook County	93.81
Flossmoor, IL (village) Cook County	93.66
Lake in the Hills, IL (village) McHenry County	93.54
Bartlett, IL (village) Du Page County	93.45

Asians Who Own Their Own Homes
Top 10 Places Sorted by Number

Place	Number
Chicago, IL (city) Cook County	16,555
Skokie, IL (village) Cook County	2,801
Naperville, IL (city) Du Page County	2,743
Schaumburg, IL (village) Cook County	1,799
Hoffman Estates, IL (village) Cook County	1,525
Glendale Heights, IL (village) Du Page County	1,263
Morton Grove, IL (village) Cook County	1,171
Glenview, IL (village) Cook County	1,115
Aurora, IL (city) Kane County	1,061
Hanover Park, IL (village) Cook County	960

Asians Who Own Their Own Homes
Top 10 Places Sorted by Percent

Place	Percent
Algonquin, IL (village) McHenry County	100.00
Burr Ridge, IL (village) Du Page County	100.00
Flossmoor, IL (village) Cook County	100.00
Gages Lake, IL (cdp) Lake County	100.00
Oak Brook, IL (village) Du Page County	100.00
South Barrington, IL (village) Cook County	100.00
Lincolnwood, IL (village) Cook County	97.79
Bartlett, IL (village) Du Page County	97.11
Orland Park, IL (village) Cook County	95.64
Morton Grove, IL (village) Cook County	95.59

Native Hawaiian and Other Pacific Islanders Who Own Their Own Homes
Top 10 Places Sorted by Number

Place	Number
Chicago, IL (city) Cook County	88

Native Hawaiian and Other Pacific Islanders Who Own Their Own Homes
Top 10 Places Sorted by Percent

Place	Percent
Chicago, IL (city) Cook County	31.65

Asian Indians Who Own Their Own Homes
Top 10 Places Sorted by Number

Place	Number
Chicago, IL (city) Cook County	2,312
Naperville, IL (city) Du Page County	1,045
Skokie, IL (village) Cook County	774
Schaumburg, IL (village) Cook County	718
Hoffman Estates, IL (village) Cook County	548
Glendale Heights, IL (village) Du Page County	511
Hanover Park, IL (village) Cook County	419
Aurora, IL (city) Kane County	393
Des Plaines, IL (city) Cook County	392
Carol Stream, IL (village) Du Page County	376

Asian Indians Who Own Their Own Homes
Top 10 Places Sorted by Percent

Place	Percent
Burr Ridge, IL (village) Du Page County	100.00
Morton Grove, IL (village) Cook County	100.00
Oak Brook, IL (village) Du Page County	100.00
South Barrington, IL (village) Cook County	100.00
Bartlett, IL (village) Du Page County	98.12
Orland Park, IL (village) Cook County	95.48
Bolingbrook, IL (village) Will County	93.84
Lincolnwood, IL (village) Cook County	91.94
Streamwood, IL (village) Cook County	91.59
Glenview, IL (village) Cook County	89.89

Bangladeshis Who Own Their Own Homes
Top 10 Places Sorted by Number

Place	Number

No places met population threshold.

Bangladeshis Who Own Their Own Homes
Top 10 Places Sorted by Percent

Place	Percent

No places met population threshold.

Cambodians Who Own Their Own Homes
Top 10 Places Sorted by Number

Place	Number
Chicago, IL (city) Cook County	129

Cambodians Who Own Their Own Homes
Top 10 Places Sorted by Percent

Place	Percent
Chicago, IL (city) Cook County	31.93

Chinese (except Taiwanese) Who Own Their Own Homes
Top 10 Places Sorted by Number

Place	Number
Chicago, IL (city) Cook County	5,029
Naperville, IL (city) Du Page County	1,026
Skokie, IL (village) Cook County	397
Schaumburg, IL (village) Cook County	300
Glenview, IL (village) Cook County	247
Hoffman Estates, IL (village) Cook County	181
Vernon Hills, IL (village) Lake County	179
Buffalo Grove, IL (village) Lake County	166
Northbrook, IL (village) Cook County	162
Palatine, IL (village) Cook County	155

Chinese (except Taiwanese) Who Own Their Own Homes
Top 10 Places Sorted by Percent

Place	Percent
Northbrook, IL (village) Cook County	95.29
Mundelein, IL (village) Lake County	90.13
Glenview, IL (village) Cook County	88.85
Vernon Hills, IL (village) Lake County	87.32
Naperville, IL (city) Du Page County	86.07
Buffalo Grove, IL (village) Lake County	81.77
Wilmette, IL (village) Cook County	78.83
Elk Grove Village, IL (village) Cook County	75.00
Aurora, IL (city) Kane County	74.75
Lisle, IL (village) Du Page County	69.41

Fijians Who Own Their Own Homes
Top 10 Places Sorted by Number

Place	Number

No places met population threshold.

Fijians Who Own Their Own Homes
Top 10 Places Sorted by Percent

Place	Percent

No places met population threshold.

Filipinos Who Own Their Own Homes
Top 10 Places Sorted by Number

Place	Number
Chicago, IL (city) Cook County	4,535
Skokie, IL (village) Cook County	615
Morton Grove, IL (village) Cook County	385
Glendale Heights, IL (village) Du Page County	369
Waukegan, IL (city) Lake County	297
Bolingbrook, IL (village) Will County	296
Hanover Park, IL (village) Cook County	284
Streamwood, IL (village) Cook County	280
Carol Stream, IL (village) Du Page County	272
Hoffman Estates, IL (village) Cook County	255

Filipinos Who Own Their Own Homes
Top 10 Places Sorted by Percent

Place	Percent
Hanover Park, IL (village) Cook County	100.00
Lincolnwood, IL (village) Cook County	100.00
Orland Park, IL (village) Cook County	100.00
Streamwood, IL (village) Cook County	97.22
Bartlett, IL (village) Du Page County	97.01
Des Plaines, IL (city) Cook County	96.21
Gurnee, IL (village) Lake County	94.95
Hoffman Estates, IL (village) Cook County	94.10
Tinley Park, IL (village) Cook County	93.02
Morton Grove, IL (village) Cook County	92.11

Guamanian or Chamorros Who Own Their Own Homes
Top 10 Places Sorted by Number

Place	Number

No places met population threshold.

Guamanian or Chamorros Who Own Their Own Homes
Top 10 Places Sorted by Percent

Place	Percent

No places met population threshold.

Notes: Please refer to the User's Guide for an explanation of data; tables reflect only those areas that meet Summary File 4 population thresholds, therefore there may be less than 10 places listed

Hawaiian, Natives Who Own Their Own Homes
Top 10 Places Sorted by Number

Place	Number
No places met population threshold.	

Hawaiian, Natives Who Own Their Own Homes
Top 10 Places Sorted by Percent

Place	Percent
No places met population threshold.	

Hmongs Who Own Their Own Homes
Top 10 Places Sorted by Number

Place	Number
No places met population threshold.	

Hmongs Who Own Their Own Homes
Top 10 Places Sorted by Percent

Place	Percent
No places met population threshold.	

Indonesians Who Own Their Own Homes
Top 10 Places Sorted by Number

Place	Number
No places met population threshold.	

Indonesians Who Own Their Own Homes
Top 10 Places Sorted by Percent

Place	Percent
No places met population threshold.	

Japanese Who Own Their Own Homes
Top 10 Places Sorted by Number

Place	Number
Chicago, IL (city) Cook County	1,487
Arlington Heights, IL (village) Cook County	93
Schaumburg, IL (village) Cook County	92
Buffalo Grove, IL (village) Lake County	84
Hoffman Estates, IL (village) Cook County	81
Mount Prospect, IL (village) Cook County	78
Elk Grove Village, IL (village) Cook County	76
Glenview, IL (village) Cook County	65
Evanston, IL (city) Cook County	64
Wilmette, IL (village) Cook County	46

Japanese Who Own Their Own Homes
Top 10 Places Sorted by Percent

Place	Percent
Glenview, IL (village) Cook County	58.56
Chicago, IL (city) Cook County	47.13
Mount Prospect, IL (village) Cook County	45.88
Buffalo Grove, IL (village) Lake County	42.86
Wilmette, IL (village) Cook County	38.98
Evanston, IL (city) Cook County	38.32
Elk Grove Village, IL (village) Cook County	36.36
Hoffman Estates, IL (village) Cook County	31.76
Schaumburg, IL (village) Cook County	23.53
Arlington Heights, IL (village) Cook County	21.23

Koreans Who Own Their Own Homes
Top 10 Places Sorted by Number

Place	Number
Chicago, IL (city) Cook County	1,049
Skokie, IL (village) Cook County	513
Glenview, IL (village) Cook County	438
Northbrook, IL (village) Cook County	413
Hoffman Estates, IL (village) Cook County	342
Schaumburg, IL (village) Cook County	271
Buffalo Grove, IL (village) Lake County	234
Mount Prospect, IL (village) Cook County	232
Morton Grove, IL (village) Cook County	218
Niles, IL (village) Cook County	216

Koreans Who Own Their Own Homes
Top 10 Places Sorted by Percent

Place	Percent
Lincolnwood, IL (village) Cook County	100.00
Morton Grove, IL (village) Cook County	93.56
Glenview, IL (village) Cook County	91.82
Northbrook, IL (village) Cook County	90.77
Buffalo Grove, IL (village) Lake County	86.03
Hoffman Estates, IL (village) Cook County	80.66
Naperville, IL (city) Du Page County	78.17
Wilmette, IL (village) Cook County	77.18
Arlington Heights, IL (village) Cook County	76.03
Vernon Hills, IL (village) Lake County	73.94

Laotians Who Own Their Own Homes
Top 10 Places Sorted by Number

Place	Number
Rockford, IL (city) Winnebago County	193
Elgin, IL (city) Kane County	137

Laotians Who Own Their Own Homes
Top 10 Places Sorted by Percent

Place	Percent
Rockford, IL (city) Winnebago County	76.59
Elgin, IL (city) Kane County	73.26

Malaysians Who Own Their Own Homes
Top 10 Places Sorted by Number

Place	Number
No places met population threshold.	

Malaysians Who Own Their Own Homes
Top 10 Places Sorted by Percent

Place	Percent
No places met population threshold.	

Pakistanis Who Own Their Own Homes
Top 10 Places Sorted by Number

Place	Number
Chicago, IL (city) Cook County	409
Skokie, IL (village) Cook County	73

Pakistanis Who Own Their Own Homes
Top 10 Places Sorted by Percent

Place	Percent
Skokie, IL (village) Cook County	75.26
Chicago, IL (city) Cook County	21.27

Samoans Who Own Their Own Homes
Top 10 Places Sorted by Number

Place	Number
No places met population threshold.	

Samoans Who Own Their Own Homes
Top 10 Places Sorted by Percent

Place	Percent
No places met population threshold.	

Sri Lankans Who Own Their Own Homes
Top 10 Places Sorted by Number

Place	Number
No places met population threshold.	

Sri Lankans Who Own Their Own Homes
Top 10 Places Sorted by Percent

Place	Percent
No places met population threshold.	

Taiwanese Who Own Their Own Homes
Top 10 Places Sorted by Number

Place	Number
Naperville, IL (city) Du Page County	113
Chicago, IL (city) Cook County	91

Taiwanese Who Own Their Own Homes
Top 10 Places Sorted by Percent

Place	Percent
Naperville, IL (city) Du Page County	81.29
Chicago, IL (city) Cook County	21.77

Thais Who Own Their Own Homes
Top 10 Places Sorted by Number

Place	Number
Chicago, IL (city) Cook County	244

Thais Who Own Their Own Homes
Top 10 Places Sorted by Percent

Place	Percent
Chicago, IL (city) Cook County	32.32

Tongans Who Own Their Own Homes
Top 10 Places Sorted by Number

Place	Number
No places met population threshold.	

Tongans Who Own Their Own Homes
Top 10 Places Sorted by Percent

Place	Percent
No places met population threshold.	

Vietnamese Who Own Their Own Homes
Top 10 Places Sorted by Number

Place	Number
Chicago, IL (city) Cook County	744
Glendale Heights, IL (village) Du Page County	185
Aurora, IL (city) Kane County	113
Champaign, IL (city) Champaign County	104
Carol Stream, IL (village) Du Page County	94
Rockford, IL (city) Winnebago County	50
Wheaton, IL (city) Du Page County	13

Vietnamese Who Own Their Own Homes
Top 10 Places Sorted by Percent

Place	Percent
Aurora, IL (city) Kane County	88.98
Glendale Heights, IL (village) Du Page County	80.43
Carol Stream, IL (village) Du Page County	77.05
Champaign, IL (city) Champaign County	76.47
Rockford, IL (city) Winnebago County	39.68
Chicago, IL (city) Cook County	30.68
Wheaton, IL (city) Du Page County	15.12

Median Gross Rent

All Specified Renter-Occupied Housing Units
Top 10 Places Sorted by Number

Place	Dollars/Month
Lincolnwood, IL (village) Cook County	2,001
South Barrington, IL (village) Cook County	2,001
Northbrook, IL (village) Cook County	1,279
Burr Ridge, IL (village) Du Page County	1,205
Lincolnshire, IL (village) Lake County	1,188
Streamwood, IL (village) Cook County	1,130
Buffalo Grove, IL (village) Lake County	1,079
Winnetka, IL (village) Cook County	1,038
Wilmette, IL (village) Cook County	1,028
Warrenville, IL (city) Du Page County	1,019

Notes: Please refer to the User's Guide for an explanation of data; tables reflect only those areas that meet Summary File 4 population thresholds, therefore there may be less than 10 places listed

Specified Housing Units Rented by Asians
Top 10 Places Sorted by Number

Place	Dollars/Month
Deerfield, IL (village) Lake County	2,001
Lincolnshire, IL (village) Lake County	2,001
Northbrook, IL (village) Cook County	2,001
Streamwood, IL (village) Cook County	1,336
Winnetka, IL (village) Cook County	1,268
Lincolnwood, IL (village) Cook County	1,266
Wilmette, IL (village) Cook County	1,236
Buffalo Grove, IL (village) Lake County	1,231
Gurnee, IL (village) Lake County	1,074
Highland Park, IL (city) Lake County	1,049

Specified Housing Units Rented by Native Hawaiian and Other Pacific Islanders
Top 10 Places Sorted by Number

Place	Dollars/Month
Chicago, IL (city) Cook County	681

Specified Housing Units Rented by Asian Indians
Top 10 Places Sorted by Number

Place	Dollars/Month
Streamwood, IL (village) Cook County	1,322
Elmhurst, IL (city) Du Page County	1,317
Darien, IL (city) Du Page County	1,297
Lincolnwood, IL (village) Cook County	1,266
Buffalo Grove, IL (village) Lake County	1,152
Gurnee, IL (village) Lake County	1,125
Bloomingdale, IL (village) Du Page County	1,111
Schaumburg, IL (village) Cook County	988
Evanston, IL (city) Cook County	977
Aurora, IL (city) Kane County	960

Specified Housing Units Rented by Bangladeshis
Top 10 Places Sorted by Number

Place	Dollars/Month

Specified Housing Units Rented by Cambodians
Top 10 Places Sorted by Number

Place	Dollars/Month
Chicago, IL (city) Cook County	676

Specified Housing Units Rented by Chinese (except Taiwanese)
Top 10 Places Sorted by Number

Place	Dollars/Month
Northbrook, IL (village) Cook County	2,001
Mundelein, IL (village) Lake County	1,375
Buffalo Grove, IL (village) Lake County	1,325
Wilmette, IL (village) Cook County	1,161
Gurnee, IL (village) Lake County	1,038
Naperville, IL (city) Du Page County	961
Schaumburg, IL (village) Cook County	882
Lisle, IL (village) Du Page County	878
Skokie, IL (village) Cook County	839
Palatine, IL (village) Cook County	826

Specified Housing Units Rented by Fijians
Top 10 Places Sorted by Number

Place	Dollars/Month

Specified Housing Units Rented by Filipinos
Top 10 Places Sorted by Number

Place	Dollars/Month
Des Plaines, IL (city) Cook County	1,125
Gurnee, IL (village) Lake County	1,125
Arlington Heights, IL (village) Cook County	1,029
Buffalo Grove, IL (village) Lake County	1,019
Schaumburg, IL (village) Cook County	986
Palatine, IL (village) Cook County	958
Lombard, IL (village) Du Page County	950
Wheeling, IL (village) Cook County	911
Hoffman Estates, IL (village) Cook County	850
Mount Prospect, IL (village) Cook County	850

Specified Housing Units Rented by Guamanian or Chamorros
Top 10 Places Sorted by Number

Place	Dollars/Month

Specified Housing Units Rented by Hawaiian, Natives
Top 10 Places Sorted by Number

Place	Dollars/Month

Specified Housing Units Rented by Hmongs
Top 10 Places Sorted by Number

Place	Dollars/Month

Specified Housing Units Rented by Indonesians
Top 10 Places Sorted by Number

Place	Dollars/Month

Specified Housing Units Rented by Japanese
Top 10 Places Sorted by Number

Place	Dollars/Month
Buffalo Grove, IL (village) Lake County	1,967
Wilmette, IL (village) Cook County	1,950
Hoffman Estates, IL (village) Cook County	1,643
Mount Prospect, IL (village) Cook County	1,583
Schaumburg, IL (village) Cook County	1,323
Arlington Heights, IL (village) Cook County	1,322
Elk Grove Village, IL (village) Cook County	1,281
Glenview, IL (village) Cook County	1,088
Evanston, IL (city) Cook County	945
Chicago, IL (city) Cook County	731

Specified Housing Units Rented by Koreans
Top 10 Places Sorted by Number

Place	Dollars/Month
Northbrook, IL (village) Cook County	2,001
Buffalo Grove, IL (village) Lake County	1,583
Morton Grove, IL (village) Cook County	1,516
Wilmette, IL (village) Cook County	1,131
Schaumburg, IL (village) Cook County	1,063
Vernon Hills, IL (village) Lake County	1,008
Naperville, IL (city) Du Page County	990
Arlington Heights, IL (village) Cook County	973
Hoffman Estates, IL (village) Cook County	952
Palatine, IL (village) Cook County	873

Specified Housing Units Rented by Laotians
Top 10 Places Sorted by Number

Place	Dollars/Month
Elgin, IL (city) Kane County	644
Rockford, IL (city) Winnebago County	466

Specified Housing Units Rented by Malaysians
Top 10 Places Sorted by Number

Place	Dollars/Month

Specified Housing Units Rented by Pakistanis
Top 10 Places Sorted by Number

Place	Dollars/Month
Skokie, IL (village) Cook County	685
Chicago, IL (city) Cook County	680

Specified Housing Units Rented by Samoans
Top 10 Places Sorted by Number

Place	Dollars/Month

Specified Housing Units Rented by Sri Lankans
Top 10 Places Sorted by Number

Place	Dollars/Month

Specified Housing Units Rented by Taiwanese
Top 10 Places Sorted by Number

Place	Dollars/Month
Naperville, IL (city) Du Page County	850
Chicago, IL (city) Cook County	713

Specified Housing Units Rented by Thais
Top 10 Places Sorted by Number

Place	Dollars/Month
Chicago, IL (city) Cook County	686

Specified Housing Units Rented by Tongans
Top 10 Places Sorted by Number

Place	Dollars/Month

Specified Housing Units Rented by Vietnamese
Top 10 Places Sorted by Number

Place	Dollars/Month
Aurora, IL (city) Kane County	1,031
Glendale Heights, IL (village) Du Page County	804
Carol Stream, IL (village) Du Page County	775
Wheaton, IL (city) Du Page County	675
Chicago, IL (city) Cook County	642
Champaign, IL (city) Champaign County	467
Rockford, IL (city) Winnebago County	425

Median Home Value

All Specified Owner-Occupied Housing Units
Top 10 Places Sorted by Number

Place	Dollars
Winnetka, IL (village) Cook County	756,500
South Barrington, IL (village) Cook County	678,800
Lake Forest, IL (city) Lake County	662,400
Oak Brook, IL (village) Du Page County	635,400
Long Grove, IL (village) Lake County	555,400
Hinsdale, IL (village) Du Page County	520,100
Burr Ridge, IL (village) Du Page County	477,800
Lincolnshire, IL (village) Lake County	442,400
Wilmette, IL (village) Cook County	441,600
River Forest, IL (village) Cook County	386,600

Specified Housing Units Owned and Occupied by Asians
Top 10 Places Sorted by Number

Place	Dollars
Winnetka, IL (village) Cook County	852,300
South Barrington, IL (village) Cook County	801,300
Oak Brook, IL (village) Du Page County	773,300
Lake Forest, IL (city) Lake County	684,700
Burr Ridge, IL (village) Du Page County	589,300
Deerfield, IL (village) Lake County	461,100
Long Grove, IL (village) Lake County	443,200
Lincolnshire, IL (village) Lake County	423,100
Highland Park, IL (city) Lake County	398,100
River Forest, IL (village) Cook County	355,600

Specified Housing Units Owned and Occupied by Native Hawaiian and Other Pacific Islanders
Top 10 Places Sorted by Number

Place	Dollars
Chicago, IL (city) Cook County	135,000

Notes: Please refer to the User's Guide for an explanation of data; tables reflect only those areas that meet Summary File 4 population thresholds, therefore there may be less than 10 places listed

Specified Housing Units Owned and Occupied by Asian Indians
Top 10 Places Sorted by Number

Place	Dollars
Oak Brook, IL (village) Du Page County	856,100
South Barrington, IL (village) Cook County	830,400
Burr Ridge, IL (village) Du Page County	613,200
Glenview, IL (village) Cook County	402,800
Rolling Meadows, IL (city) Cook County	316,700
Lincolnwood, IL (village) Cook County	294,100
Naperville, IL (city) Du Page County	271,200
Buffalo Grove, IL (village) Lake County	262,500
Orland Park, IL (village) Cook County	262,500
Darien, IL (city) Du Page County	246,300

Specified Housing Units Owned and Occupied by Bangladeshis
Top 10 Places Sorted by Number

Place	Dollars

Specified Housing Units Owned and Occupied by Cambodians
Top 10 Places Sorted by Number

Place	Dollars
Chicago, IL (city) Cook County	229,200

Specified Housing Units Owned and Occupied by Chinese (except Taiwanese)
Top 10 Places Sorted by Number

Place	Dollars
Northbrook, IL (village) Cook County	348,200
Glenview, IL (village) Cook County	297,800
Wilmette, IL (village) Cook County	290,400
Evanston, IL (city) Cook County	285,700
Vernon Hills, IL (village) Lake County	283,100
Arlington Heights, IL (village) Cook County	275,000
Buffalo Grove, IL (village) Lake County	261,100
Naperville, IL (city) Du Page County	261,000
Lisle, IL (village) Du Page County	253,800
Mundelein, IL (village) Lake County	244,100

Specified Housing Units Owned and Occupied by Fijians
Top 10 Places Sorted by Number

Place	Dollars

No places met population threshold.

Specified Housing Units Owned and Occupied by Filipinos
Top 10 Places Sorted by Number

Place	Dollars
Naperville, IL (city) Du Page County	302,000
Lincolnwood, IL (village) Cook County	278,300
Glenview, IL (village) Cook County	277,100
Gurnee, IL (village) Lake County	237,000
Darien, IL (city) Du Page County	234,400
Arlington Heights, IL (village) Cook County	233,200
Downers Grove, IL (village) Du Page County	232,000
Mundelein, IL (village) Lake County	231,800
Niles, IL (village) Cook County	222,000
Wheeling, IL (village) Cook County	216,900

Specified Housing Units Owned and Occupied by Guamanian or Chamorros
Top 10 Places Sorted by Number

Place	Dollars

No places met population threshold.

Specified Housing Units Owned and Occupied by Hawaiian, Natives
Top 10 Places Sorted by Number

Place	Dollars

No places met population threshold.

Specified Housing Units Owned and Occupied by Hmongs
Top 10 Places Sorted by Number

Place	Dollars

No places met population threshold.

Specified Housing Units Owned and Occupied by Indonesians
Top 10 Places Sorted by Number

Place	Dollars

No places met population threshold.

Specified Housing Units Owned and Occupied by Japanese
Top 10 Places Sorted by Number

Place	Dollars
Glenview, IL (village) Cook County	342,500
Schaumburg, IL (village) Cook County	296,900
Arlington Heights, IL (village) Cook County	280,200
Hoffman Estates, IL (village) Cook County	279,500
Wilmette, IL (village) Cook County	273,800
Buffalo Grove, IL (village) Lake County	246,900
Elk Grove Village, IL (village) Cook County	226,600
Evanston, IL (city) Cook County	225,000
Mount Prospect, IL (village) Cook County	217,900
Chicago, IL (city) Cook County	176,900

Specified Housing Units Owned and Occupied by Koreans
Top 10 Places Sorted by Number

Place	Dollars
Glenview, IL (village) Cook County	335,500
Northbrook, IL (village) Cook County	318,900
Wilmette, IL (village) Cook County	305,800
Palatine, IL (village) Cook County	278,300
Lincolnwood, IL (village) Cook County	278,000
Buffalo Grove, IL (village) Lake County	266,700
Arlington Heights, IL (village) Cook County	263,500
Vernon Hills, IL (village) Lake County	245,000
Morton Grove, IL (village) Cook County	239,700
Mount Prospect, IL (village) Cook County	234,000

Specified Housing Units Owned and Occupied by Laotians
Top 10 Places Sorted by Number

Place	Dollars
Elgin, IL (city) Kane County	149,700
Rockford, IL (city) Winnebago County	82,400

Specified Housing Units Owned and Occupied by Malaysians
Top 10 Places Sorted by Number

Place	Dollars

No places met population threshold.

Specified Housing Units Owned and Occupied by Pakistanis
Top 10 Places Sorted by Number

Place	Dollars
Skokie, IL (village) Cook County	199,000
Chicago, IL (city) Cook County	120,100

Specified Housing Units Owned and Occupied by Samoans
Top 10 Places Sorted by Number

Place	Dollars

No places met population threshold.

Specified Housing Units Owned and Occupied by Sri Lankans
Top 10 Places Sorted by Number

Place	Dollars

No places met population threshold.

Specified Housing Units Owned and Occupied by Taiwanese
Top 10 Places Sorted by Number

Place	Dollars
Naperville, IL (city) Du Page County	263,100
Chicago, IL (city) Cook County	95,000

Specified Housing Units Owned and Occupied by Thais
Top 10 Places Sorted by Number

Place	Dollars
Chicago, IL (city) Cook County	174,600

Specified Housing Units Owned and Occupied by Tongans
Top 10 Places Sorted by Number

Place	Dollars

No places met population threshold.

Specified Housing Units Owned and Occupied by Vietnamese
Top 10 Places Sorted by Number

Place	Dollars
Chicago, IL (city) Cook County	191,400
Carol Stream, IL (village) Du Page County	170,800
Aurora, IL (city) Kane County	157,600
Wheaton, IL (city) Du Page County	148,200
Glendale Heights, IL (village) Du Page County	146,600
Rockford, IL (city) Winnebago County	96,400
Champaign, IL (city) Champaign County	88,100

Notes: Please refer to the User's Guide for an explanation of data; tables reflect only those areas that meet Summary File 4 population thresholds, therefore there may be less than 10 places listed

Climate

ILLINOIS

PHYSICAL FEATURES. Illinois lies midway between the Continental Divide and the Atlantic Ocean and some 500 miles north of the Gulf of Mexico. Its climate is typically continental with cold winters, warm summers, and frequent short period fluctuations in temperature, humidity, cloudiness, and wind direction.

The irregular shape of the State has a width of less than 200 miles at most points, but extends for 385 miles in the north-south direction. Except for a few low hills in the extreme south and a small unglaciated area in the extreme northwest, the terrain is flat. Differences in elevation have no significant influence on the climate. River drainage is mainly toward the Mississippi River, which forms the entire western boundary of the State. From north to south the principal rivers entering the Mississippi are the Rock, Illinois, Kaskaskia, and the Big Muddy. Approximately one-seventh of the State area drains southeastward into the Wabash and Ohio Rivers. Only a small area drains into Lake Michigan.

GENERAL CLIMATE. Without the protection of natural barriers, such as mountain ranges, Illinois experiences the full sweep of the winds which are constantly bringing in the climates of other areas. Southeast and easterly winds bring mild and wet weather; southerly winds are warm and showery; westerly winds are dry with moderate temperatures; and winds from the northwest and north are cool and dry. Winds are controlled by the storm systems and weather fronts which move eastward and northeastward through this area.

Storm systems move through the State most frequently during the winter and spring months and cause a maximum of cloudiness during those seasons. Summer-season storm systems tend to be weaker and to stay farther north, leaving Illinois with much sunshine interspersed with thunderstorm situations of comparatively short duration. The retreat of the sun in autumn is associated with variable periods of pleasant dry weather of the Indian summer variety. This season ends rather abruptly with the returning storminess which usually begins in November.

TEMPERATURE. Because Illinois extends so far in a north-south direction, the contrasts in winter temperature conditions are rather strong. The extreme north has frequent snow and temperatures drop to below zero several times each winter. The soil freezes to a depth of about three feet and occasionally remains snow-covered for weeks at a time. In the extreme south snow falls only occasionally and leaves after a few days, while temperatures drop to zero on an average of only about one day each winter. The soil freezes, but only to a depth of eight to 12 inches, with great variation in the duration of soil-frost periods. The north-south range in winter mean temperatures is approximately 14°F.

During the summer season the sun heats the entire State quite strongly and uniformly. The north-south range of mean temperatures in July is only about 6°F. The annual average of days with temperatures of 90°F. or higher is near 20 in the north and near 50 in the south and west-central. Summer also brings periods of uncomfortably hot and humid weather, which are most persistent in the south. In the north the heat is usually broken after a few days by the arrival of cool air from Canada, but this cooling does not always penetrate to the southern portions of the State.

PRECIPITATION. Latitude is the principal control for both temperature and precipitation, with the northern counties averaging cooler and drier than the south. Distance from the Gulf of Mexico and lower airmass temperatures both tend to reduce the amounts of precipitation in the northern portion. Annual precipitation is approximately one and one-half times as great in the extreme south as in the extreme north, but most of the excess in the southern portion falls during winter and early spring. Mean total precipitation for the four-month period of December through March ranges from near seven inches in the extreme northwest to more than 14 inches in the extreme southeast. Precipitation during the warm season is more uniform. Totals for the six-month period of April through September range from 21 to 24 inches throughout the State. The driest month is February. The wettest months are May and June.

Precipitation during fall, winter, and spring tends to fall uniformly over large areas. In contrast, summer rainfall occurs principally as brief showers affecting relatively small areas. The erratic occurrence of summer showers results in uneven distribution. The high rates of summer rainfall also cause runoff and soil erosion. Summer showers are usually accompanied by thunder and, sometimes, by hail or destructive windstorms.

Floods occur nearly every year in at least some part of the State. The spring and early summer flood season results from a tendency for heavy general rainfall at that time of the year. The extreme north frequently has late winter or early spring flooding with the breakup of river ice, especially if there is an appreciable snow cover which is taken off by rain. River stages tend to decline during late summer, but local flash floods in minor streams, due to heavy thunderstorm rains, are common throughout the warm season. The interior rivers in the central and south have flat beds and sluggish currents so that they rise slowly and remain in flood conditions for relatively long periods.

SNOWFALL. The annual average of snowfall ranges from near 30 inches in the extreme north to only 10 inches in the extreme south. In the extreme north the most likely form of winter precipitation is snow. In contrast, more than 90% of Cairo's winter precipitation falls as rain. In a large number of winter storm situations, only a slight change in the temperature pattern would suffice to change rain to snow or vice versa. For this reason, Illinois snowfall records show great variability. Snowfalls of one inch or more occur on an average of 10 to 12 days per year in the extreme north and decrease to three or four in the far south. The two northern divisions average about 50 days annually when the ground is covered with one inch or more of snow, and this average decreases to about 15 days in the two southern divisions.

STORMS. Heavy snows of four to six inches or more average one or two per year in the north and less frequently in the south. Strong winds will drift snow and make driving hazardous. Moderate to heavy ice storms average about once every four or five years and can be quite damaging. Thunderstorms average about 35 to 50 annually, but most are quite harmless. On occasion they provide the source for hail, damaging winds, and tornadoes. Hail falls on an average of two or three days annually in the same locality, but usually causes little damage.

More than 65 percent of Illinois tornadoes occur during the months of March, April, May, and June. This "tornado season" is marked by a rapid increase in activity during March, a peak in April and May, and a decline during June. Tornadoes have occurred during each of the twelve months of the year.

INFLUENCE OF LAKE MICHIGAN. Because prevailing winds are westerly and storm systems move from the same direction, the influence of the lake on Illinois weather is not large. When the wind blows from the lake toward the shore, which it does for approximately one-fourth of the time during spring and summer and for about one-eighth of the time during fall and winter, the result is a moderation of temperature. In addition to the general occurrence of onshore winds, there is the local "sea breeze" effect on summer afternoons which is usually observable in a narrow strip near the lake shore.

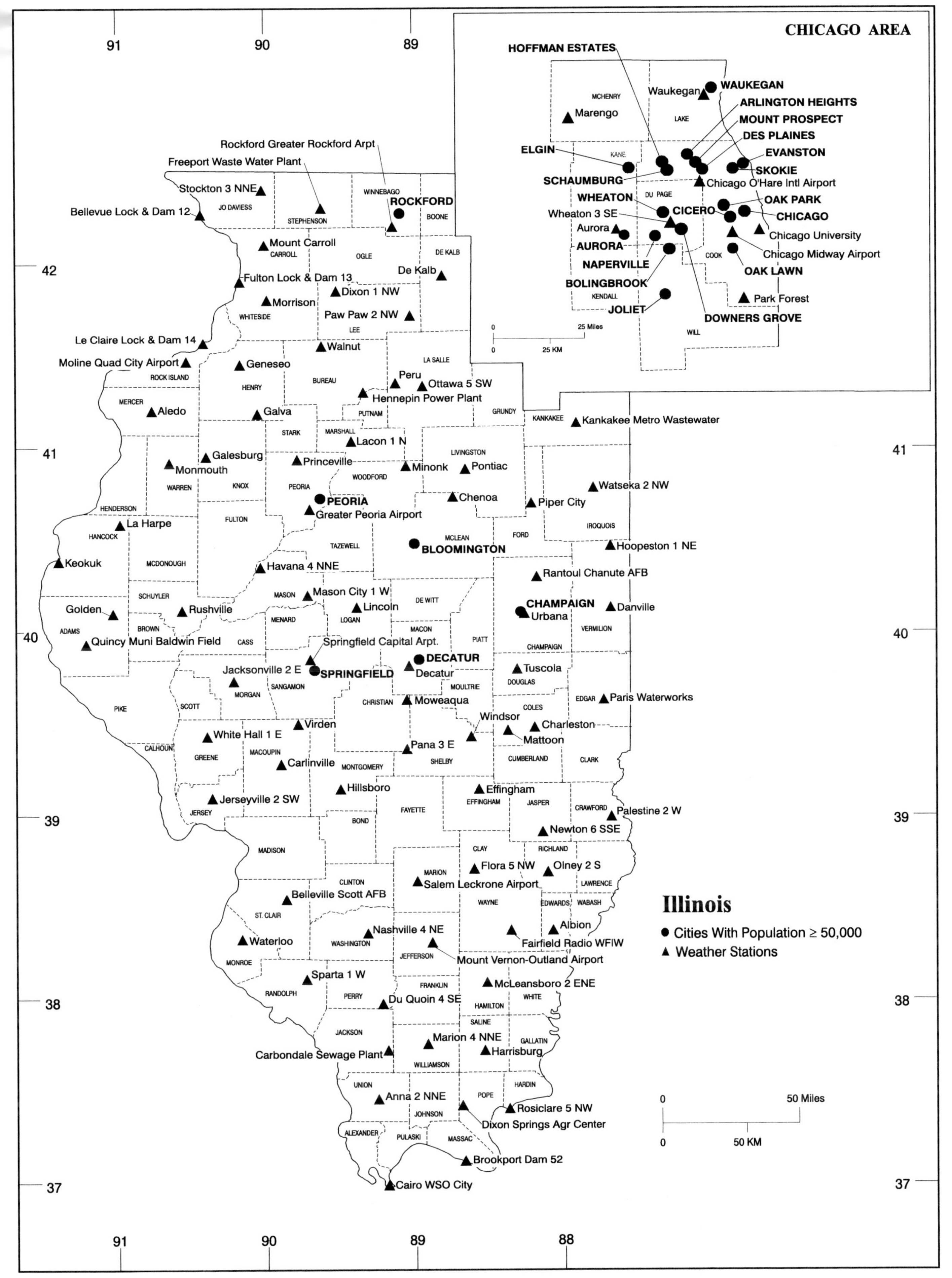
CHICAGO AREA
HOFFMAN ESTATES
Waukegan
WAUKEGAN
MCHENRY
Marengo
LAKE
ARLINGTON HEIGHTS
MOUNT PROSPECT
DES PLAINES
ELGIN
KANE
EVANSTON
SKOKIE
SCHAUMBURG
Chicago O'Hare Intl Airport
WHEATON
DU PAGE
OAK PARK
Wheaton 3 SE
CICERO
CHICAGO
Aurora
Chicago University
AURORA
NAPERVILLE
COOK
Chicago Midway Airport
OAK LAWN
BOLINGBROOK
KENDALL
Park Forest
JOLIET
DOWNERS GROVE
WILL
25 Miles
25 KM
91
90
89
88
42
41
40
39
38
37
Rockford Greater Rockford Arpt
Freeport Waste Water Plant
Stockton 3 NNE
WINNEBAGO
ROCKFORD
JO DAVIESS
STEPHENSON
BOONE
Bellevue Lock & Dam 12
Mount Carroll
CARROLL
OGLE
DE KALB
De Kalb
Fulton Lock & Dam 13
Dixon 1 NW
Morrison
WHITESIDE
Paw Paw 2 NW
LEE
Le Claire Lock & Dam 14
Walnut
Moline Quad City Airport
Geneseo
LA SALLE
ROCK ISLAND
HENRY
BUREAU
Peru
Ottawa 5 SW
Hennepin Power Plant
MERCER
Aledo
Galva
PUTNAM
GRUNDY
KANKAKEE
Kankakee Metro Wastewater
STARK
MARSHALL
Lacon 1 N
LIVINGSTON
Galesburg
Princeville
Minonk
Pontiac
Monmouth
WARREN
KNOX
PEORIA
WOODFORD
Watseka 2 NW
Chenoa
HENDERSON
PEORIA
Piper City
Greater Peoria Airport
La Harpe
FULTON
IROQUOIS
HANCOCK
MCLEAN
FORD
TAZEWELL
BLOOMINGTON
Hoopeston 1 NE
Keokuk
MCDONOUGH
Havana 4 NNE
Rantoul Chanute AFB
SCHUYLER
MASON
Mason City 1 W
DE WITT
CHAMPAIGN
Danville
Golden
Rushville
Lincoln
MENARD
LOGAN
Urbana
ADAMS
BROWN
MACON
VERMILION
Quincy Muni Baldwin Field
CASS
Springfield Capital Arpt.
PIATT
CHAMPAIGN
DECATUR
Tuscola
Jacksonville 2 E
SPRINGFIELD
Decatur
DOUGLAS
MORGAN
SANGAMON
MOULTRIE
EDGAR
Paris Waterworks
PIKE
SCOTT
CHRISTIAN
Moweaqua
COLES
Windsor
Virden
Charleston
White Hall 1 E
Mattoon
CALHOUN
MACOUPIN
Pana 3 E
GREENE
SHELBY
CUMBERLAND
CLARK
Carlinville
MONTGOMERY
Hillsboro
Effingham
Jerseyville 2 SW
EFFINGHAM
JASPER
CRAWFORD
JERSEY
FAYETTE
Palestine 2 W
BOND
Newton 6 SSE
MADISON
CLAY
RICHLAND
Flora 5 NW
Olney 2 S
MARION
CLINTON
Salem Leckrone Airport
LAWRENCE
Belleville Scott AFB
WAYNE
EDWARDS
WABASH
ST. CLAIR
Illinois
Albion
Nashville 4 NE
Cities With Population ≥ 50,000
Waterloo
Fairfield Radio WFIW
Weather Stations
WASHINGTON
JEFFERSON
MONROE
Mount Vernon-Outland Airport
Sparta 1 W
FRANKLIN
McLeansboro 2 ENE
RANDOLPH
PERRY
WHITE
Du Quoin 4 SE
HAMILTON
SALINE
JACKSON
Marion 4 NNE
GALLATIN
Harrisburg
Carbondale Sewage Plant
WILLIAMSON
UNION
HARDIN
Anna 2 NNE
POPE
Rosiclare 5 NW
50 Miles
JOHNSON
Dixon Springs Agr Center
ALEXANDER
PULASKI
MASSAC
50 KM
Brookport Dam 52
Cairo WSO City

Illinois Weather Stations by County

County	Station Name
Adams	Golden Quincy Muni Baldwin Field
Alexander	Cairo WSO City
Bureau	Walnut
Carroll	Mount Carroll
Champaign	Rantoul Chanute AFB Urbana
Christian	Pana 3 E
Clay	Flora 5 NW
Coles	Charleston Mattoon
Cook	Chicago Midway Airport Chicago O'Hare Int'l Airport Chicago University Park Forest
Crawford	Palestine 2 W
Dekalb	De Kalb
Douglas	Tuscola
Dupage	Wheaton 3 SE
Edgar	Paris Waterworks
Edwards	Albion
Effingham	Effingham
Ford	Piper City
Greene	White Hall 1 E
Hamilton	McLeansboro 2 ENE
Hancock	La Harpe
Hardin	Rosiclare 5 NW
Henry	Galva Geneseo
Iroquois	Watseka 2 NW
Jackson	Carbondale Sewage Plant
Jasper	Newton 6 SSE
Jefferson	Mount Vernon-Outland Airport
Jersey	Jerseyville 2 SW
Jo Daviess	Stockton 3 NNE
Kane	Aurora

County	Station Name
Kankakee	Kankakee Metro Wastewater
Knox	Galesburg
La Salle	Ottawa 5 SW Peru
Lake	Waukegan
Lee	Dixon 1 NW Paw Paw 2 NW
Livingston	Pontiac
Logan	Lincoln
Macon	Decatur
Macoupin	Carlinville Virden
Madison	Alton Melvin Price Lock & Dam
Marion	Salem Leckrone Airport
Marshall	Lacon 1 N
Mason	Havana 4 NNE Mason City 1 W
Massac	Brookport Dam 52
McHenry	Marengo
McLean	Chenoa
Mercer	Aledo
Monroe	Waterloo
Montgomery	Hillsboro
Morgan	Jacksonville 2 E
Peoria	Greater Peoria Airport Princeville
Perry	Du Quoin 4 SE
Pope	Dixon Springs Agr. Center
Putnam	Hennepin Power Plant
Randolph	Sparta 1 W
Richland	Olney 2 S
Rock Island	Moline Quad City Airport
Saline	Harrisburg
Sangamon	Springfield Capital Airport

County	Station Name
Schuyler	Rushville
Shelby	Moweaqua Windsor
St. Clair	Belleville Scott AFB
Stephenson	Freeport Waste Water Plant
Union	Anna 2 NNE
Vermilion	Danville Hoopeston 1 NE
Warren	Monmouth
Washington	Nashville 4 NE
Wayne	Fairfield Radio WFIW
Whiteside	Fulton Lock & Dam 13 Morrison
Williamson	Marion 4 NNE
Winnebago	Rockford Greater Rockford Arpt.
Woodford	Minonk

Illinois Weather Stations by City

City	Station Name	Miles
Arlington Heights	Chicago O'Hare Int'l Airport	8
	Waukegan	18
	Wheaton 3 SE	20
Aurora	Aurora	1
	Wheaton 3 SE	13
Bolingbrook	Aurora	13
	Chicago Midway Airport	17
	Wheaton 3 SE	8
Champaign	Rantoul Chanute AFB	14
	Urbana	1
Chicago	Chicago O'Hare Int'l Airport	15
	Chicago University	7
	Chicago Midway Airport	6
Cicero	Chicago O'Hare Int'l Airport	12
	Chicago University	9
	Chicago Midway Airport	4
	Wheaton 3 SE	16
Decatur	Decatur	4
	Moweaqua	16
Des Plaines	Chicago O'Hare Int'l Airport	4
	Chicago Midway Airport	19
	Wheaton 3 SE	17
Downers Grove	Aurora	16
	Chicago O'Hare Int'l Airport	14
	Chicago Midway Airport	14
	Wheaton 3 SE	3
Elgin	Aurora	19
	Chicago O'Hare Int'l Airport	19
	Wheaton 3 SE	19
Evanston	Chicago O'Hare Int'l Airport	12
	Chicago University	19
	Chicago Midway Airport	18
Hoffman Estates	Chicago O'Hare Int'l Airport	11
	Wheaton 3 SE	17
Joliet	Aurora	20
	Wheaton 3 SE	20
Mount Prospect	Chicago O'Hare Int'l Airport	6
	Wheaton 3 SE	18
Naperville	Aurora	9
	Chicago O'Hare Int'l Airport	20
	Wheaton 3 SE	6
Oak Lawn	Chicago University	9
	Chicago Midway Airport	5
	Park Forest	15
	Wheaton 3 SE	18
Oak Park	Chicago O'Hare Int'l Airport	9
	Chicago University	12
	Chicago Midway Airport	7
Oak Park *(cont.)*	Wheaton 3 SE	15
Peoria	Greater Peoria Airport	5
	Princeville	17
Rockford	Rockford Greater Rockford Arpt.	6
	Beloit, WI	16
Schaumburg	Chicago O'Hare Int'l Airport	9
	Wheaton 3 SE	15
Skokie	Chicago O'Hare Int'l Airport	10
	Chicago University	19
	Chicago Midway Airport	17
Springfield	Springfield Capital Airport	4
Waukegan	Waukegan	2
	Kenosha, WI	14
Wheaton	Aurora	13
	Chicago O'Hare Int'l Airport	13
	Chicago Midway Airport	19
	Wheaton 3 SE	3

Note: Miles is the distance between the geographic center of the city and the weather station.

Illinois Weather Stations by Elevation

Feet	Station Name
967	Stockton 3 NNE
948	Paw Paw 2 NW
872	De Kalb
816	Marengo
807	Galva
770	Galesburg
761	Quincy Muni Baldwin Field
754	Rantoul Chanute AFB
748	Freeport Waste Water Plant
748	Minonk
744	Monmouth
741	Urbana
734	Princeville
725	Golden
718	Aledo
715	Mattoon
711	Chenoa
708	Hoopeston 1 NE
708	Park Forest
698	Dixon 1 NW
698	La Harpe
698	Pana 3 E
698	Waukegan
688	Walnut
688	Windsor
679	Charleston
679	Paris Waterworks
679	Rockford Greater Rockford Arpt.
679	Wheaton 3 SE
672	Virden
669	Piper City
659	Rushville
656	Chicago O'Hare Int'l Airport
652	Tuscola
649	Greater Peoria Airport
649	Pontiac
649	Waterloo
639	Aurora
639	Kankakee Metro Wastewater
639	Mount Carroll
636	Geneseo
629	Carlinville
629	Hillsboro
629	Jerseyville 2 SW
620	Decatur
620	Peru
620	Watseka 2 NW
613	Moweaqua
610	Chicago Midway Airport
606	Effingham
606	Jacksonville 2 E
600	Morrison
597	Anna 2 NNE
593	Chicago University
590	Fulton Lock & Dam 13

Feet	Station Name
590	Moline Quad City Airport
583	Mason City 1 W
583	Springfield Capital Airport
580	Lincoln
577	White Hall 1 E
567	Salem Leckrone Airport
557	Danville
538	Dixon Springs Agr. Center
534	Sparta 1 W
528	Albion
524	Ottawa 5 SW
515	Nashville 4 NE
508	Newton 6 SSE
498	Flora 5 NW
479	McLeansboro 2 ENE
479	Olney 2 S
475	Marion 4 NNE
469	Palestine 2 W
465	Mount Vernon-Outland Airport
459	Havana 4 NNE
459	Hennepin Power Plant
459	Lacon 1 N
442	Belleville Scott AFB
429	Alton Melvin Price Lock & Dam
429	Fairfield Radio WFIW
419	Du Quoin 4 SE
396	Rosiclare 5 NW
387	Carbondale Sewage Plant
364	Harrisburg
328	Brookport Dam 52
311	Cairo WSO City

Chicago O'Hare Int'l Airport

Chicago is located along the southwest shore of Lake Michigan and occupies a plain which, for the most part, is only some tens of feet above the lake. Lake Michigan averages 579 feet above sea level. Natural water drainage over most of the city would be into Lake Michigan, and from areas west of the city is into the Mississippi River System. But actual drainage over most of the city is artificially channeled also into the Mississippi system.

Chicago is in a region of frequently changeable weather. The climate is predominately continental, ranging from relatively warm in summer to relatively cold in winter. In late autumn and winter however, air masses that are initially very cold often reach the city only after being tempered by passage over one or more of the lakes. Similarly, in late spring and summer, air masses reaching the city from the north, northeast, or east are cooler because of movement over the Great Lakes. Very low winter temperatures most often occur in air that flows southward to the west of Lake Superior before reaching the Chicago area. In summer the higher temperatures are with south or southwest flow and are therefore not influenced by the lakes, the only modifying effect being a local lake breeze.

During the warm season, when the lake is cold relative to land, there is frequently a lake breeze that reduces daytime temperature near the shore. When the breeze off the lake is light this effect usually reaches inland only a mile or two, but with stronger on-shore winds the whole city is cooled. On the other hand, temperatures at night are warmer near the lake.

At the O'Hare International Airport temperatures of 96 degrees or higher occur in about half the summers, while about half the winters have a minimum as low as -15 degrees. The average occurrence of the first temperature as low as 32 degrees in the fall is mid-October and the average occurrence of the last temperature as low as 32 degrees in the spring is late April.

Precipitation falls mostly from air that has passed over the Gulf of Mexico. But in winter there is sometimes snowfall, light inland but locally heavy near the lakeshore, with Lake Michigan as the principal moisture source. The effect of Lake Michigan, both on winter temperatures and lake-produced snowfall, is enhanced by non-freezing of much of the lake during the winter, even though areas and harbors are often ice-choked.

Summer thunderstorms are often locally heavy and variable, parts of the city may receive substantial rainfall and other parts none. Longer periods of continuous precipitation are mostly in autumn, winter, and spring.

Chicago O'Hare Int'l Airport *Cook County* Elevation: 656 ft. Latitude: 41° 59' N Longitude: 87° 55' W

	JAN	FEB	MAR	APR	MAY	JUN	JUL	AUG	SEP	OCT	NOV	DEC	YEAR
Mean Maximum Temp. (°F)	29.6	34.6	45.8	58.3	70.2	79.8	84.3	82.0	74.6	62.7	47.8	35.3	58.7
Mean Temp. (°F)	21.8	26.9	37.3	48.4	59.2	68.7	74.0	72.3	64.3	52.5	39.8	28.1	49.5
Mean Minimum Temp. (°F)	14.1	19.2	28.7	38.4	48.1	57.7	63.7	62.5	54.0	42.3	31.8	20.8	40.1
Extreme Maximum Temp. (°F)	65	71	88	91	93	104	104	101	99	90	78	71	104
Extreme Minimum Temp. (°F)	-27	-19	-3	7	27	36	43	42	28	17	1	-25	-27
Days Maximum Temp. ≥ 90°F	0	0	0	0	1	4	8	4	2	0	0	0	19
Days Maximum Temp. ≤ 32°F	17	12	4	0	0	0	0	0	0	0	2	10	45
Days Minimum Temp. ≤ 32°F	29	24	21	7	1	0	0	0	0	4	16	26	128
Days Minimum Temp. ≤ 0°F	6	3	0	0	0	0	0	0	0	0	0	2	11
Heating Degree Days (base 65°F)	1,332	1,069	853	503	225	46	5	8	107	391	751	1,137	6,427
Cooling Degree Days (base 65°F)	0	0	2	9	47	163	292	238	91	8	0	0	850
Mean Precipitation (in.)	1.73	1.58	2.68	3.65	3.49	3.72	3.53	4.59	3.44	2.75	3.01	2.42	36.59
Maximum Precipitation (in.)	4.1	3.5	5.9	7.7	7.1	10.0	8.3	17.1	11.4	7.4	8.2	8.6	49.3
Minimum Precipitation (in.)	0.1	0.1	0.6	1.0	0.3	0.9	1.2	0.5	trace	0.2	0.6	0.2	21.8
Maximum 24-hr. Precipitation (in.)	2.0	1.4	1.8	2.4	3.4	3.1	2.9	6.5	2.9	4.3	2.9	4.5	6.5
Days With ≥ 0.1" Precipitation	5	4	6	7	7	6	6	7	6	5	6	5	70
Days With ≥ 1.0" Precipitation	0	0	0	1	1	1	1	1	1	1	1	1	9
Mean Snowfall (in.)	11.1	8.1	6.4	1.8	trace	trace	trace	trace	0.0	0.3	1.8	7.8	37.3
Maximum Snowfall (in.)	34	26	25	11	2	0	0	0	0	7	10	35	75
Maximum 24-hr. Snowfall (in.)	15	10	9	11	2	0	0	0	0	4	5	10	15
Days With ≥ 1.0" Snow Depth	18	12	4	1	0	0	0	0	0	0	1	8	44
Thunderstorm Days	< 1	< 1	2	4	5	6	6	6	4	2	1	1	37
Foggy Days	12	11	12	10	10	8	9	12	11	11	12	13	131
Predominant Sky Cover	OVR	OVR	OVR	OVR	OVR	OVR	SCT	SCT	OVR	OVR	OVR	OVR	OVR
Mean Relative Humidity 6am (%)	77	78	79	77	77	78	82	85	85	82	81	80	80
Mean Relative Humidity 3pm (%)	66	63	59	53	51	52	54	55	55	53	62	68	58
Mean Dewpoint (°F)	14	18	27	36	46	56	62	61	54	42	31	21	39
Prevailing Wind Direction	W	W	W	NNE	NNE	SSW	SW	SSW	S	S	SSW	WNW	SSW
Prevailing Wind Speed (mph)	12	10	12	13	12	10	9	9	9	10	13	12	10
Maximum Wind Gust (mph)	58	54	84	69	58	63	76	64	58	58	62	62	84

Greater Peoria Airport

The airport station is situated on a rather level tableland surrounded by well-drained and gently rolling terrain. It is set back a mile from the rim of the Illinois River Valley and is almost 200 feet above the river bed. Exposures of all instruments are good. The climate of this area is typically continental as shown by its changeable weather and the wide range of temperature extremes.

June and September are usually the most pleasant months of the year. Then during October or the first of November, Indian Summer is often experienced with an extended period of warm, dry weather.

Precipitation is normally heaviest during the growing season and lowest during midwinter.

The earliest snowfalls have occurred in September and the latest in the spring have occurred as late as May. Heavy snowfalls have rarely exceeded 20 inches.

Based on the 1951-1980 period, the average first occurrence of 32 degrees Fahrenheit in the fall is October 20 and the average last occurrence in the spring is April 24.

Greater Peoria Airport *Peoria County* Elevation: 649 ft. Latitude: 40° 40' N Longitude: 89° 41' W

	JAN	FEB	MAR	APR	MAY	JUN	JUL	AUG	SEP	OCT	NOV	DEC	YEAR
Mean Maximum Temp. (°F)	30.4	36.3	48.9	62.0	73.0	82.2	85.8	83.4	76.6	64.3	48.9	36.0	60.7
Mean Temp. (°F)	22.3	28.0	39.5	51.3	62.1	71.3	75.4	73.3	65.7	53.5	40.4	28.4	50.9
Mean Minimum Temp. (°F)	14.2	19.5	30.1	40.6	51.0	60.4	65.0	63.1	54.6	42.8	31.8	20.8	41.2
Extreme Maximum Temp. (°F)	70	72	86	92	93	105	102	103	97	87	78	71	105
Extreme Minimum Temp. (°F)	-25	-19	-6	14	29	39	47	41	29	19	-2	-23	-25
Days Maximum Temp. ≥ 90°F	0	0	0	0	1	5	9	6	2	0	0	0	23
Days Maximum Temp. ≤ 32°F	17	11	3	0	0	0	0	0	0	0	2	11	44
Days Minimum Temp. ≤ 32°F	29	24	19	5	0	0	0	0	0	4	17	27	125
Days Minimum Temp. ≤ 0°F	6	3	0	0	0	0	0	0	0	0	0	2	11
Heating Degree Days (base 65°F)	1,318	1,040	785	416	153	18	2	6	90	360	733	1,127	6,048
Cooling Degree Days (base 65°F)	0	0	2	12	68	222	342	280	117	11	0	0	1,054
Mean Precipitation (in.)	1.49	1.63	2.83	3.71	4.17	3.84	4.14	3.24	3.42	2.85	2.92	2.41	36.65
Maximum Precipitation (in.)	8.1	4.9	6.9	8.7	11.5	11.7	10.1	8.6	13.1	10.5	7.6	6.3	55.3
Minimum Precipitation (in.)	0.1	0.1	0.4	0.7	0.5	0.4	0.3	0.3	trace	trace	0.1	0.3	22.2
Maximum 24-hr. Precipitation (in.)	4.4	2.8	2.9	5.1	5.5	4.7	3.6	4.3	4.1	3.6	4.3	2.5	5.5
Days With ≥ 0.1" Precipitation	4	4	6	7	8	6	6	6	6	6	6	5	70
Days With ≥ 1.0" Precipitation	0	0	0	1	1	1	1	1	1	1	1	1	9
Mean Snowfall (in.)	8.0	5.8	3.5	1.1	trace	0.0	trace	0.0	trace	trace	2.1	6.3	26.8
Maximum Snowfall (in.)	25	15	18	13	trace	0	0	0	1	3	11	22	52
Maximum 24-hr. Snowfall (in.)	12	9	9	6	trace	0	0	0	1	3	8	7	12
Days With ≥ 1.0" Snow Depth	16	11	3	1	0	0	0	0	0	0	1	8	40
Thunderstorm Days	< 1	1	3	5	7	9	8	7	5	2	1	1	49
Foggy Days	11	10	9	7	7	6	7	9	9	10	10	12	107
Predominant Sky Cover	OVR	OVR	OVR	OVR	OVR	OVR	SCT	CLR	CLR	OVR	OVR	OVR	OVR
Mean Relative Humidity 6am (%)	80	81	81	78	80	82	86	89	87	84	83	83	83
Mean Relative Humidity 3pm (%)	67	64	58	52	52	52	55	56	52	52	61	69	57
Mean Dewpoint (°F)	16	20	29	38	49	59	64	63	54	43	32	22	41
Prevailing Wind Direction	S	S	S	S	S	S	S	S	S	S	S	S	S
Prevailing Wind Speed (mph)	12	12	13	12	10	10	9	8	9	10	12	12	10
Maximum Wind Gust (mph)	54	53	68	69	61	75	85	54	75	48	62	59	85

Moline Quad City Airport

The locality is in the heart of the Corn Belt. Agricultural crops include many important staple products in addition to corn. Cattle, hogs, horses, and poultry produced in Iowa and Illinois rank high in the nation. Close to the Mississippi River there is large scale truck gardening and considerable dairying. Field production of grains and livestock attains greater development farther away from the large streams, where the countryside is rolling prairie. Damaging droughts are not common. This, together with the variety of agricultural products, has led to designating the section as the Bread Basket of America.

The climate is favorable for many industries as evidenced by the large number and variety of manufacturing and other enterprises which have located and developed in the community. Among these are some of the largest producers of agricultural machinery in the world.

This area has a temperate continental climate, with a wide temperature range throughout the year. There are some intensely hot, unusually humid, periods in summer and severely cold periods in winter. Maxima of 90 degrees or more have occurred in summer as frequently as 55 days and zero or lower readings have occurred during every winter.

Freezing temperatures have occurred as late in spring as late May and as early in autumn as late September. Precipitation is usually well distributed throughout the year with the greatest amounts falling during the 177-day average crop growing season. Substantial weather changes frequently occur at three or four day intervals, as a direct result of proximity to some of the most important storm tracks.

Moline Quad City Airport *Rock Island Co.* Elevation: 590 ft. Latitude: 41° 28' N Longitude: 90° 31' W

	JAN	FEB	MAR	APR	MAY	JUN	JUL	AUG	SEP	OCT	NOV	DEC	YEAR
Mean Maximum Temp. (°F)	28.9	34.9	47.5	61.5	73.1	82.6	86.1	83.6	76.1	63.9	47.7	34.5	60.0
Mean Temp. (°F)	20.5	26.4	38.1	50.5	61.6	71.2	75.3	73.0	64.8	52.7	39.0	26.7	50.0
Mean Minimum Temp. (°F)	12.0	17.8	28.6	39.4	50.1	59.8	64.5	62.3	53.4	41.5	30.2	18.8	39.9
Extreme Maximum Temp. (°F)	69	71	88	93	95	104	103	103	98	93	79	71	104
Extreme Minimum Temp. (°F)	-27	-28	-7	7	29	39	46	40	30	16	-9	-24	-28
Days Maximum Temp. ≥ 90°F	0	0	0	0	1	5	9	6	2	0	0	0	23
Days Maximum Temp. ≤ 32°F	18	11	3	0	0	0	0	0	0	0	3	12	47
Days Minimum Temp. ≤ 32°F	29	24	20	7	1	0	0	0	0	6	18	28	133
Days Minimum Temp. ≤ 0°F	7	4	0	0	0	0	0	0	0	0	0	3	14
Heating Degree Days (base 65°F)	1,376	1,085	828	443	166	17	2	7	104	386	774	1,181	6,369
Cooling Degree Days (base 65°F)	0	0	2	13	61	213	334	265	103	11	0	0	1,002
Mean Precipitation (in.)	1.55	1.42	2.98	3.83	4.47	4.52	4.08	4.48	3.46	2.81	2.71	2.19	38.50
Maximum Precipitation (in.)	4.4	2.8	7.4	11.3	11.4	13.2	11.8	15.2	14.2	8.5	6.8	5.0	56.4
Minimum Precipitation (in.)	0.3	0.2	0.3	0.7	0.3	1.0	0.4	0.3	trace	trace	0.5	0.3	20.2
Maximum 24-hr. Precipitation (in.)	1.7	1.8	2.2	4.3	3.2	4.6	5.1	4.6	6.2	4.8	2.0	3.1	6.2
Days With ≥ 0.1" Precipitation	4	4	6	7	7	7	6	7	6	5	5	5	69
Days With ≥ 1.0" Precipitation	0	0	1	1	1	1	1	2	1	1	0	0	9
Mean Snowfall (in.)	9.8	6.7	5.2	1.6	trace	trace	trace	0.0	trace	0.2	3.0	7.3	33.8
Maximum Snowfall (in.)	27	21	20	13	trace	0	0	0	0	7	16	22	63
Maximum 24-hr. Snowfall (in.)	16	9	10	8	trace	0	0	0	0	7	8	9	16
Days With ≥ 1.0" Snow Depth	19	14	5	1	0	0	0	0	0	0	2	10	51
Thunderstorm Days	< 1	< 1	2	5	7	8	8	7	5	2	1	< 1	45
Foggy Days	12	11	13	10	11	9	12	15	14	13	12	13	145
Predominant Sky Cover	OVR	OVR	OVR	OVR	OVR	OVR	CLR	CLR	CLR	CLR	OVR	OVR	OVR
Mean Relative Humidity 6am (%)	76	78	79	78	79	81	85	89	87	82	80	79	81
Mean Relative Humidity 3pm (%)	66	63	57	50	49	50	54	55	52	49	59	67	56
Mean Dewpoint (°F)	13	18	27	37	48	59	64	63	54	42	30	19	40
Prevailing Wind Direction	WNW	WNW	WNW	WNW	S	S	S	S	S	S	WNW	WNW	WNW
Prevailing Wind Speed (mph)	14	14	14	15	12	10	9	9	10	12	14	14	13
Maximum Wind Gust (mph)	59	54	69	81	66	79	66	81	59	61	60	69	81

Rockford- Greater Rockford Arpt.

The climate of Rockford is characterized by hot summers and cold winters.

When winter northeasterly winds blow across Lake Michigan, cloudiness often is increased in the Rockford area, and temperatures are somewhat higher than those westward around the Mississippi River. Conversely, in summer, the cooling effect of Lake Michigan sometimes is felt as far westward as Rockford.

While 34 percent of the precipitation occurs in the three summer months of June to August, and 64 percent in the six months, April to September, no month averages less than four percent of the annual total.

Though summers may be described as hot, seldom does oppressive heat prevail for extended periods. In general, the summers are pleasant.

Winters are cold. Snow cover is adequate for diversified winter sports, and usually is continuous from late December through February.

Based on the 1951-1980 period, the average first occurrence of 32 degrees Fahrenheit in the fall is October 11 and the average last occurrence in the spring is April 29.

Rockford-Greater Rockford Arpt. *Winnebago Co.* Elev. 679 ft. Latitude: 42° 12' N Longitude: 89° 07' W

	JAN	FEB	MAR	APR	MAY	JUN	JUL	AUG	SEP	OCT	NOV	DEC	YEAR
Mean Maximum Temp. (°F)	26.9	32.5	44.6	58.7	71.4	80.6	83.9	81.5	74.2	61.9	45.7	32.5	57.9
Mean Temp. (°F)	18.7	24.3	35.5	47.9	59.7	69.2	73.4	71.2	63.0	51.0	37.3	25.0	48.0
Mean Minimum Temp. (°F)	10.5	16.0	26.5	37.0	48.0	57.8	62.7	60.8	51.7	40.0	28.9	17.3	38.1
Extreme Maximum Temp. (°F)	63	68	85	91	95	101	102	104	95	90	75	66	104
Extreme Minimum Temp. (°F)	-27	-24	-9	5	27	37	45	41	27	17	-10	-24	-27
Days Maximum Temp. ≥ 90°F	0	0	0	0	1	3	6	3	1	0	0	0	14
Days Maximum Temp. ≤ 32°F	20	13	5	0	0	0	0	0	0	0	3	14	55
Days Minimum Temp. ≤ 32°F	30	26	23	9	1	0	0	0	1	7	20	28	145
Days Minimum Temp. ≤ 0°F	9	5	0	0	0	0	0	0	0	0	0	4	18
Heating Degree Days (base 65°F)	1,430	1,145	907	514	209	34	4	13	131	435	824	1,235	6,881
Cooling Degree Days (base 65°F)	0	0	1	8	48	171	275	215	76	6	0	0	800
Mean Precipitation (in.)	1.38	1.29	2.42	3.62	3.99	4.67	4.09	4.11	3.56	2.67	2.61	2.04	36.45
Maximum Precipitation (in.)	4.7	3.0	5.6	9.9	7.0	11.8	11.8	13.5	10.7	8.3	5.5	5.0	56.5
Minimum Precipitation (in.)	0.2	trace	0.6	1.0	0.5	0.5	0.8	0.7	0	trace	0.4	0.4	23.3
Maximum 24-hr. Precipitation (in.)	2.5	1.6	2.5	3.4	3.6	3.9	5.0	5.7	5.6	4.8	2.1	2.0	5.7
Days With ≥ 0.1" Precipitation	4	3	5	7	7	7	7	7	6	5	5	5	68
Days With ≥ 1.0" Precipitation	0	0	0	1	1	1	1	1	1	1	1	0	8
Mean Snowfall (in.)	10.1	7.6	5.7	1.6	trace	trace	trace	trace	0.0	trace	2.6	9.8	37.4
Maximum Snowfall (in.)	26	30	23	8	1	0	0	0	0	2	15	25	59
Maximum 24-hr. Snowfall (in.)	10	8	10	6	1	0	0	0	0	2	7	11	11
Days With ≥ 1.0" Snow Depth	22	17	7	1	0	0	0	0	0	0	2	14	63
Thunderstorm Days	< 1	< 1	2	4	5	8	8	6	5	2	1	< 1	41
Foggy Days	12	11	12	11	11	8	12	16	14	12	13	14	146
Predominant Sky Cover	OVR	OVR	OVR	OVR	OVR	OVR	OVR	OVR	OVR	OVR	OVR	OVR	OVR
Mean Relative Humidity 6am (%)	80	81	82	80	80	81	86	90	90	86	83	83	84
Mean Relative Humidity 3pm (%)	69	64	60	51	50	51	53	56	54	53	63	70	58
Mean Dewpoint (°F)	13	17	26	36	47	57	62	62	53	41	30	19	39
Prevailing Wind Direction	WNW	WNW	WNW	ENE	S	S	S	S	S	S	S	WNW	S
Prevailing Wind Speed (mph)	13	13	13	13	10	9	8	8	8	9	10	13	10
Maximum Wind Gust (mph)	56	54	54	64	81	67	79	67	58	59	59	62	81

Springfield Capital Airport

The location of Springfield near the center of North America gives it a typical continental climate with warm summers and fairly cold winters. The surrounding country is nearly level. There are no large hills in the vicinity, but rolling terrain is found near the Sangamon River and Spring Creek.

Monthly temperatures range from the upper 20s for January to the upper 70s for July. Considerable variation may take place within the seasons. Temperatures of 70 degrees or higher may occur in winter and temperatures near 50 degrees are sometimes recorded during the summer months.

There are no wet and dry seasons. Monthly precipitation ranges from a little over four inches in May and June to about two inches in January. There is some variation in rainfall totals from year to year. Thunderstorms are common during hot weather, and these are sometimes locally severe with brief but heavy showers. The average year has about fifty thunderstorms of which two-thirds occur during the months of May through August. Damaging hail accompanies only a few of the thunderstorms and the areas affected are usually small.

Sunshine is particularly abundant during the summer months when days are long and not very cloudy. January is the cloudiest month, with only about a third as much sunshine as July or August. March is the windiest month, and August the month with the least wind. Velocities of more than 40 mph are not unusual for brief periods in most months of the year. The prevailing wind direction is southerly during most of the year with northwesterly winds during the late fall and early spring months.

An overall description of the climate of Springfield would be one indicating pleasant conditions with sharp seasonal changes, but no extended periods of severely cold weather. Summer weather is often uncomfortably warm and humid.

Based on the 1951-1980 period, the average first occurrence of 32 degrees Fahrenheit in the fall is October 19 and the average last occurrence in the spring is April 17.

Springfield Capital Airport *Sangamon Co.* Elevation: 583 ft. Latitude: 39° 51' N Longitude: 89° 41' W

	JAN	FEB	MAR	APR	MAY	JUN	JUL	AUG	SEP	OCT	NOV	DEC	YEAR
Mean Maximum Temp. (°F)	32.8	38.7	50.9	63.8	74.8	83.6	87.0	84.7	78.6	66.7	51.2	38.6	62.6
Mean Temp. (°F)	24.8	30.3	41.6	53.1	63.8	72.8	76.5	74.3	67.1	55.5	42.6	30.9	52.8
Mean Minimum Temp. (°F)	16.8	21.8	32.2	42.4	52.7	61.9	66.0	63.9	55.5	44.3	33.8	23.2	42.9
Extreme Maximum Temp. (°F)	69	74	87	90	94	101	102	102	101	90	82	74	102
Extreme Minimum Temp. (°F)	-21	-20	-6	19	29	42	48	43	32	19	1	-21	-21
Days Maximum Temp. ≥ 90°F	0	0	0	0	1	7	11	7	3	0	0	0	29
Days Maximum Temp. ≤ 32°F	14	9	2	0	0	0	0	0	0	0	1	8	34
Days Minimum Temp. ≤ 32°F	28	22	16	4	0	0	0	0	0	4	14	25	113
Days Minimum Temp. ≤ 0°F	4	3	0	0	0	0	0	0	0	0	0	2	9
Heating Degree Days (base 65°F)	1,239	975	722	368	121	13	1	3	74	311	668	1,050	5,545
Cooling Degree Days (base 65°F)	0	0	3	16	86	254	369	307	140	22	1	0	1,198
Mean Precipitation (in.)	1.62	1.78	3.13	3.60	4.09	3.68	3.51	3.44	3.03	2.62	2.79	2.56	35.85
Maximum Precipitation (in.)	6.2	4.9	7.9	9.9	10.6	10.8	10.8	8.4	15.2	13.4	6.9	8.9	54.5
Minimum Precipitation (in.)	trace	0.3	0.2	0.7	0.3	0.2	0.3	0.1	trace	0.1	trace	0.1	22.8
Maximum 24-hr. Precipitation (in.)	2.4	2.4	3.3	4.4	3.6	5.1	4.3	4.4	5.4	4.7	2.4	4.7	5.4
Days With ≥ 0.1" Precipitation	4	4	7	7	7	6	6	5	5	5	6	5	67
Days With ≥ 1.0" Precipitation	0	0	1	1	1	1	1	1	1	1	0	1	9
Mean Snowfall (in.)	7.4	5.9	3.4	0.8	trace	0.0	trace	0.0	0.0	trace	1.6	5.0	24.1
Maximum Snowfall (in.)	21	18	23	8	1	0	0	0	0	3	9	23	48
Maximum 24-hr. Snowfall (in.)	8	10	9	6	1	0	0	0	0	3	8	11	11
Days With ≥ 1.0" Snow Depth	13	9	3	0	0	0	0	0	0	0	1	6	32
Thunderstorm Days	< 1	1	3	5	7	9	8	7	5	2	2	< 1	49
Foggy Days	9	8	8	6	6	5	6	9	8	8	8	10	91
Predominant Sky Cover	OVR	OVR	OVR	OVR	OVR	OVR	SCT	CLR	CLR	CLR	OVR	OVR	OVR
Mean Relative Humidity 6am (%)	80	81	81	79	81	82	85	89	87	83	82	82	83
Mean Relative Humidity 3pm (%)	67	65	59	52	51	51	54	56	50	50	60	69	57
Mean Dewpoint (°F)	18	22	31	41	51	61	65	64	56	44	33	24	43
Prevailing Wind Direction	S	S	S	S	S	S	S	S	S	S	S	S	S
Prevailing Wind Speed (mph)	15	14	15	15	13	12	9	9	10	13	14	15	13
Maximum Wind Gust (mph)	55	53	71	63	67	59	60	69	61	53	76	73	76

Albion *Edwards Co.* Elevation: 528 ft. Latitude: 38° 23' N Longitude: 88° 03' W

	JAN	FEB	MAR	APR	MAY	JUN	JUL	AUG	SEP	OCT	NOV	DEC	YEAR
Mean Maximum Temp. (°F)	39.5	45.5	56.0	67.3	77.0	85.9	90.0	88.3	81.8	70.7	55.4	43.9	66.8
Mean Temp. (°F)	31.3	36.2	46.0	56.3	66.2	75.2	79.1	77.3	70.3	59.0	46.3	35.7	56.6
Mean Minimum Temp. (°F)	23.0	26.9	35.9	45.3	55.4	64.5	68.1	66.3	58.7	47.3	37.1	27.5	46.3
Extreme Maximum Temp. (°F)	70	78	85	89	95	101	105	104	100	92	80	75	105
Extreme Minimum Temp. (°F)	-20	-11	2	22	34	42	50	47	36	24	9	-18	-20
Days Maximum Temp. ≥ 90°F	0	0	0	0	2	10	18	14	6	0	0	0	50
Days Maximum Temp. ≤ 32°F	9	5	1	0	0	0	0	0	0	0	1	5	21
Days Minimum Temp. ≤ 32°F	24	19	13	3	0	0	0	0	0	1	10	21	91
Days Minimum Temp. ≤ 0°F	1	1	0	0	0	0	0	0	0	0	0	1	3
Heating Degree Days (base 65°F)	1,040	807	587	282	76	5	0	1	37	217	557	902	4,511
Cooling Degree Days (base 65°F)	0	0	5	28	124	325	454	398	205	38	2	0	1,579
Mean Precipitation (in.)	2.55	2.82	4.19	5.34	4.73	4.19	3.80	3.14	2.95	3.48	4.33	3.34	44.86
Days With ≥ 0.1" Precipitation	5	5	7	8	7	6	5	5	5	5	6	6	70
Days With ≥ 1.0" Precipitation	1	1	1	2	1	1	1	1	1	1	1	1	13
Mean Snowfall (in.)	2.7	2.7	2.0	0.1	0.0	0.0	0.0	0.0	0.0	0.1	0.2	2.5	10.3
Days With ≥ 1.0" Snow Depth	4	3	1	0	0	0	0	0	0	0	0	1	9

Aledo *Mercer Co.* Elevation: 718 ft. Latitude: 41° 12' N Longitude: 90° 45' W

	JAN	FEB	MAR	APR	MAY	JUN	JUL	AUG	SEP	OCT	NOV	DEC	YEAR
Mean Maximum Temp. (°F)	30.0	35.7	48.4	62.4	73.5	82.4	85.9	83.7	76.4	64.5	47.9	34.8	60.5
Mean Temp. (°F)	21.7	27.2	38.8	51.2	62.0	71.2	74.6	72.8	64.7	53.4	39.2	27.1	50.3
Mean Minimum Temp. (°F)	13.4	18.6	29.0	39.7	50.7	60.0	63.5	61.8	53.1	42.2	30.5	19.3	40.1
Extreme Maximum Temp. (°F)	69	70	87	91	93	103	103	102	97	91	77	70	103
Extreme Minimum Temp. (°F)	-25	-28	-7	10	30	36	44	43	30	17	-6	-20	-28
Days Maximum Temp. ≥ 90°F	0	0	0	0	1	4	9	6	2	0	0	0	22
Days Maximum Temp. ≤ 32°F	17	11	3	0	0	0	0	0	0	0	3	11	45
Days Minimum Temp. ≤ 32°F	29	25	20	6	0	0	0	0	0	5	18	28	131
Days Minimum Temp. ≤ 0°F	6	3	0	0	0	0	0	0	0	0	0	3	12
Heating Degree Days (base 65°F)	1,333	1,062	806	424	151	18	3	7	103	364	766	1,170	6,207
Cooling Degree Days (base 65°F)	0	0	2	13	60	207	303	264	99	10	0	0	958
Mean Precipitation (in.)	1.28	1.25	2.46	3.63	3.97	4.37	4.10	4.40	3.44	2.76	2.51	1.95	36.12
Days With ≥ 0.1" Precipitation	3	3	6	7	8	7	6	7	6	5	5	4	67
Days With ≥ 1.0" Precipitation	0	0	1	1	1	1	1	1	1	1	0	0	8
Mean Snowfall (in.)	8.7	6.1	4.0	1.1	trace	0.0	0.0	0.0	0.0	0.2	2.2	5.8	28.1
Days With ≥ 1.0" Snow Depth	na	na	2	0	0	0	0	0	0	0	1	na	na

Alton Melvin Price Lock & Dam *Madison Co.* Elevation: 429 ft. Latitude: 38° 49' N Longitude: 90° 09' W

	JAN	FEB	MAR	APR	MAY	JUN	JUL	AUG	SEP	OCT	NOV	DEC	YEAR
Mean Maximum Temp. (°F)	35.3	41.3	52.2	64.1	74.6	83.8	88.1	86.3	79.4	67.3	52.9	41.5	63.9
Mean Temp. (°F)	27.0	32.3	42.8	54.4	64.8	74.0	78.3	76.3	68.8	56.7	44.0	33.4	54.4
Mean Minimum Temp. (°F)	18.7	23.3	33.4	44.6	54.9	64.2	68.5	66.3	58.2	46.1	35.1	25.4	44.9
Extreme Maximum Temp. (°F)	71	74	85	90	93	98	106	103	98	90	81	73	106
Extreme Minimum Temp. (°F)	-16	-15	2	20	36	44	50	46	37	25	6	-16	-16
Days Maximum Temp. ≥ 90°F	0	0	0	0	1	6	14	9	3	0	0	0	33
Days Maximum Temp. ≤ 32°F	12	7	1	0	0	0	0	0	0	0	1	6	27
Days Minimum Temp. ≤ 32°F	28	22	15	3	0	0	0	0	0	1	12	23	104
Days Minimum Temp. ≤ 0°F	2	1	0	0	0	0	0	0	0	0	0	1	4
Heating Degree Days (base 65°F)	1,172	916	684	328	96	8	1	1	50	271	622	972	5,121
Cooling Degree Days (base 65°F)	0	0	3	15	94	292	432	372	174	22	1	0	1,405
Mean Precipitation (in.)	2.00	2.14	3.49	4.40	4.29	3.23	3.49	3.13	3.08	2.73	3.83	2.95	38.76
Days With ≥ 0.1" Precipitation	5	4	7	7	7	5	6	5	5	6	7	6	70
Days With ≥ 1.0" Precipitation	0	0	1	1	1	1	1	1	1	1	1	1	10
Mean Snowfall (in.)	na	na	2.1	0.4	0.0	0.0	0.0	0.0	0.0	trace	0.3	0.4	na
Days With ≥ 1.0" Snow Depth	7	4	1	0	0	0	0	0	0	0	0	2	14

Anna 2 NNE *Union Co.* Elevation: 597 ft. Latitude: 37° 28' N Longitude: 89° 14' W

	JAN	FEB	MAR	APR	MAY	JUN	JUL	AUG	SEP	OCT	NOV	DEC	YEAR
Mean Maximum Temp. (°F)	40.9	47.3	57.5	68.4	77.1	85.2	88.9	87.7	80.8	70.2	56.8	45.6	67.2
Mean Temp. (°F)	32.1	37.4	47.0	57.2	66.0	74.3	78.3	76.6	69.6	58.4	47.1	37.0	56.8
Mean Minimum Temp. (°F)	23.3	27.5	36.4	46.0	54.9	63.4	67.6	65.5	58.3	46.5	37.4	28.4	46.3
Extreme Maximum Temp. (°F)	70	77	84	90	93	100	104	103	101	90	83	76	104
Extreme Minimum Temp. (°F)	-17	-10	1	21	31	45	49	46	32	20	9	-14	-17
Days Maximum Temp. ≥ 90°F	0	0	0	0	1	7	16	12	4	0	0	0	40
Days Maximum Temp. ≤ 32°F	8	4	1	0	0	0	0	0	0	0	0	4	17
Days Minimum Temp. ≤ 32°F	24	18	12	3	0	0	0	0	0	2	11	20	90
Days Minimum Temp. ≤ 0°F	1	0	0	0	0	0	0	0	0	0	0	1	2
Heating Degree Days (base 65°F)	1,012	773	557	254	71	4	0	0	40	226	531	860	4,328
Cooling Degree Days (base 65°F)	0	0	4	27	111	295	431	380	181	29	2	0	1,460
Mean Precipitation (in.)	3.48	3.34	4.82	4.89	5.19	4.25	3.21	3.59	3.12	3.51	4.62	4.26	48.28
Days With ≥ 0.1" Precipitation	6	6	8	8	8	6	5	5	5	6	7	7	77
Days With ≥ 1.0" Precipitation	1	1	1	1	2	1	1	1	1	1	1	1	13
Mean Snowfall (in.)	4.9	4.5	2.3	0.1	0.0	0.0	0.0	0.0	0.0	0.1	0.5	2.3	14.7
Days With ≥ 1.0" Snow Depth	6	5	1	0	0	0	0	0	0	0	0	3	15

Aurora *Kane Co.* Elevation: 639 ft. Latitude: 41° 46' N Longitude: 88° 19' W

	JAN	FEB	MAR	APR	MAY	JUN	JUL	AUG	SEP	OCT	NOV	DEC	YEAR
Mean Maximum Temp. (°F)	29.5	35.1	46.6	59.8	72.1	81.3	84.8	82.6	75.4	63.4	47.8	34.6	59.4
Mean Temp. (°F)	20.3	26.0	37.0	48.8	60.1	69.4	73.6	71.5	63.7	51.7	38.8	26.3	48.9
Mean Minimum Temp. (°F)	11.4	16.6	27.2	37.7	48.0	57.5	62.4	60.5	51.9	40.2	29.7	18.3	38.5
Extreme Maximum Temp. (°F)	66	70	83	91	95	103	102	101	95	90	77	68	103
Extreme Minimum Temp. (°F)	-26	-20	-1	8	26	35	42	43	28	15	-2	-22	-26
Days Maximum Temp. ≥ 90°F	0	0	0	0	1	5	7	4	1	0	0	0	18
Days Maximum Temp. ≤ 32°F	17	11	3	0	0	0	0	0	0	0	2	11	44
Days Minimum Temp. ≤ 32°F	30	26	23	8	1	0	0	0	0	6	19	28	141
Days Minimum Temp. ≤ 0°F	8	4	0	0	0	0	0	0	0	0	0	3	15
Heating Degree Days (base 65°F)	1,381	1,092	863	487	200	35	4	10	117	413	779	1,194	6,575
Cooling Degree Days (base 65°F)	0	0	1	6	50	176	283	224	81	6	0	0	827
Mean Precipitation (in.)	1.62	1.50	2.58	3.95	3.99	4.35	4.32	4.42	3.63	2.73	3.15	2.44	38.68
Days With ≥ 0.1" Precipitation	5	4	6	8	7	7	6	7	6	5	6	5	72
Days With ≥ 1.0" Precipitation	0	0	0	1	1	1	1	1	1	1	1	1	9
Mean Snowfall (in.)	9.9	6.9	3.8	0.9	0.0	0.0	0.0	0.0	0.0	trace	1.5	6.7	29.7
Days With ≥ 1.0" Snow Depth	20	14	5	0	0	0	0	0	0	0	1	11	51

Belleville Scott AFB *St. Clair Co.* Elevation: 442 ft. Latitude: 38° 33' N Longitude: 89° 51' W

	JAN	FEB	MAR	APR	MAY	JUN	JUL	AUG	SEP	OCT	NOV	DEC	YEAR
Mean Maximum Temp. (°F)	39.2	45.8	56.8	68.0	77.2	85.6	89.6	87.7	81.7	70.8	56.1	44.2	66.9
Mean Temp. (°F)	30.5	36.0	46.1	56.3	65.5	74.1	78.0	75.6	68.9	57.9	46.1	35.6	55.9
Mean Minimum Temp. (°F)	21.7	26.2	35.3	44.6	53.7	62.4	66.3	63.5	56.1	44.9	36.1	27.0	44.8
Extreme Maximum Temp. (°F)	72	80	89	90	94	101	105	100	101	92	82	76	105
Extreme Minimum Temp. (°F)	-27	-21	-8	19	28	38	43	39	26	20	2	-19	-27
Days Maximum Temp. ≥ 90°F	0	0	0	0	1	9	16	12	5	0	0	0	43
Days Maximum Temp. ≤ 32°F	10	5	1	0	0	0	0	0	0	0	0	4	20
Days Minimum Temp. ≤ 32°F	25	20	14	4	0	0	0	0	0	4	12	22	101
Days Minimum Temp. ≤ 0°F	2	1	0	0	0	0	0	0	0	0	0	1	4
Heating Degree Days (base 65°F)	1,064	812	586	281	85	6	1	2	50	245	563	904	4,599
Cooling Degree Days (base 65°F)	0	0	6	28	111	292	424	351	171	32	2	0	1,417
Mean Precipitation (in.)	1.98	2.15	3.55	3.96	4.15	3.82	3.31	3.34	3.06	2.92	3.80	2.99	39.03
Days With ≥ 0.1" Precipitation	4	4	7	7	7	7	5	5	5	5	6	5	67
Days With ≥ 1.0" Precipitation	0	0	1	1	1	1	1	1	1	1	1	1	10
Mean Snowfall (in.)	6.5	3.2	2.1	0.8	0.0	0.0	0.0	0.0	0.0	0.0	0.9	2.6	16.1
Days With ≥ 1.0" Snow Depth	9	5	1	0	0	0	0	0	0	0	1	4	20

Brookport Dam 52 *Massac Co.* Elevation: 328 ft. Latitude: 37° 08' N Longitude: 88° 39' W

	JAN	FEB	MAR	APR	MAY	JUN	JUL	AUG	SEP	OCT	NOV	DEC	YEAR
Mean Maximum Temp. (°F)	42.2	48.0	58.1	68.9	77.6	85.7	89.5	88.3	81.6	70.8	57.8	47.0	68.0
Mean Temp. (°F)	33.4	38.4	47.8	57.8	66.8	74.9	78.9	77.2	70.3	58.9	48.1	38.2	57.6
Mean Minimum Temp. (°F)	24.5	28.8	37.4	46.7	55.9	64.1	68.3	66.1	58.9	46.8	38.3	29.4	47.1
Extreme Maximum Temp. (°F)	72	74	83	89	94	100	105	101	99	92	82	74	105
Extreme Minimum Temp. (°F)	-21	-9	0	21	32	42	48	42	29	18	9	-13	-21
Days Maximum Temp. ≥ 90°F	0	0	0	0	1	8	17	13	5	0	0	0	44
Days Maximum Temp. ≤ 32°F	6	3	0	0	0	0	0	0	0	0	0	3	12
Days Minimum Temp. ≤ 32°F	23	17	11	2	0	0	0	0	0	2	9	19	83
Days Minimum Temp. ≤ 0°F	1	0	0	0	0	0	0	0	0	0	0	0	1
Heating Degree Days (base 65°F)	973	744	531	235	60	3	0	0	37	218	504	824	4,129
Cooling Degree Days (base 65°F)	0	0	4	24	120	306	448	393	195	35	2	0	1,527
Mean Precipitation (in.)	3.40	3.83	4.54	4.85	4.66	4.12	4.18	3.03	3.22	3.36	4.38	4.47	48.04
Days With ≥ 0.1" Precipitation	6	6	8	7	8	7	6	5	5	6	7	7	78
Days With ≥ 1.0" Precipitation	1	1	1	1	1	1	2	1	1	1	1	1	13
Mean Snowfall (in.)	3.3	3.0	1.3	trace	0.0	0.0	0.0	0.0	0.0	0.0	trace	1.0	8.6
Days With ≥ 1.0" Snow Depth	5	5	1	0	0	0	0	0	0	0	0	1	12

Cairo WSO City *Alexander Co.* Elevation: 311 ft. Latitude: 37° 00' N Longitude: 89° 10' W

	JAN	FEB	MAR	APR	MAY	JUN	JUL	AUG	SEP	OCT	NOV	DEC	YEAR
Mean Maximum Temp. (°F)	40.6	47.3	57.1	68.6	78.0	86.4	89.7	87.4	81.1	70.4	56.9	46.2	67.5
Mean Temp. (°F)	33.3	39.0	48.5	59.2	68.5	76.8	80.5	78.1	71.3	60.1	48.4	38.6	58.5
Mean Minimum Temp. (°F)	25.9	30.7	39.9	49.7	59.0	67.2	71.2	68.7	61.5	49.7	39.8	31.0	49.5
Extreme Maximum Temp. (°F)	71	77	85	91	96	100	104	102	99	89	82	79	104
Extreme Minimum Temp. (°F)	-12	-5	10	27	38	49	57	50	39	27	13	-9	-12
Days Maximum Temp. ≥ 90°F	0	0	0	0	2	10	17	11	4	0	0	0	44
Days Maximum Temp. ≤ 32°F	8	4	1	0	0	0	0	0	0	0	0	4	17
Days Minimum Temp. ≤ 32°F	23	16	7	1	0	0	0	0	0	1	6	17	71
Days Minimum Temp. ≤ 0°F	1	0	0	0	0	0	0	0	0	0	0	0	1
Heating Degree Days (base 65°F)	977	727	510	212	44	2	0	0	28	191	495	811	3,997
Cooling Degree Days (base 65°F)	0	0	8	42	152	357	487	413	212	42	2	1	1,716
Mean Precipitation (in.)	3.02	3.50	4.55	4.98	4.82	4.29	4.29	3.77	3.10	3.52	4.26	4.06	48.16
Days With ≥ 0.1" Precipitation	5	5	8	7	8	6	6	5	5	5	7	6	73
Days With ≥ 1.0" Precipitation	1	1	1	2	2	1	1	1	1	1	1	1	14
Mean Snowfall (in.)	4.0	2.7	1.7	trace	0.0	0.0	0.0	0.0	0.0	0.1	0.2	0.9	9.6
Days With ≥ 1.0" Snow Depth	6	4	1	0	0	0	0	0	0	0	0	1	12

Carbondale Sewage Plant *Jackson Co.* Elevation: 387 ft. Latitude: 37° 44' N Longitude: 89° 10' W

	JAN	FEB	MAR	APR	MAY	JUN	JUL	AUG	SEP	OCT	NOV	DEC	YEAR
Mean Maximum Temp. (°F)	39.5	45.7	55.4	67.1	76.4	84.8	88.6	87.6	80.8	69.5	56.0	44.9	66.4
Mean Temp. (°F)	30.2	35.1	44.7	55.3	64.6	73.5	77.5	75.4	68.0	55.9	45.4	35.4	55.1
Mean Minimum Temp. (°F)	20.8	24.4	34.0	43.5	52.8	62.2	66.4	63.3	55.2	42.3	34.8	25.9	43.8
Extreme Maximum Temp. (°F)	70	79	83	90	95	102	103	102	99	92	83	77	103
Extreme Minimum Temp. (°F)	-25	-11	-11	21	30	41	42	43	30	18	9	-14	-25
Days Maximum Temp. ≥ 90°F	0	0	0	0	1	7	14	12	4	0	0	0	38
Days Maximum Temp. ≤ 32°F	9	5	1	0	0	0	0	0	0	0	1	4	20
Days Minimum Temp. ≤ 32°F	26	21	15	4	0	0	0	0	0	6	14	23	109
Days Minimum Temp. ≤ 0°F	2	1	0	0	0	0	0	0	0	0	0	0	3
Heating Degree Days (base 65°F)	1,074	839	624	306	98	7	1	1	60	295	582	910	4,797
Cooling Degree Days (base 65°F)	0	0	4	20	87	268	401	334	146	19	1	0	1,280
Mean Precipitation (in.)	2.96	2.84	4.39	4.62	4.74	4.49	3.28	3.97	3.08	2.83	4.45	3.68	45.33
Days With ≥ 0.1" Precipitation	6	5	8	8	8	7	6	6	5	5	7	7	78
Days With ≥ 1.0" Precipitation	1	1	1	1	1	1	1	1	1	1	1	1	12
Mean Snowfall (in.)	4.9	3.8	2.0	0.3	0.0	0.0	0.0	0.0	0.0	0.1	0.5	2.2	13.8
Days With ≥ 1.0" Snow Depth	6	5	1	0	0	0	0	0	0	0	0	2	14

Carlinville *Macoupin Co.* Elevation: 629 ft. Latitude: 39° 17' N Longitude: 89° 53' W

	JAN	FEB	MAR	APR	MAY	JUN	JUL	AUG	SEP	OCT	NOV	DEC	YEAR
Mean Maximum Temp. (°F)	35.0	41.8	53.4	66.1	75.9	84.2	88.0	85.9	79.7	68.0	52.8	40.7	64.3
Mean Temp. (°F)	26.7	32.8	43.3	54.8	64.5	73.2	77.1	74.9	68.0	56.5	43.8	32.8	54.0
Mean Minimum Temp. (°F)	18.4	23.7	33.1	43.4	53.0	62.1	66.1	63.9	56.2	44.9	34.8	24.8	43.7
Extreme Maximum Temp. (°F)	71	78	86	90	92	99	103	105	99	92	81	74	105
Extreme Minimum Temp. (°F)	-19	-17	-9	18	30	39	45	41	31	20	1	-15	-19
Days Maximum Temp. ≥ 90°F	0	0	0	0	1	6	13	9	3	0	0	0	32
Days Maximum Temp. ≤ 32°F	13	7	1	0	0	0	0	0	0	0	1	7	29
Days Minimum Temp. ≤ 32°F	27	21	16	4	0	0	0	0	0	3	13	24	108
Days Minimum Temp. ≤ 0°F	3	2	0	0	0	0	0	0	0	0	0	1	6
Heating Degree Days (base 65°F)	1,181	903	670	323	104	10	1	2	61	280	630	992	5,157
Cooling Degree Days (base 65°F)	0	0	4	21	94	267	388	323	152	22	1	0	1,272
Mean Precipitation (in.)	1.95	1.93	3.54	4.16	4.25	3.83	3.60	3.36	3.08	2.66	3.56	2.87	38.79
Days With ≥ 0.1" Precipitation	5	4	7	8	7	6	5	5	5	6	7	5	70
Days With ≥ 1.0" Precipitation	0	0	1	1	1	1	1	1	1	0	1	1	9
Mean Snowfall (in.)	6.8	4.4	3.3	0.7	trace	0.0	0.0	0.0	0.0	trace	1.4	3.6	20.2
Days With ≥ 1.0" Snow Depth	11	6	2	0	0	0	0	0	0	0	1	4	24

Charleston *Coles Co.* Elevation: 679 ft. Latitude: 39° 29' N Longitude: 88° 10' W

	JAN	FEB	MAR	APR	MAY	JUN	JUL	AUG	SEP	OCT	NOV	DEC	YEAR
Mean Maximum Temp. (°F)	34.8	40.7	52.3	64.7	74.6	83.1	86.4	84.3	78.4	66.8	52.2	40.2	63.2
Mean Temp. (°F)	26.8	32.1	42.8	54.0	64.1	72.7	76.4	74.3	67.6	56.2	43.6	32.5	53.6
Mean Minimum Temp. (°F)	18.7	23.4	33.2	43.3	53.4	62.2	66.3	64.3	56.6	45.5	35.0	24.8	43.9
Extreme Maximum Temp. (°F)	69	74	84	88	92	102	101	102	97	89	79	71	102
Extreme Minimum Temp. (°F)	-27	-18	-5	17	30	41	49	42	32	20	3	-20	-27
Days Maximum Temp. ≥ 90°F	0	0	0	0	0	5	9	6	2	0	0	0	22
Days Maximum Temp. ≤ 32°F	13	8	2	0	0	0	0	0	0	0	1	7	31
Days Minimum Temp. ≤ 32°F	27	21	16	5	0	0	0	0	0	3	13	24	109
Days Minimum Temp. ≤ 0°F	4	2	0	0	0	0	0	0	0	0	0	1	7
Heating Degree Days (base 65°F)	1,179	925	685	340	110	12	1	2	63	290	635	1,001	5,243
Cooling Degree Days (base 65°F)	0	0	3	16	85	256	370	304	146	23	1	0	1,204
Mean Precipitation (in.)	2.16	2.35	3.36	4.10	4.18	3.74	4.53	3.27	3.13	3.21	3.77	3.21	41.01
Days With ≥ 0.1" Precipitation	5	5	8	9	7	6	6	5	5	5	7	6	74
Days With ≥ 1.0" Precipitation	0	0	1	1	1	1	1	1	1	1	1	1	10
Mean Snowfall (in.)	9.3	4.1	2.7	0.2	trace	0.0	0.0	0.0	0.0	trace	1.6	4.2	22.1
Days With ≥ 1.0" Snow Depth	13	9	3	0	0	0	0	0	0	0	1	6	32

Chenoa *McLean Co.* Elevation: 711 ft. Latitude: 40° 44' N Longitude: 88° 43' W

	JAN	FEB	MAR	APR	MAY	JUN	JUL	AUG	SEP	OCT	NOV	DEC	YEAR
Mean Maximum Temp. (°F)	31.1	37.0	49.1	62.9	74.3	83.3	85.7	83.6	77.7	65.4	49.5	36.6	61.4
Mean Temp. (°F)	23.1	28.3	39.5	51.4	62.4	71.7	74.7	72.5	65.7	54.0	40.8	29.1	51.1
Mean Minimum Temp. (°F)	14.8	19.6	29.9	39.8	50.5	59.9	63.5	61.3	53.7	42.5	31.9	21.4	40.7
Extreme Maximum Temp. (°F)	66	73	85	91	95	102	101	103	97	90	78	70	103
Extreme Minimum Temp. (°F)	-23	-19	-2	7	26	36	45	40	24	17	-2	-26	-26
Days Maximum Temp. ≥ 90°F	0	0	0	0	2	6	8	5	2	0	0	0	23
Days Maximum Temp. ≤ 32°F	16	10	2	0	0	0	0	0	0	0	2	10	40
Days Minimum Temp. ≤ 32°F	29	24	20	7	0	0	0	0	0	5	17	27	129
Days Minimum Temp. ≤ 0°F	5	3	0	0	0	0	0	0	0	0	0	2	10
Heating Degree Days (base 65°F)	1,293	1,030	783	413	147	17	3	8	87	350	721	1,106	5,958
Cooling Degree Days (base 65°F)	0	0	2	11	72	229	319	254	114	13	0	0	1,014
Mean Precipitation (in.)	1.55	1.42	3.00	3.42	3.88	4.11	3.40	3.29	3.13	2.69	2.64	2.46	34.99
Days With ≥ 0.1" Precipitation	4	4	6	7	8	7	6	5	6	6	6	5	70
Days With ≥ 1.0" Precipitation	0	0	0	1	1	1	1	1	1	0	1	1	8
Mean Snowfall (in.)	7.0	5.4	2.8	1.1	trace	0.0	0.0	0.0	0.0	trace	1.6	4.8	22.7
Days With ≥ 1.0" Snow Depth	14	10	3	0	0	0	0	0	0	0	1	6	34

Chicago Midway Airport *Cook Co.* Elevation: 610 ft. Latitude: 41° 47' N Longitude: 87° 45' W

	JAN	FEB	MAR	APR	MAY	JUN	JUL	AUG	SEP	OCT	NOV	DEC	YEAR
Mean Maximum Temp. (°F)	30.4	35.6	46.7	59.0	71.1	80.7	84.9	82.6	75.4	63.3	48.3	36.2	59.5
Mean Temp. (°F)	23.1	28.3	38.6	49.7	60.9	70.8	75.7	73.8	66.1	54.1	41.0	29.4	51.0
Mean Minimum Temp. (°F)	15.9	20.9	30.4	40.4	50.8	60.7	66.3	65.0	56.7	44.8	33.6	22.6	42.3
Extreme Maximum Temp. (°F)	67	75	86	91	95	104	106	102	98	92	79	71	106
Extreme Minimum Temp. (°F)	-25	-17	0	10	28	40	46	46	34	20	0	-20	-25
Days Maximum Temp. ≥ 90°F	0	0	0	0	1	5	9	5	2	0	0	0	22
Days Maximum Temp. ≤ 32°F	16	11	3	0	0	0	0	0	0	0	2	10	42
Days Minimum Temp. ≤ 32°F	28	23	19	6	0	0	0	0	0	2	14	25	117
Days Minimum Temp. ≤ 0°F	5	2	0	0	0	0	0	0	0	0	0	2	9
Heating Degree Days (base 65°F)	1,291	1,031	814	465	190	31	2	4	82	347	715	1,098	6,070
Cooling Degree Days (base 65°F)	0	0	2	12	69	213	349	290	122	13	0	0	1,070
Mean Precipitation (in.)	1.93	1.76	2.88	3.89	3.79	4.23	3.77	3.91	3.46	2.89	3.25	2.72	38.48
Days With ≥ 0.1" Precipitation	5	5	7	7	7	6	6	6	6	6	7	5	73
Days With ≥ 1.0" Precipitation	0	0	0	1	1	1	1	1	1	1	1	1	9
Mean Snowfall (in.)	13.0	10.2	6.6	1.8	trace	0.0	trace	0.0	trace	0.1	2.4	8.7	42.8
Days With ≥ 1.0" Snow Depth	20	13	5	1	0	0	0	0	0	0	1	10	50

Chicago University *Cook Co.* Elevation: 593 ft. Latitude: 41° 47' N Longitude: 87° 36' W

	JAN	FEB	MAR	APR	MAY	JUN	JUL	AUG	SEP	OCT	NOV	DEC	YEAR
Mean Maximum Temp. (°F)	31.4	36.3	46.9	58.9	70.4	80.4	84.5	82.8	76.1	64.1	49.4	36.9	59.8
Mean Temp. (°F)	24.7	29.4	39.4	50.2	60.8	70.6	75.7	74.3	67.3	55.6	42.8	30.5	51.8
Mean Minimum Temp. (°F)	18.0	22.5	31.8	41.5	51.2	60.7	66.8	65.6	58.4	47.1	36.1	24.0	43.6
Extreme Maximum Temp. (°F)	62	71	84	91	94	104	102	101	97	92	77	69	104
Extreme Minimum Temp. (°F)	-24	-9	4	13	33	41	51	49	37	24	2	-20	-24
Days Maximum Temp. ≥ 90°F	0	0	0	0	1	4	8	5	2	0	0	0	20
Days Maximum Temp. ≤ 32°F	16	11	3	0	0	0	0	0	0	0	1	9	40
Days Minimum Temp. ≤ 32°F	27	22	16	4	0	0	0	0	0	1	11	24	105
Days Minimum Temp. ≤ 0°F	4	1	0	0	0	0	0	0	0	0	0	1	6
Heating Degree Days (base 65°F)	1,242	998	788	452	191	32	2	3	63	302	660	1,064	5,797
Cooling Degree Days (base 65°F)	0	0	2	16	72	211	350	309	140	15	0	0	1,115
Mean Precipitation (in.)	1.90	1.69	3.05	3.67	3.52	4.20	3.54	4.13	3.39	2.77	3.47	2.85	38.18
Days With ≥ 0.1" Precipitation	5	5	7	7	7	7	6	7	6	5	7	6	75
Days With ≥ 1.0" Precipitation	0	0	0	1	1	1	1	1	1	1	1	0	8
Mean Snowfall (in.)	na	na	na	na	na	na	na	na	na	na	na	na	na
Days With ≥ 1.0" Snow Depth	na	na	na	na	na	na	na	na	na	na	na	na	na

Danville *Vermilion Co.* Elevation: 557 ft. Latitude: 40° 08' N Longitude: 87° 39' W

	JAN	FEB	MAR	APR	MAY	JUN	JUL	AUG	SEP	OCT	NOV	DEC	YEAR
Mean Maximum Temp. (°F)	34.0	39.8	51.5	64.5	75.2	83.6	86.3	84.1	78.5	66.5	51.7	39.3	62.9
Mean Temp. (°F)	25.5	30.7	41.4	52.8	63.0	71.8	75.4	73.4	66.7	54.9	42.8	31.5	52.5
Mean Minimum Temp. (°F)	17.0	21.6	31.3	41.1	50.7	60.0	64.3	62.5	54.9	43.2	33.8	23.5	42.0
Extreme Maximum Temp. (°F)	68	71	84	90	94	102	102	102	96	89	79	72	102
Extreme Minimum Temp. (°F)	-26	-22	-8	12	28	38	45	41	29	18	5	-25	-26
Days Maximum Temp. ≥ 90°F	0	0	0	0	1	6	9	5	2	0	0	0	23
Days Maximum Temp. ≤ 32°F	14	8	2	0	0	0	0	0	0	0	1	7	32
Days Minimum Temp. ≤ 32°F	27	23	17	6	0	0	0	0	0	5	15	24	117
Days Minimum Temp. ≤ 0°F	4	3	0	0	0	0	0	0	0	0	0	2	9
Heating Degree Days (base 65°F)	1,217	962	726	374	132	16	2	4	73	323	659	1,034	5,522
Cooling Degree Days (base 65°F)	0	0	2	14	75	230	338	276	127	17	1	0	1,080
Mean Precipitation (in.)	2.00	1.93	3.18	4.10	4.51	4.53	4.54	3.95	3.03	3.13	3.46	2.75	41.11
Days With ≥ 0.1" Precipitation	5	5	7	8	8	7	7	6	5	6	7	6	77
Days With ≥ 1.0" Precipitation	0	0	1	1	1	1	1	1	1	1	1	0	9
Mean Snowfall (in.)	6.2	4.1	3.1	0.3	trace	0.0	0.0	0.0	0.0	0.2	1.2	4.7	19.8
Days With ≥ 1.0" Snow Depth	10	6	2	0	0	0	0	0	0	0	1	5	24

De Kalb *Dekalb Co.* Elevation: 872 ft. Latitude: 41° 56' N Longitude: 88° 47' W

	JAN	FEB	MAR	APR	MAY	JUN	JUL	AUG	SEP	OCT	NOV	DEC	YEAR
Mean Maximum Temp. (°F)	26.8	33.3	45.1	59.3	71.7	81.3	84.5	82.0	75.6	63.1	46.4	33.6	58.5
Mean Temp. (°F)	18.9	25.2	36.1	48.5	60.1	70.0	73.7	71.4	64.2	52.0	38.1	26.3	48.7
Mean Minimum Temp. (°F)	10.9	17.1	27.2	37.6	48.4	58.6	62.8	60.7	52.7	40.8	29.8	18.9	38.8
Extreme Maximum Temp. (°F)	60	68	81	91	95	101	102	103	94	89	76	66	103
Extreme Minimum Temp. (°F)	-27	-23	-6	8	24	34	45	42	27	13	-8	-22	-27
Days Maximum Temp. ≥ 90°F	0	0	0	0	1	4	6	4	1	0	0	0	16
Days Maximum Temp. ≤ 32°F	21	13	4	0	0	0	0	0	0	0	3	12	53
Days Minimum Temp. ≤ 32°F	30	26	23	9	1	0	0	0	1	6	18	28	142
Days Minimum Temp. ≤ 0°F	8	4	0	0	0	0	0	0	0	0	0	3	15
Heating Degree Days (base 65°F)	1,425	1,118	888	499	200	31	5	14	112	406	800	1,194	6,692
Cooling Degree Days (base 65°F)	0	0	1	9	46	185	279	220	92	8	0	0	840
Mean Precipitation (in.)	1.54	1.35	2.49	3.49	4.25	4.46	4.35	4.48	3.68	2.65	2.79	2.16	37.69
Days With ≥ 0.1" Precipitation	4	3	6	7	8	7	6	7	6	6	6	5	71
Days With ≥ 1.0" Precipitation	0	0	0	1	1	1	1	1	1	0	1	0	7
Mean Snowfall (in.)	9.7	7.1	5.1	1.3	trace	0.0	0.0	0.0	0.0	0.1	2.1	8.6	34.0
Days With ≥ 1.0" Snow Depth	23	16	6	1	0	0	0	0	0	0	2	12	60

Decatur *Macon Co.* Elevation: 620 ft. Latitude: 39° 49' N Longitude: 89° 01' W

	JAN	FEB	MAR	APR	MAY	JUN	JUL	AUG	SEP	OCT	NOV	DEC	YEAR
Mean Maximum Temp. (°F)	34.0	40.5	52.0	65.1	75.9	84.5	87.8	85.8	79.9	67.6	52.0	40.0	63.8
Mean Temp. (°F)	25.4	31.2	41.8	53.5	63.6	72.5	76.1	74.3	67.4	55.7	42.7	31.8	53.0
Mean Minimum Temp. (°F)	16.7	21.8	31.5	41.8	51.3	60.4	64.4	62.7	54.9	43.7	33.4	23.4	42.2
Extreme Maximum Temp. (°F)	67	76	86	93	95	103	104	106	100	91	80	72	106
Extreme Minimum Temp. (°F)	-23	-20	-10	15	27	39	46	42	29	18	0	-22	-23
Days Maximum Temp. ≥ 90°F	0	0	0	0	2	7	13	8	4	0	0	0	34
Days Maximum Temp. ≤ 32°F	13	7	2	0	0	0	0	0	0	0	1	7	30
Days Minimum Temp. ≤ 32°F	28	23	17	5	0	0	0	0	0	4	15	25	117
Days Minimum Temp. ≤ 0°F	5	3	0	0	0	0	0	0	0	0	0	1	9
Heating Degree Days (base 65°F)	1,222	950	714	356	120	13	1	4	67	303	664	1,025	5,439
Cooling Degree Days (base 65°F)	0	0	2	17	78	245	360	309	144	21	1	0	1,177
Mean Precipitation (in.)	2.10	1.91	3.28	3.83	4.58	3.94	4.41	4.04	3.01	2.78	3.09	2.84	39.81
Days With ≥ 0.1" Precipitation	5	4	7	7	7	6	6	5	5	5	6	6	69
Days With ≥ 1.0" Precipitation	0	0	1	1	1	1	1	1	1	1	1	0	9
Mean Snowfall (in.)	7.8	5.1	2.7	0.4	trace	0.0	0.0	0.0	0.0	trace	1.1	5.4	22.5
Days With ≥ 1.0" Snow Depth	13	9	3	0	0	0	0	0	0	0	1	6	32

Dixon 1 NW *Lee Co.* Elevation: 698 ft. Latitude: 41° 51' N Longitude: 89° 30' W

	JAN	FEB	MAR	APR	MAY	JUN	JUL	AUG	SEP	OCT	NOV	DEC	YEAR
Mean Maximum Temp. (°F)	27.5	33.4	45.5	59.8	71.6	80.6	83.9	81.9	74.7	62.9	46.7	33.3	58.5
Mean Temp. (°F)	18.7	24.4	36.2	48.8	60.2	69.4	73.2	71.0	63.1	51.3	37.8	25.3	48.3
Mean Minimum Temp. (°F)	9.7	15.4	26.9	37.7	48.7	58.0	62.5	60.1	51.4	39.6	28.8	17.3	38.0
Extreme Maximum Temp. (°F)	59	69	87	93	95	100	101	103	99	91	77	68	103
Extreme Minimum Temp. (°F)	-27	-26	-6	8	27	36	45	40	28	17	-8	-25	-27
Days Maximum Temp. ≥ 90°F	0	0	0	0	1	3	7	5	2	0	0	0	18
Days Maximum Temp. ≤ 32°F	19	12	4	0	0	0	0	0	0	0	3	13	51
Days Minimum Temp. ≤ 32°F	30	26	22	9	1	0	0	0	1	7	20	29	145
Days Minimum Temp. ≤ 0°F	9	5	0	0	0	0	0	0	0	0	0	4	18
Heating Degree Days (base 65°F)	1,432	1,140	886	490	198	32	6	15	131	428	811	1,224	6,793
Cooling Degree Days (base 65°F)	0	0	1	7	47	160	258	202	70	8	0	0	753
Mean Precipitation (in.)	1.56	1.36	2.56	3.57	4.43	4.79	3.36	4.41	3.47	2.78	2.80	2.12	37.21
Days With ≥ 0.1" Precipitation	4	4	6	7	7	7	6	7	5	6	6	5	70
Days With ≥ 1.0" Precipitation	0	0	1	1	1	1	1	1	1	1	0	0	8
Mean Snowfall (in.)	11.1	6.8	4.6	1.2	0.0	0.0	0.0	0.0	0.0	trace	2.1	8.4	34.2
Days With ≥ 1.0" Snow Depth	20	15	5	0	0	0	0	0	0	0	1	12	53

Dixon Springs Agr. Center *Pope Co.* Elevation: 538 ft. Latitude: 37° 26' N Longitude: 88° 40' W

	JAN	FEB	MAR	APR	MAY	JUN	JUL	AUG	SEP	OCT	NOV	DEC	YEAR
Mean Maximum Temp. (°F)	41.8	48.3	58.8	69.4	77.6	85.4	89.0	88.1	82.0	71.5	57.9	47.0	68.1
Mean Temp. (°F)	33.0	38.4	48.2	58.0	66.2	74.2	78.0	76.6	70.1	59.1	48.3	38.4	57.4
Mean Minimum Temp. (°F)	24.2	28.5	37.5	46.5	54.8	63.1	67.0	65.0	58.1	46.7	38.6	29.6	46.6
Extreme Maximum Temp. (°F)	70	78	83	89	92	100	101	102	100	91	83	77	102
Extreme Minimum Temp. (°F)	-20	-10	-3	21	29	39	46	46	32	17	6	-9	-20
Days Maximum Temp. ≥ 90°F	0	0	0	0	1	8	15	13	5	0	0	0	42
Days Maximum Temp. ≤ 32°F	7	4	0	0	0	0	0	0	0	0	0	3	14
Days Minimum Temp. ≤ 32°F	23	17	11	3	0	0	0	0	0	3	10	18	85
Days Minimum Temp. ≤ 0°F	1	1	0	0	0	0	0	0	0	0	0	0	2
Heating Degree Days (base 65°F)	984	745	521	239	74	5	0	1	39	216	500	820	4,144
Cooling Degree Days (base 65°F)	0	0	8	36	125	304	433	388	200	43	4	1	1,542
Mean Precipitation (in.)	3.18	3.30	4.68	4.90	5.22	4.07	3.74	3.61	3.23	3.31	4.64	4.34	48.22
Days With ≥ 0.1" Precipitation	6	6	8	8	8	7	6	5	5	5	7	7	78
Days With ≥ 1.0" Precipitation	1	1	1	1	2	1	1	1	1	1	1	1	13
Mean Snowfall (in.)	3.8	3.3	1.5	0.1	0.0	0.0	0.0	0.0	0.0	0.2	trace	0.8	9.7
Days With ≥ 1.0" Snow Depth	6	5	1	0	0	0	0	0	0	0	0	1	13

Du Quoin 4 SE *Perry Co.* Elevation: 419 ft. Latitude: 37° 59' N Longitude: 89° 12' W

	JAN	FEB	MAR	APR	MAY	JUN	JUL	AUG	SEP	OCT	NOV	DEC	YEAR
Mean Maximum Temp. (°F)	38.9	45.6	56.3	67.6	77.0	85.5	89.7	87.8	81.1	70.0	55.6	43.7	66.6
Mean Temp. (°F)	30.2	35.9	45.9	56.4	65.8	74.4	78.5	76.1	69.0	57.5	45.7	35.0	55.9
Mean Minimum Temp. (°F)	21.5	26.1	35.4	45.1	54.5	63.2	67.3	64.3	56.7	45.0	35.7	26.6	45.1
Extreme Maximum Temp. (°F)	70	77	85	92	94	106	106	106	100	92	84	75	106
Extreme Minimum Temp. (°F)	-20	-16	-10	22	30	41	49	43	31	20	8	-14	-20
Days Maximum Temp. ≥ 90°F	0	0	0	0	2	9	16	12	5	0	0	0	44
Days Maximum Temp. ≤ 32°F	9	5	1	0	0	0	0	0	0	0	0	5	20
Days Minimum Temp. ≤ 32°F	26	19	13	3	0	0	0	0	0	3	12	22	98
Days Minimum Temp. ≤ 0°F	2	1	0	0	0	0	0	0	0	0	0	1	4
Heating Degree Days (base 65°F)	1,072	816	588	279	81	5	0	1	48	254	576	923	4,643
Cooling Degree Days (base 65°F)	0	0	4	25	110	301	429	358	164	29	2	0	1,422
Mean Precipitation (in.)	2.73	2.57	4.31	4.27	4.83	4.09	3.52	3.18	3.31	3.28	4.36	3.41	43.86
Days With ≥ 0.1" Precipitation	5	5	7	8	7	7	5	5	5	5	6	6	71
Days With ≥ 1.0" Precipitation	1	1	1	1	2	1	1	1	1	1	1	1	13
Mean Snowfall (in.)	5.1	3.4	1.2	0.5	0.0	0.0	0.0	0.0	0.0	0.2	0.8	2.5	13.7
Days With ≥ 1.0" Snow Depth	8	5	1	0	0	0	0	0	0	0	0	3	17

Effingham *Effingham Co.* Elevation: 606 ft. Latitude: 39° 09' N Longitude: 88° 33' W

	JAN	FEB	MAR	APR	MAY	JUN	JUL	AUG	SEP	OCT	NOV	DEC	YEAR
Mean Maximum Temp. (°F)	34.2	39.8	51.7	64.0	74.2	83.5	87.4	85.2	78.6	66.5	52.7	40.3	63.2
Mean Temp. (°F)	25.8	30.3	42.0	53.3	63.1	72.5	76.6	74.3	66.9	55.0	43.4	31.9	52.9
Mean Minimum Temp. (°F)	17.4	20.9	32.2	42.4	52.0	61.4	65.8	63.3	55.2	43.3	34.1	23.3	42.6
Extreme Maximum Temp. (°F)	69	78	84	89	94	102	102	103	100	92	81	71	103
Extreme Minimum Temp. (°F)	-24	-19	-11	21	29	40	48	44	34	20	5	-16	-24
Days Maximum Temp. ≥ 90°F	0	0	0	0	1	6	12	9	3	0	0	0	31
Days Maximum Temp. ≤ 32°F	14	8	2	0	0	0	0	0	0	0	1	7	32
Days Minimum Temp. ≤ 32°F	28	23	17	5	0	0	0	0	0	5	14	24	116
Days Minimum Temp. ≤ 0°F	4	3	0	0	0	0	0	0	0	0	0	2	9
Heating Degree Days (base 65°F)	1,209	972	709	363	128	14	1	4	76	324	642	1,021	5,463
Cooling Degree Days (base 65°F)	0	0	3	17	74	254	381	307	135	17	1	0	1,189
Mean Precipitation (in.)	2.11	2.37	3.67	4.00	4.22	4.21	4.32	2.88	3.17	3.04	4.01	3.36	41.36
Days With ≥ 0.1" Precipitation	5	5	7	8	7	7	7	5	5	5	7	6	74
Days With ≥ 1.0" Precipitation	0	1	1	1	1	1	1	1	1	1	1	1	11
Mean Snowfall (in.)	7.3	5.2	2.9	0.2	0.0	0.0	0.0	0.0	0.0	trace	1.3	3.8	20.7
Days With ≥ 1.0" Snow Depth	10	na	2	0	0	0	0	0	0	0	1	4	na

Fairfield Radio WFIW *Wayne Co.* Elevation: 429 ft. Latitude: 38° 23' N Longitude: 88° 20' W

	JAN	FEB	MAR	APR	MAY	JUN	JUL	AUG	SEP	OCT	NOV	DEC	YEAR
Mean Maximum Temp. (°F)	37.6	43.8	54.9	66.5	76.1	84.8	88.2	86.6	80.3	68.6	54.3	42.8	65.4
Mean Temp. (°F)	29.3	34.5	44.7	55.2	64.6	73.2	77.0	75.0	68.2	56.7	45.0	34.5	54.8
Mean Minimum Temp. (°F)	21.0	25.2	34.4	43.8	53.1	61.6	65.7	63.4	56.1	44.7	35.6	26.2	44.2
Extreme Maximum Temp. (°F)	72	78	84	89	94	102	102	104	100	91	81	74	104
Extreme Minimum Temp. (°F)	-23	-16	-8	17	30	39	46	43	32	19	7	-18	-23
Days Maximum Temp. ≥ 90°F	0	0	0	0	1	8	14	10	4	0	0	0	37
Days Maximum Temp. ≤ 32°F	11	6	1	0	0	0	0	0	0	0	1	5	24
Days Minimum Temp. ≤ 32°F	26	21	14	4	0	0	0	0	0	4	13	22	104
Days Minimum Temp. ≤ 0°F	2	1	0	0	0	0	0	0	0	0	0	1	4
Heating Degree Days (base 65°F)	1,100	855	626	310	99	8	1	2	58	277	595	937	4,868
Cooling Degree Days (base 65°F)	0	0	3	20	95	263	384	323	150	25	1	0	1,264
Mean Precipitation (in.)	2.75	2.62	4.63	4.90	4.71	4.01	3.80	3.22	2.89	3.43	4.28	3.45	44.69
Days With ≥ 0.1" Precipitation	6	5	8	9	8	7	6	5	5	5	7	7	78
Days With ≥ 1.0" Precipitation	1	1	1	1	1	1	1	1	1	1	1	1	12
Mean Snowfall (in.)	5.2	3.7	2.4	0.3	0.0	0.0	0.0	0.0	0.0	trace	0.7	2.9	15.2
Days With ≥ 1.0" Snow Depth	7	5	1	0	0	0	0	0	0	0	0	2	15

Flora 5 NW *Clay Co.* Elevation: 498 ft. Latitude: 38° 43' N Longitude: 88° 35' W

	JAN	FEB	MAR	APR	MAY	JUN	JUL	AUG	SEP	OCT	NOV	DEC	YEAR
Mean Maximum Temp. (°F)	38.1	43.9	55.3	67.2	76.9	85.5	89.2	87.5	81.1	69.6	55.1	43.1	66.0
Mean Temp. (°F)	29.4	34.4	44.7	55.4	64.8	73.5	77.3	75.3	68.5	57.2	45.3	34.5	55.0
Mean Minimum Temp. (°F)	20.6	24.7	34.2	43.5	52.7	61.5	65.4	63.1	55.8	44.8	35.4	25.8	44.0
Extreme Maximum Temp. (°F)	70	79	85	97	94	104	104	105	100	93	82	73	105
Extreme Minimum Temp. (°F)	-24	-25	-14	18	29	38	44	39	29	17	5	-21	-25
Days Maximum Temp. ≥ 90°F	0	0	0	0	1	8	15	11	5	0	0	0	40
Days Maximum Temp. ≤ 32°F	10	6	1	0	0	0	0	0	0	0	0	5	22
Days Minimum Temp. ≤ 32°F	26	20	15	4	0	0	0	0	0	4	12	22	103
Days Minimum Temp. ≤ 0°F	3	2	0	0	0	0	0	0	0	0	0	1	6
Heating Degree Days (base 65°F)	1,097	859	626	306	97	8	1	2	55	263	588	939	4,841
Cooling Degree Days (base 65°F)	0	0	5	24	100	282	404	339	162	32	2	0	1,350
Mean Precipitation (in.)	2.55	2.38	4.04	4.29	4.23	4.24	3.77	3.17	3.15	3.02	4.01	3.31	42.16
Days With ≥ 0.1" Precipitation	5	5	8	8	8	7	6	5	5	5	7	6	75
Days With ≥ 1.0" Precipitation	0	1	1	1	1	1	1	1	1	1	1	1	11
Mean Snowfall (in.)	2.5	2.1	1.2	0.2	trace	0.0	0.0	0.0	0.0	trace	0.8	1.5	8.3
Days With ≥ 1.0" Snow Depth	8	6	1	0	0	0	0	0	0	0	1	3	19

Freeport Waste Water Plant *Stephenson Co.* Elevation: 748 ft. Latitude: 42° 18' N Longitude: 89° 36' W

	JAN	FEB	MAR	APR	MAY	JUN	JUL	AUG	SEP	OCT	NOV	DEC	YEAR
Mean Maximum Temp. (°F)	26.4	32.2	43.9	58.1	70.5	79.9	83.8	81.0	73.5	61.6	45.6	31.9	57.4
Mean Temp. (°F)	17.7	23.2	34.5	47.3	59.1	68.6	72.8	70.0	61.7	50.0	36.7	23.9	47.1
Mean Minimum Temp. (°F)	9.0	14.1	25.1	36.4	47.6	57.2	61.8	59.0	49.8	38.2	27.8	15.9	36.8
Extreme Maximum Temp. (°F)	59	65	85	92	95	100	101	101	96	90	75	66	101
Extreme Minimum Temp. (°F)	-27	-27	-6	9	27	38	46	40	28	15	-5	-22	-27
Days Maximum Temp. ≥ 90°F	0	0	0	0	1	3	6	4	1	0	0	0	15
Days Maximum Temp. ≤ 32°F	21	14	5	0	0	0	0	0	0	0	3	14	57
Days Minimum Temp. ≤ 32°F	30	26	25	10	1	0	0	0	1	9	22	29	153
Days Minimum Temp. ≤ 0°F	9	6	1	0	0	0	0	0	0	0	0	5	21
Heating Degree Days (base 65°F)	1,460	1,176	938	533	225	41	7	21	155	465	841	1,267	7,129
Cooling Degree Days (base 65°F)	0	0	0	7	43	156	250	186	63	5	0	0	710
Mean Precipitation (in.)	1.29	1.26	2.18	3.23	3.95	4.30	3.55	4.05	3.72	2.62	2.68	1.69	34.52
Days With ≥ 0.1" Precipitation	4	4	5	6	7	7	6	6	6	5	5	4	65
Days With ≥ 1.0" Precipitation	0	0	0	1	1	1	1	1	1	1	1	0	8
Mean Snowfall (in.)	9.6	6.5	4.4	1.7	trace	0.0	0.0	0.0	0.0	trace	2.5	7.3	32.0
Days With ≥ 1.0" Snow Depth	19	15	6	1	0	0	0	0	0	0	2	13	56

Fulton Lock & Dam 13 *Whiteside Co.* Elevation: 590 ft. Latitude: 41° 54' N Longitude: 90° 09' W

	JAN	FEB	MAR	APR	MAY	JUN	JUL	AUG	SEP	OCT	NOV	DEC	YEAR
Mean Maximum Temp. (°F)	27.9	32.8	44.6	58.7	70.7	80.1	83.9	81.8	74.5	62.8	46.6	33.2	58.1
Mean Temp. (°F)	19.4	24.3	35.8	49.0	60.7	70.0	74.2	72.2	64.1	52.5	38.5	25.7	48.9
Mean Minimum Temp. (°F)	10.8	15.8	27.0	39.2	50.6	59.9	64.5	62.4	53.7	42.2	30.4	18.1	39.5
Extreme Maximum Temp. (°F)	62	68	82	91	92	98	99	102	96	90	74	66	102
Extreme Minimum Temp. (°F)	-23	-26	-7	13	30	40	47	42	30	16	-5	-21	-26
Days Maximum Temp. ≥ 90°F	0	0	0	0	0	3	5	4	1	0	0	0	13
Days Maximum Temp. ≤ 32°F	19	13	4	0	0	0	0	0	0	0	3	13	52
Days Minimum Temp. ≤ 32°F	30	26	22	6	0	0	0	0	0	4	18	28	134
Days Minimum Temp. ≤ 0°F	8	5	0	0	0	0	0	0	0	0	0	3	16
Heating Degree Days (base 65°F)	1,410	1,143	897	484	180	24	2	6	109	390	789	1,212	6,646
Cooling Degree Days (base 65°F)	0	0	0	9	45	178	292	240	87	8	0	0	859
Mean Precipitation (in.)	1.28	1.20	2.39	3.41	3.90	4.18	3.41	4.50	3.26	2.72	2.65	1.80	34.70
Days With ≥ 0.1" Precipitation	3	3	5	6	7	7	6	7	5	5	5	4	63
Days With ≥ 1.0" Precipitation	0	0	0	1	1	1	1	1	1	1	1	0	8
Mean Snowfall (in.)	6.4	3.8	2.0	0.8	0.0	0.0	0.0	0.0	0.0	trace	0.9	3.8	17.7
Days With ≥ 1.0" Snow Depth	14	14	5	0	0	0	0	0	0	0	1	9	43

Galesburg *Knox Co.* Elevation: 770 ft. Latitude: 40° 57' N Longitude: 90° 23' W

	JAN	FEB	MAR	APR	MAY	JUN	JUL	AUG	SEP	OCT	NOV	DEC	YEAR
Mean Maximum Temp. (°F)	29.2	35.3	47.6	61.1	72.3	81.5	84.9	82.4	75.4	63.5	47.6	34.6	59.6
Mean Temp. (°F)	21.2	27.1	38.3	50.7	61.9	71.2	75.1	72.8	65.1	53.2	39.3	27.2	50.3
Mean Minimum Temp. (°F)	13.1	18.8	29.1	40.2	51.4	60.9	65.3	63.1	54.7	42.9	30.8	19.7	40.8
Extreme Maximum Temp. (°F)	66	71	86	91	92	101	102	101	96	91	76	69	102
Extreme Minimum Temp. (°F)	-25	-24	-5	9	29	41	46	42	29	19	-5	-21	-25
Days Maximum Temp. ≥ 90°F	0	0	0	0	0	4	8	4	1	0	0	0	17
Days Maximum Temp. ≤ 32°F	17	11	4	0	0	0	0	0	0	0	3	12	47
Days Minimum Temp. ≤ 32°F	29	25	20	6	0	0	0	0	0	4	18	27	129
Days Minimum Temp. ≤ 0°F	7	3	0	0	0	0	0	0	0	0	0	3	13
Heating Degree Days (base 65°F)	1,352	1,064	821	434	156	18	3	7	99	371	765	1,166	6,256
Cooling Degree Days (base 65°F)	0	0	2	11	64	216	331	263	106	11	0	0	1,004
Mean Precipitation (in.)	1.40	1.51	2.84	3.90	4.03	4.15	4.44	4.21	3.72	2.52	2.70	2.28	37.70
Days With ≥ 0.1" Precipitation	4	4	6	7	8	7	7	7	6	5	6	5	72
Days With ≥ 1.0" Precipitation	0	0	1	1	1	1	1	1	1	0	1	1	9
Mean Snowfall (in.)	8.2	5.4	3.0	1.8	trace	0.0	0.0	0.0	0.0	trace	1.8	5.1	25.3
Days With ≥ 1.0" Snow Depth	18	11	4	1	0	0	0	0	0	0	1	8	43

Galva *Henry Co.* Elevation: 807 ft. Latitude: 41° 11' N Longitude: 90° 02' W

	JAN	FEB	MAR	APR	MAY	JUN	JUL	AUG	SEP	OCT	NOV	DEC	YEAR
Mean Maximum Temp. (°F)	28.1	33.9	46.3	60.2	71.9	81.5	85.0	82.7	75.8	63.3	47.0	33.8	59.1
Mean Temp. (°F)	20.0	25.5	36.9	49.5	61.2	70.5	74.5	72.2	64.5	52.3	38.6	26.0	49.3
Mean Minimum Temp. (°F)	11.8	17.1	27.4	38.7	50.4	59.5	64.0	61.6	53.1	41.3	30.1	18.2	39.4
Extreme Maximum Temp. (°F)	64	69	85	90	92	100	103	101	99	91	78	69	103
Extreme Minimum Temp. (°F)	-23	-21	-6	11	28	39	45	42	29	19	-7	-22	-23
Days Maximum Temp. ≥ 90°F	0	0	0	0	0	4	8	5	2	0	0	0	19
Days Maximum Temp. ≤ 32°F	19	12	4	0	0	0	0	0	0	0	3	13	51
Days Minimum Temp. ≤ 32°F	30	25	22	8	0	0	0	0	0	5	18	28	136
Days Minimum Temp. ≤ 0°F	8	4	0	0	0	0	0	0	0	0	0	4	16
Heating Degree Days (base 65°F)	1,389	1,109	868	469	176	23	5	9	108	396	786	1,202	6,540
Cooling Degree Days (base 65°F)	0	0	2	9	61	201	314	250	97	10	0	0	944
Mean Precipitation (in.)	1.48	1.48	2.80	3.90	4.20	4.46	4.03	4.36	3.71	2.76	2.92	2.32	38.42
Days With ≥ 0.1" Precipitation	4	4	6	7	8	7	7	6	6	5	6	4	70
Days With ≥ 1.0" Precipitation	0	0	1	1	1	1	1	2	1	1	1	1	11
Mean Snowfall (in.)	8.2	6.2	4.2	1.7	0.0	0.0	0.0	0.0	0.0	0.4	2.2	5.7	28.6
Days With ≥ 1.0" Snow Depth	19	14	6	1	0	0	0	0	0	0	2	11	53

Geneseo *Henry Co.* Elevation: 636 ft. Latitude: 41° 27' N Longitude: 90° 09' W

	JAN	FEB	MAR	APR	MAY	JUN	JUL	AUG	SEP	OCT	NOV	DEC	YEAR
Mean Maximum Temp. (°F)	28.4	34.2	47.0	61.1	73.1	82.5	85.9	83.2	75.6	63.2	47.0	33.8	59.6
Mean Temp. (°F)	20.4	26.3	37.9	50.4	62.1	71.6	75.5	72.9	64.8	52.8	38.8	26.4	50.0
Mean Minimum Temp. (°F)	12.3	18.3	28.7	39.7	51.1	60.8	65.0	62.5	53.9	42.3	30.5	18.9	40.3
Extreme Maximum Temp. (°F)	66	70	87	92	95	101	103	103	99	92	77	70	103
Extreme Minimum Temp. (°F)	-23	-24	-5	12	29	39	47	40	31	19	-7	-20	-24
Days Maximum Temp. ≥ 90°F	0	0	0	0	1	5	9	6	2	0	0	0	23
Days Maximum Temp. ≤ 32°F	18	12	4	0	0	0	0	0	0	0	3	12	49
Days Minimum Temp. ≤ 32°F	30	25	21	6	0	0	0	0	0	4	18	28	132
Days Minimum Temp. ≤ 0°F	7	3	0	0	0	0	0	0	0	0	0	3	13
Heating Degree Days (base 65°F)	1,377	1,087	836	443	155	16	2	7	103	385	781	1,191	6,383
Cooling Degree Days (base 65°F)	0	0	1	12	68	225	339	263	100	11	0	0	1,019
Mean Precipitation (in.)	1.50	1.52	2.70	3.76	4.36	4.18	4.00	4.32	3.23	3.04	2.85	2.15	37.61
Days With ≥ 0.1" Precipitation	4	4	6	7	7	7	6	6	5	5	6	5	68
Days With ≥ 1.0" Precipitation	0	0	1	1	1	1	1	1	1	1	1	0	9
Mean Snowfall (in.)	7.8	5.1	3.7	1.7	0.0	0.0	0.0	0.0	0.0	trace	2.2	6.6	27.1
Days With ≥ 1.0" Snow Depth	19	14	5	1	0	0	0	0	0	0	2	10	51

Golden *Adams Co.* Elevation: 725 ft. Latitude: 40° 06' N Longitude: 91° 01' W

	JAN	FEB	MAR	APR	MAY	JUN	JUL	AUG	SEP	OCT	NOV	DEC	YEAR
Mean Maximum Temp. (°F)	31.9	38.2	50.6	63.3	73.9	83.3	87.1	85.0	78.1	66.6	50.2	37.5	62.1
Mean Temp. (°F)	23.6	29.2	40.7	52.3	63.0	72.5	76.2	74.0	66.4	55.1	41.2	29.5	52.0
Mean Minimum Temp. (°F)	15.2	20.2	30.8	41.3	52.1	61.5	65.3	63.0	54.7	43.5	32.1	21.3	41.8
Extreme Maximum Temp. (°F)	67	76	84	93	92	101	102	103	98	93	79	71	103
Extreme Minimum Temp. (°F)	-23	-20	-14	13	31	41	46	43	30	19	-2	-22	-23
Days Maximum Temp. ≥ 90°F	0	0	0	0	1	6	11	8	3	0	0	0	29
Days Maximum Temp. ≤ 32°F	15	9	3	0	0	0	0	0	0	0	2	9	38
Days Minimum Temp. ≤ 32°F	29	24	19	5	0	0	0	0	0	4	16	27	124
Days Minimum Temp. ≤ 0°F	5	3	0	0	0	0	0	0	0	0	0	2	10
Heating Degree Days (base 65°F)	1,278	1,004	747	390	130	14	2	5	82	320	709	1,095	5,776
Cooling Degree Days (base 65°F)	0	0	2	14	70	244	357	299	125	17	0	0	1,128
Mean Precipitation (in.)	1.15	1.52	2.69	3.61	5.01	3.71	4.31	3.69	3.86	3.05	2.96	2.14	37.70
Days With ≥ 0.1" Precipitation	4	4	6	7	8	7	6	6	6	6	6	4	70
Days With ≥ 1.0" Precipitation	0	0	1	1	1	1	1	1	1	1	1	1	10
Mean Snowfall (in.)	6.0	4.9	2.0	0.6	0.0	0.0	0.0	0.0	0.0	trace	1.6	3.9	19.0
Days With ≥ 1.0" Snow Depth	9	6	2	0	0	0	0	0	0	0	1	4	22

Harrisburg *Saline Co.* Elevation: 364 ft. Latitude: 37° 44' N Longitude: 88° 31' W

	JAN	FEB	MAR	APR	MAY	JUN	JUL	AUG	SEP	OCT	NOV	DEC	YEAR
Mean Maximum Temp. (°F)	39.8	46.9	57.3	69.0	78.4	86.3	90.2	88.5	82.1	70.8	57.2	46.3	67.7
Mean Temp. (°F)	31.2	36.9	46.7	57.3	66.6	75.0	78.9	77.0	69.9	58.1	47.2	37.5	56.9
Mean Minimum Temp. (°F)	22.6	27.0	36.1	45.5	54.7	63.6	67.5	65.3	57.6	45.3	37.2	28.6	45.9
Extreme Maximum Temp. (°F)	71	79	85	90	95	101	105	104	100	90	83	78	105
Extreme Minimum Temp. (°F)	-22	-8	-7	22	32	41	45	43	32	18	9	-10	-22
Days Maximum Temp. ≥ 90°F	0	0	0	0	2	10	18	14	6	0	0	0	50
Days Maximum Temp. ≤ 32°F	9	4	1	0	0	0	0	0	0	0	0	3	17
Days Minimum Temp. ≤ 32°F	25	19	13	3	0	0	0	0	0	3	11	20	94
Days Minimum Temp. ≤ 0°F	2	1	0	0	0	0	0	0	0	0	0	0	3
Heating Degree Days (base 65°F)	1,040	786	565	258	69	4	0	1	43	239	530	846	4,381
Cooling Degree Days (base 65°F)	0	0	5	26	117	302	434	378	185	29	2	0	1,478
Mean Precipitation (in.)	2.99	2.73	4.45	4.76	4.82	4.43	4.02	3.22	3.09	3.14	4.09	3.96	45.70
Days With ≥ 0.1" Precipitation	6	6	8	8	7	6	6	5	5	5	7	7	76
Days With ≥ 1.0" Precipitation	1	1	1	1	1	1	1	1	1	1	1	1	12
Mean Snowfall (in.)	4.8	3.8	2.3	0.4	0.0	0.0	0.0	0.0	0.0	trace	0.6	1.7	13.6
Days With ≥ 1.0" Snow Depth	7	5	1	0	0	0	0	0	0	0	0	1	14

Havana 4 NNE *Mason Co.* Elevation: 459 ft. Latitude: 40° 21' N Longitude: 90° 01' W

	JAN	FEB	MAR	APR	MAY	JUN	JUL	AUG	SEP	OCT	NOV	DEC	YEAR
Mean Maximum Temp. (°F)	32.2	38.5	50.9	63.8	74.3	84.1	88.3	85.8	79.4	67.2	51.0	38.1	62.8
Mean Temp. (°F)	23.4	29.1	40.6	52.3	62.7	72.6	76.6	74.1	66.5	54.5	41.3	29.5	51.9
Mean Minimum Temp. (°F)	14.5	19.7	30.3	40.8	51.2	61.1	64.8	62.3	53.6	41.9	31.6	20.8	41.0
Extreme Maximum Temp. (°F)	67	75	88	95	96	104	106	106	100	92	81	72	106
Extreme Minimum Temp. (°F)	-30	-25	-13	16	31	42	46	38	28	19	1	-23	-30
Days Maximum Temp. ≥ 90°F	0	0	0	0	1	8	13	9	4	0	0	0	35
Days Maximum Temp. ≤ 32°F	15	9	2	0	0	0	0	0	0	0	2	9	37
Days Minimum Temp. ≤ 32°F	29	24	19	5	0	0	0	0	0	6	17	27	127
Days Minimum Temp. ≤ 0°F	6	4	0	0	0	0	0	0	0	0	0	2	12
Heating Degree Days (base 65°F)	1,285	1,008	752	391	138	15	1	5	80	336	705	1,092	5,808
Cooling Degree Days (base 65°F)	0	0	2	12	72	246	366	295	123	15	0	0	1,131
Mean Precipitation (in.)	1.82	1.91	2.97	3.52	4.53	3.73	3.81	3.62	3.49	2.94	3.21	2.63	38.18
Days With ≥ 0.1" Precipitation	5	4	6	7	8	6	7	6	6	5	6	5	71
Days With ≥ 1.0" Precipitation	0	0	1	1	1	1	1	1	1	1	1	1	10
Mean Snowfall (in.)	9.9	7.7	3.8	1.1	0.0	0.0	0.0	0.0	0.0	trace	1.5	6.1	30.1
Days With ≥ 1.0" Snow Depth	15	9	2	0	0	0	0	0	0	0	1	6	33

Hennepin Power Plant *Putnam Co.* Elevation: 459 ft. Latitude: 41° 18' N Longitude: 89° 19' W

	JAN	FEB	MAR	APR	MAY	JUN	JUL	AUG	SEP	OCT	NOV	DEC	YEAR
Mean Maximum Temp. (°F)	30.2	36.0	48.0	61.9	73.7	82.8	86.2	84.2	77.6	65.1	49.3	36.1	60.9
Mean Temp. (°F)	20.3	26.3	37.9	50.0	61.1	70.3	74.0	72.1	64.7	52.3	39.2	27.1	49.6
Mean Minimum Temp. (°F)	10.6	16.4	27.8	38.1	48.4	57.7	61.7	59.9	51.6	39.5	29.2	17.9	38.2
Extreme Maximum Temp. (°F)	63	72	86	93	95	104	104	104	97	89	80	70	104
Extreme Minimum Temp. (°F)	-30	-21	-8	9	27	34	43	40	28	15	-4	-25	-30
Days Maximum Temp. ≥ 90°F	0	0	0	0	2	5	10	7	2	0	0	0	26
Days Maximum Temp. ≤ 32°F	16	11	3	0	0	0	0	0	0	0	2	10	42
Days Minimum Temp. ≤ 32°F	30	26	22	9	1	0	0	0	1	8	20	28	145
Days Minimum Temp. ≤ 0°F	8	4	0	0	0	0	0	0	0	0	0	3	15
Heating Degree Days (base 65°F)	1,379	1,087	834	456	174	24	5	11	104	398	767	1,170	6,409
Cooling Degree Days (base 65°F)	0	0	2	10	56	188	291	244	95	8	0	0	894
Mean Precipitation (in.)	1.10	1.09	2.16	3.25	3.75	4.26	3.90	4.47	3.88	2.73	2.49	2.18	35.26
Days With ≥ 0.1" Precipitation	na	3	4	6	7	7	6	6	6	5	5	3	na
Days With ≥ 1.0" Precipitation	na	0	1	1	1	1	1	1	1	1	1	1	na
Mean Snowfall (in.)	na	na	na	0.4	0.0	0.0	0.0	0.0	0.0	trace	0.8	na	na
Days With ≥ 1.0" Snow Depth	na	na	na	0	0	0	0	0	0	0	1	na	na

Hillsboro *Montgomery Co.* Elevation: 629 ft. Latitude: 39° 09' N Longitude: 89° 29' W

	JAN	FEB	MAR	APR	MAY	JUN	JUL	AUG	SEP	OCT	NOV	DEC	YEAR
Mean Maximum Temp. (°F)	36.5	43.0	54.6	67.1	77.0	85.6	89.5	87.4	81.0	69.3	54.0	41.8	65.6
Mean Temp. (°F)	27.6	33.4	44.0	55.4	65.2	74.1	77.9	75.5	68.5	57.1	44.5	33.3	54.7
Mean Minimum Temp. (°F)	18.8	23.6	33.3	43.7	53.4	62.5	66.3	63.6	55.8	44.8	35.0	24.7	43.8
Extreme Maximum Temp. (°F)	70	78	88	92	95	103	104	105	101	90	81	74	105
Extreme Minimum Temp. (°F)	-21	-17	-3	20	30	43	46	39	29	20	2	-20	-21
Days Maximum Temp. ≥ 90°F	0	0	0	0	1	10	16	11	4	0	0	0	42
Days Maximum Temp. ≤ 32°F	11	6	1	0	0	0	0	0	0	0	1	6	25
Days Minimum Temp. ≤ 32°F	27	21	15	4	0	0	0	0	0	3	13	24	107
Days Minimum Temp. ≤ 0°F	3	1	0	0	0	0	0	0	0	0	0	2	6
Heating Degree Days (base 65°F)	1,153	887	648	305	91	8	1	1	54	263	610	978	4,999
Cooling Degree Days (base 65°F)	0	0	4	23	113	311	441	364	167	27	2	0	1,452
Mean Precipitation (in.)	2.08	1.96	3.54	4.36	4.31	4.04	3.49	3.38	3.24	2.88	3.73	2.97	39.98
Days With ≥ 0.1" Precipitation	4	4	7	7	7	7	6	6	5	5	7	5	70
Days With ≥ 1.0" Precipitation	0	0	1	1	1	1	1	1	1	1	1	1	10
Mean Snowfall (in.)	5.8	4.2	3.2	0.5	trace	0.0	0.0	0.0	0.0	trace	1.0	3.9	18.6
Days With ≥ 1.0" Snow Depth	na	na	na	0	0	0	0	0	0	0	0	na	na

Hoopeston 1 NE *Vermilion Co.* Elevation: 708 ft. Latitude: 40° 28' N Longitude: 87° 39' W

	JAN	FEB	MAR	APR	MAY	JUN	JUL	AUG	SEP	OCT	NOV	DEC	YEAR
Mean Maximum Temp. (°F)	31.6	37.4	49.4	62.4	73.9	82.6	85.4	83.1	77.3	64.8	49.8	37.2	61.2
Mean Temp. (°F)	24.1	29.3	40.2	51.5	62.7	71.8	75.0	72.7	66.1	54.4	41.8	30.1	51.7
Mean Minimum Temp. (°F)	16.5	21.2	31.0	40.7	51.5	61.0	64.6	62.3	54.9	43.9	33.7	23.0	42.0
Extreme Maximum Temp. (°F)	64	71	84	88	94	104	102	104	96	89	77	70	104
Extreme Minimum Temp. (°F)	-24	-17	-1	9	28	38	43	42	30	20	3	-21	-24
Days Maximum Temp. ≥ 90°F	0	0	0	0	1	5	8	4	2	0	0	0	20
Days Maximum Temp. ≤ 32°F	16	10	2	0	0	0	0	0	0	0	1	9	38
Days Minimum Temp. ≤ 32°F	28	23	18	6	1	0	0	0	0	3	14	26	119
Days Minimum Temp. ≤ 0°F	5	3	0	0	0	0	0	0	0	0	0	2	10
Heating Degree Days (base 65°F)	1,262	1,001	763	408	144	19	3	7	81	337	690	1,075	5,790
Cooling Degree Days (base 65°F)	0	0	2	11	79	239	332	263	122	15	0	0	1,063
Mean Precipitation (in.)	1.54	1.57	2.95	3.66	4.17	4.01	4.08	3.80	2.91	3.05	2.93	2.35	37.02
Days With ≥ 0.1" Precipitation	4	4	7	8	8	7	6	6	5	5	6	6	72
Days With ≥ 1.0" Precipitation	0	0	1	1	1	1	1	1	1	1	1	0	9
Mean Snowfall (in.)	5.4	4.1	2.2	0.6	trace	0.0	0.0	0.0	0.0	0.1	1.2	4.2	17.8
Days With ≥ 1.0" Snow Depth	14	11	4	0	0	0	0	0	0	0	1	7	37

Jacksonville 2 E *Morgan Co.* Elevation: 606 ft. Latitude: 39° 44' N Longitude: 90° 12' W

	JAN	FEB	MAR	APR	MAY	JUN	JUL	AUG	SEP	OCT	NOV	DEC	YEAR
Mean Maximum Temp. (°F)	33.1	39.1	50.8	63.4	73.7	82.7	86.5	84.3	78.6	66.8	51.7	39.1	62.5
Mean Temp. (°F)	24.3	29.3	40.0	51.6	62.0	71.2	75.0	72.6	65.7	54.2	41.6	30.3	51.5
Mean Minimum Temp. (°F)	15.3	19.5	29.2	39.8	50.2	59.6	63.6	60.9	52.8	41.5	31.5	21.4	40.4
Extreme Maximum Temp. (°F)	71	74	87	90	93	101	101	103	99	90	80	74	103
Extreme Minimum Temp. (°F)	-21	-21	-9	18	30	36	45	39	29	20	0	-20	-21
Days Maximum Temp. ≥ 90°F	0	0	0	0	1	5	10	6	3	0	0	0	25
Days Maximum Temp. ≤ 32°F	15	9	3	0	0	0	0	0	0	0	1	8	36
Days Minimum Temp. ≤ 32°F	29	24	20	6	0	0	0	0	0	6	17	27	129
Days Minimum Temp. ≤ 0°F	5	3	0	0	0	0	0	0	0	0	0	2	10
Heating Degree Days (base 65°F)	1,257	1,001	769	407	153	20	3	9	91	345	694	1,070	5,819
Cooling Degree Days (base 65°F)	0	0	3	11	62	212	325	260	117	16	0	0	1,006
Mean Precipitation (in.)	1.35	1.66	3.15	3.91	5.04	4.29	3.75	3.39	3.61	2.69	3.42	2.56	38.82
Days With ≥ 0.1" Precipitation	4	3	6	7	8	6	6	6	6	6	6	5	69
Days With ≥ 1.0" Precipitation	0	0	1	1	1	2	1	1	1	1	1	1	11
Mean Snowfall (in.)	7.3	5.6	3.1	0.5	0.0	0.0	0.0	0.0	0.0	trace	1.4	5.0	22.9
Days With ≥ 1.0" Snow Depth	13	10	3	0	0	0	0	0	0	0	1	6	33

Jerseyville 2 SW *Jersey Co.* Elevation: 629 ft. Latitude: 39° 06' N Longitude: 90° 21' W

	JAN	FEB	MAR	APR	MAY	JUN	JUL	AUG	SEP	OCT	NOV	DEC	YEAR
Mean Maximum Temp. (°F)	35.3	41.5	52.6	64.6	74.6	83.3	87.8	86.0	79.1	67.6	52.8	40.8	63.8
Mean Temp. (°F)	26.3	31.7	42.5	53.5	63.4	72.3	76.7	74.4	66.8	55.3	43.2	32.0	53.2
Mean Minimum Temp. (°F)	17.2	22.0	32.2	42.4	52.2	61.4	65.4	62.7	54.5	42.9	33.5	23.2	42.5
Extreme Maximum Temp. (°F)	71	80	86	91	92	100	104	104	101	90	80	73	104
Extreme Minimum Temp. (°F)	-25	-22	-10	20	28	37	44	38	27	17	-2	-19	-25
Days Maximum Temp. ≥ 90°F	0	0	0	0	1	6	13	9	3	0	0	0	32
Days Maximum Temp. ≤ 32°F	13	7	2	0	0	0	0	0	0	0	1	7	30
Days Minimum Temp. ≤ 32°F	28	22	17	5	0	0	0	0	0	5	15	25	117
Days Minimum Temp. ≤ 0°F	4	2	0	0	0	0	0	0	0	0	0	1	7
Heating Degree Days (base 65°F)	1,194	935	695	356	123	14	2	4	78	314	648	1,016	5,379
Cooling Degree Days (base 65°F)	0	0	4	17	81	249	379	306	135	16	1	0	1,188
Mean Precipitation (in.)	1.89	1.96	3.47	4.28	3.92	3.65	3.39	2.92	3.39	2.86	3.73	2.82	38.28
Days With ≥ 0.1" Precipitation	4	4	7	7	7	6	6	5	5	6	6	5	68
Days With ≥ 1.0" Precipitation	0	0	1	1	1	1	1	1	1	1	1	1	10
Mean Snowfall (in.)	5.1	3.7	2.8	0.5	0.0	0.0	0.0	0.0	0.0	trace	1.2	3.5	16.8
Days With ≥ 1.0" Snow Depth	11	7	2	0	0	0	0	0	0	0	1	5	26

Kankakee Metro Wastewater *Kankakee Co.* Elevation: 639 ft. Latitude: 41° 08' N Longitude: 87° 53' W

	JAN	FEB	MAR	APR	MAY	JUN	JUL	AUG	SEP	OCT	NOV	DEC	YEAR
Mean Maximum Temp. (°F)	30.6	36.1	47.6	60.4	72.5	82.4	85.8	83.4	77.3	64.7	49.8	36.4	60.6
Mean Temp. (°F)	21.8	26.8	37.8	49.4	60.7	70.6	74.6	72.2	64.8	52.4	40.4	28.2	50.0
Mean Minimum Temp. (°F)	12.9	17.6	27.9	38.4	48.9	58.8	63.3	60.9	52.2	40.0	30.9	20.1	39.3
Extreme Maximum Temp. (°F)	65	71	84	91	94	103	103	107	99	89	78	70	107
Extreme Minimum Temp. (°F)	-29	-21	-6	8	27	39	47	39	30	18	1	-26	-29
Days Maximum Temp. ≥ 90°F	0	0	0	0	1	6	9	5	2	0	0	0	23
Days Maximum Temp. ≤ 32°F	16	11	3	0	0	0	0	0	0	0	1	9	40
Days Minimum Temp. ≤ 32°F	29	25	21	7	0	0	0	0	0	5	17	28	132
Days Minimum Temp. ≤ 0°F	6	4	0	0	0	0	0	0	0	0	0	3	13
Heating Degree Days (base 65°F)	1,333	1,069	838	470	186	26	3	9	100	393	733	1,134	6,294
Cooling Degree Days (base 65°F)	0	0	1	7	55	202	306	237	99	7	0	0	914
Mean Precipitation (in.)	1.86	1.68	2.80	3.81	4.61	4.43	4.27	3.20	3.29	2.72	3.41	2.50	38.58
Days With ≥ 0.1" Precipitation	5	4	6	8	8	7	6	6	6	6	6	5	73
Days With ≥ 1.0" Precipitation	0	0	0	1	1	1	1	1	1	1	1	0	8
Mean Snowfall (in.)	8.9	6.4	2.9	1.0	trace	0.0	0.0	0.0	0.0	trace	1.0	5.6	25.8
Days With ≥ 1.0" Snow Depth	17	12	4	0	0	0	0	0	0	0	1	8	42

La Harpe *Hancock Co.* Elevation: 698 ft. Latitude: 40° 35' N Longitude: 90° 58' W

	JAN	FEB	MAR	APR	MAY	JUN	JUL	AUG	SEP	OCT	NOV	DEC	YEAR
Mean Maximum Temp. (°F)	31.8	38.3	50.1	63.1	73.9	83.2	87.4	84.8	77.6	66.0	50.0	37.3	62.0
Mean Temp. (°F)	22.3	28.3	39.3	51.1	62.0	71.3	75.4	72.9	65.0	53.5	39.9	28.1	50.8
Mean Minimum Temp. (°F)	12.7	18.3	28.5	39.1	50.2	59.4	63.3	60.9	52.5	41.0	29.9	18.9	39.6
Extreme Maximum Temp. (°F)	66	74	87	92	93	105	104	105	98	92	79	72	105
Extreme Minimum Temp. (°F)	-23	-22	-8	9	28	39	42	40	29	18	-1	-23	-23
Days Maximum Temp. ≥ 90°F	0	0	0	0	1	6	12	7	2	0	0	0	28
Days Maximum Temp. ≤ 32°F	15	9	2	0	0	0	0	0	0	0	2	9	37
Days Minimum Temp. ≤ 32°F	30	25	21	7	0	0	0	0	0	7	19	28	137
Days Minimum Temp. ≤ 0°F	7	3	0	0	0	0	0	0	0	0	0	3	13
Heating Degree Days (base 65°F)	1,318	1,032	790	421	151	17	3	6	99	361	746	1,137	6,081
Cooling Degree Days (base 65°F)	0	0	2	10	60	217	334	265	104	10	0	0	1,002
Mean Precipitation (in.)	1.43	1.59	2.87	3.92	4.62	4.19	4.47	3.89	4.30	2.85	3.13	2.25	39.51
Days With ≥ 0.1" Precipitation	4	4	6	7	8	7	6	6	6	5	6	5	70
Days With ≥ 1.0" Precipitation	0	0	1	1	1	1	1	1	1	1	1	1	10
Mean Snowfall (in.)	7.8	5.1	3.7	1.1	0.0	0.0	0.0	0.0	0.0	trace	1.9	5.5	25.1
Days With ≥ 1.0" Snow Depth	17	11	4	0	0	0	0	0	0	0	1	9	42

Lacon 1 N *Marshall Co.* Elevation: 459 ft. Latitude: 41° 02' N Longitude: 89° 24' W

	JAN	FEB	MAR	APR	MAY	JUN	JUL	AUG	SEP	OCT	NOV	DEC	YEAR
Mean Maximum Temp. (°F)	31.4	37.7	49.8	63.7	74.8	83.7	87.1	85.3	78.4	66.5	50.5	37.5	62.2
Mean Temp. (°F)	23.3	28.9	39.9	52.2	62.8	71.7	75.7	73.8	66.3	54.8	41.5	29.6	51.7
Mean Minimum Temp. (°F)	14.9	20.1	30.0	40.6	50.7	59.8	64.1	62.3	54.2	43.1	32.4	21.6	41.2
Extreme Maximum Temp. (°F)	70	73	81	91	92	102	103	102	99	90	78	71	103
Extreme Minimum Temp. (°F)	-27	-21	-5	11	26	36	44	45	28	18	-3	-24	-27
Days Maximum Temp. ≥ 90°F	0	0	0	0	1	6	11	7	2	0	0	0	27
Days Maximum Temp. ≤ 32°F	15	10	2	0	0	0	0	0	0	0	1	9	37
Days Minimum Temp. ≤ 32°F	28	24	19	7	0	0	0	0	0	4	16	27	125
Days Minimum Temp. ≤ 0°F	6	3	0	0	0	0	0	0	0	0	0	2	11
Heating Degree Days (base 65°F)	1,286	1,013	772	394	137	16	2	5	80	325	699	1,091	5,820
Cooling Degree Days (base 65°F)	0	0	2	14	70	231	351	298	125	16	0	0	1,107
Mean Precipitation (in.)	1.57	1.61	3.18	4.05	4.38	4.33	4.18	3.66	3.72	3.13	3.02	2.33	39.16
Days With ≥ 0.1" Precipitation	4	4	7	7	8	7	6	6	5	6	6	5	71
Days With ≥ 1.0" Precipitation	0	0	1	1	1	1	1	1	1	1	1	1	10
Mean Snowfall (in.)	7.3	4.6	2.8	0.8	trace	0.0	0.0	0.0	0.0	trace	1.7	5.4	22.6
Days With ≥ 1.0" Snow Depth	16	11	4	1	0	0	0	0	0	0	1	8	41

Lincoln *Logan Co.* Elevation: 580 ft. Latitude: 40° 08' N Longitude: 89° 22' W

	JAN	FEB	MAR	APR	MAY	JUN	JUL	AUG	SEP	OCT	NOV	DEC	YEAR
Mean Maximum Temp. (°F)	32.2	38.6	50.6	63.8	74.7	83.4	86.5	84.2	78.5	66.5	51.0	39.0	62.4
Mean Temp. (°F)	23.8	29.6	40.6	52.3	63.2	72.3	75.7	73.4	66.4	54.5	41.8	30.7	52.0
Mean Minimum Temp. (°F)	15.4	20.6	30.6	40.7	51.6	61.1	64.8	62.6	54.3	42.4	32.4	22.3	41.6
Extreme Maximum Temp. (°F)	68	75	86	91	95	102	103	104	97	89	80	72	104
Extreme Minimum Temp. (°F)	-25	-20	-4	15	25	41	47	39	28	21	2	-19	-25
Days Maximum Temp. ≥ 90°F	0	0	0	0	1	6	9	6	2	0	0	0	24
Days Maximum Temp. ≤ 32°F	15	9	2	0	0	0	0	0	0	0	1	8	35
Days Minimum Temp. ≤ 32°F	29	24	19	6	0	0	0	0	0	5	16	26	125
Days Minimum Temp. ≤ 0°F	5	3	0	0	0	0	0	0	0	0	0	2	10
Heating Degree Days (base 65°F)	1,271	992	751	389	129	16	1	5	77	334	690	1,057	5,712
Cooling Degree Days (base 65°F)	0	0	2	12	76	245	345	281	123	14	0	0	1,098
Mean Precipitation (in.)	1.69	1.47	3.09	3.79	4.56	3.97	4.24	4.01	3.21	2.93	2.96	2.61	38.53
Days With ≥ 0.1" Precipitation	4	4	7	7	7	6	6	6	5	5	6	6	69
Days With ≥ 1.0" Precipitation	0	0	0	1	1	1	1	1	1	1	1	0	8
Mean Snowfall (in.)	6.6	4.8	2.1	0.6	0.0	0.0	0.0	0.0	0.0	trace	1.2	4.6	19.9
Days With ≥ 1.0" Snow Depth	13	8	2	0	0	0	0	0	0	0	1	5	29

Marengo *McHenry Co.* Elevation: 816 ft. Latitude: 42° 15' N Longitude: 88° 36' W

	JAN	FEB	MAR	APR	MAY	JUN	JUL	AUG	SEP	OCT	NOV	DEC	YEAR
Mean Maximum Temp. (°F)	27.8	32.8	44.9	59.0	71.8	81.6	85.0	82.4	75.3	62.9	46.7	32.9	58.6
Mean Temp. (°F)	18.8	23.4	35.1	47.3	58.9	69.0	73.1	70.7	62.8	50.8	37.4	24.6	47.7
Mean Minimum Temp. (°F)	9.7	14.0	25.2	35.6	46.0	56.4	61.1	58.9	50.2	38.5	28.2	16.3	36.7
Extreme Maximum Temp. (°F)	61	68	84	91	95	105	105	103	98	90	76	64	105
Extreme Minimum Temp. (°F)	-29	-23	-10	6	26	29	39	39	25	14	-8	-23	-29
Days Maximum Temp. ≥ 90°F	0	0	0	0	1	5	8	4	1	0	0	0	19
Days Maximum Temp. ≤ 32°F	19	13	4	0	0	0	0	0	0	0	2	13	51
Days Minimum Temp. ≤ 32°F	30	27	24	12	2	0	0	0	1	8	20	29	153
Days Minimum Temp. ≤ 0°F	9	6	1	0	0	0	0	0	0	0	0	4	20
Heating Degree Days (base 65°F)	1,429	1,169	921	533	232	40	7	18	136	441	820	1,245	6,991
Cooling Degree Days (base 65°F)	0	0	0	9	44	167	267	202	71	6	0	0	766
Mean Precipitation (in.)	1.40	1.21	2.36	3.57	3.94	4.36	3.89	4.40	3.55	2.67	2.68	1.97	36.00
Days With ≥ 0.1" Precipitation	4	4	6	7	7	7	6	7	6	5	6	5	70
Days With ≥ 1.0" Precipitation	0	0	0	1	1	1	1	1	1	1	1	0	8
Mean Snowfall (in.)	11.7	7.7	4.8	1.7	0.1	0.0	0.0	0.0	0.0	trace	2.5	8.4	36.9
Days With ≥ 1.0" Snow Depth	20	16	7	1	0	0	0	0	0	0	2	11	57

Marion 4 NNE *Williamson Co.* Elevation: 475 ft. Latitude: 37° 46' N Longitude: 88° 54' W

	JAN	FEB	MAR	APR	MAY	JUN	JUL	AUG	SEP	OCT	NOV	DEC	YEAR
Mean Maximum Temp. (°F)	38.0	43.9	54.7	65.9	74.9	83.2	87.3	85.9	79.2	68.0	54.7	43.3	64.9
Mean Temp. (°F)	29.0	33.8	44.1	54.5	63.7	72.4	76.7	74.8	67.6	55.9	44.8	34.3	54.3
Mean Minimum Temp. (°F)	20.0	23.7	33.5	43.1	52.5	61.6	66.0	63.7	56.0	43.6	34.9	25.4	43.7
Extreme Maximum Temp. (°F)	70	79	85	89	93	100	103	104	100	90	82	77	104
Extreme Minimum Temp. (°F)	-22	-11	-8	19	31	40	49	43	33	19	7	-17	-22
Days Maximum Temp. ≥ 90°F	0	0	0	0	0	5	11	9	3	0	0	0	28
Days Maximum Temp. ≤ 32°F	10	6	1	0	0	0	0	0	0	0	1	5	23
Days Minimum Temp. ≤ 32°F	27	22	15	5	0	0	0	0	0	5	14	23	111
Days Minimum Temp. ≤ 0°F	2	1	0	0	0	0	0	0	0	0	0	1	4
Heating Degree Days (base 65°F)	1,109	876	643	327	115	11	1	3	67	298	602	944	4,996
Cooling Degree Days (base 65°F)	0	0	4	18	83	248	381	323	142	23	2	0	1,224
Mean Precipitation (in.)	2.98	3.03	4.62	4.67	5.03	4.08	3.80	3.81	3.26	3.14	4.91	3.68	47.01
Days With ≥ 0.1" Precipitation	6	6	8	8	8	7	6	6	5	6	7	7	80
Days With ≥ 1.0" Precipitation	0	1	1	1	2	1	1	1	1	1	1	1	12
Mean Snowfall (in.)	5.9	5.4	2.5	0.5	0.0	0.0	0.0	0.0	0.0	0.2	0.8	2.9	18.2
Days With ≥ 1.0" Snow Depth	7	6	2	0	0	0	0	0	0	0	0	3	18

Mason City 1 W *Mason Co.* Elevation: 583 ft. Latitude: 40° 12' N Longitude: 89° 42' W

	JAN	FEB	MAR	APR	MAY	JUN	JUL	AUG	SEP	OCT	NOV	DEC	YEAR
Mean Maximum Temp. (°F)	32.6	38.8	51.2	64.6	75.0	83.7	86.8	84.6	78.9	66.9	51.0	38.1	62.7
Mean Temp. (°F)	24.5	30.0	41.3	53.2	63.7	72.6	75.9	73.7	66.9	55.3	42.0	30.3	52.4
Mean Minimum Temp. (°F)	16.2	21.2	31.4	41.6	52.2	61.4	65.0	62.8	54.9	43.7	32.9	22.4	42.2
Extreme Maximum Temp. (°F)	70	75	87	91	94	103	102	103	99	90	80	73	103
Extreme Minimum Temp. (°F)	-24	-21	-8	15	29	39	48	40	28	19	-1	-23	-24
Days Maximum Temp. ≥ 90°F	0	0	0	0	1	6	10	6	3	0	0	0	26
Days Maximum Temp. ≤ 32°F	14	9	2	0	0	0	0	0	0	0	1	9	35
Days Minimum Temp. ≤ 32°F	28	23	17	5	0	0	0	0	0	4	15	25	117
Days Minimum Temp. ≤ 0°F	5	3	0	0	0	0	0	0	0	0	0	2	10
Heating Degree Days (base 65°F)	1,251	982	730	364	120	12	2	4	71	312	684	1,069	5,601
Cooling Degree Days (base 65°F)	0	0	4	16	86	254	357	294	135	19	0	0	1,165
Mean Precipitation (in.)	1.54	1.49	2.76	3.52	4.33	3.63	3.89	3.49	3.15	2.79	2.88	2.42	35.89
Days With ≥ 0.1" Precipitation	4	4	6	7	7	7	6	6	6	5	6	5	69
Days With ≥ 1.0" Precipitation	0	0	1	1	1	1	1	1	1	0	1	1	9
Mean Snowfall (in.)	6.0	4.9	2.4	0.6	trace	0.0	0.0	0.0	0.0	trace	1.3	4.6	19.8
Days With ≥ 1.0" Snow Depth	13	10	2	0	0	0	0	0	0	0	1	7	33

Mattoon *Coles Co.* Elevation: 715 ft. Latitude: 39° 28' N Longitude: 88° 21' W

	JAN	FEB	MAR	APR	MAY	JUN	JUL	AUG	SEP	OCT	NOV	DEC	YEAR
Mean Maximum Temp. (°F)	33.4	39.1	50.7	63.3	74.3	83.4	86.6	84.7	78.7	66.1	51.0	38.8	62.5
Mean Temp. (°F)	25.4	30.7	41.3	52.6	63.4	72.7	76.2	74.1	67.3	55.2	42.4	31.0	52.7
Mean Minimum Temp. (°F)	17.4	22.2	31.8	41.9	52.5	61.9	65.7	63.5	55.8	44.3	33.8	23.1	42.8
Extreme Maximum Temp. (°F)	67	73	85	89	95	103	102	104	98	90	79	71	104
Extreme Minimum Temp. (°F)	-23	-17	-3	17	30	41	49	40	33	20	4	-20	-23
Days Maximum Temp. ≥ 90°F	0	0	0	0	1	6	10	7	3	0	0	0	27
Days Maximum Temp. ≤ 32°F	14	9	2	0	0	0	0	0	0	0	1	8	34
Days Minimum Temp. ≤ 32°F	28	23	18	5	0	0	0	0	0	3	14	25	116
Days Minimum Temp. ≤ 0°F	4	2	0	0	0	0	0	0	0	0	0	2	8
Heating Degree Days (base 65°F)	1,221	963	731	378	125	13	1	3	67	314	671	1,048	5,535
Cooling Degree Days (base 65°F)	0	0	2	12	83	260	367	303	142	18	0	0	1,187
Mean Precipitation (in.)	2.01	2.03	3.07	4.01	3.91	4.13	4.07	3.12	3.09	3.03	3.65	2.72	38.84
Days With ≥ 0.1" Precipitation	5	5	7	8	7	7	7	5	5	6	6	5	73
Days With ≥ 1.0" Precipitation	0	0	1	1	1	1	1	1	1	1	1	1	10
Mean Snowfall (in.)	6.9	3.4	1.9	0.1	trace	0.0	0.0	0.0	0.0	trace	1.0	4.4	17.7
Days With ≥ 1.0" Snow Depth	11	7	2	0	0	0	0	0	0	0	1	5	26

McLeansboro 2 ENE *Hamilton Co.* Elevation: 479 ft. Latitude: 38° 06' N Longitude: 88° 30' W

	JAN	FEB	MAR	APR	MAY	JUN	JUL	AUG	SEP	OCT	NOV	DEC	YEAR
Mean Maximum Temp. (°F)	38.0	44.0	54.4	65.8	75.7	84.7	88.9	87.6	81.3	69.4	55.3	43.7	65.7
Mean Temp. (°F)	29.2	34.1	44.1	54.8	64.4	73.4	77.4	75.3	68.4	56.4	45.2	34.6	54.8
Mean Minimum Temp. (°F)	20.3	24.2	33.7	43.7	53.1	62.1	65.9	63.1	55.4	43.5	35.0	25.4	43.8
Extreme Maximum Temp. (°F)	69	79	84	90	92	102	103	103	103	92	83	75	103
Extreme Minimum Temp. (°F)	-21	-11	-5	20	31	40	45	44	32	19	9	-20	-21
Days Maximum Temp. ≥ 90°F	0	0	0	0	1	8	15	12	6	0	0	0	42
Days Maximum Temp. ≤ 32°F	10	6	1	0	0	0	0	0	0	0	0	5	22
Days Minimum Temp. ≤ 32°F	27	21	15	4	0	0	0	0	0	4	13	23	107
Days Minimum Temp. ≤ 0°F	2	1	0	0	0	0	0	0	0	0	0	1	4
Heating Degree Days (base 65°F)	1,103	866	645	321	103	9	1	2	57	283	589	937	4,916
Cooling Degree Days (base 65°F)	0	0	4	19	90	271	399	337	161	25	2	0	1,308
Mean Precipitation (in.)	3.09	2.68	4.50	4.72	4.63	3.80	3.46	3.02	2.91	3.08	4.51	3.55	43.95
Days With ≥ 0.1" Precipitation	6	6	8	8	8	6	6	6	5	5	7	7	78
Days With ≥ 1.0" Precipitation	1	0	1	1	1	1	1	1	1	1	1	1	11
Mean Snowfall (in.)	5.0	4.4	2.5	0.4	0.0	0.0	0.0	0.0	0.0	0.2	0.7	3.1	16.3
Days With ≥ 1.0" Snow Depth	8	6	2	0	0	0	0	0	0	0	0	3	19

Minonk *Woodford Co.* Elevation: 748 ft. Latitude: 40° 54' N Longitude: 89° 02' W

	JAN	FEB	MAR	APR	MAY	JUN	JUL	AUG	SEP	OCT	NOV	DEC	YEAR
Mean Maximum Temp. (°F)	29.9	35.9	47.8	61.9	73.5	83.5	86.4	84.2	78.3	65.6	49.0	35.9	61.0
Mean Temp. (°F)	21.3	27.0	38.1	50.2	61.3	71.2	74.5	72.2	65.3	53.3	39.7	27.6	50.1
Mean Minimum Temp. (°F)	12.7	18.2	28.3	38.4	49.0	58.8	62.6	60.1	52.2	40.9	30.4	19.4	39.3
Extreme Maximum Temp. (°F)	65	74	88	93	96	103	103	102	99	90	81	70	103
Extreme Minimum Temp. (°F)	-25	-22	-6	7	27	36	44	38	25	16	-3	-22	-25
Days Maximum Temp. ≥ 90°F	0	0	0	0	1	7	10	6	3	0	0	0	27
Days Maximum Temp. ≤ 32°F	17	10	4	0	0	0	0	0	0	0	2	10	43
Days Minimum Temp. ≤ 32°F	30	25	21	8	1	0	0	0	0	6	18	28	137
Days Minimum Temp. ≤ 0°F	7	4	0	0	0	0	0	0	0	0	0	3	14
Heating Degree Days (base 65°F)	1,349	1,066	829	449	176	24	5	10	97	372	752	1,152	6,281
Cooling Degree Days (base 65°F)	0	0	2	11	64	211	308	240	104	12	0	0	952
Mean Precipitation (in.)	1.76	1.89	3.22	3.67	4.35	3.70	3.83	3.42	3.29	2.88	3.33	2.39	37.73
Days With ≥ 0.1" Precipitation	5	4	7	8	7	7	6	6	5	6	7	6	74
Days With ≥ 1.0" Precipitation	0	0	1	1	1	1	1	1	1	0	1	1	9
Mean Snowfall (in.)	9.0	6.8	3.6	0.9	trace	0.0	0.0	0.0	0.0	trace	1.6	6.2	28.1
Days With ≥ 1.0" Snow Depth	15	10	5	0	0	0	0	0	0	0	1	8	39

Monmouth *Warren Co.* Elevation: 744 ft. Latitude: 40° 55' N Longitude: 90° 38' W

	JAN	FEB	MAR	APR	MAY	JUN	JUL	AUG	SEP	OCT	NOV	DEC	YEAR
Mean Maximum Temp. (°F)	31.0	37.6	50.0	63.9	74.6	83.2	86.8	84.4	77.6	65.5	49.3	36.2	61.7
Mean Temp. (°F)	22.7	28.8	40.0	52.2	62.8	71.7	75.5	73.0	65.7	54.3	40.4	28.4	51.3
Mean Minimum Temp. (°F)	14.4	20.1	30.0	40.5	50.9	60.1	64.1	61.6	53.7	43.0	31.5	20.6	40.9
Extreme Maximum Temp. (°F)	69	72	87	93	93	103	104	104	98	91	80	69	104
Extreme Minimum Temp. (°F)	-25	-24	-6	12	29	37	45	41	27	17	-3	-21	-25
Days Maximum Temp. ≥ 90°F	0	0	0	0	1	5	10	6	2	0	0	0	24
Days Maximum Temp. ≤ 32°F	16	10	2	0	0	0	0	0	0	0	2	10	40
Days Minimum Temp. ≤ 32°F	29	24	19	6	0	0	0	0	0	4	17	27	126
Days Minimum Temp. ≤ 0°F	6	3	0	0	0	0	0	0	0	0	0	3	12
Heating Degree Days (base 65°F)	1,304	1,015	769	391	136	15	2	6	87	339	731	1,127	5,922
Cooling Degree Days (base 65°F)	0	0	2	14	71	228	340	269	112	14	0	0	1,050
Mean Precipitation (in.)	1.61	1.66	2.87	3.83	4.34	4.08	4.36	4.17	3.70	2.99	2.72	2.31	38.64
Days With ≥ 0.1" Precipitation	4	4	7	7	8	7	6	6	6	6	6	5	72
Days With ≥ 1.0" Precipitation	0	0	0	1	1	1	1	1	1	1	0	1	8
Mean Snowfall (in.)	8.6	5.8	3.5	1.6	0.0	0.0	0.0	0.0	0.0	trace	2.3	6.4	28.2
Days With ≥ 1.0" Snow Depth	19	13	4	1	0	0	0	0	0	0	2	9	48

Morrison *Whiteside Co.* Elevation: 600 ft. Latitude: 41° 48' N Longitude: 89° 58' W

	JAN	FEB	MAR	APR	MAY	JUN	JUL	AUG	SEP	OCT	NOV	DEC	YEAR
Mean Maximum Temp. (°F)	28.7	34.5	46.6	60.5	72.6	82.0	85.3	83.0	76.0	64.1	47.6	34.4	59.6
Mean Temp. (°F)	19.4	25.0	36.8	49.0	60.8	70.0	73.9	71.4	63.5	51.7	38.2	25.8	48.8
Mean Minimum Temp. (°F)	10.1	15.5	27.0	37.5	48.9	58.1	62.4	59.7	50.9	39.3	28.7	17.1	37.9
Extreme Maximum Temp. (°F)	62	69	86	92	95	102	103	105	96	92	79	70	105
Extreme Minimum Temp. (°F)	-28	-25	-9	8	27	35	45	40	27	16	-7	-23	-28
Days Maximum Temp. ≥ 90°F	0	0	0	0	1	5	8	5	2	0	0	0	21
Days Maximum Temp. ≤ 32°F	18	12	3	0	0	0	0	0	0	0	2	11	46
Days Minimum Temp. ≤ 32°F	30	26	23	9	1	0	0	0	1	8	20	29	147
Days Minimum Temp. ≤ 0°F	9	5	0	0	0	0	0	0	0	0	0	4	18
Heating Degree Days (base 65°F)	1,408	1,123	867	481	183	27	4	12	121	414	799	1,209	6,648
Cooling Degree Days (base 65°F)	0	0	1	8	52	187	288	223	77	6	0	0	842
Mean Precipitation (in.)	1.49	1.44	2.79	3.68	4.68	4.19	3.76	4.78	3.09	2.86	2.90	2.13	37.79
Days With ≥ 0.1" Precipitation	4	4	6	7	8	7	6	7	5	5	6	5	70
Days With ≥ 1.0" Precipitation	0	0	0	1	1	1	1	1	1	1	1	0	8
Mean Snowfall (in.)	10.7	6.8	4.6	1.4	0.0	0.0	0.0	0.0	0.0	trace	2.2	8.3	34.0
Days With ≥ 1.0" Snow Depth	22	17	6	1	0	0	0	0	0	0	2	14	62

Mount Carroll *Carroll Co.* Elevation: 639 ft. Latitude: 42° 06' N Longitude: 89° 59' W

	JAN	FEB	MAR	APR	MAY	JUN	JUL	AUG	SEP	OCT	NOV	DEC	YEAR
Mean Maximum Temp. (°F)	27.8	33.7	45.6	59.6	71.7	81.0	84.7	82.4	75.0	62.9	46.6	33.5	58.7
Mean Temp. (°F)	17.6	23.2	35.0	47.2	58.9	67.8	71.6	69.5	61.2	49.5	36.6	24.0	46.8
Mean Minimum Temp. (°F)	7.5	12.7	24.4	34.7	45.9	54.4	58.7	56.5	47.3	35.9	26.5	14.5	34.9
Extreme Maximum Temp. (°F)	60	65	85	91	93	100	101	102	95	91	77	69	102
Extreme Minimum Temp. (°F)	-29	-30	-13	-2	24	31	39	32	23	5	-15	-24	-30
Days Maximum Temp. ≥ 90°F	0	0	0	0	1	4	7	4	1	0	0	0	17
Days Maximum Temp. ≤ 32°F	18	12	4	0	0	0	0	0	0	0	2	12	48
Days Minimum Temp. ≤ 32°F	30	27	25	13	2	0	0	0	2	13	22	30	164
Days Minimum Temp. ≤ 0°F	11	7	1	0	0	0	0	0	0	0	0	5	24
Heating Degree Days (base 65°F)	1,464	1,173	922	535	227	48	11	26	169	482	844	1,264	7,165
Cooling Degree Days (base 65°F)	0	0	1	7	38	133	217	167	58	4	0	0	625
Mean Precipitation (in.)	1.41	1.44	2.66	3.65	4.50	4.56	3.71	4.51	3.65	2.77	2.82	2.01	37.69
Days With ≥ 0.1" Precipitation	4	4	6	7	7	7	6	7	6	6	6	5	71
Days With ≥ 1.0" Precipitation	0	0	0	1	1	1	1	1	1	1	1	0	8
Mean Snowfall (in.)	10.5	6.7	4.3	1.6	trace	0.0	0.0	0.0	trace	0.2	2.6	7.0	32.9
Days With ≥ 1.0" Snow Depth	22	17	7	1	0	0	0	0	0	0	2	14	63

Mount Vernon-Outland Airport *Jefferson Co.* Elevation: 465 ft. Latitude: 38° 19' N Longitude: 88° 52' W

	JAN	FEB	MAR	APR	MAY	JUN	JUL	AUG	SEP	OCT	NOV	DEC	YEAR
Mean Maximum Temp. (°F)	37.3	43.2	53.9	65.4	75.2	84.2	88.3	86.6	79.8	68.4	54.3	42.7	65.0
Mean Temp. (°F)	28.4	33.5	43.8	54.6	64.0	73.2	77.4	75.3	68.0	56.1	44.7	33.9	54.4
Mean Minimum Temp. (°F)	19.6	23.8	33.6	43.7	52.9	62.1	66.5	64.0	56.1	43.7	35.1	25.0	43.8
Extreme Maximum Temp. (°F)	69	79	83	90	94	101	103	102	98	93	81	78	103
Extreme Minimum Temp. (°F)	-21	-12	-10	19	31	41	49	42	29	18	8	-19	-21
Days Maximum Temp. ≥ 90°F	0	0	0	0	1	7	14	10	4	0	0	0	36
Days Maximum Temp. ≤ 32°F	11	6	1	0	0	0	0	0	0	0	1	5	24
Days Minimum Temp. ≤ 32°F	27	21	15	4	0	0	0	0	0	5	13	24	109
Days Minimum Temp. ≤ 0°F	3	1	0	0	0	0	0	0	0	0	0	1	5
Heating Degree Days (base 65°F)	1,127	884	653	326	110	9	0	2	62	292	603	959	5,027
Cooling Degree Days (base 65°F)	0	0	3	18	78	257	384	319	144	21	1	0	1,225
Mean Precipitation (in.)	2.45	2.59	4.01	4.44	4.52	3.53	3.50	3.24	3.18	2.98	4.27	3.18	41.89
Days With ≥ 0.1" Precipitation	5	5	8	8	7	7	6	5	5	5	7	6	74
Days With ≥ 1.0" Precipitation	1	1	1	1	1	1	1	1	1	1	1	1	12
Mean Snowfall (in.)	6.4	4.8	1.9	0.4	0.0	0.0	0.0	0.0	0.0	0.2	0.7	2.9	17.3
Days With ≥ 1.0" Snow Depth	9	5	1	0	0	0	0	0	0	0	0	3	18

Moweaqua *Shelby Co.* Elevation: 613 ft. Latitude: 39° 38' N Longitude: 89° 02' W

	JAN	FEB	MAR	APR	MAY	JUN	JUL	AUG	SEP	OCT	NOV	DEC	YEAR
Mean Maximum Temp. (°F)	34.0	40.2	52.2	64.7	75.4	84.0	87.4	85.5	79.9	67.9	52.1	39.7	63.6
Mean Temp. (°F)	25.4	30.8	41.8	53.0	63.5	72.4	75.9	73.7	67.1	55.5	42.6	31.3	52.8
Mean Minimum Temp. (°F)	16.8	21.3	31.3	41.2	51.6	60.8	64.4	61.9	54.2	43.1	33.1	22.8	41.9
Extreme Maximum Temp. (°F)	68	76	86	89	93	104	103	104	99	91	80	72	104
Extreme Minimum Temp. (°F)	-26	-21	-9	17	29	41	46	40	29	19	3	-21	-26
Days Maximum Temp. ≥ 90°F	0	0	0	0	1	7	12	8	4	0	0	0	32
Days Maximum Temp. ≤ 32°F	13	8	2	0	0	0	0	0	0	0	1	7	31
Days Minimum Temp. ≤ 32°F	28	23	18	5	0	0	0	0	0	5	16	26	121
Days Minimum Temp. ≤ 0°F	4	2	0	0	0	0	0	0	0	0	0	2	8
Heating Degree Days (base 65°F)	1,219	960	715	369	120	14	1	4	72	308	667	1,035	5,484
Cooling Degree Days (base 65°F)	0	0	2	13	74	245	348	285	135	18	0	0	1,120
Mean Precipitation (in.)	1.70	1.94	2.87	3.93	4.22	4.21	4.02	3.33	2.99	2.83	3.55	2.24	37.83
Days With ≥ 0.1" Precipitation	4	4	6	8	7	7	6	5	5	5	6	4	67
Days With ≥ 1.0" Precipitation	0	0	1	1	1	1	1	1	1	1	1	0	9
Mean Snowfall (in.)	na	na	0.9	0.2	trace	0.0	0.0	0.0	0.0	trace	0.5	na	na
Days With ≥ 1.0" Snow Depth	na	na	1	0	0	0	0	0	0	0	0	3	na

Nashville 4 NE *Washington Co.* Elevation: 515 ft. Latitude: 38° 22' N Longitude: 89° 18' W

	JAN	FEB	MAR	APR	MAY	JUN	JUL	AUG	SEP	OCT	NOV	DEC	YEAR
Mean Maximum Temp. (°F)	37.6	43.7	55.1	66.5	76.0	84.7	88.4	86.5	80.1	68.8	54.4	42.8	65.4
Mean Temp. (°F)	29.5	34.9	45.2	55.9	65.5	74.3	78.1	75.9	69.1	58.0	45.5	34.9	55.6
Mean Minimum Temp. (°F)	21.4	26.0	35.2	45.3	55.0	63.8	67.7	65.2	58.1	47.1	36.6	27.0	45.7
Extreme Maximum Temp. (°F)	69	76	84	90	93	101	106	105	100	91	82	73	106
Extreme Minimum Temp. (°F)	-18	-13	2	22	32	43	52	46	33	25	6	-21	-21
Days Maximum Temp. ≥ 90°F	0	0	0	0	1	7	13	9	4	0	0	0	34
Days Maximum Temp. ≤ 32°F	10	6	1	0	0	0	0	0	0	0	1	5	23
Days Minimum Temp. ≤ 32°F	26	20	13	3	0	0	0	0	0	2	11	21	96
Days Minimum Temp. ≤ 0°F	2	1	0	0	0	0	0	0	0	0	0	1	4
Heating Degree Days (base 65°F)	1,093	844	610	290	85	5	1	1	47	242	579	926	4,723
Cooling Degree Days (base 65°F)	0	0	3	22	108	297	418	355	170	31	1	0	1,405
Mean Precipitation (in.)	2.15	2.30	3.54	3.92	4.09	3.59	3.41	2.73	3.22	3.07	3.74	2.98	38.74
Days With ≥ 0.1" Precipitation	5	5	7	7	7	6	6	5	5	5	6	6	70
Days With ≥ 1.0" Precipitation	0	0	1	1	1	1	1	1	1	1	1	1	10
Mean Snowfall (in.)	5.8	4.3	1.5	0.6	0.0	0.0	0.0	0.0	0.0	trace	0.9	3.2	16.3
Days With ≥ 1.0" Snow Depth	10	6	2	0	0	0	0	0	0	0	1	3	22

Newton 6 SSE *Jasper Co.* Elevation: 508 ft. Latitude: 38° 55' N Longitude: 88° 07' W

	JAN	FEB	MAR	APR	MAY	JUN	JUL	AUG	SEP	OCT	NOV	DEC	YEAR
Mean Maximum Temp. (°F)	34.9	40.8	51.7	63.4	74.0	83.2	87.1	85.2	79.4	67.5	53.0	40.7	63.4
Mean Temp. (°F)	26.6	31.7	42.2	52.8	63.0	72.5	76.2	73.8	67.0	55.2	43.5	32.5	53.1
Mean Minimum Temp. (°F)	18.3	22.4	32.6	42.2	52.0	61.7	65.3	62.3	54.5	42.9	34.1	24.3	42.7
Extreme Maximum Temp. (°F)	68	77	83	88	94	103	102	104	98	91	81	73	104
Extreme Minimum Temp. (°F)	-28	-21	-12	21	30	41	47	39	31	20	6	-19	-28
Days Maximum Temp. ≥ 90°F	0	0	0	0	1	6	10	8	3	0	0	0	28
Days Maximum Temp. ≤ 32°F	13	8	2	0	0	0	0	0	0	0	1	7	31
Days Minimum Temp. ≤ 32°F	27	22	16	5	0	0	0	0	0	5	14	24	113
Days Minimum Temp. ≤ 0°F	3	2	0	0	0	0	0	0	0	0	0	1	6
Heating Degree Days (base 65°F)	1,184	935	703	372	127	14	1	3	71	317	638	1,001	5,366
Cooling Degree Days (base 65°F)	0	0	2	12	74	248	361	282	130	20	1	0	1,130
Mean Precipitation (in.)	2.38	2.26	3.81	3.94	4.38	3.65	4.19	3.29	3.22	2.82	3.92	2.88	40.74
Days With ≥ 0.1" Precipitation	5	5	7	8	8	7	6	5	5	5	6	6	73
Days With ≥ 1.0" Precipitation	0	0	1	1	1	1	1	1	1	1	1	1	10
Mean Snowfall (in.)	4.9	3.2	2.2	0.1	trace	0.0	0.0	0.0	0.0	0.1	0.9	3.4	14.8
Days With ≥ 1.0" Snow Depth	9	7	2	0	0	0	0	0	0	0	1	5	24

Olney 2 S *Richland Co.* Elevation: 479 ft. Latitude: 38° 42' N Longitude: 88° 05' W

	JAN	FEB	MAR	APR	MAY	JUN	JUL	AUG	SEP	OCT	NOV	DEC	YEAR
Mean Maximum Temp. (°F)	37.2	43.2	54.5	66.3	76.4	84.9	88.4	86.7	80.8	69.2	54.7	42.6	65.4
Mean Temp. (°F)	28.9	34.1	44.5	55.3	64.9	73.7	77.4	75.4	68.8	57.2	45.4	34.5	55.0
Mean Minimum Temp. (°F)	20.6	24.9	34.5	44.2	53.4	62.4	66.3	64.1	56.8	45.2	36.0	26.3	44.6
Extreme Maximum Temp. (°F)	70	78	85	89	93	103	101	103	98	92	81	74	103
Extreme Minimum Temp. (°F)	-24	-21	-15	21	29	38	46	46	32	18	6	-19	-24
Days Maximum Temp. ≥ 90°F	0	0	0	0	1	7	13	9	4	0	0	0	34
Days Maximum Temp. ≤ 32°F	11	6	1	0	0	0	0	0	0	0	1	5	24
Days Minimum Temp. ≤ 32°F	25	20	14	4	0	0	0	0	0	4	12	22	101
Days Minimum Temp. ≤ 0°F	3	2	0	0	0	0	0	0	0	0	0	1	6
Heating Degree Days (base 65°F)	1,113	866	631	306	95	7	0	0	50	264	584	940	4,856
Cooling Degree Days (base 65°F)	0	0	4	19	100	280	400	338	166	28	1	0	1,336
Mean Precipitation (in.)	2.84	2.60	4.31	4.64	4.56	3.97	3.89	3.25	3.05	3.33	4.41	3.60	44.45
Days With ≥ 0.1" Precipitation	6	5	8	8	7	7	6	5	5	5	7	6	75
Days With ≥ 1.0" Precipitation	1	1	1	1	1	1	1	1	1	1	1	1	12
Mean Snowfall (in.)	4.2	3.3	1.9	0.2	0.0	0.0	0.0	0.0	0.0	trace	0.8	2.9	13.3
Days With ≥ 1.0" Snow Depth	na	na	0	0	0	0	0	0	0	0	0	1	na

Ottawa 5 SW *La Salle Co.* Elevation: 524 ft. Latitude: 41° 20' N Longitude: 88° 55' W

	JAN	FEB	MAR	APR	MAY	JUN	JUL	AUG	SEP	OCT	NOV	DEC	YEAR
Mean Maximum Temp. (°F)	30.6	36.9	48.7	62.5	74.0	82.4	85.4	83.6	77.4	65.6	49.6	36.5	61.1
Mean Temp. (°F)	22.3	28.1	39.2	51.3	62.4	71.5	75.0	73.1	65.9	54.0	40.8	28.6	51.0
Mean Minimum Temp. (°F)	13.8	19.2	29.7	40.0	50.7	60.5	64.6	62.5	54.3	42.5	32.0	20.6	40.9
Extreme Maximum Temp. (°F)	64	72	82	92	96	100	104	102	99	93	80	70	104
Extreme Minimum Temp. (°F)	-25	-21	-2	12	29	39	47	46	30	19	-2	-20	-25
Days Maximum Temp. ≥ 90°F	0	0	0	0	2	5	8	6	2	0	0	0	23
Days Maximum Temp. ≤ 32°F	16	9	3	0	0	0	0	0	0	0	2	9	39
Days Minimum Temp. ≤ 32°F	29	24	19	6	0	0	0	0	0	4	16	27	125
Days Minimum Temp. ≤ 0°F	6	3	0	0	0	0	0	0	0	0	0	3	12
Heating Degree Days (base 65°F)	1,319	1,037	794	419	148	19	3	6	85	347	719	1,122	6,018
Cooling Degree Days (base 65°F)	0	0	2	12	68	207	312	256	107	12	0	0	976
Mean Precipitation (in.)	1.48	1.33	2.62	3.51	4.13	4.22	3.66	3.78	3.70	2.62	2.90	2.25	36.20
Days With ≥ 0.1" Precipitation	4	3	6	7	7	7	6	6	6	5	6	5	68
Days With ≥ 1.0" Precipitation	0	0	0	1	1	1	1	1	1	0	1	1	8
Mean Snowfall (in.)	8.6	5.0	3.2	0.8	0.0	0.0	0.0	0.0	0.0	trace	1.0	5.4	24.0
Days With ≥ 1.0" Snow Depth	19	12	4	0	0	0	0	0	0	0	1	8	44

Palestine 2 W *Crawford Co.* Elevation: 469 ft. Latitude: 39° 00' N Longitude: 87° 39' W

	JAN	FEB	MAR	APR	MAY	JUN	JUL	AUG	SEP	OCT	NOV	DEC	YEAR
Mean Maximum Temp. (°F)	36.8	42.6	54.1	65.9	76.2	84.8	88.1	86.2	80.1	68.3	54.1	42.3	64.9
Mean Temp. (°F)	28.6	34.0	44.5	55.1	65.1	73.5	77.2	75.6	67.8	56.6	45.1	34.4	54.8
Mean Minimum Temp. (°F)	20.4	25.2	34.9	44.4	54.0	62.3	66.4	64.9	55.5	44.9	36.2	26.5	44.6
Extreme Maximum Temp. (°F)	70	77	86	94	98	102	104	107	98	92	82	74	107
Extreme Minimum Temp. (°F)	-21	-18	-9	21	32	34	44	44	30	20	7	-23	-23
Days Maximum Temp. ≥ 90°F	0	0	0	0	1	8	13	9	4	0	0	0	35
Days Maximum Temp. ≤ 32°F	11	6	1	0	0	0	0	0	0	0	0	5	23
Days Minimum Temp. ≤ 32°F	26	20	13	3	0	0	0	0	0	3	12	22	99
Days Minimum Temp. ≤ 0°F	3	1	0	0	0	0	0	0	0	0	0	1	5
Heating Degree Days (base 65°F)	1,121	870	633	312	94	11	1	0	60	276	590	942	4,910
Cooling Degree Days (base 65°F)	0	0	3	20	107	282	400	354	142	22	1	0	1,331
Mean Precipitation (in.)	2.53	2.49	3.79	4.10	4.63	3.82	3.94	3.66	3.26	2.92	3.87	3.11	42.12
Days With ≥ 0.1" Precipitation	5	5	7	8	8	7	6	6	5	5	6	6	74
Days With ≥ 1.0" Precipitation	0	0	1	1	1	1	1	1	1	1	1	1	10
Mean Snowfall (in.)	6.4	4.5	2.6	0.2	0.0	0.0	0.0	0.0	0.0	trace	1.0	3.8	18.5
Days With ≥ 1.0" Snow Depth	10	7	2	0	0	0	0	0	0	0	1	3	23

Pana 3 E *Christian Co.* Elevation: 698 ft. Latitude: 39° 22' N Longitude: 89° 02' W

	JAN	FEB	MAR	APR	MAY	JUN	JUL	AUG	SEP	OCT	NOV	DEC	YEAR
Mean Maximum Temp. (°F)	34.7	40.7	52.6	65.4	75.0	83.6	87.2	84.9	78.9	67.0	52.7	40.3	63.6
Mean Temp. (°F)	26.6	32.0	42.8	54.1	63.9	72.7	76.5	74.2	67.4	55.9	43.8	32.4	53.5
Mean Minimum Temp. (°F)	18.5	23.2	32.9	42.8	52.8	61.8	65.7	63.4	55.8	44.7	34.8	24.5	43.4
Extreme Maximum Temp. (°F)	70	75	87	90	98	103	103	104	102	90	80	72	104
Extreme Minimum Temp. (°F)	-21	-13	-5	20	31	42	48	41	28	23	4	-20	-21
Days Maximum Temp. ≥ 90°F	0	0	0	0	1	6	11	7	3	0	0	0	28
Days Maximum Temp. ≤ 32°F	13	7	1	0	0	0	0	0	0	0	1	7	29
Days Minimum Temp. ≤ 32°F	28	22	16	4	0	0	0	0	0	3	13	24	110
Days Minimum Temp. ≤ 0°F	3	1	0	0	0	0	0	0	0	0	0	1	5
Heating Degree Days (base 65°F)	1,184	925	684	337	110	11	1	2	64	296	631	1,004	5,249
Cooling Degree Days (base 65°F)	0	0	3	17	84	263	382	308	142	20	1	0	1,220
Mean Precipitation (in.)	2.23	2.23	3.54	4.00	3.98	4.46	3.94	2.98	3.06	2.94	3.77	3.22	40.35
Days With ≥ 0.1" Precipitation	5	5	8	8	7	7	6	5	5	6	7	6	75
Days With ≥ 1.0" Precipitation	0	0	1	1	1	2	1	1	1	1	1	1	11
Mean Snowfall (in.)	7.4	5.0	4.2	0.9	trace	0.0	0.0	0.0	0.0	0.1	1.8	5.4	24.8
Days With ≥ 1.0" Snow Depth	13	10	3	0	0	0	0	0	0	0	1	6	33

Paris Waterworks *Edgar Co.* Elevation: 679 ft. Latitude: 39° 38' N Longitude: 87° 42' W

	JAN	FEB	MAR	APR	MAY	JUN	JUL	AUG	SEP	OCT	NOV	DEC	YEAR
Mean Maximum Temp. (°F)	34.0	40.0	51.5	63.8	74.7	83.2	86.5	84.3	78.5	66.3	51.8	39.6	62.9
Mean Temp. (°F)	26.0	31.3	42.1	53.2	63.9	72.7	76.2	74.0	67.5	55.6	43.2	32.0	53.2
Mean Minimum Temp. (°F)	17.9	22.6	32.6	42.6	53.1	62.2	65.9	63.7	56.5	44.9	34.6	24.2	43.4
Extreme Maximum Temp. (°F)	66	74	85	88	94	104	104	101	97	91	80	73	104
Extreme Minimum Temp. (°F)	-22	-17	-4	17	28	40	48	42	31	22	2	-22	-22
Days Maximum Temp. ≥ 90°F	0	0	0	0	1	6	10	6	2	0	0	0	25
Days Maximum Temp. ≤ 32°F	14	8	2	0	0	0	0	0	0	0	1	7	32
Days Minimum Temp. ≤ 32°F	27	22	16	5	0	0	0	0	0	3	14	24	111
Days Minimum Temp. ≤ 0°F	4	2	0	0	0	0	0	0	0	0	0	1	7
Heating Degree Days (base 65°F)	1,204	945	707	362	116	13	1	3	66	304	647	1,018	5,386
Cooling Degree Days (base 65°F)	0	0	3	14	89	255	359	293	145	20	1	0	1,179
Mean Precipitation (in.)	2.21	2.16	3.28	4.08	4.23	4.07	4.43	4.36	2.96	2.81	3.63	3.09	41.31
Days With ≥ 0.1" Precipitation	6	5	8	8	8	7	7	6	5	5	7	6	78
Days With ≥ 1.0" Precipitation	0	0	0	1	1	1	1	1	1	1	1	1	9
Mean Snowfall (in.)	10.4	6.6	3.6	0.3	0.0	0.0	0.0	0.0	0.0	0.1	1.3	5.9	28.2
Days With ≥ 1.0" Snow Depth	13	9	2	0	0	0	0	0	0	0	1	6	31

Park Forest *Cook Co.* Elevation: 708 ft. Latitude: 41° 30' N Longitude: 87° 41' W

	JAN	FEB	MAR	APR	MAY	JUN	JUL	AUG	SEP	OCT	NOV	DEC	YEAR
Mean Maximum Temp. (°F)	29.0	34.5	45.4	58.4	70.1	80.1	83.8	81.5	74.6	62.9	47.9	35.2	58.6
Mean Temp. (°F)	21.1	26.4	36.8	48.5	59.6	69.4	73.9	71.9	64.4	52.4	39.9	27.8	49.3
Mean Minimum Temp. (°F)	13.2	18.1	28.1	38.4	49.0	58.7	63.9	62.1	54.0	41.9	31.8	20.3	40.0
Extreme Maximum Temp. (°F)	64	70	83	89	94	102	102	103	95	89	77	70	103
Extreme Minimum Temp. (°F)	-27	-18	-2	9	28	36	45	41	29	18	1	-21	-27
Days Maximum Temp. ≥ 90°F	0	0	0	0	1	4	6	3	1	0	0	0	15
Days Maximum Temp. ≤ 32°F	18	12	4	0	0	0	0	0	0	0	2	11	47
Days Minimum Temp. ≤ 32°F	30	25	22	8	1	0	0	0	0	4	17	27	134
Days Minimum Temp. ≤ 0°F	6	3	0	0	0	0	0	0	0	0	0	2	11
Heating Degree Days (base 65°F)	1,355	1,085	869	499	218	41	7	11	110	393	747	1,148	6,483
Cooling Degree Days (base 65°F)	0	0	1	9	56	184	295	238	95	10	0	0	888
Mean Precipitation (in.)	1.76	1.62	2.75	3.85	4.19	4.55	4.15	3.86	3.31	2.82	3.40	2.54	38.80
Days With ≥ 0.1" Precipitation	4	4	6	8	7	7	6	6	6	6	6	5	71
Days With ≥ 1.0" Precipitation	0	0	0	1	1	1	1	1	1	1	1	0	8
Mean Snowfall (in.)	10.6	7.6	4.7	1.0	trace	0.0	0.0	0.0	0.0	0.2	1.0	5.7	30.8
Days With ≥ 1.0" Snow Depth	20	14	6	0	0	0	0	0	0	0	1	9	50

Paw Paw 2 NW *Lee Co.* Elevation: 948 ft. Latitude: 41° 43' N Longitude: 89° 00' W

	JAN	FEB	MAR	APR	MAY	JUN	JUL	AUG	SEP	OCT	NOV	DEC	YEAR
Mean Maximum Temp. (°F)	26.1	31.4	43.1	57.6	70.1	79.7	82.9	80.1	73.7	61.6	45.3	32.0	57.0
Mean Temp. (°F)	18.1	23.4	34.3	46.9	58.9	68.6	72.3	69.8	62.6	50.5	36.8	24.4	47.2
Mean Minimum Temp. (°F)	10.2	15.3	25.4	36.1	47.5	57.4	61.7	59.4	51.4	39.3	28.3	16.7	37.4
Extreme Maximum Temp. (°F)	61	68	83	90	94	101	100	99	93	88	75	65	101
Extreme Minimum Temp. (°F)	-25	-33	-9	9	26	36	43	37	29	17	-7	-23	-33
Days Maximum Temp. ≥ 90°F	0	0	0	0	0	3	4	2	1	0	0	0	10
Days Maximum Temp. ≤ 32°F	21	14	6	0	0	0	0	0	0	0	4	15	60
Days Minimum Temp. ≤ 32°F	30	27	25	10	1	0	0	0	0	7	20	29	149
Days Minimum Temp. ≤ 0°F	8	5	0	0	0	0	0	0	0	0	0	4	17
Heating Degree Days (base 65°F)	1,447	1,168	945	543	230	40	9	19	135	450	839	1,252	7,077
Cooling Degree Days (base 65°F)	0	0	0	4	41	158	243	174	65	5	0	0	690
Mean Precipitation (in.)	1.40	1.21	2.32	3.54	4.33	4.54	3.60	4.17	4.15	2.72	2.98	2.15	37.11
Days With ≥ 0.1" Precipitation	4	3	6	8	8	7	6	6	6	5	6	5	70
Days With ≥ 1.0" Precipitation	0	0	0	1	1	1	1	1	1	1	1	0	8
Mean Snowfall (in.)	9.0	5.8	4.2	1.0	trace	0.0	0.0	0.0	0.0	0.2	2.6	7.4	30.2
Days With ≥ 1.0" Snow Depth	20	13	5	0	0	0	0	0	0	0	2	11	51

Peru *La Salle Co.* Elevation: 620 ft. Latitude: 41° 21' N Longitude: 89° 06' W

	JAN	FEB	MAR	APR	MAY	JUN	JUL	AUG	SEP	OCT	NOV	DEC	YEAR
Mean Maximum Temp. (°F)	29.3	35.3	47.4	61.5	73.4	82.6	85.9	83.7	77.1	65.1	48.7	35.8	60.5
Mean Temp. (°F)	20.7	26.5	37.7	49.9	61.4	70.6	74.6	72.4	64.7	53.1	39.7	27.7	49.9
Mean Minimum Temp. (°F)	12.2	17.7	28.1	38.4	49.3	58.7	63.2	61.0	52.2	41.0	30.8	19.6	39.3
Extreme Maximum Temp. (°F)	64	72	82	91	93	101	104	103	96	90	78	69	104
Extreme Minimum Temp. (°F)	-26	-21	-4	13	25	38	42	40	27	16	-5	-21	-26
Days Maximum Temp. ≥ 90°F	0	0	0	0	2	5	10	6	2	0	0	0	25
Days Maximum Temp. ≤ 32°F	17	11	4	0	0	0	0	0	0	0	2	10	44
Days Minimum Temp. ≤ 32°F	30	26	21	8	1	0	0	0	0	6	18	28	138
Days Minimum Temp. ≤ 0°F	8	4	0	0	0	0	0	0	0	0	0	3	15
Heating Degree Days (base 65°F)	1,366	1,080	839	456	173	24	4	10	103	373	751	1,149	6,328
Cooling Degree Days (base 65°F)	0	0	1	8	63	202	308	249	94	9	0	0	934
Mean Precipitation (in.)	1.38	1.40	2.76	3.82	4.82	4.24	4.12	4.25	3.82	3.06	2.78	2.27	38.72
Days With ≥ 0.1" Precipitation	4	4	6	7	8	7	6	6	6	6	6	5	71
Days With ≥ 1.0" Precipitation	0	0	0	1	1	1	1	1	1	1	1	1	9
Mean Snowfall (in.)	8.0	4.5	3.6	0.6	trace	0.0	0.0	0.0	0.0	0.1	1.3	5.6	23.7
Days With ≥ 1.0" Snow Depth	20	10	3	0	0	0	0	0	0	0	1	8	42

Piper City *Ford Co.* Elevation: 669 ft. Latitude: 40° 42' N Longitude: 88° 11' W

	JAN	FEB	MAR	APR	MAY	JUN	JUL	AUG	SEP	OCT	NOV	DEC	YEAR
Mean Maximum Temp. (°F)	30.7	36.7	48.9	62.7	74.9	83.9	86.4	83.9	78.2	65.5	49.4	36.7	61.5
Mean Temp. (°F)	22.3	27.9	38.9	50.6	62.3	71.6	74.7	72.0	65.3	53.5	40.4	28.7	50.7
Mean Minimum Temp. (°F)	13.8	19.0	29.0	38.4	49.5	59.2	63.0	60.1	52.4	41.3	31.3	20.6	39.8
Extreme Maximum Temp. (°F)	66	72	86	93	97	106	105	108	98	90	80	70	108
Extreme Minimum Temp. (°F)	-25	-20	-4	7	25	37	42	37	26	17	0	-23	-25
Days Maximum Temp. ≥ 90°F	0	0	0	0	3	8	10	6	2	0	0	0	29
Days Maximum Temp. ≤ 32°F	16	10	3	0	0	0	0	0	0	0	2	10	41
Days Minimum Temp. ≤ 32°F	29	25	22	8	1	0	0	0	0	6	18	27	136
Days Minimum Temp. ≤ 0°F	6	3	0	0	0	0	0	0	0	0	0	2	11
Heating Degree Days (base 65°F)	1,318	1,042	803	436	154	21	4	10	92	365	733	1,118	6,096
Cooling Degree Days (base 65°F)	0	0	2	9	70	225	322	239	102	13	0	0	982
Mean Precipitation (in.)	1.84	1.73	2.75	3.44	4.24	3.74	4.18	3.88	3.03	2.60	2.87	2.50	36.80
Days With ≥ 0.1" Precipitation	5	4	6	7	8	7	6	6	5	5	6	5	70
Days With ≥ 1.0" Precipitation	0	0	1	1	1	1	1	1	1	1	1	0	9
Mean Snowfall (in.)	9.4	6.2	3.4	1.1	trace	0.0	0.0	0.0	0.0	0.2	2.0	5.8	28.1
Days With ≥ 1.0" Snow Depth	14	10	5	0	0	0	0	0	0	0	1	6	36

Pontiac *Livingston Co.* Elevation: 649 ft. Latitude: 40° 53' N Longitude: 88° 38' W

	JAN	FEB	MAR	APR	MAY	JUN	JUL	AUG	SEP	OCT	NOV	DEC	YEAR
Mean Maximum Temp. (°F)	29.9	36.3	48.2	61.9	73.5	82.3	85.1	82.9	77.3	64.9	48.9	36.0	60.6
Mean Temp. (°F)	22.1	27.9	38.8	50.8	62.1	71.4	74.8	72.6	65.8	53.7	40.5	28.6	50.8
Mean Minimum Temp. (°F)	14.2	19.4	29.5	39.7	50.7	60.5	64.5	62.3	54.4	42.5	31.9	21.1	40.9
Extreme Maximum Temp. (°F)	65	72	81	89	95	103	101	104	96	91	77	71	104
Extreme Minimum Temp. (°F)	-23	-18	-8	11	25	39	45	47	31	19	1	-20	-23
Days Maximum Temp. ≥ 90°F	0	0	0	0	1	5	8	5	2	0	0	0	21
Days Maximum Temp. ≤ 32°F	17	10	3	0	0	0	0	0	0	0	2	10	42
Days Minimum Temp. ≤ 32°F	29	25	20	7	0	0	0	0	0	4	17	27	129
Days Minimum Temp. ≤ 0°F	6	3	0	0	0	0	0	0	0	0	0	2	11
Heating Degree Days (base 65°F)	1,325	1,041	806	432	155	21	3	7	85	358	729	1,122	6,084
Cooling Degree Days (base 65°F)	0	0	2	11	64	211	311	247	109	11	0	0	966
Mean Precipitation (in.)	1.64	1.38	2.81	3.49	3.99	4.13	4.07	3.60	3.23	2.68	2.94	2.48	36.44
Days With ≥ 0.1" Precipitation	4	4	6	7	8	7	6	6	5	5	6	5	69
Days With ≥ 1.0" Precipitation	0	0	0	1	1	1	1	1	1	0	0	0	6
Mean Snowfall (in.)	8.9	5.7	3.3	1.0	0.0	0.0	0.0	0.0	0.0	trace	1.7	5.2	25.8
Days With ≥ 1.0" Snow Depth	11	7	2	0	0	0	0	0	0	0	1	4	25

Princeville *Peoria Co.* Elevation: 734 ft. Latitude: 40° 56' N Longitude: 89° 46' W

	JAN	FEB	MAR	APR	MAY	JUN	JUL	AUG	SEP	OCT	NOV	DEC	YEAR
Mean Maximum Temp. (°F)	29.9	36.3	48.7	62.4	73.0	81.4	85.0	82.7	76.3	64.5	49.0	35.6	60.4
Mean Temp. (°F)	20.5	26.5	37.8	50.0	60.7	69.5	73.1	70.8	63.5	52.1	39.0	26.7	49.2
Mean Minimum Temp. (°F)	11.1	16.7	26.9	37.4	48.2	57.4	61.1	58.9	50.7	39.7	28.9	17.8	37.9
Extreme Maximum Temp. (°F)	65	72	87	93	94	101	104	105	99	90	82	70	105
Extreme Minimum Temp. (°F)	-26	-26	-7	5	22	35	44	36	26	12	-3	-26	-26
Days Maximum Temp. ≥ 90°F	0	0	0	0	1	4	8	5	2	0	0	0	20
Days Maximum Temp. ≤ 32°F	17	11	3	0	0	0	0	0	0	0	2	10	43
Days Minimum Temp. ≤ 32°F	30	25	23	10	1	0	0	0	1	8	19	28	145
Days Minimum Temp. ≤ 0°F	8	5	0	0	0	0	0	0	0	0	0	4	17
Heating Degree Days (base 65°F)	1,373	1,080	837	455	182	31	7	16	125	402	774	1,179	6,461
Cooling Degree Days (base 65°F)	0	0	1	8	45	158	250	191	73	7	0	0	733
Mean Precipitation (in.)	1.74	1.65	3.07	3.86	4.66	3.94	3.97	3.74	3.72	2.86	2.96	2.48	38.65
Days With ≥ 0.1" Precipitation	4	3	6	7	8	7	7	7	6	6	6	5	72
Days With ≥ 1.0" Precipitation	0	0	1	1	1	1	1	1	1	1	1	1	10
Mean Snowfall (in.)	6.4	5.6	2.9	0.7	trace	0.0	0.0	0.0	0.0	0.1	2.1	5.5	23.3
Days With ≥ 1.0" Snow Depth	10	6	1	0	0	0	0	0	0	0	1	3	21

Quincy Muni Baldwin Field *Adams Co.* Elevation: 761 ft. Latitude: 39° 56' N Longitude: 91° 12' W

	JAN	FEB	MAR	APR	MAY	JUN	JUL	AUG	SEP	OCT	NOV	DEC	YEAR
Mean Maximum Temp. (°F)	31.9	38.0	50.1	62.8	72.8	82.1	86.5	84.2	77.1	65.3	50.1	37.5	61.5
Mean Temp. (°F)	24.2	29.9	41.1	52.8	63.0	72.2	76.6	74.2	66.6	55.0	41.7	30.0	52.3
Mean Minimum Temp. (°F)	16.4	21.7	32.1	42.9	53.1	62.3	66.6	64.3	56.0	44.6	33.3	22.6	43.0
Extreme Maximum Temp. (°F)	72	76	85	92	91	101	105	103	100	92	78	71	105
Extreme Minimum Temp. (°F)	-21	-18	-8	17	32	42	48	42	32	20	0	-22	-22
Days Maximum Temp. ≥ 90°F	0	0	0	0	0	5	10	7	2	0	0	0	24
Days Maximum Temp. ≤ 32°F	15	9	2	0	0	0	0	0	0	0	2	10	38
Days Minimum Temp. ≤ 32°F	28	22	16	4	0	0	0	0	0	3	14	26	113
Days Minimum Temp. ≤ 0°F	5	3	0	0	0	0	0	0	0	0	0	2	10
Heating Degree Days (base 65°F)	1,258	986	736	373	129	14	1	4	81	322	692	1,077	5,673
Cooling Degree Days (base 65°F)	0	0	3	15	68	236	367	303	132	17	1	0	1,142
Mean Precipitation (in.)	1.35	1.72	3.14	3.85	5.02	3.55	3.87	3.63	4.13	3.25	3.23	2.41	39.15
Days With ≥ 0.1" Precipitation	3	4	6	7	8	6	6	6	6	6	6	5	69
Days With ≥ 1.0" Precipitation	0	0	1	1	2	1	1	1	1	1	1	1	11
Mean Snowfall (in.)	7.6	6.0	2.9	0.9	trace	trace	trace	trace	trace	trace	2.2	4.8	24.4
Days With ≥ 1.0" Snow Depth	15	11	3	0	0	0	0	0	0	0	1	6	36

Rantoul Chanute AFB *Champaign Co.* Elevation: 754 ft. Latitude: 40° 18' N Longitude: 88° 09' W

	JAN	FEB	MAR	APR	MAY	JUN	JUL	AUG	SEP	OCT	NOV	DEC	YEAR
Mean Maximum Temp. (°F)	32.2	37.3	48.6	62.2	73.9	83.3	86.6	84.3	78.5	66.0	50.3	37.9	61.7
Mean Temp. (°F)	23.2	27.9	38.8	50.6	62.1	71.7	75.2	72.8	65.9	53.7	40.7	29.5	51.0
Mean Minimum Temp. (°F)	14.2	18.6	29.0	39.0	50.2	60.1	63.7	61.2	53.3	41.4	31.1	21.0	40.2
Extreme Maximum Temp. (°F)	65	72	85	90	97	104	105	102	98	90	78	70	105
Extreme Minimum Temp. (°F)	-27	-19	-13	10	27	38	46	38	31	21	3	-22	-27
Days Maximum Temp. ≥ 90°F	0	0	0	0	2	7	10	6	3	0	0	0	28
Days Maximum Temp. ≤ 32°F	15	10	2	0	0	0	0	0	0	0	1	8	36
Days Minimum Temp. ≤ 32°F	29	25	21	7	0	0	0	0	0	6	18	27	133
Days Minimum Temp. ≤ 0°F	6	3	0	0	0	0	0	0	0	0	0	2	11
Heating Degree Days (base 65°F)	1,290	1,041	808	434	155	21	3	7	87	356	723	1,095	6,020
Cooling Degree Days (base 65°F)	0	0	2	9	64	231	330	256	113	12	0	0	1,017
Mean Precipitation (in.)	1.72	1.79	3.13	3.88	4.16	3.92	4.52	4.33	3.17	2.94	3.10	2.64	39.30
Days With ≥ 0.1" Precipitation	5	4	6	8	7	7	6	6	5	6	6	6	72
Days With ≥ 1.0" Precipitation	0	0	1	1	1	1	2	1	1	1	1	1	11
Mean Snowfall (in.)	na	na	1.9	0.4	trace	0.0	0.0	0.0	0.0	trace	0.5	na	na
Days With ≥ 1.0" Snow Depth	na	9	1	0	0	0	0	0	0	0	0	4	na

Rosiclare 5 NW *Hardin Co.* Elevation: 396 ft. Latitude: 37° 25' N Longitude: 88° 21' W

	JAN	FEB	MAR	APR	MAY	JUN	JUL	AUG	SEP	OCT	NOV	DEC	YEAR
Mean Maximum Temp. (°F)	41.5	47.9	58.1	68.9	76.8	84.2	88.0	87.1	80.8	70.4	57.5	46.7	67.3
Mean Temp. (°F)	31.9	37.0	46.6	56.2	64.7	72.9	77.0	75.5	68.5	57.3	46.8	36.9	55.9
Mean Minimum Temp. (°F)	22.3	26.0	35.2	43.5	52.9	61.4	66.0	64.0	56.2	44.2	36.1	27.1	44.6
Extreme Maximum Temp. (°F)	72	77	84	90	92	100	102	101	100	90	83	76	102
Extreme Minimum Temp. (°F)	-22	-12	3	16	31	39	47	36	32	18	3	-17	-22
Days Maximum Temp. ≥ 90°F	0	0	0	0	0	5	13	10	4	0	0	0	32
Days Maximum Temp. ≤ 32°F	7	3	1	0	0	0	0	0	0	0	0	3	14
Days Minimum Temp. ≤ 32°F	25	20	14	5	0	0	0	0	0	4	12	21	101
Days Minimum Temp. ≤ 0°F	2	1	0	0	0	0	0	0	0	0	0	0	3
Heating Degree Days (base 65°F)	1,019	785	569	281	92	7	0	1	51	257	540	864	4,466
Cooling Degree Days (base 65°F)	0	0	6	20	87	247	385	337	152	22	2	0	1,258
Mean Precipitation (in.)	3.34	3.56	4.81	4.96	5.04	4.27	4.22	3.48	3.18	3.37	4.34	4.25	48.82
Days With ≥ 0.1" Precipitation	6	6	8	8	8	7	6	5	5	5	6	7	77
Days With ≥ 1.0" Precipitation	1	1	1	1	1	1	1	1	1	1	1	1	12
Mean Snowfall (in.)	4.3	3.3	1.4	0.1	0.0	0.0	0.0	0.0	0.0	0.2	0.1	1.3	10.7
Days With ≥ 1.0" Snow Depth	7	5	1	0	0	0	0	0	0	0	0	1	14

Rushville *Schuyler Co.* Elevation: 659 ft. Latitude: 40° 07' N Longitude: 90° 33' W

	JAN	FEB	MAR	APR	MAY	JUN	JUL	AUG	SEP	OCT	NOV	DEC	YEAR
Mean Maximum Temp. (°F)	32.6	39.0	50.6	63.7	74.1	82.7	87.2	85.2	78.2	66.5	50.7	38.0	62.4
Mean Temp. (°F)	24.0	29.9	40.7	52.7	62.9	71.9	76.3	74.0	66.5	54.9	41.4	29.9	52.1
Mean Minimum Temp. (°F)	15.4	20.7	30.8	41.7	51.7	61.0	65.3	62.8	54.7	43.3	32.1	21.6	41.8
Extreme Maximum Temp. (°F)	69	78	86	91	93	101	102	103	98	91	79	76	103
Extreme Minimum Temp. (°F)	-21	-20	-7	15	30	41	46	42	30	17	-1	-19	-21
Days Maximum Temp. ≥ 90°F	0	0	0	0	0	5	11	7	2	0	0	0	25
Days Maximum Temp. ≤ 32°F	15	9	2	0	0	0	0	0	0	0	2	8	36
Days Minimum Temp. ≤ 32°F	29	24	18	4	0	0	0	0	0	4	16	26	121
Days Minimum Temp. ≤ 0°F	5	3	0	0	0	0	0	0	0	0	0	2	10
Heating Degree Days (base 65°F)	1,265	985	749	378	130	16	1	3	79	321	702	1,083	5,712
Cooling Degree Days (base 65°F)	0	0	3	15	68	228	364	294	128	17	0	0	1,117
Mean Precipitation (in.)	1.54	1.84	3.06	4.04	5.19	4.04	3.79	3.69	3.96	3.27	3.14	2.45	40.01
Days With ≥ 0.1" Precipitation	3	3	6	7	7	6	6	5	5	5	5	5	63
Days With ≥ 1.0" Precipitation	0	0	1	1	2	1	1	1	1	1	1	1	11
Mean Snowfall (in.)	5.6	4.6	2.3	0.7	0.0	0.0	0.0	0.0	0.0	trace	1.0	3.7	17.9
Days With ≥ 1.0" Snow Depth	10	8	2	0	0	0	0	0	0	0	1	5	26

Salem Leckrone Airport *Marion Co.* Elevation: 567 ft. Latitude: 38° 39' N Longitude: 88° 58' W

	JAN	FEB	MAR	APR	MAY	JUN	JUL	AUG	SEP	OCT	NOV	DEC	YEAR
Mean Maximum Temp. (°F)	37.6	43.9	55.1	67.0	76.7	85.3	89.1	87.3	80.7	69.2	54.7	42.9	65.8
Mean Temp. (°F)	29.1	34.5	44.8	55.6	65.2	74.0	78.0	76.0	68.9	57.3	45.2	34.5	55.3
Mean Minimum Temp. (°F)	20.5	25.0	34.4	44.3	53.7	62.7	66.9	64.6	57.1	45.4	35.7	26.1	44.7
Extreme Maximum Temp. (°F)	70	78	85	91	94	101	104	105	99	90	82	74	105
Extreme Minimum Temp. (°F)	-23	-23	-8	20	31	42	49	45	33	21	6	-20	-23
Days Maximum Temp. ≥ 90°F	0	0	0	0	1	8	15	11	4	0	0	0	39
Days Maximum Temp. ≤ 32°F	10	6	1	0	0	0	0	0	0	0	0	5	22
Days Minimum Temp. ≤ 32°F	27	20	14	4	0	0	0	0	0	3	12	23	103
Days Minimum Temp. ≤ 0°F	2	1	0	0	0	0	0	0	0	0	0	1	4
Heating Degree Days (base 65°F)	1,107	856	625	299	89	6	1	1	48	259	589	938	4,818
Cooling Degree Days (base 65°F)	0	0	4	22	103	293	425	358	167	28	1	0	1,401
Mean Precipitation (in.)	2.42	2.45	3.95	4.16	4.25	4.21	3.79	3.31	3.23	3.11	3.98	3.23	42.09
Days With ≥ 0.1" Precipitation	5	5	7	8	8	7	5	6	5	5	7	6	74
Days With ≥ 1.0" Precipitation	0	0	1	1	1	1	1	1	1	1	1	1	10
Mean Snowfall (in.)	5.4	3.5	1.1	0.3	0.0	0.0	0.0	0.0	0.0	trace	0.7	2.7	13.7
Days With ≥ 1.0" Snow Depth	9	5	1	0	0	0	0	0	0	0	0	4	19

Sparta 1 W *Randolph Co.* Elevation: 534 ft. Latitude: 38° 07' N Longitude: 89° 43' W

	JAN	FEB	MAR	APR	MAY	JUN	JUL	AUG	SEP	OCT	NOV	DEC	YEAR
Mean Maximum Temp. (°F)	38.8	46.0	56.7	67.9	77.2	85.8	89.6	87.9	81.2	70.2	55.6	44.0	66.8
Mean Temp. (°F)	30.4	36.4	46.1	56.6	65.7	74.8	78.5	76.5	69.5	58.3	46.2	35.7	56.2
Mean Minimum Temp. (°F)	21.9	26.7	35.5	45.1	54.2	63.6	67.4	65.1	57.6	46.4	36.7	27.2	45.6
Extreme Maximum Temp. (°F)	72	81	86	92	94	103	108	105	99	92	85	76	108
Extreme Minimum Temp. (°F)	-16	-11	0	23	29	43	48	41	31	23	8	-16	-16
Days Maximum Temp. ≥ 90°F	0	0	0	0	2	9	17	12	4	0	0	0	44
Days Maximum Temp. ≤ 32°F	10	5	1	0	0	0	0	0	0	0	1	4	21
Days Minimum Temp. ≤ 32°F	26	19	13	3	0	0	0	0	0	3	11	21	96
Days Minimum Temp. ≤ 0°F	2	0	0	0	0	0	0	0	0	0	0	1	3
Heating Degree Days (base 65°F)	1,067	802	583	277	83	6	0	1	48	235	560	903	4,565
Cooling Degree Days (base 65°F)	0	0	6	28	110	310	426	368	180	33	2	0	1,463
Mean Precipitation (in.)	2.37	2.49	4.16	4.14	4.47	3.74	3.88	3.25	2.93	3.35	4.13	3.27	42.18
Days With ≥ 0.1" Precipitation	4	5	7	7	7	6	6	5	5	5	6	6	69
Days With ≥ 1.0" Precipitation	0	0	1	1	1	1	1	1	1	1	1	1	10
Mean Snowfall (in.)	5.1	3.5	2.0	0.5	0.0	0.0	0.0	0.0	0.0	trace	1.0	2.7	14.8
Days With ≥ 1.0" Snow Depth	8	5	1	0	0	0	0	0	0	0	1	3	18

Stockton 3 NNE *Jo Daviess Co.* Elevation: 967 ft. Latitude: 42° 24' N Longitude: 90° 00' W

	JAN	FEB	MAR	APR	MAY	JUN	JUL	AUG	SEP	OCT	NOV	DEC	YEAR
Mean Maximum Temp. (°F)	25.7	31.5	43.0	57.7	70.0	78.8	82.0	79.8	72.3	60.7	44.2	31.1	56.4
Mean Temp. (°F)	17.4	23.2	34.2	47.1	59.0	68.2	71.8	69.7	61.6	50.1	36.0	23.4	46.8
Mean Minimum Temp. (°F)	8.8	14.8	25.4	36.5	47.9	57.4	61.6	59.5	50.8	39.5	27.9	15.7	37.2
Extreme Maximum Temp. (°F)	57	62	84	91	93	99	99	99	95	87	75	66	99
Extreme Minimum Temp. (°F)	-28	-30	-8	7	24	37	40	39	27	13	-8	-24	-30
Days Maximum Temp. ≥ 90°F	0	0	0	0	0	2	4	2	0	0	0	0	8
Days Maximum Temp. ≤ 32°F	21	14	5	0	0	0	0	0	0	0	4	16	60
Days Minimum Temp. ≤ 32°F	31	26	24	10	1	0	0	0	1	8	21	29	151
Days Minimum Temp. ≤ 0°F	9	5	1	0	0	0	0	0	0	0	0	5	20
Heating Degree Days (base 65°F)	1,471	1,175	947	537	226	41	10	22	156	460	863	1,282	7,190
Cooling Degree Days (base 65°F)	0	0	1	6	41	143	223	173	56	5	0	0	648
Mean Precipitation (in.)	1.16	1.31	2.38	3.52	3.82	4.58	3.16	4.30	3.85	2.77	2.70	1.60	35.15
Days With ≥ 0.1" Precipitation	3	4	5	7	8	7	6	7	6	6	5	4	68
Days With ≥ 1.0" Precipitation	0	0	0	1	1	2	1	1	1	1	1	0	9
Mean Snowfall (in.)	8.8	6.5	4.8	2.0	trace	0.0	0.0	0.0	0.0	0.3	2.6	7.4	32.4
Days With ≥ 1.0" Snow Depth	na	13	5	1	0	0	0	0	0	0	2	11	na

Tuscola *Douglas Co.* Elevation: 652 ft. Latitude: 39° 48' N Longitude: 88° 17' W

	JAN	FEB	MAR	APR	MAY	JUN	JUL	AUG	SEP	OCT	NOV	DEC	YEAR
Mean Maximum Temp. (°F)	34.2	40.2	52.3	65.5	76.5	85.4	88.2	86.1	80.5	68.2	52.1	40.3	64.1
Mean Temp. (°F)	25.7	31.1	42.2	53.7	64.5	73.5	76.5	74.3	67.9	56.1	42.8	32.3	53.4
Mean Minimum Temp. (°F)	17.3	22.0	31.9	41.7	52.5	61.6	64.9	62.5	55.2	43.9	33.4	24.2	42.6
Extreme Maximum Temp. (°F)	67	73	86	90	95	104	104	104	99	91	79	70	104
Extreme Minimum Temp. (°F)	-24	-18	-5	15	30	40	46	43	31	20	1	-26	-26
Days Maximum Temp. ≥ 90°F	0	0	0	0	2	9	13	9	4	0	0	0	37
Days Maximum Temp. ≤ 32°F	13	8	1	0	0	0	0	0	0	0	1	6	29
Days Minimum Temp. ≤ 32°F	28	23	17	5	0	0	0	0	0	4	15	24	116
Days Minimum Temp. ≤ 0°F	4	2	0	0	0	0	0	0	0	0	0	1	7
Heating Degree Days (base 65°F)	1,211	950	703	349	106	10	1	2	59	292	661	1,009	5,353
Cooling Degree Days (base 65°F)	0	0	2	14	99	280	379	310	153	22	0	0	1,259
Mean Precipitation (in.)	2.12	2.08	3.18	4.03	3.96	4.05	4.72	3.74	3.23	2.92	3.76	3.00	40.79
Days With ≥ 0.1" Precipitation	5	5	7	8	8	7	6	5	5	6	7	6	75
Days With ≥ 1.0" Precipitation	0	1	0	1	1	1	1	1	1	1	1	1	10
Mean Snowfall (in.)	8.0	4.8	2.5	0.3	trace	0.0	0.0	0.0	0.0	trace	1.7	4.8	22.1
Days With ≥ 1.0" Snow Depth	10	7	2	0	0	0	0	0	0	0	0	5	24

Urbana *Champaign Co.* Elevation: 741 ft. Latitude: 40° 06' N Longitude: 88° 14' W

	JAN	FEB	MAR	APR	MAY	JUN	JUL	AUG	SEP	OCT	NOV	DEC	YEAR
Mean Maximum Temp. (°F)	31.7	37.4	49.2	62.3	73.7	82.7	85.3	83.2	77.7	65.0	49.7	37.4	61.3
Mean Temp. (°F)	24.1	29.4	40.2	51.8	62.8	71.8	75.1	73.0	66.2	54.2	41.4	30.1	51.7
Mean Minimum Temp. (°F)	16.5	21.5	31.1	41.0	51.9	61.0	64.8	62.8	54.7	43.3	33.1	22.8	42.0
Extreme Maximum Temp. (°F)	66	71	84	91	94	103	101	102	97	90	78	71	103
Extreme Minimum Temp. (°F)	-25	-17	-1	16	29	41	47	40	30	19	4	-20	-25
Days Maximum Temp. ≥ 90°F	0	0	0	0	1	6	7	5	2	0	0	0	21
Days Maximum Temp. ≤ 32°F	16	10	2	0	0	0	0	0	0	0	2	9	39
Days Minimum Temp. ≤ 32°F	29	24	18	5	0	0	0	0	0	4	15	26	121
Days Minimum Temp. ≤ 0°F	4	2	0	0	0	0	0	0	0	0	0	2	8
Heating Degree Days (base 65°F)	1,261	998	763	405	138	17	2	4	78	343	701	1,074	5,784
Cooling Degree Days (base 65°F)	0	0	1	9	72	232	329	269	120	13	0	0	1,045
Mean Precipitation (in.)	1.86	1.96	3.23	3.81	4.65	4.16	4.74	4.35	3.31	2.82	3.37	2.73	40.99
Days With ≥ 0.1" Precipitation	5	5	7	8	8	6	7	7	5	6	6	6	76
Days With ≥ 1.0" Precipitation	0	0	1	1	1	1	1	1	1	1	1	0	9
Mean Snowfall (in.)	8.5	5.7	3.3	0.6	trace	0.0	0.0	0.0	0.0	0.1	2.1	5.6	25.9
Days With ≥ 1.0" Snow Depth	14	9	3	0	0	0	0	0	0	0	1	6	33

Virden *Macoupin Co.* Elevation: 672 ft. Latitude: 39° 30' N Longitude: 89° 46' W

	JAN	FEB	MAR	APR	MAY	JUN	JUL	AUG	SEP	OCT	NOV	DEC	YEAR
Mean Maximum Temp. (°F)	34.5	40.2	52.5	65.6	75.8	84.2	88.0	86.2	80.2	68.1	52.4	40.0	64.0
Mean Temp. (°F)	26.3	31.7	42.7	54.6	64.7	73.3	76.9	74.8	68.1	56.6	43.4	32.1	53.8
Mean Minimum Temp. (°F)	18.0	23.0	32.9	43.6	53.5	62.4	65.7	63.3	55.9	45.1	34.4	24.1	43.5
Extreme Maximum Temp. (°F)	70	75	85	90	93	100	102	105	99	90	80	74	105
Extreme Minimum Temp. (°F)	-22	-19	-7	19	30	40	44	39	30	18	-1	-20	-22
Days Maximum Temp. ≥ 90°F	0	0	0	0	1	7	13	9	4	0	0	0	34
Days Maximum Temp. ≤ 32°F	13	8	2	0	0	0	0	0	0	0	1	7	31
Days Minimum Temp. ≤ 32°F	27	21	16	4	0	0	0	0	0	3	14	24	109
Days Minimum Temp. ≤ 0°F	4	2	0	0	0	0	0	0	0	0	0	1	7
Heating Degree Days (base 65°F)	1,195	936	687	327	101	10	1	2	61	278	641	1,015	5,254
Cooling Degree Days (base 65°F)	0	0	3	21	100	276	392	330	162	25	1	0	1,310
Mean Precipitation (in.)	1.84	2.03	3.27	3.80	4.41	3.90	3.53	3.06	3.02	2.54	3.26	2.47	37.13
Days With ≥ 0.1" Precipitation	4	4	7	7	7	6	5	5	5	5	6	4	65
Days With ≥ 1.0" Precipitation	0	0	1	1	1	1	1	1	1	1	1	1	10
Mean Snowfall (in.)	6.5	6.5	3.9	0.7	0.0	0.0	0.0	0.0	0.0	trace	1.5	4.7	23.8
Days With ≥ 1.0" Snow Depth	12	8	3	0	0	0	0	0	0	0	1	6	30

Walnut *Bureau Co.* Elevation: 688 ft. Latitude: 41° 33' N Longitude: 89° 36' W

	JAN	FEB	MAR	APR	MAY	JUN	JUL	AUG	SEP	OCT	NOV	DEC	YEAR
Mean Maximum Temp. (°F)	28.3	34.0	46.4	60.5	72.8	81.8	85.1	82.9	75.9	64.0	47.0	34.0	59.4
Mean Temp. (°F)	19.5	25.4	37.0	49.4	61.4	70.5	74.1	71.8	64.2	52.4	38.3	25.9	49.2
Mean Minimum Temp. (°F)	10.6	16.7	27.5	38.2	50.0	59.1	63.1	60.7	52.4	40.7	29.6	17.8	38.9
Extreme Maximum Temp. (°F)	63	69	87	93	95	101	103	104	97	90	77	68	104
Extreme Minimum Temp. (°F)	-27	-23	-6	6	25	38	46	39	29	15	-8	-22	-27
Days Maximum Temp. ≥ 90°F	0	0	0	0	1	4	8	4	1	0	0	0	18
Days Maximum Temp. ≤ 32°F	18	12	4	0	0	0	0	0	0	0	3	12	49
Days Minimum Temp. ≤ 32°F	30	26	23	8	1	0	0	0	1	7	19	29	144
Days Minimum Temp. ≤ 0°F	8	5	0	0	0	0	0	0	0	0	0	4	17
Heating Degree Days (base 65°F)	1,406	1,112	863	472	173	23	4	11	111	395	793	1,204	6,567
Cooling Degree Days (base 65°F)	0	0	1	9	63	192	293	229	84	9	0	0	880
Mean Precipitation (in.)	1.31	1.34	2.67	3.50	4.43	4.62	3.60	4.44	3.64	2.93	2.61	2.04	37.13
Days With ≥ 0.1" Precipitation	4	4	6	7	8	7	6	7	6	6	6	5	72
Days With ≥ 1.0" Precipitation	0	0	0	1	1	1	1	1	1	1	0	0	7
Mean Snowfall (in.)	10.8	6.7	4.3	1.3	trace	0.0	0.0	0.0	0.0	0.1	1.9	7.8	32.9
Days With ≥ 1.0" Snow Depth	19	13	4	0	0	0	0	0	0	0	1	10	47

Waterloo *Monroe Co.* Elevation: 649 ft. Latitude: 38° 20' N Longitude: 90° 09' W

	JAN	FEB	MAR	APR	MAY	JUN	JUL	AUG	SEP	OCT	NOV	DEC	YEAR
Mean Maximum Temp. (°F)	37.9	44.2	54.9	66.5	76.0	84.7	88.9	87.0	80.5	68.8	54.7	42.9	65.6
Mean Temp. (°F)	29.4	34.9	45.0	55.7	65.4	74.1	78.3	76.3	69.4	57.7	45.7	34.5	55.5
Mean Minimum Temp. (°F)	20.9	25.6	35.0	44.9	54.7	63.5	67.6	65.6	58.2	46.7	36.6	26.2	45.4
Extreme Maximum Temp. (°F)	75	81	88	93	95	103	105	105	102	92	89	75	105
Extreme Minimum Temp. (°F)	-16	-12	0	21	30	42	47	46	34	22	6	-18	-18
Days Maximum Temp. ≥ 90°F	0	0	0	0	1	8	15	12	5	0	0	0	41
Days Maximum Temp. ≤ 32°F	11	6	1	0	0	0	0	0	0	0	1	6	25
Days Minimum Temp. ≤ 32°F	26	20	13	3	0	0	0	0	0	2	11	23	98
Days Minimum Temp. ≤ 0°F	2	1	0	0	0	0	0	0	0	0	0	1	4
Heating Degree Days (base 65°F)	1,096	843	620	301	90	8	1	2	51	251	576	939	4,778
Cooling Degree Days (base 65°F)	0	0	6	29	109	296	427	367	185	32	4	0	1,455
Mean Precipitation (in.)	2.27	2.35	3.75	4.22	4.04	3.79	3.96	3.12	3.30	3.08	4.03	3.41	41.32
Days With ≥ 0.1" Precipitation	4	4	7	7	7	6	6	5	5	5	7	6	69
Days With ≥ 1.0" Precipitation	1	0	1	1	1	1	1	1	1	1	1	1	11
Mean Snowfall (in.)	4.5	3.2	2.0	0.7	0.0	0.0	0.0	0.0	0.0	0.0	1.2	3.0	14.6
Days With ≥ 1.0" Snow Depth	8	5	2	0	0	0	0	0	0	0	1	3	19

Watseka 2 NW *Iroquois Co.* Elevation: 620 ft. Latitude: 40° 47' N Longitude: 87° 46' W

	JAN	FEB	MAR	APR	MAY	JUN	JUL	AUG	SEP	OCT	NOV	DEC	YEAR
Mean Maximum Temp. (°F)	30.2	36.1	47.6	60.3	72.4	82.0	84.8	82.7	77.1	64.4	49.2	36.3	60.3
Mean Temp. (°F)	22.1	27.2	38.2	49.2	60.7	70.3	73.7	71.3	64.6	52.4	40.3	28.6	49.9
Mean Minimum Temp. (°F)	14.0	18.2	28.8	38.2	49.0	58.6	62.5	59.8	51.9	40.3	31.4	20.8	39.5
Extreme Maximum Temp. (°F)	65	71	78	88	93	104	102	105	97	89	79	70	105
Extreme Minimum Temp. (°F)	-28	-27	-13	3	26	36	43	43	27	18	0	-26	-28
Days Maximum Temp. ≥ 90°F	0	0	0	0	1	5	7	4	1	0	0	0	18
Days Maximum Temp. ≤ 32°F	17	10	3	0	0	0	0	0	0	0	2	10	42
Days Minimum Temp. ≤ 32°F	29	25	21	8	1	0	0	0	0	7	18	27	136
Days Minimum Temp. ≤ 0°F	6	4	0	0	0	0	0	0	0	0	0	2	12
Heating Degree Days (base 65°F)	1,323	1,063	824	473	187	28	5	12	104	397	734	1,123	6,273
Cooling Degree Days (base 65°F)	0	0	1	5	60	203	290	221	95	12	0	0	887
Mean Precipitation (in.)	1.67	1.64	3.48	4.05	4.20	4.67	4.18	3.75	3.58	2.81	3.32	2.57	39.92
Days With ≥ 0.1" Precipitation	4	4	7	8	7	7	7	6	6	5	6	5	72
Days With ≥ 1.0" Precipitation	0	0	1	1	1	1	1	1	1	1	1	1	10
Mean Snowfall (in.)	6.9	4.6	2.5	0.9	0.0	0.0	0.0	0.0	0.0	trace	1.3	5.2	21.4
Days With ≥ 1.0" Snow Depth	14	9	3	0	0	0	0	0	0	0	1	7	34

Waukegan *Lake Co.* Elevation: 698 ft. Latitude: 42° 21' N Longitude: 87° 53' W

	JAN	FEB	MAR	APR	MAY	JUN	JUL	AUG	SEP	OCT	NOV	DEC	YEAR
Mean Maximum Temp. (°F)	28.5	32.7	42.5	54.3	66.5	76.6	81.4	79.6	72.4	60.9	46.8	34.1	56.4
Mean Temp. (°F)	20.3	24.5	34.1	45.0	56.2	66.0	71.4	70.0	62.4	50.9	38.5	26.6	47.2
Mean Minimum Temp. (°F)	12.2	16.3	25.6	35.7	45.8	55.2	61.4	60.4	52.3	40.9	30.1	19.0	37.9
Extreme Maximum Temp. (°F)	64	69	81	90	93	101	102	102	96	89	76	66	102
Extreme Minimum Temp. (°F)	-27	-22	-5	8	28	34	45	40	29	18	-3	-23	-27
Days Maximum Temp. ≥ 90°F	0	0	0	0	0	2	4	3	1	0	0	0	10
Days Maximum Temp. ≤ 32°F	19	13	5	0	0	0	0	0	0	0	2	13	52
Days Minimum Temp. ≤ 32°F	29	26	24	10	1	0	0	0	0	5	18	28	141
Days Minimum Temp. ≤ 0°F	7	4	0	0	0	0	0	0	0	0	0	3	14
Heating Degree Days (base 65°F)	1,379	1,138	952	598	299	79	16	21	138	437	789	1,186	7,032
Cooling Degree Days (base 65°F)	0	0	1	5	33	116	228	192	65	6	0	0	646
Mean Precipitation (in.)	1.58	1.34	2.18	3.65	3.44	3.62	3.40	4.18	3.53	2.46	2.67	2.05	34.10
Days With ≥ 0.1" Precipitation	4	4	5	7	7	6	6	6	6	5	6	5	67
Days With ≥ 1.0" Precipitation	0	0	1	1	1	1	1	1	1	0	0	0	7
Mean Snowfall (in.)	12.0	9.2	5.7	1.7	trace	0.0	0.0	0.0	0.0	0.1	1.9	7.3	37.9
Days With ≥ 1.0" Snow Depth	na	na	5	1	0	0	0	0	0	0	1	na	na

Wheaton 3 SE *Dupage Co.* Elevation: 679 ft. Latitude: 41° 49' N Longitude: 88° 04' W

	JAN	FEB	MAR	APR	MAY	JUN	JUL	AUG	SEP	OCT	NOV	DEC	YEAR
Mean Maximum Temp. (°F)	31.0	37.0	48.9	62.1	74.2	83.4	86.7	84.7	77.8	65.8	49.4	36.9	61.5
Mean Temp. (°F)	22.3	27.6	38.5	49.8	60.8	70.3	74.7	73.0	65.4	53.7	40.4	28.8	50.4
Mean Minimum Temp. (°F)	13.5	18.2	27.9	37.4	47.3	57.2	62.6	61.2	53.0	41.5	31.4	20.6	39.3
Extreme Maximum Temp. (°F)	65	70	85	90	94	103	105	100	97	90	78	68	105
Extreme Minimum Temp. (°F)	-26	-21	-3	4	26	32	42	42	27	14	-3	-21	-26
Days Maximum Temp. ≥ 90°F	0	0	0	0	1	7	10	7	2	0	0	0	27
Days Maximum Temp. ≤ 32°F	16	10	2	0	0	0	0	0	0	0	1	9	38
Days Minimum Temp. ≤ 32°F	29	25	21	9	2	0	0	0	0	6	17	26	135
Days Minimum Temp. ≤ 0°F	6	4	0	0	0	0	0	0	0	0	0	2	12
Heating Degree Days (base 65°F)	1,318	1,050	817	461	184	28	3	6	92	359	731	1,116	6,165
Cooling Degree Days (base 65°F)	0	0	2	11	61	203	326	278	113	13	0	0	1,007
Mean Precipitation (in.)	1.83	1.58	2.65	3.81	3.99	3.86	3.93	4.68	3.46	2.65	3.15	2.42	38.01
Days With ≥ 0.1" Precipitation	5	4	6	7	7	7	6	7	6	5	6	5	71
Days With ≥ 1.0" Precipitation	0	0	0	1	1	1	1	1	1	1	1	1	9
Mean Snowfall (in.)	11.1	7.8	4.8	0.8	trace	0.0	0.0	0.0	0.0	trace	1.9	6.1	32.5
Days With ≥ 1.0" Snow Depth	18	12	4	0	0	0	0	0	0	0	1	8	43

White Hall 1 E *Greene Co.* Elevation: 577 ft. Latitude: 39° 26' N Longitude: 90° 23' W

	JAN	FEB	MAR	APR	MAY	JUN	JUL	AUG	SEP	OCT	NOV	DEC	YEAR
Mean Maximum Temp. (°F)	34.7	41.0	52.4	64.7	74.7	83.4	87.4	85.2	78.8	67.7	52.6	40.3	63.6
Mean Temp. (°F)	25.7	31.2	41.9	53.5	63.5	72.5	76.5	74.3	67.0	55.8	42.9	31.6	53.0
Mean Minimum Temp. (°F)	16.7	21.3	31.4	42.1	52.3	61.5	65.5	63.3	55.1	43.8	33.2	22.8	42.4
Extreme Maximum Temp. (°F)	71	79	85	92	92	100	104	101	99	90	80	73	104
Extreme Minimum Temp. (°F)	-20	-19	-13	21	27	39	44	42	33	19	0	-20	-20
Days Maximum Temp. ≥ 90°F	0	0	0	0	1	6	12	8	3	0	0	0	30
Days Maximum Temp. ≤ 32°F	13	7	2	0	0	0	0	0	0	0	1	7	30
Days Minimum Temp. ≤ 32°F	28	23	18	5	0	0	0	0	0	4	15	26	119
Days Minimum Temp. ≤ 0°F	4	3	0	0	0	0	0	0	0	0	0	2	9
Heating Degree Days (base 65°F)	1,212	949	711	358	118	13	1	4	72	301	657	1,029	5,425
Cooling Degree Days (base 65°F)	0	0	3	15	72	243	362	299	131	18	1	0	1,144
Mean Precipitation (in.)	1.61	1.72	3.26	3.78	4.53	3.56	3.28	2.99	3.10	2.61	3.21	2.54	36.19
Days With ≥ 0.1" Precipitation	4	4	7	7	7	6	5	6	5	5	6	5	67
Days With ≥ 1.0" Precipitation	0	0	1	1	1	1	1	1	1	0	1	1	9
Mean Snowfall (in.)	na	na	2.0	0.5	0.0	0.0	0.0	0.0	0.0	trace	0.7	2.9	na
Days With ≥ 1.0" Snow Depth	na	na	1	0	0	0	0	0	0	0	0	3	na

Windsor *Shelby Co.* Elevation: 688 ft. Latitude: 39° 26' N Longitude: 88° 36' W

	JAN	FEB	MAR	APR	MAY	JUN	JUL	AUG	SEP	OCT	NOV	DEC	YEAR
Mean Maximum Temp. (°F)	34.5	40.7	52.3	65.1	75.4	83.8	87.3	85.5	80.0	67.8	52.3	40.1	63.7
Mean Temp. (°F)	26.6	32.0	42.6	54.1	64.4	72.9	76.5	74.5	68.2	56.5	43.6	32.5	53.7
Mean Minimum Temp. (°F)	18.6	23.3	32.9	42.9	53.2	61.9	65.6	63.4	56.4	45.2	34.8	24.8	43.6
Extreme Maximum Temp. (°F)	67	75	84	87	92	102	102	102	99	89	79	71	102
Extreme Minimum Temp. (°F)	-22	-18	-3	19	30	38	48	38	32	20	3	-20	-22
Days Maximum Temp. ≥ 90°F	0	0	0	0	1	6	11	7	3	0	0	0	28
Days Maximum Temp. ≤ 32°F	13	8	2	0	0	0	0	0	0	0	1	7	31
Days Minimum Temp. ≤ 32°F	27	21	16	4	0	0	0	0	0	3	13	24	108
Days Minimum Temp. ≤ 0°F	3	2	0	0	0	0	0	0	0	0	0	1	6
Heating Degree Days (base 65°F)	1,185	926	690	338	106	10	1	2	55	279	636	1,002	5,230
Cooling Degree Days (base 65°F)	0	0	3	16	93	263	375	312	153	24	0	0	1,239
Mean Precipitation (in.)	1.97	1.87	3.31	3.93	3.96	3.94	3.96	3.10	3.02	2.99	3.73	2.95	38.73
Days With ≥ 0.1" Precipitation	5	4	7	8	7	7	6	5	5	5	6	6	71
Days With ≥ 1.0" Precipitation	0	0	1	1	1	1	1	1	1	1	1	1	10
Mean Snowfall (in.)	7.9	4.3	3.0	0.3	0.0	0.0	0.0	0.0	0.0	trace	1.3	5.0	21.8
Days With ≥ 1.0" Snow Depth	12	8	2	0	0	0	0	0	0	0	1	5	28

Note: *See User's Guide for explanation of data.*

Annual Extreme Maximum Temperature

Highest Rank	Station Name	°F	Lowest Rank	Station Name	°F
1	Piper City	108	1	Stockton 3 NNE	99
1	Sparta 1 W	108	2	Freeport Waste Water Plant	101
3	Kankakee Metro Wastewater	107	2	Paw Paw 2 NW	101
3	Palestine 2 W	107	4	Charleston	102
5	Alton Melvin Price Lock & Dam	106	4	Danville	102
5	Chicago Midway Airport	106	4	Dixon Springs Agr. Center	102
5	Decatur	106	4	Fulton Lock & Dam 13	102
5	Du Quoin 4 SE	106	4	Galesburg	102
5	Havana 4 NNE	106	4	Mount Carroll	102
5	Nashville 4 NE	106	4	Rosiclare 5 NW	102
11	Albion	105	4	Springfield Capital Airport	102
11	Belleville Scott AFB	105	4	Waukegan	102
11	Brookport Dam 52	105	4	Windsor	102
11	Carlinville	105	14	Aledo	103
11	Flora 5 NW	105	14	Aurora	103
11	Greater Peoria Airport	105	14	Carbondale Sewage Plant	103
11	Harrisburg	105	14	Chenoa	103
11	Hillsboro	105	14	De Kalb	103
11	La Harpe	105	14	Dixon 1 NW	103
11	Marengo	105	14	Effingham	103
11	Morrison	105	14	Galva	103
11	Princeville	105	14	Geneseo	103
11	Quincy Muni Baldwin Field	105	14	Golden	103
11	Rantoul Chanute AFB	105	14	Jacksonville 2 E	103
11	Salem Leckrone Airport	105	14	Lacon 1 N	103

Annual Mean Maximum Temperature

Highest Rank	Station Name	°F	Lowest Rank	Station Name	°F
1	Dixon Springs Agr. Center	68.1	1	Stockton 3 NNE	56.4
2	Brookport Dam 52	68.0	1	Waukegan	56.4
3	Harrisburg	67.7	3	Paw Paw 2 NW	57.0
4	Cairo WSO City	67.5	4	Freeport Waste Water Plant	57.4
5	Rosiclare 5 NW	67.3	5	Rockford Greater Rockford Arpt.	57.9
6	Anna 2 NNE	67.2	6	Fulton Lock & Dam 13	58.1
7	Belleville Scott AFB	66.9	7	De Kalb	58.5
8	Albion	66.8	7	Dixon 1 NW	58.5
8	Sparta 1 W	66.8	9	Marengo	58.6
10	Du Quoin 4 SE	66.6	9	Park Forest	58.6
11	Carbondale Sewage Plant	66.4	11	Chicago O'Hare Int'l Airport	58.7
12	Flora 5 NW	66.0	11	Mount Carroll	58.7
13	Salem Leckrone Airport	65.8	13	Galva	59.1
14	McLeansboro 2 ENE	65.7	14	Aurora	59.4
15	Hillsboro	65.6	14	Walnut	59.4
15	Waterloo	65.6	16	Chicago Midway Airport	59.5
17	Fairfield Radio WFIW	65.4	17	Galesburg	59.6
17	Nashville 4 NE	65.4	17	Geneseo	59.6
17	Olney 2 S	65.4	17	Morrison	59.6
20	Mount Vernon-Outland Airport	65.0	20	Chicago University	59.8
21	Marion 4 NNE	64.9	21	Moline Quad City Airport	60.0
21	Palestine 2 W	64.9	22	Watseka 2 NW	60.3
23	Carlinville	64.3	23	Princeville	60.4
24	Tuscola	64.1	24	Aledo	60.5
25	Virden	64.0	24	Peru	60.5

Annual Mean Temperature

Highest

Rank	Station Name	°F
1	Cairo WSO City	58.5
2	Brookport Dam 52	57.6
3	Dixon Springs Agr. Center	57.4
4	Harrisburg	56.9
5	Anna 2 NNE	56.8
6	Albion	56.6
7	Sparta 1 W	56.2
8	Belleville Scott AFB	55.9
8	Du Quoin 4 SE	55.9
8	Rosiclare 5 NW	55.9
11	Nashville 4 NE	55.6
12	Waterloo	55.5
13	Salem Leckrone Airport	55.3
14	Carbondale Sewage Plant	55.1
15	Flora 5 NW	55.0
15	Olney 2 S	55.0
17	Fairfield Radio WFIW	54.8
17	McLeansboro 2 ENE	54.8
17	Palestine 2 W	54.8
20	Hillsboro	54.7
21	Alton Melvin Price Lock & Dam	54.4
21	Mount Vernon-Outland Airport	54.4
23	Marion 4 NNE	54.3
24	Carlinville	54.0
25	Virden	53.8

Lowest

Rank	Station Name	°F
1	Mount Carroll	46.8
1	Stockton 3 NNE	46.8
3	Freeport Waste Water Plant	47.1
4	Paw Paw 2 NW	47.2
4	Waukegan	47.2
6	Marengo	47.7
7	Rockford Greater Rockford Arpt.	48.0
8	Dixon 1 NW	48.3
9	De Kalb	48.7
10	Morrison	48.8
11	Aurora	48.9
11	Fulton Lock & Dam 13	48.9
13	Princeville	49.2
13	Walnut	49.2
15	Galva	49.3
15	Park Forest	49.3
17	Chicago O'Hare Int'l Airport	49.5
18	Hennepin Power Plant	49.6
19	Peru	49.9
19	Watseka 2 NW	49.9
21	Geneseo	50.0
21	Kankakee Metro Wastewater	50.0
21	Moline Quad City Airport	50.0
24	Minonk	50.1
25	Aledo	50.3

Annual Mean Minimum Temperature

Highest

Rank	Station Name	°F
1	Cairo WSO City	49.5
2	Brookport Dam 52	47.1
3	Dixon Springs Agr. Center	46.6
4	Albion	46.3
4	Anna 2 NNE	46.3
6	Harrisburg	45.9
7	Nashville 4 NE	45.7
8	Sparta 1 W	45.6
9	Waterloo	45.4
10	Du Quoin 4 SE	45.1
11	Alton Melvin Price Lock & Dam	44.9
12	Belleville Scott AFB	44.8
13	Salem Leckrone Airport	44.7
14	Olney 2 S	44.6
14	Palestine 2 W	44.6
14	Rosiclare 5 NW	44.6
17	Fairfield Radio WFIW	44.2
18	Flora 5 NW	44.0
19	Charleston	43.9
20	Carbondale Sewage Plant	43.8
20	Hillsboro	43.8
20	McLeansboro 2 ENE	43.8
20	Mount Vernon-Outland Airport	43.8
24	Carlinville	43.7
24	Marion 4 NNE	43.7

Lowest

Rank	Station Name	°F
1	Mount Carroll	34.9
2	Marengo	36.7
3	Freeport Waste Water Plant	36.8
4	Stockton 3 NNE	37.2
5	Paw Paw 2 NW	37.4
6	Morrison	37.9
6	Princeville	37.9
6	Waukegan	37.9
9	Dixon 1 NW	38.0
10	Rockford Greater Rockford Arpt.	38.1
11	Hennepin Power Plant	38.2
12	Aurora	38.5
13	De Kalb	38.8
14	Walnut	38.9
15	Kankakee Metro Wastewater	39.3
15	Minonk	39.3
15	Peru	39.3
15	Wheaton 3 SE	39.3
19	Galva	39.4
20	Fulton Lock & Dam 13	39.5
20	Watseka 2 NW	39.5
22	La Harpe	39.6
23	Piper City	39.8
24	Moline Quad City Airport	39.9
25	Park Forest	40.0

Annual Extreme Minimum Temperature

Highest

Rank	Station Name	°F
1	Cairo WSO City	-12
2	Alton Melvin Price Lock & Dam	-16
2	Sparta 1 W	-16
4	Anna 2 NNE	-17
5	Waterloo	-18
6	Carlinville	-19
7	Albion	-20
7	Dixon Springs Agr. Center	-20
7	Du Quoin 4 SE	-20
7	White Hall 1 E	-20
11	Brookport Dam 52	-21
11	Hillsboro	-21
11	Jacksonville 2 E	-21
11	McLeansboro 2 ENE	-21
11	Mount Vernon-Outland Airport	-21
11	Nashville 4 NE	-21
11	Pana 3 E	-21
11	Rushville	-21
11	Springfield Capital Airport	-21
20	Harrisburg	-22
20	Marion 4 NNE	-22
20	Paris Waterworks	-22
20	Quincy Muni Baldwin Field	-22
20	Rosiclare 5 NW	-22
20	Virden	-22

Lowest

Rank	Station Name	°F
1	Paw Paw 2 NW	-33
2	Havana 4 NNE	-30
2	Hennepin Power Plant	-30
2	Mount Carroll	-30
2	Stockton 3 NNE	-30
6	Kankakee Metro Wastewater	-29
6	Marengo	-29
8	Aledo	-28
8	Moline Quad City Airport	-28
8	Morrison	-28
8	Newton 6 SSE	-28
8	Watseka 2 NW	-28
13	Belleville Scott AFB	-27
13	Charleston	-27
13	Chicago O'Hare Int'l Airport	-27
13	De Kalb	-27
13	Dixon 1 NW	-27
13	Freeport Waste Water Plant	-27
13	Lacon 1 N	-27
13	Park Forest	-27
13	Rantoul Chanute AFB	-27
13	Rockford Greater Rockford Arpt.	-27
13	Walnut	-27
13	Waukegan	-27
25	Aurora	-26

July Mean Maximum Temperature

Highest

Rank	Station Name	°F
1	Harrisburg	90.2
2	Albion	90.0
3	Cairo WSO City	89.7
3	Du Quoin 4 SE	89.7
5	Belleville Scott AFB	89.6
5	Sparta 1 W	89.6
7	Brookport Dam 52	89.5
7	Hillsboro	89.5
9	Flora 5 NW	89.2
10	Salem Leckrone Airport	89.1
11	Dixon Springs Agr. Center	89.0
12	Anna 2 NNE	88.9
12	McLeansboro 2 ENE	88.9
12	Waterloo	88.9
15	Carbondale Sewage Plant	88.6
16	Nashville 4 NE	88.4
16	Olney 2 S	88.4
18	Havana 4 NNE	88.3
18	Mount Vernon-Outland Airport	88.3
20	Fairfield Radio WFIW	88.2
20	Tuscola	88.2
22	Alton Melvin Price Lock & Dam	88.1
22	Palestine 2 W	88.1
24	Carlinville	88.0
24	Rosiclare 5 NW	88.0

Lowest

Rank	Station Name	°F
1	Waukegan	81.4
2	Stockton 3 NNE	82.0
3	Paw Paw 2 NW	82.9
4	Freeport Waste Water Plant	83.8
4	Park Forest	83.8
6	Dixon 1 NW	83.9
6	Fulton Lock & Dam 13	83.9
6	Rockford Greater Rockford Arpt.	83.9
9	Chicago O'Hare Int'l Airport	84.3
10	Chicago University	84.5
10	De Kalb	84.5
12	Mount Carroll	84.7
13	Aurora	84.8
13	Watseka 2 NW	84.8
15	Chicago Midway Airport	84.9
15	Galesburg	84.9
17	Galva	85.0
17	Marengo	85.0
17	Princeville	85.0
20	Pontiac	85.1
20	Walnut	85.1
22	Morrison	85.3
22	Urbana	85.3
24	Hoopeston 1 NE	85.4
24	Ottawa 5 SW	85.4

January Mean Minimum Temperature

Highest

Rank	Station Name	°F
1	Cairo WSO City	25.9
2	Brookport Dam 52	24.5
3	Dixon Springs Agr. Center	24.2
4	Anna 2 NNE	23.3
5	Albion	23.0
6	Harrisburg	22.6
7	Rosiclare 5 NW	22.3
8	Sparta 1 W	21.9
9	Belleville Scott AFB	21.7
10	Du Quoin 4 SE	21.5
11	Nashville 4 NE	21.4
12	Fairfield Radio WFIW	21.0
13	Waterloo	20.9
14	Carbondale Sewage Plant	20.8
15	Flora 5 NW	20.6
15	Olney 2 S	20.6
17	Salem Leckrone Airport	20.5
18	Palestine 2 W	20.4
19	McLeansboro 2 ENE	20.3
20	Marion 4 NNE	20.0
21	Mount Vernon-Outland Airport	19.6
22	Hillsboro	18.8
23	Alton Melvin Price Lock & Dam	18.7
23	Charleston	18.7
25	Windsor	18.6

Lowest

Rank	Station Name	°F
1	Mount Carroll	7.5
2	Stockton 3 NNE	8.8
3	Freeport Waste Water Plant	9.0
4	Dixon 1 NW	9.7
4	Marengo	9.7
6	Morrison	10.1
7	Paw Paw 2 NW	10.2
8	Rockford Greater Rockford Arpt.	10.5
9	Hennepin Power Plant	10.6
9	Walnut	10.6
11	Fulton Lock & Dam 13	10.8
12	De Kalb	10.9
13	Princeville	11.1
14	Aurora	11.4
15	Galva	11.8
16	Moline Quad City Airport	12.0
17	Peru	12.2
17	Waukegan	12.2
19	Geneseo	12.3
20	La Harpe	12.7
20	Minonk	12.7
22	Kankakee Metro Wastewater	12.9
23	Galesburg	13.1
24	Park Forest	13.2
25	Aledo	13.4

Number of Annual Heating Degree Days

Highest

Rank	Station Name	Num.
1	Stockton 3 NNE	7,190
2	Mount Carroll	7,165
3	Freeport Waste Water Plant	7,129
4	Paw Paw 2 NW	7,077
5	Waukegan	7,032
6	Marengo	6,991
7	Rockford Greater Rockford Arpt.	6,881
8	Dixon 1 NW	6,793
9	De Kalb	6,692
10	Morrison	6,648
11	Fulton Lock & Dam 13	6,646
12	Aurora	6,575
13	Walnut	6,567
14	Galva	6,540
15	Park Forest	6,483
16	Princeville	6,461
17	Chicago O'Hare Int'l Airport	6,427
18	Hennepin Power Plant	6,409
19	Geneseo	6,383
20	Moline Quad City Airport	6,369
21	Peru	6,328
22	Kankakee Metro Wastewater	6,294
23	Minonk	6,281
24	Watseka 2 NW	6,273
25	Galesburg	6,256

Lowest

Rank	Station Name	Num.
1	Cairo WSO City	3,997
2	Brookport Dam 52	4,129
3	Dixon Springs Agr. Center	4,144
4	Anna 2 NNE	4,328
5	Harrisburg	4,381
6	Rosiclare 5 NW	4,466
7	Albion	4,511
8	Sparta 1 W	4,565
9	Belleville Scott AFB	4,599
10	Du Quoin 4 SE	4,643
11	Nashville 4 NE	4,723
12	Waterloo	4,778
13	Carbondale Sewage Plant	4,797
14	Salem Leckrone Airport	4,818
15	Flora 5 NW	4,841
16	Olney 2 S	4,856
17	Fairfield Radio WFIW	4,868
18	Palestine 2 W	4,910
19	McLeansboro 2 ENE	4,916
20	Marion 4 NNE	4,996
21	Hillsboro	4,999
22	Mount Vernon-Outland Airport	5,027
23	Alton Melvin Price Lock & Dam	5,121
24	Carlinville	5,157
25	Windsor	5,230

Number of Annual Cooling Degree Days

Highest

Rank	Station Name	Num.
1	Cairo WSO City	1,716
2	Albion	1,579
3	Dixon Springs Agr. Center	1,542
4	Brookport Dam 52	1,527
5	Harrisburg	1,478
6	Sparta 1 W	1,463
7	Anna 2 NNE	1,460
8	Waterloo	1,455
9	Hillsboro	1,452
10	Du Quoin 4 SE	1,422
11	Belleville Scott AFB	1,417
12	Alton Melvin Price Lock & Dam	1,405
12	Nashville 4 NE	1,405
14	Salem Leckrone Airport	1,401
15	Flora 5 NW	1,350
16	Olney 2 S	1,336
17	Palestine 2 W	1,331
18	Virden	1,310
19	McLeansboro 2 ENE	1,308
20	Carbondale Sewage Plant	1,280
21	Carlinville	1,272
22	Fairfield Radio WFIW	1,264
23	Tuscola	1,259
24	Rosiclare 5 NW	1,258
25	Windsor	1,239

Lowest

Rank	Station Name	Num.
1	Mount Carroll	625
2	Waukegan	646
3	Stockton 3 NNE	648
4	Paw Paw 2 NW	690
5	Freeport Waste Water Plant	710
6	Princeville	733
7	Dixon 1 NW	753
8	Marengo	766
9	Rockford Greater Rockford Arpt.	800
10	Aurora	827
11	De Kalb	840
12	Morrison	842
13	Chicago O'Hare Int'l Airport	850
14	Fulton Lock & Dam 13	859
15	Walnut	880
16	Watseka 2 NW	887
17	Park Forest	888
18	Hennepin Power Plant	894
19	Kankakee Metro Wastewater	914
20	Peru	934
21	Galva	944
22	Minonk	952
23	Aledo	958
24	Pontiac	966
25	Ottawa 5 SW	976

Annual Precipitation

Highest

Rank	Station Name	Inches
1	Rosiclare 5 NW	48.82
2	Anna 2 NNE	48.28
3	Dixon Springs Agr. Center	48.22
4	Cairo WSO City	48.16
5	Brookport Dam 52	48.04
6	Marion 4 NNE	47.01
7	Harrisburg	45.70
8	Carbondale Sewage Plant	45.33
9	Albion	44.86
10	Fairfield Radio WFIW	44.69
11	Olney 2 S	44.45
12	McLeansboro 2 ENE	43.95
13	Du Quoin 4 SE	43.86
14	Sparta 1 W	42.18
15	Flora 5 NW	42.16
16	Palestine 2 W	42.12
17	Salem Leckrone Airport	42.09
18	Mount Vernon-Outland Airport	41.89
19	Effingham	41.36
20	Waterloo	41.32
21	Paris Waterworks	41.31
22	Danville	41.11
23	Charleston	41.01
24	Urbana	40.99
25	Tuscola	40.79

Lowest

Rank	Station Name	Inches
1	Waukegan	34.10
2	Freeport Waste Water Plant	34.52
3	Fulton Lock & Dam 13	34.70
4	Chenoa	34.99
5	Stockton 3 NNE	35.15
6	Hennepin Power Plant	35.26
7	Springfield Capital Airport	35.85
8	Mason City 1 W	35.89
9	Marengo	36.00
10	Aledo	36.12
11	White Hall 1 E	36.19
12	Ottawa 5 SW	36.20
13	Pontiac	36.44
14	Rockford Greater Rockford Arpt.	36.45
15	Chicago O'Hare Int'l Airport	36.59
16	Greater Peoria Airport	36.65
17	Piper City	36.80
18	Hoopeston 1 NE	37.02
19	Paw Paw 2 NW	37.11
20	Virden	37.13
20	Walnut	37.13
22	Dixon 1 NW	37.21
23	Geneseo	37.61
24	De Kalb	37.69
24	Mount Carroll	37.69

Number of Days Annually With ≥ 0.1" Precipitation

Highest

Rank	Station Name	Days
1	Marion 4 NNE	80
2	Brookport Dam 52	78
2	Carbondale Sewage Plant	78
2	Dixon Springs Agr. Center	78
2	Fairfield Radio WFIW	78
2	McLeansboro 2 ENE	78
2	Paris Waterworks	78
8	Anna 2 NNE	77
8	Danville	77
8	Rosiclare 5 NW	77
11	Harrisburg	76
11	Urbana	76
13	Chicago University	75
13	Flora 5 NW	75
13	Olney 2 S	75
13	Pana 3 E	75
13	Tuscola	75
18	Charleston	74
18	Effingham	74
18	Minonk	74
18	Mount Vernon-Outland Airport	74
18	Palestine 2 W	74
18	Salem Leckrone Airport	74
24	Cairo WSO City	73
24	Chicago Midway Airport	73

Lowest

Rank	Station Name	Days
1	Fulton Lock & Dam 13	63
1	Rushville	63
3	Freeport Waste Water Plant	65
3	Virden	65
5	Aledo	67
5	Belleville Scott AFB	67
5	Moweaqua	67
5	Springfield Capital Airport	67
5	Waukegan	67
5	White Hall 1 E	67
11	Geneseo	68
11	Jerseyville 2 SW	68
11	Ottawa 5 SW	68
11	Rockford Greater Rockford Arpt.	68
11	Stockton 3 NNE	68
16	Decatur	69
16	Jacksonville 2 E	69
16	Lincoln	69
16	Mason City 1 W	69
16	Moline Quad City Airport	69
16	Pontiac	69
16	Quincy Muni Baldwin Field	69
16	Sparta 1 W	69
16	Waterloo	69
25	Albion	70

Number of Days Annually With ≥ 1.0" Precipitation

Highest

Rank	Station Name	Days
1	Cairo WSO City	14
2	Albion	13
2	Anna 2 NNE	13
2	Brookport Dam 52	13
2	Dixon Springs Agr. Center	13
2	Du Quoin 4 SE	13
7	Carbondale Sewage Plant	12
7	Fairfield Radio WFIW	12
7	Harrisburg	12
7	Marion 4 NNE	12
7	Mount Vernon-Outland Airport	12
7	Olney 2 S	12
7	Rosiclare 5 NW	12
14	Effingham	11
14	Flora 5 NW	11
14	Galva	11
14	Jacksonville 2 E	11
14	McLeansboro 2 ENE	11
14	Pana 3 E	11
14	Quincy Muni Baldwin Field	11
14	Rantoul Chanute AFB	11
14	Rushville	11
14	Waterloo	11
24	Alton Melvin Price Lock & Dam	10
24	Belleville Scott AFB	10

Lowest

Rank	Station Name	Days
1	Pontiac	6
2	De Kalb	7
2	Walnut	7
2	Waukegan	7
5	Aledo	8
5	Chenoa	8
5	Chicago University	8
5	Dixon 1 NW	8
5	Freeport Waste Water Plant	8
5	Fulton Lock & Dam 13	8
5	Kankakee Metro Wastewater	8
5	Lincoln	8
5	Marengo	8
5	Monmouth	8
5	Morrison	8
5	Mount Carroll	8
5	Ottawa 5 SW	8
5	Park Forest	8
5	Paw Paw 2 NW	8
5	Rockford Greater Rockford Arpt.	8
21	Aurora	9
21	Carlinville	9
21	Chicago Midway Airport	9
21	Chicago O'Hare Int'l Airport	9
21	Danville	9

Annual Snowfall

Highest Rank	Station Name	Inches	Lowest Rank	Station Name	Inches
1	Chicago Midway Airport	42.8	1	Flora 5 NW	8.3
2	Waukegan	37.9	2	Brookport Dam 52	8.6
3	Rockford Greater Rockford Arpt.	37.4	3	Cairo WSO City	9.6
4	Chicago O'Hare Int'l Airport	37.3	4	Dixon Springs Agr. Center	9.7
5	Marengo	36.9	5	Albion	10.3
6	Dixon 1 NW	34.2	6	Rosiclare 5 NW	10.7
7	De Kalb	34.0	7	Olney 2 S	13.3
7	Morrison	34.0	8	Harrisburg	13.6
9	Moline Quad City Airport	33.8	9	Du Quoin 4 SE	13.7
10	Mount Carroll	32.9	9	Salem Leckrone Airport	13.7
10	Walnut	32.9	11	Carbondale Sewage Plant	13.8
12	Wheaton 3 SE	32.5	12	Waterloo	14.6
13	Stockton 3 NNE	32.4	13	Anna 2 NNE	14.7
14	Freeport Waste Water Plant	32.0	14	Newton 6 SSE	14.8
15	Park Forest	30.8	14	Sparta 1 W	14.8
16	Paw Paw 2 NW	30.2	16	Fairfield Radio WFIW	15.2
17	Havana 4 NNE	30.1	17	Belleville Scott AFB	16.1
18	Aurora	29.7	18	McLeansboro 2 ENE	16.3
19	Galva	28.6	18	Nashville 4 NE	16.3
20	Monmouth	28.2	20	Jerseyville 2 SW	16.8
20	Paris Waterworks	28.2	21	Mount Vernon-Outland Airport	17.3
22	Aledo	28.1	22	Fulton Lock & Dam 13	17.7
22	Minonk	28.1	22	Mattoon	17.7
22	Piper City	28.1	24	Hoopeston 1 NE	17.8
25	Geneseo	27.1	25	Rushville	17.9

Note: See User's Guide for explanation of data.

Deadliest Storm Events in Illinois: June 1983 - May 2008

Rank	Location or County	Date	Storm Event	Fatalities	Injuries	Property Damage ($mil.)	Crop Damage ($mil.)
1	Northeast Illinois	7/12/1995	Heat	583	0	0.0	0.0
2	Chicago Metropolitan Area	7/28/1999	Excessive Heat	99	0	0.0	0.0
3	Will County	8/28/1990	Tornado (F5)	29	350	250.0	0.0
4	Cook County	8/11/1995	Heat	27	0	0.0	0.0
5	Cook County	8/1/2006	Excessive Heat	24	0	0.0	0.0
6	Cook County	6/21/1997	Excessive Heat	16	0	0.0	0.0
7	Cook County	8/6/2001	Excessive Heat	14	0	0.0	0.0
8	Chicago Metropolitan Area	7/21/1999	Excessive Heat	13	0	0.0	0.0
9	Cook County	7/29/1995	Heat	12	0	0.0	0.0
10	Cook County	7/1/2002	Excessive Heat	12	0	0.0	0.0
11	Cook County	7/15/2002	Excessive Heat	11	0	0.0	0.0
12	Cook County	6/24/1998	Excessive Heat	10	0	0.0	0.0
13	Cook County	7/21/2001	Excessive Heat	10	0	0.0	0.0
14	Cook County	2/1/2007	Extreme Cold/Wind Chill	10	0	0.0	0.0
15	Cook County	7/15/2006	Excessive Heat	9	0	0.0	0.0
16	Adams, Bond, Brown, Calhoun, Clinton, Fayette, Greene, Jersey, Macoupin, Madison, Marion, Monroe, Montgomery, Pike, Randolph, St. Clair, and Washington Counties	7/18/1999	Excessive Heat	8	119	0.0	0.0
17	Peru	4/20/2004	Tornado (F3)	8	7	0.0	0.0
18	Cook County	6/21/2002	Excessive Heat	7	0	0.0	0.0
19	Cook County	12/2/2006	Extreme Cold/Wind Chill	7	5	0.0	0.0
20	Cook County	7/29/2001	Excessive Heat	6	0	0.0	0.0
21	Cook County	8/5/1996	Excessive Heat	5	0	0.0	0.0
22	Northern Illinois	1/15/1997	Winter Storm	5	0	0.0	0.0
23	Cook County	7/14/1997	Excessive Heat	5	0	0.0	0.0
24	Cook County	1/22/2008	Extreme Cold/Wind Chill	5	0	0.0	0.0

Source: National Climatic Data Center, Storm Events Database

Most Destructive Storm Events in Illinois: June 1983 - May 2008

Rank	Location or County	Date	Storm Event	Fatalities	Injuries	Property Damage ($mil.)	Crop Damage ($mil.)
1	Adams, Calhoun and Jersey Counties	8/31/1993	River Flood	0	0	5,000.0	5,000.0
2	Will County	8/28/1990	Tornado (F5)	29	350	250.0	0.0
3	Central Illinois	4/11/1994	Flash Flooding	2	0	50.0	0.0
4	Central Illinois	4/12/1994	Flooding	0	0	50.0	0.0
5	Henry County	7/21/2003	Tstm Wind (80 kts.)	0	0	50.0	25.0
6	Southern Illinois	7/17/1996	Flash Flood	0	0	44.7	0.0
7	Cook County	8/2/2001	Flash Flood	0	0	37.0	0.0
8	Wabash County	1/7/1989	Tornado (F4)	0	50	25.0	0.0
9	Will County	3/27/1991	Tornado (F3)	0	0	25.0	0.0
10	Will County	3/27/1991	Tornado (F3)	0	0	25.0	0.0
11	Cook County	3/27/1991	Tornado (F3)	0	7	25.0	0.0
12	Williamson County	11/19/1991	Tornado (F3)	0	16	25.0	0.0
13	Rockford	9/4/2006	Flash Flood	0	0	20.0	0.0
14	Galatia	3/18/2008	Flood	0	0	16.8	0.0
15	Mississippi River Valley	5/9/1995	River Flood	0	0	15.0	12.0
16	Warsaw	4/8/1999	Tornado (F3)	0	0	15.0	0.0
17	Southern and Central Illinois	7/17/1996	Flash Flood	0	0	14.5	0.0
18	Will County	7/27/2003	Flash Flood	0	0	14.0	0.0
19	Jefferson County	7/21/2006	Tstm Wind (78 kts.)	0	5	13.0	0.0
20	Lincoln	5/9/1995	Hail (2.25 in.)	0	0	12.0	0.0
21	Cantrall	5/9/1995	Tornado (F3)	0	6	10.0	0.0
22	Niota	5/13/1995	Tornado (F4)	0	7	10.0	0.0
23	Bishop Hill	4/19/1996	Tornado (F3)	0	4	10.0	0.0
24	Galva	4/19/1996	Tornado (F0)	0	4	10.0	0.0
25	Mercer County	4/30/2003	Flash Flood	0	0	10.0	0.0
26	Henry County	4/30/2003	Flash Flood	0	0	10.0	0.0
27	Hillerman	5/6/2003	Tornado (F4)	1	20	10.0	0.0
28	Gladstone	5/8/2003	Hail (4.00 in.)	0	0	10.0	0.0
29	South Pekin	5/10/2003	Tornado (F3)	0	32	10.0	0.0
30	Mercer County	7/20/2003	Tstm Wind (70 kts.)	0	0	10.0	3.0
31	Mattoon	9/26/2003	Tornado (F1)	0	1	10.0	0.0

Source: National Climatic Data Center, Storm Events Database

Demographic and Reference Maps

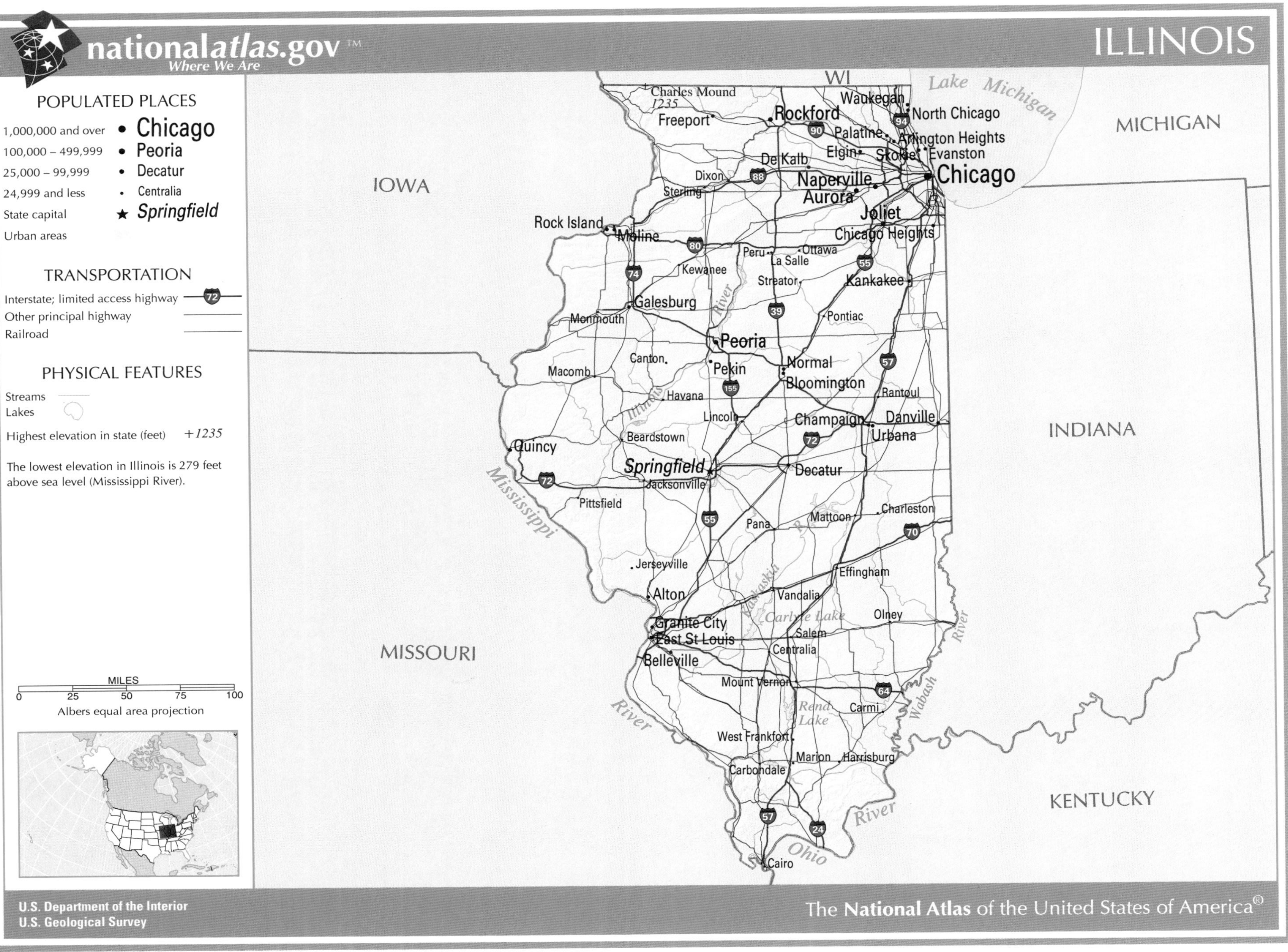
nationalatlas.gov™
Where We Are
ILLINOIS
POPULATED PLACES
1,000,000 and over • Chicago
100,000 – 499,999 • Peoria
25,000 – 99,999 • Decatur
24,999 and less · Centralia
State capital ★ Springfield
Urban areas
TRANSPORTATION
Interstate; limited access highway
Other principal highway
Railroad
PHYSICAL FEATURES
Streams
Lakes
Highest elevation in state (feet) +1235
The lowest elevation in Illinois is 279 feet above sea level (Mississippi River).
MILES
0 25 50 75 100
Albers equal area projection
U.S. Department of the Interior
U.S. Geological Survey
The National Atlas of the United States of America®
IOWA
MICHIGAN
INDIANA
MISSOURI
KENTUCKY
WI
Lake Michigan
Mississippi
Illinois River
Ohio River
Wabash River
Kaskaskia
Carlyle Lake
Rend Lake
Charles Mound 1235
Freeport
Rockford
Waukegan
North Chicago
Palatine
Arlington Heights
Elgin
Skokie
Evanston
De Kalb
Chicago
Dixon
Sterling
Naperville
Aurora
Joliet
Rock Island
Moline
Chicago Heights
Peru
Ottawa
La Salle
Kewanee
Streator
Kankakee
Galesburg
Pontiac
Monmouth
Peoria
Canton
Macomb
Pekin
Normal
Bloomington
Havana
Rantoul
Lincoln
Champaign
Danville
Urbana
Beardstown
Quincy
Springfield
Decatur
Jacksonville
Pittsfield
Charleston
Mattoon
Pana
Jerseyville
Effingham
Alton
Vandalia
Olney
Granite City
East St Louis
Salem
Centralia
Belleville
Mount Vernon
Carmi
West Frankfort
Marion
Harrisburg
Carbondale
Cairo
90
94
88
80
74
55
39
57
155
72
70
64
24

nationalatlas.gov™
Where We Are

ILLINOIS

FEDERAL LANDS AND INDIAN RESERVATIONS

- Department of Defense (includes Army Corps of Engineers lakes)
- Fish and Wildlife Service / Wilderness
- Forest Service / Wilderness
- Other agencies

Some small sites are not shown, especially in urban areas.

MILES
0 25 50 75 100
Albers equal area projection

Abbreviations

NWR National Wildlife Refuge

U.S. Department of the Interior
U.S. Geological Survey

The National Atlas of the United States of America®

ILLINOIS - Core Based Statistical Areas, Counties, and Independent City

U.S. DEPARTMENT OF COMMERCE Economics and Statistics Administration U.S. Census Bureau

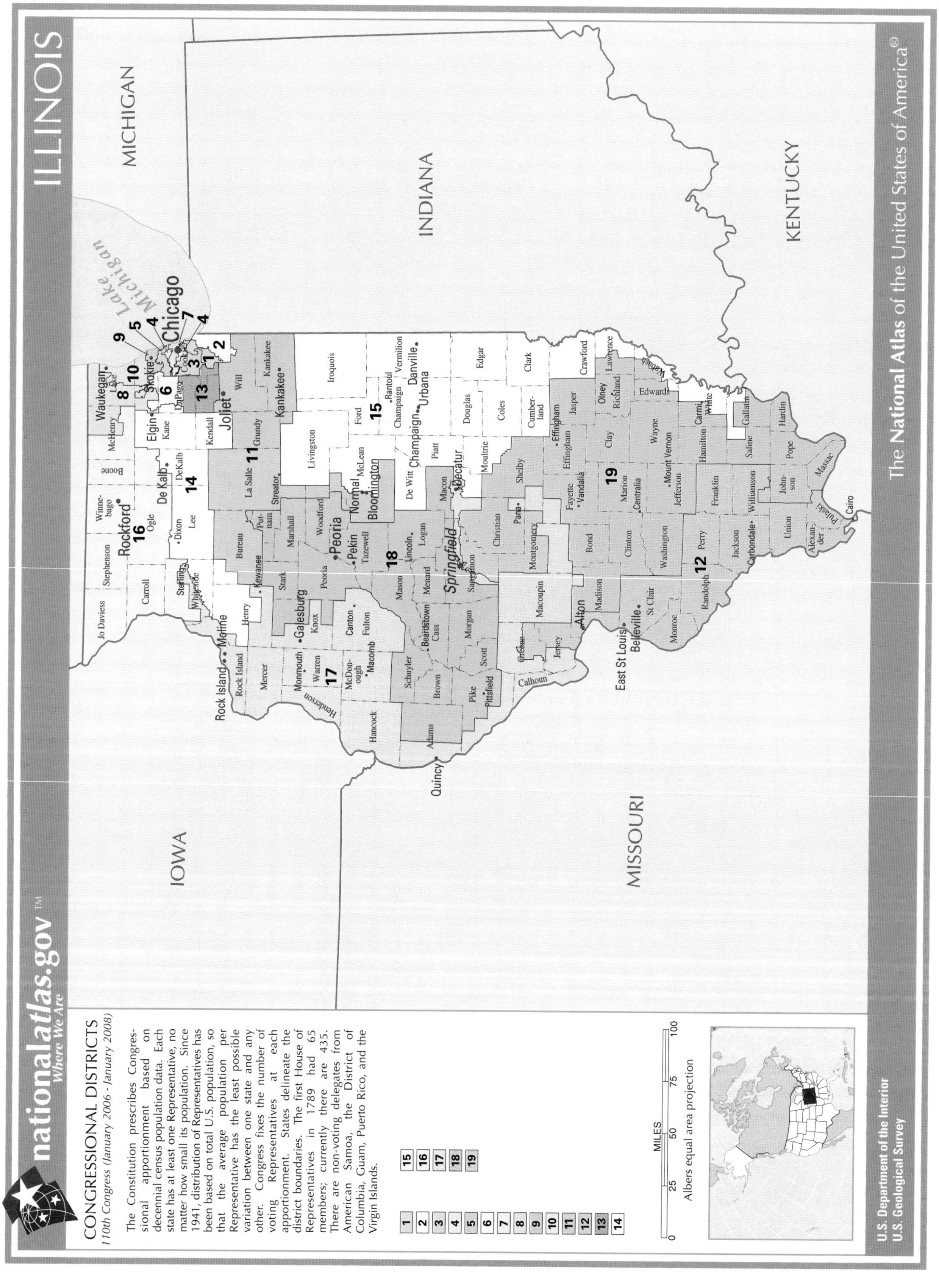
ILLINOIS
nationalatlas.gov™
Where We Are
CONGRESSIONAL DISTRICTS
110th Congress (January 2006 - January 2008)
The Constitution prescribes Congressional apportionment based on decennial census population data. Each state has at least one Representative, no matter how small its population. Since 1941, distribution of Representatives has been based on total U.S. population, so that the average population per Representative has the least possible variation between one state and any other. Congress fixes the number of voting Representatives at each apportionment. States delineate the district boundaries. The first House of Representatives in 1789 had 65 members; currently there are 435. There are non-voting delegates from American Samoa, the District of Columbia, Guam, Puerto Rico, and the Virgin Islands.
1 2 3 4 5 6 7 8 9 10 11 12 13 14 15 16 17 18 19
MILES
0 25 50 75 100
Albers equal area projection
U.S. Department of the Interior
U.S. Geological Survey
The National Atlas of the United States of America®
MICHIGAN
INDIANA
KENTUCKY
IOWA
MISSOURI
Lake Michigan
Chicago
Rockford
Springfield
Peoria
Joliet
Elgin
Waukegan
Skokie
De Kalb
Dixon
Sterling
Moline
Rock Island
Galesburg
Kewanee
Monmouth
Macomb
Canton
Pekin
Normal
Bloomington
Streator
Kankakee
Rantoul
Champaign
Urbana
Danville
Decatur
Lincoln
Beardstown
Pittsfield
Quincy
Pana
Effingham
Vandalia
Centralia
Mount Vernon
Carmi
Olney
Alton
East St Louis
Belleville
Carbondale
Cairo
Jo Daviess
Stephenson
Winnebago
Boone
McHenry
Lake
Carroll
Ogle
DeKalb
Kane
DuPage
Cook
Whiteside
Lee
Kendall
Will
Henry
Bureau
La Salle
Grundy
Mercer
Stark
Put-nam
Marshall
Livingston
Iroquois
Warren
Knox
Peoria
Woodford
Ford
Vermilion
Henderson
McDon-ough
Fulton
Tazewell
McLean
Hancock
Schuyler
Mason
Logan
De Witt
Piatt
Adams
Brown
Cass
Menard
Sangamon
Macon
Douglas
Edgar
Pike
Scott
Morgan
Christian
Moultrie
Coles
Clark
Calhoun
Greene
Macoupin
Montgomery
Shelby
Cumber-land
Jersey
Madison
Bond
Fayette
Jasper
Crawford
Clinton
Marion
Clay
Richland
Lawrence
St Clair
Washington
Jefferson
Wayne
Edwards
Wabash
Monroe
Randolph
Perry
Franklin
Hamilton
White
Jackson
Williamson
Saline
Gallatin
Union
John-son
Pope
Hardin
Alexan-der
Pulaski
Massac

Population (2007)

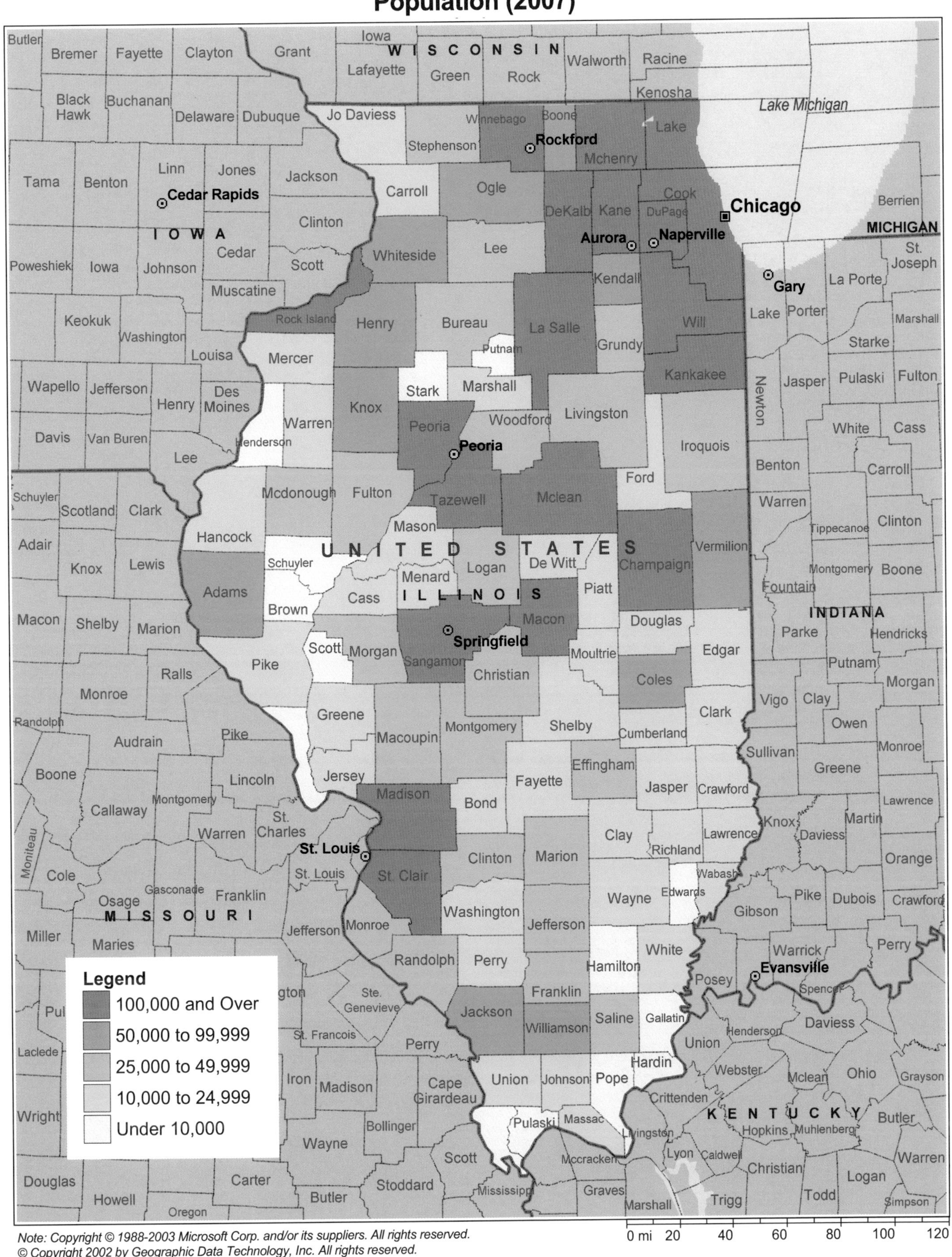

Percent White (2007)

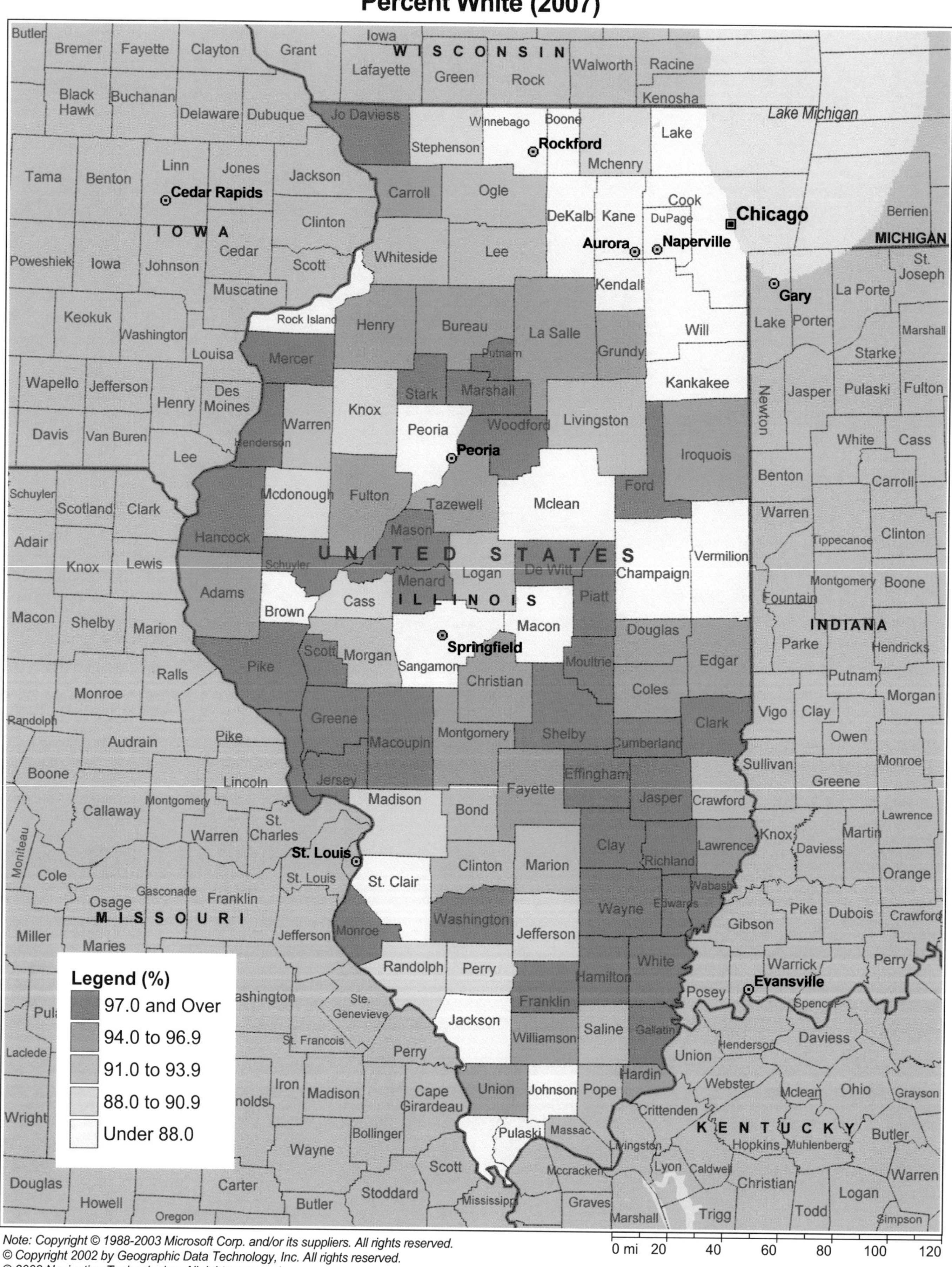

Percent Black (2007)

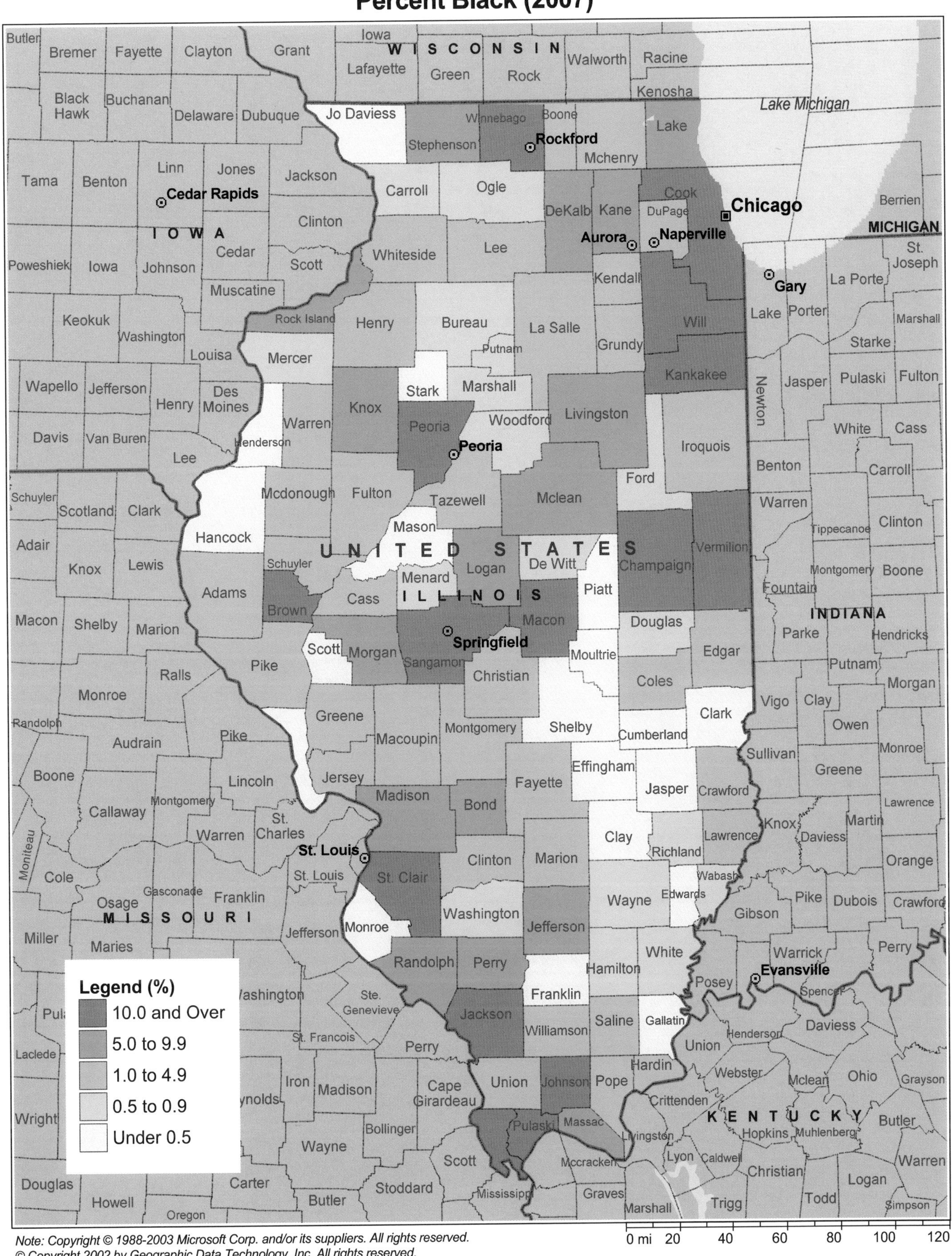

Percent Asian (2007)

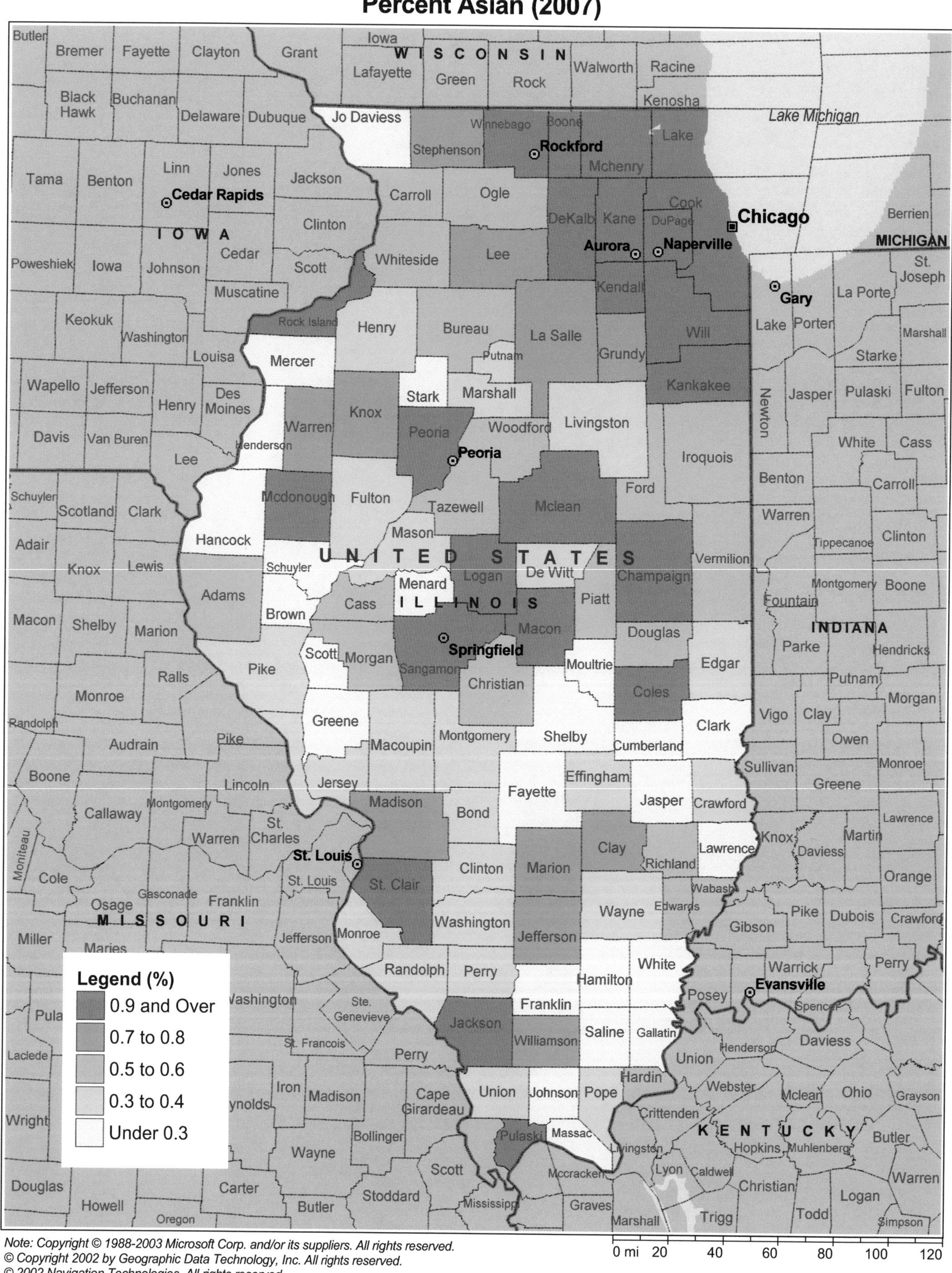

Percent Hispanic (2007)

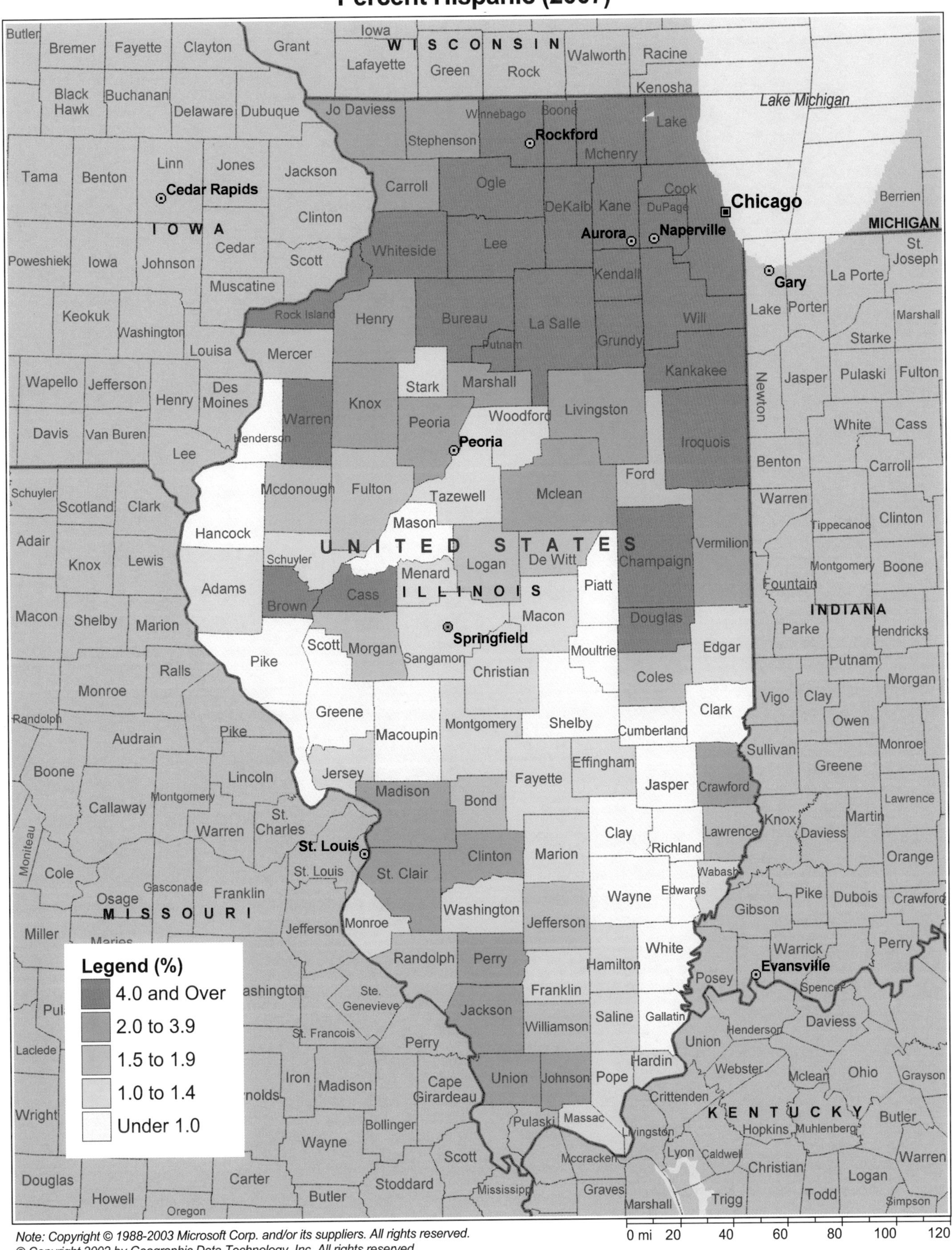

Median Age (2007)

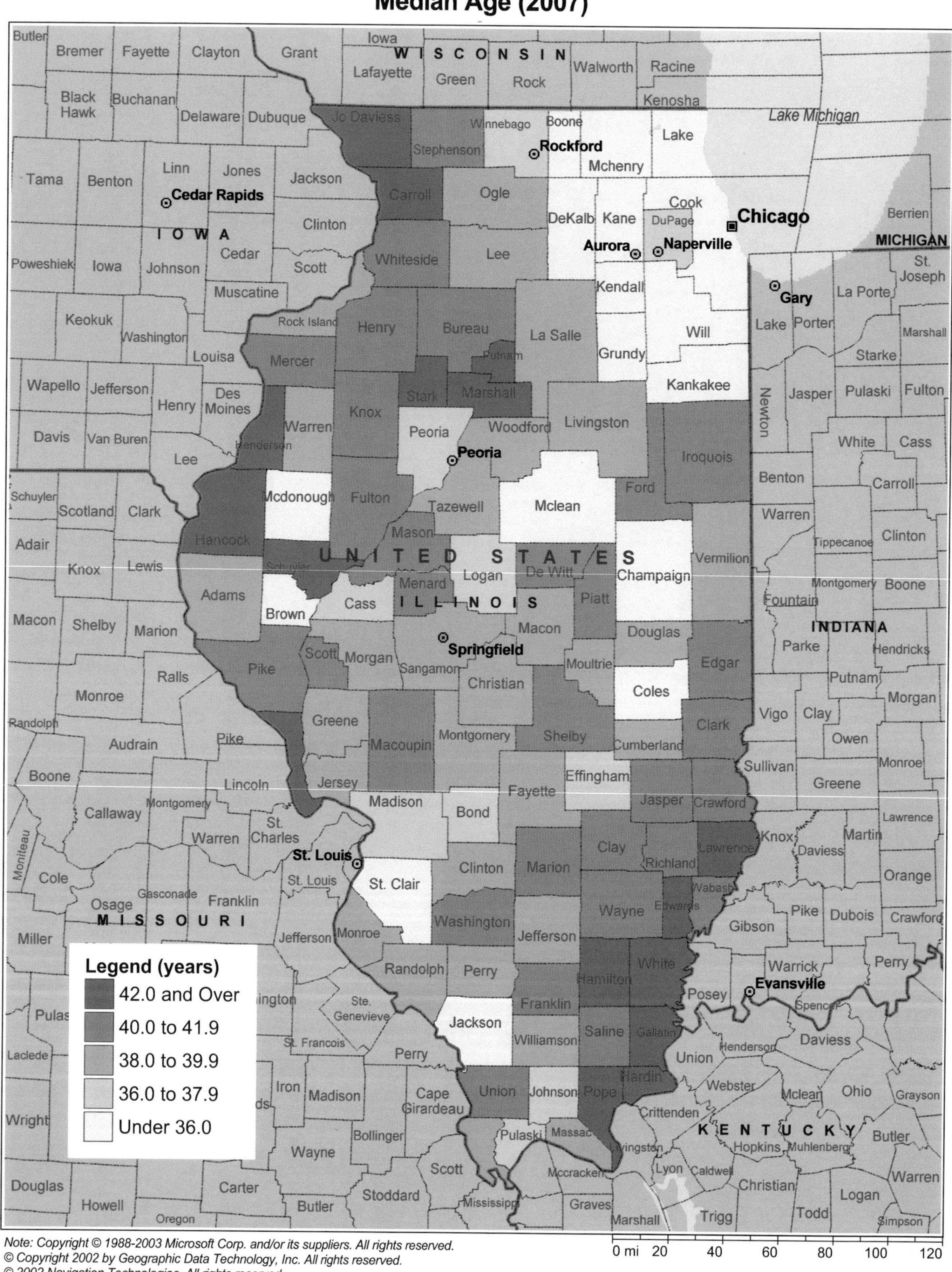

Median Household Income (2007)

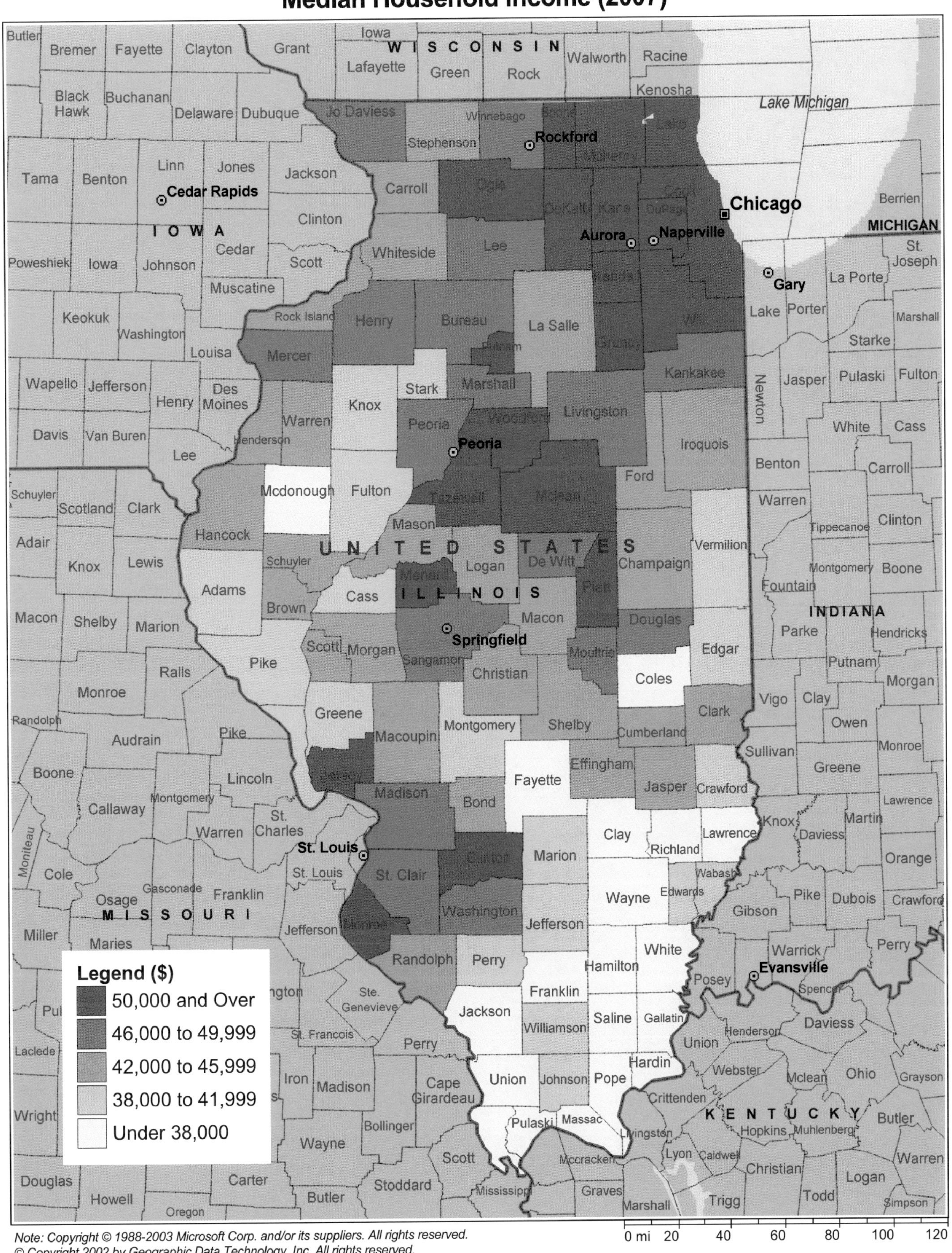

Median Home Value (2007)

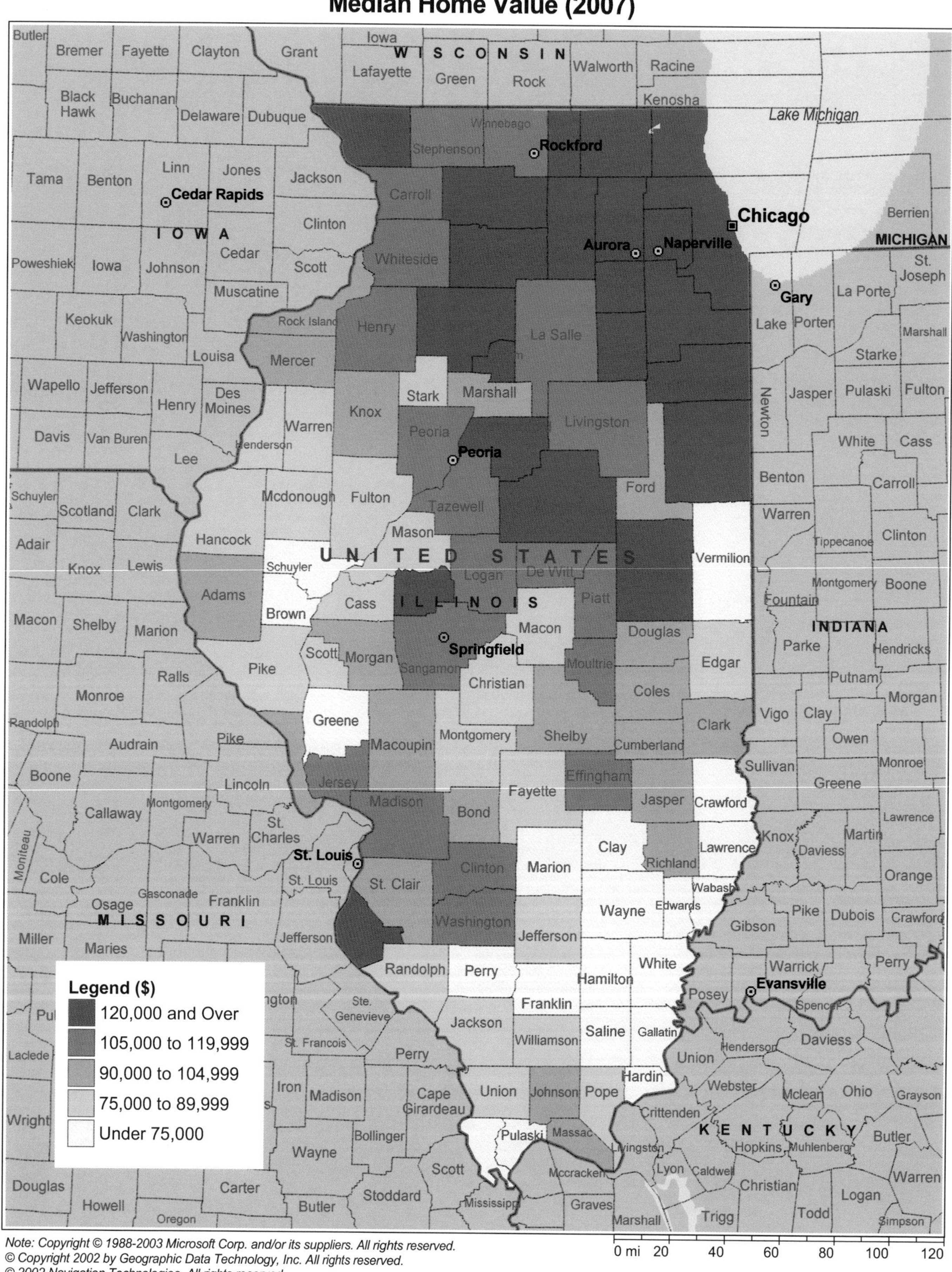

Percent of Population Who are Homeowners (2007)

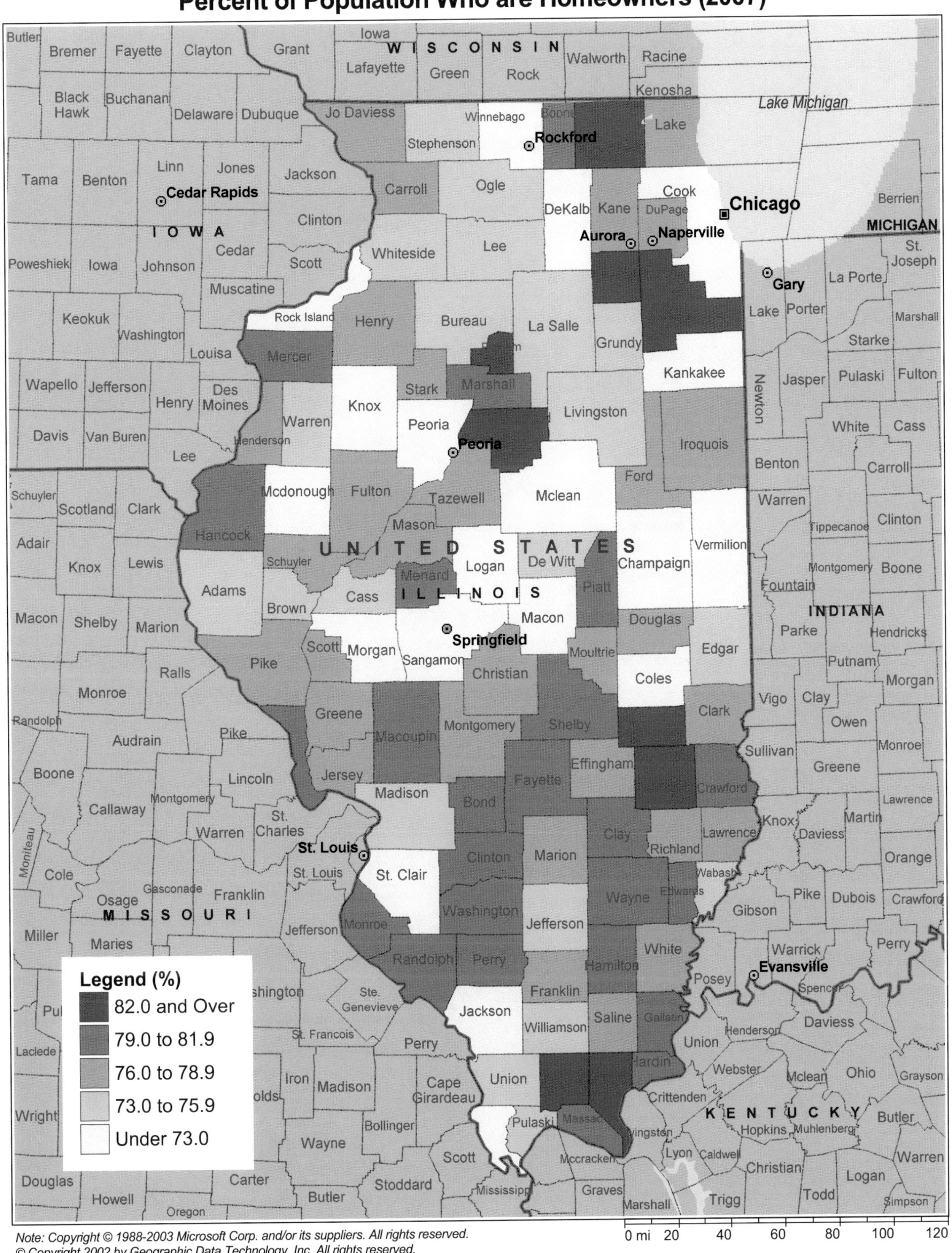

High School Graduates* (2007)

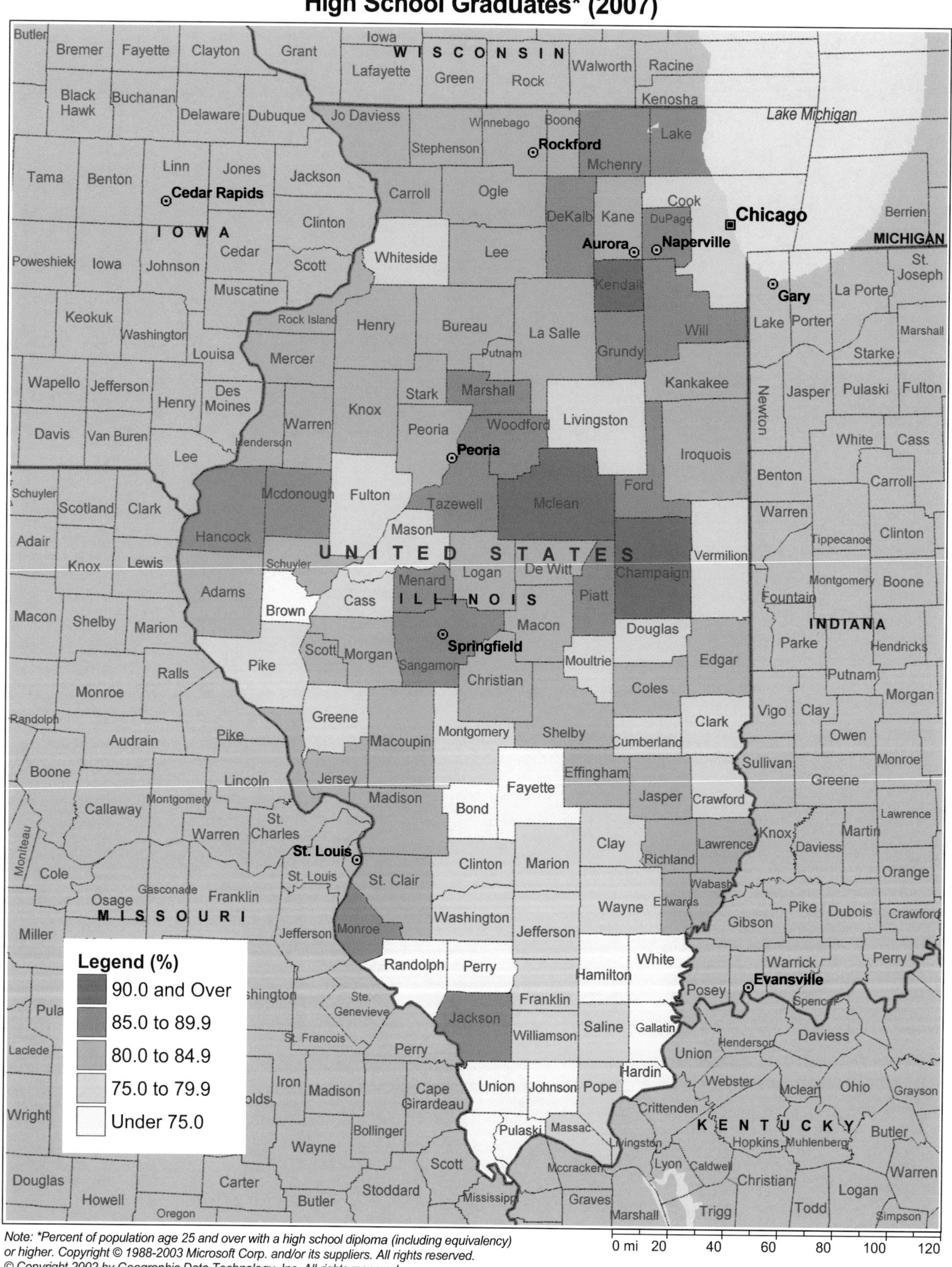

Note: *Percent of population age 25 and over with a high school diploma (including equivalency) or higher.

College Graduates* (2007)

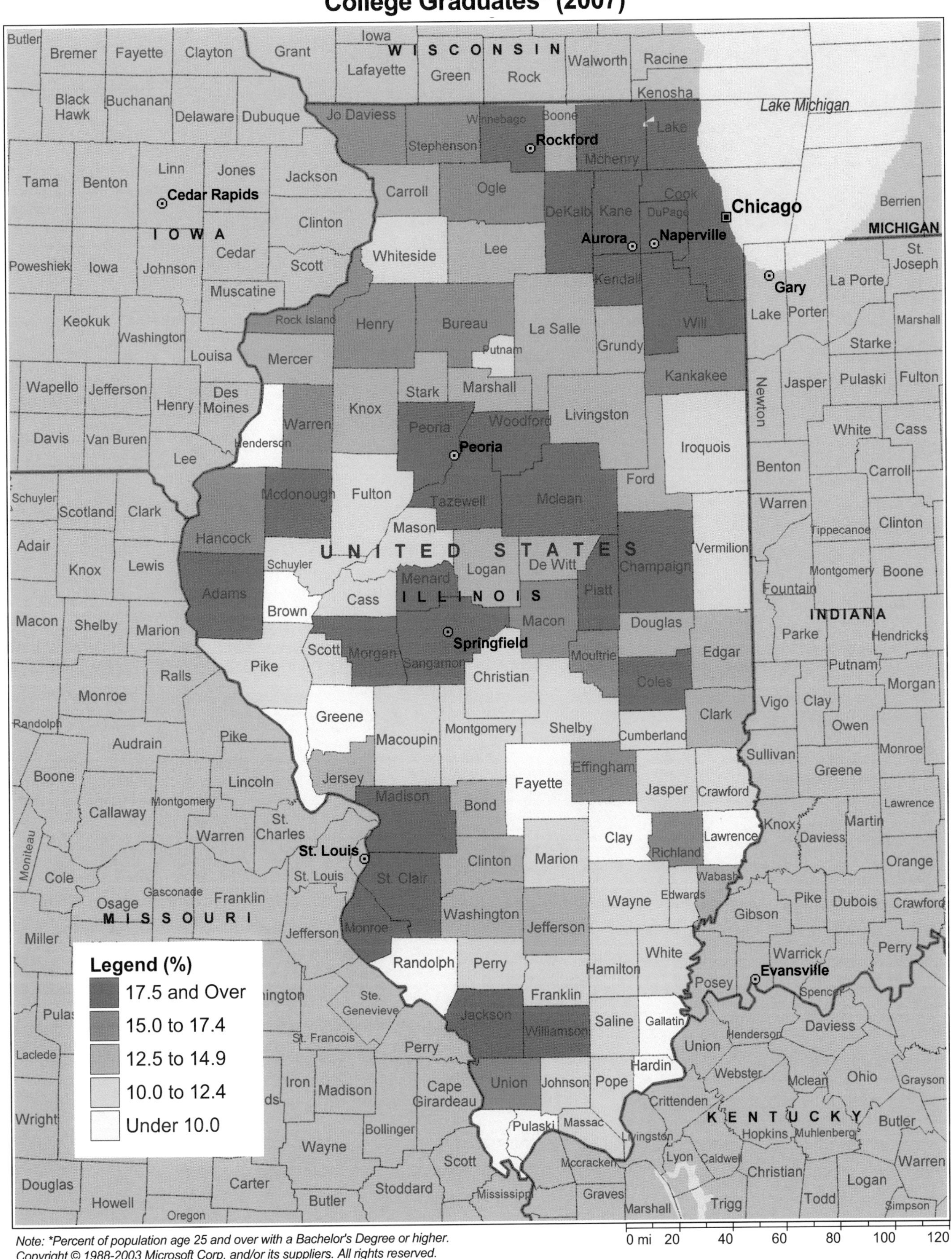

Note: *Percent of population age 25 and over with a Bachelor's Degree or higher.

Percent of Population Who Voted for George Bush in 2004

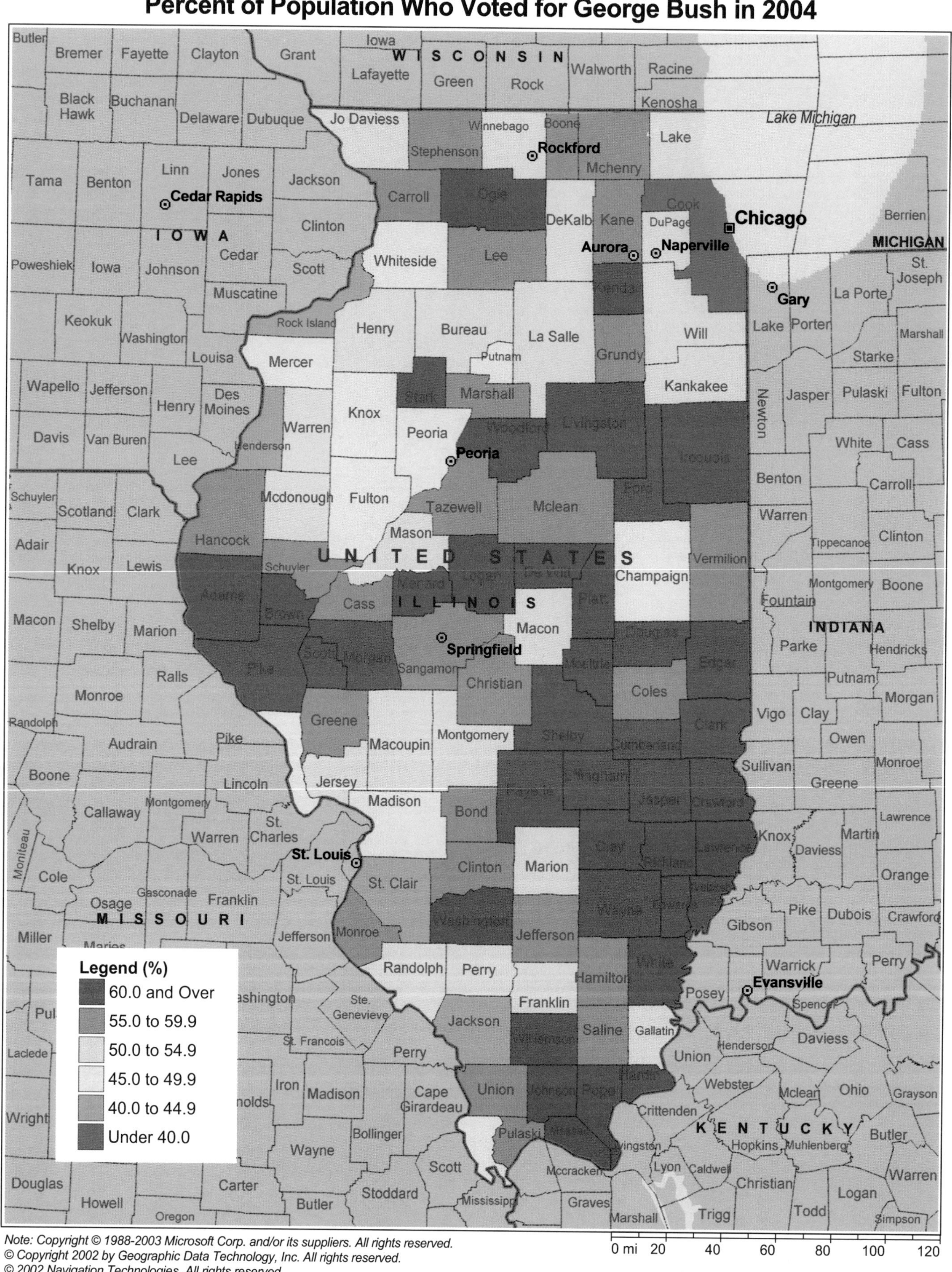

The Directory of Business Information Resources, 2008

With 100% verification, over 1,000 new listings and more than 12,000 updates, *The Directory of Business Information Resources* is the most up-to-date source for contacts in over 98 business areas – from advertising and agriculture to utilities and wholesalers. This carefully researched volume details: the Associations representing each industry; the Newsletters that keep members current; the Magazines and Journals - with their "Special Issues" - that are important to the trade, the Conventions that are "must attends," Databases, Directories and Industry Web Sites that provide access to must-have marketing resources. Includes contact names, phone & fax numbers, web sites and e-mail addresses. This one-volume resource is a gold mine of information and would be a welcome addition to any reference collection.

"This is a most useful and easy-to-use addition to any researcher's library." –The Information Professionals Institute

Softcover ISBN 978-1-59237-193-8, 2,500 pages, $195.00 | Online Database $495.00

Hudson's Washington News Media Contacts Directory, 2008

With 100% verification of data, Hudson's Washington News Media Contacts Directory is the most accurate, most up-to-date source for media contacts in our nation's capital. With the largest concentration of news media in the world, having access to Washington's news media will get your message heard by these key media outlets. Published for over 40 years, Hudson's Washington News Media Contacts Directory brings you immediate access to: News Services & Newspapers, News Service Syndicates, DC Newspapers, Foreign Newspapers, Radio & TV, Magazines & Newsletters, and Freelance Writers & Photographers. The easy-to-read entries include contact names, phone & fax numbers, web sites and e-mail and more. For easy navigation, Hudson's Washington News Media Contacts Directory contains two indexes: Entry Index and Executive Index. This kind of comprehensive and up-to-date information would cost thousands of dollars to replicate or countless hours of searching to find. Don't miss this opportunity to have this important resource in your collection, and start saving time and money today. Hudson's Washington News Media Contacts Directory is the perfect research tool for Public Relations, Marketing, Networking and so much more. This resource is a gold mine of information and would be a welcome addition to any reference collection.

Softcover ISBN 978-1-59237-393-2, 800 pages, $289.00

Nations of the World, 2009 A Political, Economic and Business Handbook

This completely revised edition covers all the nations of the world in an easy-to-use, single volume. Each nation is profiled in a single chapter that includes Key Facts, Political & Economic Issues, a Country Profile and Business Information. In this fast-changing world, it is extremely important to make sure that the most up-to-date information is included in your reference collection. This edition is just the answer. Each of the 200+ country chapters have been carefully reviewed by a political expert to make sure that the text reflects the most current information on Politics, Travel Advisories, Economics and more. You'll find such vital information as a Country Map, Population Characteristics, Inflation, Agricultural Production, Foreign Debt, Political History, Foreign Policy, Regional Insecurity, Economics, Trade & Tourism, Historical Profile, Political Systems, Ethnicity, Languages, Media, Climate, Hotels, Chambers of Commerce, Banking, Travel Information and more. Five Regional Chapters follow the main text and include a Regional Map, an Introductory Article, Key Indicators and Currencies for the Region. As an added bonus, an all-inclusive CD-ROM is available as a companion to the printed text. Noted for its sophisticated, up-to-date and reliable compilation of political, economic and business information, this brand new edition will be an important acquisition to any public, academic or special library reference collection.

"A useful addition to both general reference collections and business collections." –RUSQ

Softcover ISBN 978-1-59237-273-7, 1,700 pages, $155.00

The Directory of Venture Capital & Private Equity Firms, 2008

This edition has been extensively updated and broadly expanded to offer direct access to over 2,800 Domestic and International Venture Capital Firms, including address, phone & fax numbers, e-mail addresses and web sites for both primary and branch locations. Entries include details on the firm's Mission Statement, Industry Group Preferences, Geographic Preferences, Average and Minimum Investments and Investment Criteria. You'll also find details that are available nowhere else, including the Firm's Portfolio Companies and extensive information on each of the firm's Managing Partners, such as Education, Professional Background and Directorships held, along with the Partner's E-mail Address. *The Directory of Venture Capital & Private Equity Firms* offers five important indexes: Geographic Index, Executive Name Index, Portfolio Company Index, Industry Preference Index and College & University Index. With its comprehensive coverage and detailed, extensive information on each company, The Directory of Venture Capital & Private Equity Firms is an important addition to any finance collection.

"The sheer number of listings, the descriptive information and the outstanding indexing make this directory a better value than …Pratt's Guide to Venture Capital Sources. Recommended for business collections in large public, academic and business libraries." –Choice

Softcover ISBN 978-1-59237-272-0, 1,300 pages, $565/$450 Library | Online Database $889.00

The Encyclopedia of Emerging Industries

*Published under an exclusive license from the Gale Group, Inc.

The fifth edition of the *Encyclopedia of Emerging Industries* details the inception, emergence, and current status of nearly 120 flourishing U.S. industries and industry segments. These focused essays unearth for users a wealth of relevant, current, factual data previously accessible only through a diverse variety of sources. This volume provides broad-based, highly-readable, industry information under such headings as Industry Snapshot, Organization & Structure, Background & Development, Industry Leaders, Current Conditions, America and the World, Pioneers, and Research & Technology. Essays in this new edition, arranged alphabetically for easy use, have been completely revised, with updated statistics and the most current information on industry trends and developments. In addition, there are new essays on some of the most interesting and influential new business fields, including Application Service Providers, Concierge Services, Entrepreneurial Training, Fuel Cells, Logistics Outsourcing Services, Pharmacogenomics, and Tissue Engineering. Two indexes, General and Industry, provide immediate access to this wealth of information. Plus, two conversion tables for SIC and NAICS codes, along with Suggested Further Readings, are provided to aid the user. *The Encyclopedia of Emerging Industries* pinpoints emerging industries while they are still in the spotlight. This important resource will be an important acquisition to any business reference collection.

"This well-designed source...should become another standard business source, nicely complementing Standard & Poor's Industry Surveys. It contains more information on each industry than Hoover's Handbook of Emerging Companies, is broader in scope than The Almanac of American Employers 1998-1999, but is less expansive than the Encyclopedia of Careers & Vocational Guidance. Highly recommended for all academic libraries and specialized business collections." –Library Journal

Hardcover ISBN 978-1-59237-242-3, 1,400 pages, $325.00

Encyclopedia of American Industries

*Published under an exclusive license from the Gale Group, Inc.

The Encyclopedia of American Industries is a major business reference tool that provides detailed, comprehensive information on a wide range of industries in every realm of American business. A two volume set, Volume I provides separate coverage of nearly 500 manufacturing industries, while Volume II presents nearly 600 essays covering the vast array of services and other non-manufacturing industries in the United States. Combined, these two volumes provide individual essays on every industry recognized by the U.S. Standard Industrial Classification (SIC) system. Both volumes are arranged numerically by SIC code, for easy use. Additionally, each entry includes the corresponding NAICS code(s). The *Encyclopedia's* business coverage includes information on historical events of consequence, as well as current trends and statistics. Essays include an Industry Snapshot, Organization & Structure, Background & Development, Current Conditions, Industry Leaders, Workforce, America and the World, Research & Technology along with Suggested Further Readings. Both SIC and NAICS code conversion tables and an all-encompassing Subject Index, with cross-references, complete the text. With its detailed, comprehensive information on a wide range of industries, this resource will be an important tool for both the industry newcomer and the seasoned professional.

"Encyclopedia of American Industries contains detailed, signed essays on virtually every industry in contemporary society. ... Highly recommended for all but the smallest libraries." -American Reference Books Annual

Two Volumes, Hardcover ISBN 978-1-59237-244-7, 3,000 pages, $650.00

Encyclopedia of Global Industries

*Published under an exclusive license from the Gale Group, Inc.

This fourth edition of the acclaimed *Encyclopedia of Global Industries* presents a thoroughly revised and expanded look at more than 125 business sectors of global significance. Detailed, insightful articles discuss the origins, development, trends, key statistics and current international character of the world's most lucrative, dynamic and widely researched industries – including hundreds of profiles of leading international corporations. Beginning researchers will gain from this book a solid understanding of how each industry operates and which countries and companies are significant participants, while experienced researchers will glean current and historical figures for comparison and analysis. The industries profiled in previous editions have been updated, and in some cases, expanded to reflect recent industry trends. Additionally, this edition provides both SIC and NAICS codes for all industries profiled. As in the original volumes, *The Encyclopedia of Global Industries* offers thorough studies of some of the biggest and most frequently researched industry sectors, including Aircraft, Biotechnology, Computers, Internet Services, Motor Vehicles, Pharmaceuticals, Semiconductors, Software and Telecommunications. An SIC and NAICS conversion table and an all-encompassing Subject Index, with cross-references, are provided to ensure easy access to this wealth of information. These and many others make the *Encyclopedia of Global Industries* the authoritative reference for studies of international industries.

"Provides detailed coverage of the history, development, and current status of 115 of "the world's most lucrative and high-profile industries." It far surpasses the Department of Commerce's U.S. Global Trade Outlook 1995-2000 (GPO, 1995) in scope and coverage. Recommended for comprehensive public and academic library business collections." -Booklist

Hardcover ISBN 978-1-59237-243-0, 1,400 pages, $495.00

The Directory of Mail Order Catalogs, 2008

Published since 1981, *The Directory of Mail Order Catalogs* is the premier source of information on the mail order catalog industry. It is the source that business professionals and librarians have come to rely on for the thousands of catalog companies in the US. Since the 2007 edition, *The Directory of Mail Order Catalogs* has been combined with its companion volume, *The Directory of Business to Business Catalogs*, to offer all 13,000 catalog companies in one easy-to-use volume. Section I: Consumer Catalogs, covers over 9,000 consumer catalog companies in 44 different product chapters from Animals to Toys & Games. Section II: Business to Business Catalogs, details 5,000 business catalogs, everything from computers to laboratory supplies, building construction and much more. Listings contain detailed contact information including mailing address, phone & fax numbers, web sites, e-mail addresses and key contacts along with important business details such as product descriptions, employee size, years in business, sales volume, catalog size, number of catalogs mailed and more. Three indexes are included for easy access to information: Catalog & Company Name Index, Geographic Index and Product Index. *The Directory of Mail Order Catalogs*, now with its expanded business to business catalogs, is the largest and most comprehensive resource covering this billion-dollar industry. It is the standard in its field. This important resource is a useful tool for entrepreneurs searching for catalogs to pick up their product, vendors looking to expand their customer base in the catalog industry, market researchers, small businesses investigating new supply vendors, along with the library patron who is exploring the available catalogs in their areas of interest.

"This is a godsend for those looking for information." –Reference Book Review

Softcover ISBN 978-1-59237-202-7, 1,700 pages, $350/$250 Library | Online Database $495.00

Sports Market Place Directory, 2008

For over 20 years, this comprehensive, up-to-date directory has offered direct access to the Who, What, When & Where of the Sports Industry. With over 20,000 updates and enhancements, the *Sports Market Place Directory* is the most detailed, comprehensive and current sports business reference source available. In 1,800 information-packed pages, *Sports Market Place Directory* profiles contact information and key executives for: Single Sport Organizations, Professional Leagues, Multi-Sport Organizations, Disabled Sports, High School & Youth Sports, Military Sports, Olympic Organizations, Media, Sponsors, Sponsorship & Marketing Event Agencies, Event & Meeting Calendars, Professional Services, College Sports, Manufacturers & Retailers, Facilities and much more. The Sports Market Place Directory provides organization's contact information with detailed descriptions including: Key Contacts, physical, mailing, email and web addresses plus phone and fax numbers. *Sports Market Place Directory* provides a one-stop resources for this billion-dollar industry. This will be an important resource for large public libraries, university libraries, university athletic programs, career services or job placement organizations, and is a must for anyone doing research on or marketing to the US and Canadian sports industry.

"Grey House is the new publisher and has produced an excellent edition...highly recommended for public libraries and academic libraries with sports management programs or strong interest in athletics." -Booklist

Softcover ISBN 978-1-59237-348-2, 1,800 pages, $225.00 | Online Database $479.00

Food and Beverage Market Place, 2008

Food and Beverage Market Place is bigger and better than ever with thousands of new companies, thousands of updates to existing companies and two revised and enhanced product category indexes. This comprehensive directory profiles over 18,000 Food & Beverage Manufacturers, 12,000 Equipment & Supply Companies, 2,200 Transportation & Warehouse Companies, 2,000 Brokers & Wholesalers, 8,000 Importers & Exporters, 900 Industry Resources and hundreds of Mail Order Catalogs. Listings include detailed Contact Information, Sales Volumes, Key Contacts, Brand & Product Information, Packaging Details and much more. *Food and Beverage Market Place* is available as a three-volume printed set, a subscription-based Online Database via the Internet, on CD-ROM, as well as mailing lists and a licensable database.

"An essential purchase for those in the food industry but will also be useful in public libraries where needed. Much of the information will be difficult and time consuming to locate without this handy three-volume ready-reference source." –ARBA

3 Vol Set, Softcover ISBN 978-1-59237-198-3, 8,500 pages, $595 | Online Database $795 | Online Database & 3 Vol Set Combo, $995

The Grey House Performing Arts Directory, 2007

The Grey House Performing Arts Directory is the most comprehensive resource covering the Performing Arts. This important directory provides current information on over 8,500 Dance Companies, Instrumental Music Programs, Opera Companies, Choral Groups, Theater Companies, Performing Arts Series and Performing Arts Facilities. Plus, this edition now contains a brand new section on Artist Management Groups. In addition to mailing address, phone & fax numbers, e-mail addresses and web sites, dozens of other fields of available information include mission statement, key contacts, facilities, seating capacity, season, attendance and more. This directory also provides an important Information Resources section that covers hundreds of Performing Arts Associations, Magazines, Newsletters, Trade Shows, Directories, Databases and Industry Web Sites. Five indexes provide immediate access to this wealth of information: Entry Name, Executive Name, Performance Facilities, Geographic and Information Resources. *The Grey House Performing Arts Directory* pulls together thousands of Performing Arts Organizations, Facilities and Information Resources into an easy-to-use source – this kind of comprehensiveness and extensive detail is not available in any resource on the market place today.

"Immensely useful and user-friendly ... recommended for public, academic and certain special library reference collections." –Booklist

Softcover ISBN 978-1-59237-138-9, 1,500 pages, $185.00 | Online Database $335.00

New York State Directory, 2008/09

The New York State Directory, published annually since 1983, is a comprehensive and easy-to-use guide to accessing public officials and private sector organizations and individuals who influence public policy in the state of New York. *The New York State Directory* includes important information on all New York state legislators and congressional representatives, including biographies and key committee assignments. It also includes staff rosters for all branches of New York state government and for federal agencies and departments that impact the state policy process. Following the state government section are 25 chapters covering policy areas from agriculture through veterans' affairs. Each chapter identifies the state, local and federal agencies and officials that formulate or implement policy. In addition, each chapter contains a roster of private sector experts and advocates who influence the policy process. The directory also offers appendices that include statewide party officials; chambers of commerce; lobbying organizations; public and private universities and colleges; television, radio and print media; and local government agencies and officials.

"This comprehensive directory covers not only New York State government offices and key personnel but pertinent U.S. government agencies and non-governmental entities. This directory is all encompassing... recommended." -Choice

New York State Directory - Softcover ISBN 978-1-59237-358-1, 800 pages, $145.00
New York State Directory with *Profiles of New York* – 2 Volumes, Softcover ISBN 978-1-59237-359-8, 1,600 pages, $225.00

The Grey House Homeland Security Directory, 2008

This updated edition features the latest contact information for government and private organizations involved with Homeland Security along with the latest product information and provides detailed profiles of nearly 1,000 Federal & State Organizations & Agencies and over 3,000 Officials and Key Executives involved with Homeland Security. These listings are incredibly detailed and include Mailing Address, Phone & Fax Numbers, Email Addresses & Web Sites, a complete Description of the Agency and a complete list of the Officials and Key Executives associated with the Agency. Next, *The Grey House Homeland Security Directory* provides the go-to source for Homeland Security Products & Services. This section features over 2,000 Companies that provide Consulting, Products or Services. With this Buyer's Guide at their fingertips, users can locate suppliers of everything from Training Materials to Access Controls, from Perimeter Security to BioTerrorism Countermeasures and everything in between – complete with contact information and product descriptions. A handy Product Locator Index is provided to quickly and easily locate suppliers of a particular product. This comprehensive, information-packed resource will be a welcome tool for any company or agency that is in need of Homeland Security information and will be a necessary acquisition for the reference collection of all public libraries and large school districts.

"Compiles this information in one place and is discerning in content. A useful purchase for public and academic libraries." –Booklist

Softcover ISBN 978-1-59237-196-6, 800 pages, $195.00 | Online Database $385.00

The Grey House Safety & Security Directory, 2008

The Grey House Safety & Security Directory is the most comprehensive reference tool and buyer's guide for the safety and security industry. Arranged by safety topic, each chapter begins with OSHA regulations for the topic, followed by Training Articles written by top professionals in the field and Self-Inspection Checklists. Next, each topic contains Buyer's Guide sections that feature related products and services. Topics include Administration, Insurance, Loss Control & Consulting, Protective Equipment & Apparel, Noise & Vibration, Facilities Monitoring & Maintenance, Employee Health Maintenance & Ergonomics, Retail Food Services, Machine Guards, Process Guidelines & Tool Handling, Ordinary Materials Handling, Hazardous Materials Handling, Workplace Preparation & Maintenance, Electrical Lighting & Safety, Fire & Rescue and Security. Six important indexes make finding information and product manufacturers quick and easy: Geographical Index of Manufacturers and Distributors, Company Profile Index, Brand Name Index, Product Index, Index of Web Sites and Index of Advertisers. This comprehensive, up-to-date reference will provide every tool necessary to make sure a business is in compliance with OSHA regulations and locate the products and services needed to meet those regulations.

"Presents industrial safety information for engineers, plant managers, risk managers, and construction site supervisors…" –Choice

Softcover ISBN 978-1-59237-205-8, 1,500 pages, $165.00

The Grey House Transportation Security Directory & Handbook

This is the only reference of its kind that brings together current data on Transportation Security. With information on everything from Regulatory Authorities to Security Equipment, this top-flight database brings together the relevant information necessary for creating and maintaining a security plan for a wide range of transportation facilities. With this current, comprehensive directory at the ready you'll have immediate access to: Regulatory Authorities & Legislation; Information Resources; Sample Security Plans & Checklists; Contact Data for Major Airports, Seaports, Railroads, Trucking Companies and Oil Pipelines; Security Service Providers; Recommended Equipment & Product Information and more. Using the *Grey House Transportation Security Directory & Handbook*, managers will be able to quickly and easily assess their current security plans; develop contacts to create and maintain new security procedures; and source the products and services necessary to adequately maintain a secure environment. This valuable resource is a must for all Security Managers at Airports, Seaports, Railroads, Trucking Companies and Oil Pipelines.

"Highly recommended. Library collections that support all levels of readers, including professionals/practitioners; and schools/organizations offering education and training in transportation security." -Choice

Softcover ISBN 978-1-59237-075-7, 800 pages, $195.00

The Grey House Biometric Information Directory

This edition offers a complete, current overview of biometric companies and products – one of the fastest growing industries in today's economy. Detailed profiles of manufacturers of the latest biometric technology, including Finger, Voice, Face, Hand, Signature, Iris, Vein and Palm Identification systems. Data on the companies include key executives, company size and a detailed, indexed description of their product line. Information in the directory includes: Editorial on Advancements in Biometrics; Profiles of 700+ companies listed with contact information; Organizations, Trade & Educational Associations, Publications, Conferences, Trade Shows and Expositions Worldwide; Web Site Index; Biometric & Vendors Services Index by Types of Biometrics; and a Glossary of Biometric Terms. This resource will be an important source for anyone who is considering the use of a biometric product, investing in the development of biometric technology, support existing marketing and sales efforts and will be an important acquisition for the business reference collection for large public and business libraries.

"This book should prove useful to agencies or businesses seeking companies that deal with biometric technology. Summing Up: Recommended. Specialized collections serving researchers/faculty and professionals/practitioners." -Choice

Softcover ISBN 978-1-59237-121-1, 800 pages, $225.00

The Environmental Resource Handbook, 2008/09

The Environmental Resource Handbook is the most up-to-date and comprehensive source for Environmental Resources and Statistics. Section I: Resources provides detailed contact information for thousands of information sources, including Associations & Organizations, Awards & Honors, Conferences, Foundations & Grants, Environmental Health, Government Agencies, National Parks & Wildlife Refuges, Publications, Research Centers, Educational Programs, Green Product Catalogs, Consultants and much more. Section II: Statistics, provides statistics and rankings on hundreds of important topics, including Children's Environmental Index, Municipal Finances, Toxic Chemicals, Recycling, Climate, Air & Water Quality and more. This kind of up-to-date environmental data, all in one place, is not available anywhere else on the market place today. This vast compilation of resources and statistics is a must-have for all public and academic libraries as well as any organization with a primary focus on the environment.

"...the intrinsic value of the information make it worth consideration by libraries with environmental collections and environmentally concerned users." –Booklist

Softcover ISBN 978-1-59237-195-2, 1,000 pages, $155.00 | Online Database $300.00

The Rauch Guide to the US Adhesives & Sealants, Cosmetics & Toiletries, Ink, Paint, Plastics, Pulp & Paper and Rubber Industries

The Rauch Guides save time and money by organizing widely scattered information and providing estimates for important business decisions, some of which are available nowhere else. Within each Guide, after a brief introduction, the ECONOMICS section provides data on industry shipments; long-term growth and forecasts; prices; company performance; employment, expenditures, and productivity; transportation and geographical patterns; packaging; foreign trade; and government regulations. Next, TECHNOLOGY & RAW MATERIALS provide market, technical, and raw material information for chemicals, equipment and related materials, including market size and leading suppliers, prices, end uses, and trends. PRODUCTS & MARKETS provide information for each major industry product, including market size and historical trends, leading suppliers, five-year forecasts, industry structure, and major end uses. Next, the COMPANY DIRECTORY profiles major industry companies, both public and private. Information includes complete contact information, web address, estimated total and domestic sales, product description, and recent mergers and acquisitions. *The Rauch Guides* will prove to be an invaluable source of market information, company data, trends and forecasts that anyone in these fast-paced industries.

"An invaluable and affordable publication. The comprehensive nature of the data and text offers considerable insights into the industry, market sizes, company activities, and applications of the products of the industry. The additions that have been made have certainly enhanced the value of the Guide." –Adhesives & Sealants Newsletter of the Rauch Guide to the US Adhesives & Sealants Industry

Paint Industry: Softcover ISBN 978-1-59237-127-3 $595 | Plastics Industry: Softcover ISBN 978-1-59237-128-0 $595 | Adhesives and Sealants Industry: Softcover ISBN 978-1-59237-129-7 $595 | Ink Industry: Softcover ISBN 978-1-59237-126-6 $595 | Rubber Industry: Softcover ISBN 978-1-59237-130-3 $595 | Pulp and Paper Industry: Softcover ISBN 978-1-59237-131-0 $595 | Cosmetic & Toiletries Industry: Softcover ISBN 978-1-59237-132-7 $895

Research Services Directory: Commercial & Corporate Research Centers

This ninth edition provides access to well over 8,000 independent Commercial Research Firms, Corporate Research Centers and Laboratories offering contract services for hands-on, basic or applied research. Research Services Directory covers the thousands of types of research companies, including Biotechnology & Pharmaceutical Developers, Consumer Product Research, Defense Contractors, Electronics & Software Engineers, Think Tanks, Forensic Investigators, Independent Commercial Laboratories, Information Brokers, Market & Survey Research Companies, Medical Diagnostic Facilities, Product Research & Development Firms and more. Each entry provides the company's name, mailing address, phone & fax numbers, key contacts, web site, e-mail address, as well as a company description and research and technical fields served. Four indexes provide immediate access to this wealth of information: Research Firms Index, Geographic Index, Personnel Name Index and Subject Index.

"An important source for organizations in need of information about laboratories, individuals and other facilities." –ARBA

Softcover ISBN 978-1-59237-003-0, 1,400 pages, $465.00

International Business and Trade Directories

Completely updated, the Third Edition of *International Business and Trade Directories* now contains more than 10,000 entries, over 2,000 more than the last edition, making this directory the most comprehensive resource of the worlds business and trade directories. Entries include content descriptions, price, publisher's name and address, web site and e-mail addresses, phone and fax numbers and editorial staff. Organized by industry group, and then by region, this resource puts over 10,000 industry-specific business and trade directories at the reader's fingertips. Three indexes are included for quick access to information: Geographic Index, Publisher Index and Title Index. Public, college and corporate libraries, as well as individuals and corporations seeking critical market information will want to add this directory to their marketing collection.

"Reasonably priced for a work of this type, this directory should appeal to larger academic, public and corporate libraries with an international focus." –Library Journal

Softcover ISBN 978-1-930956-63-6, 1,800 pages, $225.00

TheStreet.com Ratings Guide to Health Insurers

TheStreet.com Ratings Guide to Health Insurers is the first and only source to cover the financial stability of the nation's health care system, rating the financial safety of more than 6,000 health insurance providers, health maintenance organizations (HMOs) and all of the Blue Cross Blue Shield plans – updated quarterly to ensure the most accurate information. The Guide also provides a complete listing of all the major health insurers, including all Long-Term Care and Medigap insurers. Our *Guide to Health Insurers* includes comprehensive, timely coverage on the financial stability of HMOs and health insurers; the most accurate insurance company ratings available–the same quality ratings heralded by the U.S. General Accounting Office; separate listings for those companies offering Medigap and long-term care policies; the number of serious consumer complaints filed against most HMOs so you can see who is actually providing the best (or worst) service and more. The easy-to-use layout gives you a one-line summary analysis for each company that we track, followed by an in-depth, detailed analysis of all HMOs and the largest health insurers. The guide also includes a list of TheStreet.com Ratings Recommended Companies with information on how to contact them, and the reasoning behind any rating upgrades or downgrades.

"With 20 years behind its insurance-advocacy research [the rating guide] continues to offer a wealth of information that helps consumers weigh their healthcare options now and in the future." -Today's Librarian

Issues published quarterly, Softcover, 550 pages, $499.00 for four quarterly issues, $249.00 for a single issue

TheStreet.com Ratings Guide to Life & Annuity Insurers

TheStreet.com Safety Ratings are the most reliable source for evaluating an insurer's financial solvency risk. Consequently, policy-holders have come to rely on TheStreet.com's flagship publication, *TheStreet.com Ratings Guide to Life & Annuity Insurers*, to help them identify the safest companies to do business with. Each easy-to-use edition delivers TheStreet.com's independent ratings and analyses on more than 1,100 insurers, updated every quarter. Plus, your patrons will find a complete list of TheStreet.com Recommended Companies, including contact information, and the reasoning behind any rating upgrades or downgrades. This guide is perfect for those who are considering the purchase of a life insurance policy, placing money in an annuity, or advising clients about insurance and annuities. A life or health insurance policy or annuity is only as secure as the insurance company issuing it. Therefore, make sure your patrons have what they need to periodically monitor the financial condition of the companies with whom they have an investment. The TheStreet.com Ratings product line is designed to help them in their evaluations.

"Weiss has an excellent reputation and this title is held by hundreds of libraries. This guide is recommended for public and academic libraries." -ARBA

Issues published quarterly, Softcover, 360 pages, $499.00 for four quarterly issues, $249.00 for a single issue

TheStreet.com Ratings Guide to Property & Casualty Insurers

TheStreet.com Ratings Guide to Property and Casualty Insurers provides the most extensive coverage of insurers writing policies, helping consumers and businesses avoid financial headaches. Updated quarterly, this easy-to-use publication delivers the independent, unbiased TheStreet.com Safety Ratings and supporting analyses on more than 2,800 U.S. insurance companies, offering auto & homeowners insurance, business insurance, worker's compensation insurance, product liability insurance, medical malpractice and other professional liability insurance. Each edition includes a list of TheStreet.com Recommended Companies by type of insurance, including a contact number, plus helpful information about the coverage provided by the State Guarantee Associations.

"In contrast to the other major insurance rating agencies...Weiss does not have a financial relationship worth the companies it rates. A GAO study found that Weiss identified financial vulnerability earlier than the other rating agencies." -ARBA

Issues published quarterly, Softcover, 455 pages, $499.00 for four quarterly issues, $249.00 for a single issue

TheStreet.com Ratings Consumer Box Set

Deliver the critical information your patrons need to safeguard their personal finances with *TheStreet.com Ratings' Consumer Guide Box Set*. Each of the eight guides is packed with accurate, unbiased information and recommendations to help your patrons make sound financial decisions. TheStreet.com Ratings Consumer Guide Box Set provides your patrons with easy to understand guidance on important personal finance topics, including: *Consumer Guide to Variable Annuities, Consumer Guide to Medicare Supplement Insurance, Consumer Guide to Elder Care Choices, Consumer Guide to Automobile Insurance, Consumer Guide to Long-Term Care Insurance, Consumer Guide to Homeowners Insurance, Consumer Guide to Term Life Insurance, and Consumer Guide to Medicare Prescription Drug Coverage*. Each guide provides an easy-to-read overview of the topic, what to look out for when selecting a company or insurance plan to do business with, who are the recommended companies to work with and how to navigate through these often-times difficult decisions. Custom worksheets and step-by-step directions make these resources accessible to all types of users. Packaged in a handy custom display box, these helpful guides will prove to be a much-used addition to any reference collection.

Issues published twice per year, Softcover, 600 pages, $499.00 for two biennial issues

TheStreet.com Ratings Guide to Stock Mutual Funds

TheStreet.com Ratings Guide to Stock Mutual Funds offers ratings and analyses on more than 8,800 equity mutual funds – more than any other publication. The exclusive TheStreet.com Investment Ratings combine an objective evaluation of each fund's performance and risk to provide a single, user-friendly, composite rating, giving your patrons a better handle on a mutual fund's risk-adjusted performance. Each edition identifies the top-performing mutual funds based on risk category, type of fund, and overall risk-adjusted performance. TheStreet.com's unique investment rating system makes it easy to see exactly which stocks are on the rise and which ones should be avoided. For those investors looking to tailor their mutual fund selections based on age, income, and tolerance for risk, we've also assigned two component ratings to each fund: a performance rating and a risk rating. With these, you can identify those funds that are best suited to meet your - or your client's – individual needs and goals. Plus, we include a handy Risk Profile Quiz to help you assess your personal tolerance for risk. So whether you're an investing novice or professional, the *Guide to Stock Mutual Funds* gives you everything you need to find a mutual fund that is right for you.

"There is tremendous need for information such as that provided by this Weiss publication. This reasonably priced guide is recommended for public and academic libraries serving investors." -ARBA

Issues published quarterly, Softcover, 655 pages, $499 for four quarterly issues, $249 for a single issue

TheStreet.com Ratings Guide to Exchange-Traded Funds

TheStreet.com Ratings editors analyze hundreds of mutual funds each quarter, condensing all of the available data into a single composite opinion of each fund's risk-adjusted performance. The intuitive, consumer-friendly ratings allow investors to instantly identify those funds that have historically done well and those that have under-performed the market. Each quarterly edition identifies the top-performing exchange-traded funds based on risk category, type of fund, and overall risk-adjusted performance. The rating scale, A through F, gives you a better handle on an exchange-traded fund's risk-adjusted performance. Other features include Top & Bottom 200 Exchange-Traded Funds; Performance and Risk: 100 Best and Worst Exchange- Traded Funds; Investor Profile Quiz; Performance Benchmarks and Fund Type Descriptions. With the growing popularity of mutual fund investing, consumers need a reliable source to help them track and evaluate the performance of their mutual fund holdings. Plus, they need a way of identifying and monitoring other funds as potential new investments. Unfortunately, the hundreds of performance and risk measures available, multiplied by the vast number of mutual fund investments on the market today, can make this a daunting task for even the most sophisticated investor. This Guide will serve as a useful tool for both the first-time and seasoned investor.

Editions published quarterly, Softcover, 440 pages, $499.00 for four quarterly issues, $249.00 for a single issue

TheStreet.com Ratings Guide to Bond & Money Market Mutual Funds

TheStreet.com Ratings Guide to Bond & Money Market Mutual Funds has everything your patrons need to easily identify the top-performing fixed income funds on the market today. Each quarterly edition contains TheStreet.com's independent ratings and analyses on more than 4,600 fixed income funds – more than any other publication, including corporate bond funds, high-yield bond funds, municipal bond funds, mortgage security funds, money market funds, global bond funds and government bond funds. In addition, the fund's risk rating is combined with its three-year performance rating to get an overall picture of the fund's risk-adjusted performance. The resulting TheStreet.com Investment Rating gives a single, user-friendly, objective evaluation that makes it easy to compare one fund to another and select the right fund based on the level of risk tolerance. Most investors think of fixed income mutual funds as "safe" investments. That's not always the case, however, depending on the credit risk, interest rate risk, and prepayment risk of the securities owned by the fund. TheStreet.com Ratings assesses each of these risks and assigns each fund a risk rating to help investors quickly evaluate the fund's risk component. Plus, we include a handy Risk Profile Quiz to help you assess your personal tolerance for risk. So whether you're an investing novice or professional, the *Guide to Bond and Money Market Mutual Funds* gives you everything you need to find a mutual fund that is right for you.

"Comprehensive... It is easy to use and consumer-oriented, and can be recommended for larger public and academic libraries." -ARBA

Issues published quarterly, Softcover, 470 pages, $499.00 for four quarterly issues, $249.00 for a single issue

TheStreet.com Ratings Guide to Banks & Thrifts

Updated quarterly, for the most up-to-date information, *TheStreet.com Ratings Guide to Banks and Thrifts* offers accurate, intuitive safety ratings your patrons can trust; supporting ratios and analyses that show an institution's strong & weak points; identification of the TheStreet.com Recommended Companies with branches in your area; a complete list of institutions receiving upgrades/downgrades; and comprehensive coverage of every bank and thrift in the nation – more than 9,000. TheStreet.com Safety Ratings are then based on the analysts' review of publicly available information collected by the federal banking regulators. The easy-to-use layout gives you: the institution's TheStreet.com Safety Rating for the last 3 years; the five key indexes used to evaluate each institution; along with the primary ratios and statistics used in determining the company's rating. *TheStreet.com Ratings Guide to Banks & Thrifts* will be a must for individuals who are concerned about the safety of their CD or savings account; need to be sure that an existing line of credit will be there when they need it; or simply want to avoid the hassles of dealing with a failing or troubled institution.

"Large public and academic libraries most definitely need to acquire the work. Likewise, special libraries in large corporations will find this title indispensable." -ARBA

Issues published quarterly, Softcover, 370 pages, $499.00 for four quarterly issues, $249.00 for a single issue

TheStreet.com Ratings Guide to Common Stocks

TheStreet.com Ratings Guide to Common Stocks gives your patrons reliable insight into the risk-adjusted performance of common stocks listed on the NYSE, AMEX, and Nasdaq – over 5,800 stocks in all – more than any other publication. TheStreet.com's unique investment rating system makes it easy to see exactly which stocks are on the rise and which ones should be avoided. In addition, your patrons also get supporting analysis showing growth trends, profitability, debt levels, valuation levels, the top-rated stocks within each industry, and more. Plus, each stock is ranked with the easy-to-use buy-hold-sell equivalents commonly used by Wall Street. Whether they're selecting their own investments or checking up on a broker's recommendation, TheStreet.com Ratings can help them in their evaluations.

"Users... will find the information succinct and the explanations readable, easy to understand, and helpful to a novice." -Library Journal

Issues published quarterly, Softcover, 440 pages, $499.00 for four quarterly issues, $249.00 for a single issue

TheStreet.com Ratings Ultimate Guided Tour of Stock Investing

This important reference guide from TheStreet.com Ratings is just what librarians around the country have asked for: a step-by-step introduction to stock investing for the beginning to intermediate investor. This easy-to-navigate guide explores the basics of stock investing and includes the intuitive TheStreet.com Investment Rating on more than 5,800 stocks, complete with real-world investing information that can be put to use immediately with stocks that fit the concepts discussed in the guide; informative charts, graphs and worksheets; easy-to-understand explanations on topics like P/E, compound interest, marked indices, diversifications, brokers, and much more; along with financial safety ratings for every stock on the NYSE, American Stock Exchange and the Nasdaq. This consumer-friendly guide offers complete how-to information on stock investing that can be put to use right away; a friendly format complete with our "Wise Guide" who leads the reader on a safari to learn about the investing jungle; helpful charts, graphs and simple worksheets; the intuitive TheStreet.com Investment rating on over 6,000 stocks — every stock found on the NYSE, American Stock Exchange and the NASDAQ; and much more.

"Provides investors with an alternative to stock broker recommendations, which recently have been tarnished by conflicts of interest. In summary, the guide serves as a welcome addition for all public library collections." -ARBA

Issues published quarterly, Softcover, 370 pages, $499.00 for four quarterly issues, $249.00 for a single issue

TheStreet.com Ratings' Reports & Services

- Ratings Online — An on-line summary covering an individual company's TheStreet.com Financial Strength Rating or an investment's unique TheStreet.com Investment Rating with the factors contributing to that rating; available 24 hours a day by visiting www.thestreet.com/tscratings or calling (800) 289-9222.
- Unlimited Ratings Research — The ultimate research tool providing fast, easy online access to the very latest TheStreet.com Financial Strength Ratings and Investment Ratings. Price: $559 per industry.

Contact TheStreet.com for more information about Reports & Services at www.thestreet.com/tscratings or call (800) 289-9222

TheStreet.com Ratings' Custom Reports

TheStreet.com Ratings is pleased to offer two customized options for receiving ratings data. Each taps into TheStreet.com's vast data repositories and is designed to provide exactly the data you need. Choose from a variety of industries, companies, data variables, and delivery formats including print, Excel, SQL, Text or Access.

- Customized Reports - get right to the heart of your company's research and data needs with a report customized to your specifications.
- Complete Database Download – TheStreet.com will design and deliver the database; from there you can sort it, recalculate it, and format your results to suit your specific needs.

Contact TheStreet.com for more information about Custom Reports at www.thestreet.com/tscratings or call (800) 289-9222

The Value of a Dollar 1600-1859, The Colonial Era to The Civil War

Following the format of the widely acclaimed, *The Value of a Dollar, 1860-2004, The Value of a Dollar 1600-1859, The Colonial Era to The Civil War* records the actual prices of thousands of items that consumers purchased from the Colonial Era to the Civil War. Our editorial department had been flooded with requests from users of our *Value of a Dollar* for the same type of information, just from an earlier time period. This new volume is just the answer – with pricing data from 1600 to 1859. Arranged into five-year chapters, each 5-year chapter includes a Historical Snapshot, Consumer Expenditures, Investments, Selected Income, Income/Standard Jobs, Food Basket, Standard Prices and Miscellany. There is also a section on Trends. This informative section charts the change in price over time and provides added detail on the reasons prices changed within the time period, including industry developments, changes in consumer attitudes and important historical facts. This fascinating survey will serve a wide range of research needs and will be useful in all high school, public and academic library reference collections.

"The Value of a Dollar: Colonial Era to the Civil War, 1600-1865 will find a happy audience among students, researchers, and general browsers. It offers a fascinating and detailed look at early American history from the viewpoint of everyday people trying to make ends meet. This title and the earlier publication, The Value of a Dollar, 1860-2004, complement each other very well, and readers will appreciate finding them side-by-side on the shelf." -Booklist

Hardcover ISBN 978-1-59237-094-8, 600 pages, $145.00 | Ebook ISBN 978-1-59237-169-3 www.gale.com/gvrl/partners/grey.htm

The Value of a Dollar 1860-2004, Third Edition

A guide to practical economy, *The Value of a Dollar* records the actual prices of thousands of items that consumers purchased from the Civil War to the present, along with facts about investment options and income opportunities. This brand new Third Edition boasts a brand new addition to each five-year chapter, a section on Trends. This informative section charts the change in price over time and provides added detail on the reasons prices changed within the time period, including industry developments, changes in consumer attitudes and important historical facts. Plus, a brand new chapter for 2000-2004 has been added. Each 5-year chapter includes a Historical Snapshot, Consumer Expenditures, Investments, Selected Income, Income/Standard Jobs, Food Basket, Standard Prices and Miscellany. This interesting and useful publication will be widely used in any reference collection.

"Business historians, reporters, writers and students will find this source... very helpful for historical research. Libraries will want to purchase it." –ARBA

Hardcover ISBN 978-1-59237-074-0, 600 pages, $145.00 | Ebook ISBN 978-1-59237-173-0 www.gale.com/gvrl/partners/grey.htm

Working Americans 1880-1999
Volume I: The Working Class, Volume II: The Middle Class, Volume III: The Upper Class

Each of the volumes in the *Working Americans* series focuses on a particular class of Americans, The Working Class, The Middle Class and The Upper Class over the last 120 years. Chapters in each volume focus on one decade and profile three to five families. Family Profiles include real data on Income & Job Descriptions, Selected Prices of the Times, Annual Income, Annual Budgets, Family Finances, Life at Work, Life at Home, Life in the Community, Working Conditions, Cost of Living, Amusements and much more. Each chapter also contains an Economic Profile with Average Wages of other Professions, a selection of Typical Pricing, Key Events & Inventions, News Profiles, Articles from Local Media and Illustrations. The *Working Americans* series captures the lifestyles of each of the classes from the last twelve decades, covers a vast array of occupations and ethnic backgrounds and travels the entire nation. These interesting and useful compilations of portraits of the American Working, Middle and Upper Classes during the last 120 years will be an important addition to any high school, public or academic library reference collection.

"These interesting, unique compilations of economic and social facts, figures and graphs will support multiple research needs. They will engage and enlighten patrons in high school, public and academic library collections." –Booklist

Volume I: The Working Class Hardcover ISBN 978-1-891482-81-6, 558 pages, $145.00 | Volume II: The Middle Class Hardcover ISBN 978-1-891482-72-4, 591 pages, $145.00 | Volume III: The Upper Class Hardcover ISBN 978-1-930956-38-4, 567 pages, $145.00 | Ebooks www.gale.com/gvrl/partners/grey.htm

Working Americans 1880-1999 Volume IV: Their Children

This Fourth Volume in the highly successful *Working Americans* series focuses on American children, decade by decade from 1880 to 1999. This interesting and useful volume introduces the reader to three children in each decade, one from each of the Working, Middle and Upper classes. Like the first three volumes in the series, the individual profiles are created from interviews, diaries, statistical studies, biographies and news reports. Profiles cover a broad range of ethnic backgrounds, geographic area and lifestyles – everything from an orphan in Memphis in 1882, following the Yellow Fever epidemic of 1878 to an eleven-year-old nephew of a beer baron and owner of the New York Yankees in New York City in 1921. Chapters also contain important supplementary materials including News Features as well as information on everything from Schools to Parks, Infectious Diseases to Childhood Fears along with Entertainment, Family Life and much more to provide an informative overview of the lifestyles of children from each decade. This interesting account of what life was like for Children in the Working, Middle and Upper Classes will be a welcome addition to the reference collection of any high school, public or academic library.

Hardcover ISBN 978-1-930956-35-3, 600 pages, $145.00 | Ebook ISBN 978-1-59237-166-2 www.gale.com/gvrl/partners/grey.htm

Working Americans 1880-2003 Volume V: Americans At War

Working Americans 1880-2003 Volume V: Americans At War is divided into 11 chapters, each covering a decade from 1880-2003 and examines the lives of Americans during the time of war, including declared conflicts, one-time military actions, protests, and preparations for war. Each decade includes several personal profiles, whether on the battlefield or on the homefront, that tell the stories of civilians, soldiers, and officers during the decade. The profiles examine: Life at Home; Life at Work; and Life in the Community. Each decade also includes an Economic Profile with statistical comparisons, a Historical Snapshot, News Profiles, local News Articles, and Illustrations that provide a solid historical background to the decade being examined. Profiles range widely not only geographically, but also emotionally, from that of a girl whose leg was torn off in a blast during WWI, to the boredom of being stationed in the Dakotas as the Indian Wars were drawing to a close. As in previous volumes of the *Working Americans* series, information is presented in narrative form, but hard facts and real-life situations back up each story. The basis of the profiles come from diaries, private print books, personal interviews, family histories, estate documents and magazine articles. For easy reference, *Working Americans 1880-2003 Volume V: Americans At War* includes an in-depth Subject Index. The Working Americans series has become an important reference for public libraries, academic libraries and high school libraries. This fifth volume will be a welcome addition to all of these types of reference collections.

Hardcover ISBN 978-1-59237-024-5, 600 pages, $145.00 | Ebook ISBN 978-1-59237-167-9 www.gale.com/gvrl/partners/grey.htm

Working Americans 1880-2005 Volume VI: Women at Work

Unlike any other volume in the *Working Americans* series, this Sixth Volume, is the first to focus on a particular gender of Americans. *Volume VI: Women at Work*, traces what life was like for working women from the 1860's to the present time. Beginning with the life of a maid in 1890 and a store clerk in 1900 and ending with the life and times of the modern working women, this text captures the struggle, strengths and changing perception of the American woman at work. Each chapter focuses on one decade and profiles three to five women with real data on Income & Job Descriptions, Selected Prices of the Times, Annual Income, Annual Budgets, Family Finances, Life at Work, Life at Home, Life in the Community, Working Conditions, Cost of Living, Amusements and much more. For even broader access to the events, economics and attitude towards women throughout the past 130 years, each chapter is supplemented with News Profiles, Articles from Local Media, Illustrations, Economic Profiles, Typical Pricing, Key Events, Inventions and more. This important volume illustrates what life was like for working women over time and allows the reader to develop an understanding of the changing role of women at work. These interesting and useful compilations of portraits of women at work will be an important addition to any high school, public or academic library reference collection.

Hardcover ISBN 978-1-59237-063-4, 600 pages, $145.00 | Ebook ISBN 978-1-59237-168-6 www.gale.com/gvrl/partners/grey.htm

Working Americans 1880-2005 Volume VII: Social Movements

Working Americans series, Volume VII: Social Movements explores how Americans sought and fought for change from the 1880s to the present time. Following the format of previous volumes in the Working Americans series, the text examines the lives of 34 individuals who have worked -- often behind the scenes --- to bring about change. Issues include topics as diverse as the Anti-smoking movement of 1901 to efforts by Native Americans to reassert their long lost rights. Along the way, the book will profile individuals brave enough to demand suffrage for Kansas women in 1912 or demand an end to lynching during a March on Washington in 1923. Each profile is enriched with real data on Income & Job Descriptions, Selected Prices of the Times, Annual Incomes & Budgets, Life at Work, Life at Home, Life in the Community, along with News Features, Key Events, and Illustrations. The depth of information contained in each profile allow the user to explore the private, financial and public lives of these subjects, deepening our understanding of how calls for change took place in our society. A must-purchase for the reference collections of high school libraries, public libraries and academic libraries.

Hardcover ISBN 978-1-59237-101-3, 600 pages, $145.00 | Ebook ISBN 978-1-59237-174-7 www.gale.com/gvrl/partners/grey.htm

Working Americans 1880-2005 Volume VIII: Immigrants

Working Americans 1880-2007 Volume VIII: Immigrants illustrates what life was like for families leaving their homeland and creating a new life in the United States. Each chapter covers one decade and introduces the reader to three immigrant families. Family profiles cover what life was like in their homeland, in their community in the United States, their home life, working conditions and so much more. As the reader moves through these pages, the families and individuals come to life, painting a picture of why they left their homeland, their experiences in setting roots in a new country, their struggles and triumphs, stretching from the 1800s to the present time. Profiles include a seven-year-old Swedish girl who meets her father for the first time at Ellis Island; a Chinese photographer's assistant; an Armenian who flees the genocide of his country to build Ford automobiles in Detroit; a 38-year-old German bachelor cigar maker who settles in Newark NJ, but contemplates tobacco farming in Virginia; a 19-year-old Irish domestic servant who is amazed at the easy life of American dogs; a 19-year-old Filipino who came to Hawaii against his parent's wishes to farm sugar cane; a French-Canadian who finds success as a boxer in Maine and many more. As in previous volumes, information is presented in narrative form, but hard facts and real-life situations back up each story. With the topic of immigration being so hotly debated in this country, this timely resource will prove to be a useful source for students, researchers, historians and library patrons to discover the issues facing immigrants in the United States. This title will be a useful addition to reference collections of public libraries, university libraries and high schools.

Hardcover ISBN 978-1-59237-197-6, 600 pages, $145.00 | Ebook ISBN 978-1-59237-232-4 www.gale.com/gvrl/partners/grey.htm

The Encyclopedia of Warrior Peoples & Fighting Groups

Many military groups throughout the world have excelled in their craft either by fortuitous circumstances, outstanding leadership, or intense training. This new second edition of *The Encyclopedia of Warrior Peoples and Fighting Groups* explores the origins and leadership of these outstanding combat forces, chronicles their conquests and accomplishments, examines the circumstances surrounding their decline or disbanding, and assesses their influence on the groups and methods of warfare that followed. Readers will encounter ferocious tribes, charismatic leaders, and daring militias, from ancient times to the present, including Amazons, Buffalo Soldiers, Green Berets, Iron Brigade, Kamikazes, Peoples of the Sea, Polish Winged Hussars, Teutonic Knights, and Texas Rangers. With over 100 alphabetical entries, numerous cross-references and illustrations, a comprehensive bibliography, and index, the *Encyclopedia of Warrior Peoples and Fighting Groups* is a valuable resource for readers seeking insight into the bold history of distinguished fighting forces.

"Especially useful for high school students, undergraduates, and general readers with an interest in military history." –Library Journal

Hardcover ISBN 978-1-59237-116-7, 660 pages, $135.00 | Ebook ISBN 978-1-59237-172-3 www.gale.com/gvrl/partners/grey.htm

The Encyclopedia of Invasions & Conquests, From the Ancient Times to the Present

This second edition of the popular *Encyclopedia of Invasions & Conquests*, a comprehensive guide to over 150 invasions, conquests, battles and occupations from ancient times to the present, takes readers on a journey that includes the Roman conquest of Britain, the Portuguese colonization of Brazil, and the Iraqi invasion of Kuwait, to name a few. New articles will explore the late 20th and 21st centuries, with a specific focus on recent conflicts in Afghanistan, Kuwait, Iraq, Yugoslavia, Grenada and Chechnya. In addition to covering the military aspects of invasions and conquests, entries cover some of the political, economic, and cultural aspects, for example, the effects of a conquest on the invade country's political and monetary system and in its language and religion. The entries on leaders – among them Sargon, Alexander the Great, William the Conqueror, and Adolf Hitler – deal with the people who sought to gain control, expand power, or exert religious or political influence over others through military means. Revised and updated for this second edition, entries are arranged alphabetically within historical periods. Each chapter provides a map to help readers locate key areas and geographical features, and bibliographical references appear at the end of each entry. Other useful features include cross-references, a cumulative bibliography and a comprehensive subject index. This authoritative, well-organized, lucidly written volume will prove invaluable for a variety of readers, including high school students, military historians, members of the armed forces, history buffs and hobbyists.

"Engaging writing, sensible organization, nice illustrations, interesting and obscure facts, and useful maps make this book a pleasure to read." –ARBA

Hardcover ISBN 978-1-59237-114-3, 598 pages, $135.00 | Ebook ISBN 978-1-59237-171-6 www.gale.com/gvrl/partners/grey.htm

Encyclopedia of Prisoners of War & Internment

This authoritative second edition provides a valuable overview of the history of prisoners of war and interned civilians, from earliest times to the present. Written by an international team of experts in the field of POW studies, this fascinating and thought-provoking volume includes entries on a wide range of subjects including the Crusades, Plains Indian Warfare, concentration camps, the two world wars, and famous POWs throughout history, as well as atrocities, escapes, and much more. Written in a clear and easily understandable style, this informative reference details over 350 entries, 30% larger than the first edition, that survey the history of prisoners of war and interned civilians from the earliest times to the present, with emphasis on the 19th and 20th centuries. Medical conditions, international law, exchanges of prisoners, organizations working on behalf of POWs, and trials associated with the treatment of captives are just some of the themes explored. Entries are arranged alphabetically, plus illustrations and maps are provided for easy reference. The text also includes an introduction, bibliography, appendix of selected documents, and end-of-entry reading suggestions. This one-of-a-kind reference will be a helpful addition to the reference collections of all public libraries, high schools, and university libraries and will prove invaluable to historians and military enthusiasts.

"Thorough and detailed yet accessible to the lay reader. Of special interest to subject specialists and historians; recommended for public and academic libraries." - Library Journal

Hardcover ISBN 978-1-59237-120-4, 676 pages, $135.00 | Ebook ISBN 978-1-59237-170-9 www.gale.com/gvrl/partners/grey.htm

The Encyclopedia of Rural America: the Land & People

History, sociology, anthropology, and public policy are combined to deliver the encyclopedia destined to become the standard reference work in American rural studies. From irrigation and marriage to games and mental health, this encyclopedia is the first to explore the contemporary landscape of rural America, placed in historical perspective. With over 300 articles prepared by leading experts from across the nation, this timely encyclopedia documents and explains the major themes, concepts, industries, concerns, and everyday life of the people and land who make up rural America. Entries range from the industrial sector and government policy to arts and humanities and social and family concerns. Articles explore every aspect of life in rural America. *Encyclopedia of Rural America*, with its broad range of coverage, will appeal to high school and college students as well as graduate students, faculty, scholars, and people whose work pertains to rural areas.

"This exemplary encyclopedia is guaranteed to educate our highly urban society about the uniqueness of rural America. Recommended for public and academic libraries." -Library Journal

Two Volumes, Hardcover, ISBN 978-1-59237-115-0, 800 pages, $250.00

The Religious Right, A Reference Handbook

Timely and unbiased, this third edition updates and expands its examination of the religious right and its influence on our government, citizens, society, and politics. From the fight to outlaw the teaching of Darwin's theory of evolution to the struggle to outlaw abortion, the religious right is continually exerting an influence on public policy. This text explores the influence of religion on legislation and society, while examining the alignment of the religious right with the political right. A historical survey of the movement highlights the shift to "hands-on" approach to politics and the struggle to present a unified front. The coverage offers a critical historical survey of the religious right movement, focusing on its increased involvement in the political arena, attempts to forge coalitions, and notable successes and failures. The text offers complete coverage of biographies of the men and women who have advanced the cause and an up to date chronology illuminate the movement's goals, including their accomplishments and failures. This edition offers an extensive update to all sections along with several brand new entries. Two new sections complement this third edition, a chapter on legal issues and court decisions and a chapter on demographic statistics and electoral patterns. To aid in further research, *The Religious Right*, offers an entire section of annotated listings of print and non-print resources, as well as of organizations affiliated with the religious right, and those opposing it. Comprehensive in its scope, this work offers easy-to-read, pertinent information for those seeking to understand the religious right and its evolving role in American society. A must for libraries of all sizes, university religion departments, activists, high schools and for those interested in the evolving role of the religious right.

" Recommended for all public and academic libraries." - Library Journal

Hardcover ISBN 978-1-59237-113-6, 600 pages, $135.00 | Ebook ISBN 978-1-59237-226-3 www.gale.com/gvrl/partners/grey.htm

From Suffrage to the Senate, America's Political Women

From Suffrage to the Senate is a comprehensive and valuable compendium of biographies of leading women in U.S. politics, past and present, and an examination of the wide range of women's movements. Up to date through 2006, this dynamically illustrated reference work explores American women's path to political power and social equality from the struggle for the right to vote and the abolition of slavery to the first African American woman in the U.S. Senate and beyond. This new edition includes over 150 new entries and a brand new section on trends and demographics of women in politics. The in-depth coverage also traces the political heritage of the abolition, labor, suffrage, temperance, and reproductive rights movements. The alphabetically arranged entries include biographies of every woman from across the political spectrum who has served in the U.S. House and Senate, along with women in the Judiciary and the U.S. Cabinet and, new to this edition, biographies of activists and political consultants. Bibliographical references follow each entry. For easy reference, a handy chronology is provided detailing 150 years of women's history. This up-to-date reference will be a must-purchase for women's studies departments, high schools and public libraries and will be a handy resource for those researching the key players in women's politics, past and present.

"An engaging tool that would be useful in high school, public, and academic libraries looking for an overview of the political history of women in the US." –Booklist

Two Volumes, Hardcover ISBN 978-1-59237-117-4, 1,160 pages, $195.00 | Ebook ISBN 978-1-59237-227-0
www.gale.com/gvrl/partners/grey.htm

An African Biographical Dictionary

This landmark second edition is the only biographical dictionary to bring together, in one volume, cultural, social and political leaders – both historical and contemporary – of the sub-Saharan region. Over 800 biographical sketches of prominent Africans, as well as foreigners who have affected the continent's history, are featured, 150 more than the previous edition. The wide spectrum of leaders includes religious figures, writers, politicians, scientists, entertainers, sports personalities and more. Access to these fascinating individuals is provided in a user-friendly format. The biographies are arranged alphabetically, cross-referenced and indexed. Entries include the country or countries in which the person was significant and the commonly accepted dates of birth and death. Each biographical sketch is chronologically written; entries for cultural personalities add an evaluation of their work. This information is followed by a selection of references often found in university and public libraries, including autobiographies and principal biographical works. Appendixes list each individual by country and by field of accomplishment – rulers, musicians, explorers, missionaries, businessmen, physicists – nearly thirty categories in all. Another convenient appendix lists heads of state since independence by country. Up-to-date and representative of African societies as a whole, An African Biographical Dictionary provides a wealth of vital information for students of African culture and is an indispensable reference guide for anyone interested in African affairs.

"An unquestionable convenience to have these concise, informative biographies gathered into one source, indexed, and analyzed by appendixes listing entrants by nation and occupational field." –Wilson Library Bulletin

Hardcover ISBN 978-1-59237-112-9, 667 pages, $135.00 | Ebook ISBN 978-1-59237-229-4 www.gale.com/gvrl/partners/grey.htm

American Environmental Leaders, From Colonial Times to the Present

A comprehensive and diverse award winning collection of biographies of the most important figures in American environmentalism. Few subjects arouse the passions the way the environment does. How will we feed an ever-increasing population and how can that food be made safe for consumption? Who decides how land is developed? How can environmental policies be made fair for everyone, including multiethnic groups, women, children, and the poor? *American Environmental Leaders* presents more than 350 biographies of men and women who have devoted their lives to studying, debating, and organizing these and other controversial issues over the last 200 years. In addition to the scientists who have analyzed how human actions affect nature, we are introduced to poets, landscape architects, presidents, painters, activists, even sanitation engineers, and others who have forever altered how we think about the environment. The easy to use A–Z format provides instant access to these fascinating individuals, and frequent cross references indicate others with whom individuals worked (and sometimes clashed). End of entry references provide users with a starting point for further research.

"Highly recommended for high school, academic, and public libraries needing environmental biographical information." –Library Journal/Starred Review

Two Volumes, Hardcover ISBN 978-1-59237-119-8, 900 pages $195.00 | Ebook ISBN 978-1-59237-230-0
www.gale.com/gvrl/partners/grey.htm

World Cultural Leaders of the Twentieth & Twenty-First Centuries

World Cultural Leaders of the Twentieth & Twenty-First Centuries is a window into the arts, performances, movements, and music that shaped the world's cultural development since 1900. A remarkable around-the-world look at one-hundred-plus years of cultural development through the eyes of those that set the stage and stayed to play. This second edition offers over 120 new biographies along with a complete update of existing biographies. To further aid the reader, a handy fold-out timeline traces important events in all six cultural categories from 1900 through the present time. Plus, a new section of detailed material and resources for 100 selected individuals is also new to this edition, with further data on museums, homesteads, websites, artwork and more. This remarkable compilation will answer a wide range of questions. Who was the originator of the term "documentary"? Which poet married the daughter of the famed novelist Thomas Mann in order to help her escape Nazi Germany? Which British writer served as an agent in Russia against the Bolsheviks before the 1917 revolution? A handy two-volume set that makes it easy to look up 450 worldwide cultural icons: novelists, poets, playwrights, painters, sculptors, architects, dancers, choreographers, actors, directors, filmmakers, singers, composers, and musicians. *World Cultural Leaders of the Twentieth & Twenty-First Centuries* provides entries (many of them illustrated) covering the person's works, achievements, and professional career in a thorough essay and offers interesting facts and statistics. Entries are fully cross-referenced so that readers can learn how various individuals influenced others. An index of leaders by occupation, a useful glossary and a thorough general index complete the coverage. This remarkable resource will be an important acquisition for the reference collections of public libraries, university libraries and high schools.

"Fills a need for handy, concise information on a wide array of international cultural figures."-ARBA

Two Volumes, Hardcover ISBN 978-1-59237-118-1, 900 pages, $195.00 | Ebook ISBN 978-1-59237-231-7
www.gale.com/gvrl/partners/grey.htm

Political Corruption in America: An Encyclopedia of Scandals, Power, and Greed

The complete scandal-filled history of American political corruption, focusing on the infamous people and cases, as well as society's electoral and judicial reactions. Since colonial times, there has been no shortage of politicians willing to take a bribe, skirt campaign finance laws, or act in their own interests. Corruption like the Whiskey Ring, Watergate, and Whitewater cases dominate American life, making political scandal a leading U.S. industry. From judges to senators, presidents to mayors, *Political Corruption in America* discusses the infamous people throughout history who have been accused of and implicated in crooked behavior. In this new second edition, more than 250 A–Z entries explore the people, crimes, investigations, and court cases behind 200 years of American political scandals. This unbiased volume also delves into the issues surrounding Koreagate, the Chinese campaign scandal, and other ethical lapses. Relevant statutes and terms, including the Independent Counsel Statute and impeachment as a tool of political punishment, are examined as well. Students, scholars, and other readers interested in American history, political science, and ethics will appreciate this survey of a wide range of corrupting influences. This title focuses on how politicians from all parties have fallen because of their greed and hubris, and how society has used electoral and judicial means against those who tested the accepted standards of political conduct. A full range of illustrations including political cartoons, photos of key figures such as Abe Fortas and Archibald Cox, graphs of presidential pardons, and tables showing the number of expulsions and censures in both the House and Senate round out the text. In addition, a comprehensive chronology of major political scandals in U.S. history from colonial times until the present. For further reading, an extensive bibliography lists sources including archival letters, newspapers, and private manuscript collections from the United States and Great Britain. With its comprehensive coverage of this interesting topic, *Political Corruption in America: An Encyclopedia of Scandals, Power, and Greed* will prove to be a useful addition to the reference collections of all public libraries, university libraries, history collections, political science collections and high schools.

"...this encyclopedia is a useful contribution to the field. Highly recommended." - CHOICE
"Political Corruption should be useful in most academic, high school, and public libraries." Booklist

Two Volumes, Hardcover ISBN 978-1-59237-297-3, 500 pages, $195.00

Religion and Law: A Dictionary

This informative, easy-to-use reference work covers a wide range of legal issues that affect the roles of religion and law in American society. Extensive A–Z entries provide coverage of key court decisions, case studies, concepts, individuals, religious groups, organizations, and agencies shaping religion and law in today's society. This *Dictionary* focuses on topics involved with the constitutional theory and interpretation of religion and the law; terms providing a historical explanation of the ways in which America's ever increasing ethnic and religious diversity contributed to our current understanding of the mandates of the First and Fourteenth Amendments; terms and concepts describing the development of religion clause jurisprudence; an analytical examination of the distinct vocabulary used in this area of the law; the means by which American courts have attempted to balance religious liberty against other important individual and social interests in a wide variety of physical and regulatory environments, including the classroom, the workplace, the courtroom, religious group organization and structure, taxation, the clash of "secular" and "religious" values, and the relationship of the generalized idea of individual autonomy of the specific concept of religious liberty. Important legislation and legal cases affecting religion and society are thoroughly covered in this timely volume, including a detailed Table of Cases and Table of Statutes for more detailed research. A guide to further reading and an index are also included. This useful resource will be an important acquisition for the reference collections of all public libraries, university libraries, religion reference collections and high schools.

Hardcover ISBN 978-1-59237-298-0, 500 pages, $135.00

Human Rights in the United States: A Dictionary and Documents

This two volume set offers easy to grasp explanations of the basic concepts, laws, and case law in the field, with emphasis on human rights in the historical, political, and legal experience of the United States. Human rights is a term not fully understood by many Americans. Addressing this gap, the new second edition of *Human Rights in the United States: A Dictionary and Documents* offers a comprehensive introduction that places the history of human rights in the United States in an international context. It surveys the legal protection of human dignity in the United States, examines the sources of human rights norms, cites key legal cases, explains the role of international governmental and non-governmental organizations, and charts global, regional, and U.N. human rights measures. Over 240 dictionary entries of human rights terms are detailed—ranging from asylum and cultural relativism to hate crimes and torture. Each entry discusses the significance of the term, gives examples, and cites appropriate documents and court decisions. In addition, a Documents section is provided that contains 59 conventions, treaties, and protocols related to the most up to date international action on ethnic cleansing; freedom of expression and religion; violence against women; and much more. A bibliography, extensive glossary, and comprehensive index round out this indispensable volume. This comprehensive, timely volume is a must for large public libraries, university libraries and social science departments, along with high school libraries.

"...invaluable for anyone interested in human rights issues ... highly recommended for all reference collections."
- American Reference Books Annual

Two Volumes, Hardcover ISBN 978-1-59237-290-4, 750 pages, $225.00

The Comparative Guide to American Elementary & Secondary Schools, 2008

The only guide of its kind, this award winning compilation offers a snapshot profile of every public school district in the United States serving 1,500 or more students – more than 5,900 districts are covered. Organized alphabetically by district within state, each chapter begins with a Statistical Overview of the state. Each district listing includes contact information (name, address, phone number and web site) plus Grades Served, the Numbers of Students and Teachers and the Number of Regular, Special Education, Alternative and Vocational Schools in the district along with statistics on Student/Classroom Teacher Ratios, Drop Out Rates, Ethnicity, the Numbers of Librarians and Guidance Counselors and District Expenditures per student. As an added bonus, *The Comparative Guide to American Elementary and Secondary Schools* provides important ranking tables, both by state and nationally, for each data element. For easy navigation through this wealth of information, this handbook contains a useful City Index that lists all districts that operate schools within a city. These important comparative statistics are necessary for anyone considering relocation or doing comparative research on their own district and would be a perfect acquisition for any public library or school district library.

"This straightforward guide is an easy way to find general information. Valuable for academic and large public library collections." –ARBA

Softcover ISBN 978-1-59237-223-2, 2,400 pages, $125.00 | Ebook ISBN 978-1-59237-238-6 www.gale.com/gvrl/partners/grey.htm

The Complete Learning Disabilities Directory, 2008

The Complete Learning Disabilities Directory is the most comprehensive database of Programs, Services, Curriculum Materials, Professional Meetings & Resources, Camps, Newsletters and Support Groups for teachers, students and families concerned with learning disabilities. This information-packed directory includes information about Associations & Organizations, Schools, Colleges & Testing Materials, Government Agencies, Legal Resources and much more. For quick, easy access to information, this directory contains four indexes: Entry Name Index, Subject Index and Geographic Index. With every passing year, the field of learning disabilities attracts more attention and the network of caring, committed and knowledgeable professionals grows every day. This directory is an invaluable research tool for these parents, students and professionals.

"Due to its wealth and depth of coverage, parents, teachers and others... should find this an invaluable resource." -Booklist

Softcover ISBN 978-1-59237-207-2, 900 pages, $145.00 | Online Database $195.00 | Online Database & Directory Combo $280.00

Educators Resource Directory, 2007/08

Educators Resource Directory is a comprehensive resource that provides the educational professional with thousands of resources and statistical data for professional development. This directory saves hours of research time by providing immediate access to Associations & Organizations, Conferences & Trade Shows, Educational Research Centers, Employment Opportunities & Teaching Abroad, School Library Services, Scholarships, Financial Resources, Professional Consultants, Computer Software & Testing Resources and much more. Plus, this comprehensive directory also includes a section on Statistics and Rankings with over 100 tables, including statistics on Average Teacher Salaries, SAT/ACT scores, Revenues & Expenditures and more. These important statistics will allow the user to see how their school rates among others, make relocation decisions and so much more. For quick access to information, this directory contains four indexes: Entry & Publisher Index, Geographic Index, a Subject & Grade Index and Web Sites Index. *Educators Resource Directory* will be a well-used addition to the reference collection of any school district, education department or public library.

"Recommended for all collections that serve elementary and secondary school professionals." –Choice

Softcover ISBN 978-1-59237-179-2, 800 pages, $145.00 | Online Database $195.00 | Online Database & Directory Combo $280.00

Profiles of New York | Profiles of Florida | Profiles of Texas | Profiles of Illinois | Profiles of Michigan | Profiles of Ohio | Profiles of New Jersey | Profiles of Massachusetts | Profiles of Pennsylvania | Profiles of Wisconsin | Profiles of Connecticut & Rhode Island | Profiles of Indiana | Profiles of North Carolina & South Carolina | Profiles of Virginia | Profiles of California

The careful layout gives the user an easy-to-read snapshot of every single place and county in the state, from the biggest metropolis to the smallest unincorporated hamlet. The richness of each place or county profile is astounding in its depth, from history to weather, all packed in an easy-to-navigate, compact format. Each profile contains data on History, Geography, Climate, Population, Vital Statistics, Economy, Income, Taxes, Education, Housing, Health & Environment, Public Safety, Newspapers, Transportation, Presidential Election Results, Information Contacts and Chambers of Commerce. As an added bonus, there is a section on Selected Statistics, where data from the 100 largest towns and cities is arranged into easy-to-use charts. Each of 22 different data points has its own two-page spread with the cities listed in alpha order so researchers can easily compare and rank cities. A remarkable compilation that offers overviews and insights into each corner of the state, each volume goes beyond Census statistics, beyond metro area coverage, beyond the 100 best places to live. Drawn from official census information, other government statistics and original research, you will have at your fingertips data that's available nowhere else in one single source.

"The publisher claims that this is the 'most comprehensive portrait of the state of Florida ever published,' and this reviewer is inclined to believe it...Recommended. All levels." –Choice on Profiles of Florida

Each Profiles of... title ranges from 400-800 pages, priced at $149.00 each

America's Top-Rated Cities, 2008

America's Top-Rated Cities provides current, comprehensive statistical information and other essential data in one easy-to-use source on the 100 "top" cities that have been cited as the best for business and living in the U.S. This handbook allows readers to see, at a glance, a concise social, business, economic, demographic and environmental profile of each city, including brief evaluative comments. In addition to detailed data on Cost of Living, Finances, Real Estate, Education, Major Employers, Media, Crime and Climate, city reports now include Housing Vacancies, Tax Audits, Bankruptcy, Presidential Election Results and more. This outstanding source of information will be widely used in any reference collection.

"The only source of its kind that brings together all of this information into one easy-to-use source. It will be beneficial to many business and public libraries." –ARBA

Four Volumes, Softcover ISBN 978-1-59237-349-9, 2,500 pages, $195.00 | Ebook ISBN 978-1-59237-233-1
www.gale.com/gvrl/partners/grey.htm

America's Top-Rated Smaller Cities, 2008/09

A perfect companion to *America's Top-Rated Cities*, *America's Top-Rated Smaller Cities* provides current, comprehensive business and living profiles of smaller cities (population 25,000-99,999) that have been cited as the best for business and living in the United States. Sixty cities make up this 2004 edition of America's Top-Rated Smaller Cities, all are top-ranked by Population Growth, Median Income, Unemployment Rate and Crime Rate. City reports reflect the most current data available on a wide-range of statistics, including Employment & Earnings, Household Income, Unemployment Rate, Population Characteristics, Taxes, Cost of Living, Education, Health Care, Public Safety, Recreation, Media, Air & Water Quality and much more. Plus, each city report contains a Background of the City, and an Overview of the State Finances. *America's Top-Rated Smaller Cities* offers a reliable, one-stop source for statistical data that, before now, could only be found scattered in hundreds of sources. This volume is designed for a wide range of readers: individuals considering relocating a residence or business; professionals considering expanding their business or changing careers; general and market researchers; real estate consultants; human resource personnel; urban planners and investors.

"Provides current, comprehensive statistical information in one easy-to-use source... Recommended for public and academic libraries and specialized collections." –Library Journal

Two Volumes, Softcover ISBN 978-1-59237-284-3, 1,100 pages, $195.00 | Ebook ISBN 978-1-59237-234-8
www.gale.com/gvrl/partners/grey.htm

Profiles of America: Facts, Figures & Statistics for Every Populated Place in the United States

Profiles of America is the only source that pulls together, in one place, statistical, historical and descriptive information about every place in the United States in an easy-to-use format. This award winning reference set, now in its second edition, compiles statistics and data from over 20 different sources – the latest census information has been included along with more than nine brand new statistical topics. This Four-Volume Set details over 40,000 places, from the biggest metropolis to the smallest unincorporated hamlet, and provides statistical details and information on over 50 different topics including Geography, Climate, Population, Vital Statistics, Economy, Income, Taxes, Education, Housing, Health & Environment, Public Safety, Newspapers, Transportation, Presidential Election Results and Information Contacts or Chambers of Commerce. Profiles are arranged, for ease-of-use, by state and then by county. Each county begins with a County-Wide Overview and is followed by information for each Community in that particular county. The Community Profiles within the county are arranged alphabetically. *Profiles of America* is a virtual snapshot of America at your fingertips and a unique compilation of information that will be widely used in any reference collection.

A Library Journal Best Reference Book "An outstanding compilation." –Library Journal

Four Volumes, Softcover ISBN 978-1-891482-80-9, 10,000 pages, $595.00

The Comparative Guide to American Suburbs, 2007/08

The Comparative Guide to American Suburbs is a one-stop source for Statistics on the 2,000+ suburban communities surrounding the 50 largest metropolitan areas – their population characteristics, income levels, economy, school system and important data on how they compare to one another. Organized into 50 Metropolitan Area chapters, each chapter contains an overview of the Metropolitan Area, a detailed Map followed by a comprehensive Statistical Profile of each Suburban Community, including Contact Information, Physical Characteristics, Population Characteristics, Income, Economy, Unemployment Rate, Cost of Living, Education, Chambers of Commerce and more. Next, statistical data is sorted into Ranking Tables that rank the suburbs by twenty different criteria, including Population, Per Capita Income, Unemployment Rate, Crime Rate, Cost of Living and more. *The Comparative Guide to American Suburbs* is the best source for locating data on suburbs. Those looking to relocate, as well as those doing preliminary market research, will find this an invaluable timesaving resource.

"Public and academic libraries will find this compilation useful...The work draws together figures from many sources and will be especially helpful for job relocation decisions." – Booklist

Softcover ISBN 978-1-59237-180-8, 1,700 pages, $130.00 | Ebook ISBN 978-1-59237-235-5 www.gale.com/gvrl/partners/grey.htm

The American Tally: Statistics & Comparative Rankings for U.S. Cities with Populations over 10,000

This important statistical handbook compiles, all in one place, comparative statistics on all U.S. cities and towns with a 10,000+ population. *The American Tally* provides statistical details on over 4,000 cities and towns and profiles how they compare with one another in Population Characteristics, Education, Language & Immigration, Income & Employment and Housing. Each section begins with an alphabetical listing of cities by state, allowing for quick access to both the statistics and relative rankings of any city. Next, the highest and lowest cities are listed in each statistic. These important, informative lists provide quick reference to which cities are at both extremes of the spectrum for each statistic. Unlike any other reference, *The American Tally* provides quick, easy access to comparative statistics – a must-have for any reference collection.

"A solid library reference." -Bookwatch

Softcover ISBN 978-1-930956-29-2, 500 pages, $125.00 | Ebook ISBN 978-1-59237-241-6 www.gale.com/gvrl/partners/grey.htm

The Asian Databook: Statistics for all US Counties & Cities with Over 10,000 Population

This is the first-ever resource that compiles statistics and rankings on the US Asian population. *The Asian Databook* presents over 20 statistical data points for each city and county, arranged alphabetically by state, then alphabetically by place name. Data reported for each place includes Population, Languages Spoken at Home, Foreign-Born, Educational Attainment, Income Figures, Poverty Status, Homeownership, Home Values & Rent, and more. Next, in the Rankings Section, the top 75 places are listed for each data element. These easy-to-access ranking tables allow the user to quickly determine trends and population characteristics. This kind of comparative data can not be found elsewhere, in print or on the web, in a format that's as easy-to-use or more concise. A useful resource for those searching for demographics data, career search and relocation information and also for market research. With data ranging from Ancestry to Education, *The Asian Databook* presents a useful compilation of information that will be a much-needed resource in the reference collection of any public or academic library along with the marketing collection of any company whose primary focus in on the Asian population.

"This useful resource will help those searching for demographics data, and market research or relocation information... Accurate and clearly laid out, the publication is recommended for large public library and research collections." -Booklist

Softcover ISBN 978-1-59237-044-3, 1,000 pages, $150.00

The Hispanic Databook: Statistics for all US Counties & Cities with Over 10,000 Population

Previously published by Toucan Valley Publications, this second edition has been completely updated with figures from the latest census and has been broadly expanded to include dozens of new data elements and a brand new Rankings section. The Hispanic population in the United States has increased over 42% in the last 10 years and accounts for 12.5% of the total US population. For ease-of-use, *The Hispanic Databook* presents over 20 statistical data points for each city and county, arranged alphabetically by state, then alphabetically by place name. Data reported for each place includes Population, Languages Spoken at Home, Foreign-Born, Educational Attainment, Income Figures, Poverty Status, Homeownership, Home Values & Rent, and more. Next, in the Rankings Section, the top 75 places are listed for each data element. These easy-to-access ranking tables allow the user to quickly determine trends and population characteristics. This kind of comparative data can not be found elsewhere, in print or on the web, in a format that's as easy-to-use or more concise. A useful resource for those searching for demographics data, career search and relocation information and also for market research. With data ranging from Ancestry to Education, *The Hispanic Databook* presents a useful compilation of information that will be a much-needed resource in the reference collection of any public or academic library along with the marketing collection of any company whose primary focus in on the Hispanic population.

"This accurate, clearly presented volume of selected Hispanic demographics is recommended for large public libraries and research collections."-Library Journal

Softcover ISBN 978-1-59237-008-5, 1,000 pages, $150.00

Ancestry in America: A Comparative Guide to Over 200 Ethnic Backgrounds

This brand new reference work pulls together thousands of comparative statistics on the Ethnic Backgrounds of all populated places in the United States with populations over 10,000. Never before has this kind of information been reported in a single volume. Section One, Statistics by Place, is made up of a list of over 200 ancestry and race categories arranged alphabetically by each of the 5,000 different places with populations over 10,000. The population number of the ancestry group in that city or town is provided along with the percent that group represents of the total population. This informative city-by-city section allows the user to quickly and easily explore the ethnic makeup of all major population bases in the United States. Section Two, Comparative Rankings, contains three tables for each ethnicity and race. In the first table, the top 150 populated places are ranked by population number for that particular ancestry group, regardless of population. In the second table, the top 150 populated places are ranked by the percent of the total population for that ancestry group. In the third table, those top 150 populated places with 10,000 population are ranked by population number for each ancestry group. These easy-to-navigate tables allow users to see ancestry population patterns and make city-by-city comparisons as well. This brand new, information-packed resource will serve a wide-range or research requests for demographics, population characteristics, relocation information and much more. *Ancestry in America: A Comparative Guide to Over 200 Ethnic Backgrounds* will be an important acquisition to all reference collections.

"This compilation will serve a wide range of research requests for population characteristics ... it offers much more detail than other sources." –*Booklist*

Softcover ISBN 978-1-59237-029-0, 1,500 pages, $225.00

Weather America, A Thirty-Year Summary of Statistical Weather Data and Rankings

This valuable resource provides extensive climatological data for over 4,000 National and Cooperative Weather Stations throughout the United States. Weather America begins with a new Major Storms section that details major storm events of the nation and a National Rankings section that details rankings for several data elements, such as Maximum Temperature and Precipitation. The main body of Weather America is organized into 50 state sections. Each section provides a Data Table on each Weather Station, organized alphabetically, that provides statistics on Maximum and Minimum Temperatures, Precipitation, Snowfall, Extreme Temperatures, Foggy Days, Humidity and more. State sections contain two brand new features in this edition – a City Index and a narrative Description of the climatic conditions of the state. Each section also includes a revised Map of the State that includes not only weather stations, but cities and towns.

"Best Reference Book of the Year." –*Library Journal*

Softcover ISBN 978-1-891482-29-8, 2,013 pages, $175.00 | Ebook ISBN 978-1-59237-237-9 www.gale.com/gvrl/partners/grey.htm

Crime in America's Top-Rated Cities

This volume includes over 20 years of crime statistics in all major crime categories: violent crimes, property crimes and total crime. *Crime in America's Top-Rated Cities* is conveniently arranged by city and covers 76 top-rated cities. Crime in America's Top-Rated Cities offers details that compare the number of crimes and crime rates for the city, suburbs and metro area along with national crime trends for violent, property and total crimes. Also, this handbook contains important information and statistics on Anti-Crime Programs, Crime Risk, Hate Crimes, Illegal Drugs, Law Enforcement, Correctional Facilities, Death Penalty Laws and much more. A much-needed resource for people who are relocating, business professionals, general researchers, the press, law enforcement officials and students of criminal justice.

"Data is easy to access and will save hours of searching." –*Global Enforcement Review*

Softcover ISBN 978-1-891482-84-7, 832 pages, $155.00

The Complete Directory for People with Disabilities, 2008

A wealth of information, now in one comprehensive sourcebook. Completely updated, this edition contains more information than ever before, including thousands of new entries and enhancements to existing entries and thousands of additional web sites and e-mail addresses. This up-to-date directory is the most comprehensive resource available for people with disabilities, detailing Independent Living Centers, Rehabilitation Facilities, State & Federal Agencies, Associations, Support Groups, Periodicals & Books, Assistive Devices, Employment & Education Programs, Camps and Travel Groups. Each year, more libraries, schools, colleges, hospitals, rehabilitation centers and individuals add *The Complete Directory for People with Disabilities* to their collections, making sure that this information is readily available to the families, individuals and professionals who can benefit most from the amazing wealth of resources cataloged here.

"No other reference tool exists to meet the special needs of the disabled in one convenient resource for information." –Library Journal

Softcover ISBN 978-1-59237-194-5, 1,200 pages, $165.00 | Online Database $215.00 | Online Database & Directory Combo $300.00

The Complete Learning Disabilities Directory, 2008

The Complete Learning Disabilities Directory is the most comprehensive database of Programs, Services, Curriculum Materials, Professional Meetings & Resources, Camps, Newsletters and Support Groups for teachers, students and families concerned with learning disabilities. This information-packed directory includes information about Associations & Organizations, Schools, Colleges & Testing Materials, Government Agencies, Legal Resources and much more. For quick, easy access to information, this directory contains four indexes: Entry Name Index, Subject Index and Geographic Index. With every passing year, the field of learning disabilities attracts more attention and the network of caring, committed and knowledgeable professionals grows every day. This directory is an invaluable research tool for these parents, students and professionals.

"Due to its wealth and depth of coverage, parents, teachers and others... should find this an invaluable resource." -Booklist

Softcover ISBN 978-1-59237-207-2, 900 pages, $145.00 | Online Database $195.00 | Online Database & Directory Combo $280.00

The Complete Directory for People with Chronic Illness, 2007/08

Thousands of hours of research have gone into this completely updated edition – several new chapters have been added along with thousands of new entries and enhancements to existing entries. Plus, each chronic illness chapter has been reviewed by a medical expert in the field. This widely-hailed directory is structured around the 90 most prevalent chronic illnesses – from Asthma to Cancer to Wilson's Disease – and provides a comprehensive overview of the support services and information resources available for people diagnosed with a chronic illness. Each chronic illness has its own chapter and contains a brief description in layman's language, followed by important resources for National & Local Organizations, State Agencies, Newsletters, Books & Periodicals, Libraries & Research Centers, Support Groups & Hotlines, Web Sites and much more. This directory is an important resource for health care professionals, the collections of hospital and health care libraries, as well as an invaluable tool for people with a chronic illness and their support network.

"A must purchase for all hospital and health care libraries and is strongly recommended for all public library reference departments." –ARBA

Softcover ISBN 978-1-59237-183-9, 1,200 pages, $165.00 | Online Database $215.00 | Online Database & Directory Combo $300.00

The Complete Mental Health Directory, 2008/09

This is the most comprehensive resource covering the field of behavioral health, with critical information for both the layman and the mental health professional. For the layman, this directory offers understandable descriptions of 25 Mental Health Disorders as well as detailed information on Associations, Media, Support Groups and Mental Health Facilities. For the professional, The Complete Mental Health Directory offers critical and comprehensive information on Managed Care Organizations, Information Systems, Government Agencies and Provider Organizations. This comprehensive volume of needed information will be widely used in any reference collection.

"... the strength of this directory is that it consolidates widely dispersed information into a single volume." –Booklist

Softcover ISBN 978-1-59237-285-0, 800 pages, $165.00 | Online Database $215.00 | Online & Directory Combo $300.00

The Comparative Guide to American Hospitals, Second Edition

This new second edition compares all of the nation's hospitals by 24 measures of quality in the treatment of heart attack, heart failure, pneumonia, and, new to this edition, surgical procedures and pregnancy care. Plus, this second edition is now available in regional volumes, to make locating information about hospitals in your area quicker and easier than ever before. The Comparative Guide to American Hospitals provides a snapshot profile of each of the nations 4,200+ hospitals. These informative profiles illustrate how the hospital rates when providing 24 different treatments within four broad categories: Heart Attack Care, Heart Failure Care, Surgical Infection Prevention (NEW), and Pregnancy Care measures (NEW). Each profile includes the raw percentage for that hospital, the state average, the US average and data on the top hospital. For easy access to contact information, each profile includes the hospital's address, phone and fax numbers, email and web addresses, type and accreditation along with 5 top key administrations. These profiles will allow the user to quickly identify the quality of the hospital and have the necessary information at their fingertips to make contact with that hospital. Most importantly, *The Comparative Guide to American Hospitals* provides easy-to-use Regional State by State Statistical Summary Tables for each of the data elements to allow the user to quickly locate hospitals with the best level of service. Plus, a new 30-Day Mortality Chart, Glossary of Terms and Regional Hospital Profile Index make this a must-have source. This new, expanded edition will be a must for the reference collection at all public, medical and academic libraries.

"These data will help those with heart conditions and pneumonia make informed decisions about their healthcare and encourage hospitals to improve the quality of care they provide. Large medical, hospital, and public libraries are most likely to benefit from this weighty resource."-Library Journal

Four Volumes Softcover ISBN 978-1-59237-182-2, 3,500 pages, $325.00 | Regional Volumes $135.00 | Ebook ISBN 978-1-59237-239-3 www.gale.com/gvrl/partners/grey.htm

Older Americans Information Directory, 2008

Completely updated for 2008, this sixth edition has been completely revised and now contains 1,000 new listings, over 8,000 updates to existing listings and over 3,000 brand new e-mail addresses and web sites. You'll find important resources for Older Americans including National, Regional, State & Local Organizations, Government Agencies, Research Centers, Libraries & Information Centers, Legal Resources, Discount Travel Information, Continuing Education Programs, Disability Aids & Assistive Devices, Health, Print Media and Electronic Media. Three indexes: Entry Index, Subject Index and Geographic Index make it easy to find just the right source of information. This comprehensive guide to resources for Older Americans will be a welcome addition to any reference collection.

"Highly recommended for academic, public, health science and consumer libraries…" –Choice

1,200 pages; Softcover ISBN 978-1-59237-357-4, $165.00 | Online Database $215.00 | Online Database & Directory Combo $300.00

The Complete Directory for Pediatric Disorders, 2008

This important directory provides parents and caregivers with information about Pediatric Conditions, Disorders, Diseases and Disabilities, including Blood Disorders, Bone & Spinal Disorders, Brain Defects & Abnormalities, Chromosomal Disorders, Congenital Heart Defects, Movement Disorders, Neuromuscular Disorders and Pediatric Tumors & Cancers. This carefully written directory offers: understandable Descriptions of 15 major bodily systems; Descriptions of more than 200 Disorders and a Resources Section, detailing National Agencies & Associations, State Associations, Online Services, Libraries & Resource Centers, Research Centers, Support Groups & Hotlines, Camps, Books and Periodicals. This resource will provide immediate access to information crucial to families and caregivers when coping with children's illnesses.

"Recommended for public and consumer health libraries." –Library Journal

Softcover ISBN 978-1-59237-150-1, 1,200 pages, $165.00 | Online Database $215.00 | Online Database & Directory Combo $300.00

The Directory of Drug & Alcohol Residential Rehabilitation Facilities

This brand new directory is the first-ever resource to bring together, all in one place, data on the thousands of drug and alcohol residential rehabilitation facilities in the United States. The Directory of Drug & Alcohol Residential Rehabilitation Facilities covers over 1,000 facilities, with detailed contact information for each one, including mailing address, phone and fax numbers, email addresses and web sites, mission statement, type of treatment programs, cost, average length of stay, numbers of residents and counselors, accreditation, insurance plans accepted, type of environment, religious affiliation, education components and much more. It also contains a helpful chapter on General Resources that provides contact information for Associations, Print & Electronic Media, Support Groups and Conferences. Multiple indexes allow the user to pinpoint the facilities that meet very specific criteria. This time-saving tool is what so many counselors, parents and medical professionals have been asking for. *The Directory of Drug & Alcohol Residential Rehabilitation Facilities* will be a helpful tool in locating the right source for treatment for a wide range of individuals. This comprehensive directory will be an important acquisition for all reference collections: public and academic libraries, case managers, social workers, state agencies and many more.

"This is an excellent, much needed directory that fills an important gap…" –Booklist

Softcover ISBN 978-1-59237-031-3, 300 pages, $135.00

The Directory of Hospital Personnel, 2008

The Directory of Hospital Personnel is the best resource you can have at your fingertips when researching or marketing a product or service to the hospital market. A "Who's Who" of the hospital universe, this directory puts you in touch with over 150,000 key decision-makers. With 100% verification of data you can rest assured that you will reach the right person with just one call. Every hospital in the U.S. is profiled, listed alphabetically by city within state. Plus, three easy-to-use, cross-referenced indexes put the facts at your fingertips faster and more easily than any other directory: Hospital Name Index, Bed Size Index and Personnel Index. *The Directory of Hospital Personnel* is the only complete source for key hospital decision-makers by name. Whether you want to define or restructure sales territories... locate hospitals with the purchasing power to accept your proposals... keep track of important contacts or colleagues... or find information on which insurance plans are accepted, *The Directory of Hospital Personnel* gives you the information you need – easily, efficiently, effectively and accurately.

"Recommended for college, university and medical libraries." -ARBA

Softcover ISBN 978-1-59237-286-7, 2,500 pages, $325.00 | Online Database $545.00 | Online Database & Directory Combo, $650.00

The Directory of Health Care Group Purchasing Organizations, 2008

This comprehensive directory provides the important data you need to get in touch with over 800 Group Purchasing Organizations. By providing in-depth information on this growing market and its members, *The Directory of Health Care Group Purchasing Organizations* fills a major need for the most accurate and comprehensive information on over 800 GPOs – Mailing Address, Phone & Fax Numbers, E-mail Addresses, Key Contacts, Purchasing Agents, Group Descriptions, Membership Categorization, Standard Vendor Proposal Requirements, Membership Fees & Terms, Expanded Services, Total Member Beds & Outpatient Visits represented and more. Five Indexes provide a number of ways to locate the right GPO: Alphabetical Index, Expanded Services Index, Organization Type Index, Geographic Index and Member Institution Index. With its comprehensive and detailed information on each purchasing organization, *The Directory of Health Care Group Purchasing Organizations* is the go-to source for anyone looking to target this market.

"The information is clearly arranged and easy to access...recommended for those needing this very specialized information." –ARBA

1,000 pages; Softcover ISBN 978-1-59237-287-4, $325.00 | Online Database, $650.00 | Online Database & Directory Combo, $750.00

The HMO/PPO Directory, 2008

The HMO/PPO Directory is a comprehensive source that provides detailed information about Health Maintenance Organizations and Preferred Provider Organizations nationwide. This comprehensive directory details more information about more managed health care organizations than ever before. Over 1,100 HMOs, PPOs, Medicare Advantage Plans and affiliated companies are listed, arranged alphabetically by state. Detailed listings include Key Contact Information, Prescription Drug Benefits, Enrollment, Geographical Areas served, Affiliated Physicians & Hospitals, Federal Qualifications, Status, Year Founded, Managed Care Partners, Employer References, Fees & Payment Information and more. Plus, five years of historical information is included related to Revenues, Net Income, Medical Loss Ratios, Membership Enrollment and Number of Patient Complaints. Five easy-to-use, cross-referenced indexes will put this vast array of information at your fingertips immediately: HMO Index, PPO Index, Other Providers Index, Personnel Index and Enrollment Index. *The HMO/PPO Directory* provides the most comprehensive data on the most companies available on the market place today.

"Helpful to individuals requesting certain HMO/PPO issues such as co-payment costs, subscription costs and patient complaints. Individuals concerned (or those with questions) about their insurance may find this text to be of use to them." -ARBA

Softcover ISBN 978-1-59237-204-1, 600 pages, $325.00 | Online Database, $495.00 | Online Database & Directory Combo, $600.00

Medical Device Register, 2008

The only one-stop resource of every medical supplier licensed to sell products in the US. This award-winning directory offers immediate access to over 13,000 companies - and more than 65,000 products – in two information-packed volumes. This comprehensive resource saves hours of time and trouble when searching for medical equipment and supplies and the manufacturers who provide them. Volume I: The Product Directory, provides essential information for purchasing or specifying medical supplies for every medical device, supply, and diagnostic available in the US. Listings provide FDA codes & Federal Procurement Eligibility, Contact information for every manufacturer of the product along with Prices and Product Specifications. Volume 2 - Supplier Profiles, offers the most complete and important data about Suppliers, Manufacturers and Distributors. Company Profiles detail the number of employees, ownership, method of distribution, sales volume, net income, key executives detailed contact information medical products the company supplies, plus the medical specialties they cover. Four indexes provide immediate access to this wealth of information: Keyword Index, Trade Name Index, Supplier Geographical Index and OEM (Original Equipment Manufacturer) Index. *Medical Device Register* is the only one-stop source for locating suppliers and products; looking for new manufacturers or hard-to-find medical devices; comparing products and companies; know who's selling what and who to buy from cost effectively. This directory has become the standard in its field and will be a welcome addition to the reference collection of any medical library, large public library, university library along with the collections that serve the medical community.

"A wealth of information on medical devices, medical device companies... and key personnel in the industry is provide in this comprehensive reference work... A valuable reference work, one of the best hardcopy compilations available." -Doody Publishing

Two Volumes, Hardcover ISBN 978-1-59237-206-5, 3,000 pages, $325.00

Canadian Almanac & Directory, 2008

The Canadian Almanac & Directory contains sixteen directories in one – giving you all the facts and figures you will ever need about Canada. No other single source provides users with the quality and depth of up-to-date information for all types of research. This national directory and guide gives you access to statistics, images and over 100,000 names and addresses for everything from Airlines to Zoos - updated every year. It's Ten Directories in One! Each section is a directory in itself, providing robust information on business and finance, communications, government, associations, arts and culture (museums, zoos, libraries, etc.), health, transportation, law, education, and more. Government information includes federal, provincial and territorial - and includes an easy-to-use quick index to find key information. A separate municipal government section includes every municipality in Canada, with full profiles of Canada's largest urban centers. A complete legal directory lists judges and judicial officials, court locations and law firms across the country. A wealth of general information, the *Canadian Almanac & Directory* also includes national statistics on population, employment, imports and exports, and more. National awards and honors are presented, along with forms of address, Commonwealth information and full color photos of Canadian symbols. Postal information, weights, measures, distances and other useful charts are also incorporated. Complete almanac information includes perpetual calendars, five-year holiday planners and astronomical information. Published continuously for 160 years, *The Canadian Almanac & Directory* is the best single reference source for business executives, managers and assistants; government and public affairs executives; lawyers; marketing, sales and advertising executives; researchers, editors and journalists.

Hardcover ISBN 978-1-59237-220-1, 1,600 pages, $315.00

Associations Canada, 2008

The Most Powerful Fact-Finder to Business, Trade, Professional and Consumer Organizations

Associations Canada covers Canadian organizations and international groups including industry, commercial and professional associations, registered charities, special interest and common interest organizations. This annually revised compendium provides detailed listings and abstracts for nearly 20,000 regional, national and international organizations. This popular volume provides the most comprehensive picture of Canada's non-profit sector. Detailed listings enable users to identify an organization's budget, founding date, scope of activity, licensing body, sources of funding, executive information, full address and complete contact information, just to name a few. Powerful indexes help researchers find information quickly and easily. The following indexes are included: subject, acronym, geographic, budget, executive name, conferences & conventions, mailing list, defunct and unreachable associations and registered charitable organizations. In addition to annual spending of over $1 billion on transportation and conventions alone, Canadian associations account for many millions more in pursuit of membership interests. *Associations Canada* provides complete access to this highly lucrative market. *Associations Canada* is a strong source of prospects for sales and marketing executives, tourism and convention officials, researchers, government officials - anyone who wants to locate non-profit interest groups and trade associations.

Hardcover ISBN 978-1-59237-277-5, 1,600 pages, $315.00

Financial Services Canada, 2008/09

Financial Services Canada is the only master file of current contacts and information that serves the needs of the entire financial services industry in Canada. With over 18,000 organizations and hard-to-find business information, Financial Services Canada is the most up-to-date source for names and contact numbers of industry professionals, senior executives, portfolio managers, financial advisors, agency bureaucrats and elected representatives. Financial Services Canada incorporates the latest changes in the industry to provide you with the most current details on each company, including: name, title, organization, telephone and fax numbers, e-mail and web addresses. *Financial Services Canada* also includes private company listings never before compiled, government agencies, association and consultant services - to ensure that you'll never miss a client or a contact. Current listings include: banks and branches, non-depository institutions, stock exchanges and brokers, investment management firms, insurance companies, major accounting and law firms, government agencies and financial associations. Powerful indexes assist researchers with locating the vital financial information they need. The following indexes are included: alphabetic, geographic, executive name, corporate web site/e-mail, government quick reference and subject. *Financial Services Canada* is a valuable resource for financial executives, bankers, financial planners, sales and marketing professionals, lawyers and chartered accountants, government officials, investment dealers, journalists, librarians and reference specialists.

Hardcover ISBN 978-1-59237-278-2, 900 pages, $315.00

Directory of Libraries in Canada, 2008/09

The Directory of Libraries in Canada brings together almost 7,000 listings including libraries and their branches, information resource centers, archives and library associations and learning centers. The directory offers complete and comprehensive information on Canadian libraries, resource centers, business information centers, professional associations, regional library systems, archives, library schools and library technical programs. *The Directory of Libraries in Canada* includes important features of each library and service, including library information; personnel details, including contact names and e-mail addresses; collection information; services available to users; acquisitions budgets; and computers and automated systems. Useful information on each library's electronic access is also included, such as Internet browser, connectivity and public Internet/CD-ROM/subscription database access. The directory also provides powerful indexes for subject, location, personal name and Web site/e-mail to assist researchers with locating the crucial information they need. *The Directory of Libraries in Canada* is a vital reference tool for publishers, advocacy groups, students, research institutions, computer hardware suppliers, and other diverse groups that provide products and services to this unique market.

Hardcover ISBN 978-1-59237-279-9, 850 pages, $315.00

Canadian Environmental Directory, 2008 /09

The Canadian Environmental Directory is Canada's most complete and only national listing of environmental associations and organizations, government regulators and purchasing groups, product and service companies, special libraries, and more! The extensive Products and Services section provides detailed listings enabling users to identify the company name, address, phone, fax, e-mail, Web address, firm type, contact names (and titles), product and service information, affiliations, trade information, branch and affiliate data. The Government section gives you all the contact information you need at every government level – federal, provincial and municipal. We also include descriptions of current environmental initiatives, programs and agreements, names of environment-related acts administered by each ministry or department PLUS information and tips on who to contact and how to sell to governments in Canada. The Associations section provides complete contact information and a brief description of activities. Included are Canadian environmental organizations and international groups including industry, commercial and professional associations, registered charities, special interest and common interest organizations. All the Information you need about the Canadian environmental industry: directory of products and services, special libraries and resource, conferences, seminars and tradeshows, chronology of environmental events, law firms and major Canadian companies, *The Canadian Environmental Directory* is ideal for business, government, engineers and anyone conducting research on the environment.

Softcover ISBN 978-1-59237-224-9, 900 pages, $315.00

Canadian Parliamentary Guide, 2008

An indispensable guide to government in Canada, the annual *Canadian Parliamentary Guide* provides information on both federal and provincial governments, courts, and their elected and appointed members. The Guide is completely bilingual, with each record appearing both in English and then in French. The Guide contains biographical sketches of members of the Governor General's Household, the Privy Council, members of Canadian legislatures (federal, including both the House of Commons and the Senate, provincial and territorial), members of the federal superior courts (Supreme, Federal, Federal Appeal, Court Martial Appeal and Tax Courts) and the senior staff for these institutions. Biographies cover personal data, political career, private career and contact information. In addition, the Guide provides descriptions of each of the institutions, including brief historical information in text and chart format and significant facts (i.e. number of members and their salaries). The Guide covers the results of all federal general elections and by-elections from Confederations to the present and the results of the most recent provincial elections. A complete name index rounds out the text, making information easy to find. No other resources presents a more up-to-date, more complete picture of Canadian government and her political leaders. A must-have resource for all Canadian reference collections.

Hardcover ISBN 978-1-59237-310-9, 800 pages, $184.00